Contents

CONTENTS

INDEXES

A Note from the Peterson's® Editors

Billions of dollars in financial aid are made available by private donors and governmental agencies to students and their families every year to help pay for college. Yet, to the average person, the task of finding financial aid awards in this huge network of scholarships, grants, and prizes appears to be nearly impossible.

For nearly forty years, Peterson's® has given students and parents the most comprehensive, up-to-date information on how to get their fair share of the financial aid pie. *Peterson's® Scholarships, Grants & Prizes* was created to help students and their families pinpoint those specific private financial aid programs that best match students' backgrounds, interests, talents, or abilities.

In *Peterson's® Scholarships, Grants & Prizes,* you will find nearly 2,700 award programs and resources that are providing financial awards to undergraduates in the 2018-19 academic year. Foundations, fraternal and ethnic organizations, community service clubs, churches and religious groups, philanthropies, companies and industry groups, labor unions and public employees' associations, veterans' groups, and trusts and bequests are all possible sources.

For those seeking to enter college, *Peterson's® Scholarships, Grants & Prizes* includes information needed to make financing a college education as seamless as possible.

The **How to Find an Award That's Right for You** section paints a complete picture of the financial aid landscape, discusses strategies for finding financial awards, provides important tips on how to avoid scholarship scams, and offers insight into how to make scholarship management organizations work for you.

Also found in **How to Find an Award That's Right for You** is the "How to Use This Guide" article, which describes how the nearly 3,500 awards in the guide are profiled, along with information on how to search for an award in one of eleven categories.

If you would like to compare awards quickly, refer to the **Quick-Reference Chart.** Here you can search through the "Scholarships, Grants & Prizes At-a-Glance" chart and select awards by the highest dollar amount.

In the **Profiles of Scholarships, Grants & Prizes** section you'll find updated award programs, along with information about award sponsors. The profile section is divided into three categories: *Academic Fields/Career Goals, Nonacademic/Noncareer Criteria,* and *Miscellaneous Criteria.* Each profile provides all of the need-to-know information about available scholarships, grants, and prizes.

Finally, the back of the book features thirteen **Indexes** listing scholarships, grants, and prizes based on award name; sponsor; academic fields/career goals; civic, professional, social, or union affiliation; corporate affiliation; employment/volunteer experience; impairment; military service; nationality or ethnic background; religious affiliation; residence; location of study; and talent/interest area.

Peterson's® publishes a full line of books—financial aid, career preparation, test prep, and education exploration. Peterson's® publications can be found at high school guidance offices, college libraries and career centers, and your local bookstore and library. Peterson's® books are also available at www.petersonsbooks.com. To search for scholarships online, check out www.petersons.com/college-search/scholarship-search.aspx.

We welcome any comments or suggestions you may have about this publication. Your feedback will help us make educational dreams possible for you—and others like you.

HOW TO FIND AN AWARD THAT'S RIGHT FOR YOU

All About Scholarships

Dr. Gary M. Bell
Former Academic Dean, Honors College, Texas Tech University

During the next four (or more) years you will spend your time earning your college baccalaureate degree, think of the learning task as your primary employment. It is helpful to think of a scholarship as part of the salary for undertaking your job of learning. One of your first inquiries as you examine a potential college setting is about the type of assistance it might provide given your interests, academic record, and personal history. Talk to a financial aid officer or a scholarship coordinator at the school. At most schools, these are special officers—people specifically employed to assist you in your quest for financial assistance. Virtually all schools also have brochures or publications and specific information on their website that show the scholarship opportunities at their institution. Take a close look at this scholarship information.

Also, high school counselors often have keen insight into resources available at colleges, especially for the schools in your area. These people are the key points of contact between institutions of higher education and you.

In general, it is not a good idea to use a private company that promises to provide you with a list of scholarships for which you might be eligible. Such lists are often very broad, and you can secure the same results by using available high school, university, web-based, and published information. The scholarship search you perform online will probably be more fruitful than what any private company can do for you.

What do we mean by the word *scholarship*, anyway? In the very broadest sense, scholarships consist of outright grants of monetary assistance to eligible students to help them attend college. The money is applied to tuition or the cost of living while in school. Scholarships do not need to be repaid. They do, however, often carry stringent criteria for maintaining them, such as the achievement of a certain grade point average, the carrying of a given number of class hours, matriculation in a specific program, or membership in a designated group. Scholarships at many schools may be combined with college work-study programs, in which some work is also required. Often, scholarships are combined with other forms of financial aid so that collectively they provide you with a truly attractive financial aid package. This may include low-interest loan programs to make the school of your choice financially feasible.

Scholarships generally fall into three major categories: *need-based scholarships*, predicated on income; *merit-based scholarships*, based on your academic and sometimes extracurricular achievements; and *association-based scholarships*, which are dependent on as many different associations as you can imagine (for instance, your home county, your identification with a particular group, fraternal and religious organizations, or the company for which a parent may work). The range of reasons for which scholarships are given is almost infinite.

Most schools accommodate students who have financial need. The largest and best grant programs are the U.S. government-sponsored Federal Pell Grants and the Federal Supplemental Educational Opportunity Grants, which you might want to explore with your financial aid counselor. Also inquire about state-sponsored scholarship and grant programs.

Merit-based scholarships come from a variety of sources—the university, individual departments or colleges within the university, state scholarship programs, or special donors who want to assist worthy students. Remember this as you meet with your financial aid officer because he or she knows that different opportunities may be available for you as a petroleum engineering, agriculture, accounting, pre-veterinary, or performing arts major. Merit-based scholarships are typically designed to reward the highest performers on such precollege measures as standardized tests (the SAT° or ACT°) and high school grades. Because repeated performance on standardized tests often leads to higher scores, it may be financially advantageous for you to take these college admission tests several times.

Inquire about each of the three categories of scholarships. The association-based scholarships can sometimes be particularly helpful and quite surprising. Employers of parents, people from specific geographic locations, or organizations (churches, civic groups, unions, special interest clubs, and even family name associations) may provide assistance for college students. Campus scholarship literature is the key to unlocking the mysteries of association-based financial assistance (and the other two categories as well), but personal interviews with financial officers are also crucial.

There are several issues to keep in mind as you seek scholarship assistance. Probably the most important is to determine deadlines that apply to a scholarship for which you may be eligible. It's wise to begin your search early, so that your eligibility is not nullified by missing a published deadline. Most scholarship opportunities require that you complete an application form, and it is time well spent to make sure your answers are neat (if using a paper application), grammatically correct, and logical. Correct spelling is essential. Have someone proofread your application. Keep in mind that if applications require essays, fewer students typically take the time to complete these essays, and this gives those students who do so a better chance of winning that particular scholarship. Always be truthful in these applications, but at the same time provide the most positive self-portrayal to enhance your chances of being considered. Most merit-based and association-based scholarships are awarded competitively.

Finally, let the people who offer you assistance know whether you will accept their offer. Too many students simply assume that a scholarship offer means automatic acceptance. This is not the case! In most instances, you must send a letter of acknowledgement and acceptance. Virtually all schools have agreed that students must make up their minds about scholarship acceptance no later than May 1, but earlier deadlines may apply.

As you probably know, tuition at private schools is typically higher than tuition at state colleges and universities. Scholarships can narrow this gap. Many private institutions have a great deal of money to spend on scholarship assistance, so you may find that with a scholarship, going to a private college will cost no more than attending a state-supported college or university. **Note:** A substantial scholarship from a private school may still leave you with a very large annual bill to cover the difference between the scholarship amount and the actual cost of tuition, fees, and living expenses.

When you evaluate a scholarship, take into account your final out-of-pocket costs. Also consider the length of time for which the school extends scholarship support. Be cautious about schools that promise substantial assistance for the first year to get you there, but then provide little or nothing in subsequent years. The most attractive and meaningful scholarships are offered for four to five years. Do not abandon the scholarship search once you are enrolled at the school of your choice. Often, a number of additional scholarship opportunities are available for you once you're enrolled, especially as you prove your ability and interest in a given field.

It's Never Too Early to Look for College Scholarships

Many high school students make the mistake of thinking that their race to the top of the scholarship mountain begins during their senior year. Some have the forethought to begin their hunt for college money in their junior year. But even that may be too late. Rising costs of college tuition, the increasing number of people attending college for the first time, and the reduction in federal, state, and local grants for college goers have made paying for college without student loan debt a competitive sport. And only those who are prepared are coming out unscathed and debt free.

The importance of securing scholarships and grants to help pay for college cannot be overestimated. The nation is currently in the midst of a student-loan debt crisis that is crippling the earning power of millions of college graduates. If you need any further convincing to get serious about finding money for college other than student loans, check out these sobering statistics:*

- In recent years, college students borrowed more than $100 billion to pay for college, the highest amount of student borrowing ever.

- In 2018, the outstanding balance of student loan debt reached nearly $1.48 trillion (yes, that's with a "T"), surpassing credit card debt of $620 billion.

- Nearly every student who earns a four-year degree graduates with student loan debt, which currently averages about $28,000.

Student loan debt may be inevitable, but it doesn't have to be crippling. And the more money you can get that doesn't require repayment, the better your financial future will be once you do get your college degree. Here are some tips on how to get ahead of the college money rat race and come out a winner:

1. **Make a Family College Payment Plan.** While 70 percent of parents surveyed by an investment group said their students are so brilliant that they will win enormous amounts of scholarships to pay for college, the reality is paying for college without student loans doesn't happen by chance. Paying for college takes planning, and the sooner you begin the better off you'll be. But a student cannot plan for college payments alone. Parents must meet with their children to develop a college payment plan. In their discussions, they need to discuss all family college payment plan options, including parental tax credits, college saving accounts, trusts, savings bonds, and even stock options. At the meeting, parents and their children should do the following:

- Calculate the real costs of attending college.

- Decide who is going to pay and how much.

- Develop a strategy to meet those payment commitments.

Making a family college payment plan is an essential first step. The outcome of this plan gives students a clear scholarship money goal and provides an excellent starting point for your scholarship sojourn.

2. **Start scholarship research on day one.** While most scholarships and grants require you to be a junior or senior in high school, this does not preclude you from creating an application strategy the day you enter high school—or even before! In truth, the minute you decide to go to college you should start researching the best ways to pay for it. Talk to guidance counselors, do research online, learn what the scholarship requirements are, and develop a plan to apply when ready. By searching for scholarships as early as possible, you will be able to zero in on the ones that match with your skills, abilities, characteristics, and passions. In addition to finding scholarships, use this preliminary time to learn the scholarship rules. Build a checklist of all the accompanying documents you're going to need to

---

* Statistics are derived from the Student Loan Report's "Student Loan Debt Statistics 2018." www.studentloans.net/student-loan-debt-statistics; https://www.federalreserve.gov/publications/2019-economic-well-being-of-us-households-in-2018-student-loans-and-other-education-debt.htm

accompany your scholarship application. Save items that you think would work well in your personal statement or essay. Develop a list of people who could be references or write letters of recommendations. Organize, organize, organize—the more organized you are, the easier it will be to apply for multiple scholarships.

3. **Be Your Guidance Counselor's Best Friend.** Long the butt of jokes, guidance counselors are the most maligned members of a high school system. But they can be your best ally when it comes to securing scholarships and grants for college. Get to know your guidance counselor well. Offer your counselor a proactive strategy for getting money for college. Your guidance counselor is more apt to help you with planning your high school career if he or she knows you are serious about going to college.

4. **Rack up scholarships as you go along.** College savings bonds may seem like a blast from the 1950s, but believe it or not there are still essay, speech, and music contests all over the nation that offer them to winners. You can earn these types of rewards as well as cold hard cash at anytime—even before you get into high school. Check out contests such as the Ayn Rand Institute's Anthem and Atlas Shrugged Essay Contests or the American Legion National High School Oratorical Contest. These are open to all high school-age students.

5. **Plan Your High School Years with College in Mind.** As you do your research on college scholarships, you will see that many have academic requirements. You need to start early on developing a course of study to help you hit those necessary academic marks. Few students wake up one day and score 31 on the ACT or start a charity out of the blue. So plan your classes, extracurricular events, and charity activities with college in mind. To be sure, you need to do what appeals to you, but keep in mind that every class you attend, every test you take, and every club you join can be an asset to your scholarship hunt. Be deliberate about your school choices and start with the end goal in mind.

Filling out a scholarship application is the end, not the beginning of a long process to earn money for college. Fortunately, you can begin all the organization and planning necessary to secure scholarship money well before the scholarship is due. Do not wait. It's never too early to start your scholarship journey. The earlier you begin, the better your journey will be!

A Strategy for Finding Awards

Private scholarships and awards can be characterized by unpredictable, sometimes seemingly bizarre, criteria. Before you begin your award search, write a personal profile of yourself to help establish as many criteria as possible that might form a basis for your scholarship award. Here is a basic checklist of fifteen questions you should consider:

1. **What are your career goals?**

   Be both narrow and broad in your designations. If, for example, you aim to be a TV news reporter, you will find many awards specific to this field in the *TV/Radio Broadcasting* section. However, collegiate broadcasting courses are offered in departments or schools of communication. So, be sure that you consider *Communications* as a relevant section for your search. Consider *Journalism*, too, for the same reasons. Then look under other broadly inclusive but possibly relevant areas, such as *Trade/Technical Specialties*. Or check a related but different field, such as *Performing Arts*. Finally, look under marginally related basic academic fields, such as *Humanities*, *Social Sciences*, or *Political Science*. Peterson's makes every attempt to provide the best cross-reference aids, but the nuances of specific awards can be difficult to capture even with the most flexible cross-referencing systems. You will need to be broadly associative in your thinking to get the most out of this wealth of information.

   If you have no clear career goal, browsing the huge variety of academic/career awards may well spark new interest in a career path. Be open to imagining yourself filling different career roles that you previously may not have considered.

2. **In what academic fields might you major?**

   Your educational experiences or your sense about your personal talents or interests may have given you a good idea of what academic discipline you wish to pursue. Again, use both broad and narrow focuses in designing your search, and look at related subject fields. For example, if you want to major in history, check the *History* section, but be sure to check out *Social Sciences* and *Humanities* as well, and maybe *Area/Ethnic Studies*. *Education*, for example, could suggest the perfect scholarship for a future historian.

3. **In which jobs, industries, or occupations have your parents or other members of your immediate family been employed? What employment experiences do you have?**

   Individual companies, employee organizations, trade unions, government agencies, and industry associations frequently establish scholarships for workers, children of workers, or other relatives of workers from specific companies or industries. These awards might require that you stay in the same career field, but most are offered regardless of the field of study you wish to undertake. Also, if one of your parents is a public service employee, especially a firefighter or police officer, you have many relevant awards from which to choose.

4. **Do you have any hobbies or special interests? Have you ever been an officer or leader of a group? Do you possess special skills or talents? Have you won any competitions? Are you a good writer?**

   From gardening to clarinet playing, from caddying to playing basketball, your special interests can win awards for you from groups that wish to promote and/or reward these pursuits. Many scholarships are targeted to "student leaders," including sports team captains; yearbook or newspaper editors; student government officers; and club, organization, and community activists.

5. **Where do you live? Where have you lived? Where will you go to college?**

   Residence criteria are among the most common qualifications for scholarship aid. Local clubs and companies provide millions of dollars in scholarship aid to students who live in a particular state, province, region, or section of a state. This means that your residential identity puts you at the head of the line for these grants. State of residence can—depending on the sponsor's criteria—include the place of your official residence, the place you attend college, the place you were born, or anywhere you have lived for more than a year.

6. **What is your family's ethnic heritage?**

   Hundreds of scholarships have been endowed for students who can claim a particular nationality or racial or ethnic descent. Partial ethnic descent frequently qualifies, so don't be put off if you do not think of your identity as a specific "ethnic" entity.

Awards are available for Colonial American, English, Polish, Welsh, Scottish, European, and other backgrounds that students may not consider especially "ethnic." One is even available for descendants of the signers of the Declaration of Independence, whatever ethnicity that might have turned out to be some ten generations later.

7. **Do you have a physical disability?**
Many awards are available to individuals with physical disabilities. Of course, commonly recognized impairments of mobility, sight, communication, and hearing are recognized, but learning disabilities and chronic diseases, such as asthma and epilepsy, are also criteria for some awards.

8. **Do you currently or have you ever served in the Armed Forces? Did one of your parents serve in a** war? **Was one of your parents lost or disabled while serving in the Armed Forces?**
Hundreds of awards use these qualifications.

9. **Do you belong to a civic association, union, or religious organization? Do your parents belong to such groups?**
Hundreds of clubs and religious groups provide scholarship assistance to members or children of members.

10. **Are you male or female?**

11. **What is your age?**

12. **Do you qualify for need-based aid?**

13. **Did you graduate in the upper one-half, upper one-third, or upper one-quarter of your class?**

14. **Do you plan to attend a two-year college, a four-year college, or a trade/technical school?**

15. **In what academic year will you be entering?**

Be expansive when considering your possible qualifications. Although some awards may be small, you may qualify for more than one award—and these can add up to significant amounts in the end.

Who Wants to Be a College Scholarship Millionaire?

There are high school seniors around the country who are becoming rich beyond their wildest dreams even before stepping inside the hallowed halls of higher education. These college upstarts are not start-up kings and queens, á la Mark Zuckerberg of Facebook fame. But they may be just as innovative. They're a part of small, but growing, elite—the College Scholarship Millionaire Club.

The concept of earning a million dollars for college sounds like the premise of a television game show. And to be honest, such a goal remains incredibly lofty for some and downright impossible for others. But what was once a fantasy of every would-be college student is now fast becoming a reality for those willing to work incredibly hard to make it happen.

So just what is the College Scholarship Millionaire Club? It's a group of students who have won $1 million or more in scholarship commitments from universities and colleges and private scholarship funds. The definition should clue you in on at least one prerequisite for joining this club—you have to apply for scholarships—a LOT of them. Still, a quick analysis of some college scholarship millionaires and how they secured their awards can offer any pre-college student great advice on how to get the most out of their scholarship application season.

While there is no sure-fire way to ensure that you earn big bucks in the college scholarship process—anyone promising that is just running a scam—there are steps you can take to increase your odds of having a big scholarship haul. Here are some valuable tips.

MAKE HIGH-ACHIEVING A GROUP SPORT

More than a decade ago James Ralph Sparks, a calculus teacher at Whitehaven High School (WHS) in Memphis, Tennessee, wanted to find a way to get more of his students into college. Back in 2002, the public school located on Elvis Presley Blvd. wasn't exactly known for its academic aptitude. Back then, graduating seniors were bringing in less than $5 million in scholarship offers for the entire school. But Sparks felt the school could do better. So he created a competition. The 30+ club was the first weapon in the battle to get students more money for college. There was only one criterion for membership: a score of 30 or higher on the ACT. By encouraging students to score high on the national standardized test, Sparks ensured that his students would be in the running for top scholarships. Students who achieved entrance into the club had their scholarship offer letters and scores posted on bulletin boards in the school.

But Sparks wasn't finished. He created the Fortune 500 club, providing exclusive membership only to students who could achieve more than $100,000 in scholarships. The combination of the 30+ club and the Fortune 500 club helped to spur students to achieve. The WHS graduating senior class brought in more than $30 million in scholarship offers in 2010–11.

APPLY, APPLY, AND APPLY AGAIN

Another facet of the Whitehaven High School's scholarship program was playing the odds. Anyone who has guided students through a college scholarship application understands that the process can become a numbers game. The more applications you complete, the better your chances of securing a scholarship. While the average high school student applies for two to three scholarships, WHS' millionaire club members applied for ten times that number—about thirty or forty.

BECOME A SUPER COLLEGE CANDIDATE

By now everyone applying to college knows you have to do more than get good grades to stand out. If you want to rise to the top of the scholarship heap, you're going to have to be extraordinary. You can't just volunteer at your local soup kitchen—that's a given. You might have to start your *own* soup kitchen to be considered above your peers. To be a part of the million-dollar scholarship club, you're going to have to go above and beyond to pull down that six-figure college gift.

So let's break down what it takes to be a million-dollar scholar:

- **Start early.** It's never too early to research scholarship opportunities as well as plan your scholarship strategy. Practice writing your personal statement, essay, interviewing skills, and so on to get yourself acquainted with the scholarship process.

- **Make applying a group activity.** Everyone loves a good competition, and it seems earning scholarship money is no exception. At Whitehaven High School, teachers publicly listed the scholarship earnings of students with more than $100,000. WHS also had a scoreboard in front of its school that highlighted scholarship amounts, not just football scores.

- **Don't forget the academics.** Many scholarships have an academic threshold, so you want to make sure to get above that to open more opportunities.

- **Keep Your Options Open.** There are critics who say that applying for scholarships you have no intention of using is not appropriate. But how do you know where you want to go until you figure out how to pay for it? Don't pigeon-hole yourself into one option. If you don't get your first-choice, you'll at least have something to fall back upon.

- **Be sincere.** You may think it's all about the numbers, but you become a million-dollar scholar through authenticity not fakery. Apply to scholarships that fit your passion, purpose, and educational prowess. And apply to schools you actually want to attend. Applying for scholarships and grants take time, and you don't want to waste it on pipe dreams.

Snap and Chat: Use Your Fingertips and Social Media to Pay for College

Felecia Hatcher
Author of *The C Student's Guide to Scholarships* **and** *Start Your Business on a Ramen Noodle Budget*

Snapchat, Instagram, Facebook, Twitter—every day a new social media platform is being launched to suck more of our precious time away. As a prospective college student trying to snag scholarship dollars, every second counts. But what if I told you that you don't have to sacrifice your time on social media and that you could find thousands of scholarship dollars and opportunities by using your smartphone and your thumbs!

It's said that more than $1 billion in scholarships goes un-awarded each year. You may think that this money is being hidden on purpose. I promise you that colleges and scholarship committees are not trying to hide the money from you; they are actually starting to use social media more and more to get the information directly to you. Currently, there are thousands of social media sites on the Internet, and these sites could possibly bring you one step closer to paying for college. Keep reading to find out how you can use social media and crowd funding sites to get creative with your search and not only think outside the box, but also think outside the application.

TWITTER

Twitter allows you to send and receive short messages of 280 characters or less in real time. The one thing that is great about Twitter is that it has a search bar that allows you to search for tweets from anyone or any entity that belongs to the social network. By using special keywords in the search bar, you should be able to find scholarship information the organization tweeted about and direct links to scholarship applications.

Go to the search bar in Twitter and type in the following keywords:

"Scholarship Deadline"

"Scholarship + [Your State]"

"Scholarship PDF"

"Scholarship Deadline http"

GOOGLE IT!

I jokingly tell people that I feel like I can rule the world with my smartphone, 2 safety pins, a rubber band, and Google. Need a restaurant recommendation? Google it! Need to research the best place to get school supplies for a project? Google it! Need to find money for your college education? Google it! Yes, believe it or not, it may be just that simple. But in order to not be bombarded with thousands of useless results, you must use the right keywords. Here is a short list of some keyword combinations that will yield great results in your scholarship search.

You can use the same search terms previously used for your Twitter searches for Google, as well as the following:

Scholarship + 2018

Scholarship + 2019

Scholarship + Deadline + Current Month

Scholarship + [your city/hometown]

Scholarship + [your race/ethnicity/religion]

Scholarship + [your talent]

You can also replace the word *scholarship* with *grant* or *fellowship*.

CROWD FUNDING

So, you applied but didn't win that big $25,000 scholarship. Don't despair—put the power of your network of family, friends, and social media followers to work, and create your own scholarship through crowd funding! With crowd funding, you can get 5,000 strangers to donate $5 each, which equals $25,000 . . . right?

No, I'm not talking about standing on a busy corner and playing your guitar. The following websites allow you to reach out to your friends and family or total strangers; pitch your need through a profile, pictures, and compelling video; and creatively fundraise your way to funding your college education.

Paypal.com

commonbond.co

ScholarMatch.org

Gofundme.com

Indiegogo.com

TIPS TO HELP YOU MAXIMIZE YOUR CHANCES OF GETTING FUNDING

Tell a compelling story through video: Writing an essay is one way to let your personality shine through, but nothing is better than seeing you! Use social media platforms like Instagram and YouTube to create short videos that showcase who you are and why you deserve the scholarships, and get as many people as you can to share them. Scholarship committees know that you need money, that's a given. But you want to captivate the committee with an exciting story that will keep them viewing and opening up their wallets with each word. Tell them who you are and what makes you and your needs different from other students. Most importantly, tell them why they should care enough to part with their money. Get creative!

Create an exciting profile: Photos and video go a long way when you are creating profiles on crowd-funding sites, or even on an application that asks for additional information. Take the time to capture great pictures that really let your personality show through. There are an increasing number of applications asking for video submissions. This is your time to shine, so take out your camera and start shooting testimonials from teachers, coaches, and guidance counselors raving about how fabulous you are instead of (or in addition to) submitting the traditional recommendation letter. Capture video when you are doing community service work, working at your part-time job, playing sports, or engaging in your hobbies. Remember photos and video paint the best picture and make the need *real.*

Tip: Use WordPress.com to create a portfolio that not only showcases your education and your resume but also your talents and hobbies. Colleges and Scholarship committees are always searching for well-rounded students!

Don't be afraid to ask for help: Let me put it frankly: The truth is you only get what you ask for! Networks like Facebook, Twitter, LinkedIn, and YouCaring.com allow you to amplify your message, so put the message out there. If you don't ask for the help and let everyone know, then you can't expect anyone to assist you.

So, the next time your parents tell you to get off Facebook or Twitter or to put down your phone, tell them that you are tweeting or searching for scholarship dollars.

CLEAN UP YOUR ACT: SPRUCE UP YOUR INTERNET AND SOCIAL MEDIA PRESENCE

Social media is a huge part of today's social realm. There is a good chance that you probably communicate with your friends on Facebook and Twitter more then you do in person. While these social networks are great for connecting with friends and family, and even meeting new people, they can hurt your scholarship efforts if you are not careful. Having this information in mind, set aside some time before, or directly after, you mail out that first scholarship application to investigate and (if necessary) clean up your online presence.

Are you wondering why this is necessary? I bet you think that your Facebook page has nothing to do with your scholarship application. Well, if these are your thoughts, you are unfortunately very wrong. There's an excellent chance that a scholarship organization will spend time searching for you on the Internet. If you're shuddering at the thought of the scholarship committee members seeing anything on your page, I recommend you follow these tips for "scrubbing" your web reputation squeaky clean.

1. **Google yourself.**

   Search for every possible variation of your name on Google. If anything unbecoming pops up in the search results, do what you can to have it taken down.

2. **Check your social media sites.**

   This includes Facebook, LinkedIn, Twitter, Flickr, Instagram, Tumblr, WordPress, and so on. Make sure all the content on these sites is dignified and academic, meaning that it's serious and grammatically correct. It would be wise to include blog posts about social issues, quotes from famous people you admire, poetry you've written (not including dirty limericks), and so on. Your social media pages need to present you as being smart, mature, and hardworking. If they don't do those things, then clean up your pages, and replace them with content that does. I am not saying that you have to be boring; just be cautious of how everything you post on the Internet *looks* because it's like a tattoo—once it is posted, it's difficult to remove.

3. **Web pages that can't be scrubbed should be hidden.**

   Try to use nicknames when creating your social profiles, and always use the highest privacy settings so that people must be approved in order to see the page. After doing these things, you should still log out and check what information appears on your default profile page. If a picture that depicts you partying or anything else that would be unflattering to a scholarship committee appears, log back in and replace it with something else.

4. **Take those videos off YouTube.**
   Do this right now. You know which ones I mean.

5. **Remain vigilant.**
   Just because you cleaned up your web presence today doesn't mean it will be clean as a whistle next week. Be aware of what others are posting and tagging with your name. Some search engines even allow you to set up "alerts" to warn you every time your name shows up on the web. I would recommend taking advantage of these helpful alerts.

6. **Check your voicemail.**
   This is very important. If you have an inappropriate ring-back tone or voicemail greeting, you need to either replace it with something professional and appropriate, or kiss your scholarship chances goodbye.

ABOUT THE AUTHOR

Felecia Hatcher-Pearson is a trailblazing social entrepreneur with an authentic voice for change. For the past decade, Felecia has dedicated her life to inspiring a new generation of leaders through her conversational talks on entrepreneurship, college funding, and personal branding.

As an author and social entrepreneur, Felecia Hatcher-Pearson has been honored by the White House as a 2014 Champion of Change for STEM Access & Diversity, Black Enterprise Innovator of the Week, and featured *Essence Magazine* Tech Master. She has been featured on NBC's *Today Show,* MSNBC, The Cooking Channel, and Grio's "100 African American's Making History" for her very successful company, Feverish Ice Cream & Gourmet Pops, where she is former Chief Popsicle.

As a "C" student in high school, Felicia beat the odds and won over $100,000 in scholarships to attend college by getting creative. She used her experience and knack for personal marketability to start her first business called Urban Excellence as a freshman in college. She built and ran innovative college-prep programs for DeVry University and companies such as MECA, AMPS Institute, the YMCA, the TED Center, and the Urban League.

In 2008, after falling flat on her face while attempting to chase an ice cream truck in heels, Felecia started her own gourmet ice pops and dessert catering company, Feverish Pops. Felecia has presented engaging talks like "Embracing Failure" at Google London and "Entrepreneurship and Managing Investor Relations" at SXSW. She has spoken as part of the White House Young America Series, at Coca-Cola's headquarters, and at TEDxMiami and TEDxJamaica. Felecia is also the author of three books, *Start Your Business on a Ramen Noodle Budget, The C Students Guide to Scholarships,* and *Focused.*

Aside from being a successful entrepreneur and author, Felecia Hatcher-Pearson has dedicated her life to turning kids and young adults from undeserved communities into entrepreneurs and exposing them to careers and entrepreneurial opportunities in technology with her Code Fever program and Black Tech Week initiatives that help to increase tech entrepreneurship funding and training to underserved Florida communities.

Ask the Experts: College Scholarships

Here are some frequently asked scholarship-related questions of college planning and admissions experts. You may have some of the same questions too.

Q: When college representatives visit high schools, do they offer a certain amount of scholarships to students who may be interested in attending that institution?

College reps do visit many high schools on recruiting trips, usually in the early to mid-fall and sometimes in the late spring. Watch your guidance office bulletin board or school website to see when representatives from the colleges you might be interested in are visiting your school or a location near your home. Colleges do not offer a limited amount of scholarships based on where you go to high school. School representatives will discuss both need-based and, often, merit-based financial awards their college may provide. Scholarships might be available to students from your area for one reason or another, but, generally there aren't a specific number based on a particular high school. You should apply to the colleges in which you are interested and apply for both need-based financial aid and possible additional merit (non-need-based) scholarships for which you might qualify.

Q: How do I get a scholarship through the PSAT/NMSQT®?

The "NMSQT" in "PSAT/NMSQT" stands for the National Merit Scholarship Qualifying Test. About 55,000 of the more than 1.3 million students taking that test each year will be selected as National Merit Commended Students. Going into senior year, in September, smaller proportions of students will be selected as Semifinalists, then Finalists, and, finally, Merit Scholars (who can earn $2,500 awards). See www.nationalmerit.org for more information on these programs.

Q: I am a 4.0 student and I'm in the National Honor Society. Do you know the level of difficulty of getting an NHS scholarship?

The National Honor Society (www.NHS.us) awards 200 scholarships of $1,000 each year. Your NHS chapter can nominate two students to compete for the scholarships, so the first hurdle is to get one of your chapter's nominations. It's pretty competitive after that, since some highly talented students across the country are in the pool for these merit-based awards. But go for it—you could be one of the lucky winners.

Q: What do I need to do to qualify for a merit scholarship?

It is important to research the colleges you are interested in and determine their merit scholarship criteria. For example, a school might state that it will guarantee a scholarship as long as the student has a certain grade point average, minimum SAT®/ACT® scores, and a specific rank in high school. It is critical to make an in-person appointment with an admissions representative to find out all of the details and requirements for obtaining any of the institution's scholarships. You can also search for merit-based scholarships online.

Q: What are some requirements for athletic scholarships?

The website www.ncaa.org is a good place to look into the differences between Division I, II, and III colleges and universities, and recruiting prospects. Division I and II schools (except the Ivies) offer athletic scholarships. Division III colleges do not. Minimum requirements for scholarships are actually quite low on the whole. However, particular colleges and universities have their own admission and scholarship requirements that you'll need to meet in order to be recruited and admitted.

As you begin the athletic recruiting process and talk with coaches, ask them about their college's recruiting and admission requirements, as well as typical scholarship packages for athletes. If you visit a school's campus on an "official visit," talk with other players about their recruiting experiences and scholarship packages. There are typically minimum college GPA and "reasonable academic progress" requirements that you must meet in order to maintain your eligibility to play college sports and keep your scholarship.

If you want to scope out some athletic scholarships, you can take a look through the scholarship search tool at www.petersons.com and also in this book.

Q: Are grants better than scholarships?

Grants and scholarships are both "free money," in the sense that you don't need to repay them. Grants are usually need-based, while scholarships are based on merit of some kind, or they are a basic discounting of tuition. They are equal, though a hitch with scholarships is that sometimes you have to meet conditions, such as participation in a sport or another activity or maintaining a certain GPA, in order to renew the scholarship. Always read the fine print when evaluating scholarship offers to

see how long they last, if they are annually renewable, and what the conditions are that are associated with them.

Q: Will my SAT® or ACT® score qualify me for a scholarship?

It's possible that a high score on these college admission tests will qualify you for a scholarship, though typically colleges like to see the score plus a certain GPA in combination for many of their merit-based scholarship opportunities. Sometimes colleges will elaborate on award criteria on their websites and in their informational materials, explaining that a certain SAT, or SAT/GPA, or GPA level will qualify all or a selection of students for certain levels of awards. Other times, it will be apparent that if your scores are in the top third or so of a college's range, you will likely qualify for a merit-based award (aka a discount on tuition) if that institution has a non-need-based aid program. Most do.

Winning the Scholarship with a Winning Essay

Who knew it was going to be this hard? You've already dealt with SO much: the SAT®, doing community service, excelling in your AP® class, etc. Convincing your parents that you will be fine 1,500 miles from home and that each and every one of those college application fees are, yes, absolutely necessary! You even learned calculus for goodness sake!

And now in front of you—yet, for right now, somehow out of reach—the golden ticket to make it all come true. Just 500 words (more or less) separate you from those hallowed halls: It's the scholarship essay.

IT HAS TO BE EASY, RIGHT?

Much as you may feel like, c'mon, I'm worth it, just give me the scholarship money, we all know it just doesn't work like that. Because you know what—lots of students are worth it! And lots of students are special, just like you! And where does that leave a scholarship selection committee in deciding to whom their money should be awarded? Yes, now you are catching on—they will pore over *everyone*'s scholarship essay.

So, first and foremost, write your scholarship essay in a way that makes it EASY for the scholarship-awarding committees to do their job! It's almost like a partnership—you show them (in 500 words, more or less) why YOU ARE THE MOST WORTHY RECIPIENT, and they say, thank you, you're right, here is a scholarship for you, and everyone wins! Easy, right?

SORRY—IT REALLY ISN'T THAT EASY

What? You are still sitting there in front of a blank computer screen with nary a thought or sentence? Understood. It's really not that easy. That, too, is part of the point.

No doubt that your GPA, SAT scores, volunteer efforts, leadership roles, and community service are immensely important, but again, you must remember that, during the process of selecting an award recipient, pretty much all the applicants are going to be stellar on some level. And so the scholarship-awarding committee uses your essay to see what sets you apart from the crowd. They are looking for a reason to select you over everyone else.

Your scholarship essay serves many purposes. You have to convince the scholarship-awarding committee you are able to do the following:

- Effectively communicate through the written word
- Substantiate your merit and unique qualities
- Follow directions and adhere to guidelines

A winning scholarship essay can mean up to tens of thousands of dollars for your college education, so let's get started on putting that money in YOUR hands!

EFFECTIVE WRITTEN COMMUNICATION

Be Passionate

Let's face it—you have already written lots of essays. And, we won't tell, but most were probably about topics that were as interesting to you as watching paint dry, right? But you plowed through them and even managed to get some good grades along the way. You may think about just "plowing through" your scholarship essay the same way—mustering up the same amount of excitement you feel when you have to watch old videos of your Aunt Monica on her summer camping trips. But that would be a huge mistake!

An important feature of all winning essays is that they are written on subjects about which the author is truly passionate. Think about it—it actually takes a good bit of effort to fake passion for a subject. But when you are genuinely enthusiastic about something, the words and thoughts flow much more easily, and your passion and energy naturally shine through in your writing. Therefore, when you are choosing your scholarship essay topic, be sure it is something about which you truly care and for which you can show affinity—keeping both you and your reader interested and intrigued!

Be Positive

You've probably heard the expression: "If you don't have anything nice to say, don't say anything at all." Try to steer clear of essays that are too critical, pessimistic, or antagonistic. This doesn't mean that your essay shouldn't acknowledge a serious problem or that everything has to have a happy ending. But it does mean that you should not just write about the negative. If you are writing about a problem, present solutions. If your story doesn't have a happy ending, write about what you learned from the experience and how you would do things differently if faced with a similar situation in the future. Your optimism is what makes the scholarship-awarding committee excited about giving you money to pursue your dreams. Use positive language and be proud to share yourself and your accomplishments. Everyone likes an uplifting story, and even scholarship judges want to feel your enthusiasm and zest for life.

Be Clear and Concise

Don't fall into the common essay-writing trap of using general statements instead of specific ones. All scholarship judges read at least one essay that starts with "Education is the key to success." And that means nothing to them. What does mean something is writing about how your tenth-grade English teacher opened your eyes to the understated beauty and simplicity of haiku—how less can be more—and how that then translated into you donating some of your old video games to a homeless shelter where you now volunteer once a month. That's powerful stuff! It's a very real story, clearly correlating education to a successful outcome. Focusing on a specific and concise example from your life helps readers relate to you and your experiences. It also guarantees you bonus points for originality!

Edit and Proofread and Then Edit and Proofread

There is an old saying: "Behind every good writer is an even better editor." Find people (friends, siblings, coaches, teachers, guidance counselors) to read your essay, provide feedback on how to make it better, and edit it for silly, sloppy mistakes. Some people will read your essay and find issues with your grammar. Others will read your essay and point out how one paragraph doesn't make sense in relation to another paragraph. Some people will tell you how to give more examples to better make your point. All of those people are giving you great information, and you need to take it all in and use it to your advantage! However, don't be overwhelmed by it, and don't let it become all about what everyone else thinks. It's your essay and your thoughts—the goal of editing and proofreading is to clean up the rough edges and make the entire essay shine!

And when you do get to that magical point where you think "DONE!"—instead, just put the essay aside for a few days. Come back to it with an open mind and read, edit, and proofread it one last time. Check it one last time

for spelling and grammar fumbles. Check it one last time for clarity and readability (reading it out loud helps!). Check it one last time to ensure it effectively communicates why you are absolutely the winning scholarship candidate.

YOUR UNIQUE QUALITIES

It's one thing to help out at the local library a few hours a week; it's a completely different thing if you took it upon yourself to suggest, recruit, organize, and lead a fundraising campaign to buy 10 new laptops for kids to use at the library!

And don't simply rattle off all your different group memberships. Write about things you did that demonstrate leadership and initiative within those groups. Did you recruit new members or offer to head up a committee? Did you find a way for the local news station to cover your event or reach out to another organization and collaborate on an activity? Think about your unique qualities and how you have used them to bring about change.

A SLICE OF YOUR LIFE

While one goal of your essay is surely to explain why you should win the scholarship money, an equally important goal is to reveal something about you, something that makes it easy to see why you should win. Notice we said to reveal "something" about you and not "everything" about you. Most likely, the rest of the scholarship application gathers quite a bit of information about you. The essay is where you need to hone in on just one aspect of your unique talents, one aspect of an experience, one aspect of reaching a goal. It's not about listing all your accomplishments in your essay (again, you probably did that on the application). It's about sharing a slice of your life—telling your story and giving your details about what makes YOU memorable.

YOUR ACCOMPLISHMENTS, LOUD AND PROUD

Your extracurricular activities illustrate your personal priorities and let the scholarship selection committee know what's important to you. Being able to elaborate on your accomplishments and awards within those activities certainly bolsters your chances of winning the scholarship. Again, though, be careful to not just repeat what is already on the application itself. Use your essay to focus on a specific accomplishment (or activity or talent or award) of which you are most proud.

Did your community suffer through severe flooding last spring? And did you organize a clothing drive for neighbors who were in need? How did that make you feel? What feedback did you get? How did it inspire your desire to become a climatologist?

Were school budget cuts going to mean the disbanding of some afterschool clubs? Did you work with teachers and parents to write a proposal to present to the school board, addressing how new funds could be raised in order to save the clubs? How did that make you feel? What feedback did you get? How did it inspire you to start a writing lab for junior high kids?

You have done great things—think about that one special accomplishment and paint the picture of how it has made you wiser, stronger, or more compassionate to the world around you. Share the details!

But Don't Go Overboard

A five-hanky story may translate into an Oscar-worthy movie, but rarely does it translate into winning a scholarship. If your main reason for applying for the scholarship is that you feel you deserve the money because of how much suffering you have been through, you need a better reason. Scholarship selection committees are not really interested in awarding money to people with problems; they want to award money to people who solve problems. While it's just fine to write about why you need the scholarship money to continue your education, it's not fine for your essay to simply be a laundry list of family tragedies and hardships.

So, instead of presenting a sob story, present how you have succeeded and what you have accomplished despite the hardships and challenges you faced. Remember that everyone has faced difficulties. What's unique about you is how YOU faced your difficulties and overcame them. That is what makes your essay significant and memorable.

FOLLOWING DIRECTIONS

Does Your Essay Really Answer the Question?

Have you ever been asked one question but felt like there was another question that was really being asked? Maybe your dad said something like, "Tell me about your new friend Logan." But what he really meant to ask you was, "Tell me about your new friend Logan. Do his lip rings and tattoos mean he's involved in things I don't want you involved in?"

The goal of every scholarship judge is to determine the best applicant out of a pool of applicants who are all rather similar. Pay attention and you'll find that the essay question is an alternate way for you to answer the real question the scholarship-awarding committee wants to ask. For instance, an organization giving an award to students who plan to study business might ask, "Why do you want to study business?" But their real underlying question is, "Why are you the best future business person to whom we should give our money?" If there is a scholarship for students who want to become doctors, you can bet that 99 percent of the students applying want to become doctors. And if you apply for that scholarship with an essay simply delving into your lifelong desire to be a potter, well, that doesn't make you unique, it makes you pretty much unqualified for that opportunity. Be sure to connect your personal skills, characteristics, and experiences with the objectives of the scholarship and its awarding organization.

Does Your Essay Theme Tie In?

Let's say that you are applying for a community service-based award and, on the application, you go ahead and list all the community service groups you belong to and all the awards you have won. But in your essay, you write about how homeless people should find a job instead of sitting on street corners begging for money. Hey—everyone is entitled to their opinion, but would you agree that there is some sort of disconnect between your application and your essay? And no doubt you have made the scholarship-awarding committee wonder the same thing.

So how do you ensure your essay doesn't create a conflicting message? You need to examine the theme of your essay and how it relates both to your application and the reason the scholarship exists in the first place. If the scholarship-funding organization seeks to give money to someone who wants a career in public relations and your essay focuses on how you are not really a "people person," well, you can see how that sends a mixed message to your reader.

Think about it this way: The theme of your essay should naturally flow around the overarching purpose or goal of the organization awarding the scholarship money. Once you have clarified this nugget, you can easily see if and how your words tie in to the organization's vision of whom their scholarship winner is.

Three More Pieces of Advice

1. **Follow the essay length guidelines closely.** You certainly don't want your essay disqualified simply because it was too long or too short!

2. **The deadline is the deadline.** A day late and you could certainly be more than a dollar short in terms of the award money that isn't going to be awarded to you if your application is not received by the due date. Begin the essay writing process well in advance of the scholarship deadline. Writing and editing and rewriting takes time so you should probably allow yourself at least 2 weeks to write your scholarship essay.

3. **Tell the truth.** No need to say anything further on that, right? Right.

Getting in the Minority Scholarship Mix

Did you know that a great duck call can win you scholarship money in the Chick and Sophie Major Memorial Duck Calling Contest?

Website: http://www.stuttgartarkansas.org/scholarship-contest.html

Perhaps duck-calling is not your calling but creativity with Duck° brand duct tape is. If so, the "Stuck at Prom" scholarship may be just for you—design prom ware for you and your date and win some moola!

Website: http://www.stuckatprom.com

How about this tall order? Tall Clubs International awards scholarships to men who are taller than 6'2" or women who are taller than 5'10".

Website: http://www.tallclubfoundation.org/ scholarship-program.html

Oh? Not necessarily the minority group you had in mind? That's OK because guess what? In this day and age, just about everyone is a minority of some sort. It all depends on a scholarship benefactor's definition of minority.

In the college realm, the word "minority" takes on a myriad of meanings. One definition of a minority that often springs to mind is of someone of an underrepresented ethnicity, such as Native Americans, African Americans, or Hispanic Americans. No question there. Similarly though, a minority can be someone pursuing an underrepresented college major, such as paranormal research. Think that all scholarships for minorities target United States–specific groups? Think again. For example, Canadian students, whether they plan to study at home or abroad, can qualify for scholarships for aboriginals. Getting the picture? The key is to use your own unique qualities as you search for scholarships. Think about your gender, your family's economic status, your religious background, and your geographic locale just to start the ball rolling. Once you broadly frame your search along those lines, you'll quickly see how easily you can qualify for a scholarship!

AM I REALLY A MINORITY?

No matter the source—federal, state, professional organization, private endowment, corporate donor, college, or university—they all offer minority scholarships, looking to create diversity and inclusion in an increasingly global marketplace.

It's more than probable that you fit into at least one of the ever-expanding minority scholarship categories—nearly everyone does—by some broadly based definition of minority. Some of the niche scholarship "minorities" have already been mentioned. Now let's take a look at some of the broader categories—one of which likely fits you!

African American Students

While African Americans make up a large U.S. minority group, they are still met with one of the biggest barriers to college enrollment—money. To combat that challenge, scholarships for African American students have grown over the years, with some of the best sources of funding found within partnerships between minority organizations and corporate sponsors.

As the nation's largest minority education organization, the United Negro College Fund (UNCF) provides operating funds for 38-member historically black colleges and universities (HBCUs), along with scholarships and internships for students at about 900 institutions. The UNCF has helped more than 400,000 students attend and graduate college with the more than $3.3 billion it has raised—more funds helping minorities attend college than any other entity outside of the U.S. government.

United Negro College Fund
8260 Willow Oaks Corporate Drive
P.O. Box 10444
Fairfax, VA 22031-8044
Phone: 800-331-2244
Website: www.uncf.org

Hispanic American Students

Fortunately, over the years, the U.S. government has contributed millions of dollars toward startup costs for the development of Hispanic universities and colleges and toward already established Hispanic universities and colleges. The effort has been paying off with dramatic increases in college enrollment by Hispanic American students. Scholarship programs for Hispanic American students look to increase the number of Hispanic students studying in subject areas most underrepresented by them, for instance, the sciences, engineering, math, and technology.

As the nation's leading Hispanic higher-education fund, the Hispanic Scholarship Fund (HSF) works to remove the barriers keeping many Hispanic American students from earning a college degree. Over the past 35 years, HSF has awarded more than $430 million in scholarships (over 150 types of scholarships) and supported a wide range of outreach and education programs for both college students and their families.

Hispanic Scholarship Fund
55 Second Street, Suite 1500
San Francisco, CA 94105
Phone: 877-HSF-INFO (877-473-4636)
E-mail: scholar1@hsf.net
Website: www.hsf.net

Asian American Students

Identifying yourself as Asian American means you probably consider yourself Cambodian, Hmong, Laotian, Malaysian, Okinawan, Tahitian, or Thai—just to name a few possibilities. As a somewhat smaller, yet growing, minority group, Asian Americans attend college more than any other minority group and tend to stay in college once they have enrolled. Excellent merit-based aid sources for Asian American students include cultural organizations, university departments such as law and journalism, and professional organizations.

The Asian & Pacific Islander American Scholarship Fund (APIASF), founded in 2003, has provided more than $50 million in scholarships to Asian and Pacific Islander Americans with financial need.

The Asian & Pacific Islander American
    Scholarship Fund
2025 M Street NW, Suite 610
Washington, DC 20036

Phone: 202-986-6892
Phone (toll-free): 877-808-7032
Fax: 202-530-0643
E-mail: info@apiasf.org
Website: http://www.apiasf.org/

Native American Students

Native American (inclusive of American Indians and Native Alaskans) students make up the smallest minority population on college campuses. As you explore scholarship opportunities for Native Americans, you may find that you'll need proof of your Native American status, which means your Certificate of Indian Blood (CIB), as well as belonging to a well-recognized tribe. If you are like most Native American descendants, though, you will probably not have this proof, as many tribes change names and have nonexistent documentation records. If somehow you do have a CIB and belong to a tribe, you may have an upper hand in qualifying for some more esoteric scholarship and grant programs.

American Indian College Fund

Located in Denver, Colorado, the mission of the American Indian College Fund (AICF) is threefold: to spread awareness of the Fund and of tribal colleges and universities; to raise college scholarship funds for American Indian students attending tribal and mainstream colleges; and to raise money for other needs and projects of the tribal schools.

The AICF awards approximately 5,000 college scholarships a year. Monies given to individual schools are used to award Tribal College Scholarships to candidates of each school's choosing. Other undergraduate scholarships are awarded directly from the AICF to American Indian students attending both tribal and mainstream colleges and universities.

The American Indian College Fund
8333 Greenwood Boulevard
Denver, CO 80221
Phone: 303-426-8900
Phone (toll-free): 800-776-3863
Website: www.collegefund.org

American Indian Graduate Center

Another large source of student scholarships and financial aid for Native Americans is the American

Indian Graduate Center (AIGC), which provides monies to both undergraduate and graduate students.

The mission of the AIGC is to improve the cultural and economic well-being of American Indians and Native Alaskans both individually and tribally. Their efforts focus on developing educated and forward-thinking leaders who will steer their communities into an era of prosperity, productivity, and self-reliance.

The AIGC, with the generous support of the Tommy Hilfiger Corporation Foundation, also administers the All Native American High School Academic Team, a program recognizing Native American/Alaska Native students who demonstrate superior success in academics, leadership, and American Indian community service.

As part of the AIGC's overall mission, this program promotes academic excellence and the pursuit of higher education among Native American and Alaska Native students, with the goal of preparing them for future roles as community leaders and role models. All of the students recognized by this program receive financial awards to pay for the cost of attending the college or university of their choice.

The American Indian Graduate Center
3701 San Mateo Boulevard NE #200
Albuquerque, NM 87110
Phone: 505-881-4584
Website: www.aigcs.org/aigc-scholarship-fellowship-
opportunities

Other Opportunities

In addition to the AICF and the AIGC, there are several other organizations that provide various student scholarships to Native Americans:

- **American Indian Science and Engineering Society (AISES):** With the goal of substantially increasing "the representation of American Indian and Alaskan Natives in engineering, science and other related technology disciplines," the AISES awards university scholarships to Native American undergraduate and graduate students pursuing degrees in various areas of engineering and science. (www.aises.org/scholarships)
- **Association on American Indian Affairs (AAIA):** Offers college scholarship opportunities to both undergraduate and graduate students demonstrating financial need. (https://www.indian-affairs.org/scholarships.html)

- **Indian Health Service (IHS):** As an arm of the U.S. Department of Health and Human Services, the IHS awards university scholarships to pay for the education and training of undergraduate, graduate, and doctoral students pursuing degrees in healthcare related areas. (https://www.ihs.gov/scholarship/)
- **Intertribal Timber Council (ITC):** Dedicated to improving the management of natural resources that are important to Native American communities, the ITC sponsors a variety of different undergraduate scholarships and fellowship opportunities each year. (www.itcnet.org/about_us/scholarships.html)

Interracial Students

There is an interesting trend in minority scholarships where scholarship-funding organizations seek to include students of mixed heritage, blended cultures, and students whose ethnic backgrounds don't fit neatly into one particular category. Search for prizes tagged as "interracial scholarships," "multicultural scholarships," or "multiethnic scholarships."

Lesbian, Gay, Bisexual, and Transgender Students

Lesbian, gay, bisexual, and transgender (LGBT) students are recognized as a legitimate minority, and many colleges and organizations offer scholarships to this group. As an LGBT student, also be on the lookout for scholarship opportunities for sons and daughters of gay and lesbian parents, as well as friends and allies of the LGBT community.

Since its inception in 2001, the Point Foundation has invested more than $3 million in outstanding gay, lesbian, bisexual, and transgender students. An average Point Scholarship is about $13,600 and covers tuition, books, supplies, room and board, transportation, and living expenses.

Point Foundation
5055 Wilshire Boulevard, Suite 501
Los Angeles, CA 90036
Phone: 323-933-1234
Fax: 866-397-6468
E-mail: info@pointfoundation.org
Website: www.pointfoundation.org

EVERYONE NEEDS A GOOD RESOURCE

From specialized databases to award programs serving as umbrella organizations for numerous other organizations and awards, many resources are out there for criteria-based scholarships, all with one goal—to help you find the money you need to get you on your college path.

CHCI (Congressional Hispanic Caucus Institute)

CHCI provides a free, comprehensive list of scholarships, internships, and fellowships for Hispanic students.

Congressional Hispanic Caucus Institute
1128 16th Street NW
Washington, DC 20036
Phone: 202-543-1771
Phone: (toll-free) 800-EXCEL-DC (392-3532)
Fax: 202-548-8799
Websites: www.chci.org
www.chcinextopp.net

Gates Millennium Scholars

The Gates Millennium Scholars program was founded by a grant from the Bill and Melinda Gates Foundation with the intention of increasing the number of African Americans, Native Americans, Asian Americans, and Hispanic Americans enrolling in and completing undergraduate and graduate degree programs.

Gates Millennium Scholars
P.O. Box 10500
Fairfax, VA 22031-8044
Phone (toll-free): 877-690-4677
Website: www.gmsp.org

GETTING CREATIVE WITH MINORITY SCHOLARSHIPS

Now that you are really thinking outside of the box, you may consider one or more of your outstanding features as the conduit to classifying yourself as a minority. And if you still need some more inspiration:

- Juniata College in Pennsylvania offers a scholarship for left-handed students.
- Little People of America offers a scholarship to adult students who are 4'10" or shorter.
- There are even scholarships for white males offered by The Former Majority Association for Equality, a nonprofit group in Texas.

Be creative and get in the mix! To which minority groups do *you* belong?

What to Do If You Don't Win a Scholarship, Grant, or Prize

More than 20 million students will enroll in the nation's colleges and universities this year, and you can bet nearly all of them will be vying for the more than $4 billion in private scholarship money that's available. In fact, 85 percent of all first-time undergraduate students attending a four-year college receive some type of financial aid—including scholarships, grants, awards, and student loans.

Yet, even though billions of dollars are out there for the grasping, the average scholarship award may just be a few thousand dollars. That's only going to put a minor dent in the more than $20,000 annual price tag for in-state tuition, room, and board at a public four-year institution (over $40,000 for private). So, unless you started working as a toddler you're going to have to do something spectacular to avoid buckling under a mountain of student loan debt to get your degree.

Applying for grants and private scholarships is a given. But what if your living room table is filling up with denial letters? What do you do then? Well, the first thing is not to panic. There are plenty of ways to pay for college without going into an enormous amount of debt. Here are some tips and suggestions that will help you to formulate a back-up plan if you miss out on the college scholarship lottery.

IF AT FIRST YOU DON'T SUCCEED

A rejection letter doesn't mean no, it really means, "Not right now." There is nothing wrong with applying for a private scholarship, fellowship, or grant again, even if you've been rejected. Just think, you'll have a leg up on everyone who is coming to the competition cold, as you've been there before. Before you dust off your essay from last year and shove it into an envelope this year, be sure to contact the organization and ask for feedback.

Sure, some may not be willing to speak to you, but you won't lose any sleep by trying. Often the best advice comes from the unlikeliest places, and asking pointed, mature questions about why your first application failed can only serve you in your college money hunt. In addition, the counsel might help you to improve an application for another organization. So follow up on those who've said no—you never know what kind of great tips and suggestions they will have for you. Here are some questions you may ask when you seek feedback:

- Did my application get rejected because of a procedural mistake? Did I mess up the application process? Did I meet the deadline? Were all my documents included?
- Was my personal statement/essay well done? How could it have been improved?
- Could you give me suggestions on how best to apply for your scholarship again?

Note: You, of course, can't do any of this if you waited until the last minute to fill out your scholarship application, so it pays to start your quest for college treasure early.

YOU CAN APPLY FOR SCHOLARSHIPS WHILE IN COLLEGE

Even if you've already started your college career with your scholarship coffers empty and your student loan debt toppling over, do not fret. You can still apply for grants, scholarships, and programs that do not require you go into debt while you're attending school. Many scholarships are not automatically renewed, and if students do not apply for them, there may be more cash for you. Create an application cycle for every year you attend school. You never know what opportunity you may be missing if you do not at least try to apply while attending school.

WORK NOW, NOT LATER

It used to be that flipping burgers at the local fast-food joint was the way most college students paid for college. And to be sure that option is still open. But the recent technology boom fueled by the monetization of the Internet has allowed even the youngest among us to become entrepreneurs. From teenage search engine app maker Nick D'Alosio, who has raised capital from one of China's billionaires, to the pre-adolescent Mallory Kiveman, who invented a lollipop to cure the hiccups, the spirit of innovation runs deep among the young. Use technology to start your version of a lemonade stand, and you may make enough in your senior year to pay for college and beyond. Technology has allowed people to think better, smarter, and bigger than ever before. As you're working on that latest science project, think about ways to monetize it. It could be your ticket to a full-ride to college.

DON'T LEAVE MONEY ON THE TABLE

Did you know that only 1 in 10 undergraduate students receive a scholarship award? This isn't because there aren't enough scholarships available. On the contrary, millions of dollars in scholarship money go unclaimed because students do not apply for them.

Yes, that's right. College students, desperate to incur massive amounts of debts forget to apply for grants, miss deadlines, and sloppily fill out scholarship applications to ensure they get rejected and leave money on the table. You, of course, would never do that. But some people will.

Do not be one of those people. Make sure you are taking advantage of all your opportunities to gain debt-free money for college. In addition to applying for private scholarships, make sure you go beyond the Federal Pell Grant. Remember, there are state grants, local grants, need-based grants, merit grants, and college university grants that are available for students. Be sure to check with your admitting institution to make sure you haven't overlooked grants—many of which are automatically offered to students regardless of income.

PRACTICE SOME ALTRUISM

Though it may seem to have gone the way of milkshakes and quaint small-town post offices, there are still some programs that will help pay for your college education as long as you commit to performing public service. From AmeriCorps, which defrays college costs for students who work for nonprofits, or in high-need areas to the Public Service Loan Forgiveness Program, in which borrowers may qualify for forgiveness of the remaining balance of their Direct Loans after they make 120 qualifying payments on those loans while employed full time by certain public service employers, there are dozens of programs that will lower your college costs in exchange for public service. Even top-tier universities such as Harvard and Princeton are offering free tuition (Harvard

for just one year) for students who choose to work in public service careers. There are loan forgiveness programs for virtually every public service profession from state-appointed prosecutors, teachers, primary care doctors, and law enforcement officers; members of the armed forces; nurses and healthcare workers; and even Peace Corps volunteers. But beware—the programs have strict guidelines; one misstep and you could end up footing the bill for your entire college dream. And, as always, consult your tax advisor as current law categorizes the loan amount that is forgiven as income.

Here are some contacts for programs that pay down college costs for volunteerism or public service:

AmeriCorps

More than 75,000 adults work with thousands of non-profits around the country providing tutoring, mentoring, housing management, and a host of other services to the disadvantaged through AmeriCorps. In exchange they receive money to pay for college or graduate school, or they obtain forgiveness on student loans plus a pay check.

AmeriCorps
1201 New York Avenue, NW
Washington, DC 20525
Phone: 202-606-5000
TTY: 800-833-3722 (toll-free)
Website: www.nationalservice.gov/programs/
    americorps

National Health Service Corps

The National Health Service Corps awards scholarships to students who are pursuing careers in primary care. Students must be pursuing degrees in medicine, dentistry, nursing, and physician assistant studies.

National Health Corps
Phone: 800-221-9393 (toll-free)
Website: http://nhsc.hrsa.gov

Public Service Loan Forgiveness

Congress created the Public Service Loan Forgiveness Program in 2007 as an incentive for people to enter fields that focused on public service. The beneficial program offers qualified borrowers the opportunity to have their federal loans forgiven if they work in certain public service areas.

Website: www.studentaid.gov.

How to Use This Guide

The more than 3,500 award programs described in this book are organized into eleven broad categories that represent the major factors used to determine eligibility for scholarships, awards, and prizes. To build a basic list of awards available to you, look under the broad category or categories that fit your particular academic goals, skills, personal characteristics, or background. The categories are:

- Academic Fields/Career Goals
- Civic, Professional, Social, or Union Affiliation
- Corporate Affiliation
- Employment/Volunteer Experience
- Impairment
- Military Service
- Nationality or Ethnic Heritage
- Religious Affiliation
- Residence/Location of Study
- Talent/Interest Area
- Miscellaneous Criteria

The **Academic Fields/Career Goals** category is subdivided into 131 subject areas that are organized alphabetically by award sponsor. The **Military Service** category is subdivided alphabetically by branch of service. All other categories are organized alphabetically by the name of the award sponsor.

Full descriptive profiles appear in only one location in the book. Cross-references to the name and page number of the full descriptive profile appear at other locations under the other relevant categories for the award. The full description appears in the first relevant location in the book and cross-references later locations, so you will always be redirected toward the front of the book.

Your major field of study and career goals have central importance in college planning. As a result, we have combined these into a single category and have given this category precedence over the others. The **Academic Fields/Career Goals** section appears first in the book. If an academic major or career area is a criterion for a scholarship, the description of this award will appear in this section.

Within the **Academic Fields/Career Goals** section, cross-references are only from and to other academic fields or career areas. You will be able to locate relevant awards from nonacademic or noncareer criteria through the indexes in the back of this book.

For example, the full descriptive profile of a scholarship for any type of engineering student who resides in Ohio might appear under *Aviation/Aerospace*, which is the first engineering category heading in the **Academic Fields/Career Goals** section. Cross-references to this first listing may occur from any other relevant engineering or technological academic field subject area, such as *Chemical Engineering, Civil Engineering, Electrical Engineering/Electronics, Engineering-Related Technologies, Engineering/Technology, Mechanical Engineering,* or *Nuclear Science*. There would not be a cross-reference from the *Residence* category. However, the name of the award will appear in the Residence index under Ohio.

Within the major category sections, descriptive profiles are organized alphabetically by the name of the sponsoring organization. If more than one award from the same organization appears in a particular section, the awards are listed alphabetically under the sponsor name, which appears only once, by the name of the first award.

HOW THE PROFILES ARE ORGANIZED

Here are the elements of a full profile:

Name of Sponsoring Organization

These appear alphabetically under the appropriate category. In most instances, acronyms are given as full names. However, occasionally a sponsor will refer to itself by an acronym. In these instances, we present the sponsor's name as an acronym.

Website Address

Award Name

Brief Textual Description of the Award

Academic Fields/Career Goals (only in the Academic Fields/Career Goals section of the book)

This is a list of all academic or career subject terms that are assigned to this award.

Award

Is it a scholarship? A prize for winning a competition? A forgivable loan? For what type and for what years of college can it be used? Is it renewable or is it for only one year?

Eligibility Requirements

Application Requirements

What information do you need to supply to be considered? What are the deadlines?

Contact

If provided by the sponsor, this element includes the name, mailing address, phone and fax numbers, and e-mail address of the person to contact for information about a specific award.

USING THE INDEXES

The alphabetical indexes in the back of the book are designed to aid your search. Two are name indexes. One lists scholarships alphabetically by academic fields and career goals. The other ten indexes supply access by nonacademic and noncareer criteria. The indexes give you the page number of the descriptions of relevant awards regardless of the part of the book in which they appear.

These are the indexes:

Award Name

Sponsor

Academic Fields/Career Goals

> [131 subject areas, from Academic Advising to Women's Studies]

Civic, Professional, Social, or Union Affiliation

Corporate Affiliation

Employment/Volunteer Experience

Impairment

Military Service

Nationality or Ethnic Heritage

Religious Affiliation

Residence

Location of Study
Talent/Interest Area

In general, when using the indexes, writing down the names and page numbers of the awards that you are interested in is an effective technique.

DATA COLLECTION PROCEDURES

Peterson's takes its responsibility to its readers, as a provider of trustworthy information, very seriously. Peterson's administered an electronic survey between November 2017 and April 2018 in order to update information from all programs listed within this guide. All collected data was updated between November 2017 and April 2018. Additional award program data was obtained between January 2013 and April 2018. Peterson's research staff makes every effort to verify unusual figures and resolve discrepancies. Nonetheless, errors and omissions are possible in a data collection endeavor of this scope. Also, facts and figures, such as number and amount of awards, can suddenly change, or awards can be discontinued by a sponsoring organization. Therefore, readers should verify data with the specific sponsoring agency responsible for administering these awards before applying.

CRITERIA FOR INCLUSION IN THIS BOOK

The programs listed in this book have the primary characteristics of legitimate scholarships: verifiable sponsor addresses and phone numbers, appropriate descriptive materials, and fees that, if required, are not exorbitant. Peterson's assumes that these fees are used to defray administrative expenses and are not major sources of income.

QUICK REFERENCE CHART

Scholarships, Grants & Prizes At-a-Glance

This chart lists award programs that indicate that their largest award provides $2000 or more. The awards are ranked in descending order on the basis of the dollar amount of the largest award. Because the award criteria in the Academic Fields/Career Goals and Nonacademic/Noncareer Criteria column may represent only some of the criteria or limitations that affect eligibility for the award, you should refer to the full description in the award profiles to ascertain all relevant details.

Award Name	Page Number	Highest Dollar Amount	Lowest Dollar Amount	Number of Awards	Academic Fields/Career Goals and Nonacademic/Noncareer Criteria
Regeneron Science Talent Search	696	$250,000	$25,000	40	Must be in high school.
U.S. Army ROTC Four-Year College Scholarship	492	$150,000	$9000	1,000–2,500	Military Service: Army; Army National Guard. Studying in Alabama; Alaska; Arizona; Arkansas; California; Colorado; Connecticut; Delaware; District of Columbia; Florida; Georgia; Guam; Hawaii; Idaho; Illinois; Indiana; Iowa; Kansas; Kentucky; Louisiana; Maine; Maryland; Massachusetts; Michigan; Minnesota; Mississippi; Missouri; Montana; Nebraska; Nevada; New Hampshire; New Jersey; New Mexico; New York; North Carolina; North Dakota; Ohio; Oklahoma; Oregon; Pennsylvania; Puerto Rico; Rhode Island; South Carolina; South Dakota; Tennessee; Texas; Utah; Vermont; Virginia; Washington; West Virginia; Wisconsin; Wyoming. Must be in high school.
Army (ROTC) Reserve Officers Training Corps Two-, Three-, Four-Year Campus-Based Scholarships	492	$120,000	$10,000	2,000–3,500	Military Service: Army. Studying in Alabama; Alaska; Arizona; Arkansas; California; Colorado; Connecticut; Delaware; District of Columbia; Florida; Georgia; Guam; Hawaii; Idaho; Illinois; Indiana; Iowa; Kansas; Kentucky; Louisiana; Maine; Maryland; Massachusetts; Michigan; Minnesota; Mississippi; Missouri; Montana; Nebraska; Nevada; New Hampshire; New Jersey; New Mexico; New York; North Carolina; North Dakota; Ohio; Oklahoma; Oregon; Pennsylvania; Puerto Rico; Rhode Island; South Carolina; South Dakota; Tennessee; Texas; Utah; Vermont; Virginia; Washington; West Virginia; Wisconsin; Wyoming.

Award Name	Page Number	Highest Dollar Amount	Lowest Dollar Amount	Number of Awards	Academic Fields/Career Goals and Nonacademic/Noncareer Criteria
U.S. Army ROTC Guaranteed Reserve Forces Duty (GRFD), (ARNG/USAR) and Dedicated ARNG Scholarships	494	$120,000	$10,000	1,000–3,000	Military Service: Army National Guard. Studying in Alabama; Alaska; Arizona; Arkansas; California; Colorado; Connecticut; Delaware; District of Columbia; Florida; Georgia; Guam; Hawaii; Idaho; Illinois; Indiana; Iowa; Kansas; Kentucky; Louisiana; Maine; Maryland; Massachusetts; Michigan; Minnesota; Mississippi; Missouri; Montana; Nebraska; Nevada; New Hampshire; New Jersey; New Mexico; New York; North Carolina; North Dakota; Ohio; Oklahoma; Oregon; Pennsylvania; Puerto Rico; Rhode Island; Saskatchewan; South Carolina; South Dakota; Tennessee; Texas; Utah; Vermont; Virginia; Washington; West Virginia; Wisconsin; Wyoming.
Regeneron International Science and Engineering Fair	696	$75,000	$500	1–600	Must be in high school.
Indian Health Service Health Professions Pre-graduate Scholarships	108	$63,500	$23,000	50–100	Applied Sciences; Biology; Health and Medical Sciences. Residence: Alabama; Alaska; Arizona; Arkansas; California; Colorado; Connecticut; Delaware; District of Columbia; Florida; Georgia; Hawaii; Idaho; Illinois; Indiana; Iowa; Kansas; Kentucky; Louisiana; Maine; Maryland; Massachusetts; Michigan; Minnesota; Mississippi; Missouri; Montana; Nebraska; Nevada; New Hampshire; New Jersey; New Mexico; New York; North Carolina; North Dakota; Ohio; Oklahoma; Oregon; Pennsylvania; Rhode Island; South Carolina; South Dakota; Tennessee; Texas; Utah; Vermont; Virginia; Washington; West Virginia; Wisconsin; Wyoming. Limited to American Indian/Alaska Native students.
Health Professions Preparatory Scholarship Program	137	$52,600	$13,250	25–50	Behavioral Science; Biology; Health and Medical Sciences; Nursing; Optometry; Pharmacy; Psychology; Social Sciences. Residence: Alabama; Alaska; Arizona; Arkansas; California; Colorado; Connecticut; Delaware; District of Columbia; Florida; Georgia; Hawaii; Idaho; Illinois; Indiana; Iowa; Kansas; Kentucky; Louisiana; Maine; Maryland; Massachusetts; Michigan; Minnesota; Mississippi; Missouri; Montana; Nebraska; Nevada; New Hampshire; New Jersey; New Mexico; New York; North Carolina; North Dakota; Ohio; Oklahoma; Oregon; Pennsylvania; Rhode Island; South Carolina; South Dakota; Tennessee; Texas; Utah; Vermont; Virginia; Washington; West Virginia; Wisconsin; Wyoming. Limited to American Indian/Alaska Native students.

Award Name	Page Number	Highest Dollar Amount	Lowest Dollar Amount	Number of Awards	Academic Fields/Career Goals and Nonacademic/Noncareer Criteria
U.S. Army ROTC Military Junior College (MJC) Scholarship	492	$52,000	$5600	110–150	Military Service: Army; Army National Guard. Studying in Alabama; Alaska; Arizona; Arkansas; California; Colorado; Connecticut; Delaware; District of Columbia; Florida; Georgia; Guam; Hawaii; Idaho; Illinois; Indiana; Iowa; Kansas; Kentucky; Louisiana; Maine; Maryland; Massachusetts; Michigan; Minnesota; Mississippi; Missouri; Montana; Nebraska; Nevada; New Hampshire; New Jersey; New Mexico; New York; North Carolina; North Dakota; Ohio; Oklahoma; Oregon; Pennsylvania; Puerto Rico; Rhode Island; South Carolina; South Dakota; Tennessee; Texas; Utah; Vermont; Virginia; Washington; West Virginia; Wisconsin; Wyoming.
Kentucky Transportation Cabinet Civil Engineering Scholarship Program	165	$51,200	$12,400	15–30	Civil Engineering. Residence: Kentucky. Studying in Kentucky.
Elks National Foundation Most Valuable Student Scholarship Contest	617	$50,000	$4000	500	Talent/Interest Area: leadership. Must be in high school.
Miss America Organization Competition Scholarships	619	$50,000	$2000	70	Talent/Interest Area: beauty pageant.
U.S. Army ROTC Four-Year Nursing Scholarship	364	$50,000	$5000	100	Nursing. Military Service: Army; Army National Guard. Studying in Alabama; Alaska; Arizona; Arkansas; California; Colorado; Connecticut; Delaware; District of Columbia; Florida; Georgia; Guam; Hawaii; Idaho; Illinois; Indiana; Iowa; Kansas; Kentucky; Louisiana; Maine; Maryland; Massachusetts; Michigan; Minnesota; Mississippi; Missouri; Montana; Nebraska; Nevada; New Hampshire; New Jersey; New Mexico; New York; North Carolina; North Dakota; Ohio; Oklahoma; Oregon; Pennsylvania; Puerto Rico; Rhode Island; South Carolina; South Dakota; Tennessee; Texas; Utah; Vermont; Virginia; Washington; West Virginia; Wisconsin; Wyoming.
Veterans United Foundation Scholarship	508	$50,000	N/A	1–10	Military Service: General.
Tuition Exchange Scholarships	471	$49,750	$4190	7,400–9,000	Employment/Volunteer Experience: teaching/education.

Award Name	Page Number	Highest Dollar Amount	Lowest Dollar Amount	Number of Awards	Academic Fields/Career Goals and Nonacademic/Noncareer Criteria
Hagan Scholarship	572	$48,000	N/A	375–500	Residence: Alabama; Alberta; Arizona; British Columbia; California; Colorado; Connecticut; Delaware; District of Columbia; Florida; Guam; Hawaii; Idaho; Illinois; Indiana; Iowa; Kansas; Kentucky; Louisiana; Manitoba; Maryland; Massachusetts; Michigan; Minnesota; Mississippi; Missouri; Montana; Nebraska; Nevada; New Brunswick; Newfoundland; New Hampshire; New Jersey; New Mexico; North Carolina; Nova Scotia; Ohio; Ontario; Oregon; Quebec; Saskatchewan; South Carolina; South Dakota; Tennessee; Texas; Utah; Vermont; Virginia; Washington; West Virginia; Wisconsin. Studying in Alabama; Alaska; Arizona; Arkansas; California; Colorado; Connecticut; Delaware; District of Columbia; Florida; Georgia; Hawaii; Idaho; Illinois; Indiana; Iowa; Kansas; Kentucky; Louisiana; Maine; Maryland; Massachusetts; Michigan; Minnesota; Mississippi; Missouri; Montana; Nebraska; Nevada; New Hampshire; New Jersey; New Mexico; New York; North Carolina; North Dakota; Ohio; Oklahoma; Oregon; Pennsylvania; Rhode Island; South Carolina; South Dakota; Tennessee; Texas; Utah; Vermont; Virginia; Washington; West Virginia; Wisconsin; Wyoming. Must be in high school.
LEADS! Scholarship	593	$40,000	$1500	200–250	Residence: Michigan; Ohio. Studying in Michigan; Ohio. Must be in high school.
Mas Family Scholarship Award	149	$40,000	$8000	5–10	Business/Consumer Services; Chemical Engineering; Civil Engineering; Communications; Economics; Electrical Engineering/Electronics; Engineering-Related Technologies; International Studies; Journalism; Materials Science, Engineering, and Metallurgy; Mechanical Engineering. Limited to Hispanic students.
Ron Brown Scholar Program	530	$40,000	$10,000	10–20	Must be in high school. Limited to Black (non-Hispanic) students.
U.S. Army ROTC Four-Year Historically Black College/University Scholarship	492	$40,000	$9000	20–200	Military Service: Army; Army National Guard. Studying in Alabama; Alaska; Arizona; Arkansas; California; Colorado; Connecticut; Delaware; District of Columbia; Florida; Georgia; Guam; Hawaii; Idaho; Illinois; Indiana; Iowa; Kansas; Kentucky; Louisiana; Maine; Maryland; Massachusetts; Michigan; Minnesota; Mississippi; Missouri; Montana; Nebraska; Nevada; New Hampshire; New Jersey; New Mexico; New York; North Carolina; North Dakota; Ohio; Oklahoma; Oregon; Pennsylvania; Puerto Rico; Rhode Island; South Carolina; South Dakota; Tennessee; Texas; Utah; Vermont; Virginia; Washington; West Virginia; Wisconsin; Wyoming.

Award Name	Page Number	Highest Dollar Amount	Lowest Dollar Amount	Number of Awards	Academic Fields/Career Goals and Nonacademic/Noncareer Criteria
Master's Scholarship Program	158	$32,000	$25,000	1–15	Chemical Engineering; Computer Science/Data Processing; Electrical Engineering/Electronics; Engineering/Technology; Materials Science, Engineering, and Metallurgy. Limited to American Indian/Alaska Native; Black (non-Hispanic); Hispanic students.
Baer Reintegration Scholarship	642	$30,000	$1000	20–30	N/A
National Security Agency Stokes Educational Scholarship Program	181	$30,000	$1000	15–20	Computer Science/Data Processing; Electrical Engineering/Electronics. Must be in high school.
Voice of Democracy Program	625	$30,000	$1000	54	Talent/Interest Area: public speaking; writing. Must be in high school.
National FFA Collegiate Scholarship Program	447	$29,000	$500	1,700–1,800	Civic Affiliation: Future Farmers of America.
Florida Space Research Program	131	$25,000	$12,500	13–15	Aviation/Aerospace; Earth Science; Education; Electrical Engineering/Electronics; Engineering/Technology; Marine/Ocean Engineering; Materials Science, Engineering, and Metallurgy; Mathematics; Mechanical Engineering; Meteorology/Atmospheric Science; Physical Sciences. Residence: Florida. Studying in Florida.
Ford Opportunity Program	567	$25,000	$1000	30–50	Residence: California; Oregon. Studying in California; Oregon.
Ford ReStart Program	567	$25,000	$1000	46	Residence: California; Oregon. Studying in California; Oregon.
Ford Scholars Program	567	$25,000	$1000	100–120	Residence: California; Oregon. Studying in California; Oregon.
General Study Scholarships	532	$25,000	$4000	6–12	N/A
Henry Salvatori Scholarship for General Study	532	$25,000	$4000	1	Must be in high school.
Horatio Alger Association Scholarship Programs	662	$25,000	$7000	1,009	Must be in high school.
Italian Language Scholarship	169	$25,000	$4000	1	Classics; Foreign Language.
National Honor Society Scholarship Program	446	$25,000	$3200	600	Civic Affiliation: National Honor Society. Must be in high school.
Princess Grace Awards in Dance, Theater, and Film	259	$25,000	$5000	15–25	Filmmaking/Video; Performing Arts.
Young Entrepreneur Awards	623	$25,000	$2000	100	Talent/Interest Area: entrepreneurship. Must be in high school.
Pride Foundation Scholarship Program	598	$24,000	$1000	85–125	Residence: Alaska; Idaho; Montana; Oregon; Washington. Talent/Interest Area: LGBT issues.
Coca-Cola Scholars Program	644	$20,000	$10,000	250	Must be in high school.

Award Name	Page Number	Highest Dollar Amount	Lowest Dollar Amount	Number of Awards	Academic Fields/Career Goals and Nonacademic/Noncareer Criteria
Hub Foundation Scholarships	88	$20,000	$5000	1–15	African Studies; Anthropology; Area/Ethnic Studies; Art History; Asian Studies; Child and Family Studies; Foreign Language; History; International Migration; International Studies; Journalism; Law/Legal Services; Literature/English/Writing; Near and Middle East Studies; Political Science; Psychology; Religion/Theology; Social Sciences; Women's Studies.
Jesse Brown Memorial Youth Scholarship Program	462	$20,000	$5000	8	Employment/Volunteer Experience: community service; helping people with disabilities.
Los Alamos Employees' Scholarship	580	$20,000	$1000	113–152	Residence: New Mexico.
Milton Fisher Scholarship for Innovation and Creativity	598	$20,000	$250	1–7	Residence: Alabama; Alberta; Arizona; British Columbia; California; Colorado; Connecticut; Delaware; District of Columbia; Florida; Guam; Hawaii; Idaho; Illinois; Indiana; Iowa; Kansas; Kentucky; Louisiana; Manitoba; Maryland; Massachusetts; Michigan; Minnesota; Mississippi; Missouri; Montana; Nebraska; New Brunswick; Newfoundland; New Hampshire; New Jersey; New Mexico; North Carolina; Nova Scotia; Ohio; Ontario; Oregon; Quebec; Saskatchewan; South Carolina; South Dakota; Tennessee; Texas; Utah; Vermont; Virginia; Washington; West Virginia; Wisconsin. Studying in Alabama; Alaska; Arizona; Arkansas; California; Colorado; Connecticut; Delaware; District of Columbia; Florida; Georgia; Hawaii; Idaho; Illinois; Indiana; Iowa; Kansas; Kentucky; Louisiana; Maine; Maryland; Massachusetts; Michigan; Minnesota; Mississippi; Missouri; Montana; Nebraska; Nevada; New Hampshire; New Jersey; New Mexico; New York; North Carolina; North Dakota; Ohio; Oklahoma; Oregon; Pennsylvania; Rhode Island; South Carolina; South Dakota; Tennessee; Texas; Utah; Vermont; Virginia; Washington; West Virginia; Wisconsin; Wyoming.
National Security Education Program (NSEP) David L. Boren Undergraduate Scholarships	119	$20,000	$8000	130–170	Area/Ethnic Studies; Business/Consumer Services; Economics; Engineering-Related Technologies; Environmental Science; Foreign Language; International Studies; Peace and Conflict Studies; Social Sciences.
NIH Undergraduate Scholarship Program for Students from Disadvantaged Backgrounds	101	$20,000	$2000	10–15	Animal/Veterinary Sciences; Behavioral Science; Biology; Environmental Health; Environmental Science; Health and Medical Sciences; Neurobiology; Nuclear Science; Nursing; Physical Sciences; Public Health; Women's Studies.
RARE Scholars	472	$20,000	$2500	1–5	Disability: learning disabled; physically disabled.
Georgia Public Safety Memorial Grant	464	$18,000	$2000	N/A	Employment/Volunteer Experience: police/firefighting. Residence: Florida. Studying in Georgia.

Award Name	Page Number	Highest Dollar Amount	Lowest Dollar Amount	Number of Awards	Academic Fields/Career Goals and Nonacademic/Noncareer Criteria
5 Strong Scholars Scholarship	511	$16,000	$10,000	25	Residence: Georgia. Studying in Georgia. Must be in high school. Limited to ethnic minority students.
Scholarship for Engineering Education for Minorities (MSEE)	518	$15,750	$5250	N/A	Residence: Florida. Studying in Georgia. Limited to ethnic minority students.
Barnes Scholarship	604	$15,000	$1000	1–4	Residence: Florida. Must be in high school.
First in Family Scholarship	577	$15,000	$12,500	10	Residence: Alabama. Studying in Alabama. Must be in high school.
Francis Ouimet Scholarship	567	$15,000	$1000	N/A	Residence: Massachusetts. Talent/Interest Area: golf.
Jeffrey L. Esser Career Development Scholarship	75	$15,000	$5000	1–2	Accounting; Business/Consumer Services; Finance; Public Policy and Administration.
Life Lessons Scholarship Program	672	$15,000	$5000	20–50	N/A
Margaret McNamara Education Grants	673	$15,000	$7000	27–35	N/A
National Beta Club Scholarship	447	$15,000	$1000	221	Civic Affiliation: National Beta Club. Must be in high school.
National Black MBA Association Graduate Scholarship Program	677	$15,000	$2500	10–25	N/A
St. Andrew's Society of Washington DC Scholarships	531	$15,000	$500	1–8	Residence: Delaware; District of Columbia; Maryland; New Jersey; North Carolina; Pennsylvania; Virginia; West Virginia.
Sallie Mae® Make College Happen Challenge	641	$15,000	$1000	10	N/A
Saul T. Wilson, Jr., Scholarship Program (STWJS)	103	$15,000	$7500	N/A	Animal/Veterinary Sciences; Biology.
Scholarship America Dream Award	691	$15,000	$5000	8–10	N/A
Scholarship for Students Pursuing a Business or STEM Degree	80	$15,000	$2500	35–120	Accounting; Advertising/Public Relations; Agribusiness; Agriculture; Animal/Veterinary Sciences; Applied Sciences; Archaeology; Architecture; Audiology; Aviation/Aerospace; Biology; Business/Consumer Services; Chemical Engineering; Civil Engineering; Computer Science/Data Processing; Dental Health/Services; Earth Science; Economics; Electrical Engineering/Electronics; Energy and Power Engineering; Engineering-Related Technologies; Engineering/Technology; Environmental Science; Finance; Food Science/Nutrition; Geography; Health Administration; Health and Medical Sciences; Health Information Management/Technology; Hospitality Management; Human Resources; Insurance and Actuarial Science; Marine Biology; Marine/Ocean Engineering; Marketing; Materials Science, Engineering, and Metallurgy; Mathematics; Mechanical Engineering; Meteorology/Atmospheric Science; Natural Sciences; Neurobiology; Nuclear Science; Nursing; Oceanography; Oncology; Optometry; Osteopathy; Pharmacy; Physical Sciences; Sports-Related/Exercise Science; Therapy/Rehabilitation. Residence: Tennessee.

Award Name	Page Number	Highest Dollar Amount	Lowest Dollar Amount	Number of Awards	Academic Fields/Career Goals and Nonacademic/Noncareer Criteria
Sterbenz-Ryan Scholarship	601	$15,000	$5000	44	Residence: Minnesota; Wisconsin.
Tailhook Educational Foundation Scholarship	496	$15,000	$2500	100	Military Service: Coast Guard.
Tribal Priority Award	521	$15,000	$2500	1–5	Limited to American Indian/Alaska Native students.
American Angus Auxiliary Scholarship	679	$14,000	$1000	10	Must be in high school.
Safety Officers' Survivor Grant Program	467	$13,840	N/A	1–10	Employment/Volunteer Experience: police/firefighting. Residence: Minnesota. Studying in Minnesota.
CSAC Cal Grant B Award	554	$13,665	$700	20,500	Residence: British Columbia. Studying in California.
National Space Grant Consortium Scholarships	110	$13,333	$1250	1–50	Applied Sciences; Aviation/Aerospace; Chemical Engineering; Civil Engineering; Computer Science/Data Processing; Earth Science; Engineering/Technology; Mathematics; Mechanical Engineering; Natural Sciences; Physical Sciences. Residence: Nevada. Studying in Nevada.
Environmental Protection Scholarship	142	$13,000	$10,000	1–4	Biology; Chemical Engineering; Civil Engineering; Earth Science; Environmental Science; Hydrology; Mechanical Engineering; Natural Sciences. Residence: Kentucky. Studying in Kentucky.
Law Enforcement Officers/Firemen Scholarship	467	$12,854	$2010	11–30	Employment/Volunteer Experience: police/firefighting. Residence: Mississippi. Studying in Mississippi.
CSAC Cal Grant A Award	554	$12,192	$5472	1,000–2,000	Residence: British Columbia. Studying in California.
Law Enforcement Personnel Dependents Grant Program	461	$12,192	$100	N/A	Employment/Volunteer Experience: police/firefighting. Residence: British Columbia. Studying in California.
Airline Pilots Association Scholarship Program	429	$12,000	$1000	1–3	Civic Affiliation: Airline Pilots Association.
Herman O. West Foundation Scholarship Program	459	$12,000	$3000	1–14	Corporate Affiliation: West Pharmaceuticals. Must be in high school.
National Federation of the Blind of California Merit Scholarships	481	$12,000	$3000	3	Disability: visually impaired. Residence: British Columbia.
National Italian American Foundation Category II Scholarship	118	$12,000	$2500	N/A	Area/Ethnic Studies. Talent/Interest Area: Italian language.
National Italian American Foundation Scholarship Program	526	$12,000	$2500	40–70	N/A
Police Officers and Firefighters Survivors Education Assistance Program-Alabama	542	$12,000	$1600	15–30	Residence: Alabama. Studying in Alabama.
United States Society on Dams Student Scholarship Award	168	$12,000	$2000	4	Civil Engineering; Engineering/Technology; Environmental Science. Civic Affiliation: United States Society on Dams.
Minnesota State Grant Program	585	$11,334	$100	71,000–120,000	Residence: Minnesota. Studying in Minnesota.
Global Study Awards	700	$11,215	$11,215	1–9	N/A

Award Name	Page Number	Highest Dollar Amount	Lowest Dollar Amount	Number of Awards	Academic Fields/Career Goals and Nonacademic/Noncareer Criteria
Reisher Family Scholarship Fund	562	$11,000	$4000	N/A	Residence: Colorado. Studying in Colorado.
SPIE Educational Scholarships in Optical Science and Engineering	108	$11,000	$2000	100–150	Applied Sciences; Chemical Engineering; Electrical Engineering/Electronics; Engineering-Related Technologies; Engineering/Technology; Materials Science, Engineering, and Metallurgy; Mechanical Engineering.
AFE Floriculture Scholarships	634	$10,000	$500	2–25	N/A
AIAA Foundation Undergraduate Scholarships	127	$10,000	$500	11	Aviation/Aerospace; Electrical Engineering/Electronics; Engineering-Related Technologies; Engineering/Technology; Materials Science, Engineering, and Metallurgy; Mechanical Engineering; Physical Sciences; Science, Technology, and Society. Civic Affiliation: American Institute of Aeronautics and Astronautics.
Anne Ford and Allegra Ford Thomas Scholarship	479	$10,000	$2500	2	Disability: learning disabled. Must be in high school.
AREMA Graduate and Undergraduate Scholarships	162	$10,000	$1000	30–40	Civil Engineering; Computer Science/Data Processing; Construction Engineering/Management; Electrical Engineering/Electronics; Engineering-Related Technologies; Engineering/Technology; Mechanical Engineering.
Arkansas Governor's Scholars Program	552	$10,000	$4000	75–375	Residence: Arizona. Studying in Arkansas. Must be in high school.
Association of State Dam Safety Officials (ASDSO) Senior Undergraduate Scholarship	140	$10,000	$5000	1–3	Biology; Civil Engineering; Computer Science/Data Processing; Construction Engineering/Management; Earth Science; Electrical Engineering/Electronics; Energy and Power Engineering; Engineering-Related Technologies; Engineering/Technology; Environmental Science; Geography; Materials Science, Engineering, and Metallurgy; Mechanical Engineering; Natural Resources; Natural Sciences; Science, Technology, and Society; Surveying, Surveying Technology, Cartography, or Geographic Information Science; Urban and Regional Planning.
Automotive Aftermarket Scholarships	146	$10,000	$1000	N/A	Business/Consumer Services; Marketing; Mechanical Engineering; Trade/Technical Specialties.
CBCF Louis Stokes Health Scholars Program	516	$10,000	$5000	4	Limited to Black (non-Hispanic) students.
Center for Architecture, Women's Auxiliary Eleanor Allwork Scholarship	114	$10,000	$4000	1–5	Architecture. Studying in New York.
Charles and Melva T. Owen Memorial Scholarship	479	$10,000	$3000	2	Disability: visually impaired.
CTIA Wireless Foundation Drive Smart Digital Short Contest	641	$10,000	$1000	6	N/A
Cystic Fibrosis Scholarship	474	$10,000	$1000	40–50	Disability: physically disabled.

Award Name	Page Number	Highest Dollar Amount	Lowest Dollar Amount	Number of Awards	Academic Fields/Career Goals and Nonacademic/Noncareer Criteria
DC Tuition Assistance Grant Program (DCTAG)	562	$10,000	$2500	5,999–6,000	Residence: District of Columbia.
Duck Brand Duct Tape "Stuck at Prom" Scholarship Contest	573	$10,000	$1000	1–11	Residence: Alabama; Alaska; Alberta; Arizona; Arkansas; British Columbia; California; Connecticut; Delaware; District of Columbia; Florida; Georgia; Guam; Hawaii; Idaho; Illinois; Indiana; Iowa; Kansas; Kentucky; Louisiana; Maine; Manitoba; Massachusetts; Michigan; Minnesota; Mississippi; Missouri; Montana; Nebraska; Nevada; New Brunswick; Newfoundland; New Hampshire; New Jersey; New Mexico; New York; North Carolina; North Dakota; Northwest Territories; Nova Scotia; Ohio; Oklahoma; Ontario; Oregon; Pennsylvania; Prince Edward Island; Puerto Rico; Rhode Island; Saskatchewan; South Carolina; South Dakota; Tennessee; Texas; Utah; Virginia; Washington; West Virginia; Wisconsin; Wyoming; Yukon. Must be in high school.
ESA Youth Scholarship Program	462	$10,000	$500	N/A	Employment/Volunteer Experience: police/firefighting. Must be in high school.
Executive Women International Scholarship Program	653	$10,000	$1000	75–100	Must be in high school.
ExploraVision Science Competition	625	$10,000	$5000	N/A	Talent/Interest Area: science.
Foundation Fund Scholarship	97	$10,000	$2000	1–100	Agriculture. Residence: Washington.
Fred and Lena Meijer Scholarship	659	$10,000	$4000	N/A	N/A
Health Care Profession Scholarship	195	$10,000	$1000	1–5	Dental Health/Services; Environmental Health; Food Science/Nutrition; Health Administration; Health and Medical Sciences; Health Information Management/Technology; Nursing; Occupational Safety and Health; Pharmacy; Psychology; Public Health; Radiology; Therapy/Rehabilitation. Residence: North Carolina. Studying in North Carolina.
Hellenic Times Scholarship Fund	518	$10,000	$500	30–40	N/A

Award Name	Page Number	Highest Dollar Amount	Lowest Dollar Amount	Number of Awards	Academic Fields/Career Goals and Nonacademic/Noncareer Criteria
HENAAC Scholarship Program	100	$10,000	$500	100–120	Animal/Veterinary Sciences; Applied Sciences; Architecture; Audiology; Aviation/Aerospace; Biology; Chemical Engineering; Civil Engineering; Computer Science/Data Processing; Construction Engineering/Management; Earth Science; Electrical Engineering/Electronics; Energy and Power Engineering; Engineering-Related Technologies; Engineering/Technology; Entomology; Environmental Health; Environmental Science; Food Science/Nutrition; Horticulture/Floriculture; Hydrology; Industrial Design; Marine Biology; Marine/Ocean Engineering; Materials Science, Engineering, and Metallurgy; Mathematics; Mechanical Engineering; Meteorology/Atmospheric Science; Natural Resources; Natural Sciences; Neurobiology; Nuclear Science; Nursing; Oceanography; Oncology; Optometry; Osteopathy; Paper and Pulp Engineering; Pharmacy; Physical Sciences; Statistics. Studying in Alabama; Alaska; Arizona; Arkansas; California; Colorado; Connecticut; Delaware; District of Columbia; Florida; Georgia; Hawaii; Idaho; Illinois; Indiana; Iowa; Kansas; Kentucky; Louisiana; Maine; Maryland; Massachusetts; Michigan; Minnesota; Mississippi; Missouri; Montana; Nebraska; Nevada; New Hampshire; New Jersey; New Mexico; New York; North Carolina; North Dakota; Ohio; Oklahoma; Oregon; Pennsylvania; Puerto Rico; Rhode Island; South Carolina; South Dakota; Tennessee; Texas; Utah; Vermont; Virginia; Washington; West Virginia; Wisconsin; Wyoming. Limited to Hispanic students.
High School Senior Scholarship	552	$10,000	$1000	1–25	Residence: North Carolina. Studying in North Carolina. Must be in high school.
The Hirsch Family Scholarship	648	$10,000	$2000	N/A	N/A
HORIZONS Scholarship	346	$10,000	$500	5–6	Military and Defense Studies.
Illinois Restaurant Association Educational Foundation Scholarships	190	$10,000	$1000	50–70	Culinary Arts; Food Science/Nutrition; Food Service/Hospitality; Hospitality Management. Employment/Volunteer Experience: food service; hospitality/hotel administration/operations. Residence: Illinois.
James R. Hoffa Memorial Scholarship Fund	442	$10,000	$1000	1–100	Civic Affiliation: International Brotherhood of Teamsters. Must be in high school.

Award Name	Page Number	Highest Dollar Amount	Lowest Dollar Amount	Number of Awards	Academic Fields/Career Goals and Nonacademic/Noncareer Criteria
Jules Cohen Scholarship	218	$10,000	$5000	1–13	Electrical Engineering/Electronics; Engineering-Related Technologies; Science, Technology, and Society. Studying in Alabama; Alaska; Arizona; Arkansas; California; Colorado; Connecticut; Delaware; District of Columbia; Florida; Georgia; Guam; Hawaii; Idaho; Illinois; Indiana; Iowa; Kansas; Kentucky; Louisiana; Maine; Maryland; Massachusetts; Michigan; Minnesota; Mississippi; Missouri; Montana; Nebraska; Nevada; New Hampshire; New Jersey; New Mexico; New York; North Carolina; North Dakota; Ohio; Oklahoma; Oregon; Pennsylvania; Puerto Rico; Rhode Island; South Carolina; South Dakota; Tennessee; Texas; Utah; Vermont; Virginia; Washington; West Virginia; Wisconsin; Wyoming.
Lee-Jackson Educational Foundation Scholarship Competition	579	$10,000	$1000	27	Residence: Virginia. Talent/Interest Area: writing. Must be in high school.
Louie Family Foundation Scholarship	669	$10,000	$1000	25–35	N/A
Marine Corps Scholarship Foundation	673	$10,000	$1500	2,000–2,300	N/A
Medicus Student Exchange	533	$10,000	$2000	1–10	Talent/Interest Area: foreign language.
Nancy Lorraine Jensen Memorial Scholarship	160	$10,000	$2500	1–6	Chemical Engineering; Electrical Engineering/Electronics; Mechanical Engineering. Talent/Interest Area: science.
National Restaurant Association Educational Foundation Undergraduate Scholarships for College Students	95	$10,000	$2500	150–300	Agriculture; Business/Consumer Services; Culinary Arts; Food Science/Nutrition; Food Service/Hospitality; Horticulture/Floriculture; Hospitality Management; Marketing.
New York Women in Communications Scholarships	591	$10,000	$1000	1–22	Residence: Connecticut; New Jersey; New York; Pennsylvania. Studying in New York.
Order Sons and Daughters of Italy in America - General Study Scholarships	529	$10,000	$4000	9–10	N/A
Order Sons and Daughters of Italy - Italian Language Scholarship	271	$10,000	$4000	1	Foreign Language.
PG&E Better Together STEM Scholarship Program	181	$10,000	$1000	40	Computer Science/Data Processing; Electrical Engineering/Electronics; Environmental Science; Mechanical Engineering. Residence: California. Studying in California.
Profile in Courage Essay Contest	667	$10,000	$500	7	Must be in high school.
SAE International Scholarships Program	230	$10,000	$1000	15	Engineering-Related Technologies; Engineering/Technology.
Scholastic Art and Writing Awards	632	$10,000	$500	89	Must be in high school.
SHRM Foundation Student Scholarships	297	$10,000	$2500	44	Human Resources. Civic Affiliation: Society for Human Resource Management.
Single Working Parent Scholarship	552	$10,000	$1000	1–5	Residence: North Carolina. Studying in North Carolina.

Award Name	Page Number	Highest Dollar Amount	Lowest Dollar Amount	Number of Awards	Academic Fields/Career Goals and Nonacademic/Noncareer Criteria
The Soroptimist Live Your Dream: Education and Training Awards for Women	697	$10,000	$500	N/A	N/A
Spencer Educational Foundation Scholarship	301	$10,000	$5000	30–40	Insurance and Actuarial Science.
State Tuition Assistance	488	$10,000	N/A	1–200	Military Service: Air Force National Guard; Army National Guard. Studying in Delaware.
Swanson Scholarship	272	$10,000	$1000	1–10	Funeral Services/Mortuary Science. Residence: Nebraska.
Technical Minority Scholarship	161	$10,000	$1000	128	Chemical Engineering; Computer Science/Data Processing; Electrical Engineering/Electronics; Engineering-Related Technologies; Engineering/Technology; Materials Science, Engineering, and Metallurgy; Mechanical Engineering; Physical Sciences. Limited to ethnic minority students.
Teletoon Animation Scholarship	123	$10,000	$5000	9	Arts; Filmmaking/Video. Residence: Alberta; British Columbia; Manitoba; New Brunswick; Newfoundland; Northwest Territories; Nova Scotia; Ontario; Prince Edward Island; Quebec; Saskatchewan.
Television Academy Foundation	701	$10,000	$3000	9	N/A
Theodore R. and Vivian M. Johnson Scholarship Program for Children of UPS Employees or UPS Retirees	459	$10,000	$1000	1–205	Corporate Affiliation: Universal American Financial Corporation. Residence: Florida. Studying in Florida.
Vectorworks Design Scholarship	117	$10,000	$3000	15–18	Architecture; Arts; Civil Engineering; Construction Engineering/Management; Drafting; Engineering-Related Technologies; Engineering/Technology; Graphics/Graphic Arts/Printing; Industrial Design; Interior Design; Landscape Architecture; Urban and Regional Planning.
Walter J. Clore Scholarship	97	$10,000	$1000	1–100	Agriculture; Food Science/Nutrition. Residence: Washington. Studying in Washington.
Wine Group Scholarships	601	$10,000	$1000	1–10	Residence: California.
Young American Creative Patriotic Art Awards Program	621	$10,000	$500	8	Talent/Interest Area: art. Must be in high school.
Frank O'Bannon Grant Program	575	$9200	$650	N/A	Residence: Illinois. Studying in Indiana.
Canadian Nurses Foundation Scholarships	363	$9000	$1500	50–60	Nursing. Employment/Volunteer Experience: nursing. Nationality: Canadian.
Nissan Scholarship	586	$8718	$4409	2–2	Residence: Mississippi. Studying in Mississippi. Must be in high school.
Undergraduate STEM Research Scholarships	110	$8500	$3000	1–35	Applied Sciences; Aviation/Aerospace; Biology; Chemical Engineering; Computer Science/Data Processing; Electrical Engineering/Electronics; Engineering-Related Technologies; Materials Science, Engineering, and Metallurgy; Mathematics; Mechanical Engineering; Physical Sciences; Science, Technology, and Society. Residence: Virginia. Studying in Virginia.

Award Name	Page Number	Highest Dollar Amount	Lowest Dollar Amount	Number of Awards	Academic Fields/Career Goals and Nonacademic/Noncareer Criteria
CBC Spouses Education Scholarship	98	$8200	$1500	250–300	American Studies; Criminal Justice/Criminology; Economics; Law/Legal Services; Political Science; Public Policy and Administration; Social Sciences; Urban and Regional Planning. Studying in Alabama; Alaska; Arizona; Arkansas; California; Colorado; Connecticut; Delaware; District of Columbia; Florida; Georgia; Guam; Hawaii; Idaho; Illinois; Indiana; Iowa; Kansas; Kentucky; Louisiana; Maine; Maryland; Massachusetts; Michigan; Minnesota; Mississippi; Missouri; Montana; Nebraska; Nevada; New Hampshire; New Jersey; New Mexico; New York; North Carolina; North Dakota; Ohio; Oklahoma; Oregon; Pennsylvania; Puerto Rico; Rhode Island; South Carolina; South Dakota; Tennessee; Texas; Utah; Vermont; Virginia; Washington; West Virginia; Wisconsin; Wyoming. Limited to Black (non-Hispanic) students.
AACE International Competitive Scholarship	112	$8000	$2000	10–20	Architecture; Aviation/Aerospace; Business/Consumer Services; Chemical Engineering; Civil Engineering; Construction Engineering/Management; Electrical Engineering/Electronics; Engineering-Related Technologies; Engineering/Technology; Mechanical Engineering.
California Wine Grape Growers Foundation Scholarship	553	$8000	$2000	7–7	Residence: California. Studying in California. Must be in high school.
Demonstration of Energy and Efficiency Developments Technical Design Project	154	$8000	$5000	1	Chemical Engineering; Civil Engineering; Electrical Engineering/Electronics; Energy and Power Engineering; Engineering-Related Technologies; Engineering/Technology; Environmental Science; Mechanical Engineering; Natural Resources.
Don't Mess With Texas Scholarship Program	562	$8000	$2000	4	Residence: Texas. Studying in Texas. Must be in high school.
Helping Educate Reservists and their Offspring (HERO) Scholarship	570	$8000	$2000	N/A	Residence: Florida. Studying in Georgia.
Hispanic Metropolitan Chamber Scholarships	520	$8000	$2000	45–50	Residence: Oregon. Limited to Hispanic students.
Jewish Federation of Metropolitan Chicago Academic Scholarship Program	522	$8000	$1000	100–125	Religion: Jewish.
Licensed Vocational Nurse to Associate Degree Nursing Scholarship Program	368	$8000	$4000	N/A	Nursing. Residence: British Columbia.
American Legion Department of Pennsylvania High School Oratorical Contest	549	$7500	$4000	3	Residence: Pennsylvania. Talent/Interest Area: public speaking. Must be in high school.
Civil Air Patrol Academic Scholarships	438	$7500	$1000	40	Civic Affiliation: Civil Air Patrol.

Award Name	Page Number	Highest Dollar Amount	Lowest Dollar Amount	Number of Awards	Academic Fields/Career Goals and Nonacademic/Noncareer Criteria
Epsilon Sigma Alpha Foundation Scholarships	517	$7500	$350	125–175	Limited to ethnic minority students.
Foundation of the National Student Nurses' Association General Scholarships	366	$7500	$1000	N/A	Nursing.
FSCNY Young Leaders Scholarship	564	$7500	$2000	1–10	Residence: New York. Talent/Interest Area: leadership. Must be in high school.
International Violoncello Competition	626	$7500	$2500	3	Talent/Interest Area: music.
Military Order of the Purple Heart Scholarship	504	$7500	$2500	84–87	Military Service: General.
Palmetto Fellows Scholarship Program	602	$7500	$6700	4,846	Residence: South Carolina. Studying in South Carolina. Must be in high school.
Promise of Nursing Scholarship	367	$7500	$1000	N/A	Nursing. Studying in Arizona; California; Florida; Georgia; Illinois; Maryland; Massachusetts; Michigan; New Jersey; Oregon; Pennsylvania; South Carolina; Tennessee; Texas; Washington.
Samuel Robinson Award	541	$7500	$2000	2	Religion: Presbyterian.
TELACU Education Foundation	563	$7500	$500	350–600	Residence: California; Illinois; New York; Texas.
William Faulkner-William Wisdom Creative Writing Competition	339	$7500	$250	8	Mathematics. Employment/Volunteer Experience: human services. Talent/Interest Area: English language; writing.
Higher Education Legislative Plan (HELP)	585	$7344	$340	3,357	Residence: Mississippi. Studying in Mississippi.
Teaching Assistant Program in France	98	$7280	$1040	1,120	American Studies; Art History; Education; European Studies; Foreign Language; History; Humanities; International Studies; Literature/English/Writing; Political Science; Social Sciences. Talent/Interest Area: English language; foreign language; French language; international exchange.
Charles & Lucille King Family Foundation Scholarships	171	$7000	$3500	10–20	Communications; Filmmaking/Video; TV/Radio Broadcasting.
Freeman Awards for Study in Asia	706	$7000	$3000	N/A	N/A
Jerry McDowell Fund	156	$7000	$1500	1–7	Chemical Engineering; Civil Engineering; Construction Engineering/Management; Earth Science; Electrical Engineering/Electronics; Energy and Power Engineering; Engineering-Related Technologies; Engineering/Technology; Environmental Science; Fire Sciences; Law Enforcement/Police Administration; Materials Science, Engineering, and Metallurgy; Mechanical Engineering; Military and Defense Studies; Natural Resources; Nuclear Science; Occupational Safety and Health; Physical Sciences; Science, Technology, and Society; Trade/Technical Specialties.
Northern Cheyenne Tribal Education Department	528	$7000	$100	90	Limited to American Indian/Alaska Native students.

Award Name	Page Number	Highest Dollar Amount	Lowest Dollar Amount	Number of Awards	Academic Fields/Career Goals and Nonacademic/Noncareer Criteria
Selby Scholar Program	611	$7000	$1000	40	Residence: Florida. Talent/Interest Area: leadership.
Women's jewelry association student scholarship	124	$7000	$500	5–12	Arts; Trade/Technical Specialties. Employment/Volunteer Experience: fine arts. Talent/Interest Area: art.
Armenian Students Association of America Inc. Scholarships	512	$6700	$3300	35	N/A
Pennsylvania Burglar and Fire Alarm Association Youth Scholarship Program	469	$6500	$500	6–8	Employment/Volunteer Experience: police/firefighting. Residence: Pennsylvania. Must be in high school.
Pinnacol Foundation Scholarship Program	686	$6500	$2500	100	N/A
AHLEF Annual Scholarship Grant Program	267	$6000	$500	N/A	Food Service/Hospitality; Hospitality Management; Recreation, Parks, Leisure Studies; Travel/Tourism.
American Jewish League for Israel Scholarship Program	634	$6000	$4000	5–15	N/A
American Montessori Society Teacher Education Scholarship Fund	206	$6000	$425	12–24	Education.
Conditional Grant Program	167	$6000	$3000	10–20	Civil Engineering; Computer Science/Data Processing; Occupational Safety and Health. Residence: Texas. Studying in Texas.
Contemporary Record Society National Competition for Performing Artists	616	$6000	$2000	1	Talent/Interest Area: music/singing.
Elements Behavioral Health College Tuition Scholarship	652	$6000	$1000	3	N/A
Foster Care to Success Scholarship Program	655	$6000	$1000	100	N/A
Friends of 440 Scholarship Fund, Inc.	568	$6000	$500	1–60	Residence: Florida.
GCSAA Scholars Competition	314	$6000	$500	N/A	Landscape Architecture. Civic Affiliation: Golf Course Superintendents Association of America.
Golden Gate Restaurant Association Scholarship Foundation	190	$6000	$1000	9–15	Culinary Arts; Hospitality Management. Residence: California.
Jackie Robinson Scholarship	466	$6000	$6000	40–60	Employment/Volunteer Experience: community service. Talent/Interest Area: leadership. Must be in high school. Limited to ethnic minority students.
Jo Anne J. Trow Scholarships	632	$6000	$1000	1–36	N/A
Marion Huber Learning Through Listening Awards	444	$6000	$2000	6	Civic Affiliation: Learning Ally. Disability: learning disabled. Must be in high school.
Mary P. Oenslager Scholastic Achievement Awards	445	$6000	$1000	3–9	Civic Affiliation: Learning Ally. Disability: visually impaired.
National Competition for Composers' Recordings	616	$6000	$2000	1	Talent/Interest Area: music/singing.
Needham & Company September 11th Scholarship Fund	681	$6000	$1500	20–50	N/A
New Jersey State Golf Association Caddie Scholarship	469	$6000	$3500	145	Employment/Volunteer Experience: private club/caddying. Residence: New Jersey.

Award Name	Page Number	Highest Dollar Amount	Lowest Dollar Amount	Number of Awards	Academic Fields/Career Goals and Nonacademic/Noncareer Criteria
Office and Professional Employees International Union Howard Coughlin Memorial Scholarship Fund	449	$6000	$2400	18	Civic Affiliation: Office and Professional Employees International Union.
RehabCenter.net	598	$6000	$3000	1–3	Residence: Alabama; Alaska; Alberta; Arizona; Arkansas; California; Colorado; Connecticut; Delaware; District of Columbia; Florida; Georgia; Hawaii; Idaho; Illinois; Indiana; Iowa; Kansas; Kentucky; Louisiana; Maine; Manitoba; Maryland; Massachusetts; Michigan; Minnesota; Mississippi; Missouri; Montana; Nebraska; Nevada; New Brunswick; Newfoundland; New Hampshire; New Jersey; New Mexico; New York; North Carolina; North Dakota; Ohio; Oklahoma; Oregon; Pennsylvania; Prince Edward Island; Puerto Rico; Rhode Island; South Carolina; South Dakota; Tennessee; Texas; Utah; Vermont; Virginia; Washington; West Virginia; Wisconsin; Wyoming.
Society of Plastics Engineers Scholarship Program	159	$6000	$1000	35–40	Chemical Engineering; Electrical Engineering/Electronics; Engineering/Technology; Industrial Design; Materials Science, Engineering, and Metallurgy; Trade/Technical Specialties.
Texas Mutual Insurance Company Scholarship Program	702	$6000	$600	1–25	N/A
Texas Educational Opportunity Grant (TEOG)	605	$5876	N/A	N/A	Residence: Tennessee. Studying in Texas.
UNCF/Travelers Insurance Scholarship	151	$5850	$3000	N/A	Business/Consumer Services; Insurance and Actuarial Science. Residence: California; Colorado; Florida; Georgia; Illinois; Massachusetts; Missouri; North Carolina; Texas; Washington. Limited to Black (non-Hispanic) students.
Academic Scholars Program	594	$5500	$2200	N/A	Residence: Ohio. Studying in Oklahoma. Must be in high school.
Governor's Scholarship Program—Need/Merit Scholarship	559	$5250	$2275	1,967	Residence: Connecticut. Studying in Connecticut.
New York State Tuition Assistance Program	590	$5165	$500	350,000–360,000	Residence: New Mexico. Studying in New York.
Tuition Equalization Grant (TEG) Program	702	$5130	N/A	N/A	Studying in Texas.
Academy of Motion Picture Arts and Sciences Student Academy Awards	257	$5000	$2000	3–15	Filmmaking/Video.
AFCEA STEM Majors Scholarships for Undergraduate Students	106	$5000	$2500	1–10	Applied Sciences; Computer Science/Data Processing; Electrical Engineering/Electronics; Engineering-Related Technologies; Engineering/Technology; Materials Science, Engineering, and Metallurgy; Mathematics; Military and Defense Studies; Physical Sciences; Statistics.

Award Name	Page Number	Highest Dollar Amount	Lowest Dollar Amount	Number of Awards	Academic Fields/Career Goals and Nonacademic/Noncareer Criteria
AG Bell College Scholarship Program	472	$5000	$1500	20–40	Disability: hearing impaired. Residence: Alabama; Alaska; Alberta; American Samoa; Arizona; Arkansas; British Columbia; California; Colorado; Connecticut; Delaware; District of Columbia; Florida; Georgia; Guam; Hawaii; Idaho; Illinois; Indiana; Iowa; Kansas; Kentucky; Louisiana; Maine; Manitoba; Maryland; Massachusetts; Michigan; Minnesota; Mississippi; Missouri; Montana; Nebraska; Nevada; New Brunswick; Newfoundland; New Hampshire; New Jersey; New Mexico; New York; North Carolina; North Dakota; Northern Mariana Islands; Northwest Territories; Nova Scotia; Ohio; Oklahoma; Ontario; Oregon; Pennsylvania; Prince Edward Island; Puerto Rico; Quebec; Rhode Island; Saskatchewan; South Carolina; South Dakota; Tennessee; Texas; Utah; Vermont; Virginia; Washington; West Virginia; Wisconsin; Wyoming; Yukon. Studying in Alabama; Alaska; Alberta; American Samoa; Arizona; Arkansas; British Columbia; California; Colorado; Connecticut; Delaware; District of Columbia; Florida; Georgia; Guam; Hawaii; Idaho; Illinois; Indiana; Iowa; Kansas; Kentucky; Louisiana; Maine; Manitoba; Maryland; Massachusetts; Michigan; Minnesota; Mississippi; Missouri; Montana; Nebraska; Nevada; New Brunswick; Newfoundland; New Hampshire; New Jersey; New Mexico; New York; North Carolina; North Dakota; Northern Mariana Islands; Northwest Territories; Nova Scotia; Ohio; Oklahoma; Ontario; Oregon; Pennsylvania; Prince Edward Island; Puerto Rico; Quebec; Rhode Island; Saskatchewan; South Carolina; South Dakota; Tennessee; Texas; Utah; Vermont; Virginia; Washington; West Virginia; Wisconsin; Wyoming; Yukon.
AICPA Scholarship Award for Minority Accounting Students	511	$5000	$3000	N/A	Limited to ethnic minority students.
Alabama Student Assistance Program	542	$5000	$300	3,500–4,500	Residence: Alabama. Studying in Alabama.
Alabama Student Assistance Program	542	$5000	$300	3,500–4,500	Residence: Alabama. Studying in Alabama.
Allen Chi Gaming Scholarship	631	$5000	$1000	25	N/A
All-Ink.com College Scholarship Program	632	$5000	$1000	5–10	N/A
AMA EBSCO Marketing Scholar Award	635	$5000	$2000	3	N/A

Award Name	Page Number	Highest Dollar Amount	Lowest Dollar Amount	Number of Awards	Academic Fields/Career Goals and Nonacademic/Noncareer Criteria
American Chemical Society Scholars Program	153	$5000	$1000	100–130	Chemical Engineering; Environmental Science; Materials Science, Engineering, and Metallurgy; Natural Sciences; Paper and Pulp Engineering; Trade/Technical Specialties. Limited to American Indian/Alaska Native; Black (non-Hispanic); Hispanic students.
American Legion Auxiliary's Children of Warriors National Presidents' Scholarship	498	$5000	$2500	15	Military Service: General. Must be in high school.
American Welding Society Foundation Scholarships	225	$5000	$500	200–900	Engineering-Related Technologies; Trade/Technical Specialties.
Anchor Scholarship Foundation	509	$5000	$2000	35–43	Military Service: Navy.
Angus Foundation Scholarships	447	$5000	$250	75–90	Civic Affiliation: American Angus Association.
Arkansas Academic Challenge Scholarship	551	$5000	$1000	30,000–35,000	Residence: Arizona. Studying in Arkansas.
ARTBA-TDF Lanford Family Highway Workers Memorial Scholarship Program	461	$5000	$1000	N/A	Employment/Volunteer Experience: construction; roadway work; transportation industry.
Ashby B. Carter Memorial Scholarship Fund Founders Award	445	$5000	$2000	3	Civic Affiliation: National Alliance of Postal and Federal Employees. Must be in high school.
Associated General Contractors NYS Scholarship Program	163	$5000	$1500	15–25	Civil Engineering; Construction Engineering/Management; Surveying, Surveying Technology, Cartography, or Geographic Information Science; Transportation. Residence: New York.
Audria M. Edwards Scholarship Fund	596	$5000	$1000	8–15	Residence: Oregon; Washington.
BURGER KING Scholars Program	640	$5000	$1000	N/A	Must be in high school.
Caterpillar Scholars Award Fund	244	$5000	$1000	1–15	Engineering/Technology.
Center for Architecture Design Scholarship	114	$5000	$2000	1–2	Architecture; Civil Engineering; Electrical Engineering/Electronics; Engineering/Technology; Industrial Design; Interior Design; Landscape Architecture; Mechanical Engineering. Studying in New York.
Center for Architecture, Douglas Haskell Award for Student Journals	238	$5000	$1000	1–3	Engineering/Technology; Landscape Architecture; Urban and Regional Planning.
Citrix RightSignature Signature Stories Scholarship Contest	644	$5000	$2000	3	N/A

Award Name	Page Number	Highest Dollar Amount	Lowest Dollar Amount	Number of Awards	Academic Fields/Career Goals and Nonacademic/Noncareer Criteria
Classic Scholarships	607	$5000	$2500	300–350	Residence: Alabama; Alaska; Arizona; Arkansas; California; Colorado; Connecticut; Delaware; Florida; Georgia; Hawaii; Idaho; Illinois; Indiana; Iowa; Kansas; Kentucky; Louisiana; Maine; Maryland; Massachusetts; Michigan; Minnesota; Mississippi; Missouri; Montana; Nebraska; Nevada; New Hampshire; New Jersey; New Mexico; New York; North Carolina; North Dakota; Ohio; Oklahoma; Oregon; Pennsylvania; Puerto Rico; Rhode Island; South Carolina; South Dakota; Tennessee; Texas; Utah; Vermont; Virginia; Washington; West Virginia; Wisconsin; Wyoming. Studying in Alabama; Alaska; Arizona; Arkansas; California; Colorado; Connecticut; Delaware; Florida; Georgia; Hawaii; Idaho; Illinois; Indiana; Iowa; Kansas; Kentucky; Louisiana; Maine; Maryland; Massachusetts; Michigan; Minnesota; Mississippi; Missouri; Montana; Nebraska; Nevada; New Hampshire; New Jersey; New Mexico; New York; North Carolina; North Dakota; Ohio; Oklahoma; Oregon; Pennsylvania; Puerto Rico; Rhode Island; South Carolina; South Dakota; Tennessee; Texas; Utah; Vermont; Virginia; Washington; West Virginia; Wisconsin; Wyoming.
College Photographer of the Year Competition	386	$5000	$600	10	Photojournalism/Photography.
Colorado Contractors Association Scholarship Program	185	$5000	$1000	N/A	Construction Engineering/Management. Studying in Colorado.
Colorado Student Grant	557	$5000	$300	N/A	Residence: Colorado. Studying in Colorado.
Common Scholarship Application	600	$5000	$1000	900–1,100	Residence: California.
Course Hero $5,000 Monthly Scholarship	646	$5000	$1000	1	N/A
Culinary Trust Scholarship Program for Culinary Study and Research	190	$5000	$1000	21	Culinary Arts; Food Science/Nutrition; Food Service/Hospitality.
Darooge Family Scholarship for Construction Trades	185	$5000	$1000	1–5	Construction Engineering/Management; Trade/Technical Specialties. Employment/Volunteer Experience: construction. Residence: Massachusetts. Studying in Michigan.
Doran/Blair Scholarships	439	$5000	$1000	1–20	Civic Affiliation: Fleet Reserve Association/Auxiliary. Military Service: Coast Guard.
EDSF Board of Directors Scholarships	274	$5000	$1000	1–40	Graphics/Graphic Arts/Printing.
Elie Wiesel Prize in Ethics Essay Contest	617	$5000	$500	1–5	Talent/Interest Area: writing.
Environmental Litigation Group, P.C. Asbestos Scholarship	653	$5000	$2000	3	N/A

Award Name	Page Number	Highest Dollar Amount	Lowest Dollar Amount	Number of Awards	Academic Fields/Career Goals and Nonacademic/Noncareer Criteria
Eric J. Gennuso and LeRoy D. (Bud) Loy, Jr. Scholarship Program	153	$5000	$2500	1–3	Chemical Engineering; Civil Engineering; Construction Engineering/Management; Electrical Engineering/Electronics; Energy and Power Engineering; Engineering-Related Technologies; Engineering/Technology; Environmental Science; Marine/Ocean Engineering; Materials Science, Engineering, and Metallurgy; Mechanical Engineering; Surveying, Surveying Technology, Cartography, or Geographic Information Science; Transportation. Residence: Pennsylvania.
Esther R. Sawyer Research Award	76	$5000	$3000	1–3	Accounting; Business/Consumer Services.
Explosive Ordnance Disposal Memorial Scholarship	463	$5000	$1000	25–75	Employment/Volunteer Experience: explosive ordnance disposal. Military Service: General.
Federated Garden Clubs of Connecticut Inc. Scholarships	142	$5000	$1000	2–5	Biology; Horticulture/Floriculture; Landscape Architecture. Residence: Connecticut. Studying in Connecticut.
Feeding Tomorrow Undergraduate General Education Scholarships	264	$5000	$1500	8	Food Science/Nutrition. Talent/Interest Area: leadership.
Fleet Reserve Association Education Foundation Scholarships	496	$5000	$1000	1–10	Military Service: Coast Guard.
Foundation for Seacoast Health Scholarships	282	$5000	$1000	2–6	Health and Medical Sciences. Residence: Maine; New Hampshire.
Frame My Future Scholarship Contest	643	$5000	$500	1–3	N/A
Franz Stenzel M.D. and Kathryn Stenzel Scholarship Fund	283	$5000	$2000	70	Health and Medical Sciences; Nursing. Residence: Oregon.
General John Ratay Educational Fund Grants	674	$5000	$4000	1–5	N/A
Georgia Engineering Foundation Scholarship Program	240	$5000	$1000	45	Engineering/Technology. Residence: Georgia.
Geraldo Rivera Scholarship	307	$5000	$1000	N/A	Journalism; TV/Radio Broadcasting.
Gilman Scholarship	706	$5000	$1000	1,000–1,100	N/A
Girls Impact the World Scholarship Program	646	$5000	$1000	12	N/A
Greater Cincinnati HSF Scholarship	520	$5000	$500	N/A	Residence: Illinois; Kansas; Nova Scotia. Limited to Hispanic students.
Great Falls Broadcasters Association Scholarship	424	$5000	$2000	1	TV/Radio Broadcasting. Residence: Montana. Studying in Montana.

Award Name	Page Number	Highest Dollar Amount	Lowest Dollar Amount	Number of Awards	Academic Fields/Career Goals and Nonacademic/Noncareer Criteria
Greenhouse Scholars	571	$5000	$500	15–30	Residence: California; Florida; Idaho; Newfoundland. Studying in Alabama; Alaska; Arizona; Arkansas; California; Colorado; Connecticut; Delaware; District of Columbia; Florida; Georgia; Hawaii; Idaho; Illinois; Indiana; Iowa; Kansas; Kentucky; Louisiana; Maine; Maryland; Massachusetts; Michigan; Minnesota; Mississippi; Missouri; Montana; Nebraska; Nevada; New Hampshire; New Jersey; New Mexico; New York; North Carolina; North Dakota; Ohio; Oklahoma; Oregon; Pennsylvania; Rhode Island; South Carolina; South Dakota; Tennessee; Texas; Utah; Vermont; Virginia; Washington; West Virginia; Wisconsin; Wyoming. Must be in high school.
Harry A. Applegate Scholarship	73	$5000	$1000	20–25	Accounting; Business/Consumer Services; Education; Fashion Design; Finance; Food Service/Hospitality; Hospitality Management; Marketing. Civic Affiliation: Distribution Ed Club or Future Business Leaders of America.
Harry Ludwig Scholarship Fund	482	$5000	$500	1–3	Disability: visually impaired.
Harvard Travellers Club Permanent Fund	660	$5000	$1000	1–4	N/A
Hispanic Association of Colleges and Universities Scholarship Program	661	$5000	$1000	1	N/A
Hispanic Scholarship Fund Scholarship	520	$5000	$500	N/A	Limited to Hispanic students.
Houston Symphony Ima Hogg Competition	349	$5000	$300	5	Music. Talent/Interest Area: music.
IAAO Academic Partnership Program	664	$5000	$1000	1–5	N/A
IABA Scholarship	521	$5000	$3000	25–35	Limited to Black (non-Hispanic) students.
IFMA Foundation Scholarships	116	$5000	$1500	25–35	Architecture; Construction Engineering/ Management; Engineering-Related Technologies; Engineering/Technology; Interior Design; Urban and Regional Planning.
Indiana Health Care Policy Institute Nursing Scholarship	368	$5000	$750	1–5	Nursing. Residence: Indiana. Studying in Illinois; Indiana; Kentucky; Michigan; Ohio.
Indian American Scholarship Fund	521	$5000	$500	N/A	Residence: Georgia. Must be in high school. Limited to Asian/Pacific Islander students.
Ingersoll Rand Scholarship	537	$5000	$2000	N/A	Must be in high school. Limited to Asian/ Pacific Islander students.
ISA Educational Foundation Scholarships	227	$5000	$500	15–16	Engineering-Related Technologies.
ISF National Scholarship	104	$5000	$2000	1–40	Anthropology; Filmmaking/Video; History; International Studies; Journalism; Law Enforcement/Police Administration; Law/ Legal Services; Near and Middle East Studies; TV/Radio Broadcasting. Religion: Muslim faith.

Award Name	Page Number	Highest Dollar Amount	Lowest Dollar Amount	Number of Awards	Academic Fields/Career Goals and Nonacademic/Noncareer Criteria
John L. Dales Scholarship Program	692	$5000	$1000	1–16	N/A
Joseph Shinoda Memorial Scholarship	292	$5000	$1000	8–15	Horticulture/Floriculture.
Judith McManus Price Scholarship	427	$5000	$2000	N/A	Urban and Regional Planning. Limited to American Indian/Alaska Native; Black (non-Hispanic); Hispanic students.
JVS Scholarship Program	522	$5000	$750	150–200	Residence: California. Religion: Jewish.
Louis F. Wolf Jr. Memorial Scholarship	175	$5000	$1000	1	Communications; Electrical Engineering/Electronics; Engineering-Related Technologies; Engineering/Technology; Filmmaking/Video; Science, Technology, and Society; TV/Radio Broadcasting. Civic Affiliation: Society of Motion Picture and Television Engineers.
L. Ron Hubbard's Illustrators of the Future Contest	614	$5000	$500	12	Talent/Interest Area: art.
L. Ron Hubbard's Writers of the Future Contest	614	$5000	$500	12	Talent/Interest Area: writing.
Mary McMillan Scholarship Award	207	$5000	$3000	1–6	Education; Health and Medical Sciences; Therapy/Rehabilitation. Employment/Volunteer Experience: physical therapy/rehabilitation.
Math, Engineering, Science, Business, Education, Computers Scholarships	146	$5000	$500	180	Business/Consumer Services; Computer Science/Data Processing; Education; Engineering/Technology; Humanities; Physical Sciences; Science, Technology, and Society; Social Sciences. Limited to American Indian/Alaska Native students.
Media Plan Case Competition	88	$5000	$3000	4	Advertising/Public Relations; Business/Consumer Services; Communications; Journalism; Marketing; Political Science; Public Policy and Administration; TV/Radio Broadcasting.
Minority Teacher Incentive Grant Program	209	$5000	$2500	87	Education. Residence: Connecticut. Studying in Connecticut. Limited to ethnic minority students.
MOAA American Patriot Scholarship	674	$5000	$2500	1–60	N/A
National Asphalt Pavement Association Research and Education Foundation Scholarship Program	165	$5000	$500	51	Civil Engineering; Construction Engineering/Management.
Native American Leadership in Education (NALE)	146	$5000	$500	30	Business/Consumer Services; Education; Humanities; Physical Sciences; Science, Technology, and Society. Limited to American Indian/Alaska Native students.
New England Employee Benefits Council Scholarship Program	78	$5000	$1000	1–3	Accounting; Business/Consumer Services; Economics; Health Administration; Human Resources; Insurance and Actuarial Science; Law/Legal Services; Public Health; Public Policy and Administration. Residence: Connecticut; Maine; Massachusetts; New Hampshire; Rhode Island; Vermont. Studying in Connecticut; Maine; Massachusetts; New Hampshire; Rhode Island; Vermont.

Award Name	Page Number	Highest Dollar Amount	Lowest Dollar Amount	Number of Awards	Academic Fields/Career Goals and Nonacademic/Noncareer Criteria
NGWA Foundation's Len Assante Scholarship	202	$5000	$1000	1–10	Earth Science; Environmental Science; Hydrology.
Norm Manly—YMTA Maritime Educational Scholarships	326	$5000	$1000	6–7	Marine Biology; Marine/Ocean Engineering; Oceanography; Trade/Technical Specialties. Residence: Washington. Must be in high school.
North Carolina Association of CPAs Foundation Scholarships	78	$5000	$1000	50–60	Accounting. Residence: North Carolina. Studying in North Carolina.
North Carolina Education and Training Voucher Program	682	$5000	N/A	N/A	N/A
NurseRecruiter.com Scholarship	683	$5000	$1000	1–10	N/A
Osage Nation Higher Education Scholarship	529	$5000	$150	1–1,200	Limited to American Indian/Alaska Native students.
Outdoor Writers Association of America - Bodie McDowell Scholarship Award	174	$5000	$1000	2–6	Communications; Environmental Science; Filmmaking/Video; Journalism; Literature/English/Writing; Natural Resources; Photojournalism/Photography; TV/Radio Broadcasting. Talent/Interest Area: amateur radio; art; athletics/sports; photography/photogrammetry/filmmaking; writing.
Pellegrini Scholarship Grants	533	$5000	$500	50	Residence: Connecticut; Delaware; New Jersey; New York; Pennsylvania.
PepsiCo Hallmark Scholarships	537	$5000	$2000	1	Must be in high school. Limited to Asian/Pacific Islander students.
Print and Graphics Scholarships Foundation	174	$5000	$1500	150–200	Communications; Graphics/Graphic Arts/Printing.
Regional and Restricted Scholarship Award Program	559	$5000	$2000	200–300	Residence: Connecticut.
The Risk Management Association Foundation Scholarship Program	690	$5000	$2000	40	N/A
Scholarship Program for Sons and Daughters of Employees of Roseburg Forest Products Co.	458	$5000	$3000	30–47	Corporate Affiliation: Roseburg Forest Products.
Screen Actors Guild Foundation/John L. Dales Scholarship Fund (Standard)	692	$5000	$1000	100–135	N/A
SEMA Memorial Scholarship Fund	81	$5000	$2000	50–60	Accounting; Advertising/Public Relations; Business/Consumer Services; Communications; Computer Science/Data Processing; Electrical Engineering/Electronics; Engineering/Technology; Finance; Marketing; Mechanical Engineering; Trade/Technical Specialties; Transportation. Talent/Interest Area: automotive.
Sigma Delta Chi Scholarships	311	$5000	$3000	4–7	Journalism. Studying in District of Columbia; Maryland; Virginia.
Society of Physics Students Leadership Scholarships	392	$5000	$2000	17–22	Physical Sciences. Civic Affiliation: Society of Physics Students.

Award Name	Page Number	Highest Dollar Amount	Lowest Dollar Amount	Number of Awards	Academic Fields/Career Goals and Nonacademic/Noncareer Criteria
TAC Foundation Scholarships	168	$5000	$2500	30–45	Civil Engineering; Construction Engineering/Management; Economics; Engineering-Related Technologies; Engineering/Technology; Urban and Regional Planning. Nationality: Canadian. Residence: Alberta; British Columbia; Manitoba; New Brunswick; Newfoundland; Northwest Territories; Nova Scotia; Ontario; Prince Edward Island; Quebec; Saskatchewan; Yukon.
Taylor Michaels Scholarship Fund	467	$5000	$1000	N/A	Employment/Volunteer Experience: community service. Must be in high school. Limited to ethnic minority students.
Theta Delta Chi Educational Foundation Inc. Scholarship	702	$5000	$1000	15	N/A
TLMI 4 Year College Degree Scholarship Program	262	$5000	$2500	1–6	Flexography; Graphics/Graphic Arts/Printing.
Tombow's Create Your Best Work Art Scholarship	123	$5000	$2500	3	Arts. Residence: Alabama; Alaska; Arizona; Arkansas; California; Colorado; Connecticut; Delaware; District of Columbia; Florida; Georgia; Hawaii; Idaho; Illinois; Indiana; Iowa; Kansas; Kentucky; Louisiana; Maine; Maryland; Massachusetts; Michigan; Minnesota; Mississippi; Missouri; Montana; Nebraska; Nevada; New Brunswick; New Hampshire; New Jersey; New Mexico; New York; North Carolina; North Dakota; Ohio; Oklahoma; Oregon; Pennsylvania; Puerto Rico; Rhode Island; South Carolina; South Dakota; Tennessee; Texas; Utah; Vermont; Virginia; Virgin Islands; Washington; West Virginia; Wisconsin; Wyoming.
Tribal Business Management Program (TBM)	72	$5000	$500	35	Accounting; Business/Consumer Services; Computer Science/Data Processing; Economics; Electrical Engineering/Electronics; Engineering-Related Technologies. Limited to American Indian/Alaska Native students.
Tuskegee Airmen Scholarship	134	$5000	$1500	40	Aviation/Aerospace; Science, Technology, and Society. Must be in high school.

Award Name	Page Number	Highest Dollar Amount	Lowest Dollar Amount	Number of Awards	Academic Fields/Career Goals and Nonacademic/Noncareer Criteria
Two Ten Footwear Foundation Scholarship	471	$5000	$2500	300–350	Employment/Volunteer Experience: leather/footwear industry. Residence: Alabama; Alaska; Arizona; Arkansas; California; Colorado; Connecticut; Delaware; Florida; Georgia; Hawaii; Idaho; Illinois; Indiana; Iowa; Kansas; Kentucky; Louisiana; Maine; Maryland; Massachusetts; Michigan; Minnesota; Mississippi; Missouri; Montana; Nebraska; Nevada; New Hampshire; New Jersey; New Mexico; New York; North Carolina; North Dakota; Ohio; Oklahoma; Ontario; Oregon; Pennsylvania; Puerto Rico; Rhode Island; South Carolina; South Dakota; Tennessee; Texas; Utah; Vermont; Virginia; Washington; West Virginia; Wisconsin; Wyoming. Studying in Alabama; Alaska; Arizona; Arkansas; California; Colorado; Connecticut; Delaware; Florida; Georgia; Hawaii; Idaho; Illinois; Indiana; Iowa; Kansas; Kentucky; Louisiana; Maine; Maryland; Massachusetts; Michigan; Minnesota; Mississippi; Missouri; Montana; Nebraska; Nevada; New Hampshire; New Jersey; New Mexico; New York; North Carolina; North Dakota; Ohio; Oklahoma; Oregon; Pennsylvania; Puerto Rico; Rhode Island; South Carolina; South Dakota; Tennessee; Texas; Utah; Vermont; Virginia; Washington; West Virginia; Wisconsin; Wyoming.
Udall Undergraduate Scholarship	675	$5000	N/A	50	N/A
UPS Hallmark Scholarships	538	$5000	$2000	N/A	Must be in high school. Limited to Asian/Pacific Islander students.
Varian Radiation Therapy Advancement Scholarship	378	$5000	$2500	9	Oncology. Civic Affiliation: American Society of Radiologic Technologists.
Vermont Space Grant Consortium	92	$5000	$2500	6–9	Agribusiness; Applied Sciences; Aviation/Aerospace; Biology; Civil Engineering; Computer Science/Data Processing; Earth Science; Electrical Engineering/Electronics; Energy and Power Engineering; Engineering-Related Technologies; Engineering/Technology; Materials Science, Engineering, and Metallurgy; Mathematics; Mechanical Engineering; Physical Sciences; Science, Technology, and Society; Trade/Technical Specialties. Residence: Vermont. Studying in Vermont.
Vertical Flight Foundation Scholarship	126	$5000	$1500	10–19	Aviation/Aerospace; Electrical Engineering/Electronics; Engineering-Related Technologies; Engineering/Technology; Mechanical Engineering. Talent/Interest Area: aviation.
VSCPA Educational Foundation Accounting Scholarships	83	$5000	$1000	26	Accounting. Residence: Virginia. Studying in Virginia.
Warner Norcross and Judd LLP Scholarship for Students of Color	318	$5000	$1000	1–3	Law/Legal Services. Residence: Massachusetts. Studying in Michigan. Limited to ethnic minority students.

Award Name	Page Number	Highest Dollar Amount	Lowest Dollar Amount	Number of Awards	Academic Fields/Career Goals and Nonacademic/Noncareer Criteria
Washington Crossing Foundation Scholarship	395	$5000	$500	N/A	Political Science; Public Policy and Administration. Must be in high school.
WinWin Products, Inc. Scholarship	538	$5000	$2000	N/A	Must be in high school. Limited to Asian/Pacific Islander students.
Women in Cybersecurity Scholarships	180	$5000	$1000	3	Computer Science/Data Processing.
Women in Defense HORIZONS-Michigan Scholarship	612	$5000	$1500	1–4	Residence: Michigan. Studying in Michigan.
WWIN Education Grant Program	610	$5000	$1000	20–200	Residence: Washington. Studying in Washington.
Young Artist Competition	618	$5000	$500	8	Talent/Interest Area: music.
Youth Activity Fund Grants	103	$5000	$500	N/A	Anthropology; Archaeology; Biology; Environmental Science; Marine Biology; Natural Sciences; Science, Technology, and Society.
Toward EXcellence, Access, and Success (TEXAS) Grant	605	$4896	N/A	N/A	Residence: Tennessee. Studying in Texas.
AIA West Virginia Scholarship	118	$4500	$3500	N/A	Architecture. Residence: West Virginia.
American Council of the Blind Scholarships	472	$4500	$1000	16–20	Disability: visually impaired.
Brook Hollow Golf Club Scholarship	648	$4500	$2000	N/A	Must be in high school.
Ernest Alan and Barbara Park Meyer Scholarship Fund	595	$4500	$1000	5	Residence: Oregon.
Glenn Miller Instrumental Scholarship	618	$4500	$1000	3	Talent/Interest Area: music/singing. Must be in high school.
Greater Washington Society of CPAs Scholarship	75	$4500	$2000	3–5	Accounting. Residence: District of Columbia. Studying in District of Columbia.
Hawaii Association of Broadcasters Scholarship	423	$4500	$500	20–30	TV/Radio Broadcasting.
Roberta B. Willis Scholarship Program—Need-Based Grant	559	$4500	N/A	N/A	Residence: Connecticut. Studying in Connecticut.
Swiss Benevolent Society of San Francisco Scholarships	533	$4500	$2000	N/A	Residence: California.
Nebraska Opportunity Grant	588	$4458	$100	N/A	Residence: Nebraska. Studying in Nebraska.
Actuarial Diversity Scholarship	300	$4000	$1000	N/A	Insurance and Actuarial Science; Mathematics; Statistics. Limited to ethnic minority students.
Alexander and Maude Hadden Scholarship	471	$4000	$2500	96–108	Employment/Volunteer Experience: community service.
American Legion Auxiliary Department of California Past Presidents' Parley Nursing Scholarships	361	$4000	$4000	1–2	Nursing. Military Service: General. Residence: California.
American Society for Enology and Viticulture Scholarships	92	$4000	$500	30	Agriculture; Chemical Engineering; Food Science/Nutrition; Horticulture/Floriculture.

Award Name	Page Number	Highest Dollar Amount	Lowest Dollar Amount	Number of Awards	Academic Fields/Career Goals and Nonacademic/Noncareer Criteria
American Society of Naval Engineers Scholarship	106	$4000	$3000	8–14	Applied Sciences; Aviation/Aerospace; Civil Engineering; Electrical Engineering/Electronics; Energy and Power Engineering; Engineering/Technology; Marine/Ocean Engineering; Materials Science, Engineering, and Metallurgy; Mechanical Engineering; Nuclear Science; Physical Sciences.
Bridging Scholarship for Study Abroad in Japan	633	$4000	$2500	70–120	N/A
C.A.R. Scholarship Foundation Award	400	$4000	$2000	10–25	Real Estate. Residence: California. Studying in California.
College Now Greater Cleveland Adult Learner Program Scholarship	557	$4000	$1000	100–200	Residence: Ohio. Studying in Ohio.
Community Bankers Assoc. of IL Essay Contest	558	$4000	$500	12–24	Residence: Illinois. Must be in high school.
Elks Emergency Educational Grants	438	$4000	$1000	N/A	Civic Affiliation: Elks Club.
Fifth/Graduate Year Student Scholarship	77	$4000	$2000	16–25	Accounting. Studying in Michigan.
General Henry H. Arnold Education Grant Program	486	$4000	$500	3,000	Military Service: Air Force; Air Force National Guard.
GMP Memorial Scholarship Program	440	$4000	$2000	10	Civic Affiliation: Glass, Molders, Pottery, Plastics and Allied Workers International Union. Must be in high school.
Governors' Scholarship for Foster Youth Program	557	$4000	$2000	30–50	Residence: Washington. Studying in Washington. Must be in high school.
Higher Education Success Stipend Program	608	$4000	$300	N/A	Residence: Utah. Studying in Utah.
Illinois CPA Society Accounting Scholarship Program	76	$4000	$500	12–35	Accounting. Residence: Illinois. Studying in Illinois.
Incoming Freshman Scholarships	268	$4000	$2000	5–10	Food Service/Hospitality; Hospitality Management; Recreation, Parks, Leisure Studies; Travel/Tourism. Must be in high school.
John F. and Anna Lee Stacey Scholarship Fund	620	$4000	$1000	3–5	Talent/Interest Area: art.
Minority Student Summer Scholarship	112	$4000	$1500	2	Archaeology; Arts; Classics; Foreign Language; History. Limited to ethnic minority students.
Mississippi Press Association Education Foundation Scholarship	306	$4000	$1000	1	Journalism. Residence: Mississippi.
New Mexico Vietnam Veteran Scholarship	590	$4000	$3500	100	Residence: New Mexico. Studying in New Mexico.
New Mexico Wartime Veterans Scholarship	505	$4000	$3500	100	Military Service: General. Residence: New Mexico. Studying in New Mexico.
NGPA Education Fund, Inc.	133	$4000	$3000	3–4	Aviation/Aerospace. Employment/Volunteer Experience: community service. Talent/Interest Area: aviation; LGBT issues.
Part-Time Grant Program	576	$4000	$20	4,680–6,700	Residence: Indiana. Studying in Indiana.
South Florida Fair College Scholarship	603	$4000	$1000	10	Residence: Florida.

Award Name	Page Number	Highest Dollar Amount	Lowest Dollar Amount	Number of Awards	Academic Fields/Career Goals and Nonacademic/Noncareer Criteria
SSPI International Scholarships	134	$4000	$2500	1–4	Aviation/Aerospace; Communications; Law/Legal Services; Meteorology/Atmospheric Science; Military and Defense Studies.
Student-View Scholarship program	699	$4000	$500	13	Must be in high school.
Texas Gridiron Club Scholarships	177	$4000	$500	10–15	Communications; Journalism; Photojournalism/Photography; TV/Radio Broadcasting.
Union Plus Credit Card Scholarship Program	430	$4000	$500	N/A	Civic Affiliation: American Federation of State, County, and Municipal Employees.
Union Plus Scholarship Program	446	$4000	$500	3	Civic Affiliation: National Association of Letter Carriers. Must be in high school.
University Film and Video Association Carole Fielding Student Grants	260	$4000	$1000	2–5	Filmmaking/Video.
Veterans Education (VetEd) Reimbursement Grant	485	$4000	$1340	N/A	Disability: hearing impaired; learning disabled; physically disabled; visually impaired. Military Service: Air Force; Air Force National Guard; Army; Army National Guard; Coast Guard; General. Residence: Wisconsin. Studying in Minnesota; Wisconsin.
Wenderoth Undergraduate Scholarship	450	$4000	$1750	1–4	Civic Affiliation: Phi Sigma Kappa.
William L. Cullison Scholarship	354	$4000	$2000	1–2	Natural Resources; Paper and Pulp Engineering.
WRI Foundation College Scholarship Program	168	$4000	$2000	2–5	Civil Engineering; Construction Engineering/Management.
Taylor Opportunity Program for Students Tech Award	581	$3985	$436	1,671	Residence: Kentucky. Studying in Louisiana.
Virginia Tuition Assistance Grant Program (Private Institutions)	609	$3900	$850	N/A	Residence: Vermont. Studying in Virginia.
Taylor Opportunity Program for Students Honors Award	580	$3836	$793	N/A	Residence: Kentucky. Studying in Louisiana.
Taylor Opportunity Program for Students Performance Award	581	$3836	$793	N/A	Residence: Kentucky. Studying in Louisiana.
LAGRANT Foundation Scholarship for Graduates	85	$3750	$3250	N/A	Advertising/Public Relations; Business/Consumer Services; Communications; Graphics/Graphic Arts/Printing; Marketing. Limited to ethnic minority students.
Taylor Opportunity Program for Students Opportunity Level	581	$3731	$793	N/A	Residence: Kentucky. Studying in Louisiana.
Georgia HOPE Grant Program	569	$3600	$420	100,000	Residence: Florida. Studying in Georgia.
HOPE Scholarship	570	$3600	$420	200,000	Residence: Florida. Studying in Georgia.
Stella Blum Student Research Grant	118	$3600	$2000	1	Area/Ethnic Studies; Art History; Arts; Historic Preservation and Conservation; History; Home Economics; Museum Studies; Performing Arts. Civic Affiliation: Costume Society of America.

Award Name	Page Number	Highest Dollar Amount	Lowest Dollar Amount	Number of Awards	Academic Fields/Career Goals and Nonacademic/Noncareer Criteria
AFIO Undergraduate and Graduate Scholarships	98	$3500	$1000	4	American Studies; Aviation/Aerospace; Computer Science/Data Processing; Criminal Justice/Criminology; Foreign Language; History; International Studies; Law Enforcement/Police Administration; Military and Defense Studies; Natural Sciences; Near and Middle East Studies; Peace and Conflict Studies; Political Science; Public Policy and Administration.
American Legion Department of Arkansas High School Oratorical Contest	546	$3500	$1250	4	Residence: Arkansas. Talent/Interest Area: public speaking. Must be in high school.
Annual Award Program	540	$3500	$800	6–8	Religion: Muslim faith.
Changemaker In Your Community Documentary Competition	629	$3500	$3100	1	N/A
David Hudak Memorial Essay Contest for Freethinking Students of Color	656	$3500	$200	10	N/A
Dwight D. Gardner Scholarship	441	$3500	$3000	6	Civic Affiliation: Institute of Industrial Engineers. Talent/Interest Area: leadership.
Freedom Alliance Scholarship Fund	656	$3500	$500	300–400	N/A
Hispanic Heritage Foundation Youth Awards	519	$3500	$1000	190–200	Must be in high school. Limited to Hispanic students.
Idaho Opportunity Scholarship	573	$3500	N/A	700–2,500	Residence: Idaho. Studying in Idaho.
Michael Hakeem Memorial Essay Contest for Ongoing College Students	656	$3500	$200	10	N/A
National Defense Transportation Association, Scott Air Force Base-St. Louis Area Chapter Scholarship	588	$3500	$2000	6	Residence: Illinois; Missouri. Studying in Colorado; Illinois; Indiana; Iowa; Kansas; Michigan; Minnesota; Missouri; Montana; Nebraska; North Dakota; South Dakota; Wisconsin; Wyoming.
OAB Foundation Scholarship	174	$3500	$2500	4	Communications; Journalism; TV/Radio Broadcasting. Residence: Oregon.
Ohio College Opportunity Grant	593	$3500	$69	N/A	Residence: Nova Scotia. Studying in Ohio; Pennsylvania.
Order Of The Golden Rule Foundation Awards of Excellence Scholarship Program	272	$3500	$2000	2	Funeral Services/Mortuary Science.
Robert Guthrie PKU Scholarship and Awards	482	$3500	$500	4–8	Disability: physically disabled.
Unmet NEED Grant Program	527	$3500	$1000	10–500	Residence: Pennsylvania. Limited to Black (non-Hispanic) students.
William J. Schulz Memorial Essay Contest for College-Bound High School Seniors	656	$3500	$200	10	Must be in high school.
North Carolina National Guard Tuition Assistance Program	490	$3440	$100	N/A	Military Service: Air Force National Guard; Army National Guard. Residence: North Carolina. Studying in North Carolina.
American Legion Department of Indiana High School Oratorical Contest	547	$3400	$200	N/A	Residence: Illinois. Must be in high school.
Dolphin Scholarships	651	$3400	$2000	25–30	N/A

Award Name	Page Number	Highest Dollar Amount	Lowest Dollar Amount	Number of Awards	Academic Fields/Career Goals and Nonacademic/Noncareer Criteria
Wisconsin HEAB Grant - UW system, Technical Colleges, Tribal Colleges (WG-UW,TC,TR)	611	$3150	$250	N/A	Residence: West Virginia. Studying in Wisconsin.
The Alexander Foundation Scholarship Program	544	$3000	$300	6–35	Residence: Colorado. Studying in Colorado. Talent/Interest Area: LGBT issues.
AMA Social Impact Scholarship	635	$3000	$2000	2–2	N/A
American Hotel & Lodging Educational Foundation Pepsi Scholarship	189	$3000	$500	N/A	Culinary Arts; Food Service/Hospitality; Hospitality Management; Recreation, Parks, Leisure Studies; Travel/Tourism. Residence: District of Columbia.
American Legion Department of Tennessee High School Oratorical Contest	550	$3000	$1000	1–3	Residence: Tennessee. Talent/Interest Area: public speaking. Must be in high school.
American Physical Society Corporate-Sponsored Scholarship for Minority Undergraduate Students Who Major in Physics	391	$3000	$2000	N/A	Physical Sciences. Limited to ethnic minority students.
American Water Ski Educational Foundation Scholarship	436	$3000	$1500	5	Civic Affiliation: USA Water Ski.
Arizona Nursery Association Foundation Scholarship	291	$3000	$500	12–16	Horticulture/Floriculture.
Armed Forces Communications and Electronics Association ROTC Scholarship Program	179	$3000	$2500	1–6	Computer Science/Data Processing; Electrical Engineering/Electronics; Engineering-Related Technologies; Engineering/Technology; Mathematics; Physical Sciences. Military Service: Air Force; Army; Marine Corps; Navy.
Astrid G. Cates and Myrtle Beinhauer Scholarship Funds	454	$3000	$1000	2–7	Civic Affiliation: Mutual Benefit Society.
AWG Ethnic Minority Scholarship	200	$3000	$500	1–5	Earth Science; Education; Environmental Science; Gemology; Geography; Hydrology; Meteorology/Atmospheric Science; Museum Studies; Natural Resources; Natural Sciences; Oceanography; Physical Sciences. Limited to American Indian/Alaska Native; Black (non-Hispanic); Hispanic students.
Bright Flight Program	586	$3000	$1000	N/A	Residence: Mississippi. Studying in Missouri.
Calcot-Seitz Scholarship	93	$3000	$500	1–30	Agriculture. Residence: Arizona; California; New Mexico; Texas.
Chief Master Sergeants of the Air Force Scholarship Program	487	$3000	$500	30	Military Service: Air Force; Air Force National Guard.
CollegeBound Last Dollar Grant	556	$3000	$500	60–70	Residence: Manitoba. Must be in high school.
Developmental Disabilities Scholastic Achievement Scholarship for College Students who are Lutheran	195	$3000	$500	2–3	Dental Health/Services; Education; Health Administration; Health and Medical Sciences; Health Information Management/Technology; Humanities; Religion/Theology; Social Services; Special Education; Therapy/Rehabilitation. Religion: Lutheran.

Award Name	Page Number	Highest Dollar Amount	Lowest Dollar Amount	Number of Awards	Academic Fields/Career Goals and Nonacademic/Noncareer Criteria
The Donaldson Company, Inc. Scholarship Program	458	$3000	$2000	N/A	Corporate Affiliation: Donaldson Company.
GAPA Scholarships	618	$3000	$1000	3–5	Talent/Interest Area: leadership; LGBT issues.
GO Grant	580	$3000	$300	N/A	Residence: Kentucky.
Humana Foundation Scholarship Program	662	$3000	$1500	74–75	N/A
Illinois PTA Scholarship	210	$3000	$2000	2	Education. Residence: Illinois. Must be in high school.
Joseph S. Rumbaugh Historical Oration Contest	622	$3000	$1000	1–3	Talent/Interest Area: public speaking.
Lone Star Rising Career Scholarship	200	$3000	N/A	1–2	Earth Science; Education; Environmental Science; Gemology; Hydrology; Meteorology/Atmospheric Science; Museum Studies; Natural Resources; Natural Sciences; Oceanography; Physical Sciences; Science, Technology, and Society. Employment/Volunteer Experience: physical or natural sciences.
Millie Brother Scholarship for Children of Deaf Adults	644	$3000	$1000	2–5	N/A
Minnesota GI Bill Program	585	$3000	$50	N/A	Residence: Minnesota. Studying in Minnesota.
Moody Research Grants	99	$3000	$600	10–15	American Studies; History; International Studies; Military and Defense Studies; Museum Studies; Political Science.
MRCA Foundation Scholarship Program	116	$3000	$500	40	Architecture; Civil Engineering; Construction Engineering/Management; Drafting; Engineering/Technology; Industrial Design; Materials Science, Engineering, and Metallurgy; Trade/Technical Specialties. Employment/Volunteer Experience: construction.
NASA Idaho Space Grant Consortium Scholarship Program	109	$3000	$500	1–50	Applied Sciences; Biology; Chemical Engineering; Civil Engineering; Computer Science/Data Processing; Earth Science; Electrical Engineering/Electronics; Energy and Power Engineering; Engineering-Related Technologies; Engineering/Technology; Environmental Science; Fire Sciences; Geography; Materials Science, Engineering, and Metallurgy; Mathematics; Mechanical Engineering; Meteorology/Atmospheric Science; Natural Resources; Natural Sciences; Nuclear Science; Physical Sciences; Science, Technology, and Society. Studying in Idaho.
National Federation of Paralegal Associates Inc. Thomson Reuters Scholarship	320	$3000	$2000	2	Law/Legal Services.
National High School Journalist of the Year/Sister Rita Jeanne Scholarships	668	$3000	$850	1–7	Must be in high school.
Ohio American Legion Scholarships	434	$3000	$2000	15–18	Civic Affiliation: American Legion or Auxiliary. Military Service: General.

Award Name	Page Number	Highest Dollar Amount	Lowest Dollar Amount	Number of Awards	Academic Fields/Career Goals and Nonacademic/Noncareer Criteria
OSCPA Educational Foundation Scholarship Program	80	$3000	$500	45–75	Accounting. Studying in Oregon.
Rama Scholarship for the American Dream	268	$3000	$500	N/A	Food Service/Hospitality; Hospitality Management; Recreation, Parks, Leisure Studies; Travel/Tourism. Studying in California; Florida; Georgia; New York; North Carolina; South Carolina; Texas; Virginia. Limited to ethnic minority students.
Rockefeller State Wildlife Scholarship	325	$3000	$2000	N/A	Marine Biology; Marine/Ocean Engineering; Natural Resources; Oceanography. Residence: Kentucky. Studying in Louisiana.
Roothbert Fund Inc. Scholarship	599	$3000	$2000	50–60	Residence: Connecticut; Delaware; District of Columbia; Maine; Maryland; Massachusetts; New Hampshire; New Jersey; New York; North Carolina; Ohio; Pennsylvania; Rhode Island; Virginia; West Virginia. Studying in Connecticut; Delaware; District of Columbia; Maryland; Massachusetts; New Hampshire; New Jersey; New York; Ohio; Pennsylvania; Rhode Island; Vermont; Virginia; West Virginia.
Scholar Serve Awards	691	$3000	$500	5–10	N/A
Scholarships for Education, Business and Religion	147	$3000	$500	N/A	Business/Consumer Services; Education; Religion/Theology. Residence: California.
Simplilearn Student Ambassador Scholarship	694	$3000	$1000	1–3	N/A
Sonne Scholarship	368	$3000	$1000	2–4	Nursing. Residence: Illinois. Studying in Illinois.
Student Design Competition	103	$3000	$1000	6	Anthropology.
Tortoise Young Entrepreneurs Scholarship	606	$3000	$1000	3	Residence: Kansas; Missouri. Studying in Kansas; Missouri.
Traub-Dicker Rainbow Scholarship	698	$3000	$1000	3–4	N/A
Undergraduate Marketing Education Merit Scholarships	146	$3000	$500	7	Business/Consumer Services; Marketing. Studying in Maryland.
William P. Willis Scholarship	594	$3000	$2000	N/A	Residence: Ohio. Studying in Oklahoma.
Women in Logistics Scholarship	152	$3000	$1000	1–3	Business/Consumer Services; Trade/Technical Specialties; Transportation. Civic Affiliation: Women in Logistics. Residence: California. Studying in California.
Women's Independence Scholarship Program	710	$3000	$500	350–500	N/A
Writer's Digest Annual Writing Competition	627	$3000	$100	501	Talent/Interest Area: writing.
Writer's Digest Self-Published Book Awards	627	$3000	$1000	45	Talent/Interest Area: writing.
Access Missouri Financial Assistance Program	586	$2850	$300	N/A	Residence: Mississippi. Studying in Missouri.
Postsecondary Child Care Grant Program-Minnesota	585	$2800	$100	1–3,500	Residence: Minnesota. Studying in Minnesota.

Award Name	Page Number	Highest Dollar Amount	Lowest Dollar Amount	Number of Awards	Academic Fields/Career Goals and Nonacademic/Noncareer Criteria
Florida Postsecondary Student Assistance Grant	565	$2610	$200	N/A	Residence: Florida. Studying in Florida.
Florida Private Student Assistance Grant	565	$2610	$200	N/A	Residence: District of Columbia. Studying in Florida.
Florida Public Student Assistance Grant	565	$2610	$200	N/A	Residence: District of Columbia. Studying in Florida.
Florida Student Assistance Grant-Career Education	566	$2610	$200	N/A	Residence: Florida. Studying in Florida.
Adult Students in Scholastic Transition	653	$2500	$250	100–150	N/A
Agnes Jones Jackson Scholarship	445	$2500	$2000	20–40	Civic Affiliation: National Association for the Advancement of Colored People. Limited to ethnic minority students.
AHIMA Foundation Student Merit Scholarship	285	$2500	$1000	1	Health Information Management/Technology. Civic Affiliation: American Health Information Management Association.
Alaska Geological Society Scholarship	199	$2500	$500	3–8	Earth Science. Studying in Alaska.
American Legion Auxiliary Department of North Dakota National President's Scholarship	460	$2500	$1000	3	Employment/Volunteer Experience: community service. Military Service: General. Residence: North Dakota. Studying in North Dakota. Must be in high school.
American Legion Auxiliary Department of Oregon National President's Scholarship	545	$2500	$1000	3	Residence: Oregon. Must be in high school.
American Legion Auxiliary Department of Utah National President's Scholarship	431	$2500	$1000	15	Civic Affiliation: American Legion or Auxiliary. Military Service: General. Residence: Utah. Must be in high school.
American Legion Baseball Scholarship	613	$2500	$500	1–51	Talent/Interest Area: athletics/sports. Must be in high school.
American Legion Department of North Carolina High School Oratorical Contest	549	$2500	$1000	5	Residence: North Carolina. Talent/Interest Area: public speaking. Must be in high school.
American Legion Department of Washington Children and Youth Scholarships	434	$2500	$1500	2	Civic Affiliation: American Legion or Auxiliary. Residence: Washington. Must be in high school.
American-Scandinavian Foundation Translation Prize	323	$2500	$2000	2	Literature/English/Writing. Talent/Interest Area: Scandinavian language.
ASCPA Educational Foundation Scholarship	542	$2500	$1500	34–38	Residence: Alabama. Studying in Alabama.
Assured Life Association Endowment Scholarship Program	637	$2500	$500	65–75	N/A
Breakthrough to Nursing Scholarships for Racial/Ethnic Minorities	366	$2500	$1000	N/A	Nursing. Limited to ethnic minority students.
Career Journalism Scholarship	176	$2500	$1000	1–3	Communications; Journalism; Photojournalism/Photography; TV/Radio Broadcasting. Residence: Florida. Must be in high school.

Award Name	Page Number	Highest Dollar Amount	Lowest Dollar Amount	Number of Awards	Academic Fields/Career Goals and Nonacademic/Noncareer Criteria
Clem Judd, Jr. Memorial Scholarship	294	$2500	$1000	2	Hospitality Management. Residence: Hawaii. Limited to Asian/Pacific Islander students.
CrossLites Scholarship Award	617	$2500	$100	33	Talent/Interest Area: writing.
Delaware Solid Waste Authority John P. "Pat" Healy Scholarship	238	$2500	$1500	2	Engineering/Technology; Environmental Science. Residence: Delaware. Studying in Delaware. Talent/Interest Area: leadership.
Excellence in Accounting Scholarship	81	$2500	$1000	5–15	Accounting. Studying in South Dakota.
Foreclosure.com Scholarship Program	655	$2500	$500	3–2,500	N/A
Foundation for Accounting Education Scholarship	79	$2500	$500	1–60	Accounting. Residence: New York. Studying in New York.
Foundation of the National Student Nurses' Association Career Mobility Scholarship	366	$2500	$1000	N/A	Nursing.
Foundation of the National Student Nurses' Association Specialty Scholarship	367	$2500	$1000	N/A	Nursing.
Friends of Bill Rutherford Education Fund	595	$2500	$1000	1–2	Residence: Oregon.
Fulfilling Our Dreams Scholarship Fund	531	$2500	$500	50–60	Residence: California. Studying in California. Limited to Hispanic students.
Graphic Communications Scholarship Fund of New England	275	$2500	$1350	16–35	Graphics/Graphic Arts/Printing. Residence: Connecticut; Maine; Massachusetts; New Hampshire; Rhode Island; Vermont.
Hungry To Lead Scholarship	193	$2500	$500	4	Culinary Arts; Food Science/Nutrition; Food Service/Hospitality.
Institute of Management Accountants Memorial Education Fund Scholarships	148	$2500	$1000	N/A	Business/Consumer Services.
International Association of Fire Chiefs Foundation Scholarship Award	261	$2500	$500	20–30	Fire Sciences.
Jackson-Stricks Scholarship	479	$2500	$1500	1–2	Disability: physically disabled. Studying in New York.
Joseph S. Garske Collegiate Grant Program	440	$2500	$500	1–5	Civic Affiliation: Golf Course Superintendents Association of America. Employment/Volunteer Experience: community service. Talent/Interest Area: leadership. Must be in high school.
Kentucky Society of Certified Public Accountants College Scholarship	77	$2500	$1000	10–40	Accounting. Residence: Kentucky. Studying in Kentucky.
Korean-American Scholarship Foundation Northeastern Region Scholarships	523	$2500	$1000	60	Studying in Connecticut; Maine; Massachusetts; New Hampshire; New Jersey; New York; Rhode Island; Vermont. Limited to Asian/Pacific Islander students.
LAGRANT Foundation Scholarship for Undergraduates	85	$2500	$2000	N/A	Advertising/Public Relations; Business/Consumer Services; Communications; Graphics/Graphic Arts/Printing; Marketing. Limited to ethnic minority students.

Award Name	Page Number	Highest Dollar Amount	Lowest Dollar Amount	Number of Awards	Academic Fields/Career Goals and Nonacademic/Noncareer Criteria
LEAGUE Foundation Academic Scholarship	621	$2500	$1500	4–8	Talent/Interest Area: LGBT issues. Must be in high school.
Leveraging Educational Assistance Partnership	551	$2500	$100	N/A	Residence: Arizona. Studying in Arizona.
Literacy Grant Competition	440	$2500	$300	1–18	Civic Affiliation: Phi Kappa Phi.
Maine State Society Foundation Scholarship	582	$2500	$1000	5–15	Residence: Maine. Studying in Maine.
Minnesota Space Grant Consortium Scholarship Program	131	$2500	$500	40–70	Aviation/Aerospace; Computer Science/Data Processing; Earth Science; Electrical Engineering/Electronics; Engineering/Technology; Environmental Science; Mathematics; Mechanical Engineering; Meteorology/Atmospheric Science; Natural Sciences; Nuclear Science; Oceanography; Physical Sciences. Studying in Minnesota.
Minority Undergraduate Retention Grant-Wisconsin	538	$2500	$250	N/A	Residence: West Virginia. Studying in Wisconsin. Limited to ethnic minority students.
Mississippi Eminent Scholars Grant	585	$2500	$1157	2,908	Residence: Mississippi. Studying in Mississippi.
Missouri Broadcasters Association Scholarship Program	424	$2500	$1000	3–5	TV/Radio Broadcasting. Residence: Missouri. Studying in Missouri.
Missouri Insurance Education Foundation Scholarship	300	$2500	$2000	6	Insurance and Actuarial Science. Residence: Missouri. Studying in Missouri.
National Federation of the Blind of Missouri Scholarship Program for Legally Blind Students	481	$2500	$500	1–3	Disability: visually impaired. Residence: Missouri. Studying in Missouri.
New Hampshire Society of Certified Public Accountants Scholarship Fund	79	$2500	$500	1–7	Accounting. Residence: New Hampshire.
New Jersey Association of Realtors Educational Foundation Scholarship Program	400	$2500	$1000	20–32	Real Estate. Civic Affiliation: New Jersey Association of Realtors. Residence: New Jersey. Must be in high school.
Noplag Scholarship Essay Contest	682	$2500	$300	3	N/A
North Carolina Hispanic College Fund Scholarship	528	$2500	$500	N/A	Residence: North Carolina. Limited to Hispanic students.
Ohio Environmental Science & Engineering Scholarships	255	$2500	$1250	18	Environmental Science. Studying in Ohio.
Optimist International Oratorical Contest	623	$2500	$1000	N/A	Talent/Interest Area: public speaking.
Polish Heritage Scholarship	530	$2500	$1500	1–9	Residence: Maryland.
Professional Advancement Scholarship	276	$2500	$1200	7	Health Administration; Health and Medical Sciences; Health Information Management/Technology; Oncology; Radiology. Civic Affiliation: American Society of Radiologic Technologists.
Robert P. Sheppard Leadership Award for NSHSS Members	448	$2500	$1000	5	Civic Affiliation: National Society of High School Scholars. Talent/Interest Area: leadership. Must be in high school.
Robert T. Kenney Scholarship Program at the American Savings Foundation	551	$2500	$1000	400	Residence: Connecticut.

Award Name	Page Number	Highest Dollar Amount	Lowest Dollar Amount	Number of Awards	Academic Fields/Career Goals and Nonacademic/Noncareer Criteria
SCACPA Educational Fund Scholarships	81	$2500	$500	19–25	Accounting. Residence: South Carolina. Studying in South Carolina.
Scholarships for Orphans of Veterans	505	$2500	$1000	1	Military Service: General. Residence: New Hampshire. Studying in New Hampshire.
Simon Youth Foundation Community Scholarship Program	694	$2500	$1400	100–200	Must be in high school.
Society of Physics Students Outstanding Student in Research	392	$2500	$500	1–2	Physical Sciences. Civic Affiliation: Society of Physics Students.
South Carolina Need-Based Grants Program	602	$2500	$1250	1–26,730	Residence: South Carolina. Studying in South Carolina.
South Carolina Tourism and Hospitality Educational Foundation Scholarships	193	$2500	$750	5–16	Culinary Arts; Food Service/Hospitality; Hospitality Management. Residence: South Carolina. Studying in South Carolina.
Sussman-Miller Educational Assistance Fund	543	$2500	$500	25–30	Residence: New Mexico.
Swiss Benevolent Society of Chicago Scholarships	533	$2500	$500	30	Residence: Illinois; Wisconsin.
Tennessee Society of CPA Scholarship	82	$2500	$250	120–130	Accounting. Residence: Tennessee.
Tilford Field Studies Scholarship	199	$2500	$500	4–5	Earth Science. Civic Affiliation: Association of Engineering Geologists.
U.S. Scholarship Program	674	$2500	$600	100–150	N/A
Writer's Digest Popular Fiction Awards	627	$2500	$500	7	Talent/Interest Area: writing.
CSAC Cal Grant C Award	554	$2462	$576	N/A	Residence: British Columbia. Studying in California.
South Dakota Opportunity Scholarship	603	$2300	$1300	1,000–4,100	Residence: South Dakota. Studying in South Dakota. Must be in high school.
South Dakota Retailers Association Scholarship Program	91	$2250	$500	10–15	Agribusiness.
Menominee Indian Tribe of Wisconsin Higher Education Grants	525	$2200	$100	136	Limited to American Indian/Alaska Native students.

PROFILES OF SCHOLARSHIPS, GRANTS & PRIZES

Academic Fields/Career Goals

ACCOUNTING

AICPA INSTITUTE
https://www.aicpa.org/

AICPA/ACCOUNTEMPS STUDENT SCHOLARSHIP
AICPA/Accountemps Student Scholarship is one of four awards provided through the AICPA Legacy Scholars program. All applications must be completed and submitted by the deadline to be considered. Students interested in being considered for more than one AICPA Legacy Scholarship award need only complete one application--applicants will be evaluated for all awards for which they are eligible. Scholarship aid may be used only for the payment of expenses that directly relate to obtaining an accounting education (e.g.; tuition, fees, room and board, and/or books and materials). Awards are non-renewable and past recipients may not re-apply. Payments are sent directly to the student's financial aid office on behalf of the student. When available, publication and application details for this award can be found at https://thiswaytocpa.com/education/aicpa-legacy-scholarships/

Academic Fields/Career Goals: Accounting.

Award: Scholarship for use in sophomore, junior, senior, or graduate years; not renewable. *Number:* 4. *Amount:* $10,000.

Eligibility Requirements: Applicant must be enrolled or expecting to enroll full-time at a four-year institution or university. Available to U.S. citizens.

Application Requirements: Application form, application form may be submitted online (https://thiswaytocpa.com/education/aicpa-legacy-scholarships/), essay, recommendations or references, resume, transcript. *Deadline:* March 1.

Contact: Scholarship Manager
AICPA Institute
220 Leigh Farm Road
AICPA / Academic & Student Engagement
Durham, NC 27707-8110
E-mail: scholarships@aicpa.org

ALASKA SOCIETY OF CERTIFIED PUBLIC ACCOUNTANTS
http://www.akcpa.org/

PAUL HAGELBARGER MEMORIAL FUND SCHOLARSHIP
Scholarships open to all junior, senior, and graduate students who are majoring in accounting and attending institutions in Alaska.

Academic Fields/Career Goals: Accounting.

Award: Scholarship for use in junior, senior, or graduate years; not renewable. *Number:* 2–3. *Amount:* $2000.

Eligibility Requirements: Applicant must be enrolled or expecting to enroll full-time at a four-year institution or university and studying in Alaska. Available to U.S. citizens.

Application Requirements: Application form, recommendations or references, resume, transcript. *Deadline:* November 15.

Contact: Linda Plimpton, Executive Director
Alaska Society of Certified Public Accountants
341 West Tudor Road, Suite 105
Anchorage, AK 99503
Phone: 907-562-4334
Fax: 907-562-4025
E-mail: akcpa@ak.net

AMERICAN SOCIETY OF WOMEN ACCOUNTANTS
http://www.afwa.org/

ACCOUNTING & FINANCIAL WOMEN'S ALLIANCE UNDERGRADUATE SCHOLARSHIP
Scholarship awards are presented to support the costs of attending 3rd, 4th, or 5th year when pursuing an accounting or finance degree. Candidates will be reviewed on leadership, character, communication skills, scholastic average, and financial need.

Academic Fields/Career Goals: Accounting; Finance.

Award: Scholarship for use in junior, senior, or graduate years; not renewable.

Eligibility Requirements: Applicant must be enrolled or expecting to enroll full- or part-time at a four-year institution or university; female and must have an interest in leadership. Available to U.S. and non-U.S. citizens.

Application Requirements: Application form, essay, financial need analysis. *Deadline:* April 1.

Contact: Kristin Edwards, Administrator
Phone: 703-506-3265
Fax: 703-506-3266
E-mail: kedwards@aswa.org

ASSOCIATION OF CERTIFIED FRAUD EXAMINERS
http://www.acfe.com/

RITCHIE-JENNINGS MEMORIAL SCHOLARSHIP
Applicant must be an undergraduate or graduate student, currently enrolled full-time (12 semester hours undergraduate; 9 semester hours graduate, or equivalent) at an accredited four-year college or university (or equivalent) with a declared major or minor in accounting or criminal justice.

Academic Fields/Career Goals: Accounting; Criminal Justice/Criminology.

Award: Scholarship for use in freshman, sophomore, junior, or senior years; not renewable. *Number:* up to 30. *Amount:* $1000.

Eligibility Requirements: Applicant must be enrolled or expecting to enroll full-time at a four-year institution or university. Available to U.S. and non-U.S. citizens.

Application Requirements: Application form, essay, recommendations or references, transcript. *Deadline:* April 16.

Contact: Keely Miers, Scholarship Coordinator
Association of Certified Fraud Examiners
The Gregor Building, 716 West Avenue
Austin, TX 78701
Phone: 800-245-3321
Fax: 512-478-9297
E-mail: scholarships@acfe.com

AUTOMOTIVE WOMEN'S ALLIANCE FOUNDATION
http://awafoundation.org/index.php

AUTOMOTIVE WOMEN'S ALLIANCE FOUNDATION SCHOLARSHIPS
Scholarships are the root of our purpose in Automotive Women's Alliance Foundation (AWAF). As an active professional foundation dedicated to supporting the advancement of automotive professionals, AWAF strives to motivate current and future students studying an automotive related field. Scholarships are selected by the Scholarship

Committee and awarded quarterly to the women that solicit passion and drive for the automotive industry. It is our hope that with these scholarships, we can lessen the burden on students and allow them to focus on gaining knowledge and development in automotive related fields and thus enhance their potential career path and the future of the industry. Scholarships are awarded to female, North American citizens, with a passion for a career or advancement in the automotive and its related industries. While AWAF members and family members are encouraged to apply for scholarships, we encourage applicants who are not affiliated with the organization to apply as well. In order to be eligible for a scholarship applicants should be already accepted to or enrolled in an accredited collegiate program, with a 3.0 or higher GPA.

Academic Fields/Career Goals: Accounting; Advertising/Public Relations; Applied Sciences; Business/Consumer Services; Chemical Engineering; Civil Engineering; Communications; Computer Science/Data Processing; Economics; Electrical Engineering/Electronics; Energy and Power Engineering; Engineering-Related Technologies; Engineering/Technology; Environmental Science; Finance; Graphics/Graphic Arts/Printing; Human Resources; Industrial Design; International Studies; Law/Legal Services; Marketing; Materials Science, Engineering, and Metallurgy; Mathematics; Mechanical Engineering; Meteorology/Atmospheric Science; Science, Technology, and Society; Statistics; Transportation.

Award: Scholarship for use in freshman, sophomore, junior, senior, graduate, or postgraduate years; not renewable. *Number:* 15–24. *Amount:* $2500.

Eligibility Requirements: Applicant must be Canadian, Latin American/Caribbean, Mexican citizen; enrolled or expecting to enroll full- or part-time at a two-year or four-year institution or university; female and resident of Mississippi. Available to U.S. and Canadian citizens.

Application Requirements: Application form. *Deadline:* continuous.

Contact: RoseAnn Nicolai, Administrator
Automotive Women's Alliance Foundation
AWAF Scholarships
Box 4305
Troy, MI 48099
Phone: 877-393-2923
E-mail: admin@AWAFoundation.org

CATCHING THE DREAM

http://www.catchingthedream.org/

TRIBAL BUSINESS MANAGEMENT PROGRAM (TBM)

Renewable scholarships available for Native American and Alaska Native students to study business administration, economic development, and related subjects, with the goal to provide experts in business management to Native American tribes in the U.S. Must be at least one-quarter Native American from a federally recognized, state recognized, or terminated tribe. Must demonstrate high academic achievement, depth of character, leadership, seriousness of purpose, and service orientation.

Academic Fields/Career Goals: Accounting; Business/Consumer Services; Computer Science/Data Processing; Economics; Electrical Engineering/Electronics; Engineering-Related Technologies.

Award: Scholarship for use in freshman, sophomore, junior, senior, graduate, or postgraduate years; renewable. *Number:* 35. *Amount:* $500–$5000.

Eligibility Requirements: Applicant must be American Indian/Alaska Native and enrolled or expecting to enroll full-time at a four-year institution or university. Available to U.S. citizens.

Application Requirements: Application form, essay, financial need analysis, personal photograph.

Contact: Joy Noll, Student Services
Catching the Dream
8200 Mountain Road, NE, Suite 103
Albuquerque, NM 87110
Phone: 505-262-2351
E-mail: nscholarsh@aol.com

COLORADO SOCIETY OF CERTIFIED PUBLIC ACCOUNTANTS EDUCATIONAL FOUNDATION

http://www.cocpa.org/

COLORADO COLLEGE AND UNIVERSITY SCHOLARSHIPS

Award available to declared accounting majors at Colorado colleges and universities with accredited accounting programs. Must have completed at least 8 semester hours of accounting courses. Overall GPA and accounting GPA must be at least 3.0. Must be Colorado resident.

Academic Fields/Career Goals: Accounting.

Award: Scholarship for use in junior, senior, graduate, or postgraduate years; not renewable. *Number:* 15–20. *Amount:* $2500.

Eligibility Requirements: Applicant must be enrolled or expecting to enroll full- or part-time at a four-year institution or university; resident of Colorado and studying in Colorado. Available to U.S. citizens.

Application Requirements: Application form, recommendations or references, transcript. *Deadline:* June 1.

Contact: Gena Mantz, Membership Coordinator
Phone: 303-741-8613
Fax: 303-773-6344
E-mail: gmantz@cocpa.org

CONNECTICUT SOCIETY OF CERTIFIED PUBLIC ACCOUNTANTS

http://www.ctcpas.org/

CT SOCIETY OF CPAS RISING SOPHOMORE ACCOUNTING SCHOLARSHIP

The Educational Trust Fund of the Connecticut Society of CPAs (CTCPA) has established this scholarship to assist Connecticut accounting majors entering into their sophomore year of study at a four-year college or university in financing their education.

Academic Fields/Career Goals: Accounting.

Award: Scholarship for use in sophomore year; not renewable. *Number:* 1–4. *Amount:* $1500.

Eligibility Requirements: Applicant must be enrolled or expecting to enroll full-time at a four-year institution or university; resident of Connecticut and studying in Connecticut. Available to U.S. citizens.

Application Requirements: Application form, driver's license, essay. *Deadline:* April 17.

Contact: Mrs. Jill Brightman, Program Coordinator
Connecticut Society of Certified Public Accountants
716 Brook Street, Suite 100
Rocky Hill, CT 06067
Phone: 860-258-0329
E-mail: jillb@ctcpas.org

EDUCATIONAL TRUST FUND OF THE CTCPA - CANDIDATE'S SCHOLARSHIP

Scholarship of $5000 that assists students in complying with the 150-hour requirement of the Connecticut State Board of Accountancy to sit for the Uniform Certified Public Accountant Examination. An overall GPA of 3.0.

Academic Fields/Career Goals: Accounting.

Award: Scholarship for use in senior or graduate years; not renewable. *Number:* 1. *Amount:* $5000.

Eligibility Requirements: Applicant must be enrolled or expecting to enroll full- or part-time at a four-year institution or university; resident of Connecticut and studying in Connecticut. Available to U.S. citizens.

Application Requirements: Application form, driver's license, essay. *Deadline:* April 17.

Contact: Mrs. Jill Brightman, Program Coordinator
Connecticut Society of Certified Public Accountants
716 Brook Street, Suite 100
Rocky Hill, CT 06067
Phone: 860-258-0239
E-mail: jillb@ctcpas.org

DECA (DISTRIBUTIVE EDUCATION CLUBS OF AMERICA)

http://www.deca.org/

HARRY A. APPLEGATE SCHOLARSHIP

Scholarship available to current DECA or Collegiate DECA members for undergraduate study in marketing education, marketing, entrepreneurship, finance, hospitality or management. Nonrenewable merit-based award for current DECA members based on DECA activities, grades, and leadership.

Academic Fields/Career Goals: Accounting; Business/Consumer Services; Education; Fashion Design; Finance; Food Service/Hospitality; Hospitality Management; Marketing.

Award: Scholarship for use in freshman, sophomore, junior, or senior years; not renewable. *Number:* 20–25. *Amount:* $1000–$5000.

Eligibility Requirements: Applicant must be enrolled or expecting to enroll full-time at a two-year or four-year institution or university. Applicant or parent of applicant must be member of Distribution Ed Club or Future Business Leaders of America. Available to U.S. and non-U.S. citizens.

Application Requirements: Application form. *Deadline:* January 19.

Contact: Cameron Brown, Corporate and External Affairs Assistant
DECA (Distributive Education Clubs of America)
1908 Association Drive
Reston, VA 20191
Phone: 703-860-5000 Ext. 303
E-mail: cameron_burrell@deca.org

EDUCATIONAL FOUNDATION FOR WOMEN IN ACCOUNTING (EFWA)

https://www.efwa.org/

MICHELE L. MCDONALD MEMORIAL SCHOLARSHIP

An annual scholarship will be awarded in the amount of $1,000 for the purpose of earning a degree in Accounting, with preference being given to a woman returning to college from the work force or after raising children.

Academic Fields/Career Goals: Accounting.

Award: Scholarship for use in freshman, sophomore, junior, or senior years; not renewable. *Amount:* $1000.

Eligibility Requirements: Applicant must be enrolled or expecting to enroll full- or part-time at an institution or university and married female. Available to U.S. citizens.

Application Requirements: Application form, application form may be submitted online, financial need analysis. *Deadline:* April 30.

Contact: Foundation Administrator
Educational Foundation for Women in Accounting (EFWA)
136 South Keowee St.
Dayton, OH 45402
Phone: 937-424-3391
Fax: 937-222-5794
E-mail: info@efwa.org

RHONDA J. B. O'LEARY MEMORIAL SCHOLARSHIP (SEATTLE CHAPTER AFWA)

A one-year scholarship for an amount up to $2,000 will be awarded to an undergraduate or graduate student attending an accredited school within the State of Washington.

Academic Fields/Career Goals: Accounting.

Award: Scholarship for use in freshman, sophomore, junior, senior, or graduate years; renewable. *Amount:* $2000.

Eligibility Requirements: Applicant must be enrolled or expecting to enroll full- or part-time at an institution or university; female and studying in Washington. Available to U.S. citizens.

Application Requirements: Application form, application form may be submitted online, financial need analysis. *Deadline:* April 30.

Contact: Foundation Administrator
Educational Foundation for Women in Accounting (EFWA)
136 South Keowee St.
Dayton, OH 45402
Phone: 937-424-3391
Fax: 937-222-5794
E-mail: info@efwa.org

ROWLING, DOLD & ASSOCIATES LLP SCHOLARSHIP

One year $1000 scholarship award for minority women enrolled in an accounting program at an accredited college or university. Women returning to school with undergraduate status; incoming, current, or reentry juniors or seniors; or minority women are all eligible.

Academic Fields/Career Goals: Accounting.

Award: Scholarship for use in junior, senior, or graduate years; not renewable. *Amount:* $1000.

Eligibility Requirements: Applicant must be American Indian/Alaska Native, Asian/Pacific Islander, Black (non-Hispanic), Hispanic; enrolled or expecting to enroll full- or part-time at a four-year institution or university and female. Available to U.S. citizens.

Application Requirements: Application form, financial need analysis, transcript. *Deadline:* April 15.

Contact: Foundation Administrator
Educational Foundation for Women in Accounting (EFWA)
136 South Keowee St.
Dayton, OH 45402
Phone: 937-424-3391
Fax: 937-222-5794
E-mail: info@efwa.org

WOMEN IN NEED SCHOLARSHIP

This scholarship is for a woman who is the primary source of support for her family and is completing her sophomore year of academic pursuit to earn a Bachelors degree in Accounting. It is awarded in the amount of $2,000 per year for two years and will be renewed for the second year upon completion of satisfactory course work as evidenced by a 3.0 GPA.

Academic Fields/Career Goals: Accounting.

Award: Scholarship for use in junior year; renewable. *Number:* 1. *Amount:* $2000.

Eligibility Requirements: Applicant must be enrolled or expecting to enroll full- or part-time at an institution or university and female. Available to U.S. citizens.

Application Requirements: Application form, application form may be submitted online, financial need analysis. *Deadline:* April 30.

Contact: Foundation Administrator
Educational Foundation for Women in Accounting (EFWA)
136 South Keowee St.
Dayton, OH 45402
Phone: 937-424-3391
Fax: 937-222-5794
E-mail: info@efwa.org

WOMEN IN TRANSITION SCHOLARSHIP

Renewable award available to incoming or current freshmen and women returning to school with a freshman status. Scholarship value may be up to $16,000 over four years.

Academic Fields/Career Goals: Accounting.

Award: Scholarship for use in freshman year; renewable. *Number:* 1. *Amount:* up to $4000.

Eligibility Requirements: Applicant must be enrolled or expecting to enroll full- or part-time at a four-year institution or university and female. Available to U.S. citizens.

Application Requirements: Application form, financial need analysis, transcript. *Deadline:* April 15.

Contact: Foundation Administrator
Educational Foundation for Women in Accounting (EFWA)
136 South Keowee St.
Dayton, OH 45402
Phone: 937-424-3391
Fax: 937-222-5794
E-mail: info@efwa.org

EDUCATIONAL FOUNDATION OF THE MASSACHUSETTS SOCIETY OF CERTIFIED PUBLIC ACCOUNTANTS

https://www.cpatrack.com/

KATHLEEN M. PEABODY, CPA, MEMORIAL SCHOLARSHIP

Sponsored by Wolf & Company PC, the Kathleen M. Peabody, CPA, Memorial Scholarship is to encourage individuals who have demonstrated academic excellence and financial need to pursue a career in public accounting in Massachusetts. Information on website at http://www.cpatrack.com.

Academic Fields/Career Goals: Accounting.

Award: Scholarship for use in junior or senior years; not renewable. *Number:* 1. *Amount:* $2500.

Eligibility Requirements: Applicant must be enrolled or expecting to enroll full-time at an institution or university; resident of Maryland and studying in Massachusetts. Available to U.S. citizens.

Application Requirements: Application form, application form may be submitted online, essay, financial need analysis. *Deadline:* February 3.

Contact: Erica DeBiase, Director of Academic & Career Development
Educational Foundation of the Massachusetts Society of
Certified Public Accountants
105 Chauncy Street, 10th Floor
Boston, MA 02111
Phone: 617-303-2403
E-mail: edebiase@mscpaonline.org

MSCPA/ALPFA SCHOLARSHIP

To encourage Hispanic and Latino students who have demonstrated academic excellence and financial need to pursue a career in accounting in Massachusetts. Must be a ALPFA Boston student member.

Academic Fields/Career Goals: Accounting.

Award: Scholarship for use in sophomore, junior, senior, or graduate years; not renewable. *Amount:* $2500.

Eligibility Requirements: Applicant must be Hispanic and enrolled or expecting to enroll full-time at an institution or university. Available to U.S. citizens.

Application Requirements: Application form, application form may be submitted online, essay. *Deadline:* February 3.

Contact: Erica DeBiase, Director of Academic & Career Development
Educational Foundation of the Massachusetts Society of
Certified Public Accountants
105 Chauncy Street, 10th Floor
Boston, MA 02111
Phone: 617-303-2403
E-mail: edebiase@mscpaonline.org

MSCPA FIRM SCHOLARSHIP

Scholarship to encourage individuals who have demonstrated academic excellence and financial need to pursue a career in public accounting in Massachusetts.

Academic Fields/Career Goals: Accounting.

Award: Scholarship for use in junior, senior, or graduate years; not renewable. *Number:* 12–16. *Amount:* $2500.

Eligibility Requirements: Applicant must be enrolled or expecting to enroll full-time at a four-year institution or university and resident of Massachusetts. Available to U.S. citizens.

Application Requirements: Application form, essay, financial need analysis, recommendations or references, transcript. *Deadline:* April 1.

Contact: Erica DeBiase, Director of Academic & Career Development
Educational Foundation of the Massachusetts Society of
Certified Public Accountants
105 Chauncy Street, 10th Floor
Boston, MA 02111
Phone: 617-303-2403
E-mail: edebiase@mscpaonline.org

MSCPA/NABA SCHOLARSHIP

To encourage Black and African American students who have demonstrated academic excellence and financial need to pursue a career in accounting in Massachusetts.

Academic Fields/Career Goals: Accounting.

Award: Scholarship for use in junior, senior, or graduate years; not renewable.

Eligibility Requirements: Applicant must be Black (non-Hispanic); enrolled or expecting to enroll full-time at an institution or university and studying in Massachusetts. Applicant or parent of applicant must be member of National Association of Black Accountants. Available to U.S. citizens.

Application Requirements: Application form, application form may be submitted online, essay, interview. *Deadline:* June 21.

Contact: Whitney Russell, ERSC Scholarship Committee Chair
E-mail: scholarship@nabaer.org

WOMEN IN ACCOUNTING SCHOLARSHIP

The purpose of these scholarships is to encourage women who have demonstrated academic excellence and financial need to pursue an accounting career in Massachusetts.

Academic Fields/Career Goals: Accounting.

Award: Scholarship for use in junior, senior, or graduate years; not renewable. *Number:* 3–4. *Amount:* $2500.

Eligibility Requirements: Applicant must be enrolled or expecting to enroll full-time at an institution or university; female and resident of Maryland. Available to U.S. citizens.

Application Requirements: Application form, application form may be submitted online, essay, financial need analysis. *Deadline:* February 3.

Contact: Erica DeBiase, Director of Academic & Career Development
Educational Foundation of the Massachusetts Society of
Certified Public Accountants
105 Chauncy Street, 10th Floor
Boston, MA 02111
Phone: 617-303-2403
E-mail: edebiase@mscpaonline.org

FLORIDA INSTITUTE OF CERTIFIED PUBLIC ACCOUNTANTS SCHOLARSHIP FOUNDATION, INC.

http://www.ficpa.org/

1040K RUN/WALK SCHOLARSHIPS

1. Applicant(s) must be a citizen of the United States or hold permanent residency status and be a resident of Miami-Dade County, Broward County, Monroe County, or Palm Beach County. a. The Lewis Davis scholarship is to be awarded to an African-American student. b. One scholarship is to be awarded to a minority student. (May or not be African-American) c. One scholarship is to be awarded to a student based on need. (May or not be African-American) See website for details http://www1.ficpa.org/ficpa/Visitors/Careers/EdFoundation/Scholar.ships/Availa.

Academic Fields/Career Goals: Accounting.

Award: Scholarship for use in senior or graduate years; not renewable. *Number:* up to 3. *Amount:* up to $3000.

Eligibility Requirements: Applicant must be enrolled or expecting to enroll full-time at a four-year institution or university; resident of Florida and studying in Florida. Available to U.S. citizens.

Application Requirements: Application form, must be recommended by accounting faculty committee at Florida college or university attended, recommendations or references, transcript. *Deadline:* February 15.

Contact: Mrs. Carol Kearney, Stewardship Coordinator
Florida Institute of Certified Public Accountants Scholarship
Foundation, Inc.
3800 Esplanade Way
Suite 210
Tallahassee, FL 32311
Phone: 800-3423197 Ext. 415
Fax: 850-222-8190
E-mail: ficpascholarship@ficpa.org

FICPA SCHOLARSHIP FOUNDATION SCHOLARSHIPS

Scholarship for full-time or part-time (minimum of six credit hours), fourth- or fifth-year accounting major at participating Florida colleges or universities. Must be a member of the Florida Institute of CPAs, a Florida resident and plan to practice accounting in Florida. See website for list of institutions http://www1.ficpa.org/ficpa/Visitors/Careers/EdFoundation/Scholarships.

Academic Fields/Career Goals: Accounting.

Award: Scholarship for use in senior or graduate years; not renewable. *Number:* up to 63. *Amount:* $1000–$2000.

Eligibility Requirements: Applicant must be enrolled or expecting to enroll full- or part-time at a four-year institution or university; resident of Florida and studying in Florida. Available to U.S. citizens.

Application Requirements: Application form, must be recommended by faculty committee at school attended, recommendations or references, transcript. *Deadline:* March 4.

Contact: Mrs. Carol Kearney, Stewardship Coordinator
Florida Institute of Certified Public Accountants Scholarship Foundation, Inc.
3800 Esplanade Way
Suite 210
Tallahassee, FL 32311
Phone: 800-3423197
Fax: 850-222-8190
E-mail: ficpascholarship@ficpa.org

GOVERNMENT FINANCE OFFICERS ASSOCIATION

https://www.gfoa.org/

FRANK L. GREATHOUSE GOVERNMENT ACCOUNTING SCHOLARSHIP

Two scholarships awarded to undergraduate or graduate students enrolled full-time, preparing for a career in state or local government finance.

Academic Fields/Career Goals: Accounting; Finance.

Award: Scholarship for use in junior, senior, or graduate years; not renewable. *Number:* 2. *Amount:* $10,000.

Eligibility Requirements: Applicant must be enrolled or expecting to enroll full-time at an institution or university. Available to U.S. and Canadian citizens.

Application Requirements: Application form, essay. *Deadline:* January 26.

Contact: Genevieve Carter, Consultant/Analyst
Government Finance Officers Association
203 N. LaSalle Street, Suite 2700
Chicago, IL 60601-1210
Phone: 312-977-9700
Fax: 312-977-4806
E-mail: gcarter@gfoa.org

JEFFREY L. ESSER CAREER DEVELOPMENT SCHOLARSHIP

Award for part-time student pursuing an Associate's degree or Bachelor's degree in public administration, (governmental) accounting, finance or business administration, and a career plan in state/provincial or local government finance. Must be currently employed at least 3 years by one or more state or local governments.

Academic Fields/Career Goals: Accounting; Business/Consumer Services; Finance; Public Policy and Administration.

Award: Scholarship for use in freshman, sophomore, junior, or senior years; not renewable. *Number:* 1–2. *Amount:* $5000–$15,000.

Eligibility Requirements: Applicant must be enrolled or expecting to enroll part-time at a two-year institution or university. Available to U.S. and Canadian citizens.

Application Requirements: Application form, essay. *Deadline:* January 26.

Contact: Genevieve Carter, Consultant/Analyst
Government Finance Officers Association
203 N. LaSalle Street, Suite 2700
Chicago, IL 60601-1210
Phone: 312-977-9700
Fax: 312-977-4806
E-mail: gcarter@gfoa.org

MINORITIES IN GOVERNMENT FINANCE SCHOLARSHIP

Awards upper-division undergraduate or graduate students of public administration, governmental accounting, finance, political science, economics, or business administration to recognize outstanding performance by minority students preparing for a career in state and local government finance.

Academic Fields/Career Goals: Accounting; Business/Consumer Services; Economics; Finance; Political Science; Public Policy and Administration.

Award: Scholarship for use in junior, senior, or graduate years; not renewable. *Number:* 1. *Amount:* $10,000.

Eligibility Requirements: Applicant must be American Indian/Alaska Native, Asian/Pacific Islander, Black (non-Hispanic), Hispanic and enrolled or expecting to enroll full- or part-time at an institution or university. Available to U.S. and Canadian citizens.

Application Requirements: Application form, essay. *Deadline:* January 26.

Contact: Genevieve Carter, Consultant/Analyst
Government Finance Officers Association
203 N. LaSalle Street, Suite 2700
Chicago, IL 60601-1210
Phone: 312-977-9700
Fax: 312-977-4806
E-mail: gcarter@gfoa.org

GREATER WASHINGTON SOCIETY OF CPAS

http://www.gwscpa.org/

GREATER WASHINGTON SOCIETY OF CPAS SCHOLARSHIP

Scholarship available to accounting students. School must offer an accounting degree that qualifies graduates to sit for the CPA exam (must meet the 150-hour rule). Minimum 3.0 GPA in major courses required. Application details on our website http://www.gwscpa.org.

Academic Fields/Career Goals: Accounting.

Award: Scholarship for use in junior, senior, or graduate years; not renewable. *Number:* 3–5. *Amount:* $2000–$4500.

Eligibility Requirements: Applicant must be enrolled or expecting to enroll full-time at a four-year institution or university; resident of District of Columbia and studying in District of Columbia. Available to U.S. citizens.

Application Requirements: Application form, essay, financial need analysis, recommendations or references, resume, transcript. *Deadline:* February 15.

Contact: Mr. Brian Calvary, Membership Director
Greater Washington Society of CPAs
1140 Connecticut Avenue, NW
Suite 606
Washington, DC 20036
Phone: 202-601-0569
E-mail: info@gwscpa.org

HAWAII SOCIETY OF CERTIFIED PUBLIC ACCOUNTANTS

http://www.hscpa.org/

HSCPA SCHOLARSHIP PROGRAM FOR ACCOUNTING STUDENTS

Scholarship for Hawaii resident currently attending an accredited Hawaii college or university. Minimum 3.0 GPA required. Must be majoring, or concentrating, in accounting with the intention to sit for the CPA exam, and have completed an intermediate accounting course. Number of awards vary from year to year.

Academic Fields/Career Goals: Accounting.

Award: Scholarship for use in freshman, sophomore, junior, or senior years; not renewable. *Amount:* $500–$1500.

Eligibility Requirements: Applicant must be enrolled or expecting to enroll full-time at a four-year institution or university; resident of Hawaii and studying in Hawaii. Available to U.S. citizens.

Application Requirements: Application form, community service, recommendations or references, test scores, transcript. *Deadline:* January 31.

Contact: Kathy Castillo, Executive Director
Hawaii Society of Certified Public Accountants
900 Fort Street Mall, Suite 850
Honolulu, HI 96813
Phone: 808-537-9475
Fax: 808-537-3520
E-mail: info@hscpa.org

ILLINOIS CPA SOCIETY/CPA ENDOWMENT FUND OF ILLINOIS

http://www.icpas.org/

ILLINOIS CPA SOCIETY ACCOUNTING SCHOLARSHIP PROGRAM

The Illinois CPA Society has numerous scholarships available to support accounting students who are studying accounting and planning to become a CPA. Candidates must demonstrate a course of study which reflects a goal to sit for the CPA exam in Illinois. The scholarship program supports diversity of students, investing in their success and helping them to realize their dream of becoming CPAs. Scholarship recipients have studied at a variety of schools throughout the state, from large state universities to small private schools to community colleges. Some scholarships have supported students with their graduate studies, while others support a fifth year of undergraduate education.

Academic Fields/Career Goals: Accounting.

Award: Scholarship for use in junior, senior, graduate, or postgraduate years; not renewable. *Number:* 12–35. *Amount:* $500–$4000.

Eligibility Requirements: Applicant must be enrolled or expecting to enroll full- or part-time at a four-year institution or university; resident of Illinois and studying in Illinois. Available to U.S. citizens.

Application Requirements: Application form, application form may be submitted online (https://thiswaytocpa.com/education/scholarship-search/illinois-cpa-society-accounting-scholarship-program/), essay, recommendations or references, resume, transcript. *Deadline:* April 1.

Contact: Elizabeth Anderson, Student Engagement & Diversity
Specialist
Phone: 312-517-7652
E-mail: andersone@icpas.org

INDEPENDENT COLLEGE FUND OF NEW JERSEY

http://www.njcolleges.org/

COHNREZNICK ACCOUNTING SCHOLARSHIP

The CohnReznick Scholarship recognizes and rewards high achieving students preparing for careers in public accounting. CohnReznick seeks to support candiates who align with its mission to provide forward thinking solutions, service that exceeds expectations, and creates opportunity, value and trust for their clients, people and the community. Applicant must be be enrolled as a full-time student at an ICFNJ member college or university; majoring in Accounting with a demonstrated desire to pursue a career in public accounting including a commitment and plan for attaining 150 credit hours); must be a junior year during award period; and possess a minimum cunulative GPA of 3.2 on 4.0 scale. Candidates should be engaged as a leader, or otherwise demonstrate leadership abilities, potential or qualities, through academic work, special project activities and/or other extracurricular experiences.

Academic Fields/Career Goals: Accounting.

Award: Scholarship for use in junior year; renewable. *Number:* 3. *Amount:* $2000.

Eligibility Requirements: Applicant must be enrolled or expecting to enroll full-time at an institution or university.

Application Requirements: Application form, essay.

Contact: Yvette Panella
Summit, NJ 07901
Phone: 908-277-3424
Fax: 908-277-0851
E-mail: ypanella@njcolleges.org

MARTIN R. SULLIVAN MEMORIAL/PRICEWATERHOUSECOOPERS SCHOLARSHIP

The scholarship was created in memory of the late Martin R. Sullivan, a partner at Coopers & Lybrand, who had an interest in accounting education at New Jersey's independent colleges and in the preparation of students entering the accounting profession. The scholarship assists high achieving students to prepare for careers in public accounting. Applicant must be entering your junior or senior year; possess a minimum cumulative grade point average of 3.3 on a 4.0 scale; be majoring in accounting; demonstrate superior academic performance and promise for a career in public accounting.

Academic Fields/Career Goals: Accounting.

Award: Scholarship for use in junior or senior years. *Number:* 2–4. *Amount:* $1000–$2000.

Eligibility Requirements: Applicant must be enrolled or expecting to enroll at an institution or university.

Application Requirements: Application form, essay. *Deadline:* October 1.

Contact: Yvette Panella
Summit, NJ 07901
Phone: 908-277-3424
Fax: 908-277-0851
E-mail: ypanella@njcolleges.org

INSTITUTE OF MANAGEMENT ACCOUNTANTS

https://www.imanet.org/students/scholarships-and-awards/scholarships?ssopc=1

STUART CAMERON AND MARGARET MCLEOD MEMORIAL SCHOLARSHIP

Scholarships for IMA undergraduate or graduate student members studying at accredited institutions in the U.S. and Puerto Rico and carrying 12 credits per semester. Must be pursuing a career in management accounting, financial management, or information technology, and have a minimum GPA of 3.0. Awards based on academic merit, IMA participation, strength of recommendations, and quality of written statements.

Academic Fields/Career Goals: Accounting; Business/Consumer Services.

Award: Scholarship for use in junior, senior, or graduate years; not renewable. *Number:* 1. *Amount:* $5000.

Eligibility Requirements: Applicant must be enrolled or expecting to enroll full- or part-time at a two-year or four-year institution or university. Available to U.S. citizens.

Application Requirements: Application form, essay, resume, transcript. *Deadline:* February 15.

Contact: Kerry Butkera, Research & Academic Relations Administrator
Institute of Management Accountants
IMA
10 Paragon Drive, Suite 1
Montvale, NJ 07628
Phone: 800-638-4427 Ext. 1546
E-mail: kbutkera@imanet.org

INTERNAL AUDIT FOUNDATION

http://www.theiia.org/

ESTHER R. SAWYER RESEARCH AWARD

Awarded to a student entering or currently enrolled in an Internal Auditing Education Partnership (IAEP) program at an IIA-affiliated school. Awarded based on submission of an original manuscript on a specific topic related to modern internal auditing.

Academic Fields/Career Goals: Accounting; Business/Consumer Services.

Award: Prize for use in freshman, sophomore, junior, senior, or graduate years; not renewable. *Number:* 1–3. *Amount:* $3000–$5000.

Eligibility Requirements: Applicant must be enrolled or expecting to enroll full-time at a four-year institution or university. Available to U.S. and non-U.S. citizens.

Application Requirements: Application form, essay. *Deadline:* March 1.

Contact: Benjamin Bouchillon, Director of Publishing and Retail
Internal Audit Foundation
1035 Greenwood Blvd., Suite 401
Lake Mary, FL 32746
Phone: 407-937-1352
E-mail: foundation@theiia.org

KENTUCKY SOCIETY OF CERTIFIED PUBLIC ACCOUNTANTS

http://www.kycpa.org/

KENTUCKY SOCIETY OF CERTIFIED PUBLIC ACCOUNTANTS COLLEGE SCHOLARSHIP

Nonrenewable award for accounting majors at a Kentucky college or university. Must rank in upper third of class or have a minimum 3.0 GPA. Must be a Kentucky resident.

Academic Fields/Career Goals: Accounting.

Award: Scholarship for use in sophomore, junior, or senior years; not renewable. *Number:* 10–40. *Amount:* $1000–$2500.

Eligibility Requirements: Applicant must be enrolled or expecting to enroll part-time at a two-year or four-year institution or university; resident of Kentucky and studying in Kentucky. Available to U.S. citizens.

Application Requirements: Application form, essay. *Deadline:* February 18.

Contact: Julie Salvaggio, Educational Foundation Manager
Kentucky Society of Certified Public Accountants
1735 Alliant Avenue
Louisville, KY 40299-6326
Phone: 502-736-1360
E-mail: jsalvaggio@kycpa.org

MARYLAND ASSOCIATION OF CERTIFIED PUBLIC ACCOUNTANTS EDUCATIONAL FOUNDATION

https://www.macpa.org/for-students/

MACPA EDUCATIONAL FOUNDATION SCHOLARSHIP AWARD

Award for Maryland residents who will have completed at least 60 credit hours at a Maryland college or university by the time of the award. Must have 3.0 GPA, demonstrate commitment to 150 semester hours of education, and intend to pursue a career as a certified public accountant. Number of awards varies. Must be a student member with the Maryland Association of CPAs. U.S. citizenship required. See website at for further details. https://www.macpa.org/for-students/

Academic Fields/Career Goals: Accounting.

Award: Scholarship for use in junior, senior, or graduate years; renewable. *Number:* 10–12. *Amount:* $500–$1500.

Eligibility Requirements: Applicant must be enrolled or expecting to enroll full-time at a four-year institution or university; resident of Maryland and studying in Maryland. Available to U.S. citizens.

Application Requirements: Application form, financial need analysis. *Deadline:* April 15.

Contact: Margaret DeRoose, Staff Accountant
Maryland Association of Certified Public Accountants
Educational Foundation
901 Dulaney Valley Road
Suite 800
Towson, MD 21204
Phone: 443-632-2327
E-mail: margaret@macpa.org

MICHIGAN ASSOCIATION OF CPAS

http://www.michcpa.org/

FIFTH/GRADUATE YEAR STUDENT SCHOLARSHIP

Scholarship for a full-time student in senior year, or a student with a combination of education and employment (defined as a minimum of two classes per term and 20 hours per week of employment). Must be majoring in accounting, and a U.S. citizen.

Academic Fields/Career Goals: Accounting.

Award: Scholarship for use in senior year; not renewable. *Number:* 16–25. *Amount:* $2000–$4000.

Eligibility Requirements: Applicant must be enrolled or expecting to enroll full- or part-time at a four-year institution or university and studying in Michigan. Available to U.S. citizens.

Application Requirements: Application form, application form may be submitted online (http://www.mafonline.org), essay, financial need analysis, recommendations or references, transcript. *Deadline:* January 31.

Contact: MACPA Academic Services Specialist
Michigan Association of CPAs
5480 Corporate Drive, Suite 200
Troy, MI 48007-5068
Phone: 248-267-3700
Fax: 248-267-3737
E-mail: macpa@michcpa.org

MONTANA SOCIETY OF CERTIFIED PUBLIC ACCOUNTANTS

http://www.mscpa.org/

MONTANA SOCIETY OF CERTIFIED PUBLIC ACCOUNTANTS SCHOLARSHIP

Scholarship available to one student in each of the following five schools: Montana State University Billings, MSU Bozeman, Carroll College, Montana Tech and University of Montana. Must be: 1. Accounting Major 2. At least a junior standing with at least one semester of coursework remaining 3. Minimum GPA of 3.0 4. Graduate students eligible 5. Must be a student member of the MSCPA 6. Graduate of a Montana high school and currently a Montana resident. Two additional scholarships are awarded through our Endowment Fund and may be applied for through the Montana Community Foundation.

Academic Fields/Career Goals: Accounting.

Award: Scholarship for use in junior, senior, or graduate years; not renewable. *Number:* 7. *Amount:* $1000.

Eligibility Requirements: Applicant must be enrolled or expecting to enroll full-time at a four-year institution or university; resident of Montana and studying in Montana. Available to U.S. citizens.

Application Requirements: Application form, essay. *Deadline:* March 17.

Contact: Mrs. Margaret Herriges, Communications Director
Montana Society of Certified Public Accountants
1534 9th Avenue
Helena, MT 59601
Phone: 406-442-7301
E-mail: mscpa@mscpa.org

NATIONAL SOCIETY OF ACCOUNTANTS

http://www.nsacct.org/

NATIONAL SOCIETY OF ACCOUNTANTS SCHOLARSHIP

One-time award of $500 to $1000 available to undergraduate students. Applicants must maintain a 3.0 GPA and have declared a major in accounting. Must submit an appraisal form and transcripts in addition to application. Must be U.S. or Canadian citizen attending an accredited U.S. school.

Academic Fields/Career Goals: Accounting.

Award: Scholarship for use in freshman, sophomore, junior, or senior years; not renewable. *Number:* up to 40. *Amount:* $500–$1000.

Eligibility Requirements: Applicant must be enrolled or expecting to enroll full- or part-time at a two-year or four-year institution or university. Available to U.S. and Canadian citizens.

Application Requirements: Application form, appraisal form, financial need analysis, transcript. *Deadline:* March 10.

Contact: Susan Noell, Director of Education Programs
National Society of Accountants
1010 North Fairfax Street
Alexandria, VA 22314-1574
Phone: 703-549-6400 Ext. 1312
Fax: 703-549-2984 Ext. 1312
E-mail: snoell@nsacct.org

STANLEY H. STEARMAN SCHOLARSHIP

One award for accounting major who is a relative of an active, retired, or deceased member of National Society of Accountants. Must be citizen of the United States or Canada and attend school in the United States. Minimum GPA of 3.0 required. Not available for freshman year. Submit application, appraisal form, and letter of intent.

Academic Fields/Career Goals: Accounting.

Award: Scholarship for use in freshman, sophomore, junior, senior, or graduate years; renewable. *Number:* 1. *Amount:* up to $2000.

Eligibility Requirements: Applicant must be enrolled or expecting to enroll full- or part-time at a two-year or four-year institution or university. Applicant or parent of applicant must be member of National Society of Accountants. Available to U.S. and Canadian citizens.

Application Requirements: Application form, appraisal form, essay, financial need analysis, transcript. *Deadline:* March 10.

Contact: Sally Brasse, Director of Education Programs
National Society of Accountants
1010 North Fairfax Street
Alexandria, VA 22314-1574
Phone: 703-549-6400 Ext. 1307
Fax: 703-549-2984
E-mail: sbrasse@nsacct.org

NC CPA FOUNDATION INC.

http://www.ncacpa.org/ncacpa-foundation/

NORTH CAROLINA ASSOCIATION OF CPAS FOUNDATION SCHOLARSHIPS

Scholarship available for North Carolina residents enrolled in a program leading to a degree in accounting or its equivalent in a North Carolina college or university. Must have completed at least one college or university level accounting course and have completed at least 36 semester hours (or equivalent) by the start of the spring semester of the year of application. The applicant must be sponsored by one accounting faculty members. Application and information at http://csbapp.csb.uncw.edu/nccpa.

Academic Fields/Career Goals: Accounting.

Award: Scholarship for use in sophomore, junior, senior, or graduate years; not renewable. *Number:* 50–60. *Amount:* $1000–$5000.

Eligibility Requirements: Applicant must be enrolled or expecting to enroll full- or part-time at a two-year or four-year institution or university; resident of North Carolina and studying in North Carolina. Available to U.S. citizens.

Application Requirements: Application form, application form may be submitted online (http://www.ncacpa.org/Member_Connections/Students/Foundation.aspx), essay, transcript. *Deadline:* February 10.

Contact: Mr. Jim Ahler, Chief Executive Officer
NC CPA Foundation Inc.
PO Box 80188
Raleigh, NC 27623
Phone: 919-469-1040 Ext. 130
E-mail: jtahler@ncacpa.org

NEBRASKA SOCIETY OF CERTIFIED PUBLIC ACCOUNTANTS

http://www.nescpa.org/

THE FOUNDATION OF THE NEBRASKA SOCIETY OF CERTIFIED PUBLIC ACCOUNTANTS 150-HOUR SCHOLARSHIP

The scholarship is for accounting majors who have completed their junior year and are enrolled in a fifth-year (150-hour) program at a Nebraska college or university; accounting students who plan to sit for the CPA exam; accounting students who have the interest and capabilities of becoming a successful accountant and who are considering an accounting career in Nebraska. When candidates are reviewed, scholarship, personality, leadership and character should be considered by the accounting instructional staff at each college or university. Scholarship criteria & applications are available through the qualifying college or university's Accounting Department's Chair.

Academic Fields/Career Goals: Accounting.

Award: Scholarship for use in senior or graduate years; not renewable.

Eligibility Requirements: Applicant must be enrolled or expecting to enroll full-time at a four-year institution or university and studying in Nebraska. Available to U.S. citizens.

Application Requirements: Application form. *Deadline:* April 1.

NEBRASKA SOCIETY OF CPAS GENERAL ACCOUNTING SCHOLARSHIP

Scholarship awards are presented to accounting students who have completed their junior year; accounting majors who plan to sit for the CPA exam; students who have the interest and capabilities of becoming a successful accountant and who are considering an accounting career in Nebraska are to be considered. Recipients need not necessarily have the highest scholastic average. Amounts vary every year. Scholarship criteria & applications are available through the qualifying college or university's Accounting Department's Chair.

Academic Fields/Career Goals: Accounting.

Award: Scholarship for use in senior year; not renewable.

Eligibility Requirements: Applicant must be enrolled or expecting to enroll full-time at a four-year institution or university and studying in Nebraska. Available to U.S. citizens.

Application Requirements: Application form. *Deadline:* August 1.

NEW ENGLAND EMPLOYEE BENEFITS COUNCIL

http://www.neebc.org/

NEW ENGLAND EMPLOYEE BENEFITS COUNCIL SCHOLARSHIP PROGRAM

Renewable award designed to encourage undergraduate or graduate students to pursue a course of study leading to a bachelor's degree or higher in the employee benefits field. Must be a resident of/or studying in Maine, Massachusetts, New Hampshire, Rhode Island, Connecticut or Vermont. Must have demonstrated interest in the fields of employee benefits, human resources, business law.

Academic Fields/Career Goals: Accounting; Business/Consumer Services; Economics; Health Administration; Human Resources; Insurance and Actuarial Science; Law/Legal Services; Public Health; Public Policy and Administration.

Award: Scholarship for use in freshman, sophomore, junior, senior, graduate, or postgraduate years; renewable. *Number:* 1–3. *Amount:* $1000–$5000.

Eligibility Requirements: Applicant must be enrolled or expecting to enroll full- or part-time at a two-year or four-year institution or university; resident of Connecticut, Maine, Massachusetts, New Hampshire, Rhode Island, Vermont and studying in Connecticut, Maine, Massachusetts, New Hampshire, Rhode Island, Vermont. Available to U.S. citizens.

Application Requirements: Application form, essay. *Deadline:* April 1.

Contact: Ms. Linda Viens, Manager of Operations and Member Services
New England Employee Benefits Council
240 Bear Hill Road
Suite 102
Waltham, MA 02451
Phone: 781-684 Ext. 8700
E-mail: linda@neebc.org

NEW HAMPSHIRE SOCIETY OF CERTIFIED PUBLIC ACCOUNTANTS

http://www.nhscpa.org/

NEW HAMPSHIRE SOCIETY OF CERTIFIED PUBLIC ACCOUNTANTS SCHOLARSHIP FUND

Applicant must be a U.S. citizen, a New Hampshire resident, and an accounting or business major entering their senior year at an accredited four-year college or university; a graduate student pursuing a Master's degree in accounting or business in an accredited program; or those seeking the additional 30 hours of education to become eligible for a CPA license in New Hampshire. Must be recommended by a teacher or person responsible for the accounting or business program where the applicant is presently enrolled. Complete and return the application provided by the New Hampshire Society of Certified Public Accountants by the due date. Must have at least 90 credits or have senior- standing. Must have taken at least 3 courses of upper level accounting courses which would exclude introductory financial and managerial classes or the first 6 credits in accounting courses.

Academic Fields/Career Goals: Accounting.

Award: Scholarship for use in senior or graduate years; not renewable. *Number:* 1–7. *Amount:* $500–$2500.

Eligibility Requirements: Applicant must be enrolled or expecting to enroll full-time at a four-year institution or university and resident of New Hampshire. Available to U.S. citizens.

Application Requirements: Application form, recommendations or references, transcript. *Deadline:* November 30.

Contact: Roberta Daly, CPE and Events Manager
Phone: 603-622-1999 Ext. 201

NEW JERSEY SOCIETY OF CERTIFIED PUBLIC ACCOUNTANTS

http://www.njcpa.org/

NEW JERSEY SOCIETY OF CERTIFIED PUBLIC ACCOUNTANTS COLLEGE SCHOLARSHIP PROGRAM

Award for college juniors or those entering an accounting-related graduate program. Must be a New Jersey resident attending a four-year New Jersey institution. Must be nominated by accounting department chair or submit application directly. Minimum 3.2 GPA required. Award values at $6,000

Academic Fields/Career Goals: Accounting.

Award: Scholarship for use in junior or senior years; not renewable. *Number:* 40–50. *Amount:* $6000.

Eligibility Requirements: Applicant must be enrolled or expecting to enroll full- or part-time at a four-year institution or university; resident of New Jersey and studying in New Jersey. Available to U.S. citizens.

Application Requirements: Application form, application form may be submitted online (https://njcpa.org/become-a-cpa/scholarships/one-year), essay, interview. *Deadline:* January 5.

Contact: Ms. Pam Isenburg, Membership Coordinator, NextGen
Outreach
New Jersey Society of Certified Public Accountants
425 Eagle Rock Avenue, Suite 100
Roseland, NJ 07068-1723
Phone: 973-226-4494 Ext. 241
E-mail: pisenburg@njcpa.org

NEW JERSEY SOCIETY OF CERTIFIED PUBLIC ACCOUNTANTS HIGH SCHOOL SCHOLARSHIP PROGRAM

Renewable scholarship for New Jersey high school seniors who wish to pursue a degree in accounting. Must be resident of New Jersey. Scholarship value is $7,000. Deadline is in December.

Academic Fields/Career Goals: Accounting.

Award: Scholarship for use in freshman, sophomore, junior, or senior years; renewable. *Number:* 15–20. *Amount:* $7000.

Eligibility Requirements: Applicant must be high school student; planning to enroll or expecting to enroll full-time at a four-year institution or university and resident of New Jersey. Available to U.S. citizens.

Application Requirements: Application form, application form may be submitted online (https://njcpa.org/become-a-cpa/scholarships/four-year), essay, interview. *Deadline:* December 8.

Contact: Ms. Pam Isenburg, Membership Coordinator, NextGen
Outreach
New Jersey Society of Certified Public Accountants
425 Eagle Rock Avenue, Suite 100
Roseland, NJ 07068-1723
Phone: 973-226-4494 Ext. 241
E-mail: pisenburg@njcpa.org

NEW YORK STATE SOCIETY OF CERTIFIED PUBLIC ACCOUNTANTS FOUNDATION FOR ACCOUNTING EDUCATION

http://www.nysscpa.org/page/future-cpas/college-students

FOUNDATION FOR ACCOUNTING EDUCATION SCHOLARSHIP

Awards up to $500 to $2500 scholarships to college students to encourage them to pursue a career in accounting. Must be a New York resident studying in New York and maintaining a 3.0 GPA.

Academic Fields/Career Goals: Accounting.

Award: Scholarship for use in junior, senior, or graduate years; not renewable. *Number:* 1–60. *Amount:* $500–$2500.

Eligibility Requirements: Applicant must be enrolled or expecting to enroll full- or part-time at a four-year institution or university; resident of New York and studying in New York. Available to U.S. citizens.

Application Requirements: Application form, application form may be submitted online (http://www.nysscpa.org), essay, financial need analysis, recommendations or references, transcript. *Deadline:* April 1.

Contact: Ms. Lisa Axisa, Associate Director, Recruitment and Retention
New York State Society of Certified Public Accountants
Foundation for Accounting Education
3 Park Avenue, 18th Floor
New York, NY 10016
Phone: 212-719-8362
E-mail: laxisa@nysspca.org

OREGON ASSOCIATION OF PUBLIC ACCOUNTANTS SCHOLARSHIP FOUNDATION

http://www.oaia.net/

OAIA SCHOLARSHIP

Scholarships of $1000 to $2000 are awarded to full-time students. Must be a resident of the state of Oregon and major in accounting studies at an accredited school in the state of Oregon. The scholarship may be used for tuition, fees, books or other academic expenses incurred during the term.

Academic Fields/Career Goals: Accounting.

Award: Scholarship for use in freshman, sophomore, junior, or senior years; not renewable. *Number:* 5. *Amount:* $1000–$2000.

Eligibility Requirements: Applicant must be enrolled or expecting to enroll full-time at a two-year or four-year institution or university; resident of Oregon and studying in Oregon. Available to U.S. citizens.

Application Requirements: Application form, financial need analysis. *Deadline:* April 1.

Contact: Sue Robertson, Treasurer
Oregon Association of Public Accountants
Scholarship Foundation
1804 NE 43rd Ave.
Portland, OR 97213
Phone: 503-282-7247
E-mail: srobertson4oaia@aol.com

OSCPA EDUCATIONAL FOUNDATION

http://www.orcpa.org/

OSCPA EDUCATIONAL FOUNDATION SCHOLARSHIP PROGRAM

Full-time Oregon college/university undergraduate accounting majors, post baccalaureate and master's program students are eligible to apply. Scholarships will be awarded based on student's academic performance, intent to pursue a CPA career and work within the state of Oregon. Scholarships are for tuition and books. Minimum required GPA is 3.2 in accounting/business classes and an overall cumulative 3.2 GPA.

Academic Fields/Career Goals: Accounting.

Award: Scholarship for use in sophomore, junior, senior, or graduate years; not renewable. *Number:* 45–75. *Amount:* $500–$3000.

Eligibility Requirements: Applicant must be enrolled or expecting to enroll full-time at a two-year or four-year or technical institution or university and studying in Oregon. Available to U.S. citizens.

Application Requirements: Application form. *Deadline:* January 15.

Contact: Tonna Hollis, Senior Manager, Member Services &
Professional Development
OSCPA Educational Foundation
PO Box 4555
Beaverton, OR 97076-4555
Phone: 503-641-7200 Ext. 29
E-mail: thollis@orcpa.org

RHODE ISLAND FOUNDATION

http://www.rifoundation.org/

CARL W. CHRISTIANSEN SCHOLARSHIP

$1000 scholarship for Rhode Island residents pursuing full-time study in accounting or related fields. Must maintain a minimum 3.0 GPA.

Academic Fields/Career Goals: Accounting.

Award: Scholarship for use in freshman, sophomore, junior, senior, or graduate years; not renewable. *Amount:* $1000.

Eligibility Requirements: Applicant must be enrolled or expecting to enroll full-time at a two-year or four-year institution or university and resident of Rhode Island. Available to U.S. citizens.

Application Requirements: Application form. *Deadline:* January 11.

Contact: Denise Jacobson
E-mail: djacobson@riscpa.org

CHERYL A. RUGGIERO SCHOLARSHIP

Award for female Rhode Island residents pursuing full-time study in public accounting. Must maintain a minimum 3.0 GPA.

Academic Fields/Career Goals: Accounting.

Award: Scholarship for use in freshman, sophomore, junior, senior, or graduate years; not renewable. *Amount:* $1000.

Eligibility Requirements: Applicant must be enrolled or expecting to enroll full-time at a two-year or four-year institution or university; female and resident of Rhode Island. Available to U.S. citizens.

Application Requirements: Application form, essay, interview, proof of U.S. citizenship, proof of RI residency, recommendations or references, transcript. *Deadline:* January 11.

Contact: Denise Jacobson
E-mail: djacobson@riscpa.org

RHODE ISLAND SOCIETY OF CERTIFIED PUBLIC ACCOUNTANTS

http://www.riscpa.org/

RHODE ISLAND SOCIETY OF CERTIFIED PUBLIC ACCOUNTANTS SCHOLARSHIP

Annual scholarship for graduates and undergraduates majoring in accounting, who are legal residents of Rhode Island and U.S. citizens. Must have interest in a career in public accounting, and submit one-page memo outlining that interest. Minimum GPA of 3.0 required. For more information, see website http://www.riscpa.org.

Academic Fields/Career Goals: Accounting.

Award: Scholarship for use in freshman, sophomore, junior, senior, or graduate years; not renewable.

Eligibility Requirements: Applicant must be enrolled or expecting to enroll full-time at a four-year institution or university and resident of Rhode Island. Available to U.S. citizens.

Application Requirements: Application form, recommendations or references, resume, test scores, transcript. *Deadline:* January 15.

Contact: Robert Mancini, Executive Director
Phone: 401-331-5720
Fax: 401-454-5780
E-mail: rmancini@riscpa.org

SCARLETT FAMILY FOUNDATION SCHOLARSHIP PROGRAM

http://www.scarlettfoundation.org/

SCHOLARSHIP FOR STUDENTS PURSUING A BUSINESS OR STEM DEGREE

Each year, the Scarlett Family Foundation will award scholarships in varying amounts based on financial need and merit, that is directly tied to the cost of the college the student attends. The minimum scholarship award is $2,500 per academic year. The maximum award is $15,000 per academic year. The scholarship is applied to tuition, books and fees. Scholarships are renewable awards for up to 4 years or until the recipient completes their undergraduate degree, whichever comes first. The scholarships are open to high school seniors and college freshmen, sophomores, and juniors who will graduate or have graduated from a public, independent or homeschool association high school in 40 Middle Tennessee counties. Also eligible are individuals who have obtained a GED.

Academic Fields/Career Goals: Accounting; Advertising/Public Relations; Agribusiness; Agriculture; Animal/Veterinary Sciences; Applied Sciences; Archaeology; Architecture; Audiology; Aviation/Aerospace; Biology; Business/Consumer Services; Chemical Engineering; Civil Engineering; Computer Science/Data Processing; Dental Health/Services; Earth Science; Economics; Electrical Engineering/Electronics; Energy and Power Engineering; Engineering-Related Technologies; Engineering/Technology; Environmental Science; Finance; Food Science/Nutrition; Geography; Health Administration; Health and Medical Sciences; Health Information Management/Technology; Hospitality Management; Human Resources; Insurance and Actuarial Science; Marine Biology; Marine/Ocean Engineering; Marketing; Materials Science, Engineering, and Metallurgy; Mathematics; Mechanical Engineering; Meteorology/Atmospheric Science; Natural Sciences; Neurobiology; Nuclear Science; Nursing; Oceanography; Oncology; Optometry; Osteopathy; Pharmacy; Physical Sciences; Sports-Related/Exercise Science; Therapy/Rehabilitation.

Award: Scholarship for use in freshman, sophomore, junior, or senior years; renewable. *Number:* 35–120. *Amount:* $2500–$15,000.

Eligibility Requirements: Applicant must be enrolled or expecting to enroll full-time at a four-year institution or university and resident of Tennessee. Available to U.S. citizens.

Application Requirements: Application form, driver's license, essay, financial need analysis. *Deadline:* December 15.

Contact: Tom Parrish, Chief Operating Officer
Scarlett Family Foundation Scholarship Program
4117 Hillsboro Pike
Suite 103255
Nashville, TN 37215-2728
E-mail: TomParrish@ScarlettFoundation.org

SOCIETY OF AUTOMOTIVE ANALYSTS

http://saaauto.com/

SOCIETY OF AUTOMOTIVE ANALYSTS SCHOLARSHIP

A scholarship of $1500 awarded to students in economics, finance, business administration or marketing management. Minimum 3.0 GPA required. Must submit two letters of recommendation.

Academic Fields/Career Goals: Accounting; Business/Consumer Services; Economics.

Award: Scholarship for use in freshman, sophomore, junior, or senior years; not renewable. *Number:* 2. *Amount:* $1500.

Eligibility Requirements: Applicant must be enrolled or expecting to enroll full-time at a two-year or four-year or technical institution or university. Available to U.S. and non-U.S. citizens.

Application Requirements: Application form, recommendations or references, transcript. *Deadline:* June 1.

Contact: Lynne Hall, Awards and Scholarships
Phone: 313-240-4000
Fax: 313-240-8641

SOCIETY OF LOUISIANA CERTIFIED PUBLIC ACCOUNTANTS

http://www.lcpa.org/

SOCIETY OF LOUISIANA CPAS SCHOLARSHIPS

One-time award for accounting majors. Applicant must be a Louisiana resident attending a four-year college or university in Louisiana. For full-time undergraduates entering their junior or senior year, or full-time graduate students. Minimum 3.0 GPA for accounting courses and 2.5 GPA overall required. Deadline varies. Must be U.S. citizen.

Academic Fields/Career Goals: Accounting.

Award: Scholarship for use in junior, senior, or graduate years; not renewable. *Amount:* $500–$2000.

Eligibility Requirements: Applicant must be enrolled or expecting to enroll full-time at a four-year institution or university; resident of Louisiana and studying in Louisiana. Available to U.S. citizens.

Application Requirements: Application form, essay. *Deadline:* November 2.

Contact: Lisa Richardson, Member Services Manager
Phone: 504-904-1139
Fax: 504-469-7930
E-mail: lrichardson@lcpa.org

SOUTH CAROLINA ASSOCIATION OF CERTIFIED PUBLIC ACCOUNTANTS

http://www.scacpa.org

SCACPA EDUCATIONAL FUND SCHOLARSHIPS

These scholarships are awarded to South Carolina residents who are rising juniors or seniors majoring in accounting, or master's degree students at a South Carolina college or university. Applicants must have a GPA of no less than 3.25 overall and a GPA in accounting no less than 3.5 (on a 4.0 scale).

Academic Fields/Career Goals: Accounting.

Award: Scholarship for use in junior, senior, or graduate years; not renewable. *Number:* 19–25. *Amount:* $500–$2500.

Eligibility Requirements: Applicant must be enrolled or expecting to enroll full-time at a four-year institution or university; resident of South Carolina and studying in South Carolina. Available to U.S. and non-U.S. citizens.

Application Requirements: Application form, driver's license, essay, financial need analysis, recommendations or references, resume, transcript. *Deadline:* May 31.

Contact: Ms. Jacque Curtin, COO/CFO
South Carolina Association of Certified Public Accountants
1300 12th Street, Suite D
Cayce, SC 29033
Phone: 803-791-4181 Ext. 408
Fax: 803-791-4196
E-mail: jcurtin@scacpa.org

SOUTH DAKOTA CPA SOCIETY

http://www.sdcpa.org/

EXCELLENCE IN ACCOUNTING SCHOLARSHIP

Scholarships available for senior undergraduate and graduate students majoring in accounting. Must have completed 90 credit hours, demonstrated excellence in academics and leadership potential. Application available online at http://www.sdcpa.org.

Academic Fields/Career Goals: Accounting.

Award: Scholarship for use in senior or graduate years; not renewable. *Number:* 5–15. *Amount:* $1000–$2500.

Eligibility Requirements: Applicant must be enrolled or expecting to enroll full-time at a four-year institution or university and studying in South Dakota. Available to U.S. citizens.

Application Requirements: Application form, personal photograph. *Deadline:* April 30.

Contact: Laura Coome, Executive Director
South Dakota CPA Society
5024 South Bur Oak Place, #108
Sioux Falls, SD 57108
Phone: 605-334-3848
E-mail: laura@sdcpa.org

SPECIALTY EQUIPMENT MARKET ASSOCIATION

http://www.sema.org/

SEMA MEMORIAL SCHOLARSHIP FUND

Scholarships for college students pursuing careers in or related to the automotive industry. All applicants must be U.S. citizens who are currently attending U.S. institutions. Minimum 2.5 GPA required. For more information and to apply, please visit: http://www.SEMA.org/scholarships.

Academic Fields/Career Goals: Accounting; Advertising/Public Relations; Business/Consumer Services; Communications; Computer Science/Data Processing; Electrical.Engineering/Electronics; Engineering/Technology; Finance; Marketing; Mechanical Engineering; Trade/Technical Specialties; Transportation.

Award: Scholarship for use in junior, senior, graduate, or postgraduate years; not renewable. *Number:* 50–60. *Amount:* $2000–$5000.

Eligibility Requirements: Applicant must be enrolled or expecting to enroll full-time at a two-year or four-year or technical institution or university and must have an interest in automotive. Available to U.S. citizens.

Application Requirements: Application form, essay. *Deadline:* March 1.

Contact: Ms. Juliet Marshall, Education Manager
Phone: 909-978-6655
Fax: 909-860-0184
E-mail: julietm@sema.org

STRAIGHT NORTH

https://www.straightnorth.com/

STRAIGHT NORTH STEM SCHOLARSHIP

With Internet marketing becoming more complex and challenging by the day, successful execution requires a solid education. As an industry leader, Straight North supports students pursuing degrees in science, technology, engineering and math (STEM) disciplines.

Academic Fields/Career Goals: Accounting; Applied Sciences; Aviation/Aerospace; Biology; Chemical Engineering; Civil Engineering; Computer Science/Data Processing; Construction Engineering/Management; Earth Science; Electrical Engineering/Electronics; Energy and Power Engineering; Engineering-Related Technologies; Engineering/Technology; Environmental Health; Environmental Science; Finance; Flexography; Gemology; Health and Medical Sciences; Health Information Management/Technology; Heating, Air-Conditioning, and Refrigeration Mechanics; Hydrology; Insurance and Actuarial Science; Marine Biology; Marine/Ocean Engineering; Marketing; Materials Science, Engineering, and Metallurgy; Mathematics; Mechanical Engineering;

Meteorology/Atmospheric Science; Natural Resources; Natural Sciences; Neurobiology; Nuclear Science; Nursing; Occupational Safety and Health; Oncology; Optometry; Osteopathy; Paper and Pulp Engineering; Physical Sciences; Science, Technology, and Society.

Award: Scholarship for use in freshman, sophomore, junior, senior, graduate, or postgraduate years; not renewable. *Number:* 3. *Amount:* $250–$1000.

Eligibility Requirements: Applicant must be enrolled or expecting to enroll full- or part-time at a two-year or four-year institution or university. Available to U.S. and non-U.S. citizens.

Application Requirements: Application form, autobiography. *Deadline:* August 1.

Contact: Tammy Barry, Director of Human Resources
    E-mail: tbarry@straightnorth.com

TAU KAPPA EPSILON EDUCATION FOUNDATION

https://www.tke.org/

HARRY J. DONNELLY MEMORIAL SCHOLARSHIP

Mrs. Ellanor Donnelly established the scholarship in loving member of her husband for the benefit of members of Tau Kappa Epsilon. This scholarship is awarded in recognition of academic achievement with GPA of at least 3.0 or higher, and recognizes outstanding leadership within the chapter, on campus and within the community. The applicant must be pursuing an undergraduate degree in accounting or a graduate degree in law, and plans to be a full-time student the following year.

Academic Fields/Career Goals: Accounting; Law/Legal Services.

Award: Scholarship for use in freshman, sophomore, junior, senior, or graduate years. *Number:* 1.

Eligibility Requirements: Applicant must be enrolled or expecting to enroll full-time at an institution or university and male. Applicant or parent of applicant must be member of Tau Kappa Epsilon. Available to U.S. citizens.

Application Requirements: Application form, application form may be submitted online, personal photograph. *Deadline:* March 15.

Contact: Rachel Stevenson, Foundation Communications Manager
    Tau Kappa Epsilon Education Foundation
    7439 Woodland Drive
    Suite 100
    Indianapolis, IN 46278
    Phone: 317-872-6533 Ext. 246
    E-mail: rstevenson@tke.org

W. ALLAN HERZOG SCHOLARSHIP

This scholarship is available to an undergraduate member of Nu Chapter of TKE, with a 2.75 GPA, who is a full-time student pursuing a degree in accounting, finance or economics. If no one qualifies, any other undergraduate member of Nu Chapter with a 2.75 Grade Point Average will be accepted. If Nu Chapter has no applicants with a 2.75 average, then applicants from other TKE chapters in accounting, finance or economics may be considered. Any applicant must have at least one full year of undergraduate study remaining.

Academic Fields/Career Goals: Accounting; Economics; Finance.

Award: Scholarship for use in sophomore, junior, or senior years. *Number:* 1.

Eligibility Requirements: Applicant must be enrolled or expecting to enroll full-time at an institution or university and male. Applicant or parent of applicant must be member of Tau Kappa Epsilon. Available to U.S. citizens.

Application Requirements: Application form, application form may be submitted online, personal photograph. *Deadline:* March 15.

Contact: Rachel Stevenson, Foundation Communications Manager
    Tau Kappa Epsilon Education Foundation
    7439 Woodland Drive
    Suite 100
    Indianapolis, IN 46278
    Phone: 317-872-6533 Ext. 246
    E-mail: rstevenson@tke.org

TENNESSEE SOCIETY OF CPAS

http://www.tscpa.com/

TENNESSEE SOCIETY OF CPA SCHOLARSHIP

Scholarships are available only to full-time students who have completed introductory courses in accounting and/or students majoring in accounting. Applicants must be legal residents of Tennessee.

Academic Fields/Career Goals: Accounting.

Award: Scholarship for use in freshman, sophomore, junior, senior, or graduate years; not renewable. *Number:* 120–130. *Amount:* $250–$2500.

Eligibility Requirements: Applicant must be enrolled or expecting to enroll full-time at a four-year institution or university and resident of Tennessee. Available to U.S. citizens.

Application Requirements: Application form, financial need analysis, recommendations or references, transcript. *Deadline:* June 1.

Contact: Wendy Garvin, Member Services Manager
    Phone: 615-377-3825
    Fax: 390-377-3904
    E-mail: wgarvin@tscpa.com

TRIANGLE PEST CONTROL

http://www.trianglepest.com

TRIANGLE PEST CONTROL SCHOLARSHIP

riangle Pest Control has been a trusted name in pest control in the Raleigh and Charlotte areas for the past ten years. In 2017, Triangle Pest Control completed an expansion to serve pest control to residents of Greenville, SC, and to celebrate, they created a merit-based scholarship fund for individuals seeking education in business management and business administration studies. With this goal in mind, Donnie Shelton, the CEO of Triangle Pest Control, has created a scholarship fund for the 2018 fall academic semester. The $500 scholarship will be awarded to an individual who has displayed academic excellence, in addition to a passionate pursuit of furthered business education at an accredited college or university in North or South Carolina. The purpose of The Triangle Pest Control Scholarship Fund is to encourage commitment by students to a career in business administration, management, marketing or other business-related fields. Entrepreneurship and small business ownership are important principles in the pest control industry, as well as the local community. Triangle Pest Control is constantly seeking new ways to be a leading voice in the pest control industry and to foster growth and opportunity in the communities they serve. This scholarship offers financial assistance to individuals with proven merit and serves to reward students pursuing a degree in business in North or South Carolina schools.

Academic Fields/Career Goals: Accounting; Business/Consumer Services; Marketing.

Award: Scholarship for use in freshman, sophomore, junior, or senior years; not renewable. *Number:* 1. *Amount:* $500.

Eligibility Requirements: Applicant must be enrolled or expecting to enroll full-time at a four-year institution or university and studying in North Carolina, South Carolina. Available to U.S. citizens.

Application Requirements: Application form. *Deadline:* August 31.

Contact: Mr. Frank Andolina
    Triangle Pest Control
    131 S. Wilmington St.
    Raleigh, NC 27601

UNITED NEGRO COLLEGE FUND

http://www.uncf.org/

DISCOVER FINANCIAL SERVICES SCHOLARSHIP

Scholarship and internship opportunities to students who are first semester sophomores enrolled at any UNCF member institution or other accredited HBCU, major in Computer Engineering, Computer Information System, Computer Science, Computer Science/MIS, Engineering Technology, Information Management System, Information Technology, Software Engineering, System Engineering, Finance, Accounting, Marketing, Analytics Risk Management, Supply Chain Logistics, Economics or other STEM related majors. The selected finalists are required to accept internship positions located in Riverwoods, IL.

Academic Fields/Career Goals: Accounting; Applied Sciences; Computer Science/Data Processing; Economics; Engineering-Related Technologies; Engineering/Technology; Finance; Marketing.

Award: Scholarship for use in sophomore year; renewable. *Amount:* $7500.

Eligibility Requirements: Applicant must be Black (non-Hispanic) and enrolled or expecting to enroll full-time at a four-year institution or university. Available to U.S. citizens.

Application Requirements: Application form, essay. *Deadline:* September 21.

Contact: Larry Griffith, Senior Vice President, Programs and Student Services
Phone: 800-331-2244

HCN/APRICITY RESOURCES SCHOLARS PROGRAM

Scholarship and internship at TN Apricity Resources, The intent of the internship program is to hire exceptional talent in hopes of converting to full-time hires upon graduation based on performance and business need. The focus is on African American undergraduates at HBCU(s) available during the summer before their senior year. Targeted majors: Accounting, Business, Business (Sales Interest), Computer Engineering, Computer Science, Counseling, English, Finance, Healthcare Administration, Healthcare Management, Management Information Systems, Marketing, Nursing, Pre-Nursing, Psychology, Social Work, Sociology.

Academic Fields/Career Goals: Accounting; Business/Consumer Services; Computer Science/Data Processing; Finance; Health Administration; Literature/English/Writing; Marketing; Nursing; Psychology; Social Sciences; Social Services; Therapy/Rehabilitation.

Award: Scholarship for use in senior year; not renewable.

Eligibility Requirements: Applicant must be Black (non-Hispanic) and enrolled or expecting to enroll at a four-year institution or university. Available to U.S. citizens.

Application Requirements: Application form. *Deadline:* February 22.

Contact: Crystal Terry
E-mail: crystal.terry@uncf.org

NASCAR WENDELL SCOTT SR. SCHOLARSHIP

NASCAR has partnered with UNCF to recognize the achievement of Wendell Scott, Sr. in NASCAR. Candidates must be enrolled full-time at a four-year college or university and must have a major in business related disciplines, communications, engineering, information technology or public relations. Award up to $10,000.

Academic Fields/Career Goals: Accounting; Business/Consumer Services; Communications; Computer Science/Data Processing; Electrical Engineering/Electronics; Finance; Marketing; Mechanical Engineering.

Award: Scholarship for use in freshman, sophomore, junior, senior, or graduate years; not renewable.

Eligibility Requirements: Applicant must be Black (non-Hispanic) and enrolled or expecting to enroll full-time at a four-year institution or university. Available to U.S. citizens.

Application Requirements: Application form, recommendations or references, resume, transcript, video. *Deadline:* July 25.

Contact: William Dunham
E-mail: william.dunham@uncf.org

NATIONAL BLACK MCDONALD'S OWNERS ASSOCIATION HOSPITALITY SCHOLARS PROGRAM

Scholarship of up to $5000 for a student majoring in restaurant/hotel/hospitality management, accounting, business, or marketing as full-time students at an accredited Historically Black College or University (HBCU) that have an interest in hospitality management. Minimum 2.8 GPA required. Dependents of either McDonald's executives or NBMOA owners are ineligible for this opportunity as are former recipients of the NBMOA scholarship.

Academic Fields/Career Goals: Accounting; Business/Consumer Services; Food Service/Hospitality; Hospitality Management; Marketing.

Award: Scholarship for use in sophomore, junior, or senior years; not renewable.

Eligibility Requirements: Applicant must be Black (non-Hispanic) and enrolled or expecting to enroll full-time at a two-year or four-year institution or university. Available to U.S. citizens.

Application Requirements: Application form. *Deadline:* June 16.

Contact: Larry Griffith, Senior Vice President, Programs and Student Services
Phone: 800-331-2244

VOYA SCHOLARS

Award for current juniors who are enrolled full-time at a UNCF member college or university in a restricted major in accounting, actuarial science, business/business management, finance/investment, marketing, mathematics, or quants/quantitative. Preference will be given to students with a home residence in Atlanta, GA; Hartford, CT; Jackson, Mississippi; Minneapolis, MN New York City; and Philadelphia, PA.

Academic Fields/Career Goals: Accounting; Business/Consumer Services; Finance; Insurance and Actuarial Science; Marketing; Mathematics; Statistics.

Award: Scholarship for use in junior year; not renewable.

Eligibility Requirements: Applicant must be enrolled or expecting to enroll full-time at a four-year institution or university. Available to U.S. citizens.

Application Requirements: Application form, essay, financial need analysis. *Deadline:* November 30.

Contact: Larry Griffith, Senior Vice President, Programs and Student Services
Phone: 800-331-2244

VIRCHOW, KRAUSE & COMPANY, LLP

http://www.virchowkrause.com/

VIRCHOW, KRAUSE AND COMPANY SCHOLARSHIP

One-time scholarship for students enrolled either full-time or part-time in accredited colleges or universities of Wisconsin, majoring in accounting.

Academic Fields/Career Goals: Accounting.

Award: Scholarship for use in freshman, sophomore, junior, or senior years; not renewable. *Number:* up to 3. *Amount:* up to $1000.

Eligibility Requirements: Applicant must be enrolled or expecting to enroll full- or part-time at a two-year or four-year institution or university and studying in Wisconsin. Available to U.S. citizens.

Application Requirements: Application form, transcript. *Deadline:* varies.

Contact: Darbie Miller, Human Resources Coordinator
Virchow, Krause & Company, LLP
4600 American Parkway, PO Box 7398
Madison, WI 53707-7398
Phone: 608-240-2474
Fax: 608-249-1411
E-mail: dmiller@virchowkrause.com

VIRGINIA SOCIETY OF CERTIFIED PUBLIC ACCOUNTANTS EDUCATIONAL FOUNDATION

http://www.vscpa.com/

VSCPA EDUCATIONAL FOUNDATION ACCOUNTING SCHOLARSHIPS

All applicants must be U.S. citizens; successfully complete 3 credit hours of accounting prior to the fall semester; be currently enrolled in an accredited Virginia college or university with the intent to pursue a degree in accounting; and enrollment in an accredited Virginia college or university accounting program in the fall semester.

Academic Fields/Career Goals: Accounting.

Award: Scholarship for use in sophomore, junior, senior, graduate, or postgraduate years; not renewable. *Number:* up to 26. *Amount:* $1000–$5000.

Eligibility Requirements: Applicant must be enrolled or expecting to enroll full- or part-time at a two-year or four-year institution or university; resident of Virginia and studying in Virginia. Available to U.S. citizens.

Application Requirements: Application form, application form may be submitted online (http://www.vscpa.com/Scholarships), essay, recommendations or references, resume, transcript. *Deadline:* April 1.

Contact: Tracey Zink, Academic and Career Development Coordinator
Phone: 800-612-9427
E-mail: tzink@vscpa.com

WASHINGTON SOCIETY OF CERTIFIED PUBLIC ACCOUNTANTS

http://www.wscpa.org/

WA CPA FOUNDATION SCHOLARSHIPS

The Washington CPA Foundation is a 501(c)(3) not-for-profit foundation committed to ensuring that Washington's diverse communities have awareness of and access to both high quality accounting education and the resources required to make sound financial decisions. In order to make our vision a reality, the Foundation funds education and research in the field of accountancy, scholarships for accounting students, programs designed to improve accounting education and expand knowledge within the profession, and initiatives designed to improve the public's skills in personal financial management.

Academic Fields/Career Goals: Accounting.

Award: Scholarship for use in sophomore, junior, senior, graduate, or postgraduate years; not renewable. *Number:* 70. *Amount:* $5000.

Eligibility Requirements: Applicant must be enrolled or expecting to enroll full- or part-time at a four-year institution or university and studying in Washington. Available to U.S. and non-U.S. citizens.

Application Requirements: Application form, essay. *Deadline:* February 14.

Contact: Ms. Monette Anderson, Manager of Student Initiatives
Washington Society of Certified Public Accountants
902 140th Ave NE
Bellevue, WA 98005
Phone: 425-586-1118
E-mail: manderson@wscpa.org

WYOMING TRUCKING ASSOCIATION SCHOLARSHIP FUND TRUST

http://www.wytruck.org/

WYOMING TRUCKING ASSOCIATION SCHOLARSHIP TRUST FUND

To qualify, students must (1) be a graduate of a Wyoming high school; (2) plan to pursue a course of study which will lead to a career in the Highway Transportation Industry with the following approved courses of study: business management, computer skills, accounting, office procedures and management, safety, diesel mechanics and truck driving; (3) attend a Wyoming school (University, Community College or trade school) approved by the WTA Scholarship Committee.

Academic Fields/Career Goals: Accounting; Business/Consumer Services; Communications; Computer Science/Data Processing; Marketing; Trade/Technical Specialties; Transportation.

Award: Scholarship for use in freshman, sophomore, junior, or senior years; not renewable. *Number:* 4–8. *Amount:* $500–$1500.

Eligibility Requirements: Applicant must be enrolled or expecting to enroll full-time at a two-year or four-year or technical institution or university; resident of Wyoming and studying in Wyoming. Available to U.S. citizens.

Application Requirements: Application form, community service, essay, financial need analysis. *Deadline:* March 5.

Contact: Kathy Cundall, Administrative Assistant
Phone: 307-234-1579
E-mail: khcundall@aol.com

ADVERTISING/PUBLIC RELATIONS

ASIAN AMERICAN JOURNALISTS ASSOCIATION, SEATTLE CHAPTER

http://www.aajaseattle.org/

NORTHWEST JOURNALISTS OF COLOR SCHOLARSHIP

One-time award for Washington state high school and college students seeking careers in journalism. Awardees are also paired with a mentor, expected to join AAJA, and participate in AAJA activities. The program also offers The Founder's Scholarship, which pays for registration and airfare so a student may attend the AAJA National Convention.

Academic Fields/Career Goals: Advertising/Public Relations; Communications; Filmmaking/Video; Journalism; Photojournalism/Photography; TV/Radio Broadcasting.

Award: Scholarship for use in freshman, sophomore, junior, or senior years; not renewable. *Number:* 1–5. *Amount:* $250–$1000.

Eligibility Requirements: Applicant must be of African, Chinese, Hispanic, Indian, Japanese, Korean, Lao/Hmong, Latin American/Caribbean, Lebanese, Mexican, Mongolian, Sub-Saharan African, Syrian, Turkish, Vietnamese, Yemeni heritage; American Indian/Alaska Native, Asian/Pacific Islander, Black (non-Hispanic); enrolled or expecting to enroll full- or part-time at a two-year or four-year or technical institution or university and resident of Washington. Applicant or parent of applicant must have employment or volunteer experience in journalism/broadcasting. Available to U.S. citizens.

Application Requirements: Application form, community service, essay, financial need analysis. *Deadline:* May 1.

Contact: Ms. Mai Hoang, AAJA Chapter Treasurer
Asian American Journalists Association, Seattle Chapter
Yakima Herald Republic
114 North Fourth Street
Yakima, WA 98909
Phone: 509-577-7724
E-mail: mhoang@yakimaherald.com

AUTOMOTIVE WOMEN'S ALLIANCE FOUNDATION

http://awafoundation.org/index.php

AUTOMOTIVE WOMEN'S ALLIANCE FOUNDATION SCHOLARSHIPS

• *See page 71*

DIGITAL THIRD COAST INTERNET MARKETING

http://www.digitalthirdcoast.net/

DIGITAL MARKETING SCHOLARSHIP

In a 500+ word essay, share how you think digital marketing will develop in the next five to ten years, and what you think the industry will be like when you're out of school and working in the marketing industry. You may focus on how one aspect of digital marketing will change, or you can address how each branch of digital marketing will grow to interact with the others.

Academic Fields/Career Goals: Advertising/Public Relations; Business/Consumer Services; Marketing.

Award: Scholarship for use in freshman, sophomore, junior, or senior years; not renewable. *Number:* 1. *Amount:* $500.

Eligibility Requirements: Applicant must be enrolled or expecting to enroll full-time at a four-year institution. Available to U.S. citizens.

Application Requirements: Application form may be submitted online (http://www.digitalthirdcoast.net/blog/dtc-digital-marketing-scholarship), essay, personal photograph. *Deadline:* March 1.

Contact: Barry Dyke, Account Manager
Digital Third Coast Internet Marketing
2035 West Wabansia Avenue
Chicago, IL 60647
Phone: 773-897-0572
E-mail: bdyke@digitalthirdcoast.net

HOUSE OF BLUES MUSIC FORWARD FOUNDATION

https://hobmusicforward.org/

TIFFANY GREEN OPERATOR SCHOLARSHIP AWARD

Established in the memory of Tiffany Green, US Concerts division supports women pursuing careers in live event operations, production and music engineering related fields of study. The $10,000 scholarship will expand the student's training and professional interactions through participation in educational opportunities.

Academic Fields/Career Goals: Advertising/Public Relations; Audiology; Business/Consumer Services; Communications; Economics; Hospitality Management; Human Resources; Marketing; Music.

Award: Scholarship for use in junior or senior years; not renewable. *Number:* 1. *Amount:* $10,000.

Eligibility Requirements: Applicant must be enrolled or expecting to enroll full-time at a four-year institution or university; female and must have an interest in music or music/singing.

Application Requirements: Application form, essay. *Deadline:* March 31.

Contact: Ms. Nazanin Fatemian, House of Blues Music Forward Foundation
House of Blues Music Forward Foundation
7060 Hollywood Boulevard, Floor 2
Los Angeles, CA 90028
Phone: 323-821-3946
E-mail: nfatemian@hobmusicforward.org

THE LAGRANT FOUNDATION

http://www.lagrantfoundation.org/

LAGRANT FOUNDATION SCHOLARSHIP FOR GRADUATES

Awards are for graduate minority students who are attending accredited four-year institutions and are pursuing careers in the fields of advertising, graphic design, marketing, and public relations. Must have a minimum of two academic semesters or one year left to complete his/her Master's degree from the time the scholarship is awarded. The applicant must make a one-year commitment to maintain contact with TLF to receive professional guidance and academic support. Minimum 3.2 GPA required.

Academic Fields/Career Goals: Advertising/Public Relations; Business/Consumer Services; Communications; Graphics/Graphic Arts/Printing; Marketing.

Award: Scholarship for use in sophomore, junior, senior, graduate, or postgraduate years; not renewable. *Amount:* $3250–$3750.

Eligibility Requirements: Applicant must be American Indian/Alaska Native, Asian/Pacific Islander, Black (non-Hispanic), Hispanic and enrolled or expecting to enroll full-time at an institution or university. Available to U.S. citizens.

Application Requirements: Application form, application form may be submitted online (https://www.lagrantfoundation.org/Scholarship%20Program), essay, recommendations or references, resume, transcript. *Deadline:* February 28.

Contact: Programs & Communications Associate
The LAGRANT Foundation
633 W. 5th Street, 48th Floor
Los Angeles, CA 90071
Phone: 323-469-8680 Ext. 223
E-mail: tlfinfo@lagrant.com

LAGRANT FOUNDATION SCHOLARSHIP FOR UNDERGRADUATES

Awards are for undergraduate minority students who are attending accredited four-year institutions and are pursuing careers in the fields of advertising, graphic design, marketing, and public relations. Must have at least one year to complete his/her degree from the time the scholarships are awarded. The applicant must make a one-year commitment to maintain contact with TLF to receive professional guidance and academic support. Minimum 3.0 GPA required.

Academic Fields/Career Goals: Advertising/Public Relations; Business/Consumer Services; Communications; Graphics/Graphic Arts/Printing; Marketing.

Award: Scholarship for use in freshman, sophomore, junior, or senior years; not renewable. *Amount:* $2000–$2500.

Eligibility Requirements: Applicant must be American Indian/Alaska Native, Asian/Pacific Islander, Black (non-Hispanic), Hispanic and enrolled or expecting to enroll full-time at a four-year institution or university. Available to U.S. citizens.

Application Requirements: Application form, application form may be submitted online (https://www.lagrantfoundation.org/Scholarship%20Program), essay, personal photograph, recommendations or references, resume, transcript. *Deadline:* February 28.

Contact: Programs & Communications Associate
The LAGRANT Foundation
633 W. 5th Street, 48th Floor
Los Angeles, CA 90071
Phone: 323-469-8680 Ext. 223
E-mail: tlfinfo@lagrant.com

NATIONAL ACADEMY OF TELEVISION ARTS AND SCIENCES, MICHIGAN CHAPTER

http://natasmichigan.org

DR. LYNNE BOYLE/JOHN SCHIMPF UNDERGRADUATE SCHOLARSHIP

This scholarship is for tuition for undergraduate school. Only Michigan residents are eligible for the scholarship. The university or college attended does not have to be a Michigan institution. Work submitted must be that done by the student which is representative of the students ability. Scholarships are awarded on the basis of merit. Student must be enrolled in a undergraduate program of an accredited 4-year college or university for their Junior and Senior years of study.

Academic Fields/Career Goals: Advertising/Public Relations; Communications; Filmmaking/Video; Journalism; Performing Arts; TV/Radio Broadcasting.

Award: Scholarship for use in junior or senior years; not renewable. *Number:* 1. *Amount:* $5000.

Eligibility Requirements: Applicant must be enrolled or expecting to enroll full- or part-time at a four-year institution or university and resident of Michigan. Available to U.S. citizens.

Application Requirements: Application form, essay. *Deadline:* April 8.

Contact: Adm. Stacia Mottley, Executive Director
National Academy of Television Arts and Sciences, Michigan Chapter
24903 Lois Lane
Southfield, MI 48075
Phone: 248-827-0931
E-mail: smottley@comcast.net

NATIVE AMERICAN JOURNALISTS ASSOCIATION

http://www.naja.com/

NATIVE AMERICAN JOURNALISTS ASSOCIATION SCHOLARSHIPS

One-time award for undergraduate study leading to journalism career at accredited colleges and universities. Applicants must be current members of Native-American Journalists Association or may join at time of application. Applicants must have proof of tribal association. Send cover letter, letters of reference, and work samples with application. Financial need considered.

Academic Fields/Career Goals: Advertising/Public Relations; Journalism; Photojournalism/Photography..

Award: Scholarship for use in freshman, sophomore, junior, senior, or graduate years; renewable. *Number:* 1–10. *Amount:* $500–$2000.

Eligibility Requirements: Applicant must be American Indian/Alaska Native; enrolled or expecting to enroll full-time at a two-year or four-year institution or university and must have an interest in writing. Applicant or parent of applicant must be member of Native American Journalists Association. Available to U.S. and Canadian citizens.

Application Requirements: Application form, community service, essay, financial need analysis, interview, personal photograph, portfolio. *Deadline:* June 30.

Contact: Jeffrey Palmer, Education Director
     Phone: 405-325-9008
     Fax: 866-325-7565
     E-mail: jeffrey.p.palmer@ou.edu

NEBRASKA PRESS ASSOCIATION
http://www.nebpress.com/

NEBRASKA PRESS ASSOCIATION FOUNDATION SCHOLARSHIP

Award for graduates of Nebraska high schools who have a minimum GPA of 2.5. Preference will be given to students who will be pursuing community journalism education at a Nebraska college or university.

Academic Fields/Career Goals: Advertising/Public Relations; Communications; Graphics/Graphic Arts/Printing; Journalism; Marketing; Photojournalism/Photography.

Award: Scholarship for use in freshman, sophomore, or junior years; not renewable. *Number:* 2–4. *Amount:* $2000.

Eligibility Requirements: Applicant must be enrolled or expecting to enroll full-time at a four-year institution or university; resident of Nebraska and studying in Nebraska. Available to U.S. citizens.

Application Requirements: Application form, essay. *Deadline:* February 20.

Contact: Allen Beermann, Executive Director
     Phone: 402-476-2851
     Fax: 402-476-2942
     E-mail: abeermann@nebpress.com

OHIO NEWS MEDIA FOUNDATION
http://www.ohionews.org

HAROLD K. DOUTHIT SCHOLARSHIP

$1500 scholarship for student enrolled as a sophomore, junior or senior at an Ohio college or university. Must be majoring in journalism, marketing, communications, or advertising. Minimum 3.0 GPA required.

Academic Fields/Career Goals: Advertising/Public Relations; Communications; Journalism; Marketing.

Award: Scholarship for use in sophomore, junior, or senior years; not renewable. *Number:* 1. *Amount:* $1500.

Eligibility Requirements: Applicant must be enrolled or expecting to enroll full-time at a four-year institution or university; resident of Ohio and studying in Ohio. Available to U.S. citizens.

Application Requirements: Application form, application form may be submitted online(mwidner@ohionews.org), essay, financial need analysis, transcript. *Deadline:* April 19.

Contact: Ms. Michelle Widner, Administrative Assistant
     Ohio News Media Foundation
     1335 Dublin Road, Suite 216B
     Columbus, OH 43215
     Phone: 614-486-6677 Ext. 1010
     E-mail: mwidner@ohionews.org

OHIO NEWS MEDIA FOUNDATION MINORITY SCHOLARSHIP

One scholarship for a minority high school senior in Ohio who plans to major in a field relevant to the newspaper industry, particularly journalism, advertising, marketing, or a communications degree program. Applicants must plan to enroll for fall classes at an accredited college or university within the United States. Must be African-American, Hispanic, Asian-American or American-Indian. A minimum high school GPA of 2.5 required.

Academic Fields/Career Goals: Advertising/Public Relations; Communications; Journalism; Marketing.

Award: Scholarship for use in freshman year; not renewable. *Number:* 1. *Amount:* $1500.

Eligibility Requirements: Applicant must be American Indian/Alaska Native, Asian/Pacific Islander, Black (non-Hispanic), Hispanic; high school student; planning to enroll or expecting to enroll full-time at a four-year institution or university and resident of Ohio. Available to U.S. citizens.

Application Requirements: Application form, application form may be submitted online(mwidner@ohionews.org), essay, transcript. *Deadline:* April 19.

Contact: Ms. Michelle "Mike" Widner, Admin. Asst.
     Ohio News Media Foundation
     1335 Dublin Road, Suite 216B
     Columbus, OH 43215
     Phone: 614-486-6677 Ext. 1010
     E-mail: mwidner@ohionews.org

OHIO NEWS MEDIA FOUNDATION UNIVERSITY JOURNALISM SCHOLARSHIP

The Foundation will award 2 scholarships of $2,000 each for a student currently enrolled in an Ohio college or university and majoring in a field relevant to the newspaper industry, particularly journalism, advertising, marketing, or communications degree program. Preference will be given to students demonstrating a career commitment to newspaper journalism. A minimum GPA of 2.5 required.

Academic Fields/Career Goals: Advertising/Public Relations; Communications; Journalism; Marketing.

Award: Scholarship for use in sophomore, junior, or senior years; not renewable. *Number:* 2. *Amount:* $2000.

Eligibility Requirements: Applicant must be enrolled or expecting to enroll full-time at a four-year institution or university; resident of Ohio and studying in Ohio. Available to U.S. citizens.

Application Requirements: Application form, application form may be submitted online(mwidner@ohionews.org), essay, transcript. *Deadline:* April 19.

Contact: Ms. Michelle Widner, Administrative Assistant
     Ohio News Media Foundation
     1335 Dublin Road, Suite 216B
     Columbus, OH 43215
     Phone: 614-486-6677 Ext. 1010
     E-mail: mwidner@ohionews.org

ONWA ANNUAL SCHOLARSHIP

One-time scholarship. Applicant may be a male or female student enrolled as a junior or senior in an Ohio college or university and majoring in a field relevant to the newspaper industry, particularly journalism, advertising, marketing, or communications degree program. Must be U.S. citizen.

Academic Fields/Career Goals: Advertising/Public Relations; Communications; Journalism; Marketing.

Award: Scholarship for use in junior or senior years; not renewable. *Number:* 1. *Amount:* $2000.

Eligibility Requirements: Applicant must be enrolled or expecting to enroll full-time at a four-year institution or university; resident of Ohio and studying in Ohio. Available to U.S. citizens.

Application Requirements: Application form, application form may be submitted online(mwidner@ohionews.org), essay, financial need analysis, transcript. *Deadline:* April 19.

Contact: Ms. Michelle "Mike" Widner, Admin. Asst.
     Ohio News Media Foundation
     1335 Dublin Road, Suite 216B
     Columbus, OH 43215
     Phone: 614-486-6677 Ext. 1010
     E-mail: mwidner@ohionews.org

PUBLIC RELATIONS STUDENT SOCIETY OF AMERICA

http://www.prssa.org/

PUBLIC RELATIONS SOCIETY OF AMERICA MULTICULTURAL AFFAIRS SCHOLARSHIP

Two, one-time $1500 awards for members of a principal minority group who are in their junior or senior year at an accredited four-year college or university. Must have at least a 3.0 GPA and be preparing for career in public relations or communications. Must be a full-time student and U.S. citizen.

Academic Fields/Career Goals: Advertising/Public Relations; Communications.

Award: Scholarship for use in freshman, sophomore, junior, or senior years; not renewable. *Number:* 2. *Amount:* $1500.

Eligibility Requirements: Applicant must be American Indian/Alaska Native, Asian/Pacific Islander, Black (non-Hispanic), Hispanic and enrolled or expecting to enroll full-time at a four-year institution or university. Available to U.S. citizens.

Application Requirements: Application form, essay, financial need analysis. *Deadline:* April 18.

Contact: Dora Tovar, Chair, Multicultural Communications Section
Public Relations Student Society of America
33 Maiden Lane, 11th Floor
New York, NY 10038-5150
Phone: 212-460-1476
E-mail: jeneen.garcia@prsa.org

RHODE ISLAND FOUNDATION

http://www.rifoundation.org/

J. D. EDSAL SCHOLARSHIP

Award to benefit Rhode Island residents studying advertising (public relations, marketing, graphic design, film, video, television, or broadcast production) with the expectation of pursuing a career in one of more of these fields. Applicants must be college undergraduates, sophomore or above.

Academic Fields/Career Goals: Advertising/Public Relations; Communications; Filmmaking/Video; Graphics/Graphic Arts/Printing; Marketing; TV/Radio Broadcasting.

Award: Scholarship for use in sophomore, junior, or senior years; renewable. *Amount:* $500–$1000.

Eligibility Requirements: Applicant must be enrolled or expecting to enroll full-time at a four-year institution or university and resident of Rhode Island. Available to U.S. citizens.

Application Requirements: Application form, essay, financial need analysis, recommendations or references, self-addressed stamped envelope with application, transcript.

Contact: Kelly Riley, Donor Services Administrator
Phone: 401-427-4028
E-mail: kriley@rifoundation.org

SCARLETT FAMILY FOUNDATION SCHOLARSHIP PROGRAM

http://www.scarlettfoundation.org/

SCHOLARSHIP FOR STUDENTS PURSUING A BUSINESS OR STEM DEGREE
• See page 80

SIMMONS AND FLETCHER, P.C.

https://www.simmonsandfletcher.com/

MARKETING SCHOLARSHIP

Our Marketing Scholarship offers a $1,000 scholarship for the winner and a $500 scholarship for one runner up who have an interest in marketing and advertising.

Academic Fields/Career Goals: Advertising/Public Relations; Marketing.

Award: Scholarship for use in freshman, sophomore, junior, or senior years; not renewable. *Number:* 1–2. *Amount:* $500–$1000.

Eligibility Requirements: Applicant must be enrolled or expecting to enroll full- or part-time at a two-year or four-year institution or university. Available to U.S. citizens.

Application Requirements: Essay. *Deadline:* July 1.

Contact: Administrative Assistant
Simmons and Fletcher, P.C.
9821 Katy Freeway, Suite 925
Houston, TX 77024
Phone: 713-7139320777
E-mail: info@simmonsandfletcher.com

SPECIALTY EQUIPMENT MARKET ASSOCIATION

http://www.sema.org/

SEMA MEMORIAL SCHOLARSHIP FUND
• See page 81

STRAIGHTFORWARD MEDIA

http://www.straightforwardmedia.com/

STRAIGHTFORWARD MEDIA BUSINESS SCHOOL SCHOLARSHIP

Scholarship of $500 for undergraduate and graduate students pursuing a business-related degree, including but not limited to economics, finance, marketing, and management. Students pursuing an online business degree are also eligible. Awarded four times per year. Deadlines: March 31, June 30, September 30, and December 31.

Academic Fields/Career Goals: Advertising/Public Relations; Business/Consumer Services; Economics; Finance; Marketing.

Award: Scholarship for use in freshman, sophomore, junior, senior, or graduate years; not renewable. *Number:* 4. *Amount:* $500.

Eligibility Requirements: Applicant must be enrolled or expecting to enroll full- or part-time at a two-year or four-year or technical institution or university. Available to U.S. and non-U.S. citizens.

Application Requirements: Essay. *Deadline:* varies.

Contact: Scholarship Committee
Phone: 605-348-3042

STRAIGHTFORWARD MEDIA MEDIA & COMMUNICATIONS SCHOLARSHIP

Scholarship of $500 available to students of media and communications. Must be majoring in programs such as journalism, broadcasting, advertising, speech, mass communications, or marketing. Awarded four times per year. Deadlines are March 31, June 30, September 30, and December 31. For more information, visit website at http://www.straightforwardmedia.com/media/form.php.

Academic Fields/Career Goals: Advertising/Public Relations; Communications; Journalism; Marketing; Photojournalism/Photography; TV/Radio Broadcasting.

Award: Scholarship for use in freshman, sophomore, junior, or senior years; not renewable. *Number:* 4. *Amount:* $500.

Eligibility Requirements: Applicant must be enrolled or expecting to enroll full- or part-time at a two-year or four-year or technical institution or university. Available to U.S. and non-U.S. citizens.

Application Requirements: Essay. *Deadline:* varies.

Contact: Scholarship Committee
Phone: 605-348-3042

TAMPA BAY TIMES FUND, INC.

http://www.tampabay.com/fund

TAMPA BAY TIMES FUND CAREER JOURNALISM SCHOLARSHIPS

Scholarship to high school seniors in the Tampa Bay Times' audience area who have a demonstrated interest in pursuing journalism/media major in college and career after graduation.

Academic Fields/Career Goals: Advertising/Public Relations; Communications; Journalism; Marketing; Photojournalism/Photography; TV/Radio Broadcasting.

Award: Scholarship for use in freshman, sophomore, junior, or senior years; renewable. *Number:* 3. *Amount:* $2500.

Eligibility Requirements: Applicant must be high school student; age 18-22; planning to enroll or expecting to enroll full-time at a four-year institution or university; single and resident of Florida. Available to U.S. citizens.

Application Requirements: Application form, essay, portfolio. *Deadline:* January 23.

Contact: Nancy Waclawek, Scholarship Administrator
  Phone: 813-340-4125
  E-mail: tbtschls@gmail.com

UNITED NEGRO COLLEGE FUND

http://www.uncf.org/

UNCF/ALLIANCE DATA SCHOLARSHIP AND INTERNSHIP PROGRAM

Up to $5000 scholarship; summer internship; stipend and travel expenses to the UNCF Student Leadership Conference. Applicant must be an under-represented minority college student enrolled at an accredited four-year college or university with preference given to students attending private or public historically black colleges and universities. (Students residing in/or attending school near Plano, TX and Atlanta, GA will receive priority consideration for internships designated in those locations). Must be classified as sophomores (rising juniors) or juniors (rising seniors) at time of application and demonstrate unmet financial need. For internships in the Plano, TX location, students must major in Management Information Systems or Computer Science. For internships in the Atlanta, GA Epsilon location, students must major in Communications, Marketing or Advertising. For internships in the Columbus, OH Card Services location, students must major in Marketing or Computer Science.

Academic Fields/Career Goals: Advertising/Public Relations; Business/Consumer Services; Communications; Computer Science/Data Processing; Human Resources; Marketing.

Award: Scholarship for use in junior or senior years; not renewable.

Eligibility Requirements: Applicant must be American Indian/Alaska Native, Asian/Pacific Islander, Black (non-Hispanic), Hispanic and enrolled or expecting to enroll at a four-year institution or university. Available to U.S. citizens.

Application Requirements: Application form, application form may be submitted online, financial need analysis, personal statement of career interest, recommendations or references, resume, transcript. *Deadline:* January 26.

Contact: Crystal Terry
  E-mail: crystal.terry@uncf.org

WASHINGTON MEDIA SCHOLARS FOUNDATION

www.mediascholars.org

MEDIA PLAN CASE COMPETITION

Case Competition Teams of two create a strategic media plan based on a hypothetical public policy issue. Students work with actual, real-world data from leading national research and ratings firms to create a media plan that effectively reaches their target audience. Finalists come to Washington DC on an all expenses paid trip where they will compete, network with top media executives and take part in professional development.

Academic Fields/Career Goals: Advertising/Public Relations; Business/Consumer Services; Communications; Journalism; Marketing; Political Science; Public Policy and Administration; TV/Radio Broadcasting.

Award: Scholarship for use in sophomore, junior, or senior years; not renewable. *Number:* 4. *Amount:* $3000–$5000.

Eligibility Requirements: Applicant must be age 18 and over and enrolled or expecting to enroll full-time at a four-year institution or university. Available to U.S. and non-U.S. citizens.

Application Requirements: Answers and media plan for case study scenario., application form may be submitted online (https://www.mediascholars.org/media-scholars/). *Deadline:* February 1.

AFRICAN STUDIES

ABO CAPITAL

http://www.abocapital.net/

CHANGE AFRICA IMPROVE THE WORLD SCHOLARSHIP

Africa is a continent bursting with economic opportunities. Under the right circumstances, it could become a global leader across industries including technology, sustainability, and agriculture. Show us how you can change Africa to change the world. In 500 words or less, demonstrate your knowledge of Africa and explain your deep conceptual ideas for tapping into its economic potential and bettering the continent. These ideas could be your own or showcase your support of projects already in development. The Grand Prize essay will win a scholarship for one full semester of college, up to $30,000. The top three essays will win a 5-night all-expenses paid trip to Angola. Entries will be due February 28, 2018. Finalists will be notified by March 31, 2018. Participants can submit their essays to scholarship@abocapital.net. Must be 18 years or older and currently enrolled in undergraduate, graduate, or university program to enter. Please attach the essay as a word document. Include contact information, proof of enrollment, declared major, and age.

Academic Fields/Career Goals: African Studies.

Award: Prize for use in freshman, sophomore, junior, senior, graduate, or postgraduate years; not renewable. *Number:* 3. *Amount:* $30,000.

Eligibility Requirements: Applicant must be age 18 and over and enrolled or expecting to enroll full-time at a four-year institution or university. Available to U.S. and Canadian citizens.

Application Requirements: Application form, essay. *Deadline:* February 28.

Contact: Meghan Busch, Senior Account Executive
  New York, NY
  E-mail: scholarship@abocapital.net

HUB FOUNDATION

https://hub-foundation.org

HUB FOUNDATION SCHOLARSHIPS

Hub Foundation accepts scholarship applications from graduate and undergraduate students with a 3.5 grade point average who study Islam and Muslims in the fields of Islamic Studies, Religious Studies, Comparative Religious Studies, Near or Middle Eastern Studies, Central and South Asian Studies, African Studies, Sociology, Anthropology, Political Science, Law, Media, or Journalism. For application deadlines and more information visit https://hub-foundation.org/scholarships.

Academic Fields/Career Goals: African Studies; Anthropology; Area/Ethnic Studies; Art History; Asian Studies; Child and Family Studies; Foreign Language; History; International Migration; International Studies; Journalism; Law/Legal Services; Literature/English/Writing; Near and Middle East Studies; Political Science; Psychology; Religion/Theology; Social Sciences; Women's Studies.

Award: Scholarship for use in junior, senior, or graduate years; not renewable. *Number:* 1–15. *Amount:* $5000–$20,000.

Eligibility Requirements: Applicant must be enrolled or expecting to enroll full-time at a four-year institution or university. Available to U.S. and non-U.S. citizens.

Application Requirements: Application form, application form may be submitted online (https://www.hub-foundation.org/forms/scholarship-application), essay, One (1) page description of your major, thesis, or dissertation., recommendations or references, resume. *Deadline:* continuous.

Contact: Zachary Markwith, Executive Director
  Phone: (925) 271-5332
  E-mail: information@hub-foundation.org

UNITED NEGRO COLLEGE FUND

http://www.uncf.org/

THE OSSIE DAVIS LEGACY AWARD SCHOLARSHIP

Need-based scholarship of up to $6800 for a high school senior planning to attend a four-year HBCU. Applicants must demonstrate the ability and desire to use artistic activism to proactively address the concerns of humanity. Eligible majors include African American studies, communications, education, fine arts, humanities, performing arts, political science, social sciences, theater arts/drama and visual arts. The scholarship is renewable for up to 4 years, provided that students continue to meet the scholarship criteria. Minimum 3.0 GPA required. Eligible colleges are Benedict College, Bethune Cookman University, Claflin University, Clark Atlanta University, Florida Memorial University, Howard University, Lane College, Miles College, Morehouse College, Spelman College, Virginia Union University or Xavier University of Louisiana.

Academic Fields/Career Goals: African Studies; Arts; Communications; Humanities; Performing Arts; Political Science; Social Sciences.

Award: Scholarship for use in freshman, sophomore, junior, or senior years; renewable.

Eligibility Requirements: Applicant must be Black (non-Hispanic); high school student and planning to enroll or expecting to enroll full-time at a four-year institution or university. Available to U.S. citizens.

Application Requirements: Application form, application form may be submitted online, essay, financial need analysis, portfolio, recommendations or references. *Deadline:* October 9.

Contact: Girmu Habte
    E-mail: Girmu.Habte@uncf.org

AGRIBUSINESS

ABBIE SARGENT MEMORIAL SCHOLARSHIP INC.

http://www.nhfarmbureau.org/

ABBIE SARGENT MEMORIAL SCHOLARSHIP

Up to three awards between $400 and $700 will be provided to deserving New Hampshire residents, planning to attend an institution of higher learning. Must be a U.S. citizen.

Academic Fields/Career Goals: Agribusiness; Agriculture; Animal/Veterinary Sciences; Environmental Science; Home Economics; Horticulture/Floriculture.

Award: Scholarship for use in freshman, sophomore, junior, senior, graduate, or postgraduate years; not renewable. *Number:* 1–5. *Amount:* $400–$700.

Eligibility Requirements: Applicant must be enrolled or expecting to enroll full- or part-time at a two-year or four-year or technical institution or university and resident of New Hampshire. Applicant or parent of applicant must have employment or volunteer experience in agriculture. Available to U.S. citizens.

Application Requirements: Application form, driver's license, financial need analysis, personal photograph. *Deadline:* March 15.

Contact: Diane Clary, Administrator
    Abbie Sargent Memorial Scholarship Inc.
    Abbie Sargent Scholarship
    295 Sheep Davis Road
    Concord, NH 03301
    Phone: 603-224-1934
    E-mail: dianec@nhfarmbureau.org

CHS FOUNDATION

http://www.chsfoundation.org/

CHS FOUNDATION HIGH SCHOOL SCHOLARSHIPS

Scholarships available to graduating high school seniors who plan to enroll in an agricultural-related program of study in a two-year or four-year college or university. Student must be a U.S. citizen. For additional information and an application, see website http://www.chsfoundation.org.

Academic Fields/Career Goals: Agribusiness; Agriculture; Horticulture/Floriculture.

Award: Scholarship for use in freshman year; not renewable. *Number:* 50. *Amount:* $1000.

Eligibility Requirements: Applicant must be high school student and planning to enroll or expecting to enroll full- or part-time at a two-year or four-year or technical institution or university. Available to U.S. citizens.

Application Requirements: Application form, essay, recommendations or references, transcript. *Deadline:* April 1.

Contact: Scholarship Committee
    Phone: 800-814-0506
    E-mail: info@chsfoundation.org

CHS FOUNDATION TWO-YEAR COLLEGE SCHOLARSHIPS

Non-renewable scholarship available to first-year agricultural students at a two-year college. Must be studying an agricultural-related major; scholarship is intended for the second year of study. Must be a U.S. citizen. For additional information and application, see website http://www.chsfoundation.org.

Academic Fields/Career Goals: Agribusiness; Agriculture; Horticulture/Floriculture.

Award: Scholarship for use in sophomore year; not renewable. *Number:* 25. *Amount:* $1000.

Eligibility Requirements: Applicant must be enrolled or expecting to enroll full- or part-time at a two-year or technical institution. Available to U.S. citizens.

Application Requirements: Application form, essay, recommendations or references, transcript. *Deadline:* April 1.

Contact: Scholarship Committee
    Phone: 800-814-0506
    E-mail: info@chsfoundation.org

CHS FOUNDATION UNIVERSITY SCHOLARSHIPS

Renewable scholarship available for students in sophomore, junior, or senior year currently studying agriculture at select universities around the nation. Preference given to students interested in a career in or studying agricultural-based cooperatives and working towards a degree in agribusiness or production agriculture. Students apply to the School of Agriculture or Financial Aid Office at one of the participating universities and follow individual procedures and deadlines for that institution. For additional information and a list of participating universities, see website http://www.chsfoundation.org.

Academic Fields/Career Goals: Agribusiness; Agriculture.

Award: Scholarship for use in sophomore, junior, or senior years; not renewable. *Number:* up to 150. *Amount:* $1000.

Eligibility Requirements: Applicant must be enrolled or expecting to enroll full- or part-time at a four-year institution or university. Available to U.S. citizens.

Application Requirements: Application form, essay, recommendations or references, transcript.

Contact: Scholarship Committee
    Phone: 800-814-0506
    E-mail: info@chsfoundation.org

HOLSTEIN ASSOCIATION USA INC.

http://www.holsteinusa.com/

ROBERT H. RUMLER SCHOLARSHIP

Awards to encourage deserving and qualified persons with an established interest in the dairy field, who have demonstrated leadership qualities and managerial abilities to pursue a master's degree in business administration.

Academic Fields/Career Goals: Agribusiness; Business/Consumer Services.

Award: Scholarship for use in freshman, sophomore, junior, senior, or graduate years; not renewable. *Number:* 1. *Amount:* $3000.

Eligibility Requirements: Applicant must be enrolled or expecting to enroll full-time at an institution or university and must have an interest in leadership. Available to U.S. and non-U.S. citizens.

Application Requirements: Application form, essay, personal photograph, recommendations or references, transcript. *Deadline:* April 15.

Contact: John Meyer, Chief Executive Officer
Holstein Association USA Inc.
One Holstein Place, PO Box 808
Brattleboro, VT 05302-0808
Phone: 802-254-4551
Fax: 802-254-8251
E-mail: jmeyer@holstein.com

MAINE DEPARTMENT OF AGRICULTURE, FOOD AND RURAL RESOURCES

http://www.maine.gov/agriculture

MAINE RURAL REHABILITATION FUND SCHOLARSHIP PROGRAM

One-time scholarship open to Maine residents enrolled in or accepted by any school, college, or university. Must be full-time and demonstrate financial need. Those opting for a Maine institution given preference. Major must lead to an agricultural career. Minimum 3.0 GPA required.

Academic Fields/Career Goals: Agribusiness; Agriculture; Animal/Veterinary Sciences.

Award: Scholarship for use in freshman, sophomore, junior, senior, graduate, or postgraduate years; not renewable. *Number:* 10–20. *Amount:* $800–$2000.

Eligibility Requirements: Applicant must be enrolled or expecting to enroll full-time at a two-year or four-year or technical institution or university and resident of Maine. Available to U.S. citizens.

Application Requirements: Application form, driver's license, financial need analysis, transcript. *Deadline:* June 15.

Contact: Jane Aiudi, Director of Marketing
Phone: 207-287-7628
Fax: 207-287-5576
E-mail: jane.aiudi@maine.gov

NATIONAL CATTLEMEN'S FOUNDATION

http://www.nationalcattlemensfoundation.org/

CME BEEF INDUSTRY SCHOLARSHIP

Ten $1500 scholarships will be awarded to students who intend to pursue a career in the beef industry, including areas such as agricultural education, communications, production, or research. Applicant must be a graduating high school senior or full-time undergraduate student enrolled at a two or four-year institution.

Academic Fields/Career Goals: Agribusiness; Agriculture; Communications.

Award: Scholarship for use in freshman, sophomore, junior, or senior years; not renewable. *Number:* 10. *Amount:* $1500.

Eligibility Requirements: Applicant must be enrolled or expecting to enroll full-time at a four-year institution or university. Available to U.S. citizens.

Application Requirements: Application form, essay.

Contact: RoxAnn Johnson, Executive Director
Phone: 303-850-3388
Fax: 303-694-7372
E-mail: mcf@beef.org

NATIONAL POULTRY AND FOOD DISTRIBUTORS ASSOCIATION

http://www.npfda.org/

NATIONAL POULTRY AND FOOD DISTRIBUTORS ASSOCIATION SCHOLARSHIP FOUNDATION

The scholarships are awarded to full-time students in their junior or senior years at a U.S. college pursuing degrees in poultry science, food science, Food Marketing, agricultural business, or other related areas of study pertaining to the poultry and food industries. Dietetics does not qualify. Must attend U.S. College or university full time.

Academic Fields/Career Goals: Agribusiness; Agriculture; Animal/Veterinary Sciences; Food Science/Nutrition; Food Service/Hospitality.

Award: Scholarship for use in junior or senior years; not renewable. *Number:* 5. *Amount:* $4000.

Eligibility Requirements: Applicant must be enrolled or expecting to enroll full-time at a four-year institution or university. Available to U.S. citizens.

Application Requirements: Application form, essay. *Deadline:* May 31.

Contact: Kristin McWhorter, Executive Director
National Poultry and Food Distributors Association
2014 Osborne Road
Saint Marys, GA 31558
Phone: 770-535-9901
E-mail: kkm@npfda.org

NEW YORK STATE ASSOCIATION OF AGRICULTURAL FAIRS

http://www.nyfairs.org/

NEW YORK STATE ASSOCIATION OF AGRICULTURAL FAIRS AND NEW YORK STATE SHOWPEOPLE'S ASSOCIATION ANNUAL SCHOLARSHIP

Scholarship of $1000 given to New York high school seniors and students attending college and planning to pursue, or already pursuing a degree in an agricultural field, a fair management related field or an outdoor amusement related field.

Academic Fields/Career Goals: Agribusiness; Agriculture.

Award: Scholarship for use in freshman, sophomore, junior, senior, or graduate years; not renewable. *Number:* 6. *Amount:* $1000.

Eligibility Requirements: Applicant must be enrolled or expecting to enroll full-time at a two-year or four-year institution or university and resident of New York. Available to U.S. citizens.

Application Requirements: Application form, essay, recommendations or references, transcript. *Deadline:* April 9.

Contact: Mark St. Jacques, President
Phone: 518-692-2464
E-mail: markwashfair@aol.com

OHIO FARMERS UNION

http://www.ohfarmersunion.org/

VIRGIL THOMPSON MEMORIAL SCHOLARSHIP CONTEST

Award available to members of Ohio Farmers Union who are enrolled as full-time college sophomores, juniors or seniors. Awards of $1000 to winner and $500 each to two runners-up.

Academic Fields/Career Goals: Agribusiness; Agriculture.

Award: Scholarship for use in sophomore, junior, or senior years; not renewable. *Number:* 1–3. *Amount:* $500–$1000.

Eligibility Requirements: Applicant must be enrolled or expecting to enroll full-time at a four-year institution or university and resident of Ohio. Applicant or parent of applicant must be member of Ohio Farmers Union. Available to U.S. citizens.

Application Requirements: Application form, entry in a contest, essay. *Deadline:* December 31.

Contact: Ms. Linda Borton, Executive Director
Ohio Farmers Union
PO Box 363
Ottawa, OH 45875
Phone: 419-523-5300
E-mail: lborton@ohfarmersunion.org

SCARLETT FAMILY FOUNDATION SCHOLARSHIP PROGRAM

http://www.scarlettfoundation.org/

SCHOLARSHIP FOR STUDENTS PURSUING A BUSINESS OR STEM DEGREE
• *See page 80*

SOIL AND WATER CONSERVATION SOCIETY

http://www.swcs.org

DONALD A. WILLIAMS SCHOLARSHIP SOIL CONSERVATION SCHOLARSHIP

The scholarship provides financial assistance to members who are employed but wish to improve their technical or administrative competence in a conservation-related field. Applicants must be an SWCS member for at least 1 year and has completed at least one year of full-time employment in a natural resource conservation endeavor.

Academic Fields/Career Goals: Agribusiness; Agriculture; Biology; Earth Science; Environmental Science; Food Science/Nutrition; Hydrology; Natural Resources; Natural Sciences; Science, Technology, and Society.

Award: Scholarship for use in freshman, sophomore, junior, senior, graduate, or postgraduate years; not renewable. *Number:* 1–3. *Amount:* $700–$1000.

Eligibility Requirements: Applicant must be enrolled or expecting to enroll full- or part-time at a two-year or four-year or technical institution or university. Applicant or parent of applicant must be member of Soil and Water Conservation Society. Applicant or parent of applicant must have employment or volunteer experience in agriculture, environmental-related field. Available to U.S. and non-U.S. citizens.

Application Requirements: Application form, essay, recommendations or references. *Deadline:* February 13.

Contact: SWCS Scholarships Program Coordinator
Soil and Water Conservation Society
945 SW Ankeny Road
Ankeny, IA 50023-9723
Phone: 515-289-2331 Ext. 114
E-mail: scholarships@swcs.org

SOIL AND WATER CONSERVATION SOCIETY-NEW JERSEY CHAPTER

http://www.geocities.com/njswcs

EDWARD R. HALL SCHOLARSHIP

Two $500 scholarships awarded annually to students attending a New Jersey accredited college or New Jersey residents attending any out-of-state college. Undergraduate students, with the exception of freshmen, are eligible. Must be enrolled in a curriculum related to natural resources. Other areas related to conservation may qualify.

Academic Fields/Career Goals: Agribusiness; Agriculture; Animal/Veterinary Sciences; Biology; Earth Science; Environmental Science; Horticulture/Floriculture; Natural Resources; Natural Sciences.

Award: Scholarship for use in sophomore, junior, or senior years; not renewable. *Number:* 2. *Amount:* $500.

Eligibility Requirements: Applicant must be enrolled or expecting to enroll full-time at a two-year or four-year institution or university and resident of New Jersey. Available to U.S. and non-U.S. citizens.

Application Requirements: Application form, essay, financial need analysis, list of clubs and organizations related to natural resources of which applicant is a member, recommendations or references, transcript. *Deadline:* April 15.

Contact: Fireman E. Bear Chapter, c/o USDA-NRCS
Soil and Water Conservation Society-New Jersey Chapter
220 Davidson Avenue, Fourth Floor
Somerset, NJ 08873
Phone: 732-932-9295
E-mail: njswcs@yahoo.com

SOUTH DAKOTA BOARD OF REGENTS

http://www.sdbor.edu/

SOUTH DAKOTA BOARD OF REGENTS BJUGSTAD SCHOLARSHIP

Scholarship for graduating North or South Dakota high school senior who is a Native American. Must demonstrate academic achievement, character and leadership abilities. Must submit proof of tribal enrollment. One-time award of $500. Must rank in upper half of class or have a minimum 2.5 GPA. Must be pursuing studies in agriculture, agribusiness, or natural resources.

Academic Fields/Career Goals: Agribusiness; Agriculture; Natural Resources.

Award: Scholarship for use in freshman year; not renewable. *Number:* 2. *Amount:* $500.

Eligibility Requirements: Applicant must be American Indian/Alaska Native; high school student; planning to enroll or expecting to enroll full-time at a four-year institution or university; resident of North Dakota, South Dakota and must have an interest in leadership. Available to U.S. citizens.

Application Requirements: Application form. *Deadline:* February 23.

Contact: Kerri Richards, Student Services Coordinator
South Dakota Board of Regents
306 E. Capital Ave.
Suite 200
Pierre, SD 57501
Phone: 605-773-3455
E-mail: kerri.richards@sdbor.edu

SOUTH DAKOTA RETAILERS ASSOCIATION

http://www.sdra.org

SOUTH DAKOTA RETAILERS ASSOCIATION SCHOLARSHIP PROGRAM

Scholarships for students studying for a career in retailing. See application for eligible fields of study. Applicants must have graduated from a South Dakota high school or be enrolled in postsecondary school in South Dakota. Must complete required number of college or vocational school prior to receiving award, or have work experience in lieu of education.

Academic Fields/Career Goals: Agribusiness.

Award: Scholarship for use in sophomore, junior, senior, graduate, or postgraduate years; not renewable. *Number:* 10–15. *Amount:* $500–$2250.

Eligibility Requirements: Applicant must be enrolled or expecting to enroll full- or part-time at a two-year or four-year or technical institution or university. Available to U.S. and non-U.S. citizens.

Application Requirements: Application form, essay. *Deadline:* April 17.

Contact: Donna Leslie, Communications Director
South Dakota Retailers Association
SDRA
PO Box 638
Pierre, SD 57501
Phone: 800-658-5545
Fax: 605-224-2059
E-mail: donna@sdra.org

VERMONT SPACE GRANT CONSORTIUM

http://www.cems.uvm.edu/vsgc

VERMONT SPACE GRANT CONSORTIUM

Applicant must be a U.S. citizen, Vermont resident, graduating senior in a Vermont high school, or current undergraduate with a minimum 3.0 GPA enrolled full-time for the following academic year in a degree program in a Vermont institution of higher education. Must plan to pursue a professional career which has direct relevance to the U.S. aerospace industry and the goals of NASA. Three awards will be given to students enrolled in the Burlington Technical College Aviation Technology Program.

Academic Fields/Career Goals: Agribusiness; Applied Sciences; Aviation/Aerospace; Biology; Civil Engineering; Computer Science/Data Processing; Earth Science; Electrical Engineering/Electronics; Energy and Power Engineering; Engineering-Related Technologies; Engineering/Technology; Materials Science, Engineering, and Metallurgy; Mathematics; Mechanical Engineering; Physical Sciences; Science, Technology, and Society; Trade/Technical Specialties.

Award: Scholarship for use in freshman, sophomore, junior, or senior years; not renewable. *Number:* 6–9. *Amount:* $2500–$5000.

Eligibility Requirements: Applicant must be enrolled or expecting to enroll full-time at a two-year or four-year or technical institution or university; resident of Vermont and studying in Vermont. Available to U.S. citizens.

Application Requirements: Application form, essay. *Deadline:* March 1.

Contact: Ms. Debra Fraser, Program Coordinator
Vermont Space Grant Consortium
University of Vermont -Vermont Space Grant Consortium
210 Colchester Avenue, Room 120
Burlington, VT 05405-0156
Phone: 802-656-1429
E-mail: dfraser1@uvm.edu

AGRICULTURE

ABBIE SARGENT MEMORIAL SCHOLARSHIP INC.

http://www.nhfarmbureau.org/

ABBIE SARGENT MEMORIAL SCHOLARSHIP
• *See page 89*

ALABAMA GOLF COURSE SUPERINTENDENTS ASSOCIATION

http://www.agcsa.org/

ALABAMA GOLF COURSE SUPERINTENDENT'S ASSOCIATION'S DONNIE ARTHUR MEMORIAL SCHOLARSHIP

One-time award for students majoring in agriculture with an emphasis on turf-grass management. Must have a minimum 2.0 GPA. Applicant must be a full-time student. High school students not considered. Award available to U.S. citizens.

Academic Fields/Career Goals: Agriculture; Horticulture/Floriculture.

Award: Scholarship for use in freshman, sophomore, junior, or senior years; not renewable. *Number:* 1. *Amount:* $2000.

Eligibility Requirements: Applicant must be enrolled or expecting to enroll full-time at a two-year or four-year institution or university. Available to U.S. citizens.

Application Requirements: Application form, essay. *Deadline:* October 15.

Contact: Melanie Bonds, Secretary
Phone: 205-967-0397
E-mail: agcsa@charter.net

AMERICAN OIL CHEMISTS' SOCIETY

www.aocs.org/

AOCS BIOTECHNOLOGY STUDENT EXCELLENCE AWARD

Award to recognize an outstanding paper in the field of biotechnology presented by a student at the AOCS Annual Meeting and Expo. Graduate students presenting within the Biotechnology Division technical program are eligible for the award.

Academic Fields/Career Goals: Agriculture; Chemical Engineering; Food Science/Nutrition.

Award: Prize for use in junior, senior, or graduate years; not renewable. *Number:* 1–3. *Amount:* $100–$300.

Eligibility Requirements: Applicant must be enrolled or expecting to enroll full- or part-time at a four-year institution or university. Available to U.S. and non-U.S. citizens.

Application Requirements: Essay, extended abstract, recommendations or references. *Deadline:* February 1.

Contact: Barbara Semeraro, Area Manager, Membership
American Oil Chemists' Society
AOCS
PO Box 17190
Urbana, IL 61803
Phone: 217-693-4804
Fax: 217-693-4849
E-mail: awards@aocs.org

AMERICAN SOCIETY FOR ENOLOGY AND VITICULTURE

http://www.asev.org/

AMERICAN SOCIETY FOR ENOLOGY AND VITICULTURE SCHOLARSHIPS

One-time award for college juniors, seniors, and graduate students residing in North America and enrolled in a program studying viticulture, enology, or any field related to the wine and grape industry. Minimum 3.0 GPA for undergraduates; minimum 3.2 GPA for graduate students. Must be a resident of the United States, Canada, or Mexico.

Academic Fields/Career Goals: Agriculture; Chemical Engineering; Food Science/Nutrition; Horticulture/Floriculture.

Award: Scholarship for use in junior, senior, or graduate years; not renewable. *Number:* up to 30. *Amount:* $500–$4000.

Eligibility Requirements: Applicant must be enrolled or expecting to enroll full-time at a four-year institution or university. Available to U.S. and non-U.S. citizens.

Application Requirements: Application form, essay, financial need analysis, recommendations or references, transcript. *Deadline:* March 1.

Contact: Karli Kolb, Administrative Assistant
Phone: 530-753-3142
Fax: 530-753-3318
E-mail: society@asev.org

AMERICAN SOCIETY OF AGRICULTURAL AND BIOLOGICAL ENGINEERS

http://www.asabe.org/

WILLIAM J. ADAMS, JR. AND MARIJANE E. ADAMS SCHOLARSHIP

One-time award for a full-time U.S. or Canadian undergraduate who is a student member of the American Society of Agricultural Engineers and a declared major in biological or agricultural engineering. Must be at least a sophomore and have minimum 2.5 GPA. Must be interested in agricultural machinery product design or development. Application procedures can be found on http://www.asabe.org website.

Academic Fields/Career Goals: Agriculture; Biology.

Award: Scholarship for use in sophomore, junior, or senior years; not renewable. *Number:* 1. *Amount:* $1200.

Eligibility Requirements: Applicant must be enrolled or expecting to enroll full-time at a four-year institution or university. Applicant or parent of applicant must be member of Other Student Academic Clubs. Available to U.S. and Canadian citizens.

Application Requirements: Application form, essay, financial need analysis, recommendations or references, resume. *Deadline:* March 15.

Contact: Carol Flautt, Scholarship Program
American Society of Agricultural and Biological Engineers
2950 Niles Road
St. Joseph, MI 49085-9659
Phone: 269-932-7036
Fax: 269-429-3852
E-mail: flautt@asabe.org

ASSOCIATION ON AMERICAN INDIAN AFFAIRS, INC.

http://www.indian-affairs.org/

ELIZABETH AND SHERMAN ASCHE MEMORIAL SCHOLARSHIP FUND

Scholarship of up to $1500 available for undergraduate and graduate students seeking a Bachelor's or Master's degree in science or public health. Students must apply each year. Must be a Native American. See website for details http://www.indian-affairs.org. Must be seeking an Associate's degree or higher at an accredited school.

Academic Fields/Career Goals: Agriculture; Animal/Veterinary Sciences; Biology; Chemical Engineering; Dental Health/Services; Earth Science; Health and Medical Sciences; Marine Biology; Natural Sciences; Nursing; Physical Sciences; Public Health.

Award: Scholarship for use in freshman, sophomore, junior, senior, or graduate years; not renewable. *Number:* 6–8. *Amount:* up to $1500.

Eligibility Requirements: Applicant must be American Indian/Alaska Native and enrolled or expecting to enroll full-time at a two-year or four-year or technical institution or university. Available to U.S. citizens.

Application Requirements: Application form, essay, Tribal Enrollment. *Deadline:* June 1.

Contact: Lisa Wyzlic, Director of Scholarship Programs
Association on American Indian Affairs, Inc.
966 Hungerford Drive, Suite 12-B
Rockville, MD 20850
Phone: 240-314-7155
Fax: 240-314-7159
E-mail: lw.aaia@indian-affairs.org

CALCOT-SEITZ FOUNDATION

http://www.calcot.com/

CALCOT-SEITZ SCHOLARSHIP

Scholarship for young students from Arizona, New Mexico, Texas, and California who plan to attend a college or are attending a college offering at least a four-year degree in agriculture.

Academic Fields/Career Goals: Agriculture.

Award: Scholarship for use in freshman, sophomore, junior, senior, or graduate years; not renewable. *Number:* 1–30. *Amount:* $500–$3000.

Eligibility Requirements: Applicant must be enrolled or expecting to enroll full-time at a four-year institution or university and resident of Arizona, California, New Mexico, Texas. Available to U.S. and non-U.S. citizens.

Application Requirements: Application form, community service, essay, interview, personal photograph. *Deadline:* March 31.

Contact: Marci Cunningham, Scholarship Committee
Calcot-Seitz Foundation
PO Box 259
Bakersfield, CA 93302
Phone: 661-327-5961
E-mail: mcunningham@calcot.com

CHS FOUNDATION

http://www.chsfoundation.org/

CHS FOUNDATION HIGH SCHOOL SCHOLARSHIPS
• *See page 89*

CHS FOUNDATION TWO-YEAR COLLEGE SCHOLARSHIPS
• *See page 89*

CHS FOUNDATION UNIVERSITY SCHOLARSHIPS
• *See page 89*

COUPONBIRDS

https://www.couponbirds.com/

HELP TO SAVE SCHOLARSHIP

To assist students in reducing their tuition fee burden and collect their smart ways of saving money, couponbirds starts the Couponbirds "Help to Save" Scholarship program. The most sparkling idea and response will be drawn to present at our site and rewarded with prize. Please be free to contact us if you have any further questions about the site or the scholarship.

Academic Fields/Career Goals: Agriculture.

Award: Scholarship for use in freshman, sophomore, junior, or senior years; renewable. *Amount:* $1–$1000.

Eligibility Requirements: Applicant must be Disciple of Christ; Armenian citizen; American Indian/Alaska Native or Asian/Pacific Islander; enrolled or expecting to enroll full- or part-time at a two-year or four-year or technical institution or university; resident of Montana; studying in Utah and must have an interest in art. Applicant or parent of applicant must have employment or volunteer experience in computer science. Available to U.S. and non-U.S. citizens.

Application Requirements: Application form, autobiography, community service, essay, interview, personal photograph, portfolio. *Deadline:* October 10.

Contact: Steven Ruff
Couponbirds
2443 Fillmore Street, #380-3240
San Francisco, CA 94115
Phone: 6164269997
E-mail: scholarship@couponbirds.com

FEEDING TOMORROW: THE FOUNDATION OF THE INSTITUTE OF FOOD TECHNOLOGISTS

http://www.feedingtomorrow.org

EVAN TUREK MEMORIAL SCHOLARSHIP

Two $1500 awards for students studying food science, nutrition, agricultural engineering, biochemistry, chemical engineering, dairy science, food chemistry, food engineering, food packaging, non-thermal processing or related discipline. Minimum 3.0 GPA.

Academic Fields/Career Goals: Agriculture; Chemical Engineering; Food Science/Nutrition.

Award: Scholarship for use in sophomore, junior, or senior years; not renewable. *Number:* 2. *Amount:* $1500.

Eligibility Requirements: Applicant must be enrolled or expecting to enroll full- or part-time at a four-year institution or university and must have an interest in leadership. Available to U.S. and non-U.S. citizens.

Application Requirements: Application form, application form may be submitted online, transcript. *Deadline:* February 28.

Contact: Feeding Tomorrow Manager
Feeding Tomorrow: The Foundation of the Institute of Food Technologists
525 West Van Buren, Suite 1000
Chicago, IL 60607
Phone: 312-604-0256
E-mail: feedingtomorrow@ift.org

IFT FOOD LAWS AND REGULATIONS DIVISION UNDERGRADUATE SCHOLARSHIP

One $1500 scholarship for a student planning to enroll full-time or part-time as a rising sophomore, junior, or senior student pursuing an undergraduate degree in food science with an interest in food laws, regulation, food policy, agricultural policy, or nutrition policy. Minimum 3.0 GPA.

Academic Fields/Career Goals: Agriculture; Food Science/Nutrition.

Award: Scholarship for use in sophomore, junior, or senior years; not renewable. *Number:* 1. *Amount:* $1500.

Eligibility Requirements: Applicant must be enrolled or expecting to enroll full- or part-time at a four-year institution or university and must have an interest in leadership. Available to U.S. and non-U.S. citizens.

Application Requirements: Application form, application form may be submitted online, transcript. *Deadline:* February 28.

Contact: Feeding Tomorrow Manager
Feeding Tomorrow: The Foundation of the Institute of Food Technologists
525 West Van Buren, Suite 1000
Chicago, IL 60607
Phone: 312-604-0256
E-mail: feedingtomorrow@ift.org

JAPANESE AMERICAN CITIZENS LEAGUE (JACL)
http://www.jacl.org/

NATIONAL JACL HEADQUARTERS SCHOLARSHIP
Scholarship offers over 30 awards to qualified students nationwide. Scholarships are provided to students at the entering freshman, undergraduate, graduate, law, financial need and creative & performing arts. All scholarships are one-time awards. Every applicant must be an active National JACL member at either an Individual or Student/Youth Level.

Academic Fields/Career Goals: Agriculture; Journalism; Law/Legal Services; Literature/English/Writing; Public Policy and Administration.

Award: Scholarship for use in freshman, sophomore, junior, senior, or graduate years; not renewable. *Number:* 30.

Eligibility Requirements: Applicant must be of Japanese heritage; Asian/Pacific Islander and enrolled or expecting to enroll full-time at a two-year or four-year institution or university. Available to U.S. and non-U.S. citizens.

Application Requirements: Application form, essay, financial need analysis. *Deadline:* March 1.

Contact: Scholarship Committee
Phone: 415-921-5225
E-mail: jacl@jacl.org

LES DAMES D'ESCOFFIER INTERNATIONAL, COLORADO CHAPTER
www.lesdamescolorado.org/scholarship

LES DAMES D'ESCOFFIER INTERNATIONAL, COLORADO CHAPTER SCHOLARSHIP
Les Dames d'Escoffier International, Colorado Chapter, will award two $1,000 scholarships in 2019 to qualified female students in food-related fields and attending schools in Colorado. The awards are based on financial need, academic performance, and personal/professional accomplishments. The deadline is April 5, 2019.

Academic Fields/Career Goals: Agriculture; Animal/Veterinary Sciences; Culinary Arts; Food Science/Nutrition; Food Service/Hospitality; Home Economics.

Award: Scholarship for use in freshman, sophomore, junior, senior, or graduate years; not renewable. *Number:* 2. *Amount:* $1000.

Eligibility Requirements: Applicant must be enrolled or expecting to enroll full- or part-time at a two-year or four-year or technical institution or university; female and studying in Colorado. Available to U.S. and non-U.S. citizens.

Application Requirements: Application form, application form may be submitted online(www.lesdamescolorado.org/scholarship), essay, financial need analysis, recommendations or references, resume, transcript. *Deadline:* April 5.

Contact: Carol Fenster
Les Dames d'Escoffier International, Colorado Chapter
5397 E Mineral Circle
Centennial, CO 80122
Phone: 303-741-0313
E-mail: carol@carolfenster.com

MAINE DEPARTMENT OF AGRICULTURE, FOOD AND RURAL RESOURCES
http://www.maine.gov/agriculture

MAINE RURAL REHABILITATION FUND SCHOLARSHIP PROGRAM
• *See page 90*

MICHIGAN STATE HORTICULTURAL SOCIETY
http://www.mihortsociety.com

FRUITS INDUSTRIES SCHOLARSHIPS
This scholarship is only for students who intend to pursue careers in or connected to the Midwest fruit industry.

Academic Fields/Career Goals: Agriculture.

Award: Scholarship for use in junior, senior, or graduate years; not renewable. *Number:* 4–7. *Amount:* $1500.

Eligibility Requirements: Applicant must be enrolled or expecting to enroll full-time at a two-year or four-year institution or university. Applicant or parent of applicant must have employment or volunteer experience in agriculture. Available to U.S. citizens.

Application Requirements: Application form. *Deadline:* September 30.
Contact: Ben Smith

NATIONAL CATTLEMEN'S FOUNDATION
http://www.nationalcattlemensfoundation.org/

CME BEEF INDUSTRY SCHOLARSHIP
• *See page 90*

NATIONAL COUNCIL OF STATE GARDEN CLUBS INC. SCHOLARSHIP
http://www.gardenclub.org/

NATIONAL COUNCIL OF STATE GARDEN CLUBS INC. SCHOLARSHIP
Scholarship to students for study in agriculture education, horticulture, floriculture, landscape design, botany, biology, plant pathology/science, forestry, agronomy, environmental concerns.

Academic Fields/Career Goals: Agriculture; Biology; Environmental Science; Horticulture/Floriculture.

Award: Scholarship for use in sophomore, junior, senior, or graduate years; not renewable. *Number:* 34. *Amount:* $3500.

Eligibility Requirements: Applicant must be enrolled or expecting to enroll full-time at a two-year or four-year institution or university. Available to U.S. citizens.

Application Requirements: Application form, financial need analysis, recommendations or references, transcript. *Deadline:* March 1.

Contact: Kathy Romine, National Headquarters
Phone: 314-776-7574 Ext. 15
Fax: 314-776-5108
E-mail: headquarters@gardenclub.org

NATIONAL GARDEN CLUBS INC.
http://www.gardenclub.org/

NATIONAL GARDEN CLUBS INC. SCHOLARSHIP PROGRAM
One-time award for full-time students in plant sciences, agriculture and related or allied subjects. Applicants must have at least a 3.25 GPA.

Academic Fields/Career Goals: Agriculture; Biology; Earth Science; Environmental Science; Horticulture/Floriculture; Landscape Architecture.

Award: Scholarship for use in junior, senior, or graduate years; not renewable. *Number:* 41. *Amount:* $4000.

Eligibility Requirements: Applicant must be enrolled or expecting to enroll full-time at a four-year institution or university. Available to U.S. citizens.

Application Requirements: Application form, financial need analysis, personal photograph. *Deadline:* February 1.

Contact: Sandra Robinson, Vice President for Scholarship
Phone: 606-878-7281
E-mail: sandyr@kayandkay.com

NATIONAL POULTRY AND FOOD DISTRIBUTORS ASSOCIATION

http://www.npfda.org/

NATIONAL POULTRY AND FOOD DISTRIBUTORS ASSOCIATION SCHOLARSHIP FOUNDATION
• *See page 90*

NATIONAL RESTAURANT ASSOCIATION EDUCATIONAL FOUNDATION

http://www.chooserestaurants.org

NATIONAL RESTAURANT ASSOCIATION EDUCATIONAL FOUNDATION UNDERGRADUATE SCHOLARSHIPS FOR COLLEGE STUDENTS

Merit-based scholarship awards for students pursuing degrees related to the restaurant/foodservice/hospitality industry.

Academic Fields/Career Goals: Agriculture; Business/Consumer Services; Culinary Arts; Food Science/Nutrition; Food Service/Hospitality; Horticulture/Floriculture; Hospitality Management; Marketing.

Award: Scholarship for use in freshman, sophomore, junior, or senior years; not renewable. *Number:* 150–300. *Amount:* $2500–$10,000.

Eligibility Requirements: Applicant must be enrolled or expecting to enroll full- or part-time at a two-year or four-year or technical institution or university. Available to U.S. citizens.

Application Requirements: Application form, application form may be submitted online(www.chooserestaurants.org/scholarships), community service, essay, recommendations or references, transcript. *Deadline:* March 15.

Contact: Matt Rosales, Program Manager
National Restaurant Association Educational Foundation
2055 L Street NW, Suite 700
Washington, DC 20036
Phone: 202-973-3672
E-mail: scholars@nraef.org

NEW YORK STATE ASSOCIATION OF AGRICULTURAL FAIRS

http://www.nyfairs.org/

NEW YORK STATE ASSOCIATION OF AGRICULTURAL FAIRS AND NEW YORK STATE SHOWPEOPLE'S ASSOCIATION ANNUAL SCHOLARSHIP
• *See page 90*

NEW YORK STATE GRANGE

http://www.nysgrange.org/

HOWARD F. DENISE SCHOLARSHIP

Awards for undergraduates under 21 years old to pursue studies in agriculture. Must be a New York resident with a minimum 3.0 GPA. One-time award of $1000.

Academic Fields/Career Goals: Agriculture.

Award: Scholarship for use in freshman, sophomore, junior, or senior years; not renewable. *Number:* 1–6. *Amount:* $1000.

Eligibility Requirements: Applicant must be age 21 or under; enrolled or expecting to enroll full-time at a two-year or four-year institution and resident of New York. Available to U.S. citizens.

Application Requirements: Application form, financial need analysis. *Deadline:* April 15.

Contact: Scholarship Committee
New York State Grange
100 Grange Place
Cortland, NY 13045
Phone: 607-756-7553
E-mail: nysgrange@nysgrange.org

OHIO FARMERS UNION

http://www.ohfarmersunion.org/

JOSEPH FITCHER SCHOLARSHIP CONTEST

Scholarship available to member of Ohio Farmers Union who is a high school junior or senior, or enrolled as a college freshman. Participants are to submit an application obtained from OFU and a typed essay. Essay subject matter changes annually. Award of $1000 to winner and $250 to two runners-up.

Academic Fields/Career Goals: Agriculture.

Award: Scholarship for use in freshman year; not renewable. *Number:* 1–3. *Amount:* $250–$1000.

Eligibility Requirements: Applicant must be high school student; planning to enroll or expecting to enroll full-time at a four-year institution or university and resident of Ohio. Applicant or parent of applicant must be member of Ohio Farmers Union. Available to U.S. citizens.

Application Requirements: Application form, entry in a contest, essay. *Deadline:* December 31.

Contact: Ms. Linda Borton, Executive Director
Ohio Farmers Union
PO Box 363
Ottawa, OH 45875
Phone: 419-523-5300
E-mail: lborton@ohfarmersunion.org

VIRGIL THOMPSON MEMORIAL SCHOLARSHIP CONTEST
• *See page 90*

SCARLETT FAMILY FOUNDATION SCHOLARSHIP PROGRAM

http://www.scarlettfoundation.org/

SCHOLARSHIP FOR STUDENTS PURSUING A BUSINESS OR STEM DEGREE
• *See page 80*

SOIL AND WATER CONSERVATION SOCIETY

http://www.swcs.org

DONALD A. WILLIAMS SCHOLARSHIP SOIL CONSERVATION SCHOLARSHIP
• *See page 91*

SOIL AND WATER CONSERVATION SOCIETY–NEW JERSEY CHAPTER

http://www.geocities.com/njswcs

EDWARD R. HALL SCHOLARSHIP
• *See page 91*

SOUTH DAKOTA BOARD OF REGENTS

http://www.sdbor.edu/

SOUTH DAKOTA BOARD OF REGENTS BJUGSTAD SCHOLARSHIP

• *See page 91*

SOUTH FLORIDA FAIR AND PALM BEACH COUNTY EXPOSITIONS INC.

http://www.southfloridafair.com/

SOUTH FLORIDA FAIR AGRICULTURAL COLLEGE SCHOLARSHIP

Renewable award of $2000 for students pursuing a degree in agriculture. Must be a permanent resident of Florida.

Academic Fields/Career Goals: Agriculture.

Award: Scholarship for use in freshman, sophomore, junior, or senior years; renewable. *Number:* 2. *Amount:* $2000.

Eligibility Requirements: Applicant must be enrolled or expecting to enroll full- or part-time at a four-year institution or university and resident of Florida. Available to U.S. and non-U.S. citizens.

Application Requirements: Application form, community service, essay, recommendations or references, test scores, transcript. *Deadline:* October 15.

Contact: Agriculture Committee
South Florida Fair and Palm Beach County Expositions Inc.
PO Box 210367
West Palm Beach, FL 33421-0367
Phone: 561-790-5245

TAILOR MADE LAWNS

http://www.tailormadelawns.com

2017 TAILOR MADE LAWNS SCHOLARSHIP FUND

This $1,000 scholarship will be awarded to a student based on merit and passion for the enhancement of their local and global environment. Candidates will be evaluated according to letters of recommendation, academic records, and their passion for the environment. These qualifications will be demonstrated through faculty references, academic transcripts, SAT/ACT scores, and most importantly, a letter of intent written by the student. All eligible North Carolina students are encouraged to apply online or through the mail.

Academic Fields/Career Goals: Agriculture; Environmental Science; Nuclear Science; Physical Sciences.

Award: Scholarship for use in freshman, sophomore, junior, or senior years; not renewable. *Number:* 1. *Amount:* $1000.

Eligibility Requirements: Applicant must be age 16 and over; enrolled or expecting to enroll full-time at a four-year institution or university; resident of North Carolina and studying in North Carolina. Available to U.S. citizens.

Application Requirements: Application form, essay. *Deadline:* May 31.

Contact: Damon Milotte, General Manager & Vice President
Tailor Made Lawns
1003 1st Street West
Conover, NC 28613
Phone: 828-465-4070
E-mail: scholarship@tailormadelawns.com

TURF AND ORNAMENTAL COMMUNICATORS ASSOCIATION

http://www.toca.org/

TURF AND ORNAMENTAL COMMUNICATORS ASSOCIATION SCHOLARSHIP PROGRAM

One-time award for undergraduate students majoring or minoring in technical communications or in a green industry field such as horticulture, plant sciences, botany, or agronomy. The applicant must also demonstrate an interest in using this course of study in the field of communications. An overall GPA of 3.0 is required in major area of study.

Academic Fields/Career Goals: Agriculture; Communications; Horticulture/Floriculture.

Award: Scholarship for use in freshman, sophomore, junior, or senior years; not renewable. *Number:* 1. *Amount:* $2500.

Eligibility Requirements: Applicant must be enrolled or expecting to enroll full-time at a two-year or four-year institution or university. Available to U.S. and non-U.S. citizens.

Application Requirements: Application form, essay, portfolio, recommendations or references, resume, transcript. *Deadline:* March 1.

Contact: Den Gardner, Executive Director
Phone: 952-758-6340
E-mail: toca@gardnerandgardnercommunications.com

UNITED NEGRO COLLEGE FUND

http://www.uncf.org/

LEIDOS STEM SCHOLARSHIP

Leidos STEM Scholarship was established by UNCF and Leidos Holdings Inc. to provide merit-based scholarships to assist students majoring in STEM related fields attending an HBCU or any other accredited four-year college or university. See the UNCF website for full list of majors. https://scholarships.uncf.org/Program/Details/96ac2ba5-76e4-4aae-b166-19472fe06747

Academic Fields/Career Goals: Agriculture; Animal/Veterinary Sciences; Anthropology; Applied Sciences; Aviation/Aerospace; Biology; Chemical Engineering; Civil Engineering; Computer Science/Data Processing; Construction Engineering/Management; Earth Science; Electrical Engineering/Electronics; Energy and Power Engineering; Engineering-Related Technologies; Engineering/Technology; Environmental Science; Food Science/Nutrition; Geography; Health and Medical Sciences; Health Information Management/Technology; Horticulture/Floriculture; Hydrology; Marine Biology; Marine/Ocean Engineering; Materials Science, Engineering, and Metallurgy; Mathematics; Mechanical Engineering; Meteorology/Atmospheric Science; Natural Sciences; Neurobiology; Nuclear Science; Nursing; Oceanography; Paper and Pulp Engineering; Pharmacy; Physical Sciences; Radiology; Social Sciences; Statistics; Surveying, Surveying Technology, Cartography, or Geographic Information Science.

Award: Scholarship for use in freshman, sophomore, junior, or senior years; not renewable.

Eligibility Requirements: Applicant must be Black (non-Hispanic) and enrolled or expecting to enroll at a four-year institution or university. Available to U.S. citizens.

Application Requirements: Application form, application form may be submitted online, recommendations or references, statement of career interest, transcript. *Deadline:* July 30.

Contact: Girmu Habte
E-mail: Girmu.Habte@uncf.org

UNITED STATES DEPARTMENT OF AGRICULTURE

http://www.usda.gov/

USDA/1994 TRIBAL SCHOLARS PROGRAM

Scholarships for applicants attending 1994 Land Grant Tribal Colleges and Universities seeking careers in food, agriculture, and natural resource sciences, and/or other related disciplines. The program offers support for an Associate's degree (up to 2 Years of support) or Bachelor's of Science Degree (up to 4 Years of support).

Academic Fields/Career Goals: Agriculture; Food Science/Nutrition; Natural Resources.

Award: Scholarship for use in freshman, sophomore, junior, or senior years; renewable.

Eligibility Requirements: Applicant must be American Indian/Alaska Native and enrolled or expecting to enroll full- or part-time at an institution or university. Available to U.S. citizens.

Application Requirements: *Deadline:* February 1.

WILLIAM HELMS SCHOLARSHIP PROGRAM (WHSP)

The USDA APHIS is the agency responsible for safeguarding America's agricultural and natural resources from exotic plant and animal pests and diseases. APHIS' PPQ program deals specifically with plant health issues. Scholarship benefits include: financial aid while pursuing a degree; mentoring; paid work experience during school breaks; possible permanent employment upon graduation. Applicants must be enrolled in programs related to agriculture or the biological sciences and must maintain at least a 2.5 GPA.

Academic Fields/Career Goals: Agriculture; Biology.

Award: Scholarship for use in junior or senior years; renewable. *Number:* up to 5,000.

Eligibility Requirements: Applicant must be enrolled or expecting to enroll full- or part-time at a four-year institution or university. Available to U.S. citizens.

Application Requirements: *Deadline:* March 1.

Contact: United States Department of Agriculture
United States Department of Agriculture
1400 Independence Avenue, SW, Room 1710
Attention: HR/Recruitment
Washington, DC 20250
Phone: 202-690-4759

WASHINGTON WINE INDUSTRY FOUNDATION

http://washingtonwinefoundation.org/

FOUNDATION FUND SCHOLARSHIP

The Foundation Fund was endowed in June 2013 by the Board of Directors. Several family funds, including the Charles Lill, Michael Manz, Glenn Coogan and John Farmer funds, plus the Industry Need and Rainy Day Funds, were combined to create the initial endowment. With this larger endowed fund, WWIF can make a bigger impact on the industry's need for an educated workforce. Individual gifts and dedicated auction revenues continue to grow the endowment. The number of awards is determined annually, ranging from $2,000 to $10,000.

Academic Fields/Career Goals: Agriculture.

Award: Scholarship for use in freshman, sophomore, junior, senior, graduate, or postgraduate years; not renewable. *Number:* 1–100. *Amount:* $2000–$10,000.

Eligibility Requirements: Applicant must be enrolled or expecting to enroll full-time at a two-year or four-year institution or university and resident of Washington. Available to U.S. and non-U.S. citizens.

Application Requirements: Application form, essay, financial need analysis, personal photograph, recommendations or references, transcript. *Deadline:* March 29.

Contact: Rachel Burgoon, Program Assistant
Washington Wine Industry Foundation
PO Box 716
Cashmere, WA 98815
Phone: 509-7821108
E-mail: rachel@washingtonwinefoundation.org

GEORGE & SUSAN CARTER SCHOLARSHIP

The George & Susan Carter Scholarship was established in 2017 as an endowed fund in honor of WSU researcher and winemaker George Carter and his wife, Susan. George Carter worked side by side with Dr. Walter Clore and the two were close friends. As part of his day-to-day activities, Carter developed a system for classifying American, European and hybrid grape varietals. In recognition of his wine making accomplishments, Carter was elevated to a Supreme Knight in the International Brotherhood of the Knights of the Vine. This scholarship was established to assist students of limited means to attain associates, bachelors and graduate level degrees in viticulture and enology and will offer one (1) $1,000 auto-renewing scholarship per year.

Academic Fields/Career Goals: Agriculture.

Award: Scholarship for use in freshman, sophomore, junior, senior, graduate, or postgraduate years; renewable. *Number:* 1. *Amount:* $1000.

Eligibility Requirements: Applicant must be enrolled or expecting to enroll full-time at a two-year or four-year institution or university; resident of Washington and studying in Washington. Available to U.S. citizens.

Application Requirements: Application form, essay, financial need analysis, recommendations or references, transcript. *Deadline:* March 29.

Contact: Rachel Burgoon, Program Assistant
Washington Wine Industry Foundation
PO Box 716
Cashmere, WA 98815
Phone: 509-782-1108
E-mail: rachel@washingtonwinefoundation.org

WALTER J. CLORE SCHOLARSHIP

The Walter J. Clore Scholarship was established in 1997 by the Washington Winegrowers Association in honor of Dr. Clore's grape research and lifetime achievements in the field of viticulture and enology. Working with growers, Dr. Clore and his colleagues published information on grape varieties, diseases, insects, mineral nutrition, irrigation, cover crops, weed control and climatological effects, including winter injury. He tested various trellis designs, which eventually led to the widespread adoption of mechanical harvesting. More than any other individual, Dr. Clore has had a profound and lasting impact on the Washington wine industry. The number of awards is determined annually and scholarships start at $1,000.

Academic Fields/Career Goals: Agriculture; Food Science/Nutrition.

Award: Scholarship for use in freshman, sophomore, junior, senior, or graduate years; not renewable. *Number:* 1–100. *Amount:* $1000–$10,000.

Eligibility Requirements: Applicant must be enrolled or expecting to enroll full- or part-time at a two-year or four-year institution or university; resident of Washington and studying in Washington. Available to U.S. and non-U.S. citizens.

Application Requirements: Application form, essay, financial need analysis, recommendations or references, transcript. *Deadline:* March 29.

Contact: Rachel Burgoon, Program Assistant
Washington Wine Industry Foundation
PO Box 716
Cashmere, WA 98815
Phone: 509-7821108
E-mail: rachel@washingtonwinefoundation.org

WOMEN GROCERS OF AMERICA

http://www.nationalgrocers.org/

MARY MACEY SCHOLARSHIP

Award for students intending to pursue a career in the independent sector of the grocery industry. One-time award for students who have completed freshman year. Submit statement and recommendation from sponsor in the grocery industry. Applicant should have a minimum 2.0 GPA.

Academic Fields/Career Goals: Agriculture; Business/Consumer Services; Food Service/Hospitality.

Award: Scholarship for use in sophomore, junior, senior, graduate, or postgraduate years; not renewable. *Number:* 2–7. *Amount:* $1000.

Eligibility Requirements: Applicant must be enrolled or expecting to enroll full-time at a two-year or four-year institution or university. Available to U.S. citizens.

Application Requirements: Application form, personal statement, recommendations or references, transcript. *Deadline:* May 15.

Contact: Kristen Comley, Director of Administration
Women Grocers of America
1005 North Glebe Road, Suite 250
Arlington, VA 22201-5758
Phone: 703-516-0700
Fax: 703-516-0115
E-mail: kcomley@nationalgrocers.org

AMERICAN STUDIES

AMERICAN FEDERATION OF STATE, COUNTY, AND MUNICIPAL EMPLOYEES

https://www.afscme.org/

AFSCME/UNCF UNION SCHOLARS PROGRAM

One-time award for a sophomore or junior majoring in ethnic studies, women's studies, labor studies, American studies, sociology, anthropology, history, political science, psychology, social work or economics. Must be African-American, Hispanic-American, Asian Pacific Islander, or American-Indian/Alaska Native. Minimum 2.5 GPA.

Academic Fields/Career Goals: American Studies; Anthropology; Economics; History; Political Science; Psychology; Social Sciences; Social Services; Women's Studies.

Award: Scholarship for use in sophomore or junior years; not renewable. *Number:* 10. *Amount:* $5000.

Eligibility Requirements: Applicant must be American Indian/Alaska Native, Asian/Pacific Islander, Black (non-Hispanic), Hispanic and enrolled or expecting to enroll full-time at an institution or university. Available to U.S. citizens.

Application Requirements: Application form, essay, interview. *Deadline:* February 28.

ASSOCIATION OF FORMER INTELLIGENCE OFFICERS

www.afio.com

AFIO UNDERGRADUATE AND GRADUATE SCHOLARSHIPS

The type of institution attended is less important than the clarity that the course of study being undertaken leads to a career in the U.S. Intelligence Community. This includes law enforcement, foreign policy, intelligence analysis, counter-terrorism, homeland security, some foreign language mastery (Farsi, Tagalog, Pashto, Urdu, Mandarin, Arabic, Hindi, etc.—NOT Spanish or French), and related disciplines. Applicants seeking funding for law or medical school are not eligible. Applicant must be a U.S. citizen studying at a U.S. Institution. Advanced knowledge and corroboration of claims of near-native performance in one of the mission-critical languages mentioned above puts applicants at top of consideration. Applicants going to online-only schools are acceptable, but only institutions that are on a nationally accredited list maintained by the U.S. Dept. of Education.

Academic Fields/Career Goals: American Studies; Aviation/Aerospace; Computer Science/Data Processing; Criminal Justice/Criminology; Foreign Language; History; International Studies; Law Enforcement/Police Administration; Military and Defense Studies; Natural Sciences; Near and Middle East Studies; Peace and Conflict Studies; Political Science; Public Policy and Administration.

Award: Scholarship for use in junior, senior, graduate, or postgraduate years; not renewable. *Number:* 4. *Amount:* $1000–$3500.

Eligibility Requirements: Applicant must be age 19-35 and enrolled or expecting to enroll full-time at a four-year institution or university. Available to U.S. citizens.

Application Requirements: Application form, application form may be submitted online (https://afio.formstack.com/forms/scholarships_2019), essay, personal photograph, resume, transcript. *Deadline:* June 1.

Contact: Mrs. Eileen Doughty, Coordinator, AFIO Scholarship Program
Association of Former Intelligence Officers
7700 Leesburg Pike, Suite 324
Falls Church, VA 22043
Phone: 703-790-0320
E-mail: scholarships@afio.com

CONGRESSIONAL BLACK CAUCUS FOUNDATION, INC.

http://www.cbcfinc.org/

CBC SPOUSES EDUCATION SCHOLARSHIP

This opportunity awards scholarships to academically talented and highly motivated African-American or Black students pursuing an associates, undergraduate, graduate, or doctoral degree.

Academic Fields/Career Goals: American Studies; Criminal Justice/Criminology; Economics; Law/Legal Services; Political Science; Public Policy and Administration; Social Sciences; Urban and Regional Planning.

Award: Scholarship for use in freshman, sophomore, junior, senior, or graduate years; not renewable. *Number:* 250–300. *Amount:* $1500–$8200.

Eligibility Requirements: Applicant must be of African heritage; Black (non-Hispanic); enrolled or expecting to enroll full-time at a two-year institution or university and studying in Alabama, Alaska, Arizona, Arkansas, California, Colorado, Connecticut, Delaware, District of Columbia, Florida, Georgia, Guam, Hawaii, Idaho, Illinois, Indiana, Iowa, Kansas, Kentucky, Louisiana, Maine, Maryland, Massachusetts, Michigan, Minnesota, Mississippi, Missouri, Montana, Nebraska, Nevada, New Hampshire, New Jersey, New Mexico, New York, North Carolina, North Dakota, Ohio, Oklahoma, Oregon, Pennsylvania, Puerto Rico, Rhode Island, South Carolina, South Dakota, Tennessee, Texas, Utah, Vermont, Virginia, Washington, West Virginia, Wisconsin, Wyoming. Available to U.S. citizens.

Application Requirements: Application form, application form may be submitted online, essay, personal photograph. *Deadline:* April 30.

Contact: Ms. Katrina Finch, Program Administrator, Scholarships
Phone: 202-263-2800
E-mail: scholarships@cbcfinc.org

CULTURAL SERVICES OF THE FRENCH EMBASSY

http://www.frenchculture.org/

TEACHING ASSISTANT PROGRAM IN FRANCE

Grants support American students as they teach English for 7 months in the French school system. Monthly stipend of about 790 euros (net) supports recipient in the life-style of a typical French student. Must be U.S. citizen or a permanent resident (not a French citizen). Proficiency in French is required. May not have received a similar grant from the French government for the last three years. For additional information and application, visit website http://highereducation.frenchculture.org/teach-in-france.

Academic Fields/Career Goals: American Studies; Art History; Education; European Studies; Foreign Language; History; Humanities; International Studies; Literature/English/Writing; Political Science; Social Sciences.

Award: Grant for use in junior, senior, graduate, or postgraduate years; not renewable. *Number:* 1,120. *Amount:* $1040–$7280.

Eligibility Requirements: Applicant must be age 20-30; enrolled or expecting to enroll full- or part-time at a four-year institution or university and must have an interest in English language, foreign language, French language, or international exchange. Available to U.S. citizens.

Application Requirements: Application form, application form may be submitted online, essay, passport, personal photograph, recommendations or references, transcript. *Fee:* $40. *Deadline:* January 15.

Contact: Ms. Carolyn Collins, Educational Affairs Program Officer
Cultural Services of the French Embassy
Embassy of France
4101 Reservoir Road, NW
Washington, DC 20007
Phone: 202-944-6011
Fax: 202-944-6268
E-mail: assistant.washington-amba@diplomatie.gouv.fr

THE GEORGIA TRUST FOR HISTORIC PRESERVATION

http://www.georgiatrust.org/

B. PHINIZY SPALDING, HUBERT B. OWENS, AND THE NATIONAL SOCIETY OF THE COLONIAL DAMES OF AMERICA IN THE STATE OF GEORGIA ACADEMIC SCHOLARSHIPS

The Georgia Trust annually awards two $1000 and two $1,500 scholarships to encourage the study of historic preservation and related fields. Recipients are chosen on the basis of leadership and academic achievement. Applicants must be residents of Georgia enrolled in an accredited Georgia institution.

Academic Fields/Career Goals: American Studies; Historic Preservation and Conservation; History; Landscape Architecture.

Award: Scholarship for use in sophomore, junior, senior, or graduate years; not renewable. *Number:* 4. *Amount:* $1000–$1500.

Eligibility Requirements: Applicant must be enrolled or expecting to enroll full-time at a four-year institution or university; resident of Georgia and studying in Georgia. Available to U.S. citizens.

Application Requirements: Application form, essay. *Deadline:* February 9.

Contact: Mr. Neale Nickels, Director of Preservation
The Georgia Trust for Historic Preservation
1516 Peachtree Street, NW
Atlanta, GA 30309
Phone: 404-885-7817
E-mail: nnickels@georgiatrust.org

THE LYNDON BAINES JOHNSON FOUNDATION

http://www.lbjlibrary.org/page/foundation/

MOODY RESEARCH GRANTS

Grants to defray travel and other expenses incurred while conducting research at LBJ Library. September 15 deadline for spring term (January 1 - August 31), March 15 deadline for fall term (June 1 - December 31). Must contact Archives regarding availability of material. Should state clearly how Library's holdings will contribute to completion of project.

Academic Fields/Career Goals: American Studies; History; International Studies; Military and Defense Studies; Museum Studies; Political Science.

Award: Grant for use in senior, graduate, or postgraduate years; not renewable. *Number:* 10–15. *Amount:* $600–$3000.

Eligibility Requirements: Applicant must be enrolled or expecting to enroll full- or part-time at an institution or university. Available to U.S. and non-U.S. citizens.

Application Requirements: Application form. *Deadline:* March 15.

Contact: Mrs. Samantha Stone, Deputy Director
Phone: 512-721-0265
Fax: 512-721-0220
E-mail: samantha@lbjfoundation.org

ANIMAL/VETERINARY SCIENCES

101ST AIRBORNE DIVISION ASSOCIATION

http://www.screamingeaglefoundation.org/

AL & WILLIAMARY VISTE SCHOLARSHIP

Scholarship to provide financial assistance to students who have the potential to become assets to our nation. The major factors to be considered in the evaluation and rating of applicants are eligibility, career objectives, academic record, and insight gained from the letter requesting consideration and letters of recommendation. Preference will be given, but is not limited, to obtaining a degree in one of the physical sciences, medical, or scientific research fields. Must be an upperclassman and have a minimum 3.75 GPA. Applicants parents, grandparent, husband or wife is (or if deceased was) a regular or life (not Associate) member of the 101st Airborne Division Association.

Academic Fields/Career Goals: Animal/Veterinary Sciences; Applied Sciences; Audiology; Behavioral Science; Biology; Chemical Engineering; Dental Health/Services; Environmental Science; Food Science/Nutrition; Mathematics; Neurobiology; Nursing; Pharmacy; Physical Sciences; Radiology; Sports-Related/Exercise Science; Therapy/Rehabilitation.

Award: Scholarship for use in junior, senior, or graduate years; not renewable. *Number:* 1–2. *Amount:* $1000–$2000.

Eligibility Requirements: Applicant must be enrolled or expecting to enroll full-time at a four-year institution or university. Available to U.S. citizens.

Application Requirements: Application form, essay, personal photograph. *Deadline:* May 11.

Contact: Mr. Randal Underhill, Executive Director
101st Airborne Division Association
PO Box 929
Fort Campbell, KY 42223
Phone: 931-431-0199
E-mail: 101exec@comcast.net

ABBIE SARGENT MEMORIAL SCHOLARSHIP INC.

http://www.nhfarmbureau.org/

ABBIE SARGENT MEMORIAL SCHOLARSHIP
• *See page 89*

AMERICAN LEGION DEPARTMENT OF MARYLAND

http://www.mdlegion.org/

AMERICAN LEGION DEPARTMENT OF MARYLAND MATH-SCIENCE SCHOLARSHIP

Nonrenewable scholarship for veterans or children of veterans who served in the Armed Forces during dates of eligibility for American Legion membership. Proof of service and application required for eligibility. Merit-based award. Application available on website http://mdlegion.org.

Academic Fields/Career Goals: Animal/Veterinary Sciences; Applied Sciences; Biology; Earth Science; Environmental Science; Health and Medical Sciences; Mathematics; Natural Sciences; Nuclear Science; Physical Sciences.

Award: Scholarship for use in freshman, sophomore, junior, or senior years; not renewable. *Number:* 1–3. *Amount:* $500–$1500.

Eligibility Requirements: Applicant must be high school student; planning to enroll or expecting to enroll full-time at a two-year or four-year institution or university and resident of Maryland. Applicant or parent of applicant must be member of American Legion or Auxiliary. Available to U.S. citizens.

Application Requirements: Application form, essay, financial need analysis, Proof of Active Duty Service of parent during American Legion membership eligibility periods. *Deadline:* April 1.

Contact: Steve Tatro, Assistant Adjutant
American Legion Department of Maryland
101 North Gay, Room E
Baltimore, MD 21202
Phone: 410-752-1405 Ext. 101
E-mail: hdqtrs@mdlegion.org

APPALOOSA HORSE CLUB-APPALOOSA YOUTH PROGRAM

http://www.appaloosayouth.com/

LEW AND JOANN EKLUND EDUCATIONAL SCHOLARSHIP

One-time award for college juniors and seniors and graduate students studying a field related to the equine industry. Must be member or dependent of member of the Appaloosa Horse Club.

Academic Fields/Career Goals: Animal/Veterinary Sciences.

Award: Scholarship for use in junior, senior, or graduate years; not renewable. *Number:* 1. *Amount:* $2000.

Eligibility Requirements: Applicant must be enrolled or expecting to enroll full-time at a four-year institution or university. Applicant or parent of applicant must be member of Appaloosa Horse Club/Appaloosa Youth Association. Available to U.S. and non-U.S. citizens.

Application Requirements: Application form, entry in a contest, essay, personal photograph, recommendations or references, transcript. *Deadline:* June 1.

Contact: Anna Brown, AYF Coordinator
Appaloosa Horse Club-Appaloosa Youth Program
2720 West Pullman Road
Moscow, ID 83843
Phone: 208-882-5578 Ext. 264
Fax: 208-882-8150
E-mail: youth@appaloosa.com

ASSOCIATION OF ZOO VETERINARY TECHNICIANS

LAURIE PAGE-PECK SCHOLARSHIPS FUND

This award is for veterinary technician students currently enrolled in an AVMA accredited program.

Academic Fields/Career Goals: Animal/Veterinary Sciences.

Award: Scholarship for use in senior year; not renewable. *Number:* 1. *Amount:* $1500.

Eligibility Requirements: Applicant must be enrolled or expecting to enroll full- or part-time at a two-year or four-year or technical institution. Available to U.S. and Canadian citizens.

Application Requirements: *Deadline:* March 1.

Contact: Kimberly Olson Aubuchon
St. Louis, MO
Phone: 314-646-4854
E-mail: kolson@stlzoo.org

ASSOCIATION ON AMERICAN INDIAN AFFAIRS, INC.

http://www.indian-affairs.org/

ELIZABETH AND SHERMAN ASCHE MEMORIAL SCHOLARSHIP FUND

• *See page 93*

AVACARE MEDICAL

https://avacaremedical.com

AVACARE MEDICAL SCHOLARSHIP

The AvaCare Medical Scholarship recognizes those who are working to better the lives of our customers, students who are pursuing a degree in the medical field, with a prize of $1000 toward college tuition. This scholarship is awarded annually to one submission that tells about a truly inspiring act of kindness. AvaCare Medical judges will choose five to ten finalists, whose work will then be posted on our website. Voting will be open on our website, and the scholarship winner will be chosen based on a combination of judges' scores and the number of votes.

Academic Fields/Career Goals: Animal/Veterinary Sciences; Behavioral Science; Cosmetology; Dental Health/Services; Food Science/Nutrition; Health Administration; Health and Medical Sciences; Health Information Management/Technology; Neurobiology; Nursing; Oncology; Optometry; Osteopathy; Pharmacy; Psychology; Public Health; Therapy/Rehabilitation.

Award: Scholarship for use in freshman, sophomore, junior, senior, graduate, or postgraduate years; not renewable. *Number:* 1. *Amount:* $1000.

Eligibility Requirements: Applicant must be enrolled or expecting to enroll full- or part-time at a two-year or four-year institution or university. Available to U.S. citizens.

Application Requirements: Photo, writing or video of an inspirational act of kindness; personal info, transcript. *Deadline:* December 15.

Contact: Scholarship Department
AvaCare Medical
1665 Corporate Road West
Lakewood, NJ 08701
Phone: 877-813-7799
E-mail: scholarship@avacaremedical.com

GREAT MINDS IN STEM

http://www.greatmindsinstem.org/college/scholarship-application-information

HENAAC SCHOLARSHIP PROGRAM

Scholarships available to Hispanic students maintaining a 3.0 GPA. Must be studying science, technology, engineering or math-related discipline in the United States or Puerto Rico. Some health-related fields qualify.

Academic Fields/Career Goals: Animal/Veterinary Sciences; Applied Sciences; Architecture; Audiology; Aviation/Aerospace; Biology; Chemical Engineering; Civil Engineering; Computer Science/Data Processing; Construction Engineering/Management; Earth Science; Electrical Engineering/Electronics; Energy and Power Engineering; Engineering-Related Technologies; Engineering/Technology; Entomology; Environmental Health; Environmental Science; Food Science/Nutrition; Horticulture/Floriculture; Hydrology; Industrial Design; Marine Biology; Marine/Ocean Engineering; Materials Science, Engineering, and Metallurgy; Mathematics; Mechanical Engineering; Meteorology/Atmospheric Science; Natural Resources; Natural Sciences; Neurobiology; Nuclear Science; Nursing; Oceanography; Oncology; Optometry; Osteopathy; Paper and Pulp Engineering; Pharmacy; Physical Sciences; Statistics.

Award: Scholarship for use in freshman, sophomore, junior, senior, or graduate years; not renewable. *Number:* 100–120. *Amount:* $500–$10,000.

Eligibility Requirements: Applicant must be of Hispanic heritage; enrolled or expecting to enroll full-time at a two-year or four-year institution or university and studying in Alabama, Alaska, Arizona, Arkansas, California, Colorado, Connecticut, Delaware, District of Columbia, Florida, Georgia, Hawaii, Idaho, Illinois, Indiana, Iowa, Kansas, Kentucky, Louisiana, Maine, Maryland, Massachusetts, Michigan, Minnesota, Mississippi, Missouri, Montana, Nebraska, Nevada, New Hampshire, New Jersey, New Mexico, New York, North Carolina, North Dakota, Ohio, Oklahoma, Oregon, Pennsylvania, Puerto Rico, Rhode Island, South Carolina, South Dakota, Tennessee, Texas, Utah, Vermont, Virginia, Washington, West Virginia, Wisconsin, Wyoming. Available to U.S. and non-U.S. citizens.

Application Requirements: Application form, community service, essay, personal photograph. *Deadline:* April 1.

Contact: Dr. Gary Cruz
Great Minds in STEM
2465 Whittier Boulevard, Suite 202
Montebello, CA 90640
Phone: 323-262-0997 Ext. 775
E-mail: scholars@greatmindsinstem.org

LES DAMES D'ESCOFFIER INTERNATIONAL, COLORADO CHAPTER

www.lesdamescolorado.org/scholarship

LES DAMES D'ESCOFFIER INTERNATIONAL, COLORADO CHAPTER SCHOLARSHIP

• *See page 94*

MAINE COMMUNITY FOUNDATION, INC.

http://www.mainecf.org/

RONALD P. GUERRETTE FFA SCHOLARSHIP FUND

The Ronald P. Guerrette FFA Scholarship Fund was created in the spring of 1998 by friends and family to honor the life and work of Ronald P. Guerrette of Caribou. The fund will provide one $1,000 scholarship per year. Eligible applicants are graduating seniors at Maine high schools who are FFA members and have a demonstrated interest and motivation to pursue a career in farming and agriculture/natural resources.

Academic Fields/Career Goals: Animal/Veterinary Sciences.

Award: Scholarship for use in freshman year; not renewable. *Amount:* $1000.

Eligibility Requirements: Applicant must be high school student; planning to enroll or expecting to enroll at a two-year or technical institution or university and resident of Louisiana. Applicant or parent of applicant must be member of Future Farmers of America. Applicant or parent of applicant must have employment or volunteer experience in farming. Available to U.S. citizens.

Application Requirements: Application form, essay, financial need analysis. *Deadline:* March 1.

Contact: State FFA Advisor
Maine Community Foundation, Inc.
Department of Education
23 State House Station
Augusta, ME 04333-0023
Phone: 877-700-6800
E-mail: info@mainecf.org

MAINE DEPARTMENT OF AGRICULTURE, FOOD AND RURAL RESOURCES

http://www.maine.gov/agriculture

MAINE RURAL REHABILITATION FUND SCHOLARSHIP PROGRAM

• *See page 90*

NATIONAL INSTITUTES OF HEALTH

https://www.training.nih.gov/programs/ugsp

NIH UNDERGRADUATE SCHOLARSHIP PROGRAM FOR STUDENTS FROM DISADVANTAGED BACKGROUNDS

Awarded to financially disadvantaged students who come from a family with an annual income at or below a level based on low-income thresholds according to family size, as published by the U.S. Bureau of the Census. Must be enrolled full-time at a postsecondary institution and have a GPA of 3.3 or higher. Visit website https://www.training.nih.gov/programs/ugsp for more details.

Academic Fields/Career Goals: Animal/Veterinary Sciences; Behavioral Science; Biology; Environmental Health; Environmental Science; Health and Medical Sciences; Neurobiology; Nuclear Science; Nursing; Physical Sciences; Public Health; Women's Studies.

Award: Scholarship for use in freshman, sophomore, or junior years; renewable. *Number:* 10–15. *Amount:* $2000–$20,000.

Eligibility Requirements: Applicant must be enrolled or expecting to enroll full-time at a four-year institution or university. Available to U.S. citizens.

Application Requirements: Application form, essay, financial need analysis. *Deadline:* March 15.

Contact: Adrian Warren, Administrative Assistant
National Institutes of Health
Two Center Drive, Room 2W11A, MSC 0230
Bethesda, MD 20892-0230
Phone: 301-402-3831
E-mail: wardron@mail.nih.gov

NATIONAL POULTRY AND FOOD DISTRIBUTORS ASSOCIATION

http://www.npfda.org/

NATIONAL POULTRY AND FOOD DISTRIBUTORS ASSOCIATION SCHOLARSHIP FOUNDATION

• *See page 90*

NOVUS BIOLOGICALS, LLC

https://www.novusbio.com

NOVUS BIOLOGICALS SCHOLARSHIP PROGRAM

Applicants must have a major declared in a science related field and must be enrolled or accepted for enrollment (Baccalaureate, graduate, associate degree, or diploma) with a declared major in a science related field. Fill out the scholarship application form and submit a transcript of all college/post-secondary coursework (if high school student submit high school transcript). This may be an official or unofficial copy. Submit a written statement addressing the following topics: Submit a 200 character (including spaces) statement on what you wish to teach others using your degree. Write a personal statement of 500 words or less on where you see yourself in 10 years in your field of interest using the degree you are working towards.

Academic Fields/Career Goals: Animal/Veterinary Sciences; Applied Sciences; Behavioral Science; Biology; Dental Health/Services; Earth Science; Entomology; Environmental Health; Environmental Science; Food Science/Nutrition; Health Administration; Health and Medical Sciences; Health Information Management/Technology; Marine Biology; Marine/Ocean Engineering; Materials Science, Engineering, and Metallurgy; Natural Sciences; Neurobiology; Nuclear Science; Nursing; Occupational Safety and Health; Oceanography; Oncology; Optometry; Osteopathy; Pharmacy; Physical Sciences; Psychology; Public Health; Radiology; Science, Technology, and Society; Sports-Related/Exercise Science; Therapy/Rehabilitation.

Award: Scholarship for use in freshman, sophomore, junior, senior, graduate, or postgraduate years; not renewable. *Number:* 1. *Amount:* $1500.

Eligibility Requirements: Applicant must be enrolled or expecting to enroll full- or part-time at a two-year or four-year institution or university. Available to U.S. and non-U.S. citizens.

Application Requirements: Application form, application form may be submitted online (https://www.novusbio.com/scholarship-program), entry in a contest, essay, transcript. *Deadline:* July 31.

Contact: Leah Perkins
Novus Biologicals, LLC
10730 E. Briarwood Ave
Centennial, CO 80112
Phone: 303-7301950
E-mail: scholarship@bio-techne.com

R&D SYSTEMS SCHOLARSHIP

Applicants must have a major declared in a science related field and must be enrolled or accepted for enrollment (Baccalaureate, graduate, associate degree, or diploma) with a declared major in a science related field. Fill out the scholarship application form and submit a transcript of all college/post-secondary coursework (if high school student submit high school transcript). This may be an official or unofficial copy. Submit a written statement addressing the following topics: Submit a 200 character (including spaces) statement on what extra curricular activities you partake in that are related to your field of study. Write a personal statement of 500 words or less on the impact you strive to make using a degree in your field of interest.

Academic Fields/Career Goals: Animal/Veterinary Sciences; Applied Sciences; Audiology; Behavioral Science; Biology; Dental Health/Services; Earth Science; Entomology; Environmental Health; Environmental Science; Food Science/Nutrition; Health Administration; Health and Medical Sciences; Health Information Management/Technology; Marine Biology; Marine/Ocean Engineering; Materials Science, Engineering, and Metallurgy; Natural Sciences; Neurobiology; Nuclear Science; Nursing; Occupational Safety and Health; Oceanography; Oncology; Optometry; Osteopathy; Pharmacy; Physical Sciences; Psychology; Public Health; Radiology; Science, Technology, and Society; Sports-Related/Exercise Science; Therapy/Rehabilitation.

Award: Scholarship for use in freshman, sophomore, junior, senior, graduate, or postgraduate years; not renewable. *Number:* 1. *Amount:* $1500.

Eligibility Requirements: Applicant must be high school student and planning to enroll or expecting to enroll full- or part-time at a two-year or four-year institution or university. Available to U.S. and non-U.S. citizens.

Application Requirements: Application form, application form may be submitted online (https://www.rndsystems.com/grants-scholarships/scholarship-application), entry in a contest, essay, transcript. *Deadline:* July 31.

Contact: Leah Perkins
Novus Biologicals, LLC
10730 E. Briarwood Ave
Centennial, CO 80112
Phone: 303-7301950
E-mail: scholarship@bio-techne.com

TOCRIS BIOSCIENCE SCHOLARSHIP

Tocris is proud to support students who plan to pursue a science related degree. The Tocris Scholarship Program has been established to award a $1500 scholarship (or international currency equivalent) twice a year for the fall and spring semesters. This scholarship is open to students accepted/enrolled in a university and plan to pursue a science related degree. The deadline is July 31, 2019 at 11:59 p.m. MST. Winners will be notified the week following the deadline. Applicants will need to fill out the application form on the Tocris site, and include the following written statements: Write a personal statement of 500 words or less on how you plan to use your degree to further advance science in your field of interest. What is your favorite show or movie that is related to your field of interest and why?

Academic Fields/Career Goals: Animal/Veterinary Sciences; Applied Sciences; Audiology; Biology; Dental Health/Services; Earth Science; Entomology; Environmental Health; Environmental Science; Food Science/Nutrition; Health Administration; Health and Medical Sciences; Health Information Management/Technology; Marine Biology; Marine/Ocean Engineering; Materials Science, Engineering, and Metallurgy; Natural Resources; Natural Sciences; Neurobiology; Nuclear Science; Nursing; Occupational Safety and Health; Oceanography; Oncology; Optometry; Osteopathy; Pharmacy; Physical Sciences; Psychology; Public Health; Radiology; Science, Technology, and Society; Social Sciences; Sports-Related/Exercise Science; Therapy/Rehabilitation.

Award: Scholarship for use in freshman, sophomore, junior, senior, graduate, or postgraduate years; not renewable. *Number:* 1. *Amount:* $1500.

Eligibility Requirements: Applicant must be high school student and planning to enroll or expecting to enroll full- or part-time at a two-year or four-year institution or university. Available to U.S. and non-U.S. citizens.

Application Requirements: Application form, application form may be submitted online (https://www.tocris.com/scholarship), entry in a contest, essay, transcript. *Deadline:* July 31.

Contact: Leah Perkins
Novus Biologicals, LLC
10730 E. Briarwood Ave
Centennial, CO 80112
Phone: 303-730-1950
E-mail: scholarship@bio-techne.com

PLATINUM EDUCATIONAL GROUP

www.platinumed.com

PLATINUM EDUCATIONAL GROUP SCHOLARSHIPS PROGRAM FOR EMS, NURSING, AND ALLIED HEALTH

Applicants must be attending an EMS, nursing, or Allied Health Program. All information, downloading, and submissions can be found at www.platinumed.com/scholarships.

Academic Fields/Career Goals: Animal/Veterinary Sciences; Dental Health/Services; Fire Sciences; Health and Medical Sciences; Nursing; Pharmacy; Public Health; Radiology; Trade/Technical Specialties.

Award: Scholarship for use in freshman, sophomore, junior, senior, graduate, or postgraduate years; not renewable. *Number:* 3. *Amount:* $1000.

Eligibility Requirements: Applicant must be age 17-99 and enrolled or expecting to enroll full- or part-time at a two-year or technical institution or university. Available to U.S. and non-U.S. citizens.

Application Requirements: Application form, application form may be submitted online, essay. *Deadline:* June 1.

Contact: Jeremy Johnson, Director of Marketing
Platinum Educational Group
4370 Chicago Dr SW
Ste B#205
Grandville, MI 49418
Phone: 616-818-7877 Ext. 2904
E-mail: marketing@platinumed.com

RKT PUBLISHING

http://www.rktpublishing.com/

EMPATHY FOR ANIMALS (EFA) SCHOLARSHIP AWARD FOR VETERINARY STUDENTS

This is a new scholarship that will be awarded annually in the amount of $500 to undergraduate students enrolled in veterinary or animal science studies, who are in good academic standing and have demonstrated a passion for animal advocacy and fighting animal cruelty. Applicants in good academic standing, with extracurricular community experience or demonstrated passion for animal advocacy and an interest in working to fight animal cruelty. We are looking for applicants with an educational and personal history of working to educate the public about the mistreatment of animals in today's society and a commitment to reshaping the treatment of animals in local communities across the nation. To be eligible, you must meet the following criteria: 1. Currently enrolled, and in good standing, in an accredited pre-veterinary or animal sciences undergraduate program in the United States, 2. Minimum GPA of 3.0, 3. Proven history of advocacy for animals, 4. Demonstrated community involvement, 5. Demonstrated financial need.

Academic Fields/Career Goals: Animal/Veterinary Sciences.

Award: Scholarship for use in freshman, sophomore, junior, or senior years; not renewable. *Number:* 1. *Amount:* $500.

Eligibility Requirements: Applicant must be enrolled or expecting to enroll full-time at a four-year institution and must have an interest in wildlife conservation/animal rescue. Available to U.S. and non-U.S. citizens.

Application Requirements: Essay. *Deadline:* December 31.

Contact: Ken Lyons, Co-Founder
E-mail: efascholarship@petlifetoday.com

SCARLETT FAMILY FOUNDATION SCHOLARSHIP PROGRAM

http://www.scarlettfoundation.org/

SCHOLARSHIP FOR STUDENTS PURSUING A BUSINESS OR STEM DEGREE

• See page 80

SOIL AND WATER CONSERVATION SOCIETY-NEW JERSEY CHAPTER

http://www.geocities.com/njswcs

EDWARD R. HALL SCHOLARSHIP

• See page 91

UNITED NEGRO COLLEGE FUND

http://www.uncf.org/

LEIDOS STEM SCHOLARSHIP

• See page 96

UNITED STATES DEPARTMENT OF AGRICULTURE

http://www.usda.gov/

SAUL T. WILSON, JR., SCHOLARSHIP PROGRAM (STWJS)

Undergraduate student applicants must have completed at least 2 years (60 semester or 90 quarter hours) of a 4-year pre-veterinary medicine or other biomedical science curriculum. Graduate student applicants must have completed not more than 1 full academic year of study in veterinary medicine. Awards up to $7500 per year for undergraduate studies, up to $15000 for graduate studies. Benefits include paid employment during summers and school breaks, possible full-time employment with APHIS upon successful completion of the program with a D.V.M. degree, training and other work requirements.

Academic Fields/Career Goals: Animal/Veterinary Sciences; Biology.

Award: Scholarship for use in junior, senior, or graduate years; renewable. *Amount:* $7500–$15,000.

Eligibility Requirements: Applicant must be enrolled or expecting to enroll full-time at a four-year institution or university. Available to U.S. citizens.

Application Requirements: *Deadline:* March 10.

Contact: Lin Chambers, Saul T. Wilson, Jr. Scholarship
United States Department of Agriculture
USDA, APHIS, Human Resources Division/Office of
   Recruitment
1400 Independence Avenue, SW, Room 1710
Washington, DC 20250
Phone: 202-690-4759
E-mail: Lin.S.Chambers@usda.gov

WILSON ORNITHOLOGICAL SOCIETY

http://www.wilsonsociety.org/

GEORGE A. HALL/HAROLD F. MAYFIELD AWARD

One-time award for scientific research on birds. Available to independent researchers without access to funds or facilities at a college or university. Must be a nonprofessional to apply. Submit research proposal.

Academic Fields/Career Goals: Animal/Veterinary Sciences; Biology; Natural Resources.

Award: Grant for use in freshman, sophomore, junior, or senior years; not renewable. *Number:* 1. *Amount:* $1000.

Eligibility Requirements: Applicant must be enrolled or expecting to enroll full- or part-time at a four-year institution or university. Available to U.S. and non-U.S. citizens.

Application Requirements: Application form. *Deadline:* February 1.

Contact: Dr. Jameson Chace, Research Grants Coordinator
Wilson Ornithological Society
Salve Regina University
Newport, RI 02840
Phone: 401-341-3204
E-mail: wos@salve.edu

PAUL A. STEWART AWARDS

One-time award for studies of bird movements based on banding, analysis of recoveries, and returns of banded birds, or research with an emphasis on economic ornithology. Submit research proposal.

Academic Fields/Career Goals: Animal/Veterinary Sciences; Biology; Natural Resources.

Award: Grant for use in freshman, sophomore, junior, or senior years; not renewable. *Number:* 1–4. *Amount:* up to $500.

Eligibility Requirements: Applicant must be enrolled or expecting to enroll full- or part-time at a four-year institution or university. Available to U.S. and non-U.S. citizens.

Application Requirements: Application form, proposal, recommendations or references. *Deadline:* February 1.

Contact: Dr. Jameson Chace, Research Grants Coordinator
Wilson Ornithological Society
Salve Regina University
Newport, RI 02840
Phone: 401-341-3204
E-mail: wos@salve.edu

ANTHROPOLOGY

AMERICAN FEDERATION OF STATE, COUNTY, AND MUNICIPAL EMPLOYEES

https://www.afscme.org/

AFSCME/UNCF UNION SCHOLARS PROGRAM
• *See page 98*

EXPLORERS CLUB

http://www.explorers.org/

YOUTH ACTIVITY FUND GRANTS

Award given to college students or high school students pursuing a research project in the field of science. Applicants must have two letters of recommendation, one-page description of project, a budget or plan, and proof of student enrollment with dates.

Academic Fields/Career Goals: Anthropology; Archaeology; Biology; Environmental Science; Marine Biology; Natural Sciences; Science, Technology, and Society.

Award: Grant for use in freshman, sophomore, junior, or senior years; not renewable. *Amount:* $500–$5000.

Eligibility Requirements: Applicant must be enrolled or expecting to enroll full-time at a four-year institution or university. Available to U.S. and non-U.S. citizens.

Application Requirements: Application form, essay, financial need analysis. *Deadline:* November 5.

Contact: Annie Lee, Member Services
Explorers Club
46 East 70th Street
New York, NY 10021
E-mail: alee@explorers.org

HUB FOUNDATION

https://hub-foundation.org

HUB FOUNDATION SCHOLARSHIPS
• *See page 88*

INTERNATIONAL HOUSEWARES ASSOCIATION

http://www.housewares.org

STUDENT DESIGN COMPETITION

Industrial design students invent a new product and must submit user research, market research, concept drawings, exploded views and narrative.

Academic Fields/Career Goals: Anthropology.

Award: Prize for use in freshman, sophomore, junior, or senior years; not renewable. *Number:* 6. *Amount:* $1000–$3000.

Eligibility Requirements: Applicant must be enrolled or expecting to enroll full- or part-time at an institution or university. Available to U.S. and non-U.S. citizens.

Application Requirements: Application form. *Deadline:* December 15.

Contact: Ms. Victoria Matranga, Design Programs Coordinator
International Housewares Association
6400 Shafer Court
Suite 650
Rosemont, IL 60302
Phone: 847-692-0136
Fax: 847-292-4200
E-mail: vmatranga@housewares.org

ISLAMIC SCHOLARSHIP FUND

http://islamicscholarshipfund.org/

ISF NATIONAL SCHOLARSHIP

ISF is a non-profit 501 (c)(3) organization with the mission to improve the understanding and acceptance of Islam by supporting students and increasing Muslim American representation in the professions that influence public policy and public opinion through academic scholarships, film grants and networking opportunities. Award is available to both U.S. citizens and green card holders and may be renewed if reapplying. Minimum 3.0 GPA required.

Academic Fields/Career Goals: Anthropology; Filmmaking/Video; History; International Studies; Journalism; Law Enforcement/Police Administration; Law/Legal Services; Near and Middle East Studies; TV/Radio Broadcasting.

Award: Scholarship for use in sophomore, junior, senior, graduate, or postgraduate years; not renewable. *Number:* 1–40. *Amount:* $2000–$5000.

Eligibility Requirements: Applicant must be Muslim faith and enrolled or expecting to enroll full-time at a two-year or four-year institution or university. Available to U.S. citizens.

Application Requirements: Application form, essay. *Deadline:* March 21.

Contact: Ms. Somayeh Nikooei, Director of Operations
Islamic Scholarship Fund
540 Shattuck Avenue
Suite 706
Berkeley, CA 94704
Phone: 650-995-6782
E-mail: admin@islamicscholarshipfund.org

LAMBDA ALPHA NATIONAL ANTHROPOLOGY HONOR SOCIETY

https://laanthro.org/

LAMBDA ALPHA NATIONAL ANTHROPOLOGY HONOR SOCIETY SCHOLARSHIP AWARD

Award to give academic recognition to undergraduate students and to encourage the pursuit of careers in anthropology. Must submit statement of future plans. Must include four copies of complete application packet. Minimum 3.00 GPA. For further information applicant should contact their department's Lambda Alpha faculty sponsor or visit the web page laanthro.org.

Academic Fields/Career Goals: Anthropology.

Award: Scholarship for use in senior year; not renewable. *Number:* 1–3. *Amount:* $5000.

Eligibility Requirements: Applicant must be enrolled or expecting to enroll full-time at a four-year institution or university. Applicant or parent of applicant must be member of Lambda Alpha National Collegiate Honor Society for Anthropology. Available to U.S. citizens.

Application Requirements: Application form, driver's license, essay. *Deadline:* March 15.

Contact: Dr. Mark Groover, National Executive Secretary
Lambda Alpha National Anthropology Honor Society
Department of Anthropology, Ball State University
2000 W University Avenue
Muncie, IN 47306-0435
Phone: 765-285-3567
E-mail: mdgroover@bsu.edu

LA-PHILOSOPHIE.COM

http://la-philosophie.com

LA-PHILOSOPHIE.COM SCHOLARSHIP

Since 2008, the mission of La-Philosophie.com is the democratisation of the philosophical knowledge. That is why we want to support a student every year to help him/her by a $200 fund to pursue his/her studies in social sciences. An essay on the interest of philosophy today will have to show their motivation. This essay will attempt to answer the following question: Why Philosophy Matters in Today's World. Your essay should include at least 2,000 words and a maximum of 5,000 words. The essay selected by the editors will be published on the site la-philosophie.com.

Applications open December 1st. Deadline for registration is December 31st. Review of applications by the editorial committee takes place from January 1st to 15th. Announcement of the winner takes place January 16th. Application should include your full name, a few words about your course (diploma in progress, etc.), the school of your choice (may be private or public), your essay (2000 to 5000 words) in word or pdf format. Send your application before December 31st to laphilosophie.com@gmail.com. Official page: http://la-philosophie.com/bourse-detudes-la-philosophie-com

Academic Fields/Career Goals: Anthropology; History; Humanities; Journalism; Philosophy; Political Science; Psychology; Religion/Theology; Social Sciences.

Award: Scholarship for use in freshman, sophomore, junior, senior, graduate, or postgraduate years; renewable. *Number:* 1. *Amount:* $200.

Eligibility Requirements: Applicant must be enrolled or expecting to enroll full- or part-time at a four-year institution or university. Available to U.S. and non-U.S. citizens.

Application Requirements: Essay. *Deadline:* December 31.

Contact: Mr. Julien Josset
La-Philosophie.com
139 rue de saussure
Paris
FRA
E-mail: laphilosophie.com@gmail.com

MEDICAL SCRUBS COLLECTION

http://medicalscrubscollection.com

MEDICAL SCRUBS COLLECTION SCHOLARSHIP

Medical Scrubs Collection is dedicated to recognizing the individuals who go above and beyond to help others every day. To show our appreciation for these hard working individuals, MSC has decided to Pay it Forward by creating an annual scholarship opportunity for students studying in any health or medical-related field. MSC's scholarship will provide each applicant with a chance to win $1000 towards their college tuition by answering one question: What Inspired You To Pursue A Career In Helping Others? The Medical Scrubs Collection Scholarship will be awarded to the applicant with the winning submission for the thousand dollar question. When the deadline has passed, Medical Scrubs Collection judges will choose five to ten submissions that best fit the criteria for the MSC Scholarship question: What inspired you to pursue a career in helping others? The submissions of these finalists will be posted on Medical Scrubs Collection's website, https://medicalscrubscollection.com/scholarship-program where voting will be open to the public. The final winner will be determined by a combination of judges' scores and the number of votes.

Academic Fields/Career Goals: Anthropology; Applied Sciences; Archaeology; Audiology; Behavioral Science; Biology; Chemical Engineering; Cosmetology; Dental Health/Services; Earth Science; Entomology; Food Science/Nutrition; Health Administration; Health and Medical Sciences; Health Information Management/Technology; Marine Biology; Materials Science, Engineering, and Metallurgy; Natural Sciences; Neurobiology; Nursing; Oncology; Optometry; Osteopathy; Pharmacy; Physical Sciences; Psychology; Public Health; Radiology; Therapy/Rehabilitation.

Award: Scholarship for use in freshman, sophomore, junior, senior, graduate, or postgraduate years; renewable. *Number:* 1. *Amount:* $1000.

Eligibility Requirements: Applicant must be enrolled or expecting to enroll full- or part-time at a two-year or four-year or technical institution or university. Available to U.S. citizens.

Application Requirements: Application form. *Deadline:* December 15.

Contact: Program Manager
Medical Scrubs Collection
1665 Corporate Road West
Lakewood, NJ 08701
Phone: 888-567-2782
E-mail: scholarships@medicalscrubscollection.com

NEXTSTEPU

http://www.nextstepu.com/

$1,500 STEM SCHOLARSHIP

NextStepU.com will award one $1,500 scholarship to one randomly selected winner three times a year. Applicants must enter online at http://www.nextstepu.com/nextstepu-scholarships. Winner must be enrolled in college within 3 years from the time the prize is awarded. 3 Awards: DEADLINE (1): January 31 DEADLINE (2): May 31 DEADLINE (3) September 30

Academic Fields/Career Goals: Anthropology; Applied Sciences; Architecture; Aviation/Aerospace; Behavioral Science; Biology; Chemical Engineering; Civil Engineering; Computer Science/Data Processing; Construction Engineering/Management; Earth Science; Electrical Engineering/Electronics; Energy and Power Engineering; Engineering-Related Technologies; Engineering/Technology; Environmental Health; Environmental Science; Food Science/Nutrition; Health and Medical Sciences; Health Information Management/Technology; Marine Biology; Marine/Ocean Engineering; Materials Science, Engineering, and Metallurgy; Mathematics; Mechanical Engineering; Meteorology/Atmospheric Science; Natural Sciences; Neurobiology; Nuclear Science; Nursing; Oceanography; Oncology; Optometry; Osteopathy; Paper and Pulp Engineering; Pharmacy; Physical Sciences; Radiology; Science, Technology, and Society; Sports-Related/Exercise Science; Statistics; Surveying, Surveying Technology, Cartography, or Geographic Information Science; Trade/Technical Specialties.

Award: Scholarship for use in freshman, sophomore, junior, senior, or graduate years; not renewable. *Number:* 2–3. *Amount:* $1500.

Eligibility Requirements: Applicant must be age 16 and over and enrolled or expecting to enroll full- or part-time at a two-year or four-year or technical institution or university. Available to U.S. and Canadian citizens.

Application Requirements: Application form, essay. *Deadline:* continuous.

Contact: Web Department
    E-mail: webcopy@nextstepu.com

THE SOCIETY FOR THE SCIENTIFIC STUDY OF SEXUALITY

http://www.sexscience.org/

THE SOCIETY FOR THE SCIENTIFIC STUDY OF SEXUALITY STUDENT RESEARCH GRANT

Award to support students doing scientific research related to sexuality. Purpose of research can be master's thesis or doctoral dissertation, but this is not a requirement. Must be enrolled in degree-granting program. Deadlines: February 1 and June 1. All applicants MUST be a member of the SSSS organization. A one-time award of $1000.

Academic Fields/Career Goals: Anthropology; Behavioral Science; Biology; Education; Health and Medical Sciences; Nursing; Psychology; Public Health; Religion/Theology; Social Sciences; Women's Studies.

Award: Grant for use in freshman, sophomore, junior, senior, or graduate years; not renewable. *Number:* 2. *Amount:* $1000.

Eligibility Requirements: Applicant must be enrolled or expecting to enroll full- or part-time at a four-year institution or university. Available to U.S. and non-U.S. citizens.

Application Requirements: Application form, essay.

Contact: Mandy Peters, Executive Director
    The Society for the Scientific Study of Sexuality
    881 Third Street, Suite B5
    Whitehall, PA 18052
    Phone: 610-443-3100
    E-mail: thesociety@sexscience.org

UNITED NEGRO COLLEGE FUND

http://www.uncf.org/

LEIDOS STEM SCHOLARSHIP
• *See page 96*

APPLIED SCIENCES

101ST AIRBORNE DIVISION ASSOCIATION

http://www.screamingeaglefoundation.org/

AL & WILLIAMARY VISTE SCHOLARSHIP
• *See page 99*

AMERICAN CHEMICAL SOCIETY, RUBBER DIVISION

http://www.rubber.org/

AMERICAN CHEMICAL SOCIETY, RUBBER DIVISION UNDERGRADUATE SCHOLARSHIP

Candidate must be majoring in a technical discipline relevant to the rubber industry with a "B" or better overall academic average. Two scholarships are awarded to juniors and seniors enrolled in an accredited college or university in the United States, Canada, Mexico, India or Brazil.

Academic Fields/Career Goals: Applied Sciences; Aviation/Aerospace; Chemical Engineering; Electrical Engineering/Electronics; Energy and Power Engineering; Engineering-Related Technologies; Engineering/Technology; Materials Science, Engineering, and Metallurgy; Mechanical Engineering; Nuclear Science.

Award: Scholarship for use in junior or senior years; not renewable. *Number:* 3. *Amount:* $5000.

Eligibility Requirements: Applicant must be enrolled or expecting to enroll full-time at a four-year institution or university. Available to U.S. and non-U.S. citizens.

Application Requirements: Application form, essay, interview. *Deadline:* March 1.

Contact: Christie Robinson, Training and Development Director
    American Chemical Society, Rubber Division
    411 Wolf Ledges Parkway
    Suite 201
    Akron, OH 44311
    Phone: 330-595-7602
    E-mail: crobinson@rubber.org

AMERICAN INDIAN SCIENCE AND ENGINEERING SOCIETY

http://www.aises.org/

A.T. ANDERSON MEMORIAL SCHOLARSHIP PROGRAM

Award for full-time students majoring in Mathematics, Medical Sciences, Physical Science, Technology, Science, Engineering, or Natural Resources. Must be a member of the AISES and an enrolled member/citizen or a decedent of an enrolled member/citizen of a federally or state recognized American Indian Tribe or Alaskan Native Village (or be Native Hawaiian or decedent from a Native Hawaiian). Must have minimum 3.0 GPA.

Academic Fields/Career Goals: Applied Sciences; Biology; Business/Consumer Services; Chemical Engineering; Civil Engineering; Computer Science/Data Processing; Construction Engineering/Management; Dental Health/Services; Earth Science; Electrical Engineering/Electronics; Energy and Power Engineering; Engineering-Related Technologies; Engineering/Technology; Entomology; Environmental Health; Environmental Science; Food Science/Nutrition; Gemology; Geography; Health and Medical Sciences; Heating, Air-Conditioning, and Refrigeration Mechanics; Horticulture/Floriculture; Hydrology; Marine Biology; Marine/Ocean Engineering; Materials Science, Engineering, and Metallurgy; Mathematics; Mechanical Engineering; Meteorology/Atmospheric Science; Natural Resources; Natural Sciences; Neurobiology; Nuclear Science; Nursing; Occupational Safety and Health; Oceanography; Oncology; Optometry; Osteopathy; Paper and Pulp Engineering; Pharmacy; Physical Sciences; Radiology; Science, Technology, and Society; Social Sciences; Sports-Related/Exercise Science; Statistics; Surveying, Surveying Technology, Cartography, or Geographic Information Science; Therapy/Rehabilitation; Transportation.

Award: Scholarship for use in freshman, sophomore, junior, or graduate years; not renewable. *Amount:* $1000–$2000.

Eligibility Requirements: Applicant must be American Indian/Alaska Native and enrolled or expecting to enroll full-time at a two-year or four-year institution or university. Available to U.S. citizens.

Application Requirements: Application form, essay. *Deadline:* May 1.

Contact: Kyle Coulon, Program Officer
Phone: 720-552-6123 Ext. 108
E-mail: kcoulon@aises.org

AMERICAN LEGION DEPARTMENT OF MARYLAND

http://www.mdlegion.org/

AMERICAN LEGION DEPARTMENT OF MARYLAND MATH-SCIENCE SCHOLARSHIP
• *See page 99*

AMERICAN SOCIETY OF NAVAL ENGINEERS

http://www.navalengineers.org/

AMERICAN SOCIETY OF NAVAL ENGINEERS SCHOLARSHIP

Award for naval engineering students or students in related disciplines in the final year of an undergraduate program or for one year of graduate study at an accredited institution. Must be full-time student and a U.S. citizen. Award of $3000 for undergraduates and $4000 for graduate students.

Academic Fields/Career Goals: Applied Sciences; Aviation/Aerospace; Civil Engineering; Electrical Engineering/Electronics; Energy and Power Engineering; Engineering/Technology; Marine/Ocean Engineering; Materials Science, Engineering, and Metallurgy; Mechanical Engineering; Nuclear Science; Physical Sciences.

Award: Scholarship for use in senior or graduate years; not renewable. *Number:* 8–14. *Amount:* $3000–$4000.

Eligibility Requirements: Applicant must be enrolled or expecting to enroll full-time at a four-year institution or university. Available to U.S. citizens.

Application Requirements: Application form, personal photograph. *Deadline:* February 15.

Contact: Erica Cox, Senior Manager for Education and Business Development
American Society of Naval Engineers
1452 Duke Street
Alexandria, VA 22314
Phone: 703-836-6727
Fax: 703-836-7491
E-mail: asnehq@navalengineers.org

ARMED FORCES COMMUNICATIONS AND ELECTRONICS ASSOCIATION, EDUCATIONAL FOUNDATION

https://foundation.afcea.org

AFCEA STEM MAJORS SCHOLARSHIPS FOR UNDERGRADUATE STUDENTS

Scholarships for full-time students currently working toward a undergraduate degree in the following STEM majors related to the mission of AFCEA include: Biometry/Biometrics, Computer Engineering, Computer Forensics Science, Computer Programming, Computer Science, Computer Systems, Cybersecurity, Electrical Engineering, Electronics Engineering, Geospatial Science, Information Science, Information Technology, Information Resource, Management, Intelligence, Mathematics, Network Engineering, Network Security, Operations, Research, Physics, Robotics Engineering, Robotics Technology, Statistics, Strategic Intelligence, and Telecommunications Engineering at an accredited college or university in the United States.

Academic Fields/Career Goals: Applied Sciences; Computer Science/Data Processing; Electrical Engineering/Electronics; Engineering-Related Technologies; Engineering/Technology; Materials Science, Engineering, and Metallurgy; Mathematics; Military and Defense Studies; Physical Sciences; Statistics.

Award: Scholarship for use in sophomore or junior years; not renewable. *Number:* 1–10. *Amount:* $2500–$5000.

Eligibility Requirements: Applicant must be enrolled or expecting to enroll full-time at a four-year institution or university. Available to U.S. citizens.

Application Requirements: Application form, application form may be submitted online (https://www.afcea.org/site/foundation/stem-majors), essay, transcript. *Deadline:* April 12.

Contact: Mrs. Casmere Kistner, Manager, Scholarship and Awards
Phone: 703-631-6147
Fax: 703-631-4693
E-mail: edfoundation@afcea.org

ASSOCIATION FOR WOMEN GEOSCIENTISTS (AWG)

http://www.awg.org/

AWG UNDERGRADUATE EXCELLENCE IN PALEONTOLOGY AWARD

The Association for Women Geoscientists is pleased to announce the AWG Undergraduate Paleontology Award. The award, which consists of a $1000 cash prize and membership in the Paleontological Society and AWG for the tenure of the awardee's schooling, will be presented to an outstanding female undergraduate student pursuing a career in paleontology.

Academic Fields/Career Goals: Applied Sciences; Archaeology; Biology; Earth Science; Marine Biology; Natural Sciences.

Award: Scholarship for use in freshman, sophomore, junior, or senior years; not renewable. *Number:* 1. *Amount:* $1000.

Eligibility Requirements: Applicant must be enrolled or expecting to enroll full- or part-time at a two-year or four-year institution or university and female. Available to U.S. and non-U.S. citizens.

Application Requirements: Application form, essay. *Deadline:* April 15.

Contact: Dr. Erin Saupe, Co-Chair
E-mail: goldring@awg.org

ASSOCIATION OF CALIFORNIA WATER AGENCIES

http://www.acwa.com/

ASSOCIATION OF CALIFORNIA WATER AGENCIES SCHOLARSHIPS

Two $3500 awards available to juniors and seniors who are California residents attending California universities. Must be in a water-related field of study. Community college transfers are also eligible as long as they will hold junior class standing as of the fall.

Academic Fields/Career Goals: Applied Sciences; Biology; Civil Engineering; Environmental Science; Hydrology; Natural Resources; Natural Sciences; Surveying, Surveying Technology, Cartography, or Geographic Information Science.

Award: Scholarship for use in junior or senior years; not renewable. *Number:* 2. *Amount:* $3500.

Eligibility Requirements: Applicant must be enrolled or expecting to enroll full-time at a four-year institution or university; resident of California and studying in California. Available to U.S. citizens.

Application Requirements: Application form, essay. *Deadline:* March 1.

Contact: Marie Meade, Outreach Specialist
Association of California Water Agencies
901 K Street, Suite 100
Sacramento, CA 95814
Phone: 916-441-4545
E-mail: mariem@acwa.com

CLAIR A. HILL SCHOLARSHIP

Scholarship is administered by a different member agency each year and guidelines vary based on the administrator. Contact ACWA for current information. Applicants must be in a water-related field of study and must be a resident of California enrolled in a California four-year college or university.

Academic Fields/Career Goals: Applied Sciences; Biology; Civil Engineering; Environmental Science; Hydrology; Natural Resources; Natural Sciences; Surveying, Surveying Technology, Cartography, or Geographic Information Science.

Award: Scholarship for use in junior or senior years; not renewable. *Number:* 1. *Amount:* $5000.

Eligibility Requirements: Applicant must be enrolled or expecting to enroll full-time at a four-year institution or university; resident of California and studying in California. Available to U.S. citizens.

Application Requirements: Application form, essay. *Deadline:* February 1.

Contact: Marie Meade, Outreach Specialist
Association of California Water Agencies
910 K Street, Suite 100
Sacramento, CA 95814
Phone: 916-441-4545
E-mail: mariem@acwa.com

ASTRONAUT SCHOLARSHIP FOUNDATION

http://www.astronautscholarship.org/

ASTRONAUT SCHOLARSHIP

Scholarship candidates must be nominated by the faculty members. Students may not apply directly for the scholarship. Must be U.S. citizens. Scholarship nominees must be seeking a STEM degree with intentions to pursue research or advance their field upon completion of their final degrees. They must be enrolled in one of the participating universities in the Scholarship Program.

Academic Fields/Career Goals: Applied Sciences; Aviation/Aerospace; Biology; Chemical Engineering; Computer Science/Data Processing; Earth Science; Electrical Engineering/Electronics; Engineering-Related Technologies; Materials Science, Engineering, and Metallurgy; Mechanical Engineering; Meteorology/Atmospheric Science.

Award: Scholarship for use in sophomore, junior, senior, or graduate years; renewable. *Amount:* $10,000.

Eligibility Requirements: Applicant must be enrolled or expecting to enroll full-time at a four-year institution or university. Available to U.S. citizens.

Application Requirements: Financial need analysis. *Deadline:* March 25.

AUTOMOTIVE WOMEN'S ALLIANCE FOUNDATION

http://awafoundation.org/index.php

AUTOMOTIVE WOMEN'S ALLIANCE FOUNDATION SCHOLARSHIPS
• *See page 71*

BARRY GOLDWATER SCHOLARSHIP AND EXCELLENCE IN EDUCATION FOUNDATION

https://goldwater.scholarsapply.org

BARRY M. GOLDWATER SCHOLARSHIP AND EXCELLENCE IN EDUCATION PROGRAM

One-time award to college juniors and seniors who will pursue advanced degrees in mathematics, natural sciences, or engineering. Students planning to study medicine are eligible if they plan a career in research. Candidates must be nominated by their college or university. Minimum 3.0 GPA required. Nomination deadline: February 1.

Academic Fields/Career Goals: Applied Sciences; Biology; Chemical Engineering; Computer Science/Data Processing; Earth Science; Electrical Engineering/Electronics; Energy and Power Engineering; Engineering-Related Technologies; Engineering/Technology; Entomology; Environmental Science; Hydrology; Marine Biology; Marine/Ocean Engineering; Materials Science, Engineering, and Metallurgy; Mathematics; Mechanical Engineering;

Meteorology/Atmospheric Science; Natural Sciences; Neurobiology; Nuclear Science; Oceanography; Pharmacy; Physical Sciences.

Award: Scholarship for use in junior or senior years; renewable. *Number:* 300. *Amount:* $7500.

Eligibility Requirements: Applicant must be enrolled or expecting to enroll full-time at a two-year or four-year institution or university. Available to U.S. citizens.

Application Requirements: Application form, essay. *Deadline:* January 31.

Contact: Ms. Lucy Decher, Executive Administrator
Phone: 703-756-6012
Fax: 703-756-6015
E-mail: goldh2o@vacoxmail.com

BHW GROUP

https://thebhwgroup.com/

BHW WOMEN IN STEM SCHOLARSHIP

The Women In STEM Scholarship is available to undergraduate and graduate female students. You must be pursuing a degree in science, technology, engineering, or mathematics to be eligible for this award.

Academic Fields/Career Goals: Applied Sciences; Archaeology; Architecture; Aviation/Aerospace; Behavioral Science; Biology; Chemical Engineering; Civil Engineering; Computer Science/Data Processing; Construction Engineering/Management; Dental Health/Services; Earth Science; Electrical Engineering/Electronics; Energy and Power Engineering; Engineering-Related Technologies; Engineering/Technology; Entomology; Environmental Health; Environmental Science; Food Science/Nutrition; Gemology; Geography; Health Administration; Health and Medical Sciences; Health Information Management/Technology; Heating, Air-Conditioning, and Refrigeration Mechanics; Horticulture/Floriculture; Hydrology; Industrial Design; Insurance and Actuarial Science; Landscape Architecture; Marine/Ocean Engineering; Materials Science, Engineering, and Metallurgy; Mathematics; Mechanical Engineering; Meteorology/Atmospheric Science; Military and Defense Studies; Natural Resources; Natural Sciences; Near and Middle East Studies; Neurobiology; Nuclear Science; Nursing; Occupational Safety and Health; Oceanography; Oncology; Optometry; Osteopathy; Paper and Pulp Engineering; Pharmacy; Physical Sciences; Psychology; Science, Technology, and Society; Social Sciences.

Award: Scholarship for use in freshman, sophomore, junior, senior, graduate, or postgraduate years; not renewable. *Number:* 1. *Amount:* $3000.

Eligibility Requirements: Applicant must be enrolled or expecting to enroll full-time at a two-year or four-year or technical institution or university and female. Available to U.S. and non-U.S. citizens.

Application Requirements: Essay. *Deadline:* April 15.

Contact: Mr. Paul Francis, Partner
BHW Group
6011 W. Courtyard Dr.
Suite 410
Austin, TX 78730
Phone: 512-220-0035
E-mail: scholarship@thebhwgroup.com

CARDS AGAINST HUMANITY

https://cardsagainsthumanity.com/

SCIENCE AMBASSADOR SCHOLARSHIP

The Science Ambassador Scholarship is a full-ride scholarship for undergraduate women studying science, technology, engineering, or math, funded by Cards Against Humanity. To apply, applicants must submit a three minute video explaining a scientific topic they're passionate about. Applications are now open! The deadline is December 11th, 2017. Apply now at ScienceAmbassadorScholarship.org. If you have questions, you're welcome to email SAS@CardsAgainstHumanity.com.

Academic Fields/Career Goals: Applied Sciences; Aviation/Aerospace; Biology; Chemical Engineering; Civil Engineering; Computer Science/Data Processing; Dental Health/Services; Earth Science; Electrical Engineering/Electronics; Energy and Power Engineering; Engineering-Related Technologies; Engineering/Technology;

Environmental Science; Insurance and Actuarial Science; Mathematics; Mechanical Engineering; Meteorology/Atmospheric Science; Natural Sciences; Neurobiology; Nuclear Science; Oceanography; Oncology; Optometry; Osteopathy; Paper and Pulp Engineering; Physical Sciences.

Award: Scholarship for use in freshman, sophomore, junior, or senior years; renewable. *Number:* 1.

Eligibility Requirements: Applicant must be enrolled or expecting to enroll full-time at a four-year institution or university and female. Available to U.S. and non-U.S. citizens.

Application Requirements: Application form. *Deadline:* December 11.

Contact: Maria Ranahan, Community Manager
E-mail: maria@cardsagainsthumanity.com

DISTIL NETWORKS
http://www.distilnetworks.com

WOMEN FORWARD IN TECHNOLOGY SCHOLARSHIP PROGRAM

The Woman Forward in Technology scholarship is to empower women entering the STEM field. The STEM career field workforce is currently only 24% women. Our mission is to help women who are pursuing undergraduate and graduate degrees in STEM programs to achieve their education goals, an objective which has the added long-term benefit of improving the diversity in STEM careers at large. Women, both U.S. citizen and non-citizen, who are attending at U.S. accredited university are encouraged to apply for a number of $3,000 scholarships being given out. Applicants can be either undergraduate or graduate students with a minimum GPA of 3.5 and a major in a STEM field.

Academic Fields/Career Goals: Applied Sciences; Biology; Chemical Engineering; Civil Engineering; Computer Science/Data Processing; Economics; Electrical Engineering/Electronics; Energy and Power Engineering; Engineering-Related Technologies; Engineering/Technology; Environmental Science; Finance; Marine Biology; Marine/Ocean Engineering; Materials Science, Engineering, and Metallurgy; Mathematics; Mechanical Engineering; Meteorology/Atmospheric Science; Natural Resources; Natural Sciences; Neurobiology; Nuclear Science; Oceanography; Pharmacy; Physical Sciences; Science, Technology, and Society.

Award: Scholarship for use in freshman, sophomore, junior, senior, graduate, or postgraduate years; not renewable. *Number:* 15–25. *Amount:* $3000.

Eligibility Requirements: Applicant must be enrolled or expecting to enroll full- or part-time at a two-year or four-year institution or university and female. Available to U.S. and non-U.S. citizens.

Application Requirements: Application form, essay. *Deadline:* June 15.

Contact: Ms. Laura Leatherman, Operations Manager
Phone: 703-9979674
E-mail: laura.leatherman@distilnetworks.com

GREAT MINDS IN STEM
http://www.greatmindsinstem.org/college/scholarship-application-information

HENAAC SCHOLARSHIP PROGRAM
• *See page 100*

INDIAN HEALTH SERVICES, UNITED STATES DEPARTMENT OF HEALTH AND HUMAN SERVICES
http://www.ihs.gov/scholarship

INDIAN HEALTH SERVICE HEALTH PROFESSIONS PRE-GRADUATE SCHOLARSHIPS

Scholarship for American Indian/Alaska Native students who are enrolled part-time or full-time in courses leading to a bachelor degree in the areas of pre-medicine, pre-dentistry, pre-optometry, or pre-podiatry. Minimum 2.0 GPA required to apply. Must intend to serve AI/AN people upon completion of professional healthcare education.

Academic Fields/Career Goals: Applied Sciences; Biology; Health and Medical Sciences.

Award: Scholarship for use in junior or senior years; not renewable. *Number:* 50–100. *Amount:* $23,000–$63,500.

Eligibility Requirements: Applicant must be of English heritage; American Indian/Alaska Native; enrolled or expecting to enroll full- or part-time at a four-year institution or university and resident of Alabama, Alaska, Arizona, Arkansas, California, Colorado, Connecticut, Delaware, District of Columbia, Florida, Georgia, Hawaii, Idaho, Illinois, Indiana, Iowa, Kansas, Kentucky, Louisiana, Maine, Maryland, Massachusetts, Michigan, Minnesota, Mississippi, Missouri, Montana, Nebraska, Nevada, New Hampshire, New Jersey, New Mexico, New York, North Carolina, North Dakota, Ohio, Oklahoma, Oregon, Pennsylvania, Rhode Island, South Carolina, South Dakota, Tennessee, Texas, Utah, Vermont, Virginia, Washington, West Virginia, Wisconsin, Wyoming. Available to U.S. citizens.

Application Requirements: Application form, essay. *Deadline:* March 28.

Contact: Ms. Reta Brewer, Branch Chief
Indian Health Services, United States Department of Health and Human Services
5600 Fishers Lane
Mail Stop: OHR 11E53A
Rockville, MD 20857
Phone: 301-443-6197
Fax: 301-443-6048
E-mail: reta.brewer@ihs.gov

INTERNATIONAL SOCIETY FOR OPTICAL ENGINEERING-SPIE
http://www.spie.org/scholarships

SPIE EDUCATIONAL SCHOLARSHIPS IN OPTICAL SCIENCE AND ENGINEERING

Scholarships for high school seniors, undergraduate and graduate students who are SPIE student member. High school students will receive a one-year complimentary student membership. Undergraduate and graduate students must be enrolled in an optics, photonics, imaging, optoelectronics program or related discipline for the full year. More details on eligibility and application requirements/forms can be found at http://spie.org/scholarships.

Academic Fields/Career Goals: Applied Sciences; Chemical Engineering; Electrical Engineering/Electronics; Engineering-Related Technologies; Engineering/Technology; Materials Science, Engineering, and Metallurgy; Mechanical Engineering.

Award: Scholarship for use in freshman, sophomore, junior, senior, or graduate years; not renewable. *Number:* 100–150. *Amount:* $2000–$11,000.

Eligibility Requirements: Applicant must be enrolled or expecting to enroll full- or part-time at a two-year or four-year or technical institution or university. Available to U.S. and non-U.S. citizens.

Application Requirements: Application form, essay, recommendations or references. *Deadline:* January 15.

Contact: Scholarship Committee
International Society for Optical Engineering-SPIE
PO Box 10
Bellingham, WA 98227-0010
Phone: 360-676-3290 Ext. 5452
Fax: 360-647-1445
E-mail: scholarships@spie.org

THE JACKSON LABORATORY
https://www.jax.org

THE JACKSON LABORATORY COLLEGE SCHOLARSHIP PROGRAM

The Jackson Laboratory, through the JAX College Scholarship Program, will award a $10,000 scholarship to three students from underserved backgrounds who will pursue a college degree and aspire to a career in biomedicine. This program is open to graduating high school seniors who reside in Connecticut, Maine, or in Sacramento County, California. One student from each location will be awarded this scholarship. The mission of The Jackson Laboratory is to discover precise genomic solutions for disease, and the scholarships will be awarded to students who share this goal by pursuing a career in research or medicine. In addition to the financial award, JAX will facilitate internship programs for scholarship recipients throughout their college career and sponsor annual campus visits to Bar Harbor, Maine and Farmington, CT. Scholarship recipients are expected to maintain strong academic performance and provide periodic updates on their college experience through blog posts and presentations.

Academic Fields/Career Goals: Applied Sciences; Behavioral Science; Biology; Computer Science/Data Processing; Environmental Health; Health and Medical Sciences; Nursing; Pharmacy; Public Health; Science, Technology, and Society.

Award: Scholarship for use in freshman or sophomore years; not renewable. *Number:* 3. *Amount:* $10,000.

Eligibility Requirements: Applicant must be high school student; planning to enroll or expecting to enroll full-time at a two-year or four-year institution or university and resident of California, Connecticut, Maine. Available to U.S. citizens.

Application Requirements: Application form, application form may be submitted online (https://www.jax.org/scholarship), essay, financial need analysis, recommendations or references, transcript. *Deadline:* February 1.

Contact: Michael McKernan, Program Director, STEM and Undergraduate Education
The Jackson Laboratory
The Jackson Laboratory
600 Main St.
Bar Harbor, ME 04609
Phone: 207-288-6000
E-mail: scholarship@jax.org

LOGMEIN

https://www.logmeininc.com

LASTPASS STEM SCHOLARSHIP

At LastPass we recently celebrated 10 years of providing seamless password security for individuals and businesses. Our customers have given us so much over the years — their time, their feedback, their trust — that we've been inspired to give back. That's why LastPass and LogMeIn's corporate social responsibility program, Mission Possible, have partnered to offer the LastPass STEM Scholarship. With this scholarship, we aim to provide STEM students with resources to support their education. Students entering and currently attending college who plan on studying or currently study within the STEM fields are eligible to apply to win a scholarship of $12,000 ($10,000 for tuition and $2,000 for books). We will select a winner based on the quality and substance of their submitted essay and video. If you meet the below criteria, please apply via the application on this page. If you are associated with a high school or university, please spread the word to your students. LastPass STEM Scholarship Details: 1. Students must be high school seniors or be currently enrolled in a college or university. 2. Only students enrolled in high schools, colleges and universities in the U.S. are eligible. 3. Student must be majoring in a STEM field or planning to major in a STEM field. 4. An applicant's GPA must be above a 3.0 to qualify. 5. Each applicant must submit a 500-word essay to apply and, if chosen to proceed to the second round, each applicant must submit a video. Video topic to be disclosed upon notification. 6. Essay submission deadline is April 30, 2019. And the winner will be announced July 2019. Essay topic: Being in the cybersecurity industry, we're fascinated by its constantly evolving nature, which can include shocking data breaches and innovative new technology. An unexpected factor here is human behavior. Even when one of their accounts is involved in a data breach, over 50% of people do not change their password. What is the link between human behavior and technology, and what does that say about the future of security?

Academic Fields/Career Goals: Applied Sciences; Aviation/Aerospace; Chemical Engineering; Civil Engineering; Computer Science/Data Processing; Construction Engineering/Management; Electrical Engineering/Electronics; Engineering/Technology; Mathematics; Mechanical Engineering; Physical Sciences; Science, Technology, and Society; Statistics.

Award: Scholarship for use in freshman, sophomore, junior, or senior years; not renewable. *Number:* 1. *Amount:* $12,000.

Eligibility Requirements: Applicant must be enrolled or expecting to enroll full-time at a four-year institution or university and studying in Alabama, Alaska, Arizona, Arkansas, California, Colorado, Connecticut, Delaware, District of Columbia, Florida, Georgia, Hawaii, Idaho, Illinois, Indiana, Iowa, Kansas, Kentucky, Louisiana, Maine, Maryland, Massachusetts, Michigan, Minnesota, Mississippi, Missouri, Montana, Nebraska, Nevada, New Hampshire, New Jersey, New Mexico, New York, North Carolina, North Dakota, Ohio, Oklahoma, Oregon, Pennsylvania, Rhode Island, South Carolina, South Dakota, Tennessee, Texas, Utah, Vermont, Virginia, Washington, West Virginia, Wisconsin, Wyoming. Available to U.S. and non-U.S. citizens.

Application Requirements: Application form, application form may be submitted online (https://www.lastpass.com/scholarship), essay, GPA. *Deadline:* April 30.

Contact: LastPass Scholarship Committee
LogMeIn
320 Summer St.
Boston, MA 02110
Phone: 866-560-9165
E-mail: scholarship@lastpass.com

MEDICAL SCRUBS COLLECTION

http://medicalscrubscollection.com

MEDICAL SCRUBS COLLECTION SCHOLARSHIP
• *See page 104*

NASA IDAHO SPACE GRANT CONSORTIUM

http://www.idahospacegrant.org

NASA IDAHO SPACE GRANT CONSORTIUM SCHOLARSHIP PROGRAM

Applicants must attend an Idaho accredited institution and maintain a 3.0 GPA. Major/career interest in engineering, mathematics, science or secondary education in math or science. Applicants must be a U.S. citizen. Specifics of the program change from year to year. Please check our website for the most up to date information.

Academic Fields/Career Goals: Applied Sciences; Biology; Chemical Engineering; Civil Engineering; Computer Science/Data Processing; Earth Science; Electrical Engineering/Electronics; Energy and Power Engineering; Engineering-Related Technologies; Engineering/Technology; Environmental Science; Fire Sciences; Geography; Materials Science, Engineering, and Metallurgy; Mathematics; Mechanical Engineering; Meteorology/Atmospheric Science; Natural Resources; Natural Sciences; Nuclear Science; Physical Sciences; Science, Technology, and Society.

Award: Scholarship for use in freshman or sophomore years; not renewable. *Number:* 1–50. *Amount:* $500–$3000.

Eligibility Requirements: Applicant must be enrolled or expecting to enroll full-time at a two-year institution and studying in Idaho. Available to U.S. citizens.

Application Requirements: Application form, essay. *Deadline:* March 5.

Contact: Susie Johnson, Program Manager
NASA Idaho Space Grant Consortium
875 Perimeter Drive
Moscow, ID 83844-1026
Phone: 208-885-4934
Fax: 208-885-1399
E-mail: susiej@uidaho.edu

NASA/MARYLAND SPACE GRANT CONSORTIUM

https://md.spacegrant.org

NASA MARYLAND SPACE GRANT CONSORTIUM SCHOLARSHIPS

Scholarships for full-time undergraduate students pursuing studies in math, science, engineering, or technology, who are interested in aerospace and/or NASA-relevant careers. Eligibility requirements: (1) U.S. citizenship (2) attending a Maryland Space Grant Consortium affiliate institution (3) pursuing a relevant major (4) maintaining a 3.0 or higher GPA. Award amounts vary.

Academic Fields/Career Goals: Applied Sciences; Aviation/Aerospace; Biology; Chemical Engineering; Computer Science/Data Processing; Earth Science; Electrical Engineering/Electronics; Engineering/Technology; Environmental Science; Materials Science,

Engineering, and Metallurgy; Mathematics; Mechanical Engineering; Physical Sciences.

Award: Scholarship for use in freshman, sophomore, junior, or senior years; renewable.

Eligibility Requirements: Applicant must be enrolled or expecting to enroll full-time at a two-year or four-year institution or university; studying in Maryland and must have an interest in designated field specified by sponsor. Available to U.S. citizens.

Application Requirements: Application form, application form may be submitted online (https://md.spacegrant.org/document-center/scholarship-application/), essay. *Deadline:* continuous.

Contact: Ms. Cheryl Dillard-Ewing
NASA/Maryland Space Grant Consortium
The Johns Hopkins University - Maryland Space Grant Consortium
3400 N. Charles St., Bloomberg Center 145
Baltimore, MD 21218
Phone: 410-516-7351

NASA'S VIRGINIA SPACE GRANT CONSORTIUM

http://www.vsgc.odu.edu/

COMMUNITY COLLEGE STEM SCHOLARSHIPS

This scholarship is designated for Virginia community college students studying STEM fields involving science, technology, engineering and math with aerospace relevance. Applicant must be U.S. citizen with a minimum GPA of 3.0 currently enrolled full time with at least one semester of coursework (minimum of 12 credit hours) completed.

Academic Fields/Career Goals: Applied Sciences; Biology; Computer Science/Data Processing; Construction Engineering/Management; Drafting; Electrical Engineering/Electronics; Engineering/Technology; Environmental Science; Industrial Design; Materials Science, Engineering, and Metallurgy; Mathematics; Mechanical Engineering.

Award: Scholarship for use in sophomore year; not renewable. *Number:* 1–12. *Amount:* $2000–$2000.

Eligibility Requirements: Applicant must be U.S. Colonial citizen; enrolled or expecting to enroll full-time at a two-year institution; resident of Virginia and studying in Virginia. Available to U.S. citizens.

Application Requirements: Application form, application form may be submitted online (http://vsgc.odu.edu/communitycollegescholarships/), essay, recommendations or references, resume, transcript. *Deadline:* March 11.

Contact: Mr. Chris Carter, Deputy Director
NASA's Virginia Space Grant Consortium
VSGC ODU, PHEC 600 Butler Farm Road
Hampton, VA 23666
Phone: 757-766-5210
Fax: 757-766-5205
E-mail: cxcarter@odu.edu

UNDERGRADUATE STEM RESEARCH SCHOLARSHIPS

Scholarships designated for undergraduate students pursuing any field of study with aerospace relevance. Must attend one of the five Virginia Space Grant colleges and universities. Must have minimum 3.0 GPA. Please refer to website for further details http://www.vsgc.odu.edu.

Academic Fields/Career Goals: Applied Sciences; Aviation/Aerospace; Biology; Chemical Engineering; Computer Science/Data Processing; Electrical Engineering/Electronics; Engineering-Related Technologies; Materials Science, Engineering, and Metallurgy; Mathematics; Mechanical Engineering; Physical Sciences; Science, Technology, and Society.

Award: Scholarship for use in junior or senior years; not renewable. *Number:* 1–35. *Amount:* $3000–$8500.

Eligibility Requirements: Applicant must be enrolled or expecting to enroll full-time at a four-year institution or university; resident of Virginia and studying in Virginia. Available to U.S. citizens.

Application Requirements: Application form, application form may be submitted online (http://vsgc.odu.edu/undergraduatescholarships/), essay, recommendations or references, resume, transcript. *Deadline:* January 28.

Contact: Mr. Chris Carter, Deputy Director
NASA's Virginia Space Grant Consortium
VSGC PHEC 600 Butler Farm Road
Hampton, VA 23666
Phone: 757-766-5210
Fax: 757-766-5205
E-mail: cxcarter@odu.edu

NEVADA NASA SPACE GRANT CONSORTIUM

https://nasa.epscorspo.nevada.edu/

NATIONAL SPACE GRANT CONSORTIUM SCHOLARSHIPS

Scholarships provide financial support to undergraduate and graduate students pursuing science, technology, engineering, and mathematics (STEM) degrees and provide the opportunity for students to deepen their inquiry within STEM through a myriad of channels including research experience, technical collaborations and professional development.

Academic Fields/Career Goals: Applied Sciences; Aviation/Aerospace; Chemical Engineering; Civil Engineering; Computer Science/Data Processing; Earth Science; Engineering/Technology; Mathematics; Mechanical Engineering; Natural Sciences; Physical Sciences.

Award: Scholarship for use in freshman, sophomore, junior, senior, or graduate years; not renewable. *Number:* 1–50. *Amount:* $1250–$13,333.

Eligibility Requirements: Applicant must be enrolled or expecting to enroll full-time at a two-year or four-year institution or university; resident of Nevada and studying in Nevada. Available to U.S. citizens.

Application Requirements: Application form, essay. *Deadline:* continuous.

Contact: Leone Thierman, Program Coordinator
Nevada NASA Space Grant Consortium
2601 Enterprise Way
Reno, NV 89512
Phone: 775-784-3476
Fax: 775-784-1127
E-mail: nvspacegrant@nshe.nevada.edu

NEXTSTEPU

http://www.nextstepu.com/

$1,500 STEM SCHOLARSHIP
• *See page 104*

NOVUS BIOLOGICALS, LLC

https://www.novusbio.com

NOVUS BIOLOGICALS SCHOLARSHIP PROGRAM
• *See page 101*

R&D SYSTEMS SCHOLARSHIP
• *See page 101*

TOCRIS BIOSCIENCE SCHOLARSHIP
• *See page 102*

OREGON OFFICE OF STUDENT ACCESS AND COMPLETION

https://oregonstudentaid.gov/

SEHAR SALEHA AHMAD AND ABRAHIM EKRAMULLAH ZAFAR FOUNDATION SCHOLARSHIP

Scholarship available to female graduating seniors of Oregon high schools (including GED recipients and home schooled students). Minimum 3.8 GPA. Must be a mathematics or science major at a 4-year public or nonprofit college or university. Scholarship is automatically renewable if renewal criteria met. Based on financial need.

Academic Fields/Career Goals: Applied Sciences; Biology; Earth Science; Mathematics; Natural Sciences; Physical Sciences.

Award: Scholarship for use in freshman year; renewable.

Eligibility Requirements: Applicant must be high school student; planning to enroll or expecting to enroll full-time at a four-year institution or university; female and resident of Oregon. Available to U.S. citizens.

Application Requirements: Application form, financial need analysis. *Deadline:* March 1.

Contact: Melissa Adams, Scholarship Processing Coordinator
Phone: 541-687-7409
E-mail: melissa.adams@state.or.us

SCARLETT FAMILY FOUNDATION SCHOLARSHIP PROGRAM

http://www.scarlettfoundation.org/

SCHOLARSHIP FOR STUDENTS PURSUING A BUSINESS OR STEM DEGREE

• *See page 80*

SINO-AMERICAN PHARMACEUTICAL PROFESSIONALS ASSOCIATION

http://www.sapaweb.org

SAPA SCHOLARSHIP AND EXCELLENCE IN EDUCATION PROGRAM

$1000 award for a high school senior who is planning to attend a full-time undergraduate program at an accredited four-year college/university with a major related to life sciences. Must have a minimum GPA of 3.3, a minimum SAT score of 2000 out of 2400 (or 1400 out of 1600 for new SAT) or ACT score of 30, and be a United States citizen or a legal resident alien.

Academic Fields/Career Goals: Applied Sciences.

Award: Scholarship for use in freshman year; not renewable. *Number:* 2. *Amount:* $1000.

Eligibility Requirements: Applicant must be high school student and planning to enroll or expecting to enroll full-time at a four-year institution or university. Available to U.S. citizens.

Application Requirements: Application form, essay. *Deadline:* June 30.

STRAIGHT NORTH

https://www.straightnorth.com/

STRAIGHT NORTH STEM SCHOLARSHIP

• *See page 81*

UNITED NEGRO COLLEGE FUND

http://www.uncf.org/

DAVIS SCHOLARSHIP FOR WOMEN IN STEM

One-time award of up to $5000 for minority female students to pursue a future career in the STEM fields. Must be at least sophomore standing. Preference will be given to students from Massachusetts, although all eligible students are encouraged to apply. Must be a U.S. citizen or permanent resident and have a minimum 3.0 GPA.

Academic Fields/Career Goals: Applied Sciences; Aviation/Aerospace; Chemical Engineering; Computer Science/Data Processing; Electrical Engineering/Electronics; Energy and Power Engineering; Engineering/Technology; Environmental Science; Materials Science, Engineering, and Metallurgy; Mathematics; Mechanical Engineering; Meteorology/Atmospheric Science.

Award: Scholarship for use in sophomore, junior, or senior years; not renewable. *Number:* 2.

Eligibility Requirements: Applicant must be Black (non-Hispanic); enrolled or expecting to enroll full-time at a four-year institution or university and female. Available to U.S. citizens.

Application Requirements: Application form, essay, financial need analysis. *Deadline:* June 8.

Contact: Kenya Gray
E-mail: kenya.gray@uncf.org

DISCOVER FINANCIAL SERVICES SCHOLARSHIP

• *See page 82*

GALACTIC UNITE BYTHEWAY SCHOLARSHIP

Scholarship of up to $7500 for a first-year female college student pursuing STEM degrees at any accredited four-year college or university in the United States. Minimum 3.2 GPA required. The selected recipients will be required to participate in the Galactic Unite mentorship program.

Academic Fields/Career Goals: Applied Sciences; Chemical Engineering; Computer Science/Data Processing; Electrical Engineering/Electronics; Energy and Power Engineering; Engineering-Related Technologies; Engineering/Technology; Environmental Science; Health and Medical Sciences; Materials Science, Engineering, and Metallurgy; Mathematics; Mechanical Engineering; Science, Technology, and Society.

Award: Scholarship for use in freshman year; renewable.

Eligibility Requirements: Applicant must be Black (non-Hispanic); high school student; planning to enroll or expecting to enroll full-time at a four-year institution or university and female. Available to U.S. citizens.

Application Requirements: Application form, recommendations or references, resume, transcript. *Deadline:* June 12.

Contact: William Dunham
E-mail: william.dunham@uncf.org

LEIDOS STEM SCHOLARSHIP

• *See page 96*

VERMONT SPACE GRANT CONSORTIUM

http://www.cems.uvm.edu/vsgc

VERMONT SPACE GRANT CONSORTIUM

• *See page 92*

ARCHAEOLOGY

ASSOCIATION FOR WOMEN GEOSCIENTISTS (AWG)

http://www.awg.org/

AWG MARIA LUISA CRAWFORD FIELD CAMP SCHOLARSHIP

The Crawford Scholarship encourages promising young women to pursue geoscience careers through attendance at field camp. Two $750 scholarships are awarded annually through a competitive process.

Academic Fields/Career Goals: Archaeology; Earth Science; Education; Energy and Power Engineering; Environmental Science; Gemology; Hydrology; Meteorology/Atmospheric Science; Natural Resources; Natural Sciences; Oceanography; Physical Sciences.

Award: Scholarship for use in freshman, sophomore, junior, or senior years; not renewable. *Number:* 2. *Amount:* $750.

Eligibility Requirements: Applicant must be enrolled or expecting to enroll full-time at a four-year institution or university and female. Available to U.S. citizens.

Application Requirements: Application form, essay. *Deadline:* February 14.

Contact: Sarah Hunt, Crawford Scholarship Coordinator
E-mail: crawford@awg.org

AWG SALT LAKE CHAPTER (SLC) RESEARCH SCHOLARSHIP

Offered by AWG's Salt Lake Chapter, this scholarship will help defray the costs of presenting geoscience research results at national, or regional, science conventions and meetings. It is awarded based upon the quality and importance of the research being conducted and reported.

Academic Fields/Career Goals: Archaeology; Earth Science; Education; Environmental Science; Geography; Hydrology;

Meteorology/Atmospheric Science; Museum Studies; Natural Resources; Natural Sciences; Oceanography; Physical Sciences.

Award: Scholarship for use in freshman, sophomore, junior, senior, or graduate years; not renewable. *Number:* 1. *Amount:* $1–$1000.

Eligibility Requirements: Applicant must be enrolled or expecting to enroll full- or part-time at a two-year or four-year institution or university; female and studying in Utah. Available to U.S. citizens.

Application Requirements: Application form, letter from applicant summarizing research, purpose and importance of research, recommendations or references. *Deadline:* March 12.

Contact: Janae Wallace, AWG Salt Lake Chapter Scholarship
Coordinator
Association for Women Geoscientists (AWG)
AWG Salt Lake Chapter
PO Box 58691
Salt Lake City, UT 84152
Phone: 801-537-3387
E-mail: janaewallace@utah.gov

AWG UNDERGRADUATE EXCELLENCE IN PALEONTOLOGY AWARD
• *See page 106*

JANET CULLEN TANAKA GEOSCIENCES UNDERGRADUATE SCHOLARSHIP

This scholarship is for undergraduate women who are committed to completing a Bachelor's degree and pursuing a career or graduate work in the geosciences.

Academic Fields/Career Goals: Archaeology; Earth Science; Environmental Science; Hydrology; Meteorology/Atmospheric Science; Natural Resources; Natural Sciences; Oceanography; Physical Sciences.

Award: Scholarship for use in sophomore, junior, or senior years; not renewable. *Number:* 1–2. *Amount:* $1–$1500.

Eligibility Requirements: Applicant must be enrolled or expecting to enroll full-time at a two-year or four-year institution or university; female and studying in Oregon, Washington. Available to U.S. citizens.

Application Requirements: Essay, financial need analysis, recommendations or references, transcript. *Deadline:* December 15.

Contact: Jenny Saltonstall, AWG PNW Scholarship Chair
Association for Women Geoscientists (AWG)
AWG Pacific Northwest Chapter
PO Box 28391
Seattle, WA 98118
Phone: 425-827-7701
Fax: 425-827-5424
E-mail: scholarship@awg-ps.org

OSAGE CHAPTER UNDERGRADUATE SERVICE SCHOLARSHIP

This Service Scholarship provides an undergraduate student in the geosciences with funding for research, tuition or books. The recipient will be required to participate in two service events (e.g. AWG outreach activities) within a year following receipt of the award.

Academic Fields/Career Goals: Archaeology; Earth Science; Environmental Science; Gemology; Geography; Hydrology; Meteorology/Atmospheric Science; Museum Studies; Natural Resources; Oceanography; Physical Sciences.

Award: Scholarship for use in freshman, sophomore, junior, or senior years; not renewable. *Number:* 1. *Amount:* $500.

Eligibility Requirements: Applicant must be enrolled or expecting to enroll full-time at a four-year institution or university and studying in Kansas, Missouri, Nebraska. Available to U.S. citizens.

Application Requirements: Application form, personal statement, transcript. *Deadline:* April 15.

Contact: Sarah Morton, AWG Osage Chapter President
Association for Women Geoscientists (AWG)
University of Kansas
1475 Jayhawk Boulevard, Room 120
Lawrence, KS 66045
E-mail: awgosage@gmail.com

BHW GROUP
https://thebhwgroup.com/

BHW WOMEN IN STEM SCHOLARSHIP
• *See page 107*

EXPLORERS CLUB
http://www.explorers.org/

YOUTH ACTIVITY FUND GRANTS
• *See page 103*

MEDICAL SCRUBS COLLECTION
http://medicalscrubscollection.com

MEDICAL SCRUBS COLLECTION SCHOLARSHIP
• *See page 104*

SCARLETT FAMILY FOUNDATION SCHOLARSHIP PROGRAM
http://www.scarlettfoundation.org/

SCHOLARSHIP FOR STUDENTS PURSUING A BUSINESS OR STEM DEGREE
• *See page 80*

SOCIETY FOR CLASSICAL STUDIES
http://www.classicalstudies.org/

MINORITY STUDENT SUMMER SCHOLARSHIP

Award to minority undergraduate students for a scholarship to further an undergraduate's preparation for graduate work in classics or archaeology. Applicants should be current students of classics. Eligible proposals might include (but are not limited to) participation in summer programs or field schools in Italy, Greece, Egypt, or language training at institutions in the U.S, Canada, or Europe. Amount of the award will range from $1,500 to $4,000. Application must be supported by a member of the SCS.

Academic Fields/Career Goals: Archaeology; Arts; Classics; Foreign Language; History.

Award: Scholarship for use in freshman, sophomore, junior, or senior years; not renewable. *Number:* 2. *Amount:* $1500–$4000.

Eligibility Requirements: Applicant must be American Indian/Alaska Native, Asian/Pacific Islander, Black (non-Hispanic), Hispanic and enrolled or expecting to enroll full-time at a four-year institution or university. Available to U.S. and non-U.S. citizens.

Application Requirements: Application form, application form may be submitted online (http://www.classicalstudies.org), essay, financial need analysis, recommendations or references, transcript. *Deadline:* December 15.

Contact: Dr. Adam Blistein, Executive Director
Phone: 215-898-4975
Fax: 215-573-7874
E-mail: scsclassics@sas.upenn.edu

ARCHITECTURE

AACE INTERNATIONAL
http://www.aacei.org/

AACE INTERNATIONAL COMPETITIVE SCHOLARSHIP
AACE International scholarships are available in amounts ranging from $2000 to $8000. Specific awards will be determined based on overall scholarship and collegiate accomplishments. Applications are only

available on line and are accepted from mid-December through February 7th. Applicants should attach an unofficial transcript in a PDF format to their application.

Academic Fields/Career Goals: Architecture; Aviation/Aerospace; Business/Consumer Services; Chemical Engineering; Civil Engineering; Construction Engineering/Management; Electrical Engineering/Electronics; Engineering-Related Technologies; Engineering/Technology; Mechanical Engineering.

Award: Scholarship for use in freshman, sophomore, junior, senior, or graduate years; not renewable. *Number:* 10–20. *Amount:* $2000–$8000.

Eligibility Requirements: Applicant must be enrolled or expecting to enroll full-time at a two-year or four-year institution or university. Available to U.S. and non-U.S. citizens.

Application Requirements: Application form, application form may be submitted online (http://www.aacei.org/awards/scholarships/application.shtml), essay, recommendations or references, transcript. *Deadline:* February 7.

Contact: Mr. John Hines, Manager, Education
AACE International
1265 Suncrest Towne Centre Drive
Morgantown, WV 26505-1876
Phone: 304-296-8444 Ext. 119
E-mail: jhines@aacei.org

ACI FOUNDATION

http://www.acifoundation.org

ACI FOUNDATION SCHOLARSHIP PROGRAM

Awards available for full-time graduate students in their first or second year of study in a concrete-related field. Must be enrolled in a program in a U.S. or Canadian institution. For more details visit http://www.concrete.org.

Academic Fields/Career Goals: Architecture; Civil Engineering; Engineering/Technology; Materials Science, Engineering, and Metallurgy.

Award: Scholarship for use in freshman, sophomore, junior, senior, or graduate years; not renewable. *Number:* 5. *Amount:* $5000.

Eligibility Requirements: Applicant must be enrolled or expecting to enroll full-time at a four-year institution or university. Available to U.S. and non-U.S. citizens.

Application Requirements: Application form, essay. *Deadline:* continuous.

Contact: Ashley Mayra, Scholarship Coordinator
ACI Foundation
38800 Country Club Drive
Farmington Hills, MI 48331
Phone: 248-848-3737
E-mail: scholarships@concrete.org

ARCHITECTS FOUNDATION

https://architectsfoundation.org/

ARCHITECTS FOUNDATION DIVERSITY ADVANCEMENT SCHOLARSHIP

Maybe you chose architecture because you want to design a better world. Or you can't imagine doing anything else. One thing's for certain: You love this work. And we'd love to help fund your college experience with a multiyear scholarship, up to $20,000. We created the Diversity Advancement Scholarship to help more minority students pursue a successful career in architecture. Multiple scholarships are available. We're looking for minority students whose imagination and design thinking will influence the future of the built environment and the architecture profession. Eligible students must be a U.S. citizen, have a minimum 3.0 GPA, and be a high school student planning to enroll in a NAAB-accredited architecture degree program; or, a rising second-year college student in a NAAB-accredited architecture degree program; or a technical school or community college student who has completed high school or its equivalent and intends to transfer to a NAAB-accredited architecture program. NAAB-accredited degree programs may be a five-year Bachelor of Architecture degree, or a four-year pre-professional bachelor degree followed by a Master of Architecture degree. Scholarships may be renewed for up to 5 years (up to a $20,000 total award—multiple scholarships are available).

Academic Fields/Career Goals: Architecture.

Award: Scholarship for use in freshman, sophomore, junior, senior, or graduate years; renewable. *Number:* 3–10. *Amount:* $4000.

Eligibility Requirements: Applicant must be American Indian/Alaska Native, Asian/Pacific Islander, Black (non-Hispanic), Hispanic and enrolled or expecting to enroll full-time at a two-year or four-year or technical institution or university. Available to U.S. citizens.

Application Requirements: Application form, essay, financial need analysis, portfolio. *Deadline:* January 17.

Contact: Amanda Malloy, Development Manager
Architects Foundation
The Architects Foundation
1735 New York Avenue, NW
Washington, DC 20006-5292
Phone: 202-626-7577
E-mail: scholarships@architectsfoundation.org

ARCHITECTS FOUNDATION PAYETTE SHO-PING CHIN MEMORIAL ACADEMIC SCHOLARSHIP

The Payette Sho-Ping Chin Memorial Academic Scholarship was established with the architecture firm Payette to support a woman studying architecture within a NAAB-accredited Bachelor's or Master's degree program. Sho-Ping, a fellow and leader in the AIA, was a long-time principal and healthcare practice leader at Payette. She was a talented and compassionate architect who was fiercely determined to design healthcare architecture of the highest caliber for those in need. Sho-Ping was a wonderful mentor and instilled in her teams a sense of camaraderie and commitment to design. As a founder of the AIA Women's Leadership Summit, held biennially, Sho-Ping was instrumental in defining the national discourse for Women in Design. The $10,000 scholarship will be awarded to a student who will be entering at least their third year of undergraduate or any level of graduate study within an accredited architecture program. Previous Payette Sho-Ping Chin Memorial Academic Scholarship recipients are eligible to reapply in subsequent years. To help the scholarship recipient establish contacts within the profession, she will be assigned a senior mentor from Payette for the scholarship year.

Academic Fields/Career Goals: Architecture.

Award: Scholarship for use in junior, senior, graduate, or postgraduate years; not renewable. *Number:* 1. *Amount:* $10,000.

Eligibility Requirements: Applicant must be enrolled or expecting to enroll full-time at a four-year institution or university and female. Available to U.S. citizens.

Application Requirements: Application form, essay, financial need analysis, portfolio. *Deadline:* January 17.

Contact: Amanda Malloy, Development Manager
Architects Foundation
1735 New York Avenue NW
Washington, DC 20006
Phone: 202-626-7577
E-mail: scholarships@architectsfoundation.org

BHW GROUP

https://thebhwgroup.com/

BHW WOMEN IN STEM SCHOLARSHIP
• *See page 107*

BRASKEM ODEBRECHT

http://www.odebrechtaward.com

ODEBRECHT AWARD FOR SUSTAINABLE DEVELOPMENT

Award for undergraduate students in all engineering fields, architecture, building and construction management, and chemistry. By submitting a paper that outlines contributions to sustainability, students have an opportunity to win $65,000 in cash prizes for themselves, their faculty advisors and their universities. Ideas can be related to efficient, real-world uses of sustainable materials, new chemical and petrochemical processes or new building techniques. Must register at website to enter.

Academic Fields/Career Goals: Architecture; Chemical Engineering; Civil Engineering; Construction Engineering/Management; Electrical

Engineering/Electronics; Energy and Power Engineering; Mechanical Engineering.

Award: Prize for use in freshman, sophomore, junior, or senior years; not renewable.

Eligibility Requirements: Applicant must be enrolled or expecting to enroll full- or part-time at a four-year institution or university. Available to U.S. citizens.

Application Requirements: Application form, application form may be submitted online, recommendations or references, university identification. *Deadline:* May 31.

CENTER FOR ARCHITECTURE

www.centerforarchitecture.org

CENTER FOR ARCHITECTURE DESIGN SCHOLARSHIP

Merit-based scholarships that support deserving students studying architecture, design, engineering, planning or a related discipline in an accredited program within New York State.

Academic Fields/Career Goals: Architecture; Civil Engineering; Electrical Engineering/Electronics; Engineering/Technology; Industrial Design; Interior Design; Landscape Architecture; Mechanical Engineering.

Award: Scholarship for use in freshman, sophomore, junior, senior, or graduate years; not renewable. *Number:* 1–2. *Amount:* $2000–$5000.

Eligibility Requirements: Applicant must be enrolled or expecting to enroll full-time at a two-year or technical institution or university and studying in New York. Available to U.S. and non-U.S. citizens.

Application Requirements: Application form, essay, portfolio. *Deadline:* March 20.

Contact: Anna Marcum, Grants and Foundation Relations Manager
Center for Architecture
536 LaGuardia Place
New York, NY 10012
Phone: 212-683-0023
E-mail: amarcum@centerforarchitecture.org

CENTER FOR ARCHITECTURE, WOMEN'S AUXILIARY ELEANOR ALLWORK SCHOLARSHIP

Students seeking their first degree in architecture from an NAAB accredited school within the State of New York are eligible. The Dean or Chair of the architectural school shall nominate up to three students from their respective college or university to apply. Nominated students will have a high level of academic performance and evidence of financial need. The financial need of each student shall be determined by the guidelines of the Financial Aid Officer of the school nominating the candidate. Students need not be U.S. citizens.

Academic Fields/Career Goals: Architecture.

Award: Scholarship for use in freshman, sophomore, junior, senior, or graduate years; not renewable. *Number:* 1–5. *Amount:* $4000–$10,000.

Eligibility Requirements: Applicant must be enrolled or expecting to enroll full-time at an institution or university and studying in New York. Available to U.S. and non-U.S. citizens.

Application Requirements: Application form, portfolio. *Deadline:* March 20.

Contact: Anna Marcum, Grants and Foundation Relations Manager
Center for Architecture
536 LaGuardia Place
New York, NY 10012
Phone: 212-683-0023
E-mail: amarcum@centerforarchitecture.org

THE WALTER A. HUNT, JR. SCHOLARSHIP

To promote and encourage the study of architecture by New York City public high school students through a two-year scholarship to supplement tuition and related costs during their freshman and sophomore years at Architecture School in the U.S.

Academic Fields/Career Goals: Architecture.

Award: Scholarship for use in freshman or sophomore years; not renewable. *Number:* 1. *Amount:* $10,000.

Eligibility Requirements: Applicant must be high school student; planning to enroll or expecting to enroll full-time at an institution or university and resident of New Mexico. Available to U.S. and non-U.S. citizens.

Application Requirements: Application form, essay, interview, portfolio. *Deadline:* May 15.

Contact: Anna Marcum, Grants and Foundation Relations Manager
Center for Architecture
536 LaGuardia Place
New York, NY 10012
Phone: 212-683-0023
E-mail: amarcum@centerforarchitecture.org

CONNECTICUT BUILDING CONGRESS SCHOLARSHIP FUND, INC.

http://www.cbc-ct.org

CBC SCHOLARSHIP FUND

The Connecticut Building Congress Scholarship Fund (CBCSF) announces that it will once again be offering scholarships to graduating Connecticut high school students entering college-level programs in architecture, construction-related engineering, construction management, surveying, planning or other courses of study leading to Associate, Baccalaureate, or Masters degrees in the construction field. The awards will be given for academic merit, extracurricular activities, potential and financial need. The scholarships may be renewable each year based on performance in school and available resources. The number of awards as well as the amounts may vary at the discretion of the CBCSF Board of Directors. In the past, scholarships have ranged from $500 to $2,000 per year.

Academic Fields/Career Goals: Architecture; Civil Engineering; Construction Engineering/Management; Engineering-Related Technologies; Engineering/Technology; Landscape Architecture; Mechanical Engineering.

Award: Scholarship for use in freshman, sophomore, junior, or senior years; renewable. *Number:* 2–4. *Amount:* $500–$2000.

Eligibility Requirements: Applicant must be high school student; planning to enroll or expecting to enroll full-time at a four-year institution or university and resident of Connecticut. Available to U.S. citizens.

Application Requirements: Application form, essay, financial need analysis. *Deadline:* March 9.

Contact: Mr. Thomas DiBlasi, President
Connecticut Building Congress Scholarship Fund, Inc.
500 Purdy Hill Road
Monroe, CT 06468
Phone: 203-452-1331 Ext. 108
Fax: 203-268-8103
E-mail: TomD@DiBlasi-Engrs.com

THE DALLAS FOUNDATION

http://www.dallasfoundation.org/

DALLAS CENTER FOR ARCHITECTURE FOUNDATION—HKS/JOHN HUMPHRIES SCHOLARSHIP

The scholarship must be used in the year it is awarded. If the funds are not used in this time period, they will be forfeited. The funds are intended to be used for college tuition towards a degree in architecture, and as such, will be routed directly to the appropriate college office for credit towards tuition. Must be a Dallas city resident.

Academic Fields/Career Goals: Architecture.

Award: Scholarship for use in freshman year; not renewable. *Amount:* $2000.

Eligibility Requirements: Applicant must be high school student; planning to enroll or expecting to enroll full-time at a four-year institution or university and resident of Texas.

Application Requirements: Application form, essay, portfolio, recommendations or references, transcript. *Deadline:* March 31.

Contact: Rachel Lasseter, Program Associate
Phone: 214-741-9898
E-mail: scholarships@dallasfoundation.org

WHITLEY PLACE SCHOLARSHIP

Established in 2009, the Whitley Place Scholarship seeks to provide aid to graduating seniors in Prosper ISD who plan to study civil engineering, construction science, construction management, architecture, landscape architecture, planning, public administration, mechanical engineering or other math/science related fields.

Academic Fields/Career Goals: Architecture; Civil Engineering; Engineering/Technology; Landscape Architecture; Mathematics; Mechanical Engineering; Physical Sciences; Public Policy and Administration.

Award: Scholarship for use in freshman, sophomore, junior, or senior years; renewable. *Amount:* $2500.

Eligibility Requirements: Applicant must be high school student; planning to enroll or expecting to enroll full-time at a two-year or four-year institution or university and resident of Texas.

Application Requirements: Application form, driver's license, financial need analysis, recommendations or references, resume, transcript. *Deadline:* March 31.

Contact: Rachel Lasseter, Program Associate
Phone: 214-741-9898
E-mail: scholarships@dallasfoundation.org

FLORIDA EDUCATIONAL FACILITIES PLANNERS' ASSOCIATION

http://www.fefpa.org/

FEFPA ASSISTANTSHIP

Renewable scholarship for full-time sophomores, juniors, seniors and graduate students enrolled in an accredited four-year Florida university or community college, majoring in facilities planning or a field related to facilities planning. Must be a resident of Florida with a 3.0 GPA.

Academic Fields/Career Goals: Architecture; Construction Engineering/Management.

Award: Scholarship for use in sophomore, junior, senior, or graduate years; renewable. *Number:* 2. *Amount:* $3000.

Eligibility Requirements: Applicant must be enrolled or expecting to enroll full-time at a four-year institution or university; resident of Florida and studying in Florida. Available to U.S. and non-U.S. citizens.

Application Requirements: Application form, essay, financial need analysis, recommendations or references, test scores, transcript. *Deadline:* June 1.

Contact: Robert Griffith, Selection Committee Chair
Phone: 305-348-4070 Ext. 4002
Fax: 305-341-3377
E-mail: griffith@fiu.edu

THE GEORGIA TRUST FOR HISTORIC PRESERVATION

http://www.georgiatrust.org/

J. NEEL REID PRIZE

A $4000 fellowship is given to an architecture student, architecture intern or a recently-registered architect residing, studying or working in Georgia. Proposed projects should involve the study of an aspect of classic architecture.

Academic Fields/Career Goals: Architecture; Historic Preservation and Conservation; Landscape Architecture.

Award: Prize for use in sophomore, junior, senior, graduate, or postgraduate years; not renewable. *Number:* 1. *Amount:* $4000.

Eligibility Requirements: Applicant must be enrolled or expecting to enroll full- or part-time at a four-year institution or university and resident of Georgia. Available to U.S. and non-U.S. citizens.

Application Requirements: Application form, essay, portfolio. *Deadline:* February 9.

Contact: Mr. Neale Nickels, Director of Preservation
The Georgia Trust for Historic Preservation
1516 Peachtree Street, NW
Atlanta, GA 30309
Phone: 404-885-7817
E-mail: nnickels@georgiatrust.org

GREAT MINDS IN STEM

http://www.greatmindsinstem.org/college/scholarship-application-information

HENAAC SCHOLARSHIP PROGRAM

• *See page 100*

HOUZZ

http://houzz.com

RESIDENTIAL DESIGN SCHOLARSHIP

Houzz has been connecting homeowners with home industry professionals for years and we are dedicated to supporting and strengthening our growing community. We are looking for residential design students who share our passion. Open to students studying interior design, architecture or landscape architecture at the undergraduate or graduate level who want to pursue residential design professionally.

Academic Fields/Career Goals: Architecture; Interior Design; Landscape Architecture.

Award: Scholarship for use in freshman, sophomore, junior, senior, or graduate years; not renewable. *Number:* 1. *Amount:* $2500.

Eligibility Requirements: Applicant must be age 17 and over; enrolled or expecting to enroll full- or part-time at a two-year or technical institution or university and studying in Alabama, Alaska, Arizona, Arkansas, California, Colorado, Connecticut, Delaware, District of Columbia, Florida, Georgia, Hawaii, Idaho, Illinois, Indiana, Iowa, Kansas, Kentucky, Louisiana, Maine, Maryland, Massachusetts, Michigan, Minnesota, Mississippi, Missouri, Montana, Nebraska, Nevada, New Hampshire, New Jersey, New Mexico, New York, North Carolina, North Dakota, Ohio, Oklahoma, Oregon, Pennsylvania, Puerto Rico, Rhode Island, South Carolina, South Dakota, Tennessee, Texas, Utah, Vermont, Virginia, Washington, West Virginia, Wisconsin, Wyoming. Available to U.S. and non-U.S. citizens.

Application Requirements: Application form, application form may be submitted online, essay. *Deadline:* March 31.

Contact: Emily Hurley, Community Manager
Houzz
285 Hamilton Avenue
Palo Alto, CA 94301
Phone: 800-368-4268
E-mail: scholarships@houzz.com

SUSTAINABLE RESIDENTIAL DESIGN SCHOLARSHIP

Sustainability and green design are part of our core values at Houzz. We want to encourage practices that will reduce negative impacts on the environment by supporting students passionate about green building initiatives. Open to students studying architecture, interior design or landscape architecture at the undergraduate or graduate level who want to pursue sustainable residential design professionally.

Academic Fields/Career Goals: Architecture; Interior Design; Landscape Architecture.

Award: Scholarship for use in freshman, sophomore, junior, senior, or graduate years; not renewable. *Number:* 1. *Amount:* $2500.

Eligibility Requirements: Applicant must be age 17 and over; enrolled or expecting to enroll full- or part-time at a two-year or technical institution or university and studying in Alabama, Alaska, Arizona, Arkansas, California, Colorado, Connecticut, Delaware, District of Columbia, Florida, Georgia, Hawaii, Idaho, Illinois, Indiana, Iowa, Kansas, Kentucky, Louisiana, Maine, Maryland, Massachusetts, Michigan, Minnesota, Mississippi, Missouri, Montana, Nebraska, Nevada, New Hampshire, New Jersey, New Mexico, New York, North Carolina, North Dakota, Ohio, Oklahoma, Oregon, Pennsylvania, Puerto Rico, Rhode Island, South Carolina, South Dakota, Tennessee, Texas, Utah, Vermont, Virginia, Washington, West Virginia, Wisconsin, Wyoming. Available to U.S. and non-U.S. citizens.

Application Requirements: Application form, application form may be submitted online, essay. *Deadline:* March 31.

Contact: Emily Hurley, Community Manager
Houzz
285 Hamilton Avenue
Palo Alto, CA 94301
Phone: 800-368-4268
E-mail: scholarships@houzz.com

WOMEN IN ARCHITECTURE SCHOLARSHIP

Houzz is committed to supporting and encouraging women architecture students as they pursue their educational endeavors and enter the world of residential design. Open to female students studying architecture/architectural engineering at the undergraduate or graduate level.

Academic Fields/Career Goals: Architecture.

Award: Scholarship for use in freshman, sophomore, junior, senior, or graduate years; not renewable. *Number:* 1. *Amount:* $2500.

Eligibility Requirements: Applicant must be enrolled or expecting to enroll full- or part-time at a two-year or technical institution or university; female and studying in Alabama, Alaska, Arizona, Arkansas, California, Colorado, Connecticut, Delaware, District of Columbia, Florida, Georgia, Hawaii, Idaho, Illinois, Indiana, Iowa, Kansas, Kentucky, Louisiana, Maine, Maryland, Massachusetts, Michigan, Minnesota, Mississippi, Missouri, Montana, Nebraska, Nevada, New Hampshire, New Jersey, New Mexico, New York, North Carolina, North Dakota, Ohio, Oklahoma, Oregon, Pennsylvania, Rhode Island, South Carolina, South Dakota, Tennessee, Texas, Utah, Vermont, Virginia, Washington, West Virginia, Wisconsin, Wyoming. Available to U.S. and non-U.S. citizens.

Application Requirements: Application form, application form may be submitted online, essay. *Deadline:* March 31.

Contact: Emily Hurley, Community Manager
Houzz
285 Hamilton Avenue
Palo Alto, CA 94301
Phone: 800-368-4268
E-mail: scholarships@houzz.com

ILLUMINATING ENGINEERING SOCIETY OF NORTH AMERICA

http://www.ies.org/

ROBERT W. THUNEN MEMORIAL SCHOLARSHIPS

One-time award for juniors, seniors, or graduate students enrolled at four-year colleges and universities in northern California, Nevada, Oregon, or Washington pursuing lighting career. Must submit statement describing proposed lighting course work or project and three recommendations, at least one from someone involved professionally or academically with lighting. Curriculum must be accredited by ABET, ACSA, or FIDER.

Academic Fields/Career Goals: Architecture; Engineering-Related Technologies; Engineering/Technology; Interior Design; Performing Arts; TV/Radio Broadcasting.

Award: Scholarship for use in junior, senior, or graduate years; not renewable. *Number:* 2. *Amount:* $2500.

Eligibility Requirements: Applicant must be enrolled or expecting to enroll full-time at a four-year institution or university and studying in California, Nevada, Oregon, Washington. Available to U.S. and non-U.S. citizens.

Application Requirements: Application form, recommendations or references, transcript. *Deadline:* April 1.

Contact: Phil Hall, Chairman
Phone: 510-864-0204
Fax: 510-248-5017
E-mail: mrcatisbac@aol.com

ILLUMINATING ENGINEERING SOCIETY OF NORTH AMERICA–GOLDEN GATE SECTION

http://www.iesgg.org/

ALAN LUCAS MEMORIAL EDUCATIONAL SCHOLARSHIP

Scholarship available to full-time student for pursuit of lighting education or research as part of undergraduate, graduate, or doctoral studies. Scholarships may be made by those who will be a junior, senior, or graduate student in an accredited four-year college or university located in Northern California. The scholarships to be awarded will be at least $1500.

Academic Fields/Career Goals: Architecture; Electrical Engineering/Electronics; Filmmaking/Video; Interior Design.

Award: Scholarship for use in junior, senior, or graduate years; not renewable. *Number:* 1. *Amount:* $1500.

Eligibility Requirements: Applicant must be enrolled or expecting to enroll full-time at a four-year institution or university and studying in California. Available to U.S. citizens.

Application Requirements: Application form, recommendations or references, statement of purpose, description of work in progress, scholar agreement form, transcript. *Deadline:* April 1.

Contact: Phil Hall, Scholarship Committee
Phone: 510-864-0204
Fax: 510-864-8511
E-mail: iesggthunenfund@aol.com

INTERNATIONAL FACILITY MANAGEMENT ASSOCIATION FOUNDATION

http://www.ifmafoundation.org/

IFMA FOUNDATION SCHOLARSHIPS

One-time scholarships of up to $5000 awarded to students currently enrolled in full-time facility management programs or related programs. Minimum 3.2 GPA required for undergraduates and 3.5 for graduate students.

Academic Fields/Career Goals: Architecture; Construction Engineering/Management; Engineering-Related Technologies; Engineering/Technology; Interior Design; Urban and Regional Planning.

Award: Scholarship for use in junior, senior, graduate, or postgraduate years; not renewable. *Number:* 25–35. *Amount:* $1500–$5000.

Eligibility Requirements: Applicant must be enrolled or expecting to enroll full-time at a four-year institution or university. Available to U.S. and non-U.S. citizens.

Application Requirements: Application form. *Deadline:* April 20.

Contact: Amy Arnold, Foundation Administrator
International Facility Management Association Foundation
800 Gessner
Suite 900
Houston, TX 77024
Phone: 713-623-4362
E-mail: amy.arnold@ifma.org

MIDWEST ROOFING CONTRACTORS ASSOCIATION

http://www.mrca.org/

MRCA FOUNDATION SCHOLARSHIP PROGRAM

Renewable scholarships for full-time students enrolled or intending to enroll in an accredited university, college, community college, or trade school. Applicant must be pursuing a curriculum leading to a career in the construction industry or related. Award amount ranges from $500 to $3000.

Academic Fields/Career Goals: Architecture; Civil Engineering; Construction Engineering/Management; Drafting; Engineering/Technology; Industrial Design; Materials Science, Engineering, and Metallurgy; Trade/Technical Specialties.

Award: Scholarship for use in freshman, sophomore, junior, or senior years; not renewable. *Number:* up to 40. *Amount:* $500–$3000.

Eligibility Requirements: Applicant must be enrolled or expecting to enroll full-time at a two-year or four-year or technical institution or university. Applicant or parent of applicant must have employment or volunteer experience in construction. Available to U.S. citizens.

Application Requirements: Application form, community service, essay, financial need analysis, recommendations or references, transcript. *Deadline:* June 20.

Contact: Ms. Peggy Doherty, Operations Manager
Midwest Roofing Contractors Association
4700 West Lake Avenue
Glenview, IL 60025
Phone: 847-375-6378
Fax: 847-375-6473

NATIONAL ASSOCIATION OF WOMEN IN CONSTRUCTION

http://www.nawic.org/

NAWIC UNDERGRADUATE SCHOLARSHIPS

One-time award for any student having at least one year of study remaining in a construction-related program leading to an Associate or higher degree. Awards range from $500 to $2000. Submit application and transcript of grades.

Academic Fields/Career Goals: Architecture; Civil Engineering; Drafting; Electrical Engineering/Electronics; Engineering-Related Technologies; Engineering/Technology; Interior Design; Landscape Architecture; Mechanical Engineering; Trade/Technical Specialties.

Award: Scholarship for use in sophomore or junior years; not renewable. *Number:* 40–50. *Amount:* $500–$2000.

Eligibility Requirements: Applicant must be enrolled or expecting to enroll full-time at a two-year or four-year or technical institution or university. Available to U.S. and Canadian citizens.

Application Requirements: Application form, essay, financial need analysis, interview, transcript. *Deadline:* March 15.

Contact: Scholarship Committee
National Association of Women in Construction
327 South Adams Street
Fort Worth, TX 76104
Phone: 817-877-5551
Fax: 817-877-0324

NEXTSTEPU

http://www.nextstepu.com/

$1,500 STEM SCHOLARSHIP

• See page 104

RHODE ISLAND FOUNDATION

http://www.rifoundation.org/

NORTON E. SALK SCHOLARSHIP

Scholarship for a student enrolled in an accredited school in Rhode Island and pursuing the study of architecture. Must have completed at least one academic year and demonstrate financial need.

Academic Fields/Career Goals: Architecture.

Award: Scholarship for use in sophomore, junior, or senior years; not renewable.

Eligibility Requirements: Applicant must be enrolled or expecting to enroll full-time at a four-year institution or university and studying in Rhode Island. Available to U.S. citizens.

Application Requirements: Application form, essay, financial need analysis, letter of eligibility for financial aid, recommendations or references. *Deadline:* June 15.

Contact: Executive Director, Rhode Island AIA Architectural Forum
Phone: 401-272-6418
E-mail: execdir@aia-ri.org

SCARLETT FAMILY FOUNDATION SCHOLARSHIP PROGRAM

http://www.scarlettfoundation.org/

SCHOLARSHIP FOR STUDENTS PURSUING A BUSINESS OR STEM DEGREE

• See page 80

SUPPORT CREATIVITY

http://wesupportcreativity.org

SUPPORT CREATIVITY SCHOLARSHIP

The Support Creativity Scholarship is for (but not limited to) passionate designers, animators, editors, photographers, artists, illustrators, and painters, who wish to develop their skills at higher education institutions. The student must submit a project that illustrates their passion for their specific creative field in any medium. The student must also submit an essay describing their project as well as any financial hardships.

Academic Fields/Career Goals: Architecture; Art History; Arts; Communications; Culinary Arts; Drafting; Fashion Design; Filmmaking/Video; Graphics/Graphic Arts/Printing; Industrial Design; Interior Design; Landscape Architecture; Marketing; Photojournalism/Photography.

Award: Scholarship for use in freshman, sophomore, junior, senior, or graduate years; not renewable. *Number:* 3. *Amount:* $1000.

Eligibility Requirements: Applicant must be enrolled or expecting to enroll full- or part-time at a two-year or four-year institution or university and studying in Connecticut, New Jersey, New York. Available to U.S. and non-U.S. citizens.

Application Requirements: Application form, essay. *Deadline:* May 1.

Contact: Steve Lucin, Founder
Support Creativity
244 West 54th Street, Suite 800
New York, NY 10019
E-mail: lucin@wesupportcreativity.org

TURNER CONSTRUCTION COMPANY

http://www.turnerconstruction.com/

YOUTHFORCE 2020 SCHOLARSHIP PROGRAM

The scholarship will be awarded to five graduating high school seniors from New York City schools and in the amount of $2000 per year; totaling $8000 after the completion of four years in college. As a scholarship recipient, students must maintain a 2.80 GPA and complete a four-year summer internship at Turner Construction that begins immediately following their first full year of college.

Academic Fields/Career Goals: Architecture; Civil Engineering; Construction Engineering/Management; Electrical Engineering/Electronics; Engineering-Related Technologies; Engineering/Technology; Interior Design; Landscape Architecture; Materials Science, Engineering, and Metallurgy; Mechanical Engineering.

Award: Scholarship for use in freshman, sophomore, junior, or senior years; renewable. *Number:* 5. *Amount:* $8000.

Eligibility Requirements: Applicant must be American Indian/Alaska Native, Asian/Pacific Islander, Black (non-Hispanic), Hispanic; high school student; planning to enroll or expecting to enroll full-time at a four-year institution or university; resident of New York and studying in New York. Available to U.S. citizens.

Application Requirements: Application form, community service, essay, financial need analysis, interview, personal photograph, recommendations or references, resume, test scores, transcript. *Deadline:* April 30.

Contact: Stephanie Burns, Community Affairs Director
Turner Construction Company
375 Hudson Street
6th Floor
New York, NY 10014
Phone: 212-229-6000 Ext. 6480
Fax: 212-229-6083
E-mail: yf2020@tcco.com

VECTORWORKS, INC.

http://www.vectorworks.net

VECTORWORKS DESIGN SCHOLARSHIP

Nemetschek Vectorworks is inviting talented students across all design disciplines to submit their best individual or group work to the Vectorworks Design Scholarship for the chance to win up to $10,000! Additionally, winners' schools receive free Vectorworks design software, as well as free in-person or virtual training for faculty and students. Submissions can be created in any software, and can even be a project previously completed for school. Entering is simple. Answer three short questions by August 31.

Academic Fields/Career Goals: Architecture; Arts; Civil Engineering; Construction Engineering/Management; Drafting; Engineering-Related Technologies; Engineering/Technology; Graphics/Graphic Arts/Printing;

Industrial Design; Interior Design; Landscape Architecture; Urban and Regional Planning.

Award: Scholarship for use in freshman, sophomore, junior, senior, or graduate years; not renewable. *Number:* 15–18. *Amount:* $3000–$10,000.

Eligibility Requirements: Applicant must be enrolled or expecting to enroll full- or part-time at a two-year or four-year or technical institution or university. Available to U.S. and non-U.S. citizens.

Application Requirements: Application form, application form may be submitted online (http://www.vectorworks.net/scholarship/en), CAD or Drawn Design submission, entry in a contest. *Deadline:* August 31.

Contact: Marissa Diehl, Marketing Intern
Vectorworks, Inc.
7150 Riverwood Drive
Columbia, MD 21046
Phone: 443-542-0275 Ext. 275
E-mail: mdiehl97@vectorworks.net

THE WALTER J. TRAVIS SOCIETY

http://www.travissociety.com

THE WALTER J. TRAVIS MEMORIAL SCHOLARSHIP AND THE WALTER J. TRAVIS-RUDY ZOCCHI MEMORIAL SCHOLARSHIP

This scholarship is awarded to students who are pursuing a career in one of the following golf-related professions: golf course architecture, golf course superintendent/turfgrass manager, sports journalism, or professional golf management. Also, any college student who is an outstanding amateur golfer is eligible. Awards based on academic record, extracurricular activities including volunteer service, work experience, and golf-related interests and accomplishments. Award may be used for any educational expenses.

Academic Fields/Career Goals: Architecture; Landscape Architecture; Recreation, Parks, Leisure Studies; Sports-Related/Exercise Science.

Award: Scholarship for use in freshman, sophomore, junior, senior, or graduate years; not renewable. *Number:* 1–5. *Amount:* $1000.

Eligibility Requirements: Applicant must be enrolled or expecting to enroll full-time at a four-year or technical institution or university and must have an interest in athletics/sports or golf. Available to U.S. and non-U.S. citizens.

Application Requirements: Application form, community service, essay. *Deadline:* June 1.

Contact: Mr. Edward Homsey, Scholarship Chairman
The Walter J. Travis Society
24 Sandstone Drive
Rochester, NY 14616
Phone: 585-663-6120
E-mail: TravisSociety@yahoo.com

WEST VIRGINIA SOCIETY OF ARCHITECTS/AIA

http://www.aiawv.org/

AIA WEST VIRGINIA SCHOLARSHIP

Award for a West Virginia resident who has completed at least their sixth semester of an NAAB-accredited undergraduate architectural program or accepted to a NAAB-accredited graduate architectural program by application deadline. Must submit resume and letter stating need, qualifications, and portfolio of work.

Academic Fields/Career Goals: Architecture.

Award: Scholarship for use in junior, senior, graduate, or postgraduate years; not renewable. *Amount:* $3500–$4500.

Eligibility Requirements: Applicant must be enrolled or expecting to enroll full-time at an institution or university and resident of West Virginia. Available to U.S. citizens.

Application Requirements: Application form, portfolio. *Deadline:* October 16.

Contact: William Yoke, Scholarship Committee Chair
West Virginia Society of Architects/AIA
PO Box 813
Charleston, WV 25323
Phone: 304-344-9872
E-mail: aiawv@aiawv.org

AREA/ETHNIC STUDIES

COSTUME SOCIETY OF AMERICA

http://www.costumesocietyamerica.com/

ADELE FILENE STUDENT PRESENTER GRANT

Adele Filene Student Presenter Grants provide financial assistance to students who have been selected to present oral research papers or research exhibits at the CSA National Symposium. These grants of up to $500 award, $100 travel stipend and a day-of-presentation registration fee, funded by the CSA Endowment, are intended to encourage student participation in both the symposium and CSA.

Academic Fields/Career Goals: Area/Ethnic Studies; Art History; Arts; Historic Preservation and Conservation; History; Home Economics; Museum Studies; Performing Arts.

Award: Grant for use in freshman, sophomore, junior, senior, or graduate years; not renewable. *Number:* 2. *Amount:* $500–$600.

Eligibility Requirements: Applicant must be enrolled or expecting to enroll full-time at a two-year or four-year or technical institution or university. Applicant or parent of applicant must be member of Costume Society of America. Available to U.S. and non-U.S. citizens.

Application Requirements: Application form, essay. *Deadline:* October 15.

Contact: Michelle Finamore
E-mail: MFinamore@mfa.org

STELLA BLUM STUDENT RESEARCH GRANT

The Stella Blum Student Research Grant is intended to assist the research of a current undergraduate or graduate student who is a member of the Costume Society of America and conducting original research in the field of North American costume. This $3,000 grant, funded by the CSA Endowment, is awarded annually to provide a student with financial assistance with research. An additional stipend of up to $600 and a day-of-presentation registration fee, also funded by the CSA Endowment, is awarded to allow the recipient to present the completed research at a CSA National Symposium.

Academic Fields/Career Goals: Area/Ethnic Studies; Art History; Arts; Historic Preservation and Conservation; History; Home Economics; Museum Studies; Performing Arts.

Award: Grant for use in freshman, sophomore, junior, senior, or graduate years; not renewable. *Number:* 1. *Amount:* $2000–$3600.

Eligibility Requirements: Applicant must be enrolled or expecting to enroll full- or part-time at a two-year or four-year or technical institution or university. Applicant or parent of applicant must be member of Costume Society of America. Available to U.S. and non-U.S. citizens.

Application Requirements: Application form, essay. *Deadline:* May 1.

Contact: Ann Wass
Costume Society of America
5903 60th Avenue
Riverdale, MD 20737
E-mail: annbwass@aol.com

HUB FOUNDATION

https://hub-foundation.org

HUB FOUNDATION SCHOLARSHIPS
• See page 88

NATIONAL ITALIAN AMERICAN FOUNDATION

http://www.niaf.org/

NATIONAL ITALIAN AMERICAN FOUNDATION CATEGORY II SCHOLARSHIP

Award available to students majoring or minoring in Italian language, Italian Studies, Italian-American Studies or a related field who have outstanding potential and high academic achievements. Minimum 3.5 GPA required. Must be a U.S. citizen and be enrolled in an accredited institution of higher education. Application can only be submitted online.

For further information, deadlines, and online application visit website http://www.niaf.org/scholarships/index.asp.

Academic Fields/Career Goals: Area/Ethnic Studies.

Award: Scholarship for use in freshman, sophomore, junior, senior, or graduate years; not renewable. *Amount:* $2500–$12,000.

Eligibility Requirements: Applicant must be enrolled or expecting to enroll full-time at a two-year or four-year institution or university and must have an interest in Italian language. Available to U.S. citizens.

Application Requirements: Application form, essay, recommendations or references, transcript. *Deadline:* March 6.

Contact: Serena Cantoni, Director, Culture and Education
National Italian American Foundation
The National Italian American Foundation
1860 19th Street, NW
Washington, DC 20009
Phone: 202-939-3107
E-mail: serena@niaf.org

NATIONAL SECURITY EDUCATION PROGRAM

http://www.iie.org/

NATIONAL SECURITY EDUCATION PROGRAM (NSEP) DAVID L. BOREN UNDERGRADUATE SCHOLARSHIPS

The Boren Scholarships provide funding to American undergraduate students for study abroad in regions critical to U.S. national interests. Emphasized world areas include Africa, Asia, Central and Eastern Europe, the NIS, Latin America and the Caribbean, and the Middle East. NSEP scholarship recipients incur a federal service agreement. Must be a U.S. citizen. Program must have a foreign language component.

Academic Fields/Career Goals: Area/Ethnic Studies; Business/Consumer Services; Economics; Engineering-Related Technologies; Environmental Science; Foreign Language; International Studies; Peace and Conflict Studies; Social Sciences.

Award: Scholarship for use in freshman, sophomore, junior, or senior years; not renewable. *Number:* 130–170. *Amount:* $8000–$20,000.

Eligibility Requirements: Applicant must be enrolled or expecting to enroll full- or part-time at a two-year or four-year institution or university. Available to U.S. citizens.

Application Requirements: Application form, essay, financial need analysis. *Deadline:* February 8.

Contact: Boren Awards Program
Phone: 800-618-6737
E-mail: boren@iie.org

SONS OF NORWAY FOUNDATION

http://www.sonsofnorway.com/foundation

KING OLAV V NORWEGIAN-AMERICAN HERITAGE FUND

Scholarship available to American students interested in studying Norwegian heritage or modern Norway, or Norwegian students 18 or older interested in studying North American culture. Selection of applicants is based on a 500-word essay, educational and career goals, community service, work experience, and GPA. Must have minimum 3.0 GPA.

Academic Fields/Career Goals: Area/Ethnic Studies.

Award: Scholarship for use in freshman, sophomore, junior, or senior years; not renewable. *Number:* 4–8. *Amount:* $1000–$1500.

Eligibility Requirements: Applicant must be of Norwegian heritage and Norwegian citizen; age 18-30 and enrolled or expecting to enroll full-time at a two-year or four-year or technical institution or university. Available to U.S. and non-Canadian citizens.

Application Requirements: Application form, application form may be submitted online (http://www.sonsofnorway.com/foundation), community service, essay, recommendations or references, transcript. *Deadline:* March 1.

Contact: Scholarship Coordinator
Sons of Norway Foundation
1455 West Lake Street
Minneapolis, MN 55408-2666
Phone: 612-827-3611
Fax: 612-827-0658

STRAIGHTFORWARD MEDIA

http://www.straightforwardmedia.com/

STRAIGHTFORWARD MEDIA LIBERAL ARTS SCHOLARSHIP

Scholarship of $500 available exclusively to liberal arts students. Awarded four times per year. For more information, see web http://www.straightforwardmedia.com/liberal-arts/form.php.

Academic Fields/Career Goals: Area/Ethnic Studies; Art History; Classics; Economics; Foreign Language; History; Humanities; Literature/English/Writing; Philosophy; Political Science; Psychology; Social Sciences.

Award: Scholarship for use in freshman, sophomore, junior, or senior years; not renewable. *Number:* 4. *Amount:* $500.

Eligibility Requirements: Applicant must be enrolled or expecting to enroll full- or part-time at a two-year or four-year or technical institution or university. Available to U.S. and non-U.S. citizens.

Application Requirements: Essay. *Deadline:* varies.

Contact: Scholarship Committee
Phone: 605-348-3042

WILLIAMS LAW GROUP

https://familylawyersnewjersey.com/

WILLIAMS LAW GROUP OPPORTUNITY TO GROW SCHOLARSHIP

Are you a New Jersey student who will be enrolled in a New Jersey two-year to five-year institution in 2018-2019? Do you need help paying for schooling or supplies? You are not alone. College is not cheap, but we don't want that to stop you from pursuing this irreplaceable experience. At Williams Law Group, we have experienced the benefits of higher education. That is why we are offering a $1500 scholarship to help one New Jersey student go to college, law school, or other institute of higher education. To apply for this scholarship, you must be a New Jersey high school or college student and are enrolled in a two-year to five-year institution in New Jersey in 2018-2019. Additionally, the student must want to pursue their Juris Doctor, a degree in Social Work or a closely related field. The student must be well-rounded and demonstrate a commitment to their school and community. A minimum GPA is not required. To apply, create a short (30-120 second) video and essay, telling us the following things: 1. What does your community mean to you?, and 2. How have you demonstrated a commitment to both your school and larger community? Upload your video to YouTube. Fill out the application, and include a link to your video on YouTube. Applications are due May 11, 2018.

Academic Fields/Career Goals: Area/Ethnic Studies; Behavioral Science; Child and Family Studies; Criminal Justice/Criminology; Law/Legal Services; Political Science; Psychology; Social Sciences; Social Services; Women's Studies.

Award: Scholarship for use in freshman, sophomore, junior, senior, or graduate years; not renewable. *Number:* 1. *Amount:* $1500.

Eligibility Requirements: Applicant must be enrolled or expecting to enroll full- or part-time at a two-year or four-year institution or university; resident of New Jersey and studying in New Jersey. Available to U.S. citizens.

Application Requirements: Application form, essay. *Deadline:* May 11.

Contact: Scholarship Coordinator
Phone: 513-444-2016
E-mail: coordinator@ourscholarship.io

ART HISTORY

CONGRESSIONAL BLACK CAUCUS FOUNDATION, INC.

http://www.cbcfinc.org/

CBC SPOUSES VISUAL ARTS SCHOLARSHIP

This award is for students with majors in the visual arts including, but not limited to, architecture, ceramics, drawing, fashion, graphic design, illustration, interior design, painting, photography, sketching, video production and other decorative arts.

Academic Fields/Career Goals: Art History; Arts; Fashion Design; Filmmaking/Video; Graphics/Graphic Arts/Printing.

Award: Scholarship for use in freshman, sophomore, junior, senior, or graduate years; not renewable. *Number:* 10. *Amount:* $3000.

Eligibility Requirements: Applicant must be Black (non-Hispanic); enrolled or expecting to enroll full-time at a two-year institution or university; studying in Alabama, Alaska, Arizona, Arkansas, California, Colorado, Connecticut, Delaware, District of Columbia, Florida, Georgia, Guam, Hawaii, Idaho, Illinois, Indiana, Iowa, Kansas, Kentucky, Louisiana, Maine, Maryland, Massachusetts, Michigan, Minnesota, Mississippi, Missouri, Montana, Nebraska, Nevada, New Hampshire, New Jersey, New Mexico, New York, North Carolina, North Dakota, Ohio, Oklahoma, Oregon, Pennsylvania, Puerto Rico, Rhode Island, South Carolina, South Dakota, Tennessee, Texas, Utah, Vermont, Virginia, Washington, West Virginia, Wisconsin, Wyoming and must have an interest in art. Applicant or parent of applicant must have employment or volunteer experience in fine arts. Available to U.S. citizens.

Application Requirements: Application form, application form may be submitted online, essay, personal photograph, portfolio. *Deadline:* April 30.

Contact: Ms. Katrina Finch, Program Administrator, Scholarships
Phone: 202-263-2800
E-mail: scholarships@cbcfinc.org

COSTUME SOCIETY OF AMERICA

http://www.costumesocietyamerica.com/

ADELE FILENE STUDENT PRESENTER GRANT
• *See page 118*

STELLA BLUM STUDENT RESEARCH GRANT
• *See page 118*

CULTURAL SERVICES OF THE FRENCH EMBASSY

http://www.frenchculture.org/

TEACHING ASSISTANT PROGRAM IN FRANCE
• *See page 98*

HUB FOUNDATION

https://hub-foundation.org

HUB FOUNDATION SCHOLARSHIPS
• *See page 88*

QUALITY BATH

www.qualitybath.com

QUALITYBATH.COM SCHOLARSHIP PROGRAM

Convey the beauty of humanity, e.g. a good deed you witnessed or envision, in a way that will inspire others. Original, unpublished content only. Submit one of the following: Essay up to 1,500 words; image up to 8.5 x 11, with description; video up to 90 seconds long, in one of the following formats:.mov,.mp4,.m4v,.flv,.3gp,.avi,.wmv. Submissions containing grammatical or spelling errors, or any inappropriate language or content, may be disqualified. Save a digital copy in case we decide to publish your work. Must be a U.S. citizen or permanent resident alien, high school senior or enrolled in accredited U.S. college or university, achieved minimum cumulative GPA of 3.0, currently pursuing a degree in the arts or design field. Applicant must not have a professional or familial relation with QualityBath.com and its management. Email to scholarships@qualitybath.com or mail to Scholarship Contest, c/o Quality Bath, 1144 East County Line Road, Unit 200, Lakewood, NJ 08701. Include submission; copy of transcript; your name, email address, phone number; degree you are pursuing; proof of citizenship/alien status. Deadline: March 1, 2017.

Academic Fields/Career Goals: Art History; Arts; Fashion Design; Filmmaking/Video; Graphics/Graphic Arts/Printing; Interior Design; Landscape Architecture; Music; Performing Arts; Photojournalism/Photography.

Award: Prize for use in freshman, sophomore, junior, senior, or graduate years; not renewable. *Number:* 1. *Amount:* $1500.

Eligibility Requirements: Applicant must be enrolled or expecting to enroll full- or part-time at a two-year or four-year or technical institution or university. Available to U.S. citizens.

Application Requirements: Application form. *Deadline:* April 9.

Contact: Fay Friedman, Director of SEO/Marketing
Quality Bath
1144 East County Line Road
Lakewood, NJ 08701
Phone: 800-554-3210
E-mail: scholarships@qualitybath.com

STRAIGHTFORWARD MEDIA

http://www.straightforwardmedia.com/

STRAIGHTFORWARD MEDIA LIBERAL ARTS SCHOLARSHIP
• *See page 119*

SUPPORT CREATIVITY

http://wesupportcreativity.org

SUPPORT CREATIVITY SCHOLARSHIP
• *See page 117*

ARTS

AMERICAN INSTITUTE OF POLISH CULTURE INC.

http://www.ampolinstitute.org/

HARRIET IRSAY SCHOLARSHIP GRANT

Merit-based $1000 scholarships for students studying communications, public relations, and/or journalism. All U.S. citizens may apply, but preference will be given to U.S. citizens of Polish heritage. Must submit three letters of recommendation on appropriate letterhead with application mailed directly to AIPC. For study in the United States only. Non-refundable fee of $10 will be collected.

Academic Fields/Career Goals: Arts; Communications; Education; Foreign Language; Journalism; Public Policy and Administration.

Award: Scholarship for use in freshman, sophomore, junior, senior, or graduate years; not renewable. *Number:* 10–15. *Amount:* $1000.

Eligibility Requirements: Applicant must be enrolled or expecting to enroll full-time at a two-year or four-year institution or university. Available to U.S. citizens.

Application Requirements: Application form, recommendations or references, resume, self-addressed stamped envelope with application, transcript. *Fee:* $10. *Deadline:* April 20.

Contact: Scholarship Committee
Phone: 305-864-2349
Fax: 305-865-5150
E-mail: info@ampolinstitute.org

BULKOFFICESUPPLY.COM

http://www.bulkofficesupply.com

OFFICE SUPPLY SCHOLARSHIP

If you have an interest in teaching, art or owning your own business you are eligible to apply for our scholarship program. The program is open to all high school students as well as College Freshmen and Sophomores.

Academic Fields/Career Goals: Arts; Business/Consumer Services; Education.

Award: Scholarship for use in freshman or sophomore years; not renewable. *Number:* 1. *Amount:* $1000.

Eligibility Requirements: Applicant must be enrolled or expecting to enroll full- or part-time at a two-year or four-year or technical institution or university. Available to U.S. and non-U.S. citizens.

Application Requirements: Application form may be submitted online(www.bulkofficesupply.com/scholarships-in-new-york), entry in a contest, essay. *Deadline:* February 1.

Contact: Mr. Harrison Blackhurst, Online Marketing Manager
BulkOfficeSupply.com
1614 Hereford Road
Hewlett, NY 11557
Phone: 800-658 -1488
E-mail: webteam.bulkofficesupply@gmail.com

CONGRESSIONAL BLACK CAUCUS FOUNDATION, INC.

http://www.cbcfinc.org/

CBC SPOUSES VISUAL ARTS SCHOLARSHIP
• See page 120

COSTUME SOCIETY OF AMERICA

http://www.costumesocietyamerica.com/

ADELE FILENE STUDENT PRESENTER GRANT
• See page 118

STELLA BLUM STUDENT RESEARCH GRANT
• See page 118

GOLDEN KEY INTERNATIONAL HONOUR SOCIETY

http://www.goldenkey.org/

VISUAL AND PERFORMING ARTS ACHIEVEMENT AWARDS

Award of $500 will be given to winners in each of the following nine categories: painting, drawing, photography, sculpture, computer-generated art/graphic design/illustration, mixed media, instrumental performance, vocal performance, and dance.

Academic Fields/Career Goals: Arts; Graphics/Graphic Arts/Printing.

Award: Prize for use in freshman, sophomore, junior, senior, graduate, or postgraduate years; not renewable. *Number:* 9. *Amount:* $500.

Eligibility Requirements: Applicant must be enrolled or expecting to enroll full- or part-time at a four-year institution or university and must have an interest in art. Available to U.S. and non-U.S. citizens.

Application Requirements: Application form, artwork, cover letter, entry in a contest. *Deadline:* April 1.

Contact: Scholarship Program Administrators
Golden Key International Honour Society
PO Box 23737
Nashville, TN 37202
Phone: 800-377-2401

GRAND RAPIDS COMMUNITY FOUNDATION

http://www.grfoundation.org/

ARTS COUNCIL OF GREATER GRAND RAPIDS MINORITY SCHOLARSHIP

Scholarship is for students of color (African American, Asian, Hispanic, Native American, Pacific Islander) attending a non-profit public or private college/university majoring in Fine Arts including all visual and performing art forms. Must have financial need, be a Kent County resident, and have a minimum 2.5 GPA.

Academic Fields/Career Goals: Arts; Performing Arts.

Award: Scholarship for use in freshman, sophomore, junior, or senior years; not renewable. *Number:* 2. *Amount:* $5000.

Eligibility Requirements: Applicant must be American Indian/Alaska Native, Asian/Pacific Islander, Black (non-Hispanic), Hispanic; enrolled or expecting to enroll full-time at a two-year institution or university; resident of Massachusetts; studying in Michigan and must have an interest in art, photography/photogrammetry/filmmaking, or theater. Available to U.S. citizens.

Application Requirements: Application form, application form may be submitted online, essay, financial need analysis. *Deadline:* April 1.

Contact: Ms. Ruth Bishop, Education Program Officer
Grand Rapids Community Foundation
185 Oakes Street SW
Grand Rapids, MI 49503
Phone: 616-454-1751 Ext. 103
E-mail: rbishop@grfoundation.org

HEMOPHILIA FOUNDATION OF SOUTHERN CALIFORNIA

http://www.hemosocal.org/

DR. EARL JAMES FAHRINGER PERFORMING ARTS SCHOLARSHIP

Due to the extreme generosity of the late Dr. Earl James Fahringer, the Hemophilia Foundation of Southern California is thrilled to have a scholarship fund known as the Dr. Earl James Fahringer Performing Arts Scholarship, which will be awarded each year to 1-2 students pursuing a major in music, arts, drama, or dance. Dr. Fahringer was a lifelong musician, and music educator in the Pomona School District and served as a violinist, violist, percussionist, Assistant Conductor, Music Director, and Co-Conductor of the Claremont Symphony Orchestra. We hope to provide the means for young musicians and artists to pursue their education through this scholarship.

Academic Fields/Career Goals: Arts; Filmmaking/Video; Music; Performing Arts.

Award: Scholarship for use in freshman, sophomore, junior, senior, graduate, or postgraduate years; not renewable. *Number:* 1–5. *Amount:* $500–$1000.

Eligibility Requirements: Applicant must be enrolled or expecting to enroll full- or part-time at a two-year or four-year or technical institution or university; resident of California and studying in California. Applicant must be physically disabled. Available to U.S. citizens.

Application Requirements: Application form, essay. *Deadline:* June 28.

Contact: Laura Desai, Operations Manager
Hemophilia Foundation of Southern California
959 East Walnut Street, Suite 114
Pasadena, CA 91106
Phone: 626-765-6656
Fax: 626-765-6657
E-mail: info@hemosocal.org

NATIONAL OPERA ASSOCIATION

http://www.noa.org/

NOA VOCAL COMPETITION/LEGACY AWARD PROGRAM

Awards granted based on competitive audition to support study and career development. Singers compete in Scholarship and Artist Division. Legacy Awards are granted for study and career development in any opera-related career to those who further NOA's goal of increased minority participation in the profession.

Academic Fields/Career Goals: Arts; Performing Arts.

Award: Prize for use in freshman, sophomore, junior, senior, graduate, or postgraduate years; not renewable. *Number:* 3–8. *Amount:* $500–$2000.

Eligibility Requirements: Applicant must be age 18-24; enrolled or expecting to enroll full- or part-time at a two-year or four-year or technical institution or university and must have an interest in music or music/singing. Available to U.S. and non-U.S. citizens.

Application Requirements: Application form, audition tape/proposal, driver's license, entry in a contest, personal photograph, recommendations or references. *Fee:* $25. *Deadline:* October 15.

Contact: Robert Hansen, Executive Secretary
National Opera Association
2403 Russell Long Boulevard, PO Box 60869
Canyon, TX 79016-0001
Phone: 806-651-2857
Fax: 806-651-2958
E-mail: hansen@mail.wtamu.edu

ONLINE LOGO MAKER

http://onlinelogomaker.com

OLM MALALA YOUSAFZAI SCHOLARSHIP 2017-2018

Online Logo Maker is proud to announce its own Scholarship named after the great activist from the actual time: Malala Yousafzai, known for fighting for education. And from now on, we are going to provide an annual scholarship for minorities as an act for education. Acknowledging the difficulty that women face on a sexist society, the 2017–2018 scholarship will provide a $1000 scholarship to a woman. All women, from all over the world, who has 30 years old or more and want the opportunity to go back to school to start or continue interrupted studies in the Arts and Design field can apply. The OLM Malala Yousafzai Scholarship 2017–2018 application requires a 500–1000 words essay written in English about a challenge you have faced and how you overcame it. Fill out the online form including your essay and good luck! For more info, see website http://www.onlinelogomaker.com/scholarships-for-women

Academic Fields/Career Goals: Arts; Drafting; Industrial Design; Interior Design; Performing Arts.

Award: Scholarship for use in freshman, sophomore, junior, senior, graduate, or postgraduate years; not renewable. *Number:* 1. *Amount:* $1000.

Eligibility Requirements: Applicant must be Baha'i faith, Baptist, Brethren, Buddhist faith, Christian, Disciple of Christ, Eastern Orthodox, Episcopalian, Friends, Hindu faith, Jewish, Latter-day Saints, Lutheran, Methodist, Muslim faith, Pentecostal, Presbyterian, Protestant, Roman Catholic, Seventh-Day Adventist, Unitarian Universalist; of African, Albanian, Arab, Armenian, Arumanian/Ulacedo-Romanian, Australian, Belgian, Bulgarian, Canadian, Central European, Chinese, Croatian/Serbian, Cypriot, Danish, Dutch, Eastern European, English, European Union, Finnish, former Soviet Union, French, German, Greek, Haitian, Hispanic, Hungarian, Icelandic, Indian, Irish, Israeli, Italian, Japanese, Jewish, Korean, Lao/Hmong, Latin American/Caribbean, Latvian, Lebanese, Lithuanian, Mexican, Mongolian, New Zealander, Nicaraguan, Norwegian, Polish, Portuguese, Rumanian, Russian, Scandinavian, Scottish, Slavic/Czech, Spanish, Sub-Saharan African, Swedish, Swiss, Syrian, Turkish, Ukrainian, Vietnamese, Welsh, Yemeni heritage and African, Albanian, Arab, Armenian, Arumanian/Ulacedo-Romanian, Australian, Belgian, Bulgarian, Canadian, Central European, Chinese, Croatian/Serbian, Cypriot, Danish, Dutch, Eastern European, English, European Union, Finnish, former Soviet Union, French, German, Greek, Haitian, Hispanic, Hungarian, Icelandic, Indian, Irish, Israeli, Italian, Japanese, Jewish, Korean, Lao/Hmong, Latin American/Caribbean, Latvian, Lebanese, Lithuanian, Mexican, Mongolian, New Zealander, Nicaraguan, Norwegian, Polish, Portuguese, Rumanian, Russian, Scandinavian, Scottish, Slavic/Czech, Spanish, Sub-Saharan African, Swedish, Swiss, Syrian, Turkish, Ukrainian, Vietnamese, Welsh, Yemeni citizen; American Indian/Alaska Native, Asian/Pacific Islander, Black (non-Hispanic); age 30-70; enrolled or expecting to enroll full- or part-time at a two-year or four-year or technical institution or university and female. Available to U.S. and non-U.S. citizens.

Application Requirements: Application form, essay. *Deadline:* December 1.

Contact: OLM Malala Yousafzai Scholarship
E-mail: scholarship@onlinelogomaker.com

POLISH ARTS CLUB OF BUFFALO SCHOLARSHIP FOUNDATION

http://www.pacb.bfn.org/

POLISH ARTS CLUB OF BUFFALO SCHOLARSHIP FOUNDATION TRUST

Provides educational scholarships to students of Polish background who are legal residents of New York. Must be enrolled at the junior level or above in an accredited college or university in NY during the upcoming year of application. Must be a U.S. citizen. For application and additional information, visit website http://www.pacb.bfn.org.

Academic Fields/Career Goals: Arts; Communications; Filmmaking/Video; Music; Performing Arts; TV/Radio Broadcasting.

Award: Scholarship for use in junior, senior, graduate, or postgraduate years; not renewable. *Number:* 1–3. *Amount:* $1000.

Eligibility Requirements: Applicant must be of Polish heritage; enrolled or expecting to enroll full- or part-time at a four-year institution or university and resident of New York. Available to U.S. citizens.

Application Requirements: Application form, essay, interview, portfolio. *Deadline:* April 14.

Contact: Anne Flansburg, Selection Chair
Polish Arts Club of Buffalo Scholarship Foundation
24 Amherston Drive
Williamsville, NY 14221-7002
Phone: 716-863-3631
E-mail: anneflanswz@aol.com

QUALITY BATH

www.qualitybath.com

QUALITYBATH.COM SCHOLARSHIP PROGRAM
• *See page 120*

RHODE ISLAND FOUNDATION

http://www.rifoundation.org/

PATRICIA W. EDWARDS MEMORIAL ART SCHOLARSHIP

Award to further education of young Rhode Island artists (such as art lessons for high school students in two-dimensional art) and/or scholarships for Rhode Island art students (freshmen, sophomores, and juniors) at Rhode Island institutions.

Academic Fields/Career Goals: Arts.

Award: Scholarship for use in freshman year; not renewable. *Amount:* up to $425.

Eligibility Requirements: Applicant must be high school student; planning to enroll or expecting to enroll full- or part-time at a two-year or four-year institution or university; resident of Rhode Island and studying in Rhode Island. Available to U.S. citizens.

Application Requirements: Application form. *Deadline:* March 4.

Contact: Kelly Riley, Donor Services Administrator
Phone: 401-427-4028
E-mail: kriley@rifoundation.org

ROBERT H. MOLLOHAN FAMILY CHARITABLE FOUNDATION, INC.

http://www.mollohanfoundation.org/

MARY OLIVE EDDY JONES ART SCHOLARSHIP

The Mary Olive Eddy Jones Art Scholarship is a $1,000 scholarship offered to a sophomore or junior student in attendance at a college or University in West Virginia who is currently majoring in an art-related field.

Academic Fields/Career Goals: Arts; Graphics/Graphic Arts/Printing.

Award: Scholarship for use in sophomore or junior years; not renewable. *Number:* 1–3. *Amount:* $1000.

Eligibility Requirements: Applicant must be enrolled or expecting to enroll full- or part-time at an institution or university; resident of Washington and studying in West Virginia. Available to U.S. citizens.

Application Requirements: Application form, essay, portfolio. *Deadline:* March 31.

SERVICE EMPLOYEES INTERNATIONAL UNION (SEIU)

http://www.seiu.org/

SEIU MOE FONER SCHOLARSHIP PROGRAM FOR VISUAL AND PERFORMING ARTS

Scholarship for students pursuing a degree or training full-time in the visual or performing arts. Scholarship funding must be applied to tuition at a two- or four-year college, university, or an accredited community college, technical or trade school in an arts-related field.

Academic Fields/Career Goals: Arts; Performing Arts.

Award: Scholarship for use in freshman, sophomore, junior, or senior years; not renewable. *Number:* 1. *Amount:* $5000.

Eligibility Requirements: Applicant must be enrolled or expecting to enroll full-time at a two-year or four-year or technical institution or university. Applicant or parent of applicant must be member of Service Employees International Union. Available to U.S. citizens.

Application Requirements: 6 copies of a single original creative work, application form, essay, transcript. *Deadline:* March 1.

Contact: c/o Scholarship Program Administrators, Inc.
　　　Phone: 615-320-3149
　　　Fax: 615-320-3151
　　　E-mail: info@spaprog.com

SOCIETY FOR CLASSICAL STUDIES

http://www.classicalstudies.org/

MINORITY STUDENT SUMMER SCHOLARSHIP
• See page 112

SOUTHEASTERN THEATRE CONFERENCE

http://www.setc.org

POLLY HOLLIDAY SCHOLARSHIP

The Polly Holliday Scholarship is awarded each year to a qualified High School Senior planning to major in Theatre Arts at an accredited college or university within the 10 SETC regional states (Alabama, Florida, Georgia, Kentucky, Mississippi, North Carolina, South Carolina, Tennessee, Virginia, West Virginia). All applicants must reside in the SETC region as well as attend college there. Applicant criteria for the Polly Holliday Award is based on financial need, talent, and the potential for academic success in college. https://www.setc.org/scholarships-awards/undergraduate-studies/polly-holliday-award/

Academic Fields/Career Goals: Arts; Performing Arts.

Award: Scholarship for use in freshman year; not renewable. *Number:* 1. *Amount:* $1000.

Eligibility Requirements: Applicant must be high school student; planning to enroll or expecting to enroll full-time at a two-year or four-year or technical institution or university; resident of Alabama, Florida, Georgia, Kentucky, Mississippi, North Carolina, South Carolina, Tennessee, Virginia, West Virginia; studying in Alabama, Florida, Georgia, Kentucky, Mississippi, North Carolina, South Carolina, Tennessee, Virginia, West Virginia and must have an interest in theater. Available to U.S. citizens.

Application Requirements: Application form. *Deadline:* April 1.

Contact: Claire Wisniewski, Educational Services Manager
　　　Phone: 336-272-3645
　　　E-mail: info@setc.org

STRAIGHTFORWARD MEDIA

http://www.straightforwardmedia.com/

STRAIGHTFORWARD MEDIA ART SCHOOL SCHOLARSHIP

Award of $500 for students pursuing a degree in any art-related field. May be used for full- or part-time study. Scholarship is awarded four times per year. Deadlines: November 30, February 28, May 31, and August 31. For more information, visit website http://www.straightforwardmedia.com/art/form.php.

Academic Fields/Career Goals: Arts.

Award: Scholarship for use in freshman, sophomore, junior, or senior years; not renewable. *Number:* 4. *Amount:* $500.

Eligibility Requirements: Applicant must be enrolled or expecting to enroll full- or part-time at a two-year or four-year or technical institution or university. Available to U.S. and non-U.S. citizens.

Application Requirements: Essay. *Deadline:* varies.

Contact: Scholarship Committee
　　　Phone: 605-348-3042

SUPPORT CREATIVITY

http://wesupportcreativity.org

SUPPORT CREATIVITY SCHOLARSHIP
• See page 117

TELETOON

http://www.teletoon.com/

TELETOON ANIMATION SCHOLARSHIP

Scholarship competition created by TELETOON to encourage creative, original, and imaginative animation by supporting Canadians studying in the animation field or intending to pursue studies in animation. One-time award. Must submit portfolio.

Academic Fields/Career Goals: Arts; Filmmaking/Video.

Award: Scholarship for use in freshman, sophomore, junior, senior, graduate, or postgraduate years; not renewable. *Number:* 9. *Amount:* $5000–$10,000.

Eligibility Requirements: Applicant must be enrolled or expecting to enroll full-time at a two-year or four-year or technical institution or university and resident of Alberta, British Columbia, Manitoba, New Brunswick, Newfoundland, Northwest Territories, Nova Scotia, Ontario, Prince Edward Island, Quebec, Saskatchewan. Available to Canadian citizens.

Application Requirements: 5-minute film, application form, driver's license, essay, portfolio, transcript. *Deadline:* June 15.

Contact: Denise Vaughan, Senior Coordinator, Public Relations
　　　Phone: 416-956-2060
　　　Fax: 416-956-2070
　　　E-mail: denisev@teletoon.com

TOMBOW

https://www.tombowusa.com/

TOMBOW'S CREATE YOUR BEST WORK ART SCHOLARSHIP

At Tombow, we know that it takes the best products to create your best work -- and we want to help equip young artists with the tools to flourish in their industry. We are proud to announce the Create Your Best Work Art Scholarship to aid three promising art students with tuition costs. Tombow's Create Your Best Work Art Scholarship is available to high school seniors (graduating by May 2019) and college freshman and sophomore students. Employees of American Tombow Inc., as well as immediate family and household members of each such employee, are not eligible. Members of Tombow's Design Team and Brand Ambassador Program are also not eligible. Find out more information and download an application at TombowUSA.com.

Academic Fields/Career Goals: Arts.

Award: Scholarship for use in freshman or sophomore years; not renewable. *Number:* 3. *Amount:* $2500–$5000.

Eligibility Requirements: Applicant must be enrolled or expecting to enroll full-time at a two-year or four-year or technical institution or university and resident of Alabama, Alaska, Arizona, Arkansas, California, Colorado, Connecticut, Delaware, District of Columbia, Florida, Georgia, Hawaii, Idaho, Illinois, Indiana, Iowa, Kansas, Kentucky, Louisiana, Maine, Maryland, Massachusetts, Michigan, Minnesota, Mississippi, Missouri, Montana, Nebraska, Nevada, New Brunswick, New Hampshire, New Jersey, New Mexico, New York, North Carolina, North Dakota, Ohio, Oklahoma, Oregon, Pennsylvania, Puerto Rico, Rhode Island, South Carolina, South Dakota, Tennessee, Texas, Utah, Vermont, Virginia, Virgin Islands, Washington, West Virginia, Wisconsin, Wyoming. Available to U.S. citizens.

Application Requirements: Application form, application form may be submitted online (https://www.tombowusa.com/art-scholarship), Artist's Statement, portfolio, transcript. *Deadline:* March 31.

Contact: Marketing Department
Tombow
355 Satellite Blvd NE
Suite 300
Suwanee, GA 30024
Phone: 800-835-3232
E-mail: marketing@tombowusa.com

UNITARIAN UNIVERSALIST ASSOCIATION
http://www.uua.org/

STANFIELD AND D'ORLANDO ART SCHOLARSHIP
Scholarships for both Master's and undergraduate Unitarian Universalist students studying the fields of art and law.

Academic Fields/Career Goals: Arts; Law/Legal Services.

Award: Scholarship for use in freshman, sophomore, junior, senior, or graduate years; not renewable.

Eligibility Requirements: Applicant must be Unitarian Universalist and enrolled or expecting to enroll full- or part-time at a four-year institution or university. Available to U.S. citizens.

Application Requirements: Application form. *Deadline:* February 15.

Contact: Ms. Hillary Goodridge, Program Director
Phone: 617-971-9600
Fax: 617-971-0029
E-mail: uufp@aol.com

UNITED NEGRO COLLEGE FUND
http://www.uncf.org/

THE OSSIE DAVIS LEGACY AWARD SCHOLARSHIP
• *See page 89*

VECTORWORKS, INC.
http://www.vectorworks.net

VECTORWORKS DESIGN SCHOLARSHIP
• *See page 117*

WARNER BROS. ENTERTAINMENT
http://www.warnerbros.com/

WARNER BROS. ANIMATION/HANNA-BARBERA HONORSHIP
The Honorship will be awarded annually to a graduating high school senior enrolling in a college, university, or trade school to study animation. Applicants must have (1) a passion and talent for a career in animation; (2) a minimum GPA of 3.0 upon graduation; and (3) demonstrate financial need. Each cash scholarship will be for $10,000, disbursed annually in equal amounts over the course of enrollment. In addition, the winner will have the opportunity to receive (4) consecutive, paid summer internships at Warner Bros. Studios in Burbank while at university.

Academic Fields/Career Goals: Arts.

Award: Scholarship for use in freshman, sophomore, junior, or senior years; renewable. *Number:* 1. *Amount:* $10,000.

Eligibility Requirements: Applicant must be high school student and planning to enroll or expecting to enroll full- or part-time at a four-year or technical institution or university. Available to U.S. citizens.

Application Requirements: *Deadline:* March 1.

WOMEN'S JEWELRY ASSOCIATION
http://www.womensjewelryassociation.com

WOMEN'S JEWELRY ASSOCIATION STUDENT SCHOLARSHIP
This is a student scholarship for a woman studying in the jewelry, gem and watch fields.

Academic Fields/Career Goals: Arts; Trade/Technical Specialties.

Award: Scholarship for use in freshman, sophomore, junior, senior, graduate, or postgraduate years; renewable. *Number:* 5–12. *Amount:* $500–$7000.

Eligibility Requirements: Applicant must be enrolled or expecting to enroll full-time at a two-year or four-year or technical institution or university; female and must have an interest in art. Applicant or parent of applicant must have employment or volunteer experience in fine arts. Available to U.S. and non-U.S. citizens.

Application Requirements: Application form, essay, personal photograph, portfolio. *Fee:* $10. *Deadline:* April 1.

Contact: Jenny Calleri
E-mail: Jennyo@tbirdjewels.com

ASIAN STUDIES

HUB FOUNDATION
https://hub-foundation.org

HUB FOUNDATION SCHOLARSHIPS
• *See page 88*

UNITED NATIONS ASSOCIATION OF CONNECTICUT
http://www.unausa.org

UNITED NATIONS ASSOCIATION OF CONNECTICUT SCHOLARSHIP
Scholarship to encourage and support students with a demonstrated interest in promoting world peace through work in international relations and diplomatic service to cultivate an understanding of and support for the work of the UN in the United States. At least one award of $1000 will be made in the Spring of each year to assist the selected student with his or her college expenses. Applicants must be graduating seniors of a public high school in Connecticut. The scholarship is based on demonstrated academic excellence, evidence of engagement in international issues, progress in developing proficiency in a foreign language, commitment to social advancement as documented through community service or related activities, and participation in a Model UN or similar intercultural program. The e-mail application (postmarked not later than March 31) must be sent to UNACT.studentfund@gmail.com.

Academic Fields/Career Goals: Asian Studies; Foreign Language; Health and Medical Sciences; International Migration; International Studies; Natural Sciences; Near and Middle East Studies; Nuclear Science; Peace and Conflict Studies; Political Science; Women's Studies.

Award: Scholarship for use in freshman year; not renewable. *Number:* 1–3. *Amount:* $1000.

Eligibility Requirements: Applicant must be high school student; planning to enroll or expecting to enroll full-time at a two-year or four-year institution or university and resident of Connecticut. Available to U.S. and non-U.S. citizens.

Application Requirements: Application form, essay. *Deadline:* March 31.

Contact: Ms. Barbara Bacewicz
Phone: 860-9274333
E-mail: jjbaxer@icloud.com

AUDIOLOGY

101ST AIRBORNE DIVISION ASSOCIATION

http://www.screamingeaglefoundation.org/

AL & WILLIAMARY VISTE SCHOLARSHIP
• *See page 99*

AMERICAN LEGION AUXILIARY DEPARTMENT OF COLORADO

http://www.alacolorado.com

AMERICAN LEGION AUXILIARY DEPARTMENT OF COLORADO PAST PRESIDENTS' PARLEY HEALTH CARE PROFESSIONAL SCHOLARSHIPNURSES SCHOLARSHIP

Open to children, spouses, grandchildren, and great-grandchildren of American Legion veterans, and veterans who served in the armed forces during eligibility dates for membership in the American Legion. Must be Colorado residents who have been accepted by an accredited health care professional school in Colorado.

Academic Fields/Career Goals: Audiology; Dental Health/Services; Health Administration; Health and Medical Sciences; Health Information Management/Technology; Nursing; Oncology; Optometry; Osteopathy; Pharmacy; Therapy/Rehabilitation.

Award: Scholarship for use in freshman, sophomore, junior, senior, or graduate years; not renewable. *Number:* 3–5. *Amount:* $500–$1500.

Eligibility Requirements: Applicant must be enrolled or expecting to enroll full- or part-time at a two-year or four-year institution or university; resident of Colorado and studying in Colorado. Available to U.S. citizens.

Application Requirements: Application form, essay, financial need analysis. *Deadline:* March 15.

Contact: Rhonda Larkowski, Department Secretary and Treasurer
American Legion Auxiliary Department of Colorado
7465 East First Avenue, Suite D
Denver, CO 80230
Phone: 303-367-5388
E-mail: www.dept-sec@alacolorado.com

GREAT MINDS IN STEM

http://www.greatmindsinstem.org/college/scholarship-application-information

HENAAC SCHOLARSHIP PROGRAM
• *See page 100*

HOUSE OF BLUES MUSIC FORWARD FOUNDATION

https://hobmusicforward.org/

TIFFANY GREEN OPERATOR SCHOLARSHIP AWARD
• *See page 85*

INTERMOUNTAIN MEDICAL IMAGING

https://www.aboutimi.com/

INTERMOUNTAIN MEDICAL IMAGING SCHOLARSHIP

Intermountain Medical Imaging (IMI) provides outpatient radiology services such as x-ray, computed tomography (CT), magnetic resonance imaging (MRI), ultrasound, and interventional radiology procedures that are competitively priced and generally far less expensive than the average hospital price. Providing excellence in both quality and experience, with locations in Boise, Meridian, and Eagle Idaho.

Academic Fields/Career Goals: Audiology; Behavioral Science; Dental Health/Services; Health Administration; Health and Medical Sciences; Health Information Management/Technology; Neurobiology; Occupational Safety and Health; Oncology; Optometry; Osteopathy; Psychology; Public Health; Therapy/Rehabilitation.

Award: Scholarship for use in freshman year; not renewable. *Number:* 1. *Amount:* $1000.

Eligibility Requirements: Applicant must be enrolled or expecting to enroll full-time at a four-year institution or university and resident of Idaho. Available to U.S. citizens.

Application Requirements: Essay. *Deadline:* April 30.

Contact: Rachel Bergmann
E-mail: community@aboutimi.com

MEDICAL SCRUBS COLLECTION

http://medicalscrubscollection.com

MEDICAL SCRUBS COLLECTION SCHOLARSHIP
• *See page 104*

NEW YORK STATE GRANGE

http://www.nysgrange.org/

CAROLINE KARK AWARD

Award available to a Grange member who is preparing for a career working with the deaf, or a deaf individual who is furthering his or her education beyond high school. The recipient must be a New York State resident. The award is based on funds available.

Academic Fields/Career Goals: Audiology.

Award: Scholarship for use in freshman year; not renewable. *Number:* 1.

Eligibility Requirements: Applicant must be high school student; planning to enroll or expecting to enroll full- or part-time at a four-year institution or university and resident of New York. Applicant or parent of applicant must be member of Grange Association. Applicant must be hearing impaired. Available to U.S. citizens.

Application Requirements: Application form. *Deadline:* April 15.

Contact: Program Manager
New York State Grange
100 Grange Place
Cortland, NY 13045
Phone: 607-756-7553
E-mail: nysgrange@nysgrange.com

NOVUS BIOLOGICALS, LLC

https://www.novusbio.com

R&D SYSTEMS SCHOLARSHIP
• *See page 101*

TOCRIS BIOSCIENCE SCHOLARSHIP
• *See page 102*

SCARLETT FAMILY FOUNDATION SCHOLARSHIP PROGRAM

http://www.scarlettfoundation.org/

SCHOLARSHIP FOR STUDENTS PURSUING A BUSINESS OR STEM DEGREE
• *See page 80*

AVIATION/AEROSPACE

AACE INTERNATIONAL

http://www.aacei.org/

AACE INTERNATIONAL COMPETITIVE SCHOLARSHIP
• *See page 112*

AHS INTERNATIONAL—THE VERTICAL FLIGHT TECHNICAL SOCIETY

http://www.vtol.org/

VERTICAL FLIGHT FOUNDATION SCHOLARSHIP

This award is available for undergraduate (must be at least a second semester freshman), graduate, or doctoral study in aerospace, electrical, or mechanical engineering. Applicants must demonstrate an interest in vertical flight technology through contribution to the vertical flight technical community such as technical papers presented at technical meetings, submission to technical journals, participating in aerospace engineering design competitions, etc. All students must attend for the entire year following acceptance of the scholarship.

Academic Fields/Career Goals: Aviation/Aerospace; Electrical Engineering/Electronics; Engineering-Related Technologies; Engineering/Technology; Mechanical Engineering.

Award: Scholarship for use in sophomore, junior, senior, graduate, or postgraduate years; not renewable. *Number:* 10–19. *Amount:* $1500–$5000.

Eligibility Requirements: Applicant must be enrolled or expecting to enroll full-time at a four-year institution or university and must have an interest in aviation. Available to U.S. and non-U.S. citizens.

Application Requirements: Application form, essay, recommendations or references, resume, transcript. *Deadline:* February 1.

Contact: Ms. Holly Cafferelli, VFF Scholarship Coordinator
AHS International—The Vertical Flight Technical Society
217 North Washington Street
Alexandria, VA 22314
Phone: 703-684-6777 Ext. 100
Fax: 703-739-9279
E-mail: hcafferelli@vtol.org

AIRCRAFT ELECTRONICS ASSOCIATION EDUCATIONAL FOUNDATION

http://www.aea.net/

L-3 AVIONICS SYSTEMS SCHOLARSHIP

Scholarship of $2500 available to high school seniors and college students who plan to attend or are attending an avionics or aircraft repair program in an accredited school. Minimum 2.5 GPA required.

Academic Fields/Career Goals: Aviation/Aerospace.

Award: Scholarship for use in freshman, sophomore, junior, or senior years; not renewable. *Number:* 1. *Amount:* $2500.

Eligibility Requirements: Applicant must be enrolled or expecting to enroll full- or part-time at a two-year or four-year or technical institution or university. Available to U.S. citizens.

Application Requirements: Application form, essay, transcript. *Deadline:* February 15.

Contact: Geoff Hill, Director of Communications
Phone: 816-366-5107
E-mail: geoffh@aea.net

LOWELL GAYLOR MEMORIAL SCHOLARSHIP

Scholarship for high school seniors and college students who plan to attend or are attending an avionics or aircraft repair program in an accredited school. Minimum 2.5 GPA required.

Academic Fields/Career Goals: Aviation/Aerospace; Trade/Technical Specialties.

Award: Scholarship for use in freshman, sophomore, junior, or senior years; not renewable. *Number:* 1. *Amount:* $1000.

Eligibility Requirements: Applicant must be enrolled or expecting to enroll full- or part-time at a two-year or four-year or technical institution or university. Available to U.S. and non-U.S. citizens.

Application Requirements: Application form, essay, recommendations or references, test scores, transcript. *Deadline:* February 15.

Contact: Geoff Hill, Director of Communications
Phone: 816-366-5107
E-mail: geoffh@aea.net

MONTE R. MITCHELL GLOBAL SCHOLARSHIP

Scholarship of $1000 available to European students pursuing a degree in aviation maintenance technology, avionics, or aircraft repair at an accredited school located in Europe or the United States.

Academic Fields/Career Goals: Aviation/Aerospace.

Award: Scholarship for use in freshman, sophomore, junior, or senior years; not renewable. *Number:* 1. *Amount:* $1000.

Eligibility Requirements: Applicant must be enrolled or expecting to enroll full- or part-time at a two-year or four-year or technical institution or university. Available to citizens of countries other than the U.S. or Canada.

Application Requirements: Application form, essay, recommendations or references, transcript. *Deadline:* February 15.

Contact: Geoff Hill, Director of Communications
Phone: 816-366-5107
E-mail: geoffh@aea.net

AIRPORT MINORITY ADVISORY COUNCIL EDUCATIONAL AND SCHOLARSHIP PROGRAM

http://www.amac-org.com/

AMACESP STUDENT SCHOLARSHIPS

Applicant must be seeking a BS or BA with interest and desire to pursue a career in the aviation/airport industry and seeking a degree in Aviation, Business Administration, Accounting, Architecture, Engineering or Finance and admitted by an accredited school or university for the current school term in which you are applying for a scholarship. Demonstration of a cumulative 3.0 GPA and involvement in community activities and extracurricular activities. Applicants must be a U.S. citizen. A commitment to involvement in furthering the mission of the Airport Minority Advisory Council (AMAC) by participating in the AMAC Student Program. AMAC Member Scholarship Awards are offered to Airport Minority Advisory Council (AMAC) members, their spouses, and their children. The AMAC Aviation & Professional Development Committee grant four $2000 scholarships each year to a number of students who are enrolled in an aviation related program and have a grade point average 3.0 or higher.

Academic Fields/Career Goals: Aviation/Aerospace.

Award: Scholarship for use in sophomore, junior, or senior years; not renewable. *Number:* 1–3. *Amount:* $2000.

Eligibility Requirements: Applicant must be enrolled or expecting to enroll full-time at a four-year institution or university. Available to U.S. citizens.

Application Requirements: Application form, autobiography, essay, personal photograph, recommendations or references, transcript. *Deadline:* May 18.

Contact: Miss. Jennifer Ibe, AMACESP Intern
Airport Minority Advisory Council Educational and
Scholarship Program
2345 Crystal Drive, Suite 902
Arlington, VA 22202
Phone: 703-414-2622 Ext. 1
Fax: 703-414-2686
E-mail: gene.roth@amac-org.com

ALASKAN AVIATION SAFETY FOUNDATION

http://www.aasfonline.org

ALASKAN AVIATION SAFETY FOUNDATION MEMORIAL SCHOLARSHIP FUND

Scholarships for undergraduate or graduate study in aviation. Must be a resident of Alaska and a U.S. citizen. Write for deadlines and details.

Academic Fields/Career Goals: Aviation/Aerospace.

Award: Scholarship for use in freshman, sophomore, junior, senior, or graduate years; not renewable. *Number:* 1–3. *Amount:* $500–$750.

Eligibility Requirements: Applicant must be enrolled or expecting to enroll full- or part-time at a two-year or four-year or technical institution or university; resident of Alaska and must have an interest in aviation. Available to U.S. citizens.

Application Requirements: Application form, driver's license, financial need analysis, recommendations or references, test scores, transcript. *Deadline:* May 30.

Contact: Scholarship Committee
Alaskan Aviation Safety Foundation
c/o Aviation Technology Division UAA
2811 Merril Field Drive
Anchorage, AK 99501
Phone: 907-243-7237

AMERICAN ASSOCIATION OF AIRPORT EXECUTIVES-SOUTHWEST CHAPTER

http://www.swaaae.org/

SWAAAE ACADEMIC SCHOLARSHIPS

A scholarship of $1500 for students pursuing an undergraduate or graduate degree in airport management may apply annually for an academic scholarship. Applicant must attend a college in Arizona, California, Nevada, Utah, or Hawaii.

Academic Fields/Career Goals: Aviation/Aerospace.

Award: Scholarship for use in sophomore, junior, senior, or graduate years; not renewable. *Number:* 5. *Amount:* $500–$1500.

Eligibility Requirements: Applicant must be enrolled or expecting to enroll full- or part-time at a four-year institution or university and studying in Arizona, California, Hawaii, Nevada, Utah. Available to U.S. and non-U.S. citizens.

Application Requirements: Application form. *Deadline:* September 29.

Contact: Charles Mangum, Scholarship Committee
American Association of Airport Executives-Southwest
Chapter
8565 North Sand Dune Place
Tucson, AZ 85743
Phone: 520-682-9565
E-mail: cman2122@comcast.net

AMERICAN CHEMICAL SOCIETY, RUBBER DIVISION

http://www.rubber.org/

AMERICAN CHEMICAL SOCIETY, RUBBER DIVISION UNDERGRADUATE SCHOLARSHIP

• *See page 105*

AMERICAN INSTITUTE OF AERONAUTICS AND ASTRONAUTICS

https://www.aiaa.org/

AIAA FOUNDATION UNDERGRADUATE SCHOLARSHIPS

Available to college students that will be sophomores, juniors, and seniors enrolled full-time in an accredited college/university. Must be AIAA student member to apply. Course of study must provide entry into some field of science or engineering encompassed by an AIAA technical committee. Minimum 3.3 GPA required.

Academic Fields/Career Goals: Aviation/Aerospace; Electrical Engineering/Electronics; Engineering-Related Technologies; Engineering/Technology; Materials Science, Engineering, and Metallurgy; Mechanical Engineering; Physical Sciences; Science, Technology, and Society.

Award: Scholarship for use in sophomore, junior, or senior years; not renewable. *Number:* 11. *Amount:* $500–$10,000.

Eligibility Requirements: Applicant must be enrolled or expecting to enroll full-time at a two-year institution or university. Applicant or parent of applicant must be member of American Institute of Aeronautics and Astronautics. Available to U.S. and non-U.S. citizens.

Application Requirements: Application form, application form may be submitted online, essay. *Deadline:* January 31.

Contact: Patricia Carr, Manager, AIAA Honors and Awards
American Institute of Aeronautics and Astronautics
12700 Sunrise Valley Drive
Suite 200
Reston, VA 20191
Phone: 703-264-7523
E-mail: patriciac@aiaa.org

LEATRICE GREGORY PENDRAY SCHOLARSHIP

Available to female college students that will be sophomores, juniors, and seniors enrolled full-time in an accredited college/university. Must be AIAA student member to apply. Course of study must provide entry into some field of science or engineering encompassed by AIAA. Minimum 3.3 GPA required.

Academic Fields/Career Goals: Aviation/Aerospace; Electrical Engineering/Electronics; Engineering-Related Technologies; Engineering/Technology; Materials Science, Engineering, and Metallurgy; Mechanical Engineering; Physical Sciences; Science, Technology, and Society.

Award: Scholarship for use in sophomore, junior, or senior years; not renewable. *Number:* 1. *Amount:* $1250.

Eligibility Requirements: Applicant must be enrolled or expecting to enroll full-time at a two-year institution or university and female. Applicant or parent of applicant must be member of American Institute of Aeronautics and Astronautics. Available to U.S. and non-U.S. citizens.

Application Requirements: Application form, application form may be submitted online, essay. *Deadline:* January 31.

Contact: Patricia Carr, Manager, AIAA Honors and Awards
American Institute of Aeronautics and Astronautics
12700 Sunrise Valley Drive
Suite 200
Reston, VA 20191-5807
Phone: 703-264-7523
E-mail: patriciac@aiaa.org

AMERICAN SOCIETY OF NAVAL ENGINEERS

http://www.navalengineers.org/

AMERICAN SOCIETY OF NAVAL ENGINEERS SCHOLARSHIP

• *See page 106*

ASSOCIATION OF FORMER INTELLIGENCE OFFICERS

www.afio.com

AFIO UNDERGRADUATE AND GRADUATE SCHOLARSHIPS

• *See page 98*

ASTRONAUT SCHOLARSHIP FOUNDATION

http://www.astronautscholarship.org/

ASTRONAUT SCHOLARSHIP

• *See page 107*

AVIATION COUNCIL OF PENNSYLVANIA

http://www.acpfly.com/

AVIATION COUNCIL OF PENNSYLVANIA SCHOLARSHIP PROGRAM

Sponsored by the Aviation Council of Pennsylvania, awards for Pennsylvania residents are available in the following categories: Aviation Technology, Aviation Management, and Aviation Pilot.

Academic Fields/Career Goals: Aviation/Aerospace.

Award: Scholarship for use in freshman, sophomore, junior, or senior years; not renewable. *Number:* 1–3. *Amount:* $500–$1000.

Eligibility Requirements: Applicant must be enrolled or expecting to enroll full- or part-time at a two-year or four-year or technical institution or university; resident of Pennsylvania and studying in Pennsylvania. Available to U.S. citizens.

Application Requirements: Application form, financial need analysis. *Deadline:* July 8.

Contact: Debra Bowman, Executive Director
Aviation Council of Pennsylvania
3915 Union Deposit Road, #935
Harrisburg, PA 17109
Phone: 717-850-0227
Fax: 717-850-0228
E-mail: dbowman@acpfly.com

AVIATION DISTRIBUTORS AND MANUFACTURERS ASSOCIATION INTERNATIONAL

ADMA SCHOLARSHIP

Scholarship to provide assistance to students pursuing careers in the aviation field. Those enrolled in an accredited Aviation program may be eligible.

Academic Fields/Career Goals: Aviation/Aerospace.

Award: Scholarship for use in junior or senior years; not renewable. *Number:* 1. *Amount:* up to $2000.

Eligibility Requirements: Applicant must be enrolled or expecting to enroll full-time at a two-year or four-year institution or university and must have an interest in aviation. Available to U.S. citizens.

Application Requirements: Application form, essay, financial need analysis, recommendations or references, transcript. *Deadline:* March 28.

Contact: Scholarship Committee
Aviation Distributors and Manufacturers Association
International
100 North 20th Street, Fourth Floor
Philadelphia, PA 19103-1443
Phone: 215-564-3484
Fax: 215-963-9785
E-mail: adma@fernley.com

BHW GROUP

https://thebhwgroup.com/

BHW WOMEN IN STEM SCHOLARSHIP

• *See page 107*

CARDS AGAINST HUMANITY

https://cardsagainsthumanity.com/

SCIENCE AMBASSADOR SCHOLARSHIP

• *See page 107*

CHARLIE WELLS MEMORIAL SCHOLARSHIP FUND

http://www.wellsscholarship.com/

CHARLIE WELLS MEMORIAL AVIATION SCHOLARSHIP

Scholarship(s) of varying amounts will be awarded each year when funds are available. The applicant must be a resident of the United States or one of its territories. Must be a full-time student majoring in an aviation-oriented curriculum.

Academic Fields/Career Goals: Aviation/Aerospace.

Award: Scholarship for use in freshman, sophomore, junior, senior, or graduate years; not renewable.

Eligibility Requirements: Applicant must be enrolled or expecting to enroll full-time at a four-year institution or university. Available to U.S. citizens.

Application Requirements: Application form, recommendations or references, transcript. *Deadline:* April 30.

Contact: Roger Thompson, Manager
Phone: 217-899-3263
E-mail: rog@wellsscholarship.com

CHICAGO AREA BUSINESS AVIATION ASSOCIATION

http://www.cabaa.com

CABAA/FLIGHTSAFETY CITATION EXCEL PROFESSIONAL PILOT TRAINING AWARDS

CABAA together with FlightSafety and CAE, will award two 2020 applicants with advanced training to enhance each individual's progress toward a career in Business Aviation. The awards will only be available for students who will have graduated with a pilot degree Spring / Summer 2020 and within the last five years The retail value of each award is approximately $22,200 per scholarship. CABAA will also provide a $1,000 travel stipend to assist in the cost of travel, additional funds may be approved on a case by case basis.

Academic Fields/Career Goals: Aviation/Aerospace.

Award: Scholarship for use in senior year; not renewable. *Number:* 2. *Amount:* $22,000.

Eligibility Requirements: Applicant must be age 21 and over and enrolled or expecting to enroll full- or part-time at an institution or university. Available to U.S. citizens.

Application Requirements: Application form, essay, interview. *Deadline:* May 15.

Contact: Alex Kwiatkowski
Chicago Area Business Aviation Association
2164 Tower Rd. Unit #3
West Chicago, IL 60185
E-mail: cabaascholarships@gmail.com

CABAA/FLIGHTSAFETY MAINTENANCE PROFESSIONAL TRAINING AWARD

One recipient will be awarded the Citation Sovereign Maintenance Initial course with a retail value of approximately $18,000. The recipient of the award must be a college student who graduated with a degree in Aircraft Maintenance and holds a current A&P license. CABAA will also provide a $1000 travel stipend to assist in the cost of travel; additional funds will be considered on a case by case basis.

Academic Fields/Career Goals: Aviation/Aerospace.

Award: Scholarship for use in senior year; not renewable. *Number:* 1. *Amount:* $18,000.

Eligibility Requirements: Applicant must be age 22 and over and enrolled or expecting to enroll full- or part-time at a two-year or technical institution or university. Available to U.S. citizens.

Application Requirements: Application form, essay, interview. *Deadline:* May 15.

Contact: Alex Kwiatkowski
Chicago Area Business Aviation Association
2164 Tower Rd. Unit #3
West Chicago, IL 60185
E-mail: cabaascholarships@gmail.com

CABAA MAINTENANCE COMMITTEE FINANCIAL AWARD

One scholarship will be awarded in the amount $8000. This scholarship is open to both high school seniors graduating in 2020 and college level students. Scholarship funds will be paid to the student and college or university of which the recipient is enrolled and are to be used to pay tuition or fees for aviation specific programs.

Academic Fields/Career Goals: Aviation/Aerospace.

Award: Scholarship for use in freshman, sophomore, junior, or senior years; not renewable. *Number:* 1. *Amount:* $8000.

Eligibility Requirements: Applicant must be enrolled or expecting to enroll full- or part-time at a two-year or technical institution or university. Available to U.S. citizens.

Application Requirements: Application form, essay. *Deadline:* May 15.

Contact: Alex Kwiatkowski
Chicago Area Business Aviation Association
2164 Tower Rd. Unit #3
West Chicago, IL 60185
E-mail: cabaascholarships@gmail.com

CABAA SCHOLARSHIP

Up to four (4) scholarships will be awarded in the amount of $7500 per recipient. These scholarships are open to both high school seniors graduating in 2017 and college level students. Scholarship funds will be paid to the student and college or university of which the recipient is enrolled and are to be used to pay tuition or fees for aviation specific programs. CABAA offers this award to promote professional development for a career in business aviation. The winner will be notified by phone and presented the award at the annual CABAA Golf Classic held on August 7th, 2017. The recipient's presence is required at the time of award presentation. For more information about CABAA, including membership visit http://www.cabaa.com.

Academic Fields/Career Goals: Aviation/Aerospace.

Award: Scholarship for use in freshman, sophomore, junior, or senior years; not renewable. *Number:* 4. *Amount:* $7500.

Eligibility Requirements: Applicant must be enrolled or expecting to enroll full- or part-time at a two-year or four-year or technical institution or university and resident of Illinois, Indiana, Iowa, Michigan, Missouri, Wisconsin. Available to U.S. citizens.

Application Requirements: Application form, essay. *Deadline:* May 1.

Contact: Brian Zankowski
Lake Villa, IL 60046
Phone: 224-931-8064
E-mail: scholarships@cabaa.com

KEN JOHNSON MEMORIAL SCHOLARSHIP

One scholarship will be awarded in the amount of $8000 to a 2020 graduating high school student seeking a degree in aviation. Scholarship funds will be paid to the student and college or university of which the recipient is enrolled and are to be used to pay tuition or fees for aviation specific programs.

Academic Fields/Career Goals: Aviation/Aerospace.

Award: Scholarship for use in freshman year; not renewable. *Number:* 1. *Amount:* $8000.

Eligibility Requirements: Applicant must be high school student; age 19 or under and planning to enroll or expecting to enroll full- or part-time at a two-year or technical institution or university. Available to U.S. citizens.

Application Requirements: Application form, essay. *Deadline:* May 15.

Contact: Alex Kwiatkowski
Chicago Area Business Aviation Association
2164 Tower Rd. Unit #3
West Chicago, IL 60185
E-mail: cabaascholarships@gmail.com

CIVIL AIR PATROL, USAF AUXILIARY

http://www.gocivilairpatrol.com/

MAJOR GENERAL LUCAS V. BEAU FLIGHT SCHOLARSHIPS SPONSORED BY THE ORDER OF DAEDALIANS

One-time scholarships for active cadets of the Civil Air Patrol who desire a career in military aviation. Award is to be used toward flight training for a private pilot license. Must be 15 1/2 to 18 1/2 years of age on April 1st of the year for which applying. Must be an active CAP cadet officer. Not open to the general public.

Academic Fields/Career Goals: Aviation/Aerospace.

Award: Scholarship for use in freshman year; not renewable. *Number:* 5. *Amount:* $2100.

Eligibility Requirements: Applicant must be high school student; planning to enroll or expecting to enroll full- or part-time at a four-year institution or university; single and must have an interest in aviation. Applicant or parent of applicant must be member of Civil Air Patrol. Available to U.S. citizens.

Application Requirements: Application form, essay, interview, personal photograph, recommendations or references, test scores, transcript. *Deadline:* March 1.

Contact: Kelly Easterly, Assistant Program Manager
Civil Air Patrol, USAF Auxiliary
105 South Hansell Street, Building 714
Maxwell Air Force Base, AL 36112-6332
Phone: 334-953-8640
Fax: 334-953-6699
E-mail: cpr@capnhq.gov

DAEDALIAN FOUNDATION

http://www.daedalians.org/

DAEDALIAN FOUNDATION MATCHING SCHOLARSHIP PROGRAM

Scholarship program, wherein the foundation matches amounts given by flights, or chapters of the Order of Daedalians, to deserving college and university students who are pursuing a career as a military aviator.

Academic Fields/Career Goals: Aviation/Aerospace.

Award: Scholarship for use in freshman, sophomore, junior, senior, or graduate years; not renewable. *Number:* 75–80. *Amount:* up to $2500.

Eligibility Requirements: Applicant must be enrolled or expecting to enroll full-time at a four-year institution or university. Available to U.S. citizens.

Application Requirements: Application form, flight/ROTC/CAP recommendation, personal photograph, test scores. *Deadline:* December 31.

Contact: Kristi Cavenaugh, Program Executive Secretary
Daedalian Foundation
55 Main Circle, Building 676
Randolph AFB, TX 78148
Phone: 210-945-2111
Fax: 210-945-2112
E-mail: kristi@daedalians.org

EAA AVIATION FOUNDATION, INC.

http://www.eaa.org/

HANSEN SCHOLARSHIP

Renewable scholarship of $1000 for a student enrolled in an accredited institution and pursuing a degree in aerospace engineering or aeronautical engineering. Student must be in good standing; financial need not a requirement. Must be an EAA member. Applications may be downloaded from the website http://www.youngeagles.org.

Academic Fields/Career Goals: Aviation/Aerospace.

Award: Scholarship for use in freshman, sophomore, junior, or senior years; not renewable. *Number:* up to 1. *Amount:* up to $1000.

Eligibility Requirements: Applicant must be enrolled or expecting to enroll full-time at a two-year or four-year or technical institution or university. Applicant or parent of applicant must be member of Experimental Aircraft Association. Available to U.S. and non-U.S. citizens.

Application Requirements: Application form. *Deadline:* February 28.

Contact: Jane Smith, Scholarship Coordinator
EAA Aviation Foundation, Inc.
PO Box 3086
Oshkosh, WI 54903-3086
Phone: 920-426-6823
Fax: 920-426-4873
E-mail: jsmith@eaa.org

PAYZER SCHOLARSHIP

Scholarship for a student accepted or enrolled in an accredited college, university, or postsecondary school with an emphasis on technical information. Awarded to an individual who is seeking a major and declares an intention to pursue a professional career in engineering, mathematics, or the physical/biological sciences. Visit http://www.youngeagles.org for criteria and to download official application. Must be an EAA member or recommended by an EAA member.

Academic Fields/Career Goals: Aviation/Aerospace; Biology; Engineering/Technology; Physical Sciences.

Award: Scholarship for use in freshman, sophomore, junior, or senior years; not renewable. *Number:* up to 1. *Amount:* up to $5000.

Eligibility Requirements: Applicant must be enrolled or expecting to enroll full-time at a two-year or four-year or technical institution or university. Applicant or parent of applicant must be member of Experimental Aircraft Association. Available to U.S. and non-U.S. citizens.

Application Requirements: Application form. *Deadline:* February 28.

Contact: Jane Smith, Scholarship Coordinator
EAA Aviation Foundation, Inc.
PO Box 3086
Oshkosh, WI 54903-3086
Phone: 920-426-6823
Fax: 920-426-4873
E-mail: jsmith@eaa.org

GENERAL AVIATION MANUFACTURERS ASSOCIATION

http://www.gama.aero/

EDWARD W. STIMPSON "AVIATION EXCELLENCE" AWARD

One-time scholarship award for students who are graduating from high school and have been accepted to attend aviation college or university in the upcoming year. See website at http://www.gama.aero for more details.

Academic Fields/Career Goals: Aviation/Aerospace.

Award: Scholarship for use in freshman year; not renewable. *Number:* 1. *Amount:* $500.

Eligibility Requirements: Applicant must be high school student; planning to enroll or expecting to enroll full-time at a four-year institution or university and must have an interest in aviation. Available to U.S. citizens.

Application Requirements: Application form, essay, recommendations or references, transcript. *Deadline:* April 28.

Contact: Katie Pribyl, Director, Communications
Phone: 202-393-1500
Fax: 202-842-4063
E-mail: kpribyl@gama.aero

HAROLD S. WOOD AWARD FOR EXCELLENCE

One-time scholarship award for an university student who is attending a National Intercollegiate Flying Association (NIFA) school. Must have completed at least one semester of coursework. See website at http://www.gama.aero for additional details.

Academic Fields/Career Goals: Aviation/Aerospace.

Award: Scholarship for use in freshman, sophomore, junior, or senior years; not renewable. *Number:* 1. *Amount:* $1000.

Eligibility Requirements: Applicant must be enrolled or expecting to enroll full-time at a four-year institution or university. Available to U.S. citizens.

Application Requirements: Application form, nomination, recommendations or references, transcript. *Deadline:* February 24.

Contact: Katie Pribyl, Director, Communications
Phone: 202-393-1500
Fax: 202-842-4063
E-mail: kpribyl@gama.aero

GRAND RAPIDS COMMUNITY FOUNDATION

http://www.grfoundation.org/

JOSHUA ESCH MITCHELL AVIATION SCHOLARSHIP

Student must be a US citizen, enrolled full or part-time at a college or university in the United States providing an accredited flight science curriculum. Applicants must be second year students or above or a first year student graduating from West Michigan Aviation Academy with a minimum 2.75 GPA pursuing undergraduate studies in the field of professional pilot with an emphasis in general aviation, Aviation Management, or Aviation Safety. A valid pilot's certificate (not to include a Student Certificate) is required. A letter of recommendation from a professional in the aviation field is required.

Academic Fields/Career Goals: Aviation/Aerospace.

Award: Scholarship for use in sophomore, junior, or senior years; not renewable. *Number:* 1–4. *Amount:* $1000.

Eligibility Requirements: Applicant must be enrolled or expecting to enroll full- or part-time at an institution or university. Applicant or parent of applicant must have employment or volunteer experience in transportation industry. Available to U.S. citizens.

Application Requirements: Application form, application form may be submitted online, essay, financial need analysis. *Deadline:* April 1.

Contact: Ms. Ruth Bishop, Education Program Officer
Grand Rapids Community Foundation
185 Oakes Street SW
Grand Rapids, MI 49503
Phone: 616-454-1751 Ext. 103
E-mail: rbishop@grfoundation.org

GREAT MINDS IN STEM

http://www.greatmindsinstem.org/college/scholarship-application-information

HENAAC SCHOLARSHIP PROGRAM
• *See page 100*

INTERNATIONAL SOCIETY OF WOMEN AIRLINE PILOTS (ISA+21)

http://www.iswap.org/

INTERNATIONAL SOCIETY OF WOMEN AIRLINE PILOTS FIORENZA DE BERNARDI MERIT SCHOLARSHIP

Financial award will aid those pilots endeavoring to fill some of the basic squares, i.e. a CFI, CFII, MEI or any international equivalents. Must have flight time in a fixed wing aircraft commensurate with the rating sought. Must have flight time in a fixed wing aircraft commensurate with the rating sought.

Academic Fields/Career Goals: Aviation/Aerospace.

Award: Scholarship for use in freshman, sophomore, junior, or senior years; not renewable. *Number:* 1.

Eligibility Requirements: Applicant must be age 21 and over; enrolled or expecting to enroll full- or part-time at a four-year institution or university and female. Available to U.S. and non-U.S. citizens.

Application Requirements: Application form, copies of income tax forms, logbook pages, pilot licenses, medical certificates, driver's license, financial need analysis, interview, personal photograph, recommendations or references, resume, transcript. *Deadline:* December 10.

Contact: Ms. Julie Clippard, Scholarship Chairwoman
E-mail: scholarship@iswap.org

INTERNATIONAL SOCIETY OF WOMEN AIRLINE PILOTS GRACE MCADAMS HARRIS SCHOLARSHIP

Scholarship may fund any ISA scholarship if the applicant has demonstrated an exceptionally spirited and ingenious attitude under difficult circumstances in the field of aviation. Applicants must have an U.S. FAA Commercial Pilot Certificate with an Instrument Rating and First Class Medical Certificate. Visit website http://www.iswap.org for more details.

Academic Fields/Career Goals: Aviation/Aerospace.

Award: Scholarship for use in freshman, sophomore, junior, or senior years; not renewable. *Number:* 1.

Eligibility Requirements: Applicant must be age 21 and over; enrolled or expecting to enroll full-time at a four-year institution or university; female and must have an interest in aviation. Available to U.S. and non-U.S. citizens.

Application Requirements: Application form, copies of income tax forms, logbook pages, pilot licenses, medical certificates, driver's license, financial need analysis, interview, personal photograph, recommendations or references, transcript. *Deadline:* December 10.

Contact: Ms. Julie Clippard, Scholarship Chairwoman
E-mail: scholarship@iswap.org

INTERNATIONAL SOCIETY OF WOMEN AIRLINE PILOTS HOLLY MULLENS MEMORIAL SCHOLARSHIP

Financial award is reserved for that applicant who is a single mother. Applicants must have an U.S. FAA Commercial Pilot Certificate with an Instrument Rating and First Class Medical Certificate. Visit website, http://www.iswap.org, for more details.

Academic Fields/Career Goals: Aviation/Aerospace.

Award: Scholarship for use in freshman, sophomore, junior, or senior years; not renewable. *Number:* 1.

Eligibility Requirements: Applicant must be age 21 and over; enrolled or expecting to enroll full-time at a four-year institution or university and single female. Available to U.S. and non-U.S. citizens.

Application Requirements: Application form, copies of income tax forms, logbook pages, pilot licenses, medical certificates, driver's license, financial need analysis, interview, recommendations or references, transcript. *Deadline:* December 10.

Contact: Ms. Julie Clippard, Scholarship Chairwoman
E-mail: scholarship@iswap.org

INTERNATIONAL SOCIETY OF WOMEN AIRLINE PILOTS NORTH CAROLINA FINANCIAL SCHOLARSHIP

Scholarships for a woman pilot from North Carolina interested in a career in the airline world. Must have flight time in a fixed wing aircraft commensurate with the rating sought. Must have flight time in a fixed wing aircraft commensurate with the rating sought.

Academic Fields/Career Goals: Aviation/Aerospace.

Award: Scholarship for use in freshman, sophomore, junior, or senior years; not renewable. *Number:* 1.

Eligibility Requirements: Applicant must be age 21 and over; enrolled or expecting to enroll full-time at a four-year institution or university; female and resident of North Carolina. Available to U.S. and non-U.S. citizens.

Application Requirements: Application form, copies of income tax forms, logbook pages, pilot licenses, medical certificates, driver's license, financial need analysis, interview, personal photograph, recommendations or references, resume, transcript. *Deadline:* December 10.

Contact: Ms. Julie Clippard, Scholarship Chairwoman
E-mail: scholarship@iswap.org

LOGMEIN

https://www.logmeininc.com

LASTPASS STEM SCHOLARSHIP
• *See page 109*

MANUFACTURERS ASSOCIATION OF MAINE

http://www.mainemfg.com/

MAINE MANUFACTURING CAREER AND TRAINING FOUNDATION SCHOLARSHIP

Maine Manufacturing Career and Training Foundation offers scholarship awards to individuals seeking education in the manufacturing field of study. Any Maine student or worker can apply for tuition assistance at any Maine institute of higher learning. All applicants must be full-time students and maintain a minimum of a C average.

Academic Fields/Career Goals: Aviation/Aerospace; Engineering-Related Technologies; Engineering/Technology; Industrial Design; Marine/Ocean Engineering; Materials Science, Engineering, and Metallurgy; Mechanical Engineering; Trade/Technical Specialties.

Award: Scholarship for use in freshman, sophomore, junior, senior, graduate, or postgraduate years; not renewable. *Number:* 5–25. *Amount:* $250–$1000.

Eligibility Requirements: Applicant must be enrolled or expecting to enroll full- or part-time at a two-year or four-year or technical institution or university; resident of Maine and studying in Maine. Available to U.S. citizens.

Application Requirements: Application form, essay. *Deadline:* April 30.

Contact: Marion Sprague, Outreach Communications Director
Manufacturers Association of Maine
101 Mcalister Farm Raod
Portland, ME 04103
Phone: 207-747-4406
E-mail: marion@mainemfg.com

NASA FLORIDA SPACE GRANT CONSORTIUM

http://www.floridaspacegrant.org/

FLORIDA SPACE RESEARCH PROGRAM

Grants for faculty researchers from Florida public and private universities and community colleges. One-time award for aerospace and technology research. Submit research proposal with budget.

Academic Fields/Career Goals: Aviation/Aerospace; Earth Science; Education; Electrical Engineering/Electronics; Engineering/Technology; Marine/Ocean Engineering; Materials Science, Engineering, and Metallurgy; Mathematics; Mechanical Engineering; Meteorology/Atmospheric Science; Physical Sciences.

Award: Grant for use in junior, senior, graduate, or postgraduate years; not renewable. *Number:* 13–15. *Amount:* $12,500–$25,000.

Eligibility Requirements: Applicant must be enrolled or expecting to enroll full- or part-time at a two-year or four-year institution or university; resident of Florida and studying in Florida. Available to U.S. citizens.

Application Requirements: Application form. *Deadline:* May 17.

Contact: Dr. Jaydeep Mukherjee, FSGC Director
NASA Florida Space Grant Consortium
PO Box 160650, 12354 Research Parkway, Room 218
Orlando, FL 32826
Phone: 407-823-6177
E-mail: fsgc@ucf.edu

NASA/MARYLAND SPACE GRANT CONSORTIUM

https://md.spacegrant.org

NASA MARYLAND SPACE GRANT CONSORTIUM SCHOLARSHIPS
• *See page 109*

NASA MINNESOTA SPACE GRANT CONSORTIUM

https://www.mnspacegrant.org/

MINNESOTA SPACE GRANT CONSORTIUM SCHOLARSHIP PROGRAM

Scholarships for full-time undergraduates attending higher education institutions that are affiliates of the Minnesota Space Grant Consortium—institution list on the website. Preference given to students studying aerospace engineering, space science, and NASA-related math, science, or engineering fields. Minimum 3.0 GPA required. Must be a U.S. citizen. For more details go to https://www.mnspacegrant.org/ then explore the Opportunities menu.

Academic Fields/Career Goals: Aviation/Aerospace; Computer Science/Data Processing; Earth Science; Electrical

Engineering/Electronics; Engineering/Technology; Environmental Science; Mathematics; Mechanical Engineering; Meteorology/Atmospheric Science; Natural Sciences; Nuclear Science; Oceanography; Physical Sciences.

Award: Scholarship for use in freshman, sophomore, junior, or senior years; not renewable. *Number:* 40–70. *Amount:* $500–$2500.

Eligibility Requirements: Applicant must be enrolled or expecting to enroll full-time at a two-year or four-year institution or university and studying in Minnesota. Available to U.S. citizens.

Application Requirements: Application form, MN Space Grant "Student Information Form" (posted on website), recommendations or references, transcript. *Deadline:* continuous.

Contact: Minnesota Space Grant, Department of Aerospace Engineering
NASA Minnesota Space Grant Consortium
107 Akerman Hall, 110 Union Street, SE
Minneapolis, MN 55455
Phone: 612-626-9295
E-mail: mnsgc@umn.edu

NASA MONTANA SPACE GRANT CONSORTIUM

http://www.spacegrant.montana.edu/

MONTANA SPACE GRANT SCHOLARSHIP PROGRAM

Awards are made on a competitive basis to students enrolled in fields of study relevant to the aerospace sciences and engineering. Must be U.S. citizen enrolled as full-time student at a Montana Consortium campus.

Academic Fields/Career Goals: Aviation/Aerospace; Biology; Chemical Engineering; Civil Engineering; Computer Science/Data Processing; Electrical Engineering/Electronics; Engineering/Technology; Mathematics; Mechanical Engineering.

Award: Scholarship for use in freshman, sophomore, junior, or senior years; not renewable. *Number:* 15–20. *Amount:* $1000–$2000.

Eligibility Requirements: Applicant must be enrolled or expecting to enroll full-time at a two-year or four-year institution or university and studying in Montana. Available to U.S. citizens.

Application Requirements: Application form, application form may be submitted online (http://spacegrant.montana.edu), essay, recommendations or references, transcript. *Deadline:* April 1.

Contact: Chris Harmon, Program Coordinator
Phone: 406-994-4223
Fax: 406-994-4452

NASA RHODE ISLAND SPACE GRANT CONSORTIUM

http://brown/initiatives/ri-space-grant

NASA RHODE ISLAND SPACE GRANT CONSORTIUM UNDERGRADUATE RESEARCH SCHOLARSHIP

Scholarship for undergraduate students for study and/or outreach related to NASA and space sciences, engineering and/or technology. Must attend a Rhode Island Space Grant Consortium participating school. Recipients are expected to devote a maximum of 4 hours per week in science education for K-12 children and teachers. See website for additional information http://www.spacegrant.brown.edu.

Academic Fields/Career Goals: Aviation/Aerospace; Engineering/Technology; Meteorology/Atmospheric Science.

Award: Scholarship for use in sophomore, junior, or senior years; not renewable. *Number:* up to 2. *Amount:* up to $4000.

Eligibility Requirements: Applicant must be enrolled or expecting to enroll full-time at a four-year institution or university and studying in Rhode Island. Available to U.S. citizens.

Application Requirements: Application form, essay, recommendations or references, resume, transcript. *Deadline:* varies.

Contact: Nancy Ciminelli, Program Manager
NASA Rhode Island Space Grant Consortium
Brown University
Box 1846, Lincoln Field
Providence, RI 02912
Phone: 401-863-1151
Fax: 401-863-3978
E-mail: nancy_ciminelli@brown.edu

NASA RISGC SCIENCE EN ESPANOL SCHOLARSHIP FOR UNDERGRADUATE STUDENTS

Award for undergraduate students attending a Rhode Island Space Grant Consortium participating school and studying in any space-related field of science, math, engineering, or other field with applications in space study. Recipients are expected to devote a maximum of 8 hours per week in outreach activities, supporting ESL teachers with science instruction.

Academic Fields/Career Goals: Aviation/Aerospace; Engineering/Technology; Mathematics.

Award: Scholarship for use in sophomore, junior, or senior years; not renewable. *Number:* 2. *Amount:* up to $4000.

Eligibility Requirements: Applicant must be enrolled or expecting to enroll full-time at a four-year institution or university and studying in Rhode Island. Available to U.S. citizens.

Application Requirements: Application form, essay, resume, transcript. *Deadline:* varies.

Contact: Nancy Ciminelli, Program Manager
NASA Rhode Island Space Grant Consortium
Brown University
Box 1846, Lincoln Field
Providence, RI 02912
Phone: 401-863-1151
Fax: 401-863-3978
E-mail: nancy_ciminelli@brown.edu

NASA RISGC SUMMER SCHOLARSHIP FOR UNDERGRADUATE STUDENTS

Scholarship for full-time summer study. Students are expected to devote 75 percent of their time to a research project with a faculty adviser and 25 percent to outreach activities in science education for K-12 students and teachers. Must attend a Rhode Island Space Grant Consortium participating school. See website for additional information http://www.spacegrant.brown.edu.

Academic Fields/Career Goals: Aviation/Aerospace; Education.

Award: Scholarship for use in sophomore, junior, or senior years; not renewable. *Number:* up to 2. *Amount:* up to $4000.

Eligibility Requirements: Applicant must be enrolled or expecting to enroll full-time at a four-year institution or university and studying in Rhode Island. Available to U.S. citizens.

Application Requirements: Application form, letter of interest, recommendations or references, resume. *Deadline:* varies.

Contact: Nancy Ciminelli, Program Manager
NASA Rhode Island Space Grant Consortium
Brown University
Box 1846, Lincoln Field
Providence, RI 02912
Phone: 401-863-1151
Fax: 401-863-3978
E-mail: nancy_ciminelli@brown.edu

NASA'S VIRGINIA SPACE GRANT CONSORTIUM

http://www.vsgc.odu.edu/

UNDERGRADUATE STEM RESEARCH SCHOLARSHIPS
• *See page 110*

NASA WISCONSIN SPACE GRANT CONSORTIUM

https://spacegrant.carthage.edu/

WISCONSIN SPACE GRANT CONSORTIUM UNDERGRADUATE SCHOLARSHIP PROGRAM

Scholarship of up to $2000 for a U.S. citizen enrolled full-time in, admitted to, or applying to any undergraduate program at a Wisconsin Space Grant Consortium college or university. Awards will be given to students with outstanding potential in programs of aerospace, space science, or other interdisciplinary space-related studies. Minimum 3.0 GPA required. Refer to website for more information https://spacegrant.carthage.edu/funding-programs/undergraduate/scholarship/.

Academic Fields/Career Goals: Aviation/Aerospace.

Award: Scholarship for use in freshman, sophomore, junior, or senior years; not renewable. *Number:* 15. *Amount:* $2000.

Eligibility Requirements: Applicant must be enrolled or expecting to enroll full-time at a two-year or four-year institution or university; resident of Wisconsin and studying in Wisconsin. Available to U.S. citizens.

Application Requirements: Application form, essay. *Deadline:* February 5.

Contact: Christine Bolz, Assistant Director
NASA Wisconsin Space Grant Consortium
2001 Alford Park Drive
Kenosha, WI 53140
Phone: 262-551-2120
E-mail: cthompson2@carthage.edu

NATIONAL GAY PILOTS ASSOCIATION EDUCATION FUND

http://www.ngpa.org/

NGPA EDUCATION FUND, INC.

Scholarship for candidates pursuing a career as a professional pilot. Funds cannot be used to pay for the basic private certificate; they must be applied towards advanced fight training at a government certified flight school or to college tuition if enrolled in an accredited aviation degree program. Applicants must provide evidence of their contribution to the gay and lesbian community.

Academic Fields/Career Goals: Aviation/Aerospace.

Award: Scholarship for use in freshman, sophomore, junior, or senior years; not renewable. *Number:* 3–4. *Amount:* $3000–$4000.

Eligibility Requirements: Applicant must be age 18 and over; enrolled or expecting to enroll full- or part-time at a two-year or four-year or technical institution or university and must have an interest in aviation or LGBT issues. Applicant or parent of applicant must have employment or volunteer experience in community service. Available to U.S. and non-U.S. citizens.

Application Requirements: Application form, copies of the applicant's pilot certificate, medical certificate, recent logbook page, essay, recommendations or references, transcript. *Deadline:* March 31.

Contact: David Pettet, Executive Director
National Gay Pilots Association Education Fund
PO Box 11313
Norfolk, VA 23517
E-mail: ExecDir@ngpa.org

NEVADA NASA SPACE GRANT CONSORTIUM

https://nasa.epscorspo.nevada.edu/

NATIONAL SPACE GRANT CONSORTIUM SCHOLARSHIPS

• *See page 110*

NEXTSTEPU

http://www.nextstepu.com/

$1,500 STEM SCHOLARSHIP

• *See page 104*

PALWAUKEE AIRPORT PILOTS ASSOCIATION

http://www.pwkpilots.org

PAPA SCHOLARSHIP & SAFETY FOUNDATION

Scholarship offered to Illinois residents who are attending accredited programs at Illinois institutions. Must be pursuing a course of study in an aviation-related program. Minimum GPA of 2.0. Applications available on website www.pwkpilots.org.

Academic Fields/Career Goals: Aviation/Aerospace.

Award: Scholarship for use in freshman, sophomore, junior, or senior years; not renewable. *Number:* 2. *Amount:* $1000.

Eligibility Requirements: Applicant must be age 18 and over; enrolled or expecting to enroll full- or part-time at a two-year or four-year or technical institution or university; resident of Illinois and studying in Illinois. Available to U.S. citizens.

Application Requirements: Application form, driver's license, essay, personal photograph. *Deadline:* May 1.

Contact: Jason Simpson, Chairman, Scholarship Committee
Palwaukee Airport Pilots Association
1005 South Wolf Road, Suite 106
Wheeling, IL 60090
Phone: 773-842-5088
E-mail: scholarship@pwkpilots.org

RHODE ISLAND PILOTS ASSOCIATION

http://www.ripilots.com/

RHODE ISLAND PILOTS ASSOCIATION SCHOLARSHIP

A scholarship open to Rhode Island residents to begin or advance a career in aviation. Must be age 16 or above.

Academic Fields/Career Goals: Aviation/Aerospace.

Award: Scholarship for use in freshman, sophomore, junior, or senior years; not renewable. *Number:* 2–4. *Amount:* $500–$1500.

Eligibility Requirements: Applicant must be age 16 and over; enrolled or expecting to enroll full- or part-time at a two-year or four-year or technical institution; resident of Rhode Island and must have an interest in aviation. Available to U.S. citizens.

Application Requirements: Application form, essay, financial need analysis. *Deadline:* February 28.

Contact: Marilyn Biagetti, Scholarship Chair
Phone: 401-568-3497
E-mail: biagettim@aol.com

ROBERT H. MOLLOHAN FAMILY CHARITABLE FOUNDATION, INC.

http://www.mollohanfoundation.org/

MID-ATLANTIC AEROSPACE SCHOLARSHIP

The Mid-Atlantic Aerospace Complex Scholarship provides scholarship opportunities to students who wish to pursue one of the following aerospace programs offered at the Robert C. Byrd National Aerospace Education Center which awards degrees through Fairmont State University and Pierpont Community and Technical College: BS in Aviation Administration Management, BS in Aviation Administration-Professional Flight, BS in Aviation Maintenance Management, AAS in Airframe & Aerospace Electronics Technology, AAS in Aviation Maintenance Technology. The student must have at least a 2.5 GPA, and will be expected to remain actively involved in an aviation program upon receipt of the scholarship.

Academic Fields/Career Goals: Aviation/Aerospace.

Award: Scholarship for use in freshman, sophomore, junior, or senior years. *Amount:* $1000.

Eligibility Requirements: Applicant must be high school student; planning to enroll or expecting to enroll full-time at a four-year institution or university; resident of West Virginia and studying in West Virginia. Available to U.S. citizens.

Application Requirements: Application form, essay, recommendations or references, resume, test scores, transcript.

SCARLETT FAMILY FOUNDATION SCHOLARSHIP PROGRAM

http://www.scarlettfoundation.org/

SCHOLARSHIP FOR STUDENTS PURSUING A BUSINESS OR STEM DEGREE

• *See page 80*

SOCIETY OF SATELLITE PROFESSIONALS INTERNATIONAL

http://www.sspi.org/

SSPI INTERNATIONAL SCHOLARSHIPS

Scholarship open to students majoring or planning to major in fields related to satellite communications. Selection is based on academic and leadership achievement, commitment to pursue education and career opportunities in the satellite industry or a field making direct use of satellite technology. Available to members of SSPI.

Academic Fields/Career Goals: Aviation/Aerospace; Communications; Law/Legal Services; Meteorology/Atmospheric Science; Military and Defense Studies.

Award: Scholarship for use in freshman, sophomore, junior, senior, or graduate years; not renewable. *Number:* 1–4. *Amount:* $2500–$4000.

Eligibility Requirements: Applicant must be enrolled or expecting to enroll full- or part-time at a two-year or four-year institution or university. Available to U.S. and non-U.S. citizens.

Application Requirements: Essay, financial need analysis. *Deadline:* April 15.

Contact: Ms. Tamara Bond-Williams, Membership Director
Society of Satellite Professionals International
250 Park Avenue, 7th Floor
New York, NY 10177
Phone: 212-809-5199 Ext. 103
Fax: 212-825-0075
E-mail: tbond-williams@sspi.org

SOCIETY OF WOMEN ENGINEERS

https://swe.org/

GE'S WOMEN'S NETWORK PAULA MARTIN SCHOLARSHIP

One $5000 scholarship for female applicants planning to study a full-time ABET-accredited program in engineering, technology, or computing in the upcoming academic year. This scholarship is renewable for all years of a four-year college program. Sponsorship to work in the US is not required now nor will it be in the future. Preference given to students who are from underrepresented backgrounds in STEM and/or those who demonstrate financial need.

Academic Fields/Career Goals: Aviation/Aerospace; Computer Science/Data Processing; Electrical Engineering/Electronics; Materials Science, Engineering, and Metallurgy; Mechanical Engineering.

Award: Scholarship for use in freshman year; renewable. *Number:* 1. *Amount:* $5000.

Eligibility Requirements: Applicant must be enrolled or expecting to enroll full-time at a four-year institution or university and female. Available to U.S. citizens.

Application Requirements: Application form, financial need analysis, recommendations or references, transcript. *Deadline:* May 1.

Contact: Scholarship Committee.
Phone: 312-596-5223
E-mail: scholarships@swe.org

STRAIGHT NORTH

https://www.straightnorth.com/

STRAIGHT NORTH STEM SCHOLARSHIP
• *See page 81*

TUSKEGEE AIRMEN SCHOLARSHIP FOUNDATION

http://www.taisf.org/

TUSKEGEE AIRMEN SCHOLARSHIP

Each year the Foundation grants scholarship awards to deserving young men and women. The number of available scholarship awards is directly related to income received from investments. The selection committee uses academic achievement, extracurricular and community activities,

relative financial need, recommendations, and two essays in order to competitively rank applicants.

Academic Fields/Career Goals: Aviation/Aerospace; Science, Technology, and Society.

Award: Scholarship for use in freshman year; not renewable. *Number:* 40. *Amount:* $1500–$5000.

Eligibility Requirements: Applicant must be high school student and planning to enroll or expecting to enroll full-time at a two-year or four-year institution or university. Available to U.S. citizens.

Application Requirements: Application form, community service, essay, financial need analysis, recommendations or references, test scores, transcript. *Deadline:* January 26.

Contact: Mr. Errol Lewis
E-mail: lewisei@aol.com

UNITED NEGRO COLLEGE FUND

http://www.uncf.org/

DAVIS SCHOLARSHIP FOR WOMEN IN STEM
• *See page 111*

LEIDOS STEM SCHOLARSHIP
• *See page 96*

UNIVERSITY AVIATION ASSOCIATION

http://www.uaa.aero/

CAE SIMUFLITE CITATION TYPE RATING SCHOLARSHIP

Scholarship open to undergraduate seniors and post-Baccalaureate graduates of aviation degree programs up to two years after graduation. Must have a minimum 3.25 GPA. Students must attend, or must have graduated from, a University Aviation Association member institution. The application is posted at the University Aviation Association website at http://www.uaa.aero. There are extensive aviation flight certification and flight time requirements for this application so please consult the application directly for more details.

Academic Fields/Career Goals: Aviation/Aerospace.

Award: Scholarship for use in senior year; not renewable. *Number:* 6. *Amount:* $10,500.

Eligibility Requirements: Applicant must be enrolled or expecting to enroll full-time at a four-year institution or university and must have an interest in aviation. Available to U.S. citizens.

Application Requirements: Application form, essay, FAA first class medical certificate, recommendations or references, resume, transcript. *Deadline:* March 31.

Contact: Dr. David NewMyer, Professor and Department Chair, Aviation Management and Flight
University Aviation Association
Transportation Education Center, 545 North Airport Road
Southern Illinois University Carbondale
Murphysboro, IL 62966
Phone: 616-453-8898
Fax: 618-453-5230
E-mail: newmyer@siu.edu

CHICAGO AREA BUSINESS AVIATION ASSOCIATION SCHOLARSHIP

One-time awards of $2500 for U.S. citizens who are Illinois residents. Minimum GPA of 2.5. Priority given to Chicagoland residents followed by Illinois residents who are attending, or will attend, a postsecondary aviation degree program in such fields as Aerospace Engineering, Air Traffic Control, Aircraft Charter, Aircraft Maintenance, Aviation Administration/Management, Aviation Flight, Avionics/Aviation Electronics, etc. At least three letters of recommendation required; at least one of these must be from a person currently employed in the field of Business Aviation. The financial statement that is included in the CABAA Scholarship Application must be completed and attached to the application. Application is posted at the website of the University Aviation Association at http://www.uaa.aero.

Academic Fields/Career Goals: Aviation/Aerospace.

Award: Scholarship for use in freshman, sophomore, junior, senior, graduate, or postgraduate years; not renewable. *Number:* 8. *Amount:* $4000.

Eligibility Requirements: Applicant must be enrolled or expecting to enroll full-time at a two-year or four-year or technical institution or university and resident of Illinois. Available to U.S. citizens.

Application Requirements: Application form, essay, recommendations or references. *Deadline:* April 20.

Contact: Dr. David Newmyer, Department Chair, Aviation Management and Flight
University Aviation Association
Southern Illinois University at Carbondale, College of Applied Sciences and Arts
1365 Douglas Drive
Carbondale, IL 62901-6623
Phone: 618-453-8898
Fax: 618-453-7286
E-mail: newmyer@siu.edu

JOSEPH FRASCA EXCELLENCE IN AVIATION SCHOLARSHIP

Established to encourage those who demonstrate the highest level of commitment to and achievement in aviation studies. Applicant must be a junior or senior currently enrolled in a University Aviation Association member institution. Must be FAA certified/qualified in either aviation maintenance or flight, have membership in at least one aviation organization (such as National Intercollegiate Flying Association flying team, Alpha Eta Rho, Warbirds of America, Experimental Aircraft Association, etc.), and be involved in aviation activities, projects, and events. Minimum 3.0 GPA required. Application is posted at http://www.uaa.aero and applications are due on the second Monday of April each year.

Academic Fields/Career Goals: Aviation/Aerospace.

Award: Scholarship for use in junior or senior years; not renewable. *Number:* 2. *Amount:* $2000.

Eligibility Requirements: Applicant must be enrolled or expecting to enroll full- or part-time at a four-year institution or university and must have an interest in aviation. Available to U.S. and non-U.S. citizens.

Application Requirements: Application form, essay, FAA certification as a pilot or mechanic or both, financial need analysis, recommendations or references, transcript. *Deadline:* April 10.

Contact: Dr. David Newmyer, Department Chair, Aviation Management and Flight
University Aviation Association
1365 Douglas Drive
Carbondale, IL 62901-6623
Phone: 618-453-8898
Fax: 618-453-4850
E-mail: newmyer@siu.edu

PAUL A. WHELAN AVIATION SCHOLARSHIP

One-time award of $2000 given to sophomore, junior, senior or graduate. Must be a U.S. citizen. Must be enrolled in University Aviation Association member institution. 2.5 GPA required. Current or past military service (active duty, reserves or national guard, FAA certification, membership in aviation-related association preferred. Application is posted at the University Aviation Association website at http://www.uaa.aero

Academic Fields/Career Goals: Aviation/Aerospace.

Award: Scholarship for use in sophomore, junior, senior, or graduate years; not renewable. *Number:* 1. *Amount:* $2000.

Eligibility Requirements: Applicant must be enrolled or expecting to enroll full-time at a two-year or four-year institution or university and must have an interest in aviation. Available to U.S. citizens.

Application Requirements: Application form, essay, FAA certification, recommendations or references, transcript. *Deadline:* May 15.

Contact: David Newmyer, Department Chair, Aviation Management and Flight
University Aviation Association
Southern Illinois University at Carbondale, College of Applied Sciences and Arts
1365 Douglas Drive
Carbondale, IL 62901-6623
Phone: 618-453-8898
Fax: 618-453-7268
E-mail: newmyer@siu.edu

VERMONT SPACE GRANT CONSORTIUM

http://www.cems.uvm.edu/vsgc

VERMONT SPACE GRANT CONSORTIUM
• *See page 92*

VIRGINIA AVIATION AND SPACE EDUCATION FORUM

http://www.doav.virginia.gov/

JOHN R. LILLARD VIRGINIA AIRPORT OPERATORS COUNCIL SCHOLARSHIP PROGRAM

Scholarship of $3000 offered to high school seniors planning a career in the field of aviation. Must be enrolled or accepted into an aviation-related program at an accredited college. Minimum 3.75 unweighted GPA.

Academic Fields/Career Goals: Aviation/Aerospace.

Award: Scholarship for use in freshman year; not renewable. *Number:* 1. *Amount:* $3000.

Eligibility Requirements: Applicant must be high school student; planning to enroll or expecting to enroll full-time at a four-year institution or university and must have an interest in aviation. Available to U.S. and non-U.S. citizens.

Application Requirements: Application form, essay, financial need analysis, recommendations or references, transcript. *Deadline:* February 20.

Contact: Betty Wilson, Program Coordinator
Phone: 804-236-3624
Fax: 804-236-3636
E-mail: betty.wilson@doav.virginia.gov

WILLARD G. PLENTL AVIATION SCHOLARSHIP PROGRAM

Scholarship of $1000 awarded to a high school senior who is planning an aviation career in a non-engineering area.

Academic Fields/Career Goals: Aviation/Aerospace.

Award: Scholarship for use in freshman year; not renewable. *Number:* 1. *Amount:* $1000.

Eligibility Requirements: Applicant must be high school student; planning to enroll or expecting to enroll full-time at a four-year institution or university and must have an interest in aviation. Available to U.S. and non-U.S. citizens.

Application Requirements: Application form, essay, financial need analysis, recommendations or references, transcript. *Deadline:* February 20.

Contact: Betty Wilson, Program Coordinator
Virginia Aviation and Space Education Forum
5702 Gulfstream Road
Richmond, VA 23250-2422
E-mail: betty.wilson@doav.virginia.gov

WOMEN IN AEROSPACE FOUNDATION

https://www.womeninaerospace.org/

THE WOMEN IN AEROSPACE FOUNDATION SCHOLARSHIP

The WIA Foundation is pleased to provide scholarships to women interested in a career in the aerospace field to pursue higher education degrees in engineering, math or science. One or more awards will be given each year to a rising junior or senior in college, to be applied during the upcoming academic year. To be eligible for the WIA Foundation

Scholarship, an applicant must be interested in pursuing a career in the aerospace field and be a rising junior or senior working towards a Bachelor's degree in engineering, math or science. An applicant must have completed at least two and a half academic years of full-time college work at the time of application and must be currently enrolled in an accredited college or university in the United States or its territories, and plan to be enrolled in the subsequent academic year. Each applicant must have a college grade point average of at least 3.0 on a 4.0 scale. Applicants must be female of any nationality. To apply, please send in one merged PDF the following materials to info@ womeninaerospace.org: the application form found on the website, high school and college transcripts, two letters of recommendation from a professor, or a supervisor of summer or Co-op work experience, or a supervisor of research work. Recommendations from relatives will not be accepted. References or transcripts may be emailed separately, if necessary. Additionally, please include a 500-1000 word essay responding to the following: "Imagine that you are trying to explain to someone with no interest in aerospace why aerospace is important. How would approach this explanation and what would you say?"

Academic Fields/Career Goals: Aviation/Aerospace; Engineering-Related Technologies; Engineering/Technology; Mathematics; Science, Technology, and Society.

Award: Scholarship for use in junior or senior years; not renewable. *Number:* 4. *Amount:* $2000.

Eligibility Requirements: Applicant must be enrolled or expecting to enroll full-time at a four-year institution or university and female. Available to U.S. and non-U.S. citizens.

Application Requirements: Application form, application form may be submitted online (https://www.womeninaerospace.org/forms/foundation/scholarship_app.pdf), essay, recommendations or references, transcript. *Deadline:* June 18.

Contact: Ms. Torrie Nickerson, Program and Event Specialist
Women in Aerospace Foundation
204 E Street NE
Washington, DC 20002
Phone: 202-547-0229
E-mail: tnickerson@womeninaerospace.org

WOMEN IN AVIATION, INTERNATIONAL

http://www.wai.org/

THE BOEING COMPANY CAREER ENHANCEMENT SCHOLARSHIP

The Boeing Company will award a scholarship to a woman who wishes to advance her career in the aerospace industry in the fields of engineering, technology development or management. The award is to be used for educational purposes only and may not be applied toward flight hours. Applicants may be full-time or part-time employees currently in the aerospace industry or a related field. Also eligible are students pursuing aviation and aerospace-related degrees that are at the sophomore level with a minimum GPA of 2.5 (on a 4.0 scale).

Academic Fields/Career Goals: Aviation/Aerospace; Engineering-Related Technologies; Engineering/Technology.

Award: Scholarship for use in junior or senior years; not renewable. *Number:* 2. *Amount:* $5000.

Eligibility Requirements: Applicant must be enrolled or expecting to enroll full- or part-time at an institution or university and female. Applicant or parent of applicant must be member of Women in Aviation, International. Available to U.S. and non-U.S. citizens.

Application Requirements: Application form, essay. *Deadline:* November 12.

Contact: Donna Wallace, Exhibit Coordinator/Scholarship Coordinator
Women in Aviation, International
3647 State Route 503 South
West Alexandria, OH 45381
Phone: 937-839-4647
Fax: 937-839-4645
E-mail: dwallace@wai.org

DELTA AIR LINES AIRCRAFT MAINTENANCE TECHNOLOGY SCHOLARSHIP

Scholarship of $5000 available to a student currently enrolled in an Aviation Maintenance Technician Program (A&P) or a degree in Aviation Maintenance Technology. Applicant must be a full-time student with a minimum of two semesters left, with a minimum GPA of 3.0 or better (on

a 4.0 scale). Must be a member of WAI. Must be an U.S. citizen or eligible non-citizen.

Academic Fields/Career Goals: Aviation/Aerospace; Engineering/Technology.

Award: Scholarship for use in freshman, sophomore, or junior years; not renewable. *Number:* 1. *Amount:* $5000.

Eligibility Requirements: Applicant must be enrolled or expecting to enroll full-time at a two-year or technical institution or university. Applicant or parent of applicant must be member of Women in Aviation, International. Available to U.S. and non-U.S. citizens.

Application Requirements: Application form, essay. *Deadline:* November 12.

Contact: Donna Wallace, Exhibit Coordinator/Scholarship Coordinator
Women in Aviation, International
3647 State Route 503 South
West Alexandria, OH 45381
Phone: 937-839-4647
Fax: 937-839-4645
E-mail: dwallace@wai.org

DELTA AIR LINES AVIATION MAINTENANCE MANAGEMENT/AVIATION BUSINESS MANAGEMENT SCHOLARSHIP

Scholarship to a student currently enrolled in an Associate or Baccalaureate degree in Aviation Maintenance Management or Aviation Business Management. Applicant must be a full-time college student, with a minimum of two semesters left. Must have a minimum GPA of 3.0 (on a 4.0 scale) or better. Must be a member of WAI and be a U.S. citizen or eligible non-citizen.

Academic Fields/Career Goals: Aviation/Aerospace.

Award: Scholarship for use in freshman, sophomore, or junior years; not renewable. *Number:* 1. *Amount:* $5000.

Eligibility Requirements: Applicant must be enrolled or expecting to enroll full-time at a two-year institution or university. Applicant or parent of applicant must be member of Women in Aviation, International. Available to U.S. and non-U.S. citizens.

Application Requirements: Application form, essay. *Deadline:* November 12.

Contact: Donna Wallace, Exhibit Coordinator/Scholarship Coordinator
Women in Aviation, International
3647 State Route 503 South
West Alexandria, OH 45381
Phone: 937-839-4647
Fax: 937-839-4645
E-mail: dwallace@wai.org

DELTA AIR LINES ENGINEERING SCHOLARSHIP

Student must be currently enrolled in a Baccalaureate degree in Aerospace / Aeronautical, Electrical, or Mechanical Engineering. Applicants must be full-time students at the junior or senior level with a minimum of two semesters left, with a cumulative GPA of 3.0 (on a 4.0 scale) or better. Must be a member of WAI and be U.S. citizen or eligible non-citizen.

Academic Fields/Career Goals: Aviation/Aerospace; Electrical Engineering/Electronics; Engineering/Technology; Mechanical Engineering.

Award: Scholarship for use in junior or senior years; not renewable. *Number:* 1. *Amount:* $5000.

Eligibility Requirements: Applicant must be enrolled or expecting to enroll full-time at an institution or university. Applicant or parent of applicant must be member of Women in Aviation, International. Available to U.S. and non-U.S. citizens.

Application Requirements: Application form, essay. *Deadline:* November 12.

Contact: Donna Wallace, Exhibit Coordinator/Scholarship Coordinator
Women in Aviation, International
3647 State Route 503 South
West Alexandria, OH 45381
Phone: 937-839-4647
Fax: 937-839-4645
E-mail: dwallace@wai.org

KEEP FLYING SCHOLARSHIP

One scholarship of up to $3000 will be awarded to an individual working on an instrument or multi engine rating, commercial or initial flight instructor certificate. Flight training must be completed within one year. Minimum requirements: private pilot certificate, 100 hours of flight time, and a copy of a current written test (with passing grade) for the certificate/rating sought. One letter of recommendation must be from a pilot that you have flown with. Finalist will only be interviewed at the annual Women in Aviation Conference. Must be a member of WAI.

Academic Fields/Career Goals: Aviation/Aerospace.

Award: Scholarship for use in freshman year; not renewable. *Number:* 1. *Amount:* $3000.

Eligibility Requirements: Applicant must be enrolled or expecting to enroll full- or part-time at a technical institution. Applicant or parent of applicant must be member of Women in Aviation, International. Available to U.S. and non-U.S. citizens.

Application Requirements: Application form, essay. *Deadline:* November 12.

Contact: Donna Wallace, Exhibit Coordinator/Scholarship Coordinator
Women in Aviation, International
3647 State Route 503 South
West Alexandria, OH 45381
Phone: 937-839-4647
Fax: 937-839-4645
E-mail: dwallace@wai.org

WOMEN MILITARY AVIATORS DREAM OF FLIGHT SCHOLARSHIP

This will be awarded to a woman pursuing her flight ratings at an accredited institution or FAA Part 141 approved flight school. Must demonstrate persistence and determination to flight. Training must be completed within one year of the award and be a member of WAI.

Academic Fields/Career Goals: Aviation/Aerospace.

Award: Scholarship for use in freshman, sophomore, junior, or senior years; not renewable. *Number:* 1. *Amount:* $2500.

Eligibility Requirements: Applicant must be enrolled or expecting to enroll full- or part-time at a two-year or technical institution or university and female. Applicant or parent of applicant must be member of Women in Aviation, International. Available to U.S. and non-U.S. citizens.

Application Requirements: Application form, financial need analysis. *Deadline:* November 12.

Contact: Donna Wallace, Exhibit Coordinator/Scholarship Coordinator
Women in Aviation, International
3647 State Route 503 South
West Alexandria, OH 45381
Phone: 937-839-4647
Fax: 937-839-4645
E-mail: dwallace@wai.org

WRIGHT CHAPTER, WOMEN IN AVIATION, INTERNATIONAL, ELISHA HALL MEMORIAL SCHOLARSHIP

Scholarship offered to a woman seeking to further the aviation career in flight training, aircraft scheduling or dispatch, aviation management, aviation maintenance, or avionics. Preference will be given to applicants from Cincinnati Ohio/Tri-State area, but all applicants will be considered based upon character, need, community involvement, and accomplishments. Must be a member of WAI, but does not have to be member of Cincinnati Chapter.

Academic Fields/Career Goals: Aviation/Aerospace.

Award: Scholarship for use in freshman, sophomore, junior, or senior years; not renewable. *Number:* 1. *Amount:* $1500.

Eligibility Requirements: Applicant must be enrolled or expecting to enroll full- or part-time at a two-year or technical institution or university and female. Applicant or parent of applicant must be member of Women in Aviation, International. Applicant or parent of applicant must have employment or volunteer experience in community service. Available to U.S. and non-U.S. citizens.

Application Requirements: Application form, essay. *Deadline:* November 12.

Contact: Donna Wallace, Exhibit Coordinator/Scholarship Coordinator
Women in Aviation, International
3647 State Route 503 South
West Alexandria, OH 45381
Phone: 937-839-4647
Fax: 937-839-4645
E-mail: dwallace@wai.org

BEHAVIORAL SCIENCE

101ST AIRBORNE DIVISION ASSOCIATION

http://www.screamingeaglefoundation.org/

AL & WILLIAMARY VISTE SCHOLARSHIP
• *See page 99*

AVACARE MEDICAL

https://avacaremedical.com

AVACARE MEDICAL SCHOLARSHIP
• *See page 100*

BHW GROUP

https://thebhwgroup.com/

BHW WOMEN IN STEM SCHOLARSHIP
• *See page 107*

INDIAN HEALTH SERVICES, UNITED STATES DEPARTMENT OF HEALTH AND HUMAN SERVICES

http://www.ihs.gov/scholarship

HEALTH PROFESSIONS PREPARATORY SCHOLARSHIP PROGRAM

Scholarship for undergraduate American Indian/Alaska Native students enrolled part-time or full-time in programs related to health and allied health professions. Minimum 2.0 GPA required to apply. Applicant must demonstrate a desire to serve AI/AN people when their health or allied health profession education/ training is complete. The dollar amount and number of awards varies annually.

Academic Fields/Career Goals: Behavioral Science; Biology; Health and Medical Sciences; Nursing; Optometry; Pharmacy; Psychology; Social Sciences.

Award: Scholarship for use in junior, senior, or graduate years; not renewable. *Number:* 25–50. *Amount:* $13,250–$52,600.

Eligibility Requirements: Applicant must be of English heritage; American Indian/Alaska Native; enrolled or expecting to enroll full- or part-time at a four-year institution or university and resident of Alabama, Alaska, Arizona, Arkansas, California, Colorado, Connecticut, Delaware, District of Columbia, Florida, Georgia, Hawaii, Idaho, Illinois, Indiana, Iowa, Kansas, Kentucky, Louisiana, Maine, Maryland, Massachusetts, Michigan, Minnesota, Mississippi, Missouri, Montana, Nebraska, Nevada, New Hampshire, New Jersey, New Mexico, New York, North Carolina, North Dakota, Ohio, Oklahoma, Oregon, Pennsylvania, Rhode Island, South Carolina, South Dakota, Tennessee, Texas, Utah, Vermont, Virginia, Washington, West Virginia, Wisconsin, Wyoming. Available to U.S. citizens.

Application Requirements: Application form, essay. *Deadline:* March 28.

Contact: Ms. Reta Brewer, Branch Chief
Indian Health Services, United States Department of Health and Human Services
5600 Fishers Lane
Mail Stop: OHR 11E53A
Rockville, MD 20857
Phone: 301-443-6197
Fax: 301-443-6048
E-mail: reta.brewer@ihs.gov

INTERMOUNTAIN MEDICAL IMAGING

https://www.aboutimi.com/

INTERMOUNTAIN MEDICAL IMAGING SCHOLARSHIP
• *See page 125*

THE JACKSON LABORATORY

https://www.jax.org

THE JACKSON LABORATORY COLLEGE SCHOLARSHIP PROGRAM
• *See page 108*

KETAMINE CLINICS OF LOS ANGELES

http://www.ketamineclinics.com/

KETAMINE CLINICS OF LOS ANGELES SCHOLARSHIP PROGRAM

To be eligible, students must be planning to enroll in medical school, or a degree program that leads to medical school, in the following academic year, or already be enrolled in a medical degree program and plan to return in the next academic year. The scholarship is available to all students ages 18 and over, at all levels from high school to graduate school.

Academic Fields/Career Goals: Behavioral Science; Biology; Health and Medical Sciences; Neurobiology; Nursing; Optometry; Psychology; Therapy/Rehabilitation.

Award: Scholarship for use in freshman, sophomore, junior, senior, graduate, or postgraduate years; renewable. *Number:* 1. *Amount:* $1000.

Eligibility Requirements: Applicant must be enrolled or expecting to enroll full-time at a two-year or four-year or technical institution or university. Available to U.S. and non-U.S. citizens.

Application Requirements: Essay. *Deadline:* December 1.

Contact: Mr. Sam Mandel, Chief Operating Officer
Ketamine Clinics of Los Angeles
11645 Wilshire Blvd.
Suite 852
Los Angeles, CA 90025
Phone: 310-270-0625
E-mail: scholarship@ketamineclinics.com

MEDICAL SCRUBS COLLECTION

http://medicalscrubscollection.com

MEDICAL SCRUBS COLLECTION SCHOLARSHIP
• *See page 104*

MENTAL HEALTH ASSOCIATION IN NEW YORK STATE INC.

www.MHANYS.org

SYLVIA LASK SCHOLARSHIP

The Sylvia Lask Scholarship Committee is awarded annually by the Mental Health Association in New York State, Inc (MHANYS). It was named in honor of Sylvia Lask in 2018. Ms. Lask is a tireless Mental Health Advocate who championed the creation of New York State Mental Health Education Law from inception. This law requires Mental Health to be taught as part of health class in all K-12 classes — NYS is the first state in the nation to make this happen. Ms. Lask is known statewide for a lifetime of fighting on behalf of all New Yorkers. She is a visionary and a master mental health advocate based out of Bronx, NY. She has served in many capacities on many different boards over her career. The purpose of this scholarship is to encourage the education of individuals to assist in the prevention and treatment of mental illnesses, the promotion of mental health, and the empowerment of adults, children, and families whose lives have been affected by mental illnesses.

Academic Fields/Career Goals: Behavioral Science.

Award: Scholarship for use in junior, senior, or graduate years; not renewable. *Number:* 1. *Amount:* $2500.

Eligibility Requirements: Applicant must be enrolled or expecting to enroll full- or part-time at a four-year institution or university; resident of New York and studying in New York. Available to U.S. citizens.

Application Requirements: Application form, essay, financial need analysis, recommendations or references, transcript. *Deadline:* June 30.

Contact: Awards Committee
E-mail: scholarship@mhanys.org

NATIONAL INSTITUTES OF HEALTH

https://www.training.nih.gov/programs/ugsp

NIH UNDERGRADUATE SCHOLARSHIP PROGRAM FOR STUDENTS FROM DISADVANTAGED BACKGROUNDS
• *See page 101*

NEXTSTEPU

http://www.nextstepu.com/

$1,500 STEM SCHOLARSHIP
• *See page 104*

NOVUS BIOLOGICALS, LLC

https://www.novusbio.com

NOVUS BIOLOGICALS SCHOLARSHIP PROGRAM
• *See page 101*

R&D SYSTEMS SCHOLARSHIP
• *See page 101*

THE SOCIETY FOR THE SCIENTIFIC STUDY OF SEXUALITY

http://www.sexscience.org/

THE SOCIETY FOR THE SCIENTIFIC STUDY OF SEXUALITY STUDENT RESEARCH GRANT
• *See page 105*

WILLIAMS LAW GROUP

https://familylawyersnewjersey.com/

WILLIAMS LAW GROUP OPPORTUNITY TO GROW SCHOLARSHIP
• *See page 119*

BIOLOGY

101ST AIRBORNE DIVISION ASSOCIATION

http://www.screamingeaglefoundation.org/

AL & WILLIAMARY VISTE SCHOLARSHIP
• *See page 99*

AIST FOUNDATION

http://www.aistfoundation.org/

ASSOCIATION FOR IRON AND STEEL TECHNOLOGY OHIO VALLEY CHAPTER SCHOLARSHIP

Scholarship of $1000 per year for up to four years provided that applicant continues to meet requirements and reapplies for scholarship. Applicant must be a dependent of Ohio Valley Chapter member, or student or Young Professional member. Must attend or plan to attend an accredited school full-time and pursue a degree in any technological field, including engineering, physics, computer sciences, chemistry or other fields approved by the scholarship committee.

Academic Fields/Career Goals: Biology; Computer Science/Data Processing; Electrical Engineering/Electronics; Engineering-Related Technologies; Engineering/Technology; Materials Science, Engineering, and Metallurgy; Physical Sciences.

Award: Scholarship for use in freshman, sophomore, junior, or senior years; not renewable. *Number:* 1–2. *Amount:* $1000.

Eligibility Requirements: Applicant must be enrolled or expecting to enroll full-time at a four-year institution or university. Applicant or parent of applicant must be member of Association for Iron and Steel Technology. Available to U.S. and non-U.S. citizens.

Application Requirements: Application form, essay, recommendations or references, resume, test scores, transcript. *Deadline:* March 31.

Contact: Jeff McKain, Scholarship Chairman
AIST Foundation
11451 Reading Road
Cincinnati, OH 45241
Phone: 724-776-6040
E-mail: jeff.mckain@xtek.com

ALBERTA HERITAGE SCHOLARSHIP FUND

http://www.alis.alberta.ca/

ABORIGINAL HEALTH CAREERS BURSARY

Award between CAN$2000 and CAN$11,000 for aboriginal students in Alberta, entering their second or subsequent year of postsecondary education in a health field. Must be Indian, Inuit, or Metis students who have been living in Alberta for at least the last three years, and are enrolled full-time at the technical, college, or university level. Students are selected on the basis of financial need, previous academic record, program of study, involvement in the aboriginal community, and experience in the health care field. For additional information and an application, visit website http://alis.alberta.ca.

Academic Fields/Career Goals: Biology; Dental Health/Services; Health Administration; Health and Medical Sciences; Nursing; Therapy/Rehabilitation.

Award: Scholarship for use in sophomore, junior, or senior years; not renewable.

Eligibility Requirements: Applicant must be Canadian citizen; American Indian/Alaska Native; enrolled or expecting to enroll full-time at a two-year or four-year or technical institution or university and resident of Alberta.

Application Requirements: Application form, essay, financial need analysis, proof of Aboriginal status, recommendations or references, transcript. *Deadline:* May 1.

AMERICAN ASSOCIATION OF BLOOD BANKS-SBB SCHOLARSHIP AWARDS

http://www.aabb.org/

AABB-FENWAL SCHOLARSHIP AWARD

Scholarship for an individual enrolled, accepted for enrollment in, or having recently completed a program leading to Specialist in Blood Banking certification in an AABB-accredited institution.

Academic Fields/Career Goals: Biology.

Award: Scholarship for use in freshman, sophomore, junior, senior, or graduate years; not renewable. *Number:* 2.

Eligibility Requirements: Applicant must be enrolled or expecting to enroll full- or part-time at an institution or university. Available to U.S. citizens.

Application Requirements: Application form. *Deadline:* June 1.

Contact: Scholarship Coordinator
E-mail: rsinger@aabb.org

AMERICAN INDIAN SCIENCE AND ENGINEERING SOCIETY

http://www.aises.org/

A.T. ANDERSON MEMORIAL SCHOLARSHIP PROGRAM
• *See page 105*

AMERICAN LEGION DEPARTMENT OF MARYLAND

http://www.mdlegion.org/

AMERICAN LEGION DEPARTMENT OF MARYLAND MATH-SCIENCE SCHOLARSHIP
• *See page 99*

AMERICAN PHYSIOLOGICAL SOCIETY

https://www.physiology.org/

BARBARA A. HORWITZ AND JOHN M. HOROWITZ UNDERGRADUATE RESEARCH AWARDS

These awards recognize excellence in undergraduate physiology research. The applicant must be the first author on an abstract submitted to the Experimental Biology meeting and must be working with an APS member who attests that the student is deserving of the first authorship. The student must be enrolled as an undergraduate student at the time of abstract submission. There are two types of awards: 1) Barbara A. Horwitz and John M. Horowitz Outstanding Undergraduate Abstract Award for best abstract and student letter. This award provides $100, a certificate and a two-year complimentary APS membership; and 2) Barbara A. Horwitz and John M. Horowitz Excellence in Undergraduate Research Award for the best poster and presentation. Recipient receives $400 and a certificate. The candidate must be an Outstanding Undergraduate Abstract awardee. The top ranked Excellence in Undergraduate Research awardee receives an additional $250. For more information, go to www.the-aps.org/EB-undergrad.

Academic Fields/Career Goals: Biology; Environmental Science; Health and Medical Sciences; Marine Biology; Natural Sciences; Neurobiology; Science, Technology, and Society; Sports-Related/Exercise Science.

Award: Prize for use in freshman, sophomore, junior, or senior years; not renewable. *Number:* 12–30. *Amount:* $100–$500.

Eligibility Requirements: Applicant must be enrolled or expecting to enroll full-time at a two-year institution or university. Available to U.S. and non-U.S. citizens.

Application Requirements: Application form, application form may be submitted online, essay. *Deadline:* January 12.

Contact: Dr. Marsha Matyas, Director of Education Programs
American Physiological Society
6120 Executive Boulevard
Suite 600
Rockville, MD 20852-4911
Phone: 301-634-7164
Fax: 301-634-7241
E-mail: education@physiology.org

AMERICAN SOCIETY OF AGRICULTURAL AND BIOLOGICAL ENGINEERS

http://www.asabe.org/

WILLIAM J. ADAMS, JR. AND MARIJANE E. ADAMS SCHOLARSHIP
• *See page 92*

AMERICAN SOCIETY OF ICHTHYOLOGISTS AND HERPETOLOGISTS

http://www.asih.org/

GAIGE FUND AWARD

Funds are used to provide support to young herpetologists for museum or laboratory study, travel, fieldwork, or any other activity that will effectively enhance their professional careers and their contributions to the science of herpetology. Applicants must be members of ASIH and be enrolled for an advanced degree. Visit website at http://www.asih.org for additional information.

Academic Fields/Career Goals: Biology.

Award: Grant for use in freshman, sophomore, junior, senior, or graduate years; not renewable. *Number:* 5–10. *Amount:* $400–$1000.

Eligibility Requirements: Applicant must be enrolled or expecting to enroll full-time at a four-year institution or university. Applicant or parent of applicant must be member of American Society of Ichthyologists and Herpetologists. Available to U.S. and non-U.S. citizens.

Application Requirements: Application form, financial need analysis, recommendations or references. *Deadline:* March 1.

Contact: Maureen Donnelly, Secretary
Phone: 305-348-1235
Fax: 305-348-1986
E-mail: asih@fiu.edu

RANEY FUND AWARD

Applications are solicited for grants awarded from the Raney Fund for ichthyology. Funds are used to provide support for young ichthyologists for museums or laboratory study, travel, fieldwork, or any activity that will effectively enhance their professional careers and their contributions to the sciences of ichthyology. Must be a member of ASIH and be enrolled for an advanced degree. Visit website at http://www.asih.org for additional information.

Academic Fields/Career Goals: Biology.

Award: Grant for use in freshman, sophomore, junior, senior, or graduate years; not renewable. *Number:* 5–10. *Amount:* $400–$1000.

Eligibility Requirements: Applicant must be enrolled or expecting to enroll full-time at a four-year institution or university. Applicant or parent of applicant must be member of American Society of Ichthyologists and Herpetologists. Available to U.S. and non-U.S. citizens.

Application Requirements: Application form, financial need analysis, recommendations or references. *Deadline:* March 1.

Contact: Maureen Donnelly, Secretary
Phone: 305-348-1235
Fax: 305-348-1986
E-mail: asih@fiu.edu

ASSOCIATION FOR WOMEN GEOSCIENTISTS (AWG)

http://www.awg.org/

AWG UNDERGRADUATE EXCELLENCE IN PALEONTOLOGY AWARD

• *See page 106*

ASSOCIATION OF CALIFORNIA WATER AGENCIES

http://www.acwa.com/

ASSOCIATION OF CALIFORNIA WATER AGENCIES SCHOLARSHIPS

• *See page 106*

CLAIR A. HILL SCHOLARSHIP

• *See page 106*

ASSOCIATION OF STATE DAM SAFETY OFFICIALS (ASDSO)

http://www.DamSafety.org

ASSOCIATION OF STATE DAM SAFETY OFFICIALS (ASDSO) SENIOR UNDERGRADUATE SCHOLARSHIP

Scholarships will be awarded for the 2019/2020 school year and have ranged from $5,000 to $10,000 in recent years. Successful recipients must be U.S. citizens and enrolled full-time at the senior level (during the 2019/2020 school year) in an accredited civil engineering program, or in a related field as determined by ASDSO, and must demonstrate an interest in pursuing a career in hydraulics, hydrology or geotechnical disciplines, or in another discipline related to the design, construction and operation of dams. Undergraduate students planning to graduate in May/December 2020 will be eligible for the scholarship. Applicants must have a cumulative grade point average of 2.5 for the first three years of college and be recommended by their academic advisor. The basis for selection will generally follow these guidelines: academic scholarship, financial need, work experience/activities, essay. Announcement of successful candidates will be made in July 2019. https://damsafety.org/apply-scholarship

Academic Fields/Career Goals: Biology; Civil Engineering; Computer Science/Data Processing; Construction Engineering/Management; Earth Science; Electrical Engineering/Electronics; Energy and Power Engineering; Engineering-Related Technologies; Engineering/Technology; Environmental Science; Geography; Materials Science, Engineering, and Metallurgy; Mechanical Engineering; Natural Resources; Natural Sciences; Science, Technology, and Society; Surveying, Surveying Technology, Cartography, or Geographic Information Science; Urban and Regional Planning.

Award: Scholarship for use in senior year; not renewable. *Number:* 1–3. *Amount:* $5000–$10,000.

Eligibility Requirements: Applicant must be enrolled or expecting to enroll full-time at a four-year institution or university. Available to U.S. citizens.

Application Requirements: Application form, essay, financial need analysis, recommendations or references, transcript. *Deadline:* March 29.

Contact: Student Outreach Coordinator
Association of State Dam Safety Officials (ASDSO)
239 S Limestone
Lexington, KY 40508
Phone: 859-550-2788
Fax: 859-550-2795
E-mail: info@damsafety.org

ASSOCIATION ON AMERICAN INDIAN AFFAIRS, INC.

http://www.indian-affairs.org/

ELIZABETH AND SHERMAN ASCHE MEMORIAL SCHOLARSHIP FUND

• *See page 93*

ASTRONAUT SCHOLARSHIP FOUNDATION

http://www.astronautscholarship.org/

ASTRONAUT SCHOLARSHIP

• *See page 107*

BARRY GOLDWATER SCHOLARSHIP AND EXCELLENCE IN EDUCATION FOUNDATION

https://goldwater.scholarsapply.org

BARRY M. GOLDWATER SCHOLARSHIP AND EXCELLENCE IN EDUCATION PROGRAM

• *See page 107*

BHW GROUP

https://thebhwgroup.com/

BHW WOMEN IN STEM SCHOLARSHIP
• *See page 107*

B.O.G. PEST CONTROL

http://www.bogpestcontrol.com/

B.O.G. PEST CONTROL SCHOLARSHIP FUND

B.O.G. Pest Control has established a merit-based scholarship fund for individuals seeking undergraduate or graduate level education in chemistry, chemical engineering, biology, environmental studies or related fields. The winner of the scholarship will be a person who demonstrates academic excellence, as well as a passion for the pursuit of further study in environmental education at an accredited college or university.

Academic Fields/Career Goals: Biology; Chemical Engineering; Earth Science; Environmental Science; Natural Resources; Natural Sciences.

Award: Scholarship for use in freshman, sophomore, junior, senior, or graduate years; not renewable. *Number:* 1. *Amount:* $1000.

Eligibility Requirements: Applicant must be enrolled or expecting to enroll full-time at a four-year institution or university. Available to U.S. citizens.

Application Requirements: Application form, essay. *Deadline:* March 15.

Contact: Angela Hieronimus
B.O.G. Pest Control
645 Central Avenue East
Edgewater, MD 21037
Phone: 410-867-1002
E-mail: ahieronimus@bladesofgreen.com

BROWN AND CALDWELL

http://www.brownandcaldwell.com

ECKENFELDER SCHOLARSHIP

Dr. Wesley Eckenfelder, Jr.'s career as an environmental trailblazer spanned more than 50 years, during which time he trained thousands of graduate students and professionals in the science and art of industrial wastewater treatment. To honor his dedication to the environmental industry, we offer a $5,000 Dr. Wesley Eckenfelder, Jr. Scholarship to support students who are interested in pursuing a career in the environmental profession. Applicant must be a United States citizen or permanent resident; a full-time student enrolled in his/her junior, senior, or graduate program at an accredited college/university; must have declared a major in civil, chemical or environmental engineering, or one of the environmental sciences (e.g. geology, hydrogeology, ecology); must have a cumulative GPA of 3.0 or higher on a 4.0 scale (or equivalent on a 5.0 scale). All candidates must submit with a completed application; resume; an essay of 250 words minimum, "Tell us about a personal experience that influenced your decision to focus on environmental studies"; two written recommendations, with at least one from a university official (e.g. advisor, professor); and an official transcript of your academic record. Scholarship funds my only be used for university/college billed expenses such as tuition. We will be accepting 2017 applications starting at the end of March 2017. Applications will closed and materials must be postmarked by April 30th 2017 to be considered for our 2017 scholarships.

Academic Fields/Career Goals: Biology; Chemical Engineering; Civil Engineering; Construction Engineering/Management; Earth Science; Electrical Engineering/Electronics; Energy and Power Engineering; Engineering-Related Technologies; Engineering/Technology; Environmental Health; Environmental Science; Geography; Hydrology; Marine/Ocean Engineering; Mechanical Engineering; Meteorology/Atmospheric Science; Natural Resources; Natural Sciences; Oceanography; Paper and Pulp Engineering; Science, Technology, and Society; Surveying, Surveying Technology, Cartography, or Geographic Information Science.

Award: Scholarship for use in junior, senior, graduate, or postgraduate years; not renewable. *Number:* 1. *Amount:* $5000.

Eligibility Requirements: Applicant must be enrolled or expecting to enroll full-time at a four-year institution or university. Available to U.S. citizens.

Application Requirements: Application form, essay. *Deadline:* April 30.

Contact: BC Scholarships Committee
Brown and Caldwell
1527 Cole Boulevard
Suite 300
Lakewood, CO 80401
E-mail: Scholarships@brwncald.com

MINORITY SCHOLARSHIP PROGRAM

At Brown and Caldwell, we value diversity in the workplace, supporting organizations like the National Society of Black Engineers and the Society for Hispanic Professional Engineers. We also offer a $5,000 Minority Scholarship to support students who identify as minorities and are interested in pursuing a career in the environmental profession. Applicant must be a United States citizen or permanent resident; a full-time student enrolled in his/her junior, senior, or graduate program at an accredited college/university; declared a major in civil, chemical, or environmental engineering or one of the environmental sciences (e.g. geology, hydrogeology, ecology); have a cumulative GPA of 3.0 or higher on a 4.0 scale (or equivalent on a 5.0 scale); identify as a member of a minority group (e.g. African American, Hispanic, Asian or Pacific American or Alaska Native). All candidates must submit with a completed application; resume; an essay of 250 words minimum, "Tell us about a personal experience that influenced your decision to focus on environmental studies"; two written recommendations, with at least one from a university official (e.g. advisor, professor); and an official transcript of your academic record. Scholarship funds my only be used for university/college billed expenses such as tuition. We will be accepting 2017 applications starting at the end of March 2017. Applications will closed and materials must be postmarked by April 30th 2017 to be considered for our 2017 scholarships

Academic Fields/Career Goals: Biology; Chemical Engineering; Civil Engineering; Construction Engineering/Management; Earth Science; Electrical Engineering/Electronics; Energy and Power Engineering; Engineering-Related Technologies; Engineering/Technology; Environmental Health; Environmental Science; Geography; Hydrology; Marine/Ocean Engineering; Materials Science, Engineering, and Metallurgy; Mechanical Engineering; Meteorology/Atmospheric Science; Natural Resources; Natural Sciences; Oceanography; Paper and Pulp Engineering; Surveying, Surveying Technology, Cartography, or Geographic Information Science.

Award: Scholarship for use in junior, senior, graduate, or postgraduate years; not renewable. *Number:* 1. *Amount:* $5000.

Eligibility Requirements: Applicant must be American Indian/Alaska Native, Asian/Pacific Islander, Black (non-Hispanic), Hispanic and enrolled or expecting to enroll full-time at a four-year institution or university. Available to U.S. citizens.

Application Requirements: Application form, essay. *Deadline:* April 30.

Contact: BC Scholarships Committee
Brown and Caldwell
1527 Cole Boulevard
Suite 300
Lakewood, CO 80401
E-mail: scholarships@brwncald.com

CARDS AGAINST HUMANITY

https://cardsagainsthumanity.com/

SCIENCE AMBASSADOR SCHOLARSHIP
• *See page 107*

CUSHMAN FOUNDATION FOR FORAMINIFERAL RESEARCH

http://www.cushmanfoundation.org/index.php

LOEBLICH AND TAPPAN STUDENT RESEARCH AWARD

Research award given to both graduate and undergraduates interested in foraminiferal research. The maximum dollar value for the award is $2000.

Academic Fields/Career Goals: Biology; Marine Biology.

Award: Grant for use in freshman, sophomore, junior, senior, or graduate years; not renewable. *Number:* 1–57. *Amount:* $100–$2000.

Eligibility Requirements: Applicant must be enrolled or expecting to enroll full- or part-time at a four-year institution or university. Available to U.S. and non-U.S. citizens.

Application Requirements: Proposal for research, recommendations or references, resume. *Deadline:* September 15.

Contact: Jennifer Jett, Secretary and Treasurer
Cushman Foundation for Foraminiferal Research
MRC-121 Department of Paleobiology
PO Box 37012
Washington, DC 20013-7012
E-mail: jettje@si.edu

DISTIL NETWORKS

http://www.distilnetworks.com

WOMEN FORWARD IN TECHNOLOGY SCHOLARSHIP PROGRAM

• *See page 108*

EAA AVIATION FOUNDATION, INC.

http://www.eaa.org/

PAYZER SCHOLARSHIP

• *See page 130*

THE EXPERT INSTITUTE

https://www.theexpertinstitute.com

ANNUAL HEALTHCARE AND LIFE SCIENCES SCHOLARSHIP

The scholarship is available to students who are interested in or are already pursuing an undergraduate or graduate-level degree in healthcare or the life sciences. Applicants must have a 3.0 GPA or higher, and must also submit a 1,000-2,000 word essay on how their specialized knowledge could be applied to improving the practice of law.

Academic Fields/Career Goals: Biology; Dental Health/Services; Health and Medical Sciences; Marine Biology; Neurobiology; Nursing; Oncology; Optometry; Public Health; Therapy/Rehabilitation.

Award: Scholarship for use in freshman, sophomore, junior, senior, or graduate years; not renewable. *Number:* 1. *Amount:* $1000.

Eligibility Requirements: Applicant must be enrolled or expecting to enroll full- or part-time at a two-year or four-year or technical institution or university. Available to U.S. and non-U.S. citizens.

Application Requirements: Essay. *Deadline:* December 31.

Contact: Mr. Joseph O'Neill, Associate Director, Marketing
The Expert Institute
48 Wall Street
32nd Floor
New York, NY 10005
Phone: 646-216-2339
E-mail: joe@theexpertinstitute.com

EXPLORERS CLUB

http://www.explorers.org/

YOUTH ACTIVITY FUND GRANTS

• *See page 103*

FEDERATED GARDEN CLUBS OF CONNECTICUT

http://www.ctgardenclubs.org/

FEDERATED GARDEN CLUBS OF CONNECTICUT INC. SCHOLARSHIPS

One-time award for Connecticut residents entering his or her junior, senior, or graduate year at a Connecticut college or university and pursuing studies in gardening, landscaping, or biology. Minimum 3.0 GPA. Ph.D. candidates are not eligible.

Academic Fields/Career Goals: Biology; Horticulture/Floriculture; Landscape Architecture.

Award: Scholarship for use in junior, senior, or graduate years; not renewable. *Number:* 2–5. *Amount:* $1000–$5000.

Eligibility Requirements: Applicant must be enrolled or expecting to enroll full-time at a four-year institution or university; resident of Connecticut and studying in Connecticut. Available to U.S. citizens.

Application Requirements: Application form, driver's license, financial need analysis, recommendations or references, self-addressed stamped envelope with application, test scores, transcript. *Deadline:* July 1.

Contact: Barbara Bomblad, Office Manager
Phone: 203-488-5528
Fax: 203-488-5528 Ext. 51
E-mail: fgcctoff@hotmail.com

GREAT MINDS IN STEM

http://www.greatmindsinstem.org/college/scholarship-application-information

HENAAC SCHOLARSHIP PROGRAM

• *See page 100*

INDIAN HEALTH SERVICES, UNITED STATES DEPARTMENT OF HEALTH AND HUMAN SERVICES

http://www.ihs.gov/scholarship

HEALTH PROFESSIONS PREPARATORY SCHOLARSHIP PROGRAM

• *See page 137*

INDIAN HEALTH SERVICE HEALTH PROFESSIONS PRE-GRADUATE SCHOLARSHIPS

• *See page 108*

THE JACKSON LABORATORY

https://www.jax.org

THE JACKSON LABORATORY COLLEGE SCHOLARSHIP PROGRAM

• *See page 108*

KENTUCKY ENERGY AND ENVIRONMENT CABINET

http://dep.ky.gov

ENVIRONMENTAL PROTECTION SCHOLARSHIP

Renewable awards for college juniors, seniors, and graduate students for in-state tuition, fees, room and board, and a book allowance at a Kentucky public university. Minimum 3.0 GPA required. Must work full-time for the Kentucky Department for Environmental Protection upon graduation (six months for each semester of scholarship support received). Interview required. Program not generally appropriate for non-residents.

Academic Fields/Career Goals: Biology; Chemical Engineering; Civil Engineering; Earth Science; Environmental Science; Hydrology; Mechanical Engineering; Natural Sciences.

Award: Scholarship for use in junior, senior, or graduate years; renewable. *Number:* 1–4. *Amount:* $10,000–$13,000.

Eligibility Requirements: Applicant must be enrolled or expecting to enroll full-time at a four-year institution or university; resident of Kentucky and studying in Kentucky. Available to U.S. citizens.

Application Requirements: Application form, essay, interview. *Deadline:* February 15.

Contact: James Kipp, Scholarship Program Coordinator
Kentucky Energy and Environment Cabinet
233 Mining/Mineral Resources Building
Lexington, KY 40506-0107
Phone: 859-257-1299
E-mail: kipp@uky.edu

KETAMINE CLINICS OF LOS ANGELES

http://www.ketamineclinics.com/

KETAMINE CLINICS OF LOS ANGELES SCHOLARSHIP PROGRAM
• *See page 138*

THE LAND CONSERVANCY OF NEW JERSEY

http://www.tlc-nj.org/

ROGERS FAMILY SCHOLARSHIP

The Scholarship Program is administered by the Board of Trustees of The Land Conservancy of New Jersey and is awarded annually to deserving individuals who plan careers in environmental science, natural resource management, conservation, horticulture, park administration, or a related field. An applicant must be a student in good standing with at least 15 credits completed, have an academic average equivalent to a 3.0 or higher, be a resident of New Jersey and considering a career in New Jersey that is consistent with the goals of the Conservancy. Selected finalists will have to attend an interview in late May or early June. Scholarship funds are paid only directly to the institution in which the recipient is enrolled, not to the individual.

Academic Fields/Career Goals: Biology; Earth Science; Environmental Science; Geography; Horticulture/Floriculture; Hydrology; Marine Biology; Meteorology/Atmospheric Science; Natural Resources; Oceanography; Physical Sciences; Recreation, Parks, Leisure Studies; Surveying, Surveying Technology, Cartography, or Geographic Information Science; Urban and Regional Planning.

Award: Scholarship for use in sophomore, junior, senior, or graduate years; not renewable. *Number:* 1. *Amount:* $7500.

Eligibility Requirements: Applicant must be enrolled or expecting to enroll full-time at a four-year institution or university and resident of New Jersey. Available to U.S. citizens.

Application Requirements: Application form, essay. *Deadline:* April 1.

Contact: Scholarship Program
The Land Conservancy of New Jersey
19 Boonton Avenue
Boonton, NJ 07005
Phone: 973-541-1010 Ext. 10
E-mail: info@tlc-nj.org

RUSSELL W. MYERS SCHOLARSHIP

The Scholarship Program is administered by the Board of Trustees of The Land Conservancy of New Jersey and is awarded annually to deserving individuals who plan careers in environmental science, natural resource management, conservation, horticulture, park administration, or a related field. An applicant must be a student in good standing with at least 15 credits completed, have an academic average equivalent to a 3.0 or higher, be a resident of New Jersey and considering a career in New Jersey that is consistent with the goals of the Conservancy. Selected finalists will have to attend an interview with The Committee in late May or early June. Scholarship funds are paid only directly to the institution where the recipient is enrolled, not to the individual.

Academic Fields/Career Goals: Biology; Earth Science; Environmental Science; Hydrology; Landscape Architecture; Marine Biology; Natural Resources; Oceanography; Recreation, Parks, Leisure Studies; Surveying, Surveying Technology, Cartography, or Geographic Information Science; Urban and Regional Planning.

Award: Scholarship for use in sophomore, junior, senior, or graduate years; not renewable. *Number:* 1. *Amount:* $7500.

Eligibility Requirements: Applicant must be enrolled or expecting to enroll full-time at a four-year institution or university and resident of New Jersey. Available to U.S. citizens.

Application Requirements: Application form, essay. *Deadline:* April 1.

Contact: Scholarship Program
The Land Conservancy of New Jersey
19 Boonton Avenue
Boonton, NJ 07005
Phone: 973-541-1010

MEDICAL SCRUBS COLLECTION

http://medicalscrubscollection.com

MEDICAL SCRUBS COLLECTION SCHOLARSHIP
• *See page 104*

NASA IDAHO SPACE GRANT CONSORTIUM

http://www.idahospacegrant.org

NASA IDAHO SPACE GRANT CONSORTIUM SCHOLARSHIP PROGRAM
• *See page 109*

NASA/MARYLAND SPACE GRANT CONSORTIUM

https://md.spacegrant.org

NASA MARYLAND SPACE GRANT CONSORTIUM SCHOLARSHIPS
• *See page 109*

NASA MONTANA SPACE GRANT CONSORTIUM

http://www.spacegrant.montana.edu/

MONTANA SPACE GRANT SCHOLARSHIP PROGRAM
• *See page 132*

NASA'S VIRGINIA SPACE GRANT CONSORTIUM

http://www.vsgc.odu.edu/

COMMUNITY COLLEGE STEM SCHOLARSHIPS
• *See page 110*

UNDERGRADUATE STEM RESEARCH SCHOLARSHIPS
• *See page 110*

NATIONAL COUNCIL OF STATE GARDEN CLUBS INC. SCHOLARSHIP

http://www.gardenclub.org/

NATIONAL COUNCIL OF STATE GARDEN CLUBS INC. SCHOLARSHIP
• *See page 94*

NATIONAL GARDEN CLUBS INC.

http://www.gardenclub.org/

NATIONAL GARDEN CLUBS INC. SCHOLARSHIP PROGRAM
• *See page 94*

NATIONAL INSTITUTES OF HEALTH

https://www.training.nih.gov/programs/ugsp

NIH UNDERGRADUATE SCHOLARSHIP PROGRAM FOR STUDENTS FROM DISADVANTAGED BACKGROUNDS
• *See page 101*

NEXTSTEPU

http://www.nextstepu.com/

$1,500 STEM SCHOLARSHIP
• *See page 104*

NOVUS BIOLOGICALS, LLC

https://www.novusbio.com

NOVUS BIOLOGICALS SCHOLARSHIP PROGRAM
• *See page 101*

R&D SYSTEMS SCHOLARSHIP
• *See page 101*

TOCRIS BIOSCIENCE SCHOLARSHIP
• *See page 102*

OREGON OFFICE OF STUDENT ACCESS AND COMPLETION

https://oregonstudentaid.gov/

SEHAR SALEHA AHMAD AND ABRAHIM EKRAMULLAH ZAFAR FOUNDATION SCHOLARSHIP
• *See page 110*

SCARLETT FAMILY FOUNDATION SCHOLARSHIP PROGRAM

http://www.scarlettfoundation.org/

SCHOLARSHIP FOR STUDENTS PURSUING A BUSINESS OR STEM DEGREE
• *See page 80*

SOCIETY FOR INTEGRATIVE AND COMPARATIVE BIOLOGY

http://www.sicb.org/

LIBBIE H. HYMAN MEMORIAL SCHOLARSHIP

Scholarship provides assistance to students to take courses or to carry on research on invertebrates at a marine freshwater or terrestrial field station. For more information and/or an application see website, http://www.sicb.org.

Academic Fields/Career Goals: Biology; Marine Biology.

Award: Scholarship for use in senior year; not renewable. *Number:* 1. *Amount:* $750–$1200.

Eligibility Requirements: Applicant must be enrolled or expecting to enroll full- or part-time at a four-year institution or university. Available to U.S. and non-U.S. citizens.

Application Requirements: Application form, essay, financial need analysis, recommendations or references, transcript. *Deadline:* March 6.

Contact: Bruno Pernet, Chair, Scholarship Committee
Society for Integrative and Comparative Biology
California State University
Long Beach, CA 90840
Phone: 562-985-5378
Fax: 562-985-8878
E-mail: bpernet@csulb.edu

THE SOCIETY FOR THE SCIENTIFIC STUDY OF SEXUALITY

http://www.sexscience.org/

THE SOCIETY FOR THE SCIENTIFIC STUDY OF SEXUALITY STUDENT RESEARCH GRANT
• *See page 105*

SOIL AND WATER CONSERVATION SOCIETY

http://www.swcs.org

DONALD A. WILLIAMS SCHOLARSHIP SOIL CONSERVATION SCHOLARSHIP
• *See page 91*

SOIL AND WATER CONSERVATION SOCIETY-NEW JERSEY CHAPTER

http://www.geocities.com/njswcs

EDWARD R. HALL SCHOLARSHIP
• *See page 91*

STRAIGHT NORTH

https://www.straightnorth.com/

STRAIGHT NORTH STEM SCHOLARSHIP
• *See page 81*

TAU KAPPA EPSILON EDUCATION FOUNDATION

https://www.tke.org/

TIMOTHY L. TASCHWER SCHOLARSHIP

This scholarship is awarded in recognition of academic achievement, with a cumulative grade point average of 2.75 or higher and recognizes outstanding leadership within the chapter, having served as a chapter officer or committee chairman. The applicant must be pursuing an undergraduate degree in natural resources, environmental sciences, earth sciences, biology or any of the pure sciences (geology, physics, chemistry, etc.).

Academic Fields/Career Goals: Biology; Earth Science; Environmental Science; Natural Resources; Science, Technology, and Society.

Award: Scholarship for use in freshman, sophomore, junior, or senior years. *Number:* 1.

Eligibility Requirements: Applicant must be enrolled or expecting to enroll at an institution or university and male. Applicant or parent of applicant must be member of Tau Kappa Epsilon. Available to U.S. citizens.

Application Requirements: Application form, application form may be submitted online, personal photograph. *Deadline:* March 15.

Contact: Rachel Stevenson, Foundation Communications Manager
Tau Kappa Epsilon Education Foundation
7439 Woodland Drive
Suite 100
Indianapolis, IN 46278
Phone: 317-872-6533 Ext. 246
E-mail: rstevenson@tke.org

UNITED NEGRO COLLEGE FUND

http://www.uncf.org/

LEIDOS STEM SCHOLARSHIP
• *See page 96*

UNITED STATES DEPARTMENT OF AGRICULTURE

http://www.usda.gov/

SAUL T. WILSON, JR., SCHOLARSHIP PROGRAM (STWJS)
• *See page 103*

WILLIAM HELMS SCHOLARSHIP PROGRAM (WHSP)
• *See page 96*

VERMONT SPACE GRANT CONSORTIUM

http://www.cems.uvm.edu/vsgc

VERMONT SPACE GRANT CONSORTIUM
• *See page 92*

WILSON ORNITHOLOGICAL SOCIETY

http://www.wilsonsociety.org/

GEORGE A. HALL/HAROLD F. MAYFIELD AWARD
• *See page 103*

PAUL A. STEWART AWARDS
• *See page 103*

BUSINESS/CONSUMER SERVICES

AACE INTERNATIONAL

http://www.aacei.org/

AACE INTERNATIONAL COMPETITIVE SCHOLARSHIP
• *See page 112*

ALICE L. HALTOM EDUCATIONAL FUND

http://www.alhef.org/

ALICE L. HALTOM EDUCATIONAL FUND

Award for students pursuing a career in information and records management. Up to $1000 for those in an associate degree program, and up to $2000 for students in a baccalaureate or advanced degree program. Students must be citizens of the United States or Canada.

Academic Fields/Career Goals: Business/Consumer Services; Computer Science/Data Processing; Health Administration; Health Information Management/Technology; Library and Information Sciences.

Award: Scholarship for use in freshman, sophomore, junior, senior, graduate, or postgraduate years; not renewable. *Number:* 5–15. *Amount:* $1000–$2000.

Eligibility Requirements: Applicant must be Canadian citizen and enrolled or expecting to enroll full- or part-time at a two-year or four-year institution or university. Available to U.S. and Canadian citizens.

Application Requirements: Application form, application form may be submitted online (http://www.alhef.org/scholarship/), essay, financial need analysis, recommendations or references. *Deadline:* May 1.

Contact: Executive Director
E-mail: contact@alhef.org

AMERICAN CONGRESS ON SURVEYING AND MAPPING

http://landsurveyorsunited.com/acsm

TRI-STATE SURVEYING AND PHOTOGRAMMETRY KRIS M. KUNZE MEMORIAL SCHOLARSHIP

One-time award of $1000 for students pursuing college-level courses in business administration or business management. Candidates, in order of priority, include professional land surveyors and certified photogrammetrists, land survey interns and students enrolled in a two- or four-year program in surveying and mapping. Must be ACSM member.

Academic Fields/Career Goals: Business/Consumer Services; Surveying, Surveying Technology, Cartography, or Geographic Information Science.

Award: Scholarship for use in freshman, sophomore, junior, or senior years; not renewable. *Number:* 1. *Amount:* $1000.

Eligibility Requirements: Applicant must be enrolled or expecting to enroll full- or part-time at a two-year or four-year institution or university. Applicant or parent of applicant must be member of American Congress on Surveying and Mapping. Available to U.S. citizens.

Application Requirements: Application form, essay, membership proof, recommendations or references, transcript. *Deadline:* October 1.

Contact: Ilse Genovese, Communications Director
American Congress on Surveying and Mapping
6 Montgomery Village Avenue, Suite 403
Gaithersburg, MD 20879
Phone: 240-632-9716 Ext. 113
Fax: 240-632-1321
E-mail: ilse.genovese@acsm.net

AMERICAN INDIAN SCIENCE AND ENGINEERING SOCIETY

http://www.aises.org/

A.T. ANDERSON MEMORIAL SCHOLARSHIP PROGRAM
• *See page 105*

AMERICAN WHOLESALE MARKETERS ASSOCIATION

http://www.awmanet.org/

RAY FOLEY MEMORIAL YOUTH EDUCATION FOUNDATION SCHOLARSHIP

Scholarship program annually offers two $5000 scholarships to deserving students. Awards are based on academic merit and a career interest in the candy/tobacco/ convenience-products wholesale industry. Must be employed by an AWMA wholesaler distributor member or be an immediate family member. Must be enrolled full-time in an undergraduate or graduate program. For details visit website http://www.awmanet.org/.

Academic Fields/Career Goals: Business/Consumer Services.

Award: Scholarship for use in freshman, sophomore, junior, senior, or graduate years; not renewable. *Number:* 2. *Amount:* $5000.

Eligibility Requirements: Applicant must be enrolled or expecting to enroll full-time at a four-year institution or university. Available to U.S. citizens.

Application Requirements: Application form, essay, recommendations or references. *Deadline:* May 21.

Contact: Kathy Trost, Manager of Education
American Wholesale Marketers Association
2750 Prosperity Avenue, Suite 530
Fairfax, VA 22031
Phone: 800-482-2962 Ext. 648
Fax: 703-573-5738
E-mail: kathyt@awmanet.org

AUTOMOTIVE AFTERMARKET SCHOLARSHIPS

http://www.automotivescholarships.com/

AUTOMOTIVE AFTERMARKET SCHOLARSHIPS

To receive a scholarship, applicants must be a high school graduate enrolled in a full time college-level program or an ASE/NATEF certified postsecondary automotive technical program, and planning a career in the automotive aftermarket.

Academic Fields/Career Goals: Business/Consumer Services; Marketing; Mechanical Engineering; Trade/Technical Specialties.

Award: Scholarship for use in freshman, sophomore, junior, senior, graduate, or postgraduate years; not renewable. *Amount:* $1000–$10,000.

Eligibility Requirements: Applicant must be enrolled or expecting to enroll full-time at a two-year or four-year or technical institution or university. Available to U.S. and non-U.S. citizens.

Application Requirements: Application form, essay. *Deadline:* March 31.

Contact: Jennifer Hollar, Scholarship Committee Chairman
Automotive Aftermarket Scholarships
PO Box 13966
Research Triangle Park, NC 27709-3966
Phone: 919-406-8811
E-mail: media@mema.org

AUTOMOTIVE WOMEN'S ALLIANCE FOUNDATION

http://awafoundation.org/index.php

AUTOMOTIVE WOMEN'S ALLIANCE FOUNDATION SCHOLARSHIPS
• *See page 71*

BALTIMORE CHAPTER OF THE AMERICAN MARKETING ASSOCIATION

http://www.amabaltimore.org/

UNDERGRADUATE MARKETING EDUCATION MERIT SCHOLARSHIPS

Scholarship of $3000 awarded for first place, two $1000 second place, and four $500 third place awards for full-time students in marketing. Must be attending a 4-year college or university in Maryland with credits equivalent to the status of a junior or senior as of September. Minimum 3.0 GPA required.

Academic Fields/Career Goals: Business/Consumer Services; Marketing.

Award: Scholarship for use in sophomore or junior years; not renewable. *Number:* 7. *Amount:* $500–$3000.

Eligibility Requirements: Applicant must be enrolled or expecting to enroll full-time at a four-year institution or university and studying in Maryland. Available to U.S. and non-U.S. citizens.

Application Requirements: Application form, test scores. *Deadline:* February 16.

Contact: Marisa O'Brien, Scholarship Committee
Phone: 410-467-2529
E-mail: scholarship@amabaltimore.org

BULKOFFICESUPPLY.COM

http://www.bulkofficesupply.com

OFFICE SUPPLY SCHOLARSHIP
• *See page 121*

CATCHING THE DREAM

http://www.catchingthedream.org/

MATH, ENGINEERING, SCIENCE, BUSINESS, EDUCATION, COMPUTERS SCHOLARSHIPS

Renewable scholarships for Native American students planning to study math, engineering, science, business, education, and computers, or presently studying in these fields. Study of social science, humanities and liberal arts also funded. Scholarships are awarded on merit and on the basis of likelihood of recipient improving the lives of Native American people. Scholarships are available nationwide.

Academic Fields/Career Goals: Business/Consumer Services; Computer Science/Data Processing; Education; Engineering/Technology; Humanities; Physical Sciences; Science, Technology, and Society; Social Sciences.

Award: Scholarship for use in freshman, sophomore, junior, senior, graduate, or postgraduate years; renewable. *Number:* 180. *Amount:* $500–$5000.

Eligibility Requirements: Applicant must be American Indian/Alaska Native and enrolled or expecting to enroll full-time at a two-year or four-year institution or university. Available to U.S. citizens.

Application Requirements: Application form, essay, financial need analysis, personal photograph. *Deadline:* continuous.

Contact: Joy Noll, Student Services
Catching the Dream
8200 Mountain Road, NE, Suite 103
Albuquerque, NM 87110
Phone: 505-262-2351
E-mail: nscholarsh@aol.com

NATIVE AMERICAN LEADERSHIP IN EDUCATION (NALE)

Renewable scholarships available for Native American and Alaska Native students. Must be at least one-quarter Native American from a federally recognized, state recognized, or terminated tribe. Must be U.S. citizen. Must demonstrate high academic achievement, depth of character, leadership, seriousness of purpose, and service orientation.

Academic Fields/Career Goals: Business/Consumer Services; Education; Humanities; Physical Sciences; Science, Technology, and Society.

Award: Scholarship for use in freshman, sophomore, junior, senior, graduate, or postgraduate years; renewable. *Number:* 30. *Amount:* $500–$5000.

Eligibility Requirements: Applicant must be American Indian/Alaska Native and enrolled or expecting to enroll full-time at a four-year institution or university. Available to U.S. citizens.

Application Requirements: Application form, essay, financial need analysis, personal photograph.

Contact: Joy Noll, Student Services
Catching the Dream
8200 Mountain Road, NE, Suite 103
Albuquerque, NM 87110
Phone: 505-262-2351
E-mail: nscholarsh@aol.com

TRIBAL BUSINESS MANAGEMENT PROGRAM (TBM)
• *See page 72*

DECA (DISTRIBUTIVE EDUCATION CLUBS OF AMERICA)

http://www.deca.org/

HARRY A. APPLEGATE SCHOLARSHIP
• *See page 73*

DELTA SIGMA PI LEADERSHIP FOUNDATION

http://www.dsp.org/

DELTA SIGMA PI UNDERGRADUATE SCHOLARSHIP

Applicant must be a member of Delta Sigma Pi in good standing with at least one full semester or quarter of college remaining in the fall following application.

Academic Fields/Career Goals: Business/Consumer Services.

Award: Scholarship for use in sophomore, junior, or senior years; not renewable. *Number:* 1–8. *Amount:* $1000.

Eligibility Requirements: Applicant must be enrolled or expecting to enroll full-time at a four-year institution or university. Applicant or parent of applicant must be member of Greek Organization. Available to U.S. and non-U.S. citizens.

Application Requirements: Application form, community service, essay, financial need analysis. *Deadline:* June 15.

Contact: Tyler Wash, Executive Vice President
Delta Sigma Pi Leadership Foundation
330 South Campus Avenue
Oxford, OH 45056
Phone: 513-523-1907
E-mail: foundation@dsp.org

DIGITAL THIRD COAST INTERNET MARKETING

http://www.digitalthirdcoast.net/

DIGITAL MARKETING SCHOLARSHIP

• *See page 84*

EASTERN STAR-GRAND CHAPTER OF CALIFORNIA

http://www.oescal.org/

SCHOLARSHIPS FOR EDUCATION, BUSINESS AND RELIGION

Scholarship of $500 to $3000 awarded to students residing in California for post-secondary study. These scholarships are awarded for the study of business, education or religion.

Academic Fields/Career Goals: Business/Consumer Services; Education; Religion/Theology.

Award: Scholarship for use in freshman, sophomore, junior, or senior years; renewable. *Amount:* $500–$3000.

Eligibility Requirements: Applicant must be enrolled or expecting to enroll full-time at a two-year or four-year or technical institution or university and resident of California. Available to U.S. citizens.

Application Requirements: Application form, financial need analysis, personal photograph, proof of acceptance to college or university, recommendations or references, self-addressed stamped envelope with application, transcript. *Deadline:* March 8.

Contact: Maryann Barrios, Grand Secretary
Eastern Star-Grand Chapter of California
16960 Bastanchury Road, Suite E
Yorba Linda, CA 92886-1711
Phone: 714-986-2380
Fax: 714-986-2385
E-mail: gsecretary@oescal.org

ELECTRONIC DOCUMENT SYSTEMS FOUNDATION

http://www.edsf.org/

LYNDA BABOYIAN MEMORIAL SCHOLARSHIP

$2000 award for full-time students whose academic focus includes all document management and graphic communications careers. Minimum 3.0 GPA required.

Academic Fields/Career Goals: Business/Consumer Services; Computer Science/Data Processing; Graphics/Graphic Arts/Printing.

Award: Scholarship for use in freshman, sophomore, junior, or senior years; not renewable. *Number:* 1. *Amount:* $2000.

Eligibility Requirements: Applicant must be enrolled or expecting to enroll full-time at a two-year or four-year institution or university. Available to U.S. and non-U.S. citizens.

Application Requirements: Application form, community service, essay. *Deadline:* May 1.

Contact: Ms. Brenda Kai, Executive Director
Phone: 817-849-1145
E-mail: brenda.kai@edsf.org

FAMILY, CAREER AND COMMUNITY LEADERS OF AMERICA-TEXAS ASSOCIATION

http://www.texasfccla.org/

FCCLA REGIONAL SCHOLARSHIPS

One-time award for graduating high school seniors enrolled in full-time program in family and consumer sciences. Must be Texas resident and should study in Texas. Must have minimum GPA of 2.5.

Academic Fields/Career Goals: Business/Consumer Services; Home Economics.

Award: Scholarship for use in freshman year; not renewable. *Number:* up to 5. *Amount:* $1000.

Eligibility Requirements: Applicant must be high school student; planning to enroll or expecting to enroll full-time at a four-year institution or university; single; resident of Texas and studying in Texas. Applicant or parent of applicant must be member of Family, Career and Community Leaders of America. Available to U.S. citizens.

Application Requirements: Application form, essay, recommendations or references, test scores, transcript. *Deadline:* March 1.

Contact: Staff
Family, Career and Community Leaders of America-Texas Association
1107 West 45th
Austin, TX 78756
Phone: 512-306-0099
Fax: 512-442-7100
E-mail: fccla@texasfccla.org

FCCLA TEXAS FARM BUREAU SCHOLARSHIP

One-time award for a graduating high school senior enrolled in full-time program in family and consumer sciences. Must be a Texas resident and must study in Texas. Must have minimum GPA of 2.5. The award value is $5000.

Academic Fields/Career Goals: Business/Consumer Services; Home Economics.

Award: Scholarship for use in freshman year; not renewable. *Number:* 1. *Amount:* $1000.

Eligibility Requirements: Applicant must be high school student; planning to enroll or expecting to enroll full-time at a four-year institution or university; single; resident of Texas and studying in Texas. Applicant or parent of applicant must be member of Family, Career and Community Leaders of America. Available to U.S. citizens.

Application Requirements: Application form, driver's license, essay, recommendations or references, test scores, transcript. *Deadline:* March 1.

Contact: Staff
Family, Career and Community Leaders of America-Texas Association
1107 West 45th
Austin, TX 78756
Phone: 512-306-0099
Fax: 512-442-7100
E-mail: fccla@texasfccla.org

GOLDEN KEY INTERNATIONAL HONOUR SOCIETY

http://www.goldenkey.org/

BUSINESS ACHIEVEMENT AWARD

Award to members who excel in the study of business. Applicants will be asked to respond to a problem posed by an honorary member within the discipline. The response will be in the form of a professional business report. One winner will receive a $1000 award. The second place winner will receive $750 and the third place winner will receive $500.

Academic Fields/Career Goals: Business/Consumer Services.

Award: Prize for use in freshman, sophomore, junior, senior, graduate, or postgraduate years; not renewable. *Number:* 3. *Amount:* $500–$1000.

Eligibility Requirements: Applicant must be enrolled or expecting to enroll full- or part-time at a four-year institution or university. Available to U.S. and non-U.S. citizens.

Application Requirements: Application form, business-related report, entry in a contest, essay, recommendations or references, transcript. *Deadline:* March 3.

Contact: Scholarship Program Administrators
Golden Key International Honour Society
PO Box 23737
Nashville, TN 37202-3737
Phone: 800-377-2401
E-mail: scholarships@goldenkey.org

GOVERNMENT FINANCE OFFICERS ASSOCIATION

https://www.gfoa.org/

JEFFREY L. ESSER CAREER DEVELOPMENT SCHOLARSHIP
• *See page 75*

MINORITIES IN GOVERNMENT FINANCE SCHOLARSHIP
• *See page 75*

GREENPAL

GREENPAL BUSINESS SCHOLARSHIP

$2000 scholarship open to any high school senior, college freshman, or sophomore who owns and operates his/her own small business, or has put together a business plan to start a business while in college. The student must enter their freshman year at an accredited two- or four-year university, college or vocational/technical institute. Must be graduating high school senior or currently enrolled in a college of business with a 3.0 or higher GPA.

Academic Fields/Career Goals: Business/Consumer Services.

Award: Scholarship for use in freshman or sophomore years; not renewable. *Amount:* $2000.

Eligibility Requirements: Applicant must be enrolled or expecting to enroll full-time at a four-year or technical institution or university. Available to U.S. citizens.

Application Requirements: Application form, essay, recommendations or references, transcript. *Deadline:* February 28.

HOLSTEIN ASSOCIATION USA INC.

http://www.holsteinusa.com/

ROBERT H. RUMLER SCHOLARSHIP
• *See page 89*

HOUSE OF BLUES MUSIC FORWARD FOUNDATION

https://hobmusicforward.org/

STEVEN J. FINKEL SERVICE EXCELLENCE SCHOLARSHIP

Established in the memory of Steven J. Finkel, Live Nation's US Concerts division seeks to support the ever growing customer service expectation within the entertainment industry. The $10,000 scholarship will award students who are passionate about improving the live music customer experience for fans, artists, and employees.

Academic Fields/Career Goals: Business/Consumer Services; Communications; Economics; Hospitality Management; Music.

Award: Scholarship for use in junior or senior years; not renewable. *Number:* 1. *Amount:* $10,000.

Eligibility Requirements: Applicant must be enrolled or expecting to enroll full-time at a four-year institution or university and must have an interest in music or music/singing.

Application Requirements: Application form, essay. *Deadline:* March 31.

Contact: Ms. Nazanin Fatemian, House of Blues Music Forward Foundation
House of Blues Music Forward Foundation
7060 Hollywood Boulevard, Floor 2
Los Angeles, CA 90028
Phone: 323-821-3946
E-mail: nfatemian@hobmusicforward.org

TIFFANY GREEN OPERATOR SCHOLARSHIP AWARD
• *See page 85*

IDAHO STATE BROADCASTERS ASSOCIATION

http://www.idahobroadcasters.org/

WAYNE C. CORNILS MEMORIAL SCHOLARSHIP

Scholarship for students enrolled in an Idaho school on a full-time basis. Must be majoring in a broadcasting related field. Must have minimum GPA of 2.0 if in the first two years of school or 2.5 in the last two years of school.

Academic Fields/Career Goals: Business/Consumer Services; Communications; Engineering/Technology; Journalism; Marketing; TV/Radio Broadcasting.

Award: Scholarship for use in sophomore, junior, or senior years; not renewable. *Number:* 3. *Amount:* $1000.

Eligibility Requirements: Applicant must be enrolled or expecting to enroll full-time at a four-year institution or university; resident of Idaho and studying in Idaho. Available to U.S. citizens.

Application Requirements: Application form, essay. *Deadline:* March 15.

Contact: Connie Searles, President and CEO
Idaho State Broadcasters Association
1674 Hill Road
Suite 3
Boise, ID 83702
Phone: 208-345-3072
E-mail: isba@qwestoffice.net

INSTITUTE OF MANAGEMENT ACCOUNTANTS

https://www.imanet.org/students/scholarships-and-awards/scholarships?ssopc=1

INSTITUTE OF MANAGEMENT ACCOUNTANTS MEMORIAL EDUCATION FUND SCHOLARSHIPS

Scholarships for IMA undergraduate or graduate student members studying at accredited institutions in the U.S. and Puerto Rico. Must be pursuing a career in management accounting, financial management, or information technology, and have a minimum GPA of 3.0. Awards based on academic merit, IMA participation, strength of recommendations, and quality of written statements.

Academic Fields/Career Goals: Business/Consumer Services.

Award: Scholarship for use in sophomore, junior, senior, or graduate years; not renewable. *Amount:* $1000–$2500.

Eligibility Requirements: Applicant must be enrolled or expecting to enroll full- or part-time at a two-year institution or university. Available to U.S. citizens.

Application Requirements: Application form, application form may be submitted online, essay. *Deadline:* March 10.

Contact: Kerry Butkera, Research & Academic Relations Administrator
Institute of Management Accountants
IMA
10 Paragon Drive, Suite 1
Montvale, NJ 07628
Phone: 800-638-4427 Ext. 1546
E-mail: kbutkera@imanet.org

STUART CAMERON AND MARGARET MCLEOD MEMORIAL SCHOLARSHIP
• *See page 76*

INTERNAL AUDIT FOUNDATION
http://www.theiia.org/

ESTHER R. SAWYER RESEARCH AWARD
• *See page 76*

JORGE MAS CANOSA FREEDOM FOUNDATION
http://masscholarships.org/

MAS FAMILY SCHOLARSHIP AWARD
Scholarship for Cuban American student who is a direct descendant of those who left Cuba or was born in Cuba. Minimum 3.5 GPA in college. Scholarships available only in the fields of engineering, business, international relations, economics, communications and journalism.

Academic Fields/Career Goals: Business/Consumer Services; Chemical Engineering; Civil Engineering; Communications; Economics; Electrical Engineering/Electronics; Engineering-Related Technologies; International Studies; Journalism; Materials Science, Engineering, and Metallurgy; Mechanical Engineering.

Award: Scholarship for use in freshman, sophomore, junior, senior, or graduate years; renewable. *Number:* 5–10. *Amount:* $8000–$40,000.

Eligibility Requirements: Applicant must be of Latin American/Caribbean heritage; Hispanic and enrolled or expecting to enroll full-time at a two-year or four-year institution or university. Available to U.S. and non-U.S. citizens.

Application Requirements: Application form, essay, financial need analysis, proof of Cuban descent, recommendations or references, test scores, transcript. *Deadline:* April 15.

Contact: Mr. Daniel Lafuente, Mas Scholarship Coordinator
Jorge Mas Canosa Freedom Foundation
1312 SW 27th Avenue
Miami, FL 33145
Phone: 305-592-7768
E-mail: dlafuente@canf.org

THE LAGRANT FOUNDATION
http://www.lagrantfoundation.org/

LAGRANT FOUNDATION SCHOLARSHIP FOR GRADUATES
• *See page 85*

LAGRANT FOUNDATION SCHOLARSHIP FOR UNDERGRADUATES
• *See page 85*

LEAGUE OF UNITED LATIN AMERICAN CITIZENS NATIONAL EDUCATIONAL SERVICE CENTERS INC.
http://www.lnesc.org/

GE/LULAC SCHOLARSHIP
The scholarship for business and engineering students offers outstanding minority or low-income students entering their sophomore year in pursuit of an undergraduate degree a renewable scholarship up to 3 years.

Academic Fields/Career Goals: Business/Consumer Services; Engineering/Technology.

Award: Scholarship for use in sophomore, junior, or senior years; renewable. *Number:* up to 9. *Amount:* up to $5000.

Eligibility Requirements: Applicant must be American Indian/Alaska Native, Asian/Pacific Islander, Black (non-Hispanic), Hispanic and enrolled or expecting to enroll full-time at a four-year institution or university. Available to U.S. citizens.

Application Requirements: Application form, personal statement with career goals, recommendations or references, transcript. *Deadline:* July 15.

Contact: Scholarship Administrator
League of United Latin American Citizens National Educational Service Centers Inc.
2000 L Street, NW, Suite 610
Washington, DC 20036
Phone: 202-835-9646 Ext. 10
Fax: 202-835-9685

NATIONAL RESTAURANT ASSOCIATION EDUCATIONAL FOUNDATION
http://www.chooserestaurants.org

NATIONAL RESTAURANT ASSOCIATION EDUCATIONAL FOUNDATION UNDERGRADUATE SCHOLARSHIPS FOR COLLEGE STUDENTS
• *See page 95*

NATIONAL SECURITY EDUCATION PROGRAM
http://www.iie.org/

NATIONAL SECURITY EDUCATION PROGRAM (NSEP) DAVID L. BOREN UNDERGRADUATE SCHOLARSHIPS
• *See page 119*

NEBRASKA DECA
http://www.nedeca.org/

NEBRASKA DECA LEADERSHIP SCHOLARSHIP
Awards applicants who intend to pursue a full-time two- or four-year course of study in a marketing or business-related field. Applicant must be active in DECA and involved in community service activities.

Academic Fields/Career Goals: Business/Consumer Services.

Award: Scholarship for use in freshman year; not renewable. *Number:* 2–9. *Amount:* $250–$1000.

Eligibility Requirements: Applicant must be high school student; planning to enroll or expecting to enroll full-time at a two-year or four-year or technical institution or university and resident of Nebraska. Applicant or parent of applicant must be member of Distribution Ed Club or Future Business Leaders of America. Available to U.S. citizens.

Application Requirements: Application form, DECA participation and accomplishment documents, essay, recommendations or references, resume, test scores, transcript. *Deadline:* February 1.

Contact: Scholarship Review Committee
Nebraska DECA
301 Centennial Mall South, PO Box 94987
Lincoln, NE 68509-4987
Phone: 402-471-4803
Fax: 402-471-0117
E-mail: nedeca@nedeca.org

NEW ENGLAND EMPLOYEE BENEFITS COUNCIL

http://www.neebc.org/

NEW ENGLAND EMPLOYEE BENEFITS COUNCIL SCHOLARSHIP PROGRAM
• *See page 78*

NEW ENGLAND WATER WORKS ASSOCIATION

https://www.newwa.org/

FRANCIS X. CROWLEY SCHOLARSHIP

Scholarships are awarded to eligible civil engineering, environmental and business management students on the basis of merit, character, and need. Preference given to those students whose programs are considered by a committee as beneficial to water works practice in New England. NEWWA student membership is required to receive a scholarship award. Applicants for scholarships should be residents or attend school in New England. (Maine, New Hampshire, Vermont, Massachusetts, Rhode Island and Connecticut).

Academic Fields/Career Goals: Business/Consumer Services; Civil Engineering; Engineering/Technology; Environmental Science.

Award: Scholarship for use in freshman, sophomore, junior, senior, or graduate years; not renewable. *Number:* 1. *Amount:* $3000.

Eligibility Requirements: Applicant must be enrolled or expecting to enroll full-time at an institution or university. Applicant or parent of applicant must be member of New England Water Works Association. Available to U.S. citizens.

Application Requirements: Application form, application form may be submitted online, essay, financial need analysis. *Fee:* $30. *Deadline:* April 1.

Contact: Stephen Donovan, Scholarship Committee Chair
New England Water Works Association
125 Hopping Brook Road
Holliston, MA 01746
Phone: 508-248-2893
Fax: 508-893-9898
E-mail: sdonovan@rhwhite.com

JOSEPH MURPHY SCHOLARSHIP

Scholarships are awarded to students enrolled in a civil or environmental engineering program, or a related science or business program applicable to public water supply on the basis of merit, character, and need. Preference given to those students whose programs are considered by a committee as beneficial to water works practice in New England. NEWWA student membership is required to receive a scholarship award.

Academic Fields/Career Goals: Business/Consumer Services; Civil Engineering; Engineering/Technology; Environmental Science.

Award: Scholarship for use in freshman, sophomore, junior, senior, or graduate years; not renewable. *Number:* 1. *Amount:* $1500.

Eligibility Requirements: Applicant must be enrolled or expecting to enroll full-time at an institution or university. Applicant or parent of applicant must be member of New England Water Works Association. Available to U.S. citizens.

Application Requirements: Application form, application form may be submitted online, essay, financial need analysis. *Fee:* $30. *Deadline:* April 1.

Contact: Stephen Donovan, Scholarship Committee Chair
New England Water Works Association
125 Hopping Brook Road
Holliston, MA 01746
Phone: 508-248-2893
Fax: 508-893-9898
E-mail: sdonovan@rhwhite.com

NORTH AMERICAN VAN LINES

https://www.northamerican.com/

NORTH AMERICAN VAN LINES 2020 LOGISTICS SCHOLARSHIP COMPETITION

NO PROGRAM DESCRIPTION

Academic Fields/Career Goals: Business/Consumer Services; Economics.

Award: Scholarship for use in freshman, sophomore, junior, senior, or graduate years; not renewable. *Number:* 3. *Amount:* $1000.

Eligibility Requirements: Applicant must be enrolled or expecting to enroll full-time at a two-year or technical institution or university. Available to U.S. citizens.

Application Requirements: Application form, application form may be submitted online, essay. *Deadline:* December 15.

Contact: Ann Crislip
North American Van Lines
8000 Centerview Parkway, Suite 203
Memphis, TN 38018
Phone: 901-6727243

ROBERT H. MOLLOHAN FAMILY CHARITABLE FOUNDATION, INC.

http://www.mollohanfoundation.org/

TEAMING TO WIN BUSINESS SCHOLARSHIP

Scholarship for a rising college sophomore or junior pursuing a degree in business administration at a West Virginia college or university.

Academic Fields/Career Goals: Business/Consumer Services.

Award: Scholarship for use in sophomore or junior years; not renewable. *Number:* 2. *Amount:* up to $1000.

Eligibility Requirements: Applicant must be enrolled or expecting to enroll full- or part-time at a four-year institution or university; resident of West Virginia; studying in West Virginia and must have an interest in leadership. Available to U.S. citizens.

Application Requirements: Application form, essay, interview, recommendations or references, resume, test scores, transcript. *Deadline:* February 9.

Contact: Aime Shaffer, Program Manager
Robert H. Mollohan Family Charitable Foundation, Inc.
1000 Technology Drive, Suite 2000
Fairmont, WV 26554
Phone: 304-333-6783
Fax: 304-333-3900
E-mail: ashaffer@wvhtf.org

SALES PROFESSIONALS-USA

http://www.salesprofessionals-usa.com/

SALES PROFESSIONALS-USA SCHOLARSHIP

Scholarships are awarded to students furthering their degree or obtaining a degree in business or marketing. The scholarships are initiated and awarded by the individual Sales Pros Clubs (located in Colorado, Kansas and Missouri) and are not nationally awarded. A listing of local clubs can be found at http://www.salesprofessionals-usa.com.

Academic Fields/Career Goals: Business/Consumer Services.

Award: Scholarship for use in freshman, sophomore, junior, or senior years; not renewable. *Number:* 3–5. *Amount:* $600–$1000.

Eligibility Requirements: Applicant must be enrolled or expecting to enroll full- or part-time at a two-year or four-year institution or university; resident of Colorado, Indiana, Kansas and studying in Colorado, Kansas, Missouri. Available to U.S. citizens.

Application Requirements: Application form, essay. *Deadline:* varies.

Contact: Jay Berg, National President
Sales Professionals-USA
2870 North Speer Boulevard
Denver, CO 80001
Phone: 303-433-1051
E-mail: jberg@spacelogic.net

SCARLETT FAMILY FOUNDATION SCHOLARSHIP PROGRAM

http://www.scarlettfoundation.org/

SCHOLARSHIP FOR STUDENTS PURSUING A BUSINESS OR STEM DEGREE
• *See page 80*

SOCIETY OF AUTOMOTIVE ANALYSTS

http://saaauto.com/

SOCIETY OF AUTOMOTIVE ANALYSTS SCHOLARSHIP
• *See page 81*

SPECIALTY EQUIPMENT MARKET ASSOCIATION

http://www.sema.org/

SEMA MEMORIAL SCHOLARSHIP FUND
• *See page 81*

STRAIGHTFORWARD MEDIA

http://www.straightforwardmedia.com/

STRAIGHTFORWARD MEDIA BUSINESS SCHOOL SCHOLARSHIP
• *See page 87*

TRIANGLE PEST CONTROL

http://www.trianglepest.com

TRIANGLE PEST CONTROL SCHOLARSHIP
• *See page 82*

UNITED NEGRO COLLEGE FUND

http://www.uncf.org/

EDWARD M. NAGEL ENDOWED SCHOLARSHIP

The Edward M Nagel Scholarship is open to undergraduate students pursuing studies in business (and business related majors). Up to $3000. Requires full time enrollment at an accredited 4-year college or university and demonstrated financial need.

Academic Fields/Career Goals: Business/Consumer Services.

Award: Scholarship for use in freshman, sophomore, junior, or senior years; renewable.

Eligibility Requirements: Applicant must be Black (non-Hispanic) and enrolled or expecting to enroll full-time at a four-year institution or university. Available to U.S. citizens.

Application Requirements: Application form, essay, financial need analysis. *Deadline:* September 18.

Contact: Larry Griffith, Senior Vice President, Programs and Student Services
Phone: 800-331-2244

HCN/APRICITY RESOURCES SCHOLARS PROGRAM
• *See page 83*

NASCAR WENDELL SCOTT SR. SCHOLARSHIP
• *See page 83*

NATIONAL BLACK MCDONALD'S OWNERS ASSOCIATION HOSPITALITY SCHOLARS PROGRAM
• *See page 83*

RYDER SYSTEM CHARITABLE FOUNDATION SCHOLARSHIP PROGRAM

Applicant must have a minimum GPA of 2.75; be a woman from an educationally under-represented racial group who is in her junior or senior year who is enrolled full time at any accredited four-year college or university; pursuing a declared major in logistics, supply chain management or business marketing. Preference will be given to students who have served in the U.S. Military.

Academic Fields/Career Goals: Business/Consumer Services; Marketing.

Award: Scholarship for use in junior or senior years; not renewable. *Number:* 5. *Amount:* $9000.

Eligibility Requirements: Applicant must be American Indian/Alaska Native, Black (non-Hispanic), Hispanic; enrolled or expecting to enroll full-time at a four-year institution or university and female. Available to U.S. citizens.

Application Requirements: Application form, application form may be submitted online, personal statement of career interest, recommendations or references, transcript. *Deadline:* August 15.

Contact: Yvonne Nash
E-mail: yvonne.nash@uncf.org

UNCF/ALLIANCE DATA SCHOLARSHIP AND INTERNSHIP PROGRAM
• *See page 88*

UNCF/CARNIVAL CORPORATE SCHOLARS PROGRAM

Up to $5000 scholarship and paid summer internship for minority college sophomores and juniors with an interest in pursuing a career in the hospitality industry and whose experience in their first two years of college demonstrates leadership and strategic and analytical ability. Minimum 3.0 GPA. Open to transfer students from community colleges that have been accepted into an accredited four-year college or university. Majoring in business, communications, culinary arts, hospitality management and/or administration, tourism, finance, marketing, information technology, statistics or other related field.

Academic Fields/Career Goals: Business/Consumer Services; Communications; Culinary Arts; Finance; Hospitality Management; Marketing; Travel/Tourism.

Award: Scholarship for use in sophomore or junior years; renewable.

Eligibility Requirements: Applicant must be American Indian/Alaska Native, Asian/Pacific Islander, Black (non-Hispanic), Hispanic and enrolled or expecting to enroll full-time at a four-year institution or university. Available to U.S. citizens.

Application Requirements: Application form, application form may be submitted online, personal statement of career goals, recommendations or references, transcript. *Deadline:* January 19.

Contact: Melissa Jordan
E-mail: melissa.jordan@uncf.org

UNCF/TRAVELERS INSURANCE SCHOLARSHIP

Scholarship for African-American students with unmet financial need. Selected Scholars shall be expected to participate in Travelers-sponsored online and/or on site career readiness opportunities. Applicants must be pursuing a major in a business-related field, risk management or insurance.

Academic Fields/Career Goals: Business/Consumer Services; Insurance and Actuarial Science.

Award: Scholarship for use in sophomore, junior, or senior years. *Amount:* $3000–$5850.

Eligibility Requirements: Applicant must be Black (non-Hispanic); enrolled or expecting to enroll at a four-year institution or university and resident of California, Colorado, Florida, Georgia, Illinois, Massachusetts, Missouri, North Carolina, Texas, Washington. Available to U.S. citizens.

Application Requirements: Application form, essay, financial need analysis. *Deadline:* September 30.

Contact: Larry Griffith, Senior Vice President, Programs and Student Services
Phone: 800-331-2244

VOYA SCHOLARS
• *See page 83*

WASHINGTON MEDIA SCHOLARS FOUNDATION

www.mediascholars.org

MEDIA PLAN CASE COMPETITION
• *See page 88*

WOMEN GROCERS OF AMERICA

http://www.nationalgrocers.org/

MARY MACEY SCHOLARSHIP
• *See page 97*

WOMEN IN LOGISTICS, NORTHERN CALIFORNIA

http://www.womeninlogistics.org/

WOMEN IN LOGISTICS SCHOLARSHIP
Award for students (undergraduate/graduate, male/female) studying and eventually planning careers in logistics/supply chain management. Applicants must be enrolled in a degree program at an institution within the 9 counties comprising the San Francisco Bay Area and have at least one semester left, as this award goes directly to the institution towards tuition/fees. Deadlines typically fall on November 1st. While student need may considered, awards are based primarily on merit, work experience and demonstrated interest in the field.

Academic Fields/Career Goals: Business/Consumer Services; Trade/Technical Specialties; Transportation.

Award: Scholarship for use in freshman, sophomore, junior, senior, or graduate years; not renewable. *Number:* 1–3. *Amount:* $1000–$3000.

Eligibility Requirements: Applicant must be enrolled or expecting to enroll full- or part-time at a two-year or four-year institution or university; resident of California and studying in California. Applicant or parent of applicant must be member of Women in Logistics. Available to U.S. and non-U.S. citizens.

Application Requirements: Application form, essay. *Deadline:* November 1.

Contact: Dr. Susan Cholette, Scholarship Director
Phone: 415-405-2173
E-mail: cholette@sfsu.edu

WYOMING TRUCKING ASSOCIATION SCHOLARSHIP FUND TRUST

http://www.wytruck.org/

WYOMING TRUCKING ASSOCIATION SCHOLARSHIP TRUST FUND
• *See page 84*

Y'S MEN INTERNATIONAL

http://www.ysmen.org/

ALEXANDER SCHOLARSHIP LOAN FUND
The purpose of the fund is to promote the training of staff of the YMCA and/or those seeking to become members or staff of the YMCA. Deadlines are May 30 for fall semester and October 30 for spring semester.

Academic Fields/Career Goals: Business/Consumer Services; Child and Family Studies; Education; Human Resources; Social Sciences; Social Services; Sports-Related/Exercise Science.

Award: Scholarship for use in freshman, sophomore, junior, or senior years; renewable.

Eligibility Requirements: Applicant must be enrolled or expecting to enroll full- or part-time at a two-year or four-year institution or university. Available to U.S. citizens.

Application Requirements: Application form. *Fee:* $1. *Deadline:* varies.

Contact: Dean Currie, Area Service Director
Phone: 908-753-9493
Fax: 602-935-6322
E-mail: kidcurrie@adelphia.net

CAMPUS ACTIVITIES

NATIONAL ASSOCIATION FOR CAMPUS ACTIVITIES

http://www.naca.org/

NATIONAL ASSOCIATION FOR CAMPUS ACTIVITIES NORTHERN PLAINS REGION SCHOLARSHIP FOR STUDENT LEADERS
The NACA Northern Plains Regional Student Leadership Scholarship is designed to assist students pursuing graduate or undergraduate study leading toward a career in student activities or a related student services field.

Academic Fields/Career Goals: Campus Activities.

Award: Scholarship for use in freshman, sophomore, junior, senior, or graduate years; not renewable. *Number:* 1. *Amount:* $300.

Eligibility Requirements: Applicant must be enrolled or expecting to enroll full- or part-time at a two-year institution or university; studying in Alberta, Iowa, Manitoba, Michigan, Minnesota, Montana, Nebraska, North Dakota, Ontario, Saskatchewan, South Dakota, Wisconsin, Wyoming and must have an interest in leadership. Applicant or parent of applicant must have employment or volunteer experience in community service. Available to U.S. citizens.

Application Requirements: Application form, application form may be submitted online, essay. *Deadline:* November 30.

Contact: Sarah Keeling, Director of Education and Research
Phone: 803-217-3485
E-mail: scholarships@naca.org

CHEMICAL ENGINEERING

101ST AIRBORNE DIVISION ASSOCIATION

http://www.screamingeaglefoundation.org/

AL & WILLIAMARY VISTE SCHOLARSHIP
• *See page 99*

AACE INTERNATIONAL

http://www.aacei.org/

AACE INTERNATIONAL COMPETITIVE SCHOLARSHIP
• *See page 112*

AIST FOUNDATION

http://www.aistfoundation.org/

ASSOCIATION FOR IRON AND STEEL TECHNOLOGY BENJAMIN F. FAIRLESS SCHOLARSHIP (AIME)
Scholarship for full-time students of metallurgy, materials science, chemical, mechanical, electrical, environmental, computer science, and industrial engineering. Students must have an interest in a career in the steel industry as demonstrated by an internship or related experience, or who have plans to pursue such experiences during college. Student may apply after first term of freshman year of college. Applications are accepted from 1 Sep through 31 Dec each year. Note: High school students do not qualify but are encouraged to learn about the steel industry and the career opportunities available therein, during their freshman year.

Academic Fields/Career Goals: Chemical Engineering; Electrical Engineering/Electronics; Engineering-Related Technologies; Materials Science, Engineering, and Metallurgy; Mechanical Engineering.

Award: Scholarship for use in sophomore, junior, or senior years; not renewable. *Number:* 2. *Amount:* $3000.

Eligibility Requirements: Applicant must be enrolled or expecting to enroll full-time at a four-year institution or university. Available to U.S. and non-U.S. citizens.

Application Requirements: Application form, essay, recommendations or references, resume, transcript. *Deadline:* December 31.

Contact: Lori Wharrey, AIST Manager, Board Services
AIST Foundation
186 Thorn Hill Road
Warrendale, PA 15086
Phone: 724-814-3044
E-mail: lwharrey@aist.org

ASSOCIATION FOR IRON AND STEEL TECHNOLOGY WILLY KORF MEMORIAL SCHOLARSHIP

Scholarships are available for full-time students of metallurgy, chemical, materials science, mechanical, electrical, computer science, industrial and environmental engineering who have a genuine demonstrated interest in a career in the steel industry as demonstrated by an internship or related experience, or who have plans to pursue such experiences during college. Student may apply first during the freshman year of college. Applications are accepted 1 Sep through 31 Dec each year. Note: High school seniors are not eligible though are encouraged to learn and investigate the steel industry and the career opportunities available, during their freshman year.

Academic Fields/Career Goals: Chemical Engineering; Computer Science/Data Processing; Electrical Engineering/Electronics; Environmental Science; Industrial Design; Materials Science, Engineering, and Metallurgy; Mechanical Engineering.

Award: Scholarship for use in sophomore, junior, senior, or graduate years; not renewable. *Number:* 2. *Amount:* $3000.

Eligibility Requirements: Applicant must be enrolled or expecting to enroll full-time at a four-year institution or university. Applicant or parent of applicant must have employment or volunteer experience in engineering/technology. Available to U.S. and non-U.S. citizens.

Application Requirements: Application form, essay, recommendations or references, resume, transcript. *Deadline:* December 31.

Contact: Lori Wharrey, AIST Manager, Board Services
AIST Foundation
186 Thorn Hill Road
Warrendale, PA 15086
Phone: 724-814-3044 Ext. 621
E-mail: lwharrey@aist.org

AMERICAN CHEMICAL SOCIETY

http://www.acs.org/

AMERICAN CHEMICAL SOCIETY SCHOLARS PROGRAM

Renewable scholarship to underrepresented minority students majoring in a chemistry-related discipline and are also intending to pursue a career in chemistry-related fields. Must be U.S. citizen or legal permanent resident and have minimum 3.0 GPA. Must be African-American/Black, Hispanic/Latino or American Indian.

Academic Fields/Career Goals: Chemical Engineering; Environmental Science; Materials Science, Engineering, and Metallurgy; Natural Sciences; Paper and Pulp Engineering; Trade/Technical Specialties.

Award: Scholarship for use in freshman, sophomore, or junior years; renewable. *Number:* 100–130. *Amount:* $1000–$5000.

Eligibility Requirements: Applicant must be American Indian/Alaska Native, Black (non-Hispanic), Hispanic and enrolled or expecting to enroll full-time at a two-year or four-year or technical institution or university. Available to U.S. citizens.

Application Requirements: Application form, application form may be submitted online(www.acs.org/scholars), essay, financial need analysis, recommendations or references, resume, test scores, transcript. *Deadline:* March 1.

Contact: Dr. Racquel Jemison, Manager, ACS Scholars Program
American Chemical Society
1155 16th Street, NW
Washington, DC 20036
Phone: 202-872-6048
E-mail: scholars@acs.org

AMERICAN CHEMICAL SOCIETY, RUBBER DIVISION

http://www.rubber.org/

AMERICAN CHEMICAL SOCIETY, RUBBER DIVISION UNDERGRADUATE SCHOLARSHIP
• See page 105

AMERICAN COUNCIL OF ENGINEERING COMPANIES OF PENNSYLVANIA (ACEC/PA)

http://www.acecpa.org/

ERIC J. GENNUSO AND LEROY D. (BUD) LOY, JR. SCHOLARSHIP PROGRAM

Scholarship for full-time engineering students enrolled in accredited colleges or universities. Must be a Must be a United States Citizen. Must be a full-time sophomore or junior student as of the school year in which the scholarship is awarded, pursuing a bachelor degree in engineering or environmental sciences. Must meet at least one of these criteria: Attend a college or university located in Pennsylvania or be a Pennsylvania Resident. Up to three awards are granted annually.

Academic Fields/Career Goals: Chemical Engineering; Civil Engineering; Construction Engineering/Management; Electrical Engineering/Electronics; Energy and Power Engineering; Engineering-Related Technologies; Engineering/Technology; Environmental Science; Marine/Ocean Engineering; Materials Science, Engineering, and Metallurgy; Mechanical Engineering; Surveying, Surveying Technology, Cartography, or Geographic Information Science; Transportation.

Award: Scholarship for use in sophomore or junior years; not renewable. *Number:* 1–3. *Amount:* $2500–$5000.

Eligibility Requirements: Applicant must be enrolled or expecting to enroll full-time at a four-year institution or university and resident of Pennsylvania. Available to U.S. citizens.

Application Requirements: Application form, community service, essay. *Deadline:* May 15.

Contact: Jenna Earley, Director of Marketing
American Council of Engineering Companies of Pennsylvania (ACEC/PA)
800 N. 3rd Street
Suite 301
Harrisburg, PA 17102
Phone: 800-651-1946
E-mail: jearley@acecpa.org

AMERICAN INDIAN SCIENCE AND ENGINEERING SOCIETY

http://www.aises.org/

A.T. ANDERSON MEMORIAL SCHOLARSHIP PROGRAM
• See page 105

AMERICAN INSTITUTE OF CHEMICAL ENGINEERS

http://www.aiche.org/

MINORITY AFFAIRS COMMITTEE AWARD FOR OUTSTANDING SCHOLASTIC ACHIEVEMENT

Award recognizing the outstanding achievements of a chemical engineering student who serves as a role model for minority students. Offers $1000 award and $500 travel allowance to attend AICHE meeting. Must be nominated.

Academic Fields/Career Goals: Chemical Engineering.

Award: Scholarship for use in freshman, sophomore, junior, senior, or graduate years; not renewable. *Number:* 1. *Amount:* $1500.

Eligibility Requirements: Applicant must be American Indian/Alaska Native, Asian/Pacific Islander, Black (non-Hispanic), Hispanic and enrolled or expecting to enroll full-time at a four-year institution or university. Available to U.S. and non-U.S. citizens.

Application Requirements: Application form. *Deadline:* May 15.

Contact: Dr. Emmanuel Dada, Scholarship Administrator
American Institute of Chemical Engineers
PO Box 8
Princeton, NJ 08543
Phone: 212-591-7107
E-mail: emmanuel_dada@fmc.com

NATIONAL STUDENT DESIGN COMPETITION-INDIVIDUAL

Three cash prizes for student contest problem that typifies a real, working, chemical engineering design situation. Competition statements are distributed online to student chapter advisors and department heads.

Academic Fields/Career Goals: Chemical Engineering.

Award: Prize for use in freshman, sophomore, junior, senior, or graduate years; not renewable. *Number:* 3. *Amount:* $200–$500.

Eligibility Requirements: Applicant must be enrolled or expecting to enroll full-time at a four-year institution or university. Available to U.S. and non-U.S. citizens.

Application Requirements: Entry in a contest, essay. *Deadline:* June 6.

Contact: AIChE Awards Administrator
American Institute of Chemical Engineers
Three Park Avenue
New York, NY 10016
Phone: 212-591-7107
Fax: 212-591-8882
E-mail: awards@aiche.org

SAFETY AND CHEMICAL ENGINEERING EDUCATION (SACHE) STUDENT ESSAY AWARD FOR SAFETY

Awards individuals or a team submitting the best essays on the topic of chemical process safety. Essays may focus on process safety in education, relevance of safety in undergraduate education, or integrating safety principles into the undergraduate chemical engineering curriculum.

Academic Fields/Career Goals: Chemical Engineering.

Award: Prize for use in freshman, sophomore, junior, or senior years; not renewable. *Number:* up to 4. *Amount:* $500.

Eligibility Requirements: Applicant must be enrolled or expecting to enroll full-time at a four-year institution or university. Available to U.S. and non-U.S. citizens.

Application Requirements: Entry in a contest, essay. *Deadline:* June 5.

Contact: AIChE Awards Administrator
American Institute of Chemical Engineers
Three Park Avenue
New York, NY 10016
Phone: 212-591-7107
Fax: 212-591-8880
E-mail: awards@aiche.org

AMERICAN OIL CHEMISTS' SOCIETY

www.aocs.org/

AOCS BIOTECHNOLOGY STUDENT EXCELLENCE AWARD

• *See page 92*

AOCS PROCESSING DIVISION AWARDS

Award and certificate to recognize graduate students presenting an outstanding paper at the Society's annual meeting. All graduate students presenting a paper at any of the AOCS Annual Meeting Processing Division sessions are eligible for the award.

Academic Fields/Career Goals: Chemical Engineering; Food Science/Nutrition.

Award: Prize for use in junior, senior, or graduate years; not renewable. *Number:* 1. *Amount:* $1000.

Eligibility Requirements: Applicant must be enrolled or expecting to enroll full-time at a four-year institution or university. Available to U.S. and non-U.S. citizens.

Application Requirements: Essay, extended abstract, recommendations or references. *Deadline:* February 1.

Contact: Barbara Semeraro, Area Manager, Membership
American Oil Chemists' Society
AOCS
PO Box 17190
Urbana, IL 61803
Phone: 217-693-4804
Fax: 217-693-4849
E-mail: awards@aocs.org

AMERICAN PUBLIC POWER ASSOCIATION

https://www.publicpower.org/deed-rd-funding

DEMONSTRATION OF ENERGY AND EFFICIENCY DEVELOPMENTS EDUCATIONAL SCHOLARSHIP

This program supports the education of students working toward lineworker and other technical careers that are in high demand by electric utilities. Applicants must be students attending or planning to attend a vocational institution, lineworker school or two to four-year college/university within the U.S. and must not be graduating within 12 months of the application deadline. Official transcripts must be submitted by the application deadline. Spring Application Cycle is every December 1st - February 15th while Fall Application Cycle is every August 1st - October 15th.

Academic Fields/Career Goals: Chemical Engineering; Civil Engineering; Electrical Engineering/Electronics; Energy and Power Engineering; Engineering-Related Technologies; Engineering/Technology; Environmental Science; Mechanical Engineering; Natural Resources.

Award: Scholarship for use in freshman, sophomore, junior, or senior years; not renewable. *Number:* 20. *Amount:* $2000.

Eligibility Requirements: Applicant must be enrolled or expecting to enroll full-time at a two-year or technical institution or university. Available to U.S. and non-U.S. citizens.

Application Requirements: Application form, essay.

Contact: Jack Miller, DEED and Engineering Services Assistant
Phone: 202-467-2942
E-mail: DEED@PublicPower.org

DEMONSTRATION OF ENERGY AND EFFICIENCY DEVELOPMENTS STUDENT INTERNSHIP

The program provides paid internships provide work experience at a participating DEED member utility. Spring Application Cycle is every December 1st - February 15th while Fall Application Cycle is every August 1st - October 15th.

Academic Fields/Career Goals: Chemical Engineering; Civil Engineering; Electrical Engineering/Electronics; Energy and Power Engineering; Engineering-Related Technologies; Engineering/Technology; Environmental Science; Mechanical Engineering; Natural Resources.

Award: Scholarship for use in freshman, sophomore, junior, senior, graduate, or postgraduate years; not renewable. *Number:* 5–10. *Amount:* $5000.

Eligibility Requirements: Applicant must be enrolled or expecting to enroll full-time at a two-year or technical institution or university. Available to U.S. and non-U.S. citizens.

Application Requirements: Application form.

Contact: Jack Miller, DEED and Engineering Services Assistant
Phone: 202-467-2942
E-mail: DEED@PublicPower.org

DEMONSTRATION OF ENERGY AND EFFICIENCY DEVELOPMENTS TECHNICAL DESIGN PROJECT

Technical Design Projects support students working on a technical project of interest to electric utilities, especially engineering students working on their senior design or a capstone project. Spring Application Cycle is every December 1st - February 15th while Fall Application Cycle is every August 1st - October 15th.

Academic Fields/Career Goals: Chemical Engineering; Civil Engineering; Electrical Engineering/Electronics; Energy and Power

Engineering; Engineering-Related Technologies; Engineering/Technology; Environmental Science; Mechanical Engineering; Natural Resources.

Award: Scholarship for use in junior, senior, or graduate years; not renewable. *Number:* 1. *Amount:* $5000–$8000.

Eligibility Requirements: Applicant must be enrolled or expecting to enroll full-time at a two-year or technical institution or university. Available to U.S. and non-U.S. citizens.

Application Requirements: Application form.

Contact: Jack Miller, DEED and Engineering Services Assistant
Phone: 202-467-2942
E-mail: DEED@PublicPower.org

AMERICAN SOCIETY FOR ENOLOGY AND VITICULTURE

http://www.asev.org/

AMERICAN SOCIETY FOR ENOLOGY AND VITICULTURE SCHOLARSHIPS
• See page 92

ASIAN PACIFIC FUND

BANATAO FAMILY FILIPINO AMERICAN EDUCATION FUND

The Banatao Family Filipino American Education Fund awards five scholarships of $5,000 each. Every student selected for the scholarship program is a California resident of Filipino heritage majoring in engineering, computer science or physical science at a four-year college or university. Each scholarship can be renewed for four years ($20,000 total) based on academic performance.

Academic Fields/Career Goals: Chemical Engineering; Civil Engineering; Computer Science/Data Processing; Electrical Engineering/Electronics; Environmental Science; Materials Science, Engineering, and Metallurgy; Mechanical Engineering; Physical Sciences.

Award: Scholarship for use in freshman, sophomore, junior, or senior years; renewable. *Number:* 5–6. *Amount:* $5000.

Eligibility Requirements: Applicant must be Asian/Pacific Islander; high school student; planning to enroll or expecting to enroll full-time at a four-year institution or university and resident of California. Available to U.S. citizens.

Application Requirements: Application form, essay, financial need analysis. *Deadline:* February 23.

ASSOCIATION ON AMERICAN INDIAN AFFAIRS, INC.

http://www.indian-affairs.org/

ELIZABETH AND SHERMAN ASCHE MEMORIAL SCHOLARSHIP FUND
• See page 93

ASTRONAUT SCHOLARSHIP FOUNDATION

http://www.astronautscholarship.org/

ASTRONAUT SCHOLARSHIP
• See page 107

AUTOMOTIVE WOMEN'S ALLIANCE FOUNDATION

http://awafoundation.org/index.php

AUTOMOTIVE WOMEN'S ALLIANCE FOUNDATION SCHOLARSHIPS
• See page 71

BARRY GOLDWATER SCHOLARSHIP AND EXCELLENCE IN EDUCATION FOUNDATION

https://goldwater.scholarsapply.org

BARRY M. GOLDWATER SCHOLARSHIP AND EXCELLENCE IN EDUCATION PROGRAM
• See page 107

BHW GROUP

https://thebhwgroup.com/

BHW WOMEN IN STEM SCHOLARSHIP
• See page 107

B.O.G. PEST CONTROL

http://www.bogpestcontrol.com/

B.O.G. PEST CONTROL SCHOLARSHIP FUND
• See page 141

BRASKEM ODEBRECHT

http://www.odebrechtaward.com

ODEBRECHT AWARD FOR SUSTAINABLE DEVELOPMENT
• See page 113

BROWN AND CALDWELL

http://www.brownandcaldwell.com

ECKENFELDER SCHOLARSHIP
• See page 141

MINORITY SCHOLARSHIP PROGRAM
• See page 141

CARDS AGAINST HUMANITY

https://cardsagainsthumanity.com/

SCIENCE AMBASSADOR SCHOLARSHIP
• See page 107

DISTIL NETWORKS

http://www.distilnetworks.com

WOMEN FORWARD IN TECHNOLOGY SCHOLARSHIP PROGRAM
• See page 108

THE ELECTROCHEMICAL SOCIETY

https://www.electrochem.org/

BATTERY DIVISION STUDENT RESEARCH AWARD SPONSORED BY MERCEDES-BENZ RESEARCH & DEVELOPMENT

Award to recognize promising young engineers and scientists in the field of electrochemical power sources. Student must be enrolled or must have been accepted for enrollment at a college or university.

Academic Fields/Career Goals: Chemical Engineering; Electrical Engineering/Electronics; Energy and Power Engineering; Engineering-Related Technologies; Engineering/Technology; Materials Science, Engineering, and Metallurgy; Mechanical Engineering; Natural Sciences; Physical Sciences; Science, Technology, and Society.

Award: Prize for use in freshman, sophomore, junior, senior, or graduate years; not renewable. *Number:* 1. *Amount:* $1000.

Eligibility Requirements: Applicant must be enrolled or expecting to enroll full-time at an institution or university. Available to U.S. and non-U.S. citizens.

Application Requirements: Application form. *Deadline:* March 15.

Contact: Ms. Marcelle Austin, Board Relations Specialist
The Electrochemical Society
The Electrochemical Society
65 South Main Street, Building D
Pennington, NJ 08534
Phone: 609-737-1902 Ext. 124
Fax: 609-737-2743
E-mail: marcelle.austin@electrochem.org

H.H. DOW MEMORIAL STUDENT ACHIEVEMENT AWARD OF THE INDUSTRIAL ELECTROLYSIS AND ELECTROCHEMICAL ENGINEERING DIVISION OF THE ELECTROCHEMICAL SOCIETY INC

Award to recognize promising young engineers and scientists in the field of electrochemical engineering and applied electrochemistry. Applicant must be enrolled or accepted for enrollment in a college or university as a graduate student. Must submit description of proposed research project and how it relates to the field of electrochemistry, a letter of recommendation from research supervisor, and biography or resume.

Academic Fields/Career Goals: Chemical Engineering; Electrical Engineering/Electronics; Energy and Power Engineering; Engineering-Related Technologies; Engineering/Technology; Physical Sciences; Science, Technology, and Society.

Award: Prize for use in freshman, sophomore, junior, senior, or graduate years; not renewable. *Number:* 1. *Amount:* $1000.

Eligibility Requirements: Applicant must be enrolled or expecting to enroll full-time at an institution or university. Available to U.S. and non-U.S. citizens.

Application Requirements: Application form. *Deadline:* September 15.

Contact: Ms. Marcelle Austin, Board Relations Specialist
The Electrochemical Society
The Electrochemical Society
65 South Main Street, Building D
Pennington, NJ 08534
Phone: 609-737-1902 Ext. 124
Fax: 609-737-2743
E-mail: marcelle.austin@electrochem.org

FEEDING TOMORROW: THE FOUNDATION OF THE INSTITUTE OF FOOD TECHNOLOGISTS

http://www.feedingtomorrow.org

EVAN TUREK MEMORIAL SCHOLARSHIP
• *See page 93*

FLORIDA ENGINEERING SOCIETY

https://www.fleng.org/page/Scholarships

DAVID F. LUDOVICI SCHOLARSHIP

One-time scholarship of $1000 given to students in their junior or senior year in any Florida university engineering program, with at least 3.0 GPA. Applicants must be interested in civil, structural, or consulting engineering.

Academic Fields/Career Goals: Chemical Engineering; Civil Engineering; Electrical Engineering/Electronics; Energy and Power Engineering; Engineering-Related Technologies; Engineering/Technology.

Award: Scholarship for use in junior or senior years; not renewable. *Number:* 1. *Amount:* $1000.

Eligibility Requirements: Applicant must be enrolled or expecting to enroll full-time at an institution or university and studying in Florida. Available to U.S. citizens.

Application Requirements: Application form. *Deadline:* February 14.

Contact: Amanda Hudson, Director of Information Technology
Florida Engineering Society
125 South Gadsden Street
Tallahassee, FL 32301
Phone: 850-224-7121
E-mail: ahudson@fleng.org

GREAT MINDS IN STEM

http://www.greatmindsinstem.org/college/scholarship-application-information

HENAAC SCHOLARSHIP PROGRAM
• *See page 100*

INTERNATIONAL SOCIETY FOR OPTICAL ENGINEERING-SPIE

http://www.spie.org/scholarships

SPIE EDUCATIONAL SCHOLARSHIPS IN OPTICAL SCIENCE AND ENGINEERING
• *See page 108*

INTERNATIONAL SOCIETY OF EXPLOSIVES ENGINEERS

http://www.isee.org/

JERRY MCDOWELL FUND

Scholarship of $1500 to $7000 to students whose field of education is related to the commercial explosives industry.

Academic Fields/Career Goals: Chemical Engineering; Civil Engineering; Construction Engineering/Management; Earth Science; Electrical Engineering/Electronics; Energy and Power Engineering; Engineering-Related Technologies; Engineering/Technology; Environmental Science; Fire Sciences; Law Enforcement/Police Administration; Materials Science, Engineering, and Metallurgy; Mechanical Engineering; Military and Defense Studies; Natural Resources; Nuclear Science; Occupational Safety and Health; Physical Sciences; Science, Technology, and Society; Trade/Technical Specialties.

Award: Scholarship for use in freshman, sophomore, junior, senior, or graduate years; not renewable. *Number:* 1–7. *Amount:* $1500–$7000.

Eligibility Requirements: Applicant must be enrolled or expecting to enroll full-time at a two-year or four-year or technical institution or university. Available to U.S. and non-U.S. citizens.

Application Requirements: Application form, application form may be submitted online(www.isee.org), essay, financial need analysis, recommendations or references, resume, transcript. *Deadline:* May 3.

Contact: Patrick Lang, Manager, Education Foundation
Phone: 440-349-4400
Fax: 440-349-3788
E-mail: isee@isee.org

JORGE MAS CANOSA FREEDOM FOUNDATION

http://masscholarships.org/

MAS FAMILY SCHOLARSHIP AWARD
• *See page 149*

KENTUCKY ENERGY AND ENVIRONMENT CABINET

http://dep.ky.gov

ENVIRONMENTAL PROTECTION SCHOLARSHIP
• *See page 142*

LOGMEIN
https://www.logmeininc.com

LASTPASS STEM SCHOLARSHIP
• See page 109

LOS ANGELES COUNCIL OF BLACK PROFESSIONAL ENGINEERS
http://www.lablackengineers.org/

AL-BEN SCHOLARSHIP FOR ACADEMIC INCENTIVE
One-time scholarship for students enrolled full-time with scholastic achievements in the academic pursuits of engineering, math, computer or scientific studies. Must be from a minority group. Scholarship value is $500 to $1000. Two scholarships are granted annually. Preference given to residents of Southern California.

Academic Fields/Career Goals: Chemical Engineering; Civil Engineering; Computer Science/Data Processing; Electrical Engineering/Electronics; Engineering-Related Technologies; Engineering/Technology; Materials Science, Engineering, and Metallurgy; Mechanical Engineering; Physical Sciences.

Award: Scholarship for use in freshman, sophomore, junior, or senior years; not renewable. *Number:* 2. *Amount:* $500–$1000.

Eligibility Requirements: Applicant must be American Indian/Alaska Native, Asian/Pacific Islander, Black (non-Hispanic), Hispanic and enrolled or expecting to enroll full-time at a four-year institution or university. Available to U.S. citizens.

Application Requirements: Application form, essay, recommendations or references, transcript. *Deadline:* April 2.

Contact: Leroy Freelon, President
Phone: 310-635-7734
E-mail: lfreelonjr@aol.com

AL-BEN SCHOLARSHIP FOR PROFESSIONAL MERIT
One-time scholarship for students enrolled full-time with scholastic achievements in the academic pursuits of engineering, math, computer or scientific studies. Must be from a minority group. Scholarship value is $500 to $1000. Two scholarships are granted annually. Preference given to residents of Southern California.

Academic Fields/Career Goals: Chemical Engineering; Civil Engineering; Computer Science/Data Processing; Electrical Engineering/Electronics; Engineering-Related Technologies; Engineering/Technology; Materials Science, Engineering, and Metallurgy; Mechanical Engineering; Physical Sciences.

Award: Scholarship for use in freshman, sophomore, junior, or senior years; not renewable. *Number:* 2. *Amount:* $500–$1000.

Eligibility Requirements: Applicant must be American Indian/Alaska Native, Asian/Pacific Islander, Black (non-Hispanic), Hispanic and enrolled or expecting to enroll full-time at a four-year institution or university. Available to U.S. citizens.

Application Requirements: Application form, essay, recommendations or references, transcript. *Deadline:* April 2.

Contact: Leroy Freelon, President
Phone: 310-635-7734
E-mail: lfreelonjr@aol.com

AL-BEN SCHOLARSHIP FOR SCHOLASTIC ACHIEVEMENT
Scholarships for students enrolled full-time with scholastic achievements in the academic pursuits of engineering, math, computer or scientific studies. Must be from a minority group.

Academic Fields/Career Goals: Chemical Engineering; Civil Engineering; Computer Science/Data Processing; Electrical Engineering/Electronics; Engineering-Related Technologies; Engineering/Technology; Materials Science, Engineering, and Metallurgy; Mechanical Engineering; Physical Sciences.

Award: Scholarship for use in freshman, sophomore, junior, or senior years; not renewable. *Number:* 2. *Amount:* $500–$1000.

Eligibility Requirements: Applicant must be American Indian/Alaska Native, Asian/Pacific Islander, Black (non-Hispanic), Hispanic and enrolled or expecting to enroll full-time at a four-year institution or university. Available to U.S. citizens.

Application Requirements: Application form, essay, recommendations or references, transcript. *Deadline:* April 2.

Contact: Leroy Freelon, President
Phone: 310-635-7734
E-mail: lfreelonjr@aol.com

MEDICAL SCRUBS COLLECTION
http://medicalscrubscollection.com

MEDICAL SCRUBS COLLECTION SCHOLARSHIP
• See page 104

NASA IDAHO SPACE GRANT CONSORTIUM
http://www.idahospacegrant.org

NASA IDAHO SPACE GRANT CONSORTIUM SCHOLARSHIP PROGRAM
• See page 109

NASA/MARYLAND SPACE GRANT CONSORTIUM
https://md.spacegrant.org

NASA MARYLAND SPACE GRANT CONSORTIUM SCHOLARSHIPS
• See page 109

NASA MONTANA SPACE GRANT CONSORTIUM
http://www.spacegrant.montana.edu/

MONTANA SPACE GRANT SCHOLARSHIP PROGRAM
• See page 132

NASA'S VIRGINIA SPACE GRANT CONSORTIUM
http://www.vsgc.odu.edu/

UNDERGRADUATE STEM RESEARCH SCHOLARSHIPS
• See page 110

NATIONAL BOARD OF BOILER AND PRESSURE VESSEL INSPECTORS
http://www.nationalboard.org/

NATIONAL BOARD TECHNICAL SCHOLARSHIP
Two $6000 scholarships to selected students meeting eligibility standards, who are pursuing a Bachelor's degree in certain engineering or related studies. Must be a child, step-child, grandchild, or great-grandchild of a past or present National Board member (living or deceased), or of a past or present Commissioned Inspector (living or deceased), employed by a member jurisdiction, or of a past or present National Board employee (living or deceased).

Academic Fields/Career Goals: Chemical Engineering; Electrical Engineering/Electronics; Mechanical Engineering.

Award: Scholarship for use in freshman, sophomore, junior, or senior years; not renewable. *Number:* 2. *Amount:* $6000.

Eligibility Requirements: Applicant must be enrolled or expecting to enroll full-time at a four-year or technical institution or university. Applicant or parent of applicant must be member of National Board of Boiler and Pressure Vessel Inspectors. Available to U.S. and Canadian citizens.

Application Requirements: Application form, essay, recommendations or references, transcript. *Deadline:* February 28.

Contact: Donald Tanner, Executive Director
   Phone: 614-888-8320
   Fax: 614-888-0750
   E-mail: dtanner@nationalboard.org

NATIONAL SOCIETY OF PROFESSIONAL ENGINEERS

http://www.nspe.org/

PAUL H. ROBBINS HONORARY SCHOLARSHIP

Awarded annually to a current engineering undergraduate student entering the junior year in an ABET-accredited engineering program and attending a college/university that participates in the NSPE Professional Engineers in Higher Education (PEHE) Sustaining University Program(SUP).

Academic Fields/Career Goals: Chemical Engineering; Civil Engineering; Electrical Engineering/Electronics; Engineering-Related Technologies; Engineering/Technology; Materials Science, Engineering, and Metallurgy; Mechanical Engineering.

Award: Scholarship for use in junior year; renewable. *Number:* 1. *Amount:* $5000.

Eligibility Requirements: Applicant must be enrolled or expecting to enroll full-time at a four-year institution or university. Applicant or parent of applicant must be member of National Society of Professional Engineers. Available to U.S. citizens.

Application Requirements: Application form, essay, recommendations or references, test scores, transcript. *Deadline:* March 1.

PROFESSIONAL ENGINEERS IN INDUSTRY SCHOLARSHIP

Applicants must be sponsored by an NSPE/PEI member. Students must have completed a minimum of two semesters or three quarters of undergraduate engineering studies (or be enrolled in graduate study) accredited by ABET.

Academic Fields/Career Goals: Chemical Engineering; Civil Engineering; Electrical Engineering/Electronics; Engineering-Related Technologies; Engineering/Technology; Materials Science, Engineering, and Metallurgy; Mechanical Engineering.

Award: Scholarship for use in sophomore, junior, or senior years; not renewable. *Number:* 1. *Amount:* $2500.

Eligibility Requirements: Applicant must be enrolled or expecting to enroll full-time at a four-year institution or university. Available to U.S. citizens.

Application Requirements: Application form, community service, essay, recommendations or references, resume, transcript, work experience certificates. *Deadline:* April 1.

Contact: Erin Reyes, Practice Division Manager
   National Society of Professional Engineers
   1420 King Street
   Alexandria, VA 22314
   Phone: 703-684-2884
   E-mail: egarcia@nspe.org

NEVADA NASA SPACE GRANT CONSORTIUM

https://nasa.epscorspo.nevada.edu/

NATIONAL SPACE GRANT CONSORTIUM SCHOLARSHIPS
• See page 110

NEXTSTEPU

http://www.nextstepu.com/

$1,500 STEM SCHOLARSHIP
• See page 104

ROBERT H. MOLLOHAN FAMILY CHARITABLE FOUNDATION, INC.

http://www.mollohanfoundation.org/

HIGH TECHNOLOGY SCHOLARS PROGRAM

The High Technology Scholars Program offers a $500 scholarship, in addition to internship and loan opportunities, to West Virginia high school seniors who plan on majoring in a technology-related field at a West Virginia University or college. The student applying must be from one of the following counties: Barbour, Brooke, Calhoun, Doddridge, Gilmer, Grant, Hancock, Harrison, Marion, Marshall, Mineral, Monongalia, Ohio, Pleasants, Preston, Ritchie, Taylor, Tucker, Tyler, Wetzel, or Wood.

Academic Fields/Career Goals: Chemical Engineering; Computer Science/Data Processing; Electrical Engineering/Electronics; Energy and Power Engineering; Engineering-Related Technologies; Engineering/Technology; Mechanical Engineering; Physical Sciences.

Award: Scholarship for use in freshman year; not renewable. *Number:* 1–60. *Amount:* $500.

Eligibility Requirements: Applicant must be high school student; planning to enroll or expecting to enroll full-time at an institution or university; resident of Washington and studying in West Virginia. Available to U.S. citizens.

Application Requirements: Application form, essay. *Deadline:* March 31.

SCARLETT FAMILY FOUNDATION SCHOLARSHIP PROGRAM

http://www.scarlettfoundation.org/

SCHOLARSHIP FOR STUDENTS PURSUING A BUSINESS OR STEM DEGREE
• See page 80

SEMICONDUCTOR RESEARCH CORPORATION (SRC)

http://www.src.org/

MASTER'S SCHOLARSHIP PROGRAM

Scholarship given to women or members of an under represented minority category (African-American, Hispanic, Native American). Scholarships are for study in disciplines related to microelectronics at U.S.-based universities having research funded by the Semiconductor Research Corporation and require U.S. citizenship or permanent resident status.

Academic Fields/Career Goals: Chemical Engineering; Computer Science/Data Processing; Electrical Engineering/Electronics; Engineering/Technology; Materials Science, Engineering, and Metallurgy.

Award: Scholarship for use in senior or graduate years; renewable. *Number:* 1–15. *Amount:* $25,000–$32,000.

Eligibility Requirements: Applicant must be American Indian/Alaska Native, Black (non-Hispanic), Hispanic and enrolled or expecting to enroll full-time at a four-year institution or university. Available to U.S. citizens.

Application Requirements: Application form, recommendations or references, resume, test scores, transcript. *Deadline:* February 15.

Contact: Virginia Wiggins, Student Relations Manager
   Phone: 919-941-9453
   E-mail: students@src.org

SOCIETY OF PLASTICS ENGINEERS FOUNDATION (SPE)

http://www.4spe.org/

FLEMING/BLASZCAK SCHOLARSHIP

Award available for a full-time undergraduate student, with a demonstrated interest in the plastics industry. Must be a U.S. citizen and provide documentation of Mexican heritage.

Academic Fields/Career Goals: Chemical Engineering; Electrical Engineering/Electronics; Engineering/Technology; Industrial Design; Materials Science, Engineering, and Metallurgy; Trade/Technical Specialties.

Award: Scholarship for use in freshman, sophomore, junior, or senior years; not renewable. *Number:* 1. *Amount:* $2000.

Eligibility Requirements: Applicant must be of Mexican heritage; Hispanic and enrolled or expecting to enroll full-time at a two-year or four-year institution or university. Available to U.S. citizens.

Application Requirements: Application form, community service, essay. *Deadline:* April 1.

Contact: Mr. Gene Havel, Scholarships Program Administrator
Society of Plastics Engineers Foundation (SPE)
6 Berkshire Blvd., Suite 306
Bethel, CT 06801-1065
Phone: 203-740-5457
E-mail: foundation@4spe.org

GULF COAST HURRICANE SCHOLARSHIP

One $6,000 scholarship for a student at a 4-year college. One $2,000 scholarship for a student at a 2-year junior college or technical institute. Must be a resident of and attending school in FL, AL, MS, LA or TX.

Academic Fields/Career Goals: Chemical Engineering; Engineering-Related Technologies; Engineering/Technology; Industrial Design; Materials Science, Engineering, and Metallurgy; Mechanical Engineering; Science, Technology, and Society; Trade/Technical Specialties.

Award: Scholarship for use in freshman, sophomore, junior, senior, or graduate years; not renewable. *Number:* 1. *Amount:* $2000.

Eligibility Requirements: Applicant must be enrolled or expecting to enroll full-time at a two-year or four-year or technical institution or university; resident of Alabama, Florida, Louisiana, Mississippi, Texas and studying in Alabama, Florida, Louisiana, Mississippi, Texas. Available to U.S. citizens.

Application Requirements: Application form, community service, essay. *Deadline:* April 1.

Contact: Mr. Gene Havel, Scholarships Program Administrator
Society of Plastics Engineers Foundation (SPE)
6 Berkshire Blvd., Suite 306
Bethel, CT 06801-1065
Phone: 203-740-5457
E-mail: foundation@4spe.org

SOCIETY OF PLASTICS ENGINEERS SCHOLARSHIP PROGRAM

Scholarships awarded to full-time students who have demonstrated or expressed an interest in the plastics industry. Major or course of study must be beneficial to a career in the plastics industry.

Academic Fields/Career Goals: Chemical Engineering; Electrical Engineering/Electronics; Engineering/Technology; Industrial Design; Materials Science, Engineering, and Metallurgy; Trade/Technical Specialties.

Award: Scholarship for use in freshman, sophomore, junior, senior, or graduate years; not renewable. *Number:* 35–40. *Amount:* $1000–$6000.

Eligibility Requirements: Applicant must be enrolled or expecting to enroll full-time at a two-year or four-year or technical institution or university. Available to U.S. and non-U.S. citizens.

Application Requirements: Application form, community service, essay. *Deadline:* April 1.

Contact: Mr. Gene Havel, Scholarship Program Administrator
Society of Plastics Engineers Foundation (SPE)
6 Berkshire Boulevard, Suite 306
Bethel, CT 06801-1065
Phone: 203-740-5457
E-mail: foundation@4spe.org

SOCIETY OF WOMEN ENGINEERS

https://swe.org/

DUPONT COMPANY SCHOLARSHIP

Two $1000 scholarship for female applicants planning to study a full-time ABET-accredited program in engineering, technology, or computing in the upcoming academic year. US Citizenship required. Preference given to those who demonstrate financial need. Geographic location based on home and collegiate address, and must be in Delaware, Pennsylvania or Virginia. Minimum GPA: 3.0.

Academic Fields/Career Goals: Chemical Engineering; Engineering/Technology; Mechanical Engineering.

Award: Scholarship for use in junior or senior years; not renewable. *Number:* 2. *Amount:* $1000.

Eligibility Requirements: Applicant must be enrolled or expecting to enroll full-time at a four-year institution or university and female. Available to U.S. citizens.

Application Requirements: Application form, financial need analysis, recommendations or references, transcript. *Deadline:* February 15.

Contact: Scholarship Committee
Phone: 312-596-5223
E-mail: scholarships@swe.org

SWE REGION E SCHOLARSHIP

One $1750 scholarship for female applicants planning to study a full-time ABET-accredited program in engineering, technology, or computing in the upcoming academic year. SWE membership required. Must be attending school within the Region E boundaries: Delaware, District of Columbia, Eastern Pennsylvania, Maryland, New Jersey, New York, and Virginia.

Academic Fields/Career Goals: Chemical Engineering; Civil Engineering; Computer Science/Data Processing; Construction Engineering/Management; Electrical Engineering/Electronics; Energy and Power Engineering; Engineering-Related Technologies; Engineering/Technology; Marine/Ocean Engineering; Mechanical Engineering; Paper and Pulp Engineering.

Award: Scholarship for use in sophomore, junior, senior, or graduate years; not renewable. *Number:* 1. *Amount:* $1750.

Eligibility Requirements: Applicant must be enrolled or expecting to enroll full-time at a four-year institution or university; female and studying in Delaware, District of Columbia, Maryland, New Jersey, New York, Pennsylvania, Virginia. Applicant or parent of applicant must be member of Society of Women Engineers. Available to U.S. citizens.

Application Requirements: Application form, recommendations or references, transcript. *Deadline:* February 15.

Contact: Scholarship Committee
Phone: 312-596-5223
E-mail: scholarships@swe.org

SWE REGION H SCHOLARSHIPS

Two scholarships, one $1500 scholarship and one $1750 scholarship, for female applicants planning to study a full-time ABET-accredited program in engineering, technology, or computing in the upcoming academic year. SWE membership required. Must attend a school within Region H boundaries: colleges in North Dakota, South Dakota, Minnesota, Iowa, Wisconsin, Illinois, Michigan, Indiana. Level of involvement in SWE should be high/amount of time spent volunteering, level of commitment, years of service.

Academic Fields/Career Goals: Chemical Engineering; Civil Engineering; Construction Engineering/Management; Electrical Engineering/Electronics; Energy and Power Engineering; Engineering/Technology; Marine/Ocean Engineering; Materials Science, Engineering, and Metallurgy; Mechanical Engineering; Paper and Pulp Engineering.

Award: Scholarship for use in sophomore, junior, senior, or graduate years; not renewable. *Number:* 2. *Amount:* $1500–$1750.

Eligibility Requirements: Applicant must be enrolled or expecting to enroll full-time at a four-year institution or university; female and studying in Illinois, Indiana, Iowa, Michigan, Minnesota, North Dakota, South Dakota, Wisconsin. Applicant or parent of applicant must be member of Society of Women Engineers. Available to U.S. citizens.

Application Requirements: Application form, recommendations or references, transcript. *Deadline:* February 15.

Contact: Scholarship Committee
Phone: 312-596-5223
E-mail: scholarships@swe.org

SWE REGION J SCHOLARSHIP

One $1250 scholarship for female applicants planning to study a full-time ABET-accredited program in engineering, technology, or computing in the upcoming academic year. SWE membership required. Must be attending school in the Region J boundaries: Alaska, Washington,

Oregon, Montana and Idaho. Renewable for 5 years. Availability dependent upon renewals.

Academic Fields/Career Goals: Chemical Engineering; Civil Engineering; Construction Engineering/Management; Electrical Engineering/Electronics; Energy and Power Engineering; Engineering/Technology; Marine/Ocean Engineering; Materials Science, Engineering, and Metallurgy; Mechanical Engineering; Paper and Pulp Engineering.

Award: Scholarship for use in sophomore, junior, senior, or graduate years; renewable. *Number:* 1. *Amount:* $1250.

Eligibility Requirements: Applicant must be enrolled or expecting to enroll full-time at a four-year institution or university; female and studying in Alaska, Idaho, Montana, Oregon, Washington. Applicant or parent of applicant must be member of Society of Women Engineers. Available to U.S. citizens.

Application Requirements: Application form, recommendations or references, transcript. *Deadline:* February 15.

Contact: Scholarship Committee
Phone: 312-596-5223
E-mail: scholarships@swe.org

TE CONNECTIVITY EXCELLENCE IN ENGINEERING SCHOLARSHIP

20 scholarships of $5000 for women pursuing ABET-accredited Baccalaureate programs in preparation for careers in engineering, engineering technology, and computer science in the United States and Mexico. Must be a U.S. citizen and have a minimum 3.0 GPA. Preference given to students who are from underrepresented backgrounds in STEM and/or those who demonstrate financial need.

Academic Fields/Career Goals: Chemical Engineering; Civil Engineering; Construction Engineering/Management; Electrical Engineering/Electronics; Engineering-Related Technologies; Engineering/Technology; Marine/Ocean Engineering; Materials Science, Engineering, and Metallurgy; Mechanical Engineering; Paper and Pulp Engineering.

Award: Scholarship for use in junior or senior years; not renewable. *Number:* 20. *Amount:* $5000.

Eligibility Requirements: Applicant must be enrolled or expecting to enroll full-time at a four-year institution or university and female. Available to U.S. citizens.

Application Requirements: Application form. *Deadline:* February 15.

Contact: Scholarship Committee
Phone: 312-596-5223
E-mail: scholarships@swe.org

SONS OF NORWAY FOUNDATION

http://www.sonsofnorway.com/foundation

NANCY LORRAINE JENSEN MEMORIAL SCHOLARSHIP

Scholarship available for full-time undergraduate study in chemistry, physics, or in chemical, electrical, or mechanical engineering by a female student who is a U.S. citizen, and a current member, daughter, or granddaughter of a current member of Sons of Norway. The annual award will be at least 50 percent of the tuition for one semester and no more than 100 percent of the tuition for one year. Must have attained a SAT score of at least 1800, a math score of 600 or better, or an ACT score of at least 26. Applicant must have completed at least one term of studies in the above fields. The award will be made jointly payable to the student and her institution. The award is renewable two times during undergraduate study.

Academic Fields/Career Goals: Chemical Engineering; Electrical Engineering/Electronics; Mechanical Engineering.

Award: Scholarship for use in sophomore, junior, or senior years; not renewable. *Number:* 1–6. *Amount:* $2500–$10,000.

Eligibility Requirements: Applicant must be of Norwegian heritage; age 17-35; enrolled or expecting to enroll full-time at a four-year institution or university; female and must have an interest in science. Available to U.S. citizens.

Application Requirements: Application form, essay, personal photograph, recommendations or references, test scores, transcript. *Deadline:* April 1.

Contact: Scholarship Coordinator
Sons of Norway Foundation
1455 West Lake Street
Minneapolis, MN 55408-2666
Phone: 612-827-3611
Fax: 612-827-0658
E-mail: foundation@sofn.com

STRAIGHTFORWARD MEDIA

http://www.straightforwardmedia.com/

STRAIGHTFORWARD MEDIA ENGINEERING SCHOLARSHIP

Scholarship of $500 to students attending or planning to enroll in a postsecondary engineering program in the United States or abroad. Scholarship is awarded four times per year. Deadlines: March 31, June 30, September 30, and December 31. For more information, see web http://www.straightforwardmedia.com/engineering/form.php.

Academic Fields/Career Goals: Chemical Engineering; Civil Engineering; Electrical Engineering/Electronics; Energy and Power Engineering; Engineering-Related Technologies; Engineering/Technology; Materials Science, Engineering, and Metallurgy; Mechanical Engineering; Paper and Pulp Engineering.

Award: Scholarship for use in freshman, sophomore, junior, or senior years; not renewable. *Number:* 4. *Amount:* $500.

Eligibility Requirements: Applicant must be enrolled or expecting to enroll full- or part-time at a two-year or four-year or technical institution or university. Available to U.S. and non-U.S. citizens.

Application Requirements: Essay. *Deadline:* varies.

Contact: Scholarship Committee
Phone: 605-348-3042

STRAIGHT NORTH

https://www.straightnorth.com/

STRAIGHT NORTH STEM SCHOLARSHIP
• *See page 81*

TAU KAPPA EPSILON EDUCATION FOUNDATION

https://www.tke.org/

STEVEN J. MUIR SCHOLARSHIP

This scholarship is awarded in recognition of academic achievement with a Grade Point Average of at least 3.0 or higher, and must be at least a sophomore or above, and recognizes outstanding leadership within the chapter, having served as a chapter officer or committee chair. The applicant must be pursuing an undergraduate degree in engineering or any of the pure sciences (i.e., chemistry, mathematics, physics, geology, etc.). Preference will first be given to a member of Beta-Eta Chapter but, if there is no qualified applicant, the scholarship will be open to any other qualified Teke.

Academic Fields/Career Goals: Chemical Engineering; Engineering/Technology; Mathematics; Science, Technology, and Society.

Award: Scholarship for use in sophomore, junior, or senior years. *Number:* 1.

Eligibility Requirements: Applicant must be enrolled or expecting to enroll at an institution or university and male. Applicant or parent of applicant must be member of Tau Kappa Epsilon. Available to U.S. citizens.

Application Requirements: Application form, application form may be submitted online, personal photograph. *Deadline:* March 15.

Contact: Rachel Stevenson, Foundation Communications Manager
Tau Kappa Epsilon Education Foundation
7439 Woodland Drive
Suite 100
Indianapolis, IN 46278
Phone: 317-872-6533 Ext. 246
E-mail: rstevenson@tke.org

UNITED NEGRO COLLEGE FUND

http://www.uncf.org/

DAVIS SCHOLARSHIP FOR WOMEN IN STEM
• *See page 111*

GALACTIC UNITE BYTHEWAY SCHOLARSHIP
• *See page 111*

LEIDOS STEM SCHOLARSHIP
• *See page 96*

XEROX

http://www.xerox.com//

TECHNICAL MINORITY SCHOLARSHIP

Scholarships are made available to minority students enrolled in technical degree programs at the Bachelor's degree level or above. Eligible students must have a GPA of 3.0 or higher and show financial need. Refer to website http://www.studentcareers-xerox-com.tmpqa.com/ for details.

Academic Fields/Career Goals: Chemical Engineering; Computer Science/Data Processing; Electrical Engineering/Electronics; Engineering-Related Technologies; Engineering/Technology; Materials Science, Engineering, and Metallurgy; Mechanical Engineering; Physical Sciences.

Award: Scholarship for use in freshman, sophomore, junior, senior, graduate, or postgraduate years; not renewable. *Number:* up to 128. *Amount:* $1000–$10,000.

Eligibility Requirements: Applicant must be American Indian/Alaska Native, Asian/Pacific Islander, Black (non-Hispanic), Hispanic and enrolled or expecting to enroll full-time at a four-year institution or university. Available to U.S. citizens.

Application Requirements: Application form, financial need analysis, resume. *Deadline:* September 30.

Contact: Stephanie Michalowski
Xerox
150 State Street
Rochester, NY 14614
Fax: 585-482-3095
E-mail: xtmsp@rballiance.com

CHILD AND FAMILY STUDIES

CALIFORNIA STUDENT AID COMMISSION

http://www.csac.ca.gov/

CHILD DEVELOPMENT TEACHER AND SUPERVISOR GRANT PROGRAM

Award is for those students pursuing an approved course of study leading to a Child Development Permit issued by the California Commission on Teacher Credentialing. In exchange for each year funding is received, recipients agree to provide one year of service in a licensed childcare center.

Academic Fields/Career Goals: Child and Family Studies; Education.

Award: Grant for use in freshman, sophomore, junior, senior, or graduate years; renewable. *Number:* up to 300. *Amount:* $1000–$2000.

Eligibility Requirements: Applicant must be enrolled or expecting to enroll full- or part-time at a two-year or four-year institution or university; resident of California and studying in California. Applicant or parent of applicant must have employment or volunteer experience in teaching/education. Available to U.S. citizens.

Application Requirements: Application form, financial need analysis, GPA verification, recommendations or references. *Deadline:* April 16.

Contact: Catalina Mistler, Deputy Director, Program Administration & Services Division
California Student Aid Commission
PO Box 419027
Rancho Cordova, CA 95741-9027
Phone: 888-224-7268
Fax: 916-526-8004
E-mail: catalina.mistler@csac.ca.gov

HUB FOUNDATION

https://hub-foundation.org

HUB FOUNDATION SCHOLARSHIPS
• *See page 88*

SOCIETY OF PEDIATRIC NURSES

http://www.pedsnurses.org/

SOCIETY OF PEDIATRIC NURSES EDUCATIONAL SCHOLARSHIP

Award to a member engaged in a BSN completion program or a graduate program that will advance the health of children. Nominee must be a current Society of Pediatric Nurses member.

Academic Fields/Career Goals: Child and Family Studies; Health and Medical Sciences; Nursing.

Award: Scholarship for use in freshman, sophomore, junior, senior, or graduate years; not renewable. *Number:* 1. *Amount:* $500.

Eligibility Requirements: Applicant must be enrolled or expecting to enroll full-time at a four-year institution or university. Applicant or parent of applicant must be member of Society of Pediatric Nurses. Applicant or parent of applicant must have employment or volunteer experience in nursing. Available to U.S. citizens.

Application Requirements: Application form, essay, recommendations or references, resume. *Deadline:* November 14.

Contact: Scholarship Committee
Phone: 800-723-2902
Fax: 850-484-8762
E-mail: spn@puetzamc.com

WILLIAMS LAW GROUP

https://familylawyersnewjersey.com/

WILLIAMS LAW GROUP OPPORTUNITY TO GROW SCHOLARSHIP
• *See page 119*

Y'S MEN INTERNATIONAL

http://www.ysmen.org/

ALEXANDER SCHOLARSHIP LOAN FUND
• *See page 152*

CIVIL ENGINEERING

AACE INTERNATIONAL

http://www.aacei.org/

AACE INTERNATIONAL COMPETITIVE SCHOLARSHIP
• *See page 112*

ACI FOUNDATION

http://www.acifoundation.org

ACI FOUNDATION SCHOLARSHIP PROGRAM
• See page 113

AMERICAN COUNCIL OF ENGINEERING COMPANIES OF PENNSYLVANIA (ACEC/PA)

http://www.acecpa.org/

ERIC J. GENNUSO AND LEROY D. (BUD) LOY, JR. SCHOLARSHIP PROGRAM
• See page 153

AMERICAN INDIAN SCIENCE AND ENGINEERING SOCIETY

http://www.aises.org/

A.T. ANDERSON MEMORIAL SCHOLARSHIP PROGRAM
• See page 105

AMERICAN PUBLIC POWER ASSOCIATION

https://www.publicpower.org/deed-rd-funding

DEMONSTRATION OF ENERGY AND EFFICIENCY DEVELOPMENTS EDUCATIONAL SCHOLARSHIP
• See page 154

DEMONSTRATION OF ENERGY AND EFFICIENCY DEVELOPMENTS STUDENT INTERNSHIP
• See page 154

DEMONSTRATION OF ENERGY AND EFFICIENCY DEVELOPMENTS STUDENT RESEARCH GRANTS
Student grants provide funding to support research in an energy project sponsored by a DEED member utility. Spring Application Cycle is every December 1st - February 15th while Fall Application Cycle is every August 1st - October 15th.

Academic Fields/Career Goals: Civil Engineering; Electrical Engineering/Electronics; Energy and Power Engineering; Engineering-Related Technologies; Engineering/Technology; Environmental Science; Mechanical Engineering; Natural Resources.

Award: Scholarship for use in freshman, sophomore, junior, senior, graduate, or postgraduate years; not renewable. *Number:* 5–10. *Amount:* $5000.

Eligibility Requirements: Applicant must be Hispanic and enrolled or expecting to enroll full-time at a two-year or technical institution or university. Available to U.S. and non-U.S. citizens.

Application Requirements: Application form.

Contact: Jack Miller, DEED and Engineering Services Assistant
Phone: 202-467-2942
E-mail: DEED@PublicPower.org

DEMONSTRATION OF ENERGY AND EFFICIENCY DEVELOPMENTS TECHNICAL DESIGN PROJECT
• See page 154

AMERICAN PUBLIC TRANSPORTATION FOUNDATION

https://www.aptfd.org/

TRANSIT HALL OF FAME SCHOLARSHIP AWARD PROGRAM
Renewable award for sophomores, juniors, seniors or graduate students studying transportation or rail transit engineering. Must be sponsored by APTA member organization and complete an internship program with a member organization. Must have a minimum 3.0 GPA and be a U.S. or Canadian citizen.

Academic Fields/Career Goals: Civil Engineering; Electrical Engineering/Electronics; Engineering-Related Technologies; Engineering/Technology; Mechanical Engineering; Transportation.

Award: Scholarship for use in sophomore, junior, senior, or graduate years; renewable. *Number:* 1. *Amount:* $2500.

Eligibility Requirements: Applicant must be enrolled or expecting to enroll full-time at a two-year or four-year institution or university. Available to U.S. and Canadian citizens.

Application Requirements: Application form, essay, financial need analysis, nomination by APTA member, verification of enrollment, copy of fee schedule from the college/university for the academic year, recommendations or references, transcript. *Deadline:* June 16.

Contact: Pamela Boswell, Vice President of Program Management
American Public Transportation Foundation
1666 K Street, NW
Washington, DC 20006-1215
Phone: 202-496-4803
Fax: 202-496-4323

AMERICAN RAILWAY ENGINEERING AND MAINTENANCE OF WAY ASSOCIATION

http://www.aremafoundation.org/

AREMA GRADUATE AND UNDERGRADUATE SCHOLARSHIPS
Railroad interest - Applicants must be enrolled as a student in a Graduate or Undergraduate program leading to a degree in Engineering or Engineering Technology in a curriculum which has been accredited by the Accreditation Board of Engineering and Technology (or comparable accreditation in Canada and Mexico). The applicant must have at least a 2.00 GPA (out of 4.00).

Academic Fields/Career Goals: Civil Engineering; Computer Science/Data Processing; Construction Engineering/Management; Electrical Engineering/Electronics; Engineering-Related Technologies; Engineering/Technology; Mechanical Engineering.

Award: Scholarship for use in freshman, sophomore, junior, senior, or graduate years; not renewable. *Number:* 30–40. *Amount:* $1000–$10,000.

Eligibility Requirements: Applicant must be enrolled or expecting to enroll full- or part-time at a four-year institution or university. Available to U.S. and Canadian citizens.

Application Requirements: Application form. *Deadline:* December 9.

Contact: Alayne Bell, Manager, Committees & Technical Services
Phone: 301-459-3200 Ext. 708
E-mail: abell@arema.org

AMERICAN SOCIETY OF CERTIFIED ENGINEERING TECHNICIANS

http://www.ascet.org/

KURT H. AND DONNA M. SCHULER SMALL GRANT
The small Cash Grant program was suggested by students and faculty advisors who recommended that several grants be awarded to deserving students and that these awards carry as few restrictions as possible. Each award shall be in the amount of $400 to be used to offset the cost of educational expenses as desired. Such grants may be awarded to one or more students each year. Must be either a student, certified, regular, registered or associate member of ASCET, or be a high school senior in the last five months of the academic year who will be enrolled in an Engineering Technology curriculum no later than six months following selection for award. Must also achieve passing grades in present curriculum.

Academic Fields/Career Goals: Civil Engineering; Construction Engineering/Management; Drafting; Electrical Engineering/Electronics; Energy and Power Engineering; Engineering-Related Technologies; Engineering/Technology; Fire Sciences; Landscape Architecture; Marine/Ocean Engineering; Materials Science, Engineering, and Metallurgy; Mechanical Engineering; Surveying, Surveying Technology, Cartography, or Geographic Information Science; Trade/Technical Specialties; Transportation.

Award: Grant for use in freshman, sophomore, junior, or senior years; not renewable. *Number:* 1–4. *Amount:* $400.

Eligibility Requirements: Applicant must be enrolled or expecting to enroll full- or part-time at a two-year or four-year or technical institution or university. Available to U.S. citizens.

Application Requirements: Application form, financial need analysis. *Deadline:* February 28.

Contact: Mr. Jimmy Lynch, Financial Aid Committee Chair
American Society of Certified Engineering Technicians
15621 West 87th Street Parkway, #205
Lenexa, KS 66219
Phone: 773-242-7238
E-mail: financialaid@ascet.org

AMERICAN SOCIETY OF NAVAL ENGINEERS

http://www.navalengineers.org/

AMERICAN SOCIETY OF NAVAL ENGINEERS SCHOLARSHIP
• *See page 106*

ASIAN PACIFIC FUND

BANATAO FAMILY FILIPINO AMERICAN EDUCATION FUND
• *See page 155*

ASSOCIATED GENERAL CONTRACTORS EDUCATION AND RESEARCH FOUNDATION

https://www.agc.org/

JAMES L. ALLHANDS ESSAY COMPETITION
The competition is open to any senior&-level student in a four or five&-year ABET or ACCE&-accredited university construction management or construction&-related engineering program. The First Place essay author receives $1,000. His/her faculty sponsor receives $500. Second place wins $500 and third place, $300. Both the recipient and sponsor are invited as guests of the Foundation to the AGC Annual Convention.

Academic Fields/Career Goals: Civil Engineering.

Award: Prize for use in senior year; not renewable. *Number:* 3. *Amount:* $300–$1000.

Eligibility Requirements: Applicant must be enrolled or expecting to enroll full-time at an institution or university. Available to U.S. citizens.

Application Requirements: Application form, essay. *Deadline:* November 15.

Contact: Melinda Patrician, Director
Associated General Contractors Education and Research Foundation
2300 Wilson Boulevard, Suite 300
Arlington, VA 22201
Phone: 703-837-5342
E-mail: patricianm@agc.org

UNDERGRADUATE SCHOLARSHIP
Scholarships are for a maximum of $2,500 per student per year and may be renewable for up to three years of undergraduate study in construction-related engineering, construction, or a dual degree with construction or construction-related engineering as one part. College sophomores and juniors enrolled or planning to enroll in a full-time, four or five-year ABET or ACCE-accredited construction management or construction-related engineering program are eligible to apply. High school are not eligible.

Academic Fields/Career Goals: Civil Engineering.

Award: Scholarship for use in sophomore, junior, or senior years; renewable.

Eligibility Requirements: Applicant must be enrolled or expecting to enroll full-time at an institution or university. Available to U.S. citizens.

Application Requirements: Application form, interview. *Deadline:* November 1.

Contact: Courtney Bishop, Associate Director
Associated General Contractors Education and Research Foundation
2300 Wilson Boulevard, Suite 300
Arlington, VA 22201
Phone: 703-837-5356
E-mail: courtney.bishop@agc.org

ASSOCIATED GENERAL CONTRACTORS OF NEW YORK STATE, LLC

https://www.agcnys.org/programs/scholarship/

ASSOCIATED GENERAL CONTRACTORS NYS SCHOLARSHIP PROGRAM
Scholarship for students enrolled full-time study in civil engineering, construction management and construction technology and diesel technology. Must have minimum GPA of 2.5. Scholarship value is from $1500 to $5000. Must be resident of New York.

Academic Fields/Career Goals: Civil Engineering; Construction Engineering/Management; Surveying, Surveying Technology, Cartography, or Geographic Information Science; Transportation.

Award: Scholarship for use in sophomore, junior, senior, or graduate years; not renewable. *Number:* 15–25. *Amount:* $1500–$5000.

Eligibility Requirements: Applicant must be enrolled or expecting to enroll full-time at a two-year or four-year institution or university and resident of New York. Available to U.S. citizens.

Application Requirements: Application form, financial need analysis, recommendations or references, transcript. *Deadline:* May 15.

Contact: Mr. Brendan Manning, Vice President, Education and Environment
Associated General Contractors of New York State, LLC
10 Airline Drive
Suite 203
Albany, NY 12205
Phone: 518-456-1134
E-mail: bmanning@agcnys.org

ASSOCIATION OF CALIFORNIA WATER AGENCIES

http://www.acwa.com/

ASSOCIATION OF CALIFORNIA WATER AGENCIES SCHOLARSHIPS
• *See page 106*

CLAIR A. HILL SCHOLARSHIP
• *See page 106*

ASSOCIATION OF STATE DAM SAFETY OFFICIALS (ASDSO)

http://www.DamSafety.org

ASSOCIATION OF STATE DAM SAFETY OFFICIALS (ASDSO) SENIOR UNDERGRADUATE SCHOLARSHIP
• *See page 140*

AUTOMOTIVE WOMEN'S ALLIANCE FOUNDATION

http://awafoundation.org/index.php

AUTOMOTIVE WOMEN'S ALLIANCE FOUNDATION SCHOLARSHIPS
• *See page 71*

BHW GROUP

https://thebhwgroup.com/

BHW WOMEN IN STEM SCHOLARSHIP
• *See page 107*

BRASKEM ODEBRECHT

http://www.odebrechtaward.com

ODEBRECHT AWARD FOR SUSTAINABLE DEVELOPMENT
• *See page 113*

BROWN AND CALDWELL

http://www.brownandcaldwell.com

ECKENFELDER SCHOLARSHIP
• *See page 141*

MINORITY SCHOLARSHIP PROGRAM
• *See page 141*

CARDS AGAINST HUMANITY

https://cardsagainsthumanity.com/

SCIENCE AMBASSADOR SCHOLARSHIP
• *See page 107*

CENTER FOR ARCHITECTURE

www.centerforarchitecture.org

CENTER FOR ARCHITECTURE DESIGN SCHOLARSHIP
• *See page 114*

CONNECTICUT BUILDING CONGRESS SCHOLARSHIP FUND, INC.

http://www.cbc-ct.org

CBC SCHOLARSHIP FUND
• *See page 114*

THE DALLAS FOUNDATION

http://www.dallasfoundation.org/

JERE W. THOMPSON, JR., SCHOLARSHIP FUND
Renewable scholarships awarded to full-time undergraduate juniors or seniors with disadvantaged backgrounds, who are pursuing a degree in civil engineering and closely related disciplines at Texas colleges and universities. Up to $2000 awarded each semester, beginning with junior year. Must maintain 2.5 GPA. Special consideration given to students from Collin, Dallas, Denton, and Tarrant Counties, Texas.
Academic Fields/Career Goals: Civil Engineering.
Award: Scholarship for use in junior or senior years; renewable. *Number:* 1–2. *Amount:* up to $4000.
Eligibility Requirements: Applicant must be enrolled or expecting to enroll full-time at a four-year institution or university; resident of Texas and studying in Texas. Available to U.S. citizens.
Application Requirements: Application form, essay, financial need analysis, recommendations or references, test scores, transcript. *Deadline:* April 1.

Contact: Rachel Lasseter, Program Associate
The Dallas Foundation
900 Jackson Street, Suite 705
Dallas, TX 75202
Phone: 214-741-9898
Fax: 214-741-9848
E-mail: scholarships@dallasfoundation.org

WHITLEY PLACE SCHOLARSHIP
• *See page 114*

DISTIL NETWORKS

http://www.distilnetworks.com

WOMEN FORWARD IN TECHNOLOGY SCHOLARSHIP PROGRAM
• *See page 108*

FLORIDA ENGINEERING SOCIETY

https://www.fleng.org/page/Scholarships

DAVID F. LUDOVICI SCHOLARSHIP
• *See page 156*

FECON SCHOLARSHIP
One-time scholarship of $1000 given to Florida citizens in their junior or senior year, who are enrolled or accepted into a Florida university engineering program. Minimum 3.0 GPA required. Applicant must be interested in pursuing a career in the field of construction.
Academic Fields/Career Goals: Civil Engineering; Construction Engineering/Management; Engineering/Technology.
Award: Scholarship for use in junior or senior years; not renewable. *Number:* 1. *Amount:* $1000.
Eligibility Requirements: Applicant must be enrolled or expecting to enroll full-time at an institution or university; resident of District of Columbia and studying in Florida. Available to U.S. citizens.
Application Requirements: Application form, essay. *Deadline:* April 20.
Contact: Meridith Glass, Event Coordinator
Florida Engineering Society
125 South Gadsden Street
Tallahassee, FL 32301
Phone: 850-224-7121
E-mail: mglass@fleng.org

GREAT MINDS IN STEM

http://www.greatmindsinstem.org/college/scholarship-application-information

HENAAC SCHOLARSHIP PROGRAM
• *See page 100*

INTERNATIONAL SOCIETY OF EXPLOSIVES ENGINEERS

http://www.isee.org/

JERRY MCDOWELL FUND
• *See page 156*

JORGE MAS CANOSA FREEDOM FOUNDATION

http://masscholarships.org/

MAS FAMILY SCHOLARSHIP AWARD
• *See page 149*

KENTUCKY ENERGY AND ENVIRONMENT CABINET

http://dep.ky.gov

ENVIRONMENTAL PROTECTION SCHOLARSHIP
• See page 142

KENTUCKY TRANSPORTATION CABINET

http://transportation.ky.gov/Education/Pages/Scholarships.aspx

KENTUCKY TRANSPORTATION CABINET CIVIL ENGINEERING SCHOLARSHIP PROGRAM

Scholarships awarded to qualified Kentucky residents who wish to study civil engineering at University of Kentucky, Western Kentucky University, University of Louisville or Kentucky State University. Applicant should be a graduate of an accredited Kentucky high school or a Kentucky resident. Scholarship recipients are given opportunities to work for the Cabinet during summers and job opportunities upon graduation within the state of KY.

Academic Fields/Career Goals: Civil Engineering.

Award: Scholarship for use in freshman, sophomore, junior, or senior years; renewable. *Number:* 15–30. *Amount:* $12,400–$51,200.

Eligibility Requirements: Applicant must be enrolled or expecting to enroll full-time at a four-year institution or university; resident of Kentucky and studying in Kentucky. Available to U.S. and non-U.S. citizens.

Application Requirements: Application form, essay, interview. *Deadline:* February 1.

Contact: Cherie Mertz, Scholarship Program Coordinator
Kentucky Transportation Cabinet
200 Mero Street, 6th Floor East
Frankfort, KY 40622
Phone: 502-564-3730
E-mail: Cherie.Mertz@ky.gov

LOGMEIN

https://www.logmeininc.com

LASTPASS STEM SCHOLARSHIP
• See page 109

LOS ANGELES COUNCIL OF BLACK PROFESSIONAL ENGINEERS

http://www.lablackengineers.org/

AL-BEN SCHOLARSHIP FOR ACADEMIC INCENTIVE
• See page 157

AL-BEN SCHOLARSHIP FOR PROFESSIONAL MERIT
• See page 157

AL-BEN SCHOLARSHIP FOR SCHOLASTIC ACHIEVEMENT
• See page 157

MIDWEST ROOFING CONTRACTORS ASSOCIATION

http://www.mrca.org/

MRCA FOUNDATION SCHOLARSHIP PROGRAM
• See page 116

NASA IDAHO SPACE GRANT CONSORTIUM

http://www.idahospacegrant.org

NASA IDAHO SPACE GRANT CONSORTIUM SCHOLARSHIP PROGRAM
• See page 109

NASA MONTANA SPACE GRANT CONSORTIUM

http://www.spacegrant.montana.edu/

MONTANA SPACE GRANT SCHOLARSHIP PROGRAM
• See page 132

NATIONAL ASPHALT PAVEMENT ASSOCIATION RESEARCH AND EDUCATION FOUNDATION

http://www.asphaltpavement.org

NATIONAL ASPHALT PAVEMENT ASSOCIATION RESEARCH AND EDUCATION FOUNDATION SCHOLARSHIP PROGRAM

Our Scholarship program provides funding for undergraduate and graduate students who are U.S. citizens enrolled in a full time civil engineering, construction management, or construction engineering curriculum at an accredited four year college/university or two-year technical institution. The NAPAREF Scholarship Program was initiated in 1994 to encourage young people to take elective courses in asphalt technology and management and to encourage institutions to make such courses available. The Scholarship Program is the keystone for assuring the future of the Asphalt industry through the education of tomorrow's industry leaders and the establishment of opportunities to expand knowledge and training in asphalt technology. Our scholarships provide an incentive for engineering students to select courses in asphalt technology; a workforce with training in asphalt technology; and an incentive for colleges/universities to offer training in asphalt technology. The NAPAREF Scholarship Program ensures the future of the asphalt industry and that of asphalt as America's leading choice in paving materials.

Academic Fields/Career Goals: Civil Engineering; Construction Engineering/Management.

Award: Scholarship for use in freshman, sophomore, junior, senior, graduate, or postgraduate years; not renewable. *Number:* 51. *Amount:* $500–$5000.

Eligibility Requirements: Applicant must be enrolled or expecting to enroll full-time at a two-year or four-year or technical institution or university. Available to U.S. citizens.

Application Requirements: Application form, essay. *Deadline:* continuous.

Contact: Mrs. Carolyn Wilson, Vice President, Finance and Operations
National Asphalt Pavement Association Research and Education Foundation
5100 Forbes Boulevard, Suite 200
Lanham, MD 20706
Phone: 301-731-4748 Ext. 127
Fax: 301-731-4621
E-mail: cwilson@asphaltpavement.org

NATIONAL ASSOCIATION OF WOMEN IN CONSTRUCTION

http://www.nawic.org/

NAWIC UNDERGRADUATE SCHOLARSHIPS
• See page 117

NATIONAL SOCIETY OF PROFESSIONAL ENGINEERS

http://www.nspe.org/

MAUREEN L. & HOWARD N. BLITMAN, P.E., SCHOLARSHIP TO PROMOTE DIVERSITY IN ENGINEERING

Award two disbursements of $2,500 each to a high school senior from an ethnic minority who has been accepted into an ABET-accredited engineering program at a four-year college or university.

Academic Fields/Career Goals: Civil Engineering; Electrical Engineering/Electronics; Engineering-Related Technologies; Engineering/Technology; Materials Science, Engineering, and Metallurgy; Mechanical Engineering.

Award: Scholarship for use in freshman year; not renewable. *Number:* 2. *Amount:* $2500.

Eligibility Requirements: Applicant must be American Indian/Alaska Native, Black (non-Hispanic), Hispanic; high school student and planning to enroll or expecting to enroll full-time at an institution or university. Available to U.S. citizens.

Application Requirements: Application form. *Deadline:* March 1.

PAUL H. ROBBINS HONORARY SCHOLARSHIP
• See page 158

PROFESSIONAL ENGINEERS IN INDUSTRY SCHOLARSHIP
• See page 158

NEVADA NASA SPACE GRANT CONSORTIUM

https://nasa.epscorspo.nevada.edu/

NATIONAL SPACE GRANT CONSORTIUM SCHOLARSHIPS
• See page 110

NEW ENGLAND WATER WORKS ASSOCIATION

https://www.newwa.org/

ELSON T. KILLAM MEMORIAL SCHOLARSHIP

Scholarships are awarded to eligible civil and environmental engineering students on the basis of merit, character, and need. Preference given to those students whose programs are considered by a committee as beneficial to water works practice in New England. NEWWA student membership is required to receive a scholarship award. Applicants for scholarships should be residents or attend school in New England. (Maine, New Hampshire, Vermont, Massachusetts, Rhode Island and Connecticut).

Academic Fields/Career Goals: Civil Engineering; Engineering/Technology; Environmental Science.

Award: Scholarship for use in freshman, sophomore, junior, senior, or graduate years; not renewable. *Number:* 1. *Amount:* $1500.

Eligibility Requirements: Applicant must be enrolled or expecting to enroll full-time at an institution or university. Applicant or parent of applicant must be member of New England Water Works Association. Available to U.S. citizens.

Application Requirements: Application form, application form may be submitted online, essay, financial need analysis. *Fee:* $30. *Deadline:* April 1.

Contact: Stephen Donovan, Scholarship Committee Chair
New England Water Works Association
125 Hopping Brook Road
Holliston, MA 01746
Phone: 508-248-2893
Fax: 508-893-9898
E-mail: sdonovan@rhwhite.com

FRANCIS X. CROWLEY SCHOLARSHIP
• See page 150

GEORGE E. WATTERS MEMORIAL SCHOLARSHIP

Scholarships are awarded to eligible Civil Engineering students on the basis of merit, character, and need. Preference given to those students whose programs are considered by a committee as beneficial to water works practice in New England. NEWWA student membership is required to receive a scholarship award. Applicants for scholarships should be residents or attend school in New England. (Maine, New Hampshire, Vermont, Massachusetts, Rhode Island and Connecticut).

Academic Fields/Career Goals: Civil Engineering.

Award: Scholarship for use in freshman, sophomore, junior, senior, or graduate years; not renewable. *Number:* 1. *Amount:* $5000.

Eligibility Requirements: Applicant must be enrolled or expecting to enroll full-time at an institution or university. Applicant or parent of applicant must be member of New England Water Works Association. Available to U.S. citizens.

Application Requirements: Application form, application form may be submitted online, essay, financial need analysis. *Fee:* $30. *Deadline:* April 1.

Contact: Stephen Donovan, Scholarship Committee Chair
New England Water Works Association
125 Hopping Brook Road
Holliston, MA 01746
Phone: 508-248-2893
Fax: 508-893-9898
E-mail: sdonovan@rhwhite.com

JOSEPH MURPHY SCHOLARSHIP
• See page 150

NEXTSTEPU

http://www.nextstepu.com/

$1,500 STEM SCHOLARSHIP
• See page 104

PROFESSIONAL CONSTRUCTION ESTIMATORS ASSOCIATION

http://www.pcea.org/

TED G. WILSON MEMORIAL SCHOLARSHIP FOUNDATION

Amount up to $1000 to a deserving student (high school senior, college freshman, sophomore, or junior) based on their academic ability, need, and desire to enter the construction industry.

Academic Fields/Career Goals: Civil Engineering; Construction Engineering/Management; Drafting; Electrical Engineering/Electronics; Engineering/Technology; Heating, Air-Conditioning, and Refrigeration Mechanics; Landscape Architecture; Mechanical Engineering; Surveying, Surveying Technology, Cartography, or Geographic Information Science; Trade/Technical Specialties.

Award: Scholarship for use in freshman, sophomore, junior, or senior years; not renewable. *Number:* 5. *Amount:* up to $1000.

Eligibility Requirements: Applicant must be enrolled or expecting to enroll full-time at a two-year or four-year or technical institution or university; resident of Florida, Georgia, North Carolina, South Carolina, Virginia and studying in Florida, Georgia, North Carolina, South Carolina, Virginia. Available to U.S. and non-U.S. citizens.

Application Requirements: Application form, financial need analysis, interview, recommendations or references, transcript. *Deadline:* March 15.

Contact: Kim Lybrand, National Office Manager
Professional Construction Estimators Association
PO Box 680336
Charlotte, NC 28216-0336
Phone: 704-987-9978
Fax: 704-987-9979
E-mail: pcea@pcea.org

ROCKY MOUNTAIN COAL MINING INSTITUTE

http://www.rmcmi.org/

ROCKY MOUNTAIN COAL MINING INSTITUTE SCHOLARSHIP

Must be full-time college sophomore or junior at time of application, pursuing a degree in mining-related fields or engineering disciplines such as mining, geology, mineral processing, or metallurgy. For residents of Arizona, Colorado, Montana, New Mexico, North Dakota, Texas, Utah, and Wyoming. Scholarship value is $2500 per year for two-years sent directly to school for tuition.

Academic Fields/Career Goals: Civil Engineering; Earth Science; Engineering-Related Technologies; Engineering/Technology; Materials Science, Engineering, and Metallurgy.

Award: Scholarship for use in junior or senior years; renewable. *Number:* 8. *Amount:* $2500.

Eligibility Requirements: Applicant must be enrolled or expecting to enroll full-time at a four-year institution or university and resident of Arizona, Colorado, Montana, New Mexico, North Dakota, Texas, Utah, Wyoming. Available to U.S. citizens.

Application Requirements: Application form, interview, recommendations or references. *Deadline:* February 1.

Contact: Karen Inzano, Executive Director
Phone: 303-948-3300
E-mail: mail@rmcmi.org

SCARLETT FAMILY FOUNDATION SCHOLARSHIP PROGRAM

http://www.scarlettfoundation.org/

SCHOLARSHIP FOR STUDENTS PURSUING A BUSINESS OR STEM DEGREE
• *See page 80*

SOCIETY OF WOMEN ENGINEERS

https://swe.org/

SWE REGION E SCHOLARSHIP
• *See page 159*

SWE REGION H SCHOLARSHIPS
• *See page 159*

SWE REGION J SCHOLARSHIP
• *See page 159*

TE CONNECTIVITY EXCELLENCE IN ENGINEERING SCHOLARSHIP
• *See page 160*

STRAIGHTFORWARD MEDIA

http://www.straightforwardmedia.com/

STRAIGHTFORWARD MEDIA ENGINEERING SCHOLARSHIP
• *See page 160*

STRAIGHT NORTH

https://www.straightnorth.com/

STRAIGHT NORTH STEM SCHOLARSHIP
• *See page 81*

TEXAS DEPARTMENT OF TRANSPORTATION

http://www.txdot.gov/

CONDITIONAL GRANT PROGRAM

Renewable award to students who are considered economically disadvantaged based on federal guidelines. The maximum amount awarded per semester is $3,000 not to exceed $6000 per academic year. Students already enrolled in an undergraduate program should have minimum GPA 2.5 and students newly enrolling should have minimum GPA 3.0.

Academic Fields/Career Goals: Civil Engineering; Computer Science/Data Processing; Occupational Safety and Health.

Award: Grant for use in freshman, sophomore, junior, or senior years; renewable. *Number:* 10–20. *Amount:* $3000–$6000.

Eligibility Requirements: Applicant must be enrolled or expecting to enroll full-time at a four-year institution or university; resident of Texas and studying in Texas. Available to U.S. citizens.

Application Requirements: Application form, essay, financial need analysis, interview. *Deadline:* March 1.

Contact: Sheila Brooks, Program Coordinator
Texas Department of Transportation
125 East 11th Street
Austin, TX 78701-2483
Phone: 512-416-4979
E-mail: hrd_recruitment@txdot.gov

TIMOTION

http://www.timotion.com/

TIMOTION ENGINEERING AND EXCELLENCE SCHOLARSHIP

In 2005, TiMOTION entered the world of electric linear actuators, quickly becoming the premier global designer and manufacturer of complete motion system solutions. Since its inception, the company has earned a reputation for reliable, high quality, competitively priced products that satisfy the needs of worldwide medical, furniture, ergonomic, and industrial markets. TiMOTION established this annual scholarship opportunity for aspiring engineers, ergonomists, or technology students to continue their education in hopes of powering the worlds towards a better future. Must be a full-time student enrolled in an engineering, ergonomics, or technology-focused program at an accredited undergraduate university or college. Must provide transcripts indicating strong academic performance with a GPA of 3.0 or higher. Must provide information regarding extracurricular activities, volunteering opportunities, or other community-involvement experience. We advise reading all information listed on our website prior to submitting your application, so that you can be better prepared. You will need to submit: 1. a transcript. You will need this as a record of proof to the course level and grades that you received since your freshman year in high school; 2. contact information. You must be prepared to provide us with your name, email address, and phone number so that we may contact you if your application is selected; 3. a school profile. We have an area of the application that asks you to give us the details of the university or college you will attend; 4.the essay. In 500-700 words, you will need to provide us with a comprehensive look into what inspired you to pursue your field of study. Check out sample applications for ideas.

Academic Fields/Career Goals: Civil Engineering; Electrical Engineering/Electronics; Energy and Power Engineering; Engineering-Related Technologies; Engineering/Technology; Industrial Design; Mechanical Engineering.

Award: Scholarship for use in freshman, sophomore, junior, senior, or postgraduate years; renewable. *Number:* 5. *Amount:* $2000.

Eligibility Requirements: Applicant must be enrolled or expecting to enroll full-time at a four-year institution or university. Available to U.S. and non-U.S. citizens.

Application Requirements: Application form, essay. *Deadline:* December 1.

Contact: Samantha Rosenfeld, Senior Marketing Associate
TiMOTION
1535 Center Park Drive
Charlotte, NC 28217
Phone: 704-708-6924 Ext. 914
E-mail: scholarships@timotion.com

TRANSPORTATION ASSOCIATION OF CANADA FOUNDATION

http://www.tac-foundation.ca

TAC FOUNDATION SCHOLARSHIPS

The TAC Foundation's primary focus for educational support (scholarships) is on the planning, design, construction, operations, maintenance and program management of transportation infrastructure, including urban transit. Scholarships are supported through annual donations to the TAC Foundation from donor organizations and individuals that support the Foundation's mandate. Candidates must be Canadian citizens or permanent residents; enrolled at a post-secondary institution (university or college) in an academic program related to the planning, design, construction, operations, maintenance and program management of transportation infrastructure, including urban transit; are limited to being awarded one TAC Foundation scholarship at each stage of their education (community college, university undergraduate, graduate. TAC Foundation entrance scholarships are not included in this restriction); must have achieved an overall B average or equivalent average mark in their previous academic year; may apply for and receive scholarships from other sources.

Academic Fields/Career Goals: Civil Engineering; Construction Engineering/Management; Economics; Engineering-Related Technologies; Engineering/Technology; Urban and Regional Planning.

Award: Scholarship for use in senior or graduate years; not renewable. *Number:* 30–45. *Amount:* $2500–$5000.

Eligibility Requirements: Applicant must be Canadian citizen; enrolled or expecting to enroll full-time at a two-year or four-year institution or university and resident of Alberta, British Columbia, Manitoba, New Brunswick, Newfoundland, Northwest Territories, Nova Scotia, Ontario, Prince Edward Island, Quebec, Saskatchewan, Yukon.

Application Requirements: Application form. *Deadline:* February 28.

Contact: Ms. Erica Andersen, Secretary-Treasurer
Phone: 613-736-1350 Ext. 235
Fax: 613-736-1395
E-mail: foundation@tac-atc.ca

TURNER CONSTRUCTION COMPANY

http://www.turnerconstruction.com/

YOUTHFORCE 2020 SCHOLARSHIP PROGRAM
• *See page 117*

UNITED NEGRO COLLEGE FUND

http://www.uncf.org/

DELL CORPORATE SCHOLARS PROGRAM

Scholarship of up to $2500 for a student majoring or having an academic focus in Engineering, Supply Chain Management, Computer Science or Information Technology. Must be a minority student enrolled full-time at a U.S. located accredited four year institution as a junior during the application and interview process. Must possess a demonstrated unmet financial need as verified by their institution/college (for scholarship award) and have a minimum 3.0 GPA. All applicants for the UNCF/Dell Corporate Scholars Program may be considered for summer internship opportunities at Dell HQ in Round Rock TX.

Academic Fields/Career Goals: Civil Engineering; Computer Science/Data Processing; Electrical Engineering/Electronics; Energy and Power Engineering; Engineering-Related Technologies; Engineering/Technology.

Award: Scholarship for use in junior year; not renewable.

Eligibility Requirements: Applicant must be American Indian/Alaska Native, Asian/Pacific Islander, Black (non-Hispanic), Hispanic and enrolled or expecting to enroll full-time at a four-year institution or university. Available to U.S. citizens.

Application Requirements: Application form, essay, financial need analysis. *Deadline:* September 22.

Contact: Larry Griffith, Senior Vice President, Programs and Student Services
Phone: 800-331-2244

LEIDOS STEM SCHOLARSHIP
• *See page 96*

UNITED STATES SOCIETY ON DAMS

http://www.ussdams.org/

UNITED STATES SOCIETY ON DAMS STUDENT SCHOLARSHIP AWARD

USSD annually awards scholarships to students whose academic program has a potential for developing practical solutions to dam-related issues. Applicants must be U.S. citizens enrolled full-time in U.S. academic institutions.

Academic Fields/Career Goals: Civil Engineering; Engineering/Technology; Environmental Science.

Award: Prize for use in senior or graduate years; not renewable. *Number:* 4. *Amount:* $2000–$12,000.

Eligibility Requirements: Applicant must be enrolled or expecting to enroll full-time at a four-year institution or university. Applicant or parent of applicant must be member of United States Society on Dams. Available to U.S. citizens.

Application Requirements: Application form, application form may be submitted online (https://www.ussdams.org/about/scholarships/), transcript. *Deadline:* January 26.

Contact: Tina Stanard, Awards Committee Chair
Phone: 512-617-3120
E-mail: ces@freese.com

VECTORWORKS, INC.

http://www.vectorworks.net

VECTORWORKS DESIGN SCHOLARSHIP
• *See page 117*

VERMONT SPACE GRANT CONSORTIUM

http://www.cems.uvm.edu/vsgc

VERMONT SPACE GRANT CONSORTIUM
• *See page 92*

WIRE REINFORCEMENT INSTITUTE EDUCATION FOUNDATION

http://www.wirereinforcementinstitute.org/

WRI FOUNDATION COLLEGE SCHOLARSHIP PROGRAM

Academic scholarships for qualified current undergraduate and graduate level students officially declared as or presently pursuing four-year or graduate-level degrees in structural and/or civil engineering at accredited four-year universities or colleges in the U.S. or Canada. Scholarship recipients will also participate in the WRI Mentor Program for the year in which the scholarship is awarded.

Academic Fields/Career Goals: Civil Engineering; Construction Engineering/Management.

Award: Scholarship for use in sophomore, junior, senior, or graduate years; not renewable. *Number:* 2–5. *Amount:* $2000–$4000.

Eligibility Requirements: Applicant must be enrolled or expecting to enroll full-time at a four-year institution or university. Available to U.S. and non-U.S. citizens.

Application Requirements: Application form, essay. *Deadline:* April 15.

Contact: Scholarship Selection Committee
Wire Reinforcement Institute Education Foundation
942 Main Street
Hartford, CT 06103
Phone: 860-240-9545
E-mail: wrischolar@wirereinforcementinstitute.org

CLASSICS

ACL/NJCL NATIONAL LATIN EXAM

http://www.nle.org/

NATIONAL LATIN EXAM SCHOLARSHIP

Scholarships to high school seniors who are gold medal winners in Latin III, III-IV Prose, III-IV Poetry, or Latin V-VI their senior year. Applicants must agree to take at least one year of Latin or classical Greek language in college.

Academic Fields/Career Goals: Classics; Foreign Language.

Award: Scholarship for use in freshman, sophomore, junior, or senior years; renewable. *Number:* 21. *Amount:* $2000.

Eligibility Requirements: Applicant must be high school student; planning to enroll or expecting to enroll full-time at a four-year institution or university and must have an interest in Greek language or Latin language. Available to U.S. and non-U.S. citizens.

Application Requirements: Application form, essay. *Deadline:* May 16.

Contact: Mrs. Ephy Howard, Scholarship Chairperson
Phone: 888-378-7721

AMERICAN CLASSICAL LEAGUE/NATIONAL JUNIOR CLASSICAL LEAGUE

http://www.aclclassics.org/

NATIONAL JUNIOR CLASSICAL LEAGUE SCHOLARSHIP

A one-time award available to graduating high school seniors, who are members of the Junior Classical League. Preference is given to students who plan to major in the classics.

Academic Fields/Career Goals: Classics; Foreign Language; Humanities.

Award: Scholarship for use in freshman year; not renewable. *Number:* 7. *Amount:* $1000–$2000.

Eligibility Requirements: Applicant must be high school student; planning to enroll or expecting to enroll full-time at a two-year or four-year institution or university and must have an interest in foreign language. Applicant or parent of applicant must be member of Junior Classical League. Available to U.S. and non-U.S. citizens.

Application Requirements: Application form, essay. *Deadline:* April 1.

Contact: Sherwin Little, Executive Director
American Classical League/National Junior Classical League
860 NW Washington Boulevard
Suite A
Hamilton, OH 45013
Phone: 513-529-7741
E-mail: info@aclclassics.org

SOCIETY FOR CLASSICAL STUDIES

http://www.classicalstudies.org/

MINORITY STUDENT SUMMER SCHOLARSHIP

• *See page 112*

SONS OF ITALY FOUNDATION

https://www.osia.org/programs/scholarships/

ITALIAN LANGUAGE SCHOLARSHIP

Through the Sons of Italy Foundation (SIF), and hundreds of thousands of family members located in all fifty states and the District of Columbia, the Order Sons and Daughters of Italy in America (OSDIA) has awarded nearly $61 million in scholarships to date. In past years, the SIF has offered 10 to 12 merit-based scholarships (National Leadership Grants), ranging from $4,000 to $25,000, in a nationwide competition. These figures and the number of scholarships may vary according to funding each year. U.S. citizens of Italian descent in their junior or senior year of undergraduate study for the fall 2018 term, majoring or minoring in Italian language studies at an accredited academic institution are eligible for this award.

Academic Fields/Career Goals: Classics; Foreign Language.

Award: Scholarship for use in junior or senior years; not renewable. *Number:* 1. *Amount:* $4000–$25,000.

Eligibility Requirements: Applicant must be of Italian heritage and enrolled or expecting to enroll full-time at a four-year institution or university. Available to U.S. citizens.

Application Requirements: Application form, essay. *Fee:* $35. *Deadline:* February 28.

Contact: Carly Jerome, Director of Programming
Sons of Italy Foundation
219 E Street NE
Washington, DC 20002
Phone: 202-547-2900
E-mail: scholarships@osia.org

STRAIGHTFORWARD MEDIA

http://www.straightforwardmedia.com/

STRAIGHTFORWARD MEDIA LIBERAL ARTS SCHOLARSHIP

• *See page 119*

COMMUNICATIONS

ADC RESEARCH INSTITUTE

http://www.adc.org/

JACK SHAHEEN MASS COMMUNICATIONS SCHOLARSHIP AWARD

Awarded to Arab-American students who excel in the mass communications field (journalism, radio, television or film). Must be a junior or senior undergraduate or graduate student. Must be U.S. citizen. Minimum 3.0 GPA required.

Academic Fields/Career Goals: Communications; Filmmaking/Video; Journalism; TV/Radio Broadcasting.

Award: Scholarship for use in junior, senior, or graduate years; not renewable. *Number:* 4. *Amount:* $2500.

Eligibility Requirements: Applicant must be of Arab heritage and enrolled or expecting to enroll full-time at a four-year institution or university. Available to U.S. citizens.

Application Requirements: Application form, essay. *Deadline:* June 15.

Contact: Mr. Nabil Mohamad, Vice President
ADC Research Institute
1705 Desales street NW, 5th Floor
Washington, DC 20036
Phone: 202-244-2990
E-mail: nmohamad@adc.org

AMERICAN INSTITUTE OF POLISH CULTURE INC.

http://www.ampolinstitute.org/

HARRIET IRSAY SCHOLARSHIP GRANT

• See page 120

AMERICAN LEGION AUXILIARY DEPARTMENT OF ARIZONA

http:/wwwaladeptaz.org

AMERICAN LEGION AUXILIARY DEPARTMENT OF ARIZONA WILMA HOYAL-MAXINE CHILTON MEMORIAL SCHOLARSHIP

Annual scholarship to a student in second year or higher in one of the three state universities in Arizona. Must be enrolled in a program of study in political science, public programs, or special education. Must be a citizen of United States and of Arizona for at least one year. Honorably discharged veterans or immediate family members are given preference.

Academic Fields/Career Goals: Communications; Public Policy and Administration; Social Services; Special Education.

Award: Scholarship for use in freshman, sophomore, junior, senior, graduate, or postgraduate years; not renewable. *Number:* 3. *Amount:* $1000.

Eligibility Requirements: Applicant must be enrolled or expecting to enroll full- or part-time at a four-year institution or university; resident of Arizona and studying in Arizona. Available to U.S. citizens.

Application Requirements: Application form, essay, financial need analysis, personal photograph. *Deadline:* May 15.

Contact: Barbara Matteson, Department Secretary/Treasurer
American Legion Auxiliary Department of Arizona
4701 North 19th Avenue, Suite 100
Phoenix, AZ 85015
Phone: 602-241-1080
E-mail: secretary@aladeptaz.org

AMERICAN QUARTER HORSE FOUNDATION (AQHF)

https://aqhfoundation.smapply.io/

AQHF JOURNALISM OR COMMUNICATIONS SCHOLARSHIP

Ideal candidate is an AQHA or AQHYA member pursuing a college degree in journalism or communications. Recipient must pursue a career in news, editorial or print journalism, photojournalism or a related field.

Academic Fields/Career Goals: Communications; Journalism; Photojournalism/Photography.

Award: Scholarship for use in freshman, sophomore, junior, senior, or graduate years; renewable. *Number:* 1. *Amount:* $8000.

Eligibility Requirements: Applicant must be enrolled or expecting to enroll full-time at a two-year or four-year institution or university and must have an interest in animal/agricultural competition or writing. Applicant or parent of applicant must be member of American Quarter Horse Association. Available to U.S. and non-U.S. citizens.

Application Requirements: Application form, financial need analysis. *Deadline:* December 1.

Contact: Scholarship Office
American Quarter Horse Foundation (AQHF)
2601 East Interstate 40
Amarillo, TX 79104
Phone: 806-378-5029
E-mail: foundation@aqha.org

ARAB AMERICAN SCHOLARSHIP FOUNDATION

http://www.lahc.org/

LEBANESE AMERICAN HERITAGE CLUB'S SCHOLARSHIP FUND

Scholarship for high school, undergraduate, or graduate students who are of Arab descent. Minimum 3.0 GPA required for high school and undergraduate applicants, 3.5 GPA for graduate student applicants. Must be U.S. citizens.

Academic Fields/Career Goals: Communications; Political Science.

Award: Scholarship for use in freshman, sophomore, junior, senior, or graduate years; not renewable. *Number:* 1. *Amount:* $1000.

Eligibility Requirements: Applicant must be of Arab heritage; enrolled or expecting to enroll full-time at a four-year institution or university and resident of Michigan. Available to U.S. citizens.

Application Requirements: Application form, essay, financial need analysis, recommendations or references, Student Aid Report (SAR), transcript. *Deadline:* April 6.

Contact: Suehalia Amen, Communications Chair
Phone: 313-846-8480
Fax: 313-846-2710
E-mail: sueamen@lahc.org

ASIAN AMERICAN JOURNALISTS ASSOCIATION

http://www.aaja.org/

CIC/ANNA CHENNAULT SCHOLARSHIP

$5,000 is available to current high school seniors or college students committed to and/or interested in the field of journalism as a career or area of study. The selected student will receive travel, lodging and registration to attend the 2018 AAJA national annual convention August 8-11 in Houston. Depending on the winner's area of study, the student will also be paired with a professional print, online or broadcast mentor at the convention to help them network.

Academic Fields/Career Goals: Communications; Filmmaking/Video; Journalism; Photojournalism/Photography; TV/Radio Broadcasting.

Award: Scholarship for use in freshman, sophomore, junior, senior, or graduate years; not renewable. *Number:* 1. *Amount:* $5000.

Eligibility Requirements: Applicant must be American Indian/Alaska Native, Asian/Pacific Islander, Black (non-Hispanic), Hispanic; age 18 and over and enrolled or expecting to enroll full-time at a two-year or four-year institution or university. Available to U.S. citizens.

Application Requirements: Application form, essay, financial need analysis. *Deadline:* April 8.

Contact: Justin Seiter, Program Coordinator
Asian American Journalists Association
5 Third Street
Suite 1108
San Francisco, CA 94103
Phone: 415-346-2051 Ext. 107
E-mail: justins@aaja.org

MARY QUON MOY ING MEMORIAL SCHOLARSHIP AWARD

One-time award of up to $2000 for a deserving high school senior or current undergraduate or graduate student. Must intend to pursue a journalism career and must show a commitment to the Asian-American community. Visit website http://www.aaja.org for application and details.

Academic Fields/Career Goals: Communications; Journalism; Photojournalism/Photography; TV/Radio Broadcasting.

Award: Scholarship for use in freshman, sophomore, junior, senior, or graduate years; not renewable. *Number:* 1. *Amount:* $2000.

Eligibility Requirements: Applicant must be Asian/Pacific Islander; age 18 and over and enrolled or expecting to enroll full-time at a two-year or four-year institution or university. Available to U.S. and non-U.S. citizens.

Application Requirements: Application form, essay, financial need analysis. *Deadline:* April 8.

Contact: Justin Seiter, Program Coordinator
Asian American Journalists Association
5 Third Street
Suite 1108
San Francisco, CA 94103
Phone: 415-346-2051 Ext. 107
E-mail: justins@aaja.org

VINCENT CHIN MEMORIAL SCHOLARSHIP

$500 award to a journalism student committed to keeping Vincent Chin's memory alive. Minimum GPA of 2.5.

Academic Fields/Career Goals: Communications; Journalism; Photojournalism/Photography; TV/Radio Broadcasting.

Award: Scholarship for use in freshman, sophomore, junior, senior, or graduate years; not renewable. *Number:* 1. *Amount:* $500.

Eligibility Requirements: Applicant must be Asian/Pacific Islander; age 18 and over and enrolled or expecting to enroll full-time at a two-year or four-year or technical institution or university. Available to U.S. and non-U.S. citizens.

Application Requirements: Application form, essay, financial need analysis. *Deadline:* April 8.

Contact: Justin Seiter, Program Coordinator
Asian American Journalists Association
5 Third Street
Suite 1108
San Francisco, CA 94103
Phone: 415-346-2051 Ext. 107
E-mail: justins@aaja.org

ASIAN AMERICAN JOURNALISTS ASSOCIATION, SEATTLE CHAPTER

http://www.aajaseattle.org/

NORTHWEST JOURNALISTS OF COLOR SCHOLARSHIP

• *See page 84*

AUTOMOTIVE WOMEN'S ALLIANCE FOUNDATION

http://awafoundation.org/index.php

AUTOMOTIVE WOMEN'S ALLIANCE FOUNDATION SCHOLARSHIPS

• *See page 71*

BIOCOMMUNICATIONS ASSOCIATION

www.bca.org

ENDOWMENT FUND FOR EDUCATION GRANT

The EFFE Scholarship supports educational opportunities for students pursuing a career in scientific/biomedical visual communications.

Academic Fields/Career Goals: Communications; Health and Medical Sciences.

Award: Scholarship for use in sophomore, junior, senior, graduate, or postgraduate years; not renewable. *Number:* 2. *Amount:* $500.

Eligibility Requirements: Applicant must be enrolled or expecting to enroll full-time at a two-year or four-year or technical institution or university. Available to U.S. and non-U.S. citizens.

Application Requirements: Application form, essay, portfolio. *Deadline:* February 1.

Contact: EFFE Chair
BioCommunications Association
389 Newport Ave.
Attleboro, MA 02703
E-mail: office@bca.org

CCNMA: LATINO JOURNALISTS OF CALIFORNIA

http://www.ccnma.org/

CCNMA SCHOLARSHIPS

Scholarships for Latinos interested in pursuing a career in journalism. Awards based on scholastic achievement, financial need, and cultural awareness. Submit sample of work. Award limited to California residents or those attending school in California.

Academic Fields/Career Goals: Communications; Graphics/Graphic Arts/Printing; Journalism; Photojournalism/Photography; TV/Radio Broadcasting.

Award: Scholarship for use in freshman, sophomore, junior, senior, or graduate years; not renewable. *Number:* 5–10. *Amount:* $500–$1000.

Eligibility Requirements: Applicant must be of Latin American/Caribbean heritage; Hispanic; enrolled or expecting to enroll full-time at a two-year or four-year institution or university and resident of California. Available to U.S. and non-U.S. citizens.

Application Requirements: Application form, application form may be submitted online (http://www.ccnma.org), essay, financial need analysis, interview, portfolio, recommendations or references, resume, transcript. *Deadline:* April 1.

Contact: Mr. Julio Moran, Executive Director
CCNMA: Latino Journalists of California
ASU Walter Cronkite School of Journalism and Mass
Communication
725 Arizona Avenue, Suite 406
Santa Monica, CA 90401-1723
Phone: 424-229-9482
Fax: 424-238-0271
E-mail: ccnmainfo@ccnma.org

CHARLES AND LUCILLE KING FAMILY FOUNDATION, INC.

http://www.kingfoundation.org/

CHARLES & LUCILLE KING FAMILY FOUNDATION SCHOLARSHIPS

Renewable award for college undergraduates at junior or senior level pursuing television, film, or communication studies to further their education. Must attend a four-year undergraduate institution in USA. Minimum 3.0 GPA required to renew scholarship. Must have completed at least two years of study and be currently enrolled in a U.S. college or university. Application may be downloaded on website.

Academic Fields/Career Goals: Communications; Filmmaking/Video; TV/Radio Broadcasting.

Award: Scholarship for use in junior or senior years; renewable. *Number:* 10–20. *Amount:* $3500–$7000.

Eligibility Requirements: Applicant must be enrolled or expecting to enroll full-time at a four-year institution or university. Available to U.S. and non-U.S. citizens.

Application Requirements: Application form, application form may be submitted online (http://www.kingfoundation.org), Current official college/university transcript, essay, financial need analysis. *Deadline:* April 15.

Contact: Mr. Michael Donovan, Educational Director, The Charles and
Lucille King Family Foundation
Charles and Lucille King Family Foundation, Inc.
P.O. Box 3450
New York, NY 10163-3450
Phone: 212-682-2913
E-mail: info@kingfoundation.org

CONNECTICUT CHAPTER OF SOCIETY OF PROFESSIONAL JOURNALISTS

http://www.ctspj.org/

CONNECTICUT SPJ BOB EDDY SCHOLARSHIP PROGRAM

One-time awards of $250 to $2000 for college juniors or seniors planning a career in journalism. Must be a Connecticut resident attending a four year college or any student attending a four year college in Connecticut.

Academic Fields/Career Goals: Communications; Journalism; Photojournalism/Photography.

Award: Scholarship for use in junior or senior years; not renewable. *Number:* 5. *Amount:* $250–$2000.

Eligibility Requirements: Applicant must be enrolled or expecting to enroll full-time at a four-year institution or university; resident of Connecticut; studying in Connecticut and must have an interest in writing. Available to U.S. and non-U.S. citizens.

Application Requirements: Application form, entry in a contest, essay, financial need analysis, transcript. *Deadline:* April 4.

Contact: Debra Estock, Scholarship Committee Chairman
Connecticut Chapter of Society of Professional Journalists
71 Kenwood Avenue
Fairfield, CT 06824
Phone: 203-255-2127
E-mail: debae@optonline.net

HOUSE OF BLUES MUSIC FORWARD FOUNDATION

https://hobmusicforward.org/

STEVEN J. FINKEL SERVICE EXCELLENCE SCHOLARSHIP
• *See page 148*

TIFFANY GREEN OPERATOR SCHOLARSHIP AWARD
• *See page 85*

IDAHO STATE BROADCASTERS ASSOCIATION

http://www.idahobroadcasters.org/

WAYNE C. CORNILS MEMORIAL SCHOLARSHIP
• *See page 148*

INTERNATIONAL COMMUNICATIONS INDUSTRIES FOUNDATION

http://www.infocomm.org/scholarships

ICIF SCHOLARSHIP FOR EMPLOYEES AND DEPENDENTS OF MEMBER ORGANIZATIONS

Scholarship for a spouse, child, stepchild or grandchild of an employee of an InfoComm International member organization or for an employee of an InfoComm International member organization. Must be majoring in audiovisual related fields, such as audio, video, audiovisual, electronics, telecommunications, technical theatre, data networking, software development, and information technology. Minimum of 2.75 GPA required. Must show evidence of AV experience (completed course, job, internship, etc.).

Academic Fields/Career Goals: Communications; Computer Science/Data Processing; Electrical Engineering/Electronics; Filmmaking/Video.

Award: Scholarship for use in freshman, sophomore, junior, senior, or graduate years; not renewable. *Number:* 1–50. *Amount:* $1500.

Eligibility Requirements: Applicant must be enrolled or expecting to enroll full-time at a two-year or four-year or technical institution or university. Available to U.S. and non-U.S. citizens.

Application Requirements: Application form, essay, recommendations or references, transcript. *Deadline:* May 10.

Contact: Ms. Shana Rieger, Membership and Social Media Program Manager
International Communications Industries Foundation
11242 Waples Mill Road, Suite 200
Fairfax, VA 22030
Phone: 703-273-7200 Ext. 3690
Fax: 703-278-8082
E-mail: srieger@infocomm.org

INTERNATIONAL COMMUNICATIONS INDUSTRIES FOUNDATION AV SCHOLARSHIP

Scholarship for students majoring in audiovisual related fields such as audio, video, audiovisual, electronics, telecommunications, technical theatre, data networking, software development, information and technology. Minimum 2.75 GPA required. Must provide evidence of audiovisual knowledge (completed course, job, internship, etc.).

Academic Fields/Career Goals: Communications; Computer Science/Data Processing; Electrical Engineering/Electronics; Filmmaking/Video.

Award: Scholarship for use in freshman, sophomore, junior, senior, or graduate years; not renewable. *Number:* 1–50. *Amount:* $1200.

Eligibility Requirements: Applicant must be enrolled or expecting to enroll full-time at a two-year or four-year or technical institution or university. Available to U.S. and Canadian citizens.

Application Requirements: Application form, essay, recommendations or references, transcript. *Deadline:* May 10.

Contact: Ms. Shana Rieger, Membership and Social Media Program Manager
International Communications Industries Foundation
11242 Waples Mill Road, Suite 200
Fairfax, VA 22030
Phone: 703-273-7200 Ext. 3690
Fax: 703-278-8082
E-mail: srieger@infocomm.org

IOWA NEWSPAPER ASSOCIATION

https://inanews.com/

SHAW SCHOLARSHIP

Funded by a contribution from Shaw Newspapers. An annual scholarship award will go to an incoming college freshman preparing for a journalism or communications career at an accredited two or four-year college or university in the United States. This scholarship is awarded to students who are dependents of men or women who work for Iowa newspapers. The amount of each Shaw scholarship will be based on fund earnings and will be determined in early 2020

Academic Fields/Career Goals: Communications; Journalism.

Award: Scholarship for use in freshman year; not renewable.

Eligibility Requirements: Applicant must be enrolled or expecting to enroll at a two-year institution or university. Available to U.S. citizens.

Application Requirements: Application form. *Deadline:* February 14.

Contact: Jana Shepherd, Program Director
Iowa Newspaper Association
319 E. 5th Street
Des Moines, IA 50309
Phone: 515-244-2145 Ext. 159
Fax: 515-244-4855
E-mail: jshepherd@inanews.com

WOODWARD SCHOLARSHIP

Funded by a contribution from Woodward Communications, Inc. An annual scholarship award will go to a student studying journalism, communications, mass communications, photojournalism, graphic design, marketing or public relations at a college or university in Iowa, Illinois, or Wisconsin. The amount of each Woodward scholarship will be based on fund earnings and will be determined in early 2020.

Academic Fields/Career Goals: Communications; Graphics/Graphic Arts/Printing; Journalism; Marketing; Photojournalism/Photography.

Award: Scholarship for use in freshman, sophomore, junior, or senior years; not renewable.

Eligibility Requirements: Applicant must be enrolled or expecting to enroll at an institution or university and studying in Illinois, Iowa, Wisconsin. Available to U.S. citizens.

Application Requirements: Application form. *Deadline:* February 14.

Contact: Jana Shepherd, Program Director
Iowa Newspaper Association
319 E. 5th Street
Des Moines, IA 50309
Phone: 515-244-2145 Ext. 159
Fax: 515-244-4855
E-mail: jshepherd@inanews.com

JORGE MAS CANOSA FREEDOM FOUNDATION

http://masscholarships.org/

MAS FAMILY SCHOLARSHIP AWARD
• *See page 149*

THE LAGRANT FOUNDATION

http://www.lagrantfoundation.org/

LAGRANT FOUNDATION SCHOLARSHIP FOR GRADUATES
• *See page 85*

LAGRANT FOUNDATION SCHOLARSHIP FOR UNDERGRADUATES
• *See page 85*

NATIONAL ACADEMY OF TELEVISION ARTS AND SCIENCES

https://theemmys.tv/

DOUGLAS W. MUMMERT SCHOLARSHIP
Awarded to a student pursuing a career in any aspect of the television industry, who has made a positive impact through community service.
Academic Fields/Career Goals: Communications; Filmmaking/Video; Journalism; Music; Performing Arts; Photojournalism/Photography; Public Policy and Administration; TV/Radio Broadcasting.
Award: Scholarship for use in freshman year; not renewable. *Number:* 1. *Amount:* $10,000.
Eligibility Requirements: Applicant must be high school student and planning to enroll or expecting to enroll full-time at a two-year institution or university. Available to U.S. citizens.
Application Requirements: Application form, application form may be submitted online, community service, essay, portfolio. *Deadline:* March 22.
Contact: Paul Pillitteri, SVP, Communications
Phone: 626-296-3757
E-mail: ppillitteri@emmyonline.tv

NATIONAL ACADEMY OF TELEVISION ARTS AND SCIENCES, MICHIGAN CHAPTER

http://natasmichigan.org

DR. LYNNE BOYLE/JOHN SCHIMPF UNDERGRADUATE SCHOLARSHIP
• *See page 85*

NATIONAL ACADEMY OF TELEVISION ARTS & SCIENCES—OHIO VALLEY CHAPTER

http://ohiovalleyemmy.org/

DAVID J. CLARKE MEMORIAL SCHOLARSHIP
One $3000 scholarship offered to a full-time undergraduate student, with a journalism, multimedia broadcast or production-related major at an accredited college or university in the designated market areas serving the Ohio Valley Chapter of the National Academy of Television Arts and Sciences. The award will be given to a student who has achieved academic excellence; who is involved in co-curricular television activities (through student media, internships, or related employment); who possesses a desire to engage in television as a career; and who has high integrity and personal character. Financial need may also be considered.
Academic Fields/Career Goals: Communications; Filmmaking/Video; Journalism; TV/Radio Broadcasting.
Award: Scholarship for use in freshman, sophomore, junior, or senior years; not renewable. *Number:* 1. *Amount:* $3000.
Eligibility Requirements: Applicant must be enrolled or expecting to enroll full-time at a four-year institution or university. Available to U.S. citizens.
Application Requirements: Application form, application form may be submitted online (https://ohiovalleyemmy.org/students/scholarship-application/), essay, portfolio, recommendations or references, resume, transcript. *Deadline:* April 30.

NATIONAL ASSOCIATION OF BROADCASTERS

http://www.nab.org/

NATIONAL ASSOCIATION OF BROADCASTERS GRANTS FOR RESEARCH IN BROADCASTING
Award program is intended to fund research on economic, business, social, and policy issues important to station managers and other decision-makers in the United States commercial broadcast industry. Competition is open to all academic personnel. Graduate students and senior undergraduates are invited to submit proposals. For details refer to website http://www.nab.org.
Academic Fields/Career Goals: Communications; Journalism; TV/Radio Broadcasting.
Award: Grant for use in senior, graduate, or postgraduate years; not renewable. *Number:* 2. *Amount:* $5000.
Eligibility Requirements: Applicant must be enrolled or expecting to enroll full-time at a four-year institution or university. Available to U.S. and non-U.S. citizens.
Application Requirements: Application form, recommendations or references, research proposal, budget. *Deadline:* February 1.
Contact: Debbie Milman, Research Director
National Association of Broadcasters
1771 N Street, NW
Washington, DC 20036
Phone: 202-429-5383
Fax: 202-429-4199
E-mail: dmilman@nab.org

NATIONAL ASSOCIATION OF HISPANIC JOURNALISTS (NAHJ)

http://www.nahj.org/

NATIONAL ASSOCIATION OF HISPANIC JOURNALISTS SCHOLARSHIP
One-time award for high school seniors, college undergraduates, and first-year graduate students who are pursuing careers in English- or Spanish-language print, photo, broadcast, or online journalism. Students may major or plan to major in any subject, but must demonstrate a sincere desire to pursue a career in journalism. Must submit resume and work samples. Applications available only on website http://www.nahj.org.
Academic Fields/Career Goals: Communications; Journalism; Photojournalism/Photography; TV/Radio Broadcasting.
Award: Scholarship for use in freshman, sophomore, junior, senior, or graduate years; not renewable. *Amount:* $1000–$2000.
Eligibility Requirements: Applicant must be enrolled or expecting to enroll full-time at a four-year institution or university and must have an interest in photography/photogrammetry/filmmaking or writing. Available to U.S. citizens.
Application Requirements: Application form, essay, financial need analysis, recommendations or references, resume, transcript, work samples. *Deadline:* March 31.

Contact: Alberto Mendoza, Executive Director
Phone: 202-662-7145
E-mail: abmendoza@nahj.org

NATIONAL CATTLEMEN'S FOUNDATION

http://www.nationalcattlemensfoundation.org/

CME BEEF INDUSTRY SCHOLARSHIP
• See page 90

NEBRASKA PRESS ASSOCIATION

http://www.nebpress.com/

NEBRASKA PRESS ASSOCIATION FOUNDATION SCHOLARSHIP
• See page 86

OHIO NEWS MEDIA FOUNDATION

http://www.ohionews.org

HAROLD K. DOUTHIT SCHOLARSHIP
• See page 86

OHIO NEWS MEDIA FOUNDATION MINORITY SCHOLARSHIP
• See page 86

OHIO NEWS MEDIA FOUNDATION UNIVERSITY JOURNALISM SCHOLARSHIP
• See page 86

ONWA ANNUAL SCHOLARSHIP
• See page 86

OREGON ASSOCIATION OF BROADCASTERS

http://www.theoab.org/

OAB FOUNDATION SCHOLARSHIP
Award for students to begin or continue their education in broadcast and related studies. Must have a minimum GPA of 3.25. Must be a resident of Oregon studying in Oregon. For more details, refer to website at http//www.TheOAB.org.

Academic Fields/Career Goals: Communications; Journalism; TV/Radio Broadcasting.

Award: Scholarship for use in freshman, sophomore, junior, senior, graduate, or postgraduate years; renewable. *Number:* 4. *Amount:* $2500–$3500.

Eligibility Requirements: Applicant must be enrolled or expecting to enroll full-time at a two-year or four-year institution or university and resident of Oregon. Available to U.S. citizens.

Application Requirements: Application form, essay, financial need analysis, recommendations or references, resume, transcript. *Deadline:* May 3.

Contact: Mr. Bill Johnstone, President and Chief Executive Officer
Oregon Association of Broadcasters
9020 SW Washington Square Road
Suite 140
Portland, OR 97223-4433
Phone: 503-443-2299
Fax: 503-443-2488
E-mail: theoab@theoab.org

OUTDOOR WRITERS ASSOCIATION OF AMERICA

http://www.owaa.org/

OUTDOOR WRITERS ASSOCIATION OF AMERICA - BODIE MCDOWELL SCHOLARSHIP AWARD
One-time award for undergraduate and graduate students who demonstrate outdoor communications talent and intend to make a career in this field. Applicants must include a letter of recommendation from their institution and samples of their outdoor communications work.

Academic Fields/Career Goals: Communications; Environmental Science; Filmmaking/Video; Journalism; Literature/English/Writing; Natural Resources; Photojournalism/Photography; TV/Radio Broadcasting.

Award: Scholarship for use in freshman, sophomore, junior, senior, graduate, or postgraduate years; not renewable. *Number:* 2–6. *Amount:* $1000–$5000.

Eligibility Requirements: Applicant must be enrolled or expecting to enroll full-time at a two-year or four-year or technical institution or university and must have an interest in amateur radio, art, athletics/sports, photography/photogrammetry/filmmaking, or writing. Available to U.S. and non-U.S. citizens.

Application Requirements: Application form, essay. *Deadline:* March 15.

Contact: Ms. Jessica Seitz, Membership and Conference Director
Outdoor Writers Association of America
615 Oak St.
Suite 201
Missoula, MT 59801
Phone: 406-728-7434
Fax: 406-728-7445
E-mail: info@owaa.org

POLISH ARTS CLUB OF BUFFALO SCHOLARSHIP FOUNDATION

http://www.pacb.bfn.org/

POLISH ARTS CLUB OF BUFFALO SCHOLARSHIP FOUNDATION TRUST
• See page 122

PRINT AND GRAPHIC SCHOLARSHIP FOUNDATION

http://www.printing.org/

PRINT AND GRAPHICS SCHOLARSHIPS FOUNDATION
Applicant must be interested in a career in graphic communications, printing technology or management, or publishing. Selection is based on academic record, recommendations, biographical information, and extracurricular activities. All applications and letters of recommendation must be submitted online at www.pgsf.org. All applications high school and college applicants must be submitted by March 1. Awards are available to applicants outside United States, as long as they are attending a U.S. institution and meet the basic criteria of the Print and Graphics Scholarship Foundation.

Academic Fields/Career Goals: Communications; Graphics/Graphic Arts/Printing.

Award: Scholarship for use in freshman, sophomore, junior, senior, or graduate years; renewable. *Number:* 150–200. *Amount:* $1500–$5000.

Eligibility Requirements: Applicant must be enrolled or expecting to enroll full-time at a two-year or four-year or technical institution or university. Available to U.S. and non-U.S. citizens.

Application Requirements: Application form, essay. *Deadline:* March 1.

Contact: Bernie Eckert, Administrator
Print and Graphic Scholarship Foundation
301 Brush Creek Road
Warrendale, PA 15086
Phone: 412-259-1740
E-mail: pgsf@printing.org

PRINTING INDUSTRY MIDWEST EDUCATION FOUDNATION

http://www.pimw.org/scholarships

PRINTING INDUSTRY MIDWEST EDUCATION FOUNDATION SCHOLARSHIP FUND

The fund offers $1000 renewable scholarships to full-time students enrolled in two- or four-year institutions and technical colleges offering degrees in the print communications discipline. Applicant must be a Minnesota resident and be committed to a career in the print communications industry. Minimum 3.0 GPA required. Priority given to children of PIM member company employees.

Academic Fields/Career Goals: Communications; Flexography; Graphics/Graphic Arts/Printing; Journalism; Marketing; Photojournalism/Photography.

Award: Scholarship for use in freshman, sophomore, junior, or senior years; renewable. *Number:* 5–10. *Amount:* $1000.

Eligibility Requirements: Applicant must be enrolled or expecting to enroll full-time at a two-year or four-year or technical institution or university and resident of Iowa, Minnesota, Nebraska, North Dakota, South Dakota. Available to U.S. citizens.

Application Requirements: Application form, essay. *Deadline:* April 1.

Contact: Kristin Pilling-Davis, Education Director
Printing Industry Midwest Education Foudnation
PIM
1300 Godward Street, NE, Suite 2650
Minneapolis, MN 55413
Phone: 612-400-6200
E-mail: kdavis@pimw.org

PUBLIC RELATIONS STUDENT SOCIETY OF AMERICA

http://www.prssa.org/

PUBLIC RELATIONS SOCIETY OF AMERICA MULTICULTURAL AFFAIRS SCHOLARSHIP

• *See page 87*

RHODE ISLAND FOUNDATION

http://www.rifoundation.org/

J. D. EDSAL SCHOLARSHIP

• *See page 87*

ROBERT H. MOLLOHAN FAMILY CHARITABLE FOUNDATION, INC.

http://www.mollohanfoundation.org/

HARRY C. HAMM FAMILY SCHOLARSHIP

The Harry C. Hamm Family Scholarship is awarded to a sophomore, junior, or senior college student who is in serious pursuit of a B.A. in Journalism or Communications at a West Virginia four-year institution. Mr. Hamm was a 50 year veteran reporter/editor with Ogden Newspapers. The applicant must be a graduate of a high school in West Virginia and must have at least a 3.0 GPA.

Academic Fields/Career Goals: Communications; Journalism.

Award: Scholarship for use in sophomore, junior, or senior years; not renewable. *Amount:* $1000.

Eligibility Requirements: Applicant must be high school student; planning to enroll or expecting to enroll full-time at a four-year institution or university; resident of West Virginia and studying in West Virginia. Available to U.S. citizens.

Application Requirements: Application form, essay, recommendations or references, resume, test scores, transcript.

SOCIETY FOR TECHNICAL COMMUNICATION

http://www.stc.org/

SOCIETY FOR TECHNICAL COMMUNICATION SCHOLARSHIP PROGRAM

Award for study relating to communication of information about technical subjects. Applicants must be full-time graduate students working toward a Master's or Doctoral degree, or undergraduate students working toward a Bachelor's degree. Must have completed at least one year of postsecondary education and have at least one full year of academic work remaining. Two awards available for undergraduate students, two available for graduate students.

Academic Fields/Career Goals: Communications; Science, Technology, and Society.

Award: Scholarship for use in sophomore, junior, senior, or graduate years; not renewable. *Number:* up to 4. *Amount:* up to $1500.

Eligibility Requirements: Applicant must be enrolled or expecting to enroll full-time at a four-year institution or university. Available to U.S. and non-U.S. citizens.

Application Requirements: Application form, essay, recommendations or references, transcript. *Deadline:* February 15.

Contact: Scott DeLoach, Manager, Scholarship Selection Committee
Society for Technical Communication
834 C Dekalb Avenue, NE
Atlanta, GA 30307

SOCIETY OF MOTION PICTURE AND TELEVISION ENGINEERS

https://www.smpte.org/

LOUIS F. WOLF JR. MEMORIAL SCHOLARSHIP

This scholarship was established to help students further their undergraduate or graduate studies in motion pictures and television, with an emphasis on technology. Open To Currently Enrolled, Full-Time Undergraduate Student Members;, Extra Credit May Be Awarded For Volunteer Work/Leadership.

Academic Fields/Career Goals: Communications; Electrical Engineering/Electronics; Engineering-Related Technologies; Engineering/Technology; Filmmaking/Video; Science, Technology, and Society; TV/Radio Broadcasting.

Award: Scholarship for use in freshman, sophomore, junior, senior, graduate, or postgraduate years; not renewable. *Number:* up to 1. *Amount:* $1000–$5000.

Eligibility Requirements: Applicant must be enrolled or expecting to enroll full-time at a two-year or four-year or technical institution or university. Applicant or parent of applicant must be member of Society of Motion Picture and Television Engineers. Available to U.S. and non-U.S. citizens.

Application Requirements: Application form, essay, financial need analysis, recommendations or references, transcript. *Deadline:* June 1.

Contact: Sally-Ann DAmato, Director of Operations
Society of Motion Picture and Television Engineers
SMPTE, 3 Barker Avenue
White Plains, NY 10601
Phone: 914-761-1100 Ext. 2375
E-mail: sdamato@smpte.org

STUDENT PAPER AWARD

Contest for best paper by a current Student Member of SMPTE. Paper must deal with some technical phase of motion pictures, television, photographic instrumentation, or their closely allied arts and sciences. For more information see website http://www.smpte.org.

Academic Fields/Career Goals: Communications; Electrical Engineering/Electronics; Engineering-Related Technologies; Engineering/Technology; Filmmaking/Video; Science, Technology, and Society; TV/Radio Broadcasting.

Award: Prize for use in freshman, sophomore, junior, senior, graduate, or postgraduate years; not renewable. *Number:* 1–2. *Amount:* $1–$1500.

Eligibility Requirements: Applicant must be enrolled or expecting to enroll full- or part-time at a two-year or four-year or technical institution or university. Applicant or parent of applicant must be member of Society of Motion Picture and Television Engineers. Available to U.S. and non-U.S. citizens.

Application Requirements: Application form, entry in a contest, essay, student ID card, transcript. *Deadline:* May 1.

Contact: Sally-Ann DAmato, Director of Operations
Society of Motion Picture and Television Engineers
SMPTE, 3 Barker Avenue
White Plains, NY 10601
Phone: 914-761-1100 Ext. 2375
E-mail: sdamato@smpte.org

SOCIETY OF SATELLITE PROFESSIONALS INTERNATIONAL

http://www.sspi.org/

SSPI INTERNATIONAL SCHOLARSHIPS
• *See page 134*

SPECIALTY EQUIPMENT MARKET ASSOCIATION

http://www.sema.org/

SEMA MEMORIAL SCHOLARSHIP FUND
• *See page 81*

STRAIGHTFORWARD MEDIA

http://www.straightforwardmedia.com/

STRAIGHTFORWARD MEDIA MEDIA & COMMUNICATIONS SCHOLARSHIP
• *See page 87*

SUPPORT CREATIVITY

http://wesupportcreativity.org

SUPPORT CREATIVITY SCHOLARSHIP
• *See page 117*

TAMPA BAY TIMES FUND, INC.

http://company.tampabay.com:2052/times-fund/scholarships

CAREER JOURNALISM SCHOLARSHIP

These scholarships target high school seniors in the Times audience area who have a demonstrated interest in pursuing journalism/media as a major in college and as a career. The scholarship is worth up to $2,500 per year and may be renewed annually. Up to 3 winners are selected each year. Students from these Florida counties are eligible to apply: Pinellas, Hillsborough, Pasco, Hernando. Application deadline: January 20. Winners are notified by the end of February. On-line applications only.

Academic Fields/Career Goals: Communications; Journalism; Photojournalism/Photography; TV/Radio Broadcasting.

Award: Scholarship for use in freshman, sophomore, junior, or senior years; not renewable. *Number:* 1–3. *Amount:* $1000–$2500.

Eligibility Requirements: Applicant must be high school student; age 17-19; planning to enroll or expecting to enroll full-time at a four-year institution or university; single and resident of Florida. Available to U.S. citizens.

Application Requirements: Application form, essay, portfolio. *Deadline:* January 20.

Contact: Ms. Nancy Waclawek, Scholarship Administrator
Tampa Bay Times Fund, Inc.
PO Box 1121
St. Petersburg, FL 33731-1121
E-mail: tbtschls@gmail.com

TAMPA BAY TIMES FUND CAREER JOURNALISM SCHOLARSHIPS
• *See page 87*

TEXAS ASSOCIATION OF BROADCASTERS

https://www.tab.org/scholarships/available-scholarships

TEXAS ASSOCIATION OF BROADCASTERS - BELO SCHOLARSHIP

Scholarship of $3000 to undergraduate and graduate students enrolled in a fully accredited program of instruction that emphasizes radio or television broadcasting or communications at a four-year college or university in Texas. Student must be a member of the Texas Association of Broadcasters. Must have a GPA of 3.0 minimum.

Academic Fields/Career Goals: Communications; TV/Radio Broadcasting.

Award: Scholarship for use in junior, senior, or graduate years; not renewable. *Number:* 1. *Amount:* $3000.

Eligibility Requirements: Applicant must be enrolled or expecting to enroll full-time at an institution or university and studying in Texas. Applicant or parent of applicant must be member of Texas Association of Broadcasters. Available to U.S. and non-U.S. citizens.

Application Requirements: Application form, essay, financial need analysis. *Deadline:* May 3.

Contact: Craig Bean, Public Service Manager
Texas Association of Broadcasters
502 East 11th Street, Suite 200
Austin, TX 78701
Phone: 512-322-9944
Fax: 512-322-0522
E-mail: craig@tab.org

TEXAS ASSOCIATION OF BROADCASTERS - TWO-YEAR/TECHNICAL SCHOOL SCHOLARSHIP

Scholarship of $3000 for a student enrolled in a program that emphasizes radio or TV broadcasting or communications at a two-year or technical school in Texas. Student must be a member of the Texas Association of Broadcasters. Must have a GPA of 3.0 minimum.

Academic Fields/Career Goals: Communications; Journalism; TV/Radio Broadcasting.

Award: Scholarship for use in freshman, sophomore, junior, or senior years; not renewable. *Number:* 1. *Amount:* $3000.

Eligibility Requirements: Applicant must be enrolled or expecting to enroll full-time at a two-year or technical institution and studying in Texas. Applicant or parent of applicant must be member of Texas Association of Broadcasters. Available to U.S. and non-U.S. citizens.

Application Requirements: Application form, essay, financial need analysis. *Deadline:* May 3.

Contact: Craig Bean, Public Service Manager
Texas Association of Broadcasters
502 East 11th Street, Suite 200
Austin, TX 78701
Phone: 512-322-9944
Fax: 512-322-0522
E-mail: craig@tab.org

TEXAS ASSOCIATION OF BROADCASTERS - UNDERGRADUATE SCHOLARSHIP

Scholarship of $3000 available to an undergraduate student enrolled in a fully accredited program of instruction that emphasizes radio or television broadcasting or communications at a four-year college or university in Texas. Student must be a member of the Texas Association of Broadcasters. Must have a GPA of 3.0 minimum.

Academic Fields/Career Goals: Communications; Journalism; TV/Radio Broadcasting.

Award: Scholarship for use in freshman or sophomore years; not renewable. *Number:* 1. *Amount:* $3000.

Eligibility Requirements: Applicant must be enrolled or expecting to enroll full-time at an institution or university and studying in Texas. Applicant or parent of applicant must be member of Texas Association of Broadcasters. Available to U.S. and non-U.S. citizens.

Application Requirements: Application form, essay, financial need analysis. *Deadline:* May 3.

Contact: Craig Bean, Public Service Manager
Texas Association of Broadcasters
502 East 11th Street, Suite 200
Austin, TX 78701
Phone: 512-322-9944
Fax: 512-322-0522
E-mail: craig@tab.org

TEXAS ASSOCIATION OF BROADCASTERS - VANN KENNEDY SCHOLARSHIP

Scholarship of $3000 to a undergraduate or graduate student enrolled in a fully accredited program of instruction that emphasizes radio or television broadcasting or communications at college or university in Texas. Student must be a member of the Texas Association of Broadcasters. Must have a GPA of 3.0 minimum.

Academic Fields/Career Goals: Communications; Journalism; TV/Radio Broadcasting.

Award: Scholarship for use in freshman, sophomore, junior, senior, or graduate years; not renewable. *Number:* 1. *Amount:* $3000.

Eligibility Requirements: Applicant must be enrolled or expecting to enroll full-time at a two-year institution or university and studying in Texas. Applicant or parent of applicant must be member of Texas Association of Broadcasters. Available to U.S. and non-U.S. citizens.

Application Requirements: Application form, essay, financial need analysis. *Deadline:* May 3.

Contact: Craig Bean, Public Service Manager
Texas Association of Broadcasters
502 East 11th Street, Suite 200
Austin, TX 78701
Phone: 512-322-9944
Fax: 512-322-0522
E-mail: craig@tab.org

TEXAS GRIDIRON CLUB INC.

http://www.spjfw.org/

TEXAS GRIDIRON CLUB SCHOLARSHIPS

$500 to $4000 scholarships for full-time or part-time college juniors, seniors, or graduate students majoring in newspaper, photojournalism, or broadcast fields. Must be Texas resident or going to school in Texas.

Academic Fields/Career Goals: Communications; Journalism; Photojournalism/Photography; TV/Radio Broadcasting.

Award: Scholarship for use in sophomore, junior, senior, or graduate years; not renewable. *Number:* 10–15. *Amount:* $500–$4000.

Eligibility Requirements: Applicant must be enrolled or expecting to enroll full- or part-time at a four-year institution or university. Available to U.S. citizens.

Application Requirements: Application form, essay, financial need analysis. *Deadline:* December 1.

Contact: Angie Summers, Scholarships Coordinator
Texas Gridiron Club Inc.
709 Houston Street
Arlington, TX 76012
E-mail: asummers@star-telegram.com

TURF AND ORNAMENTAL COMMUNICATORS ASSOCIATION

http://www.toca.org/

TURF AND ORNAMENTAL COMMUNICATORS ASSOCIATION SCHOLARSHIP PROGRAM

• See page 96

UNITED METHODIST COMMUNICATIONS

http://www.umcom.org/

LEONARD M. PERRYMAN COMMUNICATIONS SCHOLARSHIP FOR ETHNIC MINORITY STUDENTS

One-time award to assist United Methodist ethnic minority students who are college students intending to pursue careers in religious communications.

Academic Fields/Career Goals: Communications; Journalism; Photojournalism/Photography; Religion/Theology; TV/Radio Broadcasting.

Award: Scholarship for use in junior or senior years; not renewable. *Number:* 1. *Amount:* $2500.

Eligibility Requirements: Applicant must be Methodist; American Indian/Alaska Native, Asian/Pacific Islander, Black (non-Hispanic), Hispanic and enrolled or expecting to enroll full-time at a two-year or four-year institution or university. Available to U.S. citizens.

Application Requirements: Application form, essay, personal photograph, recommendations or references, transcript. *Deadline:* March 15.

Contact: Michael Neff, Executive Director
Phone: 703-836-4606 Ext. 325
Fax: 703-836-2024
E-mail: mwneff@ashs.org

UNITED NEGRO COLLEGE FUND

http://www.uncf.org/

DIVERSE VOICES IN STORYTELLING SCHOLARSHIP

Need-based program open to full-time, African American students with an interest in a career focused on storytelling in the media/entertainment field. Applicants must attend an accredited HBCU with a declared major in film, creative writing, communications or journalism. Up to $5625.

Academic Fields/Career Goals: Communications; Filmmaking/Video; Journalism; Literature/English/Writing.

Award: Scholarship for use in junior year; renewable.

Eligibility Requirements: Applicant must be Black (non-Hispanic) and enrolled or expecting to enroll full-time at a four-year institution or university. Available to U.S. citizens.

Application Requirements: Application form, essay, financial need analysis. *Deadline:* December 17.

Contact: Larry Griffith, Senior Vice President, Programs and Student Services
Phone: 800-331-2244

NASCAR WENDELL SCOTT SR. SCHOLARSHIP

• See page 83

THE OSSIE DAVIS LEGACY AWARD SCHOLARSHIP

• See page 89

UNCF/ALLIANCE DATA SCHOLARSHIP AND INTERNSHIP PROGRAM

• See page 88

UNCF/CARNIVAL CORPORATE SCHOLARS PROGRAM

• See page 151

WALT DISNEY COMPANY UNCF CORPORATE SCHOLARS PROGRAM

Up to $1000 scholarships for underrepresented African American freshmen, enrolled full-time at a four-year college or university. Preference will be given to students attending a Historically Black College or University (HBCU). Must have a demonstrated financial need as verified by college or university. Must have an interest in pursuing an off-camera career in the entertainment industry (e.g. film, television, hospitality management, journalism, media production, digital media, etc.) as demonstrated by submission of an initial essay. Minimum 2.5 GPA required.

Academic Fields/Career Goals: Communications; Filmmaking/Video; Hospitality Management; Journalism.

Award: Scholarship for use in freshman year; not renewable. *Number:* 40. *Amount:* $1000.

Eligibility Requirements: Applicant must be Black (non-Hispanic); high school student and planning to enroll or expecting to enroll full-time at a four-year institution or university. Available to U.S. citizens.

Application Requirements: Application form, essay. *Deadline:* May 15.

Contact: Larry Griffith, Senior Vice President, Programs and Student Services
Phone: 800-331-2244

VALLEY PRESS CLUB

http://www.valleypressclub.com/

VALLEY PRESS CLUB SCHOLARSHIPS, THE REPUBLICAN SCHOLARSHIP, CHANNEL 22 SCHOLARSHIP

Nonrenewable award for graduating high school seniors from Connecticut and Massachusetts, who are interested in television journalism, photojournalism, broadcast journalism, or print journalism.

Academic Fields/Career Goals: Communications; Journalism; Photojournalism/Photography; TV/Radio Broadcasting.

Award: Scholarship for use in freshman year; not renewable. *Number:* 4–6. *Amount:* $1000.

Eligibility Requirements: Applicant must be high school student; planning to enroll or expecting to enroll full-time at a four-year institution or university; resident of Connecticut, Massachusetts and must have an interest in writing. Available to U.S. citizens.

Application Requirements: Application form, community service, financial need analysis, interview. *Deadline:* April 1.

Contact: Noreen Tassinari, Scholarship Committee Chair
Valley Press Club
PO Box 5475
Springfield, MA 01101
Phone: 413-205-5037
E-mail: ntassinari@thebige.com

VIRGINIA ASSOCIATION OF BROADCASTERS

http://www.vabonline.com/

VIRGINIA ASSOCIATION OF BROADCASTERS SCHOLARSHIP AWARD

Scholarships are available to entering juniors and seniors majoring in mass communications-related courses. Must either be a resident of Virginia or be enrolled at a Virginia college or university. Must be U.S. citizen and enrolled full-time.

Academic Fields/Career Goals: Communications.

Award: Scholarship for use in junior or senior years; renewable. *Number:* 4. *Amount:* $500–$1000.

Eligibility Requirements: Applicant must be enrolled or expecting to enroll full-time at a four-year institution or university; resident of Virginia and studying in Virginia. Available to U.S. and non-U.S. citizens.

Application Requirements: Application form, essay, financial need analysis, transcript. *Deadline:* February 15.

Contact: Ruby Seal, Director of Administration
Phone: 434-977-3716
Fax: 434-979-2439
E-mail: ruby.seal@easterassociates.com

WASHINGTON MEDIA SCHOLARS FOUNDATION

www.mediascholars.org

MEDIA PLAN CASE COMPETITION
• *See page 88*

WISCONSIN BROADCASTERS ASSOCIATION FOUNDATION

http://www.wi-broadcasters.org/

WISCONSIN BROADCASTERS ASSOCIATION FOUNDATION SCHOLARSHIP

Four $2000 scholarships offered to assist students enrolled in broadcasting-related educational programs at four-year public or private institutions. Applicants must either have graduated from a Wisconsin high school, or be attending a Wisconsin college or university, must have completed at least 60 credits, and must be planning a career in radio or television broadcasting.

Academic Fields/Career Goals: Communications; TV/Radio Broadcasting.

Award: Scholarship for use in freshman, sophomore, junior, or senior years; not renewable. *Number:* 4. *Amount:* $2000.

Eligibility Requirements: Applicant must be enrolled or expecting to enroll full-time at a four-year institution or university and studying in Wisconsin. Available to U.S. citizens.

Application Requirements: Application form, essay. *Deadline:* October 20.

Contact: John Laabs, President
Phone: 608-255-2600
Fax: 608-256-3986
E-mail: contact@wi-broadcasters.org

WOMEN'S BASKETBALL COACHES ASSOCIATION

http://www.wbca.org/

ROBIN ROBERTS/WBCA SPORTS COMMUNICATIONS SCHOLARSHIP AWARD

One-time award for female student athletes who have completed their eligibility and plan to go to graduate school. Must major in communications. Must be nominated by the head coach of women's basketball who is a member of the WBCA.

Academic Fields/Career Goals: Communications; Journalism.

Award: Scholarship for use in senior, graduate, or postgraduate years; not renewable. *Number:* 1. *Amount:* $4000.

Eligibility Requirements: Applicant must be enrolled or expecting to enroll full- or part-time at a four-year institution or university; female and must have an interest in athletics/sports. Available to U.S. and non-U.S. citizens.

Application Requirements: Application form, recommendations or references, statistics. *Deadline:* February 15.

Contact: Betty Jaynes, Consultant
Phone: 770-279-8027 Ext. 102
Fax: 770-279-6290
E-mail: bettyj@wbca.org

WYOMING TRUCKING ASSOCIATION SCHOLARSHIP FUND TRUST

http://www.wytruck.org/

WYOMING TRUCKING ASSOCIATION SCHOLARSHIP TRUST FUND
• *See page 84*

COMPUTER SCIENCE/ DATA PROCESSING

AIST FOUNDATION

http://www.aistfoundation.org/

ASSOCIATION FOR IRON AND STEEL TECHNOLOGY OHIO VALLEY CHAPTER SCHOLARSHIP
• *See page 138*

ASSOCIATION FOR IRON AND STEEL TECHNOLOGY WILLY KORF MEMORIAL SCHOLARSHIP
• *See page 153*

ALICE L. HALTOM EDUCATIONAL FUND

http://www.alhef.org/

ALICE L. HALTOM EDUCATIONAL FUND
• *See page 145*

AMERICAN FOUNDATION FOR THE BLIND

http://www.afb.org/

PAUL W. RUCKES SCHOLARSHIP
Scholarship of $1000 to an undergraduate or graduate student studying in the field of engineering or in computer, physical, or life sciences. For more information and application requirements, please visit http://www.afb.org/scholarships.asp.
Academic Fields/Career Goals: Computer Science/Data Processing; Electrical Engineering/Electronics; Engineering/Technology; Natural Sciences; Physical Sciences.
Award: Scholarship for use in freshman, sophomore, junior, or senior years; not renewable. *Number:* 1. *Amount:* $1000.
Eligibility Requirements: Applicant must be enrolled or expecting to enroll full-time at a two-year or four-year institution or university. Applicant must be visually impaired. Available to U.S. citizens.
Application Requirements: Application form, essay, proof of post-secondary acceptance and legal blindness, proof of citizenship, FAFSA, recommendations or references, transcript. *Deadline:* April 30.
Contact: Dawn Bodrogi, Information Center
American Foundation for the Blind
11 Penn Plaza, Suite 300
New York, NY 10001
Phone: 212-502-7661
Fax: 212-502-7771
E-mail: afbinfo@afb.net

AMERICAN INDIAN SCIENCE AND ENGINEERING SOCIETY

http://www.aises.org/

A.T. ANDERSON MEMORIAL SCHOLARSHIP PROGRAM
• *See page 105*

AMERICAN RAILWAY ENGINEERING AND MAINTENANCE OF WAY ASSOCIATION

http://www.aremafoundation.org/

AREMA GRADUATE AND UNDERGRADUATE SCHOLARSHIPS
• *See page 162*

ARMED FORCES COMMUNICATIONS AND ELECTRONICS ASSOCIATION, EDUCATIONAL FOUNDATION

https://foundation.afcea.org

AFCEA STEM MAJORS SCHOLARSHIPS FOR UNDERGRADUATE STUDENTS
• *See page 106*

ARMED FORCES COMMUNICATIONS AND ELECTRONICS ASSOCIATION ROTC SCHOLARSHIP PROGRAM
Award for ROTC students in their sophomore or junior years enrolled in four-year accredited colleges or universities in the United States. Eligible C4I-related fields of study or majors that align with the mission statement of AFCEA Educational Foundation. The list of acceptable majors can be found on the website. Must exhibit academic excellence and potential to serve as an officer in the armed forces of the United States. Nominations are submitted by professors of military science, naval science, or aerospace studies.
Academic Fields/Career Goals: Computer Science/Data Processing; Electrical Engineering/Electronics; Engineering-Related Technologies; Engineering/Technology; Mathematics; Physical Sciences.
Award: Scholarship for use in sophomore or junior years; not renewable. *Number:* 1–6. *Amount:* $2500–$3000.
Eligibility Requirements: Applicant must be enrolled or expecting to enroll full-time at a four-year institution or university. Available to U.S. citizens. Applicant must have served in the Air Force, Army, Marine Corps, or Navy.
Application Requirements: Application form, application form may be submitted online (https://www.afcea.org/site/foundation/scholarships/rotc-scholarships), essay, recommendations or references, transcript. *Deadline:* February 22.
Contact: Mrs. Casmere Kistner, Manager, Scholarship and Awards
Phone: 703-631-6147
Fax: 703-631-4693
E-mail: edfoundation@afcea.org

ASIAN PACIFIC FUND

BANATAO FAMILY FILIPINO AMERICAN EDUCATION FUND
• *See page 155*

ASSOCIATION OF FORMER INTELLIGENCE OFFICERS

www.afio.com

AFIO UNDERGRADUATE AND GRADUATE SCHOLARSHIPS
• *See page 98*

ASSOCIATION OF STATE DAM SAFETY OFFICIALS (ASDSO)

http://www.DamSafety.org

ASSOCIATION OF STATE DAM SAFETY OFFICIALS (ASDSO) SENIOR UNDERGRADUATE SCHOLARSHIP
• *See page 140*

ASTRONAUT SCHOLARSHIP FOUNDATION

http://www.astronautscholarship.org/

ASTRONAUT SCHOLARSHIP
• *See page 107*

AUTOMOTIVE WOMEN'S ALLIANCE FOUNDATION

http://awafoundation.org/index.php

AUTOMOTIVE WOMEN'S ALLIANCE FOUNDATION SCHOLARSHIPS
• *See page 71*

BARRY GOLDWATER SCHOLARSHIP AND EXCELLENCE IN EDUCATION FOUNDATION

https://goldwater.scholarsapply.org

BARRY M. GOLDWATER SCHOLARSHIP AND EXCELLENCE IN EDUCATION PROGRAM
• *See page 107*

BHW GROUP

https://thebhwgroup.com/

BHW WOMEN IN STEM SCHOLARSHIP
• See page 107

CARDS AGAINST HUMANITY

https://cardsagainsthumanity.com/

SCIENCE AMBASSADOR SCHOLARSHIP
• See page 107

CATCHING THE DREAM

http://www.catchingthedream.org/

MATH, ENGINEERING, SCIENCE, BUSINESS, EDUCATION, COMPUTERS SCHOLARSHIPS
• See page 146

TRIBAL BUSINESS MANAGEMENT PROGRAM (TBM)
• See page 72

DISTIL NETWORKS

http://www.distilnetworks.com

WOMEN FORWARD IN TECHNOLOGY SCHOLARSHIP PROGRAM
• See page 108

ELECTRONIC DOCUMENT SYSTEMS FOUNDATION

http://www.edsf.org/

LYNDA BABOYIAN MEMORIAL SCHOLARSHIP
• See page 147

GREAT MINDS IN STEM

http://www.greatmindsinstem.org/college/scholarship-application-information

HENAAC SCHOLARSHIP PROGRAM
• See page 100

INTERNATIONAL COMMUNICATIONS INDUSTRIES FOUNDATION

http://www.infocomm.org/scholarships

ICIF SCHOLARSHIP FOR EMPLOYEES AND DEPENDENTS OF MEMBER ORGANIZATIONS
• See page 172

INTERNATIONAL COMMUNICATIONS INDUSTRIES FOUNDATION AV SCHOLARSHIP
• See page 172

THE JACKSON LABORATORY

https://www.jax.org

THE JACKSON LABORATORY COLLEGE SCHOLARSHIP PROGRAM
• See page 108

LOGMEIN

https://www.logmeininc.com

LASTPASS STEM SCHOLARSHIP
• See page 109

LOS ANGELES COUNCIL OF BLACK PROFESSIONAL ENGINEERS

http://www.lablackengineers.org/

AL-BEN SCHOLARSHIP FOR ACADEMIC INCENTIVE
• See page 157

AL-BEN SCHOLARSHIP FOR PROFESSIONAL MERIT
• See page 157

AL-BEN SCHOLARSHIP FOR SCHOLASTIC ACHIEVEMENT
• See page 157

MICROSOFT CORPORATION

http://www.microsoft.com/

YOU CAN MAKE A DIFFERENCE SCHOLARSHIP
Scholarship for high school students who want make an impact with technology. All students who submit proposals will receive a free copy of Microsoft Visual Studio NET Academic Edition.

Academic Fields/Career Goals: Computer Science/Data Processing.

Award: Scholarship for use in freshman year; not renewable. *Number:* 10. *Amount:* $5000.

Eligibility Requirements: Applicant must be high school student and planning to enroll or expecting to enroll full- or part-time at a four-year institution or university. Available to U.S. citizens.

Application Requirements: Application form, transcript. *Deadline:* April 30.

Contact: Scholarship Committee
    E-mail: scholars@microsoft.com

MORPHISEC

https://www.morphisec.com

WOMEN IN CYBERSECURITY SCHOLARSHIPS
Women are underrepresented in the field of cybersecurity to the detriment, we believe, of the industry as a whole. To encourage young women to explore a career in this field, we founded an annual scholarship program. At Morphisec, we believe that diversity drives innovation and we strive to increase the number of women employed in cybersecurity and related fields. Our current scholarship opportunities are open to female students who are studying for degrees in cybersecurity, information assurance, information security, information systems security, an other sub-disciplines of computer science.

Academic Fields/Career Goals: Computer Science/Data Processing.

Award: Scholarship for use in freshman, sophomore, junior, senior, graduate, or postgraduate years; not renewable. *Number:* 3. *Amount:* $1000–$5000.

Eligibility Requirements: Applicant must be enrolled or expecting to enroll full-time at a two-year or four-year institution or university and female. Available to U.S. and non-Canadian citizens.

Application Requirements: Application form, application form may be submitted online (https://engage.morphisec.com/womens-cyber-scholarship-2019), cyber challenge, essay. *Deadline:* June 15.

Contact: Ursula Ron, Director of Marketing
    Morphisec
    275 Grove Street Suite 2-400
    Newton, MA 02466
    Phone: 617-209-2552
    E-mail: scholarships@morphisec.com

NASA IDAHO SPACE GRANT CONSORTIUM

http://www.idahospacegrant.org

NASA IDAHO SPACE GRANT CONSORTIUM SCHOLARSHIP PROGRAM
• *See page 109*

NASA/MARYLAND SPACE GRANT CONSORTIUM

https://md.spacegrant.org

NASA MARYLAND SPACE GRANT CONSORTIUM SCHOLARSHIPS
• *See page 109*

NASA MINNESOTA SPACE GRANT CONSORTIUM

https://www.mnspacegrant.org/

MINNESOTA SPACE GRANT CONSORTIUM SCHOLARSHIP PROGRAM
• *See page 131*

NASA MONTANA SPACE GRANT CONSORTIUM

http://www.spacegrant.montana.edu/

MONTANA SPACE GRANT SCHOLARSHIP PROGRAM
• *See page 132*

NASA'S VIRGINIA SPACE GRANT CONSORTIUM

http://www.vsgc.odu.edu/

COMMUNITY COLLEGE STEM SCHOLARSHIPS
• *See page 110*

UNDERGRADUATE STEM RESEARCH SCHOLARSHIPS
• *See page 110*

NATIONAL SECURITY AGENCY

http://www.nsa.gov/Careers

NATIONAL SECURITY AGENCY STOKES EDUCATIONAL SCHOLARSHIP PROGRAM

Renewable awards for high school students planning to attend a four-year undergraduate institution to study computer science, electrical engineering, or computer engineering. Must be at least 16 to apply. Must be a U.S. citizen. Minimum 3.0 GPA required, and minimum SAT score of 1600. For application visit website http://www.nsa.gov/careers

Academic Fields/Career Goals: Computer Science/Data Processing; Electrical Engineering/Electronics.

Award: Scholarship for use in freshman, sophomore, junior, or senior years; renewable. *Number:* 15–20. *Amount:* $1000–$30,000.

Eligibility Requirements: Applicant must be high school student; age 16 and over and planning to enroll or expecting to enroll full-time at a four-year institution or university. Available to U.S. citizens.

Application Requirements: Application form, application form may be submitted online (http://www.nsa.gov/careers), essay, interview, recommendations or references, resume, test scores, transcript. *Deadline:* October 31.

Contact: Anne Clark, Program Manager
National Security Agency
9800 Savage Road, Suite 6779
Fort Meade, MD 20755-6779
Phone: 866-672-4473
Fax: 410-854-3002
E-mail: amclark@nsa.gov

NEVADA NASA SPACE GRANT CONSORTIUM

https://nasa.epscorspo.nevada.edu/

NATIONAL SPACE GRANT CONSORTIUM SCHOLARSHIPS
• *See page 110*

NEXTSTEPU

http://www.nextstepu.com/

$1,500 STEM SCHOLARSHIP
• *See page 104*

NORTH AMERICAN NETWORK OPERATORS GROUP (NANOG)

http://www.scholarshipamerica.org

NANOG SCHOLARSHIP PROGRAM

The North American Network Operator' Group (NANOG), is the professional association for Internet engineering, architecture and operations. Our core focus is on continuous improvement of the data transmission technologies, practices, and facilities that make the Internet function. In an effort to support the next generation of network operators, NANOG has established a scholarship program to assist current undergraduate and graduate level students pursuing a degree in computer engineering, computer science, electrical engineering, network engineering or telecommunications (at the graduate-level only) with $10,000 scholarships. To apply, students must plan to enroll part-time (at least six credits) or full-time in undergraduate or graduate study at an accredited two- or four-year college or university for the entire 2017–2018 academic year. Applicants must have a minimum 3.0 grade point average on a 4.0 scale or its equivalent. Qualified students are encouraged to apply early!

Academic Fields/Career Goals: Computer Science/Data Processing.

Award: Scholarship for use in freshman, sophomore, junior, senior, or graduate years; not renewable. *Number:* 4. *Amount:* $10,000.

Eligibility Requirements: Applicant must be enrolled or expecting to enroll full- or part-time at a two-year or four-year institution. Available to U.S. citizens.

Application Requirements: Application form, essay. *Deadline:* June 2.

Contact: Program Manager
North American Network Operators Group (NANOG)
One Scholarship Way
Saint Peter, MN 56082
Phone: 800-537-4180
E-mail: nanog@scholarshipamerica.org

PACIFIC GAS AND ELECTRIC COMPANY

http://www.scholarshipamerica.org

PG&E BETTER TOGETHER STEM SCHOLARSHIP PROGRAM

PG&E believes in helping students interested in being a part of California's clean energy future, giving them opportunities to learn and succeed in higher education. PG&E is awarding scholarships to help further STEM studies of students in California. Twenty scholarships of $10,000 each and 20 scholarships of $1,000 each are available to high school seniors, current college students, veterans and adults returning to school who are PG&E customers at the time of application and are pursuing a degree in one of the following STEM disciplines: Engineering (electrical, mechanical, computer, industrial or environmental),

Computer Science/Information Systems, Cyber Security or Environmental Sciences. Applicants must plan to enroll in full-time undergraduate study for the entire 2018-2019 academic year and be pursuing their first postsecondary degree at a school in California. Scholarships will be awarded based on academic achievement, demonstrated participation and leadership in school and community activities and financial need. Applicable majors include Engineering (electrical, mechanical, computer, industrial or environmental), Computer Science/Information Systems, Cyber Security, and Environmental Sciences.

Academic Fields/Career Goals: Computer Science/Data Processing; Electrical Engineering/Electronics; Environmental Science; Mechanical Engineering.

Award: Scholarship for use in freshman, sophomore, junior, or senior years; not renewable. *Number:* 40. *Amount:* $1000–$10,000.

Eligibility Requirements: Applicant must be enrolled or expecting to enroll full-time at a two-year or four-year or technical institution or university; resident of California and studying in California. Available to U.S. citizens.

Application Requirements: Application form, financial need analysis. *Deadline:* February 5.

Contact: Program Manager
Pacific Gas and Electric Company
Scholarship America
One Scholarship Way
Saint Peter, MN 56082
Phone: 800-537-4180 Ext. 437
E-mail: pge@scholarshipamerica.org

ROBERT H. MOLLOHAN FAMILY CHARITABLE FOUNDATION, INC.

http://www.mollohanfoundation.org/

HIGH TECHNOLOGY SCHOLARS PROGRAM
• See page 158

RURAL TECHNOLOGY FUND

http://ruraltechfund.org/

SOCIAL ENTREPRENEURSHIP SCHOLARSHIP

This scholarship is open to students from schools in Kentucky who have a passion for using technology skills to make a positive social change in the world or at home in their communities. Applicants must be an active member of the Student Technology Leadership Program at his or her respective high school.

Academic Fields/Career Goals: Computer Science/Data Processing.

Award: Scholarship for use in freshman year; not renewable. *Number:* 1. *Amount:* $500.

Eligibility Requirements: Applicant must be high school student; planning to enroll or expecting to enroll full- or part-time at a four-year institution and studying in Kentucky. Available to U.S. citizens.

Application Requirements: Application form, essay. *Deadline:* April 15.

SCARLETT FAMILY FOUNDATION SCHOLARSHIP PROGRAM

http://www.scarlettfoundation.org/

SCHOLARSHIP FOR STUDENTS PURSUING A BUSINESS OR STEM DEGREE
• See page 80

SEMICONDUCTOR RESEARCH CORPORATION (SRC)

http://www.src.org/

MASTER'S SCHOLARSHIP PROGRAM
• See page 158

SOCIETY OF WOMEN ENGINEERS

https://swe.org/

GE'S WOMEN'S NETWORK PAULA MARTIN SCHOLARSHIP
• See page 134

LIEBHERR MINING SCHOLARSHIP

One $1250 scholarship for female applicants planning to study a full-time ABET-accredited program in engineering, technology, or computing in the upcoming academic year. US Citizenship required. Geographic location based on home address and must be from Virginia. Minimum GPA: 3.0.

Academic Fields/Career Goals: Computer Science/Data Processing; Electrical Engineering/Electronics; Engineering-Related Technologies; Engineering/Technology; Mechanical Engineering.

Award: Scholarship for use in freshman year; not renewable. *Number:* 1. *Amount:* $1250.

Eligibility Requirements: Applicant must be enrolled or expecting to enroll full-time at a four-year institution or university; female and resident of Virginia. Available to U.S. citizens.

Application Requirements: Application form, transcript. *Deadline:* May 1.

Contact: Scholarship Committee
Phone: 312-596-5223
E-mail: scholarships@swe.org

SWE REGION E SCHOLARSHIP
• See page 159

SOCIETY OF WOMEN ENGINEERS-DALLAS SECTION

http://www.dallaswe.org/

DALLAS SWE ANNIE COLACO COLLEGIATE LEADER SCHOLARSHIP

The scholarship is named in honor of Annie Colaco (1899-1991), the grandmother to SWE lifetime member Nandika D'Souza. Annie Colaco epitomized selfless service and lifelong learning, which is reflected in the SWE mission. $100 award to a student leader and $150 to the SWE student section where the student serves. A maximum of 2 (two) award recipients may be from the same SWE section. The maximum number of awards given annually is 4 (four).

Academic Fields/Career Goals: Computer Science/Data Processing; Engineering/Technology.

Award: Scholarship for use in sophomore, junior, senior, graduate, or postgraduate years; not renewable. *Number:* 1–4. *Amount:* $100–$250.

Eligibility Requirements: Applicant must be enrolled or expecting to enroll full-time at a two-year or four-year institution or university; resident of Texas and studying in Texas. Available to U.S. and non-U.S. citizens.

Application Requirements: Application form, essay, personal photograph. *Deadline:* April 30.

Contact: Shelley Stracener, FY18 President
E-mail: dallas.swe@gmail.com

SOCIETY OF WOMEN ENGINEERS-TWIN TIERS SECTION

http://twintiers.swe.org/scholarship-information.html

SOCIETY OF WOMEN ENGINEERS-TWIN TIERS SECTION SCHOLARSHIP

Scholarship available to female students who reside or attend school in the Twin Tiers SWE section of New York. This is limited to zip codes that begin with 148, 149, 169 and residents of Bradford County, Pennsylvania. Applicant must be accepted or enrolled in an undergraduate degree program in engineering or computer science at an ABET-, CSAB- or SWE-accredited school.

Academic Fields/Career Goals: Computer Science/Data Processing; Engineering-Related Technologies; Engineering/Technology.

Award: Scholarship for use in freshman year; not renewable. *Number:* 5. *Amount:* $2000.

Eligibility Requirements: Applicant must be high school student; planning to enroll or expecting to enroll full-time at a four-year institution or university; female and resident of New York, Pennsylvania. Available to U.S. citizens.

Application Requirements: Application form, essay, test scores, transcript. *Deadline:* March 22.

Contact: Jessica Ortiz
    E-mail: scholarship@swetwintiers.org

SPECIALTY EQUIPMENT MARKET ASSOCIATION

http://www.sema.org/

SEMA MEMORIAL SCHOLARSHIP FUND
• *See page 81*

STRAIGHT NORTH

https://www.straightnorth.com/

STRAIGHT NORTH STEM SCHOLARSHIP
• *See page 81*

TAU KAPPA EPSILON EDUCATION FOUNDATION

https://www.tke.org/

THOMAS H. DUNNING, SR., MEMORIAL SCHOLARSHIP

This scholarship is awarded in recognition of academic achievement with a Grade Point Average of at least 2.75 or higher and must be at least a sophomore or higher, and recognizes active involvement within the chapter, as an officer and/or committee chairman. The applicant must be pursuing an undergraduate degree in engineering, computer science, or any of the pure sciences (chemistry, mathematics, physics, geology, etc.). Preference will be given to Tekes at Missouri University of Science and Technology. If there are no qualified candidates from Beta-Eta Chapter, this scholarship will be open to any Frater who meets the criteria.

Academic Fields/Career Goals: Computer Science/Data Processing; Mathematics; Science, Technology, and Society.

Award: Scholarship for use in sophomore, junior, or senior years. *Number:* 1.

Eligibility Requirements: Applicant must be enrolled or expecting to enroll at an institution or university and male. Applicant or parent of applicant must be member of Tau Kappa Epsilon. Available to U.S. citizens.

Application Requirements: Application form, application form may be submitted online, personal photograph. *Deadline:* March 15.

Contact: Rachel Stevenson, Foundation Communications Manager
    Tau Kappa Epsilon Education Foundation
    7439 Woodland Drive
    Suite 100
    Indianapolis, IN 46278
    Phone: 317-872-6533 Ext. 246
    E-mail: rstevenson@tke.org

TECHNOLOGY FIRST

https://technologyfirst.org/

ROBERT V. MCKENNA SCHOLARSHIPS

Must have at least sophomore standing (30 semester hours) at his/her respective university or college and currently be enrolled as an undergraduate student as defined by the applicant's institution. Must be able to prove that his/her major relates to the information technology field. Approved majors include but are not limited to the following: computer systems, computer science, computer information systems, management information systems, and industrial/computer engineering. Must have a minimum cumulative GPA of 3.0 and a minimum major

GPA of 3.25 on a 4.0 scale at the date of submission. Must have a strong interest in pursuing an IT career in Southwest Ohio. Must be a permanent resident of or attend a North Central accredited degree-granting college within the Southwest Ohio region including Adams, Brown, Butler, Champaign, Clark, Clermont, Clinton, Darke, Greene, Hamilton, Logan, Miami, Montgomery, Preble, Shelby and Warren counties. Financial need, character, and personal work ethic will be important selection criteria.

Academic Fields/Career Goals: Computer Science/Data Processing; Engineering-Related Technologies; Engineering/Technology; Health Information Management/Technology; Science, Technology, and Society.

Award: Scholarship for use in sophomore or junior years; not renewable. *Number:* 2–4. *Amount:* $750–$1500.

Eligibility Requirements: Applicant must be enrolled or expecting to enroll full-time at a four-year institution; resident of Ohio and studying in Ohio. Available to U.S. citizens.

Application Requirements: Application form. *Deadline:* March 15.

TEXAS DEPARTMENT OF TRANSPORTATION

http://www.txdot.gov/

CONDITIONAL GRANT PROGRAM
• *See page 167*

UNITED NEGRO COLLEGE FUND

http://www.uncf.org/

DAVIS SCHOLARSHIP FOR WOMEN IN STEM
• *See page 111*

DELL CORPORATE SCHOLARS PROGRAM
• *See page 168*

DISCOVER FINANCIAL SERVICES SCHOLARSHIP
• *See page 82*

GALACTIC UNITE BYTHEWAY SCHOLARSHIP
• *See page 111*

HCN/APRICITY RESOURCES SCHOLARS PROGRAM
• *See page 83*

LEIDOS STEM SCHOLARSHIP
• *See page 96*

NASCAR WENDELL SCOTT SR. SCHOLARSHIP
• *See page 83*

ORACLE COMMUNITY IMPACT SCHOLARSHIP

Provides scholarship support to African American and Hispanic American students majoring in computer science, computer engineering or mathematics. Applicant must be a matriculating student attending any accredited four-year college or university. Preference is given to students attending a UNCF member institution or other HBCU. Candidates can be either a resident of Northern California or a graduate of a Chicago Public School. Eligible counties include; Alameda, Contra Costa, Marin, San Francisco, San Mateo, Santa Clara, and Solano

Academic Fields/Career Goals: Computer Science/Data Processing; Mathematics.

Award: Scholarship for use in freshman, sophomore, junior, or senior years; not renewable.

Eligibility Requirements: Applicant must be Black (non-Hispanic), Hispanic and enrolled or expecting to enroll at a four-year institution or university. Available to U.S. citizens.

Application Requirements: Application form, essay, recommendations or references, transcript. *Deadline:* February 28.

Contact: David Ray
    E-mail: david.ray@uncf.org

UNCF/ALLIANCE DATA SCHOLARSHIP AND INTERNSHIP PROGRAM
• *See page 88*

UNCF-NORTHROP GRUMMAN SCHOLARSHIP
Scholarship available for a freshman, sophomore, or junior in college who is a U.S. citizen, an African- American, and enrolled full-time as a college undergraduate. Minimum 3.0 GPA required. Must be pursuing a major in computer science, computer engineering, electrical engineering, software engineering, or systems engineering. Must have an unmet financial need.

Academic Fields/Career Goals: Computer Science/Data Processing; Electrical Engineering/Electronics; Engineering/Technology.

Award: Scholarship for use in freshman, sophomore, or junior years; not renewable.

Eligibility Requirements: Applicant must be Black (non-Hispanic) and enrolled or expecting to enroll full-time at a four-year institution or university. Available to U.S. citizens.

Application Requirements: Application form, FAFSA, financial need analysis. *Deadline:* January 21.

Contact: David Ray
      E-mail: David.ray@uncf.org

VERMONT SPACE GRANT CONSORTIUM
http://www.cems.uvm.edu/vsgc

VERMONT SPACE GRANT CONSORTIUM
• *See page 92*

WYOMING TRUCKING ASSOCIATION SCHOLARSHIP FUND TRUST
http://www.wytruck.org/

WYOMING TRUCKING ASSOCIATION SCHOLARSHIP TRUST FUND
• *See page 84*

XEROX
http://www.xerox.com//

TECHNICAL MINORITY SCHOLARSHIP
• *See page 161*

CONSTRUCTION ENGINEERING/ MANAGEMENT

AACE INTERNATIONAL
http://www.aacei.org/

AACE INTERNATIONAL COMPETITIVE SCHOLARSHIP
• *See page 112*

AMERICAN COUNCIL OF ENGINEERING COMPANIES OF PENNSYLVANIA (ACEC/PA)
http://www.acecpa.org/

ERIC J. GENNUSO AND LEROY D. (BUD) LOY, JR. SCHOLARSHIP PROGRAM
• *See page 153*

AMERICAN INDIAN SCIENCE AND ENGINEERING SOCIETY
http://www.aises.org/

A.T. ANDERSON MEMORIAL SCHOLARSHIP PROGRAM
• *See page 105*

AMERICAN RAILWAY ENGINEERING AND MAINTENANCE OF WAY ASSOCIATION
http://www.aremafoundation.org/

AREMA GRADUATE AND UNDERGRADUATE SCHOLARSHIPS
• *See page 162*

AMERICAN SOCIETY OF CERTIFIED ENGINEERING TECHNICIANS
http://www.ascet.org/

KURT H. AND DONNA M. SCHULER SMALL GRANT
• *See page 162*

ASSOCIATED GENERAL CONTRACTORS OF NEW YORK STATE, LLC
https://www.agcnys.org/programs/scholarship/

ASSOCIATED GENERAL CONTRACTORS NYS SCHOLARSHIP PROGRAM
• *See page 163*

ASSOCIATION OF STATE DAM SAFETY OFFICIALS (ASDSO)
http://www.DamSafety.org

ASSOCIATION OF STATE DAM SAFETY OFFICIALS (ASDSO) SENIOR UNDERGRADUATE SCHOLARSHIP
• *See page 140*

BHW GROUP
https://thebhwgroup.com/

BHW WOMEN IN STEM SCHOLARSHIP
• *See page 107*

BRASKEM ODEBRECHT
http://www.odebrechtaward.com

ODEBRECHT AWARD FOR SUSTAINABLE DEVELOPMENT
• *See page 113*

BROWN AND CALDWELL
http://www.brownandcaldwell.com

ECKENFELDER SCHOLARSHIP
• *See page 141*

MINORITY SCHOLARSHIP PROGRAM
• *See page 141*

COLORADO CONTRACTORS ASSOCIATION INC.

http://www.coloradocontractors.org/

COLORADO CONTRACTORS ASSOCIATION SCHOLARSHIP PROGRAM

Scholarships for junior and senior students who are interested in pursuing a career in heavy-highway-municipal-utility construction. Scholarships are only awarded to students who attend the following institutions: Colorado School of Mines, Colorado State University-Fort Collins or Pueblo, CU-Boulder and Colorado Mesa University.

Academic Fields/Career Goals: Construction Engineering/Management.

Award: Scholarship for use in junior or senior years; not renewable. *Amount:* $1000–$5000.

Eligibility Requirements: Applicant must be enrolled or expecting to enroll full- or part-time at a four-year institution or university and studying in Colorado. Available to U.S. citizens.

Application Requirements: Application form. *Deadline:* May 14.

Contact: Scholarship Program Coordinator
Phone: 290-290-6611
Fax: 290-290-9141
E-mail: info@coloradocontractors.org

CONNECTICUT BUILDING CONGRESS SCHOLARSHIP FUND, INC.

http://www.cbc-ct.org

CBC SCHOLARSHIP FUND
• *See page 114*

FLORIDA EDUCATIONAL FACILITIES PLANNERS' ASSOCIATION

http://www.fefpa.org/

FEFPA ASSISTANTSHIP
• *See page 115*

FLORIDA ENGINEERING SOCIETY

https://www.fleng.org/page/Scholarships

FECON SCHOLARSHIP
• *See page 164*

GRAND RAPIDS COMMUNITY FOUNDATION

http://www.grfoundation.org/

DAROOGE FAMILY SCHOLARSHIP FOR CONSTRUCTION TRADES

Student is a high school senior residing in Kent County Michigan pursuing an undergrad degree in a construction-related field at an accredited 2 or 4 year college/university/trade school in Michigan. Must have financial need.

Academic Fields/Career Goals: Construction Engineering/Management; Trade/Technical Specialties.

Award: Scholarship for use in freshman, sophomore, junior, or senior years; not renewable. *Number:* 1–5. *Amount:* $1000–$5000.

Eligibility Requirements: Applicant must be enrolled or expecting to enroll full-time at a two-year or technical institution or university; resident of Massachusetts and studying in Michigan. Applicant or parent of applicant must have employment or volunteer experience in construction. Available to U.S. citizens.

Application Requirements: Application form, application form may be submitted online, essay, financial need analysis. *Deadline:* April 1.

Contact: Ms. Ruth Bishop, Education Program Officer
Grand Rapids Community Foundation
185 Oakes Street SW
Grand Rapids, MI 49503
Phone: 616-454-1751 Ext. 103
E-mail: rbishop@grfoundation.org

GREAT MINDS IN STEM

http://www.greatmindsinstem.org/college/scholarship-application-information

HENAAC SCHOLARSHIP PROGRAM
• *See page 100*

HOUZZ

http://houzz.com

RESIDENTIAL CONSTRUCTION MANAGEMENT SCHOLARSHIP

Houzz is committed to supporting the next generation of construction professionals as they enter the world of residential construction. Open to students studying construction management at the undergraduate or graduate level who want to pursue residential construction management professionally.

Academic Fields/Career Goals: Construction Engineering/Management.

Award: Scholarship for use in freshman, sophomore, junior, senior, or graduate years; not renewable. *Number:* 1. *Amount:* $2500.

Eligibility Requirements: Applicant must be age 17 and over; enrolled or expecting to enroll full- or part-time at a two-year or technical institution or university and studying in Alabama, Alaska, Arizona, Arkansas, California, Colorado, Connecticut, Delaware, District of Columbia, Florida, Georgia, Hawaii, Idaho, Illinois, Indiana, Iowa, Kansas, Kentucky, Louisiana, Maine, Maryland, Massachusetts, Michigan, Minnesota, Mississippi, Missouri, Montana, Nebraska, Nevada, New Hampshire, New Jersey, New Mexico, New York, North Carolina, North Dakota, Ohio, Oklahoma, Oregon, Pennsylvania, Rhode Island, South Carolina, South Dakota, Tennessee, Texas, Utah, Vermont, Virginia, Washington, West Virginia, Wisconsin, Wyoming. Available to U.S. and non-U.S. citizens.

Application Requirements: Application form, application form may be submitted online, essay. *Deadline:* March 31.

Contact: Emily Hurley, Community Manager
Houzz
285 Hamilton Avenue
Palo Alto, CA 94301
Phone: 800-368-4268
E-mail: scholarships@houzz.com

INTERNATIONAL FACILITY MANAGEMENT ASSOCIATION FOUNDATION

http://www.ifmafoundation.org/

IFMA FOUNDATION SCHOLARSHIPS
• *See page 116*

INTERNATIONAL SOCIETY OF EXPLOSIVES ENGINEERS

http://www.isee.org/

JERRY MCDOWELL FUND
• *See page 156*

LOGMEIN

https://www.logmeininc.com

LASTPASS STEM SCHOLARSHIP
* *See page 109*

MIDWEST ROOFING CONTRACTORS ASSOCIATION

http://www.mrca.org/

MRCA FOUNDATION SCHOLARSHIP PROGRAM
* *See page 116*

NASA'S VIRGINIA SPACE GRANT CONSORTIUM

http://www.vsgc.odu.edu/

COMMUNITY COLLEGE STEM SCHOLARSHIPS
* *See page 110*

NATIONAL ASPHALT PAVEMENT ASSOCIATION RESEARCH AND EDUCATION FOUNDATION

http://www.asphaltpavement.org

NATIONAL ASPHALT PAVEMENT ASSOCIATION RESEARCH AND EDUCATION FOUNDATION SCHOLARSHIP PROGRAM
* *See page 165*

NATIONAL CONSTRUCTION EDUCATION FOUNDATION

http://www.abc.org/

TRIMMER EDUCATION FOUNDATION SCHOLARSHIPS FOR CONSTRUCTION MANAGEMENT

Scholarships are available to students in a major related to the construction industry. Applicants must be enrolled at an educational institution with an ABC student chapter, and be current, active members or employed by an ABC member firm. Architecture and most engineering programs are excluded. Applicants must have a minimum overall GPA of 2.85 and 3.0 in the major. If no courses have been taken in the major, a minimum overall GPA of 3.0 is required. Visit website http://www.abc.org.

Academic Fields/Career Goals: Construction Engineering/Management.

Award: Scholarship for use in sophomore, junior, or senior years; not renewable. *Number:* 10–15. *Amount:* up to $5000.

Eligibility Requirements: Applicant must be enrolled or expecting to enroll full-time at a two-year or four-year institution or university. Available to U.S. citizens.

Application Requirements: Application form, essay, financial need analysis, recommendations or references, Student Aid Report (SAR), transcript. *Deadline:* May 22.

Contact: John Strock, Director, Career and Constructions
    Phone: 703-812-2008
    E-mail: strock@abc.org

NEXTSTEPU

http://www.nextstepu.com/

$1,500 STEM SCHOLARSHIP
* *See page 104*

PROFESSIONAL CONSTRUCTION ESTIMATORS ASSOCIATION

http://www.pcea.org/

TED G. WILSON MEMORIAL SCHOLARSHIP FOUNDATION
* *See page 166*

SOCIETY OF WOMEN ENGINEERS

https://swe.org/

SWE REGION E SCHOLARSHIP
* *See page 159*

SWE REGION H SCHOLARSHIPS
* *See page 159*

SWE REGION J SCHOLARSHIP
* *See page 159*

TE CONNECTIVITY EXCELLENCE IN ENGINEERING SCHOLARSHIP
* *See page 160*

STRAIGHT NORTH

https://www.straightnorth.com/

STRAIGHT NORTH STEM SCHOLARSHIP
* *See page 81*

TRANSPORTATION ASSOCIATION OF CANADA FOUNDATION

http://www.tac-foundation.ca

TAC FOUNDATION SCHOLARSHIPS
* *See page 168*

TURNER CONSTRUCTION COMPANY

http://www.turnerconstruction.com/

YOUTHFORCE 2020 SCHOLARSHIP PROGRAM
* *See page 117*

UNITED NEGRO COLLEGE FUND

http://www.uncf.org/

LEIDOS STEM SCHOLARSHIP
* *See page 96*

VECTORWORKS, INC.

http://www.vectorworks.net

VECTORWORKS DESIGN SCHOLARSHIP
* *See page 117*

WIRE REINFORCEMENT INSTITUTE EDUCATION FOUNDATION

http://www.wirereinforcementinstitute.org/

WRI FOUNDATION COLLEGE SCHOLARSHIP PROGRAM
* *See page 168*

COSMETOLOGY

AVACARE MEDICAL

https://avacaremedical.com

AVACARE MEDICAL SCHOLARSHIP
• *See page 100*

JOE FRANCIS HAIRCARE SCHOLARSHIP FOUNDATION

http://www.joefrancis.com

JOE FRANCIS HAIRCARE SCHOLARSHIP FOUNDATION
Cosmetology or Barber School scholarships are awarded for $1200 each, with 26 to 28 scholarships awarded annually. Applicants are evaluated for their potential to successfully complete school, their financial need, and commitment to a long-term career in cosmetology. Window to apply is January 1st to June 1st. Deadline to apply is June 1st. Students who graduate before September of the award year are not eligible to apply. Applications are found on our website (apply online) www.joefrancis.com.

Academic Fields/Career Goals: Cosmetology.

Award: Scholarship for use in freshman year; not renewable. *Number:* 26–28. *Amount:* $1200.

Eligibility Requirements: Applicant must be enrolled or expecting to enroll full- or part-time at a technical institution. Available to U.S. citizens.

Application Requirements: Application form, essay, financial need analysis. *Deadline:* June 1.

Contact: Kim Larson, Administrator
Joe Francis Haircare Scholarship Foundation
PO Box 50625
Minneapolis, MN 55405
Phone: 651-769-1757
E-mail: kimlarsonmn@gmail.com

MEDICAL SCRUBS COLLECTION

http://medicalscrubscollection.com

MEDICAL SCRUBS COLLECTION SCHOLARSHIP
• *See page 104*

CRIMINAL JUSTICE/ CRIMINOLOGY

AMERICAN SOCIETY OF CRIMINOLOGY

http://www.asc41.com/

AMERICAN SOCIETY OF CRIMINOLOGY GENE CARTE STUDENT PAPER COMPETITION
Award for full-time undergraduate or graduate students. Must submit a conceptual or empirical paper on a subject directly relating to criminology. Papers must be 7500 words or less.

Academic Fields/Career Goals: Criminal Justice/Criminology; Law Enforcement/Police Administration; Law/Legal Services; Social Sciences.

Award: Prize for use in freshman, sophomore, junior, senior, or graduate years; not renewable. *Number:* 3. *Amount:* $200–$500.

Eligibility Requirements: Applicant must be enrolled or expecting to enroll full-time at a four-year institution or university and must have an interest in writing. Available to U.S. and non-U.S. citizens.

Application Requirements: Conceptual or empirical paper on a subject directly relating to criminology, entry in a contest. *Deadline:* April 15.

Contact: Andrew Hochstetlet, Scholarship Committee
American Society of Criminology
Iowa State University, 203D East Hall
Ames, IA 50011-4504
Phone: 515-294-2841
E-mail: hochstet@iastate.edu

ASSOCIATION OF CERTIFIED FRAUD EXAMINERS

http://www.acfe.com/

RITCHIE-JENNINGS MEMORIAL SCHOLARSHIP
• *See page 71*

ASSOCIATION OF FORMER INTELLIGENCE OFFICERS

www.afio.com

AFIO UNDERGRADUATE AND GRADUATE SCHOLARSHIPS
• *See page 98*

CANTOR CRANE INJURY LAW

https://cantorcrane.com

CANTOR CRANE PERSONAL INJURY LAWYER $1,000 SCHOLARSHIP
In order to help make a college education more affordable opportunity and to help spread awareness about Driving Under the Influence and Distracted Driving, the Arizona law firm of Cantor Crane is offering a $1,000 law student scholarship to help current, or soon-to-be, law students ease the burden of higher education costs. The scholarship funds may be used for law school tuition at a college or university. It is not required that the applicant be enrolled in an educational program at the time of his or her application. The winner will have one year from the date of the award to provide a tuition invoice from the school of their choice. A check for $1,000 will then be sent to the educational institution. Submitting the application is easy. Simply take the pledge to not drive under the influence and to not drive while distracted by things such as texting and fill out the contact information.

Academic Fields/Career Goals: Criminal Justice/Criminology; Law/Legal Services.

Award: Scholarship for use in freshman, sophomore, junior, senior, graduate, or postgraduate years; renewable. *Number:* 1. *Amount:* $1000.

Eligibility Requirements: Applicant must be enrolled or expecting to enroll full- or part-time at a two-year or four-year institution or university. Available to U.S. and non-U.S. citizens.

Application Requirements: Application form. *Deadline:* July 31.

Contact: Tristan Petricca, Media Director
Cantor Crane Injury Law
1 East Washington Street
Suite 1800
Phoenix, AZ 85004
Phone: 602-254-2701
E-mail: t.petricca@dmcantor.com

CONGRESSIONAL BLACK CAUCUS FOUNDATION, INC.

http://www.cbcfinc.org/

CBC SPOUSES EDUCATION SCHOLARSHIP
• *See page 98*

CONNECTICUT ASSOCIATION OF WOMEN POLICE

http://www.cawp.net/

CONNECTICUT ASSOCIATION OF WOMEN POLICE SCHOLARSHIP

Available to Connecticut residents graduating from an accredited high school, and entering a college or university in Connecticut as a criminal justice major.

Academic Fields/Career Goals: Criminal Justice/Criminology; Law Enforcement/Police Administration.

Award: Scholarship for use in freshman year; not renewable. *Number:* 1–3. *Amount:* $200–$500.

Eligibility Requirements: Applicant must be high school student; planning to enroll or expecting to enroll full-time at a two-year or four-year institution or university; resident of Connecticut and studying in Connecticut. Available to U.S. citizens.

Application Requirements: Application form, essay, financial need analysis, recommendations or references, transcript. *Deadline:* April 30.

Contact: Gail McDonnell, Scholarship Committee
Connecticut Association of Women Police
PO Box 1653
Hartford, CT 06144
Phone: 860-527-7300

CONTINENTAL SOCIETY, DAUGHTERS OF INDIAN WARS

http://www.csdiw.org/

CONTINENTAL SOCIETY, DAUGHTERS OF INDIAN WARS SCHOLARSHIP

Award for a certified Indian tribal member enrolled in an undergraduate degree program in education or social service. Must maintain minimum 3.0 GPA and work with Native Americans in a social service or educational role after graduation. Preference given to those in or entering junior year.

Academic Fields/Career Goals: Criminal Justice/Criminology; Dental Health/Services; Education; Food Science/Nutrition; Health Administration; Health and Medical Sciences; Home Economics; Nursing; Occupational Safety and Health; Oncology; Optometry; Osteopathy; Pharmacy; Public Health; Social Services; Special Education; Therapy/Rehabilitation.

Award: Scholarship for use in sophomore, junior, or senior years; renewable. *Number:* 1. *Amount:* $5000.

Eligibility Requirements: Applicant must be American Indian/Alaska Native and enrolled or expecting to enroll full-time at a two-year or four-year institution or university. Available to U.S. citizens.

Application Requirements: Application form, essay, financial need analysis. *Deadline:* June 15.

Contact: Mrs. J.B. Richards, II, National Scholarship Chairman
Continental Society, Daughters of Indian Wars
PO Box 6695
Chesterfield, MO 63006-6695
Phone: 636-220-2442
E-mail: leslie@khs65.com

LIVSECURE

https://www.livsecure.com

LIVSECURE STUDENT SCHOLARSHIP

At LivSecure, we are proud to support those who are studying to make our neighborhoods a safer place. If you are currently studying law enforcement, law, criminal justice, or a related field, then you are eligible to submit a security-focused essay for a chance to win a $1,000 scholarship to put toward your college tuition.

Academic Fields/Career Goals: Criminal Justice/Criminology; Law Enforcement/Police Administration; Law/Legal Services.

Award: Scholarship for use in freshman or sophomore years; not renewable. *Number:* 1–3. *Amount:* $500–$1000.

Eligibility Requirements: Applicant must be enrolled or expecting to enroll full- or part-time at a two-year or four-year or technical institution or university.

Application Requirements: Essay. *Deadline:* July 1.

Contact: Megan Nonemacher, Marketing Manager
LivSecure
3803 West Chester Pike
Suite 100
Newtown Square, PA 19073
Phone: 484-420-0314
E-mail: megan.nonemacher@myalarmcenter.com

NATIONAL BLACK POLICE ASSOCIATION

http://www.blackpolice.org/

ALPHONSO DEAL SCHOLARSHIP AWARD

$500 scholarship for high school senior and U.S. citizen to attend a two-year college or university. Must study law enforcement or other related criminal justice field. Minimum 2.5 GPA required.

Academic Fields/Career Goals: Criminal Justice/Criminology; Law Enforcement/Police Administration; Law/Legal Services; Social Sciences; Social Services.

Award: Scholarship for use in freshman year; not renewable. *Number:* 4. *Amount:* $500.

Eligibility Requirements: Applicant must be high school student and planning to enroll or expecting to enroll full-time at a two-year or four-year institution or university. Available to U.S. citizens.

Application Requirements: Application form, letter of acceptance, personal photograph, recommendations or references, transcript. *Deadline:* June 1.

Contact: Ronald Hampton, Executive Director
National Black Police Association
30 Kennedy Street, NW, Suite 101
Washington, DC 20011
Phone: 202-986-2070
Fax: 202-986-0410
E-mail: nbpanatofc@worldnet.att.net

NORTH CAROLINA STATE EDUCATION ASSISTANCE AUTHORITY

http://www.ncseaa.edu/

NORTH CAROLINA SHERIFFS' ASSOCIATION UNDERGRADUATE CRIMINAL JUSTICE SCHOLARSHIPS

One-time award for full-time North Carolina resident undergraduate students majoring in criminal justice at a University of North Carolina school. Priority given to child of any North Carolina law enforcement officer. Letter of recommendation from county sheriff required. Deadline determined by FA Office.

Academic Fields/Career Goals: Criminal Justice/Criminology; Law Enforcement/Police Administration.

Award: Scholarship for use in freshman, sophomore, junior, or senior years; not renewable. *Number:* 12. *Amount:* up to $2000.

Eligibility Requirements: Applicant must be enrolled or expecting to enroll full-time at a four-year institution or university; resident of North Carolina and studying in North Carolina. Applicant or parent of applicant must have employment or volunteer experience in police/firefighting. Available to U.S. citizens.

Application Requirements: Application form, financial need analysis, recommendations or references, transcript. *Deadline:* continuous.

Contact: Maxine Hicklin, Program Assistant, Grants, Training & Outreach Division
Phone: 866-866-2362
E-mail: programinformation@cfnc.org

OREGON ASSOCIATION CHIEFS OF POLICE

http://www.policechief.org/

LAW ENFORCEMENT AND CRIMINAL JUSTICE COLLEGE SCHOLARSHIP PROGRAM

Each year, the Oregon Association Chiefs of Police (OACP) provides $1000 college scholarships to students who plan to enter a law enforcement or other criminal justice career. The OACP is committed to promoting professionalism and we value the presence and contributions of educated men and women in Law Enforcement and Criminal Justice. To further our commitment, the OACP provides competitive college scholarships for qualifying students. The following information will help you determine if you qualify for scholarship consideration and will help you understand the application process. Each year, the Oregon Association Chiefs of Police (OACP) provides $1000 college scholarships to students who plan to enter a law enforcement or other criminal justice career. The OACP is committed to promoting professionalism and we value the presence and contributions of educated men and women in Law Enforcement and Criminal Justice. To further our commitment, the OACP provides competitive college scholarships for qualifying students. The following information will help you determine if you qualify for scholarship consideration and will help you understand the application process. 1. Have you completed at least 36 college credit hours or 30 semester hours? In lieu of 36 college credit hours have you logged at least 240 hours of service over the last year as a cadet, explorer, or reserve police officer? 2. Have you maintained a grade point average (GPA) of at least 2.5? 3. Do you plan to enter a law enforcement or other criminal justice career? Preference will be given to immediate family members of an Oregon Police Officer killed or disabled in the line of duty, as well as dependents of OACP members.

Academic Fields/Career Goals: Criminal Justice/Criminology.

Award: Scholarship for use in freshman, sophomore, junior, senior, graduate, or postgraduate years; not renewable. *Number:* 5. *Amount:* $1000.

Eligibility Requirements: Applicant must be enrolled or expecting to enroll full- or part-time at a two-year or four-year institution or university and resident of Oregon. Available to U.S. citizens.

Application Requirements: Application form, autobiography, personal photograph. *Deadline:* December 31.

Contact: Mrs. Marie Campbell, Association Executive
Oregon Association Chiefs of Police
1191 Capitol Street, NE
Salem, OR 97301
Phone: 503-315-1411
Fax: 503-315-1416
E-mail: marie@victorygrp.com

WASHINGTON STATE ASSOCIATION FOR JUSTICE

http://www.washingtonjustice.org/

WASHINGTON STATE ASSOCIATION FOR JUSTICE AMERICAN JUSTICE ESSAY & VIDEO SCHOLARSHIP

As part of the Washington State Association for Justice's (WSAJ) commitment to foster an awareness and understanding of the important role that the civil justice system plays in our society, WSAJ sponsors an annual statewide student essay and video scholarship program. For 2017, WSAJ will award two, $3,750 scholarships, one to an essayist and one to a videographer. The video scholarship winner's piece will be posted on WSAJ's Facebook and Twitter accounts, and may be aired on TV. This scholarship is available to high school seniors who are residents attending high school in Washington state. Students need not attend a Washington college, but must start college within the next two years to receive the funds. If you have questions about the prompt or the practice of law, please contact anita@washingtonjustice.org and we will connect you with an attorney to answer your questions. The prompt for both scholarships is—Forced arbitration clauses in consumer contracts: How do they affect us? Essay option: Write a 700-800 word essay on this subject. Video option: Create a video of no more than 60 seconds in length on this subject in the format of a Public Service Announcement, as well as writing a 300-400 word summary on this subject and the

inspiration for the video. The video must be uploaded on YouTube or Vimeo and the link shared with the scholarship committee. WSAJ reserves the right to make the winning video available to the general public. By submitting a video, you grant WSAJ a royalty-free license to copy, distribute, modify, display and perform publicly and otherwise use and authorize others to use your video for any purpose. You also guarantee that no other person, corporation or organization has a copyright interest in your video. Applications must be postmarked on or before March 17, 2017.

Academic Fields/Career Goals: Criminal Justice/Criminology; Law/Legal Services; Peace and Conflict Studies; Political Science; Public Policy and Administration; Social Sciences.

Award: Scholarship for use in freshman year; not renewable. *Number:* 2. *Amount:* $3750.

Eligibility Requirements: Applicant must be high school student; planning to enroll or expecting to enroll full-time at a four-year institution or university; resident of Washington and studying in Washington. Available to U.S. and non-U.S. citizens.

Application Requirements: Application form, essay. *Deadline:* March 17.

Contact: Anita Yandle, Scholarship Coordinator
Washington State Association for Justice
1809 7th Avenue
Suite 1500
Seattle, WA 98101
Phone: 206-464-1011
E-mail: anita@washingtonjustice.org

WILLIAMS LAW GROUP

https://familylawyersnewjersey.com/

WILLIAMS LAW GROUP OPPORTUNITY TO GROW SCHOLARSHIP

• *See page 119*

CULINARY ARTS

AMERICAN HOTEL AND LODGING EDUCATIONAL FOUNDATION

https://www.ahlafoundation.org/

AMERICAN HOTEL & LODGING EDUCATIONAL FOUNDATION PEPSI SCHOLARSHIP

Scholarships of $500 to $3000 awarded to graduates of Hospitality High School in Washington, DC. The scholarship recipients are selected by Hospitality High based upon a set of minimum eligibility criteria which includes graduate of Hospitality High, a minimum 2.5 GPA, and at least 250 hours in the hotel/hospitality industry.

Academic Fields/Career Goals: Culinary Arts; Food Service/Hospitality; Hospitality Management; Recreation, Parks, Leisure Studies; Travel/Tourism.

Award: Scholarship for use in freshman, sophomore, junior, or senior years; not renewable. *Amount:* $500–$3000.

Eligibility Requirements: Applicant must be enrolled or expecting to enroll full-time at a two-year or four-year institution or university and resident of District of Columbia. Available to U.S. and non-U.S. citizens.

Application Requirements: Application form, essay, financial need analysis, nomination from Hospitality High School, resume, transcript. *Deadline:* May 1.

Contact: Ms. Kelsey Allagood, Foundation Manager
American Hotel and Lodging Educational Foundation
1201 New York Avenue, NW, Suite 600
Washington, DC 20005
Phone: 202-289-3139
Fax: 202-289-3199
E-mail: scholarships@ahlef.org

CANFIT

http://www.canfit.org/

CANFIT NUTRITION, PHYSICAL EDUCATION AND CULINARY ARTS SCHOLARSHIP

Awards undergraduate and graduate African-American, American-Indian/Alaska Native, Asian-American, Pacific Islander or Latino/Hispanic students who express financial need and are studying nutrition, physical education, or culinary arts in California. GPA of minimum 2.5 for undergraduates and 3.0 for graduates. See website for essay topic http://www.canfit.org.

Academic Fields/Career Goals: Culinary Arts; Food Science/Nutrition; Food Service/Hospitality; Health and Medical Sciences; Sports-Related/Exercise Science.

Award: Scholarship for use in junior, senior, or graduate years; not renewable. *Number:* 5–10. *Amount:* $500–$1500.

Eligibility Requirements: Applicant must be of African, Chinese, Hispanic, Indian, Japanese heritage; American Indian/Alaska Native, Asian/Pacific Islander, Black (non-Hispanic); enrolled or expecting to enroll full-time at a four-year or technical institution or university; resident of California and studying in California. Available to U.S. citizens.

Application Requirements: Application form, essay, financial need analysis, personal photograph, recommendations or references, transcript. *Deadline:* March 31.

Contact: Ms. Arnell Hinkle, Executive Director
 Phone: 510-644-1533 Ext. 12
 Fax: 510-644-1535
 E-mail: info@canfit.org

CAREERS THROUGH CULINARY ARTS PROGRAM INC.

http://www.ccapinc.org/

CAREERS THROUGH CULINARY ARTS PROGRAM COOKING COMPETITION FOR SCHOLARSHIPS

Applicants must be a senior in a C-CAP designated partner high school in Arizona; Prince George's County, Maryland; Tidewater, Virginia; or the cities of Boston, Chicago, Los Angeles, New York, Philadelphia or Washington, DC. Applicants must be accepted into the cooking competition for scholarships. Check website for local coordinator's contact information.

Academic Fields/Career Goals: Culinary Arts; Hospitality Management.

Award: Scholarship for use in freshman, sophomore, junior, or senior years; not renewable.

Eligibility Requirements: Applicant must be high school student; age 21 or under; planning to enroll or expecting to enroll full- or part-time at a two-year or four-year or technical institution and resident of Arizona, California, Illinois, Maryland, New York, Pennsylvania, Virginia. Available to U.S. and non-U.S. citizens.

Application Requirements: Application form, essay, financial need analysis, interview.

Contact: College Advisor
 Phone: 212-974-7111
 E-mail: info@ccapinc.org

THE CULINARY TRUST

http://www.theculinarytrust.org/

CULINARY TRUST SCHOLARSHIP PROGRAM FOR CULINARY STUDY AND RESEARCH

Scholarships provides funds to qualified applicants for beginning, continuing, and specialty education courses at accredited culinary schools worldwide, as well as, independent study for research projects. Applicants must have at least, a minimum 3.0 GPA, must write an essay, submit two letters of recommendation. Application fee: $35.

Academic Fields/Career Goals: Culinary Arts; Food Science/Nutrition; Food Service/Hospitality.

Award: Scholarship for use in freshman, sophomore, junior, senior, graduate, or postgraduate years; not renewable. *Number:* 21. *Amount:* $1000–$5000.

Eligibility Requirements: Applicant must be age 18 and over and enrolled or expecting to enroll full- or part-time at a two-year or four-year or technical institution or university. Available to U.S. and non-U.S. citizens.

Application Requirements: Application form, application form may be submitted online (http://www.theculinarytrust.org), essay, interview, recommendations or references, resume, transcript. *Fee:* $35. *Deadline:* March 1.

Contact: Heather Johnston, Administrator
 The Culinary Trust
 PO Box 273
 New York, NY 10013
 Phone: 888-345-4666
 Fax: 888-345-4666
 E-mail: heather@theculinarytrust.org

GOLDEN GATE RESTAURANT ASSOCIATION

http://www.ggra.org/

GOLDEN GATE RESTAURANT ASSOCIATION SCHOLARSHIP FOUNDATION

One-time award for any student pursuing a food service degree at a 501(c)(3) institution, or institutions approved by the Board of Trustees. California residency and personal interview in San Francisco is required. Minimum GPA of 2.75 required. For further information email donnalyn@ggra.org, or visit http://ggra.org/scholarships/.

Academic Fields/Career Goals: Culinary Arts; Hospitality Management.

Award: Scholarship for use in freshman, sophomore, junior, or senior years; renewable. *Number:* 9–15. *Amount:* $1000–$6000.

Eligibility Requirements: Applicant must be enrolled or expecting to enroll full- or part-time at a two-year or four-year or technical institution or university and resident of California. Available to U.S. citizens.

Application Requirements: Application form, essay, financial need analysis, interview. *Deadline:* April 30.

Contact: Donnalyn Murphy, Trustee and Secretary
 Golden Gate Restaurant Association
 220 Montgomery Street
 Suite 990
 San Francisco, CA 94104
 Phone: 415-781-5350
 E-mail: donnalyn@ggra.org

ILLINOIS RESTAURANT ASSOCIATION EDUCATIONAL FOUNDATION

http://www.illinoisrestaurants.org/

ILLINOIS RESTAURANT ASSOCIATION EDUCATIONAL FOUNDATION SCHOLARSHIPS

Scholarship available to Illinois residents enrolled in a food service management, culinary arts, or hospitality management concentration in an accredited program of a two- or four-year college or university. Must be a U.S. citizen.

Academic Fields/Career Goals: Culinary Arts; Food Science/Nutrition; Food Service/Hospitality; Hospitality Management.

Award: Scholarship for use in freshman, sophomore, junior, senior, graduate, or postgraduate years; not renewable. *Number:* 50–70. *Amount:* $1000–$10,000.

Eligibility Requirements: Applicant must be age 17-25; enrolled or expecting to enroll full- or part-time at a two-year or four-year institution or university and resident of Illinois. Applicant or parent of applicant must have employment or volunteer experience in food service, hospitality/hotel administration/operations. Available to U.S. citizens.

Application Requirements: Application form, essay, personal photograph, recommendations or references, transcript. *Deadline:* April 27.

CULINARY ARTS

Contact: Jenna Zera, IRA Educational Foundation Scholarship
Committee
Illinois Restaurant Association Educational Foundation
33 West Monroe, Suite 250
Chicago, IL 60603
Phone: 312-380-4117
Fax: 312-787-4792

JAMES BEARD FOUNDATION INC.

http://www.jamesbeard.org/

BERN LAXER MEMORIAL SCHOLARSHIP

Scholarship for students seeking careers in food service and hospitality management. Up to one scholarship will be given in one of three programs: culinary, hospitality management, and viticulture/oenology. Program and school must be accredited in accordance with the James Beard Foundation scholarship criteria. Must be resident of Florida and substantiate residency, have a high school diploma or the equivalent, and have a minimum of one-year culinary experience either as a student or employee.

Academic Fields/Career Goals: Culinary Arts; Food Science/Nutrition; Hospitality Management.

Award: Scholarship for use in freshman, sophomore, junior, or senior years; not renewable. *Number:* 1. *Amount:* $11,150.

Eligibility Requirements: Applicant must be enrolled or expecting to enroll full- or part-time at a four-year institution or university and resident of Florida. Available to U.S. and non-U.S. citizens.

Application Requirements: Application form, essay, financial need analysis. *Deadline:* May 15.

Contact: Scholarship Management Services
James Beard Foundation Inc.
One Scholarship Way
Saint Peter, MN 56082
Phone: 507-931-1682
E-mail: jamesbeard@scholarshipamerica.org

CHICAGO JBF EATS WEEK SCHOLARSHIP

$12,900 scholarship for residents of the greater Chicago area who are enrolled in an accredited program of hospitality, culinary, baking, or beverage studies. Must be able to verify residency.

Academic Fields/Career Goals: Culinary Arts; Hospitality Management.

Award: Scholarship for use in freshman, sophomore, junior, or senior years; not renewable. *Number:* 1. *Amount:* $12,900.

Eligibility Requirements: Applicant must be enrolled or expecting to enroll full- or part-time at a four-year institution or university and resident of Illinois. Available to U.S. citizens.

Application Requirements: Application form, application form may be submitted online (https://www.scholarsapply.org/jamesbeard/), essay, financial need analysis, recommendations or references, transcript. *Deadline:* May 15.

Contact: Emily Rothkrug, Impact Programs Manager
Phone: 212-675-4985 Ext. 567

CHRISTIAN WOLFFER SCHOLARSHIP

Up to one $5,000 award is available to New York residents planning to enroll or currently enrolled at a licensed or accredited culinary school or wine studies program. Minimum GPA of 3.0 required.

Academic Fields/Career Goals: Culinary Arts.

Award: Scholarship for use in freshman, sophomore, junior, or senior years; not renewable. *Number:* 1. *Amount:* $5000.

Eligibility Requirements: Applicant must be enrolled or expecting to enroll full- or part-time at a two-year or four-year institution or university and resident of New York. Available to U.S. citizens.

Application Requirements: Application form, essay, financial need analysis. *Deadline:* May 15.

Contact: Scholarship Management Services
James Beard Foundation Inc.
One Scholarship Way
Saint Peter, MN 56082
Phone: 507-931-1682
E-mail: jamesbeard@scholarshipamerica.org

CONNECTONE BANK SCHOLARSHIP

Up to one scholarship of $4,250 for high school seniors or graduates who are already enrolled at least part-time in a course of study at a licensed or accredited culinary school. Must reside and/or attend school in New Jersey.

Academic Fields/Career Goals: Culinary Arts.

Award: Scholarship for use in freshman, sophomore, junior, or senior years; not renewable. *Number:* 1. *Amount:* $4250.

Eligibility Requirements: Applicant must be enrolled or expecting to enroll full- or part-time at a two-year or four-year or technical institution or university. Available to U.S. citizens.

Application Requirements: Application form, application form may be submitted online (https://www.scholarsapply.org/jamesbeard/), essay, financial need analysis, recommendations or references, transcript. *Deadline:* May 15.

Contact: Emily Rothkrug, Impact Programs Manager
Phone: 212-675-4985 Ext. 567

JAMES BEARD LEGACY SCHOLARSHIP

Up to 10 scholarships of $10,000 each for high school seniors or graduates who plan to enroll or students who are already enrolled at least part-time in a course of study at a licensed or accredited program of food or culinary studies. Must be planning to enroll or currently enrolled in a program of study for culinary arts, wine, food history, nutrition, dietetics, continuing education, food writing, food studies, or a related field. Must also demonstrate financial need.

Academic Fields/Career Goals: Culinary Arts.

Award: Scholarship for use in freshman, sophomore, junior, or senior years; not renewable. *Number:* 10. *Amount:* $10,000.

Eligibility Requirements: Applicant must be enrolled or expecting to enroll full-time at a two-year or four-year institution or university.

Application Requirements: Application form, application form may be submitted online (https://www.scholarsapply.org/jamesbeard/), essay, financial need analysis, recommendations or references, transcript. *Deadline:* May 15.

Contact: Emily Rothkrug, Impact Programs Manager
Phone: 212-675-4985 Ext. 567

MILJENKO "MIKE" GRGICH'S AMERICAN DREAM SCHOLARSHIP

Up to one $5000 award is available to students planning to enroll or currently enrolled at an accredited wine studies program.

Academic Fields/Career Goals: Culinary Arts.

Award: Scholarship for use in freshman, sophomore, junior, senior, or graduate years; not renewable. *Number:* 1. *Amount:* $5000.

Eligibility Requirements: Applicant must be enrolled or expecting to enroll full- or part-time at a four-year institution or university. Available to U.S. and non-U.S. citizens.

Application Requirements: Application form, application form may be submitted online (https://www.scholarsapply.org/jamesbeard/), essay, financial need analysis, recommendations or references, transcript. *Deadline:* May 15.

Contact: Emily Rothkrug, Impact Programs Manager
Phone: 212-675-4985 Ext. 567

PETER KUMP MEMORIAL SCHOLARSHIP

Up to 5 scholarships of $12,500 towards tuition at an accredited or licensed culinary school of student's choice. Candidates must have a minimum of one year of experience in the culinary field, demonstrate financial need, and have at least a 3.0 GPA.

Academic Fields/Career Goals: Culinary Arts.

Award: Scholarship for use in freshman year; not renewable. *Number:* 1–5. *Amount:* $12,500.

Eligibility Requirements: Applicant must be high school student and planning to enroll or expecting to enroll full- or part-time at a four-year institution or university. Available to U.S. and non-U.S. citizens.

Application Requirements: Application form, application form may be submitted online (https://www.scholarsapply.org/jamesbeard/), essay, financial need analysis, recommendations or references, transcript. *Deadline:* May 15.

Contact: Emily Rothkrug, Impact Programs Manager
Phone: 212-675-4985 Ext. 567

www.petersons.com   191

ROBERT MONDAVI WINERY MEMORIAL SCHOLARSHIP

Up to one scholarship of $10,000 for a student planning to enroll or currently enrolled in a beverage, wine studies, or hospitality management program or a Master Sommelier program at an accredited culinary school, hospitality institution, college, or university. Must be a U.S. resident, over 21 years of age, and have a high school diploma or GED.

Academic Fields/Career Goals: Culinary Arts.

Award: Scholarship for use in freshman, sophomore, junior, or senior years; not renewable. *Number:* 1. *Amount:* $10,000.

Eligibility Requirements: Applicant must be age 21 and over and enrolled or expecting to enroll full- or part-time at a two-year or four-year institution or university. Available to U.S. citizens.

Application Requirements: Application form, application form may be submitted online (https://www.scholarsapply.org/jamesbeard/), recommendations or references, transcript. *Deadline:* May 15.

Contact: Emily Rothkrug, Impact Programs Manager
  Phone: 212-675-4985 Ext. 567

STEVEN SCHER MEMORIAL SCHOLARSHIP FOR ASPIRING RESTAURANTEURS

One award of $8,000 for a student in a culinary or hospitality management program at an accredited institution. Must detail work experience, submit essay, and include a list of top three favorite restaurants and explain why they have earned that ranking. Special consideration will be given to career changers.

Academic Fields/Career Goals: Culinary Arts.

Award: Scholarship for use in freshman, sophomore, junior, or senior years; not renewable. *Number:* 1. *Amount:* $8000.

Eligibility Requirements: Applicant must be enrolled or expecting to enroll full- or part-time at a two-year or four-year institution or university. Available to U.S. citizens.

Application Requirements: Application form, essay. *Deadline:* May 15.

Contact: Scholarship Management Services
  James Beard Foundation Inc.
  One Scholarship Way
  Saint Peter, MN 56082
  Phone: 507-931-1682
  E-mail: jamesbeard@scholarshipamerica.org

TASTE AMERICA SCHOLARSHIPS

Up to 9 scholarships of $2,500 each for students residing or attending school in the states that hosted the JBF nationwide celebration of American Taste: Arizona, California, Illinois, Louisiana, Massachusetts, Kentucky, Pennsylvania, Texas, and Washington.

Academic Fields/Career Goals: Culinary Arts.

Award: Scholarship for use in freshman, sophomore, junior, or senior years; not renewable. *Number:* 1–9. *Amount:* $2500.

Eligibility Requirements: Applicant must be enrolled or expecting to enroll full- or part-time at a two-year or four-year or technical institution or university. Available to U.S. citizens.

Application Requirements: Application form, application form may be submitted online (https://www.scholarsapply.org/jamesbeard/), essay, recommendations or references, transcript. *Deadline:* May 15.

Contact: Emily Rothkrug, Impact Programs Manager
  Phone: 212-675-4985 Ext. 567

LES DAMES D'ESCOFFIER INTERNATIONAL, COLORADO CHAPTER

www.lesdamescolorado.org/scholarship

LES DAMES D'ESCOFFIER INTERNATIONAL, COLORADO CHAPTER SCHOLARSHIP

• See page 94

MAINE RESTAURANT ASSOCIATION

http://www.mainerestaurant.com/

MAINE RESTAURANT ASSOCIATION EDUCATION FOUNDATION SCHOLARSHIP FUND

Scholarship available to students (Maine Residents Only) who wish to pursue higher education in culinary arts, restaurant, and hotel or hospitality management. Preference will be given to ProStart students.

Academic Fields/Career Goals: Culinary Arts; Hospitality Management.

Award: Scholarship for use in freshman, sophomore, junior, or senior years; not renewable. *Number:* 1–8. *Amount:* $500–$2000.

Eligibility Requirements: Applicant must be enrolled or expecting to enroll full- or part-time at a two-year or four-year or technical institution or university and resident of Maine. Available to U.S. citizens.

Application Requirements: Application form, essay. *Deadline:* April 28.

Contact: Becky Jacobson, Operations Manager
  Maine Restaurant Association
  45 Melville St.
  Augusta, ME 04330
  Phone: 207-623-2178
  E-mail: becky@mainerestaurant.com

MARYLAND RESTAURANT ASSOCIATION EDUCATION FOUNDATION

https://www.marylandrestaurants.com/about.html

THE LETITIA B. CARTER SCHOLARSHIP

The Letitia B. Carter Scholarship is presented by the Restaurant Association of Maryland Education Foundation in memory of former CEO of the Restaurant Association of Maryland. This competitive scholarship is awarded to Maryland residents interested in pursuing hospitality-related coursework. It is available to high school students and college students as well as high school, college or corporate instructors and current hospitality industry professionals. ($500 - $2000 scholarship pool)

Academic Fields/Career Goals: Culinary Arts; Food Science/Nutrition; Food Service/Hospitality; Hospitality Management.

Award: Scholarship for use in freshman, sophomore, junior, or senior years; not renewable. *Number:* 1. *Amount:* $500–$2000.

Eligibility Requirements: Applicant must be age 17 and over; enrolled or expecting to enroll full- or part-time at a two-year or four-year or technical institution or university and resident of Maryland. Applicant or parent of applicant must have employment or volunteer experience in food service, hospitality/hotel administration/operations. Available to U.S. citizens.

Application Requirements: Application form, essay. *Deadline:* March 16.

Contact: Jessica Waller, Executive Director
  Maryland Restaurant Association Education Foundation
  6301 Hillside Court
  Columbia, MD 21046
  Phone: 410-290-6800 Ext. 1025
  Fax: 410-290-6882
  E-mail: jwaller@marylandrestaurants.com

MARCIA S. HARRIS LEGACY FUND SCHOLARSHIP

The Marcia S. Harris Legacy Fund Scholarship is presented by the Restaurant Association of Maryland in memory of Marcia S. Harris former CEO of the Restaurant Association of Maryland for more than 20 years. Marcia had a love for life and a love for the foodservice industry that stood out even in the largest crowds. Her passion and dedication to promoting, protecting and improving the foodservice industry is what drove her day in and day out. Applicants should also possess the qualities of passion and dedication and have a strong desire to improve the foodservice industry through the personal pursuit of professionalism. ($500 - $2000 scholarship pool)

Academic Fields/Career Goals: Culinary Arts; Food Science/Nutrition; Food Service/Hospitality; Hospitality Management.

Award: Scholarship for use in freshman, sophomore, junior, or senior years; not renewable. *Number:* 1. *Amount:* $500–$2000.

Eligibility Requirements: Applicant must be age 17 and over; enrolled or expecting to enroll full- or part-time at a two-year or four-year or technical institution or university and resident of Maryland. Available to U.S. citizens.

Application Requirements: Application form, essay. *Deadline:* March 16.

Contact: Jessica Waller, Executive Director
Maryland Restaurant Association Education Foundation
6301 Hillside Court
Columbia, MD 21046
Phone: 410-290-6800 Ext. 1025
Fax: 410-290-6882
E-mail: jwaller@marylandrestaurants.com

NATIONAL RESTAURANT ASSOCIATION EDUCATIONAL FOUNDATION

http://www.chooserestaurants.org

NATIONAL RESTAURANT ASSOCIATION EDUCATIONAL FOUNDATION UNDERGRADUATE SCHOLARSHIPS FOR COLLEGE STUDENTS
• *See page 95*

PROFESSIONAL REPS

http://www.professionalreps.com/

HUNGRY TO LEAD SCHOLARSHIP

Those eligible to apply are high school seniors, or college students registered/pre-registered to attend an accredited school in the United States. Applicant must be pursuing a degree in a foodservice/hospitality program, or directly related. The scholarship is merit based on high school records, ACT and/or SAT scores, college transcripts if applicable, and extracurricular activities. Minimum requirements as follows: high school or college cumulative GPA of 2.5, SAT of 1300, or ACT of 18. Applicants will also be judged on their ability to demonstrate leadership capabilities. Top four finalists will be awarded scholarships in the following order: first place, The Amana Leadership Scholarship ($2,500); second place, The Hungry To Lead Scholarship ($1,500); third place, Leadership Recognition Award ($500); fourth place, Leadership Recognition Award ($500)

Academic Fields/Career Goals: Culinary Arts; Food Science/Nutrition; Food Service/Hospitality.

Award: Scholarship for use in freshman, sophomore, junior, or senior years; not renewable. *Number:* 4. *Amount:* $500–$2500.

Eligibility Requirements: Applicant must be enrolled or expecting to enroll full-time at a two-year or four-year or technical institution or university. Available to U.S. and non-U.S. citizens.

Application Requirements: Application form, essay. *Deadline:* July 1.

Contact: Tessa Bucklin
Professional Reps
750 E. Covey Lane #110
Phoenix, AZ 85024
Phone: 877-995-8922
E-mail: scholarships@professionalreps.com

SOUTH CAROLINA RESTAURANT AND LODGING ASSOCIATION

http://www.scrla.org/

SOUTH CAROLINA TOURISM AND HOSPITALITY EDUCATIONAL FOUNDATION SCHOLARSHIPS

The South Carolina Restaurant and Lodging Educational Foundation (SCRLEF) manages scholarships on behalf of a variety of organizations that support hospitality education. These scholarships are designed to assist students who demonstrate an interest in and commitment to the hospitality (restaurant, foodservice, lodging, tourism) industry.

Academic Fields/Career Goals: Culinary Arts; Food Service/Hospitality; Hospitality Management.

Award: Scholarship for use in freshman, sophomore, junior, or senior years; not renewable. *Number:* 5–16. *Amount:* $750–$2500.

Eligibility Requirements: Applicant must be enrolled or expecting to enroll full-time at a two-year or four-year or technical institution or university; resident of South Carolina and studying in South Carolina. Available to U.S. citizens.

Application Requirements: Application form, essay. *Deadline:* May 1.

Contact: Douglas OFlaherty, Vice President
South Carolina Restaurant and Lodging Association
PO Box 7577
Columbia, SC 29202
Phone: 803-765-9000

SUPPORT CREATIVITY

http://wesupportcreativity.org

SUPPORT CREATIVITY SCHOLARSHIP
• *See page 117*

TEXAS RESTAURANT ASSOCIATION

http://www.restaurantville.com/

W. PRICE, JR. MEMORIAL SCHOLARSHIP

Each year the Texas Restaurant Association awards the W. Price Jr. Memorial Scholarship to students with a growing passion for the foodservice industry. The scholarship is named for W. Price Jr., the first executive director of the Texas Restaurant Association who served from 1953 until 1974. Seven scholarships of $1,000 are awarded to students graduating high school or those currently enrolled in a postsecondary culinary programs.

Academic Fields/Career Goals: Culinary Arts; Food Service/Hospitality.

Award: Scholarship for use in freshman, sophomore, junior, senior, or graduate years; not renewable. *Number:* 5–7. *Amount:* $1000.

Eligibility Requirements: Applicant must be enrolled or expecting to enroll full-time at a two-year or four-year institution or university and resident of Texas. Applicant or parent of applicant must have employment or volunteer experience in food service, hospitality/hotel administration/operations. Available to U.S. citizens.

Application Requirements: Application form, essay. *Deadline:* February 15.

Contact: Jerrica Deloney, Program Manager
Texas Restaurant Association
PO Box 1429
Austin, TX 78767
Phone: 800-395-2872
E-mail: foundation@tramail.org

UNITED NEGRO COLLEGE FUND

http://www.uncf.org/

UNCF/CARNIVAL CORPORATE SCHOLARS PROGRAM
• *See page 151*

WISCONSIN BAKERS ASSOCIATION (WBA)

http://www.wibakers.com/

ROBERT W. HILLER SCHOLARSHIP FUND

Scholarship of $1000 awarded for students at all levels in a baking/pastry arts-related program that prepares candidates for a retail baking profession. Minimum 2.85 GPA required.

Academic Fields/Career Goals: Culinary Arts; Food Science/Nutrition; Food Service/Hospitality.

Award: Scholarship for use in freshman, sophomore, junior, senior, graduate, or postgraduate years; not renewable. *Amount:* $1000.

Eligibility Requirements: Applicant must be enrolled or expecting to enroll full-time at a two-year or four-year institution or university. Available to U.S. citizens.

Application Requirements: Application form, essay. *Deadline:* December 1.

Contact: Jessica Hoover
  Phone: 414-258-5552
  Fax: 414-258-5582
  E-mail: jessica@wibakers.com

WBA SCHOLARSHIP

The Wisconsin Bakers Association's education committee submitted recommendations to the Board of Governors on Oct. 24, 1983, to implement the WBA Scholarship Program. The first scholarship awards were later presented in 1984. Since then, the WBA has awarded more than $25,000 in WBA Scholarships! Wisconsin residents only can apply for the WBA Scholarship.

Academic Fields/Career Goals: Culinary Arts; Food Science/Nutrition; Food Service/Hospitality.

Award: Scholarship for use in freshman, sophomore, junior, senior, graduate, or postgraduate years; not renewable.

Eligibility Requirements: Applicant must be enrolled or expecting to enroll full- or part-time at a two-year or four-year or technical institution or university and resident of Wisconsin. Available to U.S. citizens.

Application Requirements: Application form, essay, interview. *Deadline:* continuous.

Contact: Jessica Hoover
  Phone: 414-258-5552
  Fax: 414-258-5582
  E-mail: jessica@wibakers.com

WOMEN CHEFS AND RESTAURATEURS

http://www.womenchefs.org/

FRENCH CULINARY INSTITUTE/ITALIAN CULINARY EXPERIENCE SCHOLARSHIP

Scholarship intended for a culinary student wishing to specialize in Italian cuisine. Recipient must be a new enrollment and satisfy all entrance requirements of the FCI. Scholarship award is applied to total program fee.

Academic Fields/Career Goals: Culinary Arts; Food Service/Hospitality.

Award: Scholarship for use in freshman, sophomore, junior, senior, graduate, or postgraduate years; not renewable. *Number:* 1. *Amount:* $5000.

Eligibility Requirements: Applicant must be enrolled or expecting to enroll full-time at a four-year institution or university. Available to U.S. and non-U.S. citizens.

Application Requirements: Application form, essay. *Fee:* $25. *Deadline:* March 31.

Contact: Dori Sacksteder, Director of Programs
  Phone: 502-581-0300 Ext. 219
  Fax: 502-589-3602
  E-mail: dsacksteder@hqtrs.com

DENTAL HEALTH/ SERVICES

101ST AIRBORNE DIVISION ASSOCIATION

http://www.screamingeaglefoundation.org/

AL & WILLIAMARY VISTE SCHOLARSHIP
• *See page 99*

ACLS CERTIFICATION INSTITUTE

https://acls.com

MEDICAL SCHOOL SCHOLARSHIP

It's no secret that medical school is stressful. Between demanding course work and long hours, many students don't have the time of resources to care for their overall well-being. Long periods of stress predisposes students for depression and anxiety. This cycle frequently continues after medical school. Roughly 1 physician commits suicide per day. It is our goal to combat this trend by improving student wellness and removing the stigma around mental health treatment. Award amount of $2,500. Post a video creatively responding to the following prompt: How would you improve student wellness? i.e.: a system you would change, a service/program that would be helpful? Videos should be 30-45 second in length. Upload the video to YouTube and submit the link with your application. Each video should include a brief description with a link to https://acls.com/scholarship and the hashtag #studentwellnessscholarship. Each video must be original. Share the scholarship page on Facebook with the hashtag #studentwellnessscholarship. Complete the application including the student survey. Open to students currently enrolled or accepted to medical school, dental school, or nursing school. Student must be a legal resident of and currently living in the United States. Winner is not based on financial need. Relatives of employees and employees of ACLS Certification Institute and its affiliates are ineligible. Applicant must complete all steps of the application process to be considered.

Academic Fields/Career Goals: Dental Health/Services; Health and Medical Sciences; Nursing; Radiology.

Award: Scholarship for use in freshman, sophomore, junior, senior, or graduate years; not renewable. *Number:* 1. *Amount:* $2500.

Eligibility Requirements: Applicant must be enrolled or expecting to enroll full- or part-time at a two-year or four-year or technical institution or university. Available to U.S. citizens.

Application Requirements: Application form. *Deadline:* November 30.

ALBERTA HERITAGE SCHOLARSHIP FUND

http://www.alis.alberta.ca/

ABORIGINAL HEALTH CAREERS BURSARY
• *See page 139*

AMERICAN ACADEMY OF ORAL & MAXILLOFACIAL RADIOLOGY

http://www.aaomr.org/

CHARLES R. MORRIS STUDENT RESEARCH AWARD

Award to applicants from accredited programs performing research in oral and maxillofacial radiology. Applicant must be a full-time undergraduate or predoctoral student at the time of research, be nominated by the institution where research was carried out, and submit a manuscript detailing the research project.

Academic Fields/Career Goals: Dental Health/Services.

Award: Grant for use in junior, senior, or graduate years; not renewable. *Number:* 1. *Amount:* $1000.

Eligibility Requirements: Applicant must be enrolled or expecting to enroll full-time at an institution or university. Available to U.S. and non-U.S. citizens.

Application Requirements: Application form, application form may be submitted online. *Deadline:* June 12.

Contact: Dr. Aruna Ramesh, Awards Committee Chair
  E-mail: aruna.ramesh@tufts.edu

AMERICAN DENTAL ASSOCIATION (ADA) FOUNDATION

http://www.adafoundation.org/

AMERICAN DENTAL ASSOCIATION FOUNDATION DENTAL HYGIENE SCHOLARSHIP PROGRAM

Applicant must be enrolled full-time with a minimum of 12 Credit hours as a student in an accredited dental hygiene program accredited by the Commission of Dental Accreditation of the American Dental Association. Must be U.S. citizen, permanent resident is ineligible to apply. Must have a minimum 3.5 GPA on a 4.0 scale. Applicants must be recommended by the dental hygiene program director and may request application materials from that same individual at the school where they are currently enrolled as an entering final year student in a dental hygiene program. Applicants must demonstrate a minimum financial need of $1000.

Academic Fields/Career Goals: Dental Health/Services.

Award: Scholarship for use in senior year; not renewable. *Number:* up to 15. *Amount:* up to $1000.

Eligibility Requirements: Applicant must be enrolled or expecting to enroll full-time at a four-year institution or university. Available to U.S. citizens.

Application Requirements: Application form, essay, financial need analysis, recommendations or references. *Deadline:* April 23.

Contact: Rose Famularo, Coordinator
Phone: 312-440-2763
E-mail: famularor@ada.org

AMERICAN DENTAL ASSOCIATION FOUNDATION DENTAL STUDENT SCHOLARSHIP PROGRAM

One-time award for entering second-year students at a dental school accredited by the American Dental Association Commission on Dental Accreditation. Must have 3.0 GPA, and be enrolled full-time (minimum of 12 hours). Must show financial need and be a U.S. citizen, a permanent resident is ineligible to apply. Applicants may request application materials from associate dean for student affairs at the dental school where they are currently enrolled. An applicant must be recommended to the ADA Foundation by the school official.

Academic Fields/Career Goals: Dental Health/Services.

Award: Scholarship for use in sophomore year; not renewable. *Number:* up to 25. *Amount:* up to $2500.

Eligibility Requirements: Applicant must be enrolled or expecting to enroll full-time at a four-year institution or university. Available to U.S. citizens.

Application Requirements: Application form, essay, financial need analysis, recommendations or references. *Deadline:* October 4.

Contact: Rose Famularo, Coordinator
Phone: 312-440-2763
E-mail: famularor@ada.org

AMERICAN DENTAL HYGIENISTS' ASSOCIATION (ADHA) INSTITUTE FOR ORAL HEALTH

https://www.adha.org/

JOHNSON & JOHNSON SCHOLARSHIP

These scholarships are awarded to applicants pursuing a certificate/associate or baccalaureate degree in dental hygiene and have completed a minimum of one year in a dental hygiene curriculum.

Academic Fields/Career Goals: Dental Health/Services.

Award: Scholarship for use in sophomore, junior, or senior years; not renewable. *Number:* 5. *Amount:* $1000.

Eligibility Requirements: Applicant must be enrolled or expecting to enroll full-time at a two-year or four-year institution or university. Available to U.S. citizens.

Application Requirements: Application form, essay. *Deadline:* February 1.

Contact: Kelsey Turner, Awards
American Dental Hygienists' Association (ADHA) Institute For Oral Health
444 North Michigan Avenue
Suite 400
Chicago, IL 60611
Phone: 312-440-8937
E-mail: kelseyt@adha.net

AMERICAN INDIAN SCIENCE AND ENGINEERING SOCIETY

http://www.aises.org/

A.T. ANDERSON MEMORIAL SCHOLARSHIP PROGRAM
• See page 105

AMERICAN LEGION AUXILIARY DEPARTMENT OF COLORADO

http://www.alacolorado.com

AMERICAN LEGION AUXILIARY DEPARTMENT OF COLORADO PAST PRESIDENTS' PARLEY HEALTH CARE PROFESSIONAL SCHOLARSHIPNURSES SCHOLARSHIP
• See page 125

ASSISTANCE LEAGUE OF THE TRIANGLE AREA

HEALTH CARE PROFESSION SCHOLARSHIP

Students must be residents of Wake, Durham, or Orange Counties in North Carolina and be attending a school in North Carolina.

Academic Fields/Career Goals: Dental Health/Services; Environmental Health; Food Science/Nutrition; Health Administration; Health and Medical Sciences; Health Information Management/Technology; Nursing; Occupational Safety and Health; Pharmacy; Psychology; Public Health; Radiology; Therapy/Rehabilitation.

Award: Scholarship for use in freshman, sophomore, junior, or senior years; not renewable. *Number:* 1–5. *Amount:* $1000–$10,000.

Eligibility Requirements: Applicant must be enrolled or expecting to enroll full- or part-time at a two-year or four-year or technical institution or university; resident of North Carolina and studying in North Carolina. Available to U.S. citizens.

Application Requirements: Application form, community service, essay, financial need analysis. *Deadline:* March 1.

Contact: Grace Fox
E-mail: altascholars@gmail.com

ASSOCIATION ON AMERICAN INDIAN AFFAIRS, INC.

http://www.indian-affairs.org/

ELIZABETH AND SHERMAN ASCHE MEMORIAL SCHOLARSHIP FUND
• See page 93

AVACARE MEDICAL

https://avacaremedical.com

AVACARE MEDICAL SCHOLARSHIP
• See page 100

BETHESDA LUTHERAN COMMUNITIES

http://www.bethesdalutherancommunities.org/scholarships

DEVELOPMENTAL DISABILITIES SCHOLASTIC ACHIEVEMENT SCHOLARSHIP FOR COLLEGE STUDENTS WHO ARE LUTHERAN

One-time award for Lutheran students who are currently enrolled in studies related to developmental disabilities. Awards of up to $3000. 3.0 GPA required.

Academic Fields/Career Goals: Dental Health/Services; Education; Health Administration; Health and Medical Sciences; Health Information Management/Technology; Humanities; Religion/Theology; Social Services; Special Education; Therapy/Rehabilitation.

Award: Scholarship for use in freshman, sophomore, junior, or senior years; not renewable. *Number:* 2–3. *Amount:* $500–$3000.

Eligibility Requirements: Applicant must be Lutheran and enrolled or expecting to enroll full-time at a four-year institution or university. Available to U.S. citizens.

Application Requirements: Application form, community service, essay. *Deadline:* May 1.

Contact: Barb Schultz, Program Coordinator
Bethesda Lutheran Communities
600 Hoffmann Drive
Watertown, WI 53094-6294
Phone: 920-206-4427
E-mail: barb.schultz@mailblc.org

BHW GROUP

https://thebhwgroup.com/

BHW WOMEN IN STEM SCHOLARSHIP
• *See page 107*

CARDS AGAINST HUMANITY

https://cardsagainsthumanity.com/

SCIENCE AMBASSADOR SCHOLARSHIP
• *See page 107*

CONTINENTAL SOCIETY, DAUGHTERS OF INDIAN WARS

http://www.csdiw.org/

CONTINENTAL SOCIETY, DAUGHTERS OF INDIAN WARS SCHOLARSHIP
• *See page 188*

DDSRANK

https://www.ddsrank.com

DDSRANK DENTAL SCHOLARSHIP
The DDSRank Dental Scholarship is awarded to one aspiring dental student to help them pay for the cost of tuition or books.

Academic Fields/Career Goals: Dental Health/Services.

Award: Scholarship for use in freshman, sophomore, junior, senior, or graduate years; not renewable. *Number:* 1. *Amount:* $500.

Eligibility Requirements: Applicant must be enrolled or expecting to enroll full-time at a four-year institution or university. Available to U.S. citizens.

Application Requirements: Essay. *Deadline:* September 23.

Contact: Scholarship Administrator
E-mail: scholarships@ddsrank.com

THE EXPERT INSTITUTE

https://www.theexpertinstitute.com

ANNUAL HEALTHCARE AND LIFE SCIENCES SCHOLARSHIP
• *See page 142*

HEALTH PROFESSIONS EDUCATION FOUNDATION

http://www.healthprofessions.ca.gov/

ALLIED HEALTHCARE SCHOLARSHIP PROGRAM
One-time award available to students enrolled in, or accepted to California accredited allied health education programs. Scholarship worth up to $8000. Deadlines: check website http://oshpd.ca.gov/HPEF. Must be resident of California. Must have GPA 2.0 or greater.

Academic Fields/Career Goals: Dental Health/Services; Health and Medical Sciences; Pharmacy; Psychology; Radiology; Social Services; Therapy/Rehabilitation.

Award: Scholarship for use in freshman, sophomore, junior, senior, graduate, or postgraduate years; not renewable. *Amount:* $8000.

Eligibility Requirements: Applicant must be enrolled or expecting to enroll full- or part-time at a two-year or technical institution or university; resident of British Columbia and studying in California. Available to U.S. citizens.

Application Requirements: Application form, application form may be submitted online, community service, driver's license, financial need analysis. *Deadline:* February 23.

Contact: Caryn Rizell, Interim Executive Director
Phone: 916-326-3640
Fax: 916-324-6585
E-mail: Caryn.Rizell@oshpd.ca.gov

HISPANIC DENTAL ASSOCIATION FOUNDATION

http://www.hdassoc.org/

DR. JUAN D. VILLARREAL/HISPANIC DENTAL ASSOCIATION FOUNDATION
Scholarship offered to Hispanic U.S. students who have been accepted into or are currently enrolled in an accredited dental or dental hygiene program in the state of Texas. Scholarship will obligate the grantees to complete the current year of their dental or dental hygiene program. Scholastic achievement, leadership skills, community service and commitment to improving the health of the Hispanic community will all be considered. Must be a current member of the Hispanic Dental Association.

Academic Fields/Career Goals: Dental Health/Services.

Award: Scholarship for use in freshman, sophomore, junior, or senior years; not renewable. *Number:* up to 3. *Amount:* $500–$1000.

Eligibility Requirements: Applicant must be of Hispanic heritage; enrolled or expecting to enroll full-time at a two-year or four-year institution or university; resident of Texas and studying in Texas. Available to U.S. citizens.

Application Requirements: Application form, essay, recommendations or references, transcript. *Deadline:* June 1.

Contact: David Pena, Executive Director
Hispanic Dental Association Foundation
1111 14th Street
Suite 1100
Washington, DC 20005
Phone: 202-629-3726
E-mail: dpena@hdassoc.org

PROCTOR AND GAMBLE ORAL CARE AND HDA FOUNDATION SCHOLARSHIP
Scholarships available to Hispanic students entering into their first year of an accredited dental, dental hygiene, dental assisting, or dental technician program. Scholastic achievement, community service, leadership, and commitment to improving health of the Hispanic community will all be considered. Must be member of the Hispanic Dental Association.

Academic Fields/Career Goals: Dental Health/Services.

Award: Scholarship for use in freshman year; not renewable. *Number:* up to 15. *Amount:* up to $1000.

Eligibility Requirements: Applicant must be high school student and planning to enroll or expecting to enroll full-time at a two-year or four-year or technical institution or university. Available to U.S. citizens.

Application Requirements: Application form, community service, essay, recommendations or references, transcript. *Deadline:* June 1.

Contact: David Pena, Executive Director
Hispanic Dental Association Foundation
1111 14th Street
Suite 1100
Washington, DC 20005
Phone: 202-629-6108
E-mail: dpena@hdassoc.org

INTERMOUNTAIN MEDICAL IMAGING

https://www.aboutimi.com/

INTERMOUNTAIN MEDICAL IMAGING SCHOLARSHIP
• *See page 125*

INTERNATIONAL ORDER OF THE KING'S DAUGHTERS AND SONS

http://www.iokds.org/

HEALTH CAREERS SCHOLARSHIP

Award for students preparing for careers in medicine, dentistry, pharmacy, physical or occupational therapy, and medical technologies. Must be a U.S. or Canadian citizen, enrolled full-time in a school accredited in the field involved and located in the U.S. or Canada. For all students, except those preparing for an RN degree, application must be for at least the third year of college. RN students must have completed the first year of schooling. Premedicine students are not eligible to apply. For those students seeking degrees of MD or DDS application must be for at least the second year of medical or dental school. Each applicant must supply proof of acceptance in the school involved.

Academic Fields/Career Goals: Dental Health/Services; Health and Medical Sciences; Nursing; Therapy/Rehabilitation.

Award: Scholarship for use in junior, senior, or graduate years; not renewable. *Number:* 20–30. *Amount:* $500–$1000.

Eligibility Requirements: Applicant must be enrolled or expecting to enroll full-time at a four-year institution or university. Available to U.S. and Canadian citizens.

Application Requirements: Application form, essay, itemized budget, recommendations or references, resume, self-addressed stamped envelope with application, transcript. *Deadline:* April 1.

Contact: Director, Health Careers Department
International Order of The King's Daughters and Sons
PO Box 1017
Chautauqua, NY 14722-1017
Phone: 716-357-4951

MEDICAL SCRUBS COLLECTION

http://medicalscrubscollection.com

MEDICAL SCRUBS COLLECTION SCHOLARSHIP
• *See page 104*

NATIONAL DENTAL ASSOCIATION FOUNDATION

http://www.ndaonline.org/

NATIONAL DENTAL ASSOCIATION FOUNDATION COLGATE-PALMOLIVE SCHOLARSHIP PROGRAM (UNDERGRADUATES)

A scholarship of up to $1000 is given to sophomores through juniors in a dental school who are under-represented minority students. Applicants should be a member of NDA. Number of scholarships granted varies.

Academic Fields/Career Goals: Dental Health/Services.

Award: Scholarship for use in sophomore, junior, or senior years; not renewable. *Number:* up to 100. *Amount:* $700–$1000.

Eligibility Requirements: Applicant must be American Indian/Alaska Native, Asian/Pacific Islander, Black (non-Hispanic), Hispanic and enrolled or expecting to enroll full-time at a four-year institution or university. Available to U.S. citizens.

Application Requirements: Application form, financial need analysis, letter of request, recommendations or references, resume, transcript. *Deadline:* May 15.

Contact: Roosevelt Brown, President
Phone: 501-681-6110
Fax: 541-376-4008
E-mail: rbndaf1@comcast.net

NOVUS BIOLOGICALS, LLC

https://www.novusbio.com

NOVUS BIOLOGICALS SCHOLARSHIP PROGRAM
• *See page 101*

R&D SYSTEMS SCHOLARSHIP
• *See page 101*

TOCRIS BIOSCIENCE SCHOLARSHIP
• *See page 102*

PLATINUM EDUCATIONAL GROUP

www.platinumed.com

PLATINUM EDUCATIONAL GROUP SCHOLARSHIPS PROGRAM FOR EMS, NURSING, AND ALLIED HEALTH
• *See page 102*

THE RECOVERY VILLAGE

https://www.therecoveryvillage.com/

RECOVERY VILLAGE HEALTHCARE SCHOLARSHIP

A $500 award will be given to a student pursuing a health-related degree program. Areas of study that will be considered include, but are not limited to, counseling, social work, emergency medicine, pre-med, nursing, psychology (with a focus on addiction counseling or a substance-abuse related field). In order to be eligible, students must meet the following criteria: U.S. citizen or permanent U.S. resident; enrolled or accepted in an accredited college or university and plan to continue enrollment; graduating high school seniors who meet the above criteria are encouraged to apply; consent to a talent release, and will provide a digital photograph and quote for display on ARS websites if notified as the winner. Selection will be based upon completed of application, originality (20%), creativity (20%), writing skills (20%), inspiration (20%), and demonstrated interest in addiction treatment and recovery (20%). The winner will be notified following the deadline and the award will be credited to the student's school. Certain information must be provided by the student to The Recovery Village in order for the school to receive the funds.

Academic Fields/Career Goals: Dental Health/Services; Nursing; Occupational Safety and Health; Psychology; Public Health; Public Policy and Administration; Therapy/Rehabilitation.

Award: Scholarship for use in freshman, sophomore, junior, senior, graduate, or postgraduate years; not renewable. *Number:* 1–2. *Amount:* $1–$1000.

Eligibility Requirements: Applicant must be enrolled or expecting to enroll full- or part-time at a two-year or four-year institution or university. Applicant or parent of applicant must have employment or volunteer experience in occupational health and safety. Available to U.S. citizens.

Application Requirements: Application form, essay. *Deadline:* June 30.
Contact: Amy Campbell
E-mail: amy.campbell@laneterralever.com

SCARLETT FAMILY FOUNDATION SCHOLARSHIP PROGRAM

http://www.scarlettfoundation.org/

SCHOLARSHIP FOR STUDENTS PURSUING A BUSINESS OR STEM DEGREE
• *See page 80*

STANLEY DENTISTRY

http://www.stanleysmiles.com

STANLEY DENTISTRY SCHOLARSHIP FUND

Drs. Robert and Bobbi Stanley have created a merit-based scholarship fund for individuals seeking undergraduate or graduate-level education in dentistry or related fields. The scholarship will be in the amount of $500 for the 2019 academic year. The scholarship will be awarded based on academic excellence, the pursuit of further study in dentistry at an accredited college or university in North Carolina, and genuine passion for further study. The scholarship will last for the duration of one year and be paid directly to the winning candidate to use towards tuition and board.

Academic Fields/Career Goals: Dental Health/Services.

Award: Scholarship for use in freshman, sophomore, junior, senior, graduate, or postgraduate years; not renewable. *Number:* 1. *Amount:* $500.

Eligibility Requirements: Applicant must be enrolled or expecting to enroll full-time at a two-year or four-year institution or university and studying in North Carolina. Available to U.S. citizens.

Application Requirements: Application form. *Deadline:* March 15.

Contact: Catherine Shireman, Scholarship Coordinator
Stanley Dentistry
3731 NW Cary Parkway
Suite 201
Cary, NC 27513
Phone: 919-371-4454
E-mail: catherine@stanleysmiles.com

STRAIGHTFORWARD MEDIA

http://www.straightforwardmedia.com/

STRAIGHTFORWARD MEDIA MEDICAL PROFESSIONS SCHOLARSHIP

Scholarship of $500 available to full-time students in any health-related field. Awarded four times per year. Deadlines: March 31, June 30, September 30, and December 31.

Academic Fields/Career Goals: Dental Health/Services; Environmental Health; Health Administration; Health and Medical Sciences; Health Information Management/Technology; Nursing; Occupational Safety and Health; Oncology; Optometry; Osteopathy; Pharmacy; Therapy/Rehabilitation.

Award: Scholarship for use in freshman, sophomore, junior, or senior years; not renewable. *Number:* 4. *Amount:* $500.

Eligibility Requirements: Applicant must be enrolled or expecting to enroll full- or part-time at a two-year or four-year or technical institution or university. Available to U.S. and non-U.S. citizens.

Application Requirements: Essay. *Deadline:* varies.

Contact: Scholarship Committee
Phone: 605-348-3042

SUPREME GUARDIAN COUNCIL, INTERNATIONAL ORDER OF JOB'S DAUGHTERS

http://www.iojd.org/

GROTTO SCHOLARSHIP

Scholarships of $1500 to aid Job's Daughters students of outstanding ability whom have a sincerity of purpose. High school seniors, or graduates, junior college, technical school, or college students who are in early graduation programs, and pursuing an education in dentistry, preferably with some training in the handicapped field are eligible to apply.

Academic Fields/Career Goals: Dental Health/Services.

Award: Scholarship for use in freshman, sophomore, junior, senior, graduate, or postgraduate years; not renewable. *Number:* 1. *Amount:* $1500.

Eligibility Requirements: Applicant must be age 18-30; enrolled or expecting to enroll full- or part-time at a two-year or four-year or technical institution or university and single female. Applicant or parent of applicant must be member of Jobs Daughters. Available to U.S. and non-U.S. citizens.

Application Requirements: Application form, community service, essay, recommendations or references, transcript. *Deadline:* April 30.

Contact: Christal Bindrich, Scholarship Committee Chairman
Supreme Guardian Council, International Order of Job's
Daughters
5351 South Butterfield Way
Greenfield, WI 53221
Phone: 414-423-0016
E-mail: christalbindrich@wi.rr.com

DRAFTING

AMERICAN SOCIETY OF CERTIFIED ENGINEERING TECHNICIANS

http://www.ascet.org/

KURT H. AND DONNA M. SCHULER SMALL GRANT
• See page 162

MIDWEST ROOFING CONTRACTORS ASSOCIATION

http://www.mrca.org/

MRCA FOUNDATION SCHOLARSHIP PROGRAM
• See page 116

NASA'S VIRGINIA SPACE GRANT CONSORTIUM

http://www.vsgc.odu.edu/

COMMUNITY COLLEGE STEM SCHOLARSHIPS
• See page 110

NATIONAL ASSOCIATION OF WOMEN IN CONSTRUCTION

http://www.nawic.org/

NAWIC UNDERGRADUATE SCHOLARSHIPS
• See page 117

ONLINE LOGO MAKER

http://onlinelogomaker.com

OLM MALALA YOUSAFZAI SCHOLARSHIP 2017-2018
• See page 122

PROFESSIONAL CONSTRUCTION ESTIMATORS ASSOCIATION

http://www.pcea.org/

TED G. WILSON MEMORIAL SCHOLARSHIP FOUNDATION
• See page 166

SUPPORT CREATIVITY

http://wesupportcreativity.org

SUPPORT CREATIVITY SCHOLARSHIP
• See page 117

VECTORWORKS, INC.

http://www.vectorworks.net

VECTORWORKS DESIGN SCHOLARSHIP
• See page 117

EARTH SCIENCE

AEG FOUNDATION

http://www.aegfoundation.org/

AEG FOUNDATION MARLIAVE FUND

One-time award to support undergraduate and graduate students studying engineering geology and geological engineering.

Academic Fields/Career Goals: Earth Science; Engineering/Technology; Science, Technology, and Society.

Award: Scholarship for use in senior or graduate years; not renewable. *Number:* 1. *Amount:* $4000.

Eligibility Requirements: Applicant must be enrolled or expecting to enroll full-time at a four-year institution or university. Available to U.S. and Canadian citizens.

Application Requirements: Application form, application form may be submitted online (http://www.aegfoundation.org), essay, recommendations or references, resume, transcript. *Deadline:* February 1.

Contact: Becky Roland, Executive Director
AEG Foundation
PO Box 460518
Denver, CO 80246
Phone: 303-757-2926
Fax: 720-230-4846
E-mail: staff@aegfoundation.org

TILFORD FIELD STUDIES SCHOLARSHIP

Scholarship of $1000 for student members of AEG. Three to four awards are granted annually. For undergraduate students, the scholarship goes toward the cost of a geology field camp course or senior thesis field research. For graduate students, the scholarship would apply to field research.

Academic Fields/Career Goals: Earth Science.

Award: Scholarship for use in freshman, sophomore, junior, senior, graduate, or postgraduate years; not renewable. *Number:* 4–5. *Amount:* $500–$2500.

Eligibility Requirements: Applicant must be enrolled or expecting to enroll full-time at a four-year institution or university. Applicant or parent of applicant must be member of Association of Engineering Geologists. Available to U.S. and non-U.S. citizens.

Application Requirements: Application form, application form may be submitted online (http://www.aegfoundation.org), essay, recommendations or references, resume, transcript. *Deadline:* February 1.

Contact: Becky Roland, AEG Foundation
AEG Foundation
PO Box 460518
Denver, CO 80246
Phone: 303-757-2926
Fax: 720-230-4846
E-mail: staff@aegfoundation.org

ALASKA GEOLOGICAL SOCIETY INC.

http://www.alaskageology.org/

ALASKA GEOLOGICAL SOCIETY SCHOLARSHIP

Scholarship available for a full-time junior or senior undergraduate or graduate student enrolled at any college or university with academic emphasis in earth sciences. Student must have a project based in Alaska or on a topic directly related to Alaskan geology.

Academic Fields/Career Goals: Earth Science.

Award: Scholarship for use in junior, senior, or graduate years; not renewable. *Number:* 3–8. *Amount:* $500–$2500.

Eligibility Requirements: Applicant must be enrolled or expecting to enroll full-time at a four-year institution or university and studying in Alaska. Available to U.S. and non-U.S. citizens.

Application Requirements: Application form, essay. *Deadline:* February 1.

Contact: Susan Karl, Chair of Scholarship Committee
Alaska Geological Society Inc.
Alaska Geological Society
PO Box 101288
Anchorage, AK 99510
Phone: 907-786-7428
E-mail: skarl@usgs.gov

AMERICAN GROUND WATER TRUST

http://www.agwt.org/

AMERICAN GROUND WATER TRUST-AMTROL INC. SCHOLARSHIP

Award for college/university entry-level students intending to pursue a career in ground water-related field. Must either have completed a science/environmental project involving ground water resources or have had vacation work experience related to the environment and natural resources. Must be U.S. citizen or legal resident with minimum 3.0 GPA. Submit two letters of recommendation and transcript.

Academic Fields/Career Goals: Earth Science; Hydrology; Natural Resources.

Award: Scholarship for use in freshman year; not renewable. *Number:* 2. *Amount:* $1500.

Eligibility Requirements: Applicant must be enrolled or expecting to enroll full-time at a four-year institution or university. Available to U.S. citizens.

Application Requirements: Application form, essay. *Deadline:* June 1.

Contact: Andrew Stone, Executive Director
American Ground Water Trust
50 Pleasant Street, Suite 2
Concord, NH 03301-4073
Phone: 603-228-5444
E-mail: trustinfo@agwt.org

AMERICAN GROUND WATER TRUST-BAROID SCHOLARSHIP

Award for entry-level students intending to pursue a career in ground water-related field. Must either have completed a science/environmental project involving ground water resources or have had vacation work experience related to the environment and natural resources. Must be a U.S. citizen or legal resident with minimum 3.0 GPA. Submit two letters of recommendation and transcript.

Academic Fields/Career Goals: Earth Science; Hydrology; Natural Resources.

Award: Scholarship for use in freshman year; not renewable. *Number:* 1. *Amount:* $2000.

Eligibility Requirements: Applicant must be enrolled or expecting to enroll full-time at a four-year institution or university. Available to U.S. citizens.

Application Requirements: Application form, essay. *Deadline:* June 1.

Contact: Andrew Stone, Executive Director
American Ground Water Trust
50 Pleasant Street, Suite 2
Concord, NH 03301-4073
Phone: 603-228-5444
E-mail: trustinfo@agwt.org

AMERICAN GROUND WATER TRUST-THOMAS STETSON SCHOLARSHIP

For students entering their freshman year in a full-time program of study at a four-year accredited university or college located west of the Mississippi River and intending to pursue a career in ground water-related field. Must be U.S. citizen or legal resident with 3.0 GPA or higher. For more information see website http://www.agwt.org.

Academic Fields/Career Goals: Earth Science; Hydrology; Natural Resources.

Award: Scholarship for use in freshman year; not renewable. *Number:* 1. *Amount:* $2000.

Eligibility Requirements: Applicant must be enrolled or expecting to enroll full-time at a four-year institution or university. Available to U.S. citizens.

Application Requirements: Application form, essay. *Deadline:* June 1.

Contact: Andrew Stone, Executive Director
American Ground Water Trust
50 Pleasant Street, Suite 2
Concord, NH 03301-4073
Phone: 603-228-5444
E-mail: trustinfo@agwt.org

AMERICAN INDIAN SCIENCE AND ENGINEERING SOCIETY

http://www.aises.org/

A.T. ANDERSON MEMORIAL SCHOLARSHIP PROGRAM
• *See page 105*

AMERICAN LEGION DEPARTMENT OF MARYLAND

http://www.mdlegion.org/

AMERICAN LEGION DEPARTMENT OF MARYLAND MATH-SCIENCE SCHOLARSHIP
• *See page 99*

AMERICAN SOCIETY OF AGRONOMY, CROP SCIENCE SOCIETY OF AMERICA, SOIL SCIENCE SOCIETY OF AMERICA

http://www.agronomy.org

J. FIELDING REED UNDERGRADUATE SOIL AND PLANT SCIENCES SCHOLARSHIP

Two scholarships of $2000 to honor an outstanding undergraduate senior pursuing a career in soil or plant sciences. Must have GPA of 3.0, or above, and nominations should contain a history of community and campus leadership activities, specifically in agriculture. For more information on nomination and eligibility criteria, visit website https://www.agronomy.org/awards

Academic Fields/Career Goals: Earth Science; Entomology; Environmental Science; Natural Resources; Natural Sciences.

Award: Scholarship for use in senior year; not renewable. *Number:* 2. *Amount:* $2000.

Eligibility Requirements: Applicant must be enrolled or expecting to enroll full-time at an institution or university. Applicant or parent of applicant must have employment or volunteer experience in community service. Available to U.S. and non-U.S. citizens.

Application Requirements: Application form. *Deadline:* April 2.

Contact: Sara Uttech, Senior Governance Manager
Phone: 608-268-4948
E-mail: suttech@agronomy.org

ARIZONA HYDROLOGICAL SOCIETY

http://www.azhydrosoc.org/

ARIZONA HYDROLOGICAL SOCIETY SCHOLARSHIP

One-time award to outstanding upper-level undergraduate or graduate students who have demonstrated academic excellence in water resources related fields as a means of encouraging them to continue to develop as water resources professionals. Must be a resident of Arizona and be enrolled in a postsecondary Arizona institution.

Academic Fields/Career Goals: Earth Science; Hydrology; Natural Resources; Nuclear Science; Science, Technology, and Society.

Award: Scholarship for use in junior, senior, or graduate years; not renewable. *Number:* 3. *Amount:* $2000.

Eligibility Requirements: Applicant must be enrolled or expecting to enroll full-time at a two-year or four-year or technical institution or university; resident of Arizona and studying in Arizona. Available to U.S. citizens.

Application Requirements: Application form, essay, financial need analysis, recommendations or references, transcript. *Deadline:* April 30.

Contact: Aregai Tecle, Professor
Phone: 928-523-6642
Fax: 928-556-7112
E-mail: aregai.tecle@nau.edu

ASSOCIATION FOR WOMEN GEOSCIENTISTS (AWG)

http://www.awg.org/

AWG ETHNIC MINORITY SCHOLARSHIP

The Minority Scholarship encourages young women of a minority background, or heritage, to pursue a major and career in the geosciences. The scholarship provides financial support for college expenses and matches the student with a mentor who has a career similar to that desired by the awardee.

Academic Fields/Career Goals: Earth Science; Education; Environmental Science; Gemology; Geography; Hydrology; Meteorology/Atmospheric Science; Museum Studies; Natural Resources; Natural Sciences; Oceanography; Physical Sciences.

Award: Scholarship for use in freshman, sophomore, junior, or senior years; not renewable. *Number:* 1–5. *Amount:* $500–$3000.

Eligibility Requirements: Applicant must be American Indian/Alaska Native, Black (non-Hispanic), Hispanic; enrolled or expecting to enroll full- or part-time at a four-year institution or university and female. Available to U.S. citizens.

Application Requirements: Application form, community service, recommendations or references, statement of academic or career goals, test scores, transcript. *Deadline:* June 30.

Contact: Christina Tapia, Ethnic Minority Scholarship Coordinator

AWG MARIA LUISA CRAWFORD FIELD CAMP SCHOLARSHIP
• *See page 111*

AWG SALT LAKE CHAPTER (SLC) RESEARCH SCHOLARSHIP
• *See page 111*

AWG UNDERGRADUATE EXCELLENCE IN PALEONTOLOGY AWARD
• *See page 106*

JANET CULLEN TANAKA GEOSCIENCES UNDERGRADUATE SCHOLARSHIP
• *See page 112*

LONE STAR RISING CAREER SCHOLARSHIP

The Lone Star Rising Career Scholarship provides professional development funding for women geoscience professionals seeking to resume their geoscience careers after having been out of the work force, or women geoscience students seeking to enter the workforce in a geoscience-related field within the next two years.

Academic Fields/Career Goals: Earth Science; Education; Environmental Science; Gemology; Hydrology; Meteorology/Atmospheric Science; Museum Studies; Natural Resources; Natural Sciences; Oceanography; Physical Sciences; Science, Technology, and Society.

Award: Scholarship for use in freshman, sophomore, junior, senior, graduate, or postgraduate years; not renewable. *Number:* 1–2. *Amount:* $1–$3000.

Eligibility Requirements: Applicant must be enrolled or expecting to enroll full- or part-time at a two-year or four-year institution or university and single female. Applicant or parent of applicant must have employment or volunteer experience in physical or natural sciences. Available to U.S. citizens.

Application Requirements: Application form, financial need analysis, recommendations or references. *Deadline:* October 31.

Contact: AWG Lone Star Rising Career Scholarship Coordinator
Association for Women Geoscientists (AWG)
AWG Lone Star Chapter
PO Box 542042
Houston, TX 77254
E-mail: awglonestar@gmail.com

OSAGE CHAPTER UNDERGRADUATE SERVICE SCHOLARSHIP
• *See page 112*

SUSAN EKDALE MEMORIAL FIELD CAMP SCHOLARSHIP

The scholarship will be awarded to a female student in the geosciences to help defray field camp expenses. Applicant must be attending a Utah institution of higher learning, or be a Utah resident attending college elsewhere.

Academic Fields/Career Goals: Earth Science; Environmental Science; Hydrology; Meteorology/Atmospheric Science; Museum Studies; Natural Resources; Natural Sciences; Oceanography; Physical Sciences.

Award: Scholarship for use in freshman, sophomore, junior, senior, or graduate years; not renewable. *Amount:* $1000–$2000.

Eligibility Requirements: Applicant must be enrolled or expecting to enroll full- or part-time at a four-year institution or university; female; resident of Utah and studying in Utah. Available to U.S. citizens.

Application Requirements: Application form, essay, letter of eligibility from the department verifying field of study, recommendations or references. *Deadline:* March 12.

Contact: Janae Wallace, Ekdale Scholarship Committee Chair
Association for Women Geoscientists (AWG)
AWG Salt Lake Chapter
PO Box 58691
Salt Lake City, UT 84158-0691
Phone: 801-537-3387
E-mail: janaewallace@utah.gov

ASSOCIATION OF STATE DAM SAFETY OFFICIALS (ASDSO)

http://www.DamSafety.org

ASSOCIATION OF STATE DAM SAFETY OFFICIALS (ASDSO) SENIOR UNDERGRADUATE SCHOLARSHIP
• *See page 140*

ASSOCIATION ON AMERICAN INDIAN AFFAIRS, INC.

http://www.indian-affairs.org/

ELIZABETH AND SHERMAN ASCHE MEMORIAL SCHOLARSHIP FUND
• *See page 93*

ASTRONAUT SCHOLARSHIP FOUNDATION

http://www.astronautscholarship.org/

ASTRONAUT SCHOLARSHIP
• *See page 107*

BARRY GOLDWATER SCHOLARSHIP AND EXCELLENCE IN EDUCATION FOUNDATION

https://goldwater.scholarsapply.org

BARRY M. GOLDWATER SCHOLARSHIP AND EXCELLENCE IN EDUCATION PROGRAM
• *See page 107*

BHW GROUP

https://thebhwgroup.com/

BHW WOMEN IN STEM SCHOLARSHIP
• *See page 107*

B.O.G. PEST CONTROL

http://www.bogpestcontrol.com/

B.O.G. PEST CONTROL SCHOLARSHIP FUND
• *See page 141*

BROWN AND CALDWELL

http://www.brownandcaldwell.com

ECKENFELDER SCHOLARSHIP
• *See page 141*

MINORITY SCHOLARSHIP PROGRAM
• *See page 141*

CARDS AGAINST HUMANITY

https://cardsagainsthumanity.com/

SCIENCE AMBASSADOR SCHOLARSHIP
• *See page 107*

GREAT MINDS IN STEM

http://www.greatmindsinstem.org/college/scholarship-application-information

HENAAC SCHOLARSHIP PROGRAM
• *See page 100*

INTERNATIONAL SOCIETY OF EXPLOSIVES ENGINEERS

http://www.isee.org/

JERRY MCDOWELL FUND
• *See page 156*

KENTUCKY ENERGY AND ENVIRONMENT CABINET

http://dep.ky.gov

ENVIRONMENTAL PROTECTION SCHOLARSHIP
• *See page 142*

THE LAND CONSERVANCY OF NEW JERSEY

http://www.tlc-nj.org/

ROGERS FAMILY SCHOLARSHIP
• *See page 143*

RUSSELL W. MYERS SCHOLARSHIP
• *See page 143*

MEDICAL SCRUBS COLLECTION

http://medicalscrubscollection.com

MEDICAL SCRUBS COLLECTION SCHOLARSHIP
• *See page 104*

MONTANA FEDERATION OF GARDEN CLUBS

http://www.mtfgc.org/

LIFE MEMBER MONTANA FEDERATION OF GARDEN CLUBS SCHOLARSHIP

Applicant must be at least a sophomore, majoring in conservation, horticulture, park or forestry, floriculture, greenhouse management, land management, or related subjects. Must be in need of assistance. Must have a potential for a successful future. Must be ranked in upper half of class or have a minimum 2.7 GPA. Must be a Montana resident and all study must be done in Montana.

Academic Fields/Career Goals: Earth Science; Horticulture/Floriculture; Landscape Architecture; Natural Resources.

Award: Scholarship for use in sophomore, junior, or senior years; not renewable. *Number:* 1. *Amount:* $1000.

Eligibility Requirements: Applicant must be enrolled or expecting to enroll full-time at a four-year institution or university; resident of Montana and studying in Montana. Available to U.S. citizens.

Application Requirements: Driver's license, recommendations or references, transcript. *Deadline:* May 1.

Contact: Joyce Backa, Life Members Scholarship Chairman
Montana Federation of Garden Clubs
513 Skyline Drive
Craig, MT 59404-8712
Phone: 406-235-4229
E-mail: rjback@bresnan.net

NASA FLORIDA SPACE GRANT CONSORTIUM

http://www.floridaspacegrant.org/

FLORIDA SPACE RESEARCH PROGRAM
• *See page 131*

NASA IDAHO SPACE GRANT CONSORTIUM

http://www.idahospacegrant.org

NASA IDAHO SPACE GRANT CONSORTIUM SCHOLARSHIP PROGRAM
• *See page 109*

NASA/MARYLAND SPACE GRANT CONSORTIUM

https://md.spacegrant.org

NASA MARYLAND SPACE GRANT CONSORTIUM SCHOLARSHIPS
• *See page 109*

NASA MINNESOTA SPACE GRANT CONSORTIUM

https://www.mnspacegrant.org/

MINNESOTA SPACE GRANT CONSORTIUM SCHOLARSHIP PROGRAM
• *See page 131*

NATIONAL ASSOCIATION OF GEOSCIENCE TEACHERS & FAR WESTERN SECTION

http://www.nagt-fws.org

NATIONAL ASSOCIATION OF GEOSCIENCE TEACHERS-FAR WESTERN SECTION SCHOLARSHIP

Academically superior students currently enrolled in school in Hawaii, Nevada, or California are eligible to apply for one of three $500 scholarships to the school of their choice. Must be a high school senior or community college student enrolling full-time (12 quarter units) in a Bachelor's degree program in geology at a four-year institution or an undergraduate geology major enrolling in an upper division field geology course of approximately 30 field mapping days.

Academic Fields/Career Goals: Earth Science.

Award: Scholarship for use in sophomore, junior, or senior years; not renewable. *Number:* 3. *Amount:* $500.

Eligibility Requirements: Applicant must be enrolled or expecting to enroll full- or part-time at a four-year institution or university and studying in California, Hawaii, Nevada. Available to U.S. citizens.

Application Requirements: Application form, endorsement signature of a regular member of NAGT-FWS in the reference letter, recommendations or references, transcript. *Deadline:* April 1.

Contact: Mike Martin, Geology Scholarship Coordinator
Phone: 951-789-5690
E-mail: mmartin@rusd.k12.ca.us

NATIONAL GARDEN CLUBS INC.

http://www.gardenclub.org/

NATIONAL GARDEN CLUBS INC. SCHOLARSHIP PROGRAM
• *See page 94*

NEVADA NASA SPACE GRANT CONSORTIUM

https://nasa.epscorspo.nevada.edu/

NATIONAL SPACE GRANT CONSORTIUM SCHOLARSHIPS
• *See page 110*

NEXTSTEPU

http://www.nextstepu.com/

$1,500 STEM SCHOLARSHIP
• *See page 104*

NGWA FOUNDATION

http://www.ngwa.org/Foundation/Pages/default.aspx

NGWA FOUNDATION'S LEN ASSANTE SCHOLARSHIP

Applicant must be in a field of study that serves, supports, or promotes the groundwater industry. Qualifying majors: geology, hydrology, hydrogeology, environmental sciences, microbiology, and well-drilling two-year associate degree programs. Minimum 2.5 GPA required.

Academic Fields/Career Goals: Earth Science; Environmental Science; Hydrology.

Award: Scholarship for use in freshman, sophomore, junior, senior, graduate, or postgraduate years; not renewable. *Number:* 1–10. *Amount:* $1000–$5000.

Eligibility Requirements: Applicant must be enrolled or expecting to enroll full-time at a two-year or four-year or technical institution or university. Available to U.S. and non-U.S. citizens.

Application Requirements: Application form, essay, personal photograph. *Deadline:* February 15.

Contact: Foundation Administrator
NGWA Foundation
601 Dempsey Road
Westerville, OH 43081
Phone: 614-898-7791 Ext. 1504
E-mail: foundation@ngwa.org

NOVUS BIOLOGICALS, LLC

https://www.novusbio.com

NOVUS BIOLOGICALS SCHOLARSHIP PROGRAM
• *See page 101*

R&D SYSTEMS SCHOLARSHIP
• *See page 101*

TOCRIS BIOSCIENCE SCHOLARSHIP
• *See page 102*

OREGON OFFICE OF STUDENT ACCESS AND COMPLETION

https://oregonstudentaid.gov/

SEHAR SALEHA AHMAD AND ABRAHIM EKRAMULLAH ZAFAR FOUNDATION SCHOLARSHIP
• *See page 110*

ROCKY MOUNTAIN COAL MINING INSTITUTE

http://www.rmcmi.org/

ROCKY MOUNTAIN COAL MINING INSTITUTE SCHOLARSHIP
• *See page 167*

SCARLETT FAMILY FOUNDATION SCHOLARSHIP PROGRAM

http://www.scarlettfoundation.org/

SCHOLARSHIP FOR STUDENTS PURSUING A BUSINESS OR STEM DEGREE
• *See page 80*

SOIL AND WATER CONSERVATION SOCIETY

http://www.swcs.org

DONALD A. WILLIAMS SCHOLARSHIP SOIL CONSERVATION SCHOLARSHIP
• *See page 91*

SOIL AND WATER CONSERVATION SOCIETY-NEW JERSEY CHAPTER

http://www.geocities.com/njswcs

EDWARD R. HALL SCHOLARSHIP
• *See page 91*

STRAIGHT NORTH

https://www.straightnorth.com/

STRAIGHT NORTH STEM SCHOLARSHIP
• *See page 81*

TAU KAPPA EPSILON EDUCATION FOUNDATION

https://www.tke.org/

TIMOTHY L. TASCHWER SCHOLARSHIP
• *See page 144*

UNITED NEGRO COLLEGE FUND

http://www.uncf.org/

LEIDOS STEM SCHOLARSHIP
• *See page 96*

VERMONT SPACE GRANT CONSORTIUM

http://www.cems.uvm.edu/vsgc

VERMONT SPACE GRANT CONSORTIUM
• *See page 92*

ECONOMICS

280 GROUP

https://280group.com/contact/280-group-product-management-scholarship/

280 GROUP PRODUCT MANAGEMENT SCHOLARSHIP

The 280 Group is a strategic consulting partner to any business that needs a proven methodology to optimize Product Management and Product Marketing functions in their company. We're excited to be offering three $500 scholarships to students pursuing a Bachelor's or Master's degree in business, economics or a related field. Students who receive the scholarships will also get full access to the Certified Product Manager — Online Course and Exam. This course is valued at $1,495 and will teach students the core skills to be a Product Manager and allow them to earn the prestigious AIPMM (Association of International Product Management and Marketing) Certified Product Manager® credential.

Academic Fields/Career Goals: Economics; Marketing.

Award: Scholarship for use in freshman, sophomore, junior, senior, or graduate years; renewable. *Number:* 3. *Amount:* $500.

Eligibility Requirements: Applicant must be enrolled or expecting to enroll full- or part-time at a four-year institution or university. Available to U.S. and non-U.S. citizens.

Application Requirements: Application form, essay. *Deadline:* November 15.

Contact: Ms. Mira Wooten, Director of Solutions
280 Group
142B Santa Cruz Avenue
Los Gatos, CA 95030
Phone: 831-419-3502
E-mail: mira@280group.com

THE ACTUARIAL FOUNDATION

www.actuarialfoundation.org

ACTUARY OF TOMORROW—STUART A. ROBERTSON MEMORIAL SCHOLARSHIP

The Actuary of Tomorrow—Stuart A. Robertson Memorial Scholarship recognizes and encourages the academic achievements of undergraduate students pursuing a career in actuarial science. Applicants must be full-time students entering as a sophomore, junior or senior, must have a minimum cumulative GPA of 3.0 (on 4.0 scale) and must have successfully completed two actuarial exams.

Academic Fields/Career Goals: Economics; Insurance and Actuarial Science; Mathematics; Statistics.

Award: Scholarship for use in sophomore, junior, or senior years; not renewable. *Amount:* $9000.

Eligibility Requirements: Applicant must be enrolled or expecting to enroll full-time at a four-year institution. Available to U.S. and non-U.S. citizens.

Application Requirements: Application form, application form may be submitted online (https://actfnd.academicworks.com/opportunities/148), essay, personal photograph, recommendations or references, resume, transcript. *Deadline:* June 1.

Contact: Actuary of Tomorrow, Stuart A. Robertson Memorial
        Scholarship
        The Actuarial Foundation
        475 North Martingale Road, Suite 600
        Schaumburg, IL 60173
        Phone: 847-706-3535
        E-mail: scholarships@actfnd.org

CURTIS E. HUNTINGTON MEMORIAL SCHOLARSHIP

The Curtis E. Huntington Memorial Scholarship (formerly the John Culver Wooddy Scholarship) is awarded annually to college seniors who have successfully completed at least one actuarial examination, rank in the top quartile of their class and are nominated by a professor at their school.

Academic Fields/Career Goals: Economics; Insurance and Actuarial Science; Mathematics; Statistics.

Award: Scholarship for use in senior year; not renewable. *Amount:* $2000.

Eligibility Requirements: Applicant must be enrolled or expecting to enroll full-time at a four-year institution or university. Available to U.S. and non-U.S. citizens.

Application Requirements: Application form, application form may be submitted online (https://actfnd.academicworks.com/opportunities/146), essay, personal photograph, resume, transcript. *Deadline:* April 1.

Contact: Curtis E. Huntington Memorial Scholarship
        The Actuarial Foundation
        475 North Martingale Road, Suite 600
        Schaumburg, IL 60173
        Phone: 847-706-3535
        E-mail: scholarships@actfnd.org

AMERICAN FEDERATION OF STATE, COUNTY, AND MUNICIPAL EMPLOYEES

https://www.afscme.org/

AFSCME/UNCF UNION SCHOLARS PROGRAM
• *See page 98*

AUTOMOTIVE WOMEN'S ALLIANCE FOUNDATION

http://awafoundation.org/index.php

AUTOMOTIVE WOMEN'S ALLIANCE FOUNDATION SCHOLARSHIPS
• *See page 71*

CATCHING THE DREAM

http://www.catchingthedream.org/

TRIBAL BUSINESS MANAGEMENT PROGRAM (TBM)
• *See page 72*

CONGRESSIONAL BLACK CAUCUS FOUNDATION, INC.

http://www.cbcfinc.org/

CBC SPOUSES EDUCATION SCHOLARSHIP
• *See page 98*

DISTIL NETWORKS

http://www.distilnetworks.com

WOMEN FORWARD IN TECHNOLOGY SCHOLARSHIP PROGRAM
• *See page 108*

GOVERNMENT FINANCE OFFICERS ASSOCIATION

https://www.gfoa.org/

MINORITIES IN GOVERNMENT FINANCE SCHOLARSHIP
• *See page 75*

HOUSE OF BLUES MUSIC FORWARD FOUNDATION

https://hobmusicforward.org/

STEVEN J. FINKEL SERVICE EXCELLENCE SCHOLARSHIP
• *See page 148*

TIFFANY GREEN OPERATOR SCHOLARSHIP AWARD
• *See page 85*

JORGE MAS CANOSA FREEDOM FOUNDATION

http://masscholarships.org/

MAS FAMILY SCHOLARSHIP AWARD
• *See page 149*

NATIONAL ASSOCIATION OF NEGRO BUSINESS AND PROFESSIONAL WOMEN'S CLUBS INC.

http://www.nanbpwc.org/

JULIANNE MALVEAUX SCHOLARSHIP

Scholarship for African-American women who are college sophomores or juniors enrolled in an accredited college or university. Applicants must be majoring in journalism, economics, or a related field. Minimum 3.0 GPA required. Must be a U.S. citizen.

Academic Fields/Career Goals: Economics; Journalism.

Award: Scholarship for use in sophomore or junior years; not renewable. *Number:* 1. *Amount:* $1000.

Eligibility Requirements: Applicant must be Black (non-Hispanic); enrolled or expecting to enroll full-time at a four-year institution or university and female. Available to U.S. citizens.

Application Requirements: Application form, essay, recommendations or references, transcript. *Deadline:* April 30.

Contact: Scholarship Program Director
        National Association of Negro Business and Professional
           Women's Clubs Inc.
        1806 New Hampshire Avenue, NW
        Washington, DC 20009-3298
        Phone: 202-483-4206
        E-mail: info@nanbpwc.org

NATIONAL SECURITY EDUCATION PROGRAM

http://www.iie.org/

NATIONAL SECURITY EDUCATION PROGRAM (NSEP) DAVID L. BOREN UNDERGRADUATE SCHOLARSHIPS
• *See page 119*

NEW ENGLAND EMPLOYEE BENEFITS COUNCIL

http://www.neebc.org/

NEW ENGLAND EMPLOYEE BENEFITS COUNCIL SCHOLARSHIP PROGRAM
• See page 78

NORTH AMERICAN VAN LINES

https://www.northamerican.com/

NORTH AMERICAN VAN LINES 2020 LOGISTICS SCHOLARSHIP COMPETITION
• See page 150

OFFICE AND PROFESSIONAL EMPLOYEES INTERNATIONAL UNION

http://www.opeiu.org/

JOHN KELLY LABOR STUDIES SCHOLARSHIP FUND

Scholarship of up to $3000 given to graduate or undergraduate students who have labor studies, social sciences, industrial relation as their major. Ten scholarships are granted. Applicants should be a member or associate member of the union.

Academic Fields/Career Goals: Economics; Social Sciences.

Award: Scholarship for use in freshman, sophomore, junior, senior, or graduate years; not renewable. *Number:* 10. *Amount:* up to $3000.

Eligibility Requirements: Applicant must be enrolled or expecting to enroll full-time at a four-year institution or university. Available to U.S. citizens.

Application Requirements: Application form, essay, transcript. *Deadline:* March 31.

Contact: Mary Mahoney, Secretary-Treasurer
Phone: 202-393-4464
Fax: 202-887-0910
E-mail: mmahoney@opeiudc.org

SCARLETT FAMILY FOUNDATION SCHOLARSHIP PROGRAM

http://www.scarlettfoundation.org/

SCHOLARSHIP FOR STUDENTS PURSUING A BUSINESS OR STEM DEGREE
• See page 80

SOCIETY OF AUTOMOTIVE ANALYSTS

http://saaauto.com/

SOCIETY OF AUTOMOTIVE ANALYSTS SCHOLARSHIP
• See page 81

STRAIGHTFORWARD MEDIA

http://www.straightforwardmedia.com/

STRAIGHTFORWARD MEDIA BUSINESS SCHOOL SCHOLARSHIP
• See page 87

STRAIGHTFORWARD MEDIA LIBERAL ARTS SCHOLARSHIP
• See page 119

TAU KAPPA EPSILON EDUCATION FOUNDATION

https://www.tke.org/

W. ALLAN HERZOG SCHOLARSHIP
• See page 82

TRANSPORTATION ASSOCIATION OF CANADA FOUNDATION

http://www.tac-foundation.ca

TAC FOUNDATION SCHOLARSHIPS
• See page 168

UNITED NEGRO COLLEGE FUND

http://www.uncf.org/

DISCOVER FINANCIAL SERVICES SCHOLARSHIP
• See page 82

EDUCATION

ALBERTA HERITAGE SCHOLARSHIP FUND

http://www.alis.alberta.ca/

NORTHERN ALBERTA DEVELOPMENT COUNCIL BURSARY

Return service bursary awards CAN$6000 per year for up to two years to increase the number of trained professionals in Northern Alberta and to encourage students from Northern Alberta to obtain a post-secondary education. Must be residents of Alberta, and planning to enroll in a full-time post-secondary program in a field in demand in Northern Alberta. Fields in demand include education, health and medical, engineering, technical fields, and social work. Applicants must also be within two years of completion of their post-secondary program. Students must live and work for one year in Northern Alberta for each year of assistance awarded. For additional information, go to website http://alis.alberta.ca.

Academic Fields/Career Goals: Education; Engineering/Technology; Health and Medical Sciences; Social Services.

Award: Scholarship for use in junior or senior years; not renewable.

Eligibility Requirements: Applicant must be Canadian citizen; enrolled or expecting to enroll full-time at a technical institution or university; resident of Alaska and studying in Alberta.

Application Requirements: Application form, application form may be submitted online, essay, financial need analysis. *Deadline:* April 30.

AMERICAN FEDERATION OF TEACHERS

http://www.aft.org/

ROBERT G. PORTER SCHOLARS PROGRAM-AFT MEMBERS

Nonrenewable grant provides continuing education for school teachers, paraprofessionals and school-related personnel, higher education faculty and professionals, employees of state and local governments, nurses and other health professionals. Must be member of the American Federation of Teachers for at least one year.

Academic Fields/Career Goals: Education.

Award: Grant for use in freshman, sophomore, junior, or senior years; not renewable. *Number:* up to 10. *Amount:* $1000.

Eligibility Requirements: Applicant must be enrolled or expecting to enroll full- or part-time at a four-year institution or university. Applicant or parent of applicant must have employment or volunteer experience in nursing, teaching/education. Available to U.S. citizens.

Application Requirements: Application form, essay, recommendations or references, statement of need. *Deadline:* March 31.

Contact: Bernadette Bailey, Scholarship Coordinator
American Federation of Teachers
555 New Jersey Avenue, NW
Washington, DC 20001
Phone: 202-879-4481
Fax: 202-879-4406
E-mail: bbailey@aft.org

AMERICAN FOUNDATION FOR THE BLIND

http://www.afb.org/

DELTA GAMMA FOUNDATION FLORENCE MARGARET HARVEY MEMORIAL SCHOLARSHIP

One scholarship of $1000 to an undergraduate or graduate student who has exhibited academic excellence, and is studying in the field of rehabilitation and/or education of persons who are blind or visually impaired. Must submit proof of legal blindness. For additional information and application requirements, refer to website http://www.afb.org/scholarships.asp.

Academic Fields/Career Goals: Education; Therapy/Rehabilitation.

Award: Scholarship for use in freshman, sophomore, junior, or senior years; not renewable. *Number:* 1. *Amount:* $1000.

Eligibility Requirements: Applicant must be enrolled or expecting to enroll full- or part-time at a two-year or four-year institution or university. Applicant must be visually impaired. Available to U.S. citizens.

Application Requirements: Application form, essay, proof of post-secondary acceptance and legal blindness, recommendations or references, transcript. *Deadline:* April 30.

Contact: Dawn Bodrogi, Information Center and Library Coordinator
American Foundation for the Blind
11 Penn Plaza, Suite 300
New York, NY 10001
Phone: 212-502-7661
Fax: 212-502-7771
E-mail: afbinfo@afb.net

RUDOLPH DILLMAN MEMORIAL SCHOLARSHIP

One-time award not open to previous recipients. Four scholarships of $2500 each to undergraduate or graduate students who are studying in the field of rehabilitation and/or education of persons who are blind or visually impaired. One of these grants is specifically for a student who meets all requirements and submits evidence of economic need. Must submit proof of legal blindness. For additional information and application requirements, visit website http://www.afb.org/scholarships.asp.

Academic Fields/Career Goals: Education; Therapy/Rehabilitation.

Award: Scholarship for use in freshman, sophomore, junior, or senior years; not renewable. *Number:* up to 4. *Amount:* $2500.

Eligibility Requirements: Applicant must be enrolled or expecting to enroll full- or part-time at a two-year or four-year institution or university. Applicant must be visually impaired. Available to U.S. citizens.

Application Requirements: Application form, essay, financial need analysis, proof of legal blindness, acceptance letter, recommendations or references, transcript. *Deadline:* April 30.

Contact: Dawn Bodrogi, Information Center and Library Coordinator
American Foundation for the Blind
11 Penn Plaza, Suite 300
New York, NY 10001
Phone: 212-502-7661
Fax: 212-502-7771
E-mail: afbinfo@afb.net

AMERICAN INSTITUTE OF POLISH CULTURE INC.

http://www.ampolinstitute.org/

HARRIET IRSAY SCHOLARSHIP GRANT

• *See page 120*

AMERICAN LEGION AUXILIARY DEPARTMENT OF IOWA

http://www.iowaala.org

AMERICAN LEGION AUXILIARY DEPARTMENT OF IOWA HARRIET HOFFMAN MEMORIAL MERIT AWARD FOR TEACHER TRAINING

One-time award for Iowa residents attending Iowa institutions who are the children, grandchildren, or great-grandchildren of veterans. Preference given to descendants of deceased veterans.

Academic Fields/Career Goals: Education.

Award: Scholarship for use in freshman, sophomore, junior, or senior years; not renewable. *Number:* 1. *Amount:* $400.

Eligibility Requirements: Applicant must be enrolled or expecting to enroll full-time at a four-year institution or university; resident of Iowa and studying in Iowa. Available to U.S. citizens. Applicant or parent must meet one or more of the following requirements: general military experience; retired from active duty; disabled or killed as a result of military service; prisoner of war; or missing in action.

Application Requirements: Application form, essay, financial need analysis, personal photograph, recommendations or references, self-addressed stamped envelope with application, test scores, transcript. *Deadline:* June 1.

Contact: Marlene Valentine, Secretary and Treasurer
American Legion Auxiliary Department of Iowa
720 Lyon Street
Des Moines, IA 50309
Phone: 515-282-7987
Fax: 515-282-7583
E-mail: alasectreas@ialegion.org

AMERICAN LEGION DEPARTMENT OF MISSOURI

http://www.missourilegion.org/

ERMAN W. TAYLOR MEMORIAL SCHOLARSHIP

The Erman W. Taylor Memorial Scholarship awards two $750 scholarships to students planning on obtaining a degree in education, in honor of this Past National Executive Committeeman from Missouri. Must be a descendant of a veteran who served 90 or more days of active duty in the armed forces and having an honorable discharge.

Academic Fields/Career Goals: Education.

Award: Scholarship for use in freshman year; not renewable. *Number:* 2. *Amount:* $750.

Eligibility Requirements: Applicant must be high school student; age 20 or under; planning to enroll or expecting to enroll full-time at a two-year institution or university; single and resident of Mississippi. Available to U.S. citizens. Applicant or parent must meet one or more of the following requirements: general military experience; retired from active duty; disabled or killed as a result of military service; prisoner of war; or missing in action.

Application Requirements: Application form, essay. *Deadline:* April 20.

Contact: Mr. John Buckwalter, Chair, Education and Scholarship Committee
American Legion Department of Missouri
P.O. Box 179
Jefferson City, MO 65102-0179
Phone: 660-627-4713

AMERICAN MONTESSORI SOCIETY

http://www.amshq.org/

AMERICAN MONTESSORI SOCIETY TEACHER EDUCATION SCHOLARSHIP FUND

One-time award for aspiring Montessori teacher candidates. Requires verification that applicant has been accepted into an AMS-affiliated Montessori Teacher Education program. Awards are considered on the basis of financial need, a compelling personal statement, and 3 letters of recommendation.

Academic Fields/Career Goals: Education.

Award: Scholarship for use in freshman, sophomore, junior, senior, or graduate years; not renewable. *Number:* 12–24. *Amount:* $425–$6000.

Eligibility Requirements: Applicant must be enrolled or expecting to enroll full-time at a two-year or four-year or technical institution or university. Available to U.S. and non-U.S. citizens.

Application Requirements: Application form, essay, financial need analysis, recommendations or references. *Deadline:* May 1.

Contact: Sophia Zamudio, Manager of Teacher Education Program
Affiliation
American Montessori Society
American Montessori Society, 116 East 16th Street, 6th Floor
New York, NY 10003
Phone: 212-358-1250 Ext. 330
E-mail: sophia@amshq.org

AMERICAN PHYSICAL THERAPY ASSOCIATION

http://www.apta.org/honorsawards

MARY MCMILLAN SCHOLARSHIP AWARD

Students may be nominated from physical therapist assistant education programs and physical therapist professional education programs accredited by the Commission on Accreditation in Physical Therapy Education (CAPTE) of the association. Physical therapist assistant education program students must be enrolled in the final year of study. For physical therapist assistant education programs that have a part-time curriculum, all nominees must be in the final year of the curriculum of that institution. Minimum 3.0 GPA required.

Academic Fields/Career Goals: Education; Health and Medical Sciences; Therapy/Rehabilitation.

Award: Scholarship for use in senior, graduate, or postgraduate years; not renewable. *Number:* 1–6. *Amount:* $3000–$5000.

Eligibility Requirements: Applicant must be enrolled or expecting to enroll full-time at a two-year or four-year institution or university. Applicant or parent of applicant must have employment or volunteer experience in physical therapy/rehabilitation. Available to U.S. citizens.

Application Requirements: Application form, community service, essay. *Deadline:* December 1.

Contact: Alissa Patanarut, Senior Honors and Awards Program
Specialist
American Physical Therapy Association
1111 North Fairfax Street
Alexandria, VA 22314
Phone: 800-999-2782 Ext. 3154
E-mail: alissapatanarut@apta.org

ARCTIC INSTITUTE OF NORTH AMERICA

http://www.arctic.ucalgary.ca/

JIM BOURQUE SCHOLARSHIP

One-time award of CAN$1000 to Canadian aboriginal student enrolled in postsecondary training in education, environmental studies, traditional knowledge or telecommunications. Must submit, in 500 words or less, a description of their intended program of study and reasons for their choice of program. Must include most recent high school or college/university transcript; a signed letter of recommendation from a community leader, a statement of financial need which indicates funding already received or expected; and proof of enrollment in, or application to, a post secondary institution. Applicants must also provide proof of Canadian Aboriginal descent. Applicants are evaluated based on need, relevance of study, achievements, return of investment and overall presentation of the application.

Academic Fields/Career Goals: Education; Environmental Science; Natural Resources; Natural Sciences.

Award: Scholarship for use in freshman, sophomore, junior, or senior years; not renewable. *Number:* 1.

Eligibility Requirements: Applicant must be of Canadian heritage and Canadian citizen; American Indian/Alaska Native; enrolled or expecting to enroll full-time at a four-year institution or university and resident of Alberta, British Columbia, Manitoba, New Brunswick, Newfoundland, Newfoundland and Labrador, Northwest Territories, Nova Scotia, Nunavut, Ontario, Prince Edward Island, Quebec, Saskatchewan, Yukon.

Application Requirements: Application form, application form may be submitted online (https://arctic.ucalgary.ca/webform/jim-bourque-scholarship), Cover Letter, description of program of study, proof of Canadian Aboriginal descent, essay, financial need analysis, recommendations or references, transcript. *Deadline:* July 12.

Contact: Melanie Paulson, Administrative Coordinator
Phone: 403-220-7515
E-mail: arctic@ucalgary.ca

ARIZONA BUSINESS EDUCATION ASSOCIATION

http://www.azbea.org/

ABEA STUDENT TEACHER SCHOLARSHIPS

Scholarships awarded to future business education teachers. Must be member of ABEA. Must be a student in last semester or two of an undergraduate Arizona business education teacher program at an accredited university or four-year college or in a post-Baccalaureate Arizona business education teacher certification program at an accredited university or four-year college.

Academic Fields/Career Goals: Education.

Award: Scholarship for use in junior or senior years; not renewable. *Number:* up to 3. *Amount:* $500.

Eligibility Requirements: Applicant must be enrolled or expecting to enroll full-time at a four-year institution or university and resident of Arizona. Applicant or parent of applicant must be member of Arizona Business Education Association. Available to U.S. citizens.

Application Requirements: Application form, recommendations or references, resume, transcript. *Deadline:* April 1.

Contact: Shirley Eittreim, Scholarships Committee Chair
Arizona Business Education Association
Northland Pioneer College
PO Box 610
Holbrook, AZ 86025
Phone: 928-532-6151
E-mail: sjeittreim@cybertrails.com

ASSOCIATION FOR EDUCATION AND REHABILITATION OF THE BLIND AND VISUALLY IMPAIRED

http://www.aerbvi.org/

WILLIAM AND DOROTHY FERRELL SCHOLARSHIP

Nonrenewable scholarship given in even years for postsecondary education leading to career in services for blind or visually impaired. Applicant must submit proof of legal blindness or visual field impairment of 20 percent or less.

Academic Fields/Career Goals: Education; Health and Medical Sciences; Occupational Safety and Health; Public Policy and Administration; Therapy/Rehabilitation.

Award: Scholarship for use in freshman, sophomore, junior, senior, or graduate years; not renewable. *Number:* 2. *Amount:* $500–$1000.

Eligibility Requirements: Applicant must be enrolled or expecting to enroll full-time at a two-year or four-year institution or university. Applicant must be visually impaired. Available to U.S. and non-U.S. citizens.

Application Requirements: Application form. *Deadline:* March 25.

Contact: Scholarship Coordinator
Association for Education and Rehabilitation of the Blind and
Visually Impaired
1703 North Beauregard Street, Suite 440
Alexandria, VA 22311-1744
Phone: 703-671-4500
E-mail: scholarships@aerbvi.org

ASSOCIATION FOR WOMEN GEOSCIENTISTS (AWG)

http://www.awg.org/

AWG ETHNIC MINORITY SCHOLARSHIP
• *See page 200*

AWG MARIA LUISA CRAWFORD FIELD CAMP SCHOLARSHIP
• *See page 111*

AWG SALT LAKE CHAPTER (SLC) RESEARCH SCHOLARSHIP
• *See page 111*

LONE STAR RISING CAREER SCHOLARSHIP
• *See page 200*

ASSOCIATION OF RETIRED TEACHERS OF CONNECTICUT

http://www.artct.org/

ARTC GLEN MOON SCHOLARSHIP

Renewable scholarship to Connecticut high school seniors, who intend to pursue a career in teaching. Must demonstrate a positive financial need.

Academic Fields/Career Goals: Education.

Award: Scholarship for use in freshman year; renewable. *Number:* 2–3. *Amount:* $1500–$2000.

Eligibility Requirements: Applicant must be high school student; planning to enroll or expecting to enroll full- or part-time at a four-year institution or university and resident of Connecticut. Available to U.S. citizens.

Application Requirements: Application form, community service, driver's license, financial need analysis, recommendations or references, test scores, transcript. *Deadline:* March 31.

Contact: Teresa Barton, Scholarship Committee
Phone: 866-343-2782
E-mail: info@ctretiredteachers.org

BETHESDA LUTHERAN COMMUNITIES

http://www.bethesdalutherancommunities.org/scholarships

DEVELOPMENTAL DISABILITIES SCHOLASTIC ACHIEVEMENT SCHOLARSHIP FOR COLLEGE STUDENTS WHO ARE LUTHERAN
• *See page 195*

BULKOFFICESUPPLY.COM

http://www.bulkofficesupply.com

OFFICE SUPPLY SCHOLARSHIP
• *See page 121*

CALIFORNIA STUDENT AID COMMISSION

http://www.csac.ca.gov/

CHILD DEVELOPMENT TEACHER AND SUPERVISOR GRANT PROGRAM
• *See page 161*

CALIFORNIA TEACHERS ASSOCIATION (CTA)

http://www.cta.org/

MARTIN LUTHER KING, JR. MEMORIAL SCHOLARSHIP

The Martin Luther King Jr. Memorial Scholarship Program encourages ethnic minority students to become educators, school nurses, school counselors or school therapists and to promote professional growth for ethnic minority teachers and ESP members.

Academic Fields/Career Goals: Education.

Award: Scholarship for use in freshman, sophomore, junior, senior, or graduate years; not renewable. *Amount:* $6000.

Eligibility Requirements: Applicant must be American Indian/Alaska Native, Asian/Pacific Islander, Black (non-Hispanic), Hispanic; enrolled or expecting to enroll full-time at a two-year institution or university and resident of British Columbia. Applicant or parent of applicant must be member of California Teachers Association. Available to U.S. citizens.

Application Requirements: Application form, application form may be submitted online, financial need analysis.

Contact: Janeya Dawson
California Teachers Association (CTA)
PO Box 921
Burlingame, CA 94011-0921
Phone: 650-552-5446
E-mail: scholarships@cta.org

CANADIAN INSTITUTE OF UKRAINIAN STUDIES

https://www.ualberta.ca/canadian-institute-of-ukrainian-studies/index.html

LEO J. KRYSA FAMILY UNDERGRADUATE SCHOLARSHIP

The Krysa Undergraduate Scholarship (up to C$3,500), non-renewable, is awarded annually to a student in the Faculty of Arts or Faculty of Education about to enter the final year of study in pursuit of an undergraduate degree. The applicant's programs must emphasize Ukrainian and/or Ukrainian-Canadian studies, through a combination of Ukrainian and East European or Canadian courses in one of the above areas. The scholarship is for an eight-month period of study at any Canadian university. Candidates must be Canadian citizens or permanent residents of Canada at the time of application

Academic Fields/Career Goals: Education; European Studies; History; Humanities; Social Sciences.

Award: Scholarship for use in senior year; not renewable. *Number:* 1.

Eligibility Requirements: Applicant must be Canadian citizen; enrolled or expecting to enroll full-time at an institution or university; resident of Alaska, Arkansas, Maine, Nevada, New York, North Dakota, Northwest Territories, Oklahoma, Pennsylvania, Puerto Rico, Rhode Island, Wyoming and studying in Alberta, British Columbia, Manitoba, New Brunswick, Newfoundland, Nova Scotia, Ontario, Prince Edward Island, Quebec, Saskatchewan. Available to U.S. and non-U.S. citizens.

Application Requirements: Application form, application form may be submitted online. *Deadline:* March 1.

Contact: Oleksandr Pankieiev, Research Communication Coordinator
Canadian Institute of Ukrainian Studies
4-30 Pembina Hall
University of Alberta
Edmonton, AB T6G 2H8
CAN
Phone: 780-492-1470
E-mail: oleksandr.pankieiev@ualberta.ca

CATCHING THE DREAM

http://www.catchingthedream.org/

MATH, ENGINEERING, SCIENCE, BUSINESS, EDUCATION, COMPUTERS SCHOLARSHIPS
• *See page 146*

NATIVE AMERICAN LEADERSHIP IN EDUCATION (NALE)
• *See page 146*

CONNECTICUT EDUCATION FOUNDATION INC.

http://www.cea.org/cef/

SCHOLARSHIP FOR ETHNIC MINORITY COLLEGE STUDENTS

An award for qualified minority candidates who have been accepted into a teacher preparation program at an accredited Connecticut college or university. Must have a 3.0 GPA.

Academic Fields/Career Goals: Education.

Award: Scholarship for use in freshman, sophomore, junior, or senior years; renewable. *Number:* 1–2. *Amount:* $1000–$2000.

Eligibility Requirements: Applicant must be American Indian/Alaska Native, Asian/Pacific Islander, Black (non-Hispanic), Hispanic; enrolled or expecting to enroll full-time at a two-year or four-year institution or university; resident of Connecticut and studying in Connecticut. Available to U.S. citizens.

Application Requirements: Application form, essay. *Deadline:* May 1.

Contact: Mr. Jeffrey Leake, President
Connecticut Education Foundation Inc.
21 Oak Street, Suite 500
Hartford, CT 06106
Phone: 860-525-5641 Ext. 6308
E-mail: jeffl@cea.org

SCHOLARSHIP FOR MINORITY HIGH SCHOOL STUDENTS

Award for qualified minority candidates who have been accepted into an accredited four-year Connecticut college or university and intend to enter the teaching profession. Must have 3.0 GPA.

Academic Fields/Career Goals: Education.

Award: Scholarship for use in freshman, sophomore, junior, or senior years; renewable. *Number:* 1–2. *Amount:* $1000–$2000.

Eligibility Requirements: Applicant must be American Indian/Alaska Native, Asian/Pacific Islander, Black (non-Hispanic), Hispanic; high school student; planning to enroll or expecting to enroll full-time at a four-year institution or university; resident of Connecticut and studying in Connecticut. Available to U.S. citizens.

Application Requirements: Application form, essay. *Deadline:* May 1.

Contact: Mr. Jeffrey Leake, President
Connecticut Education Foundation Inc.
21 Oak Street, Suite 500
Hartford, CT 06106
Phone: 860-525-5641 Ext. 6308
E-mail: jeffl@cea.org

CONNECTICUT OFFICE OF HIGHER EDUCATION

http://www.ctohe.org

MINORITY TEACHER INCENTIVE GRANT PROGRAM

Program provides up to $5,000 a year for two years of full-time study in a teacher preparation program for the junior or senior year at a Connecticut college or university. Applicant must be African-American, Hispanic/Latino, Asian American or Native American heritage and be nominated by the Education Dean. Program graduates who teach in Connecticut public schools may be eligible for loan reimbursement stipends up to $2,500 per year for up to four years.

Academic Fields/Career Goals: Education.

Award: Grant for use in junior or senior years; renewable. *Number:* 87. *Amount:* $2500–$5000.

Eligibility Requirements: Applicant must be American Indian/Alaska Native, Asian/Pacific Islander, Black (non-Hispanic), Hispanic; enrolled or expecting to enroll full-time at a four-year institution or university; resident of Connecticut and studying in Connecticut. Available to U.S. citizens.

Application Requirements: Application form. *Deadline:* October 15.

Contact: Ms. Lynne Goodwin, Executive Assistant
Connecticut Office of Higher Education
450 Columbus Boulevard
Suite 510
Hartford, CT 06103
Phone: 860-947-1855
E-mail: mtip@ctohe.org

CONTINENTAL SOCIETY, DAUGHTERS OF INDIAN WARS

http://www.csdiw.org/

CONTINENTAL SOCIETY, DAUGHTERS OF INDIAN WARS SCHOLARSHIP
• *See page 188*

CULTURAL SERVICES OF THE FRENCH EMBASSY

http://www.frenchculture.org/

TEACHING ASSISTANT PROGRAM IN FRANCE
• *See page 98*

DECA (DISTRIBUTIVE EDUCATION CLUBS OF AMERICA)

http://www.deca.org/

HARRY A. APPLEGATE SCHOLARSHIP
• *See page 73*

EASTERN STAR-GRAND CHAPTER OF CALIFORNIA

http://www.oescal.org/

SCHOLARSHIPS FOR EDUCATION, BUSINESS AND RELIGION
• *See page 147*

GENERAL BOARD OF HIGHER EDUCATION AND MINISTRY

http://www.gbhem.org

EDITH M. ALLEN SCHOLARSHIP

Scholarship for outstanding African-American graduate or undergraduate students pursuing a degree in education, social work, medicine, and/or other health professions. Must be enrolled at a United Methodist college or university and be an active, full member of the United Methodist Church for at least three years.

Academic Fields/Career Goals: Education; Health and Medical Sciences; Social Services.

Award: Scholarship for use in freshman, sophomore, junior, or senior years; not renewable. *Number:* 2. *Amount:* $1200.

Eligibility Requirements: Applicant must be Methodist; Black (non-Hispanic) and enrolled or expecting to enroll full-time at a four-year institution or university. Available to U.S. citizens.

Application Requirements: Application form, essay. *Deadline:* March 1.

Contact: Ms. Marcie Bigord, Assistant Director of Loans & Scholarships
General Board of Higher Education and Ministry
PO Box 340007
Nashville, TN 37203-0007
Phone: 615-340-7388
Fax: 615-340-7529
E-mail: mbigord@gbhem.org

GEORGIA ASSOCIATION OF EDUCATORS

http://www.gae.org/

GAE GFIE SCHOLARSHIP FOR ASPIRING TEACHERS

Scholarships will be awarded to graduating seniors who currently attend a fully accredited public Georgia high school and will attend a fully accredited Georgia college or university within the next twelve months. Must have a 3.0 GPA. Must submit three letters of recommendation. Must have plans to enter the teaching profession.

Academic Fields/Career Goals: Education.

Award: Scholarship for use in freshman year; not renewable. *Number:* up to 20. *Amount:* $1000.

Eligibility Requirements: Applicant must be enrolled or expecting to enroll full-time at a two-year or four-year institution or university; resident of Georgia and studying in Georgia. Available to U.S. citizens.

Application Requirements: Application form, recommendations or references, transcript. *Deadline:* February 1.

Contact: Sharon Henderson, Staff Associate
Phone: 678-837-1114
Fax: 678-837-1150
E-mail: sharon.henderson@gae.org

GOLDEN APPLE FOUNDATION

http://www.goldenapple.org/

GOLDEN APPLE SCHOLARS OF ILLINOIS

Applicants must be between the ages of 16 and 21 and maintain a GPA of 2.5. Eligible applicants must be residents of Illinois studying education in Illinois. Recipients must agree to teach in an Illinois school school-of-need for 5 years.

Academic Fields/Career Goals: Education.

Award: Scholarship for use in freshman, sophomore, junior, or senior years; renewable. *Number:* 200. *Amount:* $23,000.

Eligibility Requirements: Applicant must be age 16-21; enrolled or expecting to enroll full-time at a two-year or four-year institution or university; resident of Illinois and studying in Illinois. Available to U.S. citizens.

Application Requirements: Application form, essay, interview, personal photograph. *Deadline:* February 15.

Contact: Ms. Patricia Kilduff, Director of Recruitment and Placement
Phone: 312-477-7515
E-mail: kilduff@goldenapple.org

GOLDEN KEY INTERNATIONAL HONOUR SOCIETY

http://www.goldenkey.org/

EDUCATION ACHIEVEMENT AWARDS

Awards members who excel in the study of education. Eligible applicants are undergraduate, graduate and postgraduate members who are currently enrolled in classes at a degree-granting program. One winner will receive a $1000 award. The second place winner will receive $750 and the third place winner will receive $500.

Academic Fields/Career Goals: Education.

Award: Prize for use in freshman, sophomore, junior, senior, graduate, or postgraduate years; not renewable. *Number:* 3. *Amount:* $500–$1000.

Eligibility Requirements: Applicant must be enrolled or expecting to enroll full- or part-time at a four-year institution or university. Available to U.S. and non-U.S. citizens.

Application Requirements: Application form, education related paper or report, entry in a contest, essay, recommendations or references, transcript. *Deadline:* March 3.

Contact: Scholarship Program Administrators
Golden Key International Honour Society
PO Box 23737
Nashville, TN 37202-3737
Phone: 800-377-2401
E-mail: scholarships@goldenkey.org

ILLINOIS PTA

http://www.illinoispta.org

ILLINOIS PTA SCHOLARSHIP

Scholarship has evolved to encourage Illinois college-bound high school seniors entering the field of education or an education-related field at the college/university of their choice. Minimum 3.0 GPA required.

Academic Fields/Career Goals: Education.

Award: Scholarship for use in freshman year; not renewable. *Number:* 2. *Amount:* $2000–$3000.

Eligibility Requirements: Applicant must be high school student; planning to enroll or expecting to enroll full-time at a four-year institution or university and resident of Illinois. Available to U.S. citizens.

Application Requirements: Application form, application form may be submitted online (http://www.illinoispta.org), community service, essay, personal photograph, resume, test scores, transcript. *Deadline:* February 15.

Contact: Barb Miller, Scholarship Director
Illinois PTA
PO Box 907
Springfield, IL 62705-0907
Phone: 217-528-9617
Fax: 217-528-9490
E-mail: Bmiller@illinoispta.org

INDIANA RETIRED TEACHER'S ASSOCIATION (IRTA)

http://www.retiredteachers.org/

INDIANA RETIRED TEACHERS FOUNDATION SCHOLARSHIP

Scholarship available to college sophomores or juniors who are enrolled full-time in an education program at an Indiana college or university for a baccalaureate degree. The applicant must be the child, grandchild, legal dependent or spouse of an active, retired or deceased member of the Indiana State Teachers Retirement Fund and Indiana Retired Teachers Association.

Academic Fields/Career Goals: Education.

Award: Scholarship for use in sophomore or junior years; not renewable. *Number:* 10. *Amount:* $2000.

Eligibility Requirements: Applicant must be enrolled or expecting to enroll full-time at a four-year institution or university; resident of Indiana and studying in Indiana. Applicant or parent of applicant must have employment or volunteer experience in teaching/education. Available to U.S. citizens.

Application Requirements: Application form, community service, essay, financial need analysis. *Deadline:* April 28.

Contact: Executive Director
Indiana Retired Teacher's Association (IRTA)
150 West Market Street, Suite 610
Indianapolis, IN 46204-2812
Phone: 888-454-9333

INTERNATIONAL TECHNOLOGY EDUCATION ASSOCIATION

http://www.iteaconnect.org/

INTERNATIONAL TECHNOLOGY EDUCATION ASSOCIATION UNDERGRADUATE SCHOLARSHIP IN TECHNOLOGY EDUCATION

A scholarship for undergraduate students pursuing a degree in technology education and technological studies. Applicants must be members of the association.

Academic Fields/Career Goals: Education; Engineering/Technology; Science, Technology, and Society.

Award: Scholarship for use in freshman, sophomore, junior, or senior years; not renewable. *Number:* 3. *Amount:* $1000.

Eligibility Requirements: Applicant must be enrolled or expecting to enroll full-time at a four-year institution or university. Applicant or parent of applicant must be member of International Technology Education Association. Available to U.S. and non-U.S. citizens.

Application Requirements: Application form, recommendations or references, resume, transcript. *Deadline:* December 1.

Contact: Scholarship Committee
International Technology Education Association
1914 Association Drive, Suite 201
Reston, VA 20191
Phone: 703-860-2100
Fax: 703-860-0353
E-mail: iteaordr@iris.org

JACK J. ISGUR FOUNDATION

www.isgur.org

JACK J. ISGUR FOUNDATION SCHOLARSHIP

Awards scholarships to juniors, seniors, and graduate students with intentions of teaching the humanities in grades kindergarten through 8th grade, preferably in rural Missouri.

Academic Fields/Career Goals: Education; Humanities; Music.

Award: Scholarship for use in junior, senior, graduate, or postgraduate years; not renewable. *Number:* 5–100. *Amount:* $750–$1500.

Eligibility Requirements: Applicant must be enrolled or expecting to enroll full- or part-time at a four-year institution or university. Available to U.S. and non-U.S. citizens.

Application Requirements: Application form, essay, interview. *Deadline:* May 15.

Contact: Mr. Charles Jensen, Administrator, Jack J. Isgur Foundation
Jack J. Isgur Foundation
Stinson Leonard Street Law Firm
1201 Walnut Street, 29th Floor
Kansas City, MO 64106
Phone: 816-691-2760
E-mail: charles.jensen@stinson.com

KANSAS NURSES FOUNDATION

KANSAS NURSES FOUNDATION

Kansas Nurses Foundation awards scholarships and research grants to Kansas residents who are U.S. citizens. Scholarships are awarded to students in nursing programs leading to register nurse (RN), Bachelor of Science in Nursing (BSN), and Graduate Nursing (MSN, DNP, EdD, PhD) programs. Criteria for scholarships and application may be found on the Kansas Nurses Foundation tab at www.ksnurses.com

Academic Fields/Career Goals: Education; Nursing.

Award: Scholarship for use in freshman, sophomore, junior, senior, graduate, or postgraduate years; not renewable. *Number:* 18–25. *Amount:* $300–$1000.

Eligibility Requirements: Applicant must be age 18-99; enrolled or expecting to enroll full- or part-time at a two-year or four-year institution and resident of Kansas. Available to U.S. citizens.

Application Requirements: Application form, essay. *Deadline:* June 30.

NASA FLORIDA SPACE GRANT CONSORTIUM

http://www.floridaspacegrant.org/

FLORIDA SPACE RESEARCH PROGRAM
• *See page 131*

NASA RHODE ISLAND SPACE GRANT CONSORTIUM

http://brown/initiatives/ri-space-grant

NASA RISGC SUMMER SCHOLARSHIP FOR UNDERGRADUATE STUDENTS
• *See page 132*

NATIONAL ASSOCIATION FOR CAMPUS ACTIVITIES

http://www.naca.org/

NATIONAL ASSOCIATION FOR CAMPUS ACTIVITIES MID ATLANTIC HIGHER EDUCATION RESEARCH SCHOLARSHIP

The NACA Mid Atlantic Higher Education Research Scholarship was established in 1995 by the former NACA East Coast Region. The scholarship provides funds for research projects designed to add to the college student personnel knowledge base, particularly those projects which focus on campus activities, address issues challenging student affairs practitioners and/or issues challenging higher education as they relate to campus activities. The fund provides up to $500 to be awarded annually.

Academic Fields/Career Goals: Education.

Award: Scholarship for use in freshman, sophomore, junior, senior, graduate, or postgraduate years; not renewable. *Number:* 1. *Amount:* $50–$500.

Eligibility Requirements: Applicant must be enrolled or expecting to enroll full- or part-time at a two-year institution or university and studying in Delaware, District of Columbia, Maryland, New Jersey, New York, Ontario, Pennsylvania. Available to U.S. citizens.

Application Requirements: Application form, application form may be submitted online, essay. *Deadline:* June 30.

Contact: Sarah Keeling, Director of Education and Research
Phone: 803-217-3485
E-mail: scholarships@naca.org

NATIONAL COUNCIL OF TEACHERS OF MATHEMATICS

http://www.nctm.org/

PROSPECTIVE SECONDARY TEACHER COURSE WORK SCHOLARSHIPS

Grant provides financial support to college students preparing for teaching secondary school mathematics. Award of $10,000 will be granted in two phases, with $5000 for the recipient's third year of full-time study, and $5000 for fourth year. Must be student members of NCTM and cannot reapply. Must submit proposal, essay, letters of recommendation, and transcripts.

Academic Fields/Career Goals: Education; Mathematics.

Award: Scholarship for use in junior or senior years; not renewable. *Number:* 2. *Amount:* up to $5000.

Eligibility Requirements: Applicant must be enrolled or expecting to enroll full-time at a four-year institution or university. Available to U.S. and non-U.S. citizens.

Application Requirements: Application form, essay, recommendations or references, transcript, written proposal. *Deadline:* May 9.

Contact: Mathematics Education Trust
Phone: 703-620-9840 Ext. 2112
Fax: 703-476-2970
E-mail: exec@nctm.org

NORTH CAROLINA ASSOCIATION OF EDUCATORS

http://www.ncae.org/

MARY MORROW-EDNA RICHARDS SCHOLARSHIP

One-time award for junior year of study in four-year education degree program. Preference given to members of the student branch of the North Carolina Association of Educators. Must be North Carolina resident attending a North Carolina institution. Must agree to teach in North Carolina for two years after graduation. Must be a junior in college when application is filed.

Academic Fields/Career Goals: Education.

Award: Scholarship for use in senior year; not renewable. *Number:* 3–8. *Amount:* up to $1000.

Eligibility Requirements: Applicant must be enrolled or expecting to enroll full-time at a four-year institution or university; resident of North

Carolina and studying in North Carolina. Applicant or parent of applicant must be member of Other Student Academic Clubs. Available to U.S. citizens.

Application Requirements: Application form, essay, financial need analysis, recommendations or references, transcript. *Deadline:* January 13.

Contact: Annette Montgomery, Communications Secretary
Phone: 800-662-7924
Fax: 919-839-8229
E-mail: annette.montgomery@ncae.org

OREGON PTA

http://www.oregonpta.org/

TEACHER EDUCATION SCHOLARSHIP

Nonrenewable scholarships to high school seniors or college students who are Oregon residents who want to teach in Oregon at an elementary or secondary school. The scholarship may be used at any Oregon public college or university that trains teachers or that transfers credits in education.

Academic Fields/Career Goals: Education.

Award: Scholarship for use in freshman, sophomore, junior, or senior years; not renewable. *Number:* 6–13. *Amount:* $500.

Eligibility Requirements: Applicant must be enrolled or expecting to enroll full-time at a two-year or four-year institution or university; resident of Oregon and studying in Oregon. Available to U.S. citizens.

Application Requirements: Application form, essay. *Deadline:* March 21.

Contact: Scholarship Committee
Oregon PTA
4506 Southeast Belmont Street, Suite 108-B
Portland, OR 97215
E-mail: or_office@pta.org

PADDLE CANADA

http://www.paddlecanada.com

BILL MASON SCHOLARSHIP FUND

The Bill Mason Memorial Scholarship Fund is a tribute to the late Bill Mason, a Canadian recognized both nationally and internationally as an avid canoeist, environmentalist, filmmaker, photographer, artist and public speaker. The scholarship is intended to incorporate some of the characteristics that made Bill Mason unique and to help ensure that the memory, spirit and ideals that he represented are kept fresh in the minds of Canadians. Applicants must demonstrate experience and competency in any or all of the following: canoeing and kayaking skills, wilderness travel experience, wilderness leadership and guiding, environmental issues, communication skills.

Academic Fields/Career Goals: Education; Environmental Science; Natural Resources; Natural Sciences; Recreation, Parks, Leisure Studies; Sports-Related/Exercise Science.

Award: Scholarship for use in sophomore, junior, or senior years; not renewable. *Number:* 1. *Amount:* $943.

Eligibility Requirements: Applicant must be Canadian citizen; enrolled or expecting to enroll full-time at a two-year or four-year institution or university; resident of Alberta, British Columbia, Manitoba, New Brunswick, Newfoundland, Northwest Territories, Nova Scotia, Ontario, Prince Edward Island, Quebec, Saskatchewan, Yukon and studying in Alberta, British Columbia, Manitoba, New Brunswick, Newfoundland, Northwest Territories, Nova Scotia, Ontario, Prince Edward Island, Quebec, Saskatchewan, Yukon.

Application Requirements: Application form, community service, driver's license, financial need analysis. *Deadline:* September 30.

Contact: Mr. Graham Ketcheson, Executive Director
Paddle Canada
PO Box 126 Station Main
Kingston, ON K7L 4V6
CAN
Phone: 888-252-6292 Ext. 11
E-mail: graham@paddlecanada.com

PANCHOLI COSMETIC SURGERY

https://www.drpancholi.com/

PANCHOLI SCHOLARSHIP FOR NEVADA EDUCATORS

Any current Nevada resident who is interested in a career in education and is pursuing a degree is welcome to apply for the $2,000 scholarship--whether you are a high school senior, current education major, or considering returning to school. Eligible candidates must meet the following criteria: 1. Must be a Nevada resident; 2. Must be pursuing a degree or career path in an education-related field at an institution of higher learning the following semester; 3. Must submit one letter of recommendation with valid contact information; 4. Must complete the application form, provide original essay answers, and upload completed application and one letter of reference.

Academic Fields/Career Goals: Education.

Award: Scholarship for use in freshman, sophomore, junior, senior, graduate, or postgraduate years; not renewable. *Number:* 1. *Amount:* $2000.

Eligibility Requirements: Applicant must be enrolled or expecting to enroll full- or part-time at a two-year or four-year institution or university; resident of Nevada and studying in Nevada. Available to U.S. citizens.

Application Requirements: Application form, essay. *Deadline:* December 13.

Contact: Emily Bradley, Marketing Assistant
E-mail: pancholischolarship@gmail.com

PHI DELTA KAPPA INTERNATIONAL

http://www.pdkintl.org/

PHI DELTA KAPPA INTERNATIONAL PROSPECTIVE EDUCATOR SCHOLARSHIPS

High school seniors and current undergraduates who are pursuing careers in teaching are eligible for Prospective Educator Scholarships. Applicants must be connected to the PDK family of associations through membership in Educators Rising, PDK International, and/or Pi Lambda Theta.

Academic Fields/Career Goals: Education.

Award: Scholarship for use in freshman, sophomore, junior, or senior years; not renewable. *Number:* 25–35. *Amount:* $500–$2000.

Eligibility Requirements: Applicant must be enrolled or expecting to enroll full- or part-time at a four-year institution or university. Applicant or parent of applicant must be member of Phi Delta Kappa International. Available to U.S. and non-U.S. citizens.

Application Requirements: Application form, essay. *Deadline:* April 2.

Contact: Katrina Breese, Senior Director of Development &
Engagement
Phi Delta Kappa International
PO Box 13090
Arlington, VA 22219
Phone: 812-339-1156
Fax: 812-339-0018
E-mail: scholarships@pdkintl.org

PRESBYTERIAN CHURCH (USA)

https://www.presbyterianmission.org/

STUDENT OPPORTUNITY SCHOLARSHIP

Designed to assist undergraduate students with their sophomore, junior and senior year of college. Restricted to members of the Presbyterian Church (USA).

Academic Fields/Career Goals: Education; Health and Medical Sciences; Religion/Theology; Social Sciences; Social Services.

Award: Scholarship for use in sophomore, junior, or senior years; renewable. *Number:* 68. *Amount:* up to $3000.

Eligibility Requirements: Applicant must be Presbyterian and enrolled or expecting to enroll full-time at a four-year institution or university. Available to U.S. citizens.

Application Requirements: Application form, essay, financial need analysis, recommendations or references, resume, transcript. *Deadline:* June 1.

Contact: Ms. Laura Bryan, Coordinator, Financial Aid for Studies
Presbyterian Church (USA)
100 Witherspoon Street
Louisville, KY 40202
Phone: 800-728-7228 Ext. 5735
Fax: 502-569-8766
E-mail: finaid@pcusa.org

SARAH KLENKE MEMORIAL TEACHING SCHOLARSHIP

http://www.sarahklenkescholarship.org/

SARAH ELIZABETH KLENKE MEMORIAL TEACHING SCHOLARSHIP

Scholarship for deserving young adults to achieve the goal of becoming teachers. Must have a 2.0 GPA or higher, participate in JROTC or a team sport, and a desire to major in education.

Academic Fields/Career Goals: Education.

Award: Scholarship for use in freshman or senior years; not renewable. *Number:* 1. *Amount:* $1000.

Eligibility Requirements: Applicant must be enrolled or expecting to enroll full-time at a two-year or four-year institution or university. Available to U.S. and non-U.S. citizens.

Application Requirements: Application form, essay, letter from coach or teacher confirming participation in ROTC or team sport, recommendations or references. *Deadline:* April 15.

Contact: William Klenke, Scholarship Committee
Sarah Klenke Memorial Teaching Scholarship
9108 Charred Oak Drive
Bethesda, MD 20817
Phone: 202-412-2812
E-mail: wjk40@yahoo.com

THE SOCIETY FOR THE SCIENTIFIC STUDY OF SEXUALITY

http://www.sexscience.org/

THE SOCIETY FOR THE SCIENTIFIC STUDY OF SEXUALITY STUDENT RESEARCH GRANT
• *See page 105*

SOUTH DAKOTA BOARD OF REGENTS

http://www.sdbor.edu/

SOUTH DAKOTA BOARD OF REGENTS ANNIS I. FOWLER/KADEN SCHOLARSHIP

Scholarship for graduating South Dakota high school seniors to pursue a career in elementary education at a South Dakota public university. University must be one of the following: BHSU, BSU, NSU or USD. Applicants must have a cumulative GPA of 3.0 after three years of high school. One-time award.

Academic Fields/Career Goals: Education.

Award: Scholarship for use in freshman year; not renewable. *Number:* 2. *Amount:* $1000.

Eligibility Requirements: Applicant must be high school student; planning to enroll or expecting to enroll full-time at a four-year institution or university; resident of South Dakota and studying in South Dakota. Available to U.S. citizens.

Application Requirements: Application form, essay. *Deadline:* February 26.

Contact: Kerri Richards, Student Services Coordinator
South Dakota Board of Regents
306 E. Capitol Avenue
Suite 200
Pierre, SD 57501
Phone: 605-773-3455
E-mail: kerri.richards@sdbor.edu

STRAIGHTFORWARD MEDIA

http://www.straightforwardmedia.com/

STRAIGHTFORWARD MEDIA TEACHER SCHOLARSHIP

Scholarship of $500 for students planning to be teachers of any kind and at any level. Must be U.S. citizen. Awarded four times per year. Deadlines are January 14, April 14, July 14, and October 14. For more information, see website at http://www.straightforwardmedia.com/education/form.php.

Academic Fields/Career Goals: Education; Special Education.

Award: Scholarship for use in freshman, sophomore, junior, or senior years; not renewable. *Number:* 4. *Amount:* $500.

Eligibility Requirements: Applicant must be enrolled or expecting to enroll full- or part-time at a two-year or four-year or technical institution or university. Available to U.S. citizens.

Application Requirements: Essay. *Deadline:* varies.

Contact: Scholarship Committee
Phone: 605-348-3042

TAU KAPPA EPSILON EDUCATION FOUNDATION

https://www.tke.org/

CARROL C. HALL MEMORIAL SCHOLARSHIP

This scholarship is awarded in recognition of academic achievement and recognizes outstanding leadership within the chapter, on campus and in the community. The applicant must be pursuing an undergraduate degree in education or science, and have plans to be a teacher or pursue a profession in the field of science.

Academic Fields/Career Goals: Education; Science, Technology, and Society.

Award: Scholarship for use in freshman, sophomore, junior, or senior years. *Number:* 1.

Eligibility Requirements: Applicant must be enrolled or expecting to enroll at an institution or university and male. Applicant or parent of applicant must be member of Tau Kappa Epsilon. Available to U.S. citizens.

Application Requirements: Application form, application form may be submitted online, personal photograph. *Deadline:* March 15.

Contact: Rachel Stevenson, Foundation Communications Manager
Tau Kappa Epsilon Education Foundation
7439 Woodland Drive
Suite 100
Indianapolis, IN 46278
Phone: 317-872-6533 Ext. 246
E-mail: rstevenson@tke.org

FRANCIS J. FLYNN MEMORIAL SCHOLARSHIP

This scholarship is awarded in recognition of academic achievement with a Grade Point Average of at least 2.75 or higher, and recognizes outstanding leadership within the chapter. The applicant must be pursuing an undergraduate degree in mathematics or education. Preference will first be given to a member of Theta-Sigma Chapter, but if there is no qualified applicant, the scholarship will be open to any other qualified Teke.

Academic Fields/Career Goals: Education; Mathematics.

Award: Scholarship for use in freshman, sophomore, junior, or senior years. *Number:* 1.

Eligibility Requirements: Applicant must be enrolled or expecting to enroll at an institution or university and male. Applicant or parent of applicant must be member of Tau Kappa Epsilon. Available to U.S. citizens.

Application Requirements: Application form, application form may be submitted online, personal photograph. *Deadline:* March 15.

Contact: Rachel Stevenson, Foundation Communications Manager
Tau Kappa Epsilon Education Foundation
7439 Woodland Drive
Suite 100
Indianapolis, IN 46278
Phone: 317-872-6533 Ext. 246
E-mail: rstevenson@tke.org

TEACHER.ORG

http://www.teacher.org

"INSPIRE OUR FUTURE" $2,500 SCHOLARSHIP

Teacher.org offers a $2500 scholarship for college students studying to become teachers or work in the field of education.

Academic Fields/Career Goals: Education.

Award: Scholarship for use in sophomore, junior, senior, graduate, or postgraduate years; not renewable. *Number:* 1. *Amount:* $2500.

Eligibility Requirements: Applicant must be enrolled or expecting to enroll full- or part-time at a two-year or four-year or technical institution or university. Available to U.S. citizens.

Application Requirements: Application form, application form may be submitted online (http://www.teacher.org), essay, transcript. *Deadline:* April 1.

Contact: Salpy Baharian, Co-Founder
Teacher.org
7120 Hayvenhurst Avenue
Van Nuys, CA 91406
Phone: 818-860-8620
E-mail: scholarships@teacher.org

TENNESSEE EDUCATION ASSOCIATION

http://www.teateachers.org/

TEA DON SAHLI-KATHY WOODALL FUTURE TEACHERS OF AMERICA SCHOLARSHIP

Scholarship is available to a high school senior planning to major in education, attending a high school which has an FTA Chapter affiliated with TEA, and planning to enroll in a Tennessee college or university.

Academic Fields/Career Goals: Education.

Award: Scholarship for use in freshman year; not renewable. *Number:* 1. *Amount:* $1000.

Eligibility Requirements: Applicant must be high school student; planning to enroll or expecting to enroll full-time at an institution or university; resident of South Dakota and studying in Tennessee. Applicant or parent of applicant must have employment or volunteer experience in community service. Available to U.S. citizens.

Application Requirements: Application form, application form may be submitted online, essay, financial need analysis. *Deadline:* March 1.

Contact: Jeanette DeMain
Tennessee Education Association
801 Second Avenue North
Nashville, TN 37201-1099
Phone: 615-242-8392 Ext. 210
E-mail: jdemain@tnea.org

TEA DON SAHLI-KATHY WOODALL MINORITY SCHOLARSHIP

Scholarship is available to a minority high school senior planning to major in education and planning to enroll in a Tennessee college or university. Application must be made by an FTA Chapter, or by the student with the recommendation of an active TEA member.

Academic Fields/Career Goals: Education.

Award: Scholarship for use in freshman year; not renewable. *Number:* 1. *Amount:* $1000.

Eligibility Requirements: Applicant must be American Indian/Alaska Native, Asian/Pacific Islander, Black (non-Hispanic), Hispanic; high school student; planning to enroll or expecting to enroll full-time at an institution or university; resident of South Dakota and studying in Tennessee. Applicant or parent of applicant must have employment or volunteer experience in community service. Available to U.S. citizens.

Application Requirements: Application form, application form may be submitted online, essay, financial need analysis. *Deadline:* March 1.

Contact: Jeanette DeMain
Tennessee Education Association
801 Second Avenue North
Nashville, TN 37201
Phone: 615-242-8392 Ext. 210
E-mail: jdemain@tnea.org

TEA DON SAHLI-KATHY WOODALL SONS AND DAUGHTERS SCHOLARSHIP

Scholarship is available to a TEA member's child who is a high school senior, undergraduate or graduate student, and is planning to enroll, or is already enrolled, in a Tennessee college, majoring in education.

Academic Fields/Career Goals: Education.

Award: Scholarship for use in freshman, sophomore, junior, senior, or graduate years; not renewable. *Number:* 1. *Amount:* $1000.

Eligibility Requirements: Applicant must be enrolled or expecting to enroll full-time at an institution or university; resident of South Dakota and studying in Tennessee. Applicant or parent of applicant must be member of Tennessee Education Association. Applicant or parent of applicant must have employment or volunteer experience in community service, teaching/education. Available to U.S. citizens.

Application Requirements: Application form, application form may be submitted online, essay, financial need analysis. *Deadline:* March 1.

Contact: Jeanette DeMain
Tennessee Education Association
801 Second North
Nashville, TN 37201
Phone: 615-242-8392 Ext. 210
E-mail: jdemain@tnea.org

TEA DON SAHLI-KATHY WOODALL STEA SCHOLARSHIP

Scholarship is available to undergraduate students who are student TEA members. Application must be made through the local STEA Chapter. Amount varies from $500 to $1000.

Academic Fields/Career Goals: Education.

Award: Scholarship for use in freshman, sophomore, junior, or senior years; not renewable. *Number:* 4. *Amount:* $500–$1000.

Eligibility Requirements: Applicant must be enrolled or expecting to enroll full- or part-time at an institution or university; resident of South Dakota and studying in Tennessee. Applicant or parent of applicant must be member of Tennessee Education Association. Applicant or parent of applicant must have employment or volunteer experience in community service. Available to U.S. citizens.

Application Requirements: Application form, application form may be submitted online, essay, financial need analysis. *Deadline:* March 1.

Contact: Jeanette DeMain
Tennessee Education Association
801 Second Avenue North
Nashville, TN 37201-1099
Phone: 615-242-8392 Ext. 210
E-mail: jdemain@tnea.org

UNIVERSITY OF WYOMING

http://www.uwyo.edu/scholarships

SUPERIOR STUDENT IN EDUCATION SCHOLARSHIP-WYOMING

Scholarship available each year to sixteen Wyoming high school graduates who plan to teach in Wyoming. The award covers costs of undergraduate tuition at the University of Wyoming or any Wyoming community college.

Academic Fields/Career Goals: Education.

Award: Scholarship for use in freshman, sophomore, junior, or senior years; renewable. *Number:* 16–16. *Amount:* $1000.

Eligibility Requirements: Applicant must be enrolled or expecting to enroll full-time at a two-year or four-year institution or university; resident of Wyoming and studying in Wyoming. Available to U.S. citizens.

Application Requirements: Application form, recommendations or references, test scores, transcript. *Deadline:* October 31.

Contact: Tammy Mack, Assistant Director, Scholarships
University of Wyoming
Department 3335
1000 East University Avenue
Laramie, WY 82071
Phone: 307-766-2412
Fax: 307-766-3800
E-mail: FinAid@uwyo.edu

VERMONT-NEA

http://www.vtnea.org/

VERMONT-NEA/MAIDA F. TOWNSEND SCHOLARSHIP

Scholarship of $1000 to sons and daughters of Vermont-NEA members in their last year of high school, undergraduates, and graduate students. Students majoring in any discipline are eligible to apply, but preference may be given to those majoring in education, or having that intention.

Academic Fields/Career Goals: Education.

Award: Scholarship for use in freshman, sophomore, junior, senior, or graduate years; not renewable. *Number:* 5. *Amount:* $1000.

Eligibility Requirements: Applicant must be enrolled or expecting to enroll full- or part-time at a two-year or four-year or technical institution or university. Applicant or parent of applicant must be member of Vermont-NEA. Applicant or parent of applicant must have employment or volunteer experience in teaching/education. Available to U.S. and non-U.S. citizens.

Application Requirements: Application form, community service, cover letter, essay, recommendations or references, test scores, transcript. *Deadline:* February 1.

Contact: Sandy Perkins, Administrative Assistant
Vermont-NEA
10 Wheelock Street
Montpelier, VT 05602-3737
Phone: 802-223-6375
E-mail: sperkins@vtnea.org

VIRGINIA CONGRESS OF PARENTS AND TEACHERS

http://www.vapta.org/

FRIEDA L. KOONTZ SCHOLARSHIP

Scholarship of $1200 to graduating high school students planning to enter teaching or other youth-serving professions in Virginia. Must be Virginia residents graduating from a Virginia public high school with a Parent-Teacher-Student Association (PTSA) and attending a Virginia college or university. Minimum 2.5 GPA required.

Academic Fields/Career Goals: Education.

Award: Scholarship for use in freshman year; not renewable. *Number:* 1. *Amount:* $1200.

Eligibility Requirements: Applicant must be high school student; planning to enroll or expecting to enroll full-time at a four-year institution or university; resident of Virginia and studying in Virginia. Applicant or parent of applicant must be member of Parent-Teacher Association/Organization. Available to U.S. citizens.

Application Requirements: Application form, essay, recommendations or references, test scores, transcript. *Deadline:* March 1.

Contact: Daniel Phillips, Scholarship Chair
Phone: 804-264-1234
E-mail: info@vapta.org

GENERAL SCHOLARSHIPS

General scholarships in addition to the Freida L. Koontz and John S. Davis Scholarships. Only graduating students enrolled in a Virginia school that is a PTA or PTSA school may apply. See website for application details.

Academic Fields/Career Goals: Education.

Award: Scholarship for use in freshman year; not renewable. *Number:* 10–20. *Amount:* $1000.

Eligibility Requirements: Applicant must be high school student; planning to enroll or expecting to enroll full-time at a four-year institution or university and resident of Virginia. Applicant or parent of applicant must be member of Parent-Teacher Association/Organization. Available to U.S. citizens.

Application Requirements: Application form, essay, recommendations or references, test scores, transcript. *Deadline:* March 1.

Contact: Daniel Phillips, Scholarship Chair
Phone: 804-264-1234
E-mail: info@vapta.org

S. JOHN DAVIS SCHOLARSHIP

Scholarship of $1200 to Virginia residents graduating from a Virginia public school that has a Parent-Teacher-Student Association (PTSA) or PTA. Must be planning to attend a Virginia college or university and pursuing a career in teaching or qualifying for service with a youth-serving agency in Virginia. Minimum 2.5 GPA required.

Academic Fields/Career Goals: Education.

Award: Scholarship for use in freshman year; not renewable. *Number:* 1. *Amount:* $1200.

Eligibility Requirements: Applicant must be high school student; planning to enroll or expecting to enroll full-time at a four-year institution or university; resident of Virginia and studying in Virginia. Applicant or parent of applicant must be member of Parent-Teacher Association/Organization. Available to U.S. citizens.

Application Requirements: Application form, essay. *Deadline:* March 1.

Contact: Daniel Phillips, Scholarship Chair
Phone: 804-264-1234
E-mail: info@vapta.org

WISCONSIN CONGRESS OF PARENTS AND TEACHERS INC.

http://www.wisconsinpta.org/

BROOKMIRE-HASTINGS SCHOLARSHIPS

One-time award to graduating high school seniors from Wisconsin public schools. Must pursue a degree in education. High school must have an active PTA in good standing of the Wisconsin PTA.

Academic Fields/Career Goals: Education; Special Education.

Award: Scholarship for use in freshman year; not renewable. *Number:* up to 2. *Amount:* $1000.

Eligibility Requirements: Applicant must be high school student; planning to enroll or expecting to enroll full-time at a four-year institution or university and resident of Wisconsin. Available to U.S. citizens.

Application Requirements: Application form, essay, interview, recommendations or references, transcript. *Deadline:* March 1.

Contact: Kim Schwantes, Executive Administrator
Wisconsin Congress of Parents and Teachers Inc.
4797 Hayes Road, Suite 2
Madison, WI 53704-3256
Phone: 608-244-1455

WISCONSIN MATHEMATICS EDUCATION FOUNDATION

http://wmefonline.org/

ARNE ENGEBRETSEN WISCONSIN MATHEMATICS COUNCIL SCHOLARSHIP

Scholarship for Wisconsin high school senior who is planning to study mathematics education and teach mathematics at K-12 level.

Academic Fields/Career Goals: Education; Mathematics.

Award: Scholarship for use in freshman year; not renewable. *Number:* 1. *Amount:* $2000.

Eligibility Requirements: Applicant must be high school student; planning to enroll or expecting to enroll full-time at a four-year institution or university and resident of Wisconsin. Available to U.S. citizens.

Application Requirements: Application form, essay, recommendations or references, resume, transcript. *Deadline:* March 1.

ETHEL A. NEIJAHR WISCONSIN MATHEMATICS COUNCIL SCHOLARSHIP

Scholarship for a Wisconsin resident who is currently enrolled in teacher education programs in a Wisconsin institution studying mathematics education. Minimum GPA of 3.0 required.

Academic Fields/Career Goals: Education; Mathematics.

Award: Scholarship for use in junior or senior years; not renewable. *Number:* 1. *Amount:* $2000.

Eligibility Requirements: Applicant must be enrolled or expecting to enroll full-time at a four-year institution or university; resident of Wisconsin and studying in Wisconsin. Available to U.S. citizens.

Application Requirements: Application form, essay, recommendations or references, resume, transcript. *Deadline:* March 1.

SISTER MARY PETRONIA VAN STRATEN WISCONSIN MATHEMATICS COUNCIL SCHOLARSHIP

Scholarship for a Wisconsin resident who is currently enrolled in teacher education programs in Wisconsin institution studying mathematics education. Minimum GPA of 3.0 required.

Academic Fields/Career Goals: Education; Mathematics.

Award: Scholarship for use in junior or senior years; not renewable. *Number:* 1. *Amount:* $2000.

Eligibility Requirements: Applicant must be enrolled or expecting to enroll full-time at a four-year institution or university; resident of Wisconsin and studying in Wisconsin. Available to U.S. citizens.

Application Requirements: Application form, essay, recommendations or references, resume, transcript. *Deadline:* March 1.

WOMEN BAND DIRECTORS INTERNATIONAL

http://www.womenbanddirectors.org/

CHARLOTTE PLUMMER OWEN MEMORIAL SCHOLARSHIP

One-time award for women instrumental music majors enrolled in a four-year institution. Applicants must be working toward a degree in music education with the intention of becoming a band director. See website for application http://www.womenbanddirectors.org/.

Academic Fields/Career Goals: Education; Music; Performing Arts.

Award: Scholarship for use in freshman, sophomore, junior, or senior years; not renewable. *Number:* 4. *Amount:* $300.

Eligibility Requirements: Applicant must be enrolled or expecting to enroll full-time at a four-year institution or university; female and must have an interest in music/singing. Available to U.S. and non-U.S. citizens.

Application Requirements: Application form, essay, personal photograph, recommendations or references, transcript. *Deadline:* December 1.

Contact: Nicole Aakre-Rubis, Scholarship Chair
Women Band Directors International
16085 Excel Way
Rosemount, MN 55068

MARTHA ANN STARK MEMORIAL SCHOLARSHIP

One-time award for women instrumental music majors enrolled in a four-year institution. Applicants must be working toward a degree in music education with the intention of becoming a band director. Three of the scholarships are designated for college upperclassmen, and one is open to all levels. See website for application http://www.womenband directors.org/.

Academic Fields/Career Goals: Education; Music; Performing Arts.

Award: Scholarship for use in freshman, sophomore, junior, or senior years; not renewable. *Number:* 1. *Amount:* $300.

Eligibility Requirements: Applicant must be enrolled or expecting to enroll full-time at a four-year institution or university; female and must have an interest in music/singing. Available to U.S. and non-U.S. citizens.

Application Requirements: Application form, essay, personal photograph, recommendations or references, transcript. *Deadline:* December 1.

Contact: Nicole Aakre-Rubis, Scholarship Chair
Women Band Directors International
16085 Excel Way
Rosemount, MN 55068

VOLKWEIN MEMORIAL SCHOLARSHIP

One-time award for female instrumental music majors enrolled in a four-year institution. Applicants must be working toward a degree in music education with the intention of becoming a band director. Three of the

scholarships are designated for college upperclassmen, and one is open to all levels. See website for application http://www.womenband directors.org/.

Academic Fields/Career Goals: Education; Music; Performing Arts.

Award: Scholarship for use in freshman, sophomore, junior, senior, or graduate years; not renewable. *Number:* 4. *Amount:* $300–$500.

Eligibility Requirements: Applicant must be enrolled or expecting to enroll full-time at a four-year institution or university; female and must have an interest in music/singing. Available to U.S. and non-U.S. citizens.

Application Requirements: Application form, essay, personal photograph, recommendations or references, self-addressed stamped envelope with application, transcript. *Deadline:* December 1.

Contact: Nicole Aakre-Rubis, Scholarship Chair
Women Band Directors International
16085 Excel Way
Rosemount, MN 55068

WOMEN'S SPORTS FOUNDATION

http://www.womenssportsfoundation.org/

DOROTHEA DEITZ ENDOWED MEMORIAL SCHOLARSHIP

The Dorothea Deitz Endowed Memorial Scholarship was established in 2005 by the Dorothea Deitz Memorial Scholarship Fund Board of Trustees to encourage young women in New York to pursue careers in the physical education teaching profession.

Academic Fields/Career Goals: Education.

Award: Scholarship for use in freshman year; not renewable. *Number:* 1–9. *Amount:* $1000.

Eligibility Requirements: Applicant must be high school student; planning to enroll or expecting to enroll full-time at a four-year institution; female and resident of New York. Available to U.S. citizens.

Application Requirements: Application form. *Deadline:* May 31.

Contact: Elizabeth Flores
Phone: 516-307-3915
E-mail: lflores@womenssportsfoundation.org

Y'S MEN INTERNATIONAL

http://www.ysmen.org/

ALEXANDER SCHOLARSHIP LOAN FUND
• See page 152

ELECTRICAL ENGINEERING/ ELECTRONICS

AACE INTERNATIONAL

http://www.aacei.org/

AACE INTERNATIONAL COMPETITIVE SCHOLARSHIP
• See page 112

AHS INTERNATIONAL—THE VERTICAL FLIGHT TECHNICAL SOCIETY

http://www.vtol.org/

VERTICAL FLIGHT FOUNDATION SCHOLARSHIP
• See page 126

AIST FOUNDATION

http://www.aistfoundation.org/

ASSOCIATION FOR IRON AND STEEL TECHNOLOGY BENJAMIN F. FAIRLESS SCHOLARSHIP (AIME)

• See page 152

ASSOCIATION FOR IRON AND STEEL TECHNOLOGY OHIO VALLEY CHAPTER SCHOLARSHIP

• See page 138

ASSOCIATION FOR IRON AND STEEL TECHNOLOGY RONALD E. LINCOLN SCHOLARSHIP

Scholarship for full-time students of metallurgy, materials science, chemical, mechanical, electrical, environmental, computer science, and industrial engineering. Students must have an interest in a career in the steel industry as demonstrated by an internship or related experience, or who have plans to pursue such experiences during college. Student may apply after first term of freshman year of college. Applications are accepted from 1 Sep through 31 Dec each year. Note: High school students do not qualify but are encouraged to learn about the steel industry and the career opportunities available therein, during their freshman year.

Academic Fields/Career Goals: Electrical Engineering/Electronics; Materials Science, Engineering, and Metallurgy; Mechanical Engineering.

Award: Scholarship for use in sophomore, junior, or senior years; not renewable. *Number:* 2. *Amount:* $3000.

Eligibility Requirements: Applicant must be enrolled or expecting to enroll full-time at a four-year institution or university. Available to U.S. and non-U.S. citizens.

Application Requirements: Application form, essay, recommendations or references, resume, transcript. *Deadline:* December 31.

Contact: Lori Wharrey, AIST Manager, Board Services
AIST Foundation
186 Thorn Hill Road
Warrendale, PA 15086
Phone: 724-814-3044
E-mail: lwharrey@aist.org

ASSOCIATION FOR IRON AND STEEL TECHNOLOGY WILLY KORF MEMORIAL SCHOLARSHIP

• See page 153

STEEL ENGINEERING EDUCATION LINK (STEEL) SCHOLARSHIPS

Scholarships are for full-time students of chemical, electrical, mechanical, computer science, environment, and industrial engineering. Students must have an interest in a career in the steel industry as demonstrated by an internship or related experience, or who have plans to pursue such experiences during college. Students must commit to a paid summer internship at a steel producing company (placement assistance is provided) prior to receiving this scholarship. Student may apply during their sophomore and junior years. Applications are accepted from 1 Sep through 31 Dec each year.

Academic Fields/Career Goals: Electrical Engineering/Electronics; Mechanical Engineering.

Award: Scholarship for use in sophomore or junior years; not renewable. *Number:* 1–10. *Amount:* $5000.

Eligibility Requirements: Applicant must be enrolled or expecting to enroll full-time at a four-year institution or university. Available to U.S. and non-U.S. citizens.

Application Requirements: Application form, essay, recommendations or references, resume, transcript. *Deadline:* December 31.

Contact: Lori Wharrey, AIST Manager, Board Services
AIST Foundation
186 Thorn Hill Road
Warrendale, PA 15086
Phone: 724-814-3044
E-mail: lwharrey@aist.org

AMERICAN CHEMICAL SOCIETY, RUBBER DIVISION

http://www.rubber.org/

AMERICAN CHEMICAL SOCIETY, RUBBER DIVISION UNDERGRADUATE SCHOLARSHIP

• See page 105

AMERICAN COUNCIL OF ENGINEERING COMPANIES OF PENNSYLVANIA (ACEC/PA)

http://www.acecpa.org/

ERIC J. GENNUSO AND LEROY D. (BUD) LOY, JR. SCHOLARSHIP PROGRAM

• See page 153

AMERICAN FOUNDATION FOR THE BLIND

http://www.afb.org/

PAUL W. RUCKES SCHOLARSHIP

• See page 179

AMERICAN INDIAN SCIENCE AND ENGINEERING SOCIETY

http://www.aises.org/

A.T. ANDERSON MEMORIAL SCHOLARSHIP PROGRAM

• See page 105

AMERICAN INSTITUTE OF AERONAUTICS AND ASTRONAUTICS

https://www.aiaa.org/

AIAA FOUNDATION UNDERGRADUATE SCHOLARSHIPS

• See page 127

LEATRICE GREGORY PENDRAY SCHOLARSHIP

• See page 127

AMERICAN PUBLIC POWER ASSOCIATION

https://www.publicpower.org/deed-rd-funding

DEMONSTRATION OF ENERGY AND EFFICIENCY DEVELOPMENTS EDUCATIONAL SCHOLARSHIP

• See page 154

DEMONSTRATION OF ENERGY AND EFFICIENCY DEVELOPMENTS STUDENT INTERNSHIP

• See page 154

DEMONSTRATION OF ENERGY AND EFFICIENCY DEVELOPMENTS STUDENT RESEARCH GRANTS

• See page 162

DEMONSTRATION OF ENERGY AND EFFICIENCY DEVELOPMENTS TECHNICAL DESIGN PROJECT

• See page 154

AMERICAN PUBLIC TRANSPORTATION FOUNDATION

https://www.aptfd.org/

TRANSIT HALL OF FAME SCHOLARSHIP AWARD PROGRAM
• *See page 162*

AMERICAN RAILWAY ENGINEERING AND MAINTENANCE OF WAY ASSOCIATION

http://www.aremafoundation.org/

AREMA GRADUATE AND UNDERGRADUATE SCHOLARSHIPS
• *See page 162*

AMERICAN SOCIETY OF CERTIFIED ENGINEERING TECHNICIANS

http://www.ascet.org/

KURT H. AND DONNA M. SCHULER SMALL GRANT
• *See page 162*

AMERICAN SOCIETY OF NAVAL ENGINEERS

http://www.navalengineers.org/

AMERICAN SOCIETY OF NAVAL ENGINEERS SCHOLARSHIP
• *See page 106*

ARMED FORCES COMMUNICATIONS AND ELECTRONICS ASSOCIATION, EDUCATIONAL FOUNDATION

https://foundation.afcea.org

AFCEA STEM MAJORS SCHOLARSHIPS FOR UNDERGRADUATE STUDENTS
• *See page 106*

ARMED FORCES COMMUNICATIONS AND ELECTRONICS ASSOCIATION ROTC SCHOLARSHIP PROGRAM
• *See page 179*

ASIAN PACIFIC FUND

BANATAO FAMILY FILIPINO AMERICAN EDUCATION FUND
• *See page 155*

ASSOCIATION OF FEDERAL COMMUNICATIONS CONSULTING ENGINEERS

http://www.afcce.org

JULES COHEN SCHOLARSHIP

AFCCE/IEEE-BTS Scholarships provide financial assistance to students who are undertaking a full-time undergraduate or graduate program in engineering or science and demonstrate an interest in careers in telecommunications consulting or broadcast engineering. AFCCE Scholarships generally range between $500 to $2,500 per semester and the IEEE-BTS Jules Cohen Scholarships, administered by the AFCCE,

are either $5,000 or $10,000. A single application to the AFCCE will automatically enter the student for consideration for all scholarships for which you are eligible during each semester.

Academic Fields/Career Goals: Electrical Engineering/Electronics; Engineering-Related Technologies; Science, Technology, and Society.

Award: Scholarship for use in junior, senior, or graduate years; not renewable. *Number:* 1–13. *Amount:* $5000–$10,000.

Eligibility Requirements: Applicant must be enrolled or expecting to enroll full-time at a four-year institution or university and studying in Alabama, Alaska, Arizona, Arkansas, California, Colorado, Connecticut, Delaware, District of Columbia, Florida, Georgia, Guam, Hawaii, Idaho, Illinois, Indiana, Iowa, Kansas, Kentucky, Louisiana, Maine, Maryland, Massachusetts, Michigan, Minnesota, Mississippi, Missouri, Montana, Nebraska, Nevada, New Hampshire, New Jersey, New Mexico, New York, North Carolina, North Dakota, Ohio, Oklahoma, Oregon, Pennsylvania, Puerto Rico, Rhode Island, South Carolina, South Dakota, Tennessee, Texas, Utah, Vermont, Virginia, Washington, West Virginia, Wisconsin, Wyoming. Available to U.S. and non-U.S. citizens.

Application Requirements: Application form, essay. *Deadline:* April 30.

Contact: Mr. Marshall Cross, Chair, AFCCE Scholarship Committee
Association of Federal Communications Consulting Engineers
MegaWave Corporation
100 Jackson Road
Devens, MA 01434
Phone: 978-615-7200 Ext. 14
Fax: 978-615-7241
E-mail: mcross@megawave.com

ASSOCIATION OF STATE DAM SAFETY OFFICIALS (ASDSO)

http://www.DamSafety.org

ASSOCIATION OF STATE DAM SAFETY OFFICIALS (ASDSO) SENIOR UNDERGRADUATE SCHOLARSHIP
• *See page 140*

ASTRONAUT SCHOLARSHIP FOUNDATION

http://www.astronautscholarship.org/

ASTRONAUT SCHOLARSHIP
• *See page 107*

AUTOMOTIVE WOMEN'S ALLIANCE FOUNDATION

http://awafoundation.org/index.php

AUTOMOTIVE WOMEN'S ALLIANCE FOUNDATION SCHOLARSHIPS
• *See page 71*

BARRY GOLDWATER SCHOLARSHIP AND EXCELLENCE IN EDUCATION FOUNDATION

https://goldwater.scholarsapply.org

BARRY M. GOLDWATER SCHOLARSHIP AND EXCELLENCE IN EDUCATION PROGRAM
• *See page 107*

BHW GROUP

https://thebhwgroup.com/

BHW WOMEN IN STEM SCHOLARSHIP
• *See page 107*

BRASKEM ODEBRECHT

http://www.odebrechtaward.com

ODEBRECHT AWARD FOR SUSTAINABLE DEVELOPMENT
• *See page 113*

BROWN AND CALDWELL

http://www.brownandcaldwell.com

ECKENFELDER SCHOLARSHIP
• *See page 141*

MINORITY SCHOLARSHIP PROGRAM
• *See page 141*

CARDS AGAINST HUMANITY

https://cardsagainsthumanity.com/

SCIENCE AMBASSADOR SCHOLARSHIP
• *See page 107*

CATCHING THE DREAM

http://www.catchingthedream.org/

TRIBAL BUSINESS MANAGEMENT PROGRAM (TBM)
• *See page 72*

CENTER FOR ARCHITECTURE

www.centerforarchitecture.org

CENTER FOR ARCHITECTURE DESIGN SCHOLARSHIP
• *See page 114*

DISTIL NETWORKS

http://www.distilnetworks.com

WOMEN FORWARD IN TECHNOLOGY SCHOLARSHIP PROGRAM
• *See page 108*

THE ELECTROCHEMICAL SOCIETY

https://www.electrochem.org/

BATTERY DIVISION STUDENT RESEARCH AWARD SPONSORED BY MERCEDES-BENZ RESEARCH & DEVELOPMENT
• *See page 155*

H.H. DOW MEMORIAL STUDENT ACHIEVEMENT AWARD OF THE INDUSTRIAL ELECTROLYSIS AND ELECTROCHEMICAL ENGINEERING DIVISION OF THE ELECTROCHEMICAL SOCIETY INC
• *See page 156*

FLORIDA ENGINEERING SOCIETY

https://www.fleng.org/page/Scholarships

DAVID F. LUDOVICI SCHOLARSHIP
• *See page 156*

GREAT MINDS IN STEM

http://www.greatmindsinstem.org/college/scholarship-application-information

HENAAC SCHOLARSHIP PROGRAM
• *See page 100*

ILLUMINATING ENGINEERING SOCIETY OF NORTH AMERICA–GOLDEN GATE SECTION

http://www.iesgg.org/

ALAN LUCAS MEMORIAL EDUCATIONAL SCHOLARSHIP
• *See page 116*

INTERNATIONAL COMMUNICATIONS INDUSTRIES FOUNDATION

http://www.infocomm.org/scholarships

ICIF SCHOLARSHIP FOR EMPLOYEES AND DEPENDENTS OF MEMBER ORGANIZATIONS
• *See page 172*

INTERNATIONAL COMMUNICATIONS INDUSTRIES FOUNDATION AV SCHOLARSHIP
• *See page 172*

INTERNATIONAL SOCIETY FOR OPTICAL ENGINEERING-SPIE

http://www.spie.org/scholarships

SPIE EDUCATIONAL SCHOLARSHIPS IN OPTICAL SCIENCE AND ENGINEERING
• *See page 108*

INTERNATIONAL SOCIETY OF EXPLOSIVES ENGINEERS

http://www.isee.org/

JERRY MCDOWELL FUND
• *See page 156*

JORGE MAS CANOSA FREEDOM FOUNDATION

http://masscholarships.org/

MAS FAMILY SCHOLARSHIP AWARD
• *See page 149*

LOGMEIN

https://www.logmeininc.com

LASTPASS STEM SCHOLARSHIP
• *See page 109*

LOS ANGELES COUNCIL OF BLACK PROFESSIONAL ENGINEERS

http://www.lablackengineers.org/

AL-BEN SCHOLARSHIP FOR ACADEMIC INCENTIVE
• *See page 157*

AL-BEN SCHOLARSHIP FOR PROFESSIONAL MERIT
• *See page 157*

AL-BEN SCHOLARSHIP FOR SCHOLASTIC ACHIEVEMENT
• *See page 157*

NASA FLORIDA SPACE GRANT CONSORTIUM

http://www.floridaspacegrant.org/

FLORIDA SPACE RESEARCH PROGRAM
• *See page 131*

NASA IDAHO SPACE GRANT CONSORTIUM

http://www.idahospacegrant.org

NASA IDAHO SPACE GRANT CONSORTIUM SCHOLARSHIP PROGRAM
• *See page 109*

NASA/MARYLAND SPACE GRANT CONSORTIUM

https://md.spacegrant.org

NASA MARYLAND SPACE GRANT CONSORTIUM SCHOLARSHIPS
• *See page 109*

NASA MINNESOTA SPACE GRANT CONSORTIUM

https://www.mnspacegrant.org/

MINNESOTA SPACE GRANT CONSORTIUM SCHOLARSHIP PROGRAM
• *See page 131*

NASA MONTANA SPACE GRANT CONSORTIUM

http://www.spacegrant.montana.edu/

MONTANA SPACE GRANT SCHOLARSHIP PROGRAM
• *See page 132*

NASA'S VIRGINIA SPACE GRANT CONSORTIUM

http://www.vsgc.odu.edu/

COMMUNITY COLLEGE STEM SCHOLARSHIPS
• *See page 110*

UNDERGRADUATE STEM RESEARCH SCHOLARSHIPS
• *See page 110*

NATIONAL ASSOCIATION OF WOMEN IN CONSTRUCTION

http://www.nawic.org/

NAWIC UNDERGRADUATE SCHOLARSHIPS
• *See page 117*

NATIONAL BOARD OF BOILER AND PRESSURE VESSEL INSPECTORS

http://www.nationalboard.org/

NATIONAL BOARD TECHNICAL SCHOLARSHIP
• *See page 157*

NATIONAL SECURITY AGENCY

http://www.nsa.gov/Careers

NATIONAL SECURITY AGENCY STOKES EDUCATIONAL SCHOLARSHIP PROGRAM
• *See page 181*

NATIONAL SOCIETY OF PROFESSIONAL ENGINEERS

http://www.nspe.org/

MAUREEN L. & HOWARD N. BLITMAN, P.E., SCHOLARSHIP TO PROMOTE DIVERSITY IN ENGINEERING
• *See page 166*

PAUL H. ROBBINS HONORARY SCHOLARSHIP
• *See page 158*

PROFESSIONAL ENGINEERS IN INDUSTRY SCHOLARSHIP
• *See page 158*

NEXTSTEPU

http://www.nextstepu.com/

$1,500 STEM SCHOLARSHIP
• *See page 104*

PACIFIC GAS AND ELECTRIC COMPANY

http://www.scholarshipamerica.org

PG&E BETTER TOGETHER STEM SCHOLARSHIP PROGRAM
• *See page 181*

PROFESSIONAL CONSTRUCTION ESTIMATORS ASSOCIATION

http://www.pcea.org/

TED G. WILSON MEMORIAL SCHOLARSHIP FOUNDATION
• *See page 166*

ROBERT H. MOLLOHAN FAMILY CHARITABLE FOUNDATION, INC.

http://www.mollohanfoundation.org/

HIGH TECHNOLOGY SCHOLARS PROGRAM
• *See page 158*

SCARLETT FAMILY FOUNDATION SCHOLARSHIP PROGRAM

http://www.scarlettfoundation.org/

SCHOLARSHIP FOR STUDENTS PURSUING A BUSINESS OR STEM DEGREE
• *See page 80*

SEMICONDUCTOR RESEARCH CORPORATION (SRC)

http://www.src.org/

MASTER'S SCHOLARSHIP PROGRAM
• *See page 158*

SOCIETY OF MOTION PICTURE AND TELEVISION ENGINEERS

https://www.smpte.org/

LOUIS F. WOLF JR. MEMORIAL SCHOLARSHIP
• *See page 175*

STUDENT PAPER AWARD
• *See page 175*

SOCIETY OF PLASTICS ENGINEERS FOUNDATION (SPE)

http://www.4spe.org/

FLEMING/BLASZCAK SCHOLARSHIP
• *See page 158*

SOCIETY OF PLASTICS ENGINEERS SCHOLARSHIP PROGRAM
• *See page 159*

SOCIETY OF WOMEN ENGINEERS

https://swe.org/

GE'S WOMEN'S NETWORK PAULA MARTIN SCHOLARSHIP
• *See page 134*

LIEBHERR MINING SCHOLARSHIP
• *See page 182*

SWE REGION E SCHOLARSHIP
• *See page 159*

SWE REGION H SCHOLARSHIPS
• *See page 159*

SWE REGION J SCHOLARSHIP
• *See page 159*

TE CONNECTIVITY EXCELLENCE IN ENGINEERING SCHOLARSHIP
• *See page 160*

SONS OF NORWAY FOUNDATION

http://www.sonsofnorway.com/foundation

NANCY LORRAINE JENSEN MEMORIAL SCHOLARSHIP
• *See page 160*

SPECIALTY EQUIPMENT MARKET ASSOCIATION

http://www.sema.org/

SEMA MEMORIAL SCHOLARSHIP FUND
• *See page 81*

STRAIGHTFORWARD MEDIA

http://www.straightforwardmedia.com/

STRAIGHTFORWARD MEDIA ENGINEERING SCHOLARSHIP
• *See page 160*

STRAIGHT NORTH

https://www.straightnorth.com/

STRAIGHT NORTH STEM SCHOLARSHIP
• *See page 81*

TIMOTION

http://www.timotion.com/

TIMOTION ENGINEERING AND EXCELLENCE SCHOLARSHIP
• *See page 167*

TURNER CONSTRUCTION COMPANY

http://www.turnerconstruction.com/

YOUTHFORCE 2020 SCHOLARSHIP PROGRAM
• *See page 117*

UNITED NEGRO COLLEGE FUND

http://www.uncf.org/

DAVIS SCHOLARSHIP FOR WOMEN IN STEM
• *See page 111*

DELL CORPORATE SCHOLARS PROGRAM
• *See page 168*

GALACTIC UNITE BYTHEWAY SCHOLARSHIP
• *See page 111*

LEIDOS STEM SCHOLARSHIP
• *See page 96*

NASCAR WENDELL SCOTT SR. SCHOLARSHIP
• *See page 83*

UNCF-NORTHROP GRUMMAN SCHOLARSHIP
• *See page 184*

VERMONT SPACE GRANT CONSORTIUM

http://www.cems.uvm.edu/vsgc

VERMONT SPACE GRANT CONSORTIUM
• *See page 92*

WOMEN IN AVIATION, INTERNATIONAL

http://www.wai.org/

DELTA AIR LINES ENGINEERING SCHOLARSHIP
• *See page 136*

XEROX

http://www.xerox.com//

TECHNICAL MINORITY SCHOLARSHIP
• *See page 161*

ENERGY AND POWER ENGINEERING

AMERICAN CHEMICAL SOCIETY, RUBBER DIVISION

http://www.rubber.org/

AMERICAN CHEMICAL SOCIETY, RUBBER DIVISION UNDERGRADUATE SCHOLARSHIP
• *See page 105*

AMERICAN COUNCIL OF ENGINEERING COMPANIES OF PENNSYLVANIA (ACEC/PA)

http://www.acecpa.org/

ERIC J. GENNUSO AND LEROY D. (BUD) LOY, JR. SCHOLARSHIP PROGRAM
• *See page 153*

AMERICAN INDIAN SCIENCE AND ENGINEERING SOCIETY

http://www.aises.org/

A.T. ANDERSON MEMORIAL SCHOLARSHIP PROGRAM
• *See page 105*

AMERICAN PUBLIC POWER ASSOCIATION

https://www.publicpower.org/deed-rd-funding

DEMONSTRATION OF ENERGY AND EFFICIENCY DEVELOPMENTS EDUCATIONAL SCHOLARSHIP
• *See page 154*

DEMONSTRATION OF ENERGY AND EFFICIENCY DEVELOPMENTS STUDENT INTERNSHIP
• *See page 154*

DEMONSTRATION OF ENERGY AND EFFICIENCY DEVELOPMENTS STUDENT RESEARCH GRANTS
• *See page 162*

DEMONSTRATION OF ENERGY AND EFFICIENCY DEVELOPMENTS TECHNICAL DESIGN PROJECT
• *See page 154*

AMERICAN SOCIETY FOR NONDESTRUCTIVE TESTING

www.asnt.org

ASNT ENGINEERING UNDERGRADUATE SCHOLARSHIP

The Engineering Undergraduate Scholarship provides incentive to engineering undergraduate students enrolled in colleges and universities in the U.S. to choose nondestructive testing and evaluation as their field of specialization.

Academic Fields/Career Goals: Energy and Power Engineering; Engineering-Related Technologies; Engineering/Technology.

Award: Scholarship for use in freshman, sophomore, junior, or senior years; not renewable. *Number:* 3. *Amount:* $3000.

Eligibility Requirements: Applicant must be enrolled or expecting to enroll full-time at a two-year or four-year institution or university. Applicant or parent of applicant must have employment or volunteer experience in engineering/technology. Available to U.S. citizens.

Application Requirements: Application form, application form may be submitted online (https://www.asnt.org/MinorSiteSections/AboutASNT/Awards/Undergraduate.aspx), essay. *Deadline:* December 15.

Contact: Jessica Ames, Program Coordinator
American Society for Nondestructive Testing
1711 Arlingate Lane
PO Box 28518
Columbus, OH 43228
E-mail: james@asnt.org

AMERICAN SOCIETY OF CERTIFIED ENGINEERING TECHNICIANS

http://www.ascet.org/

KURT H. AND DONNA M. SCHULER SMALL GRANT
• *See page 162*

AMERICAN SOCIETY OF NAVAL ENGINEERS

http://www.navalengineers.org/

AMERICAN SOCIETY OF NAVAL ENGINEERS SCHOLARSHIP
• *See page 106*

ASSOCIATION FOR WOMEN GEOSCIENTISTS (AWG)

http://www.awg.org/

AWG MARIA LUISA CRAWFORD FIELD CAMP SCHOLARSHIP
• *See page 111*

ASSOCIATION OF STATE DAM SAFETY OFFICIALS (ASDSO)

http://www.DamSafety.org

ASSOCIATION OF STATE DAM SAFETY OFFICIALS (ASDSO) SENIOR UNDERGRADUATE SCHOLARSHIP
• *See page 140*

AUTOMOTIVE WOMEN'S ALLIANCE FOUNDATION

http://awafoundation.org/index.php

AUTOMOTIVE WOMEN'S ALLIANCE FOUNDATION SCHOLARSHIPS
• *See page 71*

BARRY GOLDWATER SCHOLARSHIP AND EXCELLENCE IN EDUCATION FOUNDATION

https://goldwater.scholarsapply.org

BARRY M. GOLDWATER SCHOLARSHIP AND EXCELLENCE IN EDUCATION PROGRAM
• *See page 107*

BHW GROUP

https://thebhwgroup.com/

BHW WOMEN IN STEM SCHOLARSHIP
• *See page 107*

BRASKEM ODEBRECHT

http://www.odebrechtaward.com

ODEBRECHT AWARD FOR SUSTAINABLE DEVELOPMENT
• *See page 113*

BROWN AND CALDWELL

http://www.brownandcaldwell.com

ECKENFELDER SCHOLARSHIP
• *See page 141*

MINORITY SCHOLARSHIP PROGRAM
• *See page 141*

CARDS AGAINST HUMANITY

https://cardsagainsthumanity.com/

SCIENCE AMBASSADOR SCHOLARSHIP
• *See page 107*

DISTIL NETWORKS

http://www.distilnetworks.com

WOMEN FORWARD IN TECHNOLOGY SCHOLARSHIP PROGRAM
• *See page 108*

THE ELECTROCHEMICAL SOCIETY

https://www.electrochem.org/

BATTERY DIVISION STUDENT RESEARCH AWARD SPONSORED BY MERCEDES-BENZ RESEARCH & DEVELOPMENT
• *See page 155*

H.H. DOW MEMORIAL STUDENT ACHIEVEMENT AWARD OF THE INDUSTRIAL ELECTROLYSIS AND

ELECTROCHEMICAL ENGINEERING DIVISION OF THE ELECTROCHEMICAL SOCIETY INC

• *See page 156*

FLORIDA ENGINEERING SOCIETY

https://www.fleng.org/page/Scholarships

DAVID F. LUDOVICI SCHOLARSHIP
• *See page 156*

GREAT MINDS IN STEM

http://www.greatmindsinstem.org/college/scholarship-application-information

HENAAC SCHOLARSHIP PROGRAM
• *See page 100*

INTERNATIONAL SOCIETY OF EXPLOSIVES ENGINEERS

http://www.isee.org/

JERRY MCDOWELL FUND
• *See page 156*

NASA IDAHO SPACE GRANT CONSORTIUM

http://www.idahospacegrant.org

NASA IDAHO SPACE GRANT CONSORTIUM SCHOLARSHIP PROGRAM
• *See page 109*

NEXTSTEPU

http://www.nextstepu.com/

$1,500 STEM SCHOLARSHIP
• *See page 104*

ROBERT H. MOLLOHAN FAMILY CHARITABLE FOUNDATION, INC.

http://www.mollohanfoundation.org/

HIGH TECHNOLOGY SCHOLARS PROGRAM
• *See page 158*

SCARLETT FAMILY FOUNDATION SCHOLARSHIP PROGRAM

http://www.scarlettfoundation.org/

SCHOLARSHIP FOR STUDENTS PURSUING A BUSINESS OR STEM DEGREE
• *See page 80*

SOCIETY OF WOMEN ENGINEERS

https://swe.org/

SWE REGION E SCHOLARSHIP
• *See page 159*

SWE REGION H SCHOLARSHIPS
• *See page 159*

SWE REGION J SCHOLARSHIP
• *See page 159*

STRAIGHTFORWARD MEDIA

http://www.straightforwardmedia.com/

STRAIGHTFORWARD MEDIA ENGINEERING SCHOLARSHIP
• See page 160

STRAIGHT NORTH

https://www.straightnorth.com/

STRAIGHT NORTH STEM SCHOLARSHIP
• See page 81

TIMOTION

http://www.timotion.com/

TIMOTION ENGINEERING AND EXCELLENCE SCHOLARSHIP
• See page 167

UNITED NEGRO COLLEGE FUND

http://www.uncf.org/

DAVIS SCHOLARSHIP FOR WOMEN IN STEM
• See page 111

DELL CORPORATE SCHOLARS PROGRAM
• See page 168

GALACTIC UNITE BYTHEWAY SCHOLARSHIP
• See page 111

LEIDOS STEM SCHOLARSHIP
• See page 96

VERMONT SPACE GRANT CONSORTIUM

http://www.cems.uvm.edu/vsgc

VERMONT SPACE GRANT CONSORTIUM
• See page 92

ENGINEERING-RELATED TECHNOLOGIES

AACE INTERNATIONAL

http://www.aacei.org/

AACE INTERNATIONAL COMPETITIVE SCHOLARSHIP
• See page 112

AHS INTERNATIONAL—THE VERTICAL FLIGHT TECHNICAL SOCIETY

http://www.vtol.org/

VERTICAL FLIGHT FOUNDATION SCHOLARSHIP
• See page 126

AIST FOUNDATION

http://www.aistfoundation.org/

ASSOCIATION FOR IRON AND STEEL TECHNOLOGY BALTIMORE CHAPTER SCHOLARSHIP

Scholarship for child, grandchild, or spouse of a member of the Baltimore Chapter of AIST. Must be high school seniors who are currently enrolled undergraduate students pursuing a career in engineering or metallurgy. Student may reapply each year for the term of their college education.

Academic Fields/Career Goals: Engineering-Related Technologies; Engineering/Technology; Materials Science, Engineering, and Metallurgy.

Award: Scholarship for use in freshman, sophomore, junior, or senior years; not renewable. *Number:* 1. *Amount:* $1500.

Eligibility Requirements: Applicant must be enrolled or expecting to enroll full-time at a four-year institution or university. Applicant or parent of applicant must be member of Association for Iron and Steel Technology. Available to U.S. citizens.

Application Requirements: Application form, essay, test scores, transcript. *Deadline:* April 30.

Contact: Thomas Russo, Program Coordinator
AIST Foundation
1430 Sparrows Point Boulevard
Sparrows Point, MD 21219-1014

ASSOCIATION FOR IRON AND STEEL TECHNOLOGY BENJAMIN F. FAIRLESS SCHOLARSHIP (AIME)
• See page 152

ASSOCIATION FOR IRON AND STEEL TECHNOLOGY OHIO VALLEY CHAPTER SCHOLARSHIP
• See page 138

AMERICAN CHEMICAL SOCIETY, RUBBER DIVISION

http://www.rubber.org/

AMERICAN CHEMICAL SOCIETY, RUBBER DIVISION UNDERGRADUATE SCHOLARSHIP
• See page 105

AMERICAN COUNCIL OF ENGINEERING COMPANIES OF PENNSYLVANIA (ACEC/PA)

http://www.acecpa.org/

ERIC J. GENNUSO AND LEROY D. (BUD) LOY, JR. SCHOLARSHIP PROGRAM
• See page 153

AMERICAN INDIAN SCIENCE AND ENGINEERING SOCIETY

http://www.aises.org/

A.T. ANDERSON MEMORIAL SCHOLARSHIP PROGRAM
• See page 105

AMERICAN INSTITUTE OF AERONAUTICS AND ASTRONAUTICS

https://www.aiaa.org/

AIAA FOUNDATION UNDERGRADUATE SCHOLARSHIPS
• See page 127

LEATRICE GREGORY PENDRAY SCHOLARSHIP
• See page 127

AMERICAN PUBLIC POWER ASSOCIATION

https://www.publicpower.org/deed-rd-funding

DEMONSTRATION OF ENERGY AND EFFICIENCY DEVELOPMENTS EDUCATIONAL SCHOLARSHIP
• *See page 154*

DEMONSTRATION OF ENERGY AND EFFICIENCY DEVELOPMENTS STUDENT INTERNSHIP
• *See page 154*

DEMONSTRATION OF ENERGY AND EFFICIENCY DEVELOPMENTS STUDENT RESEARCH GRANTS
• *See page 162*

DEMONSTRATION OF ENERGY AND EFFICIENCY DEVELOPMENTS TECHNICAL DESIGN PROJECT
• *See page 154*

AMERICAN PUBLIC TRANSPORTATION FOUNDATION

https://www.aptfd.org/

TRANSIT HALL OF FAME SCHOLARSHIP AWARD PROGRAM
• *See page 162*

AMERICAN RAILWAY ENGINEERING AND MAINTENANCE OF WAY ASSOCIATION

http://www.aremafoundation.org/

AREMA GRADUATE AND UNDERGRADUATE SCHOLARSHIPS
• *See page 162*

AMERICAN SOCIETY FOR NONDESTRUCTIVE TESTING

www.asnt.org

ASNT ENGINEERING UNDERGRADUATE SCHOLARSHIP
• *See page 222*

AMERICAN SOCIETY OF CERTIFIED ENGINEERING TECHNICIANS

http://www.ascet.org/

JOSEPH C. JOHNSON MEMORIAL GRANT

Grant for $750 given to qualified applicants in order to offset the cost of tuition, books and lab fees. Applicant must be a U.S. citizen or a legal resident of the country in which the applicant is currently living, as well as be either a student, certified, regular, registered or associate member of ASCET. Student must be enrolled in an engineering technology program. For further information, visit http://www.ascet.org.

Academic Fields/Career Goals: Engineering-Related Technologies; Engineering/Technology.

Award: Grant for use in freshman, sophomore, junior, or senior years; not renewable. *Number:* 1. *Amount:* $750.

Eligibility Requirements: Applicant must be enrolled or expecting to enroll full- or part-time at a two-year or four-year or technical institution or university. Available to U.S. citizens.

Application Requirements: Application form, financial need analysis, personal photograph. *Deadline:* February 28.

Contact: Mr. Jimmy Lynch, Scholarship Committee Chair
American Society of Certified Engineering Technicians
15621 W. 87th Street Parkway, #205
Lenexa, KS 66219
Phone: 773-242-7238
E-mail: financialaid@ascet.org

JOSEPH M. PARISH MEMORIAL GRANT

Grant of $500 will be awarded to a student to be used to offset the cost of tuition, books and lab fees. Applicant must be a student member of ASCET and be a U.S. citizen or a legal resident of the country in which the applicant is currently living. The award will be given to full time students enrolled in an engineering technology program; students pursuing a BS degree in engineering are not eligible for this grant. For more information, visit http://www.ascet.org.

Academic Fields/Career Goals: Engineering-Related Technologies; Engineering/Technology.

Award: Grant for use in freshman, sophomore, junior, or senior years; not renewable. *Number:* 1. *Amount:* $500.

Eligibility Requirements: Applicant must be enrolled or expecting to enroll full- or part-time at a two-year or four-year or technical institution or university. Available to U.S. citizens.

Application Requirements: Application form, financial need analysis, personal photograph. *Deadline:* February 28.

Contact: Mr. Jimmy Lynch, Financial Aid Chair
American Society of Certified Engineering Technicians
15621 W. 87th Street Parkway, #205
Lenexa, KS 66219
Phone: 733-242-7238
E-mail: financialaid@ascet.org

KURT H. AND DONNA M. SCHULER SMALL GRANT
• *See page 162*

AMERICAN WELDING SOCIETY

http://www.aws.org/

AMERICAN WELDING SOCIETY FOUNDATION SCHOLARSHIPS

The AWS Foundation awards over $1.3 million annually to help students achieve their dreams through education. Scholarships are available for students in welding or related programs attending trade schools, community colleges, and four-year universities.

Academic Fields/Career Goals: Engineering-Related Technologies; Trade/Technical Specialties.

Award: Scholarship for use in freshman, sophomore, junior, or senior years; not renewable. *Number:* 200–900. *Amount:* $500–$5000.

Eligibility Requirements: Applicant must be age 18 and over and enrolled or expecting to enroll full- or part-time at a two-year or four-year or technical institution or university. Available to U.S. and Canadian citizens.

Application Requirements: Application form, application form may be submitted online (https://scholarship.aws.org), essay, financial need analysis, transcript. *Deadline:* March 1.

Contact: Mr. John Douglass, Associate Director, Foundation
American Welding Society
8669 NW 36 Street, Suite 130
Miami, FL 33166
Phone: 800-443-9353 Ext. 212
E-mail: jdouglass@aws.org

MILLER ELECTRIC INTERNATIONAL WORLD SKILLS COMPETITION SCHOLARSHIP

Applicant must compete in the National Skills USA-VICA Competition for Welding, and advance to the AWS Weld Trials at the AWS International Welding and Fabricating Exposition and Convention, which is held on a bi-annual basis. The winner of the U.S. Weld Trial Competition will receive the scholarship for $10,000 and runner up will receive $1000. For additional information, see website http://www.aws.org.

Academic Fields/Career Goals: Engineering-Related Technologies; Engineering/Technology; Materials Science, Engineering, and Metallurgy; Trade/Technical Specialties.

Award: Grant for use in freshman, sophomore, junior, or senior years; renewable.

Eligibility Requirements: Applicant must be enrolled or expecting to enroll full- or part-time at a four-year institution or university. Available to U.S. citizens.

Application Requirements: Interview.

Contact: Mr. John Douglass, Associate Director, AWS Foundation
American Welding Society
8669 NW 36 Street, Suite 130
Miami, FL 33166
Phone: 800-443-9353 Ext. 212
E-mail: jdouglass@aws.org

ARMED FORCES COMMUNICATIONS AND ELECTRONICS ASSOCIATION, EDUCATIONAL FOUNDATION

https://foundation.afcea.org

AFCEA STEM MAJORS SCHOLARSHIPS FOR UNDERGRADUATE STUDENTS
• *See page 106*

ARMED FORCES COMMUNICATIONS AND ELECTRONICS ASSOCIATION ROTC SCHOLARSHIP PROGRAM
• *See page 179*

ASSOCIATED GENERAL CONTRACTORS EDUCATION AND RESEARCH FOUNDATION

https://www.agc.org/

WORKFORCE DEVELOPMENT SCHOLARSHIP

Applicant can be anyone who is planning to attend a technical school or approved craft training program in any discipline of construction, including a high school senior, military member, or postsecondary student.

Academic Fields/Career Goals: Engineering-Related Technologies; Engineering/Technology; Trade/Technical Specialties.

Award: Scholarship for use in freshman or sophomore years; renewable. *Number:* 10–20. *Amount:* $1000.

Eligibility Requirements: Applicant must be enrolled or expecting to enroll full- or part-time at a two-year or technical institution. Available to U.S. citizens.

Application Requirements: Application form, interview. *Deadline:* June 1.

Contact: Courtney Bishop, Associate Director
Associated General Contractors Education and Research
Foundation
2300 Wilson Ave.
Alexandria, VA 22201
Phone: 703-8375356
E-mail: courtney.bishop@agc.org

ASSOCIATION OF FEDERAL COMMUNICATIONS CONSULTING ENGINEERS

http://www.afcce.org

JULES COHEN SCHOLARSHIP
• *See page 218*

ASSOCIATION OF STATE DAM SAFETY OFFICIALS (ASDSO)

http://www.DamSafety.org

ASSOCIATION OF STATE DAM SAFETY OFFICIALS (ASDSO) SENIOR UNDERGRADUATE SCHOLARSHIP
• *See page 140*

ASTRONAUT SCHOLARSHIP FOUNDATION

http://www.astronautscholarship.org/

ASTRONAUT SCHOLARSHIP
• *See page 107*

AUTOMOTIVE WOMEN'S ALLIANCE FOUNDATION

http://awafoundation.org/index.php

AUTOMOTIVE WOMEN'S ALLIANCE FOUNDATION SCHOLARSHIPS
• *See page 71*

BARRY GOLDWATER SCHOLARSHIP AND EXCELLENCE IN EDUCATION FOUNDATION

https://goldwater.scholarsapply.org

BARRY M. GOLDWATER SCHOLARSHIP AND EXCELLENCE IN EDUCATION PROGRAM
• *See page 107*

BHW GROUP

https://thebhwgroup.com/

BHW WOMEN IN STEM SCHOLARSHIP
• *See page 107*

BROWN AND CALDWELL

http://www.brownandcaldwell.com

ECKENFELDER SCHOLARSHIP
• *See page 141*

MINORITY SCHOLARSHIP PROGRAM
• *See page 141*

CARDS AGAINST HUMANITY

https://cardsagainsthumanity.com/

SCIENCE AMBASSADOR SCHOLARSHIP
• *See page 107*

CATCHING THE DREAM

http://www.catchingthedream.org/

TRIBAL BUSINESS MANAGEMENT PROGRAM (TBM)
• *See page 72*

THE CLUNKER JUNKER

https://theclunkerjunker.com/

CLUNKER JUNKER CASH FOR CARS AND COLLEGE SCHOLARSHIP

This scholarship is open to all college aged females who are pursuing a degree or certification in an automotive technology field such as engineering, mechanics, design, or auto body at an accredited college or technical school in the Fall of 2017 and/or the Spring of 2018.

Academic Fields/Career Goals: Engineering-Related Technologies; Engineering/Technology; Industrial Design; Transportation.

Award: Scholarship for use in freshman, sophomore, junior, senior, graduate, or postgraduate years; renewable. *Number:* 1. *Amount:* $1000.

Eligibility Requirements: Applicant must be enrolled or expecting to enroll full- or part-time at a two-year or four-year or technical institution or university; female and studying in Alabama, Alaska, Alberta, Arizona, Arkansas, British Columbia, California, Colorado, Connecticut, Delaware, District of Columbia, Florida, Georgia, Guam, Hawaii, Idaho, Illinois, Indiana, Iowa, Kansas, Kentucky, Louisiana, Maine, Manitoba, Maryland, Massachusetts, Michigan, Minnesota, Mississippi, Missouri, Montana, Nebraska, Nevada, New Brunswick, Newfoundland, New Hampshire, New Jersey, New Mexico, New York, North Carolina, North Dakota, Northwest Territories, Nova Scotia, Ohio, Oklahoma, Ontario, Oregon, Pennsylvania, Prince Edward Island, Puerto Rico, Quebec, Rhode Island, Saskatchewan, South Carolina, South Dakota, Tennessee, Texas, Utah, Vermont, Virginia, Washington, West Virginia, Wisconsin, Wyoming, Yukon. Available to U.S. and non-U.S. citizens.

Application Requirements: Essay. *Deadline:* continuous.

Contact: Valerie Mitz, COO
E-mail: valerie@theclunkerjunker.com

CONNECTICUT BUILDING CONGRESS SCHOLARSHIP FUND, INC.

http://www.cbc-ct.org

CBC SCHOLARSHIP FUND
• *See page 114*

DISTIL NETWORKS

http://www.distilnetworks.com

WOMEN FORWARD IN TECHNOLOGY SCHOLARSHIP PROGRAM
• *See page 108*

THE ELECTROCHEMICAL SOCIETY

https://www.electrochem.org/

BATTERY DIVISION STUDENT RESEARCH AWARD SPONSORED BY MERCEDES-BENZ RESEARCH & DEVELOPMENT
• *See page 155*

H.H. DOW MEMORIAL STUDENT ACHIEVEMENT AWARD OF THE INDUSTRIAL ELECTROLYSIS AND ELECTROCHEMICAL ENGINEERING DIVISION OF THE ELECTROCHEMICAL SOCIETY INC
• *See page 156*

FLORIDA ENGINEERING SOCIETY

https://www.fleng.org/page/Scholarships

DAVID F. LUDOVICI SCHOLARSHIP
• *See page 156*

GREAT MINDS IN STEM

http://www.greatmindsinstem.org/college/scholarship-application-information

HENAAC SCHOLARSHIP PROGRAM
• *See page 100*

ILLUMINATING ENGINEERING SOCIETY OF NORTH AMERICA

http://www.ies.org/

ROBERT W. THUNEN MEMORIAL SCHOLARSHIPS
• *See page 116*

INTERNATIONAL FACILITY MANAGEMENT ASSOCIATION FOUNDATION

http://www.ifmafoundation.org/

IFMA FOUNDATION SCHOLARSHIPS
• *See page 116*

INTERNATIONAL SOCIETY FOR OPTICAL ENGINEERING-SPIE

http://www.spie.org/scholarships

SPIE EDUCATIONAL SCHOLARSHIPS IN OPTICAL SCIENCE AND ENGINEERING
• *See page 108*

INTERNATIONAL SOCIETY OF AUTOMATION

http://www.isa.org/

ISA EDUCATIONAL FOUNDATION SCHOLARSHIPS

Scholarships to graduate and undergraduate students who demonstrate outstanding potential for long-range contribution to the fields of automation, systems, and control.

Academic Fields/Career Goals: Engineering-Related Technologies.

Award: Scholarship for use in sophomore, junior, or graduate years; not renewable. *Number:* 15–16. *Amount:* $500–$5000.

Eligibility Requirements: Applicant must be enrolled or expecting to enroll full-time at a two-year or four-year or technical institution or university. Available to U.S. and non-U.S. citizens.

Application Requirements: Application form, essay. *Deadline:* February 15.

Contact: Scholarship Committee
International Society of Automation
67 TW Alexander Drive
Research Triangle Park, NC 27709

INTERNATIONAL SOCIETY OF EXPLOSIVES ENGINEERS

http://www.isee.org/

JERRY MCDOWELL FUND
• *See page 156*

JORGE MAS CANOSA FREEDOM FOUNDATION

http://masscholarships.org/

MAS FAMILY SCHOLARSHIP AWARD
• See page 149

LOGISTICS & TRANSPORTATION ASSOCIATION OF NORTH AMERICA

http://www.ltna.org

TRANSPORTATION CLUBS INTERNATIONAL FRED A. HOOPER MEMORIAL SCHOLARSHIP

Merit-based award available to currently enrolled college students majoring in traffic management, transportation, physical distribution, logistics, or a related field. Must have completed at least one year of post-high school education. One-time award of $1500. Must submit three references. Available to citizens of the United States, Canada, and Mexico.

Academic Fields/Career Goals: Engineering-Related Technologies; Transportation.

Award: Scholarship for use in freshman, sophomore, junior, or senior years; not renewable. *Number:* 1. *Amount:* $1500.

Eligibility Requirements: Applicant must be enrolled or expecting to enroll full- or part-time at a two-year or four-year or technical institution or university. Available to U.S. and non-U.S. citizens.

Application Requirements: Application form, essay, personal photograph, recommendations or references, transcript. *Deadline:* April 30.

Contact: Katie Dejonge, Executive Director
Union, WA 98592
Phone: 360-898-3344
E-mail: executive.director@ltna.org

LOS ANGELES COUNCIL OF BLACK PROFESSIONAL ENGINEERS

http://www.lablackengineers.org/

AL-BEN SCHOLARSHIP FOR ACADEMIC INCENTIVE
• See page 157

AL-BEN SCHOLARSHIP FOR PROFESSIONAL MERIT
• See page 157

AL-BEN SCHOLARSHIP FOR SCHOLASTIC ACHIEVEMENT
• See page 157

MAINE SOCIETY OF PROFESSIONAL ENGINEERS

http://www.mespe.org/

MAINE SOCIETY OF PROFESSIONAL ENGINEERS VERNON T. SWAINE-ROBERT E. CHUTE SCHOLARSHIP

Nonrenewable scholarship for full-time study for freshmen only. Must be a Maine resident. Application can also be obtained by sending e-mail to rgmglads@twi.net.

Academic Fields/Career Goals: Engineering-Related Technologies; Engineering/Technology.

Award: Scholarship for use in freshman year; not renewable. *Number:* 1–2. *Amount:* $1500.

Eligibility Requirements: Applicant must be high school student; planning to enroll or expecting to enroll full-time at a four-year institution or university; resident of Maine and studying in Maine. Available to U.S. citizens.

Application Requirements: Application form, essay, interview, recommendations or references, self-addressed stamped envelope with application, test scores, transcript. *Deadline:* March 1.

Contact: Robert Martin, Scholarship Committee Chairman
Maine Society of Professional Engineers
1387 Augusta Road
Belgrade, ME 04917
Phone: 207-495-2244
E-mail: rgmglads@twi.net

MANUFACTURERS ASSOCIATION OF MAINE

http://www.mainemfg.com/

MAINE MANUFACTURING CAREER AND TRAINING FOUNDATION SCHOLARSHIP
• See page 131

MINERALS, METALS, AND MATERIALS SOCIETY (TMS)

http://www.tms.org/

MATERIALS PROCESSING AND MANUFACTURING DIVISION SCHOLARSHIP

The applicant must be a student member of Material Advantage. Applicants must be undergraduate sophomores or junior unless otherwise noted. Applicants must be enrolled full time in a metallurgical/materials science engineering program at a qualified college or university. Relatives of members of the funding committee/division are not eligible. Submitted coursework must be relevant to the scholarship for which the student is applying.

Academic Fields/Career Goals: Engineering-Related Technologies; Engineering/Technology; Materials Science, Engineering, and Metallurgy; Science, Technology, and Society.

Award: Scholarship for use in sophomore or junior years; not renewable. *Number:* 1. *Amount:* $2500.

Eligibility Requirements: Applicant must be age 18-30 and enrolled or expecting to enroll full-time at a four-year institution or university. Available to U.S. and non-U.S. citizens.

Application Requirements: Application form, essay, recommendations or references, transcript. *Deadline:* March 15.

Contact: Ms. Bryn Simpson
E-mail: bsimpson@tms.org

TMS EXTRACTION & PROCESSING SCHOLARSHIP

The applicant must be a student member of Material Advantage. Applicants must be undergraduate sophomores or junior unless otherwise noted. Applicants must be enrolled full time in a metallurgical/materials science engineering program at a qualified college or university. Relatives of members of the funding committee/division are not eligible. Submitted coursework must be relevant to the scholarship for which the student is applying.

Academic Fields/Career Goals: Engineering-Related Technologies; Engineering/Technology; Materials Science, Engineering, and Metallurgy; Science, Technology, and Society.

Award: Scholarship for use in sophomore or junior years; not renewable. *Number:* 2. *Amount:* $2500.

Eligibility Requirements: Applicant must be age 18-30 and enrolled or expecting to enroll full-time at a four-year institution or university. Available to U.S. and non-U.S. citizens.

Application Requirements: Application form, essay, recommendations or references, transcript. *Deadline:* March 15.

Contact: Ms. Bryn Simpson
E-mail: bsimpson@tms.org

TMS FUNCTIONAL MATERIALS GILBERT CHIN SCHOLARSHIP

The applicant must be a student member of Material Advantage. Applicants must be undergraduate sophomores or junior unless otherwise noted. Applicants must be enrolled full time in a metallurgical/materials science engineering program at a qualified college or university. Relatives of members of the funding committee/division are not eligible. Submitted coursework must be relevant to the scholarship for which the student is applying.

Academic Fields/Career Goals: Engineering-Related Technologies; Engineering/Technology; Materials Science, Engineering, and Metallurgy; Science, Technology, and Society.

Award: Scholarship for use in sophomore or junior years; not renewable. *Number:* 1. *Amount:* $2500.

Eligibility Requirements: Applicant must be age 18-30 and enrolled or expecting to enroll full-time at a four-year institution or university. Available to U.S. and non-U.S. citizens.

Application Requirements: Application form, essay, recommendations or references, transcript. *Deadline:* March 15.

Contact: Ms. Bryn Simpson
  E-mail: bsimpson@tms.org

TMS/INTERNATIONAL SYMPOSIUM ON SUPERALLOYS SCHOLARSHIP PROGRAM

The applicant must be a student member of Material Advantage. Applicants must be undergraduate sophomores or junior unless otherwise noted. Applicants must be enrolled full time in a metallurgical/materials science engineering program at a qualified college or university. Relatives of members of the funding committee/division are not eligible. Submitted coursework must be relevant to the scholarship for which the student is applying.

Academic Fields/Career Goals: Engineering-Related Technologies; Engineering/Technology; Materials Science, Engineering, and Metallurgy; Science, Technology, and Society.

Award: Scholarship for use in sophomore, junior, senior, or graduate years; not renewable. *Number:* 2. *Amount:* $2000.

Eligibility Requirements: Applicant must be age 18-30 and enrolled or expecting to enroll full-time at a four-year institution or university. Available to U.S. and non-U.S. citizens.

Application Requirements: Application form, essay, recommendations or references, transcript. *Deadline:* March 15.

Contact: Ms. Bryn Simpson
  E-mail: bsimpson@tms.org

TMS/LIGHT METALS DIVISION SCHOLARSHIP PROGRAM

The applicant must be a student member of Material Advantage. Applicants must be undergraduate sophomores or junior unless otherwise noted. Applicants must be enrolled full time in a metallurgical/materials science engineering program at a qualified college or university. Relatives of members of the funding committee/division are not eligible. Submitted coursework must be relevant to the scholarship for which the student is applying.

Academic Fields/Career Goals: Engineering-Related Technologies; Engineering/Technology; Materials Science, Engineering, and Metallurgy; Science, Technology, and Society.

Award: Scholarship for use in sophomore or junior years; not renewable. *Number:* 1. *Amount:* $2500.

Eligibility Requirements: Applicant must be age 18-30 and enrolled or expecting to enroll full-time at a four-year institution or university. Available to U.S. and non-U.S. citizens.

Application Requirements: Application form, essay, recommendations or references, transcript. *Deadline:* March 15.

Contact: Ms. Bryn Simpson
  E-mail: bsimpson@tms.org

TMS OUTSTANDING STUDENT PAPER CONTEST-UNDERGRADUATE

The applicant must be a student member of Material Advantage. Applicants must be an undergraduate student enrolled full-time in a metallurgical/materials science engineering program at a qualified college or university. Papers must be unpublished as of the submission deadline date. Only one paper contest entry per student is accepted. Papers should be of a technical/research nature and may deal with any of the following disciplines: physical and mechanical metallurgy, extractive and process metallurgy, or materials science. The paper should be prepared by one author. It should be the original work of that author as far as possible. If a faculty member is listed as co-author, include a letter from the faculty member confirming that the applicant is the primary author. Papers must be written in English, utilizing good communication skills. The photocopy or digital file submitted must be easily legible. Poor copies of figures and texts are unacceptable. The paper should be neither less than 2,000 nor more than 4,000 words.

Academic Fields/Career Goals: Engineering-Related Technologies; Engineering/Technology; Materials Science, Engineering, and Metallurgy; Science, Technology, and Society.

Award: Prize for use in freshman, sophomore, junior, or senior years; not renewable. *Number:* 2.

Eligibility Requirements: Applicant must be age 18-30 and enrolled or expecting to enroll full-time at a four-year institution or university. Available to U.S. and non-U.S. citizens.

Application Requirements: Essay, photocopy or digital file of the paper for consideration, recommendations or references. *Deadline:* May 1.

Contact: Ms. Bryn Simpson
  E-mail: bsimpson@tms.org

TMS/STRUCTURAL MATERIALS DIVISION SCHOLARSHIP

The applicant must be a student member of Material Advantage. Applicants must be undergraduate sophomores or junior unless otherwise noted. Applicants must be enrolled full time in a metallurgical/materials science engineering program at a qualified college or university. Relatives of members of the funding committee/division are not eligible. Submitted coursework must be relevant to the scholarship for which the student is applying.

Academic Fields/Career Goals: Engineering-Related Technologies; Engineering/Technology; Materials Science, Engineering, and Metallurgy; Science, Technology, and Society.

Award: Scholarship for use in sophomore or junior years; not renewable. *Number:* 1. *Amount:* $2500.

Eligibility Requirements: Applicant must be age 18-30 and enrolled or expecting to enroll full-time at a four-year institution or university. Available to U.S. and non-U.S. citizens.

Application Requirements: Application form, essay, recommendations or references, transcript. *Deadline:* March 15.

Contact: Ms. Bryn Simpson
  E-mail: bsimpson@tms.org

NASA IDAHO SPACE GRANT CONSORTIUM

http://www.idahospacegrant.org

NASA IDAHO SPACE GRANT CONSORTIUM SCHOLARSHIP PROGRAM

• *See page 109*

NASA'S VIRGINIA SPACE GRANT CONSORTIUM

http://www.vsgc.odu.edu/

UNDERGRADUATE STEM RESEARCH SCHOLARSHIPS

• *See page 110*

NATIONAL ASSOCIATION FOR THE ADVANCEMENT OF COLORED PEOPLE

http://www.naacp.org/

HUBERTUS W.V. WILLEMS SCHOLARSHIP FOR MALE STUDENTS

Scholarship for a male, full-time student, majoring in one of the following: engineering, chemistry, physics, or mathematical sciences. Graduate student may be full- or part-time and have 2.5 minimum GPA. Graduating high school seniors and undergraduates must have 3.0 minimum GPA. Must demonstrate financial need. Maximum award is $3000. NAACP membership and participation is highly desirable.

Academic Fields/Career Goals: Engineering-Related Technologies; Engineering/Technology; Physical Sciences.

Award: Scholarship for use in freshman, sophomore, junior, senior, or graduate years; not renewable. *Number:* 20–40.

Eligibility Requirements: Applicant must be enrolled or expecting to enroll full- or part-time at a two-year institution or university and male. Available to U.S. citizens.

Application Requirements: Application form, application form may be submitted online, financial need analysis.

Contact: Victor Goode, Attorney
Phone: 410-580-5760
E-mail: info@naacp.org

NATIONAL ASSOCIATION OF WOMEN IN CONSTRUCTION

http://www.nawic.org/

NAWIC UNDERGRADUATE SCHOLARSHIPS
• *See page 117*

NATIONAL SECURITY EDUCATION PROGRAM

http://www.iie.org/

NATIONAL SECURITY EDUCATION PROGRAM (NSEP) DAVID L. BOREN UNDERGRADUATE SCHOLARSHIPS
• *See page 119*

NATIONAL SOCIETY OF BLACK ENGINEERS

https://connect.nsbe.org/Scholarships/Scholarship List.aspx

NSBE CORPORATE SCHOLARSHIP PROGRAM

The goals of the scholarships are to encourage and reward academic excellence for African-American students, and to promote retention is engineering studies. Scholarships are offered to chemical, mechanical, civil, electrical, environmental, and computer engineering majors who are undergraduate sophomores, juniors, and seniors.

Academic Fields/Career Goals: Engineering-Related Technologies; Engineering/Technology.

Award: Scholarship for use in freshman, sophomore, junior, or senior years; not renewable. *Number:* 3. *Amount:* $2500.

Eligibility Requirements: Applicant must be Black (non-Hispanic) and enrolled or expecting to enroll full- or part-time at a four-year institution or university. Available to U.S. citizens.

Application Requirements: Application form, essay. *Deadline:* June 30.

Contact: Raynashia Goodine, Scholarship Coordinator
National Society of Black Engineers
205 Daingerfield Road
Alexandria, VA 22314
E-mail: scholarships@nsbe.org

NATIONAL SOCIETY OF PROFESSIONAL ENGINEERS

http://www.nspe.org/

MAUREEN L. & HOWARD N. BLITMAN, P.E., SCHOLARSHIP TO PROMOTE DIVERSITY IN ENGINEERING
• *See page 166*

PAUL H. ROBBINS HONORARY SCHOLARSHIP
• *See page 158*

PROFESSIONAL ENGINEERS IN INDUSTRY SCHOLARSHIP
• *See page 158*

NATIONAL STONE, SAND AND GRAVEL ASSOCIATION (NSSGA)

http://www.nssga.org/

BARRY K. WENDT MEMORIAL SCHOLARSHIP

Scholarship is restricted to a student in an engineering school who plans to pursue a career in the aggregates industry. Eligible students will be enrolled in a mining-related degree program and will have completed at least one year of college coursework.

Academic Fields/Career Goals: Engineering-Related Technologies; Materials Science, Engineering, and Metallurgy.

Award: Scholarship for use in sophomore, junior, or senior years; not renewable. *Number:* 1. *Amount:* up to $2500.

Eligibility Requirements: Applicant must be enrolled or expecting to enroll full-time at a four-year institution or university. Available to U.S. and non-U.S. citizens.

Application Requirements: 300- to 500-word statement of plans for career in the aggregates industry, application form, application form may be submitted online (http://www.nssga.org/education/scholarships/), essay, recommendations or references. *Deadline:* May 29.

Contact: Catherine Whalen, Barry K. Wendt Memorial Scholarship
Committee, c/o NSSGA
National Stone, Sand and Gravel Association (NSSGA)
1605 King Street
Alexandria, VA 22314
Phone: 703-525-8788
Fax: 703-525-7782
E-mail: info@nssga.org

NEXTSTEPU

http://www.nextstepu.com/

$1,500 STEM SCHOLARSHIP
• *See page 104*

ROBERT H. MOLLOHAN FAMILY CHARITABLE FOUNDATION, INC.

http://www.mollohanfoundation.org/

HIGH TECHNOLOGY SCHOLARS PROGRAM
• *See page 158*

ROCKY MOUNTAIN COAL MINING INSTITUTE

http://www.rmcmi.org/

ROCKY MOUNTAIN COAL MINING INSTITUTE SCHOLARSHIP
• *See page 167*

SAE INTERNATIONAL

SAE INTERNATIONAL SCHOLARSHIPS PROGRAM

Please visit https://www.sae.org/participate/scholarships for detailed information about all SAE International Scholarships.

Academic Fields/Career Goals: Engineering-Related Technologies; Engineering/Technology.

Award: Scholarship for use in freshman, sophomore, junior, senior, graduate, or postgraduate years; not renewable. *Number:* 15. *Amount:* $1000–$10,000.

Eligibility Requirements: Applicant must be enrolled or expecting to enroll full- or part-time at a four-year institution or university. Available to U.S. citizens.

Application Requirements: Essay. *Deadline:* March 15.

SCARLETT FAMILY FOUNDATION SCHOLARSHIP PROGRAM

http://www.scarlettfoundation.org/

SCHOLARSHIP FOR STUDENTS PURSUING A BUSINESS OR STEM DEGREE
• *See page 80*

SIMPLEHUMAN

http://www.simplehuman.com/

SIMPLE SOLUTIONS DESIGN COMPETITION

IDSA-endorsed competition to promote creative problem-solving through product design and increase public awareness of industrial design. Applicants must be enrolled in an Industrial Design program or a closely related program at a design school or university and must design a new, innovative product/technology/concept for making household chores easier. Entries evaluated on utility, efficiency, innovation, research, and aesthetics. See website for details http://www.simplehuman.com/design.

Academic Fields/Career Goals: Engineering-Related Technologies; Engineering/Technology; Industrial Design.

Award: Prize for use in freshman, sophomore, junior, or senior years; not renewable. *Number:* 1. *Amount:* $5000.

Eligibility Requirements: Applicant must be enrolled or expecting to enroll full- or part-time at a two-year or four-year or technical institution or university. Available to U.S. and non-U.S. citizens.

Application Requirements: Application form, entry in a contest, one PDF or JPEG of design, specs, materials, explanation. *Deadline:* February 27.

Contact: Sarah Beachler, Marketing and Communications Associate
Phone: 310-436-2278
Fax: 310-538-9196
E-mail: sbeachler@simplehuman.com

SOCIETY OF MOTION PICTURE AND TELEVISION ENGINEERS

https://www.smpte.org/

LOUIS F. WOLF JR. MEMORIAL SCHOLARSHIP
• *See page 175*

STUDENT PAPER AWARD
• *See page 175*

SOCIETY OF PLASTICS ENGINEERS FOUNDATION (SPE)

http://www.4spe.org/

GULF COAST HURRICANE SCHOLARSHIP
• *See page 159*

SOCIETY OF WOMEN ENGINEERS

https://swe.org/

GE WOMEN'S NETWORK SHARON DALEY SCHOLARSHIP

One $5000 scholarship for female applicants planning to study a full-time ABET-accredited program in engineering, technology, or computing in the upcoming academic year. Sponsorship to work in the US is not required now nor will it be in the future. Preference given to students who are GE Girls Particiapnts, SWE members, and/or are from underrepresented backgrounds in STEM.

Academic Fields/Career Goals: Engineering-Related Technologies; Engineering/Technology.

Award: Scholarship for use in freshman, sophomore, or junior years; not renewable. *Number:* 1. *Amount:* $5000.

Eligibility Requirements: Applicant must be enrolled or expecting to enroll full-time at a four-year institution or university and female. Available to U.S. citizens.

Application Requirements: Application form, transcript. *Deadline:* February 15.

Contact: Scholarship Committee
Phone: 312-596-5223
E-mail: scholarships@swe.org

LIEBHERR MINING SCHOLARSHIP
• *See page 182*

SWE REGION E SCHOLARSHIP
• *See page 159*

TE CONNECTIVITY EXCELLENCE IN ENGINEERING SCHOLARSHIP
• *See page 160*

SOCIETY OF WOMEN ENGINEERS-TWIN TIERS SECTION

http://twintiers.swe.org/scholarship-information.html

SOCIETY OF WOMEN ENGINEERS-TWIN TIERS SECTION SCHOLARSHIP
• *See page 182*

STRAIGHTFORWARD MEDIA

http://www.straightforwardmedia.com/

STRAIGHTFORWARD MEDIA ENGINEERING SCHOLARSHIP
• *See page 160*

STRAIGHT NORTH

https://www.straightnorth.com/

STRAIGHT NORTH STEM SCHOLARSHIP
• *See page 81*

TECHNICAL ASSOCIATION OF THE PULP & PAPER INDUSTRY (TAPPI)

https://www.tappi.org/

CORRUGATED PACKAGING DIVISION SCHOLARSHIPS

Award to applicants working full time or part time in the box business and attending day/night school for a graduate or undergraduate degree or to a full-time student in a two- or four-year college, university or technical school. Information can be found at http://www.tappi.org/s_tappi/sec.asp?CID=6101&DID=546695.

Academic Fields/Career Goals: Engineering-Related Technologies; Paper and Pulp Engineering.

Award: Scholarship for use in freshman, sophomore, junior, senior, or graduate years; not renewable. *Number:* 1–4. *Amount:* $1000–$2000.

Eligibility Requirements: Applicant must be enrolled or expecting to enroll full- or part-time at a four-year or technical institution or university. Available to U.S. and non-U.S. citizens.

Application Requirements: Application form. *Deadline:* March 15.

Contact: Mr. Laurence Womack, Director of Standards and Awards
Technical Association of the Pulp & Paper Industry (TAPPI)
15 Technology Parkway South
Peachtree Corners, GA 30092
Phone: 770-209-7276
E-mail: standards@tappi.org

TECHNOLOGY FIRST

https://technologyfirst.org/

ROBERT V. MCKENNA SCHOLARSHIPS
• *See page 183*

TIMOTION

http://www.timotion.com/

TIMOTION ENGINEERING AND EXCELLENCE SCHOLARSHIP
• See page 167

TRANSPORTATION ASSOCIATION OF CANADA FOUNDATION

http://www.tac-foundation.ca

TAC FOUNDATION SCHOLARSHIPS
• See page 168

TURNER CONSTRUCTION COMPANY

http://www.turnerconstruction.com/

YOUTHFORCE 2020 SCHOLARSHIP PROGRAM
• See page 117

UNITED NEGRO COLLEGE FUND

http://www.uncf.org/

DELL CORPORATE SCHOLARS PROGRAM
• See page 168

DISCOVER FINANCIAL SERVICES SCHOLARSHIP
• See page 82

GALACTIC UNITE BYTHEWAY SCHOLARSHIP
• See page 111

LEIDOS STEM SCHOLARSHIP
• See page 96

VECTORWORKS, INC.

http://www.vectorworks.net

VECTORWORKS DESIGN SCHOLARSHIP
• See page 117

VERMONT SPACE GRANT CONSORTIUM

http://www.cems.uvm.edu/vsgc

VERMONT SPACE GRANT CONSORTIUM
• See page 92

WOMEN IN AEROSPACE FOUNDATION

https://www.womeninaerospace.org/

THE WOMEN IN AEROSPACE FOUNDATION SCHOLARSHIP
• See page 135

WOMEN IN AVIATION, INTERNATIONAL

http://www.wai.org/

THE BOEING COMPANY CAREER ENHANCEMENT SCHOLARSHIP
• See page 136

XEROX

http://www.xerox.com//

TECHNICAL MINORITY SCHOLARSHIP
• See page 161

ENGINEERING/ TECHNOLOGY

AACE INTERNATIONAL

http://www.aacei.org/

AACE INTERNATIONAL COMPETITIVE SCHOLARSHIP
• See page 112

ACI FOUNDATION

http://www.acifoundation.org

ACI FOUNDATION SCHOLARSHIP PROGRAM
• See page 113

AEG FOUNDATION

http://www.aegfoundation.org/

AEG FOUNDATION MARLIAVE FUND
• See page 199

AHS INTERNATIONAL—THE VERTICAL FLIGHT TECHNICAL SOCIETY

http://www.vtol.org/

VERTICAL FLIGHT FOUNDATION SCHOLARSHIP
• See page 126

AIST FOUNDATION

http://www.aistfoundation.org/

AIST ALFRED B. GLOSSBRENNER AND JOHN KLUSCH SCHOLARSHIPS
Scholarship intended to award high school senior who plans on pursuing a degree in metallurgy or engineering. Student must have previous academic excellence in science courses. Applicant must be a dependent of a AIST Northeastern Ohio chapter member.

Academic Fields/Career Goals: Engineering/Technology; Materials Science, Engineering, and Metallurgy.

Award: Scholarship for use in freshman year; not renewable. *Number:* 2. *Amount:* $1000.

Eligibility Requirements: Applicant must be high school student and planning to enroll or expecting to enroll full-time at a four-year institution or university. Applicant or parent of applicant must be member of Association for Iron and Steel Technology. Available to U.S. and non-U.S. citizens.

Application Requirements: Application form, essay, recommendations or references, resume, test scores, transcript. *Deadline:* April 30.

Contact: Richard Kurz, Chapter Secretary
AIST Foundation
22831 East State Street, Route 62
Alliance, OH 44601

ASSOCIATION FOR IRON AND STEEL TECHNOLOGY BALTIMORE CHAPTER SCHOLARSHIP
• See page 224

ASSOCIATION FOR IRON AND STEEL TECHNOLOGY MIDWEST CHAPTER BETTY MCKERN SCHOLARSHIP

Scholarship awarded to a graduating female high school senior, or to an undergraduate freshman, sophomore, or junior enrolled in a fully AIST-accredited college or university. Applicant must be in good academic standing. Must be a dependent of an AIST Midwest chapter member.

Academic Fields/Career Goals: Engineering/Technology.

Award: Scholarship for use in freshman, sophomore, junior, or senior years; not renewable. *Number:* 1. *Amount:* $3000.

Eligibility Requirements: Applicant must be enrolled or expecting to enroll full-time at a four-year institution or university and female. Applicant or parent of applicant must be member of Association for Iron and Steel Technology. Available to U.S. and non-U.S. citizens.

Application Requirements: Application form, essay, recommendations or references, resume, test scores, transcript. *Deadline:* March 15.

Contact: AIST Midwest Member Chapter Scholarships Chair
AIST Foundation
c/o Barry Felton
250 West U.S. Highway 12
Burns Harbor, IN 46304

ASSOCIATION FOR IRON AND STEEL TECHNOLOGY MIDWEST CHAPTER DON NELSON SCHOLARSHIP

One scholarship for a graduating high school senior, or undergraduate freshman, sophomore or junior enrolled in a fully AIST-accredited college or university. Applicant must be in good academic standing. Must be a dependent of an AIST Midwest chapter member. May reapply each year for the duration of college education.

Academic Fields/Career Goals: Engineering/Technology.

Award: Scholarship for use in freshman, sophomore, junior, or senior years; not renewable. *Number:* 1. *Amount:* up to $1000.

Eligibility Requirements: Applicant must be enrolled or expecting to enroll full-time at a four-year institution or university. Applicant or parent of applicant must be member of Association for Iron and Steel Technology. Available to U.S. and non-U.S. citizens.

Application Requirements: Application form, essay, recommendations or references, resume, test scores, transcript. *Deadline:* March 15.

Contact: AIST Midwest Member Chapter Scholarships Chair
AIST Foundation
c/o Barry Felton
250 West U.S. Highway 12
Burns Harbor, IN 46304

ASSOCIATION FOR IRON AND STEEL TECHNOLOGY MIDWEST CHAPTER ENGINEERING SCHOLARSHIP

Two four-year scholarships awarded to graduating high school senior or undergraduate freshman, sophomore or junior enrolled in a fully AIST-accredited college or university majoring engineering. Applicant must be in good academic standing. Must be a dependent of an AIST Midwest chapter member. May reapply each year for the duration of college education.

Academic Fields/Career Goals: Engineering/Technology.

Award: Scholarship for use in freshman, sophomore, or junior years; renewable. *Number:* 2. *Amount:* $1500.

Eligibility Requirements: Applicant must be enrolled or expecting to enroll full-time at a four-year institution or university. Applicant or parent of applicant must be member of Association for Iron and Steel Technology. Available to U.S. and non-U.S. citizens.

Application Requirements: Application form, essay, recommendations or references, resume, test scores, transcript. *Deadline:* March 15.

Contact: AIST Midwest Member Chapter Scholarships Chair
AIST Foundation
c/o Barry Felton
250 West U.S. Highway 12
Burns Harbor, IN 46304

ASSOCIATION FOR IRON AND STEEL TECHNOLOGY MIDWEST CHAPTER JACK GILL SCHOLARSHIP

Scholarship for a graduating high school senior, or undergraduate freshman, sophomore, or junior enrolled in a fully AIST-accredited college or university majoring engineering. Applicant must be in good academic standing. Must be a dependent of an AIST Midwest chapter member. May reapply each year for the duration of college education.

Academic Fields/Career Goals: Engineering/Technology.

years; not renewable. *Number:* 1. *Amount:* $3000.

Eligibility Requirements: Applicant must be enrolled or expecting to enroll full-time at a four-year institution or university. Applicant or parent of applicant must be member of Association for Iron and Steel Technology. Available to U.S. and non-U.S. citizens.

Application Requirements: Application form, essay, recommendations or references, resume, test scores, transcript. *Deadline:* March 15.

Contact: AIST Midwest Member Chapter Scholarships Chair
AIST Foundation
c/o Barry Felton
250 West U.S. Highway 12
Burns Harbor, IN 46304

ASSOCIATION FOR IRON AND STEEL TECHNOLOGY MIDWEST CHAPTER MEL NICKEL SCHOLARSHIP

Scholarship awarded to a graduating high school senior, or undergraduate freshman, sophomore or junior enrolled in a fully AIST-accredited college or university majoring engineering. Applicant must be in good academic standing. Must be a dependent of an AIST Midwest chapter member. May reapply each year for the term of their college education.

Academic Fields/Career Goals: Engineering/Technology.

Award: Scholarship for use in freshman, sophomore, junior, or senior years; not renewable. *Number:* 1. *Amount:* $3000.

Eligibility Requirements: Applicant must be enrolled or expecting to enroll full-time at a four-year institution or university. Applicant or parent of applicant must be member of Association for Iron and Steel Technology. Available to U.S. and non-U.S. citizens.

Application Requirements: Application form, essay, recommendations or references, resume, test scores, transcript. *Deadline:* March 15.

Contact: AIST Midwest Member Chapter Scholarships Chair
AIST Foundation
c/o Barry Felton
250 West U.S. Highway 12
Burns Harbor, IN 46304

ASSOCIATION FOR IRON AND STEEL TECHNOLOGY MIDWEST CHAPTER NON-ENGINEERING SCHOLARSHIP

Scholarship for graduating high school senior, or undergraduate freshman, sophomore, or junior enrolled in a fully AIST-accredited college or university. Applicant must be in good academic standing and dependent of an AIST Midwest chapter member. Recipients may reapply each year for the term of their college education.

Academic Fields/Career Goals: Engineering/Technology.

Award: Scholarship for use in freshman, sophomore, junior, or senior years; not renewable. *Number:* 3. *Amount:* $1500.

Eligibility Requirements: Applicant must be enrolled or expecting to enroll full-time at a four-year institution or university. Applicant or parent of applicant must be member of Association for Iron and Steel Technology. Available to U.S. and non-U.S. citizens.

Application Requirements: Application form, essay, recommendations or references, resume, test scores, transcript. *Deadline:* March 15.

Contact: AIST Midwest Member Chapter Scholarships Chair
AIST Foundation
c/o Barry Felton
250 West U.S. Highway 12
Burns Harbor, IN 46304

ASSOCIATION FOR IRON AND STEEL TECHNOLOGY MIDWEST CHAPTER WESTERN STATES SCHOLARSHIP

Scholarship of $3000 awarded to a graduating high school senior, or undergraduate freshman, sophomore, junior, or senior enrolled in a fully AIST-accredited college or university. Applicant must be in good academic standing and a dependent of an AIST Midwest chapter member. Recipients may reapply each year for the term of their college education.

Academic Fields/Career Goals: Engineering/Technology.

Award: Scholarship for use in freshman, sophomore, junior, or senior years; not renewable. *Number:* 1. *Amount:* $3000.

Eligibility Requirements: Applicant must be enrolled or expecting to enroll full-time at a four-year institution or university. Applicant or parent of applicant must be member of Association for Iron and Steel Technology. Available to U.S. and non-U.S. citizens.

Application Requirements: Application form, essay, recommendations or references, resume, test scores, transcript. *Deadline:* March 15.

Contact: AIST Midwest Member Chapter Scholarships Chair
AIST Foundation
c/o Barry Felton
250 West U.S. Highway 12
Burns Harbor, IN 46304

ASSOCIATION FOR IRON AND STEEL TECHNOLOGY OHIO VALLEY CHAPTER SCHOLARSHIP
• *See page 138*

ASSOCIATION FOR IRON AND STEEL TECHNOLOGY PITTSBURGH CHAPTER SCHOLARSHIP

Scholarships of $2500 for children, stepchildren, grandchildren, or spouse of a member in good standing of the Pittsburgh Chapter. Applicant must be a high school senior or currently enrolled undergraduate preparing for a career in engineering or metallurgy.

Academic Fields/Career Goals: Engineering/Technology; Materials Science, Engineering, and Metallurgy.

Award: Scholarship for use in freshman, sophomore, junior, or senior years; not renewable. *Number:* 2–3. *Amount:* $2500.

Eligibility Requirements: Applicant must be enrolled or expecting to enroll full-time at a four-year institution or university. Applicant or parent of applicant must be member of Association for Iron and Steel Technology. Available to U.S. citizens.

Application Requirements: Application form, essay, recommendations or references, resume, test scores, transcript. *Deadline:* April 30.

Contact: Daniel Kos, Program Coordinator
AIST Foundation
375 Saxonburg Boulevard
Saxonburg, PA 16056
E-mail: dkos@ii-vi.com

ASSOCIATION FOR IRON AND STEEL TECHNOLOGY SOUTHEAST MEMBER CHAPTER SCHOLARSHIP

Scholarship of $3000 for children, stepchildren, grandchildren, or spouse of active Southeast Chapter members who are pursuing a career in engineering, the sciences, or other majors relating to iron and steel production. Students may reapply for the scholarship each year for their term of college.

Academic Fields/Career Goals: Engineering/Technology; Materials Science, Engineering, and Metallurgy.

Award: Scholarship for use in freshman, sophomore, junior, or senior years; renewable. *Number:* 1. *Amount:* $3000.

Eligibility Requirements: Applicant must be enrolled or expecting to enroll full- or part-time at a four-year institution or university. Applicant or parent of applicant must be member of Association for Iron and Steel Technology. Available to U.S. citizens.

Application Requirements: Application form, essay, recommendations or references, resume, test scores, transcript. *Deadline:* April 30.

Contact: Mike Hutson, AIST Southeast Chapter Secretary
AIST Foundation
803 Floyd Street
Kings Mountain, NC 29086
Phone: 704-730-8320
Fax: 704-730-8321
E-mail: mike@johnhutsoncompany.com

ALBERTA HERITAGE SCHOLARSHIP FUND
http://www.alis.alberta.ca/

NORTHERN ALBERTA DEVELOPMENT COUNCIL BURSARY
• *See page 205*

AMERICAN CHEMICAL SOCIETY, RUBBER DIVISION
http://www.rubber.org/

AMERICAN CHEMICAL SOCIETY, RUBBER DIVISION UNDERGRADUATE SCHOLARSHIP
• *See page 105*

AMERICAN COUNCIL OF ENGINEERING COMPANIES OF PENNSYLVANIA (ACEC/PA)
http://www.acecpa.org/

ERIC J. GENNUSO AND LEROY D. (BUD) LOY, JR. SCHOLARSHIP PROGRAM
• *See page 153*

AMERICAN FOUNDATION FOR THE BLIND
http://www.afb.org/

PAUL W. RUCKES SCHOLARSHIP
• *See page 179*

AMERICAN INDIAN SCIENCE AND ENGINEERING SOCIETY
http://www.aises.org/

A.T. ANDERSON MEMORIAL SCHOLARSHIP PROGRAM
• *See page 105*

AMERICAN INSTITUTE OF AERONAUTICS AND ASTRONAUTICS
https://www.aiaa.org/

AIAA FOUNDATION UNDERGRADUATE SCHOLARSHIPS
• *See page 127*

LEATRICE GREGORY PENDRAY SCHOLARSHIP
• *See page 127*

AMERICAN PUBLIC POWER ASSOCIATION
https://www.publicpower.org/deed-rd-funding

DEMONSTRATION OF ENERGY AND EFFICIENCY DEVELOPMENTS EDUCATIONAL SCHOLARSHIP
• *See page 154*

DEMONSTRATION OF ENERGY AND EFFICIENCY DEVELOPMENTS STUDENT INTERNSHIP
• *See page 154*

DEMONSTRATION OF ENERGY AND EFFICIENCY DEVELOPMENTS STUDENT RESEARCH GRANTS
• *See page 162*

DEMONSTRATION OF ENERGY AND EFFICIENCY DEVELOPMENTS TECHNICAL DESIGN PROJECT
• *See page 154*

AMERICAN PUBLIC TRANSPORTATION FOUNDATION

https://www.aptfd.org/

TRANSIT HALL OF FAME SCHOLARSHIP AWARD PROGRAM
• *See page 162*

AMERICAN RAILWAY ENGINEERING AND MAINTENANCE OF WAY ASSOCIATION

http://www.aremafoundation.org/

AREMA GRADUATE AND UNDERGRADUATE SCHOLARSHIPS
• *See page 162*

AMERICAN SOCIETY FOR NONDESTRUCTIVE TESTING

www.asnt.org

ASNT ENGINEERING UNDERGRADUATE SCHOLARSHIP
• *See page 222*

AMERICAN SOCIETY OF AGRICULTURAL AND BIOLOGICAL ENGINEERS

http://www.asabe.org/

ASABE FOUNDATION SCHOLARSHIP
Award for full-time engineering undergraduate student in the U.S. or Canada. Must be active student member of the American Society of Agricultural Engineers. Must have a minimum of 3.0 GPA. Write for more information and special application procedures. One-time award of $1000. Must have completed one year of school, and must submit paper titled "My Goals in the Engineering Profession".

Academic Fields/Career Goals: Engineering/Technology.

Award: Scholarship for use in sophomore, junior, or senior years; not renewable. *Number:* 1. *Amount:* $1200.

Eligibility Requirements: Applicant must be enrolled or expecting to enroll full-time at a four-year institution or university. Applicant or parent of applicant must be member of Other Student Academic Clubs. Available to U.S. and Canadian citizens.

Application Requirements: Application form, essay, financial need analysis, recommendations or references, resume. *Deadline:* March 15.

Contact: Carol Flautt, Scholarship Program
American Society of Agricultural and Biological Engineers
2950 Niles Road
St. Joseph, MI 49085
Phone: 269-932-7036
Fax: 269-429-3852
E-mail: flautt@asabe.org

AMERICAN SOCIETY OF CERTIFIED ENGINEERING TECHNICIANS

http://www.ascet.org/

JOSEPH C. JOHNSON MEMORIAL GRANT
• *See page 225*

JOSEPH M. PARISH MEMORIAL GRANT
• *See page 225*

KURT H. AND DONNA M. SCHULER SMALL GRANT
• *See page 162*

AMERICAN SOCIETY OF MECHANICAL ENGINEERS

https://www.asme.org/

AGNES MALAKATE KEZIOS SCHOLARSHIP
Scholarship to college juniors for use in final year at a four year college. Must be majoring in mechanical engineering, be member of ASME (if available), and exhibit leadership values. Must be U.S. citizen enrolled in a college/university in the United States that has ABET accreditation. Scholarship value is $3000 and the number of awards granted varies.

Academic Fields/Career Goals: Engineering/Technology; Mechanical Engineering.

Award: Scholarship for use in junior or senior years; not renewable. *Number:* 1–2. *Amount:* $3000.

Eligibility Requirements: Applicant must be enrolled or expecting to enroll full-time at an institution or university and must have an interest in leadership. Applicant or parent of applicant must be member of American Society of Mechanical Engineers. Available to U.S. citizens.

Application Requirements: Application form, application form may be submitted online, essay, financial need analysis. *Deadline:* March 3.

Contact: RuthAnn Bigley, ASME Auxiliary Staff Coordinator
American Society of Mechanical Engineers
Two Park Avenue
Mailstop RB
New York, NY 10016
Phone: 212-591-7650
E-mail: bigleyr@asme.org

ALLEN J. BALDWIN SCHOLARSHIP
Scholarship available to college juniors for use in final year at a four year college. Must be majoring in mechanical engineering, be member of ASME (if available), and exhibit leadership values. Must be U.S. citizen enrolled in a college/university in the United States that has ABET accreditation. Scholarship value is $3000 and the number of awards granted varies.

Academic Fields/Career Goals: Engineering/Technology; Mechanical Engineering.

Award: Scholarship for use in junior or senior years; not renewable. *Number:* 1–2. *Amount:* $3000.

Eligibility Requirements: Applicant must be enrolled or expecting to enroll full-time at an institution or university and must have an interest in leadership. Applicant or parent of applicant must be member of American Society of Mechanical Engineers. Available to U.S. citizens.

Application Requirements: Application form, application form may be submitted online, essay, financial need analysis. *Deadline:* March 3.

Contact: RuthAnn Bigley, ASME Auxiliary Staff Coordinator
American Society of Mechanical Engineers
Two Park Avenue
Mailstop RB
New York, NY 10016
Phone: 212-591-7650
E-mail: bigleyr@asme.org

ASME AUXILIARY UNDERGRADUATE SCHOLARSHIP CHARLES B. SHARP
Award of $3000 available only to ASME student members to be used in final year of undergraduate study in mechanical engineering. Must be a U.S. citizen.

Academic Fields/Career Goals: Engineering/Technology.

Award: Scholarship for use in junior year; not renewable. *Number:* 1–2. *Amount:* $3000.

Eligibility Requirements: Applicant must be enrolled or expecting to enroll full-time at a four-year institution or university. Applicant or parent of applicant must be member of American Society of Mechanical Engineers. Available to U.S. citizens.

Application Requirements: Application form, application form may be submitted online(www.go.asme.org/scholarships), essay, financial need analysis, recommendations or references. *Deadline:* March 1.

Contact: RuthAnn Bigley, ASME Auxiliary Staff Coordinator
American Society of Mechanical Engineers
Two Park Avenue
Mailstop RB
New York, NY 10016
Phone: 212-591-7650
E-mail: bigleyr@asme.org

BERNA LOU CARTWRIGHT SCHOLARSHIP

Scholarship for study in the final year of undergraduate study; five-year students must apply in their fourth year. This scholarship was made possible by the ASME Auxiliary to honor Berna Lou Cartwright who was an active member of the ASME Auxiliary's Los Angeles Section.

Academic Fields/Career Goals: Engineering/Technology; Mechanical Engineering.

Award: Scholarship for use in senior year; not renewable. *Number:* 1–2. *Amount:* $3000.

Eligibility Requirements: Applicant must be enrolled or expecting to enroll full-time at an institution or university and must have an interest in leadership. Applicant or parent of applicant must be member of American Society of Mechanical Engineers. Available to U.S. citizens.

Application Requirements: Application form, application form may be submitted online, financial need analysis. *Deadline:* March 3.

Contact: RuthAnn Bigley, ASME Auxiliary Staff Coordinator
American Society of Mechanical Engineers
Two Park Avenue
Mailstop RB
New York, NY 10016
Phone: 212-591-7650
E-mail: bigleyr@asme.org

CHARLES B. SHARP SCHOLARSHIP

For study in the final (senior) year of undergraduate study. *Five-year students must apply in their fourth year. Requirements: Applicant must be a US Citizen and be enrolled in a mechanical engineering program. This scholarship is to be used in the final year of undergraduate study so a student will apply in their junior year.

Academic Fields/Career Goals: Engineering/Technology; Mechanical Engineering.

Award: Scholarship for use in senior year; not renewable. *Number:* 1. *Amount:* $3000.

Eligibility Requirements: Applicant must be enrolled or expecting to enroll full-time at an institution or university and must have an interest in leadership. Applicant or parent of applicant must be member of American Society of Mechanical Engineers. Available to U.S. citizens.

Application Requirements: Application form, application form may be submitted online, essay, financial need analysis. *Deadline:* March 3.

Contact: RuthAnn Bigley, ASME Auxiliary Staff Coordinator
American Society of Mechanical Engineers
Two Park Avenue
Mailstop RB
New York, NY 10016
Phone: 212-591-7650
E-mail: bigleyr@asme.org

LUCY AND CHARLES W.E. CLARKE SCHOLARSHIP

To recognize students whose FIRST experience has inspired an interest in pursuing an engineering career, the ASME Auxiliary will award multiple $5,000 scholarships to high school seniors active on a FIRST FTC or a FIRST FRC team, who are nominated by an ASME member, ASME Auxiliary member, or ASME student member who are also active with FIRST. This award will be for the first year of study (non-renewable) in an accredited Mechanical Engineering or Mechanical Engineering Technology program.

Academic Fields/Career Goals: Engineering/Technology; Mechanical Engineering.

Award: Scholarship for use in freshman year; not renewable. *Number:* 2–12. *Amount:* $5000.

Eligibility Requirements: Applicant must be high school student; planning to enroll or expecting to enroll full-time at an institution or university and must have an interest in leadership. Applicant or parent of applicant must have employment or volunteer experience in community service. Available to U.S. citizens.

Application Requirements: Application form, application form may be submitted online, essay, financial need analysis. *Deadline:* March 15.

Contact: RuthAnn Bigley
Phone: 212-591-7650
E-mail: bigleyr@asme.org

SYLVIA W. FARNY SCHOLARSHIP

One-time awards of $3000 to ASME student members for the final year of undergraduate study in mechanical engineering. Must be a U.S. citizen, enrolled in a college/university in the United States that has ABET accreditation. Number of scholarships granted varies.

Academic Fields/Career Goals: Engineering/Technology; Mechanical Engineering.

Award: Scholarship for use in junior or senior years; not renewable. *Number:* 1–2. *Amount:* $3000.

Eligibility Requirements: Applicant must be enrolled or expecting to enroll full-time at an institution or university and must have an interest in leadership. Applicant or parent of applicant must be member of American Society of Mechanical Engineers. Available to U.S. citizens.

Application Requirements: Application form, application form may be submitted online, essay, financial need analysis. *Deadline:* March 3.

Contact: RuthAnn Bigley, ASME Auxiliary Staff Coordinator
American Society of Mechanical Engineers
Two Park Avenue
Mailstop RB
New York, NY 10016
Phone: 212-591-7650
E-mail: bigleyr@asme.org

AMERICAN SOCIETY OF NAVAL ENGINEERS

http://www.navalengineers.org/

AMERICAN SOCIETY OF NAVAL ENGINEERS SCHOLARSHIP

• See page 106

AMERICAN SOCIETY OF PLUMBING ENGINEERS

http://www.aspe.org/

ALFRED STEELE ENGINEERING SCHOLARSHIP

Scholarships of $1000 are awarded for the members of American society of plumbing engineers towards education and professional development on plumbing engineering and designing.

Academic Fields/Career Goals: Engineering/Technology; Industrial Design.

Award: Scholarship for use in freshman, sophomore, junior, or senior years; not renewable. *Number:* 5. *Amount:* $1000.

Eligibility Requirements: Applicant must be enrolled or expecting to enroll full-time at a two-year or four-year or technical institution or university. Available to U.S. and non-U.S. citizens.

Application Requirements: Application form, community service, essay, recommendations or references, statement of personal achievement, transcript. *Deadline:* September 1.

Contact: Stacey Kidd, Membership Director
Phone: 773-693-2773
Fax: 773-695-9007
E-mail: skidd@aspe.org

AMERICAN WELDING SOCIETY

http://www.aws.org/

MILLER ELECTRIC INTERNATIONAL WORLD SKILLS COMPETITION SCHOLARSHIP

• See page 225

ANDERSON SOBEL COSMETIC SURGERY

https://www.andersonsobelcosmetic.com/

WISE (WOMEN IN STEM EXCEL) SCHOLARSHIP

The $1,500 WISE Scholarship is open to all Washingtonian women interested in pursuing a career in a STEM field. That includes high school seniors, anyone considering returning to school, and everything in between. We encourage you to apply if you meet the scholarship criteria: 1. Any female student living in Washington State who plans to attend any college or university; 2. Student must be actively pursuing a degree and career path in a STEM-related field at an institution of higher learning; 3. Must be able to provide one letter of recommendation; 4. Complete the application form and provide original essay answers

Academic Fields/Career Goals: Engineering/Technology.

Award: Scholarship for use in freshman, sophomore, junior, senior, graduate, or postgraduate years; not renewable. *Number:* 1. *Amount:* $1500.

Eligibility Requirements: Applicant must be enrolled or expecting to enroll full-time at an institution or university; female; resident of Washington and studying in Washington.

Application Requirements: Application form. *Deadline:* May 5.

Contact: Emily Bradley, Marketing Assistant
Anderson Sobel Cosmetic Surgery
230 Hilliard Ave Suite 2
Asheville, NC 28801
Phone: 828-8283508563
Fax: 28801
E-mail: womeninstemscholarship@gmail.com

ARIZONA PROFESSIONAL CHAPTER OF AISES

http://www.aises.org/scholarships

ARIZONA PROFESSIONAL CHAPTER OF AISES SCHOLARSHIP

Scholarship awarded to American Indian/Alaska Natives attending Arizona schools of higher education pursuing degrees in the sciences, engineering, medicine, natural resources, math, and technology. Student must be a full-time undergraduate student (at least 12 hours per semester) at an accredited two-year or four-year college or university.

Academic Fields/Career Goals: Engineering/Technology; Health and Medical Sciences; Natural Resources; Physical Sciences.

Award: Scholarship for use in freshman, sophomore, junior, or senior years; not renewable.

Eligibility Requirements: Applicant must be American Indian/Alaska Native; enrolled or expecting to enroll full-time at a two-year or four-year institution or university and studying in Arizona. Available to U.S. citizens.

Application Requirements: Application form, essay, portfolio, proof of tribal enrollment, copy of AISES membership card, recommendations or references, resume, transcript. *Deadline:* August 17.

Contact: Jaime Ashike, Scholarship Committee
Arizona Professional Chapter of AISES
PO Box 2528
Phoenix, AZ 85002
Phone: 480-326-0958
E-mail: amazing_butterfly@hotmail.com

ARMED FORCES COMMUNICATIONS AND ELECTRONICS ASSOCIATION, EDUCATIONAL FOUNDATION

https://foundation.afcea.org

AFCEA STEM MAJORS SCHOLARSHIPS FOR UNDERGRADUATE STUDENTS

• See page 106

ARMED FORCES COMMUNICATIONS AND ELECTRONICS ASSOCIATION ROTC SCHOLARSHIP PROGRAM

• See page 179

ASSOCIATED GENERAL CONTRACTORS EDUCATION AND RESEARCH FOUNDATION

https://www.agc.org/

WORKFORCE DEVELOPMENT SCHOLARSHIP

• See page 226

ASSOCIATION OF STATE DAM SAFETY OFFICIALS (ASDSO)

http://www.DamSafety.org

ASSOCIATION OF STATE DAM SAFETY OFFICIALS (ASDSO) SENIOR UNDERGRADUATE SCHOLARSHIP

• See page 140

AUTOMOTIVE WOMEN'S ALLIANCE FOUNDATION

http://awafoundation.org/index.php

AUTOMOTIVE WOMEN'S ALLIANCE FOUNDATION SCHOLARSHIPS

• See page 71

BARRY GOLDWATER SCHOLARSHIP AND EXCELLENCE IN EDUCATION FOUNDATION

https://goldwater.scholarsapply.org

BARRY M. GOLDWATER SCHOLARSHIP AND EXCELLENCE IN EDUCATION PROGRAM

• See page 107

BHW GROUP

https://thebhwgroup.com/

BHW WOMEN IN STEM SCHOLARSHIP

• See page 107

BOYS AND GIRLS CLUBS OF GREATER SAN DIEGO

http://www.sdyouth.org/

SPENCE REESE SCHOLARSHIP

Renewable scholarship for graduating high school seniors in the United States for study of law, medicine, engineering, and political science. Awarded based on academic standing, academic ability, financial need, and character.

Academic Fields/Career Goals: Engineering/Technology; Health and Medical Sciences; Law/Legal Services; Political Science.

Award: Scholarship for use in freshman, sophomore, junior, or senior years; not renewable. *Number:* 4. *Amount:* $6000.

Eligibility Requirements: Applicant must be high school student and planning to enroll or expecting to enroll full-time at a four-year institution or university. Available to U.S. citizens.

Application Requirements: Application form, essay, financial need analysis, interview. *Deadline:* March 30.

Contact:　Spence Reese Scholarship Administrator
　　　　　Boys and Girls Clubs of Greater San Diego
　　　　　4635 Clairemont Mesa Boulevard
　　　　　San Diego, CA 92117
　　　　　E-mail: mahazzard@sdyouth.org

BROWN AND CALDWELL

http://www.brownandcaldwell.com

ECKENFELDER SCHOLARSHIP
• *See page 141*

MINORITY SCHOLARSHIP PROGRAM
• *See page 141*

CARDS AGAINST HUMANITY

https://cardsagainsthumanity.com/

SCIENCE AMBASSADOR SCHOLARSHIP
• *See page 107*

CATCHING THE DREAM

http://www.catchingthedream.org/

MATH, ENGINEERING, SCIENCE, BUSINESS, EDUCATION, COMPUTERS SCHOLARSHIPS
• *See page 146*

CENTER FOR ARCHITECTURE

www.centerforarchitecture.org

CENTER FOR ARCHITECTURE DESIGN SCHOLARSHIP
• *See page 114*

CENTER FOR ARCHITECTURE, DOUGLAS HASKELL AWARD FOR STUDENT JOURNALS

Any journal (online or print) published by a school of architecture, landscape architecture or planning in the United States that is edited by students is eligible. The publication must have been produced in the current or previous school year.

Academic Fields/Career Goals: Engineering/Technology; Landscape Architecture; Urban and Regional Planning.

Award: Prize for use in freshman, sophomore, junior, senior, or graduate years; not renewable. *Number:* 1–3. *Amount:* $1000–$5000.

Eligibility Requirements: Applicant must be enrolled or expecting to enroll full- or part-time at a two-year or technical institution or university. Available to U.S. citizens.

Application Requirements: Application form, essay, portfolio. *Deadline:* May 15.

Contact:　Anna Marcum, Grants and Foundation Relations Manager
　　　　　Center for Architecture
　　　　　536 LaGuardia Place
　　　　　New York, NY 10012
　　　　　Phone: 212-683-0023
　　　　　E-mail: amarcum@centerforarchitecture.org

THE CLUNKER JUNKER

https://theclunkerjunker.com/

CLUNKER JUNKER CASH FOR CARS AND COLLEGE SCHOLARSHIP
• *See page 227*

CONNECTICUT BUILDING CONGRESS SCHOLARSHIP FUND, INC.

http://www.cbc-ct.org

CBC SCHOLARSHIP FUND
• *See page 114*

THE DALLAS FOUNDATION

http://www.dallasfoundation.org/

WHITLEY PLACE SCHOLARSHIP
• *See page 114*

DELAWARE HIGHER EDUCATION OFFICE

http://www.doe.k12.de.us

DELAWARE SOLID WASTE AUTHORITY JOHN P. "PAT" HEALY SCHOLARSHIP

Award for legal residents of Delaware who are U.S. citizens or eligible non-citizens. Must be high school seniors or full-time college students in their freshman or sophomore years. Must major in either environmental engineering or environmental sciences at a Delaware college. Selection based on financial need, academic performance, community and school involvement, and leadership ability.

Academic Fields/Career Goals: Engineering/Technology; Environmental Science.

Award: Scholarship for use in freshman or sophomore years; renewable. *Number:* 2. *Amount:* $1500–$2500.

Eligibility Requirements: Applicant must be enrolled or expecting to enroll full-time at a two-year or four-year institution or university; resident of Delaware; studying in Delaware and must have an interest in leadership. Available to U.S. citizens.

Application Requirements: Application form, financial need analysis. *Deadline:* March 4.

Contact:　Ms. Juliet Murawski, Program Administrator
　　　　　Delaware Higher Education Office
　　　　　401 Federal Street
　　　　　Suite 2
　　　　　Dover, DE 19901
　　　　　Phone: 302-735-4120
　　　　　Fax: 302-739-5894
　　　　　E-mail: dheo@doe.k12.de.us

DISTIL NETWORKS

http://www.distilnetworks.com

WOMEN FORWARD IN TECHNOLOGY SCHOLARSHIP PROGRAM
• *See page 108*

EAA AVIATION FOUNDATION, INC.

http://www.eaa.org/

PAYZER SCHOLARSHIP
• *See page 130*

THE ELECTROCHEMICAL SOCIETY

https://www.electrochem.org/

BATTERY DIVISION STUDENT RESEARCH AWARD SPONSORED BY MERCEDES-BENZ RESEARCH & DEVELOPMENT
• *See page 155*

H.H. DOW MEMORIAL STUDENT ACHIEVEMENT AWARD OF THE INDUSTRIAL ELECTROLYSIS AND

ELECTROCHEMICAL ENGINEERING DIVISION OF THE ELECTROCHEMICAL SOCIETY INC

• See page 156

ENGINEERS FOUNDATION OF OHIO

http://www.ohioengineer.com/

ENGINEERS FOUNDATION OF OHIO GENERAL FUND SCHOLARSHIP

Applicant must be a college junior or senior at the end of the academic year in which the application is submitted. Must be enrolled full-time at an Ohio college or university in a curriculum leading to a BS degree in engineering or its equivalent. Minimum GPA of 3.0 required. Must be a U.S. citizen and permanent resident of Ohio.

Academic Fields/Career Goals: Engineering/Technology.

Award: Scholarship for use in junior or senior years; not renewable. *Number:* 1. *Amount:* $1000.

Eligibility Requirements: Applicant must be enrolled or expecting to enroll full-time at an institution or university; resident of Nova Scotia and studying in Ohio. Available to U.S. citizens.

Application Requirements: Application form, essay, financial need analysis. *Deadline:* January 15.

Contact: Pam McClure, EFO Manager of Administration
　　　　　Phone: 614-223-1177
　　　　　E-mail: efo@ohioengineer.com

LLOYD A. CHACEY, PE-OHIO SOCIETY OF PROFESSIONAL ENGINEERS MEMORIAL SCHOLARSHIP

Scholarship available for a son, daughter, brother, sister, niece, nephew, spouse or grandchild of a current member of the Ohio Society of Professional Engineers, or of a deceased member who was in good standing at the time of his or her death. Must be enrolled full-time at an Ohio college or university in a curriculum leading to a degree in engineering or its equivalent. Must have a minimum of 3.0 GPA. Must be a U.S. citizen and permanent resident of Ohio.

Academic Fields/Career Goals: Engineering/Technology.

Award: Scholarship for use in junior or senior years; renewable. *Number:* 1–2. *Amount:* $2000.

Eligibility Requirements: Applicant must be enrolled or expecting to enroll full-time at an institution or university; resident of Nova Scotia and studying in Ohio. Available to U.S. citizens.

Application Requirements: Application form, essay, financial need analysis. *Deadline:* January 15.

Contact: Pam McClure, EFO Manager of Administration
　　　　　Phone: 614-223-1177
　　　　　E-mail: efo@ohioengineer.com

RAYMOND H. FULLER, PE MEMORIAL SCHOLARSHIP

Scholarship of $1000 to graduating high school seniors who will enter their freshman year in college the next fall. Recipients must be accepted for enrollment in an engineering program at an Ohio college or university. Must have a minimum of 3.0 GPA. Must be a U.S. citizen and permanent resident of Ohio. Consideration will be given to the prospective recipient's academic achievement, interest in a career in engineering and financial need as determined by interviews and from references.

Academic Fields/Career Goals: Engineering/Technology.

Award: Scholarship for use in freshman year; not renewable. *Number:* 1. *Amount:* $1000.

Eligibility Requirements: Applicant must be high school student; planning to enroll or expecting to enroll full-time at an institution or university; resident of Nova Scotia and studying in Ohio. Available to U.S. citizens.

Application Requirements: Application form, essay, financial need analysis, interview. *Deadline:* January 15.

Contact: Pam McClure, EFO Manager of Administration
　　　　　Phone: 614-223-1177
　　　　　E-mail: efo@ohioengineer.com

FLORIDA ENGINEERING SOCIETY

https://www.fleng.org/page/Scholarships

ACEC-FLORIDA SCHOLARSHIP

One-time scholarship of $5000 given to Florida citizen pursuing a bachelor's, master's or doctoral degree in an ABET-approved engineering program or in an accredited land surveying program. Students must be entering their junior, senior, or fifth year of college.

Academic Fields/Career Goals: Engineering/Technology; Natural Sciences; Surveying, Surveying Technology, Cartography, or Geographic Information Science.

Award: Scholarship for use in junior, senior, or graduate years; not renewable. *Number:* 1. *Amount:* $5000.

Eligibility Requirements: Applicant must be enrolled or expecting to enroll full-time at an institution or university; resident of District of Columbia and studying in Florida. Available to U.S. citizens.

Application Requirements: Application form, essay. *Deadline:* March 6.

Contact: Chad Faison, Chief Operating Officer
　　　　　Florida Engineering Society
　　　　　125 South Gadsden Street
　　　　　Tallahassee, FL 32301
　　　　　Phone: 850-224-7121
　　　　　E-mail: cfaison@fleng.org

DAVID F. LUDOVICI SCHOLARSHIP

• See page 156

ERIC PRIMAVERA MEMORIAL SCHOLARSHIP

One-time scholarship of $1000 given to students in their junior or senior year in a Florida university engineering program. Minimum 3.0 GPA required.

Academic Fields/Career Goals: Engineering/Technology.

Award: Scholarship for use in junior or senior years; not renewable. *Number:* 1. *Amount:* $1000.

Eligibility Requirements: Applicant must be enrolled or expecting to enroll full-time at an institution or university and studying in Florida. Applicant or parent of applicant must have employment or volunteer experience in engineering/technology. Available to U.S. citizens.

Application Requirements: Application form. *Deadline:* February 14.

Contact: Amanda Hudson, Director of Information Technology
　　　　　Florida Engineering Society
　　　　　125 S Gadsden Street
　　　　　Tallahassee, FL 32301
　　　　　Phone: 850-224-7121
　　　　　E-mail: ahudson@fleng.org

FECON SCHOLARSHIP

• See page 164

HIGH SCHOOL SCHOLARSHIP

One-time scholarship given to high school seniors who are residents of Florida. Minimum 3.5 GPA required. Applicant must have genuine interest in engineering.

Academic Fields/Career Goals: Engineering/Technology.

Award: Scholarship for use in freshman year; not renewable. *Number:* 6. *Amount:* $3000.

Eligibility Requirements: Applicant must be high school student; planning to enroll or expecting to enroll full-time at an institution or university; resident of District of Columbia and studying in Florida. Applicant or parent of applicant must have employment or volunteer experience in engineering/technology. Available to U.S. citizens.

Application Requirements: Application form, community service, interview. *Deadline:* February 14.

Contact: Amanda Hudson, Director of Information Technology
　　　　　Florida Engineering Society
　　　　　125 S Gadsden Street
　　　　　Tallahassee, FL 32301
　　　　　Phone: 850-224-7121
　　　　　E-mail: ahudson@fleng.org

RICHARD B. GASSETT, PE SCHOLARSHIP

One-time scholarship given to students in their junior or senior year in a Florida university engineering program. Minimum 3.0 GPA required.

Academic Fields/Career Goals: Engineering/Technology.

Award: Scholarship for use in junior or senior years; not renewable. *Number:* 1. *Amount:* $2500.

Eligibility Requirements: Applicant must be enrolled or expecting to enroll full-time at an institution or university and studying in Florida. Available to U.S. citizens.

Application Requirements: Application form. *Deadline:* February 14.

Contact: Amanda Hudson, Director of Information Technology
Florida Engineering Society
125 S Gadsden Street
Tallahassee, FL 32301
Phone: 850-224-7121
E-mail: ahudson@fleng.org

GEORGIA SOCIETY OF PROFESSIONAL ENGINEERS/GEORGIA ENGINEERING FOUNDATION

http://www.gefinc.org/

GEORGIA ENGINEERING FOUNDATION SCHOLARSHIP PROGRAM

Awards scholarships to students who are preparing for a career in engineering or engineering technology. Must be U.S. citizens and legal residents of Georgia. Must be attending or accepted in an ABET-accredited program. Separate applications are available: one for use by high school seniors and new college freshmen and one for use by college upperclassmen.

Academic Fields/Career Goals: Engineering/Technology.

Award: Scholarship for use in freshman, sophomore, junior, or senior years; not renewable. *Number:* 45. *Amount:* $1000–$5000.

Eligibility Requirements: Applicant must be enrolled or expecting to enroll full-time at a four-year institution or university and resident of Georgia. Available to U.S. citizens.

Application Requirements: Application form, personal photograph. *Deadline:* August 31.

Contact: Julie Secrist, Scholarship Committee Chairman
Georgia Society of Professional Engineers/Georgia
Engineering Foundation
233 Peachtree Street, Suite 700, Harris Tower
Atlanta, GA 30303
Phone: 678-449-5522
E-mail: scholarshipchair@gefinc.org

GOLDEN KEY INTERNATIONAL HONOUR SOCIETY

http://www.goldenkey.org/

ENGINEERING/TECHNOLOGY ACHIEVEMENT AWARD

Award to members who excel in the study of engineering or technology. Applicants will be asked to respond to a problem posed by an honorary member within the discipline. One winner will receive a $1000 award. The second place winner will receive $750 and the third place winner will receive $500.

Academic Fields/Career Goals: Engineering/Technology.

Award: Prize for use in freshman, sophomore, junior, senior, graduate, or postgraduate years; not renewable. *Number:* 3. *Amount:* $500–$1000.

Eligibility Requirements: Applicant must be enrolled or expecting to enroll full- or part-time at a four-year institution or university. Available to U.S. and non-U.S. citizens.

Application Requirements: Application form, engineering-related report, cover page from the online registration, entry in a contest, essay, recommendations or references, transcript. *Deadline:* March 3.

Contact: Scholarship Program Administrators
Golden Key International Honour Society
PO Box 23737
Nashville, TN 37202-3737
Phone: 800-377-2401
E-mail: scholarships@goldenkey.org

GREAT MINDS IN STEM

http://www.greatmindsinstem.org/college/scholarship-application-information

HENAAC SCHOLARSHIP PROGRAM
• See page 100

HELLENIC UNIVERSITY CLUB OF PHILADELPHIA

http://www.hucphiladephia.org/

DIMITRI J. VERVERELLI MEMORIAL SCHOLARSHIP FOR ARCHITECTURE AND/OR ENGINEERING

$2000 award for full-time student enrolled in an architecture or engineering degree program at an accredited four-year college or university. High school seniors accepted for enrollment in such a degree program may also apply. Must be a U.S. citizen of Greek descent and a resident of particular counties in NJ or PA.

Academic Fields/Career Goals: Engineering/Technology.

Award: Scholarship for use in freshman, sophomore, junior, or senior years; not renewable. *Amount:* $2000.

Eligibility Requirements: Applicant must be of Greek heritage; enrolled or expecting to enroll full-time at an institution or university and resident of New Hampshire, Oregon. Available to U.S. citizens.

Application Requirements: Application form, application form may be submitted online, essay, financial need analysis. *Deadline:* April 5.

Contact: Toula Bastas, Chairperson
Phone: 610-613-4310
E-mail: HucScholarship@gmail.com

IDAHO STATE BROADCASTERS ASSOCIATION

http://www.idahobroadcasters.org/

WAYNE C. CORNILS MEMORIAL SCHOLARSHIP
• See page 148

ILLINOIS SOCIETY OF PROFESSIONAL ENGINEERS

http://www.illinoisengineer.com/

ILLINOIS SOCIETY OF PROFESSIONAL ENGINEERS/MELVIN E. AMSTUTZ MEMORIAL AWARD

Applicant must attend an Illinois university approved by the Accreditation Board of Engineering. Applicant must be at least a junior in university he or she attends, and must prove financial need. Essay must address why applicant wishes to become a professional engineer. Must have a B average.

Academic Fields/Career Goals: Engineering/Technology.

Award: Scholarship for use in junior or senior years; not renewable. *Number:* 1. *Amount:* $1500.

Eligibility Requirements: Applicant must be enrolled or expecting to enroll full-time at a four-year institution and studying in Illinois. Available to U.S. and non-U.S. citizens.

Application Requirements: Application form, application form may be submitted online (http://illinoisengineer.com/scholarships.shtml), essay, financial need analysis, recommendations or references, resume, transcript. *Deadline:* March 31.

Contact: Mrs. Nicole Palmisano, Scholarship Coordinator
Phone: 217-544-7424 Ext. 238
Fax: 217-528-6545
E-mail: NicolePalmisano@illinoisengineer.com

ILLUMINATING ENGINEERING SOCIETY OF NORTH AMERICA

http://www.ies.org/

ROBERT W. THUNEN MEMORIAL SCHOLARSHIPS
• *See page 116*

INSTITUTE OF INDUSTRIAL ENGINEERS

https://www.iise.org/

SOCIETY FOR HEALTH SYSTEMS SCHOLARSHIP

Scholarship available to undergraduate students enrolled full-time in any school in the United States and its territories, Canada and Mexico, provided: (1) the school's industrial engineering program or equivalent is accredited by an agency or organization recognized by IISE; and (2) the student is pursuing a course of study in industrial engineering and operations research with a definite interest in the area of healthcare. Must be an active Society for Health Systems student member.

Academic Fields/Career Goals: Engineering/Technology; Health Administration; Health Information Management/Technology.

Award: Scholarship for use in freshman, sophomore, junior, or senior years; not renewable. *Number:* 1. *Amount:* $1000.

Eligibility Requirements: Applicant must be enrolled or expecting to enroll full-time at an institution or university. Available to U.S. citizens.

Application Requirements: Application form, essay. *Deadline:* November 15.

Contact: Bonnie Cameron, Operations Administrator
Phone: 770-449-0461 Ext. 105
E-mail: bcameron@iise.org

INTERNATIONAL FACILITY MANAGEMENT ASSOCIATION FOUNDATION

http://www.ifmafoundation.org/

IFMA FOUNDATION SCHOLARSHIPS
• *See page 116*

INTERNATIONAL SOCIETY FOR OPTICAL ENGINEERING-SPIE

http://www.spie.org/scholarships

SPIE EDUCATIONAL SCHOLARSHIPS IN OPTICAL SCIENCE AND ENGINEERING
• *See page 108*

INTERNATIONAL SOCIETY OF EXPLOSIVES ENGINEERS

http://www.isee.org/

JERRY MCDOWELL FUND
• *See page 156*

INTERNATIONAL TECHNOLOGY EDUCATION ASSOCIATION

http://www.iteaconnect.org/

INTERNATIONAL TECHNOLOGY EDUCATION ASSOCIATION UNDERGRADUATE SCHOLARSHIP IN TECHNOLOGY EDUCATION
• *See page 210*

LEAGUE OF UNITED LATIN AMERICAN CITIZENS NATIONAL EDUCATIONAL SERVICE CENTERS INC.

http://www.lnesc.org/

GE/LULAC SCHOLARSHIP
• *See page 149*

GM/LULAC SCHOLARSHIP

Renewable award for minority students who are pursuing an undergraduate degree in engineering at an accredited college or university. Must maintain a minimum 3.0 GPA. Selection is based in part on the likelihood of pursuing a successful career in engineering.

Academic Fields/Career Goals: Engineering/Technology.

Award: Scholarship for use in freshman, sophomore, junior, or senior years; renewable. *Number:* up to 20. *Amount:* up to $2000.

Eligibility Requirements: Applicant must be American Indian/Alaska Native, Asian/Pacific Islander, Black (non-Hispanic), Hispanic and enrolled or expecting to enroll full-time at a four-year institution or university. Available to U.S. citizens.

Application Requirements: Application form, essay, recommendations or references, transcript. *Deadline:* July 15.

Contact: Scholarship Administrator
League of United Latin American Citizens National
Educational Service Centers Inc.
2000 L Street, NW, Suite 610
Washington, DC 20036
Phone: 202-835-9646 Ext. 10
Fax: 202-835-9685

LOGMEIN

https://www.logmeininc.com

LASTPASS STEM SCHOLARSHIP
• *See page 109*

LOS ANGELES COUNCIL OF BLACK PROFESSIONAL ENGINEERS

http://www.lablackengineers.org/

AL-BEN SCHOLARSHIP FOR ACADEMIC INCENTIVE
• *See page 157*

AL-BEN SCHOLARSHIP FOR PROFESSIONAL MERIT
• *See page 157*

AL-BEN SCHOLARSHIP FOR SCHOLASTIC ACHIEVEMENT
• *See page 157*

MAINE SOCIETY OF PROFESSIONAL ENGINEERS

http://www.mespe.org/

MAINE SOCIETY OF PROFESSIONAL ENGINEERS VERNON T. SWAINE-ROBERT E. CHUTE SCHOLARSHIP
• *See page 228*

MANUFACTURERS ASSOCIATION OF MAINE

http://www.mainemfg.com/

MAINE MANUFACTURING CAREER AND TRAINING FOUNDATION SCHOLARSHIP
• *See page 131*

MASSACHUSETTS ASSOCIATION OF LAND SURVEYORS AND CIVIL ENGINEERS

http://www.malsce.org/

MALSCE SCHOLARSHIPS

A scholarship awarded to a student presently enrolled full time (days) as an undergraduate in an accredited college, university, junior college, technical institute or community college and majoring in land surveying, civil engineering, or environmental engineering. The MALSCE Education Trust may select one or more applicants to receive scholarships per year and currently plans to award one or two scholarships. Typically 2-3 scholarships are awarded each year with varying denominations of $500, $1000 or $2500 each. The MALSCE Education Trust Chair will contact winning applicants. Applicant must be presently enrolled full-time (days) in an accredited college, university, junior college, technical institute, or community college and majoring in land surveying, civil engineering, or environmental engineering; be a Massachusetts resident (based upon parents full-time residence, if still a dependent), however, he/she may attend an out-of-state school; complete and sign the application and give it to a qualified sponsor. A sponsor must be a department head, dean, professor, or instructor who has personal knowledge of the applicant. An applicant's employer may also be a sponsor, if that employer is a MALSCE member in good standing. Friends and relatives of the applicant may not be sponsors. The Trustees will not accept a letter of recommendation from a sponsor other than the types listed above.

Academic Fields/Career Goals: Engineering/Technology; Environmental Science; Surveying, Surveying Technology, Cartography, or Geographic Information Science.

Award: Scholarship for use in sophomore, junior, or senior years; not renewable. *Number:* 1–2. *Amount:* $500–$2000.

Eligibility Requirements: Applicant must be enrolled or expecting to enroll full- or part-time at a two-year or four-year or technical institution or university; resident of Massachusetts and studying in Massachusetts. Available to U.S. citizens.

Application Requirements: Application form, essay. *Deadline:* October 31.

Contact: Mrs. Mary Ann Corcoran, MALSCE Education Trust Chair
Massachusetts Association of Land Surveyors and Civil Engineers
One Walnut Street
Boston, MA 02108
Phone: 413-841-0355
E-mail: mcorcoran@hillengineers.com

MIDWEST ROOFING CONTRACTORS ASSOCIATION

http://www.mrca.org/

MRCA FOUNDATION SCHOLARSHIP PROGRAM
• See page 116

MINERALS, METALS, AND MATERIALS SOCIETY (TMS)

http://www.tms.org/

MATERIALS PROCESSING AND MANUFACTURING DIVISION SCHOLARSHIP
• See page 228

TMS EXTRACTION & PROCESSING SCHOLARSHIP
• See page 228

TMS FUNCTIONAL MATERIALS GILBERT CHIN SCHOLARSHIP
• See page 228

TMS/INTERNATIONAL SYMPOSIUM ON SUPERALLOYS SCHOLARSHIP PROGRAM
• See page 229

TMS/LIGHT METALS DIVISION SCHOLARSHIP PROGRAM
• See page 229

TMS OUTSTANDING STUDENT PAPER CONTEST-UNDERGRADUATE
• See page 229

TMS/STRUCTURAL MATERIALS DIVISION SCHOLARSHIP
• See page 229

NASA FLORIDA SPACE GRANT CONSORTIUM

http://www.floridaspacegrant.org/

FLORIDA SPACE RESEARCH PROGRAM
• See page 131

NASA IDAHO SPACE GRANT CONSORTIUM

http://www.idahospacegrant.org

NASA IDAHO SPACE GRANT CONSORTIUM SCHOLARSHIP PROGRAM
• See page 109

NASA/MARYLAND SPACE GRANT CONSORTIUM

https://md.spacegrant.org

NASA MARYLAND SPACE GRANT CONSORTIUM SCHOLARSHIPS
• See page 109

NASA MINNESOTA SPACE GRANT CONSORTIUM

https://www.mnspacegrant.org/

MINNESOTA SPACE GRANT CONSORTIUM SCHOLARSHIP PROGRAM
• See page 131

NASA MONTANA SPACE GRANT CONSORTIUM

http://www.spacegrant.montana.edu/

MONTANA SPACE GRANT SCHOLARSHIP PROGRAM
• See page 132

NASA RHODE ISLAND SPACE GRANT CONSORTIUM

http://brown/initiatives/ri-space-grant

NASA RHODE ISLAND SPACE GRANT CONSORTIUM UNDERGRADUATE RESEARCH SCHOLARSHIP
• See page 132

NASA RISGC SCIENCE EN ESPANOL SCHOLARSHIP FOR UNDERGRADUATE STUDENTS
• See page 132

NASA'S VIRGINIA SPACE GRANT CONSORTIUM

http://www.vsgc.odu.edu/

COMMUNITY COLLEGE STEM SCHOLARSHIPS
• *See page 110*

NATIONAL ACTION COUNCIL FOR MINORITIES IN ENGINEERING-NACME INC.

http://www.nacme.org/

NACME SCHOLARS PROGRAM
Renewable award for African-American, American-Indian, or Latino student enrolled in a Baccalaureate engineering program. Award money is given to participating institutions who select applicants and disperse funds. High school seniors must be accepted by a College of Engineering (at the end of the freshman year, NACME assumes a minimum GPA of 2.5 on a scale of 4.0). Two-year community college transfers, i.e., those accepted for their third year of engineering study, must enter with at least a 2.7 cumulative GPA on a scale of a 4.0 and an Associate's Degree in engineering science (or the equivalent program of study). Check website for details, http://www.nacme.org.

Academic Fields/Career Goals: Engineering/Technology.

Award: Scholarship for use in freshman, sophomore, junior, or senior years; renewable.

Eligibility Requirements: Applicant must be American Indian/Alaska Native, Black (non-Hispanic), Hispanic and enrolled or expecting to enroll full-time at a four-year institution or university. Available to U.S. citizens.

Application Requirements: Financial need analysis. *Deadline:* March 15.

Contact: Christopher Smith, Vice President, Scholarships, University Relations, and Research
National Action Council for Minorities in Engineering-NACME Inc.
One North Broadway
Suite 601
White Plains, NY 10601-2318
Phone: 914-539-4316
Fax: 914-539-4032
E-mail: scholars@nacme.org

NATIONAL ASSOCIATION FOR THE ADVANCEMENT OF COLORED PEOPLE

http://www.naacp.org/

HUBERTUS W.V. WILLEMS SCHOLARSHIP FOR MALE STUDENTS
• *See page 229*

NATIONAL ASSOCIATION OF WOMEN IN CONSTRUCTION

http://www.nawic.org/

NAWIC UNDERGRADUATE SCHOLARSHIPS
• *See page 117*

NATIONAL SOCIETY OF BLACK ENGINEERS

https://connect.nsbe.org/Scholarships/ScholarshipList.aspx

NSBE CORPORATE SCHOLARSHIP PROGRAM
• *See page 230*

S. D. BECHTEL JR. FOUNDATION ENGINEERING SCHOLARSHIP

The purpose of this scholarship is to provide financial scholarships for students pursuing undergraduate degrees in Engineering and collegiate members of the National Society of Black Engineers (NSBE). Applicants must be NSBE members, majoring in civil engineering or mechanical engineering.

Academic Fields/Career Goals: Engineering/Technology.

Award: Scholarship for use in freshman, sophomore, junior, or senior years; renewable. *Number:* 3. *Amount:* $15,000.

Eligibility Requirements: Applicant must be Black (non-Hispanic) and enrolled or expecting to enroll full- or part-time at a four-year institution or university. Available to U.S. citizens.

Application Requirements: *Deadline:* June 30.

Contact: Raynashia Goodine, Programs Coordinator, Scholarships
National Society of Black Engineers
205 Daingerfield Road
Alexandria, VA 22314
Phone: 703-837-2207 Ext. 214
E-mail: scholarships@nsbe.org

NATIONAL SOCIETY OF PROFESSIONAL ENGINEERS

http://www.nspe.org/

MAUREEN L. & HOWARD N. BLITMAN, P.E., SCHOLARSHIP TO PROMOTE DIVERSITY IN ENGINEERING
• *See page 166*

PAUL H. ROBBINS HONORARY SCHOLARSHIP
• *See page 158*

PROFESSIONAL ENGINEERS IN INDUSTRY SCHOLARSHIP
• *See page 158*

NEVADA NASA SPACE GRANT CONSORTIUM

https://nasa.epscorspo.nevada.edu/

NATIONAL SPACE GRANT CONSORTIUM SCHOLARSHIPS
• *See page 110*

NEW ENGLAND WATER WORKS ASSOCIATION

https://www.newwa.org/

ELSON T. KILLAM MEMORIAL SCHOLARSHIP
• *See page 166*

FRANCIS X. CROWLEY SCHOLARSHIP
• *See page 150*

JOSEPH MURPHY SCHOLARSHIP
• *See page 150*

NEXTSTEPU

http://www.nextstepu.com/

$1,500 STEM SCHOLARSHIP
• *See page 104*

PROFESSIONAL CONSTRUCTION ESTIMATORS ASSOCIATION

http://www.pcea.org/

TED G. WILSON MEMORIAL SCHOLARSHIP FOUNDATION
• See page 166

ROBERT H. MOLLOHAN FAMILY CHARITABLE FOUNDATION, INC.

http://www.mollohanfoundation.org/

HIGH TECHNOLOGY SCHOLARS PROGRAM
• See page 158

ROCKY MOUNTAIN COAL MINING INSTITUTE

http://www.rmcmi.org/

ROCKY MOUNTAIN COAL MINING INSTITUTE SCHOLARSHIP
• See page 167

SAE INTERNATIONAL

SAE INTERNATIONAL SCHOLARSHIPS PROGRAM
• See page 230

SALT RIVER PROJECT (SRP)

http://www.srpnet.com/

NAVAJO GENERATING STATION NAVAJO SCHOLARSHIP
Applicants must be enrolled members of the Navajo Nation who will be full-time students at an accredited college or university. Priority will be given to the math, engineering and environmental studies. Awards are made based on the field of study, and academic excellence and achievement. Award amounts are determined by the NGS Scholarship Committee following an evaluation of the Financial Needs Analysis of each applicant.

Academic Fields/Career Goals: Engineering/Technology; Environmental Science; Mathematics.

Award: Scholarship for use in junior year; renewable.

Eligibility Requirements: Applicant must be American Indian/Alaska Native and enrolled or expecting to enroll full-time at a four-year institution or university.

Application Requirements: *Deadline:* April 25.

SCARLETT FAMILY FOUNDATION SCHOLARSHIP PROGRAM

http://www.scarlettfoundation.org/

SCHOLARSHIP FOR STUDENTS PURSUING A BUSINESS OR STEM DEGREE
• See page 80

SEMICONDUCTOR RESEARCH CORPORATION (SRC)

http://www.src.org/

MASTER'S SCHOLARSHIP PROGRAM
• See page 158

SIMPLEHUMAN

http://www.simplehuman.com/

SIMPLE SOLUTIONS DESIGN COMPETITION
• See page 231

SOCIETY OF MANUFACTURING ENGINEERS EDUCATION FOUNDATION

http://www.smeef.org/

CATERPILLAR SCHOLARS AWARD FUND
Supports five one-time scholarships for full-time students enrolled in a manufacturing engineering program. Minority applicants may apply as incoming freshmen. Applicants must have an overall minimum GPA of 3.0.

Academic Fields/Career Goals: Engineering/Technology.

Award: Scholarship for use in freshman, sophomore, junior, or senior years; not renewable. *Number:* 1–15. *Amount:* $1000–$5000.

Eligibility Requirements: Applicant must be enrolled or expecting to enroll full-time at a four-year institution or university. Available to U.S. and Canadian citizens.

Application Requirements: Application form, essay, recommendations or references, resume, transcript. *Deadline:* February 1.

Contact: Jennifer Sperbeck, Scholarship Program Coordinator
Phone: 313-425-3300
E-mail: jsperbeck@sme.org

SOCIETY OF MOTION PICTURE AND TELEVISION ENGINEERS

https://www.smpte.org/

LOUIS F. WOLF JR. MEMORIAL SCHOLARSHIP
• See page 175

STUDENT PAPER AWARD
• See page 175

SOCIETY OF PETROLEUM ENGINEERS

http://www.spe.org/

GUS ARCHIE MEMORIAL SCHOLARSHIPS
Renewable award for students who have not attended college or university before and are planning to enroll in a petroleum engineering degree program at a four-year institution. Must have minimum 3.0 GPA.

Academic Fields/Career Goals: Engineering/Technology.

Award: Scholarship for use in freshman, sophomore, junior, or senior years; renewable. *Number:* 1–2. *Amount:* $6000.

Eligibility Requirements: Applicant must be enrolled or expecting to enroll full-time at a four-year institution or university. Available to U.S. and non-U.S. citizens.

Application Requirements: Application form, financial need analysis, personal photograph, recommendations or references, test scores, transcript. *Deadline:* April 30.

Contact: Young Member Program
Society of Petroleum Engineers
PO Box 833836
Richardson, TX 75083
Phone: 972-952-9448
Fax: 972-952-9435
E-mail: studentactivities@spe.org

SOCIETY OF PLASTICS ENGINEERS FOUNDATION (SPE)

http://www.4spe.org/

FLEMING/BLASZCAK SCHOLARSHIP
• See page 158

GULF COAST HURRICANE SCHOLARSHIP
• See page 159

SOCIETY OF PLASTICS ENGINEERS SCHOLARSHIP PROGRAM
• See page 159

SOCIETY OF WOMEN ENGINEERS
https://swe.org/

DUPONT COMPANY SCHOLARSHIP
• See page 159

GE WOMEN'S NETWORK SHARON DALEY SCHOLARSHIP
• See page 231

LIEBHERR MINING SCHOLARSHIP
• See page 182

SWE REGION E SCHOLARSHIP
• See page 159

SWE REGION H SCHOLARSHIPS
• See page 159

SWE REGION J SCHOLARSHIP
• See page 159

TE CONNECTIVITY EXCELLENCE IN ENGINEERING SCHOLARSHIP
• See page 160

SOCIETY OF WOMEN ENGINEERS-DALLAS SECTION
http://www.dallaswe.org/

DALLAS SWE ANNIE COLACO COLLEGIATE LEADER SCHOLARSHIP
• See page 182

DALLAS SWE HIGH SCHOOL SENIOR SCHOLARSHIP
Scholarship for graduating high school senior women who wish to pursue a degree in engineering. Applicant must be a Texas resident and attend a Texas Region 10 high school. Please refer to website for further details http://www.dallaswe.org/scholarships.

Academic Fields/Career Goals: Engineering/Technology.

Award: Scholarship for use in freshman year; not renewable. *Number:* 2–10. *Amount:* $500–$1500.

Eligibility Requirements: Applicant must be high school student; planning to enroll or expecting to enroll full-time at a two-year or four-year institution or university; female and resident of Texas. Available to U.S. citizens.

Application Requirements: Application form, essay, personal photograph, test scores, transcript. *Deadline:* April 15.

Contact: Shelley Stracener, FY18 President
E-mail: dallas.swe@gmail.com

SOCIETY OF WOMEN ENGINEERS-TWIN TIERS SECTION
http://twintiers.swe.org/scholarship-information.html

SOCIETY OF WOMEN ENGINEERS-TWIN TIERS SECTION SCHOLARSHIP
• See page 182

SPECIALTY EQUIPMENT MARKET ASSOCIATION
http://www.sema.org/

SEMA MEMORIAL SCHOLARSHIP FUND
• See page 81

STRAIGHTFORWARD MEDIA
http://www.straightforwardmedia.com/

STRAIGHTFORWARD MEDIA ENGINEERING SCHOLARSHIP
• See page 160

STRAIGHT NORTH
https://www.straightnorth.com/

STRAIGHT NORTH STEM SCHOLARSHIP
• See page 81

TAU KAPPA EPSILON EDUCATION FOUNDATION
https://www.tke.org/

STEVEN J. MUIR SCHOLARSHIP
• See page 160

TECHNICAL ASSOCIATION OF THE PULP & PAPER INDUSTRY (TAPPI)
https://www.tappi.org/

PAPER AND BOARD DIVISION SCHOLARSHIPS
Award to TAPPI student member or an undergraduate member of a TAPPI Student Chapter enrolled as a college or university undergraduate in an engineering or science program. Must be sophomore, junior, or senior and able to show a significant interest in the paper industry. Information can be found at http://www.tappi.org/s_tappi/sec.asp?CID=6101&DID=546695.

Academic Fields/Career Goals: Engineering/Technology; Paper and Pulp Engineering.

Award: Scholarship for use in sophomore, junior, or senior years; not renewable. *Number:* 1–4. *Amount:* $1000–$1500.

Eligibility Requirements: Applicant must be enrolled or expecting to enroll full-time at a four-year institution or university. Available to U.S. and non-U.S. citizens.

Application Requirements: Application form. *Deadline:* February 15.

Contact: Mr. Laurence Womack, Director of Standards and Awards
Technical Association of the Pulp & Paper Industry (TAPPI)
15 Technology Parkway South
Peachtree Corners, GA 30092
Phone: 770-209-7276
E-mail: standards@tappi.org

TAPPI PROCESS AND PRODUCT QUALITY DIVISION SCHOLARSHIP
The TAPPI Process and Product Quality Scholarship is awarded to TAPPI student members or student chapter members to encourage them to pursue careers in the pulp and paper industry and to develop awareness of quality management.

Academic Fields/Career Goals: Engineering/Technology.

Award: Scholarship for use in sophomore, junior, or senior years; not renewable. *Number:* 1. *Amount:* $1000.

Eligibility Requirements: Applicant must be enrolled or expecting to enroll full-time at a four-year institution or university. Available to U.S. and non-U.S. citizens.

Application Requirements: Application form. *Deadline:* February 15.

Contact: Mr. Charles Bohanan, Director of Standards and Awards
Technical Association of the Pulp & Paper Industry (TAPPI)
15 Technology Parkway South
Peachtree Corners, GA 30092
Phone: 770-209-7276
E-mail: standards@tappi.org

TECHNOLOGY FIRST
https://technologyfirst.org/

ROBERT V. MCKENNA SCHOLARSHIPS
• *See page 183*

TIMOTION
http://www.timotion.com/

TIMOTION ENGINEERING AND EXCELLENCE SCHOLARSHIP
• *See page 167*

TRANSPORTATION ASSOCIATION OF CANADA FOUNDATION
http://www.tac-foundation.ca

TAC FOUNDATION SCHOLARSHIPS
• *See page 168*

TURNER CONSTRUCTION COMPANY
http://www.turnerconstruction.com/

YOUTHFORCE 2020 SCHOLARSHIP PROGRAM
• *See page 117*

UNITED NEGRO COLLEGE FUND
http://www.uncf.org/

DAVIS SCHOLARSHIP FOR WOMEN IN STEM
• *See page 111*

DELL CORPORATE SCHOLARS PROGRAM
• *See page 168*

DISCOVER FINANCIAL SERVICES SCHOLARSHIP
• *See page 82*

GALACTIC UNITE BYTHEWAY SCHOLARSHIP
• *See page 111*

LEIDOS STEM SCHOLARSHIP
• *See page 96*

UNCF-NORTHROP GRUMMAN SCHOLARSHIP
• *See page 184*

UNITED STATES SOCIETY ON DAMS
http://www.ussdams.org/

UNITED STATES SOCIETY ON DAMS STUDENT SCHOLARSHIP AWARD
• *See page 168*

VECTORWORKS, INC.
http://www.vectorworks.net

VECTORWORKS DESIGN SCHOLARSHIP
• *See page 117*

VERMONT SPACE GRANT CONSORTIUM
http://www.cems.uvm.edu/vsgc

VERMONT SPACE GRANT CONSORTIUM
• *See page 92*

WISCONSIN SOCIETY OF PROFESSIONAL ENGINEERS
http://www.wspe.org/

WISCONSIN SOCIETY OF PROFESSIONAL ENGINEERS SCHOLARSHIPS
Scholarships are awarded each year to high school seniors having qualifications for success in engineering education. Must be a U.S. citizen and Wisconsin resident, ACT composite score and have a minimum GPA of 3.0.
Academic Fields/Career Goals: Engineering/Technology.
Award: Scholarship for use in freshman year; not renewable. *Number:* 7. *Amount:* $1000–$2000.
Eligibility Requirements: Applicant must be high school student; planning to enroll or expecting to enroll full-time at a four-year institution or university and resident of Wisconsin. Available to U.S. citizens.
Application Requirements: Application form, essay, interview, recommendations or references, self-addressed stamped envelope with application, test scores, transcript. *Deadline:* December 19.
Contact: Al Linder
E-mail: Al.lindner@graef-usa.com

WOMEN IN AEROSPACE FOUNDATION
https://www.womeninaerospace.org/

THE WOMEN IN AEROSPACE FOUNDATION SCHOLARSHIP
• *See page 135*

WOMEN IN AVIATION, INTERNATIONAL
http://www.wai.org/

THE BOEING COMPANY CAREER ENHANCEMENT SCHOLARSHIP
• *See page 136*

DELTA AIR LINES AIRCRAFT MAINTENANCE TECHNOLOGY SCHOLARSHIP
• *See page 136*

DELTA AIR LINES ENGINEERING SCHOLARSHIP
• *See page 136*

XEROX
http://www.xerox.com//

TECHNICAL MINORITY SCHOLARSHIP
• *See page 161*

ENTOMOLOGY

AMERICAN INDIAN SCIENCE AND ENGINEERING SOCIETY

http://www.aises.org/

A.T. ANDERSON MEMORIAL SCHOLARSHIP PROGRAM
• See page 105

AMERICAN SOCIETY OF AGRONOMY, CROP SCIENCE SOCIETY OF AMERICA, SOIL SCIENCE SOCIETY OF AMERICA

http://www.agronomy.org

J. FIELDING REED UNDERGRADUATE SOIL AND PLANT SCIENCES SCHOLARSHIP
• See page 200

BARRY GOLDWATER SCHOLARSHIP AND EXCELLENCE IN EDUCATION FOUNDATION

https://goldwater.scholarsapply.org

BARRY M. GOLDWATER SCHOLARSHIP AND EXCELLENCE IN EDUCATION PROGRAM
• See page 107

BHW GROUP

https://thebhwgroup.com/

BHW WOMEN IN STEM SCHOLARSHIP
• See page 107

GREAT MINDS IN STEM

http://www.greatmindsinstem.org/college/scholarship-application-information

HENAAC SCHOLARSHIP PROGRAM
• See page 100

HORTICULTURAL RESEARCH INSTITUTE

https://www.hriresearch.org/

BRYAN A. CHAMPION MEMORIAL SCHOLARSHIP
The Bryan A. Champion Memorial Scholarship awards one $1,000 scholarship to a deserving horticultural student. Applicant must be enrolled in an accredited undergraduate or graduate program in landscape, horticulture or related discipline at a two or four-year institution. Students in vocational agriculture programs will also be considered. Must have a minimum grade point average overall of 2.25 based on a scale of 4.0, and a minimum GPA of 2.7 on a scale of 4.0 in their major.

Academic Fields/Career Goals: Entomology; Horticulture/Floriculture; Landscape Architecture.

Award: Scholarship for use in sophomore, junior, senior, graduate, or postgraduate years; not renewable. *Number:* 1. *Amount:* $1000.

Eligibility Requirements: Applicant must be enrolled or expecting to enroll full- or part-time at a two-year or technical institution or university and studying in Ohio. Available to U.S. citizens.

Application Requirements: Application form, application form may be submitted online, essay, financial need analysis. *Deadline:* September 10.

Contact: Jennifer Gray, Research Programs Administrator
Horticultural Research Institute
2130 Stella Court
Columbus, OH 43215
Phone: 614-487-1117
E-mail: jenniferg@americanhort.org

CARVILLE M. AKEHURST MEMORIAL SCHOLARSHIP
The Carville M. Akehurst Memorial Scholarship provides one $5,000 scholarship to qualified students to help ensure the continuity of the nursery and landscape profession. Must have a minimum grade point average overall of 2.7 based on a scale of 4.0, and a minimum GPA of 3.0 on a scale of 4.0 in their major. Preference will be given to applicants who plan to work within the industry (including nursery operation, landscape architecture/design/construction/maintenance, interiorscape, horticultural distribution, or retail garden center) following graduation.

Academic Fields/Career Goals: Entomology; Horticulture/Floriculture; Landscape Architecture.

Award: Scholarship for use in sophomore, junior, senior, graduate, or postgraduate years; not renewable. *Number:* 1. *Amount:* $5000.

Eligibility Requirements: Applicant must be enrolled or expecting to enroll full-time at a two-year or technical institution or university and resident of Manitoba, Vermont, Washington. Available to U.S. citizens.

Application Requirements: Application form, application form may be submitted online, essay, financial need analysis. *Deadline:* September 10.

Contact: Jennifer Gray, Research Programs Administrator
Horticultural Research Institute
2130 Stella Court
Columbus, OH 43215
Phone: 614-487-1117
E-mail: jenniferg@americanhort.org

SUSIE AND BRUCE USREY EDUCATION SCHOLARSHIP
The Susie and Bruce Usrey Education Scholarship awards one $500 scholarship annually to a student enrolled in an accredited undergraduate or graduate landscape horticulture program or related discipline at a two- or four-year institution. Must have a minimum grade point average overall of 2.25 based on a scale of 4.0, and a minimum GPA of 2.7 on a scale of 4.0 in their major. Preference will be given to applicants who plan to work within the industry (including nursery operation, landscape architecture/design/construction/maintenance, interiorscape, horticultural distribution, or retail garden center) following graduation.

Academic Fields/Career Goals: Entomology; Horticulture/Floriculture; Landscape Architecture.

Award: Scholarship for use in freshman, sophomore, junior, senior, or graduate years; not renewable. *Number:* 1. *Amount:* $500.

Eligibility Requirements: Applicant must be enrolled or expecting to enroll full-time at a two-year or technical institution or university and studying in California. Available to U.S. citizens.

Application Requirements: Application form, application form may be submitted online, essay, financial need analysis. *Deadline:* September 10.

Contact: Jennifer Gray, Research Programs Administrator
Horticultural Research Institute
2130 Stella Court
Columbus, OH 43215
Phone: 614-487-1117
E-mail: jenniferg@americanhort.org

TIMOTHY S. AND PALMER W. BIGELOW, JR. SCHOLARSHIP
The Timothy S. and Palmer W. Bigelow, Jr. Scholarship awards one $3,000 scholarship to a student enrolled in an accredited undergraduate or graduate landscape/horticulture program or related discipline at a two- or four-year institution. Must have a minimum grade point average of 2.25 based on a scale of 4.0, or 3.0 on a scale of 4.0 for a graduate student. Preference will be given to an applicant who plans to work in any aspect of the nursery industry following graduation, including the desire to own one's own business. Preference will also be given to an applicant in financial need.

Academic Fields/Career Goals: Entomology; Horticulture/Floriculture; Landscape Architecture.

Award: Scholarship for use in sophomore, junior, senior, or graduate years; not renewable. *Number:* 1. *Amount:* $3000.

Eligibility Requirements: Applicant must be enrolled or expecting to enroll full-time at a two-year or technical institution or university and resident of Colorado, Louisiana, Maryland, New Brunswick, Quebec, Utah. Available to U.S. citizens.

Application Requirements: Application form, application form may be submitted online, essay, financial need analysis. *Deadline:* September 10.

Contact: Jennifer Gray, Research Programs Administrator
Horticultural Research Institute
2130 Stella Court
Columbus, OH 43215
Phone: 614-487-1117
E-mail: jenniferg@americanhort.org

USREY FAMILY SCHOLARSHIP

The Usrey Family Scholarship awards one $1,000 scholarship to a student enrolled in an accredited undergraduate or graduate landscape horticulture program or related discipline at a two- or four-year institution. Students in vocational agriculture programs will also be considered. Must have a minimum grade point average overall of 2.25 based on a scale of 4.0, and a minimum GPA of 2.7 on a scale of 4.0 in their major. Preference will be given to applicants who plan to work within the industry (including nursery operation, landscape architecture/design/construction/maintenance, interiorscape, horticultural distribution, or retail garden center) following graduation.

Academic Fields/Career Goals: Entomology; Horticulture/Floriculture; Landscape Architecture.

Award: Scholarship for use in freshman, sophomore, junior, senior, or graduate years; not renewable. *Number:* 1. *Amount:* $1000.

Eligibility Requirements: Applicant must be enrolled or expecting to enroll full-time at a two-year or technical institution or university and studying in California. Available to U.S. and non-U.S. citizens.

Application Requirements: Application form, application form may be submitted online, essay, financial need analysis. *Deadline:* September 10.

Contact: Jennifer Gray, Research Programs Administrator
Horticultural Research Institute
2130 Stella Court
Columbus, OH 43215
Phone: 614-487-1117
E-mail: jenniferg@americanhort.org

MEDICAL SCRUBS COLLECTION

http://medicalscrubscollection.com

MEDICAL SCRUBS COLLECTION SCHOLARSHIP
• See page 104

NOVUS BIOLOGICALS, LLC

https://www.novusbio.com

NOVUS BIOLOGICALS SCHOLARSHIP PROGRAM
• See page 101

R&D SYSTEMS SCHOLARSHIP
• See page 101

TOCRIS BIOSCIENCE SCHOLARSHIP
• See page 102

ENVIRONMENTAL HEALTH

AMERICAN INDIAN SCIENCE AND ENGINEERING SOCIETY

http://www.aises.org/

A.T. ANDERSON MEMORIAL SCHOLARSHIP PROGRAM
• See page 105

ASSISTANCE LEAGUE OF THE TRIANGLE AREA

HEALTH CARE PROFESSION SCHOLARSHIP
• See page 195

ASSOCIATION OF ENVIRONMENTAL HEALTH ACADEMIC PROGRAMS (AEHAP)

http://www.aehap.org/

STUDENT RESEARCH COMPETITION (SRC)

The purpose of this competition is to provide graduates and undergraduates in their junior or senior year with an opportunity to present their current, recently (within the last 3 months) completed or ongoing individual research on an environmental health related topic to environmental health professionals at the National Environmental Health Association's (NEHA) annual education conference. This is an extraordinary opportunity for students to experience a professional conference, to network with potential employers and to gain experience presenting their work in a formal session and during a poster session. Some students have even landed jobs as a result of winning the competition and meeting their future employer at the conference. Further, the scholarship provides $1,000 in cash and an all-expenses paid trip to NEHA's conference held annually each summer.

Academic Fields/Career Goals: Environmental Health.

Award: Scholarship for use in junior, senior, or graduate years; not renewable. *Amount:* $1000.

Eligibility Requirements: Applicant must be enrolled or expecting to enroll full-time at a four-year institution. Available to U.S. citizens.

Application Requirements: Application form. *Deadline:* February 28.

Contact: Clint Pinion
Association of Environmental Health Academic Programs (AEHAP)
PO Box 66057
Burien, WA 98166
Phone: 206-522-5272
E-mail: Clint.Pinion@eku.edu

BHW GROUP

https://thebhwgroup.com/

BHW WOMEN IN STEM SCHOLARSHIP
• See page 107

BROWN AND CALDWELL

http://www.brownandcaldwell.com

ECKENFELDER SCHOLARSHIP
• See page 141

MINORITY SCHOLARSHIP PROGRAM
• See page 141

CYNTHIA E. MORGAN SCHOLARSHIP FUND (CEMS)

http://www.cemsfund.com/

CYNTHIA E. MORGAN MEMORIAL SCHOLARSHIP FUND, INC.

Award for a high school junior or senior, or a current college student, who is a Maryland resident and first generation college student. No previous generation (parents or grandparents) may have attended any college/university. Scholarship for use only at a Maryland post-secondary school or medical school. Must be majoring in, or plan to enter, a medical-related field (for example: doctor, nurse, radiologist).

Academic Fields/Career Goals: Environmental Health; Health and Medical Sciences; Health Information Management/Technology; Neurobiology; Nursing; Occupational Safety and Health; Oncology; Osteopathy; Pharmacy; Psychology; Radiology; Therapy/Rehabilitation.

Award: Scholarship for use in freshman, sophomore, junior, senior, graduate, or postgraduate years; not renewable. *Number:* up to 1. *Amount:* $1000.

Eligibility Requirements: Applicant must be enrolled or expecting to enroll full- or part-time at a two-year or four-year or technical institution or university; resident of Maryland and studying in Maryland. Available to U.S. citizens.

Application Requirements: Application form, essay. *Deadline:* February 25.

Contact: Mr. John Kantorski, Founder and President
Cynthia E. Morgan Scholarship Fund (CEMS)
5516 Maudes Way
White Marsh, MD 21162-3417
Phone: 410-458-6312
Fax: 443-927-7321
E-mail: administrator@cemsfund.com

FLORIDA ENVIRONMENTAL HEALTH ASSOCIATION

http://www.feha.org/

FLORIDA ENVIRONMENTAL HEALTH ASSOCIATION EDUCATIONAL SCHOLARSHIP AWARDS

Scholarships offered to students interested in pursuing a career in the field of environmental health, or to enhance an existing career in environmental health. Applicant must be a member of FEHA in good standing. Minimum scholarship is $500.

Academic Fields/Career Goals: Environmental Health; Public Health.

Award: Scholarship for use in junior, senior, graduate, or postgraduate years; not renewable.

Eligibility Requirements: Applicant must be enrolled or expecting to enroll full- or part-time at a four-year institution or university. Applicant or parent of applicant must be member of Florida Environmental Health Association. Available to U.S. and non-U.S. citizens.

Application Requirements: Application form. *Deadline:* June 13.

Contact: Kim Duffek, Scholarship Committee Chair
Florida Environmental Health Association
400 West Robinson Street, Suite S-529
Orlando, FL 32801
Phone: 407-317-7325
E-mail: duffekkj@gmail.com

GREAT MINDS IN STEM

http://www.greatmindsinstem.org/college/scholarship-application-information

HENAAC SCHOLARSHIP PROGRAM
• *See page 100*

THE JACKSON LABORATORY

https://www.jax.org

THE JACKSON LABORATORY COLLEGE SCHOLARSHIP PROGRAM
• *See page 108*

NATIONAL ENVIRONMENTAL HEALTH ASSOCIATION/AMERICAN ACADEMY OF SANITARIANS

http://www.neha.org/

NATIONAL ENVIRONMENTAL HEALTH ASSOCIATION/AMERICAN ACADEMY OF SANITARIANS SCHOLARSHIP

One-time award for college juniors, seniors, and graduate students pursuing studies in environmental health sciences or public health. Undergraduates must be enrolled full-time in an approved program that is accredited by the Environmental Health Accreditation Council (EHAC) or a NEHA institutional/educational or sustaining member school.

Academic Fields/Career Goals: Environmental Health; Public Health.

Award: Scholarship for use in junior or senior years; renewable. *Number:* 3–4. *Amount:* $1000–$2000.

Eligibility Requirements: Applicant must be enrolled or expecting to enroll full- or part-time at a four-year institution or university. Available to U.S. citizens.

Application Requirements: Application form, recommendations or references, transcript. *Deadline:* February 1.

Contact: Cindy Dimmitt, Scholarship Coordinator
National Environmental Health Association/American
Academy of Sanitarians
720 South Colorado Boulevard, Suite 1000-N
Denver, CO 80246-1926
Phone: 303-756-9090
Fax: 303-691-9490
E-mail: cdimmitt@neha.org

NATIONAL INSTITUTES OF HEALTH

https://www.training.nih.gov/programs/ugsp

NIH UNDERGRADUATE SCHOLARSHIP PROGRAM FOR STUDENTS FROM DISADVANTAGED BACKGROUNDS
• *See page 101*

NEXTSTEPU

http://www.nextstepu.com/

$1,500 STEM SCHOLARSHIP
• *See page 104*

NOVUS BIOLOGICALS, LLC

https://www.novusbio.com

NOVUS BIOLOGICALS SCHOLARSHIP PROGRAM
• *See page 101*

R&D SYSTEMS SCHOLARSHIP
• *See page 101*

TOCRIS BIOSCIENCE SCHOLARSHIP
• *See page 102*

STRAIGHTFORWARD MEDIA

http://www.straightforwardmedia.com/

STRAIGHTFORWARD MEDIA MEDICAL PROFESSIONS SCHOLARSHIP
• *See page 198*

STRAIGHT NORTH

https://www.straightnorth.com/

STRAIGHT NORTH STEM SCHOLARSHIP
• *See page 81*

WASHINGTON STATE ENVIRONMENTAL HEALTH ASSOCIATION

http://www.wseha.org/

CIND M. TRESER MEMORIAL SCHOLARSHIP PROGRAM

Scholarships are available for undergraduate students pursuing a major in environmental health or related science and intending to practice environmental health. Must be a resident of Washington. For more details see website http://www.wseha.org.

Academic Fields/Career Goals: Environmental Health.

Award: Scholarship for use in junior or senior years; not renewable. *Number:* 1–2. *Amount:* $500–$2000.

Eligibility Requirements: Applicant must be enrolled or expecting to enroll full-time at a four-year institution or university; resident of Washington and studying in Washington. Available to U.S. citizens.

Application Requirements: Application form. *Deadline:* March 15.

Contact: Mr. Charles Treser, Principle Lecturer Emeritus
Washington State Environmental Health Association
Univ. of Washington, SPH, DEOHS
1959 NE Pacific Street, F-226D
Seattle, WA 98195-7234
Phone: 206-616-2097
E-mail: ctreser@uw.edu

WISCONSIN ASSOCIATION FOR FOOD PROTECTION

http://www.wifoodprotection.org

E.H. MARTH FOOD PROTECTION AND FOOD SCIENCES SCHOLARSHIP

Scholarship awarded to promote and sustain interest in the fields of study that may lead to a career in dairy, food, or environmental sanitation. One scholarship is awarded per year and previous applicants and recipients may reapply.

Academic Fields/Career Goals: Environmental Health; Food Science/Nutrition.

Award: Scholarship for use in sophomore, junior, senior, or graduate years; not renewable. *Number:* 1. *Amount:* $1500.

Eligibility Requirements: Applicant must be enrolled or expecting to enroll full-time at a four-year institution or university; resident of Wisconsin and studying in Wisconsin. Available to U.S. citizens.

Application Requirements: Application form, recommendations or references, transcript. *Deadline:* July 1.

Contact: Mr. Jim Wickert, Chairman, Scholarship Committee
Wisconsin Association for Food Protection
3834 Ridgeway Avenue
Madison, WI 53704
Phone: 608-241-2438
E-mail: jwick16060@tds.net

ENVIRONMENTAL SCIENCE

101ST AIRBORNE DIVISION ASSOCIATION

http://www.screamingeaglefoundation.org/

AL & WILLIAMARY VISTE SCHOLARSHIP
• *See page 99*

ABBIE SARGENT MEMORIAL SCHOLARSHIP INC.

http://www.nhfarmbureau.org/

ABBIE SARGENT MEMORIAL SCHOLARSHIP
• *See page 89*

AIR & WASTE MANAGEMENT ASSOCIATION, ALLEGHENY MOUNTAIN SECTION

http://www.ams-awma.org/

ALLEGHENY MOUNTAIN SECTION AIR & WASTE MANAGEMENT ASSOCIATION SCHOLARSHIP

Scholarships for qualified students enrolled in an undergraduate program leading to a career in a field related directly to the environment. Open to current undergraduate students or high school students accepted full-time in a four-year college or university program in Western Pennsylvania or West Virginia. Applicants must have a minimum B average or a 3.0 GPA.

Academic Fields/Career Goals: Environmental Science; Meteorology/Atmospheric Science.

Award: Scholarship for use in freshman, sophomore, junior, or senior years; not renewable. *Number:* 1–5. *Amount:* $500–$2000.

Eligibility Requirements: Applicant must be enrolled or expecting to enroll full-time at a four-year institution or university; resident of Pennsylvania, West Virginia and studying in Pennsylvania, West Virginia. Available to U.S. citizens.

Application Requirements: Application form, community service, essay. *Deadline:* March 31.

Contact: David Testa, Scholarship Chair
Air & Waste Management Association, Allegheny Mountain Section
c/o AECOM
681 Andersen Drive, Foster Plaza 6
Pittsburgh, PA 15220
Phone: 412-503-4560
E-mail: david.testa@aecom.com

AIR & WASTE MANAGEMENT ASSOCIATION–COASTAL PLAINS CHAPTER

http://www.awmacoastalplains.org/

COASTAL PLAINS CHAPTER OF THE AIR AND WASTE MANAGEMENT ASSOCIATION ENVIRONMENTAL STEWARD SCHOLARSHIP

Scholarships awarded to first- or second-year students pursuing a career in environmental science or physical science. Minimum high school and college GPA of 2.5 required. A 500-word paper on personal and professional goals must be submitted.

Academic Fields/Career Goals: Environmental Science; Physical Sciences.

Award: Scholarship for use in freshman or sophomore years; not renewable. *Number:* 5. *Amount:* $800.

Eligibility Requirements: Applicant must be enrolled or expecting to enroll full-time at a two-year or four-year institution or university. Available to U.S. citizens.

Application Requirements: 500-word paper on personal and professional goals, application form, recommendations or references, test scores. *Deadline:* varies.

Contact: Dwain Waters, Treasurer
Air & Waste Management Association–Coastal Plains Chapter
One Energy Place
Pensacola, FL 32520-0328
Phone: 850-444-6527
Fax: 850-444-6217
E-mail: gdwaters@southernco.com

AIST FOUNDATION

http://www.aistfoundation.org/

ASSOCIATION FOR IRON AND STEEL TECHNOLOGY WILLY KORF MEMORIAL SCHOLARSHIP
• *See page 153*

AMERICAN CHEMICAL SOCIETY

http://www.acs.org/

AMERICAN CHEMICAL SOCIETY SCHOLARS PROGRAM
• *See page 153*

AMERICAN COUNCIL OF ENGINEERING COMPANIES OF PENNSYLVANIA (ACEC/PA)

http://www.acecpa.org/

ERIC J. GENNUSO AND LEROY D. (BUD) LOY, JR. SCHOLARSHIP PROGRAM
• *See page 153*

AMERICAN INDIAN SCIENCE AND ENGINEERING SOCIETY

http://www.aises.org/

A.T. ANDERSON MEMORIAL SCHOLARSHIP PROGRAM
• *See page 105*

AMERICAN LEGION DEPARTMENT OF MARYLAND

http://www.mdlegion.org/

AMERICAN LEGION DEPARTMENT OF MARYLAND MATH-SCIENCE SCHOLARSHIP
• *See page 99*

AMERICAN METEOROLOGICAL SOCIETY

http://www.ametsoc.org/

FATHER JAMES B. MACELWANE ANNUAL AWARD
Student must have been enrolled as an undergraduates at the time the paper was written on a phase of atmospheric sciences. Submit a copy of the original research paper and a letter of application from the author, including mailing address and email, stating the title of the paper and the name of the university at which the paper was written. The abstract should be no more than 250 words. In addition, a letter from the department head or other faculty member within the department, confirming that the author was an undergraduate student at the time the paper was written and indicating the elements of the paper that represent original contributions by the student. Must be a U.S. citizen or be a permanent resident.

Academic Fields/Career Goals: Environmental Science; Hydrology; Meteorology/Atmospheric Science; Oceanography; Physical Sciences.

Award: Prize for use in freshman, sophomore, junior, or senior years; not renewable. *Number:* 1. *Amount:* $1000.

Eligibility Requirements: Applicant must be enrolled or expecting to enroll full-time at a two-year or four-year institution or university. Available to U.S. and Canadian citizens.

Application Requirements: Application form, application form may be submitted online (https://awards.ametsoc.org/), Undergraduate research paper, requested cover letter and faculty member letter. *Deadline:* June 7.

Contact: Donna Fernandez, Development and Student Program
Manager
American Meteorological Society
45 Beacon Street
Boston, MA 02108
Phone: 617-226-3907
Fax: 617-227-7418
E-mail: dfernandez@ametsoc.org

AMERICAN PHYSIOLOGICAL SOCIETY

https://www.physiology.org/

BARBARA A. HORWITZ AND JOHN M. HOROWITZ UNDERGRADUATE RESEARCH AWARDS
• *See page 139*

AMERICAN PUBLIC POWER ASSOCIATION

https://www.publicpower.org/deed-rd-funding

DEMONSTRATION OF ENERGY AND EFFICIENCY DEVELOPMENTS EDUCATIONAL SCHOLARSHIP
• *See page 154*

DEMONSTRATION OF ENERGY AND EFFICIENCY DEVELOPMENTS STUDENT INTERNSHIP
• *See page 154*

DEMONSTRATION OF ENERGY AND EFFICIENCY DEVELOPMENTS STUDENT RESEARCH GRANTS
• *See page 162*

DEMONSTRATION OF ENERGY AND EFFICIENCY DEVELOPMENTS TECHNICAL DESIGN PROJECT
• *See page 154*

AMERICAN SOCIETY OF AGRONOMY, CROP SCIENCE SOCIETY OF AMERICA, SOIL SCIENCE SOCIETY OF AMERICA

http://www.agronomy.org

J. FIELDING REED UNDERGRADUATE SOIL AND PLANT SCIENCES SCHOLARSHIP
• *See page 200*

ARCTIC INSTITUTE OF NORTH AMERICA

http://www.arctic.ucalgary.ca/

JIM BOURQUE SCHOLARSHIP
• *See page 207*

ASIAN PACIFIC FUND

BANATAO FAMILY FILIPINO AMERICAN EDUCATION FUND
• *See page 155*

ASSOCIATION FOR WOMEN GEOSCIENTISTS (AWG)

http://www.awg.org/

AWG ETHNIC MINORITY SCHOLARSHIP
• *See page 200*

AWG MARIA LUISA CRAWFORD FIELD CAMP SCHOLARSHIP
• *See page 111*

AWG SALT LAKE CHAPTER (SLC) RESEARCH SCHOLARSHIP
• *See page 111*

JANET CULLEN TANAKA GEOSCIENCES UNDERGRADUATE SCHOLARSHIP
• *See page 112*

LONE STAR RISING CAREER SCHOLARSHIP
• *See page 200*

OSAGE CHAPTER UNDERGRADUATE SERVICE SCHOLARSHIP
• *See page 112*

SUSAN EKDALE MEMORIAL FIELD CAMP SCHOLARSHIP
• *See page 201*

ASSOCIATION OF CALIFORNIA WATER AGENCIES
http://www.acwa.com/

ASSOCIATION OF CALIFORNIA WATER AGENCIES SCHOLARSHIPS
• *See page 106*

CLAIR A. HILL SCHOLARSHIP
• *See page 106*

ASSOCIATION OF NEW JERSEY ENVIRONMENTAL COMMISSIONS
http://www.anjec.org/

LECHNER SCHOLARSHIP
Award of $1000 scholarship for a student entering his/her junior or senior year at an accredited New Jersey college or university. Must be a New Jersey resident and have a minimum GPA of 3.0.

Academic Fields/Career Goals: Environmental Science.

Award: Scholarship for use in junior or senior years; not renewable. *Number:* 1. *Amount:* $1000.

Eligibility Requirements: Applicant must be enrolled or expecting to enroll full-time at a four-year institution or university; resident of New Jersey and studying in New Jersey. Available to U.S. citizens.

Application Requirements: Application form, essay, recommendations or references, transcript.

Contact: Jennifer Coffey, Executive Director
Phone: 973-539-7547
Fax: 973-539-7713
E-mail: jcoffey@anjec.org

ASSOCIATION OF STATE DAM SAFETY OFFICIALS (ASDSO)
http://www.DamSafety.org

ASSOCIATION OF STATE DAM SAFETY OFFICIALS (ASDSO) SENIOR UNDERGRADUATE SCHOLARSHIP
• *See page 140*

AUDUBON SOCIETY OF WESTERN PENNSYLVANIA
http://www.aswp.org/

BEULAH FREY ENVIRONMENTAL SCHOLARSHIP
Scholarship available to high school seniors pursuing studies in the environmental and natural sciences. Students who are applying to a two- or four-year college to further their studies in an environmentally-related field are eligible to apply. Scholarship is restricted to the residents of the seven counties around Pittsburgh.

Academic Fields/Career Goals: Environmental Science; Natural Sciences.

Award: Scholarship for use in freshman year; not renewable. *Number:* 1–2. *Amount:* $1000.

Eligibility Requirements: Applicant must be high school student; planning to enroll or expecting to enroll full-time at a two-year or four-year institution or university and resident of Pennsylvania. Available to U.S. citizens.

Application Requirements: Application form, essay, recommendations or references, test scores, transcript. *Deadline:* March 31.

Contact: Patricia O'Neill, Director of Education
Audubon Society of Western Pennsylvania
614 Dorseyville Road
Pittsburgh, PA 15238
Phone: 412-963-6100
Fax: 412-963-6761
E-mail: toneill@aswp.org

AUTOMOTIVE WOMEN'S ALLIANCE FOUNDATION
http://awafoundation.org/index.php

AUTOMOTIVE WOMEN'S ALLIANCE FOUNDATION SCHOLARSHIPS
• *See page 71*

BARRY GOLDWATER SCHOLARSHIP AND EXCELLENCE IN EDUCATION FOUNDATION
https://goldwater.scholarsapply.org

BARRY M. GOLDWATER SCHOLARSHIP AND EXCELLENCE IN EDUCATION PROGRAM
• *See page 107*

BHW GROUP
https://thebhwgroup.com/

BHW WOMEN IN STEM SCHOLARSHIP
• *See page 107*

B.O.G. PEST CONTROL
http://www.bogpestcontrol.com/

B.O.G. PEST CONTROL SCHOLARSHIP FUND
• *See page 141*

BROWN AND CALDWELL
http://www.brownandcaldwell.com

ECKENFELDER SCHOLARSHIP
• *See page 141*

MINORITY SCHOLARSHIP PROGRAM
• *See page 141*

CARDS AGAINST HUMANITY
https://cardsagainsthumanity.com/

SCIENCE AMBASSADOR SCHOLARSHIP
• *See page 107*

CONSERVATION FEDERATION OF MISSOURI
http://www.confedmo.org/

CHARLES P. BELL CONSERVATION SCHOLARSHIP
Eight scholarships of $250 to $600 for Missouri students and/or teachers whose studies or projects are related to natural science, resource conservation, earth resources, or environmental protection. Must be used for study in Missouri. See application for eligibility details.

Academic Fields/Career Goals: Environmental Science; Natural Resources; Natural Sciences.

Award: Scholarship for use in freshman, sophomore, junior, senior, or graduate years; not renewable. *Number:* 8. *Amount:* $250–$600.

Eligibility Requirements: Applicant must be enrolled or expecting to enroll full- or part-time at a four-year institution or university; resident of Missouri and studying in Missouri. Available to U.S. citizens.

Application Requirements: Application form, community service, financial need analysis. *Deadline:* January 31.

Contact: Laurie Coleman, Membership Director
Conservation Federation of Missouri
728 West Main Street
Jefferson City, MO 65101
Phone: 573-634-2322
Fax: 573-634-8205
E-mail: lcoleman@confedmo.org

DELAWARE HIGHER EDUCATION OFFICE

http://www.doe.k12.de.us

DELAWARE SOLID WASTE AUTHORITY JOHN P. "PAT" HEALY SCHOLARSHIP
• *See page 238*

DISTIL NETWORKS

http://www.distilnetworks.com

WOMEN FORWARD IN TECHNOLOGY SCHOLARSHIP PROGRAM
• *See page 108*

ENVIRONMENTAL PROFESSIONALS' ORGANIZATION OF CONNECTICUT

http://www.epoc.org/

EPOC ENVIRONMENTAL SCHOLARSHIP FUND

Scholarships awarded annually to junior, senior, and graduate level students (full- or part-time) enrolled in accepted programs of study leading the student to become an environmental professional in Connecticut.

Academic Fields/Career Goals: Environmental Science.

Award: Scholarship for use in junior, senior, or graduate years; not renewable. *Number:* 2–3.

Eligibility Requirements: Applicant must be enrolled or expecting to enroll full- or part-time at a four-year institution or university. Available to U.S. citizens.

Application Requirements: Application form, essay, financial need analysis, recommendations or references, transcript. *Deadline:* May 7.

Contact: John Figurelli, Scholarship Fund Coordinator
Environmental Professionals' Organization of Connecticut
PO Box 176
Amston, CT 06231-0176
Phone: 860-513-1473
Fax: 860-228-4902
E-mail: figurelj@wseinc.com

EXPLORERS CLUB

http://www.explorers.org/

YOUTH ACTIVITY FUND GRANTS
• *See page 103*

GREAT MINDS IN STEM

http://www.greatmindsinstem.org/college/scholarship-application-information

HENAAC SCHOLARSHIP PROGRAM
• *See page 100*

GREEN CHEMISTRY INSTITUTE-AMERICAN CHEMICAL SOCIETY

http://www.acs.org/greenchemistry

CIBA TRAVEL AWARDS IN GREEN CHEMISTRY

The award sponsors the participation of students (high school, undergraduate, and graduate students) in an American Chemical Society (ACS) technical meeting, conference or training program, having a significant green chemistry or sustainability component, to expand the students' education in green chemistry. The applicant must demonstrate research or educational interest in green chemistry. The award amount is based on estimated travel expenses.

Academic Fields/Career Goals: Environmental Science.

Award: Grant for use in freshman, sophomore, junior, senior, graduate, or postgraduate years; not renewable. *Number:* 3–4. *Amount:* up to $2000.

Eligibility Requirements: Applicant must be enrolled or expecting to enroll full-time at a four-year institution or university. Available to U.S. citizens.

Application Requirements: Application form, application form may be submitted online, essay, recommendations or references, resume, transcript. *Deadline:* October 12.

Contact: Ms. Joyce Kilgore, Program Manager
Green Chemistry Institute-American Chemical Society
1155 16th Street, NW
Washington, DC 20036
Phone: 202-872-6109
E-mail: gci@acs.org

KENNETH G. HANCOCK MEMORIAL AWARD IN GREEN CHEMISTRY

Award of $1000 for the students who have completed their education or research in green chemistry. The scholarship provides national recognition for outstanding student contributions to furthering the goals of green chemistry through research or education.

Academic Fields/Career Goals: Environmental Science.

Award: Prize for use in freshman, sophomore, junior, senior, or graduate years; not renewable. *Number:* 1–2. *Amount:* $1000.

Eligibility Requirements: Applicant must be enrolled or expecting to enroll full-time at a four-year institution or university. Available to U.S. and non-U.S. citizens.

Application Requirements: Application form, application form may be submitted online, essay. *Deadline:* March 1.

Contact: Mrs. Jennifer MacKellar, Program Manager
Green Chemistry Institute-American Chemical Society
1155 16th Street, NW
Washington, DC 20036
Phone: 202-872-6173
E-mail: gci@acs.org

INDIANA WILDLIFE FEDERATION ENDOWMENT

http://www.indianawildlife.org/

CHARLES A. HOLT INDIANA WILDLIFE FEDERATION ENDOWMENT SCHOLARSHIP

A $1000.00 scholarship will be award to one Indiana resident enrolled in a course of study related to resource conservation or environmental education at a sophomore level or above in an accredited college or university. The scholarship recipient will receive priority consideration for an Indiana Wildlife Federation internship position.

Academic Fields/Career Goals: Environmental Science; Natural Resources.

Award: Scholarship for use in sophomore, junior, or senior years; not renewable. *Number:* 1. *Amount:* $1000.

Eligibility Requirements: Applicant must be enrolled or expecting to enroll full-time at a four-year institution or university; resident of Indiana and studying in Indiana. Available to U.S. citizens.

Application Requirements: Application form, essay. *Deadline:* June 1.

Contact: Barbara Simpson, Executive Director
Indiana Wildlife Federation Endowment
708 East Michigan Street
Indianapolis, IN 46202
Phone: 317-875-9453
E-mail: info@indianawildlife.org

INTERNATIONAL SOCIETY OF EXPLOSIVES ENGINEERS

http://www.isee.org/

JERRY MCDOWELL FUND
• *See page 156*

KENTUCKY ENERGY AND ENVIRONMENT CABINET

http://dep.ky.gov

ENVIRONMENTAL PROTECTION SCHOLARSHIP
• *See page 142*

THE LAND CONSERVANCY OF NEW JERSEY

http://www.tlc-nj.org/

ROGERS FAMILY SCHOLARSHIP
• *See page 143*

RUSSELL W. MYERS SCHOLARSHIP
• *See page 143*

MASSACHUSETTS ASSOCIATION OF LAND SURVEYORS AND CIVIL ENGINEERS

http://www.malsce.org/

MALSCE SCHOLARSHIPS
• *See page 242*

NASA IDAHO SPACE GRANT CONSORTIUM

http://www.idahospacegrant.org

NASA IDAHO SPACE GRANT CONSORTIUM SCHOLARSHIP PROGRAM
• *See page 109*

NASA/MARYLAND SPACE GRANT CONSORTIUM

https://md.spacegrant.org

NASA MARYLAND SPACE GRANT CONSORTIUM SCHOLARSHIPS
• *See page 109*

NASA MINNESOTA SPACE GRANT CONSORTIUM

https://www.mnspacegrant.org/

MINNESOTA SPACE GRANT CONSORTIUM SCHOLARSHIP PROGRAM
• *See page 131*

NASA'S VIRGINIA SPACE GRANT CONSORTIUM

http://www.vsgc.odu.edu/

COMMUNITY COLLEGE STEM SCHOLARSHIPS
• *See page 110*

NATIONAL COUNCIL OF STATE GARDEN CLUBS INC. SCHOLARSHIP

http://www.gardenclub.org/

NATIONAL COUNCIL OF STATE GARDEN CLUBS INC. SCHOLARSHIP
• *See page 94*

NATIONAL GARDEN CLUBS INC.

http://www.gardenclub.org/

NATIONAL GARDEN CLUBS INC. SCHOLARSHIP PROGRAM
• *See page 94*

NATIONAL INSTITUTES OF HEALTH

https://www.training.nih.gov/programs/ugsp

NIH UNDERGRADUATE SCHOLARSHIP PROGRAM FOR STUDENTS FROM DISADVANTAGED BACKGROUNDS
• *See page 101*

NATIONAL SAFETY COUNCIL

http://www.cshema.org/

CAMPUS SAFETY, HEALTH AND ENVIRONMENTAL MANAGEMENT ASSOCIATION SCHOLARSHIP AWARD PROGRAM

One $2000 scholarship available to full-time undergraduate or graduate students in all majors to encourage the study of safety and environmental management. The program is open to all college undergraduate and graduate students in all majors/disciplines enrolled in 12 credit hours per semester, trimester, or quarter.

Academic Fields/Career Goals: Environmental Science; Occupational Safety and Health.

Award: Scholarship for use in freshman, sophomore, junior, senior, or graduate years; not renewable. *Number:* 1. *Amount:* $2000.

Eligibility Requirements: Applicant must be enrolled or expecting to enroll full-time at a four-year institution or university. Available to U.S. and Canadian citizens.

Application Requirements: Application form, essay, transcript. *Deadline:* March 31.

Contact: Scholarship Committee
National Safety Council
120 West 7th Street, Suite 204
Bloomington, IN 47404
Phone: 812-245-8084
Fax: 812-245-0590

NATIONAL SECURITY EDUCATION PROGRAM

http://www.iie.org/

NATIONAL SECURITY EDUCATION PROGRAM (NSEP) DAVID L. BOREN UNDERGRADUATE SCHOLARSHIPS
• *See page 119*

NEW ENGLAND WATER WORKS ASSOCIATION

https://www.newwa.org/

ELSON T. KILLAM MEMORIAL SCHOLARSHIP
• *See page 166*

FRANCIS X. CROWLEY SCHOLARSHIP
• *See page 150*

JOSEPH MURPHY SCHOLARSHIP
• *See page 150*

NEXTSTEPU

http://www.nextstepu.com/

$1,500 STEM SCHOLARSHIP
• *See page 104*

NGWA FOUNDATION

http://www.ngwa.org/Foundation/Pages/default.aspx

NGWA FOUNDATION'S LEN ASSANTE SCHOLARSHIP
• *See page 202*

NOVUS BIOLOGICALS, LLC

https://www.novusbio.com

NOVUS BIOLOGICALS SCHOLARSHIP PROGRAM
• *See page 101*

R&D SYSTEMS SCHOLARSHIP
• *See page 101*

TOCRIS BIOSCIENCE SCHOLARSHIP
• *See page 102*

OHIO ACADEMY OF SCIENCE/OHIO ENVIRONMENTAL EDUCATION FUND

http://www.ohiosci.org/

OHIO ENVIRONMENTAL SCIENCE & ENGINEERING SCHOLARSHIPS

Merit-based, non-renewable, tuition-only scholarships awarded to undergraduate students admitted to Ohio state or private colleges and universities. Must be able to demonstrate knowledge of, and commitment to, careers in environmental sciences or environmental engineering.

Academic Fields/Career Goals: Environmental Science.

Award: Scholarship for use in senior year; not renewable. *Number:* 18. *Amount:* $1250–$2500.

Eligibility Requirements: Applicant must be enrolled or expecting to enroll full- or part-time at a two-year or four-year institution or university and studying in Ohio. Available to U.S. citizens.

Application Requirements: Application form, application form may be submitted online (https://mc04.manuscriptcentral.com/oas), community service, essay, recommendations or references, resume, self-addressed stamped envelope with application, transcript. *Deadline:* April 15.

Contact: Dr. Stephen McConoughey, Chief Executive Officer
Ohio Academy of Science/Ohio Environmental Education Fund
1500 West Third Avenue, Suite 228
Columbus, OH 43212-2817
Phone: 614-488-2228
Fax: 614-488-7629
E-mail: smcconoughey@ohiosci.org

OUTDOOR WRITERS ASSOCIATION OF AMERICA

http://www.owaa.org/

OUTDOOR WRITERS ASSOCIATION OF AMERICA - BODIE MCDOWELL SCHOLARSHIP AWARD
• *See page 174*

PACIFIC GAS AND ELECTRIC COMPANY

http://www.scholarshipamerica.org

PG&E BETTER TOGETHER STEM SCHOLARSHIP PROGRAM
• *See page 181*

PADDLE CANADA

http://www.paddlecanada.com

BILL MASON SCHOLARSHIP FUND
• *See page 212*

SALT RIVER PROJECT (SRP)

http://www.srpnet.com/

NAVAJO GENERATING STATION NAVAJO SCHOLARSHIP
• *See page 244*

SCARLETT FAMILY FOUNDATION SCHOLARSHIP PROGRAM

http://www.scarlettfoundation.org/

SCHOLARSHIP FOR STUDENTS PURSUING A BUSINESS OR STEM DEGREE
• *See page 80*

SHRED NATIONS

https://www.shrednations.com/

SHRED NATIONS SCHOLARSHIP

Shred Nations Scholarship is a one time annual award of up to $5,000 to offset the costs of higher education. The scholarship award may be divided into two separate payments to be paid directly to the applicant's chosen institution of higher education, which must be an accredited university, college or trade school. Applicants must have completed secondary school, or currently be a senior in a secondary school, with a minimum GPA of 3.0 with an interest in business, environmental studies or the shredding and recycling industry. Applicants will be required to submit a nomination from a NAID member. NAID members will be comprised of any employee or owner of a NAID member company. One scholarship will be awarded for the academic year, and past recipients may re-apply to be awarded the scholarship for subsequent years. Shred Nations employees, immediate or extended families are not permitted to be awarded the scholarship. Candidates who plan to make the secure destruction industry a career and whose degree program provides the maximum potential benefit to their respective/perspective employer will be favorably considered. Priority will also be given to family and friends of members of the Shred Nations partner network. All applicants will be evaluated based on the following criteria, and such other considerations as the Selection Committee determines are meritorious to the purposes of the scholarship. The selection committee will analyze the scholar's academic achievement and rigor including high school and college/university transcripts, honors and awards. The scholar's character will be evaluated based upon the recommendation of a NAID member owner/executive. In addition, the scholar's extracurricular activities and merits related to those activities will be examined. The scholar should demonstrate through a 500 and 1,000 word essay how they can use their studies to improve business, environmental responsibility and make future contributions to the community including interest in the secure destruction industry and demonstrate what they value they can provide to a potential company that is hiring them.

Academic Fields/Career Goals: Environmental Science.

Award: Scholarship for use in freshman, sophomore, junior, senior, graduate, or postgraduate years; not renewable. *Number:* 1. *Amount:* $5000.

Eligibility Requirements: Applicant must be enrolled or expecting to enroll full- or part-time at a two-year or four-year or technical institution or university. Available to U.S. citizens.

Application Requirements: Application form, essay. *Deadline:* February 26.

Contact: Mr. Rand LeMarinel, President
Phone: 303-962-5585
E-mail: scholarship@shrednations.com

SOIL AND WATER CONSERVATION SOCIETY
http://www.swcs.org

DONALD A. WILLIAMS SCHOLARSHIP SOIL CONSERVATION SCHOLARSHIP
• *See page 91*

SOIL AND WATER CONSERVATION SOCIETY-NEW JERSEY CHAPTER
http://www.geocities.com/njswcs

EDWARD R. HALL SCHOLARSHIP
• *See page 91*

STRAIGHT NORTH
https://www.straightnorth.com/

STRAIGHT NORTH STEM SCHOLARSHIP
• *See page 81*

TAILOR MADE LAWNS
http://www.tailormadelawns.com

2017 TAILOR MADE LAWNS SCHOLARSHIP FUND
• *See page 96*

TAU KAPPA EPSILON EDUCATION FOUNDATION
https://www.tke.org/

TIMOTHY L. TASCHWER SCHOLARSHIP
• *See page 144*

TECHNICAL ASSOCIATION OF THE PULP & PAPER INDUSTRY (TAPPI)
https://www.tappi.org/

ENVIRONMENTAL WORKING GROUP SCHOLARSHIP
Scholarship for full-time students in a college program or applicants working full-time or part-time in the corrugated industry. Must demonstrate an interest in the corrugated packaging industry.

Academic Fields/Career Goals: Environmental Science; Paper and Pulp Engineering.

Award: Scholarship for use in sophomore, junior, or senior years; not renewable. *Number:* 1. *Amount:* $2500.

Eligibility Requirements: Applicant must be enrolled or expecting to enroll full-time at a four-year institution or university. Available to U.S. and non-U.S. citizens.

Application Requirements: Application form, interview. *Deadline:* February 15.

Contact: Mr. Laurence Womack, Director of Standards and Awards
Technical Association of the Pulp & Paper Industry (TAPPI)
15 Technology Parkway South
Peachtree Corners, GA 30092
Phone: 770-209-7276
E-mail: standards@tappi.org

UNITED NEGRO COLLEGE FUND
http://www.uncf.org/

DAVIS SCHOLARSHIP FOR WOMEN IN STEM
• *See page 111*

GALACTIC UNITE BYTHEWAY SCHOLARSHIP
• *See page 111*

LEIDOS STEM SCHOLARSHIP
• *See page 96*

UNITED STATES ENVIRONMENTAL PROTECTION AGENCY
http://www.epa.gov/enviroed

NATIONAL NETWORK FOR ENVIRONMENTAL MANAGEMENT STUDIES FELLOWSHIP
Fellowship program designed to provide undergraduate and graduate students with research opportunities at one of EPA's facilities nationwide. EPA awards approximately 40 NNEMS fellowships per year. Selected students receive a stipend for performing their research project. EPA develops an annual catalog of research projects available for student application. Submit a complete application package as described in the annual catalog. Minimum 3.0 GPA required.

Academic Fields/Career Goals: Environmental Science; Natural Resources.

Award: Grant for use in freshman, sophomore, junior, senior, graduate, or postgraduate years; not renewable. *Number:* 20–25.

Eligibility Requirements: Applicant must be enrolled or expecting to enroll full- or part-time at a two-year or four-year institution or university. Available to U.S. citizens.

Application Requirements: Application form, recommendations or references, resume, transcript. *Deadline:* January 22.

Contact: Michael Baker, Acting Director
United States Environmental Protection Agency
Environmental Education Division
1200 Pennsylvania Avenue, NW, MC 1704A
Washington, DC 20460
Phone: 202-564-0446
Fax: 202-564-2754
E-mail: baker.michael@epa.gov

UNITED STATES SOCIETY ON DAMS
http://www.ussdams.org/

UNITED STATES SOCIETY ON DAMS STUDENT SCHOLARSHIP AWARD
• *See page 168*

EUROPEAN STUDIES

CANADIAN INSTITUTE OF UKRAINIAN STUDIES

https://www.ualberta.ca/canadian-institute-of-ukrainian-studies/index.html

LEO J. KRYSA FAMILY UNDERGRADUATE SCHOLARSHIP
• See page 208

CULTURAL SERVICES OF THE FRENCH EMBASSY

http://www.frenchculture.org/

TEACHING ASSISTANT PROGRAM IN FRANCE
• See page 98

FASHION DESIGN

AMERICAN SHEEP INDUSTRY ASSOCIATION

http://www.sheepusa.org/

NATIONAL MAKE IT WITH WOOL COMPETITION
Awards available for entrants ages 13 years & older. Must enter at district and/or state level with home-constructed garment of at least 60 percent wool. Applicant must model garment. National entry fee is $12 for regular contest and $20 for Fashion/Apparel Design students. District and state entry fees may also apply. Complete rules available from State Director, National Coordinator, and online. www.NationalMakeItWithWool.com

Academic Fields/Career Goals: Fashion Design.

Award: Prize for use in freshman, sophomore, junior, senior, or graduate years; not renewable. *Number:* 2–26. *Amount:* $25–$1500.

Eligibility Requirements: Applicant must be enrolled or expecting to enroll full- or part-time at a two-year or four-year or technical institution or university; resident of Alberta, California, Colorado, Connecticut, Delaware, Florida, Georgia, Idaho, Illinois, Indiana, Kansas, Kentucky, Maine, Maryland, Massachusetts, Michigan, Minnesota, Missouri, Montana, Nebraska, New Hampshire, New Jersey, New York, North Carolina, North Dakota, Ohio, Oklahoma, Oregon, Pennsylvania, Rhode Island, South Dakota, Tennessee, Texas, Utah, Vermont, Washington, Wisconsin, Wyoming; studying in Alabama, Alaska, Arizona, Arkansas, California, Colorado, Connecticut, Delaware, District of Columbia, Florida, Georgia, Idaho, Illinois, Indiana, Iowa, Kansas, Kentucky, Louisiana, Maine, Maryland, Massachusetts, Michigan, Minnesota, Mississippi, Missouri, Montana, Nebraska, Nevada, New Hampshire, New Jersey, New Mexico, New York, North Carolina, North Dakota, Ohio, Oklahoma, Oregon, Pennsylvania, Rhode Island, South Carolina, South Dakota, Tennessee, Texas, Utah, Vermont, Virginia, Washington, West Virginia, Wisconsin, Wyoming and must have an interest in sewing. Available to U.S. citizens.

Application Requirements: Application form. *Fee:* $12.

Contact: Mary Roediger, National Coordinator
American Sheep Industry Association
PO Box 123
Albany, OH 45710
Phone: 740-591-5149
E-mail: wool@sewtruedesigns.com

CONGRESSIONAL BLACK CAUCUS FOUNDATION, INC.

http://www.cbcfinc.org/

CBC SPOUSES VISUAL ARTS SCHOLARSHIP
• See page 120

DECA (DISTRIBUTIVE EDUCATION CLUBS OF AMERICA)

http://www.deca.org/

HARRY A. APPLEGATE SCHOLARSHIP
• See page 73

QUALITY BATH

www.qualitybath.com

QUALITYBATH.COM SCHOLARSHIP PROGRAM
• See page 120

SUPPORT CREATIVITY

http://wesupportcreativity.org

SUPPORT CREATIVITY SCHOLARSHIP
• See page 117

FILMMAKING/VIDEO

ACADEMY FOUNDATION OF THE ACADEMY OF MOTION PICTURE ARTS AND SCIENCES

http://www.oscars.org/saa

ACADEMY OF MOTION PICTURE ARTS AND SCIENCES STUDENT ACADEMY AWARDS
Award available to students who have made a narrative, documentary, alternative, foreign or animated film of up to 60 minutes within the curricular structure of an accredited college or university. Initial entry must be on DVD-R. 16mm or larger format print, digital beta-cam tape, HD-Cam or DCP required for further rounds. Prizes awarded in four categories. Each category awards gold ($5000), silver ($3000), and bronze ($2000). Visit website for details and application http://www.oscars.org/saa.

Academic Fields/Career Goals: Filmmaking/Video.

Award: Prize for use in freshman, sophomore, junior, senior, or graduate years; not renewable. *Number:* 3–15. *Amount:* $2000–$5000.

Eligibility Requirements: Applicant must be enrolled or expecting to enroll full-time at a two-year or four-year institution or university. Available to U.S. and non-U.S. citizens.

Application Requirements: 16mm or larger format film print or NTSC digital betacam version of the entry (BetaSP format is not acceptable), DVD, application form, entry in a contest. *Deadline:* April 1.

Contact: Shawn Guthrie, Program Administrator
Academy Foundation of the Academy of Motion Picture Arts and Sciences
8949 Wilshire Boulevard
Beverly Hills, CA 90211-1972
Phone: 310-247-3000 Ext. 3306
Fax: 310-859-9619
E-mail: sguthrie@oscars.org

ADC RESEARCH INSTITUTE

http://www.adc.org/

JACK SHAHEEN MASS COMMUNICATIONS SCHOLARSHIP AWARD
• See page 169

ASIAN AMERICAN JOURNALISTS ASSOCIATION

http://www.aaja.org/

CIC/ANNA CHENNAULT SCHOLARSHIP
• See page 170

ASIAN AMERICAN JOURNALISTS ASSOCIATION, SEATTLE CHAPTER

http://www.aajaseattle.org/

NORTHWEST JOURNALISTS OF COLOR SCHOLARSHIP
• See page 84

CHARLES AND LUCILLE KING FAMILY FOUNDATION, INC.

http://www.kingfoundation.org/

CHARLES & LUCILLE KING FAMILY FOUNDATION SCHOLARSHIPS
• See page 171

CONGRESSIONAL BLACK CAUCUS FOUNDATION, INC.

http://www.cbcfinc.org/

CBC SPOUSES VISUAL ARTS SCHOLARSHIP
• See page 120

HEMOPHILIA FOUNDATION OF SOUTHERN CALIFORNIA

http://www.hemosocal.org/

DR. EARL JAMES FAHRINGER PERFORMING ARTS SCHOLARSHIP
• See page 121

ILLUMINATING ENGINEERING SOCIETY OF NORTH AMERICA–GOLDEN GATE SECTION

http://www.iesgg.org/

ALAN LUCAS MEMORIAL EDUCATIONAL SCHOLARSHIP
• See page 116

INTERNATIONAL COMMUNICATIONS INDUSTRIES FOUNDATION

http://www.infocomm.org/scholarships

ICIF SCHOLARSHIP FOR EMPLOYEES AND DEPENDENTS OF MEMBER ORGANIZATIONS
• See page 172

INTERNATIONAL COMMUNICATIONS INDUSTRIES FOUNDATION AV SCHOLARSHIP
• See page 172

ISLAMIC SCHOLARSHIP FUND

http://islamicscholarshipfund.org/

ISF NATIONAL SCHOLARSHIP
• See page 104

NATIONAL ACADEMY OF TELEVISION ARTS AND SCIENCES

https://theemmys.tv/

DOUGLAS W. MUMMERT SCHOLARSHIP
• See page 173

JIM MCKAY MEMORIAL SCHOLARSHIP

The Jim McKay Memorial Scholarship honors sports journalist Jim McKay (1921-2008) and was established in 2009 by the HBO, CBS, NBC, ABC and FOX networks. It is presented at the Sports Emmys each May. It is awarded to a college-bound applicant who demonstrates exceptional talent as a creator of video programming as well as outstanding academic achievement and potential for success in a highly competitive profession.

Academic Fields/Career Goals: Filmmaking/Video; Journalism; Music; Performing Arts; Photojournalism/Photography; TV/Radio Broadcasting.

Award: Scholarship for use in freshman year; not renewable. *Number:* 1. *Amount:* $10,000.

Eligibility Requirements: Applicant must be high school student and planning to enroll or expecting to enroll full-time at a two-year institution or university. Available to U.S. citizens.

Application Requirements: Application form, application form may be submitted online, essay, portfolio. *Deadline:* March 22.

Contact: Paul Pillitteri, SVP, Communications
    Phone: 626-296-3757
    E-mail: ppillitteri@emmyonline.tv

MIKE WALLACE MEMORIAL SCHOLARSHIP

The Mike Wallace Memorial Scholarship is funded by a grant from CBS News in honor of longtime correspondent Mike Wallace (1918-2012) and presented each year at the News and Documentary Emmys. It is awarded to a college-bound applicant who demonstrates exceptional talent as a creator of video programming as well as outstanding academic achievement and potential for success in a highly competitive profession.

Academic Fields/Career Goals: Filmmaking/Video; Journalism; Music; Performing Arts; Photojournalism/Photography; TV/Radio Broadcasting.

Award: Scholarship for use in freshman year; not renewable. *Number:* 1. *Amount:* $10,000.

Eligibility Requirements: Applicant must be high school student and planning to enroll or expecting to enroll full-time at a two-year institution or university. Available to U.S. citizens.

Application Requirements: Application form, application form may be submitted online, essay, portfolio. *Deadline:* March 22.

Contact: Paul Pillitteri, SVP, Communications
    Phone: 626-296-3757
    E-mail: ppillitteri@emmyonline.tv

NATIONAL ACADEMY OF TELEVISION ARTS AND SCIENCES TRUSTEES' LINDA GIANNECCHINI SCHOLARSHIP

The Trustees Scholarship was established by the NATAS Board of Trustees to recognize standout graduating high school seniors who intend to pursue degrees in pursuit of a career in any aspect of the television industry.

Academic Fields/Career Goals: Filmmaking/Video; Journalism; Music; Performing Arts; Photojournalism/Photography; TV/Radio Broadcasting.

Award: Scholarship for use in freshman year; not renewable. *Number:* 1. *Amount:* $10,000.

Eligibility Requirements: Applicant must be high school student and planning to enroll or expecting to enroll full-time at a two-year institution or university. Available to U.S. citizens.

Application Requirements: Application form, application form may be submitted online, essay, portfolio. *Deadline:* March 22.

Contact: Paul Pillitteri, SVP, Communications
Phone: 626-296-3757
E-mail: ppillitteri@emmyonline.tv

RANDY FALCO SCHOLARSHIP

The Falco Scholarship is awarded to a college-bound Hispanic or Latino student who demonstrates exceptional talent as a creator of video programming as well as outstanding academic achievement and potential for success in a highly competitive profession. The $10,000 annual scholarship honors the industry contributions of renowned media executive Randy Falco, currently the President and Chief Executive Officer of Univision Communications Inc. (UCI).

Academic Fields/Career Goals: Filmmaking/Video; Journalism; Music; Performing Arts; Photojournalism/Photography; TV/Radio Broadcasting.

Award: Scholarship for use in freshman year; not renewable. *Number:* 1. *Amount:* $10,000.

Eligibility Requirements: Applicant must be Hispanic; high school student and planning to enroll or expecting to enroll full-time at a two-year institution or university. Available to U.S. citizens.

Application Requirements: Application form, application form may be submitted online, essay, portfolio. *Deadline:* March 22.

Contact: Paul Pillitteri, SVP, Communications
Phone: 626-296-3757
E-mail: ppillitteri@emmyonline.tv

NATIONAL ACADEMY OF TELEVISION ARTS AND SCIENCES, MICHIGAN CHAPTER

http://natasmichigan.org

DR. LYNNE BOYLE/JOHN SCHIMPF UNDERGRADUATE SCHOLARSHIP
• *See page 85*

NATIONAL ACADEMY OF TELEVISION ARTS & SCIENCES—OHIO VALLEY CHAPTER

http://ohiovalleyemmy.org/

DAVID J. CLARKE MEMORIAL SCHOLARSHIP
• *See page 173*

NATIONAL COUNCIL OF JEWISH WOMEN - LOS ANGELES (NCJW L LA)

http://ncjwla.org/

STEPHEN L. TELLER & RICHARD HOTSON TV, CINEMA, AND THEATER SCHOLARSHIP

To qualify, applicants must be a full-time student enrolled in a COMMUNITY COLLEGE Film/ Television/ Cinema/ Theater program, and preparing for a career in film, television, or theater production (not acting). Applicant must have completed 12 units of classes in their school's Film/TV/Cinema/Theater program. Must live and attend school in the Greater Los Angeles area, including Los Angeles, Orange, Riverside, San Bernandino and Ventura Counties.

Academic Fields/Career Goals: Filmmaking/Video; TV/Radio Broadcasting.

Award: Scholarship for use in freshman, sophomore, junior, or senior years; not renewable. *Number:* 2. *Amount:* $1000.

Eligibility Requirements: Applicant must be enrolled or expecting to enroll full-time at a two-year institution; resident of British Columbia and studying in California. Available to U.S. citizens.

Application Requirements: Application form, application form may be submitted online, essay, financial need analysis. *Deadline:* May 1.

Contact: Carrie Jacoves, Director of Operations and Outreach
National Council of Jewish Women - Los Angeles (NCJW l LA)
543 N. Fairfax Ave.
Los Angeles, CA 90036
Phone: 323-651-2930
Fax: 323-651-5348
E-mail: carrie@ncjwla.org

OUTDOOR WRITERS ASSOCIATION OF AMERICA

http://www.owaa.org/

OUTDOOR WRITERS ASSOCIATION OF AMERICA - BODIE MCDOWELL SCHOLARSHIP AWARD
• *See page 174*

POLISH ARTS CLUB OF BUFFALO SCHOLARSHIP FOUNDATION

http://www.pacb.bfn.org/

POLISH ARTS CLUB OF BUFFALO SCHOLARSHIP FOUNDATION TRUST
• *See page 122*

PRINCESS GRACE FOUNDATION-USA

http://www.pgfusa.org/

PRINCESS GRACE AWARDS IN DANCE, THEATER, AND FILM

One-time scholarship for students enrolled full-time in film or video, dance, or theater program. For dance, applicant must have completed at least one year of undergraduate study; for theater, final year of study in either undergraduate or graduate level; and for film, must be in thesis program. The number of scholarships varies from ten to twelve annually.

Academic Fields/Career Goals: Filmmaking/Video; Performing Arts.

Award: Grant for use in sophomore, junior, senior, or graduate years; not renewable. *Number:* 15–25. *Amount:* $5000–$25,000.

Eligibility Requirements: Applicant must be enrolled or expecting to enroll full-time at a four-year institution or university. Available to U.S. citizens.

Application Requirements: Application form, essay, personal photograph, portfolio.

Contact: Ms. Diana Kemppainen, Program Director
Phone: 212-317-1470
E-mail: grants@pgfusa.org

QUALITY BATH

www.qualitybath.com

QUALITYBATH.COM SCHOLARSHIP PROGRAM
• *See page 120*

RHODE ISLAND FOUNDATION

http://www.rifoundation.org/

J. D. EDSAL SCHOLARSHIP
• *See page 87*

SOCIETY OF MOTION PICTURE AND TELEVISION ENGINEERS

https://www.smpte.org/

LOUIS F. WOLF JR. MEMORIAL SCHOLARSHIP
• *See page 175*

STUDENT PAPER AWARD
• *See page 175*

SUPPORT CREATIVITY

http://wesupportcreativity.org

SUPPORT CREATIVITY SCHOLARSHIP
• *See page 117*

TELETOON

http://www.teletoon.com/

TELETOON ANIMATION SCHOLARSHIP
• *See page 123*

UNITED NEGRO COLLEGE FUND

http://www.uncf.org/

DIVERSE VOICES IN STORYTELLING SCHOLARSHIP
• *See page 177*

WALT DISNEY COMPANY UNCF CORPORATE SCHOLARS PROGRAM
• *See page 177*

UNIVERSITY FILM AND VIDEO ASSOCIATION

http://www.ufva.org/

UNIVERSITY FILM AND VIDEO ASSOCIATION CAROLE FIELDING STUDENT GRANTS
Up to $4000 is available for production grants in narrative, documentary, experimental, new-media/installation, or animation. Up to $1000 is available for grants in research. Applicant must be sponsored by a faculty person who is an active member of the University Film and Video Association. Fifty percent of award distributed upon completion of project.
Academic Fields/Career Goals: Filmmaking/Video.
Award: Grant for use in freshman, sophomore, junior, senior, or graduate years; not renewable. *Number:* 2–5. *Amount:* $1000–$4000.
Eligibility Requirements: Applicant must be enrolled or expecting to enroll full- or part-time at a two-year or four-year institution or university. Available to U.S. and non-U.S. citizens.
Application Requirements: Application form, essay. *Deadline:* December 15.
Contact: Prof. Laura Vazquez
University Film and Video Association
Northern Illinois University
Department of Communication
DeKalb, IL 60115
Phone: 815-753-7107
E-mail: lvazquez@niu.edu

FINANCE

AMERICAN SOCIETY OF WOMEN ACCOUNTANTS

http://www.afwa.org/

ACCOUNTING & FINANCIAL WOMEN'S ALLIANCE UNDERGRADUATE SCHOLARSHIP
• *See page 71*

AUTOMOTIVE WOMEN'S ALLIANCE FOUNDATION

http://awafoundation.org/index.php

AUTOMOTIVE WOMEN'S ALLIANCE FOUNDATION SCHOLARSHIPS
• *See page 71*

CHECKS SUPERSTORE

http://www.checks-superstore.com/

CHECKS SUPERSTORE SCHOLARSHIP
Checks SuperStore is offering an annual $1,000 scholarship to one college/university student in the United States. The scholarship will be awarded to the student who submits the best overall essay. Essay must be between 500 and 1,000 words long and must fully answer one of the questions. Entry deadline is on August 15th.
Academic Fields/Career Goals: Finance.
Award: Scholarship for use in freshman, sophomore, junior, or senior years; renewable. *Number:* 1. *Amount:* $1000.
Eligibility Requirements: Applicant must be enrolled or expecting to enroll full-time at a four-year institution. Available to U.S. citizens.
Application Requirements: Application form may be submitted online(www.checks-superstore.com/scholarship.aspx), essay. *Deadline:* August 15.
Contact: Ryan Skidmore, Scholarship Manager
E-mail: scholarship@checks-superstore.com

DECA (DISTRIBUTIVE EDUCATION CLUBS OF AMERICA)

http://www.deca.org/

HARRY A. APPLEGATE SCHOLARSHIP
• *See page 73*

DISTIL NETWORKS

http://www.distilnetworks.com

WOMEN FORWARD IN TECHNOLOGY SCHOLARSHIP PROGRAM
• *See page 108*

GOVERNMENT FINANCE OFFICERS ASSOCIATION

https://www.gfoa.org/

FRANK L. GREATHOUSE GOVERNMENT ACCOUNTING SCHOLARSHIP
• *See page 75*

JEFFREY L. ESSER CAREER DEVELOPMENT SCHOLARSHIP
• *See page 75*

MINORITIES IN GOVERNMENT FINANCE SCHOLARSHIP
• *See page 75*

SCARLETT FAMILY FOUNDATION SCHOLARSHIP PROGRAM

http://www.scarlettfoundation.org/

SCHOLARSHIP FOR STUDENTS PURSUING A BUSINESS OR STEM DEGREE
• *See page 80*

SPECIALTY EQUIPMENT MARKET ASSOCIATION

http://www.sema.org/

SEMA MEMORIAL SCHOLARSHIP FUND
• *See page 81*

STRAIGHTFORWARD MEDIA

http://www.straightforwardmedia.com/

STRAIGHTFORWARD MEDIA BUSINESS SCHOOL SCHOLARSHIP
• *See page 87*

STRAIGHT NORTH

https://www.straightnorth.com/

STRAIGHT NORTH STEM SCHOLARSHIP
• *See page 81*

TAU KAPPA EPSILON EDUCATION FOUNDATION

https://www.tke.org/

W. ALLAN HERZOG SCHOLARSHIP
• *See page 82*

UNITED NEGRO COLLEGE FUND

http://www.uncf.org/

DISCOVER FINANCIAL SERVICES SCHOLARSHIP
• *See page 82*

HCN/APRICITY RESOURCES SCHOLARS PROGRAM
• *See page 83*

NASCAR WENDELL SCOTT SR. SCHOLARSHIP
• *See page 83*

UNCF/CARNIVAL CORPORATE SCHOLARS PROGRAM
• *See page 151*

VOYA SCHOLARS
• *See page 83*

FIRE SCIENCES

AMERICAN SOCIETY OF CERTIFIED ENGINEERING TECHNICIANS

http://www.ascet.org/

KURT H. AND DONNA M. SCHULER SMALL GRANT
• *See page 162*

GRAND RAPIDS COMMUNITY FOUNDATION

http://www.grfoundation.org/

HARRY J. MORRIS, JR. EMERGENCY SERVICES SCHOLARSHIP
Scholarship is for students who are residents of Kent, Allegan, Barry, Ionia, Ottawa, Montcalm, Muskegon, or Newaygo County pursuing an undergraduate certificate or degree at an accredited education program in Michigan in the field of emergency medical technician, paramedic, or firefighter training. Must have a 2.5 cumulative grade point average or verified GED certificate and demonstrate financial need.
Academic Fields/Career Goals: Fire Sciences; Health Administration; Health and Medical Sciences.
Award: Scholarship for use in freshman, sophomore, junior, or senior years; not renewable. *Number:* 1–4. *Amount:* $1000–$1500.
Eligibility Requirements: Applicant must be enrolled or expecting to enroll full- or part-time at a two-year or technical institution or university; resident of Massachusetts and studying in Michigan. Available to U.S. citizens.
Application Requirements: Application form, application form may be submitted online, essay, financial need analysis. *Deadline:* April 1.
Contact: Ms. Ruth Bishop, Education Program Officer
Grand Rapids Community Foundation
185 Oakes Street SW
Grand Rapids, MI 49503
Phone: 616-454-1751 Ext. 103
E-mail: rbishop@grfoundation.org

INTERNATIONAL ASSOCIATION OF FIRE CHIEFS FOUNDATION

http://www.iafcf.org/

INTERNATIONAL ASSOCIATION OF FIRE CHIEFS FOUNDATION SCHOLARSHIP AWARD
One-time award, open to any person who is an active member (volunteer or paid) of an emergency or fire department. Must use the scholarship funds for an accredited, recognized institution of higher education.
Academic Fields/Career Goals: Fire Sciences.
Award: Scholarship for use in freshman, sophomore, junior, senior, or graduate years; not renewable. *Number:* 20–30. *Amount:* $500–$2500.
Eligibility Requirements: Applicant must be enrolled or expecting to enroll full- or part-time at a two-year or four-year or technical institution or university. Available to U.S. and Canadian citizens.
Application Requirements: Application form, essay. *Deadline:* April 29.
Contact: Terry Monroe, Director, Membership and Marketing
Phone: 703-385-1610
Fax: 703-273-9363
E-mail: tmonroe@iafc.org

INTERNATIONAL SOCIETY OF EXPLOSIVES ENGINEERS

http://www.isee.org/

JERRY MCDOWELL FUND
• *See page 156*

LEARNING FOR LIFE

http://www.learning-for-life.org/

INTERNATIONAL ASSOCIATIONS OF FIRE CHIEFS FOUNDATION SCHOLARSHIP
Applicant must be a graduating high school senior in May or June of the year the application is issued and a Fire Service Explorer. The school selected by the applicant must be an accredited public or proprietary institution.
Academic Fields/Career Goals: Fire Sciences.

Award: Scholarship for use in freshman year; not renewable. *Number:* 2. *Amount:* $500.

Eligibility Requirements: Applicant must be high school student and planning to enroll or expecting to enroll full- or part-time at a two-year or four-year institution or university. Applicant or parent of applicant must be member of Explorer Program/Learning for Life. Available to U.S. citizens.

Application Requirements: Application form, essay, personal photograph, recommendations or references, transcript. *Deadline:* July 1.

Contact: William Taylor, Scholarships and Awards Coordinator
E-mail: btaylor@lflmail.org

NASA IDAHO SPACE GRANT CONSORTIUM

http://www.idahospacegrant.org

NASA IDAHO SPACE GRANT CONSORTIUM SCHOLARSHIP PROGRAM
• *See page 109*

PLATINUM EDUCATIONAL GROUP

www.platinumed.com

PLATINUM EDUCATIONAL GROUP SCHOLARSHIPS PROGRAM FOR EMS, NURSING, AND ALLIED HEALTH
• *See page 102*

FLEXOGRAPHY

FOUNDATION OF FLEXOGRAPHIC TECHNICAL ASSOCIATION

http://www.flexography.org/

FOUNDATION OF FLEXOGRAPHIC TECHNICAL ASSOCIATION SCHOLARSHIP COMPETITION

Awards students enrolled in a FFTA Flexo in Education Program with plans to attend a postsecondary institution, or be currently enrolled in a postsecondary institution offering a course of study in flexography. Must demonstrate an interest in a career in flexography, and maintain an overall GPA of at least 3.0. Must reapply.

Academic Fields/Career Goals: Flexography.

Award: Scholarship for use in freshman, sophomore, junior, or senior years; not renewable. *Number:* 6–8. *Amount:* up to $3000.

Eligibility Requirements: Applicant must be enrolled or expecting to enroll full-time at a two-year or four-year or technical institution or university. Available to U.S. and Canadian citizens.

Application Requirements: Application form, application form may be submitted online (http://www.flexography.org), essay, recommendations or references, transcript. *Deadline:* March 15.

Contact: Shelley Rubin, Manager of Educational Programs
Foundation of Flexographic Technical Association
3920 Veterans Memorial Highway, Suite 9
Bohemia, NY 11716
Phone: 631-737-6020 Ext. 36
Fax: 631-737-6813

PRINTING INDUSTRY MIDWEST EDUCATION FOUDNATION

http://www.pimw.org/scholarships

PRINTING INDUSTRY MIDWEST EDUCATION FOUNDATION SCHOLARSHIP FUND
• *See page 175*

STRAIGHT NORTH

https://www.straightnorth.com/

STRAIGHT NORTH STEM SCHOLARSHIP
• *See page 81*

TAG AND LABEL MANUFACTURERS INSTITUTE, INC.

http://www.tlmi.com/

TLMI 2 YEAR COLLEGE DEGREE SCHOLARSHIP PROGRAM

Scholarship program for students enrolled at a two-year college or in a degree technical program whose major course work includes courses appropriate for future work in the tag and label manufacturing industry. Must submit statements including personal information, financial circumstances, career and/or educational goals, employment experience, and reasons applicant should be selected for this award.

Academic Fields/Career Goals: Flexography; Graphics/Graphic Arts/Printing.

Award: Scholarship for use in freshman or sophomore years; not renewable. *Number:* 1–6. *Amount:* $500–$1000.

Eligibility Requirements: Applicant must be enrolled or expecting to enroll full-time at a two-year or technical institution. Available to U.S. and Canadian citizens.

Application Requirements: Application form, application form may be submitted online (https://www.tlmi.com/events-awards/tlmi-scholarship-programs/2019-tlmi-scholarship-application), essay, portfolio. *Deadline:* April 5.

Contact: Jessica Johnson, Program Director
Tag and Label Manufacturers Institute, Inc.
6 Main Street
Milford, OH 45150
Phone: 513-401-9454
E-mail: jessica.johnson@tlmi.com

TLMI 4 YEAR COLLEGE DEGREE SCHOLARSHIP PROGRAM

Scholarship program for students enrolled at a four-year college whose major course work includes courses appropriate for future work in the tag and label manufacturing industry. Must submit statements including personal information, financial circumstances, career and/or educational goals, employment experience, and reasons applicant should be selected for this award.

Academic Fields/Career Goals: Flexography; Graphics/Graphic Arts/Printing.

Award: Scholarship for use in junior or senior years; not renewable. *Number:* 1–6. *Amount:* $2500–$5000.

Eligibility Requirements: Applicant must be enrolled or expecting to enroll full-time at a four-year institution or university. Available to U.S. and Canadian citizens.

Application Requirements: Application form, application form may be submitted online (https://www.tlmi.com/events-awards/tlmi-scholarship-programs/2019-tlmi-scholarship-application), essay, interview, portfolio, recommendations or references, transcript. *Deadline:* April 5.

Contact: Jessica Johnson, Program Director
Tag and Label Manufacturers Institute, Inc.
6 Main Street
Milford, OH 45150
Phone: 513-401-9454
E-mail: jessica.johnson@tlmi.com

FOOD SCIENCE/ NUTRITION

101ST AIRBORNE DIVISION ASSOCIATION

http://www.screamingeaglefoundation.org/

AL & WILLIAMARY VISTE SCHOLARSHIP
• *See page 99*

AACC INTERNATIONAL

http://www.aaccnet.org/

UNDERGRADUATE SCHOLARSHIP AWARD

The purposes of the undergraduate scholarship program are to encourage scholastically outstanding advanced undergraduate students in academic preparation for a career in grain-based food science and technology, and to attract and encourage outstanding students to enter the field of grain-based food science and technology.

Academic Fields/Career Goals: Food Science/Nutrition.

Award: Scholarship for use in freshman, sophomore, junior, or senior years; not renewable. *Number:* 1. *Amount:* $825.

Eligibility Requirements: Applicant must be enrolled or expecting to enroll full-time at an institution or university. Available to U.S. and non-U.S. citizens.

Application Requirements: Application form, essay. *Deadline:* March 3.

Contact: Lauren McGinty, Membership Experience Manager
AACC International
3340 Pilot Knob Road
St. Paul, MN 55121
Phone: 651-454-7250
E-mail: lmcginty@scisoc.org

AMERICAN INDIAN SCIENCE AND ENGINEERING SOCIETY

http://www.aises.org/

A.T. ANDERSON MEMORIAL SCHOLARSHIP PROGRAM
• *See page 105*

AMERICAN OIL CHEMISTS' SOCIETY

www.aocs.org/

AOCS BIOTECHNOLOGY STUDENT EXCELLENCE AWARD
• *See page 92*

AOCS HEALTH AND NUTRITION DIVISION STUDENT EXCELLENCE AWARD

$500 award and certificate to recognize the outstanding merit and performance of a student in the health and nutrition field. Student will present a paper at the Annual Meeting of the Society.

Academic Fields/Career Goals: Food Science/Nutrition.

Award: Prize for use in senior or graduate years; not renewable. *Number:* 1. *Amount:* $500.

Eligibility Requirements: Applicant must be enrolled or expecting to enroll full-time at a four-year institution or university. Available to U.S. and non-U.S. citizens.

Application Requirements: Abstract, application form, essay, recommendations or references. *Deadline:* October 15.

Contact: Barbara Semeraro, Area Manager, Membership
American Oil Chemists' Society
AOCS
PO Box 17190
Urbana, IL 61803
Phone: 217-693-4804
Fax: 217-693-4849
E-mail: awards@aocs.org

AOCS PROCESSING DIVISION AWARDS
• *See page 154*

AMERICAN SOCIETY FOR ENOLOGY AND VITICULTURE

http://www.asev.org/

AMERICAN SOCIETY FOR ENOLOGY AND VITICULTURE SCHOLARSHIPS
• *See page 92*

ASSISTANCE LEAGUE OF THE TRIANGLE AREA

HEALTH CARE PROFESSION SCHOLARSHIP
• *See page 195*

AVACARE MEDICAL

https://avacaremedical.com

AVACARE MEDICAL SCHOLARSHIP
• *See page 100*

BHW GROUP

https://thebhwgroup.com/

BHW WOMEN IN STEM SCHOLARSHIP
• *See page 107*

CANFIT

http://www.canfit.org/

CANFIT NUTRITION, PHYSICAL EDUCATION AND CULINARY ARTS SCHOLARSHIP
• *See page 190*

CONTINENTAL SOCIETY, DAUGHTERS OF INDIAN WARS

http://www.csdiw.org/

CONTINENTAL SOCIETY, DAUGHTERS OF INDIAN WARS SCHOLARSHIP
• *See page 188*

THE CULINARY TRUST

http://www.theculinarytrust.org/

CULINARY TRUST SCHOLARSHIP PROGRAM FOR CULINARY STUDY AND RESEARCH
• *See page 190*

FEEDING TOMORROW: THE FOUNDATION OF THE INSTITUTE OF FOOD TECHNOLOGISTS

http://www.feedingtomorrow.org

BARBARA B. KEENAN SCHOLARSHIP

One $1000 award for an undergraduate student enrolled as a rising sophomore, junior, or senior pursuing an undergraduate degree in food science. Minimum 3.0 GPA required.

Academic Fields/Career Goals: Food Science/Nutrition.

Award: Scholarship for use in sophomore, junior, or senior years; not renewable. *Number:* 1. *Amount:* $1000.

Eligibility Requirements: Applicant must be enrolled or expecting to enroll full- or part-time at a four-year institution or university and must have an interest in leadership. Available to U.S. and non-U.S. citizens.

Application Requirements: Application form, application form may be submitted online, transcript. *Deadline:* February 28.

Contact: Feeding Tomorrow Manager
Feeding Tomorrow: The Foundation of the Institute of Food Technologists
525 West Van Buren, Suite 1000
Chicago, IL 60607
Phone: 312-604-0256
E-mail: feedingtomorrow@ift.org

DR. ANN C. HOLLINGSWORTH STUDENT LEADERSHIP SCHOLARSHIP

One award for an undergraduate student enrolled as a rising sophomore, junior, or senior pursuing an undergraduate degree in food science. Minimum 3.0 GPA required. Recipient must be a student leader who has demonstrated outstanding leadership at their university and the IFT student association, along with a passion for student advocacy, IFT, and their chosen profession.

Academic Fields/Career Goals: Food Science/Nutrition.

Award: Scholarship for use in sophomore, junior, or senior years; not renewable. *Number:* 1. *Amount:* $1500.

Eligibility Requirements: Applicant must be enrolled or expecting to enroll full- or part-time at a four-year institution or university and must have an interest in leadership. Available to U.S. and non-U.S. citizens.

Application Requirements: Application form, application form may be submitted online, transcript. *Deadline:* February 28.

Contact: Jaime Gutshall
Phone: 312-604-0256
E-mail: jgutshall@ift.org

EDLONG DAIRY TECHNOLOGIES SCHOLARSHIPS

One $1500 award for a rising junior or senior and one $2000 award for MS or PhD student pursuing studies in food science with an emphasis on dairy flavors and/or dairy science at an accredited college or university for the 2019-2020 academic year. Minimum of 3.0 GPA. Must demonstrate commitment in the science of food profession, such as, but not limited to IFT membership.

Academic Fields/Career Goals: Food Science/Nutrition.

Award: Scholarship for use in junior, senior, graduate, or postgraduate years; not renewable. *Number:* 2. *Amount:* $1500–$2000.

Eligibility Requirements: Applicant must be enrolled or expecting to enroll full- or part-time at a four-year institution or university and must have an interest in leadership. Available to U.S. and non-U.S. citizens.

Application Requirements: Application form, application form may be submitted online, transcript. *Deadline:* February 28.

Contact: Feeding Tomorrow Manager
Feeding Tomorrow: The Foundation of the Institute of Food Technologists
525 West Van Buren, Suite 1000
Chicago, IL 60607
Phone: 312-604-0256
E-mail: feedingtomorrow@ift.org

EVAN TUREK MEMORIAL SCHOLARSHIP
• See page 93

FEEDING TOMORROW FRESHMAN SCHOLARSHIP

Scholarship for students planning to enroll as a full-time freshman student pursuing an undergraduate degree in science of food at an approved university for the 2019-2020 academic year. Minimum 3.0 GPA required.

Academic Fields/Career Goals: Food Science/Nutrition.

Award: Scholarship for use in freshman year; not renewable. *Number:* 4. *Amount:* $1000.

Eligibility Requirements: Applicant must be enrolled or expecting to enroll full-time at a four-year institution or university and must have an interest in leadership. Available to U.S. and non-U.S. citizens.

Application Requirements: Application form, application form may be submitted online, transcript. *Deadline:* May 30.

Contact: Jaime Gutshall
Phone: 312-604-0256
E-mail: jgutshall@ift.org

FEEDING TOMORROW UNDERGRADUATE GENERAL EDUCATION SCHOLARSHIPS

Multiple scholarships for college sophomores, juniors, and seniors demonstrating exceptional scholastic achievements, leadership experience and a devotion to the food science and technology profession. Minimum 3.0 GPA required.

Academic Fields/Career Goals: Food Science/Nutrition.

Award: Scholarship for use in sophomore, junior, or senior years; not renewable. *Number:* 8. *Amount:* $1500–$5000.

Eligibility Requirements: Applicant must be enrolled or expecting to enroll full- or part-time at a four-year institution or university and must have an interest in leadership. Available to U.S. and non-U.S. citizens.

Application Requirements: Application form, application form may be submitted online, transcript. *Deadline:* February 28.

Contact: Jaime Gutshall
Phone: 312-604-0256
E-mail: jgutshall@ift.org

IFT FOOD ENGINEERING DIVISION SCHOLARSHIP

One $1500 scholarship for an undergraduate student pursuing a degree in the science of food focusing on any aspect of food process engineering. Minimum 3.0 GPA. Will submit a recommendation letter from a research mentor who is a member of the Food Engineering Division of IFT stating that the mentor will supervise the student to do research in their lab.

Academic Fields/Career Goals: Food Science/Nutrition.

Award: Scholarship for use in sophomore, junior, or senior years; not renewable. *Number:* 1. *Amount:* $1500.

Eligibility Requirements: Applicant must be enrolled or expecting to enroll full- or part-time at a four-year institution or university and must have an interest in leadership. Available to U.S. and non-U.S. citizens.

Application Requirements: Application form, application form may be submitted online, transcript. *Deadline:* February 28.

Contact: Feeding Tomorrow Manager
Feeding Tomorrow: The Foundation of the Institute of Food Technologists
525 West Van Buren, Suite 1000
Chicago, IL 60607
Phone: 312-604-0256
E-mail: feedingtomorrow@ift.org

IFT FOOD LAWS AND REGULATIONS DIVISION UNDERGRADUATE SCHOLARSHIP
• See page 93

IFT FOOD MICROBIOLOGY DIVISION UNDERGRADUATE SCHOLARSHIP

One $1000 scholarship for an undergraduate student studying food microbiology. Minimum 3.0 GPA.

Academic Fields/Career Goals: Food Science/Nutrition.

Award: Scholarship for use in sophomore, junior, or senior years; not renewable. *Number:* 1. *Amount:* $1000.

Eligibility Requirements: Applicant must be enrolled or expecting to enroll full- or part-time at a four-year institution or university and must have an interest in leadership. Available to U.S. and non-U.S. citizens.

Application Requirements: Application form, application form may be submitted online, transcript. *Deadline:* February 28.

Contact: Feeding Tomorrow Manager
Feeding Tomorrow: The Foundation of the Institute of Food Technologists
525 West Van Buren, Suite 1000
Chicago, IL 60607
Phone: 312-604-0256
E-mail: feedingtomorrow@ift.org

INGREDION SCHOLARSHIP AND INTERNSHIP

Paid summer internship with $2000 tuition scholarship provided by Feeding Tomorrow Ingredion. Applicant must be pursuing a Bachelor's or Master's degree program in Food Science. Must be familiar with experimental design, statistical data analysis and interpretation of results. Must possess unrestricted authorization to work in the United States. Ingredion does not intend to sponsor work visas with respect to this position or to provide this position as OPT or CPT. Minimum 3.0 GPA.

Academic Fields/Career Goals: Food Science/Nutrition.

Award: Scholarship for use in sophomore, junior, senior, or graduate years; not renewable. *Number:* 1. *Amount:* $2000.

Eligibility Requirements: Applicant must be enrolled or expecting to enroll full-time at a four-year institution or university. Available to U.S. and non-U.S. citizens.

Application Requirements: Application form. *Deadline:* September 15.

Contact: Feeding Tomorrow Manager
Feeding Tomorrow: The Foundation of the Institute of Food Technologists
525 West Van Buren, Suite 1000
Chicago, IL 60607
Phone: 312-604-0256
E-mail: feedingtomorrow@ift.org

INSTITUTE FOR THERMAL PROCESSING SPECIALISTS IRVING PFLUG MEMORIAL SCHOLARSHIP

One $1500 scholarship for an undergraduate student studying food science, food engineering, or food microbiology as it relates to food preservation. Minimum 3.0 GPA.

Academic Fields/Career Goals: Food Science/Nutrition.

Award: Scholarship for use in sophomore, junior, or senior years; not renewable. *Number:* 1. *Amount:* $1500.

Eligibility Requirements: Applicant must be enrolled or expecting to enroll full- or part-time at a four-year institution or university and must have an interest in leadership. Available to U.S. and non-U.S. citizens.

Application Requirements: Application form, application form may be submitted online, transcript. *Deadline:* February 28.

Contact: Feeding Tomorrow Manager
Feeding Tomorrow: The Foundation of the Institute of Food Technologists
525 West Van Buren, Suite 1000
Chicago, IL 60607
Phone: 312-604-0256
E-mail: feedingtomorrow@ift.org

JOHN POWERS SCHOLARSHIP

One award for an undergraduate student enrolled as a rising sophomore, junior, or senior pursuing an undergraduate degree in food science. Minimum 3.0 GPA required. Applicant must be a student member of IFT at the time of application.

Academic Fields/Career Goals: Food Science/Nutrition.

Award: Scholarship for use in sophomore, junior, or senior years; not renewable. *Number:* 1.

Eligibility Requirements: Applicant must be enrolled or expecting to enroll full-time at a four-year institution or university. Available to U.S. and non-U.S. citizens.

Application Requirements: Application form. *Deadline:* February 15.

Contact: Feeding Tomorrow Manager
Feeding Tomorrow: The Foundation of the Institute of Food Technologists
525 West Van Buren, Suite 1000
Chicago, IL 60607
Phone: 312-604-0256
E-mail: feedingtomorrow@ift.org

MCCORMICK & COMPANY SCHOLARSHIP

One $2000 scholarship for a student planning to enroll full-time or part-time as a rising sophomore, junior, or senior student pursuing an undergraduate degree in science of food at an approved university for the 2019-2020 academic year. Minimum 3.0 GPA.

Academic Fields/Career Goals: Food Science/Nutrition.

Award: Scholarship for use in sophomore, junior, or senior years; not renewable. *Number:* 1. *Amount:* $2000.

Eligibility Requirements: Applicant must be enrolled or expecting to enroll full- or part-time at a four-year institution or university and must have an interest in leadership. Available to U.S. and non-U.S. citizens.

Application Requirements: Application form, application form may be submitted online, transcript. *Deadline:* February 28.

Contact: Feeding Tomorrow Manager
Feeding Tomorrow: The Foundation of the Institute of Food Technologists
525 West Van Buren, Suite 1000
Chicago, IL 60607
Phone: 312-604-0256
E-mail: feedingtomorrow@ift.org

PEPSICO SCHOLARSHIP AND INTERNSHIP

One scholarship and internship at PepsiCo. Applicant must be enrolled in an IFT approved undergraduate or graduate program at the standing of junior or above, majoring in biochemistry, dairy science, food chemistry, food packaging, non-thermal processing or related discipline. Applicant must demonstrate exceptional leadership experience and be an IFT member at the time of application. Must have 3.0 cumulative GPA in food science.

Academic Fields/Career Goals: Food Science/Nutrition.

Award: Scholarship for use in junior, senior, or graduate years; not renewable. *Number:* 1. *Amount:* $1000.

Eligibility Requirements: Applicant must be enrolled or expecting to enroll full-time at a four-year institution or university. Available to U.S. citizens.

Application Requirements: Application form, interview, transcript. *Deadline:* September 15.

Contact: Feeding Tomorrow Manager
Feeding Tomorrow: The Foundation of the Institute of Food Technologists
525 West Van Buren, Suite 1000
Chicago, IL 60607
Phone: 312-604-0256
E-mail: feedingtomorrow@ift.org

GREAT MINDS IN STEM

http://www.greatmindsinstem.org/college/scholarship-application-information

HENAAC SCHOLARSHIP PROGRAM
• *See page 100*

ILLINOIS RESTAURANT ASSOCIATION EDUCATIONAL FOUNDATION

http://www.illinoisrestaurants.org/

ILLINOIS RESTAURANT ASSOCIATION EDUCATIONAL FOUNDATION SCHOLARSHIPS
• *See page 190*

JAMES BEARD FOUNDATION INC.

http://www.jamesbeard.org/

BERN LAXER MEMORIAL SCHOLARSHIP
• *See page 191*

LES DAMES D'ESCOFFIER INTERNATIONAL, COLORADO CHAPTER

www.lesdamescolorado.org/scholarship

LES DAMES D'ESCOFFIER INTERNATIONAL, COLORADO CHAPTER SCHOLARSHIP
• *See page 94*

MARYLAND RESTAURANT ASSOCIATION EDUCATION FOUNDATION

https://www.marylandrestaurants.com/about.html

THE LETITIA B. CARTER SCHOLARSHIP
• *See page 192*

MARCIA S. HARRIS LEGACY FUND SCHOLARSHIP
• *See page 192*

MEDICAL SCRUBS COLLECTION

http://medicalscrubscollection.com

MEDICAL SCRUBS COLLECTION SCHOLARSHIP
• *See page 104*

NATIONAL POULTRY AND FOOD DISTRIBUTORS ASSOCIATION

http://www.npfda.org/

NATIONAL POULTRY AND FOOD DISTRIBUTORS ASSOCIATION SCHOLARSHIP FOUNDATION
• *See page 90*

NATIONAL RESTAURANT ASSOCIATION EDUCATIONAL FOUNDATION

http://www.chooserestaurants.org

NATIONAL RESTAURANT ASSOCIATION EDUCATIONAL FOUNDATION UNDERGRADUATE SCHOLARSHIPS FOR COLLEGE STUDENTS
• *See page 95*

NEXTSTEPU

http://www.nextstepu.com/

$1,500 STEM SCHOLARSHIP
• *See page 104*

NOVUS BIOLOGICALS, LLC

https://www.novusbio.com

NOVUS BIOLOGICALS SCHOLARSHIP PROGRAM
• *See page 101*

R&D SYSTEMS SCHOLARSHIP
• *See page 101*

TOCRIS BIOSCIENCE SCHOLARSHIP
• *See page 102*

PROFESSIONAL REPS

http://www.professionalreps.com/

HUNGRY TO LEAD SCHOLARSHIP
• *See page 193*

SCARLETT FAMILY FOUNDATION SCHOLARSHIP PROGRAM

http://www.scarlettfoundation.org/

SCHOLARSHIP FOR STUDENTS PURSUING A BUSINESS OR STEM DEGREE
• *See page 80*

SCHOOL NUTRITION FOUNDATION

https://www.schoolnutritionfoundation.org/

NANCY CURRY SCHOLARSHIP

Scholarship assists members of the American School Food Service Association and their dependents to pursue educational and career advancement in school food-service or child nutrition.

Academic Fields/Career Goals: Food Science/Nutrition.

Award: Scholarship for use in freshman, sophomore, junior, senior, graduate, or postgraduate years; not renewable. *Number:* 1. *Amount:* $500.

Eligibility Requirements: Applicant must be enrolled or expecting to enroll full- or part-time at a two-year or technical institution or university. Applicant or parent of applicant must have employment or volunteer experience in food service. Available to U.S. citizens.

Application Requirements: Application form, application form may be submitted online, essay. *Deadline:* January 31.

Contact: Sarah Youssef, Program Manager
School Nutrition Foundation
2900 S. Quincy Street
Suite 700
Arlington, VA 22206
Phone: 703-824-3000
Fax: 703-824-3015
E-mail: smurphy@schoolnutrition.org

SCHWAN'S FOOD SERVICE SCHOLARSHIP

Since 1983, Schwan's Food Service, Inc., has made an annual donation to offer multiple scholarships of up to $2,500 each. Program is designed to assist members of the American School Food Service Association and their dependents as they pursue educational advancement in the field of child nutrition.

Academic Fields/Career Goals: Food Science/Nutrition.

Award: Scholarship for use in freshman, sophomore, junior, senior, graduate, or postgraduate years; not renewable. *Amount:* $2500.

Eligibility Requirements: Applicant must be enrolled or expecting to enroll full- or part-time at a two-year or technical institution or university. Applicant or parent of applicant must have employment or volunteer experience in food service. Available to U.S. citizens.

Application Requirements: Application form, application form may be submitted online, essay. *Deadline:* January 31.

Contact: Sarah Youssef, Program Manager
School Nutrition Foundation
2900 S. Quincy Street
Suite 700
Arlington, VA 22206
Phone: 703-824-3000
Fax: 703-824-3015
E-mail: smurphy@schoolnutrition.org

SNF PROFESSIONAL GROWTH SCHOLARSHIP

The SNF Professional Growth Scholarship is funded by SNA members through past special events. Scholarships of up to $2,500 each are awarded.

Academic Fields/Career Goals: Food Science/Nutrition.

Award: Scholarship for use in freshman, sophomore, junior, senior, graduate, or postgraduate years; not renewable. *Amount:* $2500.

Eligibility Requirements: Applicant must be enrolled or expecting to enroll full- or part-time at a two-year or technical institution or university. Applicant or parent of applicant must have employment or volunteer experience in food service. Available to U.S. citizens.

Application Requirements: Application form, application form may be submitted online, essay. *Deadline:* January 31.

Contact: Sarah Youssef, Program Manager
School Nutrition Foundation
2900 S. Quincy Street
Suite 700
Arlington, VA 22206
Phone: 703-824-3000
Fax: 703-824-3015
E-mail: smurphy@schoolnutrition.org

SOIL AND WATER CONSERVATION SOCIETY

http://www.swcs.org

DONALD A. WILLIAMS SCHOLARSHIP SOIL CONSERVATION SCHOLARSHIP
• *See page 91*

UNITED NEGRO COLLEGE FUND

http://www.uncf.org/

LEIDOS STEM SCHOLARSHIP
• *See page 96*

UNITED STATES DEPARTMENT OF AGRICULTURE

http://www.usda.gov/

USDA/1994 TRIBAL SCHOLARS PROGRAM
• *See page 96*

WASHINGTON WINE INDUSTRY FOUNDATION

http://washingtonwinefoundation.org/

WALTER J. CLORE SCHOLARSHIP
• *See page 97*

WHAT DETOX

http://whatdetox.com/meet-the-team/

WHAT DETOX SCHOLARSHIP
The principal aim of this scholarship program is to offer financial support to current undergraduate and graduate students and to encourage serious and deserving students to continue their studies in marketing or nutrition.
Academic Fields/Career Goals: Food Science/Nutrition; Marketing.
Award: Scholarship for use in freshman, sophomore, junior, senior, graduate, or postgraduate years; not renewable. *Number:* 1. *Amount:* $1000.
Eligibility Requirements: Applicant must be enrolled or expecting to enroll full-time at a four-year institution or university. Available to U.S. and non-U.S. citizens.
Application Requirements: Essay. *Deadline:* January 31.
Contact: Christina Johnson, CEO
E-mail: christine@whatdetox.com

WISCONSIN ASSOCIATION FOR FOOD PROTECTION

http://www.wifoodprotection.org

E.H. MARTH FOOD PROTECTION AND FOOD SCIENCES SCHOLARSHIP
• *See page 250*

WISCONSIN BAKERS ASSOCIATION (WBA)

http://www.wibakers.com/

ROBERT W. HILLER SCHOLARSHIP FUND
• *See page 193*

WBA SCHOLARSHIP
• *See page 194*

FOOD SERVICE/ HOSPITALITY

AMERICAN HOTEL AND LODGING EDUCATIONAL FOUNDATION

https://www.ahlafoundation.org/

AHLEF ANNUAL SCHOLARSHIP GRANT PROGRAM
The program is co-administered with affiliated schools that select the scholarship recipients based upon a set of minimum eligiblity criteria, which includes full-time enrollment status in a U.S. hospitality-related degree granting program, minimum cumulative GPA of 3.0 or higher, U.S. citizenship or permanent U.S. residency. A list of affiliated schools available on https://www.ahlef.org/Scholarships/Academic/AHLEF_School-Nominated_Scholarships/.
Academic Fields/Career Goals: Food Service/Hospitality; Hospitality Management; Recreation, Parks, Leisure Studies; Travel/Tourism.
Award: Scholarship for use in junior or senior years; not renewable. *Amount:* $500–$6000.
Eligibility Requirements: Applicant must be enrolled or expecting to enroll full-time at a two-year institution or university. Available to U.S. citizens.
Application Requirements: Application form, essay, financial need analysis. *Deadline:* February 15.
Contact: Kodichi Nwankwo, Foundation Coordinator
American Hotel and Lodging Educational Foundation
1250 Eye Street, NW
Suite 1100
Washington, DC 20005
Phone: 202-289-3134
E-mail: knwankwo@ahlef.org

AMERICAN HOTEL & LODGING EDUCATIONAL FOUNDATION PEPSI SCHOLARSHIP
• *See page 189*

ECOLAB SCHOLARSHIP PROGRAM
Award for students enrolled full-time in United States baccalaureate or associate program leading to degree in hospitality management.
Academic Fields/Career Goals: Food Service/Hospitality; Hospitality Management; Recreation, Parks, Leisure Studies; Travel/Tourism.
Award: Scholarship for use in freshman, sophomore, junior, or senior years; not renewable. *Number:* 10–15. *Amount:* $1000–$2000.
Eligibility Requirements: Applicant must be enrolled or expecting to enroll full-time at a two-year institution or university. Available to U.S. and non-U.S. citizens.
Application Requirements: Application form, essay, financial need analysis. *Deadline:* May 1.
Contact: Kodichi Nwankwo, Foundation Coordinator
American Hotel and Lodging Educational Foundation
1250 Eye Street, NW
Suite 1100
Washington, DC 20005
Phone: 202-289-3134
E-mail: knwankwo@ahlef.org

HYATT HOTELS FUND FOR MINORITY LODGING MANAGEMENT

Scholarship available for African-American, Hispanic, American Indian, Alaskan Native, Asian, or Pacific Islander in a baccalaureate hospitality management program. Must be at least a junior in a four-year program to receive the scholarship.

Academic Fields/Career Goals: Food Service/Hospitality; Hospitality Management; Recreation, Parks, Leisure Studies; Travel/Tourism.

Award: Scholarship for use in junior or senior years; not renewable. *Number:* 10–15. *Amount:* $3000.

Eligibility Requirements: Applicant must be American Indian/Alaska Native, Asian/Pacific Islander, Black (non-Hispanic), Hispanic and enrolled or expecting to enroll full-time at an institution or university. Available to U.S. citizens.

Application Requirements: Application form, essay, financial need analysis. *Deadline:* May 1.

Contact: Kodichi Nwankwo, Foundation Coordinator
American Hotel and Lodging Educational Foundation
1250 Eye Street, NW
Suite 1100
Washington, DC 20005
Phone: 202-289-3134
E-mail: knwankwo@ahlef.org

INCOMING FRESHMAN SCHOLARSHIPS

This program is exclusively for incoming freshman interested in pursuing hospitality-related undergraduate programs. Preference will be given to any applicant who is a graduate of the Educational Institute's Lodging Management Program (LMP, which is a two-year high school program.) Must have a minimum 2.0 GPA.

Academic Fields/Career Goals: Food Service/Hospitality; Hospitality Management; Recreation, Parks, Leisure Studies; Travel/Tourism.

Award: Scholarship for use in freshman year; not renewable. *Number:* 5–10. *Amount:* $2000–$4000.

Eligibility Requirements: Applicant must be high school student and planning to enroll or expecting to enroll full-time at a two-year institution or university. Available to U.S. citizens.

Application Requirements: Application form, essay, financial need analysis. *Deadline:* May 1.

Contact: Kodichi Nwankwo, Foundation Coordinator
American Hotel and Lodging Educational Foundation
1250 Eye Street, NW
Suite 1100
Washington, DC 20005
Phone: 202-289-3134
E-mail: knwankwo@ahlef.org

RAMA SCHOLARSHIP FOR THE AMERICAN DREAM

Schools participating in this program include Bethune-Cookman College, California State Polytechnic University, Cornell University, Florida International University, Georgia State University, Greenville Technical College, Johnson & Wales University, New York University, University of Central Florida, University of Houston, University of South Carolina, and Virginia Polytechnic Institute and State University. The participating schools select the student nominees based upon a set of minimum eligibility criteria which include: enrolled in at least 9 credit hours for the fall and spring semesters, majoring in an undergraduate or graduate hospitality management program, minimum GPA of 2.5, U.S. citizenship or permanent resident, and schools must give preference to students of Asian-Indian descent or other minority groups, as well as JHM employees and their dependents.

Academic Fields/Career Goals: Food Service/Hospitality; Hospitality Management; Recreation, Parks, Leisure Studies; Travel/Tourism.

Award: Scholarship for use in sophomore, junior, senior, or graduate years; not renewable. *Amount:* $500–$3000.

Eligibility Requirements: Applicant must be American Indian/Alaska Native, Asian/Pacific Islander, Black (non-Hispanic), Hispanic; enrolled or expecting to enroll full- or part-time at a two-year institution or university and studying in California, Florida, Georgia, New York, North Carolina, South Carolina, Texas, Virginia. Available to U.S. citizens.

Application Requirements: Application form, essay, financial need analysis. *Deadline:* May 1.

Contact: Kodichi Nwankwo, Foundation Coordinator
American Hotel and Lodging Educational Foundation
1250 Eye Street, NW
Suite 1100
Washington, DC 20005
Phone: 202-289-3134
E-mail: knwankwo@ahlef.org

CALIFORNIA RESTAURANT ASSOCIATION EDUCATIONAL FOUNDATION

http://www.calrest.org/

ACADEMIC SCHOLARSHIP FOR HIGH SCHOOL SENIORS

One-time scholarship awarded to high school seniors to support their education in the restaurant and/or food service industry. Applicants must be citizens of the United States or its territories (American Samoa, Guam, Puerto Rico, and U.S. Virgin Islands).

Academic Fields/Career Goals: Food Service/Hospitality.

Award: Scholarship for use in freshman year; not renewable. *Amount:* up to $2000.

Eligibility Requirements: Applicant must be high school student; planning to enroll or expecting to enroll full-time at a two-year or four-year or technical institution or university and resident of California. Available to U.S. and non-U.S. citizens.

Application Requirements: Application form, essay, interview, recommendations or references, resume, transcript. *Deadline:* April 15.

Contact: Mrs. Kathie Griley, Director, Industry Education
Phone: 800-765-4842 Ext. 2756
E-mail: kgriley@calrest.org

ACADEMIC SCHOLARSHIP FOR UNDERGRADUATE STUDENTS

Scholarships awarded to college students to support their education in the restaurant and food service industry. Minimum 2.75 GPA required. Individuals must be citizens of the United States or its territories (American Samoa, Guam, Puerto Rico, and U.S. Virgin Islands).

Academic Fields/Career Goals: Food Service/Hospitality.

Award: Scholarship for use in freshman, sophomore, junior, or senior years; not renewable.

Eligibility Requirements: Applicant must be enrolled or expecting to enroll full-time at a four-year institution or university and resident of California. Available to U.S. and non-U.S. citizens.

Application Requirements: Application form, essay, interview, recommendations or references, transcript. *Deadline:* March 31.

Contact: Mrs. Kathie Griley, Director, Industry Education
Phone: 800-765-4842 Ext. 2756
E-mail: kgriley@calrest.org

CANFIT

http://www.canfit.org/

CANFIT NUTRITION, PHYSICAL EDUCATION AND CULINARY ARTS SCHOLARSHIP

• *See page 190*

COLORADO RESTAURANT ASSOCIATION

http://www.coloradorestaurant.com/

CRA UNDERGRADUATE SCHOLARSHIPS

Scholarship of $1000 to $2000 for applicants intending to pursue education in the undergraduate level in the field of food service or hospitality and have a GPA of at least 2.75.

Academic Fields/Career Goals: Food Service/Hospitality.

Award: Scholarship for use in freshman, sophomore, junior, or senior years; not renewable. *Number:* 15. *Amount:* $1000–$2000.

Eligibility Requirements: Applicant must be enrolled or expecting to enroll full- or part-time at a four-year institution or university. Available to U.S. and non-U.S. citizens.

Application Requirements: Application form, recommendations or references, resume, transcript. *Deadline:* April 6.

Contact: Mary Mino, President
Phone: 800-522-2972
Fax: 303-830-2973
E-mail: info@coloradorestaurant.com

PROSTART SCHOLARSHIPS

Scholarship of $500 to $1000 for applicants currently in high school and intending to pursue education in the field of food service or hospitality and have a GPA of at least 3.0.

Academic Fields/Career Goals: Food Service/Hospitality.

Award: Scholarship for use in freshman year; not renewable. *Number:* 15. *Amount:* $500–$1000.

Eligibility Requirements: Applicant must be high school student and planning to enroll or expecting to enroll full- or part-time at a four-year institution or university. Available to U.S. and non-U.S. citizens.

Application Requirements: Application form, recommendations or references, resume, transcript. *Deadline:* April 6.

Contact: Mary Mino, President
Phone: 800-522-2972
Fax: 303-830-2973
E-mail: info@coloradorestaurant.com

THE CULINARY TRUST

http://www.theculinarytrust.org/

CULINARY TRUST SCHOLARSHIP PROGRAM FOR CULINARY STUDY AND RESEARCH
• *See page 190*

DECA (DISTRIBUTIVE EDUCATION CLUBS OF AMERICA)

http://www.deca.org/

HARRY A. APPLEGATE SCHOLARSHIP
• *See page 73*

ILLINOIS RESTAURANT ASSOCIATION EDUCATIONAL FOUNDATION

http://www.illinoisrestaurants.org/

ILLINOIS RESTAURANT ASSOCIATION EDUCATIONAL FOUNDATION SCHOLARSHIPS
• *See page 190*

INTERNATIONAL FOOD SERVICE EXECUTIVES ASSOCIATION

http://www.ifsea.com/

INTERNATIONAL FOOD SERVICE EXECUTIVES ASSOCIATION / WORTHY GOAL SCHOLARSHIP FUND

Scholarships to assist individuals in receiving food service, vocational or hospitality training beyond high school. Applicant must be enrolled or accepted as full-time student in an accredited program at an institution of higher education.

Academic Fields/Career Goals: Food Service/Hospitality.

Award: Scholarship for use in freshman, sophomore, junior, senior, graduate, or postgraduate years; not renewable. *Number:* 1–23,000. *Amount:* $1000–$2000.

Eligibility Requirements: Applicant must be enrolled or expecting to enroll full-time at a two-year or four-year or technical institution or university. Available to U.S. and non-U.S. citizens.

Application Requirements: Application form, essay, financial need analysis, financial statement summary, work experience documentation, recommendations or references, transcript. *Deadline:* March 1.

Contact: David Orosz, Chairman, Board of Trustees, Worthy Goal Foundation
International Food Service Executives Association
4435 Colchester Creek Drive
Cumming, GA 30040
Phone: 952-402-9686
Fax: 317-863-0586
E-mail: dave@orosz.us

LES DAMES D'ESCOFFIER INTERNATIONAL, COLORADO CHAPTER

www.lesdamescolorado.org/scholarship

LES DAMES D'ESCOFFIER INTERNATIONAL, COLORADO CHAPTER SCHOLARSHIP
• *See page 94*

MARYLAND RESTAURANT ASSOCIATION EDUCATION FOUNDATION

https://www.marylandrestaurants.com/about.html

THE LETITIA B. CARTER SCHOLARSHIP
• *See page 192*

MARCIA S. HARRIS LEGACY FUND SCHOLARSHIP
• *See page 192*

MISSOURI TRAVEL COUNCIL

http://www.missouritravel.com/

BOB SMITH TOURISM SCHOLARSHIP

One-time award for Missouri resident pursuing hospitality-related major such as hotel/restaurant management or tourism. Applicant must be currently enrolled in an accredited four-year college or university in the state of Missouri. Selection is based on responses to set-forth scholarship criteria.

Academic Fields/Career Goals: Food Service/Hospitality; Hospitality Management; Travel/Tourism.

Award: Scholarship for use in sophomore, junior, or senior years; not renewable. *Number:* 2. *Amount:* $1000.

Eligibility Requirements: Applicant must be enrolled or expecting to enroll full-time at a four-year institution or university; resident of Missouri and studying in Missouri. Available to U.S. citizens.

Application Requirements: Application form, essay. *Deadline:* March 1.

Contact: Mr. Chuck Martin, Executive Director
Missouri Travel Council
1505 East Riverside Drive
Cape Girardeau, MO 63701-2219
Phone: 573-803-3777
E-mail: CMartin@MissouriTravel.com

NATIONAL POULTRY AND FOOD DISTRIBUTORS ASSOCIATION

http://www.npfda.org/

NATIONAL POULTRY AND FOOD DISTRIBUTORS ASSOCIATION SCHOLARSHIP FOUNDATION
• *See page 90*

NATIONAL RESTAURANT ASSOCIATION EDUCATIONAL FOUNDATION

http://www.chooserestaurants.org

NATIONAL RESTAURANT ASSOCIATION EDUCATIONAL FOUNDATION UNDERGRADUATE SCHOLARSHIPS FOR COLLEGE STUDENTS
• *See page 95*

PROFESSIONAL REPS

http://www.professionalreps.com/

HUNGRY TO LEAD SCHOLARSHIP
• *See page 193*

SOUTH CAROLINA RESTAURANT AND LODGING ASSOCIATION

http://www.scrla.org/

SOUTH CAROLINA TOURISM AND HOSPITALITY EDUCATIONAL FOUNDATION SCHOLARSHIPS
• *See page 193*

TEXAS RESTAURANT ASSOCIATION

http://www.restaurantville.com/

W. PRICE, JR. MEMORIAL SCHOLARSHIP
• *See page 193*

UNITED NEGRO COLLEGE FUND

http://www.uncf.org/

NATIONAL BLACK MCDONALD'S OWNERS ASSOCIATION HOSPITALITY SCHOLARS PROGRAM
• *See page 83*

WISCONSIN BAKERS ASSOCIATION (WBA)

http://www.wibakers.com/

ROBERT W. HILLER SCHOLARSHIP FUND
• *See page 193*

WBA SCHOLARSHIP
• *See page 194*

WOMEN CHEFS AND RESTAURATEURS

http://www.womenchefs.org/

FRENCH CULINARY INSTITUTE/ITALIAN CULINARY EXPERIENCE SCHOLARSHIP
• *See page 194*

WOMEN GROCERS OF AMERICA

http://www.nationalgrocers.org/

MARY MACEY SCHOLARSHIP
• *See page 97*

FOREIGN LANGUAGE

ACL/NJCL NATIONAL LATIN EXAM

http://www.nle.org/

NATIONAL LATIN EXAM SCHOLARSHIP
• *See page 169*

ALBERTA HERITAGE SCHOLARSHIP FUND

http://www.alis.alberta.ca/

FELLOWSHIPS FOR FULL-TIME STUDIES IN FRENCH
Awards of between CAN$500 and CAN$1000 per semester to assist Albertans in pursuing postsecondary studies taught in French. Must be Alberta resident, Canadian citizen, or landed immigrant, and plan to register full-time in a postsecondary program in Alberta of at least one semester in length. Must be enrolled in a minimum of three courses per semester which have French as the language of instruction. For additional information and application, see website http://alis.alberta.ca.

Academic Fields/Career Goals: Foreign Language.

Award: Scholarship for use in freshman, sophomore, junior, or senior years; not renewable.

Eligibility Requirements: Applicant must be Canadian citizen; enrolled or expecting to enroll full-time at a two-year or four-year or technical institution or university; resident of Alberta and must have an interest in French language.

Application Requirements: Application form, transcript. *Deadline:* November 15.

ALPHA MU GAMMA, THE NATIONAL COLLEGIATE FOREIGN LANGUAGE SOCIETY

http://www.amgnational.org/

NATIONAL ALPHA MU GAMMA SCHOLARSHIPS
One-time award to student members of Alpha Mu Gamma with a minimum 3.5 GPA, who plan to continue study of a foreign language. Must participate in a national scholarship competition. Apply through local chapter advisers. Freshmen are not eligible. Must submit a copy of Alpha Mu Gamma membership certificate. Can study overseas if part of his/her school program.

Academic Fields/Career Goals: Foreign Language.

Award: Scholarship for use in sophomore, junior, or senior years; not renewable. *Number:* 2–3. *Amount:* $500–$1000.

Eligibility Requirements: Applicant must be enrolled or expecting to enroll full- or part-time at a two-year or four-year institution or university. Applicant or parent of applicant must be member of Alpha Mu Gamma. Available to U.S. and non-U.S. citizens.

Application Requirements: Application form, essay. *Deadline:* February 1.

Contact: Dr. Eileen Wilkinson
Fairfield, CT 06824
E-mail: ewilkinson@fairfield.edu

AMERICAN CLASSICAL LEAGUE/NATIONAL JUNIOR CLASSICAL LEAGUE

http://www.aclclassics.org/

NATIONAL JUNIOR CLASSICAL LEAGUE SCHOLARSHIP
• *See page 169*

AMERICAN INSTITUTE OF POLISH CULTURE INC.

http://www.ampolinstitute.org/

HARRIET IRSAY SCHOLARSHIP GRANT
• *See page 120*

ASSOCIATION OF FORMER INTELLIGENCE OFFICERS

www.afio.com

AFIO UNDERGRADUATE AND GRADUATE SCHOLARSHIPS
• *See page 98*

CULTURAL SERVICES OF THE FRENCH EMBASSY

http://www.frenchculture.org/

TEACHING ASSISTANT PROGRAM IN FRANCE
• *See page 98*

GERMAN ACADEMIC EXCHANGE SERVICE (DAAD)

http://www.daad.org/

DAAD UNIVERSITY SUMMER COURSE GRANT
Scholarships are awarded to full-time degree students of Canadian or U.S. colleges, sophomore/2nd year and higher, for the pursuit of summer courses at universities in Germany. It is open to applicants of any major but there is a prerequisite of at least two years of college-level German (B1) or the equivalent German language fluency. Courses are three to four weeks in duration, take place at many locations in Germany (universities), are taught in German, and topics include German language, literature, current affairs, political science, history, culture, arts, film and media, economics, linguistics, law, translation and interpretation, and test prep for German language proficiency examinations. Accommodations are arranged by the host institution.

Academic Fields/Career Goals: Foreign Language.

Award: Grant for use in sophomore, junior, or senior years; not renewable.

Eligibility Requirements: Applicant must be enrolled or expecting to enroll full-time at a four-year institution or university and must have an interest in German language/culture. Available to U.S. and non-U.S. citizens.

Application Requirements: Application form, essay.

HUB FOUNDATION

https://hub-foundation.org

HUB FOUNDATION SCHOLARSHIPS
• *See page 88*

NATIONAL SECURITY EDUCATION PROGRAM

http://www.iie.org/

NATIONAL SECURITY EDUCATION PROGRAM (NSEP) DAVID L. BOREN UNDERGRADUATE SCHOLARSHIPS
• *See page 119*

ORDER SONS AND DAUGHTERS OF ITALY IN AMERICA

http://www.osia.org/

ORDER SONS AND DAUGHTERS OF ITALY - ITALIAN LANGUAGE SCHOLARSHIP
Scholarships for undergraduate students in their junior or senior year of study who are majoring in Italian language studies. Must be a U.S. citizen of Italian descent. For more details see website http://www.osia.org.

Academic Fields/Career Goals: Foreign Language.

Award: Scholarship for use in junior or senior years; not renewable. *Number:* 1. *Amount:* $4000–$10,000.

Eligibility Requirements: Applicant must be of Italian heritage and enrolled or expecting to enroll full-time at an institution or university. Available to U.S. citizens.

Application Requirements: Application form, application form may be submitted online, essay. *Fee:* $35. *Deadline:* February 28.

Contact: Michelle Ment, Chair, Scholarship, Education and Culture Committee
Order Sons and Daughters of Italy in America
219 E St, NE
Washington, DC 20002
Phone: 202-547-2900
E-mail: scholarships@osia.org

SOCIETY FOR CLASSICAL STUDIES

http://www.classicalstudies.org/

MINORITY STUDENT SUMMER SCHOLARSHIP
• *See page 112*

SONS OF ITALY FOUNDATION

https://www.osia.org/programs/scholarships/

ITALIAN LANGUAGE SCHOLARSHIP
• *See page 169*

STRAIGHTFORWARD MEDIA

http://www.straightforwardmedia.com/

STRAIGHTFORWARD MEDIA LIBERAL ARTS SCHOLARSHIP
• *See page 119*

UNITED NATIONS ASSOCIATION OF CONNECTICUT

http://www.unausa.org

UNITED NATIONS ASSOCIATION OF CONNECTICUT SCHOLARSHIP
• *See page 124*

FUNERAL SERVICES/ MORTUARY SCIENCE

ALABAMA FUNERAL DIRECTORS ASSOCIATION INC.

http://www.alabamafda.org/

ALABAMA FUNERAL DIRECTORS ASSOCIATION SCHOLARSHIP

Two $1000 scholarships available to Alabama residents. Applicant must have been accepted by an accredited mortuary science school and be sponsored by a member of the AFDA. Must maintain a minimum 2.5 GPA. Deadline: no later than 30 days prior to the AFDA mid winter meeting and annual convention.

Academic Fields/Career Goals: Funeral Services/Mortuary Science.

Award: Scholarship for use in freshman, sophomore, junior, or senior years; not renewable. *Number:* 2. *Amount:* $1000.

Eligibility Requirements: Applicant must be enrolled or expecting to enroll full- or part-time at a four-year institution or university and resident of Alabama. Available to U.S. citizens.

Application Requirements: Application form, essay, personal photograph.

Contact: Scholarship Committee
Alabama Funeral Directors Association Inc.
PMB 380
7956 Vaughn Road
Montgomery, AL 36116
Phone: 334-956-8000
Fax: 334-956-8001

MISSOURI FUNERAL DIRECTORS & EMBALMERS ASSOCIATION

http://www.mofuneral.org/

MISSOURI FUNERAL DIRECTORS ASSOCIATION SCHOLARSHIPS

Scholarship to Missouri residents pursuing a career in funeral services or mortuary science.

Academic Fields/Career Goals: Funeral Services/Mortuary Science.

Award: Scholarship for use in freshman, sophomore, junior, or senior years; not renewable. *Number:* up to 5. *Amount:* $300–$600.

Eligibility Requirements: Applicant must be enrolled or expecting to enroll full- or part-time at a technical institution and resident of Missouri. Available to U.S. citizens.

Application Requirements: Application form, recommendations or references, resume. *Deadline:* April 15.

Contact: Don Otto, Executive Director
Missouri Funeral Directors & Embalmers Association
1105 Southwest Boulevard, Suite A
Jefferson City, MO 65109
Phone: 573-635-1661
Fax: 573-635-9494
E-mail: info@mofuneral.org

NATIONAL FUNERAL DIRECTORS AND MORTICIANS ASSOCIATION

http://www.nfdma.com/

NATIONAL FUNERAL DIRECTORS AND MORTICIANS ASSOCIATION SCHOLARSHIP

Awards for high school graduates who have preferably worked in or had one year of apprenticeship in the funeral home business.

Academic Fields/Career Goals: Funeral Services/Mortuary Science.

Award: Scholarship for use in freshman year; not renewable. *Number:* 1. *Amount:* $1500.

Eligibility Requirements: Applicant must be high school student and planning to enroll or expecting to enroll full- or part-time at a four-year institution or university. Available to U.S. citizens.

Application Requirements: Application form, recommendations or references, resume, test scores. *Deadline:* April 15.

Contact: Eva Cranford, Scholarship Coordinator
Phone: 718-625-4656
E-mail: lladyc23@aol.com

THE ORDER OF THE GOLDEN RULE FOUNDATION

http://www.ogr.org/charitable-foundation

ORDER OF THE GOLDEN RULE FOUNDATION AWARDS OF EXCELLENCE SCHOLARSHIP PROGRAM

One-time scholarship for mortuary science students to prepare for a career in funeral service. Must be enrolled in a mortuary science degree program at an accredited mortuary school, have a minimum 3.0 GPA, commit to working at an independently owned funeral home, and be scheduled to graduate within this calendar year.

Academic Fields/Career Goals: Funeral Services/Mortuary Science.

Award: Scholarship for use in junior or senior years; not renewable. *Number:* 2. *Amount:* $2000–$3500.

Eligibility Requirements: Applicant must be enrolled or expecting to enroll full- or part-time at a two-year or four-year or technical institution or university. Available to U.S. and non-U.S. citizens.

Application Requirements: Application form, application form may be submitted online (https://iogr.memberclicks.net/index.php?option=com_mc&view=mc&mcid=form_258644), community service, essay, transcript. *Deadline:* March 1.

Contact: Jessica Smith, Assistant Executive Director
The Order of the Golden Rule Foundation
9101 Burnet Road
Suite 120
Austin, TX 78758
Phone: 800-637-8030
Fax: 512-334-5514
E-mail: jsmith@ogr.org

WALLACE S. AND WILMA K. LAUGHLIN FOUNDATION TRUST

http://www.nefda.org/

SWANSON SCHOLARSHIP

Scholarship for a Nebraska student entering the mortuary science program at a Kansas City community college. Must be a US citizen, a high school graduate and have completed Nebraska pre-mortuary science hours. Scholarship value and number of awards varies annually.

Academic Fields/Career Goals: Funeral Services/Mortuary Science.

Award: Scholarship for use in junior or senior years; not renewable. *Number:* 1–10. *Amount:* $1000–$10,000.

Eligibility Requirements: Applicant must be enrolled or expecting to enroll full-time at a two-year institution and resident of Nebraska. Available to U.S. citizens.

Application Requirements: Application form, financial need analysis, interview. *Deadline:* June 30.

Contact: Craig Draucker, Chairman
Wallace S. and Wilma K. Laughlin Foundation Trust
PO Box 10
521 First Street
Milford, NE 68405
Phone: 402-761-2217
E-mail: Staff@nefda.org

GEMOLOGY

AMERICAN INDIAN SCIENCE AND ENGINEERING SOCIETY

http://www.aises.org/

A.T. ANDERSON MEMORIAL SCHOLARSHIP PROGRAM
• *See page 105*

ASSOCIATION FOR WOMEN GEOSCIENTISTS (AWG)

http://www.awg.org/

AWG ETHNIC MINORITY SCHOLARSHIP
• *See page 200*

AWG MARIA LUISA CRAWFORD FIELD CAMP SCHOLARSHIP
• *See page 111*

LONE STAR RISING CAREER SCHOLARSHIP
• *See page 200*

OSAGE CHAPTER UNDERGRADUATE SERVICE SCHOLARSHIP
• *See page 112*

BHW GROUP

https://thebhwgroup.com/

BHW WOMEN IN STEM SCHOLARSHIP
• *See page 107*

STRAIGHT NORTH

https://www.straightnorth.com/

STRAIGHT NORTH STEM SCHOLARSHIP
• *See page 81*

GEOGRAPHY

AMERICAN ASSOCIATION OF GEOGRAPHERS

http://www.aag.org/

DARREL HESS COMMUNITY COLLEGE GEOGRAPHY SCHOLARSHIPS

Two $1,000 scholarships will be awarded to students from community colleges, junior colleges, city colleges, or similar two-year educational institutions who will be transferring as geography majors to four year colleges and universities.

Academic Fields/Career Goals: Geography.
Award: Grant for use in junior year; not renewable. *Number:* 2–4. *Amount:* $1000.
Eligibility Requirements: Applicant must be enrolled or expecting to enroll full-time at a two-year institution. Available to U.S. and non-U.S. citizens.
Application Requirements: Application form, essay. *Deadline:* December 31.

Contact: Ms. Candida Mannozzi, Deputy Director for Operations
American Association of Geographers
Association of American Geographers
1710 16th Street, NW
Washington, DC 20009
Phone: 202-234-1450
E-mail: grantsawards@aag.org

AMERICAN INDIAN SCIENCE AND ENGINEERING SOCIETY

http://www.aises.org/

A.T. ANDERSON MEMORIAL SCHOLARSHIP PROGRAM
• *See page 105*

ASSOCIATION FOR WOMEN GEOSCIENTISTS (AWG)

http://www.awg.org/

AWG ETHNIC MINORITY SCHOLARSHIP
• *See page 200*

AWG SALT LAKE CHAPTER (SLC) RESEARCH SCHOLARSHIP
• *See page 111*

OSAGE CHAPTER UNDERGRADUATE SERVICE SCHOLARSHIP
• *See page 112*

ASSOCIATION OF STATE DAM SAFETY OFFICIALS (ASDSO)

http://www.DamSafety.org

ASSOCIATION OF STATE DAM SAFETY OFFICIALS (ASDSO) SENIOR UNDERGRADUATE SCHOLARSHIP
• *See page 140*

BHW GROUP

https://thebhwgroup.com/

BHW WOMEN IN STEM SCHOLARSHIP
• *See page 107*

BROWN AND CALDWELL

http://www.brownandcaldwell.com

ECKENFELDER SCHOLARSHIP
• *See page 141*

MINORITY SCHOLARSHIP PROGRAM
• *See page 141*

GAMMA THETA UPSILON-INTERNATIONAL GEOGRAPHIC HONOR SOCIETY

https://gammathetaupsilon.org/

THE BUZZARD UNDERGRADUATE AND GRADUATE SCHOLARSHIPS

Award is granted to a student who is a Gamma Theta Upsilon member, majoring in geography, will be a senior undergraduate and who has been accepted into a graduate program in geography.

Academic Fields/Career Goals: Geography.

Award: Scholarship for use in senior or graduate years; not renewable. *Number:* 2. *Amount:* $1000.

Eligibility Requirements: Applicant must be enrolled or expecting to enroll full-time at an institution or university. Applicant or parent of applicant must be member of Gamma Theta Upsilon. Available to U.S. and non-U.S. citizens.

Application Requirements: Application form, essay. *Deadline:* June 1.

Contact: Dr. Harry Wilson, First Vice President
Gamma Theta Upsilon-International Geographic Honor Society
525 S. Main St.
Ohio Northern University
Ada, OH 45810
Phone: 419-772-2608
Fax: 419-772-2593
E-mail: h-wilson.1@onu.edu

THE LAND CONSERVANCY OF NEW JERSEY

http://www.tlc-nj.org/

ROGERS FAMILY SCHOLARSHIP
• *See page 143*

NASA IDAHO SPACE GRANT CONSORTIUM

http://www.idahospacegrant.org

NASA IDAHO SPACE GRANT CONSORTIUM SCHOLARSHIP PROGRAM
• *See page 109*

SCARLETT FAMILY FOUNDATION SCHOLARSHIP PROGRAM

http://www.scarlettfoundation.org/

SCHOLARSHIP FOR STUDENTS PURSUING A BUSINESS OR STEM DEGREE
• *See page 80*

UNITED NEGRO COLLEGE FUND

http://www.uncf.org/

LEIDOS STEM SCHOLARSHIP
• *See page 96*

GRAPHICS/GRAPHIC ARTS/ PRINTING

AUTOMOTIVE WOMEN'S ALLIANCE FOUNDATION

http://awafoundation.org/index.php

AUTOMOTIVE WOMEN'S ALLIANCE FOUNDATION SCHOLARSHIPS
• *See page 71*

CCNMA: LATINO JOURNALISTS OF CALIFORNIA

http://www.ccnma.org/

CCNMA SCHOLARSHIPS
• *See page 171*

CONGRESSIONAL BLACK CAUCUS FOUNDATION, INC.

http://www.cbcfinc.org/

CBC SPOUSES VISUAL ARTS SCHOLARSHIP
• *See page 120*

ELECTRONIC DOCUMENT SYSTEMS FOUNDATION

http://www.edsf.org/

ANDY AND JULIE PLATA HONORARY SCHOLARSHIP

This scholarship is provided to a student in a graphic arts related program who displays an entrepreneurial spirit and is pursuing a career in the graphic communications / printing industry.

Academic Fields/Career Goals: Graphics/Graphic Arts/Printing.

Award: Scholarship for use in freshman, sophomore, junior, senior, or graduate years; not renewable. *Number:* 1. *Amount:* $2000.

Eligibility Requirements: Applicant must be enrolled or expecting to enroll full-time at a two-year or four-year or technical institution or university. Available to U.S. and non-U.S. citizens.

Application Requirements: Application form, community service, essay. *Deadline:* May 1.

Contact: Ms. Brenda Kai, Executive Director
Phone: 817-849-1145
E-mail: brenda.kai@edsf.org

EDSF BOARD OF DIRECTORS SCHOLARSHIPS

Scholarships awarded to full-time students who are committed to pursuing a career in the document management and graphic communications marketplace. The career choices are very broad and include, but are not limited to, computer science and engineering, graphic design, graphic communications, media communications, and business. Preference is given to college-level juniors, seniors and advanced degree students. Minimum 3.0 GPA required.

Academic Fields/Career Goals: Graphics/Graphic Arts/Printing.

Award: Scholarship for use in freshman, sophomore, junior, senior, or graduate years; not renewable. *Number:* 1–40. *Amount:* $1000–$5000.

Eligibility Requirements: Applicant must be enrolled or expecting to enroll full-time at a two-year or four-year institution or university. Available to U.S. and non-U.S. citizens.

Application Requirements: Application form, community service, essay. *Deadline:* May 1.

Contact: Ms. Brenda Kai, Executive Director
Phone: 817-849-1145
E-mail: brenda.kai@edsf.org

HOODS MEMORIAL SCHOLARSHIP

$2000 award for students whose academic focus includes all document management and graphic communications careers with special consideration given to students interested in marketing and public relations. Minimum 3.0 GPA required.

Academic Fields/Career Goals: Graphics/Graphic Arts/Printing.

Award: Scholarship for use in freshman, sophomore, junior, senior, or graduate years; not renewable. *Number:* 1. *Amount:* $2000.

Eligibility Requirements: Applicant must be enrolled or expecting to enroll full-time at a two-year or four-year institution or university. Available to U.S. and non-U.S. citizens.

Application Requirements: Application form, community service, essay. *Deadline:* May 1.

Contact: Ms. Brenda Kai, Executive Director
Phone: 817-849-1145
E-mail: brenda.kai@edsf.org

LYNDA BABOYIAN MEMORIAL SCHOLARSHIP
• *See page 147*

GOLDEN KEY INTERNATIONAL HONOUR SOCIETY

http://www.goldenkey.org/

VISUAL AND PERFORMING ARTS ACHIEVEMENT AWARDS
• See page 121

IOWA NEWSPAPER ASSOCIATION

https://inanews.com/

WOODWARD SCHOLARSHIP
• See page 172

THE LAGRANT FOUNDATION

http://www.lagrantfoundation.org/

LAGRANT FOUNDATION SCHOLARSHIP FOR GRADUATES
• See page 85

LAGRANT FOUNDATION SCHOLARSHIP FOR UNDERGRADUATES
• See page 85

NATIONAL ASSOCIATION OF HISPANIC JOURNALISTS (NAHJ)

http://www.nahj.org/

NEWHOUSE SCHOLARSHIP PROGRAM
Two-year $5000 annually award for students who are pursuing careers in the newspaper industry as reporters, editors, graphic artists, or photojournalists. Recipient is expected to participate in summer internship at a Newhouse newspaper following their junior year. Students must submit resume and writing samples.

Academic Fields/Career Goals: Graphics/Graphic Arts/Printing; Journalism; Photojournalism/Photography.

Award: Scholarship for use in junior or senior years; not renewable. *Amount:* $5000.

Eligibility Requirements: Applicant must be enrolled or expecting to enroll full-time at a four-year institution or university. Available to U.S. citizens.

Application Requirements: Application form, essay, financial need analysis, recommendations or references, resume, transcript, work samples. *Deadline:* March 31.

Contact: Alberto Mendoza, Executive Director
Phone: 202-662-7145
E-mail: abmendoza@nahj.org

NEBRASKA PRESS ASSOCIATION

http://www.nebpress.com/

NEBRASKA PRESS ASSOCIATION FOUNDATION SCHOLARSHIP
• See page 86

NEW ENGLAND PRINTING AND PUBLISHING COUNCIL

http://www.gcsfne.org/

GRAPHIC COMMUNICATIONS SCHOLARSHIP FUND OF NEW ENGLAND
Applicants must be residents of New England who have been admitted to, or are currently attending, an accredited two-year vocational or technical college or a four-year college or university that offers a degree program related to printing or graphic communications. Renewable for up to four years if student maintains 2.5 GPA.

Academic Fields/Career Goals: Graphics/Graphic Arts/Printing.

Award: Scholarship for use in freshman, sophomore, junior, or senior years; renewable. *Number:* 16–35. *Amount:* $1350–$2500.

Eligibility Requirements: Applicant must be enrolled or expecting to enroll full-time at a two-year or four-year or technical institution or university and resident of Connecticut, Maine, Massachusetts, New Hampshire, Rhode Island, Vermont. Available to U.S. citizens.

Application Requirements: Application form, financial need analysis. *Deadline:* June 15.

Contact: Tad Parker, Scholarship Administrator
New England Printing and Publishing Council
5 Crystal Pond Road
Southboro, MA 01772
E-mail: chair@gcsfne.org

PRINT AND GRAPHIC SCHOLARSHIP FOUNDATION

http://www.printing.org/

PRINT AND GRAPHICS SCHOLARSHIPS FOUNDATION
• See page 174

PRINTING INDUSTRY MIDWEST EDUCATION FOUDNATION

http://www.pimw.org/scholarships

PRINTING INDUSTRY MIDWEST EDUCATION FOUNDATION SCHOLARSHIP FUND
• See page 175

QUALITY BATH

www.qualitybath.com

QUALITYBATH.COM SCHOLARSHIP PROGRAM
• See page 120

RHODE ISLAND FOUNDATION

http://www.rifoundation.org/

J. D. EDSAL SCHOLARSHIP
• See page 87

ROBERT H. MOLLOHAN FAMILY CHARITABLE FOUNDATION, INC.

http://www.mollohanfoundation.org/

MARY OLIVE EDDY JONES ART SCHOLARSHIP
• See page 122

SUPPORT CREATIVITY

http://wesupportcreativity.org

SUPPORT CREATIVITY SCHOLARSHIP
• See page 117

TAG AND LABEL MANUFACTURERS INSTITUTE, INC.

http://www.tlmi.com/

TLMI 2 YEAR COLLEGE DEGREE SCHOLARSHIP PROGRAM
• See page 262

TLMI 4 YEAR COLLEGE DEGREE SCHOLARSHIP PROGRAM
• *See page 262*

VECTORWORKS, INC.

http://www.vectorworks.net

VECTORWORKS DESIGN SCHOLARSHIP
• *See page 117*

HEALTH ADMINISTRATION

ALBERTA HERITAGE SCHOLARSHIP FUND

http://www.alis.alberta.ca/

ABORIGINAL HEALTH CAREERS BURSARY
• *See page 139*

ALICE L. HALTOM EDUCATIONAL FUND

http://www.alhef.org/

ALICE L. HALTOM EDUCATIONAL FUND
• *See page 145*

AMERICAN LEGION AUXILIARY DEPARTMENT OF COLORADO

http://www.alacolorado.com

AMERICAN LEGION AUXILIARY DEPARTMENT OF COLORADO PAST PRESIDENTS' PARLEY HEALTH CARE PROFESSIONAL SCHOLARSHIPNURSES SCHOLARSHIP
• *See page 125*

ASRT FOUNDATION

https://foundation.asrt.org/

JERMAN-CAHOON STUDENT SCHOLARSHIP

Merit scholarship for certificate or undergraduate students. Must have completed at least one semester in the radiological sciences to apply (does not include prerequisites). Financial need is a factor. Requirements include 3.0 GPA, recommendation and several short answer essays.

Academic Fields/Career Goals: Health Administration; Health and Medical Sciences; Health Information Management/Technology; Oncology; Radiology.

Award: Scholarship for use in sophomore or junior years; not renewable. *Number:* 8. *Amount:* $2500.

Eligibility Requirements: Applicant must be enrolled or expecting to enroll full- or part-time at a two-year or technical institution or university. Available to U.S. citizens.

Application Requirements: Application form, application form may be submitted online, essay, financial need analysis. *Deadline:* February 1.

Contact: Carol Kennedy, Foundation Director
ASRT Foundation
ASRT Foundation
15000 Central Ave. SE
Albuquerque, NM 87123-3909
Phone: 800-444-2778
Fax: 505-298-5063
E-mail: foundation@asrt.org

PROFESSIONAL ADVANCEMENT SCHOLARSHIP

Open to ASRT members only who are certificate, undergraduate or graduate students pursuing any degree or certificate intended to further a career in the radiologic sciences profession. One of the following must also be true: applicant holds an unrestricted state license, is registered by the American Registry of Radiologic Technologists, or registered with an equivalent certifying body.

Academic Fields/Career Goals: Health Administration; Health and Medical Sciences; Health Information Management/Technology; Oncology; Radiology.

Award: Scholarship for use in freshman, sophomore, junior, senior, graduate, or postgraduate years; not renewable. *Number:* 7. *Amount:* $1200–$2500.

Eligibility Requirements: Applicant must be enrolled or expecting to enroll full- or part-time at a two-year or technical institution or university. Applicant or parent of applicant must be member of American Society of Radiologic Technologists. Available to U.S. citizens.

Application Requirements: Application form, application form may be submitted online, essay, financial need analysis. *Deadline:* February 1.

Contact: Carol Kennedy, Foundation Director
ASRT Foundation
ASRT Foundation
15000 Central Ave. SE
Albuquerque, NM 87123-3909
Phone: 800-444-2778
Fax: 505-298-5063
E-mail: foundation@asrt.org

ROYCE OSBORN MINORITY STUDENT SCHOLARSHIP

Minority scholarship for certificate or undergraduate students. Must have completed at least one semester in the radiological sciences to apply (does not include prerequisites). Financial need is a factor. Requirements include 3.0 GPA, recommendation and several short answer essays.

Academic Fields/Career Goals: Health Administration; Health and Medical Sciences; Health Information Management/Technology; Radiology.

Award: Scholarship for use in sophomore or junior years; not renewable. *Number:* 5. *Amount:* $4000.

Eligibility Requirements: Applicant must be American Indian/Alaska Native, Asian/Pacific Islander, Black (non-Hispanic), Hispanic and enrolled or expecting to enroll full- or part-time at a two-year or technical institution or university. Applicant or parent of applicant must be member of American Society of Radiologic Technologists. Available to U.S. citizens.

Application Requirements: Application form, application form may be submitted online, essay, financial need analysis. *Deadline:* February 1.

Contact: Carol Kennedy, Foundation Director
ASRT Foundation
ASRT Foundation
15000 Central Ave. SE
Albuquerque, NM 87123-3909
Phone: 800-444-2778
Fax: 505-298-5063
E-mail: foundation@asrt.org

ASSISTANCE LEAGUE OF THE TRIANGLE AREA

HEALTH CARE PROFESSION SCHOLARSHIP
• *See page 195*

AVACARE MEDICAL

https://avacaremedical.com

AVACARE MEDICAL SCHOLARSHIP
• *See page 100*

BETHESDA LUTHERAN COMMUNITIES

http://www.bethesdalutherancommunities.org/
scholarships

DEVELOPMENTAL DISABILITIES SCHOLASTIC ACHIEVEMENT SCHOLARSHIP FOR COLLEGE STUDENTS WHO ARE LUTHERAN
• *See page 195*

BHW GROUP

https://thebhwgroup.com/

BHW WOMEN IN STEM SCHOLARSHIP
• *See page 107*

CONTINENTAL SOCIETY, DAUGHTERS OF INDIAN WARS

http://www.csdiw.org/

CONTINENTAL SOCIETY, DAUGHTERS OF INDIAN WARS SCHOLARSHIP
• *See page 188*

GRAND RAPIDS COMMUNITY FOUNDATION

http://www.grfoundation.org/

HARRY J. MORRIS, JR. EMERGENCY SERVICES SCHOLARSHIP
• *See page 261*

HEALTHCARE INFORMATION AND MANAGEMENT SYSTEMS SOCIETY FOUNDATION

http://www.himss.org/

HIMSS FOUNDATION SCHOLARSHIP PROGRAM

The Foundation Scholarships can be awarded to undergraduate, Master's or Ph.D. students enrolled in a program related to the healthcare information and management systems field. In addition to the $5000 scholarship award, the winner also receives an all-expense paid trip to the Annual HIMSS Conference and Exhibition. Applicants must be member in good standing of HIMS. Primary occupation must be that of student in an accredited program related to the healthcare information or management systems field. The specific degree program is not a critical factor, although it is expected that programs similar to those in industrial engineering, operations research, healthcare informatics, computer science and information systems, mathematics, and quantitative programs in business administration and hospital administration will predominate. Undergraduate applicants must be at least a first-term junior when the scholarship is awarded. Previous Foundation Scholarship winners are ineligible.

Academic Fields/Career Goals: Health Administration; Health and Medical Sciences; Health Information Management/Technology; Science, Technology, and Society.

Award: Scholarship for use in junior, senior, graduate, or postgraduate years; not renewable. *Number:* 4–12. *Amount:* $5000.

Eligibility Requirements: Applicant must be enrolled or expecting to enroll full-time at a four-year institution or university. Applicant or parent of applicant must be member of Healthcare Information and Management Systems Society. Available to U.S. and non-U.S. citizens.

Application Requirements: Application form, community service, essay, recommendations or references, resume, transcript. *Deadline:* October 15.

Contact: Helen Figge, Senior Director, Professional Development, Career Services
Healthcare Information and Management Systems Society Foundation
33 West Monroe Street, Suite 1700
Chicago, IL 60603
Phone: 312-915-9548
E-mail: hfigge@himss.org

HEALTH RESEARCH COUNCIL OF NEW ZEALAND

https://gateway.hrc.govt.nz/

PACIFIC HEALTH WORKFORCE AWARD

Intended to support students studying towards a health or health-related qualification. The eligible courses of study are: health, health administration, or a recognized qualification aligned with the Pacific Island. Priority given to management training, medical, and nursing students. Applicants should be New Zealand citizens or hold residency in New Zealand at the time of application and be of Pacific Island descent. The value of the awards and dollar value will vary and for one year of study.

Academic Fields/Career Goals: Health Administration; Health and Medical Sciences; Health Information Management/Technology; Nursing.

Award: Scholarship for use in freshman, sophomore, junior, senior, graduate, or postgraduate years; not renewable.

Eligibility Requirements: Applicant must be New Zealander citizen; Asian/Pacific Islander and enrolled or expecting to enroll full-time at a two-year or four-year institution or university. Available to citizens of countries other than the U.S. or Canada.

Application Requirements: Application form, driver's license, essay, financial need analysis, recommendations or references, transcript. *Deadline:* October 10.

Contact: Ngamau Wichman Tou, Manager, Pacific Health Research
Phone: 64 9 3035255
Fax: 64 9 377 9988
E-mail: info@hrc.govt.nz

PACIFIC MENTAL HEALTH WORK FORCE AWARD

Intended to provide one year of support for students studying towards a mental health or mental health-related qualification. Eligible courses of study include: nursing, psychology, health, health administration or a recognized qualification aligned with the Pacific Island mental health priority areas. Applicants should be New Zealand citizens or hold residency in New Zealand at the time of application and be of Pacific Island descent.

Academic Fields/Career Goals: Health Administration; Health and Medical Sciences; Health Information Management/Technology; Nursing; Psychology.

Award: Scholarship for use in freshman, sophomore, junior, senior, graduate, or postgraduate years; not renewable.

Eligibility Requirements: Applicant must be New Zealander citizen; Asian/Pacific Islander and enrolled or expecting to enroll full-time at a two-year or four-year institution or university. Available to citizens of countries other than the U.S. or Canada.

Application Requirements: Application form, essay, financial need analysis, recommendations or references, resume, transcript. *Deadline:* October 10.

Contact: Ngamau Wichman Tou, Manager, Pacific Health Research
Phone: 64 9 3035255
Fax: 64 9 377 9988
E-mail: info@hrc.govt.nz

INSTITUTE OF INDUSTRIAL ENGINEERS

https://www.iise.org/

SOCIETY FOR HEALTH SYSTEMS SCHOLARSHIP
• *See page 241*

INTERMOUNTAIN MEDICAL IMAGING

https://www.aboutimi.com/

INTERMOUNTAIN MEDICAL IMAGING SCHOLARSHIP
• *See page 125*

MEDICAL SCRUBS COLLECTION

http://medicalscrubscollection.com

MEDICAL SCRUBS COLLECTION SCHOLARSHIP
• *See page 104*

THE NATIONAL SOCIETY OF THE COLONIAL DAMES OF AMERICA

http://www.nscda.org/

AMERICAN INDIAN NURSE SCHOLARSHIP PROGRAM
Since 1928 The National Society of The Colonial Dames of America has provided a small number of scholarship awards to assist students of American Indian heritage who are pursuing degrees in nursing or in the field of health care and health education. Eligible students receive $1,500 per semester and the money is to be used strictly for tuition, books or fees applicable to the student's approved program. The grant is sent to the school and credited to the student's account. Once a student is accepted, he or she may re-apply for continued funds each semester as long as the student remains in academic good standing.

Academic Fields/Career Goals: Health Administration; Nursing.

Award: Scholarship for use in freshman, sophomore, junior, senior, graduate, or postgraduate years; renewable. *Number:* 2. *Amount:* $500–$1500.

Eligibility Requirements: Applicant must be American Indian/Alaska Native and enrolled or expecting to enroll full-time at a two-year or four-year or technical institution or university. Available to U.S. citizens.

Application Requirements: Application form, autobiography, driver's license, financial need analysis, personal photograph. *Deadline:* June 1.

Contact: NSCDA Membership Manager
Phone: 202-337-2288 Ext. 227
E-mail: dames@dumbartonhouse.org

NEW ENGLAND EMPLOYEE BENEFITS COUNCIL

http://www.neebc.org/

NEW ENGLAND EMPLOYEE BENEFITS COUNCIL SCHOLARSHIP PROGRAM
• *See page 78*

NOVUS BIOLOGICALS, LLC

https://www.novusbio.com

NOVUS BIOLOGICALS SCHOLARSHIP PROGRAM
• *See page 101*

R&D SYSTEMS SCHOLARSHIP
• *See page 101*

TOCRIS BIOSCIENCE SCHOLARSHIP
• *See page 102*

SCARLETT FAMILY FOUNDATION SCHOLARSHIP PROGRAM

http://www.scarlettfoundation.org/

SCHOLARSHIP FOR STUDENTS PURSUING A BUSINESS OR STEM DEGREE
• *See page 80*

STRAIGHTFORWARD MEDIA

http://www.straightforwardmedia.com/

STRAIGHTFORWARD MEDIA MEDICAL PROFESSIONS SCHOLARSHIP
• *See page 198*

UNITED NEGRO COLLEGE FUND

http://www.uncf.org/

HCN/APRICITY RESOURCES SCHOLARS PROGRAM
• *See page 83*

HEALTH AND MEDICAL SCIENCES

ACLS CERTIFICATION INSTITUTE

https://acls.com

MEDICAL SCHOOL SCHOLARSHIP
• *See page 194*

ALBERTA HERITAGE SCHOLARSHIP FUND

http://www.alis.alberta.ca/

ABORIGINAL HEALTH CAREERS BURSARY
• *See page 139*

NORTHERN ALBERTA DEVELOPMENT COUNCIL BURSARY
• *See page 205*

ALPENA REGIONAL MEDICAL CENTER

http://www.alpenaregionalmedicalcenter.org/

THELMA ORR MEMORIAL SCHOLARSHIP
Two $1500 scholarships for students pursuing a course of study related to human medicine at any state accredited Michigan college or university.

Academic Fields/Career Goals: Health and Medical Sciences.

Award: Scholarship for use in freshman, sophomore, junior, or senior years; not renewable. *Number:* 2. *Amount:* $1500.

Eligibility Requirements: Applicant must be enrolled or expecting to enroll full-time at a four-year institution or university; resident of Michigan and studying in Michigan. Available to U.S. citizens.

Application Requirements: Application form. *Deadline:* April 15.

Contact: Marlene Pear, Director, Voluntary Services
Phone: 989-356-7351
E-mail: info@agh.org

AMERICAN INDIAN SCIENCE AND ENGINEERING SOCIETY

http://www.aises.org/

A.T. ANDERSON MEMORIAL SCHOLARSHIP PROGRAM
• *See page 105*

AMERICAN LEGION AUXILIARY DEPARTMENT OF ARIZONA

http://wwwaladeptaz.org

AMERICAN LEGION AUXILIARY DEPARTMENT OF ARIZONA HEALTH CARE OCCUPATION SCHOLARSHIPS

Award for Arizona residents enrolled at an institution in Arizona that awards degrees or certificates in health occupations. Preference given to an immediate family member of a veteran. Must be a U.S. citizen and Arizona resident for at least one year.

Academic Fields/Career Goals: Health and Medical Sciences.

Award: Scholarship for use in freshman, sophomore, junior, senior, graduate, or postgraduate years; not renewable. *Amount:* $500.

Eligibility Requirements: Applicant must be age 17-99; enrolled or expecting to enroll full- or part-time at a two-year or four-year or technical institution or university; resident of Arizona and studying in Arizona. Available to U.S. citizens.

Application Requirements: Application form, essay, financial need analysis, personal photograph. *Deadline:* May 15.

Contact: Mrs. Barbara Matteson, Department Secretary and Treasurer
American Legion Auxiliary Department of Arizona
4701 North 19th Avenue, Suite 100
Phoenix, AZ 85015-3727
Phone: 602-241-1080
E-mail: secretary@aladeptaz.org

AMERICAN LEGION AUXILIARY DEPARTMENT OF COLORADO

http://www.alacolorado.com

AMERICAN LEGION AUXILIARY DEPARTMENT OF COLORADO PAST PRESIDENTS' PARLEY HEALTH CARE PROFESSIONAL SCHOLARSHIPNURSES SCHOLARSHIP

• *See page 125*

AMERICAN LEGION AUXILIARY DEPARTMENT OF MAINE

http://www.mainelegion.org/

AMERICAN LEGION AUXILIARY DEPARTMENT OF MAINE PAST PRESIDENTS' PARLEY NURSES SCHOLARSHIP

One-time award for child, grandchild, sister, or brother of veteran. Must be resident of Maine and wishing to continue education at accredited school in medical field. Must submit photo, doctor's statement, and evidence of civic activity. Minimum 3.5 GPA required.

Academic Fields/Career Goals: Health and Medical Sciences; Nursing.

Award: Scholarship for use in freshman, sophomore, junior, or senior years; not renewable. *Number:* 1. *Amount:* $300.

Eligibility Requirements: Applicant must be age 18 and over; enrolled or expecting to enroll full-time at a two-year or four-year or technical institution or university and resident of Maine. Applicant or parent of applicant must have employment or volunteer experience in community service. Available to U.S. citizens. Applicant or parent must meet one or more of the following requirements: general military experience; retired from active duty; disabled or killed as a result of military service; prisoner of war; or missing in action.

Application Requirements: Application form, doctor's statement, personal photograph, recommendations or references, transcript. *Deadline:* March 31.

Contact: Mary Wells, Education Chairman
Phone: 207-532-6007
E-mail: aladeptsecme@verizon.net

AMERICAN LEGION AUXILIARY DEPARTMENT OF MICHIGAN

http://www.michalaux.org/

AMERICAN LEGION AUXILIARY DEPARTMENT OF MICHIGAN MEDICAL CAREER SCHOLARSHIP

Award for training in Michigan as registered nurse, licensed practical nurse, physical therapist, respiratory therapist, or in any medical career. Must be child, grandchild, great-grandchild, wife, or widow of honorably discharged or deceased veteran who has served during the eligibility dates for American Legion membership. Must be Michigan resident attending a Michigan school.

Academic Fields/Career Goals: Health and Medical Sciences; Nursing; Therapy/Rehabilitation.

Award: Scholarship for use in freshman year; not renewable. *Number:* 10–20. *Amount:* $500.

Eligibility Requirements: Applicant must be enrolled or expecting to enroll full-time at a two-year or technical institution or university; resident of Massachusetts and studying in Michigan. Available to U.S. citizens. Applicant must have general military experience.

Application Requirements: Application form, financial need analysis. *Deadline:* March 15.

Contact: Scholarship Coordinator
American Legion Auxiliary Department of Michigan
212 North Verlinden Avenue, Suite B
Lansing, MI 48915
Phone: 517-267-8809 Ext. 21
Fax: 517-371-3698
E-mail: info@michalaux.org

AMERICAN LEGION AUXILIARY DEPARTMENT OF MINNESOTA

http://www.mnala.org

AMERICAN LEGION AUXILIARY DEPARTMENT OF MINNESOTA PAST PRESIDENTS' PARLEY HEALTH CARE SCHOLARSHIP

One-time $1000 award for American Legion Auxiliary Department of Minnesota member for at least three years who is needy and deserving, to begin or continue education in any phase of the health care field. Must be a Minnesota resident, attend a vocational or postsecondary institution and maintain at least a C average in school.

Academic Fields/Career Goals: Health and Medical Sciences.

Award: Scholarship for use in freshman, sophomore, junior, or senior years; not renewable. *Number:* 1–10. *Amount:* $1000.

Eligibility Requirements: Applicant must be enrolled or expecting to enroll full-time at a two-year or four-year or technical institution or university; resident of Minnesota and studying in Minnesota. Applicant or parent of applicant must be member of American Legion or Auxiliary. Available to U.S. citizens.

Application Requirements: Application form, financial need analysis. *Deadline:* March 15.

Contact: Sandie Deutsch, Executive Secretary
American Legion Auxiliary Department of Minnesota
State Veterans Service Building
20 West 12th Street, Room 314
St. Paul, MN 55155
Phone: 651-224-7634

AMERICAN LEGION AUXILIARY DEPARTMENT OF TEXAS

http://www.alatexas.org/

AMERICAN LEGION AUXILIARY DEPARTMENT OF TEXAS PAST PRESIDENTS' PARLEY MEDICAL SCHOLARSHIP

Scholarships available for full-time students pursuing studies in human health care. Must be a resident of Texas. Must be a veteran or child, grandchild, great grandchild of a veteran who served in the Armed Forces during period of eligibility.

Academic Fields/Career Goals: Health and Medical Sciences.

Award: Scholarship for use in freshman, sophomore, junior, or senior years; not renewable. *Number:* 1–10. *Amount:* $1000.

Eligibility Requirements: Applicant must be enrolled or expecting to enroll full-time at a two-year or four-year or technical institution or university and resident of Texas. Available to U.S. citizens. Applicant must have general military experience.

Application Requirements: Application form, community service, financial need analysis, letter stating qualifications and intentions, recommendations or references, transcript. *Deadline:* June 1.

Contact: Paula Raney, State Secretary
  Phone: 512-476-7278
  Fax: 512-482-8391
  E-mail: alatexas@txlegion.org

AMERICAN LEGION DEPARTMENT OF MARYLAND

http://www.mdlegion.org/

AMERICAN LEGION DEPARTMENT OF MARYLAND MATH-SCIENCE SCHOLARSHIP
• *See page 99*

AMERICAN PHYSICAL THERAPY ASSOCIATION

http://www.apta.org/honorsawards

MARY MCMILLAN SCHOLARSHIP AWARD
• *See page 207*

AMERICAN PHYSIOLOGICAL SOCIETY

https://www.physiology.org/

BARBARA A. HORWITZ AND JOHN M. HOROWITZ UNDERGRADUATE RESEARCH AWARDS
• *See page 139*

AMERICAN RESPIRATORY CARE FOUNDATION

http://www.arcfoundation.org/

MORTON B. DUGGAN, JR. MEMORIAL EDUCATION RECOGNITION AWARD

The Morton B. Duggan, Jr. Memorial Education Recognition Award is awarded to a student currently enrolled in an accredited respiratory care education program. Preference given to candidates from Georgia and South Carolina. The American Respiratory Care Foundation may award up to $1,000 in memory of Morton B. Duggan, Jr. Applicants/nominees are accepted from all states, with preference given to candidates from Georgia and South Carolina. This award consists of a certificate of recognition, coach airfare, one night's lodging, and registration for AARC Congress.

Academic Fields/Career Goals: Health and Medical Sciences; Therapy/Rehabilitation.

Award: Scholarship for use in freshman, sophomore, junior, or senior years; not renewable. *Number:* 1. *Amount:* $1000.

Eligibility Requirements: Applicant must be enrolled or expecting to enroll full- or part-time at a two-year institution or university. Available to U.S. citizens.

Application Requirements: Application form, application form may be submitted online. *Deadline:* June 1.

Contact: Crystal Maldonado, ARCF Grants Coordinator
  E-mail: crystal.maldonado@aarc.org

SEPRACOR ACHIEVEMENT AWARD FOR EXCELLENCE IN PULMONARY DISEASE STATE MANAGEMENT

Nominations may be made by anyone by submitting a paper of not more than 1000 words describing why a nominee should be considered for the award. Must be a member of the American Association for Respiratory Care. Must be a respiratory therapist or other healthcare professional, including physician. Nominees must have demonstrated the attainment of positive healthcare outcomes as a direct result of their disease-oriented practice of respiratory care, regardless of care setting.

Academic Fields/Career Goals: Health and Medical Sciences; Therapy/Rehabilitation.

Award: Prize for use in freshman, sophomore, junior, senior, graduate, or postgraduate years; not renewable. *Number:* 1. *Amount:* up to $2500.

Eligibility Requirements: Applicant must be enrolled or expecting to enroll full- or part-time at a four-year institution or university. Applicant or parent of applicant must have employment or volunteer experience in physical therapy/rehabilitation. Available to U.S. and non-U.S. citizens.

Application Requirements: Paper describing why a nominee should be considered for the award, recommendations or references, resume. *Deadline:* June 1.

Contact: Jill Nelson, Administrative Coordinator
  American Respiratory Care Foundation
  9425 North MacArthur Boulevard, Suite 100
  Irving, TX 75063-4706
  Phone: 972-243-2272
  Fax: 972-484-2720
  E-mail: info@arcfoundation.org

ARIZONA PROFESSIONAL CHAPTER OF AISES

http://www.aises.org/scholarships

ARIZONA PROFESSIONAL CHAPTER OF AISES SCHOLARSHIP
• *See page 237*

ASRT FOUNDATION

https://foundation.asrt.org/

JERMAN-CAHOON STUDENT SCHOLARSHIP
• *See page 276*

PROFESSIONAL ADVANCEMENT SCHOLARSHIP
• *See page 276*

ROYCE OSBORN MINORITY STUDENT SCHOLARSHIP
• *See page 276*

ASSISTANCE LEAGUE OF THE TRIANGLE AREA

HEALTH CARE PROFESSION SCHOLARSHIP
• *See page 195*

ASSOCIATION FOR EDUCATION AND REHABILITATION OF THE BLIND AND VISUALLY IMPAIRED

http://www.aerbvi.org/

WILLIAM AND DOROTHY FERRELL SCHOLARSHIP
• *See page 207*

ASSOCIATION ON AMERICAN INDIAN AFFAIRS, INC.

http://www.indian-affairs.org/

ELIZABETH AND SHERMAN ASCHE MEMORIAL SCHOLARSHIP FUND
• *See page 93*

AVACARE MEDICAL

https://avacaremedical.com

AVACARE MEDICAL SCHOLARSHIP
• *See page 100*

BETHESDA LUTHERAN COMMUNITIES

http://www.bethesdalutherancommunities.org/scholarships

DEVELOPMENTAL DISABILITIES SCHOLASTIC ACHIEVEMENT SCHOLARSHIP FOR COLLEGE STUDENTS WHO ARE LUTHERAN
• *See page 195*

BHW GROUP

https://thebhwgroup.com/

BHW WOMEN IN STEM SCHOLARSHIP
• *See page 107*

BIOCOMMUNICATIONS ASSOCIATION

www.bca.org

ENDOWMENT FUND FOR EDUCATION GRANT
• *See page 171*

BOYS AND GIRLS CLUBS OF GREATER SAN DIEGO

http://www.sdyouth.org/

SPENCE REESE SCHOLARSHIP
• *See page 237*

CANFIT

http://www.canfit.org/

CANFIT NUTRITION, PHYSICAL EDUCATION AND CULINARY ARTS SCHOLARSHIP
• *See page 190*

CHRISTIANA CARE HEALTH SYSTEMS

http://www.christianacare.org/

RUTH SHAW JUNIOR BOARD SCHOLARSHIP
Offers financial assistance to students currently enrolled in nursing and selected allied health programs. Applicants are selected based on academic achievement and a proven commitment to quality patient care. Students receiving assistance are required to commit to a minimum of one year of employment with Christiana Care.
Academic Fields/Career Goals: Health and Medical Sciences; Nursing.
Award: Scholarship for use in freshman, sophomore, junior, or senior years; not renewable.
Eligibility Requirements: Applicant must be enrolled or expecting to enroll full- or part-time at a four-year institution or university. Applicant or parent of applicant must have employment or volunteer experience in nursing. Available to U.S. citizens.
Application Requirements: Application form, driver's license, recommendations or references, resume, transcript. *Deadline:* April 30.
Contact: Wendy Gable, Scholarship Committee
Christiana Care Health Systems
200 Hygeia Drive, PO Box 6001
Newark, DE 19713
Phone: 302-428-5710
E-mail: wgable@christianacare.org

CONSOLE AND HOLLAWELL

http://www.myinjuryattorney.com/legal-scholarship-2017-2018/

OVERDOSE ATTORNEY SCHOLARSHIP
Overdose Attorney is a website project created by the law firm Console & Hollawell in response to the US opioid epidemic. We started this project in 2017, to help those who lost someone due to an opioid overdose. We're committed to fighting over-prescription, a leader cause of opioid addiction. This includes shutting down pill-pushing doctors and holding drug manufacturers accountable. To raise awareness of this important cause, we're proud to offer our Overdose Lawyer Scholarship. Our hope is that students of the legal or medical professions will help us fight this epidemic. We want qualified applicants to write a brief essay (500 words) to tell us why you deserve this award.
Academic Fields/Career Goals: Health and Medical Sciences; Law/Legal Services.
Award: Scholarship for use in freshman, sophomore, junior, senior, or graduate years; not renewable. *Number:* 1. *Amount:* $1000.
Eligibility Requirements: Applicant must be enrolled or expecting to enroll full-time at a two-year or four-year institution or university. Available to U.S. citizens.
Application Requirements: Essay, personal photograph. *Deadline:* July 15.
Contact: Emily Senski, Digital Marketing Specialist
Console and Hollawell
525 NJ 73, #117
Marlton, NJ 08053

CONTINENTAL SOCIETY, DAUGHTERS OF INDIAN WARS

http://www.csdiw.org/

CONTINENTAL SOCIETY, DAUGHTERS OF INDIAN WARS SCHOLARSHIP
• *See page 188*

CROHN'S & COLITIS FOUNDATION

http://www.ccfa.org/

CROHN'S & COLITIS FOUNDATION OF AMERICA STUDENT RESEARCH FELLOWSHIP AWARDS
Student Research Fellowship Awards will be available for full time research with a mentor investigating a subject relevant to IBD. Mentors may not be a relative of the applicant and may not work in their lab. The mentor must be a faculty member who directs a research project highly relevant to the study of IBD at an accredited institution. Awards will be payable to the institution, not the individual. A complete financial statement and scientific report are due September 1 of the year of the award. All publications arising from work funded by this project must acknowledge support of CCFA. Candidates may be undergraduate, medical or graduate students (not yet engaged in thesis research) in accredited United States institutions. Candidates may not hold similar salary support from other agencies.
Academic Fields/Career Goals: Health and Medical Sciences.
Award: Scholarship for use in freshman, sophomore, junior, senior, or graduate years; not renewable. *Amount:* $2500.
Eligibility Requirements: Applicant must be enrolled or expecting to enroll full-time at a four-year institution or university. Available to U.S. and non-U.S. citizens.
Application Requirements: Application form. *Deadline:* March 15.
Contact: Mr. Moustafa Ibrahim, National Manager of Grants and Contracts
Crohn's & Colitis Foundation
733 Third Avenue
Suite 510
New York, NY 10017
Phone: 646-943-7505
E-mail: grants@ccfa.org

CYNTHIA E. MORGAN SCHOLARSHIP FUND (CEMS)

http://www.cemsfund.com/

CYNTHIA E. MORGAN MEMORIAL SCHOLARSHIP FUND, INC.
• *See page 248*

THE EXPERT INSTITUTE

https://www.theexpertinstitute.com

ANNUAL HEALTHCARE AND LIFE SCIENCES SCHOLARSHIP
• *See page 142*

FOUNDATION FOR SEACOAST HEALTH

http://www.ffsh.org

FOUNDATION FOR SEACOAST HEALTH SCHOLARSHIPS

In keeping with the mission of the organization to invest its resources to improve the health and well being of Seacoast residents, candidates must be pursuing an undergraduate or graduate degree in a health-related field of study. The awards are based primarily on scholastic aptitude and performance, personal achievements, leadership, and community involvement. The applicant's primary residence must be in one of the following towns: Portsmouth, Rye, Newcastle, Greenland, Newington, and North Hampton, New Hampshire; Kittery, Elliot and York, Maine.

Academic Fields/Career Goals: Health and Medical Sciences.

Award: Scholarship for use in freshman, sophomore, junior, senior, graduate, or postgraduate years; renewable. *Number:* 2–6. *Amount:* $1000–$5000.

Eligibility Requirements: Applicant must be enrolled or expecting to enroll full- or part-time at a two-year or four-year or technical institution or university and resident of Maine, New Hampshire. Available to U.S. citizens.

Application Requirements: Application form, essay. *Deadline:* April 1.

Contact: Noreen Hodgdon
Foundation for Seacoast Health
100 Campus Drive, Suite 1
Portsmouth, NH 03801
Phone: 603-422-8204
Fax: 603-422-8207
E-mail: nhodgdon@communitycampus.org

GENERAL BOARD OF HIGHER EDUCATION AND MINISTRY

http://www.gbhem.org

EDITH M. ALLEN SCHOLARSHIP
• *See page 209*

GEORGIA BOARD FOR PHYSICIAN WORKFORCE (GBPW)

http://www.gbpw.georgia.gov

PHYSICIANS FOR RURAL AREAS ASSISTANCE PROGRAM

Service repayable medical school scholarship for a maximum of $20,000 per year for four years available to Georgia residents enrolled in U.S. accredited medical school. Repay by practicing medicine for one year in rural Georgia for each year that the scholarship is received. Service payment begins upon completion of residency training.

Academic Fields/Career Goals: Health and Medical Sciences.

Award: Scholarship for use in freshman, sophomore, junior, or senior years; renewable. *Number:* 20–25. *Amount:* up to $20,000.

Eligibility Requirements: Applicant must be enrolled or expecting to enroll full-time at an institution or university and resident of Georgia. Available to U.S. citizens.

Application Requirements: Application form, essay, financial need analysis, interview, personal photograph, proof of GA residency, test scores, transcript. *Deadline:* June 1.

Contact: Ms. Pamela Smith, Administration Manager
Georgia Board for Physician Workforce (GBPW)
2 Peachtree Street, NW
36th Floor
Atlanta, GA 30303
Phone: 404-232-7972
E-mail: psmith@dch.ga.gov

GRAND RAPIDS COMMUNITY FOUNDATION

http://www.grfoundation.org/

HARRY J. MORRIS, JR. EMERGENCY SERVICES SCHOLARSHIP
• *See page 261*

HEALTHCARE INFORMATION AND MANAGEMENT SYSTEMS SOCIETY FOUNDATION

http://www.himss.org/

HIMSS FOUNDATION SCHOLARSHIP PROGRAM
• *See page 277*

HEALTH PROFESSIONS EDUCATION FOUNDATION

http://www.healthprofessions.ca.gov/

ALLIED HEALTHCARE SCHOLARSHIP PROGRAM
• *See page 196*

HEALTH RESEARCH COUNCIL OF NEW ZEALAND

https://gateway.hrc.govt.nz/

PACIFIC HEALTH WORKFORCE AWARD
• *See page 277*

PACIFIC MENTAL HEALTH WORK FORCE AWARD
• *See page 277*

INDIAN HEALTH SERVICES, UNITED STATES DEPARTMENT OF HEALTH AND HUMAN SERVICES

http://www.ihs.gov/scholarship

HEALTH PROFESSIONS PREPARATORY SCHOLARSHIP PROGRAM
• *See page 137*

INDIAN HEALTH SERVICE HEALTH PROFESSIONS PRE-GRADUATE SCHOLARSHIPS
• *See page 108*

INTERMOUNTAIN MEDICAL IMAGING

https://www.aboutimi.com/

INTERMOUNTAIN MEDICAL IMAGING SCHOLARSHIP
• *See page 125*

INTERNATIONAL ORDER OF THE KING'S DAUGHTERS AND SONS

http://www.iokds.org/

HEALTH CAREERS SCHOLARSHIP
• *See page 197*

THE JACKSON LABORATORY

https://www.jax.org

THE JACKSON LABORATORY COLLEGE SCHOLARSHIP PROGRAM
• *See page 108*

KETAMINE CLINICS OF LOS ANGELES

http://www.ketamineclinics.com/

KETAMINE CLINICS OF LOS ANGELES SCHOLARSHIP PROGRAM
• *See page 138*

LADIES AUXILIARY TO THE VETERANS OF FOREIGN WARS, DEPARTMENT OF MAINE

http://mainevfw.org/

FRANCES L. BOOTH MEDICAL SCHOLARSHIP SPONSORED BY LAVFW DEPARTMENT OF MAINE

Award for an undergraduate student majoring in the field of medicine who has a parent or grandparent who is a member of the Maine VFW or VFW auxiliary. Applicant must have sponsor from the VFW/Ladies Auxiliary to the Veterans of Foreign Wars.

Academic Fields/Career Goals: Health and Medical Sciences; Humanities; Nursing; Therapy/Rehabilitation.

Award: Scholarship for use in freshman, sophomore, junior, or senior years; renewable. *Number:* 1. *Amount:* $1000.

Eligibility Requirements: Applicant must be enrolled or expecting to enroll full-time at a two-year or four-year institution or university and resident of Maine. Applicant or parent of applicant must be member of Veterans of Foreign Wars or Auxiliary. Available to U.S. citizens.

Application Requirements: Application form, community service, essay, financial need analysis, personal letter, recommendations or references, resume, transcript. *Deadline:* March 31.

Contact: Sheila Webber, Chairman, FBMS
Ladies Auxiliary to the Veterans of Foreign Wars, Department of Maine
PO Box 493
Old Orchard Beach, ME 04064
Phone: 207-934-2405
E-mail: swebber2@maine.rr.com

MEDICAL SCRUBS COLLECTION

http://medicalscrubscollection.com

MEDICAL SCRUBS COLLECTION SCHOLARSHIP
• *See page 104*

NATIONAL ATHLETIC TRAINERS' ASSOCIATION RESEARCH AND EDUCATION FOUNDATION

http://www.natafoundation.org/

NATIONAL ATHLETIC TRAINERS' ASSOCIATION RESEARCH AND EDUCATION FOUNDATION SCHOLARSHIP PROGRAM

One-time award available to full-time students who are members of NATA. Minimum 3.2 GPA required. Open to undergraduate upperclassmen and graduate/postgraduate students.

Academic Fields/Career Goals: Health and Medical Sciences; Health Information Management/Technology; Sports-Related/Exercise Science; Therapy/Rehabilitation.

Award: Scholarship for use in junior, senior, graduate, or postgraduate years; not renewable. *Number:* 70. *Amount:* $2000.

Eligibility Requirements: Applicant must be enrolled or expecting to enroll full-time at a four-year institution or university. Applicant or parent of applicant must be member of National Athletic Trainers Association. Available to U.S. and non-U.S. citizens.

Application Requirements: Application form, essay, recommendations or references, transcript. *Deadline:* February 10.

Contact: Patsy Brown, Scholarship Coordinator
National Athletic Trainers' Association Research and Education Foundation
2952 Stemmons Freeway, Suite 200
Dallas, TX 75247
Phone: 214-637-6282 Ext. 151
Fax: 214-637-2206
E-mail: patsyb@nata.org

NATIONAL INSTITUTES OF HEALTH

https://www.training.nih.gov/programs/ugsp

NIH UNDERGRADUATE SCHOLARSHIP PROGRAM FOR STUDENTS FROM DISADVANTAGED BACKGROUNDS
• *See page 101*

NEXTSTEPU

http://www.nextstepu.com/

$1,500 STEM SCHOLARSHIP
• *See page 104*

NOVUS BIOLOGICALS, LLC

https://www.novusbio.com

NOVUS BIOLOGICALS SCHOLARSHIP PROGRAM
• *See page 101*

R&D SYSTEMS SCHOLARSHIP
• *See page 101*

TOCRIS BIOSCIENCE SCHOLARSHIP
• *See page 102*

OREGON COMMUNITY FOUNDATION

http://www.oregoncf.org/

FRANZ STENZEL M.D. AND KATHRYN STENZEL SCHOLARSHIP FUND

Scholarships for Oregon residents, with a focus on three types of students: (a) those pursuing any type of undergraduate degree, (b) those pursuing a nursing education through a two-year, four-year, or graduate program, and (c) medical students.

Academic Fields/Career Goals: Health and Medical Sciences; Nursing.

Award: Scholarship for use in freshman, sophomore, junior, or senior years; renewable. *Number:* up to 70. *Amount:* $2000–$5000.

Eligibility Requirements: Applicant must be enrolled or expecting to enroll full-time at a two-year or four-year institution or university and resident of Oregon. Available to U.S. citizens.

Application Requirements: Application form, recommendations or references. *Deadline:* March 1.

Contact: Dianne Causey, Program Associate for Scholarships and
    Grants
    Phone: 503-227-6846 Ext. 1418
    E-mail: dcausey@oregoncf.org

PACERS FOUNDATION INC.

http://www.pacersfoundation.org/

LINDA CRAIG MEMORIAL SCHOLARSHIP PRESENTED BY ST. VINCENT SPORTS MEDICINE

Scholarship presented by St. Vincent Sports Medicine is for currently-enrolled juniors and seniors with declared majors of medicine, sports medicine, and/or physical therapy. Students must have completed at least 4 semesters and attend a school in Indiana. Minimum 3.0 GPA required.

Academic Fields/Career Goals: Health and Medical Sciences; Sports-Related/Exercise Science; Therapy/Rehabilitation.

Award: Scholarship for use in junior, senior, graduate, or postgraduate years; renewable. *Number:* 1–2. *Amount:* $2000.

Eligibility Requirements: Applicant must be enrolled or expecting to enroll full-time at a two-year or four-year institution or university and studying in Indiana. Available to U.S. citizens.

Application Requirements: Application form, essay, recommendations or references, transcript. *Deadline:* March 1.

Contact: Jami Marsh, Executive Director
    Pacers Foundation Inc.
    125 South Pennsylvania Street
    Indianapolis, IN 46204
    Phone: 317-917-2856
    E-mail: foundation@pacers.com

PLATINUM EDUCATIONAL GROUP

www.platinumed.com

PLATINUM EDUCATIONAL GROUP SCHOLARSHIPS PROGRAM FOR EMS, NURSING, AND ALLIED HEALTH
• *See page 102*

PRESBYTERIAN CHURCH (USA)

https://www.presbyterianmission.org/

STUDENT OPPORTUNITY SCHOLARSHIP
• *See page 212*

SCARLETT FAMILY FOUNDATION SCHOLARSHIP PROGRAM

http://www.scarlettfoundation.org/

SCHOLARSHIP FOR STUDENTS PURSUING A BUSINESS OR STEM DEGREE
• *See page 80*

THE SOCIETY FOR THE SCIENTIFIC STUDY OF SEXUALITY

http://www.sexscience.org/

THE SOCIETY FOR THE SCIENTIFIC STUDY OF SEXUALITY STUDENT RESEARCH GRANT
• *See page 105*

SOCIETY OF PEDIATRIC NURSES

http://www.pedsnurses.org/

SOCIETY OF PEDIATRIC NURSES EDUCATIONAL SCHOLARSHIP
• *See page 161*

STRAIGHTFORWARD MEDIA

http://www.straightforwardmedia.com/

STRAIGHTFORWARD MEDIA MEDICAL PROFESSIONS SCHOLARSHIP
• *See page 198*

STRAIGHT NORTH

https://www.straightnorth.com/

STRAIGHT NORTH STEM SCHOLARSHIP
• *See page 81*

UNITED NATIONS ASSOCIATION OF CONNECTICUT

http://www.unausa.org

UNITED NATIONS ASSOCIATION OF CONNECTICUT SCHOLARSHIP
• *See page 124*

UNITED NEGRO COLLEGE FUND

http://www.uncf.org/

GALACTIC UNITE BYTHEWAY SCHOLARSHIP
• *See page 111*

LEIDOS STEM SCHOLARSHIP
• *See page 96*

U.S. DEPARTMENT OF HEALTH AND HUMAN SERVICES

https://www.hhs.gov/

SCHOLARSHIPS FOR DISADVANTAGED STUDENTS PROGRAM

One-time award for full-time students from disadvantaged backgrounds enrolled in health professions and nursing programs. Institution must apply for funding and must be eligible to receive SDS funds. Students must contact financial aid office to apply.

Academic Fields/Career Goals: Health and Medical Sciences; Nursing; Therapy/Rehabilitation.

Award: Scholarship for use in freshman, sophomore, junior, senior, or graduate years; not renewable. *Number:* 79.

Eligibility Requirements: Applicant must be enrolled or expecting to enroll full-time at a two-year institution or university. Available to U.S. citizens.

Application Requirements: Application form, application form may be submitted online, financial need analysis. *Deadline:* March 3.

Contact: Denise Sorrell, Senior Public Health Analyst
    U.S. Department of Health and Human Services
    Division of Health Careers and Financial Support Bureau of
        Health Workforce
    5600 Fishers Lane, Room 15N-78
    Rockville, MD 20857
    Phone: 301-443-2909
    E-mail: SDSProgram@hrsa.gov

VESALIUS TRUST FOR VISUAL COMMUNICATION IN THE HEALTH SCIENCES

http://www.vesaliustrust.org/

STUDENT RESEARCH SCHOLARSHIP

Scholarships available to students currently enrolled in an undergraduate or graduate school program of bio-communications (medical illustration) who have completed one full year of the curriculum.

Academic Fields/Career Goals: Health and Medical Sciences.

Award: Scholarship for use in junior, senior, or graduate years; not renewable. *Number:* 10–15. *Amount:* $500.

Eligibility Requirements: Applicant must be enrolled or expecting to enroll full- or part-time at a four-year institution or university and must have an interest in art. Available to U.S. and non-U.S. citizens.

Application Requirements: Application form, portfolio, recommendations or references, resume, transcript. *Deadline:* November 7.

Contact: Wendy Gee, Student Grants and Scholarships
Vesalius Trust for Visual Communication in the Health Sciences
1100 Grundy Lane
San Bruno, CA 94066
Phone: 650-244-4320
E-mail: wendy.hillergee@krames.com

WISCONSIN MEDICAL SOCIETY FOUNDATION

http://www.wisconsinmedicalsocietyfoundation.org

AMY HUNTER-WILSON, MD SCHOLARSHIP

Scholarship assists American Indians with proof of tribal membership who pursue training or advanced education as doctors of medicine, nurses, or in related health careers. Award amounts are determined based on the students field of study and financial need and will vary depending on the number of eligible applicants and funds available.

Academic Fields/Career Goals: Health and Medical Sciences.

Award: Scholarship for use in freshman, sophomore, junior, senior, or graduate years; not renewable.

Eligibility Requirements: Applicant must be American Indian/Alaska Native; enrolled or expecting to enroll full-time at a two-year or four-year or technical institution or university; resident of Wisconsin and studying in Wisconsin. Available to U.S. citizens.

Application Requirements: Application form, essay, financial need analysis. *Deadline:* February 1.

Contact: Ms. Elizabeth Ringle, Scholarship Coordinator
Phone: 866-442-3800
Fax: 608-442-3851

HEALTH INFORMATION MANAGEMENT/ TECHNOLOGY

AHIMA FOUNDATION

http://ahimafoundation.org/

AHIMA FOUNDATION STUDENT MERIT SCHOLARSHIP

Merit scholarships for undergraduate, Master's, and Doctoral health information management students. Must be a member of AHIMA. One standard application for all available scholarships. Applicant must have a minimum cumulative GPA of 3.5 (out of 4.0) or 4.5 (out of 5.0). Applications information is available at: http://ahimafoundation.org/education/MeritScholarships.aspx

Academic Fields/Career Goals: Health Information Management/Technology.

Award: Scholarship for use in sophomore, junior, senior, graduate, or postgraduate years; not renewable. *Number:* 1. *Amount:* $1000–$2500.

Eligibility Requirements: Applicant must be enrolled or expecting to enroll full- or part-time at a two-year or four-year institution or university. Applicant or parent of applicant must be member of American Health Information Management Association. Available to U.S. and non-U.S. citizens.

Application Requirements: Application form, application form may be submitted online (http://ahimafoundation.org/education/MeritScholarships.aspx), community service, essay, program director verification, recommendations or references, transcript. *Deadline:* September 30.

Contact: AHIMA Foundation
AHIMA Foundation
233 North Michigan Avenue, 21st Floor
Chicago, IL 60601-5800
Phone: 312-233-1131
E-mail: fore@ahima.org

ALICE L. HALTOM EDUCATIONAL FUND

http://www.alhef.org/

ALICE L. HALTOM EDUCATIONAL FUND
• See page 145

AMERICAN LEGION AUXILIARY DEPARTMENT OF COLORADO

http://www.alacolorado.com

AMERICAN LEGION AUXILIARY DEPARTMENT OF COLORADO PAST PRESIDENTS' PARLEY HEALTH CARE PROFESSIONAL SCHOLARSHIPNURSES SCHOLARSHIP
• See page 125

ASRT FOUNDATION

https://foundation.asrt.org/

JERMAN-CAHOON STUDENT SCHOLARSHIP
• See page 276

PROFESSIONAL ADVANCEMENT SCHOLARSHIP
• See page 276

ROYCE OSBORN MINORITY STUDENT SCHOLARSHIP
• See page 276

ASSISTANCE LEAGUE OF THE TRIANGLE AREA

HEALTH CARE PROFESSION SCHOLARSHIP
• See page 195

AVACARE MEDICAL

https://avacaremedical.com

AVACARE MEDICAL SCHOLARSHIP
• See page 100

BETHESDA LUTHERAN COMMUNITIES

http://www.bethesdalutherancommunities.org/scholarships

DEVELOPMENTAL DISABILITIES SCHOLASTIC ACHIEVEMENT SCHOLARSHIP FOR COLLEGE STUDENTS WHO ARE LUTHERAN
• *See page 195*

BHW GROUP

https://thebhwgroup.com/

BHW WOMEN IN STEM SCHOLARSHIP
• *See page 107*

CYNTHIA E. MORGAN SCHOLARSHIP FUND (CEMS)

http://www.cemsfund.com/

CYNTHIA E. MORGAN MEMORIAL SCHOLARSHIP FUND, INC.
• *See page 248*

HEALTHCARE INFORMATION AND MANAGEMENT SYSTEMS SOCIETY FOUNDATION

http://www.himss.org/

HIMSS FOUNDATION SCHOLARSHIP PROGRAM
• *See page 277*

HEALTH RESEARCH COUNCIL OF NEW ZEALAND

https://gateway.hrc.govt.nz/

PACIFIC HEALTH WORKFORCE AWARD
• *See page 277*

PACIFIC MENTAL HEALTH WORK FORCE AWARD
• *See page 277*

INSTITUTE OF INDUSTRIAL ENGINEERS

https://www.iise.org/

SOCIETY FOR HEALTH SYSTEMS SCHOLARSHIP
• *See page 241*

INTERMOUNTAIN MEDICAL IMAGING

https://www.aboutimi.com/

INTERMOUNTAIN MEDICAL IMAGING SCHOLARSHIP
• *See page 125*

MEDICAL SCRUBS COLLECTION

http://medicalscrubscollection.com

MEDICAL SCRUBS COLLECTION SCHOLARSHIP
• *See page 104*

NATIONAL ATHLETIC TRAINERS' ASSOCIATION RESEARCH AND EDUCATION FOUNDATION

http://www.natafoundation.org/

NATIONAL ATHLETIC TRAINERS' ASSOCIATION RESEARCH AND EDUCATION FOUNDATION SCHOLARSHIP PROGRAM
• *See page 283*

NEXTSTEPU

http://www.nextstepu.com/

$1,500 STEM SCHOLARSHIP
• *See page 104*

NOVUS BIOLOGICALS, LLC

https://www.novusbio.com

NOVUS BIOLOGICALS SCHOLARSHIP PROGRAM
• *See page 101*

R&D SYSTEMS SCHOLARSHIP
• *See page 101*

TOCRIS BIOSCIENCE SCHOLARSHIP
• *See page 102*

SCARLETT FAMILY FOUNDATION SCHOLARSHIP PROGRAM

http://www.scarlettfoundation.org/

SCHOLARSHIP FOR STUDENTS PURSUING A BUSINESS OR STEM DEGREE
• *See page 80*

STRAIGHTFORWARD MEDIA

http://www.straightforwardmedia.com/

STRAIGHTFORWARD MEDIA MEDICAL PROFESSIONS SCHOLARSHIP
• *See page 198*

STRAIGHT NORTH

https://www.straightnorth.com/

STRAIGHT NORTH STEM SCHOLARSHIP
• *See page 81*

TECHNOLOGY FIRST

https://technologyfirst.org/

ROBERT V. MCKENNA SCHOLARSHIPS
• *See page 183*

ULTRASOUNDTECHNICIANSCHOOLS.COM

http://www.ultrasoundtechnicianschools.com

ULTRASOUNDTECHNICIANSCHOOLS.COM SCHOLARSHIP
We are offering you the chance to win a $1,000 ultrasound technician scholarship. A winner will be selected from the list of all eligible candidates. We will be awarding two different scholarships each year. When one deadline ends, the next scholarship will begin.

Academic Fields/Career Goals: Health Information Management/Technology; Radiology.

Award: Scholarship for use in freshman, sophomore, or junior years; not renewable. *Number:* 2. *Amount:* $1000.

Eligibility Requirements: Applicant must be enrolled or expecting to enroll full-time at a two-year or four-year or technical institution or university. Available to U.S. citizens.

Application Requirements: Application form. *Deadline:* July 15.

Contact: Jennifer Moody, Website Marketing Strategist
UltrasoundTechnicianSchools.com
15500 Wes 113th Street
#200
Lenexa, KS 66219
Phone: 913-254-6000 Ext. 6063
E-mail: jennifer.moody@marketing.keypathedu.com

UNITED NEGRO COLLEGE FUND

http://www.uncf.org/

LEIDOS STEM SCHOLARSHIP
• *See page 96*

HEATING, AIR-CONDITIONING, AND REFRIGERATION MECHANICS

AIR-CONDITIONING, HEATING, AND REFRIGERATION INSTITUTE (AHRI)

http://www.reesscholarship.org/site/1/Home

REES SCHOLARSHIP FOUNDATION HVACR AND WATER HEATING TECHNICIAN PROGRAM

The Rees Scholarship Foundation's HVACR and water heating technician's program provides awards of up to $2,000 to students enrolled in an HVACR training program at an institutionally accredited school.

Academic Fields/Career Goals: Heating, Air-Conditioning, and Refrigeration Mechanics.

Award: Scholarship for use in freshman, sophomore, junior, or senior years; renewable. *Amount:* $500–$2000.

Eligibility Requirements: Applicant must be enrolled or expecting to enroll full- or part-time at a two-year or technical institution. Available to U.S. citizens.

Application Requirements: Application form, application form may be submitted online (http://www.reesscholarship.org/site/292/Apply), essay, recommendations or references, transcript. *Deadline:* June 1.

REES SCHOLARSHIP FOUNDATION VETERANS PROGRAM

The Rees Scholarship Foundation's Veteran's program awards up to $2,000 to veterans enrolled in an HVACR training program at an institutionally accredited school.

Academic Fields/Career Goals: Heating, Air-Conditioning, and Refrigeration Mechanics.

Award: Scholarship for use in freshman, sophomore, junior, or senior years; not renewable. *Amount:* $1500–$2000.

Eligibility Requirements: Applicant must be enrolled or expecting to enroll full- or part-time at a two-year or technical institution. Available to U.S. citizens. Applicant or parent must meet one or more of the following requirements: general military experience; retired from active duty; disabled or killed as a result of military service; prisoner of war; or missing in action.

Application Requirements: Application form, application form may be submitted online (http://www.reesscholarship.org/site/292/Apply), essay, recommendations or references, transcript. *Deadline:* continuous.

AMERICAN INDIAN SCIENCE AND ENGINEERING SOCIETY

http://www.aises.org/

A.T. ANDERSON MEMORIAL SCHOLARSHIP PROGRAM
• *See page 105*

BHW GROUP

https://thebhwgroup.com/

BHW WOMEN IN STEM SCHOLARSHIP
• *See page 107*

THE EGIA FOUNDATION

www.egiafoundation.org

EGIA FOUNDATION SCHOLARSHIP PROGRAM

Up to 20 eligible students will be awarded a $2500 scholarship to pursue an HVAC degree or certificate at an accredited community college, technical/vocational school, or approved technical institute during the 2019-2020 academic year. Applicants will be asked to explain what inspired them to choose an HVAC technical education and their plans upon graduating.

Academic Fields/Career Goals: Heating, Air-Conditioning, and Refrigeration Mechanics.

Award: Scholarship for use in freshman or sophomore years; not renewable. *Number:* 20. *Amount:* $2500.

Eligibility Requirements: Applicant must be enrolled or expecting to enroll full- or part-time at a two-year or technical institution. Available to U.S. citizens.

Application Requirements: Application form, application form may be submitted online(www.egiafoundation.org/scholarship), transcript. *Deadline:* April 30.

Contact: Erin McCollum, Development Director
The EGIA Foundation
3800 Watt Ave Ste 105
Sacramento, CA 95821
Phone: 916-480-7337
E-mail: info@egiafoundation.org

PROFESSIONAL CONSTRUCTION ESTIMATORS ASSOCIATION

http://www.pcea.org/

TED G. WILSON MEMORIAL SCHOLARSHIP FOUNDATION
• *See page 166*

SOUTH CAROLINA ASSOCIATION OF HEATING AND AIR CONDITIONING CONTRACTORS

http://www.schvac.org/

SOUTH CAROLINA ASSOCIATION OF HEATING AND AIR CONDITIONING CONTRACTORS SCHOLARSHIP

Scholarship of $500 to pursue a career in the heating and air conditioning industry. Participating students must maintain an overall GPA of 2.5 and a GPA of 3.0 in all major topics. Deadline varies.

Academic Fields/Career Goals: Heating, Air-Conditioning, and Refrigeration Mechanics.

Award: Scholarship for use in freshman year; renewable.

Eligibility Requirements: Applicant must be high school student and planning to enroll or expecting to enroll full- or part-time at a technical institution. Available to U.S. and non-U.S. citizens.

Application Requirements: Application form.

Contact: Leigh Faircloth, Scholarship Committee
Phone: 800-395-9276
Fax: 803-252-7799
E-mail: staff@schvac.org

STRAIGHT NORTH

https://www.straightnorth.com/

STRAIGHT NORTH STEM SCHOLARSHIP
• *See page 81*

HISTORIC PRESERVATION AND CONSERVATION

COSTUME SOCIETY OF AMERICA

http://www.costumesocietyamerica.com/

ADELE FILENE STUDENT PRESENTER GRANT
• *See page 118*

STELLA BLUM STUDENT RESEARCH GRANT
• *See page 118*

THE GEORGIA TRUST FOR HISTORIC PRESERVATION

http://www.georgiatrust.org/

B. PHINIZY SPALDING, HUBERT B. OWENS, AND THE NATIONAL SOCIETY OF THE COLONIAL DAMES OF AMERICA IN THE STATE OF GEORGIA ACADEMIC SCHOLARSHIPS
• *See page 99*

J. NEEL REID PRIZE
• *See page 115*

HISTORY

AMERICAN FEDERATION OF STATE, COUNTY, AND MUNICIPAL EMPLOYEES

https://www.afscme.org/

AFSCME/UNCF UNION SCHOLARS PROGRAM
• *See page 98*

ASSOCIATION OF FORMER INTELLIGENCE OFFICERS

www.afio.com

AFIO UNDERGRADUATE AND GRADUATE SCHOLARSHIPS
• *See page 98*

CANADIAN INSTITUTE OF UKRAINIAN STUDIES

https://www.ualberta.ca/canadian-institute-of-ukrainian-studies/index.html

LEO J. KRYSA FAMILY UNDERGRADUATE SCHOLARSHIP
• *See page 208*

COSTUME SOCIETY OF AMERICA

http://www.costumesocietyamerica.com/

ADELE FILENE STUDENT PRESENTER GRANT
• *See page 118*

STELLA BLUM STUDENT RESEARCH GRANT
• *See page 118*

CULTURAL SERVICES OF THE FRENCH EMBASSY

http://www.frenchculture.org/

TEACHING ASSISTANT PROGRAM IN FRANCE
• *See page 98*

THE GEORGIA TRUST FOR HISTORIC PRESERVATION

http://www.georgiatrust.org/

B. PHINIZY SPALDING, HUBERT B. OWENS, AND THE NATIONAL SOCIETY OF THE COLONIAL DAMES OF AMERICA IN THE STATE OF GEORGIA ACADEMIC SCHOLARSHIPS
• *See page 99*

GREATER SALINA COMMUNITY FOUNDATION

http://www.gscf.org/

KANSAS FEDERATION OF REPUBLICAN WOMEN SCHOLARSHIP

Awards female students currently attending a Kansas college or university with declared major of political science, history, or public administration. Must be entering junior or senior year of undergraduate study, or attending graduate school. Must be Kansas residents and maintain cumulative GPA of 3.0 or better. Applicants must be registered members of the Republican Party. Must be involved in extracurricular activities.

Academic Fields/Career Goals: History; Political Science; Public Policy and Administration.

Award: Scholarship for use in junior, senior, or graduate years; renewable. *Number:* 1. *Amount:* up to $1000.

Eligibility Requirements: Applicant must be enrolled or expecting to enroll full-time at a two-year or four-year institution or university; female; resident of Kansas and studying in Kansas. Available to U.S. citizens.

Application Requirements: Application form, essay. *Deadline:* March 31.

Contact: Michelle Griffin, Scholarship and Affiliate Coordinator
Greater Salina Community Foundation
PO Box 2876
Salina, KS 67402-2876
Phone: 785-823-1800
E-mail: michellegriffin@gscf.org

HUB FOUNDATION

https://hub-foundation.org

HUB FOUNDATION SCHOLARSHIPS
• *See page 88*

ISLAMIC SCHOLARSHIP FUND

http://islamicscholarshipfund.org/

ISF NATIONAL SCHOLARSHIP
• *See page 104*

LA-PHILOSOPHIE.COM

http://la-philosophie.com

LA-PHILOSOPHIE.COM SCHOLARSHIP
• *See page 104*

THE LYNDON BAINES JOHNSON FOUNDATION

http://www.lbjlibrary.org/page/foundation/

MOODY RESEARCH GRANTS
• *See page 99*

MAINE COMMUNITY FOUNDATION, INC.

http://www.mainecf.org/

KEEPERS PRESERVATION EDUCATION FUND
The Keepers Preservation Education Fund was established to support aspiring or established historic preservation professionals who wish to increase their professional knowledge or career potential. Eligibility is not limited to Maine residents. Applicants may be from anywhere in the United States. Awards are not retroactive. Please go to the Maine Community Foundation, Inc. website for application requirements. https://www.mainecf.org/

Academic Fields/Career Goals: History.

Award: Scholarship for use in freshman, sophomore, junior, senior, graduate, or postgraduate years; not renewable.

Eligibility Requirements: Applicant must be enrolled or expecting to enroll full- or part-time at an institution or university. Available to U.S. citizens.

Application Requirements: Application form. *Deadline:* continuous.

Contact: Liz Fickett, Maine Community Foundation
Maine Community Foundation, Inc.
245 Main Street
Ellsworth, ME 04605
Phone: 207-412-2015
E-mail: efickett@mainecf.org

NATIONAL SOCIETY DAUGHTERS OF THE AMERICAN REVOLUTION

http://www.dar.org/

ENID HALL GRISWOLD MEMORIAL SCHOLARSHIP
The Enid Hall Griswold Memorial Scholarship is awarded to two deserving college juniors or seniors enrolled in an accredited college or university in the United States who is pursuing a major in political science, history, government, or economics. This is a one-time award in the amount of $5,000.

Academic Fields/Career Goals: History; Political Science.

Award: Scholarship for use in junior or senior years; not renewable. *Number:* 2. *Amount:* $5000.

Eligibility Requirements: Applicant must be enrolled or expecting to enroll full-time at an institution or university. Available to U.S. citizens.

Application Requirements: Application form, application form may be submitted online, essay, financial need analysis. *Deadline:* February 15.

Contact: Lakeisha Graham, Manager, Office of the Reporter General
Phone: 202-628-1776
Fax: 202-879-3348
E-mail: nsdarscholarships@dar.org

PHI ALPHA THETA HISTORY HONOR SOCIETY, INC.

http://www.phialphatheta.org/

PHI ALPHA THETA/WESTERN FRONT ASSOCIATION PAPER PRIZE
Essay competition open to full-time undergraduate members of the association. The paper must be from 12 to 15 typed pages and must address the American experience in World War I, must be dealing with virtually any aspect of American involvement during the period from 1912 (second Moroccan crisis) to 1924 (Dawes plan). Primary source material must be used. For further details visit http://www.phialphatheta.org.

Academic Fields/Career Goals: History.

Award: Prize for use in freshman, sophomore, junior, or senior years; not renewable. *Number:* 1. *Amount:* $1000.

Eligibility Requirements: Applicant must be enrolled or expecting to enroll full-time at a four-year institution or university and must have an interest in writing. Applicant or parent of applicant must be member of Phi Alpha Theta. Available to U.S. and non-U.S. citizens.

Application Requirements: 5 copies of the paper, CD-ROM containing a file of the paper and cover letter, application form, essay. *Deadline:* December 1.

Contact: Dr. Graydon Tunstall, Executive Director
Phi Alpha Theta History Honor Society, Inc.
University of South Florida
4202 East Fowler Avenue, SOC 107
Tampa, FL 33620-8100
Phone: 800-394-8195
Fax: 813-974-8215
E-mail: info@phialphatheta.org

PHI ALPHA THETA WORLD HISTORY ASSOCIATION PAPER PRIZE
Awards one undergraduate and one graduate-level prize for papers examining any historical issue with global implications such as: exchange or interchange of cultures, comparison of civilizations or cultures. This is a joint award with the World History Association. Must be a member of the World History Association or Phi Alpha Theta. Paper must have been composed while enrolled at an accredited college or university. Must send in four copies of paper along with professor's letter.

Academic Fields/Career Goals: History; Humanities; International Studies; Social Sciences.

Award: Prize for use in freshman, sophomore, junior, senior, or graduate years; not renewable. *Number:* 2. *Amount:* $500.

Eligibility Requirements: Applicant must be enrolled or expecting to enroll full-time at a four-year institution or university. Applicant or parent of applicant must be member of Other Student Academic Clubs, Phi Alpha Theta. Available to U.S. and non-U.S. citizens.

Application Requirements: 4 copies of paper, abstract, letter from faculty member or professor, recommendations or references. *Deadline:* June 30.

Contact: Prof. Merry Wiesner-Hanks
Phi Alpha Theta History Honor Society, Inc.
Department of History
University of Wisconsin-Madison
Madison, WI 53201
E-mail: merrywh@uwm.edu

SOCIETY FOR CLASSICAL STUDIES

http://www.classicalstudies.org/

MINORITY STUDENT SUMMER SCHOLARSHIP
• *See page 112*

STRAIGHTFORWARD MEDIA

http://www.straightforwardmedia.com/

STRAIGHTFORWARD MEDIA LIBERAL ARTS SCHOLARSHIP
• *See page 119*

HOME ECONOMICS

ABBIE SARGENT MEMORIAL SCHOLARSHIP INC.

http://www.nhfarmbureau.org/

ABBIE SARGENT MEMORIAL SCHOLARSHIP
• *See page 89*

AMERICAN ASSOCIATION OF FAMILY & CONSUMER SERVICES

http://www.aafcs.org/

AMERICAN ASSOCIATION OF FAMILY & CONSUMER SCIENCES NATIONAL UNDERGRADUATE SCHOLARSHIP

The association awards scholarships to individuals who have exhibited the potential to make contributions to the family and consumer sciences profession.

Academic Fields/Career Goals: Home Economics.

Award: Scholarship for use in sophomore, junior, or senior years; not renewable. *Number:* up to 1. *Amount:* up to $5000.

Eligibility Requirements: Applicant must be enrolled or expecting to enroll full-time at a four-year institution or university. Available to U.S. citizens.

Application Requirements: Application form, application form may be submitted online (http://www.aafcs.org), recommendations or references, resume, transcript. *Deadline:* January 15.

CONTINENTAL SOCIETY, DAUGHTERS OF INDIAN WARS

http://www.csdiw.org/

CONTINENTAL SOCIETY, DAUGHTERS OF INDIAN WARS SCHOLARSHIP
• *See page 188*

COSTUME SOCIETY OF AMERICA

http://www.costumesocietyamerica.com/

ADELE FILENE STUDENT PRESENTER GRANT
• *See page 118*

STELLA BLUM STUDENT RESEARCH GRANT
• *See page 118*

FAMILY, CAREER AND COMMUNITY LEADERS OF AMERICA-TEXAS ASSOCIATION

http://www.texasfccla.org/

C.J. DAVIDSON SCHOLARSHIP FOR FCCLA

Renewable award for graduating high school seniors enrolled in full-time program in family and consumer sciences. Must be Texas resident and should study in Texas. Must have minimum GPA of 2.5.

Academic Fields/Career Goals: Home Economics.

Award: Scholarship for use in freshman year; renewable. *Number:* 1–10. *Amount:* up to $18,000.

Eligibility Requirements: Applicant must be high school student; planning to enroll or expecting to enroll full-time at a four-year institution or university; single; resident of Texas and studying in Texas. Applicant or parent of applicant must be member of Family, Career and Community Leaders of America. Available to U.S. citizens.

Application Requirements: Application form, essay, recommendations or references, test scores, transcript. *Deadline:* March 1.

Contact: Staff
Family, Career and Community Leaders of America-Texas Association
1107 West 45th
Austin, TX 78756
Phone: 512-306-0099
Fax: 512-442-7100
E-mail: fccla@texasfccla.org

FCCLA REGIONAL SCHOLARSHIPS
• *See page 147*

FCCLA TEXAS FARM BUREAU SCHOLARSHIP
• *See page 147*

LES DAMES D'ESCOFFIER INTERNATIONAL, COLORADO CHAPTER

www.lesdamescolorado.org/scholarship

LES DAMES D'ESCOFFIER INTERNATIONAL, COLORADO CHAPTER SCHOLARSHIP
• *See page 94*

HORTICULTURE/ FLORICULTURE

ABBIE SARGENT MEMORIAL SCHOLARSHIP INC.

http://www.nhfarmbureau.org/

ABBIE SARGENT MEMORIAL SCHOLARSHIP
• *See page 89*

ALABAMA GOLF COURSE SUPERINTENDENTS ASSOCIATION

http://www.agcsa.org/

ALABAMA GOLF COURSE SUPERINTENDENT'S ASSOCIATION'S DONNIE ARTHUR MEMORIAL SCHOLARSHIP
• *See page 92*

AMERICAN INDIAN SCIENCE AND ENGINEERING SOCIETY

http://www.aises.org/

A.T. ANDERSON MEMORIAL SCHOLARSHIP PROGRAM
• *See page 105*

AMERICAN SOCIETY FOR ENOLOGY AND VITICULTURE

http://www.asev.org/

AMERICAN SOCIETY FOR ENOLOGY AND VITICULTURE SCHOLARSHIPS
• *See page 92*

ARIZONA NURSERY ASSOCIATION

http://www.azna.org/

ARIZONA NURSERY ASSOCIATION FOUNDATION SCHOLARSHIP

Provides research grants and scholarships for the Green Industry. Applicant must be an Arizona resident currently or planning to be enrolled in a horticultural related curriculum at an Arizona university, community college, or continuing education program. See website for further details http://www.azna.org.

Academic Fields/Career Goals: Horticulture/Floriculture.

Award: Scholarship for use in freshman, sophomore, junior, or senior years; renewable. *Number:* 12–16. *Amount:* $500–$3000.

Eligibility Requirements: Applicant must be enrolled or expecting to enroll full- or part-time at a two-year or four-year or technical institution or university. Available to U.S. citizens.

Application Requirements: Application form, recommendations or references, transcript. *Deadline:* April 15.

Contact: Cheryl Goar, Executive Director
Phone: 480-966-1610
E-mail: cgoar@azna.org

BHW GROUP

https://thebhwgroup.com/

BHW WOMEN IN STEM SCHOLARSHIP
• *See page 107*

CHS FOUNDATION

http://www.chsfoundation.org/

CHS FOUNDATION HIGH SCHOOL SCHOLARSHIPS
• *See page 89*

CHS FOUNDATION TWO-YEAR COLLEGE SCHOLARSHIPS
• *See page 89*

ENVIRONMENTAL CARE ASSOCIATION OF IDAHO

http://www.eacofidaho.org

ECA SCHOLARSHIP

The scholarship will be given directly to the recipient. Applicants must be a son or daughter of ECA member, OR be employed in the Lawn Care, Pest Control or Grounds Management Industries, OR Applicant must be enrolled as a full-time student in an accredited college level in Pest Control, Lawn Care or related industry. A reference letter and two letters of recommendation are required along with a one-page typed essay stating the benefits of the Lawn Care or Pest Control Industries.

Academic Fields/Career Goals: Horticulture/Floriculture; Trade/Technical Specialties.

Award: Scholarship for use in freshman, sophomore, junior, or senior years; not renewable. *Number:* 1–2. *Amount:* $500.

Eligibility Requirements: Applicant must be enrolled or expecting to enroll full- or part-time at a two-year or four-year or technical institution or university and resident of Idaho.

Application Requirements: Application form, essay. *Deadline:* November 10.

Contact: Ann Bates, Executive Coordinator
Phone: 208-681-4769
E-mail: abates@ecaofidaho.org

FEDERATED GARDEN CLUBS OF CONNECTICUT

http://www.ctgardenclubs.org/

FEDERATED GARDEN CLUBS OF CONNECTICUT INC. SCHOLARSHIPS
• *See page 142*

FEDERATED GARDEN CLUBS OF MARYLAND

office@fgcofmd.org

ROBERT LEWIS BAKER SCHOLARSHIP

Scholarship awards of up to $5000 to encourage the study of ornamental horticulture, and landscape design. Applicants must be high school graduates, current college and/or graduate students, and Maryland residents. Can attend any accredited college/university in the United States.

Academic Fields/Career Goals: Horticulture/Floriculture; Landscape Architecture.

Award: Scholarship for use in freshman, sophomore, junior, senior, or graduate years; not renewable. *Number:* 1. *Amount:* $5000.

Eligibility Requirements: Applicant must be enrolled or expecting to enroll full-time at a four-year institution or university and resident of Maryland. Available to U.S. citizens.

Application Requirements: Application form. *Deadline:* June 30.

Contact: Marjorie Schiebel, Scholarship Chair
Phone: 410-296-6961
E-mail: fgcofmd@aol.com

GOLDEN STATE BONSAI FEDERATION

http://www.gsbf-bonsai.org/

HORTICULTURE SCHOLARSHIPS

Scholarship for study towards a certificate in ornamental horticulture from an accredited school. Applicant must be a current member of a GSBF member club and have a letter of recommendation from club president, or a responsible spokesperson from GSBF. Deadline varies.

Academic Fields/Career Goals: Horticulture/Floriculture.

Award: Scholarship for use in freshman, sophomore, junior, senior, graduate, or postgraduate years; not renewable. *Amount:* $400.

Eligibility Requirements: Applicant must be enrolled or expecting to enroll full-time at a two-year or four-year or technical institution or university. Applicant or parent of applicant must be member of Golden State Bonsai Federation. Available to U.S. citizens.

Application Requirements: Application form.

Contact: Abe Far, Grants and Scholarship Committee
Phone: 619-234-3434
Fax: 619-234-2420
E-mail: abefar@cox.net

GREAT MINDS IN STEM

http://www.greatmindsinstem.org/college/scholarship-application-information

HENAAC SCHOLARSHIP PROGRAM
• *See page 100*

HORTICULTURAL RESEARCH INSTITUTE

https://www.hriresearch.org/

BRYAN A. CHAMPION MEMORIAL SCHOLARSHIP
• *See page 247*

CARVILLE M. AKEHURST MEMORIAL SCHOLARSHIP
• *See page 247*

MUGGET SCHOLARSHIP

Each year Mugget Growers of America (MGA) participants meet at the American Nursery & Landscape Association's (ANLA) Management Clinic to discuss important plant issues regarding the development of a new plant called "Mugget". These Mugget supporters hope to help aspiring students from across the country obtain a degree in horticulture with this one $1,000 scholarship. Applicant must have a minimum grade point average overall of 2.25 based on a scale of 4.0, and a minimum GPA of 2.7 on a scale of 4.0 in their major. Preference will be given to applicants who plan to work within the industry (including nursery operation, landscape architecture/design/construction/maintenance, interiorscape, horticultural distribution, or retail garden center) following graduation.

Academic Fields/Career Goals: Horticulture/Floriculture; Landscape Architecture.

Award: Scholarship for use in sophomore, junior, senior, graduate, or postgraduate years; not renewable. *Number:* 1. *Amount:* $1000.

Eligibility Requirements: Applicant must be enrolled or expecting to enroll full- or part-time at a two-year or technical institution or university. Available to U.S. citizens.

Application Requirements: Application form, application form may be submitted online, essay, financial need analysis. *Deadline:* September 10.

Contact: Jennifer Gray, Research Programs Administrator
　　　　　Horticultural Research Institute
　　　　　2130 Stella Court
　　　　　Columbus, OH 43215
　　　　　Phone: 614-487-1117
　　　　　E-mail: jenniferg@americanhort.org

SPRING MEADOW NURSERY SCHOLARSHIP

The Spring Meadow Nursery's goal is to grant three $3,500 scholarships to students with an interest in woody plant production, woody plant propagation, woody plant breeding, horticultural sales and marketing. Must have a minimum grade point average overall of 2.25 based on a scale of 4.0, and a minimum GPA of 2.7 on a scale of 4.0 in their major.

Academic Fields/Career Goals: Horticulture/Floriculture; Landscape Architecture.

Award: Scholarship for use in sophomore, junior, senior, or graduate years; not renewable. *Number:* 3. *Amount:* $3500.

Eligibility Requirements: Applicant must be enrolled or expecting to enroll full-time at a two-year or technical institution or university. Available to U.S. and Canadian citizens.

Application Requirements: Application form, application form may be submitted online, essay, financial need analysis. *Deadline:* September 10.

Contact: Jennifer Gray, Research Programs Administrator
　　　　　Horticultural Research Institute
　　　　　2130 Stella Court
　　　　　Columbus, OH 43215
　　　　　Phone: 614-487-1117
　　　　　E-mail: jenniferg@americanhort.org

SUSIE AND BRUCE USREY EDUCATION SCHOLARSHIP
• *See page 247*

TIMOTHY S. AND PALMER W. BIGELOW, JR. SCHOLARSHIP
• *See page 247*

USREY FAMILY SCHOLARSHIP
• *See page 248*

IDAHO NURSERY AND LANDSCAPE ASSOCIATION

http://www.inlagrow.org/

IDAHO NURSERY AND LANDSCAPE ASSOCIATION SCHOLARSHIPS

To encourage study of Horticulture, Floriculture, Plant Pathology, Landscape Design, Turfgrass Management, Botany and other allied subjects that pertain to the green industry. Applicant must be an Idaho resident.

Academic Fields/Career Goals: Horticulture/Floriculture.

Award: Scholarship for use in freshman, sophomore, junior, or senior years; not renewable. *Number:* 1–4. *Amount:* $750.

Eligibility Requirements: Applicant must be enrolled or expecting to enroll full- or part-time at a two-year or four-year or technical institution or university; resident of Idaho and studying in Idaho. Available to U.S. citizens.

Application Requirements: Application form, community service, essay. *Deadline:* December 1.

Contact: Ann Bates, Executive Director
　　　　　Phone: 208-681-4769
　　　　　Fax: 208-529-0832
　　　　　E-mail: abates@inlagrow.org

JOSEPH SHINODA MEMORIAL SCHOLARSHIP FOUNDATION

http://www.shinodascholarship.org/

JOSEPH SHINODA MEMORIAL SCHOLARSHIP

One-time award for undergraduates in accredited colleges and universities. Must be furthering their education in the field of floriculture (production, distribution, research, or retail).

Academic Fields/Career Goals: Horticulture/Floriculture.

Award: Scholarship for use in sophomore, junior, or senior years; not renewable. *Number:* 8–15. *Amount:* $1000–$5000.

Eligibility Requirements: Applicant must be enrolled or expecting to enroll full-time at a four-year institution or university. Available to U.S. citizens.

Application Requirements: Application form, essay, financial need analysis, recommendations or references, transcript. *Deadline:* March 30.

Contact: Barbara McCaleb, Executive Secretary
　　　　　Joseph Shinoda Memorial Scholarship Foundation
　　　　　234 Via La Paz
　　　　　San Luis Obispo, CA 93401
　　　　　Phone: 805-544-0717

THE LAND CONSERVANCY OF NEW JERSEY

http://www.tlc-nj.org/

ROGERS FAMILY SCHOLARSHIP
• *See page 143*

LANDSCAPE ARCHITECTURE FOUNDATION

www.lafoundation.org

RAIN BIRD INTELLIGENT USE OF WATER SCHOLARSHIP

This award recognizes an outstanding landscape architecture, horticulture or irrigation science student. Eligible applicants are in the final two years of undergraduate study with demonstrated commitment to these professions through participation in extracurricular activities and exemplary scholastic achievements.

Academic Fields/Career Goals: Horticulture/Floriculture.

Award: Scholarship for use in junior or senior years; not renewable. *Number:* 1. *Amount:* $2500.

Eligibility Requirements: Applicant must be enrolled or expecting to enroll full- or part-time at a four-year institution or university. Available to U.S. and non-U.S. citizens.

Application Requirements: Application form, essay, personal photograph. *Fee:* $5. *Deadline:* February 1.

Contact: Ms. Danielle Carbonneau, Program Manager, Scholarships and Leadership
　　　　　Phone: 202-331-7070 Ext. 14
　　　　　E-mail: scholarships@lafoundation.org

MONTANA FEDERATION OF GARDEN CLUBS

http://www.mtfgc.org/

LIFE MEMBER MONTANA FEDERATION OF GARDEN CLUBS SCHOLARSHIP
• See page 202

NATIONAL GARDEN CLUBS SCHOLARSHIP

Scholarship for a college student majoring in some branch of horticulture. Applicants must have sophomore or higher standing and be a legal resident of Montana.

Academic Fields/Career Goals: Horticulture/Floriculture.

Award: Scholarship for use in sophomore, junior, or senior years; not renewable. *Number:* 1. *Amount:* up to $3500.

Eligibility Requirements: Applicant must be enrolled or expecting to enroll full-time at a four-year institution or university and resident of Montana. Available to U.S. citizens.

Application Requirements: Application form, financial need analysis. *Deadline:* February 28.

Contact: Margaret Yaw, Scholarship Committee, State Chairman
Montana Federation of Garden Clubs
2603 Spring Creek Drive
Bozeman, MT 59715-3621
Phone: 406-587-3621

NATIONAL COUNCIL OF STATE GARDEN CLUBS INC. SCHOLARSHIP

http://www.gardenclub.org/

NATIONAL COUNCIL OF STATE GARDEN CLUBS INC. SCHOLARSHIP
• See page 94

NATIONAL GARDEN CLUBS INC.

http://www.gardenclub.org/

NATIONAL GARDEN CLUBS INC. SCHOLARSHIP PROGRAM
• See page 94

NATIONAL RESTAURANT ASSOCIATION EDUCATIONAL FOUNDATION

http://www.chooserestaurants.org

NATIONAL RESTAURANT ASSOCIATION EDUCATIONAL FOUNDATION UNDERGRADUATE SCHOLARSHIPS FOR COLLEGE STUDENTS
• See page 95

OREGON ASSOCIATION OF NURSERIES

https://www.oan.org/

BILL EGAN MEMORIAL AWARD

$1,000 to a college student majoring in horticulture with emphasis on greenhouse/floriculture areas. Preference will be given to family members and employees of the OAN Greenhouse Chapter.

Academic Fields/Career Goals: Horticulture/Floriculture.

Award: Scholarship for use in freshman, sophomore, junior, or senior years; not renewable. *Amount:* $1000.

Eligibility Requirements: Applicant must be enrolled or expecting to enroll at an institution or university. Available to U.S. citizens.

Application Requirements: Application form. *Deadline:* April 1.

Contact: Stephanie Weihrauch, Event and Education Manager
Oregon Association of Nurseries
29751 SW Town Center Loop W
Wilsonville, OR 97070
Phone: 503-682-5089
Fax: 503-682-5099
E-mail: sweihrauch@oan.org

CLACKAMAS CHAPTER AWARD

$1,500 to a student beginning college studies in an ornamental horticulture field.

Academic Fields/Career Goals: Horticulture/Floriculture.

Award: Scholarship for use in freshman, sophomore, junior, or senior years; not renewable. *Amount:* $1500.

Eligibility Requirements: Applicant must be enrolled or expecting to enroll at an institution or university. Available to U.S. citizens.

Application Requirements: Application form. *Deadline:* April 1.

Contact: Stephanie Weihrauch, Event and Education Manager
Oregon Association of Nurseries
29751 SW Town Center Loop W
Wilsonville, OR 97070
Phone: 503-682-5089
Fax: 503-682-5099
E-mail: sweihrauch@oan.org

EMERALD EMPIRE CHAPTER AWARD

$1,000 to a junior or senior college student majoring in horticulture, landscape architecture or landscape construction who also graduated from an Oregon high school. Preference will be given to a student from the Emerald Empire (Eugene) area.

Academic Fields/Career Goals: Horticulture/Floriculture; Landscape Architecture.

Award: Scholarship for use in junior or senior years; not renewable. *Amount:* $1000.

Eligibility Requirements: Applicant must be enrolled or expecting to enroll at an institution or university. Available to U.S. citizens.

Application Requirements: Application form. *Deadline:* April 1.

Contact: Stephanie Weihrauch, Event and Education Manager
Oregon Association of Nurseries
29751 SW Town Center Loop W
Wilsonville, OR 97070
Phone: 503-682-5089
Fax: 503-682-5099
E-mail: sweihrauch@oan.org

SOIL AND WATER CONSERVATION SOCIETY-NEW JERSEY CHAPTER

http://www.geocities.com/njswcs

EDWARD R. HALL SCHOLARSHIP
• See page 91

SOUTHERN NURSERY ASSOCIATION

http://www.sna.org/

SIDNEY B. MEADOWS SCHOLARSHIP ENDOWMENT FUND

Scholarship of at least $1500 to students enrolled in an accredited undergraduate or graduate ornamental horticulture program or related discipline at a four-year institution. Student must be in a junior or senior or graduate standing at time of application. For undergraduate students minimum grade point average of 2.25 on a scale of 4.0, or 3.0 for graduate students. Students must be a US Citizen and a resident of the following states in the United States: Alabama, Arkansas, Florida, Georgia, Kentucky, Louisiana, Maryland, Mississippi, Missouri, North Carolina, Oklahoma, South Carolina, Tennessee, Texas, Virginia and West Virginia.

Academic Fields/Career Goals: Horticulture/Floriculture.

Award: Scholarship for use in junior, senior, or graduate years; not renewable. *Number:* 10–12. *Amount:* $1500.

Eligibility Requirements: Applicant must be enrolled or expecting to enroll full-time at a four-year institution or university and resident of Alabama, Arkansas, Florida, Georgia, Kentucky, Louisiana, Maryland, Mississippi, Missouri, North Carolina, Oklahoma, South Carolina, Tennessee, Texas, Virginia, West Virginia. Available to U.S. citizens.

Application Requirements: Application form. *Deadline:* May 30.

Contact: Mr. Danny Summers, Executive Vice President
Southern Nursery Association
PO Box 801513
Acworth, GA 30101
Phone: 678-813-1880
E-mail: danny@sbmsef.org

TURF AND ORNAMENTAL COMMUNICATORS ASSOCIATION

http://www.toca.org/

TURF AND ORNAMENTAL COMMUNICATORS ASSOCIATION SCHOLARSHIP PROGRAM
• *See page 96*

UNITED NEGRO COLLEGE FUND

http://www.uncf.org/

LEIDOS STEM SCHOLARSHIP
• *See page 96*

HOSPITALITY MANAGEMENT

AMERICAN HOTEL AND LODGING EDUCATIONAL FOUNDATION

https://www.ahlafoundation.org/

AHLEF ANNUAL SCHOLARSHIP GRANT PROGRAM
• *See page 267*

AMERICAN EXPRESS SCHOLARSHIP PROGRAM
Award for full- and part-time students in undergraduate program leading to degree in hospitality management. Must be employed at hotel which is a member of AHLA, and must work a minimum of 20 hours per week. Dependents of hotel employees may also apply.

Academic Fields/Career Goals: Hospitality Management.

Award: Scholarship for use in freshman, sophomore, junior, or senior years; not renewable. *Number:* 5–8. *Amount:* $500–$2000.

Eligibility Requirements: Applicant must be enrolled or expecting to enroll full- or part-time at a two-year institution or university. Applicant or parent of applicant must have employment or volunteer experience in hospitality/hotel administration/operations. Available to U.S. and non-U.S. citizens.

Application Requirements: Application form, essay, financial need analysis. *Deadline:* May 1.

Contact: Kodichi Nwankwo, Foundation Coordinator
American Hotel and Lodging Educational Foundation
1250 Eye Street, NW
Suite 1100
Washington, DC 20005
Phone: 202-289-3134
E-mail: knwankwo@ahlef.org

AMERICAN HOTEL & LODGING EDUCATIONAL FOUNDATION PEPSI SCHOLARSHIP
• *See page 189*

ECOLAB SCHOLARSHIP PROGRAM
• *See page 267*

HYATT HOTELS FUND FOR MINORITY LODGING MANAGEMENT
• *See page 268*

INCOMING FRESHMAN SCHOLARSHIPS
• *See page 268*

RAMA SCHOLARSHIP FOR THE AMERICAN DREAM
• *See page 268*

CAREERS THROUGH CULINARY ARTS PROGRAM INC.

http://www.ccapinc.org/

CAREERS THROUGH CULINARY ARTS PROGRAM COOKING COMPETITION FOR SCHOLARSHIPS
• *See page 190*

CLUB FOUNDATION

http://www.clubfoundation.org/

JOE PERDUE SCHOLARSHIP PROGRAM
Awards for candidates seeking a managerial career in the private club industry and currently attending an accredited four year college or university. Must have completed freshman year and be enrolled full-time. Must have achieved and continue to maintain a GPA of at least 2.5 on a 4.0 scale or a 4.5 on a 6.0 scale.

Academic Fields/Career Goals: Hospitality Management.

Award: Scholarship for use in sophomore, junior, or senior years; not renewable. *Number:* 8. *Amount:* $2500.

Eligibility Requirements: Applicant must be enrolled or expecting to enroll full-time at a four-year institution or university. Available to U.S. citizens.

Application Requirements: Application form, essay. *Deadline:* May 1.

Contact: Carrie Wosicki, Director of Development
E-mail: carrie.wosicki@cmaa.org

DECA (DISTRIBUTIVE EDUCATION CLUBS OF AMERICA)

http://www.deca.org/

HARRY A. APPLEGATE SCHOLARSHIP
• *See page 73*

GOLDEN GATE RESTAURANT ASSOCIATION

http://www.ggra.org/

GOLDEN GATE RESTAURANT ASSOCIATION SCHOLARSHIP FOUNDATION
• *See page 190*

HAWAII LODGING & TOURISM ASSOCIATION

http://www.hawaiilodging.org

CLEM JUDD, JR. MEMORIAL SCHOLARSHIP
Scholarship for a Hawaii resident who must be able to prove Hawaiian ancestry. Applicant must be enrolled full-time at a U.S. accredited university/college majoring in hotel management. Must have a minimum 3.0 GPA.

Academic Fields/Career Goals: Hospitality Management.

Award: Scholarship for use in junior or senior years; not renewable. *Number:* 2. *Amount:* $1000–$2500.

Eligibility Requirements: Applicant must be Asian/Pacific Islander; enrolled or expecting to enroll full-time at a four-year institution and resident of Hawaii. Available to U.S. citizens.

Application Requirements: Application form, essay, personal photograph, recommendations or references, resume. *Deadline:* July 1.

Contact: Scholarship Committee
Hawaii Lodging & Tourism Association
2270 Kalakaua Avenue, Suite 1506
Honolulu, HI 96815
Phone: 808-923-0407
Fax: 808-924-3843
E-mail: info@hawaiilodging.org

R.W. "BOB" HOLDEN SCHOLARSHIP

One $1000 award for a student attending an accredited university or college in Hawaii, majoring in hotel management. Must be a Hawaii resident and a U.S. citizen. Must have a minimum 3.0 GPA.

Academic Fields/Career Goals: Hospitality Management; Travel/Tourism.

Award: Scholarship for use in junior or senior years; not renewable. *Number:* 1–5. *Amount:* $1000.

Eligibility Requirements: Applicant must be enrolled or expecting to enroll full-time at a four-year institution or university. Available to U.S. citizens.

Application Requirements: Application form, essay, personal photograph, recommendations or references, resume, self-addressed stamped envelope with application, transcript. *Deadline:* July 1.

Contact: Dean Nakasone, Vice President
Hawaii Lodging & Tourism Association
2270 Kalakaua Avenue, Suite 1702
Honolulu, HI 96815
Phone: 808-923-0407
E-mail: info@hawaiilodging.org

HOUSE OF BLUES MUSIC FORWARD FOUNDATION

https://hobmusicforward.org/

STEVEN J. FINKEL SERVICE EXCELLENCE SCHOLARSHIP
• *See page 148*

TIFFANY GREEN OPERATOR SCHOLARSHIP AWARD
• *See page 85*

ILLINOIS RESTAURANT ASSOCIATION EDUCATIONAL FOUNDATION

http://www.illinoisrestaurants.org/

ILLINOIS RESTAURANT ASSOCIATION EDUCATIONAL FOUNDATION SCHOLARSHIPS
• *See page 190*

JAMES BEARD FOUNDATION INC.

http://www.jamesbeard.org/

BERN LAXER MEMORIAL SCHOLARSHIP
• *See page 191*

CHICAGO JBF EATS WEEK SCHOLARSHIP
• *See page 191*

MAINE RESTAURANT ASSOCIATION

http://www.mainerestaurant.com/

MAINE RESTAURANT ASSOCIATION EDUCATION FOUNDATION SCHOLARSHIP FUND
• *See page 192*

MARYLAND RESTAURANT ASSOCIATION EDUCATION FOUNDATION

https://www.marylandrestaurants.com/about.html

THE LETITIA B. CARTER SCHOLARSHIP
• *See page 192*

MARCIA S. HARRIS LEGACY FUND SCHOLARSHIP
• *See page 192*

MISSOURI TRAVEL COUNCIL

http://www.missouritravel.com/

BOB SMITH TOURISM SCHOLARSHIP
• *See page 269*

NATIONAL RESTAURANT ASSOCIATION EDUCATIONAL FOUNDATION

http://www.chooserestaurants.org

NATIONAL RESTAURANT ASSOCIATION EDUCATIONAL FOUNDATION UNDERGRADUATE SCHOLARSHIPS FOR COLLEGE STUDENTS
• *See page 95*

OHIO TRAVEL ASSOCIATION

http://www.ohiotravel.org/

BILL SCHWARTZ MEMORIAL SCHOLARSHIP

Scholarship will be granted to a qualified full-time, Ohio student after the completion of their freshman year. Must be studying hospitality management or travel/tourism with a minimum 2.5 GPA. As part of the scholarship program, the recipient will be invited to various OTA events throughout the year.

Academic Fields/Career Goals: Hospitality Management; Travel/Tourism.

Award: Scholarship for use in sophomore, junior, or senior years; not renewable. *Number:* 1. *Amount:* $1000.

Eligibility Requirements: Applicant must be enrolled or expecting to enroll full-time at a two-year or four-year or technical institution or university; resident of Ohio and studying in Ohio. Applicant or parent of applicant must have employment or volunteer experience in travel and tourism industry. Available to U.S. citizens.

Application Requirements: Application form, financial need analysis, recommendations or references, transcript. *Deadline:* June 15.

Contact: Ms. Betsy Decillis, Membership and Community Manager
Phone: 800-896-4682 Ext. 0#
E-mail: betsy@ohiotravel.org

SCARLETT FAMILY FOUNDATION SCHOLARSHIP PROGRAM

http://www.scarlettfoundation.org/

SCHOLARSHIP FOR STUDENTS PURSUING A BUSINESS OR STEM DEGREE
• *See page 80*

SOUTH CAROLINA RESTAURANT AND LODGING ASSOCIATION

http://www.scrla.org/

SOUTH CAROLINA TOURISM AND HOSPITALITY EDUCATIONAL FOUNDATION SCHOLARSHIPS
• *See page 193*

UNITED NEGRO COLLEGE FUND

http://www.uncf.org/

NATIONAL BLACK MCDONALD'S OWNERS ASSOCIATION HOSPITALITY SCHOLARS PROGRAM
• See page 83

UNCF/CARNIVAL CORPORATE SCHOLARS PROGRAM
• See page 151

WALT DISNEY COMPANY UNCF CORPORATE SCHOLARS PROGRAM
• See page 177

HUMANITIES

AMERICAN CLASSICAL LEAGUE/NATIONAL JUNIOR CLASSICAL LEAGUE

http://www.aclclassics.org/

NATIONAL JUNIOR CLASSICAL LEAGUE SCHOLARSHIP
• See page 169

BETHESDA LUTHERAN COMMUNITIES

http://www.bethesdalutherancommunities.org/scholarships

DEVELOPMENTAL DISABILITIES SCHOLASTIC ACHIEVEMENT SCHOLARSHIP FOR COLLEGE STUDENTS WHO ARE LUTHERAN
• See page 195

CANADIAN INSTITUTE OF UKRAINIAN STUDIES

https://www.ualberta.ca/canadian-institute-of-ukrainian-studies/index.html

LEO J. KRYSA FAMILY UNDERGRADUATE SCHOLARSHIP
• See page 208

CATCHING THE DREAM

http://www.catchingthedream.org/

MATH, ENGINEERING, SCIENCE, BUSINESS, EDUCATION, COMPUTERS SCHOLARSHIPS
• See page 146

NATIVE AMERICAN LEADERSHIP IN EDUCATION (NALE)
• See page 146

CULTURAL SERVICES OF THE FRENCH EMBASSY

http://www.frenchculture.org/

TEACHING ASSISTANT PROGRAM IN FRANCE
• See page 98

JACK J. ISGUR FOUNDATION

www.isgur.org

JACK J. ISGUR FOUNDATION SCHOLARSHIP
• See page 211

LADIES AUXILIARY TO THE VETERANS OF FOREIGN WARS, DEPARTMENT OF MAINE

http://mainevfw.org/

FRANCES L. BOOTH MEDICAL SCHOLARSHIP SPONSORED BY LAVFW DEPARTMENT OF MAINE
• See page 283

LA-PHILOSOPHIE.COM

http://la-philosophie.com

LA-PHILOSOPHIE.COM SCHOLARSHIP
• See page 104

NOET SCHOLARLY TOOLS

http://www.noet.com

NOET HUMANITIES SCHOLARSHIP
The Noet Humanities Scholarship seeks to award students enrolled in a humanities program at the undergraduate or graduate level. There is one scholarship available at $500. To enter, students must be currently enrolled (or enrolling in the upcoming quarter) in an undergraduate or graduate program in the humanities.

Academic Fields/Career Goals: Humanities.

Award: Scholarship for use in freshman, sophomore, junior, senior, graduate, or postgraduate years; not renewable. *Number:* up to 1. *Amount:* $500–$500.

Eligibility Requirements: Applicant must be enrolled or expecting to enroll full- or part-time at a two-year or four-year institution or university. Available to U.S. and non-U.S. citizens.

Application Requirements: Application form may be submitted online (http://noet.com/scholarships), email address, transcript. *Deadline:* varies.

Contact: Mr. Benjamin Amundgaard, Noet Brand/Product Manager
Noet Scholarly Tools
1313 Commercial Street
Bellingham, WA 98226
Phone: 360-398-5145
E-mail: ben.amundgaard@noet.com

PHI ALPHA THETA HISTORY HONOR SOCIETY, INC.

http://www.phialphatheta.org/

PHI ALPHA THETA WORLD HISTORY ASSOCIATION PAPER PRIZE
• See page 289

STRAIGHTFORWARD MEDIA

http://www.straightforwardmedia.com/

STRAIGHTFORWARD MEDIA LIBERAL ARTS SCHOLARSHIP
• See page 119

UNITED NEGRO COLLEGE FUND

http://www.uncf.org/

THE OSSIE DAVIS LEGACY AWARD SCHOLARSHIP
• See page 89

HUMAN RESOURCES

AUTOMOTIVE WOMEN'S ALLIANCE FOUNDATION

http://awafoundation.org/index.php

AUTOMOTIVE WOMEN'S ALLIANCE FOUNDATION SCHOLARSHIPS
• *See page 71*

HOUSE OF BLUES MUSIC FORWARD FOUNDATION

https://hobmusicforward.org/

TIFFANY GREEN OPERATOR SCHOLARSHIP AWARD
• *See page 85*

NEW ENGLAND EMPLOYEE BENEFITS COUNCIL

http://www.neebc.org/

NEW ENGLAND EMPLOYEE BENEFITS COUNCIL SCHOLARSHIP PROGRAM
• *See page 78*

SCARLETT FAMILY FOUNDATION SCHOLARSHIP PROGRAM

http://www.scarlettfoundation.org/

SCHOLARSHIP FOR STUDENTS PURSUING A BUSINESS OR STEM DEGREE
• *See page 80*

SHRM FOUNDATION-SOCIETY FOR HUMAN RESOURCE MANAGEMENT

http://www.shrmfoundation.org

SHRM FOUNDATION STUDENT SCHOLARSHIPS
Applicants must be SHRM members and must be pursuing a college degree in HR or a related field. Undergraduates must have a cumulative GPA of at least 3.0 on a 4.0 point scale, and graduate applicants must have at least a 3.5 GPA on a 4.0 scale. Course work in HR management is required. Awards are primarily merit-based.

Academic Fields/Career Goals: Human Resources.

Award: Scholarship for use in junior, senior, or graduate years; not renewable. *Number:* 44. *Amount:* $2500–$10,000.

Eligibility Requirements: Applicant must be enrolled or expecting to enroll full- or part-time at a four-year institution or university. Applicant or parent of applicant must be member of Society for Human Resource Management. Available to U.S. and non-U.S. citizens.

Application Requirements: Application form, community service, essay. *Deadline:* October 10.

Contact: Dorothy Mebane, Manager, Foundation Programs
SHRM Foundation-Society for Human Resource Management
1800 Duke Street
Alexandria, VA 22314
Phone: 703-535-6219
E-mail: dorothy.mebane@shrm.org

UNITED NEGRO COLLEGE FUND

http://www.uncf.org/

UNCF/ALLIANCE DATA SCHOLARSHIP AND INTERNSHIP PROGRAM
• *See page 88*

Y'S MEN INTERNATIONAL

http://www.ysmen.org/

ALEXANDER SCHOLARSHIP LOAN FUND
• *See page 152*

HYDROLOGY

AMERICAN GROUND WATER TRUST

http://www.agwt.org/

AMERICAN GROUND WATER TRUST-AMTROL INC. SCHOLARSHIP
• *See page 199*

AMERICAN GROUND WATER TRUST-BAROID SCHOLARSHIP
• *See page 199*

AMERICAN GROUND WATER TRUST-THOMAS STETSON SCHOLARSHIP
• *See page 199*

AMERICAN INDIAN SCIENCE AND ENGINEERING SOCIETY

http://www.aises.org/

A.T. ANDERSON MEMORIAL SCHOLARSHIP PROGRAM
• *See page 105*

AMERICAN METEOROLOGICAL SOCIETY

http://www.ametsoc.org/

FATHER JAMES B. MACELWANE ANNUAL AWARD
• *See page 251*

ARIZONA HYDROLOGICAL SOCIETY

http://www.azhydrosoc.org/

ARIZONA HYDROLOGICAL SOCIETY SCHOLARSHIP
• *See page 200*

ASSOCIATION FOR WOMEN GEOSCIENTISTS (AWG)

http://www.awg.org/

AWG ETHNIC MINORITY SCHOLARSHIP
• *See page 200*

AWG MARIA LUISA CRAWFORD FIELD CAMP SCHOLARSHIP
• *See page 111*

AWG SALT LAKE CHAPTER (SLC) RESEARCH SCHOLARSHIP
• *See page 111*

JANET CULLEN TANAKA GEOSCIENCES UNDERGRADUATE SCHOLARSHIP
• *See page 112*

LONE STAR RISING CAREER SCHOLARSHIP
• *See page 200*

OSAGE CHAPTER UNDERGRADUATE SERVICE SCHOLARSHIP
• *See page 112*

SUSAN EKDALE MEMORIAL FIELD CAMP SCHOLARSHIP
• *See page 201*

ASSOCIATION OF CALIFORNIA WATER AGENCIES

http://www.acwa.com/

ASSOCIATION OF CALIFORNIA WATER AGENCIES SCHOLARSHIPS
• *See page 106*

CLAIR A. HILL SCHOLARSHIP
• *See page 106*

BARRY GOLDWATER SCHOLARSHIP AND EXCELLENCE IN EDUCATION FOUNDATION

https://goldwater.scholarsapply.org

BARRY M. GOLDWATER SCHOLARSHIP AND EXCELLENCE IN EDUCATION PROGRAM
• *See page 107*

BHW GROUP

https://thebhwgroup.com/

BHW WOMEN IN STEM SCHOLARSHIP
• *See page 107*

BROWN AND CALDWELL

http://www.brownandcaldwell.com

ECKENFELDER SCHOLARSHIP
• *See page 141*

MINORITY SCHOLARSHIP PROGRAM
• *See page 141*

CALIFORNIA GROUNDWATER ASSOCIATION

http://www.groundh2o.org/

CALIFORNIA GROUNDWATER ASSOCIATION SCHOLARSHIP

Award for California residents who demonstrate an interest in some facet of groundwater technology. One to two $1000 awards. Must use for study in California. Submit letter of recommendation.

Academic Fields/Career Goals: Hydrology; Natural Resources.

Award: Scholarship for use in freshman, sophomore, junior, or senior years; not renewable. *Number:* 1–2. *Amount:* $1000.

Eligibility Requirements: Applicant must be enrolled or expecting to enroll full-time at a two-year or four-year or technical institution or university; resident of California and studying in California. Available to U.S. citizens.

Application Requirements: Application form, essay, recommendations or references, transcript. *Deadline:* April 1.

Contact: Mike Mortensson, Executive Director
California Groundwater Association
PO Box 14369
Santa Rosa, CA 95402
Phone: 707-578-4408
Fax: 707-546-4906
E-mail: wellguy@groundh2o.org

GREAT MINDS IN STEM

http://www.greatmindsinstem.org/college/scholarship-application-information

HENAAC SCHOLARSHIP PROGRAM
• *See page 100*

KENTUCKY ENERGY AND ENVIRONMENT CABINET

http://dep.ky.gov

ENVIRONMENTAL PROTECTION SCHOLARSHIP
• *See page 142*

THE LAND CONSERVANCY OF NEW JERSEY

http://www.tlc-nj.org/

ROGERS FAMILY SCHOLARSHIP
• *See page 143*

RUSSELL W. MYERS SCHOLARSHIP
• *See page 143*

NGWA FOUNDATION

http://www.ngwa.org/Foundation/Pages/default.aspx

NGWA FOUNDATION'S LEN ASSANTE SCHOLARSHIP
• *See page 202*

SOIL AND WATER CONSERVATION SOCIETY

http://www.swcs.org

DONALD A. WILLIAMS SCHOLARSHIP SOIL CONSERVATION SCHOLARSHIP
• *See page 91*

STRAIGHT NORTH

https://www.straightnorth.com/

STRAIGHT NORTH STEM SCHOLARSHIP
• *See page 81*

UNITED NEGRO COLLEGE FUND

http://www.uncf.org/

LEIDOS STEM SCHOLARSHIP
• *See page 96*

INDUSTRIAL DESIGN

AIST FOUNDATION
http://www.aistfoundation.org/

ASSOCIATION FOR IRON AND STEEL TECHNOLOGY WILLY KORF MEMORIAL SCHOLARSHIP
• See page 153

AMERICAN SOCIETY OF PLUMBING ENGINEERS
http://www.aspe.org/

ALFRED STEELE ENGINEERING SCHOLARSHIP
• See page 236

AUTOMOTIVE WOMEN'S ALLIANCE FOUNDATION
http://awafoundation.org/index.php

AUTOMOTIVE WOMEN'S ALLIANCE FOUNDATION SCHOLARSHIPS
• See page 71

BHW GROUP
https://thebhwgroup.com/

BHW WOMEN IN STEM SCHOLARSHIP
• See page 107

CENTER FOR ARCHITECTURE
www.centerforarchitecture.org

CENTER FOR ARCHITECTURE DESIGN SCHOLARSHIP
• See page 114

THE CLUNKER JUNKER
https://theclunkerjunker.com/

CLUNKER JUNKER CASH FOR CARS AND COLLEGE SCHOLARSHIP
• See page 227

GREAT MINDS IN STEM
http://www.greatmindsinstem.org/college/scholarship-application-information

HENAAC SCHOLARSHIP PROGRAM
• See page 100

INDUSTRIAL DESIGNERS SOCIETY OF AMERICA
http://www.idsa.org/

INDUSTRIAL DESIGNERS SOCIETY OF AMERICA UNDERGRADUATE SCHOLARSHIP

One-time award to a U.S. citizen or permanent U.S. resident currently enrolled in an industrial design program. Must submit twenty visual examples of work and study full-time.

Academic Fields/Career Goals: Industrial Design.

Award: Scholarship for use in junior year; not renewable. *Number:* 2. *Amount:* $2500.

Eligibility Requirements: Applicant must be enrolled or expecting to enroll full-time at an institution or university. Available to U.S. citizens.

Application Requirements: Application form, recommendations or references, transcript, twenty visual examples of work. *Deadline:* May 18.

Contact: Max Taylor, Executive Assistant
Industrial Designers Society of America
45195 Business Court, Suite 250
Dulles, VA 20166
Phone: 703-707-6000
Fax: 703-787-8501
E-mail: maxt@idsa.org

MANUFACTURERS ASSOCIATION OF MAINE
http://www.mainemfg.com/

MAINE MANUFACTURING CAREER AND TRAINING FOUNDATION SCHOLARSHIP
• See page 131

MIDWEST ROOFING CONTRACTORS ASSOCIATION
http://www.mrca.org/

MRCA FOUNDATION SCHOLARSHIP PROGRAM
• See page 116

NASA'S VIRGINIA SPACE GRANT CONSORTIUM
http://www.vsgc.odu.edu/

COMMUNITY COLLEGE STEM SCHOLARSHIPS
• See page 110

ONLINE LOGO MAKER
http://onlinelogomaker.com

OLM MALALA YOUSAFZAI SCHOLARSHIP 2017-2018
• See page 122

SIMPLEHUMAN
http://www.simplehuman.com/

SIMPLE SOLUTIONS DESIGN COMPETITION
• See page 231

SOCIETY OF PLASTICS ENGINEERS FOUNDATION (SPE)
http://www.4spe.org/

FLEMING/BLASZCAK SCHOLARSHIP
• See page 158

GULF COAST HURRICANE SCHOLARSHIP
• See page 159

SOCIETY OF PLASTICS ENGINEERS SCHOLARSHIP PROGRAM
• See page 159

SUPPORT CREATIVITY

http://wesupportcreativity.org

SUPPORT CREATIVITY SCHOLARSHIP
• *See page 117*

TIMOTION

http://www.timotion.com/

TIMOTION ENGINEERING AND EXCELLENCE SCHOLARSHIP
• *See page 167*

VECTORWORKS, INC.

http://www.vectorworks.net

VECTORWORKS DESIGN SCHOLARSHIP
• *See page 117*

INSURANCE AND ACTUARIAL SCIENCE

THE ACTUARIAL FOUNDATION

www.actuarialfoundation.org

ACTUARIAL DIVERSITY SCHOLARSHIP

The Actuarial Diversity Scholarship promotes diversity through an annual scholarship program for Black/African American, Hispanic, Native North American and Pacific Islander students. The scholarship award recognizes and encourages the academic achievements of full-time undergraduate students pursuing a degree that may lead to a career in the actuarial profession.

Academic Fields/Career Goals: Insurance and Actuarial Science; Mathematics; Statistics.

Award: Scholarship for use in freshman, sophomore, junior, or senior years; renewable. *Amount:* $1000–$4000.

Eligibility Requirements: Applicant must be American Indian/Alaska Native, Asian/Pacific Islander, Black (non-Hispanic), Hispanic and enrolled or expecting to enroll full-time at a two-year or four-year institution or university. Available to U.S. and non-U.S. citizens.

Application Requirements: Application form, application form may be submitted online (https://actfnd.academicworks.com/opportunities/144), essay, personal photograph, recommendations or references, resume, test scores, transcript. *Deadline:* March 31.

Contact: Attn: Actuarial Diversity Program Specialist
The Actuarial Foundation
475 North Martingale Road
Suite 600
Schaumburg, IL 60173-2226
Phone: 847-706-3535
E-mail: scholarships@actfnd.org

ACTUARY OF TOMORROW—STUART A. ROBERTSON MEMORIAL SCHOLARSHIP
• *See page 203*

CURTIS E. HUNTINGTON MEMORIAL SCHOLARSHIP
• *See page 204*

BHW GROUP

https://thebhwgroup.com/

BHW WOMEN IN STEM SCHOLARSHIP
• *See page 107*

CARDS AGAINST HUMANITY

https://cardsagainsthumanity.com/

SCIENCE AMBASSADOR SCHOLARSHIP
• *See page 107*

D.W. SIMPSON & COMPANY

http://www.dwsimpson.com/

D.W. SIMPSON ACTUARIAL SCIENCE SCHOLARSHIP

One-time award for full-time actuarial science students. Must be entering senior year of undergraduate study in actuarial science. GPA of 3.2 or better in actuarial science and an overall GPA of 3.0 or better required. Must have passed at least one actuarial exam and be eligible to work in the U.S. Deadlines: April 30 for fall and October 31 for spring.

Academic Fields/Career Goals: Insurance and Actuarial Science.

Award: Scholarship for use in senior year; not renewable. *Number:* 2. *Amount:* $1000.

Eligibility Requirements: Applicant must be enrolled or expecting to enroll full-time at a four-year institution or university. Available to U.S. citizens.

Application Requirements: Application form, essay.

Contact: Bethany Rave, Partner-Operations
Phone: 312-867-2300
Fax: 312-951-8386
E-mail: scholarship@dwsimpson.com

MISSOURI INSURANCE EDUCATION FOUNDATION

http://www.mief.org

MISSOURI INSURANCE EDUCATION FOUNDATION SCHOLARSHIP

One $2500 scholarship and five $2000 scholarships available to college and university students in their junior or senior year. Must be Missouri resident and attending school in Missouri.

Academic Fields/Career Goals: Insurance and Actuarial Science.

Award: Scholarship for use in junior or senior years; not renewable. *Number:* 6. *Amount:* $2000–$2500.

Eligibility Requirements: Applicant must be enrolled or expecting to enroll full-time at a four-year institution or university; resident of Missouri and studying in Missouri. Available to U.S. citizens.

Application Requirements: Application form, financial need analysis, recommendations or references, transcript. *Deadline:* March 31.

Contact: Amy Hamacher, Assistant
Missouri Insurance Education Foundation
PO Box 1654
Jefferson City, MO 65102
Phone: 573-893-4234
Fax: 573-893-4996
E-mail: miis@midamerica.net

NEW ENGLAND EMPLOYEE BENEFITS COUNCIL

http://www.neebc.org/

NEW ENGLAND EMPLOYEE BENEFITS COUNCIL SCHOLARSHIP PROGRAM
• *See page 78*

SCARLETT FAMILY FOUNDATION SCHOLARSHIP PROGRAM

http://www.scarlettfoundation.org/

SCHOLARSHIP FOR STUDENTS PURSUING A BUSINESS OR STEM DEGREE
• *See page 80*

SPENCER EDUCATIONAL FOUNDATION INC.

http://www.spencered.org/

SPENCER EDUCATIONAL FOUNDATION SCHOLARSHIP

Scholarship is available to outstanding applicants who are focused on a career in risk management, insurance, and related disciplines. If student is attending a two year college, he/she must have intentions of transferring to a four year college with proof that he or she is majoring or minoring in Risk Management as it pertains to insurance.

Academic Fields/Career Goals: Insurance and Actuarial Science.

Award: Scholarship for use in junior, senior, graduate, or postgraduate years; renewable. *Number:* 30–40. *Amount:* $5000–$10,000.

Eligibility Requirements: Applicant must be enrolled or expecting to enroll full- or part-time at a two-year or four-year institution or university. Available to U.S. and Canadian citizens.

Application Requirements: Application form, essay. *Deadline:* January 31.

Contact: Ms. Angela Sabatino, Programs Director
Spencer Educational Foundation Inc.
1065 Avenue of the Americas, 13th Floor
New York, NY 10018
Phone: 212-655-6223
E-mail: asabatino@spencered.org

STRAIGHT NORTH

https://www.straightnorth.com/

STRAIGHT NORTH STEM SCHOLARSHIP
• *See page 81*

UNITED NEGRO COLLEGE FUND

http://www.uncf.org/

UNCF/TRAVELERS INSURANCE SCHOLARSHIP
• *See page 151*

VOYA SCHOLARS
• *See page 83*

INTERIOR DESIGN

AMERICAN SOCIETY OF INTERIOR DESIGNERS (ASID) EDUCATION FOUNDATION INC.

http://www.asidfoundation.org

ASID FOUNDATION LEGACY SCHOLARSHIP FOR UNDERGRADUATES

Open to all students in their junior or senior year of undergraduate study enrolled in at least a three-year program of interior design. The award will be given to a creatively outstanding student as demonstrated through their portfolio.

Academic Fields/Career Goals: Interior Design.

Award: Scholarship for use in junior or senior years; not renewable. *Number:* 1. *Amount:* $4000.

Eligibility Requirements: Applicant must be enrolled or expecting to enroll full- or part-time at a four-year institution or university. Available to U.S. citizens.

Application Requirements: Application form, application form may be submitted online (http://www.asidfoundation.org), portfolio, recommendations or references, transcript. *Deadline:* March 12.

Contact: Valerie O'Keefe, Executive Assistant and Foundation Manager
Phone: 202-546-3480
Fax: 202-546-3240
E-mail: foundation@asid.org

CENTER FOR ARCHITECTURE

www.centerforarchitecture.org

CENTER FOR ARCHITECTURE DESIGN SCHOLARSHIP
• *See page 114*

HOUZZ

http://houzz.com

RESIDENTIAL DESIGN SCHOLARSHIP
• *See page 115*

SUSTAINABLE RESIDENTIAL DESIGN SCHOLARSHIP
• *See page 115*

ILLUMINATING ENGINEERING SOCIETY OF NORTH AMERICA

http://www.ies.org/

ROBERT W. THUNEN MEMORIAL SCHOLARSHIPS
• *See page 116*

ILLUMINATING ENGINEERING SOCIETY OF NORTH AMERICA–GOLDEN GATE SECTION

http://www.iesgg.org/

ALAN LUCAS MEMORIAL EDUCATIONAL SCHOLARSHIP
• *See page 116*

INTERNATIONAL FACILITY MANAGEMENT ASSOCIATION FOUNDATION

http://www.ifmafoundation.org/

IFMA FOUNDATION SCHOLARSHIPS
• *See page 116*

NATIONAL ASSOCIATION OF WOMEN IN CONSTRUCTION

http://www.nawic.org/

NAWIC UNDERGRADUATE SCHOLARSHIPS
• *See page 117*

ONLINE LOGO MAKER

http://onlinelogomaker.com

OLM MALALA YOUSAFZAI SCHOLARSHIP 2017-2018
• *See page 122*

QUALITY BATH

www.qualitybath.com

QUALITYBATH.COM SCHOLARSHIP PROGRAM
• *See page 120*

SUPPORT CREATIVITY

http://wesupportcreativity.org

SUPPORT CREATIVITY SCHOLARSHIP
• *See page 117*

TURNER CONSTRUCTION COMPANY

http://www.turnerconstruction.com/

YOUTHFORCE 2020 SCHOLARSHIP PROGRAM
• *See page 117*

VECTORWORKS, INC.

http://www.vectorworks.net

VECTORWORKS DESIGN SCHOLARSHIP
• *See page 117*

INTERNATIONAL MIGRATION

HUB FOUNDATION

https://hub-foundation.org

HUB FOUNDATION SCHOLARSHIPS
• *See page 88*

UNITED NATIONS ASSOCIATION OF CONNECTICUT

http://www.unausa.org

UNITED NATIONS ASSOCIATION OF CONNECTICUT SCHOLARSHIP
• *See page 124*

INTERNATIONAL STUDIES

ASSOCIATION OF FORMER INTELLIGENCE OFFICERS

www.afio.com

AFIO UNDERGRADUATE AND GRADUATE SCHOLARSHIPS
• *See page 98*

AUTOMOTIVE WOMEN'S ALLIANCE FOUNDATION

http://awafoundation.org/index.php

AUTOMOTIVE WOMEN'S ALLIANCE FOUNDATION SCHOLARSHIPS
• *See page 71*

CULTURAL SERVICES OF THE FRENCH EMBASSY

http://www.frenchculture.org/

TEACHING ASSISTANT PROGRAM IN FRANCE
• *See page 98*

HUB FOUNDATION

https://hub-foundation.org

HUB FOUNDATION SCHOLARSHIPS
• *See page 88*

ISLAMIC SCHOLARSHIP FUND

http://islamicscholarshipfund.org/

ISF NATIONAL SCHOLARSHIP
• *See page 104*

JORGE MAS CANOSA FREEDOM FOUNDATION

http://masscholarships.org/

MAS FAMILY SCHOLARSHIP AWARD
• *See page 149*

THE LYNDON BAINES JOHNSON FOUNDATION

http://www.lbjlibrary.org/page/foundation/

MOODY RESEARCH GRANTS
• *See page 99*

NATIONAL SECURITY EDUCATION PROGRAM

http://www.iie.org/

NATIONAL SECURITY EDUCATION PROGRAM (NSEP) DAVID L. BOREN UNDERGRADUATE SCHOLARSHIPS
• *See page 119*

PHI ALPHA THETA HISTORY HONOR SOCIETY, INC.

http://www.phialphatheta.org/

PHI ALPHA THETA WORLD HISTORY ASSOCIATION PAPER PRIZE
• *See page 289*

UNITED NATIONS ASSOCIATION OF CONNECTICUT

http://www.unausa.org

UNITED NATIONS ASSOCIATION OF CONNECTICUT SCHOLARSHIP
• *See page 124*

WOMEN IN INTERNATIONAL TRADE (WIIT)

http://www.wiit.org/

WIIT CHARITABLE TRUST SCHOLARSHIP PROGRAM

2 scholarships of $1500 each (one for an undergraduate female student and one for a graduate female student) may be awarded for the summer or fall semester and the spring semester of each year. Applicants must: (1) be currently enrolled or accepted at an undergraduate or graduate program at an accredited U.S. university or college, either full-time or part-time; and (2) demonstrate interest in international development, international relations, international trade, international economics, or international business. A completed application includes a 3–5 page essay, applicant information, and proof of acceptance or current enrollment in an accredited U.S. college or university. All materials should be submitted by email only to info@wiittrust.org using the following subject line-"Submission for WIIT TRUST Essay Writing Contest". Only one submission entry will be accepted from each entrant. Awards are based on the quality of the applicants' essays in response to the assigned topic for that year. Application information is available at https://www.wiit.org/wiit-charitable-trust/; click on "new scholarship program" to download the information for the current year.

Academic Fields/Career Goals: International Studies.

Award: Scholarship for use in freshman, sophomore, junior, senior, graduate, or postgraduate years; not renewable. *Number:* 1–4. *Amount:* $1500.

Eligibility Requirements: Applicant must be enrolled or expecting to enroll full- or part-time at a two-year or four-year institution or university and female. Available to U.S. citizens.

Application Requirements: Application form, essay. *Deadline:* June 15.

Contact: Nancy Travis, Chair, WIIT Charitable Trust
E-mail: info@wiittrust.org

JOURNALISM

ADC RESEARCH INSTITUTE

http://www.adc.org/

JACK SHAHEEN MASS COMMUNICATIONS SCHOLARSHIP AWARD
• *See page 169*

AMERICAN INSTITUTE OF POLISH CULTURE INC.

http://www.ampolinstitute.org/

HARRIET IRSAY SCHOLARSHIP GRANT
• *See page 120*

AMERICAN QUARTER HORSE FOUNDATION (AQHF)

https://aqhfoundation.smapply.io/

AQHF JOURNALISM OR COMMUNICATIONS SCHOLARSHIP
• *See page 170*

ASIAN AMERICAN JOURNALISTS ASSOCIATION

http://www.aaja.org/

CIC/ANNA CHENNAULT SCHOLARSHIP
• *See page 170*

MARY QUON MOY ING MEMORIAL SCHOLARSHIP AWARD
• *See page 170*

VINCENT CHIN MEMORIAL SCHOLARSHIP
• *See page 171*

ASIAN AMERICAN JOURNALISTS ASSOCIATION, SEATTLE CHAPTER

http://www.aajaseattle.org/

NORTHWEST JOURNALISTS OF COLOR SCHOLARSHIP
• *See page 84*

ASSOCIATED PRESS

http://www.aptra.org/

ASSOCIATED PRESS TELEVISION/RADIO ASSOCIATION-CLETE ROBERTS JOURNALISM SCHOLARSHIP AWARDS

Award for college undergraduates and graduate students studying in California, Nevada or Hawaii and pursuing careers in broadcast journalism. Submit application, references, and examples of broadcast-related work.

Academic Fields/Career Goals: Journalism; TV/Radio Broadcasting.

Award: Scholarship for use in freshman, sophomore, junior, or senior years; not renewable. *Number:* 3. *Amount:* $1500.

Eligibility Requirements: Applicant must be enrolled or expecting to enroll full-time at a two-year or four-year institution or university and studying in California, Hawaii, Nevada. Available to U.S. citizens.

Application Requirements: Application form, recommendations or references. *Deadline:* December 14.

Contact: Roberta Gonzales, Scholarship Committee
Associated Press
CBS 5 TV, 855 Battery Street
San Francisco, CA 94111

KATHRYN DETTMAN MEMORIAL JOURNALISM SCHOLARSHIP

One-time award of $1500 for broadcast journalism students, enrolled at a California, Hawaii, or Nevada college or university. Must submit entry form and examples of broadcast-related work.

Academic Fields/Career Goals: Journalism; TV/Radio Broadcasting.

Award: Scholarship for use in freshman, sophomore, junior, or senior years; renewable. *Number:* 1–4. *Amount:* $1500.

Eligibility Requirements: Applicant must be enrolled or expecting to enroll full-time at a two-year or four-year institution or university and studying in California, Hawaii, Nevada. Available to U.S. citizens.

Application Requirements: Application form, examples of broadcast-related work. *Deadline:* December 14.

Contact: Roberta Gonzales, Scholarship Committee
Associated Press
CBS 5 TV, 855 Battery Street
San Francisco, CA 94111

ASSOCIATION FOR WOMEN IN COMMUNICATIONS-SEATTLE PROFESSIONAL CHAPTER

http://www.seattleawc.org/

SEATTLE PROFESSIONAL CHAPTER OF THE ASSOCIATION FOR WOMEN IN COMMUNICATIONS

Scholarship of $3000 for women pursuing journalism in the state of Washington. For more details on eligibility criteria or selection procedure, refer to website at http://www.seattleawc.org/scholarships.html.

Academic Fields/Career Goals: Journalism.

Award: Scholarship for use in sophomore, junior, or senior years; not renewable. *Number:* 2. *Amount:* $3000.

Eligibility Requirements: Applicant must be enrolled or expecting to enroll full-time at a two-year or four-year or technical institution or university; female; resident of Washington and studying in Washington. Available to U.S. citizens.

Application Requirements: Application form, resume, sample of work, cover letter, transcript. *Deadline:* March 16.

Contact: Jaron Snow, Office Administrator
Phone: 425-771-4189
E-mail: awcseattle@verizon.net

CCNMA: LATINO JOURNALISTS OF CALIFORNIA

http://www.ccnma.org/

CCNMA SCHOLARSHIPS
• See page 171

CONNECTICUT CHAPTER OF SOCIETY OF PROFESSIONAL JOURNALISTS

http://www.ctspj.org/

CONNECTICUT SPJ BOB EDDY SCHOLARSHIP PROGRAM
• See page 172

DOW JONES NEWS FUND

https://dowjonesnewsfund.org/

DOW JONES NEWS FUND HIGH SCHOOL JOURNALISM WORKSHOPS WRITING, PHOTOGRAPHY AND MULTIMEDIA COMPETITION

Participants in DJNF summer workshops are nominated for writing, multimedia and photography awards based on their published work. Scholarships are presented to the best writers, digital producers and photographers to pursue media careers.

Academic Fields/Career Goals: Journalism.

Award: Scholarship for use in freshman year; not renewable. *Number:* 6. *Amount:* $1000.

Eligibility Requirements: Applicant must be high school student and planning to enroll or expecting to enroll full-time at a four-year institution or university. Available to U.S. and non-U.S. citizens.

Application Requirements: Application form, essay, portfolio. *Deadline:* October 1.

Contact: Mrs. Linda Shockley, Managing Director
Dow Jones News Fund
PO Box 300
Princeton, NJ 08543-0300
Phone: 609-452-2820
E-mail: djnf@dowjones.com

FREEDOM FORUM

http://www.newseuminstitute.org

AL NEUHARTH FREE SPIRIT AND JOURNALISM CONFERENCE PROGRAM

One-time award for high school juniors interested in pursuing a career in journalism. Must be actively involved in high school journalism and demonstrate qualities such as being a visionary, an innovative leader, an entrepreneur or a courageous achiever. One student selected from each state and the District of Columbia. Scholars come to Washington D.C. to receive their awards and participate in an all-expense paid journalism conference. See website at http://www.freespirit.org for further information.

Academic Fields/Career Goals: Journalism.

Award: Scholarship for use in freshman year; not renewable. *Number:* 51. *Amount:* $1000.

Eligibility Requirements: Applicant must be high school student; planning to enroll or expecting to enroll full-time at a two-year or four-year institution or university and must have an interest in entrepreneurship, leadership, photography/photogrammetry/filmmaking, or writing. Available to U.S. citizens.

Application Requirements: Application form, essay, personal photograph. *Deadline:* February 1.

Contact: Karen Catone, Director, Al Neuharth Free Spirit Program
Freedom Forum
555 Pennsylvania Avenue, NW
Washington, DC 20001
Phone: 202-292-6271
E-mail: kcatone@freedomforum.org

GEORGIA PRESS EDUCATIONAL FOUNDATION INC.

http://gapress.org/

DURWOOD MCALISTER SCHOLARSHIP

Established in 1992 by The Atlanta Journal, this scholarship is awarded annually to an outstanding student majoring in print journalism at a Georgia college or university. The McAlister Scholarship is named in honor of Durwood McAlister, former editor of The Atlanta Journal.

Academic Fields/Career Goals: Journalism.

Award: Scholarship for use in freshman, sophomore, junior, senior, or graduate years; not renewable. *Number:* 1. *Amount:* $500–$2000.

Eligibility Requirements: Applicant must be enrolled or expecting to enroll full-time at a two-year institution or university; resident of Florida and studying in Georgia. Available to U.S. citizens.

Application Requirements: Application form, essay, financial need analysis, interview, personal photograph. *Deadline:* March 1.

Contact: Jennifer Farmer, Scholarship and Internship Coordinator
Georgia Press Educational Foundation Inc.
3066 Mercer University Dr., Suite 200
Atlanta, GA 30341
Phone: 770-454-6776
Fax: 770-454-6778
E-mail: jfarmer@gapress.org

MORRIS NEWSPAPER CORPORATION SCHOLARSHIP

Established in 1987 by Charles Morris, Morris Newspaper Corp., Savannah, this scholarship is awarded annually to an outstanding print journalism student. Applications can be submitted through newspapers in the Morris Newspaper Corporation family and recipients are named by the GPEF Board of Trustees.

Academic Fields/Career Goals: Journalism.

Award: Scholarship for use in freshman, sophomore, junior, or senior years; not renewable. *Number:* 1. *Amount:* $500–$2000.

Eligibility Requirements: Applicant must be enrolled or expecting to enroll full-time at a two-year institution or university; resident of Florida and studying in Georgia. Available to U.S. citizens.

Application Requirements: Application form, essay, financial need analysis, interview, personal photograph. *Deadline:* March 1.

Contact: Jennifer Farmer, Scholarship and Internship Coordinator
Georgia Press Educational Foundation Inc.
3066 Mercer University Dr., Suite 200
Atlanta, GA 30341
Phone: 770-454-6776
Fax: 770-454-6778
E-mail: jfarmer@gapress.org

OTIS A. BRUMBY II SCHOLARSHIP

This scholarship is awarded annually to a college junior or senior majoring in print journalism. Priority will be given to applicants from Cobb County. The Brumby Community Scholarship is named in honor of Otis A. Brumby, Jr., longtime publisher of the Marietta Daily Journal, Neighbor Newspapers and Cherokee Tribune. He is a past president of the Georgia Press Association and frequent winner of GPA and AP Freedom of Information Awards. He is also the first recipient of the David E. Hudson Open Government Award.

Academic Fields/Career Goals: Journalism.

Award: Scholarship for use in junior or senior years; not renewable.

Eligibility Requirements: Applicant must be enrolled or expecting to enroll full-time at a two-year institution or university; resident of Florida and studying in Georgia. Available to U.S. citizens.

Application Requirements: Application form, interview. *Deadline:* March 1.

Contact: Jennifer Farmer, Scholarship and Internship Coordinator
Georgia Press Educational Foundation Inc.
3066 Mercer University Dr., Suite 200
Atlanta, GA 30341
Phone: 770-454-6776
Fax: 770-454-6778
E-mail: jfarmer@gapress.org

WILLIAM C. ROGERS SCHOLARSHIP

This scholarship was established in memory of William Curran Rogers Sr., who was editor and publisher of the Swainsboro Forest-Blade for more than 30 years. During his career, he served as president of Georgia Press Association, president of National Newspaper Association and president of National Newspaper Representatives. The William C. Rogers Scholarship granted by the Georgia Press Educational Foundation to students of the Grady College of Journalism and Mass Communication at the University of Georgia was established in his honor.

Academic Fields/Career Goals: Journalism.

Award: Scholarship for use in junior or senior years; not renewable. *Number:* 1. *Amount:* $500–$2000.

Eligibility Requirements: Applicant must be enrolled or expecting to enroll full-time at an institution or university; resident of Florida and studying in Georgia. Available to U.S. citizens.

Application Requirements: Application form, essay, financial need analysis, interview, personal photograph. *Deadline:* March 1.

Contact: Jennifer Farmer, Scholarship and Internship Coordinator
Georgia Press Educational Foundation Inc.
3066 Mercer University Dr., Suite 200
Atlanta, GA 30341
Phone: 770-454-6776
Fax: 770-454-6778
E-mail: jfarmer@gapress.org

HUB FOUNDATION

https://hub-foundation.org

HUB FOUNDATION SCHOLARSHIPS
• *See page 88*

IDAHO STATE BROADCASTERS ASSOCIATION

http://www.idahobroadcasters.org/

WAYNE C. CORNILS MEMORIAL SCHOLARSHIP
• *See page 148*

INDIANA BROADCASTERS ASSOCIATION

http://www.indianabroadcasters.org/

INDIANA BROADCASTERS FOUNDATION SCHOLARSHIP

Awards a student majoring in broadcasting, electronic media, or journalism. Must maintain a 3.0 GPA and be a resident of Indiana. One-time award for full-time undergraduate study in Indiana.

Academic Fields/Career Goals: Journalism; TV/Radio Broadcasting.

Award: Scholarship for use in freshman, sophomore, junior, or senior years; not renewable. *Number:* up to 10. *Amount:* $500–$2000.

Eligibility Requirements: Applicant must be enrolled or expecting to enroll full-time at a two-year or four-year or technical institution or university; resident of Indiana and studying in Indiana. Available to U.S. citizens.

Application Requirements: Application form, application form may be submitted online (http://www.indianabroadcasters.org), essay, recommendations or references, transcript. *Deadline:* March 4.

Contact: Gwen Piening, Scholarship Administrator
Indiana Broadcasters Association
3003 East 98th Street, Suite 161
Indianapolis, IN 46280
Phone: 317-573-0119
Fax: 317-573-0895
E-mail: indba@aol.com

IOWA NEWSPAPER ASSOCIATION

https://inanews.com/

SHAW SCHOLARSHIP
• *See page 172*

WOODWARD SCHOLARSHIP
• *See page 172*

ISLAMIC SCHOLARSHIP FUND

http://islamicscholarshipfund.org/

ISF NATIONAL SCHOLARSHIP
• *See page 104*

JAPANESE AMERICAN CITIZENS LEAGUE (JACL)

http://www.jacl.org/

NATIONAL JACL HEADQUARTERS SCHOLARSHIP
• *See page 94*

JORGE MAS CANOSA FREEDOM FOUNDATION

http://masscholarships.org/

MAS FAMILY SCHOLARSHIP AWARD
• *See page 149*

LA-PHILOSOPHIE.COM

http://la-philosophie.com

LA-PHILOSOPHIE.COM SCHOLARSHIP
• *See page 104*

MARYLAND/DELAWARE/DISTRICT OF COLUMBIA PRESS FOUNDATION

http://www.mddcpress.com/

MICHAEL J. POWELL HIGH SCHOOL JOURNALIST OF THE YEAR

Scholarship of $1500 to an outstanding high school student. Applicant must submit five samples of work, mounted on unlined paper, a letter of recommendation from the nominee's advisor, an autobiography geared to the publication activities in which the nominee participated, and the nominee should write a paragraph or two on the most important aspect of scholastic journalism.

Academic Fields/Career Goals: Journalism.

Award: Scholarship for use in freshman year; not renewable. *Number:* 1. *Amount:* $1500.

Eligibility Requirements: Applicant must be high school student; planning to enroll or expecting to enroll full-time at a four-year institution or university; resident of Delaware, District of Columbia, Maryland and must have an interest in writing. Available to U.S. citizens.

Application Requirements: Application form, driver's license, entry in a contest, five sample articles, recommendations or references. *Deadline:* January 31.

Contact: Jennifer Thornberry, Membership Services Coordinator
Maryland/Delaware/District of Columbia Press Foundation
60 West Street
Suite 107
Annapolis, MD 21401-2479
Phone: 855-721-6332 Ext. 2
Fax: 855-721-6332
E-mail: service@mddcpress.com

MISSISSIPPI ASSOCIATION OF BROADCASTERS

http://www.msbroadcasters.org/

MISSISSIPPI ASSOCIATION OF BROADCASTERS SCHOLARSHIP

Scholarship available to a student enrolled in a fully accredited broadcast curriculum at a Mississippi two- or four-year college.

Academic Fields/Career Goals: Journalism; TV/Radio Broadcasting.

Award: Scholarship for use in freshman, sophomore, junior, or senior years; not renewable. *Number:* up to 8. *Amount:* $2000.

Eligibility Requirements: Applicant must be enrolled or expecting to enroll full-time at a two-year or four-year institution or university; resident of Mississippi and studying in Mississippi. Available to U.S. citizens.

Application Requirements: Application form, extracurricular activities and community involvement also considered, financial need analysis, recommendations or references. *Deadline:* May 1.

Contact: Jackie Lett, Scholarship Coordinator
Phone: 601-957-9121
Fax: 601-957-9175
E-mail: jackie@msbroadcasters.org

MISSISSIPPI PRESS ASSOCIATION EDUCATION FOUNDATION

http://www.mspress.org/displaycommon.cfm?an=1&sub articlenbr=16

MISSISSIPPI PRESS ASSOCIATION EDUCATION FOUNDATION SCHOLARSHIP

The foundation annually offers $1000 ($500 per semester) scholarships to qualified students enrolled in print journalism, and who are residents of Mississippi. The recipient who maintains a 3.0 GPA. Total value of the scholarship can be as much as $4000 when awarded to an incoming freshman who remains qualified throughout their four years of print journalism education.

Academic Fields/Career Goals: Journalism.

Award: Scholarship for use in freshman, sophomore, junior, or senior years; renewable. *Number:* 1. *Amount:* $1000–$4000.

Eligibility Requirements: Applicant must be enrolled or expecting to enroll full-time at a two-year or four-year institution or university and resident of Mississippi. Available to U.S. citizens.

Application Requirements: Application form, recommendations or references, resume, sample of work. *Deadline:* April 1.

Contact: Beth Boone, Scholarship Coordinator
Phone: 601-981-3060
Fax: 601-981-3676
E-mail: bboone@mspress.org

NATIONAL ACADEMY OF TELEVISION ARTS AND SCIENCES

https://theemmys.tv/

DOUGLAS W. MUMMERT SCHOLARSHIP
• See page 173

JIM MCKAY MEMORIAL SCHOLARSHIP
• See page 258

MIKE WALLACE MEMORIAL SCHOLARSHIP
• See page 258

NATIONAL ACADEMY OF TELEVISION ARTS AND SCIENCES TRUSTEES' LINDA GIANNECCHINI SCHOLARSHIP
• See page 258

RANDY FALCO SCHOLARSHIP
• See page 259

NATIONAL ACADEMY OF TELEVISION ARTS AND SCIENCES, MICHIGAN CHAPTER

http://natasmichigan.org

DR. LYNNE BOYLE/JOHN SCHIMPF UNDERGRADUATE SCHOLARSHIP
• See page 85

NATIONAL ACADEMY OF TELEVISION ARTS AND SCIENCES-NATIONAL CAPITAL/CHESAPEAKE BAY CHAPTER

http://www.natasdc.org/

BETTY ENDICOTT/NTA-NCCB STUDENT SCHOLARSHIP

Scholarship for a full-time sophomore, junior or non-graduating senior student pursuing a career in communication, television or broadcast journalism. Must be enrolled in an accredited four-year college or university in Maryland, Virginia or Washington, D.C. Minimum GPA of 3.0 required. Must demonstrate an aptitude or interest in communication, television or broadcast journalism. Application URL http://capitalemmys.tv/betty_endicott.htm.

Academic Fields/Career Goals: Journalism; TV/Radio Broadcasting.

Award: Scholarship for use in sophomore, junior, or senior years; not renewable. *Number:* 1. *Amount:* $5000.

Eligibility Requirements: Applicant must be enrolled or expecting to enroll full-time at a four-year institution or university and studying in District of Columbia, Maryland, Virginia. Available to U.S. citizens.

Application Requirements: Application form, essay, recommendations or references, resume, transcript, work samples (resume tape in VHS format and radio or television broadcast scripts). *Deadline:* April 22.

Contact: Diane Bruno, Student Affairs Committee
National Academy of Television Arts and Sciences-National Capital/Chesapeake Bay Chapter
9405 Russell Road
Silver Spring, MD 20910
Phone: 301-587-3993
E-mail: capitalemmys@aol.com

NATIONAL ACADEMY OF TELEVISION ARTS & SCIENCES—OHIO VALLEY CHAPTER

http://ohiovalleyemmy.org/

DAVID J. CLARKE MEMORIAL SCHOLARSHIP
• See page 173

NATIONAL ASSOCIATION OF BLACK JOURNALISTS

http://www.nabj.org/

ALLISON FISHER SCHOLARSHIP

Scholarship for students currently attending an accredited college or university. Must be majoring in print journalism and maintain a 3.0 GPA. Recipient will attend NABJ convention and participate in the mentor program. Scholarship value and the number of awards granted varies.

Academic Fields/Career Goals: Journalism.

Award: Scholarship for use in freshman, sophomore, junior, senior, or graduate years; not renewable.

Eligibility Requirements: Applicant must be enrolled or expecting to enroll full-time at a four-year institution or university. Available to U.S. and non-U.S. citizens.

Application Requirements: Driver's license, proof of enrollment, recommendations or references. *Deadline:* March 17.

Contact: Irving Washington, Manager
Phone: 301-445-7100
Fax: 301-445-7101
E-mail: jriley@nabj.org

GERALD BOYD/ROBIN STONE NON-SUSTAINING SCHOLARSHIP

One-time scholarship for students enrolled in an accredited four-year institution. Must be enrolled as an undergraduate or graduate student and maintain a 3.0 GPA. Must major in print journalism. Must be a member of NABJ. Scholarship value and the number of awards granted annually varies.

Academic Fields/Career Goals: Journalism.

Award: Scholarship for use in freshman, sophomore, junior, senior, or graduate years; not renewable.

Eligibility Requirements: Applicant must be enrolled or expecting to enroll full-time at a four-year institution or university. Available to U.S. and non-U.S. citizens.

Application Requirements: 6 samples of work, application form, essay, personal photograph, recommendations or references, transcript. *Deadline:* March 17.

Contact: Irving Washington, Manager
Phone: 301-445-7100
Fax: 301-445-7101
E-mail: jriley@nabj.org

NABJ SCHOLARSHIP

Scholarship for a student who is currently attending an accredited four-year college or university. Must be enrolled as an undergraduate or graduate student majoring in journalism (print, radio, online, or television) or a communications-related discipline. Minimum 2.5 GPA. Must be a member of NABJ. Scholarship value and the number of awards granted varies annually.

Academic Fields/Career Goals: Journalism; TV/Radio Broadcasting.

Award: Scholarship for use in freshman, sophomore, junior, senior, or graduate years; not renewable. *Amount:* $2500.

Eligibility Requirements: Applicant must be enrolled or expecting to enroll full-time at an institution or university. Available to U.S. and non-U.S. citizens.

Application Requirements: Application form, application form may be submitted online, community service, essay, portfolio. *Deadline:* April 19.

Contact: Irving Washington, Manager
Phone: 301-445-7100
Fax: 301-445-7101
E-mail: jriley@nabj.org

NATIONAL ASSOCIATION OF BLACK JOURNALISTS AND NEWHOUSE FOUNDATION SCHOLARSHIP

Award for high school seniors planning to attend an accredited four-year college or university and major in journalism. Minimum 3.0 GPA required. Must be a member of NABJ. The scholarship value and the number of awards granted varies.

Academic Fields/Career Goals: Journalism.

Award: Scholarship for use in freshman, sophomore, junior, or senior years; not renewable.

Eligibility Requirements: Applicant must be enrolled or expecting to enroll full-time at a four-year institution or university and must have an interest in writing. Available to U.S. and non-U.S. citizens.

Application Requirements: Application form, driver's license, essay, interview, recommendations or references, transcript. *Deadline:* March 17.

Contact: Irving Washington, Manager
Phone: 301-445-7100
Fax: 301-445-7101
E-mail: jriley@nabj.org

NATIONAL ASSOCIATION OF BLACK JOURNALISTS NON-SUSTAINING SCHOLARSHIP AWARDS

One-time award for college students attending a four-year institution and majoring in journalism. Minimum 2.5 GPA required. Must be a member of NABJ. Scholarship value and the number of awards varies annually.

Academic Fields/Career Goals: Journalism; Photojournalism/Photography; TV/Radio Broadcasting.

Award: Scholarship for use in freshman, sophomore, junior, or senior years; not renewable.

Eligibility Requirements: Applicant must be enrolled or expecting to enroll full-time at a four-year institution or university and must have an interest in writing. Available to U.S. and non-U.S. citizens.

Application Requirements: Application form, driver's license, personal photograph, proof of enrollment, recommendations or references, transcript. *Deadline:* March 17.

Contact: Irving Washington, Manager
Phone: 301-445-7100
Fax: 301-445-7101
E-mail: jriley@nabj.org

NATIONAL ASSOCIATION OF BROADCASTERS

http://www.nab.org/

NATIONAL ASSOCIATION OF BROADCASTERS GRANTS FOR RESEARCH IN BROADCASTING

• *See page 173*

NATIONAL ASSOCIATION OF HISPANIC JOURNALISTS (NAHJ)

http://www.nahj.org/

GERALDO RIVERA SCHOLARSHIP

Awards available to college undergraduates and graduate students pursuing careers in English- or Spanish-language TV broadcast journalism. Applications available on website, http://www.nahj.org.

Academic Fields/Career Goals: Journalism; TV/Radio Broadcasting.

Award: Scholarship for use in senior or graduate years; not renewable. *Amount:* $1000–$5000.

Eligibility Requirements: Applicant must be enrolled or expecting to enroll full-time at a four-year institution or university. Available to U.S. citizens.

Application Requirements: Application form, financial need analysis, recommendations or references, resume, transcript. *Deadline:* March 31.

Contact: Alberto Mendoza, Executive Director
Phone: 202-662-7145
E-mail: abmendoza@nahj.org

MARIA ELENA SALINAS SCHOLARSHIP

One-time scholarship for high school seniors, college undergraduates, and first-year graduate students who are pursuing careers in Spanish-language broadcast (radio or TV) journalism. Students may major or plan to major in any subject, but must demonstrate a sincere desire to pursue a career in this field. Must submit essays and demo tapes (audio or video) in Spanish. Scholarship includes the opportunity to serve an internship with Univision Spanish-language television news network.

Academic Fields/Career Goals: Journalism; TV/Radio Broadcasting.

Award: Scholarship for use in freshman, sophomore, junior, senior, or graduate years; not renewable. *Number:* 2. *Amount:* $2500.

Eligibility Requirements: Applicant must be enrolled or expecting to enroll full-time at an institution or university. Available to U.S. citizens.

Application Requirements: Application form, application form may be submitted online, essay, financial need analysis, portfolio. *Deadline:* February 28.

Contact: Alberto Mendoza, Executive Director
Phone: 202-662-7145
E-mail: abmendoza@nahj.org

NATIONAL ASSOCIATION OF HISPANIC JOURNALISTS SCHOLARSHIP
• See page 173

NEWHOUSE SCHOLARSHIP PROGRAM
• See page 275

WASHINGTON POST YOUNG JOURNALISTS SCHOLARSHIP

Four-year award of $10,000 for high school seniors in D.C. metropolitan area. Contact educational programs manager for application and information.

Academic Fields/Career Goals: Journalism.

Award: Scholarship for use in freshman year; not renewable. *Amount:* $10,000.

Eligibility Requirements: Applicant must be high school student; planning to enroll or expecting to enroll full-time at a four-year institution or university and resident of District of Columbia, Maryland, Virginia. Available to U.S. citizens.

Application Requirements: Application form, recommendations or references, transcript. *Deadline:* March 31.

Contact: Alberto Mendoza, Executive Director
         Phone: 202-662-7145
         E-mail: abmendoza@nahj.org

NATIONAL ASSOCIATION OF NEGRO BUSINESS AND PROFESSIONAL WOMEN'S CLUBS INC.

http://www.nanbpwc.org/

JULIANNE MALVEAUX SCHOLARSHIP
• See page 204

NATIONAL PRESS CLUB

http://www.press.org/

NATIONAL PRESS CLUB SCHOLARSHIP FOR JOURNALISM DIVERSITY

Scholarship of $2500 per year awarded to a talented minority student planning to pursue a career in journalism. Applicant must be a high school senior. Must have applied to or been accepted by a college or university for the upcoming year.

Academic Fields/Career Goals: Journalism.

Award: Scholarship for use in freshman year; not renewable. *Number:* 1. *Amount:* $2500.

Eligibility Requirements: Applicant must be American Indian/Alaska Native, Asian/Pacific Islander, Black (non-Hispanic), Hispanic; high school student and planning to enroll or expecting to enroll full-time at a four-year institution or university. Available to U.S. and non-U.S. citizens.

Application Requirements: Application form, essay, financial need analysis, recommendations or references, transcript, work samples demonstrating an ongoing interest in journalism. *Deadline:* March 1.

Contact: Joann Booze, Scholarship Coordinator
         Phone: 202-662-7532
         Fax: 202-662-7512
         E-mail: jbooze@press.org

NATIONAL SCHOLASTIC PRESS ASSOCIATION

http://www.studentpress.org/

NSPA JOURNALISM HONOR ROLL SCHOLARSHIP

Scholarship to student journalists who have achieved a 3.75 or higher GPA and have worked in student media for two or more years.

Academic Fields/Career Goals: Journalism.

Award: Scholarship for use in freshman year; not renewable. *Number:* 1–3. *Amount:* $1000.

Eligibility Requirements: Applicant must be high school student and planning to enroll or expecting to enroll full-time at a four-year institution or university. Applicant or parent of applicant must have employment or volunteer experience in journalism/broadcasting. Available to U.S. and non-U.S. citizens.

Application Requirements: Application form, essay, proof of NSPA membership required, recommendations or references, resume, transcript. *Deadline:* February 15.

Contact: Marisa Dobson, Sponsorship Contest Coordinator
         Phone: 612-625-6519
         Fax: 612-626-0720
         E-mail: marisa@studentpress.org

NATIONAL WRITERS ASSOCIATION FOUNDATION

http://www.nationalwriters.com/

NATIONAL WRITERS ASSOCIATION FOUNDATION SCHOLARSHIPS

Scholarships available to talented young writers with serious interest in any writing field.

Academic Fields/Career Goals: Journalism; Literature/English/Writing.

Award: Scholarship for use in freshman, sophomore, junior, senior, graduate, or postgraduate years; not renewable. *Number:* 1–4. *Amount:* $1000.

Eligibility Requirements: Applicant must be enrolled or expecting to enroll full- or part-time at a two-year or four-year or technical institution or university and must have an interest in writing. Available to U.S. and non-U.S. citizens.

Application Requirements: Application form. *Deadline:* December 31.

Contact: Sandy Whelchel, Executive Director
         National Writers Association Foundation
         10940 South Parker Road, Suite 508
         Parker, CO 80134
         Phone: 303-841-0246
         Fax: 303-841-2607
         E-mail: natlwritersassn@hotmail.com

NATIVE AMERICAN JOURNALISTS ASSOCIATION

http://www.naja.com/

NATIVE AMERICAN JOURNALISTS ASSOCIATION SCHOLARSHIPS
• See page 85

NEBRASKA PRESS ASSOCIATION

http://www.nebpress.com/

NEBRASKA PRESS ASSOCIATION FOUNDATION SCHOLARSHIP
• See page 86

NEW JERSEY PRESS FOUNDATION

http://www.njpressfoundation.org/

BERNARD KILGORE MEMORIAL SCHOLARSHIP FOR THE NJ HIGH SCHOOL JOURNALIST OF THE YEAR

Program co-sponsored with the Garden State Scholastic Press Association. Winning student is nominated to the Journalism Education Association for the National High School Journalist of the Year Competition. Must be in high school with plans of entering a four-year college or university on a full-time basis. Minimum 3.0 GPA required.

Academic Fields/Career Goals: Journalism.

Award: Scholarship for use in freshman year; not renewable. *Number:* 1. *Amount:* $5000.

Eligibility Requirements: Applicant must be high school student; planning to enroll or expecting to enroll full-time at a four-year institution or university; resident of New Jersey and must have an interest in writing. Available to U.S. citizens.

Application Requirements: Application form, essay, portfolio.
Deadline: February 28.

Contact: Peggy Arbitell, Business Manager
   Phone: 609-406-0600 Ext. 14
   E-mail: parbitell@njpa.org

OHIO NEWS MEDIA FOUNDATION

http://www.ohionews.org

HAROLD K. DOUTHIT SCHOLARSHIP
• *See page 86*

OHIO NEWS MEDIA FOUNDATION MINORITY SCHOLARSHIP
• *See page 86*

OHIO NEWS MEDIA FOUNDATION UNIVERSITY JOURNALISM SCHOLARSHIP
• *See page 86*

ONWA ANNUAL SCHOLARSHIP
• *See page 86*

OREGON ASSOCIATION OF BROADCASTERS

http://www.theoab.org/

OAB FOUNDATION SCHOLARSHIP
• *See page 174*

OREGON COMMUNITY FOUNDATION

http://www.oregoncf.org/

JACKSON FOUNDATION JOURNALISM SCHOLARSHIP FUND

Scholarship for students attending an Oregon college or university and majoring in, or with emphasis on, journalism. For both full-time and part-time. Must be a resident of Oregon.

Academic Fields/Career Goals: Journalism.

Award: Scholarship for use in freshman, sophomore, junior, or senior years; renewable. *Number:* 5. *Amount:* $1500–$2000.

Eligibility Requirements: Applicant must be enrolled or expecting to enroll full-time at a four-year institution or university; resident of Oregon and studying in Oregon. Available to U.S. citizens.

Application Requirements: Application form. *Deadline:* March 1.

Contact: Dianne Causey, Program Associate for Scholarships and
   Grants
   Phone: 503-227-6846 Ext. 1418
   E-mail: dcausey@oregoncf.org

OREGON OFFICE OF STUDENT ACCESS AND COMPLETION

https://oregonstudentaid.gov/

JACKSON FOUNDATION JOURNALISM SCHOLARSHIP

For students of Oregon public and nonprofit colleges who are journalism majors or whose course of study emphasizes journalism. Preference given to students who have taken the SAT and have received good essay scores. Based on financial need.

Academic Fields/Career Goals: Journalism.

Award: Scholarship for use in freshman, sophomore, junior, or senior years; not renewable.

Eligibility Requirements: Applicant must be enrolled or expecting to enroll full-time at a two-year or four-year institution and studying in Oregon. Available to U.S. citizens.

Application Requirements: Application form, financial need analysis. *Deadline:* March 1.

Contact: Melissa Adams, Scholarship Processing Coordinator
   Phone: 541-687-7409
   E-mail: melissa.adams@state.or.us

OUTDOOR WRITERS ASSOCIATION OF AMERICA

http://www.owaa.org/

OUTDOOR WRITERS ASSOCIATION OF AMERICA - BODIE MCDOWELL SCHOLARSHIP AWARD
• *See page 174*

PALM BEACH ASSOCIATION OF BLACK JOURNALISTS

PALM BEACH ASSOCIATION OF BLACK JOURNALISTS SCHOLARSHIP

Scholarship of $1000 are awarded to African-American graduating high school seniors plan to pursue a degree in journalism-print, television, radio broadcasting or photography industries. Have a GPA of 2.7 or better.

Academic Fields/Career Goals: Journalism; Photojournalism/Photography; TV/Radio Broadcasting.

Award: Scholarship for use in freshman year; not renewable. *Number:* 1. *Amount:* $1000.

Eligibility Requirements: Applicant must be Black (non-Hispanic); high school student and planning to enroll or expecting to enroll full- or part-time at a four-year institution or university. Available to U.S. and non-U.S. citizens.

Application Requirements: Application form, college acceptance proof, driver's license, transcript. *Deadline:* March 30.

Contact: Christopher Smith, Scholarship Chair
   Palm Beach Association of Black Journalists
   PO Box 19533
   West Palm Beach, FL 33416

PHILADELPHIA ASSOCIATION OF BLACK JOURNALISTS

http://www.pabj.org/

PHILADELPHIA ASSOCIATION OF BLACK JOURNALISTS SCHOLARSHIP

One-time award available to deserving high school students in the Delaware Valley who are interested in becoming journalists. Must have a 2.5 GPA. All applicants must state their intention to pursue journalism careers.

Academic Fields/Career Goals: Journalism.

Award: Scholarship for use in freshman, sophomore, junior, or senior years; not renewable. *Number:* 2. *Amount:* up to $1000.

Eligibility Requirements: Applicant must be Black (non-Hispanic); enrolled or expecting to enroll full-time at a four-year institution or university; resident of Pennsylvania and must have an interest in writing. Available to U.S. citizens.

Application Requirements: Application form, driver's license, essay, recommendations or references, transcript. *Deadline:* May 1.

Contact: Manny Smith, Scholarship Committee
   Philadelphia Association of Black Journalists
   PO Box 8232
   Philadelphia, PA 19101
   E-mail: manuelsmith@gmail.com

PRINTING INDUSTRY MIDWEST EDUCATION FOUDNATION

http://www.pimw.org/scholarships

PRINTING INDUSTRY MIDWEST EDUCATION FOUNDATION SCHOLARSHIP FUND
• *See page 175*

QUILL AND SCROLL FOUNDATION

http://www.quillandscroll.org

EDWARD J. NELL MEMORIAL SCHOLARSHIP IN JOURNALISM

Merit-based award for high school seniors planning to major in journalism. Must have won a National Quill and Scroll Writing Award or a Photography or Yearbook Excellence contest. Entry forms available from journalism adviser or Quill and Scroll. Must rank in upper third of class or have a minimum 3.0 GPA.

Academic Fields/Career Goals: Journalism.

Award: Scholarship for use in freshman year; not renewable. *Number:* 1–6. *Amount:* $500–$1500.

Eligibility Requirements: Applicant must be high school student; planning to enroll or expecting to enroll full-time at a four-year institution or university and must have an interest in photography/photogrammetry/filmmaking or writing. Available to U.S. citizens.

Application Requirements: Application form, essay, personal photograph. *Deadline:* May 10.

Contact: Jeffrey Browne, Executive Director
Quill and Scroll Foundation
School of Journalism, W111 AJB
Iowa City, IA 52242-1528
Phone: 319-335-3457
E-mail: quill-scroll@uiowa.edu

RADIO TELEVISION DIGITAL NEWS ASSOCIATION

http://www.rtdna.org

CAROLE SIMPSON SCHOLARSHIP

Carole Simpson is a former RTDNF trustee and the 1996 recipient of the Leonard Zeidenberg First Amendment Award in recognition of her work to protect First Amendment Freedoms. She established the Carole Simpson Scholarship to encourage and help minority students to overcome hurdles along their career path in electronic journalism. The recipient of the Carole Simpson Scholarship will receive $2,000 and an invitation to the Excellence in Journalism conference.

Academic Fields/Career Goals: Journalism; Photojournalism/Photography; TV/Radio Broadcasting.

Award: Scholarship for use in sophomore, junior, or senior years; not renewable. *Number:* 1. *Amount:* $2000.

Eligibility Requirements: Applicant must be American Indian/Alaska Native, Asian/Pacific Islander, Black (non-Hispanic), Hispanic and enrolled or expecting to enroll full-time at an institution or university. Available to U.S. and non-U.S. citizens.

Application Requirements: Application form, application form may be submitted online, essay, portfolio. *Deadline:* January 31.

Contact: Ms. Kate McGarrity, Awards and Programs Manager
Radio Television Digital News Association
529 14th Street, NW
Suite 1240
Washington, DC 20045
Phone: 202-662-7254
E-mail: katem@rtdna.org

ED BRADLEY SCHOLARSHIP

Bradley established the Ed Bradley Scholarship in 1994. Since then, 20 young, aspiring journalists of color have received the award created by the late CBS News and 60 Minutes correspondent. Past winners have gone on to work for organizations including NPR, CNN, and Al-Jazeera America. They have enjoyed careers from reporter, anchor, and media attorney to Saturday Night Live comedy writer and White House speechwriter. The recipient of the Ed Bradley Scholarship will receive $10,000 and an invitation to the Excellence in Journalism conference.

Academic Fields/Career Goals: Journalism; Photojournalism/Photography; TV/Radio Broadcasting.

Award: Scholarship for use in sophomore, junior, or senior years; not renewable. *Number:* 1. *Amount:* $10,000.

Eligibility Requirements: Applicant must be American Indian/Alaska Native, Asian/Pacific Islander, Black (non-Hispanic), Hispanic and

enrolled or expecting to enroll full-time at an institution or university. Available to U.S. and non-U.S. citizens.

Application Requirements: Application form, application form may be submitted online, essay, portfolio. *Deadline:* January 31.

Contact: Ms. Kate McGarrity, Awards and Programs Manager
Radio Television Digital News Association
529 14th Street, NW
Suite 1240
Washington, DC 20045
Phone: 202-662-7254
E-mail: katem@rtdna.org

GEORGE FOREMAN TRIBUTE TO LYNDON B. JOHNSON SCHOLARSHIP

George Foreman is a boxing champion, Olympic gold medal winner and celebrated pitchman. As a young man, he was inspired by President Lyndon Johnson and by RTDNF founder Barney Oldfield. The scholarship is a $6,000 award given to a journalism student from the University of Texas at Austin.

Academic Fields/Career Goals: Journalism; Photojournalism/Photography; TV/Radio Broadcasting.

Award: Scholarship for use in sophomore, junior, or senior years; not renewable. *Number:* 1. *Amount:* $6000.

Eligibility Requirements: Applicant must be enrolled or expecting to enroll full-time at an institution or university and studying in Texas. Available to U.S. and non-U.S. citizens.

Application Requirements: Application form, application form may be submitted online, essay, portfolio. *Deadline:* January 31.

Contact: Ms. Kate McGarrity, Awards and Programs Manager
Radio Television Digital News Association
529 14th Street, NW
Suite 1240
Washington, DC 20045
Phone: 202-662-7254
E-mail: katem@rtdna.org

LEE THORNTON SCHOLARSHIP

Lee Thornton was the first African-American woman to cover the White House for a major news network (CBS) and the first African-American host of All Things Considered on National Public Radio. She served as a faculty member at the Howard University School of Communications, earning a tenured position. Later in her career, she taught at the University of Maryland's Philip Merrill College of Journalism and served a term as the school's interim dean. She held a Master's degree from Michigan State University and a doctorate in mass communications from Northwestern University. Ms. Thornton passed away in 2013 at age 71, and endowed in her estate this scholarship in her name. Students from the University of Maryland and Howard University will be given preference. The recipient of the Lee Thornton Scholarship will receive $2,000 and an invitation to the Excellence in Journalism conference.

Academic Fields/Career Goals: Journalism; TV/Radio Broadcasting.

Award: Scholarship for use in sophomore, junior, or senior years; not renewable. *Number:* 1. *Amount:* $2000.

Eligibility Requirements: Applicant must be enrolled or expecting to enroll full-time at an institution or university and studying in District of Columbia, Maryland. Available to U.S. and non-U.S. citizens.

Application Requirements: Application form, application form may be submitted online, essay, portfolio. *Deadline:* January 31.

Contact: Ms. Kate McGarrity, Awards and Programs Manager
Radio Television Digital News Association
529 14th Street, NW
Suite 1240
Washington, DC 20045
Phone: 202-662-7254
E-mail: katem@rtdna.org

LOU AND CAROLE PRATO SPORTS REPORTING SCHOLARSHIP

The scholarship was established in 2001 in recognition of Lou's service to RTDNA and RTDNF and his commitment to excellence in journalism. It is awarded to a journalism student who brings Lou's journalism values to covering sports. The recipient of the Lou and Carole Prato Sports Reporting Scholarship will receive $1,000 and an invitation to the Excellence in Journalism conference.

Academic Fields/Career Goals: Journalism; Photojournalism/Photography; Sports-Related/Exercise Science; TV/Radio Broadcasting.

Award: Scholarship for use in sophomore, junior, or senior years; not renewable. *Number:* 1. *Amount:* $1000.

Eligibility Requirements: Applicant must be enrolled or expecting to enroll full-time at an institution or university. Available to U.S. and non-U.S. citizens.

Application Requirements: Application form, application form may be submitted online, essay, portfolio. *Deadline:* January 31.

Contact: Ms. Kate McGarrity, Awards and Programs Manager
Radio Television Digital News Association
529 14th Street, NW
Suite 1240
Washington, DC 20045
Phone: 202-662-7254
E-mail: katem@rtdna.org

MIKE REYNOLDS JOURNALISM SCHOLARSHIP

Mike Reynolds, who died in 1988 of a brain tumor at age 45, was assignment editor and then managing editor at KCCI-TV in Des Moines, IA. This scholarship is awarded to a journalism student with a good writing ability, excellent grades, a dedication to the news business, strong interest in pursuing a career in electronic journalism and a demonstrated need for financial assistance. The recipient of the Mike Reynolds Scholarship will receive $1,000 and an invitation to the Excellence in Journalism conference.

Academic Fields/Career Goals: Journalism; Photojournalism/Photography; TV/Radio Broadcasting.

Award: Scholarship for use in sophomore, junior, or senior years; not renewable. *Number:* 1. *Amount:* $1000.

Eligibility Requirements: Applicant must be enrolled or expecting to enroll full-time at an institution or university. Available to U.S. and non-U.S. citizens.

Application Requirements: Application form, application form may be submitted online, essay, portfolio. *Deadline:* January 31.

Contact: Ms. Kate McGarrity, Awards and Programs Manager
Radio Television Digital News Association
529 14th Street, NW
Suite 1240
Washington, DC 20045
Phone: 202-662-7254
E-mail: katem@rtdna.org

PETE WILSON JOURNALISM SCHOLARSHIP

The Pete Wilson Journalism Scholarship was established in 2007 to honor the late Pete Wilson, a San Francisco television and radio journalist. The scholarship is granted to a graduate journalism student from the San Francisco Bay area or attending a college or university in the Bay Area who shares Wilson's commitment to ethical, responsible journalism. The Pete Wilson Scholarship is open to both undergraduates and graduate applicants. The recipient of the Pete Wilson Journalism Scholarship will receive $2,000 and an invitation to the Excellence in Journalism conference.

Academic Fields/Career Goals: Journalism; Photojournalism/Photography; TV/Radio Broadcasting.

Award: Scholarship for use in sophomore, junior, senior, or graduate years; not renewable. *Number:* 1. *Amount:* $2000.

Eligibility Requirements: Applicant must be enrolled or expecting to enroll full-time at an institution or university; resident of British Columbia and studying in California. Available to U.S. and non-U.S. citizens.

Application Requirements: Application form, application form may be submitted online, essay, portfolio. *Deadline:* January 31.

Contact: Ms. Kate McGarrity, Awards and Programs Manager
Radio Television Digital News Association
529 14th Street, NW
Suite 1240
Washington, DC 20045
Phone: 202-662-7254
E-mail: katem@rtdna.org

PRESIDENTS SCHOLARSHIP

Two awards are given each year in honor of former RTDNA Presidents Theodore Koop, Bruce Dennis, James McCulla, John Salisbury, Bruce Palmer, Dick Cheverton, Jim Byron, Ben Chatfield and John Hogan. The recipients of the Presidents Scholarship will each receive $2,500 and an invitation to the Excellence in Journalism conference.

Academic Fields/Career Goals: Journalism; TV/Radio Broadcasting.

Award: Scholarship for use in sophomore, junior, or senior years; not renewable. *Number:* 2. *Amount:* $2500.

Eligibility Requirements: Applicant must be enrolled or expecting to enroll full-time at an institution or university. Available to U.S. and non-U.S. citizens.

Application Requirements: Application form, application form may be submitted online, essay, portfolio. *Deadline:* January 31.

Contact: Ms. Kate McGarrity, Awards and Programs Manager
Radio Television Digital News Association
529 14th Street, NW
Suite 1240
Washington, DC 20045
Phone: 202-662-7254
E-mail: katem@rtdna.org

ROBERT H. MOLLOHAN FAMILY CHARITABLE FOUNDATION, INC.

http://www.mollohanfoundation.org/

HARRY C. HAMM FAMILY SCHOLARSHIP

• *See page 175*

SIGMA DELTA CHI FOUNDATION OF WASHINGTON D.C.

http://www.sdxdc.org

SIGMA DELTA CHI SCHOLARSHIPS

One-time award to help pay tuition for full-time students in their junior or senior year demonstrating a clear intention to become journalists. Must demonstrate financial need. Grades and skills are also considered. Must be enrolled in a college or university in the Washington, D.C., metropolitan area. Sponsored by the Society of Professional Journalists.

Academic Fields/Career Goals: Journalism.

Award: Scholarship for use in junior or senior years; not renewable. *Number:* 4–7. *Amount:* $3000–$5000.

Eligibility Requirements: Applicant must be enrolled or expecting to enroll full-time at a four-year institution or university and studying in District of Columbia, Maryland, Virginia. Available to U.S. and non-U.S. citizens.

Application Requirements: Application form, essay, financial need analysis, interview, portfolio. *Deadline:* February 28.

Contact: Maura Judkis
E-mail: scholarship@sdxdc.org

SOCIETY OF PROFESSIONAL JOURNALISTS, LOS ANGELES CHAPTER

http://www.spj.org/losangeles

BILL FARR SCHOLARSHIP

Award available to a student who is either a resident of Los Angeles, Ventura or Orange counties or is enrolled at a university in one of those counties. Must have completed sophomore year and be enrolled in or accepted to a journalism program.

Academic Fields/Career Goals: Journalism.

Award: Scholarship for use in junior, senior, or graduate years; not renewable. *Number:* 1. *Amount:* $500–$1000.

Eligibility Requirements: Applicant must be enrolled or expecting to enroll full-time at a four-year institution or university; resident of California and studying in California. Available to U.S. citizens.

Application Requirements: Application form, essay, financial need analysis, recommendations or references, resume, work samples. *Deadline:* April 15.

Contact: Daniel Garvey, Scholarship Chairman
Society of Professional Journalists, Los Angeles Chapter
1250 Bellflower
Long Beach, CA 90840
Phone: 562-985-5779

CARL GREENBERG SCHOLARSHIP

Award for a student who is either a resident of Los Angeles, Ventura or Orange counties or is enrolled at a university in one of those three California counties. Must have completed sophomore year and be enrolled in or accepted to an investigative or political journalism program.

Academic Fields/Career Goals: Journalism.

Award: Scholarship for use in junior, senior, or graduate years; not renewable. *Number:* 1. *Amount:* $1000.

Eligibility Requirements: Applicant must be enrolled or expecting to enroll full-time at a four-year institution or university; resident of California and studying in California. Available to U.S. citizens.

Application Requirements: Application form, essay, financial need analysis, recommendations or references, resume, work samples. *Deadline:* April 15.

Contact: Daniel Garvey, Scholarship Chairman
Society of Professional Journalists, Los Angeles Chapter
1250 Bellflower
Long Beach, CA 90840
Phone: 562-985-5779

HELEN JOHNSON SCHOLARSHIP

Awards are available to a student who is a resident of Los Angeles, Ventura or Orange counties or is enrolled at a university in one of those three California counties. Must have completed sophomore year and be enrolled in or accepted to a broadcast journalism program.

Academic Fields/Career Goals: Journalism; TV/Radio Broadcasting.

Award: Scholarship for use in junior, senior, or graduate years; not renewable. *Number:* 1. *Amount:* $500–$1000.

Eligibility Requirements: Applicant must be enrolled or expecting to enroll full-time at a four-year institution or university; resident of California and studying in California. Available to U.S. citizens.

Application Requirements: Application form, essay, financial need analysis, recommendations or references, resume, work samples. *Deadline:* April 15.

Contact: Daniel Garvey, Scholarship Chairman
Society of Professional Journalists, Los Angeles Chapter
1250 Bellflower
Long Beach, CA 90840
Phone: 562-985-5779

KEN INOUYE SCHOLARSHIP

Awards are available to a minority student who is either a resident of Los Angeles, Ventura, or Orange counties or is enrolled at a university in one of those three California counties. Must have completed sophomore year and be enrolled in or accepted to a journalism program.

Academic Fields/Career Goals: Journalism.

Award: Scholarship for use in junior, senior, or graduate years; renewable. *Number:* 1. *Amount:* $500–$1000.

Eligibility Requirements: Applicant must be American Indian/Alaska Native, Asian/Pacific Islander, Black (non-Hispanic), Hispanic; enrolled or expecting to enroll full-time at a four-year institution or university; resident of California and studying in California. Available to U.S. citizens.

Application Requirements: Application form, essay, financial need analysis, recommendations or references, resume, work samples. *Deadline:* April 15.

Contact: Daniel Garvey, Scholarship Chairman
Society of Professional Journalists, Los Angeles Chapter
1250 Bellflower
Long Beach, CA 90840
Phone: 562-985-5779

SOCIETY OF PROFESSIONAL JOURNALISTS MARYLAND PRO CHAPTER

http://www.spj.org/mdpro

MARYLAND SPJ PRO CHAPTER COLLEGE SCHOLARSHIP

Scholarships for journalism students whose regular home residence is in Maryland. May attend colleges or universities in Virginia, Washington D.C., or Pennsylvania.

Academic Fields/Career Goals: Journalism.

Award: Scholarship for use in freshman, sophomore, junior, or senior years; not renewable.

Eligibility Requirements: Applicant must be enrolled or expecting to enroll full- or part-time at a four-year institution or university; resident of Maryland and studying in District of Columbia, Maryland, Pennsylvania, Virginia. Available to U.S. citizens.

Application Requirements: Application form, awards or honors received, essay, financial need analysis, recommendations or references, transcript. *Deadline:* May 9.

Contact: Sue Katcef, Scholarship Chair
Society of Professional Journalists Maryland Pro Chapter
402 Fox Hollow Lane
Annapolis, MD 21403
Phone: 301-405-7526
E-mail: susiekk@aol.com

SOUTH ASIAN JOURNALISTS ASSOCIATION (SAJA)

http://www.saja.org/

SAJA JOURNALISM SCHOLARSHIP

Scholarships for students in North America who are of South Asian descent (includes Bangladesh, Bhutan, India, Maldives, Nepal, Pakistan and Sri Lanka, Indo-Caribbean) or those with a demonstrated interest in South Asia or South Asian issues. Must be interested in pursuing journalism. Applicant must be a high school senior, undergraduate student or graduate-level student.

Academic Fields/Career Goals: Journalism.

Award: Scholarship for use in freshman, sophomore, junior, senior, graduate, or postgraduate years; not renewable. *Number:* 1–4. *Amount:* $1000–$2000.

Eligibility Requirements: Applicant must be Asian/Pacific Islander and enrolled or expecting to enroll full-time at a two-year or four-year institution or university. Available to U.S. and non-U.S. citizens.

Application Requirements: Application form, essay, financial need analysis, journalism clips or work samples, portfolio, recommendations or references, resume. *Deadline:* February 15.

Contact: Amita Parashar, Student Committee and Scholarships
Phone: 202-513-2845
E-mail: students@saja.org

STRAIGHTFORWARD MEDIA

http://www.straightforwardmedia.com/

STRAIGHTFORWARD MEDIA MEDIA & COMMUNICATIONS SCHOLARSHIP

• *See page 87*

TAMPA BAY TIMES FUND, INC.

http://company.tampabay.com:2052/times-fund/scholarships

CAREER JOURNALISM SCHOLARSHIP

• *See page 176*

TAMPA BAY TIMES FUND CAREER JOURNALISM SCHOLARSHIPS

• *See page 87*

TEXAS ASSOCIATION OF BROADCASTERS

https://www.tab.org/scholarships/available-scholarships

ANN ARNOLD SCHOLARSHIP

Junior, senior or graduate student enrolled in a broadcast curriculum at a four-year college or university in Texas, demonstrating financial need.

Academic Fields/Career Goals: Journalism.

Award: Scholarship for use in junior, senior, graduate, or postgraduate years; not renewable. *Number:* 1. *Amount:* $5000.

Eligibility Requirements: Applicant must be enrolled or expecting to enroll full-time at an institution or university; resident of Tennessee and studying in Texas. Available to U.S. citizens.

Application Requirements: Application form, essay, financial need analysis. *Deadline:* April 15.

Contact: Mr. Craig Bean, Director, Public Service & EEO
Texas Association of Broadcasters
502 East 11th Street, Suite 200
Austin, TX 78701
Phone: 512-322-9944
Fax: 512-322-0522
E-mail: craig@tab.org

TEXAS ASSOCIATION OF BROADCASTERS - BONNER MCLANE SCHOLARSHIP

Scholarship of $3000 to a undergraduate and students enrolled in a fully accredited program of instruction that emphasizes radio or television broadcasting or communications at a four-year college or university in Texas. Student must be a member of the Texas Association of Broadcasters. Must have a GPA of 3.0 minimum.

Academic Fields/Career Goals: Journalism; TV/Radio Broadcasting.

Award: Scholarship for use in junior, senior, or graduate years; not renewable. *Number:* 1. *Amount:* $3000.

Eligibility Requirements: Applicant must be enrolled or expecting to enroll full-time at an institution or university and studying in Texas. Applicant or parent of applicant must be member of Texas Association of Broadcasters. Available to U.S. and non-U.S. citizens.

Application Requirements: Application form, essay, financial need analysis. *Deadline:* May 3.

Contact: Craig Bean, Public Service Manager
Texas Association of Broadcasters
502 East 11th Street, Suite 200
Austin, TX 78701
Phone: 512-322-9944
Fax: 512-322-0522
E-mail: craig@tab.org

TEXAS ASSOCIATION OF BROADCASTERS - TOM REIFF SCHOLARSHIP

Scholarship of $3000 to undergraduate and graduate students enrolled in a fully accredited program of instruction that emphasizes radio or television broadcasting or communications at a four-year college or university in Texas. Student must be a member of the Texas Association of Broadcasters. Must have a GPA of 3.0 minimum.

Academic Fields/Career Goals: Journalism; TV/Radio Broadcasting.

Award: Scholarship for use in junior, senior, or graduate years; not renewable. *Number:* 1. *Amount:* $3000.

Eligibility Requirements: Applicant must be enrolled or expecting to enroll full-time at an institution or university and studying in Texas. Applicant or parent of applicant must be member of Texas Association of Broadcasters. Available to U.S. and non-U.S. citizens.

Application Requirements: Application form, essay, financial need analysis. *Deadline:* May 3.

Contact: Craig Bean, Public Service Manager
Texas Association of Broadcasters
502 East 11th Street, Suite 200
Austin, TX 78701
Phone: 512-322-9944
Fax: 512-322-0522
E-mail: craig@tab.org

TEXAS ASSOCIATION OF BROADCASTERS - TWO-YEAR/TECHNICAL SCHOOL SCHOLARSHIP
• *See page 176*

TEXAS ASSOCIATION OF BROADCASTERS - UNDERGRADUATE SCHOLARSHIP
• *See page 176*

TEXAS ASSOCIATION OF BROADCASTERS - VANN KENNEDY SCHOLARSHIP
• *See page 177*

TEXAS GRIDIRON CLUB INC.

http://www.spjfw.org/

TEXAS GRIDIRON CLUB SCHOLARSHIPS
• *See page 177*

UNITED METHODIST COMMUNICATIONS

http://www.umcom.org/

LEONARD M. PERRYMAN COMMUNICATIONS SCHOLARSHIP FOR ETHNIC MINORITY STUDENTS
• *See page 177*

UNITED NEGRO COLLEGE FUND

http://www.uncf.org/

DIVERSE VOICES IN STORYTELLING SCHOLARSHIP
• *See page 177*

WALT DISNEY COMPANY UNCF CORPORATE SCHOLARS PROGRAM
• *See page 177*

VALLEY PRESS CLUB

http://www.valleypressclub.com/

VALLEY PRESS CLUB SCHOLARSHIPS, THE REPUBLICAN SCHOLARSHIP, CHANNEL 22 SCHOLARSHIP
• *See page 178*

WASHINGTON MEDIA SCHOLARS FOUNDATION

www.mediascholars.org

MEDIA PLAN CASE COMPETITION
• *See page 88*

WOMEN'S BASKETBALL COACHES ASSOCIATION

http://www.wbca.org/

ROBIN ROBERTS/WBCA SPORTS COMMUNICATIONS SCHOLARSHIP AWARD
• *See page 178*

LANDSCAPE ARCHITECTURE

AMERICAN SOCIETY OF CERTIFIED ENGINEERING TECHNICIANS

http://www.ascet.org/

KURT H. AND DONNA M. SCHULER SMALL GRANT
• *See page 162*

BHW GROUP

https://thebhwgroup.com/

BHW WOMEN IN STEM SCHOLARSHIP
• *See page 107*

CENTER FOR ARCHITECTURE

www.centerforarchitecture.org

CENTER FOR ARCHITECTURE DESIGN SCHOLARSHIP
• *See page 114*

CENTER FOR ARCHITECTURE, DOUGLAS HASKELL AWARD FOR STUDENT JOURNALS
• *See page 238*

CONNECTICUT BUILDING CONGRESS SCHOLARSHIP FUND, INC.

http://www.cbc-ct.org

CBC SCHOLARSHIP FUND
• *See page 114*

THE DALLAS FOUNDATION

http://www.dallasfoundation.org/

WHITLEY PLACE SCHOLARSHIP
• *See page 114*

FEDERATED GARDEN CLUBS OF CONNECTICUT

http://www.ctgardenclubs.org/

FEDERATED GARDEN CLUBS OF CONNECTICUT INC. SCHOLARSHIPS
• *See page 142*

FEDERATED GARDEN CLUBS OF MARYLAND

office@fgcofmd.org

ROBERT LEWIS BAKER SCHOLARSHIP
• *See page 291*

THE GEORGIA TRUST FOR HISTORIC PRESERVATION

http://www.georgiatrust.org/

B. PHINIZY SPALDING, HUBERT B. OWENS, AND THE NATIONAL SOCIETY OF THE COLONIAL DAMES OF AMERICA IN THE STATE OF GEORGIA ACADEMIC SCHOLARSHIPS
• *See page 99*

J. NEEL REID PRIZE
• *See page 115*

GOLF COURSE SUPERINTENDENTS ASSOCIATION OF AMERICA

https://www.gcsaa.org/

GCSAA SCHOLARS COMPETITION

Competition for outstanding students planning careers in golf course management. Must be full-time college undergraduates currently enrolled in a two-year or more accredited program related to golf course management and have completed one year of program. Must be member of GCSAA.

Academic Fields/Career Goals: Landscape Architecture.

Award: Scholarship for use in sophomore, junior, or senior years; not renewable. *Amount:* $500–$6000.

Eligibility Requirements: Applicant must be enrolled or expecting to enroll full-time at a two-year institution or university. Applicant or parent of applicant must be member of Golf Course Superintendents Association of America. Available to U.S. and non-U.S. citizens.

Application Requirements: Application form, essay. *Deadline:* June 1.

Contact: Mischia Wright, Associate Director
Golf Course Superintendents Association of America
1421 Research Park Drive
Lawrence, KS 66049
Phone: 800-472-7878 Ext. 4445
Fax: 785-832-4448
E-mail: mwright@gcsaa.org

HORTICULTURAL RESEARCH INSTITUTE

https://www.hriresearch.org/

BRYAN A. CHAMPION MEMORIAL SCHOLARSHIP
• *See page 247*

CARVILLE M. AKEHURST MEMORIAL SCHOLARSHIP
• *See page 247*

MUGGET SCHOLARSHIP
• *See page 292*

SPRING MEADOW NURSERY SCHOLARSHIP
• *See page 292*

SUSIE AND BRUCE USREY EDUCATION SCHOLARSHIP
• *See page 247*

TIMOTHY S. AND PALMER W. BIGELOW, JR. SCHOLARSHIP
• *See page 247*

USREY FAMILY SCHOLARSHIP
• *See page 248*

HOUZZ

http://houzz.com

RESIDENTIAL DESIGN SCHOLARSHIP
• *See page 115*

SUSTAINABLE RESIDENTIAL DESIGN SCHOLARSHIP
• *See page 115*

THE LAND CONSERVANCY OF NEW JERSEY

http://www.tlc-nj.org/

RUSSELL W. MYERS SCHOLARSHIP
• *See page 143*

MONTANA FEDERATION OF GARDEN CLUBS

http://www.mtfgc.org/

LIFE MEMBER MONTANA FEDERATION OF GARDEN CLUBS SCHOLARSHIP
• *See page 202*

NATIONAL ASSOCIATION OF WOMEN IN CONSTRUCTION

http://www.nawic.org/

NAWIC UNDERGRADUATE SCHOLARSHIPS
• *See page 117*

NATIONAL GARDEN CLUBS INC.

http://www.gardenclub.org/

NATIONAL GARDEN CLUBS INC. SCHOLARSHIP PROGRAM
• *See page 94*

OREGON ASSOCIATION OF NURSERIES

https://www.oan.org/

EMERALD EMPIRE CHAPTER AWARD
• *See page 293*

PROFESSIONAL CONSTRUCTION ESTIMATORS ASSOCIATION

http://www.pcea.org/

TED G. WILSON MEMORIAL SCHOLARSHIP FOUNDATION
• *See page 166*

QUALITY BATH

www.qualitybath.com

QUALITYBATH.COM SCHOLARSHIP PROGRAM
• *See page 120*

SUPPORT CREATIVITY

http://wesupportcreativity.org

SUPPORT CREATIVITY SCHOLARSHIP
• *See page 117*

TURNER CONSTRUCTION COMPANY

http://www.turnerconstruction.com/

YOUTHFORCE 2020 SCHOLARSHIP PROGRAM
• *See page 117*

VECTORWORKS, INC.

http://www.vectorworks.net

VECTORWORKS DESIGN SCHOLARSHIP
• *See page 117*

THE WALTER J. TRAVIS SOCIETY

http://www.travissociety.com

THE WALTER J. TRAVIS MEMORIAL SCHOLARSHIP AND THE WALTER J. TRAVIS-RUDY ZOCCHI MEMORIAL SCHOLARSHIP
• *See page 118*

LAW ENFORCEMENT/ POLICE ADMINISTRATION

AMERICAN SOCIETY OF CRIMINOLOGY

http://www.asc41.com/

AMERICAN SOCIETY OF CRIMINOLOGY GENE CARTE STUDENT PAPER COMPETITION
• *See page 187*

ASSOCIATION OF FORMER INTELLIGENCE OFFICERS

www.afio.com

AFIO UNDERGRADUATE AND GRADUATE SCHOLARSHIPS
• *See page 98*

CONNECTICUT ASSOCIATION OF WOMEN POLICE

http://www.cawp.net/

CONNECTICUT ASSOCIATION OF WOMEN POLICE SCHOLARSHIP
• *See page 188*

INTERNATIONAL SOCIETY OF EXPLOSIVES ENGINEERS

http://www.isee.org/

JERRY MCDOWELL FUND
• *See page 156*

ISLAMIC SCHOLARSHIP FUND

http://islamicscholarshipfund.org/

ISF NATIONAL SCHOLARSHIP
• *See page 104*

LEARNING FOR LIFE

http://www.learning-for-life.org/

CAPTAIN JAMES J. REGAN SCHOLARSHIP
Two one-time $500 scholarships are presented annually to Law Enforcement Explorers graduating from high school or from an

accredited college program. Evaluation will be based on academic record.

Academic Fields/Career Goals: Law Enforcement/Police Administration.

Award: Scholarship for use in freshman, sophomore, junior, or senior years; not renewable. *Number:* 2. *Amount:* $500.

Eligibility Requirements: Applicant must be age 20 or under and enrolled or expecting to enroll full-time at a two-year or four-year or technical institution or university. Applicant or parent of applicant must be member of Explorer Program/Learning for Life. Available to U.S. citizens.

Application Requirements: Application form, essay, personal photograph, recommendations or references, transcript. *Deadline:* March 31.

Contact: William Taylor, Scholarships and Awards Coordinator
Learning for Life
1329 West Walnut Hill Lane, PO Box 152225
Irving, TX 75015-2225
Phone: 972-580-2241
E-mail: btaylor@lflmail.org

SHERYL A. HORAK MEMORIAL SCHOLARSHIP

Award for graduating high school students who are Law Enforcement Explorers joining a program in law enforcement in accredited college or university. Provides a one-time scholarship of $1000.

Academic Fields/Career Goals: Law Enforcement/Police Administration.

Award: Scholarship for use in freshman year; not renewable. *Number:* 1. *Amount:* $1000.

Eligibility Requirements: Applicant must be enrolled or expecting to enroll full-time at a two-year or four-year institution or university. Applicant or parent of applicant must be member of Explorer Program/Learning for Life. Available to U.S. citizens.

Application Requirements: Application form, essay, personal photograph, recommendations or references, transcript. *Deadline:* March 31.

Contact: William Taylor, Scholarships and Awards Coordinator
E-mail: btaylor@lflmail.org

LIVSECURE

https://www.livsecure.com

LIVSECURE STUDENT SCHOLARSHIP
• See page 188

NATIONAL BLACK POLICE ASSOCIATION

http://www.blackpolice.org/

ALPHONSO DEAL SCHOLARSHIP AWARD
• See page 188

NORTH CAROLINA STATE EDUCATION ASSISTANCE AUTHORITY

http://www.ncseaa.edu/

NORTH CAROLINA SHERIFFS' ASSOCIATION UNDERGRADUATE CRIMINAL JUSTICE SCHOLARSHIPS
• See page 188

LAW/LEGAL SERVICES

AMERICAN SOCIETY OF CRIMINOLOGY

http://www.asc41.com/

AMERICAN SOCIETY OF CRIMINOLOGY GENE CARTE STUDENT PAPER COMPETITION
• See page 187

AUTOMOTIVE WOMEN'S ALLIANCE FOUNDATION

http://awafoundation.org/index.php

AUTOMOTIVE WOMEN'S ALLIANCE FOUNDATION SCHOLARSHIPS
• See page 71

BAURKOT & BAURKOT: THE IMMIGRATION LAW GROUP

http://nationalimmigrationlawyers.com/

ATTORNEY RAYMOND LAHOUD SCHOLAR PROGRAM

All scholarship candidates must be enrolled in a 4-year college or university program and about to embark on their sophomore, junior, or senior year; or be accepted, or already enrolled in an ABA-accredited law school and about to embark on their first, second, or third year of law school; wish to pursue, or already be pursuing a career in the legal profession; have maintained a minimum GPA of 3.0 at their current college, university, or law school; and submit an application, resume, unofficial transcripts, and an essay discussing why the candidate wishes to pursue a career in the legal profession. The essay must be no less than 3,000 words. The application deadline is March 1 of each year. Selected candidates will be notified no later than April 1 of the same year. The scholarship may be used by the selected recipient for any education related expense. To learn more, please visit: http://nationalimmigrationlawyers.com/legalscholars/ or e-mail legalscholars@baurkotlaw.com. No phone calls or faxes, please.

Academic Fields/Career Goals: Law/Legal Services.

Award: Scholarship for use in sophomore, junior, senior, graduate, or postgraduate years; not renewable. *Number:* 5. *Amount:* $10,000.

Eligibility Requirements: Applicant must be enrolled or expecting to enroll full-time at a four-year institution or university. Available to U.S. and non-U.S. citizens.

Application Requirements: Application form, essay. *Deadline:* March 1.

Contact: Yenny Bautista, Office Director
Baurkot & Baurkot: The Immigration Law Group
205 South 7th Street
Easton, PA 18042
Phone: 484-544-0022
E-mail: legalscholars@baurkotlaw.com

BENSON & BINGHAM

https://www.bensonbingham.com/

BENSON & BINGHAM ANNUAL SCHOLARSHIP

Entrants for our scholarship must submit a minimum of a 600-word typed essay on one of the following two topics to be judged by partners Joe Benson and Ben Bingham at the conclusion of the deadline: 1. Premises Security: Given the Mandalay Bay Shooting, what steps should hotels take to insure the safety and security of their guests? or 2. Consumer Product Safety: When are the affixed warnings regarding the potential risk of injury obvious enough to warrant not having them? [A product is defective for its failure to be accompanied by suitable and adequate warnings concerning its safe and proper use, if the absence of such warnings renders the product unreasonably dangerous. To be adequate a warning must be: (1) designed to reasonably catch the consumer's attention, (2) that the language be comprehensible and give a fair indication of the specific risks attendant to use of the product, and (3) that warnings be of sufficient intensity justified by the magnitude of the risk.] In order to be eligible for the scholarship award, applicants must adhere to the following scholarship criteria: currently enrolled in or recently accepted to an accredited law school; a United States citizen or permanent resident; have a cumulative GPA of 3.0 or higher. A copy of your college transcript (unofficial) must accompany the application. Proof of law school acceptance or attendance must accompany the application. Applications must be received electronically by August 31, 2018 to the following email address: scholarship@bensonbingham.com. In the subject line, please reference: Benson & Bingham Annual Scholarship Application. One grand prize winner will receive a one-time payment of $2,000 and two one-time runner up awards a payment of $250 to be applied to the law school of their admission/attendance. Essays may be published by Benson & Bingham, so please refrain from submitting anything personal, vulgar or inappropriate for the web. The winner of the award will be announced by October 31st, 2018.

Academic Fields/Career Goals: Law/Legal Services.

Award: Scholarship for use in senior or postgraduate years; not renewable. *Number:* 3–2,000. *Amount:* $250.

Eligibility Requirements: Applicant must be enrolled or expecting to enroll full-time at an institution or university and studying in Alabama, Alaska, Alberta, Arizona, Arkansas, British Columbia, California, Colorado, Connecticut, Delaware, District of Columbia, Florida, Georgia, Guam, Hawaii, Idaho, Illinois, Indiana, Iowa, Kansas, Kentucky, Louisiana, Maine, Manitoba, Maryland, Massachusetts, Michigan, Minnesota, Mississippi, Missouri, Montana, Nebraska, Nevada, New Brunswick, Newfoundland, New Hampshire, New Jersey, New Mexico, New York, North Carolina, North Dakota, Northwest Territories, Nova Scotia, Ohio, Oklahoma, Ontario, Oregon, Pennsylvania, Prince Edward Island, Puerto Rico, Quebec, Rhode Island, Saskatchewan, South Carolina, South Dakota, Tennessee, Texas, Utah, Vermont, Virginia, Washington, West Virginia, Wisconsin, Wyoming, Yukon. Available to U.S. citizens.

Application Requirements: Application form, essay. *Deadline:* August 31.

Contact: Justin Simpson, Scholarship Administrator
Benson & Bingham
11441 Allerton Park Drive, Suite #100
Las Vegas, NV 89135
Phone: 702-684-6900
E-mail: scholarship@bensonbingham.com

BLACK ENTERTAINMENT AND SPORTS LAWYERS ASSOCIATION INC.

http://www.besla.org/

BESLA SCHOLARSHIP LEGAL WRITING COMPETITION

Award for the best 1000-word, or two-page essay on a compelling legal issue facing the entertainment or sports industry. Essay must be written by law school student who has completed at least one full year at an accredited law school. Minimum GPA of 2.8 required.

Academic Fields/Career Goals: Law/Legal Services.

Award: Scholarship for use in freshman, sophomore, junior, senior, or graduate years; not renewable.

Eligibility Requirements: Applicant must be Black (non-Hispanic) and enrolled or expecting to enroll full-time at a four-year institution or university. Available to U.S. and non-U.S. citizens.

Application Requirements: Application form, essay. *Deadline:* September 28.

Contact: Rev. Phyllicia Hatton, Executive Administrator
Phone: 301-248-1818
Fax: 301-248-0700
E-mail: beslamailbox@aol.com

BLACK WYNN PLLC

2017 LAW SCHOOL SCHOLARSHIP

The scholarship is designed to defray a portion of the tuition cost for attending law school. You may apply even if you are not currently enrolled, but you must be accepted at the law school you will be attending and provide us with that information, including proof that you have been accepted, within one (1) year of being notified that you were

selected as the recipient of the scholarship. The $1,000 award will be delivered directly to the law school as a tuition payment. The law school must be a U.S. law school accredited by the American Bar Association (ABA). Applications are accepted from United States citizens who are or will be attending a U.S. law school accredited by the ABA. In order to have your application accepted, you must: fill out the online application form; upload a short statement of up to 100 words explaining why you want to obtain a law degree. (Optional) Upload an essay of 700 words or less discussing how you intend to use your law degree to make a difference in your community.

Academic Fields/Career Goals: Law/Legal Services.

Award: Scholarship for use in freshman, sophomore, junior, senior, or graduate years; not renewable. *Number:* 1. *Amount:* $1000.

Eligibility Requirements: Applicant must be enrolled or expecting to enroll full- or part-time at a four-year institution or university. Available to U.S. citizens.

Application Requirements: Application form, essay. *Deadline:* February 23.

Contact: William Wynn
Black Wynn PLLC
40 North Central Avenue, Suite 1400
Phoenix, AZ 85004
E-mail: michael@bwphoenixpersonalinjurylawyers.com

BOYS AND GIRLS CLUBS OF GREATER SAN DIEGO

http://www.sdyouth.org/

SPENCE REESE SCHOLARSHIP
• See page 237

CANLAS LAW GROUP

https://www.canlaslaw.com/

LEGAL COLLEGE SCHOLARSHIP PROGRAM

Canlas Law Group, APLC, law firm is currently accepting applications for its 2018 college scholarship program. Young people who are interested in this opportunity are challenged to write an essay on a topic of our selection. The winning applicant will be presented with a $500 college scholarship that may be used toward related education expenses.

Academic Fields/Career Goals: Law/Legal Services.

Award: Scholarship for use in freshman, sophomore, junior, or senior years; not renewable. *Number:* 1. *Amount:* $500.

Eligibility Requirements: Applicant must be enrolled or expecting to enroll full-time at a four-year institution or university. Available to U.S. citizens.

Application Requirements: Application form, essay. *Deadline:* June 1.

Contact: Christopher Canlas, Owner
Canlas Law Group
18000 Studebaker Road
Suite 350
Cerritos, CA 90703
Phone: 323-888-4325
E-mail: Canlaslawgroupmarketing@gmail.com

CANTOR CRANE INJURY LAW

https://cantorcrane.com

CANTOR CRANE PERSONAL INJURY LAWYER $1,000 SCHOLARSHIP
• See page 187

CONGRESSIONAL BLACK CAUCUS FOUNDATION, INC.

http://www.cbcfinc.org/

CBC SPOUSES EDUCATION SCHOLARSHIP
• See page 98

CONSOLE AND HOLLAWELL

http://www.myinjuryattorney.com/legal-scholarship-2017-2018/

OVERDOSE ATTORNEY SCHOLARSHIP
• See page 281

FALES & FALES, P.A.

https://www.faleslaw.com/

LAW ENFORCEMENT FAMILY MEMBER SCHOLARSHIP

This scholarship will be awarded to a student (undergraduate or graduate) enrolled at either an accredited law school or an accredited university. The student must have a family member (such as a parent, spouse or sibling) who is or was an active duty member of law enforcement, including reserve officers and retired, deceased or disabled officers. To be eligible, a candidate must submit a 1-3 page typed essay describing the impact of the law enforcement member on the candidate's life. Candidates must be full-time students with a current GPA of at least a 3.0. To apply, candidates must submit the following by 5:00 pm (CST) on August 31st, 2017 to the included address: 1. a completed application (which can be found on our website), 2. A personal essay, and 3. a certified copy of the applicant's current transcript confirming satisfaction of the eligibility requirements listed above.

Academic Fields/Career Goals: Law/Legal Services.

Award: Scholarship for use in freshman, sophomore, junior, senior, graduate, or postgraduate years; not renewable. *Number:* 1. *Amount:* $1000.

Eligibility Requirements: Applicant must be enrolled or expecting to enroll full-time at a four-year institution or university. Applicant or parent of applicant must have employment or volunteer experience in police/firefighting. Available to U.S. citizens.

Application Requirements: Application form, essay. *Deadline:* August 31.

Contact: Anthony Ferguson
Fales & Fales, P.A.
192 Lisbon Street
PO Box 889
Lewiston, ME 04240
Phone: 207-786-0606
Fax: 207-786-2514
E-mail: aferguson@faleslaw.com

FELDMAN LAW FIRM PLLC

http://www.afphoenixcriminalattorney.com/

LAW STUDENT SCHOLARSHIP

The scholarship, in the amount of $1,000, is being offered to assist in the payment of tuition to law school. It is not required that an applicant be enrolled in law school at the time of the submission of his or her application. However, the scholarship funds must be utilized within one year after the date of the announcement of the winner. The $1,000 award will be paid directly to the law school selected by the winner. The scholarship is open to citizens of the United States who are enrolled at, or who intend to enroll at a U.S. law school accredited by the American Bar Association. The application includes the online form; a statement of not more than 100 words telling us why you want to pursue a legal education; and an (optional) essay of not more than 750 words discussing how you will use your law school degree to make a difference in the world.

Academic Fields/Career Goals: Law/Legal Services.

Award: Scholarship for use in freshman, sophomore, junior, senior, or graduate years; not renewable. *Number:* 1. *Amount:* $1000.

Eligibility Requirements: Applicant must be enrolled or expecting to enroll full- or part-time at a four-year institution or university. Available to U.S. citizens.

Application Requirements: Application form, essay. *Deadline:* February 22.

Contact: John Kelly
Feldman Law Firm PLLC
1 E. Washington St., Suite 500
Phoenix, AZ 85004
E-mail: mike@jkphoenixpersonalinjuryattorney.com

GRAND RAPIDS COMMUNITY FOUNDATION

http://www.grfoundation.org/

WARNER NORCROSS AND JUDD LLP SCHOLARSHIP FOR STUDENTS OF COLOR

Financial assistance to students of color who are residents of Michigan, or attend a college/university/vocational school in Michigan, pursuing a career in law, paralegal, or a legal secretarial program. Law school scholarship ($5000), paralegal scholarship ($2000), legal secretary scholarship ($1000).

Academic Fields/Career Goals: Law/Legal Services.

Award: Scholarship for use in freshman, sophomore, junior, senior, or graduate years; not renewable. *Number:* 1–3. *Amount:* $1000–$5000.

Eligibility Requirements: Applicant must be American Indian/Alaska Native, Asian/Pacific Islander, Black (non-Hispanic), Hispanic; enrolled or expecting to enroll full-time at a two-year institution or university; resident of Massachusetts and studying in Michigan. Available to U.S. citizens.

Application Requirements: Application form, essay, financial need analysis. *Deadline:* April 1.

Contact: Ms. Ruth Bishop, Education Program Officer
Grand Rapids Community Foundation
185 Oakes Street SW
Grand Rapids, MI 49503
Phone: 616-454-1751 Ext. 103
E-mail: rbishop@grfoundation.org

HIRSCH & LYON ACCIDENT LAW PLLC

https://www.hirschandlyonaccidentlaw.com

HIRSCH & LYON ANNUAL COLLEGE SCHOLARSHIP

https://www.hirschandlyonaccidentlaw.com/college-scholarship/

Academic Fields/Career Goals: Law/Legal Services.

Award: Scholarship for use in freshman, sophomore, junior, or senior years; not renewable. *Number:* 1. *Amount:* $500.

Eligibility Requirements: Applicant must be enrolled or expecting to enroll full- or part-time at a two-year or four-year institution or university. Available to U.S. citizens.

Application Requirements: Essay. *Deadline:* July 10.

Contact: Greg Lyon, Partner
Phone: 602-535-1900
E-mail: Scholarship@hlaccidentlaw.com

HUB FOUNDATION

https://hub-foundation.org

HUB FOUNDATION SCHOLARSHIPS
• See page 88

ISLAMIC SCHOLARSHIP FUND

http://islamicscholarshipfund.org/

ISF NATIONAL SCHOLARSHIP
• See page 104

JAPANESE AMERICAN CITIZENS LEAGUE (JACL)

http://www.jacl.org/

NATIONAL JACL HEADQUARTERS SCHOLARSHIP
• See page 94

LAW OFFICE OF DAVID P. SHAPIRO

http://www.davidpshapirolaw.com/about-us/

LAW STUDENT SCHOLARSHIP

This is a single scholarship in the amount of $1,000. It will be used by the successful applicant to offset the cost of law school tuition at a United States law school accredited by the American Bar Association. You need not be enrolled in law school at the time of your application, but you must provide us, within one year of being selected as the winner of the award, the name of the ABA-approved law school you will be attending, along with proof of your acceptance at the law school. The scholarship funds will be paid directly to the law school on your behalf. The scholarship is open to applicants who are citizens of the United States who are attending law school or who plan to do so within the time frame set forth above. To be considered for the award, you must complete the online application form, prepare and upload a brief (100 words or less) statement describing why you are interested in obtaining a law degree, and (ptional) prepare and upload an essay (up to 1,000 words) that describes how obtaining your law school degree will enable you to have a positive impact on the world.

Academic Fields/Career Goals: Law/Legal Services.

Award: Scholarship for use in freshman, sophomore, junior, senior, or graduate years; not renewable. *Number:* 1. *Amount:* $1000.

Eligibility Requirements: Applicant must be enrolled or expecting to enroll full- or part-time at a four-year institution or university. Available to U.S. citizens.

Application Requirements: Application form, essay. *Deadline:* February 2.

Contact: David Shapiro
Law Office of David P. Shapiro
1501 5th Avenue, #200
San Diego, CA 92101
E-mail: michael@davidpshapirolaw.com

LAW OFFICES OF GOODWIN & SCIESZKA

http://www.1888goodwin.com/

GOODWIN & SCIESZKA INNOVATION SCHOLARSHIP

The Innovation Scholarship will be awarded to three high-achieving students intending to pursue a career in law. Applicants will be judged on their academic performance and their essay addressing one of two law-related questions provided on the application. Applicant must be either a current law student at an accredited law school within the U.S. or at an accredited undergraduate university planning to attend law school.

Academic Fields/Career Goals: Law/Legal Services.

Award: Scholarship for use in freshman, sophomore, junior, senior, or graduate years; not renewable. *Number:* 3. *Amount:* $500–$1000.

Eligibility Requirements: Applicant must be enrolled or expecting to enroll full- or part-time at a two-year or four-year institution or university. Available to U.S. citizens.

Application Requirements: Application form, essay. *Deadline:* June 1.

Contact: Michael Cianfarani
E-mail: mcianfarani@trafficdigitalagency.com

LIVSECURE

https://www.livsecure.com

LIVSECURE STUDENT SCHOLARSHIP

• See page 188

MORROW & SHEPPARD LLP

https://www.morrowsheppard.com

MORROW & SHEPPARD COLLEGE SCHOLARSHIP

Morrow & Sheppard LLP is a law firm founded by Nick Morrow and John Sheppard. Both partners are Houston lawyers representing clients with cases relating to maritime injuries, truck accidents, oil field accidents, and other types of civil and commercial litigation. It can be very difficult to pay for college, and the expense can be a heavy financial burden. Morrow & Sheppard LLP offers this legal scholarship to students starting their journey into college and to those intending to explore a legal career, as a way to provide financial assistance. The winner of this scholarship will receive $500 towards their education. Any high school senior or current college student who is interested in pursuing law within the U.S. is allowed to apply. For full details see our website: https://www.morrowsheppard.com/college-scholarship/

Academic Fields/Career Goals: Law/Legal Services.

Award: Scholarship for use in freshman, sophomore, junior, or senior years; not renewable. *Number:* 1. *Amount:* $500.

Eligibility Requirements: Applicant must be high school student; planning to enroll or expecting to enroll full- or part-time at a two-year or four-year institution or university and studying in Alabama, Alaska, Arizona, Arkansas, California, Colorado, Connecticut, Delaware, District of Columbia, Florida, Georgia, Hawaii, Idaho, Illinois, Indiana, Iowa, Kansas, Kentucky, Louisiana, Maine, Maryland, Massachusetts, Michigan, Minnesota, Mississippi, Missouri, Montana, Nebraska, Nevada, New Hampshire, New Jersey, New Mexico, New York, North Carolina, North Dakota, Ohio, Oklahoma, Oregon, Pennsylvania, Rhode Island, South Carolina, South Dakota, Tennessee, Texas, Utah, Vermont, Virginia, Washington, West Virginia, Wisconsin, Wyoming. Available to U.S. citizens.

Application Requirements: Application form, essay. *Deadline:* July 10.

Contact: Nick Morrow
Morrow & Sheppard LLP
3701 Kirby Drive, Suite 840
Houston, TX 77098
Phone: 713-489-1206
E-mail: scholarship@morrowsheppard.com

NADRICH & COHEN, LLP

http://www.personalinjurylawcal.com/

NADRICH & COHEN, LLP CIVIL JUSTICE SCHOLARSHIP

Please see website for details
http://www.personalinjurylawcal.com/nadrich-cohen-civil-justice-scholarship-fund/

Academic Fields/Career Goals: Law/Legal Services.

Award: Scholarship for use in freshman, sophomore, junior, senior, or graduate years; not renewable. *Number:* 1. *Amount:* $1000.

Eligibility Requirements: Applicant must be enrolled or expecting to enroll full-time at a four-year institution or university and resident of California. Available to U.S. citizens.

Application Requirements: Application form, essay. *Deadline:* August 1.

Contact: Jeffrey Nadrich, Attorney
Nadrich & Cohen, LLP
12100 Wilshire Blvd., #1250
Los Angeles, CA 90025
Phone: 800-7184658
Fax: 800-9952980
E-mail: info@personalinjurylawcal.com

NATIONAL BLACK POLICE ASSOCIATION

http://www.blackpolice.org/

ALPHONSO DEAL SCHOLARSHIP AWARD

• See page 188

NATIONAL COURT REPORTERS ASSOCIATION

http://ncra.org

COUNCIL ON APPROVED STUDENT EDUCATION'S SCHOLARSHIP FUND

Applicant must have a writing speed of 140 to 180 words/min; must be in an NCRA certified court reporting program; write a two-page essay on topic chosen for the year; and submit a letter of recommendation.

Academic Fields/Career Goals: Law/Legal Services.

Award: Scholarship for use in sophomore year; not renewable. *Number:* 3. *Amount:* $500–$1500.

Eligibility Requirements: Applicant must be enrolled or expecting to enroll full- or part-time at a two-year or four-year or technical institution. Available to U.S. and Canadian citizens.

Application Requirements: Application form, entry in a contest, essay, recommendations or references, transcript. *Deadline:* April 1.

Contact: Cynthia Andrews, Director, Professional Development
Programs
National Court Reporters Association
8224 Old Courthouse Road
Vienna, VA 22182
Phone: 703-584-9058
E-mail: candrews@ncra.org

FRANK SARLI MEMORIAL SCHOLARSHIP

One-time award to a student who is nearing graduation from a trade/technical school or four-year college. Must be enrolled in a court reporting program. Minimum 3.5 GPA required.

Academic Fields/Career Goals: Law/Legal Services.

Award: Scholarship for use in senior year; not renewable. *Number:* 1. *Amount:* $2000.

Eligibility Requirements: Applicant must be enrolled or expecting to enroll full- or part-time at a four-year or technical institution or university. Applicant or parent of applicant must be member of National Federation of Press Women. Available to U.S. and non-U.S. citizens.

Application Requirements: Application form. *Deadline:* February 28.

Contact: B.J. Shorak, Deputy Executive Director
National Court Reporters Association
8224 Old Courthouse Road
Vienna, VA 22182-3808
Phone: 703-556-6272 Ext. 126
Fax: 703-556-6291
E-mail: BJSHORAK@ncra.org

STUDENT MEMBER TUITION GRANT

Four $500 awards for students in good academic standing in a court reporting program. Students are required to write 120 to 200 words/min.

Academic Fields/Career Goals: Law/Legal Services.

Award: Grant for use in freshman, sophomore, junior, or senior years; not renewable. *Number:* 4. *Amount:* $500.

Eligibility Requirements: Applicant must be enrolled or expecting to enroll full- or part-time at a four-year or technical institution or university. Available to U.S. and non-U.S. citizens.

Application Requirements: Application form. *Deadline:* May 31.

Contact: Amy Davidson, Assistant Director of Membership
National Court Reporters Association
8224 Old Courthouse Road
Vienna, VA 22182
Phone: 703-556-6272 Ext. 123
E-mail: adavidson@ncrahq.org

NATIONAL FEDERATION OF PARALEGAL ASSOCIATIONS INC. (NFPA)

http://www.paralegals.org/

NATIONAL FEDERATION OF PARALEGAL ASSOCIATES INC. THOMSON REUTERS SCHOLARSHIP

Applicants must be full- or part-time students enrolled in an accredited paralegal education program or college-level program with emphasis in paralegal studies. Minimum GPA of 3.0 required. NFPA membership is not required. Travel stipend to annual convention, where recipients will receive awards, also provided.

Academic Fields/Career Goals: Law/Legal Services.

Award: Scholarship for use in freshman, sophomore, junior, senior, graduate, or postgraduate years; not renewable. *Number:* 2. *Amount:* $2000–$3000.

Eligibility Requirements: Applicant must be enrolled or expecting to enroll full- or part-time at a two-year or four-year or technical institution or university. Available to U.S. and non-U.S. citizens.

Application Requirements: Application form, application form may be submitted online(www.paralegals.org), essay, recommendations or references, resume, transcript. *Deadline:* July 1.

Contact: Allison Kastner, Administrative Assistant
National Federation of Paralegal Associations Inc. (NFPA)
9100 Purdue Road
Suite 200
Indianapolis, IN 46268
Phone: 317-454-8312
E-mail: info@paralegals.org

NEW ENGLAND EMPLOYEE BENEFITS COUNCIL

http://www.neebc.org/

NEW ENGLAND EMPLOYEE BENEFITS COUNCIL SCHOLARSHIP PROGRAM

• *See page 78*

ROBINSON & HENRY, P.C.

https://www.robinsonandhenry.com/

ROBINSON & HENRY FAMILY LAW SCHOLARSHIP

This scholarship is available to high school seniors and current college students nationwide who plan on attending, or are attending, an accredited 4-year college/university or 2-year accredited community college in the Fall of 2017. The Family Law Scholarship is open only to applicants whose parents have gone through a divorce or are planning on pursuing a career in family law.

Academic Fields/Career Goals: Law/Legal Services.

Award: Scholarship for use in freshman, sophomore, junior, or senior years; not renewable. *Number:* 1. *Amount:* $1000.

Eligibility Requirements: Applicant must be enrolled or expecting to enroll full-time at a two-year or four-year institution or university. Available to U.S. citizens.

Application Requirements: Application form, essay. *Deadline:* May 31.

Contact: Amador Cahvez
E-mail: amador@niftymarketing.com

ROBINSON & HENRY INJURY SCHOLARSHIP

This scholarship is available to high school seniors and current college students nationwide who plan on attending, or are attending, an accredited 4-year college/university or 2-year accredited community college in the Fall of 2017. The applicant or the applicant's family must have been involved in a personal injury accident. Special preferences will be given to members of a family that has recently been injured in a car accident.

Academic Fields/Career Goals: Law/Legal Services.

Award: Scholarship for use in freshman, sophomore, junior, or senior years; not renewable. *Number:* 1. *Amount:* $1500.

Eligibility Requirements: Applicant must be enrolled or expecting to enroll full-time at a two-year or four-year institution or university. Available to U.S. citizens.

Application Requirements: Application form, essay. *Deadline:* May 31.

Contact: Amador Cahvez
E-mail: amador@niftymarketing.com

SOCIETY OF SATELLITE PROFESSIONALS INTERNATIONAL

http://www.sspi.org/

SSPI INTERNATIONAL SCHOLARSHIPS

• *See page 134*

SWEET LAW GROUP

https://sweetlaw.com/

FUTURE LEGAL LEADERS SCHOLARSHIP COMPETITION

The competition is open to any post-graduate law school or undergraduate student attending a four year accredited university. To participate, complete the form posted on Sweet Law's scholarship page and respond to the prompt, "Recount a time when you faced a challenge, setback, or failure. How did it affect you, and what did you learn from the experience?" Applications will be reviewed by the Sweet Law Group's team evaluated based on originality and creativity.

Academic Fields/Career Goals: Law/Legal Services.

Award: Scholarship for use in freshman, sophomore, junior, senior, graduate, or postgraduate years; renewable. *Number:* 1. *Amount:* $2000.

Eligibility Requirements: Applicant must be age 16-100 and enrolled or expecting to enroll full- or part-time at a four-year institution or university. Available to U.S. citizens.

Application Requirements: Application form may be submitted online (https://sweetlaw.com/scholarship/), essay. *Deadline:* December 31.

TAU KAPPA EPSILON EDUCATION FOUNDATION

https://www.tke.org/

HARRY J. DONNELLY MEMORIAL SCHOLARSHIP
• *See page 82*

UNITARIAN UNIVERSALIST ASSOCIATION

http://www.uua.org/

STANFIELD AND D'ORLANDO ART SCHOLARSHIP
• *See page 124*

VIRGINIA STATE BAR

http://www.vsb.org/

LAW IN SOCIETY AWARD COMPETITION

Participants write an essay in response to a hypothetical situation dealing with legal issues. Awards are based on superior understanding of the value of law in everyday life. The top thirty essays are awarded prizes of a plaque and dictionary/thesaurus set. First place receives $2000 U.S. Savings Bond or $1000 cash; second place, $1,500 bond or $750 cash; third place, $1000 bond or $500 cash; honorable mentions, $200 bond or $100 cash.

Academic Fields/Career Goals: Law/Legal Services.

Award: Prize for use in freshman year; not renewable. *Number:* up to 10. *Amount:* $100–$1000.

Eligibility Requirements: Applicant must be high school student; age 19 or under; planning to enroll or expecting to enroll full- or part-time at a four-year institution or university; resident of Virginia and must have an interest in writing. Available to U.S. citizens.

Application Requirements: Application form, entry in a contest, essay. *Deadline:* February 1.

Contact: Sandy Adkins, Public Relations Assistant
Virginia State Bar
707 East Main Street, Suite 1500
Richmond, VA 23219-2800
Phone: 804-775-0594
Fax: 804-775-0582
E-mail: adkins@vsb.org

WARNER NORCROSS + JUDD LLP

www.wnj.com

1L DIVERSITY SCHOLARSHIP

The 1L Diversity Scholarship program is intended to promote diversity in the legal profession in Michigan by assisting first-year, minority law students in good standing attending University of Michigan Law School, Michigan State University Law School or Wayne State Law School. Warner Norcross + Judd will award one scholarship of $2,000 to a student in each of the listed law schools.

Academic Fields/Career Goals: Law/Legal Services.

Award: Scholarship for use in freshman year; not renewable. *Number:* 3. *Amount:* $2000.

Eligibility Requirements: Applicant must be enrolled or expecting to enroll full-time at an institution or university and studying in Michigan. Available to U.S. and non-U.S. citizens.

Application Requirements: Application form, One-minute video uploaded to YouTube with an explanation regarding why you should be a recipient., resume, transcript. *Deadline:* March 31.

Contact: Mrs. Courtney Failer, Community Relations
Warner Norcross + Judd LLP
1500 Warner Building
150 Ottawa Ave NW
Grand Rapids, MI 49503
Phone: 616-7522345 Ext. 2345
E-mail: cfailer@wnj.com

WASHINGTON STATE ASSOCIATION FOR JUSTICE

http://www.washingtonjustice.org/

WASHINGTON STATE ASSOCIATION FOR JUSTICE AMERICAN JUSTICE ESSAY & VIDEO SCHOLARSHIP
• *See page 189*

WASHINGTON STATE ASSOCIATION FOR JUSTICE PAST PRESIDENTS' SCHOLARSHIP

The Washington State Association for Justice (WSAJ) created the WSAJ Past President's Scholarship Fund in 1991. One $7,500 scholarship will be awarded in 2017. Winners must have 1. Demonstrated academic achievement and planned advancement toward a degree in an institution of higher learning. 2. A documented need for financial assistance. 3. A history of achievement despite having been a victim of injury or overcoming a disability, handicap, or similar challenge. 4. A record of commitment to helping people in need or protecting the rights of injured persons. 5. A plan or commitment to apply your education toward helping people. 6. Residency in Washington State. 7. High school seniors only. Application for this scholarship must be made as follows. Incomplete applications will not be reviewed or considered. 1. Send a letter (written by the student/applicant) to the scholarship committee describing the qualifications of the applicant and explaining the reasons why s/he feels they deserve the scholarship. 2. Include all high school and community college academic transcripts; name, address, and telephone number of two (2) references, at least one of which must be outside of the school environment (please do not submit more than two); brief written financial statement indicating what resources are available to the applicant and why this scholarship is necessary to fund the applicant's college education (copies of FAFSA are acceptable); name, address, telephone number and email (if they have one) of the applicant; any other documentation the applicant wishes to attach in support of their qualifications and; completed Application Checklist form. Applications must be postmarked on or before March 17, 2017.

Academic Fields/Career Goals: Law/Legal Services.

Award: Scholarship for use in freshman year; not renewable. *Number:* 1. *Amount:* $7500.

Eligibility Requirements: Applicant must be high school student; planning to enroll or expecting to enroll full-time at a four-year institution or university and resident of Washington. Applicant or parent of applicant must have employment or volunteer experience in community service. Available to U.S. citizens.

Application Requirements: Application form, driver's license, essay, financial need analysis. *Deadline:* March 17.

Contact: Anita Yandle, Scholarship Coordinator
Washington State Association for Justice
1809 7th Avenue
Suite 1500
Seattle, WA 98101
Phone: 206-464-1011
E-mail: anita@washingtonjustice.org

WILLIAMS LAW GROUP

https://familylawyersnewjersey.com/

WILLIAMS LAW GROUP OPPORTUNITY TO GROW SCHOLARSHIP
• *See page 119*

LIBRARY AND INFORMATION SCIENCES

ALICE L. HALTOM EDUCATIONAL FUND

http://www.alhef.org/

ALICE L. HALTOM EDUCATIONAL FUND
• *See page 145*

ASSOCIATION FOR INFORMATION SCIENCE AND TECHNOLOGY

https://www.asist.org/

JOHN WILEY & SONS BEST JASIST PAPER AWARD

Award of $1500 to recognize the best refereed paper published in the volume year of the JASIT preceding the ASIST annual meeting. John Wiley & Sons Inc., shall contribute $500 towards travel expenses to attend the ASIST annual meeting. No nomination procedure is used for this award. All eligible papers are considered.

Academic Fields/Career Goals: Library and Information Sciences.

Award: Prize for use in freshman, sophomore, junior, senior, graduate, or postgraduate years; not renewable. *Number:* 1. *Amount:* $2000.

Eligibility Requirements: Applicant must be enrolled or expecting to enroll full-time at an institution or university. Available to U.S. and non-U.S. citizens.

Application Requirements: Application form, essay. *Deadline:* April 27.

Contact: Lydia Middleton, Executive Director
Association for Information Science and Technology
8555 16th Street
Suite 850
Silver Spring, MD 20910
Phone: 301-495-0900 Ext. 1100
E-mail: lmiddleton@asist.org

ASSOCIATION OF MOVING IMAGE ARCHIVISTS

https://amianet.org/

AMIA SCHOLARSHIPS PROGRAM

These scholarships, each in the amount of $4,000, are given as financial assistance to students of merit who intend to pursue careers in moving image archiving. The funds are sent directly to the recipients' educational institutions to help cover the costs of tuition or registration fees. Students from any country may apply. Applicants need only submit one application form and one set of supporting documents to be eligible for all three scholarships; however, no applicant will be awarded more than one scholarship.

Academic Fields/Career Goals: Library and Information Sciences.

Award: Scholarship for use in freshman, sophomore, junior, senior, graduate, or postgraduate years; not renewable. *Number:* 4. *Amount:* $4000.

Eligibility Requirements: Applicant must be enrolled or expecting to enroll full-time at a two-year or four-year or technical institution or university. Available to U.S. and non-U.S. citizens.

Application Requirements: Application form, essay. *Deadline:* May 15.

Contact: Kristina Kersels, Events and Operations
Association of Moving Image Archivists
1313 Vine Street
Hollywood, CA 90028
Phone: 323-463-1500
E-mail: kkersels@amianet.org

BIBLIOGRAPHICAL SOCIETY OF AMERICA

http://www.bibsocamer.org/

JUSTIN G. SCHILLER PRIZE FOR BIBLIOGRAPHICAL WORK IN PRE-20TH-CENTURY CHILDREN'S BOOKS

Award for bibliographic work in the field of pre-20th century children's books. Winner will receive a cash award of $2000 and a year's membership in the Society.

Academic Fields/Career Goals: Library and Information Sciences; Literature/English/Writing.

Award: Prize for use in freshman, sophomore, junior, or senior years; not renewable. *Number:* 1. *Amount:* $2000.

Eligibility Requirements: Applicant must be enrolled or expecting to enroll full- or part-time at a four-year institution or university. Available to U.S. and non-U.S. citizens.

Application Requirements: Application form, documentation regarding the approval of a thesis or dissertation or confirming the date of publication, entry in a contest, resume. *Deadline:* September 1.

Contact: Michele Randall, Executive Secretary
Bibliographical Society of America
PO Box 1537, Lenox Hill Station
New York, NY 10021
Phone: 212-452-2710
Fax: 212-452-2710
E-mail: bsa@bibsocamer.org

CALIFORNIA SCHOOL LIBRARY ASSOCIATION

http://www.csla.net/

CSLA NORTHERN REGION PARAPROFESSIONAL SCHOLARSHIP

This scholarship is intended to assist a school library paraprofessional who is enrolled in a 2-year paraprofessional program working towards the goal of becoming a school library media technician, or enrolled in a class to support the library program through job-related skills.

Academic Fields/Career Goals: Library and Information Sciences.

Award: Scholarship for use in freshman or sophomore years; not renewable. *Number:* 1–2. *Amount:* $500.

Eligibility Requirements: Applicant must be enrolled or expecting to enroll full- or part-time at a two-year institution and resident of British Columbia. Available to U.S. citizens.

Application Requirements: Application form, application form may be submitted online, essay. *Deadline:* October 15.

Contact: Katie McNamara, President
Phone: 888-655-8480
E-mail: Katie_McNamara@kernhigh.org

FLORIDA ASSOCIATION FOR MEDIA IN EDUCATION

http://www.floridamediaed.org/ssyra.html

FAME/SANDY ULM SCHOLARSHIP

Scholarship for students studying to be school library media specialists. The scholarship awards at least $1000 to one or more students each year.

Academic Fields/Career Goals: Library and Information Sciences.

Award: Scholarship for use in freshman year; not renewable.

Eligibility Requirements: Applicant must be high school student; planning to enroll or expecting to enroll full-time at a two-year or four-year or technical institution or university and studying in Florida. Available to U.S. citizens.

Application Requirements: Application form.

Contact: Larry Bodkin, Executive Director
Phone: 850-531-8350
Fax: 850-531-8344
E-mail: lbodkin@floridamedia.org

IDAHO LIBRARY ASSOCIATION

http://www.idaholibraries.org/

IDAHO LIBRARY ASSOCIATION GARDNER HANKS SCHOLARSHIP

Scholarship for students who are beginning or continuing formal library education, pursuing a Master's of Library Science degree or Media Generalist certification. Must be an Idaho Library Association member.

Academic Fields/Career Goals: Library and Information Sciences.

Award: Scholarship for use in freshman, sophomore, junior, senior, graduate, or postgraduate years; not renewable. *Number:* 1. *Amount:* $600.

Eligibility Requirements: Applicant must be enrolled or expecting to enroll full-time at a two-year or four-year institution or university and resident of Idaho. Applicant or parent of applicant must be member of Idaho Library Association. Available to U.S. citizens.

Application Requirements: Application form, financial need analysis. *Deadline:* May 31.

Contact: Rami Attebury, Scholarships, Awards, and Recruitment
Committee Chair
E-mail: rattebur@uidaho.edu

WISCONSIN LIBRARY ASSOCIATION

https://www.wisconsinlibraries.org/

WLA CONTINUING EDUCATION SCHOLARSHIP

Scholarship awarded to employee who is planning to attend a continuing education program within or outside of Wisconsin. Applicant must be able to communicate the knowledge gained from the continuing education program to fellow librarians and information professionals in Wisconsin, employed in a library and information agency in Wisconsin.

Academic Fields/Career Goals: Library and Information Sciences.

Award: Scholarship for use in freshman, sophomore, junior, senior, graduate, or postgraduate years; not renewable. *Number:* 1.

Eligibility Requirements: Applicant must be enrolled or expecting to enroll full- or part-time at a four-year institution or university and resident of Wisconsin. Available to U.S. citizens.

Application Requirements: Application form. *Deadline:* July 17.

Contact: Ms. Brigitte Rupp Vacha, WLA Conference Liaison
Wisconsin Library Association
4610 S Biltmore Lane
Suite 100
Madison, WI 53718
Phone: 608-245-3640
Fax: 608-245-3646
E-mail: ruppvacha@wisconsinlibraries.org

LITERATURE/ENGLISH/ WRITING

AMERICAN FOUNDATION FOR THE BLIND

http://www.afb.org/

R.L. GILLETTE SCHOLARSHIP

Two scholarships of $1000 each to women who are enrolled in a four-year undergraduate degree program in literature or music. In addition to the general requirements, applicants must submit a performance tape not to exceed 30 minutes, or a creative writing sample. Must submit proof of legal blindness. For additional information and application requirements, refer to website http://www.afb.org/scholarships.asp.

Academic Fields/Career Goals: Literature/English/Writing; Music.

Award: Scholarship for use in freshman, sophomore, junior, or senior years; not renewable. *Number:* up to 2. *Amount:* $1000.

Eligibility Requirements: Applicant must be enrolled or expecting to enroll full-time at a four-year institution or university and female. Applicant must be visually impaired. Available to U.S. citizens.

Application Requirements: Application form, essay, financial need analysis, performance tape (not to exceed 30 minutes) or creative writing sample, proof of legal blindness, acceptance letter, recommendations or references, transcript. *Deadline:* April 30.

Contact: Dawn Bodrogi, Information Center and Library Coordinator
American Foundation for the Blind
11 Penn Plaza, Suite 300
New York, NY 10001
Phone: 212-502-7661
Fax: 212-502-7771
E-mail: afbinfo@afb.net

AMERICAN-SCANDINAVIAN FOUNDATION

http://www.amscan.org/

AMERICAN-SCANDINAVIAN FOUNDATION TRANSLATION PRIZE

Two prizes are awarded for outstanding English translations of poetry, fiction, drama or literary prose originally written in Danish, Finnish, Icelandic, Norwegian or Swedish. The Nadia Christensen Prize includes a $2,500 award, publication of an excerpt in Scandinavian Review, and a commemorative bronze medallion. The Leif and Inger Sjöberg Award, given to an individual whose literature translations have not previously been published, includes a $2,000 award, publication of an excerpt in Scandinavian Review, and a commemorative bronze medallion.

Academic Fields/Career Goals: Literature/English/Writing.

Award: Prize for use in freshman, sophomore, junior, senior, graduate, or postgraduate years; not renewable. *Number:* 2. *Amount:* $2000–$2500.

Eligibility Requirements: Applicant must be enrolled or expecting to enroll full- or part-time at a two-year or four-year or technical institution or university and must have an interest in Scandinavian language. Available to U.S. and non-U.S. citizens.

Application Requirements: Application form. *Deadline:* June 15.

Contact: Carl Fritscher, Fellowships and Grants Officer
Phone: 212-779-3587
E-mail: grants@amscan.org

BIBLIOGRAPHICAL SOCIETY OF AMERICA

http://www.bibsocamer.org/

JUSTIN G. SCHILLER PRIZE FOR BIBLIOGRAPHICAL WORK IN PRE-20TH-CENTURY CHILDREN'S BOOKS
• See page 322

CULTURAL SERVICES OF THE FRENCH EMBASSY

http://www.frenchculture.org/

TEACHING ASSISTANT PROGRAM IN FRANCE
• See page 98

GOLDEN KEY INTERNATIONAL HONOUR SOCIETY

http://www.goldenkey.org/

LITERARY ACHIEVEMENT AWARDS

Award of $1000 will be given to winners in each of the following four categories: fiction, non-fiction, poetry, and feature writing. Eligible applicants are undergraduate, graduate and postgraduate members who are currently enrolled in classes at a degree-granting program.

Academic Fields/Career Goals: Literature/English/Writing.

Award: Prize for use in freshman, sophomore, junior, senior, graduate, or postgraduate years; not renewable. *Number:* 4. *Amount:* $1000.

Eligibility Requirements: Applicant must be enrolled or expecting to enroll full- or part-time at a four-year institution or university and must have an interest in writing. Available to U.S. and non-U.S. citizens.

Application Requirements: Application form, entry in a contest, essay, original composition. *Deadline:* April 1.

Contact: Scholarship Program Administrators
Golden Key International Honour Society
PO Box 23737
Nashville, TN 37202-3737
Phone: 800-377-2401
E-mail: scholarships@goldenkey.org

HUB FOUNDATION

https://hub-foundation.org

HUB FOUNDATION SCHOLARSHIPS
• *See page 88*

JAPANESE AMERICAN CITIZENS LEAGUE (JACL)

http://www.jacl.org/

NATIONAL JACL HEADQUARTERS SCHOLARSHIP
• *See page 94*

NATIONAL WRITERS ASSOCIATION FOUNDATION

http://www.nationalwriters.com/

NATIONAL WRITERS ASSOCIATION FOUNDATION SCHOLARSHIPS
• *See page 308*

OUTDOOR WRITERS ASSOCIATION OF AMERICA

http://www.owaa.org/

OUTDOOR WRITERS ASSOCIATION OF AMERICA - BODIE MCDOWELL SCHOLARSHIP AWARD
• *See page 174*

STRAIGHTFORWARD MEDIA

http://www.straightforwardmedia.com/

STRAIGHTFORWARD MEDIA LIBERAL ARTS SCHOLARSHIP
• *See page 119*

UNITED NEGRO COLLEGE FUND

http://www.uncf.org/

DIVERSE VOICES IN STORYTELLING SCHOLARSHIP
• *See page 177*

HCN/APRICITY RESOURCES SCHOLARS PROGRAM
• *See page 83*

VIRTUOUS PROM

https://www.virtuousprom.com

KAREN HANSON MEMORIAL SCHOLARSHIP

This scholarship was created in loving memory of Karen Hanson, amazing mother, wife, teacher and friend. Karen was taken from us too soon, but among the many lessons she taught us, it was to face life's challenges with optimism and humor. The Karen Hanson Memorial Scholarship is for anyone planning to or currently pursuing studies in Literature, either at the undergraduate, graduate or post–graduate level. The winner will be awarded $350. In order to apply, applicants must submit a 250+ word essay responding to the following prompt: Life is full of challenges and struggles, and one of the great things literature can do is help us move through and past them with humor. In 250 words or more, describe how an education in Literature can help us move through life with greater joy. Submissions may be written in prose or may be submitted in the form of a short (hopefully humorous!) story. All essays must be submitted to scholarships@virtuousprom.com beginning each year on September 1 and received no later than November 30. Out of the pool of applicants, we will choose three finalists by January 1. Finalists will be chosen based on the coherency and persuasiveness of their essays. We will then notify the finalists and post the three finalists' essays on our blog and on our Facebook page. The winner will be announced January 31 on Facebook.

Academic Fields/Career Goals: Literature/English/Writing.

Award: Scholarship for use in freshman, sophomore, junior, senior, graduate, or postgraduate years; not renewable. *Number:* 1. *Amount:* $350.

Eligibility Requirements: Applicant must be enrolled or expecting to enroll full- or part-time at a two-year or four-year institution or university. Available to U.S. and non-U.S. citizens.

Application Requirements: Essay. *Deadline:* November 30.

Contact: Ms. Megan MacNeal, Creative Director
E-mail: megan@virtuousprom.com

MARINE BIOLOGY

AMERICAN INDIAN SCIENCE AND ENGINEERING SOCIETY

http://www.aises.org/

A.T. ANDERSON MEMORIAL SCHOLARSHIP PROGRAM
• *See page 105*

AMERICAN PHYSIOLOGICAL SOCIETY

https://www.physiology.org/

BARBARA A. HORWITZ AND JOHN M. HOROWITZ UNDERGRADUATE RESEARCH AWARDS
• *See page 139*

ASSOCIATION FOR WOMEN GEOSCIENTISTS (AWG)

http://www.awg.org/

AWG UNDERGRADUATE EXCELLENCE IN PALEONTOLOGY AWARD
• *See page 106*

ASSOCIATION ON AMERICAN INDIAN AFFAIRS, INC.

http://www.indian-affairs.org/

ELIZABETH AND SHERMAN ASCHE MEMORIAL SCHOLARSHIP FUND
• *See page 93*

BARRY GOLDWATER SCHOLARSHIP AND EXCELLENCE IN EDUCATION FOUNDATION

https://goldwater.scholarsapply.org

BARRY M. GOLDWATER SCHOLARSHIP AND EXCELLENCE IN EDUCATION PROGRAM
• *See page 107*

CUSHMAN FOUNDATION FOR FORAMINIFERAL RESEARCH

http://www.cushmanfoundation.org/index.php

LOEBLICH AND TAPPAN STUDENT RESEARCH AWARD
• See page 142

DISTIL NETWORKS

http://www.distilnetworks.com

WOMEN FORWARD IN TECHNOLOGY SCHOLARSHIP PROGRAM
• See page 108

THE EXPERT INSTITUTE

https://www.theexpertinstitute.com

ANNUAL HEALTHCARE AND LIFE SCIENCES SCHOLARSHIP
• See page 142

EXPLORERS CLUB

http://www.explorers.org/

YOUTH ACTIVITY FUND GRANTS
• See page 103

GREAT MINDS IN STEM

http://www.greatmindsinstem.org/college/scholarship-application-information

HENAAC SCHOLARSHIP PROGRAM
• See page 100

THE LAND CONSERVANCY OF NEW JERSEY

http://www.tlc-nj.org/

ROGERS FAMILY SCHOLARSHIP
• See page 143

RUSSELL W. MYERS SCHOLARSHIP
• See page 143

LOUISIANA OFFICE OF STUDENT FINANCIAL ASSISTANCE

www.osfa.la.gov/

ROCKEFELLER STATE WILDLIFE SCHOLARSHIP

For college undergraduates with a minimum of 60 credit hours who are majoring in Forestry, Wildlife, or Marine Science, and for college graduate students who are majoring in Forestry, Wildlife, or Marine Science. College undergraduates must have a grade point average of at least 2.50 to apply. College graduate students must have a grade point average of at least 3.00 in order to apply. Renewable up to three years as an undergraduate and two years as a graduate student.

Academic Fields/Career Goals: Marine Biology; Marine/Ocean Engineering; Natural Resources; Oceanography.

Award: Scholarship for use in freshman, sophomore, junior, senior, or graduate years; renewable. *Amount:* $2000–$3000.

Eligibility Requirements: Applicant must be enrolled or expecting to enroll full-time at an institution or university; resident of Kentucky and studying in Louisiana. Available to U.S. citizens.

Application Requirements: Application form. *Deadline:* July 1.
Contact: Joanna Brumfield
Baton Rouge, LA 70821-9202
Phone: 225-219-7708
E-mail: Joanna.Brumfield@la.gov

MARINE TECHNOLOGY SOCIETY

http://www.mtsociety.org/

CHARLES H. BUSSMAN UNDERGRADUATE SCHOLARSHIP

$2500 scholarship open to MTS members who are college undergraduate students currently enrolled full-time in a marine-related field.

Academic Fields/Career Goals: Marine Biology; Marine/Ocean Engineering; Oceanography.

Award: Scholarship for use in freshman, sophomore, junior, or senior years; not renewable. *Amount:* $2500.

Eligibility Requirements: Applicant must be enrolled or expecting to enroll full-time at an institution or university. Applicant or parent of applicant must be member of Marine Technology Society. Available to U.S. and non-U.S. citizens.

Application Requirements: Application form, application form may be submitted online, driver's license. *Deadline:* April 17.
Contact: Suzanne Voelker, Operations Administrator
Phone: 410-884-5330
Fax: 410-884-9060
E-mail: suzanne.voelker@mtsociety.org

MTS STUDENT SCHOLARSHIP FOR GRADUATING HIGH SCHOOL SENIORS

$2000 scholarship open to MTS student members that are high school seniors who have been accepted into a full-time undergraduate program.

Academic Fields/Career Goals: Marine Biology; Marine/Ocean Engineering.

Award: Scholarship for use in freshman year; not renewable. *Amount:* $2000.

Eligibility Requirements: Applicant must be high school student and planning to enroll or expecting to enroll full-time at an institution or university. Applicant or parent of applicant must be member of Marine Technology Society. Available to U.S. and non-U.S. citizens.

Application Requirements: Application form, application form may be submitted online, essay. *Deadline:* April 17.
Contact: Suzanne Voelker, Program Administrator
Marine Technology Society
5565 Sterrett Place, Suite 108
Columbia, MD 21044
Phone: 410-884-5330
E-mail: suzanne.voelker@mtsociety.org

THE MTS STUDENT SCHOLARSHIP FOR TWO-YEAR, TECHNICAL, ENGINEERING AND COMMUNITY COLLEGE STUDENTS

$3000 scholarship open to MTS members enrolled in a two-year, technical, engineering or community college in a marine-related field.

Academic Fields/Career Goals: Marine Biology; Marine/Ocean Engineering.

Award: Scholarship for use in freshman or sophomore years; not renewable. *Amount:* $3000.

Eligibility Requirements: Applicant must be enrolled or expecting to enroll full-time at a two-year institution. Applicant or parent of applicant must be member of Marine Technology Society. Available to U.S. and non-U.S. citizens.

Application Requirements: Application form, application form may be submitted online, essay. *Deadline:* April 17.
Contact: Suzanne Voelker, Operations Administrator
Marine Technology Society
5565 Sterrett Place, Suite 108
Columbia, MD 21044
Phone: 410-884-5330
E-mail: suzanne.voelker@mtsociety.org

MTS STUDENT SCHOLARSHIP FOR UNDERGRADUATE STUDENTS

$3000 scholarship open to MTS student members who are college undergraduate students currently enrolled full-time in a marine-related field.

Academic Fields/Career Goals: Marine Biology; Marine/Ocean Engineering; Oceanography.

Award: Scholarship for use in freshman, sophomore, junior, or senior years; not renewable. *Amount:* $3000.

Eligibility Requirements: Applicant must be enrolled or expecting to enroll full-time at an institution or university. Applicant or parent of applicant must be member of Marine Technology Society. Available to U.S. and non-U.S. citizens.

Application Requirements: Application form, application form may be submitted online, driver's license. *Deadline:* April 17.

Contact: Suzanne Voelker, Operations Administrator
Phone: 410-884-5330
Fax: 410-884-9060
E-mail: suzanne.voelker@mtsociety.org

PAROS-DIGIQUARTZ SCHOLARSHIP

$2000 scholarship open to MTS members with an interest in marine instrumentation who are undergraduate or graduate students currently enrolled full time in an academic institution.

Academic Fields/Career Goals: Marine Biology; Marine/Ocean Engineering; Oceanography.

Award: Scholarship for use in freshman, sophomore, junior, senior, or graduate years; not renewable. *Amount:* $2000.

Eligibility Requirements: Applicant must be enrolled or expecting to enroll full-time at an institution or university. Applicant or parent of applicant must be member of Marine Technology Society. Available to U.S. and non-U.S. citizens.

Application Requirements: Application form, application form may be submitted online, driver's license. *Deadline:* April 17.

Contact: Suzanne Voelker, Operations Administrator
Phone: 410-884-5330
Fax: 410-884-9060
E-mail: suzanne.voelker@mtsociety.org

MEDICAL SCRUBS COLLECTION

http://medicalscrubscollection.com

MEDICAL SCRUBS COLLECTION SCHOLARSHIP
• *See page 104*

NEXTSTEPU

http://www.nextstepu.com/

$1,500 STEM SCHOLARSHIP
• *See page 104*

NOVUS BIOLOGICALS, LLC

https://www.novusbio.com

NOVUS BIOLOGICALS SCHOLARSHIP PROGRAM
• *See page 101*

R&D SYSTEMS SCHOLARSHIP
• *See page 101*

TOCRIS BIOSCIENCE SCHOLARSHIP
• *See page 102*

SCARLETT FAMILY FOUNDATION SCHOLARSHIP PROGRAM

http://www.scarlettfoundation.org/

SCHOLARSHIP FOR STUDENTS PURSUING A BUSINESS OR STEM DEGREE
• *See page 80*

SOCIETY FOR INTEGRATIVE AND COMPARATIVE BIOLOGY

http://www.sicb.org/

LIBBIE H. HYMAN MEMORIAL SCHOLARSHIP
• *See page 144*

STRAIGHT NORTH

https://www.straightnorth.com/

STRAIGHT NORTH STEM SCHOLARSHIP
• *See page 81*

UNITED NEGRO COLLEGE FUND

http://www.uncf.org/

LEIDOS STEM SCHOLARSHIP
• *See page 96*

WOMAN'S SEAMEN'S FRIEND SOCIETY OF CONNECTICUT INC.

FINANCIAL SUPPORT FOR MARINE OR MARITIME STUDIES

Applicant must be full-time student. High school students not considered. Award available to U.S. citizens. Must be majoring in marine sciences at any college or university.

Academic Fields/Career Goals: Marine Biology; Oceanography.

Award: Scholarship for use in freshman, sophomore, junior, or senior years; not renewable.

Eligibility Requirements: Applicant must be enrolled or expecting to enroll full-time at a four-year institution or university. Available to U.S. citizens.

Application Requirements: Application form, financial need analysis, recommendations or references, resume, test scores, transcript. *Deadline:* varies.

Contact: Marshall Davidson, Executive Director
Phone: 203-777-2165
Fax: 203-777-5774
E-mail: wsfsofct@earthlink.net

YOUTH MARITIME TRAINING ASSOCIATION

http://ymta.net/

NORM MANLY—YMTA MARITIME EDUCATIONAL SCHOLARSHIPS

The scholarships may be used by students pursuing marine-related and maritime training and education in community colleges, technical and vocational programs, colleges, universities, maritime academies or other educational institutions. Scholarships will be awarded in the amounts of one $5,000, one $3,000, two $2,500, and two $1,000. In addition, Pacific Maritime Magazine will award a $500 scholarship to one of the finalists planning to pursue a seagoing maritime career. Requires 2.5 GPA or submit an additional letter of recommendation from a second teacher.

Academic Fields/Career Goals: Marine Biology; Marine/Ocean Engineering; Oceanography; Trade/Technical Specialties.

Award: Scholarship for use in freshman year; not renewable. *Number:* 6–7. *Amount:* $1000–$5000.

Eligibility Requirements: Applicant must be high school student; planning to enroll or expecting to enroll full- or part-time at a two-year or four-year or technical institution or university and resident of Washington. Available to U.S. citizens.

Application Requirements: Application form, essay. *Deadline:* March 22.

Contact: Alicia Barnes, Director
Youth Maritime Training Association
PO Box 81142
Seattle, WA 98108
Phone: 206-812-5464
E-mail: ymta@pugetmaritime.org

MARINE/OCEAN ENGINEERING

AMERICAN COUNCIL OF ENGINEERING COMPANIES OF PENNSYLVANIA (ACEC/PA)
http://www.acecpa.org/

ERIC J. GENNUSO AND LEROY D. (BUD) LOY, JR. SCHOLARSHIP PROGRAM
• *See page 153*

AMERICAN INDIAN SCIENCE AND ENGINEERING SOCIETY
http://www.aises.org/

A.T. ANDERSON MEMORIAL SCHOLARSHIP PROGRAM
• *See page 105*

AMERICAN SOCIETY OF CERTIFIED ENGINEERING TECHNICIANS
http://www.ascet.org/

KURT H. AND DONNA M. SCHULER SMALL GRANT
• *See page 162*

AMERICAN SOCIETY OF NAVAL ENGINEERS
http://www.navalengineers.org/

AMERICAN SOCIETY OF NAVAL ENGINEERS SCHOLARSHIP
• *See page 106*

BARRY GOLDWATER SCHOLARSHIP AND EXCELLENCE IN EDUCATION FOUNDATION
https://goldwater.scholarsapply.org

BARRY M. GOLDWATER SCHOLARSHIP AND EXCELLENCE IN EDUCATION PROGRAM
• *See page 107*

BHW GROUP
https://thebhwgroup.com/

BHW WOMEN IN STEM SCHOLARSHIP
• *See page 107*

BROWN AND CALDWELL
http://www.brownandcaldwell.com

ECKENFELDER SCHOLARSHIP
• *See page 141*

MINORITY SCHOLARSHIP PROGRAM
• *See page 141*

DISTIL NETWORKS
http://www.distilnetworks.com

WOMEN FORWARD IN TECHNOLOGY SCHOLARSHIP PROGRAM
• *See page 108*

GREAT MINDS IN STEM
http://www.greatmindsinstem.org/college/scholarship-application-information

HENAAC SCHOLARSHIP PROGRAM
• *See page 100*

LOUISIANA OFFICE OF STUDENT FINANCIAL ASSISTANCE
www.osfa.la.gov/

ROCKEFELLER STATE WILDLIFE SCHOLARSHIP
• *See page 325*

MANUFACTURERS ASSOCIATION OF MAINE
http://www.mainemfg.com/

MAINE MANUFACTURING CAREER AND TRAINING FOUNDATION SCHOLARSHIP
• *See page 131*

MARINE TECHNOLOGY SOCIETY
http://www.mtsociety.org/

CHARLES H. BUSSMAN UNDERGRADUATE SCHOLARSHIP
• *See page 325*

JOHN C. BAJUS SCHOLARSHIP
$1000 scholarship available to MTS members who are college undergraduates and graduate students currently enrolled full-time in a marine-related field who have shown a commitment to community service and/or volunteer activities.

Academic Fields/Career Goals: Marine/Ocean Engineering; Oceanography.

Award: Scholarship for use in freshman, sophomore, junior, senior, or graduate years; not renewable. *Amount:* $1000.

Eligibility Requirements: Applicant must be enrolled or expecting to enroll full-time at an institution or university. Applicant or parent of applicant must be member of Marine Technology Society. Applicant or parent of applicant must have employment or volunteer experience in community service. Available to U.S. and non-U.S. citizens.

Application Requirements: Application form, application form may be submitted online, driver's license. *Deadline:* April 17.

Contact: Suzanne Voelker, Operations Administrator
Phone: 410-884-5330
Fax: 410-884-9060
E-mail: suzanne.voelker@mtsociety.org

MTS STUDENT SCHOLARSHIP FOR GRADUATING HIGH SCHOOL SENIORS
• *See page 325*

THE MTS STUDENT SCHOLARSHIP FOR TWO-YEAR, TECHNICAL, ENGINEERING AND COMMUNITY COLLEGE STUDENTS
• *See page 325*

MTS STUDENT SCHOLARSHIP FOR UNDERGRADUATE STUDENTS
• *See page 326*

PAROS-DIGIQUARTZ SCHOLARSHIP
• *See page 326*

ROV SCHOLARSHIP

Scholarships of up to $8000 open to MTS student members interested in remotely operated vehicles (ROVs) or underwater work that furthers the use of ROVs. To qualify for the MATE/MTS ROV scholarship the applicant must either attend a MATE Partner college or university or have participated in a MATE ROV Competition.

Academic Fields/Career Goals: Marine/Ocean Engineering; Oceanography.

Award: Scholarship for use in freshman, sophomore, junior, senior, or graduate years; not renewable. *Amount:* $8000.

Eligibility Requirements: Applicant must be enrolled or expecting to enroll full-time at an institution or university. Applicant or parent of applicant must be member of Marine Technology Society. Available to U.S. and non-U.S. citizens.

Application Requirements: Application form, application form may be submitted online, driver's license, essay. *Deadline:* April 17.

Contact: Suzanne Voelker, Operations Administrator
Phone: 410-884-5330
Fax: 410-884-9060
E-mail: suzanne.voelker@mtsociety.org

NASA FLORIDA SPACE GRANT CONSORTIUM
http://www.floridaspacegrant.org/

FLORIDA SPACE RESEARCH PROGRAM
• *See page 131*

NEXTSTEPU
http://www.nextstepu.com/

$1,500 STEM SCHOLARSHIP
• *See page 104*

NOVUS BIOLOGICALS, LLC
https://www.novusbio.com

NOVUS BIOLOGICALS SCHOLARSHIP PROGRAM
• *See page 101*

R&D SYSTEMS SCHOLARSHIP
• *See page 101*

TOCRIS BIOSCIENCE SCHOLARSHIP
• *See page 102*

SCARLETT FAMILY FOUNDATION SCHOLARSHIP PROGRAM
http://www.scarlettfoundation.org/

SCHOLARSHIP FOR STUDENTS PURSUING A BUSINESS OR STEM DEGREE
• *See page 80*

THE SOCIETY OF NAVAL ARCHITECTS & MARINE ENGINEERS
http://www.sname.org

MANDELL AND LESTER ROSENBLATT UNDERGRADUATE SCHOLARSHIP

Mandell and Lester Rosenblatt Undergraduate Scholarship is part of the SNAME Undergraduate Scholarships Program, and open to applicants who are members of the Society of Naval Architects & Marine Engineers. Awards are made for one year of study leading to a Bachelor's Degree in naval architecture, marine engineering, ocean engineering or in other fields directly related to the maritime industry.

Academic Fields/Career Goals: Marine/Ocean Engineering.

Award: Scholarship for use in freshman, sophomore, junior, or senior years; not renewable. *Number:* 1. *Amount:* $6000.

Eligibility Requirements: Applicant must be enrolled or expecting to enroll full-time at an institution or university. Available to U.S. and non-U.S. citizens.

Application Requirements: Application form, essay. *Deadline:* June 1.

Contact: Sofia Iliogrammenou, Director of Regional Member Services
E-mail: siliogrammenou@sname.org

ROBERT N. HERBERT UNDERGRADUATE SCHOLARSHIP

Robert N. Herbert Undergraduate Scholarship is part of the SNAME Undergraduate Scholarships Program, and open to applicants who are members of the Society of Naval Architects & Marine Engineers. Awards are made for one year of study leading to a Bachelor's Degree in naval architecture, marine engineering, ocean engineering or in other fields directly related to the maritime industry.

Academic Fields/Career Goals: Marine/Ocean Engineering.

Award: Scholarship for use in freshman, sophomore, junior, or senior years; not renewable. *Amount:* $6000.

Eligibility Requirements: Applicant must be enrolled or expecting to enroll full-time at an institution or university. Available to U.S. and non-U.S. citizens.

Application Requirements: Application form, essay. *Deadline:* June 1.

Contact: Sofia Iliogrammenou, Director of Regional Member Services
E-mail: siliogrammenou@sname.org

UNDERGRADUATE GENERAL SCHOLARSHIP

The Undergraduate General Scholarship is part of the SNAME Undergraduate Scholarship Program, and open to Society of Naval Architects & Marine Engineers members. Awards are made for one year of study leading to a Bachelor's Degree in naval architecture, marine engineering, ocean engineering or in other fields directly related to the maritime industry.

Academic Fields/Career Goals: Marine/Ocean Engineering.

Award: Scholarship for use in junior or senior years; not renewable. *Amount:* $2000.

Eligibility Requirements: Applicant must be enrolled or expecting to enroll full-time at an institution or university and studying in British Columbia, California, Florida, Louisiana, Maine, Massachusetts, Michigan, Newfoundland, New York, Texas, Virginia. Available to U.S. and non-U.S. citizens.

Application Requirements: Application form, essay. *Deadline:* June 1.

Contact: Sofia Iliogrammenou, Director of Regional Member Services
E-mail: siliogrammenou@sname.org

SOCIETY OF WOMEN ENGINEERS
https://swe.org/

SWE REGION E SCHOLARSHIP
• See page 159

SWE REGION H SCHOLARSHIPS
• See page 159

SWE REGION J SCHOLARSHIP
• See page 159

TE CONNECTIVITY EXCELLENCE IN ENGINEERING SCHOLARSHIP
• See page 160

STRAIGHT NORTH
https://www.straightnorth.com/

STRAIGHT NORTH STEM SCHOLARSHIP
• See page 81

UNITED NEGRO COLLEGE FUND
http://www.uncf.org/

LEIDOS STEM SCHOLARSHIP
• See page 96

YOUTH MARITIME TRAINING ASSOCIATION
http://ymta.net/

NORM MANLY—YMTA MARITIME EDUCATIONAL SCHOLARSHIPS
• See page 326

MARKETING

280 GROUP
https://280group.com/contact/280-group-product-management-scholarship/

280 GROUP PRODUCT MANAGEMENT SCHOLARSHIP
• See page 203

AUTOMOTIVE AFTERMARKET SCHOLARSHIPS
http://www.automotivescholarships.com/

AUTOMOTIVE AFTERMARKET SCHOLARSHIPS
• See page 146

AUTOMOTIVE WOMEN'S ALLIANCE FOUNDATION
http://awafoundation.org/index.php

AUTOMOTIVE WOMEN'S ALLIANCE FOUNDATION SCHOLARSHIPS
• See page 71

BALTIMORE CHAPTER OF THE AMERICAN MARKETING ASSOCIATION
http://www.amabaltimore.org/

UNDERGRADUATE MARKETING EDUCATION MERIT SCHOLARSHIPS
• See page 146

DECA (DISTRIBUTIVE EDUCATION CLUBS OF AMERICA)
http://www.deca.org/

HARRY A. APPLEGATE SCHOLARSHIP
• See page 73

DIGITAL THIRD COAST INTERNET MARKETING
http://www.digitalthirdcoast.net/

DIGITAL MARKETING SCHOLARSHIP
• See page 84

HOUSE OF BLUES MUSIC FORWARD FOUNDATION
https://hobmusicforward.org/

TIFFANY GREEN OPERATOR SCHOLARSHIP AWARD
• See page 85

IDAHO STATE BROADCASTERS ASSOCIATION
http://www.idahobroadcasters.org/

WAYNE C. CORNILS MEMORIAL SCHOLARSHIP
• See page 148

INFINITY DENTAL WEB
http://www.infinitydentalweb.com

INTERNET MARKETING SCHOLARSHIP
This year's Infinity Dental Web scholarship seeks to assist students pursuing an education in marketing. With this scholarship, we hope to be able to assist some promising student who will make a contribution to the success of business, and to encourage them to use their skills in promoting quality dental care. Qualifying applicants will answer the essay question provided. The essay should be between 500-750 words. You may upload an essay in Word or PDF format, or you may copy and paste it into the application form. Essays will be judged on both the quality of the writing and the substance of the ideas presented. To be considered, you must submit the application and essay before the deadline. Identify a family dental practice that provides a basic level of dental care to a middle-class clientele. It can be your own dentist or any dentist, as long as the practice has a website. Please identify the practice by giving us the URL of their website. Visualize yourself as a marketing professional who has been hired to help transform this practice to a high-end practice focusing on smile makeovers and catering to a high-income clientele. Describe how you would brand this practice. Give a specific and detailed critique of what you would do to change their website.

Academic Fields/Career Goals: Marketing; Mathematics; Social Sciences; Social Services; Statistics.

Award: Scholarship for use in freshman, sophomore, junior, senior, graduate, or postgraduate years; not renewable. *Number:* 1. *Amount:* $250.

Eligibility Requirements: Applicant must be enrolled or expecting to enroll full- or part-time at a two-year or four-year institution or university. Available to U.S. citizens.

Application Requirements: Essay. *Deadline:* June 30.

Contact: Ms. Amber Mosure, Research Specialist
Infinity Dental Web
1839 South Alma School Road
Suite 200
Mesa, AZ 85210
Phone: 480-273-8888
E-mail: amber@infinitydentalweb.com

IOWA NEWSPAPER ASSOCIATION

https://inanews.com/

WOODWARD SCHOLARSHIP
• *See page 172*

THE LAGRANT FOUNDATION

http://www.lagrantfoundation.org/

LAGRANT FOUNDATION SCHOLARSHIP FOR GRADUATES
• *See page 85*

LAGRANT FOUNDATION SCHOLARSHIP FOR UNDERGRADUATES
• *See page 85*

NATIONAL RESTAURANT ASSOCIATION EDUCATIONAL FOUNDATION

http://www.chooserestaurants.org

NATIONAL RESTAURANT ASSOCIATION EDUCATIONAL FOUNDATION UNDERGRADUATE SCHOLARSHIPS FOR COLLEGE STUDENTS
• *See page 95*

NEBRASKA PRESS ASSOCIATION

http://www.nebpress.com/

NEBRASKA PRESS ASSOCIATION FOUNDATION SCHOLARSHIP
• *See page 86*

NEXT STEPS DIGITAL

https://www.nextstepsdigital.com/

NEXT STEPS DIGITAL SCHOLARSHIP
The recipient will receive a one-time $5,000 scholarship to be applied to qualified expenses, including graduate and undergraduate tuition, fees, books, and on-campus room and board for the 2017 Spring Semester. Funds are provided by Next Steps Digital. Payments are issued by Next Steps Digital and made payable to the student's approved college or university and mailed after Dec. 31, 2016 directly to the accredited college or university last designated by the student.

Academic Fields/Career Goals: Marketing.

Award: Scholarship for use in freshman, sophomore, junior, senior, or graduate years; not renewable. *Number:* 1. *Amount:* $5000.

Eligibility Requirements: Applicant must be enrolled or expecting to enroll full-time at a four-year institution or university. Available to U.S. citizens.

Application Requirements: Application form, essay. *Deadline:* December 15.

Contact: Josh Blanton, CMO
E-mail: josh@nextstepsdigital.com

OHIO NEWS MEDIA FOUNDATION

http://www.ohionews.org

HAROLD K. DOUTHIT SCHOLARSHIP
• *See page 86*

OHIO NEWS MEDIA FOUNDATION MINORITY SCHOLARSHIP
• *See page 86*

OHIO NEWS MEDIA FOUNDATION UNIVERSITY JOURNALISM SCHOLARSHIP
• *See page 86*

ONWA ANNUAL SCHOLARSHIP
• *See page 86*

PRINTING INDUSTRY MIDWEST EDUCATION FOUDNATION

http://www.pimw.org/scholarships

PRINTING INDUSTRY MIDWEST EDUCATION FOUNDATION SCHOLARSHIP FUND
• *See page 175*

RHODE ISLAND FOUNDATION

http://www.rifoundation.org/

J. D. EDSAL SCHOLARSHIP
• *See page 87*

SCARLETT FAMILY FOUNDATION SCHOLARSHIP PROGRAM

http://www.scarlettfoundation.org/

SCHOLARSHIP FOR STUDENTS PURSUING A BUSINESS OR STEM DEGREE
• *See page 80*

SIMMONS AND FLETCHER, P.C.

https://www.simmonsandfletcher.com/

MARKETING SCHOLARSHIP
• *See page 87*

SPECIALTY EQUIPMENT MARKET ASSOCIATION

http://www.sema.org/

SEMA MEMORIAL SCHOLARSHIP FUND
• *See page 81*

STRAIGHTFORWARD MEDIA

http://www.straightforwardmedia.com/

STRAIGHTFORWARD MEDIA BUSINESS SCHOOL SCHOLARSHIP
• *See page 87*

STRAIGHTFORWARD MEDIA MEDIA & COMMUNICATIONS SCHOLARSHIP
• *See page 87*

STRAIGHT NORTH

https://www.straightnorth.com/

STRAIGHT NORTH STEM SCHOLARSHIP
• *See page 81*

SUPPORT CREATIVITY

http://wesupportcreativity.org

SUPPORT CREATIVITY SCHOLARSHIP
• *See page 117*

TAMPA BAY TIMES FUND, INC.

http://www.tampabay.com/fund

TAMPA BAY TIMES FUND CAREER JOURNALISM SCHOLARSHIPS
• *See page 87*

TRIANGLE PEST CONTROL

http://www.trianglepest.com

TRIANGLE PEST CONTROL SCHOLARSHIP
• *See page 82*

UNITED NEGRO COLLEGE FUND

http://www.uncf.org/

DISCOVER FINANCIAL SERVICES SCHOLARSHIP
• *See page 82*

HCN/APRICITY RESOURCES SCHOLARS PROGRAM
• *See page 83*

NASCAR WENDELL SCOTT SR. SCHOLARSHIP
• *See page 83*

NATIONAL BLACK MCDONALD'S OWNERS ASSOCIATION HOSPITALITY SCHOLARS PROGRAM
• *See page 83*

RYDER SYSTEM CHARITABLE FOUNDATION SCHOLARSHIP PROGRAM
• *See page 151*

UNCF/ALLIANCE DATA SCHOLARSHIP AND INTERNSHIP PROGRAM
• *See page 88*

UNCF/CARNIVAL CORPORATE SCHOLARS PROGRAM
• *See page 151*

VOYA SCHOLARS
• *See page 83*

WASHINGTON MEDIA SCHOLARS FOUNDATION

www.mediascholars.org

MEDIA PLAN CASE COMPETITION
• *See page 88*

WHAT DETOX

http://whatdetox.com/meet-the-team/

WHAT DETOX SCHOLARSHIP
• *See page 267*

WYOMING TRUCKING ASSOCIATION SCHOLARSHIP FUND TRUST

http://www.wytruck.org/

WYOMING TRUCKING ASSOCIATION SCHOLARSHIP TRUST FUND
• *See page 84*

MATERIALS SCIENCE, ENGINEERING, AND METALLURGY

ACI FOUNDATION

http://www.acifoundation.org

ACI FOUNDATION SCHOLARSHIP PROGRAM
• *See page 113*

AIST FOUNDATION

http://www.aistfoundation.org/

AIST ALFRED B. GLOSSBRENNER AND JOHN KLUSCH SCHOLARSHIPS
• *See page 232*

ASSOCIATION FOR IRON AND STEEL TECHNOLOGY BALTIMORE CHAPTER SCHOLARSHIP
• *See page 224*

ASSOCIATION FOR IRON AND STEEL TECHNOLOGY BENJAMIN F. FAIRLESS SCHOLARSHIP (AIME)
• *See page 152*

ASSOCIATION FOR IRON AND STEEL TECHNOLOGY OHIO VALLEY CHAPTER SCHOLARSHIP
• *See page 138*

ASSOCIATION FOR IRON AND STEEL TECHNOLOGY PITTSBURGH CHAPTER SCHOLARSHIP
• *See page 234*

ASSOCIATION FOR IRON AND STEEL TECHNOLOGY RONALD E. LINCOLN SCHOLARSHIP
• *See page 217*

ASSOCIATION FOR IRON AND STEEL TECHNOLOGY SOUTHEAST MEMBER CHAPTER SCHOLARSHIP
• *See page 234*

ASSOCIATION FOR IRON AND STEEL TECHNOLOGY WILLY KORF MEMORIAL SCHOLARSHIP
• *See page 153*

FERROUS METALLURGY EDUCATION TODAY (FEMET)
Scholarships are for full-time students of metallurgy or materials science engineering. Students must have an interest in a career in the steel industry as demonstrated by an internship or related experience, or who

have plans to pursue such experiences during college. Students must commit to a summer internship at a steel producing company (placement assistance is provided) prior to receiving this scholarship. Student may apply during their sophomore and junior years. Applications are accepted from 1 Sep through 31 Dec each year.

Academic Fields/Career Goals: Materials Science, Engineering, and Metallurgy.

Award: Scholarship for use in sophomore or junior years; not renewable. *Number:* 1–10. *Amount:* $5000.

Eligibility Requirements: Applicant must be enrolled or expecting to enroll full-time at a four-year institution or university. Available to U.S. and non-U.S. citizens.

Application Requirements: Application form, essay, recommendations or references, resume, transcript. *Deadline:* December 31.

Contact: Lori Wharrey, AIST Manager, Board Services
AIST Foundation
186 Thorn HIll Road
Warrendale, PA 15086
Phone: 724-814-3044
E-mail: lwharrey@aist.org

AMERICAN CERAMIC SOCIETY

ELECTRONICS DIVISION LEWIS C. HOFFMAN SCHOLARSHIPS

The Lewis C. Hoffman Scholarship is a $2,000 undergraduate tuition award that is given to encourage academic interest and excellence in the area of ceramics/materials science and engineering. The 2018 essay topic is "Tailoring Material Properties through Defect Engineering for Electronic Ceramics." Deadline for applications is 15 May 2018.

Academic Fields/Career Goals: Materials Science, Engineering, and Metallurgy.

Award: Scholarship for use in junior or senior years; not renewable. *Number:* 1. *Amount:* $2000.

Eligibility Requirements: Applicant must be enrolled or expecting to enroll full-time at a four-year institution or university. Available to U.S. and non-U.S. citizens.

Application Requirements: Essay. *Deadline:* May 15.

AMERICAN CHEMICAL SOCIETY

http://www.acs.org/

AMERICAN CHEMICAL SOCIETY SCHOLARS PROGRAM
• *See page 153*

AMERICAN CHEMICAL SOCIETY, RUBBER DIVISION

http://www.rubber.org/

AMERICAN CHEMICAL SOCIETY, RUBBER DIVISION UNDERGRADUATE SCHOLARSHIP
• *See page 105*

AMERICAN COUNCIL OF ENGINEERING COMPANIES OF PENNSYLVANIA (ACEC/PA)

http://www.acecpa.org/

ERIC J. GENNUSO AND LEROY D. (BUD) LOY, JR. SCHOLARSHIP PROGRAM
• *See page 153*

AMERICAN INDIAN SCIENCE AND ENGINEERING SOCIETY

http://www.aises.org/

A.T. ANDERSON MEMORIAL SCHOLARSHIP PROGRAM
• *See page 105*

AMERICAN INSTITUTE OF AERONAUTICS AND ASTRONAUTICS

https://www.aiaa.org/

AIAA FOUNDATION UNDERGRADUATE SCHOLARSHIPS
• *See page 127*

LEATRICE GREGORY PENDRAY SCHOLARSHIP
• *See page 127*

AMERICAN SOCIETY OF CERTIFIED ENGINEERING TECHNICIANS

http://www.ascet.org/

KURT H. AND DONNA M. SCHULER SMALL GRANT
• *See page 162*

AMERICAN SOCIETY OF NAVAL ENGINEERS

http://www.navalengineers.org/

AMERICAN SOCIETY OF NAVAL ENGINEERS SCHOLARSHIP
• *See page 106*

AMERICAN WELDING SOCIETY

http://www.aws.org/

MILLER ELECTRIC INTERNATIONAL WORLD SKILLS COMPETITION SCHOLARSHIP
• *See page 225*

ARMED FORCES COMMUNICATIONS AND ELECTRONICS ASSOCIATION, EDUCATIONAL FOUNDATION

https://foundation.afcea.org

AFCEA STEM MAJORS SCHOLARSHIPS FOR UNDERGRADUATE STUDENTS
• *See page 106*

ASIAN PACIFIC FUND

BANATAO FAMILY FILIPINO AMERICAN EDUCATION FUND
• *See page 155*

ASM MATERIALS EDUCATION FOUNDATION

https://www.asmfoundation.org/

EDWARD J. DULIS SCHOLARSHIP

One award of $1,500. Established in 2003 by the family of Edward J. Dulis, who was a fellow of ASM International. Must have an intended or declared major in metallurgy or materials science engineering. Applicants majoring in related science or engineering disciplines will be considered if they demonstrate a strong academic emphasis and interest in materials science.

Academic Fields/Career Goals: Materials Science, Engineering, and Metallurgy.

Award: Scholarship for use in sophomore, junior, or senior years; not renewable. *Number:* 1. *Amount:* $1500.

Eligibility Requirements: Applicant must be enrolled or expecting to enroll full-time at an institution or university. Applicant or parent of applicant must be member of ASM International. Available to U.S. and Canadian citizens.

Application Requirements: Application form, application form may be submitted online, personal photograph. *Deadline:* May 1.

Contact: Jeane Deatherage, Program Coordinator
ASM Materials Education Foundation
ASM Materials Education Foundation
9639 Kinsman Rd.
Materials Park, OH 44073-0001
Phone: 440-338-5151
E-mail: ScholarshipsUG@asminternational.org

GEORGE A. ROBERTS SCHOLARSHIPS

Established in 1995 through a generous contribution by Dr. George A. Roberts, past president of ASM and retired CEO of Teledyne, as an expression of his commitment to education and the materials science and engineering community. Awards for college juniors or seniors studying metallurgy or materials engineering in North America. Applicants must be student members of ASM International. Awards based on need, interest in field, academics, and character.

Academic Fields/Career Goals: Materials Science, Engineering, and Metallurgy.

Award: Scholarship for use in junior or senior years; not renewable. *Number:* 1–7. *Amount:* $6000.

Eligibility Requirements: Applicant must be enrolled or expecting to enroll full-time at an institution or university. Applicant or parent of applicant must be member of ASM International. Available to U.S. and Canadian citizens.

Application Requirements: Application form, application form may be submitted online, essay, financial need analysis, personal photograph. *Deadline:* May 1.

Contact: Jeane Deatherage, Program Coordinator
ASM Materials Education Foundation
9639 Kinsman Road
Materials Park, OH 44073-0002
Phone: 440-338-5151
E-mail: jeane.deatherage@asminternational.org

JOHN M. HANIAK SCHOLARSHIP

One award of $1,500. Established in 2003 by the family of John Myron Haniak, who was a life-long dedicated member of ASM International. (Student must be a Pennsylvania resident and / or must attend a Pennsylvania university to qualify.) Must be a member of ASM International or Material Advantage student member. Must have an intended or declared major in metallurgy or materials science engineering. Applicants majoring in related science or engineering disciplines will be considered if they demonstrate a strong academic emphasis and interest in materials science.

Academic Fields/Career Goals: Materials Science, Engineering, and Metallurgy.

Award: Scholarship for use in sophomore, junior, or senior years; not renewable. *Number:* 1. *Amount:* $1500.

Eligibility Requirements: Applicant must be enrolled or expecting to enroll full-time at an institution or university. Applicant or parent of applicant must be member of ASM International. Available to U.S. and Canadian citizens.

Application Requirements: Application form, application form may be submitted online, essay, personal photograph. *Deadline:* May 1.

Contact: Jeane Deatherage, Program Coordinator
ASM Materials Education Foundation
9639 Kinsman Road
Materials Park, OH 44073-0002
Phone: 440-338-5151 Ext. 5533
E-mail: ScholarshipsUG@asminternational.org

LADISH CO. FOUNDATION SCHOLARSHIPS

Two scholarships of $2,500 (each). (Student must be a Wisconsin resident and must attend a Wisconsin university to qualify.) Must be a member of ASM International or Material Advantage student member. Must have an intended or declared major in metallurgy or materials science engineering. Applicants majoring in related science or engineering disciplines will be considered if they demonstrate a strong academic emphasis and interest in materials science.

Academic Fields/Career Goals: Materials Science, Engineering, and Metallurgy.

Award: Scholarship for use in sophomore, junior, or senior years; not renewable. *Number:* 1–2. *Amount:* $2500.

Eligibility Requirements: Applicant must be enrolled or expecting to enroll full-time at an institution or university; resident of West Virginia and studying in Wisconsin. Applicant or parent of applicant must be member of ASM International. Available to U.S. and Canadian citizens.

Application Requirements: Application form, application form may be submitted online, essay, financial need analysis, interview, personal photograph. *Deadline:* May 1.

Contact: Jeane Deatherage, Program Coordinator
ASM Materials Education Foundation
ASM Materials Education Foundation
9639 Kinsman Road
Materials Park, OH 44073
Phone: 440-338-5151 Ext. 5453
E-mail: ScholarshipsUG@asminternational.org

LUCILLE & CHARLES A. WERT SCHOLARSHIP

One year full tuition of up to $10,000. Established in 2006 through a generous bequest by Dr. & Mrs. Charles Wert. Must be a member of ASM International or Material Advantage student member. Must have an intended or declared major in metallurgy or materials science engineering. Applicants majoring in related science or engineering disciplines will be considered if they demonstrate a strong academic emphasis and interest in materials science.

Academic Fields/Career Goals: Materials Science, Engineering, and Metallurgy.

Award: Scholarship for use in sophomore, junior, or senior years; not renewable. *Number:* 1. *Amount:* $10,000.

Eligibility Requirements: Applicant must be enrolled or expecting to enroll full-time at an institution or university. Applicant or parent of applicant must be member of ASM International. Available to U.S. and Canadian citizens.

Application Requirements: Application form, application form may be submitted online, essay, financial need analysis, personal photograph. *Deadline:* May 1.

Contact: Jeane Deatherage, Program Coordinator
ASM Materials Education Foundation
ASM Materials Education Foundation
9639 Kinsman Road
Materials Park, OH 44073
Phone: 440-338-5151 Ext. 5453
E-mail: ScholarshipsUG@asminternational.org

WILLIAM PARK WOODSIDE FOUNDER'S SCHOLARSHIP

One year full tuition of up to $10,000 scholarship for college junior or senior studying metallurgy or materials engineering in North America. Must be a member of ASM International or Material Advantage student member. Award based on need, interest in field, academics, and character.

Academic Fields/Career Goals: Materials Science, Engineering, and Metallurgy.

Award: Scholarship for use in junior or senior years; not renewable. *Number:* 1. *Amount:* $10,000.

Eligibility Requirements: Applicant must be enrolled or expecting to enroll full-time at an institution or university. Applicant or parent of applicant must be member of ASM International. Available to U.S. and Canadian citizens.

Application Requirements: Application form, application form may be submitted online, essay, financial need analysis, personal photograph. *Deadline:* May 1.

Contact: Jeane Deatherage, Program Coordinator
ASM Materials Education Foundation
ASM Materials Education Foundation
9639 Kinsman Road
Materials Park, OH 44073
Phone: 440-338-5151 Ext. 5453
E-mail: ScholarshipsUG@asminternational.org

ASSOCIATION OF STATE DAM SAFETY OFFICIALS (ASDSO)

http://www.DamSafety.org

ASSOCIATION OF STATE DAM SAFETY OFFICIALS (ASDSO) SENIOR UNDERGRADUATE SCHOLARSHIP
• *See page 140*

ASTRONAUT SCHOLARSHIP FOUNDATION

http://www.astronautscholarship.org/

ASTRONAUT SCHOLARSHIP
• *See page 107*

AUTOMOTIVE WOMEN'S ALLIANCE FOUNDATION

http://awafoundation.org/index.php

AUTOMOTIVE WOMEN'S ALLIANCE FOUNDATION SCHOLARSHIPS
• *See page 71*

BARRY GOLDWATER SCHOLARSHIP AND EXCELLENCE IN EDUCATION FOUNDATION

https://goldwater.scholarsapply.org

BARRY M. GOLDWATER SCHOLARSHIP AND EXCELLENCE IN EDUCATION PROGRAM
• *See page 107*

BHW GROUP

https://thebhwgroup.com/

BHW WOMEN IN STEM SCHOLARSHIP
• *See page 107*

BROWN AND CALDWELL

http://www.brownandcaldwell.com

MINORITY SCHOLARSHIP PROGRAM
• *See page 141*

DISTIL NETWORKS

http://www.distilnetworks.com

WOMEN FORWARD IN TECHNOLOGY SCHOLARSHIP PROGRAM
• *See page 108*

THE ELECTROCHEMICAL SOCIETY

https://www.electrochem.org/

BATTERY DIVISION STUDENT RESEARCH AWARD SPONSORED BY MERCEDES-BENZ RESEARCH & DEVELOPMENT
• *See page 155*

GREAT MINDS IN STEM

http://www.greatmindsinstem.org/college/scholarship-application-information

HENAAC SCHOLARSHIP PROGRAM
• *See page 100*

INTERNATIONAL SOCIETY FOR OPTICAL ENGINEERING-SPIE

http://www.spie.org/scholarships

SPIE EDUCATIONAL SCHOLARSHIPS IN OPTICAL SCIENCE AND ENGINEERING
• *See page 108*

INTERNATIONAL SOCIETY OF EXPLOSIVES ENGINEERS

http://www.isee.org/

JERRY MCDOWELL FUND
• *See page 156*

JORGE MAS CANOSA FREEDOM FOUNDATION

http://masscholarships.org/

MAS FAMILY SCHOLARSHIP AWARD
• *See page 149*

LOS ANGELES COUNCIL OF BLACK PROFESSIONAL ENGINEERS

http://www.lablackengineers.org/

AL-BEN SCHOLARSHIP FOR ACADEMIC INCENTIVE
• *See page 157*

AL-BEN SCHOLARSHIP FOR PROFESSIONAL MERIT
• *See page 157*

AL-BEN SCHOLARSHIP FOR SCHOLASTIC ACHIEVEMENT
• *See page 157*

MANUFACTURERS ASSOCIATION OF MAINE

http://www.mainemfg.com/

MAINE MANUFACTURING CAREER AND TRAINING FOUNDATION SCHOLARSHIP
• *See page 131*

MEDICAL SCRUBS COLLECTION

http://medicalscrubscollection.com

MEDICAL SCRUBS COLLECTION SCHOLARSHIP
• *See page 104*

MIDWEST ROOFING CONTRACTORS ASSOCIATION

http://www.mrca.org/

MRCA FOUNDATION SCHOLARSHIP PROGRAM
• *See page 116*

MINERALS, METALS, AND MATERIALS SOCIETY (TMS)

http://www.tms.org/

MATERIALS PROCESSING AND MANUFACTURING DIVISION SCHOLARSHIP
• *See page 228*

TMS EXTRACTION & PROCESSING SCHOLARSHIP
• *See page 228*

TMS FUNCTIONAL MATERIALS GILBERT CHIN SCHOLARSHIP
• *See page 228*

TMS/INTERNATIONAL SYMPOSIUM ON SUPERALLOYS SCHOLARSHIP PROGRAM
• *See page 229*

TMS/LIGHT METALS DIVISION SCHOLARSHIP PROGRAM
• *See page 229*

TMS OUTSTANDING STUDENT PAPER CONTEST-UNDERGRADUATE
• *See page 229*

TMS/STRUCTURAL MATERIALS DIVISION SCHOLARSHIP
• *See page 229*

NASA FLORIDA SPACE GRANT CONSORTIUM

http://www.floridaspacegrant.org/

FLORIDA SPACE RESEARCH PROGRAM
• *See page 131*

NASA IDAHO SPACE GRANT CONSORTIUM

http://www.idahospacegrant.org

NASA IDAHO SPACE GRANT CONSORTIUM SCHOLARSHIP PROGRAM
• *See page 109*

NASA/MARYLAND SPACE GRANT CONSORTIUM

https://md.spacegrant.org

NASA MARYLAND SPACE GRANT CONSORTIUM SCHOLARSHIPS
• *See page 109*

NASA'S VIRGINIA SPACE GRANT CONSORTIUM

http://www.vsgc.odu.edu/

COMMUNITY COLLEGE STEM SCHOLARSHIPS
• *See page 110*

UNDERGRADUATE STEM RESEARCH SCHOLARSHIPS
• *See page 110*

NATIONAL SOCIETY OF PROFESSIONAL ENGINEERS

http://www.nspe.org/

MAUREEN L. & HOWARD N. BLITMAN, P.E., SCHOLARSHIP TO PROMOTE DIVERSITY IN ENGINEERING
• *See page 166*

PAUL H. ROBBINS HONORARY SCHOLARSHIP
• *See page 158*

PROFESSIONAL ENGINEERS IN INDUSTRY SCHOLARSHIP
• *See page 158*

NATIONAL STONE, SAND AND GRAVEL ASSOCIATION (NSSGA)

http://www.nssga.org/

BARRY K. WENDT MEMORIAL SCHOLARSHIP
• *See page 230*

NEXTSTEPU

http://www.nextstepu.com/

$1,500 STEM SCHOLARSHIP
• *See page 104*

NOVUS BIOLOGICALS, LLC

https://www.novusbio.com

NOVUS BIOLOGICALS SCHOLARSHIP PROGRAM
• *See page 101*

R&D SYSTEMS SCHOLARSHIP
• *See page 101*

TOCRIS BIOSCIENCE SCHOLARSHIP
• *See page 102*

ROCKY MOUNTAIN COAL MINING INSTITUTE

http://www.rmcmi.org/

ROCKY MOUNTAIN COAL MINING INSTITUTE SCHOLARSHIP
• *See page 167*

SCARLETT FAMILY FOUNDATION SCHOLARSHIP PROGRAM

http://www.scarlettfoundation.org/

SCHOLARSHIP FOR STUDENTS PURSUING A BUSINESS OR STEM DEGREE
• *See page 80*

SEMICONDUCTOR RESEARCH CORPORATION (SRC)

http://www.src.org/

MASTER'S SCHOLARSHIP PROGRAM
• *See page 158*

SOCIETY OF PLASTICS ENGINEERS FOUNDATION (SPE)

http://www.4spe.org/

FLEMING/BLASZCAK SCHOLARSHIP
• *See page 158*

GULF COAST HURRICANE SCHOLARSHIP
• *See page 159*

SOCIETY OF PLASTICS ENGINEERS SCHOLARSHIP PROGRAM
• *See page 159*

SOCIETY OF WOMEN ENGINEERS

https://swe.org/

GE'S WOMEN'S NETWORK PAULA MARTIN SCHOLARSHIP
• *See page 134*

SWE REGION H SCHOLARSHIPS
• *See page 159*

SWE REGION J SCHOLARSHIP
• *See page 159*

TE CONNECTIVITY EXCELLENCE IN ENGINEERING SCHOLARSHIP
• *See page 160*

STRAIGHTFORWARD MEDIA

http://www.straightforwardmedia.com/

STRAIGHTFORWARD MEDIA ENGINEERING SCHOLARSHIP
• *See page 160*

STRAIGHT NORTH

https://www.straightnorth.com/

STRAIGHT NORTH STEM SCHOLARSHIP
• *See page 81*

TURNER CONSTRUCTION COMPANY

http://www.turnerconstruction.com/

YOUTHFORCE 2020 SCHOLARSHIP PROGRAM
• *See page 117*

UNITED NEGRO COLLEGE FUND

http://www.uncf.org/

DAVIS SCHOLARSHIP FOR WOMEN IN STEM
• *See page 111*

GALACTIC UNITE BYTHEWAY SCHOLARSHIP
• *See page 111*

LEIDOS STEM SCHOLARSHIP
• *See page 96*

VERMONT SPACE GRANT CONSORTIUM

http://www.cems.uvm.edu/vsgc

VERMONT SPACE GRANT CONSORTIUM
• *See page 92*

XEROX

http://www.xerox.com//

TECHNICAL MINORITY SCHOLARSHIP
• *See page 161*

MATHEMATICS

101ST AIRBORNE DIVISION ASSOCIATION

http://www.screamingeaglefoundation.org/

AL & WILLIAMARY VISTE SCHOLARSHIP
• *See page 99*

THE ACTUARIAL FOUNDATION

www.actuarialfoundation.org

ACTUARIAL DIVERSITY SCHOLARSHIP
• *See page 300*

ACTUARY OF TOMORROW—STUART A. ROBERTSON MEMORIAL SCHOLARSHIP
• *See page 203*

CURTIS E. HUNTINGTON MEMORIAL SCHOLARSHIP
• *See page 204*

AMERICAN INDIAN SCIENCE AND ENGINEERING SOCIETY

http://www.aises.org/

A.T. ANDERSON MEMORIAL SCHOLARSHIP PROGRAM
• *See page 105*

AMERICAN LEGION DEPARTMENT OF MARYLAND

http://www.mdlegion.org/

AMERICAN LEGION DEPARTMENT OF MARYLAND MATH-SCIENCE SCHOLARSHIP
• *See page 99*

AMERICAN MATHEMATICAL ASSOCIATION OF TWO YEAR COLLEGES

http://www.amatyc.org/

CHARLES MILLER SCHOLARSHIP

A grand prize of $3000 for the qualified individual with the highest total score of the student mathematics league exam. Funds to continue education at an accredited four-year institution. In the case of a tie for the grand prize, the scholarship will be evenly divided.

Academic Fields/Career Goals: Mathematics.

Award: Scholarship for use in freshman or sophomore years; not renewable. *Number:* 1. *Amount:* $3000.

Eligibility Requirements: Applicant must be enrolled or expecting to enroll full-time at a two-year institution. Available to U.S. citizens.

Application Requirements: Entry in a contest, test scores. *Deadline:* September 30.

Contact: Dr. Cheryl Cleaves, Interim Executive Director
American Mathematical Association of Two Year Colleges
AMATYC c/o Southwest Tennessee CC
5983 Macon Cove
Memphis, TN 38134
Phone: 901-333-5643
Fax: 901-333-5651
E-mail: amatyc@amatyc.org

ARMED FORCES COMMUNICATIONS AND ELECTRONICS ASSOCIATION, EDUCATIONAL FOUNDATION

https://foundation.afcea.org

AFCEA STEM MAJORS SCHOLARSHIPS FOR UNDERGRADUATE STUDENTS
• *See page 106*

ARMED FORCES COMMUNICATIONS AND ELECTRONICS ASSOCIATION ROTC SCHOLARSHIP PROGRAM
• *See page 179*

ASSOCIATION FOR WOMEN IN MATHEMATICS

http://www.awm-math.org/

ALICE T. SCHAFER MATHEMATICS PRIZE FOR EXCELLENCE IN MATHEMATICS BY AN UNDERGRADUATE WOMAN

One-time merit award for women undergraduates in the math field. Based on quality of performance in math courses and special programs, ability to work independently, interest in math, and performance in competitions. Must be nominated by a professor or an adviser.

Academic Fields/Career Goals: Mathematics.

Award: Prize for use in freshman, sophomore, junior, or senior years; not renewable. *Number:* 1. *Amount:* $250–$1000.

Eligibility Requirements: Applicant must be enrolled or expecting to enroll full-time at a four-year institution or university and female. Available to U.S. citizens.

Application Requirements: Application form, application form may be submitted online (https://www.mathprograms.org). *Deadline:* October 1.

Contact: Steven Ferrucci
Association for Women in Mathematics
PO Box 40876
Providence, RI 02940
Phone: 401-455-4042
E-mail: awm@awm-math.org

AUTOMOTIVE WOMEN'S ALLIANCE FOUNDATION

http://awafoundation.org/index.php

AUTOMOTIVE WOMEN'S ALLIANCE FOUNDATION SCHOLARSHIPS
• *See page 71*

BARRY GOLDWATER SCHOLARSHIP AND EXCELLENCE IN EDUCATION FOUNDATION

https://goldwater.scholarsapply.org

BARRY M. GOLDWATER SCHOLARSHIP AND EXCELLENCE IN EDUCATION PROGRAM
• *See page 107*

BHW GROUP

https://thebhwgroup.com/

BHW WOMEN IN STEM SCHOLARSHIP
• *See page 107*

CALIFORNIA MATHEMATICS COUNCIL-SOUTH

http://www.cmc-math.org/

CALIFORNIA MATHEMATICS COUNCIL-SOUTH SECONDARY EDUCATION SCHOLARSHIPS

Scholarships for students enrolled in accredited Southern California secondary education credential programs with math as a major. Applicants must be members of the California Math Council-South.

Academic Fields/Career Goals: Mathematics.

Award: Scholarship for use in freshman, sophomore, junior, or senior years; renewable. *Number:* 2–5. *Amount:* $100–$2000.

Eligibility Requirements: Applicant must be enrolled or expecting to enroll full- or part-time at a four-year institution or university; resident of California and studying in California. Available to U.S. and non-U.S. citizens.

Application Requirements: Application form, essay, recommendations or references, transcript. *Deadline:* January 31.

Contact: Dr. Sid Kolpas, Professor of Mathematics
Phone: 818-240-1000 Ext. 5378
E-mail: sjkolpas@sprintmail.com

CARDS AGAINST HUMANITY

https://cardsagainsthumanity.com/

SCIENCE AMBASSADOR SCHOLARSHIP
• *See page 107*

THE DALLAS FOUNDATION

http://www.dallasfoundation.org/

WHITLEY PLACE SCHOLARSHIP
• *See page 114*

DISTIL NETWORKS

http://www.distilnetworks.com

WOMEN FORWARD IN TECHNOLOGY SCHOLARSHIP PROGRAM
• *See page 108*

GREAT MINDS IN STEM

http://www.greatmindsinstem.org/college/scholarship-application-information

HENAAC SCHOLARSHIP PROGRAM
• *See page 100*

INFINITY DENTAL WEB

http://www.infinitydentalweb.com

INTERNET MARKETING SCHOLARSHIP
• *See page 329*

LOGMEIN

https://www.logmeininc.com

LASTPASS STEM SCHOLARSHIP
• *See page 109*

MICHIGAN COUNCIL OF TEACHERS OF MATHEMATICS

http://www.mictm.org/

MIRIAM SCHAEFER SCHOLARSHIP

A scholarship of $2500 is given to a senior or a junior enrolled full-time in undergraduate degree with mathematics specialty. Applicants should be a resident of Michigan but citizenship does not matter.

Academic Fields/Career Goals: Mathematics.

Award: Scholarship for use in junior or senior years; not renewable. *Number:* 3–5. *Amount:* $2500.

Eligibility Requirements: Applicant must be enrolled or expecting to enroll full-time at a four-year institution or university and resident of Michigan. Available to U.S. and non-U.S. citizens.

Application Requirements: Application form, essay. *Deadline:* May 1.

Contact: Mr. Chris Berry, Executive Director
Michigan Council of Teachers of Mathematics
4767 Stadler Road
Monroe, MI 48162
Phone: 734-477-0421
Fax: 734-241-4128
E-mail: info@mictm.org

NASA FLORIDA SPACE GRANT CONSORTIUM

http://www.floridaspacegrant.org/

FLORIDA SPACE RESEARCH PROGRAM
• *See page 131*

NASA IDAHO SPACE GRANT CONSORTIUM

http://www.idahospacegrant.org

NASA IDAHO SPACE GRANT CONSORTIUM SCHOLARSHIP PROGRAM
• *See page 109*

NASA/MARYLAND SPACE GRANT CONSORTIUM

https://md.spacegrant.org

NASA MARYLAND SPACE GRANT CONSORTIUM SCHOLARSHIPS
• *See page 109*

NASA MINNESOTA SPACE GRANT CONSORTIUM

https://www.mnspacegrant.org/

MINNESOTA SPACE GRANT CONSORTIUM SCHOLARSHIP PROGRAM
• *See page 131*

NASA MONTANA SPACE GRANT CONSORTIUM

http://www.spacegrant.montana.edu/

MONTANA SPACE GRANT SCHOLARSHIP PROGRAM
• *See page 132*

NASA RHODE ISLAND SPACE GRANT CONSORTIUM

http://brown/initiatives/ri-space-grant

NASA RHODE ISLAND SPACE GRANT CONSORTIUM OUTREACH SCHOLARSHIP FOR UNDERGRADUATE STUDENTS

The NASA Rhode Island Space Grant Consortium values diversity and strongly encourages women and minorities to apply. Applicant must have a faculty mentor who will supervise your research project during the duration of the internship period, have a research project with strong NASA relevance, enrolled full time and admitted to a STEM related discipline.

Academic Fields/Career Goals: Mathematics; Science, Technology, and Society.

Award: Scholarship for use in sophomore, junior, or senior years; not renewable.

Eligibility Requirements: Applicant must be enrolled or expecting to enroll full-time at an institution or university; resident of Quebec and studying in Rhode Island. Available to U.S. citizens.

Application Requirements: Application form, application form may be submitted online, essay.

Contact: Nancy Ciminelli, Program Manager
NASA Rhode Island Space Grant Consortium
Brown University
Box 1846, Lincoln Field
Providence, RI 02912
Phone: 401-863-1151
Fax: 401-863-3978
E-mail: nancy_ciminelli@brown.edu

NASA RISGC SCIENCE EN ESPANOL SCHOLARSHIP FOR UNDERGRADUATE STUDENTS
• *See page 132*

NASA'S VIRGINIA SPACE GRANT CONSORTIUM

http://www.vsgc.odu.edu/

COMMUNITY COLLEGE STEM SCHOLARSHIPS
• *See page 110*

UNDERGRADUATE STEM RESEARCH SCHOLARSHIPS
• *See page 110*

NATIONAL COUNCIL OF TEACHERS OF MATHEMATICS

http://www.nctm.org/

PROSPECTIVE SECONDARY TEACHER COURSE WORK SCHOLARSHIPS
• *See page 211*

NEVADA NASA SPACE GRANT CONSORTIUM

https://nasa.epscorspo.nevada.edu/

NATIONAL SPACE GRANT CONSORTIUM SCHOLARSHIPS
• *See page 110*

NEXTSTEPU

http://www.nextstepu.com/

$1,500 STEM SCHOLARSHIP
• *See page 104*

OREGON OFFICE OF STUDENT ACCESS AND COMPLETION

https://oregonstudentaid.gov/

SEHAR SALEHA AHMAD AND ABRAHIM EKRAMULLAH ZAFAR FOUNDATION SCHOLARSHIP
• *See page 110*

PIRATE'S ALLEY FAULKNER SOCIETY

http://www.wordsandmusic.org/

WILLIAM FAULKNER-WILLIAM WISDOM CREATIVE WRITING COMPETITION

Prizes for unpublished manuscripts written in English. One prize awarded in each category: $7500, novel; $2500, novella; $2000, book-length narrative non-fiction; $1,500, novel-in-progress; $1500, short story; $750, essay; $750, poem; $750 high school short story-student author, $250 sponsoring teacher. Manuscripts must be submitted by e-mail; entry forms and accompanying entry fee ranging from $10 for high school category to $40 for novel must be submitted hard copy by snail mail.

Academic Fields/Career Goals: Mathematics.

Award: Prize for use in freshman, sophomore, junior, senior, graduate, or postgraduate years; not renewable. *Number:* 8. *Amount:* $250–$7500.

Eligibility Requirements: Applicant must be age 15-80; enrolled or expecting to enroll full- or part-time at a two-year or four-year institution or university and must have an interest in English language or writing. Applicant or parent of applicant must have employment or volunteer experience in human services. Available to U.S. and non-U.S. citizens.

Application Requirements: Application form. *Fee:* $25. *Deadline:* May 1.

Contact: Ms. Rosemary James, Director
Pirate's Alley Faulkner Society
624 Pirate's Alley
New Orleans, LA 70116
Phone: 504-586-1609
E-mail: faulkhouse@aol.com

SALT RIVER PROJECT (SRP)

http://www.srpnet.com/

NAVAJO GENERATING STATION NAVAJO SCHOLARSHIP
• *See page 244*

SCARLETT FAMILY FOUNDATION SCHOLARSHIP PROGRAM

http://www.scarlettfoundation.org/

SCHOLARSHIP FOR STUDENTS PURSUING A BUSINESS OR STEM DEGREE
• *See page 80*

STRAIGHT NORTH

https://www.straightnorth.com/

STRAIGHT NORTH STEM SCHOLARSHIP
• *See page 81*

TAU KAPPA EPSILON EDUCATION FOUNDATION

https://www.tke.org/

FRANCIS J. FLYNN MEMORIAL SCHOLARSHIP
• *See page 213*

STEVEN J. MUIR SCHOLARSHIP
• *See page 160*

THOMAS H. DUNNING, SR., MEMORIAL SCHOLARSHIP
• *See page 183*

UNITED NEGRO COLLEGE FUND

http://www.uncf.org/

DAVIS SCHOLARSHIP FOR WOMEN IN STEM
• *See page 111*

GALACTIC UNITE BYTHEWAY SCHOLARSHIP
• *See page 111*

LEIDOS STEM SCHOLARSHIP
• *See page 96*

ORACLE COMMUNITY IMPACT SCHOLARSHIP
• *See page 183*

VOYA SCHOLARS
• *See page 83*

VERMONT SPACE GRANT CONSORTIUM

http://www.cems.uvm.edu/vsgc

VERMONT SPACE GRANT CONSORTIUM
• *See page 92*

WISCONSIN MATHEMATICS EDUCATION FOUNDATION

http://wmefonline.org/

ARNE ENGEBRETSEN WISCONSIN MATHEMATICS COUNCIL SCHOLARSHIP
• *See page 215*

ETHEL A. NEIJAHR WISCONSIN MATHEMATICS COUNCIL SCHOLARSHIP
• *See page 215*

SISTER MARY PETRONIA VAN STRATEN WISCONSIN MATHEMATICS COUNCIL SCHOLARSHIP
• *See page 216*

WOMEN IN AEROSPACE FOUNDATION

https://www.womeninaerospace.org/

THE WOMEN IN AEROSPACE FOUNDATION SCHOLARSHIP
• *See page 135*

MECHANICAL ENGINEERING

AACE INTERNATIONAL

http://www.aacei.org/

AACE INTERNATIONAL COMPETITIVE SCHOLARSHIP

AHS INTERNATIONAL—THE VERTICAL FLIGHT TECHNICAL SOCIETY

http://www.vtol.org/

VERTICAL FLIGHT FOUNDATION SCHOLARSHIP

AIST FOUNDATION

http://www.aistfoundation.org/

ASSOCIATION FOR IRON AND STEEL TECHNOLOGY BENJAMIN F. FAIRLESS SCHOLARSHIP (AIME)

ASSOCIATION FOR IRON AND STEEL TECHNOLOGY RONALD E. LINCOLN SCHOLARSHIP

ASSOCIATION FOR IRON AND STEEL TECHNOLOGY WILLY KORF MEMORIAL SCHOLARSHIP

STEEL ENGINEERING EDUCATION LINK (STEEL) SCHOLARSHIPS

AMERICAN CHEMICAL SOCIETY, RUBBER DIVISION

http://www.rubber.org/

AMERICAN CHEMICAL SOCIETY, RUBBER DIVISION UNDERGRADUATE SCHOLARSHIP

AMERICAN COUNCIL OF ENGINEERING COMPANIES OF PENNSYLVANIA (ACEC/PA)

http://www.acecpa.org/

ERIC J. GENNUSO AND LEROY D. (BUD) LOY, JR. SCHOLARSHIP PROGRAM

AMERICAN INDIAN SCIENCE AND ENGINEERING SOCIETY

http://www.aises.org/

A.T. ANDERSON MEMORIAL SCHOLARSHIP PROGRAM

AMERICAN INSTITUTE OF AERONAUTICS AND ASTRONAUTICS

https://www.aiaa.org/

AIAA FOUNDATION UNDERGRADUATE SCHOLARSHIPS

LEATRICE GREGORY PENDRAY SCHOLARSHIP

AMERICAN PUBLIC POWER ASSOCIATION

https://www.publicpower.org/deed-rd-funding

DEMONSTRATION OF ENERGY AND EFFICIENCY DEVELOPMENTS EDUCATIONAL SCHOLARSHIP

DEMONSTRATION OF ENERGY AND EFFICIENCY DEVELOPMENTS STUDENT INTERNSHIP

DEMONSTRATION OF ENERGY AND EFFICIENCY DEVELOPMENTS STUDENT RESEARCH GRANTS

DEMONSTRATION OF ENERGY AND EFFICIENCY DEVELOPMENTS TECHNICAL DESIGN PROJECT

AMERICAN PUBLIC TRANSPORTATION FOUNDATION

https://www.aptfd.org/

LOUIS T. KLAUDER SCHOLARSHIP

Scholarships for study towards a career in the rail transit industry as an electrical or mechanical engineer. Must be sponsored by APTA member organization and complete internship with APTA member organization. Minimum GPA of 3.0 required.

Academic Fields/Career Goals: Mechanical Engineering.

Award: Scholarship for use in sophomore, junior, senior, or graduate years; renewable. *Number:* 1. *Amount:* $2500.

Eligibility Requirements: Applicant must be enrolled or expecting to enroll full-time at a two-year institution or university. Available to U.S. and Canadian citizens.

Application Requirements: Application form, application form may be submitted online, essay, financial need analysis. *Deadline:* June 15.

TRANSIT HALL OF FAME SCHOLARSHIP AWARD PROGRAM

AMERICAN RAILWAY ENGINEERING AND MAINTENANCE OF WAY ASSOCIATION

http://www.aremafoundation.org/

AREMA GRADUATE AND UNDERGRADUATE SCHOLARSHIPS

AMERICAN SOCIETY OF CERTIFIED ENGINEERING TECHNICIANS

http://www.ascet.org/

KURT H. AND DONNA M. SCHULER SMALL GRANT

AMERICAN SOCIETY OF MECHANICAL ENGINEERS

https://www.asme.org/

AGNES MALAKATE KEZIOS SCHOLARSHIP
• *See page 235*

ALLEN J. BALDWIN SCHOLARSHIP
• *See page 235*

BERNA LOU CARTWRIGHT SCHOLARSHIP
• *See page 236*

CHARLES B. SHARP SCHOLARSHIP
• *See page 236*

LUCY AND CHARLES W.E. CLARKE SCHOLARSHIP
• *See page 236*

SYLVIA W. FARNY SCHOLARSHIP
• *See page 236*

AMERICAN SOCIETY OF NAVAL ENGINEERS

http://www.navalengineers.org/

AMERICAN SOCIETY OF NAVAL ENGINEERS SCHOLARSHIP
• *See page 106*

ASIAN PACIFIC FUND

BANATAO FAMILY FILIPINO AMERICAN EDUCATION FUND
• *See page 155*

ASSOCIATION OF STATE DAM SAFETY OFFICIALS (ASDSO)

http://www.DamSafety.org

ASSOCIATION OF STATE DAM SAFETY OFFICIALS (ASDSO) SENIOR UNDERGRADUATE SCHOLARSHIP
• *See page 140*

ASTRONAUT SCHOLARSHIP FOUNDATION

http://www.astronautscholarship.org/

ASTRONAUT SCHOLARSHIP
• *See page 107*

AUTOMOTIVE AFTERMARKET SCHOLARSHIPS

http://www.automotivescholarships.com/

AUTOMOTIVE AFTERMARKET SCHOLARSHIPS
• *See page 146*

AUTOMOTIVE WOMEN'S ALLIANCE FOUNDATION

http://awafoundation.org/index.php

AUTOMOTIVE WOMEN'S ALLIANCE FOUNDATION SCHOLARSHIPS
• *See page 71*

BARRY GOLDWATER SCHOLARSHIP AND EXCELLENCE IN EDUCATION FOUNDATION

https://goldwater.scholarsapply.org

BARRY M. GOLDWATER SCHOLARSHIP AND EXCELLENCE IN EDUCATION PROGRAM
• *See page 107*

BHW GROUP

https://thebhwgroup.com/

BHW WOMEN IN STEM SCHOLARSHIP
• *See page 107*

BRASKEM ODEBRECHT

http://www.odebrechtaward.com

ODEBRECHT AWARD FOR SUSTAINABLE DEVELOPMENT
• *See page 113*

BROWN AND CALDWELL

http://www.brownandcaldwell.com

ECKENFELDER SCHOLARSHIP
• *See page 141*

MINORITY SCHOLARSHIP PROGRAM
• *See page 141*

CARDS AGAINST HUMANITY

https://cardsagainsthumanity.com/

SCIENCE AMBASSADOR SCHOLARSHIP
• *See page 107*

CENTER FOR ARCHITECTURE

www.centerforarchitecture.org

CENTER FOR ARCHITECTURE DESIGN SCHOLARSHIP
• *See page 114*

CONNECTICUT BUILDING CONGRESS SCHOLARSHIP FUND, INC.

http://www.cbc-ct.org

CBC SCHOLARSHIP FUND
• *See page 114*

THE DALLAS FOUNDATION

http://www.dallasfoundation.org/

WHITLEY PLACE SCHOLARSHIP
• *See page 114*

DISTIL NETWORKS

http://www.distilnetworks.com

WOMEN FORWARD IN TECHNOLOGY SCHOLARSHIP PROGRAM
• *See page 108*

THE ELECTROCHEMICAL SOCIETY

https://www.electrochem.org/

BATTERY DIVISION STUDENT RESEARCH AWARD SPONSORED BY MERCEDES-BENZ RESEARCH & DEVELOPMENT
• *See page 155*

GREAT MINDS IN STEM

http://www.greatmindsinstem.org/college/scholarship-application-information

HENAAC SCHOLARSHIP PROGRAM
• *See page 100*

INTERNATIONAL SOCIETY FOR OPTICAL ENGINEERING-SPIE

http://www.spie.org/scholarships

SPIE EDUCATIONAL SCHOLARSHIPS IN OPTICAL SCIENCE AND ENGINEERING
• *See page 108*

INTERNATIONAL SOCIETY OF EXPLOSIVES ENGINEERS

http://www.isee.org/

JERRY MCDOWELL FUND
• *See page 156*

JORGE MAS CANOSA FREEDOM FOUNDATION

http://masscholarships.org/

MAS FAMILY SCHOLARSHIP AWARD
• *See page 149*

KENTUCKY ENERGY AND ENVIRONMENT CABINET

http://dep.ky.gov

ENVIRONMENTAL PROTECTION SCHOLARSHIP
• *See page 142*

LOGMEIN

https://www.logmeininc.com

LASTPASS STEM SCHOLARSHIP
• *See page 109*

LOS ANGELES COUNCIL OF BLACK PROFESSIONAL ENGINEERS

http://www.lablackengineers.org/

AL-BEN SCHOLARSHIP FOR ACADEMIC INCENTIVE
• *See page 157*

AL-BEN SCHOLARSHIP FOR PROFESSIONAL MERIT
• *See page 157*

AL-BEN SCHOLARSHIP FOR SCHOLASTIC ACHIEVEMENT
• *See page 157*

MANUFACTURERS ASSOCIATION OF MAINE

http://www.mainemfg.com/

MAINE MANUFACTURING CAREER AND TRAINING FOUNDATION SCHOLARSHIP
• *See page 131*

NASA FLORIDA SPACE GRANT CONSORTIUM

http://www.floridaspacegrant.org/

FLORIDA SPACE RESEARCH PROGRAM
• *See page 131*

NASA IDAHO SPACE GRANT CONSORTIUM

http://www.idahospacegrant.org

NASA IDAHO SPACE GRANT CONSORTIUM SCHOLARSHIP PROGRAM
• *See page 109*

NASA/MARYLAND SPACE GRANT CONSORTIUM

https://md.spacegrant.org

NASA MARYLAND SPACE GRANT CONSORTIUM SCHOLARSHIPS
• *See page 109*

NASA MINNESOTA SPACE GRANT CONSORTIUM

https://www.mnspacegrant.org/

MINNESOTA SPACE GRANT CONSORTIUM SCHOLARSHIP PROGRAM
• *See page 131*

NASA MONTANA SPACE GRANT CONSORTIUM

http://www.spacegrant.montana.edu/

MONTANA SPACE GRANT SCHOLARSHIP PROGRAM
• *See page 132*

NASA'S VIRGINIA SPACE GRANT CONSORTIUM

http://www.vsgc.odu.edu/

COMMUNITY COLLEGE STEM SCHOLARSHIPS
• *See page 110*

UNDERGRADUATE STEM RESEARCH SCHOLARSHIPS
• *See page 110*

NATIONAL ASSOCIATION OF WOMEN IN CONSTRUCTION

http://www.nawic.org/

NAWIC UNDERGRADUATE SCHOLARSHIPS
• *See page 117*

NATIONAL BOARD OF BOILER AND PRESSURE VESSEL INSPECTORS

http://www.nationalboard.org/

NATIONAL BOARD TECHNICAL SCHOLARSHIP
• *See page 157*

NATIONAL SOCIETY OF PROFESSIONAL ENGINEERS

http://www.nspe.org/

MAUREEN L. & HOWARD N. BLITMAN, P.E., SCHOLARSHIP TO PROMOTE DIVERSITY IN ENGINEERING
• *See page 166*

PAUL H. ROBBINS HONORARY SCHOLARSHIP
• *See page 158*

PROFESSIONAL ENGINEERS IN INDUSTRY SCHOLARSHIP
• *See page 158*

NEVADA NASA SPACE GRANT CONSORTIUM

https://nasa.epscorspo.nevada.edu/

NATIONAL SPACE GRANT CONSORTIUM SCHOLARSHIPS
• *See page 110*

NEXTSTEPU

http://www.nextstepu.com/

$1,500 STEM SCHOLARSHIP
• *See page 104*

PACIFIC GAS AND ELECTRIC COMPANY

http://www.scholarshipamerica.org

PG&E BETTER TOGETHER STEM SCHOLARSHIP PROGRAM
• *See page 181*

PROFESSIONAL CONSTRUCTION ESTIMATORS ASSOCIATION

http://www.pcea.org/

TED G. WILSON MEMORIAL SCHOLARSHIP FOUNDATION
• *See page 166*

ROBERT H. MOLLOHAN FAMILY CHARITABLE FOUNDATION, INC.

http://www.mollohanfoundation.org/

HIGH TECHNOLOGY SCHOLARS PROGRAM
• *See page 158*

SCARLETT FAMILY FOUNDATION SCHOLARSHIP PROGRAM

http://www.scarlettfoundation.org/

SCHOLARSHIP FOR STUDENTS PURSUING A BUSINESS OR STEM DEGREE
• *See page 80*

SOCIETY OF PLASTICS ENGINEERS FOUNDATION (SPE)

http://www.4spe.org/

GULF COAST HURRICANE SCHOLARSHIP
• *See page 159*

SOCIETY OF WOMEN ENGINEERS

https://swe.org/

DUPONT COMPANY SCHOLARSHIP
• *See page 159*

GE'S WOMEN'S NETWORK PAULA MARTIN SCHOLARSHIP
• *See page 134*

LIEBHERR MINING SCHOLARSHIP
• *See page 182*

SWE REGION E SCHOLARSHIP
• *See page 159*

SWE REGION H SCHOLARSHIPS
• *See page 159*

SWE REGION J SCHOLARSHIP
• *See page 159*

TE CONNECTIVITY EXCELLENCE IN ENGINEERING SCHOLARSHIP
• *See page 160*

VIRGINIA COUNTS/BETTY IRISH SWE FOR LIFE SCHOLARSHIP

One $1500 scholarship for female applicants planning to study a full-time ABET-accredited program in engineering, technology, or computing in the upcoming academic year. SWE membership required. Preference given to applicants from Arizona or attending an Arizona school.

Academic Fields/Career Goals: Mechanical Engineering.

Award: Scholarship for use in sophomore, junior, senior, or graduate years; not renewable. *Number:* 1. *Amount:* $1500.

Eligibility Requirements: Applicant must be enrolled or expecting to enroll full-time at a four-year institution or university and female. Applicant or parent of applicant must be member of Society of Women Engineers. Available to U.S. citizens.

Application Requirements: Application form, recommendations or references, transcript. *Deadline:* February 15.

Contact: Scholarship Committee
Phone: 312-596-5223
E-mail: scholarships@swe.org

SONS OF NORWAY FOUNDATION

http://www.sonsofnorway.com/foundation

NANCY LORRAINE JENSEN MEMORIAL SCHOLARSHIP
• *See page 160*

SPECIALTY EQUIPMENT MARKET ASSOCIATION

http://www.sema.org/

SEMA MEMORIAL SCHOLARSHIP FUND
• *See page 81*

STRAIGHTFORWARD MEDIA

http://www.straightforwardmedia.com/

STRAIGHTFORWARD MEDIA ENGINEERING SCHOLARSHIP
• *See page 160*

STRAIGHT NORTH

https://www.straightnorth.com/

STRAIGHT NORTH STEM SCHOLARSHIP
• *See page 81*

TIMOTION

http://www.timotion.com/

TIMOTION ENGINEERING AND EXCELLENCE SCHOLARSHIP
• *See page 167*

TURNER CONSTRUCTION COMPANY

http://www.turnerconstruction.com/

YOUTHFORCE 2020 SCHOLARSHIP PROGRAM
• *See page 117*

UNITED NEGRO COLLEGE FUND

http://www.uncf.org/

DAVIS SCHOLARSHIP FOR WOMEN IN STEM
• *See page 111*

GALACTIC UNITE BYTHEWAY SCHOLARSHIP
• *See page 111*

LEIDOS STEM SCHOLARSHIP
• *See page 96*

NASCAR WENDELL SCOTT SR. SCHOLARSHIP
• *See page 83*

VERMONT SPACE GRANT CONSORTIUM

http://www.cems.uvm.edu/vsgc

VERMONT SPACE GRANT CONSORTIUM
• *See page 92*

WOMEN IN AVIATION, INTERNATIONAL

http://www.wai.org/

DELTA AIR LINES ENGINEERING SCHOLARSHIP
• *See page 136*

XEROX

http://www.xerox.com//

TECHNICAL MINORITY SCHOLARSHIP
• *See page 161*

METEOROLOGY/ ATMOSPHERIC SCIENCE

AIR & WASTE MANAGEMENT ASSOCIATION, ALLEGHENY MOUNTAIN SECTION

http://www.ams-awma.org/

ALLEGHENY MOUNTAIN SECTION AIR & WASTE MANAGEMENT ASSOCIATION SCHOLARSHIP
• *See page 250*

AMERICAN INDIAN SCIENCE AND ENGINEERING SOCIETY

http://www.aises.org/

A.T. ANDERSON MEMORIAL SCHOLARSHIP PROGRAM
• *See page 105*

AMERICAN METEOROLOGICAL SOCIETY

http://www.ametsoc.org/

FATHER JAMES B. MACELWANE ANNUAL AWARD
• *See page 251*

ASSOCIATION FOR WOMEN GEOSCIENTISTS (AWG)

http://www.awg.org/

AWG ETHNIC MINORITY SCHOLARSHIP
• *See page 200*

AWG MARIA LUISA CRAWFORD FIELD CAMP SCHOLARSHIP
• *See page 111*

AWG SALT LAKE CHAPTER (SLC) RESEARCH SCHOLARSHIP
• *See page 111*

JANET CULLEN TANAKA GEOSCIENCES UNDERGRADUATE SCHOLARSHIP
• *See page 112*

LONE STAR RISING CAREER SCHOLARSHIP
• *See page 200*

OSAGE CHAPTER UNDERGRADUATE SERVICE SCHOLARSHIP
• *See page 112*

SUSAN EKDALE MEMORIAL FIELD CAMP SCHOLARSHIP
• *See page 201*

ASTRONAUT SCHOLARSHIP FOUNDATION

http://www.astronautscholarship.org/

ASTRONAUT SCHOLARSHIP
- *See page 107*

AUTOMOTIVE WOMEN'S ALLIANCE FOUNDATION

http://awafoundation.org/index.php

AUTOMOTIVE WOMEN'S ALLIANCE FOUNDATION SCHOLARSHIPS
- *See page 71*

BARRY GOLDWATER SCHOLARSHIP AND EXCELLENCE IN EDUCATION FOUNDATION

https://goldwater.scholarsapply.org

BARRY M. GOLDWATER SCHOLARSHIP AND EXCELLENCE IN EDUCATION PROGRAM
- *See page 107*

BHW GROUP

https://thebhwgroup.com/

BHW WOMEN IN STEM SCHOLARSHIP
- *See page 107*

BROWN AND CALDWELL

http://www.brownandcaldwell.com

ECKENFELDER SCHOLARSHIP
- *See page 141*

MINORITY SCHOLARSHIP PROGRAM
- *See page 141*

CARDS AGAINST HUMANITY

https://cardsagainsthumanity.com/

SCIENCE AMBASSADOR SCHOLARSHIP
- *See page 107*

DISTIL NETWORKS

http://www.distilnetworks.com

WOMEN FORWARD IN TECHNOLOGY SCHOLARSHIP PROGRAM
- *See page 108*

GREAT MINDS IN STEM

http://www.greatmindsinstem.org/college/scholarship-application-information

HENAAC SCHOLARSHIP PROGRAM
- *See page 100*

THE LAND CONSERVANCY OF NEW JERSEY

http://www.tlc-nj.org/

ROGERS FAMILY SCHOLARSHIP
- *See page 143*

NASA FLORIDA SPACE GRANT CONSORTIUM

http://www.floridaspacegrant.org/

FLORIDA SPACE RESEARCH PROGRAM
- *See page 131*

NASA IDAHO SPACE GRANT CONSORTIUM

http://www.idahospacegrant.org

NASA IDAHO SPACE GRANT CONSORTIUM SCHOLARSHIP PROGRAM
- *See page 109*

NASA MINNESOTA SPACE GRANT CONSORTIUM

https://www.mnspacegrant.org/

MINNESOTA SPACE GRANT CONSORTIUM SCHOLARSHIP PROGRAM
- *See page 131*

NASA RHODE ISLAND SPACE GRANT CONSORTIUM

http://brown/initiatives/ri-space-grant

NASA RHODE ISLAND SPACE GRANT CONSORTIUM UNDERGRADUATE RESEARCH SCHOLARSHIP
- *See page 132*

NEXTSTEPU

http://www.nextstepu.com/

$1,500 STEM SCHOLARSHIP
- *See page 104*

SCARLETT FAMILY FOUNDATION SCHOLARSHIP PROGRAM

http://www.scarlettfoundation.org/

SCHOLARSHIP FOR STUDENTS PURSUING A BUSINESS OR STEM DEGREE
- *See page 80*

SOCIETY OF SATELLITE PROFESSIONALS INTERNATIONAL

http://www.sspi.org/

SSPI INTERNATIONAL SCHOLARSHIPS
- *See page 134*

STRAIGHT NORTH

https://www.straightnorth.com/

STRAIGHT NORTH STEM SCHOLARSHIP
• *See page 81*

UNITED NEGRO COLLEGE FUND

http://www.uncf.org/

DAVIS SCHOLARSHIP FOR WOMEN IN STEM
• *See page 111*

LEIDOS STEM SCHOLARSHIP
• *See page 96*

MILITARY AND DEFENSE STUDIES

ARMED FORCES COMMUNICATIONS AND ELECTRONICS ASSOCIATION, EDUCATIONAL FOUNDATION

https://foundation.afcea.org

AFCEA STEM MAJORS SCHOLARSHIPS FOR UNDERGRADUATE STUDENTS
• *See page 106*

ASSOCIATION OF FORMER INTELLIGENCE OFFICERS

www.afio.com

AFIO UNDERGRADUATE AND GRADUATE SCHOLARSHIPS
• *See page 98*

BHW GROUP

https://thebhwgroup.com/

BHW WOMEN IN STEM SCHOLARSHIP
• *See page 107*

INTERNATIONAL SOCIETY OF EXPLOSIVES ENGINEERS

http://www.isee.org/

JERRY MCDOWELL FUND
• *See page 156*

THE LYNDON BAINES JOHNSON FOUNDATION

http://www.lbjlibrary.org/page/foundation/

MOODY RESEARCH GRANTS
• *See page 99*

NATIONAL MILITARY INTELLIGENCE FOUNDATION

http://www.nmia.org/

NATIONAL MILITARY INTELLIGENCE ASSOCIATION SCHOLARSHIP

Scholarships to support the growth of professional studies in the field of military intelligence and to recognize and reward excellence in the development and transfer of knowledge about military and associated intelligence disciplines.

Academic Fields/Career Goals: Military and Defense Studies.

Award: Scholarship for use in freshman, sophomore, junior, or senior years; not renewable. *Number:* 3. *Amount:* $1000.

Eligibility Requirements: Applicant must be enrolled or expecting to enroll full-time at a four-year institution or university. Applicant or parent of applicant must be member of National Military Intelligence Association. Available to U.S. citizens.

Application Requirements: Application form, test scores. *Deadline:* August 1.

Contact: Dr. Forrest Frank, Secretary-Treasurer
National Military Intelligence Foundation
National Military Intelligence Foundation
PO Box 6844
Arlington, VA 22311
Phone: 434-542-5929
E-mail: ffrank54@comcast.net

SOCIETY OF SATELLITE PROFESSIONALS INTERNATIONAL

http://www.sspi.org/

SSPI INTERNATIONAL SCHOLARSHIPS
• *See page 134*

WOMEN IN DEFENSE (WID), A NATIONAL SECURITY ORGANIZATION

http://www.womenindefense.net/horizons/apply-for-scholarship

HORIZONS SCHOLARSHIP

Scholarships awarded to provide financial assistance to further educational objectives of women either currently employed in, or planning careers in, defense or national security arenas (not law enforcement or criminal justice). Must be U.S. citizen. Minimum 3.5 GPA required.

Academic Fields/Career Goals: Military and Defense Studies.

Award: Scholarship for use in junior, senior, graduate, or postgraduate years; not renewable. *Number:* 5–6. *Amount:* $500–$10,000.

Eligibility Requirements: Applicant must be enrolled or expecting to enroll full- or part-time at a four-year institution or university and female. Available to U.S. citizens.

Application Requirements: Application form, essay, financial need analysis. *Deadline:* July 1.

Contact: Tameka Brown
Women In Defense (WID), A National Security Organization
2101 Wilson Boulevard, Suite 700
Arlington, VA 22201-3061
Phone: 703-247-2570
E-mail: tbrown@NDIA.ORG

MUSEUM STUDIES

ASSOCIATION FOR WOMEN GEOSCIENTISTS (AWG)

http://www.awg.org/

AWG ETHNIC MINORITY SCHOLARSHIP
• See page 200

AWG SALT LAKE CHAPTER (SLC) RESEARCH SCHOLARSHIP
• See page 111

LONE STAR RISING CAREER SCHOLARSHIP
• See page 200

OSAGE CHAPTER UNDERGRADUATE SERVICE SCHOLARSHIP
• See page 112

SUSAN EKDALE MEMORIAL FIELD CAMP SCHOLARSHIP
• See page 201

COSTUME SOCIETY OF AMERICA

http://www.costumesocietyamerica.com/

ADELE FILENE STUDENT PRESENTER GRANT
• See page 118

STELLA BLUM STUDENT RESEARCH GRANT
• See page 118

THE LYNDON BAINES JOHNSON FOUNDATION

http://www.lbjlibrary.org/page/foundation/

MOODY RESEARCH GRANTS
• See page 99

MUSIC

AMERICAN FOUNDATION FOR THE BLIND

http://www.afb.org/

GLADYS C. ANDERSON MEMORIAL SCHOLARSHIP

Non-renewable award available to a legally-blind female undergraduate or graduate student studying religious or classical music. Must submit a letter from a post-secondary institution as proof of enrollment in a program in music. For online application and more information, visit website http://www.afb.org.

Academic Fields/Career Goals: Music.

Award: Scholarship for use in freshman, sophomore, junior, or senior years; not renewable. *Number:* 1. *Amount:* $1000.

Eligibility Requirements: Applicant must be enrolled or expecting to enroll full-time at a four-year institution or university and female. Applicant must be visually impaired. Available to U.S. citizens.

Application Requirements: Application form, essay, proof of enrollment letter from post secondary institution, proof of blindness letter from agency or medical doctor, recommendations or references, transcript. *Deadline:* April 30.

Contact: Dawn Bodrogi, Information Center and Library Coordinator
Phone: 212-502-7661
E-mail: dbodrogi@afb.net

R.L. GILLETTE SCHOLARSHIP
• See page 323

CENTRAL TEXAS BLUEGRASS ASSOCIATION

www.centraltexasbluegrass

WILLA BEACH-PORTER MUSIC SCHOLARSHIPS

The amount of the scholarship is set by the directors of the Central Texas Bluegrass Association and is to assist the recipient in covering the tuition at any bluegrass camp that he or she may want to attend.

Academic Fields/Career Goals: Music.

Award: Scholarship for use in freshman, sophomore, junior, or senior years; not renewable. *Number:* 4.

Eligibility Requirements: Applicant must be age 12-21; enrolled or expecting to enroll full- or part-time at a technical institution; resident of Texas and must have an interest in music or music/singing. Available to U.S. citizens. Applicant must have general military experience.

Application Requirements: Application form. *Deadline:* June 1.

Contact: Scholarship Coordindator
Central Texas Bluegrass Association
Central Texas Bluegrass Association
PO Box 9816
Austin, TX 78766-9816
E-mail: ctba@centraltexasbluegrass.org

THE CHOPIN FOUNDATION OF THE UNITED STATES

http://www.chopin.org/

SCHOLARSHIP PROGRAM FOR YOUNG AMERICAN PIANISTS

Program is open to qualified American pianists not younger than 14 and not older than 17 years of age on their first year of application. Renewable for up to four years, if eligible. Students will be assisted in preparing music repertoire required for the National Chopin Piano Competition. Must be U.S. citizens or legal residents. For more information, see website http://www.chopin.org.

Academic Fields/Career Goals: Music.

Award: Scholarship for use in freshman, sophomore, or junior years; renewable. *Number:* 1–10. *Amount:* $1000.

Eligibility Requirements: Applicant must be age 14-17; enrolled or expecting to enroll full- or part-time at a two-year or four-year institution and must have an interest in music. Available to U.S. citizens.

Application Requirements: Application form, application form may be submitted online (https://app.getacceptd.com/chopin), personal photograph. *Fee:* $25. *Deadline:* May 15.

Contact: Jadwiga Gewert, Executive Director
The Chopin Foundation of the United States
1440 79th Street Causeway, Suite 117
Miami, FL 33141
Phone: 305-868-0624
E-mail: info@chopin.org

GENERAL FEDERATION OF WOMEN'S CLUBS OF MASSACHUSETTS

http://www.gfwcma.org/

DORCHESTER WOMEN'S CLUB MUSIC SCHOLARSHIP

Scholarship for undergraduate major in voice. Applicant must be a Massachusetts resident and an undergraduate currently enrolled in a four-year accredited college, university or school of music, majoring in voice.

Academic Fields/Career Goals: Music; Performing Arts.

Award: Scholarship for use in sophomore, junior, or senior years; not renewable. *Number:* 1. *Amount:* $500.

Eligibility Requirements: Applicant must be enrolled or expecting to enroll full-time at a four-year institution or university and resident of Massachusetts. Available to U.S. citizens.

Application Requirements: Application form, driver's license, essay, interview. *Deadline:* March 1.

Contact: GFWC Massachusetts Headquarters
General Federation of Women's Clubs of Massachusetts
245 Dutton Road
Sudbury, MA 01776
Phone: 978-443-4569
E-mail: HQsecretary@gfwcma.org

GLENN MILLER BIRTHPLACE SOCIETY

http://www.glennmiller.org/

GMBS-3RD PLACE INSTRUMENTAL SCHOLARSHIP

One scholarship for a male or female instrumentalist will be awarded as a competition prize to be used for any education-related expenses. Must submit 10-minute, high-quality audio tape of pieces selected for competition or those of similar style. Applicant is responsible for travel to and lodging during the competition. One-time award for high school seniors and college freshmen.

Academic Fields/Career Goals: Music.

Award: Scholarship for use in freshman year; not renewable. *Number:* 1. *Amount:* up to $1000.

Eligibility Requirements: Applicant must be enrolled or expecting to enroll full-time at a four-year institution or university. Available to U.S. and non-U.S. citizens.

Application Requirements: Application form, essay, performance tape or CD. *Deadline:* March 10.

Contact: Arlene Leonard, Secretary
Glenn Miller Birthplace Society
PO Box 61
Clarinda, IA 51632
Phone: 712-542-2461
Fax: 712-542-2461
E-mail: gmbs@heartland.net

GMBS-BILL BAKER/HANS STARREVELD SCHOLARSHIP

One scholarship for a male or female instrumentalist will be awarded as a competition prize to be used for any education-related expenses. Must submit 10-minute, high-quality audio tape of pieces selected for competition or those of similar style. Applicant is responsible for travel to and lodging during the competition. One-time award for high school seniors and college freshmen.

Academic Fields/Career Goals: Music.

Award: Scholarship for use in freshman year; not renewable. *Number:* 1. *Amount:* up to $2000.

Eligibility Requirements: Applicant must be enrolled or expecting to enroll full-time at a four-year institution or university. Available to U.S. and non-U.S. citizens.

Application Requirements: Application form, essay, performance tape or CD. *Deadline:* March 10.

Contact: Arlene Leonard, Secretary
Glenn Miller Birthplaee Society
PO Box 61
Clarinda, IA 51632
Phone: 712-542-2461
Fax: 712-542-2461
E-mail: gmbs@heartland.net

GMBS-RAY EBERLE VOCAL SCHOLARSHIP

One scholarship for a male or female vocalist will be awarded as a competition prize to be used for any education-related expenses. Must submit 10-minute, high-quality audio tape of pieces selected for competition or those of similar style. Applicant is responsible for travel to and lodging during the competition. One-time award for high school seniors and college freshmen.

Academic Fields/Career Goals: Music.

Award: Scholarship for use in freshman year; not renewable. *Number:* 1. *Amount:* up to $4000.

Eligibility Requirements: Applicant must be enrolled or expecting to enroll full-time at a four-year institution. Available to U.S. and non-U.S. citizens.

Application Requirements: Application form, essay, performance tape or CD. *Deadline:* March 10.

Contact: Arlene Leonard, Secretary
Glenn Miller Birthplace Society
PO Box 61
Clarinda, IA 51632
Phone: 712-542-2461
Fax: 712-542-2461
E-mail: gmbs@heartland.net

GRAND RAPIDS COMMUNITY FOUNDATION

http://www.grfoundation.org/

LLEWELLYN L. CAYVAN STRING INSTRUMENT SCHOLARSHIP

Scholarship for undergraduate students studying the violin, the viola, the violoncello, and/or the bass viol. High school students not considered. To apply, submit required application form, transcript, essay, reference.

Academic Fields/Career Goals: Music.

Award: Scholarship for use in freshman, sophomore, junior, senior, or graduate years; not renewable. *Number:* 1–6. *Amount:* $1000–$2000.

Eligibility Requirements: Applicant must be enrolled or expecting to enroll full-time at an institution or university. Available to U.S. citizens.

Application Requirements: Application form, application form may be submitted online, essay. *Deadline:* April 1.

Contact: Ms. Ruth Bishop, Education Program Officer
Grand Rapids Community Foundation
185 Oakes Street SW
Grand Rapids, MI 49503
Phone: 616-454-1751 Ext. 103
E-mail: rbishop@grfoundation.org

HAPCO MUSIC FOUNDATION INC.

http://www.hapcopromo.org/

TRADITIONAL MARCHING BAND EXTRAVAGANZA SCHOLARSHIP AWARD

Scholarship is offered to deserving students who will continue their participation in any college music program. Minimum 3.0 GPA required. Applicant should have best composite score of 970 SAT or 20 ACT.

Academic Fields/Career Goals: Music.

Award: Scholarship for use in freshman year; not renewable. *Amount:* $250–$1000.

Eligibility Requirements: Applicant must be enrolled or expecting to enroll full-time at a two-year or four-year institution or university and must have an interest in music. Available to U.S. citizens.

Application Requirements: Application form, essay, personal photograph, recommendations or references, test scores, transcript. *Deadline:* varies.

Contact: Joseph McMullen, President
Phone: 407-877-2262
Fax: 407-654-0308
E-mail: hapcopromo@aol.com

HARTFORD JAZZ SOCIETY INC.

http://www.hartfordjazzsociety.com/

HARTFORD JAZZ SOCIETY SCHOLARSHIPS

Scholarship of up to $3000 is awarded to graduating high school senior attending a four-year college or university. Must be a Connecticut resident. Music major with interest in jazz required.

Academic Fields/Career Goals: Music.

Award: Scholarship for use in freshman year; not renewable. *Number:* 2–3. *Amount:* up to $3000.

Eligibility Requirements: Applicant must be high school student; planning to enroll or expecting to enroll full- or part-time at a four-year institution or university; resident of Connecticut and must have an interest in music. Available to U.S. and Canadian citizens.

Application Requirements: Application form, cassette tape or CD, recommendations or references. *Deadline:* May 1.

Contact: Scholarship Committee Chairperson
Hartford Jazz Society Inc.
116 Cottage Grove Road
Bloomfield, CT 06002
Phone: 860-242-6688
Fax: 860-243-8871
E-mail: hartjazzsocinc@aol.com

HEMOPHILIA FOUNDATION OF SOUTHERN CALIFORNIA

http://www.hemosocal.org/

DR. EARL JAMES FAHRINGER PERFORMING ARTS SCHOLARSHIP
* See page 121

HOUSE OF BLUES MUSIC FORWARD FOUNDATION

https://hobmusicforward.org/

STEVEN J. FINKEL SERVICE EXCELLENCE SCHOLARSHIP
* See page 148

TIFFANY GREEN OPERATOR SCHOLARSHIP AWARD
* See page 85

HOUSTON SYMPHONY

http://www.houstonsymphony.org/

HOUSTON SYMPHONY IMA HOGG COMPETITION
Competition for musicians ages 16 to 29 who play standard instruments of the symphony orchestra. Goal is to offer a review by panel of music professionals and further career of an advanced student or a professional musician. Participants must be U.S. citizens or studying in the United States. Application fee is $30.

Academic Fields/Career Goals: Music.

Award: Prize for use in freshman, sophomore, junior, senior, graduate, or postgraduate years; not renewable. *Number:* 5. *Amount:* $300–$5000.

Eligibility Requirements: Applicant must be age 16-29; enrolled or expecting to enroll full- or part-time at a two-year or four-year or technical institution or university and must have an interest in music. Available to U.S. and non-U.S. citizens.

Application Requirements: Application form, CD with required repertoire, entry in a contest. *Fee:* $30. *Deadline:* February 13.

Contact: Carol Wilson, Manager, Music Matters!
Houston Symphony
615 Louisiana Street, Suite 102
Houston, TX 77002
Phone: 713-238-1447
Fax: 713-224-0453
E-mail: e&o@houstonsymphony.org

HOUSTON SYMPHONY LEAGUE CONCERTO COMPETITION
Competition is open to student musicians 18 years of age or younger who have not yet graduated from high school and who play any standard orchestral instrument or piano. Must live within a 200-mile radius of Houston and submit a screening CD of one movement of their concerto.

Academic Fields/Career Goals: Music.

Award: Prize for use in freshman year; not renewable. *Number:* up to 3. *Amount:* $250–$1000.

Eligibility Requirements: Applicant must be high school student; age 18 or under; planning to enroll or expecting to enroll full-time at a two-year or four-year institution; resident of Texas and must have an interest in music. Available to U.S. citizens.

Application Requirements: Application form, CD, entry in a contest. *Fee:* $25. *Deadline:* November 18.

Contact: Carol Wilson, Manager, Music Matters!
Houston Symphony
615 Louisiana Street, Suite 102
Houston, TX 77002
Phone: 713-238-1449
Fax: 713-224-0453
E-mail: e&o@houstonsymphony.org

JACK J. ISGUR FOUNDATION

www.isgur.org

JACK J. ISGUR FOUNDATION SCHOLARSHIP
* See page 211

NATIONAL ACADEMY OF TELEVISION ARTS AND SCIENCES

https://theemmys.tv/

DOUGLAS W. MUMMERT SCHOLARSHIP
* See page 173

JIM MCKAY MEMORIAL SCHOLARSHIP
* See page 258

MIKE WALLACE MEMORIAL SCHOLARSHIP
* See page 258

NATIONAL ACADEMY OF TELEVISION ARTS AND SCIENCES TRUSTEES' LINDA GIANNECCHINI SCHOLARSHIP
* See page 258

RANDY FALCO SCHOLARSHIP
* See page 259

NATIONAL ASSOCIATION OF PASTORAL MUSICIANS

http://www.npm.org/

ELAINE RENDLER-RENE DOSOGNE-GEORGETOWN CHORALE SCHOLARSHIP
Awards NPM members enrolled full-time or part-time in a graduate or undergraduate degree program of studies related to the field of pastoral music. Applicant must intend to work at least two years in the field of pastoral music following graduation or program completion.

Academic Fields/Career Goals: Music; Religion/Theology.

Award: Scholarship for use in freshman, sophomore, junior, senior, or graduate years; not renewable. *Number:* 1. *Amount:* $1000.

Eligibility Requirements: Applicant must be enrolled or expecting to enroll full- or part-time at a two-year or four-year institution or university and must have an interest in music/singing. Applicant or parent of applicant must be member of National Association of Pastoral Musicians. Available to U.S. and non-U.S. citizens.

Application Requirements: Application form, CD of performance, essay, financial need analysis, recommendations or references, resume. *Deadline:* March 5.

Contact: Ms. Kathleen Haley, Director of Membership Services
Phone: 240-247-3000
E-mail: haley@npm.org

MUSONICS SCHOLARSHIP
Awards NPM members enrolled full-time or part-time in a graduate or undergraduate degree program of studies related to the field of pastoral music. Applicant must intend to work at least two years in the field of pastoral music following graduation or program completion. One award available for graduate study and one award available for undergraduate study.

Academic Fields/Career Goals: Music; Religion/Theology.

Award: Scholarship for use in freshman, sophomore, junior, senior, or graduate years; not renewable. *Number:* 2. *Amount:* $2000.

Eligibility Requirements: Applicant must be enrolled or expecting to enroll full- or part-time at a two-year or four-year institution or university and must have an interest in music/singing. Applicant or parent of applicant must be member of National Association of Pastoral Musicians. Available to U.S. and non-U.S. citizens.

Application Requirements: Application form, CD of performance, essay, financial need analysis, recommendations or references, resume. *Deadline:* March 5.

Contact: Ms. Kathleen Haley, Director of Membership Services
Phone: 240-247-3000
E-mail: haley@npm.org

NPM BOARD OF DIRECTORS SCHOLARSHIP

Scholarship for NPM members enrolled full- or part-time in an undergraduate or graduate pastoral music program. Must intend to work at least two years in the field of pastoral music following graduation/program completion.

Academic Fields/Career Goals: Music.

Award: Scholarship for use in freshman, sophomore, junior, senior, or graduate years; not renewable. *Number:* 1. *Amount:* $2000.

Eligibility Requirements: Applicant must be enrolled or expecting to enroll full- or part-time at a two-year or four-year institution or university and must have an interest in music/singing. Applicant or parent of applicant must be member of National Association of Pastoral Musicians. Available to U.S. and non-U.S. citizens.

Application Requirements: Application form, CD of performance, essay, financial need analysis, recommendations or references, resume. *Deadline:* March 5.

Contact: Ms. Kathleen Haley, Director of Membership Services
Phone: 240-247-3000
E-mail: haley@npm.org

NPM KOINONIA/BOARD OF DIRECTORS SCHOLARSHIP

Awards NPM members enrolled full-time or part-time in a graduate or undergraduate degree program of studies related to the field of pastoral music. Applicant must intend to work at least two years in the field of pastoral music following graduation or program completion.

Academic Fields/Career Goals: Music; Religion/Theology.

Award: Scholarship for use in freshman, sophomore, junior, senior, or graduate years; not renewable. *Number:* 1. *Amount:* $2000.

Eligibility Requirements: Applicant must be enrolled or expecting to enroll full- or part-time at a two-year or four-year institution or university and must have an interest in music/singing. Applicant or parent of applicant must be member of National Association of Pastoral Musicians. Available to U.S. and non-U.S. citizens.

Application Requirements: Application form, CD of performance, essay, financial need analysis, recommendations or references, resume. *Deadline:* March 5.

Contact: Ms. Kathleen Haley, Director of Membership Services
Phone: 240-247-3000
E-mail: haley@npm.org

NPM PERROT SCHOLARSHIP

Awards NPM members enrolled full-time or part-time in a graduate or undergraduate degree program of studies related to the field of pastoral music. Applicant must intend to work at least two years in the field of pastoral music following graduation or program completion.

Academic Fields/Career Goals: Music.

Award: Scholarship for use in freshman, sophomore, junior, senior, or graduate years; not renewable. *Number:* 1. *Amount:* $3000.

Eligibility Requirements: Applicant must be enrolled or expecting to enroll full- or part-time at a two-year or four-year institution or university. Applicant or parent of applicant must be member of National Association of Pastoral Musicians. Available to U.S. and non-U.S. citizens.

Application Requirements: Application form, CD of performance, essay, financial need analysis, recommendations or references, resume. *Deadline:* March 5.

Contact: Ms. Kathleen Haley, Director of Membership Services
Phone: 240-247-3000
E-mail: haley@npm.org

OREGON CATHOLIC PRESS SCHOLARSHIP

Awards NPM members enrolled full-time or part-time in a graduate or undergraduate degree program of studies related to the field of pastoral music. Applicant must intend to work at least two years in the field of pastoral music following graduation or program completion.

Academic Fields/Career Goals: Music; Religion/Theology.

Award: Scholarship for use in freshman, sophomore, junior, senior, or graduate years; not renewable. *Number:* 1. *Amount:* up to $2500.

Eligibility Requirements: Applicant must be enrolled or expecting to enroll full- or part-time at a two-year or four-year institution or university and must have an interest in music/singing. Available to U.S. and non-U.S. citizens.

Application Requirements: Application form, CD of performance, essay, financial need analysis, recommendations or references, resume. *Deadline:* March 5.

Contact: Ms. Kathleen Haley, Director of Membership Services
Phone: 240-247-3000
E-mail: haley@npm.org

PALUCH FAMILY FOUNDATION/WORLD LIBRARY PUBLICATIONS SCHOLARSHIP

Awards NPM members enrolled full-time or part-time in a graduate or undergraduate degree program of studies related to the field of pastoral music. Applicant must intend to work at least two years in the field of pastoral music following graduation or program completion.

Academic Fields/Career Goals: Music; Religion/Theology.

Award: Scholarship for use in freshman, sophomore, junior, senior, or graduate years; not renewable. *Number:* 1. *Amount:* up to $2500.

Eligibility Requirements: Applicant must be enrolled or expecting to enroll full- or part-time at a two-year or four-year institution or university and must have an interest in music/singing. Available to U.S. and non-U.S. citizens.

Application Requirements: Application form, CD of performance, essay, financial need analysis, recommendations or references, resume. *Deadline:* March 5.

Contact: Ms. Kathleen Haley, Director of Membership Services
Phone: 240-247-3000
E-mail: haley@npm.org

STEVEN C. WARNER SCHOLARSHIP

Scholarship for NPM members enrolled full-or part-time in an undergraduate or graduate pastoral music program. Applicant must intend to work at least two years in the field of pastoral music following graduation/program completion.

Academic Fields/Career Goals: Music.

Award: Scholarship for use in freshman, sophomore, junior, senior, or graduate years; not renewable. *Number:* 1. *Amount:* $1000.

Eligibility Requirements: Applicant must be enrolled or expecting to enroll full- or part-time at a two-year or four-year institution or university and must have an interest in music/singing. Applicant or parent of applicant must be member of National Association of Pastoral Musicians. Available to U.S. and non-U.S. citizens.

Application Requirements: Application form, CD of performance, essay, financial need analysis, recommendations or references, resume. *Deadline:* March 5.

Contact: Ms. Kathleen Haley, Director of Membership Services
Phone: 240-247-3000
E-mail: haley@npm.org

POLISH ARTS CLUB OF BUFFALO SCHOLARSHIP FOUNDATION

http://www.pacb.bfn.org/

POLISH ARTS CLUB OF BUFFALO SCHOLARSHIP FOUNDATION TRUST

• *See page 122*

QUALITY BATH

www.qualitybath.com

QUALITYBATH.COM SCHOLARSHIP PROGRAM
• *See page 120*

QUEEN ELISABETH INTERNATIONAL MUSIC COMPETITION OF BELGIUM

http://www.qeimc.be

QUEEN ELISABETH COMPETITION
Competition is open to musicians who have already completed their training and who are ready to launch their international careers. The competition covers the following musical disciplines: piano, voice and violin.

Academic Fields/Career Goals: Music.

Award: Prize for use in freshman, sophomore, junior, senior, graduate, or postgraduate years; not renewable. *Amount:* $1–$33.

Eligibility Requirements: Applicant must be age 18-32; enrolled or expecting to enroll full- or part-time at a two-year or four-year institution or university and must have an interest in music or music/singing. Available to U.S. and non-U.S. citizens.

Application Requirements: Application form, personal photograph. *Fee:* $130. *Deadline:* December 6.

Contact: Nicolas Dernoncourt, Artistic Coordinator
    Phone: 32 2 213 40 50
    E-mail: info@qeimc.be

RHODE ISLAND FOUNDATION

http://www.rifoundation.org/

BACH ORGAN AND KEYBOARD MUSIC SCHOLARSHIP
Scholarship for college music majors who are Rhode Island residents or attending college in Rhode Island. Must demonstrate good grades, financial need, and be an ABO member. Must include music sample.

Academic Fields/Career Goals: Music.

Award: Scholarship for use in freshman, sophomore, junior, or senior years; not renewable. *Amount:* $800–$1000.

Eligibility Requirements: Applicant must be enrolled or expecting to enroll full-time at a two-year or four-year institution or university; resident of Rhode Island and must have an interest in music/singing. Available to U.S. citizens.

Application Requirements: Application form, financial need analysis, recommendations or references, self-addressed stamped envelope with application, transcript. *Deadline:* June 14.

Contact: Kelly Riley, Donor Services Administrator
    Phone: 401-427-4028
    E-mail: kriley@rifoundation.org

VSA

http://www.kennedy-center.org/education/vsa/

VSA INTERNATIONAL YOUNG SOLOISTS AWARD
Each year outstanding young musicians with disabilities from around the world receive the VSA International Young Soloists Award, $2,000, and the opportunity to perform at the John F. Kennedy Center for the Performing Arts in Washington, D.C., which is live-streamed and archived on the Kennedy Center website. This program is open to soloists and ensembles of any instrument or genre including classical, jazz, hip-hop, rock, and more!

Academic Fields/Career Goals: Music; Performing Arts.

Award: Prize for use in freshman, sophomore, junior, or senior years; not renewable. *Number:* 4. *Amount:* $2000.

Eligibility Requirements: Applicant must be age 14-25; enrolled or expecting to enroll full- or part-time at a four-year institution or university and must have an interest in music or music/singing. Applicant must be hearing impaired, learning disabled, physically disabled, or visually impaired. Available to U.S. and non-U.S. citizens.

Application Requirements: Application form. *Deadline:* February 8.

Contact: Megan Bailey, Administrative Assistant
    VSA
    2700 F Street NW
    Washington, DC 20566
    Phone: 202-416-8822
    E-mail: vsainfo@kennedy-center.org

WOMEN BAND DIRECTORS INTERNATIONAL

http://www.womenbanddirectors.org/

CHARLOTTE PLUMMER OWEN MEMORIAL SCHOLARSHIP
• *See page 216*

MARTHA ANN STARK MEMORIAL SCHOLARSHIP
• *See page 216*

VOLKWEIN MEMORIAL SCHOLARSHIP
• *See page 216*

NATURAL RESOURCES

AMERICAN GROUND WATER TRUST

http://www.agwt.org/

AMERICAN GROUND WATER TRUST-AMTROL INC. SCHOLARSHIP
• *See page 199*

AMERICAN GROUND WATER TRUST-BAROID SCHOLARSHIP
• *See page 199*

AMERICAN GROUND WATER TRUST-THOMAS STETSON SCHOLARSHIP
• *See page 199*

AMERICAN INDIAN SCIENCE AND ENGINEERING SOCIETY

http://www.aises.org/

A.T. ANDERSON MEMORIAL SCHOLARSHIP PROGRAM
• *See page 105*

AMERICAN PUBLIC POWER ASSOCIATION

https://www.publicpower.org/deed-rd-funding

DEMONSTRATION OF ENERGY AND EFFICIENCY DEVELOPMENTS EDUCATIONAL SCHOLARSHIP
• *See page 154*

DEMONSTRATION OF ENERGY AND EFFICIENCY DEVELOPMENTS STUDENT INTERNSHIP
• *See page 154*

DEMONSTRATION OF ENERGY AND EFFICIENCY DEVELOPMENTS STUDENT RESEARCH GRANTS
• *See page 162*

DEMONSTRATION OF ENERGY AND EFFICIENCY DEVELOPMENTS TECHNICAL DESIGN PROJECT
• *See page 154*

AMERICAN SOCIETY OF AGRONOMY, CROP SCIENCE SOCIETY OF AMERICA, SOIL SCIENCE SOCIETY OF AMERICA

http://www.agronomy.org

J. FIELDING REED UNDERGRADUATE SOIL AND PLANT SCIENCES SCHOLARSHIP
• *See page 200*

AMERICAN WATER RESOURCES ASSOCIATION

http://www.awra.org/.

AWRA RICHARD A. HERBERT MEMORIAL SCHOLARSHIP

At least two scholarships are available: one for full-time undergraduate student and one for a full-time graduate student, each working toward a degree in water resources. All applicants must be national AWRA members.

Academic Fields/Career Goals: Natural Resources.

Award: Scholarship for use in freshman, sophomore, junior, senior, or graduate years; not renewable. *Number:* 2–6. *Amount:* $650–$2000.

Eligibility Requirements: Applicant must be enrolled or expecting to enroll full-time at a four-year institution or university. Available to U.S. and non-U.S. citizens.

Application Requirements: Application form, essay. *Deadline:* April 23.

Contact: Dresden Farrand, Executive Vice President
American Water Resources Association
4 West Federal Street, PO Box 1626
Middleburg, VA 20118-1626
Phone: 540-687-8390
E-mail: info@awra.org

ARCTIC INSTITUTE OF NORTH AMERICA

http://www.arctic.ucalgary.ca/

JIM BOURQUE SCHOLARSHIP
• *See page 207*

ARIZONA HYDROLOGICAL SOCIETY

http://www.azhydrosoc.org/

ARIZONA HYDROLOGICAL SOCIETY SCHOLARSHIP
• *See page 200*

ARIZONA PROFESSIONAL CHAPTER OF AISES

http://www.aises.org/scholarships

ARIZONA PROFESSIONAL CHAPTER OF AISES SCHOLARSHIP
• *See page 237*

ASSOCIATION FOR WOMEN GEOSCIENTISTS (AWG)

http://www.awg.org/

AWG ETHNIC MINORITY SCHOLARSHIP
• *See page 200*

AWG MARIA LUISA CRAWFORD FIELD CAMP SCHOLARSHIP
• *See page 111*

AWG SALT LAKE CHAPTER (SLC) RESEARCH SCHOLARSHIP
• *See page 111*

JANET CULLEN TANAKA GEOSCIENCES UNDERGRADUATE SCHOLARSHIP
• *See page 112*

LONE STAR RISING CAREER SCHOLARSHIP
• *See page 200*

OSAGE CHAPTER UNDERGRADUATE SERVICE SCHOLARSHIP
• *See page 112*

SUSAN EKDALE MEMORIAL FIELD CAMP SCHOLARSHIP
• *See page 201*

ASSOCIATION OF CALIFORNIA WATER AGENCIES

http://www.acwa.com/

ASSOCIATION OF CALIFORNIA WATER AGENCIES SCHOLARSHIPS
• *See page 106*

CLAIR A. HILL SCHOLARSHIP
• *See page 106*

ASSOCIATION OF STATE DAM SAFETY OFFICIALS (ASDSO)

http://www.DamSafety.org

ASSOCIATION OF STATE DAM SAFETY OFFICIALS (ASDSO) SENIOR UNDERGRADUATE SCHOLARSHIP
• *See page 140*

BHW GROUP

https://thebhwgroup.com/

BHW WOMEN IN STEM SCHOLARSHIP
• *See page 107*

B.O.G. PEST CONTROL

http://www.bogpestcontrol.com/

B.O.G. PEST CONTROL SCHOLARSHIP FUND
• *See page 141*

BROWN AND CALDWELL

http://www.brownandcaldwell.com

ECKENFELDER SCHOLARSHIP
• *See page 141*

MINORITY SCHOLARSHIP PROGRAM
• *See page 141*

CALIFORNIA GROUNDWATER ASSOCIATION

http://www.groundh2o.org/

CALIFORNIA GROUNDWATER ASSOCIATION SCHOLARSHIP
• *See page 298*

CONSERVATION FEDERATION OF MISSOURI

http://www.confedmo.org/

CHARLES P. BELL CONSERVATION SCHOLARSHIP
• *See page 252*

DISTIL NETWORKS

http://www.distilnetworks.com

WOMEN FORWARD IN TECHNOLOGY SCHOLARSHIP PROGRAM
• *See page 108*

GREAT MINDS IN STEM

http://www.greatmindsinstem.org/college/scholarship-application-information

HENAAC SCHOLARSHIP PROGRAM
• *See page 100*

INDIANA WILDLIFE FEDERATION ENDOWMENT

http://www.indianawildlife.org/

CHARLES A. HOLT INDIANA WILDLIFE FEDERATION ENDOWMENT SCHOLARSHIP
• *See page 253*

INTERNATIONAL SOCIETY OF EXPLOSIVES ENGINEERS

http://www.isee.org/

JERRY MCDOWELL FUND
• *See page 156*

INTERTRIBAL TIMBER COUNCIL

http://www.itcnet.org/

NATIVE AMERICAN NATURAL RESOURCE RESEARCH SCHOLARSHIP

The Intertribal Timber Council (ITC), in partnership with the USDA Forest Service Southern Research Station is pleased to announce scholarship opportunities for Native American students who are planning or currently conducting tribally relevant research in a natural resource issue. Deadline: January 31, 2018, 5:00 p.m. PST. Award of up to $4,000. The ITC Research Scholarship is designed to support tribally relevant, natural resource based, research being conducted by Native American scholars (graduate or undergraduate). Required Material: The ITC Research Sub-Committee will review and rank only those applications that completely address the following criteria: 1. letter of application. The letter must include your name, permanent mailing address, email address and phone number. Discuss your current educational program and how the proposed research fits into both your degree in natural resources and your future plans; 2. resume; 3. evidence of validated enrollment in a federally recognized tribe or Alaska Native Corporation, as established by the U.S. Government. A photocopy of your enrollment card, front and back, or Certificate of Indian Blood (CIB) is sufficient; 4. mini research proposal. Please keep this concise (4 page maximum not counting budget and justification). Required elements include a) abstract stating research merit and explaining how this research is relevant to tribal natural resource interests b) timeline and methodology c) dissemination plan, including a tribal component d) budget and budget justification; 5. letters of reference/support from an Academic advisor or committee member is required. Additionally, a second letter of support from a tribal resource manager or a tribal representative with tribal approval of the project or the relevancy of the project to the tribe is required. Incomplete applications will not be considered. Applications should be submitted electronically by email (itc1@teleport.com), or (fax: 503-282-1274). Questions regarding the application process can be submitted to ITC (itc1@teleport.com) (phone 503-282-4296) or Adrian Leighton, chair of the ITC Research Sub-Committee (adrian_leighton@skc.edu).

Academic Fields/Career Goals: Natural Resources; Natural Sciences.

Award: Scholarship for use in freshman, sophomore, junior, senior, or graduate years; not renewable. *Amount:* $4000.

Eligibility Requirements: Applicant must be American Indian/Alaska Native and enrolled or expecting to enroll full-time at a four-year institution or university. Available to U.S. citizens.

Application Requirements: Application form, essay. *Deadline:* January 31.

Contact: Education Committee
Intertribal Timber Council
1112 NE 21st Avenue, Suite 4
Portland, OR 97232
Phone: 503-282-4296
Fax: 503-282-1274
E-mail: itc1@teleport.com

THE LAND CONSERVANCY OF NEW JERSEY

http://www.tlc-nj.org/

ROGERS FAMILY SCHOLARSHIP
• *See page 143*

RUSSELL W. MYERS SCHOLARSHIP
• *See page 143*

LOUISIANA OFFICE OF STUDENT FINANCIAL ASSISTANCE

www.osfa.la.gov/

ROCKEFELLER STATE WILDLIFE SCHOLARSHIP
• *See page 325*

MONTANA FEDERATION OF GARDEN CLUBS

http://www.mtfgc.org/

LIFE MEMBER MONTANA FEDERATION OF GARDEN CLUBS SCHOLARSHIP
• *See page 202*

NASA IDAHO SPACE GRANT CONSORTIUM

http://www.idahospacegrant.org

NASA IDAHO SPACE GRANT CONSORTIUM SCHOLARSHIP PROGRAM
• *See page 109*

NOVUS BIOLOGICALS, LLC

https://www.novusbio.com

TOCRIS BIOSCIENCE SCHOLARSHIP
• *See page 102*

OUTDOOR WRITERS ASSOCIATION OF AMERICA

http://www.owaa.org/

OUTDOOR WRITERS ASSOCIATION OF AMERICA - BODIE MCDOWELL SCHOLARSHIP AWARD
• *See page 174*

PADDLE CANADA

http://www.paddlecanada.com

BILL MASON SCHOLARSHIP FUND
• *See page 212*

ROCKY MOUNTAIN ELK FOUNDATION

http://www.rmef.org

WILDLIFE LEADERSHIP AWARDS

Program established to recognize, encourage and promote leadership among future wildlife management professionals. Candidates must be an undergraduate in a recognized wildlife program, have at least a junior standing (completed a minimum of 56 semester hours or 108 quarter hours), and have at least one semester or two quarters remaining in their degree program.

Academic Fields/Career Goals: Natural Resources; Natural Sciences.

Award: Scholarship for use in junior or senior years; not renewable. *Number:* 1–5. *Amount:* $3000.

Eligibility Requirements: Applicant must be enrolled or expecting to enroll full-time at a four-year institution or university and must have an interest in wildlife conservation/animal rescue. Available to U.S. and Canadian citizens.

Application Requirements: Application form. *Deadline:* March 1.

Contact: Toni O'Hara, Lands & Conservation Office Administrator
E-mail: tohara@rmef.org

SOIL AND WATER CONSERVATION SOCIETY

http://www.swcs.org

DONALD A. WILLIAMS SCHOLARSHIP SOIL CONSERVATION SCHOLARSHIP
• *See page 91*

SOIL AND WATER CONSERVATION SOCIETY-NEW JERSEY CHAPTER

http://www.geocities.com/njswcs

EDWARD R. HALL SCHOLARSHIP
• *See page 91*

SOUTH DAKOTA BOARD OF REGENTS

http://www.sdbor.edu/

SOUTH DAKOTA BOARD OF REGENTS BJUGSTAD SCHOLARSHIP
• *See page 91*

STRAIGHT NORTH

https://www.straightnorth.com/

STRAIGHT NORTH STEM SCHOLARSHIP
• *See page 81*

TAU KAPPA EPSILON EDUCATION FOUNDATION

https://www.tke.org/

TIMOTHY L. TASCHWER SCHOLARSHIP
• *See page 144*

TECHNICAL ASSOCIATION OF THE PULP & PAPER INDUSTRY (TAPPI)

https://www.tappi.org/

WILLIAM L. CULLISON SCHOLARSHIP

Scholarship provides incentive for students to pursue an academic path related to the pulp and paper industry. Eligible students must meet all criteria and will have completed two years of undergraduate school with two years (or three years in a five-year program) remaining. For details, refer to website http://www.tappi.org/s_tappi/doc.asp?CID=6101&DID=561682.

Academic Fields/Career Goals: Natural Resources; Paper and Pulp Engineering.

Award: Scholarship for use in junior or senior years; renewable. *Number:* 1–2. *Amount:* $2000–$4000.

Eligibility Requirements: Applicant must be enrolled or expecting to enroll full-time at a four-year institution or university. Available to U.S. and non-U.S. citizens.

Application Requirements: Application form. *Deadline:* May 1.

Contact: Mr. Laurence Womack, Director of Standards and Awards
Technical Association of the Pulp & Paper Industry (TAPPI)
15 Technology Parkway South
Peachtree Corners, GA 30092
Phone: 770-209-7276
E-mail: standards@tappi.org

UNITED STATES DEPARTMENT OF AGRICULTURE

http://www.usda.gov/

USDA/1994 TRIBAL SCHOLARS PROGRAM
• *See page 96*

UNITED STATES ENVIRONMENTAL PROTECTION AGENCY

http://www.epa.gov/enviroed

NATIONAL NETWORK FOR ENVIRONMENTAL MANAGEMENT STUDIES FELLOWSHIP
• *See page 256*

VIRGINIA ASSOCIATION OF SOIL AND WATER CONSERVATION DISTRICTS EDUCATIONAL FOUNDATION INC.

http://www.vaswcd.org/

VASWCD EDUCATIONAL FOUNDATION INC. SCHOLARSHIP AWARDS PROGRAM

Scholarship to provide financial support to Virginia residents majoring in, or showing a strong desire to major in, a course curriculum related to natural resource conservation and/or environmental studies. Applicants must be full-time students who have applied to an undergraduate freshman-level curriculum. Must rank in the top 20 percent of graduating class or have a 3.0 or greater GPA, and demonstrate an active interest in conservation. Recipients may reapply to their individual SWCD for scholarship consideration in ensuing years.

Academic Fields/Career Goals: Natural Resources.

Award: Scholarship for use in freshman year; not renewable. *Number:* 4. *Amount:* $1000.

Eligibility Requirements: Applicant must be high school student; planning to enroll or expecting to enroll full-time at a four-year institution or university and resident of Virginia. Available to U.S. citizens.

Application Requirements: Application form, essay, financial need analysis. *Deadline:* March 1.

Contact: Jennifer Hoysa, District Manager
Phone: 540-316-6984 Ext. 6984
E-mail: jennifer.hoysa@fauquiercounty.gov

WILSON ORNITHOLOGICAL SOCIETY

http://www.wilsonsociety.org/

GEORGE A. HALL/HAROLD F. MAYFIELD AWARD
• *See page 103*

PAUL A. STEWART AWARDS
• *See page 103*

NATURAL SCIENCES

AMERICAN CHEMICAL SOCIETY

http://www.acs.org/

AMERICAN CHEMICAL SOCIETY SCHOLARS PROGRAM
• *See page 153*

AMERICAN FOUNDATION FOR THE BLIND

http://www.afb.org/

PAUL W. RUCKES SCHOLARSHIP
• *See page 179*

AMERICAN INDIAN SCIENCE AND ENGINEERING SOCIETY

http://www.aises.org/

A.T. ANDERSON MEMORIAL SCHOLARSHIP PROGRAM
• *See page 105*

AMERICAN LEGION DEPARTMENT OF MARYLAND

http://www.mdlegion.org/

AMERICAN LEGION DEPARTMENT OF MARYLAND MATH-SCIENCE SCHOLARSHIP
• *See page 99*

AMERICAN PHYSIOLOGICAL SOCIETY

https://www.physiology.org/

BARBARA A. HORWITZ AND JOHN M. HOROWITZ UNDERGRADUATE RESEARCH AWARDS
• *See page 139*

AMERICAN SOCIETY OF AGRONOMY, CROP SCIENCE SOCIETY OF AMERICA, SOIL SCIENCE SOCIETY OF AMERICA

http://www.agronomy.org

J. FIELDING REED UNDERGRADUATE SOIL AND PLANT SCIENCES SCHOLARSHIP
• *See page 200*

ARCTIC INSTITUTE OF NORTH AMERICA

http://www.arctic.ucalgary.ca/

JIM BOURQUE SCHOLARSHIP
• *See page 207*

ASSOCIATION FOR WOMEN GEOSCIENTISTS (AWG)

http://www.awg.org/

AWG ETHNIC MINORITY SCHOLARSHIP
• *See page 200*

AWG MARIA LUISA CRAWFORD FIELD CAMP SCHOLARSHIP
• *See page 111*

AWG SALT LAKE CHAPTER (SLC) RESEARCH SCHOLARSHIP
• *See page 111*

AWG UNDERGRADUATE EXCELLENCE IN PALEONTOLOGY AWARD
• *See page 106*

JANET CULLEN TANAKA GEOSCIENCES UNDERGRADUATE SCHOLARSHIP
• *See page 112*

LONE STAR RISING CAREER SCHOLARSHIP
• *See page 200*

SUSAN EKDALE MEMORIAL FIELD CAMP SCHOLARSHIP
• *See page 201*

ASSOCIATION OF CALIFORNIA WATER AGENCIES

http://www.acwa.com/

ASSOCIATION OF CALIFORNIA WATER AGENCIES SCHOLARSHIPS
• *See page 106*

CLAIR A. HILL SCHOLARSHIP
• *See page 106*

ASSOCIATION OF FORMER INTELLIGENCE OFFICERS

www.afio.com

AFIO UNDERGRADUATE AND GRADUATE SCHOLARSHIPS
• *See page 98*

ASSOCIATION OF STATE DAM SAFETY OFFICIALS (ASDSO)

http://www.DamSafety.org

ASSOCIATION OF STATE DAM SAFETY OFFICIALS (ASDSO) SENIOR UNDERGRADUATE SCHOLARSHIP
• *See page 140*

ASSOCIATION ON AMERICAN INDIAN AFFAIRS, INC.

http://www.indian-affairs.org/

ELIZABETH AND SHERMAN ASCHE MEMORIAL SCHOLARSHIP FUND
• *See page 93*

AUDUBON SOCIETY OF WESTERN PENNSYLVANIA

http://www.aswp.org/

BEULAH FREY ENVIRONMENTAL SCHOLARSHIP
• *See page 252*

BARRY GOLDWATER SCHOLARSHIP AND EXCELLENCE IN EDUCATION FOUNDATION

https://goldwater.scholarsapply.org

BARRY M. GOLDWATER SCHOLARSHIP AND EXCELLENCE IN EDUCATION PROGRAM
• *See page 107*

BHW GROUP

https://thebhwgroup.com/

BHW WOMEN IN STEM SCHOLARSHIP
• *See page 107*

B.O.G. PEST CONTROL

http://www.bogpestcontrol.com/

B.O.G. PEST CONTROL SCHOLARSHIP FUND
• *See page 141*

BROWN AND CALDWELL

http://www.brownandcaldwell.com

ECKENFELDER SCHOLARSHIP
• *See page 141*

MINORITY SCHOLARSHIP PROGRAM
• *See page 141*

CARDS AGAINST HUMANITY

https://cardsagainsthumanity.com/

SCIENCE AMBASSADOR SCHOLARSHIP
• *See page 107*

CONSERVATION FEDERATION OF MISSOURI

http://www.confedmo.org/

CHARLES P. BELL CONSERVATION SCHOLARSHIP
• *See page 252*

DISTIL NETWORKS

http://www.distilnetworks.com

WOMEN FORWARD IN TECHNOLOGY SCHOLARSHIP PROGRAM
• *See page 108*

THE ELECTROCHEMICAL SOCIETY

https://www.electrochem.org/

BATTERY DIVISION STUDENT RESEARCH AWARD SPONSORED BY MERCEDES-BENZ RESEARCH & DEVELOPMENT
• *See page 155*

EXPLORERS CLUB

http://www.explorers.org/

YOUTH ACTIVITY FUND GRANTS
• *See page 103*

FLORIDA ENGINEERING SOCIETY

https://www.fleng.org/page/Scholarships

ACEC-FLORIDA SCHOLARSHIP
• *See page 239*

GREAT MINDS IN STEM

http://www.greatmindsinstem.org/college/scholarship-application-information

HENAAC SCHOLARSHIP PROGRAM
• *See page 100*

INTERTRIBAL TIMBER COUNCIL

http://www.itcnet.org/

NATIVE AMERICAN NATURAL RESOURCE RESEARCH SCHOLARSHIP
• *See page 353*

KENTUCKY ENERGY AND ENVIRONMENT CABINET

http://dep.ky.gov

ENVIRONMENTAL PROTECTION SCHOLARSHIP
• *See page 142*

MEDICAL SCRUBS COLLECTION

http://medicalscrubscollection.com

MEDICAL SCRUBS COLLECTION SCHOLARSHIP
• *See page 104*

NASA IDAHO SPACE GRANT CONSORTIUM

http://www.idahospacegrant.org

NASA IDAHO SPACE GRANT CONSORTIUM SCHOLARSHIP PROGRAM
• *See page 109*

NASA MINNESOTA SPACE GRANT CONSORTIUM

https://www.mnspacegrant.org/

MINNESOTA SPACE GRANT CONSORTIUM SCHOLARSHIP PROGRAM
• *See page 131*

NEVADA NASA SPACE GRANT CONSORTIUM

https://nasa.epscorspo.nevada.edu/

NATIONAL SPACE GRANT CONSORTIUM SCHOLARSHIPS
• See page 110

NEXTSTEPU

http://www.nextstepu.com/

$1,500 STEM SCHOLARSHIP
• See page 104

NOVUS BIOLOGICALS, LLC

https://www.novusbio.com

NOVUS BIOLOGICALS SCHOLARSHIP PROGRAM
• See page 101

R&D SYSTEMS SCHOLARSHIP
• See page 101

TOCRIS BIOSCIENCE SCHOLARSHIP
• See page 102

OREGON OFFICE OF STUDENT ACCESS AND COMPLETION

https://oregonstudentaid.gov/

SEHAR SALEHA AHMAD AND ABRAHIM EKRAMULLAH ZAFAR FOUNDATION SCHOLARSHIP
• See page 110

PADDLE CANADA

http://www.paddlecanada.com

BILL MASON SCHOLARSHIP FUND
• See page 212

ROBERT H. MOLLOHAN FAMILY CHARITABLE FOUNDATION, INC.

http://www.mollohanfoundation.org/

JOHN M. MURPHY SCHOLARSHIP
The John M. Murphy Scholarship is a $500 scholarship that will be awarded to a Pendleton County High School senior who is planning to major in any natural science related field at a West Virginia college or university. Furthermore, the recipient will be eligible for summer internship opportunities within his or her field of study.

Academic Fields/Career Goals: Natural Sciences.

Award: Scholarship for use in senior year; not renewable. *Amount:* $500.

Eligibility Requirements: Applicant must be high school student; planning to enroll or expecting to enroll full- or part-time at a four-year institution or university; resident of West Virginia and studying in West Virginia. Available to U.S. citizens.

Application Requirements: Application form, essay, recommendations or references, resume, test scores, transcript.

ROCKY MOUNTAIN ELK FOUNDATION

http://www.rmef.org

WILDLIFE LEADERSHIP AWARDS
• See page 354

SCARLETT FAMILY FOUNDATION SCHOLARSHIP PROGRAM

http://www.scarlettfoundation.org/

SCHOLARSHIP FOR STUDENTS PURSUING A BUSINESS OR STEM DEGREE
• See page 80

SOIL AND WATER CONSERVATION SOCIETY

http://www.swcs.org

DONALD A. WILLIAMS SCHOLARSHIP SOIL CONSERVATION SCHOLARSHIP
• See page 91

SOIL AND WATER CONSERVATION SOCIETY-NEW JERSEY CHAPTER

http://www.geocities.com/njswcs

EDWARD R. HALL SCHOLARSHIP
• See page 91

STRAIGHT NORTH

https://www.straightnorth.com/

STRAIGHT NORTH STEM SCHOLARSHIP
• See page 81

UNITED NATIONS ASSOCIATION OF CONNECTICUT

http://www.unausa.org

UNITED NATIONS ASSOCIATION OF CONNECTICUT SCHOLARSHIP
• See page 124

UNITED NEGRO COLLEGE FUND

http://www.uncf.org/

LEIDOS STEM SCHOLARSHIP
• See page 96

NEAR AND MIDDLE EAST STUDIES

ASSOCIATION OF FORMER INTELLIGENCE OFFICERS

www.afio.com

AFIO UNDERGRADUATE AND GRADUATE SCHOLARSHIPS
• See page 98

BHW GROUP

https://thebhwgroup.com/

BHW WOMEN IN STEM SCHOLARSHIP

HUB FOUNDATION

https://hub-foundation.org

HUB FOUNDATION SCHOLARSHIPS

ISLAMIC SCHOLARSHIP FUND

http://islamicscholarshipfund.org/

ISF NATIONAL SCHOLARSHIP

UNITED NATIONS ASSOCIATION OF CONNECTICUT

http://www.unausa.org

UNITED NATIONS ASSOCIATION OF CONNECTICUT SCHOLARSHIP

NEUROBIOLOGY

101ST AIRBORNE DIVISION ASSOCIATION

http://www.screamingeaglefoundation.org/

AL & WILLIAMARY VISTE SCHOLARSHIP

AMERICAN INDIAN SCIENCE AND ENGINEERING SOCIETY

http://www.aises.org/

A.T. ANDERSON MEMORIAL SCHOLARSHIP PROGRAM

AMERICAN PHYSIOLOGICAL SOCIETY

https://www.physiology.org/

BARBARA A. HORWITZ AND JOHN M. HOROWITZ UNDERGRADUATE RESEARCH AWARDS

AVACARE MEDICAL

https://avacaremedical.com

AVACARE MEDICAL SCHOLARSHIP

BARRY GOLDWATER SCHOLARSHIP AND EXCELLENCE IN EDUCATION FOUNDATION

https://goldwater.scholarsapply.org

BARRY M. GOLDWATER SCHOLARSHIP AND EXCELLENCE IN EDUCATION PROGRAM

BHW GROUP

https://thebhwgroup.com/

BHW WOMEN IN STEM SCHOLARSHIP

CARDS AGAINST HUMANITY

https://cardsagainsthumanity.com/

SCIENCE AMBASSADOR SCHOLARSHIP

CYNTHIA E. MORGAN SCHOLARSHIP FUND (CEMS)

http://www.cemsfund.com/

CYNTHIA E. MORGAN MEMORIAL SCHOLARSHIP FUND, INC.

DISTIL NETWORKS

http://www.distilnetworks.com

WOMEN FORWARD IN TECHNOLOGY SCHOLARSHIP PROGRAM

THE EXPERT INSTITUTE

https://www.theexpertinstitute.com

ANNUAL HEALTHCARE AND LIFE SCIENCES SCHOLARSHIP

GREAT MINDS IN STEM

http://www.greatmindsinstem.org/college/scholarship-application-information

HENAAC SCHOLARSHIP PROGRAM

INTERMOUNTAIN MEDICAL IMAGING

https://www.aboutimi.com/

INTERMOUNTAIN MEDICAL IMAGING SCHOLARSHIP

KETAMINE CLINICS OF LOS ANGELES

http://www.ketamineclinics.com/

KETAMINE CLINICS OF LOS ANGELES SCHOLARSHIP PROGRAM

MEDICAL SCRUBS COLLECTION

http://medicalscrubscollection.com

MEDICAL SCRUBS COLLECTION SCHOLARSHIP
• *See page 104*

NATIONAL INSTITUTES OF HEALTH

https://www.training.nih.gov/programs/ugsp

NIH UNDERGRADUATE SCHOLARSHIP PROGRAM FOR STUDENTS FROM DISADVANTAGED BACKGROUNDS
• *See page 101*

NEXTSTEPU

http://www.nextstepu.com/

$1,500 STEM SCHOLARSHIP
• *See page 104*

NOVUS BIOLOGICALS, LLC

https://www.novusbio.com

NOVUS BIOLOGICALS SCHOLARSHIP PROGRAM
• *See page 101*

R&D SYSTEMS SCHOLARSHIP
• *See page 101*

TOCRIS BIOSCIENCE SCHOLARSHIP
• *See page 102*

SCARLETT FAMILY FOUNDATION SCHOLARSHIP PROGRAM

http://www.scarlettfoundation.org/

SCHOLARSHIP FOR STUDENTS PURSUING A BUSINESS OR STEM DEGREE
• *See page 80*

STRAIGHT NORTH

https://www.straightnorth.com/

STRAIGHT NORTH STEM SCHOLARSHIP
• *See page 81*

UNITED NEGRO COLLEGE FUND

http://www.uncf.org/

LEIDOS STEM SCHOLARSHIP
• *See page 96*

NUCLEAR SCIENCE

AMERICAN CHEMICAL SOCIETY, RUBBER DIVISION

http://www.rubber.org/

AMERICAN CHEMICAL SOCIETY, RUBBER DIVISION UNDERGRADUATE SCHOLARSHIP
• *See page 105*

AMERICAN INDIAN SCIENCE AND ENGINEERING SOCIETY

http://www.aises.org/

A.T. ANDERSON MEMORIAL SCHOLARSHIP PROGRAM
• *See page 105*

AMERICAN LEGION DEPARTMENT OF MARYLAND

http://www.mdlegion.org/

AMERICAN LEGION DEPARTMENT OF MARYLAND MATH-SCIENCE SCHOLARSHIP
• *See page 99*

AMERICAN SOCIETY OF NAVAL ENGINEERS

http://www.navalengineers.org/

AMERICAN SOCIETY OF NAVAL ENGINEERS SCHOLARSHIP
• *See page 106*

ARIZONA HYDROLOGICAL SOCIETY

http://www.azhydrosoc.org/

ARIZONA HYDROLOGICAL SOCIETY SCHOLARSHIP
• *See page 200*

BARRY GOLDWATER SCHOLARSHIP AND EXCELLENCE IN EDUCATION FOUNDATION

https://goldwater.scholarsapply.org

BARRY M. GOLDWATER SCHOLARSHIP AND EXCELLENCE IN EDUCATION PROGRAM
• *See page 107*

BHW GROUP

https://thebhwgroup.com/

BHW WOMEN IN STEM SCHOLARSHIP
• *See page 107*

CARDS AGAINST HUMANITY

https://cardsagainsthumanity.com/

SCIENCE AMBASSADOR SCHOLARSHIP
• *See page 107*

DISTIL NETWORKS

http://www.distilnetworks.com

WOMEN FORWARD IN TECHNOLOGY SCHOLARSHIP PROGRAM
• *See page 108*

GREAT MINDS IN STEM

http://www.greatmindsinstem.org/college/scholarship-application-information

HENAAC SCHOLARSHIP PROGRAM

INTERNATIONAL SOCIETY OF EXPLOSIVES ENGINEERS

http://www.isee.org/

JERRY MCDOWELL FUND

NASA IDAHO SPACE GRANT CONSORTIUM

http://www.idahospacegrant.org

NASA IDAHO SPACE GRANT CONSORTIUM SCHOLARSHIP PROGRAM

NASA MINNESOTA SPACE GRANT CONSORTIUM

https://www.mnspacegrant.org/

MINNESOTA SPACE GRANT CONSORTIUM SCHOLARSHIP PROGRAM

NATIONAL INSTITUTES OF HEALTH

https://www.training.nih.gov/programs/ugsp

NIH UNDERGRADUATE SCHOLARSHIP PROGRAM FOR STUDENTS FROM DISADVANTAGED BACKGROUNDS

NEXTSTEPU

http://www.nextstepu.com/

$1,500 STEM SCHOLARSHIP

NOVUS BIOLOGICALS, LLC

https://www.novusbio.com

NOVUS BIOLOGICALS SCHOLARSHIP PROGRAM

R&D SYSTEMS SCHOLARSHIP

TOCRIS BIOSCIENCE SCHOLARSHIP

SCARLETT FAMILY FOUNDATION SCHOLARSHIP PROGRAM

http://www.scarlettfoundation.org/

SCHOLARSHIP FOR STUDENTS PURSUING A BUSINESS OR STEM DEGREE

STRAIGHT NORTH

https://www.straightnorth.com/

STRAIGHT NORTH STEM SCHOLARSHIP

TAILOR MADE LAWNS

http://www.tailormadelawns.com

2017 TAILOR MADE LAWNS SCHOLARSHIP FUND

UNITED NATIONS ASSOCIATION OF CONNECTICUT

http://www.unausa.org

UNITED NATIONS ASSOCIATION OF CONNECTICUT SCHOLARSHIP

UNITED NEGRO COLLEGE FUND

http://www.uncf.org/

LEIDOS STEM SCHOLARSHIP

NURSING

101ST AIRBORNE DIVISION ASSOCIATION

http://www.screamingeaglefoundation.org/

AL & WILLIAMARY VISTE SCHOLARSHIP

ACLS CERTIFICATION INSTITUTE

https://acls.com

MEDICAL SCHOOL SCHOLARSHIP

ALBERTA HERITAGE SCHOLARSHIP FUND

http://www.alis.alberta.ca/

ABORIGINAL HEALTH CAREERS BURSARY

AMARILLO AREA FOUNDATION

http://www.amarilloareafoundation.org/

E. EUGENE WAIDE, MD MEMORIAL SCHOLARSHIP
Scholarship for graduating senior from Ochiltree, Hansford, Lipscomb, Hutchinson, Roberts or Hemphill counties. Applicant must pursue a career as LVN, BSN (junior or senior), or MSN.

Academic Fields/Career Goals: Nursing.

Award: Scholarship for use in freshman, sophomore, junior, senior, or graduate years; not renewable.

Eligibility Requirements: Applicant must be enrolled or expecting to enroll full- or part-time at a two-year or four-year or technical institution or university and resident of Texas. Available to U.S. citizens.

Application Requirements: Application form, personal photograph. *Deadline:* February 1.

Contact: Scholarship Screening Committee
Phone: 806-376-4521
Fax: 806-373-3656

NANCY GERALD MEMORIAL NURSING SCHOLARSHIP

Scholarship of $500 for graduating senior from one of the 26 counties in Texas. Applicant must be majoring in the field of nursing at Amarillo College or West Texas A & M University pursuing AAS, BSN, or MSN degree.

Academic Fields/Career Goals: Nursing.

Award: Scholarship for use in freshman, sophomore, junior, senior, or graduate years; not renewable. *Amount:* $500.

Eligibility Requirements: Applicant must be enrolled or expecting to enroll full- or part-time at a two-year or four-year institution or university; resident of Texas and studying in Texas. Available to U.S. citizens.

Application Requirements: Application form, personal photograph. *Deadline:* February 1.

Contact: Scholarship Screening Committee
Phone: 806-376-4521
Fax: 806-373-3656

AMERICAN INDIAN SCIENCE AND ENGINEERING SOCIETY

http://www.aises.org/

A.T. ANDERSON MEMORIAL SCHOLARSHIP PROGRAM
• *See page 105*

AMERICAN LEGION AUXILIARY DEPARTMENT OF ARIZONA

http://wwwaladeptaz.org

AMERICAN LEGION AUXILIARY DEPARTMENT OF ARIZONA NURSES' SCHOLARSHIPS

Award for Arizona residents enrolled in their second year at an institution in Arizona awarding degrees as a registered nurse. Preference given to immediate family member of a veteran. Must be a U.S. citizen and resident of Arizona for one year.

Academic Fields/Career Goals: Nursing.

Award: Scholarship for use in freshman, sophomore, junior, senior, or graduate years; not renewable. *Number:* 4. *Amount:* $600.

Eligibility Requirements: Applicant must be enrolled or expecting to enroll full- or part-time at a two-year or four-year or technical institution or university; resident of Arizona and studying in Arizona. Available to U.S. citizens.

Application Requirements: Application form, essay, financial need analysis, personal photograph. *Deadline:* May 15.

Contact: Mrs. Barbara Matteson, Department Secretary and Treasurer
American Legion Auxiliary Department of Arizona
4701 North 19th Avenue, Suite 100
Phoenix, AZ 85015-3727
Phone: 602-241-1080
E-mail: secretary@aladeptaz.org

AMERICAN LEGION AUXILIARY DEPARTMENT OF CALIFORNIA

http://www.calegionaux.org/

AMERICAN LEGION AUXILIARY DEPARTMENT OF CALIFORNIA PAST PRESIDENTS' PARLEY NURSING SCHOLARSHIPS

Award for student entering into or continuing studies in a nursing program.

Academic Fields/Career Goals: Nursing.

Award: Scholarship for use in freshman, sophomore, junior, or senior years; not renewable. *Number:* 1–2. *Amount:* $4000–$4000.

Eligibility Requirements: Applicant must be enrolled or expecting to enroll full- or part-time at a four-year institution or university and resident of California. Available to U.S. citizens. Applicant must have general military experience.

Application Requirements: Application form, recommendations or references, transcript. *Deadline:* April 4.

Contact: Ruby Kapsalis, Secretary/Treasurer
Phone: 415-862-5092
Fax: 415-861-8365
E-mail: calegionaux@calegionaux.org

AMERICAN LEGION AUXILIARY DEPARTMENT OF COLORADO

http://www.alacolorado.com

AMERICAN LEGION AUXILIARY DEPARTMENT OF COLORADO PAST PRESIDENTS' PARLEY HEALTH CARE PROFESSIONAL SCHOLARSHIPNURSES SCHOLARSHIP
• *See page 125*

AMERICAN LEGION AUXILIARY DEPARTMENT OF IDAHO

http://www.idahoala.org/

AMERICAN LEGION AUXILIARY DEPARTMENT OF IDAHO NURSING SCHOLARSHIP

Scholarship available to veterans or the children of veterans who are majoring in nursing. Applicants must be 17 to 35 years of age and residents of Idaho for five years prior to applying. One-time award of $1000.

Academic Fields/Career Goals: Nursing.

Award: Scholarship for use in freshman, sophomore, junior, or senior years; not renewable. *Number:* 1. *Amount:* $1000.

Eligibility Requirements: Applicant must be age 17-35; enrolled or expecting to enroll full- or part-time at a four-year institution or university and resident of Idaho. Available to U.S. citizens. Applicant or parent must meet one or more of the following requirements: general military experience; retired from active duty; disabled or killed as a result of military service; prisoner of war; or missing in action.

Application Requirements: Application form, financial need analysis, personal photograph, recommendations or references, self-addressed stamped envelope with application, transcript. *Deadline:* May 15.

Contact: Mary Sue Chase, Secretary
American Legion Auxiliary Department of Idaho
905 Warren Street
Boise, ID 83706-3825
Phone: 208-342-7066
Fax: 208-342-7066
E-mail: idalegionaux@msn.com

AMERICAN LEGION AUXILIARY DEPARTMENT OF IOWA

http://www.iowaala.org

AMERICAN LEGION AUXILIARY DEPARTMENT OF IOWA M.V. MCCRAE MEMORIAL NURSES MERIT AWARD

One-time award available to the child of an Iowa American Legion Post member or Iowa American Legion Auxiliary Unit member. Award is for full-time study in an accredited nursing program. Must be U.S. citizen and Iowa resident. Must attend an Iowa institution.

Academic Fields/Career Goals: Nursing.

Award: Scholarship for use in freshman, sophomore, junior, or senior years; not renewable. *Number:* 1. *Amount:* $400.

Eligibility Requirements: Applicant must be enrolled or expecting to enroll full-time at a two-year or four-year or technical institution or university; resident of Iowa and studying in Iowa. Applicant or parent of applicant must be member of American Legion or Auxiliary. Available to U.S. citizens. Applicant or parent must meet one or more of the following requirements: general military experience; retired from active duty;

disabled or killed as a result of military service; prisoner of war; or missing in action.

Application Requirements: Application form, essay, financial need analysis, personal photograph, recommendations or references, self-addressed stamped envelope with application, test scores, transcript. *Deadline:* June 1.

Contact: Marlene Valentine, Secretary and Treasurer
American Legion Auxiliary Department of Iowa
720 Lyon Street
Des Moines, IA 50309
Phone: 515-282-7987
Fax: 515-282-7583
E-mail: alasectreas@ialegion.org

AMERICAN LEGION AUXILIARY DEPARTMENT OF MAINE

http://www.mainelegion.org/

AMERICAN LEGION AUXILIARY DEPARTMENT OF MAINE PAST PRESIDENTS' PARLEY NURSES SCHOLARSHIP

• *See page 279*

AMERICAN LEGION AUXILIARY DEPARTMENT OF MICHIGAN

http://www.michalaux.org/

AMERICAN LEGION AUXILIARY DEPARTMENT OF MICHIGAN MEDICAL CAREER SCHOLARSHIP

• *See page 279*

AMERICAN LEGION AUXILIARY DEPARTMENT OF MISSOURI

http://www.missourilegion.org/

AMERICAN LEGION AUXILIARY DEPARTMENT OF MISSOURI PAST PRESIDENTS' PARLEY SCHOLARSHIP

Scholarship of $500 is awarded to high school graduate who has chosen to study nursing. $500 will be awarded upon receipt of verification from the college that student is enrolled. The applicant must be a resident of Missouri and a member of a veteran's family. The applicant must be validated by the sponsoring unit. Check with sponsoring unit for details on required recommendation letters.

Academic Fields/Career Goals: Nursing.

Award: Scholarship for use in freshman year; not renewable. *Number:* 2. *Amount:* $500.

Eligibility Requirements: Applicant must be high school student; planning to enroll or expecting to enroll full-time at a two-year or four-year or technical institution or university and resident of Missouri. Applicant or parent of applicant must be member of American Legion or Auxiliary. Available to U.S. citizens. Applicant or parent must meet one or more of the following requirements: general military experience; retired from active duty; disabled or killed as a result of military service; prisoner of war; or missing in action.

Application Requirements: Application form, personal photograph, resume. *Deadline:* March 1.

Contact: Karen Larson, Department Secretary/Treasurer
American Legion Auxiliary Department of Missouri
600 Ellis Boulevard
Jefferson City, MO 65101
Phone: 573-636-9133
Fax: 573-635-3467
E-mail: dptmoala@embarqmail.com

AMERICAN LEGION AUXILIARY DEPARTMENT OF NORTH DAKOTA

http://www.ndlegion.org/

AMERICAN LEGION AUXILIARY DEPARTMENT OF NORTH DAKOTA PAST PRESIDENTS' PARLEY NURSES SCHOLARSHIP

One-time award for North Dakota resident who is the child, grandchild, or great-grandchild of a member of the American Legion or Auxiliary. Must be a graduate of a North Dakota high school and attending a nursing program in North Dakota. A minimum 2.5 GPA is required.

Academic Fields/Career Goals: Nursing.

Award: Scholarship for use in freshman year; not renewable. *Number:* 5. *Amount:* $500.

Eligibility Requirements: Applicant must be enrolled or expecting to enroll full- or part-time at a four-year institution or university; resident of North Dakota and studying in North Dakota. Applicant or parent of applicant must be member of American Legion or Auxiliary. Available to U.S. citizens. Applicant or parent must meet one or more of the following requirements: general military experience; retired from active duty; disabled or killed as a result of military service; prisoner of war; or missing in action.

Application Requirements: Application form, driver's license, essay, financial need analysis, self-addressed stamped envelope with application, test scores, transcript. *Deadline:* May 15.

Contact: Myrna Ronholm, Department Secretary
American Legion Auxiliary Department of North Dakota
PO Box 1060
Jamestown, ND 58402-1060
Phone: 701-253-5992
E-mail: ala-hq@ndlegion.org

AMERICAN LEGION AUXILIARY DEPARTMENT OF OHIO

http://www.alaohio.org/

AMERICAN LEGION AUXILIARY DEPARTMENT OF OHIO PAST PRESIDENTS' PARLEY NURSES SCHOLARSHIP

One-time award worth $300 to $500 for Ohio residents who are the children or grandchildren of a veteran, living or deceased. Must enroll or be enrolled in a nursing program. Application requests must be received by May 1.

Academic Fields/Career Goals: Nursing.

Award: Scholarship for use in freshman, sophomore, junior, or senior years; not renewable. *Number:* 15–20. *Amount:* $300–$500.

Eligibility Requirements: Applicant must be enrolled or expecting to enroll full-time at a two-year or four-year institution or university and resident of Ohio. Available to U.S. citizens. Applicant or parent must meet one or more of the following requirements: general military experience; retired from active duty; disabled or killed as a result of military service; prisoner of war; or missing in action.

Application Requirements: Application form, recommendations or references. *Deadline:* May 1.

Contact: Katie Tucker, Scholarship Coordinator
Phone: 740-452-8245
Fax: 740-452-2620
E-mail: ala_katie@rrohio.com

AMERICAN LEGION AUXILIARY DEPARTMENT OF OREGON

http://www.alaoregon.org/

AMERICAN LEGION AUXILIARY DEPARTMENT OF OREGON NURSES SCHOLARSHIP

One-time award for Oregon residents who are in their senior year of high school, who are the children of veterans who served during eligibility dates for American Legion membership. Must enroll in a nursing program. Contact local units for application.

Academic Fields/Career Goals: Nursing.

Award: Scholarship for use in freshman year; not renewable. *Number:* 1. *Amount:* $1500.

Eligibility Requirements: Applicant must be high school student; planning to enroll or expecting to enroll full- or part-time at a four-year institution or university and resident of Oregon. Available to U.S. citizens.

Application Requirements: Application form, essay, financial need analysis, interview. *Deadline:* March 20.

Contact: Virginia Biddle, Secretary/Treasurer
American Legion Auxiliary Department of Oregon
PO Box 1730
Wilsonville, OR 97070
Phone: 503-682-3162
E-mail: alaor@pcez.com

AMERICAN LEGION AUXILIARY DEPARTMENT OF PENNSYLVANIA

ala.pa-legion.com

AMERICAN LEGION AUXILIARY DEPARTMENT OF PENNSYLVANIA PAST DEPARTMENT PRESIDENTS' MEMORIAL SCHOLARSHIP

Renewable award of $400 given each year to high school seniors. Must be residents of Pennsylvania. Total award $1200

Academic Fields/Career Goals: Nursing.

Award: Scholarship for use in freshman, sophomore, or junior years; renewable. *Number:* 1. *Amount:* $1200.

Eligibility Requirements: Applicant must be high school student; planning to enroll or expecting to enroll full-time at a four-year institution or university; single; resident of Pennsylvania and studying in Pennsylvania. Available to U.S. citizens.

Application Requirements: Application form. *Deadline:* March 15.

Contact: Colleen Watson, Executive Secretary and Treasurer
Phone: 717-763-7545
Fax: 717-763-0617
E-mail: paalad@hotmail.com

AMERICAN LEGION DEPARTMENT OF MISSOURI

http://www.missourilegion.org/

M.D. JACK MURPHY MEMORIAL NURSES TRAINING SCHOLARSHIP

One $1,000 award is given for two successive semesters, and may, by application, be extended for two additional successive semesters. This award is available to a Missouri boy or girl training to be a Registered Nurse, and may be used in their freshman or subsequent college years. The student must have graduated in the top forty percent of their high school class or have a "C" or equivalent standing from their last college or university semester.

Academic Fields/Career Goals: Nursing.

Award: Scholarship for use in freshman year; not renewable. *Number:* 1. *Amount:* $1000.

Eligibility Requirements: Applicant must be high school student; age 20 or under; planning to enroll or expecting to enroll full-time at a two-year institution or university; single and resident of Mississippi. Available to U.S. citizens. Applicant or parent must meet one or more of the following requirements: general military experience; retired from active duty; disabled or killed as a result of military service; prisoner of war; or missing in action.

Application Requirements: Application form, financial need analysis. *Deadline:* April 20.

Contact: Mr. John Buckwalter, Chair, Education and Scholarship Committee
American Legion Department of Missouri
P.O. Box 179
Jefferson City, MO 65102-0179
Phone: 660-627-4713

ASSISTANCE LEAGUE OF THE TRIANGLE AREA

HEALTH CARE PROFESSION SCHOLARSHIP

• See page 195

ASSOCIATION ON AMERICAN INDIAN AFFAIRS, INC.

http://www.indian-affairs.org/

ELIZABETH AND SHERMAN ASCHE MEMORIAL SCHOLARSHIP FUND

• See page 93

AVACARE MEDICAL

https://avacaremedical.com

AVACARE MEDICAL SCHOLARSHIP

• See page 100

BESTNURSINGDEGREE.COM

https://www.bestnursingdegree.com

BACK TO SCHOOL NURSING SCHOLARSHIP PROGRAM

Are you ready to chase your dream of becoming a nurse, but aren't sure how you'll pay for your education? We want to help you realize your dream of becoming a nurse by offering you the chance to win a $2,500 nursing scholarship. A winner will be randomly selected from the list of all eligible candidates. We award four different scholarships each year. When one deadline ends, the next scholarship will begin. Deadlines are as follows: January 31, April 30, July 30, and October 31. Apply for the scholarship at https://www.bestnursingdegree.com/scholarship/

Academic Fields/Career Goals: Nursing.

Award: Scholarship for use in freshman, sophomore, junior, senior, graduate, or postgraduate years; not renewable. *Number:* 1. *Amount:* $2500.

Eligibility Requirements: Applicant must be age 18 and over and enrolled or expecting to enroll full- or part-time at a two-year or four-year or technical institution or university. Available to U.S. citizens.

Application Requirements: Application form. *Deadline:* continuous.

Contact: Joann Do
BestNursingDegree.com
15500 West 113th Street, Suite 200
Lenexa, KS 66219
Phone: 913-254-6742
E-mail: Joann.Do@marketing.keypathedu.com

BHW GROUP

https://thebhwgroup.com/

BHW WOMEN IN STEM SCHOLARSHIP

• See page 107

CANADIAN NURSES FOUNDATION

http://www.cnf-fiic.ca/

CANADIAN NURSES FOUNDATION SCHOLARSHIPS

Study awards are granted annually to Canadian nurses wishing to pursue education and research. Must be a Canadian citizen or permanent resident and provide proof of citizenship. Must be studying in Canada at a Canadian institution. Baccalaureate students must be full-time, masters and doctoral students may be full- or part-time. Additional restrictions vary by specific scholarship.

Academic Fields/Career Goals: Nursing.

Award: Scholarship for use in sophomore, junior, senior, graduate, or postgraduate years; not renewable. *Number:* 50–60. *Amount:* $1500–$9000.

Eligibility Requirements: Applicant must be Canadian citizen and enrolled or expecting to enroll full- or part-time at a four-year institution or university. Applicant or parent of applicant must have employment or volunteer experience in nursing.

Application Requirements: Application form. *Fee:* $30. *Deadline:* February 22.

Contact: Foundation Coordinator
Canadian Nurses Foundation
50 Driveway
Ottawa, ON
CAN
Phone: 613-680-0879 Ext. 221
E-mail: info@cnf-fiic.ca

CHRISTIANA CARE HEALTH SYSTEMS

http://www.christianacare.org/

RUTH SHAW JUNIOR BOARD SCHOLARSHIP
• See page 281

CONTINENTAL SOCIETY, DAUGHTERS OF INDIAN WARS

http://www.csdiw.org/

CONTINENTAL SOCIETY, DAUGHTERS OF INDIAN WARS SCHOLARSHIP
• See page 188

CYNTHIA E. MORGAN SCHOLARSHIP FUND (CEMS)

http://www.cemsfund.com/

CYNTHIA E. MORGAN MEMORIAL SCHOLARSHIP FUND, INC.
• See page 248

DELAWARE COMMUNITY FOUNDATION

https://delcf.org/

MARGARET A. STAFFORD NURSING SCHOLARSHIP

Must be a resident of Delaware to apply planning on Nursing degree

Academic Fields/Career Goals: Nursing.

Award: Scholarship for use in freshman, sophomore, or junior years; not renewable. *Number:* 1–2. *Amount:* $1000–$2000.

Eligibility Requirements: Applicant must be enrolled or expecting to enroll full- or part-time at a two-year or four-year institution or university and resident of Delaware. Available to U.S. citizens.

Application Requirements: Application form, essay, financial need analysis. *Deadline:* March 15.

Contact: Kelly Sheridan, Scholarship Administrator
Delaware Community Foundation
36 The circle
Georgetown, DE 19947
Phone: 302-856-4393
E-mail: ksheridan@delcf.org

DEPARTMENT OF THE ARMY

http://www.goarmy.com/rotc

U.S. ARMY ROTC FOUR-YEAR NURSING SCHOLARSHIP

One-time award for freshman interested in nursing and accepted into an accredited nursing program. Must join ROTC program at the institution, pass physical evaluation, and have minimum GPA of 2.5. Applicant must be a U.S. citizen and have a qualifying SAT or ACT score.

Academic Fields/Career Goals: Nursing.

Award: Scholarship for use in freshman, sophomore, junior, or senior years; renewable. *Number:* 100. *Amount:* $5000–$50,000.

Eligibility Requirements: Applicant must be age 17-26; enrolled or expecting to enroll full-time at an institution or university and studying in Alabama, Alaska, Arizona, Arkansas, California, Colorado, Connecticut, Delaware, District of Columbia, Florida, Georgia, Guam, Hawaii, Idaho, Illinois, Indiana, Iowa, Kansas, Kentucky, Louisiana, Maine, Maryland, Massachusetts, Michigan, Minnesota, Mississippi, Missouri, Montana, Nebraska, Nevada, New Hampshire, New Jersey, New Mexico, New York, North Carolina, North Dakota, Ohio, Oklahoma, Oregon, Pennsylvania, Puerto Rico, Rhode Island, South Carolina, South Dakota, Tennessee, Texas, Utah, Vermont, Virginia, Washington, West Virginia, Wisconsin, Wyoming. Available to U.S. citizens. Applicant must have national guard experience.

Application Requirements: Application form, essay, interview. *Deadline:* February 4.

Contact: Mr. John Provost, U.S. Army Cadet Command
Department of the Army
204 1st Cavalry Regiment Road
Building 1002
Fort Knox, KY 40121
Phone: 502-624-2400
Fax: 502-624-1120
E-mail: john.h.provost.civ@mail.mil

DERMATOLOGY NURSES' ASSOCIATION

http://www.dnanurse.org/

CAREER MOBILITY SCHOLARSHIP

Provides financial assistance to members of the Dermatology Nurses' Association (DNA) who are pursuing an undergraduate or graduate degree. The candidate must be a DNA member for two years, and be employed in the specialty of dermatology.

Academic Fields/Career Goals: Nursing.

Award: Scholarship for use in freshman, sophomore, junior, senior, or graduate years; not renewable. *Number:* 2. *Amount:* $2500.

Eligibility Requirements: Applicant must be enrolled or expecting to enroll full- or part-time at a four-year or technical institution or university. Applicant or parent of applicant must be member of Dermatology Nurses' Association. Applicant or parent of applicant must have employment or volunteer experience in nursing. Available to U.S. and non-U.S. citizens.

Application Requirements: Application form, essay, financial need analysis, recommendations or references, transcript. *Deadline:* August 31.

Contact: DNA Recognition Program
Dermatology Nurses' Association
15000 Commerce Parkway
Suite C
Mount Laurel, NJ 08054
Phone: 800-454-4362
Fax: 856-439-0525
E-mail: dna@dnanurse.org

EXCEPTIONALNURSE.COM

http://www.exceptionalnurse.com/

CAROLINE SIMPSON MAHEADY SCHOLARSHIP AWARD

Scholarship of $250 awarded to a nursing student with a disability. Preference will be given to an undergraduate student, of Scottish descent, who has demonstrated a commitment to working with people with disabilities.

Academic Fields/Career Goals: Nursing.

Award: Scholarship for use in freshman, sophomore, junior, senior, graduate, or postgraduate years; not renewable. *Number:* 1. *Amount:* $250.

Eligibility Requirements: Applicant must be enrolled or expecting to enroll full-time at an institution or university. Applicant must be hearing impaired, learning disabled, physically disabled, or visually impaired. Available to U.S. citizens.

Application Requirements: Application form, essay. *Deadline:* June 1.

Contact: Scholarship Committee
ExceptionalNurse.com
ExceptionalNurse.com
13019 Coastal Circle
Palm Beach Gardens, FL 33410
E-mail: exceptionalnurse@aol.com

GENEVIEVE SARAN RICHMOND AWARD

Scholarship of $500 awarded to a nursing student with a disability.

Academic Fields/Career Goals: Nursing.

Award: Scholarship for use in freshman, sophomore, junior, senior, graduate, or postgraduate years; not renewable. *Number:* 1. *Amount:* $500.

Eligibility Requirements: Applicant must be enrolled or expecting to enroll full-time at an institution or university. Applicant must be hearing impaired, learning disabled, physically disabled, or visually impaired. Available to U.S. citizens.

Application Requirements: Application form, essay. *Deadline:* June 1.

Contact: Scholarship Committee
ExceptionalNurse.com
ExceptionalNurse.com
13019 Coastal Circle
Palm Beach Gardens, FL 33410
E-mail: exceptionalnurse@aol.com

JILL LAURA CREEDON SCHOLARSHIP AWARD

Scholarship of $500 awarded to a nursing student with a disability or medical challenge.

Academic Fields/Career Goals: Nursing.

Award: Scholarship for use in freshman, sophomore, junior, senior, graduate, or postgraduate years; not renewable. *Number:* 1. *Amount:* $500.

Eligibility Requirements: Applicant must be enrolled or expecting to enroll full-time at an institution or university. Applicant must be hearing impaired, learning disabled, physically disabled, or visually impaired. Available to U.S. citizens.

Application Requirements: Application form, essay. *Deadline:* June 1.

Contact: Scholarship Committee
ExceptionalNurse.com
ExceptionalNurse.com
13019 Coastal Circle
Palm Beach Gardens, FL 33410
E-mail: exceptionalnurse@aol.com

MARY SERRA GILI SCHOLARSHIP AWARD

Scholarship of $250 awarded to a nursing student with a disability.

Academic Fields/Career Goals: Nursing.

Award: Scholarship for use in freshman, sophomore, junior, senior, graduate, or postgraduate years; not renewable. *Number:* 1. *Amount:* $250.

Eligibility Requirements: Applicant must be enrolled or expecting to enroll full-time at an institution or university. Applicant must be hearing impaired, learning disabled, physically disabled, or visually impaired. Available to U.S. citizens.

Application Requirements: Application form, essay. *Deadline:* June 1.

Contact: Scholarship Committee
ExceptionalNurse.com
ExceptionalNurse.com
13019 Coastal Circle
Palm Beach Gardens, FL 33410
E-mail: exceptionalnurse@aol.com

PETER GILI SCHOLARSHIP AWARD

Scholarship of $500 awarded to a nursing student with a disability.

Academic Fields/Career Goals: Nursing.

Award: Scholarship for use in freshman, sophomore, junior, senior, graduate, or postgraduate years; not renewable. *Number:* 1. *Amount:* $500.

Eligibility Requirements: Applicant must be enrolled or expecting to enroll full-time at an institution or university. Applicant must be hearing impaired, learning disabled, physically disabled, or visually impaired. Available to U.S. citizens.

Application Requirements: Application form, essay. *Deadline:* June 1.

Contact: Scholarship Committee
ExceptionalNurse.com
ExceptionalNurse.com
13019 Coastal Circle
Palm Beach Gardens, FL 33410
E-mail: exceptionalnurse@aol.com

THE EXPERT INSTITUTE

https://www.theexpertinstitute.com

ANNUAL HEALTHCARE AND LIFE SCIENCES SCHOLARSHIP

• *See page 142*

FLORIDA NURSES ASSOCIATION

http://www.floridanurse.org/

AGNES NAUGHTON RN-BSN FUND

This fund is established to honor Agnes Naughton who was a lifelong FNA member and the mother of FNA Executive Director Paula Massey. She valued education and this scholarship will assist a RN who is continuing his or her education.

Academic Fields/Career Goals: Nursing.

Award: Scholarship for use in freshman, sophomore, junior, or senior years; not renewable. *Number:* 1. *Amount:* $500.

Eligibility Requirements: Applicant must be enrolled or expecting to enroll full- or part-time at an institution or university; resident of District of Columbia and studying in Florida. Available to U.S. citizens.

Application Requirements: Application form, application form may be submitted online, essay. *Deadline:* June 1.

Contact: Leslie Homsted, Communications Coordinator & Membership Specialist
Florida Nurses Association
1235 E. Concord St.
Orlando, FL 32803
Phone: 407-896-3261
E-mail: receptionist@floridanurse.org

EDNA HICKS FUND SCHOLARSHIP

Applicant should be enrolled in a nationally accredited nursing program. Must be in associate, baccalaureate, or master's degree nursing programs or doctoral programs. Preference given to nurse researchers from South Florida.

Academic Fields/Career Goals: Nursing.

Award: Scholarship for use in freshman, sophomore, junior, senior, graduate, or postgraduate years; not renewable. *Number:* 1. *Amount:* $500.

Eligibility Requirements: Applicant must be enrolled or expecting to enroll full- or part-time at a two-year institution or university; resident of District of Columbia and studying in Florida. Available to U.S. citizens.

Application Requirements: Application form, application form may be submitted online, driver's license. *Deadline:* June 1.

Contact: Leslie Homsted, Communications Coordinator & Membership Specialist
Florida Nurses Association
1235 E. Concord St.
Orlando, FL 32803
Phone: 407-896-3261
E-mail: receptionist@floridanurse.org

IONA PETTINGILL SCHOLARSHIP

The Iona Pettingill Scholarship is open to any nursing student interested in public health.

Academic Fields/Career Goals: Nursing.

Award: Scholarship for use in freshman, sophomore, junior, senior, graduate, or postgraduate years; not renewable.

Eligibility Requirements: Applicant must be enrolled or expecting to enroll full- or part-time at a two-year institution or university and resident of District of Columbia. Available to U.S. citizens.

Application Requirements: Application form, application form may be submitted online. *Deadline:* June 1.

Contact: Leslie Homsted, Communications Coordinator & Membership
Specialist
Florida Nurses Association
1235 E. Concord St.
Orlando, FL 32803
Phone: 407-896-3261
E-mail: receptionist@floridanurse.org

MARY YORK SCHOLARSHIP FUND

Need criteria for the Mary York Scholarship Fund is not restricted at this time.

Academic Fields/Career Goals: Nursing.

Award: Scholarship for use in freshman, sophomore, junior, senior, graduate, or postgraduate years; not renewable. *Number:* 1. *Amount:* $500.

Eligibility Requirements: Applicant must be enrolled or expecting to enroll full- or part-time at a two-year or technical institution or university; resident of District of Columbia and studying in Florida. Available to U.S. citizens.

Application Requirements: Application form, application form may be submitted online, essay, financial need analysis. *Deadline:* June 1.

Contact: Leslie Homsted, Communications Coordinator & Membership
Specialist
Florida Nurses Association
1235 E. Concord St.
Orlando, FL 32803
Phone: 407-896-3261
E-mail: receptionist@floridanurse.org

RUTH FINAMORE SCHOLARSHIP FUND

The Ruth Finamore Scholarship Fund is available to all levels of Florida nursing students.

Academic Fields/Career Goals: Nursing.

Award: Scholarship for use in freshman, sophomore, junior, senior, graduate, or postgraduate years; not renewable. *Number:* 1. *Amount:* $500.

Eligibility Requirements: Applicant must be enrolled or expecting to enroll full- or part-time at a two-year or technical institution or university; resident of District of Columbia and studying in Florida. Available to U.S. citizens.

Application Requirements: Application form, application form may be submitted online, driver's license, essay, financial need analysis. *Deadline:* June 1.

Contact: Leslie Homsted, Communications Coordinator & Membership
Specialist
Florida Nurses Association
1235 E. Concord St.
Orlando, FL 32803
Phone: 407-896-3261
E-mail: receptionist@floridanurse.org

UNDINE SAMS AND FRIENDS SCHOLARSHIP FUND

The Undine Sams and Friends Scholarship Fund is available statewide to all levels of Nursing students.

Academic Fields/Career Goals: Nursing.

Award: Scholarship for use in freshman, sophomore, junior, senior, or graduate years; not renewable. *Number:* 1. *Amount:* $500.

Eligibility Requirements: Applicant must be enrolled or expecting to enroll full- or part-time at a two-year or technical institution or university; resident of District of Columbia and studying in Florida. Available to U.S. citizens.

Application Requirements: Application form, application form may be submitted online, financial need analysis. *Deadline:* June 1.

Contact: Leslie Homsted, Communications Coordinator & Membership
Specialist
Florida Nurses Association
1235 E. Concord St.
Orlando, FL 32803
Phone: 407-896-3261
E-mail: receptionist@floridanurse.org

THE FOUNDATION OF THE NATIONAL STUDENT NURSES' ASSOCIATION, INC.

https://www.forevernursing.org

BREAKTHROUGH TO NURSING SCHOLARSHIPS FOR RACIAL/ETHNIC MINORITIES

Available to minority students enrolled in nursing or pre-nursing programs. Awards based on need, scholarship, and health-related activities. Application fee of $10. Send self-addressed stamped envelope with two stamps along with application request. Number of awards varies based on donors.

Academic Fields/Career Goals: Nursing.

Award: Scholarship for use in freshman, sophomore, junior, or senior years; not renewable. *Amount:* $1000–$2500.

Eligibility Requirements: Applicant must be American Indian/Alaska Native, Asian/Pacific Islander, Black (non-Hispanic), Hispanic and enrolled or expecting to enroll full- or part-time at a two-year or four-year institution or university. Available to U.S. citizens.

Application Requirements: Application form, financial need analysis, self-addressed stamped envelope with application, transcript. *Fee:* $10. *Deadline:* January 11.

Contact: Jasmine Melendez, Scholarship and Grants Administrator
The Foundation of the National Student Nurses' Association, Inc.
45 Main Street, Suite 606
Brooklyn, NY 11201
Phone: 718-210-0705 Ext. 118
Fax: 718-797-1186
E-mail: Jasmine@nsna.org

FOUNDATION OF THE NATIONAL STUDENT NURSES' ASSOCIATION CAREER MOBILITY SCHOLARSHIP

One-time award open to registered nurses enrolled in nursing or licensed practical or vocational nurses enrolled in a program leading to licensure as a registered nurse. The award value is $1000 to $2500 and the number of awards varies. Submit copy of license. Application fee: $10. Send self-addressed stamped envelope.

Academic Fields/Career Goals: Nursing.

Award: Scholarship for use in freshman, sophomore, junior, or senior years; not renewable. *Amount:* $1000–$2500.

Eligibility Requirements: Applicant must be enrolled or expecting to enroll full- or part-time at a two-year or four-year institution or university. Available to U.S. citizens.

Application Requirements: Application form, financial need analysis, self-addressed stamped envelope with application, transcript. *Fee:* $10. *Deadline:* January 11.

Contact: Jasmine Melendez, Scholarship and Grants Administrator
The Foundation of the National Student Nurses' Association, Inc.
45 Main Street, Suite 606
Brooklyn, NY 11201
Phone: 718-210-0705 Ext. 118
Fax: 718-797-1186
E-mail: Jasmine@nsna.org

FOUNDATION OF THE NATIONAL STUDENT NURSES' ASSOCIATION GENERAL SCHOLARSHIPS

One-time award for National Student Nurses' Association members and nonmembers enrolled in nursing programs. Graduating high school seniors are not eligible. Send self-addressed stamped envelope with two stamps for application.

Academic Fields/Career Goals: Nursing.

Award: Scholarship for use in freshman, sophomore, junior, or senior years; not renewable. *Amount:* $1000–$7500.

Eligibility Requirements: Applicant must be enrolled or expecting to enroll full- or part-time at a two-year institution or university. Available to U.S. citizens.

Application Requirements: Application form, application form may be submitted online, financial need analysis. *Fee:* $10. *Deadline:* January 17.

Contact: Jasmine Melendez, Scholarship and Grants Administrator
The Foundation of the National Student Nurses' Association, Inc.
45 Main Street, Suite 606
Brooklyn, NY 11201
Phone: 718-210-0705 Ext. 118
Fax: 718-797-1186
E-mail: Jasmine@nsna.org

FOUNDATION OF THE NATIONAL STUDENT NURSES' ASSOCIATION SPECIALTY SCHOLARSHIP

One-time award available to students currently enrolled in a state-approved school of nursing or prenursing. Must have interest in a specialty area of nursing. The award value is $1000 to $2500 and the number of awards granted varies.

Academic Fields/Career Goals: Nursing.

Award: Scholarship for use in freshman, sophomore, junior, or senior years; not renewable. *Amount:* $1000–$2500.

Eligibility Requirements: Applicant must be enrolled or expecting to enroll full- or part-time at a two-year or four-year institution or university. Available to U.S. citizens.

Application Requirements: Application form, financial need analysis, self-addressed stamped envelope with application, transcript. *Fee:* $10. *Deadline:* January 11.

Contact: Jasmine Melendez, Scholarship and Grants Administrator
The Foundation of the National Student Nurses' Association, Inc.
45 Main Street, Suite 606
Brooklyn, NY 11201
Phone: 718-210-0705 Ext. 118
Fax: 718-797-1186
E-mail: Jasmine@nsna.org

PROMISE OF NURSING SCHOLARSHIP

Applicants attending nursing school in Arizona, California, Maryland, New Jersey, Oregon, Pennsylvania, South Carolina, Tennessee, Texas and Washington are eligible. Number of awards granted varies.

Academic Fields/Career Goals: Nursing.

Award: Scholarship for use in freshman, sophomore, junior, or senior years; renewable. *Amount:* $1000–$7500.

Eligibility Requirements: Applicant must be enrolled or expecting to enroll full- or part-time at a two-year institution or university and studying in Arizona, California, Florida, Georgia, Illinois, Maryland, Massachusetts, Michigan, New Jersey, Oregon, Pennsylvania, South Carolina, Tennessee, Texas, Washington. Available to U.S. citizens.

Application Requirements: Application form, financial need analysis. *Fee:* $10. *Deadline:* January 17.

Contact: Jasmine Melendez, Scholarship and Grants Administrator
The Foundation of the National Student Nurses' Association, Inc.
45 Main Street, Suite 606
Brooklyn, NY 11201
Phone: 718-210-0705 Ext. 118
Fax: 718-797-1186
E-mail: Jasmine@nsna.org

GENESIS HEALTH SERVICES FOUNDATION

http://www.genesishealth.com/

GALA NURSING SCHOLARSHIPS

Scholarships of $6000 for up to five recipients who are seeking admission to, or have been accepted into, an undergraduate Baccalaureate program in nursing.

Academic Fields/Career Goals: Nursing.

Award: Scholarship for use in freshman, sophomore, junior, or senior years; not renewable. *Number:* up to 5. *Amount:* $6000.

Eligibility Requirements: Applicant must be enrolled or expecting to enroll full-time at a four-year institution or university; resident of Illinois, Iowa and studying in Illinois, Iowa. Available to U.S. citizens.

Application Requirements: Application form, transcript. *Deadline:* March 8.

Contact: Melinda Gowey, Executive Director
Phone: 563-421-6865
Fax: 563-421-6869
E-mail: goweym@genesishealth.com

GOOD SAMARITAN FOUNDATION

http://www.gsftx.org/

GOOD SAMARITAN BSN AND POST-BACCALAUREATE SCHOLARSHIP

Scholarship for nursing students in their clinical level of education. Must be a resident of Texas and plan to work in a U.S. health-care system. Deadlines: Spring - 5/31; Summer - 9/15; Fall - 12/31.

Academic Fields/Career Goals: Nursing.

Award: Scholarship for use in freshman, sophomore, junior, senior, graduate, or postgraduate years; renewable. *Amount:* $1000.

Eligibility Requirements: Applicant must be enrolled or expecting to enroll full-time at a four-year institution or university and resident of Texas. Available to U.S. and non-U.S. citizens.

Application Requirements: Application form, personal photograph.

Contact: Kay Crawford, Scholarship Director
Phone: 713-529-4646
Fax: 713-521-1169
E-mail: kcrawford@gsftx.org

GREAT MINDS IN STEM

http://www.greatmindsinstem.org/college/scholarship-application-information

HENAAC SCHOLARSHIP PROGRAM

• *See page 100*

GREEN LAW FIRM

https://billgreen.law

GREEN LAW FIRM NURSING HOME & ELDERLY CARE SCHOLARSHIP

Attorney Bill Green and his team at Green Law Firm are committed to improving the quality of care in nursing homes. With over 26 years of experience serving the community and many years fighting against low standards of elderly care, Bill is dedicated to promoting passionate students who are focused on making care homes a 'home' for our senior population. We are pleased to be offering a $1500 nursing scholarship to high-achieving students who are committed to elderly care and pursuing a Baccalaureate degree in nursing. Our hope is to further their professional development and continued competence, allowing them to improve the quality of life for seniors at nursing homes. Applicants will be judged on the content of their application, the essay they provide and on their academic merits. Candidates must be working at a nursing home or in an industry directly related to elderly care and pursuing a Bachelor of Science in Nursing Degree (BSN), including those who already hold a RN certification. Must submit an official copy of their transcript, application and essay. No minimum GPA required.

Academic Fields/Career Goals: Nursing.

Award: Scholarship for use in freshman, sophomore, junior, or senior years; not renewable. *Number:* 1. *Amount:* $1500.

Eligibility Requirements: Applicant must be enrolled or expecting to enroll full- or part-time at a four-year institution or university. Applicant or parent of applicant must have employment or volunteer experience in nursing. Available to U.S. and non-U.S. citizens.

Application Requirements: Application form, essay. *Deadline:* December 31.

Contact: Judi McCabe, Director of Operations
Green Law Firm
3511 Rivers Avenue
North Charleston, SC 29405
Phone: 843-747-2455
E-mail: marketing@billgreen.law

HEALTH PROFESSIONS EDUCATION FOUNDATION

http://www.healthprofessions.ca.gov/

ASSOCIATE DEGREE NURSING SCHOLARSHIP PROGRAM

One-time award to nursing students accepted to or enrolled in associate degree nursing programs. Eligible applicants may receive up to $8,000 per year in financial assistance. Deadlines: Check website http://oshpd.ca.gov/HPEF/. Must be a resident of California. Minimum 2.0 GPA.

Academic Fields/Career Goals: Nursing.

Award: Scholarship for use in freshman, sophomore, junior, or senior years; not renewable. *Amount:* $8000.

Eligibility Requirements: Applicant must be enrolled or expecting to enroll full- or part-time at a two-year institution or university; resident of British Columbia and studying in California. Available to U.S. citizens.

Application Requirements: Application form, application form may be submitted online, community service, essay, financial need analysis. *Deadline:* February 23.

Contact: Caryn Rizell, Interim Executive Director
    Phone: 916-326-3640
    Fax: 916-324-6585
    E-mail: Caryn.Rizell@oshpd.ca.gov

BACHELOR OF SCIENCE NURSING LOAN REPAYMENT PROGRAM

Repays governmental and commercial loans that were obtained for tuition expenses, books, equipment, and reasonable living expenses associated with attending college. In return for the repayment of educational debt, loan repayment recipients are required to practice full-time in direct patient care in a medically underserved area or county health facility. Must be resident of California.

Academic Fields/Career Goals: Nursing.

Award: Grant for use in senior, graduate, or postgraduate years; not renewable. *Amount:* $10,000.

Eligibility Requirements: Applicant must be enrolled or expecting to enroll full- or part-time at an institution or university; resident of British Columbia and studying in California. Available to U.S. citizens.

Application Requirements: Application form, application form may be submitted online, community service, financial need analysis. *Deadline:* October 13.

Contact: Caryn Rizell, Interim Executive Director
    Phone: 916-326-3640
    Fax: 916-324-6585
    E-mail: Caryn.Rizell@oshpd.ca.gov

BACHELOR OF SCIENCE NURSING SCHOLARSHIP PROGRAM

One-time award to nursing students accepted to or enrolled in baccalaureate degree nursing programs in California. Eligible applicants may receive up to $10,000 per year in financial assistance. Must be resident of California and a U.S. citizen. Minimum 2.0 GPA.

Academic Fields/Career Goals: Nursing.

Award: Scholarship for use in freshman, sophomore, junior, or senior years; not renewable. *Amount:* $10,000.

Eligibility Requirements: Applicant must be enrolled or expecting to enroll full- or part-time at a two-year institution or university; resident of British Columbia and studying in California. Available to U.S. citizens.

Application Requirements: Application form, application form may be submitted online, essay, financial need analysis. *Deadline:* February 23.

Contact: Caryn Rizell, Interim Executive Director
    Phone: 916-326-3640
    Fax: 916-324-6585
    E-mail: Caryn.Rizell@oshpd.ca.gov

LICENSED VOCATIONAL NURSE TO ASSOCIATE DEGREE NURSING SCHOLARSHIP PROGRAM

Scholarships are available to students who are enrolled or accepted in an accredited Vocational Nurse program. Eligible applicants may receive up to $8,000 per year in financial assistance. Deadlines: Check website http://oshpd.ca.gov/HPEF/. Must be a resident of California. Minimum 2.0 GPA.

Academic Fields/Career Goals: Nursing.

Award: Scholarship for use in freshman or sophomore years; not renewable. *Amount:* $4000–$8000.

Eligibility Requirements: Applicant must be enrolled or expecting to enroll full- or part-time at a two-year or technical institution and resident of British Columbia. Available to U.S. citizens.

Application Requirements: Application form, application form may be submitted online, community service, essay, financial need analysis. *Deadline:* February 23.

Contact: Caryn Rizell, Interim Executive Director
    Phone: 916-326-3640
    Fax: 916-324-6585
    E-mail: Caryn.Rizell@oshpd.ca.gov

HEALTH RESEARCH COUNCIL OF NEW ZEALAND

https://gateway.hrc.govt.nz/

PACIFIC HEALTH WORKFORCE AWARD
• See page 277

PACIFIC MENTAL HEALTH WORK FORCE AWARD
• See page 277

ILLINOIS NURSES ASSOCIATION

http://www.illinoisnurses.com/

SONNE SCHOLARSHIP

One-time award of up to $3000 available to nursing students. Funds may be used to cover tuition, fees, or any other cost encountered by students enrolled in Illinois state-approved nursing program. Award limited to U.S. citizens who are residents of Illinois. Recipients will receive a year's free membership in INA upon graduation.

Academic Fields/Career Goals: Nursing.

Award: Scholarship for use in freshman, sophomore, junior, or senior years; not renewable. *Number:* 2–4. *Amount:* $1000–$3000.

Eligibility Requirements: Applicant must be enrolled or expecting to enroll full-time at a four-year institution or university; resident of Illinois and studying in Illinois. Available to U.S. citizens.

Application Requirements: Application form, essay, financial need analysis, recommendations or references, transcript. *Deadline:* March 15.

Contact: Melinda Sweeney, Sonne Scholarship Committee
    Illinois Nurses Association
    105 West Adams Street, Suite 2101
    Chicago, IL 60603
    Phone: 312-419-2900 Ext. 222
    Fax: 312-419-2920
    E-mail: msweeney@illinoisnurses.com

INDIANA HEALTH CARE POLICY INSTITUTE

http://www.ihca.org/

INDIANA HEALTH CARE POLICY INSTITUTE NURSING SCHOLARSHIP

Scholarship is for students pursuing a career in long-term care. One-time award of up to $5000 for Indiana residents studying nursing at an institution in Indiana, Ohio, Kentucky, Illinois or Michigan. Minimum 2.5 GPA required. Total number of awards varies.

Academic Fields/Career Goals: Nursing.

Award: Scholarship for use in freshman, sophomore, junior, or senior years; not renewable. *Number:* 1–5. *Amount:* $750–$5000.

Eligibility Requirements: Applicant must be enrolled or expecting to enroll full- or part-time at a two-year or four-year or technical institution or university; resident of Indiana and studying in Illinois, Indiana, Kentucky, Michigan, Ohio. Available to U.S. citizens.

Application Requirements: Application form, essay, interview, recommendations or references, transcript. *Deadline:* May 13.

Contact: Dorothy Henry, Executive Director
Indiana Health Care Policy Institute
One North Capitol Avenue, Suite 100
Indianapolis, IN 46204
Phone: 317-616-9028
Fax: 877-298-3749
E-mail: dhenry@ihca.org

INDIAN HEALTH SERVICES, UNITED STATES DEPARTMENT OF HEALTH AND HUMAN SERVICES

http://www.ihs.gov/scholarship

HEALTH PROFESSIONS PREPARATORY SCHOLARSHIP PROGRAM
• *See page 137*

INTERNATIONAL ORDER OF THE KING'S DAUGHTERS AND SONS

http://www.iokds.org/

HEALTH CAREERS SCHOLARSHIP
• *See page 197*

THE JACKSON LABORATORY

https://www.jax.org

THE JACKSON LABORATORY COLLEGE SCHOLARSHIP PROGRAM
• *See page 108*

KANSAS NURSES FOUNDATION

KANSAS NURSES FOUNDATION
• *See page 211*

KETAMINE CLINICS OF LOS ANGELES

http://www.ketamineclinics.com/

KETAMINE CLINICS OF LOS ANGELES SCHOLARSHIP PROGRAM
• *See page 138*

LADIES AUXILIARY TO THE VETERANS OF FOREIGN WARS, DEPARTMENT OF MAINE

http://mainevfw.org/

FRANCES L. BOOTH MEDICAL SCHOLARSHIP SPONSORED BY LAVFW DEPARTMENT OF MAINE
• *See page 283*

LAW FIRM OF JACK TOLLIVER, MD & ASSOCIATES, PLLC

http://www.kymedicalmalpractice.com

TOLLIVER ANNUAL NURSING SCHOLARSHIP
Open to current high school seniors living in Kentucky, currently attending a Kentucky high school, and interested in pursuing a nursing degree. Applicants must be applying to a Kentucky college or university offering an accredited program of study in nursing. Apply through online application only.
Academic Fields/Career Goals: Nursing.
Award: Scholarship for use in freshman year; not renewable. *Number:* 5. *Amount:* $1000.

Eligibility Requirements: Applicant must be high school student; planning to enroll or expecting to enroll full- or part-time at a two-year or four-year institution or university; resident of Kentucky and studying in Kentucky. Available to U.S. citizens.
Application Requirements: Application form, essay. *Deadline:* March 15.
Contact: Nick Gowen
Phone: 502-827-1588
E-mail: nick@kymedicalmalpractice.com

MEDICAL SCRUBS COLLECTION

http://medicalscrubscollection.com

MEDICAL SCRUBS COLLECTION SCHOLARSHIP
• *See page 104*

MISSISSIPPI NURSES' ASSOCIATION (MNA)

http://www.msnurses.org/

MISSISSIPPI NURSES' ASSOCIATION FOUNDATION SCHOLARSHIP
Scholarship of $1000 to a Mississippi resident. Applicant should major in nursing and be a member of MASN.
Academic Fields/Career Goals: Nursing.
Award: Scholarship for use in freshman, sophomore, junior, or senior years; not renewable. *Number:* 1. *Amount:* $1000.
Eligibility Requirements: Applicant must be enrolled or expecting to enroll full- or part-time at a four-year institution or university and resident of Mississippi. Available to U.S. citizens.
Application Requirements: Application form, essay, recommendations or references, transcript. *Deadline:* October 1.
Contact: Scholarship Committee
Mississippi Nurses' Association (MNA)
31 Woodgreen Place
Madison, MS 39110
Phone: 601-898-0850
E-mail: foundation@msnurses.org

MOUNT SINAI HOSPITAL DEPARTMENT OF NURSING

http://www.mountsinai.org/

BSN STUDENT SCHOLARSHIP/WORK REPAYMENT PROGRAM
$3000 award for senior nursing student or in the last semester/year of the program. Minimum GPA is 3.25.
Academic Fields/Career Goals: Nursing.
Award: Scholarship for use in senior year; not renewable. *Amount:* $3000.
Eligibility Requirements: Applicant must be enrolled or expecting to enroll full-time at a four-year institution or university. Available to U.S. citizens.
Application Requirements: Application form, recommendations or references, resume, transcript. *Deadline:* October 1.
Contact: Maria Vezina, Director, Nursing Education and Recruitment
Mount Sinai Hospital Department of Nursing
One Gustave Levy Place, PO Box 1144
New York, NY 10029

NATIONAL AMERICAN ARAB NURSES ASSOCIATION

http://www.n-aana.org

NATIONAL AMERICAN ARAB NURSES ASSOCIATION SCHOLARSHIPS
The National American Arab Nurses Association (NAANA) annual scholarships, awarded to the most meritorious applicants who are engaged in studying nursing at the Associate degree, Bachelor degree,

RN-BSN, or BSN-MSN (Master of Science in Nursing) levels. Annually $500 to $1000 scholarships are awarded, depending on the funds available in a given year. The scholarships should be applied toward tuition and/or books in the academic year they are awarded. Applicants must be enrolled in an accredited nursing program at the time of application, and should be pursuing a nursing program during the year for which the award is made. In order to be eligible, applicants must be of Arab heritage, citizens or permanent residents of the United States, and must reside within the US or its territories; further, applicants must be members of NAANA. Major criteria to be used by the selection committee are 1. academic excellence, exemplified by achievement of a grade point average (GPA) of 3.0 or its equivalent; 2. demonstrated leadership, academic, professional, and/or through student organizations; and 3. evidence of engagement in and contribution to the health care of the Arab American community. Prior recipients of this scholarship are not eligible to apply during the same degree as the first award.

Academic Fields/Career Goals: Nursing.

Award: Scholarship for use in freshman, sophomore, junior, senior, or graduate years; not renewable. *Number:* 1–4. *Amount:* $500–$1000.

Eligibility Requirements: Applicant must be of Arab heritage and Yemeni citizen and enrolled or expecting to enroll full- or part-time at a two-year or four-year institution or university. Available to U.S. citizens.

Application Requirements: Application form, essay. *Deadline:* continuous.

Contact: Mrs. Rose Khalifa, Founder and Past President
National American Arab Nurses Association
18000 West 9 Mile Road
Suite 360
Southfield, MI 48075
Phone: 313-680-5049
E-mail: rosek@metrosolutions.us

NATIONAL ASSOCIATION OF HISPANIC NURSES

http://www.nahnnet.org

NATIONAL ASSOCIATION OF HISPANIC NURSES SCHOLARSHIPS

Awards are presented to NAHN members only (must be a member for at least 6 months) enrolled in associate, diploma, baccalaureate, graduate or practical/vocational nursing programs. Selection based on current academic standing. Scholarship award recipients are a select group of Hispanic students who demonstrate promise of future professional contributions to the nursing profession and who have the potential to act as role models for other aspiring nursing students.

Academic Fields/Career Goals: Nursing.

Award: Scholarship for use in freshman, sophomore, junior, senior, or graduate years; not renewable.

Eligibility Requirements: Applicant must be of Hispanic heritage and enrolled or expecting to enroll full-time at a four-year or technical institution or university. Available to U.S. citizens.

Application Requirements: Application form, essay.

Contact: Celia Besore, Executive Director and CEO
Phone: 202-387-2477
Fax: 202-483-7183
E-mail: info@thehispanicnurses.org

NATIONAL BLACK NURSES ASSOCIATION INC.

http://www.nbna.org/

DR. HILDA RICHARDS SCHOLARSHIP

Scholarship for nurses currently enrolled in a nursing program who are members of NBNA. Applicant must have at least one full year of school remaining.

Academic Fields/Career Goals: Nursing.

Award: Scholarship for use in freshman, sophomore, junior, senior, graduate, or postgraduate years; not renewable. *Number:* 1. *Amount:* $1000–$2000.

Eligibility Requirements: Applicant must be enrolled or expecting to enroll full-time at a two-year or four-year institution or university. Applicant or parent of applicant must be member of National Black

Nurses' Association. Applicant or parent of applicant must have employment or volunteer experience in community service. Available to U.S. and non-U.S. citizens.

Application Requirements: Application form, essay, personal photograph, recommendations or references, self-addressed stamped envelope with application, transcript. *Deadline:* April 15.

Contact: Estella Lazenby, Membership Services Manager
Phone: 301-589-3200
Fax: 301-589-3223
E-mail: elazenby@nbna.org

DR. LAURANNE SAMS SCHOLARSHIP

This $5000 scholarship is awarded to a qualified NBNA member based on scholastic achievement, financial need and community service and who is in pursuit of a baccalaureate or other advanced nursing degree. The scholarship, which is named for the Founder and First President of the NBNA, has a proud and distinguished legacy. The recipient must be an individual who truly represents the leadership, the commitment to service and the scholarship of Dr. Sams.

Academic Fields/Career Goals: Nursing.

Award: Scholarship for use in freshman, sophomore, junior, senior, graduate, or postgraduate years; not renewable. *Amount:* $5000.

Eligibility Requirements: Applicant must be enrolled or expecting to enroll full-time at a two-year institution or university and must have an interest in leadership. Applicant or parent of applicant must be member of National Black Nurses' Association. Applicant or parent of applicant must have employment or volunteer experience in community service. Available to U.S. and non-U.S. citizens.

Application Requirements: Application form, essay, financial need analysis, personal photograph. *Deadline:* April 15.

Contact: Estella Lazenby, Membership Services Manager
Phone: 301-589-3200
Fax: 301-589-3223
E-mail: elazenby@nbna.org

KAISER PERMANENTE SCHOOL OF ANESTHESIA SCHOLARSHIP

Scholarship for nurses currently enrolled in a nursing program who are active members of NBNA. Must have at least one full year of school remaining.

Academic Fields/Career Goals: Nursing.

Award: Scholarship for use in freshman, sophomore, junior, senior, graduate, or postgraduate years; not renewable. *Number:* 1. *Amount:* $1000–$2000.

Eligibility Requirements: Applicant must be enrolled or expecting to enroll full-time at a two-year or four-year institution or university. Applicant or parent of applicant must be member of National Black Nurses' Association. Available to U.S. and non-U.S. citizens.

Application Requirements: Application form, essay, recommendations or references, self-addressed stamped envelope with application, transcript. *Deadline:* April 15.

Contact: Estella Lazenby, Membership Services Manager
Phone: 301-589-3200
Fax: 301-589-3223
E-mail: elazenby@nbna.org

MARTHA DUDLEY LPN/LVN SCHOLARSHIP

Scholarship available for nurses currently enrolled full-time in a nursing program and must be a member of NBNA. Applicant must have at least one full year of school remaining. Scholarships will range from $1000 to $2000.

Academic Fields/Career Goals: Nursing.

Award: Scholarship for use in freshman, sophomore, junior, senior, graduate, or postgraduate years; not renewable. *Number:* 1. *Amount:* $1000–$2000.

Eligibility Requirements: Applicant must be Black (non-Hispanic) and enrolled or expecting to enroll full-time at a two-year institution or university. Applicant or parent of applicant must be member of National Black Nurses' Association. Applicant or parent of applicant must have employment or volunteer experience in community service. Available to U.S. and non-U.S. citizens.

Application Requirements: Application form, essay, personal photograph. *Deadline:* April 15.

Contact: Estella Lazenby, Membership Services Manager
Phone: 301-589-3200
Fax: 301-589-3223
E-mail: elazenby@nbna.org

MAYO FOUNDATIONS SCHOLARSHIP

Scholarship for nurses currently enrolled full-time in a nursing program who are members of NBNA. Applicant must have at least one full year of school remaining.

Academic Fields/Career Goals: Nursing.

Award: Scholarship for use in freshman, sophomore, junior, senior, graduate, or postgraduate years; not renewable. *Number:* 1. *Amount:* $1000–$2000.

Eligibility Requirements: Applicant must be enrolled or expecting to enroll full-time at a two-year or four-year institution or university. Applicant or parent of applicant must be member of National Black Nurses' Association. Available to U.S. and non-U.S. citizens.

Application Requirements: Application form, essay, personal photograph, recommendations or references, self-addressed stamped envelope with application, transcript. *Deadline:* April 15.

Contact: Estella Lazenby, Membership Services Manager
Phone: 301-589-3200
Fax: 301-589-3223
E-mail: elazenby@nbna.org

NBNA BOARD OF DIRECTORS SCHOLARSHIP

The scholarship enables nurses to grow and better contribute their talents to the health and healthcare of communities. Candidate must be currently enrolled in a nursing program with at least one full year of school remaining and must be a member of NBNA.

Academic Fields/Career Goals: Nursing.

Award: Scholarship for use in freshman, sophomore, junior, senior, graduate, or postgraduate years; not renewable. *Amount:* $1500.

Eligibility Requirements: Applicant must be enrolled or expecting to enroll full-time at a two-year institution or university. Applicant or parent of applicant must be member of National Black Nurses' Association. Applicant or parent of applicant must have employment or volunteer experience in community service. Available to U.S. and non-U.S. citizens.

Application Requirements: Application form, essay, personal photograph. *Deadline:* April 15.

Contact: Estella Lazenby, Membership Services Manager
Phone: 301-589-3200
Fax: 301-589-3223
E-mail: elazenby@nbna.org

NURSING SPECTRUM SCHOLARSHIP

Scholarship enables nurses to grow and better contribute their talents to the health and healthcare of communities. Candidate must be currently enrolled in a nursing program and be a member of NBNA. Applicant must have at least one full year of school remaining.

Academic Fields/Career Goals: Nursing.

Award: Scholarship for use in freshman, sophomore, junior, senior, graduate, or postgraduate years; not renewable. *Number:* 1. *Amount:* $1000–$2000.

Eligibility Requirements: Applicant must be enrolled or expecting to enroll full-time at a two-year or four-year institution or university. Applicant or parent of applicant must be member of National Black Nurses' Association. Available to U.S. and non-U.S. citizens.

Application Requirements: Application form, essay, recommendations or references, self-addressed stamped envelope with application, transcript. *Deadline:* April 15.

Contact: Estella Lazenby, Membership Services Manager
Phone: 301-589-3200
Fax: 301-589-3223
E-mail: elazenby@nbna.org

NATIONAL COUNCIL OF JEWISH WOMEN - LOS ANGELES (NCJW L LA)

http://ncjwla.org/

INGER LAWRENCE-M.R. BAUER FOUNDATION NURSING STUDIES SCHOLARSHIP

This award is given to woman or man enrolled in or accepted to a degree program in nursing. Some units toward the degree are preferred, but not required. Applicants to the Inger Lawrence-M.R. Bauer award are also eligible for the June Miller Nursing Education Scholarship. The National Council of Jewish Women l Los Angeles (NCJW l LA) provides scholarships to those who live and attend school in the Greater Los Angeles area, including Los Angeles, Orange, Riverside, and Ventura Counties.

Academic Fields/Career Goals: Nursing.

Award: Scholarship for use in freshman, sophomore, junior, senior, or graduate years; not renewable. *Number:* 2. *Amount:* $2000.

Eligibility Requirements: Applicant must be enrolled or expecting to enroll full- or part-time at an institution or university; resident of British Columbia and studying in California, Nevada. Available to U.S. citizens.

Application Requirements: Application form, application form may be submitted online, essay, financial need analysis. *Deadline:* May 1.

Contact: Carrie Jacoves, Director of Operations and Outreach
National Council of Jewish Women - Los Angeles (NCJW l LA)
543 N. Fairfax Ave.
Los Angeles, CA 90036
Phone: 323-651-2930
Fax: 323-651-5348
E-mail: carrie@ncjwla.org

JUNE MILLER NURSING EDUCATION SCHOLARSHIP

This award is given to woman or man enrolled in or accepted to a degree program in nursing. Some units toward the degree are preferred, but not required. Applicants to the June Miller Nursing Education Scholarship are also eligible for the Inger Lawrence-M.R. Bauer award. The National Council of Jewish Women l Los Angeles (NCJW l LA) provides scholarships to those who live and attend school in the Greater Los Angeles area, including Los Angeles, Orange, Riverside, and Ventura Counties.

Academic Fields/Career Goals: Nursing.

Award: Scholarship for use in freshman, sophomore, junior, senior, or graduate years; not renewable. *Number:* 4. *Amount:* $2000.

Eligibility Requirements: Applicant must be enrolled or expecting to enroll full- or part-time at a two-year institution or university; resident of British Columbia and studying in California. Available to U.S. citizens.

Application Requirements: Application form, application form may be submitted online, essay, financial need analysis. *Deadline:* May 1.

Contact: Carrie Jacoves, Director of Operations and Outreach
National Council of Jewish Women - Los Angeles (NCJW l LA)
543 N. Fairfax Ave.
Los Angeles, CA 90036
Phone: 323-651-2930
Fax: 323-651-5348
E-mail: carrie@ncjwla.org

NATIONAL INSTITUTES OF HEALTH

https://www.training.nih.gov/programs/ugsp

NIH UNDERGRADUATE SCHOLARSHIP PROGRAM FOR STUDENTS FROM DISADVANTAGED BACKGROUNDS
• *See page 101*

NATIONAL SOCIETY DAUGHTERS OF THE AMERICAN REVOLUTION

http://www.dar.org/

CAROLINE E. HOLT NURSING SCHOLARSHIP

A one-time $2,500 award is given to three students who are in financial need and who have been accepted or is currently enrolled in an accredited school of nursing. A letter of acceptance into a nursing program or a transcript stating the applicant is in a nursing program must be included with the application.

Academic Fields/Career Goals: Nursing.

Award: Scholarship for use in freshman, sophomore, junior, or senior years; not renewable. *Number:* 3. *Amount:* $2500.

Eligibility Requirements: Applicant must be enrolled or expecting to enroll full-time at a two-year institution or university. Available to U.S. citizens.

Application Requirements: Application form, application form may be submitted online, essay, financial need analysis. *Deadline:* February 15.

Contact: Lakeisha Graham, Manager, Office of the Reporter General
Phone: 202-628-1776
Fax: 202-879-3348
E-mail: nsdarscholarships@dar.org

MADELINE PICKETT (HALBERT) COGSWELL NURSING SCHOLARSHIP

Scholarship available to students who have been accepted or are currently enrolled in an accredited school of nursing, who are members of NSDAR, descendants of members of NSDAR, or are eligible to be members of NSDAR. A letter of acceptance into the nursing program or transcript showing enrollment in nursing program must be included with the application. DAR member number must be on the application.

Academic Fields/Career Goals: Nursing.

Award: Scholarship for use in freshman, sophomore, junior, or senior years; not renewable. *Number:* 2. *Amount:* $2500.

Eligibility Requirements: Applicant must be enrolled or expecting to enroll full-time at a two-year institution or university. Applicant or parent of applicant must be member of Daughters of the American Revolution. Available to U.S. and non-U.S. citizens.

Application Requirements: Application form, essay. *Deadline:* February 15.

Contact: Lakeisha Graham, Manager, Office of the Reporter General
Phone: 202-628-1776
Fax: 202-879-3348
E-mail: nsdarscholarships@dar.org

THE NATIONAL SOCIETY OF THE COLONIAL DAMES OF AMERICA

http://www.nscda.org/

AMERICAN INDIAN NURSE SCHOLARSHIP PROGRAM
• See page 278

NEW JERSEY STATE NURSES ASSOCIATION

http://www.njsna.org/

INSTITUTE FOR NURSING SCHOLARSHIP

Applicants must be New Jersey residents currently enrolled in a diploma, associate, baccalaureate, master's, or doctoral program in nursing or a related field. The amount awarded in each scholarship will be $1000 per recipient.

Academic Fields/Career Goals: Nursing.

Award: Scholarship for use in freshman, sophomore, junior, senior, graduate, or postgraduate years; not renewable. *Number:* 10. *Amount:* $1000.

Eligibility Requirements: Applicant must be high school student; planning to enroll or expecting to enroll full- or part-time at a two-year or four-year institution or university; resident of New Jersey and studying in New Jersey. Applicant or parent of applicant must have employment or volunteer experience in nursing. Available to U.S. citizens. Applicant must have general military experience.

Application Requirements: Application form, essay, financial need analysis, personal photograph. *Deadline:* February 15.

Contact: Sandy Kerr, Executive Assistant
Phone: 609-883-5335
Fax: 609-883-5343
E-mail: sandy@njsna.org

NEW YORK STATE EMERGENCY NURSES ASSOCIATION (ENA)

http://www.ena.org/

NEW YORK STATE ENA SEPTEMBER 11 SCHOLARSHIP FUND

Scholarships to rescue workers who are going to school to obtain their undergraduate nursing degree. Eligible rescue workers include prehospital care providers, fire fighters, and police officers. The scholarship is not limited geographically. The scholarship winner will also be awarded a complimentary one year ENA membership.

Academic Fields/Career Goals: Nursing.

Award: Scholarship for use in freshman, sophomore, junior, senior, graduate, or postgraduate years; not renewable. *Number:* 1. *Amount:* $2000.

Eligibility Requirements: Applicant must be enrolled or expecting to enroll full- or part-time at a four-year institution or university. Available to U.S. citizens.

Application Requirements: Application form. *Deadline:* varies.

Contact: Educational Services
Phone: 847-460-4123
Fax: 847-460-4005
E-mail: education@ena.org

NEW YORK STATE GRANGE

http://www.nysgrange.org/

JUNE GILL NURSING SCHOLARSHIP

One annual scholarship award to verified NYS Grange member pursuing a career in nursing. Selection based on verification of NYS Grange membership and enrollment in a nursing program, as well as applicant's career statement, academic records, and financial need. Payment made after successful completion of one term.

Academic Fields/Career Goals: Nursing.

Award: Scholarship for use in freshman, sophomore, junior, or senior years; not renewable. *Number:* 1. *Amount:* $1000.

Eligibility Requirements: Applicant must be enrolled or expecting to enroll full-time at a two-year or four-year institution and resident of New York. Applicant or parent of applicant must be member of Grange Association. Available to U.S. citizens.

Application Requirements: Application form, financial need analysis. *Deadline:* April 15.

Contact: Scholarship Committee
New York State Grange
100 Grange Place
Cortland, NY 13045
Phone: 607-756-7553
E-mail: nysgrange@nysgrange.org

NEXTSTEPU

http://www.nextstepu.com/

$1,500 STEM SCHOLARSHIP
• See page 104

NOVUS BIOLOGICALS, LLC

https://www.novusbio.com

NOVUS BIOLOGICALS SCHOLARSHIP PROGRAM
• See page 101

R&D SYSTEMS SCHOLARSHIP
• See page 101

TOCRIS BIOSCIENCE SCHOLARSHIP
• See page 102

ODD FELLOWS AND REBEKAHS

http://www.ioofme.org/

ODD FELLOWS AND REBEKAHS ELLEN F. WASHBURN NURSES TRAINING AWARD

Award for high school seniors and college undergraduates to attend an accredited Maine institution and pursue a registered nursing degree. Must have a minimum 2.5 GPA. Can reapply for award for up to four years.

Academic Fields/Career Goals: Nursing.

Award: Scholarship for use in freshman, sophomore, junior, or senior years; renewable. *Number:* up to 30. *Amount:* $150–$400.

Eligibility Requirements: Applicant must be enrolled or expecting to enroll full- or part-time at a two-year or four-year institution or university and studying in Maine. Available to U.S. citizens.

Application Requirements: Application form, financial need analysis, personal photograph, recommendations or references. *Deadline:* April 15.

Contact: Joyce Young, Chairman
Phone: 207-839-4723

ONCOLOGY NURSING FOUNDATION

https://www.onsfoundation.org/

ONS FOUNDATION JOSH GOTTHEIL MEMORIAL BONE MARROW TRANSPLANT CAREER DEVELOPMENT AWARDS

Awards available to any professional registered nurse in field of bone marrow transplant nursing for further study in a Bachelor's or Master's program. Submit examples of contributions to BMT nursing.

Academic Fields/Career Goals: Nursing.

Award: Scholarship for use in junior, senior, or graduate years; not renewable. *Number:* 4. *Amount:* $2000.

Eligibility Requirements: Applicant must be enrolled or expecting to enroll full- or part-time at a four-year institution or university. Available to U.S. and non-U.S. citizens.

Application Requirements: Application form, essay, recommendations or references, resume. *Deadline:* December 1.

Contact: Sloane Astorino, Director of Development
Phone: 412-859-6409
E-mail: sastorino@onfgivesback.org

ONS FOUNDATION/ONCOLOGY NURSING CERTIFICATION CORPORATION BACHELOR'S SCHOLARSHIPS

One-time awards to improve oncology nursing by assisting registered nurses in furthering their education. Applicants must hold a current license to practice and be enrolled in an undergraduate nursing degree program at an NLN-accredited school.

Academic Fields/Career Goals: Nursing; Oncology.

Award: Scholarship for use in freshman, sophomore, junior, or senior years; not renewable. *Amount:* $2000.

Eligibility Requirements: Applicant must be enrolled or expecting to enroll full- or part-time at a four-year institution or university. Available to U.S. and non-U.S. citizens.

Application Requirements: Application form, transcript. *Fee:* $5. *Deadline:* February 1.

Contact: Sloane Astorino, Director of Development
Phone: 412-859-6409
E-mail: sastorino@onfgivesback.org

ONS FOUNDATION/PEARL MOORE CAREER DEVELOPMENT AWARDS

Awards to practicing staff nurses who possess or are pursuing a BSN and have two years oncology practice experience.

Academic Fields/Career Goals: Nursing; Oncology.

Award: Prize for use in junior, senior, or graduate years; not renewable. *Number:* 3. *Amount:* $3000.

Eligibility Requirements: Applicant must be enrolled or expecting to enroll full- or part-time at a four-year institution or university. Available to U.S. citizens.

Application Requirements: Application form, recommendations or references. *Deadline:* December 1.

Contact: Sloane Astorino, Director of Development
Phone: 412-859-6409
E-mail: sastorino@onfgivesback.org

OREGON COMMUNITY FOUNDATION

http://www.oregoncf.org/

FRANZ STENZEL M.D. AND KATHRYN STENZEL SCHOLARSHIP FUND

• *See page 283*

NLN ELLA MCKINNEY SCHOLARSHIP FUND

Award for Oregon high school graduates (or the equivalent) for use in the pursuit of an undergraduate or graduate nursing education. Must attend a nonprofit college or university in Oregon accredited by the NLN Accrediting Commission. For more information, see web http://www.getcollegefunds.org.

Academic Fields/Career Goals: Nursing.

Award: Scholarship for use in freshman, sophomore, junior, or senior years; renewable. *Number:* up to 2. *Amount:* $1000–$2000.

Eligibility Requirements: Applicant must be enrolled or expecting to enroll full-time at a two-year or four-year institution or university; resident of Oregon and studying in Oregon. Available to U.S. citizens.

Application Requirements: Application form, recommendations or references. *Deadline:* March 1.

Contact: Dianne Causey, Program Associate for Scholarships and Grants
Phone: 503-227-6846 Ext. 1418
E-mail: dcausey@oregoncf.org

PILOT INTERNATIONAL

https://www.pilotinternational.org/

PILOT INTERNATIONAL SCHOLARSHIP

The Pilot International Scholarship, established in 1988 to provide financial assistance to undergraduate students preparing for a career working with youth leadership and development, helping people with brain safety or fitness, or caring for families during times of need. Scholarships are awarded for financial need, academic success, and application contents. Scholarships are awarded for one academic year. A student may re-apply and be granted the Pilot International Scholarship for no more than three additional years.

Academic Fields/Career Goals: Nursing; Psychology; Special Education; Therapy/Rehabilitation.

Award: Scholarship for use in freshman, sophomore, junior, or senior years; not renewable. *Number:* 5–10. *Amount:* $500–$1500.

Eligibility Requirements: Applicant must be enrolled or expecting to enroll full-time at an institution or university. Available to U.S. citizens.

Application Requirements: Application form, application form may be submitted online, community service, essay, financial need analysis. *Deadline:* March 15.

Contact: Founders Fund Specialist
Pilot International
102 Preston Court
Macon, GA 31210
Phone: 478-4771208 Ext. 304
Fax: 478-4776978
E-mail: piffscholarships@pilothq.org

PLATINUM EDUCATIONAL GROUP

www.platinumed.com

PLATINUM EDUCATIONAL GROUP SCHOLARSHIPS PROGRAM FOR EMS, NURSING, AND ALLIED HEALTH

• *See page 102*

THE RECOVERY VILLAGE

https://www.therecoveryvillage.com/

RECOVERY VILLAGE HEALTHCARE SCHOLARSHIP
• *See page 197*

SCARLETT FAMILY FOUNDATION SCHOLARSHIP PROGRAM

http://www.scarlettfoundation.org/

SCHOLARSHIP FOR STUDENTS PURSUING A BUSINESS OR STEM DEGREE
• *See page 80*

THE SOCIETY FOR THE SCIENTIFIC STUDY OF SEXUALITY

http://www.sexscience.org/

THE SOCIETY FOR THE SCIENTIFIC STUDY OF SEXUALITY STUDENT RESEARCH GRANT
• *See page 105*

SOCIETY OF PEDIATRIC NURSES

http://www.pedsnurses.org/

SOCIETY OF PEDIATRIC NURSES EDUCATIONAL SCHOLARSHIP
• *See page 161*

SOUTH CAROLINA NURSES FOUNDATION

http://www.scnursesfoundation.org/

EVELYN JOHNSON ENTREKIN SCHOLARSHIP
This scholarship honors the late Evelyn Johnson Entrekin, a well-known leader of public health nursing in South Carolina. She served with the SCDHEC for over 20 years and led her district to become the first in the state to receive national accreditation. Funds for the Evelyn Johnson Entrekin endowment come from her estate and contributions are designated for individuals pursuing a Baccalaureate Degree in Nursing.

Academic Fields/Career Goals: Nursing.

Award: Scholarship for use in freshman, sophomore, junior, or senior years.

Eligibility Requirements: Applicant must be enrolled or expecting to enroll at an institution or university and resident of Saskatchewan. Available to U.S. citizens.

Application Requirements: Application form, application form may be submitted online, financial need analysis. *Deadline:* May 19.

STRAIGHTFORWARD MEDIA

http://www.straightforwardmedia.com/

STRAIGHTFORWARD MEDIA MEDICAL PROFESSIONS SCHOLARSHIP
• *See page 198*

STRAIGHTFORWARD MEDIA NURSING SCHOOL SCHOLARSHIP
Scholarship of $500 available to students majoring in nursing. Awarded four times per year. Deadlines are April 14, July 14, October 14, and January 14. To apply, go to http://www.straightforwardmedia.com/nursing/form.php.

Academic Fields/Career Goals: Nursing.

Award: Scholarship for use in freshman, sophomore, junior, or senior years; not renewable. *Number:* 4. *Amount:* $500.

Eligibility Requirements: Applicant must be enrolled or expecting to enroll full- or part-time at a two-year or four-year or technical institution or university. Available to U.S. and non-U.S. citizens.

Application Requirements: Essay. *Deadline:* varies.

Contact: Scholarship Committee
Phone: 605-348-3042

STRAIGHT NORTH

https://www.straightnorth.com/

STRAIGHT NORTH STEM SCHOLARSHIP
• *See page 81*

TOUCHMARK FOUNDATION

http://www.touchmarkfoundation.org/

TOUCHMARK FOUNDATION NURSING SCHOLARSHIP
Students pursuing nursing degrees at any level are encouraged to apply, including nurses interested in pursuing advanced degrees in order to teach. Applications reviewed throughout the year. Scholarships are offered to students attending schools in the following states: WI, WA, ID, OR, ND, SD, MN, OK, MT, and AZ.

Academic Fields/Career Goals: Nursing.

Award: Scholarship for use in freshman, sophomore, junior, senior, graduate, or postgraduate years; not renewable. *Number:* 8–16. *Amount:* $1000–$2000.

Eligibility Requirements: Applicant must be enrolled or expecting to enroll full-time at a four-year institution or university; resident of Arizona, Idaho, Minnesota, Montana, North Dakota, Oklahoma, Oregon, South Dakota, Washington, Wisconsin and studying in Arizona, Idaho, Minnesota, Montana, North Dakota, Oklahoma, Oregon, South Dakota, Washington, Wisconsin. Available to U.S. citizens.

Application Requirements: Application form, essay, FAFSA, copy of school acceptance letter, recommendations or references, transcript. *Deadline:* continuous.

Contact: Bret Cope, Chairman
Touchmark Foundation
5150 SW Griffith Drive
Beaverton, OR 97005
Phone: 503-646-5186
E-mail: bjc@touchmark.com

UNITED NEGRO COLLEGE FUND

http://www.uncf.org/

HCN/APRICITY RESOURCES SCHOLARS PROGRAM
• *See page 83*

LEIDOS STEM SCHOLARSHIP
• *See page 96*

U.S. DEPARTMENT OF HEALTH AND HUMAN SERVICES

https://www.hhs.gov/

SCHOLARSHIPS FOR DISADVANTAGED STUDENTS PROGRAM
• *See page 284*

VIRGINIA DEPARTMENT OF HEALTH, OFFICE OF MINORITY HEALTH AND HEALTH EQUITY

http://www.vdh.virginia.gov/

MARY MARSHALL PRACTICAL NURSING SCHOLARSHIP (LPN)
Awards for students who are accepted or enrolled as a full-time or part-time student in a practical school of nursing in the state of Virginia. Must be a Virginia resident for at least one year and have submitted a completed application form and a recommendation from the Director regarding scholastic attainment and financial need prior to June 30.

Students pursuing a nursing degree not available in Virginia, are not eligible for the scholarship. Scholarship amount varies.

Academic Fields/Career Goals: Nursing.

Award: Scholarship for use in freshman, sophomore, junior, or senior years; not renewable. *Number:* 26–88. *Amount:* $600–$1200.

Eligibility Requirements: Applicant must be age 18 and over; enrolled or expecting to enroll full- or part-time at a two-year or four-year or technical institution or university; resident of Virginia and studying in Virginia. Available to U.S. citizens.

Application Requirements: Application form, driver's license, essay, financial need analysis, recommendations or references, transcript. *Deadline:* June 30.

Contact: Miss. Sarahbeth Jones, Communications Specialist
Virginia Department of Health, Office of Minority Health and Health Equity
PO Box 2448, 109 Governor Street, Suite 1016-E
Richmond, VA 23218-2448
Phone: 804-864-7422
Fax: 804-864-7440
E-mail: IncentivePrograms@vdh.virginia.gov

MARY MARSHALL REGISTERED NURSING SCHOLARSHIPS

Scholarship for Virginia residents who have been accepted or is enrollment as a full-time or part-time student in a school of nursing in the state of Virginia. Must demonstrate financial need, verified by the Financial Aid Office/authorized person at the applicant's nursing school. Must also be a resident of Virginia for at least one year and have a minimum 3.0 GPA in required courses. Must have submitted a completed application form and an official grade transcript to The Office of Minority Health and Public Health Policy prior to June 30. If no college courses attempted an official high school transcript or equivalent must be submitted.

Academic Fields/Career Goals: Nursing.

Award: Scholarship for use in freshman, sophomore, junior, or senior years; not renewable. *Number:* 28–95. *Amount:* $600–$2000.

Eligibility Requirements: Applicant must be age 18 and over; enrolled or expecting to enroll full- or part-time at a two-year or four-year institution or university; resident of Virginia and studying in Virginia. Available to U.S. citizens.

Application Requirements: Application form, driver's license, essay, financial need analysis, recommendations or references, transcript. *Deadline:* June 30.

Contact: Miss. Sarahbeth Jones, Communications Specialist
Virginia Department of Health, Office of Minority Health and Health Equity
PO Box 2448, 109 Governor Street, Suite 1016-E
Richmond, VA 23218-2448
Phone: 804-864-7422
Fax: 804-864-7440
E-mail: IncentivePrograms@vdh.virginia.gov

WOUND, OSTOMY AND CONTINENCE NURSES SOCIETY

http://www.wocn.org

WOCN ACCREDITED NURSING EDUCATION PROGRAM SCHOLARSHIP

Scholarships are awarded to deserving individuals committed to working within the wound, ostomy and continence nursing specialty. Applicants must agree to support the WOCN Society philosophy and scope of practice. Number of scholarships and the dollar value varies annually. Deadlines: May 1 or November 1.

Academic Fields/Career Goals: Nursing.

Award: Scholarship for use in freshman, sophomore, junior, or senior years; not renewable. *Number:* 20. *Amount:* $2000.

Eligibility Requirements: Applicant must be enrolled or expecting to enroll full-time at a two-year or four-year or technical institution or university. Applicant or parent of applicant must have employment or volunteer experience in nursing. Available to U.S. and non-U.S. citizens.

Application Requirements: Application form. *Deadline:* May 1.

Contact: Heather Martinek, Assistant Executive Director
Wound, Ostomy and Continence Nurses Society
1120 Route 73
Suite 200
Mount Laurel, NJ 08054
Phone: 888-224-9626
Fax: 856-439-0525
E-mail: info@wocn.org

OCCUPATIONAL SAFETY AND HEALTH

AMERICAN INDIAN SCIENCE AND ENGINEERING SOCIETY

http://www.aises.org/

A.T. ANDERSON MEMORIAL SCHOLARSHIP PROGRAM

ASSISTANCE LEAGUE OF THE TRIANGLE AREA

HEALTH CARE PROFESSION SCHOLARSHIP

ASSOCIATION FOR EDUCATION AND REHABILITATION OF THE BLIND AND VISUALLY IMPAIRED

http://www.aerbvi.org/

WILLIAM AND DOROTHY FERRELL SCHOLARSHIP

BHW GROUP

https://thebhwgroup.com/

BHW WOMEN IN STEM SCHOLARSHIP

CONTINENTAL SOCIETY, DAUGHTERS OF INDIAN WARS

http://www.csdiw.org/

CONTINENTAL SOCIETY, DAUGHTERS OF INDIAN WARS SCHOLARSHIP

CYNTHIA E. MORGAN SCHOLARSHIP FUND (CEMS)

http://www.cemsfund.com/

CYNTHIA E. MORGAN MEMORIAL SCHOLARSHIP FUND, INC.

INTERMOUNTAIN MEDICAL IMAGING

https://www.aboutimi.com/

INTERMOUNTAIN MEDICAL IMAGING SCHOLARSHIP

INTERNATIONAL SOCIETY OF EXPLOSIVES ENGINEERS

http://www.isee.org/

JERRY MCDOWELL FUND
• *See page 156*

NATIONAL SAFETY COUNCIL

http://www.cshema.org/

CAMPUS SAFETY, HEALTH AND ENVIRONMENTAL MANAGEMENT ASSOCIATION SCHOLARSHIP AWARD PROGRAM
• *See page 254*

NOVUS BIOLOGICALS, LLC

https://www.novusbio.com

NOVUS BIOLOGICALS SCHOLARSHIP PROGRAM
• *See page 101*

R&D SYSTEMS SCHOLARSHIP
• *See page 101*

TOCRIS BIOSCIENCE SCHOLARSHIP
• *See page 102*

THE RECOVERY VILLAGE

https://www.therecoveryvillage.com/

RECOVERY VILLAGE HEALTHCARE SCHOLARSHIP
• *See page 197*

STRAIGHTFORWARD MEDIA

http://www.straightforwardmedia.com/

STRAIGHTFORWARD MEDIA MEDICAL PROFESSIONS SCHOLARSHIP
• *See page 198*

STRAIGHT NORTH

https://www.straightnorth.com/

STRAIGHT NORTH STEM SCHOLARSHIP
• *See page 81*

TEXAS DEPARTMENT OF TRANSPORTATION

http://www.txdot.gov/

CONDITIONAL GRANT PROGRAM
• *See page 167*

OCEANOGRAPHY

AMERICAN INDIAN SCIENCE AND ENGINEERING SOCIETY

http://www.aises.org/

A.T. ANDERSON MEMORIAL SCHOLARSHIP PROGRAM
• *See page 105*

AMERICAN METEOROLOGICAL SOCIETY

http://www.ametsoc.org/

FATHER JAMES B. MACELWANE ANNUAL AWARD
• *See page 251*

ASSOCIATION FOR WOMEN GEOSCIENTISTS (AWG)

http://www.awg.org/

AWG ETHNIC MINORITY SCHOLARSHIP
• *See page 200*

AWG MARIA LUISA CRAWFORD FIELD CAMP SCHOLARSHIP
• *See page 111*

AWG SALT LAKE CHAPTER (SLC) RESEARCH SCHOLARSHIP
• *See page 111*

JANET CULLEN TANAKA GEOSCIENCES UNDERGRADUATE SCHOLARSHIP
• *See page 112*

LONE STAR RISING CAREER SCHOLARSHIP
• *See page 200*

OSAGE CHAPTER UNDERGRADUATE SERVICE SCHOLARSHIP
• *See page 112*

SUSAN EKDALE MEMORIAL FIELD CAMP SCHOLARSHIP
• *See page 201*

BARRY GOLDWATER SCHOLARSHIP AND EXCELLENCE IN EDUCATION FOUNDATION

https://goldwater.scholarsapply.org

BARRY M. GOLDWATER SCHOLARSHIP AND EXCELLENCE IN EDUCATION PROGRAM
• *See page 107*

BHW GROUP

https://thebhwgroup.com/

BHW WOMEN IN STEM SCHOLARSHIP
• *See page 107*

BROWN AND CALDWELL

http://www.brownandcaldwell.com

ECKENFELDER SCHOLARSHIP
• *See page 141*

MINORITY SCHOLARSHIP PROGRAM
• *See page 141*

CARDS AGAINST HUMANITY

https://cardsagainsthumanity.com/

SCIENCE AMBASSADOR SCHOLARSHIP
• *See page 107*

DISTIL NETWORKS

http://www.distilnetworks.com

WOMEN FORWARD IN TECHNOLOGY SCHOLARSHIP PROGRAM
• *See page 108*

GREAT MINDS IN STEM

http://www.greatmindsinstem.org/college/scholarship-application-information

HENAAC SCHOLARSHIP PROGRAM
• *See page 100*

THE LAND CONSERVANCY OF NEW JERSEY

http://www.tlc-nj.org/

ROGERS FAMILY SCHOLARSHIP
• *See page 143*

RUSSELL W. MYERS SCHOLARSHIP
• *See page 143*

LOUISIANA OFFICE OF STUDENT FINANCIAL ASSISTANCE

www.osfa.la.gov/

ROCKEFELLER STATE WILDLIFE SCHOLARSHIP
• *See page 325*

MARINE TECHNOLOGY SOCIETY

http://www.mtsociety.org/

CHARLES H. BUSSMAN UNDERGRADUATE SCHOLARSHIP
• *See page 325*

JOHN C. BAJUS SCHOLARSHIP
• *See page 327*

MTS STUDENT SCHOLARSHIP FOR UNDERGRADUATE STUDENTS
• *See page 326*

PAROS-DIGIQUARTZ SCHOLARSHIP
• *See page 326*

ROV SCHOLARSHIP
• *See page 328*

NASA MINNESOTA SPACE GRANT CONSORTIUM

https://www.mnspacegrant.org/

MINNESOTA SPACE GRANT CONSORTIUM SCHOLARSHIP PROGRAM
• *See page 131*

NEXTSTEPU

http://www.nextstepu.com/

$1,500 STEM SCHOLARSHIP
• *See page 104*

NOVUS BIOLOGICALS, LLC

https://www.novusbio.com

NOVUS BIOLOGICALS SCHOLARSHIP PROGRAM
• *See page 101*

R&D SYSTEMS SCHOLARSHIP
• *See page 101*

TOCRIS BIOSCIENCE SCHOLARSHIP
• *See page 102*

SCARLETT FAMILY FOUNDATION SCHOLARSHIP PROGRAM

http://www.scarlettfoundation.org/

SCHOLARSHIP FOR STUDENTS PURSUING A BUSINESS OR STEM DEGREE
• *See page 80*

UNITED NEGRO COLLEGE FUND

http://www.uncf.org/

LEIDOS STEM SCHOLARSHIP
• *See page 96*

WOMAN'S SEAMEN'S FRIEND SOCIETY OF CONNECTICUT INC.

FINANCIAL SUPPORT FOR MARINE OR MARITIME STUDIES
• *See page 326*

YOUTH MARITIME TRAINING ASSOCIATION

http://ymta.net/

NORM MANLY—YMTA MARITIME EDUCATIONAL SCHOLARSHIPS
• *See page 326*

ONCOLOGY

AMERICAN INDIAN SCIENCE AND ENGINEERING SOCIETY

http://www.aises.org/

A.T. ANDERSON MEMORIAL SCHOLARSHIP PROGRAM
• *See page 105*

AMERICAN LEGION AUXILIARY DEPARTMENT OF COLORADO

http://www.alacolorado.com

AMERICAN LEGION AUXILIARY DEPARTMENT OF COLORADO PAST PRESIDENTS' PARLEY HEALTH CARE PROFESSIONAL SCHOLARSHIPNURSES SCHOLARSHIP
• *See page 125*

ASRT FOUNDATION

https://foundation.asrt.org/

JERMAN-CAHOON STUDENT SCHOLARSHIP
• *See page 276*

PROFESSIONAL ADVANCEMENT SCHOLARSHIP
• *See page 276*

SIEMENS CLINICAL ADVANCEMENT SCHOLARSHIP

Open to ASRT members only who are medical imaging professionals pursuing a bachelor's or master's degree in the radiologic sciences to advance patient care skills or pursuing a certificate in a specialty discipline and seek to enhance their clinical practice skills and provide excellent patient care should apply. One of the following must also be true: applicant holds an unrestricted state license, is registered by the American Registry of Radiologic Technologists, or registered with an equivalent certifying body.

Academic Fields/Career Goals: Oncology; Radiology.

Award: Scholarship for use in sophomore, junior, senior, graduate, or postgraduate years; not renewable. *Number:* 4. *Amount:* $5000.

Eligibility Requirements: Applicant must be enrolled or expecting to enroll full- or part-time at a two-year or technical institution or university. Applicant or parent of applicant must be member of American Society of Radiologic Technologists. Available to U.S. citizens.

Application Requirements: Application form, application form may be submitted online, essay, financial need analysis. *Deadline:* February 1.

Contact: Carol Kennedy, Foundation Director
ASRT Foundation
ASRT Foundation
15000 Central Ave. SE
Albuquerque, NM 87123-3909
Phone: 800-444-2778
Fax: 505-298-5063
E-mail: foundation@asrt.org

VARIAN RADIATION THERAPY ADVANCEMENT SCHOLARSHIP

Merit scholarship for radiation therapists and medical dosimetrists or for current radiologic technologists in an entry-level radiation therapy program. Financial need is a factor. Requirements include recommendation and several short answer essays.

Academic Fields/Career Goals: Oncology.

Award: Scholarship for use in sophomore, junior, senior, graduate, or postgraduate years; not renewable. *Number:* 9. *Amount:* $2500–$5000.

Eligibility Requirements: Applicant must be enrolled or expecting to enroll full- or part-time at a two-year or technical institution or university. Applicant or parent of applicant must be member of American Society of Radiologic Technologists. Available to U.S. citizens.

Application Requirements: Application form, application form may be submitted online, essay, financial need analysis. *Deadline:* February 1.

Contact: Carol Kennedy, Foundation Director
ASRT Foundation
ASRT Foundation
15000 Central Ave. SE
Albuquerque, NM 87123-3909
Phone: 800-444-2778
Fax: 505-298-5063
E-mail: foundation@asrt.org

AVACARE MEDICAL

https://avacaremedical.com

AVACARE MEDICAL SCHOLARSHIP
• *See page 100*

BHW GROUP

https://thebhwgroup.com/

BHW WOMEN IN STEM SCHOLARSHIP
• *See page 107*

CARDS AGAINST HUMANITY

https://cardsagainsthumanity.com/

SCIENCE AMBASSADOR SCHOLARSHIP
• *See page 107*

CONTINENTAL SOCIETY, DAUGHTERS OF INDIAN WARS

http://www.csdiw.org/

CONTINENTAL SOCIETY, DAUGHTERS OF INDIAN WARS SCHOLARSHIP
• *See page 188*

CYNTHIA E. MORGAN SCHOLARSHIP FUND (CEMS)

http://www.cemsfund.com/

CYNTHIA E. MORGAN MEMORIAL SCHOLARSHIP FUND, INC.
• *See page 248*

THE EXPERT INSTITUTE

https://www.theexpertinstitute.com

ANNUAL HEALTHCARE AND LIFE SCIENCES SCHOLARSHIP
• *See page 142*

GREAT MINDS IN STEM

http://www.greatmindsinstem.org/college/scholarship-application-information

HENAAC SCHOLARSHIP PROGRAM
• *See page 100*

INTERMOUNTAIN MEDICAL IMAGING

https://www.aboutimi.com/

INTERMOUNTAIN MEDICAL IMAGING SCHOLARSHIP
• *See page 125*

MEDICAL SCRUBS COLLECTION

http://medicalscrubscollection.com

MEDICAL SCRUBS COLLECTION SCHOLARSHIP
• *See page 104*

NEXTSTEPU

http://www.nextstepu.com/

$1,500 STEM SCHOLARSHIP
• *See page 104*

NOVUS BIOLOGICALS, LLC

https://www.novusbio.com

NOVUS BIOLOGICALS SCHOLARSHIP PROGRAM
• *See page 101*

R&D SYSTEMS SCHOLARSHIP
• *See page 101*

TOCRIS BIOSCIENCE SCHOLARSHIP
• *See page 102*

ONCOLOGY NURSING FOUNDATION

https://www.onsfoundation.org/

ONS FOUNDATION/ONCOLOGY NURSING CERTIFICATION CORPORATION BACHELOR'S SCHOLARSHIPS
• *See page 373*

ONS FOUNDATION/PEARL MOORE CAREER DEVELOPMENT AWARDS
• *See page 373*

SCARLETT FAMILY FOUNDATION SCHOLARSHIP PROGRAM

http://www.scarlettfoundation.org/

SCHOLARSHIP FOR STUDENTS PURSUING A BUSINESS OR STEM DEGREE
• *See page 80*

STRAIGHTFORWARD MEDIA

http://www.straightforwardmedia.com/

STRAIGHTFORWARD MEDIA MEDICAL PROFESSIONS SCHOLARSHIP
• *See page 198*

STRAIGHT NORTH

https://www.straightnorth.com/

STRAIGHT NORTH STEM SCHOLARSHIP
• *See page 81*

OPTOMETRY

AMERICAN INDIAN SCIENCE AND ENGINEERING SOCIETY

http://www.aises.org/

A.T. ANDERSON MEMORIAL SCHOLARSHIP PROGRAM
• *See page 105*

AMERICAN LEGION AUXILIARY DEPARTMENT OF COLORADO

http://www.alacolorado.com

AMERICAN LEGION AUXILIARY DEPARTMENT OF COLORADO PAST PRESIDENTS' PARLEY HEALTH CARE PROFESSIONAL SCHOLARSHIPNURSES SCHOLARSHIP
• *See page 125*

AMERICAN OPTOMETRIC FOUNDATION

http://www.aaopt.org/

VISTAKON AWARD OF EXCELLENCE IN CONTACT LENS PATIENT CARE

Open to any fourth-year student attending any school or college of optometry. Must have 3.0 GPA. Student's knowledge of subject matter and skillful, professional clinical contact lens patient care are considered. School makes selection and sends application to AOF.

Academic Fields/Career Goals: Optometry.

Award: Scholarship for use in senior or graduate years; not renewable. *Number;* 19. *Amount:* $1000.

Eligibility Requirements: Applicant must be enrolled or expecting to enroll full-time at a four-year institution or university. Available to U.S. and non-U.S. citizens.

Application Requirements: Application form, recommendations or references. *Deadline:* September 1.

Contact: Alisa Moore, Program Administrator
    Phone: 240-880-3084
    Fax: 301-984-4737
    E-mail: alisam@aaopt.org

AVACARE MEDICAL

https://avacaremedical.com

AVACARE MEDICAL SCHOLARSHIP
• *See page 100*

BHW GROUP

https://thebhwgroup.com/

BHW WOMEN IN STEM SCHOLARSHIP
• *See page 107*

CARDS AGAINST HUMANITY

https://cardsagainsthumanity.com/

SCIENCE AMBASSADOR SCHOLARSHIP
• *See page 107*

CONTINENTAL SOCIETY, DAUGHTERS OF INDIAN WARS

http://www.csdiw.org/

CONTINENTAL SOCIETY, DAUGHTERS OF INDIAN WARS SCHOLARSHIP
• *See page 188*

THE EXPERT INSTITUTE

https://www.theexpertinstitute.com

ANNUAL HEALTHCARE AND LIFE SCIENCES SCHOLARSHIP
• *See page 142*

GREAT MINDS IN STEM

http://www.greatmindsinstem.org/college/scholarship-application-information

HENAAC SCHOLARSHIP PROGRAM
• *See page 100*

INDIAN HEALTH SERVICES, UNITED STATES DEPARTMENT OF HEALTH AND HUMAN SERVICES

http://www.ihs.gov/scholarship

HEALTH PROFESSIONS PREPARATORY SCHOLARSHIP PROGRAM
• *See page 137*

INTERMOUNTAIN MEDICAL IMAGING

https://www.aboutimi.com/

INTERMOUNTAIN MEDICAL IMAGING SCHOLARSHIP
• *See page 125*

KETAMINE CLINICS OF LOS ANGELES

http://www.ketamineclinics.com/

KETAMINE CLINICS OF LOS ANGELES SCHOLARSHIP PROGRAM
• *See page 138*

MEDICAL SCRUBS COLLECTION

http://medicalscrubscollection.com

MEDICAL SCRUBS COLLECTION SCHOLARSHIP
• *See page 104*

NEXTSTEPU

http://www.nextstepu.com/

$1,500 STEM SCHOLARSHIP
• *See page 104*

NOVUS BIOLOGICALS, LLC

https://www.novusbio.com

NOVUS BIOLOGICALS SCHOLARSHIP PROGRAM
• *See page 101*

R&D SYSTEMS SCHOLARSHIP
• *See page 101*

TOCRIS BIOSCIENCE SCHOLARSHIP
• *See page 102*

SCARLETT FAMILY FOUNDATION SCHOLARSHIP PROGRAM

http://www.scarlettfoundation.org/

SCHOLARSHIP FOR STUDENTS PURSUING A BUSINESS OR STEM DEGREE
• *See page 80*

STRAIGHTFORWARD MEDIA

http://www.straightforwardmedia.com/

STRAIGHTFORWARD MEDIA MEDICAL PROFESSIONS SCHOLARSHIP
• *See page 198*

STRAIGHT NORTH

https://www.straightnorth.com/

STRAIGHT NORTH STEM SCHOLARSHIP
• *See page 81*

OSTEOPATHY

AMERICAN INDIAN SCIENCE AND ENGINEERING SOCIETY

http://www.aises.org/

A.T. ANDERSON MEMORIAL SCHOLARSHIP PROGRAM
• *See page 105*

AMERICAN LEGION AUXILIARY DEPARTMENT OF COLORADO

http://www.alacolorado.com

AMERICAN LEGION AUXILIARY DEPARTMENT OF COLORADO PAST PRESIDENTS' PARLEY HEALTH CARE PROFESSIONAL SCHOLARSHIPNURSES SCHOLARSHIP
• *See page 125*

AVACARE MEDICAL

https://avacaremedical.com

AVACARE MEDICAL SCHOLARSHIP
• *See page 100*

BHW GROUP

https://thebhwgroup.com/

BHW WOMEN IN STEM SCHOLARSHIP
• *See page 107*

CARDS AGAINST HUMANITY

https://cardsagainsthumanity.com/

SCIENCE AMBASSADOR SCHOLARSHIP
• *See page 107*

CONTINENTAL SOCIETY, DAUGHTERS OF INDIAN WARS

http://www.csdiw.org/

CONTINENTAL SOCIETY, DAUGHTERS OF INDIAN WARS SCHOLARSHIP
• *See page 188*

CYNTHIA E. MORGAN SCHOLARSHIP FUND (CEMS)

http://www.cemsfund.com/

CYNTHIA E. MORGAN MEMORIAL SCHOLARSHIP FUND, INC.
• *See page 248*

GREAT MINDS IN STEM

http://www.greatmindsinstem.org/college/scholarship-application-information

HENAAC SCHOLARSHIP PROGRAM
• *See page 100*

INTERMOUNTAIN MEDICAL IMAGING

https://www.aboutimi.com/

INTERMOUNTAIN MEDICAL IMAGING SCHOLARSHIP
• *See page 125*

MEDICAL SCRUBS COLLECTION

http://medicalscrubscollection.com

MEDICAL SCRUBS COLLECTION SCHOLARSHIP
• *See page 104*

NEXTSTEPU

http://www.nextstepu.com/

$1,500 STEM SCHOLARSHIP
• *See page 104*

NOVUS BIOLOGICALS, LLC

https://www.novusbio.com

NOVUS BIOLOGICALS SCHOLARSHIP PROGRAM
• *See page 101*

R&D SYSTEMS SCHOLARSHIP
• *See page 101*

TOCRIS BIOSCIENCE SCHOLARSHIP
• *See page 102*

SCARLETT FAMILY FOUNDATION SCHOLARSHIP PROGRAM

http://www.scarlettfoundation.org/

SCHOLARSHIP FOR STUDENTS PURSUING A BUSINESS OR STEM DEGREE
• *See page 80*

STRAIGHTFORWARD MEDIA

http://www.straightforwardmedia.com/

STRAIGHTFORWARD MEDIA MEDICAL PROFESSIONS SCHOLARSHIP
• *See page 198*

STRAIGHT NORTH

https://www.straightnorth.com/

STRAIGHT NORTH STEM SCHOLARSHIP
• *See page 81*

PAPER AND PULP ENGINEERING

AMERICAN CHEMICAL SOCIETY

http://www.acs.org/

AMERICAN CHEMICAL SOCIETY SCHOLARS PROGRAM
• *See page 153*

AMERICAN INDIAN SCIENCE AND ENGINEERING SOCIETY

http://www.aises.org/

A.T. ANDERSON MEMORIAL SCHOLARSHIP PROGRAM
• *See page 105*

BHW GROUP

https://thebhwgroup.com/

BHW WOMEN IN STEM SCHOLARSHIP
• *See page 107*

BROWN AND CALDWELL

http://www.brownandcaldwell.com

ECKENFELDER SCHOLARSHIP
• *See page 141*

MINORITY SCHOLARSHIP PROGRAM
• *See page 141*

CARDS AGAINST HUMANITY

https://cardsagainsthumanity.com/

SCIENCE AMBASSADOR SCHOLARSHIP
• *See page 107*

GREAT MINDS IN STEM

http://www.greatmindsinstem.org/college/scholarship-application-information

HENAAC SCHOLARSHIP PROGRAM
• *See page 100*

NEXTSTEPU

http://www.nextstepu.com/

$1,500 STEM SCHOLARSHIP
• *See page 104*

SOCIETY OF WOMEN ENGINEERS

https://swe.org/

SWE REGION E SCHOLARSHIP
• *See page 159*

SWE REGION H SCHOLARSHIPS
• *See page 159*

SWE REGION J SCHOLARSHIP
• *See page 159*

TE CONNECTIVITY EXCELLENCE IN ENGINEERING SCHOLARSHIP
• *See page 160*

STRAIGHTFORWARD MEDIA

http://www.straightforwardmedia.com/

STRAIGHTFORWARD MEDIA ENGINEERING SCHOLARSHIP
• *See page 160*

STRAIGHT NORTH

https://www.straightnorth.com/

STRAIGHT NORTH STEM SCHOLARSHIP
• *See page 81*

TECHNICAL ASSOCIATION OF THE PULP & PAPER INDUSTRY (TAPPI)

https://www.tappi.org/

CORRUGATED PACKAGING DIVISION SCHOLARSHIPS
• *See page 231*

ENGINEERING DIVISION SCHOLARSHIP

Up to two $1500 scholarships offered. One may be awarded to a student who will be in his or her junior year, and the other will be offered to a student who will be in his or her senior year at the beginning of the next academic year. Information can be found at http://www.tappi.org/s_tappi/sec.asp?CID=6101&DID=546695.

Academic Fields/Career Goals: Paper and Pulp Engineering.

Award: Scholarship for use in junior or senior years; not renewable. *Number:* 1–2. *Amount:* $2000.

Eligibility Requirements: Applicant must be enrolled or expecting to enroll full-time at a four-year institution or university. Available to U.S. and non-U.S. citizens.

Application Requirements: Application form. *Deadline:* February 15.

Contact: Mr. Laurence Womack, Director of Standards and Awards
Technical Association of the Pulp & Paper Industry (TAPPI)
15 Technology Parkway South
Peachtree Corners, GA 30092
Phone: 770-209-7276
E-mail: standards@tappi.org

ENVIRONMENTAL WORKING GROUP SCHOLARSHIP
• *See page 256*

PAPER AND BOARD DIVISION SCHOLARSHIPS
• *See page 245*

TAPPI PROCESS CONTROL SCHOLARSHIP

The TAPPI Process Control Scholarship is designed to encourage talented engineering students to pursue careers in the pulp and paper industry and to develop professional skills in process control fields.

Academic Fields/Career Goals: Paper and Pulp Engineering.

Award: Scholarship for use in sophomore, junior, or senior years; not renewable. *Number:* 1. *Amount:* $1000.

Eligibility Requirements: Applicant must be high school student and planning to enroll or expecting to enroll full-time at a two-year or four-year institution or university. Available to U.S. and non-U.S. citizens.

Application Requirements: Application form. *Deadline:* February 15.

Contact: Mr. Laurence Womack, Director of Standards and Awards
Technical Association of the Pulp & Paper Industry (TAPPI)
15 Technology Parkway South
Suite 115
Peachtree Corners, GA 30092
Phone: 770-209-7276
E-mail: standards@tappi.org

WILLIAM L. CULLISON SCHOLARSHIP
• *See page 354*

UNITED NEGRO COLLEGE FUND

http://www.uncf.org/

LEIDOS STEM SCHOLARSHIP
• *See page 96*

PEACE AND CONFLICT STUDIES

ASSOCIATION OF FORMER INTELLIGENCE OFFICERS

www.afio.com

AFIO UNDERGRADUATE AND GRADUATE SCHOLARSHIPS
• *See page 98*

NATIONAL SECURITY EDUCATION PROGRAM

http://www.iie.org/

NATIONAL SECURITY EDUCATION PROGRAM (NSEP) DAVID L. BOREN UNDERGRADUATE SCHOLARSHIPS
• *See page 119*

UNITED NATIONS ASSOCIATION OF CONNECTICUT

http://www.unausa.org

UNITED NATIONS ASSOCIATION OF CONNECTICUT SCHOLARSHIP
• *See page 124*

VETERANS FOR PEACE-CHAPTER 93

VFP93.org

VETERANS FOR PEACE SCHOLARSHIP

VFP-93 Peace Scholarship is aimed to help Michigan students who are studying peace and conflict resolution, be it a degree program or course. Although originally aimed at veterans this is no longer a requirement. See VFP93.org for further description.

Academic Fields/Career Goals: Peace and Conflict Studies.

Award: Scholarship for use in freshman, sophomore, junior, senior, graduate, or postgraduate years; renewable. *Number:* 1–3. *Amount:* $500–$1000.

Eligibility Requirements: Applicant must be enrolled or expecting to enroll full- or part-time at a four-year institution and resident of Michigan. Available to U.S. citizens.

Application Requirements: Application form. *Deadline:* continuous.

Contact: Bbill Shea, Vice Chair
Veterans for Peace-Chapter 93
803 John A. Woods Drive
Ann Arbor, MI 48105
Phone: 734-662-0818
E-mail: billshea@umich.edu

WASHINGTON STATE ASSOCIATION FOR JUSTICE

http://www.washingtonjustice.org/

WASHINGTON STATE ASSOCIATION FOR JUSTICE AMERICAN JUSTICE ESSAY & VIDEO SCHOLARSHIP
• *See page 189*

PERFORMING ARTS

CONGRESSIONAL BLACK CAUCUS FOUNDATION, INC.

http://www.cbcfinc.org/

CBC SPOUSES PERFORMING ARTS SCHOLARSHIP

This award is for full-time students with majors in the performing arts including, but not limited to, drama, music, dance, opera, marching bands, and other musical ensembles.

Academic Fields/Career Goals: Performing Arts.

Award: Scholarship for use in freshman, sophomore, junior, senior, or graduate years; not renewable. *Number:* 1–10. *Amount:* $3000.

Eligibility Requirements: Applicant must be of African heritage; Black (non-Hispanic); enrolled or expecting to enroll full-time at a two-year institution or university; studying in Alabama, Alaska, Arizona, Arkansas, California, Colorado, Connecticut, Delaware, District of Columbia, Florida, Georgia, Guam, Hawaii, Idaho, Illinois, Indiana, Iowa, Kansas, Kentucky, Louisiana, Maine, Maryland, Massachusetts, Michigan, Minnesota, Mississippi, Missouri, Montana, Nebraska, Nevada, New Hampshire, New Jersey, New Mexico, New York, North Carolina, North Dakota, Ohio, Oklahoma, Oregon, Pennsylvania, Puerto Rico, Rhode Island, South Carolina, South Dakota, Tennessee, Texas, Utah, Vermont, Virginia, Washington, West Virginia, Wisconsin, Wyoming and must have an interest in music/singing or theater. Available to U.S. citizens.

Application Requirements: Application form, application form may be submitted online, essay, personal photograph, portfolio. *Deadline:* April 30.

Contact: Ms. Katrina Finch, Program Administrator, Scholarships
Phone: 202-263-2800
E-mail: scholarships@cbcfinc.org

COSTUME SOCIETY OF AMERICA

http://www.costumesocietyamerica.com/

ADELE FILENE STUDENT PRESENTER GRANT
• *See page 118*

STELLA BLUM STUDENT RESEARCH GRANT
• *See page 118*

GENERAL FEDERATION OF WOMEN'S CLUBS OF MASSACHUSETTS

http://www.gfwcma.org/

DORCHESTER WOMEN'S CLUB MUSIC SCHOLARSHIP
• *See page 347*

GRAND RAPIDS COMMUNITY FOUNDATION

http://www.grfoundation.org/

ARTS COUNCIL OF GREATER GRAND RAPIDS MINORITY SCHOLARSHIP
• *See page 121*

HEMOPHILIA FOUNDATION OF SOUTHERN CALIFORNIA

http://www.hemosocal.org/

DR. EARL JAMES FAHRINGER PERFORMING ARTS SCHOLARSHIP
• *See page 121*

HOSTESS COMMITTEE SCHOLARSHIPS/MISS AMERICA PAGEANT

http://www.missamerica.org/

EUGENIA VELLNER FISCHER AWARD FOR PERFORMING ARTS

Scholarship for Miss America contestants pursuing degree in performing arts. Award available to women who have competed within the Miss America system on the local, state, or national level from 1998 to the present, regardless of whether title was won. One or more scholarships are awarded annually, depending on qualifications of applicants. Late or incomplete applications are not accepted.

Academic Fields/Career Goals: Performing Arts.

Award: Scholarship for use in freshman, sophomore, junior, senior, or graduate years; not renewable.

Eligibility Requirements: Applicant must be enrolled or expecting to enroll full- or part-time at a four-year institution or university; female and must have an interest in beauty pageant. Available to U.S. citizens.

Application Requirements: Application form, essay, financial need analysis, recommendations or references, transcript. *Deadline:* June 30.

Contact: Doreen Gordon, Controller and Scholarship Administrator
Phone: 609-345-7571 Ext. 27
Fax: 609-347-6079
E-mail: doreen@missamerica.org

ILLUMINATING ENGINEERING SOCIETY OF NORTH AMERICA

http://www.ies.org/

ROBERT W. THUNEN MEMORIAL SCHOLARSHIPS
• *See page 116*

NATIONAL ACADEMY OF TELEVISION ARTS AND SCIENCES

https://theemmys.tv/

DOUGLAS W. MUMMERT SCHOLARSHIP
• *See page 173*

JIM MCKAY MEMORIAL SCHOLARSHIP
• *See page 258*

MIKE WALLACE MEMORIAL SCHOLARSHIP
• *See page 258*

NATIONAL ACADEMY OF TELEVISION ARTS AND SCIENCES TRUSTEES' LINDA GIANNECCHINI SCHOLARSHIP
• *See page 258*

RANDY FALCO SCHOLARSHIP
• *See page 259*

NATIONAL ACADEMY OF TELEVISION ARTS AND SCIENCES, MICHIGAN CHAPTER

http://natasmichigan.org

DR. LYNNE BOYLE/JOHN SCHIMPF UNDERGRADUATE SCHOLARSHIP
• *See page 85*

NATIONAL OPERA ASSOCIATION

http://www.noa.org/

NOA VOCAL COMPETITION/LEGACY AWARD PROGRAM
• *See page 121*

ONLINE LOGO MAKER

http://onlinelogomaker.com

OLM MALALA YOUSAFZAI SCHOLARSHIP 2017-2018
• *See page 122*

POLISH ARTS CLUB OF BUFFALO SCHOLARSHIP FOUNDATION

http://www.pacb.bfn.org/

POLISH ARTS CLUB OF BUFFALO SCHOLARSHIP FOUNDATION TRUST
• *See page 122*

PRINCESS GRACE FOUNDATION-USA

http://www.pgfusa.org/

PRINCESS GRACE AWARDS IN DANCE, THEATER, AND FILM
• *See page 259*

QUALITY BATH

www.qualitybath.com

QUALITYBATH.COM SCHOLARSHIP PROGRAM
• *See page 120*

SERVICE EMPLOYEES INTERNATIONAL UNION (SEIU)

http://www.seiu.org/

SEIU MOE FONER SCHOLARSHIP PROGRAM FOR VISUAL AND PERFORMING ARTS
• *See page 123*

SOUTHEASTERN THEATRE CONFERENCE

http://www.setc.org

POLLY HOLLIDAY SCHOLARSHIP
• *See page 123*

UNITED NEGRO COLLEGE FUND

http://www.uncf.org/

THE OSSIE DAVIS LEGACY AWARD SCHOLARSHIP
• *See page 89*

VSA

http://www.kennedy-center.org/education/vsa/

VSA INTERNATIONAL YOUNG SOLOISTS AWARD
• *See page 351*

WOMEN BAND DIRECTORS INTERNATIONAL

http://www.womenbanddirectors.org/

CHARLOTTE PLUMMER OWEN MEMORIAL SCHOLARSHIP
• *See page 216*

MARTHA ANN STARK MEMORIAL SCHOLARSHIP
• *See page 216*

VOLKWEIN MEMORIAL SCHOLARSHIP
• *See page 216*

PHARMACY

101ST AIRBORNE DIVISION ASSOCIATION

http://www.screamingeaglefoundation.org/

AL & WILLIAMARY VISTE SCHOLARSHIP
• *See page 99*

AMERICAN INDIAN SCIENCE AND ENGINEERING SOCIETY

http://www.aises.org/

A.T. ANDERSON MEMORIAL SCHOLARSHIP PROGRAM
• *See page 105*

AMERICAN LEGION AUXILIARY DEPARTMENT OF COLORADO

http://www.alacolorado.com

AMERICAN LEGION AUXILIARY DEPARTMENT OF COLORADO PAST PRESIDENTS' PARLEY HEALTH CARE PROFESSIONAL SCHOLARSHIPNURSES SCHOLARSHIP
• *See page 125*

ASSISTANCE LEAGUE OF THE TRIANGLE AREA

HEALTH CARE PROFESSION SCHOLARSHIP
• *See page 195*

ASSOCIATION FOR FOOD AND DRUG OFFICIALS

http://www.afdo.org/

ASSOCIATION FOR FOOD AND DRUG OFFICIALS SCHOLARSHIP FUND

A $1500 scholarship for students in their third year of college/university who have demonstrated a desire for a career in research, regulatory work, quality control, or teaching in an area related to some aspect of food, drugs, or consumer products safety. Minimum 3.0 GPA required in first two years of undergraduate study. For further information visit website http://www.afdo.org.

Academic Fields/Career Goals: Pharmacy.

Award: Scholarship for use in senior year; not renewable. *Number:* 3. *Amount:* $1500.

Eligibility Requirements: Applicant must be enrolled or expecting to enroll full-time at a four-year institution or university. Available to U.S. and non-U.S. citizens.

Application Requirements: Application form, essay. *Deadline:* March 1.

Contact: Dr. Joanne Brown, Association Manager
Association for Food and Drug Officials
155 W. Market Street, 3rd Floor
York, PA 17401
Phone: 717-757-2888
E-mail: afdo@afdo.org

AVACARE MEDICAL

https://avacaremedical.com

AVACARE MEDICAL SCHOLARSHIP
• *See page 100*

BARRY GOLDWATER SCHOLARSHIP AND EXCELLENCE IN EDUCATION FOUNDATION

https://goldwater.scholarsapply.org

BARRY M. GOLDWATER SCHOLARSHIP AND EXCELLENCE IN EDUCATION PROGRAM
• *See page 107*

BHW GROUP

https://thebhwgroup.com/

BHW WOMEN IN STEM SCHOLARSHIP
• *See page 107*

CONTINENTAL SOCIETY, DAUGHTERS OF INDIAN WARS

http://www.csdiw.org/

CONTINENTAL SOCIETY, DAUGHTERS OF INDIAN WARS SCHOLARSHIP
• *See page 188*

CYNTHIA E. MORGAN SCHOLARSHIP FUND (CEMS)

http://www.cemsfund.com/

CYNTHIA E. MORGAN MEMORIAL SCHOLARSHIP FUND, INC.
• *See page 248*

DISTIL NETWORKS

http://www.distilnetworks.com

WOMEN FORWARD IN TECHNOLOGY SCHOLARSHIP PROGRAM
• *See page 108*

GREAT MINDS IN STEM

http://www.greatmindsinstem.org/college/scholarship-application-information

HENAAC SCHOLARSHIP PROGRAM
• *See page 100*

HEALTH PROFESSIONS EDUCATION FOUNDATION

http://www.healthprofessions.ca.gov/

ALLIED HEALTHCARE SCHOLARSHIP PROGRAM
• *See page 196*

INDIAN HEALTH SERVICES, UNITED STATES DEPARTMENT OF HEALTH AND HUMAN SERVICES

http://www.ihs.gov/scholarship

HEALTH PROFESSIONS PREPARATORY SCHOLARSHIP PROGRAM
• *See page 137*

THE JACKSON LABORATORY

https://www.jax.org

THE JACKSON LABORATORY COLLEGE SCHOLARSHIP PROGRAM
• *See page 108*

MEDICAL SCRUBS COLLECTION

http://medicalscrubscollection.com

MEDICAL SCRUBS COLLECTION SCHOLARSHIP
• *See page 104*

NATIONAL COMMUNITY PHARMACIST ASSOCIATION (NCPA) FOUNDATION

http://www.ncpanet.org/

NATIONAL COMMUNITY PHARMACIST ASSOCIATION FOUNDATION PRESIDENTIAL SCHOLARSHIP

One-time award to student members of NCPA. Must be enrolled in an accredited U.S. school or college of pharmacy on a full-time basis. Award based on leadership qualities and accomplishments with a demonstrated interest in independent pharmacy, as well as involvement in extracurricular activities.

Academic Fields/Career Goals: Pharmacy.

Award: Scholarship for use in freshman, sophomore, junior, or senior years; not renewable. *Number:* up to 15. *Amount:* up to $2000.

Eligibility Requirements: Applicant must be enrolled or expecting to enroll full-time at a four-year institution or university and must have an interest in leadership. Available to U.S. citizens.

Application Requirements: Application form, essay, recommendations or references, resume, transcript. *Deadline:* March 15.

Contact: Jackie Lopez, Administrative Assistant
National Community Pharmacist Association (NCPA)
Foundation
100 Daingerfield Road
Alexandria, VA 22314
Phone: 703-683-8200
Fax: 703-683-3619
E-mail: jackie.lopez@ncpanet.org

NEXTSTEPU

http://www.nextstepu.com/

$1,500 STEM SCHOLARSHIP
• *See page 104*

NOVUS BIOLOGICALS, LLC

https://www.novusbio.com

NOVUS BIOLOGICALS SCHOLARSHIP PROGRAM
• *See page 101*

R&D SYSTEMS SCHOLARSHIP
• *See page 101*

TOCRIS BIOSCIENCE SCHOLARSHIP
• *See page 102*

PLATINUM EDUCATIONAL GROUP

www.platinumed.com

PLATINUM EDUCATIONAL GROUP SCHOLARSHIPS PROGRAM FOR EMS, NURSING, AND ALLIED HEALTH
• *See page 102*

SCARLETT FAMILY FOUNDATION SCHOLARSHIP PROGRAM

http://www.scarlettfoundation.org/

SCHOLARSHIP FOR STUDENTS PURSUING A BUSINESS OR STEM DEGREE
• *See page 80*

STRAIGHTFORWARD MEDIA

http://www.straightforwardmedia.com/

STRAIGHTFORWARD MEDIA MEDICAL PROFESSIONS SCHOLARSHIP
• *See page 198*

UNITED NEGRO COLLEGE FUND

http://www.uncf.org/

LEIDOS STEM SCHOLARSHIP
• *See page 96*

PHILOSOPHY

LA-PHILOSOPHIE.COM

http://la-philosophie.com

LA-PHILOSOPHIE.COM SCHOLARSHIP
• *See page 104*

STRAIGHTFORWARD MEDIA

http://www.straightforwardmedia.com/

STRAIGHTFORWARD MEDIA LIBERAL ARTS SCHOLARSHIP
• *See page 119*

PHOTOJOURNALISM/ PHOTOGRAPHY

AMERICAN QUARTER HORSE FOUNDATION (AQHF)

https://aqhfoundation.smapply.io/

AQHF JOURNALISM OR COMMUNICATIONS SCHOLARSHIP
• *See page 170*

ASIAN AMERICAN JOURNALISTS ASSOCIATION

http://www.aaja.org/

CIC/ANNA CHENNAULT SCHOLARSHIP
• *See page 170*

MARY QUON MOY ING MEMORIAL SCHOLARSHIP AWARD
• *See page 170*

VINCENT CHIN MEMORIAL SCHOLARSHIP
• *See page 171*

ASIAN AMERICAN JOURNALISTS ASSOCIATION, SEATTLE CHAPTER

http://www.aajaseattle.org/

NORTHWEST JOURNALISTS OF COLOR SCHOLARSHIP
• *See page 84*

CCNMA: LATINO JOURNALISTS OF CALIFORNIA

http://www.ccnma.org/

CCNMA SCHOLARSHIPS
• *See page 171*

COLLEGE PHOTOGRAPHER OF THE YEAR

http://www.cpoy.org/

COLLEGE PHOTOGRAPHER OF THE YEAR COMPETITION
Awards undergraduate and graduate students for juried contest of individual photographs, picture stories and photographic essay and multimedia presentations. Two financial awards in the dollar value of $500 and $1000 are granted, but multiple awards given in the form of Nikon camera equipment and workshop scholarships. Deadline varies.
Academic Fields/Career Goals: Photojournalism/Photography.
Award: Prize for use in freshman, sophomore, junior, senior, or graduate years; not renewable. *Number:* 10. *Amount:* $600–$5000.

Eligibility Requirements: Applicant must be enrolled or expecting to enroll full- or part-time at a four-year institution or university. Available to U.S. and non-U.S. citizens.

Application Requirements: Application form, essay, personal photograph, portfolio. *Deadline:* September 30.

Contact: Jackie Bell, Program Director
College Photographer of the Year
University of Missouri, School of Journalism
109 Lee Hills Hall
Columbia, MO 65211
Phone: 573-882-2198
E-mail: info@cpoy.org

CONNECTICUT CHAPTER OF SOCIETY OF PROFESSIONAL JOURNALISTS

http://www.ctspj.org/

CONNECTICUT SPJ BOB EDDY SCHOLARSHIP PROGRAM
• *See page 172*

IOWA NEWSPAPER ASSOCIATION

https://inanews.com/

WOODWARD SCHOLARSHIP
• *See page 172*

NATIONAL ACADEMY OF TELEVISION ARTS AND SCIENCES

https://theemmys.tv/

DOUGLAS W. MUMMERT SCHOLARSHIP
• *See page 173*

JIM MCKAY MEMORIAL SCHOLARSHIP
• *See page 258*

MIKE WALLACE MEMORIAL SCHOLARSHIP
• *See page 258*

NATIONAL ACADEMY OF TELEVISION ARTS AND SCIENCES TRUSTEES' LINDA GIANNECCHINI SCHOLARSHIP
• *See page 258*

RANDY FALCO SCHOLARSHIP
• *See page 259*

NATIONAL ASSOCIATION OF BLACK JOURNALISTS

http://www.nabj.org/

NATIONAL ASSOCIATION OF BLACK JOURNALISTS NON-SUSTAINING SCHOLARSHIP AWARDS
• *See page 307*

NATIONAL ASSOCIATION OF HISPANIC JOURNALISTS (NAHJ)

http://www.nahj.org/

NATIONAL ASSOCIATION OF HISPANIC JOURNALISTS SCHOLARSHIP
• *See page 173*

NEWHOUSE SCHOLARSHIP PROGRAM
• *See page 275*

NATIVE AMERICAN JOURNALISTS ASSOCIATION

http://www.naja.com/

NATIVE AMERICAN JOURNALISTS ASSOCIATION SCHOLARSHIPS
• *See page 85*

NEBRASKA PRESS ASSOCIATION

http://www.nebpress.com/

NEBRASKA PRESS ASSOCIATION FOUNDATION SCHOLARSHIP
• *See page 86*

OUTDOOR WRITERS ASSOCIATION OF AMERICA

http://www.owaa.org/

OUTDOOR WRITERS ASSOCIATION OF AMERICA - BODIE MCDOWELL SCHOLARSHIP AWARD
• *See page 174*

PALM BEACH ASSOCIATION OF BLACK JOURNALISTS

PALM BEACH ASSOCIATION OF BLACK JOURNALISTS SCHOLARSHIP
• *See page 309*

PRINTING INDUSTRY MIDWEST EDUCATION FOUDNATION

http://www.pimw.org/scholarships

PRINTING INDUSTRY MIDWEST EDUCATION FOUNDATION SCHOLARSHIP FUND
• *See page 175*

QUALITY BATH

www.qualitybath.com

QUALITYBATH.COM SCHOLARSHIP PROGRAM
• *See page 120*

RADIO TELEVISION DIGITAL NEWS ASSOCIATION

http://www.rtdna.org

CAROLE SIMPSON SCHOLARSHIP
• *See page 310*

ED BRADLEY SCHOLARSHIP
• *See page 310*

GEORGE FOREMAN TRIBUTE TO LYNDON B. JOHNSON SCHOLARSHIP
• *See page 310*

LOU AND CAROLE PRATO SPORTS REPORTING SCHOLARSHIP
• *See page 310*

MIKE REYNOLDS JOURNALISM SCHOLARSHIP
• *See page 311*

PETE WILSON JOURNALISM SCHOLARSHIP
• *See page 311*

STRAIGHTFORWARD MEDIA
http://www.straightforwardmedia.com/

STRAIGHTFORWARD MEDIA MEDIA & COMMUNICATIONS SCHOLARSHIP
• *See page 87*

SUPPORT CREATIVITY
http://wesupportcreativity.org

SUPPORT CREATIVITY SCHOLARSHIP
• *See page 117*

TAMPA BAY TIMES FUND, INC.
http://company.tampabay.com:2052/times-fund/scholarships

CAREER JOURNALISM SCHOLARSHIP
• *See page 176*

TAMPA BAY TIMES FUND CAREER JOURNALISM SCHOLARSHIPS
• *See page 87*

TEXAS GRIDIRON CLUB INC.
http://www.spjfw.org/

TEXAS GRIDIRON CLUB SCHOLARSHIPS
• *See page 177*

UNITED METHODIST COMMUNICATIONS
http://www.umcom.org/

LEONARD M. PERRYMAN COMMUNICATIONS SCHOLARSHIP FOR ETHNIC MINORITY STUDENTS
• *See page 177*

VALLEY PRESS CLUB
http://www.valleypressclub.com/

VALLEY PRESS CLUB SCHOLARSHIPS, THE REPUBLICAN SCHOLARSHIP, CHANNEL 22 SCHOLARSHIP
• *See page 178*

PHYSICAL SCIENCES

101ST AIRBORNE DIVISION ASSOCIATION
http://www.screamingeaglefoundation.org/

AL & WILLIAMARY VISTE SCHOLARSHIP
• *See page 99*

AIR & WASTE MANAGEMENT ASSOCIATION–COASTAL PLAINS CHAPTER
http://www.awmacoastalplains.org/

COASTAL PLAINS CHAPTER OF THE AIR AND WASTE MANAGEMENT ASSOCIATION ENVIRONMENTAL STEWARD SCHOLARSHIP
• *See page 250*

AIST FOUNDATION
http://www.aistfoundation.org/

ASSOCIATION FOR IRON AND STEEL TECHNOLOGY OHIO VALLEY CHAPTER SCHOLARSHIP
• *See page 138*

AMERICAN ASSOCIATION OF PHYSICS TEACHERS
http://aapt.org

BARBARA LOTZE SCHOLARSHIPS FOR FUTURE TEACHERS
Undergraduate students enrolled, or planning to enroll, in physics teacher preparation curricula and high school seniors entering such programs are eligible. Successful applicants receive a stipend of up to $2,000 and a complimentary AAPT Student Membership for one year. The scholarship may be granted to an individual for each of four years. Students who meet the following criteria are eligible to apply for the Barbara Lotze Scholarship for Future Teachers. Applicants must declare their intent to prepare for, and engage in, a career in physics teaching at the high school level and must, at the time the scholarship funds are received by the student, be an undergraduate student enrolled in an accredited two-year college, four-year college or a university; or a high school senior accepted for such enrollment. Must be pursuing, or planning to pursue, a course of study leading toward a career in physics teaching in the high schools. Must be showing promise of success in their studies, and be a citizen of the United States of America. Applications will be accepted at any time and will be considered for recommendation to the Executive Board at each AAPT Winter Meeting. All applications in which all materials, including letters of recommendation, are received by December 1 will be considered for recommendation at the winter meeting of the AAPT Executive Board.

Academic Fields/Career Goals: Physical Sciences.

Award: Scholarship for use in freshman, sophomore, junior, or senior years; not renewable. *Number:* 5–7. *Amount:* $2000.

Eligibility Requirements: Applicant must be enrolled or expecting to enroll full- or part-time at a two-year or four-year institution. Available to U.S. citizens.

Application Requirements: Application form, portfolio. *Deadline:* December 1.

Contact: Mrs. Rachel Sweeney, Executive Assistant
E-mail: rsweeney@aapt.org

AMERICAN FOUNDATION FOR THE BLIND
http://www.afb.org/

PAUL W. RUCKES SCHOLARSHIP
• *See page 179*

AMERICAN INDIAN SCIENCE AND ENGINEERING SOCIETY
http://www.aises.org/

A.T. ANDERSON MEMORIAL SCHOLARSHIP PROGRAM
• *See page 105*

AMERICAN INSTITUTE OF AERONAUTICS AND ASTRONAUTICS
https://www.aiaa.org/

AIAA FOUNDATION UNDERGRADUATE SCHOLARSHIPS
• *See page 127*

LEATRICE GREGORY PENDRAY SCHOLARSHIP
• *See page 127*

AMERICAN LEGION DEPARTMENT OF MARYLAND
http://www.mdlegion.org/

AMERICAN LEGION DEPARTMENT OF MARYLAND MATH-SCIENCE SCHOLARSHIP
• *See page 99*

AMERICAN METEOROLOGICAL SOCIETY
http://www.ametsoc.org/

FATHER JAMES B. MACELWANE ANNUAL AWARD
• *See page 251*

AMERICAN SOCIETY OF NAVAL ENGINEERS
http://www.navalengineers.org/

AMERICAN SOCIETY OF NAVAL ENGINEERS SCHOLARSHIP
• *See page 106*

ARIZONA PROFESSIONAL CHAPTER OF AISES
http://www.aises.org/scholarships

ARIZONA PROFESSIONAL CHAPTER OF AISES SCHOLARSHIP
• *See page 237*

ARMED FORCES COMMUNICATIONS AND ELECTRONICS ASSOCIATION, EDUCATIONAL FOUNDATION
https://foundation.afcea.org

AFCEA STEM MAJORS SCHOLARSHIPS FOR UNDERGRADUATE STUDENTS
• *See page 106*

ARMED FORCES COMMUNICATIONS AND ELECTRONICS ASSOCIATION ROTC SCHOLARSHIP PROGRAM
• *See page 179*

ASIAN PACIFIC FUND

BANATAO FAMILY FILIPINO AMERICAN EDUCATION FUND
• *See page 155*

ASSOCIATION FOR WOMEN GEOSCIENTISTS (AWG)
http://www.awg.org/

AWG ETHNIC MINORITY SCHOLARSHIP
• *See page 200*

AWG MARIA LUISA CRAWFORD FIELD CAMP SCHOLARSHIP
• *See page 111*

AWG SALT LAKE CHAPTER (SLC) RESEARCH SCHOLARSHIP
• *See page 111*

JANET CULLEN TANAKA GEOSCIENCES UNDERGRADUATE SCHOLARSHIP
• *See page 112*

LONE STAR RISING CAREER SCHOLARSHIP
• *See page 200*

OSAGE CHAPTER UNDERGRADUATE SERVICE SCHOLARSHIP
• *See page 112*

SUSAN EKDALE MEMORIAL FIELD CAMP SCHOLARSHIP
• *See page 201*

ASSOCIATION ON AMERICAN INDIAN AFFAIRS, INC.
http://www.indian-affairs.org/

ELIZABETH AND SHERMAN ASCHE MEMORIAL SCHOLARSHIP FUND
• *See page 93*

BARRY GOLDWATER SCHOLARSHIP AND EXCELLENCE IN EDUCATION FOUNDATION
https://goldwater.scholarsapply.org

BARRY M. GOLDWATER SCHOLARSHIP AND EXCELLENCE IN EDUCATION PROGRAM
• *See page 107*

BHW GROUP
https://thebhwgroup.com/

BHW WOMEN IN STEM SCHOLARSHIP
• *See page 107*

CARDS AGAINST HUMANITY
https://cardsagainsthumanity.com/

SCIENCE AMBASSADOR SCHOLARSHIP
• *See page 107*

CATCHING THE DREAM
http://www.catchingthedream.org/

MATH, ENGINEERING, SCIENCE, BUSINESS, EDUCATION, COMPUTERS SCHOLARSHIPS
• *See page 146*

NATIVE AMERICAN LEADERSHIP IN EDUCATION (NALE)
• See page 146

THE DALLAS FOUNDATION
http://www.dallasfoundation.org/

WHITLEY PLACE SCHOLARSHIP
• See page 114

DISTIL NETWORKS
http://www.distilnetworks.com

WOMEN FORWARD IN TECHNOLOGY SCHOLARSHIP PROGRAM
• See page 108

EAA AVIATION FOUNDATION, INC.
http://www.eaa.org/

PAYZER SCHOLARSHIP
• See page 130

THE ELECTROCHEMICAL SOCIETY
https://www.electrochem.org/

BATTERY DIVISION STUDENT RESEARCH AWARD SPONSORED BY MERCEDES-BENZ RESEARCH & DEVELOPMENT
• See page 155

H.H. DOW MEMORIAL STUDENT ACHIEVEMENT AWARD OF THE INDUSTRIAL ELECTROLYSIS AND ELECTROCHEMICAL ENGINEERING DIVISION OF THE ELECTROCHEMICAL SOCIETY INC
• See page 156

GREAT MINDS IN STEM
http://www.greatmindsinstem.org/college/scholarship-application-information

HENAAC SCHOLARSHIP PROGRAM
• See page 100

INTERNATIONAL SOCIETY OF EXPLOSIVES ENGINEERS
http://www.isee.org/

JERRY MCDOWELL FUND
• See page 156

THE LAND CONSERVANCY OF NEW JERSEY
http://www.tlc-nj.org/

ROGERS FAMILY SCHOLARSHIP
• See page 143

LOGMEIN
https://www.logmeininc.com

LASTPASS STEM SCHOLARSHIP
• See page 109

LOS ANGELES COUNCIL OF BLACK PROFESSIONAL ENGINEERS
http://www.lablackengineers.org/

AL-BEN SCHOLARSHIP FOR ACADEMIC INCENTIVE
• See page 157

AL-BEN SCHOLARSHIP FOR PROFESSIONAL MERIT
• See page 157

AL-BEN SCHOLARSHIP FOR SCHOLASTIC ACHIEVEMENT
• See page 157

MEDICAL SCRUBS COLLECTION
http://medicalscrubscollection.com

MEDICAL SCRUBS COLLECTION SCHOLARSHIP
• See page 104

NASA FLORIDA SPACE GRANT CONSORTIUM
http://www.floridaspacegrant.org/

FLORIDA SPACE RESEARCH PROGRAM
• See page 131

NASA IDAHO SPACE GRANT CONSORTIUM
http://www.idahospacegrant.org

NASA IDAHO SPACE GRANT CONSORTIUM SCHOLARSHIP PROGRAM
• See page 109

NASA/MARYLAND SPACE GRANT CONSORTIUM
https://md.spacegrant.org

NASA MARYLAND SPACE GRANT CONSORTIUM SCHOLARSHIPS
• See page 109

NASA MINNESOTA SPACE GRANT CONSORTIUM
https://www.mnspacegrant.org/

MINNESOTA SPACE GRANT CONSORTIUM SCHOLARSHIP PROGRAM
• See page 131

NASA'S VIRGINIA SPACE GRANT CONSORTIUM
http://www.vsgc.odu.edu/

UNDERGRADUATE STEM RESEARCH SCHOLARSHIPS
• See page 110

NATIONAL ASSOCIATION FOR THE ADVANCEMENT OF COLORED PEOPLE
http://www.naacp.org/

HUBERTUS W.V. WILLEMS SCHOLARSHIP FOR MALE STUDENTS
• See page 229

NATIONAL INSTITUTES OF HEALTH

https://www.training.nih.gov/programs/ugsp

NIH UNDERGRADUATE SCHOLARSHIP PROGRAM FOR STUDENTS FROM DISADVANTAGED BACKGROUNDS
• See page 101

NATIONAL SOCIETY OF BLACK PHYSICISTS

http://www.nsbp.org/

AMERICAN PHYSICAL SOCIETY CORPORATE-SPONSORED SCHOLARSHIP FOR MINORITY UNDERGRADUATE STUDENTS WHO MAJOR IN PHYSICS

Scholarship available for minority undergraduate students majoring in physics. Award of $2000 per year for new corporate scholars, and $3000 per year for renewal students. In addition, each physics department that hosts one or more APS minority undergraduate scholars and assigns a mentor for their students will receive a $500 award for programs to encourage minority students.

Academic Fields/Career Goals: Physical Sciences.

Award: Scholarship for use in freshman, sophomore, junior, or senior years; not renewable. *Amount:* $2000–$3000.

Eligibility Requirements: Applicant must be American Indian/Alaska Native, Asian/Pacific Islander, Black (non-Hispanic), Hispanic and enrolled or expecting to enroll full- or part-time at a two-year or four-year institution or university. Available to U.S. citizens.

Application Requirements: Application form, recommendations or references, transcript. *Deadline:* December 1.

Contact: Dr. Stephen Roberson, Scholarship Chairman
Phone: 703-536-4207
Fax: 703-536-4203
E-mail: adminofficer@nsbp.org

CHARLES S. BROWN SCHOLARSHIP IN PHYSICS

Scholarship providing and African-American student with financial assistance while enrolled in a physics degree program. Number of awards and dollar value varies.

Academic Fields/Career Goals: Physical Sciences.

Award: Scholarship for use in freshman, sophomore, junior, senior, or graduate years; not renewable.

Eligibility Requirements: Applicant must be Black (non-Hispanic) and enrolled or expecting to enroll full- or part-time at a four-year institution or university. Available to U.S. and non-U.S. citizens.

Application Requirements: Application form, financial need analysis, self-addressed stamped envelope with application. *Deadline:* January 12.

Contact: Scholarship Committee Chair
National Society of Black Physicists
6704G Lee Highway
Arlington, VA 22205
Phone: 703-536-4207
Fax: 703-536-4203
E-mail: scholarship@nsbp.org

ELMER S. IMES SCHOLARSHIP IN PHYSICS

Graduating high school seniors and undergraduate students already enrolled in college as physics majors may apply for the scholarship. U.S citizenship is required.

Academic Fields/Career Goals: Physical Sciences.

Award: Scholarship for use in freshman, sophomore, junior, or senior years; not renewable. *Number:* 1. *Amount:* $1000.

Eligibility Requirements: Applicant must be enrolled or expecting to enroll full-time at a two-year or four-year institution or university. Available to U.S. citizens.

Application Requirements: Application form, driver's license, essay, recommendations or references, resume, transcript. *Deadline:* January 12.

Contact: Scholarship Committee Chair
National Society of Black Physicists
6704G Lee Highway
Arlington, VA 22205
Phone: 703-536-4207
Fax: 703-536-4203
E-mail: scholarship@nsbp.org

HARVEY WASHINGTON BANKS SCHOLARSHIP IN ASTRONOMY

One-time award for an African American student pursuing an undergraduate degree in astronomy/physics.

Academic Fields/Career Goals: Physical Sciences.

Award: Scholarship for use in freshman, sophomore, junior, or senior years; not renewable. *Number:* 1. *Amount:* $1000.

Eligibility Requirements: Applicant must be Black (non-Hispanic) and enrolled or expecting to enroll full-time at a two-year or four-year institution or university. Available to U.S. citizens.

Application Requirements: Application form, essay, recommendations or references, transcript. *Deadline:* January 12.

Contact: Dr. Stephen Roberson, Scholarship Chairman
Phone: 703-536-4207
Fax: 703-536-4203
E-mail: adminofficer@nsbp.org

MICHAEL P. ANDERSON SCHOLARSHIP IN SPACE SCIENCE

One-time award for an African American undergraduate student majoring in space science/physics.

Academic Fields/Career Goals: Physical Sciences.

Award: Scholarship for use in freshman, sophomore, junior, or senior years; not renewable. *Number:* 1. *Amount:* $1000.

Eligibility Requirements: Applicant must be Black (non-Hispanic) and enrolled or expecting to enroll full-time at a two-year or four-year institution or university. Available to U.S. citizens.

Application Requirements: Application form, essay, recommendations or references, transcript. *Deadline:* January 12.

Contact: Dr. Stephen Roberson, Scholarship Chairman
Phone: 703-536-4207
Fax: 703-536-4203
E-mail: adminofficer@nsbp.org

NATIONAL SOCIETY OF BLACK PHYSICISTS AND LAWRENCE LIVERMORE NATIONAL LIBRARY UNDERGRADUATE SCHOLARSHIP

Scholarship for a graduating high school senior or undergraduate student enrolled in a physics major. Scholarship renewable up to four years if student maintains a 3.0 GPA and remains a physics major.

Academic Fields/Career Goals: Physical Sciences.

Award: Scholarship for use in freshman, sophomore, junior, or senior years; renewable. *Number:* 1. *Amount:* $5000.

Eligibility Requirements: Applicant must be Black (non-Hispanic) and enrolled or expecting to enroll full-time at a two-year or four-year institution or university. Available to U.S. citizens.

Application Requirements: Application form, essay, recommendations or references, transcript. *Deadline:* December 1.

Contact: Dr. Stephen Roberson, Scholarship Chairman
Phone: 703-536-4207
Fax: 703-536-4203
E-mail: adminofficer@nsbp.org

RONALD E. MCNAIR SCHOLARSHIP IN SPACE AND OPTICAL PHYSICS

One-time award for African American undergraduate student majoring in physics. Must be U.S. citizen.

Academic Fields/Career Goals: Physical Sciences.

Award: Scholarship for use in freshman, sophomore, junior, or senior years; not renewable. *Number:* 1. *Amount:* $1000.

Eligibility Requirements: Applicant must be Black (non-Hispanic) and enrolled or expecting to enroll full-time at a two-year or four-year institution or university. Available to U.S. citizens.

Application Requirements: Application form, essay, recommendations or references, transcript. *Deadline:* January 12.

Contact: Dr. Stephen Roberson, Scholarship Chairman
Phone: 703-536-4207
Fax: 703-536-4203
E-mail: adminofficer@nsbp.org

WALTER SAMUEL MCAFEE SCHOLARSHIP IN SPACE PHYSICS

One-time scholarship for African American full-time undergraduate student majoring in physics. Must be U.S. citizen.

Academic Fields/Career Goals: Physical Sciences.

Award: Scholarship for use in freshman, sophomore, junior, or senior years; not renewable. *Number:* 1. *Amount:* $1000.

Eligibility Requirements: Applicant must be Black (non-Hispanic) and enrolled or expecting to enroll full-time at a two-year or four-year institution or university. Available to U.S. citizens.

Application Requirements: Application form, essay, recommendations or references, transcript. *Deadline:* January 12.

Contact: Dr. Stephen Roberson, Scholarship Chairman
Phone: 703-536-4207
Fax: 703-536-4203
E-mail: adminofficer@nsbp.org

WILLIE HOBBS MOORE, HARRY L. MORRISON, AND ARTHUR B.C. WALKER PHYSICS SCHOLARSHIPS

Scholarships are intended for African American undergraduate physics majors. Applicants should be either sophomores or juniors. Award for use in junior or senior year of study.

Academic Fields/Career Goals: Physical Sciences.

Award: Scholarship for use in sophomore, junior, or senior years; not renewable. *Number:* 3. *Amount:* $1000.

Eligibility Requirements: Applicant must be Black (non-Hispanic) and enrolled or expecting to enroll full-time at a two-year or four-year institution or university. Available to U.S. citizens.

Application Requirements: Application form, essay, recommendations or references, transcript. *Deadline:* January 12.

Contact: Dr. Stephen Roberson, Scholarship Chairman
Phone: 703-536-4207
Fax: 703-536-4203
E-mail: adminofficer@nsbp.org

NEVADA NASA SPACE GRANT CONSORTIUM

https://nasa.epscorspo.nevada.edu/

NATIONAL SPACE GRANT CONSORTIUM SCHOLARSHIPS
• See page 110

NEXTSTEPU

http://www.nextstepu.com/

$1,500 STEM SCHOLARSHIP
• See page 104

NOVUS BIOLOGICALS, LLC

https://www.novusbio.com

NOVUS BIOLOGICALS SCHOLARSHIP PROGRAM
• See page 101

R&D SYSTEMS SCHOLARSHIP
• See page 101

TOCRIS BIOSCIENCE SCHOLARSHIP
• See page 102

OREGON OFFICE OF STUDENT ACCESS AND COMPLETION

https://oregonstudentaid.gov/

SEHAR SALEHA AHMAD AND ABRAHIM EKRAMULLAH ZAFAR FOUNDATION SCHOLARSHIP
• See page 110

ROBERT H. MOLLOHAN FAMILY CHARITABLE FOUNDATION, INC.

http://www.mollohanfoundation.org/

HIGH TECHNOLOGY SCHOLARS PROGRAM
• See page 158

SCARLETT FAMILY FOUNDATION SCHOLARSHIP PROGRAM

http://www.scarlettfoundation.org/

SCHOLARSHIP FOR STUDENTS PURSUING A BUSINESS OR STEM DEGREE
• See page 80

SOCIETY OF PHYSICS STUDENTS

http://www.spsnational.org/

SOCIETY OF PHYSICS STUDENTS LEADERSHIP SCHOLARSHIPS

Scholarships of $2000 to $5000 are awarded to members of Society of Physics Students (SPS) for undergraduate study. The number of awards granted ranges from 17 to 22.

Academic Fields/Career Goals: Physical Sciences.

Award: Scholarship for use in sophomore, junior, or senior years; not renewable. *Number:* 17–22. *Amount:* $2000–$5000.

Eligibility Requirements: Applicant must be enrolled or expecting to enroll full-time at a two-year or four-year institution or university. Applicant or parent of applicant must be member of Society of Physics Students. Available to U.S. and non-U.S. citizens.

Application Requirements: Application form, recommendations or references, transcript. *Deadline:* February 15.

Contact: Scholarship Committee
Society of Physics Students
One Physics Ellipse
College Park, MD 20740
Phone: 301-209-3007
Fax: 301-209-0839
E-mail: sps@aip.org

SOCIETY OF PHYSICS STUDENTS OUTSTANDING STUDENT IN RESEARCH

Available to members of the Society of Physics Students. Winners will receive a $500 honorarium and a $500 award for their SPS Chapter. In addition, expenses for transportation, room, board, and registration for the ICPS will by paid by SPS.

Academic Fields/Career Goals: Physical Sciences.

Award: Prize for use in freshman, sophomore, junior, or senior years; not renewable. *Number:* 1–2. *Amount:* $500–$2500.

Eligibility Requirements: Applicant must be enrolled or expecting to enroll full-time at a two-year or four-year institution or university. Applicant or parent of applicant must be member of Society of Physics Students. Available to U.S. and non-U.S. citizens.

Application Requirements: Abstract, application form, recommendations or references. *Deadline:* April 15.

Contact: Secretary
Society of Physics Students
One Physics Ellipse
College Park, MD 20740
Phone: 301-209-3007
Fax: 301-209-0839
E-mail: sps@aip.org

SOCIETY OF PHYSICS STUDENTS PEGGY DIXON TWO-YEAR COLLEGE SCHOLARSHIP

Scholarship available to Society of Physics Students (SPS) members. Award based on performance both in physics and overall studies, and SPS participation. Must have completed at least one semester or quarter of the introductory physics sequence, and be currently registered in the appropriate subsequent physics courses.

Academic Fields/Career Goals: Physical Sciences.

Award: Scholarship for use in freshman or sophomore years; not renewable. *Number:* 1. *Amount:* $2000.

Eligibility Requirements: Applicant must be enrolled or expecting to enroll full-time at a two-year or four-year institution or university. Applicant or parent of applicant must be member of Society of Physics Students. Available to U.S. and non-U.S. citizens.

Application Requirements: Application form, financial need analysis, letters from at least two faculty members, transcript. *Deadline:* February 15.

Contact: Sacha Purnell, Administrative Assistant
Phone: 301-209-3007
E-mail: sps@aip.org

STRAIGHT NORTH

https://www.straightnorth.com/

STRAIGHT NORTH STEM SCHOLARSHIP
• *See page 81*

TAILOR MADE LAWNS

http://www.tailormadelawns.com

2017 TAILOR MADE LAWNS SCHOLARSHIP FUND
• *See page 96*

UNITED NEGRO COLLEGE FUND

http://www.uncf.org/

LEIDOS STEM SCHOLARSHIP
• *See page 96*

VERMONT SPACE GRANT CONSORTIUM

http://www.cems.uvm.edu/vsgc

VERMONT SPACE GRANT CONSORTIUM
• *See page 92*

XEROX

http://www.xerox.com//

TECHNICAL MINORITY SCHOLARSHIP
• *See page 161*

POLITICAL SCIENCE

AMERICAN FEDERATION OF STATE, COUNTY, AND MUNICIPAL EMPLOYEES

https://www.afscme.org/

AFSCME/UNCF UNION SCHOLARS PROGRAM
• *See page 98*

JERRY CLARK MEMORIAL SCHOLARSHIP

Renewable award for a student majoring in political science for his or her junior and senior years of study. Must be a child of an AFSCME member. Minimum 2.5 GPA required. Once awarded, the scholarship will be renewed for the senior year provided the student remains enrolled full-time as a political science major.

Academic Fields/Career Goals: Political Science.

Award: Scholarship for use in junior or senior years; renewable. *Number:* 2. *Amount:* $5000.

Eligibility Requirements: Applicant must be enrolled or expecting to enroll full-time at a four-year institution or university. Applicant or parent of applicant must be member of American Federation of State, County, and Municipal Employees. Available to U.S. citizens.

Application Requirements: Application form, proof of parent, transcript. *Deadline:* July 1.

ARAB AMERICAN SCHOLARSHIP FOUNDATION

http://www.lahc.org/

LEBANESE AMERICAN HERITAGE CLUB'S SCHOLARSHIP FUND
• *See page 170*

ASSOCIATION OF FORMER INTELLIGENCE OFFICERS

www.afio.com

AFIO UNDERGRADUATE AND GRADUATE SCHOLARSHIPS
• *See page 98*

BOYS AND GIRLS CLUBS OF GREATER SAN DIEGO

http://www.sdyouth.org/

SPENCE REESE SCHOLARSHIP
• *See page 237*

CONGRESSIONAL BLACK CAUCUS FOUNDATION, INC.

http://www.cbcfinc.org/

CBC SPOUSES EDUCATION SCHOLARSHIP
• *See page 98*

CULTURAL SERVICES OF THE FRENCH EMBASSY

http://www.frenchculture.org/

TEACHING ASSISTANT PROGRAM IN FRANCE
• *See page 98*

GOVERNMENT FINANCE OFFICERS ASSOCIATION

https://www.gfoa.org/

MINORITIES IN GOVERNMENT FINANCE SCHOLARSHIP
• *See page 75*

GREATER SALINA COMMUNITY FOUNDATION

http://www.gscf.org/

KANSAS FEDERATION OF REPUBLICAN WOMEN SCHOLARSHIP
• *See page 288*

HARRY S. TRUMAN SCHOLARSHIP FOUNDATION

http://www.truman.gov/

HARRY S. TRUMAN SCHOLARSHIP

Scholarships for U.S. citizens or U.S. nationals who are college or university students with junior-level academic standing and who wish to attend professional or graduate school to prepare for careers in government or the nonprofit and advocacy sectors. Candidates must be nominated by their institution. Public service and leadership record considered. Visit website http://www.truman.gov for further information and application.

Academic Fields/Career Goals: Political Science; Public Policy and Administration.

Award: Scholarship for use in junior year; renewable. *Number:* 65. *Amount:* $30,000.

Eligibility Requirements: Applicant must be enrolled or expecting to enroll full-time at a four-year institution or university and must have an interest in leadership. Available to U.S. citizens.

Application Requirements: Application form, interview, policy proposal, recommendations or references. *Deadline:* February 5.

Contact: Tonji Wade, Program Officer
Harry S. Truman Scholarship Foundation
712 Jackson Place, NW
Washington, DC 20006
Phone: 202-395-4831
Fax: 202-395-6995
E-mail: office@truman.gov

HUB FOUNDATION

https://hub-foundation.org

HUB FOUNDATION SCHOLARSHIPS
• *See page 88*

LA-PHILOSOPHIE.COM

http://la-philosophie.com

LA-PHILOSOPHIE.COM SCHOLARSHIP
• *See page 104*

THE LYNDON BAINES JOHNSON FOUNDATION

http://www.lbjlibrary.org/page/foundation/

MOODY RESEARCH GRANTS
• *See page 99*

NATIONAL SOCIETY DAUGHTERS OF THE AMERICAN REVOLUTION

http://www.dar.org/

DR. AURA-LEE A. AND JAMES HOBBS PITTENGER AMERICAN HISTORY SCHOLARSHIP

The Dr. Aura-Lee A. and James Hobbs Pittenger American History Scholarship is awarded to graduating high school students who will pursue an undergraduate degree with a concentrated study of a minimum of 24 credit hours in American History and American Government. Renewal is conditional upon maintenance of a GPA of 3.25. This scholarship is renewable. This award is intended to promote the study of our country's history among our finest students. U.S. Citizens residing abroad may apply through a Units Overseas Chapter. Award of $2,000 each year for up to four years with annual transcript review by the National Chairman required for renewal.

Academic Fields/Career Goals: Political Science.

Award: Scholarship for use in freshman year; renewable. *Number:* 1. *Amount:* $2000.

Eligibility Requirements: Applicant must be high school student and planning to enroll or expecting to enroll full-time at an institution or university. Available to U.S. citizens.

Application Requirements: Application form, application form may be submitted online, essay. *Deadline:* February 15.

Contact: Lakeisha Graham, Manager, Office of the Reporter General
Phone: 202-628-1776
Fax: 202-879-3348
E-mail: nsdarscholarships@dar.org

ENID HALL GRISWOLD MEMORIAL SCHOLARSHIP
• *See page 289*

STRAIGHTFORWARD MEDIA

http://www.straightforwardmedia.com/

STRAIGHTFORWARD MEDIA LIBERAL ARTS SCHOLARSHIP
• *See page 119*

TAU KAPPA EPSILON EDUCATION FOUNDATION

https://www.tke.org/

BRUCE B. MELCHERT SCHOLARSHIP

This scholarship is awarded in recognition of academic achievement and outstanding leadership within the chapter, having served as Recruitment Chair, Prytanis or other major officer position in the chapter, and a leader in IFC or other campus organizations. The applicant must be pursuing an undergraduate degree in political science or government, and have a goal to serve people in a political or governmental service position. Preference will first be given to a member of Beta-Theta Chapter but, if there is no qualified applicant, the scholarship will be open to any other qualified Teke.

Academic Fields/Career Goals: Political Science.

Award: Scholarship for use in sophomore, junior, or senior years. *Number:* 1.

Eligibility Requirements: Applicant must be enrolled or expecting to enroll at an institution or university. Applicant or parent of applicant must be member of Tau Kappa Epsilon. Available to U.S. citizens.

Application Requirements: Application form, application form may be submitted online, personal photograph. *Deadline:* March 15.

Contact: Rachel Stevenson, Foundation Communications Manager
Tau Kappa Epsilon Education Foundation
7439 Woodland Drive
Suite 100
Indianapolis, IN 46278
Phone: 317-872-6533 Ext. 246
E-mail: rstevenson@tke.org

UNITED NATIONS ASSOCIATION OF CONNECTICUT

http://www.unausa.org

UNITED NATIONS ASSOCIATION OF CONNECTICUT SCHOLARSHIP
• *See page 124*

UNITED NEGRO COLLEGE FUND

http://www.uncf.org/

THE OSSIE DAVIS LEGACY AWARD SCHOLARSHIP
• *See page 89*

WASHINGTON CROSSING FOUNDATION

http://www.gwcf.org/

WASHINGTON CROSSING FOUNDATION SCHOLARSHIP
Merit-based awards available to high school seniors who are planning a career in government service. Must write an essay stating reason for deciding on a career in public service. Minimum 3.0 GPA required.
Academic Fields/Career Goals: Political Science; Public Policy and Administration.
Award: Scholarship for use in freshman year; not renewable. *Amount:* $500–$5000.
Eligibility Requirements: Applicant must be high school student and planning to enroll or expecting to enroll full-time at a four-year institution or university. Available to U.S. citizens.
Application Requirements: Application form, essay, interview, personal photograph. *Deadline:* January 15.
Contact: Washington Crossing Foundation
Washington Crossing Foundation
PO Box 503
Levittown, PA 19058-0503
Phone: 215-949-8841
E-mail: info@gwcf.org

WASHINGTON MEDIA SCHOLARS FOUNDATION

www.mediascholars.org

MEDIA PLAN CASE COMPETITION
• *See page 88*

WASHINGTON STATE ASSOCIATION FOR JUSTICE

http://www.washingtonjustice.org/

WASHINGTON STATE ASSOCIATION FOR JUSTICE AMERICAN JUSTICE ESSAY & VIDEO SCHOLARSHIP
• *See page 189*

WILLIAMS LAW GROUP

https://familylawyersnewjersey.com/

WILLIAMS LAW GROUP OPPORTUNITY TO GROW SCHOLARSHIP
• *See page 119*

PSYCHOLOGY

AMERICAN FEDERATION OF STATE, COUNTY, AND MUNICIPAL EMPLOYEES

https://www.afscme.org/

AFSCME/UNCF UNION SCHOLARS PROGRAM
• *See page 98*

ASSISTANCE LEAGUE OF THE TRIANGLE AREA

HEALTH CARE PROFESSION SCHOLARSHIP
• *See page 195*

AVACARE MEDICAL

https://avacaremedical.com

AVACARE MEDICAL SCHOLARSHIP
• *See page 100*

BHW GROUP

https://thebhwgroup.com/

BHW WOMEN IN STEM SCHOLARSHIP
• *See page 107*

CYNTHIA E. MORGAN SCHOLARSHIP FUND (CEMS)

http://www.cemsfund.com/

CYNTHIA E. MORGAN MEMORIAL SCHOLARSHIP FUND, INC.
• *See page 248*

HEALTH PROFESSIONS EDUCATION FOUNDATION

http://www.healthprofessions.ca.gov/

ALLIED HEALTHCARE SCHOLARSHIP PROGRAM
• *See page 196*

HEALTH RESEARCH COUNCIL OF NEW ZEALAND

https://gateway.hrc.govt.nz/

PACIFIC MENTAL HEALTH WORK FORCE AWARD
• *See page 277*

HUB FOUNDATION

https://hub-foundation.org

HUB FOUNDATION SCHOLARSHIPS
• *See page 88*

INDIAN HEALTH SERVICES, UNITED STATES DEPARTMENT OF HEALTH AND HUMAN SERVICES

http://www.ihs.gov/scholarship

HEALTH PROFESSIONS PREPARATORY SCHOLARSHIP PROGRAM
• *See page 137*

INTERMOUNTAIN MEDICAL IMAGING

https://www.aboutimi.com/

INTERMOUNTAIN MEDICAL IMAGING SCHOLARSHIP
• *See page 125*

KETAMINE CLINICS OF LOS ANGELES

http://www.ketamineclinics.com/

KETAMINE CLINICS OF LOS ANGELES SCHOLARSHIP PROGRAM
• *See page 138*

LA-PHILOSOPHIE.COM

http://la-philosophie.com

LA-PHILOSOPHIE.COM SCHOLARSHIP
• *See page 104*

MEDICAL SCRUBS COLLECTION

http://medicalscrubscollection.com

MEDICAL SCRUBS COLLECTION SCHOLARSHIP
• *See page 104*

NOVUS BIOLOGICALS, LLC

https://www.novusbio.com

NOVUS BIOLOGICALS SCHOLARSHIP PROGRAM
• *See page 101*

R&D SYSTEMS SCHOLARSHIP
• *See page 101*

TOCRIS BIOSCIENCE SCHOLARSHIP
• *See page 102*

PILOT INTERNATIONAL

https://www.pilotinternational.org/

PILOT INTERNATIONAL SCHOLARSHIP
• *See page 373*

THE RECOVERY VILLAGE

https://www.therecoveryvillage.com/

RECOVERY VILLAGE HEALTHCARE SCHOLARSHIP
• *See page 197*

THE SOCIETY FOR THE SCIENTIFIC STUDY OF SEXUALITY

http://www.sexscience.org/

THE SOCIETY FOR THE SCIENTIFIC STUDY OF SEXUALITY STUDENT RESEARCH GRANT
• *See page 105*

STRAIGHTFORWARD MEDIA

http://www.straightforwardmedia.com/

STRAIGHTFORWARD MEDIA LIBERAL ARTS SCHOLARSHIP
• *See page 119*

UNITED NEGRO COLLEGE FUND

http://www.uncf.org/

HCN/APRICITY RESOURCES SCHOLARS PROGRAM
• *See page 83*

VIRTUOUS PROM

https://www.virtuousprom.com

VIRTUOUS PROM PEACE SCHOLARSHIP
This scholarship is for women studying in the areas of psychology, anthropology, sociology and theology at both the undergraduate and graduate level.

Academic Fields/Career Goals: Psychology.

Award: Scholarship for use in freshman, sophomore, junior, senior, graduate, or postgraduate years; not renewable. *Number:* 1. *Amount:* $250.

Eligibility Requirements: Applicant must be enrolled or expecting to enroll full- or part-time at a two-year or four-year institution or university and female. Available to U.S. and non-U.S. citizens.

Application Requirements: Essay. *Deadline:* January 31.

Contact: Ms. Megan MacNeal, Creative Director
E-mail: megan@virtuousprom.com

WILLIAMS LAW GROUP

https://familylawyersnewjersey.com/

WILLIAMS LAW GROUP OPPORTUNITY TO GROW SCHOLARSHIP
• *See page 119*

PUBLIC HEALTH

ASSISTANCE LEAGUE OF THE TRIANGLE AREA

HEALTH CARE PROFESSION SCHOLARSHIP
• *See page 195*

ASSOCIATION ON AMERICAN INDIAN AFFAIRS, INC.

http://www.indian-affairs.org/

ELIZABETH AND SHERMAN ASCHE MEMORIAL SCHOLARSHIP FUND
• *See page 93*

AVACARE MEDICAL

https://avacaremedical.com

AVACARE MEDICAL SCHOLARSHIP
• *See page 100*

CONTINENTAL SOCIETY, DAUGHTERS OF INDIAN WARS

http://www.csdiw.org/

CONTINENTAL SOCIETY, DAUGHTERS OF INDIAN WARS SCHOLARSHIP
• *See page 188*

THE EXPERT INSTITUTE

https://www.theexpertinstitute.com

ANNUAL HEALTHCARE AND LIFE SCIENCES SCHOLARSHIP
• *See page 142*

FLORIDA ENVIRONMENTAL HEALTH ASSOCIATION

http://www.feha.org/

FLORIDA ENVIRONMENTAL HEALTH ASSOCIATION EDUCATIONAL SCHOLARSHIP AWARDS
• *See page 249*

INTERMOUNTAIN MEDICAL IMAGING

https://www.aboutimi.com/

INTERMOUNTAIN MEDICAL IMAGING SCHOLARSHIP
• *See page 125*

THE JACKSON LABORATORY

https://www.jax.org

THE JACKSON LABORATORY COLLEGE SCHOLARSHIP PROGRAM
• *See page 108*

MEDICAL SCRUBS COLLECTION

http://medicalscrubscollection.com

MEDICAL SCRUBS COLLECTION SCHOLARSHIP
• *See page 104*

NATIONAL ENVIRONMENTAL HEALTH ASSOCIATION/AMERICAN ACADEMY OF SANITARIANS

http://www.neha.org/

NATIONAL ENVIRONMENTAL HEALTH ASSOCIATION/AMERICAN ACADEMY OF SANITARIANS SCHOLARSHIP
• *See page 249*

NATIONAL INSTITUTES OF HEALTH

https://www.training.nih.gov/programs/ugsp

NIH UNDERGRADUATE SCHOLARSHIP PROGRAM FOR STUDENTS FROM DISADVANTAGED BACKGROUNDS
• *See page 101*

NEW ENGLAND EMPLOYEE BENEFITS COUNCIL

http://www.neebc.org/

NEW ENGLAND EMPLOYEE BENEFITS COUNCIL SCHOLARSHIP PROGRAM
• *See page 78*

NOVUS BIOLOGICALS, LLC

https://www.novusbio.com

NOVUS BIOLOGICALS SCHOLARSHIP PROGRAM
• *See page 101*

R&D SYSTEMS SCHOLARSHIP
• *See page 101*

TOCRIS BIOSCIENCE SCHOLARSHIP
• *See page 102*

PLATINUM EDUCATIONAL GROUP

www.platinumed.com

PLATINUM EDUCATIONAL GROUP SCHOLARSHIPS PROGRAM FOR EMS, NURSING, AND ALLIED HEALTH
• *See page 102*

THE RECOVERY VILLAGE

https://www.therecoveryvillage.com/

RECOVERY VILLAGE HEALTHCARE SCHOLARSHIP
• *See page 197*

THE SOCIETY FOR THE SCIENTIFIC STUDY OF SEXUALITY

http://www.sexscience.org/

THE SOCIETY FOR THE SCIENTIFIC STUDY OF SEXUALITY STUDENT RESEARCH GRANT
• *See page 105*

SOUTH CAROLINA PUBLIC HEALTH ASSOCIATION

http://www.scpha.com/

SOUTH CAROLINA PUBLIC HEALTH ASSOCIATION PUBLIC HEALTH SCHOLARSHIPS
Current member of the SCPHA with more than 6 hours remaining and enrolled in a accredited higher education program for public health or related field. Dantzler- exhibit significant commitment to the public health profession through volunteer and/or professional activity as indicated on the application. Public Health Scholarship- exhibit significant commitment to the public health profession through volunteer and/or professional activity as indicated on the application.

Academic Fields/Career Goals: Public Health.

Award: Scholarship for use in freshman, sophomore, junior, senior, graduate, or postgraduate years; not renewable. *Number:* 2. *Amount:* $500–$750.

Eligibility Requirements: Applicant must be enrolled or expecting to enroll full- or part-time at a four-year institution or university. Available to U.S. citizens.

Application Requirements: Application form, proof of number of hours remaining, transcript. *Deadline:* March 31.

Contact: Mr. Larry White, Scholarship Committee Chair
South Carolina Public Health Association
PO Box 3051
Conway, SC 29528
Phone: 843-488-1329 Ext. 225
Fax: 843-488-1330
E-mail: larry@smokefreehorry.org

PUBLIC POLICY AND ADMINISTRATION

AMERICAN INSTITUTE OF POLISH CULTURE INC.

http://www.ampolinstitute.org/

HARRIET IRSAY SCHOLARSHIP GRANT
• *See page 120*

AMERICAN LEGION AUXILIARY DEPARTMENT OF ARIZONA

http:/wwwaladeptaz.org

AMERICAN LEGION AUXILIARY DEPARTMENT OF ARIZONA WILMA HOYAL-MAXINE CHILTON MEMORIAL SCHOLARSHIP
• *See page 170*

ASSOCIATION FOR EDUCATION AND REHABILITATION OF THE BLIND AND VISUALLY IMPAIRED

http://www.aerbvi.org/

WILLIAM AND DOROTHY FERRELL SCHOLARSHIP
• *See page 207*

ASSOCIATION OF FORMER INTELLIGENCE OFFICERS

www.afio.com

AFIO UNDERGRADUATE AND GRADUATE SCHOLARSHIPS
• *See page 98*

CONGRESSIONAL BLACK CAUCUS FOUNDATION, INC.

http://www.cbcfinc.org/

CBC SPOUSES EDUCATION SCHOLARSHIP
• *See page 98*

THE DALLAS FOUNDATION

http://www.dallasfoundation.org/

WHITLEY PLACE SCHOLARSHIP
• *See page 114*

GOVERNMENT FINANCE OFFICERS ASSOCIATION

https://www.gfoa.org/

JEFFREY L. ESSER CAREER DEVELOPMENT SCHOLARSHIP
• *See page 75*

MINORITIES IN GOVERNMENT FINANCE SCHOLARSHIP
• *See page 75*

GREATER SALINA COMMUNITY FOUNDATION

http://www.gscf.org/

KANSAS FEDERATION OF REPUBLICAN WOMEN SCHOLARSHIP
• *See page 288*

HARRY S. TRUMAN SCHOLARSHIP FOUNDATION

http://www.truman.gov/

HARRY S. TRUMAN SCHOLARSHIP
• *See page 394*

JAPANESE AMERICAN CITIZENS LEAGUE (JACL)

http://www.jacl.org/

NATIONAL JACL HEADQUARTERS SCHOLARSHIP
• *See page 94*

NATIONAL ACADEMY OF TELEVISION ARTS AND SCIENCES

https://theemmys.tv/

DOUGLAS W. MUMMERT SCHOLARSHIP
• *See page 173*

NEW ENGLAND EMPLOYEE BENEFITS COUNCIL

http://www.neebc.org/

NEW ENGLAND EMPLOYEE BENEFITS COUNCIL SCHOLARSHIP PROGRAM
• *See page 78*

THE RECOVERY VILLAGE

https://www.therecoveryvillage.com/

RECOVERY VILLAGE HEALTHCARE SCHOLARSHIP
• *See page 197*

WASHINGTON CROSSING FOUNDATION

http://www.gwcf.org/

WASHINGTON CROSSING FOUNDATION SCHOLARSHIP
• *See page 395*

WASHINGTON MEDIA SCHOLARS FOUNDATION

www.mediascholars.org

MEDIA PLAN CASE COMPETITION
• *See page 88*

WASHINGTON STATE ASSOCIATION FOR JUSTICE

http://www.washingtonjustice.org/

WASHINGTON STATE ASSOCIATION FOR JUSTICE AMERICAN JUSTICE ESSAY & VIDEO SCHOLARSHIP
• *See page 189*

RADIOLOGY

101ST AIRBORNE DIVISION ASSOCIATION

http://www.screamingeaglefoundation.org/

AL & WILLIAMARY VISTE SCHOLARSHIP
• *See page 99*

ACLS CERTIFICATION INSTITUTE

https://acls.com

MEDICAL SCHOOL SCHOLARSHIP
• *See page 194*

AMERICAN INDIAN SCIENCE AND ENGINEERING SOCIETY

http://www.aises.org/

A.T. ANDERSON MEMORIAL SCHOLARSHIP PROGRAM
• *See page 105*

ASRT FOUNDATION

https://foundation.asrt.org/

JERMAN-CAHOON STUDENT SCHOLARSHIP
• *See page 276*

PROFESSIONAL ADVANCEMENT SCHOLARSHIP
• *See page 276*

ROYCE OSBORN MINORITY STUDENT SCHOLARSHIP
• *See page 276*

SIEMENS CLINICAL ADVANCEMENT SCHOLARSHIP
• *See page 378*

ASSISTANCE LEAGUE OF THE TRIANGLE AREA

HEALTH CARE PROFESSION SCHOLARSHIP
• *See page 195*

CYNTHIA E. MORGAN SCHOLARSHIP FUND (CEMS)

http://www.cemsfund.com/

CYNTHIA E. MORGAN MEMORIAL SCHOLARSHIP FUND, INC.
• *See page 248*

HEALTH PROFESSIONS EDUCATION FOUNDATION

http://www.healthprofessions.ca.gov/

ALLIED HEALTHCARE SCHOLARSHIP PROGRAM
• *See page 196*

MEDICAL SCRUBS COLLECTION

http://medicalscrubscollection.com

MEDICAL SCRUBS COLLECTION SCHOLARSHIP
• *See page 104*

NEXTSTEPU

http://www.nextstepu.com/

$1,500 STEM SCHOLARSHIP
• *See page 104*

NOVUS BIOLOGICALS, LLC

https://www.novusbio.com

NOVUS BIOLOGICALS SCHOLARSHIP PROGRAM
• *See page 101*

R&D SYSTEMS SCHOLARSHIP
• *See page 101*

TOCRIS BIOSCIENCE SCHOLARSHIP
• *See page 102*

PLATINUM EDUCATIONAL GROUP

www.platinumed.com

PLATINUM EDUCATIONAL GROUP SCHOLARSHIPS PROGRAM FOR EMS, NURSING, AND ALLIED HEALTH
• *See page 102*

ULTRASOUNDTECHNICIANSCHOOLS.COM

http://www.ultrasoundtechnicianschools.com

ULTRASOUNDTECHNICIANSCHOOLS.COM SCHOLARSHIP
• *See page 286*

UNITED NEGRO COLLEGE FUND

http://www.uncf.org/

LEIDOS STEM SCHOLARSHIP
• *See page 96*

REAL ESTATE

APPRAISAL INSTITUTE EDUCATION TRUST

http://www.aiedtrust.org/

AIET MINORITIES AND WOMEN EDUCATIONAL SCHOLARSHIP

Awarded to minorities and women undergraduate students pursuing academic degrees in real estate appraisal or related fields.

Academic Fields/Career Goals: Real Estate.

Award: Scholarship for use in freshman, sophomore, junior, senior, graduate, or postgraduate years; not renewable. *Amount:* $1000.

Eligibility Requirements: Applicant must be American Indian/Alaska Native, Asian/Pacific Islander, Black (non-Hispanic), Hispanic; enrolled or expecting to enroll full- or part-time at a four-year institution or university and female. Applicant must be hearing impaired, learning disabled, physically disabled, or visually impaired. Available to U.S. citizens.

Application Requirements: Application form, essay, financial need analysis, personal photograph, recommendations or references, resume, transcript. *Deadline:* April 15.

Contact: Sarah Walsh
Appraisal Institute Education Trust
200 West Madison
Suite 1500
Chicago, IL 60607
Phone: 312-335-4133
Fax: 312-335-4134
E-mail: educationtrust@appraisalinstitute.org

APPRAISAL INSTITUTE EDUCATION TRUST EDUCATION SCHOLARSHIPS

Awarded on the basis of academic excellence, this scholarship helps finance the educational endeavors of undergraduate and graduate students concentrating in real estate appraisal, land economics, real estate or allied fields.

Academic Fields/Career Goals: Real Estate.

Award: Scholarship for use in sophomore, junior, senior, or graduate years; not renewable. *Amount:* $1000–$2000.

Eligibility Requirements: Applicant must be enrolled or expecting to enroll full-time at a four-year institution or university. Available to U.S. citizens.

Application Requirements: Application form, essay, recommendations or references, resume, transcript. *Deadline:* February 15.

Contact: Sarah Walsh, Coordinator
Appraisal Institute Education Trust
200 West Madison
Suite 1500
Chicago, IL 60606
Phone: 312-335-4133
Fax: 312-335-4134
E-mail: educationtrust@appraisalinstitute.org

C.A.R. SCHOLARSHIP FOUNDATION

http://www.car.org/

C.A.R. SCHOLARSHIP FOUNDATION AWARD

Scholarships to students enrolled at a California College or University for professions which are centered on, or support a career in real estate transactional activity. Must have maintained a cumulative GPA of 2.6 or higher.

Academic Fields/Career Goals: Real Estate.

Award: Scholarship for use in sophomore, junior, senior, graduate, or postgraduate years; not renewable. *Number:* 10–25. *Amount:* $2000–$4000.

Eligibility Requirements: Applicant must be enrolled or expecting to enroll full- or part-time at a two-year or four-year institution or university; resident of California and studying in California. Available to U.S. citizens.

Application Requirements: Application form, driver's license, essay, interview. *Deadline:* April 6.

Contact: Lindsey Moss, Scholarship Coordinator
C.A.R. Scholarship Foundation
525 South Virgil Avenue
Los Angeles, CA 90020
Phone: 213-739-8217
Fax: 213-739-7278
E-mail: scholarship@car.org

ILLINOIS REAL ESTATE EDUCATIONAL FOUNDATION

http://www.ilreef.org/

ILLINOIS REAL ESTATE EDUCATIONAL FOUNDATION ACADEMIC SCHOLARSHIPS

Awards for Illinois residents attending an accredited two-or four-year junior college, college or university in Illinois. Must have completed 30 college credit hours and be pursuing a degree with an emphasis in real estate. Must be a U.S. citizen.

Academic Fields/Career Goals: Real Estate.

Award: Scholarship for use in freshman, sophomore, junior, or senior years; not renewable. *Amount:* $1000.

Eligibility Requirements: Applicant must be enrolled or expecting to enroll full-time at a two-year or four-year institution or university; resident of Illinois and studying in Illinois. Available to U.S. citizens.

Application Requirements: Application form, essay, recommendations or references, resume, transcript. *Deadline:* April 1.

Contact: Laurie Clayton, Foundation Manager
Illinois Real Estate Educational Foundation
522 South 5th Street, PO Box 2607
Springfield, IL 62708
Phone: 866-854-7333
Fax: 217-529-5893
E-mail: lclayton@iar.org

THOMAS F. SEAY SCHOLARSHIP

Award of $2000 to students pursuing a degree with an emphasis in real estate. Must be a U.S. citizen and attending any accredited U.S. college or university full-time. Must have completed at least 30 college credit hours. Minimum 3.5 GPA required.

Academic Fields/Career Goals: Real Estate.

Award: Scholarship for use in junior or senior years; not renewable. *Amount:* $2000.

Eligibility Requirements: Applicant must be enrolled or expecting to enroll full-time at a four-year institution or university; resident of Illinois and studying in Illinois. Available to U.S. citizens.

Application Requirements: Application form, community service, essay, recommendations or references, resume, transcript. *Deadline:* April 1.

Contact: Laurie Clayton, Foundation Manager
Illinois Real Estate Educational Foundation
522 South 5th Street, PO Box 2607
Springfield, IL 62708
Phone: 866-854-7333
Fax: 217-529-5893
E-mail: lclayton@iar.org

NEW JERSEY ASSOCIATION OF REALTORS

http://www.njar.com/

NEW JERSEY ASSOCIATION OF REALTORS EDUCATIONAL FOUNDATION SCHOLARSHIP PROGRAM

One-time awards for New Jersey residents who are high school seniors pursuing studies in real estate or allied fields. Preference to students considering a career in real estate. Must be member of NJAR or relative of a member. Selected candidates are interviewed in June. Must be a U.S. citizen.

Academic Fields/Career Goals: Real Estate.

Award: Scholarship for use in freshman year; not renewable. *Number:* 20–32. *Amount:* $1000–$2500.

Eligibility Requirements: Applicant must be high school student; planning to enroll or expecting to enroll full-time at a four-year institution or university and resident of New Jersey. Applicant or parent of applicant must be member of New Jersey Association of Realtors. Available to U.S. citizens.

Application Requirements: Application form, essay, financial need analysis, interview, letter of verification of realtor/realtor associate/association staff, transcript. *Deadline:* April 9.

Contact: Diane Hatley, Educational Foundation
New Jersey Association of Realtors
PO Box 2098
Edison, NJ 08818
Phone: 732-494-5616
Fax: 732-494-4723

RECREATION, PARKS, LEISURE STUDIES

AMERICAN HOTEL AND LODGING EDUCATIONAL FOUNDATION

https://www.ahlafoundation.org/

AHLEF ANNUAL SCHOLARSHIP GRANT PROGRAM
• *See page 267*

AMERICAN HOTEL & LODGING EDUCATIONAL FOUNDATION PEPSI SCHOLARSHIP
• *See page 189*

ECOLAB SCHOLARSHIP PROGRAM
• *See page 267*

HYATT HOTELS FUND FOR MINORITY LODGING MANAGEMENT
• *See page 268*

INCOMING FRESHMAN SCHOLARSHIPS
• *See page 268*

RAMA SCHOLARSHIP FOR THE AMERICAN DREAM
• *See page 268*

THE LAND CONSERVANCY OF NEW JERSEY

http://www.tlc-nj.org/

ROGERS FAMILY SCHOLARSHIP
• *See page 143*

RUSSELL W. MYERS SCHOLARSHIP
• *See page 143*

NATIONAL RECREATION AND PARK ASSOCIATION

http://www.nrpa.org/

AFRS STUDENT SCHOLARSHIP
Applicant must be currently enrolled in a NRPA accredited recreation/parks curriculum or related field. Number of awards varies.

Academic Fields/Career Goals: Recreation, Parks, Leisure Studies.

Award: Scholarship for use in freshman or sophomore years; not renewable. *Amount:* $500.

Eligibility Requirements: Applicant must be enrolled or expecting to enroll full- or part-time at a four-year institution or university. Available to U.S. citizens.

Application Requirements: Application form, essay, recommendations or references, test scores, transcript. *Deadline:* June 1.

Contact: Jessica Lytle, Senior Manager
Phone: 703-858-2150
Fax: 703-858-0974
E-mail: jlytle@nrpa.org

PADDLE CANADA

http://www.paddlecanada.com

BILL MASON SCHOLARSHIP FUND
• *See page 212*

SHAPE AMERICA

http://www.shapeamerica.org/

RUTH ABERNATHY PRESIDENTIAL SCHOLARSHIP
Three award for undergraduate students and two for graduate students in January of each year. Must be majoring in the field of health, physical education, recreation or dance. Undergraduate awards are in the amount of $1,250 each and graduate awards are in the amount of $1,750 each. Recipients also receive a complimentary three-year SHAPE America membership. Applicant must be current member of SHAPE America

Academic Fields/Career Goals: Recreation, Parks, Leisure Studies; Sports-Related/Exercise Science.

Award: Scholarship for use in junior, senior, or graduate years; not renewable. *Number:* 5. *Amount:* $1250–$1750.

Eligibility Requirements: Applicant must be enrolled or expecting to enroll full-time at a four-year institution or university and must have an interest in leadership. Available to U.S. and non-U.S. citizens.

Application Requirements: Application form. *Deadline:* October 15.

Contact: Patti Hartle, Executive Administrator
SHAPE America
1900 Association Drive
Reston, VA 20191
Phone: 703-476-3405
E-mail: phartle@shapeamerica.org

THE WALTER J. TRAVIS SOCIETY

http://www.travissociety.com

THE WALTER J. TRAVIS MEMORIAL SCHOLARSHIP AND THE WALTER J. TRAVIS-RUDY ZOCCHI MEMORIAL SCHOLARSHIP
• *See page 118*

RELIGION/THEOLOGY

BETHESDA LUTHERAN COMMUNITIES

http://www.bethesdalutherancommunities.org/scholarships

DEVELOPMENTAL DISABILITIES SCHOLASTIC ACHIEVEMENT SCHOLARSHIP FOR COLLEGE STUDENTS WHO ARE LUTHERAN
• *See page 195*

EASTERN STAR-GRAND CHAPTER OF CALIFORNIA

http://www.oescal.org/

SCHOLARSHIPS FOR EDUCATION, BUSINESS AND RELIGION
• See page 147

ED E. AND GLADYS HURLEY FOUNDATION

ED E. AND GLADYS HURLEY FOUNDATION SCHOLARSHIP

Provides scholarships up to $1000 per year per student. Applicant must be Protestant enrolled or expecting to enroll full or part-time at a two-year or four-year institution or university and studying in Texas. Available to U.S. citizens.

Academic Fields/Career Goals: Religion/Theology.

Award: Scholarship for use in freshman, sophomore, junior, senior, graduate, or postgraduate years; not renewable. *Number:* 100–150. *Amount:* up to $1000.

Eligibility Requirements: Applicant must be Protestant; enrolled or expecting to enroll full- or part-time at a two-year or four-year institution or university; resident of Arkansas, Louisiana, Texas and studying in Texas. Available to U.S. citizens.

Application Requirements: Application form, financial need analysis, recommendations or references. *Deadline:* April 30.

Contact: Rose Davis, Financial Aid Coordinator
Ed E. and Gladys Hurley Foundation
Houston Graduate School-Theology
2501 Central Parkway, Suite A19
Houston, TX 77092
Phone: 713-942-9505
E-mail: rdavis@hgst.edu

HUB FOUNDATION

https://hub-foundation.org

HUB FOUNDATION SCHOLARSHIPS
• See page 88

LA-PHILOSOPHIE.COM

http://la-philosophie.com

LA-PHILOSOPHIE.COM SCHOLARSHIP
• See page 104

NATIONAL ASSOCIATION OF PASTORAL MUSICIANS

http://www.npm.org/

ELAINE RENDLER-RENE DOSOGNE-GEORGETOWN CHORALE SCHOLARSHIP
• See page 349

FUNK FAMILY MEMORIAL SCHOLARSHIP

Awards NPM members enrolled full-time or part-time in a graduate or undergraduate degree program of studies related to the field of pastoral music. Applicant must intend to work at least two years in the field of pastoral music following graduation or program completion.

Academic Fields/Career Goals: Religion/Theology.

Award: Scholarship for use in freshman, sophomore, junior, senior, or graduate years; not renewable. *Number:* 1. *Amount:* $1000.

Eligibility Requirements: Applicant must be enrolled or expecting to enroll full- or part-time at a two-year or technical institution or university. Applicant or parent of applicant must be member of National Association of Pastoral Musicians. Available to U.S. and non-U.S. citizens.

Application Requirements: Application form, essay, financial need analysis. *Deadline:* April 7.

Contact: Karen Kane
National Association of Pastoral Musicians
962 Wayne Avenue, Suite 550
Silver Spring, MD 20910-446
E-mail: npmadmin@npm.org

GIA PASTORAL MUSICIANS SCHOLARSHIP

Awards NPM members enrolled full-time or part-time in a graduate or undergraduate degree program of studies related to the field of pastoral music. Applicant must intend to work at least two years in the field of pastoral music following graduation or program completion.

Academic Fields/Career Goals: Religion/Theology.

Award: Scholarship for use in freshman, sophomore, junior, senior, or graduate years; not renewable. *Number:* 1. *Amount:* $2000.

Eligibility Requirements: Applicant must be enrolled or expecting to enroll full- or part-time at a two-year institution or university. Applicant or parent of applicant must be member of National Association of Pastoral Musicians. Available to U.S. and non-U.S. citizens.

Application Requirements: Application form, financial need analysis. *Deadline:* April 7.

Contact: Karen Kane
National Association of Pastoral Musicians
962 Wayne Avenue, Suite 550
Silver Spring, MD 20910-4461
E-mail: npmadmin@npm.org

MUSONICS SCHOLARSHIP
• See page 349

NATIONAL ASSOCIATION OF PASTORAL MUSICIANS MEMBERS' SCHOLARSHIP

Awards NPM members enrolled full-time or part-time in a graduate or undergraduate degree program of studies related to the field of pastoral music. Applicant must intend to work at least two years in the field of pastoral music following graduation or program completion.

Academic Fields/Career Goals: Religion/Theology.

Award: Scholarship for use in freshman, sophomore, junior, senior, or graduate years; not renewable. *Number:* 1. *Amount:* $3000.

Eligibility Requirements: Applicant must be enrolled or expecting to enroll full- or part-time at a two-year or technical institution or university. Applicant or parent of applicant must be member of National Association of Pastoral Musicians. Available to U.S. and non-U.S. citizens.

Application Requirements: Application form, financial need analysis. *Deadline:* April 7.

Contact: Karen Kane
Silver Spring, MD 20910-446
E-mail: npmadmin@npm.org

NPM KOINONIA/BOARD OF DIRECTORS SCHOLARSHIP
• See page 350

OREGON CATHOLIC PRESS SCHOLARSHIP
• See page 350

PALUCH FAMILY FOUNDATION/WORLD LIBRARY PUBLICATIONS SCHOLARSHIP
• See page 350

PRESBYTERIAN CHURCH (USA)

https://www.presbyterianmission.org/

STUDENT OPPORTUNITY SCHOLARSHIP
• See page 212

THE SOCIETY FOR THE SCIENTIFIC STUDY OF SEXUALITY

http://www.sexscience.org/

THE SOCIETY FOR THE SCIENTIFIC STUDY OF SEXUALITY STUDENT RESEARCH GRANT
• See page 105

UNITED METHODIST COMMUNICATIONS

http://www.umcom.org/

LEONARD M. PERRYMAN COMMUNICATIONS SCHOLARSHIP FOR ETHNIC MINORITY STUDENTS
• *See page 177*

SCIENCE, TECHNOLOGY, AND SOCIETY

AEG FOUNDATION

http://www.aegfoundation.org/

AEG FOUNDATION MARLIAVE FUND
• *See page 199*

AMERICAN INDIAN SCIENCE AND ENGINEERING SOCIETY

http://www.aises.org/

A.T. ANDERSON MEMORIAL SCHOLARSHIP PROGRAM
• *See page 105*

AMERICAN INSTITUTE OF AERONAUTICS AND ASTRONAUTICS

https://www.aiaa.org/

AIAA FOUNDATION UNDERGRADUATE SCHOLARSHIPS
• *See page 127*

LEATRICE GREGORY PENDRAY SCHOLARSHIP
• *See page 127*

AMERICAN LEGION DEPARTMENT OF TENNESSEE

http://www.tennesseelegion.org/

JROTC SCHOLARSHIP
One scholarship of $3000 available to a Tennessee JROTC cadet who has been awarded either The American Legion General Military Excellence, or The American Legion Scholastic Award Medal and The American Legion Certificate. JROTC Senior Instructor must provide the recommendation for the award. Information and recommendation forms are provided each JROTC Unit in Tennessee. Must be U.S. citizen.

Academic Fields/Career Goals: Science, Technology, and Society.

Award: Scholarship for use in freshman, sophomore, junior, or senior years; not renewable. *Number:* 1. *Amount:* $3000.

Eligibility Requirements: Applicant must be high school student; planning to enroll or expecting to enroll full- or part-time at a four-year institution or university; resident of Tennessee and studying in Tennessee. Applicant or parent of applicant must have employment or volunteer experience in journalism/broadcasting. Available to U.S. citizens.

Application Requirements: Application form. *Deadline:* April 15.

Contact: Dean Tuttle, Department Adjutant
American Legion Department of Tennessee
318 Donelson Pike
Nashville, TN 37214
Phone: 615-391-5088
E-mail: Adjutant@TNLegion.org

AMERICAN PHYSIOLOGICAL SOCIETY

https://www.physiology.org/

BARBARA A. HORWITZ AND JOHN M. HOROWITZ UNDERGRADUATE RESEARCH AWARDS
• *See page 139*

ARIZONA HYDROLOGICAL SOCIETY

http://www.azhydrosoc.org/

ARIZONA HYDROLOGICAL SOCIETY SCHOLARSHIP
• *See page 200*

ASSOCIATION FOR WOMEN GEOSCIENTISTS (AWG)

http://www.awg.org/

LONE STAR RISING CAREER SCHOLARSHIP
• *See page 200*

ASSOCIATION OF FEDERAL COMMUNICATIONS CONSULTING ENGINEERS

http://www.afcce.org

JULES COHEN SCHOLARSHIP
• *See page 218*

ASSOCIATION OF STATE DAM SAFETY OFFICIALS (ASDSO)

http://www.DamSafety.org

ASSOCIATION OF STATE DAM SAFETY OFFICIALS (ASDSO) SENIOR UNDERGRADUATE SCHOLARSHIP
• *See page 140*

AUTOMOTIVE WOMEN'S ALLIANCE FOUNDATION

http://awafoundation.org/index.php

AUTOMOTIVE WOMEN'S ALLIANCE FOUNDATION SCHOLARSHIPS
• *See page 71*

BHW GROUP

https://thebhwgroup.com/

BHW WOMEN IN STEM SCHOLARSHIP
• *See page 107*

BROWN AND CALDWELL

http://www.brownandcaldwell.com

ECKENFELDER SCHOLARSHIP
• *See page 141*

CATCHING THE DREAM

http://www.catchingthedream.org/

MATH, ENGINEERING, SCIENCE, BUSINESS, EDUCATION, COMPUTERS SCHOLARSHIPS
• *See page 146*

NATIVE AMERICAN LEADERSHIP IN EDUCATION (NALE)
• *See page 146*

DISTIL NETWORKS
http://www.distilnetworks.com

WOMEN FORWARD IN TECHNOLOGY SCHOLARSHIP PROGRAM
• *See page 108*

THE ELECTROCHEMICAL SOCIETY
https://www.electrochem.org/

BATTERY DIVISION STUDENT RESEARCH AWARD SPONSORED BY MERCEDES-BENZ RESEARCH & DEVELOPMENT
• *See page 155*

H.H. DOW MEMORIAL STUDENT ACHIEVEMENT AWARD OF THE INDUSTRIAL ELECTROLYSIS AND ELECTROCHEMICAL ENGINEERING DIVISION OF THE ELECTROCHEMICAL SOCIETY INC
• *See page 156*

EXPLORERS CLUB
http://www.explorers.org/

YOUTH ACTIVITY FUND GRANTS
• *See page 103*

HEALTHCARE INFORMATION AND MANAGEMENT SYSTEMS SOCIETY FOUNDATION
http://www.himss.org/

HIMSS FOUNDATION SCHOLARSHIP PROGRAM
• *See page 277*

INTERNATIONAL SOCIETY OF EXPLOSIVES ENGINEERS
http://www.isee.org/

JERRY MCDOWELL FUND
• *See page 156*

INTERNATIONAL TECHNOLOGY EDUCATION ASSOCIATION
http://www.iteaconnect.org/

INTERNATIONAL TECHNOLOGY EDUCATION ASSOCIATION UNDERGRADUATE SCHOLARSHIP IN TECHNOLOGY EDUCATION
• *See page 210*

THE JACKSON LABORATORY
https://www.jax.org

THE JACKSON LABORATORY COLLEGE SCHOLARSHIP PROGRAM
• *See page 108*

LOGMEIN
https://www.logmeininc.com

LASTPASS STEM SCHOLARSHIP
• *See page 109*

MINERALS, METALS, AND MATERIALS SOCIETY (TMS)
http://www.tms.org/

MATERIALS PROCESSING AND MANUFACTURING DIVISION SCHOLARSHIP
• *See page 228*

TMS EXTRACTION & PROCESSING SCHOLARSHIP
• *See page 228*

TMS FUNCTIONAL MATERIALS GILBERT CHIN SCHOLARSHIP
• *See page 228*

TMS/INTERNATIONAL SYMPOSIUM ON SUPERALLOYS SCHOLARSHIP PROGRAM
• *See page 229*

TMS/LIGHT METALS DIVISION SCHOLARSHIP PROGRAM
• *See page 229*

TMS OUTSTANDING STUDENT PAPER CONTEST-UNDERGRADUATE
• *See page 229*

TMS/STRUCTURAL MATERIALS DIVISION SCHOLARSHIP
• *See page 229*

NASA IDAHO SPACE GRANT CONSORTIUM
http://www.idahospacegrant.org

NASA IDAHO SPACE GRANT CONSORTIUM SCHOLARSHIP PROGRAM
• *See page 109*

NASA RHODE ISLAND SPACE GRANT CONSORTIUM
http://brown/initiatives/ri-space-grant

NASA RHODE ISLAND SPACE GRANT CONSORTIUM OUTREACH SCHOLARSHIP FOR UNDERGRADUATE STUDENTS
• *See page 338*

NASA'S VIRGINIA SPACE GRANT CONSORTIUM
http://www.vsgc.odu.edu/

UNDERGRADUATE STEM RESEARCH SCHOLARSHIPS
• *See page 110*

NEXTSTEPU
http://www.nextstepu.com/

$1,500 STEM SCHOLARSHIP
• *See page 104*

NOVUS BIOLOGICALS, LLC

https://www.novusbio.com

NOVUS BIOLOGICALS SCHOLARSHIP PROGRAM
• See page 101

R&D SYSTEMS SCHOLARSHIP
• See page 101

TOCRIS BIOSCIENCE SCHOLARSHIP
• See page 102

R & D SYSTEMS INC.

https://www.rndsystems.com/

R&D SYSTEMS SCHOLARSHIP PROGRAM

Scholarship available to students with majors in a science-related field as well as high school students planning on majoring in a science field. High school students must submit a written statement addressing the following topics: Make a top ten list of your favorite emerging technologies.

Academic Fields/Career Goals: Science, Technology, and Society.

Award: Scholarship for use in freshman, sophomore, junior, senior, graduate, or postgraduate years; not renewable. *Number:* 1. *Amount:* $1500.

Eligibility Requirements: Applicant must be enrolled or expecting to enroll full- or part-time at a two-year or four-year institution or university. Available to U.S. and non-U.S. citizens.

Application Requirements: Application form, essay. *Deadline:* July 8.

Contact: Lisa Ikariyama
  E-mail: Lisa.Ikariyama@bio-techne.com

SOCIETY FOR TECHNICAL COMMUNICATION

http://www.stc.org/

SOCIETY FOR TECHNICAL COMMUNICATION SCHOLARSHIP PROGRAM
• See page 175

SOCIETY OF MOTION PICTURE AND TELEVISION ENGINEERS

https://www.smpte.org/

LOUIS F. WOLF JR. MEMORIAL SCHOLARSHIP
• See page 175

STUDENT PAPER AWARD
• See page 175

SOCIETY OF PLASTICS ENGINEERS FOUNDATION (SPE)

http://www.4spe.org/

GULF COAST HURRICANE SCHOLARSHIP
• See page 159

SOIL AND WATER CONSERVATION SOCIETY

http://www.swcs.org

DONALD A. WILLIAMS SCHOLARSHIP SOIL CONSERVATION SCHOLARSHIP
• See page 91

STRAIGHT NORTH

https://www.straightnorth.com/

STRAIGHT NORTH STEM SCHOLARSHIP
• See page 81

TAU KAPPA EPSILON EDUCATION FOUNDATION

https://www.tke.org/

CARROL C. HALL MEMORIAL SCHOLARSHIP
• See page 213

STEVEN J. MUIR SCHOLARSHIP
• See page 160

THOMAS H. DUNNING, SR., MEMORIAL SCHOLARSHIP
• See page 183

TIMOTHY L. TASCHWER SCHOLARSHIP
• See page 144

TECHNOLOGY FIRST

https://technologyfirst.org/

ROBERT V. MCKENNA SCHOLARSHIPS
• See page 183

TUSKEGEE AIRMEN SCHOLARSHIP FOUNDATION

http://www.taisf.org/

TUSKEGEE AIRMEN SCHOLARSHIP
• See page 134

UNITED NEGRO COLLEGE FUND

http://www.uncf.org/

GALACTIC UNITE BYTHEWAY SCHOLARSHIP
• See page 111

VERMONT SPACE GRANT CONSORTIUM

http://www.cems.uvm.edu/vsgc

VERMONT SPACE GRANT CONSORTIUM
• See page 92

WOMEN IN AEROSPACE FOUNDATION

https://www.womeninaerospace.org/

THE WOMEN IN AEROSPACE FOUNDATION SCHOLARSHIP
• See page 135

SOCIAL SCIENCES

AMERICAN FEDERATION OF STATE, COUNTY, AND MUNICIPAL EMPLOYEES

https://www.afscme.org/

AFSCME/UNCF UNION SCHOLARS PROGRAM

AMERICAN INDIAN SCIENCE AND ENGINEERING SOCIETY

http://www.aises.org/

A.T. ANDERSON MEMORIAL SCHOLARSHIP PROGRAM

AMERICAN SOCIETY OF CRIMINOLOGY

http://www.asc41.com/

AMERICAN SOCIETY OF CRIMINOLOGY GENE CARTE STUDENT PAPER COMPETITION

BHW GROUP

https://thebhwgroup.com/

BHW WOMEN IN STEM SCHOLARSHIP

CANADIAN INSTITUTE OF UKRAINIAN STUDIES

https://www.ualberta.ca/canadian-institute-of-ukrainian-studies/index.html

LEO J. KRYSA FAMILY UNDERGRADUATE SCHOLARSHIP

CATCHING THE DREAM

http://www.catchingthedream.org/

MATH, ENGINEERING, SCIENCE, BUSINESS, EDUCATION, COMPUTERS SCHOLARSHIPS

CONGRESSIONAL BLACK CAUCUS FOUNDATION, INC.

http://www.cbcfinc.org/

CBC SPOUSES EDUCATION SCHOLARSHIP

CULTURAL SERVICES OF THE FRENCH EMBASSY

http://www.frenchculture.org/

TEACHING ASSISTANT PROGRAM IN FRANCE

HUB FOUNDATION

https://hub-foundation.org

HUB FOUNDATION SCHOLARSHIPS

INDIAN HEALTH SERVICES, UNITED STATES DEPARTMENT OF HEALTH AND HUMAN SERVICES

http://www.ihs.gov/scholarship

HEALTH PROFESSIONS PREPARATORY SCHOLARSHIP PROGRAM

INFINITY DENTAL WEB

http://www.infinitydentalweb.com

INTERNET MARKETING SCHOLARSHIP

LA-PHILOSOPHIE.COM

http://la-philosophie.com

LA-PHILOSOPHIE.COM SCHOLARSHIP

NATIONAL BLACK POLICE ASSOCIATION

http://www.blackpolice.org/

ALPHONSO DEAL SCHOLARSHIP AWARD

NATIONAL SECURITY EDUCATION PROGRAM

http://www.iie.org/

NATIONAL SECURITY EDUCATION PROGRAM (NSEP) DAVID L. BOREN UNDERGRADUATE SCHOLARSHIPS

NOVUS BIOLOGICALS, LLC

https://www.novusbio.com

TOCRIS BIOSCIENCE SCHOLARSHIP

OFFICE AND PROFESSIONAL EMPLOYEES INTERNATIONAL UNION

http://www.opeiu.org/

JOHN KELLY LABOR STUDIES SCHOLARSHIP FUND

PARAPSYCHOLOGY FOUNDATION

http://www.parapsychology.org/

CHARLES T. AND JUDITH A. TART STUDENT INCENTIVE
An annual incentive is awarded to promote the research of an undergraduate or graduate student, who shows dedication to work within parapsychology. For more details see website http://www.parapsychology.org.

Academic Fields/Career Goals: Social Sciences.

Award: Scholarship for use in freshman, sophomore, junior, senior, graduate, or postgraduate years; not renewable. *Number:* 1. *Amount:* $500.

Eligibility Requirements: Applicant must be enrolled or expecting to enroll full-time at a two-year or four-year institution or university. Available to U.S. citizens.

Application Requirements: Application form, essay, recommendations or references, transcript. *Deadline:* October 15.

Contact: Lisette Coly, Vice President
Phone: 212-628-1550
Fax: 212-628-1559
E-mail: office@parapsychology.org

EILEEN J. GARRETT SCHOLARSHIP FOR PARAPSYCHOLOGICAL RESEARCH

Scholarship requires applicants to demonstrate academic interest in the science of parapsychology through completed research, term papers, and courses for which credit was received. Those with only a general interest will not be considered. Visit website for additional information.

Academic Fields/Career Goals: Social Sciences.

Award: Scholarship for use in freshman, sophomore, junior, senior, graduate, or postgraduate years; not renewable. *Number:* 1. *Amount:* $3000.

Eligibility Requirements: Applicant must be enrolled or expecting to enroll full-time at a two-year or four-year institution or university. Available to U.S. citizens.

Application Requirements: Application form, essay, recommendations or references, transcript. *Deadline:* July 15.

Contact: Lisette Coly, Vice President
Parapsychology Foundation
PO Box 1562
New York, NY 10021-0043
Phone: 212-628-1550
Fax: 212-628-1559
E-mail: office@parapsychology.org

PHI ALPHA THETA HISTORY HONOR SOCIETY, INC.

http://www.phialphatheta.org/

PHI ALPHA THETA WORLD HISTORY ASSOCIATION PAPER PRIZE
• *See page 289*

PRESBYTERIAN CHURCH (USA)

https://www.presbyterianmission.org/

STUDENT OPPORTUNITY SCHOLARSHIP
• *See page 212*

THE SOCIETY FOR THE SCIENTIFIC STUDY OF SEXUALITY

http://www.sexscience.org/

THE SOCIETY FOR THE SCIENTIFIC STUDY OF SEXUALITY STUDENT RESEARCH GRANT
• *See page 105*

STRAIGHTFORWARD MEDIA

http://www.straightforwardmedia.com/

STRAIGHTFORWARD MEDIA LIBERAL ARTS SCHOLARSHIP
• *See page 119*

UNITED NEGRO COLLEGE FUND

http://www.uncf.org/

HCN/APRICITY RESOURCES SCHOLARS PROGRAM
• *See page 83*

LEIDOS STEM SCHOLARSHIP
• *See page 96*

THE OSSIE DAVIS LEGACY AWARD SCHOLARSHIP
• *See page 89*

WASHINGTON STATE ASSOCIATION FOR JUSTICE

http://www.washingtonjustice.org/

WASHINGTON STATE ASSOCIATION FOR JUSTICE AMERICAN JUSTICE ESSAY & VIDEO SCHOLARSHIP
• *See page 189*

WILLIAMS LAW GROUP

https://familylawyersnewjersey.com/

WILLIAMS LAW GROUP OPPORTUNITY TO GROW SCHOLARSHIP
• *See page 119*

Y'S MEN INTERNATIONAL

http://www.ysmen.org/

ALEXANDER SCHOLARSHIP LOAN FUND
• *See page 152*

SOCIAL SERVICES

ALBERTA HERITAGE SCHOLARSHIP FUND

http://www.alis.alberta.ca/

NORTHERN ALBERTA DEVELOPMENT COUNCIL BURSARY
• *See page 205*

AMERICAN FEDERATION OF STATE, COUNTY, AND MUNICIPAL EMPLOYEES

https://www.afscme.org/

AFSCME/UNCF UNION SCHOLARS PROGRAM
• *See page 98*

AMERICAN LEGION AUXILIARY DEPARTMENT OF ARIZONA

http://wwwaladeptaz.org

AMERICAN LEGION AUXILIARY DEPARTMENT OF ARIZONA WILMA HOYAL-MAXINE CHILTON MEMORIAL SCHOLARSHIP
• *See page 170*

BETHESDA LUTHERAN COMMUNITIES

http://www.bethesdalutherancommunities.org/scholarshi.ps

DEVELOPMENTAL DISABILITIES SCHOLASTIC ACHIEVEMENT SCHOLARSHIP FOR COLLEGE STUDENTS WHO ARE LUTHERAN
• *See page 195*

COMMUNITY FOUNDATION OF WESTERN MASSACHUSETTS

http://www.communityfoundation.org/

HELEN HAMILTON SCHOLARSHIP FUND
Scholarship for students pursuing degrees in social services, housing studies, urban design, and other related fields; preference for students who have demonstrated a commitment to community service.

Academic Fields/Career Goals: Social Services; Urban and Regional Planning.

Award: Scholarship for use in freshman, sophomore, junior, senior, or graduate years; not renewable.

Eligibility Requirements: Applicant must be enrolled or expecting to enroll full- or part-time at a two-year institution or university and resident of Maryland. Applicant or parent of applicant must have employment or volunteer experience in community service. Available to U.S. citizens.

Application Requirements: Application form, application form may be submitted online, essay, financial need analysis. *Deadline:* April 17.

Contact: Nikai Fondon, Scholarship Program Associate
E-mail: NFondon@communityfoundation.org

CONTINENTAL SOCIETY, DAUGHTERS OF INDIAN WARS

http://www.csdiw.org/

CONTINENTAL SOCIETY, DAUGHTERS OF INDIAN WARS SCHOLARSHIP
• *See page 188*

GENERAL BOARD OF HIGHER EDUCATION AND MINISTRY

http://www.gbhem.org

EDITH M. ALLEN SCHOLARSHIP
• *See page 209*

HEALTH PROFESSIONS EDUCATION FOUNDATION

http://www.healthprofessions.ca.gov/

ALLIED HEALTHCARE SCHOLARSHIP PROGRAM
• *See page 196*

INFINITY DENTAL WEB

http://www.infinitydentalweb.com

INTERNET MARKETING SCHOLARSHIP
• *See page 329*

NATIONAL BLACK POLICE ASSOCIATION

http://www.blackpolice.org/

ALPHONSO DEAL SCHOLARSHIP AWARD
• *See page 188*

PRESBYTERIAN CHURCH (USA)

https://www.presbyterianmission.org/

STUDENT OPPORTUNITY SCHOLARSHIP
• *See page 212*

UNITED COMMUNITY SERVICES FOR WORKING FAMILIES

http://www.ucswf.org

TED BRICKER SCHOLARSHIP
One-time award available to child of a union member who is a parent or guardian. Must be a member of a union affiliated with the Berks County United Labor Council, AFL-CIO. Must submit essay that is clear, concise, persuasive, and shows a commitment to the community.

Academic Fields/Career Goals: Social Services.

Award: Scholarship for use in freshman year; not renewable. *Number:* 1. *Amount:* up to $250.

Eligibility Requirements: Applicant must be high school student; planning to enroll or expecting to enroll full-time at a four-year institution or university and resident of Pennsylvania. Applicant or parent of applicant must be member of AFL-CIO. Available to U.S. citizens.

Application Requirements: Application form, essay, financial need analysis, transcript. *Deadline:* July 31.

Contact: Victoria Henshaw, Executive Director
United Community Services for Working Families
1251 North Front Street
Reading, PA 19601
Phone: 610-374-3319 Ext. 104
E-mail: vhenshaw@ucswf.org

UNITED NEGRO COLLEGE FUND

http://www.uncf.org/

HCN/APRICITY RESOURCES SCHOLARS PROGRAM
• *See page 83*

WILLIAMS LAW GROUP

https://familylawyersnewjersey.com/

WILLIAMS LAW GROUP OPPORTUNITY TO GROW SCHOLARSHIP
• *See page 119*

Y'S MEN INTERNATIONAL

http://www.ysmen.org/

ALEXANDER SCHOLARSHIP LOAN FUND
• *See page 152*

SPECIAL EDUCATION

AMERICAN LEGION AUXILIARY DEPARTMENT OF ARIZONA

http:/wwwaladeptaz.org

AMERICAN LEGION AUXILIARY DEPARTMENT OF ARIZONA WILMA HOYAL-MAXINE CHILTON MEMORIAL SCHOLARSHIP
• *See page 170*

BETHESDA LUTHERAN COMMUNITIES

http://www.bethesdalutherancommunities.org/scholarships

DEVELOPMENTAL DISABILITIES SCHOLASTIC ACHIEVEMENT SCHOLARSHIP FOR COLLEGE STUDENTS WHO ARE LUTHERAN
• See page 195

CONTINENTAL SOCIETY, DAUGHTERS OF INDIAN WARS

http://www.csdiw.org/

CONTINENTAL SOCIETY, DAUGHTERS OF INDIAN WARS SCHOLARSHIP
• See page 188

PILOT INTERNATIONAL

https://www.pilotinternational.org/

PILOT INTERNATIONAL SCHOLARSHIP
• See page 373

STRAIGHTFORWARD MEDIA

http://www.straightforwardmedia.com/

STRAIGHTFORWARD MEDIA TEACHER SCHOLARSHIP
• See page 213

WISCONSIN CONGRESS OF PARENTS AND TEACHERS INC.

http://www.wisconsinpta.org/

BROOKMIRE-HASTINGS SCHOLARSHIPS
• See page 215

SPORTS-RELATED/ EXERCISE SCIENCE

101ST AIRBORNE DIVISION ASSOCIATION

http://www.screamingeaglefoundation.org/

AL & WILLIAMARY VISTE SCHOLARSHIP
• See page 99

AMERICAN INDIAN SCIENCE AND ENGINEERING SOCIETY

http://www.aises.org/

A.T. ANDERSON MEMORIAL SCHOLARSHIP PROGRAM
• See page 105

AMERICAN PHYSIOLOGICAL SOCIETY

https://www.physiology.org/

BARBARA A. HORWITZ AND JOHN M. HOROWITZ UNDERGRADUATE RESEARCH AWARDS
• See page 139

BAT AND BALL GAME

https://batandballgame.com/

BAT AND BALL GAME WOMEN'S SPORTS SCHOLARSHIP

Women in Sports: It's a theme that has been gaining popularity and momentum for decades now. While more and more female athletes are emerging, the realm of professional sports remains male-dominated. At Bat and Ball Game, we'd like to take do our part to promote greater awareness while empowering women through sports–and we're proud to announce our women's sports scholarship, which includes one award to a deserving young athlete. Write an original essay on one of the following topics: Are there women in sports today that you see as role models? Who and why?; Why is baseball important to the sporting world in general?; Where will the sport of baseball be 10 years from now?; In your perspective, how has sport changed in the last two decades? Applicants' essays will be judged on thoughtfulness, creativity, and a demonstrated knowledge of sport. All scholarship essays must be submitted in English and should be 400 to 600 words in length. Submissions will be accepted from 12/01/2017 to 05/30/2018. Submit your essay and personal details via email to scholarship@batandballgame.com. Note that in accordance with the terms and conditions of this scholarship, your bio and essay may be published on Bat and Ball Game's website, blog, and social media platforms including Twitter, and Facebook. The scholarship winner must provide the following: proof of identity and confirmation of their current enrollment at an accredited institution. Qualifying universities and colleges include accredited institutions listed on the U.S. Department of Education website. Any school transfers are subject to the same accreditation guidelines. The board of judges will make its decision by 06/15/2018 date, after which the scholarship winner will be notified. Funds are provided by Bat and Ball Game, and will be deposited directly to the winners' bank accounts or made payable to their universities' Financial Aid departments. There is no application fee for participation in this women's sports scholarship opportunity.

Academic Fields/Career Goals: Sports-Related/Exercise Science.

Award: Scholarship for use in freshman, sophomore, junior, or senior years; not renewable. *Number:* 1. *Amount:* $1000.

Eligibility Requirements: Applicant must be enrolled or expecting to enroll full- or part-time at a two-year or four-year institution and female. Applicant must be physically disabled. Available to U.S. and non-U.S. citizens.

Application Requirements: Essay. *Deadline:* May 30.

Contact: Andrew Shields
Bat and Ball Game
8345 NW 66th Street, #C7592
Miami, FL 33166-7896
Phone: 844-873-2875
E-mail: scholarship@batandballgame.com

CANFIT

http://www.canfit.org/

CANFIT NUTRITION, PHYSICAL EDUCATION AND CULINARY ARTS SCHOLARSHIP
• See page 190

NATIONAL ATHLETIC TRAINERS' ASSOCIATION RESEARCH AND EDUCATION FOUNDATION

http://www.natafoundation.org/

NATIONAL ATHLETIC TRAINERS' ASSOCIATION RESEARCH AND EDUCATION FOUNDATION SCHOLARSHIP PROGRAM
• See page 283

NEXTSTEPU

http://www.nextstepu.com/

$1,500 STEM SCHOLARSHIP
• See page 104

NOVUS BIOLOGICALS, LLC

https://www.novusbio.com

NOVUS BIOLOGICALS SCHOLARSHIP PROGRAM
• See page 101

R&D SYSTEMS SCHOLARSHIP
• See page 101

TOCRIS BIOSCIENCE SCHOLARSHIP
• See page 102

PACERS FOUNDATION INC.

http://www.pacersfoundation.org/

LINDA CRAIG MEMORIAL SCHOLARSHIP PRESENTED BY ST. VINCENT SPORTS MEDICINE
• See page 284

PADDLE CANADA

http://www.paddlecanada.com

BILL MASON SCHOLARSHIP FUND
• See page 212

RADIO TELEVISION DIGITAL NEWS ASSOCIATION

http://www.rtdna.org

LOU AND CAROLE PRATO SPORTS REPORTING SCHOLARSHIP
• See page 310

SCARLETT FAMILY FOUNDATION SCHOLARSHIP PROGRAM

http://www.scarlettfoundation.org/

SCHOLARSHIP FOR STUDENTS PURSUING A BUSINESS OR STEM DEGREE
• See page 80

SHAPE AMERICA

http://www.shapeamerica.org/

RUTH ABERNATHY PRESIDENTIAL SCHOLARSHIP
• See page 401

THE WALTER J. TRAVIS SOCIETY

http://www.travissociety.com

THE WALTER J. TRAVIS MEMORIAL SCHOLARSHIP AND THE WALTER J. TRAVIS-RUDY ZOCCHI MEMORIAL SCHOLARSHIP
• See page 118

Y'S MEN INTERNATIONAL

http://www.ysmen.org/

ALEXANDER SCHOLARSHIP LOAN FUND
• See page 152

STATISTICS

THE ACTUARIAL FOUNDATION

www.actuarialfoundation.org

ACTUARIAL DIVERSITY SCHOLARSHIP
• See page 300

ACTUARY OF TOMORROW—STUART A. ROBERTSON MEMORIAL SCHOLARSHIP
• See page 203

CURTIS E. HUNTINGTON MEMORIAL SCHOLARSHIP
• See page 204

AMERICAN INDIAN SCIENCE AND ENGINEERING SOCIETY

http://www.aises.org/

A.T. ANDERSON MEMORIAL SCHOLARSHIP PROGRAM
• See page 105

ARMED FORCES COMMUNICATIONS AND ELECTRONICS ASSOCIATION, EDUCATIONAL FOUNDATION

https://foundation.afcea.org

AFCEA STEM MAJORS SCHOLARSHIPS FOR UNDERGRADUATE STUDENTS
• See page 106

AUTOMOTIVE WOMEN'S ALLIANCE FOUNDATION

http://awafoundation.org/index.php

AUTOMOTIVE WOMEN'S ALLIANCE FOUNDATION SCHOLARSHIPS
• See page 71

GREAT MINDS IN STEM

http://www.greatmindsinstem.org/college/scholarship-application-information

HENAAC SCHOLARSHIP PROGRAM
• See page 100

INFINITY DENTAL WEB

http://www.infinitydentalweb.com

INTERNET MARKETING SCHOLARSHIP
• See page 329

LOGMEIN

https://www.logmeininc.com

LASTPASS STEM SCHOLARSHIP
• *See page 109*

NEXTSTEPU

http://www.nextstepu.com/

$1,500 STEM SCHOLARSHIP
• *See page 104*

UNITED NEGRO COLLEGE FUND

http://www.uncf.org/

LEIDOS STEM SCHOLARSHIP
• *See page 96*

VOYA SCHOLARS
• *See page 83*

SURVEYING, SURVEYING TECHNOLOGY, CARTOGRAPHY, OR GEOGRAPHIC INFORMATION SCIENCE

AMERICAN CONGRESS ON SURVEYING AND MAPPING

http://landsurveyorsunited.com/acsm

ACSM FELLOWS SCHOLARSHIP

One-time award available to a student with a junior or higher standing in any ACSM discipline (surveying, mapping, geographic information systems, and geodetic science). Must be ACSM member.

Academic Fields/Career Goals: Surveying, Surveying Technology, Cartography, or Geographic Information Science.

Award: Scholarship for use in freshman, sophomore, junior, or senior years; not renewable. *Number:* 1. *Amount:* $2000.

Eligibility Requirements: Applicant must be enrolled or expecting to enroll full- or part-time at a four-year institution or university. Applicant or parent of applicant must be member of American Congress on Surveying and Mapping. Available to U.S. citizens.

Application Requirements: Application form, essay, membership proof, recommendations or references, transcript. *Deadline:* October 1.

Contact: Ilse Genovese, Communications Director
American Congress on Surveying and Mapping
6 Montgomery Village Avenue, Suite 403
Gaithersburg, MD 20879
Phone: 240-632-9716 Ext. 113
Fax: 240-632-1321
E-mail: ilse.genovese@acsm.net

ACSM LOWELL H. AND DOROTHY LOVING UNDERGRADUATE SCHOLARSHIP

Scholarship available for a junior or senior in a college or university in the U.S. studying surveying. Program of study must include courses in two of the following areas: land surveying, geometric geodesy, photogrammetry/remote sensing, or analysis and design of spatial measurement systems.

Academic Fields/Career Goals: Surveying, Surveying Technology, Cartography, or Geographic Information Science.

Award: Scholarship for use in freshman, sophomore, junior, or senior years; not renewable. *Number:* 1. *Amount:* $2500.

Eligibility Requirements: Applicant must be enrolled or expecting to enroll full- or part-time at a four-year institution or university. Applicant or parent of applicant must be member of American Congress on Surveying and Mapping. Available to U.S. citizens.

Application Requirements: Application form, essay, membership proof, recommendations or references, transcript. *Deadline:* October 1.

Contact: Ilse Genovese, Communications Director
American Congress on Surveying and Mapping
6 Montgomery Village Avenue, Suite 403
Gaithersbutg, MD 20879
Phone: 240-632-9716
Fax: 240-632-1321
E-mail: ilse.genovese@acsm.net

AMERICAN ASSOCIATION FOR GEODETIC SURVEYING JOSEPH F. DRACUP SCHOLARSHIP AWARD

Award for students enrolled in a four-year degree program in surveying (or in closely-related degree programs such as geomatics or surveying engineering). Preference given to applicants from programs with significant focus on geodetic surveying. Must be ACSM member.

Academic Fields/Career Goals: Surveying, Surveying Technology, Cartography, or Geographic Information Science.

Award: Scholarship for use in freshman, sophomore, junior, or senior years; not renewable. *Number:* 1. *Amount:* $2000.

Eligibility Requirements: Applicant must be enrolled or expecting to enroll full- or part-time at a four-year institution or university. Applicant or parent of applicant must be member of American Congress on Surveying and Mapping. Available to U.S. and non-Canadian citizens.

Application Requirements: Application form, essay, recommendations or references, transcript. *Deadline:* October 1.

Contact: Ilse Genovese, ACSM Communications Director
American Congress on Surveying and Mapping
6 Montgomery Village Avenue, Suite 403
Gaithersburg, MD 20879
Phone: 240-632-9716 Ext. 113
Fax: 240-632-1321
E-mail: ilse.genovese@acsm.net

BERNTSEN INTERNATIONAL SCHOLARSHIP IN SURVEYING

Award of $1500 for full-time students enrolled in a four-year degree program in surveying or in a closely-related degree program, such as geomatics or surveying engineering. Must be ACSM member.

Academic Fields/Career Goals: Surveying, Surveying Technology, Cartography, or Geographic Information Science.

Award: Scholarship for use in freshman, sophomore, junior, or senior years; not renewable. *Number:* 1. *Amount:* $1500.

Eligibility Requirements: Applicant must be enrolled or expecting to enroll full-time at a four-year institution or university. Applicant or parent of applicant must be member of American Congress on Surveying and Mapping. Available to U.S. citizens.

Application Requirements: Application form, essay, recommendations or references, transcript. *Deadline:* October 1.

Contact: Ilse Genovese, ACSM Communications Director
American Congress on Surveying and Mapping
6 Montgomery Village Avenue, Suite 403
Gaithersburg, MD 20879
Phone: 240-632-9716 Ext. 113
Fax: 240-632-1321
E-mail: ilse.genovese@acsm.net

BERNTSEN INTERNATIONAL SCHOLARSHIP IN SURVEYING TECHNOLOGY

Award for full-time undergraduate students enrolled in a two-year degree program in surveying technology. For U.S. study only. Must be a member of the National Society of Professional Surveyors. Awarded in EVEN years only. See website for application and more details.

Academic Fields/Career Goals: Surveying, Surveying Technology, Cartography, or Geographic Information Science.

Award: Scholarship for use in freshman or sophomore years; not renewable.

Eligibility Requirements: Applicant must be enrolled or expecting to enroll full-time at a two-year or four-year institution. Available to U.S. and non-Canadian citizens.

Application Requirements: Application form, essay. *Deadline:* January 15.

Contact: Dawn James, ACSM Member Organizations Administrator
Phone: 240-632-9716 Ext. 113
E-mail: dawn.james@acsm.net

CADY MCDONNELL MEMORIAL SCHOLARSHIP

Award of $1000 for female surveying student. Must be a resident of one of the following western states: Alaska, Arizona, California, Colorado, Hawaii, Idaho, Montana, Nevada, New Mexico, Oregon, Utah, Washington, and Wyoming. Must provide proof of legal home residence and be a member of the American Congress on Surveying and Mapping.

Academic Fields/Career Goals: Surveying, Surveying Technology, Cartography, or Geographic Information Science.

Award: Scholarship for use in freshman, sophomore, junior, or senior years; not renewable. *Number:* 1. *Amount:* $1000.

Eligibility Requirements: Applicant must be enrolled or expecting to enroll full- or part-time at a two-year or four-year institution or university; female and resident of Alaska, Arizona, California, Colorado, Hawaii, Idaho, Montana, Nevada, New Mexico, Oregon, Utah, Washington, Wyoming. Applicant or parent of applicant must be member of American Congress on Surveying and Mapping. Available to U.S. citizens.

Application Requirements: Application form, essay, financial need analysis, proof of residence, membership proof, personal statement, recommendations or references, transcript. *Deadline:* October 1.

Contact: Ilse Genovese, ACSM Communications Director
American Congress on Surveying and Mapping
6 Montgomery Village Avenue, Suite 403
Gaithersburg, MD 20879
Phone: 240-632-9716 Ext. 113
Fax: 240-632-1321
E-mail: ilse.genovese@acsm.net

NETTIE DRACUP MEMORIAL SCHOLARSHIP

Award for undergraduate student enrolled in a four-year geodetic surveying program at an accredited college or university. Must be U.S. citizen. Must be ACSM member.

Academic Fields/Career Goals: Surveying, Surveying Technology, Cartography, or Geographic Information Science.

Award: Scholarship for use in freshman, sophomore, junior, or senior years; not renewable. *Number:* 2. *Amount:* $2000.

Eligibility Requirements: Applicant must be enrolled or expecting to enroll full-time at a four-year institution or university. Applicant or parent of applicant must be member of American Congress on Surveying and Mapping. Available to U.S. citizens.

Application Requirements: ACSM membership proof, application form, essay, financial need analysis, recommendations or references, transcript. *Deadline:* October 1.

Contact: Ilse Genovese, Communications Director
American Congress on Surveying and Mapping
6 Montgomery Village Avenue, Suite 403
Gaithersburg, MD 20879
Phone: 240-632-9716 Ext. 113
Fax: 240-632-1321
E-mail: ilse.genovese@acsm.net

SCHONSTEDT SCHOLARSHIP IN SURVEYING

Award preference given to applicants with junior or senior standing in a four-year program in surveying. Schonstedt donates magnetic locator to surveying program at each recipient's school. Must be ACSM member.

Academic Fields/Career Goals: Surveying, Surveying Technology, Cartography, or Geographic Information Science.

Award: Scholarship for use in junior or senior years; not renewable. *Number:* 2. *Amount:* $1500.

Eligibility Requirements: Applicant must be enrolled or expecting to enroll full-time at a four-year institution or university. Applicant or parent of applicant must be member of American Congress on Surveying and Mapping. Available to U.S. citizens.

Application Requirements: ACSM membership proof, application form, essay, recommendations or references, transcript. *Deadline:* October 1.

Contact: Ilse Genovese, Communications Director
American Congress on Surveying and Mapping
6 Montgomery Village Avenue, Suite 403
Gaithersburg, MD 20879
Phone: 240-632-9716 Ext. 113
Fax: 240-632-1321
E-mail: ilse.genovese@acsm.net

TRI-STATE SURVEYING AND PHOTOGRAMMETRY KRIS M. KUNZE MEMORIAL SCHOLARSHIP

• See page 145

AMERICAN COUNCIL OF ENGINEERING COMPANIES OF PENNSYLVANIA (ACEC/PA)

http://www.acecpa.org/

ERIC J. GENNUSO AND LEROY D. (BUD) LOY, JR. SCHOLARSHIP PROGRAM

• See page 153

AMERICAN INDIAN SCIENCE AND ENGINEERING SOCIETY

http://www.aises.org/

A.T. ANDERSON MEMORIAL SCHOLARSHIP PROGRAM

• See page 105

AMERICAN SOCIETY OF CERTIFIED ENGINEERING TECHNICIANS

http://www.ascet.org/

KURT H. AND DONNA M. SCHULER SMALL GRANT

• See page 162

ASPRS, THE IMAGING AND GEOSPATIAL INFORMATION SOCIETY

http://www.asprs.org/

ABRAHAM ANSON SCHOLARSHIP

Award to encourage students to pursue education in geospatial science or technology related to photogrammetry, remote sensing, surveying and mapping. Must be enrolled or intending to enroll in a U.S. college or university in geospatial science, surveying and mapping and related fields. Must submit with application a list of all applicable courses taken, a statement of work experience including internships, special projects, technical papers, and courses taught that may support the student's capabilities in this field. For additional information and online application, see website http://www.asprs.org/membership/scholar.html.

Academic Fields/Career Goals: Surveying, Surveying Technology, Cartography, or Geographic Information Science.

Award: Scholarship for use in freshman, sophomore, junior, or senior years; not renewable. *Number:* 1. *Amount:* $2000.

Eligibility Requirements: Applicant must be enrolled or expecting to enroll full-time at an institution or university. Available to U.S. citizens.

Application Requirements: Application form, application form may be submitted online, essay. *Deadline:* November 15.

Contact: Scholarship Administrator
Phone: 301-493-0290
E-mail: scholarships@asprs.org

FRANCIS H. MOFFITT SCHOLARSHIP

Award to encourage upper-division undergraduate and graduate-level students to pursue a course of study in surveying and photogrammetry leading to a career in the mapping profession. Must be enrolled or intending to enroll in a college or university in the U.S. in the field of surveying or photogrammetry. Application must include listing of all courses taken in the field, internships, special projects, courses taught, technical papers that demonstrate applicant's capabilities in the field, two letters of recommendation, and a short statement detailing contributions to the field and future career plans. For additional information, see website http://www.asprs.org.

Academic Fields/Career Goals: Surveying, Surveying Technology, Cartography, or Geographic Information Science.

Award: Scholarship for use in junior or senior years; not renewable. *Number:* 1. *Amount:* $7500.

Eligibility Requirements: Applicant must be enrolled or expecting to enroll full-time at an institution or university. Available to U.S. citizens.

Application Requirements: Application form, application form may be submitted online, essay. *Deadline:* November 15.

Contact: Jesse Winch, Scholarship Administrator
Phone: 301-493-0290
E-mail: scholarships@asprs.org

JOHN O. BEHRENS INSTITUTE FOR LAND INFORMATION MEMORIAL SCHOLARSHIP

Award to encourage study in geospatial science or technology or land information systems/records. Must be an undergraduate student enrolled or intending to enroll in a U.S. college or university in the designated field. Application must be submitted electronically and must include a list of completed courses in the field, papers, research reports, or other items produced by the applicant that demonstrate capability in the field, and internships, work experience, special projects or courses taught that support potential excellence in the field. Additional information and application on website http://www.asprs.org/membership/scholar.html.

Academic Fields/Career Goals: Surveying, Surveying Technology, Cartography, or Geographic Information Science.

Award: Scholarship for use in freshman, sophomore, junior, or senior years; not renewable. *Number:* 1. *Amount:* $2000.

Eligibility Requirements: Applicant must be enrolled or expecting to enroll full-time at an institution or university. Available to U.S. citizens.

Application Requirements: Application form, application form may be submitted online, essay. *Deadline:* November 15.

Contact: Scholarship Administrator
Phone: 301-493-0290
E-mail: scholarships@asprs.org

KENNETH J. OSBORN MEMORIAL SCHOLARSHIP

Award to encourage students who display the interest and aptitude to enter the profession of surveying, mapping, geospatial information and technology, and photogrammetry. Student must be enrolled or intending to enroll in a college or university in the U.S. in a program of study to prepare for the profession. Application must be submitted electronically. For additional requirements that must accompany electronic application, visit website http://www.asprs.org/membership/scholar.html.

Academic Fields/Career Goals: Surveying, Surveying Technology, Cartography, or Geographic Information Science.

Award: Scholarship for use in freshman, sophomore, junior, or senior years; not renewable. *Number:* 1. *Amount:* $2000.

Eligibility Requirements: Applicant must be enrolled or expecting to enroll full-time at an institution or university. Available to U.S. citizens.

Application Requirements: Application form, application form may be submitted online, essay. *Deadline:* November 15.

Contact: Scholarship Administrator
Phone: 301-493-0290
E-mail: scholarships@asprs.org

ROBERT E. ALTENHOFEN SCHOLARSHIP

One-time award of $2000 available for undergraduate or graduate study in theoretical photogrammetry. Applicant must supply a sample of work in photogrammetry and a statement of plans for future study in the field. Must be a member of ASPRS.

Academic Fields/Career Goals: Surveying, Surveying Technology, Cartography, or Geographic Information Science.

Award: Scholarship for use in junior, senior, or graduate years; not renewable. *Number:* 1. *Amount:* $2000.

Eligibility Requirements: Applicant must be enrolled or expecting to enroll full-time at an institution or university. Applicant or parent of applicant must be member of American Society for Photogrammetry and Remote Sensing. Available to U.S. and non-U.S. citizens.

Application Requirements: Application form, application form may be submitted online, essay. *Deadline:* November 15.

Contact: Program Manager
ASPRS, The Imaging and Geospatial Information Society
5410 Grosvenor Lane, Suite 210
Bethesda, MD 20814-2160
Phone: 301-493-0290
Fax: 301-493-0208
E-mail: scholarships@asprs.org

ASSOCIATED GENERAL CONTRACTORS OF NEW YORK STATE, LLC

https://www.agcnys.org/programs/scholarship/

ASSOCIATED GENERAL CONTRACTORS NYS SCHOLARSHIP PROGRAM

ASSOCIATION OF CALIFORNIA WATER AGENCIES

http://www.acwa.com/

ASSOCIATION OF CALIFORNIA WATER AGENCIES SCHOLARSHIPS

CLAIR A. HILL SCHOLARSHIP

ASSOCIATION OF STATE DAM SAFETY OFFICIALS (ASDSO)

http://www.DamSafety.org

ASSOCIATION OF STATE DAM SAFETY OFFICIALS (ASDSO) SENIOR UNDERGRADUATE SCHOLARSHIP

BROWN AND CALDWELL

http://www.brownandcaldwell.com

ECKENFELDER SCHOLARSHIP

MINORITY SCHOLARSHIP PROGRAM

FLORIDA ENGINEERING SOCIETY

https://www.fleng.org/page/Scholarships

ACEC-FLORIDA SCHOLARSHIP

THE LAND CONSERVANCY OF NEW JERSEY

http://www.tlc-nj.org/

ROGERS FAMILY SCHOLARSHIP

RUSSELL W. MYERS SCHOLARSHIP

MASSACHUSETTS ASSOCIATION OF LAND SURVEYORS AND CIVIL ENGINEERS

http://www.malsce.org/

MALSCE SCHOLARSHIPS
• See page 242

NEXTSTEPU

http://www.nextstepu.com/

$1,500 STEM SCHOLARSHIP
• See page 104

PROFESSIONAL CONSTRUCTION ESTIMATORS ASSOCIATION

http://www.pcea.org/

TED G. WILSON MEMORIAL SCHOLARSHIP FOUNDATION
• See page 166

RHODE ISLAND SOCIETY OF PROFESSIONAL LAND SURVEYORS

http://www.rispls.org/

PIERRE H. GUILLEMETTE SCHOLARSHIP
Scholarship available to any Rhode Island resident enrolled in a certificate or degree program in land surveying at a qualified institution of higher learning.

Academic Fields/Career Goals: Surveying, Surveying Technology, Cartography, or Geographic Information Science.

Award: Scholarship for use in freshman, sophomore, junior, or senior years; not renewable.

Eligibility Requirements: Applicant must be enrolled or expecting to enroll full- or part-time at a four-year institution or university and resident of Rhode Island. Available to U.S. citizens.

Application Requirements: Application form, resume, transcript. *Deadline:* October 30.

Contact: Scholarship Coordinator
 Rhode Island Society of Professional Land Surveyors
 PO Box 544
 East Greenwich, RI 02818
 Phone: 401-294-1262
 E-mail: info@rispls.org

UNITED NEGRO COLLEGE FUND

http://www.uncf.org/

LEIDOS STEM SCHOLARSHIP
• See page 96

THERAPY/ REHABILITATION

101ST AIRBORNE DIVISION ASSOCIATION

http://www.screamingeaglefoundation.org/

AL & WILLIAMARY VISTE SCHOLARSHIP
• See page 99

ALBERTA HERITAGE SCHOLARSHIP FUND

http://www.alis.alberta.ca/

ABORIGINAL HEALTH CAREERS BURSARY
• See page 139

AMERICAN FOUNDATION FOR THE BLIND

http://www.afb.org/

DELTA GAMMA FOUNDATION FLORENCE MARGARET HARVEY MEMORIAL SCHOLARSHIP
• See page 206

RUDOLPH DILLMAN MEMORIAL SCHOLARSHIP
• See page 206

AMERICAN INDIAN SCIENCE AND ENGINEERING SOCIETY

http://www.aises.org/

A.T. ANDERSON MEMORIAL SCHOLARSHIP PROGRAM
• See page 105

AMERICAN LEGION AUXILIARY DEPARTMENT OF COLORADO

http://www.alacolorado.com

AMERICAN LEGION AUXILIARY DEPARTMENT OF COLORADO PAST PRESIDENTS' PARLEY HEALTH CARE PROFESSIONAL SCHOLARSHIPNURSES SCHOLARSHIP
• See page 125

AMERICAN LEGION AUXILIARY DEPARTMENT OF MICHIGAN

http://www.michalaux.org/

AMERICAN LEGION AUXILIARY DEPARTMENT OF MICHIGAN MEDICAL CAREER SCHOLARSHIP
• See page 279

AMERICAN PHYSICAL THERAPY ASSOCIATION

http://www.apta.org/honorsawards

MARY MCMILLAN SCHOLARSHIP AWARD
• See page 207

AMERICAN RESPIRATORY CARE FOUNDATION

http://www.arcfoundation.org/

JIMMY A. YOUNG MEMORIAL EDUCATION RECOGNITION AWARD
The American Respiratory Care Foundation may award up to $1,000 in memory of Jimmy A. Young, past president of the AARC, who personally contributed greatly to respiratory care education. The foundation prefers that nominations be made by a representative of the school or an accredited respiratory training program, however, any student may initiate a request for sponsorship in order that a deserving candidate is not denied the opportunity to compete simply because the school does not initiate the application. Preference will be given to nominees of minority origin. This award consists of a certificate of recognition, coach airfare, one night's lodging, and registration for AARC Congress.

Academic Fields/Career Goals: Therapy/Rehabilitation.

Award: Prize for use in freshman, sophomore, junior, or senior years; not renewable. *Number:* 1. *Amount:* $1000.

Eligibility Requirements: Applicant must be enrolled or expecting to enroll full- or part-time at a two-year institution or university. Available to U.S. citizens.

Application Requirements: Application form, application form may be submitted online, essay. *Deadline:* June 1.

Contact: Crystal Maldonado, ARCF Grants Coordinator
E-mail: crystal.maldonado@aarc.org

MORTON B. DUGGAN, JR. MEMORIAL EDUCATION RECOGNITION AWARD
• *See page 280*

SEPRACOR ACHIEVEMENT AWARD FOR EXCELLENCE IN PULMONARY DISEASE STATE MANAGEMENT
• *See page 280*

ASSISTANCE LEAGUE OF THE TRIANGLE AREA

HEALTH CARE PROFESSION SCHOLARSHIP
• *See page 195*

ASSOCIATION FOR EDUCATION AND REHABILITATION OF THE BLIND AND VISUALLY IMPAIRED

http://www.aerbvi.org/

WILLIAM AND DOROTHY FERRELL SCHOLARSHIP
• *See page 207*

AVACARE MEDICAL

https://avacaremedical.com

AVACARE MEDICAL SCHOLARSHIP
• *See page 100*

BETHESDA LUTHERAN COMMUNITIES

http://www.bethesdalutherancommunities.org/scholarships

DEVELOPMENTAL DISABILITIES SCHOLASTIC ACHIEVEMENT SCHOLARSHIP FOR COLLEGE STUDENTS WHO ARE LUTHERAN
• *See page 195*

CONTINENTAL SOCIETY, DAUGHTERS OF INDIAN WARS

http://www.csdiw.org/

CONTINENTAL SOCIETY, DAUGHTERS OF INDIAN WARS SCHOLARSHIP
• *See page 188*

CYNTHIA E. MORGAN SCHOLARSHIP FUND (CEMS)

http://www.cemsfund.com/

CYNTHIA E. MORGAN MEMORIAL SCHOLARSHIP FUND, INC.
• *See page 248*

THE EXPERT INSTITUTE

https://www.theexpertinstitute.com

ANNUAL HEALTHCARE AND LIFE SCIENCES SCHOLARSHIP
• *See page 142*

HEALTH PROFESSIONS EDUCATION FOUNDATION

http://www.healthprofessions.ca.gov/

ALLIED HEALTHCARE SCHOLARSHIP PROGRAM
• *See page 196*

INTERMOUNTAIN MEDICAL IMAGING

https://www.aboutimi.com/

INTERMOUNTAIN MEDICAL IMAGING SCHOLARSHIP
• *See page 125*

INTERNATIONAL ORDER OF THE KING'S DAUGHTERS AND SONS

http://www.iokds.org/

HEALTH CAREERS SCHOLARSHIP
• *See page 197*

KETAMINE CLINICS OF LOS ANGELES

http://www.ketamineclinics.com/

KETAMINE CLINICS OF LOS ANGELES SCHOLARSHIP PROGRAM
• *See page 138*

LADIES AUXILIARY TO THE VETERANS OF FOREIGN WARS, DEPARTMENT OF MAINE

http://mainevfw.org/

FRANCES L. BOOTH MEDICAL SCHOLARSHIP SPONSORED BY LAVFW DEPARTMENT OF MAINE
• *See page 283*

MEDICAL SCRUBS COLLECTION

http://medicalscrubscollection.com

MEDICAL SCRUBS COLLECTION SCHOLARSHIP
• *See page 104*

NATIONAL ATHLETIC TRAINERS' ASSOCIATION RESEARCH AND EDUCATION FOUNDATION

http://www.natafoundation.org/

NATIONAL ATHLETIC TRAINERS' ASSOCIATION RESEARCH AND EDUCATION FOUNDATION SCHOLARSHIP PROGRAM
• *See page 283*

NOVUS BIOLOGICALS, LLC

https://www.novusbio.com

NOVUS BIOLOGICALS SCHOLARSHIP PROGRAM
• See page 101

R&D SYSTEMS SCHOLARSHIP
• See page 101

TOCRIS BIOSCIENCE SCHOLARSHIP
• See page 102

PACERS FOUNDATION INC.

http://www.pacersfoundation.org/

LINDA CRAIG MEMORIAL SCHOLARSHIP PRESENTED BY ST. VINCENT SPORTS MEDICINE
• See page 284

PILOT INTERNATIONAL

https://www.pilotinternational.org/

PILOT INTERNATIONAL SCHOLARSHIP
• See page 373

THE RECOVERY VILLAGE

https://www.therecoveryvillage.com/

RECOVERY VILLAGE HEALTHCARE SCHOLARSHIP
• See page 197

SCARLETT FAMILY FOUNDATION SCHOLARSHIP PROGRAM

http://www.scarlettfoundation.org/

SCHOLARSHIP FOR STUDENTS PURSUING A BUSINESS OR STEM DEGREE
• See page 80

STRAIGHTFORWARD MEDIA

http://www.straightforwardmedia.com/

STRAIGHTFORWARD MEDIA MEDICAL PROFESSIONS SCHOLARSHIP
• See page 198

UNITED NEGRO COLLEGE FUND

http://www.uncf.org/

HCN/APRICITY RESOURCES SCHOLARS PROGRAM
• See page 83

U.S. DEPARTMENT OF HEALTH AND HUMAN SERVICES

https://www.hhs.gov/

SCHOLARSHIPS FOR DISADVANTAGED STUDENTS PROGRAM
• See page 284

TRADE/TECHNICAL SPECIALTIES

AIRCRAFT ELECTRONICS ASSOCIATION EDUCATIONAL FOUNDATION

http://www.aea.net/

DUTCH AND GINGER ARVER SCHOLARSHIP

Scholarship available to high school seniors or college students who plan to attend or are attending an avionics or aircraft repair program in an accredited school. Minimum 2.5 GPA required.

Academic Fields/Career Goals: Trade/Technical Specialties.

Award: Scholarship for use in freshman, sophomore, junior, or senior years; not renewable. *Number:* 1. *Amount:* $1000.

Eligibility Requirements: Applicant must be enrolled or expecting to enroll full- or part-time at a two-year or technical institution or university. Available to U.S. citizens.

Application Requirements: Application form, application form may be submitted online, essay. *Deadline:* April 1.

Contact: Geoff Hill, Director of Communications
Phone: 816-366-5107
E-mail: geoffh@aea.net

GARMIN-JERRY SMITH MEMORIAL SCHOLARSHIP

Scholarship available for high school, college, or vocational or technical school students who plan to attend or are attending an avionics or aircraft repair program in an accredited vocational or technical school. Minimum 2.5 GPA required.

Academic Fields/Career Goals: Trade/Technical Specialties.

Award: Scholarship for use in freshman or sophomore years; not renewable. *Number:* 1. *Amount:* $1000.

Eligibility Requirements: Applicant must be enrolled or expecting to enroll full-time at a two-year or technical institution. Available to U.S. and non-U.S. citizens.

Application Requirements: Application form, application form may be submitted online, essay. *Deadline:* April 1.

Contact: Geoff Hill, Director of Communications
Phone: 816-366-5107
E-mail: geoffh@aea.net

GARMIN SCHOLARSHIP

Scholarship available to high school seniors and college students who plan to attend or are attending an avionics or aircraft repair program in an accredited school. Minimum 2.5 GPA required.

Academic Fields/Career Goals: Trade/Technical Specialties.

Award: Scholarship for use in freshman, sophomore, junior, or senior years; not renewable. *Number:* 1. *Amount:* $2000.

Eligibility Requirements: Applicant must be enrolled or expecting to enroll full- or part-time at a two-year or technical institution or university. Available to U.S. citizens.

Application Requirements: Application form, application form may be submitted online, essay. *Deadline:* April 1.

Contact: Geoff Hill, Director of Communications
Phone: 816-366-5107
E-mail: geoffh@aea.net

LEE TARBOX MEMORIAL SCHOLARSHIP

Scholarship available to high school seniors or college students who plan to attend or are attending an avionics or aircraft repair program in an accredited school.

Academic Fields/Career Goals: Trade/Technical Specialties.

Award: Scholarship for use in freshman, sophomore, junior, or senior years; not renewable. *Number:* 1. *Amount:* $2500.

Eligibility Requirements: Applicant must be enrolled or expecting to enroll full- or part-time at a two-year or technical institution or university. Available to U.S. citizens.

Application Requirements: Application form, application form may be submitted online, essay. *Deadline:* April 1.

Contact: Geoff Hill, Director of Communications
Phone: 816-366-5107
E-mail: geoffh@aea.net

LOWELL GAYLOR MEMORIAL SCHOLARSHIP
• See page 126

MID-CONTINENT INSTRUMENTS AND AVIONICS SCHOLARSHIP

Available to a high school senior or college student who plans to attend or is attending an accredited school in an avionics or aircraft maintenance program. Minimum 2.5 GPA required.

Academic Fields/Career Goals: Trade/Technical Specialties.

Award: Scholarship for use in freshman, sophomore, junior, or senior years; not renewable. Number: 1. Amount: $1000.

Eligibility Requirements: Applicant must be enrolled or expecting to enroll full- or part-time at a two-year or technical institution or university. Available to U.S. citizens.

Application Requirements: Application form, application form may be submitted online, essay. Deadline: April 1.

Contact: Geoff Hill, Director of Communications
Phone: 816-366-5107
E-mail: geoffh@aea.net

ALBERTA HERITAGE SCHOLARSHIP FUND
http://www.alis.alberta.ca/

REGISTERED APPRENTICESHIP PROGRAM/CAREER AND TECHNOLOGIES STUDIES (RAPS/CTS) SCHOLARSHIPS

Scholarships of CAN$1000 available for high school graduates who are registered as apprentices in a trade while in high school to encourage recipients to continue their apprenticeship or occupational training programs after graduation. Must be a Canadian citizen or landed immigrant and Alberta resident. For more details see website http://alis.alberta.ca.

Academic Fields/Career Goals: Trade/Technical Specialties.

Award: Scholarship for use in freshman year; not renewable. Number: 500.

Eligibility Requirements: Applicant must be enrolled or expecting to enroll full-time at a technical institution and resident of Alberta. Available to Canadian citizens.

Application Requirements: Application form, essay, recommendations or references. Deadline: June 30.

AMERICAN CHEMICAL SOCIETY
http://www.acs.org/

AMERICAN CHEMICAL SOCIETY SCHOLARS PROGRAM
• See page 153

AMERICAN LEGION DEPARTMENT OF PENNSYLVANIA
http://www.pa-legion.com/

ROBERT W. VALIMONT ENDOWMENT FUND SCHOLARSHIP (PART II)

Scholarships for any Pennsylvania high school senior seeking admission to a two-year college, post-high school trade/technical school, or training program. Must attend school in Pennsylvania. Continuation of award is based on grades. Renewable award of $600. Number of awards varies from year to year. Membership in an American Legion post in Pennsylvania is not required, but it must be documented if it does apply.

Academic Fields/Career Goals: Trade/Technical Specialties.

Award: Scholarship for use in freshman year; renewable. Amount: $600.

Eligibility Requirements: Applicant must be high school student; planning to enroll or expecting to enroll full-time at a two-year or technical institution; resident of Pennsylvania and studying in Pennsylvania. Available to U.S. citizens.

Application Requirements: Application form, financial need analysis, test scores, transcript. Deadline: May 30.

Contact: Debbie Watson, Emblem Sales Supervisor
American Legion Department of Pennsylvania
PO Box 2324
Harrisburg, PA 17105-2324
Phone: 717-730-9100
Fax: 717-975-2836
E-mail: hq@pa-legion.com

AMERICAN SOCIETY OF CERTIFIED ENGINEERING TECHNICIANS
http://www.ascet.org/

KURT H. AND DONNA M. SCHULER SMALL GRANT
• See page 162

AMERICAN WELDING SOCIETY
http://www.aws.org/

AMERICAN WELDING SOCIETY FOUNDATION SCHOLARSHIPS
• See page 225

MILLER ELECTRIC INTERNATIONAL WORLD SKILLS COMPETITION SCHOLARSHIP
• See page 225

ASSOCIATED GENERAL CONTRACTORS EDUCATION AND RESEARCH FOUNDATION
https://www.agc.org/

WORKFORCE DEVELOPMENT SCHOLARSHIP
• See page 226

AUTOMOTIVE AFTERMARKET SCHOLARSHIPS
http://www.automotivescholarships.com/

AUTOMOTIVE AFTERMARKET SCHOLARSHIPS
• See page 146

ENVIRONMENTAL CARE ASSOCIATION OF IDAHO
http://www.eacofidaho.org

ECA SCHOLARSHIP
• See page 291

GRAND RAPIDS COMMUNITY FOUNDATION
http://www.grfoundation.org/

DAROOGE FAMILY SCHOLARSHIP FOR CONSTRUCTION TRADES
• See page 185

INTERNATIONAL SOCIETY OF EXPLOSIVES ENGINEERS
http://www.isee.org/

JERRY MCDOWELL FUND
• See page 156

MANUFACTURERS ASSOCIATION OF MAINE

http://www.mainemfg.com/

MAINE MANUFACTURING CAREER AND TRAINING FOUNDATION SCHOLARSHIP
• See page 131

MIDWEST ROOFING CONTRACTORS ASSOCIATION

http://www.mrca.org/

MRCA FOUNDATION SCHOLARSHIP PROGRAM
• See page 116

NATIONAL ASSOCIATION OF WOMEN IN CONSTRUCTION

http://www.nawic.org/

NAWIC CONSTRUCTION TRADES SCHOLARSHIP

Scholarship for women pursuing a trade apprenticeship program. Only for students attending school in the United States or Canada.

Academic Fields/Career Goals: Trade/Technical Specialties.

Award: Scholarship for use in sophomore or junior years; not renewable. *Number:* 1. *Amount:* $1000–$2000.

Eligibility Requirements: Applicant must be enrolled or expecting to enroll full-time at a technical institution. Available to U.S. and Canadian citizens.

Application Requirements: Application form, essay, transcript. *Deadline:* March 15.

Contact: Scholarship Committee
National Association of Women in Construction
327 South Adams Street
Fort Worth, TX 76104
Phone: 817-877-5551
Fax: 817-877-0324

NAWIC UNDERGRADUATE SCHOLARSHIPS
• See page 117

NEXTSTEPU

http://www.nextstepu.com/

$1,500 STEM SCHOLARSHIP
• See page 104

NORTH CAROLINA COMMUNITY COLLEGE SYSTEM-STUDENT DEVELOPMENT SERVICES

http://www.nccommunitycolleges.edu/student-services

WACHOVIA TECHNICAL SCHOLARSHIP PROGRAM

One scholarship per college valued at $500 each. These scholarships are distributed among the 58 colleges in the community college system, which may be distributed in two payments: fall semester, $250; and spring semester, $250. To qualify as a candidate for these scholarships, a person must meet the following criteria: 1. Is a full-time student enrolled in the second year of a two-year educational/technical program. 2. Demonstrate financial need. 3. Demonstrate scholastic promise. 4. Use the scholarship to pay for tuition, books, and transportation. The recipients of the scholarships will be selected each year from applicants meeting the above criteria at local colleges.

Academic Fields/Career Goals: Trade/Technical Specialties.

Award: Scholarship for use in freshman or sophomore years; not renewable. *Amount:* $500.

Eligibility Requirements: Applicant must be enrolled or expecting to enroll full-time at a two-year or technical institution; resident of North Carolina and studying in North Carolina. Available to U.S. citizens.

Application Requirements: Application form, essay. *Deadline:* continuous.

Contact: Charletta Sims Evans, Associate Director of Student
Development Services
Phone: 919-807-7106
E-mail: simsc@nccommunitycolleges.edu

OIL & ENERGY SERVICE PROFESSIONALS

http://www.thinkoesp.org

DAVE NELSEN SCHOLARSHIPS

OESP is always eager to honor members who are propelling the industry, as well as supporting future energy professionals, who will one day become the backbone of our industry. Focusing on the future, The Dave Nelsen Scholarship, established in 1999, has given out more than $300,000 to students interested in pursuing careers in the energy service industry. Through our generous sponsors, OESP awards between three and six $5,000 scholarships each year. The Association seeks sponsors willing to donate $2,500 to our worthy recipients, with OESP pleased to continually provide matching funds. To be considered, scholarship candidates are asked to write a 500–word essay, highlighting how their educational background has prepared them for career success. Applicants are also asked to share their career goals for the next 5–10 years.

Academic Fields/Career Goals: Trade/Technical Specialties.

Award: Scholarship for use in freshman, sophomore, junior, or senior years; not renewable. *Number:* 3–6. *Amount:* $5000.

Eligibility Requirements: Applicant must be enrolled or expecting to enroll full- or part-time at a two-year or four-year or technical institution. Available to U.S. citizens.

Application Requirements: Application form, essay. *Deadline:* April 2.

PLATINUM EDUCATIONAL GROUP

www.platinumed.com

PLATINUM EDUCATIONAL GROUP SCHOLARSHIPS PROGRAM FOR EMS, NURSING, AND ALLIED HEALTH
• See page 102

PROFESSIONAL CONSTRUCTION ESTIMATORS ASSOCIATION

http://www.pcea.org/

TED G. WILSON MEMORIAL SCHOLARSHIP FOUNDATION
• See page 166

ROCKY MOUNTAIN COAL MINING INSTITUTE

http://www.rmcmi.org/

ROCKY MOUNTAIN COAL MINING INSTITUTE TECHNICAL SCHOLARSHIP

Scholarship for a first or second year student at a two-year technical/trade school in good standing at the time of selection. The student must be in a discipline related to potential use in the coal mining industry. Must be U.S. citizen and a legal resident of one of the Rocky Mountain Coal Mining Institute member states.

Academic Fields/Career Goals: Trade/Technical Specialties.

Award: Scholarship for use in freshman or sophomore years; not renewable. *Number:* 8. *Amount:* $1000.

Eligibility Requirements: Applicant must be enrolled or expecting to enroll full-time at a technical institution and resident of Arizona, Colorado, Montana, New Mexico, North Dakota, Texas, Utah, Wyoming. Available to U.S. citizens.

Application Requirements: Application form, essay, interview. *Deadline:* February 1.

Contact: Shahreen Salam, Executive Assistant
Rocky Mountain Coal Mining Institute
8057 South Yukon Way
Littleton, CO 80128-5510
Phone: 303-948-3300
Fax: 303-948-1132
E-mail: mail@rmcmi.org

SOCIETY OF PLASTICS ENGINEERS FOUNDATION (SPE)

http://www.4spe.org/

FLEMING/BLASZCAK SCHOLARSHIP
• *See page 158*

GULF COAST HURRICANE SCHOLARSHIP
• *See page 159*

SOCIETY OF PLASTICS ENGINEERS SCHOLARSHIP PROGRAM
• *See page 159*

SPECIALTY EQUIPMENT MARKET ASSOCIATION

http://www.sema.org/

SEMA MEMORIAL SCHOLARSHIP FUND
• *See page 81*

TRADE SCHOOL FUTURE

https://www.tradeschoolgrants.com/

FUTURE MECHANIC GRANT
This scholarship is open to any prospective student in the United States who plans to enroll in a trade or vocational school, 2 or 4 year university, accredited community college or other automotive higher education institution within the next 12 months. The applicant must complete a short essay (500 words or less) detailing why they are pursuing an automotive degree. The applicant must provide a phone number and email address for correspondence about the grant award selection process.
Academic Fields/Career Goals: Trade/Technical Specialties; Transportation.
Award: Grant for use in freshman year; not renewable. *Number:* 1. *Amount:* $1000.
Eligibility Requirements: Applicant must be age 16-75; enrolled or expecting to enroll full- or part-time at a two-year or four-year or technical institution or university and must have an interest in automotive. Available to U.S. and non-U.S. citizens.
Application Requirements: Application form, application form may be submitted online (https://www.tradeschoolgrants.com/scholarships/future-mechanic-grant/), essay. *Deadline:* December 1.

TRUCKER TO TRUCKER, LLC

http://www.truckertotrucker.com/

TRUCKER TO TRUCKER SCHOLARSHIP
$500 Scholarship to attend a commercial driver's training program in the US. Applicants will need to fill out a short online application and upload a 300-500 word essay.
Academic Fields/Career Goals: Trade/Technical Specialties.
Award: Scholarship for use in freshman, sophomore, junior, or senior years; not renewable. *Number:* 2. *Amount:* $500.
Eligibility Requirements: Applicant must be age 18-99 and enrolled or expecting to enroll full-time at a technical institution. Available to U.S. citizens.
Application Requirements: Application form, essay. *Deadline:* November 15.

Contact: Scholarship Coordinator
E-mail: scholarship@truckertotrucker.com

UNITED COMMUNITY SERVICES FOR WORKING FAMILIES

http://www.ucswf.org

RONALD LORAH MEMORIAL SCHOLARSHIP
One-time award available to a union member, spouse of a union member, or child of a union member. Must be a resident of Pennsylvania. Must submit essay that is clear, concise, persuasive and show an understanding of unions.
Academic Fields/Career Goals: Trade/Technical Specialties.
Award: Scholarship for use in freshman, sophomore, junior, or senior years; not renewable. *Number:* 2. *Amount:* $500–$750.
Eligibility Requirements: Applicant must be enrolled or expecting to enroll full-time at a two-year or four-year or technical institution or university and resident of Pennsylvania. Applicant or parent of applicant must be member of AFL-CIO. Available to U.S. citizens.
Application Requirements: Application form, essay, financial need analysis, transcript. *Deadline:* July 31.
Contact: Victoria Henshaw, Executive Director
United Community Services for Working Families
1251 North Front Street
Reading, PA 19601
E-mail: vhenshaw@ucswf.org

VERMONT SPACE GRANT CONSORTIUM

http://www.cems.uvm.edu/vsgc

VERMONT SPACE GRANT CONSORTIUM
• *See page 92*

WOMEN IN LOGISTICS, NORTHERN CALIFORNIA

http://www.womeninlogistics.org/

WOMEN IN LOGISTICS SCHOLARSHIP
• *See page 152*

WOMEN'S JEWELRY ASSOCIATION

http://www.womensjewelryassociation.com

WOMEN'S JEWELRY ASSOCIATION STUDENT SCHOLARSHIP
• *See page 124*

WYOMING TRUCKING ASSOCIATION SCHOLARSHIP FUND TRUST

http://www.wytruck.org/

WYOMING TRUCKING ASSOCIATION SCHOLARSHIP TRUST FUND
• *See page 84*

YOUTH MARITIME TRAINING ASSOCIATION

http://ymta.net/

NORM MANLY—YMTA MARITIME EDUCATIONAL SCHOLARSHIPS
• *See page 326*

TRANSPORTATION

AMERICAN BUS ASSOCIATION

https://www.buses.org/

ABA ACADEMIC MERIT SCHOLARSHIPS

Academic Merit Scholarships are open to both ABA and non-ABA Members. The applicant must be a freshman, sophomore; junior, senior, or graduate student at an accredited University (4-year university/college or junior college) and must have a declared major or course of study relevant to the transportation, travel and tourism industry and must possess a cumulative GPA of 3.4 or higher. Two scholarships are awarded, in the amount $5,000 each. Apply online between December 7th and April 6th. Create an account to submit applications, as well as check the status of your applications and make any necessary changes before the program deadline.

Academic Fields/Career Goals: Transportation; Travel/Tourism.

Award: Scholarship for use in freshman, sophomore, junior, senior, graduate, or postgraduate years; not renewable. *Number:* 2. *Amount:* $5000.

Eligibility Requirements: Applicant must be enrolled or expecting to enroll full-time at a four-year institution. Available to U.S. and Canadian citizens.

Application Requirements: Application form, essay. *Deadline:* April 6.

Contact: Zoe Deloglos, Special Projects Coordinator
American Bus Association
111 K Street NE
9th Floor
Washington, DC 20002
Phone: 202-218-7222
Fax: 202-842-0850
E-mail: zdeloglos@buses.org

ABA DIVERSITY SCHOLARSHIPS

The Diversity Scholarship focuses on broadening the number of traditionally underrepresented groups in the management and operation ranks of the transportation, travel, and tourism industry. Eligible candidates must have completed, at a minimum, their first year of college at an accredited university; must have a declared major or course of study relevant to the transportation, travel, and tourism industry; and must have a cumulative 3.0 GPA. Applicants are required to submit a 500-word essay discussing the role they hope to play in advancing the future of the transportation, motorcoach, travel, and tourism/hospitality industry.

Academic Fields/Career Goals: Transportation; Travel/Tourism.

Award: Scholarship for use in sophomore, junior, or senior years; not renewable. *Number:* 1. *Amount:* $5000.

Eligibility Requirements: Applicant must be enrolled or expecting to enroll full- or part-time at an institution or university. Available to U.S. and Canadian citizens.

Application Requirements: Application form, essay. *Deadline:* April 6.

Contact: Zoe Deloglos, Special Projects Coordinator
American Bus Association
111 K Street NE
9th Floor
Washington, DC 20002
Phone: 202-218-7222
Fax: 202-842-0850
E-mail: zdeloglos@buses.org

AMERICAN COUNCIL OF ENGINEERING COMPANIES OF PENNSYLVANIA (ACEC/PA)

http://www.acecpa.org/

ERIC J. GENNUSO AND LEROY D. (BUD) LOY, JR. SCHOLARSHIP PROGRAM

• See page 153

AMERICAN INDIAN SCIENCE AND ENGINEERING SOCIETY

http://www.aises.org/

A.T. ANDERSON MEMORIAL SCHOLARSHIP PROGRAM

• See page 105

AMERICAN PUBLIC TRANSPORTATION FOUNDATION

https://www.aptfd.org/

DAN M. REICHARD, JR. SCHOLARSHIP

Scholarship for study towards a career in the business administration/management area of the transit industry. Must be sponsored by APTA member organization and complete internship with APTA member organization. Minimum GPA of 3.0 required.

Academic Fields/Career Goals: Transportation.

Award: Scholarship for use in sophomore, junior, senior, or graduate years; renewable. *Number:* 1. *Amount:* $2500.

Eligibility Requirements: Applicant must be enrolled or expecting to enroll full-time at a two-year institution or university. Available to U.S. and Canadian citizens.

Application Requirements: Application form, application form may be submitted online, essay, financial need analysis. *Deadline:* June 15.

DONALD C. HYDE ESSAY PROGRAM

Award of $500 for the best response to the required essay component of the program.

Academic Fields/Career Goals: Transportation.

Award: Prize for use in sophomore, junior, senior, or graduate years; not renewable. *Number:* 1. *Amount:* $500.

Eligibility Requirements: Applicant must be enrolled or expecting to enroll full-time at a two-year or four-year institution or university. Available to U.S. and Canadian citizens.

Application Requirements: Application form, entry in a contest, essay, financial need analysis, recommendations or references, transcript. *Deadline:* June 16.

Contact: Pamela Boswell, Vice President of Program Management
American Public Transportation Foundation
1666 K Street, NW
Washington, DC 20006-1215
Phone: 202-496-4803
Fax: 202-496-2323
E-mail: pboswell@apta.com

JACK R. GILSTRAP SCHOLARSHIP

Awarded the APTF scholarship to the applicant with the highest score. Must be in public transportation industry-related fields of study. Must be sponsored by AFTA member organization and complete an internship program with a member organization. Minimum 3.0 GPA required.

Academic Fields/Career Goals: Transportation.

Award: Scholarship for use in sophomore, junior, senior, or graduate years; renewable. *Number:* 1. *Amount:* $2500.

Eligibility Requirements: Applicant must be enrolled or expecting to enroll full-time at a two-year institution or university. Available to U.S. and Canadian citizens.

Application Requirements: Application form, application form may be submitted online, essay, financial need analysis. *Deadline:* June 15.

TRANSIT HALL OF FAME SCHOLARSHIP AWARD PROGRAM

• See page 162

AMERICAN SOCIETY OF CERTIFIED ENGINEERING TECHNICIANS

http://www.ascet.org/

KURT H. AND DONNA M. SCHULER SMALL GRANT

• See page 162

ASSOCIATED GENERAL CONTRACTORS OF NEW YORK STATE, LLC

https://www.agcnys.org/programs/scholarship/

ASSOCIATED GENERAL CONTRACTORS NYS SCHOLARSHIP PROGRAM
• *See page 163*

AUTOMOTIVE WOMEN'S ALLIANCE FOUNDATION

http://awafoundation.org/index.php

AUTOMOTIVE WOMEN'S ALLIANCE FOUNDATION SCHOLARSHIPS
• *See page 71*

THE CLUNKER JUNKER

https://theclunkerjunker.com/

CLUNKER JUNKER CASH FOR CARS AND COLLEGE SCHOLARSHIP
• *See page 227*

LOGISTICS & TRANSPORTATION ASSOCIATION OF NORTH AMERICA

http://www.ltna.org

ALICE GLAISYER WARFIELD MEMORIAL SCHOLARSHIP
Award is available to currently enrolled students majoring in transportation, logistics, traffic management, or related fields. Available to citizens of the United States, Canada, and Mexico. See website for application, http://www.transportationclubinternational.com/.

Academic Fields/Career Goals: Transportation.

Award: Scholarship for use in freshman, sophomore, junior, or senior years; not renewable. *Number:* 1. *Amount:* $1500.

Eligibility Requirements: Applicant must be enrolled or expecting to enroll full- or part-time at a two-year or four-year or technical institution or university. Applicant or parent of applicant must be member of Transportation Club International. Available to U.S. and non-U.S. citizens.

Application Requirements: Application form, essay, personal photograph, recommendations or references, transcript. *Deadline:* April 30.

Contact: Katie Dejonge, Executive Director
Union, WA 98592
Phone: 360-898-3344
E-mail: executive.director@ltna.org

TEXAS TRANSPORTATION SCHOLARSHIP
Merit-based award for a student who is at least a sophomore studying transportation, traffic management, and related fields. Must have been enrolled in a school in Texas during some phase of education (elementary, secondary, high school). Must include photo and submit three references. One-time scholarship of $1000. See website for application http://www.transportationclubinternational.com/.

Academic Fields/Career Goals: Transportation.

Award: Scholarship for use in sophomore, junior, or senior years; not renewable. *Number:* 1. *Amount:* $1000.

Eligibility Requirements: Applicant must be enrolled or expecting to enroll full- or part-time at a two-year or four-year or technical institution or university. Applicant or parent of applicant must be member of Transportation Club International. Available to U.S. citizens.

Application Requirements: Application form, essay, personal photograph, recommendations or references, transcript. *Deadline:* April 30.

Contact: Katie Dejonge, Executive Director
Union, WA 98592
Phone: 360-898-3344
E-mail: executive.director@ltna.org

TRANSPORTATION CLUBS INTERNATIONAL CHARLOTTE WOODS SCHOLARSHIP
Award available to an enrolled college student majoring in transportation or traffic management. Must be a member or a dependent of a member of Transportation Clubs International. Must have completed at least one year of post-high school education. One-time award of $1000. See website for application http://www.transportationclubinternational.com/.

Academic Fields/Career Goals: Transportation.

Award: Scholarship for use in freshman, sophomore, junior, or senior years; not renewable. *Number:* 1. *Amount:* $1000.

Eligibility Requirements: Applicant must be enrolled or expecting to enroll full- or part-time at a two-year or four-year or technical institution or university. Applicant or parent of applicant must be member of Transportation Club International. Available to U.S. and non-U.S. citizens.

Application Requirements: Application form, essay, personal photograph, recommendations or references, transcript. *Deadline:* April 30.

Contact: Crystal Hunter, Program Manager
Phone: 800-377-2401
E-mail: awards@goldenkey.org

TRANSPORTATION CLUBS INTERNATIONAL FRED A. HOOPER MEMORIAL SCHOLARSHIP
• *See page 228*

TRANSPORTATION CLUBS INTERNATIONAL GINGER AND FRED DEINES CANADA SCHOLARSHIP
One-time award for a student of Canadian heritage, who is attending college or university in Canada or the United States and majoring in transportation, traffic management, logistics, or a related field. Academic merit is considered. See website for application http://www.transportationclubinternational.com/.

Academic Fields/Career Goals: Transportation.

Award: Scholarship for use in freshman, sophomore, junior, or senior years; not renewable. *Number:* 1. *Amount:* $1500.

Eligibility Requirements: Applicant must be of Canadian heritage and Canadian citizen and enrolled or expecting to enroll full- or part-time at a two-year or four-year or technical institution or university. Applicant or parent of applicant must be member of Transportation Club International.

Application Requirements: Application form, essay, personal photograph, recommendations or references, transcript. *Deadline:* April 30.

Contact: Katie Dejonge, Executive Director
Union, WA 98592
Phone: 360-898-3344
E-mail: executive.director@ltna.org

TRANSPORTATION CLUBS INTERNATIONAL GINGER AND FRED DEINES MEXICO SCHOLARSHIP
Scholarship of $2000 for a Mexican student who is enrolled in an accredited institution of higher learning in a vocational or degree program in the fields of transportation, logistics or traffic management, or related fields. May be enrolled in a U.S. or Canadian institution. See website for application http://www.transportationclubinternational.com/.

Academic Fields/Career Goals: Transportation.

Award: Scholarship for use in freshman, sophomore, junior, or senior years; not renewable. *Number:* 1. *Amount:* $2000.

Eligibility Requirements: Applicant must be Mexican citizen and enrolled or expecting to enroll full- or part-time at a two-year or four-year or technical institution or university. Applicant or parent of applicant must be member of Transportation Club International. Available to Canadian and non-U.S. citizens.

Application Requirements: Application form, essay, personal photograph, recommendations or references, transcript. *Deadline:* April 30.

Contact: Katie Dejonge, Executive Director
Union, WA 98592
Phone: 360-898-3344
E-mail: executive.director@ltna.org

NATIONAL CUSTOMS BROKERS AND FORWARDERS ASSOCIATION OF AMERICA

http://www.ncbfaa.org/

NATIONAL CUSTOMS BROKERS AND FORWARDERS ASSOCIATION OF AMERICA SCHOLARSHIP AWARD

One-time award for employees of National Customs Broker & Forwarders Association of America, Inc. (NCBFAA) regular member organizations and their children. Must be studying transportation logistics or international trade full time. Require minimum 2.0 GPA.

Academic Fields/Career Goals: Transportation.

Award: Scholarship for use in freshman, sophomore, junior, or senior years; not renewable. *Number:* 1. *Amount:* $5000.

Eligibility Requirements: Applicant must be enrolled or expecting to enroll full-time at a four-year institution or university. Available to U.S. citizens.

Application Requirements: Essay. *Deadline:* January 8.

Contact: Mr. Tom Mathers, Director, Communications
National Customs Brokers and Forwarders Association of America
1200 18th Street, NW, Suite 901
Washington, DC 20036
Phone: 202-466-0222
E-mail: tom@ncbfaa.org

SPECIALTY EQUIPMENT MARKET ASSOCIATION

http://www.sema.org/

SEMA MEMORIAL SCHOLARSHIP FUND
• See page 81

TRADE SCHOOL FUTURE

https://www.tradeschoolgrants.com/

FUTURE MECHANIC GRANT
• See page 419

WOMEN IN LOGISTICS, NORTHERN CALIFORNIA

http://www.womeninlogistics.org/

WOMEN IN LOGISTICS SCHOLARSHIP
• See page 152

WYOMING TRUCKING ASSOCIATION SCHOLARSHIP FUND TRUST

http://www.wytruck.org/

WYOMING TRUCKING ASSOCIATION SCHOLARSHIP TRUST FUND
• See page 84

TRAVEL/TOURISM

AMERICAN BUS ASSOCIATION

https://www.buses.org/

ABA ACADEMIC MERIT SCHOLARSHIPS
• See page 420

ABA DIVERSITY SCHOLARSHIPS
• See page 420

AMERICAN HOTEL AND LODGING EDUCATIONAL FOUNDATION

https://www.ahlafoundation.org/

AHLEF ANNUAL SCHOLARSHIP GRANT PROGRAM
• See page 267

AMERICAN HOTEL & LODGING EDUCATIONAL FOUNDATION PEPSI SCHOLARSHIP
• See page 189

ECOLAB SCHOLARSHIP PROGRAM
• See page 267

HYATT HOTELS FUND FOR MINORITY LODGING MANAGEMENT
• See page 268

INCOMING FRESHMAN SCHOLARSHIPS
• See page 268

RAMA SCHOLARSHIP FOR THE AMERICAN DREAM
• See page 268

HAWAII LODGING & TOURISM ASSOCIATION

http://www.hawaiilodging.org

R.W. "BOB" HOLDEN SCHOLARSHIP
• See page 295

MISSOURI TRAVEL COUNCIL

http://www.missouritravel.com/

BOB SMITH TOURISM SCHOLARSHIP
• See page 269

OHIO TRAVEL ASSOCIATION

http://www.ohiotravel.org/

BILL SCHWARTZ MEMORIAL SCHOLARSHIP
• See page 295

UNITED NEGRO COLLEGE FUND

http://www.uncf.org/

UNCF/CARNIVAL CORPORATE SCHOLARS PROGRAM
• See page 151

TV/RADIO BROADCASTING

ADC RESEARCH INSTITUTE

http://www.adc.org/

JACK SHAHEEN MASS COMMUNICATIONS SCHOLARSHIP AWARD
• See page 169

ALABAMA BROADCASTERS ASSOCIATION

http://www.al-ba.com/

ALABAMA BROADCASTERS ASSOCIATION SCHOLARSHIP

Scholarship available to Alabama residents studying broadcasting at any accredited Alabama technical school, 2- or 4-year college, or university.

Academic Fields/Career Goals: TV/Radio Broadcasting.

Award: Scholarship for use in junior or senior years; not renewable. *Number:* up to 4. *Amount:* up to $2500.

Eligibility Requirements: Applicant must be enrolled or expecting to enroll full-time at a two-year or four-year or technical institution or university; resident of Alabama and studying in Alabama. Available to U.S. citizens.

Application Requirements: Application form, recommendations or references. *Deadline:* April 30.

Contact: Sharon Tinsley, President
Phone: 205-982-5001
Fax: 205-982-0015
E-mail: stinsley@al-ba.com

ASIAN AMERICAN JOURNALISTS ASSOCIATION

http://www.aaja.org/

CIC/ANNA CHENNAULT SCHOLARSHIP
• See page 170

MARY QUON MOY ING MEMORIAL SCHOLARSHIP AWARD
• See page 170

VINCENT CHIN MEMORIAL SCHOLARSHIP
• See page 171

ASIAN AMERICAN JOURNALISTS ASSOCIATION, SEATTLE CHAPTER

http://www.aajaseattle.org/

NORTHWEST JOURNALISTS OF COLOR SCHOLARSHIP
• See page 84

ASSOCIATED PRESS

http://www.aptra.org/

ASSOCIATED PRESS TELEVISION/RADIO ASSOCIATION-CLETE ROBERTS JOURNALISM SCHOLARSHIP AWARDS
• See page 303

KATHRYN DETTMAN MEMORIAL JOURNALISM SCHOLARSHIP
• See page 303

CALIFORNIA BROADCASTERS FOUNDATION

http://www.cabroadcasters.org/

CALIFORNIA BROADCASTERS FOUNDATION INTERN SCHOLARSHIP

Four $1000 scholarships awarded to radio interns and four $1000 scholarships awarded to television interns each semester. Any enrolled college student working as an intern at any California Broadcasters Foundation or Association member radio or television station is eligible. No minimum number of hours per week required. Immediate family of current Foundation Board Members are not eligible.

Academic Fields/Career Goals: TV/Radio Broadcasting.

Award: Scholarship for use in freshman, sophomore, junior, senior, graduate, or postgraduate years; not renewable. *Number:* 8. *Amount:* $1000.

Eligibility Requirements: Applicant must be enrolled or expecting to enroll full- or part-time at a two-year or four-year or technical institution or university and resident of California. Available to U.S. citizens.

Application Requirements: Application form, essay.

Contact: Mark Powers, Government Affairs
Phone: 916-444-2237
E-mail: cbapowers@cabroadcasters.org

CCNMA: LATINO JOURNALISTS OF CALIFORNIA

http://www.ccnma.org/

CCNMA SCHOLARSHIPS
• See page 171

CHARLES AND LUCILLE KING FAMILY FOUNDATION, INC.

http://www.kingfoundation.org/

CHARLES & LUCILLE KING FAMILY FOUNDATION SCHOLARSHIPS
• See page 171

HAWAII ASSOCIATION OF BROADCASTERS INC.

http://www.hawaiibroadcasters.com/

HAWAII ASSOCIATION OF BROADCASTERS SCHOLARSHIP

Renewable scholarship for full-time college students with the career goal of working in the broadcast industry in Hawaii upon graduation. Minimum GPA of 2.75 required. Number of awards granted ranges between twenty and thirty. For more information, visit website http://www.hawaiibroadcasters.com.

Academic Fields/Career Goals: TV/Radio Broadcasting.

Award: Scholarship for use in freshman, sophomore, junior, or senior years; renewable. *Number:* 20–30. *Amount:* $500–$4500.

Eligibility Requirements: Applicant must be enrolled or expecting to enroll full-time at a two-year or four-year institution or university. Available to U.S. and non-U.S. citizens.

Application Requirements: Application form, recommendations or references, transcript. *Deadline:* April 30.

Contact: Scholarship Committee
Hawaii Association of Broadcasters Inc.
PO Box 61562
Honolulu, HI 96839
Phone: 808-599-1455
Fax: 808-599-7784

IDAHO STATE BROADCASTERS ASSOCIATION

http://www.idahobroadcasters.org/

WAYNE C. CORNILS MEMORIAL SCHOLARSHIP
• See page 148

ILLUMINATING ENGINEERING SOCIETY OF NORTH AMERICA

http://www.ies.org/

ROBERT W. THUNEN MEMORIAL SCHOLARSHIPS
• See page 116

INDIANA BROADCASTERS ASSOCIATION

http://www.indianabroadcasters.org/

INDIANA BROADCASTERS FOUNDATION SCHOLARSHIP
• See page 305

ISLAMIC SCHOLARSHIP FUND

http://islamicscholarshipfund.org/

ISF NATIONAL SCHOLARSHIP
• See page 104

LOUISIANA ASSOCIATION OF BROADCASTERS

http://www.broadcasters.org/

BROADCAST SCHOLARSHIP PROGRAM

Scholarship to students enrolled and attending classes, full-time, in a fully accredited broadcast curriculum at a Louisiana four-year college. Must be a Louisiana resident and maintain a minimum 2.5 GPA. Previous LAB Scholarship Award winners are eligible.

Academic Fields/Career Goals: TV/Radio Broadcasting.

Award: Scholarship for use in junior or senior years; not renewable. *Number:* 2. *Amount:* $2000.

Eligibility Requirements: Applicant must be enrolled or expecting to enroll full-time at a four-year institution or university; resident of Louisiana and studying in Louisiana. Available to U.S. citizens.

Application Requirements: Application form, essay. *Deadline:* February 1.

Contact: Polly Johnson
  Louisiana Association of Broadcasters
  660 Florida Street
  Baton Rouge, LA 70801
  Phone: 225-267-4522
  E-mail: pollyjohnson@broadcasters.org

MICHIGAN ASSOCIATION OF BROADCASTERS FOUNDATION

http://www.michmab.com/

WXYZ-TV BROADCASTING SCHOLARSHIP

One-time $1000 scholarship to assist students who are actively pursuing a career in a broadcast-related field. No limit on the number of awards within the program. Interested applicants should send a cover letter, resume, letters of recommendation, and an essay (200 to 300 words). The scholarship is open to Michigan residents currently attending college in Michigan.

Academic Fields/Career Goals: TV/Radio Broadcasting.

Award: Scholarship for use in freshman year; not renewable. *Number:* 1. *Amount:* $1000.

Eligibility Requirements: Applicant must be high school student; planning to enroll or expecting to enroll full-time at a two-year or four-year institution or university; resident of Michigan and studying in Michigan. Available to U.S. citizens.

Application Requirements: Application form, driver's license, essay, recommendations or references. *Deadline:* January 15.

Contact: Julie Sochay, Executive Vice President
  Michigan Association of Broadcasters Foundation
  819 North Washington Avenue
  Lansing, MI 48906
  Phone: 517-484-7444
  Fax: 517-484-5810
  E-mail: mabf@michmab.com

MISSISSIPPI ASSOCIATION OF BROADCASTERS

http://www.msbroadcasters.org/

MISSISSIPPI ASSOCIATION OF BROADCASTERS SCHOLARSHIP
• See page 306

MISSOURI BROADCASTERS ASSOCIATION SCHOLARSHIP PROGRAM

http://www.mbaweb.org/

MISSOURI BROADCASTERS ASSOCIATION SCHOLARSHIP PROGRAM

Scholarship for a Missouri resident enrolled or planning to enroll in a broadcast or related curriculum which provides training and expertise applicable to a broadcast operation. Must maintain a GPA of at least 3.0 or equivalent. Multiple awards may be assigned each year and the amount of the scholarship will vary.

Academic Fields/Career Goals: TV/Radio Broadcasting.

Award: Scholarship for use in freshman, sophomore, junior, or senior years; not renewable. *Number:* 3–5. *Amount:* $1000–$2500.

Eligibility Requirements: Applicant must be enrolled or expecting to enroll full-time at a two-year or four-year institution or university; resident of Missouri and studying in Missouri. Available to U.S. citizens.

Application Requirements: Application form, essay, financial need analysis. *Deadline:* March 31.

Contact: Ms. Terry Harper, Director of Member Services
  Phone: 573-636-6692
  Fax: 573-634-8258
  E-mail: tharper@mbaweb.org

MONTANA BROADCASTERS ASSOCIATION

http://www.mtbroadcasters.org/

GREAT FALLS BROADCASTERS ASSOCIATION SCHOLARSHIP

Scholarship available to a student who has graduated from a north-central Montana high school (Cascade, Meagher, Judith Basin, Fergus, Choteau, Teton, Pondera, Glacier, Toole, Liberty, Hill, Blaine, Phillips, and Valley counties) and is enrolled as at least a second year student in radio-TV at any public or private Montana college or university.

Academic Fields/Career Goals: TV/Radio Broadcasting.

Award: Scholarship for use in sophomore year; not renewable. *Number:* 1. *Amount:* $2000–$5000.

Eligibility Requirements: Applicant must be enrolled or expecting to enroll full-time at a two-year or four-year institution or university; resident of Montana and studying in Montana. Available to U.S. citizens.

Application Requirements: Application form, essay, recommendations or references, transcript. *Deadline:* March 15.

Contact: Gregory McDonald, Scholarship Coordinator
  Montana Broadcasters Association
  HC 70 PO Box 98
  Bonner, MT 59823
  Phone: 406-244-4622
  Fax: 406-244-5518
  E-mail: mba@mtbroadcasters.org

NATIONAL ACADEMY OF TELEVISION ARTS AND SCIENCES

https://theemmys.tv/

DOUGLAS W. MUMMERT SCHOLARSHIP
• *See page 173*

JIM MCKAY MEMORIAL SCHOLARSHIP
• *See page 258*

MIKE WALLACE MEMORIAL SCHOLARSHIP
• *See page 258*

NATIONAL ACADEMY OF TELEVISION ARTS AND SCIENCES TRUSTEES' LINDA GIANNECCHINI SCHOLARSHIP
• *See page 258*

RANDY FALCO SCHOLARSHIP
• *See page 259*

NATIONAL ACADEMY OF TELEVISION ARTS AND SCIENCES, MICHIGAN CHAPTER

http://natasmichigan.org

DR. LYNNE BOYLE/JOHN SCHIMPF UNDERGRADUATE SCHOLARSHIP
• *See page 85*

NATIONAL ACADEMY OF TELEVISION ARTS AND SCIENCES-NATIONAL CAPITAL/CHESAPEAKE BAY CHAPTER

http://www.natasdc.org/

BETTY ENDICOTT/NTA-NCCB STUDENT SCHOLARSHIP
• *See page 306*

NATIONAL ACADEMY OF TELEVISION ARTS & SCIENCES—OHIO VALLEY CHAPTER

http://ohiovalleyemmy.org/

DAVID J. CLARKE MEMORIAL SCHOLARSHIP
• *See page 173*

NATIONAL ASSOCIATION OF BLACK JOURNALISTS

http://www.nabj.org/

NABJ SCHOLARSHIP
• *See page 307*

NATIONAL ASSOCIATION OF BLACK JOURNALISTS NON-SUSTAINING SCHOLARSHIP AWARDS
• *See page 307*

NATIONAL ASSOCIATION OF BROADCASTERS

http://www.nab.org/

NATIONAL ASSOCIATION OF BROADCASTERS GRANTS FOR RESEARCH IN BROADCASTING
• *See page 173*

NATIONAL ASSOCIATION OF HISPANIC JOURNALISTS (NAHJ)

http://www.nahj.org/

GERALDO RIVERA SCHOLARSHIP
• *See page 307*

MARIA ELENA SALINAS SCHOLARSHIP
• *See page 307*

NATIONAL ASSOCIATION OF HISPANIC JOURNALISTS SCHOLARSHIP
• *See page 173*

NATIONAL COUNCIL OF JEWISH WOMEN - LOS ANGELES (NCJW L LA)

http://ncjwla.org/

STEPHEN L. TELLER & RICHARD HOTSON TV, CINEMA, AND THEATER SCHOLARSHIP
• *See page 259*

NORTH CAROLINA ASSOCIATION OF BROADCASTERS

http://www.ncbroadcast.com/

NCAB SCHOLARSHIP

One-time scholarship for high school seniors enrolled as full-time students in a North Carolina college or university with an interest in broadcasting. Must be between ages 17 and 20.

Academic Fields/Career Goals: TV/Radio Broadcasting.

Award: Scholarship for use in freshman year; not renewable. *Number:* 2. *Amount:* $10,000.

Eligibility Requirements: Applicant must be high school student; age 17-20; planning to enroll or expecting to enroll full-time at a two-year or four-year institution or university and studying in North Carolina. Available to U.S. citizens.

Application Requirements: Application form, essay, recommendations or references, transcript. *Deadline:* April 15.

Contact: Lisa Reynolds, Executive Manager
North Carolina Association of Broadcasters
PO Box 627
Raleigh, NC 27602
Phone: 919-821-7300
Fax: 919-839-0304

OREGON ASSOCIATION OF BROADCASTERS

http://www.theoab.org/

OAB FOUNDATION SCHOLARSHIP
• *See page 174*

OUTDOOR WRITERS ASSOCIATION OF AMERICA

http://www.owaa.org/

OUTDOOR WRITERS ASSOCIATION OF AMERICA - BODIE MCDOWELL SCHOLARSHIP AWARD
• See page 174

PALM BEACH ASSOCIATION OF BLACK JOURNALISTS

PALM BEACH ASSOCIATION OF BLACK JOURNALISTS SCHOLARSHIP
• See page 309

POLISH ARTS CLUB OF BUFFALO SCHOLARSHIP FOUNDATION

http://www.pacb.bfn.org/

POLISH ARTS CLUB OF BUFFALO SCHOLARSHIP FOUNDATION TRUST
• See page 122

RADIO TELEVISION DIGITAL NEWS ASSOCIATION

http://www.rtdna.org

CAROLE SIMPSON SCHOLARSHIP
• See page 310

ED BRADLEY SCHOLARSHIP
• See page 310

GEORGE FOREMAN TRIBUTE TO LYNDON B. JOHNSON SCHOLARSHIP
• See page 310

LEE THORNTON SCHOLARSHIP
• See page 310

LOU AND CAROLE PRATO SPORTS REPORTING SCHOLARSHIP
• See page 310

MIKE REYNOLDS JOURNALISM SCHOLARSHIP
• See page 311

PETE WILSON JOURNALISM SCHOLARSHIP
• See page 311

PRESIDENTS SCHOLARSHIP
• See page 311

RHODE ISLAND FOUNDATION

http://www.rifoundation.org/

J. D. EDSAL SCHOLARSHIP
• See page 87

SOCIETY OF MOTION PICTURE AND TELEVISION ENGINEERS

https://www.smpte.org/

LOUIS F. WOLF JR. MEMORIAL SCHOLARSHIP
• See page 175

STUDENT PAPER AWARD
• See page 175

SOCIETY OF PROFESSIONAL JOURNALISTS, LOS ANGELES CHAPTER

http://www.spj.org/losangeles

HELEN JOHNSON SCHOLARSHIP
• See page 312

STRAIGHTFORWARD MEDIA

http://www.straightforwardmedia.com/

STRAIGHTFORWARD MEDIA MEDIA & COMMUNICATIONS SCHOLARSHIP
• See page 87

TAMPA BAY TIMES FUND, INC.

http://company.tampabay.com:2052/times-fund/scholarships

CAREER JOURNALISM SCHOLARSHIP
• See page 176

TAMPA BAY TIMES FUND CAREER JOURNALISM SCHOLARSHIPS
• See page 87

TEXAS ASSOCIATION OF BROADCASTERS

https://www.tab.org/scholarships/available-scholarships

TEXAS ASSOCIATION OF BROADCASTERS - BELO SCHOLARSHIP
• See page 176

TEXAS ASSOCIATION OF BROADCASTERS - BONNER MCLANE SCHOLARSHIP
• See page 313

TEXAS ASSOCIATION OF BROADCASTERS - TOM REIFF SCHOLARSHIP
• See page 313

TEXAS ASSOCIATION OF BROADCASTERS - TWO-YEAR/TECHNICAL SCHOOL SCHOLARSHIP
• See page 176

TEXAS ASSOCIATION OF BROADCASTERS - UNDERGRADUATE SCHOLARSHIP
• See page 176

TEXAS ASSOCIATION OF BROADCASTERS - VANN KENNEDY SCHOLARSHIP
• See page 177

TEXAS GRIDIRON CLUB INC.

http://www.spjfw.org/

TEXAS GRIDIRON CLUB SCHOLARSHIPS
• See page 177

UNITED METHODIST COMMUNICATIONS

http://www.umcom.org/

LEONARD M. PERRYMAN COMMUNICATIONS SCHOLARSHIP FOR ETHNIC MINORITY STUDENTS
• See page 177

VALLEY PRESS CLUB

http://www.valleypressclub.com/

VALLEY PRESS CLUB SCHOLARSHIPS, THE REPUBLICAN SCHOLARSHIP, CHANNEL 22 SCHOLARSHIP
• *See page 178*

WASHINGTON MEDIA SCHOLARS FOUNDATION

www.mediascholars.org

MEDIA PLAN CASE COMPETITION
• *See page 88*

WISCONSIN BROADCASTERS ASSOCIATION FOUNDATION

http://www.wi-broadcasters.org/

WISCONSIN BROADCASTERS ASSOCIATION FOUNDATION SCHOLARSHIP
• *See page 178*

WOWT-TV OMAHA, NEBRASKA

http://www.wowt.com/

WOWT-TV BROADCASTING SCHOLARSHIP PROGRAM
Two annual scholarships of $1000 for high school graduates in the Channel 6 viewing area of Nebraska. Must be pursuing a full-time career in broadcasting and have a minimum GPA of 3.0.

Academic Fields/Career Goals: TV/Radio Broadcasting.

Award: Scholarship for use in freshman year; not renewable. *Number:* 2. *Amount:* $1000.

Eligibility Requirements: Applicant must be high school student; planning to enroll or expecting to enroll full-time at a two-year or four-year institution or university and resident of Nebraska. Available to U.S. citizens.

Application Requirements: Application form, community service, essay, interview. *Deadline:* March 15.

Contact: Brandy Gerry, Programming and Community Affairs Manager
WOWT-TV Omaha, Nebraska
3501 Farnam Street
Omaha, NE 68131
Phone: 402-346-6666
E-mail: scholarship@wowt.com

URBAN AND REGIONAL PLANNING

AMERICAN PLANNING ASSOCIATION

http://www.planning.org/

JUDITH MCMANUS PRICE SCHOLARSHIP
Women and minority (African American, Hispanic American, or Native American) students enrolled in an approved Planning Accreditation Board (PAB) planning program who are citizens of the United States, intend to pursue careers as practicing planners in the public sector, and are able to demonstrate a genuine financial need are eligible to apply for this scholarship. For further information visit https://www.planning.org/scholarships/apa/

Academic Fields/Career Goals: Urban and Regional Planning.

Award: Scholarship for use in freshman, sophomore, junior, senior, or graduate years; not renewable. *Amount:* $2000–$5000.

Eligibility Requirements: Applicant must be American Indian/Alaska Native, Black (non-Hispanic), Hispanic and enrolled or expecting to enroll full-time at a four-year institution or university. Available to U.S. citizens.

Application Requirements: Application form, essay, financial need analysis. *Deadline:* April 30.

Contact: Christine Rahill, Development Director
American Planning Association
205 N. Michigan Avenue
Suite 1200
Chicago, IL 60601
Phone: 312-786-6345
E-mail: crahill@planning.org

ASSOCIATION OF STATE DAM SAFETY OFFICIALS (ASDSO)

http://www.DamSafety.org

ASSOCIATION OF STATE DAM SAFETY OFFICIALS (ASDSO) SENIOR UNDERGRADUATE SCHOLARSHIP
• *See page 140*

CENTER FOR ARCHITECTURE

www.centerforarchitecture.org

CENTER FOR ARCHITECTURE, DOUGLAS HASKELL AWARD FOR STUDENT JOURNALS
• *See page 238*

COMMUNITY FOUNDATION OF WESTERN MASSACHUSETTS

http://www.communityfoundation.org/

HELEN HAMILTON SCHOLARSHIP FUND
• *See page 408*

CONGRESSIONAL BLACK CAUCUS FOUNDATION, INC.

http://www.cbcfinc.org/

CBC SPOUSES EDUCATION SCHOLARSHIP
• *See page 98*

CONNECTICUT CHAPTER OF THE AMERICAN PLANNING ASSOCIATION

http://www.ccapa.org/

DIANA DONALD SCHOLARSHIP
One-time award for full-time students enrolled in a graduate or undergraduate program in city planning or a closely related field. Must be resident of Connecticut and study in Connecticut. Deadline varies.

Academic Fields/Career Goals: Urban and Regional Planning.

Award: Scholarship for use in freshman, sophomore, junior, senior, or graduate years; not renewable. *Number:* 1. *Amount:* $3500.

Eligibility Requirements: Applicant must be enrolled or expecting to enroll full-time at a four-year institution or university; resident of Connecticut and studying in Connecticut. Available to U.S. and non-U.S. citizens.

Application Requirements: Application form, essay, financial need analysis. *Deadline:* May 4.

Contact: Mary Savage-Dunham, AICP
Phone: 860-276-6248
Fax: 860-628-3511
E-mail: savagem@southington.org

INTERNATIONAL FACILITY MANAGEMENT ASSOCIATION FOUNDATION

http://www.ifmafoundation.org/

IFMA FOUNDATION SCHOLARSHIPS
• *See page 116*

THE LAND CONSERVANCY OF NEW JERSEY

http://www.tlc-nj.org/

ROGERS FAMILY SCHOLARSHIP
• *See page 143*

RUSSELL W. MYERS SCHOLARSHIP
• *See page 143*

TRANSPORTATION ASSOCIATION OF CANADA FOUNDATION

http://www.tac-foundation.ca

TAC FOUNDATION SCHOLARSHIPS
• *See page 168*

VECTORWORKS, INC.

http://www.vectorworks.net

VECTORWORKS DESIGN SCHOLARSHIP
• *See page 117*

WOMEN'S STUDIES

AMERICAN FEDERATION OF STATE, COUNTY, AND MUNICIPAL EMPLOYEES

https://www.afscme.org/

AFSCME/UNCF UNION SCHOLARS PROGRAM
• *See page 98*

HUB FOUNDATION

https://hub-foundation.org

HUB FOUNDATION SCHOLARSHIPS
• *See page 88*

NATIONAL ASSOCIATION OF WATER COMPANIES-NEW JERSEY CHAPTER

http://www.nawc.org/chapters/new-jersey/

NATIONAL ASSOCIATION OF WATER COMPANIES-NEW JERSEY CHAPTER SCHOLARSHIP

For college students interested in a career in the water utility industry or any related field. Must be U.S. citizen, five-year resident of New Jersey, high school senior or college student attending or enrolled in a New Jersey college or university. Must maintain a 3.0 GPA.

Academic Fields/Career Goals: Women's Studies.

Award: Scholarship for use in freshman, sophomore, junior, senior, or graduate years; not renewable. *Number:* 2. *Amount:* $2500.

Eligibility Requirements: Applicant must be enrolled or expecting to enroll full- or part-time at a two-year or four-year institution or university; resident of New Jersey and studying in New Jersey. Available to U.S. citizens.

Application Requirements: Application form, essay. *Deadline:* April 1.

Contact: Gail Brady, Scholarship Committee Chairperson
National Association of Water Companies-New Jersey Chapter
Middlesex Water Company
1500 Ronson Rd.
Iselin, NJ 08830
Phone: 973-669-5807
E-mail: gbradygbconsult@verizon.net

NATIONAL INSTITUTES OF HEALTH

https://www.training.nih.gov/programs/ugsp

NIH UNDERGRADUATE SCHOLARSHIP PROGRAM FOR STUDENTS FROM DISADVANTAGED BACKGROUNDS
• *See page 101*

THE SOCIETY FOR THE SCIENTIFIC STUDY OF SEXUALITY

http://www.sexscience.org/

THE SOCIETY FOR THE SCIENTIFIC STUDY OF SEXUALITY STUDENT RESEARCH GRANT
• *See page 105*

UNITED NATIONS ASSOCIATION OF CONNECTICUT

http://www.unausa.org

UNITED NATIONS ASSOCIATION OF CONNECTICUT SCHOLARSHIP
• *See page 124*

WILLIAMS LAW GROUP

https://familylawyersnewjersey.com/

WILLIAMS LAW GROUP OPPORTUNITY TO GROW SCHOLARSHIP
• See page 119

Nonacademic/Noncareer Criteria

CIVIC, PROFESSIONAL, SOCIAL, OR UNION AFFILIATION

AIR LINE PILOTS ASSOCIATION, INTERNATIONAL

http://www.alpa.org/

AIRLINE PILOTS ASSOCIATION SCHOLARSHIP PROGRAM

Scholarship for children of medically retired, long-term disabled, or deceased pilot members of the Air Line Pilots Association. The total monetary value is $12,000 with $3000 disbursed annually to the recipient for four consecutive years, provided that a GPA of 3.0 is maintained. An additional $2000 per year is available which may be awarded to one or two additional applicants as a one-year special award, which is not renewable.

Award: Scholarship for use in freshman, sophomore, junior, or senior years; renewable. *Number:* 1–3. *Amount:* $1000–$12,000.

Eligibility Requirements: Applicant must be enrolled or expecting to enroll full-time at a four-year institution or university. Applicant or parent of applicant must be member of Airline Pilots Association. Available to U.S. and Canadian citizens.

Application Requirements: Application form, financial need analysis. *Deadline:* April 1.

Contact: Yvonne Willits, Coordinator
Phone: 703-689-4107
Fax: 703-481-5575
E-mail: Yvonne.Willits@alpa.org

ALBERTA AGRICULTURE FOOD AND RURAL DEVELOPMENT 4-H BRANCH

http://www.4h.ab.ca/

ALBERTA AGRICULTURE FOOD AND RURAL DEVELOPMENT 4-H SCHOLARSHIP PROGRAM

Awards will be given to current and incoming students attending any institute of higher learning. Must have been a member of the Alberta 4-H Program and be a Canadian citizen. Must be a resident of Alberta.

Award: Scholarship for use in freshman, sophomore, junior, senior, or graduate years; not renewable. *Number:* 115–120. *Amount:* $200–$1500.

Eligibility Requirements: Applicant must be enrolled or expecting to enroll full-time at a two-year or four-year or technical institution or university and resident of Alberta. Applicant or parent of applicant must be member of National 4-H. Available to Canadian citizens.

Application Requirements: Application form, essay, recommendations or references, transcript. *Deadline:* May 5.

Contact: Susann Stone, Scholarship Coordinator
Phone: 780-682-2153
Fax: 780-682-3784
E-mail: foundation@4hab.com

AMERICAN DENTAL HYGIENISTS' ASSOCIATION (ADHA) INSTITUTE FOR ORAL HEALTH

https://www.adha.org/

SIGMA PHI ALPHA UNDERGRADUATE SCHOLARSHIP

Awarded to an outstanding Sigma Phi Alpha member pursuing a certificate/associate or baccalaureate degree at a school with an active chapter of the Sigma Phi Alpha Dental Hygiene Honor Society. Applicant must demonstrate GPA of at least 3.5. Must have completed one year of dental hygiene curricula at an accredited dental hygiene program in United States. Must demonstrate a financial need of $1500 or more. Must be an active SADHA or ADHA member.

Award: Scholarship for use in sophomore, junior, or senior years; not renewable. *Number:* 1. *Amount:* $1000.

Eligibility Requirements: Applicant must be enrolled or expecting to enroll full-time at a two-year or technical institution or university. Applicant or parent of applicant must be member of American Dental Hygienist's Association. Available to U.S. citizens.

Application Requirements: Application form, essay. *Deadline:* February 1.

Contact: Kelsey Turner, Awards
American Dental Hygienists' Association (ADHA) Institute For Oral Health
444 North Michigan Avenue
Suite 400
Chicago, IL 60611
Phone: 312-440-8937
E-mail: kelseyt@adha.net

AMERICAN FEDERATION OF STATE, COUNTY, AND MUNICIPAL EMPLOYEES

https://www.afscme.org/

AMERICAN FEDERATION OF STATE, COUNTY, AND MUNICIPAL EMPLOYEES SCHOLARSHIP PROGRAM

Scholarship for family dependents of American Federation of State, County, and Municipal Employees members. Must be a graduating high school senior planning to pursue postsecondary education at a four-year institution. Submit proof of parent's membership. Renewable award of $2000.

Award: Scholarship for use in freshman, sophomore, junior, or senior years; renewable. *Number:* 10. *Amount:* $2000.

Eligibility Requirements: Applicant must be high school student and planning to enroll or expecting to enroll full-time at an institution or university. Applicant or parent of applicant must be member of American Federation of State, County, and Municipal Employees. Available to U.S. citizens.

Application Requirements: Application form, essay. *Deadline:* December 31.

UNION PLUS CREDIT CARD SCHOLARSHIP PROGRAM

The scholarship program is open to students attending or planning to attend a college or university, a community college, or a technical college or trade school. Applicants for scholarships are evaluated according to academic ability, social awareness, financial need and appreciation of labor. Graduate students are now eligible

Award: Scholarship for use in freshman, sophomore, junior, senior, or graduate years; not renewable. *Amount:* $500–$4000.

Eligibility Requirements: Applicant must be enrolled or expecting to enroll full-time at a two-year or technical institution or university. Applicant or parent of applicant must be member of American Federation of State, County, and Municipal Employees. Available to U.S. citizens.

Application Requirements: Application form, application form may be submitted online, driver's license, essay. *Deadline:* January 31.

AMERICAN FEDERATION OF TEACHERS

http://www.aft.org/

ROBERT G. PORTER SCHOLARS PROGRAM-AMERICAN FEDERATION OF TEACHERS DEPENDENTS

Scholarship of up to $8000 for high school seniors who are dependents of AFT members. Must submit transcript, test scores, essay, and recommendations with application. Must be U.S. citizen.

Award: Scholarship for use in freshman year; renewable. *Number:* 4. *Amount:* $8000.

Eligibility Requirements: Applicant must be high school student and planning to enroll or expecting to enroll full-time at a four-year institution or university. Applicant or parent of applicant must be member of American Federation of Teachers. Applicant or parent of applicant must have employment or volunteer experience in nursing, teaching/education. Available to U.S. citizens.

Application Requirements: Application form, community service, essay, recommendations or references, test scores, transcript. *Deadline:* March 31.

Contact: Ms. Nina Newkirk, Scholarship Coordinator
Phone: 202-393-5696
E-mail: nnewkirk@aft.org

AMERICAN LEGION AUXILIARY DEPARTMENT OF MISSOURI

http://www.missourilegion.org/

AMERICAN LEGION AUXILIARY DEPARTMENT OF MISSOURI LELA MURPHY SCHOLARSHIP

Scholarship of $500 for high school graduate. $250 will be awarded each semester. Applicant must be Missouri resident and the granddaughter or great-granddaughter of a living or deceased Auxiliary member. Sponsoring unit and department must validate application.

Award: Scholarship for use in freshman year; not renewable. *Number:* 1. *Amount:* $500.

Eligibility Requirements: Applicant must be high school student; planning to enroll or expecting to enroll full-time at a two-year or four-year or technical institution or university; female and resident of Missouri. Applicant or parent of applicant must be member of American Legion or Auxiliary. Available to U.S. citizens. Applicant or parent must meet one or more of the following requirements: general military experience; retired from active duty; disabled or killed as a result of military service; prisoner of war; or missing in action.

Application Requirements: Application form. *Deadline:* March 1.

Contact: Karen Larson, Department Secretary/Treasurer
American Legion Auxiliary Department of Missouri
600 Ellis Boulevard
Jefferson City, MO 65101
Phone: 573-636-9133
Fax: 573-635-3467
E-mail: dptmoala@embarqmail.com

AMERICAN LEGION AUXILIARY DEPARTMENT OF MISSOURI NATIONAL PRESIDENT'S SCHOLARSHIP

State-level award. Offers one $500 scholarship. Applicant must complete 50 hours of community service during their high school years. Sponsoring unit and department must validate application. Applicant must be a Missouri resident.

Award: Scholarship for use in freshman year; not renewable. *Number:* 1. *Amount:* $500.

Eligibility Requirements: Applicant must be high school student; planning to enroll or expecting to enroll full-time at a two-year or four-year or technical institution or university and resident of Missouri. Applicant or parent of applicant must be member of American Legion or Auxiliary. Available to U.S. citizens. Applicant or parent must meet one or more of the following requirements: general military experience; retired from active duty; disabled or killed as a result of military service; prisoner of war; or missing in action.

Application Requirements: Application form, community service, resume. *Deadline:* March 1.

Contact: Karen Larson, Department Secretary/Treasurer
American Legion Auxiliary Department of Missouri
600 Ellis Boulevard
Jefferson City, MO 65101
Phone: 573-636-9133
Fax: 573-635-3467
E-mail: dptmoala@embarqmail.com

AMERICAN LEGION AUXILIARY DEPARTMENT OF NEBRASKA

http://www.nebraskalegionaux.net/

AMERICAN LEGION AUXILIARY DEPARTMENT OF NEBRASKA RUBY PAUL CAMPAIGN FUND SCHOLARSHIP

One-time award for Nebraska residents who are children, grandchildren, or great-grandchildren of an American Legion Auxiliary member, or who have been members of the American Legion, American Legion Auxiliary, or Sons of the American Legion or Auxiliary for two years prior to issuing the application. Must rank in upper third of class or have minimum 3.0 GPA.

Award: Scholarship for use in freshman year; not renewable. *Number:* 1–3. *Amount:* $100–$300.

Eligibility Requirements: Applicant must be high school student; planning to enroll or expecting to enroll full-time at a four-year institution or university and resident of Nebraska. Applicant or parent of applicant must be member of American Legion or Auxiliary. Available to U.S. citizens. Applicant or parent must meet one or more of the following requirements: general military experience; retired from active duty; disabled or killed as a result of military service; prisoner of war; or missing in action.

Application Requirements: Application form, essay, financial need analysis, letter of acceptance, proof of enrollment, recommendations or references, test scores, transcript. *Deadline:* March 15.

Contact: Jacki O'Neill, Department Secretary
Phone: 402-466-1808
E-mail: neaux@alltel.net

AMERICAN LEGION AUXILIARY DEPARTMENT OF OREGON

http://www.alaoregon.org/

AMERICAN LEGION AUXILIARY DEPARTMENT OF OREGON SPIRIT OF YOUTH SCHOLARSHIP

One-time award available to Oregon high school seniors. Must be a current female junior member of the American Legion Auxiliary with a three-year membership history. Apply through local units.

Award: Scholarship for use in freshman year; not renewable. *Number:* 1. *Amount:* $1000.

Eligibility Requirements: Applicant must be high school student; planning to enroll or expecting to enroll full- or part-time at a four-year institution or university; female and resident of Oregon. Applicant or parent of applicant must be member of American Legion or Auxiliary. Available to U.S. citizens.

Application Requirements: Application form, essay, financial need analysis, interview. *Deadline:* February 1.

Contact: Virginia Biddle, Secretary/Treasurer
American Legion Auxiliary Department of Oregon
PO Box 1730
Wilsonville, OR 97070
Phone: 503-682-3162
E-mail: alaor@pcez.com

AMERICAN LEGION AUXILIARY DEPARTMENT OF SOUTH DAKOTA

http://www.sdlegion-aux.org/

AMERICAN LEGION AUXILIARY DEPARTMENT OF SOUTH DAKOTA COLLEGE SCHOLARSHIPS

One-time award of $500 to assist veterans children or auxiliary members' children from South Dakota ages 16 to 22 to secure an education at a four-year school. Write for more information.

Award: Scholarship for use in freshman, sophomore, junior, or senior years; not renewable. *Number:* 2. *Amount:* $500.

Eligibility Requirements: Applicant must be age 16-22; enrolled or expecting to enroll full-time at a four-year institution or university and resident of South Dakota. Applicant or parent of applicant must be member of American Legion or Auxiliary. Available to U.S. and non-U.S. citizens. Applicant or parent must meet one or more of the following requirements: general military experience; retired from active duty; disabled or killed as a result of military service; prisoner of war; or missing in action.

Application Requirements: Application form, entry in a contest, essay, financial need analysis, recommendations or references. *Deadline:* March 1.

Contact: Dianne Hudson, Executive Secretary
American Legion Auxiliary Department of South Dakota
PO Box 1819
Sioux Falls, SD 57101
Phone: 605-338-9774
Fax: 605-332-3032
E-mail: legionauxiliary.sd@gmail.com

AMERICAN LEGION AUXILIARY DEPARTMENT OF SOUTH DAKOTA SENIOR SCHOLARSHIP

Award of $400 for current senior member of South Dakota American Legion Auxiliary who has been a member for three years. Based on financial need.

Award: Scholarship for use in freshman year; not renewable. *Number:* 1. *Amount:* $400.

Eligibility Requirements: Applicant must be high school student; planning to enroll or expecting to enroll full-time at a two-year or four-year or technical institution; female and resident of South Dakota. Applicant or parent of applicant must be member of American Legion or Auxiliary. Available to U.S. and non-U.S. citizens. Applicant or parent must meet one or more of the following requirements: general military experience; retired from active duty; disabled or killed as a result of military service; prisoner of war; or missing in action.

Application Requirements: Application form, essay, financial need analysis, recommendations or references, transcript. *Deadline:* March 1.

Contact: Dianne Hudson, Executive Secretary
American Legion Auxiliary Department of South Dakota
PO Box 1819
Sioux Falls, SD 57101
Phone: 605-338-9774
Fax: 605-332-3032
E-mail: legionauxiliary.sd@gmail.com

AMERICAN LEGION AUXILIARY DEPARTMENT OF SOUTH DAKOTA THELMA FOSTER SCHOLARSHIP FOR SENIOR AUXILIARY MEMBERS

One-time award of $300 must be used within twelve months for a current senior member of the South Dakota American Legion Auxiliary who has been a member for three years. Applicant may be a high school senior or older and must be female.

Award: Scholarship for use in freshman year; not renewable. *Number:* 1. *Amount:* $300.

Eligibility Requirements: Applicant must be enrolled or expecting to enroll full-time at a four-year institution or university and female. Applicant or parent of applicant must be member of American Legion or Auxiliary. Available to U.S. and non-U.S. citizens. Applicant or parent must meet one or more of the following requirements: general military experience; retired from active duty; disabled or killed as a result of military service; prisoner of war; or missing in action.

Application Requirements: Application form, essay, financial need analysis, recommendations or references. *Deadline:* March 1.

Contact: Dianne Hudson, Executive Secretary
American Legion Auxiliary Department of South Dakota
PO Box 1819
Sioux Falls, SD 57101
Phone: 605-338-9774
Fax: 605-332-3032
E-mail: legionauxiliary.sd@gmail.com

AMERICAN LEGION AUXILIARY DEPARTMENT OF UTAH

http://www.legion-aux.org/

AMERICAN LEGION AUXILIARY DEPARTMENT OF UTAH NATIONAL PRESIDENT'S SCHOLARSHIP

Scholarships available for graduating high school seniors. Must be a resident of Utah, a U.S. citizen, and the direct descendant of a veteran.

Award: Scholarship for use in freshman year; not renewable. *Number:* 15. *Amount:* $1000–$2500.

Eligibility Requirements: Applicant must be high school student; planning to enroll or expecting to enroll full-time at a two-year or four-year or technical institution or university; single and resident of Utah. Applicant or parent of applicant must be member of American Legion or Auxiliary. Available to U.S. citizens. Applicant or parent must meet one or more of the following requirements: general military experience; retired from active duty; disabled or killed as a result of military service; prisoner of war; or missing in action.

Application Requirements: Application form, essay, recommendations or references, statement of parent's military service, test scores, transcript. *Deadline:* March 1.

Contact: Lucia Anderson, Public Relations Manager and Associate Editor
Phone: 801-539-1015
Fax: 801-521-9191
E-mail: landerson@legion-aux.org

AMERICAN LEGION AUXILIARY DEPARTMENT OF WISCONSIN

http://www.amlegionauxwi.org/

AMERICAN LEGION AUXILIARY DEPARTMENT OF WISCONSIN DELLA VAN DEUREN MEMORIAL SCHOLARSHIP

One-time award of $1000 for Wisconsin residents. Applicant or mother of applicant must be a member of an American Legion Auxiliary unit. Must submit certification of an American Legion Auxiliary unit president, copy of proof that veteran was in service (i.e. discharge papers), letters of recommendation, transcripts, and essay. Minimum 3.5 GPA required. Must demonstrate financial need. Applications available on website http://www.amlegionauxwi.org.

Award: Scholarship for use in freshman, sophomore, junior, or senior years; not renewable. *Number:* 2. *Amount:* $1000.

Eligibility Requirements: Applicant must be enrolled or expecting to enroll full- or part-time at a two-year or four-year or technical institution or university; female and resident of Wisconsin. Applicant or parent of applicant must be member of American Legion or Auxiliary. Available to U.S. citizens. Applicant or parent must meet one or more of the following requirements: general military experience; retired from active duty; disabled or killed as a result of military service; prisoner of war; or missing in action.

Application Requirements: Application form, essay, financial need analysis, recommendations or references, transcript, Veteran's DD214. *Deadline:* March 15.

Contact: Bonnie Dorniak, Department Secretary
American Legion Auxiliary Department of Wisconsin
PO Box 140
Portage, WI 53901
Phone: 608-745-0124
Fax: 608-745-1947
E-mail: deptsec@amlegionauxwi.org

AMERICAN LEGION DEPARTMENT OF IDAHO

http://www.idaholegion.com/

AMERICAN LEGION DEPARTMENT OF IDAHO SCHOLARSHIP

One-time award of $500 to $750 for residents of Idaho studying at an Idaho institution. Must be related to a Idaho American Member.

Award: Scholarship for use in freshman year; not renewable. *Number:* 1–3. *Amount:* $500–$750.

Eligibility Requirements: Applicant must be high school student; planning to enroll or expecting to enroll full-time at a two-year or four-year institution or university; resident of Idaho and studying in Idaho. Applicant or parent of applicant must be member of American Legion or Auxiliary. Available to U.S. citizens. Applicant or parent must meet one or more of the following requirements: general military experience; retired from active duty; disabled or killed as a result of military service; prisoner of war; or missing in action.

Application Requirements: Application form, community service, essay, financial need analysis. *Deadline:* June 1.

Contact: Abe Abrahamson, Adjutant
American Legion Department of Idaho
901 West Warren Street
Boise, ID 83706-3825
Phone: 208-342-7061
E-mail: idlegion@mindspring.com

AMERICAN LEGION DEPARTMENT OF ILLINOIS

http://www.illegion.org/

AMERICANISM ESSAY CONTEST SCHOLARSHIP

Scholarship for students in 7th to 12th grades of any accredited Illinois high school. Must write a 500-word essay on selected topic.

Award: Prize for use in freshman year; not renewable. *Number:* 1–60. *Amount:* $100–$1200.

Eligibility Requirements: Applicant must be high school student; planning to enroll or expecting to enroll full- or part-time at a two-year or four-year institution or university; resident of Illinois and must have an interest in writing. Applicant or parent of applicant must be member of American Legion or Auxiliary. Available to U.S. citizens.

Application Requirements: Application form, essay. *Deadline:* February 1.

Contact: Christy Rich, Executive Administrative Assistant
American Legion Department of Illinois
2720 East Lincoln Street
Bloomington, IL 61704
Phone: 309-663-0361
E-mail: hdqs@illegion.org

AMERICAN LEGION DEPARTMENT OF ILLINOIS BOY SCOUT/EXPLORER SCHOLARSHIP

Scholarship for a graduating high school senior who is a qualified Boy Scout or Explorer and a resident of Illinois. Must write a 500-word essay on Legion's Americanism and Boy Scout programs.

Award: Scholarship for use in freshman year; not renewable. *Number:* 1–5. *Amount:* $200–$1000.

Eligibility Requirements: Applicant must be high school student; planning to enroll or expecting to enroll full- or part-time at a four-year institution or university and resident of Illinois. Applicant or parent of applicant must be member of Boy Scouts. Available to U.S. citizens.

Application Requirements: Application form, essay. *Deadline:* April 30.

Contact: Christy Rich, Executive Administrative Assistant
American Legion Department of Illinois
2720 East Lincoln Street
Bloomington, IL 61704
Phone: 309-663-0361
E-mail: hdqs@illegion.org

AMERICAN LEGION DEPARTMENT OF INDIANA

http://www.indianalegion.org

AMERICAN LEGION FAMILY SCHOLARSHIP

Scholarship open to children and grandchildren of current members of The American Legion, American Legion Auxiliary, and The Sons of the American Legion. Also open to the children and grandchildren of deceased members who were current paid members of the above organizations at the time of their death. Applicants must be attending or planning to attend an Indiana institution of higher education.

Award: Scholarship for use in freshman, sophomore, junior, or senior years; not renewable. *Number:* 1–7.

Eligibility Requirements: Applicant must be age 20 or under; enrolled or expecting to enroll full- or part-time at a two-year or technical institution or university; resident of Illinois and studying in Indiana. Applicant or parent of applicant must be member of American Legion or Auxiliary. Available to U.S. citizens.

Application Requirements: Application form, essay. *Deadline:* April 2.

Contact: Butch Miller, Program Director
American Legion Department of Indiana
5440 Herbert Lord Road
Indianapolis, IN 46216
Phone: 317-630-1391
Fax: 317-237-9891
E-mail: bmiller@indianalegion.org

AMERICAN LEGION DEPARTMENT OF IOWA

http://www.ialegion.org/

AMERICAN LEGION DEPARTMENT OF IOWA EAGLE SCOUT OF THE YEAR SCHOLARSHIP

Three one-time award for Eagle Scouts who are residents of Iowa. For full-time study only.

Award: Scholarship for use in freshman year; not renewable. *Number:* up to 3. *Amount:* $250–$1000.

Eligibility Requirements: Applicant must be high school student; planning to enroll or expecting to enroll full-time at a two-year or four-year institution or university; male and resident of Iowa. Applicant or parent of applicant must be member of Boy Scouts. Available to U.S. citizens.

Application Requirements: Application form, entry in a contest, recommendations or references. *Deadline:* March 1.

Contact: Program Director
American Legion Department of Iowa
720 Lyon Street
Des Moines, IA 50309
Phone: 515-282-5068

AMERICAN LEGION DEPARTMENT OF MAINE

http://www.mainelegion.org/

JAMES V. DAY SCHOLARSHIP

One-time $500 award for a Maine resident whose parent is a member of the American Legion or Auxiliary in Maine, or is a member of Sons of the American Legion in Maine. Must be a U.S. citizen. Based on character and financial need.

Award: Scholarship for use in freshman, sophomore, junior, or senior years; not renewable. *Number:* 1–2. *Amount:* up to $500.

Eligibility Requirements: Applicant must be enrolled or expecting to enroll full-time at a two-year or four-year or technical institution or university and resident of Maine. Applicant or parent of applicant must be member of American Legion or Auxiliary. Available to U.S. citizens. Applicant or parent must meet one or more of the following requirements: general military experience; retired from active duty; disabled or killed as a result of military service; prisoner of war; or missing in action.

Application Requirements: Application form, recommendations or references, transcript. *Deadline:* May 1.

Contact: Mr. Paul L'Heureux, Department Adjutant
American Legion Department of Maine
PO Box 900
Waterville, ME 04903
Phone: 207-873-3229
Fax: 207-872-0501
E-mail: legionme@mainelegion.org

AMERICAN LEGION DEPARTMENT OF MARYLAND

http://www.mdlegion.org/

AMERICAN LEGION DEPARTMENT OF MARYLAND GENERAL SCHOLARSHIP FUND

Nonrenewable scholarship for children or grandchildren of veterans who served in the Armed Forces during dates of eligibility for American Legion membership. Proof of service and application required for eligibility. Merit-based award. Application available on website http://mdlegion.org.

Award: Scholarship for use in freshman, sophomore, junior, or senior years; not renewable. *Number:* 1–10. *Amount:* $500–$1000.

Eligibility Requirements: Applicant must be high school student; age 19 or under; planning to enroll or expecting to enroll full-time at a two-year institution or university and resident of Manitoba. Applicant or parent of applicant must be member of American Legion or Auxiliary. Available to U.S. citizens.

Application Requirements: Application form, essay, financial need analysis. *Deadline:* April 8.

Contact: Steve Tatro, Assistant Adjutant
American Legion Department of Maryland
War Memorial Building, Room E
101 N. Gay Street
Baltimore, MD 21202
Phone: 410-752-1405
Fax: 410-752-3822
E-mail: steve@mdlegion.org

THE AMERICAN LEGION, DEPARTMENT OF MINNESOTA

http://www.mnlegion.org/

AMERICAN LEGION DEPARTMENT OF MINNESOTA MEMORIAL SCHOLARSHIP

Scholarship available to Minnesota residents who are dependents of members of the Minnesota American Legion or Auxiliary. One-time award of $500 for study at a Minnesota institution or neighboring state with reciprocating agreement. See website for application information http://www.mnlegion.org.

Award: Scholarship for use in freshman, sophomore, junior, or senior years; not renewable. *Number:* 6. *Amount:* $500.

Eligibility Requirements: Applicant must be enrolled or expecting to enroll full- or part-time at a two-year or four-year or technical institution or university; resident of Minnesota and studying in Iowa, Minnesota, North Dakota, South Dakota, Wisconsin. Applicant or parent of applicant

must be member of American Legion or Auxiliary. Available to U.S. citizens. Applicant or parent must meet one or more of the following requirements: general military experience; retired from active duty; disabled or killed as a result of military service; prisoner of war; or missing in action.

Application Requirements: Application form, essay, financial need analysis. *Deadline:* April 1.

Contact: Jennifer Kelley, Program Coordinator
The American Legion, Department of Minnesota
20 West 12th Street, Room 300-A
St. Paul, MN 55155
Phone: 651-291-1800
E-mail: department@mnlegion.org

MINNESOTA LEGIONNAIRES INSURANCE TRUST SCHOLARSHIP

Scholarship for Minnesota residents who are veterans or dependents of veterans. One-time award of $500 for study at a Minnesota institution or neighboring state with reciprocating agreement. All applications must be approved and recommended by a post of the American Legion. See website for application information http://www.mnlegion.org.

Award: Scholarship for use in freshman, sophomore, junior, or senior years; not renewable. *Number:* 3. *Amount:* $500.

Eligibility Requirements: Applicant must be enrolled or expecting to enroll full- or part-time at a two-year or four-year or technical institution or university; resident of Minnesota and studying in Iowa, Minnesota, North Dakota, South Dakota, Wisconsin. Applicant or parent of applicant must be member of American Legion or Auxiliary. Available to U.S. citizens. Applicant or parent must meet one or more of the following requirements: general military experience; retired from active duty; disabled or killed as a result of military service; prisoner of war; or missing in action.

Application Requirements: Application form, essay, financial need analysis. *Deadline:* April 1.

Contact: Jennifer Kelley, Program Coordinator
The American Legion, Department of Minnesota
20 West 12th Street, Room 300-A
St. Paul, MN 55155
Phone: 651-291-1800
E-mail: department@mnlegion.org

AMERICAN LEGION DEPARTMENT OF MISSOURI

http://www.missourilegion.org/

CHARLES L. BACON MEMORIAL SCHOLARSHIP

The Charles L. Bacon Memorial Scholarship awards two $750 scholarships annually in memory of the first Missourian to serve as National Commander of The American Legion. Eligible are individuals who are currently members of The American Legion, the American Legion Auxiliary, or the Sons of The American Legion, or a descendant of a member of any thereof.

Award: Scholarship for use in freshman year; not renewable. *Number:* 2. *Amount:* $750.

Eligibility Requirements: Applicant must be high school student; age 20 or under; planning to enroll or expecting to enroll full-time at a two-year institution or university; single and resident of Mississippi. Applicant or parent of applicant must be member of American Legion or Auxiliary. Available to U.S. citizens. Applicant or parent must meet one or more of the following requirements: general military experience; retired from active duty; disabled or killed as a result of military service; prisoner of war; or missing in action.

Application Requirements: Application form, financial need analysis. *Deadline:* April 20.

Contact: Mr. John Buckwalter, Finance Officer
American Legion Department of Missouri
P.O. Box 179
Jefferson City, MO 65102-0179
Phone: 660-627-4713

AMERICAN LEGION DEPARTMENT OF OHIO

http://www.ohiolegion.com/

OHIO AMERICAN LEGION SCHOLARSHIPS

One-time award for full-time students attending an accredited institution. Open to students of any postsecondary academic year. Must have minimum 3.0 GPA. Must be a member of the American Legion, a direct descendent of a Legionnaire (living or deceased), or surviving spouse or child of a deceased U.S. military person who died on active duty or of injuries received on active duty.

Award: Scholarship for use in freshman, sophomore, junior, or senior years; not renewable. *Number:* 15–18. *Amount:* $2000–$3000.

Eligibility Requirements: Applicant must be enrolled or expecting to enroll full-time at a two-year or four-year or technical institution or university. Applicant or parent of applicant must be member of American Legion or Auxiliary. Available to U.S. and non-U.S. citizens. Applicant or parent must meet one or more of the following requirements: general military experience; retired from active duty; disabled or killed as a result of military service; prisoner of war; or missing in action.

Application Requirements: Application form, resume, transcript. *Deadline:* April 15.

Contact: Donald Lanthorn, Service Director
American Legion Department of Ohio
60 Big Run Road, PO Box 8007
Delaware, OH 43015
Phone: 740-362-7478
Fax: 740-362-1429
E-mail: dlanthorn@iwaynet.net

AMERICAN LEGION DEPARTMENT OF PENNSYLVANIA

http://www.pa-legion.com/

JOSEPH P. GAVENONIS COLLEGE SCHOLARSHIP (PLAN I)

Scholarships for Pennsylvania residents seeking a four-year degree from a Pennsylvania college or university. Must be the child of a member of a Pennsylvania American Legion post. Must be a graduating high school senior. Award amount and number of awards determined annually. Renewable award. Must maintain 2.5 GPA in college. Total number of awards varies.

Award: Scholarship for use in freshman year; renewable. *Amount:* $500–$1000.

Eligibility Requirements: Applicant must be high school student; planning to enroll or expecting to enroll full-time at a four-year institution or university; resident of Pennsylvania and studying in Pennsylvania. Applicant or parent of applicant must be member of American Legion or Auxiliary. Available to U.S. citizens.

Application Requirements: Application form, financial need analysis, test scores, transcript. *Deadline:* May 30.

Contact: Debbie Watson, Emblem Sales Supervisor
American Legion Department of Pennsylvania
PO Box 2324
Harrisburg, PA 17105-2324
Phone: 717-730-9100
Fax: 717-975-2836
E-mail: hq@pa-legion.com

AMERICAN LEGION DEPARTMENT OF TENNESSEE

http://www.tennesseelegion.org/

AMERICAN LEGION DEPARTMENT OF TENNESSEE EAGLE SCOUT OF THE YEAR

$3000 scholarship for graduating high school seniors who are Eagle Scouts, enrolled either part-time or full-time for study in accredited colleges or universities. Deadline varies.

Award: Scholarship for use in freshman, sophomore, junior, or senior years; not renewable. *Number:* 1. *Amount:* $3000.

Eligibility Requirements: Applicant must be high school student; age 15–18; planning to enroll or expecting to enroll full- or part-time at a four-year institution or university; male; resident of Tennessee and studying in Tennessee. Applicant or parent of applicant must be member of Boy Scouts. Available to U.S. citizens.

Application Requirements: Application form, community service, personal photograph, portfolio. *Deadline:* March 1.

Contact: Dean Tuttle, Department Adjutant
American Legion Department of Tennessee
318 Donelson Pike
Nashville, TN 37214
Phone: 615-391-5088
E-mail: Adjutant@TNLegion.org

AMERICAN LEGION DEPARTMENT OF VERMONT

http://www.vtlegion.org

AMERICAN LEGION EAGLE SCOUT OF THE YEAR

Awarded to the Boy Scout chosen for outstanding service to his religious institution, school, and community. Must receive the award and reside in Vermont.

Award: Scholarship for use in freshman year; not renewable. *Number:* 1. *Amount:* $1000.

Eligibility Requirements: Applicant must be high school student; age 18 or under; planning to enroll or expecting to enroll full-time at a two-year or four-year or technical institution or university and resident of Vermont. Applicant or parent of applicant must be member of Boy Scouts. Applicant or parent of applicant must have employment or volunteer experience in community service. Available to U.S. citizens.

Application Requirements: Application form, community service, essay, personal photograph. *Deadline:* March 1.

Contact: Ronald LaRose, Chairman
American Legion Department of Vermont
PO Box 396
Montpelier, VT 05601-0396
Phone: 802-223-7131
E-mail: alvthq@myfairpoint.net

AMERICAN LEGION DEPARTMENT OF WASHINGTON

http://www.walegion.org/

AMERICAN LEGION DEPARTMENT OF WASHINGTON CHILDREN AND YOUTH SCHOLARSHIPS

One-time award for the son or daughter of a Washington American Legion or Auxiliary member, living or deceased. Must be high school senior and Washington resident planning to attend an accredited institution of higher education in Washington. Award based on need.

Award: Scholarship for use in freshman year; not renewable. *Number:* 2. *Amount:* $1500–$2500.

Eligibility Requirements: Applicant must be high school student; planning to enroll or expecting to enroll full- or part-time at a four-year institution or university and resident of Washington. Applicant or parent of applicant must be member of American Legion or Auxiliary. Available to U.S. citizens.

Application Requirements: Application form, financial need analysis. *Deadline:* April 1.

Contact: Department Adjutant
American Legion Department of Washington
PO Box 3917
Lacey, WA 98509
Phone: 360-491-4373
E-mail: americanlegion@walegion.org

AMERICAN POSTAL WORKERS UNION

http://www.apwu.org/

E.C. HALLBECK SCHOLARSHIP FUND

Scholarship for children of American Postal Workers Union members. Applicant must be a child, grandchild, stepchild, or legally adopted child of an active member, Retirees Department member, or deceased member of American Postal Workers Union. Must be a senior attending high school or other corresponding secondary school. Must be 18 years or older. Recipient must attend accredited community college or university as a full-time student. Scholarship will be $1000 for each year of four consecutive years of college. Scholarship will provide five area winners. For additional information and to download applications go to website http://www.apwu.org.

Award: Scholarship for use in freshman year; renewable. *Number:* 5. *Amount:* $1000.

Eligibility Requirements: Applicant must be high school student; age 18 and over and planning to enroll or expecting to enroll full-time at a two-year or four-year or technical institution or university. Applicant or parent of applicant must be member of American Postal Workers Union. Applicant or parent of applicant must have employment or volunteer experience in federal/postal service. Available to U.S. citizens.

Application Requirements: Application form, essay, recommendations or references, test scores, transcript. *Deadline:* March 15.

Contact: Terry Stapleton, Secretary and Treasurer
American Postal Workers Union
1300 L Street, NW
Washington, DC 20005
Phone: 202-842-4215
Fax: 202-842-8530

VOCATIONAL SCHOLARSHIP PROGRAM

A scholarship for a child, grandchild, stepchild, or legally adopted child of an active member, Retiree's Department member, or deceased member of the American Postal Workers Union. Applicant must be a senior attending high school who plans on attending an accredited vocational school or community college vocational program as a full-time student. The award is $1000 per year consecutively or until completion of the course. For additional information see website http://www.apwu.org.

Award: Scholarship for use in freshman year; renewable. *Number:* 5. *Amount:* $1000.

Eligibility Requirements: Applicant must be high school student and planning to enroll or expecting to enroll full-time at a four-year institution or university. Applicant or parent of applicant must be member of American Postal Workers Union. Applicant or parent of applicant must have employment or volunteer experience in federal/postal service. Available to U.S. citizens.

Application Requirements: Application form, essay, recommendations or references, test scores, transcript. *Deadline:* March 15.

Contact: Terry Stapleton, Secretary and Treasurer
American Postal Workers Union
1300 L Street, NW
Washington, DC 20005
Phone: 202-842-4215
Fax: 202-842-8530

AMERICAN QUARTER HORSE FOUNDATION (AQHF)

https://aqhfoundation.smapply.io/

AQHF GENERAL SCHOLARSHIP

Ideal candidates are current AQHA or AQHYA members.

Award: Scholarship for use in sophomore, junior, senior, graduate, or postgraduate years; renewable. *Number:* 1–15. *Amount:* $4000.

Eligibility Requirements: Applicant must be enrolled or expecting to enroll full-time at a two-year or four-year or technical institution or university. Applicant or parent of applicant must be member of American Quarter Horse Association. Available to U.S. and non-U.S. citizens.

Application Requirements: Application form, financial need analysis. *Deadline:* December 1.

Contact: Scholarship Office
American Quarter Horse Foundation (AQHF)
2601 East Interstate 40
Amarillo, TX 79104
Phone: 806-378-5029
E-mail: foundation@aqha.org

AMERICAN SOCIETY OF CIVIL ENGINEERS

http://www.asce.org/

EUGENE C. FIGG JR. CIVIL ENGINEERING SCHOLARSHIP

Applicant must be a member of the Society in good standing and be enrolled in an ABET-accredited program who will be registered as an undergraduate in the fall term of the year of award, is a U.S. citizen, and have a passion for bridges.

Award: Scholarship for use in sophomore, junior, or senior years; not renewable. *Number:* 1.

Eligibility Requirements: Applicant must be enrolled or expecting to enroll full-time at an institution or university. Applicant or parent of applicant must be member of American Society of Civil Engineers. Available to U.S. citizens.

Application Requirements: Application form, essay, financial need analysis. *Deadline:* February 10.

Contact: Attn: Honors and Awards Program
American Society of Civil Engineers
American Society of Civil Engineers
1801 Alexander Bell Drive
Reston, VA 20191-4400

JOHN LENARD CIVIL ENGINEERING SCHOLARSHIP

For students engaged in the study of civil engineering with a focus on water supply or environmental engineering. Applicant must be a Society member in good standing, enrolled in an ABET-accredited program.

Award: Scholarship for use in sophomore, junior, or senior years; not renewable. *Number:* 1–2.

Eligibility Requirements: Applicant must be enrolled or expecting to enroll full-time at an institution or university. Applicant or parent of applicant must be member of American Society of Civil Engineers. Available to U.S. and non-U.S. citizens.

Application Requirements: Application form, essay, financial need analysis. *Deadline:* February 10.

Contact: Attn: Honors and Awards Program
American Society of Civil Engineers
American Society of Civil Engineers
1801 Alexander Bell Drive
Reston, VA 20191-4400

LAWRENCE W. AND FRANCIS W. COX SCHOLARSHIP

The Lawrence W. and Francis W. Cox Scholarship may be presented annually to one undergraduate civil engineering student, who will use the scholarship for their sophomore, junior or senior tuition expenses and fees. The purpose of the scholarship is to further the education of a worthy student in any civil engineering discipline.

Award: Scholarship for use in sophomore, junior, or senior years; not renewable. *Number:* 1.

Eligibility Requirements: Applicant must be enrolled or expecting to enroll full-time at an institution or university. Applicant or parent of applicant must be member of American Society of Civil Engineers. Available to U.S. and non-U.S. citizens.

Application Requirements: Application form, essay, financial need analysis. *Deadline:* February 10.

Contact: Attn: Honors and Awards Program ? ? ? ? ? ? ? ? ? ? ?
American Society of Civil Engineers
American Society of Civil Engineers
1801 Alexander Bell Drive
Reston, VA 20191-4400

ROBERT B.B. AND JOSEPHINE N. MOORMAN SCHOLARSHIP

The Robert B. B. and Josephine N. Moorman Scholarship may be presented annually to one undergraduate student, who will use the scholarship for their sophomore, junior or senior tuition expenses and fees. The purpose of the scholarship is to further the education of a worthy student in any civil engineering discipline or civil engineering related field.

Award: Scholarship for use in sophomore, junior, or senior years; not renewable. *Number:* 1.

Eligibility Requirements: Applicant must be enrolled or expecting to enroll full-time at an institution or university. Applicant or parent of applicant must be member of American Society of Civil Engineers. Available to U.S. and non-U.S. citizens.

Application Requirements: Application form, essay. *Deadline:* February 10.

Contact: Attn: Honors and Awards Program
American Society of Civil Engineers
American Society of Civil Engineers
1801 Alexander Bell Drive
Reston, VA 20191-4400

SAMUEL FLETCHER TAPMAN ASCE STUDENT CHAPTER SCHOLARSHIP

Not more than one application may be submitted from the membership of any one ASCE Student Chapter. Awards available to currently enrolled undergraduates. Must be a member of local ASCE Student Chapter and an ASCE Student Member in good standing. Selection is based on the applicant's justification of award, educational plan, academic performance and standing, potential for development, leadership capacity, ASCE activities, and financial need.

Award: Scholarship for use in sophomore, junior, or senior years; not renewable. *Number:* 1–12.

Eligibility Requirements: Applicant must be enrolled or expecting to enroll full-time at an institution or university. Applicant or parent of applicant must be member of American Society of Civil Engineers. Available to U.S. and non-U.S. citizens.

Application Requirements: Application form, essay. *Deadline:* February 10.

Contact: Attn: Honors and Awards Program
American Society of Civil Engineers
American Society of Civil Engineers
1801 Alexander Bell Drive
Reston, VA 20191-4400

Y.C. YANG CIVIL ENGINEERING SCHOLARSHIP

Applicants must be student members in good standing of the Society. Currently enrolled civil engineering students at an institution with an ABET-accredited program and an interest in structural engineering may apply.

Award: Scholarship for use in sophomore, junior, or senior years; not renewable. *Number:* 1–2. *Amount:* $2000.

Eligibility Requirements: Applicant must be enrolled or expecting to enroll full-time at an institution or university. Applicant or parent of applicant must be member of American Society of Civil Engineers. Available to U.S. and non-U.S. citizens.

Application Requirements: Application form, essay, financial need analysis. *Deadline:* February 10.

Contact: Attn: Honors and Awards Program
American Society of Civil Engineers
American Society of Civil Engineers
1801 Alexander Bell Drive
Reston, VA 20191-4400

AMERICAN WATER SKI EDUCATIONAL FOUNDATION

http://www.waterskihalloffame.com/

AMERICAN WATER SKI EDUCATIONAL FOUNDATION SCHOLARSHIP

Awards for incoming college sophomores through incoming seniors who are members of USA Water Ski. Awards are based upon academics, leadership, extracurricular activities, recommendations, essay and financial need.

Award: Scholarship for use in sophomore, junior, or senior years; renewable. *Number:* 5. *Amount:* $1500–$3000.

Eligibility Requirements: Applicant must be enrolled or expecting to enroll full-time at a two-year or four-year institution or university. Applicant or parent of applicant must be member of USA Water Ski. Available to U.S. citizens.

Application Requirements: Application form, essay, financial need analysis, recommendations or references, self-addressed stamped envelope with application, transcript. *Deadline:* March 1.

Contact: Carole Lowe, Scholarship Director
Phone: 863-324-2472 Ext. 127
Fax: 863-324-3996
E-mail: awsefhalloffame@cs.com

AMVETS AUXILIARY

http://amvetsaux.org/

AMVETS NATIONAL LADIES AUXILIARY SCHOLARSHIP

One-time award of up to $1000 for a member of AMVETS or the Auxiliary. Applicant may also be the family member of a member. Award for full-time study at any accredited U.S. institution. Minimum 2.5 GPA required.

Award: Scholarship for use in sophomore, junior, or senior years; not renewable. *Number:* up to 7. *Amount:* $750–$1000.

Eligibility Requirements: Applicant must be enrolled or expecting to enroll full-time at a two-year or four-year or technical institution. Applicant or parent of applicant must be member of AMVETS Auxiliary. Available to U.S. citizens. Applicant or parent must meet one or more of the following requirements: general military experience; retired from active duty; disabled or killed as a result of military service; prisoner of war; or missing in action.

Application Requirements: Application form, essay, recommendations or references, transcript. *Deadline:* June 1.

Contact: Kellie Haggerty, Executive Administrator
AMVETS Auxiliary
4647 Forbes Boulevard
Lanham, MD 20706-4380
Phone: 301-459-6255
Fax: 301-459-5403
E-mail: auxhdqs@amvets.org

APPALOOSA HORSE CLUB-APPALOOSA YOUTH PROGRAM

http://www.appaloosayouth.com/

APPALOOSA YOUTH EDUCATIONAL SCHOLARSHIPS

Scholarship of up to $1000 available for members or dependents of members of the Appaloosa Youth Association or Appaloosa Horse Club. Based on academics, leadership, sportsmanship, and horsemanship. Printable application is available at website, http://www.appaloosayouth.com.

Award: Scholarship for use in freshman, sophomore, junior, or senior years; not renewable. *Number:* 6–8. *Amount:* $100–$1000.

Eligibility Requirements: Applicant must be enrolled or expecting to enroll full-time at a two-year or four-year institution or university and must have an interest in animal/agricultural competition or leadership. Applicant or parent of applicant must be member of Appaloosa Horse Club/Appaloosa Youth Association. Available to U.S. citizens.

Application Requirements: Application form, entry in a contest, essay, personal photograph, recommendations or references, test scores, transcript. *Deadline:* June 1.

Contact: Anna Brown, AYF Coordinator
Appaloosa Horse Club-Appaloosa Youth Program
2720 West Pullman Road
Moscow, ID 83843
Phone: 208-882-5578 Ext. 264
Fax: 208-882-8150
E-mail: youth@appaloosa.com

ASRT FOUNDATION

https://foundation.asrt.org/

ELEKTA RADIATION THERAPY SCHOLARSHIP

Open to students in the 2nd or 3rd year of an entry-level radiation therapy program. Is a merit-based scholarship awarded on financial need, academic performance, recommendation, and essays.

Award: Scholarship for use in sophomore, junior, or senior years; not renewable. *Number:* 4. *Amount:* $5000.

Eligibility Requirements: Applicant must be enrolled or expecting to enroll full- or part-time at a two-year or technical institution or university.

Applicant or parent of applicant must be member of American Society of Radiologic Technologists. Available to U.S. citizens.

Application Requirements: Application form, application form may be submitted online, essay, financial need analysis. *Deadline:* February 1.

Contact: Carol Kennedy, Foundation Director
ASRT Foundation
ASRT Foundation
15000 Central Ave. SE
Albuquerque, NM 87123-3909
Phone: 800-444-2778
Fax: 505-298-5063
E-mail: foundation@asrt.org

AUTOMOTIVE RECYCLERS ASSOCIATION SCHOLARSHIP FOUNDATION

http://www.a-r-a.org/

AUTOMOTIVE RECYCLERS ASSOCIATION SCHOLARSHIP FOUNDATION SCHOLARSHIP

Scholarships are available for the post-high school educational pursuits of the children of employees of direct ARA member companies.

Award: Scholarship for use in freshman, sophomore, junior, or senior years; not renewable.

Eligibility Requirements: Applicant must be enrolled or expecting to enroll full-time at a two-year or four-year institution or university. Applicant or parent of applicant must be member of Automotive Recyclers Association. Available to U.S. and non-U.S. citizens.

Application Requirements: Application form, letter verifying parents' employment, personal photograph, transcript. *Deadline:* March 15.

Contact: Kelly Badillo, Director, Member Services
Automotive Recyclers Association Scholarship Foundation
3975 Fair Ridge Drive, Suite 20-North
Fairfax, VA 22033
Phone: 703-385-1001 Ext. 26
Fax: 703-385-1494
E-mail: kelly@a-r-a.org

CALIFORNIA GRANGE FOUNDATION

http://www.csgfoundation.org/

CALIFORNIA GRANGE FOUNDATION SCHOLARSHIP

Scholarship program available for Grange members residing in California who wish to attend a higher institution of learning of their choice.

Award: Scholarship for use in freshman, sophomore, junior, or senior years; renewable. *Number:* 5–8. *Amount:* $250–$1000.

Eligibility Requirements: Applicant must be enrolled or expecting to enroll full- or part-time at a two-year or four-year or technical institution or university and resident of California. Applicant or parent of applicant must be member of Grange Association. Available to U.S. citizens.

Application Requirements: Application form, community service, essay, financial need analysis, recommendations or references, transcript. *Deadline:* April 1.

Contact: Mrs. Leslie Parker, Executive Assistant
California Grange Foundation
3830 U Street
Sacramento, CA 95817
Phone: 916-454-5805 Ext. 21
Fax: 916-739-8189
E-mail: info@californiagrange.org

CALIFORNIA STATE PARENT-TEACHER ASSOCIATION

http://www.capta.org/

CONTINUING EDUCATION SCHOLARSHIP FOR PTA VOLUNTEERS

Continuing Education Scholarships for PTA Volunteers for up to $500.00 are available from California State PTA to enable PTA volunteers to continue their education. Scholarships are available annually from the California State PTA to be used for continuing education at accredited colleges, universities, trade or technical schools. These scholarships recognize volunteer service in PTA and enable PTA volunteers to continue their education.

Award: Scholarship for use in freshman, sophomore, junior, senior, or graduate years; not renewable.

Eligibility Requirements: Applicant must be enrolled or expecting to enroll full- or part-time at a two-year or technical institution or university and resident of British Columbia. Applicant or parent of applicant must be member of Parent-Teacher Association/Organization. Applicant or parent of applicant must have employment or volunteer experience in community service. Available to U.S. citizens.

Application Requirements: Application form, essay. *Deadline:* October 15.

Contact: Brenda Davis, President
Phone: 916-440-1985
Fax: 916-440-1986
E-mail: grants@capta.org

CALIFORNIA TEACHERS ASSOCIATION (CTA)

http://www.cta.org/

CALIFORNIA TEACHERS ASSOCIATION SCHOLARSHIP FOR DEPENDENT CHILDREN

The CTA Scholarship for Dependent Children offers a maximum of 35 scholarships of up to $5,000 each.

Award: Scholarship for use in freshman, sophomore, junior, or senior years; not renewable. *Number:* 36. *Amount:* $5000.

Eligibility Requirements: Applicant must be enrolled or expecting to enroll full-time at a two-year or technical institution or university. Applicant or parent of applicant must be member of California Teachers Association. Available to U.S. citizens.

Application Requirements: Application form, application form may be submitted online.

Contact: Janeya Dawson
California Teachers Association (CTA)
PO Box 921
Burlingame, CA 94011-0921
Phone: 650-552-5446
E-mail: scholarships@cta.org

CALIFORNIA TEACHERS ASSOCIATION SCHOLARSHIP FOR MEMBERS

The CTA Scholarship for Members offers a maximum of five scholarships of up to $3,000 each. One scholarship is designated as the American Indian/Alaska Native Memorial Scholarship in Honor of Alice Piper and is awarded to the highest-scoring applicant while another is designated for an ESP member who wants to transition into the teaching profession, provided an ESP member applies.

Award: Scholarship for use in freshman, sophomore, junior, or senior years; not renewable. *Number:* 5. *Amount:* $3000.

Eligibility Requirements: Applicant must be enrolled or expecting to enroll full-time at a two-year institution or university and resident of British Columbia. Applicant or parent of applicant must be member of California Teachers Association. Applicant or parent of applicant must have employment or volunteer experience in teaching/education. Available to U.S. citizens.

Application Requirements: Application form, application form may be submitted online.

Contact: Janeya Dawson
California Teachers Association (CTA)
PO Box 921
Burlingame, CA 94011-0921
Phone: 650-552-5446
E-mail: scholarships@cta.org

L. GORDON BITTLE MEMORIAL SCHOLARSHIP

The Student CTA (SCTA) Scholarship in Honor of L. Gordon Bittle offers a maximum of three scholarships of up to $5,000 each. One scholarship is designated as the Pacific Asian American Scholarship in Honor of Philip Vera Cruz and is awarded to the highest-scoring applicant.

Award: Scholarship for use in freshman, sophomore, junior, or senior years; not renewable. *Number:* 3. *Amount:* $5000.

Eligibility Requirements: Applicant must be enrolled or expecting to enroll full-time at a two-year institution or university and resident of British Columbia. Applicant or parent of applicant must be member of California Teachers Association. Available to U.S. citizens.

Application Requirements: Application form, application form may be submitted online.

Contact: Janeya Dawson
California Teachers Association (CTA)
PO Box 921
Burlingame, CA 94011-0921
Phone: 650-552-5446
E-mail: scholarships@cta.org

CIVIL AIR PATROL, USAF AUXILIARY

http://www.gocivilairpatrol.com/

CIVIL AIR PATROL ACADEMIC SCHOLARSHIPS

One-time award for active members of the Civil Air Patrol to pursue undergraduate, graduate, or trade or technical education. Must be a current CAP member. Significant restrictions apply. Not open to the general public.

Award: Scholarship for use in freshman, sophomore, junior, senior, or graduate years; not renewable. *Number:* up to 40. *Amount:* $1000–$7500.

Eligibility Requirements: Applicant must be enrolled or expecting to enroll full-time at a two-year or four-year or technical institution or university. Applicant or parent of applicant must be member of Civil Air Patrol. Available to U.S. citizens.

Application Requirements: Application form, essay, personal photograph, recommendations or references, resume, test scores, transcript. *Deadline:* January 31.

Contact: Kelly Easterly, Assistant Program Manager
Civil Air Patrol, USAF Auxiliary
105 South Hansell Street, Building 714
Maxwell Air Force Base, AL 36112-6332
Phone: 334-953-8640
Fax: 334-953-6699
E-mail: cpr@capnhq.gov

COMMUNITY BANKERS ASSOCIATION OF ILLINOIS

http://www.cbai.com/

COMMUNITY BANKERS ASSOC OF IL CHILD OF A BANKER SCHOLARSHIP

Must be a child or grandchild of an eligible CBAI member banker or be a part-time employee of an eligible CBAI member bank.

Award: Prize for use in freshman year; renewable. *Number:* 3. *Amount:* $4000.

Eligibility Requirements: Applicant must be high school student; planning to enroll or expecting to enroll full-time at a two-year or four-year or technical institution or university and resident of Illinois. Applicant or parent of applicant must be member of Community Banker Association of Illinois. Available to U.S. citizens.

Application Requirements: Application form. *Deadline:* August 15.

Contact: Ms. Bobbi Watson, Administrative Assistant
Community Bankers Association of Illinois
CBAI
901 Community Drive
Springfield, IL 62715
Phone: 800-736-2224
E-mail: bobbiw@cbai.com

COMMUNITY FOUNDATION OF WESTERN MASSACHUSETTS

http://www.communityfoundation.org/

HORACE HILL SCHOLARSHIP FUND

Scholarship for children and grandchildren of the members of the Springfield Newspapers' 25 Year Club who participated in extracurricular activities.

Award: Scholarship for use in freshman, sophomore, junior, senior, or graduate years; not renewable.

Eligibility Requirements: Applicant must be enrolled or expecting to enroll full- or part-time at a two-year institution or university and resident of Maryland. Applicant or parent of applicant must be member of Springfield Newspaper 25-Year Club. Available to U.S. citizens.

Application Requirements: Application form, application form may be submitted online, financial need analysis. *Deadline:* April 17.

Contact: Nikai Fondon, Scholarship Program Associate
E-mail: NFondon@communityfoundation.org

EASTERN ORTHODOX COMMITTEE ON SCOUTING

http://www.eocs.org/

EASTERN ORTHODOX COMMITTEE ON SCOUTING SCHOLARSHIPS

One-time award for high school seniors planning to attend a four-year institution. Must be a registered member of a Boy or Girl Scout unit, an Eagle Scout or Gold Award recipient, active member of an Eastern Orthodox Church, and recipient of the Alpha Omega religious award.

Award: Scholarship for use in freshman year; not renewable. *Number:* 2. *Amount:* $500–$1000.

Eligibility Requirements: Applicant must be Eastern Orthodox; high school student; planning to enroll or expecting to enroll full-time at a four-year institution or university and single. Applicant or parent of applicant must be member of Boy Scouts, Girl Scouts. Available to U.S. citizens.

Application Requirements: Application form, community service, recommendations or references, self-addressed stamped envelope with application, test scores, transcript. *Deadline:* May 1.

Contact: George Boulukos, Scholarship Chairman
Eastern Orthodox Committee on Scouting
862 Guy Lombardo Avenue
Freeport, NY 11520
Phone: 516-868-4050
E-mail: geobou03@aol.com

EASTERN SURFING ASSOCIATION (ESA)

http://www.surfesa.org/

ESA MARSH SCHOLARSHIP PROGRAM

Grants are awarded to ESA current members in good standing on the basis of academics and U.S. citizenship rather than athletic ability.

Award: Scholarship for use in freshman, sophomore, junior, or senior years; not renewable. *Number:* 2. *Amount:* up to $8000.

Eligibility Requirements: Applicant must be enrolled or expecting to enroll full-time at a four-year institution or university. Applicant or parent of applicant must be member of Eastern Surfing Association. Available to U.S. citizens.

Application Requirements: Application form, essay, recommendations or references, transcript. *Deadline:* May 15.

Contact: Debbie Hodges, Scholarship Committee
Phone: 757-233-1790
E-mail: centralhq@surfesa.org

ELKS NATIONAL FOUNDATION

http://www.elks.org/enf

ELKS EMERGENCY EDUCATIONAL GRANTS

Grant available to children of Elks members who are deceased or totally disabled. Disability must be proven by recent doctors note. Parent must have been a member for at least a year before the date of death or onset of disability. Applicants for the one-year renewable awards must be unmarried, under the age of 23, be a full-time undergraduate student, and demonstrate financial need. They must also maintain a minimum 2.0 GPA.

Award: Scholarship for use in freshman, sophomore, junior, or senior years; not renewable. *Amount:* $1000–$4000.

Eligibility Requirements: Applicant must be age 23 or under; enrolled or expecting to enroll full-time at a two-year or four-year institution or university and single. Applicant or parent of applicant must be member of Elks Club. Available to U.S. citizens.

Application Requirements: Application form, community service, essay, financial need analysis. *Deadline:* October 31.

Contact: Elks National Foundation Scholarship Office
Elks National Foundation
2750 North Lakeview Avenue
Chicago, IL 60614-2256
Phone: 773-755-4732
E-mail: scholarship@elks.org

ELKS NATIONAL FOUNDATION LEGACY AWARDS

$4,000 four-year scholarships available for children and grandchildren of Elks in good standing. Parent or grandparent must have been an Elk for two years and continue to be a member in good standing. Must be high school senior and apply through the related member's Elks Lodge. Applications available after September 1 online only, enf.elks.org/leg. Must be submitted online through the website.

Award: Scholarship for use in freshman, sophomore, junior, or senior years; renewable. *Number:* 250. *Amount:* $4000.

Eligibility Requirements: Applicant must be high school student and planning to enroll or expecting to enroll full-time at a four-year institution or university. Applicant or parent of applicant must be member of Elks Club. Available to U.S. citizens.

Application Requirements: Application form, community service, essay. *Deadline:* January 26.

Contact: Elks National Foundation Scholarship Office
Elks National Foundation
2750 North Lakeview Avenue
Chicago, IL 60614-2256
Phone: 773-755-4732
E-mail: scholarship@elks.org

FIRST CATHOLIC SLOVAK LADIES ASSOCIATION

http://www.fcsla.org/

FIRST CATHOLIC SLOVAK LADIES ASSOCIATION COLLEGE SCHOLARSHIPS

The First Catholic Slovak Ladies Association awards members of the Association who are enrolled full-time in a program leading to an Associate's or Bachelor's degree with a $1,250 scholarship per recipient. 60 awards will be given to Freshmen, 31 for Sophomores, 18 for Juniors, and 18 for Seniors.

Award: Scholarship for use in freshman, sophomore, junior, or senior years; not renewable. *Number:* 127. *Amount:* $1250.

Eligibility Requirements: Applicant must be of Slavic/Czech heritage and enrolled or expecting to enroll full-time at a two-year institution or university. Applicant or parent of applicant must be member of First Catholic Slovak Ladies Association. Available to U.S. and Canadian citizens.

Application Requirements: Application form, essay, personal photograph. *Deadline:* February 25.

Contact: Director of Fraternal Scholarship Aid
First Catholic Slovak Ladies Association
Scholarship Department
24950 Chagrin Blvd.
Beachwood, OH 44122
Phone: 216-464-8015 Ext. 1054
Fax: 216-464-9260
E-mail: Scholarship@fcsla.org

FLEET RESERVE ASSOCIATION EDUCATION FOUNDATION

http://www.fra.org/foundation

COLONEL HAZEL ELIZABETH BENN U.S.M.C. SCHOLARSHIP

Scholarship only for U.S. citizens who are unmarried, dependent children of a member in good standing of the FRA, currently or at time of death, who served or is now serving in the U.S. Navy as an enlisted medical rating assigned to and serving with the U.S. Marine Corps. Must be enrolled as a freshman or sophomore undergraduate at a state or regionally accredited institution of post-secondary education located in the United States.

Award: Scholarship for use in freshman or sophomore years; not renewable. *Number:* 1–5. *Amount:* $1000–$2000.

Eligibility Requirements: Applicant must be enrolled or expecting to enroll full-time at a two-year or four-year institution and married. Applicant or parent of applicant must be member of Fleet Reserve Association/Auxiliary. Available to U.S. citizens.

Application Requirements: Application form, community service, essay, financial need analysis. *Deadline:* April 15.

Contact: Mrs. Alicia Landis, Program Administrator
Phone: 703-683-1400 Ext. 107
E-mail: scholars@fra.org

DORAN/BLAIR SCHOLARSHIPS

Applicant or sponsor has to be a member in good standing of the FRA, currently or at time of death. Applicant must be an FRA member; spouse; dependent biological, step, or adoptive child; or biological, step, or adoptive grandchild; or biological, step, or adoptive great grandchild of the FRA member. Applicant must be a U.S. citizen, registered as a full time student in an accredited college located in the United States of America.

Award: Scholarship for use in freshman, sophomore, junior, senior, graduate, or postgraduate years; not renewable. *Number:* 1–20. *Amount:* $1000–$5000.

Eligibility Requirements: Applicant must be enrolled or expecting to enroll full-time at a two-year or four-year institution or university. Applicant or parent of applicant must be member of Fleet Reserve Association/Auxiliary. Available to U.S. citizens. Applicant must have served in the Coast Guard.

Application Requirements: Application form, community service, essay, financial need analysis. *Deadline:* April 15.

Contact: Mrs. Alicia Landis, Program Administrator
Phone: 703-683-1400 Ext. 107
E-mail: scholars@fra.org

GIRL SCOUTS OF CONNECTICUT

http://www.gsofct.org/

EMILY CHAISON GOLD AWARD SCHOLARSHIP

An annual scholarship of $750 is awarded each year to one Gold Award recipient from the state of Connecticut during her senior year.

Award: Scholarship for use in freshman year; not renewable. *Number:* 1. *Amount:* $750.

Eligibility Requirements: Applicant must be high school student; planning to enroll or expecting to enroll full-time at a four-year institution or university; female and resident of Connecticut. Applicant or parent of applicant must be member of Girl Scouts. Available to U.S. citizens.

Application Requirements: Application form, community service, essay, recommendations or references. *Deadline:* April 1.

Contact: Nancy Bussman, Scholarship Committee
Girl Scouts of Connecticut
340 Washington Street
Hartford, CT 06106
Phone: 203-239-2922
E-mail: nbussman@gsofct.org

GLASS, MOLDERS, POTTERY, PLASTICS AND ALLIED WORKERS INTERNATIONAL UNION

http://www.gmpiu.org/

GMP MEMORIAL SCHOLARSHIP PROGRAM

Six college scholarships of $4000 per year available to the sons and daughters of members of the union. Renewable each year for a full four-year college program if adequate academic standards are maintained. Four vocational/technical/two-year Associate degree scholarships of $2000 also available (not to exceed the cost of the program).

Award: Scholarship for use in freshman year; renewable. *Number:* 10. *Amount:* $2000–$4000.

Eligibility Requirements: Applicant must be high school student and planning to enroll or expecting to enroll full-time at a two-year or four-year or technical institution or university. Applicant or parent of applicant must be member of Glass, Molders, Pottery, Plastics and Allied Workers International Union. Available to U.S. and Canadian citizens.

Application Requirements: Application form, test scores. *Deadline:* November 1.

Contact: Bruce Smith, International Secretary and Treasurer
Glass, Molders, Pottery, Plastics and Allied Workers
International Union
608 East Baltimore Pike, PO Box 607
Media, PA 19063
Phone: 610-565-5051 Ext. 220
Fax: 610-565-0983

GOLDEN KEY INTERNATIONAL HONOUR SOCIETY

http://www.goldenkey.org/

GEICO LIFE SCHOLARSHIP

Ten $1000 awards will be given to outstanding students while balancing additional responsibilities. Must have completed at least 12 undergraduate credit hours in the previous year. Must be enrolled at the time of application and must be working toward a Baccalaureate degree.

Award: Scholarship for use in freshman, sophomore, junior, or senior years; not renewable. *Number:* 10. *Amount:* $1000.

Eligibility Requirements: Applicant must be enrolled or expecting to enroll full- or part-time at a four-year institution or university. Applicant or parent of applicant must be member of Golden Key National Honor Society. Available to U.S. and non-U.S. citizens.

Application Requirements: Application form, essay, recommendations or references, transcript. *Deadline:* April 1.

Contact: Scholarship Program Administrators
Golden Key International Honour Society
PO Box 23737
Nashville, TN 37202
Phone: 800-377-2401

GOLF COURSE SUPERINTENDENTS ASSOCIATION OF AMERICA

https://www.gcsaa.org/

GOLF COURSE SUPERINTENDENTS ASSOCIATION OF AMERICA LEGACY AWARD

Awards of $1500 for the children or grandchildren of Golf Course Superintendents Association of America members. Applicants must be enrolled full-time at an accredited institution of higher learning, or for high school seniors, they must have been accepted at such an institution for the next academic year.

Award: Scholarship for use in freshman, sophomore, junior, or senior years; not renewable. *Number:* 20. *Amount:* $1500.

Eligibility Requirements: Applicant must be enrolled or expecting to enroll full-time at a two-year or technical institution or university. Applicant or parent of applicant must be member of Golf Course Superintendents Association of America. Available to U.S. and non-U.S. citizens.

Application Requirements: Application form, essay. *Deadline:* April 20.

Contact: Mischia Wright, Associate Director
Golf Course Superintendents Association of America
1421 Research Park Drive
Lawrence, KS 66049
Phone: 800-472-7878 Ext. 4445
Fax: 785-832-4448
E-mail: mwright@gcsaa.org

JOSEPH S. GARSKE COLLEGIATE GRANT PROGRAM

Award available to children/step children of GCSAA members who have been active members for five or more consecutive years for use at an accredited college or trade school. Applicant must be a graduating high school senior and be accepted at an institution of higher learning for the upcoming year.

Award: Scholarship for use in freshman year; not renewable. *Number:* 1–5. *Amount:* $500–$2500.

Eligibility Requirements: Applicant must be high school student; planning to enroll or expecting to enroll full-time at a two-year or technical institution or university and must have an interest in leadership. Applicant or parent of applicant must be member of Golf Course Superintendents Association of America. Applicant or parent of applicant must have employment or volunteer experience in community service. Available to U.S. and non-U.S. citizens.

Application Requirements: Application form, essay. *Deadline:* March 15.

Contact: Mischia Wright, Associate Director
Golf Course Superintendents Association of America
1421 Research Park Drive
Lawrence, KS 66049
Phone: 800-472-7878 Ext. 4445
Fax: 785-832-4448
E-mail: mwright@gcsaa.org

HELLENIC UNIVERSITY CLUB OF PHILADELPHIA

http://www.hucphiladephia.org/

PAIDEIA SCHOLARSHIP

$5000 merit scholarship awarded to the child of a Hellenic University Club of Philadelphia member. Parent(s) must be current members in good standing for at least 3 years. Must be a U.S. citizen of Greek descent and a resident of particular counties in NJ or PA.

Award: Scholarship for use in freshman, sophomore, junior, or senior years; not renewable. *Number:* 1. *Amount:* $5000.

Eligibility Requirements: Applicant must be of Greek heritage; enrolled or expecting to enroll full-time at an institution or university and resident of New Hampshire, Oregon. Applicant or parent of applicant must be member of Hellenic University Club of Pennsylvania. Available to U.S. citizens.

Application Requirements: Application form, application form may be submitted online, essay. *Deadline:* April 5.

Contact: Toula Bastas, Chairperson
Phone: 610-613-4310
E-mail: HucScholarship@gmail.com

HONOR SOCIETY OF PHI KAPPA PHI

https://www.phikappaphi.org/

LITERACY GRANT COMPETITION

Grants up to $2500 are awarded to Phi Kappa Phi members for projects relating to a broad definition of literacy (math, science, music, art, reading, health, etc.). These projects should fulfill the spirit of volunteerism and community. Eligible applicants must be Active members of Phi Kappa Phi.

Award: Grant for use in freshman, sophomore, junior, senior, graduate, or postgraduate years; not renewable. *Number:* 1–18. *Amount:* $300–$2500.

Eligibility Requirements: Applicant must be enrolled or expecting to enroll full- or part-time at a two-year or technical institution or university. Applicant or parent of applicant must be member of Phi Kappa Phi. Available to U.S. and non-U.S. citizens.

Application Requirements: Application form, application form may be submitted online. *Deadline:* April 1.

Contact: Mrs. Kelli Partin, Awards Manager
Honor Society of Phi Kappa Phi
7576 Goodwood Boulevard
Baton Rouge, LA 70806
Phone: 800-804-9880 Ext. 235
E-mail: kpartin@phikappaphi.org

INDEPENDENT OFFICE PRODUCTS AND FURNITURE DEALERS ASSOCIATION

http://www.iopfda.org/

NOPA AND OFDA SCHOLARSHIP AWARD

Candidates must have graduated from high school or its equivalent before July 1 of the year in which they would use the scholarship. Must have an academic record sufficient to be accepted by an accredited college, junior college, or technical institute. Must be a relative of a member of NOPA or OFDA.

Award: Scholarship for use in freshman, sophomore, junior, or senior years; not renewable. *Number:* up to 25. *Amount:* $2000.

Eligibility Requirements: Applicant must be enrolled or expecting to enroll full- or part-time at a two-year or four-year or technical institution or university. Applicant or parent of applicant must be member of Independent Office Products and Furniture Dealers Association. Available to U.S. and non-U.S. citizens.

Application Requirements: Application form, recommendations or references, transcript. *Deadline:* March 16.

Contact: Billie Zidek, Scholarship Administrator
Phone: 703-549-9040 Ext. 121
E-mail: bzidek@iopfda.org

INSTITUTE OF INDUSTRIAL ENGINEERS

https://www.iise.org/

A.O. PUTNAM MEMORIAL SCHOLARSHIP

One $1000 scholarship available to undergraduate students enrolled in any school in the United States and its territories, Canada, and Mexico, provided: (1) the school's industrial engineering program or equivalent is accredited by an agency or organization recognized by IISE; and (2) the student is pursuing a course of study in industrial engineering. Priority is given to students who have demonstrated an interest in management consulting.

Award: Scholarship for use in freshman, sophomore, junior, or senior years; not renewable. *Number:* 1. *Amount:* $1000.

Eligibility Requirements: Applicant must be enrolled or expecting to enroll full-time at an institution or university and must have an interest in leadership. Applicant or parent of applicant must be member of Institute of Industrial Engineers. Available to U.S. and non-U.S. citizens.

Application Requirements: Application form. *Deadline:* November 15.

Contact: Bonnie Cameron, Operations Administrator
Phone: 770-449-0461 Ext. 105
E-mail: bcameron@iise.org

C.B. GAMBRELL UNDERGRADUATE SCHOLARSHIP

One $2000 scholarship available to undergraduate industrial engineering students who are U.S. citizens who have graduated from a U.S. high school and who currently have a class standing above the freshman level in an ABET accredited IE program.

Award: Scholarship for use in sophomore, junior, or senior years; not renewable. *Number:* 1. *Amount:* $2000.

Eligibility Requirements: Applicant must be enrolled or expecting to enroll full-time at an institution or university and must have an interest in leadership. Applicant or parent of applicant must be member of Institute of Industrial Engineers. Available to U.S. citizens.

Application Requirements: Application form. *Deadline:* November 15.

Contact: Bonnie Cameron, Operations Administrator
Phone: 770-449-0461 Ext. 105
E-mail: bcameron@iise.org

DWIGHT D. GARDNER SCHOLARSHIP

Scholarships available to undergraduate students enrolled in any school in the United States and its territories, Canada, and Mexico, provided: the school's industrial engineering program or equivalent is accredited by an agency or organization recognized by IISE; and the student is pursuing a course of study in industrial engineering. Six scholarships of $3,500 (4) and $3,000 (2) were awarded for the academic year 2019-20.

Award: Scholarship for use in freshman, sophomore, junior, or senior years; not renewable. *Number:* 6. *Amount:* $3000–$3500.

Eligibility Requirements: Applicant must be enrolled or expecting to enroll full-time at an institution or university and must have an interest in leadership. Applicant or parent of applicant must be member of Institute of Industrial Engineers. Available to U.S. and non-U.S. citizens.

Application Requirements: Application form, essay, financial need analysis. *Deadline:* November 15.

Contact: Bonnie Cameron, Operations Administrator
Phone: 770-449-0461 Ext. 105
E-mail: bcameron@iise.org

HAROLD AND INGE MARCUS SCHOLARSHIP

Available to undergraduate students enrolled in any school in the United States provided the school's engineering program is accredited by an agency recognized by IISE and the student is pursuing a course of study in industrial engineering. This award is intended to recognize academic excellence and noteworthy contribution to the development of the industrial engineering profession. 11 scholarships of $1,000 each were awarded for the academic year 2019-20. Must have an overall point-hour average of 3.40.

Award: Scholarship for use in freshman, sophomore, junior, or senior years; not renewable. *Number:* 11. *Amount:* $1000.

Eligibility Requirements: Applicant must be enrolled or expecting to enroll full-time at a two-year institution or university and must have an interest in leadership. Applicant or parent of applicant must be member of Institute of Industrial Engineers. Available to U.S. citizens.

Application Requirements: Application form. *Deadline:* November 15.

Contact: Bonnie Cameron, Operations Administrator
Phone: 770-449-0461 Ext. 105
E-mail: bcameron@iise.org

IISE COUNCIL OF FELLOWS UNDERGRADUATE SCHOLARSHIP

Available to undergraduate students enrolled in any school provided: (1) the school's industrial engineering program or equivalent is accredited by an agency or organization recognized by IISE; and (2) the student is pursuing a course of study in industrial engineering. This scholarship was created to reward outstanding academic scholarship and leadership at the undergraduate level. One scholarship of $1,000 was awarded for the academic year 2019-20. Must have an overall point-hour average of 3.40.

Award: Scholarship for use in freshman, sophomore, junior, or senior years; not renewable. *Number:* 1. *Amount:* $1000.

Eligibility Requirements: Applicant must be enrolled or expecting to enroll full-time at an institution or university and must have an interest in leadership. Applicant or parent of applicant must be member of Institute of Industrial Engineers. Available to U.S. and non-U.S. citizens.

Application Requirements: Application form. *Deadline:* November 15.

Contact: Bonnie Cameron, Operations Administrator
Phone: 770-449-0461 Ext. 105
E-mail: bcameron@iise.org

LISA ZAKEN AWARD FOR EXCELLENCE

Award for undergraduate and graduate students enrolled in any school, and pursuing a course of study in industrial engineering. This award is intended to recognize excellence in scholarly activities and leadership related to the industrial engineering profession on campus. Must have an overall point-hour average of 3.0.

Award: Prize for use in freshman, sophomore, junior, senior, or graduate years; not renewable. *Number:* 1. *Amount:* $1500.

Eligibility Requirements: Applicant must be enrolled or expecting to enroll full-time at an institution or university and must have an interest in leadership. Applicant or parent of applicant must be member of Institute of Industrial Engineers. Available to U.S. and non-U.S. citizens.

Application Requirements: Application form, essay. *Deadline:* November 15.

Contact: Bonnie Cameron, Operations Administrator
Phone: 770-449-0461 Ext. 105
E-mail: bcameron@iise.org

MARVIN MUNDEL MEMORIAL SCHOLARSHIP

Available to undergraduate students enrolled in any school in the United States and its territories, Canada, and Mexico, provided: (1) the school's industrial engineering program or equivalent is accredited by an agency or organization recognized by IISE; and (2) the student is pursuing a course of study in industrial engineering. Priority is given to students who have demonstrated an interest in work measurement and methods engineering. Must have an overall point-hour average of 3.40.

Award: Scholarship for use in freshman, sophomore, junior, or senior years; not renewable. *Number:* 1. *Amount:* $1500.

Eligibility Requirements: Applicant must be enrolled or expecting to enroll full-time at an institution or university and must have an interest in leadership. Applicant or parent of applicant must be member of Institute of Industrial Engineers. Available to U.S. and non-U.S. citizens.

Application Requirements: Application form. *Deadline:* November 15.

Contact: Bonnie Cameron, Operations Administrator
Phone: 770-449-0461 Ext. 105
E-mail: bcameron@iise.org

PRESIDENTS SCHOLARSHIP

The Presidents Scholarship is available to undergraduate students pursuing a course of study in industrial engineering. This award is intended to recognize excellence in scholarly activities and leadership of the industrial engineering profession. A candidate must be active in a student chapter and must have demonstrated leadership and promoted IISE involvement on campus. Must have an overall point-hour average of 3.40.

Award: Scholarship for use in freshman, sophomore, junior, or senior years; not renewable. *Number:* 5. *Amount:* $1000.

Eligibility Requirements: Applicant must be enrolled or expecting to enroll full-time at an institution or university and must have an interest in leadership. Applicant or parent of applicant must be member of Institute of Industrial Engineers. Available to U.S. citizens.

Application Requirements: Application form. *Deadline:* November 15.

Contact: Bonnie Cameron, Operations Administrator
Phone: 770-449-0461 Ext. 105
E-mail: bcameron@iise.org

UPS SCHOLARSHIP FOR FEMALE STUDENTS

Scholarship available to undergraduate students enrolled in any school in the United States and its territories, Canada, and Mexico, (1) the school's industrial engineering program or equivalent is accredited by an agency or organization recognized by IISE and (2) the student is pursuing a course of study in industrial engineering. Must have an overall point-hour average of 3.40.

Award: Scholarship for use in freshman, sophomore, junior, or senior years; not renewable. *Number:* 1. *Amount:* $4000.

Eligibility Requirements: Applicant must be enrolled or expecting to enroll full-time at a technical institution or university; female and must have an interest in leadership. Applicant or parent of applicant must be member of Institute of Industrial Engineers. Available to U.S. and non-U.S. citizens.

Application Requirements: Application form. *Deadline:* November 15.

Contact: Bonnie Cameron, Operations Administrator
Phone: 770-449-0461 Ext. 105
E-mail: bcameron@iise.org

UPS SCHOLARSHIP FOR MINORITY STUDENTS

Scholarship available to undergraduate students enrolled in any school in the United States and its territories, Canada, and Mexico, provided: (1) the school's industrial engineering program or equivalent is accredited by an agency or organization recognized by IISE; and (2) the student is pursuing a course of study in industrial engineering. Must have an overall point-hour average of 3.40.

Award: Scholarship for use in freshman, sophomore, junior, or senior years; not renewable. *Number:* 1. *Amount:* $4000.

Eligibility Requirements: Applicant must be American Indian/Alaska Native, Asian/Pacific Islander, Black (non-Hispanic), Hispanic; enrolled or expecting to enroll full-time at an institution or university and must have an interest in leadership. Applicant or parent of applicant must be member of Institute of Industrial Engineers. Available to U.S. and non-U.S. citizens.

Application Requirements: Application form. *Deadline:* November 15.

Contact: Bonnie Cameron, Operations Administrator
Phone: 770-449-0461 Ext. 105
E-mail: bcameron@iise.org

INTERNATIONAL BROTHERHOOD OF TEAMSTERS SCHOLARSHIP FUND

http://www.teamster.org/

JAMES R. HOFFA MEMORIAL SCHOLARSHIP FUND

Scholarships available to children of members of the International Brotherhood of Teamsters (in good standing). The $10,000 awards are renewed on an annual basis. Also awarded are a one-time $1000 awards (non-renewable). The recipient must plan to attend a four-year institution and must maintain 3.0 GPA.

Award: Scholarship for use in freshman, sophomore, junior, or senior years; renewable. *Number:* 1–100. *Amount:* $1000–$10,000.

Eligibility Requirements: Applicant must be high school student and planning to enroll or expecting to enroll full-time at a four-year institution or university. Applicant or parent of applicant must be member of International Brotherhood of Teamsters. Available to U.S. and Canadian citizens.

Application Requirements: Application form, entry in a contest, list of activities, recommendations or references, test scores, transcript. *Deadline:* March 31.

Contact: Mrs. Traci Jacobs, Administrative Manager
International Brotherhood of Teamsters Scholarship Fund
25 Louisiana Avenue, NW
Washington, DC 20001
Phone: 202-624-8735
Fax: 202-624-7457
E-mail: tjacobs@teamster.org

INTERNATIONAL CHEMICAL WORKERS UNION

http://www.icwuc.org/

WALTER L. MITCHELL MEMORIAL AWARDS

Award available to children of International Chemical Workers Union members. Applicants must be starting their freshman year of college.

Award: Scholarship for use in freshman year; not renewable. *Number:* 12. *Amount:* $1500.

Eligibility Requirements: Applicant must be high school student and planning to enroll or expecting to enroll full-time at a two-year or four-year or technical institution or university. Applicant or parent of applicant must be member of International Chemical Workers Union. Available to U.S. citizens.

Application Requirements: Application form, biographical questionnaire, test scores, transcript. *Deadline:* April 23.

Contact: Sue Everhart, Secretary for Research and Education
International Chemical Workers Union
1799 Akron-Peninsula Road
Akron, OH 44313
Phone: 330-926-1444 Ext. 134
Fax: 330-926-0816
E-mail: severhart@icwuc.org

ITALIAN CATHOLIC FEDERATION

http://www.icf.org/

ITALIAN CATHOLIC FEDERATION FIRST YEAR SCHOLARSHIP

Scholarship for undergraduate students of the Catholic faith and of Italian heritage (or children or grand children of non-Italian ICF members). Must have minimum 3.2 GPA. Must live in AZ, CA, IL and NV.

Award: Scholarship for use in freshman year; not renewable. *Number:* 180–200. *Amount:* $400.

Eligibility Requirements: Applicant must be Roman Catholic; high school student; planning to enroll or expecting to enroll full-time at a two-year or four-year or technical institution or university and resident of Arizona, California, Illinois, Nevada. Applicant or parent of applicant must be member of Italian Catholic Federation. Available to U.S. citizens.

Application Requirements: Application form, essay, financial need analysis, recommendations or references, test scores, transcript. *Deadline:* March 15.

Contact: Scholarship Committee
Italian Catholic Federation
ICF Central Council Office
8393 Capwell Drive, Suite 110
Oakland, CA 94621
Phone: 510-633-9058
Fax: 510-633-9758

JEWISH WAR VETERANS OF THE UNITED STATES OF AMERICA

http://www.jwv.org/

BERNARD ROTBERG MEMORIAL GRANT

This is a grant for high school seniors (at the time of application) to help them pay the costs of their tuition. Applicants must have been accepted by an accredited college, university, community college, or hospital school of nursing as a member of the freshman class entering in the fall of the year the student graduates. Applicants must be a direct descendant (children, grand-children, great-grand-children, etc.) of Jewish War Veterans members in good standing. All members, including posthumous members, must have joined before 2013.

Award: Grant for use in freshman year; not renewable. *Number:* 1. *Amount:* $1000.

Eligibility Requirements: Applicant must be high school student and planning to enroll or expecting to enroll full-time at a two-year institution or university. Applicant or parent of applicant must be member of Jewish War Veterans. Available to U.S. citizens.

Application Requirements: Application form. *Deadline:* May 22.

Contact: Cara Rinkoff, Programs Coordinator
Phone: 202-265-6280
E-mail: crinkoff@jwv.org

CHARLES KOSMUTZA MEMORIAL GRANT

Each year, the Jewish War Veterans of the USA sponsors an essay contest for current service members and veterans who plan to attend or are currently attending an accredited Associates, Bachelor's, Nursing, or Graduate degree program. The National Achievement Program is open to anyone regardless of race, religion, creed, or culture. All veterans are eligible and must be legal residents of the USA. Awards $2,500.

Award: Grant for use in freshman, sophomore, junior, senior, or graduate years; not renewable. *Amount:* $2500.

Eligibility Requirements: Applicant must be enrolled or expecting to enroll at a two-year institution or university. Applicant or parent of applicant must be member of Jewish War Veterans. Available to U.S. citizens.

Application Requirements: Essay. *Deadline:* June 1.

Contact: Cara Rinkoff, Programs Coordinator
Phone: 202-265-6280
E-mail: crinkoff@jwv.org

CLIFORD LEE KRISTAL EDUCATION GRANT

Applicants must be accepted by an accredited college, university, community college, or hospital school of nursing as a member of the freshman class entering in the fall of the year the student graduates. For high school seniors who are direct descendants of members of the Jewish War Veterans organization who joined prior to 2016. Awards $1,250. Unweighted: 92 or 3.7 or Weighted: 4.5

Award: Grant for use in freshman year; not renewable. *Amount:* $1250.

Eligibility Requirements: Applicant must be high school student and planning to enroll or expecting to enroll full- or part-time at a two-year institution or university. Applicant or parent of applicant must be member of Jewish War Veterans.

Application Requirements: Application form. *Deadline:* July 10.

Contact: Cara Rinkoff, Programs Coordinator
Phone: 202-265-6280
E-mail: crinkoff@jwv.org

EDITH, LOUIS AND MAX S. MILLEN MEMORIAL ATHLETIC GRANT

Applicants must be accepted by an accredited college, university, community college, or hospital school of nursing as a member of the freshman class entering in the fall of the year the student graduates. For high school seniors who are direct descendants of members of the Jewish War Veterans organization who joined prior to 2016. Awards $1,000. Unweighted: 92 or 3.7 or Weighted: 4.5

Award: Grant for use in freshman year; not renewable. *Amount:* $1000.

Eligibility Requirements: Applicant must be high school student and planning to enroll or expecting to enroll full-time at a two-year institution or university. Applicant or parent of applicant must be member of Jewish War Veterans. Available to U.S. citizens.

Application Requirements: Application form. *Deadline:* May 22.

Contact: Cara Rinkoff, Programs Coordinator
Phone: 202-265-6280
E-mail: crinkoff@jwv.org

LEON BROOKS MEMORIAL GRANT

Each year, the Jewish War Veterans of the USA sponsors an essay contest for current service members and veterans who plan to attend or are currently attending an accredited Associates, Bachelor's, Nursing, or Graduate degree program. The National Achievement Program is open to anyone regardless of race, religion, creed, or culture. All veterans are eligible and must be legal residents of the USA. Awards $1,000.

Award: Grant for use in freshman, sophomore, junior, senior, or graduate years; not renewable. *Amount:* $1000.

Eligibility Requirements: Applicant must be enrolled or expecting to enroll at a two-year institution or university. Applicant or parent of applicant must be member of Jewish War Veterans. Available to U.S. citizens.

Application Requirements: Essay. *Deadline:* June 1.

Contact: Cara Rinkoff, Programs Coordinator
Phone: 202-265-6280
E-mail: crinkoff@jwv.org

JUNIOR ACHIEVEMENT

http://www.ja.org/

JOE FRANCOMANO SCHOLARSHIP

Renewable award to high school seniors who have demonstrated academic achievement, leadership skills, and financial need. May be used at any accredited post secondary educational institution for any field of study resulting in a Baccalaureate degree. Must have completed JA Company Program or JA Economics.

Award: Scholarship for use in freshman year; renewable. *Number:* 1. *Amount:* $5000.

Eligibility Requirements: Applicant must be high school student; planning to enroll or expecting to enroll full-time at a four-year institution or university and must have an interest in leadership. Applicant or parent of applicant must be member of Junior Achievement. Available to U.S. citizens.

Application Requirements: Application form, essay, financial need analysis, recommendations or references, transcript. *Deadline:* February 1.

Contact: Gwen Rose, Scholarship Coordinator
Phone: 719-540-6134
E-mail: dterry@ja.org

KNIGHTS OF COLUMBUS

http://www.kofc.org/

CANADIAN UNDEGRADUATE SCHOLARSHIP

Renewable scholarships for members of Canadian Knights of Columbus councils and their children who are entering first year of study for baccalaureate degree. Based on academic excellence. Award not limited to Fourth Degree members.

Award: Scholarship for use in freshman year; renewable. *Amount:* $1500.

Eligibility Requirements: Applicant must be Roman Catholic; Canadian citizen and enrolled or expecting to enroll full-time at an institution or university. Applicant or parent of applicant must be member of Knights of Columbus.

Application Requirements: Application form, application form may be submitted online. *Deadline:* May 4.

FOURTH DEGREE PRO DEO AND PRO PATRIA SCHOLARSHIPS/JOHN W. MCDEVITT (FOURTH DEGREE) SCHOLARSHIP

Award available to students entering freshman year at a Catholic university or college in United States. Applicant must be a member or child of a member of Knights of Columbus or Columbian Squires. Scholarships are awarded on the basis of academic excellence. Minimum 3.0 GPA required. See website for additional information http://www.kofc.org.

Award: Scholarship for use in freshman, sophomore, junior, or senior years; renewable. *Amount:* $1500.

Eligibility Requirements: Applicant must be Roman Catholic and enrolled or expecting to enroll full-time at an institution or university. Applicant or parent of applicant must be member of Knights of Columbus. Available to U.S. citizens.

Application Requirements: Application form, essay. *Deadline:* March 1.

Contact: Rev. Donald Barry, Scholarship Coordinator
Knights of Columbus
Department of Scholarships, PO Box 1670
New Haven, CT 06507-0901
Phone: 203-752-4332
Fax: 203-752-4103
E-mail: scholarships@kofc.org

JOHN W. MCDEVITT (FOURTH DEGREE) SCHOLARSHIPS

Scholarship for students entering freshman year at a Catholic college or university in United States. Applicant must submit Pro Deo and Pro Patria Scholarship application. Must be a member or wife, son, or daughter of a member of the Knights of Columbus. Minimum 3.0 GPA required. See website for additional information http://www.fofc.org.

Award: Scholarship for use in freshman year; renewable.

Eligibility Requirements: Applicant must be Roman Catholic and enrolled or expecting to enroll full-time at an institution or university. Applicant or parent of applicant must be member of Knights of Columbus. Available to U.S. citizens.

Application Requirements: Application form, essay. *Deadline:* March 1.

MATTHEWS & SWIFT EDUCATIONAL TRUST SCHOLARSHIP

Available to dependent children of Knights of Columbus who died or became permanently disabled while in military service during a time of conflict, from a cause connected with military service, or who died as the result of criminal violence while in the performance of their duties as full-time law enforcement officers or firemen. The scholarship is awarded at a Catholic college in the amount not covered by other financial aid for tuition up to $25,000 annually.

Award: Scholarship for use in freshman, sophomore, junior, or senior years; renewable.

Eligibility Requirements: Applicant must be Roman Catholic and enrolled or expecting to enroll full-time at an institution or university. Applicant or parent of applicant must be member of Knights of Columbus. Available to U.S. citizens. Applicant or parent must meet one or more of the following requirements: general military experience; retired from active duty; disabled or killed as a result of military service; prisoner of war; or missing in action.

Application Requirements: Application form. *Deadline:* March 1.

PERCY J. JOHNSON ENDOWED SCHOLARSHIPS

In 1990, a bequest was received from the estate of Percy J. Johnson of Seville Council 93 in Brockton, Mass. Mr. Johnson stipulated that scholarships be awarded to young men who demonstrate financial need. Accordingly, FAFSA SAR reporting is required in the application process. Earnings of the established fund provide undergraduate scholarships of $1,500 per year to selected applicants.

Award: Scholarship for use in freshman year; renewable. *Amount:* $1500.

Eligibility Requirements: Applicant must be Roman Catholic; enrolled or expecting to enroll full-time at an institution or university and male. Applicant or parent of applicant must be member of Knights of Columbus. Available to U.S. citizens.

Application Requirements: Application form, application form may be submitted online, financial need analysis. *Deadline:* May 4.

LADIES AUXILIARY OF THE FLEET RESERVE ASSOCIATION

http://www.fra.org/

LADIES AUXILIARY OF THE FLEET RESERVE ASSOCIATION SCHOLARSHIP

Scholarship for members; spouses; dependent biological, step or adoptive child; or biological, step or adoptive grandchild of LA FRA or FRA member in good standing, currently or at time of death. Applicant must be a U.S. citizen, registered as a full-time student in an accredited college located in the United States.

Award: Scholarship for use in freshman, sophomore, junior, or senior years; not renewable. *Amount:* $1500.

Eligibility Requirements: Applicant must be enrolled or expecting to enroll full-time at a four-year institution or university and female. Applicant or parent of applicant must be member of Fleet Reserve Association/Auxiliary. Available to U.S. citizens. Applicant or parent must meet one or more of the following requirements: Coast Guard, Marine Corps, or Navy experience; retired from active duty; disabled or killed as a result of military service; prisoner of war; or missing in action.

Application Requirements: Application form, essay, recommendations or references, transcript. *Deadline:* April 15.

Contact: National Scholarship Chair
Ladies Auxiliary of the Fleet Reserve Association
PO Box 3459
Pahrump, NV 89041-3459
Phone: 775-751-3309

SAM ROSE MEMORIAL SCHOLARSHIP

Scholarship for members; spouses; dependent biological, step or adoptive child; or biological, step or adoptive grandchild of LA FRA or FRA member in good standing, currently or at time of death. Applicant must be a U.S. citizen, registered as a full-time student in an accredited college located in the United States.

Award: Scholarship for use in freshman, sophomore, junior, or senior years; not renewable. *Amount:* $1500.

Eligibility Requirements: Applicant must be enrolled or expecting to enroll full-time at a four-year institution or university. Applicant or parent of applicant must be member of Fleet Reserve Association/Auxiliary. Available to U.S. citizens. Applicant or parent must meet one or more of the following requirements: Coast Guard, Marine Corps, or Navy experience; retired from active duty; disabled or killed as a result of military service; prisoner of war; or missing in action.

Application Requirements: Application form, essay, recommendations or references, transcript. *Deadline:* April 15.

Contact: National Scholarship Chair
Ladies Auxiliary of the Fleet Reserve Association
PO Box 3459
Pahrump, NV 89041-3459
Phone: 775-751-3309

LEARNING ALLY

http://www.learningally.org

MARION HUBER LEARNING THROUGH LISTENING AWARDS

Awards presented to Learning Ally members who are high school seniors with learning disabilities, in recognition of extraordinary leadership, scholarship, enterprise and service to others. Must have minimum 3.0 GPA.

Award: Prize for use in freshman year; not renewable. *Number:* 6. *Amount:* $2000–$6000.

Eligibility Requirements: Applicant must be high school student and planning to enroll or expecting to enroll full-time at a two-year or four-year institution. Applicant or parent of applicant must be member of Learning Ally. Applicant must be learning disabled. Available to U.S. citizens.

Application Requirements: Application form, community service, essay. *Deadline:* May 31.

Contact: Jessica Kooper, Director of Engagement Marketing
Learning Ally
20 Roszel Road
Princeton, NJ 08540
Phone: 609-243-3089
E-mail: naa@learningally.org

MARY P. OENSLAGER SCHOLASTIC ACHIEVEMENT AWARDS

Award presented to Learning Ally members who are college seniors and blind or visually impaired, in recognition of extraordinary leadership, scholarship, enterprise, and service to others.

Award: Prize for use in senior or graduate years; not renewable. *Number:* 3–9. *Amount:* $1000–$6000.

Eligibility Requirements: Applicant must be enrolled or expecting to enroll full-time at a four-year institution or university. Applicant or parent of applicant must be member of Learning Ally. Applicant must be visually impaired. Available to U.S. citizens.

Application Requirements: Application form, community service, essay. *Deadline:* May 31.

Contact: Jessica Kooper, Director of Engagement Marketing
Learning Ally
20 Roszel Road
Princeton, NJ 08540
Phone: 609-243-7082
E-mail: naa@learningally.org

LOGISTICS & TRANSPORTATION ASSOCIATION OF NORTH AMERICA

http://www.ltna.org

DENNY LYDIC SCHOLARSHIP

Award is available to currently enrolled college students majoring in transportation, logistics, traffic management, or related fields. Available to citizens of the United States, Canada, and Mexico. See website for application http://www.transportationclubsinternational.com/.

Award: Scholarship for use in freshman, sophomore, junior, or senior years; not renewable. *Number:* 1. *Amount:* $1000.

Eligibility Requirements: Applicant must be enrolled or expecting to enroll full-time at a two-year or technical institution or university. Applicant or parent of applicant must be member of Transportation Club International. Available to U.S. and non-U.S. citizens.

Application Requirements: Application form, essay, personal photograph. *Deadline:* July 25.

Contact: Katie Dejonge, Executive Director
Logistics & Transportation Association of North America
LTNA Scholarships
PO Box 426
Union, WA 98592
E-mail: executive.director@ltna.org

MINNESOTA AFL-CIO

http://www.mnaflcio.org/

MARTIN DUFFY ADULT LEARNER SCHOLARSHIP AWARD

Scholarship available for union members affiliated with the Minnesota AFL-CIO or the Minnesota Joint Council 32. May be used at any postsecondary institution in Minnesota. Information available on website at http://www.mnaflcio.org.

Award: Scholarship for use in freshman, sophomore, junior, or senior years; not renewable. *Number:* 4. *Amount:* $500.

Eligibility Requirements: Applicant must be enrolled or expecting to enroll full-time at a four-year institution or university; resident of Minnesota and studying in Minnesota. Applicant or parent of applicant must be member of AFL-CIO. Available to U.S. citizens.

Application Requirements: Application form. *Deadline:* April 30.

Contact: Computer Information Specialist
Minnesota AFL-CIO
175 Aurora Avenue
St. Paul, MN 55103
Phone: 651-227-7647
Fax: 651-227-3801

MINNESOTA AFL-CIO SCHOLARSHIPS

Applicant must be attending a college or university located in Minnesota. Must have a parent or legal guardian, who has held a one year membership in a local union which is an affiliate of the Minnesota AFL-CIO. Winners are selected by lot. Academic eligibility based on a straight "B" average or better. See website http://www.mnaflcio.org for information and application.

Award: Scholarship for use in freshman year; not renewable. *Number:* up to 5. *Amount:* $1000.

Eligibility Requirements: Applicant must be high school student; planning to enroll or expecting to enroll full-time at a two-year or four-year or technical institution or university and studying in Minnesota. Applicant or parent of applicant must be member of AFL-CIO. Available to U.S. citizens.

Application Requirements: Application form, transcript. *Deadline:* April 30.

Contact: Computer Information Specialist
Minnesota AFL-CIO
175 Aurora Avenue
St. Paul, MN 55103
Phone: 651-227-7647
Fax: 651-227-3801

NATIONAL ALLIANCE OF POSTAL AND FEDERAL EMPLOYEES (NAPFE)

http://www.napfe.com/

ASHBY B. CARTER MEMORIAL SCHOLARSHIP FUND FOUNDERS AWARD

Scholarships available to high school seniors. Must be a U.S. citizen. Applicant must be a dependent of NAPFE Labor Union member with a minimum three year membership. Applicant must take the SAT on or before March 1 of the year they apply for award.

Award: Scholarship for use in freshman year; not renewable. *Number:* 3. *Amount:* $2000–$5000.

Eligibility Requirements: Applicant must be high school student and planning to enroll or expecting to enroll full-time at a four-year institution or university. Applicant or parent of applicant must be member of National Alliance of Postal and Federal Employees. Available to U.S. citizens.

Application Requirements: Application form, community service, personal photograph, recommendations or references, self-addressed stamped envelope with application, test scores, transcript. *Deadline:* April 1.

Contact: Melissa Jeffries-Stewart, Director
Phone: 202-939-6325 Ext. 239
Fax: 202-939-6389
E-mail: headquarters@napfe.org

NATIONAL ASSOCIATION FOR THE ADVANCEMENT OF COLORED PEOPLE

http://www.naacp.org/

AGNES JONES JACKSON SCHOLARSHIP

Scholarship for undergraduate and graduate students who have been members of the NAACP for at least one year, or fully paid life members. Undergraduates must have 2.5 GPA and graduate students must have 3.0 GPA. Applicant must not have reached the age of 25 by the application deadline.

Award: Scholarship for use in freshman, sophomore, junior, senior, or graduate years; not renewable. *Number:* 20–40. *Amount:* $2000–$2500.

Eligibility Requirements: Applicant must be American Indian/Alaska Native, Asian/Pacific Islander, Black (non-Hispanic), Hispanic; age 24 or under and enrolled or expecting to enroll full- or part-time at a two-year institution or university. Applicant or parent of applicant must be member of National Association for the Advancement of Colored People. Available to U.S. citizens.

Application Requirements: Application form, application form may be submitted online, essay, financial need analysis.

Contact: Victor Goode, Attorney
Phone: 410-580-5760
E-mail: info@naacp.org

NATIONAL ASSOCIATION FOR THE SELF-EMPLOYED

http://www.NASE.org/

NASE SCHOLARSHIPS

Scholarship of $4000 for high school students or college undergraduates enrolled in full-time program of study. Total number of available awards varies. Applicants must be children or dependents of NASE Members and between the ages of 16 and 24.

Award: Scholarship for use in freshman, sophomore, junior, or senior years; not renewable. *Amount:* $4000.

Eligibility Requirements: Applicant must be age 16-24; enrolled or expecting to enroll full-time at a four-year institution or university and must have an interest in leadership. Applicant or parent of applicant must be member of National Association for the Self-Employed. Available to U.S. citizens.

Application Requirements: Application form, application form may be submitted online (http://www.nase.org/Membership/MembersBenefits/BenefitDetails.aspx?BenefitId=71), essay, financial need analysis, recommendations or references, resume, transcript. *Deadline:* April 1.

Contact: Molly Nelson, Member Communications Manager
Phone: 202-466-2100
Fax: 202-466-2123
E-mail: mnelson@NASEadmin.org

NATIONAL ASSOCIATION OF ENERGY SERVICE COMPANIES

http://www.aesc.net/

ASSOCIATION OF ENERGY SERVICE COMPANIES SCHOLARSHIP PROGRAM

Applicant must be the legal dependent of an employee of an AESC member company, or an employee. Dependents of company officers are not eligible. Must submit application to local AESC chapter chairman. Application must include ACT or SAT test scores.

Award: Scholarship for use in freshman, sophomore, junior, senior, or graduate years; renewable. *Number:* 150–200. *Amount:* $1000.

Eligibility Requirements: Applicant must be enrolled or expecting to enroll full-time at a two-year or four-year or technical institution or university. Applicant or parent of applicant must be member of Association of Energy Service Companies. Available to U.S. and non-U.S. citizens.

Application Requirements: Application form, essay. *Deadline:* March 14.

Contact: Susan Dudley, Administrative Assistant
Phone: 800-692-0771
Fax: 713-781-7542
E-mail: sdudley@aesc.net

NATIONAL ASSOCIATION OF LETTER CARRIERS

http://www.nalc.org/

COSTAS G. LEMONOPOULOS SCHOLARSHIP

Scholarships to children of NALC members attending public, four-year colleges or universities supported by the state of Florida or St. Petersburg Junior College. Scholarships are renewable one time.

Award: Scholarship for use in freshman, sophomore, junior, or senior years; renewable. *Number:* 1–20.

Eligibility Requirements: Applicant must be enrolled or expecting to enroll full-time at a two-year institution or university and studying in

Florida. Applicant or parent of applicant must be member of National Association of Letter Carriers. Available to U.S. citizens.

Application Requirements: Application form. *Deadline:* June 1.

Contact: Ann Porch, Membership Committee
Phone: 202-393-4695
E-mail: nalcinf@nalc.org

JOHN T. DONELON SCHOLARSHIP

Scholarship for sons and daughters of NALC members who are high school seniors when making application. The $1000 scholarship will be renewable for four years.

Award: Scholarship for use in freshman year; renewable. *Number:* 5. *Amount:* $1000.

Eligibility Requirements: Applicant must be high school student and planning to enroll or expecting to enroll full-time at an institution or university. Applicant or parent of applicant must be member of National Association of Letter Carriers. Available to U.S. citizens.

Application Requirements: Application form. *Deadline:* December 31.

Contact: Ann Porch, Membership Committee
Phone: 202-393-4695
E-mail: nalcinf@nalc.org

UNION PLUS SCHOLARSHIP PROGRAM

One-time cash award available for undergraduate study programs. Scholarship ranges from $500 to $4000. Three awards are granted. Must be children of members of NALC.

Award: Scholarship for use in freshman year; not renewable. *Number:* 3. *Amount:* $500–$4000.

Eligibility Requirements: Applicant must be high school student and planning to enroll or expecting to enroll full-time at an institution or university. Applicant or parent of applicant must be member of National Association of Letter Carriers. Available to U.S. citizens.

Application Requirements: Application form. *Deadline:* January 31.

Contact: Ann Porch, Membership Committee
Phone: 202-393-4695
E-mail: nalcinf@nalc.org

WILLIAM C. DOHERTY SCHOLARSHIP FUND

Five scholarships of $4000 each are awarded to children of members in NALC. Renewable for three consecutive years thereafter providing the winner maintains satisfactory grades. Applicant must be a high school senior when making application.

Award: Scholarship for use in freshman year; renewable. *Number:* 5. *Amount:* $4000.

Eligibility Requirements: Applicant must be high school student and planning to enroll or expecting to enroll full-time at an institution or university. Applicant or parent of applicant must be member of National Association of Letter Carriers. Available to U.S. citizens.

Application Requirements: Application form. *Deadline:* December 31.

Contact: Ann Porch, Membership Committee
Phone: 202-393-4695
E-mail: nalcinf@nalc.org

NATIONAL ASSOCIATION OF SECONDARY SCHOOL PRINCIPALS

https://www.nhs.us/advisers/the-nhs-scholarship/

NATIONAL HONOR SOCIETY SCHOLARSHIP PROGRAM

One-time award to senior National Honor Society members who are in good standing with their active chapter. Application process opens in the fall, and members receive application instructions from their NHS adviser. Program information is available on the NHS website at https://www.nhs.us/advisers/the-nhs-scholarship.

Award: Scholarship for use in freshman year; not renewable. *Number:* 600. *Amount:* $3200–$25,000.

Eligibility Requirements: Applicant must be high school student and planning to enroll or expecting to enroll full-time at a two-year or four-year or technical institution or university. Applicant or parent of applicant must be member of National Honor Society. Available to U.S. and non-U.S. citizens.

Application Requirements: Application form, application form may be submitted online, essay. *Deadline:* December 10.

Contact: Ms. Elancia Felder, Program Manager
National Association of Secondary School Principals
1904 Association Drive
Reston, VA 20191
E-mail: scholarship@nhs.us

NATIONAL BETA CLUB

http://www.betaclub.org/

NATIONAL BETA CLUB SCHOLARSHIP

Applicant must be in twelfth grade and a member of the National Beta Club. Must be nominated by school chapter of the National Beta Club, therefore, applications will not be sent to the individual students. Renewable and nonrenewable awards available. Contact school Beta Club sponsor for more information.

Award: Scholarship for use in freshman year; renewable. *Number:* 221. *Amount:* $1000–$15,000.

Eligibility Requirements: Applicant must be high school student and planning to enroll or expecting to enroll full-time at a two-year or four-year institution or university. Applicant or parent of applicant must be member of National Beta Club. Available to U.S. citizens.

Application Requirements: Application form, application form may be submitted online, essay, recommendations or references, test scores, transcript. *Fee:* $10. *Deadline:* December 10.

Contact: Mrs. Joan Burnett, Scholarship Coordinator
Phone: 864-583-4553
Fax: 864-542-9300
E-mail: jburnett@betaclub.org

NATIONAL FFA ORGANIZATION

http://www.ffa.org

NATIONAL FFA COLLEGIATE SCHOLARSHIP PROGRAM

Scholarships to high school seniors planning to enroll in a full-time course of study at an accredited vocational/technical school, college or university. A smaller number of awards are available to currently enrolled undergraduates. Most awards require the applicant be an FFA member. Some awards are available to non-members.

Award: Scholarship for use in freshman, sophomore, junior, or senior years; not renewable. *Number:* 1,700–1,800. *Amount:* $500–$29,000.

Eligibility Requirements: Applicant must be age 17-23 and enrolled or expecting to enroll full-time at a two-year or four-year or technical institution or university. Applicant or parent of applicant must be member of Future Farmers of America. Available to U.S. citizens.

Application Requirements: Application form. *Deadline:* February 1.

Contact: Scholarship Program Manager
National FFA Organization
PO Box 68960
Indianapolis, IN 46268
Phone: 317-802-6099
E-mail: scholarships@ffa.org

NATIONAL FOSTER PARENT ASSOCIATION

http://www.nfpaonline.org/

NATIONAL FOSTER PARENT ASSOCIATION YOUTH SCHOLARSHIP

Award for high school senior who will be entering first year of college, comparable education, or training program. Six $1000 awards, three for foster children currently in foster care with an NFPA member family, and one each for birth and adopted children of foster parents. NFPA family membership required ($35 membership fee).

Award: Scholarship for use in freshman year; not renewable. *Number:* 6. *Amount:* $1000.

Eligibility Requirements: Applicant must be high school student and planning to enroll or expecting to enroll full- or part-time at a two-year or four-year or technical institution or university. Applicant or parent of applicant must be member of National Foster Parent Association. Available to U.S. citizens.

Application Requirements: Application form, driver's license, essay, recommendations or references, test scores, transcript. *Deadline:* March 31.

Contact: Karen Jorgenson, Executive Director
National Foster Parent Association
7512 Stanich Avenue, Suite 6
Gig Harbor, WA 98335
Phone: 253-853-4000
Fax: 253-853-4001
E-mail: info@nfpaonline.org

NATIONAL JUNIOR ANGUS ASSOCIATION

http://www.angus.org/njaa/

ANGUS FOUNDATION SCHOLARSHIPS

Applicants must have at one time been a National Junior Angus Association member and currently be a junior, regular or life member of the association. Must have applied to undergraduate studies in any field. Applicants must have a minimum 2.0 GPA. See website for further information and to download application.

Award: Scholarship for use in freshman, sophomore, junior, senior, or graduate years; not renewable. *Number:* 75–90. *Amount:* $250–$5000.

Eligibility Requirements: Applicant must be age 25 or under and enrolled or expecting to enroll full-time at a two-year or four-year or technical institution or university. Applicant or parent of applicant must be member of American Angus Association. Available to U.S. and Canadian citizens.

Application Requirements: Application form, recommendations or references, transcript. *Deadline:* May 1.

Contact: Mr. Milford Jenkins, Angus Foundation President
National Junior Angus Association
3201 Frederick Avenue
St. Joseph, MO 64506
Phone: 816-383-5100 Ext. 163
Fax: 816-383-5146
E-mail: mjenkins@angusfoundation.org

NATIONAL SOCIETY DAUGHTERS OF THE AMERICAN REVOLUTION

http://www.dar.org/

LILLIAN AND AUTHOR DUNN SCHOLARSHIP

A $2500 scholarship awarded for up to four years to well-qualified, deserving sons and daughters of members of the NSDAR. Outstanding recipients will be considered for an additional period of up to four years of study. Must include DAR member number.

Award: Scholarship for use in freshman, sophomore, junior, or senior years; renewable. *Amount:* $2500.

Eligibility Requirements: Applicant must be enrolled or expecting to enroll full-time at an institution or university. Applicant or parent of applicant must be member of Daughters of the American Revolution. Available to U.S. citizens.

Application Requirements: Application form, application form may be submitted online, essay, financial need analysis. *Deadline:* February 15.

Contact: Lakeisha Graham, Manager, Office of the Reporter General
Phone: 202-628-1776
Fax: 202-879-3348
E-mail: nsdarscholarships@dar.org

NATIONAL SOCIETY OF COLLEGIATE SCHOLARS (NSCS)

https://nscs.org/

NSCS EXEMPLARY SCHOLAR AWARD

Scholarship of $1000 available to outstanding undergraduates among the NSCS members for their high academic achievement as well as additional scholarly pursuits outside of the classroom. They should exemplify the NSCS mission: "Honoring and inspiring academic excellence and engaged citizenship for a lifetime" and show integrity in everything they do. Must have a completed profile and resume in NSCS database. Apply on website http://www.nscs.org/exemplary_scholar_award.

Award: Scholarship for use in freshman, sophomore, junior, or senior years; not renewable. *Number:* 3. *Amount:* $1000.

Eligibility Requirements: Applicant must be enrolled or expecting to enroll full- or part-time at a four-year institution or university and must have an interest in leadership. Applicant or parent of applicant must be member of National Society of Collegiate Scholars. Available to U.S. and non-U.S. citizens.

Application Requirements: Application form. *Deadline:* April 30.

Contact: Stephen Loflin, Executive Director
National Society of Collegiate Scholars (NSCS)
2000 M Street NW
Suite 600
Washington, DC 20036
Phone: 202-965-9000
Fax: 202-265-9200
E-mail: loflin@nscs.org

NSCS MERIT AWARD

Fifty merit awards to outstanding new NSCS members around the country. Student is chosen based upon how they exemplify the mission of NSCS. Must have a resume in the NSCS database and be a member who has joined between August of the previous year and July of the present year. Must have a minimum GPA of 3.4 and be enrolled in an accredited institution. For additional information, see website http://www.nscs.org.

Award: Scholarship for use in freshman, sophomore, junior, or senior years; not renewable. *Number:* 50. *Amount:* $1000.

Eligibility Requirements: Applicant must be enrolled or expecting to enroll full- or part-time at a two-year or four-year or technical institution or university. Applicant or parent of applicant must be member of National Society of Collegiate Scholars. Available to U.S. and non-U.S. citizens.

Application Requirements: Application form, recommendations or references, resume, transcript. *Deadline:* July 31.

Contact: Stephen Loflin, Executive Director
National Society of Collegiate Scholars (NSCS)
2000 M Street NW
Suite 600
Washington, DC 20036
Phone: 202-965-9000
Fax: 202-265-9200
E-mail: loflin@nscs.org

NSCS SCHOLAR ABROAD SPRING AND FALL AWARDS

Scholarship for an active NSCS member who has been accepted to and enrolled in an accredited study abroad program. Two $2,500 scholarships are awarded during the spring semester or summer and two $2500 scholarships for the fall semester. Deadlines: July 2 and November 4

Award: Scholarship for use in freshman, sophomore, junior, or senior years; not renewable. *Number:* 4. *Amount:* $2500.

Eligibility Requirements: Applicant must be enrolled or expecting to enroll full-time at a two-year institution or university. Applicant or parent of applicant must be member of National Society of Collegiate Scholars. Available to U.S. and non-U.S. citizens.

Application Requirements: Application form, essay. *Deadline:* July 2.

Contact: Stephen Loflin, Executive Director
National Society of Collegiate Scholars (NSCS)
2000 M Street NW
Suite 600
Washington, DC 20036
Phone: 202-965-9000
Fax: 202-265-9200
E-mail: loflin@nscs.org

NATIONAL SOCIETY OF HIGH SCHOOL SCHOLARS

http://www.nshss.org

CLAES NOBEL ACADEMIC SCHOLARSHIPS

Scholarships for high school students planning to attend four-year colleges or universities who are members of NSHSS. Minimum 3.5 GPA required.

Award: Scholarship for use in freshman year; not renewable. *Number:* 10. *Amount:* $5000.

Eligibility Requirements: Applicant must be high school student; planning to enroll or expecting to enroll full-time at a four-year institution or university and must have an interest in leadership. Applicant or parent of applicant must be member of National Society of High School Scholars. Available to U.S. and non-U.S. citizens.

Application Requirements: Application form, essay, personal photograph. *Deadline:* March 10.

Contact: Dr. Susan Thurman, Scholarship Director
National Society of High School Scholars
1936 North Druid Hills Road
Atlanta, GA 30319
Phone: 404-235-5500
E-mail: scholarships@nshss.org

NATIONAL SCHOLAR AWARDS FOR NSHSS MEMBERS

Scholarship of $1000 for undergraduate study. Applicant must be a member of NSHSS.

Award: Scholarship for use in freshman year; not renewable. *Number:* 85. *Amount:* $1000.

Eligibility Requirements: Applicant must be high school student; planning to enroll or expecting to enroll full-time at a two-year or four-year or technical institution or university and must have an interest in leadership. Applicant or parent of applicant must be member of National Society of High School Scholars. Available to U.S. and non-U.S. citizens.

Application Requirements: Application form, essay, personal photograph. *Deadline:* March 10.

Contact: Dr. Susan Thurman, Scholarship Director
National Society of High School Scholars
1936 North Druid Hills Road
Atlanta, GA 30319
Phone: 404-235-5500
E-mail: scholarships@nshss.org

ROBERT P. SHEPPARD LEADERSHIP AWARD FOR NSHSS MEMBERS

Scholarship of $1000 awarded to an NSHSS member demonstrating outstanding dedication to community service and initiative in volunteer activities.

Award: Scholarship for use in freshman year; not renewable. *Number:* 5. *Amount:* $1000–$2500.

Eligibility Requirements: Applicant must be high school student; planning to enroll or expecting to enroll full-time at a four-year institution or university and must have an interest in leadership. Applicant or parent of applicant must be member of National Society of High School Scholars. Available to U.S. and non-U.S. citizens.

Application Requirements: Application form, essay, personal photograph. *Deadline:* March 15.

Contact: Dr. Susan Thurman, Scholarship Director
National Society of High School Scholars
1936 North Druid Hills Road
Atlanta, GA 30319
Phone: 404-235-5500
E-mail: scholarships@nshss.org

NEW YORK STATE GRANGE

http://www.nysgrange.org/

SUSAN W. FREESTONE EDUCATION AWARD

Grants for members of Junior Grange and Subordinate Grange in New York State. Students must enroll in an approved two or four-year college in New York State. Second grants available with reapplication.

Award: Scholarship for use in freshman or sophomore years; not renewable. *Number:* 1–4. *Amount:* $1000.

Eligibility Requirements: Applicant must be high school student; planning to enroll or expecting to enroll full-time at a two-year or four-year institution; resident of New York and studying in New York. Applicant or parent of applicant must be member of Grange Association. Available to U.S. citizens.

Application Requirements: Application form, financial need analysis. *Deadline:* April 15.

Contact: Scholarship Committee
New York State Grange
100 Grange Place
Cortland, NY 13045
Phone: 607-756-7553
E-mail: nysgrange@nysgrange.org

NORTHEASTERN LOGGERS' ASSOCIATION INC.

http://www.northernlogger.com/

NORTHEASTERN LOGGERS' ASSOCIATION SCHOLARSHIPS

Scholarships available to those whose family is a member of the Northeastern Loggers' Association or whose family member is an employee of an Industrial or Associate Members of the Northeastern Loggers' Association. Must submit paper on topic of "What it means to grow up in the forest industry."

Award: Scholarship for use in freshman, sophomore, junior, or senior years; not renewable. *Number:* 6–10. *Amount:* $500–$1000.

Eligibility Requirements: Applicant must be enrolled or expecting to enroll full-time at a two-year or four-year or technical institution or university. Applicant or parent of applicant must be member of Northeastern Loggers Association. Available to U.S. and Canadian citizens.

Application Requirements: Application form, essay. *Deadline:* March 31.

Contact: Mona Lincoln, Director, Training and Safety
Phone: 315-369-3078
Fax: 315-369-3736
E-mail: mona@northernlogger.com

NORTH EAST ROOFING EDUCATIONAL FOUNDATION

http://www.nerca.org/

NORTH EAST ROOFING EDUCATIONAL FOUNDATION SCHOLARSHIP

Applicants must be a member of NERCA, their employees, or their respective immediate family. Immediate family is defined as self, spouse, or child. The child may be natural, legally adopted, or a stepchild. Also must be a high school senior or graduate who plans to enroll in a full-time undergraduate course of study at an accredited two-year or four-year college, university, or vocational-technical school.

Award: Scholarship for use in freshman, sophomore, junior, or senior years; not renewable. *Number:* 11. *Amount:* up to $2000.

Eligibility Requirements: Applicant must be enrolled or expecting to enroll full-time at a two-year or four-year or technical institution or university. Applicant or parent of applicant must be member of North East Roofing Contractors Association. Available to U.S. and Canadian citizens.

Application Requirements: Application form, recommendations or references, self-addressed stamped envelope with application, transcript. *Deadline:* May 1.

Contact: Patsy Sweeney, Clerk
North East Roofing Educational Foundation
150 Grossman Drive Street, Suite 313
Braintree, MA 02184
Phone: 781-849-0555
Fax: 781-849-3223
E-mail: info@nerca.org

OFFICE AND PROFESSIONAL EMPLOYEES INTERNATIONAL UNION

http://www.opeiu.org/

OFFICE AND PROFESSIONAL EMPLOYEES INTERNATIONAL UNION HOWARD COUGHLIN MEMORIAL SCHOLARSHIP FUND

Scholarship of twelve full-time awards of $6000 and six part-time awards of $2400 is given to undergraduate students. Applicants should be a member or associate member of the Union.

Award: Scholarship for use in freshman, sophomore, junior, or senior years; not renewable. *Number:* 18. *Amount:* $2400–$6000.

Eligibility Requirements: Applicant must be enrolled or expecting to enroll full- or part-time at a two-year or four-year or technical institution or university. Applicant or parent of applicant must be member of Office and Professional Employees International Union. Available to U.S. citizens.

Application Requirements: Application form, SAT/CAT scores, transcript. *Deadline:* March 31.

Contact: Mary Mahoney, Secretary-Treasurer
Phone: 202-393-4464
Fax: 202-887-0910
E-mail: mmahoney@opeiudc.org

OKLAHOMA ALUMNI & ASSOCIATES OF FHA, HERO AND FCCLA INC.

http://www.okalumni.org

OKLAHOMA ALUMNI & ASSOCIATES OF FHA, HERO, AND FCCLA INC. SCHOLARSHIP

One-time award for FCCLA members who will be pursuing a postsecondary education. Must be a resident of Oklahoma. Scholarship value is $1500. Two scholarships are granted.

Award: Scholarship for use in freshman year; not renewable. *Number:* 2. *Amount:* $1500.

Eligibility Requirements: Applicant must be high school student; planning to enroll or expecting to enroll full-time at a two-year or four-year or technical institution or university and resident of Oklahoma. Applicant or parent of applicant must be member of Family, Career and Community Leaders of America. Available to U.S. citizens.

Application Requirements: Application form, essay. *Deadline:* February 1.

Contact: Denise Morris, State FCCLA Adviser
Oklahoma Alumni & Associates of FHA, HERO and FCCLA Inc.
1500 West Seventh Avenue
Stillwater, OK 74074
Phone: 405-743-5467
E-mail: denise.morris@careertech.ok.gov

PENNSYLVANIA FEDERATION OF DEMOCRATIC WOMEN INC.

http://www.pafedofdemwomen.org

PENNSYLVANIA FEDERATION OF DEMOCRATIC WOMEN INC. ANNUAL SCHOLARSHIP AWARDS

Award of up to $1000 for any female resident of Pennsylvania who is a sophomore or junior at an accredited college or university and is a registered Democrat. Award is for their Junior or senior year. Applicants must possess a Democratic Party family background and be an active participant in activities of the Democratic Party.

Award: Scholarship for use in junior or senior years; not renewable. *Number:* 1–5. *Amount:* $250–$1000.

Eligibility Requirements: Applicant must be enrolled or expecting to enroll full-time at a four-year institution or university; female and resident of Pennsylvania. Applicant or parent of applicant must be member of Democratic Party. Available to U.S. citizens.

Application Requirements: Application form, essay. *Deadline:* April 1.

Contact: Michelle Price, Scholarship Chair
Pennsylvania Federation of Democratic Women Inc.
462 W Grant Street
Easton, PA 18042
Phone: 610-235-9599
E-mail: mbernsonprice@gmail.com

PHI ALPHA THETA HISTORY HONOR SOCIETY, INC.

http://www.phialphatheta.org/

PHI ALPHA THETA PAPER PRIZE AWARDS

Award for best graduate and undergraduate student papers. Grants $500 prize for best graduate student paper, $500 prize for best undergraduate paper, and four $400 prizes for either graduate or undergraduate papers. All applicants must be members of the association.

Award: Prize for use in freshman, sophomore, junior, senior, or graduate years; not renewable. *Number:* 6. *Amount:* $400–$500.

Eligibility Requirements: Applicant must be enrolled or expecting to enroll full-time at an institution or university. Applicant or parent of applicant must be member of Phi Alpha Theta. Available to U.S. and non-U.S. citizens.

Application Requirements: Essay. *Deadline:* July 1.

Contact: Christopher Kennedy, Office of Student Life
Phi Alpha Theta History Honor Society, Inc.
Francis Marion University
P.O. Box 100547
Florence, SC 29502-0547
E-mail: CKennedy@fmarion.edu

UNDERGRADUATE STUDENT SCHOLARSHIP

Awards of $1000 available to exceptional juniors entering the senior year and majoring in modern European history (1815 to present). Must be Phi Alpha Theta members. Based on both financial need and merit.

Award: Scholarship for use in senior year; not renewable. *Number:* 1. *Amount:* $1000.

Eligibility Requirements: Applicant must be enrolled or expecting to enroll full-time at an institution or university. Applicant or parent of applicant must be member of Phi Alpha Theta. Available to U.S. and non-U.S. citizens.

Application Requirements: Application form. *Deadline:* March 1.

Contact: Dr. Graydon Tunstall, Executive Director
Phi Alpha Theta History Honor Society, Inc.
University of South Florida
4202 East Fowler Avenue, SOC 107
Tampa, FL 33620-8100
Phone: 800-394-8195
Fax: 813-974-8215
E-mail: info@phialphatheta.org

PHILIPINO-AMERICAN ASSOCIATION OF NEW ENGLAND

http://www.pamas.org/

PAMAS RESTRICTED SCHOLARSHIP AWARD

Award of $500 for any sons or daughters of PAMAS members who are currently active in PAMAS projects and activities. Must be of Filipino descent, a resident of New England, a high school senior at the time of award, and have college acceptance letter from accredited institution. Minimum of 3.3 GPA required. For application details visit http://www.pamas.org.

Award: Scholarship for use in freshman year; not renewable. *Number:* 1. *Amount:* $500.

Eligibility Requirements: Applicant must be Asian/Pacific Islander; high school student; planning to enroll or expecting to enroll full-time at a four-year institution or university and resident of Connecticut, Maine, Massachusetts, New Hampshire, Rhode Island, Vermont. Applicant or parent of applicant must be member of Philipino-American Association. Available to U.S. citizens.

Application Requirements: Application form, college acceptance letter, essay, recommendations or references, transcript. *Deadline:* May 31.

Contact: Amanda Kalb, First Vice President
Phone: 617-471-3513
E-mail: balic2ss@comcast.net

PHI SIGMA KAPPA INTERNATIONAL HEADQUARTERS

http://www.phisigmakappa.org/

WENDEROTH UNDERGRADUATE SCHOLARSHIP

Available to sophomores and juniors on the basis of academic criteria. Must submit an essay and letter of recommendation along with the application.

Award: Scholarship for use in sophomore or junior years; not renewable. *Number:* 1–4. *Amount:* $1750–$4000.

Eligibility Requirements: Applicant must be enrolled or expecting to enroll full-time at a four-year institution or university. Applicant or parent of applicant must be member of Phi Sigma Kappa. Available to U.S. and non-U.S. citizens.

Application Requirements: Application form, essay, personal photograph, recommendations or references, resume, transcript. *Deadline:* January 31.

Contact: Michael Carey, Executive Director
Phone: 317-573-5420
Fax: 317-573-5430
E-mail: michael@phisigmakappa.org

ZETA SCHOLARSHIP

Scholarships are available following a generous gift to the Phi Sigma Kappa Foundation from the Zeta Alumni Association. Phi Sig or a child of a Phi Sig having minimum 3.0 GPA are eligible to apply.

Award: Scholarship for use in freshman, sophomore, junior, senior, or graduate years; not renewable. *Number:* 2. *Amount:* $2500.

Eligibility Requirements: Applicant must be enrolled or expecting to enroll full-time at a four-year institution or university. Applicant or parent of applicant must be member of Phi Sigma Kappa. Available to U.S. citizens.

Application Requirements: Application form, community service, personal photograph, recommendations or references, resume, test scores, transcript. *Deadline:* January 31.

Contact: Scholarship Program Coordinator
Phi Sigma Kappa International Headquarters
2925 East 96th Street
Indianapolis, IN 46240
Phone: 317-573-5420
Fax: 317-573-5430

PHI SIGMA PI NATIONAL HONOR FRATERNITY

http://www.phisigmapi.org/

RICHARD CECIL TODD AND CLAUDA PENNOCK TODD TRIPOD SCHOLARSHIP

Scholarship to promote the future academic opportunity of brothers (members) of the fraternity, who have excelled in embodying the ideals of scholarship, leadership, and fellowship. One-time award for full-time student, sophomore level or higher, with minimum 3.0 GPA.

Award: Scholarship for use in sophomore, junior, or senior years; not renewable. *Number:* 1. *Amount:* up to $1500.

Eligibility Requirements: Applicant must be enrolled or expecting to enroll full-time at a two-year or four-year or technical institution or university and must have an interest in leadership. Applicant or parent of applicant must be member of Greek Organization. Available to U.S. and non-U.S. citizens.

Application Requirements: Application form, driver's license, essay, recommendations or references, transcript. *Deadline:* April 15.

Contact: Suzanne Schaffer, Executive Director
Phone: 717-299-4710
Fax: 717-390-3054
E-mail: schaffer@phisigmapi.org

PONY OF THE AMERICAS CLUB INC.

http://www.poac.org/

POAC NATIONAL SCHOLARSHIP

Two to four renewable awards that may be used for any year or any institution but must be for full-time undergraduate study. Application and transcript required. Award restricted to those who have interest in animal or agricultural competition and active involvement in Pony Of the Americas organization.

Award: Scholarship for use in freshman, sophomore, junior, or senior years; not renewable. *Number:* 2–4. *Amount:* $500–$1000.

Eligibility Requirements: Applicant must be enrolled or expecting to enroll full- or part-time at a two-year or four-year or technical institution or university and must have an interest in animal/agricultural competition. Applicant or parent of applicant must be member of Pony of the Americas Club. Available to U.S. and non-U.S. citizens.

Application Requirements: Application form, driver's license, entry in a contest, essay, recommendations or references, transcript. *Deadline:* March 1.

Contact: Joyse Banister, Scholarship Administrator/CEO
Pony Of the Americas Club Inc.
3828 South Emerson Avenue
Indianapolis, IN 46203
Phone: 317-788-0107
Fax: 317-788-8974
E-mail: officemanager@poac.org

PROFESSIONAL HORSEMEN'S SCHOLARSHIP FUND INC.

http://www.nationalpha.com/

PROFESSIONAL HORSEMEN'S SCHOLARSHIP FUND

Scholarship provides financial assistance from a fund established for children of professional members of the Professional Horseman's Association who have been professional members for more than two years and who are enrolled in an approved school for the advancement of their education beyond the secondary level.

Award: Scholarship for use in freshman, sophomore, junior, senior, graduate, or postgraduate years; not renewable. *Number:* 10–20. *Amount:* $500–$1000.

Eligibility Requirements: Applicant must be enrolled or expecting to enroll full-time at a two-year or four-year or technical institution or university. Applicant or parent of applicant must be member of Professional Horsemen Association. Available to U.S. and non-U.S. citizens.

Application Requirements: Application form, autobiography, essay, financial need analysis, interview. *Deadline:* May 1.

Contact: Mrs. Ann Grenci, Chairman, Scholarship Committee
Phone: 561-707-9094
E-mail: foxhill33@aol.com

PROJECT BEST SCHOLARSHIP FUND

http://www.projectbest.com/

PROJECT BEST SCHOLARSHIP

One-time award of $1000 to $2000 for employees or children or spouses of employees working for a company or labor union in the construction industry that is affiliated with Project BEST. Must be residents of West Virginia, Pennsylvania, or Ohio and attend a West Virginia or Ohio postsecondary institution. Must be U.S. citizens.

Award: Scholarship for use in freshman, sophomore, junior, senior, or graduate years; renewable. *Number:* 11–22. *Amount:* $1000–$2000.

Eligibility Requirements: Applicant must be enrolled or expecting to enroll full-time at a two-year or four-year institution or university; resident of Ohio, Pennsylvania, West Virginia and studying in Ohio, West Virginia. Applicant or parent of applicant must be member of AFL-CIO. Applicant or parent of applicant must have employment or volunteer experience in construction. Available to U.S. citizens.

Application Requirements: Application form. *Deadline:* continuous.

Contact: Ginny Favede, Director
Project BEST Scholarship Fund
21 Armory Drive
Wheeling, WV 26003
Phone: 304-242-0520
E-mail: projectbest@projectbest.com

PUEBLO OF ISLETA, DEPARTMENT OF EDUCATION

http://www.isletapueblo.com/

HIGHER EDUCATION SUPPLEMENTAL SCHOLARSHIP ISLETA PUEBLO HIGHER EDUCATION DEPARTMENT

Applicants must be students seeking a postsecondary degree. The degree granting institution must be a nationally accredited vocational or postsecondary institution offering a certificate, Associate, Bachelor's, Master's, or Doctoral degree. Enrolled tribal members of the Isleta Pueblo may apply for this scholarship if they also apply for additional scholarships from different sources. Deadlines: April 1 for summer, November 1 for spring and July 1 for fall.

Award: Scholarship for use in freshman, sophomore, junior, senior, graduate, or postgraduate years; renewable.

Eligibility Requirements: Applicant must be American Indian/Alaska Native and enrolled or expecting to enroll full- or part-time at a two-year or four-year or technical institution or university. Applicant or parent of applicant must be member of Ice Skating Institute. Available to U.S. citizens.

Application Requirements: Application form, certificate of Indian blood, class schedule, financial need analysis, transcript. *Deadline:* varies.

Contact: Higher Education Director
Pueblo of Isleta, Department of Education
PO Box 1270
Isleta, NM 87022
Phone: 505-869-2680
Fax: 505-869-7690
E-mail: isletahighered@yahoo.com

RED ANGUS ASSOCIATION OF AMERICA

http://www.redangus.org/

4 RAAA/JUNIOR RED ANGUS SCHOLARSHIP

Scholarship of $500 given to active members of the National Junior Red Angus Association. Must be high school seniors or college underclassmen.

Award: Scholarship for use in freshman or sophomore years; not renewable. *Number:* 2. *Amount:* $500.

Eligibility Requirements: Applicant must be enrolled or expecting to enroll full-time at a two-year or four-year institution or university. Applicant or parent of applicant must be member of National Junior Red Angus Association. Available to U.S. citizens.

Application Requirements: Application form, personal photograph, recommendations or references, transcript. *Deadline:* March 31.

Contact: Betty Grimshaw, Association Administrative Director
Phone: 940-387-3502
Fax: 940-383-4036
E-mail: betty@redangus.org

DEE SONSTEGARD MEMORIAL SCHOLARSHIP

Scholarship of $500 given to active members of the National Junior Red Angus Association. Must be high school seniors or college underclassmen.

Award: Scholarship for use in freshman or sophomore years; not renewable. *Number:* 2. *Amount:* $500.

Eligibility Requirements: Applicant must be enrolled or expecting to enroll full-time at a two-year or four-year institution or university. Applicant or parent of applicant must be member of National Junior Red Angus Association. Available to U.S. citizens.

Application Requirements: Application form, personal photograph, recommendations or references, transcript. *Deadline:* March 31.

Contact: Betty Grimshaw, Association Administrative Director
Phone: 940-387-3502
Fax: 940-383-4036
E-mail: betty@redangus.org

FARM AND RANCH CONNECTION SCHOLARSHIP

Scholarship of $500 given to active members of the National Junior Red Angus Association. Must be high school seniors or college underclassmen.

Award: Scholarship for use in freshman or sophomore years; not renewable. *Number:* 1. *Amount:* $500.

Eligibility Requirements: Applicant must be enrolled or expecting to enroll full-time at a two-year or four-year institution or university. Applicant or parent of applicant must be member of National Junior Red Angus Association. Available to U.S. citizens.

Application Requirements: Application form, personal photograph, recommendations or references, transcript. *Deadline:* March 31.

Contact: Betty Grimshaw, Association Administrative Director
Phone: 940-387-3502
Fax: 940-383-4036
E-mail: betty@redangus.org

LEONARD A. LORENZEN MEMORIAL SCHOLARSHIP

Scholarship of $500 given to active members of the National Junior Red Angus Association. Must be high school seniors or college underclassmen.

Award: Scholarship for use in freshman or sophomore years; not renewable. *Number:* 2. *Amount:* $500.

Eligibility Requirements: Applicant must be enrolled or expecting to enroll full-time at a two-year or four-year institution or university. Applicant or parent of applicant must be member of National Junior Red Angus Association. Available to U.S. citizens.

Application Requirements: Application form, personal photograph, recommendations or references, transcript. *Deadline:* March 31.

Contact: Betty Grimshaw, Association Administrative Director
Phone: 940-387-3502
Fax: 940-383-4036
E-mail: betty@redangus.org

THE RESERVE OFFICERS ASSOCIATION

http://www.roa.org/

HENRY J. REILLY MEMORIAL SCHOLARSHIP-HIGH SCHOOL SENIORS AND FIRST YEAR FRESHMEN

One-time award for high school seniors or college freshmen who are U.S. citizens and children or grandchildren of active members of the Reserve Officers Association. Must demonstrate leadership, have minimum 3.0 GPA and 1250 on the SAT. Must submit sponsor verification. College freshmen must submit college transcript.

Award: Scholarship for use in freshman year; not renewable. *Number:* 25–30. *Amount:* $1000.

Eligibility Requirements: Applicant must be enrolled or expecting to enroll full-time at a four-year institution or university and must have an interest in leadership. Applicant or parent of applicant must be member of Reserve Officers Association. Available to U.S. citizens. Applicant or parent must meet one or more of the following requirements: general military experience; retired from active duty; disabled or killed as a result of military service; prisoner of war; or missing in action.

Application Requirements: Application form, essay, test scores, transcript. *Deadline:* May 15.

Contact: Rebecca Riedler, Executive Administrator
Phone: 202-646-7706
E-mail: scholarship@roa.org

HENRY J. REILLY MEMORIAL UNDERGRADUATE SCHOLARSHIP PROGRAM FOR COLLEGE ATTENDEES

One-time award of $1000 for members and children or grandchildren of members of the Reserve Officers Association or its Auxiliary. Must be a U.S. citizen, 26 years old or younger, and enrolled at an accredited four-year institution. Must submit sponsor verification. Minimum 3.0 GPA required. Submit SAT or ACT scores; contact for score requirements.

Award: Scholarship for use in freshman, sophomore, junior, or senior years; not renewable. *Number:* 25–30. *Amount:* $1000.

Eligibility Requirements: Applicant must be age 26 or under and enrolled or expecting to enroll full-time at a two-year or four-year institution or university. Applicant or parent of applicant must be member of Reserve Officers Association. Available to U.S. citizens. Applicant or parent must meet one or more of the following requirements: general military experience; retired from active duty; disabled or killed as a result of military service; prisoner of war; or missing in action.

Application Requirements: Application form, essay, sponsor verification, test scores, transcript. *Deadline:* May 15.

Contact: Rebecca Riedler, Executive Administrator
Phone: 202-646-7706
E-mail: scholarship@roa.org

RETAIL, WHOLESALE AND DEPARTMENT STORE UNION

http://www.rwdsu.org/

ALVIN E. HEAPS MEMORIAL SCHOLARSHIP

Scholarship for RWDSU members or members of an RWDSU family. Applicant must submit 500-word essay on the benefits of union membership. See website for application http://www.rwdsu.info/rwdsu-scholarship

Award: Scholarship for use in freshman, sophomore, junior, or senior years; not renewable.

Eligibility Requirements: Applicant must be enrolled or expecting to enroll full- or part-time at a two-year or four-year institution or university. Applicant or parent of applicant must be member of Retail, Wholesale and Department Store Union. Available to U.S. citizens.

Application Requirements: Application form, essay. *Deadline:* July 15.

Contact: Scholarship Committee
Phone: 212-684-5300
Fax: 212-779-2809

RHODE ISLAND FOUNDATION

http://www.rifoundation.org/

EDWARD LEON DUHAMEL FREEMASONS SCHOLARSHIP

Renewable scholarship for descendants of members of Franklin Lodge in Westerly Rhode Island. Must be accepted into an accredited postsecondary institution. Must demonstrate scholastic achievement, financial need, and good citizenship.

Award: Scholarship for use in freshman, sophomore, junior, or senior years; renewable. *Amount:* $500–$1000.

Eligibility Requirements: Applicant must be enrolled or expecting to enroll full-time at a four-year institution or university. Applicant or parent of applicant must be member of Freemasons. Available to U.S. citizens.

Application Requirements: Application form, essay, financial need analysis, self-addressed stamped envelope with application, transcript. *Deadline:* varies.

Contact: Kelly Riley, Donor Services Administrator
Phone: 401-427-4028
E-mail: kriley@rifoundation.org

SERVICE EMPLOYEES INTERNATIONAL UNION (SEIU)

http://www.seiu.org/

SEIU JESSE JACKSON SCHOLARSHIP PROGRAM

Renewable scholarship of $5000 given to a student whose work and aspirations for economic and social justice reflect the values and accomplishments of the Rev. Jackson.

Award: Scholarship for use in freshman, sophomore, junior, or senior years; renewable. *Number:* 1. *Amount:* $5000.

Eligibility Requirements: Applicant must be enrolled or expecting to enroll full-time at a four-year institution or university. Applicant or parent of applicant must be member of Service Employees International Union. Available to U.S. citizens.

Application Requirements: Application form, essay. *Deadline:* March 1.

Contact: c/o Scholarship Program Administrators, Inc.
Phone: 615-320-3149
Fax: 615-320-3151
E-mail: info@spaprog.com

SEIU JOHN GEAGAN SCHOLARSHIP

Scholarship to SEIU members or their children or SEIU local union staff. Priority will be given to those applicants who are not served by traditional education institutions-typically adults who have been in the workforce and have decided to go, or return to, college.

Award: Scholarship for use in freshman, sophomore, junior, or senior years; not renewable. *Number:* 1. *Amount:* $2500.

Eligibility Requirements: Applicant must be enrolled or expecting to enroll full-time at a two-year or four-year or technical institution or university. Applicant or parent of applicant must be member of Service Employees International Union. Available to U.S. citizens.

Application Requirements: Application form, essay. *Deadline:* March 1.

Contact: c/o Scholarship Program Administrators, Inc.
Phone: 615-320-3149
Fax: 615-320-3151
E-mail: info@spaprog.com

SEIU NORA PIORE SCHOLARSHIP PROGRAM

Renewable award of $4375 to SEIU members enrolled full-time in an undergraduate study. Applicant's financial need will be considered during the selection process.

Award: Scholarship for use in freshman, sophomore, junior, or senior years; renewable. *Number:* 1. *Amount:* $4375.

Eligibility Requirements: Applicant must be enrolled or expecting to enroll full-time at a four-year institution or university. Applicant or parent of applicant must be member of Service Employees International Union. Available to U.S. citizens.

Application Requirements: Application form. *Deadline:* March 1.

Contact: c/o Scholarship Program Administrators, Inc.
Phone: 615-320-3149
Fax: 615-320-3151
E-mail: info@spaprog.com

SEIU SCHOLARSHIP PROGRAM

Fifteen $1000 scholarships available in annual installments for up to four years. Applicants must graduate from a high school or GED program by August. Must be enrolled as a full-time college freshman by the fall semester at an accredited, four-year college or university.

Award: Scholarship for use in freshman year; renewable. *Number:* 15. *Amount:* $1000.

Eligibility Requirements: Applicant must be high school student and planning to enroll or expecting to enroll full-time at a four-year institution or university. Applicant or parent of applicant must be member of Service Employees International Union. Available to U.S. citizens.

Application Requirements: Application form. *Deadline:* March 1.

Contact: c/o Scholarship Program Administrators, Inc.
Phone: 615-320-3149
Fax: 615-320-3151
E-mail: info@spaprog.com

SIGMA ALPHA MU

http://www.sam-fdn.org

UNDERGRADUATE ACHIEVEMENT AWARDS

Scholarship for seniors or juniors of undergraduate students enrolled full-time study. Must be member of Sigma Alpha Mu Foundation. Scholarship value varies.

Award: Scholarship for use in junior or senior years; not renewable. *Number:* 2.

Eligibility Requirements: Applicant must be enrolled or expecting to enroll full-time at a four-year institution or university. Applicant or parent of applicant must be member of Sigma Alpha Mu Foundation. Available to U.S. citizens.

Application Requirements: Application form. *Deadline:* February 1.

Contact: Maria Mandel, Director of Scholarships and Donor Relations
Phone: 317-789-8339
Fax: 317-824-1505
E-mail: mariam@sam-fdn.org

YOUNG SCHOLARS PROGRAM

Scholarship for candidates achieving a 3.75 GPA (or equivalent) for courses taken in the academic term of the undergraduate study. Must be member of Sigma Alpha Mu Foundation. Deadline varies.

Award: Scholarship for use in freshman, sophomore, junior, or senior years; not renewable. *Amount:* $500.

Eligibility Requirements: Applicant must be enrolled or expecting to enroll full-time at a four-year institution or university. Applicant or parent of applicant must be member of Sigma Alpha Mu Foundation. Available to U.S. citizens.

Application Requirements: Application form.

Contact: Maria Mandel, Director of Scholarships and Donor Relations
Phone: 317-789-8339
Fax: 317-824-1505
E-mail: mariam@sam-fdn.org

SIGMA CHI FOUNDATION

https://sigmachi.org/

SIGMA CHI FOUNDATION - GENERAL UNDERGRADUATE SCHOLARSHIP

Applicants must have completed three semesters (or four quarters) of undergraduate study to be considered for current year awards. Funds are available for tuition/fees payments only.

Award: Scholarship for use in sophomore, junior, or senior years; not renewable. *Amount:* $1000.

Eligibility Requirements: Applicant must be enrolled or expecting to enroll full-time at an institution or university and male. Applicant or parent of applicant must be member of Sigma Chi Fraternity. Available to U.S. and non-U.S. citizens.

Application Requirements: Application form, application form may be submitted online, financial need analysis. *Deadline:* March 30.

Contact: Heidi Holley
Sigma Chi Foundation
1714 Hinman Avenue
Evanston, IL 60201
Phone: 847-425-4470
Fax: 847-869-4906
E-mail: heidi.holley@sigmachi.org

SLOVAK GYMNASTIC UNION SOKOL, USA

http://www.sokolusa.org/

SOKOL, USA/MILAN GETTING SCHOLARSHIP

Available to members of SOKOL, U.S.A who have been in good standing for at least three years. Must have plans to attend college. Renewable for a maximum of four years, based upon academic achievement. Minimum GPA 2.5 required.

Award: Grant for use in freshman, sophomore, junior, or senior years; renewable. *Number:* 4–8. *Amount:* $500.

Eligibility Requirements: Applicant must be enrolled or expecting to enroll full-time at a four-year institution or university. Applicant or parent of applicant must be member of SOKOL, USA. Available to U.S. citizens.

Application Requirements: Application form. *Deadline:* April 1.

Contact: Milan Kovac, Fraternal Secretary
Slovak Gymnastic Union SOKOL, USA
301 Pine Street
PO Box 677
Boonton, NJ 07005-0677
Phone: 973-676-0281
E-mail: sokolusahqs@aol.com

SLOVENIAN WOMEN'S UNION SCHOLARSHIP FOUNDATION

http://www.swusf.org

SLOVENIAN WOMEN'S UNION OF AMERICA SCHOLARSHIP FOUNDATION

one time award for full-time study only. Essay, transcripts, letters of recommendation from principal/teacher, financial need form, photo, civic and church activities information required. Open to high school seniors. One graduate school scholarship of $2,000 available to student majoring in education. Membership in Slovenian Women's Union not required. Applicant must be of Slovenian ancestry. One Graduate school scholarship of $2,000 available to student majoring in science, mathematics, or engineering. Membership in Slovenian Women's Union not required. Applicant must be of Slovenian ancestry.

Award: Scholarship for use in freshman, sophomore, junior, senior, or graduate years; not renewable. *Number:* 6–12. *Amount:* $1000–$2000.

Eligibility Requirements: Applicant must be enrolled or expecting to enroll full- or part-time at a two-year or four-year or technical institution or university. Applicant or parent of applicant must be member of Slovenian Women's Union of America. Available to U.S. citizens.

Application Requirements: Application form, autobiography, community service, essay, financial need analysis, personal photograph. *Deadline:* March 1.

Contact: Mary Turvey, Director
Slovenian Women's Union Scholarship Foundation
4 Lawrence Drive
Marquette, MI 49855
Phone: 906-249-4288
E-mail: mturvey@aol.com

SOIL AND WATER CONSERVATION SOCIETY

http://www.swcs.org

MELVILLE H. COHEE STUDENT LEADER CONSERVATION SCHOLARSHIP

The scholarship honors SWCS members who succeed as leaders in their studies, volunteerism, and work. Members who are in their junior or senior year of full-time undergraduate study or pursuing graduate level studies with a natural resource conservation orientation at a properly accredited college or university are eligible.

Award: Scholarship for use in junior, senior, graduate, or postgraduate years; not renewable. *Number:* 1. *Amount:* up to $500.

Eligibility Requirements: Applicant must be enrolled or expecting to enroll full-time at a four-year institution or university. Applicant or parent of applicant must be member of Soil and Water Conservation Society. Available to U.S. and non-U.S. citizens.

Application Requirements: Application form, essay, recommendations or references, transcript. *Deadline:* February 13.

Contact: SWCS Scholarships Program Coordinator
Soil and Water Conservation Society
945 SW Ankeny Road
Ankeny, IA 50023-9723
Phone: 515-289-2331 Ext. 114
E-mail: scholarships@swcs.org

SONS OF NORWAY FOUNDATION

http://www.sonsofnorway.com/foundation

ASTRID G. CATES AND MYRTLE BEINHAUER SCHOLARSHIP FUNDS

Merit award available to students ages 17 to 22 who are current members, children, or grandchildren of members of the Sons of Norway. School transcript required. Academic potential and clarity of study plan is key criterion for award. Minimum 3.0 GPA required.

Award: Scholarship for use in freshman, sophomore, junior, or senior years; not renewable. *Number:* 2–7. *Amount:* $1000–$3000.

Eligibility Requirements: Applicant must be age 17-22 and enrolled or expecting to enroll full-time at a two-year or four-year or technical institution or university. Applicant or parent of applicant must be member of Mutual Benefit Society. Available to U.S. citizens.

Application Requirements: Application form, application form may be submitted online (http://www.sonsofnorway.com/foundation), community service, essay, personal photograph, recommendations or references, test scores, transcript. *Deadline:* March 1.

Contact: Scholarship Coordinator
Sons of Norway Foundation
1455 West Lake Street
Minneapolis, MN 55408-2666
Phone: 612-827-3611
E-mail: foundation@sofn.com

SUPREME GUARDIAN COUNCIL, INTERNATIONAL ORDER OF JOB'S DAUGHTERS

http://www.iojd.org/

SUPREME GUARDIAN COUNCIL SCHOLARSHIP

Scholarships of $750 to aid Job's Daughters students of outstanding ability whom have a sincerity of purpose. High school seniors, or graduates, junior college, technical school, or college students who are in early graduation programs, are eligible to apply.

Award: Scholarship for use in freshman, sophomore, junior, senior, graduate, or postgraduate years; not renewable. *Number:* 5–10. *Amount:* $750.

Eligibility Requirements: Applicant must be age 18-30; enrolled or expecting to enroll full- or part-time at a two-year or four-year or technical institution or university and single female. Applicant or parent of applicant must be member of Jobs Daughters. Available to U.S. and non-U.S. citizens.

Application Requirements: Application form, community service, essay, financial need analysis, recommendation from Executive Bethel Guardian Council, achievements outside of Job's Daughters, recommendations or references. *Deadline:* April 30.

Contact: Christal Bindrich, Scholarship Committee Chairman
Supreme Guardian Council, International Order of Job's Daughters
5351 South Butterfield Way
Greenfield, WI 53221
Phone: 414-423-0016
E-mail: christalbindrich@wi.rr.com

SUSIE HOLMES MEMORIAL SCHOLARSHIP

Scholarships of $1000 awarded to Job's Daughters high school students with a minimum of 2.5 GPA.

Award: Scholarship for use in freshman, sophomore, junior, senior, graduate, or postgraduate years; not renewable. *Number:* 1. *Amount:* $1000.

Eligibility Requirements: Applicant must be age 18-30; enrolled or expecting to enroll full-time at a two-year or four-year or technical institution or university and single female. Applicant or parent of applicant must be member of Jobs Daughters. Available to U.S. and non-U.S. citizens.

Application Requirements: Application form, community service, essay, recommendations or references, test scores, transcript. *Deadline:* April 30.

Contact: Christal Bindrich, Scholarship Committee Chairman
Supreme Guardian Council, International Order of Job's Daughters
5351 South Butterfield Way
Greenfield, WI 53221
Phone: 414-423-0016
E-mail: christalbindrich@wi.rr.com

TAU KAPPA EPSILON EDUCATIONAL FOUNDATION

http://www.tke.org/

CHARLES J. TRABOLD SCHOLARSHIP

One-time award of $1200 given to an undergraduate member of Tau Kappa Epsilon who has demonstrated leadership ability within his chapter, campus, or community. Must be a full-time student in good standing with a GPA of 3.0 or higher. Preference will first be given to a member of Kappa-Kappa Chapter (Monmouth) but, if there is no qualified applicant, the scholarship will be open to any other qualified Teke.

Award: Scholarship for use in sophomore, junior, or senior years; not renewable. *Number:* 1. *Amount:* $1200.

Eligibility Requirements: Applicant must be enrolled or expecting to enroll full-time at a four-year institution or university; male and must have an interest in leadership. Applicant or parent of applicant must be member of Tau Kappa Epsilon. Available to U.S. and non-U.S. citizens.

Application Requirements: Application form, application form may be submitted online (http://www.tke.org/member_resources/scholarships/apply_online), essay, personal photograph, transcript. *Deadline:* March 15.

Contact: Rachel Stevenson, Foundation Communications Manager
Phone: 317-872-6533 Ext. 246
E-mail: rstevenson@tke.org

J.D. WILLIAMS SCHOLARSHIP

One-time award of $500 given to an undergraduate member of Tau Kappa Epsilon who has demonstrated leadership ability within his chapter, campus, or community. Must be a full-time student in good standing.

Award: Scholarship for use in sophomore, junior, or senior years; not renewable. *Number:* 1. *Amount:* $500.

Eligibility Requirements: Applicant must be enrolled or expecting to enroll full-time at a four-year institution or university; male and must have an interest in leadership. Applicant or parent of applicant must be member of Tau Kappa Epsilon. Available to U.S. and non-U.S. citizens.

Application Requirements: Application form, application form may be submitted online (http://www.tke.org/member_resources/scholarships/apply_online), essay, personal photograph, transcript. *Deadline:* March 15.

Contact: Rachel Stevenson, Foundation Communications Manager
Phone: 317-872-6533 Ext. 246
E-mail: rstevenson@tke.org

J. RUSSEL SALSBURY MEMORIAL SCHOLARSHIP

One-time award of $200 given to an undergraduate member of Tau Kappa Epsilon who has demonstrated leadership ability within his chapter, campus, or community. Must be a full-time student in good standing with a GPA of 3.0 or higher.

Award: Scholarship for use in sophomore, junior, or senior years; not renewable. *Number:* 1. *Amount:* $200.

Eligibility Requirements: Applicant must be enrolled or expecting to enroll full-time at a four-year institution or university; male and must have an interest in leadership. Applicant or parent of applicant must be member of Tau Kappa Epsilon. Available to U.S. and non-U.S. citizens.

Application Requirements: Application form, application form may be submitted online (http://www.tke.org/member_resources/scholarships/apply_online), essay, personal photograph, transcript. *Deadline:* March 15.

Contact: Rachel Stevenson, Foundation Communications Manager
Phone: 317-872-6533 Ext. 246
E-mail: rstevenson@tke.org

MILES GRAY MEMORIAL SCHOLARSHIP

One-time award of $300 given to an undergraduate member of Tau Kappa Epsilon who has demonstrated leadership ability within his chapter, campus, or community. Must be a full-time student in good standing with a GPA of 3.0 or higher.

Award: Scholarship for use in sophomore, junior, or senior years; not renewable. *Number:* 1. *Amount:* $300.

Eligibility Requirements: Applicant must be enrolled or expecting to enroll full-time at a four-year institution or university; male and must have an interest in leadership. Applicant or parent of applicant must be member of Tau Kappa Epsilon. Available to U.S. and non-U.S. citizens.

Application Requirements: Application form, application form may be submitted online (http://www.tke.org/member_resources/scholarships/apply_online), essay, personal photograph, transcript. *Deadline:* March 15.

Contact: Rachel Stevenson, Foundation Communications Manager
Phone: 317-872-6533 Ext. 246
E-mail: rstevenson@tke.org

TEXAS AFL-CIO

http://www.texasaflcio.org/

TEXAS AFL-CIO SCHOLARSHIP PROGRAM

Award for sons or daughters of members of unions affiliated with the Texas AFL-CIO and the appropriate Central Labor Council. Selection by interview/testing process. One-time awards of $1000. Applicant must be a graduating high school senior and Texas resident. Previous winners may apply for a limited number of continuing scholarships.

Award: Scholarship for use in freshman, sophomore, junior, or senior years; not renewable. *Number:* 20–35. *Amount:* $1000.

Eligibility Requirements: Applicant must be high school student; planning to enroll or expecting to enroll full-time at a two-year or four-year or technical institution or university and resident of Texas. Applicant or parent of applicant must be member of AFL-CIO. Available to U.S. citizens.

Application Requirements: Application form, essay, financial need analysis, interview, personal photograph. *Deadline:* January 31.

Contact: Mr. Edward Sills, Director of Communications
Texas AFL-CIO
PO Box 12727
Austin, TX 78701
Phone: 512-477-6195
Fax: 512-477-2962
E-mail: ed@texasaflcio.org

UNITED DAUGHTERS OF THE CONFEDERACY

http://www.hqudc.org/

UNITED DAUGHTERS OF THE CONFEDERACY UNDERGRADUATE SCHOLARSHIPS

Renewable award for undergraduate students who are descendants of an eligible Confederate soldier. Must be enrolled in an accredited college or university. Minimum 3.0 GPA required. Applicants must be endorsed by the President and the Second Vice President/Education Chairman of Chapter and Division, and by the Second Vice President General. Applications are submitted through local chapters.

Award: Scholarship for use in freshman, sophomore, junior, or senior years; renewable. *Number:* 18–30. *Amount:* $800–$1000.

Eligibility Requirements: Applicant must be enrolled or expecting to enroll full-time at a two-year or four-year institution or university. Applicant or parent of applicant must be member of United Daughters of the Confederacy. Available to U.S. citizens.

Application Requirements: Application form, copy of applicant's birth certificate, copy of confederate ancestor's proof of service, essay, financial need analysis, personal photograph, recommendations or references, self-addressed stamped envelope with application, test scores, transcript. *Deadline:* March 15.

Contact: Second Vice President General
Phone: 804-355-1636
E-mail: udc@hqudc.org

UNITED FOOD AND COMMERCIAL WORKERS INTERNATIONAL UNION

http://www.ufcw.org/

JAMES A. SUFFRIDGE UNITED FOOD AND COMMERCIAL WORKERS SCHOLARSHIP PROGRAM

Scholarships available to graduating high school seniors and college students during the specific program year. Must be an active member of UFCW or unmarried dependent under age 20 of a UFCW member. Scholarship is disbursed over a four-year period.

Award: Scholarship for use in freshman, sophomore, junior, or senior years; renewable. *Number:* 14–20. *Amount:* up to $8000.

Eligibility Requirements: Applicant must be age 20 or under and enrolled or expecting to enroll full- or part-time at a two-year or four-year or technical institution or university. Applicant or parent of applicant must be member of United Food and Commercial Workers. Available to U.S. and Canadian citizens.

Application Requirements: Application form, community service, essay, transcript. *Deadline:* April 15.

Contact: Field Assistant
United Food and Commercial Workers International Union
1775 K Street, NW
Washington, DC 20006
Phone: 202-223-3111
Fax: 202-721-8008
E-mail: scholarship@ufcw.org

UNITED STATES SUBMARINE VETERANS

https://www.ussvi.org/Documents.asp?Type=Scholarship|Application

UNITED STATES SUBMARINE VETERANS INC. NATIONAL SCHOLARSHIP PROGRAM

Program requires the sponsor to be a qualified Base Member or Member-at-Large in good standing. Must demonstrate financial need, have a minimum 2.5 GPA, and submit an essay. Open to children, stepchildren, and grandchildren of qualified members. Applicants must be between the ages of 17 to 23 and must be unmarried.

Award: Scholarship for use in freshman, sophomore, junior, or senior years; not renewable. *Number:* 2–18. *Amount:* $950–$1500.

Eligibility Requirements: Applicant must be age 17-23; enrolled or expecting to enroll full-time at a two-year or four-year or technical institution or university and single. Applicant or parent of applicant must be member of Veterans of Foreign Wars or Auxiliary. Applicant or parent of applicant must have employment or volunteer experience in seafaring/fishing industry. Available to U.S. citizens. Applicant or parent must meet one or more of the following requirements: Navy experience; retired from active duty; disabled or killed as a result of military service; prisoner of war; or missing in action.

Application Requirements: Application form, essay, financial need analysis, recommendations or references, transcript. *Deadline:* April 15.

Contact: Paul Orstad, National Scholarship Chairman
United States Submarine Veterans
30 Surrey Lane
Norwich, CT 06369-6541
Phone: 860-334-6457
E-mail: hogan343@aol.com

USA BMX

http://usabmx.com

BOB WARNICKE MEMORIAL SCHOLARSHIP PROGRAM

Scholarship assists students and their families in meeting the costs of undergraduate or trade school education. Applicant must be a high school senior, graduate or attending a postsecondary school at the time of application, or accepted and plan to attend an accredited postsecondary school as a full-time or part-time student for the complete award year. Must be an active member or official of USA BMX.

Award: Scholarship for use in freshman, sophomore, junior, senior, graduate, or postgraduate years; not renewable.

Eligibility Requirements: Applicant must be enrolled or expecting to enroll full- or part-time at a two-year or four-year or technical institution or university. Applicant or parent of applicant must be member of National Bicycle League. Available to U.S. and non-U.S. citizens.

Application Requirements: Application form, essay, personal photograph. *Deadline:* March 6.

Contact: Scholarship Committee
Phone: 480-961-1903

UTILITY WORKERS UNION OF AMERICA

https://www.uwua.net/

UTILITY WORKERS UNION OF AMERICA SCHOLARSHIP AWARDS PROGRAM

Renewable award for high school juniors who are children of active members of the Utility Workers Union of America. Must take the PSAT National Merit Scholarship Qualifying Test in junior year and plan to enter college in the fall after high school graduation.

Award: Scholarship for use in freshman, sophomore, junior, or senior years; renewable. *Number:* 2. *Amount:* $500–$2000.

Eligibility Requirements: Applicant must be high school student and planning to enroll or expecting to enroll full-time at a four-year institution or university. Applicant or parent of applicant must be member of Utility Workers Union of America. Available to U.S. citizens.

Application Requirements: Application form. *Deadline:* May 31.

Contact: Ms. Stacy Paulo, Executive Assistant to the National Secretary-Treasurer
Utility Workers Union of America
1300 L St. NW
Suite 1200
Washington, DC 20002
Phone: 202-899-2851
Fax: 202-899-2852
E-mail: spaulo@uwua.net

WESTERN FRATERNAL LIFE ASSOCIATION

http://www.wflains.org

WESTERN FRATERNAL LIFE NATIONAL SCHOLARSHIP

Western Fraternal Life Association is pleased to announce 26 national scholarships for its eligible members. The 26 national scholarships include the following: 1. one four-year academic scholarship, $1,000 per year for a total of $4,000; 2. two $1,000 scholarships to either community college or vocational/trade school; 3. one $1,000 community involvement scholarship; 4. one $1,000 non-traditional student scholarship. Traditional and non-traditional students are eligible. Must be a Western Fraternal Life Association member in good standing for two years prior to the application deadline. A member is an individual who has life insurance or an annuity with Western. High school seniors may apply. Members who are qualified for the National Scholarship may also qualify for state and local lodge scholarships. You are eligible to win this scholarship four times.

Award: Scholarship for use in freshman, sophomore, junior, senior, graduate, or postgraduate years; renewable. *Number:* 26. *Amount:* $1000.

Eligibility Requirements: Applicant must be enrolled or expecting to enroll full-time at a two-year or four-year or technical institution or university and resident of Colorado, Illinois, Iowa, Kansas, Louisiana, Michigan, Minnesota, Missouri, Nebraska, North Dakota, Oklahoma, Oregon, Pennsylvania, South Dakota, Texas, Washington, Wisconsin. Applicant or parent of applicant must be member of Western Fraternal Life Association. Available to U.S. citizens.

Application Requirements: Application form, application form may be submitted online (http://www.wflains.org), essay, test scores. *Deadline:* March 1.

Contact: Darcy Hilton, Member Programs Coordinator
Western Fraternal Life Association
1900 First Avenue NE
Cedar Rapids, IA 52402
Phone: 877-935-2467 Ext. 131
Fax: 319-363-8806
E-mail: dhilton@wflains.org

WISCONSIN ASSOCIATION FOR FOOD PROTECTION

http://www.wifoodprotection.org

WAFP MEMORIAL SCHOLARSHIP

Scholarship for a child or dependent of a current or deceased WAFP member, or the applicant may be a WAFP student member. Must have been accepted into an accredited degree program in a university, college, or technical institute.

Award: Scholarship for use in sophomore, junior, senior, or graduate years; not renewable. *Number:* 1. *Amount:* $1000.

Eligibility Requirements: Applicant must be enrolled or expecting to enroll full-time at a two-year or four-year or technical institution or university. Applicant or parent of applicant must be member of Wisconsin Association for Food Protection. Available to U.S. and non-U.S. citizens.

Application Requirements: Application form. *Deadline:* July 1.

Contact: Mr. Jim Wickert, Scholarship Committee Chairman
Wisconsin Association for Food Protection
3834 Ridgeway Avenue
Madison, WI 53704
Phone: 608-241-2438
E-mail: jwick16060@tds.net

WOMEN IN AVIATION, INTERNATIONAL

http://www.wai.org/

AIRBUS LEADERSHIP GRANT

One $5,000 scholarship will be awarded to a student at the college level of sophomore year or above who is pursuing a degree in an aviation-related field, who has achieved a minimum GPA of 3.0 (on a 4.0 scale) and who exhibits leadership potential. In addition to WAI requirements all applicants should submit a 500-word essay which addresses their career aspirations and clear, concise examples of how they have exhibited leadership in their academic/work/personal life.

Award: Scholarship for use in sophomore, junior, or senior years; not renewable. *Number:* 1. *Amount:* $5000.

Eligibility Requirements: Applicant must be enrolled or expecting to enroll full- or part-time at an institution or university and must have an interest in leadership. Applicant or parent of applicant must be member of Women in Aviation, International. Available to U.S. and non-U.S. citizens.

Application Requirements: Application form, essay. *Deadline:* November 12.

Contact: Donna Wallace, Exhibit Coordinator/Scholarship Coordinator
Women in Aviation, International
3647 State Route 503 South
West Alexandria, OH 45381
Phone: 937-839-4647
Fax: 937-839-4645
E-mail: dwallace@wai.org

WOMEN IN AVIATION, INTERNATIONAL ACHIEVEMENT AWARDS

One scholarship will be awarded to a full-time college or university student pursuing any type of aviation or aviation related career. A second scholarship will be awarded to an individual, not required to be a student, pursuing any type of aviation interest. Include in your essay how you plan to use the scholarship if awarded and what you have accomplished to date to reach your goals. Must be a member of WAI.

Award: Scholarship for use in freshman, sophomore, junior, or senior years; not renewable. *Number:* 2. *Amount:* $1000.

Eligibility Requirements: Applicant must be enrolled or expecting to enroll full-time at a two-year institution or university. Applicant or parent of applicant must be member of Women in Aviation, International. Available to U.S. and non-U.S. citizens.

Application Requirements: Application form. *Deadline:* November 12.

Contact: Donna Wallace, Exhibit Coordinator/Scholarship Coordinator
Women in Aviation, International
3647 State Route 503 South
West Alexandria, OH 45381
Phone: 937-839-4647
Fax: 937-839-4645
E-mail: dwallace@wai.org

WOMEN IN CORPORATE AVIATION CAREER SCHOLARSHIPS

Scholarship will be given to a person pursuing professional development or career advancement in any job classification in corporate/business aviation. Applicants should be actively working toward their goal and show financial need. Award can be used toward a specific program of education, flight training, dispatcher training, or upgrades in aviation education, and so forth, but cannot include general business course work. If you are a pilot please submit copies of pilot licenses, medical and the last three pages of logbook with your application. Must be a member of WAI.

Award: Scholarship for use in freshman, sophomore, junior, or senior years; not renewable. *Number:* 1. *Amount:* $2000.

Eligibility Requirements: Applicant must be enrolled or expecting to enroll full- or part-time at a two-year or technical institution or university

and female. Applicant or parent of applicant must be member of Women in Aviation, International. Available to U.S. and non-U.S. citizens.

Application Requirements: Application form, essay, financial need analysis. *Deadline:* November 12.

Contact: Donna Wallace, Exhibit Coordinator/Scholarship Coordinator
Women in Aviation, International
3647 State Route 503 South
West Alexandria, OH 45381
Phone: 937-839-4647
Fax: 937-839-4645
E-mail: dwallace@wai.org

WYOMING FARM BUREAU FEDERATION

http://www.wyfb.org/

LIVINGSTON FAMILY - H.J. KING MEMORIAL SCHOLARSHIP

One-time award given to graduates of Wyoming high schools. Must attend a Wyoming junior college or the University of Wyoming. Minimum 2.5 GPA required. If Applicant is under 18 years of age, the applicant must have an immediate family member or guardian that is a current member of the Wyoming Farm Bureau Federation at the time of applying.

Award: Scholarship for use in freshman, sophomore, junior, senior, or graduate years; not renewable. *Number:* 1. *Amount:* $1500.

Eligibility Requirements: Applicant must be enrolled or expecting to enroll full-time at a two-year or four-year institution or university; resident of Wyoming and studying in Wyoming. Applicant or parent of applicant must be member of Wyoming Farm Bureau. Available to U.S. and non-U.S. citizens.

Application Requirements: Application form, financial need analysis, personal photograph. *Deadline:* March 1.

Contact: McKenzi Digby, Administrative Assistant
Wyoming Farm Bureau Federation
PO Box 1348
Laramie, WY 82073
Phone: 307-721-7719
E-mail: mdigby@wyfb.org

WYOMING FARM BUREAU CONTINUING EDUCATION SCHOLARSHIPS

Award to students attending a two-year college in Wyoming or the University of Wyoming. Must be a resident of Wyoming and if 18 years or older, must be a current member of the Wyoming Farm Bureau Federation. If under 18, applicant must have an immediate family member or guardian that is a current member of the Wyoming Farm Bureau Federation at the time of applying. Must submit at least two semesters of college grade transcripts. Freshmen must submit first semester grades and proof of enrollment in second semester. Minimum 2.5 GPA.

Award: Scholarship for use in freshman, sophomore, junior, senior, or graduate years; not renewable. *Number:* 3. *Amount:* $500.

Eligibility Requirements: Applicant must be enrolled or expecting to enroll full-time at a two-year or four-year institution or university; resident of Wyoming and studying in Wyoming. Applicant or parent of applicant must be member of Wyoming Farm Bureau. Available to U.S. and non-U.S. citizens.

Application Requirements: Application form, financial need analysis, personal photograph. *Deadline:* March 1.

Contact: McKenzi Digby, Administrative Assistant
Wyoming Farm Bureau Federation
PO Box 1348
Laramie, WY 82073
Phone: 307-721-7719
E-mail: mdigby@wyfb.org

WYOMING FARM BUREAU FEDERATION SCHOLARSHIPS

Five $500 scholarships will be given to graduates of Wyoming high schools. Eligible candidates must be enrolled in a two-year college in Wyoming or the University of Wyoming and must have a minimum 2.5 GPA. If 18 years or older, applicant must be a current paid member of the Wyoming Farm Bureau Federation at the time of applying. If under 18, applicant must have an immediate family member or guardian that is a current member of the Wyoming Farm Bureau Federation.

Award: Scholarship for use in freshman, sophomore, junior, senior, or graduate years; not renewable. *Number:* 5. *Amount:* $500.

Eligibility Requirements: Applicant must be enrolled or expecting to enroll full-time at a two-year or four-year institution or university; resident of Wyoming and studying in Wyoming. Applicant or parent of applicant must be member of Wyoming Farm Bureau. Available to U.S. and non-U.S. citizens.

Application Requirements: Application form, financial need analysis, personal photograph. *Deadline:* March 1.

Contact: McKenzi Digby, Administrative Assistant
Wyoming Farm Bureau Federation
PO Box 1348
Laramie, WY 82073
Phone: 307-721-7719
E-mail: mdigby@wyfb.org

CORPORATE AFFILIATION

DEMOLAY FOUNDATION INCORPORATED
http://www.demolay.org/

FRANK S. LAND SCHOLARSHIP
Scholarship awarded to members of DeMolay International only, who have not yet reached the age of 21, to assist in financing their education. Must be U.S. resident.

Award: Scholarship for use in freshman, sophomore, junior, or senior years; not renewable. *Number:* 10–15. *Amount:* $1000.

Eligibility Requirements: Applicant must be age 21 or under; enrolled or expecting to enroll full-time at a two-year or four-year institution or university; male; resident of Alabama, Alaska, Arizona, Arkansas, California, Colorado, Connecticut, Delaware, District of Columbia, Florida, Georgia, Hawaii, Idaho, Illinois, Indiana, Iowa, Kansas, Kentucky, Louisiana, Maine, Maryland, Massachusetts, Michigan, Minnesota, Mississippi, Missouri, Montana, Nebraska, Nevada, New Hampshire, New Jersey, New Mexico, New York, North Carolina, North Dakota, Ohio, Oklahoma, Oregon, Pennsylvania, Rhode Island, South Carolina, South Dakota, Tennessee, Texas, Utah, Vermont, Virginia, Washington, West Virginia, Wisconsin, Wyoming and studying in Alabama, Alaska, Arizona, Arkansas, California, Colorado, Connecticut, Delaware, District of Columbia, Florida, Georgia, Hawaii, Idaho, Illinois, Indiana, Iowa, Kansas, Kentucky, Louisiana, Maine, Maryland, Massachusetts, Michigan, Minnesota, Mississippi, Missouri, Montana, Nebraska, Nevada, New Hampshire, New Jersey, New Mexico, New York, North Carolina, North Dakota, Ohio, Oklahoma, Oregon, Pennsylvania, Rhode Island, South Carolina, South Dakota, Tennessee, Texas, Utah, Vermont, Virginia, Washington, West Virginia, Wisconsin, Wyoming. Applicant or parent of applicant must be affiliated with DeMolay. Available to U.S. citizens.

Application Requirements: Application form, financial need analysis. *Deadline:* April 1.

Contact: Mr. Frank Kell, Scholarship Committee Chairman
DeMolay Foundation Incorporated
10200 Northwest Ambassador Drive
Kansas City, MO 64153
Phone: 800-336-6529
E-mail: scholarships@demolay.org

DONALDSON COMPANY
http://www.donaldson.com/

THE DONALDSON COMPANY, INC. SCHOLARSHIP PROGRAM
Scholarships for children of U.S. employees of Donaldson Company Inc. Any form of accredited postsecondary education is eligible. The amount of the award can range from $2000 to $3000 for each year of full-time study and may be renewed for up to a total of three years. The number of

scholarships awarded is limited to a maximum of 25 percent of the number of applicants.

Award: Scholarship for use in freshman, sophomore, junior, or senior years; renewable. *Amount:* $2000–$3000.

Eligibility Requirements: Applicant must be age 25 or under and enrolled or expecting to enroll full-time at a two-year or four-year or technical institution or university. Applicant or parent of applicant must be affiliated with Donaldson Company. Available to U.S. citizens.

Application Requirements: Application form, essay, financial need analysis. *Deadline:* March 15.

Contact: Norm Linnell, Vice President, General Counsel and Secretary
Phone: 952-887-3631
Fax: 952-887-3005
E-mail: norm.linnell@donaldson.com

THE FORD FAMILY FOUNDATION
http://www.tfff.org/scholarships

SCHOLARSHIP PROGRAM FOR SONS AND DAUGHTERS OF EMPLOYEES OF ROSEBURG FOREST PRODUCTS CO.
Kenneth W. Ford and The Ford Family Foundation established the Ford Sons & Daughters Program to provide scholarships to sons and daughters of Roseburg Forest Products Co. employees as they pursue education beyond high school. Each year, up to 10% of all eligible applicants are selected to receive the Ford Sons & Daughters Scholarship. An applicant must be a dependent child or stepchild (age 21 or younger) of an employee of Roseburg Forest Products Co. The employee must be full-time and have been employed by Roseburg Forest Products Co. for a minimum of 18 months as of March 1 of the application year.

Award: Scholarship for use in freshman, sophomore, junior, or senior years; renewable. *Number:* 30–47. *Amount:* $3000–$5000.

Eligibility Requirements: Applicant must be age 21 or under and enrolled or expecting to enroll full-time at a two-year or four-year or technical institution or university. Applicant or parent of applicant must be affiliated with Roseburg Forest Products.

Application Requirements: Application form, essay, interview. *Deadline:* March 1.

Contact: Tricia Tate, Scholarship Programs Manager
The Ford Family Foundation
44 Club Road, Suite 100
Eugene, OR 97401
Phone: 541-485-6211
Fax: 541-485-6223
E-mail: fordscholarships@tfff.org

GANNETT FOUNDATION
http://www.gannettfoundation.org/

GANNETT FOUNDATION/MADELYN P. JENNINGS SCHOLARSHIP AWARD
One-time awards for high school students whose parents are current full-time Gannett Company employees. Must be planning to attend a 4-year college or university for full-time study in the fall after graduation. Students must meet all requirements for participation in the National Merit Scholarship Program and take the PSAT/NMSQT in their junior year of high school. For more information, email the Gannett Benefits Team at Gannett Co., Inc., gannettbenefits@gannett.com.

Award: Scholarship for use in freshman year; not renewable. *Number:* 6. *Amount:* $3000.

Eligibility Requirements: Applicant must be high school student and planning to enroll or expecting to enroll full-time at a four-year institution or university. Applicant or parent of applicant must be affiliated with Gannett Company, Inc.. Available to U.S. citizens.

Application Requirements: Application form. *Deadline:* March 26.

Contact: Tiffany Sanford, Senior Benefits Analyst
Gannett Foundation
7950 Jones Branch Drive
McLean, VA 22107
Phone: 703-854-6446
E-mail: tsanford@gannett.com

GATEWAY PRESS INC. OF LOUISVILLE

http://www.gatewaypressinc.com/

GATEWAY PRESS SCHOLARSHIP

Scholarship for graduating high school seniors whose parents have been employees of Gateway Press Inc. for a minimum of 5 years. Applicant must be accepted at a college or university and maintain a minimum GPA of 2.25.

Award: Scholarship for use in freshman year; renewable. *Amount:* up to $3000.

Eligibility Requirements: Applicant must be high school student and planning to enroll or expecting to enroll full-time at a four-year institution or university. Applicant or parent of applicant must be affiliated with Gateway Press Inc.. Available to U.S. citizens.

Application Requirements: Application form, recommendations or references, transcript. *Deadline:* January 1.

Contact: Chris Georgehead, Human Resources Manager
    Phone: 502-454-0431
    Fax: 502-459-7930
    E-mail: kit@gatewaypressinc.com

HERMAN O. WEST FOUNDATION

http://www.westpharma.com/

HERMAN O. WEST FOUNDATION SCHOLARSHIP PROGRAM

Awards up to fourteen scholarships per year to high school seniors who will be attending college in the fall after graduation. The scholarship may only be applied toward tuition cost up to $3000 per year for up to four years. Available only to children of active employees of West Pharmaceutical Services, Inc.

Award: Scholarship for use in freshman, sophomore, junior, or senior years; renewable. *Number:* 1–14. *Amount:* $3000–$12,000.

Eligibility Requirements: Applicant must be high school student and planning to enroll or expecting to enroll full-time at a two-year or four-year institution or university. Applicant or parent of applicant must be affiliated with West Pharmaceuticals. Available to U.S. citizens.

Application Requirements: Application form, essay. *Deadline:* January 31.

Contact: Laura Pit, Manager, Community Affairs
    Herman O. West Foundation
    530 Herman O West Drive
    Exton, PA 19341
    Phone: 610-594-3046
    E-mail: laura.pitt@westpharma.com

ILLINOIS STUDENT ASSISTANCE COMMISSION (ISAC)

http://www.isac.org/

GRANT PROGRAM FOR DEPENDENTS OF POLICE, FIRE, OR CORRECTIONAL OFFICERS

Awards available to Illinois residents who are dependents of police, fire, and correctional officers killed or disabled in line of duty. Provides for tuition and fees at approved Illinois institutions. Number of grants and individual dollar amount awarded vary.

Award: Grant for use in freshman, sophomore, junior, senior, graduate, or postgraduate years; renewable.

Eligibility Requirements: Applicant must be enrolled or expecting to enroll full- or part-time at a two-year or four-year or technical institution or university; resident of Illinois and studying in Illinois. Applicant or parent of applicant must be affiliated with Amalgamated Sugar Company. Available to U.S. citizens. Applicant or parent must meet one or more of the following requirements: retired from active duty; disabled or killed as a result of military service; prisoner of war; or missing in action.

Application Requirements: Application form. *Deadline:* October 1.

Contact: ISAC Call Center Representative
    Illinois Student Assistance Commission (ISAC)
    1755 Lake Cook Road
    Deerfield, IL 60015-5209
    Phone: 800-899-4722
    E-mail: isac.studentservices@illinois.gov

THEODORE R. AND VIVIAN M. JOHNSON SCHOLARSHIP FOUNDATION INC.

http://www.jsf.bz/

THEODORE R. AND VIVIAN M. JOHNSON SCHOLARSHIP PROGRAM FOR CHILDREN OF UPS EMPLOYEES OR UPS RETIREES

The children of United Parcel Service employees or retirees who live in Florida are eligible for scholarship funds to attend college or vocational school in Florida. Awards are for undergraduate study only and ranges from $1000 to $10,000. Community college students and vocational school students may receive a maximum of $10,000 per year.

Award: Scholarship for use in freshman, sophomore, junior, or senior years; renewable. *Number:* 1–205. *Amount:* $1000–$10,000.

Eligibility Requirements: Applicant must be enrolled or expecting to enroll full- or part-time at a two-year or four-year or technical institution or university; resident of Florida and studying in Florida. Applicant or parent of applicant must be affiliated with Universal American Financial Corporation. Available to U.S. citizens.

Application Requirements: Application form, financial need analysis. *Deadline:* April 15.

Contact: Alexa Thelen, Program Manager
    Theodore R. and Vivian M. Johnson Scholarship Foundation
      Inc.
    Scholarship Management Services
    One Scholarship Way
    Saint Peter, MN 56082
    Phone: 507-931-1682
    E-mail: athelen@scholarshipamerica.org

TRIANGLE COMMUNITY FOUNDATION

http://www.trianglecf.org

GEORGE AND MARY NEWTON SCHOLARSHIP

Anyone between 16-25, who has received or is expecting a high school degree or equivalent and whose parent or legal guardian is an employee of Newton Instrument Company, Inc., may apply. Applicant must have applied to the institution he or she plans to attend, and must intend to enroll within one year of the application deadline. Recipients will be selected on the basis of academic achievement, financial need, school and community activities, and work experience and educational goals.

Award: Scholarship for use in freshman, sophomore, junior, or senior years; renewable. *Number:* 1. *Amount:* $1000.

Eligibility Requirements: Applicant must be age 16-25; enrolled or expecting to enroll full-time at a two-year or four-year or technical institution or university and resident of North Carolina. Applicant or parent of applicant must be affiliated with Newton Instrument Company. Available to U.S. citizens.

Application Requirements: Application form. *Deadline:* March 15.

Contact: Mrs. Sarah Battersby, Scholarships and Donor Services Officer
    Phone: 919-474-8370 Ext. 4015
    E-mail: Scholarships@trianglecf.org

WALMART FOUNDATION

http://foundation.walmart.com/

WALMART ASSOCIATE SCHOLARSHIP

The Walmart Foundation offers scholarship programs that benefit qualified Walmart associates. Applicants must be employed with any division of Walmart for at least six consecutive months prior to the application due date for the award period in which the associate is applying. Applicants must have graduated high school/home school or obtained a GED or be a graduating high school senior who intends to

enroll in a college or university upon graduation.
http://foundation.walmart.com/our-focus/associate-scholarships

Award: Scholarship for use in freshman, sophomore, junior, senior, or graduate years; renewable. *Amount:* up to $16,000.

Eligibility Requirements: Applicant must be enrolled or expecting to enroll full- or part-time at a two-year or four-year or technical institution or university. Applicant or parent of applicant must be affiliated with Wal-Mart Foundation. Available to U.S. citizens.

Application Requirements: Application form, application form may be submitted online (http://foundation.walmart.com/our-focus/associate-scholarships), community service, entry in a contest, financial need analysis. *Deadline:* varies.

Contact: Walmart Foundation Scholarship Administrator
Walmart Foundation
702 SW 8th Street
Bentonville, AR 72716-0150
Fax: 479-273-6850
E-mail: W.Mschol@wal-mart.com

WALMART DEPENDENT SCHOLARSHIP

The Walmart Foundation offers scholarship programs that benefit qualified Walmart associates and their high school senior dependents. Applicants must be the dependent of an actively employed Walmart associate (employee) within any division of Walmart for at least six consecutive months as of April 1 and must be a high school or home school senior graduating or earning a GED between August 1 and July 31. Applicants must have a cumulative high school grade point average (GPA) of at least 2.0 on a 4-point scale. See website for details, https://walmart.scholarsapply.org/dependent/

Award: Scholarship for use in freshman, sophomore, junior, or senior years; renewable. *Amount:* up to $13,000.

Eligibility Requirements: Applicant must be high school student and planning to enroll or expecting to enroll full-time at a two-year or four-year or technical institution or university. Applicant or parent of applicant must be affiliated with Wal-Mart Foundation. Available to U.S. citizens.

Application Requirements: Application form, application form may be submitted online (http://foundation.walmart.com/our-focus/associate-scholarships), entry in a contest, financial need analysis, transcript. *Deadline:* April 1.

Contact: Walmart Foundation Scholarship Administrator
Walmart Foundation
702 SW 8th Street
Bentonville, AR 72716-0150
Fax: 479-273-6850
E-mail: W.Mschol@wal-mart.com

EMPLOYMENT/ VOLUNTEER EXPERIENCE

AIR TRAFFIC CONTROL ASSOCIATION INC.

http://www.atca.org/

AIR TRAFFIC CONTROL ASSOCIATION SCHOLARSHIP

Scholarships for students in programs leading to a bachelor's degree or higher in aviation-related courses of study, and for full-time employees engaged in advanced study to improve their skills in air traffic control or aviation. Visit website for additional information http://www.atca.org.

Award: Scholarship for use in freshman, sophomore, junior, senior, graduate, or postgraduate years; not renewable.

Eligibility Requirements: Applicant must be enrolled or expecting to enroll full- or part-time at a two-year institution or university. Applicant or parent of applicant must have employment or volunteer experience in air traffic control. Available to U.S. and non-U.S. citizens.

Application Requirements: Application form, application form may be submitted online, essay, financial need analysis. *Deadline:* May 1.

Contact: Tim Wagner, Membership Manager
Air Traffic Control Association Inc.
1101 King Street, Suite 300
Alexandria, VA 22314
Phone: 703-299-2430
E-mail: info@atca.org

BUCKINGHAM MEMORIAL SCHOLARSHIP

Scholarships granted to children of air traffic control specialists pursuing a bachelor's degree or higher in any course of study. Must be the child, natural or by adoption, of a person serving, or having served as an air traffic control specialist, be it with the U.S. government, U.S. military, or in a private facility in the United States.

Award: Scholarship for use in freshman, sophomore, junior, senior, or graduate years; not renewable.

Eligibility Requirements: Applicant must be enrolled or expecting to enroll full- or part-time at an institution or university. Applicant or parent of applicant must have employment or volunteer experience in air traffic control. Available to U.S. citizens.

Application Requirements: Application form, application form may be submitted online, community service, essay, financial need analysis. *Deadline:* May 1.

Contact: Tim Wagner, Membership Manager
Air Traffic Control Association Inc.
1101 King Street
Suite 300
Alexandria, VA 22314
Phone: 703-299-2430 Ext. 314
E-mail: info@atca.org

AMERICAN FEDERATION OF TEACHERS

http://www.aft.org/

ROBERT G. PORTER SCHOLARS PROGRAM-AMERICAN FEDERATION OF TEACHERS DEPENDENTS
• See page 430

AMERICAN LEGION AUXILIARY DEPARTMENT OF NORTH DAKOTA

http://www.ndlegion.org/

AMERICAN LEGION AUXILIARY DEPARTMENT OF NORTH DAKOTA NATIONAL PRESIDENT'S SCHOLARSHIP

Three division scholarships for children of veterans who served in the Armed Forces during eligible dates for American Legion membership. Must be U.S. citizen and a high school senior with a minimum 2.5 GPA. Must be entered by local American Legion Auxiliary Unit.

Award: Scholarship for use in freshman year; not renewable. *Number:* 3. *Amount:* $1000–$2500.

Eligibility Requirements: Applicant must be high school student; planning to enroll or expecting to enroll full-time at a four-year institution or university; resident of North Dakota and studying in North Dakota. Applicant or parent of applicant must have employment or volunteer experience in community service. Available to U.S. citizens. Applicant or parent must meet one or more of the following requirements: general military experience; retired from active duty; disabled or killed as a result of military service; prisoner of war; or missing in action.

Application Requirements: Application form, essay, financial need analysis, proof of 50 hours voluntary service, recommendations or references, test scores, transcript. *Deadline:* March 1.

Contact: Myrna Runholm, Department Secretary
Phone: 701-253-5992
Fax: 701-952-5993
E-mail: ala-hq@ndlegion.org

AMERICAN LEGION DEPARTMENT OF VERMONT

http://www.vtlegion.org

AMERICAN LEGION EAGLE SCOUT OF THE YEAR
• *See page 434*

AMERICAN POSTAL WORKERS UNION

http://www.apwu.org/

E.C. HALLBECK SCHOLARSHIP FUND
• *See page 434*

VOCATIONAL SCHOLARSHIP PROGRAM
• *See page 435*

ARTBA

http://www.artbatdf.org/

ARTBA-TDF LANFORD FAMILY HIGHWAY WORKERS MEMORIAL SCHOLARSHIP PROGRAM

The ARTBA-TDF Highway Worker Memorial Scholarship Program provides financial assistance to help the sons, daughters or legally adopted children of highway workers killed or permanently disabled in the line of duty pursue post-high school education. Minimum 2.5 GPA required.

Award: Scholarship for use in freshman, sophomore, junior, senior, graduate, or postgraduate years; not renewable. *Amount:* $1000–$5000.

Eligibility Requirements: Applicant must be enrolled or expecting to enroll full- or part-time at a two-year or four-year or technical institution or university. Applicant or parent of applicant must have employment or volunteer experience in construction, roadway work, transportation industry. Available to U.S. citizens.

Application Requirements: Application form, essay, financial need analysis, personal photograph. *Deadline:* April 6.

Contact: Eileen Houlihan, District of Columbia
ARTBA
250 E Street SW
Suite 900
Washington, DC 20024
Phone: 202-683-1019
E-mail: ehoulihan@artba.org

CALIFORNIA STATE PARENT-TEACHER ASSOCIATION

http://www.capta.org/

CONTINUING EDUCATION SCHOLARSHIP FOR PTA VOLUNTEERS
• *See page 437*

GRADUATING HIGH SCHOOL SENIOR SCHOLARSHIP

Available to high school seniors graduating between January 1 and June 30 of the current academic year from high schools in California with a PTA/PTSA unit in good standing. Must be a California resident. Must have volunteered in the school and community volunteer service.

Award: Scholarship for use in freshman year; renewable. *Amount:* $500.

Eligibility Requirements: Applicant must be high school student; planning to enroll or expecting to enroll full-time at a two-year or four-year or technical institution or university and resident of California. Applicant or parent of applicant must have employment or volunteer experience in community service. Available to U.S. citizens.

Application Requirements: Application form, community service, copy of current PTA/PTSA membership card, essay, recommendations or references, transcript. *Deadline:* February 1.

Contact: Becky Reece, Scholarship and Award Chairman
California State Parent-Teacher Association
930 Georgia Street
Los Angeles, CA 90015-1322
Phone: 213-620-1100
Fax: 213-620-1411
E-mail: info@capta.org

CALIFORNIA STUDENT AID COMMISSION

http://www.csac.ca.gov/

LAW ENFORCEMENT PERSONNEL DEPENDENTS GRANT PROGRAM

The Law Enforcement Personnel Dependents Grant Program provides need-based educational grants to dependents and spouses of: California peace officers (Highway Patrol, marshals, sheriffs, police officers), Department of Corrections and California Youth Authority employees, and permanent/full-time firefighters employed by public entities who have been killed in the performance of duty or 100% disabled as a result of an accident or injury caused by external violence or physical force incurred in the performance of duty.

Award: Grant for use in freshman, sophomore, junior, or senior years; renewable. *Amount:* $100–$12,192.

Eligibility Requirements: Applicant must be enrolled or expecting to enroll full- or part-time at a two-year institution or university; resident of British Columbia and studying in California. Applicant or parent of applicant must have employment or volunteer experience in police/firefighting. Available to U.S. citizens.

Application Requirements: Application form, financial need analysis. *Deadline:* continuous.

Contact: Catalina Mistler, Deputy Director, Program Administration & Services Division
California Student Aid Commission
PO Box 419027
Rancho Cordova, CA 95741-9027
Phone: 888-224-7268
Fax: 916-526-8004
E-mail: catalina.mistler@csac.ca.gov

CALIFORNIA TABLE GRAPE COMMISSION

http://www.freshcaliforniagrapes.com/

CALIFORNIA TABLE GRAPE FARM WORKERS SCHOLARSHIP PROGRAM

Applicants must be high school graduates who plan to attend any college or university in California. The applicant, a parent, or a legal guardian must have worked in the California table grape harvest during the last season. School activities, personal references, and financial need are considered. Must be a U.S. citizen.

Award: Scholarship for use in freshman year; not renewable. *Number:* 3. *Amount:* $16,000.

Eligibility Requirements: Applicant must be enrolled or expecting to enroll full-time at a four-year institution or university and studying in California. Applicant or parent of applicant must have employment or volunteer experience in agriculture. Available to U.S. citizens.

Application Requirements: Application form, essay, recommendations or references, test scores, transcript. *Deadline:* March 19.

Contact: Scholarship Coordinator
California Table Grape Commission
392 West Fallbrook, Suite 101
Fresno, CA 93711-6150
Phone: 559-447-8350
Fax: 559-447-9184

CALIFORNIA TEACHERS ASSOCIATION (CTA)

http://www.cta.org/

CALIFORNIA TEACHERS ASSOCIATION SCHOLARSHIP FOR MEMBERS
• *See page 437*

COLLEGEBOUND FOUNDATION

http://www.collegeboundfoundation.org/

BALTIMORE RAVENS SCHOLARSHIP PROGRAM

The Baltimore Ravens established this scholarship program to enable local youth to continue their education on a collegiate level. The team has a long-standing history of service to local communities, and this fund will support those who do the same. In addition, this renewable scholarship will be based on financial need and academic achievement. You must: have a cumulative 3.0 GPA or better; demonstrate financial need (include a SAR if available); be accepted to and attend a 4-year college or university; have verifiable community service; submit one (1) reference from an individual who can attest to your commitment to helping others; submit one (1) reference from a teacher, school counselor or administrator; and submit a 1-2 page essay describing the environment in which you live, and the most meaningful contribution you have made as a volunteer to the betterment of your community.

Award: Scholarship for use in freshman, sophomore, junior, or senior years; renewable. *Number:* 1–5. *Amount:* $5000.

Eligibility Requirements: Applicant must be high school student; planning to enroll or expecting to enroll full-time at an institution or university; resident of Manitoba and studying in Maryland. Applicant or parent of applicant must have employment or volunteer experience in community service. Available to U.S. citizens.

Application Requirements: Application form, community service, essay, financial need analysis, interview. *Deadline:* March 1.

Contact: Jennifer Covahey, Director of College Success
CollegeBound Foundation
2601 Howard Street
Suite 210
Baltimore, MD 21218
Phone: 410-783-2905 Ext. 207
Fax: 410-727-5786
E-mail: jcovahey@collegeboundfoundation.org

LORENZO FELDER SCHOLARSHIP

Applicant must: be an African-American male; be a graduate of a Baltimore City public school; have a cumulative GPA of 3.0 or better; have demonstrated financial need; have verifiable community service or extracurricular activity; write an essay of 500-1,000 words describing the environment you live in and the most meaningful contribution you have made as a volunteer in your community.

Award: Scholarship for use in freshman year; not renewable. *Number:* 1–3. *Amount:* $1000–$1500.

Eligibility Requirements: Applicant must be Black (non-Hispanic); high school student; planning to enroll or expecting to enroll full-time at a two-year institution; male and resident of Manitoba. Applicant or parent of applicant must have employment or volunteer experience in community service. Available to U.S. citizens.

Application Requirements: Application form, community service, essay, financial need analysis. *Deadline:* March 1.

Contact: Jennifer Covahey, Director of College Success
CollegeBound Foundation
2601 Howard Street
Suite 210
Baltimore, MD 21218
Phone: 410-783-2905 Ext. 207
Fax: 410-727-5786
E-mail: jcovahey@collegeboundfoundation.org

DIAMANTE, INC.

http://www.diamanteinc.org/

LATINO DIAMANTE SCHOLARSHIP FUND

Awards for Hispanic high school seniors recognizing their contributions to the community and their leadership qualities. Graduating high school seniors in North Carolina who plan to enroll at North Carolina institutions of higher education, and first-year undergraduates can apply for this scholarship. Must maintain a GPA of at least 2.5.

Award: Scholarship for use in freshman year; not renewable. *Number:* 2. *Amount:* $500.

Eligibility Requirements: Applicant must be Hispanic; enrolled or expecting to enroll full- or part-time at a two-year or four-year institution or university; resident of North Carolina; studying in North Carolina and must have an interest in leadership. Applicant or parent of applicant must have employment or volunteer experience in community service. Available to U.S. citizens.

Application Requirements: Application form, community service, essay, recommendations or references, transcript.

DISABLED AMERICAN VETERANS

http://www.dav.org/

JESSE BROWN MEMORIAL YOUTH SCHOLARSHIP PROGRAM

The Jesse Brown Memorial Youth Scholarship Program honors former National Service Officer and Secretary of Veterans Affairs Jesse Brown. It is given in memory of a DAV leader dedicated to veterans, through the recognition of those who carry on his legacy of service. This scholarship is awarded to youth volunteers who are committed to serving veterans. Each year, one outstanding applicant receives the top scholarship in the amount of $20,000 to help fund their higher education. In addition, the top winner and parent/guardian receive round-trip airfare (lowest non-refundable fare), hotel accommodations, and per diem for three days to attend the DAV National Convention. The winner will be presented the award and be recognized for their dedication and commitment to veterans. Additional scholarships are awarded annually in the following amounts: second prize of $15,000, third prize of $10,000, fourth prize of $7,500 (two awarded annually), fifth prize of $5,000 (three awarded annually).

Award: Scholarship for use in freshman, sophomore, junior, senior, graduate, or postgraduate years; renewable. *Number:* 8. *Amount:* $5000–$20,000.

Eligibility Requirements: Applicant must be age 21 or under and enrolled or expecting to enroll full- or part-time at a two-year or four-year or technical institution or university. Applicant or parent of applicant must have employment or volunteer experience in community service, helping people with disabilities. Available to U.S. citizens.

Application Requirements: Application form, community service, essay. *Deadline:* February 10.

Contact: Ms. Kati Geoppinger, Supervisor of Voluntary Services
Disabled American Veterans
3725 Alexandria Pike
Cold Spring, KY 41076
Phone: 859-442-1012
E-mail: kgeoppinger@dav.org

ELECTRONIC SECURITY ASSOCIATION (ESA)

http://www.esaweb.org

ESA YOUTH SCHOLARSHIP PROGRAM

One-time award for high school seniors entering postsecondary education, who are deserving sons or daughters of police and fire officials. The number of awards granted varies annually.

Award: Scholarship for use in freshman year; not renewable. *Amount:* $500–$10,000.

Eligibility Requirements: Applicant must be high school student; age 15-20 and planning to enroll or expecting to enroll full-time at a four-year institution or university. Applicant or parent of applicant must have employment or volunteer experience in police/firefighting. Available to U.S. citizens.

Application Requirements: Application form, essay, proof of acceptance to college or university, proof of parent/guardian occupation, recommendations or references, resume, test scores, transcript. *Deadline:* March 28.

Contact: Laurie Knox, Vice President of Communications and Public Relations
Electronic Security Association (ESA)
6333 North State Highway 161
Suite 350
Irving, TX 75038
Phone: 888-447-1689 Ext. 6825
E-mail: laurie.knox@esaweb.org

EOD WARRIOR FOUNDATION

http://www.eodwarriorfoundation.org

EXPLOSIVE ORDNANCE DISPOSAL MEMORIAL SCHOLARSHIP

Award based on academic merit, community involvement, and financial need for the children, grandchildren, and spouses of military Explosive Ordnance Disposal technicians. This scholarship is for students enrolled or planning to enroll full-time as an undergraduate in a U.S. accredited two year, four year college. Applications are only available on the website at http://www.eodwarriorfoundation.org.

Award: Scholarship for use in freshman, sophomore, junior, or senior years; not renewable. *Number:* 25–75. *Amount:* $1000–$5000.

Eligibility Requirements: Applicant must be enrolled or expecting to enroll full-time at a two-year or four-year institution or university. Applicant or parent of applicant must have employment or volunteer experience in explosive ordnance disposal. Available to U.S. citizens. Applicant or parent must meet one or more of the following requirements: general military experience; retired from active duty; disabled or killed as a result of military service; prisoner of war; or missing in action.

Application Requirements: Application form, application form may be submitted online (http://www.eodmemorial.org/scholarship), community service, essay, recommendations or references, transcript. *Deadline:* March 15.

Contact: Nicole Motsek, Executive Director
EOD Warrior Foundation
33735 Snickersville Turnpike
PO Box 309
Bluemont, VA 20135
Phone: 540-554-4550
E-mail: nicole.motsek@eodmemorial.org

EXCEPTIONALNURSE.COM

http://www.exceptionalnurse.com/

BRUNO ROLANDO SCHOLARSHIP AWARD

Scholarship of $250 awarded to a nursing student with a disability. Preference will be given to a nursing student who is employed at a Veteran's Hospital.

Award: Scholarship for use in freshman, sophomore, junior, senior, graduate, or postgraduate years; not renewable. *Number:* 1. *Amount:* $250.

Eligibility Requirements: Applicant must be enrolled or expecting to enroll full-time at an institution or university. Applicant or parent of applicant must have employment or volunteer experience in nursing. Applicant must be hearing impaired, learning disabled, physically disabled, or visually impaired. Available to U.S. citizens.

Application Requirements: Application form, essay. *Deadline:* June 1.

Contact: Scholarship Committee
ExceptionalNurse.com
ExceptionalNurse.com
13019 Coastal Circle
Palm Beach Gardens, FL 33410
E-mail: exceptionalnurse@aol.com

FEDERAL RESOURCES

www.federalresources.com

WARRIOR'S LEGACY SCHOLARSHIP FUND

This scholarship is designed to recognize and financially assist college-bound high school seniors or currently enrolled college students at an accredited institution whose parent/guardian is an active, retired, or volunteer service member of Law Enforcement, the Armed Forces, or First Responders. Students must show proof of service, proof of GPA (3.0), and proof of attendance at the accredited institution. Applicant must be a US Citizen or Permanent Resident. Visit www.federalresources.com/scholarship/ to apply.

Award: Scholarship for use in freshman, sophomore, junior, or senior years; not renewable. *Number:* 1. *Amount:* $5000.

Eligibility Requirements: Applicant must be enrolled or expecting to enroll full-time at a two-year or four-year or technical institution or university. Applicant or parent of applicant must have employment or volunteer experience in police/firefighting. Available to U.S. citizens. Applicant or parent must meet one or more of the following requirements: retired from active duty; disabled or killed as a result of military service; prisoner of war; or missing in action.

Application Requirements: Application form, application form may be submitted online (http://www.federalresources.com/scholarship), essay, Parent/guardian's proof of service (Armed Forces, EMS, Law Enforcement), transcript. *Deadline:* May 1.

Contact: Scholarship Committee
Federal Resources
235G Log Canoe Circle
Stevensville, MD 21666
Phone: 800-8921099
E-mail: scholarships@federalresources.com

FINANCE AUTHORITY OF MAINE

http://www.famemaine.com/

TUITION WAIVER PROGRAMS

Provides tuition waivers for children and spouses of EMS personnel, firefighters, and law enforcement officers who have been killed in the line of duty and for students who were foster children under the custody of the Department of Human Services when they graduated from high school. Waivers valid at the University of Maine System, the Maine Technical College System, and Maine Maritime Academy. Applicant must reside and study in Maine.

Award: Grant for use in freshman, sophomore, junior, or senior years; renewable. *Number:* 30.

Eligibility Requirements: Applicant must be enrolled or expecting to enroll full- or part-time at a two-year or four-year institution or university; resident of Maine and studying in Maine. Applicant or parent of applicant must have employment or volunteer experience in police/firefighting. Available to U.S. citizens.

Application Requirements: Application form. *Deadline:* continuous.

Contact: Jennifer Lanphear, Education Programs Officer
Finance Authority of Maine
5 Community Drive
Augusta, ME 04332
Phone: 207-620-3548
E-mail: education@famemaine.com

FRATERNAL ORDER OF POLICE ASSOCIATES OF OHIO INC.

http://www.fopaohio.org/

FRATERNAL ORDER OF POLICE ASSOCIATES, STATE LODGE OF OHIO INC., SCHOLARSHIP FUND

Scholarship available to a graduating high school senior whose parent or guardian is a member in good standing of the Fraternal Order of Police, State Lodge of Ohio Inc. The amount of each scholarship will be up to $4000 payable over a four-year period. A one-time award of $500 will be given to the first runner-up. Scholarships will be awarded on the basis of scholastic merit, economic need and goals in life.

Award: Scholarship for use in freshman year; renewable. *Number:* 1–4. *Amount:* $500–$1000.

Eligibility Requirements: Applicant must be high school student; planning to enroll or expecting to enroll full-time at a four-year institution or university and resident of Ohio. Applicant or parent of applicant must have employment or volunteer experience in police/firefighting. Available to U.S. citizens.

Application Requirements: Application form, community service, essay, financial need analysis, personal photograph, proof of guardianship, recommendations or references, test scores, transcript. *Deadline:* May 1.

Contact: Mr. Michael Esposito, FOPA Scholarship Assistance Program
Fraternal Order of Police Associates of Ohio Inc.
PO Box 14564
Cincinnati, OH 45250-0564
Phone: 513-684-4755
E-mail: mje@fopaohio.org

GEORGIA STUDENT FINANCE COMMISSION

https://gsfc.georgia.gov/

GEORGIA PUBLIC SAFETY MEMORIAL GRANT

Public Safety Memorial Grant provides assistance to the dependent children of Georgia public safety officers who were permanently disabled or killed in the line of duty. Funds may be used toward the cost of attendance at eligible colleges or universities in Georgia.

Award: Grant for use in freshman, sophomore, junior, or senior years; not renewable. *Amount:* $2000–$18,000.

Eligibility Requirements: Applicant must be enrolled or expecting to enroll full-time at a two-year or technical institution or university; resident of Florida and studying in Georgia. Applicant or parent of applicant must have employment or volunteer experience in police/firefighting. Available to U.S. citizens.

Application Requirements: Application form. *Deadline:* continuous.

Contact: Ms. Pennie Strong, Vice President, Student Aid Services
Georgia Student Finance Commission
2082 East Exchange Place
Tucker, GA 30084
Phone: 770-724-9014
Fax: 770-724-9249
E-mail: pennies@gsfc.org

GOLF COURSE SUPERINTENDENTS ASSOCIATION OF AMERICA

https://www.gcsaa.org/

JOSEPH S. GARSKE COLLEGIATE GRANT PROGRAM
• *See page 440*

GREATER WASHINGTON URBAN LEAGUE

http://www.gwul.org/

SAFEWAY/GREATER WASHINGTON URBAN LEAGUE SCHOLARSHIP

Award to graduating high school students who reside in the service area of the League. Applicants must complete an essay on a subject selected by the sponsors and must have completed 90 percent of their school district's community service requirement. Minimum GPA of 2.7 required.

Award: Scholarship for use in freshman year; not renewable. *Number:* 6. *Amount:* $3000.

Eligibility Requirements: Applicant must be high school student; planning to enroll or expecting to enroll full-time at a four-year institution or university and resident of District of Columbia. Applicant or parent of applicant must have employment or volunteer experience in community service. Available to U.S. citizens.

Application Requirements: Application form, community service, entry in a contest, essay, test scores. *Deadline:* February 12.

Contact: Audrey Epperson, Director of Education
Phone: 202-265-8200
Fax: 202-387-7019
E-mail: aepperson@gwul.org

HARNESS HORSE YOUTH FOUNDATION

http://www.hhyf.org/

CURT GREENE MEMORIAL SCHOLARSHIP

One-time award with preference given to those under age 24 who have a passion for harness racing. Based on need, merit, need, and passion for harness racing. Available for study in any field. May reapply.

Award: Scholarship for use in freshman, sophomore, junior, or senior years; not renewable. *Number:* 1–2. *Amount:* $2500.

Eligibility Requirements: Applicant must be age 18-24; enrolled or expecting to enroll full-time at a two-year or four-year or technical institution or university and must have an interest in animal/agricultural competition. Applicant or parent of applicant must have employment or volunteer experience in harness racing. Available to U.S. and Canadian citizens.

Application Requirements: Application form, community service, essay, financial need analysis, personal photograph. *Deadline:* April 30.

Contact: Ellen Taylor, Executive Director
Phone: 317-908-0029
E-mail: ellen@hhyf.org

HARNESS TRACKS OF AMERICA

http://www.harnesstracks.com/

HTA/HAROLD SNYDER MEMORIAL SCHOLARSHIPS

One-time, merit-based award of $5000 for students actively involved in harness racing or the children of licensed drivers, trainers, breeders, or caretakers, living or deceased. Based on financial need, academic merit, and active harness racing involvement by applicant or family member. High school seniors may apply for the following school year award.

Award: Scholarship for use in freshman, sophomore, junior, senior, or graduate years; not renewable. *Number:* 3. *Amount:* $5000.

Eligibility Requirements: Applicant must be enrolled or expecting to enroll full-time at a two-year or four-year or technical institution or university. Applicant or parent of applicant must have employment or volunteer experience in harness racing. Available to U.S. and Canadian citizens.

Application Requirements: Application form, essay, financial need analysis. *Deadline:* June 26.

Contact: Ms. Heather McColloch, Executive Assistant
Harness Tracks of America
10705 Northfield Rd.
Northfield, OH 44067
Phone: 330-467-4101 Ext. 2204
E-mail: hmccolloch@northfieldpark.com

HISPANIC ANNUAL SALUTE

http://www.hispanicannualsalute.org/

HISPANIC ANNUAL SALUTE SCHOLARSHIP

Scholarships of $2000 are awarded to graduating high school seniors. Program is intended to help foster a strong Hispanic presence within colleges and universities that will ultimately lead to active community leadership and volunteerism. Applicant must maintain a minimum GPA of 2.5.

Award: Scholarship for use in freshman year; not renewable. *Number:* 10. *Amount:* $2000.

Eligibility Requirements: Applicant must be Hispanic; high school student and planning to enroll or expecting to enroll full-time at a four-year institution or university. Applicant or parent of applicant must have employment or volunteer experience in community service. Available to U.S. citizens.

Application Requirements: Application form, essay, recommendations or references, test scores. *Deadline:* December 4.

Contact: Dan Sandos, President
Phone: 303-699-0715
Fax: 303-627-4205
E-mail: dcsandos@aol.com

HOSPITAL CENTRAL SERVICES INC.

http://www.giveapint.org/

HOSPITAL CENTRAL SERVICES STUDENT VOLUNTEER SCHOLARSHIP

Award to a graduating high school senior. Must have completed a minimum of 135 hours of volunteer service to the Blood Center in no less than a two calendar year period. Minimum 2.5 GPA required. Children of employees of Hospital Central Services or its affiliates are not eligible.

Award: Scholarship for use in freshman year; not renewable. *Number:* up to 2. *Amount:* $1000.

Eligibility Requirements: Applicant must be high school student and planning to enroll or expecting to enroll full- or part-time at a two-year or four-year institution or university. Applicant or parent of applicant must have employment or volunteer experience in community service. Available to U.S. citizens.

Application Requirements: Application form, recommendations or references, test scores, transcript. *Deadline:* March 31.

Contact: Sandra Thomas, Director of Development and Customer
Service
Hospital Central Services Inc.
1465 Valley Center Parkway
Bethlehem, PA 18017
Phone: 610-691-5850 Ext. 292

HOSTESS COMMITTEE SCHOLARSHIPS/MISS AMERICA PAGEANT

http://www.missamerica.org/

MISS AMERICA COMMUNITY SERVICE SCHOLARSHIPS

Award to assist in the expansion of scholarship provision throughout the state and local programs. Each eligible state will receive a $1,000 scholarship for a contestant demonstrating exemplary community service initiatives. Only opened to those contestants competing at the state level.

Award: Scholarship for use in freshman, sophomore, junior, senior, or graduate years; not renewable. *Number:* 52. *Amount:* $1000.

Eligibility Requirements: Applicant must be enrolled or expecting to enroll full- or part-time at a four-year institution or university; female and must have an interest in beauty pageant. Applicant or parent of applicant must have employment or volunteer experience in community service. Available to U.S. citizens.

Application Requirements: Application form.

Contact: Doreen Gordon, Controller and Scholarship Administrator
Phone: 609-345-7571 Ext. 27
Fax: 609-347-6079
E-mail: doreen@missamerica.org

IDAHO STATE BOARD OF EDUCATION

http://www.boardofed.idaho.gov/

IDAHO GOVERNOR'S CUP SCHOLARSHIP

Idaho Governor's Cup is a renewable scholarship available to Idaho residents enrolled full-time in an undergraduate academic or career-technical program at an eligible Idaho public or private college or university. A minimum GPA of 2.8 is required. Applicants must demonstrate commitment to public service and be able to document service. Applicants must be a high school seniors and U.S. citizens.

Award: Scholarship for use in freshman year; renewable. *Number:* 20–40. *Amount:* $3000.

Eligibility Requirements: Applicant must be high school student; planning to enroll or expecting to enroll full-time at a two-year or four-year institution or university; resident of Idaho and studying in Idaho. Applicant or parent of applicant must have employment or volunteer experience in community service. Available to U.S. citizens.

Application Requirements: Application form, community service, essay, portfolio. *Deadline:* February 15.

Contact: Sarah Bettweiser
E-mail: sarah@idahogovernorscup.org

INTERNATIONAL ASSOCIATION OF FIRE FIGHTERS

http://www.iaff.org/

W. H. "HOWIE" MCCLENNAN SCHOLARSHIP

Sons, daughters, or legally adopted children of IAFF members killed in the line of duty who are planning to attend an institution of higher learning can apply. Award of $2500 for each year. Renewable up to four years. Applicant must have a GPA of 2.0.

Award: Scholarship for use in freshman year; renewable. *Number:* 20–25. *Amount:* $2500.

Eligibility Requirements: Applicant must be enrolled or expecting to enroll full- or part-time at a two-year or four-year or technical institution. Applicant or parent of applicant must have employment or volunteer experience in police/firefighting. Available to U.S. citizens.

Application Requirements: Application form, essay, financial need analysis, recommendations or references, transcript. *Deadline:* February 1.

Contact: L. Harrington, International Association of Fire Fighters
International Association of Fire Fighters
1750 New York Avenue, NW
Education Department, 3rd Floor
Washington, DC 20006-5395
Phone: 202-737-8484
Fax: 202-737-8418

INTERNATIONAL DAIRY DELI BAKERY ASSOCIATION

http://www.iddba.org

INTERNATIONAL DAIRY DELI BAKERY ASSOCIATION'S SCHOLARSHIP FOR GROWING THE FUTURE

Applicants must work for a member of IDDBA at least 13 hours per week while attending classes. Applicants are eligible for two awards per year.

Award: Scholarship for use in freshman, sophomore, junior, senior, or graduate years; not renewable. *Number:* 200–300. *Amount:* $500–$2000.

Eligibility Requirements: Applicant must be enrolled or expecting to enroll full- or part-time at a two-year or four-year or technical institution or university. Applicant or parent of applicant must have employment or volunteer experience in food service. Available to U.S. and non-U.S. citizens.

Application Requirements: Application form. *Deadline:* continuous.

Contact: Mr. Jonathan Whalley, Education Coordinator
International Dairy Deli Bakery Association
636 Science Dr.
Madison, WI 53711
Phone: 608-310-5000
E-mail: scholarships@iddba.org

INTERNATIONAL FLIGHT SERVICES ASSOCIATION

http://www.ifsanet.com

DHL AIRLINE BUSINESS SOLUTIONS SCHOLARSHIP AWARD

Individuals are selected to receive the award based on scholastic merit and dedication to an advanced education. Must be an employee of a current IFSA member company in good standing, or a relative of an employee of a current IFSA member company. Please address financial need within essay.

Award: Scholarship for use in freshman, sophomore, junior, or senior years; not renewable. *Number:* 1. *Amount:* $2250.

Eligibility Requirements: Applicant must be enrolled or expecting to enroll full- or part-time at an institution or university. Applicant or parent of applicant must have employment or volunteer experience in hospitality/hotel administration/operations. Available to U.S. and non-U.S. citizens.

Application Requirements: Application form, essay, recommendations or references, transcript. *Deadline:* May 14.

Contact: Ms. Kelly McLendon, Programs Manager
International Flight Services Association
1100 Johnson Ferry Road, NE
Suite 300
Atlanta, GA 30342
Phone: 678-303-3042
E-mail: kmclendon@kellencompany.com

FLYING FOOD GROUP SCHOLARSHIP AWARD

Individuals are selected to receive the award based on scholastic merit and dedication to an advanced education. Must be an employee of a current IFSA member company in good standing, or a relative of an employee of a current IFSA member company.

Award: Scholarship for use in freshman, sophomore, junior, or senior years; not renewable. *Number:* 1. *Amount:* $2250.

Eligibility Requirements: Applicant must be enrolled or expecting to enroll full- or part-time at an institution or university. Applicant or parent of applicant must have employment or volunteer experience in hospitality/hotel administration/operations. Available to U.S. and non-U.S. citizens.

Application Requirements: Application form, essay, recommendations or references, transcript. *Deadline:* May 14.

Contact: Ms. Kelly McLendon, Programs Manager
International Flight Services Association
1100 Johnson Ferry Road, NE
Suite 300
Atlanta, GA 30342
Phone: 678-303-3042
E-mail: kmclendon@kellencompany.com

IFSA MEMBER FAMILY SCHOLARSHIP AWARD

Individuals are selected based upon scholastic merit and dedication to pursuing an advanced degree. Must be an employee of a current IFSA member company in good standing, or a relative of an employee of a current IFSA member company.

Award: Scholarship for use in freshman, sophomore, junior, or senior years; not renewable. *Number:* 2. *Amount:* $2250.

Eligibility Requirements: Applicant must be enrolled or expecting to enroll full- or part-time at an institution or university. Applicant or parent of applicant must have employment or volunteer experience in hospitality/hotel administration/operations. Available to U.S. and non-U.S. citizens.

Application Requirements: Application form, essay, recommendations or references, transcript. *Deadline:* May 14.

Contact: Ms. Kelly McLendon, Programs Manager
International Flight Services Association
1100 Johnson Ferry Road, NE
Suite 300
Atlanta, GA 30342
Phone: 678-303-3042
E-mail: kmclendon@kellencompany.com

JOHN & GINNIE LONG SCHOLARSHIP AWARD

Individuals are selected to receive the award based on scholastic merit and dedication to an advanced education. Must be an employee of a current IFSA member company in good standing, or a relative of an employee of a current IFSA member company.

Award: Scholarship for use in freshman, sophomore, junior, or senior years; not renewable. *Number:* 1. *Amount:* $2250.

Eligibility Requirements: Applicant must be enrolled or expecting to enroll full- or part-time at an institution or university. Applicant or parent of applicant must have employment or volunteer experience in hospitality/hotel administration/operations. Available to U.S. and non-U.S. citizens.

Application Requirements: Application form, essay, recommendations or references, transcript. *Deadline:* May 14.

Contact: Ms. Kelly McLendon, Programs Manager
International Flight Services Association
1100 Johnson Ferry Road, NE
Suite 300
Atlanta, GA 30342
Phone: 678-303-3042
E-mail: kmclendon@kellencompany.com

JOHN LOUIS FOUNDATION SCHOLARSHIP AWARD

Individuals are selected to receive the award based on scholastic merit and dedication to an advanced education. Must be an employee of a current IFSA member company in good standing, or a relative of an employee of a current IFSA member company. Please address financial need within essay.

Award: Scholarship for use in freshman, sophomore, junior, or senior years; not renewable. *Number:* 1. *Amount:* $5000.

Eligibility Requirements: Applicant must be enrolled or expecting to enroll full- or part-time at an institution or university. Applicant or parent of applicant must have employment or volunteer experience in hospitality/hotel administration/operations. Available to U.S. and non-U.S. citizens.

Application Requirements: Application form, essay, recommendations or references, transcript. *Deadline:* May 14.

Contact: Ms. Kelly McLendon, Programs Manager
International Flight Services Association
1100 Johnson Ferry Road, NE
Suite 300
Atlanta, GA 30342
Phone: 678-303-3042
E-mail: kmclendon@kellencompany.com

KING NUT COMPANIES SCHOLARSHIP AWARD

Individuals are selected to receive the award based on scholastic merit and dedication to an advanced education. Must be an employee of a current IFSA member company in good standing, or a relative of an employee of a current IFSA member company. Please address financial need within essay.

Award: Scholarship for use in freshman, sophomore, junior, or senior years; not renewable. *Number:* 1. *Amount:* $2250.

Eligibility Requirements: Applicant must be enrolled or expecting to enroll full- or part-time at an institution or university. Applicant or parent of applicant must have employment or volunteer experience in hospitality/hotel administration/operations. Available to U.S. and non-U.S. citizens.

Application Requirements: Application form, essay, recommendations or references, transcript. *Deadline:* May 14.

Contact: Ms. Kelly McLendon, Programs Manager
International Flight Services Association
1100 Johnson Ferry Road, NE
Suite 300
Atlanta, GA 30342
Phone: 678-303-3042
E-mail: kmclendon@kellencompany.com

OAKFIELD FARMS SOLUTIONS SCHOLARSHIP AWARD

Individuals are selected to receive the award based on scholastic merit and dedication to pursuing a career in onboard services operations. Must be an employee of a current IFSA member company in good standing, or a relative of an employee of a current IFSA member company.

Award: Scholarship for use in freshman, sophomore, junior, or senior years; not renewable. *Number:* 1. *Amount:* $5000.

Eligibility Requirements: Applicant must be enrolled or expecting to enroll full- or part-time at an institution or university. Applicant or parent of applicant must have employment or volunteer experience in hospitality/hotel administration/operations. Available to U.S. and non-U.S. citizens.

Application Requirements: Application form, essay, recommendations or references, transcript. *Deadline:* May 14.

Contact: Ms. Kelly McLendon, Programs Manager
International Flight Services Association
1100 Johnson Ferry Road, NE
Suite 300
Atlanta, GA 30342
Phone: 678-303-3042
E-mail: kmclendon@kellencompany.com

WESSCO INTERNATIONAL SCHOLARSHIP AWARD

Individuals are selected to receive the award based on scholastic merit and dedication to an advanced education. Must be an employee of a current IFSA member company in good standing, or a relative of an employee of a current IFSA member company. Please address financial need within essay.

Award: Scholarship for use in freshman, sophomore, junior, or senior years; not renewable. *Number:* 1. *Amount:* $5000.

Eligibility Requirements: Applicant must be enrolled or expecting to enroll full- or part-time at an institution or university. Applicant or parent of applicant must have employment or volunteer experience in hospitality/hotel administration/operations. Available to U.S. and non-U.S. citizens.

Application Requirements: Application form, essay, recommendations or references, transcript. *Deadline:* May 14.

Contact: Ms. Kelly McLendon, Programs Manager
International Flight Services Association
1100 Johnson Ferry Road, NE
Suite 300
Atlanta, GA 30342
Phone: 678-303-3042
E-mail: kmclendon@kellencompany.com

JACKIE ROBINSON FOUNDATION

http://www.jackierobinson.org/

JACKIE ROBINSON SCHOLARSHIP

Scholarship for graduating high school seniors accepted to accredited four-year colleges or universities. Must be a minority student, United

States citizen, involved in community service and demonstrate leadership potential and financial need. See website for additional details.

Award: Scholarship for use in freshman, sophomore, junior, or senior years; renewable. *Number:* 40–60. *Amount:* $6000–$6000.

Eligibility Requirements: Applicant must be American Indian/Alaska Native, Asian/Pacific Islander, Black (non-Hispanic), Hispanic; high school student; age 18-22; planning to enroll or expecting to enroll full-time at a four-year institution or university and must have an interest in leadership. Applicant or parent of applicant must have employment or volunteer experience in community service. Available to U.S. citizens.

Application Requirements: Application form, application form may be submitted online (http://jackierobinson.org), community service, essay, financial need analysis, recommendations or references, test scores, transcript. *Deadline:* February 15.

Contact: Mr. John Shaw, Scholarship Application
Jackie Robinson Foundation
75 Varick Street, 2nd Floor
New York, NY 10013
Phone: 212-290-8600
Fax: 212-290-8081
E-mail: scholarships@jackierobinson.org

KOREAN AMERICAN SCHOLARSHIP FOUNDATION

http://www.kasf.org/

KOREAN-AMERICAN SCHOLARSHIP FOUNDATION EASTERN REGION SCHOLARSHIPS

Scholarships available to Korean-American and Korean students enrolled in a full-time undergraduate or graduate program in the United States. Selection based on financial need, academic achievement, school activities, and community services. Each applicant must submit an application to the respective KASF region. For more details and an application see website http://www.kasf.org.

Award: Scholarship for use in freshman, sophomore, junior, senior, or graduate years; not renewable. *Amount:* $1000.

Eligibility Requirements: Applicant must be of Korean heritage; Asian/Pacific Islander; enrolled or expecting to enroll full-time at an institution or university and studying in Delaware, District of Columbia, Kentucky, Maryland, North Carolina, Pennsylvania, Virginia, West Virginia. Applicant or parent of applicant must have employment or volunteer experience in community service. Available to U.S. and non-U.S. citizens.

Application Requirements: Application form, application form may be submitted online, essay, financial need analysis, personal photograph. *Deadline:* June 30.

Contact: Dr. Meekie Hahm, Chair, Scholarship Committee
E-mail: erc.scholarship@kasf.org

MAGIC JOHNSON FOUNDATION INC.

http://www.magicjohnson.org/

TAYLOR MICHAELS SCHOLARSHIP FUND

Scholarship to provide support for deserving minority high school students who exemplify a strong potential for academic achievement but face social-economic conditions that hinder them from reaching their full potential. Must have strong community service involvement.

Award: Scholarship for use in freshman year; renewable. *Amount:* $1000–$5000.

Eligibility Requirements: Applicant must be American Indian/Alaska Native, Asian/Pacific Islander, Black (non-Hispanic), Hispanic; high school student and planning to enroll or expecting to enroll full-time at a four-year institution or university. Applicant or parent of applicant must have employment or volunteer experience in community service. Available to U.S. and non-U.S. citizens.

Application Requirements: Application form, community service, essay, recommendations or references, transcript. *Deadline:* February 5.

Contact: Scholarship Coordinator
Magic Johnson Foundation Inc.
9100 Wilshire Boulevard, Suite 700, East Tower
Beverly Hills, CA 90212
Phone: 310-246-4400

MANA DE SAN DIEGO

http://www.manasd.org/

MANA DE SAN DIEGO SYLVIA CHAVEZ MEMORIAL SCHOLARSHIP

Scholarship for Latinas with permanent residence in San Diego County who are enrolled or about to enroll in a two-year, four-year, or graduate program. Must have a minimum 2.75 GPA and demonstrate financial need. For an application and additional information visit http://www.sdmana.org.

Award: Scholarship for use in freshman, sophomore, junior, or senior years; not renewable. *Amount:* $500–$2000.

Eligibility Requirements: Applicant must be Hispanic; enrolled or expecting to enroll full- or part-time at a two-year or four-year institution or university; female; resident of California and must have an interest in leadership. Applicant or parent of applicant must have employment or volunteer experience in community service. Available to U.S. citizens.

Application Requirements: Application form, essay, recommendations or references, transcript. *Deadline:* February 13.

Contact: Lucy Hernandez, Scholarship Director
MANA de San Diego
PO Box 81364
San Diego, CA 92138-1364
Phone: 619-225-9594
Fax: 619-225-0500
E-mail: scholarships@sdmana.org

MINNESOTA OFFICE OF HIGHER EDUCATION

http://www.ohe.state.mn.us

SAFETY OFFICERS' SURVIVOR GRANT PROGRAM

Grant for eligible survivors of Minnesota public safety officers killed in the line of duty. Safety officers who have been permanently or totally disabled in the line of duty are also eligible. Must be used at a Minnesota institution participating in State Grant Program. Write for details. Must submit proof of death or disability and Public Safety Officers Benefit Fund Certificate. Must apply for renewal each year. Five-year limit on awards.

Award: Grant for use in freshman, sophomore, junior, senior, or graduate years; not renewable. *Number:* 1–10. *Amount:* $1–$13,840.

Eligibility Requirements: Applicant must be age 23 or under; enrolled or expecting to enroll full- or part-time at a two-year or four-year or technical institution or university; resident of Minnesota and studying in Minnesota. Applicant or parent of applicant must have employment or volunteer experience in police/firefighting. Available to U.S. citizens.

Application Requirements: Application form. *Deadline:* continuous.

Contact: Brenda Larter, Program Administrator
Phone: 651-355-0612
E-mail: brenda.larter@state.mn.us

MISSISSIPPI OFFICE OF STUDENT FINANCIAL AID

http://www.msfinancialaid.org

LAW ENFORCEMENT OFFICERS/FIREMEN SCHOLARSHIP

Financial assistance to dependent children and spouses of any Mississippi law enforcement officer, full-time fire fighter or volunteer fire fighter who has suffered fatal injuries or wounds or become permanently and totally disabled as a result of injuries or wounds which occurred in the performance of the official and appointed duties of his or her office. This financial assistance is offered as an eight semester tuition and room scholarship at any state-supported college or university in Mississippi.

Award: Scholarship for use in freshman, sophomore, junior, or senior years; renewable. *Number:* 11–30. *Amount:* $2010–$12,854.

Eligibility Requirements: Applicant must be age 23 or under; enrolled or expecting to enroll full-time at a two-year or four-year institution or university; resident of Mississippi and studying in Mississippi. Applicant or parent of applicant must have employment or volunteer experience in police/firefighting. Available to U.S. citizens.

Application Requirements: Application form. *Deadline:* continuous.

Contact: Program Administrator
Mississippi Office of Student Financial Aid
3825 Ridgewood Road
Jackson, MS 39211
Phone: 601-432-6997
Fax: 601-432 Ext. 6527
E-mail: sfa@mississippi.edu

NATIONAL ASSOCIATION FOR CAMPUS ACTIVITIES

http://www.naca.org/

LORI RHETT MEMORIAL SCHOLARSHIP

The Lori Rhett Memorial Scholarship, endowed by the former NACA Pacific Northwest Region in 1996, was created to recognize the achievements of undergraduate or graduate student leaders enrolled in colleges and universities located in the former NACA Pacific Northwest Region. The fund will provide for one annual award. Awards are to be used for educational purposes, such as tuition, fees and books. Must be enrolled in a college or university within the NACA West Region.

Award: Scholarship for use in freshman, sophomore, junior, senior, or graduate years; not renewable. *Number:* 1. *Amount:* $300.

Eligibility Requirements: Applicant must be enrolled or expecting to enroll full-time at a two-year institution or university; studying in Alaska, Arizona, British Columbia, California, Colorado, Hawaii, Idaho, Nevada, New Mexico, Oregon, Utah, Washington and must have an interest in leadership. Applicant or parent of applicant must have employment or volunteer experience in community service. Available to U.S. citizens.

Application Requirements: Application form, application form may be submitted online, essay. *Deadline:* November 30.

Contact: Sarah Keeling, Director of Education and Research
Phone: 803-217-3485
E-mail: scholarships@naca.org

MARKLEY SCHOLARSHIP

The former NACA South Central region established the Markley Scholarship in 1983. The scholarship is named for Larry Markley, the acknowledged founder of the former NACA South Central Region. The purpose of this scholarship is to recognize and honor involved students who have made significant contributions to the NACA Central Region. Up to two scholarships may be awarded annually.

Award: Scholarship for use in sophomore, junior, senior, or graduate years; not renewable. *Number:* 1–2. *Amount:* $300.

Eligibility Requirements: Applicant must be enrolled or expecting to enroll full- or part-time at a two-year institution or university and studying in Arkansas, Colorado, Kansas, Louisiana, Missouri, New Mexico, Oklahoma, Texas. Applicant or parent of applicant must have employment or volunteer experience in community service. Available to U.S. citizens.

Application Requirements: Application form, application form may be submitted online, essay. *Deadline:* November 30.

Contact: Sarah Keeling, Director of Education and Research
Phone: 803-217-3485
E-mail: scholarships@naca.org

NATIONAL ASSOCIATION FOR CAMPUS ACTIVITIES MID ATLANTIC SCHOLARSHIP FOR STUDENT LEADERS

Scholarship for undergraduate students who are in good standing at the time of the application and during the academic term in which the scholarship is awarded. Applicants must maintain a 2.5 GPA, demonstrate leadership skills and abilities while holding a significant leadership position on campus or in community, and have made significant contributions via volunteer involvement. Eligible students must be attending a college or university within the NACA Mid Atlantic Region.

Award: Scholarship for use in freshman, sophomore, junior, or senior years; not renewable. *Number:* 1–2. *Amount:* $300.

Eligibility Requirements: Applicant must be enrolled or expecting to enroll full- or part-time at a two-year institution or university; studying in Delaware, District of Columbia, Maryland, New Jersey, New York, Ontario, Pennsylvania and must have an interest in leadership. Applicant

or parent of applicant must have employment or volunteer experience in community service. Available to U.S. citizens.

Application Requirements: Application form, application form may be submitted online, essay. *Deadline:* November 30.

Contact: Sarah Keeling, Director of Education and Research
Phone: 803-217-3485
E-mail: scholarships@naca.org

NATIONAL ASSOCIATION FOR CAMPUS ACTIVITIES SCHOLARSHIPS FOR STUDENT LEADERS

One means by which the NACA Foundation demonstrates its commitment to the development of professionals in the field of campus activities is through providing scholarships to undergraduate students who have demonstrated outstanding leadership abilities and made significant contributions to their campus communities. The Scholarships for Student Leaders Program, established in 1985, was created through donations to the 25 For 25 Drive, a silver anniversary fund-raising project of the NACA Foundation.

Award: Scholarship for use in freshman, sophomore, junior, or senior years; not renewable. *Number:* 1–7. *Amount:* $300.

Eligibility Requirements: Applicant must be enrolled or expecting to enroll full- or part-time at a two-year institution or university; studying in Alabama, Alaska, Alberta, Arizona, Arkansas, British Columbia, California, Colorado, Connecticut, Delaware, District of Columbia, Florida, Georgia, Hawaii, Idaho, Illinois, Indiana, Iowa, Kansas, Kentucky, Louisiana, Maine, Manitoba, Maryland, Massachusetts, Michigan, Minnesota, Mississippi, Missouri, Montana, Nebraska, Nevada, New Brunswick, New Hampshire, New Jersey, New Mexico, New York, North Carolina, North Dakota, Ohio, Oklahoma, Ontario, Oregon, Pennsylvania, Quebec, Rhode Island, Saskatchewan, South Carolina, South Dakota, Tennessee, Texas, Utah, Vermont, Virginia, Washington, West Virginia, Wisconsin, Wyoming and must have an interest in leadership. Applicant or parent of applicant must have employment or volunteer experience in community service. Available to U.S. citizens.

Application Requirements: Application form, application form may be submitted online, essay. *Deadline:* November 30.

Contact: Sarah Keeling, Director of Education and Research
Phone: 803-217-3485
E-mail: scholarships@naca.org

NATIONAL ASSOCIATION FOR CAMPUS ACTIVITIES SOUTH STUDENT LEADERSHIP SCHOLARSHIPS

The NACA South Student Leadership Scholarship, endowed by the former NACA Southeast Region, was established in 1994 to recognize the achievements of undergraduate student leaders enrolled at colleges and universities in the former NACA Southeast Region. The fund provides up to four scholarships annually. Awards are intended to be used for educational purposes, such as tuition, fees and books. Selections are made in the summer; scholarships are mailed to institutions no later than Aug. 1.

Award: Scholarship for use in freshman, sophomore, junior, or senior years; not renewable. *Number:* 1–4. *Amount:* $300.

Eligibility Requirements: Applicant must be enrolled or expecting to enroll full-time at a two-year institution or university; studying in Alabama, Florida, Georgia, Mississippi, North Carolina, South Carolina, Tennessee, Virginia and must have an interest in leadership. Applicant or parent of applicant must have employment or volunteer experience in community service. Available to U.S. citizens.

Application Requirements: Application form, application form may be submitted online, essay. *Deadline:* November 30.

Contact: Sarah Keeling, Director of Education and Research
Phone: 803-217-3485
E-mail: scholarships@naca.org

TESE CALDARELLI MEMORIAL SCHOLARSHIP

The Tese Caldarelli Memorial Scholarship was established by the former NACA Great Lakes Region to provide financial assistance to undergraduate or graduate student leaders enrolled in colleges and universities in the NACA Mid Atlantic & Mid America regions.

Award: Scholarship for use in freshman, sophomore, junior, senior, or graduate years; not renewable. *Number:* 1. *Amount:* $300.

Eligibility Requirements: Applicant must be enrolled or expecting to enroll full-time at a two-year institution or university; studying in Delaware, District of Columbia, Illinois, Indiana, Kentucky, Maryland, Michigan, New Jersey, New York, Ohio, Ontario, Pennsylvania, West

Virginia and must have an interest in leadership. Applicant or parent of applicant must have employment or volunteer experience in community service. Available to U.S. citizens.

Application Requirements: Application form, application form may be submitted online, essay. *Deadline:* November 30.

Contact: Sarah Keeling, Director of Education and Research
    Phone: 803-217-3485
    E-mail: scholarships@naca.org

NATIONAL MEDICAL FELLOWSHIPS INC.

www.nmfonline.org

THE UNITED HEALTH FOUNDATION/NMF DIVERSE MEDICAL SCHOLARS PROGRAM

The United Health Foundation and NMF are pleased to announce a new service-learning opportunity - the United Health Foundation/NMF Diverse Medical Scholars Program - to help develop the future health workforce and create healthier communities by providing an opportunity for outstanding U.S. minority medical students to engage in community service, develop critical skills, and join an active collegial network. The program's mission is to meet the need for culturally competent physician-leaders to better serve the community and ultimately improve health.

Award: Scholarship for use in sophomore, junior, senior, or graduate years; renewable. *Number:* 29. *Amount:* $7000.

Eligibility Requirements: Applicant must be American Indian/Alaska Native, Asian/Pacific Islander, Black (non-Hispanic), Hispanic and enrolled or expecting to enroll full-time at an institution or university. Applicant or parent of applicant must have employment or volunteer experience in medicine (physician/surgeon). Available to U.S. citizens.

Application Requirements: Application form, application form may be submitted online, community service, essay, financial need analysis, personal photograph. *Deadline:* September 30.

Contact: Ms. Ali Gemma, Program Manager
    Phone: 212-483-8880 Ext. 304
    Fax: 212-483-8897
    E-mail: scholarships@nmfonline.org

NATSO FOUNDATION

http://www.natso.com/

BILL MOON SCHOLARSHIP

Available to employees or dependents of NATSO-affiliated truck stops/travel plazas. Visit website at http://www.natsofoundation.org for additional information.

Award: Scholarship for use in freshman, sophomore, junior, senior, or graduate years; not renewable. *Number:* 13. *Amount:* $2500.

Eligibility Requirements: Applicant must be enrolled or expecting to enroll full- or part-time at a two-year or four-year institution or university. Applicant or parent of applicant must have employment or volunteer experience in transportation industry. Available to U.S. and non-U.S. citizens.

Application Requirements: Application form, essay, financial need analysis, recommendations or references, signature from employer, transcript. *Deadline:* April 14.

Contact: Sharon Corigliano, Executive Director
    Phone: 703-549-2100 Ext. 8561
    Fax: 703-684-9667
    E-mail: scorigliano@natso.com

NEW JERSEY STATE GOLF ASSOCIATION

NJSGA.org

NEW JERSEY STATE GOLF ASSOCIATION CADDIE SCHOLARSHIP

Caddie Scholarship Foundation, which has provided over $10 million in college tuition grants to over 2,700 deserving caddie scholars from our member clubs, since its inception in 1947.

Award: Scholarship for use in freshman, sophomore, junior, or senior years; not renewable. *Number:* 145. *Amount:* $3500–$6000.

Eligibility Requirements: Applicant must be enrolled or expecting to enroll full-time at a two-year or four-year or technical institution or university and resident of New Jersey. Applicant or parent of applicant must have employment or volunteer experience in private club/caddying. Available to U.S. citizens.

Application Requirements: Application form, financial need analysis. *Deadline:* March 1.

Contact: Ms. Sheila Menendez, Education Director
    New Jersey State Golf Association
    PO Box 6947
    Freehold, NJ 07728
    Phone: 848-8636481
    E-mail: Menendeznjsga@optonline.net

PACERS FOUNDATION INC.

http://www.pacersfoundation.org/

PACERS TEAMUP SCHOLARSHIP

Scholarship is awarded to Indiana high school seniors for their first year of undergraduate study at any accredited four-year college or university or two-year college or junior college. Primary selection criteria is student involvement in community service.

Award: Scholarship for use in freshman year; not renewable. *Number:* 5. *Amount:* $2000.

Eligibility Requirements: Applicant must be enrolled or expecting to enroll full-time at a two-year or four-year institution or university and resident of Indiana. Applicant or parent of applicant must have employment or volunteer experience in community service. Available to U.S. citizens.

Application Requirements: Application form, community service, essay, recommendations or references, transcript. *Deadline:* March 1.

Contact: Jami Marsh, Executive Director
    Pacers Foundation Inc.
    125 South Pennsylvania Street
    Indianapolis, IN 46204
    Phone: 317-917-2856
    E-mail: foundation@pacers.com

PENNSYLVANIA BURGLAR AND FIRE ALARM ASSOCIATION

http://www.pbfaa.com/

PENNSYLVANIA BURGLAR AND FIRE ALARM ASSOCIATION YOUTH SCHOLARSHIP PROGRAM

Non-renewable scholarships available to sons and daughters of active Pennsylvania police and fire personnel, and volunteer fire department personnel for full-time study at a two- or four-year college, or university. Must be a senior attending a Pennsylvania high school. Scholarship amount in the range of $500 to $6500.

Award: Scholarship for use in freshman year; not renewable. *Number:* 6–8. *Amount:* $500–$6500.

Eligibility Requirements: Applicant must be high school student; planning to enroll or expecting to enroll full-time at a two-year or four-year institution or university and resident of Pennsylvania. Applicant or parent of applicant must have employment or volunteer experience in police/firefighting. Available to U.S. citizens.

Application Requirements: Application form, essay, resume, test scores, transcript. *Deadline:* March 1.

Contact: Dale Eller, Executive Director
    Phone: 814-838-3093
    Fax: 814-838-5127
    E-mail: info@pbfaa.com

PROJECT BEST SCHOLARSHIP FUND

http://www.projectbest.com/

PROJECT BEST SCHOLARSHIP

• See page 451

PUEBLO OF SAN JUAN, DEPARTMENT OF EDUCATION

OHKAY OWINGEH TRIBAL SCHOLARSHIP

Scholarship for residents of New Mexico enrolled either full-time or part-time in accredited colleges or universities. Minimum GPA of 2.0 required. Must complete required number of hours of community service in the San Juan Pueblo. Deadline varies.

Award: Scholarship for use in freshman, sophomore, junior, or senior years; renewable.

Eligibility Requirements: Applicant must be American Indian/Alaska Native; enrolled or expecting to enroll full- or part-time at a two-year or four-year or technical institution or university and resident of New Mexico. Applicant or parent of applicant must have employment or volunteer experience in community service. Available to U.S. citizens.

Application Requirements: Application form.

Contact: Adam Garcia, Education Coordinator
Phone: 505-852-3477
Fax: 505-852-3030
E-mail: wevog68@valornet.com

POP'AY SCHOLARSHIP

Scholarship for members of Pueblo of San Juan tribe pursuing their first Associate or Baccalaureate degree. Must complete a minimum of 20 hours of community service within the San Juan Pueblo. Scholarship value is $2500. Seventeen awards are granted. Deadlines: December 30 for spring, April 30 for summer, and June 30 for fall.

Award: Scholarship for use in freshman, sophomore, junior, or senior years; renewable. *Number:* up to 17. *Amount:* $2500.

Eligibility Requirements: Applicant must be American Indian/Alaska Native; enrolled or expecting to enroll full-time at a two-year or four-year institution or university and resident of New Mexico. Applicant or parent of applicant must have employment or volunteer experience in community service. Available to U.S. citizens.

Application Requirements: Application form, letter of acceptance, transcript. *Deadline:* varies.

Contact: Adam Garcia, Education Coordinator
Phone: 505-852-3477
Fax: 505-852-3030
E-mail: wevog68@valornet.com

ST. CLAIRE REGIONAL MEDICAL CENTER

http://www.st-claire.org/

SR. MARY JEANNETTE WESS, S.N.D. SCHOLARSHIP

Scholarships available for undergraduates in their junior or senior year of study, or graduate students. Must have graduated from an eastern Kentucky high school in one of the following counties: Bath, Carter, Elliott, Fleming, Lewis, Magoffin, Menifee, Montgomery, Morgan, Rowan, or Wolfe. Must demonstrate academic achievement, leadership, service, and financial need.

Award: Scholarship for use in junior, senior, or graduate years; renewable. *Number:* 2. *Amount:* $750.

Eligibility Requirements: Applicant must be enrolled or expecting to enroll full-time at a four-year institution or university; resident of Kentucky and must have an interest in leadership. Applicant or parent of applicant must have employment or volunteer experience in community service. Available to U.S. and non-U.S. citizens.

Application Requirements: Application form, financial need analysis. *Deadline:* May 25.

Contact: Tom Lewis, Director of Development
Phone: 606-783-6511
Fax: 606-783-6795
E-mail: telewis@st-claire.org

STONEWALL COMMUNITY FOUNDATION

http://www.stonewallfoundation.org/

HARRY BARTEL MEMORIAL SCHOLARSHIP

LGBT students in New York City who are 23 years or younger with a record of community service can apply for this scholarship. Deadline varies. Applications available through Youth Program at The LGBT Center in Manhattan.

Award: Scholarship for use in freshman, sophomore, junior, senior, graduate, or postgraduate years; not renewable. *Number:* 1–2. *Amount:* $500.

Eligibility Requirements: Applicant must be age 23 or under; enrolled or expecting to enroll full-time at a two-year or four-year or technical institution or university and must have an interest in LGBT issues. Applicant or parent of applicant must have employment or volunteer experience in community service. Available to U.S. citizens.

Application Requirements: Application form. *Deadline:* continuous.

Contact: Natasha Jones, Director of Youth Leadership and Engagement
Stonewall Community Foundation
,c/o The Lesbian, Gay, Bisexual, and Transgender Community Center
208 West 13th Street
New York, NY 10011
Phone: 212-620-7310
E-mail: youth@gaycenter.org

TERRY FOX HUMANITARIAN AWARD

http://terryfoxawards.ca/

TERRY FOX HUMANITARIAN AWARD

The Terry Fox Humanitarian Award is granted to Canadian students working towards their first post-secondary degree or diploma. Criteria includes commitment to voluntary humanitarian work, courage in overcoming obstacles, excellence in academics, fitness and amateur sports. Maximum value of award is CAN$28,000 for a maximum of four years ($7000 annually, subject to renewal).

Award: Scholarship for use in freshman, sophomore, junior or senior years; renewable. *Number:* 20. *Amount:* $21,931.

Eligibility Requirements: Applicant must be Canadian citizen; enrolled or expecting to enroll full-time at a two-year or four-year institution or university; resident of Alberta, British Columbia, Manitoba, New Brunswick, Newfoundland, Northwest Territories, Nova Scotia, Ontario, Prince Edward Island, Quebec, Saskatchewan, Yukon and studying in Alberta, British Columbia, Manitoba, New Brunswick, Newfoundland, Northwest Territories, Nova Scotia, Ontario, Prince Edward Island, Quebec, Saskatchewan, Yukon. Applicant or parent of applicant must have employment or volunteer experience in community service.

Application Requirements: Application form, essay, interview. *Deadline:* February 1.

Contact: Mr. Ayden Thow, Awards Coordinator
Terry Fox Humanitarian Award
AQ 5003, 8888 University Drive
Burnaby, BC V5A 1S6
CAN
Phone: 778-782-3057
Fax: 778-782-3311
E-mail: info@terryfoxawards.ca

TRUCKER TO TRUCKER, LLC

http://www.truckertotrucker.com/

TRUCKERTOTRUCKER.COM COLLEGE SCHOLARSHIP

$500 college scholarship for individuals and their family members who are part of the transportation industry.

Award: Scholarship for use in freshman, sophomore, junior, senior, graduate, or postgraduate years; not renewable. *Number:* 2. *Amount:* $500.

Eligibility Requirements: Applicant must be age 17-99 and enrolled or expecting to enroll full-time at a two-year or four-year institution or university. Applicant or parent of applicant must have employment or volunteer experience in transportation industry. Available to U.S. citizens.

Application Requirements: Application form, essay. *Deadline:* June 1.

Contact: Scholarship Coordinator
E-mail: scholarship@truckertotrucker.com

TUITION EXCHANGE INC.

http://www.tuitionexchange.org/

TUITION EXCHANGE SCHOLARSHIPS

The Tuition Exchange is an association of over 675 colleges and universities awarding over 7400 full or substantial scholarships each year for children and other family members of faculty and staff employed at participating institutions. Students must maintain satisfactory academic progress and a cumulative GPA as established by each institution. Application procedures and deadlines vary by school. Contact Tuition Exchange Liaison Officer at home institution for details. The form does not allow posting the total value of the awards $240,000,000.

Award: Scholarship for use in freshman, sophomore, junior, senior, graduate, or postgraduate years; renewable. *Number:* 7,400–9,000. *Amount:* $4190–$49,750.

Eligibility Requirements: Applicant must be enrolled or expecting to enroll full- or part-time at a two-year or four-year institution or university. Applicant or parent of applicant must have employment or volunteer experience in teaching/education. Available to U.S. and non-U.S. citizens.

Application Requirements: Application form, application form may be submitted online (https://tuitionexchange.org). *Deadline:* continuous.

Contact: Mr. Robert Shorb, Executive Director/CEO
Tuition Exchange Inc.
3 Bethesda Metro Center
Suite 700
Bethesda, MD 20814
Phone: 301-941-1827
E-mail: info@tuitionexchange.org

TWO TEN FOOTWEAR FOUNDATION

http://www.twoten.org/

TWO TEN FOOTWEAR FOUNDATION SCHOLARSHIP

Renewable, merit and need-based award available to students who have 1000 hours work experience in footwear, leather, or allied industries during year of application, or have a parent employed in one of these fields for at least two years. Must have proof of employment and maintain 2.5 GPA. This is a needs-based scholarship.

Award: Scholarship for use in freshman, sophomore, junior, or senior years; renewable. *Number:* 300–350. *Amount:* $2500–$5000.

Eligibility Requirements: Applicant must be enrolled or expecting to enroll full- or part-time at a two-year or four-year or technical institution or university; resident of Alabama, Alaska, Arizona, Arkansas, California, Colorado, Connecticut, Delaware, Florida, Georgia, Hawaii, Idaho, Illinois, Indiana, Iowa, Kansas, Kentucky, Louisiana, Maine, Maryland, Massachusetts, Michigan, Minnesota, Mississippi, Missouri, Montana, Nebraska, Nevada, New Hampshire, New Jersey, New Mexico, New York, North Carolina, North Dakota, Ohio, Oklahoma, Ontario, Oregon, Pennsylvania, Puerto Rico, Rhode Island, South Carolina, South Dakota, Tennessee, Texas, Utah, Vermont, Virginia, Washington, West Virginia, Wisconsin, Wyoming and studying in Alabama, Alaska, Arizona, Arkansas, California, Colorado, Connecticut, Delaware, Florida, Georgia, Hawaii, Idaho, Illinois, Indiana, Iowa, Kansas, Kentucky, Louisiana, Maine, Maryland, Massachusetts, Michigan, Minnesota, Mississippi, Missouri, Montana, Nebraska, Nevada, New Hampshire, New Jersey, New Mexico, New York, North Carolina, North Dakota, Ohio, Oklahoma, Oregon, Pennsylvania, Puerto Rico, Rhode Island, South Carolina, South Dakota, Tennessee, Texas, Utah, Vermont, Virginia, Washington, West Virginia, Wisconsin, Wyoming. Applicant or parent of applicant must have employment or volunteer experience in leather/footwear industry. Available to U.S. citizens.

Application Requirements: Application form, application form may be submitted online (https://twoten.org/get-help/scholarships/higher-education-scholarships/), community service, essay, financial need analysis, personal photograph, resume, transcript. *Deadline:* April 4.

Contact: Liz Watson, Scholarship Program Manager
Phone: 781-736-1500
E-mail: scholarship@twoten.org

UNITED STATES BOWLING CONGRESS

http://www.bowl.com/

USBC ANNUAL ZEB SCHOLARSHIP

The award recognizes a USBC Youth member who achieves academic success and gives back to their community through service. Applicants must be in their junior or senior year of high school, and must be USBC Youth members in good standing. This scholarship is based mainly on community service and very strong academic success. Bowling success does not factor into the selection process. The winner receives a $2,500 scholarship and an expenses-paid trip for the winner and a parent or guardian to attend the awards ceremony, held in conjunction with the USBC Convention

Award: Scholarship for use in freshman, sophomore, junior, or senior years; not renewable. *Number:* 1. *Amount:* $2500.

Eligibility Requirements: Applicant must be high school student and planning to enroll or expecting to enroll full- or part-time at a two-year or technical institution or university. Applicant or parent of applicant must have employment or volunteer experience in community service. Available to U.S. citizens.

Application Requirements: Application form, application form may be submitted online, essay. *Deadline:* December 2.

Contact: Roger Noordhoek, Senior Director of Youth Marketing
United States Bowling Congress
621 Six Flags Drive
Arlington, TX 76011
Phone: 800-514-BOWL Ext. 8308
E-mail: contactus@ibcyouth.com

UNITED STATES SUBMARINE VETERANS

https://www.ussvi.org/Documents.asp?Type=Scholarship|Application

UNITED STATES SUBMARINE VETERANS INC. NATIONAL SCHOLARSHIP PROGRAM

• *See page 456*

YOUTH FOUNDATION INC.

http://fdnweb.org/youthfdn

ALEXANDER AND MAUDE HADDEN SCHOLARSHIP

Youth Foundation offers exceptional students with financial need an award of $2500 to $4000 per year which is renewable for four years at the foundation's discretion. Minimum GPA of 3.5 required, community service and extra curricular activities expected. Must write Foundation for information and application request form.

Award: Scholarship for use in freshman, sophomore, junior, or senior years; renewable. *Number:* 96–108. *Amount:* $2500–$4000.

Eligibility Requirements: Applicant must be enrolled or expecting to enroll full-time at a four-year institution or university. Applicant or parent of applicant must have employment or volunteer experience in community service. Available to U.S. citizens.

Application Requirements: Application form, community service, essay, financial need analysis, personal photograph. *Deadline:* February 28.

Contact: Ms. Johanna Lee, Executive Administrator
Phone: 212-840-6291
Fax: 212-840-6747
E-mail: YouthFdn@aol.com

IMPAIRMENT

ACADGILD

https://acadgild.com

ACADGILD MERIT-BASED SCHOLARSHIPS

AcadGild believes that accessing affordable and convenient eLearning options for upskilling is the smartest way to beat the high costs associated with traditional learning resulting in eventual massive college dropout rates. To make things easier for meritorious students and their families, AcadGild has decided to award $10,000 annually in scholarships to students signing up for its courses in Technology, Analytics, Design, and Digital Marketing. The majority of the scholarships are partial-course fee awards. A limited number of full-course fee awards to are also given to highly motivated students.

Award: Scholarship for use in freshman, sophomore, junior, senior, or graduate years; renewable. *Number:* 200–1,000. *Amount:* $200–$1000.

Eligibility Requirements: Applicant must be American Indian/Alaska Native, Asian/Pacific Islander, Black (non-Hispanic), Hispanic; age 13-65 and enrolled or expecting to enroll full- or part-time at a technical institution or university. Applicant must be hearing impaired, learning disabled, physically disabled, or visually impaired. Available to U.S. and non-U.S. citizens. Applicant or parent must meet one or more of the following requirements: general military experience; retired from active duty; disabled or killed as a result of military service; prisoner of war; or missing in action.

Application Requirements: Essay. *Deadline:* December 31.

Contact: Kuldeeplore Sharma
AcadGild
340 South Lemon Avenue, #9212
Walnut, CA 91789
Phone: 888-884-8355
E-mail: kuldeep@acadgild.com

ALEXANDER GRAHAM BELL ASSOCIATION FOR THE DEAF AND HARD OF HEARING

http://www.agbell.org/

AG BELL COLLEGE SCHOLARSHIP PROGRAM

Available to students with pre-lingual bilateral hearing loss in the moderate-severe to profound range who attend a mainstream and accredited college or university on a full-time basis. Specific eligibility criteria, submission guidelines, deadline and application available on AG Bell website at http://www.agbell.org.

Award: Scholarship for use in freshman, sophomore, junior, senior, graduate, or postgraduate years; not renewable. *Number:* 20–40. *Amount:* $1500–$5000.

Eligibility Requirements: Applicant must be enrolled or expecting to enroll full-time at a four-year institution or university; resident of Alabama, Alaska, Alberta, American Samoa, Arizona, Arkansas, British Columbia, California, Colorado, Connecticut, Delaware, District of Columbia, Florida, Georgia, Guam, Hawaii, Idaho, Illinois, Indiana, Iowa, Kansas, Kentucky, Louisiana, Maine, Manitoba, Maryland, Massachusetts, Michigan, Minnesota, Mississippi, Missouri, Montana, Nebraska, Nevada, New Brunswick, Newfoundland, New Hampshire, New Jersey, New Mexico, New York, North Carolina, North Dakota, Northern Mariana Islands, Northwest Territories, Nova Scotia, Ohio, Oklahoma, Ontario, Oregon, Pennsylvania, Prince Edward Island, Puerto Rico, Quebec, Rhode Island, Saskatchewan, South Carolina, South Dakota, Tennessee, Texas, Utah, Vermont, Virginia, Washington, West Virginia, Wisconsin, Wyoming, Yukon and studying in Alabama, Alaska, Alberta, American Samoa, Arizona, Arkansas, British Columbia, California, Colorado, Connecticut, Delaware, District of Columbia, Florida, Georgia, Guam, Hawaii, Idaho, Illinois, Indiana, Iowa, Kansas, Kentucky, Louisiana, Maine, Manitoba, Maryland, Massachusetts, Michigan, Minnesota, Mississippi, Missouri, Montana, Nebraska, Nevada, New Brunswick, Newfoundland, New Hampshire, New Jersey, New Mexico, New York, North Carolina, North Dakota, Northern Mariana Islands, Northwest Territories, Nova Scotia, Ohio, Oklahoma, Ontario, Oregon, Pennsylvania, Prince Edward Island, Puerto Rico, Quebec, Rhode Island, Saskatchewan, South Carolina, South Dakota, Tennessee, Texas, Utah, Vermont, Virginia, Washington, West Virginia, Wisconsin, Wyoming, Yukon. Applicant must be hearing impaired. Available to U.S. and non-U.S. citizens.

Application Requirements: Application form, essay. *Deadline:* March 8.

Contact: Ms. Lisa Chutjian, Chief Development Officer
Phone: 202-337-5220
E-mail: scholarships@agbell.org

AMERICAN COUNCIL OF THE BLIND

http://www.acb.org/

AMERICAN COUNCIL OF THE BLIND SCHOLARSHIPS

Merit-based award available to undergraduate students who are legally blind in both eyes. Submit certificate of legal blindness and proof of acceptance at an accredited postsecondary institution, as well as scholarship application, high school or college transcripts and other supporting documents (see directions on www.acb.org). Deadline: February 15.

Award: Scholarship for use in freshman, sophomore, junior, senior, graduate, or postgraduate years; not renewable. *Number:* 16–20. *Amount:* $1000–$4500.

Eligibility Requirements: Applicant must be enrolled or expecting to enroll full- or part-time at a two-year or four-year or technical institution or university. Applicant must be visually impaired. Available to U.S. citizens.

Application Requirements: Application form, application form may be submitted online (http://acb.org/2019-scholarship), community service, eye doctor's statement confirming the individual is legally blind, interview, recommendations or references, test scores. *Deadline:* February 15.

Contact: Scholarship Coordinator
American Council of the Blind
6300 Shingle Creek Pkwy
Suite 195
Brooklyn Center, MN 55430
Phone: 612-332-3242
E-mail: info@acb.org

BIOMARIN PHARMACEUTICAL INC.

http://www.biomarin.com/

RARE SCHOLARS

BioMarin Pharmaceutical Inc. has established a scholarship program to assist high school seniors, graduates, current postsecondary undergraduates, or graduate level students who have been diagnosed by a physician as having any form of mucopolysaccharidoses (MPS) disease, phenylketonuria (PKU), or Batten disease, regardless of treatment status. This program is administered by Scholarship America, the nation's largest designer and manager of scholarships, tuition assistance and other education support programs for corporations, foundations, associations, and individuals. Awards are granted without regard to race, color, creed, religion, sexual orientation, age, gender, disability, or national origin.

Award: Scholarship for use in freshman, sophomore, junior, or senior years; not renewable. *Number:* 1–5. *Amount:* $2500–$20,000.

Eligibility Requirements: Applicant must be enrolled or expecting to enroll full-time at a two-year or four-year or technical institution or university. Applicant must be learning disabled or physically disabled. Available to U.S. citizens.

Application Requirements: Application form. *Deadline:* March 30.

Contact: Allison Carleton, Senior Associate, Corporate Communications
Phone: 415-455-7588
E-mail: allison.carleton@bmrn.com

BLACK WYNN PLLC

2017 AUTISM SCHOLARSHIP

The scholarship will be in the form of a direct tuition payment to the educational institution chosen by the winning applicant. This could be a university, college, junior college, trade school or vocational school. You need not be enrolled in school at the time you submit your application, but the funds must be used within one year after the date of the award. You must be a United States citizen who has been diagnosed with ASD (DSM-V) to be eligible for the scholarship. Fill out the online application form; upload a statement of not more than 100 words describing your educational goals. (Optional) Upload a statement of not more than 650 words telling us how autism has impacted your education.

Award: Scholarship for use in freshman, sophomore, junior, or senior years; not renewable. *Number:* 1. *Amount:* $1000.

Eligibility Requirements: Applicant must be enrolled or expecting to enroll full- or part-time at a two-year or four-year or technical institution or university. Applicant must be learning disabled. Available to U.S. citizens.

Application Requirements: Application form, essay. *Deadline:* February 15.

Contact: William Wynn
Black Wynn PLLC
40 North Central Avenue, Suite 1400
Phoenix, AZ 85004
E-mail: michael@blackwynn.com

BRIDGES FOR THE DEAF AND HARD OF HEARING

http://www.bridgesfordeafandhh.org/

LINDA COWDEN MEMORIAL SCHOLARSHIP

The Linda Cowden Memorial Scholarship is awarded to Deaf or hard of hearing students or hearing students preparing to work in a profession serving the Deaf and/or hard of hearing communities. Applicants must live in the agency's 16 county service area in middle Tennessee.

Award: Scholarship for use in freshman, sophomore, junior, senior, graduate, or postgraduate years; not renewable. *Number:* 1. *Amount:* $1000.

Eligibility Requirements: Applicant must be enrolled or expecting to enroll full- or part-time at a two-year or four-year or technical institution or university and resident of Tennessee. Applicant must be hearing impaired. Available to U.S. citizens.

Application Requirements: Application form, essay, interview. *Deadline:* April 1.

Contact: Rebecca Nofi
Bridges for the Deaf and Hard of Hearing
935 Edgehill Avenue
Nashville, TN 37203
Phone: 615-248-8828
E-mail: rn@bridgesfordeafandhh.org

CALIFORNIA COUNCIL OF THE BLIND

http://www.ccbnet.org/

RHONDA KING MEMORIAL SCHOLARSHIP

The individual must be either a resident of, or attending an accredited college or university in Sacramento, Yolo, Placer, or El Dorado Counties. It is not required that a resident of Sacramento, Yolo, Placer or El Dorado Counties be attending an institution in California to submit an application.

Award: Scholarship for use in junior, senior, graduate, or postgraduate years; not renewable. *Number:* 1. *Amount:* $500.

Eligibility Requirements: Applicant must be enrolled or expecting to enroll full-time at a four-year institution or university. Applicant must be visually impaired. Available to U.S. and non-U.S. citizens.

Application Requirements: Application form, application form may be submitted online (http://www.ccbnet.org), essay, interview, recommendations or references, transcript. *Deadline:* July 17.

Contact: Leslie Thom, Scholarship Committee Chair
California Council of the Blind
ACB Capitol Chapter, California Council of the Blind
E-mail: lathom@comcast.net

COLLEGE WOMEN'S ASSOCIATION OF JAPAN

http://www.cwaj.org/

SCHOLARSHIP FOR THE VISUALLY IMPAIRED TO STUDY ABROAD

Scholarship of worth 3 million Japanese yen for visually impaired Japanese nationals or permanent residents of Japan who have been accepted into an undergraduate or graduate degree program at an accredited English-speaking university or research institution. Former recipients of CWAJ awards and members of CWAJ are ineligible. Award value is JPY3 million. Applications must be postmarked between (inclusive) November 7 and November 14.

Award: Scholarship for use in junior or senior years; not renewable. *Number:* 1.

Eligibility Requirements: Applicant must be of Japanese heritage and Japanese citizen; Asian/Pacific Islander and enrolled or expecting to enroll full-time at an institution or university. Applicant must be visually impaired. Available to citizens of countries other than the U.S. or Canada.

Application Requirements: Application form, essay. *Fee:* $19. *Deadline:* continuous.

Contact: Scholarship Committee
E-mail: scholarship@cwaj.org

SCHOLARSHIP FOR THE VISUALLY IMPAIRED TO STUDY IN JAPAN

Scholarship for visually impaired Japanese or permanent resident students for graduate or undergraduate study in Japan. Former recipients of CWAJ awards and members of CWAJ are ineligible. Award Value is JPY1.5 million. Deadline on or between November 1 and November 30.

Award: Scholarship for use in junior or senior years; not renewable. *Number:* 1–2.

Eligibility Requirements: Applicant must be of Japanese heritage and Japanese citizen and enrolled or expecting to enroll full-time at a four-year institution or university. Applicant must be visually impaired. Available to citizens of countries other than the U.S. or Canada.

Application Requirements: Application form, essay.

Contact: Scholarship Committee
E-mail: scholarship@cwaj.org

COUNCIL OF CITIZENS WITH LOW VISION INTERNATIONAL C/O AMERICAN COUNCIL OF THE BLIND

http://www.cclvi.org/

FRED SCHEIGERT SCHOLARSHIP

The Council of Citizens with Low Vision International (CCLVI) annually awards three scholarships in the amount of $3,000 each to one full-time entering freshman, undergraduate and graduate college student who are low vision, maintain a strong GPA and are involved in their school and local community. The application process annually opens January 1 at 12:01am eastern and the materials must annually be received by March 1 at 11:59pm eastern. Please see website for details. Scholarship funds will be awarded for the upcoming academic year. To read the scholarship guidelines and complete an online application, please visit https://www.cclvi.org.

Award: Scholarship for use in freshman, sophomore, junior, senior, graduate, or postgraduate years; not renewable. *Number:* 3. *Amount:* $3000.

Eligibility Requirements: Applicant must be enrolled or expecting to enroll full-time at a four-year or technical institution or university. Applicant must be visually impaired. Available to U.S. and non-U.S. citizens.

Application Requirements: Application form, application form may be submitted online (http://cclvi.org/scheigert-scholarship), interview. *Deadline:* March 15.

Contact: Lindsey Tilden, Chair
Phone: 844-460-0625
E-mail: scholarship@cclvi.org

CSA MEDICAL SUPPLY

https://csamedicalsupply.com

CSA MEDICAL SUPPLY COLLEGE SCHOLARSHIP

CSA Medical Supply.com is excited to offer our inaugural college scholarship designed to aid college students with mobility disabilities in their academic endeavors. One student will be awarded a $500 scholarship. In order to qualify for this scholarship you must submit an essay, poem, or short story about the chosen topic "Personnel Challenge". This scholarship is open to all students with mobility disabilities enrolled at an accredited 4-year institution.

Award: Scholarship for use in freshman, sophomore, junior, or senior years; renewable. *Number:* 1. *Amount:* $500.

Eligibility Requirements: Applicant must be age 18 and over and enrolled or expecting to enroll full-time at a four-year institution or university. Applicant must be physically disabled. Available to U.S. citizens.

Application Requirements: Essay. *Deadline:* May 30.

Contact: Aaron Kish, Director of Marking
CSA Medical Supply
725 North Highway A1A
Suite A106
Jupiter, FL 33477
Phone: 561-203-2191 Ext. 7018
Fax: 561-203-7932
E-mail: scholarships@csamedicalsupply.com

CYSTIC FIBROSIS SCHOLARSHIP FOUNDATION

http://www.cfscholarship.org/

CYSTIC FIBROSIS SCHOLARSHIP

One-time $1000 to $10,000 scholarships for young adults with cystic fibrosis to be used to further their education after high school. Awards may be used for tuition, books, and fees. Students may reapply in subsequent years.

Award: Scholarship for use in freshman, sophomore, junior, or senior years; not renewable. *Number:* 40–50. *Amount:* $1000–$10,000.

Eligibility Requirements: Applicant must be enrolled or expecting to enroll full-time at a two-year or four-year or technical institution or university. Applicant must be physically disabled. Available to U.S. citizens.

Application Requirements: Application form, essay, financial need analysis, recommendations or references, test scores, transcript. *Deadline:* March 21.

Contact: Mary Bottorff, President
Cystic Fibrosis Scholarship Foundation
2814 Grant Street
Evanston, IL 60201
Phone: 847-328-0127
Fax: 847-328-0127
E-mail: mkbcfsf@aol.com

DENTISTRY BY JOHN BARRAS DDS

2017 AUTISM SCHOLARSHIP

This is a scholarship, in the form of tuition assistance, that will help cover the cost of attending a college, junior college or university, or a trade or vocational school. The funds will be paid to the school chosen by the successful applicant. If you are a U.S. citizen who has been diagnosed with Autism Spectrum Disorder (DSM-V), and you wish to continue your education at a university/college/junior college or trade/vocational school, you are eligible to apply for the scholarship. You do not have to be enrolled at the time that you submit your application, but you must utilize the scholarship within a year from the date the award is announced. For a chance to win the scholarship, you must complete the application, which consists of the following: filling out the online application form, uploading a statement (200 words or less) describing your educational goals. Optional: uploading a statement (1,000 words or less) explaining how ASD or autism has impacted on your education.

Award: Scholarship for use in freshman, sophomore, junior, or senior years; not renewable. *Number:* 1. *Amount:* $1000.

Eligibility Requirements: Applicant must be enrolled or expecting to enroll full- or part-time at a two-year or four-year or technical institution or university. Applicant must be learning disabled. Available to U.S. citizens.

Application Requirements: Application form, essay. *Deadline:* February 27.

Contact: John Barras
Dentistry by John Barras DDS
1330 Post Oak Boulevard, #1300
Houston, TX 77056
E-mail: johnbarrasdds@yahoo.com

DISABLEDPERSON INC. COLLEGE SCHOLARSHIP

http://www.disabledperson.com/

DISABLEDPERSON INC. NATIONAL COLLEGE SCHOLARSHIP AWARD FOR COLLEGE STUDENTS WITH DISABILITIES

Essay contest for college students with disabilities who are enrolled and matriculated as full-time or student.in a two- or four-year accredited college or university. Students who are part-time are welcome also as long as their part-time status is because of their disability and not because of financial restraints. The essay must not exceed 1000 words. We offer two scholarships per school year. One in the fall semester and one in the spring semester since 2004.

Award: Scholarship for use in freshman, sophomore, junior, senior, graduate, or postgraduate years; not renewable. *Number:* 1. *Amount:* $2000.

Eligibility Requirements: Applicant must be enrolled or expecting to enroll full- or part-time at a two-year or four-year or technical institution or university. Applicant must be hearing impaired, learning disabled, physically disabled, or visually impaired. Available to U.S. citizens.

Application Requirements: Application form, application form may be submitted online (https://www.disABLEDperson.com), entry in a contest, essay. *Deadline:* March 31.

Contact: Michael Corso, President
disABLEDperson Inc. College Scholarship
PO Box 230636
Encinitas, CA 92023
E-mail: scholarships@disabledperson.com

ESSAYHUB

https://essayhub.com/

ESSAY WRITING CONTEST BY ESSAYHUB

Any individual choosing to participate in this contest must be undergoing high school or higher level education (university, college). Every submission must meet the minimum word count requirement of 500 words to 1000 words max. All work for this essay contest must be written in English. We understand that the world is multilingual and we would enjoy reading such interesting works in their original language, however it would make conducting such an event nearly impossible. Fill our application form located on this page to take part in the contest. Or send your works in Word or Doc type files as to allow easy access to them to the email address support@essayhub.com with subject line Essay Writing Contest. The email submission requirements need you to place your name in the work itself and in the text of the email letter itself. Example: Essay Writing Contest—Joseph Smith. Avoid continuously looking to debate whether you should be the winner or trying to convince the judges why you think you deserved to win. All judging is done anonymously and based solely on the quality of the essay writer's work. This allows for only the best essays to win. We do not accept the submission of any kind of scholarship essay. Plagiarism is a no go. All those found guilty will be disqualified without being notified. No excuses, no exceptions. There are many referencing guides available on our website for you to use in case you get stuck. In the case of a resubmission from a previous contest it will not be taken into account and regarded as plagiarism. All submissions must be given in by the 30th of April 2017 11:59 PST at the latest. Make sure to include your correct contact information so we may get a hold of you if you have won. The event begins on the 17th of February 2017 at 12:00 PST.

Award: Scholarship for use in freshman, sophomore, junior, senior, graduate, or postgraduate years; not renewable. *Number:* 3. *Amount:* $500.

Eligibility Requirements: Applicant must be American Indian/Alaska Native, Asian/Pacific Islander, Black (non-Hispanic), Hispanic; enrolled or expecting to enroll full- or part-time at a two-year or four-year institution or university and must have an interest in writing. Applicant must be hearing impaired, learning disabled, physically disabled, or visually impaired. Available to U.S. and non-U.S. citizens.

Application Requirements: Essay. *Deadline:* April 30.

Contact: Miss. Tia Moreen
  E-mail: tia.moreen@gmail.com

EXCEPTIONALNURSE.COM

http://www.exceptionalnurse.com/

ANNA MAY ROLANDO SCHOLARSHIP AWARD

Scholarship of $500 awarded to a nursing student with a disability. Preference will be given to a graduate student who has demonstrated a commitment to working with people with disabilities.

Award: Scholarship for use in freshman, sophomore, junior, senior, graduate, or postgraduate years; not renewable. *Number:* 1. *Amount:* $500.

Eligibility Requirements: Applicant must be enrolled or expecting to enroll full-time at an institution or university. Applicant must be hearing impaired, learning disabled, physically disabled, or visually impaired. Available to U.S. citizens.

Application Requirements: Application form, essay. *Deadline:* June 1.

Contact: Scholarship Committee
  ExceptionalNurse.com
  ExceptionalNurse.com
  13019 Coastal Circle
  Palm Beach Gardens, FL 33410
  E-mail: exceptionalnurse@aol.com

BRUNO ROLANDO SCHOLARSHIP AWARD

• See page 463

FELDMAN & ROYLE, ATTORNEYS AT LAW

http://www.feldmanroyle.com/

AUTISM SCHOLARSHIPS

Feldman & Royle, Attorneys at Law is pleased to announce two annual scholarships for individuals diagnosed with Autism Spectrum Disorder (ASD or Autism). The scholarships are designed to assist applicants in furthering their education. Each of the $1,000 scholarships will be for tuition at an educational institution chosen by the applicant. All those who have ASD (DSM-5) are eligible for the scholarships, which will be used to assist you in furthering your educational goals. We may request proof of your ASD diagnosis. Feldman & Royle is offering two annual scholarships. Both of them are for $1,000, and will be used to defray the cost of tuition for a secondary school, community college, trade school or college. You are eligible for a scholarship whether or not you currently attend school. After being awarded the scholarship, you will have one year within which to provide us with a tuition invoice from the educational institution you have chosen to attend. A check for $1,000 will then be issued to the institution.

Award: Scholarship for use in freshman, sophomore, junior, senior, graduate, or postgraduate years; not renewable. *Number:* 2. *Amount:* $1000.

Eligibility Requirements: Applicant must be enrolled or expecting to enroll full- or part-time at a two-year or four-year or technical institution or university. Applicant must be learning disabled. Available to U.S. citizens.

Application Requirements: Application form, essay. *Deadline:* November 7.

Contact: Adam Feldman
  E-mail: michael@feldmanroyle.com

FELDMAN LAW FIRM PLLC

http://www.afphoenixcriminalattorney.com/

AUTISM SCHOLARSHIP

The scholarship is in the amount of $1,000, and is being offered as an incentive to those persons diagnosed with ASD to continue their education. The scholarship fund will be applied to defray a portion of the tuition cost for attendance at a university or college, junior college, or vocational school. Applicants do not have to be enrolled in school at the time of submission of their application, but the scholarship fund must be used within one year from the date of the award. The scholarship being offered by The Feldman Law Firm is open to anyone who has been diagnosed with ASD (DSM-V) who would like to continue their education at a vocational school, college or university. In order to fulfill the requirements for the application process, you must fill out the online application; prepare and upload a statement (up to 100 words in length) telling us your educational goals; and (optional) prepare and upload an essay (up to 850 words in length) discussing how ASD has affected your education.

Award: Scholarship for use in freshman, sophomore, junior, or senior years; not renewable. *Number:* 1. *Amount:* $1000.

Eligibility Requirements: Applicant must be enrolled or expecting to enroll full- or part-time at a two-year or four-year or technical institution or university. Applicant must be learning disabled. Available to U.S. citizens.

Application Requirements: Application form, essay. *Deadline:* February 15.

Contact: Adam Feldman
  Feldman Law Firm PLLC
  1 E. Washington St.
  Phoenix, AZ 85004
  E-mail: mike@afphoenixcriminalattorney.com

DISABLED VETERANS SCHOLARSHIP

The Feldman Law Firm will be awarding an educational scholarship for the benefit of disabled veterans. The scholarship will be for $1,000, and it will provide tuition assistance for the successful applicant. It is being offered to encourage disabled veterans to continue their education, and provide financial assistance toward that goal. The $1,000 disabled veteran scholarship is offered to eligible applicants who wish to attend a trade or vocational school, or a college or junior college. Applicants do not have to be enrolled in a school at the time they submit their application. We do require, however, that the scholarship funds be used within a year after the date on which it is awarded. The winning applicant will provide us with a tuition invoice from the educational institution he or she has chosen, and we will pay $1,000 directly to the school. In order to apply for the scholarship, you must be a veteran of any branch of the Armed Forces of the United States. You must also have a disability rating of 30% or higher. Applicants must fill out and complete the online application form and provide us with (upload) a statement of 125 words or less discussing your educational goals. (Optional) Provide us with (upload) an essay of not more than 850 words discussing how your military service has made an impact on your life. In addition, we may request proof of your veteran status, and proof of your disability. The application, together with any upload(s), must be submitted by February 5, 2018. The winning applicant will be notified on or before March 5, 2018. The winner will be selected by Adam Feldman, founder of The Feldman Law Firm, in his sole discretion.

Award: Scholarship for use in freshman, sophomore, junior, senior, graduate, or postgraduate years; not renewable. *Number:* 1. *Amount:* $1000.

Eligibility Requirements: Applicant must be enrolled or expecting to enroll full- or part-time at a two-year or four-year or technical institution or university. Applicant must be physically disabled. Available to U.S. citizens. Applicant or parent must meet one or more of the following requirements: general military experience; retired from active duty; disabled or killed as a result of military service; prisoner of war; or missing in action.

Application Requirements: Application form, essay. *Deadline:* February 5.

Contact: Adam Feldman
  Phone: 602-540-7887
  E-mail: mike@afphoenixcriminalattorney.com

FIT SMALL BUSINESS

http://www.fitsmallbusiness.com

BUSINESS PLAN SCHOLARSHIP FOR STUDENTS WITH DISABILITIES

The Business Plan Scholarship is awarded twice a year, once during the fall semester and once during the spring semester. The winner is judged primarily on the merit of their 500-1000 word response to the essay prompt 'What I learned from writing a business plan'

Award: Scholarship for use in freshman, sophomore, junior, senior, graduate, or postgraduate years; not renewable. *Number:* 1. *Amount:* $1000.

Eligibility Requirements: Applicant must be enrolled or expecting to enroll full- or part-time at a two-year or four-year or technical institution or university. Applicant must be hearing impaired, learning disabled, physically disabled, or visually impaired. Available to U.S. and non-U.S. citizens.

Application Requirements: Essay. *Deadline:* November 1.

Contact: Mr. Marc Prosser, Publisher
E-mail: mprosser@fitsmallbusiness.com

FOUNDATION FOR SIGHT AND SOUND

http://fssny.org

HELP AMERICA HEAR SCHOLARSHIP

The scholarship is open nationally to high school seniors who have a hearing loss, which requires the use of hearing aid(s) in their daily life. The purpose of this scholarship is to help students with hearing challenges reach their full potential by giving them the gift of sound. This will further allow the students to build confidence and self-esteem as they prepare to begin their college or vocational school education. The recipient of this scholarship will be selected by an independent group of judges to be determined by the Foundation For Sight & Sound, a 501c3 Not for Profit Corporation. The scholarship will award one student per school year, currently wearing hearing aid(s). Cochlear users may enter this and will only receive the financial award. The scholarship recipient will receive two state-of-the-art ReSound Hearing Aids which best fit his/her hearing loss, along with a $1000 scholarship to the student's college or vocational school of choice.

Award: Scholarship for use in freshman year; not renewable. *Number:* 1. *Amount:* $1000.

Eligibility Requirements: Applicant must be high school student and planning to enroll or expecting to enroll full- or part-time at a two-year or four-year or technical institution or university. Applicant must be hearing impaired. Available to U.S. citizens.

Application Requirements: Application form, essay, personal photograph. *Deadline:* March 25.

Contact: Ms. Marissa Marinucci, Office Assistant
Foundation for Sight and Sound
Foundation For Sight and Sound
PO Box 1245
Smithtown, NY 11787
Phone: 631-366-3461
E-mail: info@fssny.org

GREAT LAKES HEMOPHILIA FOUNDATION

http://www.glhf.org/

GREAT LAKES HEMOPHILIA FOUNDATION EDUCATION SCHOLARSHIP

This scholarship not only targets the traditional college and vocational students, but also looks at retraining adults with bleeding disorders who are finding it difficult to function in their chosen field because of health complications. It also targets parents of children with bleeding disorders who through career advancement can better meet the financial needs of caring for their child.

Award: Scholarship for use in freshman, sophomore, junior, senior, graduate, or postgraduate years; not renewable. *Number:* 5–6. *Amount:* $500–$2000.

Eligibility Requirements: Applicant must be enrolled or expecting to enroll full- or part-time at a two-year or four-year or technical institution or university and resident of Wisconsin. Applicant must be physically disabled. Available to U.S. citizens.

Application Requirements: Application form, essay, recommendations or references, transcript. *Deadline:* May 1.

Contact: Karin Koppen, Program Services Coordinator
Great Lakes Hemophilia Foundation
638 North 18 Street, Suite 108
Milwaukee, WI 53233
Phone: 414-257-0200
Fax: 414-257-1225
E-mail: kkoppen@glhf.org

HEMOPHILIA FEDERATION OF AMERICA

http://www.hemophiliafed.org/

HFA EDUCATIONAL SCHOLARSHIP

This scholarship is for students with a bleeding disorder who are attending/planning to attend a postsecondary school.

Award: Scholarship for use in freshman, sophomore, junior, senior, graduate, or postgraduate years; not renewable. *Number:* 2. *Amount:* $2000.

Eligibility Requirements: Applicant must be enrolled or expecting to enroll full- or part-time at a two-year or four-year or technical institution or university. Applicant must be physically disabled. Available to U.S. citizens.

Application Requirements: Application form, application form may be submitted online (https://www.hemophiliafed.org/for-patient-families/resources/educational-scholarships-internships/hfa-educational-scholarships/), essay, Proof of a bleeding disorder, recommendations or references, transcript. *Deadline:* May 10.

Contact: Athenna Harrison, Educational Scholarship Committee
Hemophilia Federation of America
820 First Street NE
Suite 720
Washington, DC 20002
Phone: 202-675-6984
Fax: 972-616-6211
E-mail: scholarships@hemophiliafed.org

HFA MEDICAL/HEALTHCARE SERVICES EDUCATIONAL SCHOLARSHIP

One (1) scholarships will be awarded in the amount of $4,000.00 to a student pursuing a degree in the medical/healthcare services field.

Award: Scholarship for use in freshman, sophomore, junior, senior, graduate, or postgraduate years; not renewable. *Number:* 1. *Amount:* $4000.

Eligibility Requirements: Applicant must be enrolled or expecting to enroll full- or part-time at a two-year or four-year or technical institution or university. Applicant must be physically disabled. Available to U.S. citizens.

Application Requirements: Application form, application form may be submitted online (https://www.hemophiliafed.org/for-patient-families/resources/educational-scholarships-internships/hfa-educational-scholarships/), essay, recommendations or references, transcript. *Deadline:* May 10.

Contact: Athenna Harrison, Educational Scholarship Committee
Hemophilia Federation of America
820 First Street NE
Suite 720
Washington, DC 20002
Phone: 202-675-6984
Fax: 972-616-6211
E-mail: scholarships@hemophiliafed.org

HFA PARENT/SIBLING/CHILD EDUCATIONAL SCHOLARSHIP

This scholarship is geared towards those who are immediately related to someone with a bleeding disorder.

Award: Scholarship for use in freshman, sophomore, junior, senior, graduate, or postgraduate years; not renewable. *Number:* 1. *Amount:* $2000.

Eligibility Requirements: Applicant must be enrolled or expecting to enroll full- or part-time at a two-year or four-year or technical institution or university. Applicant must be physically disabled. Available to U.S. citizens.

Application Requirements: Application form, application form may be submitted online (https://www.hemophiliafed.org/for-patient-families/resources/educational-scholarships-internships/hfa-educational-scholarships/), essay, recommendations or references, transcript. *Deadline:* May 10.

Contact: Athenna Harrison, Educational Scholarship Committee
Hemophilia Federation of America
820 First Street NE
Suite 720
Washington, DC 20002
Phone: 202-675-6984
Fax: 972-616-6211
E-mail: scholarships@hemophiliafed.org

HEMOPHILIA FOUNDATION OF SOUTHERN CALIFORNIA

http://www.hemosocal.org/

CHRISTOPHER MARK PITKIN MEMORIAL SCHOLARSHIP

Scholarship open to all members of the hemophilia community, including spouses and siblings. Applicants must be pursuing a college or technical/trade school education. Applicants must be part of the HFSC Service Area - Counties of Los Angeles, Orange, Santa Barbara, San Luis Obispo, Riverside, San Bernardino, Ventura, Inyo, and Kern.

Award: Scholarship for use in freshman, sophomore, junior, senior, graduate, or postgraduate years; not renewable. *Number:* 5–15. *Amount:* $250–$1000.

Eligibility Requirements: Applicant must be enrolled or expecting to enroll full- or part-time at a two-year or four-year or technical institution or university; resident of California and studying in California. Applicant must be physically disabled. Available to U.S. citizens.

Application Requirements: Application form, essay, resume. *Deadline:* June 28.

Contact: Scholarship Committee
Hemophilia Foundation of Southern California
959 East Walnut St., Suite 114
c/o Christopher Mark Pitkin Memorial Scholarship
Pasadena, CA 91106
Phone: 626-765-6656
Fax: 626-765-6657
E-mail: info@hemosocal.org

HOMUS

https://homus.org

HOMUS SCHOLARSHIP PROGRAM

Since its conception in 1991, electronic commerce, or e-commerce, has made revolutionary changes in the way people do business transactions. Prior to e-commerce, consumers had to purchase items directly from a physical store. Now almost every transaction can be done online, thanks to the emergence of e-commerce. And our magazine is helping consumers to make a right decision before while shopping online. College is a big step forward in achieving student's goals and we would like to be a part of the educational life of students. That's why we are providing $3000 E-Commerce Research Scholarship program for all students currently enrolled in a college or university! Homus.org offers the opportunity for all who want to apply for the scholarship by researching and covering the following topic "E-Commerce Trends. How E-Commerce Will Change Retail Business in Next 10 Years".

Award: Scholarship for use in freshman, sophomore, junior, senior, graduate, or postgraduate years; renewable. *Number:* 1. *Amount:* $3000.

Eligibility Requirements: Applicant must be American Indian/Alaska Native, Asian/Pacific Islander, Black (non-Hispanic), Hispanic; high school student; age 18 and over and planning to enroll or expecting to enroll full- or part-time at a two-year or four-year or technical institution or university. Applicant must be hearing impaired, learning disabled, physically disabled, or visually impaired. Available to U.S. and non-U.S. citizens.

Application Requirements: Application form, essay. *Deadline:* September 15.

Contact: Mr. David Croll, Senior Manager
Homus
4318 Oakwood Avenue
New York, NY 10021
Phone: 212-639-5961
E-mail: hello@homus.org

ILLINOIS COUNCIL OF THE BLIND

http://www.icbonline.org/

FLOYD R. CARGILL SCHOLARSHIP

Award for a visually impaired Illinois resident attending or planning to attend an Illinois college. One-time award of $1000.

Award: Scholarship for use in freshman, sophomore, junior, or senior years; not renewable. *Number:* 1. *Amount:* $1000.

Eligibility Requirements: Applicant must be enrolled or expecting to enroll full-time at a two-year or four-year or technical institution or university; resident of Illinois and studying in Illinois. Applicant must be visually impaired. Available to U.S. citizens.

Application Requirements: Application form, recommendations or references, test scores, transcript. *Deadline:* July 15.

Contact: Maggie Ulrich, Office Manager
Phone: 217-523-4967
E-mail: icb@icbonline.org

KELLY LAW TEAM

http://www.jkphoenixpersonalinjuryattorney.com/

AUTISM/ASD SCHOLARSHIP

The Kelly Law Team (KLT) is pleased to announce that it will be offering a scholarship in the amount of $1,000 for individuals with autism. The scholarship will be used to assist in the pursuit secondary or post-secondary educational opportunities. The $1,000 scholarship will be in the form of a tuition payment for the attendance at a university, college, junior college, or trade or vocational school. It is not required that the individual be enrolled in an educational program at the time of the submission of his or her application, but must be used within a year after the award. The funds will be provided directly to the educational institution chosen by the winner. Applicants must be United States citizens who have been diagnosed with ASD. The completed application must be submitted to us no later than February 8, 2018. The application will consist of (a) the online application, (b) a statement of 100 words or less explaining how the scholarship will assist in achieving your educational goals, and (c) an optional essay (1,000 words or less) on how autism has affected your education. We may also ask you to provide us with evidence of your diagnosis. The winner will be chosen on or before March 8, 2018. The winner will be selected at the discretion of John Kelly, whose decision will be final.

Award: Scholarship for use in freshman, sophomore, junior, senior, graduate, or postgraduate years; not renewable. *Number:* 1. *Amount:* $1000.

Eligibility Requirements: Applicant must be enrolled or expecting to enroll full- or part-time at a two-year or four-year or technical institution or university. Applicant must be learning disabled. Available to U.S. citizens.

Application Requirements: Application form, essay. *Deadline:* February 8.

Contact: John Kelly
Phone: 602-283-4122
E-mail: michael@jkphoenixpersonalinjuryattorney.com

KITCHEN GUIDES

http://www.kitchensguides.com/

SMART KITCHEN IMPROVEMENT SCHOLARSHIP BY KITCHEN GUIDES

Under this scholarship, applicants have to write 1000 words article on the cooking related niche. Topics will provide by us, so you just need to pick one from them and start writing on it and submit it on our website

Award: Scholarship for use in freshman, sophomore, junior, senior, graduate, or postgraduate years; not renewable. *Number:* 1. *Amount:* $500.

Eligibility Requirements: Applicant must be American Indian/Alaska Native, Asian/Pacific Islander, Black (non-Hispanic), Hispanic; high school student; age 15-40 and planning to enroll or expecting to enroll full- or part-time at a two-year or four-year or technical institution or university. Applicant must be hearing impaired, learning disabled, physically disabled, or visually impaired. Available to U.S. and non-U.S. citizens. Applicant must have general military experience.

Application Requirements: Application form. *Deadline:* October 15.

Contact: Steven Burton, Kitchen Guides
Kitchen Guides
3548 Wyatt Street
Boca Raton, FL 33432
Phone: 651-3938087
E-mail: info@kitchensguides.com

LAW OFFICE OF DAVID D. WHITE, PLLC

http://www.wm-attorneys.com/

ANNUAL TRAUMATIC BRAIN INJURY SCHOLARSHIPS

The Law Office of David D. White takes pleasure in announcing the establishment of an annual scholarship program for the benefit of persons who have suffered traumatic brain injury (TBI). The scholarship program consists of two scholarships, offered annually,* both in the amount of $1,000. The scholarships will take the form of tuition payments for attendance at a school of the applicant's choosing. This may be a university, a college (or a community college), a secondary school, or a trade school. And you do not have to be enrolled as a student currently in order to apply. In order to be eligible to apply for a scholarship, you must have been diagnosed with TBI. We may ask you to provide us with proof of the diagnosis. The winners will have a year in which to provide an invoice for tuition from their school, and we will then pay $1,000 to the school toward the cost reflected in the invoice.

Award: Scholarship for use in freshman, sophomore, junior, senior, graduate, or postgraduate years; not renewable. *Number:* 2. *Amount:* $1000.

Eligibility Requirements: Applicant must be enrolled or expecting to enroll full- or part-time at a two-year or four-year or technical institution or university. Applicant must be learning disabled. Available to U.S. citizens.

Application Requirements: Application form, essay. *Deadline:* November 3.

Contact: David White
E-mail: michael@wm-attorneys.com

LAW OFFICE OF DAVID P. SHAPIRO

http://www.davidpshapirolaw.com/about-us/

AUTISM SCHOLARSHIP

This is a one-time scholarship in the amount of $1,000. It will be applied to offset the cost of tuition at a college, university, junior college, trade or vocational school, or community college. You do not have to be currently enrolled in the educational institution in order to apply for the scholarship. The winner will have one year from the date of the award in which to provide us with the name of the school you will be attending. The check for $1,000 will be issued directly to that school on the winner's behalf. Anyone who has been diagnosed with ASD (DSM-V) and is interested in furthering their educational goals is invited to apply for the scholarship. We reserve the right to request proof of the diagnosis. The application process requires the one complete the online application form, upload a brief statement (100 words or less) telling us how the money will be used for your educational plans if you are awarded the scholarship, and (optional) upload an essay (1,000 words or less) on the impact ASD has had on your education.

Award: Scholarship for use in freshman, sophomore, junior, or senior years; not renewable. *Number:* 1. *Amount:* $1000.

Eligibility Requirements: Applicant must be enrolled or expecting to enroll full- or part-time at a two-year or four-year or technical institution or university. Applicant must be learning disabled. Available to U.S. citizens.

Application Requirements: Application form, essay. *Deadline:* February 12.

Contact: David Shapiro
Law Office of David P. Shapiro
1501 5th Avenue, #200
San Diego, CA 92101
E-mail: michael@davidpshapirolaw.com

LAW OFFICES OF DAVID A. BLACK

http://www.dbphoenixcriminallawyer.com

SCHOLARSHIP FOR DISABLED VETERANS

The Law Offices of David A. Black has announced the establishment of a scholarship for disabled veterans. This is a scholarship that will assist in the payment of tuition to the educational institution chosen by the successful applicant. The scholarship is in the form of tuition assistance at a college or university, junior college, trade school or vocational school. Applicants need not be enrolled at an educational institution at the time they submit their application, but the scholarship must be utilized within one year from the date of the award. The scholarship funds will be paid directly to the school to defray a portion of the tuition cost. In order to be considered for the scholarship, you must be a veteran of the United States Armed Forces and have a 30% or higher disability rating. Your completed online application, together with all uploads, is due no later than January 15, 2018. To apply for the disabled veteran scholarship, you must 1. complete and submit the online application; 2. upload a short statement (not more than 100 words) telling us your educational goals. (Optional) Upload an essay of not more than 800 words on the topic of how your military service has affected your life. The winner will be selected at the sole discretion of David A. Black, founder of the Law Offices of David A. Black. Mr. Black's decision will be made, and the winner will be notified, on or before March 15, 2018.

Award: Scholarship for use in freshman, sophomore, junior, senior, graduate, or postgraduate years; not renewable. *Number:* 1. *Amount:* $1000.

Eligibility Requirements: Applicant must be enrolled or expecting to enroll full- or part-time at a two-year or four-year or technical institution or university. Applicant must be physically disabled. Available to U.S. citizens. Applicant or parent must meet one or more of the following requirements: general military experience; retired from active duty; disabled or killed as a result of military service; prisoner of war; or missing in action.

Application Requirements: Application form, essay. *Deadline:* January 15.

Contact: David Black
Law Offices of David A. Black
40 North Central Avenue, Suite 1400
Phoenix, AZ 85004
Phone: 480-280-8028
E-mail: michael@dbphoenixcriminallawyer.com

LAW OFFICES OF JUDD S. NEMIRO, PLLC

http://www.jnphoenixfamilylawyer.com/

ANNUAL DYSLEXIA SCHOLARSHIP

The Law Offices of Judd S. Nemiro, PLLC takes pleasure in announcing its annual dyslexia scholarship program. The program consists of two awards annually, each for $1,000, for tuition assistance at an educational institution. We offer these scholarships in order to help those with Dyslexia in continuing their education. You must be diagnosed with Dyslexia. We may ask for proof of the diagnosis. Two scholarships are being offered annually, and each is in the sum of $1,000. Each scholarship will take the form of a tuition payment for enrollment at a university, college, community college, trade school, or secondary school. You need not be currently enrolled at an educational institution at the time you submit your application. The winners, within a year from the award date, will provide us with a tuition invoice from the school they will be attending. A $1,000 check will then be forwarded to the school.

Award: Scholarship for use in freshman, sophomore, junior, senior, graduate, or postgraduate years; not renewable. *Number:* 2. *Amount:* $1000.

Eligibility Requirements: Applicant must be enrolled or expecting to enroll full- or part-time at a two-year or four-year or technical institution or university. Applicant must be learning disabled. Available to U.S. citizens.

Application Requirements: Application form, essay. *Deadline:* November 4.

Contact: Judd Nemiro
E-mail: michael@jnphoenixfamilylawyer.com

LEAD FOUNDATION OF COLORADO

https://www.leadcolorado.org

THE LEAD FOUNDATION SCHOLARSHIP

https://www.leadcolorado.org

Award: Scholarship for use in freshman, sophomore, junior, or senior years; not renewable. *Number:* 2. *Amount:* $1000.

Eligibility Requirements: Applicant must be enrolled or expecting to enroll full-time at a two-year or four-year or technical institution or university. Applicant must be learning disabled. Available to U.S. citizens.

Application Requirements: Application form, essay. *Deadline:* continuous.

Contact: Ms. Kathryn Carruth, Executive Director
LEAD Foundation of Colorado
POB 2516
Colorado Springs, CO 80901
Phone: 806-7892369
E-mail: director@leadcolorado.org

LEARNING ALLY

http://www.learningally.org

MARION HUBER LEARNING THROUGH LISTENING AWARDS

• *See page 444*

MARY P. OENSLAGER SCHOLASTIC ACHIEVEMENT AWARDS

• *See page 445*

LIGHTHOUSE GUILD

http://www.lighthouseguild.org

LIGHTHOUSE GUILD SCHOLARSHIP PROGRAM

Annual merit based scholarship program for college-bound high school and graduate school students who are legally blind. The submission deadline is March 31st. Ten - fifteen scholarships will be awarded to college bound high school seniors and one - two for graduate students.

Award: Scholarship for use in freshman, graduate, or postgraduate years; not renewable. *Number:* 15. *Amount:* $10,000.

Eligibility Requirements: Applicant must be enrolled or expecting to enroll full-time at a four-year institution or university. Applicant must be visually impaired. Available to U.S. citizens.

Application Requirements: Application form, community service, essay. *Deadline:* March 31.

Contact: Mr. Gordon Rovins, Director of Special Programs
Lighthouse Guild
250 West 64th Street
New York, NY 10023
Phone: 212-769-7801
E-mail: scholars@lighthouseguild.org

NATIONAL CENTER FOR LEARNING DISABILITIES, INC.

http://ncld.org

ANNE FORD AND ALLEGRA FORD THOMAS SCHOLARSHIP

The Allegra Ford Thomas Scholarship is a one-time $2,500 scholarship awarded to a graduating high school senior with a documented learning disability (LD) and/or ADHD who will be enrolled in a two-year community college, a vocational or technical training program, or a specialized program for students with LD and/or ADHD in the fall. The Anne Ford Scholarship is a $10,000 scholarship ($2,500/year over four years) granted to a graduating high school senior with a documented learning disability (LD) and/or ADHD who will be enrolled in a full-time Bachelor's degree program in the fall.

Award: Scholarship for use in freshman, sophomore, junior, or senior years; not renewable. *Number:* 2. *Amount:* $2500–$10,000.

Eligibility Requirements: Applicant must be high school student and planning to enroll or expecting to enroll full-time at a two-year or four-year or technical institution or university. Applicant must be learning disabled. Available to U.S. citizens.

Application Requirements: Application form, essay, financial need analysis. *Deadline:* November 1.

Contact: Natalie Tamburello, Manager
Phone: 212-545-7510
E-mail: afscholarship@ncld.org

NATIONAL COUNCIL OF JEWISH WOMEN NEW YORK SECTION

http://www.ncjwny.org/

JACKSON-STRICKS SCHOLARSHIP

Scholarship provides financial aid to a person with significant physical challenges for academic study or vocational training that leads to independent living.

Award: Scholarship for use in sophomore, junior, senior, graduate, or postgraduate years; not renewable. *Number:* 1–2. *Amount:* $1500–$2500.

Eligibility Requirements: Applicant must be enrolled or expecting to enroll full- or part-time at a two-year or four-year institution or university and studying in New York. Applicant must be physically disabled. Available to U.S. and non-U.S. citizens.

Application Requirements: Application form, essay. *Deadline:* March 31.

Contact: Naomi Skop Richter, Jackson-Stricks Scholarship Committee
National Council of Jewish Women New York Section
241 West 72 Street
New York, NY 10023
Phone: 212-687-5030 Ext. 461
E-mail: jss@ncjwny.org

NATIONAL FEDERATION OF THE BLIND (NFB)

https://www.nfb.org/

CHARLES AND MELVA T. OWEN MEMORIAL SCHOLARSHIP

Merit-based scholarship requires academic excellence and leadership, permanent residency in United States/Puerto Rico, and accredited institution's degree program (in U.S./PR) directed toward financial independence (excludes degrees in religious studies or solely for cultural education). Winner assisted to attend NFB annual convention to receive this award. Membership not required.

Award: Scholarship for use in freshman, sophomore, junior, senior, graduate, or postgraduate years; not renewable. *Number:* 2. *Amount:* $3000–$10,000.

Eligibility Requirements: Applicant must be enrolled or expecting to enroll full- or part-time at a two-year institution or university. Applicant must be visually impaired. Available to U.S. and non-U.S. citizens.

Application Requirements: Application form, application form may be submitted online, essay, interview. *Deadline:* March 31.

Contact: Cayte Mendez, Chairperson, NFB Scholarship Committee
Baltimore, MD 21230
Phone: 410-659-9314 Ext. 2415
E-mail: scholarships@nfb.org

CHARLES AND MELVA T. OWEN SCHOLARSHIP FOR $10,000

Merit-based scholarship requires academic excellence and leadership, permanently resides in United States/Puerto Rico, and accredited institution's degree program (in US/PR) directed toward financial independence (excludes degrees in religious studies or solely for cultural education). Winner assisted to attend NFB annual convention to receive this award. Membership not required. USA Citizenship is not a requirement, but if the student's home is not in the US/PR, then the student is not eligible.

Award: Scholarship for use in freshman, sophomore, junior, senior, graduate, or postgraduate years; not renewable. *Number:* 1. *Amount:* $10,000.

Eligibility Requirements: Applicant must be enrolled or expecting to enroll full- or part-time at a two-year or four-year institution or university. Applicant must be visually impaired. Available to U.S. and non-U.S. citizens.

Application Requirements: Application form, essay, interview. *Deadline:* March 31.

Contact: Ms. Patti Chang, Chairperson, NFB Scholarship Committee
National Federation of the Blind (NFB)
200 East Wells Street
Baltimore, MD 21230
Phone: 410-659-9314 Ext. 2415
E-mail: scholarships@nfb.org

KENNETH JERNIGAN SCHOLARSHIP

The American Action Fund for Blind Children & Adults $12,000 award to honor the top blind college student residing in and attending an accredited institution in the U.S. or Puerto Rico. Winner receives financial assistance to attend NFB convention to receive scholarship.

Award: Scholarship for use in freshman, sophomore, junior, senior, graduate, or postgraduate years; not renewable. *Number:* 1. *Amount:* $12,000.

Eligibility Requirements: Applicant must be enrolled or expecting to enroll full- or part-time at a two-year institution or university. Applicant must be visually impaired. Available to U.S. citizens.

Application Requirements: Application form, application form may be submitted online, essay, interview. *Deadline:* March 31.

Contact: Cayte Mendez, Chairperson
National Federation of the Blind (NFB)
NFB Scholarship Committee
200 East Wells Street
Baltimore, MD 21230
Phone: 410-659-9314 Ext. 2415
E-mail: scholarships@nfb.org

LARRY STREETER MEMORIAL SCHOLARSHIP FOR $3,000

$3000 scholarship for legally blind, permanent residents of the U.S. or Puerto Rico, pursuing a postsecondary degree at an accredited institution in U.S. or PR. Created to assist blind students to elevate their quality of life, equipping them to be active, productive participants in their family, community, and the workplace.

Award: Scholarship for use in freshman, sophomore, junior, or senior years; not renewable. *Number:* 1. *Amount:* $3000.

Eligibility Requirements: Applicant must be enrolled or expecting to enroll full- or part-time at a four-year institution or university. Applicant must be visually impaired. Available to U.S. citizens.

Application Requirements: Application form, essay, financial need analysis, proof of blindness in both eyes, transcript. *Deadline:* March 31.

Contact: Ms. Patti Chang, Chairperson, NFB Scholarship Program
National Federation of the Blind (NFB)
200 East Wells Street
Baltimore, MD 21230
Phone: 410-659-9314 Ext. 2415
E-mail: scholarships@nfb.org

NATIONAL FEDERATION OF THE BLIND SCHOLARSHIP FOR $3,000

$3000 scholarship for legally blind, permanent residents of the U.S. or Puerto Rico, pursuing a postsecondary degree at an accredited institution in U.S. or PR. Selection is merit-based on academic excellence and leadership. With NFB assistance, winner attends NFB annual convention to receive award. Membership in NFB is not required.

Award: Scholarship for use in freshman, sophomore, junior, senior, graduate, or postgraduate years; not renewable. *Number:* 20. *Amount:* $3000.

Eligibility Requirements: Applicant must be enrolled or expecting to enroll full- or part-time at a two-year or four-year institution or university. Applicant must be visually impaired. Available to U.S. and non-U.S. citizens.

Application Requirements: Application form, application form may be submitted online (https://nfb.org//scholarships), essay, interview, proof of legal blindness in both eyes, recommendations or references, test scores, transcript. *Deadline:* March 31.

Contact: Cayte Mendez, Chairperson, NFB Scholarship Committee
National Federation of the Blind (NFB)
200 East Wells Street
Baltimore, MD 21230
Phone: 410-659-9314 Ext. 2415
E-mail: scholarships@nfb.org

NATIONAL FEDERATION OF THE BLIND SCHOLARSHIP FOR $7,000

$7000 scholarship for legally blind, permanent residents of the U.S. or Puerto Rico, pursuing a postsecondary degree at an accredited institution in U.S. or PR. Selection is merit-based on academic excellence and leadership. With NFB assistance, winner attends NFB annual convention to receive award. Membership in NFB is not required.

Award: Scholarship for use in freshman, sophomore, junior, senior, graduate, or postgraduate years; not renewable. *Number:* 2. *Amount:* $7000.

Eligibility Requirements: Applicant must be enrolled or expecting to enroll full- or part-time at a two-year or four-year institution or university. Applicant must be visually impaired. Available to U.S. and non-U.S. citizens.

Application Requirements: Application form, application form may be submitted online (http://www.nfb.org//scholarships), entry in a contest, essay, interview, proof of legal blindness in both eyes, recommendations or references, test scores, transcript. *Deadline:* March 31.

Contact: Ms. Patti Chang, Chairperson, NFB Scholarship Committee
National Federation of the Blind (NFB)
200 East Wells Street
Baltimore, MD 21230
Phone: 410-659-9314 Ext. 2415
E-mail: scholarships@nfb.org

NFB SCHOLARSHIP FOR $5,000

$5000 scholarships for legally blind, permanent residents of the U.S. or Puerto Rico, pursuing a postsecondary degree at an accredited institution in U.S. or PR. Selection is merit-based on academic excellence and leadership. With NFB assistance, winner attends NFB annual convention to receive award. Membership in NFB is not required.

Award: Scholarship for use in freshman, sophomore, junior, senior, graduate, or postgraduate years; not renewable. *Number:* 4. *Amount:* $5000.

Eligibility Requirements: Applicant must be enrolled or expecting to enroll full- or part-time at a two-year or four-year institution or university. Applicant must be visually impaired. Available to U.S. and non-U.S. citizens.

Application Requirements: Application form, application form may be submitted online (http://www.nfb.org//scholarships), entry in a contest, essay, interview, proof of legal blindness in both eyes, recommendations or references, test scores, transcript. *Deadline:* March 31.

Contact: Ms. Patti Chang, Chairperson, NFB Scholarship Program
National Federation of the Blind (NFB)
200 East Wells Street
Baltimore, MD 21230
Phone: 410-659-9314 Ext. 2415
E-mail: scholarships@nfb.org

PEARSON SCHOLARSHIP

The Pearson award is funded by Pearson Education and is given to a student who plans a career in education. For Pearson, learning is a never-ending road of discovery.

Award: Scholarship for use in freshman, sophomore, junior, senior, graduate, or postgraduate years; not renewable. *Amount:* $5000.

Eligibility Requirements: Applicant must be enrolled or expecting to enroll full-time at a two-year or technical institution or university. Applicant must be visually impaired. Available to U.S. citizens.

Application Requirements: Application form, application form may be submitted online, essay, interview. *Deadline:* March 31.

Contact: Cayte Mendez, Chairperson
National Federation of the Blind (NFB)
200 E. Wells St.
Baltimore, MD 21230
Phone: 410-659-9314 Ext. 2415
E-mail: scholarships@nfb.org

NATIONAL FEDERATION OF THE BLIND OF CALIFORNIA

http://www.nfbcal.org/

GERALD DRAKE MEMORIAL SCHOLARSHIP

One-time award for legally blind students pursuing an undergraduate or graduate degree. Must be a California resident and full-time student.

Award: Scholarship for use in freshman, sophomore, junior, senior, or graduate years; not renewable. *Number:* up to 5. *Amount:* $1500.

Eligibility Requirements: Applicant must be enrolled or expecting to enroll full-time at a four-year institution or university and resident of California. Applicant must be visually impaired. Available to U.S. and non-U.S. citizens.

Application Requirements: Application form. *Deadline:* March 31.

Contact: Cricket Bidleman
    Phone: 805-372-9550
    E-mail: cricketbidleman@gmail.com

JULIE LANDUCCI SCHOLARSHIP

Award for legally blind students pursuing an undergraduate or graduate degree. Must be a California resident and full-time student. Award available to U.S. citizens.

Award: Scholarship for use in freshman, sophomore, junior, senior, or graduate years; renewable. *Number:* 1. *Amount:* up to $2000.

Eligibility Requirements: Applicant must be enrolled or expecting to enroll full-time at a four-year institution or university and resident of California. Applicant must be visually impaired. Available to U.S. citizens.

Application Requirements: Application form. *Deadline:* March 31.

Contact: Cricket Bidleman
    Phone: 805-372-9550
    E-mail: cricketbidleman@gmail.com

LA VYRL "PINKY" JOHNSON MEMORIAL SCHOLARSHIP

One-time award up to $2000 for legally blind students pursuing an undergraduate or graduate degree. Must be a California resident and full-time student.

Award: Scholarship for use in freshman, sophomore, junior, senior, or graduate years; renewable. *Number:* 1. *Amount:* $2000.

Eligibility Requirements: Applicant must be enrolled or expecting to enroll full-time at a four-year institution or university and resident of California. Applicant must be visually impaired. Available to U.S. citizens.

Application Requirements: Application form. *Deadline:* March 31.

Contact: Cricket Bidleman
    Phone: 805-372-9550
    E-mail: cricketbidleman@gmail.com

LAWRENCE "MUZZY" MARCELINO MEMORIAL SCHOLARSHIP

Scholarship provides financial assistance for graduate or undergraduate education to blind students in California. Any legally blind student may apply for a scholarship but must attend the convention of the National Federation of the Blind of California. Selection is based first on academic merit and second on financial need.

Award: Scholarship for use in freshman, sophomore, junior, senior, or graduate years; renewable. *Number:* up to 4. *Amount:* $1500.

Eligibility Requirements: Applicant must be enrolled or expecting to enroll full-time at a four-year institution or university and resident of California. Applicant must be visually impaired. Available to U.S. citizens.

Application Requirements: Application form. *Deadline:* March 15.

Contact: Cricket Bidleman
    Phone: 805-372-9550
    E-mail: cricketbidleman@gmail.com

NATIONAL FEDERATION OF THE BLIND OF CALIFORNIA MERIT SCHOLARSHIPS

The NFBCA scholarship program is our investment in the future of blind people who demonstrate scholastic aptitude, leadership, and service. All blind high school and college students are encouraged to apply! It caters to both full-time and part-time students, with the latter awarded with one scholarship when working full-time and pursuing a degree at an accredited university

Award: Scholarship for use in freshman, sophomore, junior, senior, or graduate years; renewable. *Number:* 3. *Amount:* $3000–$12,000.

Eligibility Requirements: Applicant must be enrolled or expecting to enroll full- or part-time at an institution or university and resident of British Columbia. Applicant must be visually impaired. Available to U.S. citizens.

Application Requirements: Application form, application form may be submitted online, essay, interview.

Contact: Cayte Mendez, Chairperson, NFB Scholarship Committee
    Phone: 410-659-9314 Ext. 2415
    E-mail: scholarships@nfb.org

NATIONAL FEDERATION OF THE BLIND OF MISSOURI

http://www.nfbmo.org/

NATIONAL FEDERATION OF THE BLIND OF MISSOURI SCHOLARSHIP PROGRAM FOR LEGALLY BLIND STUDENTS

Awards are based on achievement and commitment to community. Recipients must be legally blind, live in Missouri, and maintain a GPA greater than 2.5. Amount of money each year available for program will vary.

Award: Scholarship for use in sophomore or senior years; not renewable. *Number:* 1–3. *Amount:* $500–$2500.

Eligibility Requirements: Applicant must be enrolled or expecting to enroll full- or part-time at a two-year or four-year or technical institution or university; resident of Missouri and studying in Missouri. Applicant must be visually impaired. Available to U.S. citizens.

Application Requirements: Application form, essay, interview. *Deadline:* February 1.

Contact: Shelia Wright, President
    National Federation of the Blind of Missouri
    7928 NW Milrey Drive
    Kansas City, MO 64152
    Phone: 816-741-6402
    E-mail: scholarship@nfbmo.org

NATIONAL KIDNEY FOUNDATION OF INDIANA INC.

http://www.kidneyindiana.org/

NATIONAL KIDNEY FOUNDATION OF INDIANA SCHOLARSHIP

Scholarship provides financial assistance for kidney dialysis and transplant patients to pursue post-secondary education. Applicant must be resident of Indiana over the age of 18. Must have a high school diploma or its equivalent. Applications are reviewed by committee to choose awardees.

Award: Scholarship for use in freshman, sophomore, junior, or senior years; not renewable. *Number:* 2–8. *Amount:* $250–$1500.

Eligibility Requirements: Applicant must be age 18 and over; enrolled or expecting to enroll full- or part-time at a two-year or four-year or technical institution or university and resident of Indiana. Applicant must be physically disabled. Available to U.S. citizens.

Application Requirements: Application form, essay. *Deadline:* March 30.

Contact: Nicki Howard, Public Health Coordinator
    National Kidney Foundation of Indiana Inc.
    National Kidney Foundation of Indiana
    911 E. 86th Street, Suite 100
    Indianapolis, IN 46240
    Phone: 317-722-5640
    E-mail: nhoward@kidneyindiana.org

NATIONAL MULTIPLE SCLEROSIS SOCIETY

http://www.nmss.org/

NATIONAL MULTIPLE SCLEROSIS SOCIETY SCHOLARSHIP PROGRAM

Scholarships available to high school seniors and graduates (or GED) with MS, or who are children of people with MS. Must be attending a postsecondary school for the first time. All applicants must meet the basic eligibility criteria, fully complete the online application and mail supporting documents by deadline. The program is competitive in nature, and not all applicants will be selected for an award. Scholarship finalists will be selected on the basis of demonstrated financial need, academic record, leadership and participation in school or community activities, work experience, an outside appraisal, goals and aspirations, special circumstances, and an essay (written by the applicant) regarding the impact of MS on their life. More information can be found at www.nationalmssociety.org

Award: Scholarship for use in freshman year; not renewable. *Number:* 400. *Amount:* $1500.

Eligibility Requirements: Applicant must be enrolled or expecting to enroll full- or part-time at a two-year or four-year institution or university. Applicant must be physically disabled. Available to U.S. citizens.

Application Requirements: Application form, driver's license, essay, financial need analysis, personal photograph. *Deadline:* January 15.

Contact: Scholarship Management Services
Phone: 507-931-1682
E-mail: mssociety@scholarshipamerica.org

NATIONAL PKU NEWS

http://www.pkunews.org/

ROBERT GUTHRIE PKU SCHOLARSHIP AND AWARDS

Scholarship for persons with phenylketonuria (PKU) who are on a special diet for PKU treatment. Award is for full-time or part-time study at any accredited U.S. institution. Up to 8 scholarships of between $500 and $3500 are granted.

Award: Scholarship for use in freshman, sophomore, junior, or senior years; not renewable. *Number:* 4–8. *Amount:* $500–$3500.

Eligibility Requirements: Applicant must be enrolled or expecting to enroll full- or part-time at a two-year or four-year or technical institution or university. Applicant must be physically disabled. Available to U.S. and non-U.S. citizens.

Application Requirements: Application form, essay, personal photograph, recommendations or references, resume, test scores, transcript. *Deadline:* October 15.

Contact: Virginia Schuett, Director
Phone: 206-525-8140
E-mail: schuett@pkunews.org

NORTH CAROLINA DIVISION OF VOCATIONAL REHABILITATION SERVICES

http://www.dhhs.state.nc.us/

TRAINING SUPPORT FOR YOUTH WITH DISABILITIES

Public service program that helps persons with disabilities obtain competitive employment. To qualify: student must have a mental, physical or learning disability that is an impediment to employment and require post secondary training to achieve a specific employment outcome. A Rehabilitation Counselor, along with the eligible student, develops an individualized rehabilitation program outlining the specific need for post-secondary training. Financial assistance is based on NC Division of Vocational Rehabilitation demonstrated financial need and the type of program in which the student enrolls.

Award: Grant for use in freshman, sophomore, junior, senior, or graduate years; renewable.

Eligibility Requirements: Applicant must be enrolled or expecting to enroll full- or part-time at a two-year or four-year or technical institution or university and resident of North Carolina. Applicant must be hearing impaired, learning disabled, physically disabled, or visually impaired. Available to U.S. and non-U.S. citizens.

Application Requirements: Application form, Evidence of eligibility to work in the US, financial need analysis, interview. *Deadline:* continuous.

Contact: Stephanie Hanes, Program Specialist for Transition
North Carolina Division of Vocational Rehabilitation Services
2801 Mail Service Center
Raleigh, NC 27699-2801
Phone: 919-855-3576
E-mail: stephanie.hanes@dhhs.nc.gov

OPTIMIST INTERNATIONAL FOUNDATION

http://www.optimist.org/

COMMUNICATION CONTEST FOR THE DEAF AND HARD OF HEARING

College scholarship (district level) for young people through grade twelve in the U.S. and Canada, to CEGEP in Quebec and grade thirteen in the Caribbean. Students interested in participating must submit the results of an audiogram conducted no longer than twenty four months prior to the date of the contest from a qualified audiologist. Students must be certified to have a hearing loss of forty decibels or more and supported by the audiogram to be eligible to compete. Students attending either public school or schools providing special services are eligible to enter if criteria are met. The deadline to enter is determined by the sponsoring Club.

Award: Scholarship for use in freshman, sophomore, junior, or senior years; not renewable. *Amount:* $2500.

Eligibility Requirements: Applicant must be enrolled or expecting to enroll full- or part-time at a two-year or four-year or technical institution or university. Applicant must be hearing impaired. Available to U.S. and Canadian citizens.

Application Requirements: Application form.

Contact: Dana Thomas, Director of International Programs
Optimist International Foundation
4494 Lindell Boulevard
St. Louis, MO 63108
Phone: 800-500-8130
E-mail: programs@optimist.org

OREGON COMMUNITY FOUNDATION

http://www.oregoncf.org/

HARRY LUDWIG SCHOLARSHIP FUND

Scholarship for visually impaired students for use in the pursuit of a postsecondary education at a college or university. For full-time students only.

Award: Scholarship for use in freshman, sophomore, junior, or senior years; renewable. *Number:* 1–3. *Amount:* $500–$5000.

Eligibility Requirements: Applicant must be enrolled or expecting to enroll full-time at a four-year institution or university. Applicant must be visually impaired. Available to U.S. citizens.

Application Requirements: Application form, recommendations or references. *Deadline:* March 1.

Contact: Dianne Causey, Program Associate for Scholarships and Grants
Phone: 503-227-6846 Ext. 1418
E-mail: dcausey@oregoncf.org

OREGON OFFICE OF STUDENT ACCESS AND COMPLETION

https://oregonstudentaid.gov/

SALEM FOUNDATION ANSEL & MARIE SOLIE SCHOLARSHIP

Award is available to visually impaired Oregon residents planning to enroll in full-time undergraduate studies. Award may be used only at a four-year public or nonprofit Oregon college or university. Apply-compete annually. Financial need may or may not be considered.

Award: Scholarship for use in freshman, sophomore, junior, or senior years; not renewable.

Eligibility Requirements: Applicant must be enrolled or expecting to enroll full-time at a four-year institution or university; resident of Oregon and studying in Oregon. Applicant must be visually impaired. Available to U.S. citizens.

Application Requirements: Application form, financial need analysis, Letter from a physician. *Deadline:* March 1.

Contact: Melissa Adams, Scholarship Processing Coordinator
Phone: 541-687-7409
E-mail: melissa.adams@state.or.us

PENNSYLVANIA HIGHER EDUCATION ASSISTANCE AGENCY

http://www.pheaa.org/

BLIND OR DEAF BENEFICIARY GRANT PROGRAM

This state-funded program provides financial aid to blind or deaf students attending a postsecondary institution. This program awards funds on a first-come, first-served basis.

Award: Grant for use in freshman, sophomore, junior, or senior years; not renewable. *Amount:* $500.

Eligibility Requirements: Applicant must be enrolled or expecting to enroll full- or part-time at a two-year or technical institution or university and resident of Oregon. Applicant must be hearing impaired or visually impaired.

Application Requirements: Application form. *Deadline:* March 31.

Contact: Keith New, Director of Public Relations
Phone: 800-692-7392
E-mail: knew@pheaa.org

PETAZI

https://petazi.com/

2017 NURTURE FOR NATURE SCHOLARSHIP

One $1200 scholarship created to help raise everyone's awareness about protecting animals and the environment. All students located and currently studying in the United States or Canada are eligible to apply for this scholarship. Valid statements of current academic status as evidence that candidates are currently attending college. Students can apply by writing an inspirational short story about animals/ pets. Upon sharing it with us, we will then share it online via Petazi websites. The winner of the $1200 prize will be the one whose entry/story receives the most likes after we post all the entries on our Petazi Facebook page. See website for details, https://petazi.com/scholarship

Award: Scholarship for use in freshman, sophomore, junior, senior, graduate, or postgraduate years; renewable. *Number:* 1. *Amount:* $1200.

Eligibility Requirements: Applicant must be American Indian/Alaska Native, Asian/Pacific Islander, Black (non-Hispanic), Hispanic; age 13 and over and enrolled or expecting to enroll full- or part-time at a two-year or four-year institution or university. Applicant must be hearing impaired, learning disabled, physically disabled, or visually impaired. Available to U.S. and non-U.S. citizens. Applicant or parent must meet one or more of the following requirements: general military experience; retired from active duty; disabled or killed as a result of military service; prisoner of war; or missing in action.

Application Requirements: Application form, personal photograph. *Deadline:* June 30.

Contact: Ms. Rose Larson
Petazi
Petazi Scholarship Office
316A Cecil Street
Chicago, IL 60605
Phone: 331-207-4154
E-mail: scholarship@petazi.com

RJT CRIMINAL DEFENSE

http://www.sandiegocriminallawyerrt.com/

2017 AUTISM SCHOLARSHIP

RJT Criminal Defense is pleased to be offering a $1,000 educational scholarship for people who have been diagnosed with autism (now known as Autism Spectrum Disorder (ASD)). The scholarship will be used to offset a portion of the tuition at an educational institution chosen by the successful applicant. The aim of the program is to encourage those with autism to continue their education. This is a $1,000 scholarship consisting of tuition assistance at a trade or vocational school, or a college, junior college or university. The scholarship funds will be paid directly to the educational institution selected by the successful applicant. The scholarship money must be used within 1 year after the date of the award. It is not required that an applicant be enrolled in school at the time the application is submitted. The application is open to any United States citizen who has been diagnosed with ASD who wishes to continue his or her education at a trade school, vocational school, or on the college or junior college level. Complete the online application and upload a short statement (125 words or less) setting forth your educational goals. (Optional) Upload an essay (800 words or less) discussing the impact autism has had on your education. We may also require that you provide us with proof of your diagnosis. All application materials must be completed and submitted to us no later than February 5, 2018. The winner will be selected by Ryan J. Tegnelia of RJT Criminal Defense, in his sole discretion. Mr. Tegnelia will announce the winner of the scholarship on or before March 5, 2018.

Award: Scholarship for use in freshman, sophomore, junior, senior, graduate, or postgraduate years; not renewable. *Number:* 1. *Amount:* $1000.

Eligibility Requirements: Applicant must be enrolled or expecting to enroll full- or part-time at a two-year or four-year or technical institution or university. Applicant must be learning disabled. Available to U.S. citizens.

Application Requirements: Application form, essay. *Deadline:* February 5.

Contact: Ryan Tegnelia
RJT Criminal Defense
2820 Camino Del Rio South, Suite 110
San Diego, CA 92108
E-mail: mike@sandiegocriminallawyerrt.com

SCHOLARSHIP AMERICA

https://www.abbvieImmunologyScholarship.com/

ABBVIE IMMUNOLOGY SCHOLARSHIP

The AbbVie Immunology Scholarship is designed to provide financial support for exceptional students living with chronic inflammatory diseases. Scholarships of up to $15,000 each will be awarded, dependent upon type of degree pursued. Applicants must be legal residents of the U.S. and diagnosed by a healthcare professional with one of the following: ankylosing spondylitis (AS), Crohn's disease (CD), hidradenitis suppurativa (HS), juvenile idiopathic arthritis (JIA), psoriasis (Ps), psoriatic arthritis (PsA), rheumatoid arthritis (RA), ulcerative colitis (UC), or uveitis (UV). Qualified applicants must plan to enroll in undergraduate (associate's, bachelor's) or graduate (master's, MD, JD, doctorate) study at an accredited two- or four-year college, university or vocational-technical school in the U.S. for the 2018-19 academic year. Scholarships will be awarded based on academic excellence, community involvement, and ability to serve as a positive role model in the immunology community.

Award: Scholarship for use in freshman, sophomore, junior, senior, or graduate years; not renewable. *Amount:* $15,000.

Eligibility Requirements: Applicant must be enrolled or expecting to enroll full- or part-time at a two-year or four-year or technical institution or university and studying in Alabama, Alaska, Arizona, Arkansas, California, Colorado, Connecticut, Delaware, District of Columbia, Florida, Georgia, Hawaii, Idaho, Illinois, Indiana, Iowa, Kansas, Kentucky, Louisiana, Maine, Maryland, Massachusetts, Michigan, Minnesota, Mississippi, Missouri, Montana, Nebraska, Nevada, New Hampshire, New Jersey, New Mexico, New York, North Carolina, North Dakota, Ohio, Oklahoma, Oregon, Pennsylvania, Rhode Island, South Carolina, South Dakota, Tennessee, Texas, Utah, Vermont, Virginia, Washington, West Virginia, Wisconsin, Wyoming. Applicant must be physically disabled. Available to U.S. citizens.

Application Requirements: Application form. *Deadline:* January 9.

Contact: Program Manager
Scholarship America
Scholarship America
One Scholarship Way
Saint Peter, MN 56082
Phone: 507-931-0651
E-mail: AbbVieImmunology@scholarshipamerica.org

WELLS FARGO SCHOLARSHIP PROGRAM FOR PEOPLE WITH DISABILITIES

The Wells Fargo Scholarship Program for People with Disabilities is designed to help people with disabilities obtain the education or training necessary to succeed in the career path of their choice. To apply, you must have an identified disability (defined as someone who has, or considers themselves to have, a long-term or recurring issue that impacts one or more major life activity). Applicants must be high school seniors or graduates planning to enroll or who are already enrolled in full- or half-time undergraduate study at an accredited two- or four-year college or university in the United States for the 2018-2019 academic year. The program will award up to $2,500 renewable scholarships for full-time students and up to $1,250 renewable scholarships for half-time students. Visit https://scholarsapply.org/pwdscholarship for more information and to apply.

Award: Scholarship for use in freshman, sophomore, junior, or senior years; renewable. *Number:* 25. *Amount:* $2500.

Eligibility Requirements: Applicant must be enrolled or expecting to enroll full- or part-time at a two-year or four-year institution or university. Applicant must be hearing impaired, learning disabled, physically disabled, or visually impaired. Available to U.S. citizens.

Application Requirements: Application form. *Deadline:* November 28.

Contact: Program Manager
Scholarship America
Scholarship America
One Scholarship Way
Saint Peter, MN 56082
Phone: 844-402-0357
E-mail: pwdscholarship@scholarshipamerica.org

SERTOMA, INC.

http://www.sertoma.org/

SERTOMA SCHOLARSHIP FOR STUDENTS WHO ARE HARD OF HEARING OR DEAF

Applicants must have a minimum of 40dB bilateral hearing loss, as evidenced on audiogram by an SRT. Must have a minimum cumulative 3.2 GPA on a 4.0 unweighted scale.

Award: Scholarship for use in freshman, sophomore, junior, or senior years; not renewable. *Number:* 45–50. *Amount:* $1000.

Eligibility Requirements: Applicant must be enrolled or expecting to enroll full-time at a four-year institution or university. Applicant must be hearing impaired. Available to U.S. citizens.

Application Requirements: Application form, Audiogram (Proof of Hearing Loss), recommendations or references, transcript. *Deadline:* May 1.

Contact: Mrs. Bridget Almond, Mission Development Officer, Internal Marketing
Phone: 816-333-8300
E-mail: Balmond@sertomahq.org

SISTER KENNY REHABILITATION INSTITUTE

http://www.allina.com/ahs/ski.nsf

ART OF POSSIBILITIES ART SHOW & SALE

One-time award for artwork submitted by artists of any age with visual, hearing, physical, or learning impairment. This is a one-time prize, not an academic scholarship. Visit www.CourageArt.org for art show guidelines and application.

Award: Prize for use in freshman, sophomore, junior, senior, graduate, or postgraduate years; not renewable. *Number:* 25–70. *Amount:* $25–$500.

Eligibility Requirements: Applicant must be enrolled or expecting to enroll full- or part-time at a two-year or four-year or technical institution or university and must have an interest in art. Applicant must be hearing impaired, learning disabled, physically disabled, or visually impaired. Available to U.S. and non-U.S. citizens.

Application Requirements: Application form, application form may be submitted online (http://www.courageart.org), entry in a contest. *Deadline:* January 31.

Contact: Laura Brooks, Development Associate
Sister Kenny Rehabilitation Institute
Courage Kenny Rehabilitation Institute
Golden Valley, MN 55422
Phone: 612-775-2507
Fax: 612-863-8942
E-mail: laura.brooks@allina.com

SLEEP SHERPA

SLEEP SHERPA SCHOLARSHIP PROGRAM

The best part of sleep is your dreams. The Sleep Sherpa is a dreamer and wants to help students make their dreams come true. That's why we created an annual scholarship of $1,000 to be used towards furthering your education and your dreams. Scholarship Details: URL: https://sleepsherpa.com/sleep-sherpa-%20scholarship-program/. Email Id: ben@sleepsherpa.com. Award Amount: $1000. Deadline: May 31, 2018.

Award: Scholarship for use in freshman, sophomore, junior, or senior years; not renewable. *Number:* 1. *Amount:* $1000.

Eligibility Requirements: Applicant must be American Indian/Alaska Native, Asian/Pacific Islander, Black (non-Hispanic), Hispanic; age 15-80 and enrolled or expecting to enroll full- or part-time at a four-year institution or university. Applicant must be hearing impaired, learning disabled, physically disabled, or visually impaired. Available to U.S. citizens. Applicant or parent must meet one or more of the following requirements: general military experience; retired from active duty; disabled or killed as a result of military service; prisoner of war; or missing in action.

Application Requirements: Essay, portfolio. *Deadline:* May 31.

Contact: Mr. Ben Trapskin, Owner
Sleep Sherpa
7313 Washington Avenue South
Edina, MN 55343
Phone: 952-222-0752
E-mail: scholarship@sleepsherpa.com

STICKLER INVOLVED PEOPLE

https://stickler.org/

DR. GUNNAR B. STICKLER SCHOLARSHIP

Applicant must have a diagnosis of Stickler syndrome and submit letter from physician with application. Scholarship is renewable yearly with 3.0 GPA goals letter provided from school.

Award: Scholarship for use in freshman, sophomore, junior, or senior years; renewable. *Number:* 1. *Amount:* $500.

Eligibility Requirements: Applicant must be high school student and planning to enroll or expecting to enroll full-time at a four-year institution. Applicant must be hearing impaired, physically disabled, or visually impaired. Available to U.S. citizens.

Application Requirements: Application form. *Deadline:* June 15.

Contact: James Brown, Scholarship Committee Chair
Stickler Involved People
Gunnar B. Stickler Scholarship Award
PO Box 775
Cologne, NJ 08213

TITAN WEB AGENCY

THE TITAN WEB AGENCY BI-ANNUAL SCHOLARSHIP PROGRAM

At Titan Web Agency, we believe it's our responsibility to give back to the community and help those looking to build a business and are in financial need. We are specifically looking to help students who come with a desire to own their own business, and with a financial need. Recently, tuition fees have been surpassing the rate of inflation. Higher education is becoming more expensive. Once every year we will be awarding $500 to students to help them receive the education they deserve. Must be attending a two-year community college or a four year accredited university and be a U.S. resident. Students of all ethnic groups are encouraged to apply. Please submit an essay (1000 word minimum) detailing why you want to be an entrepreneur, as well as a creative photo that you feel represents you best. You can submit your application here: https://titanwebagency.com/scholarship/

Award: Scholarship for use in freshman, sophomore, junior, senior, graduate, or postgraduate years; not renewable. *Number:* 1. *Amount:* $500.

Eligibility Requirements: Applicant must be American Indian/Alaska Native, Asian/Pacific Islander, Black (non-Hispanic), Hispanic and enrolled or expecting to enroll full- or part-time at a two-year or four-year or technical institution or university. Applicant must be hearing impaired, learning disabled, physically disabled, or visually impaired. Available to U.S. citizens. Applicant must have general military experience.

Application Requirements: Essay, personal photograph. *Deadline:* December 1.

Contact: Mr. Tyson Downs
Titan Web Agency
Titan Web Agency, PO Box 1262
Riverton, UT 84065
Phone: 801-783-3101
E-mail: titanwebagency@gmail.com

TPA SCHOLARSHIP TRUST FOR THE HEARING IMPAIRED

https://www.tpahq.org/scholarshiptrust/

TPA SCHOLARSHIP TRUST FOR THE HEARING IMPAIRED

Scholarships are awarded to deaf or hearing-impaired persons of any age, race, or religion for specialized education, mechanical devices, or medical or specialized treatment. Based on financial need.

Award: Scholarship for use in freshman, sophomore, junior, senior, graduate, or postgraduate years; not renewable. *Amount:* $100–$1000.

Eligibility Requirements: Applicant must be enrolled or expecting to enroll full- or part-time at a two-year or four-year or technical institution or university. Applicant must be hearing impaired. Available to U.S. citizens.

Application Requirements: Application form, financial need analysis, personal photograph. *Deadline:* continuous.

Contact: Venita Sedodo, Trust Secretary
TPA Scholarship Trust for the Hearing Impaired
2041 Exchange Drive
Saint Charles, MO 63303
Phone: 636-724-2227
E-mail: vsedodo@tpahq.org

UNITED STATES ASSOCIATION FOR BLIND ATHLETES

http://www.usaba.org/

ARTHUR E. AND HELEN COPELAND SCHOLARSHIPS

Scholarship for a full-time college student who is blind or visually impaired. All applicants must be current members of USABA.

Award: Scholarship for use in freshman, sophomore, junior, or senior years; not renewable. *Number:* 1–2. *Amount:* $500.

Eligibility Requirements: Applicant must be enrolled or expecting to enroll full- or part-time at a four-year institution or university. Applicant must be visually impaired. Available to U.S. citizens.

Application Requirements: Application form, proof of acceptance, recommendations or references, transcript. *Deadline:* July 1.

Contact: Mark Lucas, Executive Director
United States Association for Blind Athletes
1 Olympic Plaza
Colorado Springs, CO 80909
Phone: 719-8663019
E-mail: mlucas@usaba.org

U.S. COAST GUARD

http://www.gocoastguard/cspi

COLLEGE STUDENT PRE-COMMISSIONING INITIATIVE (CSPI)

See scholarship information at the following website, http://www.gocoastguard/cspi

Award: Scholarship for use in junior or senior years; renewable. *Number:* 70. *Amount:* $12,850.

Eligibility Requirements: Applicant must be American Indian/Alaska Native, Asian/Pacific Islander, Black (non-Hispanic), Hispanic; age 19-28 and enrolled or expecting to enroll full-time at a four-year institution or university. Applicant must be physically disabled or visually impaired. Available to U.S. citizens. Applicant must have served in the Coast Guard.

Application Requirements: Application form, financial need analysis, interview. *Deadline:* continuous.

Contact: Lt. Patrick Bennett
U.S. Coast Guard
2703 Martin Luther King JR Ave SE
Washington, DC 20593
Phone: 202-795-6855
E-mail: patrick.g.bennett@uscg.mil

WHITFIELD, BRYSON & MASON LLP

DISABLED VETERANS SCHOLARSHIP

WBM will award a $1,000 scholarship to two applicants in the form of tuition assistance at an accredited four-year college or university. Applicants do not have to be currently enrolled at a college or university at the time of application, but the scholarship must be used within one year of the award. WBM LLP will pay the scholarship directly to the school chosen by the applicant to help offset the cost of tuition. The scholarship is open to all veterans of any branch of the U.S. Armed Forces who have a disability rating of 30% or higher. To be eligible for the scholarship, applicants must complete the following: required: fill out and submit the online application; optional: write an essay about how your military service has changed your life (800 words or less)

Award: Scholarship for use in freshman, sophomore, junior, or senior years; not renewable. *Number:* 2. *Amount:* $1000.

Eligibility Requirements: Applicant must be enrolled or expecting to enroll full- or part-time at a four-year institution or university. Applicant must be physically disabled. Available to U.S. citizens. Applicant or parent must meet one or more of the following requirements: general military experience; retired from active duty; disabled or killed as a result of military service; prisoner of war; or missing in action.

Application Requirements: Application form. *Deadline:* January 26.

Contact: Caroline Taylor
Whitfield, Bryson & Mason LLP
1205 4th Avenue North
Nashville, TN 37208
E-mail: caroline@wbmllp.com

WISCONSIN DEPARTMENT OF VETERANS AFFAIRS (WDVA)

http://www.dva.state.wi.us/

VETERANS EDUCATION (VETED) REIMBURSEMENT GRANT

The grant is for eligible Wisconsin veterans enrolled at approved schools who have not yet earned a BS/BA. Reimburses up to 120 credits or eight semesters at the UW Madison rate for the same number of credits taken in one semester or term. The number of credits or semesters is based on length of time serving on active duty in the armed forces (active duty for training does not apply). Application is due no later than 60 days after the course start date. The student must earn a 2.0 or better for the semester. An eligible veteran will have entered active duty as a Wisconsin resident or lived in state for twelve consecutive months since entering active duty.

Award: Grant for use in freshman, sophomore, junior, or senior years; renewable. *Amount:* $1340–$4000.

Eligibility Requirements: Applicant must be age 18-75; enrolled or expecting to enroll full- or part-time at a two-year or four-year or technical institution or university; resident of Wisconsin and studying in Minnesota, Wisconsin. Applicant must be hearing impaired, learning disabled, physically disabled, or visually impaired. Available to U.S. citizens. Applicant must have general military experience.

Application Requirements: Application form. *Deadline:* July 15.

Contact: Miss. Leslie Busby-Amegashie, Agency Liaison and Regional Coordinator
Wisconsin Department of Veterans Affairs (WDVA)
201 West Washington Street
PO Box 7843
Madison, WI 53707-7843
Phone: 800-947-8387 Ext. 63575
Fax: 608-267-0403 Ext. 3575
E-mail: leslie.busby-amegashie@dva.wisconsin.gov

WISCONSIN HIGHER EDUCATIONAL AID BOARD

http://www.heab.state.wi.us/

WI-HEAB HEARING/VISUALLY IMPAIRED STUDENT GRANT

One-time award available to residents of Wisconsin who have severe or profound hearing or visual impairment. Must be enrolled at least half-time at a nonprofit institution. If the handicap prevents the student from attending a Wisconsin school, the award may be used out-of-state in a specialized college. Refer to website for further details http://www.heab.state.wi.us.

Award: Grant for use in freshman, sophomore, junior, or senior years; not renewable. *Amount:* $250–$1800.

Eligibility Requirements: Applicant must be enrolled or expecting to enroll full- or part-time at an institution or university; resident of West Virginia and studying in Wisconsin. Applicant must be hearing impaired or visually impaired. Available to U.S. citizens.

Application Requirements: Application form, financial need analysis. *Deadline:* continuous.

Contact: Charlene Sime, Grant Specialist
Phone: 608-266-0888
E-mail: charlenek.sime@wi.gov

WONDERSHARE PDFELEMENT

https://pdf.wondershare.com

2018 PDFELEMENT $1000 SCHOLARSHIP

PDFelement is a PDF editing software that provides business solutions for universities, non-profit organizations, government entities, and small to mid-sized businesses. Our goal is provide simple PDF software that lets you work smarter with office documents. With that in mind, we want to invite you to apply for a "PDFs and I" story contest. The winning student will be awarded with $1,000, and the 10 runners-up will receive PDFelement 6 (Valued at $59.95) for free!

Award: Scholarship for use in freshman, sophomore, junior, senior, graduate, or postgraduate years; renewable. *Number:* 1–11. *Amount:* $500–$1000.

Eligibility Requirements: Applicant must be American Indian/Alaska Native; age 18-35 and enrolled or expecting to enroll full-time at a four-year institution or university. Applicant must be learning disabled. Available to U.S. and non-U.S. citizens. Applicant or parent must meet one or more of the following requirements: general military experience; retired from active duty; disabled or killed as a result of military service; prisoner of war; or missing in action.

Application Requirements: Essay, portfolio. *Deadline:* June 15.

Contact: Maggie Chou
E-mail: scholarship@wondershare.com

YORKVILLE GOODS LLC

https://www.yorkvilleblankets.com/pages/
yorkville-blankets-asd-scholarship

YORKVILLE BLANKETS ASD SCHOLARSHIP

Yorkville Blanket Company's mission to provide comfort to everybody who needs it does not end with making blankets. In order to continue pursuing our mission, we have created the Yorkville Blankets ASD

Scholarship for prospective or current college students who are living with ASD as well as students who are parents, siblings, and children of somebody on the autism spectrum to earn an award of $1000 toward continuing their education. The scholarship was created to help provide a means to pursue a post-secondary education for those whose lives have been impacted by Autism Spectrum Disorder (ASD).

Award: Scholarship for use in freshman, sophomore, junior, or senior years; not renewable. *Number:* 1. *Amount:* $1000.

Eligibility Requirements: Applicant must be enrolled or expecting to enroll full- or part-time at a two-year or four-year or technical institution or university. Applicant must be learning disabled. Available to U.S. citizens.

Application Requirements: Essay. *Deadline:* June 1.

Contact: Mr. Thomas Nolan, Owner
Yorkville Goods LLC
65 Linden Dr.
Berlin, CT 06037
Phone: 860-335-2447
E-mail: yorkvilleblankets@gmail.com

MILITARY SERVICE: AIR FORCE

AIR FORCE AID SOCIETY

http://www.afas.org/

GENERAL HENRY H. ARNOLD EDUCATION GRANT PROGRAM

Need- based grants awarded to dependent sons and daughters of active duty, Title 10 AGR/Reserve, Title 32 AGR performing full-time active duty, retired, retired reserve and deceased Air Force members; spouses of active members and Title 10 AGR/Reservist; and surviving spouses of deceased personnel for their undergraduate studies. Dependent children must be unmarried and under the age of 23. High school seniors may apply. Minimum 2.0 GPA is required. Students must reapply and compete each year. Full-time enrollment status required.

Award: Grant for use in freshman, sophomore, junior, or senior years; not renewable. *Number:* 3,000. *Amount:* $500–$4000.

Eligibility Requirements: Applicant must be enrolled or expecting to enroll full-time at a two-year or four-year or technical institution or university. Available to U.S. citizens. Applicant or parent must meet one or more of the following requirements: national guard experience; retired from active duty; disabled or killed as a result of military service; prisoner of war; or missing in action.

Application Requirements: Application form, financial need analysis. *Deadline:* April 30.

Contact: Education Programs
Air Force Aid Society
241 18th Street South, Suite 202
Arlington, VA 22202
Phone: 703-972-2647
Fax: 866-896-5637
E-mail: ED@afas-hq.org

AIR FORCE RESERVE OFFICER TRAINING CORPS

http://www.afrotc.com/

AIR FORCE ROTC COLLEGE SCHOLARSHIP TYPE 1

Pays full (100 percent) college tuition and authorized fees at any public or private institution with an Air Force ROTC detachment. Type 1 selectees will also receive a monthly living expense stipend and an annual book stipend. Applicants must pass a Department of Defense Medical Examination Review Board (DODMERB) medical exam and complete a Physical Fitness Assessment. SAT composite of 1240 or ACT composite of 26 and GPA of 3.0 or higher are also required for high school student applicants. For college applicants, the Air Force ROTC Commander will determine the minimum GPA and test scores, if applicable, for scholarship eligibility. Note: AFROTC Scholarships do not cover room and board.

Award: Scholarship for use in freshman, sophomore, junior, or senior years; renewable.

Eligibility Requirements: Applicant must be age 17-30 and enrolled or expecting to enroll full-time at a two-year institution or university. Available to U.S. citizens. Applicant or parent must meet one or more of the following requirements: Air Force experience; retired from active duty; disabled or killed as a result of military service; prisoner of war; or missing in action.

Application Requirements: Application form, application form may be submitted online, interview.

AIRMEN MEMORIAL FOUNDATION/AIR FORCE SERGEANTS ASSOCIATION

http://www.hqafsa.org/

AIRMEN MEMORIAL FOUNDATION SCHOLARSHIP

Scholarship for full-time undergraduate studies of dependent children of Air Force, Air Force Reserve Command and Air National Guard members in active duty, retired or veteran status. Must be under age of 23, have minimum combined score of 1650 on SAT or 24 on ACT, and a minimum GPA of 3.5.

Award: Scholarship for use in freshman, sophomore, junior, or senior years; not renewable. *Number:* 20. *Amount:* $500–$2000.

Eligibility Requirements: Applicant must be age 23 or under and enrolled or expecting to enroll full-time at a four-year institution or university. Available to U.S. and non-U.S. citizens. Applicant or parent must meet one or more of the following requirements: national guard experience; retired from active duty; disabled or killed as a result of military service; prisoner of war; or missing in action.

Application Requirements: Application form, essay, recommendations or references, transcript. *Deadline:* March 31.

Contact: Melanie Shirley, Scholarship Coordinator
Phone: 301-899-3500
Fax: 301-899-8136
E-mail: staff@afsahq.org

CHIEF MASTER SERGEANTS OF THE AIR FORCE SCHOLARSHIP PROGRAM

Scholarship to financially assist the full-time undergraduate studies of dependent children of Air Force, Air Force Reserve Command and Air National Guard enlisted members in active duty, retired or veteran status. Must be under age twenty-three and participate in the Airmen Memorial Foundation Scholarship Program. Must have minimum combined score of 1650 on SAT or 24 on ACT, and a minimum GPA of 3.5.

Award: Scholarship for use in freshman, sophomore, junior, or senior years; not renewable. *Number:* up to 30. *Amount:* $500–$3000.

Eligibility Requirements: Applicant must be age 23 or under and enrolled or expecting to enroll full-time at a four-year institution or university. Available to U.S. and non-U.S. citizens. Applicant or parent must meet one or more of the following requirements: national guard experience; retired from active duty; disabled or killed as a result of military service; prisoner of war; or missing in action.

Application Requirements: Application form, essay, recommendations or references, transcript. *Deadline:* March 31.

Contact: Melanie Shirley, Scholarship Coordinator
Phone: 301-899-3500
Fax: 301-899-8136
E-mail: staff@afsahq.org

DEPARTMENT OF VETERANS AFFAIRS (VA)

https://www.va.gov/

MONTGOMERY GI BILL SELECTED RESERVE

Educational assistance program for members of the selected reserve of the Army, Navy, Air Force, Marine Corps and Coast Guard, as well as the Army and Air National Guard. Available to all reservists and National Guard personnel who commit to a six-year obligation, and remain in the Reserve or Guard during the six years. Award is renewable. Monthly benefit is $309 for up to thirty-six months for full-time.

Award: Scholarship for use in freshman, sophomore, junior, senior, or postgraduate years; renewable.

Eligibility Requirements: Applicant must be enrolled or expecting to enroll full- or part-time at a two-year or technical institution or university. Available to U.S. citizens. Applicant or parent must meet one or more of the following requirements: general military experience; retired from active duty; disabled or killed as a result of military service; prisoner of war; or missing in action.

Application Requirements: Application form, application form may be submitted online. *Deadline:* continuous.

Contact: Keith Wilson, Director, Education Service
Phone: 888-442-4551

DIVERSITYCOMM, INC.

http://www.diversitycomm.net/

US VETERANS MAGAZINE SCHOLARSHIP

We would like you to tell your story in a brief narrative, starting with an introduction about who you are, your interests, and anything else you feel we should know about you. Then, please provide your entry in a 300-500 word essay about your college experience so far, and your future career plans. Graphic or creative presentations are welcome as well.

Award: Scholarship for use in freshman, sophomore, junior, or senior years; renewable. *Number:* 1. *Amount:* $500.

Eligibility Requirements: Applicant must be age 18 and over and enrolled or expecting to enroll full- or part-time at a two-year or four-year institution or university. Available to U.S. citizens. Applicant must have general military experience.

Application Requirements: Essay. *Deadline:* August 15.

IMAGINE AMERICA FOUNDATION

http://www.imagine-america.org

MILITARY AWARD PROGRAM (MAP)

The Military Award Program offers scholarships for veterans and other military students who decide to pursue career college training. This $1,000 career education award is available to any qualified active duty, reservist, honorably discharged or retired veteran of a U.S. military service branch for attendance at a participating career college.

Award: Scholarship for use in freshman, sophomore, junior, or senior years; not renewable. *Number:* 1,500. *Amount:* $1000.

Eligibility Requirements: Applicant must be enrolled or expecting to enroll full- or part-time at a two-year or four-year or technical institution. Available to U.S. citizens. Applicant must have general military experience.

Application Requirements: Application form. *Deadline:* continuous.

Contact: Lee Doubleday, Student Services Representative
Imagine America Foundation
12001 Sunrise Valley Drive, Suite 203
Reston, VA 20191
Phone: 571-267-3015
E-mail: leroyd@imagine-america.org

INDIANA DEPARTMENT OF VETERANS AFFAIRS

http://www.in.gov/dva

RESIDENT TUITION FOR ACTIVE DUTY MILITARY PERSONNEL

Applicant must be a nonresident of Indiana serving on active duty and stationed in Indiana and attending any state-supported college or university. Dependents remain eligible for the duration of their enrollment, even if the active duty person is no longer in Indiana. Entitlement is to the resident tuition rate.

Award: Grant for use in freshman, sophomore, junior, senior, graduate, or postgraduate years; renewable.

Eligibility Requirements: Applicant must be enrolled or expecting to enroll full- or part-time at a two-year or four-year or technical institution or university and studying in Indiana. Available to U.S. citizens. Applicant or parent must meet one or more of the following requirements: Air Force or Army experience; retired from active duty;

disabled or killed as a result of military service; prisoner of war; or missing in action.

Application Requirements: Application form. *Deadline:* continuous.

Contact: Michael Hamm, State Service Officer
Phone: 317-232-3910
Fax: 317-232-7721
E-mail: mhamm@dva.in.gov

KITCHEN GUIDES

http://www.kitchensguides.com/

SMART KITCHEN IMPROVEMENT SCHOLARSHIP BY KITCHEN GUIDES
• *See page 477*

PETAZI

https://petazi.com/

2017 NURTURE FOR NATURE SCHOLARSHIP
• *See page 483*

WISCONSIN DEPARTMENT OF VETERANS AFFAIRS (WDVA)

http://www.dva.state.wi.us/

VETERANS EDUCATION (VETED) REIMBURSEMENT GRANT
• *See page 485*

MILITARY SERVICE: AIR FORCE NATIONAL GUARD

AIR FORCE AID SOCIETY

http://www.afas.org/

GENERAL HENRY H. ARNOLD EDUCATION GRANT PROGRAM
• *See page 486*

AIRMEN MEMORIAL FOUNDATION/AIR FORCE SERGEANTS ASSOCIATION

http://www.hqafsa.org/

AIRMEN MEMORIAL FOUNDATION SCHOLARSHIP
• *See page 487*

CHIEF MASTER SERGEANTS OF THE AIR FORCE SCHOLARSHIP PROGRAM
• *See page 487*

ALABAMA COMMISSION ON HIGHER EDUCATION

http://www.ache.alabama.gov/

ALABAMA NATIONAL GUARD EDUCATIONAL ASSISTANCE PROGRAM
Renewable award aids Alabama residents who are members of the Alabama National Guard and are enrolled in a nationally recognized accredited college in Alabama. Forms must be signed by a representative of the Alabama Military Department and financial aid officer. Recipient must be in a degree-seeking program.

Award: Scholarship for use in freshman, sophomore, junior, senior, or graduate years; not renewable. *Number:* 400–800. *Amount:* $100–$2000.

Eligibility Requirements: Applicant must be age 17 and over; enrolled or expecting to enroll full- or part-time at a two-year or four-year or technical institution or university; resident of Alabama and studying in Alabama. Available to U.S. citizens. Applicant must have national guard experience.

Application Requirements: Application form, financial need analysis. *Deadline:* continuous.

Contact: Cheryl Newton, Grants Coordinator
Phone: 334-242-2273
Fax: 334-242-2269
E-mail: Cheryl.Newton@ache.edu

DELAWARE ARMY NATIONAL GUARD

http://www.delawarenationalguard.com/

STATE TUITION ASSISTANCE
You must enlist in the Delaware Air or Army National Guard to be eligible for this scholarship award. Award providing tuition assistance for any member of the Air or Army National Guard attending a Delaware two-year or four-year college. Awards are renewable. Applicant's minimum GPA must be 2.0.

Award: Scholarship for use in freshman, sophomore, junior, or senior years; renewable. *Number:* 1–200. *Amount:* $1–$10,000.

Eligibility Requirements: Applicant must be enrolled or expecting to enroll full- or part-time at a two-year or four-year institution or university and studying in Delaware. Available to U.S. citizens. Applicant or parent must meet one or more of the following requirements: national guard experience; retired from active duty; disabled or killed as a result of military service; prisoner of war; or missing in action.

Application Requirements: Application form. *Deadline:* continuous.

Contact: Robert Csizmadia, State Tuition Assistance Manager
Delaware Army National Guard
1 Vavala Way
New Castle, DE 19720
Phone: 302-326-7012
E-mail: robert.l.csizmadianfg@mail.mil

DEPARTMENT OF VETERANS AFFAIRS (VA)

https://www.va.gov/

MONTGOMERY GI BILL SELECTED RESERVE
• *See page 487*

RESERVE EDUCATION ASSISTANCE PROGRAM
The program provides educational assistance to members of National Guard and reserve components. Selected Reserve and Individual Ready Reserve (IRR) who are called or ordered to active duty service in response to a war or national emergency as declared by the president or Congress are eligible. For further information see website http://www.GIBILL.va.gov.

Award: Scholarship for use in freshman, sophomore, junior, senior, graduate, or postgraduate years; renewable.

Eligibility Requirements: Applicant must be enrolled or expecting to enroll full- or part-time at a two-year or four-year or technical institution or university. Available to U.S. citizens. Applicant or parent must meet one or more of the following requirements: general military experience; retired from active duty; disabled or killed as a result of military service; prisoner of war; or missing in action.

Application Requirements: Application form. *Deadline:* continuous.

Contact: Keith Wilson, Director, Education Service
Phone: 888-442-4551

DIVERSITYCOMM, INC.

http://www.diversitycomm.net/

US VETERANS MAGAZINE SCHOLARSHIP
• *See page 487*

ENLISTED ASSOCIATION OF THE NATIONAL GUARD OF NEW JERSEY

http://www.eang-nj.org/

CSM VINCENT BALDASSARI MEMORIAL SCHOLARSHIP PROGRAM

Scholarships open to the legal children of New Jersey National Guard Members who are also members of the Enlisted Association. Also open to any drilling guardsperson who is a member of the Enlisted Association. Along with application, submit proof of parent's membership and a letter stating the reason for applying and future intents.

Award: Scholarship for use in freshman, sophomore, junior, senior, graduate, or postgraduate years; not renewable. *Number:* 5. *Amount:* $1000.

Eligibility Requirements: Applicant must be enrolled or expecting to enroll full- or part-time at a two-year or four-year or technical institution or university and resident of New Jersey. Available to U.S. and non-U.S. citizens. Applicant or parent must meet one or more of the following requirements: national guard experience; retired from active duty; disabled or killed as a result of military service; prisoner of war; or missing in action.

Application Requirements: Application form, essay, personal photograph, recommendations or references, transcript. *Deadline:* May 15.

Contact: Michael Amoroso, Scholarship Committee Chairman
Phone: 609-562-0754
Fax: 609-562-0731
E-mail: michael.c@us.army.mil

USAA SCHOLARSHIP

Scholarship of $1000 open to any drilling guardsperson (need not be a member of the EANGNJ).

Award: Scholarship for use in freshman, sophomore, junior, senior, graduate, or postgraduate years; not renewable. *Number:* 1. *Amount:* $1000.

Eligibility Requirements: Applicant must be enrolled or expecting to enroll full- or part-time at a two-year or four-year or technical institution or university. Available to U.S. and non-U.S. citizens. Applicant or parent must meet one or more of the following requirements: national guard experience; retired from active duty; disabled or killed as a result of military service; prisoner of war; or missing in action.

Application Requirements: Application form, essay, personal photograph, transcript. *Deadline:* May 15.

Contact: Michael Amoroso, Scholarship Committee Chairman
Phone: 609-562-0754
Fax: 609-562-0731
E-mail: michael.c@us.army.mil

ILLINOIS STUDENT ASSISTANCE COMMISSION (ISAC)

http://www.isac.org/

ILLINOIS NATIONAL GUARD (ING) GRANT PROGRAM

Active duty members of the Illinois National Guard, or who are within 12 months of discharge, and who have completed one full year of service are eligible. May be used for study at Illinois two- or four-year public colleges for a maximum of the equivalent of four academic years of full-time enrollment. Deadlines: October 1 of the academic year for full year, March 1 for second/third term, or June 15 for the summer term.

Award: Grant for use in freshman, sophomore, junior, senior, or graduate years; not renewable.

Eligibility Requirements: Applicant must be enrolled or expecting to enroll full- or part-time at a two-year institution or university; resident of Idaho and studying in Illinois. Available to U.S. citizens. Applicant or parent must meet one or more of the following requirements: national guard experience; retired from active duty; disabled or killed as a result of military service; prisoner of war; or missing in action.

Application Requirements: Application form, application form may be submitted online. *Deadline:* continuous.

Contact: ISAC Call Center Representative
Illinois Student Assistance Commission (ISAC)
1755 Lake Cook Road
Deerfield, IL 60015-5209
Phone: 800-899-4722
E-mail: isac.studentservices@illinois.gov

IMAGINE AMERICA FOUNDATION

http://www.imagine-america.org

MILITARY AWARD PROGRAM (MAP)

• *See page 487*

INDIANA COMMISSION FOR HIGHER EDUCATION

http://www.in.gov/che

INDIANA NATIONAL GUARD TUITION SUPPLEMENT GRANT

Provides 100% of tuition and regularly assessed fees at a public Indiana institution for eligible members of the Indiana Air and Army National Guard. Students can attend either full time or part time.

Award: Grant for use in freshman, sophomore, junior, or senior years; not renewable.

Eligibility Requirements: Applicant must be enrolled or expecting to enroll full- or part-time at a two-year or technical institution or university; resident of Illinois and studying in Indiana. Available to U.S. citizens. Applicant must have national guard experience.

Application Requirements: Application form, application form may be submitted online, financial need analysis. *Deadline:* continuous.

Contact: Charlee Beasor, Communications Director
Phone: 317-232-1016
E-mail: CBeasor@che.in.gov

INDIANA DEPARTMENT OF VETERANS AFFAIRS

http://www.in.gov/dva

CHILDREN AND SPOUSE OF INDIANA NATIONAL GUARD

Award to an individual whose father, mother or spouse was a member of the Indiana National Guard and suffered a service-connected death while serving on state active duty (which includes mobilized and deployed for federal active duty). The student must be eligible to pay the resident tuition rate at the state-supported college or university and must possess the requisite academic qualifications.

Award: Grant for use in freshman, sophomore, junior, or senior years; renewable.

Eligibility Requirements: Applicant must be enrolled or expecting to enroll full- or part-time at a two-year or technical institution or university and studying in Indiana. Available to U.S. citizens. Applicant or parent must meet one or more of the following requirements: national guard experience; retired from active duty; disabled or killed as a result of military service; prisoner of war; or missing in action.

Application Requirements: Application form, application form may be submitted online. *Deadline:* continuous.

Contact: Courtney Carr, Adjutant General
Indiana Department of Veterans Affairs
2002 South Holt Road
Indianapolis, IN 46241
Phone: 317-964-7023
E-mail: c.carr@in.ngb.army.mil

NATIONAL GUARD EXTENSION SCHOLARSHIP

A scholarship extension applicant is eligible for a tuition scholarship under Indiana Code 21-13-5-4 for a period not to exceed the period of scholarship extension the applicant served on active duty as a member of the National Guard (mobilized and deployed). Must apply not later than one (1) year after the applicant ceases to be a member of the Indiana National Guard. Applicant should apply through the education officer of their last unit of assignment.

Award: Scholarship for use in freshman, sophomore, junior, or senior years; renewable.

Eligibility Requirements: Applicant must be enrolled or expecting to enroll full- or part-time at a two-year or technical institution or university; resident of Illinois and studying in Indiana. Available to U.S. citizens. Applicant must have national guard experience.

Application Requirements: Application form. *Deadline:* continuous.

Contact: Pamela Moody, National Guard Education Officer
Indiana Department of Veterans Affairs
302 West Washington Street, Room E-120
Indianapolis, IN 46204
Phone: 317-964-7017
E-mail: pamela.moody@in.ngb.army.mil

NATIONAL GUARD TUITION SUPPLEMENT GRANT

Applicant must be a member of the Indiana National Guard, in active drilling status, who has not been AWOL during the last 12 months, does not possess a bachelor's degree, possesses the requisite academic qualifications, meets the requirements of the state-supported college or university, and meets all National Guard requirements.

Award: Grant for use in freshman, sophomore, junior, or senior years; renewable.

Eligibility Requirements: Applicant must be enrolled or expecting to enroll full- or part-time at a two-year or technical institution or university; resident of Illinois and studying in Indiana. Available to U.S. citizens. Applicant must have national guard experience.

Application Requirements: Application form. *Deadline:* continuous.

Contact: ATTN: Education Services Office
Indiana Department of Veterans Affairs
Indiana Army National Guard
2002 South Holt Road
Indianapolis, IN 46241

KENTUCKY HIGHER EDUCATION ASSISTANCE AUTHORITY (KHEAA)

http://www.kheaa.com/

KENTUCKY NATIONAL GUARD TUITION AWARD

Provides tuition assistance for active members of the Kentucky National Guard to attend a Kentucky college or university. Must be a Guard member in satisfactory standing; complete basic and advanced individual training; and attend an approved accredited school to pursue a vocational, associate, bachelor or graduate program. Guard members may apply through their unit. Tuition (subject to the availability of funds) for up to $250 a credit hour, not to exceed cap outlined in National Guard Policy letter.

Award: Grant for use in freshman, sophomore, junior, or senior years; renewable.

Eligibility Requirements: Applicant must be enrolled or expecting to enroll full- or part-time at a two-year or technical institution or university; resident of Kansas and studying in Kentucky. Available to U.S. citizens. Applicant must have national guard experience.

Application Requirements: Application form. *Deadline:* continuous.

Contact: Becky Gilpatrick, Director of Student Aid
Kentucky Higher Education Assistance Authority (KHEAA)
PO Box 798
Frankfort, KY 40602-0798
Phone: 800-928-8926
Fax: 502-696-7373
E-mail: rgilpatrick@kheaa.com

KITCHEN GUIDES

http://www.kitchensguides.com/

SMART KITCHEN IMPROVEMENT SCHOLARSHIP BY KITCHEN GUIDES

• *See page 477*

LOUISIANA NATIONAL GUARD, JOINT TASK FORCE LA

http://geauxguard.com/organization/joint-force-headquarters-jfhq-la/

LOUISIANA NATIONAL GUARD STATE TUITION EXEMPTION PROGRAM

Renewable award for college undergraduates to receive tuition exemption upon satisfactory performance in the Louisiana National Guard. Applicant must attend a state-funded institution in Louisiana, be a resident and registered voter in Louisiana, meet the academic and residency requirements of the university attended, and provide documentation of Louisiana National Guard enlistment. The exemption can be used for up to 15 semesters. Minimum 2.5 GPA required.

Award: Scholarship for use in freshman, sophomore, junior, or senior years; renewable.

Eligibility Requirements: Applicant must be enrolled or expecting to enroll full- or part-time at a two-year or four-year or technical institution or university; resident of Louisiana and studying in Louisiana. Available to U.S. citizens. Applicant or parent must meet one or more of the following requirements: national guard experience; retired from active duty; disabled or killed as a result of military service; prisoner of war; or missing in action.

Application Requirements: Application form, test scores, transcript. *Deadline:* continuous.

Contact: Jona Hughes, Education Services Officer
Louisiana National Guard, Joint Task Force LA
Building 35, Jackson Barracks, JI-PD
New Orleans, LA 70146-0330
Phone: 504-278-8531 Ext. 8304
Fax: 504-278-8025
E-mail: hughesj@la-arng.ngb.army.mil

NORTH CAROLINA NATIONAL GUARD

http://nc.ng.mil/Pages/default.aspx

NORTH CAROLINA NATIONAL GUARD TUITION ASSISTANCE PROGRAM

Scholarship for members of the North Carolina Air and Army National Guard who will remain in the service for two years following the period for which assistance is provided. Must reapply for each academic period. For use at approved North Carolina institutions.

Award: Grant for use in freshman, sophomore, junior, senior, or graduate years; not renewable. *Amount:* $100–$3440.

Eligibility Requirements: Applicant must be enrolled or expecting to enroll full- or part-time at a two-year or four-year or technical institution or university; resident of North Carolina and studying in North Carolina. Available to U.S. citizens. Applicant or parent must meet one or more of the following requirements: national guard experience; retired from active duty; disabled or killed as a result of military service; prisoner of war; or missing in action.

Application Requirements: Application form. *Deadline:* continuous.

Contact: Ms. Stacy Steinmetz, NCTAP Manager
North Carolina National Guard
1636 Gold Star Drive
Raleigh, NC 27607
Phone: 919-664-6272
E-mail: stacy.m.steinmetz.nfg@mail.mil

OHIO NATIONAL GUARD

http://www.ong.ohio.gov/

OHIO NATIONAL GUARD SCHOLARSHIP PROGRAM

Scholarships are for undergraduate studies at an approved Ohio post-secondary institution. Applicants must enlist for six or three years of Selective Service Reserve Duty in the Ohio National Guard. Scholarship pays 100% instructional and general fees for public institutions and an average of cost of public universities is available for private schools. May reapply up to four years of studies (12 quarters or 8 semesters) for six year enlistment and two years of studies (6 quarters or 4 semesters) for three year enlistment. Deadlines: July 1 (fall), November 1 (winter quarter/spring semester), February 1 (spring quarter), April 1 (summer).

Award: Scholarship for use in freshman, sophomore, junior, or senior years; not renewable.

Eligibility Requirements: Applicant must be enrolled or expecting to enroll full- or part-time at a two-year or four-year or technical institution or university; resident of Ohio and studying in Ohio. Available to U.S. citizens. Applicant must have national guard experience.

Application Requirements: Application form.

Contact: Afrika Alsup, Scholarship Program Director
Phone: 614-336-7032
E-mail: akrika.k.alsup.nfg@ mail.mil

PENNSYLVANIA HIGHER EDUCATION ASSISTANCE AGENCY

http://www.pheaa.org/

POSTSECONDARY EDUCATIONAL GRATUITY PROGRAM

The program offers waiver of tuition and fees for children of Pennsylvania police officers, firefighters, rescue or ambulance squad members, corrections facility employees, or National Guard members who died in line of duty after January 1, 1976.

Award: Grant for use in freshman, sophomore, junior, or senior years; renewable.

Eligibility Requirements: Applicant must be age 25 or under; enrolled or expecting to enroll full-time at a two-year institution or university; resident of Oregon and studying in Pennsylvania. Available to U.S. citizens. Applicant or parent must meet one or more of the following requirements: national guard experience; retired from active duty; disabled or killed as a result of military service; prisoner of war; or missing in action.

Application Requirements: Application form. *Deadline:* March 31.

Contact: Keith New, Director of Public Relations
Phone: 800-692-7392
E-mail: knew@pheaa.org

PETAZI

https://petazi.com/

2017 NURTURE FOR NATURE SCHOLARSHIP
• *See page 483*

WISCONSIN DEPARTMENT OF VETERANS AFFAIRS (WDVA)

http://www.dva.state.wi.us/

VETERANS EDUCATION (VETED) REIMBURSEMENT GRANT
• *See page 485*

MILITARY SERVICE: ARMY

AMERICAN LEGION AUXILIARY DEPARTMENT OF KENTUCKY

http://www.kylegion.org/

AMERICAN LEGION AUXILIARY DEPARTMENT OF KENTUCKY LAURA BLACKBURN MEMORIAL SCHOLARSHIP

Scholarship to the child, grandchild, or great grandchild of a veteran who served in the Armed Forces. Applicant must be a Kentucky resident.

Award: Scholarship for use in freshman year; not renewable. *Number:* 1. *Amount:* $1000.

Eligibility Requirements: Applicant must be high school student; planning to enroll or expecting to enroll full-time at a four-year institution or university and resident of Kentucky. Available to U.S. citizens. Applicant or parent must meet one or more of the following requirements: Army experience; retired from active duty; disabled or killed as a result of military service; prisoner of war; or missing in action.

Application Requirements: Application form, financial need analysis, transcript. *Deadline:* March 31.

Contact: Betty Cook, Secretary and Treasurer
Phone: 270-932-7533
Fax: 270-932-7672
E-mail: secretarykyala@aol.com

ARMY OFFICERS' WIVES CLUB OF GREATER WASHINGTON AREA

http://www.aowcgwa.org/

ARMY OFFICERS WIVES CLUB OF THE GREATER WASHINGTON AREA SCHOLARSHIP

Scholarship for high school seniors, college students or children or spouses of U.S. Army personnel. Scholarship awards are based on scholastic merit and community involvement.

Award: Scholarship for use in freshman, sophomore, junior, or senior years; not renewable. *Number:* 1–3. *Amount:* $100–$500.

Eligibility Requirements: Applicant must be age 22 or under and enrolled or expecting to enroll full-time at a four-year institution or university. Available to U.S. citizens. Applicant or parent must meet one or more of the following requirements: Army experience; retired from active duty; disabled or killed as a result of military service; prisoner of war; or missing in action.

Application Requirements: Application form, essay, military dependent ID card, recommendations or references, self-addressed stamped envelope with application, transcript. *Deadline:* March 31.

Contact: Janis Waller, Scholarship Committee Chair
Army Officers' Wives Club of Greater Washington Area
12025 William and Mary Circle
Woodbridge, VA 22192-1634

DEPARTMENT OF THE ARMY

http://www.goarmy.com/rotc

ARMY ROTC GREEN TO GOLD SCHOLARSHIP PROGRAM FOR TWO-YEAR, THREE-YEAR AND FOUR-YEAR SCHOLARSHIPS, ACTIVE DUTY ENLISTED PERSONNEL

Award for junior year for use at a four-year institution for Army enlisted personnel. Merit considered. Must also be member of the school's ROTC program. Must pass physical and have completed two years of active duty. Applicant must be at least seventeen years of age by college enrollment and under thirty-one years of age in the year of graduation. Submit recommendations from Commanding Officer and Field Grade Commander. Include DODMERB Physical Forms and DA Form 2A.

Award: Scholarship for use in junior, senior, or graduate years; renewable. *Number:* 200–400.

Eligibility Requirements: Applicant must be age 17-30; enrolled or expecting to enroll full-time at a two-year institution or university and studying in Alabama, Alaska, Arizona, Arkansas, California, Colorado, Connecticut, Delaware, District of Columbia, Florida, Georgia, Guam, Hawaii, Idaho, Illinois, Indiana, Iowa, Kansas, Kentucky, Louisiana, Maine, Maryland, Massachusetts, Michigan, Minnesota, Mississippi, Missouri, Montana, Nebraska, Nevada, New Hampshire, New Jersey, New Mexico, New York, North Carolina, North Dakota, Ohio, Oklahoma, Oregon, Pennsylvania, Puerto Rico, Rhode Island, South Carolina, South Dakota, Tennessee, Texas, Utah, Vermont, Virginia, Washington, West Virginia, Wisconsin, Wyoming. Available to U.S. citizens. Applicant must have served in the Army.

Application Requirements: Application form, essay, personal photograph. *Deadline:* December 1.

Contact: Mr. John Provost, U.S. Army Cadet Command
Department of the Army
204 1st Cavalry Regiment Road
Building 1002
Fort Knox, KY 40121
Phone: 502-624-2400
Fax: 502-624-1120
E-mail: john.h.provost.civ@mail.mil

ARMY (ROTC) RESERVE OFFICERS TRAINING CORPS TWO-, THREE-, FOUR-YEAR CAMPUS-BASED SCHOLARSHIPS

One-time award for college freshmen, sophomores, or juniors or students with BA who need two years to obtain graduate degree. Must be a member of school's ROTC program. Must pass physical. Minimum 2.5 GPA required. Professor of Military Science must submit application. Must be U.S. citizen/national at time of award. Open year-round.

Award: Scholarship for use in freshman, sophomore, junior, senior, or graduate years; renewable. *Number:* 2,000–3,500. *Amount:* $10,000–$120,000.

Eligibility Requirements: Applicant must be age 17-26; enrolled or expecting to enroll full-time at an institution or university and studying in Alabama, Alaska, Arizona, Arkansas, California, Colorado, Connecticut, Delaware, District of Columbia, Florida, Georgia, Guam, Hawaii, Idaho, Illinois, Indiana, Iowa, Kansas, Kentucky, Louisiana, Maine, Maryland, Massachusetts, Michigan, Minnesota, Mississippi, Missouri, Montana, Nebraska, Nevada, New Hampshire, New Jersey, New Mexico, New York, North Carolina, North Dakota, Ohio, Oklahoma, Oregon, Pennsylvania, Puerto Rico, Rhode Island, South Carolina, South Dakota, Tennessee, Texas, Utah, Vermont, Virginia, Washington, West Virginia, Wisconsin, Wyoming. Available to U.S. citizens. Applicant or parent must meet one or more of the following requirements: Army experience; retired from active duty; disabled or killed as a result of military service; prisoner of war; or missing in action.

Application Requirements: Application form, interview. *Deadline:* continuous.

Contact: Mr. John Provost, U.S. Army Cadet Command
Department of the Army
204 1st Cavalry Regiment Road
Building 1002
Fort Knox, KY 40121
Phone: 502-624-2400
Fax: 502-624-1120
E-mail: john.h.provost.civ@mail.mil

U.S. ARMY ROTC FOUR-YEAR COLLEGE SCHOLARSHIP

One-time award for students entering college for the first time, or freshmen in a documented five-year degree program. Must join school's ROTC program, pass physical, and submit teacher evaluations. Must be a U.S. citizen and have a qualifying SAT or ACT score.

Award: Scholarship for use in freshman year; renewable. *Number:* 1,000–2,500. *Amount:* $9000–$150,000.

Eligibility Requirements: Applicant must be high school student; age 17-26; planning to enroll or expecting to enroll full-time at an institution or university and studying in Alabama, Alaska, Arizona, Arkansas, California, Colorado, Connecticut, Delaware, District of Columbia, Florida, Georgia, Guam, Hawaii, Idaho, Illinois, Indiana, Iowa, Kansas, Kentucky, Louisiana, Maine, Maryland, Massachusetts, Michigan, Minnesota, Mississippi, Missouri, Montana, Nebraska, Nevada, New Hampshire, New Jersey, New Mexico, New York, North Carolina, North Dakota, Ohio, Oklahoma, Oregon, Pennsylvania, Puerto Rico, Rhode Island, South Carolina, South Dakota, Tennessee, Texas, Utah, Vermont, Virginia, Washington, West Virginia, Wisconsin, Wyoming. Available to U.S. citizens. Applicant must have national guard experience.

Application Requirements: Application form, essay, interview. *Deadline:* February 4.

Contact: Mr. John Provost, U.S. Army Cadet Command
Department of the Army
204 1st Cavalry Regiment Road
Building 1002
Fort Knox, KY 40121
Phone: 502-624-2400
Fax: 502-624-1120
E-mail: john.h.provost.civ@mail.mil

U.S. ARMY ROTC FOUR-YEAR HISTORICALLY BLACK COLLEGE/UNIVERSITY SCHOLARSHIP

One-time award for students attending college for the first time Must attend a historically black college or university and must join school's ROTC program. Must pass physical. Must have a qualifying SAT or ACT score and minimum GPA of 2.5. Must be a U.S. citizen/national at time of award.

Award: Scholarship for use in freshman, sophomore, junior, senior, or graduate years; renewable. *Number:* 20–200. *Amount:* $9000–$40,000.

Eligibility Requirements: Applicant must be age 17-26; enrolled or expecting to enroll full-time at an institution or university and studying in Alabama, Alaska, Arizona, Arkansas, California, Colorado, Connecticut, Delaware, District of Columbia, Florida, Georgia, Guam, Hawaii, Idaho, Illinois, Indiana, Iowa, Kansas, Kentucky, Louisiana, Maine, Maryland, Massachusetts, Michigan, Minnesota, Mississippi, Missouri, Montana, Nebraska, Nevada, New Hampshire, New Jersey, New Mexico, New York, North Carolina, North Dakota, Ohio, Oklahoma, Oregon, Pennsylvania, Puerto Rico, Rhode Island, South Carolina, South Dakota, Tennessee, Texas, Utah, Vermont, Virginia, Washington, West Virginia, Wisconsin, Wyoming. Available to U.S. citizens. Applicant must have national guard experience.

Application Requirements: Application form, essay, interview. *Deadline:* February 4.

Contact: Mr. John Provost, U.S. Army Cadet Command
Department of the Army
204 1st Cavalry Regiment Road
Building 1002
Fort Knox, KY 40121
Phone: 502-624-2400
Fax: 502-624-1120
E-mail: john.h.provost.civ@mail.mil

U.S. ARMY ROTC MILITARY JUNIOR COLLEGE (MJC) SCHOLARSHIP

One-time award for high school graduates who wish to attend a two-year military junior college. Must serve simultaneously in the Army National Guard or Reserve and qualify for the ROTC Advanced Course. Must have a minimum GPA of 2.5. Must be a U.S. citizen/national at time of award. Must also be eighteen years of age by October 1 and under twenty-seven years of age on June 30 in the year of graduation. Must be used at one of five military junior colleges. See Professor of Military Science at college for application.

Award: Scholarship for use in freshman or sophomore years; renewable. *Number:* 110–150. *Amount:* $5600–$52,000.

Eligibility Requirements: Applicant must be age 18-26; enrolled or expecting to enroll full-time at a two-year institution and studying in Alabama, Alaska, Arizona, Arkansas, California, Colorado, Connecticut, Delaware, District of Columbia, Florida, Georgia, Guam, Hawaii, Idaho, Illinois, Indiana, Iowa, Kansas, Kentucky, Louisiana, Maine, Maryland, Massachusetts, Michigan, Minnesota, Mississippi, Missouri, Montana, Nebraska, Nevada, New Hampshire, New Jersey, New Mexico, New York, North Carolina, North Dakota, Ohio, Oklahoma, Oregon, Pennsylvania, Puerto Rico, Rhode Island, South Carolina, South Dakota, Tennessee, Texas, Utah, Vermont, Virginia, Washington, West Virginia, Wisconsin, Wyoming. Available to U.S. citizens. Applicant must have national guard experience.

Application Requirements: Application form, essay, interview. *Deadline:* July 25.

Contact: Mr. John Provost, U.S. Army Cadet Command
Department of the Army
204 1st Cavalry Regiment Road
Building 1002
Fort Knox, KY 40121
Phone: 502-624-2400
Fax: 502-624-1120
E-mail: john.h.provost.civ@mail.mil

DEPARTMENT OF VETERANS AFFAIRS (VA)

https://www.va.gov/

MONTGOMERY GI BILL SELECTED RESERVE
• *See page 487*

DIVERSITYCOMM, INC.

http://www.diversitycomm.net/

US VETERANS MAGAZINE SCHOLARSHIP
• *See page 487*

IMAGINE AMERICA FOUNDATION

http://www.imagine-america.org

MILITARY AWARD PROGRAM (MAP)
• *See page 487*

INDIANA DEPARTMENT OF VETERANS AFFAIRS

http://www.in.gov/dva

RESIDENT TUITION FOR ACTIVE DUTY MILITARY PERSONNEL
• *See page 487*

KITCHEN GUIDES

http://www.kitchensguides.com/

SMART KITCHEN IMPROVEMENT SCHOLARSHIP BY KITCHEN GUIDES
• *See page 477*

PETAZI

https://petazi.com/

2017 NURTURE FOR NATURE SCHOLARSHIP
• *See page 483*

SOCIETY OF DAUGHTERS OF THE UNITED STATES ARMY

SOCIETY OF DAUGHTERS OF THE UNITED STATES ARMY SCHOLARSHIPS

Scholarship for daughters or granddaughters of career warrant or commissioned officer in the U.S. Army who is on active duty; retired from active duty after 20 years of service; medically retired before 20 years of active service; died while on active duty or died after retiring from active duty. Send the following information to request an application: applicant's name, name of officer, rank, component (active, reserve, retired), dates of active duty service, and relationship to the applicant. Send information only, no documentation at this time. Send to Mary P. Maroney, DUSA Scholarship Chairman, 11804 Grey Birch Place, Reston, VA 20191. Application available.November 1 - March 1.

Award: Scholarship for use in freshman, sophomore, junior, or senior years; not renewable. *Number:* 8–12. *Amount:* $1000.

Eligibility Requirements: Applicant must be enrolled or expecting to enroll full-time at a two-year or four-year or technical institution or university and female. Available to U.S. citizens. Applicant or parent must meet one or more of the following requirements: national guard experience; retired from active duty; disabled or killed as a result of military service; prisoner of war; or missing in action.

Application Requirements: Application form, essay. *Deadline:* March 1.

Contact: Mary Maroney, Chairperson, Memorial and Scholarship Funds
Society of Daughters of the United States Army
11804 Grey Birch Place
Reston, VA 20191

STUDY.COM

http://study.com

ARMY ROTC STUDY.COM SCHOLARSHIP

A $500 academic award will be given to a student enrolled in Army ROTC at their college or university. Study.com wants to recognize students who have the dedication and strength of character necessary to be successful in the competitive ROTC program. For more information, please visit https://study.com/pages/Army_ROTC_Scholarship.html

Award: Scholarship for use in freshman, sophomore, or junior years; renewable. *Number:* 1. *Amount:* $500.

Eligibility Requirements: Applicant must be enrolled or expecting to enroll full- or part-time at a two-year or four-year institution or university. Available to U.S. citizens. Applicant must have national guard experience.

Application Requirements: Application form, personal photograph. *Deadline:* April 1.

Contact: Koby Wong, Study.com Scholarship Manager
Phone: 650-9621200
E-mail: koby@email.study.com

UNITED STATES ARMY WARRANT OFFICERS ASSOCIATION

USAWOA SCHOLARSHIP FOUNDATION

Awardee must be a dependant of a member of the USAWOA for at least 6 months when the application is received.

Award: Scholarship for use in freshman, sophomore, junior, senior, graduate, or postgraduate years; renewable. *Number:* 17–19. *Amount:* $1500–$2000.

Eligibility Requirements: Applicant must be American Indian/Alaska Native, Asian/Pacific Islander, Black (non-Hispanic), Hispanic and enrolled or expecting to enroll full-time at a two-year or four-year or technical institution or university. Available to U.S. citizens. Applicant must have national guard experience.

Application Requirements: Application form, community service, essay, personal photograph, portfolio. *Deadline:* May 1.

WISCONSIN DEPARTMENT OF VETERANS AFFAIRS (WDVA)

http://www.dva.state.wi.us/

VETERANS EDUCATION (VETED) REIMBURSEMENT GRANT
• *See page 485*

WOMEN'S ARMY CORPS VETERANS' ASSOCIATION-ARMY WOMEN UNITED

http://www.armywomen.org/

WOMEN'S ARMY CORPS VETERANS' ASSOCIATION SCHOLARSHIP

Scholarship to graduating high school senior showing academic promise. Must be a child, grandchild, niece or nephew of an Army servicewoman. Minimum cumulative GPA of 3.5 required. Applicants must plan to enroll in a degree program as a full-time student at an accredited college or university in the United States.

Award: Scholarship for use in freshman year; not renewable. *Number:* 1. *Amount:* $1500.

Eligibility Requirements: Applicant must be high school student and planning to enroll or expecting to enroll full-time at a four-year institution or university. Available to U.S. citizens. Applicant or parent must meet one or more of the following requirements: Army experience; retired from active duty; disabled or killed as a result of military service; prisoner of war; or missing in action.

Application Requirements: Application form. *Deadline:* April 1.

Contact: Ms. Eldora Engebretson, Scholarship Committee
Phone: 623-566-9299
E-mail: info@armywomen.org

MILITARY SERVICE: ARMY NATIONAL GUARD

ALABAMA COMMISSION ON HIGHER EDUCATION

http://www.ache.alabama.gov/

ALABAMA NATIONAL GUARD EDUCATIONAL ASSISTANCE PROGRAM
• *See page 488*

CONNECTICUT ARMY NATIONAL GUARD

http://ct.ng.mil/Pages/default.aspx

CONNECTICUT ARMY NATIONAL GUARD 100% TUITION WAIVER

Program is for any active member of the Connecticut Army National Guard in good standing. Must be a resident of Connecticut attending any Connecticut state (public) university, community-technical college or regional vocational-technical school. The total number of available awards is unlimited.

Award: Scholarship for use in freshman, sophomore, junior, or senior years; not renewable. *Amount:* $16,000.

Eligibility Requirements: Applicant must be age 17-65; enrolled or expecting to enroll full- or part-time at a two-year or four-year or technical institution or university; resident of Connecticut and studying in Connecticut. Available to U.S. and non-U.S. citizens. Applicant or parent must meet one or more of the following requirements: national guard experience; retired from active duty; disabled or killed as a result of military service; prisoner of war; or missing in action.

Application Requirements: Application form. *Deadline:* July 1.

Contact: Capt. Jeremy Lingenfelser, Education Services Officer
Connecticut Army National Guard
360 Broad Street
Hartford, CT 06105-3795
Phone: 860-524-4816
Fax: 860-524-4904
E-mail: education@ct.ngb.army.mil

DELAWARE ARMY NATIONAL GUARD

http://www.delawarenationalguard.com/

STATE TUITION ASSISTANCE
• *See page 488*

DEPARTMENT OF THE ARMY

http://www.goarmy.com/rotc

U.S. ARMY ROTC FOUR-YEAR COLLEGE SCHOLARSHIP
• *See page 492*

U.S. ARMY ROTC FOUR-YEAR HISTORICALLY BLACK COLLEGE/UNIVERSITY SCHOLARSHIP
• *See page 492*

U.S. ARMY ROTC GUARANTEED RESERVE FORCES DUTY (GRFD), (ARNG/USAR) AND DEDICATED ARNG SCHOLARSHIPS

One-time award for college freshmen, sophomores, and juniors, or two-year graduate degree students. Must be a member of school's ROTC program. Must pass physical. Minimum 2.5 GPA required. Must be a U.S. citizen/national at the time of award.

Award: Scholarship for use in freshman, sophomore, junior, senior, or graduate years; renewable. *Number:* 1,000–3,000. *Amount:* $10,000–$120,000.

Eligibility Requirements: Applicant must be age 17-26; enrolled or expecting to enroll full-time at an institution or university and studying in Alabama, Alaska, Arizona, Arkansas, California, Colorado, Connecticut, Delaware, District of Columbia, Florida, Georgia, Guam, Hawaii, Idaho, Illinois, Indiana, Iowa, Kansas, Kentucky, Louisiana, Maine, Maryland, Massachusetts, Michigan, Minnesota, Mississippi, Missouri, Montana, Nebraska, Nevada, New Hampshire, New Jersey, New Mexico, New York, North Carolina, North Dakota, Ohio, Oklahoma, Oregon, Pennsylvania, Puerto Rico, Rhode Island, Saskatchewan, South Carolina, South Dakota, Tennessee, Texas, Utah, Vermont, Virginia, Washington, West Virginia, Wisconsin, Wyoming. Available to U.S. citizens. Applicant must have national guard experience.

Application Requirements: Application form, essay, interview. *Deadline:* continuous.

Contact: Mr. John Provost, U.S. Army Cadet Command
Department of the Army
204 1st Cavalry Regiment Road
Building 1002
Fort Knox, KY 40121
Phone: 502-624-2400
Fax: 502-624-1120
E-mail: john.h.provost.civ@mail.mil

U.S. ARMY ROTC MILITARY JUNIOR COLLEGE (MJC) SCHOLARSHIP
• *See page 492*

DEPARTMENT OF VETERANS AFFAIRS (VA)

https://www.va.gov/

MONTGOMERY GI BILL SELECTED RESERVE
• *See page 487*

RESERVE EDUCATION ASSISTANCE PROGRAM
• *See page 488*

DIVERSITYCOMM, INC.

http://www.diversitycomm.net/

US VETERANS MAGAZINE SCHOLARSHIP
• *See page 487*

ENLISTED ASSOCIATION OF THE NATIONAL GUARD OF NEW JERSEY

http://www.eang-nj.org/

CSM VINCENT BALDASSARI MEMORIAL SCHOLARSHIP PROGRAM
• *See page 489*

USAA SCHOLARSHIP
• *See page 489*

FLEET RESERVE ASSOCIATION EDUCATION FOUNDATION

http://www.fra.org/foundation

TREADWELL/PRINGLE SCHOLARSHIPS

Scholarship for members; spouses; dependent biological, step or adoptive children; or biological, step or adoptive grandchildren of a FRA member in good standing, currently or at time of death. Applicant must be a U.S. citizen, registered as a full-time student in an accredited college located in the United States.

Award: Scholarship for use in freshman, sophomore, junior, senior, graduate, or postgraduate years; not renewable.

Eligibility Requirements: Applicant must be enrolled or expecting to enroll full-time at a two-year or four-year institution or university. Available to U.S. citizens. Applicant must have national guard experience.

Application Requirements: Application form, community service, essay, financial need analysis. *Deadline:* April 15.

Contact: Alicia Landis, Program Administrator
Phone: 703-683-1400
E-mail: scholars@fra.org

ILLINOIS STUDENT ASSISTANCE COMMISSION (ISAC)

http://www.isac.org/

ILLINOIS NATIONAL GUARD (ING) GRANT PROGRAM
• See page 489

IMAGINE AMERICA FOUNDATION

http://www.imagine-america.org

MILITARY AWARD PROGRAM (MAP)
• See page 487

INDIANA COMMISSION FOR HIGHER EDUCATION

http://www.in.gov/che

INDIANA NATIONAL GUARD TUITION SUPPLEMENT GRANT
• See page 489

INDIANA DEPARTMENT OF VETERANS AFFAIRS

http://www.in.gov/dva

CHILDREN AND SPOUSE OF INDIANA NATIONAL GUARD
• See page 489

NATIONAL GUARD EXTENSION SCHOLARSHIP
• See page 489

NATIONAL GUARD TUITION SUPPLEMENT GRANT
• See page 490

KENTUCKY HIGHER EDUCATION ASSISTANCE AUTHORITY (KHEAA)

http://www.kheaa.com/

KENTUCKY NATIONAL GUARD TUITION AWARD
• See page 490

KITCHEN GUIDES

http://www.kitchensguides.com/

SMART KITCHEN IMPROVEMENT SCHOLARSHIP BY KITCHEN GUIDES
• See page 477

LOUISIANA NATIONAL GUARD, JOINT TASK FORCE LA

http://geauxguard.com/organization/joint-force-headquarters-jfhq-la/

LOUISIANA NATIONAL GUARD STATE TUITION EXEMPTION PROGRAM
• See page 490

NEW JERSEY ARMY NATIONAL GUARD

www.njarmyguard.com

NEW JERSEY ARMY NATIONAL GUARD TUITION WAIVER

The New Jersey Army National Guard Tuition Waiver Program is available to all 6400 members of the New Jersey Army National Guard. This program waives all tuition at all public New Jersey institutions of higher learning up to 16 semester hours per semester for technical, trade, undergraduate, graduate, and professional studies. Membership in the National Guard is a requirement for this program. Minimum requirements to join the NJ Army National Guard are: be 17-35 years old, be at least a high school junior, be free of felony convictions, and generally be in good health. Call, text, or email Anthony Larobina at (908) 812-0707 Anthony.j.larobina.mil@mail.mil to find out if you are qualified.

Award: Grant for use in freshman, sophomore, junior, senior, graduate, or postgraduate years; renewable. *Number:* 6,400. *Amount:* $14,000.

Eligibility Requirements: Applicant must be age 17-35; enrolled or expecting to enroll full- or part-time at a two-year or four-year or technical institution or university and studying in New Jersey. Available to U.S. citizens. Applicant must have national guard experience.

Application Requirements: Applicant's must contact Anthony Larobina to be emailed an application. *Deadline:* continuous.

NORTH CAROLINA NATIONAL GUARD

http://nc.ng.mil/Pages/default.aspx

NORTH CAROLINA NATIONAL GUARD TUITION ASSISTANCE PROGRAM
• See page 490

OHIO NATIONAL GUARD

http://www.ong.ohio.gov/

OHIO NATIONAL GUARD SCHOLARSHIP PROGRAM
• See page 490

PENNSYLVANIA HIGHER EDUCATION ASSISTANCE AGENCY

http://www.pheaa.org/

POSTSECONDARY EDUCATIONAL GRATUITY PROGRAM
• See page 491

PETAZI

https://petazi.com/

2017 NURTURE FOR NATURE SCHOLARSHIP
• See page 483

SOCIETY OF DAUGHTERS OF THE UNITED STATES ARMY

SOCIETY OF DAUGHTERS OF THE UNITED STATES ARMY SCHOLARSHIPS
• See page 493

STUDY.COM

http://study.com

ARMY ROTC STUDY.COM SCHOLARSHIP
• See page 493

UNITED STATES ARMY WARRANT OFFICERS ASSOCIATION

USAWOA SCHOLARSHIP FOUNDATION
• *See page 493*

WISCONSIN DEPARTMENT OF VETERANS AFFAIRS (WDVA)

http://www.dva.state.wi.us/

VETERANS EDUCATION (VETED) REIMBURSEMENT GRANT
• *See page 485*

MILITARY SERVICE: COAST GUARD

DEPARTMENT OF VETERANS AFFAIRS (VA)

https://www.va.gov/

MONTGOMERY GI BILL SELECTED RESERVE
• *See page 487*

DIVERSITYCOMM, INC.

http://www.diversitycomm.net/

US VETERANS MAGAZINE SCHOLARSHIP
• *See page 487*

FLEET RESERVE ASSOCIATION EDUCATION FOUNDATION

http://www.fra.org/foundation

DORAN/BLAIR SCHOLARSHIPS
• *See page 439*

FLEET RESERVE ASSOCIATION EDUCATION FOUNDATION SCHOLARSHIPS
Applicant or sponsor has to be an FRA non-member, living, on active duty, reserve, retired, or honorably discharged veteran of the Navy, Marine Corps or Coast Guard. The applicant must be an FRA non-member; spouse; dependent biological, step, or adoptive child; or biological, step, or adoptive grandchild; or biological, step, or adoptive great grandchild of the FRA non-member. Applicant must be a U.S. citizen, registered as a full-time student in an accredited college located in the United States of America.

Award: Scholarship for use in freshman, sophomore, junior, senior, graduate, or postgraduate years; not renewable. *Number:* 1–10. *Amount:* $1000–$5000.

Eligibility Requirements: Applicant must be enrolled or expecting to enroll full-time at a two-year or four-year institution or university. Available to U.S. citizens. Applicant must have served in the Coast Guard.

Application Requirements: Application form, community service, essay, financial need analysis. *Deadline:* April 15.

Contact: Alicia Landis, Program Administrator
Phone: 703-683-1400 Ext. 107
E-mail: scholars@fra.org

TREADWELL/PRINGLE SCHOLARSHIPS
• *See page 494*

IMAGINE AMERICA FOUNDATION

http://www.imagine-america.org

MILITARY AWARD PROGRAM (MAP)
• *See page 487*

KITCHEN GUIDES

http://www.kitchensguides.com/

SMART KITCHEN IMPROVEMENT SCHOLARSHIP BY KITCHEN GUIDES
• *See page 477*

LADIES AUXILIARY OF THE FLEET RESERVE ASSOCIATION

http://www.fra.org/

LADIES AUXILIARY OF THE FLEET RESERVE ASSOCIATION SCHOLARSHIP
• *See page 444*

SAM ROSE MEMORIAL SCHOLARSHIP
• *See page 444*

PETAZI

https://petazi.com/

2017 NURTURE FOR NATURE SCHOLARSHIP
• *See page 483*

TAILHOOK EDUCATIONAL FOUNDATION

http://www.tailhook.org/

TAILHOOK EDUCATIONAL FOUNDATION SCHOLARSHIP
Applicant must be a high school graduate and the natural, step or adopted son or daughter of a current or former Naval Aviator, Naval Flight Officer or Naval Air-crewman. Individuals or children of individuals serving or having served on board a U.S. Navy Aircraft Carrier in ship's company or the Air Wing also eligible.

Award: Scholarship for use in freshman, sophomore, junior, or senior years; not renewable. *Number:* 100. *Amount:* $2500–$15,000.

Eligibility Requirements: Applicant must be enrolled or expecting to enroll full-time at a two-year or four-year institution or university. Available to U.S. citizens. Applicant or parent must meet one or more of the following requirements: Coast Guard experience; retired from active duty; disabled or killed as a result of military service; prisoner of war; or missing in action.

Application Requirements: Application form, essay. *Deadline:* March 1.

Contact: Rodger Welch, Executive Director
Tailhook Educational Foundation
9696 Businesspark Avenue
San Diego, CA 92131
Phone: 800-269-8267
Fax: 858-578-8839
E-mail: rlw@tailhook.net

U.S. COAST GUARD

http://www.gocoastguard/cspi

COLLEGE STUDENT PRE-COMMISSIONING INITIATIVE (CSPI)
• *See page 485*

WISCONSIN DEPARTMENT OF VETERANS AFFAIRS (WDVA)

http://www.dva.state.wi.us/

VETERANS EDUCATION (VETED) REIMBURSEMENT GRANT
• *See page 485*

MILITARY SERVICE: GENERAL

ACADGILD

https://acadgild.com

ACADGILD MERIT-BASED SCHOLARSHIPS
• *See page 472*

AMERICAN LEGION AUXILIARY DEPARTMENT OF ALABAMA

http://www.legional.org/

AMERICAN LEGION AUXILIARY DEPARTMENT OF ALABAMA SCHOLARSHIP PROGRAM

Merit-based scholarships for Alabama residents, preferably ages 17 to 25, who are children or grandchildren of veterans of World War I, World War II, Korea, Vietnam, Operation Desert Storm, Beirut, Grenada, or Panama. Submit proof of relationship and service record. Renewable awards of $850 each. Must send self-addressed stamped envelope for application.

Award: Scholarship for use in freshman, sophomore, junior, or senior years; renewable. *Number:* up to 40. *Amount:* $850.

Eligibility Requirements: Applicant must be age 17-25; enrolled or expecting to enroll full-time at a four-year institution or university and resident of Alabama. Available to U.S. citizens. Applicant or parent must meet one or more of the following requirements: general military experience; retired from active duty; disabled or killed as a result of military service; prisoner of war; or missing in action.

Application Requirements: Application form, birth certificate, service record, financial need analysis, personal photograph, recommendations or references, self-addressed stamped envelope with application, test scores, transcript. *Deadline:* April 1.

Contact: Education and Scholarship Chairperson
American Legion Auxiliary Department of Alabama
120 North Jackson Street
Montgomery, AL 36104-3811
Phone: 334-262-1176
Fax: 334-262-1176
E-mail: americanlegionaux1@juno.com

AMERICAN LEGION AUXILIARY DEPARTMENT OF CALIFORNIA

http://www.calegionaux.org/

AMERICAN LEGION AUXILIARY DEPARTMENT OF CALIFORNIA GENERAL SCHOLARSHIP

Award ranges from $500 to $1000 for high school senior or graduate of an accredited high school who has not been able to begin college due to circumstances of illness or finance. Student must attend a California college or university. Deadline March 16.

Award: Scholarship for use in freshman, sophomore, junior, or senior years; not renewable. *Amount:* $500–$1000.

Eligibility Requirements: Applicant must be high school student; planning to enroll or expecting to enroll full- or part-time at a two-year or four-year institution or university; resident of California and studying in California. Available to U.S. citizens. Applicant must have general military experience.

Application Requirements: Application form. *Deadline:* March 16.
Contact: Ruby Kapsalis, Secretary/Treasurer
Phone: 415-862-5092
Fax: 415-861-8365
E-mail: calegionaux@calegionaux.org

AMERICAN LEGION AUXILIARY DEPARTMENT OF IOWA

http://www.iowaala.org

AMERICAN LEGION AUXILIARY DEPARTMENT OF IOWA CHILDREN OF VETERANS MERIT AWARD

One-time award available to a high school senior, child of a veteran who served in the armed forces during eligibility dates for American Legion membership. Must be U.S. citizen and Iowa resident enrolled at an Iowa institution.

Award: Scholarship for use in freshman year; not renewable. *Number:* 10. *Amount:* $400.

Eligibility Requirements: Applicant must be high school student; planning to enroll or expecting to enroll full- or part-time at a two-year or four-year or technical institution or university; resident of Iowa and studying in Iowa. Available to U.S. citizens. Applicant or parent must meet one or more of the following requirements: general military experience; retired from active duty; disabled or killed as a result of military service; prisoner of war; or missing in action.

Application Requirements: Application form, essay, financial need analysis, personal photograph. *Deadline:* June 1.

Contact: Marlene Valentine, Executive Director
American Legion Auxiliary Department of Iowa
720 Lyon Street
Des Moines, IA 50309
Phone: 515-282-7987
E-mail: alasectreas@ialegion.org

AMERICAN LEGION AUXILIARY DEPARTMENT OF KENTUCKY

http://www.kylegion.org/

AMERICAN LEGION AUXILIARY DEPARTMENT OF KENTUCKY MARY BARRETT MARSHALL SCHOLARSHIP

Scholarship to the daughter or grand daughter of a veteran in The American Legion. Applicant must attend a Kentucky college, and demonstrate financial need.

Award: Scholarship for use in freshman year; not renewable. *Number:* 1. *Amount:* $1000.

Eligibility Requirements: Applicant must be high school student; planning to enroll or expecting to enroll full-time at a four-year institution or university; female and studying in Kentucky. Available to U.S. citizens. Applicant or parent must meet one or more of the following requirements: general military experience; retired from active duty; disabled or killed as a result of military service; prisoner of war; or missing in action.

Application Requirements: Application form, financial need analysis, transcript. *Deadline:* April 1.

Contact: Betty Cook, Secretary and Treasurer
Phone: 270-932-7533
Fax: 270-932-7672
E-mail: secretarykyala@aol.com

AMERICAN LEGION AUXILIARY DEPARTMENT OF MAINE

http://www.mainelegion.org/

AMERICAN LEGION AUXILIARY DEPARTMENT OF MAINE DANIEL E. LAMBERT MEMORIAL SCHOLARSHIP

Scholarships to assist young men and women in continuing their education beyond high school. Must demonstrate financial need, must be a resident of the State of Maine, U.S. citizen, and parent must be a veteran.

Award: Scholarship for use in freshman year; not renewable. *Number:* up to 2. *Amount:* $1000.

Eligibility Requirements: Applicant must be high school student; planning to enroll or expecting to enroll full-time at a four-year institution or university and resident of Maine. Available to U.S. citizens. Applicant or parent must meet one or more of the following requirements: general military experience; retired from active duty; disabled or killed as a result of military service; prisoner of war; or missing in action.

Application Requirements: Application form, financial need analysis. *Deadline:* May 1.

Contact: Mary Wells, Education Chairman
    Phone: 207-532-6007
    E-mail: aladeptsecme@verizon.net

AMERICAN LEGION AUXILIARY DEPARTMENT OF MICHIGAN

http://www.michalaux.org/

AMERICAN LEGION AUXILIARY DEPARTMENT OF MICHIGAN MEMORIAL SCHOLARSHIP

Scholarship for daughter, granddaughter, and great-granddaughter of any honorably discharged or deceased veteran of U.S. wars or conflicts. Must be Michigan resident for minimum of one year, female between 16 and 21 years, and attend college in Michigan. Must include copy of military discharge and copy of parent or guardian's IRS 1040 form.

Award: Scholarship for use in freshman or sophomore years; not renewable. *Number:* 10–20. *Amount:* $500.

Eligibility Requirements: Applicant must be age 16-21; enrolled or expecting to enroll full-time at a two-year or technical institution or university; female; resident of Massachusetts and studying in Michigan. Available to U.S. citizens. Applicant must have general military experience.

Application Requirements: Application form, financial need analysis. *Deadline:* February 15.

Contact: Scholarship Coordinator
    American Legion Auxiliary Department of Michigan
    212 North Verlinden Avenue, Suite B
    Lansing, MI 48915
    Phone: 517-267-8809 Ext. 119
    Fax: 517-371-3698
    E-mail: info@michalaux.org

AMERICAN LEGION AUXILIARY DEPARTMENT OF MICHIGAN SCHOLARSHIP FOR NON-TRADITIONAL STUDENT

Applicant must be a dependent of a veteran. Must be one of the following: nontraditional student returning to classroom after some period of time in which their education was interrupted, student over the age of 22 attending college for the first time to pursue a degree, or student over the age of 22 attending a trade or vocational school. Applicants must be Michigan residents only and attend Michigan institution. Judging based on need, character/leadership, scholastic standing, and initiative/goal.

Award: Scholarship for use in freshman, sophomore, junior, or senior years; renewable. *Number:* 1. *Amount:* $500.

Eligibility Requirements: Applicant must be age 22-99; enrolled or expecting to enroll full- or part-time at a two-year or technical institution or university; resident of Massachusetts and studying in Michigan. Available to U.S. citizens. Applicant must have general military experience.

Application Requirements: Application form, financial need analysis. *Deadline:* February 15.

Contact: Scholarship Coordinator
    American Legion Auxiliary Department of Michigan
    212 North Verlinden Avenue, Suite B
    Lansing, MI 48915
    Phone: 517-267-8809 Ext. 119
    Fax: 517-371-3698
    E-mail: info@michalaux.org

AMERICAN LEGION AUXILIARY'S CHILDREN OF WARRIORS NATIONAL PRESIDENTS' SCHOLARSHIP

One-time scholarship for son or daughter of veterans, who were in armed forces during the eligibility dates for American Legion membership. Must be high school senior. Only one candidate per Auxiliary Unit. Applicant must complete 50 hours of volunteer service in the community. Must submit essay of no more than 1000 words on a specified topic.

Award: Scholarship for use in freshman year; not renewable. *Number:* 15. *Amount:* $2500–$5000.

Eligibility Requirements: Applicant must be high school student and planning to enroll or expecting to enroll full-time at a two-year institution or university. Available to U.S. citizens. Applicant must have general military experience.

Application Requirements: Application form, community service, essay, financial need analysis. *Deadline:* March 1.

Contact: Scholarship Coordinator
    American Legion Auxiliary Department of Michigan
    212 North Verlinden Avenue, Suite B
    Lansing, MI 48915
    Phone: 517-267-8809 Ext. 119
    Fax: 517-371-3698
    E-mail: info@michalaux.org

AMERICAN LEGION AUXILIARY SPIRIT OF YOUTH SCHOLARSHIP FOR JUNIOR MEMBERS

Scholarship valued at $5000 is available to one Junior American Legion Auxiliary member in each division. The applicant must have held membership in the American Legion Auxiliary for the past three years, must hold a current membership card, and must continue to maintain their membership throughout the four-year scholarship period.

Award: Scholarship for use in freshman, sophomore, junior, or senior years; renewable. *Number:* 5. *Amount:* $5000.

Eligibility Requirements: Applicant must be high school student; planning to enroll or expecting to enroll full-time at a two-year or technical institution or university and female. Available to U.S. citizens. Applicant must have general military experience.

Application Requirements: Application form, essay, financial need analysis. *Deadline:* March 1.

Contact: Scholarship Coordinator
    American Legion Auxiliary Department of Michigan
    212 North Verlinden Avenue, Suite B
    Lansing, MI 48915
    Phone: 517-267-8809 Ext. 119
    Fax: 517-371-3698
    E-mail: info@michalaux.org

AMERICAN LEGION AUXILIARY DEPARTMENT OF MINNESOTA

http://www.mnala.org

AMERICAN LEGION AUXILIARY DEPARTMENT OF MINNESOTA SCHOLARSHIPS

Seven $1000 awards for the sons, daughters, grandsons, or granddaughters of veterans who served in the Armed Forces during specific eligibility dates. Must be a Minnesota resident, a high school senior or graduate, in need of financial assistance, of good character, having a good scholastic record and at least a C average. Must be planning to attend a Minnesota post secondary institution.

Award: Scholarship for use in freshman, sophomore, junior, or senior years; not renewable. *Number:* 1–7. *Amount:* $1000.

Eligibility Requirements: Applicant must be enrolled or expecting to enroll full-time at a two-year or four-year or technical institution or university; resident of Minnesota and studying in Minnesota. Available to U.S. citizens. Applicant or parent must meet one or more of the following requirements: general military experience; retired from active duty; disabled or killed as a result of military service; prisoner of war; or missing in action.

Application Requirements: Application form, essay, financial need analysis. *Deadline:* March 15.

Contact: Sandie Deutsch, Executive Secretary
American Legion Auxiliary Department of Minnesota
State Veterans Service Building
20 West 12th Street, Room 314
St. Paul, MN 55155
Phone: 651-224-7634
E-mail: sandie@mnala.org

AMERICAN LEGION AUXILIARY DEPARTMENT OF MISSOURI

http://www.missourilegion.org/

AMERICAN LEGION AUXILIARY DEPARTMENT OF MISSOURI LELA MURPHY SCHOLARSHIP
• *See page 430*

AMERICAN LEGION AUXILIARY DEPARTMENT OF MISSOURI NATIONAL PRESIDENT'S SCHOLARSHIP
• *See page 430*

AMERICAN LEGION AUXILIARY DEPARTMENT OF NEBRASKA

http://www.nebraskalegionaux.net/

AMERICAN LEGION AUXILIARY DEPARTMENT OF NEBRASKA RUBY PAUL CAMPAIGN FUND SCHOLARSHIP
• *See page 430*

AMERICAN LEGION AUXILIARY DEPARTMENT OF NORTH DAKOTA

http://www.ndlegion.org/

AMERICAN LEGION AUXILIARY DEPARTMENT OF NORTH DAKOTA NATIONAL PRESIDENT'S SCHOLARSHIP
• *See page 460*

AMERICAN LEGION AUXILIARY DEPARTMENT OF OHIO

http://www.alaohio.org/

AMERICAN LEGION AUXILIARY DEPARTMENT OF OHIO CONTINUING EDUCATION FUND

One-time award for Ohio residents who are the children or grandchildren of veterans, living or deceased, honorably discharged during eligibility dates for American Legion membership. Awards are for undergraduate use, based on need. Freshmen not eligible. Application must be signed by a unit representative.

Award: Scholarship for use in sophomore, junior, or senior years; not renewable. *Number:* 15. *Amount:* $200.

Eligibility Requirements: Applicant must be enrolled or expecting to enroll full-time at a two-year or four-year institution or university and resident of Ohio. Available to U.S. citizens. Applicant or parent must meet one or more of the following requirements: general military experience; retired from active duty; disabled or killed as a result of military service; prisoner of war; or missing in action.

Application Requirements: Application form, financial need analysis, transcript. *Deadline:* November 1.

Contact: Katie Tucker, Scholarship Coordinator
Phone: 740-452-8245
Fax: 740-452-2620
E-mail: ala_katie@rrohio.com

AMERICAN LEGION AUXILIARY DEPARTMENT OF OHIO DEPARTMENT PRESIDENT'S SCHOLARSHIP

Scholarship for children or grandchildren of veterans who served in Armed Forces during eligibility dates for American Legion membership. Must be high school senior, ages 16 to 18, Ohio resident, and U.S.

citizen. Award for full-time undergraduate study. One-time award of $1000 to $1500.

Award: Scholarship for use in freshman year; not renewable. *Number:* 2. *Amount:* $1000–$1500.

Eligibility Requirements: Applicant must be high school student; age 16-18; planning to enroll or expecting to enroll full-time at a two-year or four-year institution or university and resident of Ohio. Available to U.S. citizens. Applicant or parent must meet one or more of the following requirements: general military experience; retired from active duty; disabled or killed as a result of military service; prisoner of war; or missing in action.

Application Requirements: Application form, essay, financial need analysis, recommendations or references, transcript. *Deadline:* March 1.

Contact: Department Scholarship Coordinator
American Legion Auxiliary Department of Ohio
PO Box 2760
Zanesville, OH 43702-2760
Phone: 740-452-8245
Fax: 740-452-2620

AMERICAN LEGION AUXILIARY DEPARTMENT OF SOUTH DAKOTA

http://www.sdlegion-aux.org/

AMERICAN LEGION AUXILIARY DEPARTMENT OF SOUTH DAKOTA COLLEGE SCHOLARSHIPS
• *See page 431*

AMERICAN LEGION AUXILIARY DEPARTMENT OF SOUTH DAKOTA SENIOR SCHOLARSHIP
• *See page 431*

AMERICAN LEGION AUXILIARY DEPARTMENT OF SOUTH DAKOTA THELMA FOSTER SCHOLARSHIP FOR SENIOR AUXILIARY MEMBERS
• *See page 431*

AMERICAN LEGION AUXILIARY DEPARTMENT OF TEXAS

http://www.alatexas.org/

AMERICAN LEGION AUXILIARY DEPARTMENT OF TEXAS GENERAL EDUCATION SCHOLARSHIP

Scholarships available for Texas residents. Must be a child of a veteran who served in the Armed Forces during eligibility dates. Some additional criteria used for selection are recommendations, academics, and finances.

Award: Scholarship for use in freshman, sophomore, junior, or senior years; not renewable. *Number:* 1–10. *Amount:* $500.

Eligibility Requirements: Applicant must be enrolled or expecting to enroll full-time at a two-year or four-year or technical institution or university and resident of Texas. Available to U.S. citizens. Applicant must have general military experience.

Application Requirements: Application form, community service, financial need analysis, letter stating qualifications and intentions, recommendations or references, resume, transcript. *Deadline:* June 1.

Contact: Paula Raney, State Secretary
American Legion Auxiliary Department of Texas
PO Box 140407
Austin, TX 78714
Phone: 512-476-7278
Fax: 512-482-8391
E-mail: alatexas@txlegion.org

AMERICAN LEGION AUXILIARY DEPARTMENT OF UTAH

http://www.legion-aux.org/

AMERICAN LEGION AUXILIARY DEPARTMENT OF UTAH NATIONAL PRESIDENT'S SCHOLARSHIP
• *See page 431*

AMERICAN LEGION AUXILIARY DEPARTMENT OF WISCONSIN

http://www.amlegionauxwi.org/

AMERICAN LEGION AUXILIARY DEPARTMENT OF WISCONSIN DELLA VAN DEUREN MEMORIAL SCHOLARSHIP
• *See page 431*

AMERICAN LEGION DEPARTMENT OF IDAHO

http://www.idaholegion.com/

AMERICAN LEGION DEPARTMENT OF IDAHO SCHOLARSHIP
• *See page 432*

AMERICAN LEGION DEPARTMENT OF MAINE

http://www.mainelegion.org/

AMERICAN LEGION DEPARTMENT OF MAINE CHILDREN AND YOUTH SCHOLARSHIP

Scholarships available to high school seniors, college students, and veterans who are residents of Maine. Must be in upper half of high school class. One-time award of $500.

Award: Scholarship for use in freshman, sophomore, junior, or senior years; not renewable. *Number:* 7. *Amount:* $500.

Eligibility Requirements: Applicant must be enrolled or expecting to enroll full-time at a two-year or four-year or technical institution or university and resident of Maine. Available to U.S. citizens. Applicant or parent must meet one or more of the following requirements: general military experience; retired from active duty; disabled or killed as a result of military service; prisoner of war; or missing in action.

Application Requirements: Application form, essay, financial need analysis, recommendations or references, transcript. *Deadline:* May 1.

Contact: Mr. Paul L'Heureux, Department Adjutant
American Legion Department of Maine
PO Box 900
Waterville, ME 04903
Phone: 207-873-3229
Fax: 207-872-0501
E-mail: legionme@mainelegion.org

DANIEL E. LAMBERT MEMORIAL SCHOLARSHIP

One-time award for undergraduate and graduate student whose parents are veterans. Award is based on financial need and good character. Must be U.S. citizen. Applicant must show evidence of being enrolled, or attending accredited college or vocational technical school. Scholarship value is from $500 to $1000.

Award: Scholarship for use in freshman, sophomore, junior, or senior years; not renewable. *Number:* 1–2. *Amount:* $500–$1000.

Eligibility Requirements: Applicant must be enrolled or expecting to enroll full-time at a two-year or four-year or technical institution or university and resident of Maine. Available to U.S. citizens. Applicant or parent must meet one or more of the following requirements: general military experience; retired from active duty; disabled or killed as a result of military service; prisoner of war; or missing in action.

Application Requirements: Application form, recommendations or references. *Deadline:* May 1.

Contact: Mr. Paul L'Heureux, Department Adjutant
American Legion Department of Maine
PO Box 900
Waterville, ME 04903
Phone: 207-873-3229
Fax: 207-872-0501
E-mail: legionme@mainelegion.org

JAMES V. DAY SCHOLARSHIP
• *See page 432*

AMERICAN LEGION DEPARTMENT OF MICHIGAN

http://www.michiganlegion.org/

GUY M. WILSON SCHOLARSHIPS

Scholarship for undergraduate use at a Michigan college. Must be resident of Michigan and the son, daughter, grandchild, or great grandchild of a veteran, living or deceased. Must submit copy of veteran's honorable discharge. Must have minimum 2.5 GPA. Total number of awards given vary each year depending upon the number of applications received. Applicants have to refer the website for the deadline.

Award: Scholarship for use in freshman year; not renewable. *Number:* 9. *Amount:* $500.

Eligibility Requirements: Applicant must be high school student; planning to enroll or expecting to enroll full- or part-time at a two-year or four-year institution or university; resident of Michigan and studying in Michigan. Available to U.S. citizens. Applicant or parent must meet one or more of the following requirements: general military experience; retired from active duty; disabled or killed as a result of military service; prisoner of war; or missing in action.

Application Requirements: Application form, essay, financial need analysis. *Deadline:* January 8.

Contact: Programs Coordinator
American Legion Department of Michigan
212 North Verlinden Avenue, Suite A
Lansing, MI 48915
Phone: 517-371-4720 Ext. 23
E-mail: legion@michiganlegion.org

WILLIAM D. AND JEWELL W. BREWER SCHOLARSHIP TRUSTS

One-time award for residents of Michigan who are the son, daughter, grandchild, or great grandchild of veterans, living or deceased. Must submit copy of veteran's honorable discharge. Several scholarships of $500 each. Must have minimum 2.5 GPA. Scholarship can be applied to any college or university within the United States.

Award: Scholarship for use in freshman, sophomore, junior, or senior years; not renewable. *Number:* 4. *Amount:* $500.

Eligibility Requirements: Applicant must be enrolled or expecting to enroll full- or part-time at a two-year or four-year institution or university and resident of Michigan. Available to U.S. citizens. Applicant or parent must meet one or more of the following requirements: general military experience; retired from active duty; disabled or killed as a result of military service; prisoner of war; or missing in action.

Application Requirements: Application form, essay, financial need analysis. *Deadline:* January 8.

Contact: Programs Coordinator
American Legion Department of Michigan
212 North Verlinden Avenue, Suite A
Lansing, MI 48915
Phone: 517-371-4720 Ext. 23
E-mail: legion@michiganlegion.org

THE AMERICAN LEGION, DEPARTMENT OF MINNESOTA

http://www.mnlegion.org/

AMERICAN LEGION DEPARTMENT OF MINNESOTA MEMORIAL SCHOLARSHIP
• *See page 433*

MINNESOTA LEGIONNAIRES INSURANCE TRUST SCHOLARSHIP
• *See page 433*

AMERICAN LEGION DEPARTMENT OF MISSOURI

http://www.missourilegion.org/

CHARLES L. BACON MEMORIAL SCHOLARSHIP
• *See page 433*

LILLIE LOIS FORD SCHOLARSHIP FUND

Two awards of $1,000 each are given each year. One to a boy who has attended a full session of The American Legion Boys State of Missouri or a full session of the Department's Cadet Patrol Academy. The second award is given to a girl who has attended a full session of The American Legion Auxiliary's Girls State program or a full session of the Department's Cadet Patrol Academy.

Award: Scholarship for use in freshman year; not renewable. *Number:* 2. *Amount:* $1000.

Eligibility Requirements: Applicant must be high school student; age 20 or under; planning to enroll or expecting to enroll full-time at a two-year institution or university; single and resident of Mississippi. Available to U.S. citizens. Applicant or parent must meet one or more of the following requirements: general military experience; retired from active duty; disabled or killed as a result of military service; prisoner of war; or missing in action.

Application Requirements: Application form, financial need analysis. *Deadline:* April 20.

Contact: Mr. John Buckwalter, Chair, Education and Scholarship Committee
American Legion Department of Missouri
P.O. Box 179
Jefferson City, MO 65102-0179
Phone: 660-627-4713

AMERICAN LEGION DEPARTMENT OF OHIO

http://www.ohiolegion.com/

OHIO AMERICAN LEGION SCHOLARSHIPS
• *See page 434*

AMVETS AUXILIARY

http://amvetsaux.org/

AMVETS NATIONAL LADIES AUXILIARY SCHOLARSHIP
• *See page 436*

ARKANSAS DEPARTMENT OF HIGHER EDUCATION

http://www.adhe.edu/

MILITARY DEPENDENT'S SCHOLARSHIP PROGRAM

Renewable waiver of tuition, fees, room and board undergraduate students seeking a bachelor's degree or certificate of completion at any public college, university or technical school in Arkansas who qualify as a spouse or dependent child of an Arkansas resident who has been declared to be missing in action, killed in action, a POW, or killed on ordnance delivery, or a veteran who has been declared to be 100 percent totally and permanently disabled during, or as a result of, active military service.

Award: Scholarship for use in freshman, sophomore, junior, or senior years; renewable.

Eligibility Requirements: Applicant must be enrolled or expecting to enroll full-time at a two-year or technical institution or university; resident of Arizona and studying in Arkansas. Available to U.S. citizens. Applicant or parent must meet one or more of the following requirements: general military experience; retired from active duty; disabled or killed as a result of military service; prisoner of war; or missing in action.

Application Requirements: Application form, application form may be submitted online. *Deadline:* July 1.

Contact: Lisa Smith, Director of Financial Aid
Arkansas Department of Higher Education
423 Main Street Suite 400
Little Rock, AR 72201-3818
Phone: 501-371-2000
E-mail: lisa.smith@adhe.edu

CHARLES E. BOYK LAW OFFICES, LLC

https://www.charlesboyk-law.com/

2017 BOYK LAW VETERAN SCHOLARSHIP

As part of our Military Messages campaign, the Ohio car accident lawyers of Charles E. Boyk Law Offices, LLC are pleased to announce its first annual 2015 US Veteran Scholarship for college students. The personal injury law firm located in Toledo, Ohio represents victims of car accidents, motorcycle accidents, defective drug and medical device cases, nursing home neglect cases, dog bite injuries, and all other personal injury accident matters throughout the entire state. The scholarship has been created as part of Boyk Law's continued commitment to the service men and women of the United States Armed Forces and their continuing education. The Veteran Scholarship is $2,000.00 and will be awarded to a student who is currently attending an accredited college or university, who has either served in the Armed Forces or is the child of a US Veteran. For more information, please visit: https://www.charlesboyk-law.com/#scholarship

Award: Scholarship for use in freshman, sophomore, junior, senior, graduate, or postgraduate years; not renewable. *Number:* 1. *Amount:* $2000.

Eligibility Requirements: Applicant must be enrolled or expecting to enroll full- or part-time at a two-year or four-year or technical institution or university. Available to U.S. citizens. Applicant must have general military experience.

Application Requirements: Application form, essay. *Deadline:* May 15.

Contact: Charles Boyk
E-mail: SEO@charlesboyk-law.com

DEFENSE COMMISSARY AGENCY

http://www.militaryscholar.org/

SCHOLARSHIPS FOR MILITARY CHILDREN

One-time award to unmarried dependents of USA military personnel for full-time undergraduate study at a four-year institution. Minimum 3.0 GPA required. Further information and applications available at website http://www.militaryscholar.org.

Award: Scholarship for use in freshman, sophomore, or junior years; not renewable. *Number:* 600. *Amount:* $2000.

Eligibility Requirements: Applicant must be age 23 or under; enrolled or expecting to enroll full-time at a four-year institution or university and single. Available to U.S. citizens. Applicant or parent must meet one or more of the following requirements: general military experience; retired from active duty; disabled or killed as a result of military service; prisoner of war; or missing in action.

Application Requirements: Application form, application form may be submitted online (https://sfmc.militaryscholar.org/users/sign_in), essay. *Deadline:* February 15.

Contact: Mr. Bernard Cote
Phone: 856-573-9400
E-mail: militaryscholar@scholarshipmanagers.com

DEPARTMENT OF VETERANS AFFAIRS (VA)

https://www.va.gov/

MONTGOMERY GI BILL ACTIVE DUTY

Award provides up to thirty-six months of education benefits to eligible veterans for college, business school, technical courses, vocational courses, correspondence courses, apprenticeships/job training, or flight training. Must be an eligible veteran with an Honorable Discharge and have high school diploma or GED before applying for benefits.

Award: Scholarship for use in freshman, sophomore, junior, senior, or graduate years; renewable.

Eligibility Requirements: Applicant must be enrolled or expecting to enroll full- or part-time at a two-year or technical institution or university. Available to U.S. citizens. Applicant or parent must meet one or more of the following requirements: general military experience; retired from active duty; disabled or killed as a result of military service; prisoner of war; or missing in action.

Application Requirements: Application form, application form may be submitted online. *Deadline:* continuous.

Contact: Keith Wilson, Director, Education Service
    Phone: 888-442-4551

MONTGOMERY GI BILL SELECTED RESERVE
• *See page 487*

RESERVE EDUCATION ASSISTANCE PROGRAM
• *See page 488*

SURVIVORS AND DEPENDENTS EDUCATIONAL ASSISTANCE (CHAPTER 35)-VA

Monthly $860 benefits for up to 45 months. Must be spouses or children under age 26 of current veterans missing in action or of deceased or totally and permanently disabled (service-related) service persons. For more information visit the following website http://www.gibill.va.gov.

Award: Scholarship for use in freshman, sophomore, junior, or senior years; renewable.

Eligibility Requirements: Applicant must be age 18-26 and enrolled or expecting to enroll full- or part-time at a two-year or technical institution or university. Available to U.S. and non-U.S. citizens. Applicant or parent must meet one or more of the following requirements: general military experience; retired from active duty; disabled or killed as a result of military service; prisoner of war; or missing in action.

Application Requirements: Application form, application form may be submitted online. *Deadline:* continuous.

Contact: Keith Wilson, Director, Education Service
    Phone: 888-442-4551

DIVERSITYCOMM, INC.

http://www.diversitycomm.net/

US VETERANS MAGAZINE SCHOLARSHIP
• *See page 487*

EOD WARRIOR FOUNDATION

http://www.eodwarriorfoundation.org

EXPLOSIVE ORDNANCE DISPOSAL MEMORIAL SCHOLARSHIP
• *See page 463*

FELDMAN LAW FIRM PLLC

http://www.afphoenixcriminalattorney.com/

DISABLED VETERANS SCHOLARSHIP
• *See page 475*

FLORIDA STATE DEPARTMENT OF EDUCATION

http://www.floridastudentfinancialaid.org/

SCHOLARSHIPS FOR CHILDREN AND SPOUSES OF DECEASED OR DISABLED VETERANS

Renewable scholarships for children and spouses of deceased or disabled veterans. Children must be between the ages of 16 and 22, and attend an eligible Florida postsecondary institution and enrolled at least part-time. Must ensure that the Florida Department of Veterans Affairs certifies the applicant's eligibility. Must maintain GPA of 2.0. For more details, visit the website at
http://www.FloridaStudentFinancialAid.org/SSFAD/home/uamain.htm.

Award: Scholarship for use in freshman, sophomore, junior, or senior years; renewable.

Eligibility Requirements: Applicant must be age 16-22; enrolled or expecting to enroll full- or part-time at a two-year or technical institution or university; resident of District of Columbia and studying in Florida. Available to U.S. citizens. Applicant or parent must meet one or more of the following requirements: general military experience; retired from active duty; disabled or killed as a result of military service; prisoner of war; or missing in action.

Application Requirements: Application form, application form may be submitted online. *Deadline:* April 1.

Contact: Florida Department of Education, Office of Student Financial
    Assistance, Customer Service
    Florida State Department of Education
    325 West Gaines Street
    Tallahassee, FL 32399
    Phone: 888-827-2004
    E-mail: osfa@fldoe.org

ILLINOIS STUDENT ASSISTANCE COMMISSION (ISAC)

http://www.isac.org/

ILLINOIS VETERAN GRANT (IVG) PROGRAM

Awards qualified veterans and pays eligible tuition and fees for study in Illinois public universities or community colleges. Program eligibility units are based on the enrolled hours for a particular term, not the dollar amount of the benefits paid. Applications are available at college financial aid office and can be submitted any time during the academic year for which assistance is being requested.

Award: Grant for use in freshman, sophomore, junior, senior, or graduate years; renewable.

Eligibility Requirements: Applicant must be enrolled or expecting to enroll full- or part-time at a two-year institution or university; resident of Idaho and studying in Illinois. Available to U.S. citizens. Applicant or parent must meet one or more of the following requirements: general military experience; retired from active duty; disabled or killed as a result of military service; prisoner of war; or missing in action.

Application Requirements: Application form, application form may be submitted online. *Deadline:* continuous.

Contact: ISAC Call Center Representative
    Illinois Student Assistance Commission (ISAC)
    1755 Lake Cook Road
    Deerfield, IL 60015-5209
    Phone: 800-899-4722
    E-mail: isac.studentservices@illinois.gov

IMAGINE AMERICA FOUNDATION

http://www.imagine-america.org

MILITARY AWARD PROGRAM (MAP)
• *See page 487*

INDIANA COMMISSION FOR HIGHER EDUCATION

http://www.in.gov/che

INDIANA PURPLE HEART RECIPIENT PROGRAM

Provides 100% of tuition and regularly assessed fees for students who are Indiana veterans and Purple Heart Recipients. This program funding is limited to a maximum of 124 credit hours and may be used at the undergraduate, graduate and professional degree level.

Award: Grant for use in freshman, sophomore, junior, senior, or graduate years; renewable.

Eligibility Requirements: Applicant must be enrolled or expecting to enroll full- or part-time at a two-year or technical institution or university; resident of Illinois and studying in Indiana. Available to U.S. citizens. Applicant or parent must meet one or more of the following requirements: general military experience; retired from active duty; disabled or killed as a result of military service; prisoner of war; or missing in action.

Application Requirements: Application form, application form may be submitted online. *Deadline:* continuous.

Contact: Charlee Beasor, Communications Director
Phone: 317-232-1016
E-mail: CBeasor@che.in.gov

INDIANA DEPARTMENT OF VETERANS AFFAIRS
http://www.in.gov/dva

TUITION AND FEE EXEMPTION FOR INDIANA PURPLE HEART RECIPIENTS
Free tuition at Indiana state-supported colleges or universities for children of disabled veterans or Purple Heart recipients. Must submit form DD214 or service record. Covers tuition and mandatory fees.

Award: Grant for use in freshman, sophomore, junior, senior, graduate, or postgraduate years; renewable.

Eligibility Requirements: Applicant must be enrolled or expecting to enroll full- or part-time at a two-year institution or university; resident of Illinois and studying in Indiana. Available to U.S. citizens. Applicant must have general military experience.

Application Requirements: Application form. *Deadline:* continuous.

Contact: Michael Hamm, State Service Officer
Phone: 317-232-3910
Fax: 317-232-7721
E-mail: mhamm@dva.in.gov

TUITION AND FEE EXEMPTION FOR THE CHILD(REN) OF A DISABLED VETERAN OR POW/MIA OR PURPLE HEART RECIPIENTS
Renewable award for residents of Indiana who are the children of veterans declared missing in action or prisoner-of-war after January 1, 1960. Provides tuition at Indiana state-supported institutions for undergraduate study.

Award: Grant for use in freshman, sophomore, junior, senior, graduate, or postgraduate years; renewable.

Eligibility Requirements: Applicant must be enrolled or expecting to enroll full- or part-time at a two-year institution or university; resident of Illinois and studying in Indiana. Available to U.S. citizens. Applicant must have general military experience.

Application Requirements: Application form, application form may be submitted online. *Deadline:* continuous.

Contact: Michael Hamm, State Service Officer
Phone: 317-232-3910
Fax: 317-232-7721
E-mail: mhamm@dva.in.gov

KANSAS COMMISSION ON VETERANS AFFAIRS
http://www.kcva.org/

KANSAS EDUCATIONAL BENEFITS FOR CHILDREN OF MIA, POW, AND DECEASED VETERANS OF THE VIETNAM WAR
Scholarship awarded to students who are children of veterans. Must show proof of parent's status as missing in action, prisoner-of-war, or killed in action in the Vietnam War. Kansas residence required of veteran at time of entry to service. Must attend a state-supported postsecondary school.

Award: Scholarship for use in freshman, sophomore, junior, or senior years; not renewable. *Number:* 1.

Eligibility Requirements: Applicant must be enrolled or expecting to enroll full-time at a two-year or four-year or technical institution or university and studying in Kansas. Available to U.S. citizens. Applicant or parent must meet one or more of the following requirements: general military experience; retired from active duty; disabled or killed as a result of military service; prisoner of war; or missing in action.

Application Requirements: Application form, birth certificate, school acceptance letter, military discharge of veteran. *Deadline:* varies.

Contact: Wayne Bollig, Program Director
Phone: 785-296-3976
Fax: 785-296-1462
E-mail: wbollig@kcva.org

KITCHEN GUIDES
http://www.kitchensguides.com/

SMART KITCHEN IMPROVEMENT SCHOLARSHIP BY KITCHEN GUIDES
• *See page 477*

KNIGHTS OF COLUMBUS
http://www.kofc.org/

MATTHEWS & SWIFT EDUCATIONAL TRUST SCHOLARSHIP
• *See page 444*

LAW OFFICES OF DAVID A. BLACK
http://www.dbphoenixcriminallawyer.com

SCHOLARSHIP FOR DISABLED VETERANS
• *See page 478*

LOUISIANA DEPARTMENT OF VETERAN AFFAIRS
http://www.vetaffairs.la.gov

LOUISIANA DEPARTMENT OF VETERANS AFFAIRS STATE EDUCATIONAL AID PROGRAM
Waiver of tuition and school-imposed fees at any state supported college, university, or technical institute in Louisiana for dependent children, aged 16-25, of service connected disabled veterans, service connected deceased veterans, or veterans rated 100% service connected due to individual unemployability. Tuition waiver also available for an non-remarried surviving spouse of a service connected deceased veteran. Residency restricted to Louisiana.

Award: Scholarship for use in freshman, sophomore, junior, or senior years; not renewable.

Eligibility Requirements: Applicant must be age 16-25; enrolled or expecting to enroll full-time at a two-year or four-year or technical institution or university; resident of Louisiana and studying in Louisiana. Available to U.S. citizens. Applicant or parent must meet one or more of the following requirements: general military experience; retired from active duty; disabled or killed as a result of military service; prisoner of war; or missing in action.

Application Requirements: Application form. *Deadline:* continuous.

Contact: Mr. Barry Robinson, Regional Manager/Training Officer
Louisiana Department of Veteran Affairs
PO Box 94095, Capitol Station
Baton Rouge, LA 70804-9095
Phone: 225-219-5017
Fax: 225-219-5590
E-mail: barry.robinson@vetaffairs.la.gov

MAINE VETERANS SERVICES
http://www.maine.gov/dvem/bvs

VETERANS DEPENDENTS EDUCATIONAL BENEFITS-MAINE
Tuition waiver award for dependent children who have not reached their 22nd birthday or spouses of veterans permanently and totally disabled resulting from service-connected disability; died from a service-connected disability; at time of death was totally and permanently disabled due to service-connected disability, but whose death was not related to the service-connected disability; or member of the Armed Forces on active duty who has been listed for more than 90 days as missing in action, captured or forcibly detained or interned in the line of

duty. Benefits apply only to the University of Maine System, Maine community colleges and Maine Maritime Academy. Must be high school graduate. Must submit with application proof of veteran's VA disability along with dependent verification paperwork such as birth, marriage, or adoption certificate and proof of enrollment in degree program.

Award: Scholarship for use in freshman, sophomore, junior, or senior years; not renewable.

Eligibility Requirements: Applicant must be enrolled or expecting to enroll full- or part-time at a two-year or four-year institution or university; resident of Maine and studying in Maine. Available to U.S. citizens. Applicant or parent must meet one or more of the following requirements: general military experience; retired from active duty; disabled or killed as a result of military service; prisoner of war; or missing in action.

Application Requirements: Application form, see application.

Contact: Mrs. Paula Gagnon, Office Associate II
Maine Veterans Services
State House Station 117
Augusta, ME 04333-0117
Phone: 207-430-6035
Fax: 207-626-4471
E-mail: mainebvs@maine.gov

MICHIGAN DEPARTMENT OF TREASURY - STUDENT FINANCIAL SERVICES BUREAU

http://www.michigan.gov/mistudentaid

CHILDREN OF VETERANS TUITION GRANT

The program is designed to provide undergraduate tuition assistance to certain children older than 16 and less than 26 years of age who have been Michigan residents for the 12 months prior to application. To be eligible, a student must be the natural or adopted child of a Michigan veteran. Stepchildren of the veteran are not eligible. The veteran must have been a legal resident of Michigan immediately before entering military service and must not have later resided outside of Michigan for more than two years; or the veteran must have established legal residency in Michigan after entering military service.

Award: Grant for use in freshman, sophomore, junior, or senior years; renewable.

Eligibility Requirements: Applicant must be age 16-26; enrolled or expecting to enroll full- or part-time at an institution or university; resident of Massachusetts and studying in Michigan. Available to U.S. citizens. Applicant or parent must meet one or more of the following requirements: general military experience; retired from active duty; disabled or killed as a result of military service; prisoner of war; or missing in action.

Application Requirements: Application form.

Contact: Student Scholarships and Grants
Michigan Department of Treasury - Student Financial Services Bureau
PO Box 30462
Lansing, MI 48909
Phone: 888-447-2687
E-mail: mistudentaid@michigan.gov

MILITARY ORDER OF THE PURPLE HEART

http://www.purpleheart.org/

MILITARY ORDER OF THE PURPLE HEART SCHOLARSHIP

Scholarship for Military Order of the Purple Heart (MOPH) Members/spouses or children, stepchildren, adopted children or grandchildren, veterans killed-in-action or veterans who died of wounds and did not have the opportunity to join the MOPH. Must submit $15 application fee, essay, high school/college transcript, two letters of recommendation and list of extracurricular and volunteer activities. Must be U.S. citizen and high school graduate with minimum GPA of 2.75 and accepted or enrolled as a full-time student at a U.S. college, university or trade school at the time the scholarship is awarded.

Award: Scholarship for use in freshman, sophomore, junior, or senior years; not renewable. *Number:* 84–87. *Amount:* $2500–$7500.

Eligibility Requirements: Applicant must be enrolled or expecting to enroll full-time at a two-year or four-year or technical institution or university. Available to U.S. citizens. Applicant or parent must meet one or more of the following requirements: general military experience; retired from active duty; disabled or killed as a result of military service; prisoner of war; or missing in action.

Application Requirements: Application form, community service, essay. *Fee:* $15. *Deadline:* January 26.

Contact: Stewart Mckeown, Scholarship Coordinator
Phone: 703-642-5360
E-mail: scholarship@purpleheart.org

NATIONAL MILITARY FAMILY ASSOCIATION

http://www.MilitaryFamily.org

NATIONAL MILITARY FAMILY ASSOCIATION'S MILITARY SPOUSE SCHOLARSHIPS

Scholarships ranging from $500 to $1000 are awarded to spouses of Uniformed Services members (active duty, National Guard and Reserve, retirees, and survivors) for professional funding such as licensure and certification or any level of degree. Award number and amount varies. You must be a military spouse with a valid ID card to apply.

Award: Scholarship for use in freshman, sophomore, junior, senior, graduate, or postgraduate years; not renewable. *Number:* 400–600. *Amount:* $500–$1000.

Eligibility Requirements: Applicant must be enrolled or expecting to enroll full- or part-time at a two-year or four-year or technical institution or university and married. Available to U.S. and non-U.S. citizens. Applicant or parent must meet one or more of the following requirements: general military experience; retired from active duty; disabled or killed as a result of military service; prisoner of war; or missing in action.

Application Requirements: Application form, essay. *Deadline:* continuous.

Contact: Spouse Education + Employment Program Manager
National Military Family Association
3601 Eisenhower Avenue
Suite 425
Alexandria, VA 22304
Phone: 703-931-6632
E-mail: scholarships@militaryfamily.org

NEW JERSEY DEPARTMENT OF MILITARY AND VETERANS AFFAIRS

http://www.state.nj.us/military

NEW JERSEY WAR ORPHANS TUITION ASSISTANCE

$500 scholarship to children of those service personnel who died while in the military or due to service-connected disabilities, or who are officially listed as missing in action by the U.S. Department of Defense. Must be a resident of New Jersey for at least one year immediately preceding the filing of the application and be between the ages of 16 and 21 at the time of application.

Award: Scholarship for use in freshman, sophomore, junior, or senior years; renewable. *Amount:* $500.

Eligibility Requirements: Applicant must be age 16-21; enrolled or expecting to enroll full-time at a four-year institution or university and resident of New Jersey. Available to U.S. citizens. Applicant or parent must meet one or more of the following requirements: general military experience; retired from active duty; disabled or killed as a result of military service; prisoner of war; or missing in action.

Application Requirements: Application form.

Contact: Patricia Richter, Veterans Service Officer
New Jersey Department of Military and Veterans Affairs
PO Box 340
Trenton, NJ 08625-0340
Phone: 609-530-6854
Fax: 609-530-6970
E-mail: patty.richter@dmava.nj.gov

POW-MIA TUITION BENEFIT PROGRAM

Free undergraduate college tuition provided to any child born or adopted before or during the period of time his or her parent was officially declared a prisoner of war or person missing in action after January 1, 1960. The POW-MIA must have been a New Jersey resident at the time he or she entered the service. Child of veteran must attend either a public or private institution in New Jersey. A copy of DD 1300 must be furnished with the application. Minimum 2.5 GPA required.

Award: Scholarship for use in freshman, sophomore, junior, or senior years; renewable.

Eligibility Requirements: Applicant must be enrolled or expecting to enroll full-time at a two-year or four-year or technical institution or university; resident of New Jersey and studying in New Jersey. Available to U.S. citizens. Applicant or parent must meet one or more of the following requirements: general military experience; retired from active duty; disabled or killed as a result of military service; prisoner of war; or missing in action.

Application Requirements: Application form.

Contact: Patricia Richter, Veterans Service Officer
New Jersey Department of Military and Veterans Affairs
PO Box 340
Trenton, NJ 08625-0340
Phone: 609-530-6854
Fax: 609-530-6970
E-mail: patty.richter@dmava.nj.gov

VETERANS TUITION CREDIT PROGRAM-NEW JERSEY

Award for New Jersey resident veterans who served in the armed forces between December 31, 1960, and May 7, 1975. Must have been a New Jersey resident at time of induction or discharge or for two years immediately prior to application.

Award: Scholarship for use in freshman, sophomore, junior, or senior years; renewable. *Amount:* $200–$400.

Eligibility Requirements: Applicant must be enrolled or expecting to enroll full- or part-time at a two-year or four-year or technical institution or university and resident of New Jersey. Available to U.S. citizens. Applicant or parent must meet one or more of the following requirements: general military experience; retired from active duty; disabled or killed as a result of military service; prisoner of war; or missing in action.

Application Requirements: Application form.

Contact: Patricia Richter, Veterans Service Officer
New Jersey Department of Military and Veterans Affairs
PO Box 340
Trenton, NJ 08625-0340
Phone: 609-530-6854
Fax: 609-530-6970
E-mail: patty.richter@dmava.nj.gov

NEW MEXICO DEPARTMENT OF VETERANS' SERVICES

http://www.nmdvs.org

NEW MEXICO WARTIME VETERANS SCHOLARSHIP

Award for Wartime Veterans who have been a New Mexico resident for a minimum of ten years and are attending state-funded postsecondary schools. Must have been awarded a campaign medal such as the Southwest Asia Service Medal, Global War on Terrorism Expeditionary Medal, Iraq Campaign Medal, Afghanistan Campaign Medal or any other medal issued for service in the Armed Forces of the United States in support of any U.S. Military Campaign or armed conflict as defined by congress or presidential order or service after August 1, 1990.

Award: Scholarship for use in freshman, sophomore, junior, senior, or graduate years; renewable. *Number:* 100. *Amount:* $3500–$4000.

Eligibility Requirements: Applicant must be enrolled or expecting to enroll full- or part-time at a two-year or four-year or technical institution or university; resident of New Mexico and studying in New Mexico. Available to U.S. citizens. Applicant must have general military experience.

Application Requirements: Application form.

Contact: Mr. Dale Movius, Director, State Benefits
New Mexico Department of Veterans' Services
407 Galiesteo St, Room 134
Santa Fe, NM 87501
Phone: 505-827-6374
E-mail: dalej.movius@state.nm.us

NEW YORK STATE HIGHER EDUCATION SERVICES CORPORATION

http://www.hesc.ny.gov

NEW YORK VIETNAM/PERSIAN GULF/AFGHANISTAN VETERANS TUITION AWARDS

Vietnam, Persian Gulf, Afghanistan, or other eligible combat veterans matriculated at an undergraduate or graduate degree-granting institution or in an approved vocational training program in New York State are eligible for awards for full or part-time study.

Award: Scholarship for use in freshman, sophomore, junior, or senior years; renewable.

Eligibility Requirements: Applicant must be enrolled or expecting to enroll full- or part-time at a two-year or technical institution or university; resident of New Mexico and studying in New York. Available to U.S. citizens. Applicant or parent must meet one or more of the following requirements: general military experience; retired from active duty; disabled or killed as a result of military service; prisoner of war; or missing in action.

Application Requirements: Application form, application form may be submitted online, financial need analysis. *Deadline:* June 30.

NYS REGENTS AWARDS FOR CHILDREN OF DECEASED AND DISABLED VETERANS

Award for students whose parent, as a result of service in U.S. Armed Forces during war or national emergency, died; suffered a 40 percent or more disability; or is classified as missing in action or a prisoner of war. Veteran must be current New York State resident or have been so at time of death. Student must be a New York resident, attending, or planning to attend, college in New York State. Must establish eligibility before applying for payment.

Award: Scholarship for use in freshman, sophomore, junior, or senior years; not renewable. *Amount:* $450.

Eligibility Requirements: Applicant must be enrolled or expecting to enroll full-time at a two-year institution or university; resident of New Mexico and studying in New York. Available to U.S. citizens. Applicant or parent must meet one or more of the following requirements: general military experience; retired from active duty; disabled or killed as a result of military service; prisoner of war; or missing in action.

Application Requirements: Application form, application form may be submitted online. *Deadline:* June 30.

N.H. DEPARTMENT OF EDUCATION, DIVISION OF HIGHER EDUCATION - HIGHER EDUCATION COMMISSION

http://www.education.nh.gov/highered

SCHOLARSHIPS FOR ORPHANS OF VETERANS

Scholarship to provide financial assistance (room, board, books and supplies) to children of parents who served in World War II, Korean Conflict, Vietnam (Southeast Asian Conflict) or the Gulf Wars, or any other operation for which the armed forces expeditionary medal or theater of operations service medal was awarded to the veteran. Must be between the ages of 16 and 25 to qualify and be residents of New Hampshire studying at public New Hampshire colleges and universities.

Award: Scholarship for use in freshman, sophomore, junior, senior, graduate, or postgraduate years; renewable. *Number:* 1. *Amount:* $1000–$2500.

Eligibility Requirements: Applicant must be age 16-25; enrolled or expecting to enroll full-time at a two-year or four-year institution or university; resident of New Hampshire and studying in New Hampshire. Available to U.S. citizens. Applicant or parent must meet one or more of the following requirements: general military experience; retired from active duty; disabled or killed as a result of military service; prisoner of war; or missing in action.

Application Requirements: Application form. *Deadline:* September 1.

Contact: Mrs. Pat Moquin, Program Assistant II
N.H. Department of Education, Division of Higher Education -
Higher Education Commission
101 Pleasant Street
Concord, NH 03301
Phone: 603-271-0289
E-mail: patricia.moquin@doe.nh.gov

NORTH CAROLINA DIVISION OF VETERANS AFFAIRS

http://www.milvets.nc.gov/

NORTH CAROLINA VETERANS SCHOLARSHIPS CLASS I-A

Scholarships for children of certain deceased, disabled or POW/MIA veterans. Award value is $4500 per nine-month academic year in private colleges and junior colleges. No limit on number awarded each year.

Award: Scholarship for use in freshman, sophomore, junior, or senior years; renewable. *Amount:* $4500.

Eligibility Requirements: Applicant must be enrolled or expecting to enroll full-time at a two-year or four-year or technical institution or university; resident of North Carolina and studying in North Carolina. Available to U.S. citizens. Applicant or parent must meet one or more of the following requirements: general military experience; retired from active duty; disabled or killed as a result of military service; prisoner of war; or missing in action.

Application Requirements: Application form, financial need analysis, interview, transcript. *Deadline:* continuous.

Contact: Charles Smith, Assistant Secretary
Phone: 919-733-3851
Fax: 919-733-2834
E-mail: charlie.smith@ncmail.net

NORTH CAROLINA VETERANS SCHOLARSHIPS CLASS I-B

Awards for children of veterans rated by USDVA as 100 percent disabled due to wartime service as defined in the law, and currently or at time of death drawing compensation for such disability. Parent must have been a North Carolina resident at time of entry into service. Duration of the scholarship is four academic years (8 semesters) if used within 8 years. No limit on number awarded each year.

Award: Scholarship for use in freshman, sophomore, junior, or senior years; renewable. *Amount:* $1500.

Eligibility Requirements: Applicant must be enrolled or expecting to enroll full- or part-time at a two-year or four-year or technical institution or university; resident of North Carolina and studying in North Carolina. Available to U.S. citizens. Applicant or parent must meet one or more of the following requirements: general military experience; retired from active duty; disabled or killed as a result of military service; prisoner of war; or missing in action.

Application Requirements: Application form, financial need analysis, interview, transcript. *Deadline:* continuous.

Contact: Charles Smith, Assistant Secretary
Phone: 919-733-3851
Fax: 919-733-2834
E-mail: charlie.smith@ncmail.net

NORTH CAROLINA VETERANS SCHOLARSHIPS CLASS II

Awards for children of veterans rated by USDVA as much as 20 percent but less than 100 percent disabled due to wartime service as defined in the law, or awarded Purple Heart Medal for wounds received. Parent must have been a North Carolina resident at time of entry into service. Duration of the scholarship is four academic years (8 semesters) if used within 8 years. Free tuition and exemption from certain mandatory fees as set forth in the law in Public, Community and Technical Colleges.

Award: Scholarship for use in freshman, sophomore, junior, or senior years; renewable. *Number:* up to 100. *Amount:* $4500.

Eligibility Requirements: Applicant must be enrolled or expecting to enroll full- or part-time at a two-year or four-year or technical institution or university; resident of North Carolina and studying in North Carolina. Available to U.S. citizens. Applicant or parent must meet one or more of the following requirements: general military experience; retired from

active duty; disabled or killed as a result of military service; prisoner of war; or missing in action.

Application Requirements: Application form, financial need analysis, interview, transcript. *Deadline:* March 1.

Contact: Charles Smith, Assistant Secretary
Phone: 919-733-3851
Fax: 919-733-2834
E-mail: charlie.smith@ncmail.net

NORTH CAROLINA VETERANS SCHOLARSHIPS CLASS III

Awards for children of a deceased war veteran, who was honorably discharged and who does not qualify under any other provision within this synopsis or veteran who served in a combat zone or waters adjacent to a combat zone and received a campaign badge or medal and who does not qualify under any other provision within this synopsis. Duration of the scholarship is four academic years (8 semesters) if used within 8 years.

Award: Scholarship for use in freshman, sophomore, junior, or senior years; renewable. *Number:* up to 100. *Amount:* $4500.

Eligibility Requirements: Applicant must be enrolled or expecting to enroll full- or part-time at a two-year or four-year or technical institution or university; resident of North Carolina and studying in North Carolina. Available to U.S. citizens. Applicant or parent must meet one or more of the following requirements: general military experience; retired from active duty; disabled or killed as a result of military service; prisoner of war; or missing in action.

Application Requirements: Application form, financial need analysis, interview, transcript. *Deadline:* March 1.

Contact: Charles Smith, Assistant Secretary
Phone: 919-733-3851
Fax: 919-733-2834
E-mail: charlie.smith@ncmail.net

NORTH CAROLINA VETERANS SCHOLARSHIPS CLASS IV

Awards for children of veterans, who were prisoner of war or missing in action. Duration of the scholarship is four academic years (8 semesters) if used within 8 years. No limit on number awarded each year. Award value is $4500 per nine-month academic year in private colleges and junior colleges.

Award: Scholarship for use in freshman, sophomore, junior, or senior years; renewable. *Amount:* $4500.

Eligibility Requirements: Applicant must be enrolled or expecting to enroll full- or part-time at a two-year or four-year or technical institution or university; resident of North Carolina and studying in North Carolina. Available to U.S. citizens. Applicant or parent must meet one or more of the following requirements: general military experience; retired from active duty; disabled or killed as a result of military service; prisoner of war; or missing in action.

Application Requirements: Application form, financial need analysis, interview, transcript. *Deadline:* continuous.

Contact: Charles Smith, Assistant Secretary
Phone: 919-733-3851
Fax: 919-733-2834
E-mail: charlie.smith@ncmail.net

OHIO DEPARTMENT OF HIGHER EDUCATION

www.ohiohighered.org

OHIO WAR ORPHAN & SEVERELY DISABLED VETERANS' CHILDREN SCHOLARSHIP PROGRAM

Aids Ohio residents attending an eligible college in Ohio. Must be between the ages of 16 and 25, the child of a disabled or deceased veteran, and enrolled full-time. Must maintain a minimum GPA of 2.0. Renewable up to five years. Amount of award varies. Must include Form DD214.

Award: Scholarship for use in freshman, sophomore, junior, or senior years; renewable.

Eligibility Requirements: Applicant must be age 16-25; enrolled or expecting to enroll full-time at a two-year institution or university; resident of Nova Scotia and studying in Ohio. Available to U.S. citizens. Applicant must have general military experience.

Application Requirements: Application form. *Deadline:* May 15.

Contact: Ramah Church, Program Manager
Ohio Department of Higher Education
25 South Front Street
Columbus, OH 43215
Phone: 614-752-9528
E-mail: rchurch@highered.ohio.gov

PETAZI

https://petazi.com/

2017 NURTURE FOR NATURE SCHOLARSHIP
• *See page 483*

THE RESERVE OFFICERS ASSOCIATION

http://www.roa.org/

HENRY J. REILLY MEMORIAL SCHOLARSHIP-HIGH SCHOOL SENIORS AND FIRST YEAR FRESHMEN
• *See page 452*

HENRY J. REILLY MEMORIAL UNDERGRADUATE SCHOLARSHIP PROGRAM FOR COLLEGE ATTENDEES
• *See page 452*

RETIRED ENLISTED ASSOCIATION

http://www.trea.org/

RETIRED ENLISTED ASSOCIATION SCHOLARSHIP

One-time award for dependent children or grandchildren of a TREA member or TREA auxiliary member in good standing.

Award: Scholarship for use in freshman, sophomore, junior, senior, graduate, or postgraduate years; not renewable. *Amount:* $1000–$1500.

Eligibility Requirements: Applicant must be enrolled or expecting to enroll full-time at a two-year or four-year or technical institution or university. Available to U.S. citizens. Applicant or parent must meet one or more of the following requirements: general military experience; retired from active duty; disabled or killed as a result of military service; prisoner of war; or missing in action.

Application Requirements: Application form, copy of IRS tax forms, essay, financial need analysis, personal photograph, recommendations or references, test scores, transcript. *Deadline:* April 30.

Contact: Donnell Minnis, Executive Assistant
Phone: 303-752-0660
Fax: 303-752-0835
E-mail: execasst@trea.org

SCHOLARSHIP AMERICA

http://www.scholarshipamerica.org

WELLS FARGO VETERANS SCHOLARSHIP PROGRAM

The Wells Fargo Veterans Scholarship Program is designed to help meet the needs of veterans after military benefits and other grants and scholarships have been utilized. The scholarship program will award renewable scholarships for up to $7,000 per year to honorably-discharged veterans or spouses of disabled veterans who are high school or GED graduates and who have served in the United States military. Qualified applicants must have a minimum grade point average of 2.5 on a 4.0 scale or its equivalent and plan to enroll in full-time undergraduate or graduate (first Masters degree) study at an accredited two- or four-year college, university, or vocational-technical school for the 2017-2018 academic year. Each award renewal will increase by $1,000 over the previous year to encourage program completion. Visit www.scholarsapply.org/wellsfargoveterans for more information and to apply.

Award: Scholarship for use in freshman, sophomore, junior, senior, or graduate years; renewable.

Eligibility Requirements: Applicant must be enrolled or expecting to enroll part-time at a two-year or four-year or technical institution or university. Available to U.S. citizens. Applicant must have general military experience.

Application Requirements: Application form. *Deadline:* February 28.

Contact: Program Manager
Scholarship America
One Scholarship Way
St. Peter, MN 56082
Phone: 800-537-4180
E-mail: wellsfargoveterans@scholarshipamerica.org

SLEEP SHERPA

SLEEP SHERPA SCHOLARSHIP PROGRAM
• *See page 484*

TITAN WEB AGENCY

THE TITAN WEB AGENCY BI-ANNUAL SCHOLARSHIP PROGRAM
• *See page 484*

TONALAW

https://www.tonalaw.com/

TONALAW VETERAN'S SCHOLARSHIP

The TonaLaw Veteran's Scholarship is only open to students attending school in the United States. Students must have served in the U.S. Military and provide proof of service. Applicant must be a student at an accredited school, or be accepted to begin school at an accredited school within 6 months of application. All funds will be dispersed to scholarship recipient within 30 days of being announced as the winner.

Award: Scholarship for use in freshman, sophomore, junior, senior, graduate, or postgraduate years; not renewable. *Number:* 1–2. *Amount:* $1000–$2000.

Eligibility Requirements: Applicant must be enrolled or expecting to enroll full- or part-time at a two-year or four-year or technical institution or university. Available to U.S. citizens. Applicant must have general military experience.

Application Requirements: Application form, essay. *Deadline:* July 31.

Contact: Mackenzie Fox, Marketing Director
TonaLaw
870 Middle Country Road
St. James, NY 11780
Phone: 631-780-5355 Ext. 22
Fax: 631-780-5685
E-mail: mac@tonalaw.com

UNIVERSITY OF WYOMING

http://www.uwyo.edu/scholarships

VIETNAM VETERANS AWARD-WYOMING

Scholarship available to Wyoming residents who served in the armed forces between August 5, 1964 and May 7, 1975, and received a Vietnam service medal.

Award: Scholarship for use in freshman, sophomore, junior, or senior years; renewable.

Eligibility Requirements: Applicant must be enrolled or expecting to enroll full- or part-time at a two-year or four-year institution or university and resident of Wyoming. Available to U.S. citizens. Applicant or parent must meet one or more of the following requirements: general military experience; retired from active duty; disabled or killed as a result of military service; prisoner of war; or missing in action.

Application Requirements: Application form. *Deadline:* continuous.

Contact: Tammy Mack, Assistant Director, Scholarships
University of Wyoming
Department 3335
1000 East University Avenue
Laramie, WY 82071
Phone: 307-766-2412
Fax: 307-766-3800
E-mail: FinAid@uwyo.edu

VETERANS UNITED FOUNDATION

http://www.enhancelives.com

VETERANS UNITED FOUNDATION SCHOLARSHIP

This scholarship is for a surviving spouse or a surviving child of a deceased service member or a deceased veteran, or a veteran with 100% service connected disability currently pursuing post-secondary education. The program's primary goal is to assist veterans and their families by awarding up to ten $50,000 scholarships per semester to help pay for tuition, fees, room and board, books, and supplies pertinent to degree. For more information visit http://www.enhancelives.com/scholarships

Award: Scholarship for use in freshman, sophomore, junior, senior, graduate, or postgraduate years; not renewable. *Number:* 1–10. *Amount:* $1–$50,000.

Eligibility Requirements: Applicant must be enrolled or expecting to enroll full-time at a two-year or four-year or technical institution or university. Available to U.S. citizens. Applicant or parent must meet one or more of the following requirements: general military experience; retired from active duty; disabled or killed as a result of military service; prisoner of war; or missing in action.

Application Requirements: Application form, driver's license, essay, financial need analysis, personal photograph. *Deadline:* March 30.

Contact: Jessica Mueller, Foundation Outreach Coordinator
E-mail: foundation@veteransunited.com

VIRGINIA DEPARTMENT OF VETERANS SERVICES

http://www.dvs.virginia.gov/

VIRGINIA MILITARY SURVIVORS AND DEPENDENTS EDUCATION PROGRAM

Scholarships for post-secondary students between ages 16 and 29 to attend Virginia state-supported institutions. Must be child or surviving spouse of veteran who has either been permanently or totally disabled due to war or other armed conflict; died as a result of war or other armed conflict; or been listed as a POW or MIA. Parent must also meet Virginia residency requirements.

Award: Scholarship for use in freshman, sophomore, junior, senior, or graduate years; renewable.

Eligibility Requirements: Applicant must be age 16-29; enrolled or expecting to enroll full-time at a two-year or four-year or technical institution or university; resident of Virginia and studying in Virginia. Available to U.S. citizens. Applicant or parent must meet one or more of the following requirements: general military experience; retired from active duty; disabled or killed as a result of military service; prisoner of war; or missing in action.

Application Requirements: Application form, DD214 of service member, birth certificate of applicant, marriage certificate, acceptance letter from institution. *Deadline:* varies.

Contact: Mrs. Doris Sullivan, Coordinator
Virginia Department of Veterans Services
1351 Hershberger Road, Suite 220
Roanoke, VA 24012
Phone: 540-561-6625
Fax: 540-857-7573

WHITFIELD, BRYSON & MASON LLP

DISABLED VETERANS SCHOLARSHIP
• *See page 485*

WISCONSIN DEPARTMENT OF VETERANS AFFAIRS (WDVA)

http://www.dva.state.wi.us/

VETERANS EDUCATION (VETED) REIMBURSEMENT GRANT
• *See page 485*

WOMEN'S JEWELRY ASSOCIATION

http://www.womensjewelryassociation.com

WOMEN'S JEWELRY ASSOCIATIONS VETERANS GRANT

This award is given to a woman veteran of the US armed forces who wants to pursue a Jewelry career. It is a grant and does not have to be used for school, but could be used as a start-up grant for their business. It is essay based and is sponsored by Jewelers Mutual.

Award: Grant for use in freshman, sophomore, junior, senior, graduate, or postgraduate years; renewable. *Number:* 1. *Amount:* $5000.

Eligibility Requirements: Applicant must be enrolled or expecting to enroll full- or part-time at a two-year or four-year or technical institution or university and female. Available to U.S. citizens. Applicant or parent must meet one or more of the following requirements: general military experience; retired from active duty; disabled or killed as a result of military service; prisoner of war; or missing in action.

Application Requirements: Application form, essay. *Deadline:* April 15.

Contact: Isabel Cajulis
E-mail: icajulis@reedexpo.com

WONDERSHARE PDFELEMENT

https://pdf.wondershare.com

2018 PDFELEMENT $1000 SCHOLARSHIP
• *See page 486*

MILITARY SERVICE: MARINES

DIVERSITYCOMM, INC.

http://www.diversitycomm.net/

US VETERANS MAGAZINE SCHOLARSHIP
• *See page 487*

IMAGINE AMERICA FOUNDATION

http://www.imagine-america.org

MILITARY AWARD PROGRAM (MAP)
• *See page 487*

LADIES AUXILIARY OF THE FLEET RESERVE ASSOCIATION

http://www.fra.org/

LADIES AUXILIARY OF THE FLEET RESERVE ASSOCIATION SCHOLARSHIP
• *See page 444*

SAM ROSE MEMORIAL SCHOLARSHIP
• *See page 444*

MARINE CORPS TANKERS ASSOCIATION INC.

http://www.USMarinetankers.org/

MARINE CORPS TANKERS ASSOCIATION, JOHN CORNELIUS/MAX ENGLISH SCHOLARSHIP

Award for Marine tankers or former Marine tankers, or dependents of Marines who served in a tank unit and are on active duty, retired, reserve or have been honorably discharged. Applicant must be a high school graduate or planning to graduate in June. May be enrolled in college, undergraduate or graduate or have previously attended college. Must be a member of MCTA or intends to join in the future.

Award: Scholarship for use in freshman, sophomore, junior, senior, or graduate years; not renewable. *Number:* 10. *Amount:* up to $2000.

Eligibility Requirements: Applicant must be enrolled or expecting to enroll full-time at a two-year or four-year or technical institution or university. Available to U.S. citizens. Applicant or parent must meet one or more of the following requirements: Marine Corps experience; retired from active duty; disabled or killed as a result of military service; prisoner of war; or missing in action.

Application Requirements: Application form, essay, personal photograph, recommendations or references, test scores, transcript. *Deadline:* March 15.

Contact: Phil Morell, Scholarship Chair
Marine Corps Tankers Association Inc.
1112 Alpine Heights Road
Alpine, CA 91901-2814
Phone: 619-445-8423
Fax: 619-445-8423
E-mail: mpmorell@cox.net

PETAZI

https://petazi.com/

2017 NURTURE FOR NATURE SCHOLARSHIP
• *See page 483*

MILITARY SERVICE: NAVY

ANCHOR SCHOLARSHIP FOUNDATION

http://www.anchorscholarship.com

ANCHOR SCHOLARSHIP FOUNDATION

Must be dependent child or spouse of U.S. Navy service member (active, retired, or honorably discharged) and meet eligibility criteria which is posted on our website. Dependent child must be pursuing their first Bachelor's degree full-time at a 4-year college or university. Spouse applicants may attend either full or part-time at either a 2-year or 4-year college or university in pursuit of their first Associate's or Bachelor's degree. We use a two part on-line application (eligibility and scholarship). Once your eligibility has been confirmed, you will be given access to the scholarship application. Be prepared to submit sponsor's full name, rank/rate, list of duty stations, home-ports, ship hull numbers, dates served aboard and supporting documentation. Selection based on academics, extracurricular activities, character, and financial need.

Award: Scholarship for use in freshman, sophomore, junior, or senior years; not renewable. *Number:* 35–43. *Amount:* $2000–$5000.

Eligibility Requirements: Applicant must be enrolled or expecting to enroll full- or part-time at a two-year or four-year institution or university. Available to U.S. citizens. Applicant or parent must meet one or more of the following requirements: Navy experience; retired from active duty; disabled or killed as a result of military service; prisoner of war; or missing in action.

Application Requirements: Application form, essay, financial need analysis. *Deadline:* March 1.

Contact: Mrs. Ingrid Turner, Director of Operations
Anchor Scholarship Foundation
138 South Rosemont Road
Suite 206
Virginia Beach, VA 23452
Phone: 757-777-4724
E-mail: scholarshipadmin@anchorscholarship.com

DIVERSITYCOMM, INC.

http://www.diversitycomm.net/

US VETERANS MAGAZINE SCHOLARSHIP
• *See page 487*

GAMEWARDENS OF VIETNAM ASSOCIATION INC.

http://www.tf116.org/

GAMEWARDENS OF VIETNAM SCHOLARSHIP

Scholarship for entering freshman who is a descendant of a U.S. Navy man or woman who worked with TF-116 in Vietnam. One-time award, but applicant may reapply.

Award: Scholarship for use in freshman year; not renewable. *Number:* 1–3. *Amount:* $500.

Eligibility Requirements: Applicant must be high school student; age 16-21 and planning to enroll or expecting to enroll full-time at a two-year or four-year or technical institution or university. Available to U.S. and non-U.S. citizens. Applicant or parent must meet one or more of the following requirements: Navy experience; retired from active duty; disabled or killed as a result of military service; prisoner of war; or missing in action.

Application Requirements: Application form, recommendations or references, resume, test scores, transcript. *Deadline:* April 1.

Contact: David Ajax, Scholarship Coordinator
Gamewardens of Vietnam Association Inc.
6630 Perry Court
Arvada, CO 80003
Phone: 303-426-6385
Fax: 303-426-6186
E-mail: dpajax@comcast.net

IMAGINE AMERICA FOUNDATION

http://www.imagine-america.org

MILITARY AWARD PROGRAM (MAP)
• *See page 487*

LADIES AUXILIARY OF THE FLEET RESERVE ASSOCIATION

http://www.fra.org/

LADIES AUXILIARY OF THE FLEET RESERVE ASSOCIATION SCHOLARSHIP
• *See page 444*

SAM ROSE MEMORIAL SCHOLARSHIP
• *See page 444*

PETAZI

https://petazi.com/

2017 NURTURE FOR NATURE SCHOLARSHIP
• *See page 483*

UDT-SEAL ASSOCIATION

http://www.nswfoundation.org/

HAD RICHARDS UDT-SEAL MEMORIAL SCHOLARSHIP

One-time award for dependent children of UDT-SEAL association members. Freshmen given priority. Applicant may not be older than 22 and not married. Must be U.S. citizen.

Award: Scholarship for use in freshman, sophomore, junior, or senior years; not renewable. *Number:* 1–2.

Eligibility Requirements: Applicant must be age 22 or under; enrolled or expecting to enroll full-time at a two-year or four-year institution or university and single. Available to U.S. citizens. Applicant or parent must meet one or more of the following requirements: Navy experience; retired from active duty; disabled or killed as a result of military service; prisoner of war; or missing in action.

Application Requirements: Application form, essay, personal photograph, proof of active duty or parent/spouse's active duty, test scores, transcript. *Deadline:* varies.

Contact: Robert Rieve, President and CEO
    Phone: 757-363-7490
    E-mail: info@nswfoundation.org

NAVAL SPECIAL WARFARE SCHOLARSHIP

Awards given to active duty SEAL's, SWCC's, and other active duty military serving in a Naval Special Warfare command or their spouses and dependents.

Award: Scholarship for use in freshman, sophomore, junior, or senior years; not renewable. *Number:* 80–100.

Eligibility Requirements: Applicant must be enrolled or expecting to enroll full- or part-time at a two-year or four-year institution or university. Available to U.S. citizens. Applicant or parent must meet one or more of the following requirements: Navy experience; retired from active duty; disabled or killed as a result of military service; prisoner of war; or missing in action.

Application Requirements: Application form, essay, personal photograph, proof of active duty or parent/spouse's active duty, transcript.

Contact: Robert Rieve, President and CEO
    Phone: 757-363-7490
    E-mail: info@nswfoundation.org

UDT-SEAL SCHOLARSHIP

Award for dependent children of UDT-SEAL association members. Freshmen given priority. Applicant may not be older than 22 and not married. Must be U.S. citizen.

Award: Scholarship for use in freshman, sophomore, junior, or senior years; not renewable. *Number:* 10–20.

Eligibility Requirements: Applicant must be age 22 or under; enrolled or expecting to enroll full-time at a two-year or four-year or technical institution or university and single. Available to U.S. citizens. Applicant or parent must meet one or more of the following requirements: Navy experience; retired from active duty; disabled or killed as a result of military service; prisoner of war; or missing in action.

Application Requirements: Application form, essay, personal photograph, proof of active duty or parent/spouse's active duty, test scores, transcript. *Deadline:* varies.

Contact: Robert Rieve, President and CEO
    Phone: 757-363-7490
    E-mail: info@nswfoundation.org

UNITED STATES SUBMARINE VETERANS

https://www.ussvi.org/Documents.asp?Type=Scholarship|Application

UNITED STATES SUBMARINE VETERANS INC. NATIONAL SCHOLARSHIP PROGRAM

• See page 456

WINGS OVER AMERICA SCHOLARSHIP FOUNDATION

http://www.wingsoveramerica.us/

WINGS OVER AMERICA SCHOLARSHIP FOUNDATION

Applicant must be graduates of an accredited high school or the equivalent home school or institution and must plan to attend an accredited academic institution. Scholarship awardees must be enrolled full-time in order to receive their award. Awards may be used for tuition and tuition-related fees only.

Award: Scholarship for use in freshman, sophomore, or junior years; not renewable. *Number:* 50. *Amount:* $3000.

Eligibility Requirements: Applicant must be enrolled or expecting to enroll full-time at a two-year or four-year or technical institution or university. Available to U.S. citizens. Applicant must have served in the Navy.

Application Requirements: Application form, community service, essay. *Deadline:* February 1.

Contact: Melissa Garrison, Scholarship Administrator
    Wings Over America Scholarship Foundation
    4966 Euclid Drive
    Suite 109
    Virginia Beach, VA 23452
    Phone: 757-671-3200 Ext. 2
    E-mail: scholarship@wingsoveramerica.us

NATIONALITY OR ETHNIC HERITAGE

365 PET INSURANCE

https://365petinsurance.com/

MINORITY STUDENTS IN VETERINARY MEDICINE SCHOLARSHIP

The Minority Students in Veterinary Medicine Scholarship is for students currently enrolled in or accepted to a veterinary school in the USA. This scholarship serves to meet the economic needs of minority students to encourage enrollment in veterinary medicine programs to help diversify the population of veterinarians entering the workforce.

Award: Scholarship for use in sophomore, junior, senior, graduate, or postgraduate years; not renewable. *Number:* 1. *Amount:* $500.

Eligibility Requirements: Applicant must be of Mexican heritage; American Indian/Alaska Native, Asian/Pacific Islander, Black (non-Hispanic), Hispanic; enrolled or expecting to enroll full-time at a four-year institution or university; resident of Alabama, Alaska, Arizona, Arkansas, California, Colorado, Connecticut, Delaware, District of Columbia, Florida, Georgia, Guam, Hawaii, Idaho, Illinois, Indiana, Iowa, Kansas, Kentucky, Louisiana, Maine, Maryland, Massachusetts, Michigan, Minnesota, Mississippi, Missouri, Montana, Nebraska, Nevada, New Hampshire, New Jersey, New Mexico, New York, North Carolina, North Dakota, Ohio, Oklahoma, Oregon, Pennsylvania, Puerto Rico, Rhode Island, South Carolina, South Dakota, Tennessee, Texas, Utah, Vermont, Virginia, Washington, West Virginia, Wisconsin, Wyoming and studying in Alabama, Alaska, Arizona, Arkansas, California, Colorado, Connecticut, Delaware, District of Columbia, Florida, Georgia, Hawaii, Idaho, Illinois, Indiana, Iowa, Kansas, Kentucky, Louisiana, Maine, Maryland, Massachusetts, Michigan, Minnesota, Mississippi, Missouri, Montana, Nebraska, Nevada, New Hampshire, New Jersey, New Mexico, New York, North Carolina, North Dakota, Ohio, Oklahoma, Oregon, Pennsylvania, Rhode Island, South Carolina, South Dakota, Tennessee, Texas, Utah, Vermont, Virginia, Washington, West Virginia, Wisconsin, Wyoming. Available to U.S. citizens.

Application Requirements: Application form, essay. *Deadline:* December 31.

Contact: Mr. Jason Lee
365 Pet Insurance
10400 NE 4th Street
Bellevue, WA 98004
E-mail: jason@365petinsurance.com

THE 5 STRONG SCHOLARSHIP FOUNDATION, INC.

http://5strongscholars.org

5 STRONG SCHOLARS SCHOLARSHIP

The applicants must reside in the Metropolitan Atlanta area (Cobb, Fulton, Clayton, Fayette, Douglas, Gwinett, DeKalb, etc.). If chosen, applicants must be able to attend bi-monthly college prep sessions. Minimum requirements: GPA: 2.5 and ACT: 21, SAT: 1010

Award: Scholarship for use in freshman, sophomore, junior, or senior years; renewable. *Number:* 25. *Amount:* $10,000–$16,000.

Eligibility Requirements: Applicant must be American Indian/Alaska Native, Asian/Pacific Islander, Black (non-Hispanic), Hispanic; high school student; age 17-19; planning to enroll or expecting to enroll full-time at a four-year institution or university; resident of Georgia and studying in Georgia. Available to U.S. citizens.

Application Requirements: Application form, interview. *Deadline:* December 31.

Contact: Drew Ragland
The 5 Strong Scholarship Foundation, Inc.
103 Pinegate Rd
Peachtree City, GA 30269
E-mail: 5strongscholars@gmail.com

ACADGILD

https://acadgild.com

ACADGILD MERIT-BASED SCHOLARSHIPS

• *See page 472*

AICPA INSTITUTE

https://www.aicpa.org/

AICPA SCHOLARSHIP AWARD FOR MINORITY ACCOUNTING STUDENTS

The AICPA Scholarship Award for Minority Accounting Students is part of the AICPA Legacy Scholars program that provides financial assistance to outstanding minority students to encourage their pursuit of accounting as a major and their ultimate entry into the profession. All applications must be completed and submitted by the deadline to be considered. Students interested in being considered for more than one AICPA Legacy Scholarship award need only complete one application—applicants will be evaluated for all awards for which they are eligible. Scholarship aid may be used only for the payment of expenses that directly relate to obtaining an accounting education (e.g.; tuition, fees, room and board, and/or books and materials). Awards are renewable; however, renewals are neither automatic nor guaranteed. Students who wish to renew their scholarship award must reapply the following year. Payments are sent directly to the student's financial aid office on behalf of the student. Applications are accepted online between December 1st and March 1st on ThisWayToCPA.com

Award: Scholarship for use in sophomore, junior, senior, or graduate years; renewable. *Amount:* $3000–$5000.

Eligibility Requirements: Applicant must be American Indian/Alaska Native, Asian/Pacific Islander, Black (non-Hispanic), Hispanic and enrolled or expecting to enroll full-time at an institution or university. Available to U.S. citizens.

Application Requirements: Application form, application form may be submitted online, essay. *Deadline:* March 1.

Contact: Scholarship Manager
AICPA Institute
220 Leigh Farm Road
AICPA / ASE Team
Durham, NC 27707-8110
E-mail: scholarships@aicpa.org

ALBERTA HERITAGE SCHOLARSHIP FUND

http://www.alis.alberta.ca/

DR. ERNEST AND MINNIE MEHL SCHOLARSHIP

Award of CAN$3500 to encourage students to pursue a postsecondary education and to recognize and reward exceptional academic achievement at the senior high school level. Applicants must be Canadian citizens or landed immigrants who have completed their grade twelve in Alberta at a school that follows the Alberta Education Curriculum. Applicants must be continuing their studies at a degree granting postsecondary institution in Canada. University transfer programs are acceptable. For additional information and application, see website http://alis.alberta.ca.

Award: Scholarship for use in freshman, sophomore, junior, or senior years; not renewable. *Number:* 1.

Eligibility Requirements: Applicant must be Canadian citizen; high school student; planning to enroll or expecting to enroll full-time at a two-year or four-year or technical institution or university; resident of Alberta and studying in Alberta, British Columbia, Manitoba, New Brunswick, Newfoundland, Northwest Territories, Nova Scotia, Ontario, Prince Edward Island, Quebec, Saskatchewan.

Application Requirements: Application form, financial need analysis, transcript. *Deadline:* June 1.

EARL AND COUNTESS OF WESSEX-WORLD CHAMPIONSHIPS IN ATHLETICS SCHOLARSHIPS

Award of CAN$3000 to recognize the top male and female Alberta students who have excelled in track and field, have a strong academic record, and plan to continue their studies at the postsecondary level in Alberta. Must be Canadian citizens or landed immigrants and residents of Alberta. Must have completed grade twelve in Alberta in the same year they apply for the scholarship. Must be planning on attending University of Alberta, University of Calgary or University of Lethbridge. For additional information and application, go to website http://alis.alberta.ca.

Award: Scholarship for use in freshman year; not renewable. *Number:* 2.

Eligibility Requirements: Applicant must be Canadian citizen; high school student; planning to enroll or expecting to enroll full-time at a two-year or four-year or technical institution or university; resident of Alberta; studying in Alberta and must have an interest in athletics/sports.

Application Requirements: Application form, recommendations or references, transcript. *Deadline:* October 1.

GRANT MACEWAN UNITED WORLD COLLEGE SCHOLARSHIPS

Award to reward Alberta's best grade eleven students with a chance to complete their high school at one of the twelve United World Colleges located throughout the world. Applicants must be Alberta residents and be between the ages of 16 and 17 and a half. Applicants are normally in the process of completing their grade eleven. Scholarship is based on a student's academic record, breadth of study, personal accomplishments, community involvement, and interest in the goals of the United World Colleges. For additional information and application, see website http://alis.alberta.ca.

Award: Scholarship for use in freshman year; renewable.

Eligibility Requirements: Applicant must be Canadian citizen; high school student; age 16-17; planning to enroll or expecting to enroll full-time at a four-year institution or university and resident of Alberta.

Application Requirements: Application form, essay, interview, recommendations or references, transcript. *Deadline:* February 15.

JO-ANNE KOCH-ABC SOCIETY SCHOLARSHIP

One CAN$1500 award supporting gifted learners in their post-secondary studies. Applicants must have completed Grade 12 requirements at a publicly funded high school in Alberta and plan to pursue post-secondary studies. Applicants must meet the criteria for Giftedness as determined by their school jurisdiction. Preference will be given to applicants who have received extra support for their learning needs. For additional information, see website http://alis.alberta.ca.

Award: Scholarship for use in freshman year; not renewable. *Number:* 1.

Eligibility Requirements: Applicant must be Canadian citizen; high school student; planning to enroll or expecting to enroll full-time at a two-year institution or university and resident of Alaska.

Application Requirements: Application form. *Deadline:* December 15.

AMERICAN INDIAN GRADUATE CENTER

http://www.aigcs.org/

ACCENTURE AMERICAN INDIAN SCHOLARSHIP

Scholarships awarded to American Indian and Alaska Natives from U.S. federally recognized tribes. This program is for first year college freshmen (undergraduate) students. Must have a cumulative GPA of a 3.25 on a 4.0 scale and demonstrate financial need. Areas of study: engineering, computer science, operations management, finance, marketing and business.

Award: Scholarship for use in freshman year; renewable. *Number:* 10. *Amount:* $10,000.

Eligibility Requirements: Applicant must be American Indian/Alaska Native; high school student and planning to enroll or expecting to enroll full-time at a four-year institution or university. Available to U.S. citizens.

Application Requirements: Application form, community service, essay, financial need analysis, personal photograph. *Deadline:* May 1.

Contact: Marveline Vallo Gabbard, Program Associate
American Indian Graduate Center
3701 San Mateo Boulevard, NE, Suite 200
Albuquerque, NM 87110
Phone: 505-881-4584
E-mail: fellowships@aigcs.org

WELLS FARGO SCHOLARSHIP AMERICAN INDIAN SCHOLARSHIP

Must be an enrolled member of a U.S. federally recognized American Indian or Alaska Native tribe. Be pursuing a degree in the banking, resort management, gaming operations, management and administration, including accounting, finance, information technology and human resources. Must have a cumulative GPA of a 3.0 on a 4.0 scale and demonstrate financial need.

Award: Scholarship for use in junior, senior, or graduate years; renewable. *Number:* 2. *Amount:* $5000.

Eligibility Requirements: Applicant must be American Indian/Alaska Native and enrolled or expecting to enroll full-time at a four-year institution or university. Available to U.S. citizens.

Application Requirements: Application form, community service, essay, financial need analysis, personal photograph. *Deadline:* May 1.

Contact: Marveline Vallo Gabbard, Program Associate
American Indian Graduate Center
3701 San Mateo Boulevard, NE, Suite 200
Albuquerque, NM 87110
Phone: 505-881-4584
E-mail: fellowships@aigcs.org

AMERICAN INSTITUTE FOR FOREIGN STUDY (AIFS)

https://www.aifsabroad.com/

AIFS-HACU SCHOLARSHIPS

Scholarships to outstanding Hispanic students to study abroad with AIFS. Available to students attending HACU member schools. Students will receive scholarships of up to 50 percent of the full program fee. Students must meet all standard AIFS eligibility requirements. Deadlines: April 15 for fall, October 1 for spring, and March 15 for summer.

Award: Scholarship for use in freshman, sophomore, junior, or senior years; not renewable. *Number:* 1.

Eligibility Requirements: Applicant must be Hispanic; age 17 and over and enrolled or expecting to enroll full-time at a two-year institution or university. Available to U.S. and non-U.S. citizens.

Application Requirements: Application form, application form may be submitted online, essay, personal photograph. *Fee:* $95. *Deadline:* October 1.

Contact: Sharman Hedayati, Vice President, Director of Admissions and Operations
American Institute For Foreign Study (AIFS)
1 High Ridge Park
Stamford, CT 06905
Phone: 800-727-2437
E-mail: shedayati@aifs.com

DIVERSITY ABROAD ACHIEVEMENT SCHOLARSHIP

Scholarships are available for students studying abroad on any program offered by a DiversityAbroad.com member organization. African-American, Asian-American, Hispanic/Latino and Native-American students are strongly encouraged to apply. Deadlines: April 15 for fall, October 1 for spring. Visit https://www.aifsabroad.com/financial-aid/aifs-financial-aid.asp for more information.

Award: Scholarship for use in freshman, sophomore, junior, or senior years; not renewable. *Number:* 2–3. *Amount:* $5000.

Eligibility Requirements: Applicant must be American Indian/Alaska Native, Asian/Pacific Islander, Black (non-Hispanic), Hispanic and enrolled or expecting to enroll full-time at a two-year institution or university. Available to U.S. citizens.

Application Requirements: Application form, application form may be submitted online, community service, essay, personal photograph. *Fee:* $95. *Deadline:* October 1.

Contact: Sharman Hedayati, Vice President, Director of Admissions and Operations
American Institute For Foreign Study (AIFS)
1 High Ridge Park
Stamford, CT 06905
Phone: 800-727-2437
E-mail: shedayati@aifs.com

ARMENIAN RELIEF SOCIETY OF EASTERN USA INC.-REGIONAL OFFICE

http://www.arseastusa.org/

ARMENIAN RELIEF SOCIETY UNDERGRADUATE SCHOLARSHIP

Applicant must be an undergraduate student of Armenian heritage attending an accredited four-year college or university in the United States. Award for full-time students only. Must be U.S. or Canadian citizen. High school students may not apply.

Award: Scholarship for use in freshman, sophomore, or junior years; not renewable. *Number:* 10–25. *Amount:* $1000–$1500.

Eligibility Requirements: Applicant must be Armenian citizen and enrolled or expecting to enroll full-time at a four-year institution or university. Available to U.S. and Canadian citizens.

Application Requirements: Application form, essay, financial need analysis. *Deadline:* April 1.

Contact: Mrs. Vartouhie Chiloyan, Scholarship Committee
Armenian Relief Society of Eastern USA Inc.-Regional Office
80 Bigelow Avenue, Suite 200
Watertown, MA 02472
Phone: 617-926-3801
E-mail: arseastus@gmail.com

ARMENIAN STUDENTS ASSOCIATION OF AMERICA INC.

http://www.asainc.org/

ARMENIAN STUDENTS ASSOCIATION OF AMERICA INC. SCHOLARSHIPS

One-time award for students of Armenian descent. Must be an undergraduate in sophomore, junior, or senior years, or graduate student, attending an accredited U.S. institution. Award based on need, merit, and character. Application fee: $15.

Award: Scholarship for use in sophomore, junior, senior, or graduate years; not renewable. *Number:* 35. *Amount:* $3300–$6700.

Eligibility Requirements: Applicant must be of Armenian heritage and enrolled or expecting to enroll full-time at a four-year institution or university. Available to U.S. citizens.

Application Requirements: Application form, essay, financial need analysis. *Fee:* $15. *Deadline:* March 15.

Contact: Nathalie Yaghoobian, ASA Scholarship Committee
Phone: 401-461-6114
Fax: 401-461-6112
E-mail: asa@asainc.org

ASIAN PACIFIC COMMUNITY FUND

http://www.apcf.org/

TAIWANESE AMERICAN SCHOLARSHIP FUND

The Taiwanese American Scholarship Fund is focused on helping economically-challenged Taiwanese American youth fulfill their dreams of obtaining higher education. To be eligible, a student must be 1. a U.S. citizen or U.S. permanent resident (holders of a Permanent Resident Card) and a direct blood descendant of a Taiwanese citizen; 2. a high school senior or first year college student residing in the United States; 3. plan to attend a university or college as a full-time first or second year student in the fall of 2018 in the United States (if selected, high school seniors must submit college acceptance letter for verification); 4. have a minimum cumulative unweighted high school/college GPA of 3.0; 5. have a household income at or below the Federal/State/County Low Income Level (must be able to show 2016 or 2017 tax return should applicant be selected for award). The scholarship is open to all majors. Previous award recipients are eligible to apply as long as they meet the eligibility requirements.

Award: Scholarship for use in freshman or sophomore years; renewable. *Number:* 10. *Amount:* $5000.

Eligibility Requirements: Applicant must be of Chinese heritage; Asian/Pacific Islander and enrolled or expecting to enroll full-time at an institution or university. Available to U.S. citizens.

Application Requirements: Application form, application form may be submitted online. *Deadline:* April 17.

Contact: Karen Fan
Asian Pacific Community Fund
1145 Wilshire Boulevard
Suite 105
Los Angeles, CA 90017
Phone: 213-624-6400 Ext. 6
Fax: 213-624-6406
E-mail: kfan@apcf.org

ASSOCIATION ON AMERICAN INDIAN AFFAIRS, INC.

http://www.indian-affairs.org/

ADOLPH VAN PELT SPECIAL FUND FOR INDIAN SCHOLARSHIPS

Scholarship is open to undergraduate students pursuing a Bachelor's degree in any curriculum. Must be an American Indian/Alaska Native. See http://www.indian-affairs.org for specific details. Must be seeking an Associate's degree or higher at an accredited school.

Award: Scholarship for use in freshman, sophomore, junior, or senior years; not renewable. *Number:* 5–15. *Amount:* up to $1500.

Eligibility Requirements: Applicant must be American Indian/Alaska Native and enrolled or expecting to enroll full-time at a two-year or four-year or technical institution or university. Available to U.S. citizens.

Application Requirements: Application form, essay, Tribal Enrollment. *Deadline:* June 1.

Contact: Lisa Wyzlic, Director of Scholarship Programs
Association on American Indian Affairs, Inc.
966 Hungerford Drive, Suite 12-B
Rockville, MD 20850
Phone: 240-314-7155
Fax: 240-314-7155
E-mail: lw.aaia@indian-affairs.org

ALLOGAN SLAGLE MEMORIAL SCHOLARSHIP

Scholarship available for American Indian/Alaska Native undergraduate and graduate students who are members of tribes that are not yet recognized by the federal government. Students must apply each year. See http://www.indian-affairs.org for specific details. Must be seeking an Associate's degree or higher at an accredited school.

Award: Scholarship for use in freshman, sophomore, junior, senior, or graduate years; not renewable. *Number:* 4–8. *Amount:* $1500.

Eligibility Requirements: Applicant must be American Indian/Alaska Native and enrolled or expecting to enroll full-time at a two-year or four-year or technical institution or university. Available to U.S. citizens.

Application Requirements: Application form, essay, Tribal Enrollment. *Deadline:* June 1.

Contact: Lisa Wyzlic, Director of Scholarship Programs
Association on American Indian Affairs, Inc.
966 Hungerford Drive, Suite 12-B
Rockville, MD 20850
Phone: 240-314-7155
Fax: 240-314-7159
E-mail: lw.aaia@indian-affairs.org

DAVID RISLING EMERGENCY AID SCHOLARSHIP

This scholarship is very limited in the amount available as well as the situation covered (eviction, utility disconnection, child removed from daycare for non-payment, some very limited car expenses for commuting students). Scholarship is for acute, temporary, unexpected emergencies that would keep students from attending school. Tuition, books, computers and other expected expenses are NOT considered emergencies. Must be Native American/Alaska Native. See our website at http://www.indian-affairs.org for details AND call the Rockville office prior to submission to see if funding is available and if your situation qualifies as an emergency. We do not fund summer session or expenses incurred over the summer.

Award: Scholarship for use in freshman, sophomore, junior, senior, or graduate years; not renewable. *Amount:* $100–$400.

Eligibility Requirements: Applicant must be American Indian/Alaska Native and enrolled or expecting to enroll full-time at a two-year or four-year institution or university. Available to U.S. citizens.

Application Requirements: Application form, essay, financial need analysis, recommendations or references, transcript, Tribal Enrollment, financial aid award letter, full time class schedule, explanation of need, proof of need. *Deadline:* continuous.

Contact: Lisa Wyzlic, Director of Scholarship Programs
Association on American Indian Affairs, Inc.
966 Hungerford Drive, Suite 12-B
Rockville, MD 20850
Phone: 240-314-7155
Fax: 240-314-7159
E-mail: lw.aaia@indian-affairs.org

DISPLACED HOMEMAKER SCHOLARSHIP

This undergraduate scholarship is for men and women 30+ who would not otherwise be able to complete their educational goals due to family responsibilities. Must be an American Indian/Alaska Native. See our website http://www.indian-affairs.org for complete details. Must be an Associate's degree or higher. Must be an accredited institution.

Award: Scholarship for use in freshman, sophomore, junior, or senior years; not renewable. *Number:* 2–10. *Amount:* $1500.

Eligibility Requirements: Applicant must be American Indian/Alaska Native; age 30 and over and enrolled or expecting to enroll full-time at a two-year or four-year or technical institution or university. Available to U.S. citizens.

Application Requirements: Application form, essay, Tribal Enrollment. *Deadline:* June 3.

Contact: Lisa Wyzlic, Director of Scholarship Programs
Association on American Indian Affairs, Inc.
966 Hungerford Drive, Suite 12-B
Rockville, MD 20850
Phone: 240-314-7155
Fax: 240-314-7159
E-mail: lw.aaia@indian-affairs.org

OWANAH ANDERSON SCHOLARSHIP

This scholarship is for Native American and Alaska Native undergraduate women who are entering their Junior year of college. Students must be enrolled in a federally recognized tribe. Students must be seeking a Bachelors Degree and may be enrolled in any curriculum. This scholarship renews each semester through the student's Senior year pending satisfactory progress. Each award is $1,500 per school year. $750 is disbursed in late September and $750 is disbursed in late January. This scholarship is for two years only. See our website at www.indian-affairs.org for complete details.

Award: Scholarship for use in junior year; renewable. *Number:* 1–5. *Amount:* $1500.

Eligibility Requirements: Applicant must be American Indian/Alaska Native; enrolled or expecting to enroll full-time at a four-year institution or university and female. Available to U.S. citizens.

Application Requirements: Application form, copy of Tribal Enrollment, essay. *Deadline:* June 1.

Contact: Lisa Wyzlic, Director of Scholarship Program
Association on American Indian Affairs, Inc.
966 Hungerford Drive, Suite 12-B
Rockville, DC 20850
Phone: 240-314-7155
Fax: 240-314-7159
E-mail: lw.aaia@indian-affairs.org

BUREAU OF INDIAN AFFAIRS OFFICE OF INDIAN EDUCATION PROGRAMS

http://www.bie.edu/

BUREAU OF INDIAN EDUCATION GRANT PROGRAM

Grants are provided to supplement financial assistance to eligible American Indian/Alaska Native students entering college seeking a Baccalaureate degree. A student must be a member of, or at least one-quarter degree Indian blood descendent of a member of an American Indian tribe who are eligible for the special programs and services provided by the United States through the Bureau of Indian Affairs to Indians because of their status as Indians.

Award: Grant for use in freshman year; not renewable.

Eligibility Requirements: Applicant must be American Indian/Alaska Native; high school student and planning to enroll or expecting to enroll full-time at a two-year or four-year institution or university. Available to U.S. citizens.

Application Requirements: Application form.

Contact: Paulina Bell, Office Automation Assistant
Phone: 202-208-6123
Fax: 202-208-3312

CABRILLO CIVIC CLUBS OF CALIFORNIA INC.

http://www.cabrillocivicclubs.org/scholarship.asp

CABRILLO CIVIC CLUBS OF CALIFORNIA SCHOLARSHIP

Applicants must be graduating California high school seniors of Portuguese heritage and American citizenship, with an overall 3.5 GPA.

Award: Scholarship for use in freshman year; not renewable. *Number:* 75–100. *Amount:* $500.

Eligibility Requirements: Applicant must be of Portuguese heritage; high school student; planning to enroll or expecting to enroll full-time at a technical institution and resident of California. Available to U.S. citizens.

Application Requirements: Application form, driver's license, personal photograph, recommendations or references, resume, self-addressed stamped envelope with application, transcript. *Deadline:* March 15.

Contact: Breck Austin, Scholarship Chairperson
Cabrillo Civic Clubs of California Inc.
2174 South Coast Highway
Oceanside, CA 92054
E-mail: shampoobla@sbcglobal.net

CAFÉ BUSTELO

http://cafebustelo.com

CAFE BUSTELO EL CAFE DEL FUTURO SCHOLARSHIP ESSAY CONTEST

Café Bustelo and the Hispanic Association of Colleges and Universities (HACU) have teamed up to present El Café del Futuro Scholarship Essay Contest. Eligible students can enter for a chance to win one of nine $5,000 college scholarships. Permanent legal residents of the 50 United States and D.C., age 18 or older and of Latino decent, that are currently enrolled full-time in a college of university, are eligible to apply for the scholarship. To enter/apply, complete the online application on the HACU website: www.hacu.net; and respond to and upload your original essay on the following topic: Describe how your Latino heritage, family, and the community in which you grew up have impacted your desire and motivation to obtain a college degree. Additionally, describe what you intend to accomplish with your degree and how you will give back to your community. Attach the required supporting documents to the application.

Award: Scholarship for use in freshman, sophomore, junior, or senior years; not renewable. *Number:* 9. *Amount:* $5000.

Eligibility Requirements: Applicant must be of Hispanic heritage; age 18 and over and enrolled or expecting to enroll full-time at a four-year institution or university. Available to U.S. citizens.

Application Requirements: Application form, essay. *Deadline:* May 26.

Contact: Hispanic Association of Colleges & Universities
Café Bustelo
8415 Datapoint Drive, Suite 400
San Antonio, TX 78229
Phone: 210-692-3805
Fax: 210-692-0823
E-mail: hacu@hacu.net

CENTRAL COUNCIL, TLINGIT AND HAIDA INDIAN TRIBES OF ALASKA

http://www.hied.org/

ALUMNI STUDENT ASSISTANCE PROGRAM

The program provides annual scholarship awards to all enrolled Tlingit or Haida tribal members regardless of service area, community affiliation, origination, residence, tribal compact, or signatory status.

Award: Scholarship for use in freshman, sophomore, junior, senior, graduate, or postgraduate years; not renewable. *Number:* 1–100. *Amount:* $300–$500.

Eligibility Requirements: Applicant must be American Indian/Alaska Native and enrolled or expecting to enroll full-time at a two-year or four-year institution or university. Available to U.S. citizens.

Application Requirements: Application form, community service, essay, financial need analysis, recommendations or references, transcript, tribal enrollment certification form, letter of admission. *Deadline:* September 15.

Contact: Miss. Leslie Rae Isturis, Education Specialist
Central Council, Tlingit and Haida Indian Tribes of Alaska
3239 Hospital Drive
Juneau, AK 99801
Phone: 907-463-7375
Fax: 907-463-7173
E-mail: listuris@ccthita.org

COLLEGE STUDENT ASSISTANCE PROGRAM

A federally funded program which authorizes a program of assistance, by educational grants, to Indians seeking higher education. Awards available only to enrolled T&H members. Minimum 2.0 GPA required.

Award: Scholarship for use in freshman, sophomore, junior, senior, graduate, or postgraduate years; renewable. *Number:* 1–200. *Amount:* up to $2000.

Eligibility Requirements: Applicant must be American Indian/Alaska Native and enrolled or expecting to enroll full-time at a two-year or four-year institution or university. Available to U.S. citizens.

Application Requirements: Application form, letter of admission, test scores, transcript. *Deadline:* May 15.

Contact: Miss. Leslie Rae Isturis, Education Specialist
Central Council, Tlingit and Haida Indian Tribes of Alaska
3239 Hospital Drive
Juneau, AK 99801
Phone: 907-463-7375
Fax: 907-463-7173
E-mail: listuris@ccthita.org

CENTRAL SCHOLARSHIP

http://www.central-scholarship.org

LESSANS FAMILY SCHOLARSHIP

Scholarship available for Jewish students from Maryland who attend undergraduate colleges, universities or vocational schools full-time. Students can attend any accredited U.S. college or university. Awards are based on need and merit. The scholarship committee determines award amounts. For more information, visit website http://www.centralsb.org.

Award: Scholarship for use in freshman year; renewable. *Number:* 2. *Amount:* $2000.

Eligibility Requirements: Applicant must be Jewish; of Jewish heritage; high school student; planning to enroll or expecting to enroll full-time at a two-year or four-year institution or university and resident of Maryland. Available to U.S. citizens.

Application Requirements: Application form, essay, financial need analysis, interview. *Deadline:* April 1.

Contact: Angela Harrison, Program Manager
Phone: 410-415-5558
Fax: 410-415-5501
E-mail: aharrison@central-scholarship.org

CHEROKEE NATION OF OKLAHOMA

http://www.cherokee.org/

CHEROKEE NATION HIGHER EDUCATION SCHOLARSHIP

A supplementary program that provides financial assistance to Cherokee Nation Members only. It is a need-based program which provides assistance in seeking a Bachelor's degree.

Award: Scholarship for use in freshman, sophomore, junior, or senior years; renewable. *Number:* up to 2,800. *Amount:* $100–$1000.

Eligibility Requirements: Applicant must be American Indian/Alaska Native and enrolled or expecting to enroll full-time at a four-year institution or university. Available to U.S. citizens.

Application Requirements: Test scores, transcript, written request for application. *Deadline:* June 13.

Contact: Nita Wilson, Higher Education Specialist
Cherokee Nation of Oklahoma
PO Box 948
Tahlequah, OK 74465
Phone: 918-458-6195
E-mail: nwilson@cherokee.org

CHICANA/LATINA FOUNDATION

http://www.chicanalatina.org/

SCHOLARSHIPS FOR LATINA STUDENTS ENROLLED IN COLLEGES/UNIVERSITIES IN NORTHERN CALIFORNIA

Scholarships are awarded to female Latina students enrolled in two-year, four-year or graduate levels. Applicants must be from and/or attending colleges in the nine counties of Northern California listed on the application.

Award: Scholarship for use in freshman, sophomore, junior, or senior years; not renewable. *Number:* 25–30. *Amount:* $1500.

Eligibility Requirements: Applicant must be of Hispanic heritage; enrolled or expecting to enroll full-time at a two-year or four-year institution or university; female and resident of California. Available to U.S. citizens.

Application Requirements: Application form, essay, interview. *Deadline:* March 31.

Contact: Stephanie Segovia, Program Director
Chicana/Latina Foundation
1419 Burlingame Avenue, Suite W2
Burlingame, CA 94010
Phone: 650-548-1049
E-mail: stephanie@chicanalatina.org

CHINESE AMERICAN ASSOCIATION OF MINNESOTA

http://www.caam.org/

CHINESE AMERICAN ASSOCIATION OF MINNESOTA (CAAM) SCHOLARSHIPS

Merit and need scholarships of $1000 each are available for college and graduate students of Chinese descent and a resident of Minnesota. Applicants will be evaluated on their academic records, leadership qualities, and community service.

Award: Scholarship for use in freshman, sophomore, junior, senior, or graduate years; not renewable. *Amount:* $1000.

Eligibility Requirements: Applicant must be of Chinese heritage; Asian/Pacific Islander; enrolled or expecting to enroll full-time at a two-year or four-year or technical institution or university and resident of Minnesota. Available to U.S. citizens.

Application Requirements: Application form, financial need analysis, recommendations or references, SAT score. *Deadline:* November 15.

Contact: Scholarship Committee
Chinese American Association of Minnesota
PO Box 582584
Minneapolis, MN 55458-2584

CLOTHINGRIC.COM

http://www.clothingric.com

CLOTHINGRIC.COM ANNUAL STUDENT SCHOLARSHIP

A strong and prosperous community ClothingRIC is all set to take initiative and showed many levels of involvement in the betterment of society. And to do so, we've initiated a student reward program for students who show exceptional interest in education and have limited resources to carry it with zeal and zest. With the purpose of encouraging this highly praiseworthy value, we are pleased to announce that the winning contestant will be eligible to receive $1000 scholarship for tuition fee. The sole purpose of this scholarship program is to lend a helping hand to students who are going through financial hardships. This scholarship will surely help them to overcome their financial obstacles to a great extent

Award: Scholarship for use in freshman, sophomore, junior, senior, graduate, or postgraduate years; not renewable. *Number:* 1. *Amount:* $1000.

Eligibility Requirements: Applicant must be American Indian/Alaska Native, Asian/Pacific Islander, Black (non-Hispanic), Hispanic; age 18-35 and enrolled or expecting to enroll full-time at a two-year or four-year or technical institution or university. Available to U.S. citizens.

Application Requirements: Application form. *Deadline:* October 31.

Contact: Mr. John Spears
Phone: 004-41582965165
E-mail: johnlspears@clothingric.com

COLLEGEBOUND FOUNDATION

http://www.collegeboundfoundation.org/

LORENZO FELDER SCHOLARSHIP
• See page 462

COLLEGE WOMEN'S ASSOCIATION OF JAPAN

http://www.cwaj.org/

SCHOLARSHIP FOR THE VISUALLY IMPAIRED TO STUDY ABROAD
• See page 473

SCHOLARSHIP FOR THE VISUALLY IMPAIRED TO STUDY IN JAPAN
• See page 473

COLORADO LEGAL GROUP

https://www.coloradolegalgroup.com/

COLORADO LEGAL GROUP FUND

This scholarship is intended for undergraduate students who have an interest in moving forward with a law graduate degree. If you're interested in our scholarship please answer this question: "Why are you applying to law school and why do you want to pursue a career in the legal profession?" Please answer the question in a minimum of 250 words and a maximum of 500 words and email to scholarship@coloradolegalgroup.com

Award: Scholarship for use in freshman, sophomore, junior, or senior years; renewable. *Number:* 1. *Amount:* $1000.

Eligibility Requirements: Applicant must be American Indian/Alaska Native, Asian/Pacific Islander, Black (non-Hispanic), Hispanic; age 18-100 and enrolled or expecting to enroll full-time at a four-year institution or university. Available to U.S. and non-U.S. citizens.

Application Requirements: Essay. *Deadline:* May 30.

COMMUNITY FOUNDATION OF WESTERN MASSACHUSETTS

http://www.communityfoundation.org/

HELLESPONT SOCIETY SCHOLARSHIP FUND

Scholarship for high school graduates who attend a two or four-year college, who are persons of Greek descent; preference to descendants of past Hellespont Society members.

Award: Scholarship for use in freshman year; not renewable.

Eligibility Requirements: Applicant must be of Greek heritage; high school student; planning to enroll or expecting to enroll full- or part-time at a two-year institution and resident of Maryland. Available to U.S. citizens.

Application Requirements: Application form, application form may be submitted online, essay, financial need analysis. *Deadline:* April 17.

Contact: Nikai Fondon, Scholarship Program Associate
E-mail: NFondon@communityfoundation.org

CONGRESSIONAL BLACK CAUCUS FOUNDATION, INC.

http://www.cbcfinc.org/

CBCF LOUIS STOKES HEALTH SCHOLARS PROGRAM

The Foundation provides each scholar a minimum award between $5,000 and $10,000. The award amount is determined based on the student's cost of attendance and financial need. Louis Stokes Health Scholars renew their scholarship by maintaining their eligibility and submitting mid- and end of year reports and materials. This award will be given to 4 students who are currently enrolled in an undergraduate or graduate degree program at an accredited four-year college/university for the current academic year. Applicants must have a minimum GPA of 3.0 on a 4.0 scale, be studying a health-related field, and be a U.S. citizen or have permanent U.S. residency, and is pursuing a qualifying primary health care profession. This award is supported through our partnership with United Heath Foundation.

Award: Scholarship for use in freshman, sophomore, junior, senior, or graduate years; renewable. *Number:* 4. *Amount:* $5000–$10,000.

Eligibility Requirements: Applicant must be Black (non-Hispanic) and enrolled or expecting to enroll full-time at an institution or university. Available to U.S. citizens.

Application Requirements: Application form, application form may be submitted online, essay, financial need analysis, personal photograph. *Deadline:* April 30.

Contact: Ms. Katrina Finch, Program Administrator, Scholarships
Phone: 202-263-2800
E-mail: scholarships@cbcfinc.org

CONNECTICUT ASSOCIATION OF LATINOS IN HIGHER EDUCATION (CALAHE)

http://www.calahe.org/

CONNECTICUT ASSOCIATION OF LATINOS IN HIGHER EDUCATION SCHOLARSHIPS

Must demonstrate involvement with, and commitment to, activities that promote Latinos in pursuit of education. Must have a 2.75 GPA, be a U.S. citizen or permanent resident, be a resident of Connecticut.

Award: Scholarship for use in freshman, sophomore, junior, or senior years; not renewable. *Number:* 20. *Amount:* $1000.

Eligibility Requirements: Applicant must be of Hispanic heritage; enrolled or expecting to enroll full-time at a two-year or four-year institution or university and resident of Connecticut. Available to U.S. citizens.

Application Requirements: Application form, essay, financial need analysis. *Deadline:* May 4.

Contact: Dr. Wilson Luna, Gateway Community Technical College
Connecticut Association of Latinos in Higher Education (CALAHE)
20 Church Street
New Haven, CT 06510
Phone: 203-285-2210
E-mail: wluna@gatewayct.edu

CROATIAN SCHOLARSHIP FUND

http://www.croatianscholarship.org/

CROATIAN SCHOLARSHIP FUND

Scholarship for students of Croatian heritage. Award based on academic achievement and financial need. Must demonstrate appropriate degree selection. Scholarships are awarded depending on availability of funds and number of applicants.

Award: Scholarship for use in freshman, sophomore, junior, or senior years; renewable. *Amount:* $1500.

Eligibility Requirements: Applicant must be of Croatian/Serbian heritage; age 18-25 and enrolled or expecting to enroll full-time at a four-year institution or university. Available to U.S. and non-U.S. citizens.

Application Requirements: Application form, application form may be submitted online, autobiography, financial need analysis, personal photograph, recommendations or references, test scores, transcript. *Deadline:* May 15.

Contact: Vesna Brekalo, Scholarship Liaison
Croatian Scholarship Fund
31 Mesa Vista Court
PO Box 290
San Ramon, CA 94583
Phone: 925-556-6263
Fax: 925-556-6263
E-mail: vbrekalo@msn.com

THE DALLAS FOUNDATION

http://www.dallasfoundation.org/

DR. DAN J. AND PATRICIA S. PICKARD SCHOLARSHIP

The Dr. Dan J. and Patricia S. Pickard Scholarship Fund was established at the Dallas Foundation in 2004 to assist African-American male students in Dallas County. Dr. Pickard was an optometrist and founder of the Pickard eye clinic. He believed that if you did something nice for someone and they do something nice for someone else, you can affect the lives of many people. The Scholarship Fund is his way of "passing it on".

Award: Scholarship for use in freshman year; renewable. *Number:* 1–2. *Amount:* $1000–$2000.

Eligibility Requirements: Applicant must be Black (non-Hispanic); high school student; planning to enroll or expecting to enroll full-time at a two-year or four-year institution; male; resident of Texas and studying in Texas. Available to U.S. citizens.

Application Requirements: Application form, community service, essay, financial need analysis, recommendations or references, transcript. *Deadline:* April 1.

Contact: Ms. Rachel Lasseter, Program Associate
The Dallas Foundation
900 Jackson Street, Suite 705
Dallas, TX 75202
Phone: 214-741-9898
Fax: 214-741-9848
E-mail: scholarships@dallasfoundation.org

DIAMANTE, INC.

http://www.diamanteinc.org/

LATINO DIAMANTE SCHOLARSHIP FUND

• See page 462

DISCIPLESHIP MINISTRIES

http://umcyoungpeople.org

RICHARD S. SMITH SCHOLARSHIP

Open to racial/ethnic minority youth only. Must be a United Methodist Youth who has been active in local church for at least one year prior to application. Must be a graduating senior in high school (who maintained at least a "C" average) entering the first year of undergraduate study and be pursuing a "church-related" career.

Award: Scholarship for use in freshman year; not renewable. *Number:* 1–5. *Amount:* $100–$1300.

Eligibility Requirements: Applicant must be Methodist; American Indian/Alaska Native, Asian/Pacific Islander, Black (non-Hispanic), Hispanic; high school student and planning to enroll or expecting to enroll full-time at a two-year or four-year or technical institution or university. Available to U.S. citizens.

Application Requirements: Application form, essay, financial need analysis. *Deadline:* March 1.

Contact: Kelsey Tinker Hannum, Grant and Scholarships Administrator
Phone: 615-340-7184
E-mail: youngpeople@umcdiscipleship.org

DIVERSITYCOMM, INC.

http://www.diversitycomm.net/

BLACK EOE JOURNAL SCHOLARSHIP

For the 2018 fall semester, Black EOE Journal will be offering a $500 scholarship that is available to African–American undergraduate students. As one of the strongest growing African American publications in our nation, the Black EOE Journal informs, educates, and provides equal opportunity in corporate America. We provide the latest and most important diversity news spanning every industry, business and profession. This includes up-to-date statistics on workforce diversity, B2B trends, noteworthy conferences, business opportunities and role model spotlights. The Black EOE Journal is the ultimate African American Career & Business connection! We would like you to tell your story in a brief narrative, starting with an introduction about who you are, your interests, and anything else you feel we should know about you. Then, please provide your entry in a 300-500 word essay about your college experience so far, and your future career plans. Graphic or creative presentations are welcome as well. The scholarship will be awarded to the applicant who best demonstrates a genuine desire and goal of using the scholarship to advance in their field, and an overall passion for knowledge.

Award: Scholarship for use in freshman, sophomore, junior, or senior years. *Number:* 1. *Amount:* $500.

Eligibility Requirements: Applicant must be of African heritage; Black (non-Hispanic); age 18 and over and enrolled or expecting to enroll full- or part-time at a four-year institution or university. Available to U.S. citizens.

Application Requirements: Application form, essay. *Deadline:* August 15.

HISPANIC NETWORK MAGAZINE SCHOLARSHIP

For the 2018 Fall Semester, Hispanic Network Magazine will be offering a $500 scholarship that is available to Hispanic undergraduate students. The Hispanic Network Magazine is a valuable source to assist with your Multicultural Hiring and Supplier needs. Our goal is to create an environment of teamwork in which Latin Americans and other minorities have access to all applicable business and career opportunities. We are an information source designed to bring promising, talented people together with potential employers and customers throughout the business community. Requirements: We would like you to tell your story in a brief narrative, starting with an introduction about who you are, your interests, and anything else you feel we should know about you. Then, please provide your entry in a 300-500 word essay about your college experience so far, and your future career plans. Graphic or creative presentations are welcome as well.

Award: Scholarship for use in freshman, sophomore, junior, or senior years; renewable. *Number:* 1. *Amount:* $500.

Eligibility Requirements: Applicant must be Hispanic; age 18 and over and enrolled or expecting to enroll full- or part-time at a four-year institution or university. Available to U.S. citizens.

Application Requirements: Application form, essay. *Deadline:* August 15.

EPSILON SIGMA ALPHA

http://www.epsilonsigmaalpha.org/scholarships

EPSILON SIGMA ALPHA FOUNDATION SCHOLARSHIPS

Awards for various fields of study. Required GPA vary with scholarship. Applications must be sent to the Epsilon Sigma Alpha designated state counselor. See website at http://www.esaintl.com/esaf for further information, application forms, and a list of state counselors.

Award: Scholarship for use in freshman, sophomore, junior, senior, graduate, or postgraduate years; not renewable. *Number:* 125–175. *Amount:* $350–$7500.

Eligibility Requirements: Applicant must be American Indian/Alaska Native, Asian/Pacific Islander, Black (non-Hispanic), Hispanic and enrolled or expecting to enroll full- or part-time at a two-year or four-year or technical institution or university. Available to U.S. and non-U.S. citizens.

Application Requirements: Application form, essay, recommendations or references, test scores, transcript. *Fee:* $5. *Deadline:* February 1.

Contact: Kathy Loyd, Scholarship Chairman
Epsilon Sigma Alpha
1222 NW 651
Blairstown, MO 64726
Phone: 660-678-2611
Fax: 660-747-0807
E-mail: kloyd@knoxy.net

ESSAYHUB

https://essayhub.com/

ESSAY WRITING CONTEST BY ESSAYHUB
• See page 474

FIRST CATHOLIC SLOVAK LADIES ASSOCIATION

http://www.fcsla.org/

FIRST CATHOLIC SLOVAK LADIES ASSOCIATION COLLEGE SCHOLARSHIPS
• See page 439

FLORIDA STATE DEPARTMENT OF EDUCATION

http://www.floridastudentfinancialaid.org/

JOSE MARTI SCHOLARSHIP CHALLENGE GRANT FUND

Award available to Hispanic-American students who were born in, or whose parent was born in a Hispanic country. Must be a Florida resident, be enrolled full-time in Florida at an eligible school, and have a GPA of 3.0 or above. Must be U.S. citizen or eligible non-citizen. FAFSA must be processed by May 15. For more details, visit the website at http://www.FloridaStudentFinancialAid.org/SSFAD/home/uamain.htm.

Award: Scholarship for use in freshman, sophomore, junior, or senior years; renewable. *Amount:* $2000.

Eligibility Requirements: Applicant must be of Hispanic heritage; high school student; planning to enroll or expecting to enroll full-time at a two-year institution or university; resident of District of Columbia and studying in Florida. Available to U.S. citizens.

Application Requirements: Application form, application form may be submitted online, financial need analysis. *Deadline:* April 1.

Contact: Florida Department of Education, Office of Student Financial
Assistance, Customer Service
Florida State Department of Education
325 West Gaines Street
Tallahassee, FL 32399
Phone: 888-827-2004
E-mail: osfa@fldoe.org

GENERAL BOARD OF HIGHER EDUCATION AND MINISTRY

http://www.gbhem.org

BISHOP JOSEPH B. BETHEA SCHOLARSHIP

Undergraduate scholarship for full-time African American students. Must be a member of the Southeastern Jurisdiction Black Methodists for Church Renewal (SEJBMCR) and an active, full member of a United Methodist Church for at least one year prior to applying. Must be U.S. citizen or permanent resident, maintain a GPA of 2.8, and demonstrate financial need.

Award: Scholarship for use in freshman, sophomore, junior, or senior years; not renewable.

Eligibility Requirements: Applicant must be Methodist; Black (non-Hispanic) and enrolled or expecting to enroll full-time at a four-year institution or university. Available to U.S. citizens.

Application Requirements: Application form, essay. *Deadline:* March 1.

Contact: Ms. Marcie Bigord, Assistant Director of Loans & Scholarships
General Board of Higher Education and Ministry
PO Box 340007
Nashville, TN 37203-0007
Phone: 615-340-7388
Fax: 615-340-7529
E-mail: mbigord@gbhem.org

GEORGIA STUDENT FINANCE COMMISSION

https://gsfc.georgia.gov/

SCHOLARSHIP FOR ENGINEERING EDUCATION FOR MINORITIES (MSEE)

MSEE is a service cancelable loan available to minority upperclass students majoring in an approved program by the Engineering Accreditation Commission of the Accrediting Board for Engineering and Technology (ABET) at an eligible participating university in Georgia. Funds can be used towards educational costs. $5,250 per academic year to a maximum of nine (9) terms and $15,750. Participating universities include Georgia Institute of Technology, Georgia Southern University, University of Georgia, Kennesaw State University, and Mercer University.

Award: Scholarship for use in junior or senior years; not renewable. *Amount:* $5250–$15,750.

Eligibility Requirements: Applicant must be American Indian/Alaska Native, Asian/Pacific Islander, Black (non-Hispanic), Hispanic; enrolled or expecting to enroll full-time at an institution or university; resident of Florida and studying in Georgia. Available to U.S. citizens.

Application Requirements: Application form. *Deadline:* continuous.

Contact: Ms. Pennie Strong, Vice President, Student Aid Services
Georgia Student Finance Commission
2082 East Exchange Place
Tucker, GA 30084
Phone: 770-724-9014
Fax: 770-724-9249
E-mail: pennies@gsfc.org

HELEN DILLER FAMILY FOUNDATION

http://www.dillerteenawards.org

DILLER TEEN TIKKUN OLAM AWARDS

The Diller Teen Tikkun Olam Awards celebrate tikkun olam, or repairing the world. The Diller Family Foundation knows that supporting Jewish teen leadership today means creating and inspiring future generations of strong Jewish leaders in the global community. The Awards provide $36,000 for each recipient so that they may use it to further their project or education. If the funds will be used towards education, they will be sent directly to the college or university. Some recipients choose to divide the award between their education and philanthropic work. Applicants must demonstrate leadership via a specific community service project that is already underway. Applications presenting a project that has not yet been initiated will not be considered. Examples of past recipients' work can be found on our website, http://www.dillerteenawards.org.

Award: Prize for use in freshman, sophomore, junior, senior, graduate, or postgraduate years; not renewable. *Number:* 15. *Amount:* $36,000.

Eligibility Requirements: Applicant must be Jewish; of Jewish heritage; age 13-19 and enrolled or expecting to enroll full- or part-time at a two-year or four-year or technical institution or university. Available to U.S. citizens.

Application Requirements: Application form, community service. *Deadline:* January 8.

Contact: Ms. Lindsay Merbaum, Marketing and Outreach Coordinator
Helen Diller Family Foundation
121 Steuart Street
San Francisco, CA 94105
Phone: 415-512-6438
E-mail: lindsaym@sfjcf.org

HELLENIC TIMES SCHOLARSHIP FUND

http://www.htsf.org/

HELLENIC TIMES SCHOLARSHIP FUND

One-time award to students of Greek/Hellenic descent. Must be between the ages of 17 and 25. For use in any year of undergraduate education. Employees of the Hellenic Times and their families are not eligible.

Award: Scholarship for use in freshman, sophomore, junior, or senior years; not renewable. *Number:* 30–40. *Amount:* $500–$10,000.

Eligibility Requirements: Applicant must be of Greek heritage; age 17-25 and enrolled or expecting to enroll full-time at a two-year or four-year or technical institution or university. Available to U.S. and non-U.S. citizens.

Application Requirements: Application form, financial need analysis, recommendations or references, resume, transcript. *Deadline:* February 19.

Contact: Nick Katsoris, President of Scholarship Fund
Hellenic Times Scholarship Fund
823 11th Avenue, Fifth Floor
New York, NY 10019-3535
Phone: 212-986-6881
Fax: 212-977-3662
E-mail: htsfund@aol.com

HELLENIC UNIVERSITY CLUB OF NEW YORK

http://www.hucny.com

HELLENIC UNIVERSITY CLUB UNDERGRADUATE SCHOLARSHIP AWARDS PROGRAM

The Hellenic University Club Undergraduate Scholarship Awards are offered in recognition and honor of Greek American students who have exemplified high scholastic achievement. The Hellenic University Club of New York will offer a total of four (4) awards of $1,500 each based on academic achievement and financial need. All applicants must meet the eligibility requirements and submit a complete Hellenic University Club Undergraduate Scholarship Application to the organization. Must be a high school student that will graduate in spring 2017 from a state certified high school, or equivalent, and will enroll at an accredited university/college in the U.S. in fall 2017 as a full-time student pursuing a Bachelor's degree; must be U.S. citizens or U.S. permanent residents and living in the tri-state New York area (New York, New Jersey and Connecticut); must be of Hellenic descent, at least one great grandparent with Hellenic roots; must have a cumulative average of at least 90% (or 3.5 GPA) or be in the top 10% of their class; must have a minimum SAT score of 1800/2400 (old SAT) or 1300/1600 (new SAT) and/or minimum ACT score of 27/36; must be able to demonstrate financial need. For more information, visit our website: http://www.hucny.com

Award: Grant for use in freshman year; not renewable. *Number:* 4. *Amount:* $1500.

Eligibility Requirements: Applicant must be of Cypriot, Greek heritage; high school student; planning to enroll or expecting to enroll full-time at a four-year institution or university and resident of Connecticut, New Jersey, New York. Available to U.S. citizens.

Application Requirements: Application form, essay. *Deadline:* April 1.

HELLENIC UNIVERSITY CLUB OF PHILADELPHIA

http://www.hucphiladephia.org/

CHRISTOPHER DEMETRIS SCHOLARSHIP

$1500 scholarship for a full-time student enrolled in a degree program at an accredited four-year college or university. High school seniors accepted for enrollment in such a degree program may also apply. Must be a U.S. citizen of Greek descent and a resident of particular counties in NJ or PA.

Award: Scholarship for use in freshman, sophomore, junior, or senior years; not renewable. *Amount:* up to $1500.

Eligibility Requirements: Applicant must be of Greek heritage; enrolled or expecting to enroll full-time at a four-year institution or university and resident of New Jersey, Pennsylvania. Available to U.S. citizens.

Application Requirements: Application form, financial need analysis, transcript. *Deadline:* April 3.

Contact: Toula Bastas, Chairperson
Phone: 610-613-4310
E-mail: HucScholarship@gmail.com

DR. MICHAEL DORIZAS MEMORIAL SCHOLARSHIP

$5000 award for a full-time student enrolled in a degree program at an accredited four-year college or university. Must be a U.S. citizen of Greek descent and a resident of particular counties in NJ or PA.

Award: Scholarship for use in freshman, sophomore, junior, or senior years; not renewable. *Amount:* $5000.

Eligibility Requirements: Applicant must be of Greek heritage; enrolled or expecting to enroll full-time at an institution or university and resident of New Hampshire, Oregon. Available to U.S. citizens.

Application Requirements: Application form, application form may be submitted online, essay, financial need analysis. *Deadline:* April 5.

Contact: Toula Bastas, Chairperson
Phone: 610-613-4310
E-mail: HucScholarship@gmail.com

DR. PETER A. THEODOS MEMORIAL GRADUATE SCHOLARSHIP

$1500 scholarship awarded to a senior undergraduate or graduate student with financial need pursuing studies leading to a Doctor of Medicine degree. Must be a U.S. citizen of Greek descent and a resident of particular counties in NJ or PA.

Award: Scholarship for use in senior or graduate years; not renewable. *Number:* 1. *Amount:* $1500.

Eligibility Requirements: Applicant must be of Greek heritage; enrolled or expecting to enroll full-time at an institution or university and resident of New Hampshire, Oregon. Available to U.S. citizens.

Application Requirements: Application form, application form may be submitted online, essay, financial need analysis. *Deadline:* April 5.

Contact: Toula Bastas, Chairperson
Phone: 610-613-4310
E-mail: HucScholarship@gmail.com

FOUNDERS SCHOLARSHIP

$5000 award for a full-time student enrolled in a degree program at an accredited four-year college or university honoring the deceased founders of the Hellenic University Club of Philadelphia. Must be a U.S. citizen of Greek descent and a resident of particular counties in NJ or PA.

Award: Scholarship for use in freshman, sophomore, junior, or senior years; not renewable. *Amount:* $5000.

Eligibility Requirements: Applicant must be of Greek heritage; enrolled or expecting to enroll full-time at an institution or university and resident of New Hampshire, Oregon. Available to U.S. citizens.

Application Requirements: Application form, application form may be submitted online, essay, financial need analysis. *Deadline:* April 5.

Contact: Toula Bastas, Chairperson
Phone: 610-613-4310
E-mail: HucScholarship@gmail.com

NICHOLAS S. HETOS, DDS, MEMORIAL GRADUATE SCHOLARSHIP

$2000 scholarships for a senior undergraduate or graduate student with financial need pursuing studies leading to a Doctor of Dental Medicine or Doctor of Dental Surgery degree. Must be a U.S. citizen of Greek descent and a resident of particular counties in NJ or PA.

Award: Scholarship for use in senior or graduate years; not renewable. *Amount:* $2000.

Eligibility Requirements: Applicant must be of Greek heritage; enrolled or expecting to enroll full-time at an institution or university and resident of New Hampshire, Oregon. Available to U.S. citizens.

Application Requirements: Application form, application form may be submitted online, essay, financial need analysis. *Deadline:* April 5.

Contact: Toula Bastas, Chairperson
Phone: 610-613-4310
E-mail: HucScholarship@gmail.com

PAIDEIA SCHOLARSHIP
• See page 440

HISPANIC ANNUAL SALUTE

http://www.hispanicannualsalute.org/

HISPANIC ANNUAL SALUTE SCHOLARSHIP
• See page 464

HISPANIC HERITAGE FOUNDATION

http://hispanicheritage.org/

HISPANIC HERITAGE FOUNDATION YOUTH AWARDS

The Hispanic Heritage Foundation's Youth Awards honors Latino high school seniors who excel in the classroom and community and for their focus in various categories including: Business & Entrepreneurship, Community Service, Education, Healthcare & Science, Media & Entertainment, Science, Technology, and Engineering, & Mathematics (STEM). Three awards for each student category are given in each of the different regions across the country. In addition, one Regional Award winning student from each category will be selected as the National Youth Award recipient in his or her respective category. Youth Awards begin with a high-profile, national search through a celebrity-based multimedia campaign that includes partnerships with more than 5,000 high schools and hundreds of colleges, media, elected officials, businesses and organizations. Approximately 13,000 applications are collected from qualified juniors who are honored as seniors in the fall. Students have an average GPA of 3.5 or higher, and are promoted as role models to inspire others and shatter negative stereotypes. Youth Awardees can receive grants for education or community projects to encourage social innovation and entrepreneurship. Eligibility: Must be graduating from an accredited high school in the Spring of 2020; Must have an un-weighted 3.0 GPA on a 4.0 scale; Must be of Hispanic Heritage including (includes Spain, Brazil, Philippines); Planning to enroll full-time in a bachelor's degree program at an accredited higher education institution in the fall directly after your graduation from high school. If selected, attendance to the regional ceremony is mandatory. Travel to the ceremony will be at the recipient's expense. Completed online application including a letter of recommendation, transcript and essay questions. Applicant must be a Permanent Resident, DACA, U.S. Citizen or Eligible Non-Citizen. For more information please see www.HispanicHeritage.org.

Award: Grant for use in freshman year; not renewable. *Number:* 190–200. *Amount:* $1000–$3500.

Eligibility Requirements: Applicant must be Hispanic; high school student and planning to enroll or expecting to enroll full-time at a two-year or four-year institution or university. Available to U.S. citizens.

Application Requirements: Application form, application form may be submitted online (https://hispanicheritage.org/), essay, recommendations or references. *Deadline:* October 15.

Contact: Brenda Camarillo, Manager of Programs
Hispanic Heritage Foundation
333 S Grand Ave.
Los Angeles, CA 90071
Phone: 323-7437339
E-mail: brenda@hispanicheritage.org

HISPANIC METROPOLITAN CHAMBER SCHOLARSHIPS

http://www.hmccoregon.com/

HISPANIC METROPOLITAN CHAMBER SCHOLARSHIPS

Scholarships to encourage Hispanics to pursue higher education. Applicant must have a minimum 3.00 GPA. The award is available only to Hispanic students from Oregon and Southwest Washington.

Award: Scholarship for use in freshman, sophomore, junior, senior, graduate, or postgraduate years; not renewable. *Number:* 45–50. *Amount:* $2000–$8000.

Eligibility Requirements: Applicant must be of Hispanic heritage; enrolled or expecting to enroll full- or part-time at a two-year or four-year institution or university and resident of Oregon. Available to U.S. and non-Canadian citizens.

Application Requirements: Application form, community service, essay. *Deadline:* January 29.

Contact: MaryAnn Potter, Scholarship Director
Hispanic Metropolitan Chamber Scholarships
PO Box 1837
Portland, OR 97207
Phone: 503-222-0280
E-mail: scholarship@hmccoregon.com

HISPANIC SCHOLARSHIP FUND

HSF.net

GREATER CINCINNATI HSF SCHOLARSHIP

These scholarships are available to support Latino students from Ohio, Kentucky, and Indiana. Awards are based on merit; amounts range from $500 to $5,000, based on relative need. For High School graduating seniors, 3.0 GPA based on 4.00 scale, 2.5 GPA for Undergraduate and 2.5 GPA for Graduate students. Must be of Hispanic heritage. All majors and graduate fields accepted.

Award: Scholarship for use in freshman, sophomore, junior, senior, or graduate years. *Amount:* $500–$5000.

Eligibility Requirements: Applicant must be Hispanic; enrolled or expecting to enroll full-time at an institution or university and resident of Illinois, Kansas, Nova Scotia. Available to U.S. citizens.

Application Requirements: Application form, application form may be submitted online, financial need analysis. *Deadline:* March 5.

Contact: Mr. Daniel Edeza, Senior Vice President, Scholarship Programs
Hispanic Scholarship Fund
1411 West 190th Street
Suite 700
Gardena, CA 90248
Phone: 310-975-3700
E-mail: scholar1@hsf.net

HISPANIC SCHOLARSHIP FUND SCHOLARSHIP

Merit-based award for U.S. citizens, permanent residents, eligible non-citizens or DACA of Hispanic heritage with plans to enroll full time in an accredited U.S. 4 year university in the upcoming academic year. Applicants must have a minimum 2.5 GPA for undergraduate and graduate students and 3.0 GPA for high school students. Must complete FAFSA or state based financial aid (if available). Must include official transcript. Award ranges from $500-$5,000 depending on need. For additional information please go to HSF.net

Award: Scholarship for use in freshman, sophomore, junior, senior, or graduate years; not renewable. *Amount:* $500–$5000.

Eligibility Requirements: Applicant must be of Hispanic heritage and enrolled or expecting to enroll full-time at an institution or university. Available to U.S. citizens.

Application Requirements: Application form, application form may be submitted online, community service, essay, financial need analysis, personal photograph. *Deadline:* February 15.

Contact: Ms. Ricardo Deleon, COO
Hispanic Scholarship Fund
1411 West 190th Street
Suite 700
Gardena, CA 90248
Phone: 310-975-3700
E-mail: scholar1@hsf.net

HOME IMPROVEMENT SOLUTIONS

http://www.myhomeimprovementsolutions.com

HOME IMPROVEMENT SCHOLARSHIP BY HOME IMPROVEMENT SOLUTIONS

Under this scholarship program, an applicant needs to write 1000-1500 words on the given topics that you can check out from our site and submit your content on our site. Then our experts will analyze the quality of the content and announce the name of the winner. Winner will win $500 as a reward

Award: Scholarship for use in freshman, sophomore, junior, senior, graduate, or postgraduate years; not renewable.

Eligibility Requirements: Applicant must be American Indian/Alaska Native, Asian/Pacific Islander, Black (non-Hispanic), Hispanic and enrolled or expecting to enroll full- or part-time at a two-year or four-year or technical institution or university.

Application Requirements: Application form. *Deadline:* December 15.

Contact: Chris Diaz, Home Improvement Solutions Scholarship
Home Improvement Solutions
2389 Joes Road
Millerton, NY 12546
Phone: 518-663-0295
E-mail: info@myhomeimprovementsolutions.com

HOMUS

https://homus.org

HOMUS SCHOLARSHIP PROGRAM

• *See page 477*

HOPI TRIBE

http://www.hopi-nsn.gov/

BUREAU OF INDIAN AFFAIRS HIGHER EDUCATION GRANT

Grant provides financial support for eligible Hopi individuals pursuing postsecondary education. Deadlines: July 15 for fall, October 15 for winter and December 15 for spring. Freshmen students (0-29 credits) 2.00 CGPA; Sophomore students (30-59 credits) 2.25 CGPA; Junior-Senior students (60 credits on up) 2.50 CGPA; Graduate/Doctoral/Professional students 3.00 CGPA

Award: Grant for use in freshman, sophomore, junior, or senior years; not renewable.

Eligibility Requirements: Applicant must be American Indian/Alaska Native and enrolled or expecting to enroll full-time at a two-year institution or university. Available to U.S. citizens.

Application Requirements: Application form, financial need analysis. *Deadline:* continuous.

HOPI EDUCATION AWARD

Grant provides financial support for eligible Hopi individuals pursuing post-secondary education. Minimum 2.00 CGPA for freshmen, 2.25 CGPA for sophomores, 2.50 CGPA for juniors and seniors and 3.00 CGPA for Graduate/Doctoral/Professional. Deadlines: December 15 for winter, July 15 for fall, and December 15 for spring.

Award: Scholarship for use in freshman, sophomore, junior, or senior years; not renewable.

Eligibility Requirements: Applicant must be American Indian/Alaska Native and enrolled or expecting to enroll full-time at a two-year institution or university. Available to U.S. citizens.

Application Requirements: Application form, financial need analysis. *Deadline:* continuous.

HOPI TRIBE GRANTS AND SCHOLARSHIP PROGRAM TUITION AND BOOK AWARD

This award assists students who are attending a regionally accredited institution at Part-time status (11-1 credit hours) or who demonstrate NO unmet need. Must be an enrolled member of the Hopi Tribe. Must have 2.00 CGPA for Freshman, 2.25 CGPA for Sophommore, 2.50 CGPA for Juniors-Seniors and 3.00 CPGA for Graduate/Doctoral/Professional students. Fall deadline on July 15, Winter on October 15, Spring on December 15

Award: Scholarship for use in freshman, sophomore, junior, senior, graduate, or postgraduate years.

Eligibility Requirements: Applicant must be American Indian/Alaska Native and enrolled or expecting to enroll part-time at a two-year institution or university. Available to U.S. citizens.

Application Requirements: Application form, financial need analysis. *Deadline:* continuous.

TRIBAL PRIORITY AWARD

Scholarship provides financial support for eligible Hopi individuals pursuing postsecondary education. Minimum 3.0 GPA required.

Award: Scholarship for use in junior or senior years; not renewable. *Number:* 1–5. *Amount:* $2500–$15,000.

Eligibility Requirements: Applicant must be American Indian/Alaska Native and enrolled or expecting to enroll full-time at a two-year or four-year institution or university. Available to U.S. citizens.

Application Requirements: Application form, financial need analysis, interview, recommendations or references, test scores, transcript, verification of Hopi Indian blood. *Deadline:* July 1.

HOUSTON COMMUNITY SERVICES

AZTECA SCHOLARSHIP

Scholarships are awarded annually to a male and a female high school senior planning to attend a university or a college as first-time, first-year students. Must be a Houston Area resident.

Award: Scholarship for use in freshman year; not renewable. *Number:* 2. *Amount:* $500.

Eligibility Requirements: Applicant must be of Hispanic heritage; high school student; planning to enroll or expecting to enroll full-time at a two-year or four-year institution or university and resident of Texas. Available to U.S. citizens.

Application Requirements: Application form, essay, personal photograph. *Deadline:* April 28.

Contact: Edward Castillo, Coordinator
Houston Community Services
5115 Harrisburg Boulevard
Houston, TX 77011
Phone: 713-926-8771
Fax: 713-926-8771
E-mail: hcsaztlan@sbcglobal.net

ILLINOIS STUDENT ASSISTANCE COMMISSION (ISAC)

http://www.isac.org/

MINORITY TEACHERS OF ILLINOIS (MTI) SCHOLARSHIP PROGRAM

Award for minority students intending to become school teachers; teaching commitment attached to receipt. Number of scholarships and the individual dollar amounts vary.

Award: Scholarship for use in freshman, sophomore, junior, senior, graduate, or postgraduate years; renewable. *Amount:* $5000.

Eligibility Requirements: Applicant must be American Indian/Alaska Native, Asian/Pacific Islander, Black (non-Hispanic), Hispanic; enrolled or expecting to enroll full-time at a two-year institution or university; resident of Idaho and studying in Illinois. Available to U.S. citizens.

Application Requirements: Application form, application form may be submitted online. *Deadline:* March 1.

Contact: ISAC Call Center Representative
Illinois Student Assistance Commission (ISAC)
1755 Lake Cook Road
Deerfield, IL 60015-5209
Phone: 800-899-4722
E-mail: isac.studentservices@illinois.gov

INDIANA COMMISSION FOR HIGHER EDUCATION

http://www.in.gov/che

WILLIAM A. CRAWFORD MINORITY TEACHER SCHOLARSHIP

The William A. Crawford Minority Teacher Scholarship is available to minority students (defined as black and Hispanic individuals) who intend to pursue, or are currently pursuing, a course of study that would enable them to teach in an accredited school in Indiana. Students must agree in writing to apply for teaching positions in Indiana and, if hired, teach in Indiana for at least three years.

Award: Scholarship for use in freshman, sophomore, junior, or senior years; not renewable.

Eligibility Requirements: Applicant must be Black (non-Hispanic), Hispanic; enrolled or expecting to enroll full-time at an institution or university; resident of Illinois and studying in Indiana. Available to U.S. citizens.

Application Requirements: Application form, application form may be submitted online. *Deadline:* August 31.

Contact: Charlee Beasor, Communications Director
Phone: 317-232-1016
E-mail: CBeasor@che.in.gov

INDIAN AMERICAN CULTURAL ASSOCIATION

http://www.iasf.org/

INDIAN AMERICAN SCHOLARSHIP FUND

Scholarships for descendants of families who are from modern-day India and are graduating from public or private high schools in Georgia. They must be enrolled in four-year colleges or universities. There are both academic and need-based awards available through this program.

Award: Scholarship for use in freshman year; renewable. *Amount:* $500–$5000.

Eligibility Requirements: Applicant must be of Indian heritage; Asian/Pacific Islander; high school student; planning to enroll or expecting to enroll full-time at a four-year institution or university and resident of Georgia. Available to U.S. citizens.

Application Requirements: Application form, essay, financial need analysis.

Contact: Rajesh Kurup, Scholarship Coordinator
E-mail: rajnina@mindspring.com

INSTITUTE OF INDUSTRIAL ENGINEERS

https://www.iise.org/

UPS SCHOLARSHIP FOR MINORITY STUDENTS

• *See page 442*

INTERNATIONAL ASSOCIATION OF BLACK ACTUARIES

www.blackactuaries.org

IABA SCHOLARSHIP

The International Association of Black Actuaries scholarship program advances its mission by providing scholarships at the undergraduate and graduate level to qualified black students who are interested in pursuing an actuarial career. IABA's mission is to contribute to an increase in the number of black actuaries and to influence the successful career development, civic growth and achievement of black actuaries.

Award: Scholarship for use in freshman, sophomore, junior, senior, or graduate years; not renewable. *Number:* 25–35. *Amount:* $3000–$5000.

Eligibility Requirements: Applicant must be Black (non-Hispanic) and enrolled or expecting to enroll full-time at a two-year or four-year institution or university. Available to U.S. and non-U.S. citizens.

Application Requirements: Application form, essay. *Deadline:* March 31.

Contact: Kate Weaver, Executive Director
E-mail: iaba@blackactuaries.org

INTERNATIONAL ORDER OF THE KING'S DAUGHTERS AND SONS

http://www.iokds.org/

INTERNATIONAL ORDER OF THE KING'S DAUGHTERS AND SONS NATIVE AMERICAN SCHOLARSHIP

Scholarships available for Native American students. Proof of reservation registration, college acceptance letter, and financial aid office address required. Merit-based award. Send self-addressed stamped envelope. Must maintain minimum 2.5 GPA.

Award: Scholarship for use in freshman, sophomore, junior, or senior years; not renewable. *Amount:* $500–$700.

Eligibility Requirements: Applicant must be American Indian/Alaska Native and enrolled or expecting to enroll full-time at a two-year or four-year or technical institution or university. Available to U.S. and Canadian citizens.

Application Requirements: Application form, essay, financial need analysis. *Deadline:* April 1.

Contact: Native American Scholarship Director
Phone: 312-799-8015
E-mail: namericanindiandirector.kds@gmail.com

ITALIAN-AMERICAN CHAMBER OF COMMERCE OF CHICAGO

http://www.iacc-chicago.com/

ITALIAN-AMERICAN CHAMBER OF COMMERCE OF CHICAGO SCHOLARSHIP

One-time awards for Illinois residents of Italian descent. Available to high school seniors and college students for use at a four-year institution. Applicants must have a 3.5 GPA. Must reside in Cook, Du Page, Kane, Lake, McHenry, or Will counties of Illinois. Must submit a letter including a biographical account of themselves and two letters of recommendation, one from a teacher and one from their counselor.

Award: Scholarship for use in freshman, sophomore, junior, or senior years; not renewable. *Number:* 1. *Amount:* up to $1000.

Eligibility Requirements: Applicant must be of Italian heritage; enrolled or expecting to enroll full-time at a four-year institution and resident of Illinois. Available to U.S. and non-U.S. citizens.

Application Requirements: Application form, essay, personal photograph, recommendations or references, self-addressed stamped envelope with application, transcript. *Deadline:* May 31.

Contact: Frank Pugno, Scholarship Chairman
Italian-American Chamber of Commerce of Chicago
30 South Michigan Avenue, Suite 504
Chicago, IL 60603
Phone: 312-553-9137 Ext. 13
Fax: 312-553-9142
E-mail: info.chicago@italchambers.net

JACKIE ROBINSON FOUNDATION

http://www.jackierobinson.org/

JACKIE ROBINSON SCHOLARSHIP
• *See page 466*

JA LIVING LEGACY

http://www.jalivinglegacy.org/

TERI AND ART IWASAKI SCHOLARSHIP

The scholarship is to support the rising costs of education. Applicant must be a descendent of a Japanese-American World War II veteran that served in the United States military units. Descendants include grandchild, great grandchild, grand niece/nephew as well as extended family.

Award: Scholarship for use in freshman year; not renewable. *Number:* 1. *Amount:* $2000.

Eligibility Requirements: Applicant must be of Japanese heritage; Asian/Pacific Islander; high school student and planning to enroll or expecting to enroll full- or part-time at an institution or university. Available to U.S. citizens.

Application Requirements: *Deadline:* continuous.

JEWISH VOCATIONAL SERVICE LOS ANGELES

http://www.jvsla.org/

JVS SCHOLARSHIP PROGRAM

Need-based scholarships to support Jewish students from Los Angeles County in their pursuit of college, graduate, and vocational education. Applicants must be Jewish, permanent residents of Los Angeles, maintain a minimum 2.7 GPA for undergraduates and 3.0 GPA for graduates, and demonstrate verifiable financial need.

Award: Scholarship for use in freshman, sophomore, junior, senior, or graduate years; not renewable. *Number:* 150–200. *Amount:* $750–$5000.

Eligibility Requirements: Applicant must be Jewish; of Jewish heritage; enrolled or expecting to enroll full-time at a two-year or four-year or technical institution or university and resident of California. Available to U.S. citizens.

Application Requirements: Application form, community service, essay, financial need analysis, interview. *Deadline:* March 31.

Contact: Patricia Sills, Scholarship Program Manager
Jewish Vocational Service Los Angeles
6505 Wilshire Boulevard, Suite 200
Los Angeles, CA 90048
Phone: 323-761-8888 Ext. 8868
E-mail: scholarship@jvsla.org

JVS CHICAGO

http://jvschicago.org/

JEWISH FEDERATION OF METROPOLITAN CHICAGO ACADEMIC SCHOLARSHIP PROGRAM

Educational scholarship funds from grants administered by the Jewish Federation of Metropolitan Chicago are available for Jewish college and graduate students. Approximately $500,000 is available each year for full-time students, predominantly those legally domiciled in the metropolitan Chicago area, with career promise in their chosen fields. Assistance is available primarily for those with FINANCIAL NEED who are pursuing careers in the helping professions.

Award: Scholarship for use in junior, senior, graduate, or postgraduate years; not renewable. *Number:* 100–125. *Amount:* $1000–$8000.

Eligibility Requirements: Applicant must be Jewish; of Jewish heritage and enrolled or expecting to enroll full-time at a four-year institution or university. Available to U.S. citizens.

Application Requirements: Application form, financial need analysis. *Deadline:* February 1.

Contact: Sally Yarberry, Scholarship Administrator
JVS Chicago
216 W. Jackson Blvd.
Suite 700
Chicago, IL 60606
Phone: 312-673-3444
E-mail: jvsscholarship@jvschicago.org

KIMBO FOUNDATION

http://www.kimbofoundation.org/

KIMBO FOUNDATION SCHOLARSHIP

Scholarship available to Korean-American students only. Full time study only. Application deadline varies every year.

Award: Scholarship for use in freshman, sophomore, junior, senior, graduate, or postgraduate years; not renewable. *Amount:* $2000.

Eligibility Requirements: Applicant must be of Korean heritage; Asian/Pacific Islander and enrolled or expecting to enroll full-time at a two-year or four-year or technical institution or university. Available to citizens of countries other than the U.S. or Canada.

Application Requirements: Application form, essay.

Contact: Jennifer Chung, Program Coordinator
Phone: 415-285-4100
Fax: 415-285-4103
E-mail: info@kimbofoundation.org

KITCHEN GUIDES

http://www.kitchensguides.com/

SMART KITCHEN IMPROVEMENT SCHOLARSHIP BY KITCHEN GUIDES

• *See page 477*

KNIGHTS OF COLUMBUS

http://www.kofc.org/

CANADIAN UNDEGRADUATE SCHOLARSHIP

• *See page 443*

KOREAN AMERICAN SCHOLARSHIP FOUNDATION

http://www.kasf.org/

KOREAN-AMERICAN SCHOLARSHIP FOUNDATION EASTERN REGION SCHOLARSHIPS

• *See page 467*

KOREAN-AMERICAN SCHOLARSHIP FOUNDATION NORTHEASTERN REGION SCHOLARSHIPS

Scholarships available to Korean-American and Korean students enrolled in a full-time undergraduate or graduate program in the United States. Selection based on financial need, academic achievement, school activities, and community services. Each applicant must submit an application to the respective KASF region. For more details and an application see website http://www.kasf.org.

Award: Scholarship for use in freshman, sophomore, junior, senior, graduate, or postgraduate years; not renewable. *Number:* 60. *Amount:* $1000–$2500.

Eligibility Requirements: Applicant must be of Korean heritage; Asian/Pacific Islander; enrolled or expecting to enroll full-time at an institution or university and studying in Connecticut, Maine, Massachusetts, New Hampshire, New Jersey, New York, Rhode Island, Vermont. Available to U.S. citizens.

Application Requirements: Application form, application form may be submitted online, essay, financial need analysis, personal photograph. *Deadline:* June 30.

Contact: Dr. Meekie Hahm, Chair, Scholarship Committee
E-mail: nerc.scholarship@kasf.org

KOREAN-AMERICAN SCHOLARSHIP FOUNDATION SOUTHERN REGION SCHOLARSHIPS

Scholarships available to Korean-American and Korean students enrolled in a full-time undergraduate or graduate program in the United States. Selection based on financial need, academic achievement, school activities, and community services. Each applicant must submit an application to the respective KASF region. For more details and an application see website http://www.kasf.org.

Award: Scholarship for use in freshman, sophomore, junior, senior, or graduate years; not renewable. *Number:* 1–45. *Amount:* $1000.

Eligibility Requirements: Applicant must be of Korean heritage; Asian/Pacific Islander; enrolled or expecting to enroll full-time at an institution or university and studying in Alabama, Arkansas, Florida, Georgia, Louisiana, Mississippi, North Carolina, Oklahoma, South Carolina, Tennessee, Texas. Available to U.S. citizens.

Application Requirements: Application form, application form may be submitted online, essay, financial need analysis, personal photograph. *Deadline:* June 30.

Contact: Dr. Meekie Hahm, Chair, Scholarship Committee
E-mail: src.scholarship@kasf.org

KOREAN-AMERICAN SCHOLARSHIP FOUNDATION WESTERN REGION SCHOLARSHIPS

Scholarships available to Korean-American and Korean students enrolled in a full-time undergraduate or graduate program in the United States. Selection based on financial need, academic achievement, school activities, and community services. Each applicant must submit an application to the respective KASF region. For more details and an application see website http://www.kasf.org.

Award: Scholarship for use in freshman, sophomore, junior, senior, or graduate years; not renewable. *Amount:* $2000.

Eligibility Requirements: Applicant must be of Korean heritage; Asian/Pacific Islander; enrolled or expecting to enroll full-time at an institution or university and studying in Alaska, Arizona, California, Colorado, Hawaii, Idaho, Montana, Nevada, New Mexico, Oregon, Utah, Washington, Wyoming. Available to U.S. citizens.

Application Requirements: Application form, application form may be submitted online, essay, financial need analysis, personal photograph. *Deadline:* June 30.

Contact: Dr. Meekie Hahm, Chair, Scholarship Committee
E-mail: wrc.scholarship@kasf.org

LANDSCAPE ARCHITECTURE FOUNDATION

www.lafoundation.org

EDSA MINORITY SCHOLARSHIP

Scholarship established to help African American, Hispanic, Native American and minority students of other cultural and ethnic backgrounds to continue their landscape architecture education as they pursue a graduate degree or enter into their final two years of undergraduate study.

Award: Scholarship for use in junior, senior, or graduate years; not renewable. *Number:* 1. *Amount:* $5000.

Eligibility Requirements: Applicant must be American Indian/Alaska Native, Asian/Pacific Islander, Black (non-Hispanic), Hispanic and enrolled or expecting to enroll full- or part-time at a four-year institution or university. Available to U.S. and non-U.S. citizens.

Application Requirements: Application form, essay, personal photograph. *Fee:* $5. *Deadline:* February 1.

Contact: Ms. Danielle Carbonneau, Program Manager, Scholarships and Leadership
Phone: 202-331-7070 Ext. 14
E-mail: scholarships@lafoundation.org

LATIN AMERICAN EDUCATIONAL FOUNDATION

http://www.laef.org/

LATIN AMERICAN EDUCATIONAL FOUNDATION SCHOLARSHIPS

Scholarship for Colorado residents of Hispanic heritage. Applicant should be accepted in an accredited college, university or vocational school. Must maintain a minimum GPA of 3.0.

Award: Scholarship for use in freshman, sophomore, junior, senior, or graduate years; renewable. *Number:* 100–120. *Amount:* $500–$2000.

Eligibility Requirements: Applicant must be of Hispanic heritage; enrolled or expecting to enroll full- or part-time at a two-year or four-year institution or university and resident of Colorado. Available to U.S. citizens.

Application Requirements: Application form, community service, essay, financial need analysis, interview, personal photograph. *Deadline:* February 15.

Contact: Karley Arguello, Scholarship Selection Committee
Latin American Educational Foundation
561 Santa Fe Drive
Denver, CO 80204
Phone: 303-446-0541 Ext. 10
E-mail: karguello@laef.org

LA UNIDAD LATINA FOUNDATION

http://www.lulf.org/

LA UNIDAD LATINA FOUNDATION DREAM SCHOLARSHIP

From the beginning our scholarship has welcomed and awarded undocumented scholars. Due to the changing political climate and increased need in the community, we launched the DREAM fund in 2015 whose focus would be on DREAMERS, DACA-mented, and undocumented scholars. Since 2015 we have awarded over $15,000 in scholarships from this fund alone.

Award: Scholarship for use in sophomore, junior, senior, graduate, or postgraduate years; not renewable. *Number:* 8–12. *Amount:* $1000.

Eligibility Requirements: Applicant must be of Hispanic, Latin American/Caribbean, Mexican, Nicaraguan heritage and enrolled or expecting to enroll full- or part-time at a two-year or four-year or technical institution or university.

Application Requirements: Application form, community service. *Deadline:* October 1.

Contact: Julio Casado, President
E-mail: lulf@lulfoundation.org

LA UNIDAD LATINA FOUNDATION NATIONAL SCHOLARSHIP

Since our founding in 1999, our flagship scholarship has awarded over $200,000 in scholarships to scholars with financial needs who have demonstrated academic excellence, exceptional leadership and a commitment to impacting the Latino community. Scholarships are available on a competitive basis to undergraduate four-year college, and graduate students who meet the following criteria and abide by the following requirements: 1. must have minimum cumulative GPA above 2.80 out of a 4.0 GPA scale; 2. cumulative GPAs below 2.80 do not qualify for a scholarship; 3. must be currently enrolled in an eligible Bachelor's or Master's degree program at an accredited four-year college or university; 4. must have completed at least one full-time year of study for undergraduate applicants; 5. must reside in the United States. Required Documentation: 1. unofficial copy of University transcript. If selected as a finalist, you will be required to submit an official University-issued transcript; 2. letter of recommendation from university administrator/faculty or community leader demonstrating student leadership and commitment to civic service. (200-350 words). Only when requested by LULF: Official university-issued academic transcript(s) required and included in application. Graduate students are required to submit graduate and undergraduate transcripts. Applications are only accepted during the application period. Letters of recommendation are to be sent electronically. Mailed letters of recommendation must be postmarked by the deadline. Do not send letters of recommendation by registered mail or another delivery service that requires a signature, as we are sometimes unavailable to sign for deliveries. You will be notified when to submit an official transcript. We accept unofficial copies of transcripts both electronically and by mail. Send electronic transcripts to LULF@lulfoundation.org. Send paper transcripts to our mailing address above listed above. Applications that do not fit all of the criteria or do not meet the above mentioned requirements will be rejected.

Award: Scholarship for use in sophomore, junior, senior, graduate, or postgraduate years; not renewable. *Number:* 10–20. *Amount:* $500–$1000.

Eligibility Requirements: Applicant must be of Hispanic, Latin American/Caribbean, Mexican, Nicaraguan heritage and enrolled or expecting to enroll full- or part-time at a two-year or four-year or technical institution or university. Available to U.S. and non-U.S. citizens.

Application Requirements: Application form, community service. *Deadline:* October 1.

Contact: Julio Casado, President
E-mail: lulf@lulfoundation.org

LEAGUE OF UNITED LATIN AMERICAN CITIZENS NATIONAL EDUCATIONAL SERVICE CENTERS INC.

http://www.lnesc.org/

LULAC NATIONAL SCHOLARSHIP FUND

Awards scholarships to Hispanic students who are enrolled or planning to enroll in accredited colleges or universities in the United States. Applicants must be U.S. citizens or legal residents. Scholarships may be used for the payment of tuition, academic fees, room, board and the purchase of required educational materials. For additional information visit website http://www.lnesc.org to see a list of participating councils or send a self-addressed stamped envelope.

Award: Scholarship for use in freshman, sophomore, junior, or senior years; not renewable. *Number:* 1,000. *Amount:* $250–$2000.

Eligibility Requirements: Applicant must be Hispanic and enrolled or expecting to enroll full-time at a two-year or four-year institution or university. Available to U.S. citizens.

Application Requirements: Application form, driver's license, essay, financial need analysis, interview, recommendations or references, self-addressed stamped envelope with application, test scores, transcript. *Deadline:* March 31.

Contact: Scholarship Coordinator
League of United Latin American Citizens National
Educational Service Centers Inc.
2000 L Street, NW, Suite 610
Washington, DC 20036
Phone: 202-835-9646
Fax: 202-835-9685

LEMBERG LAW

http://www.lemberglaw.com

LEMBERG LAW AMERICAN DREAM $1,250 UNDERGRADUATE SCHOLARSHIP

Open to students who are immigrants to the U.S. and who are U.S. citizens, (Class of 2018) who plan to enroll full-time in an accredited two-year or four-year college or university in the U.S. during the 2018-2019 school year; or undergraduate students who will be enrolled full-time in an accredited two-year or four-year college or university in the U.S. during the 2018-2019 school year. Please submit an essay (maximum of 2,000 characters, or about 400 words) about interesting differences between the U.S. legal system and that of your country of origin or another country.

Award: Scholarship for use in freshman, sophomore, junior, or senior years; not renewable. *Number:* 1. *Amount:* $1250.

Eligibility Requirements: Applicant must be of African, Albanian, Arab, Armenian, Arumanian/Ulacedo-Romanian, Australian, Belgian, Bulgarian, Canadian, Central European, Chinese, Croatian/Serbian, Cypriot, Danish, Dutch, Eastern European, English, European Union, Finnish, former Soviet Union, French, German, Greek, Haitian, Hispanic, Hungarian, Icelandic, Indian, Irish, Israeli, Italian, Japanese, Jewish, Korean, Lao/Hmong, Latin American/Caribbean, Latvian, Lebanese, Lithuanian, Mexican, Mongolian, New Zealander, Nicaraguan, Norwegian, Polish, Portuguese, Rumanian, Russian, Scandinavian, Scottish, Slavic/Czech, Spanish, Sub-Saharan African, Swedish, Swiss, Syrian, Turkish, Ukrainian, Vietnamese, Welsh, Yemeni heritage and enrolled or expecting to enroll full-time at a two-year or four-year institution or university. Available to U.S. and non-U.S. citizens.

Application Requirements: Application form, essay. *Deadline:* March 31.

Contact: Ceasar DiMauro, Scholarship Manager
E-mail: scholarship2018@lemberglaw.org

MAGIC JOHNSON FOUNDATION INC.

http://www.magicjohnson.org/

TAYLOR MICHAELS SCHOLARSHIP FUND
• See page 467

MALKI MUSEUM, INC.

http://malkimuseum.org/

MALKI MUSEUM SCHOLARSHIP

Award: Scholarship for use in freshman, sophomore, junior, senior, graduate, or postgraduate years; not renewable. *Amount:* $600.

Eligibility Requirements: Applicant must be Asian/Pacific Islander, Black (non-Hispanic), Hispanic and enrolled or expecting to enroll full- or part-time at a two-year or four-year or technical institution or university. Available to U.S. and non-U.S. citizens.

Application Requirements: Application form, application form may be submitted online (http://malkimuseum.org/scholarship/), community service, essay, financial need analysis. *Deadline:* continuous.

MANA DE SAN DIEGO

http://www.manasd.org/

MANA DE SAN DIEGO SYLVIA CHAVEZ MEMORIAL SCHOLARSHIP
• *See page 467*

MENOMINEE INDIAN TRIBE OF WISCONSIN

http://www.menominee-nsn.gov/

MENOMINEE INDIAN TRIBE ADULT VOCATIONAL TRAINING PROGRAM

Renewable award for enrolled Menominee tribal members to use at vocational or technical schools. Must be at least 1/4 Menominee and show proof of Indian blood. Must complete financial aid form.

Award: Grant for use in freshman or sophomore years; renewable.

Eligibility Requirements: Applicant must be American Indian/Alaska Native and enrolled or expecting to enroll full- or part-time at a two-year or technical institution. Available to U.S. citizens.

Application Requirements: Application form, financial need analysis.

Contact: Virginia Nuske, Education Director
Phone: 715-799-5110
E-mail: vnuske@mitw.org

MENOMINEE INDIAN TRIBE OF WISCONSIN HIGHER EDUCATION GRANTS

Renewable award for only enrolled Menominee tribal members to use at a two- or four-year college or university. Must be at least 1/4 Menominee and show proof of Indian blood. Must complete the Free Application for Federal Student Aid (FAFSA)financial aid form and demonstrate financial need.

Award: Grant for use in freshman, sophomore, junior, or senior years; renewable. *Number:* 136. *Amount:* $100–$2200.

Eligibility Requirements: Applicant must be American Indian/Alaska Native and enrolled or expecting to enroll full- or part-time at a two-year or four-year institution or university. Available to U.S. citizens.

Application Requirements: Application form, financial need analysis, proof of Indian blood. *Deadline:* continuous.

Contact: Virginia Nuske, Education Director
Menominee Indian Tribe of Wisconsin
PO Box 910
Keshena, WI 54135
Phone: 715-799-5110
Fax: 715-799-5102
E-mail: vnuske@mitw.org

THE MIAMI FOUNDATION

http://www.miamifoundation.org

RODNEY THAXTON/MARTIN E. SEGAL SCHOLARSHIP

Award available to a graduating high school senior who is African American and a Miami-Dade county area resident. Must demonstrate a commitment to social justice and have financial need. For additional information and application, visit website at http://www.dadecommunityfoundation.org.

Award: Scholarship for use in freshman year; not renewable. *Number:* 11. *Amount:* $1000.

Eligibility Requirements: Applicant must be Black (non-Hispanic); high school student; planning to enroll or expecting to enroll full-time at a four-year institution or university and resident of Florida. Available to U.S. citizens.

Application Requirements: Application form, resume, transcript. *Deadline:* April 17.

Contact: Lauren Mayfield, Programs Assistant
The Miami Foundation
40 NW 3rd Street
Miami, FL 33128
Phone: 305-371-2711
E-mail: lmayfield@miamifoundation.org

SIDNEY M. ARONOVITZ SCHOLARSHIP

Award available for minority students who are seniors at a Miami-Dade county public school or GED recipient from Miami-Dade area. Must be enrolled or planning to enroll in a college or university and plan to live and work in South Florida. Must have a minimum of 3.0 GPA. Additional information and application on website http://www.dadecommunityfoundation.org.

Award: Scholarship for use in freshman year; not renewable. *Number:* 1. *Amount:* $500.

Eligibility Requirements: Applicant must be American Indian/Alaska Native, Black (non-Hispanic), Hispanic; high school student; planning to enroll or expecting to enroll full-time at a four-year institution or university and resident of Florida. Available to U.S. citizens.

Application Requirements: Application form, financial need analysis, transcript. *Deadline:* March 20.

Contact: Lauren Mayfield, Programs Assistant
The Miami Foundation
40 NW 3rd Street
Miami, FL 33128
Phone: 305-371-2711
E-mail: lmayfield@miamifoundation.org

MINNESOTA OFFICE OF HIGHER EDUCATION

http://www.ohe.state.mn.us

MINNESOTA INDIAN SCHOLARSHIP

The Minnesota Indian Scholarship Program provides postsecondary financial assistance to eligible Minnesota resident students who are of one-fourth or more American Indian ancestry and demonstrate financial need for an award. Scholarships are available to eligible American Indian undergraduate students enrolled at least 3/4 time and graduate students enrolled at least half time. The award amount is based on need up to $4,000 per year for undergraduate students and up to $6,000 for graduate students

Award: Scholarship for use in freshman, sophomore, junior, senior, graduate, or postgraduate years; not renewable.

Eligibility Requirements: Applicant must be of Arumanian/Ulacedo-Romanian heritage; American Indian/Alaska Native; high school student; planning to enroll or expecting to enroll full- or part-time at a two-year or four-year or technical institution or university; resident of Minnesota and studying in Minnesota. Available to U.S. and Canadian citizens.

Application Requirements: Application form, financial need analysis. *Deadline:* continuous.

Contact: Meghan Flores, State Grant Manager
Minnesota Office of Higher Education
1450 Energy Park Drive, Suite 350
St. Paul, MN 55108
Phone: 651-355-0610 Ext. 2
Fax: 651-642-0675
E-mail: meghan.flores@state.mn.us

NAACP LEGAL DEFENSE AND EDUCATIONAL FUND INC.

http://www.naacpldf.org/

HERBERT LEHMAN SCHOLARSHIP PROGRAM

Renewable award for successful African-American high school seniors and freshmen to attend a four-year college on a full-time basis. Candidates are required to be U.S. citizens and must have outstanding potential as evidenced by their high school academic records, test scores, and personal essays.

Award: Scholarship for use in freshman, sophomore, junior, or senior years; renewable. *Number:* 25–30. *Amount:* $2000.

Eligibility Requirements: Applicant must be Black (non-Hispanic) and enrolled or expecting to enroll full-time at a four-year institution or university. Available to U.S. citizens.

Application Requirements: Application form, community service, essay, personal photograph, recommendations or references, resume, test scores, transcript. *Deadline:* March 31.

Contact: Program Director
NAACP Legal Defense and Educational Fund Inc.
99 Hudson Street
Suite 1600
New York, NY 10013
Phone: 212-965-2225
Fax: 212-219-1595
E-mail: scholarships@naacpldf.org

NANA (NORTHWEST ALASKA NATIVE ASSOCIATION) REGIONAL CORPORATION

http://www.nana.com/

ROBERT AQQALUK NEWLIN SR. MEMORIAL TRUST SCHOLARSHIP

Scholarship for NANA shareholders, descendants of NANA shareholders, or dependents of NANA shareholders or their descendants. Applicant must be enrolled or accepted for admittance at a postsecondary educational institution or vocational school.

Award: Scholarship for use in freshman, sophomore, junior, or senior years; not renewable.

Eligibility Requirements: Applicant must be American Indian/Alaska Native and enrolled or expecting to enroll full- or part-time at a two-year or four-year or technical institution or university. Available to U.S. citizens.

Application Requirements: Application form, financial need analysis.

Contact: Erica Nelson, Education Director
Phone: 866-442-1607
E-mail: erica.nelson@nana.org

NATIONAL ASSOCIATION FOR THE ADVANCEMENT OF COLORED PEOPLE

http://www.naacp.org/

AGNES JONES JACKSON SCHOLARSHIP

• *See page 445*

THURGOOD MARSHALL COLLEGE FUND

The Thurgood Marshall College Fund (TMCF) is proud to offer financial assistance to outstanding students attending one of TMCF's 47 publicly-supported Historically Black Colleges and Universities (HBCUs) or a Predominantly Black Institutions (PBIs). Forty-seven scholars will be selected to receive a scholarship up to $7,200 for 2020-2021 academic school year ($3,600 per semester which can only be applied to verifiable costs associated with average tuition and usual fees).

Award: Scholarship for use in freshman, sophomore, junior, or senior years; not renewable. *Number:* 47.

Eligibility Requirements: Applicant must be Black (non-Hispanic) and enrolled or expecting to enroll full-time at an institution or university. Available to U.S. citizens.

Application Requirements: Application form, application form may be submitted online, essay, financial need analysis. *Deadline:* April 27.

Contact: Victor Goode, Attorney
Phone: 410-580-5760
E-mail: info@naacp.org

NATIONAL ASSOCIATION OF COLORED WOMEN'S CLUBS

http://www.nacwc.org/

HALLIE Q. BROWN SCHOLARSHIP

One-time $1000-$2000 scholarship for high school graduates who have completed at least one semester in a postsecondary accredited institution with a minimum "C" average.

Award: Scholarship for use in freshman year; not renewable. *Number:* 4–6. *Amount:* $1000–$2000.

Eligibility Requirements: Applicant must be Black (non-Hispanic); high school student and planning to enroll or expecting to enroll full-time at a two-year or four-year institution or university. Available to U.S. citizens.

Application Requirements: Application form, recommendations or references, transcript. *Deadline:* March 30.

Contact: Dr. Gerldine Jenkins, Program Coordinator
National Association of Colored Women's Clubs
Program Coordinator
Washington, DC 20009
Phone: 202-667-4080
Fax: 202-667-2574

NATIONAL ASSOCIATION OF NEGRO BUSINESS AND PROFESSIONAL WOMEN'S CLUBS INC.

http://www.nanbpwc.org/

NATIONAL SCHOLARSHIP

Scholarship for African-American graduating high school seniors with a minimum 3.0 GPA. Must submit 300-word essay on the topic "Why Education is Important to Me."

Award: Scholarship for use in freshman year; not renewable. *Number:* 6–8. *Amount:* $500–$1000.

Eligibility Requirements: Applicant must be Black (non-Hispanic); high school student and planning to enroll or expecting to enroll full-time at a four-year institution or university. Available to U.S. citizens.

Application Requirements: Application form, community service, essay, recommendations or references, test scores, transcript. *Deadline:* March 1.

Contact: Twyla Whitby, National Director of Education Scholarship Program
National Association of Negro Business and Professional Women's Clubs Inc.
1806 New Hampshire Avenue, NW
Washington, DC 20009-3298
Phone: 202-483-4206
E-mail: info@nanbpwc.org

NATIONAL ITALIAN AMERICAN FOUNDATION

http://www.niaf.org/

NATIONAL ITALIAN AMERICAN FOUNDATION SCHOLARSHIP PROGRAM

The National Italian American Foundation Award (NIAF) offers 35 categories of scholarships to Italian-American students who have outstanding potential and high academic achievements. To be considered for the NIAF Scholarship Program, applicants must be enrolled in a US-based accredited institution of higher education, have a 3.5 GPA or above, be a US citizen or permanent resident alien and be a member of NIAF or have a parent/guardian or grandparent that is an active member. The NIAF scholarship application may only be submitted online. For further information, deadlines, additional criteria and access to the Foundation's online application visit website http://www.niaf.org/programs/scholarships-overview/

Award: Scholarship for use in freshman, sophomore, junior, senior, or graduate years; not renewable. *Number:* 40–70. *Amount:* $2500–$12,000.

Eligibility Requirements: Applicant must be of Italian heritage and enrolled or expecting to enroll full-time at a four-year institution or university. Available to U.S. citizens.

Application Requirements: Application form, application form may be submitted online (https://niaf.communityforce.com/), essay, recommendations or references, resume, transcript. *Deadline:* March 1.

Contact: NIAF Education and Culture Department
National Italian American Foundation
1860 19th Street, NW
Washington, DC 20009
Phone: 202-387-0600
E-mail: scholarships@niaf.org

NATIONAL MEDICAL FELLOWSHIPS INC.

www.nmfonline.org

THE UNITED HEALTH FOUNDATION/NMF DIVERSE MEDICAL SCHOLARS PROGRAM
• *See page 469*

NATIONAL SOCIETY DAUGHTERS OF THE AMERICAN REVOLUTION

http://www.dar.org/

DAUGHTERS OF THE AMERICAN REVOLUTION AMERICAN INDIAN SCHOLARSHIP

This scholarship is awarded to help Native American students of any age, any tribe and in any state striving to get an education at the undergraduate or graduate levels. However, undergraduate students are given preference. All awards are judged based on financial need and academic achievement. Applicants must be Native Americans (proof of American Indian blood is required by letter or proof papers) in financial need and have a grade point average of 3.25 or higher. There will be no exceptions. This is a one-time $4,000 award

Award: Scholarship for use in freshman, sophomore, junior, senior, or graduate years; not renewable. *Amount:* $4000.

Eligibility Requirements: Applicant must be American Indian/Alaska Native and enrolled or expecting to enroll full-time at a two-year or technical institution or university. Available to U.S. citizens.

Application Requirements: Application form, application form may be submitted online, essay, financial need analysis. *Deadline:* February 15.

Contact: Lakeisha Graham, Manager, Office of the Reporter General
Phone: 202-628-1776
Fax: 202-879-3348
E-mail: nsdarscholarships@dar.org

FRANCES CRAWFORD MARVIN AMERICAN INDIAN SCHOLARSHIP

This scholarship is awarded once a year to one student. A candidate for this scholarship must be enrolled full time at a 2- or 4- year college or university. Applicants must be Native Americans and proof of American Indian blood is required by letter or proof papers. Students must demonstrate financial need, academic achievement, and have a 3.25 GPA or higher. A recipient may reapply for this scholarship and be considered along with other members of the applicant pool. The amount of scholarship is based on total return of the endowment, and may vary year to year

Award: Scholarship for use in freshman, sophomore, junior, or senior years; not renewable. *Number:* 1.

Eligibility Requirements: Applicant must be American Indian/Alaska Native and enrolled or expecting to enroll full-time at a two-year institution or university. Available to U.S. citizens.

Application Requirements: Application form, application form may be submitted online, essay, financial need analysis. *Deadline:* February 15.

Contact: Lakeisha Graham, Manager, Office of the Reporter General
Phone: 202-628-1776
Fax: 202-879-3348
E-mail: nsdarscholarships@dar.org

NATIVE VISION SCHOLARSHIP

http://www.nativevision.org/

NATIVEVISION

Scholarship available to any Native American high school senior who has been accepted to college.

Award: Scholarship for use in freshman year; not renewable. *Number:* 2. *Amount:* $5000.

Eligibility Requirements: Applicant must be American Indian/Alaska Native; high school student and planning to enroll or expecting to enroll full-time at a four-year institution or university. Available to U.S. and non-U.S. citizens.

Application Requirements: Application form, community service, essay, financial need analysis, recommendations or references, transcript. *Deadline:* May 10.

Contact: Marlena Hammen, Scholarship Coordinator
Native Vision Scholarship
415 North Washington Street
4th Floor
Baltimore, MD 21231
Phone: 443-287-5167
Fax: 410-955-2010
E-mail: mhammen@jhu.edu

NEED

http://www.needld.org/

UNMET NEED GRANT PROGRAM

The program provides "last dollar" funding to lower-income students that still have a need for aid after all federal, state, local and private scholarships and grants have been secured. Must be a U.S. citizen, high school graduate, resident of one of nine participating counties in Southwestern Pennsylvania (Allegheny, Armstrong, Beaver, Butler, Fayette, Greene, Lawrence, Washington or Westmoreland county), and have a minimum 2.0 GPA.

Award: Grant for use in freshman, sophomore, junior, or senior years; not renewable. *Number:* 10–500. *Amount:* $1000–$3500.

Eligibility Requirements: Applicant must be Black (non-Hispanic); enrolled or expecting to enroll full-time at a two-year or four-year or technical institution or university and resident of Pennsylvania. Available to U.S. citizens.

Application Requirements: Application form, essay, financial need analysis, personal photograph. *Deadline:* May 31.

Contact: Mrs. Rhonda Brooks, Director of Student Services
NEED
The Law and Finance Building
429 Fourth Avenue, 20th Floor
Pittsburgh, PA 15219
Phone: 412-566-2760
Fax: 412-471-6643
E-mail: rbrooks@needld.org

NEW YORK STATE HIGHER EDUCATION SERVICES CORPORATION

http://www.hesc.ny.gov

NEW YORK STATE AID TO NATIVE AMERICANS

Award for enrolled members of a New York State tribe and their children who are attending or planning to attend a New York State college and who are New York State residents. Deadlines: July 16 for the fall semester, January 4 for the spring semester, and May 20 for summer session.

Award: Scholarship for use in freshman, sophomore, junior, or senior years; renewable. *Amount:* $85–$2000.

Eligibility Requirements: Applicant must be American Indian/Alaska Native; enrolled or expecting to enroll full- or part-time at a two-year or technical institution or university; resident of New Mexico and studying in New York. Available to U.S. citizens.

Application Requirements: Application form, financial need analysis.

NORTH CAROLINA SOCIETY OF HISPANIC PROFESSIONALS

http://www.thencshp.org/

NORTH CAROLINA HISPANIC COLLEGE FUND SCHOLARSHIP

Four-year renewable scholarship for Hispanic students. Must have graduated from a North Carolina high school within the past two years, have a four-year cumulative GPA of 2.5, and be accepted into a two- or four-year college or university. Preference is given to full-time students but part-time students may apply. Preference will be given to foreign-born applicants or native-born children of foreign-born parents. Applications are available online at http://www.thencshp.org/.

Award: Scholarship for use in freshman, sophomore, junior, or senior years; renewable. *Amount:* $500–$2500.

Eligibility Requirements: Applicant must be Hispanic; enrolled or expecting to enroll full- or part-time at a two-year or four-year institution or university and resident of North Carolina. Available to U.S. and non-U.S. citizens.

Application Requirements: Application form, application form may be submitted online (http://www.thencshp.org), transcript. *Deadline:* continuous.

Contact: Marco Zarate, President
North Carolina Society of Hispanic Professionals
8450 Chapel Hill Road, Suite 209
Cary, NC 27513
Phone: 919-467-8424
Fax: 919-469-1785
E-mail: mailbox@thencshp.org

NORTHERN CHEYENNE TRIBAL EDUCATION DEPARTMENT

http://www.cheyennenation.com

NORTHERN CHEYENNE TRIBAL EDUCATION DEPARTMENT

Scholarships are provided to enrolled Northern Cheyenne members only.

Award: Scholarship for use in freshman, sophomore, junior, senior, or graduate years; renewable. *Number:* 90. *Amount:* $100–$7000.

Eligibility Requirements: Applicant must be American Indian/Alaska Native and enrolled or expecting to enroll full- or part-time at a two-year or four-year institution or university. Available to U.S. citizens.

Application Requirements: Application form, essay, financial need analysis. *Deadline:* December 1.

Contact: Norma Bixby, Director
Northern Cheyenne Tribal Education Department
Box 307
Lame Deer, MT 59043
Phone: 406-477-6602
Fax: 406-477-8150
E-mail: norma.bixby@cheyennenation.com

OCA

http://www.ocanational.org/

OCA-UPS FOUNDATION GOLD MOUNTAIN SCHOLARSHIP

Scholarships for Asian Pacific Americans who are the first person in their immediate family to attend college. Must be entering first year of college in the upcoming fall. Please check out http//www.ocanational.org for more information.

Award: Scholarship for use in freshman, sophomore, junior, or senior years; not renewable. *Number:* 15. *Amount:* $2000.

Eligibility Requirements: Applicant must be Asian/Pacific Islander; high school student and planning to enroll or expecting to enroll full-time at a two-year or four-year institution or university. Available to U.S. citizens.

Application Requirements: Application form, essay, financial need analysis. *Deadline:* continuous.

Contact: Andrew Lo, Programs Associate
OCA
1322 18th Street, NW
Washington, DC 20036
Phone: 202-223-5500
E-mail: oca@ocanational.org

OFFICE OF NAVAJO NATION SCHOLARSHIP AND FINANCIAL ASSISTANCE

http://www.onnsfa.org/

CHIEF MANUELITO SCHOLARSHIP PROGRAM

Award programs established to recognize and award undergraduate students with high test scores and GPA of 3.0. Priorities to Navajo Nation applicants. Must be enrolled as a full-time undergraduate and pursue a degree program leading to a Baccalaureate. For further details visit website http://www.onnsfa.org/docs/polproc.pdf.

Award: Scholarship for use in freshman, sophomore, junior, or senior years; not renewable. *Number:* 1. *Amount:* $7000.

Eligibility Requirements: Applicant must be American Indian/Alaska Native and enrolled or expecting to enroll full-time at a two-year or four-year institution or university. Available to U.S. citizens.

Application Requirements: Application form, financial need analysis, test scores, transcript. *Deadline:* April 1.

Contact: Maxine Damon, Financial Aid Counselor
Phone: 800-243-2956
Fax: 928-871-6561
E-mail: maxinedamon@navajo-nsn.gov

ONEIDA TRIBE OF INDIANS OF WISCONSIN

http://www.oneida-nsn.gov

ONEIDA HIGHER EDUCATION SCHOLARSHIP PROGRAM

Renewable award available to enrolled members of the Oneida Tribe of Indians of Wisconsin, who are accepted into an accredited postsecondary institution within the United States. Must have a high school diploma, HSED or GED. Maximum funding varies based on the post-secondary costs and level of degree seeking. Please see website for more details.

Award: Grant for use in freshman, sophomore, junior, senior, graduate, or postgraduate years; renewable.

Eligibility Requirements: Applicant must be American Indian/Alaska Native and enrolled or expecting to enroll full- or part-time at a two-year or four-year or technical institution or university. Available to U.S. citizens.

Application Requirements: Application form, financial need analysis. *Deadline:* continuous.

Contact: Higher Education Advisor
Oneida Tribe of Indians of Wisconsin
PO Box 365
Oneida, WI 54155
Phone: 920-869-4033
E-mail: highered@oneidanation.org

ORDER SONS AND DAUGHTERS OF ITALY IN AMERICA

http://www.osia.org/

ORDER SONS AND DAUGHTERS OF ITALY - HENRY SALVATORI SCHOLARSHIP

Scholarships for college-bound high school seniors who demonstrate exceptional leadership, distinguished scholarship, and a deep understanding and respect for the principles upon which our nation was founded: liberty, freedom, and equality. Must be a U.S. citizen of Italian descent. For more details see website http://www.osia.org.

Award: Scholarship for use in freshman year; not renewable. *Number:* 1. *Amount:* $5000.

Eligibility Requirements: Applicant must be of Italian heritage; high school student; planning to enroll or expecting to enroll full-time at an institution or university and must have an interest in leadership. Available to U.S. citizens.

Application Requirements: Application form, application form may be submitted online, community service, essay. *Fee:* $35. *Deadline:* February 28.

Contact: Michelle Ment, Chair, Scholarship, Education and Culture
            Committee
          Order Sons and Daughters of Italy in America
          219 E St, NE
          Washington, DC 20002
          Phone: 202-547-2900
          E-mail: scholarships@osia.org

ORDER SONS AND DAUGHTERS OF ITALY IN AMERICA - GENERAL STUDY SCHOLARSHIPS

Scholarships for undergraduate or graduate students who are U.S. citizens of Italian descent. Must demonstrate academic excellence. For more details see website: http://www.osia.org.

Award: Scholarship for use in freshman, sophomore, junior, senior, or graduate years; not renewable. *Number:* 9–10. *Amount:* $4000–$10,000.

Eligibility Requirements: Applicant must be of Italian heritage and enrolled or expecting to enroll full-time at an institution or university. Available to U.S. citizens.

Application Requirements: Application form, application form may be submitted online, community service, essay. *Fee:* $35. *Deadline:* February 28.

Contact: Michelle Ment, Chair, Scholarship, Education and Culture
            Committee
          Order Sons and Daughters of Italy in America
          219 E St, NE
          Washington, DC 20002
          Phone: 202-547-2900
          E-mail: scholarships@osia.org

OREGON NATIVE AMERICAN CHAMBER OF COMMERCE SCHOLARSHIP

http://www.onacc.org/

OREGON NATIVE AMERICAN CHAMBER OF COMMERCE SCHOLARSHIP

Scholarships available to Native American students studying in Oregon. Must verify Native American status and be actively involved in the Native American community.

Award: Scholarship for use in freshman, sophomore, junior, or senior years; not renewable. *Number:* 1. *Amount:* $1000.

Eligibility Requirements: Applicant must be American Indian/Alaska Native; enrolled or expecting to enroll full- or part-time at a four-year institution or university and studying in Oregon. Available to U.S. and Canadian citizens.

Application Requirements: Application form, proof of Native American descent, transcript. *Deadline:* varies.

Contact: James Parker, Director of Operations
          Phone: 503-894-4525
          E-mail: support@onacc.org

ORTHODOX UNION

http://ou.org

SARA AND MAX GOLDSAMMLER SCHOLARSHIP FUND

This award is open to any Jewish student. Applicants should write a short essay describing in 500 to 1000 words how they have demonstrated leadership ability both in and outside of school.

Award: Scholarship for use in freshman, sophomore, junior, or senior years; not renewable. *Number:* 3. *Amount:* $300–$1000.

Eligibility Requirements: Applicant must be Jewish; of Jewish heritage and enrolled or expecting to enroll full- or part-time at a two-year or four-year or technical institution or university. Available to U.S. citizens.

Application Requirements: Application form, essay. *Deadline:* August 10.

Contact: Mrs. Rachel Shammah, Alumni Assistant
          Orthodox Union
          11 Broadway
          New York, NY 10004
          Phone: 212-613-8155
          E-mail: shammahr@ncsy.org

OSAGE NATION EDUCATION DEPARTMENT

https://www.osagenation-nsn.gov/what-we-do/education-department

OSAGE NATION HIGHER EDUCATION SCHOLARSHIP

The Osage Nation provides scholarships to legally enrolled members of the Osage Nation who are attending colleges and universities throughout the United States and abroad. The annual qualifying application opens on May 15th and closes on June 15th of each year.

Award: Scholarship for use in freshman, sophomore, junior, senior, graduate, or postgraduate years; renewable. *Number:* 1–1,200. *Amount:* $150–$5000.

Eligibility Requirements: Applicant must be American Indian/Alaska Native and enrolled or expecting to enroll full- or part-time at a two-year or four-year institution or university. Available to U.S. citizens.

Application Requirements: Application form. *Deadline:* June 15.

Contact: Katie May, Program Manager
          Osage Nation Education Department
          Scholarship Management Services
          One Scholarship Way
          Saint Peter, MN 56082
          Phone: 855-758-8609
          E-mail: OsageNation@scholarshipamerica.org

PETAZI

https://petazi.com/

2017 NURTURE FOR NATURE SCHOLARSHIP
• *See page 483*

PETER DOCTOR MEMORIAL INDIAN SCHOLARSHIP FOUNDATION INC.

PETER DOCTOR MEMORIAL INDIAN SCHOLARSHIP FOUNDATION INC.

One-time award available to enrolled New York State Iroquois Indian students. Must be a full-time student at the Freshman level and above.

Award: Scholarship for use in freshman, sophomore, junior, senior, or graduate years; not renewable. *Number:* 2. *Amount:* $700–$1500.

Eligibility Requirements: Applicant must be American Indian/Alaska Native; enrolled or expecting to enroll full-time at a two-year or four-year or technical institution or university and resident of New York. Available to U.S. citizens.

Application Requirements: Application form, driver's license, financial need analysis, recommendations or references, tribal certification. *Deadline:* May 31.

Contact: Clara Hill, Treasurer
          Peter Doctor Memorial Indian Scholarship Foundation Inc.
          PO Box 431
          Basom, NY 14013
          Phone: 716-542-2025
          E-mail: ceh3936@hughes.net

PHILIPINO-AMERICAN ASSOCIATION OF NEW ENGLAND

http://www.pamas.org/

BLESSED LEON OF OUR LADY OF THE ROSARY AWARD

Award for any Filipino-American high school student. Must be of Filipino descent, and have a minimum GPA of 3.3. Application details are available at http://www.pamas.org.

Award: Scholarship for use in freshman year; not renewable. *Number:* 1. *Amount:* $250.

Eligibility Requirements: Applicant must be Asian/Pacific Islander; high school student; planning to enroll or expecting to enroll full-time at a two-year or four-year or technical institution or university and resident of Connecticut, Maine, Massachusetts, New Hampshire, Rhode Island, Vermont. Available to U.S. citizens.

Application Requirements: Application form, college acceptance letter, essay, recommendations or references, transcript. *Deadline:* May 31.

Contact: Amanda Kalb, First Vice President
　　　Phone: 617-471-3513
　　　E-mail: balic2ss@comcast.net

PAMAS RESTRICTED SCHOLARSHIP AWARD
• *See page 450*

RAVENSCROFT FAMILY AWARD

Award for any Filipino-American high school student, who is active in the Filipino community. Must be of Filipino descent, a resident of New England, and have a minimum GPA of 3.3. Application details are available at http://www.pamas.org.

Award: Scholarship for use in freshman year; not renewable. *Number:* 1. *Amount:* $250.

Eligibility Requirements: Applicant must be Asian/Pacific Islander; high school student; planning to enroll or expecting to enroll full-time at a four-year institution or university and resident of Connecticut, Maine, Massachusetts, New Hampshire, Rhode Island, Vermont. Available to U.S. citizens.

Application Requirements: Application form, college acceptance letter, essay, recommendations or references, transcript. *Deadline:* May 31.

Contact: Amanda Kalb, First Vice President
　　　Phone: 617-471-3513
　　　E-mail: balic2ss@comcast.net

POLISH HERITAGE ASSOCIATION OF MARYLAND

http://www.pha-md.org/

POLISH HERITAGE SCHOLARSHIP

$2500 scholarships given to individuals of Polish descent (at least two Polish grandparents) who demonstrates academic excellence, financial need, and promotes their Polish Heritage. Must be a legal Maryland resident.

Award: Scholarship for use in freshman, sophomore, junior, or senior years; not renewable. *Number:* 1–9. *Amount:* $1500–$2500.

Eligibility Requirements: Applicant must be of Polish heritage; enrolled or expecting to enroll full-time at a two-year or four-year institution or university and resident of Maryland. Available to U.S. citizens.

Application Requirements: Application form, essay, financial need analysis, interview, recommendations or references, transcript. *Deadline:* March 15.

Contact: Thomas Hollowak, Scholarship Chair
　　　Phone: 410-837-4268
　　　E-mail: thollowalk@ubmail.ubalt.edu

PORTUGUESE AMERICAN LEADERSHIP COUNCIL OF THE UNITED STATES

http://www.palcus.org

PALCUS NATIONAL SCHOLARSHIP PROGRAM

PALCUS has established a merit-based scholarship program to support outstanding undergraduate and graduate college students of Portuguese ancestry toward fulfilling their higher education goals. Visit www.palcus.org/scholarship for details.

Award: Scholarship for use in sophomore, junior, senior, or graduate years; not renewable. *Number:* 4. *Amount:* $1000.

Eligibility Requirements: Applicant must be of Portuguese heritage and enrolled or expecting to enroll full-time at a four-year institution or university. Available to U.S. citizens.

Application Requirements: Application form, community service, essay. *Deadline:* July 31.

Contact: Mrs. Gracielle Camilo, Executive Assistant
　　　Portuguese American Leadership Council of the United States
　　　9255 Center St., Suite 404
　　　Manassas, VA 20110
　　　Phone: 202-466-4664
　　　E-mail: palcus@palcus.org

PRESBYTERIAN CHURCH (USA)

https://www.presbyterianmission.org/

NATIVE AMERICAN SUPPLEMENTAL GRANT

Award up to $2,000 for Undergrad students who are registered Members of a Native American Tribe. Students must be members of a PC(USA) church.

Award: Grant for use in freshman, sophomore, junior, or senior years; not renewable.

Eligibility Requirements: Applicant must be Presbyterian; American Indian/Alaska Native and enrolled or expecting to enroll full-time at an institution or university. Available to U.S. citizens.

Application Requirements: Application form, application form may be submitted online, essay, financial need analysis. *Deadline:* May 15.

Contact: Ms. Laura Bryan, Coordinator, Financial Aid for Studies
　　　Presbyterian Church (USA)
　　　100 Witherspoon Street
　　　Louisville, KY 40202
　　　Phone: 800-728-7228 Ext. 5735
　　　Fax: 502-569-8766
　　　E-mail: finaid@pcusa.org

PUEBLO OF ISLETA, DEPARTMENT OF EDUCATION

http://www.isletapueblo.com/

HIGHER EDUCATION SUPPLEMENTAL SCHOLARSHIP ISLETA PUEBLO HIGHER EDUCATION DEPARTMENT
• *See page 451*

PUEBLO OF SAN JUAN, DEPARTMENT OF EDUCATION

OHKAY OWINGEH TRIBAL SCHOLARSHIP
• *See page 470*

POP'AY SCHOLARSHIP
• *See page 470*

RON BROWN SCHOLAR FUND

http://www.ronbrown.org/

RON BROWN SCHOLAR PROGRAM

The program seeks to identify African-American high school seniors who will make significant contributions to the society. Applicants must excel academically, show exceptional leadership potential, participate in community service activities, and demonstrate financial need. Must be a U.S. citizen or hold permanent resident visa. Must plan to attend a four-year college or university. Deadlines: November 1 and January 9.

Award: Scholarship for use in freshman, sophomore, junior, or senior years; renewable. *Number:* 10–20. *Amount:* $10,000–$40,000.

Eligibility Requirements: Applicant must be Black (non-Hispanic); high school student and planning to enroll or expecting to enroll full-time at a four-year institution or university. Available to U.S. citizens.

Application Requirements: Application form, community service, essay, financial need analysis, interview, personal photograph, recommendations or references, test scores, transcript. *Deadline:* January 9.

Contact: Ms. Vanessa Evans-Grevious, Vice President
Ron Brown Scholar Fund
485 Hillsdale Drive
Suite 206
Charlottesville, VA 22901
Phone: 434-964-1588
E-mail: info@ronbrown.org

RYU FAMILY FOUNDATION, INC.

http://www.ryufoundation.org/

SEOL BONG SCHOLARSHIP

A Korean-American (US citizen) or a Korean (with or without the permanent resident status), is currently enrolled as a full-time student working for a degree, such as, BA, BS, MA, MS, MBA, JD, MD, DDS, Ph.D., etc, at a legally approved college or university located in any one of the following 12 northeastern states of the United States: Connecticut, D.C., Delaware, Maine, Maryland, Massachusetts, New Hampshire, New Jersey, New York, Pennsylvania, Rhode Island, and Vermont.

Award: Scholarship for use in freshman, sophomore, junior, senior, graduate, or postgraduate years; not renewable. *Number:* 20. *Amount:* $2000.

Eligibility Requirements: Applicant must be of Korean heritage; Asian/Pacific Islander; enrolled or expecting to enroll full-time at a four-year institution or university; resident of Connecticut, Delaware, Maine, Massachusetts, New Hampshire, New Jersey, New York, Pennsylvania, Rhode Island, Vermont and studying in Connecticut, Delaware, Maine, Massachusetts, New Hampshire, New Jersey, New York, Pennsylvania, Rhode Island, Vermont. Available to U.S. and non-Canadian citizens.

Application Requirements: Application form, essay, financial need analysis, personal photograph, portfolio, recommendations or references, resume, test scores, transcript. *Deadline:* October 12.

Contact: Jenny Kang, Scholarship Secretary
Phone: 973-692-9696 Ext. 20
E-mail: jennyk@toplineus.com

SAINT ANDREW'S SOCIETY OF THE STATE OF NEW YORK

http://www.standrewsny.org/

ST. ANDREWS OF THE STATE OF NEW YORK GRADUATE SCHOLARSHIP PROGRAM

Scholarship for senior undergraduate students who will obtain a bachelor's degree from an accredited college or university in the spring and can demonstrate the significance of studying in Scotland. Proof of application to their selected school will be required for finalists. Applicant must be of Scottish descent. Applicant must be endorsed by College/University.

Award: Scholarship for use in senior year; not renewable. *Number:* 3. *Amount:* $35,000.

Eligibility Requirements: Applicant must be of Scottish heritage and enrolled or expecting to enroll full-time at a four-year institution or university. Available to U.S. citizens.

Application Requirements: Application form, essay, financial need analysis, recommendations or references, transcript. *Deadline:* December 15.

Contact: Samuel Abernethy, Scholarship Committee, Chairman

ST. ANDREW'S SOCIETY OF WASHINGTON, DC

http://www.saintandrewsociety.org/

ST. ANDREW'S SOCIETY OF WASHINGTON DC FOUNDERS' SCHOLARSHIP

In honor of the 250th Anniversary of our St. Andrew's Society's 18th c. founding, the Society has established The St. Andrew's Society Founders' Prize. Made possible by generous donations in the name of

James & Mary Dawson and Donald Malcolm MacArthur, this Scholarship is an annual award in the amount of $7,500 made to an outstanding Scottish or Scottish-American scholar. It is available for US students of Scottish descent or UK students born in Scotland to study in the UK or in the United States. Special attention will be given to applicants whose work would demonstrably contribute to enhanced knowledge of Scottish history or culture. Must be a college junior, senior, or graduate student to apply. Need for financial assistance and academic record considered. Visit website for details and application.

Award: Scholarship for use in junior, senior, or graduate years; not renewable. *Number:* 1. *Amount:* $7500.

Eligibility Requirements: Applicant must be of Scottish heritage; enrolled or expecting to enroll full-time at a four-year institution or university and resident of Delaware, District of Columbia, Maryland, New Jersey, North Carolina, Pennsylvania, Virginia, West Virginia. Available to U.S. and non-Canadian citizens.

Application Requirements: Application form, application form may be submitted online (http://www.saintandrewsociety.org/scholarships/application/), essay, financial need analysis. *Deadline:* April 30.

Contact: T.J. Holland, Chairman, Scholarships Committee
E-mail: scholarships@saintandrewsociety.org

ST. ANDREW'S SOCIETY OF WASHINGTON DC SCHOLARSHIPS

The St. Andrew's Society of Washington DC Scholarships Program awards are available for US students of Scottish descent or UK students born in Scotland to study in the UK or in the United States. Special attention will be given to applicants whose work would demonstrably contribute to enhanced knowledge of Scottish history or culture. Must be a college junior, senior, or graduate student to apply. Need for financial assistance and academic record considered. Visit website for details and application.

Award: Scholarship for use in junior, senior, or graduate years; not renewable. *Number:* 1–8. *Amount:* $500–$15,000.

Eligibility Requirements: Applicant must be of Scottish heritage; enrolled or expecting to enroll full-time at a four-year institution or university and resident of Delaware, District of Columbia, Maryland, New Jersey, North Carolina, Pennsylvania, Virginia, West Virginia. Available to U.S. and non-Canadian citizens.

Application Requirements: Application form, application form may be submitted online (http://www.saintandrewsociety.org/scholarships/application/), essay, financial need analysis. *Deadline:* April 30.

Contact: Mr. T.J. Holland, Chairman, Scholarships Committee
E-mail: scholarships@saintandrewsociety.org

SALVADORAN AMERICAN LEADERSHIP AND EDUCATIONAL FUND

http://www.salef.org/

FULFILLING OUR DREAMS SCHOLARSHIP FUND

Up to 60 scholarships ranging from $500 to $2500 will be awarded to students who come from a Latino heritage. Must have a 2.5 GPA. See website for more details, http://www.salef.org.

Award: Scholarship for use in freshman, sophomore, junior, senior, graduate, or postgraduate years; not renewable. *Number:* 50–60. *Amount:* $500–$2500.

Eligibility Requirements: Applicant must be of Hispanic, Latin American/Caribbean heritage; enrolled or expecting to enroll full- or part-time at a two-year or four-year institution or university; resident of California and studying in California. Available to U.S. and non-U.S. citizens.

Application Requirements: Application form, community service, essay, financial need analysis, interview, personal photograph, recommendations or references, resume, self-addressed stamped envelope with application, test scores, transcript. *Deadline:* June 30.

Contact: Mayra Soriano, Educational and Youth Programs Manager
Salvadoran American Leadership and Educational Fund
1625 West Olympic Boulevard, Suite 718
Los Angeles, CA 90015
Phone: 213-480-1052
Fax: 213-487-2530
E-mail: msoriano@salef.org

SANTO DOMINGO SCHOLARSHIP PROGRAM

SANTO DOMINGO SCHOLARSHIP

An organization instituted for the welfare of the Santo Domingo Pueblo enrolled members. Santo Domingo Tribe—Education Office offers scholarships in Higher Education and Adult Education. To be considered an applicant, you must fill out an application. Deadlines: Fall semester—March 1 and Spring semester—October 1.

Award: Scholarship for use in freshman, sophomore, junior, or senior years; renewable. *Amount:* $200–$1000.

Eligibility Requirements: Applicant must be American Indian/Alaska Native and enrolled or expecting to enroll full- or part-time at a two-year or four-year or technical institution or university. Available to U.S. citizens.

Application Requirements: Application form, certificate of Indian blood, financial need analysis, recommendations or references, transcript. *Deadline:* varies.

Contact: Rita Lujan, Education Director
Santo Domingo Scholarship Program
PO Box 160
Santo Domingo Pueblo, NM 87052
Phone: 505-465-2214 Ext. 2211
Fax: 505-465-2542
E-mail: rlujan@kewa-nsn.us

SLEEP SHERPA

SLEEP SHERPA SCHOLARSHIP PROGRAM
• See page 484

SNOW, CARPIO & WEEKLEY, PLC

http://workinjuryaz.com

SCW DREAMERS SCHOLARSHIP

Must be a DREAMer with a GPA of 3.0 or higher. This is a video submission scholarship. For all requirements and more info please visit our website http://workinjuryaz.com/tucson-social-security-disability-attorneys/#dreamers. Only submissions on our website will be considered.

Award: Scholarship for use in freshman or sophomore years; not renewable. *Number:* 2. *Amount:* $2500.

Eligibility Requirements: Applicant must be of Hispanic heritage; age 16-25 and enrolled or expecting to enroll full- or part-time at a two-year or four-year institution or university. Available to U.S. and non-U.S. citizens.

Application Requirements: Application form. *Deadline:* May 31.

Contact: April Snow
E-mail: snowcarpioaz@gmail.com

SOCIETY FOR APPLIED ANTHROPOLOGY

http://www.appliedanthro.org/

BEATRICE MEDICINE AWARDS

The Society for Applied Anthropology honors the memory of Dr. Beatrice Medicine with an annual student travel scholarship for Native Americans/First Nations. The scholarship provides financial support for two students (graduate or undergraduate) to attend the annual meeting of the Society. Two awards ($500 each) will be made to attend the Annual Meeting of the SfAA.

Award: Prize for use in freshman, sophomore, junior, senior, or graduate years; not renewable. *Number:* 2. *Amount:* $500.

Eligibility Requirements: Applicant must be American Indian/Alaska Native and enrolled or expecting to enroll full- or part-time at a two-year or four-year institution or university. Available to U.S. and non-U.S. citizens.

Application Requirements: Application form, essay. *Deadline:* December 20.

Contact: Trish Colvin, Office Manager
Society for Applied Anthropology
PO Box 2436
Oklahoma City, OK 73101
Phone: 405-843-5113
Fax: 405-843-8553
E-mail: info@appliedanthro.org

SONS OF ITALY FOUNDATION

https://www.osia.org/programs/scholarships/

GENERAL STUDY SCHOLARSHIPS

Through the Sons of Italy Foundation (SIF), and hundreds of thousands of family members located in all fifty states and the District of Columbia, the Order Sons and Daughters of Italy in America (OSDIA) has awarded nearly $61 million in scholarships to date. In past years, the SIF has offered 10 to 12 merit-based scholarships (National Leadership Grants), ranging from $4,000 to $25,000, in a nationwide competition. These figures and the number of scholarships may vary according to funding each year. A number of General Study Scholarships are available. Only one application is required to be eligible for all General Study Scholarships.

Award: Scholarship for use in freshman, sophomore, junior, senior, graduate, or postgraduate years; not renewable. *Number:* 6–12. *Amount:* $4000–$25,000.

Eligibility Requirements: Applicant must be of Italian heritage and enrolled or expecting to enroll full-time at a four-year institution or university. Available to U.S. citizens.

Application Requirements: Application form, essay. *Fee:* $35. *Deadline:* February 28.

Contact: Carly Jerome, Director of Programming
Sons of Italy Foundation
219 E Street NE
Washington, DC 20002
Phone: 202-547-2900
E-mail: scholarships@osia.org

HENRY SALVATORI SCHOLARSHIP FOR GENERAL STUDY

Through the Sons of Italy Foundation (SIF), and hundreds of thousands of family members located in all fifty states and the District of Columbia, the Order Sons and Daughters of Italy in America (OSDIA) has awarded nearly $61 million in scholarships to date. In past years, the SIF has offered 10 to 12 merit-based scholarships (National Leadership Grants), ranging from $4,000 to $25,000, in a nationwide competition. These figures and the number of scholarships may vary according to funding each year. Established by the late philanthropist and businessman for whom it is named, the Henry Salvatori Scholarship for General Study is a grant awarded to a college-bound high school senior who demonstrates exceptional leadership, distinguished scholarship, and a deep understanding and respect for the principles upon which our nation was founded: liberty, freedom, and equality.

Award: Scholarship for use in freshman year; not renewable. *Number:* 1. *Amount:* $4000–$25,000.

Eligibility Requirements: Applicant must be of Italian heritage; high school student and planning to enroll or expecting to enroll full-time at a four-year institution. Available to U.S. citizens.

Application Requirements: Application form, essay. *Fee:* $35. *Deadline:* February 28.

Contact: Carly Jerome, Director of Programming
Sons of Italy Foundation
219 E Street NE
Washington, DC 20002
Phone: 202-547-2900
E-mail: scholarships@osia.org

SOURCE SUPPLY COMPANY

http://sourcesupplycompany.com/

SOURCE SUPPLY SCHOLARSHIP

To apply for the 2014-2015 Source Supply Scholarship, respond to the following essay prompt in 1,000 words: Please discuss the importance of keeping the environment clean. How does recycling make an impact on the environment? And how can the systems we, as a nation, have in place be improved? To be eligible, please email your essay to info@sourcesupplycompany.com by May 31, 2015. Please be sure to reference Source Supply College Scholarship Essay Content in the subject line of your email.

Award: Scholarship for use in freshman, sophomore, or junior years; not renewable. *Number:* up to 1. *Amount:* $1000–$1000.

Eligibility Requirements: Applicant must be American Indian/Alaska Native, Asian/Pacific Islander, Black (non-Hispanic), Hispanic and enrolled or expecting to enroll full-time at a two-year or four-year or technical institution or university. Available to U.S. citizens.

Application Requirements: Entry in a contest, essay. *Deadline:* May 31.

Contact: Dave Brown, Owner
Source Supply Company
6 Bellecor Drive
Suite 104
New Castle, PA 19720
Phone: 302-328-5110
E-mail: Info@SourceSupplyCompany.com

STRAIGHTFORWARD MEDIA

http://www.straightforwardmedia.com/

STRAIGHTFORWARD MEDIA MINORITY SCHOLARSHIP

Four scholarships a year offered to students who are members of racial or ethnic minority groups and who are currently enrolled in or planning to enroll in postsecondary education. For more information, see website at http://www.straightforwardmedia.com/minority/form.php.

Award: Scholarship for use in freshman, sophomore, junior, or senior years; not renewable. *Number:* 4. *Amount:* $500.

Eligibility Requirements: Applicant must be American Indian/Alaska Native, Asian/Pacific Islander, Black (non-Hispanic), Hispanic and enrolled or expecting to enroll full- or part-time at a two-year or four-year or technical institution or university. Available to U.S. and non-U.S. citizens.

Application Requirements: Essay. *Deadline:* varies.

Contact: Scholarship Committee
Phone: 605-348-3042

SWISS BENEVOLENT SOCIETY

http://www.sbssf.com/

SWISS BENEVOLENT SOCIETY OF SAN FRANCISCO SCHOLARSHIPS

The Swiss Benevolent Society helps qualified applicants obtain a higher education in any field of endeavor at any accredited university or college in the United States. The scholarships are limited to students who are residents of Northern California. Students may apply every year while enrolled. Applicants must be of Swiss descent by demonstrating that applicant or at least one parent is a Swiss national; must be registered with the Swiss Consulate General of San Francisco (or carry a valid Swiss passport); must have resided in Northern California for a minimum of three years preceding the date of initial application; must have applied for admission to any accredited institution of higher learning in the United States offering a Baccalaureate or graduate degree. (In exceptional cases, students attending a community college or an accredited vocational school in California may be considered); and must be a full time student, 12 undergraduate or 9 graduate units per term. Additional requirements regarding scholastic merit and financial need, as well as the application form and guidelines, are available on the SBSSF website. Only complete applications, including all supporting documents, postmarked no later than April 30th, can be considered.

Award: Scholarship for use in freshman, sophomore, junior, senior, graduate, or postgraduate years; renewable. *Amount:* $2000–$4500.

Eligibility Requirements: Applicant must be of Swiss heritage; enrolled or expecting to enroll full-time at a two-year or four-year or technical institution or university and resident of California.

Application Requirements: Application form, essay, financial need analysis, recommendations or references, test scores, transcript. *Deadline:* April 30.

Contact: John Andrew, Scholarship Committee Chair
Swiss Benevolent Society
Pier 17, Suite 600
San Francisco, CA 94111
E-mail: scholarships@sbssf.com

SWISS BENEVOLENT SOCIETY OF CHICAGO

http://www.sbschicago.org/

SWISS BENEVOLENT SOCIETY OF CHICAGO SCHOLARSHIPS

Scholarship for undergraduate college students of Swiss descent, having permanent residence in Illinois or Southern Wisconsin. Must have 3.3 GPA. High school students need a 26 on ACT or 1050 on SAT.

Award: Scholarship for use in freshman, sophomore, or junior years; not renewable. *Number:* 30. *Amount:* $500–$2500.

Eligibility Requirements: Applicant must be of Swiss heritage; enrolled or expecting to enroll full-time at a four-year institution or university and resident of Illinois, Wisconsin. Available to U.S. citizens.

Application Requirements: Application form, essay. *Deadline:* April 15.

Contact: John Paluch, Chair
Swiss Benevolent Society of Chicago
PO Box 2137
Chicago, IL 60690-2137
Phone: 847-491-8081
E-mail: education@sbschicago.org

SWISS BENEVOLENT SOCIETY OF NEW YORK

http://www.sbsny.org/

MEDICUS STUDENT EXCHANGE

One-time award to students of Swiss nationality or parentage. Open to U.S. residents for study in Switzerland and to Swiss residents for study in the U.S. Must be proficient in foreign language of instruction.

Award: Grant for use in junior, senior, or graduate years; not renewable. *Number:* 1–10. *Amount:* $2000–$10,000.

Eligibility Requirements: Applicant must be of Swiss heritage; enrolled or expecting to enroll full-time at a four-year institution or university and must have an interest in foreign language. Available to U.S. and non-Canadian citizens.

Application Requirements: Application form. *Fee:* $75. *Deadline:* March 31.

Contact: Scholarship Committee
Swiss Benevolent Society of New York
500 Fifth Avenue, Suite 1800
New York, NY 10110
Phone: 212-246-0655

PELLEGRINI SCHOLARSHIP GRANTS

Award to students who have a minimum 3.0 GPA and show financial need. Must submit proof of Swiss nationality or descent. Must be a permanent resident of Connecticut, Delaware, New Jersey, New York, or Pennsylvania.

Award: Scholarship for use in freshman, sophomore, junior, senior, or graduate years; not renewable. *Number:* 50. *Amount:* $500–$5000.

Eligibility Requirements: Applicant must be of Swiss heritage; enrolled or expecting to enroll full-time at a two-year or four-year or technical institution or university and resident of Connecticut, Delaware, New Jersey, New York, Pennsylvania. Available to U.S. citizens.

Application Requirements: Application form, financial need analysis. *Fee:* $75. *Deadline:* March 31.

Contact: Scholarship Committee
Swiss Benevolent Society of New York
500 Fifth Avenue, Room 1800
New York, NY 10110
Phone: 212-246-0655

TERRY FOX HUMANITARIAN AWARD

http://terryfoxawards.ca/

TERRY FOX HUMANITARIAN AWARD
• *See page 470*

TEXAS BLACK BAPTIST SCHOLARSHIP COMMITTEE

http://www.bgct.org/

TEXAS BLACK BAPTIST SCHOLARSHIP

Renewable award for Texas residents attending a Baptist educational institution in Texas. Must be of African-American descent with a minimum 2.0 GPA. Must be a member in good standing of a Baptist church.

Award: Scholarship for use in freshman, sophomore, junior, or senior years; renewable. *Amount:* $1600.

Eligibility Requirements: Applicant must be Baptist; Black (non-Hispanic); age 18 and over; enrolled or expecting to enroll full- or part-time at a two-year or four-year institution or university; resident of Texas and studying in Texas. Available to U.S. citizens.

Application Requirements: Application form, driver's license, financial need analysis, interview, personal photograph, portfolio, recommendations or references, resume, test scores, transcript. *Deadline:* continuous.

Contact: Charlie Singleton, Director
Phone: 214-828-5130
Fax: 214-828-5284
E-mail: charlie.singleton@bgct.org

TITAN WEB AGENCY

THE TITAN WEB AGENCY BI-ANNUAL SCHOLARSHIP PROGRAM
• *See page 484*

TRANSTUTORS

http://www.transtutors.com/scholarship

TRANSTUTORS SCHOLARSHIP 2017-18

Transtutors scholarship program wants to help students get aids for their studies. We really value good education for all. We have a very simple criteria of writing an essay on your college experience, how do you see it changing and what can be done so that you get best experience. Check more information at: http://www.transtutors.com/scholarship/

Award: Scholarship for use in freshman, sophomore, junior, senior, graduate, or postgraduate years; renewable. *Number:* 3. *Amount:* $1000.

Eligibility Requirements: Applicant must be American Indian/Alaska Native, Asian/Pacific Islander, Black (non-Hispanic), Hispanic; age 13 and over and enrolled or expecting to enroll full- or part-time at a two-year or four-year institution or university. Available to U.S. and non-U.S. citizens.

Application Requirements: Essay, personal photograph. *Deadline:* November 30.

Contact: Aditya Singhal, Co-Founder
Transtutors
500startups
6th Floor Del Norte, 814 Mission Street
San Francisco, CA 94103
Phone: 415-619-1033
E-mail: aditya.singhal@transtutors.com

UNITED NEGRO COLLEGE FUND

http://www.uncf.org/

ABCNJ LEADERSHIP IMPACT SCHOLARSHIP

This scholarship program has been created to provide two merit-based scholarships (one male and one female) in the amount of $2,250 to entering college freshmen who are active members of a congregation which is in covenant with the American Baptist Churches of New Jersey (ABCNJ) member churches and who will attend any accredited four year college or university.

Award: Scholarship for use in freshman year; not renewable. *Number:* 2. *Amount:* $2250.

Eligibility Requirements: Applicant must be Baptist; Black (non-Hispanic); enrolled or expecting to enroll full-time at a four-year institution or university and resident of Florida, New Jersey, New York. Available to U.S. citizens.

Application Requirements: Application form, essay. *Deadline:* July 9.

Contact: Larry Griffith, Senior Vice President, Programs and Student Services
Phone: 800-331-2244

BLANCHE FORD ENDOWMENT SCHOLARSHIP FUND

The Blanche Ford Endowment Scholarship Fund was established in memory of Blanche Elizabeth Ford as a tribute to the love, grace, and compassion that she exemplified. The Fund provides up to $10,000 need-based scholarship awards renewable through university graduation. Applicant must be a sophomore at one of the 37 UNCF member institutions, have unmet financial need and evidence of community service commitment/involvement.

Award: Scholarship for use in junior year; renewable.

Eligibility Requirements: Applicant must be Black (non-Hispanic) and enrolled or expecting to enroll full-time at a four-year institution or university. Available to U.S. citizens.

Application Requirements: Application form, essay, financial need analysis. *Deadline:* May 29.

Contact: Larry Griffith, Senior Vice President, Programs and Student Services
Phone: 800-331-2244

BOULE' FOUNDATION SCHOLARSHIP

Annual $4000 merit-based scholarship for entering college freshmen. Must be a citizen or permanent resident of the United States, a resident of London, England, or a citizen of the Bahamas.

Award: Scholarship for use in freshman year; renewable. *Number:* up to 4,000.

Eligibility Requirements: Applicant must be Black (non-Hispanic) and enrolled or expecting to enroll at a four-year institution or university. Available to U.S. and non-U.S. citizens.

Application Requirements: Application form, application form may be submitted online, essay, participation in extra-curricular activities, academic/civic honors and awards, community service, recommendations or references. *Deadline:* March 31.

Contact: Larry Griffith, Senior Vice President, Programs and Student Services
Phone: 800-331-2244

CITY OF CHICAGO SCHOLARSHIP

Scholarship directed to students who are dependents of current or retired employees (parent, legal guardian, or foster parent) of the City of Chicago and their sister agencies. Applicants must attend HBCU or UNCF-affiliated colleges and have a financial.

Award: Scholarship for use in freshman, sophomore, junior, or senior years; not renewable.

Eligibility Requirements: Applicant must be Black (non-Hispanic) and enrolled or expecting to enroll full-time at a four-year institution or university. Available to U.S. citizens.

Application Requirements: Application form, recommendations or references. *Deadline:* February 18.

Contact: Pia Holland
E-mail: Pia.Holland@uncf.org

CYNTHIA DENISE ROBINSON HORTON SCHOLARSHIP

The Cynthia D. Horton Scholarship is open to any African American student, with a 2.5 GPA, attending an HBCU with preference given to a UNCF school, with unmet financial need.

Award: Scholarship for use in freshman, sophomore, junior, or senior years.

Eligibility Requirements: Applicant must be Black (non-Hispanic) and enrolled or expecting to enroll at a two-year or four-year institution or university. Available to U.S. citizens.

Application Requirements: Application form, essay, financial need analysis. *Deadline:* March 31.

Contact: Larry Griffith, Senior Vice President, Programs and Student Services
Phone: 800-331-2244

DEBORAH L. VINCENT/FAHRO EDUCATION SCHOLARSHIP

Up to $1500 award for residents of federally assisted housing or a recipient of assistance through the Community Development Block Grant program in Florida. Must be a high school senior and meet income requirements as defined by HUD for public/assisted housing and Community Development Block Grant targeted area recipients. Must have a sponsor that is an active member of FAHRO as a housing authority/agency or community development agency that is willing to support travel expenses to attend Annual Convention awards banquet to receive scholarship if selected. Minimum 2.5 GPA required.

Award: Scholarship for use in freshman year; renewable.

Eligibility Requirements: Applicant must be Black (non-Hispanic); high school student; planning to enroll or expecting to enroll full-time at a two-year or four-year institution and resident of Florida. Available to U.S. citizens.

Application Requirements: Application form, financial need analysis. *Deadline:* July 10.

Contact: Larry Griffith, Senior Vice President, Programs and Student Services
Phone: 800-331-2244

DELTA AIR LINES NEW YORK SCHOLARSHIPS

The Delta Air Lines Foundation in partnership with UNCF has established a scholarship program of up to $5000 for students who reside in or are permanent residents of the State of New York. The scholarship is open to freshmen through 5th year seniors, with unmet financial need. Applicant can be currently enrolled as a full-time student at any U.S located, accredited 4-year college or university. Graduating high school seniors select "freshman" as your classification.

Award: Scholarship for use in freshman, sophomore, junior, or senior years; not renewable.

Eligibility Requirements: Applicant must be Black (non-Hispanic); enrolled or expecting to enroll full-time at a four-year institution or university and resident of New York. Available to U.S. citizens.

Application Requirements: Application form, financial need analysis, recommendations or references. *Deadline:* July 27.

Contact: Jeff Darden
E-mail: Jeff.darden@uncf.org

DINWIDDIE FAMILY FOUNDATION SCHOLARSHIP

The Dinwiddie Family Foundation scholarship is being provided to reduce the financial aid gap to current graduating high school students from Los Angeles County, CA or Brooklyn, NY. This need-based scholarship will assist in providing support for pre-approved, upfront costs in addition to tuition and book expenses. Up to $20,000. Scholarship decisions will be made 6-8 weeks from the closing date of this program, where both selected and non-selected students will be notified.

Award: Scholarship for use in freshman year; not renewable.

Eligibility Requirements: Applicant must be Black (non-Hispanic); high school student; planning to enroll or expecting to enroll full-time at a four-year institution or university and resident of California, New York. Available to U.S. citizens.

Application Requirements: Application form, FAFSA, financial need analysis, transcript. *Deadline:* April 13.

Contact: JaiSun McCormick
E-mail: jaisun.mccormick@uncf.org

DR. PEPPER SNAPPLE GROUP SCHOLARSHIP

The Dr Pepper Snapple Group Scholarship is open to full-time students who are currently enrolled at an HBCU (Historically Black College or University). Candidates must possess a minimum of a 3.0 GPA on a 4.0 scale and submit a 500 word essay defining their academic achievements, accomplishments and their future career aspirations.

Award: Scholarship for use in freshman, sophomore, or junior years. *Number:* 2. *Amount:* $2500.

Eligibility Requirements: Applicant must be Black (non-Hispanic) and enrolled or expecting to enroll full-time at a four-year institution or university. Available to U.S. citizens.

Application Requirements: Application form, essay. *Deadline:* May 1.
Contact: Larry Griffith, Senior Vice President, Programs and Student Services
Phone: 800-331-2244

JAY CHARLES LEVINE SCHOLARSHIP

The Jay Charles Levine Scholarship will provide a $3,000 tuition scholarship for graduating high school seniors from the state of Michigan. Applicants must be residents of Michigan with at least a 2.75 GPA on a 4.0 scale, and must be enrolling at a UNCF member school as a full-time student.

Award: Scholarship for use in freshman year. *Amount:* $3000.

Eligibility Requirements: Applicant must be Black (non-Hispanic); high school student; planning to enroll or expecting to enroll at a four-year institution or university and resident of Michigan. Available to U.S. citizens.

Application Requirements: Application form, essay. *Deadline:* August 1.

Contact: Larry Griffith, Senior Vice President, Programs and Student Services
Phone: 800-331-2244

KAT TEAM FOUNDATION SCHOLARSHIP

The KAT Team Foundation has decided to provide 4 scholarships to graduating high school seniors who have been accepted at any accredited four-year institution. This scholarship opportunity will provide a renewable award of up to $1,000.00 for 4 years. Candidates who possess a minimum cumulative gpa of 2.8, 1 recipient will be awarded; Candidates who possess a minimum cumulative 3.2 gpa and participated in a varsity athletic sport throughout their secondary school years, 1 recipient will be awarded; Candidates who possess a minimum cumulative 3.5 gpa, 2 recipients will be awarded.

Award: Scholarship for use in freshman year; renewable. *Number:* 4.

Eligibility Requirements: Applicant must be Black (non-Hispanic); high school student and planning to enroll or expecting to enroll at a four-year institution or university. Available to U.S. citizens.

Application Requirements: Application form, application form may be submitted online, essay, recommendations or references, transcript. *Deadline:* May 11.

Contact: Jeff Darden
E-mail: jeff.darden@uncf.org

KROGER MICHIGAN SCHOLARSHIP

One-time scholarship of up to $4500 available to graduating high school seniors that reside in the Michigan area. Minimum 2.5 GPA required.

Award: Scholarship for use in freshman year; not renewable. *Number:* 1. *Amount:* $4500.

Eligibility Requirements: Applicant must be Black (non-Hispanic); high school student; planning to enroll or expecting to enroll full-time at a four-year institution or university and resident of Michigan. Available to U.S. citizens.

Application Requirements: Application form. *Deadline:* June 2.

Contact: Larry Griffith, Senior Vice President, Programs and Student Services
Phone: 800-331-2244

MAYS FAMILY SCHOLARSHIP FUND

The Mays Family Scholarship Fund has decided to provide 3 scholarships to students who reside in or are permanent residents of Arkansas, Illinois, Indiana or Michigan. Applicants must attend Howard University, other HBCU's, or one of the following institutions: University of Chicago, Michigan State University, Western Michigan University, Indiana State University, University of Arkansas, Indiana University, or the University of Illinois. Must have unmet financial need and have minimum GPA of 2.8.

Award: Scholarship for use in freshman, sophomore, or junior years; not renewable. *Number:* 3. *Amount:* $1500.

Eligibility Requirements: Applicant must be Black (non-Hispanic); enrolled or expecting to enroll at a four-year institution or university and resident of Arkansas, Illinois, Indiana, Michigan. Available to U.S. citizens.

Application Requirements: Application form, essay, financial need analysis. *Deadline:* June 16.

Contact: Larry Griffith, Senior Vice President, Programs and Student Services
Phone: 800-331-2244

NEVADA-UNCF SCHOLARSHIPS

Scholarship of up to $2500 to financially support high school seniors who plan to enroll in 4 year colleges or universities. Applicants must be permanent residents of the state of Nevada in order to be considered for this program. Candidates for this scholarship are expected to be involved in school and in their community. Ideal recipients have exhibited qualities of high character and integrity. Preference will be given to students attending an HBCU or an accredited 4 year college within the state of Nevada, although all students are encouraged to apply. Minimum 2.5 GPA required.

Award: Scholarship for use in freshman year; not renewable. *Amount:* $2500.

Eligibility Requirements: Applicant must be Black (non-Hispanic); high school student; planning to enroll or expecting to enroll full-time at a four-year institution or university and resident of Nevada. Available to U.S. citizens.

Application Requirements: Application form. *Deadline:* June 12.

Contact: Larry Griffith, Senior Vice President, Programs and Student Services
Phone: 800-331-2244

PACIFIC NORTHWEST SCHOLARSHIP

Awards available to students who are permanent residents of Washington or Oregon attending a UNCF college or university. Minimum 2.5 GPA and essay are required.

Award: Scholarship for use in freshman, sophomore, junior, or senior years; not renewable.

Eligibility Requirements: Applicant must be Black (non-Hispanic); enrolled or expecting to enroll full-time at a four-year institution or university and resident of Oregon, Washington. Available to U.S. citizens.

Application Requirements: Application form, essay. *Deadline:* March 21.

Contact: Larry Griffith, Senior Vice President, Programs and Student Services
Phone: 800-331-2244

PANDA CARES—UNCF SCHOLARS PROGRAM (PHASE I)

The program will help scholars get to and through college and support student achievement and development with a renewable scholarship to 400 students. Selected students will be awarded up to $2,500 per academic year to be used to cover the unmet costs of tuition, fees, room and board. Scholars must apply through a two-phase process. Must have a minimum cumulative 2.8 GPA on a 4.0 scale; Must participate in the online learning modules, Must participate in the online learning modules, that will provide valuable tools and information designed to empower and prepare scholars for academic and personal success, to receive renewable scholarship. After completion of Phase I, applicants will receive information regarding Phase II requirements.

Award: Scholarship for use in freshman, sophomore, junior, or senior years; renewable. *Number:* 400.

Eligibility Requirements: Applicant must be Black (non-Hispanic); enrolled or expecting to enroll full-time at a four-year institution or university and resident of Alaska, Arizona, Arkansas, California, Colorado, Florida, Georgia, Hawaii, Idaho, Illinois, Indiana, Iowa, Kansas, Maryland, Michigan, Minnesota, Missouri, Nebraska, Nevada, New Jersey, New Mexico, New York, Oklahoma, Oregon, Pennsylvania, Puerto Rico, Tennessee, Texas, Utah, Virginia, Washington, Wisconsin. Available to U.S. citizens.

Application Requirements: Application form, FAFSA, financial need analysis. *Deadline:* July 20.

Contact: Melissa Jordan
E-mail: melissa.jordan@uncf.org

PENNSYLVANIA STATE EMPLOYEES COMBINED CAMPAIGN SCHOLARSHIP (SECA)

Up to $4000 scholarship program for qualified students entering or enrolled in a UNCF member college/university. Applicant must be Pell Grant eligible and have a demonstrated financial need.

Award: Scholarship for use in freshman, sophomore, junior, senior, or graduate years; not renewable.

Eligibility Requirements: Applicant must be Black (non-Hispanic); enrolled or expecting to enroll full-time at a two-year or four-year institution or university and resident of Pennsylvania. Available to U.S. citizens.

Application Requirements: Application form, application form may be submitted online, FAFSA, financial need analysis. *Deadline:* October 14.

Contact: Lottie Evans
E-mail: lottie.evans@uncf.org

RAY CHARLES ENDOWED SCHOLARSHIP

3 scholarship awards of up to $4,500 will help African-American students with high academic promise to defray their significant financial need. Applicants must be African-American college juniors enrolled full-time at a UNCF member institution. Must have minimum cumulative GPA of 3.0 and have unmet financial need.

Award: Scholarship for use in junior year; renewable. *Number:* 3.

Eligibility Requirements: Applicant must be Black (non-Hispanic) and enrolled or expecting to enroll full-time at a four-year institution or university. Available to U.S. citizens.

Application Requirements: Application form, financial need analysis. *Deadline:* January 26.

Contact: Ms. JaiSun McCormick
E-mail: jaisun.mccormick@uncf.org

UNCF/KOCH SCHOLARS PROGRAM

Scholarships of up to $5,000 each available to African-American high school students planning to attend HBCU colleges and universities on a full-time basis. Must major in accounting, business, economics, engineering, history, philosophy, or political science. Minimum 2.7 GPA required. Must be committed to learning about how entrepreneurship, innovation, and economics contribute to well-being through participation in an online community and Annual Summit.

Award: Scholarship for use in freshman year; not renewable. *Number:* 200.

Eligibility Requirements: Applicant must be Black (non-Hispanic); high school student; planning to enroll or expecting to enroll full-time at a four-year institution or university and must have an interest in entrepreneurship. Available to U.S. citizens.

Application Requirements: Application form, essay, Financial Aid Award letter; Student Aid Report, financial need analysis, recommendations or references, transcript. *Deadline:* June 17.

Contact: Larry Griffith, Senior Vice President, Programs and Student Services
Phone: 800-331-2244

USA FUNDS SCHOLARSHIP

Scholarships of up to $5,000 to assist students and their families in gaining access to postsecondary education at UNCF or other HBCU colleges/universities in Indiana. Students must be resident of Indiana and be a U.S. citizen or permanent resident. Minimum 2.5 GPA required.

Award: Scholarship for use in freshman, sophomore, junior, or senior years; not renewable.

Eligibility Requirements: Applicant must be Black (non-Hispanic); enrolled or expecting to enroll full-time at a four-year institution or university; resident of Indiana and studying in Indiana. Available to U.S. citizens.

Application Requirements: Application form, essay. *Deadline:* August 31.

Contact: Larry Griffith, Senior Vice President, Programs and Student Services
Phone: 800-331-2244

VOYA UNCF MALE INITIATIVE

Scholarship for male, African-American colleges sophomores attending UNCF affiliated colleges or universities on a full-time basis. Must have a demonstrated unmet, financial need as verified by college or university. Minimum 2.5 GPA required.

Award: Scholarship for use in sophomore year; not renewable.

Eligibility Requirements: Applicant must be Black (non-Hispanic); enrolled or expecting to enroll full-time at a four-year institution or university and male. Available to U.S. citizens.

Application Requirements: Application form, essay, financial need analysis. *Deadline:* November 17.

Contact: Larry Griffith, Senior Vice President, Programs and Student Services
Phone: 800-331-2244

WELLS FARGO FLORIDA SCHOLARSHIP PROGRAM

Wells Fargo Florida Scholarship is restricted to permanent residents of the state of Florida pursuing an undergraduate degree. Students must be full-time, enrolled at an accredited, four-year, U.S. college or university in the state of Florida. Preference will be given to first generation college students (e.g. students whose parent(s) have not graduated from a college or university. Must have a demonstrated, unmet financial need as verified by their attending college or university.

Award: Scholarship for use in freshman, sophomore, or junior years; not renewable.

Eligibility Requirements: Applicant must be Black (non-Hispanic); enrolled or expecting to enroll full-time at a four-year institution or university; resident of Florida and studying in Florida. Available to U.S. citizens.

Application Requirements: Application form, application form may be submitted online (https://scholarships.uncf.org/Account/LogOn), financial need analysis, personal statement of career interest, recommendations or references, transcript. *Deadline:* May 18.

Contact: David Ray
E-mail: david.ray@uncf.ord

UNITED SOUTH AND EASTERN TRIBES INC.

http://www.usetinc.org/

UNITED SOUTH AND EASTERN TRIBES SCHOLARSHIP FUND

One-time scholarship for Native American students who are members of United South and Eastern Tribes, enrolled or accepted in a postsecondary educational institution.

Award: Scholarship for use in freshman, sophomore, junior, or senior years; not renewable. *Number:* 4–8. *Amount:* $500.

Eligibility Requirements: Applicant must be Indian citizen; American Indian/Alaska Native and enrolled or expecting to enroll full- or part-time at a four-year institution or university.

Application Requirements: Application form, essay, financial need analysis, proof of tribal enrollment, transcript. *Deadline:* April 30.

Contact: Theresa Embry, Executive Assistant to Director
United South and Eastern Tribes Inc.
711 Stewarts Ferry Pike, Suite 100
Nashville, TN 37214-2634
Phone: 615-872-7900
Fax: 615-872-7417

UNITED STATES ARMY WARRANT OFFICERS ASSOCIATION

USAWOA SCHOLARSHIP FOUNDATION
• See page 493

UNITED STATES HISPANIC LEADERSHIP INSTITUTE

http://www.ushli.org/

DR. JUAN ANDRADE, JR. SCHOLARSHIP

Scholarship for young Hispanic leaders. Applicants must be enrolled or accepted for enrollment as a full-time student in a four-year institution in the United States or U.S. territories, and demonstrate a verifiable need for financial support. At least one parent must be of Hispanic ancestry.

Award: Scholarship for use in freshman, sophomore, junior, or senior years; not renewable. *Number:* 30. *Amount:* $500–$1000.

Eligibility Requirements: Applicant must be Hispanic and enrolled or expecting to enroll full-time at a two-year or four-year institution or university. Available to U.S. citizens.

Application Requirements: Application form, driver's license, essay, personal photograph, recommendations or references, resume, transcript. *Deadline:* January 11.

Contact: Isabel Reyes, Scholarship Coordinator
Phone: 312-427-8683
Fax: 312-427-5183
E-mail: ireyes@ushli.org

UNIVERSITY CONSORTIUM FOR LIBERIA

http://ucliberia.com/

JOSEPH N. BOAKAI SR. HIGHER EDUCATION SCHOLARSHIP

The University Consortium for Liberia (UCL) Scholarship Program was established in 2015 by the UCL Board of Directors. A special scholarship was established on behalf of Joseph N. Boakai, Sr., the Vice President of the Republic of Liberia, in dedication of his support to educate our youth. The UCL Scholarship program is open to Liberian students and/or students of Liberian decent pursuing a post-secondary education at a U.S. College or University. Priority will be given to students applying to a UCL college/university noted below who are considered Institutional Partners.

Award: Scholarship for use in freshman, sophomore, junior, senior, graduate, or postgraduate years; not renewable. *Number:* 5–10. *Amount:* $500–$1000.

Eligibility Requirements: Applicant must be Black (non-Hispanic) and enrolled or expecting to enroll full- or part-time at a two-year or four-year or technical institution or university. Available to U.S. and non-U.S. citizens.

Application Requirements: Application form. *Deadline:* May 15.

Contact: Hon. Cynthia Blandford, University Consortium for Liberia Scholarship Committee
E-mail: uclscholarship@gmail.com

U.S. COAST GUARD

http://www.gocoastguard/cspi

COLLEGE STUDENT PRE-COMMISSIONING INITIATIVE (CSPI)
• See page 485

US PAN ASIAN AMERICAN CHAMBER OF COMMERCE EDUCATION FOUNDATION

http://www.uspaacc.com/

INGERSOLL RAND SCHOLARSHIP

The applicant should demonstrate academic achievement of 3.3 GPA or higher, leadership in extracurricular activities, involvement in community service, and financial need. The amount of the scholarship depends on the sponsors' contributions and varies between $2000 and $5000.

Award: Scholarship for use in freshman year; not renewable. *Amount:* $2000–$5000.

Eligibility Requirements: Applicant must be Asian/Pacific Islander; high school student; age 16 and over and planning to enroll or expecting to enroll full-time at a four-year institution or university. Available to U.S. citizens.

Application Requirements: Application form. *Deadline:* March 17.

Contact: Diana Yee, Program Associate
US Pan Asian American Chamber of Commerce Education Foundation
1329 18th Street NW
Washington, DC 20036
Phone: 202-378-1121
E-mail: Diana@uspaacc.com

PEPSICO HALLMARK SCHOLARSHIPS

The applicant should demonstrate academic achievement of 3.3 GPA or higher, leadership in extracurricular activities, involvement in community service, and financial need. The amount of the scholarship depends on the sponsors' contributions and varies between $2000 and $5000.

Award: Scholarship for use in freshman year; not renewable. *Number:* 1. *Amount:* $2000–$5000.

Eligibility Requirements: Applicant must be Asian/Pacific Islander; high school student; age 16 and over and planning to enroll or expecting to enroll full-time at an institution or university. Available to U.S. citizens.

Application Requirements: Application form. *Deadline:* March 17.

Contact: Diana Yee
    US Pan Asian American Chamber of Commerce Education
      Foundation
    1329 18th Street NW
    Washington, DC 20036
    Phone: 202-378-1121
    E-mail: diana@uspaacc.com

UPS HALLMARK SCHOLARSHIPS

The applicant should demonstrate academic achievement of 3.3 GPA or higher, leadership in extracurricular activities, involvement in community service, and financial need. The amount of the scholarship depends on the sponsors' contributions and varies between $2000 and $5000.

Award: Scholarship for use in freshman year; not renewable. *Amount:* $2000–$5000.

Eligibility Requirements: Applicant must be Asian/Pacific Islander; high school student; age 16 and over and planning to enroll or expecting to enroll full-time at an institution or university. Available to U.S. citizens.

Application Requirements: Application form. *Deadline:* March 17.

Contact: Diana Yee
    US Pan Asian American Chamber of Commerce Education
      Foundation
    1329 18th Street NW
    Washington, DC 20036
    Phone: 202-378-1121

WINWIN PRODUCTS, INC. SCHOLARSHIP

The applicant should demonstrate academic achievement of 3.3 GPA or higher, leadership in extracurricular activities, involvement in community service, and financial need. The amount of the scholarship depends on the sponsors' contributions and varies between $2000 and $5000.

Award: Scholarship for use in freshman year; not renewable. *Amount:* $2000–$5000.

Eligibility Requirements: Applicant must be Asian/Pacific Islander; high school student; age 16 and over and planning to enroll or expecting to enroll full-time at a four-year institution or university. Available to U.S. citizens.

Application Requirements: Application form. *Deadline:* March 13.

Contact: Diana Yee, Program Associate
    US Pan Asian American Chamber of Commerce Education
      Foundation
    1329 18th Street NW
    Washington, DC 20036
    Phone: 202-378-1121
    Fax: 202-296-5221
    E-mail: diana@uspaacc.com

WHITE EARTH TRIBAL COUNCIL

http://www.whiteearth.com/

WHITE EARTH SCHOLARSHIP PROGRAM

Renewable scholarship for students who are enrolled in postsecondary institutions. Must have a GPA of 2.5. Must be U.S. citizen.

Award: Scholarship for use in freshman, sophomore, junior, senior, graduate, or postgraduate years; renewable. *Number:* 200. *Amount:* $3000.

Eligibility Requirements: Applicant must be American Indian/Alaska Native and enrolled or expecting to enroll full- or part-time at a two-year or four-year or technical institution or university. Available to U.S. citizens.

Application Requirements: Application form, financial need analysis, transcript. *Deadline:* May 31.

Contact: Leslie Nessman, Scholarship Manager
    Phone: 218-983-3285
    Fax: 218-983-4299

WILLIAM E. DOCTER EDUCATIONAL FUND/ST. MARY ARMENIAN CHURCH

http://www.wedfund.org/

WILLIAM ERVANT DOCTER EDUCATIONAL FUND

Grant up to $2000 available to worthy students regardless of age, gender, or level of education or training. Funds given to American citizens of Armenian ancestry to pursue studies and training in the United States or Canada.

Award: Grant for use in freshman, sophomore, junior, senior, graduate, or postgraduate years; not renewable. *Number:* 20. *Amount:* $1000–$2000.

Eligibility Requirements: Applicant must be of Armenian heritage and enrolled or expecting to enroll full- or part-time at a two-year or four-year or technical institution or university. Available to U.S. citizens.

Application Requirements: Application form, essay, financial need analysis, proof of U.S. citizenship, test scores, transcript. *Deadline:* June 30.

Contact: Edward Alexander, Scholarship Committee Chairman
    Fax: 202-364-1441
    E-mail: wedfund@aol.com

WISCONSIN HIGHER EDUCATIONAL AID BOARD

http://www.heab.state.wi.us/

MINORITY UNDERGRADUATE RETENTION GRANT-WISCONSIN

The grant provides financial assistance to African-American, Native-American, Hispanic, and former citizens of Laos, Vietnam, and Cambodia, for study in Wisconsin. Must be Wisconsin resident, enrolled at least half-time in Wisconsin Technical College System schools, non-profit independent colleges and universities, and tribal colleges. Refer to website for further details http://www.heab.state.wi.us.

Award: Grant for use in sophomore, junior, or senior years; not renewable. *Amount:* $250–$2500.

Eligibility Requirements: Applicant must be American Indian/Alaska Native, Asian/Pacific Islander, Black (non-Hispanic), Hispanic; enrolled or expecting to enroll full- or part-time at a two-year or technical institution or university; resident of West Virginia and studying in Wisconsin. Available to U.S. and non-U.S. citizens.

Application Requirements: Application form, financial need analysis. *Deadline:* continuous.

Contact: Joy Dyer, Grant Specialist
    Phone: 608-267-2212
    E-mail: joy.dyer@wi.gov

WISCONSIN HEAB NATIVE AMERICAN STUDENT ASSISTANCE GRANT

Awards under this program are made to Wisconsin residents who are at least 25% Native American and are undergraduate or graduate students enrolled in degree or certificate programs at University of Wisconsin, Wisconsin Technical College, independent colleges and universities, tribal colleges, or proprietary institutions based in Wisconsin.

Award: Grant for use in freshman, sophomore, junior, or senior years; not renewable. *Amount:* $250–$1100.

Eligibility Requirements: Applicant must be American Indian/Alaska Native; enrolled or expecting to enroll full- or part-time at a two-year or technical institution or university; resident of West Virginia and studying in Wisconsin. Available to U.S. citizens.

Application Requirements: Application form, financial need analysis. *Deadline:* continuous.

Contact: Charlene Sime, Grant Specialist
    Phone: 608-266-0888
    E-mail: charlenek.sime@wi.gov

WOMEN OF THE EVANGELICAL LUTHERAN CHURCH IN AMERICA

http://www.womenoftheelca.org/

AMELIA KEMP SCHOLARSHIP

Scholarship for ELCA women who are of an ethnic minority in undergraduate, graduate, professional, or vocational courses of study. Must be at least 21 years old and hold membership in the ELCA. Must have experienced an interruption of two or more years in education since the completion of high school.

Award: Scholarship for use in freshman, sophomore, junior, senior, or graduate years; not renewable. *Number:* 1.

Eligibility Requirements: Applicant must be Lutheran; American Indian/Alaska Native, Asian/Pacific Islander, Black (non-Hispanic), Hispanic; age 21 and over; enrolled or expecting to enroll full- or part-time at a two-year or technical institution or university and female. Available to U.S. citizens.

Application Requirements: Application form. *Deadline:* February 15.

Contact: Emily Hansen, Scholarship Committee
Phone: 800-638-3522 Ext. 2736
Fax: 773-380-2419
E-mail: Women.ELCA@elca.org

WONDERSHARE PDFELEMENT

https://pdf.wondershare.com

2018 PDFELEMENT $1000 SCHOLARSHIP

• *See page 486*

ZAMI NOBLA

http://www.zaminobla.org

AUDRE LORDE SCHOLARSHIP FUND

Must be an out black lesbian or lesbian of color who is 40 years old or older attending any technical, undergraduate or graduate school located in the United States. Must be accepted or registered at a post-secondary educational institution for full or part-time attendance as defined by the institution. Must also have a cumulative high school/college/or technical school grade point average of 3.0 or higher. Please do not submit an application if you do not meet the eligibility requirements as your application will not be reviewed. No exceptions to the eligibility requirements are considered. The Fund does not offer scholarships for weekend programs, summer sessions, research, special projects, or for study out of the country.

Award: Scholarship for use in freshman, sophomore, junior, senior, graduate, or postgraduate years; renewable. *Number:* 1–6. *Amount:* $1000.

Eligibility Requirements: Applicant must be American Indian/Alaska Native, Asian/Pacific Islander, Black (non-Hispanic), Hispanic; age 40 and over; enrolled or expecting to enroll full- or part-time at a two-year or four-year or technical institution or university and female. Available to U.S. citizens.

Application Requirements: Application form, essay, interview, personal photograph.

Contact: Ms. Mary Anne Adams, Founding Director
ZAMI NOBLA
PO Box 90986
Atlanta, GA 30364
Phone: 404-647-4754
E-mail: zaminobla@zaminobla.org

RELIGIOUS AFFILIATION

AMERICAN BAPTIST FINANCIAL AID PROGRAM

http://www.abhms.org/

AMERICAN BAPTIST HOME MISSION SOCIETIES FINANCIAL AID PROGRAM

The American Baptist Financial Aid Program supports American Baptist college students, graduate students, and seminarians. Applicants must hold an active membership in an American Baptist church, maintain a GPA of 2.75 or higher, and be enrolled at an accredited institution in the United States or Puerto Rico.

Award: Scholarship for use in freshman, sophomore, junior, senior, or graduate years; not renewable. *Number:* 1–250. *Amount:* $500–$1000.

Eligibility Requirements: Applicant must be Baptist and enrolled or expecting to enroll full-time at a four-year institution or university. Available to U.S. citizens.

Application Requirements: Application form, essay, financial need analysis. *Deadline:* April 30.

Contact: Rev. Sarah Strosahl-Kagi, Director of Emerging Leaders and Scholarships Program
American Baptist Financial Aid Program
PO Box 851
Valley Forge, PA 19482-0851
Phone: 800-222-3872 Ext. 2462
Fax: 610-768-2470
E-mail: sarah.strosahl-kagi@abhms.org

AMERICAN SEPHARDI FOUNDATION

http://www.americansephardifederation.org/

BROOME AND ALLEN BOYS CAMP AND SCHOLARSHIP FUND

The Broome and Allen Scholarship is awarded to students of Sephardic origin or those working in Sephardic studies. Both graduate and undergraduate degree candidates as well as those doing research projects will be considered. It is awarded for one year and must be renewed for successive years. Enclose copy of tax returns with application.

Award: Scholarship for use in freshman, sophomore, junior, senior, graduate, or postgraduate years; not renewable. *Number:* 20–60. *Amount:* $500–$2000.

Eligibility Requirements: Applicant must be Jewish and enrolled or expecting to enroll full- or part-time at a two-year or four-year or technical institution or university. Available to U.S. and non-U.S. citizens.

Application Requirements: Application form, copy of tax returns, essay, financial need analysis, recommendations or references, transcript. *Deadline:* May 15.

Contact: Ms. Ellen Cohen, Membership and Outreach Coordinator
American Sephardi Foundation
15 West 16th Street
New York, NY 10011
Phone: 212-294-8350 Ext. 4
Fax: 212-294-8348
E-mail: ecohen@asf.cjh.org

CATHOLIC UNITED FINANCIAL

http://www.catholicunitedfinancial.org

POST HIGH SCHOOL TUITION SCHOLARSHIPS

Catholic United Financial membership requirement of 2 years by application deadline.

Award: Scholarship for use in freshman, sophomore, junior, or senior years; not renewable. *Number:* 600. *Amount:* $300–$500.

Eligibility Requirements: Applicant must be Roman Catholic and enrolled or expecting to enroll full- or part-time at a two-year or four-year or technical institution or university. Available to U.S. citizens.

Application Requirements: Application form, personal photograph. *Deadline:* April 30.

Contact: Member Engagement Department
Phone: 800-568-6670
E-mail: engage@catholicunited.org

CENTRAL SCHOLARSHIP

http://www.central-scholarship.org

LESSANS FAMILY SCHOLARSHIP
• *See page 514*

COMMUNITY FOUNDATION OF WESTERN MASSACHUSETTS

http://www.communityfoundation.org/

KIMBER RICHTER FAMILY SCHOLARSHIP FUND

Scholarship available to graduating high school seniors of the Baha'i faith from Hampden, Hampshire, Franklin or Berkshire Counties who excel in citizenship or extracurricular activities.

Award: Scholarship for use in freshman year; not renewable.

Eligibility Requirements: Applicant must be Baha'i faith; high school student; planning to enroll or expecting to enroll full- or part-time at a two-year institution or university and resident of Maryland. Available to U.S. citizens.

Application Requirements: Application form, application form may be submitted online, essay, financial need analysis. *Deadline:* April 17.

Contact: Nikai Fondon, Scholarship Program Associate
E-mail: NFondon@communityfoundation.org

DANIEL P. BUTTAFUOCO & ASSOCIATES

http://www.1800nowhurt.com

YOUNG CHRISTIAN LEADERS SCHOLARSHIP

Two awards of $1000 given each month to students under the age of 24 who are either high school seniors entering college or are currently full-time undergraduates. Must be a full-time resident of either New York, New Jersey, Connecticut, or Pennsylvania. Applications submitted by the 15th of the month will be considered in the following month's selection process. (e.g., apply by April 15th for a May award). Each applicant may receive a maximum total of three awards per 12-month period. Must be an attending, active members of a local church and have a minimum 3.0 GPA.

Award: Scholarship for use in freshman, sophomore, junior, or senior years; not renewable. *Amount:* $1000.

Eligibility Requirements: Applicant must be Christian; age 18-24; enrolled or expecting to enroll full-time at a four-year institution or university and resident of Connecticut, New Jersey, New York, Pennsylvania. Available to U.S. citizens.

Application Requirements: Application form, essay, personal photograph.

Contact: Ms. Maciel Almonte, Scholarship Administrator
Daniel P. Buttafuoco & Associates
9 Broadman Parkway
Jersey City, NJ 07305
Phone: 201-432-7300
E-mail: info@yclscholarship.org

DISCIPLESHIP MINISTRIES

http://umcyoungpeople.org

DAVID W. SELF SCHOLARSHIP

Must be a United Methodist Youth who has been active in local church for at least one year prior to application. Must be a graduating senior in high school entering the first year of undergraduate study. Must be pursuing a "church-related" career and should have maintained at least a "C" average throughout high school.

Award: Scholarship for use in freshman year; not renewable. *Number:* 1–5. *Amount:* $100–$1000.

Eligibility Requirements: Applicant must be Methodist; high school student and planning to enroll or expecting to enroll full-time at a two-year or four-year institution or university. Available to U.S. citizens.

Application Requirements: Application form, essay, financial need analysis. *Deadline:* March 1.

Contact: Kelsey Tinker Hannum, Grant and Scholarships Administrator
Phone: 615-340-7184
E-mail: youngpeople@umcdiscipleship.org

RICHARD S. SMITH SCHOLARSHIP
• *See page 517*

EASTERN ORTHODOX COMMITTEE ON SCOUTING

http://www.eocs.org/

EASTERN ORTHODOX COMMITTEE ON SCOUTING SCHOLARSHIPS
• *See page 438*

FADEL EDUCATIONAL FOUNDATION, INC.

http://www.fadelfoundation.org/

ANNUAL AWARD PROGRAM

Grants of $800 to $3500 awarded on the basis of merit and financial need.

Award: Grant for use in freshman, sophomore, junior, senior, or graduate years; renewable. *Number:* 6–8. *Amount:* $800–$3500.

Eligibility Requirements: Applicant must be Muslim faith and enrolled or expecting to enroll full- or part-time at a two-year or technical institution or university. Available to U.S. citizens.

Application Requirements: Application form, application form may be submitted online, essay, financial need analysis. *Deadline:* May 28.

Contact: Mr. Ayman Fadel, Secretary
E-mail: secretary@fadelfoundation.org

FOUNDATION FOR CHRISTIAN COLLEGE LEADERS

http://www.collegechristianleader.com/

FOUNDATION FOR COLLEGE CHRISTIAN LEADERS SCHOLARSHIP

Applicant must be accepted to or currently enrolled in an undergraduate degree program. Candidate must demonstrate Christian leadership. Combined income of parents and student must be less than $60,000. Minimum 3.0 GPA required.

Award: Scholarship for use in freshman, sophomore, junior, senior, or graduate years; not renewable.

Eligibility Requirements: Applicant must be Christian; enrolled or expecting to enroll full- or part-time at a four-year institution or university and must have an interest in leadership. Available to U.S. citizens.

Application Requirements: Application form, financial need analysis, interview, leadership assessment form, cover sheet, recommendations or references. *Deadline:* May 7.

Contact: Scholarship Committee
Phone: 858-481-0848
Fax: 858-481-0848
E-mail: lmhays@aol.com

GENERAL BOARD OF HIGHER EDUCATION AND MINISTRY

http://www.gbhem.org

BISHOP JOSEPH B. BETHEA SCHOLARSHIP
• *See page 518*

HELEN DILLER FAMILY FOUNDATION

http://www.dillerteenawards.org

DILLER TEEN TIKKUN OLAM AWARDS
• *See page 518*

ITALIAN CATHOLIC FEDERATION

http://www.icf.org/

ITALIAN CATHOLIC FEDERATION FIRST YEAR SCHOLARSHIP
• *See page 442*

JEWISH VOCATIONAL SERVICE LOS ANGELES

http://www.jvsla.org/

JVS SCHOLARSHIP PROGRAM
• *See page 522*

JVS CHICAGO

http://jvschicago.org/

JEWISH FEDERATION OF METROPOLITAN CHICAGO ACADEMIC SCHOLARSHIP PROGRAM
• *See page 522*

KNIGHTS OF COLUMBUS

http://www.kofc.org/

CANADIAN UNDEGRADUATE SCHOLARSHIP
• *See page 443*

FOURTH DEGREE PRO DEO AND PRO PATRIA SCHOLARSHIPS/JOHN W. MCDEVITT (FOURTH DEGREE) SCHOLARSHIP
• *See page 444*

JOHN W. MCDEVITT (FOURTH DEGREE) SCHOLARSHIPS
• *See page 444*

MATTHEWS & SWIFT EDUCATIONAL TRUST SCHOLARSHIP
• *See page 444*

PERCY J. JOHNSON ENDOWED SCHOLARSHIPS
• *See page 444*

ORTHODOX UNION

http://ou.org

SARA AND MAX GOLDSAMMLER SCHOLARSHIP FUND
• *See page 529*

PRESBYTERIAN CHURCH (USA)

https://www.presbyterianmission.org/

NATIONAL PRESBYTERIAN COLLEGE SCHOLARSHIP

Scholarships between $250 and $1500 available to incoming undergraduate members enrolled in full-time programs in colleges associated with the Presbyterian Church (U.S.A.). Applicants must have a minimum GPA of 2.5 and demonstrate financial need. Students are required to participate in campus ministry or a worshiping community proximate to the college they attend and respond to an annual essay question exploring aspects of vocation.

Award: Scholarship for use in freshman, sophomore, junior, or senior years; not renewable. *Number:* 25–35. *Amount:* $250–$1500.

Eligibility Requirements: Applicant must be Presbyterian and enrolled or expecting to enroll full-time at an institution or university. Available to U.S. and non-U.S. citizens.

Application Requirements: Application form, essay, financial need analysis. *Deadline:* May 15.

Contact: Ms. Laura Bryan, Coordinator, Financial Aid for Studies
Presbyterian Church (USA)
100 Witherspoon Street
Louisville, KY 40202
Phone: 800-728-7228 Ext. 5735
Fax: 502-569-8766
E-mail: finaid@pcusa.org

NATIVE AMERICAN SUPPLEMENTAL GRANT
• *See page 530*

SAMUEL ROBINSON AWARD

Prize granted to Presbyterian Church (U.S.A.) members who are full-time juniors or seniors in college and attending a Presbyterian related college or university to memorize and recite the catechism from memory and write an essay on an assigned topic.

Award: Prize for use in junior or senior years; not renewable. *Number:* 2. *Amount:* $2000–$7500.

Eligibility Requirements: Applicant must be Presbyterian and enrolled or expecting to enroll full-time at an institution or university. Available to U.S. citizens.

Application Requirements: Application form, application form may be submitted online, essay. *Deadline:* continuous.

Contact: Ms. Laura Bryan, Coordinator, Financial Aid for Studies
Presbyterian Church (USA)
100 Witherspoon Street
Louisville, KY 40202
Phone: 800-728-7228 Ext. 5735
Fax: 502-569-8766
E-mail: finaid@pcusa.org

TEXAS BLACK BAPTIST SCHOLARSHIP COMMITTEE

http://www.bgct.org/

TEXAS BLACK BAPTIST SCHOLARSHIP
• *See page 534*

UNITED NEGRO COLLEGE FUND

http://www.uncf.org/

ABCNJ LEADERSHIP IMPACT SCHOLARSHIP
• *See page 534*

WOMEN OF THE EVANGELICAL LUTHERAN CHURCH IN AMERICA

http://www.womenoftheelca.org/

AMELIA KEMP SCHOLARSHIP
• *See page 539*

ELCA SERVICE ABROAD SCHOLARSHIP

Scholarship for women who have experienced an interruption of two or more years in education since the completion of high school. Must be member of ELCA and be at least 21 years old.

Award: Scholarship for use in freshman, sophomore, junior, senior, or graduate years; not renewable.

Eligibility Requirements: Applicant must be Lutheran; age 21 and over; enrolled or expecting to enroll full- or part-time at a two-year or technical institution or university and female. Available to U.S. citizens.

Application Requirements: Application form. *Deadline:* February 15.

Contact: Emily Hansen, Scholarship Committee
Phone: 800-638-3522 Ext. 2736
Fax: 773-380-2419
E-mail: Women.ELCA@elca.org

RESIDENCE

365 PET INSURANCE

https://365petinsurance.com/

MINORITY STUDENTS IN VETERINARY MEDICINE SCHOLARSHIP
• See page 510

THE 5 STRONG SCHOLARSHIP FOUNDATION, INC.

http://5strongscholars.org

5 STRONG SCHOLARS SCHOLARSHIP
• See page 511

ALABAMA COMMISSION ON HIGHER EDUCATION

http://www.ache.alabama.gov/

ALABAMA NATIONAL GUARD EDUCATIONAL ASSISTANCE PROGRAM
• See page 488

ALABAMA STUDENT ASSISTANCE PROGRAM

Scholarship award of $300 to $5000 per academic year given to undergraduate students residing in the state of Alabama and attending a college or university in Alabama.

Award: Grant for use in freshman, sophomore, junior, or senior years; not renewable. *Number:* 3,500–4,500. *Amount:* $300–$5000.

Eligibility Requirements: Applicant must be enrolled or expecting to enroll full- or part-time at a two-year or four-year or technical institution or university; resident of Alabama and studying in Alabama. Available to U.S. citizens.

Application Requirements: Application form, financial need analysis. *Deadline:* continuous.

Contact: Cheryl Newton, Grants Coordinator
Phone: 334-242-2273
Fax: 334-242-2269
E-mail: Cheryl.Newton@ache.edu

ALABAMA STUDENT ASSISTANCE PROGRAM

Grant award of $300 to $5000 per academic year given to undergraduate students residing in the state of Alabama and attending a college or university in Alabama.

Award: Grant for use in freshman, sophomore, junior, or senior years; not renewable. *Number:* 3,500–4,500. *Amount:* $300–$5000.

Eligibility Requirements: Applicant must be enrolled or expecting to enroll full- or part-time at a two-year or four-year or technical institution or university; resident of Alabama and studying in Alabama. Available to U.S. citizens.

Application Requirements: *Deadline:* continuous.

Contact: Cheryl Newton, Grants Coordinator
Phone: 334-242-2273
Fax: 334-242-2269
E-mail: Cheryl.Newton@ache.edu

ALABAMA STUDENT GRANT PROGRAM

Nonrenewable awards available to Alabama residents for undergraduate study at certain independent colleges within the state. Both full and half-time students are eligible. Deadlines: September 15, January 15, and February 15.

Award: Grant for use in freshman, sophomore, junior, or senior years; not renewable. *Number:* 3,500–5,500. *Amount:* $200–$1200.

Eligibility Requirements: Applicant must be enrolled or expecting to enroll full- or part-time at a four-year institution or university; resident of Alabama and studying in Alabama. Available to U.S. citizens.

Application Requirements: Application form. *Deadline:* continuous.

Contact: Cheryl Newton, Grants Coordinator
Phone: 334-242-2273
Fax: 334-242-2269
E-mail: Cheryl.Newton@ache.edu

POLICE OFFICERS AND FIREFIGHTERS SURVIVORS EDUCATION ASSISTANCE PROGRAM-ALABAMA

Provides tuition, fees, books, and supplies to dependents of full-time police officers and firefighters killed or totally disabled in the line of duty. Must attend an Alabama public college as an undergraduate. Must be Alabama resident.

Award: Scholarship for use in freshman, sophomore, junior, or senior years; renewable. *Number:* 15–30. *Amount:* $1600–$12,000.

Eligibility Requirements: Applicant must be age 21 or under; enrolled or expecting to enroll full- or part-time at a two-year or technical institution or university; resident of Alabama and studying in Alabama. Available to U.S. citizens.

Application Requirements: Application form. *Deadline:* continuous.

Contact: Cheryl Newton, Grants Coordinator
Phone: 334-242-2273
Fax: 334-242-2269
E-mail: Cheryl.Newton@ache.edu

ALABAMA DEPARTMENT OF VETERANS AFFAIRS

http://www.va.alabama.gov/

ALABAMA G.I. DEPENDENTS SCHOLARSHIP PROGRAM

The scholarship is for dependents of eligible disabled Alabama veterans. This scholarship will be the payer of last resort after all other grants and scholarships have been utilized for required education expenses. The scholarship pays up to the DoD Tuition Assistance Cap (currently $250 per credit hour) and up to $1,000 for the combination of required textbooks and laboratory fees per semester. Child or stepchild must initiate training before 26th birthday; age 30 deadline may apply in certain situations. No age deadline for spouses or widows. The veteran and the step child's parent must have been married prior the child's 19th birthday.

Award: Scholarship for use in freshman, sophomore, junior, or senior years; renewable.

Eligibility Requirements: Applicant must be age 30 or under; enrolled or expecting to enroll full- or part-time at a two-year or four-year or technical institution or university; resident of Alabama and studying in Alabama. Available to U.S. citizens.

Application Requirements: Application form.

Contact: Kayla Kyle, Department Operations Manager
Alabama Department of Veterans Affairs
PO Box 1509
Montgomery, AL 36102-1509
Phone: 334-242-5077

ALABAMA SOCIETY OF CERTIFIED PUBLIC ACCOUNTANTS

http://www.ascpa.org/

ASCPA EDUCATIONAL FOUNDATION SCHOLARSHIP

Scholarships available for students with a declared major in accounting. Must have completed intermediate accounting courses (I and II) with a 3.0 average in all accounting courses, and a 3.0 average overall. Available for fourth or fifth year of study. Must be U.S. citizen or hold permanent resident status. Must have one full year of study remaining. 300 word essay.

Award: Scholarship for use in senior or graduate years; not renewable. *Number:* 34–38. *Amount:* $1500–$2500.

Eligibility Requirements: Applicant must be enrolled or expecting to enroll full-time at a four-year institution or university; resident of Alabama and studying in Alabama. Available to U.S. citizens.

Application Requirements: Application form, essay. *Deadline:* March 16.

Contact: Ms. Diane Christy, Vice President of Communications
Alabama Society of Certified Public Accountants
1041 Longfield Court
Montgomery, AL 36117
Phone: 334-386-5752
E-mail: dchristy@ascpa.org

ALBERTA AGRICULTURE FOOD AND RURAL DEVELOPMENT 4-H BRANCH

http://www.4h.ab.ca/

ALBERTA AGRICULTURE FOOD AND RURAL DEVELOPMENT 4-H SCHOLARSHIP PROGRAM
• *See page 429*

ALBERTA HERITAGE SCHOLARSHIP FUND

http://www.alis.alberta.ca/

CHINA-ALBERTA AWARD FOR EXCELLENCE IN CHINESE

Award of CAN$500 for Canadian citizens or permanent residents who are Alberta residents currently enrolled in Grade 12. Must have taken high school Chinese Language and Culture Program 10 and 20 and currently be enrolled or have completed level 30; and have obtained an average of 80% in all courses, and a minimum average of 90% in Chinese Language and Culture 10 and 20. Applicant's parents or a parent must reside in Alberta. For more information, see website http://alis.alberta.ca/.

Award: Grant for use in freshman year; not renewable.

Eligibility Requirements: Applicant must be high school student; planning to enroll or expecting to enroll full-time at a four-year institution or university and resident of Alberta.

Application Requirements: Application form, essay, recommendations or references, transcript. *Deadline:* April 30.

DR. ERNEST AND MINNIE MEHL SCHOLARSHIP
• *See page 511*

DUKE AND DUTCHESS OF CAMBRIDGE SCHOLARSHIP

Awards of CAN$2500 available to students who have been in government care and have overcome significant challenges in their lives while pursing their postsecondary studies. Eligible students must be Advancing Futures Bursary recipients and be returning to full-time postsecondary studies. Awarded on the basis of academic achievement; the highest GPA (grade point average) while working toward a degree, diploma, or certificate. Advancing Futures Bursary recipients who are taking postsecondary upgrading courses or attending a specialized high school are also eligible. For more information, see website http://alis.alberta.ca/.

Award: Scholarship for use in freshman, sophomore, junior, or senior years; not renewable. *Number:* 25.

Eligibility Requirements: Applicant must be enrolled or expecting to enroll full-time at a four-year institution or university and resident of Alberta.

Application Requirements: Application form, transcript. *Deadline:* August 1.

EARL AND COUNTESS OF WESSEX-WORLD CHAMPIONSHIPS IN ATHLETICS SCHOLARSHIPS
• *See page 511*

GRANT MACEWAN UNITED WORLD COLLEGE SCHOLARSHIPS
• *See page 511*

JO-ANNE KOCH-ABC SOCIETY SCHOLARSHIP
• *See page 511*

ALBUQUERQUE COMMUNITY FOUNDATION

http://www.albuquerquefoundation.org/

NEW MEXICO MANUFACTURED HOUSING SCHOLARSHIP PROGRAM

The scholarship is to be used for study in a four-year college or university. The total number of available awards and the dollar value of each award varies. Deadline varies. Refer to website for details and application http://www.albuquerquefoundation.org.

Award: Scholarship for use in freshman year; not renewable. *Number:* 1–2. *Amount:* $740–$1000.

Eligibility Requirements: Applicant must be high school student; planning to enroll or expecting to enroll full-time at a four-year institution or university; resident of New Mexico and studying in New Mexico. Available to U.S. citizens.

Application Requirements: Application form, recommendations or references, resume, test scores, transcript.

Contact: Ms. Nancy Johnson, Grant Director
Albuquerque Community Foundation
PO Box 25266
Albuquerque, NM 87125
Phone: 505-883-6240
E-mail: njohnson@albuquerquefoundation.org

SUSSMAN-MILLER EDUCATIONAL ASSISTANCE FUND

The program provides financial aid to enable students to continue with an undergraduate program. This is a gap program based on financial need. Must be resident of New Mexico. Minimum 3.0 GPA required. Deadline varies. The fund requests not to write or call for information. Please visit website http://www.albuquerquefoundation.org for complete information.

Award: Scholarship for use in freshman, sophomore, junior, or senior years; not renewable. *Number:* 25–30. *Amount:* $500–$2500.

Eligibility Requirements: Applicant must be enrolled or expecting to enroll full-time at a two-year or four-year institution or university and resident of New Mexico. Available to U.S. citizens.

Application Requirements: Application form, essay, financial need analysis, recommendations or references, resume, test scores, transcript.

Contact: Ms. Nancy Johnson, Grant Director
Albuquerque Community Foundation
PO Box 25266
Albuquerque, NM 87125
Phone: 505-883-6240
E-mail: njohnson@albuquerquefoundation.org

YOUTH IN FOSTER CARE SCHOLARSHIP PROGRAM

This award is designed to support youth who have been in the New Mexico foster care system.

Award: Scholarship for use in freshman, sophomore, junior, or senior years; not renewable. *Number:* 1–4. *Amount:* $500–$1000.

Eligibility Requirements: Applicant must be age 17-21; enrolled or expecting to enroll full- or part-time at a two-year or four-year or technical institution or university and resident of New Mexico. Available to U.S. citizens.

Application Requirements: Application form, essay, resume, transcript. *Deadline:* March 18.

Contact: Ms. Nancy Johnson, Grant Director
Albuquerque Community Foundation
PO Box 25266
Albuquerque, NM 87125
Phone: 505-883-6240
E-mail: njohnson@albuquerquefoundation.org

ALERT SCHOLARSHIP

http://www.alertmagazine.org/

ALERT SCHOLARSHIP

$500 scholarship for the best essay on drug / alcohol abuse from each state. Applicant must be current high school senior in Alaska, Nebraska, Oregon, Washington, Idaho, Montana, Minnesota, Wyoming, Colorado,

North Dakota, or South Dakota. Minimum 2.5 GPA required. For more information visit: http://www.alertmagazine.org/scholarship.php.

Award: Scholarship for use in freshman year; not renewable. *Amount:* $500.

Eligibility Requirements: Applicant must be high school student; planning to enroll or expecting to enroll full- or part-time at a four-year institution or university; resident of Alaska, Colorado, Idaho, Minnesota, Montana, Nebraska, North Dakota, Oregon, South Dakota, Washington, Wyoming and must have an interest in writing. Available to U.S. citizens.

Application Requirements: Essay, personal photograph. *Deadline:* continuous.

Contact: Alert Magazine
Phone: 208-375-7911
Fax: 208-376-0770
E-mail: alertmagazine@aol.com

THE ALEXANDER FOUNDATION

http://www.thealexanderfoundation.org/

THE ALEXANDER FOUNDATION SCHOLARSHIP PROGRAM

Alexander scholarships provide financial assistance to undergraduate or graduate students accepted or enrolled in Colorado institutions of higher education. Applicants must be gay, lesbian, bisexual, or transgendered and reside in Colorado, must demonstrate financial need, and should be active/supporting/contributing members of the community.

Award: Scholarship for use in freshman, sophomore, junior, senior, graduate, or postgraduate years; not renewable. *Number:* 6–35. *Amount:* $300–$3000.

Eligibility Requirements: Applicant must be enrolled or expecting to enroll full- or part-time at a two-year or four-year or technical institution or university; resident of Colorado; studying in Colorado and must have an interest in LGBT issues. Available to U.S. citizens.

Application Requirements: Application form, essay, financial need analysis, recommendations or references, transcript. *Deadline:* April 15.

Contact: Scholarship Committee
The Alexander Foundation
PO Box 1995
Denver, CO 80201-1995
Phone: 303-331-7733
Fax: 303-331-1953
E-mail: infoalexander@thealexanderfoundation.org

ALEXANDER GRAHAM BELL ASSOCIATION FOR THE DEAF AND HARD OF HEARING

http://www.agbell.org/

AG BELL COLLEGE SCHOLARSHIP PROGRAM
• *See page 472*

ALS ASSOCIATION

http://webdc.alsa.org/site/PageServer?
pagename=DC_homepage

PAULA KOVARICK SEGALMAN FAMILY SCHOLARSHIP FUND

The Paula Kovarick Segalman Family Scholarship Fund for ALS was established by the Segalman Family to provide educational funding to students affected by ALS, also known as Lou Gehrig's disease. ALS is a fatal disease affecting families physically, emotionally and financially. The cost of care for someone with ALS can exceed $200,000 a year. The fund looks to alleviate some of the additional financial burdens that families will face when paying for college. Applicant must have a parent or legal guardian currently battling ALS or who has passed away from the disease. Annual household income must be less than $50,000. See the URL link for more about the scholarship, eligibility requirements, and the application process

http://webdc.alsa.org/site/PageNavigator/DC_Chapter/DC_6_Paula_Seg
alman_Scholarship.html

Award: Scholarship for use in freshman, sophomore, junior, or senior years; not renewable. *Amount:* up to $25,000.

Eligibility Requirements: Applicant must be age 17-25; enrolled or expecting to enroll full-time at a two-year or four-year or technical institution or university and resident of District of Columbia, Maryland, Virginia. Available to U.S. citizens.

Application Requirements: Essay. *Deadline:* May 1.

Contact: Judy Taylor
ALS Association
7507 Standish Place
Rockville, MD 20855
Phone: 240-672-3742 Ext. 213
E-mail: info@ALSinfo.org

AMERICAN LEGION AUXILIARY DEPARTMENT OF ALABAMA

http://www.legional.org/

AMERICAN LEGION AUXILIARY DEPARTMENT OF ALABAMA SCHOLARSHIP PROGRAM
• *See page 497*

AMERICAN LEGION AUXILIARY DEPARTMENT OF CALIFORNIA

http://www.calegionaux.org/

AMERICAN LEGION AUXILIARY DEPARTMENT OF CALIFORNIA GENERAL SCHOLARSHIP
• *See page 497*

AMERICAN LEGION AUXILIARY DEPARTMENT OF IOWA

http://www.iowaala.org

AMERICAN LEGION AUXILIARY DEPARTMENT OF IOWA CHILDREN OF VETERANS MERIT AWARD
• *See page 497*

AMERICAN LEGION AUXILIARY DEPARTMENT OF KENTUCKY

http://www.kylegion.org/

AMERICAN LEGION AUXILIARY DEPARTMENT OF KENTUCKY LAURA BLACKBURN MEMORIAL SCHOLARSHIP
• *See page 491*

AMERICAN LEGION AUXILIARY DEPARTMENT OF MAINE

http://www.mainelegion.org/

AMERICAN LEGION AUXILIARY DEPARTMENT OF MAINE DANIEL E. LAMBERT MEMORIAL SCHOLARSHIP
• *See page 497*

AMERICAN LEGION AUXILIARY DEPARTMENT OF MICHIGAN

http://www.michalaux.org/

AMERICAN LEGION AUXILIARY DEPARTMENT OF MICHIGAN MEMORIAL SCHOLARSHIP
• *See page 498*

AMERICAN LEGION AUXILIARY DEPARTMENT OF MICHIGAN SCHOLARSHIP FOR NON-TRADITIONAL STUDENT
• *See page 498*

AMERICAN LEGION AUXILIARY DEPARTMENT OF MINNESOTA

http://www.mnala.org

AMERICAN LEGION AUXILIARY DEPARTMENT OF MINNESOTA SCHOLARSHIPS
• *See page 498*

AMERICAN LEGION AUXILIARY DEPARTMENT OF MISSOURI

http://www.missourilegion.org/

AMERICAN LEGION AUXILIARY DEPARTMENT OF MISSOURI LELA MURPHY SCHOLARSHIP
• *See page 430*

AMERICAN LEGION AUXILIARY DEPARTMENT OF MISSOURI NATIONAL PRESIDENT'S SCHOLARSHIP
• *See page 430*

AMERICAN LEGION AUXILIARY DEPARTMENT OF NEBRASKA

http://www.nebraskalegionaux.net/

AMERICAN LEGION AUXILIARY DEPARTMENT OF NEBRASKA RUBY PAUL CAMPAIGN FUND SCHOLARSHIP
• *See page 430*

AMERICAN LEGION AUXILIARY DEPARTMENT OF NORTH DAKOTA

http://www.ndlegion.org/

AMERICAN LEGION AUXILIARY DEPARTMENT OF NORTH DAKOTA NATIONAL PRESIDENT'S SCHOLARSHIP
• *See page 460*

AMERICAN LEGION AUXILIARY DEPARTMENT OF NORTH DAKOTA SCHOLARSHIPS

One-time award for North Dakota residents who are already attending a North Dakota institution of higher learning. Contact local or nearest American Legion Auxiliary Unit for more information. Must be a U.S. citizen.

Award: Scholarship for use in sophomore, junior, senior, or graduate years; not renewable. *Number:* 3. *Amount:* $400.

Eligibility Requirements: Applicant must be enrolled or expecting to enroll full-time at a two-year or four-year or technical institution or university; resident of North Dakota and studying in North Dakota. Available to U.S. citizens.

Application Requirements: Application form, driver's license, essay, financial need analysis, recommendations or references, self-addressed stamped envelope with application, test scores, transcript. *Deadline:* January 15.

Contact: Myrna Runholm, Department Secretary
American Legion Auxiliary Department of North Dakota
PO Box 1060
Jamestown, ND 58402-1060
Phone: 701-253-5992
E-mail: ala-hq@ndlegion.org

AMERICAN LEGION AUXILIARY DEPARTMENT OF OHIO

http://www.alaohio.org/

AMERICAN LEGION AUXILIARY DEPARTMENT OF OHIO CONTINUING EDUCATION FUND
• *See page 499*

AMERICAN LEGION AUXILIARY DEPARTMENT OF OHIO DEPARTMENT PRESIDENT'S SCHOLARSHIP
• *See page 499*

AMERICAN LEGION AUXILIARY DEPARTMENT OF OREGON

http://www.alaoregon.org/

AMERICAN LEGION AUXILIARY DEPARTMENT OF OREGON DEPARTMENT GRANTS

One-time award for educational use in the state of Oregon. Must be a resident of Oregon who is the child or widow of a veteran or the wife of a disabled veteran.

Award: Scholarship for use in freshman year; not renewable. *Number:* 2. *Amount:* $1000.

Eligibility Requirements: Applicant must be enrolled or expecting to enroll full- or part-time at a two-year or four-year or technical institution or university and resident of Oregon. Available to U.S. citizens.

Application Requirements: Application form, essay, financial need analysis, interview. *Deadline:* February 10.

Contact: Virginia Biddle, Secretary/Treasurer
American Legion Auxiliary Department of Oregon
PO Box 1730
Wilsonville, OR 97070
Phone: 503-682-3162
E-mail: alaor@pcez.com

AMERICAN LEGION AUXILIARY DEPARTMENT OF OREGON NATIONAL PRESIDENT'S SCHOLARSHIP

One-time award for children of veterans who served in the Armed Forces during eligibility dates for American Legion membership. Must be high school senior and Oregon resident. Must be entered by a local American Legion auxiliary unit. Three scholarships of varying amounts.

Award: Scholarship for use in freshman year; not renewable. *Number:* 3. *Amount:* $1000–$2500.

Eligibility Requirements: Applicant must be high school student; planning to enroll or expecting to enroll full-time at a four-year institution or university and resident of Oregon. Available to U.S. citizens.

Application Requirements: Application form, essay, financial need analysis, interview. *Deadline:* February 1.

Contact: Virginia Biddle, Secretary/Treasurer
American Legion Auxiliary Department of Oregon
PO Box 1730
Wilsonville, OR 97070
Phone: 503-682-3162
E-mail: alaor@pcez.com

AMERICAN LEGION AUXILIARY DEPARTMENT OF OREGON SPIRIT OF YOUTH SCHOLARSHIP
• *See page 430*

AMERICAN LEGION AUXILIARY DEPARTMENT OF PENNSYLVANIA

ala.pa-legion.com

AMERICAN LEGION AUXILIARY DEPARTMENT OF PENNSYLVANIA SCHOLARSHIP FOR DEPENDENTS OF DISABLED OR DECEASED VETERANS

Renewable award of $600 to high school seniors who are residents of Pennsylvania. Applicants must enroll in full-time studies.

Award: Scholarship for use in freshman year; renewable. *Number:* 1. *Amount:* $600.

Eligibility Requirements: Applicant must be high school student; planning to enroll or expecting to enroll full-time at a four-year institution or university and resident of Pennsylvania. Available to U.S. citizens.

Application Requirements: Application form. *Deadline:* March 15.

Contact: Colleen Watson, Executive Secretary and Treasurer
 Phone: 717-763-7545
 Fax: 717-763-0617
 E-mail: paalad@hotmail.com

AMERICAN LEGION AUXILIARY DEPARTMENT OF PENNSYLVANIA SCHOLARSHIP FOR DEPENDENTS OF LIVING VETERANS

Renewable award of $600 for high school seniors who are residents of Pennsylvania. Applicants must enroll in a program of full-time study. Total $2,400 award.

Award: Scholarship for use in freshman, sophomore, junior, or senior years; renewable. *Number:* 1. *Amount:* $600.

Eligibility Requirements: Applicant must be high school student; planning to enroll or expecting to enroll full-time at a four-year institution or university; single; resident of Pennsylvania and studying in Pennsylvania. Available to U.S. citizens.

Application Requirements: Application form. *Deadline:* March 15.

Contact: Colleen Watson, Executive Secretary and Treasurer
 Phone: 717-763-7545
 Fax: 717-763-0617
 E-mail: paalad@hotmail.com

AMERICAN LEGION AUXILIARY DEPARTMENT OF SOUTH DAKOTA

http://www.sdlegion-aux.org/

AMERICAN LEGION AUXILIARY DEPARTMENT OF SOUTH DAKOTA COLLEGE SCHOLARSHIPS
• *See page 431*

AMERICAN LEGION AUXILIARY DEPARTMENT OF SOUTH DAKOTA SENIOR SCHOLARSHIP
• *See page 431*

AMERICAN LEGION AUXILIARY DEPARTMENT OF TEXAS

http://www.alatexas.org/

AMERICAN LEGION AUXILIARY DEPARTMENT OF TEXAS GENERAL EDUCATION SCHOLARSHIP
• *See page 499*

AMERICAN LEGION AUXILIARY DEPARTMENT OF UTAH

http://www.legion-aux.org/

AMERICAN LEGION AUXILIARY DEPARTMENT OF UTAH NATIONAL PRESIDENT'S SCHOLARSHIP
• *See page 431*

AMERICAN LEGION AUXILIARY DEPARTMENT OF WISCONSIN

http://www.amlegionauxwi.org/

AMERICAN LEGION AUXILIARY DEPARTMENT OF WISCONSIN DELLA VAN DEUREN MEMORIAL SCHOLARSHIP
• *See page 431*

AMERICAN LEGION DEPARTMENT OF ARIZONA

http://www.azlegion.org/programs

AMERICAN LEGION DEPARTMENT OF ARIZONA HIGH SCHOOL ORATORICAL CONTEST

Each student must present an 8 to 10 minute prepared oration on any part of the U.S. Constitution without any notes, podiums, or coaching. The student will then be asked to do a 3 to 5 minute oration on one of four possible topics. Which one of the four topics will not be known in advance, so students must be prepared to respond to any of the four. Open to students in grades 9 to 12.

Award: Scholarship for use in freshman year; not renewable. *Number:* 10–20. *Amount:* $50–$1500.

Eligibility Requirements: Applicant must be high school student; age 20 or under; planning to enroll or expecting to enroll full-time at a two-year or four-year institution or university; resident of Arizona and must have an interest in public speaking. Available to U.S. citizens.

Application Requirements: Application form. *Deadline:* January 1.

Contact: Roger Munchbach, Department Oratorical Chairman
 American Legion Department of Arizona
 4701 North 19th Avenue, Suite 200
 Phoenix, AZ 85015-3799
 Phone: 602-264-7706
 E-mail: legionoratoricalcontest@msn.com

AMERICAN LEGION DEPARTMENT OF ARKANSAS

http://www.arklegion.homestead.com/

AMERICAN LEGION DEPARTMENT OF ARKANSAS HIGH SCHOOL ORATORICAL CONTEST

Oratorical contest open to students in ninth to twelfth grades of any accredited Arkansas high school. Begins with finalists at the post level and proceeds through area and district levels to national contest.

Award: Prize for use in freshman year; not renewable. *Number:* 4. *Amount:* $1250–$3500.

Eligibility Requirements: Applicant must be high school student; age 19 or under; planning to enroll or expecting to enroll full-time at a four-year institution or university; resident of Arkansas and must have an interest in public speaking. Available to U.S. citizens.

Application Requirements: Application form, entry in a contest, personal photograph, recommendations or references. *Deadline:* December 15.

Contact: William Winchell, Department Adjutant
 American Legion Department of Arkansas
 PO Box 3280
 Little Rock, AR 72203-3280
 Phone: 501-375-1104
 Fax: 501-375-4236
 E-mail: alegion@swbell.net

AMERICAN LEGION DEPARTMENT OF HAWAII

http://www.legion.org/

AMERICAN LEGION DEPARTMENT OF HAWAII HIGH SCHOOL ORATORICAL CONTEST

Oratorical contest open to students in ninth to twelfth grades of any accredited Hawaii high school. Must be under 20 years of age. Speech contests begin in January at post level and continue on to the national competition. Contact local American Legion Post or department for deadlines and application details.

Award: Prize for use in freshman year; not renewable. *Number:* 1–3. *Amount:* $50–$1500.

Eligibility Requirements: Applicant must be high school student; age 14-20; planning to enroll or expecting to enroll full-time at a four-year institution or university and resident of Hawaii. Available to U.S. citizens.

Application Requirements: Application form. *Deadline:* January 1.

Contact: Adm. Bernard Lee, Department Adjutant
American Legion Department of Hawaii
612 McCully Street
Honolulu, HI 96826-3935
Phone: 808-946-6383
E-mail: aldepthi@hawaii.rr.com

AMERICAN LEGION DEPARTMENT OF IDAHO

http://www.idaholegion.com/

AMERICAN LEGION DEPARTMENT OF IDAHO SCHOLARSHIP
• *See page 432*

AMERICAN LEGION DEPARTMENT OF ILLINOIS

http://www.illegion.org/

AMERICANISM ESSAY CONTEST SCHOLARSHIP
• *See page 432*

AMERICAN LEGION DEPARTMENT OF ILLINOIS BOY SCOUT/EXPLORER SCHOLARSHIP
• *See page 432*

AMERICAN LEGION DEPARTMENT OF ILLINOIS HIGH SCHOOL ORATORICAL CONTEST
Single oratorical contest with winners advancing to the next level. Open to students in 9th to 12th grades of any accredited Illinois high school. Seniors must be in attendance as of January 1. Must contact local American Legion post or department headquarters for complete information and applications, which will be available in the fall.

Award: Scholarship for use in freshman year; not renewable. *Number:* 1–30. *Amount:* $100–$2000.

Eligibility Requirements: Applicant must be high school student; planning to enroll or expecting to enroll full- or part-time at a four-year institution or university; resident of Illinois and must have an interest in English language or public speaking. Available to U.S. citizens.

Application Requirements: Application form. *Fee:* $125.

Contact: Christy Rich, Executive Administrative Assistant
American Legion Department of Illinois
2720 East Lincoln Street
Bloomington, IL 61704
Phone: 309-663-0361
Fax: 309-663-5783
E-mail: hdqs@illegion.org

AMERICAN LEGION DEPARTMENT OF INDIANA

http://www.indianalegion.org

AMERICAN LEGION DEPARTMENT OF INDIANA, AMERICANISM AND GOVERNMENT TEST
Study guides are provided to high schools. Students take a test and write an essay. One male and one female student from each grade (10 to 12) are selected as state winners.

Award: Scholarship for use in freshman, sophomore, junior, or senior years; not renewable. *Number:* 6. *Amount:* $1000.

Eligibility Requirements: Applicant must be high school student; planning to enroll or expecting to enroll full- or part-time at a two-year or technical institution or university and resident of Illinois. Available to U.S. citizens.

Application Requirements: Application form. *Deadline:* December 1.

Contact: Butch Miller, Program Director
American Legion Department of Indiana
5440 Herbert Lord Road
Indianapolis, IN 46216
Phone: 317-630-1391
Fax: 317-237-9891
E-mail: bmiller@indianalegion.org

AMERICAN LEGION DEPARTMENT OF INDIANA HIGH SCHOOL ORATORICAL CONTEST
Oratorical contest open to students in grades nine to twelve of any accredited Indiana high school or home schooled students in an equivalent grade. All contestants must be a citizen of or lawful permanent resident of the United States. Students may only enter one district/zone/state competition. The student must compete in the district in which his/her sponsoring post is located. Contact local American Legion post for application details or visit our website at http//www.indianalegion.org.

Award: Scholarship for use in freshman, sophomore, junior, or senior years; not renewable. *Amount:* $200–$3400.

Eligibility Requirements: Applicant must be high school student; age 19 or under; planning to enroll or expecting to enroll full- or part-time at a two-year or technical institution or university and resident of Illinois. Available to U.S. citizens.

Application Requirements: Application form. *Deadline:* December 20.

Contact: Butch Miller, Program Director
American Legion Department of Indiana
5440 Herbert Lord Road
Indianapolis, IN 46216
Phone: 317-630-1391
Fax: 317-237-9891
E-mail: bmiller@indianalegion.org

AMERICAN LEGION FAMILY SCHOLARSHIP
• *See page 432*

FRANK W. MCHALE MEMORIAL SCHOLARSHIPS
One-time award for Indiana high school junior boys who participated in The American Legion Hoosier Boys State Program. Must be nominated by Boys State official while in attendance at Hoosier Boys State. Write for more information and deadline.

Award: Scholarship for use in freshman, sophomore, junior, or senior years; not renewable. *Number:* 3. *Amount:* $800.

Eligibility Requirements: Applicant must be high school student; planning to enroll or expecting to enroll full- or part-time at a two-year or four-year or technical institution or university; male; resident of Indiana and must have an interest in leadership. Available to U.S. citizens.

Application Requirements: Application form, essay.

Contact: Butch Miller, Program Director
American Legion Department of Indiana
5440 Herbert Lord Road
Indianapolis, IN 46216
Phone: 317-630-1391
Fax: 317-237-9891
E-mail: bmiller@indianalegion.org

AMERICAN LEGION DEPARTMENT OF IOWA

http://www.ialegion.org/

AMERICAN LEGION DEPARTMENT OF IOWA EAGLE SCOUT OF THE YEAR SCHOLARSHIP
• *See page 432*

AMERICAN LEGION DEPARTMENT OF IOWA HIGH SCHOOL ORATORICAL CONTEST
All contestants in the department of Iowa American Legion High School Oratorical Contest shall be citizens or lawful permanent residents of the United States. The department of Iowa American Legion High School Oratorical Contest shall consist of one contestant from each of the three area contests. The area contest shall consist of one contestant from each district in the designated Area.

Award: Prize for use in freshman year; not renewable. *Number:* 3. *Amount:* $1000–$2000.

Eligibility Requirements: Applicant must be high school student; planning to enroll or expecting to enroll full-time at a two-year or four-year institution or university; resident of Iowa and must have an interest in public speaking. Available to U.S. citizens.

Application Requirements: Application form.

Contact: Programs Director
Phone: 515-282-5068
Fax: 515-282-7583
E-mail: programs@ialegion.org

AMERICAN LEGION DEPARTMENT OF IOWA OUTSTANDING SENIOR BASEBALL PLAYER

One-time award for Iowa residents who participated in the American Legion Senior Baseball Program and display outstanding sportsmanship, athletic ability, and proven academic achievements. Must be recommended by Baseball Committee.

Award: Scholarship for use in freshman year; not renewable. *Number:* 1. *Amount:* $750–$1500.

Eligibility Requirements: Applicant must be high school student; age 15-18; planning to enroll or expecting to enroll full-time at a two-year or four-year institution or university; resident of Iowa and must have an interest in athletics/sports. Available to U.S. citizens.

Application Requirements: Application form, entry in a contest, recommendations or references. *Deadline:* July 15.

Contact: Programs Director
Phone: 515-282-5068
Fax: 515-282-7583
E-mail: programs@ialegion.org

AMERICAN LEGION DEPARTMENT OF MAINE

http://www.mainelegion.org/

AMERICAN LEGION DEPARTMENT OF MAINE CHILDREN AND YOUTH SCHOLARSHIP
• *See page 500*

DANIEL E. LAMBERT MEMORIAL SCHOLARSHIP
• *See page 500*

JAMES V. DAY SCHOLARSHIP
• *See page 432*

AMERICAN LEGION DEPARTMENT OF MARYLAND

http://www.mdlegion.org/

AMERICAN LEGION DEPARTMENT OF MARYLAND GENERAL SCHOLARSHIP FUND
• *See page 433*

AMERICAN LEGION, DEPARTMENT OF MARYLAND, HIGH SCHOOL ORATORICAL SCHOLARSHIP CONTEST

Scholarship awarded to winner of the Department of MD High School Oratorical Contest. Applicants must apply at their local Posts and compete in and win their Post, County, and District level competitions for eligibility. The winner of this contest goes on to compete at Nationals. For details http://www.legion.org/oratorical

Award: Scholarship for use in freshman, sophomore, junior, or senior years; not renewable. *Number:* 1–7. *Amount:* $500–$2000.

Eligibility Requirements: Applicant must be high school student; age 19 or under; planning to enroll or expecting to enroll full-time at a two-year institution or university and resident of Manitoba. Available to U.S. citizens.

Application Requirements: *Deadline:* January 10.

Contact: Mr. Russell Myers, Department Adjutant
American Legion Department of Maryland
101 North Gay Street, Room E
Baltimore, MD 21202
Phone: 410-752-1405
Fax: 410-752-3822
E-mail: russell@mdlegion.org

MARYLAND BOYS STATE SCHOLARSHIP

Scholarship awarded from applicants that have graduated from Maryland Boys State program. Applications must be received by May 1st of the Boys State graduate's SR year in High School. Application available at http://www.mdlegion.org/Forms/bsschol.pdf

Award: Scholarship for use in freshman, sophomore, junior, or senior years; not renewable. *Number:* 1–10. *Amount:* $500.

Eligibility Requirements: Applicant must be high school student; planning to enroll or expecting to enroll full-time at a two-year institution or university; male and resident of Manitoba. Available to U.S. citizens.

Application Requirements: Application form, essay. *Deadline:* May 1.

Contact: Russell Myers, Department Adjutant
American Legion Department of Maryland
War Memorial Building, Room E
101 N. Gay Street
Baltimore, MD 21202
Phone: 410-752-1405
Fax: 410-752-3822
E-mail: russell@mdlegion.org

AMERICAN LEGION DEPARTMENT OF MICHIGAN

http://www.michiganlegion.org/

AMERICAN LEGION DEPARTMENT OF MICHIGAN ORATORICAL SCHOLARSHIP PROGRAM

Oratorical contest open to students in ninth to twelfth grades of any accredited Michigan high school or state accredited home school. Five one-time awards of varying amounts. State winner advances to National Competition for scholarship money ranging from $14,000 to $18,000. Application Due in November

Award: Scholarship for use in freshman year; not renewable. *Number:* 5. *Amount:* $800–$1500.

Eligibility Requirements: Applicant must be high school student; planning to enroll or expecting to enroll full- or part-time at a two-year or four-year institution or university; resident of Michigan and must have an interest in public speaking. Available to U.S. citizens.

Application Requirements: Application form, essay. *Deadline:* November 18.

Contact: Programs Coordinator
American Legion Department of Michigan
212 North Verlinden Avenue
Lansing, MI 48915
Phone: 517-371-4720 Ext. 23
E-mail: legion@michiganlegion.org

GUY M. WILSON SCHOLARSHIPS
• *See page 500*

WILLIAM D. AND JEWELL W. BREWER SCHOLARSHIP TRUSTS
• *See page 500*

THE AMERICAN LEGION, DEPARTMENT OF MINNESOTA

http://www.mnlegion.org/

AMERICAN LEGION DEPARTMENT OF MINNESOTA HIGH SCHOOL ORATORICAL CONTEST

Oratorical contest open to students in ninth to twelfth grades of any accredited Minnesota high school or home-schooled students. Must be Minnesota resident. Speech must be student's original work on the general subject of the Constitution. Speech contests begin in December at local Legion post level and continue on to the national competition. See website for specific topic and application details http://www.mnlegion.org.

Award: Scholarship for use in freshman year; not renewable. *Number:* 4. *Amount:* $500–$1500.

Eligibility Requirements: Applicant must be high school student; planning to enroll or expecting to enroll full- or part-time at a two-year or four-year or technical institution or university; resident of Minnesota and must have an interest in public speaking. Available to U.S. citizens.

Application Requirements: *Deadline:* November 30.

Contact: Jennifer Kelley, Program Coordinator
The American Legion, Department of Minnesota
20 West 12th Street, Room 300-A
St. Paul, MN 55155
Phone: 651-291-1800
E-mail: department@mnlegion.org

AMERICAN LEGION DEPARTMENT OF MINNESOTA MEMORIAL SCHOLARSHIP
• *See page 433*

MINNESOTA LEGIONNAIRES INSURANCE TRUST SCHOLARSHIP
• *See page 433*

AMERICAN LEGION DEPARTMENT OF MISSOURI
http://www.missourilegion.org/

CHARLES L. BACON MEMORIAL SCHOLARSHIP
• *See page 433*

LILLIE LOIS FORD SCHOLARSHIP FUND
• *See page 501*

AMERICAN LEGION DEPARTMENT OF NEW YORK
http://www.ny.legion.org/

AMERICAN LEGION DEPARTMENT OF NEW YORK HIGH SCHOOL ORATORICAL CONTEST

Oratorical contest open to students under 20 years in 9th-12th grades of any accredited New York high school. Speech contests begin in November at post levels and continue to national competition. Must be U.S. citizen or permanent resident. Payments are made directly to college and are awarded over a four-year period. Deadline varies.

Award: Scholarship for use in freshman year; not renewable.

Eligibility Requirements: Applicant must be high school student; age 20 or under; planning to enroll or expecting to enroll full-time at a four-year institution or university; resident of New York and must have an interest in public speaking. Available to U.S. citizens.

Application Requirements: Application form.

Contact: Department Adjutant
American Legion Department of New York
112 State Street, Suite 400
Albany, NY 12207
Phone: 518-463-2215
E-mail: newyork@legion.org

AMERICAN LEGION DEPARTMENT OF NORTH CAROLINA
http://www.nclegion.org/

AMERICAN LEGION DEPARTMENT OF NORTH CAROLINA HIGH SCHOOL ORATORICAL CONTEST

This is a speaking contest. The objective of the contest is to develop a deeper knowledge and appreciation of the U.S. Constitution, develop leadership qualities, the ability to think and speak clearly and intelligently, and prepare for acceptance of duties, responsibilities, rights, and privileges of American citizenship. Open to North Carolina high

school students. Must be U.S. citizen or lawful permanent resident. The contestant must have a prepared eight to ten minute oration on some aspect of the Constitution of the United States, as well as 4 three to five minute discourses on specific assigned topics to test the speaker's knowledge of the subject.

Award: Scholarship for use in freshman year; not renewable. *Number:* 5. *Amount:* $1000–$2500.

Eligibility Requirements: Applicant must be high school student; age 20 or under; planning to enroll or expecting to enroll full-time at a two-year or four-year or technical institution or university; resident of North Carolina and must have an interest in public speaking. Available to U.S. citizens.

Application Requirements: *Deadline:* December 22.

Contact: Deborah Rose, Department Executive Secretary
American Legion Department of North Carolina
4 North Blount Street, PO Box 26657
Raleigh, NC 27611-6657
Phone: 919-832-7506
E-mail: drose-nclegion@nc.rr.com

AMERICAN LEGION DEPARTMENT OF OREGON
http://www.orlegion.org/

AMERICAN LEGION DEPARTMENT OF OREGON HIGH SCHOOL ORATORICAL CONTEST

Students give two orations, one prepared and one extemporaneous on an assigned topic pertaining to the Constitution of the United States of America. Awards are given at Post, District, and State level with the state winner advancing to the National level contest. Open to students enrolled in high schools within the state of Oregon.

Award: Scholarship for use in freshman year; not renewable. *Number:* up to 4. *Amount:* $200–$500.

Eligibility Requirements: Applicant must be high school student; planning to enroll or expecting to enroll full-time at a four-year institution or university; resident of Oregon and must have an interest in public speaking. Available to U.S. citizens.

Application Requirements: Application form, entry in a contest. *Deadline:* December 1.

Contact: Barry Snyder, Adjutant
Phone: 503-685-5006
Fax: 503-968-5432
E-mail: orlegion@aol.com

AMERICAN LEGION DEPARTMENT OF PENNSYLVANIA
http://www.pa-legion.com/

AMERICAN LEGION DEPARTMENT OF PENNSYLVANIA HIGH SCHOOL ORATORICAL CONTEST

Oratorical contest open to students in 9th-12th grades of any accredited Pennsylvania high school. Speech contests begin in January at post level and continue on to national competition. Contact local American Legion post for deadlines and application details. Three one-time awards ranging from $7500 for first place, second place $5000, and third place $4000.

Award: Prize for use in freshman year; not renewable. *Number:* 3. *Amount:* $4000–$7500.

Eligibility Requirements: Applicant must be high school student; planning to enroll or expecting to enroll full-time at a two-year or four-year or technical institution or university; resident of Pennsylvania and must have an interest in public speaking. Available to U.S. citizens.

Application Requirements: Application form.

Contact: Debbie Watson, Emblem Sales Supervisor
Phone: 717-730-9100
Fax: 717-975-2836
E-mail: hq@pa-legion.com

JOSEPH P. GAVENONIS COLLEGE SCHOLARSHIP (PLAN I)
• *See page 434*

AMERICAN LEGION DEPARTMENT OF SOUTH DAKOTA

http://www.sdlegion.org/

AMERICAN LEGION DEPARTMENT OF SOUTH DAKOTA HIGH SCHOOL ORATORICAL CONTEST

Provide an 8 to 10 minute oration on some phase of the U.S. Constitution. Be prepared to speak extemporaneously for 3 to 5 minutes on specified articles or amendments. Compete at Local, District, and State levels. State winner goes on to National Contest and opportunity to win $18,000 in scholarships. Contact local American Legion post for contest dates.

Award: Prize for use in freshman, sophomore, junior, or senior years; not renewable. *Number:* 1–4. *Amount:* $100–$1000.

Eligibility Requirements: Applicant must be enrolled or expecting to enroll full-time at a two-year or four-year or technical institution or university; resident of South Dakota and must have an interest in public speaking. Available to U.S. citizens.

Application Requirements: Application form, entry in a contest.

Contact: Travise Flisrand, Department Adjutant
American Legion Department of South Dakota
PO Box 67
Watertown, SD 57201-0067
Phone: 605-886-3604
E-mail: sdlegion@dailypost.com

AMERICAN LEGION DEPARTMENT OF TENNESSEE

http://www.tennesseelegion.org/

AMERICAN LEGION DEPARTMENT OF TENNESSEE EAGLE SCOUT OF THE YEAR
• *See page 434*

AMERICAN LEGION DEPARTMENT OF TENNESSEE HIGH SCHOOL ORATORICAL CONTEST

Scholarship for graduating Tennessee high school seniors enrolled either part-time or full-time in accredited colleges or universities.

Award: Scholarship for use in freshman, sophomore, junior, or senior years; not renewable. *Number:* 1–3. *Amount:* $1000–$3000.

Eligibility Requirements: Applicant must be high school student; planning to enroll or expecting to enroll full- or part-time at a two-year or four-year institution or university; resident of Tennessee and must have an interest in public speaking. Available to U.S. citizens.

Application Requirements: Application form, essay.

Contact: Dean Tuttle, Department Adjutant
American Legion Department of Tennessee
318 Donelson Pike
Nashville, TN 37214
Phone: 615-391-5088
E-mail: Adjutant@TNLegion.org

AMERICAN LEGION DEPARTMENT OF TEXAS

http://www.txlegion.org/

AMERICAN LEGION DEPARTMENT OF TEXAS HIGH SCHOOL ORATORICAL CONTEST

Scholarships will be given to the winners of oratorical contests. Contestants must be in high school with plans to further their education in a postsecondary institution. The winner of first place will be certified to national headquarters as the Texas representative in the quarter finals and the department will award a $2000 scholarship to the college of the applicant's choice. The department champion will receive additional scholarships each time he/she advances to the next level.

Award: Prize for use in freshman year; not renewable. *Amount:* $500–$2000.

Eligibility Requirements: Applicant must be high school student; age 20 or under; planning to enroll or expecting to enroll full-time at a two-year or four-year or technical institution or university; resident of Texas and must have an interest in public speaking. Available to U.S. citizens.

Application Requirements: Application form, essay, interview.

Contact: Director of Internal Affairs
American Legion Department of Texas
3401 Ed Bluestein Boulevard
Austin, TX 78721-2902
Phone: 512-472-4138
E-mail: michaels@txlegion.org

AMERICAN LEGION DEPARTMENT OF VERMONT

http://www.vtlegion.org

AMERICAN LEGION DEPARTMENT OF VERMONT DEPARTMENT SCHOLARSHIPS

Awards for high school seniors who attend a Vermont high school or similar school in an adjoining state whose parents are legal residents of Vermont, or reside in an adjoining state and attend a Vermont secondary school.

Award: Scholarship for use in freshman year; not renewable. *Number:* 1–12. *Amount:* $500–$1500.

Eligibility Requirements: Applicant must be high school student; planning to enroll or expecting to enroll full- or part-time at a two-year or four-year or technical institution or university and resident of New Hampshire, New York, Vermont. Available to U.S. citizens.

Application Requirements: Application form, essay, financial need analysis. *Deadline:* April 1.

Contact: Huzon "Jerry" Stewart, Chairman
American Legion Department of Vermont
PO Box 396
Montpelier, VT 05601-0396
Phone: 802-223-7131
E-mail: alvthq@myfairpoint.net

AMERICAN LEGION DEPARTMENT OF VERMONT HIGH SCHOOL ORATORICAL CONTEST

Students in grades 9 to 12 are eligible to compete. Must attend an accredited Vermont high school. Must be a U.S. citizen. Selection based on oration.

Award: Prize for use in freshman year; not renewable. *Number:* 1–2. *Amount:* $200–$1500.

Eligibility Requirements: Applicant must be high school student; planning to enroll or expecting to enroll full- or part-time at a two-year or four-year or technical institution or university; resident of Vermont and must have an interest in public speaking. Available to U.S. citizens.

Application Requirements: Application form. *Deadline:* January 1.

Contact: Karlene DeVine, Chairman
American Legion Department of Vermont
126 State Street
Montpelier, VT 05601
Phone: 802-223-7131
E-mail: alvthq@myfairpoint.net

AMERICAN LEGION EAGLE SCOUT OF THE YEAR
• *See page 434*

AMERICAN LEGION DEPARTMENT OF VIRGINIA

http://www.valegion.org/

AMERICAN LEGION DEPARTMENT OF VIRGINIA HIGH SCHOOL ORATORICAL CONTEST

Three one-time awards of up to $1100. Oratorical contest open to applicants who are winners of the Virginia department oratorical contest and who attend high school in Virginia. Competitors must demonstrate their knowledge of the U.S. Constitution. Must be students in ninth to twelfth grades at accredited Virginia high schools.

Award: Prize for use in freshman year; not renewable. *Number:* 3. *Amount:* $600–$1100.

Eligibility Requirements: Applicant must be high school student; age 20 or under; planning to enroll or expecting to enroll full-time at a four-year institution or university and resident of Virginia. Available to U.S. citizens.

Application Requirements: Application form, entry in a contest. *Deadline:* December 1.

Contact: Dale Chapman, Adjutant
American Legion Department of Virginia
1708 Commonwealth Avenue
Richmond, VA 23230
Phone: 804-353-6606
Fax: 804-358-1940
E-mail: eeccleston@valegion.org

AMERICAN LEGION DEPARTMENT OF WASHINGTON

http://www.walegion.org/

AMERICAN LEGION DEPARTMENT OF WASHINGTON CHILDREN AND YOUTH SCHOLARSHIPS
• See page 434

AMERICAN SAVINGS FOUNDATION

http://www.asfdn.org/

ROBERT T. KENNEY SCHOLARSHIP PROGRAM AT THE AMERICAN SAVINGS FOUNDATION

Scholarship awards range from $1,000 to $3,000 for students entering any year of a two- or four-year undergraduate program or technical/vocational program at an accredited institution. Applicant must be a resident of one of the 64 Connecticut towns within our service area. Minimum 2.5 GPA required.

Award: Scholarship for use in freshman, sophomore, junior, or senior years; renewable. *Number:* 400. *Amount:* $1000–$2500.

Eligibility Requirements: Applicant must be enrolled or expecting to enroll full-time at a two-year or four-year or technical institution or university and resident of Connecticut.

Application Requirements: Application form, essay, financial need analysis. *Deadline:* March 31.

Contact: Heather Hokunson, Associate Program Officer - Scholarships
Phone: 860-827-2572
Fax: 860-832-4582
E-mail: hhokunson@asfdn.org

ANTHONY MUNOZ FOUNDATION

http://www.munozfoundation.org

ANTHONY MUNOZ SCHOLARSHIP FUND

The Anthony Munoz Scholarship Fund was created by Anthony Munoz and his family to support greater Cincinnati high school youth in achieving their dreams of attending a local college or university. Applications for the scholarship fund will be accepted starting January 1st, 2018 through May 1st, 2018. Recipients of The Anthony Munoz Scholarship Fund must meet several requirements to apply for this scholarship. This includes, but is not limited to being a high school senior in our greater Cincinnati Impact Area; being enrolled in or entering an eligible greater Cincinnati/Tri-State college or university; and displaying a desire to overcome adversity and demonstrate a financial need. The scholarship fund application and eligibility requirements can be found at http://www.munozfoundation.org.

Award: Scholarship for use in freshman, sophomore, junior, or senior years; renewable. *Number:* 5. *Amount:* $20,000.

Eligibility Requirements: Applicant must be high school student; planning to enroll or expecting to enroll full-time at a four-year institution; resident of Indiana, Kentucky, Ohio and studying in Indiana, Kentucky, Ohio. Available to U.S. citizens.

Application Requirements: Application form, community service, essay, financial need analysis, interview, test scores, transcript. *Deadline:* May 1.

Contact: Mrs. Victoria Knepp, Director of Marketing and Events
Anthony Munoz Foundation
8919 Rossash Road
Cincinnati, OH 45236
Phone: 513-772-4900
Fax: 513-772-4911
E-mail: vknepp@munozfoundation.org

ARIZONA COMMISSION FOR POSTSECONDARY EDUCATION

https://highered.az.gov/

LEVERAGING EDUCATIONAL ASSISTANCE PARTNERSHIP

Grants to financially needy students, who enroll in and attend postsecondary education or training in Arizona schools. Program was formerly known as the State Student Incentive Grant or SSIG Program.

Award: Grant for use in freshman, sophomore, junior, senior, or graduate years; not renewable. *Amount:* $100–$2500.

Eligibility Requirements: Applicant must be enrolled or expecting to enroll full- or part-time at a two-year or four-year or technical institution or university; resident of Arizona and studying in Arizona. Available to U.S. citizens.

Application Requirements: Application form, financial need analysis, transcript. *Deadline:* April 30.

Contact: Mila Zaporteza, Business Manager and LEAP Financial Aid Manager
Arizona Commission for Postsecondary Education
2020 North Central Avenue, Suite 650
Phoenix, AZ 85004-4503
Phone: 602-258-2435 Ext. 102
Fax: 602-258-2483
E-mail: mila@azhighered.gov

ARIZONA PRIVATE SCHOOL ASSOCIATION

http://www.arizonapsa.org/

ARIZONA PRIVATE SCHOOL ASSOCIATION SCHOLARSHIP

Scholarships are for graduating students from Arizona and the high school determines the recipients of the awards. Each spring the Arizona Private School Association awards two $1000 scholarships to every private high school in Arizona.

Award: Scholarship for use in freshman year; not renewable. *Number:* 600. *Amount:* $1000.

Eligibility Requirements: Applicant must be high school student; planning to enroll or expecting to enroll full-time at a four-year institution or university and resident of Arizona. Available to U.S. citizens.

Application Requirements: Application form, essay. *Deadline:* April 30.

Contact: Fred Lockhart, Executive Director
Arizona Private School Association
202 East McDowell Road, Suite 273
Phoenix, AZ 85004
Phone: 602-254-5199
Fax: 602-254-5073
E-mail: apsa@eschelon.com

ARKANSAS DEPARTMENT OF HIGHER EDUCATION

http://www.adhe.edu/

ARKANSAS ACADEMIC CHALLENGE SCHOLARSHIP

The Academic Challenge Program provides scholarships to Arkansas residents pursuing a higher education. Funded in large part by the Arkansas Scholarship Lottery, the Academic Challenge Scholarship is available to students regardless of their academic status, whether just graduating from high school, currently enrolled in college, enrolling in college for the first time, or re-enrolling after a period of time out of college. Must have at least a 19 ACT composite score (or the equivalent). Renewable up to three additional years.

Award: Scholarship for use in freshman, sophomore, junior, senior, or graduate years; renewable. *Number:* 30,000–35,000. *Amount:* $1000–$5000.

Eligibility Requirements: Applicant must be enrolled or expecting to enroll full- or part-time at a two-year institution or university; resident of Arizona and studying in Arkansas. Available to U.S. citizens.

Application Requirements: Application form, application form may be submitted online, financial need analysis. *Deadline:* June 1.

Contact: Jonathan Coleman, Financial Aid Manager
Phone: 501-371-2000
E-mail: jonathan.coleman@adhe.edu

ARKANSAS GOVERNOR'S SCHOLARS PROGRAM

Awards for outstanding Arkansas high school seniors. Applicants who attain 32 or above on ACT, 1410 or above on SAT and have an academic 3.5 GPA, or are selected as National Merit or National Achievement finalists may receive an award equal to tuition, mandatory fees, room, and board up to $10,000 per year at any Arkansas institution. If any of the seventy-five (75) counties is not represented, the Department of Higher Education shall select a student from each non-represented county with the highest qualifications who was not initially qualified. Students from these counties will be awarded $5000 per year at any Arkansas institution.

Award: Scholarship for use in freshman, sophomore, junior, senior, or graduate years; renewable. *Number:* 75–375. *Amount:* $4000–$10,000.

Eligibility Requirements: Applicant must be high school student; planning to enroll or expecting to enroll full-time at a two-year institution or university; resident of Arizona and studying in Arkansas. Available to U.S. citizens.

Application Requirements: Application form, application form may be submitted online, community service. *Deadline:* February 1.

Contact: Jonathan Coleman, Financial Aid Manager
Phone: 501-371-2000
E-mail: jonathan.coleman@adhe.edu

LAW ENFORCEMENT OFFICERS' DEPENDENTS SCHOLARSHIP&-ARKANSAS

Scholarship for dependents, under 23 years old, of Arkansas law-enforcement officers killed or permanently disabled in the line of duty. Renewable award is a waiver of tuition, fees, and room at two- or four-year Arkansas institution. Submit birth certificate, death certificate, and claims commission report of findings of fact. Proof of disability from State Claims Commission may also be submitted. Must maintain a minimum GPA of 2.0 on a 4.0 scale.

Award: Scholarship for use in freshman, sophomore, junior, or senior years; renewable.

Eligibility Requirements: Applicant must be age 22 or under; enrolled or expecting to enroll full- or part-time at a two-year or technical institution or university; resident of Arizona and studying in Arkansas. Available to U.S. citizens.

Application Requirements: Application form, application form may be submitted online. *Deadline:* July 1.

Contact: Lisa Smith, Program Specialist
Arkansas Department of Higher Education
423 Main Street Suite 400
Little Rock, AR 72201-3818
Phone: 501-371-2000
E-mail: lisa.smith@adhe.edu

MILITARY DEPENDENT'S SCHOLARSHIP PROGRAM
• *See page 501*

ARRL FOUNDATION INC.

http://www.arrl.org/home

HARRY A. HODGES, W6YOO, SCHOLARSHIP

$1000 scholarship award for a student with a Technician class amateur radio license. Preference will be given to applicants from San Diego County, California. If no qualified applicant is identified, preference will be given to an applicant from California. Applicant must demonstrate activity and interest in radio service or some technical proficiency by participating in some form of radio related activities such as emergency communications, equipment construction, community radio services, scouting, etc. Must be performing at a high academic level or an at-risk youth with at least two counselor or teacher recommendationsas to how and why they have turned their lives around.

Award: Scholarship for use in freshman, sophomore, junior, or senior years; not renewable. *Number:* 1. *Amount:* $1000.

Eligibility Requirements: Applicant must be enrolled or expecting to enroll full- or part-time at a two-year or four-year or technical institution or university; resident of California and must have an interest in amateur radio. Available to U.S. citizens.

Application Requirements: Application form. *Deadline:* January 31.

Contact: Ms. Melissa Stemmer
ARRL Foundation Inc.
225 Main Street
Newington, CT 06111-1400
Phone: 860-594-0348
E-mail: foundation@arrl.org

ASIAN PACIFIC COMMUNITY FUND

http://www.apcf.org/

CATHAY BANK FOUNDATION SCHOLARSHIP PROGRAM

Twenty $1,000 Scholarships Available for High School Seniors. Planning to Attend College as a Full-Time, Degree-Seeking Student in the Fall of 2020. Cathay Bank Foundation is committed to supporting youth residing in its business service territories to fulfill their dreams of obtaining a higher education. The scholarship awards will only be used to cover the cost of tuition for attending a college/university, as defined by the institution attended. Employees of Cathay Bank and their immediate family members are NOT eligible.

Award: Scholarship for use in freshman year. *Number:* 20–1,000.

Eligibility Requirements: Applicant must be high school student; planning to enroll or expecting to enroll full-time at a two-year institution or university; resident of British Columbia, Idaho, Manitoba, Maryland, Nebraska, New Hampshire, New Mexico, Tennessee, Virginia and studying in California, Illinois, Maryland, Massachusetts, Nevada, New Jersey, Texas, Washington. Available to U.S. citizens.

Application Requirements: Application form, application form may be submitted online. *Deadline:* April 17.

Contact: Karen Fan
Asian Pacific Community Fund
1145 Wilshire Boulevard
Suite 105
Los Angeles, CA 90017
Phone: 213-624-6400 Ext. 6
Fax: 213-624-6406
E-mail: kfan@apcf.org

ASSISTANCE LEAGUE OF THE TRIANGLE AREA

HIGH SCHOOL SENIOR SCHOLARSHIP

Applicants must be residents of Wake, Durham, or Orange counties in North Carolina and be attending a school in North Carolina.

Award: Scholarship for use in freshman year; not renewable. *Number:* 1–25. *Amount:* $1000–$10,000.

Eligibility Requirements: Applicant must be high school student; planning to enroll or expecting to enroll full-time at a two-year or four-year or technical institution or university; resident of North Carolina and studying in North Carolina. Available to U.S. citizens.

Application Requirements: Application form, community service, essay, financial need analysis. *Deadline:* March 1.

Contact: Grace Fox
E-mail: altascholars@gmail.com

SINGLE WORKING PARENT SCHOLARSHIP

Applicants must be residents of Wake, Durham or Orange counties in North Carolina and be attending a school in North Carolina.

Award: Scholarship for use in freshman, sophomore, junior, or senior years; not renewable. *Number:* 1–5. *Amount:* $1000–$10,000.

Eligibility Requirements: Applicant must be enrolled or expecting to enroll full- or part-time at a two-year or four-year or technical institution or university; resident of North Carolina and studying in North Carolina. Available to U.S. citizens.

Application Requirements: Application form, community service, essay, financial need analysis. *Deadline:* March 1.

Contact: Grace Fox
E-mail: altascholars@gmail.com

BARSKI LAW FIRM

http://www.barskilaw.com

BARSKI LAW FIRM SCHOLARSHIP

Scholarship for student(s) to attend an Arizona institution of higher education based upon merit, need and community service.

Award: Scholarship for use in freshman, sophomore, junior, or senior years; not renewable. *Number:* 2,500.

Eligibility Requirements: Applicant must be enrolled or expecting to enroll full-time at a two-year or four-year or technical institution or university; resident of Arizona and studying in Arizona. Available to U.S. and non-U.S. citizens.

Application Requirements: Application form, financial need analysis. *Deadline:* June 1.

Contact: Chris Barski
Barski Law Firm
8700 E. Via de Ventura, Suite 140
Scottsdale, AZ 85258
Phone: 602-441-4700
E-mail: cbarski@barskilaw.com

BLUE GRASS ENERGY

http://www.bgenergy.com/

BLUE GRASS ENERGY ACADEMIC SCHOLARSHIP

Scholarships for Kentucky high school seniors living with parents or guardians who are members of Blue Grass Energy. Must have minimum GPA of 3.0 and have demonstrated academic achievement, extracurricular involvement and financial need. For application and information, visit website http://www.bgenergy.com/forStudents.aspx.

Award: Scholarship for use in freshman year; not renewable. *Number:* 10. *Amount:* $1000.

Eligibility Requirements: Applicant must be high school student; planning to enroll or expecting to enroll full-time at a two-year or four-year or technical institution or university and resident of Kentucky. Available to U.S. citizens.

Application Requirements: Application form, essay, explanation of how scholarship is necessary to further education, financial need analysis, resume, test scores, transcript. *Deadline:* April 1.

Contact: Ms. Magen Howard, Communications Adviser
Phone: 859-885-2104
E-mail: magenh@bgenergy.com

BOUNCE ENERGY

http://www.bounceenergy.com

BE MORE SCHOLARSHIP

Bounce Energy is excited to announce its fourth annual "BE More" Scholarship! The scholarship is open to all high school senior and college students who live or attend school in the state of Texas. The $2,500 scholarship will be awarded to three qualifying students. In order to be eligible for the scholarship, students must meet the requirements below, submit an online application, and write a short essay of no more than 500 words.

Award: Scholarship for use in freshman, sophomore, junior, senior, graduate, or postgraduate years; not renewable. *Number:* 3. *Amount:* $2500.

Eligibility Requirements: Applicant must be age 13-24; enrolled or expecting to enroll full- or part-time at a two-year or four-year or technical institution or university; resident of Texas and studying in Texas. Available to U.S. and non-U.S. citizens.

Application Requirements: Application form, essay. *Deadline:* June 30.

Contact: Scholarship Coordinator
Bounce Energy
12 Greenway Plaza
Suite 250
Houston, TX 77046
Phone: 855-4526862
E-mail: BEscholarship@directenergy.com

BRIDGES FOR THE DEAF AND HARD OF HEARING

http://www.bridgesfordeafandhh.org/

LINDA COWDEN MEMORIAL SCHOLARSHIP
• *See page 473*

CABRILLO CIVIC CLUBS OF CALIFORNIA INC.

http://www.cabrillocivicclubs.org/scholarship.asp

CABRILLO CIVIC CLUBS OF CALIFORNIA SCHOLARSHIP
• *See page 514*

CALIFORNIA ASSOCIATION OF WINE GRAPE GROWERS FOUNDATION

http://www.cawgfoundation.org/

CALIFORNIA WINE GRAPE GROWERS FOUNDATION SCHOLARSHIP

Scholarship for high school seniors whose parents or legal guardians are vineyard employees of wine grape growers. Recipients may study the subject of their choice at any campus of the University of California system, the California State University system, or the California Community College system.

Award: Scholarship for use in freshman year; renewable. *Number:* 7–7. *Amount:* $2000–$8000.

Eligibility Requirements: Applicant must be high school student; planning to enroll or expecting to enroll full-time at a two-year or four-year institution or university; resident of California and studying in California.

Application Requirements: Application form, community service, essay, financial need analysis, test scores. *Deadline:* March 8.

Contact: Carolee Williams, Assistant Executive Director
California Association of Wine Grape Growers Foundation
1121 L Street, #304
Sacramento, CA 95814
Phone: 916-379-8995
E-mail: carolee@cawg.org

CALIFORNIA COMMUNITY COLLEGES

http://www.ccccco.edu/

EOPS (EXTENDED OPPORTUNITY PROGRAMS AND SERVICES)/CARE (COOPERATIVE AGENCIES RESOURCES FOR EDUCATION)

Renewable award available to California residents and individuals who are exempt from paying nonresident tuition. Individuals must be enrolled as a full-time student at a two-year publicly-funded California community college. EOPS students must fulfill program-specific income and educational disadvantage eligibility requirements. CARE students must be in EOPS, currently receive CalWORKs/TANF, have at least one child under fourteen years of age at time of acceptance into CARE program, be a single head of household, and age 18 or older. EOPS students may also qualify for CARE if their dependent child(ren) receive CalWORKs/TANF cash aid even if the student (i.e., parent) is not a cash aid recipient. Contact local college EOPS/CARE office for an application and more information about supportive services and grants. To locate nearest community college campus, see http://www.ccccco.edu/

Award: Grant for use in freshman or sophomore years; renewable. *Number:* 10,000–85,000. *Amount:* $100–$1000.

Eligibility Requirements: Applicant must be age 18 and over; enrolled or expecting to enroll full-time at a two-year institution; single; resident of California and studying in California. Available to U.S. citizens.

Application Requirements: Application form, financial need analysis. *Deadline:* continuous.

Contact: Contact local community college EOPS/CARE program.

CALIFORNIA GRANGE FOUNDATION

http://www.csgfoundation.org/

CALIFORNIA GRANGE FOUNDATION SCHOLARSHIP
• *See page 437*

CALIFORNIA INTERSCHOLASTIC FEDERATION

http://www.cifstate.org/

CIF SCHOLAR-ATHLETE OF THE YEAR

Honors one male and one female statewide and is based on excellence in athletics, academics and character.

Award: Scholarship for use in freshman year; not renewable. *Number:* 2. *Amount:* $5000.

Eligibility Requirements: Applicant must be high school student; planning to enroll or expecting to enroll full-time at a four-year institution or university; resident of California and must have an interest in athletics/sports. Available to U.S. citizens.

Application Requirements: Application form, community service, essay. *Deadline:* February 11.

Contact: Jade Chin, Assistant to the Executive Director
California Interscholastic Federation
4658 Duckhorn Dr
Sacramento, CA 95624
Phone: 916-239-4477
E-mail: jchin@cifstate.org

CIF SPIRIT OF SPORT AWARD

This award seeks to recognize student-athletes who display good sportsmanship and school leadership, regardless of athletic ability.

Award: Scholarship for use in freshman year; not renewable. *Number:* 6. *Amount:* $500.

Eligibility Requirements: Applicant must be high school student; planning to enroll or expecting to enroll full-time at a four-year institution or university; resident of California and must have an interest in athletics/sports. Available to U.S. citizens.

Application Requirements: Application form, community service, essay. *Deadline:* continuous.

Contact: Jade Chin, Assistant to the Executive Director
California Interscholastic Federation
4658 Duckhorn Dr.
Sacramento, CA 95624
Phone: 916-239-4477
E-mail: jchin@cifstate.org

CALIFORNIA JUNIOR MISS SCHOLARSHIP PROGRAM

http://www.ajm.org/

DISTINGUISHED YOUNG WOMEN OF CALIFORNIA SCHOLARSHIP PROGRAM

Scholarship program to recognize and reward outstanding high school junior females in the areas of academics, leadership, athletics, public speaking, and the performing arts. Must be single, U.S. citizen, and resident of California. Must participate in a Distinguished Young Women program. Minimum 3.0 GPA required.

Award: Scholarship for use in freshman year; not renewable.

Eligibility Requirements: Applicant must be high school student; age 15-17; planning to enroll or expecting to enroll full-time at a four-year institution or university; single female; resident of California and must have an interest in beauty pageant, leadership, or public speaking. Available to U.S. citizens.

Application Requirements: Application form, essay, interview.

Contact: Joan McDonald, Chairman
Phone: 760-420-4177
E-mail: jmcdonald@bellmicro.com

CALIFORNIA STATE PARENT-TEACHER ASSOCIATION

http://www.capta.org/

CONTINUING EDUCATION SCHOLARSHIP FOR PTA VOLUNTEERS
• *See page 437*

GRADUATING HIGH SCHOOL SENIOR SCHOLARSHIP
• *See page 461*

CALIFORNIA STUDENT AID COMMISSION

http://www.csac.ca.gov/

CSAC CAL GRANT A AWARD

Award for California residents who are not recent high school graduates attending an approved college or university within the state. Must show financial need and meet minimum 3.00 GPA requirement.

Award: Grant for use in freshman, sophomore, junior, or senior years; renewable. *Number:* 1,000–2,000. *Amount:* $5472–$12,192.

Eligibility Requirements: Applicant must be enrolled or expecting to enroll full- or part-time at a two-year institution or university; resident of British Columbia and studying in California. Available to U.S. citizens.

Application Requirements: Application form, financial need analysis. *Deadline:* March 2.

Contact: Catalina Mistler, Deputy Director, Program Administration & Services Division
California Student Aid Commission
PO Box 419027
Rancho Cordova, CA 95741-9027
Phone: 888-224-7268
Fax: 916-526-8004
E-mail: catalina.mistler@csac.ca.gov

CSAC CAL GRANT B AWARD

The Cal Grant B Award is awarded to California residents who are enrolled in an undergraduate academic program of not less than one academic year at a qualifying postsecondary institution. Must show financial need and meet the minimum 2.00 GPA requirement.

Award: Grant for use in sophomore, junior, or senior years; renewable. *Number:* 20,500. *Amount:* $700–$13,665.

Eligibility Requirements: Applicant must be enrolled or expecting to enroll full- or part-time at a two-year or technical institution or university; resident of British Columbia and studying in California. Available to U.S. citizens.

Application Requirements: Application form, financial need analysis. *Deadline:* March 2.

Contact: Catalina Mistler, Deputy Director, Program Administration & Services Division
California Student Aid Commission
PO Box 419027
Rancho Cordova, CA 95741-9027
Phone: 888-224-7268
Fax: 916-526-8004
E-mail: catalina.mistler@csac.ca.gov

CSAC CAL GRANT C AWARD

Award for California residents who are enrolled in a short-term vocational training program. Program must lead to a recognized degree or certificate. Course length must be a minimum of 4 months and no longer than 24 months. Students must be attending an approved California institution and show financial need.

Award: Grant for use in freshman or sophomore years; renewable. *Amount:* $576–$2462.

Eligibility Requirements: Applicant must be enrolled or expecting to enroll full- or part-time at a two-year or technical institution; resident of British Columbia and studying in California. Available to U.S. citizens.

Application Requirements: Application form, financial need analysis. *Deadline:* March 2.

Contact: Catalina Mistler, Deputy Director, Program Administration & Services Division
California Student Aid Commission
PO Box 419027
Rancho Cordova, CA 95741-9027
Phone: 888-224-7268
Fax: 916-526-8004
E-mail: catalina.mistler@csac.ca.gov

LAW ENFORCEMENT PERSONNEL DEPENDENTS GRANT PROGRAM
• See page 461

CALIFORNIA TEACHERS ASSOCIATION (CTA)

http://www.cta.org/

CALIFORNIA TEACHERS ASSOCIATION SCHOLARSHIP FOR MEMBERS
• See page 437

L. GORDON BITTLE MEMORIAL SCHOLARSHIP
• See page 437

CAREER COLLEGES AND SCHOOLS OF TEXAS

http://www.ccst.org/

CAREER COLLEGES AND SCHOOLS OF TEXAS SCHOLARSHIP PROGRAM

One-time award available to graduating high school seniors who plan to attend a Texas trade or technical institution. Must be a Texas resident. Criteria selection, which is determined independently by each school's guidance counselors, may be based on academic excellence, financial need, or student leadership. Must be U.S. citizen. Deadline: continuous.

Award: Scholarship for use in freshman year; not renewable. *Number:* up to 27,770. *Amount:* $1000.

Eligibility Requirements: Applicant must be high school student; planning to enroll or expecting to enroll full- or part-time at a technical institution; resident of Texas and studying in Texas. Available to U.S. citizens.

Application Requirements: Application form, recommendations or references. *Deadline:* continuous.

Contact: Jennifer George, Association Manager
Career Colleges and Schools of Texas
823 Congress Avenue, Suite 230
Austin, TX 78701
Phone: 512-479-0425 Ext. 17
Fax: 512-495-9031
E-mail: jgeorge@eami.com

CARROT-TOP INDUSTRIES, INC.

https://carrot-top.com

BEACON SCHOLARSHIP FOR RURAL AMERICA

The Beacon Scholarship for Rural America helps low-income students living in rural areas with their college endeavors. College-bound graduating high school seniors, current college students or adult learners may apply. Three $1,000 scholarships are awarded every year. Two Fall scholarships are awarded every year in July (applications are due by June 30) and one Spring scholarship is awarded every year in November (applications are due by October 31). Applicants must reside in a rural area and meet low-income criteria outlined in our online application at https://carrot-top.com/beacon-scholarship

Award: Scholarship for use in freshman, sophomore, junior, senior, graduate, or postgraduate years; not renewable. *Number:* 1–2. *Amount:* $1000.

Eligibility Requirements: Applicant must be enrolled or expecting to enroll full- or part-time at a two-year or technical institution or university; resident of Alabama, Alberta, American Samoa, Arizona, British Columbia, California, Colorado, Connecticut, Delaware, District of Columbia, Florida, Guam, Hawaii, Idaho, Illinois, Indiana, Iowa, Kansas, Kentucky, Louisiana, Manitoba, Maryland, Massachusetts, Michigan, Minnesota, Mississippi, Missouri, Montana, Nebraska, New Brunswick, Newfoundland, New Hampshire, New Jersey, New Mexico, North Carolina, Northern Mariana Islands, Nova Scotia, Ohio, Ontario, Oregon, Quebec, Saskatchewan, South Carolina, South Dakota, Tennessee, Texas, Utah, Vermont, Virginia, Washington, West Virginia, Wisconsin and studying in Alabama, Alaska, American Samoa, Arizona, Arkansas, California, Colorado, Connecticut, Delaware, District of Columbia, Florida, Georgia, Hawaii, Idaho, Illinois, Indiana, Iowa, Kansas, Kentucky, Louisiana, Maine, Maryland, Massachusetts, Michigan, Minnesota, Mississippi, Missouri, Montana, Nebraska, Nevada, New Hampshire, New Jersey, New Mexico, New York, North Carolina, North Dakota, Northern Mariana Islands, Ohio, Oklahoma, Oregon, Pennsylvania, Rhode Island, South Carolina, South Dakota, Tennessee, Texas, Utah, Vermont, Virginia, Washington, West Virginia, Wisconsin, Wyoming. Available to U.S. citizens.

Application Requirements: Application form, application form may be submitted online, essay, personal photograph. *Deadline:* June 30.

Contact: Tina Williamson, Content Marketing Specialist
Carrot-Top Industries, Inc.
328 Elizabeth Brady Rd.
Hillsborough, NC 27278
Phone: 800-628-3524 Ext. 240
Fax: 919-732-5526
E-mail: twilliamson@carrot-top.com

CENTRAL SCHOLARSHIP

http://www.central-scholarship.org

LESSANS FAMILY SCHOLARSHIP
• See page 514

THE STRAUS SCHOLARS GRANTS

Scholarship provides assistance to Maryland residents who are full-time undergraduate students in their sophomore, junior, or senior years at an accredited college or university. Renewable grants of up to $5000 each per year will be awarded. If the recipient graduates within four years with a cumulative GPA of 2.0 or higher, an additional $5000 grant will be awarded to apply toward student loan debt.

Award: Scholarship for use in sophomore, junior, or senior years; renewable.

Eligibility Requirements: Applicant must be enrolled or expecting to enroll full-time at an institution or university and resident of Manitoba. Available to U.S. citizens.

Application Requirements: Application form, application form may be submitted online, essay, financial need analysis, interview. *Deadline:* April 1.

Contact: Angela Harrison, Program Manager
Phone: 410-415-5558
Fax: 410-415-5501
E-mail: aharrison@central-scholarship.org

CHICAGO AREA BUSINESS AVIATION ASSOCIATION

http://www.cabaa.com

CABAA/FLIGHTSAFETY CORPORATE SCHEDULER AND DISPATCHER TRAINING AWARD

The CABAA Education Foundation, along with FlightSafety, will award a 2018 applicant a FlightSafety Corporate Scheduler/Dispatcher Initial. This approved course addresses the unique needs of individuals serving, or planning to serve as corporate aircraft schedulers/dispatchers. The course is designed to provide individuals with practical information, which will enable them to function as integral members of the corporate travel team. All subject matter is approached from a scheduler/dispatcher's perspective, using real-world examples and scenarios. CABAA and FlightSafety have teamed up to offer this award to promote professional development for a career in business aviation. The winner will be notified by phone and presented the award at the annual CABAA Golf Classic held on August 7th, 2018. The recipients presence is required at the time of award presentation. For more information about the course visit resources.flightsafety.com

Award: Scholarship for use in senior year; not renewable. *Number:* 1. *Amount:* $4000.

Eligibility Requirements: Applicant must be age 21 and over; enrolled or expecting to enroll full- or part-time at a two-year or four-year or technical institution or university and resident of Illinois, Indiana, Iowa, Michigan, Missouri, Wisconsin. Available to U.S. citizens.

Application Requirements: Application form, essay. *Deadline:* May 1.

Contact: Brian Zankowski
Lake Villa, IL 60046
Phone: 224-931-8064
E-mail: scholarships@cabaa.com

CHICANA/LATINA FOUNDATION

http://www.chicanalatina.org/

SCHOLARSHIPS FOR LATINA STUDENTS ENROLLED IN COLLEGES/UNIVERSITIES IN NORTHERN CALIFORNIA
• *See page 515*

CHINESE AMERICAN ASSOCIATION OF MINNESOTA

http://www.caam.org/

CHINESE AMERICAN ASSOCIATION OF MINNESOTA (CAAM) SCHOLARSHIPS
• *See page 515*

COLLEGEBOUND FOUNDATION

http://www.collegeboundfoundation.org/

BALTIMORE RAVENS SCHOLARSHIP PROGRAM
• *See page 462*

COLLEGEBOUND LAST DOLLAR GRANT

The CollegeBound Last Dollar Grant is a need-based award for Baltimore City public high school graduates whose expected family contribution and financial aid package total less than the cost to attend college. Students who are awarded a CollegeBound Foundation Last Dollar Grant are eligible to receive a grant of up to $3,000 per year, renewable for up to six (6) years of college or the maximum amount of $18,000. These Grants are gift money that does not have to be repaid. Approximately 70 awards are given each year.

Award: Grant for use in freshman, sophomore, junior, or senior years; renewable. *Number:* 60–70. *Amount:* $500–$3000.

Eligibility Requirements: Applicant must be high school student; planning to enroll or expecting to enroll full-time at an institution or university and resident of Manitoba. Available to U.S. citizens.

Application Requirements: Application form, application form may be submitted online, financial need analysis. *Deadline:* June 1.

Contact: Jennifer Covahey, Director of College Success
CollegeBound Foundation
2601 Howard Street
Suite 210
Baltimore, MD 21218
Phone: 410-783-2905 Ext. 207
Fax: 410-727-5786
E-mail: jcovahey@collegeboundfoundation.org

DUNBAR CLASS OF 1958 SCHOLARSHIP

The Dunbar Class of 1958 established this scholarship with the intention to give back to the community in which they were raised and went to school. The Class of 1958 views Dunbar as the source of their many successes, and hopes to provide financial assistance so that current graduates have the same opportunities to succeed. Applicant must be a senior at Paul Laurence Dunbar High School; have a cumulative high school GPA of at least a 2.0; and demonstrate financial need.

Award: Scholarship for use in freshman, sophomore, junior, or senior years; not renewable. *Number:* 1–3. *Amount:* $1–$1000.

Eligibility Requirements: Applicant must be high school student; planning to enroll or expecting to enroll full-time at a two-year institution or university and resident of Manitoba. Available to U.S. citizens.

Application Requirements: Application form, essay, financial need analysis. *Deadline:* March 1.

Contact: Jennifer Covahey, Director of College Success
CollegeBound Foundation
2601 Howard Street
Suite 210
Baltimore, MD 21218
Phone: 410-783-2905 Ext. 207
Fax: 410-727-5786
E-mail: jcovahey@collegeboundfoundation.org

HY ZOLET STUDENT ATHLETE SCHOLARSHIP

You must be a Baltimore City public high school student-athlete; have a cumulative 2.5 GPA or better; submit at least two (2) letters verifying your participation in high school athletics and evidence you possess the qualities Hy Zolet exemplified, including a good work ethic, fairness and courage, in addition to outstanding leadership and athletic skills; and submit an essay describing your academic and professional goals, why you have chosen them and what you have done to prepare yourself thus far (500-1,000 words; 2-4 pages).

Award: Scholarship for use in freshman, sophomore, junior, or senior years; renewable. *Number:* 4. *Amount:* $1000.

Eligibility Requirements: Applicant must be high school student; planning to enroll or expecting to enroll full-time at an institution or university; resident of Manitoba and must have an interest in athletics/sports or leadership. Available to U.S. citizens.

Application Requirements: Application form, essay. *Deadline:* March 1.

Contact: Jennifer Covahey, Director of College Success
CollegeBound Foundation
2601 Howard Street
Suite 210
Baltimore, MD 21218
Phone: 410-783-2905 Ext. 207
Fax: 410-727-5786
E-mail: jcovahey@collegeboundfoundation.org

KHIA "DJ K-SWIFT" EDGERTON MEMORIAL SCHOLARSHIP

One scholar will be chosen from each of the following areas: Baltimore City or Baltimore County. Applicant must: have a cumulative 2.5 GPA or better; submit SAT (CR+M) scores; demonstrate financial need; and submit an essay (500 words) describing the importance of a college education and why you should receive this award.

Award: Scholarship for use in freshman year; not renewable. *Number:* 1–2. *Amount:* $1000.

Eligibility Requirements: Applicant must be high school student; planning to enroll or expecting to enroll full-time at a two-year institution and resident of Manitoba. Available to U.S. citizens.

Application Requirements: Application form, essay, financial need analysis. *Deadline:* March 1.

Contact: Jennifer Covahey, Director of College Success
CollegeBound Foundation
2601 Howard Street
Suite 210
Baltimore, MD 21218
Phone: 410-783-2905 Ext. 207
Fax: 410-727-5786
E-mail: jcovahey@collegeboundfoundation.org

LORENZO FELDER SCHOLARSHIP
• *See page 462*

MANAGERIAL AND PROFESSIONAL SOCIETY (MAPS) OF BALTIMORE MERIT SCHOLARSHIP

Applicant must: have a cumulative 3.0 GPA or better; an SAT (CR+M) score of at least 950; verifiable community service; and submit an essay (500-1,000 words) describing the importance of a college education and community service you have been involved in. Only dues-paying MAPS members and their immediate family members are eligible to apply. Winners must attend a MAPS quarterly meeting.

Award: Scholarship for use in freshman year; not renewable. *Number:* 1–3. *Amount:* $1000.

Eligibility Requirements: Applicant must be high school student; planning to enroll or expecting to enroll full-time at a two-year institution and resident of Manitoba. Available to U.S. citizens.

Application Requirements: Application form, community service, essay. *Deadline:* March 1.

Contact: Jennifer Covahey, Director of College Success
CollegeBound Foundation
2601 Howard Street
Suite 210
Baltimore, MD 21218
Phone: 410-783-2905 Ext. 207
Fax: 410-727-5786
E-mail: jcovahey@collegeboundfoundation.org

COLLEGE NOW GREATER CLEVELAND, INC.

http://www.collegenowgc.org/

COLLEGE NOW GREATER CLEVELAND ADULT LEARNER PROGRAM SCHOLARSHIP

Scholarship for students pursuing first associate or bachelor's degree in an eligible two- or four-year program. Individuals already having a bachelor's degree are not eligible. Students must be 19 years old or older and must have interrupted the education for at least one year. Applicants must be a resident of Ashtabula, Cuyahoga, Geauga, Lake, Lorain, Mahoning, Medina, Portage, Stark, Summit or Trumbull County. Student must meet income guidelines and maintain a 2.5 GPA. Student must be attending a public or private not for profit institution.

Award: Scholarship for use in freshman, sophomore, junior, or senior years; renewable. *Number:* 100–200. *Amount:* $1000–$4000.

Eligibility Requirements: Applicant must be age 19 and over; enrolled or expecting to enroll full- or part-time at a two-year or four-year or technical institution or university; resident of Ohio and studying in Ohio. Available to U.S. citizens.

Application Requirements: Application form, application form may be submitted online(www.collegenowgc.org), essay, financial need analysis, interview. *Deadline:* April 14.

Contact: Mr. Robert Durham, Director of Scholarship Services and Financial Aid
College Now Greater Cleveland, Inc.
50 Public Square, Suite 1800
Cleveland, OH 44113
Phone: 216-635-0450
E-mail: rdurham@collegenowgc.org

COLLEGE SUCCESS FOUNDATION

http://www.collegesuccessfoundation.org/

GOVERNORS' SCHOLARSHIP FOR FOSTER YOUTH PROGRAM

The Washington State Governor's Scholarship for Foster Youth is a scholarship program that helps young men and women from foster care continue their education and earn a college degree from Washington state. Eligible students must meet specific criteria. The program has been supported by the current and former governors in Proceeds from the Governor's Cup, an annual golf tournament, provide funding for approximately 30-50 new scholars each year. Scholarship award amounts range from $2000 to $4000 depending on the college of attendance. The scholarship can be accessed for up to five years to complete an undergraduate study. Students much be enrolled full-time and maintain satisfactory academic progress in order to renew the scholarship each year.

Award: Scholarship for use in freshman, sophomore, junior, or senior years; renewable. *Number:* 30–50. *Amount:* $2000–$4000.

Eligibility Requirements: Applicant must be high school student; planning to enroll or expecting to enroll full- or part-time at a two-year or four-year institution or university; resident of Washington and studying in Washington. Available to U.S. citizens.

Application Requirements: Application form, application form may be submitted online (http://www.collegesuccessfoundation.org/wa/students/governors-eligibility), essay, recommendations or references, transcript. *Deadline:* March 9.

Contact: Erica Meier, Director, Scholarship Services
Phone: 425-416-2000
Fax: 425-416-2001
E-mail: info@collegesuccessfoundation.org

COLORADO COMMISSION ON HIGHER EDUCATION

http://highered.colorado.gov/cche/mission.html

COLORADO STUDENT GRANT

Grants for Colorado residents attending eligible public, private, or vocational institutions within the state. Students must complete a Free Application for Federal Student Aid (FAFSA) and demonstrate need. Application deadlines vary by institution. Renewable award for undergraduates. Contact the financial aid office at the college/institution for application and more information.

Award: Grant for use in freshman, sophomore, junior, or senior years; not renewable. *Amount:* $300–$5000.

Eligibility Requirements: Applicant must be enrolled or expecting to enroll full- or part-time at a two-year or four-year or technical institution; resident of Colorado and studying in Colorado. Available to U.S. citizens.

Application Requirements: Application form, financial need analysis. *Deadline:* continuous.

Contact: Celina Duran, Financial Aid Administrator
Colorado Commission on Higher Education
1560 Broadway
Suite 1600
Denver, CO 80202
Phone: 303-866-2723
E-mail: celina.duran@dhe.state.co.us

COLORADO EDUCATIONAL SERVICES AND DEVELOPMENT ASSOCIATION

http://www.cesda.org

CESDA DIVERSITY SCHOLARSHIPS

Award for underrepresented, economically, and disadvantaged high school seniors planning to pursue undergraduate studies at a Colorado college or university. Must be Colorado resident. Applicant must be a first generation student, or member of an underrepresented ethnic or racial minority, and/or show financial need. Minimum 2.8 GPA required.

Award: Scholarship for use in freshman year; not renewable. *Number:* 6. *Amount:* $1000.

Eligibility Requirements: Applicant must be high school student; planning to enroll or expecting to enroll full- or part-time at a two-year or four-year or technical institution or university; resident of Colorado and studying in Colorado. Available to U.S. and non-Canadian citizens.

Application Requirements: Application form, essay, financial need analysis. *Deadline:* April 1.

Contact: Maria Castro Barajas, CESDA Chair
Colorado Educational Services and Development Association
Center for Community, Suite 485
108 UCB
Boulder, CO 80309
Phone: 303-492-2178
E-mail: maria.barajas@colorado.edu

COMMUNITY BANKERS ASSOCIATION OF GEORGIA

http://www.cbaofga.com/

JULIAN AND JAN HESTER MEMORIAL SCHOLARSHIP

Scholarship available to Georgia high school seniors who will be entering a Georgia two- or four-year college or university, or a program at a technical institution. Recipients will be named on the basis of merit, and family financial need is not considered. Application must be sponsored by a local community bank, and must include an essay on community banking and what it represents.

Award: Scholarship for use in freshman year; not renewable. *Number:* 4. *Amount:* $1000.

Eligibility Requirements: Applicant must be high school student; planning to enroll or expecting to enroll full-time at a two-year or four-year or technical institution or university; resident of Georgia and studying in Georgia. Available to U.S. citizens.

Application Requirements: Application form, community service, recommendations or references, test scores, transcript. *Deadline:* March 30.

Contact: Lauren Dismuke, Public Relations and Marketing Coordinator
Phone: 770-541-4490
Fax: 770-541-4496
E-mail: lauren@cbaofga.com

COMMUNITY BANKERS ASSOCIATION OF ILLINOIS

http://www.cbai.com/

COMMUNITY BANKERS ASSOC OF IL CHILD OF A BANKER SCHOLARSHIP
• *See page 438*

COMMUNITY BANKERS ASSOC. OF IL ESSAY CONTEST

Open to Illinois high school seniors who are sponsored by a CBAI member bank. Student bank employees, immediate families of bank employees, board members, stockholders, CBAI employees, and judges are ineligible. Twelve awards are available at $1,000/year for up to four years of higher education; 12 additional one-time $500 awards are also available. For more details see website http://www.cbai.com.

Award: Prize for use in freshman year; renewable. *Number:* 12–24. *Amount:* $500–$4000.

Eligibility Requirements: Applicant must be high school student; planning to enroll or expecting to enroll full-time at a two-year or four-year or technical institution or university and resident of Illinois. Available to U.S. citizens.

Application Requirements: Application form, essay. *Deadline:* February 7.

Contact: Ms. Bobbi Watson, Administrative Assistant
Community Bankers Association of Illinois
CBAI
901 Community Drive
Springfield, IL 62703-5184
Phone: 800-736-2224
E-mail: bobbiw@cbai.com

COMMUNITY FOUNDATION OF WESTERN MASSACHUSETTS

http://www.communityfoundation.org/

CALEB L. BUTLER SCHOLARSHIP FUND

Scholarship for graduating high school seniors from Berkshire, Franklin, Hampden or Hampshire Counties who are in the custody of the Department of Children and Families (DCF), formerly the Department of Social Services (DSS); preference to former or current residents of Hillcrest Educational Centers.

Award: Scholarship for use in freshman year; not renewable.

Eligibility Requirements: Applicant must be high school student; planning to enroll or expecting to enroll full- or part-time at a two-year institution or university and resident of Maryland. Available to U.S. citizens.

Application Requirements: Application form, application form may be submitted online, essay, financial need analysis. *Deadline:* April 17.

Contact: Nikai Fondon, Scholarship Program Associate
E-mail: NFondon@communityfoundation.org

CHRISTINE MITUS ROSE MEMORIAL SCHOLARSHIP FUND

The Christine Mitus Rose Memorial Scholarship Fund is awarded to students who have a deceased parent, preference to those who have lost a parent to cancer.

Award: Scholarship for use in freshman, sophomore, junior, senior, or graduate years; not renewable.

Eligibility Requirements: Applicant must be enrolled or expecting to enroll full- or part-time at a two-year institution or university and resident of Maryland. Available to U.S. citizens.

Application Requirements: Application form, application form may be submitted online, essay, financial need analysis. *Deadline:* April 17.

Contact: Nikai Fondon, Scholarship Program Associate
E-mail: NFondon@communityfoundation.org

DIANA AND LEON FEFFER SCHOLARSHIP FUND

Scholarship available to residents of of Hampden, Hampshire or Franklin Counties, Massachusetts. For more information, please see website http://communityfoundation.org/.

Award: Scholarship for use in freshman, sophomore, junior, senior, or graduate years; not renewable.

Eligibility Requirements: Applicant must be enrolled or expecting to enroll full- or part-time at a two-year institution or university and resident of Maryland. Available to U.S. citizens.

Application Requirements: Application form, application form may be submitted online, essay, financial need analysis. *Deadline:* April 17.

Contact: Nikai Fondon, Scholarship Program Associate
E-mail: NFondon@communityfoundation.org

FRED K. LANE SCHOLARSHIP FUND

Scholarship for graduating high school seniors who are past or current members (individual or family) or former/current employees at the Orchards Golf Course or residents of South Hadley who participate in athletics, with a preference for graduating high school seniors who play golf.

Award: Scholarship for use in freshman year; not renewable.

Eligibility Requirements: Applicant must be high school student; planning to enroll or expecting to enroll full- or part-time at a two-year institution or university; resident of Maryland and must have an interest in golf. Available to U.S. citizens.

Application Requirements: Application form, application form may be submitted online, essay, financial need analysis. *Deadline:* April 17.

Contact: Nikai Fondon, Scholarship Program Associate
E-mail: NFondon@communityfoundation.org

HELLESPONT SOCIETY SCHOLARSHIP FUND
• *See page 516*

HORACE HILL SCHOLARSHIP FUND
• *See page 438*

JAMES L. SHRIVER SCHOLARSHIP FUND

Awarded to graduating seniors from Hampden, Hampshire or Franklin Counties to pursue a technical career through higher education including college, trade school or technical school and participated in extracurricular activities.

Award: Scholarship for use in freshman, sophomore, junior, senior, or graduate years; not renewable.

Eligibility Requirements: Applicant must be enrolled or expecting to enroll full- or part-time at an institution or university and resident of Maryland. Available to U.S. citizens.

Application Requirements: Application form, application form may be submitted online, essay, financial need analysis. *Deadline:* April 17.

Contact: Nikai Fondon, Scholarship Program Associate
E-mail: NFondon@communityfoundation.org

KIMBER RICHTER FAMILY SCHOLARSHIP FUND
• *See page 540*

VIRGINILLO-FALVO SCHOLARSHIP FUND

Scholarship for students age 24 or younger with independent status from Berkshire, Franklin, Hampden or Hampshire Counties, Massachusetts.

Award: Scholarship for use in freshman, sophomore, junior, senior, or graduate years; not renewable.

Eligibility Requirements: Applicant must be age 24 or under; enrolled or expecting to enroll full- or part-time at a two-year institution or university and resident of Maryland. Available to U.S. citizens.

Application Requirements: Application form, application form may be submitted online, essay, financial need analysis. *Deadline:* April 17.

Contact: Nikai Fondon, Scholarship Program Associate
E-mail: NFondon@communityfoundation.org

WILLIAM A. AND VINNIE E. DEXTER SCHOLARSHIP FUND

Scholarship for graduating high school seniors in Berkshire, Franklin, Hampden and Hampshire Counties, Massachusetts.

Award: Scholarship for use in freshman year; not renewable.

Eligibility Requirements: Applicant must be high school student; planning to enroll or expecting to enroll full- or part-time at a two-year institution or university and resident of Maryland. Available to U.S. citizens.

Application Requirements: Application form, application form may be submitted online, essay, financial need analysis. *Deadline:* April 17.

Contact: Nikai Fondon, Scholarship Program Associate
E-mail: NFondon@communityfoundation.org

WILLIAM J. (BILL) AND LORETTA M. O'NEIL SCHOLARSHIP FUND

Scholarship available to residents from Western Massachusetts particularly from Berkshire, Franklin, Hampden and Hampshire Counties, pursuing English, journalism or a related field.

Award: Scholarship for use in freshman, sophomore, junior, senior, or graduate years; not renewable.

Eligibility Requirements: Applicant must be enrolled or expecting to enroll full- or part-time at a two-year institution or university and resident of Maryland. Available to U.S. citizens.

Application Requirements: Application form, application form may be submitted online, essay, financial need analysis. *Deadline:* April 17.

Contact: Nikai Fondon, Scholarship Program Associate
E-mail: NFondon@communityfoundation.org

CONNECTICUT ARMY NATIONAL GUARD

http://ct.ng.mil/Pages/default.aspx

CONNECTICUT ARMY NATIONAL GUARD 100% TUITION WAIVER

• *See page 494*

CONNECTICUT ASSOCIATION OF LATINOS IN HIGHER EDUCATION (CALAHE)

http://www.calahe.org/

CONNECTICUT ASSOCIATION OF LATINOS IN HIGHER EDUCATION SCHOLARSHIPS

• *See page 516*

CONNECTICUT COMMUNITY FOUNDATION

http://www.conncf.org/

REGIONAL AND RESTRICTED SCHOLARSHIP AWARD PROGRAM

Supports accredited college or university study for residents of the Connecticut community twenty-one town service area. In addition, a variety of restricted award programs are based on specific fund criteria (residency, school, course of study, etc.). Scholarships are awarded on a competitive basis with consideration given to academic record, extracurricular activities, work experience, financial need, reference letter, and an essay.

Award: Scholarship for use in freshman, sophomore, junior, or senior years; renewable. *Number:* 200–300. *Amount:* $2000–$5000.

Eligibility Requirements: Applicant must be enrolled or expecting to enroll full-time at a two-year or four-year institution or university and resident of Connecticut. Available to U.S. citizens.

Application Requirements: Application form, community service, essay, financial need analysis. *Deadline:* March 15.

Contact: Ms. Tallitha Richardson, Program and Scholarship Associate
Connecticut Community Foundation
43 Field Street
Waterbury, CT 06702
Phone: 203-753-1315 Ext. 126
E-mail: scholarships@conncf.org

CONNECTICUT OFFICE OF HIGHER EDUCATION

http://www.ctohe.org

GOVERNOR'S SCHOLARSHIP PROGRAM—NEED/MERIT SCHOLARSHIP

This program provides scholarships to eligible Connecticut residents attending eligible institutions of higher education in Connecticut. Eligibility is based on a minimum SAT score of 1800, or a minimum ACT score of 27 and/or top 20% ranking in the students junior year high school class. Applications must be filed through the students high school counseling office. In addition, all students must file a Free Application for Federal Student Aid (FAFSA) and, as a result, have an Expected Family Contribution (EFC) equal to or less than the annual allowable maximum EFC. Both the application and FAFSA must be processed by February 15th.

Award: Scholarship for use in sophomore, junior, or senior years; renewable. *Number:* 1,967. *Amount:* $2275–$5250.

Eligibility Requirements: Applicant must be enrolled or expecting to enroll full- or part-time at a two-year or four-year institution or university; resident of Connecticut and studying in Connecticut. Available to U.S. citizens.

Application Requirements: Application form, financial need analysis. *Deadline:* February 15.

Contact: Ms. Lynne Goodwin, Student Financial Aid Consultant
Connecticut Office of Higher Education
450 Columbus Boulevard
Suite 510
Hartford, CT 06103
Phone: 860-947-1855
E-mail: sfa@ctohe.org

ROBERTA B. WILLIS SCHOLARSHIP PROGRAM—NEED-BASED GRANT

This program provides need-based grants to eligible Connecticut residents attending eligible institutions of higher education in Connecticut. Students must file a Free Application for Federal Student Aid (FAFSA) by their college's deadline, if applicable. Students, as a result of filing the FAFSA, must have an Expected Family Contribution (EFC) equal to or less than the allowable annual EFC. There is no application to fill out.

Award: Grant for use in freshman, sophomore, junior, or senior years; renewable. *Amount:* $1–$4500.

Eligibility Requirements: Applicant must be enrolled or expecting to enroll full- or part-time at a two-year or four-year institution or university; resident of Connecticut and studying in Connecticut. Available to U.S. citizens.

Application Requirements: Financial need analysis. *Deadline:* continuous.

Contact: Ms. Lynne Goodwin, Financial Aid Consultant
Connecticut Office of Higher Education
450 Columbus Boulevard
Suite 510
Hartford, CT 06103
Phone: 860-947-1855
E-mail: sfa@ctohe.org

CORPORATION FOR OHIO APPALACHIAN DEVELOPMENT (COAD)

http://www.coadinc.org/

DAVID V. STIVISON APPALACHIAN COMMUNITY ACTION SCHOLARSHIP FUND

Provides financial assistance to students who are residents in the Corporation for Ohio Appalachian Development's service area and want to attend college but lack the required resources. Individual income must not exceed 200 percent of Federal Poverty Level. See website for application information - http://www.coadinc.org/scholarships

Award: Scholarship for use in freshman, sophomore, junior, or senior years; not renewable. *Number:* 1–30. *Amount:* $500–$1500.

Eligibility Requirements: Applicant must be enrolled or expecting to enroll full-time at a two-year or four-year institution or university and resident of Ohio. Available to U.S. citizens.

Application Requirements: Application form, financial need analysis, personal photograph. *Deadline:* April 1.

Contact: Allyssa Mefford, Operations Director
Phone: 740-594-8499 Ext. 213
E-mail: amefford@coadinc.org

THE DALLAS FOUNDATION

http://www.dallasfoundation.org/

THE AKIN AYODELE SCHOLARSHIP IN MEMORY OF MICHAEL TILMON

Michael Tilmon was a best friend and teammate of Dallas Cowboy Akin Ayodele while at MacArthur High School. Sadly, he passed away in a car accident in March of 1997. This scholarship program is intended to honor those who demonstrate the type of character and integrity that Michael possessed.

Award: Scholarship for use in freshman year; not renewable. *Amount:* $10,000.

Eligibility Requirements: Applicant must be high school student; planning to enroll or expecting to enroll full-time at a two-year or four-year institution or university and resident of Texas.

Application Requirements: Application form, transcript. *Deadline:* April 15.

Contact: Rachel Lasseter, Program Associate
Phone: 214-741-9898
E-mail: scholarships@dallasfoundation.org

DR. DAN J. AND PATRICIA S. PICKARD SCHOLARSHIP

• See page 516

DR. DON AND ROSE MARIE BENTON SCHOLARSHIP

Award is available to students, parents of students and volunteers who have been affiliated with Trinity River Mission in Dallas, Texas. Must be enrolled in a graduate or undergraduate program in a regionally accredited college or university. Scholarship is renewable for two years if the student maintains a specified grade point average and fulfills all reporting requirements as determined by the Scholarship Committee.

Award: Scholarship for use in freshman, sophomore, junior, senior, graduate, or postgraduate years; renewable. *Number:* 1–3. *Amount:* $1500.

Eligibility Requirements: Applicant must be enrolled or expecting to enroll full-time at a two-year or four-year institution or university and resident of Texas.

Application Requirements: Application form, transcript. *Deadline:* April 1.

Contact: Ms. Dolores Sosa Green, Trinity River Mission
The Dallas Foundation
2060 Singleton Boulevard, Suite 104
Dallas, TX 75212
Phone: 214-744-5648

THE LANDON RUSNAK SCHOLARSHIP

The Landon Rusnak Scholarship Fund was established at The Dallas Foundation in 2007. This scholarship is established by the employees of LEAM Drilling Systems, Inc. and Conroe Machine, LLC in memory of Landon Rusnak, son of David and Janet Rusnak and brother of Cady Rusnak. Landon's sister Cady is an active member of the Mexia High School Black Cat Band.

Award: Scholarship for use in freshman year; not renewable. *Number:* 1. *Amount:* $3000.

Eligibility Requirements: Applicant must be high school student; planning to enroll or expecting to enroll full-time at a two-year or four-year institution or university; resident of Texas and must have an interest in music.

Application Requirements: Application form, financial need analysis, transcript. *Deadline:* February 28.

Contact: Rachel Lasseter, Program Associate
Phone: 214-741-9898
E-mail: scholarships@dallasfoundation.org

THE MAYOR'S CHESAPEAKE ENERGY SCHOLARSHIP

The Mayor's Chesapeake Energy Scholarship was established at The Dallas Foundation by Chesapeake Energy Corporation. The goal of the Fund is to make a college degree or vocational certification possible for minority and socially disadvantaged youth. Graduating students in the Dallas ISD are eligible to apply. Applicants should be female or a member of a minority group. Applicants must have participated in the Education is Freedom program.

Award: Scholarship for use in freshman, sophomore, junior, or senior years; renewable. *Amount:* $20,000.

Eligibility Requirements: Applicant must be high school student; planning to enroll or expecting to enroll full-time at a two-year or four-year or technical institution or university and resident of Texas. Available to U.S. citizens.

Application Requirements: Application form, financial need analysis, test scores, transcript. *Deadline:* April 15.

Contact: Rachel Lasseter, Program Associate
Phone: 214-741-9898
E-mail: scholarships@dallasfoundation.org

TOMMY TRANCHIN AWARD

Established at The Dallas Foundation to support students with physical, emotional or intellectual disabilities who have excelled or shown promise in a chosen field of interest. Tommy's family wants to recognize his creativity and his refusal to allow his disability to limit his personal growth by helping others to develop their own talents. Applicants should be residents of North Texas.

Award: Scholarship for use in freshman year; not renewable. *Amount:* $1500.

Eligibility Requirements: Applicant must be high school student; planning to enroll or expecting to enroll full-time at a two-year or four-year or technical institution or university and resident of Texas.

Application Requirements: Application form, physical, proof of physical, emotional or intellectual disability. *Deadline:* March 5.

Contact: Rachel Lasseter, Program Associate
Phone: 214-741-9898
E-mail: scholarships@dallasfoundation.org

DANIEL P. BUTTAFUOCO & ASSOCIATES

http://www.1800nowhurt.com

YOUNG CHRISTIAN LEADERS SCHOLARSHIP

• See page 540

DANIELS FUND

http://www.danielsfund.org

BOUNDLESS OPPORTUNITY SCHOLARSHIP

The Boundless Opportunity Scholarship (BOS) is designed to benefit highly-motivated non-traditional students who recognize the power of education to create a better life for themselves and their families. The scholarship is available at select two- and four-year colleges and universities in Colorado, New Mexico, Utah, and Wyoming. The Daniels Fund, the legacy of cable television pioneer Bill Daniels, awards grants to partnering colleges and universities who then provide need-based scholarships to successful student applicants. The BOS program serves seven non-traditional student populations, and is intended to help students able to demonstrate the need for financial assistance as they invest in themselves through continued education. Partnering schools choose to offer the BOS program to one or more of these defined student populations: adults entering or returning to college, GED recipients, former foster care youth, former juvenile justice youth, returning military, individuals pursuing EMT/paramedic training, individuals pursuing Early Childhood Education (ECE) certification. Not all schools will offer Boundless Opportunity Scholarships to all student populations; please check with your school.

Award: Scholarship for use in freshman, sophomore, junior, or senior years; renewable.

Eligibility Requirements: Applicant must be age 24 and over; enrolled or expecting to enroll full- or part-time at a two-year or four-year institution or university; resident of Colorado, New Mexico, Utah, Wyoming and studying in Colorado, New Mexico, Utah, Wyoming. Available to U.S. citizens.

Application Requirements: Application form, essay, interview. *Deadline:* continuous.

Contact: Laura Steffen, Vice President, Scholar Recruitment & Selection
Daniels Fund
101 Monroe Street
Denver, CO 80206
Phone: 720-941-4455
E-mail: lsteffen@danielsfund.org

DANIELS SCHOLARSHIP PROGRAM

The Daniels Scholarship Program provides a four-year, annually-renewable college scholarship for graduating high school seniors in Colorado, New Mexico, Utah, and Wyoming who demonstrate exceptional character, leadership, and a commitment to serving their communities. It is a "last dollar" scholarship that pays toward tuition and fees, room and board, books and supplies, and miscellaneous educational expenses. Scholars may attend any nonprofit accredited school in the United States. For more information, visit www.DanielsFund.org/Scholarships.

Award: Scholarship for use in freshman, sophomore, junior, or senior years; renewable. *Number:* 230.

Eligibility Requirements: Applicant must be high school student; planning to enroll or expecting to enroll full-time at a two-year or four-year institution or university and resident of Colorado, New Mexico, Utah, Wyoming. Available to U.S. citizens.

Application Requirements: Application form, community service, essay, financial need analysis, interview, personal photograph. *Deadline:* November 30.

Contact: Laura Steffen, Vice President, Scholar Recruitment & Selection
Daniels Fund
101 Monroe Street
Denver, CO 80206
Phone: 720-941-4455
E-mail: lsteffen@danielsfund.org

DAVID J. CROUSE & ASSOCIATES

https://crouselawgroup.com/

DAVID J. CROUSE & ASSOCIATES PUBLIC SERVICE SCHOLARSHIP FOR COLLEGE STUDENTS

If you are a college student (Washington State resident) who is planning to pursue a career in public service and are enrolled in a 2-5 year U.S. institution in 2018-2019, apply today for the $2,000 David J. Crouse & Associates Public Service Scholarship. This scholarship will be awarded annually to one college student (which can be any college in the United States) who is a Washington State resident. This scholarship is designed for the student who desires to serve their community through joining the military, police, fire, or any other form of public service (medical, humanitarian, charitable, ministry, etc.). There is no preference to the form of public service intended. We look forward to helping one college student each year to continue his or her education. David J. Crouse previously served in the United States Air Force, Washington Air National Guard and as a city police officer. He and the rest of the team here at David J. Crouse & Associates are excited to help someone else pursue their public service dream. To apply, create a short (30-120 second) video telling us how you plan to better your community through service in the military, police, or another form of public service. Also, please tell us how continuing your education will help you achieve your goals. Upload your video to YouTube. Fill out the application and include a link to your video on YouTube. Applications are due June 1, 2018 for the 2018-2019 college year. For all future years, applications are due by May 1 for the following school year.

Award: Scholarship for use in sophomore, junior, senior, or graduate years; not renewable. *Number:* 1. *Amount:* $2000.

Eligibility Requirements: Applicant must be enrolled or expecting to enroll full- or part-time at a two-year or four-year or technical institution or university and resident of Washington. Available to U.S. citizens.

Application Requirements: Application form. *Deadline:* June 1.

Contact: Scholarship Coordinator
Phone: 513-444-2016
E-mail: coordinator@ourscholarship.io

DAVID J. CROUSE & ASSOCIATES PUBLIC SERVICE SCHOLARSHIP FOR HIGH SCHOOL STUDENTS

If you are a graduating Washington State high school student planning to enroll in a 2-5-year institution to pursue a career in public service, apply today for the $2,000 David J. Crouse & Associates Public Service Scholarship. This scholarship will be awarded annually to a graduating student of any Washington high school. This scholarship is designed for the student who desires to serve their community through joining the military, police, fire, or any other form of public service (medical, humanitarian, charitable, ministry, etc.). There is no preference to the form of public service intended. We look forward to helping one high school student each year to continue his or her education. David J. Crouse previously served in the United States Air Force, Washington Air National Guard and as a city police officer. He and the rest of the team here at David J. Crouse & Associates are excited to help someone else pursue their public service dream. To apply, create a short (30-120 second) video telling us how you plan to better your community through service in the military, police, or another form of public service. Also, please tell us how continuing your education will help you achieve your goals! Upload your video to YouTube. Fill out the application and include a link to your video on YouTube. Applications are due June 1, 2018 for the 2018-2019 college year. For all future years, applications are due by May 1 for the following school year.

Award: Scholarship for use in freshman year; not renewable. *Number:* 1. *Amount:* $2000.

Eligibility Requirements: Applicant must be high school student; planning to enroll or expecting to enroll full- or part-time at a two-year or four-year or technical institution or university and resident of Washington. Available to U.S. citizens.

Application Requirements: Application form. *Deadline:* June 1.

Contact: Scholarship Coordinator
Phone: 513-444-2016
E-mail: coordinator@ourscholarship.io

DEBT.COM

https://www.debt.com/

DEBT.COM SCHOLARSHIP

Debt.com will give you $500 simply for applying for other scholarships. Debt.com's mission is to encourage Americans to fight their way to financial independence from college freshmen to senior citizens and everyone in between. Sadly, many college students don't apply for all the scholarships available to them. Winners are chosen every two (2) months.

Award: Scholarship for use in freshman, sophomore, junior, senior, graduate, or postgraduate years; renewable. *Number:* 1–6. *Amount:* $500.

Eligibility Requirements: Applicant must be enrolled or expecting to enroll full- or part-time at a two-year or four-year or technical institution or university; female and resident of Alabama, Alaska, Alberta, Arizona, Arkansas, California, Colorado, Connecticut, Delaware, District of Columbia, Florida, Georgia, Guam, Hawaii, Idaho, Illinois, Indiana, Iowa, Kansas, Kentucky, Louisiana, Maine, Maryland, Massachusetts, Michigan, Minnesota, Mississippi, Missouri, Montana, Nebraska, Nevada, New Hampshire, New Jersey, New Mexico, New York, North Carolina, North Dakota, Northern Mariana Islands, Ohio, Oklahoma, Oregon, Pennsylvania, Puerto Rico, Rhode Island, South Carolina, South Dakota, Tennessee, Texas, Utah, Vermont, Virginia, Washington, West Virginia, Wisconsin, Wyoming. Available to U.S. citizens.

Application Requirements: Essay. *Deadline:* continuous.

Contact: Miss. Michelle Bryan, Publicist
Debt.com
5769 W. Sunrise Blvd.
Plantation, FL 33313
Phone: 954-377-9054
E-mail: mbryan@debt.com

DELAWARE HIGHER EDUCATION OFFICE

http://www.doe.k12.de.us

FIRST STATE MANUFACTURED HOUSING ASSOCIATION SCHOLARSHIP

Award for legal residents of Delaware who are high school seniors or former graduates seeking to further their education. Must have been a resident of a manufactured home for at least one year prior to the application. Evaluated on scholastic record, financial need, essay, and recommendations. Award for any type of accredited two- or four-year degree program, or for any accredited training, licensing, or certification program.

Award: Scholarship for use in freshman, sophomore, junior, or senior years; not renewable. *Number:* 1. *Amount:* $1000.

Eligibility Requirements: Applicant must be enrolled or expecting to enroll full- or part-time at a two-year or four-year or technical institution or university and resident of Delaware. Available to U.S. citizens.

Application Requirements: Application form, financial need analysis, recommendations or references. *Deadline:* March 4.

Contact: Ms. Juliet Murawski, Program Administrator
Delaware Higher Education Office
401 Federal Street
Suite 2
Dover, DE 19901
Phone: 302-735-4120
Fax: 302-739-5894
E-mail: dheo@doe.k12.de.us

DEMOLAY FOUNDATION INCORPORATED

http://www.demolay.org/

FRANK S. LAND SCHOLARSHIP
• *See page 458*

DENVER FOUNDATION

http://www.denverfoundation.org/

REISHER FAMILY SCHOLARSHIP FUND

Scholarships awarded to Colorado residents who attend Metropolitan State College, the University of Northern Colorado, and the University of Colorado at Denver. Sophomores or transferring juniors who do not have sufficient funding to otherwise complete their degrees are eligible to apply. Must have at least a 3.0 GPA.

Award: Scholarship for use in sophomore or junior years; not renewable. *Amount:* $4000–$11,000.

Eligibility Requirements: Applicant must be enrolled or expecting to enroll full-time at a four-year institution or university; resident of Colorado and studying in Colorado. Available to U.S. citizens.

Application Requirements: Application form.

Contact: Karla Bieniulis, Scholarship Committee
Phone: 303-300-1790 Ext. 103
Fax: 303-300-6547
E-mail: info@denverfoundation.org

DIAMANTE, INC.

http://www.diamanteinc.org/

LATINO DIAMANTE SCHOLARSHIP FUND
• *See page 462*

DISTRICT OF COLUMBIA OFFICE OF THE STATE SUPERINTENDENT OF EDUCATION

http://www.osse.dc.gov/

DC TUITION ASSISTANCE GRANT PROGRAM (DCTAG)

Grant pays the difference between in-state and out-of-state tuition and fees at any public college or university in the United States, Guam, Puerto Rico or U.S. Virgin Islands, up to $10,000 per year. It also pays up to $2500 per year of tuition and fees at private colleges and universities in the Washington metropolitan area and at historically black colleges and universities throughout the United States. Students must be enrolled in a degree-granting program at an eligible institution, and be domiciled in the District of Columbia.

Award: Grant for use in freshman, sophomore, junior, or senior years; not renewable. *Number:* 5,999–6,000. *Amount:* $2500–$10,000.

Eligibility Requirements: Applicant must be age 24 or under; enrolled or expecting to enroll full- or part-time at a two-year or four-year institution or university and resident of District of Columbia. Available to U.S. citizens.

Application Requirements: Application form, financial need analysis. *Deadline:* June 30.

Contact: Dr. Antoinette Mitchell, Assistant Superintendent, Postsecondary and Career Education
District of Columbia Office of the State Superintendent of Education
810 First Street, NE, 3rd Floor
Washington, DC 20002
Phone: 202-727-2824
E-mail: antoinette.mitchell@dc.gov

DIXIE BOYS BASEBALL

http://www.dixie.org/boys

DIXIE YOUTH SCHOLARSHIP PROGRAM

Scholarships are presented annually to deserving high school seniors who participated in the Dixie Youth Baseball program while age 12 and under. Financial need is considered. Scholarship value is $2000.

Award: Scholarship for use in freshman year; not renewable. *Number:* 70. *Amount:* $2000.

Eligibility Requirements: Applicant must be high school student; planning to enroll or expecting to enroll full-time at a two-year or four-year or technical institution or university; resident of Alabama, Arkansas, Florida, Georgia, Louisiana, Mississippi, North Carolina, South Carolina, Tennessee, Texas, Virginia and must have an interest in athletics/sports. Available to U.S. citizens.

Application Requirements: Application form, essay, financial need analysis, personal photograph. *Deadline:* March 15.

Contact: Scholarship Chairman
Dixie Boys Baseball
PO Box 877
Marshall, TX 75671-0877
E-mail: dyb@dixie.org

DON'T MESS WITH TEXAS

http://www.dontmesswithtexas.org/

DON'T MESS WITH TEXAS SCHOLARSHIP PROGRAM

Scholarship for Texas graduating high school seniors who have taken a leadership role to prevent litter in their school and/or community. Participants must plan to attend accredited two- or four-year colleges or public or private universities in Texas

Award: Scholarship for use in freshman year; not renewable. *Number:* 4. *Amount:* $2000–$8000.

Eligibility Requirements: Applicant must be high school student; planning to enroll or expecting to enroll full- or part-time at a two-year or four-year institution or university; resident of Texas and studying in Texas. Available to U.S. citizens.

Application Requirements: Application form, application form may be submitted online (http://www.dontmesswithtexas.org/education-overview/scholarships/), community service, essay, personal photograph. *Deadline:* March 29.

Contact: Brenda Flores-Dollar, Programs Manager
Don't Mess With Texas
Texas Department of Transportation
150 E. Riverside Dr.
Austin, TX 78704
Phone: 512-486-5904
E-mail: scholarship@dontmesswithtexas.org

EAST BAY COLLEGE FUND

http://www.eastbaycollegefund.org/

GREAT EXPECTATIONS AWARD

Program provides renewable scholarships, mentoring, college counseling, and life skills training. Must have at least 3.0 cumulative GPA. Restricted to graduating seniors of Oakland, California public high schools.

Award: Scholarship for use in freshman, sophomore, junior, or senior years; renewable. *Number:* 50. *Amount:* $16,000.

Eligibility Requirements: Applicant must be high school student; planning to enroll or expecting to enroll full-time at a four-year institution or university and resident of California. Available to U.S. citizens.

Application Requirements: Application form, application form may be submitted online (https://www.scholarselect.com/scholarships/13454-2014-east-bay-college-fund-great-expectations-scholarship-program), essay, financial need analysis, interview, recommendations or references, transcript. *Deadline:* February 13.

Contact: Yancie Davis, College Access and Success Manager
East Bay College Fund
2201 Broadway, Suite 208
Oakland, CA 94612
Phone: 510-836-8900
Fax: 510-550-7876
E-mail: yancie@eastbaycollegefund.org

EAST LOS ANGELES COMMUNITY UNION (TELACU) SCHOLARSHIP PROGRAM

http://www.telacu.com/

TELACU EDUCATION FOUNDATION

Applicant must be a first-generation college student from a low-income family and have a minimum GPA of 2.5. Must attend partnering colleges and universities and be enrolled full-time for the entire academic year. California applicants: Must be permanent resident of unincorporated East Los Angeles, Bell Gardens, Commerce, Huntington Park, City of Los Angeles, Montebello, Monterey Park, Pico Rivera, Pomona and the Inland Empire, Santa Ana, South Gate, or other communities selected by foundation. Texas applicants: Must be permanent resident of San Antonio or Austin. Illinois Applicants: Must be permanent resident of Greater Chicagoland Area. New York applicants: Must be permanent resident of the state of New York.

Award: Scholarship for use in freshman, sophomore, junior, or senior years; not renewable. *Number:* 350–600. *Amount:* $500–$7500.

Eligibility Requirements: Applicant must be enrolled or expecting to enroll full-time at a two-year or four-year institution or university and resident of California, Illinois, New York, Texas. Available to U.S. citizens.

Application Requirements: Application form, essay, financial need analysis, interview, recommendations or references, resume, test scores, transcript. *Deadline:* March 14.

Contact: Mr. Daniel Garcia, Associate Director
East Los Angeles Community Union (TELACU) Scholarship Program
5400 East Olympic Boulevard
Los Angeles, CA 90022
Phone: 323-721-1655 Ext. 486
E-mail: dgarcia@TELACU.com

ELECTRICITYPLANS.COM

https://electricityplans.com/

ENERGIZE YOUR EDUCATION SCHOLARSHIP

Here at ElectricityPlans.com we make a positive difference for our customers' lives by helping them save money on their electricity bill. We are looking to reward students that make a positive difference in their cummunity. Let us know how you use your positive energy in the community to make a difference in the lives of others. You could win a $500 scholarship towards your college education.

Award: Scholarship for use in freshman year; not renewable. *Number:* 1. *Amount:* $500.

Eligibility Requirements: Applicant must be high school student; age 17-25; planning to enroll or expecting to enroll full-time at a two-year or four-year institution or university and resident of Connecticut, Ohio, Texas. Available to U.S. citizens.

Application Requirements: Application form, application form may be submitted online (https://electricityplans.com/scholarship/), essay, transcript. *Deadline:* May 1.

ELEVATE PEST CONTROL

https://elevatepestcontrol.com/

COLORADO ROFL SCHOLARSHIP

Make us laugh the hardest and you could be awarded a $500 scholarship. Take a minute from your serious academic life and make us laugh. Submit a joke, a story, a quick video (3 minutes or less), anything. All submissions need to be homemade by you. Do not copy funny jokes, stories, or videos from the internet. We want to see your personal creativity. This is the main submission for the scholarship and also what we will weigh the most heavily when choosing our recipient.

Award: Scholarship for use in freshman year; not renewable. *Number:* 1. *Amount:* $500.

Eligibility Requirements: Applicant must be enrolled or expecting to enroll full-time at a two-year or four-year or technical institution or university and resident of Colorado. Available to U.S. citizens.

Application Requirements: Application form. *Deadline:* April 30.

UTAH ROFL SCHOLARSHIP

Make us laugh the hardest and you could be awarded a $500 scholarship. Take a minute from your serious academic life and make us laugh. Submit a joke, a story, a quick video (3 minutes or less), anything. All submissions need to be homemade by you. Do not copy funny jokes, stories, or videos from the internet. We want to see your personal creativity. This is the main submission for the scholarship and also what we will weigh the most heavily when choosing our recipient.

Award: Scholarship for use in freshman year; not renewable. *Number:* 1. *Amount:* $500.

Eligibility Requirements: Applicant must be enrolled or expecting to enroll full-time at a two-year or four-year or technical institution or university and resident of Utah. Available to U.S. citizens.

Application Requirements: Application form. *Deadline:* April 30.

ENLISTED ASSOCIATION OF THE NATIONAL GUARD OF NEW JERSEY

http://www.eang-nj.org/

CSM VINCENT BALDASSARI MEMORIAL SCHOLARSHIP PROGRAM

• *See page 489*

FINALLY SOLD

http://www.finallysold.com

FINALLY SOLD IMPACT MAKER SCHOLARSHIP

The Finally Sold Impact Maker Scholarships are merit based scholarships designed for those who really feel that they can make a lasting impact in their chosen career. We are looking for passionate candidates who can articulate why going to their chosen school will allow them to ultimately make a difference in their field. Don't worry about your grades or SAT scores, because we won't look at those. Rather, we are looking for people who can demonstrate that they possess such traits and characteristics as: creativity, ambition, passion, resourcefulness, entrepreneurship, influence and persuasion. All you need to do is submit a short video and write a short essay pitching why you think we should pick you. We even award bonus points and extra credit for applicants such as our Influencer and Recruitment BONUS that rewards those who cross promote their video and our program. We also have bonuses for those who submit their application early or pass a short quiz about our company. Please see our site for more details, http://www.finallysold.com/scholarship-programs.html

Award: Scholarship for use in freshman, sophomore, junior, senior, graduate, or postgraduate years; renewable. *Number:* 6. *Amount:* $500.

Eligibility Requirements: Applicant must be age 16-99; enrolled or expecting to enroll full- or part-time at a two-year or four-year or technical institution or university; resident of Alabama, Alaska, Arizona, Arkansas, California, Colorado, Connecticut, Delaware, District of Columbia, Florida, Georgia, Hawaii, Idaho, Illinois, Indiana, Iowa, Kansas, Kentucky, Louisiana, Maine, Maryland, Massachusetts, Michigan, Minnesota, Mississippi, Missouri, Montana, Nebraska, Nevada, New Hampshire, New Jersey, New Mexico, New York, North Carolina, North Dakota, Ohio, Oklahoma, Oregon, Pennsylvania, Rhode Island, South Carolina, South Dakota, Tennessee, Texas, Utah, Vermont, Virginia, Washington, West Virginia, Wisconsin, Wyoming and studying in Arizona, Arkansas, California, Colorado, Connecticut, Delaware, District of Columbia, Florida, Georgia, Hawaii, Idaho, Illinois, Indiana, Iowa, Kansas, Kentucky, Louisiana, Maine, Maryland, Massachusetts, Michigan, Minnesota, Mississippi, Missouri, Montana, Nebraska, Nevada, New Hampshire, New Jersey, New Mexico, New York, North Carolina, North Dakota, Ohio, Oklahoma, Oregon, Pennsylvania, Rhode Island, South Carolina, South Dakota, Tennessee, Texas, Utah, Vermont, Virginia, Washington, West Virginia, Wisconsin, Wyoming. Available to U.S. citizens.

Application Requirements: Application form, essay. *Deadline:* continuous.

Contact: Douglas Schwartz, Scholarship Manager

FINANCE AUTHORITY OF MAINE

http://www.famemaine.com/

MAINE STATE GRANT PROGRAM

The Maine State Grant Program provides need-based grants to Maine undergraduate students. For the 2019-2020 academic year and the 2020–2021 academic year, the maximum grant award amount is $1,500. You must be enrolled at least half-time in an undergraduate program at an eligible institution. Because this is a need-based grant, your expected family contribution (EFC) must not exceed the maximum EFC set in any given year. The EFC for the 2019-2020 academic year is 5,800. The EFC for the 2020-2021 academic year is 4,500.* You must attend an eligible college/university in Maine. Students enrolled in NEBHE's Tuition Break Program, the New England Regional Student Program, may also be eligible. Contact FAME or your financial aid office for more information. You must attend an eligible college/university in Maine. Students enrolled in NEBHE's Tuition Break Program, the New England Regional Student Program, may also be eligible. Contact FAME or your financial aid office for more information.

Award: Grant for use in freshman, sophomore, junior, or senior years; not renewable.

Eligibility Requirements: Applicant must be enrolled or expecting to enroll full- or part-time at a two-year or technical institution or university; resident of Louisiana and studying in Connecticut, Maine, Massachusetts, New Hampshire, Rhode Island, Vermont. Available to U.S. citizens.

Application Requirements: Financial need analysis. *Deadline:* May 1.

Contact: Jennifer Lanphear, Education Programs Officer
Finance Authority of Maine
5 Community Drive
Augusta, ME 04332
Phone: 207-620-3548
E-mail: education@famemaine.com

TUITION WAIVER PROGRAMS
• See page 463

FINANCIAL SERVICE CENTERS OF NEW YORK

http://www.fscny.org

FSCNY YOUNG LEADERS SCHOLARSHIP

Applicants will be considered based on the following criteria: academic achievement; demonstrated leadership in their school; and demonstrated involvement in their community, contributing at least 50 valuable hours of volunteer service each year of high school. Applicants must be seniors attending public high schools in New York City's five boroughs or surrounding New York counties. After an initial review of all applications, the finalists will be selected for interviews with the Selection Committee. Interviews will be scheduled in late March for selected candidates. Students will be notified if they have been selected to receive an award by April 13, 2018. Award recipients may be invited to receive their awards at FSCNY's 26th Annual Conference Scholarship Luncheon, to be held at the Brooklyn Marriott Hotel April 26, 2018. Additional details will be made available to scholarship winners at a later date. Several scholarships will be issued to selected recipients consisting of a one-time cash award to be applied towards the cost of their freshman year of study at an accredited two- or four-year college or university. The cash award for each of the selected winners will range between $2,000 and $7,500 based on the recommendations of the Selection Committee.

Award: Scholarship for use in freshman year; not renewable. *Number:* 1–10. *Amount:* $2000–$7500.

Eligibility Requirements: Applicant must be high school student; planning to enroll or expecting to enroll full- or part-time at a two-year or four-year institution or university; resident of New York and must have an interest in leadership. Available to U.S. citizens.

Application Requirements: Application form, community service, essay, interview. *Deadline:* March 9.

Contact: LeeAnn Thomson
E-mail: lthompson@fisca.org

FLORIDA ASSOCIATION FOR MEDIA IN EDUCATION

http://www.floridamediaed.org/ssyra.html

INTELLECTUAL FREEDOM STUDENT SCHOLARSHIP

Scholarship in the amount of $1000 is awarded annually to a graduating senior from a high school in Florida. Only students whose library media specialists are members of FAME are eligible. Essays written by senior students will be submitted to the FAME Intellectual Freedom Committee.

Award: Scholarship for use in freshman year; not renewable. *Number:* 1. *Amount:* $1000.

Eligibility Requirements: Applicant must be high school student; planning to enroll or expecting to enroll full-time at a two-year or four-year or technical institution or university and resident of Florida. Available to U.S. citizens.

Application Requirements: Application form, essay. *Deadline:* March 15.

Contact: Larry Bodkin, Executive Director
Phone: 850-531-8350
Fax: 850-531-8344
E-mail: lbodkin@floridamedia.org

FLORIDA SOCIETY, SONS OF THE AMERICAN REVOLUTION

http://www.flssar.org/

GEORGE S. AND STELLA M. KNIGHT ESSAY CONTEST

Award for the best essay about an event, person, philosophy, or ideal associated with the American Revolution, the Declaration of Independence, or the framing of the U.S. Constitution. Due by December 31. Must be a high school student and resident of Florida and U.S. citizen or legal resident. State winner may enter the national contest. For more information, see website www.flssar.org or http://flssar.org/FLSSAR/KnightEssay1.htm. See also nssar.org for rules.

Award: Prize for use in freshman year; not renewable. *Number:* 3. *Amount:* $250–$1000.

Eligibility Requirements: Applicant must be high school student; planning to enroll or expecting to enroll full- or part-time at an institution or university and resident of Florida. Available to U.S. citizens.

Application Requirements: Application form, application form may be submitted online(1965uva@gmail.com), Bibliography (see Rules) and short Biography, essay. *Deadline:* December 31.

Contact: Mr. John Stewart
Florida Society, Sons of the American Revolution
1121 32 Avenue North
St. Petersburg, FL 33704
E-mail: 1965uva@gmail.com

FLORIDA STATE DEPARTMENT OF EDUCATION

http://www.floridastudentfinancialaid.org/

ACCESS TO BETTER LEARNING AND EDUCATION GRANT

Grant program provides tuition assistance to Florida undergraduate students enrolled in degree programs at eligible private Florida colleges or universities. Must be a U.S. citizen or eligible non-citizen and must meet Florida residency requirements. The participating institution determines application procedures, deadlines, and student eligibility. An eligible student must complete and submit the FAFSA in order to receive program funding. For more details, visit the website at http://www.FloridaStudentFinancialAid.org/SSFAD/home/uamain.htm.

Award: Grant for use in freshman, sophomore, junior, or senior years; renewable.

Eligibility Requirements: Applicant must be enrolled or expecting to enroll full-time at an institution or university; resident of District of Columbia and studying in Florida. Available to U.S. citizens.

Application Requirements: Application form, application form may be submitted online.

Contact: Florida Department of Education, Office of Student Financial
Assistance, Customer Service
Florida State Department of Education
325 West Gaines Street
Tallahassee, FL 32399
Phone: 888-827-2007
E-mail: osfa@fldoe.org

FIRST GENERATION MATCHING GRANT PROGRAM

Need-based grants to Florida resident undergraduate students who are enrolled in state universities and community colleges in Florida and whose parents have not earned baccalaureate degrees. Available state funds are contingent upon matching contributions from private sources on a dollar-for-dollar basis. Institutions determine application procedures, deadlines, and student eligibility. For more details, visit the website at http://www.FloridaStudentFinancialAid.org/SSFAD/home/uamain.htm.

Award: Grant for use in freshman, sophomore, junior, or senior years; renewable.

Eligibility Requirements: Applicant must be enrolled or expecting to enroll full- or part-time at a two-year institution or university; resident of District of Columbia and studying in Florida. Available to U.S. citizens.

Application Requirements: Application form, application form may be submitted online, financial need analysis.

Contact: Florida Department of Education, Office of Student Financial
Assistance, Customer Service
Florida State Department of Education
325 West Gaines Street
Tallahassee, FL 32399
Phone: 888-827-2004
E-mail: osfa@fldoe.org

FLORIDA BRIGHT FUTURES SCHOLARSHIP PROGRAM

Three lottery-funded scholarships reward Florida high school graduates for high academic achievement. Program is comprised of the following three awards: Florida Academic Scholars Award, Florida Medallion Scholars Award and Florida Gold Seal Vocational Scholars Award. An eligible student must complete and submit the FAFSA in order to receive program funding. For more details, visit the website at http://www.FloridaStudentFinancialAid.org/SSFAD/home/uamain.htm.

Award: Scholarship for use in freshman, sophomore, junior, or senior years; renewable.

Eligibility Requirements: Applicant must be high school student; planning to enroll or expecting to enroll full- or part-time at a two-year or technical institution or university; resident of District of Columbia and studying in Florida. Available to U.S. citizens.

Application Requirements: Application form, application form may be submitted online, community service, financial need analysis. *Deadline:* August 31.

Contact: Florida Department of Education, Office of Student Financial
Assistance, Customer Service
Florida State Department of Education
325 West Gaines Street
Tallahassee, FL 32399
Phone: 888-827-2004
E-mail: osfa@fldoe.org

FLORIDA POSTSECONDARY STUDENT ASSISTANCE GRANT

Scholarships to degree-seeking, resident, undergraduate students who demonstrate substantial financial need and are enrolled in eligible degree-granting private colleges and universities not eligible under the Florida Private Student Assistance Grant. FSAG is a decentralized program, and each participating institution determines application procedures, deadlines and student eligibility. Number of awards varies. For more details, visit the website at http://www.FloridaStudentFinancialAid.org/SSFAD/home/uamain.htm.

Award: Grant for use in freshman, sophomore, junior, or senior years; renewable. *Amount:* $200–$2610.

Eligibility Requirements: Applicant must be enrolled or expecting to enroll full-time at a two-year or four-year institution or university; resident of Florida and studying in Florida. Available to U.S. citizens.

Application Requirements: Financial need analysis.

Contact: Florida Department of Education, Office of Student Financial
Assistance, Customer Service
Florida State Department of Education
325 West Gaines Street
Tallahassee, FL 32399
Phone: 888-827-2004
E-mail: osfa@fldoe.org

FLORIDA PRIVATE STUDENT ASSISTANCE GRANT

Grants for Florida residents who are U.S. citizens or eligible non-citizens attending eligible private, nonprofit, four-year colleges and universities in Florida. Must be a full-time student and demonstrate substantial financial need. For renewal, must have earned a minimum cumulative GPA of 2.0 at the last institution attended. For more details, visit the website at http://www.FloridaStudentFinancialAid.org/SSFAD/home/uamain.htm.

Award: Grant for use in freshman, sophomore, junior, or senior years; renewable. *Amount:* $200–$2610.

Eligibility Requirements: Applicant must be enrolled or expecting to enroll full-time at an institution or university; resident of District of Columbia and studying in Florida. Available to U.S. citizens.

Application Requirements: Application form, application form may be submitted online, financial need analysis.

Contact: Florida Department of Education, Office of Student Financial
Assistance, Customer Service
Florida State Department of Education
325 West Gaines Street
Tallahassee, FL 32399
Phone: 888-827-2004
E-mail: osfa@fldoe.org

FLORIDA PUBLIC STUDENT ASSISTANCE GRANT

Grants for Florida residents, U.S. citizens or eligible non-citizens who attend state universities and public community colleges and demonstrate substantial financial need. For renewal, must have earned a minimum cumulative GPA of 2.0 at the last institution attended. For more details, visit the website at http://www.FloridaStudentFinancialAid.org/SSFAD/home/uamain.htm.

Award: Grant for use in freshman, sophomore, junior, or senior years; renewable. *Amount:* $200–$2610.

Eligibility Requirements: Applicant must be enrolled or expecting to enroll full- or part-time at a two-year institution or university; resident of District of Columbia and studying in Florida. Available to U.S. citizens.

Application Requirements: Application form, application form may be submitted online, financial need analysis.

Contact: Florida Department of Education, Office of Student Financial
Assistance, Customer Service
Florida State Department of Education
325 West Gaines Street
Tallahassee, FL 32399
Phone: 888-827-2004
E-mail: osfa@fldoe.org

Contact: Florida Department of Education, Office of Student Financial
Assistance, Customer Service
Florida State Department of Education
325 West Gaines Street
Tallahassee, FL 32399
Phone: 888-827-2004
E-mail: osfa@fldoe.org

FLORIDA STUDENT ASSISTANCE GRANT-CAREER EDUCATION

Need-based grant program available to Florida residents enrolled in certificate programs of 450 or more clock hours at participating community colleges or career centers operated by district school boards. FSAG-CE is a decentralized state of Florida program, which means that each participating institution determines application procedures, deadlines, student eligibility, and award amounts. For more details, visit the website at http://www.FloridaStudentFinancialAid.org/SSFAD/home/uamain.htm.

Award: Grant for use in freshman, sophomore, junior, or senior years; renewable. *Amount:* $200–$2610.

Eligibility Requirements: Applicant must be enrolled or expecting to enroll full- or part-time at a two-year or technical institution; resident of Florida and studying in Florida. Available to U.S. citizens.

Application Requirements: Application form may be submitted online, financial need analysis.

Contact: Florida Department of Education, Office of Student Financial
Assistance, Customer Service
Florida State Department of Education
325 West Gaines Street
Tallahassee, FL 32399
Phone: 888-827-2004
E-mail: osfa@fldoe.org

FLORIDA WORK EXPERIENCE PROGRAM

Need-based program providing eligible Florida residents work experiences that will complement and reinforce their educational and career goals. Must maintain GPA of 2.0. Postsecondary institution will determine applicant's eligibility, number of hours to be worked per week, and the award amount. For more details, visit the website at http://www.FloridaStudentFinancialAid.org/SSFAD/home/uamain.htm.

Award: Grant for use in freshman, sophomore, junior, or senior years; renewable.

Eligibility Requirements: Applicant must be enrolled or expecting to enroll full- or part-time at a two-year institution or university; resident of District of Columbia and studying in Florida. Available to U.S. citizens.

Application Requirements: Financial need analysis.

Contact: Florida Department of Education, Office of Student Financial
Assistance, Customer Service
Florida State Department of Education
325 West Gaines Street
Tallahassee, FL 32399
Phone: 888-827-2004
E-mail: osfa@fldoe.com

JOSE MARTI SCHOLARSHIP CHALLENGE GRANT FUND

• *See page 517*

MARY MCLEOD BETHUNE SCHOLARSHIP

Renewable award to Florida residents with a GPA of 3.0 or above, who will attend Bethune-Cookman University, Edward Waters College, Florida and University, or Florida Memorial University. Must not have previously received a baccalaureate degree. Must demonstrate financial need as specified by the institution. For more details, visit the website at http://www.FloridaStudentFinancialAid.org/SSFAD/home/uamain.htm.

Award: Scholarship for use in freshman, sophomore, junior, or senior years; renewable. *Amount:* $3000.

Eligibility Requirements: Applicant must be enrolled or expecting to enroll full-time at an institution or university; resident of District of Columbia and studying in Florida. Available to U.S. citizens.

Application Requirements: Application form, application form may be submitted online, financial need analysis.

Contact: Florida Department of Education, Office of Student Financial
Assistance, Customer Service
Florida State Department of Education
325 West Gaines Street
Tallahassee, FL 32399
Phone: 888-827-2004
E-mail: osfa@fldoe.org

SCHOLARSHIPS FOR CHILDREN AND SPOUSES OF DECEASED OR DISABLED VETERANS

• *See page 502*

WILLIAM L. BOYD IV FLORIDA RESIDENT ACCESS GRANT

Renewable awards to Florida undergraduate residents attending an eligible private, nonprofit Florida college or university. Postsecondary institution will determine applicant's eligibility. Renewal applicant must have earned a minimum institutional GPA of 2.0. An eligible student must complete and submit the FAFSA in order to receive program funding. For more details, visit the website at http://www.FloridaStudentFinancialAid.org/SSFAD/home/uamain.htm.

Award: Grant for use in freshman, sophomore, junior, or senior years; renewable. *Amount:* up to $3000.

Eligibility Requirements: Applicant must be enrolled or expecting to enroll full-time at a four-year institution or university; resident of Florida and studying in Florida. Available to U.S. citizens.

Application Requirements: Application form.

Contact: Florida Department of Education, Office of Student Financial
Assistance, Customer Service
Florida State Department of Education
325 West Gaines Street
Tallahassee, FL 32399
Phone: 888-827-2004
E-mail: osfa@fldoe.org

FLORIDA WOMEN'S STATE GOLF ASSOCIATION

CLUB EMPLOYEES AND DEPENDENTS SCHOLARSHIP

Scholarship was designed to employees, and dependents of employees, of FSGA Member Clubs that utilize the GHIN Handicap System.

Award: Scholarship for use in freshman, sophomore, junior, or senior years; renewable. *Number:* 1. *Amount:* $500–$2000.

Eligibility Requirements: Applicant must be enrolled or expecting to enroll full-time at a two-year or four-year or technical institution or university; resident of Florida and must have an interest in golf. Available to U.S. citizens.

Application Requirements: Application form, application form may be submitted online (http://www.fsga.org/sections/Foundation/College-Scholarships/38), community service, essay, financial need analysis, personal photograph, recommendations or references, test scores, transcript. *Deadline:* June 1.

Contact: Kyle Walkiewicz, Director of Junior Golf
Florida Women's State Golf Association
12630 Telecom Drive
Tampa, FL 33637
Phone: 813-632-3742
Fax: 813-910-2125
E-mail: kyle@fsga.org

FSGA SCHOLARS

FSGA Scholars is a scholarship program made possible by the Florida State Golf Association and our Future of Golf Foundation. In the Spring each year, the FSGA selects a minimum of five golfers from the FJT's graduating class to be awarded a renewable four-year scholarship. A total of $10,000 in college scholarships will be awarded each year, resulting in $40,000 granted to each graduating class.

Award: Scholarship for use in freshman, sophomore, junior, or senior years; renewable. *Number:* 1–8. *Amount:* $500–$2000.

Eligibility Requirements: Applicant must be high school student; planning to enroll or expecting to enroll full-time at a two-year or four-year or technical institution or university; resident of Florida and must have an interest in golf. Available to U.S. citizens.

Application Requirements: Application form, application form may be submitted online (http://www.fsga.org/sections/Foundation/College-Scholarships/38), community service, essay, financial need analysis, personal photograph, recommendations or references, test scores, transcript. *Deadline:* July 1.

Contact: Kyle Walkiewica, Director of Junior Golf
Florida Women's State Golf Association
12630 Telecom Drive
Tampa, FL 33637
Phone: 813-632-3742
Fax: 813-910-2125
E-mail: kyle@fsga.org

SARAH E. HUNEYCUTT SCHOLARSHIP

This four-year scholarship of $5000 per academic year ($20,000 total) is awarded annually to a deserving high school senior woman who is a Florida resident, will be attending an accredited Florida college or university, has demonstrated an interest in golf but is not eligible for a golf athletic scholarship, shows financial need, and maintains a grade point average of 3.0 or higher.

Award: Scholarship for use in freshman, sophomore, junior, or senior years; renewable. *Number:* 1–5. *Amount:* $5000.

Eligibility Requirements: Applicant must be high school student; planning to enroll or expecting to enroll full-time at a two-year or four-year or technical institution or university; female; resident of Florida; studying in Florida and must have an interest in golf. Available to U.S. citizens.

Application Requirements: Application form, application form may be submitted online (http://www.jggsf.org/), community service, essay, financial need analysis, personal photograph, test scores, transcript. *Deadline:* June 1.

Contact: Jan Demarco, President
E-mail: jan@jggsf.org

THE FORD FAMILY FOUNDATION

http://www.tfff.org/scholarships

FORD OPPORTUNITY PROGRAM

Hallie E. Ford and The Ford Family Foundation established the Ford Opportunity Scholarship Program to provide scholarships to college students who are single parents with custody of dependent children (18 years of age or younger) and be the head of household as defined by IRS regulations. Recipients must have at least one year remaining in their undergraduate program and attend college in their home start of Oregon or California and plan to pursue an associate or bachelor's degree. Minimum 3.0 GPA required.

Award: Scholarship for use in freshman, sophomore, junior, senior, graduate, or postgraduate years; renewable. *Number:* 30–50. *Amount:* $1000–$25,000.

Eligibility Requirements: Applicant must be enrolled or expecting to enroll full-time at a two-year or four-year institution or university; single; resident of California, Oregon and studying in California, Oregon. Available to U.S. citizens.

Application Requirements: Application form, essay, financial need analysis, interview. *Deadline:* March 1.

Contact: Tricia Tate, Scholarship Programs Manager
The Ford Family Foundation
44 Club Road, Suite 100
Eugene, OR 97401
Phone: 541-485-6211
Fax: 541-485-6223
E-mail: fordscholarships@tfff.org

FORD RESTART PROGRAM

The Ford Family Foundation established the Ford ReStart Scholarship Program to encourage adults, age 25 or older, to begin or return to full-time, post-secondary education. Each year, up to 46 applicants are selected from Oregon and Siskiyou County, California to receive a Ford ReStart scholarship. An applicant must be at least 25 years old by March 1 of the application year, be no more than halfway through their degree program, and seek an associate's degree or a bachelor's degree at an eligible institution in CA or OR (and not previously have earned a bachelor's degree).

Award: Scholarship for use in freshman, sophomore, junior, senior, graduate, or postgraduate years; renewable. *Number:* 46. *Amount:* $1000–$25,000.

Eligibility Requirements: Applicant must be age 25 and over; enrolled or expecting to enroll full-time at a two-year or four-year institution or university; resident of California, Oregon and studying in California, Oregon. Available to U.S. citizens.

Application Requirements: Application form, essay, financial need analysis, interview. *Deadline:* March 1.

Contact: Tricia Tate, Scholarship Programs Manager
The Ford Family Foundation
44 Club Road, Suite 100
Eugene, OR 97401
Phone: 541-485-6211
Fax: 541-485-6223
E-mail: fordscholarships@tfff.org

FORD SCHOLARS PROGRAM

The Ford Scholars Program is need-based and open to 1) graduating high school seniors and, 2) entering college freshmen and (3) continuing community college students ready to transfer to a four-year college, who are seeking a bachelor's degree in Oregon or California. This program is available to residents of Oregon and Siskiyou County, California. The Ford Scholars Program was created by Kenneth W. Ford (1908-1997), a founder of The Ford Family Foundation, to assist students who otherwise would find it impossible, or at least very difficult, to obtain a college degree without financial assistance.

Award: Scholarship for use in freshman, sophomore, junior, senior, graduate, or postgraduate years; renewable. *Number:* 100–120. *Amount:* $1000–$25,000.

Eligibility Requirements: Applicant must be enrolled or expecting to enroll full-time at a two-year or four-year institution or university; resident of California, Oregon and studying in California, Oregon. Available to U.S. citizens.

Application Requirements: Application form, essay, financial need analysis, interview. *Deadline:* March 1.

Contact: Tricia Tate, Scholarship Programs Manager
The Ford Family Foundation
44 Club Road, Suite 100
Eugene, OR 97401
Phone: 541-485-6211
Fax: 541-485-6223
E-mail: fordscholarships@tfff.org

FRANCIS OUIMET SCHOLARSHIP FUND

http://www.ouimet.org

FRANCIS OUIMET SCHOLARSHIP

Since 1949, The Francis Ouimet Scholarship Fund has awarded nearly $34 Million in need-based college tuition assistance to students who have given at least two years of service to golf as caddies, pro shop work, or course superintendent operations at a Massachusetts golf course. The Ouimet Scholarship is unique in that it is renewable for up to four years. Ouimet awards range from $1,000 to $15,000 per year, depending on financial need and ranking in our competitive evaluation process. The value of the award over four years can be $10,000 to $40,000, or more. Nearly 5,700 young people have received Ouimet Scholarships, and many have gone on to prestigious positions of leadership in business and professional careers.

Award: Scholarship for use in freshman, sophomore, junior, or senior years; not renewable. *Amount:* $1000–$15,000.

Eligibility Requirements: Applicant must be enrolled or expecting to enroll full-time at a two-year or four-year institution or university; resident of Massachusetts and must have an interest in golf. Available to U.S. citizens.

Application Requirements: Application form, community service, essay, financial need analysis, interview, personal photograph. *Deadline:* December 1.

Contact: Mrs. Michelle Edwards, Director of Scholarships
Francis Ouimet Scholarship Fund
300 Arnold Palmer Boulevard
Norton, MA 02766
Phone: 774-4309090
Fax: 774-4307474
E-mail: MichelleE@ouimet.org

FRATERNAL ORDER OF POLICE ASSOCIATES OF OHIO INC.

http://www.fopaohio.org/

FRATERNAL ORDER OF POLICE ASSOCIATES, STATE LODGE OF OHIO INC., SCHOLARSHIP FUND

• *See page 463*

THE FREDERICK B. ABRAMSON MEMORIAL FOUNDATION

http://www.abramsonfoundation.org/

THE FREDERICK B. ABRAMSON MEMORIAL FOUNDATION SCHOLARSHIPS

The Abramson Scholarship Foundation offers financial and mentoring support to DC public high school graduates who demonstrate academic promise, financial need, and a commitment to community service. To be eligible for an Abramson Scholarship, you must: - Be graduating in June 2019 from a public high school located in the District of Columbia (D.C.) - Be a D.C. resident - Have admission to and commitment to attend an accredited four-year college in the United States as a candidate for a degree - Have a demonstrated commitment to community service - Have an economic need for financial assistance and a family income of less than $70,000 Have a solid academic record demonstrated by an overall 2.75 GPA or better, at least 1000 combined SAT scores among evidence-based reading plus writing and math, and a combined score of 12 or above if you've taken the optional SAT essay, or at least 20 combined ACT scores.

Award: Scholarship for use in freshman, sophomore, junior, or senior years; renewable. *Amount:* $2000.

Eligibility Requirements: Applicant must be high school student; planning to enroll or expecting to enroll full-time at a four-year institution and resident of District of Columbia. Available to U.S. and non-U.S. citizens.

Application Requirements: Application form, application form may be submitted online (http://www.abramsonfoundation.org), community service, essay, financial need analysis, interview, recommendations or references, test scores, transcript. *Deadline:* April 26.

Contact: Lisa Richards Toney, Executive Director
The Frederick B. Abramson Memorial Foundation
PO Box 7810
Washington, DC 20044-7810
Phone: 202-470-5425
Fax: 202-318-2482
E-mail: info@abramsonfoundation.org

FRIENDS OF 440 SCHOLARSHIP FUND INC.

http://www.440scholarship.org/

FRIENDS OF 440 SCHOLARSHIP FUND, INC.

Scholarships to students who are dependents of workers who were injured or killed in the course and scope of their employment and who are eligible to receive benefits under the Florida Workers' Compensation system, or are dependents of those primarily engaged in the administration of the Florida Workers' Compensation Law.

Award: Scholarship for use in freshman, sophomore, junior, or senior years; renewable. *Number:* 1–60. *Amount:* $500–$6000.

Eligibility Requirements: Applicant must be enrolled or expecting to enroll full-time at a two-year or four-year or technical institution or university and resident of Florida. Available to U.S. and non-U.S. citizens.

Application Requirements: Application form, copy of tax return, transcript. *Deadline:* February 28.

Contact: Ms. Lori Gerson, Managing Director
Phone: 305-423-8710
Fax: 305-670-0716
E-mail: info@440scholarship.org

FULFILLMENT FUND

http://www.fulfillment.org/

FULFILLMENT FUND SCHOLARSHIPS

Award is for undergraduates. Serving students in seven partner high schools, Fremont, Hamilton, Locke, Los Angeles, Manual Arts, Crenshaw and Wilson. Only students who participated in the Fulfillment Fund High School Program for at least two years are eligible to apply for the scholarship.

Award: Scholarship for use in freshman, sophomore, junior, or senior years; not renewable. *Amount:* $1000–$1500.

Eligibility Requirements: Applicant must be enrolled or expecting to enroll full- or part-time at a four-year institution or university and resident of California. Available to U.S. citizens.

Application Requirements: Application form. *Deadline:* varies.

Contact: Darcine Thomas, Community Outreach Manager
Phone: 323-900-8753
Fax: 323-525-3095

GATTI, KELTNER, BIENVENU & MONTESI

https://www.gkbm.com/

MONTESI SCHOLARSHIP

$2500 scholarship for a student who submits an original essay on how Driving and Texting has affected their life or an experience of how it has impacted someone they know. Winner must show proof of acceptance or active enrollment in undergrad school.

Award: Scholarship for use in freshman, sophomore, junior, or senior years; not renewable. *Number:* 1. *Amount:* $2500.

Eligibility Requirements: Applicant must be enrolled or expecting to enroll full-time at a two-year or four-year or technical institution or university and resident of Arkansas, Mississippi, Tennessee. Available to U.S. citizens.

Application Requirements: Essay. *Deadline:* May 30.

Contact: Chloe Zollinger
E-mail: gkbmlaw@gmail.com

GENERAL FEDERATION OF WOMEN'S CLUBS OF MASSACHUSETTS

http://www.gfwcma.org/

CATHERINE E. PHILBIN SCHOLARSHIP

One scholarship of up to $500 will be awarded to a graduate or undergraduate student studying public health. Eligible applicants will be residents of Massachusetts. Along with the application, students must send a personal statement of no more than 500 words addressing professional goals and financial need.

Award: Scholarship for use in freshman, sophomore, junior, senior, or graduate years; not renewable. *Number:* 1. *Amount:* $500.

Eligibility Requirements: Applicant must be enrolled or expecting to enroll full-time at an institution or university and resident of Maryland. Available to U.S. citizens.

Application Requirements: Application form, driver's license, essay. *Deadline:* March 1.

Contact: Darlene Coutu, Scholarship Chairman
General Federation of Women's Clubs of Massachusetts
PO Box 679
Sudbury, MA 01776-0679
E-mail: darlenepwc@charter.net

EDUCATION - TEACHING SCHOLARSHIP

Applicant must be a senior in a Massachusetts high school or home schooled and has achieved the standards for graduation set by the town of residence, who will enroll in a four-year accredited college or university in a teacher training program that leads to certification to teach.

Award: Scholarship for use in freshman year; not renewable. *Number:* 1. *Amount:* $500.

Eligibility Requirements: Applicant must be high school student; planning to enroll or expecting to enroll full-time at an institution or university and resident of Maryland. Available to U.S. citizens.

Application Requirements: Application form, driver's license, essay. *Deadline:* March 1.

Contact: Darlene Coutu, Scholarship Chairman
General Federation of Women's Clubs of Massachusetts
PO Box 679
Sudbury, MA 01776-0679
E-mail: darlenepwc@charter.net

MUSIC SCHOLARSHIP "NICKLES FOR NOTES"

Scholarship for high school seniors majoring in piano, instrument, music education, music therapy or voice. Applicant must be a senior in a Massachusetts High School.

Award: Scholarship for use in freshman year; not renewable. *Number:* 1. *Amount:* $500.

Eligibility Requirements: Applicant must be high school student; planning to enroll or expecting to enroll full-time at an institution or university and resident of Maryland. Available to U.S. citizens.

Application Requirements: Application form, driver's license, essay. *Deadline:* March 1.

Contact: Sandy Higgins, Music Chairman
General Federation of Women's Clubs of Massachusetts
PO Box 679
Sudbury, MA 01776-0679
Phone: 978-443-4569
E-mail: s.a.sandy@comcast.net

PENNIES FOR ART SCHOLARSHIP

Scholarship for graduating high school senior who is resident of Massachusetts majoring in art. Must submit three (3) pieces of original artwork in three (3) different mediums (no sculpture). Matting is required except for oil on stretched canvas.

Award: Scholarship for use in freshman year; not renewable. *Number:* 1. *Amount:* $500.

Eligibility Requirements: Applicant must be high school student; planning to enroll or expecting to enroll full-time at an institution or university and resident of Maryland. Available to U.S. citizens.

Application Requirements: Application form, driver's license, essay, portfolio. *Deadline:* March 1.

Contact: Darlene Coutu, Scholarship Chairman
General Federation of Women's Clubs of Massachusetts
PO Box 679
Sudbury, MA 01776
E-mail: darlenepwc@charter.net

GENERAL FEDERATION OF WOMEN'S CLUBS OF VERMONT

BARBARA JEAN BARKER MEMORIAL SCHOLARSHIP

Applicants must be Vermont residents who need addition education to advance their position in the workplace.

Award: Grant for use in freshman, sophomore, junior, senior, or graduate years; renewable. *Number:* 2. *Amount:* $1000.

Eligibility Requirements: Applicant must be enrolled or expecting to enroll full- or part-time at a two-year or four-year or technical institution or university; female and resident of Vermont. Available to U.S. citizens.

Application Requirements: Application form, driver's license, financial need analysis, interview. *Deadline:* March 15.

Contact: Mrs. Betty Haggerty
General Federation of Women's Clubs of Vermont
16 Taylor Street
Bellows Falls, VT 05101
Phone: 802-463-4159
E-mail: hubett@hotmail.com

GEORGIA PRESS EDUCATIONAL FOUNDATION INC.

http://gapress.org/

KIRK SUTLIVE SCHOLARSHIP

Scholarship awarded annually to a student majoring in either the news-editorial or public relations sequence.

Award: Scholarship for use in freshman, sophomore, junior, or senior years; not renewable. *Number:* 1. *Amount:* $500–$2000.

Eligibility Requirements: Applicant must be enrolled or expecting to enroll full-time at a four-year institution or university; resident of Georgia and studying in Georgia. Available to U.S. citizens.

Application Requirements: Application form, essay, financial need analysis, interview, personal photograph. *Deadline:* March 1.

Contact: Jennifer Farmer, Scholarship and Internship Coordinator
Georgia Press Educational Foundation Inc.
3066 Mercer University Dr., Suite 200
Atlanta, GA 30341
Phone: 770-454-6776
Fax: 770-454-6778
E-mail: jfarmer@gapress.org

GEORGIA STUDENT FINANCE COMMISSION

https://gsfc.georgia.gov/

GEORGIA HOPE GRANT PROGRAM

HOPE Grant is available to Georgia residents who are pursuing a certificate or technical diploma. A HOPE Grant recipient must maintain a minimum 2.0 cumulative postsecondary grade point average to remain eligible. The grant provides tuition assistance to students enrolled at an eligible college or university in Georgia. A student who received a high school diploma (High School Postsecondary Graduation Opportunity Plan) by earning a technical college diploma or two technical college certificates, in one career pathway identified by the Technical College System of Georgia (TCSG), may be eligible for the HOPE Grant, up to 30 degree hours. The student must be enrolled in an associate degree program at a TCSG institution in order to receive the HOPE Grant.

Award: Grant for use in freshman, sophomore, junior, or senior years; renewable. *Number:* 100,000. *Amount:* $420–$3600.

Eligibility Requirements: Applicant must be enrolled or expecting to enroll full- or part-time at a two-year or technical institution or university; resident of Florida and studying in Georgia. Available to U.S. citizens.

Application Requirements: Application form, financial need analysis.

Contact: Ms. Pennie Strong, Vice President, Student Aid Services
Georgia Student Finance Commission
2082 East Exchange Place
Tucker, GA 30084
Phone: 770-724-9014
Fax: 770-724-9249
E-mail: pennies@gsfc.org

GEORGIA PUBLIC SAFETY MEMORIAL GRANT

• *See page 464*

GEORGIA TUITION EQUALIZATION GRANT (GTEG) PROGRAM

The Georgia Tuition Equalization Grant (GTEG) provides grant assistance toward educational costs to Georgia residents enrolled at an eligible private college or university. Students must be enrolled full-time in an undergraduate program of study leading to an undergraduate

Award: Grant for use in freshman, sophomore, junior, or senior years; renewable. *Amount:* $317–$475.

Eligibility Requirements: Applicant must be enrolled or expecting to enroll full-time at a two-year institution or university; resident of Florida and studying in Georgia. Available to U.S. citizens.

Application Requirements: Application form.

Contact: Ms. Pennie Strong, Vice President, Student Aid Services
Georgia Student Finance Commission
2082 East Exchange Place
Tucker, GA 30084
Phone: 770-724-9014
Fax: 770-724-9249
E-mail: pennies@gsfc.org

HELPING EDUCATE RESERVISTS AND THEIR OFFSPRING (HERO) SCHOLARSHIP

Provides assistance with cost of attendance to members of the Georgia National Guard and U.S. Military Reservists who were deployed overseas on active duty service, on or after February 1, 2003, to a location designated as a combat zone, and the children and spouses of such members of the Georgia National Guard and U.S. Military Reserves. Students must be attending an eligible college or university in Georgia.

Award: Scholarship for use in freshman, sophomore, junior, or senior years; not renewable. *Amount:* $2000–$8000.

Eligibility Requirements: Applicant must be enrolled or expecting to enroll full- or part-time at a two-year or technical institution or university; resident of Florida and studying in Georgia. Available to U.S. citizens.

Application Requirements: Application form.

Contact: Ms. Pennie Strong, Vice President, Student Aid Services
Georgia Student Finance Commission
2082 East Exchange Place
Tucker, GA 30084
Phone: 770-724-9014
Fax: 770-724-9249
E-mail: pennies@gsfc.org

HOPE SCHOLARSHIP

HOPE Scholarship is a merit-based award available to Georgia residents who have demonstrated academic achievement. A Hope Scholarship recipient must graduate from high school with a minimum 3.0 HOPE Calculated (approved core courses) grade point average and earned 4 credits of academic rigor. Students must maintain a minimum 3.0 cumulative postsecondary grade point average to remain eligible. The scholarship provides tuition assistance to students pursuing an undergraduate degree at a HOPE Scholarship eligible college or university in Georgia.

Award: Scholarship for use in freshman, sophomore, junior, or senior years; renewable. *Number:* 200,000. *Amount:* $420–$3600.

Eligibility Requirements: Applicant must be enrolled or expecting to enroll full- or part-time at a two-year or technical institution or university; resident of Florida and studying in Georgia. Available to U.S. citizens.

Application Requirements: Application form.

Contact: Georgia Student Finance Commission Program Administration
Georgia Student Finance Commission
2082 East Exchange Place
Tucker, GA 30084
Phone: 800-505-4732
E-mail: ProgramAdmin@gsfc.org

SCHOLARSHIP FOR ENGINEERING EDUCATION FOR MINORITIES (MSEE)

• *See page 518*

ZELL MILLER SCHOLARSHIP

Zell Miller Scholarship is a merit-based award available to Georgia residents, similar to the HOPE Scholarship, but with more stringent academic requirements and a higher level of tuition assistance. A Zell Miller Scholarship recipient must graduate from high school with a minimum 3.7 HOPE Calculated (approved core courses) grade point average combined and earned 4 credits of academic rigor, with a minimum SAT score of 1,200 on the math and reading portions or a minimum composite ACT score of 26 in single national test administration. Students must maintain a minimum 3.3 cumulative postsecondary grade point average to remain eligible. Students are provided full-tuition assistance while pursuing an undergraduate degree and they must attend an eligible college or university in Georgia. A seven-year limit exists for students first receiving the Zell Miller Scholarship during the 2011-2012 academic year (FY12) or later.

Award: Scholarship for use in freshman, sophomore, junior, or senior years; renewable.

Eligibility Requirements: Applicant must be enrolled or expecting to enroll full- or part-time at a two-year or technical institution or university; resident of Florida and studying in Georgia. Available to U.S. citizens.

Application Requirements: Application form.

Contact: Georgia Student Finance Commission
Georgia Student Finance Commission
Program Administration
2082 East Exchange Place
Tucker, GA 30084
Phone: 800-505-4732
E-mail: ProgramAdmin@gsfc.org

GIRL SCOUTS OF CONNECTICUT

http://www.gsofct.org/

EMILY CHAISON GOLD AWARD SCHOLARSHIP

• *See page 439*

GOLDBERG & OSBORNE

https://1800theeagle.com

ARIZONA DON'T TEXT AND DRIVE SCHOLARSHIP

We invite anyone who lives in the United States and knows someone who lives in Arizona currently attending college or trade school, or getting ready to attend one, to make the pledge not to text and drive. That means you can pledge not to text and drive and enter the scholarship drawing either on your behalf or on behalf of someone else. We award one (1) $1,000 scholarship every month. New scholarships begin on the first day of each month and close on the last day of each month. Applications do not carry forward from month to month so please return and take the don't text and drive pledge again to apply for a new month. Winners are announced on our Facebook and Twitter feeds.

Award: Scholarship for use in freshman, sophomore, junior, senior, graduate, or postgraduate years; not renewable. *Number:* 1. *Amount:* $1000.

Eligibility Requirements: Applicant must be enrolled or expecting to enroll full- or part-time at a two-year or four-year or technical institution or university; resident of Arizona and studying in Arizona. Available to U.S. citizens.

Application Requirements: Application form. *Deadline:* continuous.

Contact: Mr. Dan Bradley, Marketing Director
Goldberg & Osborne
2815 South Alma School Road
Mesa, AZ 85210
Phone: 602-808-6600
E-mail: scholarships@1800theeagle.com

NATIONAL DON'T TEXT AND DRIVE SCHOLARSHIP

Applicants for the Second Quarter 2017 National Goldberg & Osborne Don't Text and Drive College Scholarship must either be attending college or trade school currently or planning to attend college or trade school this semester or the fall 2017 semester. You can pledge not to text and drive and enter the scholarship drawing either on your behalf or on behalf of someone else. We award one (1) $1,000 scholarship every over month (bimonthly) for a total of six scholarships per year. New scholarships begin on the first day of every other month and close on the last day of every other month. Applications do not carry forward from one bimonthly period to the next so please return and take the don't text and drive pledge again to apply for a new period. Winners are announced on our Facebook and Twitter feeds.

Award: Scholarship for use in freshman, sophomore, junior, senior, graduate, or postgraduate years; not renewable. *Number:* 1. *Amount:* $1000.

Eligibility Requirements: Applicant must be enrolled or expecting to enroll full- or part-time at a two-year or four-year or technical institution or university and resident of Alabama, Alaska, Arizona, Arkansas, California, Colorado, Connecticut, Delaware, District of Columbia, Florida, Georgia, Hawaii, Idaho, Illinois, Indiana, Iowa, Kansas, Kentucky, Louisiana, Maine, Maryland, Massachusetts, Michigan, Minnesota, Mississippi, Missouri, Montana, Nebraska, Nevada, New Hampshire, New Jersey, New Mexico, New York, North Carolina, North Dakota, Ohio, Oklahoma, Oregon, Pennsylvania, Rhode Island, South Carolina, South Dakota, Tennessee, Texas, Utah, Vermont, Virginia,

Washington, West Virginia, Wisconsin, Wyoming. Available to U.S. citizens.

Application Requirements: Application form. *Deadline:* continuous.

Contact: Mr. Dan Bradley, Marketing Director
Goldberg & Osborne
2815 South Alma School Road
Mesa, AZ 85210
Phone: 602-808-6600
E-mail: scholarships@1800theeagle.com

GRANITE BAY COSMETIC SURGERY

https://www.granitebaycosmetic.com/

S.P.R.O.W.T. SCHOLARSHIP

The S.P.R.O.W.T. Scholarship is open to female California residents pursuing education at a California higher education institution who meet the following criteria: 1. Must be a female California resident intending to pursue education at a California college or university; 2. Must be a nontraditional student as defined by the National Center for Education Statistics by meeting one or more of the criteria; 3. Must complete application form and provide original essay answers. Eligible students may pursue any vocational or degree path of their choosing.

Award: Scholarship for use in freshman, sophomore, junior, senior, graduate, or postgraduate years; not renewable. *Number:* 1. *Amount:* $2500.

Eligibility Requirements: Applicant must be enrolled or expecting to enroll full- or part-time at a two-year or four-year or technical institution or university; female; resident of California and studying in California. Available to U.S. citizens.

Application Requirements: Application form, essay. *Deadline:* August 31.

Contact: Emily Bradley, Outreach Coordinator
Granite Bay Cosmetic Surgery
5220 Douglas Boulevard
Granite Bay, CA 95746
E-mail: emily@cakewebsites.com

GRANT LAW OFFICE

https://www.grantlawoffice.com/

BEST FOOT FORWARD SCHOLARSHIP

This scholarship is open to graduating high school seniors and current undergraduate college students with a 3.0 or higher GPA who are bettering themselves through education. In the essay section for this scholarship, please let us know about something you love to do, and explain why. When did you take your first steps towards this passion? How will college help you pursue this passion? The essay is to be 500-1000 words. The winner will be announced on June 27th, 2019. The application must be submitted by May 30th, 2019. Additional information and applications can be found on our website, https://www.grantlawoffice.com/scholarship/

Award: Scholarship for use in freshman, sophomore, junior, or senior years; not renewable. *Number:* 1. *Amount:* $1000.

Eligibility Requirements: Applicant must be high school student; planning to enroll or expecting to enroll full- or part-time at a two-year or four-year institution or university and resident of Georgia. Available to U.S. citizens.

Application Requirements: Application form, essay. *Deadline:* May 30.

Contact: Daniel Mateo
Grant Law Office
65 N Raymond Ave #230
Pasadena, CA 91103
Phone: 323-254-1510
E-mail: DMateo@slsconsulting.com

GREATER KANAWHA VALLEY FOUNDATION

http://www.tgkvf.org/

DRS. CHARLENE AND CHARLES BYRD SCHOLARSHIP

Renewable award for a West Virginia resident pursuing full-time postsecondary studies. Minimum 2.5 GPA required.

Award: Scholarship for use in freshman, sophomore, junior, or senior years; renewable. *Number:* 2. *Amount:* $1000.

Eligibility Requirements: Applicant must be enrolled or expecting to enroll full-time at an institution or university and resident of Washington. Available to U.S. citizens.

Application Requirements: Application form, application form may be submitted online. *Deadline:* January 15.

Contact: Susan Hoover, Scholarship Program Officer
Greater Kanawha Valley Foundation
900 Lee Street East, 16th Floor
Charleston, WV 25301
Phone: 304-346-3620
E-mail: shoover@tgkvf.org

O'HAIR SCHOLARSHIP

Renewable award for West Virginia residents pursuing full-time post-secondary studies. Must demonstrate academic ability. Minimum 2.5 GPA required.

Award: Scholarship for use in freshman, sophomore, junior, or senior years; renewable. *Number:* 1. *Amount:* $1800.

Eligibility Requirements: Applicant must be enrolled or expecting to enroll full-time at an institution or university and resident of Washington. Available to U.S. citizens.

Application Requirements: Application form, application form may be submitted online, financial need analysis. *Deadline:* January 15.

Contact: Susan Hoover, Scholarship Program Officer
Greater Kanawha Valley Foundation
900 Lee Street East, 16th Floor
Charleston, WV 25301
Phone: 304-346-3620
E-mail: shoover@tgkvf.org

GREATER WASHINGTON URBAN LEAGUE

http://www.gwul.org/

SAFEWAY/GREATER WASHINGTON URBAN LEAGUE SCHOLARSHIP

• See page 464

GREAT LAKES HEMOPHILIA FOUNDATION

http://www.glhf.org/

GREAT LAKES HEMOPHILIA FOUNDATION EDUCATION SCHOLARSHIP

• See page 476

GREENHOUSE SCHOLARS

https://greenhousescholars.org/

GREENHOUSE SCHOLARS

Greenhouse Scholars' vision is to create a community of leaders who will evolve the communities of the world. We are not a typical scholarship: we support each Scholar through a special community and with a unique program that provides critical personal and professional support, plus financial subsidies. Our Whole Person approach, consisting of 8 program components, is designed to connect our Scholars to opportunities and experiences, while also cultivating skill sets and meaningful relationships. We look for high-performing high school seniors who come from low-income communities and have demonstrated true leadership and positive community contributions. Applicants must be/have: 1) a graduating high school senior who is planning to attend a 4-year, accredited institution, 2) a resident of selected states, 3) a minimum un-weighted, cumulative GPA of 3.5, and 4) an annual household income no greater than $70,000 for a family of four. For application information, please visit: https://greenhousescholars.org/apply.

Award: Scholarship for use in freshman, sophomore, junior, or senior years; renewable. *Number:* 15–30. *Amount:* $500–$5000.

Eligibility Requirements: Applicant must be high school student; planning to enroll or expecting to enroll full-time at an institution or university; resident of California, Florida, Idaho, Newfoundland and studying in Alabama, Alaska, Arizona, Arkansas, California, Colorado, Connecticut, Delaware, District of Columbia, Florida, Georgia, Hawaii, Idaho, Illinois, Indiana, Iowa, Kansas, Kentucky, Louisiana, Maine, Maryland, Massachusetts, Michigan, Minnesota, Mississippi, Missouri, Montana, Nebraska, Nevada, New Hampshire, New Jersey, New Mexico, New York, North Carolina, North Dakota, Ohio, Oklahoma, Oregon, Pennsylvania, Rhode Island, South Carolina, South Dakota, Tennessee, Texas, Utah, Vermont, Virginia, Washington, West Virginia, Wisconsin, Wyoming. Available to U.S. citizens.

Application Requirements: Application form, application form may be submitted online, community service, essay, financial need analysis, interview, personal photograph. *Deadline:* November 18.

Contact: Leah Granzotto, Associate - Program
Greenhouse Scholars
1820 Folsom Street
Boulder, CO 80302
Phone: 720-459-5482
E-mail: scholars@greenhousescholars.org

HAGAN SCHOLARSHIP FOUNDATION

https://haganscholarships.org/

HAGAN SCHOLARSHIP

The Hagan Scholarship is a nationwide need-based merit scholarship for high achieving, self-motivated students. The scholarship provides up to $6,000 each semester to help recipients graduate college debt free, up to $48,000 over eight consecutive semesters. Hagan Scholars from 42 states currently attend 324 colleges and universities. Recipients must graduate from a public high school having fewer than 100 students in the high school graduating class; or will graduate from a public high school located in a county having fewer than 50,000 residents. Recipients must enroll at a four-year college or university the first semester following high school graduation. Scholarship benefits include Free Workshops, Schwab Accounts, and Study Abroad. Workshops provide recipients with a practical understanding of important life skills not typically taught as a part of the school curriculum.

Award: Scholarship for use in freshman, sophomore, junior, senior, or graduate years; renewable. *Number:* 375–500. *Amount:* $1–$48,000.

Eligibility Requirements: Applicant must be high school student; planning to enroll or expecting to enroll full-time at an institution or university; resident of Alabama, Alberta, Arizona, British Columbia, California, Colorado, Connecticut, Delaware, District of Columbia, Florida, Guam, Hawaii, Idaho, Illinois, Indiana, Iowa, Kansas, Kentucky, Louisiana, Manitoba, Maryland, Massachusetts, Michigan, Minnesota, Mississippi, Missouri, Montana, Nebraska, Nevada, New Brunswick, Newfoundland, New Hampshire, New Jersey, New Mexico, North Carolina, Nova Scotia, Ohio, Ontario, Oregon, Quebec, Saskatchewan, South Carolina, South Dakota, Tennessee, Texas, Utah, Vermont, Virginia, Washington, West Virginia, Wisconsin and studying in Alabama, Alaska, Arizona, Arkansas, California, Colorado, Connecticut, Delaware, District of Columbia, Florida, Georgia, Hawaii, Idaho, Illinois, Indiana, Iowa, Kansas, Kentucky, Louisiana, Maine, Maryland, Massachusetts, Michigan, Minnesota, Mississippi, Missouri, Montana, Nebraska, Nevada, New Hampshire, New Jersey, New Mexico, New York, North Carolina, North Dakota, Ohio, Oklahoma, Oregon, Pennsylvania, Rhode Island, South Carolina, South Dakota, Tennessee, Texas, Utah, Vermont, Virginia, Washington, West Virginia, Wisconsin, Wyoming. Available to U.S. citizens.

Application Requirements: Application form, application form may be submitted online, driver's license, essay, financial need analysis, personal photograph. *Deadline:* November 15.

Contact: Mr. Dan Hagan, Trustee
Hagan Scholarship Foundation
PO Box 1225
Columbia, MO 65205

HAWAII SCHOOLS FEDERAL CREDIT UNION

http://www.hawaiischoolsfcu.org/

EDWIN KUNIYUKI MEMORIAL SCHOLARSHIP

Annual scholarship for an incoming college freshman in recognition of academic excellence. Applicant must be Hawaii Schools Federal Credit Union member at the time the application is submitted.

Award: Scholarship for use in freshman year; not renewable. *Number:* 1. *Amount:* $1000.

Eligibility Requirements: Applicant must be high school student; planning to enroll or expecting to enroll full-time at a two-year or four-year or technical institution or university and resident of Hawaii. Available to U.S. citizens.

Application Requirements: Application form, essay. *Deadline:* February 16.

Contact: Mr. Stuart Asahina, Vice President
Hawaii Schools Federal Credit Union
233 Vineyard Street
Honolulu, HI 96813
Phone: 808-521-0302 Ext. 6236
Fax: 808-538-3231
E-mail: sasahina@hawaiischoolsfcu.org

HAWAII STATE POSTSECONDARY EDUCATION COMMISSION

HAWAII STATE STUDENT INCENTIVE GRANT

Grants are given to residents of Hawaii who are enrolled in a participating Hawaiian state school. Funds are for undergraduate tuition only. Applicants must submit a financial need analysis.

Award: Grant for use in freshman, sophomore, junior, or senior years; renewable. *Number:* 470. *Amount:* $200–$2000.

Eligibility Requirements: Applicant must be enrolled or expecting to enroll full- or part-time at a two-year or four-year or technical institution or university; resident of Hawaii and studying in Hawaii. Available to U.S. citizens.

Application Requirements: Application form, financial need analysis. *Deadline:* continuous.

Contact: Janine Oyama, Financial Aid Specialist
Hawaii State Postsecondary Education Commission
University of Hawaii
Honolulu, HI 96822
Phone: 808-956-6066

HELLENIC UNIVERSITY CLUB OF NEW YORK

http://www.hucny.com

HELLENIC UNIVERSITY CLUB UNDERGRADUATE SCHOLARSHIP AWARDS PROGRAM

• *See page 518*

HELLENIC UNIVERSITY CLUB OF PHILADELPHIA

http://www.hucphiladephia.org/

CHRISTOPHER DEMETRIS SCHOLARSHIP

• *See page 519*

DR. MICHAEL DORIZAS MEMORIAL SCHOLARSHIP

• *See page 519*

DR. PETER A. THEODOS MEMORIAL GRADUATE SCHOLARSHIP

• *See page 519*

FOUNDERS SCHOLARSHIP

• *See page 519*

NICHOLAS S. HETOS, DDS, MEMORIAL GRADUATE SCHOLARSHIP
• *See page 519*

PAIDEIA SCHOLARSHIP
• *See page 440*

HEMOPHILIA FOUNDATION OF SOUTHERN CALIFORNIA
http://www.hemosocal.org/

CHRISTOPHER MARK PITKIN MEMORIAL SCHOLARSHIP
• *See page 477*

HENKEL CONSUMER ADHESIVES INC.
http://www.ducktapeclub.com/

DUCK BRAND DUCT TAPE "STUCK AT PROM" SCHOLARSHIP CONTEST
Contest is open to residents of the United States and Canada. Must be 14 years or older. The Grand Prize winners will each receive a $10000 scholarship, the second place students will each receive $5000, and third place winners will each receive $3000. The remaining seven "runner-up" couples will each receive a $1000 prize. Additionally, the Singles Category winner will receive a $1000 prize.

Award: Prize for use in freshman, sophomore, junior, or senior years; not renewable. *Number:* 1–11. *Amount:* $1000–$10,000.

Eligibility Requirements: Applicant must be high school student; age 14 and over; planning to enroll or expecting to enroll full- or part-time at a two-year or four-year or technical institution or university and resident of Alabama, Alaska, Alberta, Arizona, Arkansas, British Columbia, California, Connecticut, Delaware, District of Columbia, Florida, Georgia, Guam, Hawaii, Idaho, Illinois, Indiana, Iowa, Kansas, Kentucky, Louisiana, Maine, Manitoba, Massachusetts, Michigan, Minnesota, Mississippi, Missouri, Montana, Nebraska, Nevada, New Brunswick, Newfoundland, New Hampshire, New Jersey, New Mexico, New York, North Carolina, North Dakota, Northwest Territories, Nova Scotia, Ohio, Oklahoma, Ontario, Oregon, Pennsylvania, Prince Edward Island, Puerto Rico, Rhode Island, Saskatchewan, South Carolina, South Dakota, Tennessee, Texas, Utah, Virginia, Washington, West Virginia, Wisconsin, Wyoming, Yukon. Available to U.S. and Canadian citizens.

Application Requirements: Application form, personal photograph. *Deadline:* May 31.

Contact: ShurTech Brands Consumer Relations Department
Henkel Consumer Adhesives Inc.
32150 Just Imagine Drive
Avon, OH 44011-1355
Phone: 800-321-1733

HERB KOHL EDUCATIONAL FOUNDATION INC.
http://www.kohleducation.org/

HERB KOHL EXCELLENCE SCHOLARSHIP PROGRAM
Scholarships of $10,000 to Wisconsin high school graduates awarded annually in a competitive selection process. Applicants must be Wisconsin residents. Recipients are chosen for their demonstrated academic potential, outstanding leadership, citizenship, community service, integrity and other special talents.

Award: Scholarship for use in freshman, sophomore, junior, or senior years; not renewable. *Number:* 100. *Amount:* $10,000.

Eligibility Requirements: Applicant must be high school student; planning to enroll or expecting to enroll full- or part-time at a two-year or four-year or technical institution or university and resident of Wisconsin. Available to U.S. and non-U.S. citizens.

Application Requirements: Application form, community service, essay. *Deadline:* November 4.

Contact: Ms. Kim Marggraf, Director
Phone: 920-457-1727
E-mail: marggraf@excel.net

HISPANIC METROPOLITAN CHAMBER SCHOLARSHIPS
http://www.hmccoregon.com/

HISPANIC METROPOLITAN CHAMBER SCHOLARSHIPS
• *See page 520*

HISPANIC SCHOLARSHIP FUND
HSF.net

GREATER CINCINNATI HSF SCHOLARSHIP
• *See page 520*

HOUSTON COMMUNITY SERVICES

AZTECA SCHOLARSHIP
• *See page 521*

HUMANE SOCIETY OF THE UNITED STATES
http://www.hsus.org/

SHAW-WORTH MEMORIAL SCHOLARSHIP
Scholarship for a New England high school senior, who has made a meaningful contribution to animal protection over a significant amount of time. Passive liking of animals or the desire to enter an animal care field does not justify the award.

Award: Scholarship for use in freshman year; not renewable. *Number:* 1. *Amount:* $2000.

Eligibility Requirements: Applicant must be high school student; planning to enroll or expecting to enroll full-time at a four-year institution or university and resident of Connecticut, Maine, Massachusetts, New Hampshire, Rhode Island, Vermont. Available to U.S. citizens.

Application Requirements: Essay, recommendations or references. *Deadline:* March 17.

Contact: Administrator
Humane Society of the United States
PO Box 619
Jacksonville, VT 05342-0619
Phone: 802-368-2790
Fax: 802-368-2756

IDAHO STATE BOARD OF EDUCATION
http://www.boardofed.idaho.gov/

IDAHO GOVERNOR'S CUP SCHOLARSHIP
• *See page 465*

IDAHO OPPORTUNITY SCHOLARSHIP
The Idaho Opportunity Scholarship is an award open to Idaho citizens who have graduated from Idaho high schools or equivalent. The application is open to any high school or college students who attended an Idaho high school, are Idaho residents, and are attending or who are planning on attending an eligible Idaho college or university. Students must be earning their first undergraduate degree. The required GPA is a 2.7 and applicants must show need by completing the FAFSA by March 1 each year. The award is renewable for a total of 4 years.

Award: Scholarship for use in freshman, sophomore, junior, or senior years; renewable. *Number:* 700–2,500. *Amount:* $1–$3500.

Eligibility Requirements: Applicant must be enrolled or expecting to enroll full- or part-time at a two-year or four-year or technical institution or university; resident of Idaho and studying in Idaho. Available to U.S. citizens.

Application Requirements: Application form, financial need analysis. *Deadline:* March 1.

Contact: Joy Miller, Scholarships Program Manager
Idaho State Board of Education
650 W. State St., #307
Boise, ID 83720
Phone: 208-332-1595
E-mail: joy.miller@osbe.idaho.gov

ILLINOIS AMVETS
http://www.ilamvets.org/

ILLINOIS AMVETS JUNIOR ROTC SCHOLARSHIPS
One year, $1000 scholarship (non-renewal) for high school seniors who have taken the ACT or SAT tests and are children or grandchildren of veterans or active-duty. Student must be enrolled in JROTC program.

Award: Scholarship for use in freshman year; not renewable. *Amount:* $1000.

Eligibility Requirements: Applicant must be high school student; planning to enroll or expecting to enroll full-time at a two-year or four-year or technical institution or university and resident of Illinois. Available to U.S. citizens.

Application Requirements: Application form, essay, financial need analysis. *Deadline:* March 1.

Contact: Ashley Murphy, Communications Director
Illinois AMVETS
2200 South Sixth St.
Springfield, IL 62703
Phone: 217-528-4713
E-mail: ashley@ilamvets.org

ILLINOIS AMVETS SERVICE FOUNDATION SCHOLARSHIP
Applicant must be an Illinois high school senior and be the child or grandchild of veteran or active duty.

Award: Scholarship for use in freshman year; not renewable. *Amount:* $1000.

Eligibility Requirements: Applicant must be high school student; planning to enroll or expecting to enroll full-time at a two-year or four-year or technical institution or university; resident of Illinois and studying in Illinois. Available to U.S. citizens.

Application Requirements: Application form, community service, essay, financial need analysis. *Deadline:* March 1.

Contact: Ashley Murphy, Communications Director
Illinois AMVETS
2200 South Sixth St.
Springfield, IL 62703
Phone: 217-528-4713
E-mail: ashley@ilamvets.org

ILLINOIS AMVETS TRADE SCHOOL SCHOLARSHIP
Applicant must be an Illinois high school senior who has been accepted in a pre-approved trade school program. Must be a child or grandchild of a veteran or active-duty.

Award: Scholarship for use in freshman year; not renewable. *Amount:* $1000.

Eligibility Requirements: Applicant must be high school student; planning to enroll or expecting to enroll full-time at a technical institution and resident of Illinois. Available to U.S. citizens.

Application Requirements: Application form, essay. *Deadline:* March 1.

Contact: Ashley Murphy, Communications Director
Illinois AMVETS
2200 South Sixth St.
Springfield, IL 62703
Phone: 217-528-4713
E-mail: ashley@ilamvets.org

ILLINOIS COUNCIL OF THE BLIND
http://www.icbonline.org/

FLOYD R. CARGILL SCHOLARSHIP
• See page 477

ILLINOIS STUDENT ASSISTANCE COMMISSION (ISAC)
http://www.isac.org/

GRANT PROGRAM FOR DEPENDENTS OF POLICE, FIRE, OR CORRECTIONAL OFFICERS
• See page 459

HIGHER EDUCATION LICENSE PLATE (HELP) PROGRAM
Grants for students who attend Illinois colleges for which the special collegiate license plates are available. The Illinois Secretary of State issues the license plates, and part of the proceeds are used for grants for undergraduate students attending these colleges, to pay tuition and mandatory fees.

Award: Grant for use in freshman, sophomore, junior, or senior years; not renewable.

Eligibility Requirements: Applicant must be enrolled or expecting to enroll full- or part-time at a two-year institution or university; resident of Idaho and studying in Illinois. Available to U.S. citizens.

Application Requirements: Application form, financial need analysis. *Deadline:* continuous.

Contact: ISAC Call Center Representative
Illinois Student Assistance Commission (ISAC)
1755 Lake Cook Road
Deerfield, IL 60015-5209
Phone: 800-899-4722
E-mail: isac.studentservices@illinois.gov

ILLINOIS NATIONAL GUARD (ING) GRANT PROGRAM
• See page 489

ILLINOIS SPECIAL EDUCATION TEACHER TUITION WAIVER (SETTW) PROGRAM
Teachers or students who are pursuing a career in special education as public, private or parochial preschool, elementary or secondary school teachers in Illinois may be eligible for this program. This program will exempt such individuals from paying tuition and mandatory fees at an eligible institution, for up to four years. The individual dollar amount awarded are subject to sufficient annual appropriations by the Illinois General Assembly.

Award: Scholarship for use in freshman, sophomore, junior, senior, or graduate years; renewable.

Eligibility Requirements: Applicant must be enrolled or expecting to enroll full- or part-time at an institution or university; resident of Idaho and studying in Illinois. Available to U.S. citizens.

Application Requirements: Application form. *Deadline:* March 1.

Contact: Illinois Student Assistance Commission Dept. D
Illinois Student Assistance Commission (ISAC)
1755 Lake Cook Road
Deerfield, IL 60015-5209
Phone: 800-899-4722
E-mail: isac.studentservices@illinois.gov

ILLINOIS VETERAN GRANT (IVG) PROGRAM
• See page 502

MINORITY TEACHERS OF ILLINOIS (MTI) SCHOLARSHIP PROGRAM
• See page 521

MONETARY AWARD PROGRAM (MAP)
Awards to Illinois residents enrolled in a minimum of 3 hours per term in a degree program at an approved Illinois institution. See website for complete list of participating schools. Must demonstrate financial need, based on the information provided on the Free Application for Federal Student Aid. Number of grants and the individual dollar amount awarded vary. Deadline: As soon as possible after October 1 of the year before the student will enter college.

Award: Grant for use in freshman, sophomore, junior, or senior years; renewable.

Eligibility Requirements: Applicant must be enrolled or expecting to enroll full- or part-time at a two-year or technical institution or university; resident of Idaho and studying in Illinois. Available to U.S. citizens.

Application Requirements: Application form, financial need analysis. *Deadline:* December 1.

Contact: ISAC Call Center Representative
Illinois Student Assistance Commission (ISAC)
1755 Lake Cook Road
Deerfield, IL 60015-5209
Phone: 800-899-4722
E-mail: isac.studentservices@illinois.gov

INDIANA COMMISSION FOR HIGHER EDUCATION

http://www.in.gov/che

21ST CENTURY SCHOLARSHIP

Started in 1990, 21st Century Scholars is Indiana's early college promise program. It offers income-eligible Hoosier students up to four years of paid tuition at an eligible Indiana college or university after they graduate from high school. Students enroll in seventh or eighth grade, and in high school they participate in the Scholar Success Program and are connected to programs and resources to help them prepare for college and career success. Once in college, Scholars receive support to complete their college degrees and connect to career opportunities.

Award: Scholarship for use in freshman, sophomore, junior, or senior years; renewable.

Eligibility Requirements: Applicant must be enrolled or expecting to enroll full-time at a two-year or technical institution or university; resident of Illinois and studying in Indiana. Available to U.S. citizens.

Application Requirements: Application form, financial need analysis. *Deadline:* continuous.

Contact: Charlee Beasor, Communications Director
Phone: 317-232-1016
E-mail: CBeasor@che.in.gov

ADULT STUDENT GRANT

The Adult Student Grant, part of the Indiana's You Can. Go Back. program, offers a renewable $2,000 grant to assist returning adult students in starting or completing an associate degree, bachelor's degree or certificate. To qualify, students must be financially independent as determined by the FAFSA, demonstrate financial need and be enrolled in at least six credit hours.

Award: Grant for use in freshman, sophomore, junior, or senior years; renewable. *Amount:* $2000.

Eligibility Requirements: Applicant must be enrolled or expecting to enroll full- or part-time at a two-year institution or university; resident of Illinois and studying in Indiana. Available to U.S. citizens.

Application Requirements: Application form, application form may be submitted online, financial need analysis. *Deadline:* continuous.

Contact: Charlee Beasor, Communications Director
Phone: 317-232-1016
E-mail: CBeasor@che.in.gov

CHILD OF DECEASED OR DISABLED VETERAN

Provides tuition and regularly assessed fees for children of deceased or disabled veterans. This program funding is limited to a maximum of 124 credit hours and may be used at the undergraduate and professional degree level.

Award: Grant for use in freshman, sophomore, junior, senior, or graduate years; renewable.

Eligibility Requirements: Applicant must be enrolled or expecting to enroll full- or part-time at a two-year or technical institution or university; resident of Illinois and studying in Indiana. Available to U.S. citizens.

Application Requirements: Application form, application form may be submitted online. *Deadline:* continuous.

Contact: Charlee Beasor, Communications Director
Phone: 317-232-1016
E-mail: CBeasor@che.in.gov

CHILD OF PURPLE HEART RECIPIENT OR WOUNDED VETERAN

Provides regularly assessed fees for children of Purple Heart recipients or wounded veterans. This program funding is limited to a maximum of 124 credit hours and may be used at the undergraduate and professional degree level.

Award: Grant for use in freshman, sophomore, junior, senior, or graduate years; renewable.

Eligibility Requirements: Applicant must be enrolled or expecting to enroll full- or part-time at a two-year or technical institution or university; resident of Illinois and studying in Indiana. Available to U.S. citizens.

Application Requirements: Application form, application form may be submitted online. *Deadline:* continuous.

Contact: Charlee Beasor, Communications Director
Phone: 317-232-1016
E-mail: CBeasor@che.in.gov

CHILDREN AND SPOUSE OF INDIANA NATIONAL GUARD PROGRAM

Provides 100% of tuition and regularly assessed fees for students who are the child or spouse of a member of the Indiana National Guard who suffered a service-connected death while serving on state active duty. This program funding is limited to a maximum of 124 credit hours.

Award: Grant for use in freshman, sophomore, junior, senior, or graduate years; renewable.

Eligibility Requirements: Applicant must be enrolled or expecting to enroll full- or part-time at a two-year or technical institution or university; resident of Illinois and studying in Indiana. Available to U.S. citizens.

Application Requirements: Application form, application form may be submitted online. *Deadline:* continuous.

Contact: Charlee Beasor, Communications Director
Phone: 317-232-1016
E-mail: CBeasor@che.in.gov

CHILDREN AND SPOUSE OF PUBLIC SAFETY OFFICERS PROGRAM

Provides 100% of tuition and regularly assessed fees for students who are the child or spouse of certain Indiana public safety officers (PSO) who were killed in the line of duty or are a permanently disabled state trooper.

Award: Grant for use in freshman, sophomore, junior, or senior years; renewable.

Eligibility Requirements: Applicant must be enrolled or expecting to enroll full-time at a two-year or technical institution or university; resident of Illinois and studying in Indiana. Available to U.S. citizens.

Application Requirements: Application form, application form may be submitted online. *Deadline:* continuous.

Contact: Charlee Beasor, Communications Director
Phone: 317-232-1016
E-mail: CBeasor@che.in.gov

FRANK O'BANNON GRANT PROGRAM

The Frank O'Bannon Grant, which includes the Higher Education Award and the Freedom of Choice Award, is Indiana's primary need-based financial aid program. It is designed to provide access for Hoosier students to attend eligible public, private and proprietary colleges and universities. Eligibility is based on a student's FAFSA, and the grant may be used toward tuition and regularly assessed fees.

Award: Grant for use in freshman, sophomore, junior, or senior years; renewable. *Amount:* $650–$9200.

Eligibility Requirements: Applicant must be enrolled or expecting to enroll full-time at a two-year or technical institution or university; resident of Illinois and studying in Indiana. Available to U.S. citizens.

Application Requirements: Application form, financial need analysis. *Deadline:* April 15.

Contact: Charlee Beasor, Communications Director
Phone: 317-232-1016
E-mail: CBeasor@che.in.gov

INDIANA NATIONAL GUARD TUITION SUPPLEMENT GRANT

• *See page 489*

INDIANA PURPLE HEART RECIPIENT PROGRAM
• *See page 502*

MITCH DANIELS EARLY GRADUATION SCHOLARSHIP

The Mitch Daniels Early Graduation Scholarship is a one-time, $4,000 scholarship for students who graduate at least one year early from a publicly supported Indiana high school. To claim this scholarship, students must enroll at an eligible Indiana institution no later than the fall semester in the academic year immediately following the year they graduate high school.

Award: Scholarship for use in freshman year; not renewable. *Amount:* $4000.

Eligibility Requirements: Applicant must be high school student; planning to enroll or expecting to enroll full-time at a two-year or technical institution or university; resident of Illinois and studying in Indiana. Available to U.S. citizens.

Application Requirements: Application form, application form may be submitted online. *Deadline:* August 31.

Contact: Charlee Beasor, Communications Director
Phone: 317-232-1016
E-mail: CBeasor@che.in.gov

NEXT GENERATION HOOSIER EDUCATORS SCHOLARSHIP

The Next Generation Hoosier Educators Scholarship provides 200 high-achieving high school and college students interested in pursuing a career in education the opportunity to earn a renewable scholarship of up to $7,500 a year for four academic years. In exchange, students agree to teach for five years at an eligible Indiana school or repay the corresponding, prorated amount of the scholarship.

Award: Scholarship for use in freshman, sophomore, junior, or senior years; renewable. *Number:* 200. *Amount:* $7500.

Eligibility Requirements: Applicant must be enrolled or expecting to enroll full-time at an institution or university; resident of Illinois and studying in Indiana. Available to U.S. citizens.

Application Requirements: Application form, application form may be submitted online, essay, interview. *Deadline:* November 30.

Contact: Charlee Beasor, Communications Director
Phone: 317-232-1016
E-mail: CBeasor@che.in.gov

PART-TIME GRANT PROGRAM

Program is designed to encourage part-time undergraduates to start and complete their Associate or Baccalaureate degrees or certificates by subsidizing part-time tuition costs. It is a term-based award that is based on need. State residency requirements must be met and a FAFSA must be filed. Eligibility is determined at the institutional level subject to approval by SSACI.

Award: Grant for use in freshman, sophomore, junior, or senior years; not renewable. *Number:* 4,680–6,700. *Amount:* $20–$4000.

Eligibility Requirements: Applicant must be enrolled or expecting to enroll part-time at a two-year or four-year or technical institution or university; resident of Indiana and studying in Indiana. Available to U.S. citizens.

Application Requirements: Application form, financial need analysis. *Deadline:* continuous.

Contact: Grants Counselor
Indiana Commission for Higher Education
150 West Market Street, Suite 500
Indianapolis, IN 46204-2805
Phone: 317-232-2350
Fax: 317-232-3260
E-mail: grants@ssaci.state.in.us

WILLIAM A. CRAWFORD MINORITY TEACHER SCHOLARSHIP
• *See page 521*

INDIANA DEPARTMENT OF VETERANS AFFAIRS
http://www.in.gov/dva

NATIONAL GUARD EXTENSION SCHOLARSHIP
• *See page 489*

NATIONAL GUARD TUITION SUPPLEMENT GRANT
• *See page 490*

TUITION AND FEE EXEMPTION FOR INDIANA PURPLE HEART RECIPIENTS
• *See page 503*

TUITION AND FEE EXEMPTION FOR THE CHILD(REN) OF A DISABLED VETERAN OR POW/MIA OR PURPLE HEART RECIPIENTS
• *See page 503*

INDIANA LIBRARY FEDERATION
http://www.ilfonline.org/

SUE MARSH WELLER SCHOLARSHIP FUND

Scholarships are provided for undergraduate or graduate students entering or currently enrolled in a program to receive educational certification in the field of school library media services. For more details, visit http//www.ilfonline.org.

Award: Scholarship for use in freshman, sophomore, junior, senior, or graduate years; not renewable.

Eligibility Requirements: Applicant must be enrolled or expecting to enroll full-time at a four-year institution or university; resident of Indiana and studying in Indiana. Available to U.S. citizens.

Application Requirements: Application form, essay. *Deadline:* June 30.

Contact: Tisa Davis, Communications Manager
Indiana Library Federation
941 E. 86th St.
Suite 260
Indianapolis, IN 46240
Phone: 317-257-2040 Ext. 104
Fax: 317-257-1389
E-mail: tdavis@ilfonline.org

INDIAN AMERICAN CULTURAL ASSOCIATION
http://www.iasf.org/

INDIAN AMERICAN SCHOLARSHIP FUND
• *See page 521*

INTER-COUNTY ENERGY
http://www.intercountyenergy.net/

INTER-COUNTY ENERGY SCHOLARSHIP

One $1,000 scholarship given to a high school senior in each of Inter-County Energy's six directorial districts: Boyle, Lincoln, Mercer, Garrard, Casey and Marion. Applicant's parent or legal guardian must be a member of Inter-County Energy with the primary residence being on the cooperative lines.

Award: Scholarship for use in freshman year; not renewable. *Number:* 6. *Amount:* $1000.

Eligibility Requirements: Applicant must be high school student; planning to enroll or expecting to enroll full-time at a four-year institution or university and resident of Kentucky. Available to U.S. citizens.

Application Requirements: Application form, autobiography, community service, financial need analysis. *Deadline:* March 20.

Contact: April Burgess, Member Services Advisor
Inter-County Energy
PO Box 87
Danville, KY 40423
Phone: 859-936-7822
Fax: 859-236-5012
E-mail: april@intercountyenergy.net

IOWA NEWSPAPER ASSOCIATION

https://inanews.com/

INF SCHOLARSHIPS

The Iowa Newspaper Foundation will award scholarships to Iowa students preparing for an Iowa newspaper career at in-state colleges or universities.

Award: Scholarship for use in freshman, sophomore, junior, or senior years; not renewable.

Eligibility Requirements: Applicant must be enrolled or expecting to enroll at an institution or university; resident of Indiana and studying in Iowa. Available to U.S. citizens.

Application Requirements: Application form. *Deadline:* February 14.

Contact: Jana Shepherd, Program Director
Iowa Newspaper Association
319 E. 5th Street
Des Moines, IA 50309
Phone: 515-244-2145 Ext. 159
Fax: 515-244-4855
E-mail: jshepherd@inanews.com

ITALIAN-AMERICAN CHAMBER OF COMMERCE OF CHICAGO

http://www.iacc-chicago.com/

ITALIAN-AMERICAN CHAMBER OF COMMERCE OF CHICAGO SCHOLARSHIP

• *See page 522*

ITALIAN CATHOLIC FEDERATION

http://www.icf.org/

ITALIAN CATHOLIC FEDERATION FIRST YEAR SCHOLARSHIP

• *See page 442*

JACKSON ENERGY COOPERATIVE

http://www.jacksonenergy.com/

JACKSON ENERGY SCHOLARSHIP ESSAY CONTEST

Applicant must be a high school senior. Scholarships are awarded to winners in an essay contest. Applicants, their parents, or legal guardians must be members of Jackson Energy Cooperative; may not be a spouse or an employee or director of Jackson Energy. Scholarships are paid directly to winner's college, university, or institution of higher education.

Award: Scholarship for use in freshman, sophomore, junior, or senior years; not renewable. *Number:* 8. *Amount:* $2000.

Eligibility Requirements: Applicant must be high school student; planning to enroll or expecting to enroll full-time at a two-year or four-year or technical institution or university and resident of Kentucky. Available to U.S. citizens.

Application Requirements: Application form, essay. *Deadline:* November 25.

Contact: Karen Combs, Manager of Member Services
Jackson Energy Cooperative
115 Jackson Energy Lane
McKee, KY 40447
Phone: 606-364-9223
E-mail: karencombs@jacksonenergy.com

J. CRAIG AND PAGE T. SMITH SCHOLARSHIP FOUNDATION

http://www.jcraigsmithfoundation.org/

FIRST IN FAMILY SCHOLARSHIP

Scholarships are available for graduating Alabama high school seniors. Must be planning to enroll in an Alabama institution in fall and pursue a four-year degree. Students who apply must want to give back to their community by volunteer and civic work. Special consideration will be given to applicants who would be the first in either their mother's or father's family (or both) to attend college.

Award: Scholarship for use in freshman year; renewable. *Number:* 10. *Amount:* $12,500–$15,000.

Eligibility Requirements: Applicant must be high school student; planning to enroll or expecting to enroll full-time at a four-year institution or university; resident of Alabama and studying in Alabama. Available to U.S. citizens.

Application Requirements: Application form, community service, essay, financial need analysis, recommendations or references, test scores, transcript. *Deadline:* January 15.

Contact: Ahrian Tyler, Administrator/Chairman of the Board
Phone: 205-250-6669
Fax: 205-328-7234
E-mail: ahrian@jcraigsmithfoundation.org

JEWISH VOCATIONAL SERVICE LOS ANGELES

http://www.jvsla.org/

JVS SCHOLARSHIP PROGRAM

• *See page 522*

KAUFMAN & STIGGER, PLLC

http://www.getthetiger.com/

THE ALBERTA C. KAUFMAN SCHOLARSHIP

In order to honor his late mother, Attorney Marshall Kaufman of Kentucky's Kaufman & Stigger, PLLC wished to offer a scholarship to graduating high school seniors and current college students. Alberta C. Kaufman encouraged her son to further his education and to eventually attend law school. It is in that spirit of support that we are sponsoring The Alberta C. Kaufman Scholarship.

Award: Scholarship for use in freshman, sophomore, junior, or senior years; not renewable. *Number:* 1. *Amount:* $500.

Eligibility Requirements: Applicant must be enrolled or expecting to enroll full- or part-time at a two-year or four-year institution or university and resident of Kentucky. Available to U.S. citizens.

Application Requirements: Application form, essay. *Deadline:* May 9.

Contact: Linda Brumleve
Kaufman & Stigger, PLLC
7513 New La Grange Road
Louisville, KY 40222
Phone: 502-458-5555
Fax: 502-458-9101
E-mail: lbrumleve@kstrial.com

KENTUCKY DEPARTMENT OF VETERANS AFFAIRS

http://www.veterans.ky.gov/

DEPARTMENT OF VETERANS AFFAIRS TUITION WAIVER-KY KRS 164-507

Scholarship available to college students who are residents of Kentucky under the age of 26.

Award: Scholarship for use in freshman, sophomore, junior, or senior years; not renewable. *Number:* 400.

Eligibility Requirements: Applicant must be age 26 or under; enrolled or expecting to enroll full- or part-time at a two-year or four-year institution or university and resident of Kentucky. Available to U.S. citizens.

Application Requirements: Application form. *Deadline:* varies.

Contact: Barbara Sipek, Tuition Waiver Coordinator
Phone: 502-595-4447
E-mail: barbaraa.sipek@ky.gov

KENTUCKY HIGHER EDUCATION ASSISTANCE AUTHORITY (KHEAA)

http://www.kheaa.com/

COLLEGE ACCESS PROGRAM (CAP) GRANT

Award up to $2,000 for U.S. citizens and Kentucky residents seeking their first undergraduate degree. Applicants enrolled in sectarian institutions are not eligible. Must submit Free Application for Federal Student Aid to demonstrate financial need. Funding is limited. Awards are made on a first-come, first-serve basis.

Award: Grant for use in freshman, sophomore, junior, or senior years; not renewable.

Eligibility Requirements: Applicant must be enrolled or expecting to enroll full- or part-time at a two-year or technical institution or university; resident of Kansas and studying in Kentucky. Available to U.S. citizens.

Application Requirements: Application form, financial need analysis. *Deadline:* continuous.

Contact: Becky Gilpatrick, Director of Student Aid
Kentucky Higher Education Assistance Authority (KHEAA)
PO Box 798
Frankfort, KY 40602-0798
Phone: 800-928-8926
Fax: 502-696-7373
E-mail: rgilpatrick@kheaa.com

EARLY CHILDHOOD DEVELOPMENT SCHOLARSHIP

The scholarship provides financial aid to Kentucky students pursuing Child Development Associate Credential, Associate's degree in early childhood education. Bachelor's degree in interdisciplinary early childhood education or a related program approved by the Early Childhood Development Authority, Kentucky Early Childhood Development Director's Certificate. Awards up to $1,800 scholarship with conditional service commitment for part-time students currently employed by participating ECD facility or providing training in ECD for an approved organization. For more information, visit website http://www.kheaa.com.

Award: Scholarship for use in freshman, sophomore, junior, or senior years; not renewable.

Eligibility Requirements: Applicant must be enrolled or expecting to enroll part-time at a two-year institution or university; resident of Kansas and studying in Kentucky. Available to U.S. citizens.

Application Requirements: Application form, application form may be submitted online. *Deadline:* continuous.

Contact: Becky Gilpatrick, Director of Student Aid
Kentucky Higher Education Assistance Authority (KHEAA)
PO Box 798
Frankfort, KY 40602-0798
Phone: 800-928-8926
Fax: 502-696-7373
E-mail: rgilpatrick@kheaa.com

KENTUCKY EDUCATIONAL EXCELLENCE SCHOLARSHIP (KEES)

Annual award based on yearly high school GPA and highest ACT or SAT score received by high school graduation. Awards are renewable, if required cumulative GPA is maintained at a Kentucky postsecondary school. Must be a Kentucky resident, and a graduate of a Kentucky high school. Low-income students who qualify for the free/reduced lunch program at least one year of high school may receive supplemental awards for passing scores on Advanced Placement (AP) or International Baccalaureate (IB) exams.

Award: Scholarship for use in freshman, sophomore, junior, or senior years; renewable. *Amount:* $125–$500.

Eligibility Requirements: Applicant must be enrolled or expecting to enroll full- or part-time at a two-year or technical institution or

university; resident of Kansas and studying in British Columbia. Available to U.S. citizens.

Application Requirements: Application form. *Deadline:* continuous.

Contact: Becky Gilpatrick, Director of Student Aid
Kentucky Higher Education Assistance Authority (KHEAA)
PO Box 798
Frankfort, KY 40602-0798
Phone: 800-928-8926
Fax: 502-696-7373
E-mail: rgilpatrick@kheaa.com

KENTUCKY NATIONAL GUARD TUITION AWARD
• *See page 490*

KENTUCKY TUITION GRANT (KTG)

Grants up to $3,000 available to Kentucky residents who are full-time undergraduates at an independent college within the state. Based on financial need. Must submit FAFSA.

Award: Grant for use in freshman, sophomore, junior, or senior years; not renewable.

Eligibility Requirements: Applicant must be enrolled or expecting to enroll full-time at a two-year institution or university; resident of Kansas and studying in Kentucky. Available to U.S. citizens.

Application Requirements: Application form, financial need analysis. *Deadline:* continuous.

Contact: Becky Gilpatrick, Director of Student Aid
Kentucky Higher Education Assistance Authority (KHEAA)
PO Box 798
Frankfort, KY 40602-0798
Phone: 800-928-8926
Fax: 502-696-7373
E-mail: rgilpatrick@kheaa.com

LANDSCAPE ARCHITECTURE FOUNDATION

www.lafoundation.org

HAWAII CHAPTER/DAVID T. WOOLSEY SCHOLARSHIP

The award provides funds for educational or professional development purposes for a third-, fourth-, or fifth-year undergraduate or graduate student of landscape architecture in a Landscape Architecture Accreditation Board (LAAB) accredited program. Student must be a permanent resident of Hawaii.

Award: Scholarship for use in junior, senior, or graduate years; not renewable. *Number:* 1–2,000.

Eligibility Requirements: Applicant must be enrolled or expecting to enroll full- or part-time at a four-year institution or university and resident of Hawaii. Available to U.S. and non-U.S. citizens.

Application Requirements: Application form, essay, personal photograph. *Fee:* $5. *Deadline:* February 1.

Contact: Ms. Danielle Carbonneau, Program Manager, Scholarships and Leadership
Phone: 202-331-7070 Ext. 14
E-mail: scholarships@lafoundation.org

LATIN AMERICAN EDUCATIONAL FOUNDATION

http://www.laef.org/

LATIN AMERICAN EDUCATIONAL FOUNDATION SCHOLARSHIPS
• *See page 523*

LAW OFFICE OF MANNING & ZIMMERMAN PLLC

https://www.manningzimmermanlaw.com/

MANNING & ZIMMERMAN DISTRACTED DRIVING SCHOLARSHIP

The Law Office of Manning & Zimmerman PLLC is pleased to award $1,000 scholarships to two New Hampshire high school students who plan to pursue any type of secondary education or vocational/technical school (in-state or out-of-state). The students who submit the best video or written essay on the topic of distracted driving will be selected as the recipients of a Manning & Zimmerman Distracted Driving Scholarship:

Award: Prize for use in freshman, sophomore, junior, or senior years; not renewable. *Number:* 2. *Amount:* $1000.

Eligibility Requirements: Applicant must be age 18-25; enrolled or expecting to enroll full- or part-time at a two-year or four-year or technical institution or university and resident of New Hampshire. Available to U.S. citizens.

Application Requirements: Application form may be submitted online (https://www.manningzimmermanlaw.com/scholarships/), essay. *Deadline:* May 1.

LEE-JACKSON EDUCATIONAL FOUNDATION

http://www.lee-jackson.org/

LEE-JACKSON EDUCATIONAL FOUNDATION SCHOLARSHIP COMPETITION

Essay contest for junior and senior Virginia high school students. Must demonstrate appreciation for the exemplary character and soldierly virtues of Generals Robert E. Lee and Thomas J. "Stonewall" Jackson. Three one-time awards of $1000 in each of Virginia's eight regions. A bonus scholarship of $1000 will be awarded to the author of the best essay in each of the eight regions. An additional award of $8000 will go to the essay judged the best in the state.

Award: Scholarship for use in freshman, sophomore, junior, or senior years; not renewable. *Number:* 27. *Amount:* $1000–$10,000.

Eligibility Requirements: Applicant must be high school student; planning to enroll or expecting to enroll full-time at a four-year institution or university; resident of Virginia and must have an interest in writing. Available to U.S. citizens.

Application Requirements: Application form, entry in a contest, essay, transcript. *Deadline:* December 21.

Contact: Stephanie Leech, Administrator
Lee-Jackson Educational Foundation
PO Box 8121
Charlottesville, VA 22906
Phone: 434-977-1861
E-mail: salp_leech@yahoo.com

LEPENDORF & SILVERSTEIN, P.C.

http://www.lependorf.com/

RIDING INTO THE FUTURE SCHOLARSHIP 2019

This scholarship is open to graduating high school seniors and current undergraduate college students with a 3.0 or higher GPA who have demonstrated a commitment to bettering their community. The application includes an essay section to tell us about your greatest personal achievement; something difficult that you overcame. How can you apply the same lessons you learned to other challenges in life? The essay is to be 500-1000 words. The winner will be announced Thursday, May 30th 2019. Additional information and applications can be found on our website.

Award: Scholarship for use in freshman, sophomore, junior, or senior years; not renewable. *Number:* 1. *Amount:* $500.

Eligibility Requirements: Applicant must be enrolled or expecting to enroll full- or part-time at a two-year or four-year institution or university and resident of New Jersey. Available to U.S. citizens.

Application Requirements: Application form, essay. *Deadline:* May 2.

Contact: Daniel Mateo
Lependorf & Silverstein, P.C.
65 N Raymond Ave
Pasadena, CA 91103, CA 91103
Phone: 323-254-1510 Ext. 119
E-mail: DMateo@slsconsulting.com

LEP FOUNDATION FOR YOUTH EDUCATION

http://www.lepfoundation.org/applications

JOHN LEPPING MEMORIAL SCHOLARSHIP

The Lep Foundation for Youth Education was formed in 2009 with the specific mission of providing financial assistance to support disabled students who demonstrate academic success and the motivation to move forward despite their disabilities. In addition, the Foundation was proud to have introduced the Cure Cancer Support Scholarship in 2016 to assist students diagnosed with childhood and adolescent cancers. The Lep Foundation is a non-profit charity with 501c3 tax exempt status (E.I.N. #27-0817346).

Award: Scholarship for use in freshman, sophomore, junior, senior, graduate, or postgraduate years; not renewable. *Number:* 1–5. *Amount:* $5000.

Eligibility Requirements: Applicant must be enrolled or expecting to enroll full- or part-time at a two-year or four-year or technical institution or university and resident of New Jersey, New York, Pennsylvania. Available to U.S. citizens.

Application Requirements: Application form, essay, financial need analysis. *Deadline:* May 1.

Contact: Scholarship Committee
Lep Foundation for Youth Education
9 Whispering Spring Dr.
Millstone Township, NJ 08510
E-mail: lepfoundation@aol.com

LEVY LAW OFFICES

https://levylawoffices.com/

LEVY LAW OFFICES CINCINNATI SAFE DRIVER SCHOLARSHIP

If you are a high school senior in Ohio or Kentucky or college student enrolled in a two to five-year institution in Ohio or Kentucky in 2018 apply today for the $2500 Levy Law Offices Cincinnati Safe Driver Scholarship. A minimum GPA is not required. Read the Instructions and Terms and Conditions for more eligibility information. To apply for this scholarship, create a short (2-3 minute video) telling us about one of the following things: 1. Explain why you do not support or promote distracted driving (i.e. driving while texting or drinking); 2. Explain how you prevent distracted driving and promote safe driving practices for yourself, friends, or family by providing specific examples. As you're submitting a video application, upload your video to YouTube. Fill out the application with supporting essay, and include a link to your video on YouTube. Applications are due March 30, 2018.

Award: Scholarship for use in freshman, sophomore, junior, senior, or graduate years; not renewable. *Number:* 1. *Amount:* $2500.

Eligibility Requirements: Applicant must be enrolled or expecting to enroll full- or part-time at a two-year or four-year or technical institution or university; resident of Kentucky, Ohio and studying in Kentucky, Ohio. Available to U.S. citizens.

Application Requirements: Application form. *Deadline:* March 30.

Contact: Scholarship Coordinator
E-mail: coordinator@ourscholarship.io

LIBERTY GRAPHICS INC.

http://www.lgtees.com

ANNUAL LIBERTY GRAPHICS ART CONTEST

One-time scholarship to the successful student who submits the winning artwork depicting appreciation of the natural environment of Maine. Applicants must be residents of Maine and be a high school seniors. Original works in traditional flat media are the required format. Photography, sculpture and computer-generated work cannot be considered. Multiple submissions are allowed.

Award: Prize for use in freshman year; not renewable. *Number:* 1. *Amount:* $1000.

Eligibility Requirements: Applicant must be high school student; planning to enroll or expecting to enroll full- or part-time at a two-year or four-year or technical institution or university; resident of Maine and must have an interest in art. Available to U.S. citizens.

Application Requirements: Application form. *Deadline:* March 12.

Contact: Mr. Jay Sproul, Scholarship Coordinator
Liberty Graphics Inc.
PO Box 5
44 Main Street
Liberty, ME 04949
Phone: 207-589-4596
E-mail: jay@lgtees.com

LOGAN TELEPHONE CO-OP

LOGAN TELEPHONE COOPERATIVE EDUCATIONAL SCHOLARSHIP

Students will receive half of the money their first semester and must maintain a 2.5 GPA in order to receive the second half of their money.

Award: Scholarship for use in freshman year; not renewable. *Number:* 3. *Amount:* $2000.

Eligibility Requirements: Applicant must be high school student; planning to enroll or expecting to enroll full-time at a two-year or four-year or technical institution or university and resident of Kentucky. Available to U.S. citizens.

Application Requirements: Application form, essay, personal photograph. *Deadline:* April 18.

Contact: Kristen Herndon, Marketing/PR Manager
Phone: 270-542-4121 Ext. 229
E-mail: kherndon@loganphone.com

LOS ALAMOS NATIONAL LABORATORY FOUNDATION

http://www.lanlfoundation.org/

LOS ALAMOS EMPLOYEES' SCHOLARSHIP

Scholarship supports students in Northern New Mexico who are pursuing undergraduate degrees in fields that will serve the region. Financial need, diversity, and regional representation are integral components of the selections process. Applicant should be a permanent resident of Northern New Mexico with at least a 3.25 cumulative GPA and 18 ACT or 940 SAT score.

Award: Scholarship for use in freshman, sophomore, junior, or senior years; renewable. *Number:* 113–152. *Amount:* $1000–$20,000.

Eligibility Requirements: Applicant must be enrolled or expecting to enroll full- or part-time at a two-year or four-year institution or university and resident of New Mexico. Available to U.S. and non-U.S. citizens.

Application Requirements: Application form, application form may be submitted online(www.lanlfoundation.org/Scholarships), community service, essay, interview, recommendations or references, test scores, transcript. *Deadline:* January 22.

Contact: John McDermon, Scholarship Program Manager
Phone: 505-753-8890 Ext. 15
Fax: 505-753-8915
E-mail: scholarships@lanlfoundation.org

LOUISIANA DEPARTMENT OF VETERAN AFFAIRS

http://www.vetaffairs.la.gov

LOUISIANA DEPARTMENT OF VETERANS AFFAIRS STATE EDUCATIONAL AID PROGRAM

• See page 503

LOUISIANA NATIONAL GUARD, JOINT TASK FORCE LA

http://geauxguard.com/organization/joint-force-headquarters-jfhq-la/

LOUISIANA NATIONAL GUARD STATE TUITION EXEMPTION PROGRAM

• See page 490

LOUISIANA OFFICE OF STUDENT FINANCIAL ASSISTANCE

www.osfa.la.gov/

GO GRANT

This program is to provide a need-based component to the state's financial aid plan to support nontraditional and low to moderate-income students who need additional aid to afford the cost of attending college. To be eligible for Louisiana GO Grant, a student must: Be a Louisiana Resident; File a Free Application for Federal Student Aid (FAFSA); Receive a federal Pell grant; Have remaining financial need after deducting Estimated Family Contribution (EFC) and all federal/state/institutional grant or scholarship aid ("gift aid") from student's Cost of Attendance (COA); Be a student enrolled in an eligible Louisiana institution on at least a half-time basis (minimum 6 hours at semester school or 4 hours at a quarter school).

Award: Grant for use in freshman, sophomore, junior, or senior years; renewable. *Amount:* $300–$3000.

Eligibility Requirements: Applicant must be enrolled or expecting to enroll full- or part-time at a two-year or technical institution or university and resident of Kentucky.

Application Requirements: Application form.

Contact: LA Office of Student Financial Assistance
Louisiana Office of Student Financial Assistance
602 North 5th Street
Baton Rouge, LA 70802
Phone: 800-259-5626
Fax: 225-208-1496
E-mail: custserv@la.gov

TAYLOR OPPORTUNITY PROGRAM FOR STUDENTS HONORS AWARD

Program awards 8 semesters or 12 terms of tuition to any Louisiana State postsecondary institution plus $400 stipend per semester. Program awards 8 semesters or 12 terms of an amount equal to the weighted average public tuition to students attending a LAICU (Louisiana Association of Independent Colleges and Universities) institution plus $400 stipend per semester. Program awards 8 semesters or 12 terms of an amount equal to the weighted average public tuition to two out-of-state Institutions for Hearing Impaired Students: Gallaudet University and Rochester Institute of Technology plus $400 stipend per semester. When you submit the FAFSA, you have automatically applied for all four levels of TOPS, for Federal Pell Grants and Go Grants and for Federal Student Loans. Please do not send separate letters of application to the TOPS office.

Award: Scholarship for use in freshman year; renewable. *Amount:* $793–$3836.

Eligibility Requirements: Applicant must be enrolled or expecting to enroll full-time at a two-year or technical institution or university; resident of Kentucky and studying in Louisiana. Available to U.S. citizens.

Application Requirements: Application form, application form may be submitted online. *Deadline:* October 29.

Contact: LA Office of Student Financial Assistance
Louisiana Office of Student Financial Assistance
602 North 5th Street
Baton Rouge, LA 70802
Phone: 800-259-5626
Fax: 225-208-1496
E-mail: custserv@la.gov

TAYLOR OPPORTUNITY PROGRAM FOR STUDENTS OPPORTUNITY LEVEL

Program awards 8 semesters or 12 terms of tuition to any Louisiana State postsecondary institution. Program awards 8 semesters or 12 terms of an amount equal to the weighted average public tuition to students attending a LAICU (Louisiana Association of Independent Colleges and Universities) institution. Program awards 8 semesters or 12 terms of an amount equal to the weighted average public tuition to two out-of-state Institutions for Hearing Impaired Students: Gallaudet University and Rochester Institute of Technology. When you submit the FAFSA, you have automatically applied for all four levels of TOPS, and for Federal Pell Grants and Go Grants. Please do not send separate letters of application to the TOPS office.

Award: Scholarship for use in freshman year; renewable. *Amount:* $793–$3731.

Eligibility Requirements: Applicant must be enrolled or expecting to enroll full-time at a two-year or technical institution or university; resident of Kentucky and studying in Louisiana. Available to U.S. citizens.

Application Requirements: Application form, application form may be submitted online. *Deadline:* July 1.

Contact: LA Office of Student Financial Assistance
Louisiana Office of Student Financial Assistance
602 North 5th Street
Baton Rouge, LA 70802
Phone: 800-259-5626
Fax: 225-208-1496
E-mail: custserv@la.gov

TAYLOR OPPORTUNITY PROGRAM FOR STUDENTS PERFORMANCE AWARD

Program awards 8 semesters or 12 terms of tuition to any Louisiana State postsecondary institution plus $200 stipend per semester. Program awards 8 semesters or 12 terms of an amount equal to the weighted average public tuition to students attending a LAICU (Louisiana Association of Independent Colleges and Universities) institution plus $200 stipend per semester. Program awards 8 semesters or 12 terms of an amount equal to the weighted average public tuition to two out-of-state Institutions for Hearing Impaired Students: Gallaudet University and Rochester Institute of Technology plus $200 stipend per semester. When you submit the FAFSA, you have automatically applied for all four levels of TOPS, for Federal Pell Grants and Go Grants and for Federal Student Loans. Please do not send separate letters of application to the TOPS office.

Award: Scholarship for use in freshman, sophomore, junior, or senior years; renewable. *Amount:* $793–$3836.

Eligibility Requirements: Applicant must be enrolled or expecting to enroll full-time at a two-year or technical institution or university; resident of Kentucky and studying in Louisiana. Available to U.S. citizens.

Application Requirements: Application form, application form may be submitted online. *Deadline:* October 29.

Contact: LA Office of Student Financial Assistance
Louisiana Office of Student Financial Assistance
602 North 5th Street
Baton Rouge, LA 70802
Phone: 800-259-5626
Fax: 225-208-1496
E-mail: custserv@la.gov

TAYLOR OPPORTUNITY PROGRAM FOR STUDENTS TECH AWARD

Program awards an amount equal to tuition for up to 4 semesters and two summers of technical training at a Louisiana postsecondary institution that offers a vocational or technical education certificate or diploma program, or a non-academic degree program; or up to $1744 to an approved Proprietary or Cosmetology school. Must have completed the TOPS Opportunity core curriculum or the TOPS Tech core curriculum, must have achieved a 2.50 grade point average over the core curriculum only, and must have achieved an ACT score of 17 or an SAT score of 810. Program awards an amount equal to the weighted average public tuition for technical programs to students attending a LAICU private institution for technical training. When you submit the FAFSA, you have automatically applied for all four levels of TOPS, for Federal Pell Grants and Go Grants and Federal Student Loans. Please do not send separate letters of application to the TOPS office.

Award: Scholarship for use in freshman year; renewable. *Number:* 1,671. *Amount:* $436–$3985.

Eligibility Requirements: Applicant must be enrolled or expecting to enroll full-time at a technical institution; resident of Kentucky and studying in Louisiana. Available to U.S. citizens.

Application Requirements: Application form, application form may be submitted online. *Deadline:* October 29.

Contact: LA Office of Student Financial Assistance
Louisiana Office of Student Financial Assistance
602 North 5th Street
Baton Rouge, LA 70802
Phone: 800-259-5626
Fax: 225-208-1496
E-mail: custserv@la.gov

MAINE COMMUNITY COLLEGE SYSTEM

http://www.mccs.me.edu/

EMBARK-SUPPORT FOR THE COLLEGE JOURNEY

Scholarship for high school students who in their junior year have not made plans for college but are academically capable of success in college. Recipients are selected by their school principal or Guidance Director. Students must be entering a Maine Community College. Refer to website http://www.mccs.me.edu/our-programs/programs-for-high-school-students/early-college/

Award: Scholarship for use in freshman or sophomore years; renewable. *Number:* 425–500. *Amount:* $2000.

Eligibility Requirements: Applicant must be high school student; planning to enroll or expecting to enroll full-time at a two-year institution; resident of Maine and studying in Maine. Available to U.S. citizens.

Application Requirements: Application form, financial need analysis. *Deadline:* April 15.

Contact: Mercedes Pour, Director of College Access
Maine Community College System
54 Lighthouse Circle
South Portland, ME 04106
Phone: 207-699-4897
E-mail: mpour@mccs.me.edu

MAINE COMMUNITY FOUNDATION, INC.

http://www.mainecf.org/

AGNES FREYER GIBBS SCHOLARSHIP FUND

The Agnes Freyer Gibbs Scholarship Fund was established in 2018 to provide renewable support for students majoring in journalism or a field reasonably related, including all forms of print, broadcast or electronic media. Recipients must be graduating seniors at Maine high schools or home-schooled in a Maine community during their last year of secondary education, with a GPA of at least 3.0. Students will be chosen based on demonstrated interest in journalism, financial need and academic achievement. There is a preference for female applicants. Those interested in careers in Marketing, Public Relations and Advertising are not eligible for consideration. Please go to the Maine Community Foundation, Inc. website for application requirements. https://www.mainecf.org/

Award: Scholarship for use in freshman year; renewable.

Eligibility Requirements: Applicant must be high school student; planning to enroll or expecting to enroll at a two-year or technical institution or university; female and resident of Louisiana. Available to U.S. citizens.

Application Requirements: Application form, application form may be submitted online. *Deadline:* June 1.

Contact: Liz Fickett
Maine Community Foundation, Inc.
MaineCF
Phone: 207-412-2015
E-mail: efickett@mainecf.org

CHET JORDAN LEADERSHIP AWARD

Eligible applicants are graduating seniors at all Maine high schools who are pursuing post-secondary study in a certificate, two-year or four-year undergraduate program at the following schools: University of Maine system; Maine Community College System; Maine Maritime Academy; All vocational/technical post-secondary schools in Maine. Recipients will demonstrate leadership, independent thinking, initiative, hard work, and the ability to rally others to the cause in their communities. Please go to the Maine Community Foundation, Inc. website for application requirements. https://www.mainecf.org/

Award: Scholarship for use in freshman year; not renewable.

Eligibility Requirements: Applicant must be high school student; planning to enroll or expecting to enroll at a two-year or technical institution or university; resident of Louisiana and studying in Maine. Available to U.S. citizens.

Application Requirements: Application form, application form may be submitted online. *Deadline:* May 15.

Contact: Liz Fickett
Maine Community Foundation, Inc.
MaineCF
Phone: 207-412-2015
E-mail: efickett@mainecf.org

GUY P. GANNETT SCHOLARSHIP FUND

Scholarship for students majoring in journalism or a field reasonably related, including all forms of print, broadcast, or electronic media. Please go to the Maine Community Foundation, Inc. website for application requirements. https://www.mainecf.org/

Award: Scholarship for use in freshman year; not renewable.

Eligibility Requirements: Applicant must be high school student; planning to enroll or expecting to enroll full-time at an institution or university and resident of Louisiana. Available to U.S. citizens.

Application Requirements: Application form, application form may be submitted online, financial need analysis. *Deadline:* June 1.

Contact: Liz Fickett
Maine Community Foundation, Inc.
MaineCF
Phone: 207-412-2015
E-mail: efickett@mainecf.org

JOSEPH W. MAYO ALS SCHOLARSHIP FUND

This scholarship was established to assist men and women who are children, step-children, grandchildren, spouses, domestic partners or the primary care givers of ALS patients. Please go to the Maine Community Foundation, Inc. website for application requirements. https://www.mainecf.org/

Award: Scholarship for use in freshman, sophomore, junior, or senior years; not renewable.

Eligibility Requirements: Applicant must be enrolled or expecting to enroll full-time at a two-year institution or university and resident of Louisiana. Available to U.S. citizens.

Application Requirements: Application form. *Deadline:* May 1.

Contact: Joseph Pietroski
Maine Community Foundation, Inc.
Joseph W. Mayo ALS Scholarship Committee
37 Sherwood Forest Dr.
Winthrop, ME 04364
E-mail: joepietroski@gmail.com

LYDIA R. LAURENDEAU SCHOLARSHIP FUND

Established in 2013, the Lydia R. Laurendeau Scholarship Fund provides renewable scholarship support to young women who are pursuing post-secondary education in either science or engineering at a four-year university. There is a preference for applicants demonstrating a connection to their Franco-American heritage. Eligible applicants will be female graduating seniors from a Maine high school who are pursuing a major in science or engineering at a four-year university. Please go to the Maine Community Foundation, Inc. website for application requirements. https://www.mainecf.org/

Award: Scholarship for use in freshman year; renewable.

Eligibility Requirements: Applicant must be high school student; planning to enroll or expecting to enroll at an institution or university; female and resident of Louisiana. Available to U.S. citizens.

Application Requirements: Application form, application form may be submitted online. *Deadline:* June 1.

Contact: Liz Fickett
Maine Community Foundation, Inc.
MaineCF
Phone: 207-412-2015
E-mail: efickett@mainecf.org

MAINE VIETNAM VETERANS SCHOLARSHIP FUND

The Maine Vietnam Veterans Scholarship Fund, founded in 1985, provides scholarship support to Maine veterans of the United States Armed Services who served in the Vietnam Theater and their descendants. As a second priority, the scholarship may be awarded to children of veterans of the United States Armed Services. Please go to the Maine Community Foundation, Inc. website for application requirements. https://www.mainecf.org/

Award: Scholarship for use in freshman, sophomore, junior, or senior years; not renewable.

Eligibility Requirements: Applicant must be enrolled or expecting to enroll at an institution or university and resident of Louisiana. Available to U.S. citizens.

Application Requirements: Application form, application form may be submitted online. *Deadline:* May 1.

Contact: Liz Fickett
Maine Community Foundation, Inc.
MaineCF
Phone: 207-412-2015
E-mail: efickett@mainecf.org

PATRIOT EDUCATION SCHOLARSHIP FUND

Eligible students are graduating seniors of Maine high schools, or graduates within four years of the date of application, who are currently enrolled in a college or university in Maine pursuing a degree in business as a part time (minimum of 9 credit hours per semester) or full-time student. There is a preference for applicants who have a demonstrated interest in personal and commercial insurance professions. Please go to the Maine Community Foundation, Inc. website for application requirements. https://www.mainecf.org/

Award: Scholarship for use in freshman, sophomore, junior, or senior years; not renewable.

Eligibility Requirements: Applicant must be enrolled or expecting to enroll full- or part-time at a two-year institution or university; resident of Louisiana and studying in Maine. Available to U.S. citizens.

Application Requirements: Application form, application form may be submitted online. *Deadline:* June 1.

Contact: Liz Fickett
Maine Community Foundation, Inc.
MaineCF
Phone: 207-412-2015
E-mail: efickett@mainecf.org

MAINE STATE SOCIETY FOUNDATION OF WASHINGTON, DC INC.

http://mainestatesociety.org/foundation/

MAINE STATE SOCIETY FOUNDATION SCHOLARSHIP

Merit-based scholarship(s) awarded to full-time students enrolled in undergraduate courses at a four-year degree-granting, nonprofit institution in Maine. Applicants must have been born in or have been a legal resident of the State of Maine for at least four years; or have at least one parent who was born in or has been a legal resident of the State of Maine for at least four years. Applicant must be 25 or younger.

Award: Scholarship for use in sophomore or junior years; not renewable. *Number:* 5–15. *Amount:* $1000–$2500.

Eligibility Requirements: Applicant must be age 25 or under; enrolled or expecting to enroll full-time at a four-year institution or university; resident of Maine and studying in Maine. Available to U.S. citizens.

Application Requirements: Application form, essay, resume. *Deadline:* March 15.

Contact: Jessica Stewart
E-mail: mssfscholarship@gmail.com

MAINE VETERANS SERVICES

http://www.maine.gov/dvem/bvs

VETERANS DEPENDENTS EDUCATIONAL BENEFITS-MAINE
• *See page 503*

MANA DE SAN DIEGO

http://www.manasd.org/

MANA DE SAN DIEGO SYLVIA CHAVEZ MEMORIAL SCHOLARSHIP
• *See page 467*

MASSACHUSETTS OFFICE OF STUDENT FINANCIAL ASSISTANCE

http://www.osfa.mass.edu/

DSS ADOPTED CHILDREN TUITION WAIVER
Need-based tuition waiver for Massachusetts residents who are full-time undergraduate students. Must attend a Massachusetts public institution of higher education and be under 24 years of age. File the FAFSA after January 1. Contact school financial aid office for more information.

Award: Scholarship for use in freshman, sophomore, junior, or senior years; renewable.

Eligibility Requirements: Applicant must be age 24 or under; enrolled or expecting to enroll full-time at a two-year or four-year institution; resident of Massachusetts and studying in District of Columbia, Massachusetts, Pennsylvania, Vermont. Available to U.S. and non-Canadian citizens.

Application Requirements: Application form.

Contact: Clantha McCurdy, Senior Deputy Commissioner
Malden, MA 02148
Phone: 617-391-6098
Fax: 617-391-6085
E-mail: cmccurdy@dhe.mass.edu

MASSACHUSETTS ASSISTANCE FOR STUDENT SUCCESS PROGRAM
Provides need-based financial assistance to Massachusetts residents to attend undergraduate postsecondary institutions in Massachusetts, Pennsylvania, Vermont, and District of Columbia. High school seniors may apply. Expected Family Contribution (EFC) should be $3850. Timely filing of FAFSA required.

Award: Grant for use in freshman, sophomore, junior, or senior years; not renewable. *Number:* 47,000–50,000. *Amount:* $400–$1600.

Eligibility Requirements: Applicant must be enrolled or expecting to enroll full-time at a two-year or four-year or technical institution or university; resident of Massachusetts and studying in District of Columbia, Massachusetts, Pennsylvania, Vermont. Available to U.S. citizens.

Application Requirements: Financial need analysis. *Deadline:* May 1.

Contact: Clantha McCurdy, Senior Deputy Commissioner
Malden, MA 02148
Phone: 617-391-6098
Fax: 617-391-6085
E-mail: cmccurdy@dhe.mass.edu

MCCURRY FOUNDATION INC.

http://www.mccurryfoundation.org/

MCCURRY FOUNDATION SCHOLARSHIP
Scholarship open to all public high school seniors, with preference given to applicants from Clay, Duval, Nassau, and St. Johns Counties, Florida and from Glynn County, Georgia. Scholarship emphasizes leadership, work ethic, and academic excellence. A minimum GPA of 3.0 is required and family income cannot exceed a maximum of $75,000 (AGI).

Award: Scholarship for use in freshman, sophomore, junior, or senior years; renewable. *Number:* 1–10. *Amount:* $1000–$1500.

Eligibility Requirements: Applicant must be high school student; planning to enroll or expecting to enroll full-time at a two-year or four-year or technical institution or university; single; resident of Florida, Georgia and must have an interest in leadership. Available to U.S. citizens.

Application Requirements: Application form, essay, financial need analysis, interview. *Deadline:* February 15.

Contact: Leslie Fine, Scholarship Selection Committee
Phone: 904-910-4414
E-mail: info@mccurryfoundation.org

THE MIAMI FOUNDATION

http://www.miamifoundation.org

ALAN R. EPSTEIN SCHOLARSHIP
Award available for a high school senior who is a Dade county resident. Must have a 3.0 GPA and attach a copy of acceptance letter to two- or four-year college or university. For additional information and application, visit website at http://www.dadecommunityfoundation.org.

Award: Scholarship for use in freshman year; not renewable.

Eligibility Requirements: Applicant must be high school student; planning to enroll or expecting to enroll full-time at a two-year or four-year institution or university and resident of Florida. Available to U.S. citizens.

Application Requirements: Acceptance letter, personal statement, application form, financial need analysis, recommendations or references, transcript. *Deadline:* April 10.

Contact: Lauren Mayfield, Programs Assistant
The Miami Foundation
40 NW 3rd Street
Miami, FL 33128
Phone: 305-371-2711
E-mail: lmayfield@miamifoundation.org

RODNEY THAXTON/MARTIN E. SEGAL SCHOLARSHIP
• *See page 525*

SIDNEY M. ARONOVITZ SCHOLARSHIP
• *See page 525*

MICHIGAN DEPARTMENT OF TREASURY - STUDENT FINANCIAL SERVICES BUREAU

http://www.michigan.gov/mistudentaid

CHILDREN OF VETERANS TUITION GRANT
• *See page 504*

MICHIGAN COMPETITIVE SCHOLARSHIP
Renewable awards for Michigan resident to pursue undergraduate study at a Michigan institution. Awards are restricted to tuition and mandatory fees and pay up to a maximum of $1,000 for the academic year at participating institutions. It is the responsibility of the college financial aid office to coordinate all sources of aid for which a student may be eligible. Other gift aid may reduce or cancel this award. Must attain SAT score of at least 1200. Must maintain at least a 2.0 grade point average and meet the college's academic progress requirements. Must file Free Application for Federal Student Aid

Award: Scholarship for use in freshman, sophomore, junior, or senior years; renewable.

Eligibility Requirements: Applicant must be enrolled or expecting to enroll full- or part-time at a two-year institution or university; resident of Massachusetts and studying in Michigan. Available to U.S. citizens.

Application Requirements: Application form, financial need analysis. *Deadline:* March 1.

Contact: Student Scholarships and Grants
Michigan Department of Treasury - Student Financial Services Bureau
PO Box 30462
Lansing, MI 48909
Phone: 888-447-2687
E-mail: mistudentaid@michigan.gov

MICHIGAN TUITION GRANT

Need-based program. Students must be Michigan residents and attend a Michigan private, nonprofit, degree-granting college. Must file the Free Application for Federal Student Aid and meet the college's academic progress requirements.

Award: Grant for use in freshman, sophomore, junior, or senior years; renewable.

Eligibility Requirements: Applicant must be enrolled or expecting to enroll full- or part-time at an institution or university; resident of Massachusetts and studying in Michigan. Available to U.S. citizens.

Application Requirements: Application form, financial need analysis. *Deadline:* March 1.

Contact: Student Scholarships and Grants
Michigan Department of Treasury - Student Financial Services Bureau
PO Box 30462
Lansing, MI 48909
Phone: 888-447-2687
E-mail: mistudentaid@michigan.gov

TUITION INCENTIVE PROGRAM

The Tuition Incentive Program (TIP) was established in 1987 under the Annual Higher Education Appropriations Act as an incentive program that encourages eligible students to complete high school by providing tuition assistance for the first two years of college and beyond. Students must be enrolled in courses leading to an associate degree or certificate. Certificate courses are defined as at least a one-year training program that leads to a certificate (or other recognized educational credential), which prepares students for gainful employment in a recognized occupation. Students must meet a Medicaid eligibility history requirement. Eligible students must apply prior to high school graduation (high school diploma or its recognized equivalent). The program targets students with financial need so students are encouraged to also complete the FAFSA. Funds are appropriated annually in the Higher Education Appropriations Act. This program is administered by the Student Scholarships and Grants Division. http://www.michigan.gov/mistudentaid/0,4636,7-128-60969_61016-274565—,00.html

Award: Grant for use in freshman, sophomore, junior, or senior years; renewable.

Eligibility Requirements: Applicant must be enrolled or expecting to enroll full- or part-time at a two-year institution or university; resident of Massachusetts and studying in Michigan. Available to U.S. citizens.

Application Requirements: Application form, financial need analysis. *Deadline:* continuous.

Contact: Student Scholarships and Grants
Michigan Department of Treasury - Student Financial Services Bureau
PO Box 30462
Lansing, MI 48909
Phone: 888-447-2687
E-mail: mistudentaid@michigan.gov

MINNESOTA AFL-CIO

http://www.mnaflcio.org/

MARTIN DUFFY ADULT LEARNER SCHOLARSHIP AWARD

• *See page 445*

MINNESOTA MASONIC CHARITIES

http://www.mnmasoniccharities.org

MINNESOTA MASONIC CHARITIES HERITAGE SCHOLARSHIP

Heritage Scholarships are provided each year to Minnesota high school students with a GPA of 3.0-3.59. Applicants must plan to enroll in a four-year college program.

Award: Scholarship for use in freshman, sophomore, junior, or senior years; renewable. *Number:* 20. *Amount:* $3000.

Eligibility Requirements: Applicant must be high school student; planning to enroll or expecting to enroll full-time at an institution or university and resident of Michigan. Available to U.S. citizens.

Application Requirements: Application form, essay. *Deadline:* February 15.

Contact: Ms. Deb Cutsinger, Scholarships Manager
Minnesota Masonic Charities
11501 Masonic Home Drive
Bloomington, MN 55437
Phone: 952-948-6206
E-mail: info@mnmasonic.org

MINNESOTA MASONIC CHARITIES LEGACY SCHOLARSHIP

Legacy Scholarships are provided each year to students graduating from a Minnesota high school with a GPA of 3.6 to 3.89. Applicants must plan to enroll in a four-year college program.

Award: Scholarship for use in freshman, sophomore, junior, or senior years; renewable. *Number:* 10. *Amount:* $4000.

Eligibility Requirements: Applicant must be high school student; planning to enroll or expecting to enroll full-time at an institution or university and resident of Michigan. Available to U.S. citizens.

Application Requirements: Application form, essay. *Deadline:* February 15.

Contact: Ms. Deb Cutsinger, Scholarships Manager
Minnesota Masonic Charities
11501 Masonic Home Drive
Bloomington, MN 55437
Phone: 952-948-6206
E-mail: deb.cutsinger@mnmasonic.org

MINNESOTA MASONIC CHARITIES SIGNATURE SCHOLARSHIP

Signature Scholarships are provided each year to students attending a Minnesota high school with a GPA of 3.9 or higher. Applicants must plan to enroll in a four-year college program.

Award: Scholarship for use in freshman, sophomore, junior, or senior years; renewable. *Number:* 6. *Amount:* $5000.

Eligibility Requirements: Applicant must be high school student; planning to enroll or expecting to enroll full-time at an institution or university and resident of Michigan. Available to U.S. citizens.

Application Requirements: Application form, essay. *Deadline:* February 15.

Contact: Ms. Deb Cutsinger, Scholarships Manager
Minnesota Masonic Charities
11501 Masonic Home Drive
Bloomington, MN 55437
Phone: 952-948-6206
E-mail: deb.cutsinger@mnmasonic.org

MINNESOTA MASONIC CHARITIES UNDERGRADUATE SCHOLARSHIP

Undergraduate Scholarships are provided each year to current college freshman, sophomores or juniors who graduated from a Minnesota high school and have a GPA of 3.0 or above. Applicants must be enrolled in a four-year college program.

Award: Scholarship for use in sophomore, junior, or senior years; renewable. *Number:* 25. *Amount:* $2500.

Eligibility Requirements: Applicant must be enrolled or expecting to enroll full-time at an institution or university and resident of Michigan. Available to U.S. citizens.

Application Requirements: Application form, essay. *Deadline:* February 15.

Contact: Ms. Deb Cutsinger, Scholarships Manager
Minnesota Masonic Charities
11501 Masonic Home Drive
Bloomington, MN 55437
Phone: 952-948-6206
E-mail: deb.cutsinger@mnmasonic.org

MINNESOTA MASONIC CHARITIES VOCATIONAL/TECHNICAL/TRADE SCHOLARSHIP

Vocational Scholarships are provided each year to individuals who have graduated from a Minnesota high school and are interested in completing a two-year higher education program or technical degree.

Award: Scholarship for use in freshman year; renewable. *Number:* 30. *Amount:* $1500.

Eligibility Requirements: Applicant must be enrolled or expecting to enroll full-time at a two-year or technical institution and resident of Michigan. Available to U.S. citizens.

Application Requirements: Application form. *Deadline:* February 15.

Contact: Ms. Deb Cutsinger, Scholarships Manager
Minnesota Masonic Charities
11501 Masonic Home Drive
Bloomington, MN 55437
Phone: 952-948-6206
E-mail: deb.cutsinger@mnmasonic.org

MINNESOTA OFFICE OF HIGHER EDUCATION

http://www.ohe.state.mn.us

MINNESOTA GI BILL PROGRAM

The Minnesota GI Bill program provides postsecondary financial assistance to eligible Minnesota veterans and service members as well as eligible spouses and children of deceased or severely disabled eligible Minnesota veterans. Full-time undergraduate or graduate students may be eligible to receive up to $1,000 per semester or term and part-time students may be eligible to receive up to $500 per semester or term. Eligible students may receive up to $3,000 per award year and up to the lifetime maximum of $10,000.

Award: Grant for use in freshman, sophomore, junior, senior, graduate, or postgraduate years; not renewable. *Amount:* $50–$3000.

Eligibility Requirements: Applicant must be enrolled or expecting to enroll full- or part-time at a two-year or four-year or technical institution or university; resident of Minnesota and studying in Minnesota. Available to U.S. citizens.

Application Requirements: Application form. *Deadline:* continuous.

Contact: Meghan Flores, State Grant Manager
Minnesota Office of Higher Education
1450 Energy Park Drive, Suite 350
St. Paul, MN 55108
Phone: 651-355-0610 Ext. 2
Fax: 651-642-0675
E-mail: meghan.flores@state.mn.us

MINNESOTA INDIAN SCHOLARSHIP

• *See page 525*

MINNESOTA STATE GRANT PROGRAM

Need-based grant program available for Minnesota residents attending Minnesota colleges. Student covers 50% of cost with remainder covered by Pell Grant, parent contribution and state grant. Students apply with FAFSA and colleges administer the program on campus.

Award: Grant for use in freshman, sophomore, junior, or senior years; not renewable. *Number:* 71,000–120,000. *Amount:* $100–$11,334.

Eligibility Requirements: Applicant must be age 17 and over; enrolled or expecting to enroll full- or part-time at a two-year or four-year or technical institution or university; resident of Minnesota and studying in Minnesota. Available to U.S. citizens.

Application Requirements: Application form, financial need analysis. *Deadline:* continuous.

Contact: Grant Staff
Minnesota Office of Higher Education
1450 Energy Park Drive, Suite 350
St. Paul, MN 55108
Phone: 651-642-0567 Ext. 2

MINNESOTA STATE VETERANS' DEPENDENTS ASSISTANCE PROGRAM

Tuition assistance to dependents of persons considered to be prisoner-of-war or missing in action after August 1, 1958. Must be Minnesota resident attending Minnesota two- or four-year school.

Award: Scholarship for use in freshman, sophomore, junior, or senior years; renewable. *Number:* 100–200. *Amount:* $249–$250.

Eligibility Requirements: Applicant must be enrolled or expecting to enroll full- or part-time at a two-year or four-year institution; resident of Minnesota and studying in Minnesota. Available to U.S. citizens.

Application Requirements: Application form. *Deadline:* continuous.

Contact: Meghan Flores, State Grant Manager
Minnesota Office of Higher Education
1450 Energy Park Drive, Suite 350
St. Paul, MN 55108
Phone: 651-355-0610 Ext. 2
Fax: 651-642-0675
E-mail: meghan.flores@state.mn.us

POSTSECONDARY CHILD CARE GRANT PROGRAM-MINNESOTA

Grant available for students who are not receiving MFIP (TANF) and have children in day care. Based on financial need. Cannot exceed actual child care costs or maximum award chart (based on income). Must be Minnesota resident. For use at Minnesota two- or four-year school, including public technical colleges. Available until student has attended college for the equivalent of four full-time academic years.

Award: Grant for use in freshman, sophomore, junior, or senior years; not renewable. *Number:* 1–3,500. *Amount:* $100–$2800.

Eligibility Requirements: Applicant must be enrolled or expecting to enroll full- or part-time at a two-year or four-year or technical institution or university; resident of Minnesota and studying in Minnesota. Available to U.S. citizens.

Application Requirements: Application form, financial need analysis. *Deadline:* continuous.

Contact: Brenda Larter, Program Administrator
Minnesota Office of Higher Education
1450 Energy Park Drive, Suite 350
St. Paul, MN 55108-5227
Phone: 651-355-0612
E-mail: brenda.larter@state.mn.us

SAFETY OFFICERS' SURVIVOR GRANT PROGRAM

• *See page 467*

MISSISSIPPI OFFICE OF STUDENT FINANCIAL AID

http://www.msfinancialaid.org

HIGHER EDUCATION LEGISLATIVE PLAN (HELP)

Eligible applicant must be resident of Mississippi and apply for the first time as a freshman and/or sophomore student who graduated from high school within the immediate past two years. Must demonstrate need as determined by the results of the FAFSA, documenting an average family adjusted gross income of $36,500 or less over the prior two years. Must be enrolled full-time at a Mississippi college or university, have a GPA of 2.5, have completed a specific high school core curriculum, and have scored 20 on the ACT.

Award: Grant for use in freshman, sophomore, junior, or senior years; renewable. *Number:* 3,357. *Amount:* $340–$7344.

Eligibility Requirements: Applicant must be enrolled or expecting to enroll full-time at a two-year or four-year institution or university; resident of Mississippi and studying in Mississippi. Available to U.S. citizens.

Application Requirements: Application form, financial need analysis. *Deadline:* March 31.

Contact: Program Administrator
Mississippi Office of Student Financial Aid
3825 Ridgewood Road
Jackson, MS 39211
Phone: 601-432-6997
Fax: 601-432 Ext. 6527
E-mail: sfa@mississippi.edu

LAW ENFORCEMENT OFFICERS/FIREMEN SCHOLARSHIP

• *See page 467*

MISSISSIPPI EMINENT SCHOLARS GRANT

Award for an entering freshmen or as a renewal for sophomore, junior or senior, who are residents of Mississippi. Applicants must achieve a GPA of 3.5 and must have scored 29 on the ACT. Must enroll full-time at an eligible Mississippi college or university.

Award: Grant for use in freshman, sophomore, junior, or senior years; not renewable. *Number:* 2,908. *Amount:* $1157–$2500.

Eligibility Requirements: Applicant must be enrolled or expecting to enroll full-time at a two-year or four-year institution or university; resident of Mississippi and studying in Mississippi. Available to U.S. citizens.

Application Requirements: Application form. *Deadline:* September 15.

Contact: Program Administrator
Mississippi Office of Student Financial Aid
3825 Ridgewood Road
Jackson, MS 39211
Phone: 601-432-6997
Fax: 601-432 Ext. 6527
E-mail: sfa@mississippi.edu

MISSISSIPPI RESIDENT TUITION ASSISTANCE GRANT

Must be a resident of Mississippi enrolled full-time at an eligible Mississippi college or university. Must maintain a minimum 2.5 GPA each semester. MTAG awards may be up to $500 per academic year for freshman and sophomores and $1000 per academic year for juniors and seniors.

Award: Grant for use in freshman, sophomore, junior, or senior years; not renewable. *Number:* 18,244–18,244. *Amount:* $17–$1000.

Eligibility Requirements: Applicant must be enrolled or expecting to enroll full-time at a two-year or four-year institution or university; resident of Mississippi and studying in Mississippi. Available to U.S. citizens.

Application Requirements: Application form. *Deadline:* September 15.

Contact: Program Administrator
Mississippi Office of Student Financial Aid
3825 Ridgewood Road
Jackson, MS 39211
Phone: 601-432-6997
Fax: 601-432 Ext. 6527
E-mail: sfa@mississippi.edu

NISSAN SCHOLARSHIP

Renewable award for Mississippi residents attending a Mississippi institution. Must be graduating from a Mississippi high school in the current year. The scholarship will pay full tuition and a book allowance. Minimum GPA of 2.5 as well as an ACT composite of at least 20 or combined SAT scores of 940 or better. Must demonstrate financial need and leadership abilities.

Award: Scholarship for use in freshman, sophomore, junior, or senior years; renewable. *Number:* 2–2. *Amount:* $4409–$8718.

Eligibility Requirements: Applicant must be high school student; planning to enroll or expecting to enroll full-time at a two-year or four-year institution or university; resident of Mississippi and studying in Mississippi. Available to U.S. citizens.

Application Requirements: Application form, essay, financial need analysis. *Deadline:* March 1.

Contact: Program Administrator
Mississippi Office of Student Financial Aid
3825 Ridgewood Road
Jackson, MS 39211
Phone: 601-432-6997
Fax: 601-432 Ext. 6527
E-mail: sfa@mississippi.edu

MISSOURI CONSERVATION AGENTS ASSOCIATION SCHOLARSHIP

http://www.moagent.com/

MISSOURI CONSERVATION AGENTS ASSOCIATION SCHOLARSHIP

Scholarship of up to $500 per student per year for full-time undergraduate students who reside in the state of Missouri. The applicant must be a U.S. citizen.

Award: Scholarship for use in freshman, sophomore, junior, or senior years; not renewable. *Amount:* up to $500.

Eligibility Requirements: Applicant must be enrolled or expecting to enroll full-time at a four-year or technical institution or university and resident of Missouri. Available to U.S. citizens.

Application Requirements: Essay, transcript. *Deadline:* February 1.

Contact: Brian Ham, Scholarship Committee
Phone: 573-896-8628

MISSOURI DEPARTMENT OF HIGHER EDUCATION

https://dhewd.mo.gov/

ACCESS MISSOURI FINANCIAL ASSISTANCE PROGRAM

Need-based program that provides awards to students who are enrolled full time and have an expected family contribution (EFC) of $12,000 or less based on their Free Application for Federal Student Aid (FAFSA). Awards vary depending on EFC and the type of post-secondary school. Applicant must not be pursuing a degree or certificate in theology or divinity and not have received your first bachelor's degree, completed the required hours for a bachelor's degree, or completed 150 semester credit hours.

Award: Grant for use in freshman, sophomore, junior, or senior years; not renewable. *Amount:* $300–$2850.

Eligibility Requirements: Applicant must be enrolled or expecting to enroll full-time at a two-year or technical institution or university; resident of Mississippi and studying in Missouri. Available to U.S. citizens.

Application Requirements: *Deadline:* April 1.

Contact: Information Center
Phone: 800-473-6757 Ext. 4
Fax: 573-751-6635
E-mail: info@dhe.mo.gov

BRIGHT FLIGHT PROGRAM

Program encourages top-ranked high school seniors to attend approved Missouri post-secondary schools. Must be a Missouri resident and a U.S. citizen or permanent resident. Must have a composite score on the ACT or SAT in the top 5 percent of all Missouri students taking those tests. Students with scores in the top 3 percent are eligible for an annual award of up to $3000 (up to $1500 each semester). Students with scores in the top 4% and 5% are eligible for an annual award of up to $1000 (up to $500 each semester). Award amounts, and the availability of the award for students in the 4% and 5%, are subject to change based on the amount of funding allocated for the program in the legislative session. Applicant must also not be pursuing a degree or certificate in theology or divinity.

Award: Scholarship for use in freshman, sophomore, junior, or senior years; renewable. *Amount:* $1000–$3000.

Eligibility Requirements: Applicant must be enrolled or expecting to enroll full-time at a two-year or technical institution or university; resident of Mississippi and studying in Missouri. Available to U.S. citizens.

Application Requirements: *Deadline:* July 31.

Contact: Information Center
Phone: 800-473-6757 Ext. 4
Fax: 573-751-6635
E-mail: info@dhe.mo.gov

MARGUERITE ROSS BARNETT MEMORIAL SCHOLARSHIP

Scholarship was established for students who are employed while attending school part-time. Must be enrolled at least half-time but less than full-time at a participating Missouri postsecondary school, be employed and compensated for at least 20 hours per week, be 18 years of age, be a Missouri resident and a U.S. citizen or a permanent resident. Applicant must also not be pursuing a degree or certificate in theology or divinity, not received their first bachelor's degree or completed 150 semester credit hours, or an employee under the Title IV College Work Study program.

Award: Scholarship for use in freshman, sophomore, junior, or senior years; renewable.

Eligibility Requirements: Applicant must be age 18 and over; enrolled or expecting to enroll part-time at a two-year or technical institution or university; resident of Mississippi and studying in Missouri. Available to U.S. citizens.

Application Requirements: *Deadline:* August 1.

Contact: Information Center
Phone: 800-473-6757 Ext. 4
Fax: 573-751-6635
E-mail: info@dhe.mo.gov

MODERN LAW

https://mymodernlaw.com

DIVORCE PREVENTION SCHOLARSHIP

https://mymodernlaw.com/scholarship/

Award: Scholarship for use in freshman year; not renewable. *Number:* 1. *Amount:* $500.

Eligibility Requirements: Applicant must be enrolled or expecting to enroll full- or part-time at a two-year or four-year or technical institution or university and resident of Arizona. Available to U.S. citizens.

Application Requirements: Application form, essay. *Deadline:* March 1.

MOUNT VERNON URBAN RENEWAL AGENCY

http://www.ci.mount-vernon.ny.us/

MAYORS EDUCATIONAL ASSISTANCE PROGRAM

Awards offered only to the low and moderate income residents of the city of Mount Vernon for the purpose of pursuing higher education at a vocational/technical school or college.

Award: Grant for use in freshman, sophomore, junior, or senior years; renewable.

Eligibility Requirements: Applicant must be enrolled or expecting to enroll full-time at a two-year or four-year or technical institution or university and resident of New York. Available to U.S. citizens.

Application Requirements: Application form, essay, financial need analysis. *Deadline:* July 1.

Contact: Mary Fleming, Director, Scholarship Programs
Mount Vernon Urban Renewal Agency
Department of Planning, One Roosevelt Square, City Hall
Mount Vernon, NY 10550
Phone: 914-699-7230
E-mail: mfleming@ci.mount-vernon.ny.us

NATIONAL COUNCIL OF JEWISH WOMEN - LOS ANGELES (NCJW L LA)

http://ncjwla.org/

DODELL WOMEN'S EMPOWERMENT SCHOLARSHIP

To qualify, an applicant must be re-entering or continuing school in order to learn a marketable skill which will lead to economic self-sufficiency. The applicant must be a woman 25 years of age or older for whom the opportunity to return to school will lead to economic independence. The applicant can be either married or single, with or without children. The National Council of Jewish Women l Los Angeles (NCJW l LA) provides scholarships to those who live and attend school in the Greater Los Angeles area, including Los Angeles, Orange, Riverside, and Ventura Counties.

Award: Scholarship for use in freshman, sophomore, junior, senior, or graduate years; not renewable. *Number:* 2. *Amount:* $1000.

Eligibility Requirements: Applicant must be age 25 and over; enrolled or expecting to enroll full- or part-time at a two-year or technical institution or university; female; resident of British Columbia and studying in California. Available to U.S. citizens.

Application Requirements: Application form, application form may be submitted online, essay, financial need analysis. *Deadline:* May 1.

Contact: Carrie Jacoves, Director of Operations and Outreach
National Council of Jewish Women - Los Angeles (NCJW l LA)
543 N. Fairfax Ave.
Los Angeles, CA 90036
Phone: 323-651-2930
Fax: 323-651-5348
E-mail: carrie@ncjwla.org

SHERMAN & FRANCES L. TELLER TEACHING CREDENTIAL SCHOLARSHIP

Applicants must be a K-12 educator pursuing a multiple or single subject TEACHING CREDENTIAL (includes special education and ESL). The applicant must be enrolled at a University of California or California State University campus in the greater Los Angeles area, including Los Angeles, Orange, Riverside, San Bernandino and Ventura Counties, and the University of Nevada Las Vegas.

Award: Scholarship for use in freshman, sophomore, junior, or senior years; not renewable. *Number:* 2. *Amount:* $2000.

Eligibility Requirements: Applicant must be enrolled or expecting to enroll full- or part-time at an institution or university; resident of British Columbia and studying in California, Nevada. Available to U.S. citizens.

Application Requirements: Application form, application form may be submitted online, essay, financial need analysis. *Deadline:* May 1.

Contact: Carrie Jacoves, Director of Operations and Outreach
National Council of Jewish Women - Los Angeles (NCJW l LA)
543 N. Fairfax Ave.
Los Angeles, CA 90036
Phone: 323-651-2930
Fax: 323-651-5348
E-mail: carrie@ncjwla.org

SOPHIE GREENSTADT SCHOLARSHIP FOR MID-LIFE WOMEN

To qualify, an applicant must be re-entering or continuing school in order to learn a marketable skill which will lead to economic self-sufficiency. The applicant must be a woman 35 years of age or older for whom the opportunity to return to school will lead to economic independence. The applicant can be either married or single, with or without children. The National Council of Jewish Women l Los Angeles (NCJW l LA) provides scholarships to those who live and attend school in the Greater Los Angeles area, including Los Angeles, Orange, Riverside, and Ventura Counties.

Award: Scholarship for use in freshman, sophomore, junior, senior, or graduate years; not renewable. *Number:* 1. *Amount:* $1000.

Eligibility Requirements: Applicant must be age 35 and over; enrolled or expecting to enroll full- or part-time at a two-year or four-year or technical institution or university; female; resident of California and studying in California. Available to U.S. citizens.

Application Requirements: Application form, essay, financial need analysis. *Deadline:* continuous.

Contact: Stephanie Flax, Scholarship and Program Coordinator
National Council of Jewish Women - Los Angeles (NCJW l LA)
543 North Fairfax Avenue
Los Angeles, CA 90036
Phone: 323-852-8515
E-mail: scholarship@ncjala.org

SUSAN SCHULMAN BEGLEY MEMORIAL SCHOLARSHIP

To qualify, applicants must identify as a woman, who is establishing herself as a head of household and a single parent, and due to extreme circumstances, following the dissolution of an abusive or emtionally traumatic relationship, has no other adequate financial means, and requires funds to meet immediate needs for herself and her children, including rent & food. Must live and attend school in the Greater Los Angeles area, including Los Angeles, Orange, Riverside, San Bernandino and Ventura Counties.

Award: Scholarship for use in freshman, sophomore, junior, senior, graduate, or postgraduate years; not renewable. *Number:* 1. *Amount:* $1000.

Eligibility Requirements: Applicant must be enrolled or expecting to enroll full- or part-time at a two-year or technical institution or university; single female; resident of British Columbia and studying in California. Available to U.S. citizens.

Application Requirements: Application form, application form may be submitted online, essay, financial need analysis. *Deadline:* May 1.

Contact: Carrie Jacoves, Director of Operations and Outreach
National Council of Jewish Women - Los Angeles (NCJW l LA)
543 N. Fairfax Ave.
Los Angeles, CA 90036
Phone: 323-651-2930
Fax: 323-651-5348
E-mail: carrie@ncjwla.org

SYLVIA AND SAMUEL SCHULMAN MEMORIAL SCHOLARSHIP

To qualify, an applicant must be a single mother entering or continuing school in an accredited institution in order to learn a marketable skill, which will lead to economic independence. The award is made in two payments of $500.00. The second payment will be received after written confirmation of status and current school transcripts from the recipient. The National Council of Jewish Women l Los Angeles (NCJW l LA) provides scholarships to those who live and attend school in the Greater Los Angeles area, including Los Angeles, Orange, Riverside, and Ventura Counties.

Award: Scholarship for use in freshman, sophomore, junior, or senior years; not renewable. *Number:* 1. *Amount:* $1000.

Eligibility Requirements: Applicant must be enrolled or expecting to enroll full- or part-time at a two-year or four-year or technical institution or university; single female; resident of California and studying in California. Available to U.S. citizens.

Application Requirements: Application form, essay, financial need analysis. *Deadline:* continuous.

Contact: Carrie Jacoves, Director of Operations and Outreach
National Council of Jewish Women - Los Angeles (NCJW l LA)
543 N. Fairfax Ave.
Los Angeles, CA 90036
Phone: 323-651-2930
Fax: 323-651-5348
E-mail: carrie@ncjwla.org

NATIONAL DEFENSE TRANSPORTATION ASSOCIATION-SCOTT ST. LOUIS CHAPTER

http://www.ndtascottstlouis.org/

NATIONAL DEFENSE TRANSPORTATION ASSOCIATION, SCOTT AIR FORCE BASE-ST. LOUIS AREA CHAPTER SCHOLARSHIP

The Scott/St. Louis Chapter of the NDTA intends to award a minimum of two (2) scholarships of $3500 each and four (4) scholarships of $2000 each. Additional awards may be granted pending availability of funds. Scholarships are open to any high school student that meets the eligibility criteria. High school students must be reside and go to school in Illinois or Missouri. College applicants must be a full-time student in the following states: CO, IA, IL, IN, KS, MI, MN, MO, MT, ND, NE, SD, WI, or WY.

Award: Scholarship for use in freshman, sophomore, junior, or senior years; not renewable. *Number:* 6. *Amount:* $2000–$3500.

Eligibility Requirements: Applicant must be enrolled or expecting to enroll full-time at a two-year or four-year institution or university; resident of Illinois, Missouri and studying in Colorado, Illinois, Indiana, Iowa, Kansas, Michigan, Minnesota, Missouri, Montana, Nebraska, North Dakota, South Dakota, Wisconsin, Wyoming. Available to U.S. citizens.

Application Requirements: Application form, community service, essay, recommendations or references, test scores, transcript. *Deadline:* March 1.

Contact: Mr. Michael Carnes, Chairman, Professional Development Committee
National Defense Transportation Association-Scott St. Louis Chapter
PO Box 25486
Scott AFB, IL 62225
Phone: 618-229-4756
E-mail: michael.carnes.ctr@ustranscom.mil

NATIONAL FEDERATION OF THE BLIND OF CALIFORNIA

http://www.nfbcal.org/

GERALD DRAKE MEMORIAL SCHOLARSHIP
• See page 481

JULIE LANDUCCI SCHOLARSHIP
• See page 481

LA VYRL "PINKY" JOHNSON MEMORIAL SCHOLARSHIP
• See page 481

LAWRENCE "MUZZY" MARCELINO MEMORIAL SCHOLARSHIP
• See page 481

NATIONAL FEDERATION OF THE BLIND OF CALIFORNIA MERIT SCHOLARSHIPS
• See page 481

NATIONAL FEDERATION OF THE BLIND OF MISSOURI

http://www.nfbmo.org/

NATIONAL FEDERATION OF THE BLIND OF MISSOURI SCHOLARSHIP PROGRAM FOR LEGALLY BLIND STUDENTS
• See page 481

NATIONAL KIDNEY FOUNDATION OF INDIANA INC.

http://www.kidneyindiana.org/

NATIONAL KIDNEY FOUNDATION OF INDIANA SCHOLARSHIP
• See page 481

NEBRASKA'S COORDINATING COMMISSION FOR POSTSECONDARY EDUCATION

https://ccpe.nebraska.gov/

NEBRASKA OPPORTUNITY GRANT

Available to undergraduates attending a participating postsecondary institution in Nebraska. Must demonstrate financial need. Nebraska residency required. Awards determined by each participating institution. Student must complete the Free Application for Federal Student Aid (FAFSA) to apply. Contact financial aid office at institution for additional information.

Award: Grant for use in freshman, sophomore, junior, or senior years; not renewable. *Amount:* $100–$4458.

Eligibility Requirements: Applicant must be enrolled or expecting to enroll full- or part-time at a two-year or four-year or technical institution or university; resident of Nebraska and studying in Nebraska. Available to U.S. citizens.

Application Requirements: Application form may be submitted online (https://studentaid.ed.gov/sa/fafsa), financial need analysis. *Deadline:* continuous.

Contact: Mr. J. Ritchie Morrow, Financial Aid Officer
Nebraska's Coordinating Commission for Postsecondary Education
140 North 8th Street, Suite 300
PO Box 95005
Lincoln, NE 68509-5005
Phone: 402-471-2847
E-mail: Ritchie.Morrow@nebraska.gov

NEED

http://www.needld.org/

UNMET NEED GRANT PROGRAM
• See page 527

NEVADA OFFICE OF THE STATE TREASURER

http://www.nevadatreasurer.gov/

GOVERNOR GUINN MILLENNIUM SCHOLARSHIP

Scholarship for Nevada residents. Student must graduate from a public or private high school within Nevada with a minimum GPA of 3.25. Must complete core curriculum. Maximum award is $10,000 paid on a per-credit hour basis, up to 15 credits each semester. Student must acknowledge award and use it within 6 years of high school graduation.

Award: Scholarship for use in freshman, sophomore, junior, or senior years; renewable.

Eligibility Requirements: Applicant must be enrolled or expecting to enroll full-time at a two-year or four-year institution or university; resident of Nevada and studying in Nevada. Available to U.S. citizens.

Contact: Linda English, Executive Director
Phone: 702-486-3889
Fax: 702-486-3246
E-mail: info@nevadatreasurer.gov

NEW ENGLAND BOARD OF HIGHER EDUCATION

http://www.nebhe.org/tuitionbreak

NEW ENGLAND REGIONAL STUDENT PROGRAM-TUITION BREAK

Tuition discount for residents of six New England states (Connecticut, Maine, Massachusetts, New Hampshire, Rhode Island, Vermont). Students pay reduced out-of-state tuition at public colleges or universities in other New England states when enrolling in eligible majors and programs. Details are available at http://www.nebhe.org/tuitionbreak.

Award: Scholarship for use in freshman, sophomore, junior, senior, or graduate years; renewable.

Eligibility Requirements: Applicant must be enrolled or expecting to enroll full- or part-time at a two-year or four-year institution or university; resident of Connecticut, Maine, Massachusetts, New Hampshire, Rhode Island, Vermont and studying in Connecticut, Maine, Massachusetts, New Hampshire, Rhode Island, Vermont. Available to U.S. citizens.

Application Requirements: Application form. *Deadline:* continuous.

Contact: Wendy Lindsay, Senior Director of Regional Student Program
New England Board of Higher Education
45 Temple Place
Boston, MA 02111
Phone: 617-533-9511
E-mail: tuitionbreak@nebhe.org

NEW HAMPSHIRE CHARITABLE FOUNDATION

https://www.nhcf.org/

FISHER CATS SCHOLAR ATHLETES

Candidates for the Fisher Cats Scholarship must be residents of New Hampshire or Massachusetts who are graduating from high school in 2020. Candidates must be planning to enroll in a four-year degree program or planning to attend a local community college or technical school in the fall. In 2020, ten (10) scholarships, each in the amount of $2,500, will be awarded to New Hampshire students. Two (2) scholarships, each in the amount of $2,500, will be awarded to Massachusetts students.

Award: Scholarship for use in freshman year; not renewable. *Number:* 2–10. *Amount:* $2500.

Eligibility Requirements: Applicant must be enrolled or expecting to enroll at a two-year or technical institution or university and resident of Maryland, New Brunswick. Available to U.S. citizens.

Application Requirements: Application form, application form may be submitted online, essay, financial need analysis. *Deadline:* May 1.

Contact: Jessica Kierstead, Student Aid Officer
Phone: 603-225-6641 Ext. 226
E-mail: jessica.kierstead@nhcf.org

MEDALLION FUND SCHOLARSHIP

This is a competitive program and there are not sufficient funds to award all applicants. Typically we make awards to approximately 50% of those who apply. Award sizes are individualized and are determined by evaluating the costs of the training program, examining any financial aid offered, and taking in to account the student's family finances. The maximum award amount is $2500. Students enrolled in a Bachelor's Degree program or graduate level are not eligible to apply.

Award: Scholarship for use in freshman or sophomore years; renewable.

Eligibility Requirements: Applicant must be enrolled or expecting to enroll at a two-year or technical institution and resident of New Brunswick. Available to U.S. citizens.

Application Requirements: Application form. *Deadline:* continuous.

Contact: Jessica Kierstead, Student Aid Officer
Phone: 603-225-6641 Ext. 226
E-mail: jessica.kierstead@nhcf.org

NEW JERSEY DEPARTMENT OF MILITARY AND VETERANS AFFAIRS

http://www.state.nj.us/military

NEW JERSEY WAR ORPHANS TUITION ASSISTANCE
• *See page 504*

POW-MIA TUITION BENEFIT PROGRAM
• *See page 505*

VETERANS TUITION CREDIT PROGRAM-NEW JERSEY
• *See page 505*

NEW JERSEY HALL OF FAME

http://njhalloffame.org/

NJHOF ARETE SCHOLARSHIP AWARD

The New Jersey Hall of Fame is proud to announce the renewal of the Arete Scholarship Fund. The Arête Scholarships will be awarded to a deserving male and female student graduating in 2019 from a New Jersey high school. Each recipient will receive a $5,000 scholarship from the New Jersey Hall of Fame (NJHOF). Arête is a concept that Plato referred to more than 3,000 years ago that refers to the act of actualizing one's highest sense of self. The term Arête essentially means that the individual should strive to pursue their passions in life, and realize their dreams regardless of their circumstances or the adversities that they are likely to face on the path to greatness. The successful applicants will embody the meaning of Arête, and will distinguish themselves as New Jerseyans who are on their way to realizing their dreams. The NJHOF Arête Scholarship Award will be one of the highest honors that the NJHOF and the state of NJ. can bestow upon a student, and each student will be recognized at the NJHOF's annual Induction Ceremony! The recipients of the Arête scholarship are young people who demonstrate that sense of Jersey pride and that willingness to go above and beyond the call of duty. The successful applicants must demonstrate the qualities such as academic engagement, moral character, and a commitment to their community. These recipients do not necessarily have to be at the very top of their school class from an academic standpoint, but should demonstrate a focus in school and life, and have a well thought out plan on how they intend to realize their highest sense of self: their Arête.

Award: Scholarship for use in freshman year; not renewable. *Number:* 2. *Amount:* $5000.

Eligibility Requirements: Applicant must be high school student; planning to enroll or expecting to enroll full-time at a two-year or four-year institution or university and resident of New Jersey.

Application Requirements: Application form, application form may be submitted online, transcript. *Deadline:* March 17.

Contact: Ms. Emaleigh Kaithern
E-mail: emaleigh@princetonscgroup.com

NEW JERSEY STATE GOLF ASSOCIATION

NJSGA.org

NEW JERSEY STATE GOLF ASSOCIATION CADDIE SCHOLARSHIP
• *See page 469*

NEW JERSEY VIETNAM VETERANS' MEMORIAL FOUNDATION

http://www.njvvmf.org/college-scholarships

NEW JERSEY VIETNAM VETERANS' MEMORIAL FOUNDATION SCHOLARSHIP

Applicant must be a New Jersey resident, be a graduating high school senior, and visited the New Jersey Vietnam Veteran's Memorial (on their own /class trip/ scholarship tour).

Award: Scholarship for use in freshman year; not renewable. *Number:* 2. *Amount:* $2500.

Eligibility Requirements: Applicant must be high school student; planning to enroll or expecting to enroll full-time at a two-year or four-year or technical institution or university and resident of New Jersey. Available to U.S. citizens.

Application Requirements: Application form, essay. *Deadline:* April 14.

NEW MEXICO DEPARTMENT OF VETERANS' SERVICES

http://www.nmdvs.org

CHILDREN OF DECEASED VETERANS SCHOLARSHIP-NEW MEXICO

Award for New Mexico residents who are children of veterans killed as a result of service, prisoner of war, or veterans missing in action. Must be between ages 16 and 26. For use at New Mexico schools for undergraduate study. Must submit parent's death certificate and DD form 214.

Award: Scholarship for use in freshman, sophomore, junior, or senior years; not renewable. *Number:* 49–50. *Amount:* $300.

Eligibility Requirements: Applicant must be age 16-26; enrolled or expecting to enroll full- or part-time at a two-year or four-year or technical institution or university; resident of New Mexico and studying in New Mexico. Available to U.S. citizens.

Application Requirements: Application form.

Contact: Mr. Dale Movius, Director, State Benefits
New Mexico Department of Veterans' Services
407 Galisteo Street, Room 134
Santa Fe, NM 87501
Phone: 505-827-6300
E-mail: dalej.movius@state.nm.us

NEW MEXICO VIETNAM VETERAN SCHOLARSHIP

Award for Vietnam veterans who have been New Mexico residents for a minimum of ten years and are attending state-funded postsecondary schools. Must have been awarded the Vietnam Campaign medal. Must submit DD 214 and discharge papers.

Award: Scholarship for use in freshman, sophomore, junior, or senior years; renewable. *Number:* 100. *Amount:* $3500–$4000.

Eligibility Requirements: Applicant must be enrolled or expecting to enroll full- or part-time at a two-year or four-year or technical institution or university; resident of New Mexico and studying in New Mexico. Available to U.S. citizens.

Application Requirements: Application form.

Contact: Mr. Dale Movius, Director, State Benefits
New Mexico Department of Veterans' Services
407 Galisteo Street, Room 134
Santa Fe, NM 87501
Phone: 505-827-6300
E-mail: Dalej.movius@state.nm.us

NEW MEXICO WARTIME VETERANS SCHOLARSHIP
• *See page 505*

NEW YORK STATE EDUCATION DEPARTMENT

http://www.highered.nysed.gov/

SCHOLARSHIP FOR ACADEMIC EXCELLENCE

Renewable award for New York residents. Scholarship winners must attend a college or university in New York. 2000 scholarships are for $1500 and 6000 are for $500. The selection criteria used are based on Regents test scores or rank in class or local exam. Must be U.S. citizen or permanent resident.

Award: Scholarship for use in freshman year; renewable. *Number:* up to 8,000. *Amount:* $500–$1500.

Eligibility Requirements: Applicant must be high school student; planning to enroll or expecting to enroll full-time at a two-year or four-year institution or university; resident of New York and studying in New York. Available to U.S. citizens.

Application Requirements: Application form. *Deadline:* December 19.

Contact: Lewis Hall, Supervisor
Phone: 518-486-1319
Fax: 518-486-5346
E-mail: scholar@nysed.gov

NEW YORK STATE GRANGE

http://www.nysgrange.org/

SUSAN W. FREESTONE EDUCATION AWARD
• *See page 448*

NEW YORK STATE HIGHER EDUCATION SERVICES CORPORATION

http://www.hesc.ny.gov

NEW YORK STATE AID TO NATIVE AMERICANS
• *See page 527*

NEW YORK STATE PART-TIME SCHOLARSHIP

The New York State Part-Time Scholarship Award Program provides scholarship awards to students who attend a SUNY or CUNY Community College part-time and maintain a 2.0 GPA. Students can receive $1,500 per semester for up to 2 years.

Award: Grant for use in freshman, sophomore, junior, or senior years; renewable. *Amount:* $1500.

Eligibility Requirements: Applicant must be enrolled or expecting to enroll part-time at a two-year institution or university; resident of New Mexico and studying in New York. Available to U.S. citizens.

Application Requirements: Application form, financial need analysis.

NEW YORK STATE TUITION ASSISTANCE PROGRAM

The New York State Tuition Assistance Program (TAP) helps eligible New York residents pay tuition at approved schools in New York State. Depending on the academic year in which you begin study, an annual TAP award can be up to $5,165. Because TAP is a grant, it does not have to be paid back.

Award: Grant for use in freshman, sophomore, junior, or senior years; renewable. *Number:* 350,000–360,000. *Amount:* $500–$5165.

Eligibility Requirements: Applicant must be enrolled or expecting to enroll full-time at a two-year institution or university; resident of New Mexico and studying in New York. Available to U.S. citizens.

Application Requirements: Application form, application form may be submitted online, financial need analysis. *Deadline:* May 1.

NEW YORK VIETNAM/PERSIAN GULF/AFGHANISTAN VETERANS TUITION AWARDS
• *See page 505*

NYS MEMORIAL SCHOLARSHIP FOR FAMILIES OF DECEASED FIREFIGHTERS, VOLUNTEER FIREFIGHTERS, POLICE OFFICERS, PEACE OFFICERS, AND EMERGENCY MEDICAL SERVICE WORKERS

This scholarship provides financial aid to children, spouses and financial dependents of deceased firefighters, volunteer firefighters, police officers, peace officers, and emergency medical service workers who have died as the result of injuries sustained in the line of duty in service to the State of New York. For study in New York State.

Award: Scholarship for use in freshman, sophomore, junior, or senior years; renewable.

Eligibility Requirements: Applicant must be enrolled or expecting to enroll full-time at an institution or university; resident of New Mexico and studying in New York. Available to U.S. citizens.

Application Requirements: Application form, application form may be submitted online, financial need analysis. *Deadline:* May 1.

NYS REGENTS AWARDS FOR CHILDREN OF DECEASED AND DISABLED VETERANS

• *See page 505*

SCHOLARSHIPS FOR ACADEMIC EXCELLENCE

This program provides scholarship assistance to outstanding New York State high school graduates. Each year, 8,000 scholarships are awarded - up to 2,000 scholarships of $1,500 and 6,000 scholarships of $500 to top scholars from registered New York State high schools. Awards are based on student grades in certain Regents exams. For up to five years of undergraduate study in New York State. Recipients can also receive other non-loan student aid, but the total cannot exceed the cost of attendance.

Award: Scholarship for use in freshman, sophomore, junior, or senior years; renewable. *Number:* 8,000. *Amount:* $500–$1500.

Eligibility Requirements: Applicant must be high school student; planning to enroll or expecting to enroll full-time at an institution or university; resident of New Mexico and studying in New York. Available to U.S. citizens.

Application Requirements: Application form. *Deadline:* June 30.

WORLD TRADE CENTER MEMORIAL SCHOLARSHIP

The World Trade Center Memorial Scholarship (WTC) provides access to a college education for children, spouses, and financial dependents of innocent victims who died or were severely and permanently disabled as a result of the September 11, 2001 terrorist attacks on the United States of America - at the World Trade Center, the Pentagon, and on airline flights 11, 77, 93, and 175 - and the resulting rescue and recovery efforts.

Award: Scholarship for use in freshman, sophomore, junior, or senior years; renewable.

Eligibility Requirements: Applicant must be enrolled or expecting to enroll full-time at an institution or university; resident of New Mexico and studying in New York. Available to U.S. and non-U.S. citizens.

Application Requirements: Application form, application form may be submitted online, financial need analysis. *Deadline:* June 30.

NEW YORK WOMEN IN COMMUNICATIONS

https://nywici.org/

NEW YORK WOMEN IN COMMUNICATIONS SCHOLARSHIPS

New York Women in Communications, Inc, cultivates leaders in our field by providing financial support, opportunities for professional development and mentoring to a diverse community of communications professionals. We are the largest foundation for women's communications scholarships in the U.S.

Award: Scholarship for use in freshman, sophomore, junior, senior, or graduate years; not renewable. *Number:* 1–22. *Amount:* $1000–$10,000.

Eligibility Requirements: Applicant must be enrolled or expecting to enroll full-time at a four-year institution or university; resident of Connecticut, New Jersey, New York, Pennsylvania and studying in New York. Available to U.S. citizens.

Application Requirements: Application form, application form may be submitted online (https://scholarships.nywici.org/), essay, resume, transcript. *Deadline:* January 25.

Contact: Anna McManus, Membership Director
New York Women in Communications
355 Lexington Avenue
Floor 15
New York, NY 10017
Phone: 212-297-2133
E-mail: info@nywici.org

N.H. DEPARTMENT OF EDUCATION, DIVISION OF HIGHER EDUCATION - HIGHER EDUCATION COMMISSION

http://www.education.nh.gov/highered

SCHOLARSHIPS FOR ORPHANS OF VETERANS

• *See page 505*

NORTH CAROLINA ASSOCIATION OF EDUCATORS

http://www.ncae.org/

NORTH CAROLINA ASSOCIATION OF EDUCATORS MARTIN LUTHER KING JR. SCHOLARSHIP

One-time award for high school seniors who are North Carolina residents to attend a postsecondary institution. Must be a U.S. citizen. Based upon financial need, GPA, and essay. Must have a GPA of at least 3.5 on a 5.0 scale or a 2.5 on a 4.0 scale.

Award: Scholarship for use in freshman year; not renewable. *Number:* 2–4. *Amount:* $500–$1000.

Eligibility Requirements: Applicant must be high school student; age 16-18; planning to enroll or expecting to enroll full-time at a two-year or four-year institution or university and resident of North Carolina. Available to U.S. citizens.

Application Requirements: Application form, community service, essay, financial need analysis. *Deadline:* February 5.

Contact: Derevana Leach, Scholarship Coordinator
North Carolina Association of Educators
700 S Salisbury St.
Raleigh, NC 27601
Phone: 919-832-3000 Ext. 203
E-mail: derevana.leach@ncae.org

NORTH CAROLINA BAR FOUNDATION

http://www.ncbar.org/

NORTH CAROLINA BAR ASSOCIATION YOUNG LAWYERS DIVISION SCHOLARSHIP

Renewable award for children or step-children of North Carolina Law Enforcement Officers killed or permanently disabled in the line of duty, studying full-time in accredited colleges or universities. Must be resident of North Carolina and under 26 years of age for first time application. The number of awards and the dollar value of the award varies annually.

Award: Scholarship for use in freshman, sophomore, junior, senior, graduate, or postgraduate years; renewable.

Eligibility Requirements: Applicant must be age 27 or under; enrolled or expecting to enroll full-time at a two-year or four-year or technical institution or university and resident of North Carolina. Available to U.S. citizens.

Application Requirements: Application form, essay, financial need analysis, personal photograph. *Deadline:* June 1.

Contact: Ms. Jacquelyn Terrell, Director of Divisions Activities, YLD
Staff Liaison
North Carolina Bar Foundation
PO Box 3688
Cary, NC 27519
Phone: 919-657-0561
E-mail: jterrell@ncbar.org

NORTH CAROLINA DIVISION OF VETERANS AFFAIRS

http://www.milvets.nc.gov/

NORTH CAROLINA VETERANS SCHOLARSHIPS CLASS I-A

• *See page 506*

NORTH CAROLINA VETERANS SCHOLARSHIPS CLASS I-B
• See page 506

NORTH CAROLINA VETERANS SCHOLARSHIPS CLASS II
• See page 506

NORTH CAROLINA VETERANS SCHOLARSHIPS CLASS III
• See page 506

NORTH CAROLINA VETERANS SCHOLARSHIPS CLASS IV
• See page 506

NORTH CAROLINA DIVISION OF VOCATIONAL REHABILITATION SERVICES
http://www.dhhs.state.nc.us/

TRAINING SUPPORT FOR YOUTH WITH DISABILITIES
• See page 482

NORTH CAROLINA NATIONAL GUARD
http://nc.ng.mil/Pages/default.aspx

NORTH CAROLINA NATIONAL GUARD TUITION ASSISTANCE PROGRAM
• See page 490

NORTH CAROLINA SOCIETY OF HISPANIC PROFESSIONALS
http://www.thencshp.org/

NORTH CAROLINA HISPANIC COLLEGE FUND SCHOLARSHIP
• See page 528

NORTH CAROLINA STATE EDUCATION ASSISTANCE AUTHORITY
http://www.ncseaa.edu/

AUBREY LEE BROOKS SCHOLARSHIPS

A renewable scholarship for graduating high school seniors who are residents of designated North Carolina counties: Alamance, Bertie, Caswell, Durham. Forsyth, Granville, Guilford, Orange, Person, Rockingham, Stokes, Surry, Swain and Warren counties. The scholarship may be used at North Carolina State University, the University of North Carolina at Chapel Hill or the University of North Carolina at Greensboro. Scholarship is renewable, provided the recipient has continued financial need, remains enrolled full-time at an eligible institution and maintains specified academic standards. Additional details and application at http://www.CFNC.org/Brooks

Award: Scholarship for use in freshman, sophomore, junior, or senior years; renewable. *Number:* 17. *Amount:* up to $12,000.

Eligibility Requirements: Applicant must be high school student; planning to enroll or expecting to enroll full-time at a four-year institution or university; resident of North Carolina and studying in North Carolina. Available to U.S. citizens.

Application Requirements: Application form, essay, financial need analysis, interview, recommendations or references, test scores, transcript. *Deadline:* January 31.

Contact: Michelle Hemmer, Forgivable Loans Higher Ed Program Manager
North Carolina State Education Assistance Authority
PO Box 13663
Research Triangle Park, NC 27709-3663
Phone: 919-549-8614
Fax: 919-549-8481
E-mail: info@ncseaa.edu

JAGANNATHAN SCHOLARSHIP

Available to graduating high school seniors who plan to enroll as college freshmen in a full-time degree program at one of the constituent institutions of The University of North Carolina. Applicant must be resident of North Carolina. Applicant must document financial need. Deadline determined by financial aid office.

Award: Scholarship for use in freshman year; not renewable.

Eligibility Requirements: Applicant must be enrolled or expecting to enroll full-time at a four-year institution or university; resident of North Carolina and studying in North Carolina. Available to U.S. citizens.

Application Requirements: Application form, financial need analysis, test scores. *Deadline:* continuous.

Contact: Edna Williams, Manager, Award and Loan Origination Services
Phone: 866-866-CFNC
E-mail: programinformation@cfnc.org

NORTH CAROLINA COMMUNITY COLLEGE GRANT PROGRAM

Grants are available to North Carolina residents who demonstrate financial need and are enrolled at NC community colleges. The applicant must be a NC resident for tuition purposes; enroll for at least six credit hours per semester in a curriculum program; meet the Satisfactory Academic Progress requirements of the institution. Eligibility is determined based on the same criteria as the Federal Pell Grant; students not eligible for the Federal Pell Grant may be considered for the grant based on the expected family contribution (EFC). Student who have earned a Bachelor's (four-year) degree already are ineligible. Applicants must complete the Free Application for Federal Student Aid (FAFSA). Consideration is automatic once the FAFSA is filed. Please contact the financial aid office at the local community college for more specific information regarding institutional processes.

Award: Grant for use in freshman or sophomore years; not renewable.

Eligibility Requirements: Applicant must be enrolled or expecting to enroll full- or part-time at a two-year or technical institution; resident of North Carolina and studying in North Carolina. Available to U.S. citizens.

Application Requirements: Financial need analysis. *Deadline:* continuous.

Contact: Michelle Hemmer, Forgivable Loans Higher Ed Program Manager
North Carolina State Education Assistance Authority
PO Box 13663
Research Triangle Park, NC 27709-3663
Phone: 919-549-8614
Fax: 919-549-8481
E-mail: info@ncseaa.edu

UNIVERSITY OF NORTH CAROLINA NEED-BASED GRANT

Applicants must be enrolled in at least 6 credit hours at one of sixteen UNC system universities. Eligibility based on need; award varies, consideration for grant automatic when FAFSA is filed. Applicants should meet priority deadlines established by their institution. Late applications may be denied if insufficient funds are available. Q4 d: Total dollar value of awards given in 2018 = $123,672,458.00

Award: Grant for use in freshman, sophomore, junior, or senior years; renewable.

Eligibility Requirements: Applicant must be enrolled or expecting to enroll full- or part-time at an institution or university; resident of North Carolina and studying in North Carolina. Available to U.S. citizens.

Application Requirements: Application form, financial need analysis. *Deadline:* continuous.

Contact: Edna Williams, Manager, Award and Loan Origination Services
Phone: 866-866-2362
E-mail: programinformation@cfnc.org

NORTH CAROLINA VIETNAM VETERANS, INC.

www.ncvvi.org

NC VIETNAM VETERANS, INC., SCHOLARSHIP PROGRAM

Scholarship is awarded to Vietnam Veterans, their spouses or their offspring including adopted. Students who successfully attend a Lessons of Vietnam class prior to or during the year of submission are eligible. A 600-900 word essay on a different topic each year relating to the Vietnam War era is required.

Award: Scholarship for use in freshman, sophomore, junior, or senior years; not renewable. *Number:* 1–6. *Amount:* $500–$1500.

Eligibility Requirements: Applicant must be enrolled or expecting to enroll full-time at a two-year or four-year or technical institution or university and resident of North Carolina. Available to U.S. and non-U.S. citizens.

Application Requirements: Application form, application form may be submitted online(ncvvi.org), DD214 of family member, essay. *Deadline:* February 28.

Contact: Ms. Bonnie Kuhr, Scholarship Administrator and Secretary
North Carolina Vietnam Veterans, Inc.
7316 Ray Road
Raleigh, NC 27613
Phone: 919-844-3970
E-mail: bkuhr@nc.rr.com

NORTH DAKOTA FARMERS UNION

http://www.ndfu.org

STANLEY MOORE FUI FOUNDATION REGIONAL SCHOLARSHIP

Written essay or oral presentation outlining personal and professional goals and involvement with Farmers Union. Priority given to ag-related study.

Award: Scholarship for use in freshman, sophomore, junior, or senior years; not renewable. *Number:* 1–3. *Amount:* $1500.

Eligibility Requirements: Applicant must be enrolled or expecting to enroll full-time at a two-year or four-year or technical institution or university and resident of Minnesota, Montana, North Dakota, South Dakota, Wisconsin. Available to U.S. citizens.

Application Requirements: Application form, community service, essay, interview. *Deadline:* April 22.

Contact: David Velde
North Dakota Farmers Union
1118 Broadway
Alexandria, MN 56308
Phone: 320-763-6561

OHIO DEPARTMENT OF HIGHER EDUCATION

www.ohiohighered.org

CHOOSE OHIO FIRST SCHOLARSHIP

Choose Ohio First awards competitive scholarship funding to Ohio's colleges and universities to support undergraduate and qualifying graduate students in innovative STEMM academic programs. Designated Choose Ohio First programs are integrated with regional economies, meeting statewide educational needs, facilitating the completion of baccalaureate degrees in cost effective manners, and recruiting underrepresented STEMM student groups including women and students of color.

Award: Scholarship for use in freshman, sophomore, junior, or senior years; renewable.

Eligibility Requirements: Applicant must be enrolled or expecting to enroll full- or part-time at a two-year institution or university; resident of Nova Scotia and studying in Ohio. Available to U.S. and non-U.S. citizens.

Application Requirements: Application form. *Deadline:* continuous.

Contact: Corey Dixon, Project Manager
Ohio Department of Higher Education
Ohio Department of Higher Education
25 South Front Street
Columbus, OH 43215
Phone: 614-644-5704
E-mail: CDixon@highered.ohio.gov

OHIO COLLEGE OPPORTUNITY GRANT

OCOG provides grant money to Ohio residents who demonstrate the highest levels of financial need (as determined by the results of the FAFSA) who are enrolled at Ohio public colleges or universities; Ohio private, non-profit colleges or universities; Ohio private, for-profit institutions; or eligible Pennsylvania institutions.

Award: Grant for use in freshman, sophomore, junior, or senior years; not renewable. *Amount:* $69–$3500.

Eligibility Requirements: Applicant must be enrolled or expecting to enroll full- or part-time at a two-year institution or university; resident of Nova Scotia and studying in Ohio, Pennsylvania.

Application Requirements: *Deadline:* October 1.

Contact: Tamika Braswell, Director
Ohio Department of Higher Education
25 South Front Street
Columbus, OH 43215
Phone: 614-728-8862
E-mail: ocog_admin@highered.ohio.gov

OHIO SAFETY OFFICERS COLLEGE MEMORIAL FUND

Renewable award covering up to full tuition is available to children and surviving spouses of peace officers, other safety officers and fire fighters killed in the line of duty in any state. Children must be under 26 years of age. Dollar value of each award varies. Must be an Ohio resident and enroll full-time or part-time at an Ohio college or university. Any spouse/child of a member of the armed services of the U.S., who has been killed in the line duty during Operation Enduring Freedom, Operation Iraqi Freedom or a combat zone designated by the President of the United States. Dollar value of each award varies.

Award: Scholarship for use in freshman, sophomore, junior, or senior years; renewable. *Amount:* $7942.

Eligibility Requirements: Applicant must be enrolled or expecting to enroll full- or part-time at a two-year institution or university; resident of Nova Scotia and studying in Ohio. Available to U.S. citizens.

Contact: Ramah Church, Program Manager
Ohio Department of Higher Education
25 South Front Street
Columbus, OH 43215
Phone: 614-752-9528
E-mail: osom_admin@highered.ohio.gov

OHIO WAR ORPHAN & SEVERELY DISABLED VETERANS' CHILDREN SCHOLARSHIP PROGRAM
• *See page 506*

OHIO-MICHIGAN ASSOCIATION OF CAREER COLLEGES AND SCHOOLS

http://www.omaccs.org/

LEADS! SCHOLARSHIP

One-time scholarship for graduating high school seniors enrolling in a career college or school that is a participating member of OMACCS. The applicant must be an Ohio or Michigan high school student with a 2.0 GPA or better and does not have to demonstrate a financial need. The scholarship amount and the number of scholarships granted varies.

Award: Scholarship for use in freshman, sophomore, junior, or senior years; not renewable. *Number:* 200–250. *Amount:* $1500–$40,000.

Eligibility Requirements: Applicant must be high school student; planning to enroll or expecting to enroll full- or part-time at a two-year or four-year or technical institution; resident of Michigan, Ohio and studying in Michigan, Ohio. Available to U.S. and non-U.S. citizens.

Application Requirements: Application form, essay. *Deadline:* April 6.

Contact: Denise Putigano, Admin Asst
Ohio-Michigan Association of Career Colleges and Schools
2109 Stella Court
Suite 125
Columbus, OH 43215
Phone: 614-487-8180
E-mail: admin@omaccs.org

OHIO NATIONAL GUARD

http://www.ong.ohio.gov/

OHIO NATIONAL GUARD SCHOLARSHIP PROGRAM
• *See page 490*

OKLAHOMA ALUMNI & ASSOCIATES OF FHA, HERO AND FCCLA INC.

http://www.okalumni.org

OKLAHOMA ALUMNI & ASSOCIATES OF FHA, HERO, AND FCCLA INC. SCHOLARSHIP
• *See page 449*

OKLAHOMA STATE REGENTS FOR HIGHER EDUCATION

http://www.okhighered.org/

ACADEMIC SCHOLARS PROGRAM

Awards for students of high academic ability to attend institutions in Oklahoma. Renewable up to four years. ACT or SAT scores must fall between 99.5 and 100th percentiles, or applicant must be designated as a National Merit scholar or finalist. Oklahoma public institutions can also select institutional nominees.

Award: Scholarship for use in freshman, sophomore, junior, senior, or graduate years; renewable. *Amount:* $2200–$5500.

Eligibility Requirements: Applicant must be high school student; planning to enroll or expecting to enroll full-time at a two-year institution or university; resident of Ohio and studying in Oklahoma. Available to U.S. citizens.

Application Requirements: Application form.

Contact: Linette McMurtrey, Scholarship Programs Coordinator
Oklahoma State Regents for Higher Education
P.O. Box 108850
Oklahoma City, OK 73101-8850
Phone: 800-858-1840
E-mail: lmcmurtrey@osrhe.edu

FUTURE TEACHER SCHOLARSHIP-OKLAHOMA

Open to outstanding Oklahoma high school graduates who agree to teach in shortage areas. Must have a GPA or ACT/SAT score ranking in the top 15% of the high school graduating class. Students nominated by institution. Reapply to renew. Must attend college/university in Oklahoma.

Award: Scholarship for use in freshman, sophomore, junior, senior, or graduate years; not renewable. *Amount:* $500–$1500.

Eligibility Requirements: Applicant must be enrolled or expecting to enroll full- or part-time at a two-year institution or university; resident of Ohio and studying in Oklahoma. Available to U.S. citizens.

Application Requirements: Application form, essay.

Contact: Linette McMurtrey, Scholarship Programs Coordinator
Oklahoma State Regents for Higher Education
P.O. Box 108850
655 Research Parkway, Suite 200
Oklahoma City, OK 73104
Phone: 405-225-9131
E-mail: lmcmurtrey@osrhe.edu

OKLAHOMA TUITION AID GRANT PROGRAM

Award for Oklahoma residents enrolled at an Oklahoma institution at least part time each semester in a degree program. May be enrolled in two- or four-year or approved vocational-technical institution. Award for students attending public institutions or private colleges. Application is made through FAFSA.

Award: Grant for use in freshman, sophomore, junior, or senior years; not renewable. *Amount:* $1000–$1300.

Eligibility Requirements: Applicant must be enrolled or expecting to enroll full- or part-time at a two-year or technical institution or university; resident of Ohio and studying in Oklahoma. Available to U.S. citizens.

Application Requirements: Application form, financial need analysis.

Contact: Linette McMurtrey, Scholarship Programs Coordinator
Oklahoma State Regents for Higher Education
P.O. Box 108850
655 Research Parkway, Suite 200
Oklahoma City, OK 73104
Phone: 405-225-9131
E-mail: lmcmurtrey@osrhe.edu

REGIONAL UNIVERSITY BACCALAUREATE SCHOLARSHIP

Renewable award for Oklahoma residents attending one of 11 participating Oklahoma public universities. Must have an ACT composite score of at least 30 or be a National Merit semifinalist or commended student. In addition to the award amount, each recipient will receive a resident tuition waiver from the institution. Must maintain a 3.25 GPA. Deadlines vary depending upon the institution attended.

Award: Scholarship for use in freshman, sophomore, junior, or senior years; renewable. *Amount:* $3000.

Eligibility Requirements: Applicant must be enrolled or expecting to enroll full-time at an institution or university; resident of Ohio and studying in Oklahoma. Available to U.S. citizens.

Application Requirements: Application form.

Contact: Linette McMurtrey, Scholarship Programs Coordinator
Oklahoma State Regents for Higher Education
P.O. Box 108850
655 Research Parkway, Suite 200
Oklahoma City, OK 73104
Phone: 405-225-9131
E-mail: lmcmurtrey@osrhe.edu

WILLIAM P. WILLIS SCHOLARSHIP

Renewable award for low-income Oklahoma residents attending an Oklahoma institution. Must be a full-time undergraduate. Deadline varies.

Award: Scholarship for use in freshman, sophomore, junior, or senior years; renewable. *Amount:* $2000–$3000.

Eligibility Requirements: Applicant must be enrolled or expecting to enroll full-time at a two-year institution or university; resident of Ohio and studying in Oklahoma. Available to U.S. citizens.

Application Requirements: Application form.

Contact: Linette McMurtrey, Scholarship Programs Coordinator
Oklahoma State Regents for Higher Education
P.O. Box 108850
655 Research Parkway, Suite 200
Oklahoma City, OK 73104
Phone: 405-225-9131
E-mail: lmcmurtrey@osrhe.edu

ONE MILLION DEGREES

http://www.onemilliondegrees.org

ONE MILLION DEGREES SCHOLARSHIP SUPPORT PROGRAM

The One Million Degrees Scholarship Program offers groundbreaking, whole-student programming to low-income, highly motivated community college students. OMD provides scholars with financial, academic, personal and professional supports to ensure students are on track to graduate and prepared for their next step. One Million Degrees currently partners with all seven City Colleges of Chicago, Harper College, Prairie State College and South Suburban College.

Award: Scholarship for use in freshman, sophomore, junior, or senior years; renewable. *Number:* 400–500. *Amount:* $1000.

Eligibility Requirements: Applicant must be enrolled or expecting to enroll full-time at a two-year institution; resident of Illinois and studying in Illinois. Available to U.S. and non-Canadian citizens.

Application Requirements: Application form, essay, financial need analysis. *Deadline:* May 16.

Contact: Magali Perez, Scholar Recruitment Manager
E-mail: apply@onemilliondegrees.org

ONLINEPSYCHOLOGYDEGREES.COM

http://www.onlinepsychologydegrees.com/

ONLINEPSYCHOLOGYDEGREES.COM EDUCATION SCHOLARSHIPS

If you're ready to begin your career of helping change lives, get started by applying for the OnlinePsychologyDegrees.com $1,000 scholarship. Apply now, and then find the psychology programs that fit your career path.

Award: Scholarship for use in freshman, sophomore, junior, senior, graduate, or postgraduate years; renewable. *Number:* 2. *Amount:* $1000.

Eligibility Requirements: Applicant must be enrolled or expecting to enroll full- or part-time at a two-year or four-year or technical institution or university and resident of Alabama, Alaska, Arizona, Arkansas, California, Colorado, Connecticut, Delaware, District of Columbia, Georgia, Hawaii, Idaho, Illinois, Indiana, Iowa, Kansas, Kentucky, Louisiana, Maine, Manitoba, Maryland, Massachusetts, Michigan, Minnesota, Mississippi, Missouri, Montana, Nebraska, Nevada, New Hampshire, New Jersey, New Mexico, North Carolina, North Dakota, Northwest Territories, Ohio, Oklahoma, Ontario, Oregon, Pennsylvania, South Carolina, South Dakota, Tennessee, Texas, Utah, Vermont, Virginia, Washington, West Virginia, Wisconsin, Wyoming. Available to U.S. citizens.

Application Requirements: Application form, essay. *Deadline:* January 15.

Contact: Jennifer Moody, Site Manager
OnlinePsychologyDegrees.com
15500 Wes 113th Street
#200
Lenexa, KS 66219
Phone: 913-254-6000
E-mail: jennifer.moody@marketing.keypathedu.com

OREGON COMMUNITY FOUNDATION

http://www.oregoncf.org/

ERNEST ALAN AND BARBARA PARK MEYER SCHOLARSHIP FUND

Scholarship for Oregon high school graduates for use in the pursuit of a postsecondary education (undergraduate or graduate) at a nonprofit two- or four-year college or university.

Award: Scholarship for use in freshman, sophomore, junior, or senior years; renewable. *Number:* up to 5. *Amount:* $1000–$4500.

Eligibility Requirements: Applicant must be enrolled or expecting to enroll full-time at a two-year or four-year or technical institution or university and resident of Oregon. Available to U.S. citizens.

Application Requirements: Application form, recommendations or references. *Deadline:* March 1.

Contact: Dianne Causey, Program Associate for Scholarships and Grants
Phone: 503-227-6846 Ext. 1418
E-mail: dcausey@oregoncf.org

FRIENDS OF BILL RUTHERFORD EDUCATION FUND

Scholarship for Oregon high school graduates or GED recipients who are dependent children of individuals holding statewide elected office or currently serving in the Oregon State Legislature. Students must be enrolled full-time in a two- or four-year college or university. For more information, see web http://www.getcollegefunds.org.

Award: Scholarship for use in freshman, sophomore, junior, or senior years; renewable. *Number:* 1–2. *Amount:* $1000–$2500.

Eligibility Requirements: Applicant must be enrolled or expecting to enroll full-time at a two-year or four-year institution or university and resident of Oregon. Available to U.S. citizens.

Application Requirements: Application form, recommendations or references. *Deadline:* March 1.

Contact: Dianne Causey, Program Associate for Scholarships and Grants
Phone: 503-227-6846 Ext. 1418
E-mail: dcausey@oregoncf.org

MARY E. HORSTKOTTE SCHOLARSHIP FUND

Award available for academically talented and financially needy students for use in the pursuit of a postsecondary education. Must be an Oregon resident. For full-time study only.

Award: Scholarship for use in freshman, sophomore, junior, or senior years; not renewable. *Number:* 1–10. *Amount:* $2000.

Eligibility Requirements: Applicant must be enrolled or expecting to enroll full-time at a two-year or four-year or technical institution or university and resident of Oregon. Available to U.S. citizens.

Application Requirements: Application form, recommendations or references. *Deadline:* March 1.

Contact: Dianne Causey, Program Associate for Scholarships and Grants
Phone: 503-227-6846 Ext. 1418
E-mail: dcausey@oregoncf.org

RUBE AND MINAH LESLIE EDUCATIONAL FUND

Scholarship for Oregon residents for the pursuit of a postsecondary education. Selection is based on financial need.

Award: Scholarship for use in freshman, sophomore, junior, or senior years; renewable. *Number:* up to 50. *Amount:* $2000.

Eligibility Requirements: Applicant must be enrolled or expecting to enroll full-time at a two-year or four-year institution or university and resident of Oregon. Available to U.S. citizens.

Application Requirements: Application form, financial need analysis. *Deadline:* March 1.

Contact: Dianne Causey, Program Associate for Scholarships and Grants
Phone: 503-227-6846 Ext. 1418
E-mail: dcausey@oregoncf.org

OREGON OFFICE OF STUDENT ACCESS AND COMPLETION

https://oregonstudentaid.gov/

OREGON STUDENT ACCESS COMMISSION EMPLOYEE AND DEPENDENTS SCHOLARSHIP

Award for eligible employees of the Office of Student Access and Completion and their dependents. Children and dependents must be 23 or under as of the March scholarship deadline. Employees must enroll at least half time. Apply/compete annually.

Award: Scholarship for use in freshman, sophomore, junior, or senior years; not renewable.

Eligibility Requirements: Applicant must be enrolled or expecting to enroll full- or part-time at a four-year institution or university and resident of Oregon. Available to U.S. citizens.

Application Requirements: Application form. *Deadline:* March 1.

Contact: Melissa Adams, Scholarship Processing Coordinator
Phone: 541-687-7409
E-mail: melissa.adams@state.or.us

PETER CROSSLEY MEMORIAL SCHOLARSHIP

Scholarship for graduating seniors of Oregon public alternative high schools. Must be highly motivated to succeed despite overcoming a severe personal obstacle or challenge during high school career. Must plan to enroll at least half-time in an Oregon college or university. Preferred GPA is between 2.0 and 3.5. Based on financial need.

Award: Scholarship for use in freshman year; not renewable.

Eligibility Requirements: Applicant must be high school student; planning to enroll or expecting to enroll full- or part-time at a four-year institution or university; resident of Oregon and studying in Oregon. Available to U.S. citizens.

Application Requirements: Application form, essay, financial need analysis. *Deadline:* March 1.

Contact: Melissa Adams, Scholarship Processing Coordinator
Phone: 541-687-7409
E-mail: melissa.adams@state.or.us

SALEM FOUNDATION ANSEL & MARIE SOLIE SCHOLARSHIP
• See page 482

PACERS FOUNDATION INC.
http://www.pacersfoundation.org/

PACERS TEAMUP SCHOLARSHIP
• See page 469

PACIFIC AND ASIAN AFFAIRS COUNCIL
http://www.paachawaii.org/

PAAC ACADEMIC SCHOLARSHIPS
PAAC's academic scholarships are available to college-bound seniors and underclassmen attending Hawaii public or private high school. Applicants must be active in PAAC's high school program (PAAC clubs or PAAC After-School Classes).

Award: Scholarship for use in freshman year; not renewable. *Number:* 5. *Amount:* $300–$1000.

Eligibility Requirements: Applicant must be high school student; planning to enroll or expecting to enroll full-time at a two-year or four-year or technical institution or university and resident of Hawaii. Available to U.S. and non-U.S. citizens.

Application Requirements: Application form, essay. *Deadline:* April 2.

Contact: Jason Shon, High School Program Director
Pacific and Asian Affairs Council
1601 East-West Road, 4th Floor
Honolulu, HI 96848
Phone: 808-944-7759
E-mail: hs@paachawaii.org

PEACOCK PRODUCTIONS, INC.
http://amefund.com

AUDRIA M. EDWARDS SCHOLARSHIP FUND
Peacock Productions, Inc. administers the Audria M. Edwards Scholarship Fund, and is funded by donations, variety show proceeds, and community fundraisers. Individuals are eligible for scholarships if they 1. will be pursuing post-secondary, under-graduate education in an accredited institution or program during the coming school year; 2. are lesbian, gay, bisexual, or transgender or have a LGBT parent; 3. have resided for at least one year in the state of Oregon or in Clark, Cowlitz, Skamania, or Wahkiakum counties in Washington. To apply, complete the application form, compile a one-page essay, and submit two letters of recommendation and a transcript. Read and sign the affidavit at the end of the application form and mail the form and enclosures on or before May 1st to: The Audria M. Edwards Scholarship Fund, P.O. Box 16337, Portland, OR 97292. A committee appointed by Peacock Productions, Inc. will review materials from all applicants and select finalists on the basis of the following qualifications: clarity of career and educational goals; potential to succeed in an educational program; experience as a volunteer or service-oriented leader; commitment to the LGBTQ community; capacity for overcoming difficult circumstances and making the most of personal assets. All finalists will be interviewed before the Review Committee who determines who will receive scholarships and how much funding each will receive. Checks will be mailed to students's schools and credited to their student accounts before the beginning of the school year. Funds can be used for tuition, fees, and on-campus room and board charges, but cannot be applied toward off-campus housing, transportation, dependent care, or other personal expenses. Awards are presented annually at Peacock in the Park in Portland, Oregon. For more information visit http://www.amefund.org.

Award: Scholarship for use in freshman, sophomore, junior, or senior years; not renewable. *Number:* 8–15. *Amount:* $1000–$5000.

Eligibility Requirements: Applicant must be enrolled or expecting to enroll full- or part-time at a two-year or four-year or technical institution or university and resident of Oregon, Washington. Available to U.S. citizens.

Application Requirements: Application form, community service, essay, financial need analysis, interview. *Deadline:* May 1.

Contact: Kimberlee Van Patten, Co-Founder
Peacock Productions, Inc.
PO Box 16337
Portland, OR 97292
E-mail: info@peacockinthepark.org

PENNSYLVANIA BURGLAR AND FIRE ALARM ASSOCIATION
http://www.pbfaa.com/

PENNSYLVANIA BURGLAR AND FIRE ALARM ASSOCIATION YOUTH SCHOLARSHIP PROGRAM
• See page 469

PENNSYLVANIA FEDERATION OF DEMOCRATIC WOMEN INC.
http://www.pafedofdemwomen.org

PENNSYLVANIA FEDERATION OF DEMOCRATIC WOMEN INC. ANNUAL SCHOLARSHIP AWARDS
• See page 449

PENNSYLVANIA HIGHER EDUCATION ASSISTANCE AGENCY
http://www.pheaa.org/

BLIND OR DEAF BENEFICIARY GRANT PROGRAM
• See page 483

PENNSYLVANIA CHAFEE EDUCATION AND TRAINING GRANT PROGRAM
This federally funded program offers grants to Pennsylvania undergraduate students aging out of foster care who are attending an eligible post-secondary institution. The maximum award under this program for 2019-20 is $5,000; award maximum for the 2020-21 year has not yet been determined.

Award: Grant for use in freshman, sophomore, junior, or senior years; not renewable.

Eligibility Requirements: Applicant must be enrolled or expecting to enroll full- or part-time at a two-year or technical institution or university and resident of Oregon. Available to U.S. citizens.

Application Requirements: Application form. *Deadline:* December 31.

Contact: Keith New, Director of Public Relations
Phone: 800-692-7392
E-mail: knew@pheaa.org

PENNSYLVANIA STATE GRANT PROGRAM
Award for Pennsylvania residents attending an approved postsecondary institution as undergraduates in a program of at least two years duration. Renewable for up to eight semesters if applicants show continued need and academic progress. Must submit FAFSA. Number of awards granted varies annually.

Award: Grant for use in freshman, sophomore, junior, or senior years; renewable. *Amount:* $500–$800.

Eligibility Requirements: Applicant must be enrolled or expecting to enroll full- or part-time at a two-year or technical institution or university and resident of Oregon. Available to U.S. citizens.

Application Requirements: Application form, application form may be submitted online, financial need analysis. *Deadline:* August 15.

Contact: Keith New, Director of Public Relations
Pennsylvania Higher Education Assistance Agency
1200 North Seventh Street
Harrisburg, PA 17102-1444
Phone: 800-692-7392

POSTSECONDARY EDUCATIONAL GRATUITY PROGRAM
• See page 491

READY TO SUCCEED SCHOLARSHIP PROGRAM

RTSS provides scholarships to high academic achievers that, in combination with the Pennsylvania State Grant Program, offer a total award up to $2,000 for full-time and $1,000 for part-time students. The minimum award is $500. Awards can be used to cover tuition, books, fees, supplies, and living expenses. Students must be nominated by their post-secondary institution for participation in the program. Funding is limited for the program and awards are made on a first-come, first-served basis. The program, which is funded by the Pennsylvania General Assembly, provides awards to high-achieving students whose annual family income does not exceed $110,000.

Award: Scholarship for use in sophomore, junior, or senior years; not renewable. *Amount:* $500–$2000.

Eligibility Requirements: Applicant must be enrolled or expecting to enroll full- or part-time at a two-year or technical institution or university; resident of Oregon and studying in Pennsylvania.

Application Requirements: Application form, financial need analysis.

Contact: Keith New, Director of Public Relations
 Phone: 800-692-7392
 E-mail: knew@pheaa.org

PETER DOCTOR MEMORIAL INDIAN SCHOLARSHIP FOUNDATION INC.

PETER DOCTOR MEMORIAL INDIAN SCHOLARSHIP FOUNDATION INC.
• *See page 529*

PHILIPINO-AMERICAN ASSOCIATION OF NEW ENGLAND

http://www.pamas.org/

BLESSED LEON OF OUR LADY OF THE ROSARY AWARD
• *See page 530*

PAMAS RESTRICTED SCHOLARSHIP AWARD
• *See page 450*

RAVENSCROFT FAMILY AWARD
• *See page 530*

PINE TREE STATE 4-H CLUB FOUNDATION/4-H POSTSECONDARY SCHOLARSHIP

http://www.umaine.edu/

PARKER-LOVEJOY SCHOLARSHIP

One-time scholarship of $1000 is available to a graduating high school senior. Applicants must be residents of Maine.

Award: Scholarship for use in freshman year; not renewable. *Number:* 1. *Amount:* $1000.

Eligibility Requirements: Applicant must be high school student; planning to enroll or expecting to enroll full-time at a two-year or four-year institution or university and resident of Maine. Available to U.S. citizens.

Application Requirements: Application form. *Deadline:* March 14.

Contact: Angela Martin, Administrative Assistant
 Phone: 207-581-3739
 Fax: 207-581-1387
 E-mail: angela.martin@maine.edu

WAYNE S. RICH SCHOLARSHIP

Scholarship for an outstanding Maine or New Hampshire 4-H member for postsecondary study. Awarded to a Maine student in odd numbered years and a New Hampshire student in even numbered years.

Award: Scholarship for use in freshman year; not renewable. *Number:* 1. *Amount:* up to $1000.

Eligibility Requirements: Applicant must be high school student; planning to enroll or expecting to enroll full-time at a two-year or four-year institution or university and resident of Maine, New Hampshire. Available to U.S. citizens.

Application Requirements: Application form. *Deadline:* March 14.

Contact: Angela Martin, Administrative Assistant
 Phone: 207-581-3739
 Fax: 207-581-1387
 E-mail: angela.martin@maine.edu

POINTE PEST CONTROL

http://pointepestcontrol.net

GREEN PEST SERVICES SCHOLARSHIP

$750 scholarship available to graduating high school seniors and college freshman who are residents of D.C. and Maryland. Minimum 3.0 GPA required.

Award: Scholarship for use in freshman year; not renewable. *Number:* 4. *Amount:* $750.

Eligibility Requirements: Applicant must be enrolled or expecting to enroll full- or part-time at a two-year or four-year or technical institution or university; resident of Maryland and studying in District of Columbia. Available to U.S. citizens.

Application Requirements: Application form, financial need analysis. *Deadline:* April 14.

Contact: Jodelle Maglaya, Communications Manager
 E-mail: pr@pointepestcontrol.net

ILLINOIS SCHOLARSHIP

$750 scholarship available to graduating high school seniors and college freshman who are residents of Illinois. Minimum 3.0 GPA required.

Award: Scholarship for use in freshman year; not renewable. *Number:* 4. *Amount:* $750.

Eligibility Requirements: Applicant must be enrolled or expecting to enroll full- or part-time at a two-year or four-year or technical institution or university and resident of Illinois. Available to U.S. citizens.

Application Requirements: Application form, financial need analysis. *Deadline:* April 14.

Contact: Jodelle Maglaya, Communications Manager
 E-mail: pr@pointepestcontrol.net

VIRGINIA GREEN PEST SERVICES

$750 scholarship available to graduating high school seniors and college freshman who are residents of Virginia. Minimum 3.0 GPA required.

Award: Scholarship for use in freshman year; not renewable. *Number:* 4. *Amount:* $750.

Eligibility Requirements: Applicant must be enrolled or expecting to enroll full- or part-time at a two-year or four-year or technical institution or university and resident of Virginia. Available to U.S. citizens.

Application Requirements: Application form, financial need analysis. *Deadline:* April 14.

Contact: Jodelle Maglaya, Communications Manager
 E-mail: pr@pointepestcontrol.net

POLISH HERITAGE ASSOCIATION OF MARYLAND

http://www.pha-md.org/

POLISH HERITAGE SCHOLARSHIP
• *See page 530*

PORTUGUESE FOUNDATION INC.

https://www.facebook.com/pfict/

PORTUGUESE FOUNDATION SCHOLARSHIP PROGRAM

Eligibility: Student must be of Portuguese ancestry, resident of Connecticut, U.S. citizen or a permanent resident, applying for, or currently in college, full-time student in an undergraduate degree conferring program or a part-time student in a master's or doctorate program.

Award: Scholarship for use in freshman, sophomore, junior, senior, graduate, or postgraduate years; not renewable. *Number:* 1–4. *Amount:* $4000.

Eligibility Requirements: Applicant must be high school student; planning to enroll or expecting to enroll full- or part-time at a two-year or four-year or technical institution or university and resident of Connecticut. Available to U.S. citizens.

Application Requirements: Application form, community service, essay, personal photograph. *Deadline:* April 15.

Contact: Gabe Serrano
Portuguese Foundation Inc.
PO Box 331441
West Hartford, CT 06133-1441
Phone: 860-236-9350
E-mail: pfict90@gmail.com

PRESCOTT AUDUBON SOCIETY

http://prescottaudubon.org

ENVIRONMENTAL SCHOLARSHIP

A $1000 scholarship awarded to a degree-seeking, continuing college student who is passionate about the environment and/or conservation. Must be from Mohave or Yavapai County (home residence), and/or enrolled at a college operating in Yavapai or Mohave County, Arizona.

Award: Scholarship for use in freshman, sophomore, junior, or senior years; not renewable. *Number:* 1. *Amount:* $1000.

Eligibility Requirements: Applicant must be enrolled or expecting to enroll full- or part-time at a two-year or four-year institution or university and resident of Arizona. Available to U.S. citizens.

Application Requirements: Application form, essay. *Deadline:* December 8.

Contact: Scholarship Committee
E-mail: scholarship@prescottaudubon.org

PRIDE FOUNDATION

http://www.PrideFoundation.org/

PRIDE FOUNDATION SCHOLARSHIP PROGRAM

Pride Foundation provides scholarships to current and future lesbian, gay, bisexual, transgender, and straight-ally student leaders from Alaska, Idaho, Montana, Oregon, and Washington. Our scholarships cover most accredited post-secondary schools, including community colleges; 4-year public or private colleges and universities; trade or certificate programs; and graduate, medical, or law school.

Award: Scholarship for use in freshman, sophomore, junior, senior, graduate, or postgraduate years; not renewable. *Number:* 85–125. *Amount:* $1000–$24,000.

Eligibility Requirements: Applicant must be enrolled or expecting to enroll full- or part-time at a two-year or four-year or technical institution or university; resident of Alaska, Idaho, Montana, Oregon, Washington and must have an interest in LGBT issues. Available to U.S. and non-U.S. citizens.

Application Requirements: Application form, essay. *Deadline:* January 15.

Contact: Craig Williams, Office Manager
Pride Foundation
2014 E. Madison Street
Suite 300
Seattle, WA 98122
Phone: 206-323-3318
Fax: 206-323-1017
E-mail: scholarships@pridefoundation.org

PROJECT BEST SCHOLARSHIP FUND

http://www.projectbest.com/

PROJECT BEST SCHOLARSHIP
• *See page 451*

PUEBLO OF SAN JUAN, DEPARTMENT OF EDUCATION

OHKAY OWINGEH TRIBAL SCHOLARSHIP
• *See page 470*

POP'AY SCHOLARSHIP
• *See page 470*

REHABCENTER.NET

http://www.rehabcenter.net/

REHABCENTER.NET

RehabCenter.net is proud to award $10,000 in scholarships this year to three students, who share their vision on the dangers of drug and alcohol abuse. The scholarship award monies may only be used toward tuition, or expenses related to your education. There is no cost to enter the contest. Scholarship winners will be notified via email, and we'll make a public announcement of each winner within 30 days of the announcement. Three awards will be given to qualifying students who write the winning essays for first, second, and third places. We're looking for essays that describe the views of those passionate about drug and alcohol addiction and the effects it has on people, their health, society, and more. Maybe you have a loved one who has struggled with drug or alcohol abuse, or maybe you have struggled in the past, maybe you're currently struggling and trying to find the help you need. We welcome and encourage you to enter the contest, share your story, and profess your dedication to addiction awareness efforts. It's not necessary that you have a history with drug and alcohol addiction to enter the contest. The only thing necessary is your commitment to expressing your views for: 1. The ways in which addiction affects society today. 2. What can we do to reduce these effects, help people, and lessen the burden of addiction on society? Essay submissions should be no longer than 1,200 words. Applicants will be awarded based on the quality of the content, degree of originality, and personal style. Contest judges will be in search of essays that are not only structured and organized well, but with strong, logical arguments.

Award: Scholarship for use in freshman, sophomore, junior, senior, graduate, or postgraduate years; renewable. *Number:* 1–3. *Amount:* $3000–$6000.

Eligibility Requirements: Applicant must be age 18 and over; enrolled or expecting to enroll full-time at a two-year or four-year or technical institution or university and resident of Alabama, Alaska, Alberta, Arizona, Arkansas, California, Colorado, Connecticut, Delaware, District of Columbia, Florida, Georgia, Hawaii, Idaho, Illinois, Indiana, Iowa, Kansas, Kentucky, Louisiana, Maine, Manitoba, Maryland, Massachusetts, Michigan, Minnesota, Mississippi, Missouri, Montana, Nebraska, Nevada, New Brunswick, Newfoundland, New Hampshire, New Jersey, New Mexico, New York, North Carolina, North Dakota, Ohio, Oklahoma, Oregon, Pennsylvania, Prince Edward Island, Puerto Rico, Rhode Island, South Carolina, South Dakota, Tennessee, Texas, Utah, Vermont, Virginia, Washington, West Virginia, Wisconsin, Wyoming. Available to U.S. citizens.

Application Requirements: Essay. *Deadline:* continuous.

Contact: Joe Belfry, Outreach Coordinator
RehabCenter.net
483 Mandalay Avenue
Clearwater, FL 33767
Phone: 231-360-2055
E-mail: joe@rehabcenter.net

RENEE B. FISHER FOUNDATION

http://www.rbffoundation.org/

MILTON FISHER SCHOLARSHIP FOR INNOVATION AND CREATIVITY

The scholarship is open to exceptionally Innovative and Creative High School Juniors, Seniors and College Freshmen who are from Connecticut or the New York City metro area (and plan to attend or are attending college anywhere in the U.S.) OR from any part of the U.S. who plan to attend (or are attending) college in CT or NYC. Apply for this scholarship if you are a student who has solved an artistic, scientific, or technical problem in a new or unusual way OR a student who has come up with a distinctive solution to problems faced by your school, community or family

Award: Scholarship for use in freshman, sophomore, junior, or senior years; renewable. *Number:* 1–7. *Amount:* $250–$20,000.

Eligibility Requirements: Applicant must be enrolled or expecting to enroll full-time at a technical institution or university; resident of Alabama, Alberta, Arizona, British Columbia, California, Colorado, Connecticut, Delaware, District of Columbia, Florida, Guam, Hawaii, Idaho, Illinois, Indiana, Iowa, Kansas, Kentucky, Louisiana, Manitoba, Maryland, Massachusetts, Michigan, Minnesota, Mississippi, Missouri, Montana, Nebraska, New Brunswick, Newfoundland, New Hampshire, New Jersey, New Mexico, North Carolina, Nova Scotia, Ohio, Ontario, Oregon, Quebec, Saskatchewan, South Carolina, South Dakota, Tennessee, Texas, Utah, Vermont, Virginia, Washington, West Virginia, Wisconsin and studying in Alabama, Alaska, Arizona, Arkansas, California, Colorado, Connecticut, Delaware, District of Columbia, Florida, Georgia, Hawaii, Idaho, Illinois, Indiana, Iowa, Kansas, Kentucky, Louisiana, Maine, Maryland, Massachusetts, Michigan, Minnesota, Mississippi, Missouri, Montana, Nebraska, Nevada, New Hampshire, New Jersey, New Mexico, New York, North Carolina, North Dakota, Ohio, Oklahoma, Oregon, Pennsylvania, Rhode Island, South Carolina, South Dakota, Tennessee, Texas, Utah, Vermont, Virginia, Washington, West Virginia, Wisconsin, Wyoming. Available to U.S. and non-U.S. citizens.

Application Requirements: Application form, application form may be submitted online, essay, financial need analysis. *Deadline:* June 1.

Contact: Noah Barnett, Scholarship Assistant
Renee B. Fisher Foundation
70 Audubon Street
2nd Floor
New Haven, CT 06510
Phone: 203-7722788
E-mail: info@mfscholarship.org

RHODE ISLAND FOUNDATION

http://www.rifoundation.org/

ANDREW BELL SCHOLARSHIP

Scholarships to high school graduates pursuing a post-secondary education. Must demonstrate financial need.

Award: Scholarship for use in freshman, sophomore, junior, or senior years; not renewable.

Eligibility Requirements: Applicant must be enrolled or expecting to enroll full-time at a two-year or four-year or technical institution or university and resident of Rhode Island. Available to U.S. citizens.

Application Requirements: Application form, financial need analysis. *Deadline:* continuous.

Contact: Urban League of Rhode Island
Phone: 401-351-5000

ROBERT H. MOLLOHAN FAMILY CHARITABLE FOUNDATION, INC.

http://www.mollohanfoundation.org/

DR. ROBERTO F. CUNANAN MEMORIAL SCHOLARSHIP

The Dr. Roberto F. Cunanan Memorial Scholarship was created to honor Dr. Cunanan's energetic spirit and loving heart. This $1000 scholarship is awarded to a Bridgeport High School student who is enrolled or planning to enroll at a West Virginia college or university, and who is an active participant in both academics and athletics.

Award: Scholarship for use in freshman, sophomore, junior, or senior years; not renewable. *Number:* 1–60. *Amount:* $1000.

Eligibility Requirements: Applicant must be high school student; planning to enroll or expecting to enroll full-time at a four-year institution or university; resident of West Virginia and must have an interest in athletics/sports. Available to U.S. citizens.

Application Requirements: Application form, essay, recommendations or references, resume, test scores, transcript.

HELEN HOLT MOLLOHAN SCHOLARSHIP

The Helen Holt Mollohan Scholarship is a $1,000 scholarship offered to a West Virginia female who is currently attending, or a senior student who is planning to attend, Glenville State College.

Award: Scholarship for use in freshman, sophomore, junior, or senior years; renewable. *Amount:* $1000.

Eligibility Requirements: Applicant must be high school student; planning to enroll or expecting to enroll full-time at an institution or university; female; resident of Washington and studying in West Virginia. Available to U.S. citizens.

Application Requirements: Application form, essay. *Deadline:* March 31.

ROOTHBERT FUND INC.

http://www.roothbertfund.org/

ROOTHBERT FUND INC. SCHOLARSHIP

Scholarships are open to all in the United States regardless of sex, age, color, nationality or religious background. The award must be used in the following states: CT, DC, DE, MA, MD, ME, NC, NH, NJ, NY, OH, PA, RI, VA, VT, or WV. Preference will be given to those who can satisfy high scholastic requirements and are considering careers in education. The Fund seeks candidates who are motivated by spiritual values, and works to foster fellowship among them.

Award: Scholarship for use in freshman, sophomore, junior, senior, or graduate years; renewable. *Number:* 50–60. *Amount:* $2000–$3000.

Eligibility Requirements: Applicant must be enrolled or expecting to enroll full-time at a two-year or four-year or technical institution or university; resident of Connecticut, Delaware, District of Columbia, Maine, Maryland, Massachusetts, New Hampshire, New Jersey, New York, North Carolina, Ohio, Pennsylvania, Rhode Island, Virginia, West Virginia and studying in Connecticut, Delaware, District of Columbia, Maryland, Massachusetts, New Hampshire, New Jersey, New York, Ohio, Pennsylvania, Rhode Island, Vermont, Virginia, West Virginia. Available to U.S. and non-U.S. citizens.

Application Requirements: Application form, essay, financial need analysis, interview, personal photograph. *Deadline:* February 1.

Contact: Percy Preston, Office Manager
Roothbert Fund Inc.
475 Riverside Drive, Room 1622
New York, NY 10115
Phone: 212-870-3116
E-mail: office@roothbertfund.org

RYU FAMILY FOUNDATION, INC.

http://www.ryufoundation.org/

SEOL BONG SCHOLARSHIP
• *See page 531*

ST. ANDREW'S SOCIETY OF WASHINGTON, DC

http://www.saintandrewsociety.org/

ST. ANDREW'S SOCIETY OF WASHINGTON DC FOUNDERS' SCHOLARSHIP
• *See page 531*

ST. ANDREW'S SOCIETY OF WASHINGTON DC SCHOLARSHIPS
• *See page 531*

ST. CLAIRE REGIONAL MEDICAL CENTER

http://www.st-claire.org/

SR. MARY JEANNETTE WESS, S.N.D. SCHOLARSHIP
• *See page 470*

SALT RIVER ELECTRIC COOPERATIVE CORPORATION

http://www.srelectric.com/

SALT RIVER ELECTRIC SCHOLARSHIP PROGRAM

Scholarships available to Kentucky high school seniors who reside in Salt River Electric Service area or the primary residence of their parents/guardian is in the service area. Must be enrolled or plan to enroll in a postsecondary institution. Minimum GPA of 2.5 required. Must demonstrate financial need. Must submit a 500-word essay on a topic chosen from the list on the website. Application and additional information available on website http://www.srelectric.com.

Award: Scholarship for use in freshman year; not renewable. *Number:* 4. *Amount:* $1000.

Eligibility Requirements: Applicant must be high school student; planning to enroll or expecting to enroll full- or part-time at a two-year or four-year or technical institution or university and resident of Kentucky. Available to U.S. citizens.

Application Requirements: Application form, community service, essay, financial need analysis, personal photograph, transcript. *Deadline:* April 4.

Contact: Nicky Rapier, Scholarship Coordinator
Phone: 502-348-3931
Fax: 502-348-1993
E-mail: nickyr@srelectric.com

SALUTE TO EDUCATION, INC.

http://www.stescholarships.org/

SALUTE TO EDUCATION SCHOLARSHIP

Through a unique partnership with the community in South Florida, the Miami-Dade and Broward County Ford and Lincoln Dealers and Ford Motor Company have awarded over $3.7 million in scholarships to more than 4,300 deserving public and private high school seniors in both counties. Salute to Education, Inc., established in 1994, is a non-profit organization funded through dealership contributions, corporate support from Ford Motor Company and other fundraising events & efforts. Salute to Education is one of South Florida's largest private scholarship foundations. In June 2018, Salute to Education will be granting $168,000 in scholarships and brand new laptops to 112 graduating high school seniors in Miami-Dade and Broward County (South Florida). For more information about the scholarship and the application criteria, please visit the website at http://www.stescholarships.org/

Award: Scholarship for use in freshman year; not renewable. *Number:* 112. *Amount:* $1500.

Eligibility Requirements: Applicant must be high school student; age 16-19; planning to enroll or expecting to enroll full-time at a four-year institution or university and resident of Florida. Available to U.S. citizens.

Application Requirements: Application form, community service, essay, financial need analysis. *Deadline:* February 9.

Contact: Rebecca Klein, Program Coordinator
Salute to Education, Inc.
PO Box 833425
Miami, FL 33173
Phone: 305-799-6726
E-mail: steinfo@stescholarships.org

SALVADORAN AMERICAN LEADERSHIP AND EDUCATIONAL FUND

http://www.salef.org/

FULFILLING OUR DREAMS SCHOLARSHIP FUND

• *See page 531*

THE SAN DIEGO FOUNDATION

http://www.sdfoundation.org/students

COMMON SCHOLARSHIP APPLICATION

The Common Scholarship Application uses one online form to access more than 100 scholarships. Scholarships are available for graduating high school seniors, undergraduates, graduate students and adult re-entry students who are attending 2-year colleges, 4-year universities, trade/vocational schools, graduate, medical and professional schools and teaching credential programs. Scholarships range from $1000 to more than $5,000 and, depending on the scholarship, can pay for tuition, room and board, books, fees and other related expenses. Note that almost all of our scholarships require San Diego County residency.

Award: Scholarship for use in freshman, sophomore, junior, senior, or graduate years; renewable. *Number:* 900–1,100. *Amount:* $1000–$5000.

Eligibility Requirements: Applicant must be enrolled or expecting to enroll full- or part-time at a two-year or four-year or technical institution or university and resident of California. Available to U.S. citizens.

Application Requirements: Application form, application form may be submitted online (https://app.smarterselect.com/matching/444/start_page), essay, financial need analysis. *Deadline:* February 5.

Contact: Jessica Jasso, Scholarships Administrator
E-mail: scholarships@sdfoundation.org

SCHOLARSHIPOWL.COM

http://www.scholarshipowl.com

YOU DESERVE IT! SCHOLARSHIP

Everyone 16 years of age or older is eligible to apply who is enrolled or plans to be enrolled next semester to college. The scholarship renews every month and expires on the 29th of each month. See website for details. For an application, please go to https://scholarshipowl.com/awards/you-deserve-it-scholarship.

Award: Scholarship for use in freshman, sophomore, junior, senior, graduate, or postgraduate years; not renewable. *Number:* 12. *Amount:* $1000.

Eligibility Requirements: Applicant must be age 16 and over; enrolled or expecting to enroll full- or part-time at a two-year or four-year or technical institution or university; resident of Alabama, Alaska, Alberta, Arizona, Arkansas, British Columbia, California, Colorado, Connecticut, Delaware, District of Columbia, Florida, Georgia, Guam, Hawaii, Idaho, Illinois, Indiana, Iowa, Kansas, Kentucky, Louisiana, Maine, Manitoba, Maryland, Massachusetts, Michigan, Minnesota, Mississippi, Missouri, Montana, Nebraska, Nevada, New Brunswick, Newfoundland, New Hampshire, New Jersey, New Mexico, New York, North Carolina, North Dakota, Northwest Territories, Nova Scotia, Ohio, Oklahoma, Ontario, Oregon, Pennsylvania, Prince Edward Island, Puerto Rico, Quebec, Saskatchewan, South Carolina, South Dakota, Tennessee, Texas, Utah, Vermont, Virginia, Washington, West Virginia, Wisconsin, Wyoming, Yukon and studying in Alabama, Alaska, Alberta, Arizona, Arkansas, British Columbia, California, Colorado, Connecticut, Delaware, District of Columbia, Florida, Georgia, Guam, Hawaii, Idaho, Illinois, Indiana, Iowa, Kansas, Kentucky, Louisiana, Maine, Manitoba, Maryland, Massachusetts, Michigan, Minnesota, Mississippi, Missouri, Montana, Nebraska, Nevada, New Brunswick, Newfoundland, New Hampshire, New Jersey, New Mexico, New York, North Carolina, North Dakota, Northwest Territories, Nova Scotia, Ohio, Oklahoma, Oregon, Pennsylvania, Prince Edward Island, Puerto Rico, Quebec, Saskatchewan, South Carolina, South Dakota, Tennessee, Texas, Utah, Vermont, Virginia, Washington, West Virginia, Wisconsin, Wyoming, Yukon. Available to U.S. citizens.

Application Requirements: Application form. *Deadline:* continuous.

Contact: Mr. Mark Galea
ScholarshipOwl.com
210/2, Manwel Dimech Street
Slimena slm1050
MLT
E-mail: contact@scholarshipowl.com

SELECTBLINDS.COM

http://www.selectblinds.com

SELECTBLINDS.COM 2019 $1000 COLLEGE SCHOLARSHIP

We want your innovative design ideas on how to create the perfect space, for you or someone you want to design for. Could be a dorm room, bedroom, office, she-shed or man cave; go crazy. Your design plan must include: -Description of space you are designing -An inspiration/idea board for the space using actual samples from our site -Visuals of how you envision the "big reveal" — what will the completed space look like? -Show us your creativity and design process via video, photos or images, infographic, etc. Order up to 10 FREE samples to use in your project here. (No purchase required. We ship them to you for free, too.) Bonus points for including some creative ideas for using them when you're done! Along with your design project, the only other thing you need to send us is a cover letter describing who you are, what you're passionate about, the dreams/goals you're pursuing through your major in college — basically, why you think you should receive this scholarship.

Award: Scholarship for use in freshman, sophomore, junior, senior; graduate, or postgraduate years; not renewable. *Number:* 1. *Amount:* $1000.

Eligibility Requirements: Applicant must be high school student; planning to enroll or expecting to enroll full- or part-time at a two-year or four-year or technical institution or university; resident of Alberta, American Samoa, British Columbia, Federated States of Micronesia, Guam, Manitoba, Marshall Islands, New Brunswick, Newfoundland, Newfoundland and Labrador, Northern Mariana Islands, Northwest Territories, Nova Scotia, Nunavut, Ontario, Palau, Prince Edward Island, Puerto Rico, Quebec, Saskatchewan, Virgin Islands, Yukon and studying in Alberta, American Samoa, British Columbia, Federated States of Micronesia, Guam, Manitoba, Marshall Islands, New Brunswick, Newfoundland, Newfoundland and Labrador, Northern Mariana Islands, Northwest Territories, Nova Scotia, Nunavut, Ontario, Palau, Prince Edward Island, Puerto Rico, Quebec, Saskatchewan, Virgin Islands, Yukon. Available to U.S. citizens.

Application Requirements: Personal photograph. *Deadline:* June 14.

Contact: Mark Anderson, Digital Marketing Specialist
SelectBlinds.com
7420 S Kyrene Rd
Suite 119
Tempe, AZ 85283
Phone: 888-2571840
E-mail: scholarship@selectshops.com

SHELBY ENERGY COOPERATIVE

http://www.shelbyenergy.com/

SHELBY ENERGY COOPERATIVE SCHOLARSHIPS

Scholarships for high school seniors in Kentucky, whose parents or guardians are Shelby Energy members. Award based on financial need, academic excellence, community and school involvement, and essay.

Award: Scholarship for use in freshman year; not renewable. *Number:* 6. *Amount:* $1000.

Eligibility Requirements: Applicant must be high school student; planning to enroll or expecting to enroll full-time at a four-year institution or university and resident of Kentucky. Available to U.S. citizens.

Application Requirements: Application form, community service, financial need analysis. *Deadline:* March 10.

Contact: Ms. Candi Waford, Manager, Member Services
Shelby Energy Cooperative
620 Old Finchville Road
Shelbyville, KY 40065
Phone: 502-633-4420
Fax: 502-633-2387
E-mail: candi@shelbyenergy.com

SHERBENZ-RYAN EDUCATION FOUNDATION

http://www.scholarshipamerica.org

STERBENZ-RYAN SCHOLARSHIP

The Sterbenz-Ryan Scholarship is to assist students residing in Minnesota and Wisconsin who plan to enroll full-time in undergraduate study at an accredited two- or four- year college, university, or vocational-technical school in the United States for the entire upcoming academic year. Qualified applicants must be high school seniors, high school graduates or current postsecondary undergraduates residing in Minnesota or Wisconsin with a grade point average of 2.5 to 3.5 on a 4.0 scale, or its equivalent. Scholarships up to $15,000 are available for students attending four-year schools and up to $5,000 for students attending two-

year schools. Awards are renewable on the basis of satisfactory academic performance. Qualified students are encouraged to apply early!

Award: Scholarship for use in freshman, sophomore, or junior years; renewable. *Number:* 44. *Amount:* $5000–$15,000.

Eligibility Requirements: Applicant must be enrolled or expecting to enroll full-time at a two-year or four-year or technical institution or university and resident of Minnesota, Wisconsin. Available to U.S. citizens.

Application Requirements: Application form. *Deadline:* June 15.

Contact: Program Manager
Sherbenz-Ryan Education Foundation
Scholarship America
One Scholarship Way
St. Peter, MN 56082
Phone: 507-931-1682
E-mail: sterbenz-ryan@scholarshipamerica.org

SILICON VALLEY COMMUNITY FOUNDATION

http://www.siliconvalleycf.org

WINE GROUP SCHOLARSHIPS

The Wine Group Scholarship Fund was established in 2009 by a group of owners of The Wine Group LLC (TWG). Its mission is to provide the children, grandchildren or legal dependents of TWG's employees with financial assistance to pursue or continue postsecondary education in any area of study. Must be a child, legal dependent or grandchild of a full-time employee of TWG. Employee must have at least one year of continuous, full-time service with TWG as of Feb. 28 of the year in which the scholarship will be awarded. Employee must be employed with TWG at the time scholarship award selections are made. Children, legal dependents and grandchildren of current and former owners of TWG are not eligible. Scholarship winners of TWG Merit Scholarship will demonstrate a desirable mix of a high level of academic performance, strong communication and leadership skills, and participation in extra-curricular activities. Current graduating high school senior planning to attend a two- or four-year college/university program on a full-time (12 or more units/credits per quarter/semester) or part-time (a minimum of 6 to a maximum of 11 units/credits per quarter/semester) basis or current full-time or part-time college student. Minimum cumulative grade point average of 3.0 on a 4.0 scale. Scholarship winners of TWG Opportunity Scholarship will demonstrate a desirable mix of educational motivation, perseverance and demonstrated financial need or hardship. Applicant must be planning to enroll or currently enrolled in a two- or four-year college or vocational school on a part-time or full-time basis (as defined by the school of attendance). Must have demonstrated financial need or hardship with a maximum family income of $150,000.

Award: Scholarship for use in freshman, sophomore, junior, or senior years; not renewable. *Number:* 1–10. *Amount:* $1000–$10,000.

Eligibility Requirements: Applicant must be enrolled or expecting to enroll full- or part-time at a two-year or four-year or technical institution or university and resident of California. Available to U.S. citizens.

Application Requirements: Application form, application form may be submitted online (https://apply.siliconvalleycf.org/s_Login.jsp), essay, FAFSA, financial need analysis, recommendations or references, transcript. *Deadline:* March 4.

Contact: Scholarships Team
Silicon Valley Community Foundation
2440 West El Camino Real
Suite 300
Mountain View, CA 94040
Phone: 650-450-5487
E-mail: scholarships@siliconvalleycf.org

SIMON FOUNDATION FOR EDUCATION AND HOUSING

http://www.sfeh.org/

SIMON SCHOLARS PROGRAM

Scholarships are given to high school seniors at qualified high schools in Atlanta, GA, Santa Fe and Albuquerque, NM, and Anaheim, Santa Ana, Oceanside, or Garden Grove, CA. Deadlines vary for each region. For more details visit website http://www.simonscholars.org.

Award: Scholarship for use in freshman year; not renewable. *Number:* 100. *Amount:* $16,000.

Eligibility Requirements: Applicant must be high school student; planning to enroll or expecting to enroll full-time at a two-year or four-year institution or university and resident of California, Georgia, New Mexico. Available to U.S. citizens.

Application Requirements: Application form, community service, essay, financial need analysis, interview, recommendations or references, test scores, transcript. *Deadline:* varies.

Contact: Dr. Heather Huntley, Director of Partnerships and
      Development
    Phone: 949-270-3622
    Fax: 949-729-8072
    E-mail: heatherh@simonscholars.org

SOUTH CAROLINA COMMISSION ON HIGHER EDUCATION

http://www.che.sc.gov/

PALMETTO FELLOWS SCHOLARSHIP PROGRAM

Renewable award for qualified high school seniors in South Carolina to attend a four-year South Carolina institution. The scholarship must be applied directly towards the cost of attendance, less any other gift aid received.

Award: Scholarship for use in freshman year; renewable. *Number:* 4,846. *Amount:* $6700–$7500.

Eligibility Requirements: Applicant must be high school student; planning to enroll or expecting to enroll full-time at a four-year institution or university; resident of South Carolina and studying in South Carolina. Available to U.S. citizens.

Application Requirements: Application form, test scores, transcript. *Deadline:* December 15.

Contact: Dr. Karen Woodfaulk, Director of Student Services
    South Carolina Commission on Higher Education
    1333 Main Street, Suite 200
    Columbia, SC 29201
    Phone: 803-737-2244
    Fax: 803-737-3610
    E-mail: kwoodfaulk@che.sc.gov

SOUTH CAROLINA HOPE SCHOLARSHIP

A merit-based scholarship for eligible first-time entering freshman attending a four-year South Carolina institution. Minimum GPA of 3.0 required. Must be a resident of South Carolina.

Award: Scholarship for use in freshman year; not renewable. *Number:* 2,605. *Amount:* $2800.

Eligibility Requirements: Applicant must be high school student; planning to enroll or expecting to enroll full-time at a four-year institution or university; resident of South Carolina and studying in South Carolina. Available to U.S. citizens.

Application Requirements: Transcript. *Deadline:* continuous.

Contact: Gerrick Hampton, Scholarship Coordinator
    South Carolina Commission on Higher Education
    1333 Main Street, Suite 200
    Columbia, SC 29201
    Phone: 803-737-4544
    Fax: 803-737-3610
    E-mail: ghampton@che.sc.gov

SOUTH CAROLINA NEED-BASED GRANTS PROGRAM

Award based on FAFSA. A student may receive up to $2500 annually for full-time and up to $1250 annually for part-time study. The grant must be applied directly towards the cost of college attendance for a maximum of eight full-time equivalent terms.

Award: Grant for use in freshman, sophomore, junior, senior, or graduate years; renewable. *Number:* 1–26,730. *Amount:* $1250–$2500.

Eligibility Requirements: Applicant must be enrolled or expecting to enroll full- or part-time at a two-year or four-year or technical institution or university; resident of South Carolina and studying in South Carolina. Available to U.S. citizens.

Application Requirements: Application form, financial need analysis. *Deadline:* continuous.

Contact: Dr. Karen Woodfaulk, Director of Student Service
    South Carolina Commission on Higher Education
    1333 Main Street, Suite 200
    Columbia, SC 29201
    Phone: 803-737-2244
    Fax: 803-737-2297
    E-mail: kwoodfaulk@che.sc.gov

SOUTH CAROLINA NURSES FOUNDATION

http://www.scnursesfoundation.org/

NURSES CARE SCHOLARSHIP

The Nurses Care Specialty License Plate Initiative was created in 2002 to provide an opportunity for nurses and the supporters of nursing to make a contribution to the profession and to increase the public's awareness of the contribution of nurses. "Nurses Care" specialty license plates are available from the Department of Motor Vehicles. The proceeds are used to fund both graduate and undergraduate scholarships.

Award: Scholarship for use in freshman, sophomore, junior, senior, or graduate years; renewable.

Eligibility Requirements: Applicant must be enrolled or expecting to enroll at an institution or university and resident of Saskatchewan. Available to U.S. citizens.

Application Requirements: Application form, application form may be submitted online, financial need analysis. *Deadline:* May 19.

VIRGINIA C. PHILLIPS SCHOLARSHIPS

The Virginia C. Phillips Scholarship Fund was established in 1979 to honor Ms. Phillips, a nursing leader in SC whose contributions to nursing and to public health nursing are many and varied. She held numerous leadership positions in SCDHEC including State Director of Public Health Nursing from 1972-1979. She also served as President of SCNA from 1963-1965. A scholarship is awarded to an undergraduate and a graduate nursing student committed to pursuing a career in community health nursing/public health nursing. For more information about these scholarships, please contact the Office of Public Health Nursing at SCDHEC: (803) 989-0801.

Award: Scholarship for use in freshman, sophomore, junior, senior, or graduate years; renewable.

Eligibility Requirements: Applicant must be enrolled or expecting to enroll at an institution or university and resident of Saskatchewan. Available to U.S. citizens.

Application Requirements: Application form, application form may be submitted online, financial need analysis. *Deadline:* May 19.

SOUTH CAROLINA STATE EMPLOYEES ASSOCIATION

http://www.scsea.com

ANNE A. AGNEW SCHOLARSHIP

Scholarships available to SCSEA members or their relatives, with priority given to Richland-Lexington Chapter members, spouses and/or children of Chapter members. The awardees must be currently enrolled at a recognized and accredited college, university, trade school or other institution of higher learning and must have completed at least one academic semester/quarter.

Award: Scholarship for use in sophomore, junior, senior, graduate, or postgraduate years; not renewable. *Number:* 3. *Amount:* $1000.

Eligibility Requirements: Applicant must be enrolled or expecting to enroll full-time at a two-year or four-year institution or university and resident of South Carolina. Available to U.S. citizens.

Application Requirements: Application form, essay, recommendations or references, transcript. *Deadline:* April 31.

Contact: Ms. OunJanice McClam, Office Manager
    South Carolina State Employees Association
    PO Box 8447
    Columbia, SC 29202-8447
    Phone: 803-765-0680
    Fax: 803-779-6558
    E-mail: omcclam@scsea.com

SOUTH DAKOTA BOARD OF REGENTS

http://www.sdbor.edu/

SOUTH DAKOTA OPPORTUNITY SCHOLARSHIP

Renewable scholarship may be worth up to $6200 over four years to students who take a rigorous college-prep curriculum while in high school and stay in the state for their postsecondary education.

Award: Scholarship for use in freshman, sophomore, junior, or senior years; renewable. *Number:* 1,000–4,100. *Amount:* $1300–$2300.

Eligibility Requirements: Applicant must be high school student; planning to enroll or expecting to enroll full-time at a two-year or four-year or technical institution or university; resident of South Dakota and studying in South Dakota. Available to U.S. citizens.

Application Requirements: Application form. *Deadline:* September 1.

Contact: Kerri Richards, Student Services Coordinator
South Dakota Board of Regents
306 East Capitol, Suite 200
Pierre, SD 57501
Phone: 605-773-3455
E-mail: info@sdbor.edu

SOUTH FLORIDA FAIR AND PALM BEACH COUNTY EXPOSITIONS INC.

http://www.southfloridafair.com/

SOUTH FLORIDA FAIR COLLEGE SCHOLARSHIP

Renewable award of up to $4000 for students who might not otherwise have an opportunity to pursue a college education. Must be a permanent resident of Florida.

Award: Scholarship for use in freshman, sophomore, junior, or senior years; renewable. *Number:* 10. *Amount:* $1000–$4000.

Eligibility Requirements: Applicant must be enrolled or expecting to enroll full- or part-time at a four-year institution or university and resident of Florida. Available to U.S. and non-U.S. citizens.

Application Requirements: Application form, community service, essay, recommendations or references, self-addressed stamped envelope with application, test scores, transcript. *Deadline:* October 15.

Contact: Scholarship Committee
South Florida Fair and Palm Beach County Expositions Inc.
PO Box 210367
West Palm Beach, FL 33421-0367
Phone: 561-790-5245

STATE EMPLOYEES ASSOCIATION OF NORTH CAROLINA (SEANC)

http://www.seanc.org/

STATE EMPLOYEES ASSOCIATION OF NORTH CAROLINA (SEANC) SCHOLARSHIPS

Scholarships available to SEANC members, their spouses and dependents seeking postsecondary education. Awarded in three categories: based on academic merit, financial need, and awards for SEANC members only. For application and more information visit http://www.seanc.org/.

Award: Scholarship for use in freshman, sophomore, junior, or senior years; not renewable. *Number:* 47. *Amount:* $500–$1000.

Eligibility Requirements: Applicant must be enrolled or expecting to enroll full-time at a two-year or four-year or technical institution or university and resident of North Carolina. Available to U.S. citizens.

Application Requirements: Application form, financial need analysis. *Deadline:* April 15.

Contact: Renee Vaughan
Phone: 919-833-6436

STEPHEN T. MARCHELLO SCHOLARSHIP FOUNDATION

http://www.stmfoundation.org/

A LEGACY OF HOPE SCHOLARSHIPS FOR SURVIVORS OF CHILDHOOD CANCER

Scholarship of up to $2,000 of a one time grant for postsecondary undergraduate education. Applicant must be a survivor of childhood cancer. Must submit a letter from doctor, clinic, or hospital where cancer treatment was received. Residents of CO and MT are eligible. Must be U.S. citizen. Minimum 2.5 GPA required.

Award: Scholarship for use in freshman year; not renewable. *Number:* 1–10. *Amount:* $200–$1500.

Eligibility Requirements: Applicant must be high school student; age 17-20; planning to enroll or expecting to enroll full- or part-time at a two-year or four-year or technical institution or university and resident of Colorado, Montana. Available to U.S. citizens.

Application Requirements: Application form, essay. *Deadline:* March 15.

Contact: Mr. Mario Marchello, Secretary
Stephen T. Marchello Scholarship Foundation
1170 East Long Place
Centennial, CO 80122
Phone: 303-886-5018
E-mail: stmfoundation@hotmail.com

STEVEN TITUS & ASSOCIATES, P.C.

http://www.steventituslaw.com/

FIND YOUR PATH SCHOLARSHIP 2019

This scholarship is open to graduating high school seniors and current undergraduate college students with a 3.0 or higher GPA who are bettering themselves through education. The application includes an essay section. Tell us about a time in your life when you were facing hardship and someone helped you. Who was this person? Why and how did they help you? What lessons did you learn from this experience? The essay is to be 500-1000 words. The winner will be announced on June 25th, 2019, and the application must be submitted no later than 11:59 on May 28th, 2019. Additional information and applications can be found on our website: http://www.steventituslaw.com/scholarship

Award: Scholarship for use in freshman, sophomore, junior, or senior years; not renewable. *Number:* 1. *Amount:* $500.

Eligibility Requirements: Applicant must be enrolled or expecting to enroll full- or part-time at a two-year or four-year institution or university and resident of Wyoming. Available to U.S. citizens.

Application Requirements: Application form, application form may be submitted online (https://www.steventituslaw.com/scholarship/application.php), essay. *Deadline:* May 28.

Contact: Daniel Mateo
Steven Titus & Associates, P.C.
65 N Raymond Ave #230
Pasadena, CA 91103
Phone: 323-254-1510
E-mail: DMateo@slsconsulting.com

SWISS BENEVOLENT SOCIETY

http://www.sbssf.com/

SWISS BENEVOLENT SOCIETY OF SAN FRANCISCO SCHOLARSHIPS

• See page 533

SWISS BENEVOLENT SOCIETY OF CHICAGO

http://www.sbschicago.org/

SWISS BENEVOLENT SOCIETY OF CHICAGO SCHOLARSHIPS

• See page 533

SWISS BENEVOLENT SOCIETY OF NEW YORK

http://www.sbsny.org/

PELLEGRINI SCHOLARSHIP GRANTS
• *See page 533*

TAMPA BAY TIMES FUND, INC.

http://company.tampabay.com:2052/times-fund/scholarships

BARNES SCHOLARSHIP

The Barnes Scholarships were established in 1999 to help college-bound teens who are high academic achievers, who have overcome significant obstacles in their lives and who have financial need. Each of the four winners is eligible to receive up to $15,000 per year for four years to attend any nationally accredited non-profit college or university. The scholarship may be used to pay for expenses related to the cost of college attendance. The students must be enrolled full-time and remain in good academic standing to continue to receive the scholarship. High school seniors from these Florida counties are eligible to apply: Hernando, Pasco, Pinellas, Hillsborough. Application period: August 1 to October 21. On-line applications only.

Award: Scholarship for use in freshman, sophomore, junior, or senior years; renewable. *Number:* 1–4. *Amount:* $1000–$15,000.

Eligibility Requirements: Applicant must be high school student; age 17-19; planning to enroll or expecting to enroll full-time at a four-year institution or university; single and resident of Florida. Available to U.S. citizens.

Application Requirements: Application form, community service, essay, interview. *Deadline:* October 21.

Contact: Ms. Nancy Waclawek, Scholarship Administrator
Tampa Bay Times Fund, Inc.
PO Box 1121
St. Petersburg, FL 33731-1121
E-mail: tbtschls@gmail.com

TAMPA BAY TIMES FUND BARNES SCHOLARSHIP

Four high school seniors from the Tampa Bay Times' audience area are selected each year and each are awarded up to $15,000 annually for four years to attend any nationally accredited college or university. Criteria for the scholarship include high academic achievement, financial need, evidence of having overcome significant obstacles in life, and community service.

Award: Scholarship for use in freshman, sophomore, junior, or senior years; renewable. *Number:* 4. *Amount:* $15,000.

Eligibility Requirements: Applicant must be high school student; age 18-22; planning to enroll or expecting to enroll full-time at a four-year institution or university; single and resident of Florida. Available to U.S. citizens.

Application Requirements: Application form, community service, essay, financial need analysis, interview. *Deadline:* October 15.

Contact: Nancy Waclawek, Scholarship Administrator
Phone: 813-340-4125
E-mail: tbtschls@gmail.com

TELIOS LAW PLLC

http://telioslaw.com

TELIOS LAW EXCELSIOR SCHOLARSHIP

The Telios Law Excelsior Scholarship application is open to any high school student or recent high school graduate who is a Colorado resident and will be enrolled full-time for the 2018-2019 school year as a freshman or sophomore at a college or university that has an emphasis on spiritual formation in the Christian faith. For complete information, please visit http://telioslaw.com/scholarships. Excelsior is a Latin word meaning "ever higher". It evokes the pursuit of excellence (think of the inspiring passages of Philippians 3:1-16 and 4:8) and is particularly fitting given the mountain regions of Colorado. Whether it be climbing a Fourteener, studying a 500-page treatise, writing a novel, creating a work of art, performing at a recital, or leading a team to victory, the desire to climb higher, think deeper, run faster, write better, or improve any other laudable skill is summed up in the phrase "ever higher". Telios Law believes that this desire to excel can be used as a gift to benefit and love those around us. Telios Law also believes that striving to excel simply and only for one's own sake is vanity. We seek to excel in the work we do while also encouraging and supporting that attitude in others with the Telios Law Excelsior Scholarship.

Award: Scholarship for use in freshman, sophomore, junior, or senior years; renewable. *Number:* 1. *Amount:* $1000.

Eligibility Requirements: Applicant must be enrolled or expecting to enroll full-time at a two-year or four-year institution or university and resident of Colorado.

Application Requirements: Application form, essay. *Deadline:* January 15.

Contact: Mr. Joshua Romero, Outreach Coordinator
Telios Law PLLC
PO Box 3488
Monument, CO 80132
Phone: 855-748-4201
E-mail: tell@telioslaw.com

TERRY FOUNDATION

www.terryfoundation.org/

TERRY FOUNDATION TRADITIONAL SCHOLARSHIP

Scholarships to Texas high school seniors who have been admitted to: University of Texas at Austin; Texas A&M University at College Station; University of Houston; Texas State University; University of Texas at San Antonio; University of Texas at Dallas; University of North Texas; Texas Tech University; Texas Woman's University; Texas A&M University at Galveston; Sam Houston State University; University of Texas at El Paso; or University of Texas at Arlington. Scholarship is based upon leadership potential and character, scholastic record and ability, and financial need.

Award: Scholarship for use in freshman, sophomore, junior, or senior years; renewable. *Number:* 238.

Eligibility Requirements: Applicant must be high school student; planning to enroll or expecting to enroll full-time at a four-year institution or university; resident of Texas; studying in Texas and must have an interest in leadership. Available to U.S. citizens.

Application Requirements: Application form, application form may be submitted online, essay, financial need analysis, interview, recommendations or references, transcript. *Deadline:* continuous.

Contact: Jodie Koszegi, Scholarship Program Director
Terry Foundation
3104 Edloe, Suite 205
Houston, TX 77027
Phone: 713-552-0002
Fax: 713-622-6352
E-mail: jkoszegi@terryfoundation.org

TERRY FOUNDATION TRANSFER SCHOLARSHIP

Scholarships for non-traditional Texas students who are transferring from a junior or community college to one of our 13 Terry-affiliated Texas public universities: University of Texas at Austin; Texas A&M University at College Station; University of Houston; Texas State University; University of Texas at San Antonio; University of Texas at Dallas; University of North Texas; Texas Tech University; Texas Woman's University; Texas A&M University at Galveston; Sam Houston State University; University of Texas at El Paso; University of Texas at Arlington. Scholarship is based upon leadership potential and character; scholastic record and ability; and financial need.

Award: Scholarship for use in sophomore, junior, or senior years; renewable. *Number:* 84. *Amount:* $13,500.

Eligibility Requirements: Applicant must be age 20 and over; enrolled or expecting to enroll full-time at a four-year institution or university; resident of Texas; studying in Texas and must have an interest in leadership. Available to U.S. citizens.

Application Requirements: Application form, application form may be submitted online, essay, financial need analysis, interview, transcript. *Deadline:* continuous.

Contact: Jodie Koszegi, Scholarship Program Director
Terry Foundation
3104 Edloe, Suite 205
Houston, TX 77027
Phone: 713-552-0002
Fax: 713-622-6352
E-mail: jkoszegi@terryfoundation.org

TERRY FOX HUMANITARIAN AWARD

http://terryfoxawards.ca/

TERRY FOX HUMANITARIAN AWARD
• *See page 470*

TEXAS 4-H YOUTH DEVELOPMENT FOUNDATION

http://texas4hfoundation.org/

TEXAS 4-H OPPORTUNITY SCHOLARSHIP

Renewable award for Texas 4-H members to attend a Texas college or university. Minimum GPA of 2.5 required. Must attend full-time.

Award: Scholarship for use in freshman, sophomore, junior, or senior years; renewable. *Amount:* $3000.

Eligibility Requirements: Applicant must be enrolled or expecting to enroll full-time at a two-year or four-year or technical institution; resident of Texas; studying in Texas and must have an interest in animal/agricultural competition. Available to U.S. citizens.

Application Requirements: Application form, essay, financial need analysis, interview.

Contact: Jim Reeves, Executive Director
Phone: 979-845-1213
Fax: 979-845-6495
E-mail: jereeves@ag.tamu.edu

TEXAS AFL-CIO

http://www.texasaflcio.org/

TEXAS AFL-CIO SCHOLARSHIP PROGRAM
• *See page 455*

TEXAS ASSOCIATION OF DEVELOPING COLLEGES

http://www.txadc.org

THE URBAN SCHOLARSHIPS FUND

Eligibility - United States citizen or eligible non-citizen (permanent resident card I-551 front and back copy) Texas resident, graduate of high school from 29 urban cities: Abilene, Amarillo, Arlington, Austin, Beaumont, Brownsville, Carrollton, Corpus Christi, Dallas, Denton, El Paso, Fort Worth, Frisco, Garland, Grand Prairie, Houston, Irving, Killeen, Laredo, Lubbock, McAllen, McKinney, Mesquite, Midland, Pasadena, Plano, San Antonio, Waco and Wichita Falls

Award: Scholarship for use in freshman, sophomore, junior, or senior years; not renewable. *Number:* 450–500. *Amount:* $700–$1000.

Eligibility Requirements: Applicant must be age 16-65; enrolled or expecting to enroll full-time at a two-year or four-year or technical institution or university and resident of Texas. Available to U.S. citizens.

Application Requirements: Financial need analysis. *Deadline:* July 10.

Contact: Ms. Janice Jackson, Office Programs Administrator
Texas Association of Developing Colleges
1140 Empire Central Drive 550
Dallas, TX 75247
Phone: 214-630-2511
E-mail: janice.jackson@txadc.org

TEXAS BLACK BAPTIST SCHOLARSHIP COMMITTEE

http://www.bgct.org/

TEXAS BLACK BAPTIST SCHOLARSHIP
• *See page 534*

TEXAS HIGHER EDUCATION COORDINATING BOARD

http://www.collegeforalltexans.com/

TEXAS EDUCATIONAL OPPORTUNITY GRANT (TEOG)

Provides grant aid to students with financial need attending public two-year colleges. For initial award, student must be enrolled at least half-time and awarded in the first 30 hours (or its equivalent) of an associate's degree or certificate program (excluding credits for dual enrollment or by examination). For renewal award, student must also maintain a minimum overall GPA of 2.50 and successfully complete a minimum of 75% of classes attempted during the school year.

Award: Grant for use in freshman, sophomore, junior, or senior years; renewable. *Amount:* $1–$5876.

Eligibility Requirements: Applicant must be enrolled or expecting to enroll full- or part-time at a two-year institution; resident of Tennessee and studying in Texas. Available to U.S. citizens.

Application Requirements: Financial need analysis. *Deadline:* continuous.

Contact: Student Financial Aid Programs
Phone: 888-311-8881

TOP 10% SCHOLARSHIP PROGRAM

Funding for Initial Awards is not available for the 2018-19 academic year and only renewal award students are eligible for this program. Renewal students must demonstrate financial need and complete the FAFSA by the state priority deadline of March 15. Renewal students must maintain a minimum overall GPA of 3.25, successfully complete at least 30 SCH each year, and successfully complete at least 75% of the hours attempted each year.

Award: Scholarship for use in junior or senior years; renewable. *Amount:* up to $2000.

Eligibility Requirements: Applicant must be enrolled or expecting to enroll full-time at a two-year or four-year institution or university; resident of Texas and studying in Texas. Available to U.S. citizens.

Application Requirements: Financial need analysis.

Contact: Student Financial Aid Programs
Phone: 888-311-8881

TOWARD EXCELLENCE, ACCESS, AND SUCCESS (TEXAS) GRANT

Renewable aid for students enrolled at least three-quarter time in a public four-year college or university in Texas within sixteen months of graduation from high school. Must demonstrate financial need and have completed the Foundation, Recommended, or DAP Curriculum in high school. For renewal awards, must also maintain a minimum GPA of 2.5 and complete a minimum of 24 SCH's each year. Amount of award is determined by the financial aid office of each school. Priority FAFSA completion deadline is January 15. Contact the college/university financial aid office for additional eligibility information.

Award: Grant for use in freshman, sophomore, junior, or senior years; renewable. *Amount:* $1–$4896.

Eligibility Requirements: Applicant must be enrolled or expecting to enroll full- or part-time at an institution or university; resident of Tennessee and studying in Texas. Available to U.S. citizens.

Application Requirements: Financial need analysis. *Deadline:* January 15.

Contact: Student Financial Aid Programs
Phone: 888-311-8881

TEXAS OUTDOOR WRITERS ASSOCIATION

http://www.towa.org/

TEXAS OUTDOOR WRITERS ASSOCIATION SCHOLARSHIP

Annual merit award available to students attending an accredited Texas college or university preparing for a career which would incorporate communications skills about the outdoors, environmental conservation, or resource management. Minimum 2.5 GPA required. Submit writing/photo samples.

Award: Scholarship for use in freshman, sophomore, junior, senior, or graduate years; not renewable. *Number:* 1–2. *Amount:* $2000.

Eligibility Requirements: Applicant must be enrolled or expecting to enroll full- or part-time at a two-year or four-year institution or university; resident of Texas; studying in Texas and must have an interest in writing. Available to U.S. citizens.

Application Requirements: Application form, application form may be submitted online, essay, portfolio, recommendations or references, transcript. *Deadline:* February 1.

Contact: Judy Mills, Scholarship Co-Chair
Texas Outdoor Writers Association
14871 Estrellita
Houston, TX 77060
Phone: 281-448-5811
E-mail: offtheroad.mills@earthlink.net

TEXAS SOCIETY, MILITARY ORDER OF THE STARS AND BARS

http://www.texasmosb.com/

TEXAS SOCIETY, MILITARY ORDER OF THE STARS AND BARS SCHOLARSHIP

The award is given on the basis of scholastics, extracurricular activities, recommendations, and financial need. Applicants must prove genealogical descent or blood relationship to a Confederate Officer, or government official of the Confederacy. Application and complete rules may be found on the Texas Society, Military Order of the Stars and Bars website.

Award: Scholarship for use in freshman, sophomore, junior, or senior years; not renewable. *Number:* 1. *Amount:* $500–$500.

Eligibility Requirements: Applicant must be enrolled or expecting to enroll full- or part-time at a two-year or four-year or technical institution or university and resident of Texas. Available to U.S. citizens.

Application Requirements: Application form, community service, essay, financial need analysis, genealogical proof, recommendations or references, transcript. *Deadline:* March 1.

Contact: Mr. James Templin, Texas Society Scholarship Chairman
Texas Society, Military Order of the Stars and Bars
2500 Woodlawn Drive
Ennis, TX 75119-7644
Phone: 972-878-2752
E-mail: hjtemp@sbcglobal.net

TEXAS TENNIS FOUNDATION

http://www.texastennisfoundation.com/

TEXAS TENNIS FOUNDATION SCHOLARSHIPS AND ENDOWMENTS

College scholarships for highly recommended students residing in Texas, with an interest in tennis. Financial need is considered. Must be between the ages of 17 and 19. Refer to website for details http://www.texastennisfoundation.com/web90/scholarships/tenniscampsscholarships.asp.

Award: Scholarship for use in freshman, sophomore, junior, or senior years; not renewable. *Number:* 10. *Amount:* $1000.

Eligibility Requirements: Applicant must be age 17-19; enrolled or expecting to enroll full-time at a two-year or four-year or technical institution or university; resident of Texas and must have an interest in athletics/sports. Available to U.S. citizens.

Application Requirements: Application form, copy of parent or guardian's federal tax return, essay, financial need analysis, personal photograph, recommendations or references, test scores, transcript. *Deadline:* April 15.

Contact: Van Barry, Executive Director
Phone: 512-443-1334 Ext. 201
Fax: 512-443-4748
E-mail: vbarry@texas.usta.com

THEODORE R. AND VIVIAN M. JOHNSON SCHOLARSHIP FOUNDATION INC.

http://www.jsf.bz/

THEODORE R. AND VIVIAN M. JOHNSON SCHOLARSHIP PROGRAM FOR CHILDREN OF UPS EMPLOYEES OR UPS RETIREES

• See page 459

TIDEWATER SCHOLARSHIP FOUNDATION

http://www.accesscollege.org/

ACCESS SCHOLARSHIP/LAST DOLLAR AWARD

A renewable scholarship of $500 to $1000 for the undergraduates participating in Norfolk, Portsmouth, and Virginia Beach, Virginia secure scholarships and financial aid for college.

Award: Scholarship for use in freshman year; renewable. *Amount:* $500–$1000.

Eligibility Requirements: Applicant must be high school student; planning to enroll or expecting to enroll full-time at a two-year or four-year institution or university and resident of Virginia. Available to U.S. citizens.

Application Requirements: Application form, financial need analysis. *Deadline:* May 1.

Contact: Bonnie Sutton, President and Chief Executive Officer
Phone: 757-962-6113
Fax: 757-962-7314
E-mail: bsutton@accesscollege.org

TIGER WOODS FOUNDATION

http://www.tigerwoodsfoundation.org/

ALFRED "TUP" HOLMES MEMORIAL SCHOLARSHIP

Given yearly to one worthy Atlanta metropolitan area graduating high school senior who has displayed high moral character while demonstrating leadership potential and academic excellence. Must be U.S. citizen. Minimum 3.0 GPA required.

Award: Scholarship for use in freshman year; not renewable. *Number:* 1. *Amount:* $2500.

Eligibility Requirements: Applicant must be high school student; planning to enroll or expecting to enroll full-time at a two-year or four-year institution or university and resident of Georgia. Available to U.S. citizens.

Application Requirements: Application form, community service, essay, recommendations or references, test scores, transcript. *Deadline:* April 1.

Contact: Michelle Kim, Scholarship and Grant Coordinator
Phone: 949-725-3003
Fax: 949-725-3002
E-mail: grants@tigerwoodsfoundation.org

TORTOISE CAPITAL ADVISORS, LLC

http://www.tortoiseadvisors.com

TORTOISE YOUNG ENTREPRENEURS SCHOLARSHIP

The program is designed to give deserving students a leg up in their academic endeavors. In turn, we hope their educational experience will help them mold an entrepreneurial mindset that helps them conceive or support firms that create innovative products, processes and solutions. To be eligible, applicants must: be a permanent resident of Kansas or Missouri who is enrolled or plans to enroll in a full-time undergraduate course of study towards a Bachelor's degree, or; be a non-resident of either state who is enrolled or plans to enroll as a full-time student in a four-year Bachelor's program at a Kansas or Missouri accredited university or college, and; have a minimum 3.3 grade-point average (on a 4.0 scale or equivalent) and a minimum ACT score of 24 or minimum SAT score of 1680 (includes writing section).

Award: Scholarship for use in freshman, sophomore, junior, or senior years; not renewable. *Number:* 3. *Amount:* $1000–$3000.

Eligibility Requirements: Applicant must be enrolled or expecting to enroll full-time at a four-year institution or university; resident of Kansas, Missouri and studying in Kansas, Missouri. Available to U.S. citizens.

Application Requirements: Application form, application form may be submitted online (http://www.tortoiseadvisors.com/scholarship), community service, essay, recommendations or references, test scores, transcript. *Deadline:* February 28.

Contact: Ben Fraser, Scholarship Coordinator
E-mail: scholarship@tortoiseadvisors.com

TOWNSHIP OFFICIALS OF ILLINOIS

http://www.toi.org/

TOWNSHIP OFFICIALS OF ILLINOIS SCHOLARSHIP PROGRAM

The scholarships are awarded to graduating Illinois high school seniors who have a B average or above, have demonstrated an active interest in school activities, who have submitted an essay on "The Importance of Township Government", high school transcript, and letters of recommendation. Students must attend Illinois institutions, either four-year or junior colleges. Must be full-time student. Must complete an interview with a current township official.

Award: Scholarship for use in freshman year; not renewable. *Number:* 7. *Amount:* $1500.

Eligibility Requirements: Applicant must be high school student; planning to enroll or expecting to enroll full-time at a two-year or four-year institution or university; resident of Illinois and studying in Illinois. Available to U.S. citizens.

Application Requirements: Application form, essay, interview. *Deadline:* March 1.

Contact: Amy Rourke, Associate Editor
Township Officials of Illinois
3217 Northfield Drive
Springfield, IL 62701-1804
Phone: 217-744-2212
E-mail: amy@toi.org

TRIANGLE COMMUNITY FOUNDATION

http://www.trianglecf.org

GEORGE AND MARY NEWTON SCHOLARSHIP
• *See page 459*

TWO TEN FOOTWEAR FOUNDATION

http://www.twoten.org/

CLASSIC SCHOLARSHIPS

Two Ten offers footwear employees and their families higher education scholarships to two or four year undergraduate programs based on financial need, academic ability and personal promise. This is a need-based scholarship.

Award: Scholarship for use in freshman, sophomore, junior, or senior years; renewable. *Number:* 300–350. *Amount:* $2500–$5000.

Eligibility Requirements: Applicant must be enrolled or expecting to enroll full- or part-time at a two-year or four-year or technical institution or university; resident of Alabama, Alaska, Arizona, Arkansas, California, Colorado, Connecticut, Delaware, Florida, Georgia, Hawaii, Idaho, Illinois, Indiana, Iowa, Kansas, Kentucky, Louisiana, Maine, Maryland, Massachusetts, Michigan, Minnesota, Mississippi, Missouri, Montana, Nebraska, Nevada, New Hampshire, New Jersey, New Mexico, New York, North Carolina, North Dakota, Ohio, Oklahoma, Oregon, Pennsylvania, Puerto Rico, Rhode Island, South Carolina, South Dakota, Tennessee, Texas, Utah, Vermont, Virginia, Washington, West Virginia, Wisconsin, Wyoming and studying in Alabama, Alaska, Arizona, Arkansas, California, Colorado, Connecticut, Delaware, Florida,

Georgia, Hawaii, Idaho, Illinois, Indiana, Iowa, Kansas, Kentucky, Louisiana, Maine, Maryland, Massachusetts, Michigan, Minnesota, Mississippi, Missouri, Montana, Nebraska, Nevada, New Hampshire, New Jersey, New Mexico, New York, North Carolina, North Dakota, Ohio, Oklahoma, Oregon, Pennsylvania, Puerto Rico, Rhode Island, South Carolina, South Dakota, Tennessee, Texas, Utah, Vermont, Virginia, Washington, West Virginia, Wisconsin, Wyoming. Available to U.S. citizens.

Application Requirements: Application form, application form may be submitted online (https://twoten.org/get-help/scholarships/higher-education-scholarships/), community service, essay, financial need analysis, personal photograph, resume, transcript. *Deadline:* April 4.

Contact: Liz Watson, Scholarship Program Manager
Phone: 781-736-1500
E-mail: scholarship@twoten.org

TWO TEN FOOTWEAR FOUNDATION SCHOLARSHIP
• *See page 471*

TWO TEN FOUNDATION FOOTWEAR DESIGN SCHOLARSHIP

Unlike our traditional college scholarships, the Footwear Design Scholarship is available to any student who is studying design with a focus on footwear. This program was created in 2003 to assist students with a demonstrated interest and skill in pursuing a career in footwear design. Applicants are evaluated by design potential and financial need. Awards of up to $4,000 annually are renewable for up to four years of undergraduate study.

Award: Scholarship for use in freshman, sophomore, junior, or senior years; renewable. *Number:* 5. *Amount:* $4000.

Eligibility Requirements: Applicant must be enrolled or expecting to enroll full- or part-time at a two-year or four-year or technical institution or university; resident of Alabama, Alaska, Arizona, Arkansas, California, Colorado, Connecticut, Delaware, Florida, Georgia, Hawaii, Idaho, Illinois, Indiana, Iowa, Kansas, Kentucky, Louisiana, Maine, Maryland, Massachusetts, Michigan, Minnesota, Mississippi, Missouri, Montana, Nebraska, Nevada, New Hampshire, New Jersey, New Mexico, New York, North Carolina, North Dakota, Ohio, Oklahoma, Oregon, Pennsylvania, Puerto Rico, Rhode Island, South Carolina, South Dakota, Tennessee, Texas, Utah, Vermont, Virginia, Washington, West Virginia, Wisconsin, Wyoming and studying in Alabama, Alaska, Arizona, Arkansas, California, Colorado, Connecticut, Delaware, Florida, Georgia, Hawaii, Idaho, Illinois, Indiana, Iowa, Kansas, Kentucky, Louisiana, Maine, Maryland, Massachusetts, Michigan, Minnesota, Mississippi, Missouri, Montana, Nebraska, Nevada, New Hampshire, New Jersey, New Mexico, New York, North Carolina, North Dakota, Nova Scotia, Ohio, Oklahoma, Oregon, Pennsylvania, Puerto Rico, Rhode Island, South Carolina, South Dakota, Tennessee, Texas, Utah, Vermont, Virginia, Washington, West Virginia, Wisconsin, Wyoming. Available to U.S. citizens.

Application Requirements: Application form, application form may be submitted online (https://twoten.org/get-help/scholarships/higher-education-scholarships/), essay, financial need analysis, personal photograph, portfolio, resume, transcript. *Deadline:* April 4.

Contact: Liz Watson, Scholarship Program Manager
Phone: 781-736-1500
E-mail: scholarship@twoten.org

ULMAN CANCER FUND FOR YOUNG ADULTS

http://www.ulmanfund.org/scholarships

VERA YIP MEMORIAL SCHOLARSHIP

The Vera Yip Memorial Scholarship Award was established to support the financial needs of young adults who are impacted by cancer and seeking higher education. Vera was committed to promoting a love of learning and helped to inspire and empower others to pursue their personal, educational and professional dreams in the face of adversity. This award seeks to honor the applicant who best demonstrates the courage, determination, motivation and dedication that Vera displayed during her lifetime.

Award: Scholarship for use in freshman, sophomore, junior, senior, graduate, or postgraduate years; not renewable. *Amount:* $2500.

Eligibility Requirements: Applicant must be age 17-35; enrolled or expecting to enroll full- or part-time at an institution or university; resident of Delaware, Manitoba, Vermont and studying in District of Columbia, Maryland, Virginia. Available to U.S. citizens.

Application Requirements: Application form, essay, financial need analysis. *Deadline:* May 1.

Contact: Lauriann Parker, Scholarship Coordinator
Ulman Cancer Fund for Young Adults
1215 E. Fort Ave.
Suite 104
Baltimore, MD 21230
Phone: 410-964-0202 Ext. 105
E-mail: scholarship@ulmanfund.org

UNITED NEGRO COLLEGE FUND

http://www.uncf.org/

ABCNJ LEADERSHIP IMPACT SCHOLARSHIP
• *See page 534*

DEBORAH L. VINCENT/FAHRO EDUCATION SCHOLARSHIP
• *See page 535*

DELTA AIR LINES NEW YORK SCHOLARSHIPS
• *See page 535*

DINWIDDIE FAMILY FOUNDATION SCHOLARSHIP
• *See page 535*

JAY CHARLES LEVINE SCHOLARSHIP
• *See page 535*

KROGER MICHIGAN SCHOLARSHIP
• *See page 535*

MAYS FAMILY SCHOLARSHIP FUND
• *See page 535*

NEVADA-UNCF SCHOLARSHIPS
• *See page 536*

PACIFIC NORTHWEST SCHOLARSHIP
• *See page 536*

PANDA CARES—UNCF SCHOLARS PROGRAM (PHASE I)
• *See page 536*

PENNSYLVANIA STATE EMPLOYEES COMBINED CAMPAIGN SCHOLARSHIP (SECA)
• *See page 536*

USA FUNDS SCHOLARSHIP
• *See page 536*

WELLS FARGO FLORIDA SCHOLARSHIP PROGRAM
• *See page 537*

UNIVERSITY OF WYOMING

http://www.uwyo.edu/scholarships

VIETNAM VETERANS AWARD-WYOMING
• *See page 507*

UTAH HIGHER EDUCATION ASSISTANCE AUTHORITY

http://www.uheaa.org/

HIGHER EDUCATION SUCCESS STIPEND PROGRAM

Award available to students with substantial financial need for use at any of the participating Utah institutions. The student must be a Utah resident. Contact the financial aid office of the participating institution for requirements and deadlines.

Award: Grant for use in freshman, sophomore, junior, or senior years; not renewable. *Amount:* $300–$4000.

Eligibility Requirements: Applicant must be enrolled or expecting to enroll full- or part-time at a two-year or four-year or technical institution or university; resident of Utah and studying in Utah. Available to U.S. citizens.

Application Requirements: Financial need analysis. *Deadline:* continuous.

Contact: Financial Office
Utah Higher Education Assistance Authority
Participating college or university

VANILLA PILGRIM FOUNDATION

https://www.vanillapilgrim.com/

2018 OPEN ESSAY COMPETITION

There are plenty of scholarships for the athletic, the intelligent, minorities, the handicapped, the needy. We think it is time to have a scholarship for the "Everyday Joe" or "Plain Jane." We think you are just as special. In 400-500 words, tell us what makes you the most vanilla/boring person in the world. Each month we establish a winner and announce the name as well as post the essay to serve as a model for others. Every May we will judge the 12 winners to see who wins the $700 dollar scholarship.

Award: Scholarship for use in freshman, sophomore, junior, senior, graduate, or postgraduate years; not renewable. *Number:* 1. *Amount:* $700.

Eligibility Requirements: Applicant must be age 17 and over; enrolled or expecting to enroll full- or part-time at a two-year or four-year or technical institution or university and resident of Alabama, Alaska, Arizona, Arkansas, California, Colorado, Connecticut, Delaware, District of Columbia, Florida, Georgia, Hawaii, Idaho, Illinois, Indiana, Iowa, Kansas, Kentucky, Louisiana, Maine, Maryland, Massachusetts, Michigan, Minnesota, Mississippi, Missouri, Montana, Nebraska, Nevada, New Hampshire, New Jersey, New Mexico, New York, North Carolina, North Dakota, Ohio, Oklahoma, Oregon, Pennsylvania, Rhode Island, South Carolina, South Dakota, Tennessee, Texas, Utah, Vermont, Virginia, Washington, West Virginia, Wisconsin, Wyoming. Available to U.S. citizens.

Application Requirements: Essay. *Fee:* $4. *Deadline:* May 1.

Contact: Mr. John Allred
E-mail: vanillapilgrimfoundation@gmail.com

VERMONT STUDENT ASSISTANCE CORPORATION

http://www.vsac.org/

VERMONT INCENTIVE GRANTS

Grants for Vermont residents based on financial need. Must meet needs test. Must be college undergraduate enrolled full-time at an approved post secondary institution. Only available to Vermont residents. Grant amounts vary by student and by year, depending on available funding. During the 2019-2020 academic year, eligible students received awards ranging from $1,000 to $12,300.

Award: Grant for use in freshman, sophomore, junior, or senior years; not renewable.

Eligibility Requirements: Applicant must be enrolled or expecting to enroll full-time at a two-year or technical institution or university and resident of Utah. Available to U.S. citizens.

Application Requirements: Application form, application form may be submitted online, financial need analysis. *Deadline:* continuous.

Contact: Grant Program
Vermont Student Assistance Corporation
PO Box 2000
Winooski, VT 05404-2000
Phone: 800-882-4166

VERMONT PART-TIME GRANT

For undergraduates carrying less than twelve credits per semester who have not received a bachelor's degree. Must be Vermont resident. Based on financial need. Complete Vermont Financial Aid Packet to apply. May be used at any approved post-secondary institution. Grant amounts vary by student and by year, depending on available funding. During the 2019-2020 academic year, eligible students received awards ranging from $500 to $9,230.

Award: Grant for use in freshman, sophomore, junior, or senior years; not renewable.

Eligibility Requirements: Applicant must be enrolled or expecting to enroll part-time at a two-year or technical institution or university and resident of Utah. Available to U.S. citizens.

Application Requirements: Application form, application form may be submitted online, financial need analysis. *Deadline:* continuous.

Contact: Grant Program
Vermont Student Assistance Corporation
PO Box 2000
Winooski, VT 05404-2000
Phone: 888-882-4166

VIRGINIA DEPARTMENT OF EDUCATION

http://www.doe.virginia.gov

GRANVILLE P. MEADE SCHOLARSHIP

The Granville P. Meade Scholarship provides financial assistance to students who have achieved academically, but who are financially unable to attend college. High school seniors only are eligible to apply for scholarship. Students are selected based upon GPA, standardized test scores, letters of recommendations, extra curricular activities, and financial need. Interested students are asked to submit scholarship applications to their high school principals by March 16.

Award: Scholarship for use in freshman year; renewable. *Amount:* $2000.

Eligibility Requirements: Applicant must be high school student; planning to enroll or expecting to enroll full-time at a two-year or four-year institution or university and resident of Virginia. Available to U.S. citizens.

Application Requirements: Application form, financial need analysis. *Deadline:* March 16.

Contact: Mr. Joseph Wharff, School Counseling Connections Specialist
Virginia Department of Education
101 North 14th Street
Richmond, VA 23218
Phone: 804-225-3370
E-mail: joseph.wharff@doe.virginia.gov

VIRGINIA DEPARTMENT OF VETERANS SERVICES

http://www.dvs.virginia.gov/

VIRGINIA MILITARY SURVIVORS AND DEPENDENTS EDUCATION PROGRAM

• *See page 508*

VIRGINIA STATE COUNCIL OF HIGHER EDUCATION

http://www.schev.edu/

VIRGINIA COMMONWEALTH AWARD

Need-based award for undergraduate or graduate study at a Virginia public two- or four-year college, or university. Undergraduates must be Virginia residents. The application and awards process are administered by the financial aid office at the Virginia public institution where the student is enrolled. Dollar value of each award varies. Contact college financial aid office for application and deadlines.

Award: Grant for use in freshman, sophomore, junior, or senior years; not renewable.

Eligibility Requirements: Applicant must be enrolled or expecting to enroll full- or part-time at a two-year institution or university; resident of Vermont and studying in Virginia. Available to U.S. citizens.

Application Requirements: Financial need analysis.

Contact: Contact the financial aid office of participating Virginia public college.

VIRGINIA GUARANTEED ASSISTANCE PROGRAM

Awards to undergraduate students proportional to their need, up to full tuition, fees and book allowance. Must be a graduate of a Virginia high school. High school GPA of 2.5 required. Must be enrolled full-time in a public Virginia two- or four-year institution and demonstrate financial need. Must maintain minimum college GPA of 2.0 for renewal awards.

Award: Grant for use in freshman, sophomore, junior, or senior years; not renewable.

Eligibility Requirements: Applicant must be enrolled or expecting to enroll full-time at a two-year institution or university; resident of Vermont and studying in Virginia. Available to U.S. citizens.

Application Requirements: Financial need analysis.

Contact: Contact the financial aid office of participating Virginia public college.

VIRGINIA TUITION ASSISTANCE GRANT PROGRAM (PRIVATE INSTITUTIONS)

Awards for undergraduate students. Also available to graduate and first professional degree students pursuing a health-related degree program. Not to be used for religious study. Must be U.S. citizen or eligible non-citizen, Virginia domiciled, and enrolled full-time at an approved private, nonprofit college within Virginia. Information and application available from participating Virginia colleges financial aid office. Visit http://www.schev.edu and click on Financial Aid.

Award: Grant for use in freshman, sophomore, junior, senior, or graduate years; renewable. *Amount:* $850–$3900.

Eligibility Requirements: Applicant must be enrolled or expecting to enroll full-time at an institution or university; resident of Vermont and studying in Virginia. Available to U.S. citizens.

Application Requirements: Application form. *Deadline:* July 31.

Contact: Contact the financial aid office of the participating private nonprofit Virginia college or university.

WASHINGTON HOSPITAL HEALTHCARE SYSTEM

http://www.whhs.com/

WASHINGTON HOSPITAL EMPLOYEE ASSOCIATION SCHOLARSHIP

Scholarship for a dependent of a Washington Hospital Employee. Must be a graduating senior, community college student, transferring community college student, or a student attending a four-year institution.

Award: Scholarship for use in freshman, sophomore, junior, or senior years; not renewable. *Number:* 1. *Amount:* $2000.

Eligibility Requirements: Applicant must be enrolled or expecting to enroll full- or part-time at a two-year or four-year or technical institution or university and resident of California. Available to U.S. citizens.

Application Requirements: Application form, driver's license, essay, recommendations or references, test scores, transcript. *Deadline:* March 5.

Contact: Scholarship Chair, c/o Personnel Department
Washington Hospital Healthcare System
2500 Mowry Avenue
Fremont, CA 94538
Phone: 510-818-6220

WASHINGTON STATE PARENT TEACHER ASSOCIATION SCHOLARSHIP PROGRAM

http://www.wastatepta.org/

WASHINGTON STATE PARENT TEACHER ASSOCIATION SCHOLARSHIPS FOUNDATION

One-time scholarships for students who have graduated from a public high school in the state of Washington, and who greatly need financial help to begin full-time postsecondary education.

Award: Scholarship for use in freshman year; not renewable. *Number:* 60–80. *Amount:* $1000–$2000.

Eligibility Requirements: Applicant must be high school student; planning to enroll or expecting to enroll full-time at a four-year institution or university and resident of Washington. Available to U.S. citizens.

Application Requirements: Application form, community service, essay, financial need analysis, recommendations or references, transcript. *Deadline:* March 31.

Contact: Mr. Bill Williams, Executive Director
Phone: 253-565-2153
Fax: 253-565-7753
E-mail: jcarpenter@wastatepta.org

WASHINGTON STUDENT ACHIEVEMENT COUNCIL

https://wsac.wa.gov/

WASHINGTON STUDENT ACHIEVEMENT COUNCIL COLLEGE BOUND SCHOLARSHIP

This program provides financial assistance to low-income students who want to achieve the dream of a college education. The application is a two-step process. Eligible students should complete an application during their 7th or 8th grade year via www.collegebound.wa.gov. The second step requires students to submit a financial aid application their senior year of high school and every year of college for income verification. Additional scholarship pledge requirements can be found at www.collegebound.wa.gov.

Award: Scholarship for use in freshman, sophomore, junior, or senior years; renewable.

Eligibility Requirements: Applicant must be enrolled or expecting to enroll full- or part-time at a two-year or technical institution or university; resident of Virginia and studying in Washington.

Application Requirements: Application form. *Deadline:* June 30.

Contact: Weiya Liang, Director of College Access & Support
Phone: 360-753-7884
E-mail: weiyal@wsac.wa.gov

WASHINGTON WOMEN IN NEED

http://www.wwin.org

WWIN EDUCATION GRANT PROGRAM

WWIN selects grantees who are ready for transformational life change. Our grantees are determined and driven and have a deep desire to build a better future for themselves and their families. They are prepared to work towards a college degree, sparking positive change for themselves, their families, and their communities for generations to come.In addition to being ready to transform their lives, applicants must meet all of WWIN's eligibility criteria and submit all required documentation to be considered.

Award: Grant for use in freshman, sophomore, junior, or senior years; renewable. *Number:* 20–200. *Amount:* $1000–$5000.

Eligibility Requirements: Applicant must be age 18 and over; enrolled or expecting to enroll full- or part-time at a two-year or four-year or technical institution or university; female; resident of Washington and studying in Washington. Available to U.S. and non-U.S. citizens.

Application Requirements: Application form, application form may be submitted online (http://www.wwin.org), driver's license, essay, financial need analysis, interview. *Deadline:* continuous.

WESTERN FRATERNAL LIFE ASSOCIATION

http://www.wflains.org

WESTERN FRATERNAL LIFE NATIONAL SCHOLARSHIP

• See page 456

WESTERN INTERSTATE COMMISSION FOR HIGHER EDUCATION

http://www.wiche.edu/

WICHE'S WESTERN UNDERGRADUATE EXCHANGE (WUE)

Students from designated states can enroll in two- and four-year undergraduate programs at some 160+ public institutions in participating Western states and pay 150 percent of resident tuition, or less. Applicants apply directly to the admissions office at participating institutions. Applicants must indicate that they want to be considered for the WUE tuition savings. Participating institutions and the majors available at the WUE rate are listed at http://wiche.edu/wue.

Award: Scholarship for use in freshman, sophomore, junior, or senior years; renewable.

Eligibility Requirements: Applicant must be enrolled or expecting to enroll full-time at a two-year institution or university; resident of Alabama, Alberta, American Samoa, British Columbia, California, Georgia, Guam, Hawaii, Missouri, Nebraska, New Jersey, North Carolina, Ontario, South Carolina, Texas, Virginia, Wisconsin and studying in Alaska, Arizona, California, Colorado, Guam, Hawaii, Idaho, Montana, Nevada, New Mexico, North Dakota, Northern Mariana Islands, Oregon, South Dakota, Utah, Washington, Wyoming. Available to U.S. citizens.

Application Requirements: Application form, driver's license. *Deadline:* continuous.

Contact: Ms. Margo Colalancia, Director, Student Access Programs
Western Interstate Commission for Higher Education
3035 Center Green Drive
Suite 200
Boulder, CO 80301
Phone: 303-541-0270
E-mail: info-sep@wiche.edu

WILLIAM D. SQUIRES EDUCATIONAL FOUNDATION INC.

http://www.wmdsquiresfoundation.org/

WILLIAM D. SQUIRES SCHOLARSHIP

$4000 Scholarship award. Renewable up to $16,000. For graduating high school seniors from Ohio planning to pursue a four year program. The William D. Squires Scholarship is primarily financial need based but students must also have a clear career goal and be highly motivated. Minimum 3.2 GPA is required. Free to apply: www.wmdsquiresfoundation.org

Award: Scholarship for use in freshman, sophomore, junior, or senior years; renewable. *Number:* 15. *Amount:* $4000.

Eligibility Requirements: Applicant must be high school student; planning to enroll or expecting to enroll full-time at a four-year institution or university and resident of Ohio. Available to U.S. citizens.

Application Requirements: Application form, essay, financial need analysis, recommendations or references, test scores. *Deadline:* April 5.

Contact: Scholarship Director
William D. Squires Educational Foundation Inc.
PO Box 2940
Jupiter, FL 33468
Phone: 561-741-7751
E-mail: info@wmdsquiresfoundation.org

WILLIAM F. COOPER SCHOLARSHIP TRUST

WILLIAM F. COOPER SCHOLARSHIP

Scholarship to provide financial assistance to women living within the state of Georgia for undergraduate studies. Cannot be used for law, theology or medicine fields of study. Nursing is an approved area of study. For more details visit website http://www.wachoviascholars.com.

Award: Scholarship for use in freshman, sophomore, junior, or senior years; renewable. *Amount:* $1000.

Eligibility Requirements: Applicant must be enrolled or expecting to enroll full- or part-time at a four-year institution or university; female and resident of Georgia. Available to U.S. citizens.

Application Requirements: Application form, federal tax form 1040, W-2 forms, financial need analysis, recommendations or references, test scores, transcript. *Deadline:* April 1.

Contact: Sally King, Program Coordinator
Phone: 800-576-5135
Fax: 864-268-7160
E-mail: sallyking@bellsouth.net

WILLIAM G. AND MARIE SELBY FOUNDATION

http://www.selbyfdn.org/

SELBY SCHOLAR PROGRAM

Must be a resident of Sarasota, Manatee, Charlotte, or Desoto counties in Florida. Scholarships awarded up to $7,000 annually, not to exceed 1/3 of individual's financial need. Renewable for four years if student is full-time undergraduate at accredited college or university and maintains 3.0 GPA. Must demonstrate financial need and values of leadership and service to the community. STUDENTS WHO ARE ALREADY ATTENDING A 4-YEAR COLLEGE ARE NOT ELIGIBLE TO APPLY.

Award: Scholarship for use in freshman, sophomore, junior, or senior years; renewable. *Number:* 40. *Amount:* $1000–$7000.

Eligibility Requirements: Applicant must be enrolled or expecting to enroll full-time at a four-year institution or university; resident of Florida and must have an interest in leadership. Available to U.S. citizens.

Application Requirements: Application form, essay, financial need analysis, interview. *Deadline:* April 1.

Contact: Evan Jones, Grants and Scholarships Manager
William G. and Marie Selby Foundation
1800 Second Street, Suite 954
Sarasota, FL 34236
Phone: 941-957-0442
E-mail: ejones@selbyfdn.org

WISCONSIN DEPARTMENT OF VETERANS AFFAIRS (WDVA)

http://www.dva.state.wi.us/

VETERANS EDUCATION (VETED) REIMBURSEMENT GRANT

• *See page 485*

WISCONSIN HIGHER EDUCATIONAL AID BOARD

http://www.heab.state.wi.us/

MINORITY UNDERGRADUATE RETENTION GRANT-WISCONSIN

• *See page 538*

TALENT INCENTIVE PROGRAM GRANT - WI

Grant assists residents of Wisconsin who are attending a nonprofit institution in Wisconsin, and who have substantial financial need. Must meet income criteria, be considered economically and educationally disadvantaged, and be enrolled at least half-time. Refer to website for further details http://www.heab.state.wi.us.

Award: Grant for use in freshman, sophomore, junior, or senior years; renewable. *Amount:* $600–$1800.

Eligibility Requirements: Applicant must be enrolled or expecting to enroll full- or part-time at a two-year or technical institution or university; resident of West Virginia and studying in Wisconsin. Available to U.S. citizens.

Application Requirements: Application form, financial need analysis. *Deadline:* continuous.

Contact: Cassie Weisensel, Grant Specialist
Phone: 608-267-2213
E-mail: cassie.weisensel@wi.gov

WI-HEAB HEARING/VISUALLY IMPAIRED STUDENT GRANT

• *See page 486*

WISCONSIN ACADEMIC EXCELLENCE SCHOLARSHIP

Renewable award for high school seniors with the highest GPA in graduating class. Must be a Wisconsin resident attending a nonprofit Wisconsin institution full-time. Scholarship value is $2250 toward tuition each year for up to four years. Must maintain 3.0 GPA for renewal. Refer to your high school counselor for more details.

Award: Scholarship for use in freshman year; renewable. *Amount:* $2250.

Eligibility Requirements: Applicant must be high school student; planning to enroll or expecting to enroll full-time at a two-year or technical institution or university; resident of West Virginia and studying in Wisconsin. Available to U.S. citizens.

Application Requirements: Application form, financial need analysis. *Deadline:* continuous.

Contact: Cassie Weisensel, Grant Specialist
Phone: 608-267-2213
E-mail: cassie.weisensel@wi.gov

WISCONSIN HEAB GRANT - UW SYSTEM, TECHNICAL COLLEGES, TRIBAL COLLEGES (WG-UW,TC,TR)

Grants for residents of Wisconsin enrolled at least half-time in degree or certificate programs at a University of Wisconsin Institution, Wisconsin Technical College or an approved Tribal College. Must show financial need. Refer to website for further details http://www.heab.wi.gov.

Award: Grant for use in freshman, sophomore, junior, or senior years; not renewable. *Amount:* $250–$3150.

Eligibility Requirements: Applicant must be enrolled or expecting to enroll full- or part-time at a two-year or technical institution or university; resident of West Virginia and studying in Wisconsin. Available to U.S. citizens.

Application Requirements: Application form, financial need analysis. *Deadline:* continuous.

Contact: Charlene Sime, Grant Specialist
Phone: 608-266-0888
E-mail: charlenek.sime@wi.gov

WISCONSIN HEAB NATIVE AMERICAN STUDENT ASSISTANCE GRANT

• *See page 538*

WISCONSIN LIBRARY ASSOCIATION

https://www.wisconsinlibraries.org/

WLAF GLORIA HOEGH MEMORIAL FUND EDUCATION FOR RURAL LIBRARIANS SCHOLARSHIP

The purpose of this scholarship is to support Wisconsin librarians or library support staff working in rural communities who plan to attend a continuing education program. Applicant must be a WLA member who is a library employee working in a Wisconsin community with a current population of 5,000 or less, or who works with library employees in those communities and planning to attend a workshop, conference, or other continuing education program within or outside Wisconsin.

Award: Scholarship for use in freshman, sophomore, junior, senior, or graduate years; not renewable. *Number:* 1. *Amount:* $900.

Eligibility Requirements: Applicant must be enrolled or expecting to enroll full- or part-time at an institution or university and resident of West Virginia. Available to U.S. citizens.

Application Requirements: Application form, application form may be submitted online. *Deadline:* June 15.

Contact: Scholarship Committee Chair
Wisconsin Library Association
WLA Foundation, Inc.
4610 South Biltmore Lane Suite 100
Madison, WI 53718-2153

WISCONSIN SCHOOL COUNSELOR ASSOCIATION

http://www.wscaweb.org/

WISCONSIN SCHOOL COUNSELOR ASSOCIATION HIGH SCHOOL SCHOLARSHIP

Scholarship is available to high school seniors in Wisconsin who plan to attend a two-year or four-year postsecondary institution in the fall. Students are asked to submit an essay that describes how a school counselor or school counseling program has impacted their life.

Award: Scholarship for use in freshman year; not renewable. *Number:* 2–4. *Amount:* $1000.

Eligibility Requirements: Applicant must be high school student; planning to enroll or expecting to enroll full-time at a two-year or four-year institution or university and resident of Wisconsin. Available to U.S. citizens.

Application Requirements: Application form, essay. *Deadline:* November 1.

Contact: Katie Nechodom, WSCA Professional Recognition and Scholarship Coordinator
E-mail: nechodomk@gmail.com

WOLTERMAN LAW OFFICE, LPA

https://www.woltermanlaw.com/

WOLTERMAN LAW OFFICE LPA HOPE FOR THE FUTURE SCHOLARSHIP

Are you an Ohio student who will be enrolled in an Ohio two-year to five-year institution in 2017-2018? Do you need help paying for schooling or supplies? You are not alone. College is not cheap, but we don't want that to stop you from pursuing this irreplaceable experience. At Wolterman Law Office LPA, we have experienced first-hand the benefits of higher education. That is why we are offering a $1500 scholarship to help one Ohio student go to college, law school, or other institute of higher education. To apply, create a short (30–120 second) video and accompanying essay or submit an essay (must be at least 1,000 words), telling us the following things: 1. What does community leadership mean to you?; 2. How have you made your Ohio community a better place? Please provide specific examples showing your commitment to community service and leadership. Applications are due May 6th, 2018.

Award: Scholarship for use in freshman, sophomore, junior, senior, or graduate years; not renewable. *Number:* 1. *Amount:* $1500.

Eligibility Requirements: Applicant must be enrolled or expecting to enroll full- or part-time at a two-year or four-year or technical institution or university; resident of Ohio and studying in Ohio. Available to U.S. citizens.

Application Requirements: Application form, essay. *Deadline:* May 6.

Contact: Scholarship Coordinator
E-mail: coordinator@ourscholarship.io

WOMEN IN DEFENSE MICHIGAN

http://wid-mi.org/

WOMEN IN DEFENSE HORIZONS-MICHIGAN SCHOLARSHIP

The program focuses on the following preferred fields of study: security studies, military history, government relations, engineering, computer science, physics, mathematics, business (as it relates to national security or defense), law (as it relates to national security or defense), international relations, political science, economics. Others will be considered if the applicant can successfully demonstrate relevance to a career in the areas of national security or defense. Awards are based on academic achievement, participation in defense and national security activities, field of study, work experience, statements of objectives, recommendations, and financial need. Awards are made without regard to race, creed, color, or religion. HORIZONS-Michigan reserves the right to revise, suspend or discontinue this program without notice.

Award: Scholarship for use in junior, senior, graduate, or postgraduate years; not renewable. *Number:* 1–4. *Amount:* $1500–$5000.

Eligibility Requirements: Applicant must be enrolled or expecting to enroll full- or part-time at a two-year or four-year or technical institution or university; female; resident of Michigan and studying in Michigan. Available to U.S. citizens.

Application Requirements: Application form, driver's license, essay, financial need analysis. *Deadline:* May 12.

Contact: Melanie Stager, Director of Scholarships
E-mail: scholarships@wid-mi.org

WYOMING FARM BUREAU FEDERATION

http://www.wyfb.org/

LIVINGSTON FAMILY - H.J. KING MEMORIAL SCHOLARSHIP
• See page 457

WYOMING FARM BUREAU CONTINUING EDUCATION SCHOLARSHIPS
• See page 457

WYOMING FARM BUREAU FEDERATION SCHOLARSHIPS
• See page 457

TALENT/INTEREST AREA

ALBERTA HERITAGE SCHOLARSHIP FUND

http://www.alis.alberta.ca/

EARL AND COUNTESS OF WESSEX-WORLD CHAMPIONSHIPS IN ATHLETICS SCHOLARSHIPS
• See page 511

ALERT SCHOLARSHIP

http://www.alertmagazine.org/

ALERT SCHOLARSHIP
• See page 543

THE ALEXANDER FOUNDATION

http://www.thealexanderfoundation.org/

THE ALEXANDER FOUNDATION SCHOLARSHIP PROGRAM
• See page 544

AMERICAN INSTITUTE FOR FOREIGN STUDY (AIFS)

https://www.aifsabroad.com/

AIFS GENERATION STUDY ABROAD SCHOLARSHIPS

Awards available to undergraduates on an AIFS study abroad program. Applicants must demonstrate leadership potential, have a minimum 3.0 cumulative GPA, and meet program requirements. The program application fee is $95. Deadlines: April 15 for fall, October 1 for spring, and March 1 for summer.

Award: Scholarship for use in freshman, sophomore, junior, or senior years; not renewable. *Amount:* $500–$1000.

Eligibility Requirements: Applicant must be age 17 and over; enrolled or expecting to enroll full-time at a two-year institution or university and must have an interest in leadership. Available to U.S. and non-U.S. citizens.

Application Requirements: Application form, essay, personal photograph. *Fee:* $95. *Deadline:* October 1.

Contact: Sharman Hedayati, Vice President, Director of Admissions and Operations
American Institute For Foreign Study (AIFS)
1 High Ridge Park
Stamford, CT 06905
Phone: 800-727-2437
E-mail: shedayati@aifs.com

AMERICAN LEGION BASEBALL

http://www.legion.org/baseball

AMERICAN LEGION BASEBALL SCHOLARSHIP

Awarded to graduated seniors who were nominated by American Legion Baseball coach who demonstrate outstanding academics, citizenship, community spirit, leadership and financial need.

Award: Scholarship for use in freshman, sophomore, junior, senior, graduate, or postgraduate years; not renewable. *Number:* 1–51. *Amount:* $500–$2500.

Eligibility Requirements: Applicant must be high school student; planning to enroll or expecting to enroll full-time at a two-year or four-year or technical institution or university and must have an interest in athletics/sports. Available to U.S. and non-Canadian citizens.

Application Requirements: Application form, personal photograph. *Deadline:* July 15.

Contact: Mr. Steve Cloud, Assistant National Program Coordinator
American Legion Baseball
PO Box 1055
Indianapolis, IN 46206
Phone: 317-630-1213
E-mail: baseball@legion.org

AMERICAN LEGION DEPARTMENT OF ARIZONA

http://www.azlegion.org/programs

AMERICAN LEGION DEPARTMENT OF ARIZONA HIGH SCHOOL ORATORICAL CONTEST
• *See page 546*

AMERICAN LEGION DEPARTMENT OF ARKANSAS

http://www.arklegion.homestead.com/

AMERICAN LEGION DEPARTMENT OF ARKANSAS HIGH SCHOOL ORATORICAL CONTEST
• *See page 546*

AMERICAN LEGION DEPARTMENT OF ILLINOIS

http://www.illegion.org/

AMERICANISM ESSAY CONTEST SCHOLARSHIP
• *See page 432*

AMERICAN LEGION DEPARTMENT OF ILLINOIS HIGH SCHOOL ORATORICAL CONTEST
• *See page 547*

AMERICAN LEGION DEPARTMENT OF INDIANA

http://www.indianalegion.org

FRANK W. MCHALE MEMORIAL SCHOLARSHIPS
• *See page 547*

AMERICAN LEGION DEPARTMENT OF IOWA

http://www.ialegion.org/

AMERICAN LEGION DEPARTMENT OF IOWA HIGH SCHOOL ORATORICAL CONTEST
• *See page 547*

AMERICAN LEGION DEPARTMENT OF IOWA OUTSTANDING SENIOR BASEBALL PLAYER
• *See page 548*

AMERICAN LEGION DEPARTMENT OF MICHIGAN

http://www.michiganlegion.org/

AMERICAN LEGION DEPARTMENT OF MICHIGAN ORATORICAL SCHOLARSHIP PROGRAM
• *See page 548*

THE AMERICAN LEGION, DEPARTMENT OF MINNESOTA

http://www.mnlegion.org/

AMERICAN LEGION DEPARTMENT OF MINNESOTA HIGH SCHOOL ORATORICAL CONTEST
• *See page 548*

AMERICAN LEGION DEPARTMENT OF NEW YORK

http://www.ny.legion.org/

AMERICAN LEGION DEPARTMENT OF NEW YORK HIGH SCHOOL ORATORICAL CONTEST
• *See page 549*

AMERICAN LEGION DEPARTMENT OF NORTH CAROLINA

http://www.nclegion.org/

AMERICAN LEGION DEPARTMENT OF NORTH CAROLINA HIGH SCHOOL ORATORICAL CONTEST
• *See page 549*

AMERICAN LEGION DEPARTMENT OF OREGON

http://www.orlegion.org/

AMERICAN LEGION DEPARTMENT OF OREGON HIGH SCHOOL ORATORICAL CONTEST
• *See page 549*

AMERICAN LEGION DEPARTMENT OF PENNSYLVANIA

http://www.pa-legion.com/

AMERICAN LEGION DEPARTMENT OF PENNSYLVANIA HIGH SCHOOL ORATORICAL CONTEST
• See page 549

AMERICAN LEGION DEPARTMENT OF SOUTH DAKOTA

http://www.sdlegion.org/

AMERICAN LEGION DEPARTMENT OF SOUTH DAKOTA HIGH SCHOOL ORATORICAL CONTEST
• See page 550

AMERICAN LEGION DEPARTMENT OF TENNESSEE

http://www.tennesseelegion.org/

AMERICAN LEGION DEPARTMENT OF TENNESSEE HIGH SCHOOL ORATORICAL CONTEST
• See page 550

AMERICAN LEGION DEPARTMENT OF TEXAS

http://www.txlegion.org/

AMERICAN LEGION DEPARTMENT OF TEXAS HIGH SCHOOL ORATORICAL CONTEST
• See page 550

AMERICAN LEGION DEPARTMENT OF VERMONT

http://www.vtlegion.org

AMERICAN LEGION DEPARTMENT OF VERMONT HIGH SCHOOL ORATORICAL CONTEST
• See page 550

AMERICAN MUSEUM OF NATURAL HISTORY

https://www.amnh.org/

YOUNG NATURALIST AWARDS

Essay contest open to students in grades 7-12 who are currently enrolled in a public, private, parochial, or home school in the United States, Canada, the U.S. territories, or a U.S.-sponsored school abroad. Essays must be based on an original scientific investigation conducted by the student. See website for guidelines http://www.amnh.org/nationalcenter/youngnaturalistawards/read.html.

Award: Prize for use in freshman year; not renewable. *Number:* 1.

Eligibility Requirements: Applicant must be high school student; planning to enroll or expecting to enroll part-time at a four-year institution or university and must have an interest in writing. Available to Canadian citizens.

Application Requirements: Application form, essay, personal photograph. *Deadline:* March 1.

Contact: Maria Rios, Assistant Director, Fellowships and Student Affairs
American Museum of Natural History
200 Central Park West
New York, NY 10024-5102
Phone: 212-769-5017
E-mail: fellowships-rggs@amnh.org

APPALOOSA HORSE CLUB-APPALOOSA YOUTH PROGRAM

http://www.appaloosayouth.com/

APPALOOSA YOUTH EDUCATIONAL SCHOLARSHIPS
• See page 436

ARRL FOUNDATION INC.

http://www.arrl.org/home

HARRY A. HODGES, W6YOO, SCHOLARSHIP
• See page 552

AUTHOR SERVICES, INC.

http://www.writersofthefuture.com/

L. RON HUBBARD'S ILLUSTRATORS OF THE FUTURE CONTEST

An ongoing competition for new and amateur artists judged by professional artists. Eligible submissions consist of three science fiction or fantasy illustrations. Prize amount ranges from $500 to $5000. Quarterly deadlines: December 31, March 31, June 30 and September 30. All entrants retain rights to artwork.

Award: Prize for use in freshman, sophomore, junior, senior, graduate, or postgraduate years; not renewable. *Number:* 12. *Amount:* $500–$5000.

Eligibility Requirements: Applicant must be enrolled or expecting to enroll full- or part-time at a two-year or four-year or technical institution or university and must have an interest in art. Available to U.S. and non-U.S. citizens.

Application Requirements: Application form. *Deadline:* continuous.

Contact: Joni Labaqui, Contest Administrator
Author Services, Inc.
7051 Hollywood Boulevard
Los Angeles, CA 90028
Phone: 323-466-3310
E-mail: contests@authorservicesinc.com

L. RON HUBBARD'S WRITERS OF THE FUTURE CONTEST

An ongoing competition for new and amateur writers judged by professional writers. Eligible submissions are short stories and novelettes of science fiction or fantasy. Deadlines: 31 March, 30 June, 30 September, 31 December annually. Prize amount ranges from $500 to $5000.

Award: Prize for use in freshman, sophomore, junior, senior, graduate, or postgraduate years; not renewable. *Number:* 12. *Amount:* $500–$5000.

Eligibility Requirements: Applicant must be enrolled or expecting to enroll full- or part-time at a two-year or four-year or technical institution or university and must have an interest in writing. Available to U.S. and non-U.S. citizens.

Application Requirements: Application form. *Deadline:* continuous.

Contact: Joni Labaqui, Contest Administrator
Author Services, Inc.
Author Services, Inc
7051 Hollywood Boulevard
Los Angeles, CA 90028
Phone: 323-466-3310
E-mail: contests@authorservicesinc.com

AUTOMOTIVE HALL OF FAME

http://www.automotivehalloffame.org/

AUTOMOTIVE HALL OF FAME EDUCATIONAL FUNDS

Award for full-time undergraduate and graduate students pursuing studies in automotive and related technologies. Must submit two letters of recommendation supporting automotive interests. Minimum 3.0 cumulative GPA required. Student must study in the United States and either be a United States citizen or on a student visa.

Award: Scholarship for use in freshman, sophomore, junior, senior, or graduate years; renewable. *Number:* 20. *Amount:* $500–$2000.

Eligibility Requirements: Applicant must be enrolled or expecting to enroll full-time at a two-year or four-year or technical institution or university and must have an interest in automotive. Available to U.S. and non-U.S. citizens.

Application Requirements: Application form, essay, financial need analysis, recommendations or references, self-addressed stamped envelope with application, transcript. *Deadline:* June 30.

Contact: Sue Lauster
Automotive Hall of Fame
21400 Oakwood Boulevard
Dearborn, MI 48124-4078
Phone: 313-240-4000
Fax: 313-240-8641

BABE RUTH LEAGUE INC.

http://www.baberuthleague.org/

BABE RUTH SCHOLARSHIP PROGRAM

Program to provide assistance to individuals (former Babe Ruth Baseball, Cal Ripken Baseball or Babe Ruth Softball players) who plan on furthering their education beyond high school. Outstanding student athletes will receive $1000 each towards their college tuition.

Award: Scholarship for use in freshman year; not renewable. *Number:* 1–10. *Amount:* $1000.

Eligibility Requirements: Applicant must be high school student; planning to enroll or expecting to enroll full- or part-time at a two-year or four-year institution or university and must have an interest in athletics/sports. Available to U.S. citizens.

Application Requirements: Application form, application form may be submitted online (http://www.baberuthleague.org), recommendations or references, transcript. *Deadline:* September 1.

Contact: Mr. Joseph Smiegocki, Scholarship Committee
Phone: 800-880-3142
Fax: 609-695-2505
E-mail: info@baberuthleague.org

CALIFORNIA INTERSCHOLASTIC FEDERATION

http://www.cifstate.org/

CIF SCHOLAR-ATHLETE OF THE YEAR
• *See page 554*

CIF SPIRIT OF SPORT AWARD
• *See page 554*

CALIFORNIA JUNIOR MISS SCHOLARSHIP PROGRAM

http://www.ajm.org/

DISTINGUISHED YOUNG WOMEN OF CALIFORNIA SCHOLARSHIP PROGRAM
• *See page 554*

CANADA ICELAND FOUNDATION INC. SCHOLARSHIPS

http://www.canadaicelandfoundation.com/

CANADA ICELAND FOUNDATION SCHOLARSHIP PROGRAM

Several scholarships awarded annually. To be offered to a university student studying towards a degree in any Canadian university.

Award: Scholarship for use in freshman, sophomore, junior, senior, or graduate years; not renewable.

Eligibility Requirements: Applicant must be enrolled or expecting to enroll full-time at an institution or university; studying in Alberta, British Columbia, Manitoba, New Brunswick, Newfoundland, Nova Scotia, Ontario, Quebec, Saskatchewan and must have an interest in leadership. Available to Canadian citizens.

Application Requirements: Application form, community service. *Deadline:* September 28.

Contact: Karen Bowman, Administrative Assistant
Phone: 204-284-5686
Fax: 204-284-7099
E-mail: karen@lh-inc.ca

CARROT-TOP INDUSTRIES, INC.

https://carrot-top.com

BEACON SCHOLARSHIP FOR RURAL AMERICA
• *See page 555*

CHRISTOPHERS

http://www.christophers.org/

POSTER CONTEST FOR HIGH SCHOOL STUDENTS

Contest invites students in grades nine through twelve to interpret the theme "You can make a difference." Posters must include this statement and illustrate the idea that one person can change the world for the better. Judging is based on overall impact, content, originality, and artistic merit. More information can be found at http://www.christophers.org.

Award: Prize for use in freshman, sophomore, junior, or senior years; not renewable. *Number:* up to 8. *Amount:* $100–$1000.

Eligibility Requirements: Applicant must be high school student; planning to enroll or expecting to enroll full-time at a four-year institution or university and must have an interest in art. Available to U.S. citizens.

Application Requirements: Application form, entry in a contest, poster. *Deadline:* February 13.

Contact: Sarah Holinski, Youth Coordinator
Christophers
5 Hanover Square, 22nd Floor
New York, NY 10004
Phone: 212-759-4050 Ext. 240
Fax: 212-838-5073
E-mail: youth@christophers.org

VIDEO CONTEST FOR COLLEGE STUDENTS

Contest requires college students to use any style or format to express the following theme "One person can make a difference." Entries can be up to 5 minutes in length and must be submitted in standard, full-sized DVD format. Entries will be judged on content, artistic and technical proficiency, and adherence to contest rules. More information is available at http://www.christophers.org.

Award: Prize for use in freshman, sophomore, junior, senior, graduate, or postgraduate years; not renewable. *Number:* 2–6. *Amount:* $1000–$2000.

Eligibility Requirements: Applicant must be enrolled or expecting to enroll full- or part-time at a two-year or four-year or technical institution or university and must have an interest in art. Available to U.S. citizens.

Application Requirements: Application form, DVD, entry in a contest. *Deadline:* February 13.

Contact: Sarah Holinski, Youth Coordinator
Christophers
5 Hanover Square, 22nd Floor
New York, NY 10004
Phone: 212-759-4050 Ext. 240
Fax: 212-838-5073
E-mail: s.holinski@christophers.org

CIRKLED IN

https://www.cirkledin.com

THE "NO SWEAT" SCHOLARSHIP

Cirkled In is a digital profile and portfolio platform for students. It's like LinkedIn for students. They compile all their activities and accomplishments on this secure cloud-based platform and cam share with any application from college and scholarships to jobs and internships. Cirkled In portfolio stays with students forever and is FREE to them

Award: Scholarship for use in junior year; not renewable. *Number:* 1. *Amount:* $2500.

Eligibility Requirements: Applicant must be high school student and planning to enroll or expecting to enroll full- or part-time at a two-year or technical institution or university. Available to U.S. citizens.

Application Requirements: Application form may be submitted online. *Deadline:* June 30.

Contact: Mrs. Reetu Gupta, CEO
Cirkled In
15405 SE 37th St,
Bellevue, WA 98006
Phone: 206-6041968
E-mail: reetu@cirkledin.com

CLAGS: CENTER FOR LGBTQ STUDIES

https://clags.org/

SYLVIA RIVERA AWARD IN TRANSGENDER STUDIES

This award, which honors the memory of Rivera, a transgender activist, will be given for the best book or article to appear in transgender studies this past year. Applications may be submitted by the author of the work or by nomination. Adjudicated by the CLAGS fellowships committee.

Award: Prize for use in freshman, sophomore, junior, senior, graduate, or postgraduate years; not renewable. *Number:* 1. *Amount:* $1000.

Eligibility Requirements: Applicant must be enrolled or expecting to enroll full- or part-time at a two-year institution or university and must have an interest in LGBT issues or writing. Available to U.S. and non-U.S. citizens.

Application Requirements: Application form. *Deadline:* June 1.

Contact: Justin Brown, Executive Director
CLAGS: Center for LGBTQ Studies
CUNY Graduate Center
365 Fifth Avenue, Room 7115
New York, NY 10016
Phone: 212-817-1955
Fax: 212-817-1567
E-mail: info@clags.org

UNDERGRADUATE STUDENT PAPER AWARD

Each year, CLAGS sponsors a student paper competition open to all undergraduate students enrolled in the CUNY or SUNY system. A cash prize is awarded to the best paper written in a CUNY or SUNY undergraduate class on any topic related to gay, lesbian, bisexual, queer, or transgender experiences and scholarship. Essays should be between 12 and 30 pages, well thought-out, and fully realized.

Award: Prize for use in freshman, sophomore, junior, or senior years; not renewable. *Number:* 1. *Amount:* $250.

Eligibility Requirements: Applicant must be enrolled or expecting to enroll full- or part-time at an institution or university; studying in New York and must have an interest in LGBT issues. Available to U.S. and non-U.S. citizens.

Application Requirements: Application form, essay. *Deadline:* June 1.

Contact: Justin Brown, Executive Director
CLAGS: Center for LGBTQ Studies
CUNY Graduate Center
365 Fifth Avenue, Room 7115
New York, NY 10016
Phone: 212-817-1955
Fax: 212-817-1567
E-mail: info@clags.org

COLLEGEBOUND FOUNDATION

http://www.collegeboundfoundation.org/

HY ZOLET STUDENT ATHLETE SCHOLARSHIP
• See page 556

COLLEGEWEEKLIVE

http://www.collegeweeklive.com/

COLLEGEWEEKLIVE.COM SCHOLARSHIP

$1,000 scholarship to students for visiting colleges on CollegeWeekLive. Students must submit an online registration and visit 5 schools on the site. For more information, see website http://www.college weeklive.com/sign-up?refcode=PAR_PETERSONS_SCHOLARSHIP

Award: Scholarship for use in freshman year; not renewable. *Number:* 1. *Amount:* $1000.

Eligibility Requirements: Applicant must be enrolled or expecting to enroll full- or part-time at a two-year or four-year or technical institution or university and must have an interest in writing. Available to U.S. and non-U.S. citizens.

Application Requirements: Application form.

Contact: Melissa King, Vice President, Marketing
Phone: 617-938-6018
E-mail: info@collegeweeklive.com

COMMUNITY FOUNDATION OF WESTERN MASSACHUSETTS

http://www.communityfoundation.org/

FRED K. LANE SCHOLARSHIP FUND
• See page 558

CONTEMPORARY RECORD SOCIETY

http://www.crsnews.org/

CONTEMPORARY RECORD SOCIETY NATIONAL COMPETITION FOR PERFORMING ARTISTS

There are no age restrictions to participate. Applicant may submit one performance tape of varied length including music of any period of music with each application. The applicant may use any number of instrumentalists and voices. First prize is a commercial distribution of the winner's recording. Application fee is $50 for each recording submitted. Submit self-addressed stamped envelope with the application for returns. The winning applicant will participate in a CD recording released by CRS. (This prize is not applicable toward tuition.)

Award: Prize for use in freshman, sophomore, junior, senior, graduate, or postgraduate years; not renewable. *Number:* 1. *Amount:* $2000–$6000.

Eligibility Requirements: Applicant must be enrolled or expecting to enroll full- or part-time at a two-year or four-year or technical institution or university and must have an interest in music/singing. Available to U.S. and non-U.S. citizens.

Application Requirements: Application form. *Fee:* $50. *Deadline:* February 29.

Contact: Ms. Caroline Hunt, Administrator
Contemporary Record Society
724 Winchester Rd.
Broomall, PA 19008
Phone: 610-2059897
E-mail: crsnews@verizon.net

NATIONAL COMPETITION FOR COMPOSERS' RECORDINGS

First prize is a CD recording grant (not tuition). Limited to nine performers and twenty-five minutes duration. Works with additional performers will be accepted provided there is a release of the original recorded master for CD reproduction. Must submit a musical composition that is non-published and not commercially recorded. Limit of 5 works per applicant.

Award: Prize for use in freshman, sophomore, junior, senior, graduate, or postgraduate years; not renewable. *Number:* 1. *Amount:* $2000–$6000.

Eligibility Requirements: Applicant must be enrolled or expecting to enroll full- or part-time at a two-year or four-year or technical institution or university and must have an interest in music/singing. Available to U.S. and non-U.S. citizens.

Application Requirements: Application form. *Fee:* $50. *Deadline:* February 29.

Contact: Ms. Caroline Hunt, Administrator
Contemporary Record Society
724 Winchester Rd.
Broomall, PA 19008
Phone: 610-2059897
E-mail: crsnews@verizon.net

CROSSLITES

http://www.crosslites.com/

CROSSLITES SCHOLARSHIP AWARD

Scholarship contest is open to high school, college and graduate school students. There are no minimum GPA, SAT, ACT, GMAT, GRE, or any other test score requirements.

Award: Prize for use in freshman, sophomore, junior, senior, or graduate years; not renewable. *Number:* 33. *Amount:* $100–$2500.

Eligibility Requirements: Applicant must be enrolled or expecting to enroll full- or part-time at a two-year or four-year or technical institution or university and must have an interest in writing. Available to U.S. and non-U.S. citizens.

Application Requirements: Application form, entry in a contest, essay. *Deadline:* December 15.

Contact: Samuel Certo, Scholarship Committee
CrossLites
1000 Holt Avenue
Winter Park, FL 32789

THE DALLAS FOUNDATION

http://www.dallasfoundation.org/

THE LANDON RUSNAK SCHOLARSHIP
• *See page 560*

DIAMANTE, INC.

http://www.diamanteinc.org/

LATINO DIAMANTE SCHOLARSHIP FUND
• *See page 462*

DIXIE BOYS BASEBALL

http://www.dixie.org/boys

DIXIE YOUTH SCHOLARSHIP PROGRAM
• *See page 562*

DO SUPPLY, INC.

https://www.dosupply.com/

DO SUPPLY, INC. ACADEMIC SCHOLARSHIP

DO Supply, Inc. is offering a $1,000 scholarship award to the student who best demonstrates his/her passion for small business in the United States by creating a well-researched and personal account of a small business that has impacted his/her life, or of a dream he/she may have to establish their own business. This will be awarded to one student for the purposes of funding a full or part time education in a college or university during the fall semester in the year 2020. The essay must be submitted in completion by June 1st, 2020. A final winner will be selected by June 20th, 2020. All decisions are final and may not be appealed. There will only be one winner, who will receive the full scholarship amount ($1000.00). The award will be sent directly to the financial aid office of the winner's institution. Applicant must: be an undergrad student; only send one entry (multiple entries will be ignored); be over 18; provide their student identification number; provide the name and address to which the scholarship award would be sent; notify their institution's financial aid office of the scholarship application; submit documents in English; submit an essay should be between 800 and 1200 words, students should include their name and the name of the institution in the top margin of the essay, along with their course of study, college email address, and student ID elsewhere on the page. Misleading/false information is reason for immediate disqualification with no further notice. Friends and relatives of DO Supply, Inc. are not eligible for this contest. By entering the student is authorizing DO Supply, Inc. to use all submitted content at our discretion for publishing or marketing purposes without requiring explicit permission from the author. Students personal details excluding first and last name will not be disclosed to other parties of published. For questions or concerns email Isaac Wittenberg at Iwittenb@dosupply.com

Award: Scholarship for use in freshman, sophomore, junior, or senior years; not renewable. *Number:* 1. *Amount:* $1000.

Eligibility Requirements: Applicant must be age 18 and over and enrolled or expecting to enroll full- or part-time at a two-year or technical institution or university. Available to U.S. and non-U.S. citizens.

Application Requirements: Application form may be submitted online, essay. *Deadline:* June 1.

ELIE WIESEL FOUNDATION FOR HUMANITY

http://www.eliewieselfoundation.org/

ELIE WIESEL PRIZE IN ETHICS ESSAY CONTEST

Scholarship for full-time junior or senior at a four-year accredited college or university in the United States. Up to five awards are granted.

Award: Prize for use in junior or senior years; not renewable. *Number:* 1–5. *Amount:* $500–$5000.

Eligibility Requirements: Applicant must be enrolled or expecting to enroll full-time at a four-year institution or university and must have an interest in writing. Available to U.S. and non-U.S. citizens.

Application Requirements: Application form, essay. *Deadline:* December 14.

Contact: Ms. Christina Burner, Essay Contest Coordinator
Elie Wiesel Foundation for Humanity
555 Madison Avenue, 20th Floor
New York, NY 10022
Phone: 212-490-7788
E-mail: christina@eliewieselfoundation.org

ELKS NATIONAL FOUNDATION

http://www.elks.org/enf

ELKS NATIONAL FOUNDATION MOST VALUABLE STUDENT SCHOLARSHIP CONTEST

Five hundred awards ranging from $1,000 to $12,500 per year, renewable for four years, are allocated nationally by state quota for graduating high school seniors. Based on scholarship, leadership, and financial need. Must be a U.S. citizen pursuing a 4-year degree full-time at an accredited, degree granting U.S. college or university. For more information, visit http://www.elks.org/scholars.

Award: Scholarship for use in freshman, sophomore, junior, or senior years; renewable. *Number:* 500. *Amount:* $4000–$50,000.

Eligibility Requirements: Applicant must be high school student; planning to enroll or expecting to enroll full-time at a four-year institution or university and must have an interest in leadership. Available to U.S. citizens.

Application Requirements: Application form, community service, essay, financial need analysis. *Deadline:* November 27.

Contact: Elks National Foundation Scholarship Office
Elks National Foundation
2750 North Lakeview Avenue
Chicago, IL 60614-2256
Phone: 773-755-4732
E-mail: scholarship@elks.org

ESSAYHUB

https://essayhub.com/

ESSAY WRITING CONTEST BY ESSAYHUB
• *See page 474*

FINANCIAL SERVICE CENTERS OF NEW YORK

http://www.fscny.org

FSCNY YOUNG LEADERS SCHOLARSHIP
• *See page 564*

FLORIDA WOMEN'S STATE GOLF ASSOCIATION

CLUB EMPLOYEES AND DEPENDENTS SCHOLARSHIP
• *See page 566*

FSGA SCHOLARS
• *See page 566*

SARAH E. HUNEYCUTT SCHOLARSHIP
• *See page 567*

FOREST ROBERTS THEATRE
http://www.nmu.edu/

MILDRED AND ALBERT PANOWSKI PLAYWRITING AWARD
Prize designed to encourage and stimulate artistic growth among playwrights. Winner receives a cash prize and a world premiere of their play.

Award: Prize for use in freshman, sophomore, junior, senior, graduate, or postgraduate years; not renewable. *Number:* 1. *Amount:* $2000.

Eligibility Requirements: Applicant must be enrolled or expecting to enroll full- or part-time at a two-year or four-year or technical institution or university and must have an interest in theater or writing. Available to U.S. and non-U.S. citizens.

Application Requirements: Application form, entry in a contest, manuscript in English, self-addressed stamped envelope with application. *Deadline:* October 31.

Contact: Matt Hudson, Playwriting Award Coordinator
Forest Roberts Theatre
Northern Michigan University
1401 Presque Isle Avenue
Marquette, MI 49855-5364
Phone: 906-227-2559
Fax: 906-227-2567

FOUNDATION FOR CHRISTIAN COLLEGE LEADERS
http://www.collegechristianleader.com/

FOUNDATION FOR COLLEGE CHRISTIAN LEADERS SCHOLARSHIP
• *See page 540*

FRANCIS OUIMET SCHOLARSHIP FUND
http://www.ouimet.org

FRANCIS OUIMET SCHOLARSHIP
• *See page 567*

FRIENDS OF THE MINNESOTA ORCHESTRA (FORMERLY WAMSO)
https://friendsofminnesotaorchestra.org/

YOUNG ARTIST COMPETITION
Awards of $500 to $5000 and/or performnce awards for graduates, undergraduates, and early career artists through age 25 as of 1/20/2019. Applicant must reside or study in U.S. or Canada.

Award: Prize for use in freshman, sophomore, junior, senior, graduate, or postgraduate years; not renewable. *Number:* 8. *Amount:* $500–$5000.

Eligibility Requirements: Applicant must be age 15-25; enrolled or expecting to enroll full- or part-time at a two-year or four-year or technical institution or university and must have an interest in music. Available to U.S. and non-U.S. citizens.

Application Requirements: Application form. *Fee:* $75. *Deadline:* September 30.

Contact: James Waldo, Young Artist Competition Co-Chair
E-mail: yac@mnorch.org

GAY ASIAN PACIFIC ALLIANCE FOUNDATION
http://gapafoundation.org/

GAPA SCHOLARSHIPS
The purpose of the Gay Asian Pacific Alliance (GAPA) Foundation Scholarship is to provide financial assistance to students in high school; undergraduate, graduate or professional school; or trade or vocational school who express activism in the Asian and Pacific Islander (API) and/or lesbian, gay, bisexual, transgender, and queer (LGBTQ) communities.

Award: Scholarship for use in freshman, sophomore, junior, senior, graduate, or postgraduate years; not renewable. *Number:* 3–5. *Amount:* $1000–$3000.

Eligibility Requirements: Applicant must be enrolled or expecting to enroll full- or part-time at a two-year or four-year or technical institution or university and must have an interest in leadership or LGBT issues. Available to U.S. and non-U.S. citizens.

Application Requirements: Application form, essay. *Deadline:* June 30.

Contact: Mr. Drew Ho, Philanthropy Co-Chair
E-mail: programs@gapafoundation.org

GLAMOUR
http://www.glamour.com/

TOP 10 COLLEGE WOMEN COMPETITION
Female students with leadership experience on and off campus, excellence in field of study, and inspiring goals can apply for this competition. Winners will be awarded $3000 along with a trip to New York City. Must be a junior studying full-time with a minimum GPA of 3.0. in either the United States or Canada. Non-U.S. citizens may apply if attending U.S. postsecondary institutions.

Award: Prize for use in junior year; not renewable. *Number:* 10. *Amount:* $3000.

Eligibility Requirements: Applicant must be enrolled or expecting to enroll full-time at a four-year institution or university; female and must have an interest in leadership. Available to U.S. and non-U.S. citizens.

Application Requirements: Application form, essay, personal photograph, recommendations or references, transcript. *Deadline:* February 2.

Contact: Lynda Laux-Bachand, Reader Services Editor
Glamour
Four Times Square, 16th Floor
New York, NY 10036-6593
Phone: 212-286-6667
Fax: 212-286-6922

GLENN MILLER BIRTHPLACE SOCIETY
http://www.glennmiller.org/

GLENN MILLER INSTRUMENTAL SCHOLARSHIP
One-time awards for high school seniors and college freshmen. Scholarships are awarded as competition prizes and must be used for any education-related expenses. Must submit 10-minute, high-quality audio tape of pieces selected for competition or those of similar style. Applicant is responsible for travel to and lodging during the competition.

Award: Scholarship for use in freshman year; not renewable. *Number:* 3. *Amount:* $1000–$4500.

Eligibility Requirements: Applicant must be high school student; planning to enroll or expecting to enroll full-time at a four-year institution or university and must have an interest in music/singing. Available to U.S. and non-U.S. citizens.

Application Requirements: Application form, entry in a contest, essay, performance tape or CD. *Deadline:* March 15.

Contact: Arlene Leonard, Secretary
Glenn Miller Birthplace Society
107 East Main Street, PO Box 61
Clarinda, IA 51632-0061
Phone: 712-542-2461
Fax: 712-542-2461
E-mail: gmbs@heartland.net

JACK PULLAN MEMORIAL SCHOLARSHIP

One scholarship for a male or female vocalist, awarded as competition prize and, to be used for any education-related expenses. Must submit 10 minute, high-quality audio tape of pieces selected for competition or those of similar style. Applicant is responsible for travel to and lodging during the competition. One-time award for high school seniors and college freshmen. More information on http://www.glenn miller.org/scholar.htm.

Award: Scholarship for use in freshman year; not renewable. *Number:* 1. *Amount:* $1000.

Eligibility Requirements: Applicant must be high school student; planning to enroll or expecting to enroll full-time at a four-year institution or university and must have an interest in music/singing. Available to U.S. and non-U.S. citizens.

Application Requirements: Application form, entry in a contest, essay, performance tape or CD. *Deadline:* March 15.

Contact: Arlene Leonard, Secretary
Glenn Miller Birthplace Society
107 East Main Street, PO Box 61
Clarinda, IA 51632-0061
Phone: 712-542-2461
Fax: 712-542-2461
E-mail: gmbs@heartland.net

RALPH BREWSTER VOCAL SCHOLARSHIP

One scholarship for a male or female vocalist, awarded as competition prize and, to be used for any education-related expenses. Must submit 10 minute, high-quality audio tape of pieces selected for competition or those of similar style. Applicant is responsible for travel to and lodging during the competition. One-time award for high school seniors and college freshmen.

Award: Scholarship for use in freshman year; not renewable. *Number:* 1. *Amount:* $2000.

Eligibility Requirements: Applicant must be high school student; planning to enroll or expecting to enroll full-time at a four-year institution or university and must have an interest in music/singing. Available to U.S. and non-U.S. citizens.

Application Requirements: Application form, entry in a contest, essay, performance tape of competition or concert quality (up to 5 minutes duration). *Deadline:* March 15.

Contact: Arlene Leonard, Secretary
Glenn Miller Birthplace Society
107 East Main Street, PO Box 61
Clarinda, IA 51632-0061
Phone: 712-542-2461
Fax: 712-542-2461
E-mail: gmbs@heartland.net

GOLF COURSE SUPERINTENDENTS ASSOCIATION OF AMERICA

https://www.gcsaa.org/

JOSEPH S. GARSKE COLLEGIATE GRANT PROGRAM
• See page 440

GREENHOUSE SCHOLARS

https://greenhousescholars.org/

GREENHOUSE SCHOLARS
• See page 571

HAGAN SCHOLARSHIP FOUNDATION

https://haganscholarships.org/

HAGAN SCHOLARSHIP
• See page 572

HARNESS HORSE YOUTH FOUNDATION

http://www.hhyf.org/

CURT GREENE MEMORIAL SCHOLARSHIP
• See page 464

HOSTESS COMMITTEE SCHOLARSHIPS/MISS AMERICA PAGEANT

http://www.missamerica.org/

MISS AMERICA COMMUNITY SERVICE SCHOLARSHIPS
• See page 465

MISS AMERICA ORGANIZATION COMPETITION SCHOLARSHIPS

Scholarship competition open to 70 contestants, each serving as state representative. Women will be judged in Private Interview, Swimsuit, Evening Wear and Talent competition. Other awards may be based on points assessed by judges during competitions. Upon reaching the National level, award values range from $2000 to $50,000. Additional awards not affecting the competition can be won with values from $1000 to $10,000.

Award: Prize for use in freshman, sophomore, junior, senior, or graduate years; not renewable. *Number:* 70. *Amount:* $2000–$50,000.

Eligibility Requirements: Applicant must be age 17-24; enrolled or expecting to enroll full- or part-time at a two-year or four-year or technical institution or university; female and must have an interest in beauty pageant. Available to U.S. citizens.

Application Requirements: Application form, entry in a contest. *Deadline:* varies.

Contact: Doreen Gordon, Controller and Scholarship Administrator
Phone: 609-345-7571 Ext. 27
Fax: 609-347-6079
E-mail: doreen@missamerica.org

MISS AMERICA SCHOLAR AWARD

$1000 award offered to one woman in each state, District of Columbia and U.S. Virgin Islands, competing at the state level, for academic excellence. Competition is opened only to those competing at the state level. Must submit official transcripts of the immediate prior two years (4 semesters) of academic study, along with application.

Award: Scholarship for use in freshman, sophomore, junior, senior, graduate, or postgraduate years; not renewable.

Eligibility Requirements: Applicant must be enrolled or expecting to enroll full- or part-time at a four-year institution or university; female and must have an interest in beauty pageant. Available to U.S. citizens.

Application Requirements: Application form, transcript. *Deadline:* varies.

Contact: Doreen Gordon, Controller and Scholarship Administrator
Phone: 609-345-7571 Ext. 27
Fax: 609-347-6079
E-mail: doreen@missamerica.org

HOUSE OF BLUES MUSIC FORWARD FOUNDATION

https://hobmusicforward.org/

LIVE NATION—US CONCERTS SCHOLARSHIP AWARD

This $10,000 scholarship is open to students interested in the five core areas of the Live Nation business: concert promotion and venue operation, sponsorship and advertising, ticketing, e-commerce and artist management. Finalists for this scholarship will also be considered for an internship opportunity with Live Nation Entertainment.

Award: Scholarship for use in junior or senior years; not renewable. *Number:* 1. *Amount:* $10,000.

Eligibility Requirements: Applicant must be enrolled or expecting to enroll full-time at a four-year institution or university and must have an interest in music or music/singing.

Application Requirements: Application form, essay. *Deadline:* March 31.

Contact: Ms. Nazanin Fatemian, House of Blues Music Forward
Foundation
House of Blues Music Forward Foundation
7060 Hollywood Boulevard, Floor 2
Los Angeles, CA 90028
Phone: 323-821-3946
E-mail: nfatemian@hobmusicforward.org

INSTITUTE OF INDUSTRIAL ENGINEERS

https://www.iise.org/

A.O. PUTNAM MEMORIAL SCHOLARSHIP

• See page 441

C.B. GAMBRELL UNDERGRADUATE SCHOLARSHIP

• See page 441

CISE UNDERGRADUATE SCHOLARSHIP

$2000 scholarship will be awarded to an undergraduate industrial engineering student for the best application of corporate social responsibility, resilience, or sustainability principals aligned with classic industrial engineering techniques to a project for an enterprise. Interested candidates must complete an application form, as well as submit a complete description of the project, including provision of a financial analysis using the triple-bottom line definitions of sustainability, showing a positive cash flow or return on investment to the enterprise over the project life. Applicants should have at least a 3.4 GPA.

Award: Scholarship for use in freshman, sophomore, junior, or senior years; not renewable. *Number:* 1. *Amount:* $2000.

Eligibility Requirements: Applicant must be enrolled or expecting to enroll full-time at an institution or university and must have an interest in leadership. Available to U.S. citizens.

Application Requirements: Application form. *Deadline:* February 1.

Contact: Bonnie Cameron, Headquarters Operations Administrator
E-mail: bcameron@iise.org

DWIGHT D. GARDNER SCHOLARSHIP

• See page 441

HAROLD AND INGE MARCUS SCHOLARSHIP

• See page 441

IISE COUNCIL OF FELLOWS UNDERGRADUATE SCHOLARSHIP

• See page 441

JOHN L. IMHOFF SCHOLARSHIP

Available to a student pursuing an industrial engineering degree who, by academic, employment and/or professional achievements, has made noteworthy contributions to the development of the industrial engineering profession through international understanding. Note that IISE membership is not required. Must have an overall point-hour average of 3.40.

Award: Scholarship for use in freshman, sophomore, junior, or senior years; not renewable. *Number:* 2. *Amount:* $1000.

Eligibility Requirements: Applicant must be enrolled or expecting to enroll full-time at an institution or university and must have an interest in leadership. Available to U.S. citizens.

Application Requirements: Application form, essay. *Deadline:* November 15.

Contact: Bonnie Cameron, Operations Administrator
Phone: 770-449-0461 Ext. 105
E-mail: bcameron@iise.org

LISA ZAKEN AWARD FOR EXCELLENCE

• See page 441

MARVIN MUNDEL MEMORIAL SCHOLARSHIP

• See page 442

PRESIDENTS SCHOLARSHIP

• See page 442

UPS SCHOLARSHIP FOR FEMALE STUDENTS

• See page 442

UPS SCHOLARSHIP FOR MINORITY STUDENTS

• See page 442

JACKIE ROBINSON FOUNDATION

http://www.jackierobinson.org/

JACKIE ROBINSON SCHOLARSHIP

• See page 466

JOHN F. AND ANNA LEE STACEY SCHOLARSHIP FUND

http://www.nationalcowboymuseum.org/

JOHN F. AND ANNA LEE STACEY SCHOLARSHIP FUND

Scholarships for artists who are high school graduates between the ages of 18 and 35, who are U.S. citizens, and whose work is devoted to the classical or conservative tradition of Western culture. Awards are for drawing or painting only. Must submit no more than six color digital images of work.

Award: Scholarship for use in freshman, sophomore, junior, senior, graduate, or postgraduate years; not renewable. *Number:* 3–5. *Amount:* $1000–$4000.

Eligibility Requirements: Applicant must be age 18-35; enrolled or expecting to enroll full- or part-time at a two-year or four-year or technical institution or university and must have an interest in art. Available to U.S. citizens.

Application Requirements: Application form. *Deadline:* February 1.

Contact: Ms. Melissa Owens, Registrar & Exhibits Coordinator
John F. and Anna Lee Stacey Scholarship Fund
National Cowboy and Western Heritage Museum
1700 NE 63rd Street
Oklahoma City, OK 73111
Phone: 405-478-2250 Ext. 220
Fax: 405-478-4714
E-mail: registrar@nationalcowboymuseum.org

JUNIOR ACHIEVEMENT

http://www.ja.org/

JOE FRANCOMANO SCHOLARSHIP

• See page 443

KNIGHTS OF PYTHIAS

http://www.pythias.org/

KNIGHTS OF PYTHIAS POSTER CONTEST

Poster contest open to all high school students in the U.S. and Canada. Contestants must submit an original drawing. Eight winners are chosen. The winners are not required to attend institution of higher education.

Award: Prize for use in freshman year; not renewable. *Number:* 8. *Amount:* $100–$1000.

Eligibility Requirements: Applicant must be high school student; planning to enroll or expecting to enroll full- or part-time at a four-year institution or university and must have an interest in art. Available to U.S. and Canadian citizens.

Application Requirements: Entry in a contest. *Deadline:* April 30.

Contact: Alfred Saltzman, Supreme Secretary
Phone: 617-472-8800
Fax: 617-376-0363
E-mail: kop@earthlink.net

LADIES AUXILIARY TO THE VETERANS OF FOREIGN WARS

http://www.ladiesauxvfw.org/

YOUNG AMERICAN CREATIVE PATRIOTIC ART AWARDS PROGRAM

One-time awards for high school students in grades 9 through 12. Must submit an original work of art expressing their patriotism. First place state-level winners go on to national competition. Eight awards of varying amounts. Must reside in same state as sponsoring organization.

Award: Scholarship for use in freshman, sophomore, junior, or senior years; not renewable. *Number:* up to 8. *Amount:* $500–$10,000.

Eligibility Requirements: Applicant must be high school student; planning to enroll or expecting to enroll full-time at a two-year or four-year or technical institution or university; single and must have an interest in art. Available to U.S. citizens.

Application Requirements: Application form, artwork, entry in a contest. *Deadline:* March 31.

Contact: Connie Wahlen, Programs Coordinator
Phone: 816-561-8655
E-mail: cwahlen@ladiesauxvfw.org

LEAGUE FOUNDATION

http://www.leaguefoundation.org/

LEAGUE FOUNDATION ACADEMIC SCHOLARSHIP

The LEAGUE Foundation provides financial resources for U.S. Citizens that are self- identified as Gay, Lesbian, Bisexual, and Transgender high school seniors entering their first year of institutions of higher learning. The scholarship application opens annually in January and closes in April with awards distributed in the summer of each year. For scholarship criteria: www.leaguefoundation.org.

Award: Scholarship for use in freshman year; not renewable. *Number:* 4–8. *Amount:* $1500–$2500.

Eligibility Requirements: Applicant must be high school student; planning to enroll or expecting to enroll full-time at a two-year or four-year or technical institution or university and must have an interest in LGBT issues. Available to U.S. citizens.

Application Requirements: Application form, community service, essay, personal photograph. *Deadline:* April 30.

Contact: Mr. Mark Patterson, Executive Director
LEAGUE Foundation
208 South Akard Street
Room 20th Floor
Dallas, TX 75202
Phone: 469-571-2279
E-mail: info@leaguefoundation.org

LEE-JACKSON EDUCATIONAL FOUNDATION

http://www.lee-jackson.org/

LEE-JACKSON EDUCATIONAL FOUNDATION SCHOLARSHIP COMPETITION

• *See page 579*

LIBERTY GRAPHICS INC.

http://www.lgtees.com

ANNUAL LIBERTY GRAPHICS ART CONTEST

• *See page 579*

THE LINCOLN FORUM

http://www.thelincolnforum.org/

PLATT FAMILY SCHOLARSHIP PRIZE ESSAY CONTEST

The Platt Family Scholarship Prize Essay Contest is designed for students who are full-time students in an American college or university. You do not have to be an American citizen, but you do need to be attending an AMERICAN COLLEGE OR UNIVERSITY during the eligibility period. For details, refer to website http://thelincolnforum.org/scholarship-essay-contest.php

Award: Prize for use in freshman, sophomore, junior, or senior years; not renewable. *Number:* 3. *Amount:* $500–$1500.

Eligibility Requirements: Applicant must be enrolled or expecting to enroll full-time at a two-year or four-year institution or university and must have an interest in writing. Available to U.S. and non-U.S. citizens.

Application Requirements: Entry in a contest, essay. *Deadline:* July 31.

Contact: Don McCue, Director
Phone: 909-798-7632
E-mail: archives@akspl.org

MANA DE SAN DIEGO

http://www.manasd.org/

MANA DE SAN DIEGO SYLVIA CHAVEZ MEMORIAL SCHOLARSHIP

• *See page 467*

MARTIN D. ANDREWS SCHOLARSHIP

http://www.mdascholarship.tripod.com/

MARTIN D. ANDREWS MEMORIAL SCHOLARSHIP FUND

One-time award for student seeking undergraduate or graduate degree. Recipient must have been in a Drum Corp for at least three years. Must submit essay and two recommendations. Must be U.S. citizen.

Award: Scholarship for use in freshman, sophomore, junior, senior, or graduate years; not renewable. *Number:* 2–5. *Amount:* $300–$1000.

Eligibility Requirements: Applicant must be enrolled or expecting to enroll full- or part-time at a two-year or four-year institution or university and must have an interest in drum corps. Available to U.S. citizens.

Application Requirements: Application form, essay. *Deadline:* June 1.

Contact: Peter Andrews, Scholarship Committee
Martin D. Andrews Scholarship
2069 Perkins Street
Bristol, CT 06010
Phone: 860-250-4757
E-mail: psandrews@charter.net

MCCURRY FOUNDATION INC.

http://www.mccurryfoundation.org/

MCCURRY FOUNDATION SCHOLARSHIP

• *See page 583*

NATIONAL AMATEUR BASEBALL FEDERATION (NABF)

http://www.nabf.com/

NATIONAL AMATEUR BASEBALL FEDERATION SCHOLARSHIP FUND

Scholarships are awarded to candidates who are enrolled in an accredited college or university. Applicant must be a bona fide participant in a federation event and be sponsored by an NABF-franchised member association. Self-nominated candidates are not eligible for this scholarship award.

Award: Scholarship for use in freshman, sophomore, junior, or senior years; not renewable.

Eligibility Requirements: Applicant must be enrolled or expecting to enroll full-time at a two-year or four-year or technical institution or university and must have an interest in athletics/sports. Available to U.S. citizens.

Application Requirements: Application form, community service, essay, letter of acceptance, recommendations or references, transcript. *Deadline:* November 15.

Contact: Awards Committee Chairman
National Amateur Baseball Federation (NABF)
PO Box 705
Bowie, MD 20718

NATIONAL ASSOCIATION F OR CAMPUS ACTIVITIES

http://www.naca.org/

ALAN DAVIS SCHOLARSHIP

This scholarship is an annual award for one outstanding undergraduate. The Alan Davis Scholarship recipient possesses an inspired spirit and creative spark. This individual is innovative and forward thinking in regards to the events and opportunities available to the student body. The awarded scholar embodies the core qualities of both NACA and Riddle & Bloom: creativity, originality, pride for his/her school and unparalleled ambition and vision.

Award: Scholarship for use in sophomore, junior, or senior years; not renewable. *Number:* 1. *Amount:* $5000.

Eligibility Requirements: Applicant must be enrolled or expecting to enroll full-time at an institution or university and must have an interest in leadership. Available to U.S. citizens.

Application Requirements: Application form, application form may be submitted online, essay. *Deadline:* November 30.

Contact: Sarah Keeling, Director of Education and Research
Phone: 803-217-3485
E-mail: scholarships@naca.org

LORI RHETT MEMORIAL SCHOLARSHIP
• *See page 468*

NATIONAL ASSOCIATION FOR CAMPUS ACTIVITIES MID ATLANTIC SCHOLARSHIP FOR STUDENT LEADERS
• *See page 468*

NATIONAL ASSOCIATION FOR CAMPUS ACTIVITIES SCHOLARSHIPS FOR STUDENT LEADERS
• *See page 468*

NATIONAL ASSOCIATION FOR CAMPUS ACTIVITIES SOUTH STUDENT LEADERSHIP SCHOLARSHIPS
• *See page 468*

TESE CALDARELLI MEMORIAL SCHOLARSHIP
• *See page 468*

ZAGUNIS STUDENT LEADER SCHOLARSHIP

The Zagunis Student Leader Scholarship was established by the former NACA Great Lakes Region to provide financial assistance to undergraduate or graduate student leaders enrolled in colleges and universities located in the Mid Atlantic & Mid America regions. Current undergraduate or graduate students attending a school in these regions are eligible to apply.

Award: Scholarship for use in freshman, sophomore, junior, senior, or graduate years; not renewable. *Number:* 1. *Amount:* $300.

Eligibility Requirements: Applicant must be enrolled or expecting to enroll full-time at a two-year institution or university; studying in Delaware, District of Columbia, Illinois, Indiana, Kentucky, Maryland, Michigan, New Jersey, New York, Ohio, Ontario, Pennsylvania, West Virginia and must have an interest in leadership. Available to U.S. citizens.

Application Requirements: Application form, application form may be submitted online, essay. *Deadline:* November 30.

Contact: Sarah Keeling, Director of Education and Research
Phone: 803-217-3485
E-mail: scholarships@naca.org

NATIONAL ASSOCIATION FOR THE SELF-EMPLOYED

http://www.NASE.org/

NASE SCHOLARSHIPS
• *See page 446*

NATIONAL COSTUMERS ASSOCIATION SCHOLARSHIPS

http://www.costumers.org

NATIONAL COSTUMERS ASSOCIATION SCHOLARSHIPS

The National Costumers Association offers two types of scholarships. The Memorial scholarship is an annual scholarship based on a brief bio and essay and GPA. The Creative scholarship is offered in odd number years is and consists of a hands on project submitted for judging.

Award: Scholarship for use in freshman, sophomore, junior, senior, graduate, or postgraduate years; not renewable. *Number:* 1–5. *Amount:* $250–$1000.

Eligibility Requirements: Applicant must be age 17 and over; enrolled or expecting to enroll full-time at a two-year or four-year institution or university and must have an interest in museum/preservation work, sewing, or theater. Available to U.S. and non-U.S. citizens.

Application Requirements: Application form, autobiography, essay, personal photograph. *Deadline:* April 1.

Contact: Linda Adams Foat, Past President
National Costumers Association Scholarships
1321 South Demeter Drive
Freeport, IL 61032
Phone: 815-233-1861
E-mail: ipp@costumers.org

NATIONAL SOCIETY OF COLLEGIATE SCHOLARS (NSCS)

https://nscs.org/

NSCS EXEMPLARY SCHOLAR AWARD
• *See page 447*

NATIONAL SOCIETY OF HIGH SCHOOL SCHOLARS

http://www.nshss.org

CLAES NOBEL ACADEMIC SCHOLARSHIPS
• *See page 448*

NATIONAL SCHOLAR AWARDS FOR NSHSS MEMBERS
• *See page 448*

ROBERT P. SHEPPARD LEADERSHIP AWARD FOR NSHSS MEMBERS
• *See page 448*

NATIONAL SOCIETY OF THE SONS OF THE AMERICAN REVOLUTION

http://www.sar.org/

JOSEPH S. RUMBAUGH HISTORICAL ORATION CONTEST

Prize ranging from $1000 to $3000 is awarded to a sophomore, junior, or senior. The oration must be original and not less than five minutes or more than six minutes in length.

Award: Prize for use in sophomore, junior, or senior years; not renewable. *Number:* 1–3. *Amount:* $1000–$3000.

Eligibility Requirements: Applicant must be enrolled or expecting to enroll full-time at a two-year or four-year or technical institution or university and must have an interest in public speaking. Available to U.S. and non-U.S. citizens.

Application Requirements: Application form, entry in a contest. *Deadline:* June 15.

Contact: Lawrence Mckinley, National Chairman
National Society of the Sons of the American Revolution
12158 Holly Knoll Circle
Great Fall, VA 22066
E-mail: dustoff@bellatlantic.net

NFIB YOUNG ENTREPRENEUR FOUNDATION

http://www.nfib.com/yef

YOUNG ENTREPRENEUR AWARDS

The Young Entrepreneur Awards program was designed to identify and reward students who have demonstrated entrepreneurial spirit and initiative by running their own entrepreneurial venture. Since 2003, YEF has awarded over 2,500 scholarships worth more than $2.5 million to graduating high school seniors. We award students who have demonstrated entrepreneurial talent by owning and/or operating their own business. Young Entrepreneur Awards range from $2,000 to $25,000 and enable students to further their studies in a two-year or four-year institution of higher learning while encouraging them to consider joining the ranks of America's independent business owners. For more information visit www.nfib.com/yea.

Award: Scholarship for use in freshman year; not renewable. *Number:* 100. *Amount:* $2000–$25,000.

Eligibility Requirements: Applicant must be high school student; planning to enroll or expecting to enroll full- or part-time at a two-year or four-year or technical institution or university and must have an interest in entrepreneurship. Available to U.S. citizens.

Application Requirements: Application form, essay, interview.

Contact: Molly young, Director, Young Entrepreneur Foundation
NFIB Young Entrepreneur Foundation
1201 F Street NW
Suite 200
Washington, DC 20004
Phone: 202-314-2042
E-mail: yef@nfib.org

OPTIMIST INTERNATIONAL FOUNDATION

http://www.optimist.org/

OPTIMIST INTERNATIONAL ESSAY CONTEST

Essay contest for youth under the age of 19 who have not graduated high school or its equivalent. U.S. students attending school on a military installation outside the United States are eligible to enter in their last U.S. home of record. Club winners advance to the District contest to compete for a college scholarship.

Award: Scholarship for use in freshman, sophomore, junior, or senior years; not renewable. *Amount:* $2500.

Eligibility Requirements: Applicant must be age 18 or under; enrolled or expecting to enroll full- or part-time at a two-year or four-year or technical institution or university and must have an interest in writing. Available to U.S. and non-U.S. citizens.

Application Requirements: Application form, essay.

Contact: Ms. Danielle Baugher, International Programs Manager
Phone: 800-500-8130 Ext. 235
E-mail: programs@optimist.org

OPTIMIST INTERNATIONAL ORATORICAL CONTEST

Contest for youth to gain experience in public speaking and to provide them with the opportunity to compete for college scholarships. The contest is open to youth under the age of 19 before graduating high school or the equivalent. Students must first compete at the Club level. Club winners are then entered into the Zone contest and those winners compete in the District contest. District winners are awarded scholarships. District winners will be able to compete in a Regional

Contest then be able to compete in the World Championships at St. Louis University in St. Louis, Missouri USA.

Award: Scholarship for use in freshman, sophomore, junior, or senior years; not renewable. *Amount:* $1000–$2500.

Eligibility Requirements: Applicant must be age 18 or under; enrolled or expecting to enroll full- or part-time at a two-year or four-year or technical institution or university and must have an interest in public speaking. Available to U.S. and non-U.S. citizens.

Application Requirements: Application form.

Contact: Dana Thomas, Director of International Programs
Optimist International Foundation
4494 Lindell Boulevard
St. Louis, MO 63108
Phone: 800-500-8130
E-mail: programs@optimist.org

ORDER SONS AND DAUGHTERS OF ITALY IN AMERICA

http://www.osia.org/

ORDER SONS AND DAUGHTERS OF ITALY - HENRY SALVATORI SCHOLARSHIP

• See page 528

OREGON COMMUNITY FOUNDATION

http://www.oregoncf.org/

DOROTHY S. CAMPBELL MEMORIAL SCHOLARSHIP FUND

Scholarship for female graduates of Oregon high schools with a strong and continuing interest in the game of golf. For use in the pursuit of a postsecondary education at a four-year college or university in Oregon.

Award: Scholarship for use in freshman, sophomore, junior, or senior years; renewable. *Number:* 9. *Amount:* $1000.

Eligibility Requirements: Applicant must be enrolled or expecting to enroll full-time at a four-year institution or university; female and must have an interest in golf. Available to U.S. citizens.

Application Requirements: Application form, recommendations or references. *Deadline:* March 1.

Contact: Dianne Causey, Program Associate for Scholarships and Grants
Phone: 503-227-6846 Ext. 1418
E-mail: dcausey@oregoncf.org

PENGUIN GROUP

http://www.penguin.com/services-academic/essayhome/

SIGNET CLASSIC SCHOLARSHIP ESSAY CONTEST

Open to 11th and 12th grade full-time matriculated students who are attending high schools located in the fifty United States and the District of Columbia, or home-schooled students between the ages of 16 to 18 who are residents of the fifty United States and the District of Columbia. Students should submit four copies of a two- to three-page double-spaced essay answering one of three possible questions on a designated novel. Entries must be submitted by a high school English teacher.

Award: Scholarship for use in freshman year; not renewable. *Number:* 5. *Amount:* $1000.

Eligibility Requirements: Applicant must be high school student; planning to enroll or expecting to enroll full-time at a four-year institution or university and must have an interest in writing. Available to U.S. citizens.

Application Requirements: Entry in a contest, essay, recommendations or references. *Deadline:* April 15.

Contact: Kym Giacoppe, Academic Marketing Assistant
Phone: 212-366-2377
E-mail: academic@penguin.com

PET LIFESTYLE AND YOU (P.L.A.Y.)

https://www.petplay.com/

SCHOLARS HELPING COLLARS SCHOLARSHIP

Students from across the U.S. are invited to apply for P.L.A.Y.'s annual Scholars Helping Collars Scholarship. This $1,000 scholarship rewards one student who can tell the best story, describing the impact he or she made in the life of a rescue animal or animal welfare cause in general. The contest is open to U.S. residents. No purchase necessary. All participants must be enrolled as a full-time high school senior. Entries are limited to one submission per person. Immediate family members of P.L.A.Y. employees are excluded from this contest. All essay submissions must be received by 11:59pm PT on Wednesday, February 28, 2018. To apply, students will submit an essay with 2-3 photos of their volunteer efforts to help animals in need and how that involvement has changed their lives or shaped their perceptions on the importance of animal welfare by February 28, 2018. The essay should be between 500-1000 words. Send a Word doc attachment to SCHOLARSHIP@ PETPLAY.COM with your essay submission. The file name should be your full name, state, and date of birth. For example, Chipper-Jones-GA-4-24-1992. 2-3 photos of your volunteer efforts to help animals in need. In the body of your email, include student's full name, date of birth, email address, postal address, high school they are currently enrolled in, and a phone number to contact. P.L.A.Y. will select the winner based on the best essay as determined by our internal panel of judges. Selection criteria will include, but is not limited to: compelling and engaging description of volunteer efforts and their impact on the personal life of the student; thematic consistency throughout the submission around the central thesis; proper spelling and grammar usage throughout the submission. Following the February 28th deadline, P.L.A.Y. will select the winner during the month of March and will announce the winner in April 2018 on the website pending notification of the student and his or her family. Please note that winner must provide proof of acceptance to college/university of choice prior to receiving the grand prize.

Award: Scholarship for use in freshman year; not renewable. *Number:* 1. *Amount:* $1000.

Eligibility Requirements: Applicant must be high school student; planning to enroll or expecting to enroll full-time at a four-year institution or university and must have an interest in wildlife conservation/animal rescue. Available to U.S. citizens.

Application Requirements: Essay. *Deadline:* February 28.

Contact: Scholarships
    E-mail: scholarship@petplay.com

PHI SIGMA PI NATIONAL HONOR FRATERNITY

http://www.phisigmapi.org/

RICHARD CECIL TODD AND CLAUDA PENNOCK TODD TRIPOD SCHOLARSHIP
• See page 450

PONY OF THE AMERICAS CLUB INC.

http://www.poac.org/

POAC NATIONAL SCHOLARSHIP
• See page 451

PRIDE FOUNDATION

http://www.PrideFoundation.org/

PRIDE FOUNDATION SCHOLARSHIP PROGRAM
• See page 598

PRO BOWLERS ASSOCIATION

http://www.pba.com/

BILLY WELU BOWLING SCHOLARSHIP

Scholarship awarded annually, recognizing exemplary qualities in male and female college students who compete in the sport of bowling. Winner will receive $1000. Candidates must be amateur bowlers who are currently in college (preceding the application deadline) and maintain at least a 2.5 GPA or equivalent.

Award: Scholarship for use in freshman, sophomore, junior, or senior years; not renewable. *Number:* 1. *Amount:* $1000.

Eligibility Requirements: Applicant must be enrolled or expecting to enroll full-time at a two-year or four-year institution or university and must have an interest in bowling. Available to U.S. citizens.

Application Requirements: Application form, essay, transcript. *Deadline:* May 31.

Contact: Karen Day, Controller
    Phone: 206-332-9688
    Fax: 206-332-9722
    E-mail: karen.day@pba.com

THE RESERVE OFFICERS ASSOCIATION

http://www.roa.org/

HENRY J. REILLY MEMORIAL SCHOLARSHIP-HIGH SCHOOL SENIORS AND FIRST YEAR FRESHMEN
• See page 452

ROBERT H. MOLLOHAN FAMILY CHARITABLE FOUNDATION, INC.

http://www.mollohanfoundation.org/

DR. ROBERTO F. CUNANAN MEMORIAL SCHOLARSHIP
• See page 599

ST. CLAIRE REGIONAL MEDICAL CENTER

http://www.st-claire.org/

SR. MARY JEANNETTE WESS, S.N.D. SCHOLARSHIP
• See page 470

SISTER KENNY REHABILITATION INSTITUTE

http://www.allina.com/ahs/ski.nsf

ART OF POSSIBILITIES ART SHOW & SALE
• See page 484

SOUTH DAKOTA BOARD OF REGENTS

http://www.sdbor.edu/

SOUTH DAKOTA BOARD OF REGENTS MARLIN R. SCARBOROUGH MEMORIAL SCHOLARSHIP

One-time merit-based award for a student who is a junior at a South Dakota university. Must be nominated by the university and must have community service and leadership experience. Minimum 3.5 GPA required. Application deadline varies.

Award: Scholarship for use in junior year; not renewable. *Number:* 1. *Amount:* $1000.

Eligibility Requirements: Applicant must be enrolled or expecting to enroll full- or part-time at an institution or university; studying in South Dakota and must have an interest in leadership. Available to U.S. citizens.

Application Requirements: Application form, essay.

Contact: Dr. Paul Turman, System Vice President for Research and
    Economic Development
    South Dakota Board of Regents
    301 East Capital Avenue, Suite 200
    Pierre, SD 57501
    Phone: 605-773-3455
    Fax: 605-773-2422
    E-mail: paul.turman@sdbor.edu

STONEWALL COMMUNITY FOUNDATION

http://www.stonewallfoundation.org/

HARRY BARTEL MEMORIAL SCHOLARSHIP
• *See page 470*

LEVIN-GOFFE SCHOLARSHIP FOR LGBTQI IMMIGRANTS

The Levin-Goffe Scholarship Fund was established to cover up to two years of schooling for immigrants here in New York City who identify as LGBTQI. Scholarships from this fund are intended to provide a measure of economic stability for those who stand at the intersection of marginalization that can be created by being both LGBTQI and an immigrant.

Award: Scholarship for use in sophomore or junior years; renewable. *Number:* 3. *Amount:* $25,000.

Eligibility Requirements: Applicant must be enrolled or expecting to enroll full-time at a four-year institution or university; studying in New York and must have an interest in LGBT issues.

Application Requirements: Application form, application form may be submitted online (http://stonewallfoundation.org/scholarships).

Contact: Program Manager
Stonewall Community Foundation
Stonewall Community Foundation
446 West 33rd Street
New York, NY 10001
Phone: 212-457.1341
E-mail: scholarships@stonewallfoundation.org

SWISS BENEVOLENT SOCIETY OF NEW YORK

http://www.sbsny.org/

MEDICUS STUDENT EXCHANGE
• *See page 533*

TAU KAPPA EPSILON EDUCATIONAL FOUNDATION

http://www.tke.org/

CHARLES J. TRABOLD SCHOLARSHIP
• *See page 454*

J.D. WILLIAMS SCHOLARSHIP
• *See page 455*

J. RUSSEL SALSBURY MEMORIAL SCHOLARSHIP
• *See page 455*

MILES GRAY MEMORIAL SCHOLARSHIP
• *See page 455*

TERRY FOUNDATION

www.terryfoundation.org/

TERRY FOUNDATION TRADITIONAL SCHOLARSHIP
• *See page 604*

TERRY FOUNDATION TRANSFER SCHOLARSHIP
• *See page 604*

TEXAS 4-H YOUTH DEVELOPMENT FOUNDATION

http://texas4hfoundation.org/

TEXAS 4-H OPPORTUNITY SCHOLARSHIP
• *See page 605*

TEXAS OUTDOOR WRITERS ASSOCIATION

http://www.towa.org/

TEXAS OUTDOOR WRITERS ASSOCIATION SCHOLARSHIP
• *See page 606*

TEXAS TENNIS FOUNDATION

http://www.texastennisfoundation.com/

TEXAS TENNIS FOUNDATION SCHOLARSHIPS AND ENDOWMENTS
• *See page 606*

TOSHIBA/NSTA

http://www.exploravision.org/

EXPLORAVISION SCIENCE COMPETITION

Competition for students in grades K-12 who enter as small teams by grade level and work on a science project. In each group, first place team members are each awarded a savings bond worth $10,000 at maturity, second place, a $5000 savings bond. Deadline varies.

Award: Prize for use in freshman year; not renewable. *Amount:* $5000–$10,000.

Eligibility Requirements: Applicant must be enrolled or expecting to enroll full- or part-time at a four-year institution or university and must have an interest in science. Available to U.S. citizens.

Application Requirements: Application form, entry in a contest. *Deadline:* varies.

Contact: Paloma Olbes, Media Contact
Phone: 212-388-1400
E-mail: polbes@dba-pr.com

UNITED NEGRO COLLEGE FUND

http://www.uncf.org/

UNCF/KOCH SCHOLARS PROGRAM
• *See page 536*

VETERANS OF FOREIGN WARS OF THE UNITED STATES

http://www.vfw.org/

VOICE OF DEMOCRACY PROGRAM

Student must be sponsored by a local VFW Post. Student submits a three to five minute audio essay on a contest theme (changes each year). Open to high school students (9th to 12th grade). Award available for all levels of postsecondary study in an American institution. Open to permanent U.S. residents only. Competition starts at local level. No entries are to be submitted to the National Headquarters. Visit website https://www.vfw.org/VOD/ for more information.

Award: Scholarship for use in freshman, sophomore, junior, senior, graduate, or postgraduate years; not renewable. *Number:* 54. *Amount:* $1000–$30,000.

Eligibility Requirements: Applicant must be high school student; age 14-19; planning to enroll or expecting to enroll full- or part-time at a two-year or four-year or technical institution or university and must have an interest in public speaking or writing. Available to U.S. citizens.

Application Requirements: Application form, essay. *Deadline:* October 31.

Contact: Kris Harmer, Program Coordinator
Veterans of Foreign Wars of the United States
406 West 34th Street
Kansas City, MO 64111
Phone: 816-968-1117
Fax: 816-968-1149
E-mail: kharmer@vfw.org

VSA

http://www.kennedy-center.org/education/vsa/

VSA PLAYWRIGHT DISCOVERY AWARD

Young writers with disabilities and collaborative groups that include students with disabilities, in U.S. grades 6-12 (or equivalents) or ages 11-18 for non-U.S. students, are invited to explore the disability experience through the art of writing for performance: plays, screenplays, spoken word poetry (for single performer or a group), or music theater. Writers are encouraged to craft short works from their own experiences and observations, create fictional characters and settings, or choose to write metaphorically or abstractly about the disability experience.

Award: Prize for use in freshman year; not renewable. *Number:* 1.

Eligibility Requirements: Applicant must be high school student; age 18 or under; planning to enroll or expecting to enroll full- or part-time at an institution or university and must have an interest in theater or writing. Available to U.S. citizens.

Application Requirements: Application form. *Deadline:* February 1.

Contact: Megan Bailey, Administrative Assistant
VSA
2700 F Street NW
Washington, DC 20566
Phone: 202-416-8822
E-mail: vsainfo@kennedy-center.org

WALTER W. NAUMBURG FOUNDATION

http://www.naumburg.org/

INTERNATIONAL VIOLONCELLO COMPETITION

Prizes of $2500 to $7500 awarded to violoncellists between the ages of 17 and 31. Application fee is $125.

Award: Prize for use in freshman, sophomore, junior, senior, graduate, or postgraduate years; not renewable. *Number:* 3. *Amount:* $2500–$7500.

Eligibility Requirements: Applicant must be age 17-31; enrolled or expecting to enroll full- or part-time at a two-year or four-year or technical institution or university and must have an interest in music. Available to U.S. and non-U.S. citizens.

Application Requirements: Applicant's audio track (CD) of no less than 30 minutes, application form, entry in a contest, recommendations or references, self-addressed stamped envelope with application. *Fee:* $125. *Deadline:* March 1.

Contact: Lucy Mann, Executive Director
Phone: 212-362-9877
Fax: 212-362-9877
E-mail: luciamann@aol.com

WESTERN INTERSTATE COMMISSION FOR HIGHER EDUCATION

http://www.wiche.edu/

WICHE'S WESTERN UNDERGRADUATE EXCHANGE (WUE)

• See page 610

WILLIAM G. AND MARIE SELBY FOUNDATION

http://www.selbyfdn.org/

SELBY SCHOLAR PROGRAM

• See page 611

WILLIAM RANDOLPH HEARST FOUNDATION

http://www.hearstfdn.org/

UNITED STATES SENATE YOUTH PROGRAM

Scholarship for high school juniors and seniors holding elected student offices. Two students selected from each state. Selection process will vary by state. Contact school principal or state department of education for information. Deadlines: early fall of each year for most states, but specific date will vary by state (see website www.ussenateyouth.org). Program is open to citizens of the United States Department of Defense schools overseas and the District of Columbia (not the territories).

Award: Scholarship for use in freshman, sophomore, junior, or senior years; not renewable. *Number:* 104. *Amount:* $10,000.

Eligibility Requirements: Applicant must be high school student; planning to enroll or expecting to enroll full-time at a two-year or four-year institution or university; single; studying in Alabama, Alaska, Arizona, Arkansas, California, Colorado, Connecticut, Delaware, District of Columbia, Florida, Georgia, Hawaii, Idaho, Illinois, Indiana, Iowa, Kansas, Kentucky, Louisiana, Maine, Maryland, Massachusetts, Michigan, Minnesota, Mississippi, Missouri, Montana, Nebraska, Nevada, New Hampshire, New Jersey, New Mexico, New York, North Carolina, North Dakota, Ohio, Oklahoma, Oregon, Pennsylvania, Rhode Island, South Carolina, South Dakota, Tennessee, Texas, Utah, Vermont, Virginia, Washington, West Virginia, Wisconsin, Wyoming and must have an interest in leadership or public speaking. Available to U.S. citizens.

Application Requirements: Application form, essay, interview.

Contact: Lynn DeSmet, Deputy Program Director
William Randolph Hearst Foundation
90 New Montgomery Street
Suite 1212
San Francisco, CA 94105
Phone: 415-908-4540
E-mail: ussyp@hearstfdn.org

WOMEN IN AVIATION, INTERNATIONAL

http://www.wai.org/

AIRBUS LEADERSHIP GRANT

• See page 457

WOMEN'S BASKETBALL COACHES ASSOCIATION

http://www.wbca.org/

WBCA SCHOLARSHIP AWARD

One-time award for two women's basketball players who have demonstrated outstanding commitment to the sport of women's basketball and to academic excellence. Minimum 3.5 GPA required. Must be nominated by the head coach of women's basketball who is WBCA member.

Award: Scholarship for use in freshman, sophomore, junior, senior, or graduate years; not renewable. *Number:* up to 2. *Amount:* up to $1000.

Eligibility Requirements: Applicant must be enrolled or expecting to enroll full- or part-time at a four-year institution or university; female and must have an interest in athletics/sports. Available to U.S. and non-U.S. citizens.

Application Requirements: Application form, recommendations or references, statistics. *Deadline:* February 15.

Contact: Betty Jaynes, Consultant
Phone: 770-279-8027 Ext. 102
Fax: 770-279-6290
E-mail: bettyj@wbca.org

WOMEN'S WESTERN GOLF FOUNDATION

http://www.wwga.org/foundation.htm

WOMEN'S WESTERN GOLF FOUNDATION SCHOLARSHIP

Scholarships for female high school seniors for use at a four-year college or university. Based on academic record, financial need, character, and involvement in golf. Golf skill not a criteria. Must continue to have financial need. Award is $2000 per student per year. Must be 17 to 18 years of age.

Award: Scholarship for use in freshman year; renewable. *Number:* 20–70. *Amount:* $2000.

Eligibility Requirements: Applicant must be high school student; age 17-18; planning to enroll or expecting to enroll full-time at a four-year institution or university; female and must have an interest in golf. Available to U.S. citizens.

Application Requirements: Application form. *Deadline:* March 1.

Contact: David Grady, President
    Phone: 817-265-4074
    E-mail: grady@orderofomega.org

WRITER'S DIGEST

http://www.writersdigest.com/

WRITER'S DIGEST ANNUAL WRITING COMPETITION

Annual writing competition. Only original, unpublished entries in any of the ten categories accepted. Visit http://www.writersdigest.com/competitions/writers-digest-annual-competition for guidelines and entry form. Application fee.

Award: Prize for use in freshman, sophomore, junior, senior, or graduate years; not renewable. *Number:* 501. *Amount:* $100–$3000.

Eligibility Requirements: Applicant must be enrolled or expecting to enroll full- or part-time at a two-year or four-year or technical institution or university and must have an interest in writing. Available to U.S. and non-U.S. citizens.

Application Requirements: Application form, application form may be submitted online, entry in a contest. *Deadline:* May 1.

Contact: Nicole Howard, Customer Service Representative
    Phone: 715-445-4612
    Fax: 513-531-0798
    E-mail: writing-competitions@fwmedia.com

WRITER'S DIGEST POPULAR FICTION AWARDS

Writing contest accepts as many manuscripts as the applicant likes in each of the following categories: romance, mystery/crime fiction, sci-fi/fantasy, thriller/suspense and horror. Manuscripts must not be more than 4,000 words. http://www.writersdigest.com/popularfictionawards

Award: Prize for use in freshman, sophomore, junior, senior, graduate, or postgraduate years; not renewable. *Number:* 7. *Amount:* $500–$2500.

Eligibility Requirements: Applicant must be enrolled or expecting to enroll full- or part-time at a two-year or four-year or technical institution or university and must have an interest in writing. Available to U.S. and non-U.S. citizens.

Application Requirements: Application form, entry in a contest, manuscript. *Fee:* $20. *Deadline:* September 1.

Contact: Nicole Howard, Customer Service Representative
    Phone: 715-445-4612 Ext. 13430
    Fax: 513-531-0798
    E-mail: writing-competitions@fwmedia.com

WRITER'S DIGEST SELF-PUBLISHED BOOK AWARDS

Awards open to self-published books for which the author has paid full cost. Visit http://www.writersdigest.com/competitions/selfpublished/ for guidelines and entry form. Application fee: $99.

Award: Prize for use in freshman, sophomore, junior, senior, graduate, or postgraduate years; not renewable. *Number:* 45. *Amount:* $1000–$3000.

Eligibility Requirements: Applicant must be enrolled or expecting to enroll full- or part-time at a two-year or four-year or technical institution or university and must have an interest in writing. Available to U.S. and non-U.S. citizens.

Application Requirements: Application form, entry in a contest. *Fee:* $99. *Deadline:* April 1.

Contact: Nicole Howard, Customer Service Representative
    Phone: 715-445-4612 Ext. 13430
    Fax: 513-531-0798
    E-mail: writing-competitions@fwmedia.com

Miscellaneous Criteria

101ST AIRBORNE DIVISION ASSOCIATION

http://www.screamingeaglefoundation.org/

101ST AIRBORNE DIVISION ASSOCIATION CHAPPIE HALL SCHOLARSHIP PROGRAM

Scholarship to provide financial assistance to students who have the potential to become assets to our nation. The major factors to be considered in the evaluation and rating of applicants are eligibility, career objectives, academic record, financial need, and insight gained from the letter and/or essay requesting consideration, and letters of recommendation. Applicant's parents, grandparents, or spouse, living or deceased must be/had been a regular member with 101st Airborne Division Association in good standing. Dollar amount and total number of awards varies.

Award: Scholarship for use in freshman, sophomore, junior, or senior years; not renewable. *Number:* 15–30. *Amount:* $1000–$2000.

Eligibility Requirements: Applicant must be enrolled or expecting to enroll full-time at a two-year or four-year or technical institution or university. Available to U.S. and non-U.S. citizens.

Application Requirements: Application form, community service, essay, personal photograph. *Deadline:* May 11.

Contact: Mr. Randal Underhill, Executive Director
    101st Airborne Division Association
    PO Box 929
    Fort Campbell, KY 42223-0929
    Phone: 931-431-0199 Ext. 35
    E-mail: 101exec@comcast.net

1800WHEELCHAIR.COM

http://www.1800wheelchair.com/

1800WHEELCHAIR.COM SCHOLARSHIP

Established in 2006, the 1800wheelchair scholarship fund now bestows two $500 awards each year. We are going to repeat our visual contest. Please submit a 'visual poem', in a style of your choosing, on the theme of overcoming a personal challenge. Limit your 'visual poem' to an 8.5in x 11in piece of paper. You can choose to represent words, images, or both. It can abstract or representational. Please include a personal statement that gives us an idea of who you are and how your poem relates to a challenge you've faced. The poem and essay (combined) should be between 500 and 1,000 words, but feel free to write a little more or less. http://www.1800wheelchair.com/scholarship/

Award: Prize for use in freshman, sophomore, junior, or senior years; renewable. *Number:* 1. *Amount:* $500.

Eligibility Requirements: Applicant must be enrolled or expecting to enroll full-time at a two-year or four-year or technical institution or university. Available to U.S. citizens.

Application Requirements: Essay, personal photograph, portfolio. *Deadline:* May 1.

Contact: Mr. Joseph Piekarski, President
    1800Wheelchair.com
    320 Roebling Street
    Suite 515
    Brooklyn, NY 11211
    E-mail: scholarship@1800wheelchair.com

1DENTAL.COM

https://www.1dental.com/

1DENTAL SCHOLARSHIP

1Dental is offering a $500 college scholarship to eligible high school seniors and college students who apply. You can apply by visiting 1Dental's scholarship page (https://www.1dental.com/scholarship/) and filling out our scholarship. We offer this scholarship every year. Deadline is December 21, 2018.

Award: Scholarship for use in freshman, sophomore, junior, senior, or graduate years; not renewable. *Number:* 1. *Amount:* $500.

Eligibility Requirements: Applicant must be enrolled or expecting to enroll full-time at a two-year or four-year or technical institution or university. Available to U.S. citizens.

Application Requirements: Application form. *Deadline:* December 21.

Contact: Natasha G., 1Dental Scholarship Coordinator
E-mail: scholarships@1dental.com

37TH DIVISION VETERANS ASSOCIATION

http://www.37thdva.org/

37TH DIVISION VETERANS ASSOCIATION SCHOLARSHIP GRANT PROGRAM

Must be a current member of the organization in good standing or be the direct lineal descendant (to the third generation) of such a member. Please visit http://www.37thdva.org to see a copy of the application and to determine eligibility. Please note that the 37th Infantry Division was part of the U.S. Army.

Award: Scholarship for use in freshman, sophomore, junior, senior, graduate, or postgraduate years; not renewable.

Eligibility Requirements: Applicant must be enrolled or expecting to enroll full-time at a two-year or four-year or technical institution or university. Available to U.S. citizens.

Application Requirements: Application form, community service, essay. *Deadline:* May 1.

Contact: Mandy Oberyszyn, Executive Director
37th Division Veterans Association
35 East Chestnut Street, Suite 512
Columbus, OH 43215
Phone: 614-228-3788
E-mail: mandy@37thdva.org

4MYCASH.COM, LLC

https://www.4mycash.com

4MYCASH ST. LOUIS HARD MONEY SCHOLARSHIP

The 4MyCash St. Louis Hard Money Scholarship was created to help students interested in higher education reach their goal of attending college or university. Each year students who have lived in St. Louis, MO, at some point in their lives, will have the chance to provide a short essay. Applicants are asked to explain how their experience living in St. Louis has shaped them as individuals. St. Louis is a dynamic and historic city faced with many challenges, but it is also one of opportunity and growth. We encourage applicants to consider some of those challenges and opportunities in their essay. A committee will select a winner by the end of November. One winner will be selected and receive $1000 towards higher education.

Award: Scholarship for use in freshman, sophomore, junior, senior, graduate, or postgraduate years; renewable. *Number:* 1. *Amount:* $1000.

Eligibility Requirements: Applicant must be enrolled or expecting to enroll full- or part-time at a two-year or four-year or technical institution or university. Available to U.S. citizens.

Application Requirements: Application form, essay. *Deadline:* November 30.

Contact: Mr. Andrew Polsky, Manager
4MyCash.com, LLC
7750 Maryland Avenue
#50004
St. Louis, MO 63105
Phone: 310-764-7656
E-mail: andrew@4mycash.com

A-1 AUTO TRANSPORT, INC.

https://www.a1autotransport.com/a-1-auto-transport-scholarship/

A-1 AUTO TRANSPORT SCHOLARSHIP

The scholarship will be sent directly to the school/university/college financial aid office. 3 awards of $1000, $500 and $250.

Award: Scholarship for use in freshman, sophomore, junior, senior, graduate, or postgraduate years; renewable. *Number:* 3. *Amount:* $250–$1000.

Eligibility Requirements: Applicant must be enrolled or expecting to enroll full- or part-time at a two-year or four-year or technical institution or university. Available to U.S. and non-U.S. citizens.

Application Requirements: Essay. *Deadline:* March 10.

Contact: Joe Webster
Phone: 831-778-4529
E-mail: scholarships@a1autotransport.com

A1 GARAGE DOOR SERVICE

http://www.phoenixazgaragedoorrepair.com/

A1 GARAGE DOOR SERVICE COLLEGE SCHOLARSHIP

Ongoing scholarship for $1000, that will be awarded twice annually. In addition to the online application, the applicant must submit a an essay (600 words or more) or video which shows a students best idea for a marketing campaign in the service industry. One submission, per student, per semester. Essays/Videos may be features on our website, Facebook page, blog or other social media accounts.

Award: Scholarship for use in freshman, sophomore, junior, or senior years; not renewable. *Number:* 1. *Amount:* $1000.

Eligibility Requirements: Applicant must be enrolled or expecting to enroll full-time at a four-year institution. Available to U.S. citizens.

Application Requirements: Application form, essay. *Deadline:* continuous.

Contact: Tommy Mello
E-mail: tommy.mello.social@gmail.com

ACBL EDUCATIONAL FOUNDATION

https://sites.google.com/site/acbleducationfoundationorg/

KING OR QUEEN OF BRIDGE SCHOLARSHIP

The King or Queen of Bridge Scholarship is a merit program available to a graduating high school senior that is a member of The American Contract Bridge League (ACBL) and who plays and promotes bridge. The ACBL Educational Foundation will present a scholarship up to $2000 to the King or Queen of Bridge. Recent winners have been cited for outstanding tournament performances plus administrative, recreational and promotional activities related to bridge. Application can be found at http://www.acbl.org/kingofbridge

Award: Scholarship for use in freshman year; not renewable. *Number:* 1–2. *Amount:* $1000–$2000.

Eligibility Requirements: Applicant must be high school student and planning to enroll or expecting to enroll full- or part-time at a two-year or four-year or technical institution or university. Available to U.S. and non-U.S. citizens.

Application Requirements: Application form. *Deadline:* May 31.

Contact: Flo Belford, Grant Administrator
E-mail: edfoundation@acbl.org

ACOUSTICAL SOCIETY OF AMERICA

http://www.acousticalsociety.org

ROBERT W. YOUNG AWARD FOR UNDERGRADUATE STUDENT RESEARCH IN ACOUSTICS

A gift to the Acoustical Society Foundation made by the family of the late Robert W. Young in his honor has been established to grant undergraduate student research awards.

Award: Grant for use in freshman, sophomore, junior, or senior years; not renewable.

Eligibility Requirements: Applicant must be enrolled or expecting to enroll at an institution or university. Available to U.S. citizens.

Application Requirements: Application form.

Contact: Ms. Elaine Moran, Director of Operations
Acoustical Society of America
Acoustical Society of America
1305 Walt Whitman Road, Suite 300
Melville, NY 11747
Phone: 516-576-2360
Fax: 631-923-2875
E-mail: asa@acousticalsociety.org

ACTUALITY MEDIA, LLC

http://www.actualitymedia.org

CHANGEMAKER IN YOUR COMMUNITY DOCUMENTARY COMPETITION

On a Documentary Outreach with Actuality Media, crews work in groups of 3-5 people to research, write, shoot and edit a 10-minute-or-less Documentary Short focused on the work of a local changemaker. Crew members serve as Producer, Director, Editor, Cinematographer or Sound Design. In 2018, our Outreach locations are Guatemala, India, Cambodia and Zambia. The winner of the Changemaker in Your Community Documentary Competition will be able to select any one Outreach location to participate in, to have the full Participation Fee covered by your scholarship.

Award: Scholarship for use in freshman, sophomore, junior, senior, graduate, or postgraduate years; not renewable. *Number:* 1. *Amount:* $3100–$3500.

Eligibility Requirements: Applicant must be age 18 and over and enrolled or expecting to enroll part-time at a technical institution. Available to U.S. and non-U.S. citizens.

Application Requirements: Application form. *Deadline:* March 1.

Contact: Robin Canfield, International Programs Director
Phone: 503-208-5042
E-mail: ROBIN@ACTUALITYMEDIA.ORG

ACUITY TRAINING LIMITED

http://www.acuitytraining.co.uk

ACUITY TRAINING SCHOLARSHIP FOR OUTSTANDING LEADERSHIP AWARD

You have a chance to win a scholarship for $1000. Your video entry should ideally be three to four minutes in length. We want you to include some of the following ideas: A) What is leadership? Why is it valuable and how can it be developed? What is the difference between leadership, management and assertiveness?, B) Examples of how and when you have shown leadership and the benefits that have flowed from that, and C) The importance of leadership qualities in the 21st century workplace? The best submission will be awarded $1000 that can be used to further their education. This award is only available to students that are currently enrolled at a college, university, high school or trade school.

Award: Scholarship for use in freshman, sophomore, junior, senior, graduate, or postgraduate years; not renewable. *Number:* 1. *Amount:* $1000.

Eligibility Requirements: Applicant must be enrolled or expecting to enroll full- or part-time at a two-year or four-year or technical institution or university. Available to U.S. and non-U.S. citizens.

Application Requirements: Application form may be submitted online (http://www.acuitytraining.co.uk/scholarships/), video. *Deadline:* December 31.

Contact: Ben Richardson
Phone: 44-1483688488
E-mail: scholarships@acuitytraining.co.uk

AICPA INSTITUTE

https://www.aicpa.org/

AICPA FOUNDATION TWO-YEAR TRANSFER SCHOLARSHIP AWARD

This scholarship award is available to students looking to transfer from a two-year college to a four-year institution to complete their degree in accounting or an accounting-related field. Up to 25 students per academic year $5,000 per recipient for one year. Payments are sent directly to the school for credit to the account of the student. This scholarship is a non-renewable award. Applicants must have a GPA of at least 3.0 (on a 4.0 scale) and be a U.S. citizen or permanent resident.

Award: Scholarship for use in freshman or sophomore years; not renewable. *Amount:* $5000.

Eligibility Requirements: Applicant must be enrolled or expecting to enroll full-time at a two-year institution. Available to U.S. citizens.

Application Requirements: Application form, application form may be submitted online, essay. *Deadline:* March 1.

Contact: Scholarship Manager
AICPA Institute
220 Leigh Farm Road
AICPA / Academic & Student Engagement
Durham, NC 27707
E-mail: scholarships@aicpa.org

AWSCPA SCHOLARSHIP AWARD

The AWSCPA Scholarship Award is part of the AICPA Legacy Scholars program. This award provides financial assistance to outstanding female students majoring in accounting or an accounting-related field. All applications must be completed and submitted by the deadline to be considered. Students interested in being considered for more than one AICPA Legacy Scholarship awards need only complete one application—applicants will be evaluated for all awards for which they are eligible.

Award: Scholarship for use in sophomore, junior, senior, or graduate years; not renewable. *Number:* 4. *Amount:* $5000.

Eligibility Requirements: Applicant must be enrolled or expecting to enroll full-time at an institution or university and female. Available to U.S. citizens.

Application Requirements: Application form, application form may be submitted online, essay. *Deadline:* March 1.

Contact: Scholarship Manager
AICPA Institute
220 Leigh Farm Road
AICPA / Academic & Student Engagement
Durham, NC 27707
E-mail: scholarships@aicpa.org

AIRCRAFT ELECTRONICS ASSOCIATION EDUCATIONAL FOUNDATION

http://www.aea.net/

CHUCK PEACOCK MEMORIAL SCHOLARSHIP

Scholarship of $1000 for high school seniors or college students who plan to attend or are attending an aviation management program in an accredited school. Minimum 2.5 GPA required.

Award: Scholarship for use in freshman, sophomore, junior, or senior years; not renewable. *Number:* 1. *Amount:* $1000.

Eligibility Requirements: Applicant must be enrolled or expecting to enroll full- or part-time at a two-year or technical institution or university. Available to U.S. citizens.

Application Requirements: Application form, application form may be submitted online, essay. *Deadline:* April 1.

Contact: Geoff Hill, Director of Communications
Phone: 816-366-5107
E-mail: geoffh@aea.net

DAVID ARVER MEMORIAL SCHOLARSHIP

Scholarship of $1000 available to high school seniors and college students who plan to or are attending an avionics or aircraft repair program in an accredited school. Restricted to use for study in the following states: Iowa, Illinois, Indiana, Kansas, Michigan, Minnesota,

Mississippi, North Dakota, Nebraska, South Dakota, and Wisconsin. Minimum 2.5 GPA required.

Award: Scholarship for use in freshman, sophomore, junior, or senior years; not renewable. *Number:* 1. *Amount:* $1000.

Eligibility Requirements: Applicant must be enrolled or expecting to enroll full- or part-time at a two-year or technical institution or university. Available to U.S. and non-U.S. citizens.

Application Requirements: Application form, application form may be submitted online, essay. *Deadline:* April 1.

Contact: Geoff Hill, Director of Communications
Phone: 816-366-5107
E-mail: geoffh@aea.net

FIELD AVIATION COMPANY INC. SCHOLARSHIP

Scholarship for high school seniors and college students who plan to or are attending an avionics or aircraft repair program in an accredited college/university. The educational institution must be located in Canada.

Award: Scholarship for use in freshman, sophomore, junior, or senior years; not renewable. *Number:* 1. *Amount:* $1000.

Eligibility Requirements: Applicant must be enrolled or expecting to enroll full-time at a two-year or technical institution or university. Available to Canadian citizens.

Application Requirements: Application form, application form may be submitted online, essay. *Deadline:* April 1.

Contact: Geoff Hill, Director of Communications
Phone: 816-366-5107
E-mail: geoffh@aea.net

JOHNNY DAVIS MEMORIAL SCHOLARSHIP

Scholarship of $1000 available to high school seniors and college students who plan to or are attending an avionics or aircraft repair program in an accredited school. Minimum 2.5 GPA required.

Award: Scholarship for use in freshman, sophomore, junior, or senior years; not renewable. *Number:* 1. *Amount:* $1000.

Eligibility Requirements: Applicant must be enrolled or expecting to enroll full- or part-time at a two-year or technical institution or university. Available to U.S. citizens.

Application Requirements: Application form, application form may be submitted online, essay. *Deadline:* April 1.

Contact: Geoff Hill, Director of Communications
Phone: 816-366-5107
E-mail: geoffh@aea.net

AIR FORCE RESERVE OFFICER TRAINING CORPS

http://www.afrotc.com/

AIR FORCE ROTC COLLEGE SCHOLARSHIP TYPE 2

Pays up to $18,000 per year in college tuition and authorized fees at any public or private institution with an Air Force ROTC detachment. Scholarship payment is further capped at $9,000 per semester or $6,000 per quarter. Type 2 selectees will also receive a monthly living expense stipend and an annual book stipend. Applicants must pass a Department of Defense Medical Examination Review Board (DODMERB) medical exam and complete a Physical Fitness Assessment. SAT composite of 1240 or ACT composite of 26 and GPA of 3.0 or higher are also required for high school student applicants. For college applicants, the Air Force ROTC Commander will determine the minimum GPA and test scores, if applicable, for scholarship eligibility. Note: AFROTC Scholarships do not cover room and board.

Award: Scholarship for use in freshman, sophomore, junior, or senior years.

Eligibility Requirements: Applicant must be enrolled or expecting to enroll at a two-year institution or university. Available to U.S. citizens.

Application Requirements: Application form, application form may be submitted online.

AIR FORCE ROTC COLLEGE SCHOLARSHIP TYPE 7

Pays full (100 percent) college tuition and authorized fees (capped at the in-state tuition rate) at a public institution with an Air Force ROTC detachment. Type 7 selectees will also receive a monthly living expense stipend and an annual book stipend. Students offered a Type 7 scholarship will be given the option to convert their scholarship to a three-year Type 2 scholarship that can be used at out-of-state or private schools. A three-year Type 2 scholarship will start during the sophomore year of school. Applicants must pass a Department of Defense Medical Examination Review Board (DODMERB) medical exam and complete a Physical Fitness Assessment. SAT composite of 1240 or ACT composite of 26 and GPA of 3.0 or higher are also required for high school student applicants. For college applicants, the Air Force ROTC Commander will determine the minimum GPA and test scores, if applicable, for scholarship eligibility. Note: AFROTC Scholarships do not cover room and board

Award: Scholarship for use in freshman, sophomore, junior, or senior years.

Eligibility Requirements: Applicant must be enrolled or expecting to enroll at a two-year institution or university. Available to U.S. citizens.

Application Requirements: Application form, application form may be submitted online.

AIR FORCE ROTC FOUR-YEAR NURSING SCHOLARSHIP

If you're interested in becoming a nurse, Air Force ROTC offers the Nursing Scholarship Program on a competitive basis to undergraduate sophomores and juniors. Applicants must be accepted to a nursing program at a college or university accredited by the National League for Nursing Accreditation Commission (NLNAC) or Commission on Collegiate Nursing Education (CCNE). Applicants must pass a Department of Defense Medical Examination Review Board (DODMERB) medical exam and complete a Physical Fitness Assessment. In addition, the Air Force ROTC Commander will determine the minimum GPA and test scores, if applicable, for scholarship eligibility. Note: AFROTC Scholarships do not cover room and board

Award: Scholarship for use in sophomore, junior, or senior years; not renewable.

Eligibility Requirements: Applicant must be enrolled or expecting to enroll full-time at an institution or university. Available to U.S. citizens.

Application Requirements: Application form.

AIR TRAFFIC CONTROL ASSOCIATION INC.

http://www.atca.org/

GABRIEL A. HARTL SCHOLARSHIP

Awarded to students enrolled in an two-year or greater air traffic control program at an institution approved and/or listed by the FAA as supporting the FAA's college training initiative.

Award: Scholarship for use in freshman, sophomore, junior, or senior years; not renewable.

Eligibility Requirements: Applicant must be enrolled or expecting to enroll full- or part-time at a two-year institution or university and studying in Arkansas. Available to U.S. and non-U.S. citizens.

Application Requirements: Application form, application form may be submitted online, essay. *Deadline:* May 1.

Contact: Tim Wagner, Membership Manager
Air Traffic Control Association Inc.
1101 King Street
Suite 300
Alexandria, VA 22314
Phone: 703-299-2430 Ext. 314
E-mail: info@atca.org

LAWRENCE C. FORTIER MEMORIAL SCHOLARSHIP

Awarded to students enrolled in an aviation related program of study leading to a Bachelor's degree.

Award: Scholarship for use in freshman, sophomore, junior, or senior years; not renewable.

Eligibility Requirements: Applicant must be enrolled or expecting to enroll full- or part-time at a two-year institution or university. Available to U.S. and non-U.S. citizens.

Application Requirements: Application form, application form may be submitted online, essay. *Deadline:* May 1.

Contact: Tim Wagner, Membership Manager
Air Traffic Control Association Inc.
1101 King Street
Suite 300
Alexandria, VA 22314
Phone: 703-299-2430 Ext. 314
E-mail: info@atca.org

ALERTONE SERVICES, LLC

https://www.alert-1.com/

ALERT1 STUDENT FOR SENIORS SCHOLARSHIP

Plan to help seniors in the future? You could be grandma's caregiver or the next great innovator for seniors. Whether you're pursuing technology or the arts, you're committed to improve senior care. To reward your hard work, Alert1 wants to give you a helping hand. As America's #1 medical alert, we're all about helping future leaders in senior care. Alert1 is offering a $250 scholarship to a student attending an accredited U.S. college or university who wants to help seniors. To apply for this scholarship, follow the instructions below. Submit the online application form and answer the following three questions (under 300 words each): What is your experience with seniors? What is the most important lesson you've learned from seniors? How will you help seniors in your chosen career?

Award: Scholarship for use in freshman, sophomore, junior, senior, or graduate years; not renewable. *Number:* 1. *Amount:* $250.

Eligibility Requirements: Applicant must be age 18 and over and enrolled or expecting to enroll full-time at a two-year or four-year institution or university. Available to U.S. citizens.

Application Requirements: Application form, application form may be submitted online (https://docs.google.com/forms/d/1G5Hk0xarAMiQTFIUSysT-7_MtCDWk5gWQDA6oo0w7ro/closedform), essay, personal photograph. *Deadline:* January 5.

Contact: Marketing Associate
AlertOne Services, LLC
1000 Commerce Park Drive
Williamsport, PA 17701
Phone: 800-693-5433 Ext. 6129
E-mail: abigial.delker@alert1.com

ALFRED G. AND ELMA M. MILOTTE SCHOLARSHIP FUND

http://www.milotte.org/

ALFRED G. AND ELMA M. MILOTTE SCHOLARSHIP

Grant of up to $4000 to high school graduate or students holding the GED. Applicants must have been accepted at a trade school, art school, two-year or four-year college or university for undergraduate or graduate studies.

Award: Scholarship for use in freshman, sophomore, junior, senior, or graduate years; not renewable. *Amount:* up to $4000.

Eligibility Requirements: Applicant must be enrolled or expecting to enroll full- or part-time at a two-year or four-year or technical institution or university. Available to U.S. citizens.

Application Requirements: Application form, recommendations or references, samples of work expressing applicant's observations of the natural world, transcript. *Deadline:* March 1.

Contact: Sean Ferguson, Assistant Vice President
Phone: 800-832-9071
Fax: 800-552-3182
E-mail: info@milotte.org

ALGAECAL INC.

https://www.algaecal.com/

ALGAECAL SCHOLARSHIP

The 2017 AlgaeCal Scholarship originated from the desire to financially assist students in pursuit of higher education as they face the challenge of significantly rising costs of obtaining a college degree. Also, it stemmed from the need for greater focus on the critical issue of health and well-being. With two-thirds of the U.S. reported to be overweight, and one-third obese, more dialogue and solutions are obviously still in need to manage and correct this huge rising health crisis. Applicants will download and fill out an AlgaeCal Health Scholarships Application Form and write an essay up to 750 words, describing "If you could, what, if any, changes to programs, policies, and education etc. would you implement for the general health/ well being of the average modern person? "

Award: Scholarship for use in freshman, sophomore, junior, senior, graduate, or postgraduate years; not renewable. *Number:* 1. *Amount:* $1000.

Eligibility Requirements: Applicant must be age 18-99 and enrolled or expecting to enroll full- or part-time at a two-year or four-year or technical institution or university. Available to U.S. and non-U.S. citizens.

Application Requirements: Essay. *Deadline:* June 30.

Contact: Mr. Philip Wong
Phone: 877-9165901
E-mail: philip@algaecal.com

ALL ABOUT CATS

http://www.allaboutcats.com

A VOICE FOR CATS ESSAY CONTEST SCHOLARSHIP

We at All About Cats are pleased to announce our very first annual A Voice For Cats scholarship contest with a prize of $1000. In our online cat community we strongly believe that enabling access to continuing higher education is very important. We strive to educate and inform our followers, so as to mitigate feline suffering and make the lives of our beloved pets better. Small steps are often necessary to achieve this ideal goal of minimizing pain and distress for our beloved kitties. We at All About Cats will grant a scholarship to one student who will provide the most outstanding essay about any topic, that would give us interesting insight with relation to our community interests. The winning essay will be published on our blog and accredited to the author. There are a growing number of incidents where the mistreatment and suffering of both outdoor and domesticated cats is being overlooked. Help us raise awareness about this issue that is dear to us, by entering the contest and submitting your essay on how to best promote the most humane treatment of felines.

Award: Scholarship for use in freshman, sophomore, junior, senior, graduate, or postgraduate years; not renewable. *Number:* 1. *Amount:* $1000.

Eligibility Requirements: Applicant must be age 18 and over and enrolled or expecting to enroll full- or part-time at an institution or university. Available to U.S. and non-U.S. citizens.

Application Requirements: Essay. *Deadline:* April 30.

Contact: Ron Wolff
Phone: 844-873-2876
E-mail: scholarships@wwwallaboutcats.com

ALLEN CHI

https://allenchi.org/

ALLEN CHI GAMING SCHOLARSHIP

The eSports arena is taking over. Gamers are rubbing elbows with conventional athletes, showing the world that gaming is as challenging as any other sport. As a gaming consultant, Allen always believes that the gamer's mentality of perseverance is exactly what the professional world needs, and he is working to provide students with unique opportunities in eSports and gaming through sponsorship and scholarship programs. As for the 2019 Allen Chi Gaming Scholarship, there will be a total of up to 25 awards available with individual award ranging from $1000 to $5000. In order to participate in this scholarship contest, the student must be studying for build a gaming related career or passionate about finding ways to promote gamification. For more information about the scholarship application, please visit: https://allenchi.org/allen-chi-gaming-scholarship/

Award: Scholarship for use in freshman, sophomore, junior, senior, or graduate years; not renewable. *Number:* 25. *Amount:* $1000–$5000.

Eligibility Requirements: Applicant must be age 13 and over and enrolled or expecting to enroll full-time at a two-year or four-year or technical institution or university. Available to U.S. and non-U.S. citizens.

Application Requirements: Application form, application form may be submitted online (https://allenchi.org/allen-chi-gaming-scholarship/), essay, interview. *Deadline:* April 30.

ALLIANCE FOR YOUNG ARTISTS AND WRITERS INC.

http://www.artandwriting.org/

SCHOLASTIC ART AND WRITING AWARDS

Public, private, or home-school students in the U.S., Canada, or American schools abroad enrolled in grades 7–12 are eligible to participate in the Scholastic Awards in 29 categories of art and wiring. The Scholastic Awards are adjudicated without knowledge of the artists/writers identity using three criteria: originality, technical skill, and emergence of personal voice or vision.

Award: Scholarship for use in freshman year; not renewable. *Number:* 89. *Amount:* $500–$10,000.

Eligibility Requirements: Applicant must be high school student and planning to enroll or expecting to enroll full- or part-time at a two-year or four-year or technical institution or university. Available to U.S. and non-U.S. citizens.

Application Requirements: Application form, essay, personal photograph, portfolio. *Fee:* $5. *Deadline:* continuous.

Contact: General Information
Alliance for Young Artists and Writers Inc.
557 Broadway
New York, NY 10012
Phone: 212-343-7700
E-mail: info@artandwriting.org

ALL-INK.COM PRINTER SUPPLIES ONLINE

ALL-INK.COM COLLEGE SCHOLARSHIP PROGRAM

One-time award for any level of postsecondary education. Minimum 2.5 GPA. Must apply online only at website http://www.all-ink.com. Recipients selected annually.

Award: Scholarship for use in freshman, sophomore, junior, senior, graduate, or postgraduate years; not renewable. *Number:* 5–10. *Amount:* $1000–$5000.

Eligibility Requirements: Applicant must be enrolled or expecting to enroll full-time at a two-year or four-year or technical institution or university. Available to U.S. and non-U.S. citizens.

Application Requirements: Application form, entry in a contest, essay. *Deadline:* December 31.

Contact: Aaron Gale, President
All-Ink.com Printer Supplies Online
1460 North Main Street, Suite 2
Spanish Fork, UT 84660
Phone: 801-794-0123
Fax: 801-794-0124
E-mail: scholarship@all-ink.com

ALLMAND LAW FIRM

https://www.allmandlaw.com/

ALLMAND LAW SCHOLARSHIP CONTEST

Every year, our firm grants a $1,000 scholarship to the American college student who creates the best video essay. This year's topic is how bankruptcy helps small businesses.

Award: Prize for use in freshman, sophomore, junior, or senior years; not renewable. *Number:* 1. *Amount:* $1000.

Eligibility Requirements: Applicant must be age 18-25 and enrolled or expecting to enroll full- or part-time at a two-year or four-year institution or university. Available to U.S. citizens.

Application Requirements: Application form may be submitted online (https://www.allmandlaw.com/scholarship-for-college-students/), essay. *Deadline:* August 15.

ALLTHEROOMS

http://alltherooms.com

ROOM TO TRAVEL - STUDY ABROAD SCHOLARSHIP

University students enrolled in or enrolling in a study abroad program with their university must submit a 600-800 worded essay on what inspires them to travel and the benefits they stand to gain from their study abroad experience. Winning submission receives $1,000 to be used on study abroad costs. Submissions must be received no later than August 1st, 2018 and winner will be announced prior to the 2018 Fall semester. Eligible students have U.S. citizenship or residency and is enrolled in or enrolling in a study abroad program at an accredited university.

Award: Prize for use in freshman, sophomore; junior, or senior years; renewable. *Number:* 1. *Amount:* $1000.

Eligibility Requirements: Applicant must be enrolled or expecting to enroll full-time at a four-year institution or university. Available to U.S. citizens.

Application Requirements: Essay. *Deadline:* August 1.

Contact: Victor Bosselaar
AllTheRooms
712 5th Avenue, 14th FL
New York, NY 10019
Phone: 203-561-9767
E-mail: victor.bosselaar@gmail.com

ALPHA LAMBDA DELTA

http://www.nationalald.org/

JO ANNE J. TROW SCHOLARSHIPS

One-time award for initiated members of Alpha Lambda Delta. Minimum 3.5 GPA required. Must be nominated by chapter.

Award: Scholarship for use in junior year; not renewable. *Number:* 1–36. *Amount:* $1000–$6000.

Eligibility Requirements: Applicant must be enrolled or expecting to enroll full-time at a four-year institution or university. Available to U.S. and non-U.S. citizens.

Application Requirements: Application form, essay. *Deadline:* April 1.

Contact: Eileen Merberg, Executive Director
Alpha Lambda Delta
6800 Pittsford Palmyra Road
Suite 340
Fairport, NY 14450
Phone: 585-364-0840
E-mail: eileen@nationalald.org

ALSANDOR LAW FIRM

https://www.alsandorlaw.com/scholarship-for-college-students/

ALSANDOR LAW FIRM SCHOLARSHIP CONTEST

Every year, our firm grants a $1,000 scholarship to the U.S. college student who creates the best video essay that elaborates on why they want to be a lawyer.

Award: Prize for use in freshman, sophomore, junior, or senior years; not renewable. *Number:* 1. *Amount:* $1000.

Eligibility Requirements: Applicant must be age 18-25 and enrolled or expecting to enroll full- or part-time at a two-year or four-year institution or university. Available to U.S. citizens.

Application Requirements: Application form may be submitted online (https://www.alsandorlaw.com/scholarship-for-college-students/), essay. *Deadline:* August 15.

ALZHEIMER'S FOUNDATION OF AMERICA

https://alzfdn.org/

AFA TEENS FOR ALZHEIMER'S AWARENESS COLLEGE SCHOLARSHIP

Alzheimer's disease doesn't just affect the people who have been diagnosed with it; it also affects their loved ones, caregivers and people of all ages, including children. Each year, AFA holds a scholarship essay contest which asks students to describe how Alzheimer's disease changed or impacted their lives. Whether they've had a loved one with the disease, volunteered or worked as a caretaker or are just passionate about the cause, the next generation of leaders in the fight against Alzheimer's have a story tell. We want to hear it! All high school seniors who are U.S. citizens or permanent residents and plan to enter a four year college/university in 2018 are invited to take part in the 2018 contest. In 2017, AFA awarded $25,000 in college scholarships to students across the country through the program. In addition to the scholarships, the grand prize winner and runners up had their essays featured in AFA's Care Quarterly magazine, which has a national readership of approximately 250,000 people.

Award: Scholarship for use in freshman year; not renewable. *Number:* 25–5,000. *Amount:* $500.

Eligibility Requirements: Applicant must be high school student and planning to enroll or expecting to enroll full-time at a four-year institution or university. Available to U.S. citizens.

Application Requirements: Application form. *Deadline:* February 15.

Contact: Sherry Cheng

AMERICAN ALPINE CLUB

https://americanalpineclub.org/

AMERICAN ALPINE CLUB RESEARCH GRANTS

AAC Research Grants support scientific endeavors in mountains and crags around the world. We fund projects that contribute vital knowledge of our climbing environment, enrich our understanding of global climber impacts and support and improve the health and sustainability of mountain environments and habitats. AAC Research Grants are powered by the Alliance for Sustainable Energy and supported by the following endowments: Lara-Karena Bitenieks Kellogg Memorial Fund, Scott Fischer Memorial Fund, Arthur K. Gilkey Memorial Fund and the Bedayn Research Fund. In addition to their relevance, applications are considered in terms of their scientific or technical quality and merit: qualifications of the applicant, strength of the research framework, dissemination plans, merit of the investigation, financial contribution the AAC grant would make to the total research budget. Application Period: November 15 to January 15 each year. Each grant recipient becomes an AAC Researcher, sharing their experiences, lessons learned, and findings with fellow climbers and the research community.

Award: Grant for use in sophomore, junior, senior, graduate, or postgraduate years; not renewable. *Number:* 8–15. *Amount:* $1500.

Eligibility Requirements: Applicant must be enrolled or expecting to enroll full- or part-time at a four-year institution or university. Available to U.S. and non-U.S. citizens.

Application Requirements: Application form. *Deadline:* January 15.

Contact: Anna Kramer, Grants Manager
        E-mail: grants@americanalpineclub.org

AMERICAN ASSOCIATION OF TEACHERS OF JAPANESE BRIDGING CLEARINGHOUSE FOR STUDY ABROAD IN JAPAN

http://www.aatj.org

BRIDGING SCHOLARSHIP FOR STUDY ABROAD IN JAPAN

Scholarships for U.S. students studying abroad in Japan on semester or year-long programs. Deadlines: April 10 and October 10.

Award: Scholarship for use in sophomore, junior, or senior years; not renewable. *Number:* 70–120. *Amount:* $2500–$4000.

Eligibility Requirements: Applicant must be age 18 and over and enrolled or expecting to enroll full-time at a two-year or four-year institution or university. Available to U.S. citizens.

Application Requirements: Application form, essay. *Deadline:* April 10.

Contact: Susan Schmidt
        E-mail: susan.schmidt@colorado.edu

AMERICAN BULLION, INC.

http://www.americanbullion.com

AMERICAN BULLION SCHOLARSHIP

The American Bullion Scholarship is offered to current college students. Applicants are asked to write a 500-1,000 word essay answering a question regarding precious metals ownership. Winning submissions are selected by a team of executives at American Bullion.

Award: Scholarship for use in freshman, sophomore, junior, senior, graduate, or postgraduate years; not renewable. *Number:* 5. *Amount:* $500.

Eligibility Requirements: Applicant must be enrolled or expecting to enroll full- or part-time at a four-year institution or university. Available to U.S. citizens.

Application Requirements: Application form, application form may be submitted online (https://www.americanbullion.com/scholarship/), essay. *Deadline:* October 31.

Contact: Orkan Ozkan, Chief Executive Officer
        American Bullion, Inc.
        12301 Wilshire Boulevard, #650
        Los Angeles, CA 90025
        Phone: 310-689-7720
        E-mail: scholarship@americanbullion.com

AMERICAN DENTAL HYGIENISTS' ASSOCIATION (ADHA) INSTITUTE FOR ORAL HEALTH

https://www.adha.org/

HU-FRIEDY/ESTHER WILKINS INSTRUMENT SCHOLARSHIP

These scholarships are awarded to applicants at the certificate/associate or baccalaureate degree level who have completed a minimum of one year in a dental hygiene curriculum. The program awards recipients with the Hu-Friedy dental hygiene instruments of their choice, equivalent to a retail value of $1,000.

Award: Scholarship for use in sophomore, junior, or senior years; not renewable. *Number:* 1–5. *Amount:* $1000.

Eligibility Requirements: Applicant must be enrolled or expecting to enroll full-time at a two-year institution or university. Available to U.S. citizens.

Application Requirements: Application form, essay. *Deadline:* February 1.

Contact: Kelsey Turner, Awards
        American Dental Hygienists' Association (ADHA) Institute
            For Oral Health
        444 North Michigan Avenue
        Suite 400
        Chicago, IL 60611
        Phone: 312-440-8937
        E-mail: kelseyt@adha.net

KARLA GIRTS MEMORIAL COMMUNITY OUTREACH SCHOLARSHIP

These scholarships are awarded to students enrolled in an associate, baccalaureate or degree completion program and completed a minimum of one year in a dental hygiene curriculum. Applicants will display a commitment to improving oral health within the geriatric population.

Award: Scholarship for use in sophomore, junior, or senior years; not renewable. *Number:* 2. *Amount:* $2000.

Eligibility Requirements: Applicant must be enrolled or expecting to enroll full-time at a two-year institution or university. Available to U.S. citizens.

Application Requirements: Application form, essay. *Deadline:* February 1.

Contact: Kelsey Turner, Awards
American Dental Hygienists' Association (ADHA) Institute
For Oral Health
444 North Michigan Avenue
Suite 400
Chicago, IL 60611
Phone: 312-440-8937
E-mail: kelseyt@adha.net

WILMA E. MOTLEY SCHOLARSHIP

This scholarship is awarded to applicant(s) pursuing a Baccalaureate degree at an accredited dental hygiene program and will have completed a minimum of one year in a dental hygiene curriculum.

Award: Scholarship for use in sophomore, junior, or senior years; not renewable. *Number:* 1. *Amount:* $1000.

Eligibility Requirements: Applicant must be enrolled or expecting to enroll full-time at an institution or university. Available to U.S. citizens.

Application Requirements: Application form, essay. *Deadline:* February 1.

Contact: Kelsey Turner, Awards
American Dental Hygienists' Association (ADHA) Institute
For Oral Health
444 North Michigan Avenue
Suite 400
Chicago, IL 60611
Phone: 312-440-8937
E-mail: kelseyt@adha.net

AMERICAN FLORAL ENDOWMENT

http://endowment.org

AFE FLORICULTURE SCHOLARSHIPS

Awarding scholarships for floriculture and horticulture students is a primary function of AFE. We understand the financial burden students face and are doing our part to help! AFE has more than 20 scholarships awarded annually. Online applications and supporting documents are due by May 1 each year.

Award: Scholarship for use in sophomore, junior, senior, graduate, or postgraduate years; not renewable. *Number:* 2–25. *Amount:* $500–$10,000.

Eligibility Requirements: Applicant must be enrolled or expecting to enroll full-time at a two-year or four-year or technical institution or university. Available to U.S. citizens.

Application Requirements: Application form, essay. *Deadline:* May 1.

Contact: Debi Chedester, Executive Director
American Floral Endowment
1001 North Fairfax Street, Suite 201
Alexandria, VA 22324
E-mail: dchedester@afeendowment.org

AMERICAN INSTITUTE FOR FOREIGN STUDY (AIFS)

https://www.aifsabroad.com/

AIFS AFFILIATE GRANT

Over 400 colleges and universities are affiliated with AIFS, which helps make the process of applying for an AIFS program easy, and may provide access to special affiliate scholarships. Students from affiliate institutions may automatically receive $400 grants for semester programs and $200 grants for summer and January Term programs. Application fee: $95. For more details, visit http://www.aifsabroad.com/scholarships.asp.

Award: Scholarship for use in freshman, sophomore, junior, or senior years; not renewable. *Amount:* $200–$400.

Eligibility Requirements: Applicant must be enrolled or expecting to enroll full-time at a two-year institution or university. Available to U.S. and non-U.S. citizens.

Application Requirements: Application form, application form may be submitted online, essay, personal photograph. *Fee:* $95. *Deadline:* October 1.

Contact: Sharman Hedayati, Vice President, Director of Admissions and
Operations
American Institute For Foreign Study (AIFS)
1 High Ridge Park
Stamford, CT 06905
Phone: 800-727-2437
E-mail: shedayati@aifs.com

AIFS GILMAN SCHOLARSHIP MATCH

AIFS will award an additional $500 to each student who receives a Benjamin A. Gilman International Scholarship and uses it toward an AIFS semester or academic year catalog program, or $250 toward a summer catalog program. More information is available at http://www.iie.org/gilman.

Award: Scholarship for use in freshman, sophomore, junior, or senior years; not renewable. *Amount:* $250–$500.

Eligibility Requirements: Applicant must be age 17 and over and enrolled or expecting to enroll full-time at an institution or university. Available to U.S. and non-U.S. citizens.

Application Requirements: Application form, application form may be submitted online, essay, personal photograph. *Fee:* $95.

Contact: Sharman Hedayati, Vice President, Director of Admissions and
Operations
American Institute For Foreign Study (AIFS)
1 High Ridge Park
Stamford, CT 06905
Phone: 800-727-2437
E-mail: shedayati@aifs.com

AIFS STUDY AGAIN SCHOLARSHIPS

Students who studied abroad on an AIFS summer program will receive a $1000 scholarship to study abroad on an AIFS semester or academic year catalog program or a $500 scholarship toward a summer catalog program. Students who studied abroad on an AIFS semester or academic year program will receive a $500 scholarship toward a summer catalog program or a $1000 scholarship toward a semester program in a different academic year. Deadlines: April 15 for fall, October 1 for spring, and March 1 for summer.

Award: Scholarship for use in freshman, sophomore, junior, or senior years; not renewable. *Amount:* $500–$1000.

Eligibility Requirements: Applicant must be age 17 and over and enrolled or expecting to enroll full-time at a two-year institution or university. Available to U.S. and non-U.S. citizens.

Application Requirements: Application form, application form may be submitted online, essay, personal photograph. *Fee:* $95. *Deadline:* October 1.

Contact: Sharman Hedayati, Vice President, Director of Admissions and
Operations
American Institute For Foreign Study (AIFS)
1 High Ridge Park
Stamford, CT 06905
Phone: 800-727-2437
E-mail: shedayati@aifs.com

AMERICAN JEWISH LEAGUE FOR ISRAEL

http://www.americanjewishleague.org/

AMERICAN JEWISH LEAGUE FOR ISRAEL SCHOLARSHIP PROGRAM

Tuition scholarship established 1957 for American students studying at one of Israel's Universities. Students must be accepted for credit and can not apply the scholarship to non-tuition costs. Students studying at a university not listed on the website are encouraged to send a description of their program with their application materials. More information is available at http://www.americanjewishleague.com/scholarships/ or by emailing ajlischolarships@gmail.com

Award: Scholarship for use in freshman, sophomore, junior, senior, graduate, or postgraduate years; not renewable. *Number:* 5–15. *Amount:* $4000–$6000.

Eligibility Requirements: Applicant must be enrolled or expecting to enroll full-time at a two-year or four-year or technical institution or university. Available to U.S. citizens.

Application Requirements: Application form, application form may be submitted online (http://www.americanjewishleague.com/scholarships/), essay, recommendations or references, transcript. *Deadline:* April 1.

Contact: Jeffrey Scheckner, Executive Director
Phone: 212-371-1583
E-mail: ajlijms@aol.com

AMERICAN LEGION AUXILIARY DEPARTMENT OF COLORADO

http://www.alacolorado.com

AMERICAN LEGION AUXILIARY DEPARTMENT OF COLORADO DEPARTMENT PRESIDENT'S SCHOLARSHIP AND SCHOLARSHIP FOR JUNIOR MEMBER

Open to children, spouses, grandchildren, and great-grandchildren of veterans, and veterans who served in the Armed Forces during eligibility dates for membership in the American Legion. Applicants must have been accepted by an accredited school.

Award: Scholarship for use in freshman year; not renewable. *Number:* 2–5. *Amount:* $500–$1000.

Eligibility Requirements: Applicant must be high school student and planning to enroll or expecting to enroll full- or part-time at a two-year or four-year institution or university. Available to U.S. citizens.

Application Requirements: Application form, essay. *Deadline:* March 15.

Contact: Rhonda Larkowski, Department Secretary and Treasurer
American Legion Auxiliary Department of Colorado
7465 East First Avenue, Suite D
Denver, CO 80230
Phone: 303-367-5388
E-mail: www.dept-sec@alacolorado.com

AMERICAN MARKETING ASSOCIATION FOUNDATION

http://www.ama.org/

AMA EBSCO MARKETING SCHOLAR AWARD

In deciding the relative merit of applicants and final selection(s), the candidate(s) will submit a 400-700 word essay on the following topic: Describe your participation in various forms of professional development through AMA and other venues (e.g., internships, jobs, etc.). Include comments on how these experiences have prepared you to make contributions as a leader in the marketing profession and society.

Award: Scholarship for use in junior year; not renewable. *Number:* 3. *Amount:* $2000–$5000.

Eligibility Requirements: Applicant must be enrolled or expecting to enroll full-time at a four-year institution. Available to U.S. and non-U.S. citizens.

Application Requirements: Application form may be submitted online (https://www.ama.org/students/Pages/AMA-EBSCO-Marketing-Scholar-Award.aspx), essay, recommendations or references, resume, transcript. *Deadline:* March 1.

Contact: Julie Schnidman, Director of Strategic Alliances and
Foundation Relations
American Marketing Association Foundation
130 East Randolph Street
22nd Floor
Chicago, IL 60601
Phone: 312-542-9015
E-mail: jschnidman@ama.org

AMA SOCIAL IMPACT SCHOLARSHIP

Award winners will be selected on the basis of a 400-700 word essay that describes the significant difference they have made in terms of the environment, social justice, economic fairness, improved health, quality of life, or another area of concern. Although all altruistic and philanthropic efforts are valued and encouraged, higher points will be earned by students who accomplished their goals by utilizing their marketing skills and techniques.

Award: Scholarship for use in junior or senior years; not renewable. *Number:* 2–2. *Amount:* $2000–$3000.

Eligibility Requirements: Applicant must be enrolled or expecting to enroll full-time at a four-year institution or university. Available to U.S. and non-U.S. citizens.

Application Requirements: Application form, application form may be submitted online (https://www.ama.org/students/Pages/Social-Impact-Scholarship.aspx), community service, essay, recommendations or references, resume. *Deadline:* March 1.

Contact: Julie Schnidman, Director of Strategic Alliances and
Foundation Relations
American Marketing Association Foundation
130 East Randolph Street
22nd Floor
Chicago, IL 60601
Phone: 312-542-9015
E-mail: jschnidman@ama.org

AMERICAN PUBLIC TRANSPORTATION FOUNDATION

https://www.aptfd.org/

DR. GEORGE M. SMERK SCHOLARSHIP

Scholarship for study towards a career in career in public transit management. Must be sponsored by APTA member organization. Minimum GPA of 3.0 required. College sophomores (30 hours or more satisfactorily completed), juniors, seniors, or those seeking advanced degrees may apply.

Award: Scholarship for use in sophomore, junior, senior, or graduate years; not renewable. *Number:* 1. *Amount:* $2500.

Eligibility Requirements: Applicant must be enrolled or expecting to enroll full-time at a two-year institution or university. Available to U.S. citizens.

Application Requirements: Application form, application form may be submitted online, essay, financial need analysis. *Deadline:* June 15.

PARSONS BRINCKERHOFF / JIM LAMMIE SCHOLARSHIP

Scholarship for study in public transportation engineering field. Must be sponsored by APTA member organization and complete internship with APTA member organization. Minimum GPA of 3.0 required.

Award: Scholarship for use in sophomore, junior, senior, or graduate years; renewable. *Number:* 1. *Amount:* $2500.

Eligibility Requirements: Applicant must be enrolled or expecting to enroll full-time at a two-year institution or university. Available to U.S. and Canadian citizens.

Application Requirements: Application form, application form may be submitted online, essay, financial need analysis. *Deadline:* June 15.

AMERICAN SOCIETY FOR NONDESTRUCTIVE TESTING

www.asnt.org

ASNT ROBERT B. OLIVER SCHOLARSHIP

The Robert B. Oliver Scholarship is an incentive to students currently enrolled in course work related to NDT in a program of study leading to an associate degree or post-secondary certificate at a U.S. university, college, technical school or company whose primary purpose is workforce education.

Award: Scholarship for use in freshman, sophomore, junior, or senior years; not renewable. *Number:* 3. *Amount:* $2500.

Eligibility Requirements: Applicant must be enrolled or expecting to enroll full-time at a two-year or technical institution. Available to U.S. citizens.

Application Requirements: Application form, application form may be submitted online (https://www.asnt.org/MinorSiteSections/AboutASNT/Awards/Oliver-Scholarship.aspx), essay. *Deadline:* February 15.

Contact: Jessica Ames, Program Coordinator
American Society for Nondestructive Testing
1711 Arlingate Lane
PO Box 28518
Columbus, OH 43228
E-mail: james@asnt.org

ANKIN LAW

http://ankinlaw.com

ANKIN LAW OFFICE ANNUAL COLLEGE SCHOLARSHIP

Ankin Law understands the financial challenges college students face. Every year we offer a scholarship to an undergraduate or law school student. The submission deadline is July 15, 2019. Qualified applicants will: Submit a fully completed application no later than July 15, 2019. Be enrolled as a full-time student in an accredited community college, college or university, or an accredited law school or graduate school starting in the fall of 2019. Submit his or her own original work. Provide proof of full-time enrollment should his/her submission be selected.

Award: Scholarship for use in freshman, sophomore, junior, senior, or graduate years; not renewable. *Number:* 1. *Amount:* $2500.

Eligibility Requirements: Applicant must be enrolled or expecting to enroll full-time at a two-year or four-year institution or university. Available to U.S. and Canadian citizens.

Application Requirements: Application form, application form may be submitted online (https://ankinlaw.com/academic-scholarship/), essay. *Deadline:* July 15.

Contact: Mr. Howard Ankin, Partner
Ankin Law
10 North Dearborn, Suite 500
Chicago, IL 60602
Phone: 844-600-0000
E-mail: ankinlaw123@gmail.com

APPALACHIAN STUDIES ASSOCIATION

http://www.appalachianstudies.org/

CARL A. ROSS STUDENT PAPER AWARD

All papers must adhere to guidelines for scholarly research. Middle/high school papers should be 8–15 pages in length. Undergraduate/graduate papers should be 15–30 pages in length. Nominations should be submitted by emailing a Microsoft Word copy of the paper to the chair of the selection committee before January 15. Papers submitted to the undergraduate/graduate competition must have been completed during the current or previous academic year. Submissions must include proof of student status during the current or previous academic year; documentation may consist of a copy of a schedule of classes or (unofficial or official) transcript or a letter from a faculty advisor (which should include the faculty advisor's e-mail address, phone number, and mailing address). Students who wish to present their papers at the conference must also submit a proposal for participation by the submission deadline (generally in October). Costs of attending the conference are the winner's responsibility.

Award: Prize for use in freshman, sophomore, junior, senior, or graduate years; not renewable. *Number:* 2. *Amount:* $100.

Eligibility Requirements: Applicant must be enrolled or expecting to enroll full- or part-time at a two-year or four-year institution or university. Available to U.S. and non-U.S. citizens.

Application Requirements: Essay. *Deadline:* January 15.

Contact: Casey LaFrance
E-mail: TC-Lafrance@wiu.edu

APPLYKIT

http://applykit.com

APPLYKIT SCHOLARSHIP $500 NO ESSAY!

The $500 ApplyKit Scholarship is awarded to one user who registers for free at ApplyKit.com. Registration is available at the following website: http://www.applykit.com/user/registration/?partner=petersons. Open to undergraduate students pursuing both full and part-time studies.

Award: Scholarship for use in freshman, sophomore, junior, or senior years; not renewable. *Number:* 1. *Amount:* $500.

Eligibility Requirements: Applicant must be age 15-19 and enrolled or expecting to enroll full- or part-time at a two-year or four-year or technical institution or university. Available to U.S. and non-U.S. citizens.

Application Requirements: Application form may be submitted online (http://www.applykit.com/user/registration/?partner=petersons), . *Deadline:* December 1.

Contact: Alex Hollis, Chief Marketing Officer
ApplyKit
844 Elm Street
Manchester, NH 03101
E-mail: alex@applykit.com

ARCHITECTURAL PRECAST ASSOCIATION

http://www.archprecast.org

TOM CORY MEMORIAL SCHOLARSHIP

One $2000 scholarship available to college upperclassmen, Master's, and doctoral students. Must be studying architecture and have a minimum 3.0 GPA.

Award: Scholarship for use in junior, senior, graduate, or postgraduate years; not renewable. *Number:* 1. *Amount:* $2000.

Eligibility Requirements: Applicant must be enrolled or expecting to enroll full-time at a four-year institution or university. Available to U.S. and Canadian citizens.

Application Requirements: Application form. *Deadline:* March 31.

Contact: Mrs. Lisa Collier, Meeting Planner/Program Manager
Architectural Precast Association
325 John Knox Road
Suite L103
Tallahassee, FL 32303
Phone: 850-224-0711
E-mail: info@archprecast.org

THE ARIZONA CITY/COUNTY MANAGEMENT ASSOCIATION

http://azmanagement.org/index.cfm?area=about.main

MARVIN A. ANDREWS SCHOLARSHIP

The Andrews Scholarship was initiated in 1990 in honor of the dedicated years of service by Marvin Andrews, former City Manager of Phoenix, to local government in Arizona. The Andrews Scholarship is sponsored by ACMA and is designed to honor and financially assist Arizona students in public administration, public policy or undergrad students working towards their Masters of Public Administration degree who aspire to a career in local government management. A scholarship is awarded to a full-time student attending either Arizona State University, Northern Arizona University, University of Arizona or Grand Canyon University who has exhibited strong academic achievement. In addition to the monetary award, the Andrews Scholarship recipient will be given the opportunity for a paid internship stipend of $6,000 with a participating Arizona city, town, or county. The purpose of the internship is to provide the scholarship recipient with professional experience and training in an Arizona city or town with a population of less than 50,000 or a county with a population of less than 200,000. This paid summer internship is provided through ACMA Scholarship funds and matching funds from the city, town, or county providing the internship.The Andrews Scholarship recipient will also be awarded a complimentary year of ACMA Student Membership. Scholarship Criteria Who may apply? Masters of Public Administration and Masters of Public Policy students as well as undergraduates in political science, planning, sustainability programs and the universities' honors colleges at Arizona State University, Northern Arizona University, the University of Arizona, and Grand Canyon University are eligible to apply for the ACMA scholarships. Master students must be enrolled in a graduate program or have completed their first semester. Undergraduate students must have completed at least 72 hours by December. Those completing the fall semester in time to graduate are also eligible. Students not selected as the recipient will have the opportunity to interview with hosts that are not selected by the scholarship recipient. If this opportunity is available, students that applied and interviewed for the internship will be notified in March. How are the scholarships to be used? The scholarships are intended to assist promising undergraduate/graduate students or recent graduates with funding to continue their studies or job search. What qualities does an ACMA Scholarship recipient possess? ACMA scholarship recipients demonstrate a strong commitment to pursuing a career in public administration at the local level in Arizona, a willingness to accept the challenges of a vigorous academic program, and a desire to succeed in their professional and/or personal endeavors. Internship The selected

Andrews Scholarship recipient will have the opportunity to interview prospective cities, towns and counties that have submitted an application to host the Andrews intern. The recipient must be able to accept a paid summer internship in 2019. Depending on the location the recipient must be able to travel.

Award: Scholarship for use in junior, senior, or graduate years; not renewable. *Number:* 1.

Eligibility Requirements: Applicant must be enrolled or expecting to enroll full-time at an institution or university and studying in Arizona.

Application Requirements: Application form, application form may be submitted online (https://azfoundation.wufoo.com/forms/acma-marvin-a-andrews-scholarshipinternship/). *Deadline:* November 19.

Contact: Samantha Womer
  Phone: 602-258-5786
  E-mail: info@azmanagement.org

ASIAN PACIFIC COMMUNITY FUND

http://www.apcf.org/

MEGA BANK SCHOLARSHIP PROGRAM

Mega Bank is committed to supporting youth residing in its business service territories to fulfill their dreams of obtaining a higher education. High school seniors who reside in Los Angeles County and Orange County, California. Plan to attend a U.S. Accredited 4-Year College/University of California or a Community College as a 1st year student in the Fall of 2020 (if selected, must submit college acceptance letter for verification).

Award: Scholarship for use in freshman year. *Number:* 10. *Amount:* $1000.

Eligibility Requirements: Applicant must be high school student and planning to enroll or expecting to enroll full-time at a two-year or technical institution or university.

Application Requirements: Application form, application form may be submitted online. *Deadline:* April 17.

Contact: Karen Fan
  Asian Pacific Community Fund
  1145 Wilshire Boulevard
  Suite 105
  Los Angeles, CA 90017
  Phone: 213-624-6400 Ext. 6
  Fax: 213-624-6406
  E-mail: kfan@apcf.org

ROYAL BUSINESS BANK SCHOLARSHIP PROGRAM

Royal Business Bank is committed to supporting economically-challenged youth residing in its business service territories to fulfill their dreams of obtaining a higher education. Applicants must be High school seniors who reside in the East Coast – (New York): New York County, Kings County, Queens County, and Richmond County or the West Coast – (Southern California and Nevada): Los Angeles County, Orange County, Ventura County, and Clark County-Nevada or the Midwest (Illinois) – Cook County.

Award: Scholarship for use in freshman year; not renewable. *Number:* 4. *Amount:* $2000.

Eligibility Requirements: Applicant must be high school student and planning to enroll or expecting to enroll full-time at a two-year institution or university. Available to U.S. citizens.

Application Requirements: Application form, application form may be submitted online, community service. *Deadline:* April 17.

Contact: Karen Fan
  Asian Pacific Community Fund
  1145 Wilshire Boulevard
  Suite 105
  Los Angeles, CA 90017
  Phone: 213-624-6400 Ext. 6
  Fax: 213-624-6406
  E-mail: kfan@apcf.org

ASSOCIATED MEDICAL SERVICES INC.

http://www.ams-inc.on.ca/

AMS HISTORY OF MEDICINE HANNAH SUMMER STUDENTSHIPS

The Hannah Summer Studentship offers four undergraduate students each summer an opportunity to learn the techniques of historical research and to encourage their serious future study of medical history. The studentships are jointly administered with the Canadian Society for the History of Medicine.

Award: Scholarship for use in freshman, sophomore, junior, senior, or graduate years; not renewable. *Number:* 4. *Amount:* $5500.

Eligibility Requirements: Applicant must be enrolled or expecting to enroll full- or part-time at an institution or university. Available to Canadian citizens.

Application Requirements: Application form.

Contact: Anne Avery, Director of Communications
  Associated Medical Services Inc.
  #228-162 Cumberland Street
  Toronto, ON
  CAN
  Phone: 416-924-3368
  Fax: 416-323-3338
  E-mail: anne.avery@ams-inc.on.ca

ASSOCIATION OF ENVIRONMENTAL HEALTH ACADEMIC PROGRAMS (AEHAP)

http://www.aehap.org/

NSF INTERNATIONAL SCHOLAR PROGRAM

Award available for college junior or senior in an AEHAP Environmental Health Academic Program. Student will spend summer on an independent research project in conjunction with their home university and NSF International and the AEHAP Office. Must have consent and commitment from advisor to help develop and oversee research project. Stipend will be paid in two sums, and advisor will receive $500 stipend.

Award: Scholarship for use in junior or senior years; not renewable. *Number:* 1. *Amount:* $3500.

Eligibility Requirements: Applicant must be enrolled or expecting to enroll full-time at a four-year institution or university. Available to U.S. citizens.

Application Requirements: Application form, essay. *Deadline:* December 31.

Contact: Clint Pinion, AEHAP - NSF Scholarship Committee
  Association of Environmental Health Academic Programs
    (AEHAP)
  PO Box 66057
  Burien, WA 98166
  Phone: 206-522-5272
  E-mail: Clint.Pinion@eku.edu

ASSURED LIFE ASSOCIATION

http://assuredlife.org

ASSURED LIFE ASSOCIATION ENDOWMENT SCHOLARSHIP PROGRAM

Award for full-time study at a trade/technical school, two-year college, four-year college or university. Applicant must be a benefit member, or a child or grandchild of a benefit member, of Assured Life Association of Colorado. Applicant may reapply each year he/she is a full-time student.

Award: Scholarship for use in freshman, sophomore, junior, senior, or graduate years; not renewable. *Number:* 65–75. *Amount:* $500–$2500.

Eligibility Requirements: Applicant must be enrolled or expecting to enroll full-time at a two-year or four-year or technical institution or university. Available to U.S. and Canadian citizens.

Application Requirements: Application form, community service, essay, personal photograph. *Deadline:* March 15.

Contact: Mr. Jerome Christensen, Vice President
Assured Life Association
PO Box 3169
Englewood, CO 80155
Phone: 303-468-3820
E-mail: jlc@assuredlife.org

AUTOHAUSAZ

https://www.autohausaz.com/

AUTOHAUSAZ SCHOLARSHIP ESSAY

AutohausAZ is offering a scholarship opportunity for full-time and part-time students attending college or university. We are providing three awards to three different students ranging from $1,000 for first place, $500 for second place, and $250 for third place. The requirements for submitting are the following: Must be a US citizen or permanent resident, Must be a full time or part time student attending or accepted into an undergraduate college or university (in the U.S.), only one entry per person, and write a 750-1,000 word essay on one of the prompts listed on our scholarship page.

Award: Scholarship for use in freshman, sophomore, junior, or senior years; not renewable. *Number:* 3. *Amount:* $250–$1000.

Eligibility Requirements: Applicant must be enrolled or expecting to enroll full- or part-time at a two-year or four-year or technical institution or university. Available to U.S. citizens.

Application Requirements: Essay. *Deadline:* March 15.

AWEBER COMMUNICATIONS

http://www.aweber.com/

AWEBER DEVELOPING FUTURES SCHOLARSHIP

The AWeber Developing Futures Scholarship, which grants a $2,500 scholarship to one college student each year, is awarded to undergraduate students studying in the Business/Marketing/Communications fields, as they pursue their educational and professional goals. It is AWeber's mission to help entrepreneurs and small business owners be successful as they connect with and grow their communities. As part of that mission, we know that drive is something that is nurtured over time—and it all begins with investing in the young individuals who will be the entrepreneurs, business owners and hard-working professionals of the future. See more at http://www.aweber.com/email-marketing-scholarship.htm#sthash.SVlP9Kh4.dpuf

Award: Scholarship for use in freshman, sophomore, junior, or senior years; not renewable. *Number:* 1. *Amount:* $2500.

Eligibility Requirements: Applicant must be enrolled or expecting to enroll full- or part-time at a four-year institution or university. Available to U.S. and non-U.S. citizens.

Application Requirements: Essay. *Deadline:* May 31.

Contact: Ms. Rebecca Pollard
E-mail: rebeccap@aweber.com

BAPTIST JOINT COMMITTEE FOR RELIGIOUS LIBERTY

http://www.BJConline.org

RELIGIOUS LIBERTY ESSAY SCHOLARSHIP CONTEST

To enter, students submit an essay based on the year's topic. All high school juniors and seniors are eligible, and they must have an essay adviser (a teacher or church staff member) to verify that the student's work is his or her own. http://www.BJConline.org/contest.

Award: Scholarship for use in freshman year; not renewable. *Number:* 1–3. *Amount:* $500–$2000.

Eligibility Requirements: Applicant must be high school student and planning to enroll or expecting to enroll full-time at a two-year or four-year or technical institution or university. Available to U.S. citizens.

Application Requirements: Application form, essay. *Deadline:* March 9.

Contact: Charles Watson, Education and Outreach Specialist
Baptist Joint Committee for Religious Liberty
200 Maryland Ave., NE
Washington, DC 20002
Phone: 202-544-4226
Fax: 202-544-2094
E-mail: cwatson@BJConline.org

BENSON LAW FIRM

https://bensonbankruptcyattorney.com/

BENSON LAW FIRM SCHOLARSHIP CONTEST

Every year, our firm grants a $1,000 scholarship to the American college student who creates the best video essay. This year's topic is how bankruptcy helps small businesses.

Award: Prize for use in freshman, sophomore, junior, or senior years; not renewable. *Number:* 1. *Amount:* $1000.

Eligibility Requirements: Applicant must be age 18-25 and enrolled or expecting to enroll full- or part-time at a two-year or four-year institution or university. Available to U.S. citizens.

Application Requirements: Application form may be submitted online (https://bensonbankruptcyattorney.com/scholarship-for-college-students/), essay. *Deadline:* August 15.

BEST ESSAY EDUCATION COMPANY

https://bestessay.education/

BEST ESSAY SCHOLARSHIP CONTEST

Best Essay Education has created a scholarship essay competition to encourage students to produce their own great essays and have the opportunity to win a sizeable financial award to help with their own educational expenses. To apply, you must be a student at an accredited college, university, community college, oct-tech certificate program, or any graduate or equivalent professional program. High school students who have just enrolled in college, are certainly eligible. Entrants must choose one of the following three prompts: Should students have the right to evaluate their teachers? Why or why not? If so, how should this be done? What new innovations promise to significantly change your life in college? How will they change your life? Of all of the environment threats, which do you see as the most dangerous right now? All eligible essays will be evaluated by a panel of Best Essay Education writers and editors. The following criteria will be used: originality of thought and structure; quality of grammar and composition, including organization, vocabulary, etc.; creativity and depth of thought. The panel shall determine the top three winners, based upon a scored rubric, and will then publish those winner names on its site, and social media pages, as it deems appropriate. Winners will receive notification via email and will be required to reply to those emails. Should a winner fail to respond to the email or, for any reason, refuse the prize award, the award will be provided to the entrant who is next in line.

Award: Scholarship for use in freshman, sophomore, junior, or senior years; not renewable. *Amount:* $400–$1000.

Eligibility Requirements: Applicant must be enrolled or expecting to enroll full- or part-time at a two-year or four-year or technical institution or university. Available to U.S. and non-U.S. citizens.

Application Requirements: Essay. *Deadline:* November 30.

Contact: Lauren Gartner
E-mail: bestessay.education@gmail.com

BILLINGS & BARRETT

https://billingsandbarrett.com/

BILLINGS & BARRETT FIRST IN FAMILY SCHOLARSHIP

Being blessed enough to graduate from college, as well as law school, Billings and Barrett recognize that while many people may have the talent and fortitude to go onto higher education, many lack the opportunity to do so simply due to their family situation. And yet, a select number of Americans are able to overcome those obstacles and become the first member of their family to go off to college. But, while they were able to walk the difficult road to get there, there is still a difficult road ahead. With that in mind, to help them on that road, Billings and Barrett are excited to introduce their First in Family Scholarship, designed to support individuals who want to further their education and are the first members of their families to attend college. For more information, please visit: https://billingsandbarrett.com/#scholarship

Award: Scholarship for use in freshman, sophomore, junior, senior, graduate, or postgraduate years; not renewable. *Number:* 1. *Amount:* $1000.

Eligibility Requirements: Applicant must be enrolled or expecting to enroll full- or part-time at a two-year or four-year or technical institution or university. Available to U.S. and non-U.S. citizens.

Application Requirements: Application form, essay. *Deadline:* September 30.

Contact: Peter Billings
E-mail: info@billingsandbarrett.com

BLADES OF GREEN

http://bladesofgreen.com

BLADES OF GREEN SCHOLARSHIP

Blades of Green has created a merit-based scholarship fund for individuals seeking undergraduate or graduate level education in environmental studies or related fields. Mark and Brad Leahy have created a $1,000 scholarship for the 2018 academic year. The scholarship will be awarded based on academic excellence, pursuit of further study in environmental education at an accredited college or university, and passion for further study. The scholarship will last for the duration of one year and be paid directly to the winning candidate to use towards tuition and board during the fall semester.

Award: Scholarship for use in freshman, sophomore, junior, senior, or graduate years; not renewable. *Number:* 1. *Amount:* $1000.

Eligibility Requirements: Applicant must be enrolled or expecting to enroll full-time at a four-year institution or university. Available to U.S. citizens.

Application Requirements: Application form, essay. *Deadline:* March 15.

Contact: Angela Hieronimus, HR Manager
Blades of Green
645 Central Avenue East
Edgewater, MD 21037
Phone: 410-867-8873
E-mail: ahieronimus@bladesofgreen.com

BLAKE FAMILY-US METRIC ASSOCIATION AWARD

www.us-metric.org

USMA/BLAKE FAMILY METRIC SCHOLARSHIP

The USMA/Blake scholarship is designed to help promote American metrication by providing partial funding for the first year in college to a high school student who has shown an interest in American metrication. Award of the scholarship will be given to a student who submits an application essay showing what they have done to help promote increased usage of the SI Metric System in the United States.

Award: Scholarship for use in freshman year; not renewable. *Number:* 1. *Amount:* $2500.

Eligibility Requirements: Applicant must be high school student and planning to enroll or expecting to enroll full-time at a four-year institution. Available to U.S. and non-U.S. citizens.

Application Requirements: Application form, application form may be submitted online(www.us-metric.org/usma-blake-family-foundation-metric-awards/), essay. *Deadline:* April 15.

Contact: Mr. Mark Henschel
Phone: 779-537-5611
E-mail: mw-henschel1@gmail.com

BLINDED VETERANS ASSOCIATION

http://www.bva.org/

KATHERN F. GRUBER SCHOLARSHIP

Award for undergraduate or graduate study is available to dependent children, grandchildren and spouses of legally blind veterans to include Active Duty legally blinded Armed Forces members. The veteran's blindness may be either service or non-service connected. High school seniors may apply. Applicant must be enrolled or accepted for admission as a full-time student in an accredited institution of higher learning, business, secretarial, or vocational school. Six awards of $2000 each are given.

Award: Scholarship for use in freshman, sophomore, junior, senior, or graduate years; not renewable. *Number:* 6. *Amount:* $2000.

Eligibility Requirements: Applicant must be enrolled or expecting to enroll full-time at a two-year or four-year or technical institution or university. Available to U.S. citizens.

Application Requirements: Application form, essay. *Deadline:* April 21.

Contact: Scholarship Coordinator
Blinded Veterans Association
125 N. West St.
Suite 300
Alexandria, VA 22314
Phone: 202-371-8880
E-mail: bva@bva.org

BOUNDLESS IMMIGRATION INC.

https://www.boundless.co

BOUNDLESS AMERICAN DREAM SCHOLARSHIP

The Boundless American Dream Scholarship will provide financial support to an exceptionally promising student who fulfills the requirements of Deferred Action for Childhood Arrivals (DACA) or Temporary Protected Status (TPS) and who wants to make the world a better place through technology. Boundless will provide a scholarship of $1,500 to improve this student's ability to design and build technology that solves real problems, based on the student's own vision and needs (including but not limited to support for college/university/graduate studies tuition, attending a coding boot camp, taking an online course, attending a professional conference, or building an early-stage prototype product for a startup idea). The 2018 Boundless American Dream Scholar will be selected for their academic excellence, entrepreneurial spirit, and dedication to community service. Additional details and online application can be found at https://www.boundless.co/boundless-american-dream-scholarship/.

Award: Scholarship for use in freshman, sophomore, junior, senior, graduate, or postgraduate years; not renewable. *Number:* 1. *Amount:* $1500.

Eligibility Requirements: Applicant must be enrolled or expecting to enroll full- or part-time at a two-year or four-year or technical institution or university. Available to Canadian and non-U.S. citizens.

Application Requirements: Application form, essay. *Deadline:* May 31.

Contact: Xiao Wang, CEO
Phone: 855-268-6353
E-mail: help@boundless.co

BRADLEY CORBETT LAW

http://www.bradleycorbettlaw.com/scholarship

LAW OFFICE OF BRADLEY R. CORBETT SCHOLARSHIP

$2000 award for a college or university student in the United States. Scholarship will be awarded to the student who submits the best overall essay; details are available at the website http://www.bradleycorbettlaw.com/scholarship/. Must be a U.S. citizen and submit proof of college enrollment.

Award: Scholarship for use in freshman, sophomore, junior, senior, graduate, or postgraduate years; not renewable. *Number:* 1. *Amount:* $2000.

Eligibility Requirements: Applicant must be enrolled or expecting to enroll full-time at a two-year or four-year or technical institution or university. Available to U.S. citizens.

Application Requirements: Essay, proof of enrollment. *Deadline:* July 15.

Contact: Mr. Cameron Cox, Scholarship Outreach Manager
Bradley Corbett Law
620 South Melrose
Suite 101
Vista, CA 92081
Phone: 619-800-4449
E-mail: ccox@scholarassociation.org

BRIGHT!TAX

https://brighttax.com

BRIGHT!TAX GLOBAL SCHOLAR INITIATIVE

The Bright!Tax Global Scholar Initiative provides assistance with fees for Americans who are or who wish to study abroad.

Award: Scholarship for use in freshman, sophomore, junior, senior, graduate, or postgraduate years; not renewable. *Number:* 2. *Amount:* $1000–$2000.

Eligibility Requirements: Applicant must be enrolled or expecting to enroll full- or part-time at an institution or university. Available to U.S. citizens.

Application Requirements: Application form, application form may be submitted online (https://brighttax.com/scholarships.html), essay, personal photograph. *Deadline:* continuous.

Contact: Greg Dewald
E-mail: inquiries@brighttax.com

BRISTOL-MYERS SQUIBB

BRISTOL-MYERS SQUIBB SCHOLARSHIP FOR CANCER SURVIVORS

The Bristol-Myers Squibb Scholarship for Cancer Survivors program was created to assist cancer survivors who plan to continue their education in college or vocational school programs. Scholarships of up to $10,000 will be awarded to up to 25 qualified students. Applicants must be cancer survivors (diagnosed by a physician as having treatment of cancer and survived), age 25 and under, who are high school seniors or graduates or postsecondary undergraduates. Qualified applicants must plan to enroll in a full-time undergraduate study at an accredited two- or four-year college, university, or vocational-technical school for the entire 2018-19 academic year. They must have a minimum grade point average of 3.5 on a 4.0 scale (or the equivalent). Scholarships will be awarded based on applicants' academic record, demonstrated leadership and participation in school and community activities, honors, work experience, statement of goals and aspirations, personal impact statement and an outside appraisal. Financial need is not considered. Students may reapply to the program each year they meet eligibility requirements.

Award: Scholarship for use in freshman year; not renewable.

Eligibility Requirements: Applicant must be age 17-25 and enrolled or expecting to enroll full-time at a two-year or four-year or technical institution or university. Available to U.S. citizens.

Application Requirements: Application form, community service. *Deadline:* March 31.

BRITISH COLUMBIA MINISTRY OF ADVANCED EDUCATION

http://www.studentaidbc.ca/

IRVING K. BARBER BRITISH COLUMBIA SCHOLARSHIP PROGRAM (FOR STUDY IN BRITISH COLUMBIA)

Scholarship to students who, after completing two years at a British Columbia public community college, university college or institute, must transfer to another public postsecondary institution in British Columbia to complete their degree. Students must demonstrate merit as well as exceptional involvement in their institution and community. Must have a GPA of at least 3.5. For more details, visit http://www.aved.gov.bc.ca/studentaidbc/specialprograms/irvingkbarber/bc_scholarship.htm.

Award: Scholarship for use in junior or senior years; not renewable. *Number:* up to 150. *Amount:* up to $5000.

Eligibility Requirements: Applicant must be enrolled or expecting to enroll full-time at a four-year institution or university and studying in British Columbia. Available to Canadian citizens.

Application Requirements: Application form, community service, essay, recommendations or references, test scores, transcript. *Deadline:* March 31.

Contact: Victoria Thibeau, Loan Remission and Management Unit
Phone: 250-387-6100
E-mail: victoria.thibeau@gov.bc.ca

BRYLAK LAW SAFETY

https://www.brylaklaw.com/

BRYLAK LAW SAFETY SCHOLARSHIP CONTEST

Every year, our firm grants a $1,000 scholarship to the U.S. college student who creates the best video essay that elaborates on how lawyers make the world a safer place.

Award: Prize for use in freshman, sophomore, junior, or senior years; not renewable. *Number:* 1. *Amount:* $1000.

Eligibility Requirements: Applicant must be age 18-25 and enrolled or expecting to enroll full- or part-time at a four-year institution or university. Available to U.S. citizens.

Application Requirements: Application form may be submitted online (https://www.brylaklaw.com/safety-scholarship-for-law-students/), essay. *Deadline:* August 15.

BURGER KING MCLAMORE FOUNDATION

https://bkmclamorefoundation.org/

BURGER KING SCHOLARS PROGRAM

Created in memory of BURGER KING® Co-founder James W. McLamore, the BURGER KING Scholars program has awarded $28.3 million in scholarships to more than 26,800 high school students, BK® employees and their families across the U.S., Canada and Puerto Rico since 2000. In 2016 alone, the Foundation awarded $3 million to more than 2,800 students in North America. Scholarship grants range from $1,000 to $50,000 and are intended to help students offset the cost of attending college or post-secondary vocational/technical school. Recipients are selected based on their grade point average (GPA), work experience, extracurricular activities and community service. Primarily funded by the BURGER KING® system and guests through annual fundraising activities, scholarships are awarded in the spring of each year. Our ultimate goal? To provide one $1,000 scholarship for every BURGER KING® restaurant in North America that's more than $7 million each year! The application period for the 2018-2019 school year begins on Oct. 15, 2017 and closes Dec. 15, 2017.

Award: Scholarship for use in freshman year; not renewable. *Amount:* $1000–$5000.

Eligibility Requirements: Applicant must be high school student and planning to enroll or expecting to enroll full-time at a two-year or four-year or technical institution or university. Available to U.S. and Canadian citizens.

Application Requirements: Application form, community service, personal photograph. *Deadline:* December 15.

Contact: Scholarship Management Services
Phone: 507-931-1682
E-mail: burgerkingscholars@scholarshipamerica.org

BUSSEY LAW FIRM, P.C.

https://www.thebusseylawfirm.com/

NEW HEIGHTS SCHOLARSHIP 2019

This scholarship is open to graduating high school seniors and current undergraduate college students with a 3.0 or higher GPA who are bettering themselves through education. The application includes an essay section, the introduction is to be 100-200 words, and the essay is to be 500-1000 words. the prompt is: How will attending college help you achieve your future goals? How do you plan on leaving your mark on the world, and in what way will a college education help you achieve your intended goals? The winner will be announced on June 26th, 2019, and the application must be submitted no later than 11:59 on May 29th, 2019. Additional information and applications can be found on our website: https://www.thebusseylawfirm.com/scholarship/

Award: Scholarship for use in freshman, sophomore, junior, or senior years; not renewable. *Number:* 1. *Amount:* $500.

Eligibility Requirements: Applicant must be enrolled or expecting to enroll full- or part-time at a two-year or four-year institution or university. Available to U.S. citizens.

Application Requirements: Application form, essay. *Deadline:* May 29.

Contact: Daniel Mateo
Bussey Law Firm, P.C.
65 N Raymond Ave #230
Pasadena, CA 91103
Phone: 323-254-1510
E-mail: DMateo@slsconsulting.com

BUY-RITE BEAUTY

https://www.buyritebeauty.com/

BUY-RITES ANNUAL BEAUTY SCHOOL SCHOLARSHIP

Buy-Rite Beauty will be awarding a $1,000 scholarship to a hairstylist or cosmetology student who best exemplifies our core beliefs. We want to hear about their most meaningful achievement and how it relates to your future as a hairstylist. The contest is open to U.S. residents. No purchase necessary. All participants must have applied to or be enrolled in as full-time beautician/cosmetology students. To apply, students will submit an essay detailing their most meaningful achievement and how it relates to their future as a hairstylist. The essay should be between 500-1000 words. Send a Word doc attachment to scholarship@buyritebeauty.com with your essay submission. The file name should be your full name, state, and date of birth. For example, Chipper-Jones-GA-4-24-1972. All submission emails must contain the student's full name, date of birth, email address, postal address, school they are currently enrolled in and/or applied to, and a phone number to contact. Buy-Rite Beauty will select the winner based on the best essay as determined by our internal panel of judges. Selection criteria will include, but is not limited to: Compelling and engaging description of essay topic; Thematic consistency throughout the submission around the central thesis; Proper spelling and grammar usage throughout the submission. Buy-Rite Beauty will select the winner during the month of December and will announce the winner on the website pending notification of the student and his or her family.

Award: Scholarship for use in freshman, sophomore, junior, or senior years; not renewable. *Number:* 1. *Amount:* $1000.

Eligibility Requirements: Applicant must be enrolled or expecting to enroll full-time at a two-year or four-year or technical institution or university. Available to U.S. citizens.

Application Requirements: Essay. *Deadline:* December 1.

Contact: Scholarships
E-mail: scholarship@buyritebeauty.com

BY KIDS FOR KIDS, CO.

http://bkfkeducation.com

CTIA WIRELESS FOUNDATION DRIVE SMART DIGITAL SHORT CONTEST

Create a digital short to help combat distracted driving. This contest is for legal residents of the 50 United States, the District of Columbia and Puerto Rico who are between the ages of 13 and 18. Distracted driving is a serious problem, but you can help. Create a 15-60 second digital short to persuade your peers to not drive distracted, and earn a chance to win $10,000! Scholarships and grants will be awarded to students and teachers. http://drivesmartnow.com

Award: Prize for use in freshman, sophomore, junior, or senior years; not renewable. *Number:* 6. *Amount:* $1000–$10,000.

Eligibility Requirements: Applicant must be age 13-18 and enrolled or expecting to enroll full- or part-time at a two-year or four-year or technical institution or university. Available to U.S. citizens.

Application Requirements: Application form. *Deadline:* January 6.

Contact: Operations and Events Manager
Phone: 203-321-1226
E-mail: info@bkfk.com

SALLIE MAE® MAKE COLLEGE HAPPEN CHALLENGE

Students are challenged to creatively answer the question, "How do you plan to pay for college?" Entries can be in the form of a video, photo, essay, song, or poem (be creative!).To enter, answer a few questions then either share a link to your creative entry or upload it. Registration is currently open. The contest launches November 1, 2016 at noon (12:00 p.m.) ET and ends December 31, 2016 at 5:00 p.m. (ET). See website for details, http://www.makecollegehappenchallenge.com

Award: Prize for use in freshman, sophomore, junior, or senior years; not renewable. *Number:* 10. *Amount:* $1000–$15,000.

Eligibility Requirements: Applicant must be age 14-18 and enrolled or expecting to enroll full- or part-time at a two-year or four-year or technical institution or university. Available to U.S. citizens.

Application Requirements: Application form. *Deadline:* December 31.

Contact: Operations and Events Manager
Phone: 203-321-1226
E-mail: info@bkfk.com

CALIFORNIA CONTRACTORS INSURANCE SERVICES, INC.

www.ccisbonds.com

FUTURE CONTRACTORS SCHOLARSHIP

Scholarship is offered for both Spring and Fall semesters.

Award: Scholarship for use in freshman, sophomore, junior, or senior years; not renewable. *Number:* 1. *Amount:* $750.

Eligibility Requirements: Applicant must be enrolled or expecting to enroll full-time at a two-year or technical institution or university. Available to U.S. citizens.

Application Requirements: Application form, application form may be submitted online, essay, personal photograph. *Deadline:* July 1.

CAMP NETWORK

https://www.campnetwork.com/

CAMP COUNSELOR APPRECIATION SCHOLARSHIP

All applicants must be U.S. citizens and current high school seniors attending school in the United States; anticipating completion of high school diploma at time of application; carrying a minimum 3.0 GPA currently. Please create a short, exciting video (3-5 minutes max) that explains your experience as a camp counselor, how you exhibit the 5 qualities above, and how you intend to use your college degree. Upload your video to DropBox.com, YouTube, Vimeo, or another reputable file sharing service (make sure the visibility is set to public). To submit your application send an email to scholarships@campnetwork.com. Please include your full name, school year, name of the college you plan to or are already attending, and a link to your video. By submitting this form you agree to allow Camp Network to use your video for promotional purposes.

Award: Scholarship for use in freshman year; not renewable. *Number:* 1–2. *Amount:* $1000.

Eligibility Requirements: Applicant must be high school student and planning to enroll or expecting to enroll full-time at an institution or university. Available to U.S. citizens.

Application Requirements: Application form. *Deadline:* November 1.

Contact: Andrew Downing
Camp Network
1033 Demonbreun Street
Suite 300
Nashville, TN 37203
E-mail: scholarships@campnetwork.com

CANADIAN FEDERATION OF UNIVERSITY WOMEN

http://www.cfuw.org/

CFUW ABORIGINAL WOMEN'S AWARD

For the 2020-2021 academic year, the value range of the award is $10,000 - $25,000. An applicant for the CFUW AWA will be considered eligible on the basis of the following criteria: Canadian Aboriginal woman; Studying in Canada; Holds or will hold an undergraduate university degree or equivalent before the CFUW AWA for which she has applied is granted. Must have applied to be a full-time student in any year of an eligible program at a recognized or accredited Canadian postsecondary degree-granting institution. There is a filing fee of $60.

Award: Scholarship for use in freshman, sophomore, junior, or senior years.

Eligibility Requirements: Applicant must be enrolled or expecting to enroll full-time at an institution or university and female.

Application Requirements: Application form, application form may be submitted online. *Deadline:* January 14.

Contact: Chair, CFUW Fellowships Committee
Canadian Federation of University Women
Canadian Federation of University Women
331 Cooper Street, Suite 502
Ottawa, ON K2P 0G5
Phone: 613-234-8252 Ext. 104
E-mail: fellowships@cfuw.org

CAREERVILLAGE.ORG

https://www.careervillage.org/

CAREERVILLAGE.ORG SCHOLARSHIP

CareerVillage.org is a website that students visit to get their college and career questions answered by actual working professionals. Getting guidance from people who have once been in your shoes enables you to better prepare for the future you want. We're hosting a monthly $1,000 scholarship giveaway that will be awarded to one student who posts two (eligible) questions onto the site by the end of the month. Here's what you need to know: To participate in this scholarship giveaway we're asking you to post two questions of your own on CareerVillage.org. By posting your questions, you're not only getting personalized information, insight, and advice from industry experts, but you're surfacing the answers to questions thousands of other students like you also want to know (aka killing two birds!). The winner will be selected based on question quality and financial need. You must ask college and/or career-related questions that require an answer from an actual human being! In other words, post more subjective questions. Don't post a question like "what is an architect?" because the answer can easily be found with a quick Google search. Instead, ask something like "what was the hardest part about becoming an architect?". This is the type of question that any architect can answer, and their answers will provide you with a ton of valuable insight into what their career path was like! If you ask questions you can find the answer to with a 10 second Google search, or off-topic questions (e.g. "why is the sky blue?") they will be removed from the site and you will not be considered when we choose a scholarship winner! Before you post your questions, it's a good idea to search CareerVillage.org first to make sure your question hasn't already been asked and answered. "Duplicate" questions usually get removed by moderators. But fear not: it's rare that two students ask for the exact same piece of advice. Don't have questions? Come on, everyone has questions! Especially when it comes to your future. Here are some ideas: Ask about what it takes to get a particular job, or about a "day in the life" of a career you find interesting. Visit CareerVillage.org to get more inspiration or watch this: https://www.youtube.com/watch?v=boMJKKBeNo4&t=

Award: Scholarship for use in freshman, sophomore, junior, senior, graduate, or postgraduate years; not renewable. *Number:* 1. *Amount:* $1000.

Eligibility Requirements: Applicant must be enrolled or expecting to enroll full- or part-time at a two-year or four-year or technical institution or university. Available to U.S. and non-U.S. citizens.

Application Requirements: *Deadline:* continuous.

Contact: Jordan Rivera
CareerVillage.org
1003 Clark Way
Palo Alto, CA 94304
Phone: 669-223-0979
E-mail: jordan@careervillage.org

CARING.COM

http://caring.com

CARING.COM STUDENT-CAREGIVER BI-ANNUAL SCHOLARSHIP

There are two deadlines for this scholarship every calendar year, one in December and one over the summer. The application can always be found at caring.com/scholarship. Additionally, previous winners' submissions can be found at caring.com/scholars. We encourage applicants to view previous winners' submissions when completing their own applications.

Award: Scholarship for use in freshman, sophomore, junior, senior, graduate, or postgraduate years; not renewable. *Number:* 2. *Amount:* $1500.

Eligibility Requirements: Applicant must be enrolled or expecting to enroll full- or part-time at a two-year or four-year or technical institution or university. Available to U.S. and non-U.S. citizens.

Application Requirements: Application form. *Deadline:* continuous.

Contact: Daniel Tachna-Fram, Product Management Intern
E-mail: tfram@caring.com

CASTLE INK

CASTLE INK PAPERLESS SCHOLARSHIP 2014

The goal of this award is to promote awareness around the importance of recycling. To apply, use social media to post something about recycling and/or how you reduce, reuse and recycle. Post something inspirational about recycling on YouTube, Pinterest, Twitter, Tumblr, or Facebook and be sure to use the hashtag #CastleInk.

Award: Scholarship for use in freshman, sophomore, junior, or senior years; not renewable. *Number:* 1. *Amount:* $1000–$1000.

Eligibility Requirements: Applicant must be enrolled or expecting to enroll full-time at a two-year or four-year or technical institution or university. Available to U.S. citizens.

Application Requirements: Application form, application form may be submitted online (http://www.castleink.com/category/717/Castle-Ink-Paperless-Scholarship.html). *Deadline:* May 1.

Contact: Bill Elward, President
Castle Ink
37 Wyckoff Street
Greenlawn, NY 11740
Phone: 917-364-6232
E-mail: bill@castleink.com

CASUALTY ACTUARIES OF THE SOUTHEAST

http://www.casact.org/community/affiliates/case/

CASUALTY ACTUARIES OF THE SOUTHEAST SCHOLARSHIP PROGRAM

Scholarships available for undergraduate students in the southeastern states for the study of actuarial science. Must be studying in Alabama, Arkansas, Florida, Georgia, Kentucky, Louisiana, Mississippi, North Carolina, South Carolina, Tennessee, or Virginia. Incoming freshmen/first-year students are not eligible for the scholarship. Must have demonstrated strong interest in mathematics or mathematics-related field and high scholastic achievement. Applicants should demonstrate interest in the actuarial profession, mathematical aptitude, and communication skills.

Award: Scholarship for use in sophomore, junior, or senior years; not renewable. *Number:* 2–4. *Amount:* $1000–$1500.

Eligibility Requirements: Applicant must be enrolled or expecting to enroll full-time at a four-year institution or university and studying in Alabama, Arkansas, Florida, Georgia, Kentucky, Louisiana, Mississippi, North Carolina, South Carolina, Tennessee, Virginia. Available to U.S. and Canadian citizens.

Application Requirements: Application form, essay, recommendations or references, transcript. *Deadline:* May 1.

Contact: Karen Jordan
Casualty Actuaries of the Southeast
3274 Medlock Bridge Road
Peachtree Corners, GA 30092
Phone: 678-684-4877
E-mail: kjordan@merlinosinc.com

CENTER FOR REINTEGRATION

http://www.reintegration.com

BAER REINTEGRATION SCHOLARSHIP

The goal of the Baer Reintegration Scholarship is to help people with schizophrenia, schizoaffective disorder or bipolar disorder acquire the educational and vocational skills necessary to reintegrate into society, secure jobs, and regain their lives

Award: Scholarship for use in freshman, sophomore, junior, senior, graduate, or postgraduate years; renewable. *Number:* 20–30. *Amount:* $1000–$30,000.

Eligibility Requirements: Applicant must be age 18 and over and enrolled or expecting to enroll full- or part-time at a two-year or four-year or technical institution or university. Available to U.S. citizens.

Application Requirements: Application form, essay, financial need analysis. *Deadline:* January 31.

Contact: Baer Reintegration Scholarship
Center for Reintegration
PO Box 35218
Phildelphia, PA 19128
E-mail: baerscholarships@reintegration.com

CENTRAL NATIONAL BANK & TRUST COMPANY OF ENID TRUSTEE

http://cnb-ok.com/

MAY T. HENRY SCHOLARSHIP FOUNDATION

A $1000 scholarship renewed annually for four years. Awarded to any student enrolled in an Oklahoma state-supported college, university or tech school. Based on need, scholastic performance and personal traits valued by May T. Henry. Minimum 3.0 GPA required.

Award: Scholarship for use in freshman, sophomore, junior, senior, graduate, or postgraduate years; renewable. *Amount:* $1000.

Eligibility Requirements: Applicant must be enrolled or expecting to enroll full-time at a two-year or four-year or technical institution or university and studying in Oklahoma. Available to U.S. and non-U.S. citizens.

Application Requirements: Application form, essay, financial need analysis, recommendations or references, test scores, transcript. *Deadline:* April 1.

Contact: Trust Department
Central National Bank & Trust Company of Enid Trustee
PO Box 3448
Enid, OK 73702-3448
Phone: 580-213-1700
Fax: 580-249-5911
E-mail: cfelix@cnb-enid.com

THE CE SHOP

https://www.theceshop.com

THE GIVE BACK SCHOLARSHIP

Application Deadline is July 31, 2018, at 11:59:59 CST - late entries will not be accepted. Students must complete a 250-word essay on "What does it mean to you to give back and why is it important?" Applicants must be a legal U.S Resident. Applicants are eligible to submit one entry per year. No purchase or payment of any kind is necessary to enter or win this scholarship, a purchase does not improve your chances of winning. The scholarship winner will be directly contacted and have 1 week to submit proof of enrollment and other required materials. Funds will be distributed directly to the winner's university.

Award: Scholarship for use in freshman, sophomore, junior, or senior years; not renewable. *Number:* 1. *Amount:* $1000.

Eligibility Requirements: Applicant must be enrolled or expecting to enroll full-time at a four-year institution or university. Available to U.S. citizens.

Application Requirements: Essay. *Deadline:* July 31.

Contact: Keeton Hayes
The CE Shop
5670 Greenwood Plaza Boulevard, #420
Greenwood Village, CO 80111
Phone: 888-8270777
E-mail: support@theceshop.com

CGTRADER

https://www.cgtrader.com/

ANNUAL CGTRADER SCHOLARSHIP

Every year CGTrader challenges students to dig into the field of technology by writing an essay on how innovative technologies are transforming our lives.

Award: Scholarship for use in senior year; not renewable. *Number:* 1–3. *Amount:* $500–$2000.

Eligibility Requirements: Applicant must be age 18 and over and enrolled or expecting to enroll full-time at a four-year institution or university. Available to U.S. and non-U.S. citizens.

Application Requirements: Essay. *Deadline:* December 14.

Contact: Ms. Erika Venckute
CGTrader
Antakalnio g. 17, LT-10312
Vilnius
LTU
E-mail: erika@cgtrader.com

ANNUAL CGTRADER SCHOLARSHIP

Each semester CGTrader challenges students to dig into the field of technology writing an essay on how innovative technologies are transforming our lives. Enter the CGTrader Scholarship challenge to win $3,000 for your education bills. The best submission will be awarded $2,000 while the two runners-up will receive $500 each. How to enter? Write and submit an original essay on the topic "The future of technology in education". Visit our Scholarship website: https://www.cgtrader.com/scholarships

Award: Scholarship for use in freshman, sophomore, junior, senior, graduate, or postgraduate years; renewable. *Number:* 3. *Amount:* $500–$2000.

Eligibility Requirements: Applicant must be high school student; age 18-99; planning to enroll or expecting to enroll full- or part-time at a two-year or four-year or technical institution or university and studying in Alabama, Alaska, Alberta, Arizona, Arkansas, British Columbia, California, Colorado, Connecticut, Delaware, District of Columbia, Florida, Georgia, Guam, Hawaii, Idaho, Illinois, Indiana, Iowa, Kansas, Kentucky, Louisiana, Maine, Manitoba, Maryland, Massachusetts, Michigan, Minnesota, Mississippi, Missouri, Montana, Nebraska, Nevada, New Brunswick, Newfoundland, New Hampshire, New Jersey, New Mexico, New York, North Carolina, North Dakota, Northwest Territories, Nova Scotia, Ohio, Oklahoma, Ontario, Oregon, Pennsylvania, Prince Edward Island, Puerto Rico, Quebec, Rhode Island, Saskatchewan, South Carolina, South Dakota, Tennessee, Texas, Utah, Vermont, Virginia, Washington, West Virginia, Wisconsin, Wyoming, Yukon. Available to U.S. and non-U.S. citizens.

Application Requirements: Essay. *Deadline:* June 1.

Contact: Laura Paskauskaite, Scholarship Adminsitrator
CGTrader
Antakalnio st. 17
Vilnius 10312
LTU
E-mail: laura@cgtrader.com

CHURCH HILL CLASSICS

http://www.diplomaframe.com/

FRAME MY FUTURE SCHOLARSHIP CONTEST

Submit an original creation that communicates: This is how I want to Frame My Future. Some examples of creative entry pieces are: photos, collages, drawings, poem, painting, graphic design piece, short typed essay, or anything you can create in an image.

Award: Scholarship for use in freshman, sophomore, junior, senior, graduate, or postgraduate years; not renewable. *Number:* 1–3. *Amount:* $500–$5000.

Eligibility Requirements: Applicant must be enrolled or expecting to enroll full-time at a two-year or four-year or technical institution or university. Available to U.S. citizens.

Application Requirements: Application form. *Deadline:* March 1.

Contact: Chris Angelone, Digital Marketing Associate
Church Hill Classics
594 Pepper Street
Monroe, CT 06468
Phone: 203-268-1598 Ext. 186
E-mail: christopher@diplomaframe.com

CITIZENSHIPTESTS.ORG

https://citizenshiptests.org

CITIZENSHIPTESTS.ORG SCHOLARSHIP

Create a video or submit an essay answering the following question: Discuss the top 3 issues affecting immigrants and how we as a society can change to make it easier for immigrants to integrate into our society. Once the video is created, upload it to your YouTube or Vimeo account. Entrants for the scholarship must be a registered member of YouTube or Vimeo in order to submit a video entry. Videos and essay should try to address the most pressing issues facing immigrants trying to integrate into our society. Videos must be 3-7 minutes long and be original. If the video includes music, then the music must be original music created by the entrant or permission obtained to use the music. Essays must be between 500 and 1000 words.

Award: Scholarship for use in freshman, sophomore, junior, senior, graduate, or postgraduate years; not renewable. *Number:* 1. *Amount:* $1000.

Eligibility Requirements: Applicant must be enrolled or expecting to enroll full-time at a two-year or four-year institution or university. Available to U.S. and non-U.S. citizens.

Application Requirements: Essay. *Deadline:* April 30.

Contact: Mr. Jonathan Lum
　　　　Phone: 4242430375
　　　　E-mail: info@citizenshiptests.org

CITRIX SYSTEMS

CITRIX RIGHTSIGNATURE SIGNATURE STORIES SCHOLARSHIP CONTEST

Citrix RightSignature will award $10,000 in scholarship awards to the top three students who submit the best essays. Finalists will be chosen by a panel of judges, including RightSignature founder Daryl Bernstein. 1st Place - $5,000; 2nd Place - $3,000; 3rd Place - $2,000. Deadline: Submissions are due by May 15th, 2017. Winners will be announced in late June. Essay Prompt: A signature has many uses. Whether it is being used to finalize a contract, serve as a souvenir, or sign a petition, your signature is an indelible symbol of your individuality and personal integrity. Tell us about a signature you have either given or received that was important in your life. Application Tips: Essays should be 600-800 words. Be creative, use proper grammar, check your spelling and "most importantly" be yourself!

Award: Scholarship for use in freshman, sophomore, junior, senior, or graduate years; not renewable. *Number:* 3. *Amount:* $2000–$5000.

Eligibility Requirements: Applicant must be enrolled or expecting to enroll full-time at a two-year or four-year or technical institution or university. Available to U.S. citizens.

Application Requirements: Essay. *Deadline:* May 15.

CLARICODE

http://www.claricode.com/

CLARICODE MEDICAL SOFTWARE SCHOLARSHIP ESSAY

One awards of $1250 available to full-time undergraduate or graduate students attending a U.S. accredited college or university. Must be at least 18 years old at time of entry and submit a 500 to 1000-word essay on the topic chosen by Claricode (and listed on the website). All majors/concentrations are welcome to apply. For additional information visit website http://www.claricode.com/scholarship.

Award: Scholarship for use in freshman, sophomore, junior, senior, graduate, or postgraduate years; not renewable. *Number:* 1. *Amount:* $1250.

Eligibility Requirements: Applicant must be age 18 and over and enrolled or expecting to enroll full-time at a two-year or four-year or technical institution or university. Available to U.S. citizens.

Application Requirements: Application form, application form may be submitted online (http://www.claricode.com/scholarship/), essay. *Deadline:* October 31.

Contact: Chief Executive Officer
　　　　E-mail: scholarship@claricode.com

COCA-COLA SCHOLARS FOUNDATION INC.

http://www.coca-colascholars.org/

COCA-COLA SCHOLARS PROGRAM

Renewable scholarship for graduating high school seniors enrolled either full-time or part-time in accredited colleges or universities. Minimum 3.0 GPA required. 252 awards are granted annually.

Award: Scholarship for use in freshman, sophomore, junior, senior, or graduate years; renewable. *Number:* 250. *Amount:* $10,000–$20,000.

Eligibility Requirements: Applicant must be high school student and planning to enroll or expecting to enroll full- or part-time at a two-year or four-year or technical institution or university. Available to U.S. citizens.

Application Requirements: Application form, application form may be submitted online (http://www.coca-colascholars.org), community service, essay, interview, recommendations or references, test scores, transcript. *Deadline:* October 31.

Contact: Mark Davis, President
　　　　Coca-Cola Scholars Foundation Inc.
　　　　PO Box 442
　　　　Atlanta, GA 30301-0442
　　　　Phone: 800-306-2653
　　　　Fax: 404-733-5439
　　　　E-mail: scholars@na.ko.com

CODA INTERNATIONAL

http://www.coda-international.org

MILLIE BROTHER SCHOLARSHIP FOR CHILDREN OF DEAF ADULTS

Scholarship awarded to any higher education student who is the hearing child of deaf parents. One-time award based on transcripts, letters of reference, and an essay.

Award: Scholarship for use in freshman, sophomore, junior, senior, or graduate years; not renewable. *Number:* 2–5. *Amount:* $1000–$3000.

Eligibility Requirements: Applicant must be enrolled or expecting to enroll full- or part-time at a two-year or four-year or technical institution or university. Available to U.S. and non-U.S. citizens.

Application Requirements: Application form, essay. *Deadline:* April 1.

Contact: Dr. Jennie Pyers, Chair, CODA Scholarship Committee
　　　　CODA International
　　　　Wellesley College, 106 Central Street
　　　　Wellesley, MA 02481
　　　　Phone: 413-650-2632
　　　　E-mail: scholarships@coda-international.org

COIT SERVICES, INC.

http://www.coit.com/

COIT 2018 CLEAN GIF SCHOLARSHIP CONTEST

This graphic design-centric scholarship challenges you to create a lightly animated GIF that shows us a fast way to get your space cleaned. When you are short on time, what is something unique or clever that makes your place feel or look clean quickly. Your GIF should be designed for posting on social media and can be as many frames as you like, just keep it short and sweet. We will give extra attention to clever submissions with a real sense of humor or brilliant cleaning hack. The most important criterion, though, is fantastic graphic design. The meme should be easy to read and visually appealing- something worth sharing!

Award: Scholarship for use in freshman, sophomore, junior, senior, graduate, or postgraduate years; not renewable. *Number:* 1. *Amount:* $2000.

Eligibility Requirements: Applicant must be enrolled or expecting to enroll full- or part-time at a two-year or four-year or technical institution or university. Available to U.S. and non-U.S. citizens.

Application Requirements: *Deadline:* August 31.

Contact: Tina Youngstein
　　　　Phone: 650-697-6190
　　　　E-mail: coit.scholarship.2017@gmail.com

COLLEGE INSIDER RESOURCES

http://www.ezcir.com/

COLLEGE INSIDER SCHOLARSHIP PROGRAM

Scholarship offered to undergraduate students with a minimum GPA of 2.5. International students attending college in the United States are also eligible. Refer to website for additional information, http://www.ezcir.com/college_request.asp.

Award: Scholarship for use in freshman, sophomore, junior, or senior years; renewable. *Number:* 1. *Amount:* $1000.

Eligibility Requirements: Applicant must be age 13 and over and enrolled or expecting to enroll full-time at a two-year or four-year or technical institution or university. Available to U.S. and non-U.S. citizens.

Application Requirements: Application form. *Deadline:* varies.

Contact: Mr. Cliff deQuilettes, CEO
  Phone: 406-652-8900
  E-mail: cliff@ezcir.com

COLLEGE JUMPSTART SCHOLARSHIP FUND

http://www.jumpstart-scholarship.net

COLLEGE JUMPSTART SCHOLARSHIP

The College JumpStart Scholarship is an annual, merit-based competition—financial need is not considered—that is open to 10th-12th graders, college students and non-traditional students. The main requirement is that you are committed to going to school and can express your goals for getting a higher education.

Award: Scholarship for use in freshman, sophomore, junior, senior, or graduate years; not renewable. *Number:* 6. *Amount:* $750–$1500.

Eligibility Requirements: Applicant must be high school student and planning to enroll or expecting to enroll full- or part-time at a two-year or four-year or technical institution or university. Available to U.S. citizens.

Application Requirements: Application form, essay. *Deadline:* October 17.

Contact: Scholarship Administrator
  E-mail: admin@jumpstart-scholarship.net

COLWELL LAW GROUP

https://www.colwell-law.org/

COLWELL LAW GROUP SINGLE PARENT SCHOLARSHIP

Colwell Law Group is proud to announce our sponsorship of the Colwell Law Group Single Parent Scholarship. As family lawyers in Albany, NY, we understand how difficult it can be for a single parent to go to college, or for a single parent to come up with enough money so that their child can go to college. That's why we've decided to sponsor this scholarship. Divorce hurts and while your situation may seem hopeless in the short-term, we are committed to bringing you hope for a better future in the long-term.

Award: Prize for use in freshman, sophomore, junior, or senior years; not renewable. *Number:* 1. *Amount:* $1000.

Eligibility Requirements: Applicant must be age 18-25 and enrolled or expecting to enroll full- or part-time at a two-year or four-year institution or university. Available to U.S. citizens.

Application Requirements: Application form may be submitted online (https://www.colwell-law.org/scholarship/), essay. *Deadline:* May 31.

COMEDY DEFENSIVE DRIVING

http://comedydefensivedriving.com/

GETTING REAL ABOUT DISTRACTED DRIVING SCHOLARSHIP

At Comedy Defensive Driving, we believe that quality education is too damn expensive for many students and should be obtainable for everyone. If you are up for trying something meaningful to help achieve your goal of a college education, then design an advertisement against distracted driving. You will be judged based on the quality of the content in terms of marketability, and how it effectively convinces drivers to stay focused on the road. To qualify, you must like the Comedy Defensive Driving Facebook fan page, take the pledge to not use your phone while driving, and definitely not to drive while you're buzzed. And definitely don't use your phone if driving. All forms of ads are accepted including PSA, music, billboards, media, graphics, etc. No time restraints, however, keep in mind that you are making an advertisement, not a Ridley Scott movie. Overt profanity, and nudity of any kind will not be allowed. Plagiarism automatically disqualified. There is no GPA requirement, financial requirement, or any other kind of requirement—just knowing you are making the effort to get out of bed and do something positive before noon qualifies. Please submit files (all formats accepted) to scholarships@comedydefensivedriving.com only. We will not be judging based on anything other than the advertisement, so don't sweat over an introductory email; just give us your name, and the best way to reach you if you win. Submission deadline is 4/30/16 and the recipient will be announced by 5/31/16.

Award: Scholarship for use in freshman, sophomore, junior, or senior years; not renewable. *Number:* 1. *Amount:* $1000.

Eligibility Requirements: Applicant must be enrolled or expecting to enroll full- or part-time at a two-year or four-year or technical institution or university. Available to U.S. and Canadian citizens.

Application Requirements: Application form. *Deadline:* May 31.

Contact: Richard Schiller
  Comedy Defensive Driving
  1825 W. Walnut Hill Lane
  Suite 101
  Irving, TX 75038
  E-mail: scholarships@comedydefensivedriving.com

COMMON KNOWLEDGE SCHOLARSHIP FOUNDATION

http://www.cksf.org/

COMMON KNOWLEDGE SCHOLARSHIP

The Common Knowledge Scholarship Foundation (CKSF) is a 501(c)(3) nonprofit organization that creates Internet-based quiz competition for students of all ages. There is no essay, long application, or GPA requirement. A single CKSF registration is good from high school all the way through college and graduate school.

Award: Scholarship for use in freshman, sophomore, junior, senior, graduate, or postgraduate years; renewable. *Number:* 1–15. *Amount:* $250–$1000.

Eligibility Requirements: Applicant must be enrolled or expecting to enroll full- or part-time at a two-year or four-year or technical institution or university. Available to U.S. and non-U.S. citizens.

Application Requirements: Application form may be submitted online (http://www.cksf.org), online registration and quiz competition, portfolio. *Deadline:* continuous.

Contact: Daryl Hulce, President
  Phone: 954-262-8553

COMPARECARDS.COM

http://www.comparecards.com

EDU SCHOLARSHIP AWARD

Each month, CompareCards will award $2500 to any qualifying college (or college bound) student in need who can answer a tricky trivia question. Using their best pop culture and math skills, and probably a bit of help from Professor Google, students should be able to answer a series of questions to arrive at a final answer in no time. After the submission deadline, CompareCards will gather all the correct answers and a tiebreaker question will be emailed with a link to submit the answer. Students who submit the correct tiebreaker answer will be entered into a random drawing and one winner will be selected.

Award: Scholarship for use in freshman, sophomore, junior, senior, graduate, or postgraduate years; not renewable. *Number:* 1–12. *Amount:* $2500.

Eligibility Requirements: Applicant must be enrolled or expecting to enroll full- or part-time at a two-year or four-year or technical institution or university. Available to U.S. citizens.

Application Requirements: Application form may be submitted online (http://www.comparecards.com/scholarship-award). *Deadline:* continuous.

Contact: Sarah Meyer
E-mail: sarah@comparecards.com

CONNECTHER
http://www.connecther.org/

GIRLS IMPACT THE WORLD SCHOLARSHIP PROGRAM

The Girls Impact the World Film Festival, presented by Connecther, is a film festival and scholarship program in which high school and undergraduate college students submit 3-6 minute short films that focus on a variety of global women's issues, including maternal health, misrepresentation of beauty, athletes against assault of women, violence against women, child-marriage, sex-trafficking, poverty alleviation, environmental issues, etc.

Award: Scholarship for use in freshman, sophomore, junior, or senior years; renewable. *Number:* 12. *Amount:* $1000–$5000.

Eligibility Requirements: Applicant must be age 13-25 and enrolled or expecting to enroll full- or part-time at a two-year or four-year or technical institution or university. Available to U.S. and non-U.S. citizens.

Application Requirements: Application form. *Deadline:* January 20.

Contact: Lila Igram
Connecther
12301 Zeller Lane
Austin, TX 78753
E-mail: filmfest@connecther.org

CONSTITUTING AMERICA
http://www.constitutingamerica.org

WE THE FUTURE CONTEST

We The Future Contest offers a $1000 scholarship for high school students, $2000 scholarship for college students plus a mentoring trip. Contest information about how to enter, and prizes including scholarships, may be found at http://www.constitutingamerica.org/downloads.php. Entry topics are based on the U.S. Constitution.

Award: Scholarship for use in freshman, sophomore, junior, senior, or graduate years; not renewable. *Number:* 12–12. *Amount:* $1000–$2000.

Eligibility Requirements: Applicant must be enrolled or expecting to enroll full- or part-time at a two-year or four-year institution or university. Available to U.S. citizens.

Application Requirements: Application form may be submitted online (http://www.constitutingamerica.org/docs/WeTheFutureContestPermission.pdf), contest entry form, entry in a contest. *Deadline:* September 17.

Contact: Ms. Amanda Hughes, Outreach Director
Constituting America
PO Box 1988
Colleyville, TX 76034
Phone: 888-937-0917
E-mail: wethepeople917@yahoo.com

CORES & ASSOCIATES
https://amysaracores.com/

CORES & ASSOCIATES SCHOLARSHIP CONTEST

Every year, our firm grants a $500 scholarship to the American college student who creates the best video essay. This year's topic is: What experiences have influenced your desire to help families who have to deal with family law matters?

Award: Prize for use in freshman, sophomore, junior, or senior years; not renewable. *Number:* 1. *Amount:* $1000.

Eligibility Requirements: Applicant must be age 18-25 and enrolled or expecting to enroll full- or part-time at a two-year or four-year institution or university. Available to U.S. citizens.

Application Requirements: Application form may be submitted online (https://amysaracores.com/scholarship-for-college-students/), essay. *Deadline:* August 15.

COUPONCHIEF.COM
https://www.couponchief.com/

COUPONCHIEF.COM SCHOLARSHIP PROGRAM

We at CouponChief.com want to support young leaders that understand frugality and saving money, and how the skills and knowledge of using coupons can contribute to that end. We will award 1 scholarship winner with $1000 to put towards education every year.

Award: Scholarship for use in freshman, sophomore, junior, senior, graduate, or postgraduate years; not renewable. *Number:* 1. *Amount:* $1000.

Eligibility Requirements: Applicant must be enrolled or expecting to enroll full- or part-time at a two-year or four-year or technical institution or university. Available to U.S. citizens.

Application Requirements: *Deadline:* July 31.

Contact: Angela Thompson
CouponChief.com
774 Mays Boulevard, #10-528
Incline Village, NV 89451
Phone: 858-342-5970
E-mail: angela@eouponchief.com

COUPONSURF.COM
http://couponsurf.com/

COUPONSURF ENTREPRENEURS SCHOLARSHIP

CouponSurf understands the importance of entrepreneurship towards building a better future. To that end, we are proud to announce a $1,000 scholarship to be awarded to a student who shows exceptional entrepreneurial skills and passion. The money can go towards financing the student's entrepreneurial idea, tuition for the 2017 fall semester, or towards attending a special entrepreneurial conference or boot camp. This scholarship is open to high school seniors and university students in accredited school programs and is for the 2017-2018 spring semester. Please review the eligibility requirements and application process below and remember, there will only be one winner. All applicants must include your full name, email, phone number, mailing address, 500 to 1,000 word essay; and a recommendation letter from a mentor, teacher or a professor. This scholarship is available to all applicants who meet the following criteria: 1. Must not have a college degree from a 4-year institution; 2. Must be enrolled in a 4-year institution or have a high school diploma. Please submit a 500 to 1,000-word essay in PDF or Word Doc format to the attached submission form along with your full name, address and contact details. We also require an unofficial copy of your high school transcript or college transcript. The essay topic is as follows: We want to hear about your entrepreneurial passion and idea. Therefore, we request you write an essay explaining what the entrepreneurial venture is and what the return on investment could be. In the essay, explain why you would be the best candidate for this scholarship Why do you want to obtain a college degree? And how will this scholarship help you achieve your goals? Alternatively, you can send a video (less than 5 minutes) talking about the venture. Please submit through the CouponSurf.com Scholarship Application Form.

Award: Scholarship for use in freshman, sophomore, junior, or senior years; not renewable. *Number:* 1. *Amount:* $1000.

Eligibility Requirements: Applicant must be enrolled or expecting to enroll full- or part-time at a two-year or four-year or technical institution or university. Available to U.S. and non-U.S. citizens.

Application Requirements: Essay. *Deadline:* December 31.

Contact: Scott Smith, Digital Product Manager
CouponSurf.com
402 Main Street, Suite 100-224
Metuchen, NJ 08840

COURSE HERO, INC.
http://www.coursehero.com

COURSE HERO $5,000 MONTHLY SCHOLARSHIP

While Course Hero can help you study smarter, we can also help you pay for school with a $5,000 monthly scholarship. It only takes a few minutes to apply! Just sign up for a free account and respond to our creative short-answer question

Award: Scholarship for use in freshman, sophomore, junior, senior, graduate, or postgraduate years; not renewable. *Number:* 1. *Amount:* $1000–$5000.

Eligibility Requirements: Applicant must be age 16 and over and enrolled or expecting to enroll full- or part-time at a two-year or four-year institution or university. Available to U.S. citizens.

Application Requirements: *Deadline:* continuous.

Contact: Sura Hussain, Marketing Manager
Course Hero, Inc.
1400B Seaport Boulevard, Floor 2
Redwood City, CA 94063
Phone: 888-634-9397
E-mail: scholarships@coursehero.com

COZZY.ORG

https://cozzy.org

COZZY.ORG CUSTOMER SUPPORT SCHOLARSHIP

The Cozzy team is excited to offer a $2,500 scholarship to one winner. The scholarship is available to any undergraduate and postgraduate college student. The $2,500 scholarship grant can be used toward course materials, books, and other educational resources. To participate in our scholarship program, you need to research and cover the following topic The future of the commerce. How the internet will change the consumption in 10 years? The essay should include title, 1000-1500 words, at least 3 research materials used. You must be a student pursuing any degree or majors in any degree. You must be above 18 years. We reserve all rights to verify your date of college enrollment or high school/college graduation. Essay must be unique, demonstrate deep understanding of the topic and research skills. We would like to see your expertise supported by data and statistics.

Award: Scholarship for use in freshman, junior, senior, graduate, or postgraduate years; renewable. *Number:* 1. *Amount:* $2500.

Eligibility Requirements: Applicant must be age 18-99 and enrolled or expecting to enroll full- or part-time at a four-year institution or university. Available to U.S. and non-U.S. citizens.

Application Requirements: Essay. *Deadline:* October 30.

Contact: Mr. Brian Landarson
E-mail: finance@cozzy.org

CRESCENT ELECTRIC SUPPLY COMPANY

http://www.cesco.com/

CRESCENT ELECTRIC SUPPLY COMPANY'S ENERGY EFFICIENT SCHOLARSHIP

If you are currently enrolled in college or headed there in 2017 and want to win a $1000 scholarship to help cover expenses, consider entering the Crescent Electric College Scholarship Contest. Crescent Electric Supply Company will award a $1000 scholarship to a highly motivated student who can thoughtfully share a photo of their effort to minimize energy usage on social media.

Award: Scholarship for use in freshman, sophomore, or junior years; not renewable. *Number:* 1. *Amount:* $1000.

Eligibility Requirements: Applicant must be age 16-22 and enrolled or expecting to enroll full-time at a two-year or four-year or technical institution or university. Available to U.S. and Canadian citizens.

Application Requirements: Personal photograph. *Deadline:* August 8.

Contact: Scholarship Director
E-mail: jessie@elitefixtures.com

CROSLEY LAW FIRM

https://crosleylaw.com

CROSLEY LAW FIRM DISTRACTED DRIVING SCHOLARSHIP

We understand how challenging it can be to finance a college education, especially while juggling classes, work, extra-curricular activities, and more. To help students get some relief and focus on their education, Crosley Law Firm is proud to offer a $500 scholarship twice a year to a currently enrolled college student or high school senior. The focus of the scholarship is distracted driving. Every single day, distracted driving kills 8 and injures 1,161 people nationwide, according to the Centers for Disease Control and Prevention. These staggering and eye-opening statistics are why we advocate for safe driving habits and why we are offering this scholarship. Applicants must have a 3.0 or higher GPA to apply. In order to apply, scholarship applicants must submit the following materials at the time of submission: confirmation of enrollment at a community college or 4-year institution, and an essay that is between 750 and 2,000 words in length and discusses how distracted driving has impacted your life. The scholarship is offered twice per year, and applications are accepted year-round. The two deadlines each year are: December 31 at 11:59 p.m. and June 30 at 11:59 p.m. https://crosleylaw.com/500-scholarship-college-student-high-school-senior-national/

Award: Scholarship for use in freshman, sophomore, junior, senior, graduate, or postgraduate years; renewable. *Number:* 2. *Amount:* $500.

Eligibility Requirements: Applicant must be enrolled or expecting to enroll full- or part-time at a two-year or four-year institution or university. Available to U.S. citizens.

Application Requirements: Application form, essay. *Deadline:* continuous.

Contact: Chip LaFleur, Marketing Manager
Crosley Law Firm
2632 Broadway Street
Suite 101 South
San Antonio, TX 78215
Phone: 210-529-3000
Fax: 210-444-1561
E-mail: info@crosleylawscholarship.com

CSA FRATERNAL LIFE

http://www.csalife.com

CSA FRATERNAL LIFE SCHOLARSHIP

CSA Scholarship Applicants must be a member in good standing of CSA Fraternal Life for a minimum of two (2) continuous years at the time of application. Must also have at least $5,000 face value in permanent life insurance or $1,000 cash value in an annuity with CSA Fraternal Life; be pursuing an undergraduate degree at an accredited junior college, college, or university on a full-time basis (full-time is defined as a minimum 12 credit hours per semester for at least two semesters per academic year). Students planning on attending a technical/vocation school full time are also eligible for an award. Must have a cumulative 3.0 or higher GPA (based on a 4.0 scale) upon graduation from high school. Students already attending college must submit college transcripts which indicate a 3.0 GPA (based on a 4.0 scale). Students applying for a scholarship who have not yet completed a full year of undergraduate studies must submit their high school transcripts indicating a 3.0 or better GPA. ACT or SAT score sheets must be included in your application. Must remain a CSA member in good standing throughout the period covered by the award. Determining factors in qualification include: grade point average (25 points), college test scores (30 points), extracurricular activities including CSA activities (15 points), and essay (30 points). Essays will be evaluated by an independent party. Total points will determine the monetary amount of each award.

Award: Scholarship for use in freshman, sophomore, junior, or senior years; not renewable.

Eligibility Requirements: Applicant must be enrolled or expecting to enroll full-time at a four-year or technical institution or university. Available to U.S. citizens.

Application Requirements: Application form, essay, personal photograph. *Deadline:* March 23.

Contact: Ms. Amanda Lovell, Fraternal Director
CSA Fraternal Life
2050 Finley Road
Suite 70
Lombard, IL 60148
Phone: 630-472-0500 Ext. 4352
Fax: 630-472-1100
E-mail: alovell@csalife.com

THE DALLAS FOUNDATION

http://www.dallasfoundation.org/

BROOK HOLLOW GOLF CLUB SCHOLARSHIP

Established in 2007 to benefit children or grandchildren of full- or part-time employees of Brook Hollow Golf Club. Applicants must be a child or grandchild of an active employee in good standing of Brook Hollow Golf Club and a graduating high school senior who has been accepted in, or a student already enrolled in, an undergraduate program of study in pursuit of a degree from a public or private, regionally accredited community college, college, university, or vocational or trade institute. Applicants must demonstrate financial need.

Award: Scholarship for use in freshman or sophomore years; renewable. *Amount:* $2000–$4500.

Eligibility Requirements: Applicant must be high school student and planning to enroll or expecting to enroll full-time at a two-year or four-year or technical institution or university.

Application Requirements: Application form, financial need analysis, transcript. *Deadline:* April 1.

Contact: Rachel Lasseter, Program Associate
Phone: 214-741-9898
E-mail: scholarships@dallasfoundation.org

THE HIRSCH FAMILY SCHOLARSHIP

The Hirsch Family Scholarship was established as a scholarship fund in 2009 to benefit dependent children of active employees of Eagle Materials, Performance Chemicals and Ingredients, Martin Fletcher, Hadlock Plastics, Highlander Partners and any of their majority-owned subsidiaries.

Award: Scholarship for use in freshman, sophomore, junior, or senior years; not renewable. *Amount:* $2000–$10,000.

Eligibility Requirements: Applicant must be enrolled or expecting to enroll full-time at a two-year or four-year or technical institution or university.

Application Requirements: Application form, transcript. *Deadline:* March 15.

Contact: Rachel Lasseter, Program Associate
Phone: 214-741-9898
E-mail: scholarships@dallasfoundation.org

KRISTOPHER KASPER MEMORIAL SCHOLARSHIP

Award for a child of a Centex Homes Texas Region employee. Based on the eligibility criteria, one scholarship of at least $1000 will be awarded annually. The scholarship may be used for tuition, fees, or books, and will be paid directly to the school. There will be an opportunity for renewal if renewal requirements are met.

Award: Scholarship for use in freshman, sophomore, junior, or senior years; renewable. *Number:* 1. *Amount:* $1000.

Eligibility Requirements: Applicant must be high school student and planning to enroll or expecting to enroll full-time at a two-year or four-year or technical institution or university.

Application Requirements: Application form, community service, recommendations or references, resume, transcript. *Deadline:* April 15.

Contact: Rachel Lasseter, Program Associate
Phone: 214-741-9898
E-mail: scholarships@dallasfoundation.org

DANLEY'S GARAGE BUILDERS

https://www.danleysgarageworld.com/

DANLEY'S GARAGE BUILDERS SCHOLARSHIP

Tell us about a teacher that has inspired you in your life and how that has affected you. Give us an introduction to who you are and how this teacher inspired you to be who you are today and who you will be moving forward. Acceptable essays will be between 700 and 1,000 words long that answer the question, "What Teacher Has Inspired You?". All entries should be sent to scholarship@danleys.com. Each scholarship entry must include a photo of yourself, your phone number, your home address and proof of enrollment/acceptance to a college or university.

Award: Scholarship for use in freshman, sophomore, junior, or senior years; not renewable. *Number:* 1. *Amount:* $1000.

Eligibility Requirements: Applicant must be enrolled or expecting to enroll full- or part-time at a two-year or four-year institution or university. Available to U.S. citizens.

Application Requirements: Essay, personal photograph. *Deadline:* November 15.

Contact: Carl K
Phone: 7084374100 ext. 4029
E-mail: scholarship@danleys.com

DARIN C. BANKS FOUNDATION

http://www.dcbfoundation.org

DCBF COLLEGE SCHOLARSHIP

DCBF's Annual Scholarship Competition awards (3) $1000 scholarships to high school seniors selected by the DCBF Scholarship Committee. The competition commences November 1, 2018 and closes on January 31, 2019. More details can be found on our website, www.dcbfoundation.org or by contacting DCBF@DCBFoundation.org.

Award: Scholarship for use in freshman year; not renewable. *Number:* 3. *Amount:* $1000.

Eligibility Requirements: Applicant must be high school student; age 16-19 and planning to enroll or expecting to enroll full-time at a four-year institution or university. Available to U.S. citizens.

Application Requirements: Application form, community service, interview, portfolio. *Deadline:* January 31.

THE DAVID & DOVETTA WILSON SCHOLARSHIP FUND

http://www.wilsonfund.org/

THE DAVID & DOVETTA WILSON SCHOLARSHIP

The mission of the David & Dovetta Wilson Scholarship Fund is to award scholarships to selected Seniors attending Public High Schools in the United States and to promote academic achievement and excellence. DDWSF Scholarship Recipients excel academically, engage in civic and religious acts of service, and demonstrate a commitment to use their education to give back to our local, state and national communities. DDWSF provides nine scholarships annually in the support of education and leadership.

Award: Scholarship for use in freshman year; not renewable. *Number:* 9. *Amount:* $500–$1000.

Eligibility Requirements: Applicant must be high school student and planning to enroll or expecting to enroll full-time at a two-year institution or university. Available to U.S. citizens.

Application Requirements: Application form, application form may be submitted online, community service, essay, financial need analysis, personal photograph. *Deadline:* March 1.

Contact: Scholarship Committee
The David & Dovetta Wilson Scholarship Fund
115-67 237th Street
Elmont, NY 11003
E-mail: submissions@wilsonfund.org

DEFENSIVEDRIVING.COM

http://defensivedriving.com

DEFENSIVEDRIVING.COM SCHOLARSHIP

This award will be given to the high school senior or college student who submits the most unique video following the prompt under the Make A Video tab on https://www.defensivedriving.com/scholarship. Applicants are also required to like DefensiveDriving.com's Facebook page to be considered. See detailed instructions here: https://www.defensivedriving.com/scholarship

Award: Scholarship for use in freshman, sophomore, junior, or senior years; not renewable. *Number:* 1. *Amount:* $1000.

Eligibility Requirements: Applicant must be enrolled or expecting to enroll full- or part-time at a two-year or four-year or technical institution or university. Available to U.S. citizens.

Application Requirements: *Deadline:* May 30.

DELETE CYBERBULLYING

http://www.deletecyberbullying.org

DELETE CYBERBULLYING SCHOLARSHIP

The application form is only available online. The purpose of this scholarship is to get students committed to the cause of deleting cyberbullying.

Award: Scholarship for use in freshman, sophomore, junior, senior, or graduate years; not renewable. *Number:* 2. *Amount:* $1500.

Eligibility Requirements: Applicant must be enrolled or expecting to enroll full- or part-time at a two-year or four-year or technical institution or university. Available to U.S. citizens.

Application Requirements: Application form, essay. *Deadline:* June 30.

Contact: Scholarship Coordinator
E-mail: help@deletecyberbullying.org

DENTAL INSURANCE SHOP

https://www.dentalinsuranceshop.com/index.html

DENTAL INSURANCE SHOP MERIT SCHOLARSHIP

We know saving up for school can be tough. At The Dental Insurance Shop, we believe that scholarships can give ambitious students the opportunity to focus on his or her studies instead of worrying about the cost of books and tuition. With that little extra help, we believe you can achieve greatness. The Dental Insurance Shop is offering a $1,000 non-renewable scholarship to enable one student chosen from all entries to pursue his or her education. All entries must be made by using the application on https://www.dentalinsuranceshop.com/scholarship.html.

Award: Scholarship for use in freshman year; not renewable. *Number:* 1. *Amount:* $1000.

Eligibility Requirements: Applicant must be high school student and planning to enroll or expecting to enroll full-time at a two-year or four-year institution or university. Available to U.S. citizens.

Application Requirements: Application form. *Deadline:* June 30.

Contact: Kevin Knutson
Dental Insurance Shop
12280 Nicollet Avenue
Suite #104
Burnsville, MN 55306
Phone: 855-871-2242
E-mail: scholarship@dentalinsuranceshop.com

DESERVE MODERN

http://www.DeserveModern.com

DESERVE MODERN SCHOLARSHIP

Deserve Modern Scholarship is open to high school juniors & seniors, all college, and graduate level students. There are no other exclusionary criteria. Applications are rolling (you can apply any time) and finalists will be announced the week of May 1st annually with the winner announced later in May. Apply online at http://www.DeserveModern.com

Award: Scholarship for use in freshman, sophomore, junior, senior, graduate, or postgraduate years; not renewable. *Number:* 1. *Amount:* $250.

Eligibility Requirements: Applicant must be age 16-99 and enrolled or expecting to enroll full- or part-time at a two-year or four-year or technical institution or university. Available to U.S. and non-U.S. citizens.

Application Requirements: Application form. *Deadline:* continuous.

Contact: Craig Brooker
E-mail: deservemodern@gmail.com

DESIGN MY COSTUME

http://designmycostume.com/

DESIGN MY COSTUME SCHOLARSHIP

Design My Costume are offering a $2,000 scholarship fund for U.S. high school students intending to pursue further study in fashion or similar subjects and trades. We understand how the ever rising costs of education are weighing heavily on students, and how taking on part or full time jobs to make ends meet can interfere with the pursuit of your chosen career. With this scholarship fund we hope to reduce some of this burden and free you up to focus exclusively on your studies. The scholarship fund will be divided up as follows: The winner will receive $1,000, the runner-up will receive $500, the second and third runners-up will receive $250 each. The amount awarded will be paid out as an education related expenditure in the form of either bank transfer or check. We are looking for students to submit essays on subjects related to clothing and sewing, preferably with a focus on embroidery machines, sewing machines, embroidery and sewing combo machines or the latest sewing and embroidery machines reviews. The scholarship prizes will be awarded based on the quality, resourcefulness, and unique content of the essay. More details and reference links are available on the scholarship page of our website. If you are a current high school student intending to study fashion or a similar trade through an accredited university, college or fashion school in the U.S. in 2017, then you're eligible to apply for the Design My Costume Scholarship. If you would like to submit an application for this scholarship, then go to our website, where you will find the application form available for download on our scholarship page. You will need to fill out your name and mailing details, and the essay should be a minimum of 400 words. You will need to attach a copy of your school or undergraduate transcript along with the application. To be considered for this year's scholarship, your application must be submitted by the 30th December 2017. The winners will be made public on the 15th January 2018. The process for accepting applications for the 2018 scholarship will open on the 1st January 2018. By applying for the Design My Costume Scholarship, you will be agreeing to have your name, photograph and essay published on our website, in our monthly newsletter, and on our social media pages, should you be awarded one of the prizes.

Award: Scholarship for use in freshman, junior, or senior years; renewable. *Number:* 1. *Amount:* $2000.

Eligibility Requirements: Applicant must be enrolled or expecting to enroll full- or part-time at a two-year or four-year or technical institution or university. Available to U.S. and non-U.S. citizens.

Application Requirements: Application form, essay, personal photograph. *Deadline:* December 30.

Contact: Denis Lubojanski, Design My Costume Scholarship
Design My Costume
Flat C, 7 Gloucester Street
London, ON SW1V 2DB
CAN
Phone: 11-7554447547
E-mail: denislubojanski@gmail.com

DEVRIES & ASSOCIATES

https://devriespc.com/

DEVRIES LAW SCHOLARSHIP CONTEST

Every year, our firm grants a $1,000 scholarship to the American college student who creates the best video essay. This year's topic is how lawyers help businesses thrive.

Award: Prize for use in freshman, sophomore, junior, or senior years; not renewable. *Number:* 1. *Amount:* $1000.

Eligibility Requirements: Applicant must be age 18-25 and enrolled or expecting to enroll full- or part-time at a two-year or four-year institution or university. Available to U.S. citizens.

Application Requirements: Application form may be submitted online (https://devriespc.com/scholarship-for-college-students/), essay. *Deadline:* August 15.

DIGITAL RESPONSIBILITY

http://www.digitalresponsibility.org

DIGITAL PRIVACY SCHOLARSHIP

The purpose of this scholarship is to help you understand why you should be cautious about what you post on the Internet. You must be a high school freshman, sophomore, junior, or senior or a current or entering college or graduate school student of any level. Home schooled students are also eligible. There is no age limit. Complete the application form including a 140-character message about digital privacy. The top 10 applications will be selected as finalists. The finalists will be asked to write a full length 500- to 1,000-word essay about digital privacy

Award: Scholarship for use in freshman, sophomore, junior, senior, graduate, or postgraduate years; not renewable. *Number:* 1. *Amount:* $1000–$1500.

Eligibility Requirements: Applicant must be enrolled or expecting to enroll full- or part-time at a two-year or technical institution or university. Available to U.S. citizens.

Application Requirements: Application form, application form may be submitted online, essay. *Deadline:* June 30.

Contact: Scholarship Coordinator
E-mail: scholarship@digitalresponsibility.org

DON'T TEXT AND DRIVE SCHOLARSHIP

The purpose of this scholarship is to help you understand the risks of texting while driving. You must be a high school freshman, sophomore, junior, or senior or a current or entering college or graduate school student of any level. Home schooled students are also eligible. There is no age limit. Complete the application form including a 140-character message about texting while driving. The top 10 applications will be selected as finalists. The finalists will be asked to write a full length 500- to 1,000-word essay about texting while driving

Award: Scholarship for use in freshman, sophomore, junior, senior, graduate, or postgraduate years; not renewable. *Number:* 1. *Amount:* $1000.

Eligibility Requirements: Applicant must be enrolled or expecting to enroll full- or part-time at a two-year or technical institution or university. Available to U.S. citizens.

Application Requirements: Application form, application form may be submitted online, essay. *Deadline:* September 30.

Contact: Scholarship Coordinator
E-mail: scholarship@digitalresponsibility.org

E-WASTE SCHOLARSHIP

The purpose of this scholarship is to help you understand the impact of e-waste and what can be done to reduce e-waste. You must be a high school freshman, sophomore, junior, or senior or a current or entering college or graduate school student of any level. Home schooled students are also eligible. There is no age limit. Complete the application form including a 140-character message about e-waste. The top 10 applications will be selected as finalists. The finalists will be asked to write a full length 500- to 1,000-word essay about e-waste

Award: Scholarship for use in freshman, sophomore, junior, senior, graduate, or postgraduate years; not renewable. *Number:* 1. *Amount:* $1000.

Eligibility Requirements: Applicant must be enrolled or expecting to enroll full- or part-time at a two-year or technical institution or university. Available to U.S. citizens.

Application Requirements: Application form, application form may be submitted online, essay. *Deadline:* April 30.

Contact: Scholarship Coordinator
E-mail: scholarship@digitalresponsibility.org

TECHNOLOGY ADDICTION AWARENESS SCHOLARSHIP

With technology always at the ready at your fingertips, it can be a challenge to unplug. But taking a break from technology is healthy for both the mind and body. The purpose of this scholarship is to help you understand the negative effects of too much screen time. You must be a high school freshman, sophomore, junior, or senior or a current or entering college or graduate school student of any level. Home schooled students are also eligible. There is no age limit. Complete the application form below including a 140-character message about technology addiction. The top 10 applications will be selected as finalists. The finalists will be asked to write a full length 500- to 1,000-word essay about technology addiction

Award: Scholarship for use in freshman, sophomore, junior, senior, graduate, or postgraduate years; not renewable. *Number:* 1. *Amount:* $1000.

Eligibility Requirements: Applicant must be enrolled or expecting to enroll full- or part-time at a two-year or technical institution or university. Available to U.S. citizens.

Application Requirements: Application form, application form may be submitted online, essay. *Deadline:* January 30.

Contact: Scholarship Coordinator
E-mail: scholarship@digitalresponsibility.org

DISTINGUISHED YOUNG WOMEN

http://www.distinguishedyw.org/our-scholarships/

DISTINGUISHED YOUNG WOMEN

We are a non-profit organization that offers Life Skills Workshops to prepare young women for life after high school and over $1 billion in college scholarships opportunities. Plus, it is free to participate. Awards are given to participants in the local, state, and national levels of competition. Must be female, high school juniors or seniors, U.S. citizens, and legal residents of the county and state of competition. Participants are evaluated on scholastic achievement, interview, talent, fitness, and public speaking. The number of awards and their amount vary from year to year.

Award: Scholarship for use in freshman, sophomore, junior, senior, or graduate years; not renewable.

Eligibility Requirements: Applicant must be high school student; age 15-19; planning to enroll or expecting to enroll full-time at a two-year or four-year or technical institution or university and married female. Available to U.S. citizens.

Application Requirements: Application form, application form may be submitted online (http://distinguishedyw.org/scholarships/our-scholarships/), interview, personal photograph. *Deadline:* continuous.

Contact: Lisa Lawley Burnette, National Field Director
Distinguished Young Women
751 Government Street
Mobile, AL 36602
Phone: 251-438-3621
Fax: 251-431-0063
E-mail: lisa@distinguishedyw.org

DIVERSITYCOMM, INC.

http://www.diversitycomm.net/

DIVERSEABILITY MAGAZINE SCHOLARSHIP

For the 2018 fall semester, DIVERSEability Magazine will be offering a $500 scholarship that is available to disabled undergraduate students. DIVERSEability is a diversity & inclusion magazine featuring individuals with all types of diverse abilities. It's more than just a magazine raising awareness and providing educational, employment and business opportunities–it's a movement celebrating advancements and achievements that inspires the world. We would like you to tell your story in a brief narrative, starting with an introduction about who you are, your interests, and anything else you feel we should know about you. Then, please provide your entry in a 300-500 word essay about your college experience so far, and your future career plans. Graphic or creative presentations are welcome as well. The scholarship will be awarded to the applicant who best demonstrates a genuine desire and goal of using the scholarship to advance in their field, and an overall passion for knowledge. We are now accepting submissions. The deadline for submitting essays is August 15. You may send us your entry either as a link or attachment to your email. Include your name, mobile phone number and contact information in the email.

Award: Scholarship for use in freshman, sophomore, junior, or senior years; renewable. *Number:* 1. *Amount:* $500.

Eligibility Requirements: Applicant must be age 18 and over and enrolled or expecting to enroll full- or part-time at a four-year institution or university. Available to U.S. citizens.

Application Requirements: Application form, essay. *Deadline:* August 15.

PROFESSIONAL WOMAN'S MAGAZINE SCHOLARSHIP

For the 2018 Fall Semester, Professional Woman's Magazine will be offering a $500 scholarship that is available to female undergraduate students. We would like you to tell your story in a brief narrative, starting with an introduction about who you are, your interests, and anything else you feel we should know about you. Then, please provide your entry in a 300-500 word essay about your college experience so far, and your future career plans. Graphic or creative presentations are welcome as well.

Award: Scholarship for use in freshman, sophomore, junior, or senior years; renewable. *Number:* 1. *Amount:* $500.

Eligibility Requirements: Applicant must be age 18 and over; enrolled or expecting to enroll full- or part-time at a two-year or four-year institution or university and female. Available to U.S. citizens.

Application Requirements: Application form, essay. *Deadline:* August 15.

DR. EDWARD JACOBSON, MD

https://www.greenwichgynecology.com/

DR. EDWARD JACOBSON HEALTHY LIVING SCHOLARSHIP

Applicants must submit a 750 word essay describing their approach to healthy living.

Award: Scholarship for use in freshman, sophomore, junior, senior, graduate, or postgraduate years; not renewable. *Number:* 1. *Amount:* $500.

Eligibility Requirements: Applicant must be enrolled or expecting to enroll full- or part-time at a two-year or four-year institution or university. Available to U.S. and non-U.S. citizens.

Application Requirements: Application form may be submitted online (https://www.greenwichgynecology.com/2018-healthy-living-scholarship/), essay, resume, transcript. *Deadline:* March 31.

DOLPHIN SCHOLARSHIP FOUNDATION

http://www.dolphinscholarship.org/

DOLPHIN SCHOLARSHIPS

Renewable award for undergraduate and vocational study. Applicant's sponsor must meet one of the following requirements: be current/former member of the U.S. Navy who qualified in submarines and served in the Submarine Force for at least eight years; current or former member of the Navy who served in submarine support activities for at least ten years; Medically discharged or; died while on active duty in the Submarine Force. Must be single, under age 24.

Award: Scholarship for use in freshman, sophomore, junior, or senior years; renewable. *Number:* 25–30. *Amount:* $2000–$3400.

Eligibility Requirements: Applicant must be age 24 or under; enrolled or expecting to enroll full-time at a two-year or four-year or technical institution or university and married. Available to U.S. citizens.

Application Requirements: Application form, community service, essay, financial need analysis, personal photograph. *Deadline:* March 15.

Contact: Mr. Andrew Clark, Executive Director
Dolphin Scholarship Foundation
4966 Euclid Road
Suite 109
Virginia Beach, VA 23462
Phone: 757-671-3200 Ext. 4
E-mail: scholars@dolphinscholarship.org

DOMNICK CUNNINGHAM AND WHALEN

https://www.dcwlaw.com/

DOMNICK CUNNINGHAM & WHALEN WATER SAFETY SCHOLARSHIP

An original essay of approximately 750-1,000 words outlining a water safety need in your community and how safe water practices will help the situation. Provide possible solutions to the hazard and explain how this plan will help save lives in the water

Award: Scholarship for use in freshman, sophomore, junior, senior, graduate, or postgraduate years; not renewable. *Number:* 1. *Amount:* $1000.

Eligibility Requirements: Applicant must be enrolled or expecting to enroll full- or part-time at a two-year or four-year or technical institution or university. Available to U.S. and non-U.S. citizens.

Application Requirements: Application form may be submitted online (https://www.dcwlaw.com/water-safety-scholarship/), essay, resume, transcript. *Deadline:* October 31.

Contact: Sean Domnick
E-mail: info@dcwlaw.com

DONTPAYFULL.COM

https://www.dontpayfull.com/

$1000 ANNUAL STUDENT SCHOLARSHIP - FRIENDS DONTPAYFULL PRICE

We want to invest in students who need financial help. This is why we are glad to announce the third edition of the DontPayFull Student Scholarship, sponsored exclusively by DontPayFull.com. We offer $1000 every year (not renewable) to one eligible student across each institution type (High School, College or University) in the United States.

Award: Scholarship for use in freshman, junior, graduate, or postgraduate years; not renewable. *Number:* 1. *Amount:* $1000.

Eligibility Requirements: Applicant must be enrolled or expecting to enroll full- or part-time at a two-year or four-year or technical institution or university. Available to U.S. citizens.

Application Requirements: Application form, application form may be submitted online (https://www.dontpayfull.com/page/scholarships-for-college-students), essay, student ID card. *Deadline:* October 31.

Contact: Ms. Irina Vasilescu
DontPayFull.com
str. Zece Mese no 9
Bucharest
ROU
E-mail: irinav@dontpayfull.com

DRONE PILOT GROUND SCHOOL

https://www.dronepilotgroundschool.com

DRONE TECHNOLOGY COLLEGE SCHOLARSHIP

The Drone Technology College Scholarship will be awarded to current U.S. undergraduates who have an interest in pushing the drone industry forward, as demonstrated in an essay of 750-1,000 words. Successful applicants will write thorough, thoughtful essays that dive deeply into the topic, and will have a strong letter of support. Visit the scholarship webpage to learn more and to apply. https://www.dronepilotgroundschool.com/scholarship/

Award: Prize for use in freshman, sophomore, junior, or senior years; not renewable. *Number:* 2. *Amount:* $1000.

Eligibility Requirements: Applicant must be age 18 and over and enrolled or expecting to enroll full- or part-time at a two-year or four-year institution or university. Available to U.S. and non-U.S. citizens.

Application Requirements: Application form, essay. *Deadline:* May 1.

Contact: Mr. Alan Perlman
Drone Pilot Ground School
746 Harpeth Knoll Road
Nashville, TN 37221
Phone: 888-3828053
E-mail: support@dronepilotgroundschool.com

EASON & TAMBORNINI, A LAW CORPORATION

https://www.capcitylaw.com/

"INJURY TO OPPORTUNITY" SCHOLARSHIP

The "Injury to Opportunity" Scholarship provides a $2,000 benefit to the children of persons who have suffered or perished from a Personal Injury Accident, or a work related injury. Applicants must apply before their 21st birthday; must have had a parent who suffered an injury, resulting in a permanent disability or wrongful death. Application and information are available here: https://www.capcitylaw.com/injury-to-opportunity-scholarship/

Award: Scholarship for use in freshman, sophomore, junior, or senior years; not renewable. *Number:* 1. *Amount:* $2000.

Eligibility Requirements: Applicant must be age 17-20 and enrolled or expecting to enroll full- or part-time at a two-year or four-year or technical institution or university. Available to U.S. and non-U.S. citizens.

Application Requirements: Application form. *Deadline:* continuous.

Contact: Matthew Eason, Partner & Senior Trial Attorney
Eason & Tambornini, A Law Corporation
1234 H Street
Suite 200
Sacramento, CA 95814
Phone: 916-438-1819
Fax: 916-438-1820
E-mail: matthew@capcitylaw.com

E-COLLEGEDEGREE.COM

http://www.e-collegedegree.com/

E-COLLEGEDEGREE.COM ONLINE EDUCATION SCHOLARSHIP AWARD

The award is to be used for online education. Application must be submitted online. Visit website for more information and application, http://www.e-collegedegree.com.

Award: Scholarship for use in freshman, sophomore, junior, senior, graduate, or postgraduate years; renewable. *Number:* 1. *Amount:* $1000.

Eligibility Requirements: Applicant must be age 18 and over and enrolled or expecting to enroll full- or part-time at a two-year or four-year or technical institution or university. Available to U.S. citizens.

Application Requirements: Application form, entry in a contest, essay. *Deadline:* December 31.

Contact: Chris Lee, Site Manager
e-CollegeDegree.com
9109 West 101st Terrace
Overland Park, KS 66212
Phone: 913-341-6949
E-mail: scholarship@e-collegedegree.com

EDUBIRDIE

https://edubirdie.com/scholarship-for-orphans

EDUBIRDIE SCHOLARSHIP FOR ORPHANS AND HALF-ORPHANS

This generous and helpful scholarship from EduBirdie comes in the form of an essay writing contest. Quite fitting for the company who offers essay writing help to college and high school students. The target students are those who have tragically lost their parents and are either orphans or half-orphans - we feel this is an extremely worthy cause. The scholarship can change lives and it is fantastic to see EduBirdie offering a chance to those who may be less fortunate. How much is the scholarship worth? It gives students the chance to win a whopping $1000! When is the application deadline? Students must submit their application no later than the 1st of April. Who can enter? Full-time students (either college, high school, or university) over the age of 17 who are either orphans or live with a single parent. What do you have to do to enter? As this is an essay writing competition, students must write a paper of 500-800 words on one of the following subjects: " Do we still need grades in modern educational system?", " Information overload: the bane of modern world. How can we help the students to deal with it?", or " Standardized testing: a conventional way of checking the results of education or a new caste system?". The essay has to be unique and written in the English language. EduBirdie really have given a brilliant scholarship that is within anyone's reach!

Award: Scholarship for use in freshman, sophomore, junior, or senior years; not renewable. *Number:* 1. *Amount:* $1000.

Eligibility Requirements: Applicant must be high school student; age 17 and over and planning to enroll or expecting to enroll full- or part-time at a two-year or four-year or technical institution or university. Available to U.S. citizens.

Application Requirements: Application form may be submitted online (https://docs.google.com/forms/d/e/1FAIpQLSfQkAvnT-Bt8Q3LwTAF910tRxNxRezJ1go7EjNHHKUy-1JwlQ/viewform), essay, Links to social media accounts, share information about scholarship on social media, resume. *Deadline:* April 1.

EDUCATOR, INC.

https://www.educator.com/

ANNUAL $2,400 STUDENT SCHOLARSHIP

Both current college students and rising freshmen are eligible for this scholarship. The scholarships will be awarded to two students ($1000 for 1st and $500 for 2nd), and the money will be transferred to their University to go towards the tuition fee. 3rd/4th/5th place winners will be emailed a login for their Annual Educator.com subscription. The students will be chosen based on their academic achievements and essay. The choice will be made by a scholarship committee of two Educator Co-Founders, and two Educator.com Instructors. To apply, applicants need to submit a scan of their most recent transcript (High School is ok for rising freshmen) plus one 500-1000 word essay on "What is the greatest problem in education today and how would you change it?" Educator.com will only consider the work for this scholarship, and will not use it for any other purposes. Application Deadline: August 31st, 2018. Application Results Announcement: October 1st, 2018. Scholarship Amount: 1st place: $1000, 2nd place: $500, 3rd/4th/5th: 1 Annual Subscription to Educator.com ($300 value each). Requirements: Most recent transcript (High School is ok for rising freshmen) plus 500–1000 word essay on "What is the greatest problem in education today and how would you change it?"

Award: Scholarship for use in freshman, sophomore, or junior years; renewable. *Number:* 5. *Amount:* $300–$1000.

Eligibility Requirements: Applicant must be enrolled or expecting to enroll full- or part-time at a two-year or four-year or technical institution or university. Available to U.S. and non-U.S. citizens.

Application Requirements: Application form, essay. *Deadline:* August 31.

Contact: Sarah Woods
E-mail: sarah@educator.com

ELEARNERS.COM

http://www.elearners.com

ELEARNERS ONLINE STUDENT SCHOLARSHIP

Entering to win our free scholarship for college is fast and easy. All you have to do is complete a short form to tell us a little about yourself and answer one essay question in 250 words or less. What is the essay question you ask? We want you to tell us: How has choosing an online college enabled you to finish your education?

Award: Scholarship for use in freshman, sophomore, junior, senior, graduate, or postgraduate years; not renewable. *Number:* 1–2. *Amount:* $1000.

Eligibility Requirements: Applicant must be enrolled or expecting to enroll full- or part-time at a two-year or four-year or technical institution or university. Available to U.S. citizens.

Application Requirements: Application form, driver's license, essay. *Deadline:* February 28.

Contact: Scholarship Organizer
E-mail: militaryscholarships@elearners.com

ELEMENTS BEHAVIORAL HEALTH

https://www.elementsbehavioralhealth.com

ELEMENTS BEHAVIORAL HEALTH COLLEGE TUITION SCHOLARSHIP

Write a 500-word essay responding to the following prompt: The new edition of the Associated Press's Stylebook states the word 'addict' should no longer be used as a noun. In short, a person should be identified separate from their disease. Essay Option: Explain why describing someone as addicted rather than nn addict is important to society in combatting addiction. Design Option: If you prefer, feel free to interpret this topic via an infographic or illustration.

Award: Scholarship for use in freshman, sophomore, junior, or senior years; not renewable. *Number:* 3. *Amount:* $1000–$6000.

Eligibility Requirements: Applicant must be enrolled or expecting to enroll full- or part-time at a four-year institution or university. Available to U.S. citizens.

Application Requirements: Application form, essay. *Deadline:* December 31.

EMPLOYMENT BOOST

https://employmentboost.com

EMPLOYMENT BOOST COLLEGE SCHOLARSHIPS

4 of our scholarships are reserved for STEM students. Students must be currently enrolled in a U.S.-based high school or college. Students graduating from high school must plan to attend college during the fall semester in the same year as the application. Eligible colleges include two-year and four-year universities in the United States. Students who apply must have a minimum GPA of 3.6. Current (unofficial) transcripts must be sent with the application. High school students who are applying must have a letter of acceptance from the college they intend to attend. A copy of this letter must be included in the application. One letter of reference must be included in the application. This letter must come from one of the following sources: a current or former teacher of the student, or a current or former employer of the student.

Award: Scholarship for use in freshman, sophomore, junior, or senior years; not renewable. *Number:* 8. *Amount:* $1000.

Eligibility Requirements: Applicant must be enrolled or expecting to enroll full-time at a two-year or four-year or technical institution or university. Available to U.S. and non-U.S. citizens.

Application Requirements: Application form, application form may be submitted online (https://employmentboost.com/scholarship/), essay, recommendations or references, transcript. *Deadline:* continuous.

Contact: EB Team
Employment BOOST
755 West Big Beaver Road
Suite 2100
Troy, MI 48084
Phone: 888-468-6495
E-mail: ebteam@employmentboost.com

ENVIRONMENTAL LITIGATION GROUP P.C.

https://www.elglaw.com/

ENVIRONMENTAL LITIGATION GROUP, P.C. ASBESTOS SCHOLARSHIP

The eligibility requirements for our 2018 Scholarship Program are the following: must be 18 years old and a U.S. citizen; must be enrolled full-time in a U.S. based accredited two-year or four-year university, community college, junior college, or a graduate degree program; must have a minimum Grade Point Average of 3.0 or higher; must be a student who witnessed a parent, sibling, immediate family member or close friend fighting cancer; must apply to the contest via online form available on our website at https://www.elglaw.com/scholarship/. Must provide the written essay by the deadline of July 31, 2018. The three winners will be chosen by the end of August 2018 and notified by email.

Award: Scholarship for use in freshman, sophomore, junior, senior, or graduate years; not renewable. *Number:* 3. *Amount:* $2000–$5000.

Eligibility Requirements: Applicant must be age 18 and over and enrolled or expecting to enroll full-time at a two-year or four-year institution or university. Available to U.S. citizens.

Application Requirements: Essay, personal photograph. *Deadline:* July 31.

Contact: Ciprian Oltean
Environmental Litigation Group P.C.
2160 Highland Avenue
Suite 200
Birmingham, AL 35205
Phone: 760-696-7959
E-mail: ciprian@elglaw.com

EVANS SCHOLARS FOUNDATION

http://www.wgaesf.org

CHICK EVANS SCHOLARSHIP FOR CADDIES

Full tuition and housing scholarship renewable up to four years for high school seniors who have worked at least two years as a caddie at a Western Golf Association member club. Must demonstrate financial need, excellent academics and outstanding character. Visit www.wgaesf.org for more information.

Award: Scholarship for use in freshman, sophomore, junior, or senior years; renewable. *Number:* 270. *Amount:* $100,000.

Eligibility Requirements: Applicant must be high school student; age 17-19; planning to enroll or expecting to enroll full-time at a four-year institution or university; single and studying in Colorado, Illinois, Indiana, Kansas, Michigan, Minnesota, Missouri, Ohio, Oregon, Pennsylvania, Washington, Wisconsin. Available to U.S. and non-U.S. citizens.

Application Requirements: Application form, essay, financial need analysis, interview, personal photograph. *Deadline:* September 30.

Contact: Scholarship Committee
Phone: 847-724-4600
E-mail: applications@wgaesf.org

EVANS WARNCKE ROBINSON, LLC

https://www.disabilityinsurancelawfirm.com/

EVANS WARNCKE ROBINSON SCHOLARSHIP CONTEST

Every year, our firm grants a $1,000 scholarship to the U.S. college student who creates the best video essay that elaborates on why they want to be a lawyer.

Award: Prize for use in freshman, sophomore, junior, or senior years; not renewable. *Number:* 1. *Amount:* $1000.

Eligibility Requirements: Applicant must be age 18-25 and enrolled or expecting to enroll full- or part-time at a two-year or four-year institution or university. Available to U.S. citizens.

Application Requirements: Application form may be submitted online (https://www.disabilityinsurancelawfirm.com/scholarship-for-college-students/), essay. *Deadline:* August 15.

EXECUTIVE WOMEN INTERNATIONAL

http://www.ewiconnect.com/

ADULT STUDENTS IN SCHOLASTIC TRANSITION

Scholarship for adult students at transitional points in their lives. Applicants may be single parents, individuals just entering the workforce, or displaced homemakers. Applications are available on the organization's website, http://www.ewiconnect.com.

Award: Scholarship for use in freshman, sophomore, junior, or senior years; not renewable. *Number:* 100–150. *Amount:* $250–$2500.

Eligibility Requirements: Applicant must be enrolled or expecting to enroll full-time at a two-year or four-year or technical institution or university. Available to U.S. and non-U.S. citizens.

Application Requirements: Application form, essay, financial need analysis, interview, personal photograph, recommendations or references, self-addressed stamped envelope with application, tax information, transcript.

EXECUTIVE WOMEN INTERNATIONAL SCHOLARSHIP PROGRAM

Competitive award to high school juniors planning careers in any business or professional field of study which requires a four-year college degree. Award is renewable based on continuing eligibility. All awards are given through local Chapters of the EWI. Applicant must apply through nearest Chapter and live within the Chapter's boundaries. Student must have a sponsoring teacher and school to be considered, and only one applicant per school. For more details visit http://www.ewiconnect.com.

Award: Scholarship for use in freshman, sophomore, junior, or senior years; renewable. *Number:* 75–100. *Amount:* $1000–$10,000.

Eligibility Requirements: Applicant must be high school student; age 15-17 and planning to enroll or expecting to enroll full-time at a four-year institution or university. Available to U.S. and non-U.S. citizens.

Application Requirements: Application form, community service, essay, interview, personal photograph, recommendations or references, self-addressed stamped envelope with application, transcript.

Contact: Mr. James Pollan, Executive Director and Trustee
E-mail: stuhrstudents@earthlink.net

EXPRESSVPN

https://www.expressvpn.com

EXPRESSVPN FUTURE OF PRIVACY SCHOLARSHIP

Introduction: The ExpressVPN Future of Privacy Scholarship was created to raise awareness of internet privacy and security. The internet is transforming our education system. The technologies used by schools across the world are not fully secure or private, and schools themselves have implemented their own surveillance systems to track what their students do online. As internet-ready devices proliferate in classrooms worldwide, so do threats to the privacy of the individuals who use them. Awareness of online security and an understanding of fundamental privacy rights are more important than ever. How to enter Revelations over the past year have stoked concern over the power that technology companies wield globally. With net neutrality repealed in the United States, the General Data Protection Regulation taking force in Europe, and governments demanding backdoors into personal devices, one thing is certain: The battle over who controls the technology we use is far from over. This year's essay topic: Technology companies can self-regulate to provide optimal privacy to internet users. The free market will choose the winners to be those companies that best protect their users, without the need for government interference. Do you agree or disagree? Your essay should be no longer than 800 words and submitted to scholarship@expressvpn.com by August 31, 2019. Why you should enter You could win cash or a year's worth of free VPN service. The winner will be featured on multiple communications platforms. This is a great résumé-builder for a career in journalism, law, computer science, or any relevant field of study. This is an opportunity to become a leading voice in the growing debate over encryption, digital rights, internet privacy, and the fight against censorship. Awards and selection process Scholarship award amount The winner of the 2019 Scholarship will receive a $5,000 cash prize. ExpressVPN will also select five runners-up to be rewarded with a 12-month VPN subscription. Selection process The winning essay shall be determined using the following criteria: Level of creativity, originality, and detail of the submission Student's ability to formulate an opinion Clear and articulate writing Contest rules Essays must be written in English. Applicants must be currently enrolled in either a high school, undergraduate school, or graduate school located in the United States, Canada, the United Kingdom, the European Union, Australia, New Zealand, or South Africa. There is no age or citizenship requirement. Essays must be sent via email only, to this address: scholarship@expressvpn.com. To be valid, the application email must include the following information: Your name The name, address, and contact details of your school Your current grade level One entry per student. Multiple entries per student will be disregarded. Essays must be submitted online by August 31, 2019, no later than 11:59 p.m., Pacific Standard Time. The winner will be announced by the end of October 2019. The prize will be awarded by international wire transfer. The winner will be required to provide his/her bank information in order to complete the bank transfer. The winner must submit a valid ID and proof of enrollment in a high school, undergraduate school, or graduate school located in the United States, Canada, the United Kingdom, the European Union, Australia, New Zealand, or South Africa. Employees of ExpressVPN and their immediate family members are not eligible for this contest. All entries become the property of ExpressVPN. The contest winner agrees to allow ExpressVPN to publish or print his/her name and essay. Winners will be solely responsible for any federal, state, or local taxes. The prize is listed and paid in United States Dollars (USD). The decision of ExpressVPN in respect of any dispute arising out of this program shall be final.

Award: Scholarship for use in freshman, sophomore, junior, senior, graduate, or postgraduate years; renewable. *Number:* 1. *Amount:* $5000.

Eligibility Requirements: Applicant must be enrolled or expecting to enroll full- or part-time at a two-year or four-year or technical institution or university. Available to U.S. and non-U.S. citizens.

Application Requirements: Essay. *Deadline:* August 31.

Contact: Scholarship Manager
E-mail: scholarship@expressvpn.com

FELDCO WINDOWS, SIDING AND DOORS

http://www.4feldco.com

FELDCO WINDOWS, SIDING AND DOORS SCHOLARSHIP

Acceptable essays will be between 700-1,000 words long that answer the question: How has your family contributed to who you are today? All entries should be sent to scholarship@4feldco.com. Send your entry to us as an email attachment and include your full name, a headshot of yourself (.png or.jpg format), mobile phone number and address in the email. The scholarship will be awarded to the applicant that best demonstrates in their own words, how their family has contributed to who they are today. Please use the full word limit (700-1,000 words) to best describe how your family has shaped your life. Deadlines to submit are January 15th and July 15th of each year indefinitely. Applications received after the deadline will be considered for the following deadline. Proof of enrollment must be provided with your email submission. This can include a digital scan of your unofficial transcript, letter from admissions or acceptance letter on a school letterhead.

Award: Scholarship for use in freshman, sophomore, junior, or senior years; renewable. *Number:* 1. *Amount:* $1000.

Eligibility Requirements: Applicant must be enrolled or expecting to enroll full-time at a four-year institution or university. Available to U.S. citizens.

Application Requirements: Essay, personal photograph. *Deadline:* continuous.

Contact: Carl Krzeczkowski
E-mail: carlk@4feldco.com

FIELDING LAW GROUP

https://www.fieldinglawgroup.com/

FIELDING LAW GROUP SCHOLARSHIP CONTEST

Every year, our firm grants a $1,000 scholarship to the U.S. college student who creates the best video essay that elaborates on why they want to be a lawyer.

Award: Prize for use in freshman, sophomore, junior, or senior years; not renewable. *Number:* 1. *Amount:* $1000.

Eligibility Requirements: Applicant must be age 18-25 and enrolled or expecting to enroll full- or part-time at a two-year or four-year institution or university.

Application Requirements: Application form may be submitted online (https://www.fieldinglawgroup.com/scholarship-for-college-students.html), essay. *Deadline:* August 15.

FIRST CHOICE COLLEGE PLACEMENT LLC

http://www.firstchoicecollege.com/

ADMISSIONHOOK.COM ESSAY CONTEST

This award is part of our ongoing mission to help students get into and pay for the college of their dreams. There are two ways to win the scholarship. First, you can create an account and submit your essay. If your essay is one of the top 5 vote recipients, your essay will be reviewed by a committee and the winner will be notified within 14 days of the close of the scholarship contest. Second, you can create an account and vote on other student's essays (you can also vote on your own). The registered user who votes on the most essays as of the scholarship deadline will receive a $500 scholarship.

Award: Prize for use in freshman, sophomore, junior, or senior years; not renewable. *Number:* 2–4. *Amount:* $500–$1000.

Eligibility Requirements: Applicant must be enrolled or expecting to enroll full-time at a two-year or four-year institution or university. Available to U.S. citizens.

Application Requirements: Application form, essay.

Contact: Mr. James Maroney, Managing Member
First Choice College Placement LLC
50 Cherry Street
Milford, CT 06460
Phone: 203-878-7998
Fax: 203-878-6087
E-mail: james@admissionhook.com

FIRST MARINE DIVISION ASSOCIATION

http://www.1stmarinedivisionassociation.org/

FIRST MARINE DIVISION ASSOCIATION SCHOLARSHIP FUND

Scholarship to assist dependents of deceased or 100 percent permanently disabled veterans of service with the 1st Marine Division in furthering their education towards a bachelor's degree. Awarded to full-time, undergraduate students who are attending an accredited college, university, or higher technical trade school, up to a maximum of four years.

Award: Scholarship for use in freshman, sophomore, junior, or senior years; renewable. *Number:* 15–25. *Amount:* $1750.

Eligibility Requirements: Applicant must be age 22 or under; enrolled or expecting to enroll full-time at a two-year or four-year or technical institution or university and single. Available to U.S. citizens.

Application Requirements: Application form, essay. *Deadline:* continuous.

Contact: Col. Len Hayes, Executive Director
Phone: 760-712-7088
E-mail: lenhayes@cox.net

FLORIDA ENGINEERING SOCIETY

https://www.fleng.org/page/Scholarships

RAYMOND W. MILLER, PE SCHOLARSHIP

One-time scholarship given to students in their junior or senior year in a Florida university engineering program. Minimum 3.0 GPA required.

Award: Scholarship for use in junior or senior years; not renewable. *Number:* 1. *Amount:* $2500.

Eligibility Requirements: Applicant must be enrolled or expecting to enroll full-time at an institution or university and studying in Florida. Available to U.S. citizens.

Application Requirements: Application form. *Deadline:* February 14.

Contact: Amanda Hudson, Director of Information Technology
Florida Engineering Society
125 S Gadsden Street
Tallahassee, FL 32301
Phone: 850-224-7121
E-mail: ahudson@fleng.org

FLORIDA OUTDOOR WRITERS ASSOCIATION

www.fowa.org

FLORIDA OUTDOOR WRITERS ASSOCIATION SCHOLARSHIPS

The Florida Outdoor Writers Association Scholarship is competitive and open to students at Florida colleges and universities, or to any college student whose application is endorsed by a FOWA member or a faculty advisor. These scholarships are intended for college-aged students whose career goals are to communicate to the public appreciation for hunting, fishing and other aspects of the outdoor experience.

Award: Scholarship for use in junior, senior, graduate, or postgraduate years; not renewable. *Number:* 2–3. *Amount:* $500–$1000.

Eligibility Requirements: Applicant must be enrolled or expecting to enroll full- or part-time at a two-year or four-year institution or university. Available to U.S. and non-U.S. citizens.

Application Requirements: Application form, essay, portfolio, resume. *Deadline:* May 14.

FLORIDA STATE DEPARTMENT OF EDUCATION

http://www.floridastudentfinancialaid.org/

FLORIDA STUDENT ASSISTANCE GRANT-CAREER EDUCATION

Need-based grant program available to degree-seeking, resident, undergraduate students who demonstrate substantial financial need and are enrolled in participating post-secondary institutions.

Award: Grant for use in freshman, sophomore, junior, or senior years; renewable. *Number:* 200.

Eligibility Requirements: Applicant must be enrolled or expecting to enroll full- or part-time at an institution or university. Available to U.S. citizens.

Application Requirements: Application form, application form may be submitted online, financial need analysis.

Contact: Customer Service
Phone: 888-827-2004
E-mail: osfa@fldoe.org

ROSEWOOD FAMILY SCHOLARSHIP FUND

Renewable award for eligible direct descendants of African-American Rosewood families affected by the incident of January 1923. The annual award amount may not exceed $6,100. The per term award amount a student may receive includes tuition and fees for up to 15 semester hours or up to 450 clock hours for undergraduate study. Must not have previously received a baccalaureate degree. For more details, visit the website at http://www.FloridaStudentFinancialAid.org/SSFAD/home/uamain.htm.

Award: Scholarship for use in freshman, sophomore, junior, or senior years; renewable.

Eligibility Requirements: Applicant must be enrolled or expecting to enroll full- or part-time at a two-year or technical institution or university and studying in Florida. Available to U.S. citizens.

Application Requirements: Application form, application form may be submitted online, financial need analysis. *Deadline:* April 1.

Contact: Florida Department of Education, Office of Student Financial Assistance, Customer Service
Florida State Department of Education
325 West Gaines Street
Tallahassee, FL 32399
Phone: 888-827-2004
E-mail: osfa@fldoe.org

FORECLOSURE.COM

https://www.foreclosure.com/

FORECLOSURE.COM SCHOLARSHIP PROGRAM

The Foreclosure.com Scholarship Program encourages students to offer innovative ideas and solutions to a specific yearly topic base don real estate in the form of an essay. Essay submissions must be between 800 and 2,000 words and all accepted freshman and enrolled under-graduate students are eligible to apply. First place prize is $2,500 and second through third place will be awarded $500 each. Checks will be made out to the college or university attended in the form of a non-renewable scholarship grant.

Award: Scholarship for use in freshman, sophomore, junior, or senior years; not renewable. *Number:* 3–2,500. *Amount:* $500–$2500.

Eligibility Requirements: Applicant must be enrolled or expecting to enroll full-time at a two-year or four-year or technical institution or university. Available to U.S. citizens.

Application Requirements: Application form, application form may be submitted online(www.foreclosure.com/scholarship), essay. *Deadline:* December 15.

Contact: Mrs. Linda Yates, Director of Education
Phone: 561-988-9669 Ext. 7383
E-mail: lyates@foreclosure.com

FOSTER CARE TO SUCCESS

http://www.fc2success.org/

FOSTER CARE TO SUCCESS SCHOLARSHIP PROGRAM

Award of up to $6000 to young people under the age of 25 who spent the 12 consecutive months prior to their 18th birthday in foster care or who were adopted or placed into legal guardianship from foster care after their 16th birthday. Scholarships are awarded for the pursuit of postsecondary education, including vocational/technical training, and are renewable for up to five years based on satisfactory progress and financial need.

Award: Scholarship for use in freshman, sophomore, junior, or senior years; not renewable. *Number:* 100. *Amount:* $1000–$6000.

Eligibility Requirements: Applicant must be age 25 or under and enrolled or expecting to enroll full- or part-time at a two-year or four-year or technical institution or university. Available to U.S. citizens.

Application Requirements: Application form, essay, financial need analysis. *Deadline:* March 31.

Contact: Dana Brown, Manager, Scholarships and Student Programs
Foster Care to Success
Foster Care To Success
23811 Chagrin Boulevard, Suite 210
Cleveland, OH 44122
Phone: 571-203-0270 Ext. 130
E-mail: dana@fc2success.org

FOUNDATION FOR OUTDOOR ADVERTISING RESEARCH AND EDUCATION (FOARE)

http://www.oaaa.org/

FOARE SCHOLARSHIP PROGRAM

One-time award of $2000 for 6 students. High school seniors, undergraduates, and graduate students enrolled in or accepted to an accredited institution are eligible to apply. Selections are based on financial need, academic performance, and career goals.

Award: Scholarship for use in freshman, sophomore, junior, senior, or graduate years; not renewable. *Number:* 6. *Amount:* $2000.

Eligibility Requirements: Applicant must be enrolled or expecting to enroll full-time at a four-year institution or university. Available to U.S. citizens.

Application Requirements: Application form, essay, financial need analysis, transcript. *Deadline:* June 15.

Contact: Scholarship Program
Foundation for Outdoor Advertising Research and Education (FOARE)
c/o Thomas M. Smith & Associates
4601 Tilden Street, NW
Washington, DC 20016
Phone: 202-364-7130
E-mail: tmfsmith@starpower.net

FREEDOM ALLIANCE

https://freedomalliance.org

FREEDOM ALLIANCE SCHOLARSHIP FUND

Freedom Alliance Scholarship Fund applicants must be one of the following: the dependent son or daughter of a U.S. soldier, sailor, airman, guardsman or Marine who has become 100% permanently disabled as a result of an combat mission or training accident; the dependent son or daughter of a U.S. soldier, sailor, airman, guardsman or Marine who has been killed in action; the dependent son or daughter of a U.S. soldier, sailor, airman, guardsman or Marine who has been classified as a Prisoner of War (POW) or Missing in Action (MIA). All applicants must also meet the following eligibility requirements in order to qualify for a Freedom Alliance scholarship: currently in their senior year of high school, a high school graduate or a currently enrolled full time undergraduate student; under the age of 26 at the time of application; have a GPA of 2.0 or higher. Eligible students can visit our website, http://www.fascholarship.com, and complete the application to start the process.

Award: Scholarship for use in freshman, sophomore, junior, or senior years; renewable. *Number:* 300–400. *Amount:* $500–$3500.

Eligibility Requirements: Applicant must be age 17-25 and enrolled or expecting to enroll full-time at a two-year or four-year or technical institution or university. Available to U.S. citizens. Applicant or parent must meet one or more of the following requirements: retired from active duty; disabled or killed as a result of military service; prisoner of war; or missing in action.

Application Requirements: Application form, essay, Military service documents fro eligible parent, personal photograph, transcript. *Deadline:* continuous.

Contact: Wanda Cruz, Programs Assistant
Freedom Alliance
22570 Markey Court
Suite 240
Dulles, VA 20166
Phone: 800-475-6620
E-mail: info@fascholarship.com

FREEDOM FROM RELIGION FOUNDATION

http://www.ffrf.org/

DAVID HUDAK MEMORIAL ESSAY CONTEST FOR FREETHINKING STUDENTS OF COLOR

Open only to freethinking students of color ages 17-21, who are either high school seniors graduating in spring 2020 who will be attending a North American college or university in fall 2020, or who are currently enrolled in a college or university. If you will be graduating from college in the spring or summer 2020, you remain eligible to enter this contest. This contest is offered to provide support and acknowledgment for freethinking students of color, as a minority within a minority. People of Color refers to all racial groups that are not white. Specifically, any person who is not considered white, including African-Americans, Hispanic- Americans, Asian-Americans and others. FFRF offers other essay contests open to all students in your age group. Students may only enter one FFRF contest annually. Applicant must submit a 400-600 words essay with the topic "Living and Thriving Without Religion".

Award: Prize for use in freshman, sophomore, junior, or senior years; not renewable. *Number:* 10. *Amount:* $200–$3500.

Eligibility Requirements: Applicant must be age 17-21 and enrolled or expecting to enroll at a two-year institution or university. Available to U.S. and Canadian citizens.

Application Requirements: Application form, application form may be submitted online, essay. *Deadline:* July 15.

Contact: Annie Laurie Gaylor, Foundation Co-President
Phone: 608-256-8900
E-mail: info@ffrf.org

MICHAEL HAKEEM MEMORIAL ESSAY CONTEST FOR ONGOING COLLEGE STUDENTS

Open to all ongoing undergraduate college students up to age 24 already attending a North American college or university. You remain eligible to enter this contest if you will graduate from college by spring or summer of 2020. If you're entering college in Fall 2020 for the first time, please enter FFRF's contest for college-bound high school seniors. If you're a student of color up to age 21, who is currently enrolled in college, you may enter this contest or the David Hudak Student of Color Contest, but you may not enter both contests. Applicant must submit a 450-650 words essay using the topic "The Necessity of Freethought — Why I am Not Religious."

Award: Scholarship for use in freshman, sophomore, junior, or senior years; not renewable. *Number:* 10. *Amount:* $200–$3500.

Eligibility Requirements: Applicant must be age 16-24 and enrolled or expecting to enroll full- or part-time at a two-year or technical institution or university. Available to U.S. and Canadian citizens.

Application Requirements: Application form, application form may be submitted online, essay. *Deadline:* July 1.

Contact: FFRF College Essay Contest
Freedom From Religion Foundation
PO Box 750
Madison, WI 53701

WILLIAM J. SCHULZ MEMORIAL ESSAY CONTEST FOR COLLEGE-BOUND HIGH SCHOOL SENIORS

College-bound high school seniors write on the topic: "Why I'm an unabashed atheist/agnostic/choose your favorite appellation" June 1 deadline. Word limits of 350 words, with winners announced in July. See all rules at: https://ffrf.org/outreach/ffrf-student-scholarship-essay-contests

Award: Scholarship for use in freshman year; not renewable. *Number:* 10. *Amount:* $200–$3500.

Eligibility Requirements: Applicant must be high school student; age 15-20 and planning to enroll or expecting to enroll full- or part-time at a two-year or technical institution or university. Available to U.S. and Canadian citizens.

Application Requirements: Application form, application form may be submitted online, essay. *Deadline:* June 1.

Contact: High School Essay Competition
Freedom From Religion Foundation
PO Box 750
Madison, WI 53701

THE FREEMAN FOUNDATION/INSTITUTE OF INTERNATIONAL EDUCATION

https://www.iie.org/

FREEMAN AWARDS FOR STUDY IN ASIA

The Freeman-ASIA program is designed to support U.S.-based undergraduates with demonstrated financial need who are planning to study abroad in East or Southeast Asia. The program's goal is to increase the number of U.S. citizens and permanent residents with first-hand exposure to and understanding of Asia and its peoples and cultures. Award recipients are required to share their experiences with their home campuses or communities to encourage study abroad by others and fulfill the program's goal of increasing understanding of Asia in the United States. Award amounts vary from $3,000 to $7,000 depending on the study abroad program length and financial need. More information can be found on the program's website: https://www.iie.org/Programs/Freeman-ASIA/

Award: Scholarship for use in freshman, sophomore, junior, or senior years; not renewable. *Amount:* $3000.

Eligibility Requirements: Applicant must be enrolled or expecting to enroll full- or part-time at a two-year or four-year institution or university. Available to U.S. citizens.

Application Requirements: Application form, essay, financial need analysis. *Deadline:* continuous.

GERMAN ACADEMIC EXCHANGE SERVICE (DAAD)

http://www.daad.org/

DAAD GROUP STUDY VISITS

Grants are available for an information visit of seven to twelve days to groups of 10 to 15 students, accompanied by a faculty member. They are intended to encourage contact with academic institutions, groups and individuals in Germany, and offer insight into current issues in the academic, scientific, economic, political and cultural realms. All departments/disciplines are eligible, preference is given to groups with a homogeneous academic background and may be drawn from more than one institution. Applications are possible around November, February and May. Groups will not be eligible for funding in successive years.

Award: Grant for use in junior, senior, or graduate years; not renewable.

Eligibility Requirements: Applicant must be enrolled or expecting to enroll full-time at a four-year institution. Available to U.S. and non-U.S. citizens.

Application Requirements: Application form.

DAAD STUDY SCHOLARSHIP

DAAD's flagship competitive scholarship awarded for study at all public universities in Germany. Open to all fields. Study Scholarships are granted for one academic year with the possibility of a one-year extension for students completing a full degree program in Germany (between 10 and 24 months)

Award: Scholarship for use in senior or graduate years; renewable.

Eligibility Requirements: Applicant must be enrolled or expecting to enroll full-time at a four-year institution or university. Available to U.S. and non-U.S. citizens.

Application Requirements: Application form.

GERSOWITZ LIBO & KOREK, P.C.

https://www.lawyertime.com

GARDINER FOUNDATION SCHOLARSHIP

For a young person, losing a family member can be a devastating experience. However, losing multiple family members all at once is almost unthinkable. That's what happened to Dexter Gardiner, who on July 9, 2006 lost six family members in a tragic car accident on the Bronx River Parkway. Yet despite the loss, Dexter chose to use the tragedy as a way to help others who have experienced similar situations in losing beloved family members unexpectedly. Needless to say, for those left behind, especially children whose college education may suddenly be in doubt due to financial concerns, the world can suddenly seem very uncertain.

Award: Scholarship for use in sophomore or senior years; renewable. *Number:* 4–5. *Amount:* $1500.

Eligibility Requirements: Applicant must be enrolled or expecting to enroll full-time at an institution or university. Available to U.S. citizens.

Application Requirements: Application form, essay. *Deadline:* July 15.

Contact: Mr. Bryan Powell
E-mail: scholarship@lawyertime.com

GETEDUCATED.COM

https://www.geteducated.com/

$1,000 EXCELLENCE IN ONLINE EDUCATION SCHOLARSHIP

Scholarships for distance education available only to U.S. citizens enrolled in a CHEA-accredited online degree program located in the USA with a minimum cumulative GPA of 3.0. Provide a copy of your most recent grade transcripts, completed application, a copy of your most recent FAFSA or 1040 tax return, and submit a 500-word essay: "What a College Degree Means to Me."

Award: Scholarship for use in freshman, sophomore, junior, senior, or graduate years; not renewable. *Number:* 1–6. *Amount:* $1000.

Eligibility Requirements: Applicant must be enrolled or expecting to enroll full- or part-time at a two-year or four-year institution or university. Available to U.S. citizens.

Application Requirements: Application form, essay, financial need analysis. *Deadline:* March 15.

Contact: Tony Huffman, CEO of GetEducated.com
GetEducated.com
PO Box 458
Monterey, VA 24465
Phone: 802-899-4866
E-mail: thuffman@perdiaeducation.com

GIBSONSINGLETON VIRGINIA INJURY ATTORNEYS

https://www.gibsonsingleton.com/

TEXTS=WRECKS SCHOLARSHIP 2019

We are offering a $1,000 scholarship for one deserving high school or college student who has a 3.0 or higher GPA and are committed to making good choices. Last year, we launched our Texts = Wrecks campaign in hopes of saving teenagers' lives. The application includes an essay section, we want to hear your best ideas –- including things you've already tried that have worked –- to help yourself, your family members, and your friends drive more safely. The introduction is to be 100-200 words, and the essay is to be 500-1000 words. The deadline to apply is May 16, 2019, and we will announce our winner on June 13, 2019. Additional information and applications can be found on our website: https://www.gibsonsingleton.com/scholarship/

Award: Scholarship for use in freshman, sophomore, junior, or senior years; not renewable. *Number:* 1. *Amount:* $1000.

Eligibility Requirements: Applicant must be enrolled or expecting to enroll full- or part-time at a two-year or four-year or technical institution or university. Available to U.S. citizens.

Application Requirements: Application form, essay. *Deadline:* May 16.

Contact: Daniel Mateo
GibsonSingleton Virginia Injury Attorneys
65 N Raymond Ave #230
Pasadena, CA 91103
Phone: 323-254-1510
E-mail: DMateo@slsconsulting.com

GIFT BASKETS PLUS

http://www.giftbasketsplus.com

2017 HIGH SCHOOL GRADUATE SCHOLARSHIP CONTEST

We are announcing the Gift Baskets Plus 2017 college scholarship contest for $500. The rules are simple. Seniors in high school will submit an essay of at least 600 words, entitled "The perfect high school graduation gift." Each essay must be submitted by email to

2017scholarship@giftbasketsplus.com. To qualify, each submission must contain a PDF of the essay; student's full name; destination college (or colleges if not yet selected); email address; mailing address; date of birth. Qualifying essays will be published on GiftBasketsPlus.com. Essays must be submitted by May 1st, 2017 to be considered. The winner will be announced on June 1, 2017. Once qualified, one essay will be selected for a $500 scholarship based on the number of social shares that essay gets. Winners will be notified by email and scholarships will be mailed by check. Good luck, students!

Award: Prize for use in freshman, sophomore, junior, senior, or graduate years; not renewable. *Number:* 1. *Amount:* $500.

Eligibility Requirements: Applicant must be enrolled or expecting to enroll full-time at a two-year or four-year or technical institution or university. Available to U.S. citizens.

Application Requirements: Essay. *Deadline:* May 1.

Contact: Tamara Watson, Marketing Manager
Phone: 800-520-6657

GIRLTEREST ONLINE MAGAZINE

http://girlterest.com/

GIRLTEREST SCHOLARSHIP PROGRAM FOR YOUNG WOMEN

Girlterest Online Magazine is offering an annual scholarship to undergraduate and postgraduate female students. As strong advocates for higher learning and women's empowerment, we are proud to give back to aspiring women through the Girlterest Yearly Scholarship. This scholarship is merit based, requires an essay submission, and the winning student will receive $1,000 towards their costs of education. All of the application details and terms, as well as the 2017 essay topics are available on our website at girlterest.com/scholarship/.

Award: Scholarship for use in freshman, sophomore, junior, senior, graduate, or postgraduate years; renewable. *Number:* 1. *Amount:* $1000.

Eligibility Requirements: Applicant must be enrolled or expecting to enroll full- or part-time at a two-year or four-year or technical institution or university and female. Available to U.S. and non-U.S. citizens.

Application Requirements: Essay, personal photograph. *Deadline:* December 30.

Contact: Mrs. Maureen Mizrahi, Co-Founder
Girlterest Online Magazine
33 Burla Street 75736
Rishon leZion
ISR
Phone: 66-958570634
E-mail: scholarships@girlterest.com

GOASSIGNMENTHELP

https://www.goassignmenthelp.com.au

GO ASSIGNMENT HELP SCHOLARSHIP

3 Scholarships for $1000 each. Scholarship application is available on website. Scholarship open for all institutions, all majors are eligible. Participant should be at least 13 years of age. For other official rules visit: https://www.goassignmenthelp.com.au/scholarship/official-rules/. Since the essay question pertains to rising students debt, the scholarship is open to students from all majors and across geographies.

Award: Scholarship for use in freshman, sophomore, junior, senior, graduate, or postgraduate years; not renewable. *Number:* 3. *Amount:* $1000.

Eligibility Requirements: Applicant must be age 13-65 and enrolled or expecting to enroll full- or part-time at a two-year or four-year or technical institution or university. Available to U.S. and non-U.S. citizens.

Application Requirements: Essay. *Deadline:* December 15.

Contact: Go-Assignment Scholarship Program
GoAssignmentHelp
187 Wolf Road
Albany, NY 12205
Phone: 617-933-5480
E-mail: scholarships@goassignmenthelp.com.au

GOENNOUNCE, LLC

http://GoEnnounce.com/about

GOENNOUNCE YOURSELF $500 MONTHLY SCHOLARSHIP

Our $500 monthly scholarship is a monthly scholarship open to all high school students and college freshmen, sophomores, and juniors. Once you apply, you're considered every month based on the updates you're posting. Not essay or GPA–based. Who are you as a student? An athlete, a history ace, a star on the drums, class treasurer, a student volunteer, or something completely different? We want to reward you for being you and for e–announcing your school progress and accomplishments each month.

Award: Prize for use in freshman, sophomore, or junior years; renewable. *Number:* 12. *Amount:* $500.

Eligibility Requirements: Applicant must be age 13 and over and enrolled or expecting to enroll full-time at a two-year or four-year institution or university. Available to U.S. citizens.

Application Requirements: *Deadline:* continuous.

GOLDEN KEY INTERNATIONAL HONOUR SOCIETY

http://www.goldenkey.org/

GOLDEN KEY SERVICE AWARD

One award totaling $500, disbursed as $250 to the recipient and $250 to the charity of the recipient's choice. Undergraduate and graduate members who were enrolled as students during the previous academic year are eligible.

Award: Scholarship for use in sophomore, junior, senior, or graduate years; not renewable. *Number:* 1. *Amount:* $500.

Eligibility Requirements: Applicant must be enrolled or expecting to enroll full- or part-time at a four-year institution or university. Available to Canadian and non-U.S. citizens.

Application Requirements: Application form, community service, cover page from the online registration, statement of project, essay, recommendations or references. *Deadline:* March 3.

Contact: Crystal Hunter, Program Manager
Phone: 800-377-2401
E-mail: awards@goldenkey.org

GOLDSTEIN AND BASHNER

https://www.eglaw.com/

COMBATING CAMPUS ISSUES SCHOLARSHIP

$1,000 award will be presented to an especially promising higher education student who shares our determination and articulates a clear vision about how he or she will work to advance advocacy initiatives and solutions for on-campus problems. For more information, please visit: http://www.eglaw.com/nassau-county-injury/#scholarship

Award: Scholarship for use in freshman, sophomore, junior, senior, graduate, or postgraduate years; not renewable. *Number:* 1. *Amount:* $1000.

Eligibility Requirements: Applicant must be enrolled or expecting to enroll full- or part-time at a two-year or four-year or technical institution or university. Available to U.S. and non-U.S. citizens.

Application Requirements: Application form may be submitted online (https://www.eglaw.com/2019-combating-campus-issues-scholarship/), essay, resume, transcript. *Deadline:* August 31.

Contact: Neal Goldstein
E-mail: help.eglaw@gmail.com

GOODCALL LLC

http://www.goodcall.com

GOODCALL BEST DECISION SCHOLARSHIP

At GoodCall, we try to help people make smarter decisions by giving them access to important data. We want to know about a great decision you've made in your life. Write an essay between 400 and 500 words detailing one of the most important decisions you've made in your life.

What information did you rely on? What decision did you make? How did you know it was the right choice? Please apply through our website; do not email.

Award: Scholarship for use in freshman, sophomore, or senior years; not renewable. *Number:* 1. *Amount:* $2500.

Eligibility Requirements: Applicant must be enrolled or expecting to enroll full-time at a two-year or four-year or technical institution or university. Available to U.S. citizens.

Application Requirements: Essay. *Deadline:* July 31.

GOODSHOP

https://www.goodsearch.com/

GOODSHOP ANNUAL SCHOLARSHIP

Here at Goodshop, we give shoppers instant access to the very best coupons for all their favorite online stores. Simultaneously, we donate a percentage of cashback earned to various charities at no extra cost to our users. This year (and every year) we want to take it one step further by giving money directly to promising students. In keeping with our mission, we're offering a $2000 scholarship towards one talented student every single year. https://www.goodsearch.com/scholarship/

Award: Prize for use in freshman, sophomore, junior, senior, graduate, or postgraduate years; renewable. *Number:* 1. *Amount:* $2000.

Eligibility Requirements: Applicant must be enrolled or expecting to enroll full- or part-time at a two-year or four-year or technical institution or university. Available to U.S. citizens.

Application Requirements: Application form. *Deadline:* December 31.

Contact: Matthew Bienz, Representative
E-mail: matthew.bienz@goodsearch.com

GRAND RAPIDS COMMUNITY FOUNDATION

http://www.grfoundation.org/

FRED AND LENA MEIJER SCHOLARSHIP

Applicants must be an employee of Meijer, Inc. or child of a Meijer, Inc employee who has been employed for at least one year by the application deadline of March 1. Children of Team Members must be full-time students. Team Members may be part or full-time students.

Award: Scholarship for use in freshman, sophomore, junior, or senior years; not renewable. *Amount:* $4000–$10,000.

Eligibility Requirements: Applicant must be enrolled or expecting to enroll full- or part-time at a two-year or technical institution or university. Available to U.S. citizens.

Application Requirements: Application form, application form may be submitted online, essay, financial need analysis. *Deadline:* March 1.

Contact: Ms. Ruth Bishop, Education Program Officer
Grand Rapids Community Foundation
185 Oakes Street SW
Grand Rapids, MI 49503
Phone: 616-454-1751 Ext. 103
E-mail: rbishop@grfoundation.org

GRUNGO COLARULO

https://gcinjurylaw.com/

GRUNGO COLARULO GIVING BACK TO THE COMMUNITY SCHOLARSHIP

The Giving Back to the Community scholarship is open to apply to for any student who is currently enrolled in an accredited community college, undergraduate, or graduate program in the United States. Students who are currently incoming first-year college students and have graduated high school or possesses a GED may also apply. For complete information on this scholarship, please visit https://gcinjurylaw.com/#scholarship

Award: Scholarship for use in freshman, sophomore, junior, senior, graduate, or postgraduate years; not renewable. *Number:* 1. *Amount:* $1000.

Eligibility Requirements: Applicant must be enrolled or expecting to enroll full- or part-time at a two-year or four-year or technical institution or university. Available to U.S. and non-U.S. citizens.

Application Requirements: Application form may be submitted online (https://gcinjurylaw.com/2019-giving-back-to-the-community-scholarship/), essay, resume, transcript. *Deadline:* July 31.

Contact: Richard Grungo
E-mail: info@gcinjurylaw.com

GUARDIAN DEBT RELIEF

https://www.guardiandebtrelief.com/

GUARDIAN DEBT RELIEF SCHOLARSHIP

Guardian Debt Relief is offering a scholarship for students entering into or already enrolled in college. Guardian Debt Relief realizes the importance of higher education and wants to lend our aid to those who pursue a degree. We want to do our part in lowering the amount of debt with which young adults leave college. We will award five (5) scholarships of $1000 each to impressive college students who qualify. Eligible applicants will be required to submit a 2,000 word essay based on one of the three essay topics listed below. The five (5) most impressive and informative essays will be selected for the awards. The applicants must be enrolled in an accredited 4-year university or college located in the United States. Open to both graduate and undergraduate students. Graduating high school seniors with a GPA of 3.0 or higher are eligible to apply for the scholarship. You must have a cumulative GPA of 3.0 if you are already enrolled in college. You must successfully complete the application form and written essay. The essay must be double spaced and submitted through email. Word Documents and PDF (.doc,.docx,.pdf) formats will be accepted. All other formats will not be considered. All essays must be at least 2000 words in length and must include a heading with your full name and date on the first page. Essays totaling less than 2000 words will not be considered. See website for details, https://www.guardiandebtrelief.com/guardian-debt-relief-scholarship/

Award: Scholarship for use in freshman, sophomore, junior, senior, or graduate years; not renewable. *Number:* 1–5. *Amount:* $1–$1000.

Eligibility Requirements: Applicant must be enrolled or expecting to enroll full- or part-time at a two-year or four-year or technical institution or university. Available to U.S. citizens.

Application Requirements: Application form, essay. *Deadline:* December 31.

Contact: Michael Milington
Phone: 212-592-0300
E-mail: scholarships@guardiandebtrelief.com

G.W. NETWORKS INC.

http://mmanuts.com

PRINT IT SCHOLARSHIP FOR ASPIRING CONTENT CREATORS

Please contact us to submit your entry or with any questions you may have by sending an email to scholarships@mmanuts.com with Scholarship Inquiry in the subject line. You may also reach us at our main office at (773) 599-1662.

Award: Scholarship for use in freshman, sophomore, junior, or senior years; not renewable. *Number:* 1. *Amount:* $250.

Eligibility Requirements: Applicant must be age 18-50 and enrolled or expecting to enroll full- or part-time at a two-year or four-year or technical institution or university. Available to U.S. citizens.

Application Requirements: Application form. *Deadline:* March 8.

Contact: Mr. Ingo Weigold, President and Owner
G.W. Networks Inc.
112 East Sunset
Lombard, IL 60148
Phone: 630-379-7673
E-mail: ingo.weigold@mmanuts.com

HANSCOM FEDERAL CREDIT UNION

https://www.hfcu.org/

JOHN F. CONDON MEMORIAL SCHOLARSHIP

To qualify, you must be a member at the time of application and you must be planning to enroll in an accredited program of higher education. Other considerations include academic performance, extracurricular activities, community service and financial need.

Award: Prize for use in freshman year; not renewable. *Number:* 5. *Amount:* $1500.

Eligibility Requirements: Applicant must be high school student and planning to enroll or expecting to enroll full- or part-time at a two-year or four-year institution or university. Available to U.S. citizens.

Application Requirements: Application form, essay. *Deadline:* March 11.

Contact: Cara Powers, Scholarship Administrator
Hanscom Federal Credit Union
1610 Eglin Street
Hanscom AFB, MA 01731
Phone: 781-698-2203
E-mail: cpowers@hfcu.org

HARVARD TRAVELLERS CLUB PERMANENT FUND

http://www.travellersfund.org/

HARVARD TRAVELLERS CLUB PERMANENT FUND

From one to three grants made each year to persons with projects that involve intelligent travel and exploration. The travel must be intimately involved with research and/or exploration. Prefer applications from persons working on advanced degrees.

Award: Grant for use in freshman, sophomore, junior, senior, graduate, or postgraduate years; not renewable. *Number:* 1–4. *Amount:* $1000–$5000.

Eligibility Requirements: Applicant must be age 18 and over and enrolled or expecting to enroll full- or part-time at a four-year institution or university. Available to U.S. and non-U.S. citizens.

Application Requirements: Application form, application form may be submitted online (http://www.travellersfund.org), financial need analysis. *Deadline:* March 31.

Contact: Mr. Jack Deary, Trustee
Harvard Travellers Club Permanent Fund
170 Hubbard St.
Lenox, MA 01240
E-mail: Jackdeary@harvardtravellersclub.org

HEALTHLINE

http://www.healthline.com/

HEALTHLINE STRONGER SCHOLARSHIP PROGRAM

This year's scholarship is dedicated to the advancement of rare and chronic diseases, either through research, patient advocacy, raising awareness, or community building. Together, we're launching our 2018 scholarship program, which aims to assist and empower college students making a positive impact on rare and/or chronic diseases. If you have demonstrated involvement in the advancement of rare and/or chronic disease(s), either through research, patient advocacy, raising awareness, or community building, tell us about it in your application. For further information, go to https://corp.healthline.com/scholarship-program.

Award: Scholarship for use in junior or senior years; not renewable. *Number:* 4. *Amount:* $5000.

Eligibility Requirements: Applicant must be enrolled or expecting to enroll full-time at a four-year institution or university. Available to U.S. and non-Canadian citizens.

Application Requirements: Application form, essay. *Deadline:* May 1.

HEALTH PRODUCTS FOR YOU

https://www.healthproductsforyou.com/

HPFY DISABILITY SCHOLARSHIP

This scholarship of $1000 will be awarded to a deserving high school senior who plans to attend a vocational or academic college. Applicant can also be a student currently enrolled in college. Must be a current high school senior or a college student living with a documented disability. If the applicant is a high school student, then he or she should be planning to attend an undergraduate program in a 2 or 4 -year University/College or Technical College in the fall of the academic year following high-school graduation. Schools must be in the USA. Enrollment status in school or college must be full time or half time. To apply for the HPFY Disability Scholarship, email the following to scholarship@ healthproductsforyou.comby August 15th: personal information, including full name, date of birth, mailing address and phone number; proof of enrollment which can be a enrollment certificate or transcript of your most recent GPA (does not affect the selection); medical documents to prove the disability; an essay of minimum 500 words that speaks about your personal trials and triumphs in life related to your illness or disability and how that has defined the person you are today; any supporting documents or letters of recommendations from teachers, mentors or advisers that you would like the selection committee to consider. If all the eligibility requirements are met, the recipient will be selected on the basis of their essay and the supporting documents. The selected recipient of the $500 scholarship will be notified by email and featured on the Giving Day page on our website by the second week of September.

Award: Scholarship for use in freshman, sophomore, junior, senior, graduate, or postgraduate years; not renewable. *Number:* 1. *Amount:* $1000.

Eligibility Requirements: Applicant must be enrolled or expecting to enroll full- or part-time at a two-year or four-year or technical institution or university. Available to U.S. and non-U.S. citizens.

Application Requirements: Application form, essay. *Deadline:* August 15.

Contact: Mrs. Gazala Bohra
E-mail: gazala@hpfy.com

HERBERT LAW OFFICE

https://www.herbertlawoffice.com/

HERBERT LAW OFFICE SCHOLARSHIP CONTEST

Every year, our firm grants a $1,000 scholarship to the U.S. college student who creates the best video essay that elaborates on why they want to be a lawyer.

Award: Prize for use in freshman, sophomore, junior, or senior years; not renewable. *Number:* 1. *Amount:* $1000.

Eligibility Requirements: Applicant must be age 18-25 and enrolled or expecting to enroll full- or part-time at a two-year or four-year institution or university. Available to U.S. citizens.

Application Requirements: Application form may be submitted online (https://www.herbertlawoffice.com/scholarship-for-college-students/), essay. *Deadline:* August 15.

HERMANN LAW GROUP, PLLC

https://www.nymetrodisability.com/

HERMANN LAW GROUP, PLLC SAFETY SCHOLARSHIP CONTEST

Every year, our firm grants a $1,000 scholarship to the U.S. college student who creates the best video essay that elaborates on why they want to be a lawyer.

Award: Prize for use in freshman, sophomore, junior, or senior years; not renewable. *Number:* 1. *Amount:* $1000.

Eligibility Requirements: Applicant must be age 18-25 and enrolled or expecting to enroll full- or part-time at a two-year or four-year institution or university. Available to U.S. citizens.

Application Requirements: Application form may be submitted online (https://www.nymetrodisability.com/safety-scholarship-for-law-students/), essay. *Deadline:* August 15.

THE HIGGINS FIRM

https://www.thehigginsfirm.com

JUDGE BILL HIGGINS PUBLIC SERVICE SCHOLARSHIP

The applicant must be currently enrolled in an accredited community college, undergraduate, or graduate program. This also includes incoming first- year college students who are high school graduates or possess a GED. For more information visit: https://www.thehigginsfirm.com/medical-malpractice.html#scholarship.

Award: Scholarship for use in freshman, sophomore, junior, senior, graduate, or postgraduate years; not renewable. *Number:* 1. *Amount:* $500.

Eligibility Requirements: Applicant must be enrolled or expecting to enroll full- or part-time at a two-year or four-year or technical institution or university. Available to U.S. and non-U.S. citizens.

Application Requirements: Application form, community service, essay. *Deadline:* July 21.

Contact: Jim Higgins
E-mail: info@higginsfirm.com

HIGH CLASS VAPE CO.

https://highclassvapeco.com/

HIGH CLASS VAPE CO. SCHOLARSHIP PROGRAM

Two Lucky Students a year will receive a $1000 scholarship by simply applying to our scholarship program. Before applying please read our requirements for our scholarships. Must be an full-time undergrad or graduate student at an accredited college or university (will verify by contacting your school) and maintain at least a 2.5 overall GPA. Submission for the first $1000 scholarship is due by December 30th, 2017. The winner will be announced on Jan. 30th, 2018. Submission for the second $1000 scholarship is due by Jun. 1st, 2018. The winner will be announced on Aug. 1st, 2018. All we're looking for is for you to write a compelling paper (maximum 1000 words) on one the following prompts to be considered: How will this money help your educational goals? Tell us about how one particular person changed your life for the better. Everyone has undergone a great deal of adversity in their lives, how have you dealt with an especially difficult scenario and overcome it?

Award: Scholarship for use in freshman, sophomore, junior, senior, or graduate years; renewable. *Number:* 2. *Amount:* $4000.

Eligibility Requirements: Applicant must be enrolled or expecting to enroll full-time at a two-year or four-year or technical institution or university. Available to U.S. and non-U.S. citizens.

Application Requirements: Application form, essay, personal photograph. *Deadline:* December 30.

Contact: Mr. Bill Brink, Marketing Manager
High Class Vape Co.
2322 La Mirada Drive
Vista, CA 92081
Phone: 760-801-0256
E-mail: marketing@highclassvapeco.com

HIGH INCOME PARENTS.COM

http://www.highincomeparents.com

MELISSA READ MEMORIAL SCHOLARSHIP

Here at High Income Parents, we value education, and we especially value education at a reduced cost. The value of the scholarship is currently at $2000. Students at technical, community and four-year colleges are welcome to apply. Your enrollment and good standing will be verified if you are selected as a finalist. There will be five finalists selected by me and then judged by a select group of teachers. This year's topic question is: What is the worst financial decision you have made and what did you learn from it? Send the essay with other information in a.doc file (written in Microsoft Word) as an email attachment to tom@highincomeparents.com with the subject line Melissa Read Memorial Scholarship. You can start to submit the applications May 1st.

Award: Scholarship for use in freshman, sophomore, junior, or senior years; not renewable. *Number:* 1. *Amount:* $2000.

Eligibility Requirements: Applicant must be enrolled or expecting to enroll full-time at a two-year or four-year or technical institution or university. Available to U.S. citizens.

Application Requirements: Essay. *Deadline:* July 1.
Contact: Dr. Tom Rairdon
E-mail: Tom@highincomeparents.com

HISPANIC ASSOCIATION OF COLLEGES AND UNIVERSITIES (HACU)

http://www.hacu.net/scholarships

HISPANIC ASSOCIATION OF COLLEGES AND UNIVERSITIES SCHOLARSHIP PROGRAM

The scholarship programs are sponsored by corporate organizations. To be eligible, students must attend a HACU member college or university and meet all additional criteria. Visit website http//www.hacu.net for details.

Award: Scholarship for use in freshman, sophomore, junior, senior, or graduate years; not renewable. *Number:* 1. *Amount:* $1000–$5000.

Eligibility Requirements: Applicant must be enrolled or expecting to enroll full- or part-time at a two-year or four-year institution or university. Available to U.S. citizens.

Application Requirements: Application form, application form may be submitted online (https://www.hacu.net/hacu/Scholarships.asp), enrollment certification form, essay, resume, transcript. *Deadline:* May 24.

Contact: Scholarship Department
Phone: 210-692-3805
Fax: 210-692-0823
E-mail: scholarship@hacu.net

HISPANIC SCHOLARSHIP FUND

HSF.net

VAMOS SCHOLARSHIP

This scholarship was made for high school seniors from Hidalgo, Starr and Cameron County. To qualify, students must be a high school senior in Hidalgo, Starr or Cameron County graduating in the spring, enrolled as a full-time student for four academic years at a U.S. accredited college or university, have a GPA of at least 80/100 or 2.5/4.0 and/or rank in the top 30% of their graduating high school class, have met the minimum SAT or ACT score requirements for the student's college or university of choice, students must be eligible for Pell Grant.

Award: Scholarship for use in freshman year; renewable.

Eligibility Requirements: Applicant must be enrolled or expecting to enroll full-time at an institution or university.

Application Requirements: Application form, application form may be submitted online, essay, financial need analysis. *Deadline:* April 15.

Contact: Mr. Daniel Edeza, Senior Vice President, Scholarship Programs
Hispanic Scholarship Fund
1411 West 190th Street
Suite 700
Gardena, CA 90248
Phone: 310-975-3700
E-mail: scholar1@hsf.net

HONOR SOCIETY OF PHI KAPPA PHI

https://www.phikappaphi.org/

STUDY ABROAD GRANT COMPETITION

Phi Kappa Phi Study Abroad Grants are designed to help support undergraduates as they seek knowledge and experience in their academic fields by studying abroad. Seventy-five $1,000 grants are awarded each year.

Award: Grant for use in freshman, sophomore, junior, or senior years; not renewable. *Number:* 75. *Amount:* $1000.

Eligibility Requirements: Applicant must be enrolled or expecting to enroll full-time at an institution or university. Available to U.S. and non-U.S. citizens.

Application Requirements: Application form, application form may be submitted online, community service, essay. *Deadline:* March 15.

Contact: Mrs. Kelli Partin, Awards Manager
Honor Society of Phi Kappa Phi
7576 Goodwood Boulevard
Baton Rouge, LA 70806
Phone: 800-804-9880 Ext. 235
E-mail: kpartin@phikappaphi.org

HORATIO ALGER ASSOCIATION OF DISTINGUISHED AMERICANS

https://scholars.horatioalger.org/

HORATIO ALGER ASSOCIATION SCHOLARSHIP PROGRAMS

The Association provides financial assistance to high school seniors (U.S citizens only) who have faced adversity, have financial need (family adjusted gross income under $55,000), and are pursuing higher education. Recipients must pursue a bachelor's degree, however, students may start their studies at a 2 year school and then transfer to a 4 year university. Minimum 2.0 GPA required.

Award: Scholarship for use in freshman, sophomore, junior, or senior years; renewable. *Number:* 1,009. *Amount:* $7000–$25,000.

Eligibility Requirements: Applicant must be high school student; age 19 or under and planning to enroll or expecting to enroll full-time at a four-year institution or university. Available to U.S. and Canadian citizens.

Application Requirements: Application form, community service, essay, financial need analysis. *Deadline:* October 25.

Contact: Ms. Colin Dixon, Educational Programs Assistant
Horatio Alger Association of Distinguished Americans
99 Canal Center Plaza, Suite 320
Alexandria, VA 22314
Phone: 703-684-9444
E-mail: programs@horatioalger.org

HORATIO ALGER NATIONAL CAREER & TECHNICAL SCHOLARSHIP PROGRAM

Must have completed high school or plan to complete high school by spring 2016 with plans to enroll at a non-profit post-secondary institution by fall 2016; exhibit a strong commitment to pursue and complete a career or technical program at an accredited non-profit postsecondary institution in the United States; demonstrated critical financial need (must be eligible to receive the Federal Pell grant as determined by completion of the FAFSA); demonstrated perseverance in overcoming adversity; be involved in community service activities; be younger than 30 years old, and a United States citizen. The application will be open with a rolling deadline until all awards have been given out. Applications will be reviewed monthly.

Award: Scholarship for use in freshman or sophomore years; not renewable. *Number:* 510. *Amount:* $2500.

Eligibility Requirements: Applicant must be high school student; age 30 or under and planning to enroll or expecting to enroll full-time at a technical institution. Available to U.S. citizens.

Application Requirements: Application form, essay, financial need analysis. *Deadline:* continuous.

Contact: Mr. Colin Dixon, Educational Programs Administrator
Horatio Alger Association of Distinguished Americans
99 Canal Center Plaza, Suite 320
Alexandria, VA 22314
Phone: 703-684-9444
E-mail: scholarships@horatioalger.org

HOSTGATOR

https://www.hostgator.com/

HOSTGATOR WEBSITE SCHOLARSHIP

Three $1,500 scholarships are available to students of all majors currently enrolled in 2- or 4-year university programs who answer the essay question, "How has the internet impacted your education?" Please see website for more details, https://www.hostgator.com/blog/hostgator-website-scholarship/

Award: Scholarship for use in freshman, sophomore, junior, senior, or graduate years; not renewable. *Number:* 3. *Amount:* $1500.

Eligibility Requirements: Applicant must be enrolled or expecting to enroll full- or part-time at a two-year or four-year institution or university. Available to U.S. citizens.

Application Requirements: Essay. *Deadline:* November 30.

HUBSHOUT

http://hubshout.com/

HUBSHOUT INTERNET MARKETING SCHOLARSHIP

The HubShout Internet Marketing Scholarship is designed to help students who are on the path to any type of technical, business, or marketing career that will involve online marketing. Students who have completed at least one year of post-secondary education and have at least a 3.0 GPA are encouraged to apply. Graduate students are also welcome to apply. This is an ongoing scholarship and applications are reviewed twice per year.

Award: Scholarship for use in sophomore, junior, senior, graduate, or postgraduate years; not renewable. *Number:* 1. *Amount:* $1000.

Eligibility Requirements: Applicant must be age 18 and over and enrolled or expecting to enroll full-time at a two-year or four-year or technical institution or university. Available to U.S. citizens.

Application Requirements: Application form. *Deadline:* continuous.

Contact: Chad Hill
HubShout
200 Little Falls Street
Suite 207
Falls Church, VA 22046
Phone: 888-266-6432
E-mail: chad@hubshout.com

HUMANA FOUNDATION

http://www.humanafoundation.org/

HUMANA FOUNDATION SCHOLARSHIP PROGRAM

Applicants must be under 25 years of age and a United States citizen. Must be a dependent of a Humana Inc. employee. For more information, visit website http://www.humanafoundation.org.

Award: Scholarship for use in freshman, sophomore, junior, or senior years; renewable. *Number:* 74–75. *Amount:* $1500–$3000.

Eligibility Requirements: Applicant must be age 25 or under and enrolled or expecting to enroll full-time at a two-year or four-year institution or university. Available to U.S. citizens.

Application Requirements: Application form, financial need analysis. *Deadline:* April 17.

Contact: Charles Jackson, Consultant
Humana Foundation
500 West Main Street, Room 208
Louisville, KY 40202
Phone: 502-580-1245
E-mail: cjackson@humana.com

IMAGINE AMERICA FOUNDATION

http://www.imagine-america.org

ADULT SKILLS EDUCATION PROGRAM (ASEP)

The Adult Skills Education Program (ASEP) offers scholarships to non-traditional students who decide to pursue career college training. This $1,000 award is available to any qualified adult student for attendance at a participating career college.

Award: Scholarship for use in freshman, sophomore, junior, or senior years; not renewable. *Number:* 10,000. *Amount:* $1000.

Eligibility Requirements: Applicant must be age 19 and over and enrolled or expecting to enroll full-time at a two-year or four-year or technical institution. Available to U.S. citizens.

Application Requirements: Application form. *Deadline:* continuous.

Contact: Lee Doubleday, Student Services Representative
Imagine America Foundation
12001 Sunrise Valley Drive, Suite 203
Reston, VA 20191
Phone: 571-267-3015
E-mail: leroyd@imagine-america.org

IMAGINE AMERICA HIGH SCHOOL SCHOLARSHIP

Imagine America, sponsored by the Imagine America Foundation (IAF), is a $1,000 career education award that is available to recent high school graduates who are pursuing postsecondary education at participating career colleges across the United States. Only recent high school graduates who meet the following recommended guidelines should apply: likelihood of successful completion of postsecondary education; high school grade point average of 2.5 or greater; financial need; demonstrated voluntary community service during senior year.

Award: Scholarship for use in freshman, sophomore, junior, or senior years; not renewable. *Number:* 15,000. *Amount:* $1000.

Eligibility Requirements: Applicant must be age 16-19 and enrolled or expecting to enroll full- or part-time at a two-year or four-year or technical institution. Available to U.S. citizens.

Application Requirements: Application form. *Deadline:* December 31.

Contact: Lee Doubleday, Student Services Representative
Imagine America Foundation
12001 Sunrise Valley Drive, Suite 203
Reston, VA 20191
Phone: 571-267-3015
E-mail: leroyd@imagine-america.org

INDEPENDENT COLLEGE FUND OF NEW JERSEY

http://www.njcolleges.org/

BD/C.R. BARD FOUNDATION NURSING SCHOLARSHIP

Applicant must be entering at least the second semester of their sophomore year or the second semester of the second year of their nursing program and be enrolled full time at an ICFNJ member college or university. Must maintain a minimum GPA of 3.0.

Award: Scholarship for use in sophomore, junior, or senior years; not renewable. *Number:* 10. *Amount:* $2500.

Eligibility Requirements: Applicant must be enrolled or expecting to enroll full-time at an institution or university and studying in New Jersey. Available to U.S. citizens.

Application Requirements: Application form, essay, financial need analysis.

Contact: Ms. Yvette Panella, Scholarship Coordinator
Independent College Fund of New Jersey
797 Springfield Avenue
Summit, NJ 07901
Phone: 908-277-3424
Fax: 908-277-0851
E-mail: ypanella@njcolleges.org

CELGENE'S SOL J. BARER SCHOLARSHIP FOR LIFE SCIENCES

Named in honor of Celgene's former Chairman and Chief Executive Officer, the Sol J. Barer Scholarship in Life Sciences assists high achieving students to prepare for careers in the Life Sciences. Applicant must be enrolled as a full-time student at any ICFNJ member institution; entering either junior or senior year; be majoring in one of the life sciences; possess a minimum cumulative GPA of 3.25 on 4.0 scale; demonstrate superior academic performance and promise for a career in life sciences.

Award: Scholarship for use in junior or senior years; not renewable. *Number:* 6. *Amount:* $2500.

Eligibility Requirements: Applicant must be enrolled or expecting to enroll full-time at an institution or university.

Application Requirements: Application form, essay. *Deadline:* September 15.

Contact: Yvette Panella
Summit, NJ 07901
Phone: 908-277-3424
Fax: 908-277-0851
E-mail: ypanella@njcolleges.org

KINGS SUPER MARKETS, INC. INDEPENDENT COLLEGE FUND SCHOLARSHIP

The Kings Super Markets, Inc. Independent College Fund Scholarship provides an opportunity for Kings' associates and their children who wish to attend any one of the private college or universities in New Jersey to receive financial assistance. The competitive scholarship program is part of an incentive to attract and retain associates. The scholarship emphasizes the importance of family by assisting the children of Kings' associates in the pursuit of their educational goals. Any ICFNJ member college or university may receive up to $1,000.

Award: Scholarship for use in freshman, sophomore, junior, senior, graduate, or postgraduate years; not renewable.

Eligibility Requirements: Applicant must be enrolled or expecting to enroll full- or part-time at a two-year or technical institution or university.

Application Requirements: Application form, essay.

Contact: Yvette Panella
Summit, NJ 07901
Phone: 908-277-3424
Fax: 908-277-0851
E-mail: ypanella@njcolleges.org

NOVARTIS SCIENCE SCHOLARSHIP

The Novartis Science Scholarship recognizes and rewards undergraduate science majors engaged in research at ICFNJ's member colleges and universities by awarding $3,000 scholarships to qualifying students. Applicants must be be enrolled full-time at an ICFNJ member college or university; a rising junior or senior; majoring in a science field; possess a cumulative minimum GPA of 3.5 or better; conducting (or planning to conduct) independent scientific research. All Novartis Science Scholarship applicants must submit a brief explanation of a scientific research project being conducted or to be conducted in the coming academic year. Applicants' independent research will be given special consideration in the review process.

Award: Scholarship for use in junior or senior years. *Number:* 10–15. *Amount:* $3000.

Eligibility Requirements: Applicant must be enrolled or expecting to enroll full-time at an institution or university.

Application Requirements: Application form, essay. *Deadline:* October 1.

Contact: Yvette Panella
Summit, NJ 07901
Phone: 908-277-3424
Fax: 908-277-0851
E-mail: ypanella@njcolleges.org

NOVO NORDISK SCHOLARS PROGRAM

The Novo Nordisk Scholarship recognizes outstanding students who demonstrate academic excellence while inspiring them to consider careers in research, education and treatment of diabetes or hemophilia and bleeding disorders. Applicant must be enrolled full time at an ICFNJ member institution; entering junior or senior year; special consideration will be given to nursing, nutrition and life science majors; possess a minimum 3.0 cumulative GPA on a 4.0 scale; demonstrate a history of work or life experience with a diabetic population or population with hemophilia or bleeding disorders; interested in pursuing a career in the health industry (show a commitment to continued work in the care, education, treatment or research of diabetes or hemophilia and bleeding disorders); demonstrate financial need as determined by your financial aid director; a U.S. citizen or eligible to work in the U.S.

Award: Scholarship for use in junior or senior years. *Number:* 5. *Amount:* $4000.

Eligibility Requirements: Applicant must be enrolled or expecting to enroll full-time at an institution or university. Available to U.S. citizens.

Application Requirements: Application form, essay. *Deadline:* October 15.

Contact: Yvette Panella
Summit, NJ 07901
Phone: 908-277-3424
Fax: 908-277-0851
E-mail: ypanella@njcolleges.org

PNC-BARRY GILLMAN HUMANITARIAN SCHOLARSHIP

The PNC – Barry Gillman Humanitarian Scholarship recognizes outstanding students who demonstrate a commitment to serving the community through volunteer service. The Barry Gillman Humanitarian Scholarship honors the compassion and spirit of volunteerism embodied by the late Barry Gillman by encouraging undergraduate students to continue in their humanitarian work while attending college. The applicants must be enrolled full-time at an ICFNJ member college or university; be entering junior or senior year; possess a cumulative minimum GPA of 3.0 or better on a 4.0 scale; must be actively engaged in a volunteer service project; must demonstrate the highest ideals and qualities of citizenship and humanitarian service as evidenced in their personal statement, resume and letters of recommendation; preference will be given to those students with plans to pursue a career in the legal profession.

Award: Scholarship for use in junior or senior years. *Number:* 2. *Amount:* $5000.

Eligibility Requirements: Applicant must be enrolled or expecting to enroll full-time at an institution or university.

Application Requirements: Application form, essay. *Deadline:* November 1.

Contact: Yvette Panella
    Summit, NJ 07901
    Phone: 908-277-3424
    Fax: 908-277-0851
    E-mail: ypanella@njcolleges.org

PSEG SCHOLARSHIP FOR ADVANCING STEM MAJORS

PSEG introduced this award to support exceptional students who share in their commitment to building environmental stewardship and developing meaningful sustainability initiatives. While enhancing the educational and learning opportuntiies in areas of importance to PSEG – science (environmental), technology, engineering and math, the scholarship contributes to an educated citizenry for New Jersey which supports the economic and cultural development of local communities and neighborhoods. Applicants must be enrolled as a full-time student at any ICFNJ member institution;

Award: Scholarship for use in junior or senior years. *Number:* 6. *Amount:* $2500.

Eligibility Requirements: Applicant must be enrolled or expecting to enroll full-time at an institution or university.

Application Requirements: Application form, essay. *Deadline:* June 15.

Contact: Yvette Panella
    Summit, NJ 07901
    Phone: 908-277-3424
    Fax: 908-277-0851
    E-mail: ypanella@njcolleges.org

INSUREON

http://www.insureon.com

INSUREON SMALL BUSINESS SCHOLARSHIP

Two $2500 scholarships for undergraduate students attending four-year colleges or universities.

Award: Scholarship for use in freshman, sophomore, junior, or senior years; renewable. *Number:* 2. *Amount:* $2500.

Eligibility Requirements: Applicant must be enrolled or expecting to enroll full-time at a four-year institution. Available to U.S. and non-U.S. citizens.

Application Requirements: Application form. *Deadline:* April 30.

Contact: Mr. Alexander Williamson, Business Analyst
    E-mail: alex@insureon.com

THE INTERNATIONAL ASSOCIATION OF ASSESSING OFFICERS

http://www.iaao.org

IAAO ACADEMIC PARTNERSHIP PROGRAM

IAAO provides financial support for students to complete research in areas related to property appraisal, assessment administration, and property tax policy. The grant carries with it an obligation to submit a satisfactory report for publication by the editor of any IAAO publication and/or a presentation at an IAAO conference.

Award: Grant for use in junior, senior, graduate, or postgraduate years; not renewable. *Number:* 1–5. *Amount:* $1000–$5000.

Eligibility Requirements: Applicant must be enrolled or expecting to enroll full- or part-time at a four-year institution or university. Available to U.S. and non-U.S. citizens.

Application Requirements: Application form, application form may be submitted online (http://www.iaao.org/APPGrant), essay, recommendations or references. *Deadline:* February 15.

Contact: Tami Knight, Director of Research
    The International Association of Assessing Officers
    314 West 10th Street
    Kansas City, MO 64105
    Phone: 816-701-8132
    Fax: 816-701-8149
    E-mail: knight@iaao.org

INTERNATIONAL COLLEGE COUNSELORS

http://www.internationalcollegecounselors.com

INTERNATIONAL COLLEGE COUNSELORS SCHOLARSHIP

International College Counselors is giving away two (2) $250 scholarships. High school freshmen, sophomores or juniors must write an essay that addresses the following topic: Brag about your high school or homeschool experience. What do you like best about it?Essays must not exceed 500 words. Two winning essays will be selected: one (1) from a student in Miami Dade County, Broward County, or Palm Beach County; and one (1) at large winner from anywhere in the world, domestic or international, including home schooled students. Each winner will receive a $250 check. The goal of the International College Counselors Scholarship is to increase awareness of the value of higher education among students.

Award: Scholarship for use in freshman year; not renewable. *Number:* 2. *Amount:* $250.

Eligibility Requirements: Applicant must be high school student and planning to enroll or expecting to enroll full-time at a two-year or four-year or technical institution or university. Available to U.S. and non-U.S. citizens.

Application Requirements: Application form, essay. *Deadline:* March 30.

Contact: Cheree Liebowitz, Director of Marketing
    International College Counselors
    3107 Stirling Road
    Suite 208
    Ft. Lauderdale, FL 33312
    E-mail: info@internationalcollegecounselors.com

INTERNATIONAL FLIGHT SERVICES ASSOCIATION

http://www.ifsanet.com

AMI SCHOLARSHIP AWARD

Individuals are selected based on scholastic merit and dedication to an advanced education. Priority is given to those with an onboard hospitality focus, or relationship with member company.

Award: Scholarship for use in freshman, sophomore, junior, senior, graduate, or postgraduate years; not renewable. *Number:* 1. *Amount:* $4500.

Eligibility Requirements: Applicant must be enrolled or expecting to enroll full- or part-time at an institution or university. Available to U.S. and non-U.S. citizens.

Application Requirements: Application form, essay, financial need analysis. *Deadline:* April 30.

Contact: Ms. Kelly McLendon, Programs Manager
    International Flight Services Association
    1100 Johnson Ferry Road
    Suite 300
    Atlanta, GA 30342
    Phone: 678-303-3042
    E-mail: kmclendon@kellencompany.com

GOURMET FOODS SCHOLARSHIP AWARD

Individuals are selected to receive the award based on scholastic merit and dedication to an advanced education. Must be an employee of a current IFSA member company in good standing, or a relative of an employee of a current IFSA member company. Please address financial need within essay.

Award: Scholarship for use in freshman, sophomore, junior, or senior years; not renewable. *Number:* 1. *Amount:* $5000.

Eligibility Requirements: Applicant must be enrolled or expecting to enroll full- or part-time at an institution or university. Available to U.S. and non-U.S. citizens.

Application Requirements: Application form, essay, recommendations or references, transcript. *Deadline:* May 14.

Contact: Ms. Kelly McLendon, Programs Manager
International Flight Services Association
1100 Johnson Ferry Road, NE
Suite 300
Atlanta, GA 30342
Phone: 678-303-3042
E-mail: kmclendon@kellencompany.com

HARVEY & LAURA ALPERT SCHOLARSHIP AWARD

Individuals are selected to receive this award based on scholastic merit and dedication to pursuing a career in onboard services operations. Must be an employee of a current IFSA member company in good standing, or a relative of an IFSA member company employee.

Award: Scholarship for use in freshman, sophomore, junior, or senior years; not renewable. *Number:* 1. *Amount:* $5000.

Eligibility Requirements: Applicant must be enrolled or expecting to enroll full-time at an institution or university. Available to U.S. and non-U.S. citizens.

Application Requirements: Application form, essay, recommendations or references, transcript. *Deadline:* May 14.

Contact: Ms. Kelly McLendon, Programs Manager
International Flight Services Association
1100 Johnson Ferry Road, NE
Suite 300
Atlanta, GA 30342
Phone: 678-303-3042
E-mail: kmclendon@kellencompany.com

INTERNATIONAL FRANCHISE ASSOCIATION FRANCHISE EDUCATION AND RESEARCH FOUNDATION

http://www.franchise.org

DON DEBOLT FRANCHISING SCHOLARSHIP PROGRAM

Scholarship award to students with a focus on law, marketing, business and franchise management.

Award: Scholarship for use in junior, senior, graduate, or postgraduate years; not renewable. *Number:* 1. *Amount:* $2500.

Eligibility Requirements: Applicant must be enrolled or expecting to enroll full-time at a two-year or four-year institution or university. Available to U.S. and non-U.S. citizens.

Application Requirements: Application form, essay. *Deadline:* continuous.

Contact: Miriam Brewer, Senior Director
International Franchise Association Franchise Education and Research Foundation
1900 K Street, NW Suite 700
Washington, DC 20006
Phone: 202-662-0784
E-mail: mbrewer@franchise.org

INTERNATIONAL LITERACY ASSOCIATION

https://literacyworldwide.org/home

CONSTANCE MCCULLOUGH INTERNATIONAL RESEARCH GRANT

The International Literacy Association (ILA) sponsors the Constance McCullough International Research Grant (up to US$2,000) to encourage international professional development activities and to assist in the investigation of reading-related problems in countries outside of the United States or Canada. There are no restrictions regarding age or setting (preschool, school, adult centers, etc.).

Award: Grant for use in freshman, sophomore, junior, senior, graduate, or postgraduate years; not renewable.

Eligibility Requirements: Applicant must be enrolled or expecting to enroll full- or part-time at a two-year or technical institution or university.

Application Requirements: Application form, application form may be submitted online. *Deadline:* June 1.

Contact: Dawn Roberts
E-mail: ILAAwards@reading.org

INTERNATIONAL SOCIETY OF WOMEN AIRLINE PILOTS (ISA+21)

http://www.iswap.org/

INTERNATIONAL SOCIETY OF WOMEN AIRLINE PILOTS AIRLINE SCHOLARSHIPS

Scholarships are available to women who are pursuing careers as airline pilots. Applicants must demonstrate financial need. Must have an U.S. FAA Commercial Pilot Certificate with an Instrument Rating and First Class Medical Certificate. Must have flight time in a fixed wing aircraft commensurate with the rating sought.

Award: Scholarship for use in freshman, sophomore, junior, or senior years; not renewable. *Number:* 2. *Amount:* $10,000.

Eligibility Requirements: Applicant must be age 21 and over; enrolled or expecting to enroll full-time at an institution or university and female. Available to U.S. and non-U.S. citizens.

Application Requirements: Application form, driver's license, financial need analysis, interview, personal photograph.

Contact: Ms. Julie Clippard, Scholarship Chairwoman
E-mail: scholarship@iswap.org

INTERNATIONAL SOCIETY OF WOMEN AIRLINE PILOTS FINANCIAL SCHOLARSHIP

Scholarships are available to women who are pursuing careers as airline pilots. Must have flight time in a fixed wing aircraft commensurate with the rating sought. Must have flight time in a fixed wing aircraft commensurate with the rating sought.

Award: Scholarship for use in freshman, sophomore, junior, or senior years; not renewable. *Number:* 2. *Amount:* $5000.

Eligibility Requirements: Applicant must be age 21 and over; enrolled or expecting to enroll full-time at an institution or university and female. Available to U.S. and non-U.S. citizens.

Application Requirements: Application form, driver's license, financial need analysis, interview, personal photograph. *Deadline:* November 10.

Contact: Ms. Julie Clippard, Scholarship Chairwoman
E-mail: scholarship@iswap.org

IOWA NEWSPAPER ASSOCIATION

https://inanews.com/

CARTER PITTS SCHOLARSHIPS

The Le Mars Daily Sentinel funds an annual Carter Pitts scholarship in the amount of $500. The scholarship is named for the Daily Sentinel's longtime publisher/owner. The late Carter Pitts was also the first president of the Iowa Newspaper Foundation and the organization's first professional fundraiser.

Award: Scholarship for use in freshman, sophomore, junior, or senior years; not renewable. *Amount:* $500.

Eligibility Requirements: Applicant must be enrolled or expecting to enroll at an institution or university. Available to U.S. citizens.

Application Requirements: Application form. *Deadline:* February 14.

Contact: Jana Shepherd, Program Director
Iowa Newspaper Association
319 E. 5th Street
Des Moines, IA 50309
Phone: 515-244-2145 Ext. 159
Fax: 515-244-4855
E-mail: jshepherd@inanews.com

JACK KENT COOKE FOUNDATION
http://www.jkcf.org/

COLLEGE SCHOLARSHIP PROGRAM

Scholarships to high-performing high school seniors with financial need who seek to attend and graduate from the nation's best accredited four-year colleges/universities. Candidates are selected based on academic achievement, financial need, persistence, leadership, and desire to help others. Awards vary by individual.

Award: Scholarship for use in freshman, sophomore, junior, or senior years; renewable. *Number:* 40. *Amount:* up to $40,000.

Eligibility Requirements: Applicant must be high school student and planning to enroll or expecting to enroll full-time at a four-year institution or university. Available to U.S. and non-U.S. citizens.

Application Requirements: Application form, application form may be submitted online, essay, financial need analysis, recommendations or references, test scores, transcript.

Contact: Gaby Ruess, Scholarship Committee
    Phone: 800-498-6478
    Fax: 319-337-1204
    E-mail: jkc-g@act.org

JACK KENT COOKE FOUNDATION UNDERGRADUATE TRANSFER SCHOLARSHIP PROGRAM

Scholarships to students and recent alumni from community colleges to complete Bachelor's degrees at accredited four-year colleges/universities in the United States. Candidates are selected based on academic achievement, financial need, persistence, leadership, and desire to help others. Minimum 3.5 GPA required.

Award: Scholarship for use in sophomore, junior, or senior years; renewable. *Number:* 85. *Amount:* up to $40,000.

Eligibility Requirements: Applicant must be enrolled or expecting to enroll full-time at a four-year institution or university. Available to U.S. and non-U.S. citizens.

Application Requirements: Application form, application form may be submitted online (http://www.jkcf.org/scholarship-programs/undergraduate-transfer/), essay, financial need analysis, recommendations or references, resume, transcript.

Contact: Gaby Ruess, Scholarship Committee
    Phone: 800-498-6478
    Fax: 319-337-1204
    E-mail: jkc-g@act.org

JACKSONWHITE ATTORNEYS AT LAW
http://www.jacksonwhitelaw.com/

JACKSONWHITE BI-ANNUAL LABOR LAW SCHOLARSHIP

JacksonWhite seeks to encourage personal and professional growth through higher education. The JacksonWhite Labor Law Bi-Annual Scholarship has been established to support hardworking individuals of any educational background. Education is essential to a successful future and JacksonWhite Law is proud to support determined students.

Award: Scholarship for use in freshman, sophomore, junior, senior, graduate, or postgraduate years; not renewable. *Number:* 1–2. *Amount:* $1000–$2000.

Eligibility Requirements: Applicant must be enrolled or expecting to enroll full-time at a two-year or four-year or technical institution or university. Available to U.S. and non-U.S. citizens.

Application Requirements: Essay. *Deadline:* December 1.

Contact: Miss. Kelsey Misseldine, Client Services Coordinator
    JacksonWhite Attorneys at Law
    40 North Center Street
    Mesa, AZ 85201
    Phone: 480-464-1111
    E-mail: scholarship@jacksonwhitelaw.com

JACKSONWHITE CRIMINAL LAW BI-ANNUAL SCHOLARSHIP

JacksonWhite understands the financial burden that comes with pursuing your goals in higher education. The JacksonWhite Criminal Law Bi-Annual Scholarship has been established in hopes of contributing to the investment of students and future leaders. Education is essential to a successful future and JacksonWhite Law is proud to support determined students. No application is required to apply for this scholarship.

Award: Scholarship for use in freshman, sophomore, junior, senior, graduate, or postgraduate years; not renewable. *Number:* 1. *Amount:* $1000.

Eligibility Requirements: Applicant must be enrolled or expecting to enroll full-time at a two-year or four-year or technical institution or university. Available to U.S. and non-U.S. citizens.

Application Requirements: Essay. *Deadline:* December 1.

Contact: Ms. Kelsey Misseldine, Client Services Coordinator
    JacksonWhite Attorneys at Law
    40 North Center Street
    Suite 200
    Mesa, AZ 85201
    E-mail: scholarship@jacksonwhitelaw.com

JACKSONWHITE FAMILY LAW BI-ANNUAL SCHOLARSHIP

Attorney Tim Durkin of JacksonWhite Attorneys at Law is offering the Family Law Bi-Annual Scholarship to honor the importance of higher education. In spite of rising costs to receive a college education, JacksonWhite believes in its value and is proud to support students in their pursuits. Please visit our website for scholarship details.

Award: Scholarship for use in freshman, sophomore, junior, senior, graduate, or postgraduate years; not renewable. *Number:* 1–2. *Amount:* $1000–$2000.

Eligibility Requirements: Applicant must be enrolled or expecting to enroll full-time at a two-year or four-year or technical institution or university. Available to U.S. citizens.

Application Requirements: Essay. *Deadline:* April 30.

Contact: Kelsey Misseldine
    JacksonWhite Attorneys at Law
    40 North Center Street
    Suite 200
    Mesa, AZ 85201
    Phone: 480-464-1111
    E-mail: scholarship@jacksonwhitelaw.com

JACKSONWHITE PERSONAL INJURY BI-ANNUAL SCHOLARSHIP

Aspiring professionals should all have access to higher education. With the increasing costs of universities, this is has become more difficult. JacksonWhite Attorneys at Law believes in the importance of education and is proud to support students in hopes of enriching their future. Please visit our website for scholarship details.

Award: Scholarship for use in freshman, sophomore, junior, senior, graduate, or postgraduate years; not renewable. *Number:* 1–2. *Amount:* $1000–$2000.

Eligibility Requirements: Applicant must be enrolled or expecting to enroll full-time at a two-year or four-year or technical institution or university. Available to U.S. and non-U.S. citizens.

Application Requirements: Essay. *Deadline:* April 30.

Contact: Ms. Kelsey Misseldine, Client Services Coordinator
    JacksonWhite Attorneys at Law
    40 North Center Street
    Suite 200
    Mesa, AZ 85201
    E-mail: scholarship@jacksonwhitelaw.com

JEANNETTE RANKIN WOMEN'S SCHOLARSHIP FUND
http://www.rankinfoundation.org/

JEANNETTE RANKIN WOMEN'S SCHOLARSHIP FUND

Applicants must be low-income women, age 35 or older, who are U.S. citizens or permanent residents of the U.S. pursuing a technical/vocational education, an associate degree, or a first bachelor's degree at a regionally or ACICS accredited college. Applications are available on our website http://www.rankinfoundation.org/students/application/ from November through March.

Award: Scholarship for use in freshman, sophomore, junior, or senior years; renewable. *Number:* 25–50. *Amount:* $2000.

Eligibility Requirements: Applicant must be age 35 and over; enrolled or expecting to enroll full- or part-time at a two-year or four-year or technical institution or university and female. Available to U.S. citizens.

Application Requirements: Application form, essay, financial need analysis. *Deadline:* March 1.

Contact: LaTrena Stokes, Program Scholarship Manager
Jeannette Rankin Women's Scholarship Fund
1 Huntington Road, #701
Athens, GA 30606
Phone: 706-208-1211
E-mail: info@rankinfoundation.org

JEWISH WAR VETERANS OF THE UNITED STATES OF AMERICA
http://www.jwv.org/

MAX R. AND IRENE RUBENSTEIN MEMORIAL GRANT

Each year, the Jewish War Veterans of the USA sponsors an essay contest for current service members and veterans who plan to attend or are currently attending an accredited Associates, Bachelor's, Nursing, or Graduate degree program. The National Achievement Program is open to anyone regardless of race, religion, creed, or culture. All veterans are eligible and must be legal residents of the USA. Awards $1,500.

Award: Grant for use in freshman, sophomore, junior, senior, or graduate years; not renewable. *Amount:* $1500.

Eligibility Requirements: Applicant must be enrolled or expecting to enroll at a two-year institution or university. Available to U.S. citizens.

Application Requirements: Essay. *Deadline:* June 1.

Contact: Cara Rinkoff, Programs Coordinator
Phone: 202-265-6280
E-mail: crinkoff@jwv.org

JOHN B. FABRIELE, III, LLC
https://www.fabrielelaw.com/

FABRIELE DISABILITY AWARENESS SCHOLARSHIP

Applicants must have a minimum cumulative GPA of 3.3 or higher. Applicants must be enrolled in an institution of higher education in the fall semester of 2017. If the applicant is still awaiting admission or deciding on a school when submitting the application, that is fine. However, before granting the scholarship we will need to ensure that the applicant is enrolled for the fall of 2017. Applicants must submit a 500-word statement in response to the following the prompt. Mail your application to 214 Route 18 #2A, East Brunswick, NJ 08816. Address your letter to The Fabriele Disability Awareness Scholarship. Please visit https://www.fabrielelaw.com/#scholarship for complete information.

Award: Scholarship for use in freshman, sophomore, junior, senior, graduate, or postgraduate years; not renewable. *Number:* 1. *Amount:* $1000.

Eligibility Requirements: Applicant must be enrolled or expecting to enroll full- or part-time at a two-year or four-year or technical institution or university. Available to U.S. and non-U.S. citizens.

Application Requirements: Application form, essay. *Deadline:* May 31.

Contact: John Fabriele
John B. Fabriele, III, LLC
214 Route 18, Suite 2A
East Brunswick, NJ 08816

JOHN F. KENNEDY LIBRARY FOUNDATION
http://www.jfklibrary.org/

PROFILE IN COURAGE ESSAY CONTEST

Essay contest open to all high school students, grades nine to twelve. Students in U.S. territories and U.S. citizens attending schools overseas may also apply. All essays will be judged on the overall originality of topic and the clear communication of ideas through language. Winner and their nominating teacher are invited to Kennedy Library to accept award. Winner receives $3000, nomination teacher receives grant of $500; second place receives $1000 and five finalists receive $500.

Award: Prize for use in freshman year; not renewable. *Number:* 7. *Amount:* $500–$10,000.

Eligibility Requirements: Applicant must be high school student; age 19 or under and planning to enroll or expecting to enroll full-time at a four-year institution. Available to U.S. citizens.

Application Requirements: Application form, essay. *Deadline:* continuous.

Contact: Esther Kohn, Essay Contest Coordinator
John F. Kennedy Library Foundation
Columbia Point
Boston, MA 02125
Phone: 617-514-1649
E-mail: profiles@nara.gov

JONATHAN DE ARAUJO REAL ESTATE
http://www.searchmasshomes.com

REAL ESTATE SCHOLARSHIP

Lexington MA Realtor Jonathan de Araujo at Century 21 Commonwealth is committed to continuing efforts to help students who have the ambition and drive to succeed. He is sponsoring an annual scholarship of $1,000 to award one College student with the financial assistance to accomplish their educational goals and prepare for future potential career aspirations related to Real Estate.

Award: Scholarship for use in freshman, sophomore, junior, senior, graduate, or postgraduate years; not renewable. *Number:* 1. *Amount:* $1000.

Eligibility Requirements: Applicant must be enrolled or expecting to enroll full-time at a two-year or four-year institution or university. Available to U.S. citizens.

Application Requirements: Application form, essay. *Deadline:* November 1.

Contact: Jonathan de Araujo, Principal
E-mail: jonathan@searchmasshomes.com

JONATHAN M. FEIGENBAUM, ESQUIRE
https://www.erisaattorneys.com/

CITY OF BOSTON DISABILITY SCHOLARSHIP CONTEST

Beginning with the fall of each school year Jonathan M. Feigenbaum, a leading ERISA and disability insurance attorney helping individuals with their insurance disability claims will award up to three (3) $1,000.00 scholarships to college students who submit the best video essay explaining what they have learned from a family member or loved one suffering with a disability.

Award: Prize for use in freshman, sophomore, junior, or senior years; not renewable. *Number:* 3. *Amount:* $1000.

Eligibility Requirements: Applicant must be age 18-25 and enrolled or expecting to enroll full- or part-time at a two-year or four-year institution or university. Available to U.S. citizens.

Application Requirements: Application form may be submitted online (https://www.erisaattorneys.com/city-boston-disability-scholarship-college-students-family-member-suffering-disability/), essay. *Deadline:* August 15.

MASSACHUSETTS NURSES ASSOCIATION DISABILITY SCHOLARSHIP CONTEST

Beginning with the fall of each school year Jonathan M. Feigenbaum, a leading ERISA and disability insurance attorney helping individuals with their insurance disability claims will award up to three (3) $1,000.00 scholarships to college students who submit the best video essay explaining what they have learned from a family member or loved one suffering with a disability.

Award: Prize for use in freshman, sophomore, junior, or senior years; not renewable. *Number:* 3. *Amount:* $1000.

Eligibility Requirements: Applicant must be age 18-25 and enrolled or expecting to enroll full- or part-time at a two-year or four-year institution or university. Available to U.S. citizens.

Application Requirements: Application form may be submitted online (https://www.erisaattorneys.com/massachusetts-nurses-association-disability-scholarship-for-college-students-with-family-member-suffering-with-a-disability/), essay. *Deadline:* August 15.

JOURNALISM EDUCATION ASSOCIATION

http://www.jea.org/

NATIONAL HIGH SCHOOL JOURNALIST OF THE YEAR/SISTER RITA JEANNE SCHOLARSHIPS

One-time award recognizes the nation's top high school journalists. Open to graduating high school seniors who have worked at least two years on school media. Applicants must have JEA member as adviser. Minimum 3.0 GPA required. Submit digital portfolio to state contest coordinator by the deadline set by the state organization (usually between Feb. 1 and March 1).

Award: Scholarship for use in freshman year; not renewable. *Number:* 1–7. *Amount:* $850–$3000.

Eligibility Requirements: Applicant must be high school student; age 17-19 and planning to enroll or expecting to enroll full-time at a four-year institution or university. Available to U.S. citizens.

Application Requirements: Application form, essay, personal photograph, portfolio. *Deadline:* March 15.

Contact: Connie Fulkerson, Administrative Assistant
          Journalism Education Association
          105 Kedzie Hall
          828 Mid-Campus Drive South
          Manhattan, KS 66506-1500
          Phone: 785-532-5532
          Fax: 785-532-5563
          E-mail: staff@jea.org

JRC INSURANCE GROUP

http://www.jrcinsurancegroup.com/scholarship/

JRC INSURANCE GROUP SCHOLARSHIP

The JRC Insurance Group Scholarship awards one $1,000 prize each semester to the high school senior or college student who best explains why the family breadwinner's income should be protected by life insurance, and the characteristics displayed by those who put their family first. The winner will be the person who best demonstrates the need for life insurance in U.S. households. Two $1,000 cash scholarships will be awarded. One scholarship will be awarded in the fall, and another in the spring. Essays will be reviewed by a selection committee made up of members of the JRC Insurance Group executive team. The winning essay will be selected based on originality and quality of writing. Submission deadlines: February 1, 2018 (spring) and October 15 (fall).

Award: Scholarship for use in freshman, sophomore, junior, senior, or graduate years; not renewable. *Number:* 2. *Amount:* $1000.

Eligibility Requirements: Applicant must be age 18-26 and enrolled or expecting to enroll full-time at a four-year institution or university. Available to U.S. citizens.

Application Requirements: Essay. *Deadline:* October 15.

Contact: Ms. Delia Noto
          JRC Insurance Group
          3914 Murphy Canyon Road
          Suite A236
          San Diego, CA 92123
          Phone: 855-225-5063
          Fax: 858-537-1090
          E-mail: info@jrcinsurancegroup.com

JUNK A CAR

https://www.junkacar.com/

JUNK A CAR 2018 SCHOLARSHIP

Junk A Car recognizes the importance of a secondary education. As a part of our ongoing commitment to community service, we are offering a $1,000 scholarship. Junk A Car uses the profits from our Cash for Junk Cars business to finance this scholarship opportunity. Incoming freshman must be enrolled full-time in a U.S. high school or in a home school program. High school graduates planning to become a full time student at an accredited college or university are also eligible. Existing college students must be full-time students enrolled in an accredited U.S. college or university. Send us an email to scholarships@junkacarworldwide.com and include the following information: your full name, address, phone number and email address; a 350 to 500 word essay explaining why you feel you deserve a scholarship from Junk A Car. If your education has been interrupted and you are not currently enrolled in high school or college, please include an explanation in your essay; the name of the high school or college in which you are currently enrolled. If you are currently not in high school or college, please include an explanation in your application essay; if you are an incoming freshman, restarting your education or not currently enrolled in a high school or college, please include the name of the college you plan to attend. If you are an incoming freshman you must be planning to be a full-time student. We will reply to all applications within 24 hours to confirm receipt of your application. We may require additional information after your application has been received. All payments will be made directly to your college or university. If you are selected, you may be asked to allow us to feature your story on our website. Participation is not required and you will not be asked to participate in a feature article until after the scholarship has been awarded. All applications are confidential. You will find the complete scholarship information by going to our website: https://www.junkacar.com/scholarships

Award: Scholarship for use in freshman, sophomore, junior, or senior years; not renewable. *Number:* 1. *Amount:* $1000.

Eligibility Requirements: Applicant must be enrolled or expecting to enroll full-time at a four-year institution or university. Available to U.S. citizens.

Application Requirements: Application form, essay. *Deadline:* June 1.

Contact: Peter Greenblum
          Junk A Car
          483 Kings Highway
          3rd Floor
          Brooklyn, NY 11223
          Phone: 888-323-7128
          E-mail: scholarships@junkacarworldwide.com

J. WALTER THOMPSON

https://wundermanthompson.com

HELEN LANSDOWNE RESOR SCHOLARSHIP

The Helen Lansdowne Resor Scholarship is an international opportunity that awards up to $10,000 for five creative women. Winners also get an internship at Wunderman Thompson, one-on-one mentorship and first-look placement upon graduation. So, who is Helen? A game changer, that's who. It started in 1908, when Helen Lansdowne was hired by J. Walter Thompson Cincinnati as the industry's first female copywriter. She soon moved to the New York office, where she rose through the ranks as a creative powerhouse. She hired and mentored dozens of creative women, ensuring that the female voice was represented in J. Walter Thompson's work. Who's eligible? Female students registered at an undergraduate, graduate, and/or portfolio school with at least 12 months of school left as of May 14, 2018. To throw your headband into the ring, apply! Visit http://www.jwt.com/ https://www.jwt.com/hlrscholarship/

Award: Scholarship for use in freshman, sophomore, junior, senior, graduate, or postgraduate years; not renewable. *Number:* 5. *Amount:* $10,000.

Eligibility Requirements: Applicant must be enrolled or expecting to enroll full- or part-time at a two-year or four-year or technical institution or university and female. Available to U.S. and non-U.S. citizens.

Application Requirements: Application form, application form may be submitted online (https://www.jwt.com/en/hlrscholarship/), essay, portfolio. *Deadline:* June 3.

Contact: Jessica Watson, HR Project Manager
          J. Walter Thompson
          466 Lexington Avenue
          2nd Floor, J. Walter Thompson
          New York, NY 10017
          Phone: 212-210-6072
          E-mail: hlrscholarship@jwt.com

KAHN ROVEN, LLP

http://www.kahnroven.com/

KAHN ROVEN, LLP SCHOLARSHIP

What does post-secondary education mean to you? How is it going to help you achieve your future goals? Application needs to be mailed in, but can be found at the following website: http://www.kahnroven.com/scholarship.html

Award: Scholarship for use in freshman year; not renewable. *Number:* 1. *Amount:* $500.

Eligibility Requirements: Applicant must be high school student and planning to enroll or expecting to enroll full-time at a four-year institution or university. Available to U.S. citizens.

Application Requirements: Application form, essay. *Deadline:* April 15.

Contact: Mr. Johnathan Roven
E-mail: kahnroven@gmail.com

KELLER LAW OFFICES

http://www.kellerlawoffices.com/

KELLER LAW OFFICES SCHOLARSHIP FOR HIGHER EDUCATION

The goal of this scholarship is to provide financial assistance to a worthy student. We understand that there are a lot of outstanding young people who, without financial assistance would not be able to go to college. Medical, social or financial obstacles can make higher education a mere dream to some students. Every year, to help open the door to the world of higher education, Keller Law Offices will offer a $1,000 scholarship to a student who submits the strongest essay focusing on the given topic.

Award: Scholarship for use in freshman, sophomore, junior, senior, or graduate years; not renewable. *Number:* 1. *Amount:* $1000.

Eligibility Requirements: Applicant must be enrolled or expecting to enroll full-time at a two-year or four-year institution or university. Available to U.S. citizens.

Application Requirements: Application form, application form may be submitted online (http://kellerlawoffices.com/academic-scholarship/), essay. *Deadline:* July 15.

Contact: Anni Hemsing
E-mail: anni@marketjd.com

KENNEDY FOUNDATION

http://uskennedyfoundation.org/scholarships/kennedy-foundation-scholarship/

KENNEDY FOUNDATION SCHOLARSHIPS

Renewable scholarships for current high school students for up to four years of undergraduate study. Renewal contingent upon academic performance. Must maintain a GPA of 2.5. Send self-addressed stamped envelope for application. See website for details http://www.columbinecorp.com/kennedyfoundation to download an application.

Award: Scholarship for use in freshman year; renewable. *Number:* 8–14. *Amount:* $2000.

Eligibility Requirements: Applicant must be high school student and planning to enroll or expecting to enroll full-time at a two-year or four-year institution or university. Available to U.S. citizens.

Application Requirements: Application form, self-addressed stamped envelope with application, test scores, transcript. *Deadline:* June 30.

Contact: Jonathan Kennedy, Vice President

KEVIN'S REVIEW

http://www.kevinsreview.com

KEVIN'S REVIEW NCLEX ASSISTANCE SCHOLARSHIP

In order to stay true to our student-centered intent and mission, KevinsReview.com is introducing a new and very unique scholarship. Platinum Tests and Feuer Nursing Review has also joined us in this mission. Both have graciously contributed for each award recipient! The scholarship is awarded on a quarterly basis, meaning there will be 4 award recipients each year. Each recipient of the scholarship will receive 1.an award of $250, enough to cover half or more of the cost of an NCLEX Review Course or an NCLEX Application; 2. lifetime access to Platinum Tests, a Computerized Adaptive Testing simulator that can predict your NCLEX readiness ($80 value); 3. three months of access to Feuer Nursing Review's Comprehensive NCLEX Review ($375 value).

Drawings will take place February 1st, May 1st, August 1st, and November 1st of each year. This money is meant to help pay for remedial classes, if necessary, or to help allay the costs of re-registration and re-application. Students must upload proof that they have unsuccessfully attempted the NCLEX. This can be in the form of NCLEX "Quick Results" (a screenshot from the Pearson Vue website), or a photo or photocopy of your NCLEX notification letter in the mail. Students must upload proof that they are either attempting the NCLEX again or are undergoing a paid NCLEX Review or remedial course. This can be in the form of a receipt or confirmation email from Pearson Vue, your State Board of Nursing, or an NCLEX Review company. Apply and upload your documents here! http://www.kevinsreview.com/nclex/nclex-assistance.php

Award: Prize for use in sophomore or senior years; renewable. *Number:* 4. *Amount:* $715.

Eligibility Requirements: Applicant must be enrolled or expecting to enroll full- or part-time at a two-year or four-year or technical institution or university. Available to U.S. and non-U.S. citizens.

Application Requirements: Application form. *Deadline:* continuous.

Contact: Kevin Pan
Phone: 630-776-5801
E-mail: kevin@kevinsreview.com

KIDGUARD

http://www.kidguard.com/

KIDGUARD FOR EDUCATION ESSAY SCHOLARSHIP FOR HIGH SCHOOL

Statistics show that 42% of teenagers with tech access have been cyberbullied over the past year and that 1 in 4 have been bullied more than once. We believe that you as high school students can give us invaluable feedback. We want to hear your honest opinion. The personal opinion expressed in your essay will in no way affect whether or not you are awarded the scholarship. We respect that everyone has their own opinions on the topic and want to hear what you have to say. There are two parts in the application: essay contest and survey questions (optional.) Please visit our site for more information.

Award: Scholarship for use in freshman, sophomore, junior, or senior years; not renewable. *Number:* 1–3. *Amount:* $500–$1000.

Eligibility Requirements: Applicant must be high school student and planning to enroll or expecting to enroll full-time at a two-year or four-year institution or university. Available to U.S. and non-U.S. citizens.

Application Requirements: Essay. *Deadline:* March 31.

Contact: Jessica Chang
KidGuard
117 West 9th Street, Suite 1009
Los Angeles, CA 90015
E-mail: jessica@kidguard.com

KIM AND HAROLD LOUIE FAMILY FOUNDATION

http://www.louiefamilyfoundation.org

LOUIE FAMILY FOUNDATION SCHOLARSHIP

Please visit www.louiefamilyfoundation.org for scholarship details.

Award: Scholarship for use in freshman year; not renewable. *Number:* 25–35. *Amount:* $1000–$10,000.

Eligibility Requirements: Applicant must be enrolled or expecting to enroll full-time at a two-year or four-year or technical institution or university. Available to U.S. and non-U.S. citizens.

Application Requirements: Application form, essay, personal photograph. *Deadline:* March 31.

Contact: Stan Sze, Director
Kim and Harold Louie Family Foundation
1325 Howard Ave., #949
Burlingame, CA 94010
Phone: 650-491-3434
E-mail: scholarships@louiefamilyfoundation.org

KOGAN AND DISALVO, P.A.

https://www.kogan-disalvo.com/

KOGAN & DISALVO PERSONAL INJURY LAW AUTONOMOUS VEHICLES SCHOLARSHIP

Kogan & DiSalvo Personal Injury Law is honored to offer the Kogan & DiSalvo Law Firm Autonomous Vehicles Scholarship to a worthy and enthusiastic student. Eligibility for this $1,000 scholarship requires the applicant to meet each of the following criteria: applicant must be accepted to/enrolled in an accredited undergraduate college, university or graduate school, and pursuing an education in the legal field; applicant must demonstrate strong academic standing with a minimum GPA of 3.0; applicant has demonstrated an academic career inclusive of outstanding service to the community, strong initiative to pursue higher education and superlative leadership. For more information, please visit: https://masseyattorneys.com/#scholarship

Award: Scholarship for use in freshman, sophomore, junior, senior, graduate, or postgraduate years; not renewable. *Number:* 1. *Amount:* $1000.

Eligibility Requirements: Applicant must be enrolled or expecting to enroll full- or part-time at a two-year or four-year or technical institution or university. Available to U.S. and non-U.S. citizens.

Application Requirements: Application form, essay. *Deadline:* July 31.

Contact: Darryl Kogan
　　　　E-mail: scholarship@koganinjurylaw.com

LANDSCAPE ARCHITECTURE FOUNDATION

www.lafoundation.org

LANDSCAPE FORMS DESIGN FOR PEOPLE SCHOLARSHIP

This $3,000 scholarship honors landscape architecture students with a proven contribution to the design of public spaces that integrate landscape design and the use of amenities to promote social interaction.

Award: Scholarship for use in senior year; not renewable. *Number:* 1. *Amount:* $3000.

Eligibility Requirements: Applicant must be enrolled or expecting to enroll full-time at a four-year institution or university. Available to U.S. and non-U.S. citizens.

Application Requirements: Application form, essay, personal photograph. *Fee:* $5. *Deadline:* February 1.

Contact: Ms. Danielle Carbonneau, Program Manager, Scholarships and Leadership
　　　　Phone: 202-331-7070 Ext. 14
　　　　E-mail: scholarships@lafoundation.org

STEVEN G. KING PLAY ENVIRONMENTS SCHOLARSHIP

This $5,000 scholarship, created by Steven G. King, FASLA, founder and Chairman of Landscape Structures Inc., recognizes a student who has high potential in the design of play environments. This student must show an interest in the value of integrating playgrounds into parks, schools and other play environments and understand the significant social and educational value of play. Key qualities in the student receiving the Scholarship are creativity, openness to innovation, and a demonstrated interest in park and playground planning.

Award: Scholarship for use in junior, senior, or graduate years; not renewable. *Number:* 1. *Amount:* $5000.

Eligibility Requirements: Applicant must be enrolled or expecting to enroll full- or part-time at a four-year institution or university. Available to U.S. and non-U.S. citizens.

Application Requirements: Application form, essay, personal photograph. *Fee:* $5. *Deadline:* February 1.

Contact: Ms. Danielle Carbonneau, Program Manager, Scholarships and Leadership
　　　　Phone: 202-331-7070 Ext. 14
　　　　E-mail: scholarships@lafoundation.org

LASIKPLUS

https://www.lasikplus.com/location/orlando-lasik-center

THE LASIKPLUS "MY VISION" ESSAY SCHOLARSHIP

ELIGIBILITY CRITERIA: Entrants must: Be a full-time freshman, sophomore, junior, senior, or graduate student currently enrolled at an accredited university in the U.S. or its territories. Have a minimum 2.5 GPA on a 4.0 scale. Be a citizen or legal permanent resident of the United States or its territories. HOW TO APPLY: Entrants must submit their essay electronically by sending it, via email, to scholarship@lasikplus.com. To be eligible for consideration, each entry must include the essay, the entrant's contact information (including, at a minimum, the entrants full name, the name of the University or College of enrollment, current major, email address and phone number where the entrant can be contacted). The winner will be selected from all of the eligible entries received, based upon evaluation of the essay. Essays will be judged based on the following five catergories: spelling and grammar; contest theme relevancy; focus on the topic; content logicality and relevancy; adherence to essay guidelines.

Award: Scholarship for use in freshman, sophomore, junior, senior, graduate, or postgraduate years; not renewable. *Number:* 1. *Amount:* $2500.

Eligibility Requirements: Applicant must be enrolled or expecting to enroll full-time at a two-year or four-year institution or university. Available to U.S. citizens.

Application Requirements: Essay. *Deadline:* continuous.

Contact: Shay O'Brien
　　　　LasikPlus
　　　　155 Cranes Roost Boulevard
　　　　Suite 1060
　　　　Altamonte Springs, FL 32701
　　　　Phone: 866- 921-2406
　　　　E-mail: scholarships@lasikplus.com

LAW OFFICE OF HENRY QUEENER

https://queenerlaw.com/

LAW OFFICE OF HENRY QUEENER ANNUAL SCHOLARSHIP

Scott Foster Memorial Scholarship Benjamin Franklin once said: "An investment in knowledge pays the best interest." The Law Office of Henry Queener is proud to announce our investment in knowledge. We are again offering a $2,500 scholarship to an exceptional student who submits the strongest essay focusing on the given topic.

Award: Scholarship for use in freshman, sophomore, junior, or senior years; not renewable. *Number:* 1. *Amount:* $2500.

Eligibility Requirements: Applicant must be high school student and planning to enroll or expecting to enroll full-time at a two-year or four-year institution or university. Available to U.S. citizens.

Application Requirements: Application form, essay. *Deadline:* July 15.

Contact: Anni Hemsing, Scholarship Coordinator
　　　　Law Office of Henry Queener
　　　　PO Box 1596
　　　　Northbrook, IL 60065
　　　　Phone: 847-940-4000
　　　　E-mail: anni@marketjd.com

LAW OFFICES OF MARK SHERMAN, LLC

markshermanlaw.com

MARK SHERMAN LAW JUVENILE JUSTICE SCHOLARSHIP

The Law Offices of Mark Sherman, based in Stamford, Connecticut, is pleased to announce that we are offering a scholarship in the amount of $1,000 to one student who has an interest in working with young people who have already been convicted of a crime and been sent to jail. We want to support them in seizing new opportunities and giving them the means to be a success in their community. This student may have also experienced and overcome adversity in their life and can relate to these juveniles who are rebuilding their lives once out of jail. For more information, please visit: https://www.markshermanlaw.com/#scholarship

Award: Scholarship for use in freshman, sophomore, junior, senior, graduate, or postgraduate years; not renewable. *Number:* 1. *Amount:* $1000.

Eligibility Requirements: Applicant must be enrolled or expecting to enroll full- or part-time at a two-year or four-year or technical institution or university. Available to U.S. and non-U.S. citizens.

Application Requirements: Application form may be submitted online (https://markshermanlaw.com/2019-juvenile-justice-scholarship/), essay, resume, transcript. *Deadline:* September 30.

Contact: Mark Sherman
E-mail: info@markshermanlaw.com

LAW OFFICES OF SEAN M. CLEARY

https://www.seanclearypa.com/

LAW OFFICES OF SEAN M. CLEARY 2017 SCHOLARSHIP

The Offices of Sean M. Cleary is not interested just in helping people recover compensation after suffering an accident, but we are also happy to provide financial help for students who pursue higher education. Approximately 3 out of 100,000 people were killed during 2015 in DUI accidents in the United States, with one of those three people being under the age of 21; the numbers being even higher if we are talking about the state of Florida. With this in mind, in 2018 we are offering a $1,000 scholarship for the student who will help bring more attention over the dangerous consequences of teens driving under the influence of alcohol. To submit your essay or if you are searching for more information on the subject, go to https://www.seanclearypa.com/scholarship/

Award: Scholarship for use in freshman, sophomore, junior, or senior years; renewable. *Number:* 1. *Amount:* $1000.

Eligibility Requirements: Applicant must be age 18 and over and enrolled or expecting to enroll full-time at a four-year institution or university. Available to U.S. citizens.

Application Requirements: Application form may be submitted online (https://www.seanclearypa.com/scholarship/), essay, personal photograph. *Deadline:* August 31.

Contact: Mr. Sean Cleary, Attorney
Law Offices of Sean M. Cleary
19 West Flagler Street, #618
Miami, FL 33130
Phone: 305-416-9805
E-mail: sean@seanclearypa.com

LAW OFFICES OF SHERYL R. RENTZ, P.C.

http://www.srrentzlaw.com/

KEY TO A BRIGHT FUTURE SCHOLARSHIP 2019

The KEY TO A BRIGHT FUTURE SCHOLARSHIP 2019 is our way of thanking those students who have gone above and beyond in order to give back to their local communities. Students who have earned at least a 3.0 GPA in the classroom while pursuing the betterment of the world outside of the classroom are welcome to apply to this scholarship. Applicants should be graduating high school seniors or current undergraduate students. U.S. Citizenship or Permanent Residency is required. Please visit our website for additional information and to submit an application today: http://www.srrentzlaw.com/scholarship/

Award: Scholarship for use in freshman, sophomore, junior, or senior years; not renewable. *Number:* 1. *Amount:* $500.

Eligibility Requirements: Applicant must be enrolled or expecting to enroll full- or part-time at a two-year or four-year institution or university. Available to U.S. citizens.

Application Requirements: Application form, essay. *Deadline:* April 30.

Contact: Mr. Daniel Mateo, Scholarship Manager
Law Offices of Sheryl R. Rentz, P.C.
65 N. Raymond Avenue, Suite 230
Pasadena, CA 91103
Phone: 323-254-1510 Ext. 119
E-mail: DMateo@slsconsulting.com

LAW OFFICES OF TRAGOS, SARTES AND TRAGOS

https://tragoslaw.com/

TRAGOS WRITE YOUR OWN LAW SCHOLARSHIP

This scholarship is offered to any student currently enrolled in an accredited community college, undergraduate, or graduate program in the United States. This includes incoming first-year college students who are high school graduates or possess a GED. All eligible candidates must be in good academic standing, with a minimum cumulative GPA of 3.0 or above. For more complete information, visit https://tragoslaw.com/#scholarship.

Award: Scholarship for use in freshman, sophomore, junior, senior, graduate, or postgraduate years; not renewable. *Number:* 1. *Amount:* $500.

Eligibility Requirements: Applicant must be enrolled or expecting to enroll full- or part-time at a two-year or four-year or technical institution or university. Available to U.S. and non-U.S. citizens.

Application Requirements: Application form, essay. *Deadline:* May 31.

Contact: George Tragos
E-mail: info@tragoslaw.com

LEGALZOOM.COM

legalzoom.com

EMERGING ENTREPRENEUR GRANT

We want to help entrepreneurial students get their business off the ground and are awarding a $5000 scholarship grant and other cool startup business perks for the student with the most innovative business idea. Find information and submission form here: https://www.legalzoom.com/scholarship-grant.html

Award: Grant for use in freshman, sophomore, junior, senior, graduate, or postgraduate years; not renewable. *Number:* 1. *Amount:* $5000.

Eligibility Requirements: Applicant must be age 18 and over and enrolled or expecting to enroll full- or part-time at a two-year or four-year or technical institution or university. Available to U.S. citizens.

Application Requirements: Application form. *Deadline:* September 10.

Contact: Mr. Christian Neeser, Outreach Coordinator
LegalZoom.com
101 North Brand Boulevard
Glendale, CA 91203
Phone: 323-428-3694
E-mail: cneeser@legalzoom.com

LEOPOLD SCHEPP FOUNDATION

http://www.scheppfoundation.org/

LEOPOLD SCHEPP SCHOLARSHIP

Scholarship for undergraduates under 30 years of age and graduate students under 40 years of age at the time of application. Applicants must have a minimum GPA of 3.0. High school seniors are not eligible. All applicants must either be enrolled in college or have completed at least one year of college at the time of issuing the application. Must be citizens or permanent residents of the United States. Deadline varies.

Award: Scholarship for use in sophomore, junior, senior, or graduate years; renewable. *Number:* 1–30. *Amount:* up to $8500.

Eligibility Requirements: Applicant must be enrolled or expecting to enroll full-time at a four-year institution or university. Available to U.S. citizens.

Application Requirements: Application form, financial need analysis, interview, recommendations or references, transcript. *Deadline:* varies.

Contact: Scholarship Committee
Leopold Schepp Foundation
551 Fifth Avenue, Suite 3000
New York, NY 10176
Phone: 212-692-0191

LEP FOUNDATION FOR YOUTH EDUCATION

http://www.lepfoundation.org/applications

CURE--CANCER SUPPORT SCHOLARSHIP

The Lep Foundation for Youth Education was formed in 2009 with the specific mission of providing financial assistance to support disabled students who demonstrate academic success and the motivation to move forward despite their disabilities. In addition, the Foundation was proud to have introduced the Cure Cancer Support Scholarship in 2016 to assist students diagnosed with childhood and adolescent cancers. The Lep Foundation is a non-profit charity with 501c3 tax exempt status (E.I.N. #27-0817346).

Award: Scholarship for use in freshman, sophomore, junior, senior, graduate, or postgraduate years; not renewable. *Number:* 1. *Amount:* $5000.

Eligibility Requirements: Applicant must be enrolled or expecting to enroll full- or part-time at a two-year or four-year or technical institution or university. Available to U.S. citizens.

Application Requirements: Application form, essay, financial need analysis. *Deadline:* June 1.

Contact: Scholarship Committee
Lep Foundation for Youth Education
9 Whispering Spring Dr.
Millstone Township, NJ 08510
E-mail: lepfoundation@aol.com

LIFE HAPPENS

http://www.lifehappens.org

LIFE LESSONS SCHOLARSHIP PROGRAM

The Life Lessons Scholarship Program is for college students and college-bound high school seniors who have experienced the death of a parent or legal guardian. To apply students must complete and submit an online application (www.lifehappens.org/scholarship), including an essay of no more than 500 words or a 3 minutes video discussing how the death of a parent or guardian affected his or her life financially and emotionally. Applicants must explain how the lack of adequate life insurance coverage (or no coverage at all) impacted their family's financial situation. Please make sure to review the Scholarship Program rules at www.lifehappens.org/scholarship-program-rules.

Award: Scholarship for use in freshman, sophomore, junior, senior, or graduate years; not renewable. *Number:* 20–50. *Amount:* $5000–$15,000.

Eligibility Requirements: Applicant must be age 17-24 and enrolled or expecting to enroll full- or part-time at a two-year or four-year or technical institution or university. Available to U.S. citizens.

Application Requirements: Application form, essay. *Deadline:* March 1.

Contact: Julie Holsinger, Manager of Programs
Life Happens
1530 Wison Boulvard
Suite 1060
Arlington, VA 22209
Phone: 703-888-5000 Ext. 4446
E-mail: scholarship@lifehappens.org

LIFESAVER ESSAYS

https://lifesaveressays.com

LIFE SAVER ESSAYS ESSAY WRITING CONTEST

Lifesaver Essays, an academic help platform, announces its third Essay Writing Contest. We welcome entries from passionate writers. So feel free to pick up your laptop, activate your caudate nucleus and get the juices flowing! Anyone, from any country, is free to apply. Apply online via https://lifesaveressays.com. There is no entry fee. The essay should be at least 900 words and not over 1300 words. Our team of writers have come out with a list of topics that are interesting, engaging and fun to write on. Choose one topic. All essays must be absolutely original and in your own words. Images are allowed. You are free to use images but they must be copyright-free or appropriately cited. Submissions are accepted only in Microsoft Word documents (doc or docx). The cover page of your essay must contain your complete details such as your full name, phone number, and email. The essay must be written in English. Multiple entries are allowed. The Essay Writing Contest is open from August 9 to 11:59 PM to November 30, PDT. The top three winners will be announced on December 15. One winner will be chosen every week as a Surprise Winner and they will get a consolation prize. You can send as many entries as you like.

Award: Prize for use in freshman, sophomore, junior, senior, graduate, or postgraduate years; not renewable. *Number:* 5–11. *Amount:* $10–$200.

Eligibility Requirements: Applicant must be enrolled or expecting to enroll full- or part-time at a two-year or four-year or technical institution or university. Available to U.S. and non-U.S. citizens.

Application Requirements: Essay. *Deadline:* November 30.

Contact: Mr. John Paulson, Co-Founder, Lifesaver Essays
Lifesaver Essays
505, Oakland City Center
14th Street, Suite 900
Oakland, CA 94612
Phone: 510-775-1061
E-mail: help@lifesaveressays.com

LOUISIANA OFFICE OF STUDENT FINANCIAL ASSISTANCE

www.osfa.la.gov/

CHAFEE EDUCATIONAL AND TRAINING VOUCHER (ETV) PROGRAM

The Chafee Educational and Training Voucher (ETV) Program awards up to $5,000 annually during the academic year to qualified students who have been in the foster care system so they can pursue an academic college education or technical and skill training in college to be prepared to enter the workforce. The actual award amount is determined by the student's financial need, which is calculated in accordance with the Higher Education Act of 1965, as amended.

Award: Scholarship for use in freshman, sophomore, junior, or senior years; renewable.

Eligibility Requirements: Applicant must be age 14-26 and enrolled or expecting to enroll at a two-year or technical institution or university.

Application Requirements: Application form.

Contact: LA Office of Student Financial Assistance
Louisiana Office of Student Financial Assistance
602 North 5th Street
Baton Rouge, LA 70802
Phone: 800-259-5626
Fax: 225-208-1496
E-mail: custserv@la.gov

MAINOR WORTH INJURY LAWYERS

https://mainorwirth.com/

MAINOR WIRTH INJURY LAWYERS SCHOLARSHIP

Mainor Wirth Injury Lawyers, located in Las Vegas, Nevada, is dedicated to helping members of our community become successful and achieve their goals. Medical, social or financial obstacles can make higher education a mere dream to some students. Therefore, every year we offer a $1,000 scholarship to the student who submits the strongest essay focusing on the given topic.

Award: Scholarship for use in freshman, sophomore, junior, or senior years; not renewable. *Number:* 1. *Amount:* $1000.

Eligibility Requirements: Applicant must be enrolled or expecting to enroll full-time at a two-year or four-year institution or university. Available to U.S. citizens.

Application Requirements: Application form, application form may be submitted online (https://mainorwirth.com/academic-scholarship/), essay. *Deadline:* July 15.

Contact: Anni Hemsing
E-mail: anni@marketjd.com

MANGUM & ASSOCIATES PC

https://mangumlaw.net/

MANGUM & ASSOCIATES PC SCHOLARSHIP CONTEST

Every year, our firm grants a $1,000 scholarship to the American college student who creates the best video essay. This year's topic is how lawyers help businesses thrive.

Award: Prize for use in freshman, sophomore, junior, or senior years; not renewable. *Number:* 1. *Amount:* $1000.

Eligibility Requirements: Applicant must be age 18-25 and enrolled or expecting to enroll full- or part-time at a two-year or four-year institution or university. Available to U.S. citizens.

Application Requirements: Application form may be submitted online (https://mangumlaw.net/scholarship-for-college-students/), essay. *Deadline:* August 15.

MARGARET MCNAMARA EDUCATION GRANTS

http://www.mmeg.org

MARGARET MCNAMARA EDUCATION GRANTS

One-time award for female students from developing countries already enrolled in accredited universities in the USA/Canada and selected universities in Latin America and South Africa (see MMEG.org for details). Candidates must articulate prior and future commitment to improve wellbeing of women and children; plan to return to their countries or a developing country within two years. Must be over 25 years of age. U.S. citizens not eligible except for the Trinity-Washington University program.

Award: Grant for use in sophomore, junior, senior, graduate, or postgraduate years; not renewable. *Number:* 27–35. *Amount:* $7000–$15,000.

Eligibility Requirements: Applicant must be age 25 and over; enrolled or expecting to enroll full- or part-time at a four-year institution or university and female. Available to citizens of countries other than the U.S. or Canada.

Application Requirements: Application form, application form may be submitted online(www.mmeg.org), entry in a contest, essay, financial need analysis, interview, personal photograph, recommendations or references. *Deadline:* January 15.

Contact: Chairman, Selection Committee
Washington, DC 20433
E-mail: mmeg@worldbank.org

MARINE CORPS SCHOLARSHIP FOUNDATION, INC.

http://www.mcsf.org/

MARINE CORPS SCHOLARSHIP FOUNDATION

Applicants for the Marine Corps Scholarship Foundation must be the child of an active duty or reserve U.S. Marine, a veteran U.S. Marine who has received an honorable discharge, or who was killed while serving in the U.S. Marine Corps. Children of U.S. Navy Corpsmen, Chaplains, or Religious Programs Specialists attached to a Marine unit may also qualify. Additionally, applicants must have at least a 2.0 GPA and must be able to demonstrate financial need. Must be planning to attend an accredited undergraduate college or career technical education (CTE) in the upcoming academic year. All who qualify and submit a completed application will receive an award. Award amounts range from $1,500 to $10,000 per year and are renewable. The undergraduate application is open January 1 to March 1 each year. The CTE application deadline is rolling for career training programs less than 12 months in length. For more information, or to apply, please visit www.mcsf.org/apply.

Award: Scholarship for use in freshman, sophomore, junior, or senior years; not renewable. *Number:* 2,000–2,300. *Amount:* $1500–$10,000.

Eligibility Requirements: Applicant must be enrolled or expecting to enroll full- or part-time at a two-year or technical institution or university. Available to U.S. citizens.

Application Requirements: Application form, application form may be submitted online, essay, financial need analysis. *Deadline:* March 1.

Contact: Scholarship Department
Marine Corps Scholarship Foundation, Inc.
909 N Washington Street
Suite 400
Alexandria, VA 22314
Phone: 866-4965462
E-mail: scholarship@mcsf.org

MARYLAND ASSOCIATION OF PRIVATE COLLEGES AND CAREER SCHOOLS

http://www.mapccs.org/

MARYLAND ASSOCIATION OF PRIVATE COLLEGES AND CAREER SCHOOLS SCHOLARSHIP

Awards for study at Maryland private colleges and career schools only. Must enroll in private college or career school same year high school is completed.

Award: Scholarship for use in freshman year; not renewable. *Number:* 50–75. *Amount:* $500–$2000.

Eligibility Requirements: Applicant must be high school student; planning to enroll or expecting to enroll full- or part-time at a technical institution and studying in Maryland. Available to U.S. and non-U.S. citizens.

Application Requirements: Application form, essay. *Deadline:* continuous.

Contact: Frank Russell, Administrative Manager
Maryland Association of Private Colleges and Career Schools
5305 Village Center Drive
Suite 295
Columbia, MD 21044
Phone: 410-282-4012
E-mail: info@mapccs.org

MASSEY AND ASSOCIATES, PC

https://www.masseyattorneys.com/

MASSEY & ASSOCIATES: JUSTICE FOR ALL SCHOLARSHIP

Massey & Associates, personal injury attorneys based in Chattanooga, Tennessee, is pleased to announce that we are offering a scholarship in the amount of $1,000 to one student who has experienced and overcome adversity in their life and justice was served - we would like to hear about the positive effects this justice had on yourself and your community. For more information, please visit: https://masseyattorneys.com/#scholarship

Award: Scholarship for use in freshman, sophomore, junior, senior, graduate, or postgraduate years; not renewable. *Number:* 1. *Amount:* $1000.

Eligibility Requirements: Applicant must be enrolled or expecting to enroll full- or part-time at a two-year or four-year or technical institution or university. Available to U.S. and non-U.S. citizens.

Application Requirements: Application form, essay. *Deadline:* July 31.

Contact: Gary Massey
E-mail: info@masseyattorneys.com

MCNEELY STEPHENSON

http://www.indianapilaw.com/

COMMUNITY INVOLVEMENT SCHOLARSHIP AWARD

This scholarship is designed to encourage and reward dedication of an exemplary individual who is deeply involved in the community that surrounds them. McNeely Stephenson believes in good citizenship and recognition for those who support their local communities through direct involvement, meaningful commitment and generosity of their time and efforts. Scholarship applicants must submit a detailed report of their community service efforts during their high school careers. This should be submitted in the form of an essay describing the involvement and how they feel this award will further both their college career and their continued dedication to helping others.

Award: Scholarship for use in freshman year; not renewable. *Amount:* $1000.

Eligibility Requirements: Applicant must be high school student and planning to enroll or expecting to enroll full- or part-time at a four-year institution or university. Available to U.S. citizens.

Application Requirements: Application form, essay. *Deadline:* May 1.

Contact: Hallie Huff
Phone: 606-371-8575
E-mail: hallie@gladiatorlawmarketing.com

MEDIGO GMBH
https://www.medigo.com/en

MEDIGO SCHOLARSHIP PROGRAM

MEDIGO strives to remove barriers to healthcare for our patients. We firmly believe that education should be equally as accessible for students. We are proud to offer a scholarship of $2,000, with the aim of supporting one promising student through their college or university degree. We are looking to reward a student who best aligns with our values of diversity and inclusion. Applicants are asked to write an essay on diversity in the workplace.

Award: Scholarship for use in freshman, sophomore, junior, or senior years; renewable. *Number:* 1. *Amount:* $2000.

Eligibility Requirements: Applicant must be enrolled or expecting to enroll full- or part-time at a four-year institution or university. Available to U.S. and non-U.S. citizens.

Application Requirements: Essay. *Deadline:* September 1.

Contact: Mr. Samuel Rucker, MEDIGO
Medigo GMBH
Rosenthaler Str. 13
Berlin, NY 10119
Phone: 49-1632212215
E-mail: scholarship@medigo.com

MENSA FOUNDATION
mensafoundation.org

U.S. SCHOLARSHIP PROGRAM

The scholarship program is an essay based program open to students of all ages. Mensa membership is not required.

Award: Scholarship for use in freshman, sophomore, junior, senior, graduate, or postgraduate years; not renewable. *Number:* 100–150. *Amount:* $600–$2500.

Eligibility Requirements: Applicant must be enrolled or expecting to enroll full- or part-time at a two-year or four-year institution or university. Available to U.S. citizens.

Application Requirements: Application form, application form may be submitted online (https://www.mensafoundation.org), essay. *Deadline:* January 15.

Contact: Jill Beckham
Mensa Foundation
1200 E Copeland Rd Ste 550
Arlington, TX 76011
Phone: 817-607-5577
E-mail: info@mensafoundation.org

MICHIGAN CONSUMER CREDIT LAWYERS
http://www.micreditlawyer.com/

MCCL THOUGHT LEADERSHIP SCHOLARSHIP

The scholarship is an essay writing competition. Students are to write on the topic of the student loan debt crisis and what possible solutions there might be to fixing the issue. When the student's application is written and submitted, it is immediately received and reviewed.

Award: Scholarship for use in freshman, sophomore, junior, senior, graduate, or postgraduate years; renewable. *Number:* 1–3. *Amount:* $250–$1000.

Eligibility Requirements: Applicant must be enrolled or expecting to enroll full-time at a four-year institution or university. Available to U.S. citizens.

Application Requirements: Application form may be submitted online (http://www.micreditlawyer.com/mccl-thought-leadership-scholarship/), entry in a contest, essay, transcript. *Deadline:* continuous.

Contact: Philip Rudy, Webmaster
Michigan Consumer Credit Lawyers
211 East 9 Mile Road
Ferndale, MI 48220
Phone: 616-238-3838
E-mail: philip@beshapeless.com

MIE SOLUTIONS
https://www.mie-solutions.com/

MIE SOLUTIONS SCHOLARSHIP

For the 2018 Fall Semester, MIE Solutions will be offering a $500 scholarship to a student who writes a winning essay regarding their future career and educational objectives in computer science and/or computer engineering.

Award: Scholarship for use in freshman, sophomore, junior, or senior years; renewable. *Number:* 1. *Amount:* $500.

Eligibility Requirements: Applicant must be age 18 and over and enrolled or expecting to enroll full- or part-time at a four-year institution or university. Available to U.S. citizens.

Application Requirements: *Deadline:* August 15.

MILA BOYD LAW OFFICES
https://www.milaboydlaw.com/

MILA BOYD LAW OFFICES SCHOLARSHIP CONTEST

Every year, our firm grants a $1,000 scholarship to the U.S. college student who creates the best video essay that elaborates on why they want to be a lawyer.

Award: Prize for use in freshman, sophomore, junior, or senior years; not renewable. *Number:* 1. *Amount:* $1000.

Eligibility Requirements: Applicant must be age 18-25 and enrolled or expecting to enroll full- or part-time at a two-year or four-year institution or university. Available to U.S. citizens.

Application Requirements: Application form may be submitted online (https://www.milaboydlaw.com/scholarship-for-college-students/), essay. *Deadline:* August 15.

MILITARY OFFICERS ASSOCIATION OF AMERICA (MOAA) SCHOLARSHIP FUND
http://www.moaa.org/scholarshipfund

GENERAL JOHN RATAY EDUCATIONAL FUND GRANTS

Grants available to the children of the surviving spouse of retired officers. Must be under 24 years old and the child of a deceased retired officer who was a member of MOAA. For more details and an application go to website http://www.moaa.org/education.

Award: Grant for use in freshman, sophomore, junior, or senior years; renewable. *Number:* 1–5. *Amount:* $4000–$5000.

Eligibility Requirements: Applicant must be age 24 or under and enrolled or expecting to enroll full-time at a two-year or four-year institution or university. Available to U.S. citizens.

Application Requirements: Application form, financial need analysis. *Deadline:* March 1.

Contact: Program Director
Phone: 800-234-6622
E-mail: edassist@moaa.org

MOAA AMERICAN PATRIOT SCHOLARSHIP

Students under the age of 24 and who are children of MOAA members and children of active-duty, reserve, National Guard, or enlisted personnel whose military parent has died on active service or whose military parent is severely wounded (as defined as Traumatic SGLI) are eligible to apply. For more information and to access the online application go to website http://www.moaa.org/education.

Award: Grant for use in freshman, sophomore, junior, or senior years; renewable. *Number:* 1–60. *Amount:* $2500–$5000.

Eligibility Requirements: Applicant must be age 24 or under and enrolled or expecting to enroll full-time at a two-year or four-year institution or university. Available to U.S. citizens.

Application Requirements: Application form, financial need analysis. *Deadline:* March 1.

Contact: Program Director
Phone: 800-234-6622
E-mail: edassist@moaa.org

MILITARY ORDER OF THE STARS AND BARS

http://www.militaryorderofthestarsandbars.org/

MILITARY ORDER OF THE STARS AND BARS SCHOLARSHIPS

Applicants must be accepted to a degree-granting junior college or four-year college or university or already enrolled in such a facility. Awards shall be made annually, and the total amount of the scholarship money to be awarded each year to each recipient shall not exceed $1000. Applicants must be sponsored by a local MOS&B Chapter or MOS&B State Society. Applicants must be able to prove they are a descendant of a commissioned officer or civil servant of the Confederate States of America. Preference is given to relatives of currently active MOS&B members. All application information is found on the MOS&B website.

Award: Scholarship for use in freshman, sophomore, junior, senior, graduate, or postgraduate years; not renewable. *Number:* 3–6. *Amount:* $1000.

Eligibility Requirements: Applicant must be enrolled or expecting to enroll full-time at a two-year or four-year institution or university. Available to U.S. and non-U.S. citizens.

Application Requirements: Application form, personal photograph. *Deadline:* March 1.

Contact: Ewell Loudermilk, Scholarship Chairman
Military Order of the Stars and Bars
6730 Treece Rd.
San Angelo, TX 76905
E-mail: rebelboy264@yahoo.com

MINDSUMO

http://www.mindsumo.com

MINDSUMO 15-MINUTE SCHOLARSHIP

This is the first year we are launching this scholarship program to run in conjunction with our standard MindSumo platform. In terms of total payouts we have provided to college students for merit-based performance on solving business and engineering challenges, we have paid out $600,000 over the last 4 years. Now we want to convert a portion of our prize pool to be dedicated to scholarships. Our reward structure is unique in that the number of winners and the award amount depends on the number of submissions. Our objective is to reward a larger proportion of applicants to encourage them through the tough scholarship application process rather than limit winners to a small select few. Please see website for details, http://www.mindsumo.com/scholarships.

Award: Scholarship for use in freshman, sophomore, junior, senior, graduate, or postgraduate years; not renewable. *Number:* 250–500. *Amount:* $40–$200.

Eligibility Requirements: Applicant must be age 18 and over and enrolled or expecting to enroll full- or part-time at a two-year or four-year or technical institution or university. Available to U.S. and non-U.S. citizens.

Application Requirements: *Deadline:* continuous.

Contact: Mr. John Huang, Manager
MindSumo
33 New Montgomery
Suite 220
San Francisco, CA 94105
Phone: 843-453-5176
E-mail: john@mindsumo.com

MINICK LAW

http://www.minicklaw.com/

THOMAS MORE SCHOLARSHIP

In an age when many political leaders seem to have gone from bending the truth, to abandoning it, and when the media is constantly on trial for fake news our country is desperately in need for young leaders who are willing to speak and stand up for the truth.

Award: Scholarship for use in freshman, sophomore, junior, or senior years; not renewable. *Number:* 1. *Amount:* $500.

Eligibility Requirements: Applicant must be enrolled or expecting to enroll full- or part-time at a two-year or four-year institution or university. Available to U.S. and non-U.S. citizens.

Application Requirements: Application form. *Deadline:* June 22.

Contact: Mr. James Minick
Phone: 828-333-5024
E-mail: james@minicklaw.com

MLD WEALTH MANAGEMENT GROUP

http://mywealthmanagement.ca/

ANNUAL MLD SCHOLASTIC SCHOLARSHIP

MLD Wealth Management is offering an annual scholarship to all the students from that meet our qualifications. This scholarship is based on merit, financial need, and community participation. The winning applicant will receive $3000 towards their education costs. The application deadline is May 10, 2017. Scholarship details: http://mywealthmanagement.ca/scholarsip2017/

Award: Scholarship for use in freshman, sophomore, junior, senior, graduate, or postgraduate years; not renewable. *Number:* 1. *Amount:* $3000.

Eligibility Requirements: Applicant must be enrolled or expecting to enroll full-time at a two-year or four-year institution or university. Available to U.S. and Canadian citizens.

Application Requirements: Application form, essay, interview, personal photograph. *Deadline:* May 10.

Contact: Mr. Chris Hilliard, PR Manager
MLD Wealth Management Group
239 - 8th Avenue SW
Suite 200
Calgary, AB T2P 1B9
CAN
Phone: 604-360-5161
Fax: 403-410-9668
E-mail: pr@mywealthmanagement.ca

THE MORRIS K. UDALL AND STEWART L. UDALL FOUNDATION

http://www.udall.gov/

UDALL UNDERGRADUATE SCHOLARSHIP

Fifty one-time scholarships and fifty one-time honorable mention awards to full-time college sophomores or juniors with demonstrated commitment to careers related to the environment, tribal public policy (Native American/Alaska Native students only), or Native American health care (Native American/Alaska Native students only). Students from all fields and disciplines are encouraged to apply. Students must be nominated by their college or university. Visit http://www.udall.gov for additional information.

Award: Scholarship for use in junior or senior years; not renewable. *Number:* 50. *Amount:* $1–$5000.

Eligibility Requirements: Applicant must be enrolled or expecting to enroll full-time at a two-year or four-year institution or university. Available to U.S. and Canadian citizens.

Application Requirements: Application form, application form may be submitted online (http://udall.gov), essay, nomination by campus faculty representative, recommendations or references, transcript. *Deadline:* March 4.

Contact: Paula Randler, Scholarship Program Manager
Phone: 520-901-8564
Fax: 520-901-8570
E-mail: randler@udall.gov

MYSTERY WEEKLY MAGAZINE

https://www.mysteryweekly.com

2018 EMERGING MYSTERY WRITER SCHOLARSHIP

Selection of the Mystery Weekly Magazine scholarship recipient will be based entirely on the creative writing requirement. Your story submission must be a previously unpublished 1000-6000 word mystery. Any mystery fiction sub-genre is acceptable. The final decision will be made by independent judges respected in the crime writing community.

Award: Scholarship for use in freshman, sophomore, junior, senior, graduate, or postgraduate years; not renewable. *Number:* 1. *Amount:* $250.

Eligibility Requirements: Applicant must be enrolled or expecting to enroll full- or part-time at a two-year or four-year or technical institution or university. Available to U.S. and Canadian citizens.

Application Requirements: Application form. *Deadline:* May 30.

Contact: Kerry Carter, Editor
Mystery Weekly Magazine
3-35 Stone Church Road
Suite 213
Ancaster, ON L9K 1S5
CAN
E-mail: info@mysteryweekly.com

MY TRAVEL LUGGAGE

ADVANCE SCHOLARSHIP PROGRAM BY MY TRAVEL LUGGAGE

Advance Scholarship Program By My Travel Luggage is for those students who are passionate about traveling and can express themselves in front of the entire world by showing their writing talent. Under this scholarship program, applicants need to write 1000-1500 words on the given topic and submit to our website. Then our experts will examine the quality of your provided article and announce the name of the winner, and he/she win $500. Applicant must be a student of graduate or postgraduate courses, write 1000-1500 words on given topic, and must have an ability to write creative and unique content. Scholarship deadline is October 10th and award is announced January 1st. Here is our scholarship link: http://www.my-travel-luggage.com/scholarship

Award: Scholarship for use in senior, graduate, or postgraduate years; renewable. *Number:* 1–2. *Amount:* $500–$501.

Eligibility Requirements: Applicant must be enrolled or expecting to enroll full- or part-time at a four-year institution or university. Available to U.S. and non-U.S. citizens.

Application Requirements: Personal photograph, portfolio. *Deadline:* October 10.

NATIONAL AIDS MEMORIAL

www.aidsmemorial.org

PEDRO ZAMORA YOUNG LEADERS SCHOLARSHIP

The Pedro Zamora Young Leaders Scholarship is open to all current high school seniors, and college freshman, sophomores and juniors (ages 27 and younger) who demonstrate an active commitment to fighting HIV/AIDS and taking on roles of public service and leadership. Examples include (but are not limited to): serving in peer-education and prevention programs; working in the reproductive-health and sexual health field; pursuing a medical degree to work with HIV-positive individuals; international service providing AIDS-related care and/or HIV-prevention education; research in established and emerging technologies designed to mitigate the epidemic; or activism and social change efforts that address issues contributing to the epidemic, like education and drug sentencing reform, employment and economic justice issues, housing and homelessness. All applicants must describe their current leadership efforts/experience, its significance to the HIV/AIDS epidemic, as well as how their future career plans or public service will be an extension of their current efforts. Applicants must provide at least one letter of recommendation from a teacher, program coordinator, supervisor/ally/community leader who is directly involved in their HIV/AIDS-related service, leadership, or field of study. A panel of community leaders will judge the applications. Submissions must include the following five items: 1. A complete application; 2. A brief personal statement (not to exceed 500 words) describing some of the ways that you provide service and/or leadership in the fight against HIV/AIDS and how your studies, career plans, or public service will contribute to the fight against HIV/AIDS; 3. A written essay, not to exceed 1,500 words, in which you reflect on the ways in which your life has been impacted by HIV/AIDS; explore and describe the ways in which you are providing public service or leadership that makes a difference in the lives of people with HIV/AIDS, or people at risk; and detail how the scholarship will help you in your career path and how that career will allow you to continue to fight HIV/AIDS in a way that makes a difference; 4. At least one written letter of recommendation from a teacher, program coordinator, supervisor/ally/community leader or other adult who is directly involved in your HIV/AIDS-related service, leadership, or field of study; 5. A transcript from current high school or college that demonstrates a minimum 2.5 GPA overall, or in the immediate past two semesters or three trimesters. Application/Personal Statement deadline is 5:00 PM, PST, Wednesday, May 1st, 2019. Essay/Letter(s) of Recommendation/Transcript deadline is 5:00 PM, PST, Friday, May 31st, 2019.

Award: Scholarship for use in freshman, sophomore, junior, or senior years; not renewable. *Number:* 8–10. *Amount:* $5000.

Eligibility Requirements: Applicant must be age 27 or under; enrolled or expecting to enroll full- or part-time at a two-year or four-year institution or university and studying in Alabama, Alaska, Arizona, Arkansas, California, Colorado, Connecticut, Delaware, District of Columbia, Florida, Georgia, Hawaii, Idaho, Illinois, Indiana, Iowa, Kansas, Kentucky, Louisiana, Maine, Maryland, Massachusetts, Michigan, Minnesota, Mississippi, Missouri, Montana, Nebraska, Nevada, New Hampshire, New Jersey, New Mexico, New York, North Carolina, North Dakota, Ohio, Oklahoma, Oregon, Pennsylvania, Puerto Rico, Rhode Island, South Carolina, South Dakota, Tennessee, Texas, Utah, Vermont, Virginia, Washington, West Virginia, Wisconsin, Wyoming. Available to U.S. and non-U.S. citizens.

Application Requirements: Application form, essay, recommendations or references, transcript. *Deadline:* May 31.

Contact: Mr. Matthew Kennedy, Operations Associate
National AIDS Memorial
National AIDS Memorial
870 Market Street, Suite 965
San Francisco, CA 94102
Phone: 415-765-0446
Fax: 415-707-6150
E-mail: mkennedy@aidsmemorial.org

NATIONAL AIR TRANSPORTATION FOUNDATION

http://www.nata.aero

DAN L. MEISINGER, SR. MEMORIAL LEARN TO FLY SCHOLARSHIP

The Dan L. Meisinger Sr. Memorial Learn to Fly Scholarship, in the amount is $2,500, is to be used for the express purpose of initial or primary flight training. Applicants must be college student currently enrolled in an aviation program, a high academic achiever with a "B" average or better, ecommended by an aviation professional, although direct applications are acceptable and residents of Kansas, Missouri or Illinois will be given preference.

Award: Scholarship for use in freshman, sophomore, junior, or senior years; not renewable. *Number:* 1. *Amount:* $2500.

Eligibility Requirements: Applicant must be age 18 and over and enrolled or expecting to enroll full-time at a two-year institution or university. Available to U.S. citizens.

Application Requirements: Application form, application form may be submitted online. *Deadline:* November 27.

Contact: Ms. Elizabeth Nicholson, Manager, Safety 1st Programs
Phone: 703-845-9000
E-mail: kblankenship@nata.aero

NATIONAL AIR TRANSPORTATION ASSOCIATION BUSINESS SCHOLARSHIP

Scholarship available for education or training to establish a career in the business aviation industry. Applicable education includes any aviation-related two-year, four-year or graduate degree program at an accredited college or university. Must be 18 years of age or older, be nominated and endorsed by a representative of a regular or associate member company of the NATA. Applicable training includes any aviation maintenance program under the aegis of Part 147 or 65, any pilot certificate or rating under Part 61 or 141, and any aviation-related two-year, four-year or graduate degree program at an accredited college or university. Visit website for more information http://www.nata.aero/Scholarships/NATA-Business-Scholarship.aspx.

Award: Scholarship for use in freshman, sophomore, junior, senior, graduate, or postgraduate years; not renewable. *Number:* 1. *Amount:* $2500.

Eligibility Requirements: Applicant must be age 18 and over and enrolled or expecting to enroll full- or part-time at a two-year or technical institution or university. Available to U.S. citizens.

Application Requirements: Application form, application form may be submitted online, essay. *Deadline:* December 25.

Contact: Ms. Elizabeth Nicholson, Manager, Safety 1st Programs
Phone: 703-845-9000
E-mail: kblankenship@nata.aero

NAVIGATE YOUR FUTURE SCHOLARSHIP

$2500 scholarship for a high school senior planning a career in the general aviation field to be used for one year of full-time undergraduate study. One award will be granted each year. Must be enrolled or accepted into an aviation-related program at an accredited college or university and be able to demonstrate an interest in pursuing a career in general aviation.

Award: Scholarship for use in freshman year; not renewable. *Number:* 1. *Amount:* $2500.

Eligibility Requirements: Applicant must be high school student and planning to enroll or expecting to enroll full-time at an institution or university. Available to U.S. citizens.

Application Requirements: Application form, application form may be submitted online. *Deadline:* June 26.

Contact: Ms. Elizabeth Nicholson, Manager, Safety 1st Programs
Phone: 703-845-9000
E-mail: kblankenship@nata.aero

PIONEERS OF FLIGHT SCHOLARSHIP

Scholarship recipients will be notified in writing by the end of April. Interested students must complete the attached application and submit it along with a complete transcript of grades, a letter of recommendation, an essay on general aviation and a paper indicating career goals in general aviation postmarked no later than the last Friday in December. For more information, visit website http://www.nata.aero/Scholarships/Pioneers-of-Flight-Scholarship-Program.aspx

Award: Scholarship for use in sophomore or junior years; not renewable. *Number:* 2. *Amount:* $1000.

Eligibility Requirements: Applicant must be age 18 and over and enrolled or expecting to enroll full-time at an institution or university. Available to U.S. citizens.

Application Requirements: Application form, application form may be submitted online, essay. *Deadline:* December 25.

Contact: Ms. Elizabeth Nicholson, Manager, Safety 1st Programs
Phone: 703-845-9000
E-mail: kblankenship@nata.aero

RICHARD L. TAYLOR FLIGHT TRAINING SCHOLARSHIP

The Richard L. Taylor Flight Training Scholarship applicant must: be enrolled in an accredited college/university; be enrolled in a flight program through the college/university with aspirations to become a pilot (general or commercial aviation); have a private pilot's license - a copy must be included in application the packet; have a GPA of 3.0 or greater; show junior and senior grade point averages from high school, if applying as an incoming freshman; submit an essay about aviation, your goals and dreams and why you should receive this scholarship; complete the official application

Award: Scholarship for use in freshman, sophomore, junior, or senior years; not renewable. *Number:* 1. *Amount:* $1500.

Eligibility Requirements: Applicant must be enrolled or expecting to enroll full- or part-time at a two-year institution or university. Available to U.S. citizens.

Application Requirements: Application form, application form may be submitted online, essay. *Deadline:* March 27.

Contact: Ms. Elizabeth Nicholson, Manager, Safety 1st Programs
Phone: 703-845-9000
E-mail: kblankenship@nata.aero

NATIONAL ASSOCIATION OF BLACK JOURNALISTS

http://www.nabj.org/

NABJ VISUAL TASK FORCE SCHOLARSHIP

Scholarship for students attending an accredited four-year college or university and majoring in visual journalism. Minimum 3.0 GPA required. Must be a member of NABJ. Scholarship value and the number of scholarships granted varies annually.

Award: Scholarship for use in freshman, sophomore, junior, senior, or graduate years; not renewable.

Eligibility Requirements: Applicant must be enrolled or expecting to enroll full-time at an institution or university. Available to U.S. and non-U.S. citizens.

Application Requirements: Application form, application form may be submitted online, driver's license, essay, interview. *Deadline:* December 31.

Contact: Irving Washington, Manager
Phone: 301-445-7100
Fax: 301-445-7101
E-mail: jriley@nabj.org

NATIONAL ASSOCIATION OF RAILWAY BUSINESS WOMEN

http://www.narbw.org/

NARBW SCHOLARSHIP

Scholarship awarded to the members of NARBW and their relatives. The number of awards varies every year. Applications are judged on scholastic ability, ambition and potential, and financial need.

Award: Scholarship for use in freshman, sophomore, junior, or senior years; not renewable. *Number:* 8. *Amount:* $2000.

Eligibility Requirements: Applicant must be enrolled or expecting to enroll full-time at a two-year or four-year or technical institution or university and female. Available to U.S. citizens.

Application Requirements: Application form, essay, financial need analysis. *Deadline:* March 1.

Contact: Scholarship Chairman
E-mail: narbwinfo@narbw.org

NATIONAL BLACK MBA ASSOCIATION

http://www.nbmbaa.org/

NATIONAL BLACK MBA ASSOCIATION GRADUATE SCHOLARSHIP PROGRAM

Program's mission is to identify and increase the pool of Black talent for business, public, private and non-profit sectors.

Award: Scholarship for use in freshman, sophomore, junior, or senior years; not renewable. *Number:* 10–25. *Amount:* $2500–$15,000.

Eligibility Requirements: Applicant must be enrolled or expecting to enroll full-time at a four-year institution or university. Available to U.S. and non-U.S. citizens.

Application Requirements: Application form, community service, essay, interview, resume, transcript. *Deadline:* April 17.

Contact: Ms. Lori Johnson, Program Administrator, University Relations
National Black MBA Association
180 North Michigan Avenue, Suite 1400
Chicago, IL 60601
Phone: 312-580-8086
E-mail: scholarship@nbmbaa.org

NATIONAL BUSINESS AVIATION ASSOCIATION INC.

http://www.nbaa.org/

AL CONKLIN AND BILL DE DECKER BUSINESS AVIATION MANAGEMENT SCHOLARSHIP

$5000 scholarship for students pursuing a career in business aviation management at NBAA and UAA institutions. Minimum 3.0 GPA required. Must be a U.S. citizen.

Award: Scholarship for use in sophomore, junior, or senior years; not renewable. *Amount:* $5000.

Eligibility Requirements: Applicant must be age 18 and over and enrolled or expecting to enroll full-time at an institution or university. Available to U.S. citizens.

Application Requirements: Application form, application form may be submitted online, essay. *Deadline:* July 26.

Contact: Molly Hitch
Phone: 202-783-9353
E-mail: scholarships@nbaa.org

NBAA INTERNATIONAL OPERATORS SCHOLARSHIP

Awards up to $9,000. Include with application 500-word essay explaining how this scholarship will help the applicant achieve their international aviation career goals, statement of the funds required to achieve these goals, and at least one professional letter of recommendation, preferably from an NBAA member company employee.

Award: Scholarship for use in freshman, sophomore, junior, senior, or graduate years; not renewable. *Number:* 1.

Eligibility Requirements: Applicant must be age 18 and over and enrolled or expecting to enroll full- or part-time at a two-year or technical institution or university. Available to U.S. and non-U.S. citizens.

Application Requirements: Application form, application form may be submitted online, essay. *Deadline:* December 20.

Contact: Molly Hitch
Phone: 202-783-9353
E-mail: scholarships@nbaa.org

NBAA LAWRENCE GINOCCHIO AVIATION SCHOLARSHIP

One-time $4500 scholarship for students officially enrolled in NBAA/UAA programs. Must be officially enrolled in aviation-related program with 3.0 minimum GPA. Include with application a 500- to 1000-word essay describing interest in and goals for a career in the business aviation industry while demonstrating strength of character. Must also have two letters of recommendation, including one from member of aviation department faculty at institution where applicant is enrolled.

Award: Scholarship for use in sophomore, junior, or senior years; not renewable. *Number:* 5. *Amount:* $4500.

Eligibility Requirements: Applicant must be age 18 and over and enrolled or expecting to enroll full-time at an institution or university. Available to U.S. and Canadian citizens.

Application Requirements: Application form, application form may be submitted online, essay. *Deadline:* July 26.

Contact: Molly Hitch
Phone: 202-783-9353
E-mail: scholarships@nbaa.org

NBAA WILLIAM M. FANNING MAINTENANCE SCHOLARSHIP

One-time award given to two students pursuing careers as maintenance technicians. One award will benefit a student who is currently enrolled in an accredited Airframe and Power-plant (A&P) program at an approved FAR Part 147 school. The second award will benefit an individual who is not currently enrolled but has been accepted into an A&P program. Include with application a 250-word essay describing applicant's interest in and goals for a career in the aviation maintenance field. A letter of recommendation from an NBAA Member Company representative is encouraged.

Award: Scholarship for use in freshman, sophomore, junior, or senior years; not renewable. *Number:* 2. *Amount:* $2500.

Eligibility Requirements: Applicant must be enrolled or expecting to enroll full-time at a two-year or technical institution or university. Available to U.S. citizens.

Application Requirements: Application form, application form may be submitted online, essay. *Deadline:* July 26.

Contact: Molly Hitch
Phone: 202-783-9353
E-mail: scholarships@nbaa.org

UAA JANICE K. BARDEN AVIATION SCHOLARSHIP

Minimum of $1000 scholarships for students officially enrolled in NBAA/UAA programs. Must be U.S. citizen, officially enrolled in an aviation-related program with 3.0 minimum GPA. Include with application an essay describing the applicant's interest and goals for a career in the business aviation industry, and a letter of recommendation from member of aviation department faculty at institution where applicant is enrolled.

Award: Scholarship for use in sophomore, junior, senior, graduate, or postgraduate years; not renewable. *Amount:* $1000.

Eligibility Requirements: Applicant must be age 18 and over and enrolled or expecting to enroll full-time at a two-year institution or university. Available to U.S. citizens.

Application Requirements: Application form, application form may be submitted online, essay. *Deadline:* January 10.

Contact: Molly Hitch
Phone: 202-783-9353
E-mail: scholarships@nbaa.org

NATIONAL COLLEGIATE CANCER FOUNDATION

http://collegiatecancer.org/

NATIONAL COLLEGIATE CANCER FOUNDATION SCHOLARSHIPS

The National Collegiate Cancer Foundation was established to provide services and support to young adults whose lives have been impacted by cancer and who have continued with their education throughout treatment or after their treatment. The NCCF Survivor Scholarship Program $1,000 competitive awards will be judged based on the criteria listed below. Applicants must meet all of the requirements listed: 1. Must be a cancer survivor or current patient; 2. Must be between the ages of 18-35. An exception will be made if you are 17 and entering college in the fall following application; 3. U.S. citizen or permanent resident; 4. Attending or planning to attend an accredited college, university or vocational institution in pursuit of an Associate, Bachelor, Master's, doctorate or certificate. Applicants will be evaluated based on six criteria: displaying a "Will Win" attitude with respect to his or her cancer experience; quality of essays; financial need; overall story of cancer survivorship; commitment to education; quality of recommendations. The National Collegiate Cancer Foundation is proud to provide financial assistance to young adults pursuing their education who have lost a parent or guardian to cancer. The Legacy Scholarship Program $1,000 competitive awards will be judged based on the criteria listed below. Applicants must meet all of the requirements listed below: 1. Must have lost a parent or guardian to cancer; 2. Must be between the ages of 18-35. An exception will be made if you are 17 and entering college; 3. U.S. citizen or permanent resident; 4. Attending or planning to attend an accredited college, university, or vocational institution in pursuit of an Associate, Bachelor, Master's, doctorate or certificate. Applicants will be evaluated based on the following criteria: journey, encouragement, financial need, notable accomplishments, quality of recommendations.

Award: Scholarship for use in freshman, sophomore, junior, senior, graduate, or postgraduate years; not renewable. *Number:* 50. *Amount:* $1000.

Eligibility Requirements: Applicant must be age 17-35 and enrolled or expecting to enroll full- or part-time at a two-year or four-year or technical institution or university. Available to U.S. citizens.

Application Requirements: Application form, essay, financial need analysis. *Deadline:* May 15.

Contact: Meghan Rodgers
National Collegiate Cancer Foundation
8334 N. Brook Lane
Bethesda, MD 20814
Phone: 240-515-6262
E-mail: info@collegiatecancer.org

NATIONAL EXPRESS AUTO TRANSPORT

https://nxautotransport.com

NATIONAL EXPRESS AUTO TRANSPORT SCHOLARSHIP

Those wishing to apply must submit 1000 words or more regarding auto transport. Examples of this type of writing would include but not be limited to topics such as open carrier transport, enclosed auto transport, door-to-door car shipping, classic cars, exotic cars, green auto transport solutions, to name a few that are related to the industry. Applicants are encouraged to dig deep when making these essays. You can provide interviews, links to authoritative sources, etc. Each submission will be placed on this page with attribution to the author. The work must be completely original and not submitted or be found anywhere else. Any plagiarized / copied articles will be rejected. Applicants are also encouraged to share their article link as much as possible through social media or through other venues that will help the article gain traction and be seen by others. Winners will have their submission converted to a blog post with them as a guest author on our site using that same url and it will remain on our site the the main blog. The submissions for those that did not win but are well written will remain on our scholarship page as well. https://nxautotransport.com/scholarship

Award: Scholarship for use in freshman, sophomore, junior, senior, graduate, or postgraduate years; not renewable. *Number:* 2. *Amount:* $400–$1100.

Eligibility Requirements: Applicant must be age 18-99 and enrolled or expecting to enroll full- or part-time at a two-year or four-year or technical institution or university. Available to U.S. citizens.

Application Requirements: Essay. *Deadline:* February 4.

Contact: Mr. Carl Rodriguez, General Manager
National Express Auto Transport
7950 NW 53rd Street
#337
MiamI, FL 33173
Phone: 800-284-7177 Ext. 404
Fax: 305-459-3305
E-mail: admin@neatransport.com

NATIONAL FOUNDATION FOR WOMEN LEGISLATORS

http://www.womenlegislators.org/

NFWL NRA SCHOLARSHIP

For 20 years now, the National Foundation for Women Legislators and the National Rifle Association have joined forces for the Annual Bill of Rights Essay Scholarship Contest, which provides six female high school juniors or seniors a $3,000 college scholarship, an all-expense-paid trip to NFWL's Annual Conference, and an award that will be presented at the event. To apply for the scholarship, students must write an essay on one of three topics announced each spring, get a letter of recommendation from a currently elected woman (on the state, county, or municipal level), receive a letter of recommendation from a school employee, and submit a resume. The essay topics change each year but always pertain to the constitution. For more information, students should visit https://www.womenlegislators.org/programs/scholarships/.

Award: Scholarship for use in freshman year; not renewable. *Number:* 6. *Amount:* $3000.

Eligibility Requirements: Applicant must be age 13-19; enrolled or expecting to enroll full-time at a two-year or four-year institution or university and female. Available to U.S. citizens.

Application Requirements: Application form, essay. *Deadline:* July 14.

Contact: Jody Thomas, Executive Director
National Foundation for Women Legislators
1727 King Street
Suite 300
Alexandria, VA 22314
Phone: 703-518-7931
E-mail: nfwl@womenlegislators.org

NATIONAL HEMOPHILIA FOUNDATION

http://www.hemophilia.org/

KEVIN CHILD SCHOLARSHIP

Scholarship applicants must be individuals diagnosed with either hemophilia A or B, and a high school senior with aspirations of attending an institute of higher education (college, university or vocational-technical school), a college student already pursuing a post-secondary education, or a student in a graduate-level program. Interested students need to submit an application along with a current official transcript of their grades and one letter of recommendation from a person familiar with their personal and academic achievements (ex. teacher, mentor). The Kevin Child Scholarship recipient will be chosen on the basis of their academic performance, participation in school or community activities and the personal application essay detailing their educational and career goals.

Award: Scholarship for use in freshman, sophomore, junior, senior, or graduate years; not renewable. *Number:* 1. *Amount:* up to $1000.

Eligibility Requirements: Applicant must be enrolled or expecting to enroll full- or part-time at a two-year or four-year or technical institution or university. Available to U.S. citizens.

Application Requirements: Application form, community service, essay, recommendations or references, transcript. *Deadline:* June 3.

Contact: NHF/HANDI
National Hemophilia Foundation
116 West 32nd Street, 11th Floor
New York, NY 10001-3212
Phone: 212-328-3700 Ext. 2
E-mail: handi@hemophilia.org

NATIONAL JUNIOR ANGUS ASSOCIATION

http://www.angus.org/njaa/

AMERICAN ANGUS AUXILIARY SCHOLARSHIP

Scholarship available to graduating high school senior. May apply only in one state. Any unmarried girl or unmarried boy recommended by a state or regional Auxiliary is eligible.

Award: Scholarship for use in freshman year; not renewable. *Number:* 10. *Amount:* $1000–$14,000.

Eligibility Requirements: Applicant must be high school student; planning to enroll or expecting to enroll full-time at a two-year or four-year or technical institution or university and single. Available to U.S. and Canadian citizens.

Application Requirements: Application form, entry in a contest, personal photograph, recommendations or references, test scores, transcript. *Deadline:* May 1.

Contact: Mrs. Anne Lampe, American Angus Auxiliary Scholarship Chairman
National Junior Angus Association
5201 East Road 110
Scott City, KS 67871
Phone: 620-872-3915

NATIONAL PRESS FOUNDATION

http://www.nationalpress.org/

EVERT CLARK/SETH PAYNE AWARD

Award to recognize outstanding reporting and writing in any field of science. Limited to non-technical, print journalism only. Articles published in newspapers (including college newspapers), magazines, and newsletters are eligible. Both freelancers and staff writers are eligible. THIS IS FOR WRITERS 30 YEARS OF AGE OR YOUNGER.,

Award: Prize for use in freshman, sophomore, junior, senior, graduate, or postgraduate years; not renewable. *Number:* 1,000.

Eligibility Requirements: Applicant must be age 30 or under and enrolled or expecting to enroll full- or part-time at a two-year or four-year or technical institution or university. Available to U.S. and Canadian citizens.

Application Requirements: Application form, portfolio. *Deadline:* June 30.

Contact: Dianeq McGurgan, Administrator
National Press Foundation
PO Box 910
Hedgesville, WV 25427
Phone: 304-754-6786
E-mail: diane@casw.org

NATIONAL SOCIETY DAUGHTERS OF THE AMERICAN REVOLUTION

http://www.dar.org/

MILDRED NUTTING NURSING SCHOLARSHIP

A one-time $2,000 scholarship for two students who are in financial need and who have been accepted or are currently enrolled in an accredited school of nursing. A letter of acceptance into the Nursing Program or the transcript stating that the applicant is in the Nursing Program must be enclosed with the application. Preference will be given to candidates from the Lowell, MA area.

Award: Scholarship for use in freshman, sophomore, junior, or senior years; not renewable. *Number:* 2. *Amount:* $2000.

Eligibility Requirements: Applicant must be enrolled or expecting to enroll full-time at a two-year institution or university. Available to U.S. citizens.

Application Requirements: Application form, application form may be submitted online, essay, financial need analysis. *Deadline:* February 15.

Contact: Lakeisha Graham, Manager, Office of the Reporter General
Phone: 202-628-1776
Fax: 202-879-3348
E-mail: nsdarscholarships@dar.org

OCCUPATIONAL/PHYSICAL THERAPY SCHOLARSHIP

The Occupational/Physical Therapy Scholarship, in the amount of $2,000, is awarded to two students who are in financial need and have been accepted or are attending an accredited school of occupational therapy (including art, music, or physical therapy).

Award: Scholarship for use in freshman, sophomore, junior, senior, or graduate years; not renewable. *Number:* 2. *Amount:* $1000.

Eligibility Requirements: Applicant must be enrolled or expecting to enroll full- or part-time at a two-year institution or university. Available to U.S. citizens.

Application Requirements: Application form, application form may be submitted online, essay, financial need analysis. *Deadline:* February 15.

Contact: Lakeisha Graham, Manager, Office of the Reporter General
Phone: 202-628-1776
Fax: 202-879-3348
E-mail: nsdarscholarships@dar.org

NATIONAL SOCIETY FOR HISTOTECHNOLOGY

http://nsh.org/

IRWIN S. LERNER STUDENT SCHOLARSHIPS

Student scholarships support the educational endeavors of aspiring histotechnologists.

Award: Scholarship for use in freshman, sophomore, junior, or senior years; not renewable. *Number:* 5. *Amount:* $500.

Eligibility Requirements: Applicant must be enrolled or expecting to enroll full- or part-time at a two-year or four-year institution or university. Available to U.S. and non-U.S. citizens.

Application Requirements: Application form. *Deadline:* March 1.

Contact: Natalie Paskoski
Phone: 4435354060
E-mail: natalie@nsh.org

NATIONAL SOCIETY OF NEWSPAPER COLUMNISTS EDUCATION FOUNDATION

https://columnisteducation.org/

DEAR ABBY COLLEGE COLUMNIST SCHOLARSHIP CONTEST

Undergraduates (including seniors) writing bylined general interest, editorial or specialized (humor, sports, business, arts, culture, etc.) columns appearing in print or online editions of college publications.

Award: Scholarship for use in freshman, sophomore, junior, or senior years; not renewable. *Number:* 3–5. *Amount:* $5000.

Eligibility Requirements: Applicant must be enrolled or expecting to enroll full- or part-time at a two-year or four-year institution or university. Available to U.S. and non-U.S. citizens.

Application Requirements: Application form. *Deadline:* June 29.

Contact: Mike Leonard, Scholarship chair
National Society of Newspaper Columnists Education Foundation
818 S. Park Ave.
Bloomington, IN 47401
E-mail: leonardbtown@gmail.com

NATIONAL SOCIETY OF PROFESSIONAL ENGINEERS

http://www.nspe.org/

NSPE EDUCATION FOUNDATION AUXILIARY LEGACY SCHOLARSHIP

The NSPE Education Foundation Auxiliary Legacy Scholarship is awarded annually to a female undergraduate entering or continuing their junior year of a four-year ABET-accredited engineering program. The scholarship is awarded in one disbursement of $2,500 at the beginning of the junior year.

Award: Scholarship for use in junior or senior years; not renewable. *Number:* 1. *Amount:* $2500.

Eligibility Requirements: Applicant must be enrolled or expecting to enroll at an institution or university and female. Available to U.S. citizens.

Application Requirements: Application form, essay. *Deadline:* March 1.

NSPE EDUCATION FOUNDATION AUXILIARY LEGACY SCHOLARSHIP

The NSPE Education Foundation Auxiliary Legacy Scholarship is awarded annually to a female undergraduate entering or continuing their junior year of a four-year ABET-accredited engineering program. The scholarship is awarded in one disbursement of $2,500 at the beginning of the junior year.

Award: Scholarship for use in junior year; renewable. *Number:* 1. *Amount:* $2500.

Eligibility Requirements: Applicant must be enrolled or expecting to enroll at an institution or university. Available to U.S. citizens.

Application Requirements: Application form, essay. *Deadline:* March 1.

NAVAL SERVICE TRAINING COMMAND/NROTC

http://www.nrotc.navy.mil/

NROTC SCHOLARSHIP PROGRAM

Scholarships are based on merit and are awarded through a highly competitive national selection process. NROTC scholarships pay for college tuition, fees, uniforms, a book stipend, a monthly allowance and other financial benefits. Room and board expenses are not covered. Scholarship nominees must be medically qualified. Upon graduation scholarship recipients have an obligation of eight years commissioned service, five of which must be active duty. For more information, visit our website at https://www.nrotc.navy.mil.

Award: Scholarship for use in freshman, sophomore, junior, or senior years; renewable. *Number:* 2,400–2,900.

Eligibility Requirements: Applicant must be age 17-23 and enrolled or expecting to enroll full-time at a four-year institution or university. Available to U.S. citizens.

Application Requirements: Application form, essay, interview, recommendations or references, test scores, transcript. *Deadline:* January 31.

Contact: NROTC Scholarship Selection Office (OD2)
   Phone: 800-628-7682
   E-mail: pnsc_nrotc.scholarship@navy.mil

NEEDHAM & COMPANY SEPTEMBER 11TH SCHOLARSHIP FUND
http://www.needhamco.com/

NEEDHAM & COMPANY SEPTEMBER 11TH SCHOLARSHIP FUND

The Fund is designed to benefit the children and dependents of the victims who lost their lives as a result of the September 11th, 2001 terror attacks. The purpose of the Fund is to ensure that the victims' children are provided with an opportunity for a private secondary and/or college-level education. Awarding of funds is based upon a combination of the applicant's financial need, scholastic abilities, and community/civic involvement. To be considered for an award, an applicant must have a current cumulative GPA of 2.50 or equivalent, and household pre-September 11th adjusted gross income must be less than $125,000. Applications are reviewed on a case-by-case basis in an objective, non-discriminatory manner.

Award: Scholarship for use in freshman, sophomore, junior, senior, or graduate years; not renewable. *Number:* 20–50. *Amount:* $1500–$6000.

Eligibility Requirements: Applicant must be enrolled or expecting to enroll full- or part-time at a two-year or four-year or technical institution or university. Available to U.S. citizens.

Application Requirements: Application form, essay, financial need analysis. *Deadline:* July 1.

Contact: Ms. Kathleen Mumma, Secretary and Treasurer
   Needham & Company September 11th Scholarship Fund
   The Needham Group, Inc.
   250 Park Avenue, 10th Floor
   New York, NY 10177
   Phone: 212-705-0293
   E-mail: kmumma@needhamco.com

NERDIFY
https://gonerdify.com/

NERDY BOT SCHOLARSHIP

High school and university students from all over the world are eligible to participate. To participate send your essay to scholarship@nerdy-bot.com. The essay should be written in English and contain no more than 500 words. Number of entries is limited. One person can send only one essay. Submitted essays should not contain any form of plagiarism. In case of the plagiarism detections the entry will be disqualified without any prior notice. We will evaluate your content, grammar and writing skills. Therefore, before, submitting the application, you should take your time to edit and review your essay thoroughly. Your essay should be authentic; polished up in terms of structure, style and grammar; demonstrate depth of your ideas. Three essays with the highest score based on the criteria above will win the Nerdy Bot essay contest. The results will be published on the website and on our official Facebook page. Only the scholarship winners will be contacted by Nerdify team members via email.

Award: Scholarship for use in freshman, sophomore, junior, senior, graduate, or postgraduate years; renewable. *Number:* 3. *Amount:* $1000.

Eligibility Requirements: Applicant must be enrolled or expecting to enroll full- or part-time at a four-year institution or university. Available to U.S. and non-U.S. citizens.

Application Requirements: Essay. *Deadline:* February 28.

Contact: Nerdify Scholarship Committee
   Nerdify
   995 Market Street
   San Francisco, CA 94103
   Phone: 1224-444-6373
   E-mail: scholarship@nerdy-bot.com

NEXTSTEPU
http://www.nextstepu.com/

WIN FREE COLLEGE TUITION GIVEAWAY

NextStepU.com will award one $2,500 scholarship to one randomly selected winner twice a year. Applicants must enter online at http://www.nextstepu.com/winfreetuition. Winner must be enrolled in college within 3 years of when the prize is awarded. DEADLINE (1): June 30 DEADLINE (2): December 31.

Award: Scholarship for use in freshman, sophomore, junior, senior, or graduate years; not renewable. *Number:* 2. *Amount:* $2500.

Eligibility Requirements: Applicant must be age 15 and over and enrolled or expecting to enroll full- or part-time at a two-year or four-year or technical institution or university. Available to U.S. and Canadian citizens.

Application Requirements: Application form. *Deadline:* continuous.

Contact: Web Department
   E-mail: webcopy@nextstepu.com

NICHE
http://www.niche.com

$2,000 NO ESSAY SCHOLARSHIP

Scholarships don't get easier than this. Simply complete the form (found here https://colleges.niche.com/scholarship/no-essay-scholarship/), and you could be the next winner! No GPA, no essay—apply in minutes! The scholarship is awarded monthly, so make sure you apply every month!

Award: Scholarship for use in freshman, sophomore, junior, senior, graduate, or postgraduate years; not renewable. *Number:* 12. *Amount:* $2000.

Eligibility Requirements: Applicant must be age 13 and over and enrolled or expecting to enroll full- or part-time at a two-year or four-year or technical institution or university. Available to U.S. citizens.

Application Requirements: Application form. *Deadline:* continuous.

Contact: Karisa Fernandez
   Phone: 4124508840
   E-mail: kfernandez@niche.com

NITRO COLLEGE
https://www.nitrocollege.com/

$2,018 NITRO COLLEGE SCHOLARSHIP

Nitro cares about providing you the resources you need to successfully navigate financing college. That's why we're offering you the opportunity to earn a $2,018 scholarship from Nitro. We know that college is a big step forward in achieving your goals and we want to help you get there using all the tools Nitro has to offer. To apply, complete the scholarship survey questions, participate in our social media activity, and submit the application when completed.

Award: Scholarship for use in freshman, sophomore, junior, senior, or graduate years; not renewable. *Number:* 1. *Amount:* $2018.

Eligibility Requirements: Applicant must be enrolled or expecting to enroll full-time at a two-year or four-year institution or university. Available to U.S. citizens.

Application Requirements: Application form. *Deadline:* continuous.

Contact: Mike Brown
   Nitro College
   1105 North Market Street, Suite 1600
   Wilmington, DE 19801
   E-mail: support@nitrocollege.com

NO BULL SPORTS
http://nobullsports.org/

NO BULL SPORTS SCHOLARSHIP

No Bull Sports is a non-profit organization dedicated to uniting, educating, and empowering young women. When we set out to build a community of female athletes from all walks of life, a cornerstone of our mission was to offer scholarships to deserving high school students. No Bull Sports provides smart, trailblazing, talented young women the financial resources they need to achieve their academic and athletic goals. No Bull Sports is excited to award our quarterly scholarships of $5,000 in March, June, and December of 2017 to a deserving female high school sophomore, junior or senior to pursue her dreams on and off the field. We will award $15,000 worth of scholarships over the course of a calendar year; awarded 3xs/year, each scholarship is worth $5,000.

Award: Scholarship for use in freshman year; not renewable.

Eligibility Requirements: Applicant must be high school student and planning to enroll or expecting to enroll full- or part-time at a two-year or four-year or technical institution or university. Available to U.S. citizens.

Application Requirements: Application form, essay. *Deadline:* continuous.

Contact: Bridget W.
No Bull Sports
653 W Fallbrook Ave. #101
Fresno, CA 93711
Phone: 877-307-1451
E-mail: hello@nobullsports.org

NOPLAG PLAGIARISM CHECKER

http://noplag.com/

NOPLAG SCHOLARSHIP ESSAY CONTEST

We are happy to announce the start of the Noplag Scholarship Essay contest. In comparison with other writing contests our goal is to help you become successful and nowadays proper education is a key component. We hope that our aid in the amount of $3500 will help the winner in his education in full or partially. Plus, you will have a good chance to test your writing skills and maybe pump them up by participating in this contest.

Award: Scholarship for use in freshman, sophomore, junior, or senior years; not renewable. *Number:* 3. *Amount:* $300–$2500.

Eligibility Requirements: Applicant must be age 16 and over and enrolled or expecting to enroll full- or part-time at a two-year or four-year or technical institution or university. Available to U.S. and non-U.S. citizens.

Application Requirements: Application form, essay. *Deadline:* June 25.

Contact: CEO
E-mail: aleks@noplag.com

NORTH CAROLINA STATE DEPARTMENT OF HEALTH AND HUMAN SERVICES/DIVISION OF SOCIAL SERVICES

http://www.ncdhhs.gov/dss

NORTH CAROLINA EDUCATION AND TRAINING VOUCHER PROGRAM

Four-year scholarship for NC foster youth and former foster youth. Must have been accepted into or be enrolled in a degree, certificate or other accredited program at a college, university, technical or vocational school and show progress towards a degree or certificate. Must be a U.S. citizen or qualified non-citizen. Applications available at: www.statevoucher.org.

Award: Grant for use in freshman, sophomore, junior, or senior years; renewable. *Amount:* $1–$5000.

Eligibility Requirements: Applicant must be age 18-23 and enrolled or expecting to enroll part-time at a two-year or four-year or technical institution or university. Available to U.S. citizens.

Application Requirements: Application form, essay. *Deadline:* continuous.

Contact: Ms. Danielle McConaga, NC DSS LINKS Independent Living Coordinator
North Carolina State Department of Health and Human Services/Division of Social Services
820 South Boylan Drive
Raleigh, NC 27603
Phone: 919-527-6343
E-mail: Danielle.McConaga@dhhs.nc.gov

NORTH DAKOTA FARMERS UNION

http://www.ndfu.org

HUBERT K. & JOANN SEYMOUR SCHOLARSHIP

Must be a Farmers Union members to apply. Scholarship is open to high school seniors pursuing a two- or four-year degree in any area of study.

Award: Scholarship for use in freshman year; not renewable. *Number:* 1–2. *Amount:* $1000–$2000.

Eligibility Requirements: Applicant must be high school student and planning to enroll or expecting to enroll full-time at a two-year or four-year institution. Available to U.S. citizens.

Application Requirements: Application form, community service, essay. *Deadline:* April 1.

Contact: Melissa Miller
North Dakota Farmers Union
20 F Street NW, Suite 300
Washington, DC 20001
Phone: 202-559-9882
E-mail: melissamiller@nfudc.org

NORTH DAKOTA FARMERS UNION SCHOLARSHIP

Applicants must be pursuing a career important to rural America, but not limited to agribusiness, farm operation or production agriculture. Must be a Farmers Union member to apply.

Award: Scholarship for use in freshman, sophomore, junior, or senior years; not renewable. *Number:* 1–10. *Amount:* $500.

Eligibility Requirements: Applicant must be enrolled or expecting to enroll full-time at a two-year or four-year or technical institution or university. Available to U.S. citizens.

Application Requirements: Application form, financial need analysis. *Deadline:* January 31.

Contact: Pam Musland
North Dakota Farmers Union
1415 12th Avenue, SE
Jamestown, ND 58401
Phone: 800-366-8331

NORTHWESTERN MUTUAL FOUNDATION

http://www.scholarshipamerica.org

NORTHWESTERN MUTUAL CHILDHOOD CANCER SURVIVOR SCHOLARSHIP

Ten $5,000 scholarship renewable up to one year or until a Bachelor's degree is earned, whichever occurs first, on the basis of maintaining full-time enrollment and a cumulative GPA of 2.5 on a 4.0 scale (or equivalent). The Northwestern Mutual Childhood Cancer Sibling Scholarship program assists siblings of individuals affected by childhood cancer, and who plan to continue their education in college or vocational school programs. The scholarship program will award up to 10 renewable $5,000 scholarships. To apply, students must be U.S. citizens and siblings of individuals who are in current treatment, have survived or passed away from pediatric childhood cancer. Applicants must be age 25 or under and planning to enroll in full-time undergraduate study at an accredited two- or four-year college, university or vocational-technical school for the entire upcoming academic year. Applicants must have a minimum grade point average of 2.5 on a 4.0 scale (or the equivalent) and demonstrate financial need.

Award: Scholarship for use in freshman, sophomore, junior, or senior years; renewable. *Number:* 10. *Amount:* $5000.

Eligibility Requirements: Applicant must be age 25 or under and enrolled or expecting to enroll full-time at a two-year or four-year or technical institution or university. Available to U.S. citizens.

Application Requirements: Application form. *Deadline:* March 30.

Contact: Program Manager
Northwestern Mutual Foundation
One Scholarship Way
Saint Peter, MN 56082
Phone: 800-537-4180
E-mail: jsowder@scholarshipamerica.org

NURSERECRUITER.COM

https://www.nurserecruiter.com

NURSERECRUITER.COM SCHOLARSHIP

For over 18 years, NurseRecruiter.com has connected hundreds of thousands of nurses with jobs nationwide. We're all aware of the nursing shortage and its impact on healthcare in America and we want to help. As part of our commitment to attract the best and the brightest to the nursing profession we are proud to announce that we are founding the NurseRecruiter.com Scholarship with an initial $10,000 in nursing scholarships to people who want to further their education and make the world a better place at the same time. Do you know someone who wants to become a nurse? If you know someone interested in pursuing a career in nursing please let them know about our scholarship, we would be happy to help them along their path to becoming a nurse. It is the policy and practice of the NurseRecruiter.com scholarship program to treat all scholarship applicants with dignity and respect and to provide equal opportunity to all persons without regard to color, race, religion, sex, national origin, citizenship, age, disability, marital status, pregnancy, sexual orientation, military status or any other category protected by law.

Award: Scholarship for use in freshman, sophomore, junior, senior, graduate, or postgraduate years; not renewable. *Number:* 1–10. *Amount:* $1000–$5000.

Eligibility Requirements: Applicant must be enrolled or expecting to enroll full- or part-time at a two-year or four-year institution or university. Available to U.S. and non-U.S. citizens.

Application Requirements: Application form, essay. *Deadline:* continuous.

Contact: Peter Frouman, Scholarship Coordinator
NurseRecruiter.com
c/o Nurse Recruiter
113 Cherry Street, #26760
Seattle, WA 98104
Phone: 800-243-3407
Fax: 866-608-1781
E-mail: support@nurserecruiter.com

ONE LOVE FOUNDATION

http://www.joinonelove.org

ONE LOVE FOUNDATION PETS VS. PARTNERS SCHOLARSHIP

Pets can and will take advantage of our love. And we forgive them because they're cute and fluffy and don't know any better. But people should know better. Help us highlight the gray areas between love and control by creating your own #OKforpetsnotpartners meme the educates others about unhealthy relationship behaviors. Yep,.. it's that fun and easy! www.petsvspartners.com

Award: Scholarship for use in freshman, sophomore, junior, senior, graduate, or postgraduate years; not renewable. *Number:* 3. *Amount:* $500.

Eligibility Requirements: Applicant must be age 18-26 and enrolled or expecting to enroll full- or part-time at a two-year or four-year or technical institution or university. Available to U.S. and non-U.S. citizens.

Application Requirements: *Deadline:* December 31.

Contact: April Wright
One Love Foundation
119 Pondfield Road
PO Box 368
Bronxville, NY 10708
E-mail: thatsnotlove@joinonelove.org

ONLINECOLLEGEPLANNING.COM

http://onlinecollegeplanning.com

ONLINECOLLEGEPLANNINGSCHOLARSHIP.COM

This scholarship is part of our mission to make college accessible to students. We give two scholarships a year. The scholarship requires a 250 word essay on the biggest influence in making you want to go to college. Value of the scholarship is $1,000. Applications are only accepted online and can be submitted at http://onlinecollegeplanningscholarship.com/

Award: Scholarship for use in freshman year; not renewable. *Number:* 2. *Amount:* $1000.

Eligibility Requirements: Applicant must be high school student; age 13-21 and planning to enroll or expecting to enroll full-time at a four-year institution or university. Available to U.S. citizens.

Application Requirements: Application form, essay. *Deadline:* June 30.

Contact: Mr. James Maroney
OnlineCollegePlanning.com
56 Payne Road
Lebanon, NJ 08833
E-mail: james@onlinecollegeplanningscholarship.com

OPTIMAL

http://www.sreducationgroup.org

COMMUNITY COLLEGE SCHOLARSHIP

Community college can be one of the most cost-effective options for people looking to start or change their careers; however, tuition can still be a large burden for many individuals. To help those with high financial need, SR Education Group is awarding $2,500 community college scholarships. To provide our judges with a true understanding of each applicant, he or she must answer two open-ended, personal, and thought-provoking questions. The students whose responses are the most persuasive, compelling, and well-written, as judged by our panel, will be considered finalists.

Award: Scholarship for use in freshman, sophomore, junior, senior, graduate, or postgraduate years; not renewable. *Number:* 2–6. *Amount:* $2500.

Eligibility Requirements: Applicant must be age 17 and over and enrolled or expecting to enroll full- or part-time at a two-year or technical institution. Available to U.S. citizens.

Application Requirements: Application form. *Deadline:* continuous.

Contact: SR Education Group
Kirkland, WA 98033
Phone: 425-605-8898
Fax: 425-968-9384
E-mail: scholarships@sreducationgroup.org

OREGON OFFICE OF STUDENT ACCESS AND COMPLETION

https://oregonstudentaid.gov/

BEN SELLING SCHOLARSHIP

Award for Oregon residents enrolling as undergraduate sophomores, juniors, or seniors. Minimum college GPA of 3.5 required. Recipients must attend any Oregon or U.S. Rabbinical public and nonprofit college. Apply/compete annually.

Award: Scholarship for use in sophomore, junior, or senior years; not renewable.

Eligibility Requirements: Applicant must be enrolled or expecting to enroll full-time at a two-year or four-year institution. Available to U.S. citizens.

Application Requirements: Application form, essay, financial need analysis, transcript. *Deadline:* March 1.

Contact: Melissa Adams, Scholarship Processing Coordinator
Phone: 541-687-7409
E-mail: melissa.adams@state.or.us

BETTER A LIFE SCHOLARSHIP

Scholarship award available to single parents age 17-25. High schools seniors must have at least 3.0 GPA and college students must have at least a 2.5 GPA or GED equivalent. For use at Oregon public and nonprofit colleges and universities. Applicants may not already possess a Bachelor's degree. May reapply for one additional year of funding. Financial need may or may not be considered.

Award: Scholarship for use in freshman, sophomore, junior, or senior years; not renewable.

Eligibility Requirements: Applicant must be age 17-25; enrolled or expecting to enroll full- or part-time at a two-year or four-year institution or university; single and studying in Oregon. Available to U.S. citizens.

Application Requirements: Application form, financial need analysis. *Deadline:* March 1.

Contact: Melissa Adams, Scholarship Processing Coordinator
Phone: 541-687-7409
E-mail: melissa.adams@state.or.us

OREGON TRAWL COMMISSION JOE EASLEY MEMORIAL SCHOLARSHIP

Award for students in any accredited U.S. college or university who are dependents of licensed Oregon Trawl fishermen or crew. Full-time enrollment required. Based on financial need.

Award: Scholarship for use in freshman, sophomore, junior, or senior years; not renewable.

Eligibility Requirements: Applicant must be enrolled or expecting to enroll full-time at a four-year institution or university. Available to U.S. citizens.

Application Requirements: Application form, financial need analysis. *Deadline:* March 1.

Contact: Melissa Adams, Scholarship Processing Coordinator
Phone: 541-687-7409
E-mail: melissa.adams@state.or.us

PITB SERVICES SCHOLARSHIP

Scholarship for PITB Services members or dependents of PITB Services members. Must enroll at least half time.

Award: Scholarship for use in freshman, sophomore, junior, or senior years; not renewable.

Eligibility Requirements: Applicant must be enrolled or expecting to enroll full- or part-time at a four-year institution or university. Available to U.S. citizens.

Application Requirements: Application form. *Deadline:* March 1.

Contact: Melissa Adams, Scholarship Processing Coordinator
Phone: 541-687-7409
E-mail: melissa.adams@state.or.us

PITB TRANSPORTATION SCHOLARSHIP

Scholarship for high school graduates (including home schooled graduates) who are dependents of PITB Transportation employees or dependents of PITB Transportation members. Must be enrolled in college at least half-time and have a minimum 3.0 GPA.

Award: Scholarship for use in freshman, sophomore, junior, or senior years; not renewable.

Eligibility Requirements: Applicant must be enrolled or expecting to enroll full- or part-time at a four-year institution or university. Available to U.S. citizens.

Application Requirements: Application form. *Deadline:* March 1.

Contact: Melissa Adams, Scholarship Processing Coordinator
Phone: 541-687-7409
E-mail: melissa.adams@state.or.us

REGISTER-GUARD FEDERAL CREDIT UNION SCHOLARSHIP

Award is available to current members of the Register-Guard Federal Credit Union, or those eligible for membership, with preference in the following order: (1) current employees, independent contractors of The Register-Guard including members of their immediate families or households, (2) retired persons as pensioners or annuitants, (3) spouses of persons who died within membership, (4) organizations of such persons, (5) members of the Confederated Tribes of Grande Ronde or their immediate family members, and (6) employees or contracted employees of the law office of Donald Slayton and Alan Seglison or their immediate family members. Minimum 2.5 GPA, or GED of 2500+. Financial need may or may not be considered.

Award: Scholarship for use in freshman, sophomore, junior, or graduate years; not renewable.

Eligibility Requirements: Applicant must be enrolled or expecting to enroll full-time at a two-year or four-year institution or university. Available to U.S. citizens.

Application Requirements: Application form, essay, financial need analysis. *Deadline:* March 1.

Contact: Melissa Adams, Scholarship Processing Coordinator
Phone: 541-687-7409
E-mail: melissa.adams@state.or.us

ORGONE BIOPHYSICAL RESEARCH LABORATORY

http://www.orgonelab.org/hochberg.htm

LOU HOCHBERG-UNIVERSITY/COLLEGE ESSAY AWARDS

An award of up to $500 will be given for the best university/college-level student research paper, addressing Wilhelm Reich's sociological discoveries.

Award: Prize for use in freshman, sophomore, junior, senior, graduate, or postgraduate years; not renewable. *Number:* 1. *Amount:* $100–$500.

Eligibility Requirements: Applicant must be enrolled or expecting to enroll full- or part-time at a two-year or four-year or technical institution or university. Available to U.S. and Canadian citizens.

Application Requirements: Essay. *Deadline:* continuous.

Contact: James DeMeo, Director
E-mail: demeo@orgonelab.org

ORTHO DERMATOLOGICS

www.ortho-dermatologics.com

ORTHO DERMATOLOGICS ASPIRE HIGHER SCHOLARSHIPS

Ortho Dermatologics Aspire Higher Scholarships will award scholarships of up to $10,000 each to nine individual students who will be attending an undergraduate or graduate education program during the 2020 to 2021 school year. The scholarships recognize students who have been diagnosed and treated for a dermatologic condition and are pursuing a higher education degree. Three scholarships will be awarded in three different categories: Undergraduate Scholar Awards for students pursuing an undergraduate degree, Graduate Scholar Awards for students pursuing a graduate degree and Today's Woman Scholar Awards for students who are mothers pursuing either a graduate or undergraduate degree.

Award: Scholarship for use in freshman, sophomore, junior, senior, or graduate years; not renewable. *Number:* 9. *Amount:* $10,000.

Eligibility Requirements: Applicant must be enrolled or expecting to enroll full- or part-time at an institution or university. Available to U.S. citizens.

Application Requirements: Application form, application form may be submitted online, essay. *Deadline:* May 31.

Contact: Mark Smith, Executive Director
E-mail: mark.smith@ortho-dermatologics.com

OTA GUIDE

http://occupational-therapy-assistant.org/

COTA SCHOLARSHIP FOR OCCUPATIONAL THERAPY ASSISTANTS

The Occupational Therapy profession is experiencing a huge increase in demand. In an effort to encourage more bright students down the path to becoming a COTA to help serve this increase in demand, we created this scholarship for COTA students. Each year we will award one COTA student with a $500 scholarship.

Award: Scholarship for use in freshman, sophomore, junior, senior, graduate, or postgraduate years; not renewable. *Number:* 1–2. *Amount:* $1–$500.

Eligibility Requirements: Applicant must be enrolled or expecting to enroll full- or part-time at a two-year or four-year or technical institution or university. Available to U.S. and non-U.S. citizens.

Application Requirements: Essay. *Deadline:* December 1.

Contact: Kelly Clark
OTA Guide
2801 Oak Crest Avenue
Austin, TX 78704

OWEN SOFTWARE

http://www.pathevo.com/

$2,000 NO ESSAY SCHOLARSHIP

$2,000 "No Essay" Scholarship. Each quarter Pathevo Prep (Owen Software) awards $2,000 to a high school junior or senior upon acceptance in an accredited four year college or university. The award is a random drawing and will be announced to all entrants. The award is given four times a year, renewing quarterly.

Award: Scholarship for use in freshman year; renewable. *Number:* 1. *Amount:* $2000.

Eligibility Requirements: Applicant must be high school student and planning to enroll or expecting to enroll full-time at a four-year institution. Available to U.S. citizens.

Application Requirements: Driver's license. *Deadline:* December 31.

Contact: Susan Hughes
Owen Software
700 King Farm Blvd
#610
Rockville, MD 20850
Phone: 240-453-0030
E-mail: susan.hughes@pathevo.com

PAPERCHECK

https://www.papercheck.com/

PAPERCHECK, LLC—CHARLES SHAFAE' SCHOLARSHIP FUND

Awards one $1,000 scholarships each year to winners of the Papercheck essay contest. Must be enrolled at an accredited four-year college or university. Must maintain a cumulative GPA of at least 3.2. Scholarship guidelines available at https://www.papercheck.com/papercheck-scholarship/.

Award: Scholarship for use in freshman, sophomore, junior, or senior years; not renewable. *Number:* 1. *Amount:* $1000.

Eligibility Requirements: Applicant must be enrolled or expecting to enroll full-time at a four-year institution or university. Available to U.S. citizens.

Application Requirements: Application form, essay. *Deadline:* January 31.

Contact: Mr. Darren Shafae, Scholarship Coordinator
Papercheck
3905 State Street
Suite 7-516
Santa Barbara, CA 93105
Phone: 866-693-3348
E-mail: scholarships@papercheck.com

PARIAN LAW FIRM, LLC

https://westgalawyer.com/

CADE PARIAN EDUCATION EQUALITY SCHOLARSHIP

A 750-word creative essay on how to close the financial gap to education and why access to higher education is important for all.

Award: Scholarship for use in freshman, sophomore, junior, senior, graduate, or postgraduate years; not renewable. *Number:* 1. *Amount:* $1000.

Eligibility Requirements: Applicant must be enrolled or expecting to enroll full- or part-time at a two-year or four-year or technical institution or university. Available to U.S. citizens.

Application Requirements: Application form may be submitted online (https://westgalawyer.com/scholarship-2019/), essay, resume, transcript. *Deadline:* September 30.

Contact: Cade Parian
E-mail: marketing@westgalawyer.com

THE EDUCATIONAL JUSTICE SCHOLARSHIP

We are offering $1,000.00 to a student currently enrolled in a community college, junior college, undergraduate, or graduate program. The Education Equality Scholarship rewards hard-working individuals seeking future education, security, and financial stability. The Education Equality Scholarship is available regardless of a student's major selection and current educational year. For more information, please visit: https://westgalawyer.com/#scholarship

Award: Scholarship for use in freshman, sophomore, junior, senior, graduate, or postgraduate years; not renewable. *Number:* 1. *Amount:* $1000.

Eligibility Requirements: Applicant must be enrolled or expecting to enroll full- or part-time at a two-year or four-year or technical institution or university. Available to U.S. and non-U.S. citizens.

Application Requirements: Application form, essay. *Deadline:* May 15.

Contact: Cade Parian
E-mail: marketing@westgalawyer.com

PATIENT ADVOCATE FOUNDATION

http://www.patientadvocate.org/

SCHOLARSHIP FOR SURVIVORS

Four years after Patient Advocate Foundation's inception, founder Nancy Davenport-Ennis created Patient Advocate Foundation's Scholarship for Survivors program after witnessing multiple recurring counts of patients whose post-secondary education had been impacted due to their life-threatening, chronic or debilitating illness. Despite their condition, these students excelled academically, served the community, and demonstrated the drive and desire to attend college. The purpose of our scholarship program is to provide support to individuals, under the age of 25, who have been diagnosed with or treated for cancer and/or a chronic/life threatening disease within the past five years.

Award: Scholarship for use in freshman, sophomore, junior, senior, or graduate years; renewable. *Number:* 12. *Amount:* $3000.

Eligibility Requirements: Applicant must be age 25 or under and enrolled or expecting to enroll full-time at a two-year or four-year institution or university. Available to U.S. citizens.

Application Requirements: Application form, essay, financial need analysis. *Deadline:* February 25.

Contact: Ms. Shawn Nason, Director, Events, Travel, Admin Services
Patient Advocate Foundation
421 Butler Farm Road
Hampton, VA 23666
Phone: 800-532-5274
E-mail: scholarship@patientadvocate.org

PENNSYLVANIA HIGHER EDUCATION ASSISTANCE AGENCY

http://www.pheaa.org/

PENNSYLVANIA TARGETED INDUSTRY PROGRAM (PA-TIP)

The Pennsylvania General Assembly created PA-TIP in 2012 to prepare students with the skills in high demand by today's employers. The Program, which is funded by the Pennsylvania General Assembly and administered by PHEAA, provides awards to students enrolled in programs of study in Energy, Advanced Materials and Diversified Manufacturing, and Agriculture and Food Production. PA-TIP provides need-based awards up to $4,123 or 75% of the student's total direct educational costs after gift aid and employers' aid, whichever is less (approved veteran applicants may receive up to 100% of the student's total educational costs or the max award, whichever is less). Awards can be used to cover tuition, books, fees, supplies, and a $4,000 living expense allowance.

Award: Scholarship for use in freshman, sophomore, junior, or senior years; not renewable.

Eligibility Requirements: Applicant must be enrolled or expecting to enroll part-time at a two-year institution or university. Available to U.S. citizens.

Application Requirements: Application form, financial need analysis. *Deadline:* May 1.

Contact: Keith New, Director of Public Relations
Phone: 800-692-7392
E-mail: knew@pheaa.org

PHI BETA SIGMA FRATERNITY INC.

http://www.pbs1914.org/

PHI BETA SIGMA FRATERNITY NATIONAL PROGRAM OF EDUCATION

Scholarships are awarded to both graduate and undergraduate students. Applicants must have minimum 3.0 GPA.

Award: Scholarship for use in freshman, sophomore, junior, senior, or graduate years; not renewable.

Eligibility Requirements: Applicant must be enrolled or expecting to enroll full-time at a four-year institution or university and male. Available to U.S. citizens.

Application Requirements: Application form, essay, personal photograph, recommendations or references, resume, transcript. *Deadline:* June 15.

Contact: Emile Pitre, Chairman
Phi Beta Sigma Fraternity Inc.
2 Belmonte Circle, SW
Atlanta, GA 30311
Phone: 404-759-6827
E-mail: mikewhines@aol.com

PILOT INTERNATIONAL

https://www.pilotinternational.org/

BECKY BURROWS MEMORIAL SCHOLARSHIP

The Becky Burrows Memorial Scholarships are for graduate or undergraduate students who are re-entering the job market, beginning "second careers", or seeking to improve their professional skills for their current occupation by continuing their education in that field. Students must pursue courses of study that further Pilot International's mission to transform communities through education and service in the area of preparing youth for service, encouraging brain safety and health, and supporting those who care for others.

Award: Scholarship for use in freshman, sophomore, junior, senior, graduate, or postgraduate years; not renewable. *Number:* 1–5. *Amount:* $500–$1000.

Eligibility Requirements: Applicant must be enrolled or expecting to enroll full-time at an institution or university. Available to U.S. citizens.

Application Requirements: Application form, application form may be submitted online, community service, essay, financial need analysis, personal photograph. *Deadline:* March 15.

Contact: Founders Fund Specialist
Phone: 478-477-1208 Ext. 304
E-mail: piffscholarships@pilothq.org

KC INTERNATIONAL SCHOLARSHIP

Scholarship for International Students ONLY. The KC International Scholarship funded by an anonymous donor was established in 2017 to provide financial assistance to international students pursuing careers that further the mission of Pilot International by seeking to influence positive change in communities throughout the world. The applicant must have a record of active participation in volunteer service and show outstanding leadership ability. The applicant should reflect on their cumulative community service, leadership ability, and career choice when completing the application. Scholarships are based on community service, leadership roles, career choice, academic success, and application content. Scholarships are awarded for one academic year. Award amount will not exceed $2,500 per year for full time students. Two individual scholarships will be awarded each year. The applicant must be a full-time student and remain a full-time student for the duration of the scholarship

Award: Scholarship for use in freshman, sophomore, junior, or senior years; not renewable. *Amount:* $2500.

Eligibility Requirements: Applicant must be enrolled or expecting to enroll full-time at an institution or university. Available to citizens of countries other than the U.S. or Canada.

Application Requirements: Application form, application form may be submitted online, community service, essay, financial need analysis, personal photograph. *Deadline:* March 15.

Contact: Founders Fund Specialist
Pilot International
102 Preston Court
Macon, GA 31210
Phone: 478-4771208 Ext. 304
Fax: 478-4776978
E-mail: piffscholarships@pilothq.org

PINNACOL FOUNDATION

www.pinnacolfoundation.org

PINNACOL FOUNDATION SCHOLARSHIP PROGRAM

Our scholarship program ensures that the children of seriously injured and killed Colorado workers have the opportunity to pursue their dreams by continuing their education. Applicants must be the natural child, adopted child, stepchild or full dependent of a worker who was injured or killed in a compensable work-related accident during the course and scope of employment with a Colorado-based employer and was entitled to receive benefits under the Colorado Workers' Compensation Act. It doesn't matter which insurance company covered the parent's workers' compensation claim. The applicant must be between the ages of 16 and 25 at the time of the application deadline, have and maintain a minimum cumulative GPA of 2.0 or higher, have a high school diploma or GED, or be a high school senior. Doesn't have to be repaid. No specific school needs to be attended. It may be used for four-year, two-year or trade programs at accredited colleges, universities, community colleges and vocational schools. They average $4,500 per student per year, and may only be used for the costs of attending school.

Award: Scholarship for use in freshman, sophomore, junior, or senior years; renewable. *Number:* 100. *Amount:* $2500–$6500.

Eligibility Requirements: Applicant must be age 16-25 and enrolled or expecting to enroll full- or part-time at a two-year or four-year or technical institution or university. Available to U.S. citizens.

Application Requirements: Application form, essay, financial need analysis. *Deadline:* February 15.

Contact: Chris Sautter, Pinnacol Foundation Director
Pinnacol Foundation
7501 E. Lowry Blvd.
Denver, CO 80230
Phone: 303-361-4775 Ext. 4775
E-mail: pinnacol.foundation@pinnacol.com

PLAINTIFF RELIEF

http://plaintiffrelief.com/

PLAINTIFF RELIEF SCHOLARSHIP

We are excited to offer one $1,000 scholarship to a high school senior who demonstrates academic achievement, exhibits leadership ability, participates in community service activities, and demonstrates financial need. Applicants must be U.S. citizens or permanent residents and current high school seniors at the time of their application. Current college students are not eligible to apply.

Award: Scholarship for use in senior year; not renewable. *Number:* 1. *Amount:* $1000.

Eligibility Requirements: Applicant must be high school student and planning to enroll or expecting to enroll full-time at a four-year institution or university. Available to U.S. citizens.

Application Requirements: Application form. *Deadline:* November 1.

Contact: Alex Miller
Plaintiff Relief
3379 Peachtree Road NE, Suite 555
Atlanta, GA 30326
Phone: 866-301-0084
E-mail: alex@plaintiffrelief.com

POLSON AND POLSON, P.C.

https://www.polsonlawfirm.com/

POLSON & POLSON, P.C. CONQUERING ADVERSITY SCHOLARSHIP

The Polson & Polson, P.C. Conquering Adversity Scholarship is available to individuals currently enrolled in a course of study at any duly accredited community or junior college, undergraduate or graduate degree program anywhere in the United States. Also eligible are high school graduates or GED holders who are about to embark on college-level studies. For full details, please visit https://www.polsonlawfirm.com/#scholarship.

Award: Scholarship for use in freshman, sophomore, junior, senior, graduate, or postgraduate years; not renewable. *Number:* 1. *Amount:* $500.

Eligibility Requirements: Applicant must be enrolled or expecting to enroll full- or part-time at a two-year or four-year or technical institution or university. Available to U.S. and non-U.S. citizens.

Application Requirements: Application form may be submitted online (https://polsonlawfirm.com/scholarship), essay, resume, transcript. *Deadline:* October 31.

Contact: Mark Polson
E-mail: info@alabamaduidefense.com

POSITIVE COACHING ALLIANCE

https://positivecoach.org/

TRIPLE-IMPACT COMPETITOR SCHOLARSHIP

PCA awards scholarships of $1,000-$2,000 (depending on location) to high school athletes, based on their responses to questions pertaining to how they meet the standard defined in Elevating Your Game: Becoming a Triple-Impact Competitor by PCA Founder Jim Thompson. Eligibility extends to any high school junior residing anywhere in the U.S. and playing for a high school team or in club sports. All details can be found on our website and you may begin an application there as well.

Award: Scholarship for use in freshman year; not renewable. *Number:* 50–150. *Amount:* $1000–$2000.

Eligibility Requirements: Applicant must be high school student and planning to enroll or expecting to enroll full-time at a two-year or four-year institution. Available to U.S. citizens.

Application Requirements: Application form. *Deadline:* May 31.

Contact: Jennie Wulbrun, Program Administrator
Positive Coaching Alliance
1001 N. Rengstorff Avenue, Suite 100
Mountain View, CA 94043
Phone: 650-210-0815
E-mail: jennie_wulbrun@positivecoach.org

PRICE BENOWITZ LLP

http://pricebenowitz.com/

AMATO SANITA BRIGHTER FUTURE SCHOLARSHIP

For more information please visit https://criminallawpennsylvania.com/2017-amato-sanita-brighter-future-scholarship/

Award: Scholarship for use in freshman, sophomore, junior, senior, or graduate years; not renewable. *Number:* 1. *Amount:* $500.

Eligibility Requirements: Applicant must be enrolled or expecting to enroll full- or part-time at a two-year or four-year or technical institution or university. Available to U.S. citizens.

Application Requirements: Essay. *Deadline:* March 31.

Contact: Amato Sanita
E-mail: info@criminallawpennsylvania.com

ANGIE DIPIETRO WOMEN IN BUSINESS SCHOLARSHIP

This scholarship is available to any female student who is pursuing post-secondary education (community college, undergraduate college, graduate school, business school, or law school) at an accredited U.S. institution. Please visit http://marylandcriminallaws.com/#scholarship for more information on this opportunity.

Award: Scholarship for use in freshman, sophomore, junior, senior, or graduate years; not renewable. *Number:* 1. *Amount:* $500.

Eligibility Requirements: Applicant must be enrolled or expecting to enroll full- or part-time at a two-year or four-year institution or university and female. Available to U.S. citizens.

Application Requirements: Essay. *Deadline:* March 31.

Contact: Angie DiPietro
E-mail: info@marylandcriminallaws.com

KAREN RILEY PORTER GOOD WORKS SCHOLARSHIP

Karin Riley Porter believes strongly in advancing the cause of the criminal justice system and criminal defense services by ensuring that everyone within the Commonwealth of Virginia receives fair representation and that those who are dedicated to that calling can realize their full academic potential. For more information, please visit https://www.virginia-criminallawyer.com/#scholarship.

Award: Scholarship for use in freshman, sophomore, junior, senior, graduate, or postgraduate years; not renewable. *Number:* 1. *Amount:* $500.

Eligibility Requirements: Applicant must be enrolled or expecting to enroll full-time at a two-year or four-year institution or university. Available to U.S. and non-U.S. citizens.

Application Requirements: Application form may be submitted online (https://www.virginia-criminallawyer.com/2019-good-works-scholarship/), essay, resume, transcript. *Deadline:* October 15.

Contact: Karin Riley Porter
E-mail: scholarships@virginia-criminallawyer.com

KERRI CASTELLINI WOMEN'S LEADERSHIP SCHOLARSHIP

This scholarship is open to any female student enrolled full-time in a community college, private or public undergraduate college or university, graduate program, business school, or law school in the United States. All candidates who apply for this scholarship must be in good academic standing and possess a minimum cumulative GPA of 3.0 or higher. For more information, please visit: https://trustandestateslawyers.com/#scholarship

Award: Scholarship for use in freshman, sophomore, junior, senior, graduate, or postgraduate years; not renewable. *Number:* 1. *Amount:* $500.

Eligibility Requirements: Applicant must be enrolled or expecting to enroll full-time at a two-year or four-year institution or university and female. Available to U.S. and non-U.S. citizens.

Application Requirements: Essay. *Deadline:* December 15.

Contact: Kerri Castellini
E-mail: info@trustandestateslawyers.com

KUSH ARORA FEDERAL CRIMINAL JUSTICE REFORM SCHOLARSHIP

Mr. Arora understands that the success of the criminal justice system depends on the success of the bright young women and men who are pursuing their academic and professional dreams today. To help them achieve their goals, and to further bolster the system that he so proudly serves, Mr. Arora has established the Kush Arora Criminal Justice Reform Scholarship. For more information, please visit https://maryland-criminallawyer.com/#scholarship.

Award: Scholarship for use in freshman, sophomore, junior, senior, graduate, or postgraduate years; not renewable. *Number:* 1. *Amount:* $500.

Eligibility Requirements: Applicant must be enrolled or expecting to enroll full-time at a two-year or four-year institution or university. Available to U.S. and non-U.S. citizens.

Application Requirements: Application form may be submitted online (https://maryland-criminallawyer.com/2019-federal-justice-reform-scholarship/), essay, resume, transcript. *Deadline:* December 15.

Contact: Kush Arora
E-mail: scholarships@maryland-criminallawyer.com

PRICE BENOWITZ SOCIAL JUSTICE SCHOLARSHIP

To further this vision of making the world a better and more equitable place, our firm offers a scholarship to individuals who have demonstrated an outstanding commitment to social justice and community outreach. For more information, please visit https://pricebenowitz.com/#scholarship.

Award: Scholarship for use in freshman, sophomore, junior, senior, graduate, or postgraduate years; not renewable. *Number:* 1. *Amount:* $2000.

Eligibility Requirements: Applicant must be enrolled or expecting to enroll full- or part-time at a two-year or four-year institution or university. Available to U.S. and non-U.S. citizens.

Application Requirements: Application form may be submitted online (https://pricebenowitz.com/2019-price-benowitz-social-justice-scholarship/), essay, resume, transcript. *Deadline:* September 30.

Contact: David Benowitz
E-mail: scholarships@pricebenowitz.com

THOMAS SOLDAN HEALTHY COMMUNITIES SCHOLARSHIP

To further champion the cause of developing healthy communities, Mr. Soldan is investing in the future and has offered a scholarship of $500 to any student in a post-secondary education seeking means to encourage sustainable and local health-initiatives in his or her own community. For more information, visit http://virginialawfirm.net/#scholarship.

Award: Scholarship for use in freshman, sophomore, junior, senior, or graduate years; not renewable. *Number:* 1. *Amount:* $500.

Eligibility Requirements: Applicant must be enrolled or expecting to enroll full- or part-time at a two-year or four-year institution or university. Available to U.S. citizens.

Application Requirements: Essay. *Deadline:* September 30.

Contact: Thomas Soldan
E-mail: info@virginialawfirm.net

PROMOCODESFORYOU.COM

https://www.promocodesforyou.com

PROMOCODESFORYOU.COM STUDENT SAVINGS SCHOLARSHIP

At PromoCodesForYou.com, our goal is to provide a resource to help you save money. We know that the financial burden of college can be overwhelming, so we are here with a scholarship to help you reach your career goals. In 750 words or less, tell us what you wish to achieve once you have earned your college degree and why you believe that you will succeed in accomplishing that goal.

Award: Scholarship for use in freshman, sophomore, or junior years; not renewable. *Number:* 1. *Amount:* $1000.

Eligibility Requirements: Applicant must be age 16-22 and enrolled or expecting to enroll full-time at a two-year or four-year or technical institution or university. Available to U.S. and Canadian citizens.

Application Requirements: Application form, essay. *Deadline:* December 10.

Contact: Manager of Scholarship
E-mail: scholarship@promocodesforyou.com

PROOFREADINGSERVICES.COM

http://www.proofreadingservices.com/

HIGH SCHOOL AND UNIVERSITY WRITING SCHOLARSHIPS

Applicants must respond to the following writing prompt: Write about a defining moment in your life in the style of your favorite children's author. Three scholarships will be awarded to high school seniors and three will be awarded to university students. See more at: http://www.proofreadingservices.com/pages/scholarship#sthash.A7Jv5CsH.dpuf.

Award: Scholarship for use in freshman, sophomore, junior, senior, or graduate years; not renewable. *Number:* 6. *Amount:* $100–$500.

Eligibility Requirements: Applicant must be enrolled or expecting to enroll full- or part-time at a two-year or four-year or technical institution or university. Available to U.S. and non-U.S. citizens.

Application Requirements: Application form, essay. *Deadline:* June 1.

Contact: Mr. Luke Palder, CEO
ProofreadingServices.com
1 Broadway
14th Floor
Cambridge, MA 02142
Phone: 800-492-6773
E-mail: scholarship@proofreadingservices.com

PRUDENT PUBLISHING COMPANY INC.

http://www.gallerycollection.com/

10TH ANNUAL CREATE-A-GREETING-CARD $10,000 SCHOLARSHIP CONTEST

Students must submit an original photo, piece of artwork, or computer graphic for the front of a greeting card. The student with the best design will win a $10,000 scholarship and have his or her entry made into an actual greeting card to be sold in The Gallery Collection's line. The winning student's school will also receive a $1000 prize for helping to promote the contest. For complete details visit http://www.gallerycollection.com/greeting-cards-scholarship.htm.

Award: Scholarship for use in freshman, sophomore, junior, senior, or graduate years; not renewable. *Number:* 1. *Amount:* $10,000.

Eligibility Requirements: Applicant must be age 14 and over and enrolled or expecting to enroll full- or part-time at a two-year or four-year or technical institution or university. Available to U.S. citizens.

Application Requirements: Application form, entry in a contest, greeting card design. *Deadline:* December 31.

Contact: Scholarship Administrator
Prudent Publishing Company Inc.
Prudent Publishing Company
65 Challenger Road
Ridgefield Park, NJ 07660
Phone: 201-641-7900
E-mail: scholarshipadmin@gallerycollection.com

PUSH FOR EXCELLENCE

http://www.pushexcel.org/

ORA LEE SANDERS SCHOLARSHIP

U.S. citizens who will be freshmen, sophomores, juniors, or seniors are eligible. The scholarship is renewable up to 4 years based upon GPA. Full time study with minimum 2.5 GPA.

Award: Scholarship for use in freshman, sophomore, junior, or senior years; renewable. *Amount:* $1000.

Eligibility Requirements: Applicant must be enrolled or expecting to enroll full-time at a four-year institution or university. Available to U.S. citizens.

Application Requirements: Application form, essay, proof of current enrollment or acceptance in a college or university, recommendations or references, self-addressed stamped envelope with application, transcript. *Deadline:* April 30.

Contact: Scholarship Committee
Push for Excellence
930 East 50th Street
Chicago, IL 60615
Phone: 773-373-3366
E-mail: info@pushexcel.org

QUALITY FORMATIONS LTD.

https://www.qualitycompanyformations.co.uk/

QUALITY COMPANY FORMATIONS SCHOLARSHIP

Our scholarship is open to all students studying at an officially recognised or listed UK and US higher learning or further education institution, and it is specifically designed to supplement each student's annual income, to enable them to spend more time pursuing and developing a new business idea. Whether you would like to attend a trade show, invest in new materials for a prototype, or you simply need some financial help to set up your first company, our scholarship seeks to provide you with all the support you need to succeed.

Award: Scholarship for use in freshman, sophomore, junior, senior, graduate, or postgraduate years; renewable. *Number:* 6. *Amount:* $1250.

Eligibility Requirements: Applicant must be age 18 and over and enrolled or expecting to enroll full- or part-time at an institution or university. Available to U.S. and non-U.S. citizens.

Application Requirements: Application form, essay. *Deadline:* July 27.

Contact: Mr. Chris Wilson, Scholarship Manager
Quality Formations Ltd.
71-75 Shelton Street
Covent Garden
London, ON WC2H 9JQ
CAN
Phone: 203-908-0044
E-mail: c.woodley@qualityformations.co.uk

RATINGLE

http://ratingle.com

RATINGLE SCHOLARSHIP PROGRAM

The Ratingle Scholarship subject is product reviews. Students should choose a unique gadget that made their last year different. The gadget could be of any field (studies/electronics/fun etc.). The video should introduce the product and answer the most important questions others may have before purchasing this product. $1000 prize available.

Award: Prize for use in freshman, sophomore, junior, senior, graduate, or postgraduate years; not renewable.

Eligibility Requirements: Applicant must be enrolled or expecting to enroll full- or part-time at an institution or university. Available to U.S. citizens.

Application Requirements: Essay. *Deadline:* April 18.

Contact: Miss. Hana Renolds, Marketing Manager, Ratingle
Ratingle
8345 NW 66 Street, #C7592
Miami, FL 33166
Phone: 844-873-2875
E-mail: ratinglereview@gmail.com

REELGOOD

REELGOOD $2,500 NO ESSAY COLLEGE SCHOLARSHIP

The $2,500 No-Essay Scholarship is a randomly drawn scholarship with no essay required for those who meet the terms of eligibility! The scholarship can be used to cover tuition, housing, books, or any expenses related to your education. The winner will be determined by randomized drawing and contacted directly by the Reelgood team. You can only apply once: scholarships@reelgood.io, Reelgood, 110 South Park St, San Francisco, CA 94107

Award: Scholarship for use in freshman, sophomore, junior, or senior years; not renewable. *Number:* 1. *Amount:* $2500.

Eligibility Requirements: Applicant must be enrolled or expecting to enroll full- or part-time at a two-year or four-year or technical institution or university. Available to U.S. citizens.

Application Requirements: Application form. *Deadline:* June 1.

Contact: Catharine Burhenne
E-mail: catharine@reelgood.io

RENOVISO

https://renoviso.com

RENOVISO DREAM HOME DESIGN SCHOLARSHIP

The Renoviso Dream Home Design Scholarship enables students to describe their ideal home improvement project. The scholarship will be awarding one student $2,000 to put towards his or her education. From tuition costs to dining and textbooks, the scholarship money can be used to cover any expenses. Eligible students should submit an essay to scholarships@renoviso.com answering the prompt: "If you were a homeowner, what's the one home improvement project you'd choose to complete and why?" This can be a fictional or real example. For instance, would you upgrade your kitchen cabinets and counters because you love entertaining? Would you fix your roof because of your area's harsh winters? Or would you buy a set of new windows for energy-efficiency? Essays will be judged based on the following criteria: content, style, and creativity. One essay per entrant only. Please include your name, mailing, email address, phone number and documentation of your current or upcoming enrollment in an accredited U.S. college or university. The deadline to apply for the scholarship is August 15, 2018. The winner will be featured on Renoviso's blog. We will post his or her name, photo,

school they are attending, along with the winning essay. Completed applications must be sent no later than August 15, 2018. Application materials should be emailed to scholarships@renoviso.com. One applicant is awarded a $2,000 scholarship. Renoviso scholarship award recipient will be notified of the selection on or before August 31, 2018.

Award: Scholarship for use in freshman, sophomore, junior, senior, graduate, or postgraduate years; not renewable. *Number:* 1. *Amount:* $2000.

Eligibility Requirements: Applicant must be age 18 and over and enrolled or expecting to enroll full- or part-time at a two-year or four-year or technical institution or university. Available to U.S. and non-U.S. citizens.

Application Requirements: Essay. *Deadline:* August 15.

Contact: Paul Buonopane
Renoviso
2 S Market Street
Floor 4
Boston, MA 02109
Phone: 888-867-1660
E-mail: scholarships@renoviso.com

REWARDEXPERT

https://www.rewardexpert.com/

REWARDEXPERT FINANCIAL WELLNESS SCHOLARSHIP

The RewardExpert Financial Wellness Scholarship is established to help undergraduate students pursuing degrees in Finance, Accounting, Business, and Mathematics to prepare for careers in personal finance and financial fields. The scholarship is designed to assist with the cost of tuition, room, or board. One $1,000 scholarship will be awarded twice annually to deserving undergraduate students with outstanding academic achievement who are attending an accredited 2- or 4-year college within the United States of America.

Award: Scholarship for use in freshman, sophomore, junior, or senior years; not renewable. *Number:* 2. *Amount:* $1000.

Eligibility Requirements: Applicant must be age 18 and over and enrolled or expecting to enroll full- or part-time at a two-year or four-year or technical institution or university. Available to U.S. and non-U.S. citizens.

Application Requirements: Application form, essay. *Deadline:* November 15.

Contact: Mr. Andrew Purfield
RewardExpert
149 Madison Avenue, Suite 804
New York
New York, NY 10016
E-mail: andrew.p@rewardexpert.com

RHINE LAW FIRM, P.C.

https://www.carolinaaccidentattorneys.com/

STRIVE FOR EXCELLENCE SCHOLARSHIP 2018

This scholarship is open to graduating high school seniors and current undergraduate college students with a 3.0 or higher GPA who are bettering themselves through education. The application includes an essay section to tell us about your academic goals and how those goals will help you leave your mark on the world; the introduction is to be 100-200 words, and the essay is to be 500-1000 words. The winner will be announced September 26th, 2018, and the application must be submitted no later than 11:59 on August 29th, 2018. Additional information and applications can be found on our website at https://www.carolinaaccidentattorneys.com/scholarship

Award: Scholarship for use in freshman, sophomore, junior, or senior years; not renewable. *Number:* 1. *Amount:* $500.

Eligibility Requirements: Applicant must be enrolled or expecting to enroll full- or part-time at a two-year or four-year institution or university. Available to U.S. citizens.

Application Requirements: Application form, essay. *Deadline:* August 29.

Contact: Mr. Joel Rhine, Attorney
Rhine Law Firm, P.C.
1612 Military Cutoff Road
Suite 300
Wilmington, NC 28403
Phone: 910-772-9960
Fax: 910-772-9062

RISK MANAGEMENT ASSOCIATION FOUNDATION

http://www.scholarshipamerica.org

THE RISK MANAGEMENT ASSOCIATION FOUNDATION SCHOLARSHIP PROGRAM

The Risk Management Association (RMA) Foundation scholarship program is awarding over $200,000 in renewable scholarships, ranging from $2,000 to $5,000 each, to current undergraduates interested in pursuing a career in the banking industry. To be eligible, student must be a citizen or permanent resident of the United States or Canada and have completed a minimum of two years of college. All applicants must be currently enrolled full-time at an accredited four-year college or university in the United States or Canada and have a minimum grade point average (GPA) of 3.0 on a 4.0 scale overall. Applicants do not have to be a current RMA member, but they must join (free) and remain a member to receive and renew their scholarship. Website: https://www.scholarsapply.org/rma/.

Award: Scholarship for use in junior or senior years; renewable. *Number:* 40. *Amount:* $2000–$5000.

Eligibility Requirements: Applicant must be enrolled or expecting to enroll full-time at a four-year institution. Available to U.S. and Canadian citizens.

Application Requirements: Application form. *Deadline:* October 22.

Contact: Program Manager
Risk Management Association Foundation
One Scholarship Way
Scholarship America
Saint Peter, MN 56082
Phone: 800-537-4180
E-mail: rma@scholarshipamerica.org

ROBERT H. MOLLOHAN FAMILY CHARITABLE FOUNDATION, INC.

http://www.mollohanfoundation.org/

CARL R. MORRIS MEMORIAL SCHOLARSHIP

The Carl R. Morris Memorial Scholarship is a $1,000 scholarship offered to Calhoun County students who are committed to education and community, and currently attend, or are planning to attend, either Alderson-Broaddus College, Glenville State College or West Virginia University. The student must also have a minimum 3.0 GPA and demonstrate financial need.

Award: Scholarship for use in freshman, sophomore, junior, or senior years; not renewable. *Number:* 1–60. *Amount:* $1000.

Eligibility Requirements: Applicant must be enrolled or expecting to enroll full-time at an institution or university and studying in West Virginia. Available to U.S. citizens.

Application Requirements: Application form, essay, financial need analysis. *Deadline:* March 31.

ROMANIAN ORTHODOX EPISCOPATE OF AMERICA

https://www.roea.org/

ARFORA UNDERGRADUATE SCHOLARSHIP FOR WOMEN

The ARFORA Undergraduate Scholarship for Women was offered for the first time in 1994. A scholarship of $1000 may be awarded annually to selected students who have successfully completed their first year of an undergraduate program. Applicant must be a communicant member, or daughter of a communicant member, of a parish/mission of The Romanian Orthodox Episcopate of America for at least one year prior to application.

Award: Scholarship for use in sophomore year; not renewable. *Amount:* $1000.

Eligibility Requirements: Applicant must be enrolled or expecting to enroll at an institution or university and female. Available to U.S. citizens.

Application Requirements: Application form, essay, personal photograph. *Deadline:* May 10.

Contact: Corina Phillips
Phone: 330-241-4775
E-mail: corina5dan@aol.com

PAMFIL AND MARIA BUJEA SEMINARIAN SCHOLARSHIP

The Pamfil and Maria Bujea Seminarian Scholarship is a scholarship given once only to a male or female Canadian or American Orthodox Christian citizen studying with the intention of serving, for a given period of time, the Romanian Orthodox Episcopate of America in Canada.

Award: Scholarship for use in freshman, sophomore, junior, or senior years; not renewable. *Amount:* $10,000.

Eligibility Requirements: Applicant must be enrolled or expecting to enroll at an institution or university and studying in Massachusetts, New York, Pennsylvania. Available to U.S. and Canadian citizens.

Application Requirements: Application form, essay, personal photograph. *Deadline:* May 31.

WILLIAM R STANITZ/AROY SCHOLARSHIP

In August of 1971, the Constantin J Stanitz family of Chicago established a Scholarship Fund in memory of their son, William Robert Stanitz, who met a premature tragic death in California. At least two scholarships of $1,000.00 each will be offered for the upcoming school year. Applicant must be an active member of their church community - partaking in services, showing themselves to be a leader and an example among peers in their parish's young religious community.

Award: Scholarship for use in freshman, sophomore, junior, or senior years; not renewable. *Number:* 2. *Amount:* $1000.

Eligibility Requirements: Applicant must be enrolled or expecting to enroll full- or part-time at an institution or university. Available to U.S. citizens.

Application Requirements: Application form, personal photograph. *Deadline:* June 1.

ROVER.COM

https://www.rover.com/

ROVER SITTER SCHOLARSHIP CONTEST

At Rover, we are passionate about helping people achieve their educational goals. Whether you are living off of insta-coffee or insta-noodles, we get it--and we would like to help fund your brain fuel for the coming school year. Just write a 400–500 word essay for your chance to win $500! If you're not already, become a sitter on Rover.com to gain eligibility for the scholarship!

Award: Scholarship for use in freshman, sophomore, junior, senior, or graduate years; not renewable. *Number:* 2. *Amount:* $500.

Eligibility Requirements: Applicant must be age 18 and over and enrolled or expecting to enroll full- or part-time at a two-year or four-year institution or university. Available to U.S. citizens.

Application Requirements: Application form, essay. *Deadline:* August 31.

RUSSELL & LAZARUS

https://www.russellandlazarus.com/

RUSSELL & LAZARUS SAFETY SCHOLARSHIP CONTEST

Every year, our firm grants a $1,000 scholarship to the U.S. college student who creates the best video essay that elaborates on how lawyers make the world a safer place.

Award: Prize for use in freshman, sophomore, junior, or senior years; not renewable. *Number:* 1. *Amount:* $1000.

Eligibility Requirements: Applicant must be age 18-25 and enrolled or expecting to enroll full- or part-time at a two-year or four-year institution or university. Available to U.S. citizens.

Application Requirements: Application form may be submitted online (https://www.russellandlazarus.com/our-firm/safety-scholarship-for-law-students/), essay. *Deadline:* August 15.

THE RYAN LAW GROUP

https://theryanlawgroup.com/

THE RYAN LAW GROUP $1,000 COLLEGE SCHOLARSHIP

The Ryan Law Group is awarding one $1,000 scholarship to the student who writes an essay that best demonstrates their aspirations and how it relates to the theme of this year's scholarship, Future Advocates of Justice.

Award: Scholarship for use in freshman, sophomore, junior, or senior years; not renewable. *Number:* 1. *Amount:* $1000.

Eligibility Requirements: Applicant must be enrolled or expecting to enroll full-time at a four-year institution or university. Available to U.S. citizens.

Application Requirements: Essay. *Deadline:* July 31.

Contact: Mr. Frank Eybsen, Marketing Manager
The Ryan Law Group
2101 Rosecrans Avenue
Suite 5290
El Segundo, CA 90245
Phone: 310-321-4800
E-mail: frank@theryanlawgroup.com

SCHOLAR SERVE

https://www.scholarserve.org

SCHOLAR SERVE AWARDS

Scholar Serve recognizes and supports college and graduate students who apply their knowledge to serving others in their communities. In addition to the recognition, the organization matches recipients to mentors who assist with their service initiatives and provide career guidance. Any full-time undergraduate or graduate student in the United States is eligible to apply. Scholar Serve recipients may receive up to $3,000. Scholar Serve reserves the right to review applications and select recipients at its discretion. The number and amount of awards may vary over time. We do not give preference to graduate students over undergraduates. We look for students who have done well in their academic studies. This does not mean you have to have a 4.0. All of our previous recipients have had a cumulative GPA of 3.0 or better, but we do not have a minimum GPA requirement. When reviewing applications we are looking for students who are volunteering and leading in ways that will enable them to engage in service and advance their career goals beyond the time when they are in school. Most recipients have used the funding they receive for their service efforts and volunteer projects. However, this is not required and is at the discretion of the recipient. U.S. citizenship is not required. All recipients for the 2018 Scholar Serve awards will be notified by March 15, 2018. We make every effort to contact each applicant to provide notification that their application has been received. We thoroughly review every application that is submitted. Late submission will not be considered.

Award: Scholarship for use in freshman, sophomore, junior, senior, graduate, or postgraduate years; not renewable. *Number:* 5–10. *Amount:* $500–$3000.

Eligibility Requirements: Applicant must be enrolled or expecting to enroll full-time at a four-year institution or university. Available to U.S. and non-U.S. citizens.

Application Requirements: Application form, community service. *Deadline:* February 15.

Contact: Angela Courtney, President
E-mail: contact@scholarserve.org

SCHOLARSHIP AMERICA

http://www.scholarshipamerica.org

SCHOLARSHIP AMERICA DREAM AWARD

Scholarship America's Dream Award is to assist students across the nation entering their second year or higher of education beyond high school. Renewable scholarships are offered for full-time study at an accredited institution of the student's choice with the awards growing in amount each year, allowing students to receive aid throughout their college careers.

Award: Scholarship for use in sophomore, junior, or senior years; renewable. *Number:* 8–10. *Amount:* $5000–$15,000.

Eligibility Requirements: Applicant must be enrolled or expecting to enroll full-time at a two-year or four-year or technical institution or university. Available to U.S. citizens.

Application Requirements: Application form. *Deadline:* October 15.

SCHOLARSHIP APPLICATION SERVICES LLC

http://celebrityscholarship.com

CELEBRITY SCHOLARSHIP

Are you tired of writing essays? Looking to show off your talents? Applying for financial aid doesn't have to be boring. Unlike traditional scholarships, we're offering something new and creative. Through costume, role-playing, props and self-expression, we are looking for the person who can give us the funniest, quirkiest and most authentic celebrity impersonation. Tell us about your celebrity and why you chose them. Send us your picture or video for a chance to win $500 in scholarship funds. Feel free to use makeup, funky clothing and a smart caption. Remember, if you are impersonating someone, you are paying respect to them. We won't accept submissions that are inappropriate or belittling.

Award: Scholarship for use in freshman, sophomore, junior, senior, graduate, or postgraduate years; not renewable. *Number:* 1. *Amount:* $500.

Eligibility Requirements: Applicant must be age 16 and over and enrolled or expecting to enroll full- or part-time at a two-year or four-year or technical institution or university. Available to U.S. citizens.

Application Requirements: Personal photograph. *Deadline:* December 31.

Contact: Eran Blecher, Director
Scholarship Application Services LLC
420 Veneto
Irvine, CA 92614
Phone: 714-627-9252
E-mail: contact@celebrity-scholarship.com

SCHOOLSOUP.COM

$1,000 I AM APPLYING SCHOLARSHIP

SchoolSoup.com encourages all students and prospective students to research and evaluate all scholarship opportunities and then apply for those that have the greatest probability of success. That's why SchoolSoup.com has been accumulating scholarship information for over 15 years. Now instead of just providing you with information, we want to award a $1000 scholarship to help pay for college. High school students, adults looking to head back to school, current college students, and anyone else looking to attend college or graduate school within 12 months may apply.

Award: Prize for use in freshman, sophomore, junior, senior, graduate, or postgraduate years; not renewable. *Number:* 2. *Amount:* $1000.

Eligibility Requirements: Applicant must be enrolled or expecting to enroll full- or part-time at a two-year or four-year or technical institution or university. Available to U.S. citizens.

Application Requirements: Application form, application form may be submitted online (http://schoolsoup.com/housescholarships/i-am-applying/), entry in a contest. *Deadline:* continuous.

Contact: Hartley Miller, President
SchoolSoup.com
305-171 Donald Street
Winnipeg, MN R3P0R9
CAN
Phone: 204-488-0215
E-mail: hmiller@amplifiedmediagroup.com

SCREEN ACTORS' GUILD FOUNDATION

http://www.sagfoundation.org/

JOHN L. DALES SCHOLARSHIP PROGRAM

Applicant must have ten vested years of pension credits with the SAG AFTRA union or lifetime earnings of $150,000. Must be U.S. citizen. Scholarship amount ranges between $1000 and $5000. Consult office or website for more information.

Award: Scholarship for use in freshman, sophomore, junior, senior, graduate, or postgraduate years; not renewable. *Number:* 1–16. *Amount:* $1000–$5000.

Eligibility Requirements: Applicant must be enrolled or expecting to enroll full- or part-time at a two-year or four-year institution or university. Available to U.S. citizens.

Application Requirements: Application form, community service, essay, financial need analysis, recommendations or references, resume, test scores, transcript. *Deadline:* March 15.

Contact: Davidson Lloyd, Director of Assistance Programs
Screen Actors' Guild Foundation
5757 Wilshire Boulevard
Suite 124
Los Angeles, CA 90036
Phone: 323-549-6649
Fax: 323-549-6710
E-mail: dlloyd@sagfoundation.org

SCREEN ACTORS GUILD FOUNDATION/JOHN L. DALES SCHOLARSHIP FUND (STANDARD)

Applicant must be a member of SAG AFTRA Union or the child of a member of SAG AFTRA Union. Member under the age of twenty-one must have been a member of AFTRA SAG Union for five years and have a lifetime earnings of $30,000. Parent of an applicant must have ten vested years of pension credits OR lifetime earnings of $150,000. Consult office or website for more information. Number and amount of awards vary.

Award: Scholarship for use in freshman, sophomore, junior, senior, graduate, or postgraduate years; not renewable. *Number:* 100–135. *Amount:* $1000–$5000.

Eligibility Requirements: Applicant must be enrolled or expecting to enroll full-time at a two-year or four-year or technical institution or university. Available to U.S. citizens.

Application Requirements: Application form, community service, essay, financial need analysis, recommendations or references, resume, test scores, transcript. *Deadline:* March 15.

Contact: Davidson Lloyd, Director of Assistance Programs
Screen Actors' Guild Foundation
5757 Wilshire Boulevard
Suite 124
Los Angeles, CA 90036
Phone: 323-549-6649
Fax: 323-549-6710
E-mail: dlloyd@sagfoundation.org

SEABEE MEMORIAL SCHOLARSHIP ASSOCIATION, INC.

http://www.seabee.org/

SEABEE MEMORIAL ASSOCIATION SCHOLARSHIP

Award available to children or grandchildren of current or former members of the Naval Construction Force (Seabees) or Naval Civil Engineer Corps. Not available for graduate study or for great-grandchildren of Seabees.

Award: Scholarship for use in freshman, sophomore, junior, or senior years; renewable. *Number:* 127. *Amount:* $3200.

Eligibility Requirements: Applicant must be enrolled or expecting to enroll full-time at a two-year or four-year institution or university. Available to U.S. citizens.

Application Requirements: Application form, essay, financial need analysis. *Deadline:* April 15.

Contact: Sheryl Chiogioji, Administrative Assistant
Seabee Memorial Scholarship Association, Inc.
PO Box 6574
Silver Spring, MD 20916
Phone: 301-570-2850
E-mail: smsa@seabee.org

SEASONS IN MALIBU

https://seasonsmalibu.com

SEASONS IN MALIBU 2018 ANNUAL SCHOLARSHIP

Write an 800-word essay about the importance of mental health and what you hope to do with your career as a mental health professional.

Award: Scholarship for use in freshman, sophomore, junior, senior, graduate, or postgraduate years; not renewable. *Number:* 1. *Amount:* $1500.

Eligibility Requirements: Applicant must be high school student and planning to enroll or expecting to enroll full- or part-time at a two-year or four-year or technical institution or university. Available to U.S. citizens.

Application Requirements: Essay. *Deadline:* March 31.

Contact: Don Varden, CEO
Seasons In Malibu
32223 Pacific Coast Highway Malibu, CA 90265
Malibu, CA 90265
Phone: 424-610-5402
E-mail: seasons.malibu.ca@gmail.com

SECOND MARINE DIVISION ASSOCIATION

http://www.2dmardiv.com/

SECOND MARINE DIVISION ASSOCIATION MEMORIAL SCHOLARSHIP FUND

Renewable award for students who are unmarried, dependent sons, daughters or grandchildren of former or current members of Second Marine Division or attached units. Must submit proof of parent's or grandparent's service. Family adjusted gross income must not exceed $94,000. Award is merit-based. Minimum 2.5 GPA required.

Award: Scholarship for use in freshman, sophomore, junior, or senior years; renewable. *Number:* 35–42. *Amount:* $1200–$1500.

Eligibility Requirements: Applicant must be enrolled or expecting to enroll full-time at a two-year or four-year or technical institution or university and single. Available to U.S. and non-U.S. citizens.

Application Requirements: Application form, essay, financial need analysis, personal photograph. *Deadline:* April 1.

Contact: Mr. Richard Van Horne, Chairman, Board of Trustees, SMDA Memorial Scholarship Fund
Second Marine Division Association
6178 Seven Lakes West
West End, NC 27376
Phone: 910-673-3123
E-mail: rvanhorne@embarqmail.com

SENIORADVISOR.COM

http://www.senioradvisor.com

FUTURE OF ASSISTED LIVING SCHOLARSHIP

Three $2,000 scholarships available to students enrolled in an associate's degree, bachelor's degree or graduate level program at an accredited 2-year college or 4-year university. Each eligible student must submit a 500-750 word essay response to the question: How can your major of study improve the lives of seniors in assisted living facilities in your town? Deadline is December 31, 2017. Scholarship award recipients will be announced January 31, 2018.

Award: Scholarship for use in freshman, sophomore, junior, senior, or graduate years; not renewable. *Number:* 3. *Amount:* $2000.

Eligibility Requirements: Applicant must be enrolled or expecting to enroll full- or part-time at a two-year or four-year institution or university. Available to U.S. citizens.

Application Requirements: Essay. *Deadline:* December 31.

SERVICESCAPE INCORPORATED

https://www.servicescape.com/

SERVICESCAPE SCHOLARSHIP 2019

Are you enrolled or about to enroll in a college, university, or trade school? Are you looking for a little extra help in funding your education to cover expenses that other scholarships and financial aid don't cover? If your answer is "yes," we have a solution that could help out with books, supplies, or anything else you need to cover your educational expenses. Apply now to our ServiceScape Scholarship, which will be in the amount of $1,000.00 USD to be paid toward the educational certification/degree program of your choice. The chosen topic is as follows: How does writing impact today's world? Think about it, write about it, and let us know your thoughts. To apply for the ServiceScape Scholarship, all scholarship applicants should fill out the application form and submit a 300 word essay on this topic. Rules and exclusions apply. Contest is open to students who are attending or who will attend an accredited college, university, or trade school in 2019/2020. In order to qualify as a contest participant, a person must successfully submit the application form below and must be at least 18 years of age.

Award: Scholarship for use in freshman, sophomore, junior, senior, graduate, or postgraduate years; renewable. *Number:* 1. *Amount:* $1000.

Eligibility Requirements: Applicant must be age 18 and over and enrolled or expecting to enroll full- or part-time at a two-year or four-year or technical institution or university. Available to U.S. and non-U.S. citizens.

Application Requirements: Application form, application form may be submitted online (https://www.servicescape.com/scholarship), essay, personal photograph. *Deadline:* November 30.

Contact: Mr. David Costello, CEO
ServiceScape Incorporated
33 Pasho Street
Andover, MA 01810
E-mail: support@servicescape.com

SEXNER & ASSOCIATES LLC

http://www.sexner.com/personal-injury/

MITCHELL S. SEXNER & ASSOCIATES LLC SCHOLARSHIP

This scholarship opportunity is available to graduating high school students or currently enrolled undergraduate college students who have maintained a 3.0 or higher GPA and are current U.S. Citizens or current U.S. Permanent Residents. Students must complete the application and a short essay demonstrating their commitment to their education and improving their community; both items, as well as additional information are available on our website: http://www.sexner.com/personal-injury/scholarship/

Award: Scholarship for use in freshman, sophomore, junior, or senior years; not renewable. *Number:* 1. *Amount:* $500.

Eligibility Requirements: Applicant must be enrolled or expecting to enroll full-time at a two-year or four-year institution. Available to U.S. citizens.

Application Requirements: Application form, essay. *Deadline:* May 15.

Contact: Mitch Sexner
Sexner & Associates LLC
2126 West Van Buren St.
Chicago, IL 60612
E-mail: mitch@sexner.com

SGM LAW GROUP PLLC

http://www.immi-usa.com/

SGM LAW GROUP BI-ANNUAL SCHOLARSHIP

This award recognizes outstanding achievements in academics and as a law firm, we seek to reward a passionate and determined student interested in the field of law. As attorneys, we have all benefited from scholarships throughout our academic careers and now we hope to play a small role in helping a deserving student realize his or her academic goals. This scholarship is open to students who are currently enrolled in an accredited university, college or law school within the U.S. Must have a cumulative GPA of 3.0 or higher and must be a full time student

enrolled in classes for spring 2017. Students will have the opportunity to earn $1,000 towards their education by submitting a 500–1000 word essay, which can be written on any of the topics listed below. Please be aware that anything over 1000 words will not be considered. Once the winner of this award is chosen, a check for $1,000 will be made to the scholarship recipient's school of choice to help cover education expenses. 1. What hardship did you conquer to achieve your goal of pursuing law studies? 2. Explain your motivation for becoming a lawyer and what about the law inspires you. 3. Discuss the impact of employment immigration on U.S. economy, including the effects of related immigration reforms. 4. What field of law are you interested in and how will you help others with your earned law degree?

Award: Scholarship for use in freshman, sophomore, junior, senior, or graduate years; not renewable. *Number:* 1–2. *Amount:* $1000.

Eligibility Requirements: Applicant must be enrolled or expecting to enroll full- or part-time at a two-year or four-year or technical institution or university. Available to U.S. and non-U.S. citizens.

Application Requirements: Essay. *Deadline:* December 15.

SHAWN SUKUMAR ATTORNEY AT LAW

https://www.washingtondccriminallawyer.net/

SHAWN SUKUMAR CRIMINAL JUSTICE REFORM SCHOLARSHIP

This scholarship is offered to any student currently enrolled in an accredited community college, undergraduate, or graduate program in the United States. This includes incoming first-year college students who are high school graduates or possess a GED. The scholarship candidate must possess an interest in social justice, as demonstrated by past and present volunteer, professional, and educational experiences. For more information, please visit
http://www.washingtondccriminallawyer.net/#scholarship

Award: Scholarship for use in freshman, sophomore, junior, senior, graduate, or postgraduate years; not renewable. *Number:* 1. *Amount:* $500.

Eligibility Requirements: Applicant must be enrolled or expecting to enroll full- or part-time at a two-year or four-year or technical institution or university. Available to U.S. and non-U.S. citizens.

Application Requirements: Application form, essay. *Deadline:* May 31.

Contact: Shawn Sukumar
E-mail: scholarships@washingtondccriminallawyer.net

SHELVING.COM

http://www.shelving.com/

2017 SHELVING.COM BUSINESS SCHOLARSHIP

This scholarship offers three prizes ranging from $500–$1500 to any currently-enrolled student taking a business-related line of study, ranging from MBAs to retail/warehouse management and any other relevant fields.

Award: Prize for use in freshman, sophomore, junior, or senior years; not renewable. *Number:* 3. *Amount:* $500–$1500.

Eligibility Requirements: Applicant must be enrolled or expecting to enroll full-time at a four-year institution or university. Available to U.S. citizens.

Application Requirements: Application form, essay. *Deadline:* June 30.

Contact: Mr. Timothy Allen, SEO Analyst
Shelving.com
340 E. Big Beaver Road
Troy, MI 48084
Phone: 248-234-1221
E-mail: tallen@trafficdigitalagency.com

SHOPKO STORES, INC.

http://www.shopko.com/foundation

SHOPKO FOUNDATION TEAMMATE & FAMILY MEMBER SCHOLARSHIP PROGRAM

The Shopko Foundation Teammate and Family Member Scholarship Program, qualified grant winners receive up to $2,500 for a given academic year. The scholarships, awarded through a competitive process, include post-secondary accredited programs: 2- or 4-year colleges and universities, vocational schools, and technical schools. Applicants must be currently enrolled, or planning to enroll, in a full-time course of study for the entire academic year during which the scholarship is awarded. The program is open to full- or part-time Shopko teammates and their dependent children under the age of 24 (as of July 1 of the year scholarships are awarded). Applicants who are children of Shopko teammates must be dependent on a Shopko teammate for over 50% of their cost of living. Shopko teammates must have at least one year of continuous service as of January 1 of the scholarship year.

Award: Scholarship for use in freshman, sophomore, junior, senior, or graduate years; not renewable. *Number:* 30. *Amount:* $2500.

Eligibility Requirements: Applicant must be enrolled or expecting to enroll full-time at a two-year or four-year or technical institution or university. Available to U.S. citizens.

Application Requirements: Application form. *Deadline:* March 1.

SIMON YOUTH FOUNDATION

http://www.sms.scholarshipamerica.org/simonyouth

SIMON YOUTH FOUNDATION COMMUNITY SCHOLARSHIP PROGRAM

Scholarships available to high school seniors attending school and living in close proximity of a Simon Property Mall or Community Center. Recipients should reside within 50 miles of a Simon Mall. Must be planning to enroll in a full-time undergraduate course of study at an accredited two- or four-year college, university, or vocational/technical school.

Award: Scholarship for use in freshman year; not renewable. *Number:* 100–200. *Amount:* $1400–$2500.

Eligibility Requirements: Applicant must be high school student and planning to enroll or expecting to enroll full-time at a two-year or four-year or technical institution or university. Available to U.S. citizens.

Application Requirements: Application form, community service, copy of page 1 of parent's tax Form 1040, financial need analysis, test scores, transcript. *Deadline:* March 1.

Contact: Casey Rubischko, Program Manager
      Phone: 507-931-1682

SIMPLILEARN AMERICAS LLC

https://www.simplilearn.com/

SIMPLILEARN STUDENT AMBASSADOR SCHOLARSHIP

Getting a college degree is a huge accomplishment, but it does not necessarily prepare you for the best jobs in today's digital economy. That is where Simplilearn comes in. We provide online training in today's hottest careers--from digital marketing, to cyber security, to cloud computing. As a Simplilearn Ambassador, you can help us spread the word and help your classmates launch their careers. Participation is free. For every visitor you bring to Simplilearn.com, via your unique referral URL, you will get another entry to our $1,000 cash Ambassador Scholarship. Simply fill out the brief form below, select the skills training that you are most interested in, get your unique link to Simplilearn, along with some tips on how to promote us, and start racking up entries to our $1,000 payout. See https://www.simplilearn.com/student-ambassador-scholarship-program for more details.

Award: Scholarship for use in freshman, sophomore, junior, senior, graduate, or postgraduate years; not renewable. *Number:* 1–3. *Amount:* $1000–$3000.

Eligibility Requirements: Applicant must be enrolled or expecting to enroll full- or part-time at a two-year or four-year institution or university. Available to U.S. citizens.

Application Requirements: Application form, personal photograph. *Deadline:* March 17.

Contact: Mr. Nirmal Kumar, Simplilearn Americas LLC
      Simplilearn Americas LLC
      201 Spear Street
      Suite 1100
      San Francisco, CA 94105
      Phone: 844-532-7688 Ext. 1025
      E-mail: scholarship@simplilearn.com

SKYLIGHTS FOR LESS

https://www.skylightsforless.com/

THE SKYLIGHT EFFECT SCHOLARSHIP CONTEST

The scholarship will reward a prospective student who plans on or is currently majoring in Photography, Art, Graphic Design, Architecture, or Interior Design, but is open to all majors. Students will be asked to capture the before and after effects of a skylight installation in a building using photos, photo edited mock-ups, digitized sketches, drawings, or paintings. The sky's the limit with this project! Some ideas to consider are: take a photo of a room with skylights and a room without; sketch/draw a room or place that could be improved with the addition of natural light provided by a skylight or sun tunnel. Photoshopped images showing before and after scenarios are acceptable. Eligibility: applicants who are considering the 2019-2020 Skylights for Less Scholarship must meet the following criteria: must be planning to enroll or be enrolled in an undergraduate or graduate program at any accredited college or university within the United States for the 2019-2020 academic school year; applicant must have a GPA greater than 2.5 on a 4.0 scale; must be an American citizen or have a student visa. Application Process: qualified students may e-mail their submissions to the address provided. The requirements for the submission are: a description of your completed work (150-400 words); a brief biography or statement of your goals in college (150-400 words); your legal name; mailing address; telephone number; email address; name of your college or university and proposed year of graduation. Follow us on Facebook or Instagram. The deadline to apply is October 1, 2019. Winner Selection: each qualified selection will be carefully reviewed by our selection panel. The most interesting submissions will be posted to our Skylights For Less Facebook Page. The selection panel will award the scholarship no later than October 1, 2019. The winner will be notified by e-mail or phone and will have 15 days to respond, after which the next best submission will be rewarded the scholarship. Terms: you are required to supply personal information to Skylights For Less to verify your submission and provide a means of contact should you become the winner of this scholarship. Submitted works will become the property of Skylights For Less and could be displayed on the website or used in any other promotional materials online or offline. We wish you the best of luck and are very excited to see your submissions! If you have any additional questions, please email us at the address provided.

Award: Scholarship for use in freshman, sophomore, junior, senior, or graduate years; not renewable. *Number:* 1. *Amount:* $1000.

Eligibility Requirements: Applicant must be enrolled or expecting to enroll full-time at a four-year institution or university. Available to U.S. citizens.

Application Requirements: Capture the before and after effects of a skylight installation using various forms of media., entry in a contest, essay. *Deadline:* October 1.

Contact: Melissa Pistor
      Skylights For Less
      20 Lewis St
      Oneonta, NY 13820
      Phone: 800-284-5194
      E-mail: scholarship@skylightsforless.com

SLOTOZILLA

http://www.slotozilla.com/

INTERNET MARKETING SCHOLARSHIP

Slotozilla is interested in attracting our players as well as helping future marketing experts. Just like ads on the internet, you never know when and where the next marketing genius will pop-out. That is why we created an annual Internet Marketing Scholarship. This scholarship is available for full-time students doing Bachelor or Master course at any accredited college or university. See website for more information, http://www.slotozilla.com/

Award: Scholarship for use in freshman, sophomore, junior, senior, graduate, or postgraduate years; not renewable. *Number:* 1. *Amount:* $500.

Eligibility Requirements: Applicant must be enrolled or expecting to enroll full- or part-time at a two-year or four-year or technical institution or university. Available to U.S. and Canadian citizens.

Application Requirements: Essay. *Deadline:* August 31.

Contact: Vanessa Skadi
      E-mail: scholarship@slotozilla.com

SMARTPAPERHELP

http://www.smartpaperhelp.com/

SMART PAPER HELP SCHOLARSHIP

SmartPaperHelp invites students to participate in our Smart Scholarship program. All you have to do is to show off your writing skills and write an essay on one of the given topics: 1. Problems Of Modern Educational System And Their Solutions; 2. Difficulties We Face In College; 3. What Problems Do You See In Your College And How Do They Affect You Personally? Participate and win cash prizes. Full guidelines you can find on the following page: http://www.smartpaperhelp.com/blog/scholarship-program-for-students

Award: Scholarship for use in freshman, sophomore, junior, senior, graduate, or postgraduate years; not renewable. *Number:* 1–3. *Amount:* $400–$1000.

Eligibility Requirements: Applicant must be enrolled or expecting to enroll full- or part-time at a two-year or four-year institution or university. Available to U.S. citizens.

Application Requirements: Application form, essay. *Deadline:* February 29.

Contact: Sheri Aldridge
　　　　　E-mail: contest@smartpaperhelp.com

SNOW, CARPIO & WEEKLEY, PLC

http://workinjuryaz.com

SCW ACADEMIC SCHOLARSHIP

Video submissions required. High school senior or recent graduate seeking a degree with a 3.0 GPA. To be awarded the fall semester of 2016. Applications must be submitted on our website http://workinjuryaz.com/tucson-workers-compensation-lawyers/#academic See all requirement and info on our website as well.

Award: Scholarship for use in freshman or sophomore years; not renewable. *Number:* 2. *Amount:* $2500.

Eligibility Requirements: Applicant must be enrolled or expecting to enroll full- or part-time at a two-year or four-year or technical institution or university. Available to U.S. citizens.

Application Requirements: Application form. *Deadline:* May 31.

Contact: April Snow
　　　　　E-mail: snowcarpioaz@gmail.com

SOCIETY FOR APPLIED ANTHROPOLOGY

http://www.appliedanthro.org/

ANNUAL SFAA STUDENT ENDOWED AWARD

The Student Endowed Award consists of a $500 travel stipend to cover costs of attending the annual meeting, plus a one-year SfAA membership, (which includes a one year subscription to the journals Human Organization and Practicing Anthropology).

Award: Prize for use in freshman, sophomore, junior, senior, graduate, or postgraduate years; not renewable. *Number:* 1. *Amount:* $500.

Eligibility Requirements: Applicant must be enrolled or expecting to enroll full- or part-time at a two-year or four-year institution or university. Available to U.S. and non-U.S. citizens.

Application Requirements: Application form, essay. *Deadline:* December 20.

Contact: Trish Colvin, Office Manager
　　　　　Society for Applied Anthropology
　　　　　PO Box 2436
　　　　　Oklahoma City, OK 73101
　　　　　Phone: 405-843-5113
　　　　　Fax: 405-843-8553
　　　　　E-mail: info@appliedanthro.org

DEL JONES AWARD

Del Jones was a distinguished member of SfAA and an African American anthropologist who developed perspectives that could assist and transform the lives of oppressed and disadvantaged peoples. Following his death in 1999, close friends and members of the Society established the Del Jones Memorial Fund. This Fund supports a travel grant of $500 for a student to attend the annual meeting of the Society. The Del Jones

Travel Award is intended to increase minority participation in SfAA, particularly African American participation, but also to honor the life and work of Del Jones independently of the minority criterion. The winning paper will best reflect the contributions and/or life experiences of Del Jones.

Award: Prize for use in freshman, sophomore, junior, senior, or graduate years; not renewable. *Number:* 2–500.

Eligibility Requirements: Applicant must be enrolled or expecting to enroll full- or part-time at a two-year or four-year institution or university. Available to U.S. and non-U.S. citizens.

Application Requirements: Application form, essay. *Deadline:* December 20.

Contact: Trish Colvin, Office Manager
　　　　　Society for Applied Anthropology
　　　　　PO Box 2436
　　　　　Oklahoma City, OK 73101
　　　　　Phone: 405-843-5113
　　　　　Fax: 405-843-8553
　　　　　E-mail: info@appliedanthro.org

EDWARD H. AND ROSAMOND B. SPICER TRAVEL AWARDS

The Awards commemorate the lifelong concern of Edward H. and Rosamond B. Spicer in furthering the maturation of students in the social sciences, both intellectually and practically, and their lifelong interest in the nature of community as both cause of, and solution to, problems in the human condition.

Award: Prize for use in freshman, sophomore, junior, senior, or graduate years; not renewable. *Number:* 2. *Amount:* $500.

Eligibility Requirements: Applicant must be enrolled or expecting to enroll full- or part-time at a two-year or four-year institution or university. Available to U.S. and non-U.S. citizens.

Application Requirements: Application form, essay. *Deadline:* December 20.

Contact: Trish Colvin, Office Manager
　　　　　Society for Applied Anthropology
　　　　　PO Box 2436
　　　　　Oklahoma City, OK 73101
　　　　　Phone: 405-843-5113
　　　　　Fax: 405-843-8553
　　　　　E-mail: info@appliedanthro.org

GIL KUSHNER MEMORIAL TRAVEL AWARD

Scholarship of $500 to attend the SfAA annual meeting. Abstracts (paper or poster) should be concerned with the persistence of cultural groups.

Award: Prize for use in freshman, sophomore, junior, senior, or graduate years; not renewable. *Number:* 2. *Amount:* $500.

Eligibility Requirements: Applicant must be enrolled or expecting to enroll full- or part-time at a two-year or four-year institution or university. Available to U.S. and non-U.S. citizens.

Application Requirements: Essay. *Deadline:* December 20.

Contact: Trish Colvin, Office Manager
　　　　　Society for Applied Anthropology
　　　　　PO Box 2436
　　　　　Oklahoma City, OK 73101
　　　　　Phone: 405-843-5113
　　　　　Fax: 405-843-8553
　　　　　E-mail: info@appliedanthro.org

HUMAN RIGHTS DEFENDER STUDENT AWARD

The Human Rights Defender Travel Award provides a $500 travel scholarship each year for a student to attend the annual meetings of the Society. This award was made possible by a generous contribution from Michael Cavendish, a Sustaining Member of the Society who is a practicing attorney in Florida and a strong advocate of human rights. As a graduate student, he was first exposed to the link between applied anthropology and disciplines like law, journalism and social work.

Award: Prize for use in freshman, sophomore, junior, senior, or graduate years; not renewable. *Number:* 1. *Amount:* $500.

Eligibility Requirements: Applicant must be enrolled or expecting to enroll full- or part-time at a two-year or four-year institution or university. Available to U.S. and non-U.S. citizens.

Application Requirements: Essay. *Deadline:* December 20.

Contact: Trish Colvin, Office Manager
Society for Applied Anthropology
PO Box 2436
Oklahoma City, OK 73101
Phone: 405-843-5113
Fax: 405-843-8553
E-mail: info@appliedanthro.org

VALENE SMITH PRIZE

The posters which are submitted for the Valene Smith Competition will be set up and exhibited with all other posters at the Annual Meeting of the Society for Applied Anthropology and should be concerned in some way with the applied social science of tourism.

Award: Prize for use in freshman, sophomore, junior, senior, or graduate years; not renewable. *Number:* 3. *Amount:* $250–$500.

Eligibility Requirements: Applicant must be enrolled or expecting to enroll full- or part-time at a two-year or four-year institution or university. Available to U.S. and non-U.S. citizens.

Application Requirements: *Deadline:* October 15.

Contact: Trish Colvin, Office Manager
Society for Applied Anthropology
PO Box 2436
Oklahoma City, OK 73101
Phone: 405-843-5113
Fax: 405-843-8553
E-mail: info@appliedanthro.org

SOCIETY FOR SCIENCE & THE PUBLIC

societyforscience.org

REGENERON INTERNATIONAL SCIENCE AND ENGINEERING FAIR

The Regeneron International Science and Engineering Fair (ISEF) is the culminating event in a series of local, regional, state and international science fairs. Students, grades 9 - 12, who compete successfully at a Regeneron ISEF-affiliated fair can advance and ultimately participate at the Regeneron ISEF.

Award: Prize for use in freshman, sophomore, junior, or senior years; not renewable. *Number:* 1–600. *Amount:* $500–$75,000.

Eligibility Requirements: Applicant must be high school student; age 12-20 and planning to enroll or expecting to enroll full- or part-time at a two-year institution or university. Available to U.S. and non-U.S. citizens.

Application Requirements: Application form, application form may be submitted online, interview. *Deadline:* April 12.

Contact: Ms. Michele Glidden, Chief, Science Education Programs
Society for Science & the Public
1719 N Street, NW
Washington, DC 20036
Phone: 202-785-2255 Ext. 137
E-mail: mglidden@societyforscience.org

REGENERON SCIENCE TALENT SEARCH

The Regeneron Science Talent Search (STS), a program of Society for Science and the Public, is the nation's most prestigious pre-college science competition. Alumni of STS have made extraordinary contributions to science and hold more than 100 of the world's most distinguished science and math honors, including the Nobel Prize and the National Medal of Science. Each year, 300 Regeneron STS Scholars and their schools are recognized. From the select pool of scholars, 40 student finalists are invited to Washington, DC in March to participate in final judging, display their work to the public, meet with notable scientists, and compete for the top award of $250,000.

Award: Prize for use in freshman, sophomore, junior, senior, or graduate years; not renewable. *Number:* 40. *Amount:* $25,000–$250,000.

Eligibility Requirements: Applicant must be high school student; age 13 and over and planning to enroll or expecting to enroll full- or part-time at a two-year institution or university. Available to U.S. citizens.

Application Requirements: Application form, application form may be submitted online, essay. *Deadline:* November 12.

Contact: Allison Stifel, Director, Regeneron STS
Society for Science & the Public
1719 N Street, NW
Washington, DC 20036
Phone: 202-785-2255 Ext. 140
E-mail: astifel@societyforscience.org

SOCIETY OF SATELLITE PROFESSIONALS INTERNATIONAL

http://www.sspi.org/

SSPI NORTHEAST CHAPTER SCHOLARSHIP

Students from or studying in the Northeast US region.

Award: Scholarship for use in freshman, sophomore, junior, senior, or graduate years; not renewable. *Number:* 1. *Amount:* $2500.

Eligibility Requirements: Applicant must be enrolled or expecting to enroll full-time at a two-year or four-year institution or university. Available to U.S. and non-U.S. citizens.

Application Requirements: Essay, financial need analysis. *Deadline:* April 15.

Contact: Ms. Tamara Bond-Williams, Membership Director
Society of Satellite Professionals International
250 Park Avenue, 7th Floor
New York, NY 10177
Phone: 212-809-5199 Ext. 103
Fax: 212-825-0075
E-mail: tbond-williams@sspi.org

SODOWSKY LAW FIRM

https://www.sodowskylaw.com/

SODOWSKY LAW FIRM SCHOLARSHIP

Every year this firm offers a $1,000 scholarship to a U.S. college student who creates the best video essay. The video will discuss one of the following: the importance of consulting a business attorney before starting one's own business, or how tax attorneys improve modern society.

Award: Prize for use in freshman, sophomore, junior, or senior years; not renewable. *Number:* 1. *Amount:* $1000.

Eligibility Requirements: Applicant must be age 18-25 and enrolled or expecting to enroll full- or part-time at a two-year or four-year institution or university. Available to U.S. citizens.

Application Requirements: Application form may be submitted online (https://www.sodowskylaw.com/safety-scholarship-for-law-students/), essay. *Deadline:* August 15.

SOFT SURROUNDINGS

https://www.softsurroundings.com/

SOFT SURROUNDINGS COLLEGE SCHOLARSHIP

If you are a college student or high school senior interested in fashion design, merchandising, visual presentation, or fashion marketing, Soft Surroundings invites you to apply for this scholarship. To enter, please submit an essay between 500-750 words on the topic of who inspired you to pursue this field of study. Many people working in fashion chose this career path because of the influence of a teacher, family member, or other mentor, and we want to hear your story!

Award: Scholarship for use in freshman, sophomore, junior, senior, or graduate years; renewable. *Number:* 1. *Amount:* $1000.

Eligibility Requirements: Applicant must be enrolled or expecting to enroll full- or part-time at a two-year or four-year institution or university. Available to U.S. citizens.

Application Requirements: Essay. *Deadline:* November 30.

SOLANO LAW FIRM

https://solanofirm.com/

SOLANO LAW FIRM SCHOLARSHIP CONTEST

Every year, our firm grants a $1,000 scholarship to the U.S. college student who creates the best video essay on overcoming obstacles in the immigrant community or why they want to be a lawyer.

Award: Prize for use in freshman, sophomore, junior, or senior years; not renewable. *Number:* 1. *Amount:* $1000.

Eligibility Requirements: Applicant must be age 18-25 and enrolled or expecting to enroll full- or part-time at a two-year or four-year institution or university. Available to U.S. citizens.

Application Requirements: Application form may be submitted online (https://solanofirm.com/immigration-resources/scholarship-college-students/), essay. *Deadline:* August 15.

SOMNISHOP

INTERNATIONAL RESEARCH SCHOLARSHIP ON PRIMARY SNORING

The scholarship is awarded by SomniShop, an international startup specialized in anti-snoring products. We would like to draw more attention of the scientific community to the huge problem of primary snoring. Primary snoring is very common it affects tens of millions worldwide every day. About 5% of those who are affected suffer from a pathological form of snoring. Pathological snoring, however, already receives considerable attention by the medical research community. For 95% of the individuals who are affected it is a different situation their non-pathological snoring, which is also referred to as simple (habitual) snoring, is still relatively little explored. That is what we would like to change with our scholarship. Scholarship Application Requirements: The scholarship application must present a sound scientific approach which has the potential to improve the diagnosis or therapy of non-pathological snoring. The idea should be creative and not already be published until the application deadline of July 31, 2018. A jury of medical experts will select the scholarship winner. You will be notified of the outcome of your application by end of August 2018. Of course, there are no application fees. Eligibility: Open to all applicants who are enrolled at a university / college, do their doctorate there or participate in a research project at a university or university clinic. You may participate on your own or as a team. In case of team applications, only one team member has to meet one of these requirements. Application deadline is July 31, 2018. All applications must be submitted per e-mail to scholarship@ somnishop.net. One winner (team) will receive a scholarship award of USD 1,000. Privacy policy: We will treat applicant's data strictly confidential, will not share them with third parties and will use applicant's contact details only for notifying him / her about the outcome of the application.

Award: Scholarship for use in freshman, sophomore, junior, senior, graduate, or postgraduate years; renewable. *Number:* 1. *Amount:* $1000.

Eligibility Requirements: Applicant must be enrolled or expecting to enroll full- or part-time at a two-year or four-year or technical institution or university. Available to U.S. and non-U.S. citizens.

Application Requirements: Application form. *Deadline:* July 31.

Contact: Dr. Daniel Gratz
       E-mail: scholarship@somnishop.net

SOROPTIMIST INTERNATIONAL OF THE AMERICAS

https://www.soroptimist.org

THE SOROPTIMIST LIVE YOUR DREAM: EDUCATION AND TRAINING AWARDS FOR WOMEN

You are eligible to apply for a Live Your Dream Award if you are a woman who provides the primary financial support for yourself and your dependent(s), has financial need, and is enrolled in or has been accepted to an educational program (such as vocational/skills training program, or an undergraduate degree program.) An award can be used to cover any expense related to pursuing your education, such as books, tuition, transportation, or childcare. For a full list of eligibility requirements, please visit our website: https://www.soroptimist.org/our-work/live-your-dream-awards/apply-for-the-live-your-dream-awards.html#eligibility

Award: Prize for use in freshman, sophomore, junior, or senior years; not renewable. *Amount:* $500–$10,000.

Eligibility Requirements: Applicant must be enrolled or expecting to enroll full- or part-time at a two-year or technical institution or university and female. Available to U.S. and non-U.S. citizens.

Application Requirements: Application form, application form may be submitted online, essay, financial need analysis. *Deadline:* November 15.

Contact: Program Assistant
       E-mail: lydawards@soroptimist.org

SOUND MONEY DEFENSE LEAGUE

http://soundmoneydefense.org

MONEY METALS EXCHANGE SCHOLARSHIP PROGRAM

Money Metals Exchange, a national precious dealer recently ranked Best in the USA, has teamed up with the Sound Money Defense League to help qualified students pay for the ever-rising costs of higher education. These groups have just introduced the first gold-backed scholarship of the modern era, setting aside 100 oz. of physical gold for scholarships to outstanding undergraduate and graduate students who display deep understanding of economics and monetary policy. Money Metals Exchange and the Sound Money Defense League will be awarding this scholarship to two incoming or current undergraduate students and two graduate students each year. Judged Scholarship Award: Undergraduate Student First Place: $2,000, Undergraduate Student Runner Up: $1,000, Graduate Student First Place: $2,000, Graduate Student Runner Up: $1,000; People's Choice Award, First Place: $500. Application, resume, and essay must be submitted by September 30, 2017. For more information, visit moneymetals.com/scholarship

Award: Scholarship for use in freshman, sophomore, junior, senior, or graduate years; not renewable. *Number:* 5. *Amount:* $500–$2000.

Eligibility Requirements: Applicant must be enrolled or expecting to enroll full-time at a two-year or four-year or technical institution or university. Available to U.S. and non-U.S. citizens.

Application Requirements: Application form, essay. *Deadline:* September 30.

Contact: Mr. Jp Cortez, Assistant Director
       Sound Money Defense League
       15720 Brixham Hill Avenue
       Charlotte, NC 28277
       E-mail: jp.cortez@soundmoneydefense.org

SOUTHWESTERN RUGS DEPOT

https://www.southwesternrugsdepot.com/

SOUTHWESTERN RUGS DEPOT SCHOLARSHIP

Minimum 300 word essay on why decor matters to you. Open to all college students. Deadline Jan. 2nd. Apply here: https://www.southwesternrugsdepot.com/scholarship/

Award: Scholarship for use in freshman, sophomore, junior, senior, or graduate years; not renewable. *Number:* 1. *Amount:* $500.

Eligibility Requirements: Applicant must be age 18 and over and enrolled or expecting to enroll full- or part-time at a two-year or four-year or technical institution or university. Available to U.S. and non-U.S. citizens.

Application Requirements: Essay. *Deadline:* January 2.

Contact: Mr. Connor Butterworth
       Phone: 770-773-6416
       E-mail: contact@southwesternrugsdepot.com

SPINE SURGEON DR. VICTOR HAYES

https://tampabaybackpaindoctor.com/

TAMPA BAY SPINE CENTER ROAD TO RECOVERY SCHOLARSHIP

Submit a 750-word essay that thoughtfully describes a time in your life in which you suffered a physical or emotional setback in which you recovered and what that recovery has meant to you. Current official transcript from the applicant's school (first-year college students may submit an official transcript from their most recent school, as well as an unofficial transcript from their current post-secondary institution). For more complete information, please visit: http://tampabaybackpaindoctor.com/#scholarship

Award: Scholarship for use in freshman, sophomore, junior, senior, graduate, or postgraduate years; not renewable. *Number:* 1. *Amount:* $1000.

Eligibility Requirements: Applicant must be enrolled or expecting to enroll full- or part-time at a two-year or four-year or technical institution or university. Available to U.S. and non-U.S. citizens.

Application Requirements: Application form may be submitted online (https://tampabaybackpaindoctor.com/the-2019-tampa-spine-center-road-to-recovery-scholarship/), essay, resume, transcript. *Deadline:* August 31.

Contact: Dr. Victor Hayes
E-mail: info@tampabaybackpaindoctor.com

STATE DEPARTMENT FEDERAL CREDIT UNION ANNUAL SCHOLARSHIP PROGRAM

http://www.sdfcu.org/

STATE DEPARTMENT FEDERAL CREDIT UNION ANNUAL SCHOLARSHIP PROGRAM

Scholarships available to members who are currently enrolled in a degree program and have completed 12 credit hours of coursework at an accredited college or university. Must have own account in good standing with SDFCU, have a minimum 2.5 GPA, submit official cumulative transcripts, and describe need for financial assistance to continue their education. Scholarship only open to members of State Department Federal Credit Union.

Award: Scholarship for use in sophomore, junior, senior, or graduate years; not renewable. *Amount:* $2500.

Eligibility Requirements: Applicant must be enrolled or expecting to enroll full-time at a four-year institution or university. Available to U.S. and non-U.S. citizens.

Application Requirements: Application form, financial need analysis. *Deadline:* April 29.

Contact: Scholarship Coordinator
Phone: 703-706-5000
E-mail: sdfcu@sdfcu.org

STEALTHY AND WEALTHY

http://stealthyandwealthy.com

STEALTHY AND WEALTHY STUDENT ENTREPRENEUR GRANT

Whether you have an idea for an app, a blog or a vlog, a talent for creating products that you want to sell online, a savvy method for investing, or a technological innovation that you want to get off the ground, we want to help. This grant is for anyone interested in building their own business or side hustle to help them get ahead while they are in school. The money can be used for marketing your business, purchasing materials, setting up at a trade show, launching an online store, or whatever your business or idea needs to help you succeed. To give back to the next generation of entrepreneurs and brilliant minds, we have created a grant that will go directly to the student who will be working to build their future. There is one grant that will be awarded each fall to a college student in the United States. This grant will be a $250 one-time gift given to the student who is selected. The money is intended to be used as an investment or to help build a personal side business for the future entrepreneur.

Award: Grant for use in freshman, sophomore, junior, senior, graduate, or postgraduate years; not renewable. *Number:* 1–2. *Amount:* $250–$1000.

Eligibility Requirements: Applicant must be enrolled or expecting to enroll full- or part-time at a two-year or four-year or technical institution or university. Available to U.S. and non-U.S. citizens.

Application Requirements: Application form, essay. *Deadline:* August 21.

Contact: Scott Patten, Editor in Chief
E-mail: scott@stealthyandwealthy.com

STEINBERG, GOODMAN AND KALISH

https://www.sgklawyers.com/

STEINBERG, GOODMAN AND KALISH SCHOLARSHIP

Steinberg, Goodman & Kalish is pleased to announce that every year we will offer a $1,000 scholarship to the student who submits the strongest essay focusing on the given topic. The current topic is "Should pharmaceutical companies be allowed to promote drugs for uses that were not FDA approved?" The application must be completed online and the deadline is July 15, 2018.

Award: Scholarship for use in freshman, sophomore, junior, or senior years; not renewable. *Number:* 1. *Amount:* $1000.

Eligibility Requirements: Applicant must be enrolled or expecting to enroll full-time at a two-year or four-year institution or university. Available to U.S. citizens.

Application Requirements: Application form, application form may be submitted online (http://sgklawyers.com/academic-scholarship/), essay. *Deadline:* July 15.

Contact: Anni Hemsing
E-mail: anni@marketjd.com

STONEWALL COMMUNITY FOUNDATION

http://www.stonewallfoundation.org/

TRAUB-DICKER RAINBOW SCHOLARSHIP

Non-renewable scholarships available to women-identified lesbians who are involved in LGBTQ activism. Must be graduating high school seniors planning to attend a recognized college, or already matriculated college students in any year of study, including graduate school.

Award: Scholarship for use in freshman, sophomore, junior, senior, graduate, or postgraduate years; not renewable. *Number:* 3–4. *Amount:* $1000–$3000.

Eligibility Requirements: Applicant must be enrolled or expecting to enroll full- or part-time at a four-year institution or university and female. Available to U.S. citizens.

Application Requirements: Application form, application form may be submitted online (http://stonewallfoundation.org/scholarships), essay.

Contact: Program Manager
Stonewall Community Foundation
Stonewall Community Foundation
1270 Broadway, Suite 501
New York, NY 10001
Phone: 212-457.1341
E-mail: scholarships@stonewallfoundation.org

STRAIGHTFORWARD MEDIA

http://www.straightforwardmedia.com/

DALE E. FRIDELL MEMORIAL SCHOLARSHIP

Scholarships are open to anyone aspiring to attend a university, college, trade school, technical institute, vocational training, or other postsecondary education program. Eligible students may not have already been awarded a full tuition scholarship or waiver from another source. International students are welcome to apply. For more information, visit website http://www.straightforwardmedia.com/fridell/form.php.

Award: Scholarship for use in freshman, sophomore, junior, or senior years; not renewable. *Number:* 2. *Amount:* $1000.

Eligibility Requirements: Applicant must be enrolled or expecting to enroll full- or part-time at a two-year or four-year or technical institution or university. Available to U.S. and non-U.S. citizens.

Application Requirements: Essay. *Deadline:* varies.

Contact: Scholarship Committee
Phone: 605-348-3042

HELPING HAND SCHOLARSHIP

Annual award to help students hampered by debt to continue their studies. Must be attending or planning to attend a college, trade school, technical institute, vocational program or other postsecondary education program. For more information, see web http://www.straightforwardmedia.com/debt2/debt-apply.html.

Award: Scholarship for use in freshman, sophomore, junior, or senior years; not renewable. *Number:* 4. *Amount:* $500.

Eligibility Requirements: Applicant must be enrolled or expecting to enroll full- or part-time at a two-year or four-year or technical institution or university. Available to U.S. and non-U.S. citizens.

Application Requirements: Essay. *Deadline:* varies.

Contact: Scholarship Committee
   Phone: 605-348-3042

MESOTHELIOMA MEMORIAL SCHOLARSHIP

Open to all students attending or planning to attend a postsecondary educational program, including 2- or 4-year college or university, vocational school, continuing education, ministry training, and job skills training. Refer to website for details http://www.straightforwardmedia.com/meso/.

Award: Scholarship for use in freshman, sophomore, junior, or senior years; not renewable. *Number:* 4. *Amount:* $500.

Eligibility Requirements: Applicant must be enrolled or expecting to enroll full- or part-time at a two-year or four-year or technical institution or university. Available to U.S. and non-U.S. citizens.

Application Requirements: Essay. *Deadline:* varies.

Contact: Scholarship Committee
   Phone: 605-348-3042

STROLLER DEPOT

https://www.strollerdepot.com/

$1,000 STROLLER DEPOT SCHOLARSHIP

Stroller Depot is offering one $1,000 scholarship to a student who is currently enrolled or accepted to a higher education program; is a young parent (age 18-30), with 1 or more children; and has a GPA of at least 3.5. The scholarship submissions must be received by December 15, 2017.

Award: Scholarship for use in freshman, sophomore, junior, senior, graduate, or postgraduate years; not renewable. *Number:* 1. *Amount:* $1000.

Eligibility Requirements: Applicant must be age 18-30 and enrolled or expecting to enroll full- or part-time at a two-year or four-year institution or university. Available to U.S. and non-U.S. citizens.

Application Requirements: Essay. *Deadline:* December 15.

STROM & ASSOCIATES

https://stromlawyers.com

STROM & ASSOCIATES ANNUAL SCHOLARSHIP

Strom & Associates understands the increasing costs of college tuition makes it more difficult to graduate college for many outstanding students across the nation. Therefore, we are offering one $1,000 scholarship. The scholarship committee will select the student who submits the best essay focusing on the given topic.

Award: Scholarship for use in freshman, sophomore, junior, or senior years; not renewable. *Number:* 1. *Amount:* $1000.

Eligibility Requirements: Applicant must be enrolled or expecting to enroll full-time at a two-year or four-year institution or university. Available to U.S. citizens.

Application Requirements: Application form, application form may be submitted online (https://stromlawyers.com/academic-scholarship/), essay. *Deadline:* July 15.

Contact: Neal Strom, Partner
   Strom & Associates
   180 N. LaSalle, Suite #2510
   Chicago, IL 60601
   Phone: 312-609-0400

STUDENT INSIGHTS

http://www.studentinsights.com

STUDENT-VIEW SCHOLARSHIP PROGRAM

Scholarship available by random drawing from the pool of entrants who respond to an online survey from Student Insights marketing organization. Parental permission to participate required for applicants under age 18.

Award: Scholarship for use in freshman year; not renewable. *Number:* 13. *Amount:* $500–$4000.

Eligibility Requirements: Applicant must be high school student and planning to enroll or expecting to enroll full-time at a two-year or four-year or technical institution or university. Available to U.S. citizens.

Application Requirements: Application form. *Deadline:* April 22.

Contact: Mr. John Becker, Program Coordinator
   Student Insights
   136 Justice Drive
   Valencia, PA 16059
   Phone: 724-903-0439
   E-mail: contact@studentinsights.com

STUDY.COM

http://study.com

STUDY.COM CLEP SCHOLARSHIP

Study.com will be supporting three students pursuing CLEP credit. CLEP exams are a proven and efficient way for both traditional and non-traditional students from all walks of life to gain college credit. For more information, please visit https://study.com/academy/popular/studycom-clep-scholarship-application-form-information.html

Award: Scholarship for use in freshman, sophomore, or junior years; renewable. *Number:* 1–3. *Amount:* $250–$500.

Eligibility Requirements: Applicant must be enrolled or expecting to enroll full- or part-time at a two-year or four-year institution or university. Available to U.S. citizens.

Application Requirements: Application form, personal photograph. *Deadline:* April 1.

Contact: Koby Wong, Study.com Scholarship Manager
   Phone: 650-9621200
   E-mail: koby@email.study.com

STUDY.COM SCHOLARSHIP FOR FLORIDA STUDENTS

The Study.com Scholarship for Florida Students provides a $500 academic award to a student pursuing their undergraduate college degree from a college or university in Florida. At Study.com, we believe every student has a right to an affordable, high-quality education, and with this scholarship we hope to ease the heavy burden of college tuition. Please visit the following link for more info: https://study.com/pages/Scholarship_for_Florida_Students.html

Award: Scholarship for use in freshman, sophomore, or junior years; renewable. *Number:* 1. *Amount:* $500.

Eligibility Requirements: Applicant must be enrolled or expecting to enroll full- or part-time at a two-year or four-year institution or university and studying in Florida. Available to U.S. citizens.

Application Requirements: Application form, personal photograph. *Deadline:* April 1.

Contact: Koby Wong, Study.com Scholarship Manager
   Phone: 650-9621200
   E-mail: koby@email.study.com

STUDY.COM SCHOLARSHIP FOR TEXAS STUDENTS

The Study.com Scholarship for Texas Students provides a $500 academic award to a student pursuing their undergraduate college degree from any college or university in Texas. At Study.com, we believe every student has a right to an affordable, high-quality education, and with this scholarship we hope to ease the heavy burden of college tuition. For more info, please visit https://study.com/pages/Scholarship_for_Texas_Students.html.

Award: Scholarship for use in freshman, sophomore, or junior years; renewable. *Number:* 1–500.

Eligibility Requirements: Applicant must be enrolled or expecting to enroll full- or part-time at a two-year or four-year institution or university and studying in Texas. Available to U.S. citizens.

Application Requirements: Application form, personal photograph. *Deadline:* April 1.

Contact: Koby Wong, Study.com Scholarship Manager
   Phone: 650-9621200
   E-mail: koby@email.study.com

STUDYPORTALS

http://www.studyportals.eu/

GLOBAL STUDY AWARDS

We want to ultimately encourage young people to study abroad as part of their tertiary studies in order to experience and explore new countries, cultures and languages. The Global Study Awards recognizes studying abroad as a positively life changing experience for many students, opening their minds to alternative ways of personal life and professional career, as well as promoting intercultural understanding and tolerance. The Award prize will be applied toward the cost of tuition fees in the first instance, paid directly to the Higher Education Institution that the successful candidate will attend. If tuition fees are below the maximum individual award fund of €10,000, the remaining funds may be allocated per diem for living costs for a maximum of 52 weeks starting from when the student first registered at the higher education institution.

Award: Scholarship for use in freshman, sophomore, junior, senior, graduate, or postgraduate years; not renewable. *Number:* 1–9. *Amount:* $11,215–$11,215.

Eligibility Requirements: Applicant must be enrolled or expecting to enroll full- or part-time at a two-year or four-year institution or university. Available to U.S. and non-U.S. citizens.

Application Requirements: Application form, application form may be submitted online(www.studyportals.com/scholarship), essay, transcript. *Deadline:* varies.

Contact: Ms. Sissy Bottcher, Community Manager
StudyPortals
Torenallee 45 - 4.02
Eindhoven 5617 BA
NLD
Phone: 3-140 218 0238
Fax: 3-140 292 0075
E-mail: students@studyportals.com

STUDYSOUP

FUTURE INNOVATOR SCHOLARSHIP

As a company driven to help students succeed, we know that college is an important step along many career paths, but it can be expensive. Students can upload notes to StudySoup to lighten their financial burden. However, we still felt like we could do more to give back to the future leaders of the world. Therefore, we are offering a $500 scholarship each month to outstanding students who exemplify one or more of StudySoup's core values: Be a Knight Make an Impact Succeed Together You may have mentored a fellow student, organized a fundraiser for charity, or gone on a humanitarian trip abroad. Whatever your achievements, we want to hear from you!

Award: Scholarship for use in freshman, sophomore, junior, senior, graduate, or postgraduate years; renewable. *Number:* 1–7. *Amount:* $200–$500.

Eligibility Requirements: Applicant must be age 18 and over and enrolled or expecting to enroll full-time at a two-year or four-year institution or university. Available to U.S. and non-U.S. citizens.

Application Requirements: Application form. *Deadline:* continuous.

Contact: Katy Tripses
E-mail: katy@studysoup.com

SUNTRUST BANK

http://www.suntrusteducation.com/

OFF TO COLLEGE SCHOLARSHIP SWEEPSTAKES AWARD

Award of $1000 to a high school senior planning to attend college in the fall. Must complete an online entry form by accessing the website, http://www.offtocollege.info. Scholarship sweepstakes drawings are random and occur every other week from October 31 to May 15.

Award: Scholarship for use in freshman year; not renewable. *Number:* 15. *Amount:* $1000.

Eligibility Requirements: Applicant must be high school student; age 13 and over and planning to enroll or expecting to enroll full- or part-time at a two-year or four-year or technical institution or university. Available to U.S. citizens.

Application Requirements: Application form. *Deadline:* continuous.

Contact: Joy Blauvelt, Scholarship Coordinator
Phone: 800-552-3006

SUPPORT COLLECTORS

https://www.supportcollectors.com/

SUPPORT COLLECTORS SCHOLARSHIP

We want to provide financial assistance to a selected college student who has either been affected by family separation in their own life, or who intends to pursue a career that will have a positive impact on separated families. The selected student will receive an award of $500 for use toward tuition, books, or living expenses. Selection date is December 14.

Award: Scholarship for use in freshman, sophomore, junior, or senior years; not renewable. *Number:* 1. *Amount:* $500.

Eligibility Requirements: Applicant must be enrolled or expecting to enroll full-time at a four-year institution or university. Available to U.S. citizens.

Application Requirements: Application form, essay. *Deadline:* December 7.

TALL CLUBS INTERNATIONAL FOUNDATION, INC.

http://www.tall.org

KAE SUMNER EINFELDT SCHOLARSHIP

Females 5'10", or males 6'2" (minimum heights), are eligible to apply for the scholarship. Interested individuals should contact their local Tall Clubs Chapter. Canadian and U.S. winners are selected from finalists submitted by each local chapter.

Award: Scholarship for use in freshman year; not renewable. *Number:* 2–6. *Amount:* $1000.

Eligibility Requirements: Applicant must be age 17-21 and enrolled or expecting to enroll full- or part-time at a two-year or four-year institution or university. Available to U.S. and Canadian citizens.

Application Requirements: Application form, essay, personal photograph, recommendations or references, transcript, verification of height. *Deadline:* March 1.

Contact: Carolyn Goldstein, TCI Foundation Scholarship Contact
E-mail: tcischolarships@hotmail.com

TECHNICAL ASSOCIATION OF THE PULP & PAPER INDUSTRY (TAPPI)

https://www.tappi.org/

TAPPI PLACE (POLYMERS, LAMINATIONS, ADHESIVES, COATINGS AND EXTRUSIONS) SCHOLARSHIP

Awarded only in even numbered years, the TAPPI PLACE (Polymers, Laminations, Adhesives, Coatings and Extrusions) Scholarship is designed to encourage talented science and engineering students to pursue careers in the packaging industry and to develop awareness of the industry, and of the TAPPI Polymers, Laminations, Adhesives, Coatings, and Extrusions (PLACE) Division. Membership in a TAPPI Student Chapter is required.

Award: Scholarship for use in freshman, sophomore, junior, or senior years; not renewable. *Number:* 1. *Amount:* $4000.

Eligibility Requirements: Applicant must be enrolled or expecting to enroll full-time at a two-year or four-year institution or university. Available to U.S. and non-U.S. citizens.

Application Requirements: Application form. *Deadline:* February 14.

Contact: Mr. Laurence Womack, Director of Standards and Awards
Technical Association of the Pulp & Paper Industry (TAPPI)
15 Technology Parkway South
Suite 115
Peachtree Corners, GA 30092
Phone: 770-209-7276
E-mail: standards@tappi.org

TECHNOSOFT INNOVATIONS, INC.

https://www.technosoftinv.com/

TECHNOSOFT INNOVATIONS SCHOLARSHIP PROGRAM

Technosoft Innovations is glad to inform you that we are offering a scholarship of $500 to the students of your university for the academic year 2017-2018. Please send the scholarship application before May 31, 2018 on innovations@technosofteng.com with the subject line "Application for Scholarship Program 2017-18." Visit https://www.technosoftinv.com/electronic-products.html#scholarship for detailed information. To apply for the scholarship you need to submit a 1000 words essay on either one of these topics: 1. Recent Developments in the Medical Industry; or 2. Recent Developments in the Electronics Industry. We will accept only 100% original essay. Any plagiarism will instantly lead to disqualification. Each applicant can make only one submission. Applicants under the age of 18 years will be disqualified. Winner of the scholarship will be declared on June 15, 2018.

Award: Scholarship for use in freshman, sophomore, junior, senior, graduate, or postgraduate years; renewable. *Number:* 1. *Amount:* $500.

Eligibility Requirements: Applicant must be high school student; age 18 and over and planning to enroll or expecting to enroll full- or part-time at a two-year or four-year or technical institution or university. Available to U.S. and Canadian citizens.

Application Requirements: Essay, personal photograph. *Deadline:* May 31.

Contact: Rayburn Rozario, Marketing Head
Technosoft Innovations, Inc.
900 Perimeter Park Drive
Suite C
Morrisville, NC 27590
Phone: 313-265-2622
E-mail: innovations@technosofteng.coml

TELEVISION ACADEMY FOUNDATION

http://www.televisionacademy.com/foundation

TELEVISION ACADEMY FOUNDATION

A competition for excellence in college student video, digital, and film productions. Rules and guidelines are updated annually in the fall at televisionacademyfoundation.org. Awards of up to $10,000. Open to those students who have produced their video while enrolled in a community college, college, or university in the United States.

Award: Prize for use in freshman, sophomore, junior, senior, graduate, or postgraduate years; not renewable. *Number:* 9. *Amount:* $3000–$10,000.

Eligibility Requirements: Applicant must be age 18 and over and enrolled or expecting to enroll full- or part-time at a two-year or four-year or technical institution or university. Available to U.S. citizens.

Application Requirements: Application form, application form may be submitted online (http://www.emmys.com/foundation/programs/cta), entry in a contest, video and plot summaries.

Contact: Liz Korda, Director, Awards Dept
Television Academy Foundation
5220 Lankershim Boulevard
North Hollywood, CA 91601
Phone: 818-754-2800
E-mail: ctasupport@televisionacademy.com

TELIOS LAW PLLC

http://telioslaw.com

TELIOS LAW SOJOURNER SCHOLARSHIP

The Telios Law Sojourner Scholarship application is open to any high school student or recent high school graduate who has spent three or more years of his or her life as a third-culture missionary kid and will be enrolled full-time for the 2018-2019 school year as a freshman or sophomore at a college or university that has an emphasis on spiritual formation in the Christian faith. For complete information, please visit http://telioslaw.com/scholarships. A sojourner lives between cultures, and this is often the experience of a third-culture missionary kid. For MKs, a key to transitioning back "home" is figuring out how to flourish in a new culture. Behind this struggle is the desire put into pop culture terms by singer and songwriter Adele, who wrote, "But I want to live / And not just survive." We all have a longing for what ancient Greek philosophers called eudaimonia, which roughly translates to "happiness, welfare, or human flourishing." Telios Law believes that we as humans were made to flourish, and we want to contribute to that flourishing, not only through doing our legal work well, but by helping MKs in particular pursue their flourishing as they transition back.

Award: Scholarship for use in freshman, sophomore, junior, or senior years; renewable. *Number:* 1. *Amount:* $1000.

Eligibility Requirements: Applicant must be enrolled or expecting to enroll full-time at a two-year or four-year institution or university.

Application Requirements: Application form, essay. *Deadline:* January 15.

Contact: Mr. Joshua Romero, Outreach Coordinator
Telios Law PLLC
PO Box 3488
Monument, CO 80132
Phone: 855-748-4201
E-mail: tell@telioslaw.com

TETHERBOX

http://www.tetherbox.com/

$1,000 CREATIVE VIDEO CHALLENGE COLLEGE SCHOLARSHIP

Make a creative funny, heartwarming, or informational video for the opportunity to win a $1,000 college scholarship. The assignment for the TetherBox Creative Video Challenge College Scholarship is to make a commercial about TetherBox College Care Packages or a video related to care packages, being away from home, etc. Video length should be at least 1 minute but no longer than 4 minutes. You have full creative control on how you storyboard and shoot your video, but here is a few thoughts to help add context: Situation: Think of unique situations, locations, occurrences, etc. or think of common situations, occurrences and locations that you can put a creative, humorous or heartwarming twist on; Dialogue/Narrative: Develop hilarious or touching dialogue and/or narratives; Perspective: Find creative and unique angles and shots; Effects: Try and make use of different video styles and effects to get the video just the way you want it; Think Creatively: Think back on your favorite commercials and the most popular viral commercials on the web and see what unique ideas you can come up with. Go to www.tetherbox.com/scholarship and complete the brief application. When your commercial is ready, upload your video to a file sharing site like Dropbox or Google Drive and send the link to info@tetherbox.com, along with a short bio including your name, year in school, and expected graduation date and a brief overview explaining your video concept. Submission deadline: March 31, 2017. Your personal safety is paramount so please be safe. Entry is subject to the official rules and conditions. By submitting your video to TetherBox for scholarship consideration you agree to assign all rights and ownership of the video to TetherBox and you grant TetherBox full permission to re-publish, edit and otherwise freely use your video in any manner without notice or compensation.

Award: Scholarship for use in freshman, sophomore, junior, or senior years; not renewable. *Number:* 1. *Amount:* $1000.

Eligibility Requirements: Applicant must be enrolled or expecting to enroll full-time at a four-year or technical institution or university. Available to U.S. citizens.

Application Requirements: Application form. *Deadline:* March 31.

Contact: Lynn Holdsworth, Co-Founder
TetherBox
5 Walter E. Foran Blvd.
Suite 2002
Flemington, NJ 08822
Phone: 908-246-3934
Fax: 866-302-2255
E-mail: lynn.holdsworth@tetherbox.com

TEXAS HIGHER EDUCATION COORDINATING BOARD

http://www.collegeforalltexans.com/

GOOD NEIGHBOR SCHOLARSHIP PROGRAM

Provides assistance for tuition to students from other nations of the Western Hemisphere (other than Cuba). Students must have lived for at least five years in the Western Hemisphere, scholastically qualify for admission, and must intend to return to their country upon completion of their program of study. Students that apply for Permanent Resident status or have dual citizenship are not eligible. Renewal awards require student meet the institution's minimum GPA requirement. Contact your institution for more information.

Award: Scholarship for use in freshman, sophomore, junior, senior, or graduate years; renewable.

Eligibility Requirements: Applicant must be enrolled or expecting to enroll full- or part-time at a two-year institution or university and studying in Texas. Available to Canadian and non-U.S. citizens.

Application Requirements: Application form, application form may be submitted online. *Deadline:* May 1.

Contact: Student Financial Aid Office at the institution
Phone: 844-792-2640

TEXAS PUBLIC EDUCATIONAL GRANT PROGRAM (TPEG)

To provide grant assistance to students with financial need. Public colleges or universities in Texas make TPEG awards from their own resources. Only in-state (Texas) colleges or universities may participate in the program. Only public colleges or universities participate in the program (no private, non-profit or career colleges or universities).

Award: Grant for use in freshman, sophomore, junior, or senior years; renewable.

Eligibility Requirements: Applicant must be enrolled or expecting to enroll full- or part-time at a two-year institution or university. Available to U.S. and non-U.S. citizens.

Application Requirements: Financial need analysis. *Deadline:* continuous.

Contact: Student Financial Aid Office at the institution

TUITION EQUALIZATION GRANT (TEG) PROGRAM

Renewable award for Texas residents enrolled at least three-quarter time at an independent college or private university in Texas in a degree program that does not lead to ordination or licensure to preach. Awards are based on financial need. Renewal awards also require the student to maintain a minimum overall college GPA of at least 2.5, complete at least 24 SCH's each year (18 SCH's for students in graduate programs), and complete a minimum of 75% of classes attempted each year. Must not be receiving athletic scholarship concurrently. Contact college/university financial aid office for application information.

Award: Grant for use in freshman, sophomore, junior, senior, or graduate years; renewable. *Amount:* $1–$5130.

Eligibility Requirements: Applicant must be enrolled or expecting to enroll full- or part-time at an institution or university and studying in Texas. Available to U.S. citizens.

Application Requirements: Financial need analysis. *Deadline:* continuous.

Contact: Student Financial Aid Programs
Phone: 888-311-8881

TEXAS MUTUAL INSURANCE COMPANY

http://www.texasmutual.com/

TEXAS MUTUAL INSURANCE COMPANY SCHOLARSHIP PROGRAM

A scholarship program open to qualified family members of policyholder employees who died from on-the-job injuries or accidents, policyholder employees who qualify for lifetime income benefits pursuant to the Texas Workers Compensation Act, and family members of injured employees who qualify for lifetime income benefits.

Award: Scholarship for use in freshman, sophomore, junior, or senior years; not renewable. *Number:* 1–25. *Amount:* $600–$6000.

Eligibility Requirements: Applicant must be age 25 or under and enrolled or expecting to enroll full-time at a two-year or four-year or technical institution or university. Available to U.S. and non-U.S. citizens.

Application Requirements: Application form, financial need analysis. *Deadline:* continuous.

Contact: Temetria McVea, Executive Assistant to the President
Texas Mutual Insurance Company
6210 East Highway 290
Austin, TX 78723
Phone: 512-224-3907
E-mail: tmcvea@texasmutual.com

THE10PRO

THE10PRO SCHOLARSHIP PROGRAM

1 - Scholarship Purpose: We understand that there are intelligent students who is struggling economically with their school fees or upkeep money. This scholarship is aimed at assisting such students to further their education for a better tomorrow. For that reason, we will be awarding any eligible student who proves to having unique writing skills with an amount of USD 2,000. 2 - Eligibility: The entrance fee for this scholarship is FREE. You need to be A STUDENT from any country/area. Show that you are currently studying or pursuing any field of study. 3 - How to Apply for This Scholarship? Choose a topic (there are 3 topics available) and write an essay about it (1,000-1,500 words). Send your essay (PDF) and contact information to scholarship@the10pro.com. 4 - Awards:The amount of USD 2,000 (Two Thousands US Dollars) will be given to the number one contestant. 5 - Scholarship Timelines (EDT): Jul 07 2017: Start accepting essays. Oct 15 2017: Deadline of essay submission. Nov 05 2017: Winner will be announced on the10pro.com/scholarship/. (For more information, please visit www.the10pro.com/scholarship/)

Award: Prize for use in freshman, sophomore, junior, senior, graduate, or postgraduate years; not renewable. *Number:* 1. *Amount:* $2000.

Eligibility Requirements: Applicant must be enrolled or expecting to enroll full- or part-time at an institution or university.

Application Requirements: Essay. *Deadline:* October 15.

Contact: Vincent Hill
The10Pro
3535 1st St North
Dolomite, AL 35061
Phone: 205-201-5413
E-mail: scholarship@the10pro.com

THEPENNYHOARDER.COM

http://www.thepennyhoarder.com/

FRUGAL STUDENT

You just need to tell us in 150 words or less the craziest, funniest, most interesting, unique, or creative way you've ever saved or made extra money.

Award: Scholarship for use in freshman, sophomore, junior, or senior years; renewable. *Number:* 1. *Amount:* $2000.

Eligibility Requirements: Applicant must be enrolled or expecting to enroll full- or part-time at a two-year or four-year institution or university. Available to U.S. citizens.

Application Requirements: Application form, application form may be submitted online (http://www.thepennyhoarder.com/frugal-student-scholarship/), entry in a contest, essay. *Deadline:* December 31.

Contact: Cynthia Moll
E-mail: scholarships@thepennyhoarder.com

THETA DELTA CHI EDUCATIONAL FOUNDATION INC.

http://www.tdx.org/

THETA DELTA CHI EDUCATIONAL FOUNDATION INC. SCHOLARSHIP

Scholarships for undergraduate or graduate students enrolled in an accredited institution. Awards are based on candidate's history of service to the fraternity, scholastic achievement, and need. See website for application and additional information http://www.tdx.org/scholarship/scholarship.html.

Award: Scholarship for use in freshman, sophomore, junior, senior, or graduate years; renewable. *Number:* 15. *Amount:* $1000–$5000.

Eligibility Requirements: Applicant must be enrolled or expecting to enroll full-time at a four-year institution or university. Available to U.S. and non-U.S. citizens.

Application Requirements: Application form, financial need analysis, recommendations or references, transcript. *Deadline:* May 15.

Contact: William McClung, Executive Director
    Phone: 617-742-8886
    Fax: 617-742-8868
    E-mail: execdir@tdx.org

THURGOOD MARSHALL COLLEGE FUND

http://www.tmcf.org/

THURGOOD MARSHALL COLLEGE FUND

Merit & Need-based scholarships for students attending one of the 47 member-schools which are HBCUs (historically black colleges and universities) including 5 member law schools. Must maintain an average GPA of 3.0, demonstrate financial need, and be a U.S. citizen/permanent resident. For further details refer to website, http://www.tmcf.org.

Award: Scholarship for use in freshman, sophomore, junior, senior, or graduate years; renewable. *Amount:* up to $6200.

Eligibility Requirements: Applicant must be enrolled or expecting to enroll full-time at a four-year institution or university. Available to U.S. and Canadian citizens.

Application Requirements: Application form, community service, essay, financial need analysis, interview, personal photograph. *Deadline:* June 1.

Contact: Ms. Deshuandra Walker, Senior Manager of Scholarship
        Programs
    Thurgood Marshall College Fund
    1770 Saint James Place, Suite 414
    Houston, TX 77056
    Phone: 713-955-1073
    Fax: 202-448-1017
    E-mail: deshuandra.walker@tmcf.org

TOPPRODUCTS.COM

http://topproducts.com/

TOPPRODUCTS SINGLE MOTHER SCHOLARSHIP

At TopProducts, we firmly believe in the power of education and giving back to the local community, especially single parent families. We understand the financial strain going to college can place on any family, let alone mothers who not only want to go further their education, but also must raise their children and run the household every day on their own. As strong advocates of both higher education and family values, we are pleased to help single moms who have shown strong scholastic ability throughout their high school or college years get the financial help they need to create a secure future for their children. Please review the eligibility requirements and application process below and remember, there will only be one winner. All applicants must include your full name, mail, phone number, mailing address, and 1,200 to 1,500 word essay. Application Deadline: Dec 31, 2017. This scholarship is available to all single mothers who meet the following criteria: 1. Must be a single parent and have custodial care of one or more children under 18, 2. Must not have a college degree from a 4-year institution, 3. Must be enrolled in a 4-year institution or have a high school diploma. Please submit a 1,200 to 1,500 word essay in PDF or Word Doc format to the attached submission form along with your full name, address, and contact details. We also require an unofficial copy of your high school transcript or college transcript. The essay topic is as follows: We want to hear your story. Therefore, we request you write a personal narrative describing yourself, your family and what education means to you. Why do you want to obtain a college degree? And how will this scholarship help you achieve your goals? Please submit through the TopProducts.com Scholarship Application Form.

Award: Scholarship for use in freshman, sophomore, junior, or senior years; not renewable. *Number:* 1. *Amount:* $1000.

Eligibility Requirements: Applicant must be enrolled or expecting to enroll full- or part-time at a two-year or four-year or technical institution or university and single female. Available to U.S. and non-U.S. citizens.

Application Requirements: Essay. *Deadline:* December 31.

TORHOERMAN LAW LLC

http://torhoermanlaw.com

TORHOERMAN LAW DISTRACTED DRIVING ESSAY SCHOLARSHIP

In accordance with our End Distracted Driving campaign, student contestants will be asked to discuss the dangers of distracted driving and what steps our society can take to put an end to this issue. The student with the best overall response will receive $1,000 to go towards their education costs. Contestants can choose to submit either a written essay or a video response to our essay topic prompt.

Award: Scholarship for use in freshman, sophomore, junior, or senior years; not renewable. *Number:* 1. *Amount:* $1000.

Eligibility Requirements: Applicant must be enrolled or expecting to enroll full-time at a two-year or four-year institution or university. Available to U.S. citizens.

Application Requirements: Autobiography, essay. *Deadline:* April 1.

Contact: Mr. Jordan Terry, Marketing Team
    Phone: 618-656-4400
    E-mail: JTerry@THLawyer.com

TRAVELNURSESOURCE.COM

https://www.travelnursesource.com/

FUTURE U.S. NURSE SCHOLARSHIP

Travel Nurse Source is awarding a $2,000 scholarship to a nursing student who composes a winning essay to our scholarship essay contest. We would like you to author your personal narrative including a brief introduction about yourself, your interests, and anything else you feel explains your story and reason for wanting this scholarship. Then in a 750-1000 word essay, please tell us about (1) your desire to become a registered nurse and how you plan to contribute to society as an RN, and (2) the significance that receiving this scholarship would have on you.

Award: Scholarship for use in freshman, sophomore, junior, or senior years; not renewable. *Number:* 1. *Amount:* $2000.

Eligibility Requirements: Applicant must be enrolled or expecting to enroll full- or part-time at a two-year or four-year or technical institution or university. Available to U.S. citizens.

Application Requirements: Essay. *Deadline:* October 13.

Contact: Troy Diffenderfer
    E-mail: troy@track5media.com

TURBOSQUID

https://www.turbosquid.com/

TURBOSQUID 2017 SPRING SCHOLARSHIP

TurboSquid has established a scholarship program to help identify and nurture future talent in the 3D industry. The topic for our initial scholarship is The Importance of Diversity for the 3D Industry. We want to hear from the future artists (or fans) of our industry. Let us know why you think it's important for 3D companies to diversify their workforce, or tell us what the 3D industry can do to better meet the needs of diverse consumers for whom they produce content or both. Research and write an essay on the following topic, The Importance of Diversity for the 3D Industry. Essay length should be 500-1000 words. You must be an active and graduating high school senior, or currently and actively enrolled as a full-time undergraduate or graduate college student with a minimum 3.0 minimum GPA.

Award: Scholarship for use in freshman, sophomore, junior, senior, or graduate years; not renewable. *Number:* 1. *Amount:* $5000.

Eligibility Requirements: Applicant must be enrolled or expecting to enroll full-time at a two-year or four-year or technical institution or university. Available to U.S. and non-U.S. citizens.

Application Requirements: Essay. *Deadline:* July 31.

Contact: DeLonna Day, Content Marketing Associate
    E-mail: scholarships@turbosquid.com

UNIGO

https://www.unigo.com

DO-OVER SCHOLARSHIP

Applicants must: Be thirteen years of age or older at the time of application. Be legal residents of the fifty United States or the District of Columbia. Be currently enrolled (or enroll no later than the fall of 2021) in an accredited post-secondary institution of higher education. Submit an online short written response (250 words or less) for the question: "If you could get one 'do over' in life, what would it be and why?"

Award: Scholarship for use in freshman, sophomore, junior, senior, graduate, or postgraduate years; not renewable. *Number:* 1. *Amount:* $1500.

Eligibility Requirements: Applicant must be age 13 and over and enrolled or expecting to enroll full- or part-time at a two-year or technical institution or university. Available to U.S. citizens.

Application Requirements: Application form, application form may be submitted online, essay. *Deadline:* June 30.

Contact: Scholarship Committee
Unigo
10751 Deerwood Park Boulevard, #125
Jacksonville, FL 32256
Phone: 904-483-2939
Fax: 904-483-2934
E-mail: info@scholarshipexperts.com

EDUCATION MATTERS SCHOLARSHIP

Applicants must: Complete a profile on the ScholarshipExperts.com website. Be thirteen years of age or older at the time of application. Be legal residents of the fifty United States or the District of Columbia. Be currently enrolled (or enroll no later than the fall of 2021) in an accredited post-secondary institution of higher education. Submit an online short written response (250 words or less) for the question: 'What would you say to someone who thinks education doesn't matter, or that college is a waste of time and money?'

Award: Scholarship for use in freshman, sophomore, junior, senior, graduate, or postgraduate years; not renewable. *Number:* 1. *Amount:* $5000.

Eligibility Requirements: Applicant must be age 13 and over and enrolled or expecting to enroll full- or part-time at a two-year or technical institution or university. Available to U.S. citizens.

Application Requirements: Application form, application form may be submitted online, essay. *Deadline:* November 30.

Contact: Scholarship Committee
Unigo
10751 Deerwood Park Boulevard, #125
Jacksonville, FL 32256
Phone: 904-483-2939
Fax: 904-483-2934
E-mail: info@scholarshipexperts.com

FIFTH MONTH SCHOLARSHIP

Applicants must: Be thirteen years of age or older at the time of application. Be legal residents of the fifty United States or the District of Columbia. Be currently enrolled (or enroll no later than the fall of 2021) in an accredited post-secondary institution of higher education and submit an online short written response (250 words or less) for the topic: 'May is the fifth month of the year. Write a letter to the number five explaining why five is important. Be serious or be funny. Either way, here's a high five to you just for being original.'

Award: Scholarship for use in freshman, sophomore, junior, senior, graduate, or postgraduate years; not renewable. *Number:* 1. *Amount:* $1500.

Eligibility Requirements: Applicant must be age 13 and over and enrolled or expecting to enroll full- or part-time at a two-year or technical institution or university. Available to U.S. citizens.

Application Requirements: Application form, application form may be submitted online, essay. *Deadline:* May 31.

Contact: Scholarship Committee
Unigo
10751 Deerwood Park Boulevard, #125
Jacksonville, FL 32256
Phone: 904-483-2939
Fax: 904-483-2934
E-mail: info@scholarshipexperts.com

I HAVE A DREAM SCHOLARSHIP

Applicants must: Be thirteen years of age or older at the time of application. Be legal residents of the fifty United States or the District of Columbia. Be currently enrolled (or enroll no later than the fall of 2027) in an accredited post-secondary institution of higher education and submit an online short written response (250 words or less) for the topic: 'We want to know, what do you dream about? Whether it's some bizarre dream from last week, or your hopes for the future, share your dreams with us for a chance to win $1,500 for college.'

Award: Scholarship for use in freshman, sophomore, junior, senior, graduate, or postgraduate years; not renewable. *Number:* 1. *Amount:* $1500.

Eligibility Requirements: Applicant must be age 13 and over and enrolled or expecting to enroll full- or part-time at a two-year or technical institution or university. Available to U.S. citizens.

Application Requirements: Application form, application form may be submitted online, essay. *Deadline:* January 31.

Contact: Scholarship Committee
Unigo
10751 Deerwood Park Boulevard, #125
Jacksonville, FL 32256
Phone: 904-483-2939
Fax: 904-483-2934
E-mail: info@scholarshipexperts.com

SHOUT IT OUT SCHOLARSHIP

Applicants must: Be thirteen years of age or older at the time of application. Be legal residents of the fifty United States or the District of Columbia. Be currently enrolled (or enroll no later than the fall of 2026) in an accredited post-secondary institution of higher education and submit an online short written response (250 words or less) for the topic: 'If you could say one thing to the entire world at once, what would it be and why?'

Award: Scholarship for use in freshman, sophomore, junior, senior, graduate, or postgraduate years; not renewable. *Number:* 1. *Amount:* $1500.

Eligibility Requirements: Applicant must be age 13 and over and enrolled or expecting to enroll full- or part-time at a two-year or technical institution or university. Available to U.S. citizens.

Application Requirements: Application form, application form may be submitted online, essay. *Deadline:* September 30.

Contact: Scholarship Committee
Unigo
10751 Deerwood Park Boulevard, #125
Jacksonville, FL 32256
Phone: 904-483-2939
Fax: 904-483-2934
E-mail: info@scholarshipexperts.com

SUPERPOWER SCHOLARSHIP

Applicants must: Be thirteen years of age or older at the time of application. Be legal residents of the fifty United States or the District of Columbia. Be currently enrolled (or enroll no later than the fall of 2027) in an accredited post-secondary institution of higher education. Submit an online short written response (250 words or less) for the question: 'Which superhero or villain would you want to changes places with for a day and why?'

Award: Scholarship for use in freshman, sophomore, junior, or senior years; not renewable. *Number:* 1. *Amount:* $2500.

Eligibility Requirements: Applicant must be age 13 and over and enrolled or expecting to enroll full- or part-time at a two-year or technical institution or university. Available to U.S. citizens.

Application Requirements: Application form, application form may be submitted online, essay. *Deadline:* March 31.

Contact: Scholarship Committee
Unigo
10751 Deerwood Park Boulevard, #125
Jacksonville, FL 32256
Phone: 904-483-2939
Fax: 904-483-2934
E-mail: info@scholarshipexperts.com

SWEET AND SIMPLE SCHOLARSHIP

Applicants must: Be thirteen years of age or older at the time of application. Be legal residents of the fifty United States or the District of Columbia. Be currently enrolled (or enroll no later than the fall of 2027) in an accredited post-secondary institution of higher education and submit an online short written response (250 words or less) for the topic: ???Not every gift has to be expensive or extravagant. In fact, sometimes it???s the sweet and simple things that make a real difference in our lives. Think back and tell us about something you received as a gift and why it meant so much to you.???'

Award: Scholarship for use in freshman, sophomore, junior, senior, graduate, or postgraduate years; not renewable. *Number:* 1. *Amount:* $1500.

Eligibility Requirements: Applicant must be age 13 and over and enrolled or expecting to enroll full- or part-time at a two-year or technical institution or university. Available to U.S. citizens.

Application Requirements: Application form, application form may be submitted online, essay. *Deadline:* February 28.

Contact: Scholarship Committee
Unigo
10751 Deerwood Park Boulevard, #125
Jacksonville, FL 32256
Phone: 904-483-2939
Fax: 904-483-2934
E-mail: info@scholarshipexperts.com

TOP TEN LIST SCHOLARSHIP

Applicants must: Be thirteen years of age or older at the time of application. Be legal residents of the fifty United States or the District of Columbia. Be currently enrolled (or enroll no later than the fall of 2026) in an accredited post-secondary institution of higher education. Submit an online short written response (250 words or less) for the topic: 'Create a Top Ten List of the top ten reasons you should get this scholarship.'

Award: Scholarship for use in freshman, sophomore, junior, senior, graduate, or postgraduate years; not renewable. *Number:* 1. *Amount:* $1500.

Eligibility Requirements: Applicant must be age 13 and over and enrolled or expecting to enroll full- or part-time at a two-year or technical institution or university. Available to U.S. citizens.

Application Requirements: Application form, application form may be submitted online, essay. *Deadline:* December 31.

Contact: Scholarship Committee
Unigo
10751 Deerwood Park Boulevard, #125
Jacksonville, FL 32256
Phone: 904-483-2939
Fax: 904-483-2934
E-mail: info@scholarshipexperts.com

UNIGO $10K SCHOLARSHIP

The Unigo.com Unigo $10K Scholarship Program contest is open only to those legal residents of the fifty (50) United States and the District of Columbia who are thirteen (13) years of age or older at the time of application and who are currently enrolled (or enroll no later than the fall of 2026) in an accredited post-secondary institution of higher learning (college, university or trade school).

Award: Scholarship for use in freshman, sophomore, junior, or senior years. *Number:* 1. *Amount:* $10,000.

Eligibility Requirements: Applicant must be enrolled or expecting to enroll full- or part-time at a two-year or technical institution or university. Available to U.S. citizens.

Application Requirements: Application form, application form may be submitted online, essay. *Deadline:* December 31.

Contact: Scholarship Committee
Phone: 904-483-2939
Fax: 904-483-2934
E-mail: info@scholarshipexperts.com

UNITED STATES ACHIEVEMENT ACADEMY

http://www.usaa-academy.com/

DR. GEORGE A. STEVENS FOUNDER'S AWARD

One $10,000 scholarship cash grant to enhance the intellectual and personal growth of students who demonstrate a genuine interest in learning. Award must be used for educational purposes. Must maintain a minimum GPA of 3.0.

Award: Grant for use in freshman year; not renewable. *Number:* 1. *Amount:* $10,000.

Eligibility Requirements: Applicant must be high school student and planning to enroll or expecting to enroll full-time at a four-year institution or university. Available to U.S. and non-U.S. citizens.

Application Requirements: Application form.

Contact: Scholarship Committee
Phone: 859-269-5674
Fax: 859-268-9068
E-mail: usaa@usaa-academy.com

NATIONAL SCHOLARSHIP CASH GRANT

The Foundation awards 400 national scholarship cash grants of $1500. All scholarship winners are determined by an independent selection committee. Winners are selected based on GPA, school activities, SAT scores (if applicable), honors and awards. All students in grades 6 to 12 are eligible.

Award: Grant for use in freshman year; not renewable. *Number:* 400. *Amount:* $1500.

Eligibility Requirements: Applicant must be high school student and planning to enroll or expecting to enroll full-time at a four-year institution or university. Available to U.S. and non-U.S. citizens.

Application Requirements: Application form, application form may be submitted online (http://www.fs22.formsite.com/USAA/form23/index.html). *Deadline:* June 1.

Contact: Scholarship Committee
Phone: 859-269-5674
Fax: 859-268-9068
E-mail: usaa@usaa-academy.com

UNITED STATES BOWLING CONGRESS

http://www.bowl.com/

GIFT FOR LIFE SCHOLARSHIP

The Gift for Life Scholarships are available to any USBC Youth member currently in high school and holding a GPA of 2.5 or better who can demonstrate financial need. Two of the six awards are reserved annually for children of fire department, emergency rescue or police personnel. Selected finalists may be asked to provide evidence of their financial need. Award winners receive a $1,000 college scholarship.

Award: Scholarship for use in freshman year; not renewable. *Number:* 12. *Amount:* $1000.

Eligibility Requirements: Applicant must be high school student and planning to enroll or expecting to enroll full- or part-time at a two-year or technical institution or university. Available to U.S. citizens.

Application Requirements: Application form, application form may be submitted online, essay, financial need analysis. *Deadline:* December 2.

Contact: Roger Noordhoek, Senior Director of Youth Marketing
United States Bowling Congress
621 Six Flags Drive
Arlington, TX 76011
Phone: 800-514-2695 Ext. 8308
E-mail: contactus@ibcyouth.com

USBC ALBERTA E. CROWE STAR OF TOMORROW AWARD

This award annually recognizes star qualities in a female high school senior or college student who competes in the sport of bowling. Star qualities include distinguished bowling performance on the local, regional, state and national levels, academic achievement and extracurricular and civic involvement. The award winner receives a $6,000 scholarship. Must be a member of United States Bowling Congress Youth.

Award: Scholarship for use in freshman, sophomore, junior, or senior years; not renewable. *Number:* 1. *Amount:* $6000.

Eligibility Requirements: Applicant must be enrolled or expecting to enroll full-time at a two-year or technical institution or university and female. Available to U.S. citizens.

Application Requirements: Application form, application form may be submitted online, essay. *Deadline:* December 2.

Contact: Roger Noordhoek, Senior Director of Youth Marketing
United States Bowling Congress
621 Six Flags Drive
Arlington, TX 76011
Phone: 800-514-BOWL Ext. 8308
E-mail: contactus@ibcyouth.com

USBC CHUCK HALL STAR OF TOMORROW

This award annually recognizes star qualities in a male high school senior or college student who competes in the sport of bowling. Star qualities include distinguished certified bowling performance on the local, regional, state and national levels, academic achievement and extracurricular and civic involvement. The award winner receives a $6,000 scholarship.

Award: Scholarship for use in freshman, sophomore, junior, or senior years; renewable. *Number:* 1. *Amount:* $6000.

Eligibility Requirements: Applicant must be enrolled or expecting to enroll full-time at a two-year or technical institution or university and male. Available to U.S. citizens.

Application Requirements: Application form, application form may be submitted online, essay. *Deadline:* December 2.

Contact: Roger Noordhoek, Senior Director of Youth Marketing
United States Bowling Congress
621 Six Flags Drive
Arlington, TX 76011
Phone: 800-514-BOWL Ext. 8308
E-mail: contactus@ibcyouth.com

USBC EARL ANTHONY MEMORIAL SCHOLARSHIP

If you are a senior in high school or a college student with a record of strong community involvement and academic achievements as well as financial need, you are eligible for this scholarship. Bowling success is not considered in awarding this scholarship. USBC presents this prestigious scholarship in honor of legendary pro bowler Earl Anthony. USBC will award five USBC Youth members with a $5,000 scholarship. Candidates must be enrolled in their senior year of high school or presently attending college and must be current USBC Youth members in good standing. In addition, candidates must have a minimum cumulative GPA of 3.0 based on a 4.0 scale (or equivalent). Individuals may win this award only once

Award: Scholarship for use in freshman, sophomore, junior, or senior years; not renewable. *Number:* 5. *Amount:* $5000.

Eligibility Requirements: Applicant must be high school student and planning to enroll or expecting to enroll full- or part-time at a two-year or technical institution or university. Available to U.S. citizens.

Application Requirements: Application form, application form may be submitted online, community service, essay. *Deadline:* December 2.

Contact: Roger Noordhoek, Senior Director of Youth Marketing
United States Bowling Congress
621 Six Flags Drive
Arlington, TX 76011
Phone: 800-514-BOWL Ext. 8308
E-mail: contactus@ibcyouth.com

USBC YOUTH AMBASSADOR OF THE YEAR

This award annually recognizes one male and one female USBC Youth bowler for his/her exemplary contributions in the sport of bowling outside of league or tournament play, academic accomplishments and community involvement. Each award winner will receive a $1,500 scholarship and an expenses-paid trip to the awards ceremony held in conjunction with the USBC Convention in the spring. One of the winners may serve on the IBC Youth Committee and be eligible for additional scholarship funds. Youth Ambassadors selected to serve on Youth Committee must be at least 18 years old as of Aug. 1 in year of selection

Award: Scholarship for use in freshman year; not renewable. *Number:* 2. *Amount:* $1500.

Eligibility Requirements: Applicant must be high school student and planning to enroll or expecting to enroll full- or part-time at a two-year or technical institution or university. Available to U.S. citizens.

Application Requirements: Application form, application form may be submitted online, essay, personal photograph. *Deadline:* December 2.

Contact: Roger Noordhoek, Senior Director of Youth Marketing
United States Bowling Congress
621 Six Flags Drive
Arlington, TX 76011
Phone: 800-514-BOWL Ext. 8308
E-mail: contactus@ibcyouth.com

UNITED STATES DEPARTMENT OF STATE

http://www.fulbrightexchanges.org/

FREEMAN AWARDS FOR STUDY IN ASIA

The Freeman-ASIA program is designed to support U.S.-based undergraduates with demonstrated financial need who are planning to study abroad in East or Southeast Asia. The program's goal is to increase the number of U.S. citizens and permanent residents with first-hand exposure to and understanding of Asia and its peoples and cultures. Award recipients are required to share their experiences with their home campuses or communities to encourage study abroad by others and fulfill the program's goal of increasing understanding of Asia in the United States. From its inception in 2001, Freeman-ASIA has made study abroad in East and Southeast Asia possible for over 4,600 U.S. undergraduates from more than 600 institutions.

Award: Scholarship for use in freshman, sophomore, junior, or senior years; not renewable. *Amount:* $3000–$7000.

Eligibility Requirements: Applicant must be enrolled or expecting to enroll full- or part-time at a two-year or four-year institution or university. Available to U.S. citizens.

Application Requirements: Application form, essay, financial need analysis. *Deadline:* continuous.

Contact: Ann Koepke, Outreach Specialist
Phone: 202-314-3537
Fax: 202-479-6806
E-mail: fulbright@grad.usda.gov

GILMAN SCHOLARSHIP

The U.S. Department of State's Benjamin A. Gilman International Scholarship is a grant program that enables students of limited financial means to study or intern abroad, thereby gaining skills critical to our national security and economic competitiveness. The Gilman Scholarship Program broadens the student population that studies and interns abroad by supporting undergraduates who might not otherwise participate due to financial constraints. The program aims to encourage students to study and intern in a diverse array of countries and world regions. The program also encourages students to study languages, especially critical need languages (those deemed important to national security). Veterans of military service are encouraged to apply, and preference is given to veterans when other factors are equivalent. By supporting undergraduate students who have high financial need, the program has been successful in supporting students who have been historically underrepresented in education abroad, including but not limited to first-generation college students, students in STEM fields, ethnic minority students, students with disabilities, students attending HBCUs or other minority-serving institutions, students attending community colleges, and students coming from U.S. states with less study abroad participation.

Award: Scholarship for use in freshman, sophomore, junior, or senior years; not renewable. *Number:* 1,000–1,100. *Amount:* $1000–$5000.

Eligibility Requirements: Applicant must be enrolled or expecting to enroll full- or part-time at a two-year or four-year or technical institution or university. Available to U.S. citizens.

Application Requirements: Application form, essay, financial need analysis. *Deadline:* continuous.

Contact: Ann Koepke, Outreach Specialist
Phone: 202-314-3537
Fax: 202-479-6806
E-mail: fulbright@grad.usda.gov

UNITED STATES-INDONESIA SOCIETY

http://www.usindo.org/

UNITED STATES-INDONESIA SOCIETY TRAVEL GRANTS

Grants are provided to fund travel to Indonesia or the United States for American and Indonesian students and professors to conduct research, language training or other independent study/research. Must have a minimum 3.0 GPA.

Award: Grant for use in freshman, sophomore, junior, senior, graduate, or postgraduate years; not renewable. *Number:* 1–15. *Amount:* $1000–$2000.

Eligibility Requirements: Applicant must be enrolled or expecting to enroll full- or part-time at a four-year institution or university. Available to U.S. and non-Canadian citizens.

Application Requirements: Application form, basic budget, recommendations or references, resume, transcript. *Deadline:* continuous.

Contact: Thomas Spooner, Educational Officer
   Phone: 202-232-1400
   Fax: 202-232-7300
   E-mail: tspooner@usindo.org

UNITED TRANSPORTATION UNION INSURANCE ASSOCIATION

http://www.utuia.org/

UTUIA SCHOLARSHIP

Scholarships of $2000 awarded to undergraduate students. Requirements of a UTUIA scholarship applicant are that he or she be a U.S. citizen, at least a high school senior or equivalent, and age 25 or under. Applicants must be associated with the UTUIA by either owning a UTUIA insurance policy, or by being the child or grandchild of a current UTUIA policyholder. Scholarship applicants must also be associated with the SMART Transportation Division by belonging to the union, or by being the child or grandchild of an active or lifetime SMART Transportation Division member. Applicants also must be accepted for admittance, or already enrolled, for at least 12 credit hours per quarter or semester at a recognized institution of higher learning (university, college or junior college, nursing or technical school offering college credit).

Award: Scholarship for use in freshman, sophomore, junior, or senior years; renewable. *Number:* 50. *Amount:* $2000.

Eligibility Requirements: Applicant must be age 25 or under and enrolled or expecting to enroll full-time at a two-year or four-year or technical institution or university. Available to U.S. citizens.

Application Requirements: Application form. *Deadline:* March 31.

Contact: Beth Thomas, Compensation Specialist
   Phone: 216-227-5254

UNPAKT LLC

https://www.unpakt.com/

UNPAKT COLLEGE SCHOLARSHIP

Dream big and tell us where you see yourself moving to start your professional life after college. Dreaming of startups in Redwood City or helping urban development in Buffalo? Focusing on intelligence and politics in Washington, D.C. or educating Bostonian minds? Whether you are planning on moving out of state or staying local, we want to know about it. In no more than 500 words, let us know where you plan to move once you finish your education and why. Winners will be chosen by committee review. Judges will be looking for passion and commitment to the dream. Applicant must be a current college student or recent college graduate (within one year) at time of award announcement on December 31, 2017. Apply online. www.unpakt.com/scholarship

Award: Prize for use in freshman, sophomore, junior, or senior years; not renewable. *Number:* 1. *Amount:* $1000.

Eligibility Requirements: Applicant must be enrolled or expecting to enroll full-time at a four-year institution or university. Available to U.S. citizens.

Application Requirements: Application form, essay. *Deadline:* December 15.

Contact: Scholarship Coordinator
   Phone: 212-677-5333 Ext. 107
   E-mail: scholarship@unpakt.com

UPLIFT LEGAL FUNDING

https://upliftlegalfunding.com/

UPLIFT LEGAL FUNDING COLLEGE SCHOLARSHIP PROGRAM

Eligibility is based on the following criteria: United States citizen, accepted to or enrolled in a college or university within the United States. In the spirit of personal injury legal funding, applicants should demonstrate a strong willingness to succeed despite challenges. See more information on our website (upliftlegalfunding.com).

Award: Prize for use in freshman, sophomore, junior, or senior years; not renewable. *Number:* 1. *Amount:* $1500.

Eligibility Requirements: Applicant must be enrolled or expecting to enroll full- or part-time at a two-year or four-year institution or university. Available to U.S. citizens.

Application Requirements: Application form, essay. *Deadline:* continuous.

Contact: Ms. Taylor Williams
   Uplift Legal Funding
   21515 Hawthorne Boulevard
   Suite 200, Office 101
   Torrance, CA 90503
   Phone: 800-385-3660
   E-mail: taylor@upliftlegalfunding.com

USATTORNEYS.COM

USATTORNEYS.COM IMMIGRATION SCHOLARSHIP ESSAY CONTEST

The award amount was decreased from 2,500 to 1,500 starting in 2017. We have two different deadlines, each with one scholarship being awarded per deadline. The two deadlines are February 1st and July 1st.

Award: Scholarship for use in freshman, sophomore, junior, senior, graduate, or postgraduate years; not renewable. *Number:* 2. *Amount:* $1500.

Eligibility Requirements: Applicant must be enrolled or expecting to enroll full- or part-time at a two-year or four-year or technical institution or university. Available to U.S. citizens.

Application Requirements: Essay. *Deadline:* July 1.

Contact: Peyton Mathews
   Phone: 954-357-0894
   E-mail: pmathews@damg.com

USATTORNEYS.COM NATIONAL SCHOLARSHIP ESSAY CONTEST

See the following website for scholarship details, http://divorce.usattorneys.com/scholarship-program/

Award: Scholarship for use in freshman, sophomore, junior, senior, graduate, or postgraduate years; not renewable. *Number:* 2. *Amount:* $1500.

Eligibility Requirements: Applicant must be enrolled or expecting to enroll full- or part-time at a two-year or four-year or technical institution or university. Available to U.S. citizens.

Application Requirements: Essay. *Deadline:* June 1.

Contact: Peyton Mathews
   Phone: 954-357-0894
   E-mail: pmathews@damg.com

U.S. BANK INTERNET SCHOLARSHIP PROGRAM

http://www.usbank.com/

U.S. BANK INTERNET SCHOLARSHIP PROGRAM

A high school senior planning to enroll or a current college freshmen, sophomore or junior at an eligible four-year college or university participating in the U.S. Bank No Fee Education Loan Program. Apply online at usbank.com/student banking from October through March. No paper applications accepted.

Award: Scholarship for use in freshman, sophomore, or junior years; not renewable. *Number:* up to 40. *Amount:* up to $1000.

Eligibility Requirements: Applicant must be enrolled or expecting to enroll full- or part-time at a four-year institution or university. Available to U.S. and non-U.S. citizens.

Application Requirements: Application form. *Deadline:* March 31.

Contact: Mary Ennis, Scholarship Coordinator
Phone: 800-242-1200
E-mail: mary.ennis@usbank.com

U.S. DEPARTMENT OF HEALTH AND HUMAN SERVICES

https://www.hhs.gov/

NURSE CORPS SCHOLARSHIP PROGRAM

As a student accepted or enrolled in a diploma, associate, baccalaureate, or graduate degree nursing program, you can receive funding for tuition, fees, and other educational costs. In exchange, you must work at an eligible facility with a critical shortage of nurses-a Critical Shortage Facility (CSF)-upon graduation. Learn more at: https://bhw.hrsa.gov/loansscholarships/nursecorps/scholarship

Award: Scholarship for use in freshman, sophomore, junior, senior, graduate, or postgraduate years; renewable.

Eligibility Requirements: Applicant must be enrolled or expecting to enroll full- or part-time at a two-year or technical institution or university. Available to U.S. citizens.

Application Requirements: Application form, application form may be submitted online, essay. *Deadline:* April 30.

Contact: Andrea Stampone, Scholarship Coordinator
Phone: 301-443-4776
Fax: 301-443-0846
E-mail: astampone@hrsa.gov

UTAH ADVOCATES

ADVOCATES SCHOLARSHIP

ourselves and our communities. Understanding the financial burden higher education can bring to students and their families, we are offering our help to you through our Advocates Scholarship. Scholarship Application: Write 300-500 word essay on the following topic: What are some of the daily problems bicyclists face on the roads? How aware are we of bicyclists and the laws associated with them? How can you contribute to improving awareness and road safety for bicyclists? Scholarship Eligibility: All prospective or current students enrolled in an accredited university or college, located within the United States may submit an application. Scholarship Amount: $1000 is offered biannually. Scholarship Deadline: This scholarship is ongoing and awards are offered biannually. Fall Term: December 15th. Spring Term: May 30th. Scholarship Terms and Conditions: By submitting your essay, you agree to our terms and conditions. Only your email and phone number will be used to contact you concerning the scholarship. We will not provide this information to any 3rd party. Your name and the name of your school may be used if you are selected as a prizewinner, or if you are part of our honorable mentions. If you do not fill out all necessary information you will forfeit your consideration for this scholarship. As previously mentioned, if you are selected as the prizewinner, we will contact you through email or phone, and the award will be sent to your accredited institution. If you are selected as the scholarship winner, we will contact you for a profile photo to be included with your scholarship on our scholarship page.

Award: Scholarship for use in freshman, sophomore, junior, or senior years; not renewable. *Number:* 1. *Amount:* $1000.

Eligibility Requirements: Applicant must be enrolled or expecting to enroll full-time at a two-year or four-year institution or university. Available to U.S. citizens.

Application Requirements: Essay. *Deadline:* December 15.

Contact: Clayton Coombs, Marketing Manager
E-mail: ccoombs@lawdbd.com

VALUEPENGUIN

http://www.valuepenguin.com

2017 VALUEPENGUIN SCHOLARSHIP

The cost of education in the U.S. is on the rise. In addition, the National Center for Education Statistics reports that only 12.8% of undergraduate students receive private grants. These facts illustrate how difficult it is for many students across the nation to afford basic necessities, such as textbooks and transportation. let alone tuition. In our coverage of personal finance, we've discovered how these issues have far reaching effects on an individual's financial well being. Oftentimes, they continue to be a burden well after graduation. That's why ValuePenguin is offering a $2,000 scholarship to eligible undergraduate students in the U.S. To be considered for the scholarship, submit a 500 to 750 word response (for a total word count of 1,000 to 1,500) to each of the following two questions: 1) What is a non-essential item or activity you splurge on regularly in college? How much do you think you have spent on it since starting college and do you think it's worthwhile? 2) If you had to teach a personal finance class to college students, what are the top three topics you would cover and why?

Award: Scholarship for use in freshman, sophomore, junior, or senior years; not renewable. *Number:* 1. *Amount:* $2000.

Eligibility Requirements: Applicant must be enrolled or expecting to enroll full- or part-time at a two-year or four-year institution or university and studying in Alabama, Alaska, Arizona, Arkansas, California, Colorado, Connecticut, Delaware, District of Columbia, Florida, Georgia, Guam, Hawaii, Idaho, Illinois, Indiana, Iowa, Kansas, Kentucky, Louisiana, Maine, Maryland, Massachusetts, Michigan, Minnesota, Mississippi, Missouri, Montana, Nebraska, Nevada, New Hampshire, New Jersey, New Mexico, New York, North Carolina, North Dakota, Ohio, Oklahoma, Oregon, Pennsylvania, Puerto Rico, Rhode Island, South Carolina, South Dakota, Tennessee, Texas, Utah, Vermont, Virginia, Washington, West Virginia, Wisconsin, Wyoming. Available to U.S. and non-U.S. citizens.

Application Requirements: Application form, essay. *Deadline:* December 15.

Contact: Rebecca Wessell, Scholarship Manager
ValuePenguin
597 5th Avenue
Floor 5
New York, NY 10017
Phone: 646-248-5684
E-mail: scholarships@valuepenguin.com

VELVETJOBS LLC

http://www.velvetjobs.com

EMPLOYEE MORALE SCHOLARSHIP

Are you an undergraduate or graduate college or university student? VelvetJobs is proud to announce a $1000 scholarship for students studying in the USA or overseas. The "Employee Morale Scholarship" aims to get students thinking about their own potential future management position and how their decisions can affect employee morale. Through our own outplacement services we've dealt with thousands of employers on the issues that affect them most when it comes to retaining employees and keeping them happy. We're looking for students to write about their favorite idea on how to boost and maintain employee morale. Open to U.S. or international students. Entrants must 18 years or older. No GPA requirement. The piece should include a headline of the morale boosting idea and then should include at least 500 words on how to effectively deploy the strategy. Email your essay and the morale boosting idea to scholarship@velvetjobs.com. We will be judging the strategy on both it's uniqueness and it's practicality. That means the idea should stand out from the crowd but also be easily implemented into the workforce. The idea does not have to be overarching to all types of workforce but can be individualized to a specific workforce such as (office based, manufacturing, mobile workers, etc.). The winner will be announced by January 15th. Scholarship funds will be released for the Spring 2018 semester.

Award: Scholarship for use in freshman, sophomore, junior, senior, graduate, or postgraduate years; renewable. *Number:* 1. *Amount:* $1000.

Eligibility Requirements: Applicant must be age 18 and over and enrolled or expecting to enroll full- or part-time at a two-year or four-year or technical institution or university. Available to U.S. and non-U.S. citizens.

Application Requirements: Essay. *Deadline:* December 16.

Contact: Christina Murphy, Scholarship Coordinator
VelvetJobs LLC
1400 North Martel Avenue, Suite 108
Los Angeles, CA 90046
Phone: 877-370-7552
E-mail: scholarship@velvetjobs.com

VERMONT STUDENT ASSISTANCE CORPORATION

http://www.vsac.org/

ARMED SERVICES SCHOLARSHIP

This program was created by the Vermont Legislature to provide free tuition for the families of Vermont National Guard (VTNG), or U.S. active reserve or active armed services members who have died while on active or inactive duty. Applicants are reviewed by VSAC. Selection is based on eligibility and available funds. An Armed Services Scholarship may be used for the number of academic credits needed to graduate, up to a maximum of 130 credits. If you receive a federal Pell Grant, the amount of the grant will be deducted from the amount you can receive under the Armed Services Scholarship.

Award: Scholarship for use in freshman, sophomore, junior, or senior years.

Eligibility Requirements: Applicant must be enrolled or expecting to enroll full-time at a two-year or technical institution or university.

Application Requirements: Application form, application form may be submitted online, essay, portfolio. *Deadline:* continuous.

EMILY LESTER VERMONT OPPORTUNITY SCHOLARSHIP

If you've experienced foster care and you're ready to go to college, this scholarship—funded by the State of Vermont—may be right for you. Under this scholarship, you must be enrolled in an undergraduate associate's or bachelor's degree program. There are no requirements as to the number of credits that you must take. Scholarships generally range from $1,000 to $2,000 and may not exceed $3,000. The amount disbursed cannot exceed your total costs (tuition, fees, room, and board) minus your expected family contribution (EFC) and all other sources of gift aid combined.

Award: Scholarship for use in freshman, sophomore, junior, or senior years.

Eligibility Requirements: Applicant must be age 18-24 and enrolled or expecting to enroll full- or part-time at a two-year institution or university.

Application Requirements: Application form, application form may be submitted online. *Deadline:* continuous.

VERTICAL MEASURES

https://www.verticalmeasures.com/

VERTICAL MEASURES DIGITAL MARKETING SCHOLARSHIP

Our team is pleased to announce the Vertical Measures Digital Marketing Scholarship. A $1000 scholarship will be awarded bi-annually to students in the United States interested in pursuing an education in digital marketing. The deadline for the first scholarship is March 31, 2019, and the deadline for the second scholarship is September 30, 2019. There is no minimum SAT/ACT or GPA required United States Resident 5-minute video max Questions to answer What are your career goals? Why are you interested in digital marketing? What will the landscape look like in the future? How do you plan on shaping the industry? $1000 awarded twice annually

Award: Scholarship for use in freshman, sophomore, junior, or senior years; not renewable. *Number:* 2. *Amount:* $1000.

Eligibility Requirements: Applicant must be enrolled or expecting to enroll full- or part-time at a two-year or four-year or technical institution or university. Available to U.S. citizens.

Application Requirements: Application form may be submitted online (https://www.verticalmeasures.com/scholarship/), interview, Video. *Deadline:* September 30.

VETERANAID.ORG

https://www.veteranaid.org

VETERAN BENEFITS SCHOLARSHIP

VeteranAid.org Veterans Benefits Scholarship: Three $2,000 scholarships available to students enrolled in an Associate's degree, Bachelor's degree, or graduate level program at an accredited 2-year college or 4-year university. Each eligible student will submit a 500-750 word essay on the following essay topic: give an example of one veterans benefit and explain how it helps senior veterans, then propose your own benefit to help senior veterans.

Award: Scholarship for use in freshman, sophomore, junior, senior, graduate, or postgraduate years; not renewable. *Number:* 3. *Amount:* $2000.

Eligibility Requirements: Applicant must be enrolled or expecting to enroll full-time at a two-year or four-year institution or university. Available to U.S. citizens.

Application Requirements: Essay. *Deadline:* December 31.

Contact: Sarah Johnson
Phone: 888-907-3272
E-mail: scholarship@veteranaid.org

VICEROY AUTO TRANS

https://ViceroyAutoTrans.com

VICEROY AUTO TRANS SCHOLARSHIP PROGRAM

Five awards in the amounts of $1000, $750, $500, $250 & 100 will be issued by Viceroy Auto Trans every year for the advancement of educating aspiring students pursuing a positive future through schooling. All scholarship awards will be sent directly to the financial aid office of the school or university or college of the student. Any and all current, full time or part-time student of an accredited or non accredited institute, truck driver academy or other transport logistics program, must have a minimum cumulative GPA of 3.0 to become eligible. There is no minimum age requirement. Applying for this scholarship will require applicants to write an essay/article (consisting of 1000 words or more and may NOT be published anywhere on the internet) about a topic regarding the Auto Transportation industry or any detail related to our site

Award: Prize for use in freshman, sophomore, junior, senior, graduate, or postgraduate years; renewable. *Number:* 5–1,000. *Amount:* $100–$1000.

Eligibility Requirements: Applicant must be age 16-90 and enrolled or expecting to enroll full- or part-time at a two-year or four-year or technical institution or university. Available to U.S. citizens.

Application Requirements: Driver's license, personal photograph. *Deadline:* March 8.

Contact: Mr. Charles Church, Owner
Viceroy Auto Trans
7930 NW 20 Ct.
Sunrise, FL 33322
Phone: 754-333-3596
E-mail: Management@viceroyautotrans.com

WARD LAW GROUP, PL

http://thecoveragelawyer.com/

WARD LAW GROUP BETTER FUTURE SCHOLARSHIP

This scholarship is offered to any student currently enrolled in an accredited community college, undergraduate, or graduate program in the United States. This includes incoming first-year college students who are high school graduates or possess a GED. For more information please visit following webpage: http://thecoveragelawyer.com/#scholarship

Award: Scholarship for use in freshman, sophomore, junior, senior, graduate, or postgraduate years; not renewable. *Number:* 1. *Amount:* $500.

Eligibility Requirements: Applicant must be enrolled or expecting to enroll full- or part-time at a two-year or four-year or technical institution or university. Available to U.S. and non-U.S. citizens.

Application Requirements: Application form, essay. *Deadline:* January 31.

Contact: Gregory Ward
E-mail: info@thecoveragelawyer.com

WATERLOGIC

https://www.waterlogic.com/en-us/

WATERLOGIC SCHOLARSHIP

Waterlogic is thrilled to announce this year's scholarship opportunity, open to all current or incoming college students. As a company committed to increasing global access to clean water, we believe this scholarship will foster an increased awareness of issues related to such access, as well as reward a student who has demonstrated a sincere interest in the matter. As such, we look forward to issuing a prize of $1,500 to the student who best outlines their response to the following prompt: Accessible clean water–how can we achieve it? 783 million people worldwide do not have access to safe, clean water. In developing countries, as much as 80% of illnesses are linked to poor water and sanitation conditions. Given the resources of today's technological age, how can the problem of clean water be resolved? Choose one solution and explain how this idea would specifically impact developing countries. The minimum and maximum requirement regarding the length of the essay response is 600-800 words. To be eligible, the applicant must be entering or currently enrolled in an undergraduate degree, be a U.S. citizen, national, or permanent resident, plan on attending an accredited US institution (two- or four-year college), and have a minimum 3.00 GPA. Applications must be sent via the Waterlogic website https://www.waterlogic.com/en-us/scholarship-competition/. The deadline for this scholarship application is May 31, 2018.

Award: Prize for use in freshman, sophomore, junior, or senior years; not renewable. *Number:* 1. *Amount:* $1500.

Eligibility Requirements: Applicant must be high school student and planning to enroll or expecting to enroll full-time at a two-year or four-year or technical institution or university. Available to U.S. citizens.

Application Requirements: Essay. *Deadline:* May 31.

Contact: Mr. Edward Hull
Waterlogic
77 McCullough Drive, Suite 9
New Castle, DE 19720
Phone: 49-8935856946
E-mail: edward@waterlogic-email.com

WINGATE, RUSSOTTI, SHAPIRO & HALPERIN, LLP

https://www.wrshlaw.com/

FOUNDATION FOR YOUR FUTURE SCHOLARSHIP 2019

This scholarship is open to graduating high school seniors and current undergraduate college students with a 3.0 or higher GPA who are bettering themselves through education. The application includes an essay section with the following prompt: Who do you look up to, and why? The essay must be 500-1000 words. The deadline to submit the scholarship is July 24, 2019. The winner will be announced on August 21, 2019. Additional information and applications can be found on our website, https://www.wrshlaw.com/scholarship/

Award: Scholarship for use in freshman, sophomore, junior, or senior years; not renewable. *Number:* 1. *Amount:* $2500.

Eligibility Requirements: Applicant must be enrolled or expecting to enroll full- or part-time at a two-year or four-year institution or university. Available to U.S. citizens.

Application Requirements: Application form, application form may be submitted online (https://www.wrshlaw.com/scholarship/application.php), essay. *Deadline:* July 24.

Contact: Daniel Mateo
Wingate, Russotti, Shapiro & Halperin, LLP
65 N Raymond Ave #230
Pasadena, CA 91103
Phone: 323-254-1510
E-mail: DMateo@slsconsulting.com

WISCONSIN LIBRARY ASSOCIATION

https://www.wisconsinlibraries.org/

WISCONSIN ASSOCIATION OF ACADEMIC LIBRARIANS CONFERENCE SCHOLARSHIP

The WAAL Professional Development Committee has created three scholarship application forms for individuals wanting to apply for a scholarship to attend the annual WAAL conference; Undergraduate, Graduate and Paraprofessional staff. Scholarship covers registration fee, and expenses up to $250 which may include meal expenses (to an acknowledge meal provider), hotel room and transportation services.

Award: Scholarship for use in sophomore, junior, senior, or graduate years; not renewable.

Eligibility Requirements: Applicant must be enrolled or expecting to enroll full- or part-time at an institution or university.

Application Requirements: Application form, application form may be submitted online. *Deadline:* March 15.

Contact: Ms. Brigitte Rupp Vacha, WLA Conference Liaison
Wisconsin Library Association
4610 S Biltmore Lane
Suite 100
Madison, WI 53718
Phone: 608-245-3640
Fax: 608-245-3646
E-mail: ruppvacha@wisconsinlibraries.org

WOMEN'S INDEPENDENCE SCHOLARSHIP PROGRAM, INC.

http://www.wispinc.org/

WOMEN'S INDEPENDENCE SCHOLARSHIP PROGRAM

Scholarship for female survivors of intimate partner abuse, separated from their abusive partner a minimum of one year but not more than seven years, and sponsored by a domestic violence service agency they have worked with for a minimum of six months. Funding is available for US citizens and permanent legal residents attending an accredited course of study at a U.S. institution. The application is only available online and must be submitted electronically.

Award: Scholarship for use in freshman, sophomore, junior, senior, or graduate years; renewable. *Number:* 350–500. *Amount:* $500–$3000.

Eligibility Requirements: Applicant must be enrolled or expecting to enroll full- or part-time at a two-year or four-year or technical institution or university and female. Available to U.S. citizens.

Application Requirements: Application form, application form may be submitted online (http://wispinc.org), essay, financial need analysis, recommendations or references. *Deadline:* continuous.

Contact: Ms. Nancy Soward, Executive Director
Women's Independence Scholarship Program, Inc.
4900 Randall Parkway, Suite H
Wilmington, NC 28403
Phone: 910-397-7742 Ext. 101
Fax: 910-397-0023
E-mail: nancy@wispinc.org

WOMEN'S JEWELRY ASSOCIATION

http://www.womensjewelryassociation.com

MEMBER GRANTS

This grant is available to WJA Members only and is valid towards any type of professional growth.

Award: Grant for use in freshman, sophomore, junior, senior, graduate, or postgraduate years; renewable. *Number:* 12–25. *Amount:* $500–$1000.

Eligibility Requirements: Applicant must be enrolled or expecting to enroll full- or part-time at a two-year or four-year or technical institution or university and female. Available to U.S. and non-U.S. citizens.

Application Requirements: Application form, essay. *Deadline:* January 31.

Contact: Sue Elliott
E-mail: Selliott@gia.edu

WOMEN'S SPORTS FOUNDATION

http://www.womenssportsfoundation.org/

LINDA RIDDLE/SGMA ENDOWED SCHOLARSHIP

One $1,500 scholarship to provide female student-athletes of limited financial means the opportunity to continue to pursue their sport in addition to their college studies. If you plan to participate in intercollegiate sports at a Division I school, consult with your college compliance office to determine whether this scholarship will affect your eligibility. Please check website for application procedures.

Award: Scholarship for use in freshman year; not renewable. *Number:* 1. *Amount:* $1500.

Eligibility Requirements: Applicant must be high school student; planning to enroll or expecting to enroll full-time at a two-year or four-year institution and female. Available to U.S. citizens.

Application Requirements: Application form. *Deadline:* May 31.

Contact: Elizabeth Flores
Phone: 516-307-3915
E-mail: LFlores@WomensSportsFoundation.org

WORTHY, INC.

WORTHY WOMEN'S PROFESSIONAL STUDIES SCHOLARSHIP

Helping women get a fresh start is one of the things we take the most pride in. The ability for women to sell their diamond jewelry in a safe, transparent, value-adding way, allows for more possibilities and greater control in the process. We want to take this idea further with our Worthy Women Scholarship. Women who have decided to enroll in school and pursue their passions are eligible to win one of three scholarships. To apply, please review the requirements and select one of the accompanying writing assignments.

Award: Scholarship for use in freshman, sophomore, junior, senior, graduate, or postgraduate years; renewable. *Number:* 5,000. *Amount:* $1000.

Eligibility Requirements: Applicant must be age 30 and over; enrolled or expecting to enroll full-time at a two-year or four-year institution or university and female. Available to U.S. citizens.

Application Requirements: Application form, essay. *Deadline:* November 26.

Contact: Jonathan Dotan
Worthy, Inc.
20 West 37 Street
12th Floor
New York, NY 10018
Phone: 888-222-0208
E-mail: jonathan@worthy.com

WYZANT INC.

WYZANT COLLEGE SCHOLARSHIPS

Each individual who applies (Applicant) will be required to write an essay in English of no more than 300 words answering the question: "Who has been most important tutor, teacher or coach in my life and why?" As part of the application, Applicant may use tools and services provided by WyzAnt to promote the essay to friends and family. Contest runs from October 1 through May 1 each year.

Award: Scholarship for use in freshman, sophomore, junior, or senior years; not renewable.

Eligibility Requirements: Applicant must be enrolled or expecting to enroll full- or part-time at a four-year institution or university. Available to U.S. citizens.

Application Requirements: Essay. *Deadline:* May 1.

YTA.SE

https://yta.se

YTA.SE CLIMATE SCHOLARSHIP

The yta.se Climate Scholarship shall be used to catalyze and bring progress to promising projects and research within real estate sustainability. Anyone who studies on a university-level can apply. Apply by submitting the application form on https://yta.se/blogg/scholarship/ which includes a motivation, description of the project or research and what the scholarship can help achieve in terms of next actions.

Award: Scholarship for use in freshman, sophomore, junior, senior, graduate, or postgraduate years; not renewable. *Number:* 1. *Amount:* $1230.

Eligibility Requirements: Applicant must be enrolled or expecting to enroll full- or part-time at a two-year or four-year or technical institution or university. Available to U.S. and non-U.S. citizens.

Application Requirements: *Deadline:* December 15.

Contact: Mr. Alexander Åquist, Co-Founder
yta.se
Svevägen 64
Stockholm 111 34
SWE
Phone: 46-73-512 59 78
E-mail: alexander@yta.se

ZELUS RECOVERY

http://zelusrecovery.com/

ZELUS RECOVERY $1000 COLLEGE SCHOLARSHIP

Zelus Recovery specializes in treating adolescents and young adults with substance abuse problems. Our goal is to help young people find their way back to health and happiness so they can become contributing members of society. We have created the Zelus Recovery Scholarship for undergraduate and postgraduates students to further that message.

Award: Scholarship for use in freshman, sophomore, junior, senior, graduate, or postgraduate years; not renewable. *Number:* 1. *Amount:* $1000.

Eligibility Requirements: Applicant must be age 18 and over and enrolled or expecting to enroll full- or part-time at a two-year or four-year or technical institution or university. Available to U.S. citizens.

Application Requirements: Essay. *Deadline:* August 1.

Contact: Jason Zelus, Executive Director
Zelus Recovery
1965 S. Eagle Road Suite 140
Meridian, ID 83642
Phone: 208-957-6514
Fax: 208-957-6506
E-mail: info@zelusrecovery.com

ZIPRECRUITER

https://www.ziprecruiter.com/

ZIPRECRUITER $3,000 SCHOLARSHIP

Starting July 2017, ZipRecruiter is offering $3,000 to the college or university student with the most creative entry about their home or college town. The Grand Prize Winner will receive the $3,000 scholarship. The best entries within each city will have their entries posted on our website, and will receive recognition as a ZipRecruiter Scholar Finalist. More information may be found at https://www.ziprecruiter.com/scholarship.

Award: Prize for use in freshman, sophomore, junior, senior, graduate, or postgraduate years; renewable. *Number:* 1. *Amount:* $3000.

Eligibility Requirements: Applicant must be enrolled or expecting to enroll full- or part-time at a two-year or four-year or technical institution or university. Available to U.S. citizens.

Application Requirements: Application form, essay. *Deadline:* September 30.

Contact: Richard Fendler, Marketing Associate
E-mail: richard@ziprecruiter.com

ZOOMITA

http://zoomita.com

$1,000 NOT AN ESSAY SCHOLARSHIP

Application essays are hard. Zoomita makes them easier. Create a free account and respond to the mystery question for a chance to win $1,000 toward your college expenses!

Award: Scholarship for use in freshman year; not renewable. *Number:* up to 1. *Amount:* up to $1000.

Eligibility Requirements: Applicant must be high school student; age 15-19 and planning to enroll or expecting to enroll full- or part-time at a four-year or technical institution or university. Available to U.S. and non-U.S. citizens.

Application Requirements: Application form may be submitted online (http://zoomita.com/VGhpc1NIb3VkbEJFSGlkZGVu), response to mystery question. *Deadline:* December 31.

Contact: Sandeep Chauhan
Zoomita
1440 Broadway
Oakland, CA 94612
E-mail: info@edswell.com

ZUMPER

ZUMPER SCHOLARSHIP

Scholarship details: $1,000 College Scholarship. We are looking for outstanding students who have helped their classmates or community in a tremendous way. Maybe you started a club that raised $10,000 for charity, or championed recycling and sustainable practices across campus. Whatever it is, we would love to hear about it! About Zumper: Zumper has over one million apartments for rent across the U.S., including apartments for rent in Philadelphia. https://www.zumper.com/apartments-for-rent/philadelphia-pa

Award: Scholarship for use in freshman, sophomore, junior, senior, graduate, or postgraduate years; not renewable. *Number:* 100. *Amount:* $1000.

Eligibility Requirements: Applicant must be enrolled or expecting to enroll full- or part-time at a two-year or four-year or technical institution or university. Available to U.S. and non-U.S. citizens.

Application Requirements: Application form.

INDEXES

Award Name

Allegheny Mountain Section Air & Waste Management Association Scholarship 250

Allen Chi Gaming Scholarship 631

Allen J. Baldwin Scholarship 235

Allied Healthcare Scholarship Program 196

All-Ink.com College Scholarship Program 632

Allison Fisher Scholarship 306

Allmand Law Scholarship Contest 632

Allogan Slagle Memorial Scholarship 513

Al Neuharth Free Spirit and Journalism Conference Program 304

Alphonso Deal Scholarship Award 188

Alsandor Law Firm Scholarship Contest 632

Alumni Student Assistance Program 514

Alvin E. Heaps Memorial Scholarship 452

AMACESP Student Scholarships 126

AMA EBSCO Marketing Scholar Award 635

AMA Social Impact Scholarship 635

Amato Sanita Brighter Future Scholarship 687

Amelia Kemp Scholarship 539

American Alpine Club Research Grants 633

American Angus Auxiliary Scholarship 679

American Association for Geodetic Surveying Joseph F. Dracup Scholarship Award 411

American Association of Family & Consumer Sciences National Undergraduate Scholarship 290

American Baptist Home Mission Societies Financial Aid Program 539

American Bullion Scholarship 633

American Chemical Society, Rubber Division Undergraduate Scholarship 105

American Chemical Society Scholars Program 153

American Council of the Blind Scholarships 472

American Dental Association Foundation Dental Hygiene Scholarship Program 194

American Dental Association Foundation Dental Student Scholarship Program 195

American Express Scholarship Program 294

American Federation of State, County, and Municipal Employees Scholarship Program 429

American Ground Water Trust-AMTROL Inc. Scholarship 199

American Ground Water Trust-Baroid Scholarship 199

American Ground Water Trust-Thomas Stetson Scholarship 199

American Hotel & Lodging Educational Foundation Pepsi Scholarship 189

American Indian Nurse Scholarship Program 278

Americanism Essay Contest Scholarship 432

American Jewish League for Israel Scholarship Program 634

American Legion Auxiliary Department of Alabama Scholarship Program 497

American Legion Auxiliary Department of Arizona Health Care Occupation Scholarships 279

American Legion Auxiliary Department of Arizona Nurses' Scholarships 361

American Legion Auxiliary Department of Arizona Wilma Hoyal-Maxine Chilton Memorial Scholarship 170

American Legion Auxiliary Department of California General Scholarship 497

American Legion Auxiliary Department of California Past Presidents' Parley Nursing Scholarships 361

American Legion Auxiliary Department of Colorado Department President's Scholarship and Scholarship for Junior Member 635

American Legion Auxiliary Department of Colorado Past Presidents' Parley Health Care Professional ScholarshipNurses Scholarship 125

American Legion Auxiliary Department of Idaho Nursing Scholarship 361

American Legion Auxiliary Department of Iowa Children of Veterans Merit Award 497

American Legion Auxiliary Department of Iowa Harriet Hoffman Memorial Merit Award for Teacher Training 206

American Legion Auxiliary Department of Iowa M.V. McCrae Memorial Nurses Merit Award 361

American Legion Auxiliary Department of Kentucky Laura Blackburn Memorial Scholarship 491

American Legion Auxiliary Department of Kentucky Mary Barrett Marshall Scholarship 497

American Legion Auxiliary Department of Maine Daniel E. Lambert Memorial Scholarship 497

American Legion Auxiliary Department of Maine Past Presidents' Parley Nurses Scholarship 279

American Legion Auxiliary Department of Michigan Medical Career Scholarship 279

American Legion Auxiliary Department of Michigan Memorial Scholarship 498

American Legion Auxiliary Department of Michigan Scholarship for Non-Traditional Student 498

American Legion Auxiliary Department of Minnesota Past Presidents' Parley Health Care Scholarship 279

American Legion Auxiliary Department of Minnesota Scholarships 498

American Legion Auxiliary Department of Missouri Lela Murphy Scholarship 430

American Legion Auxiliary Department of Missouri National President's Scholarship 430

American Legion Auxiliary Department of Missouri Past Presidents' Parley Scholarship 362

American Legion Auxiliary Department of Nebraska Ruby Paul Campaign Fund Scholarship 430

American Legion Auxiliary Department of North Dakota National President's Scholarship 460

American Legion Auxiliary Department of North Dakota Past Presidents' Parley Nurses Scholarship 362

American Legion Auxiliary Department of North Dakota Scholarships 545

American Legion Auxiliary Department of Ohio Continuing Education Fund 499

American Legion Auxiliary Department of Ohio Department President's Scholarship 499

American Legion Auxiliary Department of Ohio Past Presidents' Parley Nurses Scholarship 362

American Legion Auxiliary Department of Oregon Department Grants 545

American Legion Auxiliary Department of Oregon National President's Scholarship 545

American Legion Auxiliary Department of Oregon Nurses Scholarship 362

American Legion Auxiliary Department of Oregon Spirit of Youth Scholarship 430

American Legion Auxiliary Department of Pennsylvania Past Department Presidents' Memorial Scholarship 363

American Legion Auxiliary Department of Pennsylvania Scholarship for Dependents of Disabled or Deceased Veterans 545

American Legion Auxiliary Department of Pennsylvania Scholarship for Dependents of Living Veterans 546

American Legion Auxiliary Department of South Dakota College Scholarships 431

American Legion Auxiliary Department of South Dakota Senior Scholarship 431

American Legion Auxiliary Department of South Dakota Thelma Foster Scholarship for Senior Auxiliary Members 431

American Legion Auxiliary Department of Texas General Education Scholarship 499

American Legion Auxiliary Department of Texas Past Presidents' Parley Medical Scholarship 279

American Legion Auxiliary Department of Utah National President's Scholarship 431

American Legion Auxiliary Department of Wisconsin Della Van Deuren Memorial Scholarship 431

American Legion Auxiliary's Children of Warriors National Presidents' Scholarship 498

American Legion Auxiliary Spirit of Youth Scholarship for Junior Members 498

American Legion Baseball Scholarship 613

American Legion Department of Arizona High School Oratorical Contest 546

American Legion Department of Arkansas High School Oratorical Contest 546

American Legion Department of Hawaii High School Oratorical Contest 546

American Legion Department of Idaho Scholarship 432

American Legion Department of Illinois Boy Scout/Explorer Scholarship 432

American Legion Department of Illinois High School Oratorical Contest 546

American Legion Department of Indiana, Americanism and Government Test 547

American Legion Department of Indiana High School Oratorical Contest 547

American Legion Department of Iowa Eagle Scout of the Year Scholarship 432

American Legion Department of Iowa High School Oratorical Contest 547

American Legion Department of Iowa Outstanding Senior Baseball Player 548

American Legion Department of Maine Children and Youth Scholarship 500

American Legion Department of Maryland General Scholarship Fund 433

American Legion, Department of Maryland, High School Oratorical Scholarship Contest 548

American Legion Department of Maryland Math-Science Scholarship 99

American Legion Department of Michigan Oratorical Scholarship Program 548

American Legion Department of Minnesota High School Oratorical Contest 548

American Legion Department of Minnesota Memorial Scholarship 433

American Legion Department of New York High School Oratorical Contest 549

Sponsor

Jeannette Rankin Women's Scholarship Fund 666
Jewish Vocational Service Los Angeles 522, 541, 577
Jewish War Veterans of the United States of America 443, 667
Joe Francis Haircare Scholarship Foundation 187
John B. Fabriele, III, LLC 667
John F. and Anna Lee Stacey Scholarship Fund 620
John F. Kennedy Library Foundation 667
Jonathan de Araujo Real Estate 667
Jonathan M. Feigenbaum, Esquire 667
Jorge Mas Canosa Freedom Foundation 149, 156, 164, 173, 204, 219, 228, 302, 305, 334, 342
Joseph Shinoda Memorial Scholarship Foundation 292
Journalism Education Association 668
JRC Insurance Group 668
Junior Achievement 443, 620
Junk A Car 668
JVS Chicago 522, 541
J. Walter Thompson 668
Kahn Roven, LLP 668
Kansas Commission on Veterans Affairs 503
Kansas Nurses Foundation 211, 369
Kaufman & Stigger, PLLC 577
Keller Law Offices 669
Kelly Law Team 477
Kennedy Foundation 669
Kentucky Department of Veterans Affairs 577
Kentucky Energy and Environment Cabinet 142, 156, 165, 201, 254, 298, 342, 356
Kentucky Higher Education Assistance Authority (KHEAA) 490, 495, 578
Kentucky Society of Certified Public Accountants 77
Kentucky Transportation Cabinet 165
Ketamine Clinics of Los Angeles 138, 143, 283, 358, 369, 380, 396, 415
Kevin's Review 669
KidGuard 669
Kim and Harold Louie Family Foundation 669
Kimbo Foundation 523
Kitchen Guides 477, 488, 490, 493, 495, 496, 503, 523
Knights of Columbus 443, 503, 523, 541
Knights of Pythias 620
Kogan and DiSalvo, P.A. 670
Korean American Scholarship Foundation 467, 523
Ladies Auxiliary of the Fleet Reserve Association 444, 496, 508, 509
Ladies Auxiliary to the Veterans of Foreign Wars 621
Ladies Auxiliary to the Veterans of Foreign Wars, Department of Maine 283, 296, 369, 415
The LAGRANT Foundation 85, 149, 173, 275, 330
Lambda Alpha National Anthropology Honor Society 104
The Land Conservancy of New Jersey 143, 201, 254, 274, 292, 298, 315, 325, 345, 353, 377, 390, 401, 413, 428
Landscape Architecture Foundation 292, 523, 578, 670
La-Philosophie.com 104, 289, 296, 305, 386, 394, 396, 402, 406
LasikPlus 670
Latin American Educational Foundation 523, 578
La Unidad Latina Foundation 524
Law Firm of Jack Tolliver, MD & Associates, PLLC 369
Law Office of David D. White, PLLC 478
Law Office of David P. Shapiro 319, 478
Law Office of Henry Queener 670
Law Office of Manning & Zimmerman PLLC 578

Law Offices of David A. Black 478, 503
Law Offices of Goodwin & Scieszka 319
Law Offices of Judd S. Nemiro, PLLC 478
Law Offices of Mark Sherman, LLC 670
Law Offices of Sean M. Cleary 671
Law Offices of Sheryl R. Rentz, P.C. 671
Law Offices of Tragos, Sartes and Tragos 671
LEAD Foundation of Colorado 479
LEAGUE Foundation 621
League of United Latin American Citizens National Educational Service Centers Inc. 149, 241, 524
Learning Ally 444, 479
Learning for Life 261, 315
Lee-Jackson Educational Foundation 579, 621
LegalZoom.com 671
Lemberg Law 524
Leopold Schepp Foundation 671
Lependorf & Silverstein, P.C. 579
Lep Foundation for Youth Education 579, 672
Les Dames d'Escoffier International, Colorado Chapter 94, 100, 192, 266, 269, 290
Levy Law Offices 579
Liberty Graphics Inc. 579, 621
Life Happens 672
Lifesaver Essays 672
Lighthouse Guild 479
The Lincoln Forum 621
LivSecure 188, 316, 319
Logan Telephone Co-op 580
Logistics & Transportation Association of North America 228, 421, 445
LogMeIn 109, 131, 157, 165, 180, 186, 219, 241, 338, 342, 390, 404, 411
Los Alamos National Laboratory Foundation 580
Los Angeles Council of Black Professional Engineers 157, 165, 180, 219, 228, 241, 334, 342, 390
Louisiana Association of Broadcasters 424
Louisiana Department of Veteran Affairs 503, 580
Louisiana National Guard, Joint Task Force LA 490, 495, 580
Louisiana Office of Student Financial Assistance 325, 327, 353, 377, 580, 672
The Lyndon Baines Johnson Foundation 99, 289, 302, 346, 347, 394
Magic Johnson Foundation Inc. 467, 524
Maine Community College System 581
Maine Community Foundation, Inc. 101, 289, 581
Maine Department of Agriculture, Food and Rural Resources 90, 94, 101
Maine Restaurant Association 192, 295
Maine Society of Professional Engineers 228, 241
Maine State Society Foundation of Washington, DC Inc. 582
Maine Veterans Services 503, 583
Mainor Worth Injury Lawyers 672
Malki Museum, Inc. 525
MANA de San Diego 467, 525, 583, 621
Mangum & Associates PC 673
Manufacturers Association of Maine 131, 228, 241, 299, 327, 334, 342, 418
Margaret McNamara Education Grants 673
Marine Corps Scholarship Foundation, Inc. 673
Marine Corps Tankers Association Inc. 509
Marine Technology Society 325, 327, 377
Martin D. Andrews Scholarship 621
Maryland Association of Certified Public Accountants Educational Foundation 77
Maryland Association of Private Colleges and Career Schools 673
Maryland/Delaware/District of Columbia Press Foundation 305

Maryland Restaurant Association Education Foundation 192, 266, 269, 295
Massachusetts Association of Land Surveyors and Civil Engineers 242, 254, 414
Massachusetts Office of Student Financial Assistance 583
Massey and Associates, PC 673
McCurry Foundation Inc. 583, 621
McNeely Stephenson 673
Medical Scrubs Collection 104, 109, 112, 125, 138, 143, 157, 187, 197, 201, 248, 266, 278, 283, 286, 326, 334, 356, 359, 369, 378, 380, 381, 385, 390, 396, 397, 399, 415
Medigo GMBH 674
Menominee Indian Tribe of Wisconsin 525
Mensa Foundation 674
Mental Health Association in New York State Inc. 138
The Miami Foundation 525, 583
Michigan Association of Broadcasters Foundation 424
Michigan Association of CPAs 77
Michigan Consumer Credit Lawyers 674
Michigan Council of Teachers of Mathematics 338
Michigan Department of Treasury - Student Financial Services Bureau 504, 583
Michigan State Horticultural Society 94
Microsoft Corporation 180
Midwest Roofing Contractors Association 116, 165, 186, 198, 242, 299, 335, 418
MIE Solutions 674
Mila Boyd Law Offices 674
Military Officers Association of America (MOAA) Scholarship Fund 674
Military Order of the Purple Heart 504
Military Order of the Stars and Bars 675
MindSumo 675
Minerals, Metals, and Materials Society (TMS) 228, 242, 335, 404
Minick Law 675
Minnesota AFL-CIO 445, 584
Minnesota Masonic Charities 584
Minnesota Office of Higher Education 467, 525, 585
Mississippi Association of Broadcasters 306, 424
Mississippi Nurses' Association (MNA) 369
Mississippi Office of Student Financial Aid 467, 585
Mississippi Press Association Education Foundation 306
Missouri Broadcasters Association Scholarship Program 424
Missouri Conservation Agents Association Scholarship 586
Missouri Department of Higher Education 586
Missouri Funeral Directors & Embalmers Association 272
Missouri Insurance Education Foundation 300
Missouri Travel Council 269, 295, 422
MLD Wealth Management Group 675
Modern Law 587
Montana Broadcasters Association 424
Montana Federation of Garden Clubs 202, 293, 315, 353
Montana Society of Certified Public Accountants 77
Morphisec 180
The Morris K. Udall and Stewart L. Udall Foundation 675
Morrow & Sheppard LLP 319
Mount Sinai Hospital Department of Nursing 369
Mount Vernon Urban Renewal Agency 587
Mystery Weekly Magazine 676
My Travel Luggage 676

Academic Fields/Career Goals

Elizabeth and Sherman Asche Memorial
Scholarship Fund 93
Evan Turek Memorial Scholarship 93
Foundation Fund Scholarship 97
Fruits Industries Scholarships 94
George & Susan Carter Scholarship 97
Help to Save Scholarship 93
Howard F. DeNise Scholarship 95
IFT Food Laws and Regulations Division
Undergraduate Scholarship 93
Joseph Fitcher Scholarship Contest 95
Leidos STEM Scholarship 96
Les Dames d'Escoffier International, Colorado
Chapter Scholarship 94
Maine Rural Rehabilitation Fund Scholarship
Program 90
Mary Macey Scholarship 97
National Council of State Garden Clubs Inc.
Scholarship 94
National Garden Clubs Inc. Scholarship
Program 94
National JACL Headquarters Scholarship 94
National Poultry and Food Distributors
Association Scholarship Foundation 90
National Restaurant Association Educational
Foundation Undergraduate Scholarships for
College Students 95
New York State Association of Agricultural Fairs
and New York State Showpeople's Association
Annual Scholarship 90
Scholarship for Students Pursuing a Business or
STEM Degree 80
South Dakota Board of Regents Bjugstad
Scholarship 91
South Florida Fair Agricultural College
Scholarship 96
Turf and Ornamental Communicators Association
Scholarship Program 96
USDA/1994 Tribal Scholars Program 96
Virgil Thompson Memorial Scholarship
Contest 90
Walter J. Clore Scholarship 97
William Helms Scholarship Program (WHSP) 96
William J. Adams, Jr. and Marijane E. Adams
Scholarship 92

American Studies
AFIO Undergraduate and Graduate
Scholarships 98
AFSCME/UNCF Union Scholars Program 98
B. Phinizy Spalding, Hubert B. Owens, and The
National Society of the Colonial Dames of
America in the State of Georgia Academic
Scholarships 99
CBC Spouses Education Scholarship 98
Moody Research Grants 99
Teaching Assistant Program in France 98

Animal/Veterinary Sciences
Abbie Sargent Memorial Scholarship 89
Al & Williamary Viste Scholarship 99
American Legion Department of Maryland Math-
Science Scholarship 99
AvaCare Medical Scholarship 100
Edward R. Hall Scholarship 91
Elizabeth and Sherman Asche Memorial
Scholarship Fund 93
Empathy for Animals (EFA) Scholarship Award
for Veterinary Students 102
George A. Hall/Harold F. Mayfield Award 103
HENAAC Scholarship Program 100
Laurie Page-Peck Scholarships Fund 100
Leidos STEM Scholarship 96
Les Dames d'Escoffier International, Colorado
Chapter Scholarship 94
Lew and JoAnn Eklund Educational
Scholarship 100

Maine Rural Rehabilitation Fund Scholarship
Program 90
National Poultry and Food Distributors
Association Scholarship Foundation 90
NIH Undergraduate Scholarship Program for
Students from Disadvantaged
Backgrounds 101
Novus Biologicals Scholarship Program 101
Paul A. Stewart Awards 103
Platinum Educational Group Scholarships Program
for EMS, Nursing, and Allied Health 102
R&D Systems Scholarship 101
Ronald P. Guerrette FFA Scholarship Fund 101
Saul T. Wilson, Jr., Scholarship Program
(STWJS) 103
Scholarship for Students Pursuing a Business or
STEM Degree 80
Tocris Bioscience Scholarship 102

Anthropology
$1,500 STEM Scholarship 104
AFSCME/UNCF Union Scholars Program 98
Hub Foundation Scholarships 88
ISF National Scholarship 104
Lambda Alpha National Anthropology Honor
Society Scholarship Award 104
La-Philosophie.com Scholarship 104
Leidos STEM Scholarship 96
Medical Scrubs Collection Scholarship 104
The Society for the Scientific Study of Sexuality
Student Research Grant 105
Student Design Competition 103
Youth Activity Fund Grants 103

Applied Sciences
$1,500 STEM Scholarship 104
AFCEA STEM Majors Scholarships for
Undergraduate Students 106
Al & Williamary Viste Scholarship 99
American Chemical Society, Rubber Division
Undergraduate Scholarship 105
American Legion Department of Maryland Math-
Science Scholarship 99
American Society of Naval Engineers
Scholarship 106
Association of California Water Agencies
Scholarships 106
Astronaut Scholarship 107
A.T. Anderson Memorial Scholarship
Program 105
Automotive Women's Alliance Foundation
Scholarships 71
AWG Undergraduate Excellence in Paleontology
Award 106
Barry M. Goldwater Scholarship and Excellence in
Education Program 107
BHW Women in STEM Scholarship 107
Clair A. Hill Scholarship 106
Community College STEM Scholarships 110
Davis Scholarship for Women in STEM 111
Discover Financial Services Scholarship 82
Galactic Unite Bytheway Scholarship 111
HENAAC Scholarship Program 100
Indian Health Service Health Professions Pre-
graduate Scholarships 108
The Jackson Laboratory College Scholarship
Program 108
LastPass STEM Scholarship 109
Leidos STEM Scholarship 96
Medical Scrubs Collection Scholarship 104
NASA Idaho Space Grant Consortium Scholarship
Program 109
NASA Maryland Space Grant Consortium
Scholarships 109
National Space Grant Consortium
Scholarships 110
Novus Biologicals Scholarship Program 101

R&D Systems Scholarship 101
SAPA Scholarship and Excellence in Education
Program 111
Scholarship for Students Pursuing a Business or
STEM Degree 80
Science Ambassador Scholarship 107
Sehar Saleha Ahmad and Abrahim Ekramullah
Zafar Foundation Scholarship 110
SPIE Educational Scholarships in Optical Science
and Engineering 108
Straight North STEM Scholarship 81
Tocris Bioscience Scholarship 102
Undergraduate STEM Research
Scholarships 110
Vermont Space Grant Consortium 92
Women Forward in Technology Scholarship
Program 108

Archaeology
AWG Maria Luisa Crawford Field Camp
Scholarship 111
AWG Salt Lake Chapter (SLC) Research
Scholarship 111
AWG Undergraduate Excellence in Paleontology
Award 106
BHW Women in STEM Scholarship 107
Janet Cullen Tanaka Geosciences Undergraduate
Scholarship 112
Medical Scrubs Collection Scholarship 104
Minority Student Summer Scholarship 112
Osage Chapter Undergraduate Service
Scholarship 112
Scholarship for Students Pursuing a Business or
STEM Degree 80
Youth Activity Fund Grants 103

Architecture
$1,500 STEM Scholarship 104
AACE International Competitive
Scholarship 112
ACI Foundation Scholarship Program 113
AIA West Virginia Scholarship 118
Alan Lucas Memorial Educational
Scholarship 116
Architects Foundation Diversity Advancement
Scholarship 113
Architects Foundation Payette Sho-Ping Chin
Memorial Academic Scholarship 113
BHW Women in STEM Scholarship 107
CBC Scholarship Fund 114
Center for Architecture Design Scholarship 114
Center for Architecture, Women's Auxiliary
Eleanor Allwork Scholarship 114
Dallas Center for Architecture Foundation—HKS/
John Humphries Scholarship 114
FEFPA Assistantship 115
HENAAC Scholarship Program 100
IFMA Foundation Scholarships 116
J. Neel Reid Prize 115
MRCA Foundation Scholarship Program 116
NAWIC Undergraduate Scholarships 117
Norton E. Salk Scholarship 117
Odebrecht Award for Sustainable
Development 113
Residential Design Scholarship 115
Robert W. Thunen Memorial Scholarships 116
Scholarship for Students Pursuing a Business or
STEM Degree 80
Support Creativity Scholarship 117
Sustainable Residential Design Scholarship 115
Vectorworks Design Scholarship 117
The Walter A. Hunt, Jr. Scholarship 114
The Walter J. Travis Memorial Scholarship and
The Walter J. Travis-Rudy Zocchi Memorial
Scholarship 118
Whitley Place Scholarship 114
Women in Architecture Scholarship 116

Sylvia Lask Scholarship *138*
Williams Law Group Opportunity to Grow
    Scholarship *119*

Biology

$1,500 STEM Scholarship *104*
AABB-Fenwal Scholarship Award *139*
Aboriginal Health Careers Bursary *139*
Al & Williamary Viste Scholarship *99*
American Legion Department of Maryland Math-
    Science Scholarship *99*
Annual Healthcare and Life Sciences
    Scholarship *142*
Association for Iron and Steel Technology Ohio
    Valley Chapter Scholarship *138*
Association of California Water Agencies
    Scholarships *106*
Association of State Dam Safety Officials
    (ASDSO) Senior Undergraduate
    Scholarship *140*
Astronaut Scholarship *107*
A.T. Anderson Memorial Scholarship
    Program *105*
AWG Undergraduate Excellence in Paleontology
    Award *106*
Barbara A. Horwitz and John M. Horowitz
    Undergraduate Research Awards *139*
Barry M. Goldwater Scholarship and Excellence in
    Education Program *107*
BHW Women in STEM Scholarship *107*
B.O.G. Pest Control Scholarship Fund *141*
Clair A. Hill Scholarship *106*
Community College STEM Scholarships *110*
Donald A. Williams Scholarship Soil Conservation
    Scholarship *91*
Eckenfelder Scholarship *141*
Edward R. Hall Scholarship *91*
Elizabeth and Sherman Asche Memorial
    Scholarship Fund *93*
Environmental Protection Scholarship *142*
Federated Garden Clubs of Connecticut Inc.
    Scholarships *142*
Gaige Fund Award *140*
George A. Hall/Harold F. Mayfield Award *103*
Health Professions Preparatory Scholarship
    Program *137*
HENAAC Scholarship Program *100*
Indian Health Service Health Professions Pre-
    graduate Scholarships *108*
The Jackson Laboratory College Scholarship
    Program *108*
Ketamine Clinics of Los Angeles Scholarship
    Program *138*
Leidos STEM Scholarship *96*
Libbie H. Hyman Memorial Scholarship *144*
Loeblich and Tappan Student Research
    Award *142*
Medical Scrubs Collection Scholarship *104*
Minority Scholarship Program *141*
Montana Space Grant Scholarship Program *132*
NASA Idaho Space Grant Consortium Scholarship
    Program *109*
NASA Maryland Space Grant Consortium
    Scholarships *109*
National Council of State Garden Clubs Inc.
    Scholarship *94*
National Garden Clubs Inc. Scholarship
    Program *94*
NIH Undergraduate Scholarship Program for
    Students from Disadvantaged
    Backgrounds *101*
Novus Biologicals Scholarship Program *101*
Paul A. Stewart Awards *103*
Payzer Scholarship *130*
Raney Fund Award *140*
R&D Systems Scholarship *101*

Rogers Family Scholarship *143*
Russell W. Myers Scholarship *143*
Saul T. Wilson, Jr., Scholarship Program
    (STWJS) *103*
Scholarship for Students Pursuing a Business or
    STEM Degree *80*
Science Ambassador Scholarship *107*
Sehar Saleha Ahmad and Abrahim Ekramullah
    Zafar Foundation Scholarship *110*
The Society for the Scientific Study of Sexuality
    Student Research Grant *105*
Straight North STEM Scholarship *81*
Timothy L. Taschwer Scholarship *144*
Tocris Bioscience Scholarship *102*
Undergraduate STEM Research
    Scholarships *110*
Vermont Space Grant Consortium *92*
William Helms Scholarship Program (WHSP) *96*
William J. Adams, Jr. and Marijane E. Adams
    Scholarship *92*
Women Forward in Technology Scholarship
    Program *108*
Youth Activity Fund Grants *103*

Business/Consumer Services

AACE International Competitive
    Scholarship *112*
Alexander Scholarship Loan Fund *152*
Alice L. Haltom Educational Fund *145*
A.T. Anderson Memorial Scholarship
    Program *105*
Automotive Aftermarket Scholarships *146*
Automotive Women's Alliance Foundation
    Scholarships *71*
Business Achievement Award *148*
Delta Sigma Pi Undergraduate Scholarship *147*
Digital Marketing Scholarship *84*
Edward M. Nagel Endowed Scholarship *151*
Esther R. Sawyer Research Award *76*
FCCLA Regional Scholarships *147*
FCCLA Texas Farm Bureau Scholarship *147*
Francis X. Crowley Scholarship *150*
GE/LULAC Scholarship *149*
Greenpal Business Scholarship *148*
Harry A. Applegate Scholarship *73*
HCN/Apricity Resources Scholars Program *83*
Institute of Management Accountants Memorial
    Education Fund Scholarships *148*
Jeffrey L. Esser Career Development
    Scholarship *75*
Joseph Murphy Scholarship *150*
LAGRANT Foundation Scholarship for
    Graduates *85*
LAGRANT Foundation Scholarship for
    Undergraduates *85*
Lynda Baboyian Memorial Scholarship *147*
Mary Macey Scholarship *97*
Mas Family Scholarship Award *149*
Math, Engineering, Science, Business, Education,
    Computers Scholarships *146*
Media Plan Case Competition *88*
Minorities in Government Finance
    Scholarship *75*
NASCAR Wendell Scott Sr. Scholarship *83*
National Black McDonald's Owners Association
    Hospitality Scholars Program *83*
National Restaurant Association Educational
    Foundation Undergraduate Scholarships for
    College Students *95*
National Security Education Program (NSEP)
    David L. Boren Undergraduate
    Scholarships *119*
Native American Leadership in Education
    (NALE) *146*
Nebraska DECA Leadership Scholarship *149*

New England Employee Benefits Council
    Scholarship Program *78*
North American Van Lines 2020 Logistics
    Scholarship Competition *150*
Office Supply Scholarship *121*
Ray Foley Memorial Youth Education Foundation
    Scholarship *145*
Robert H. Rumler Scholarship *89*
Ryder System Charitable Foundation Scholarship
    Program *151*
Sales Professionals-USA Scholarship *150*
Scholarship for Students Pursuing a Business or
    STEM Degree *80*
Scholarships for Education, Business and
    Religion *147*
SEMA Memorial Scholarship Fund *81*
Society of Automotive Analysts Scholarship *81*
Steven J. Finkel Service Excellence
    Scholarship *148*
StraightForward Media Business School
    Scholarship *87*
Stuart Cameron and Margaret McLeod Memorial
    Scholarship *76*
Teaming to Win Business Scholarship *150*
Tiffany Green Operator Scholarship Award *85*
Triangle Pest Control Scholarship *82*
Tribal Business Management Program (TBM) *72*
Tri-State Surveying and Photogrammetry Kris M.
    Kunze Memorial Scholarship *145*
UNCF/Alliance Data Scholarship and Internship
    Program *88*
UNCF/Carnival Corporate Scholars
    Program *151*
UNCF/Travelers Insurance Scholarship *151*
Undergraduate Marketing Education Merit
    Scholarships *146*
Voya Scholars *83*
Wayne C. Cornils Memorial Scholarship *148*
Women in Logistics Scholarship *152*
Wyoming Trucking Association Scholarship Trust
    Fund *84*

Campus Activities

National Association for Campus Activities
    Northern Plains Region Scholarship for
    Student Leaders *152*

Chemical Engineering

$1,500 STEM Scholarship *104*
AACE International Competitive
    Scholarship *112*
Al & Williamary Viste Scholarship *99*
Al-Ben Scholarship for Academic Incentive *157*
Al-Ben Scholarship for Professional Merit *157*
Al-Ben Scholarship for Scholastic
    Achievement *157*
American Chemical Society, Rubber Division
    Undergraduate Scholarship *105*
American Chemical Society Scholars
    Program *153*
American Society for Enology and Viticulture
    Scholarships *92*
AOCS Biotechnology Student Excellence
    Award *92*
AOCS Processing Division Awards *154*
Association for Iron and Steel Technology
    Benjamin F. Fairless Scholarship
    (AIME) *152*
Association for Iron and Steel Technology Willy
    Korf Memorial Scholarship *153*
Astronaut Scholarship *107*
A.T. Anderson Memorial Scholarship
    Program *105*
Automotive Women's Alliance Foundation
    Scholarships *71*
Banatao Family Filipino American Education
    Fund *155*

Child and Family Studies

Civil Engineering

Classics

Communications

IFMA Foundation Scholarships *116*
Jerry McDowell Fund *156*
Kurt H. and Donna M. Schuler Small Grant *162*
LastPass STEM Scholarship *109*
Leidos STEM Scholarship *96*
Minority Scholarship Program *141*
MRCA Foundation Scholarship Program *116*
National Asphalt Pavement Association Research and Education Foundation Scholarship Program *165*
Odebrecht Award for Sustainable Development *113*
Residential Construction Management Scholarship *185*
Straight North STEM Scholarship *81*
SWE Region E Scholarship *159*
SWE Region H Scholarships *159*
SWE Region J Scholarship *159*
TAC Foundation Scholarships *168*
TE Connectivity Excellence in Engineering Scholarship *160*
Ted G. Wilson Memorial Scholarship Foundation *166*
Trimmer Education Foundation Scholarships for Construction Management *186*
Vectorworks Design Scholarship *117*
WRI Foundation College Scholarship Program *168*
YouthForce 2020 Scholarship Program *117*

Cosmetology
AvaCare Medical Scholarship *100*
Joe Francis Haircare Scholarship Foundation *187*
Medical Scrubs Collection Scholarship *104*

Criminal Justice/Criminology
AFIO Undergraduate and Graduate Scholarships *98*
Alphonso Deal Scholarship Award *188*
American Society of Criminology Gene Carte Student Paper Competition *187*
Cantor Crane Personal Injury Lawyer $1,000 Scholarship *187*
CBC Spouses Education Scholarship *98*
Connecticut Association of Women Police Scholarship *188*
Continental Society, Daughters of Indian Wars Scholarship *188*
Law Enforcement and Criminal Justice College Scholarship Program *189*
LivSecure Student Scholarship *188*
North Carolina Sheriffs' Association Undergraduate Criminal Justice Scholarships *188*
Ritchie-Jennings Memorial Scholarship *71*
Washington State Association for Justice American Justice Essay & Video Scholarship *189*
Williams Law Group Opportunity to Grow Scholarship *119*

Culinary Arts
American Hotel & Lodging Educational Foundation Pepsi Scholarship *189*
Bern Laxer Memorial Scholarship *191*
CANFIT Nutrition, Physical Education and Culinary Arts Scholarship *190*
Careers Through Culinary Arts Program Cooking Competition for Scholarships *190*
Chicago JBF Eats Week Scholarship *191*
Christian Wolffer Scholarship *191*
ConnectOne Bank Scholarship *191*
Culinary Trust Scholarship Program for Culinary Study and Research *190*
French Culinary Institute/Italian Culinary Experience Scholarship *194*

Golden Gate Restaurant Association Scholarship Foundation *190*
Hungry To Lead Scholarship *193*
Illinois Restaurant Association Educational Foundation Scholarships *190*
James Beard Legacy Scholarship *191*
Les Dames d'Escoffier International, Colorado Chapter Scholarship *94*
The Letitia B. Carter Scholarship *192*
Maine Restaurant Association Education Foundation Scholarship Fund *192*
Marcia S. Harris Legacy Fund Scholarship *192*
Miljenko "Mike"Grgich's American Dream Scholarship *191*
National Restaurant Association Educational Foundation Undergraduate Scholarships for College Students *95*
Peter Kump Memorial Scholarship *191*
Robert Mondavi Winery Memorial Scholarship *192*
Robert W. Hiller Scholarship Fund *193*
South Carolina Tourism and Hospitality Educational Foundation Scholarships *193*
Steven Scher Memorial Scholarship for Aspiring Restauranteurs *192*
Support Creativity Scholarship *117*
Taste America Scholarships *192*
UNCF/Carnival Corporate Scholars Program *151*
WBA Scholarship *194*
W. Price, Jr. Memorial Scholarship *193*

Dental Health/Services
Aboriginal Health Careers Bursary *139*
Al & Williamary Viste Scholarship *99*
Allied Healthcare Scholarship Program *196*
American Dental Association Foundation Dental Hygiene Scholarship Program *194*
American Dental Association Foundation Dental Student Scholarship Program *195*
American Legion Auxiliary Department of Colorado Past Presidents' Parley Health Care Professional ScholarshipNurses Scholarship *125*
Annual Healthcare and Life Sciences Scholarship *142*
A.T. Anderson Memorial Scholarship Program *105*
AvaCare Medical Scholarship *100*
BHW Women in STEM Scholarship *107*
Charles R. Morris Student Research Award *194*
Continental Society, Daughters of Indian Wars Scholarship *188*
DDSRank Dental Scholarship *196*
Developmental Disabilities Scholastic Achievement Scholarship for College Students who are Lutheran *195*
Dr. Juan D. Villarreal/Hispanic Dental Association Foundation *196*
Elizabeth and Sherman Asche Memorial Scholarship Fund *93*
Grotto Scholarship *198*
Health Careers Scholarship *197*
Health Care Profession Scholarship *195*
Intermountain Medical Imaging Scholarship *125*
Johnson & Johnson Scholarship *195*
Medical School Scholarship *194*
Medical Scrubs Collection Scholarship *104*
National Dental Association Foundation Colgate-Palmolive Scholarship Program (Undergraduates) *197*
Novus Biologicals Scholarship Program *101*
Platinum Educational Group Scholarships Program for EMS, Nursing, and Allied Health *102*
Proctor and Gamble Oral Care and HDA Foundation Scholarship *196*

R&D Systems Scholarship *101*
Recovery Village Healthcare Scholarship *197*
Scholarship for Students Pursuing a Business or STEM Degree *80*
Science Ambassador Scholarship *107*
Stanley Dentistry Scholarship Fund *197*
StraightForward Media Medical Professions Scholarship *198*
Tocris Bioscience Scholarship *102*

Drafting
Community College STEM Scholarships *110*
Kurt H. and Donna M. Schuler Small Grant *162*
MRCA Foundation Scholarship Program *116*
NAWIC Undergraduate Scholarships *117*
OLM Malala Yousafzai Scholarship 2017-2018 *122*
Support Creativity Scholarship *117*
Ted G. Wilson Memorial Scholarship Foundation *166*
Vectorworks Design Scholarship *117*

Earth Science
$1,500 STEM Scholarship *104*
AEG Foundation Marliave Fund *199*
Alaska Geological Society Scholarship *199*
American Ground Water Trust-AMTROL Inc. Scholarship *199*
American Ground Water Trust-Baroid Scholarship *199*
American Ground Water Trust-Thomas Stetson Scholarship *199*
American Legion Department of Maryland Math-Science Scholarship *99*
Arizona Hydrological Society Scholarship *200*
Association of State Dam Safety Officials (ASDSO) Senior Undergraduate Scholarship *140*
Astronaut Scholarship *107*
A.T. Anderson Memorial Scholarship Program *105*
AWG Ethnic Minority Scholarship *200*
AWG Maria Luisa Crawford Field Camp Scholarship *111*
AWG Salt Lake Chapter (SLC) Research Scholarship *111*
AWG Undergraduate Excellence in Paleontology Award *106*
Barry M. Goldwater Scholarship and Excellence in Education Program *107*
BHW Women in STEM Scholarship *107*
B.O.G. Pest Control Scholarship Fund *141*
Donald A. Williams Scholarship Soil Conservation Scholarship *91*
Eckenfelder Scholarship *141*
Edward R. Hall Scholarship *91*
Elizabeth and Sherman Asche Memorial Scholarship Fund *93*
Environmental Protection Scholarship *142*
Florida Space Research Program *131*
HENAAC Scholarship Program *100*
Janet Cullen Tanaka Geosciences Undergraduate Scholarship *112*
Jerry McDowell Fund *156*
J. Fielding Reed Undergraduate Soil and Plant Sciences Scholarship *200*
Leidos STEM Scholarship *96*
Life Member Montana Federation of Garden Clubs Scholarship *202*
Lone Star Rising Career Scholarship *200*
Medical Scrubs Collection Scholarship *104*
Minnesota Space Grant Consortium Scholarship Program *131*
Minority Scholarship Program *141*
NASA Idaho Space Grant Consortium Scholarship Program *109*

Energy and Power Engineering

Engineering-Related Technologies

Engineering/Technology

Entomology

Environmental Health

Environmental Science

Nebraska Press Association Foundation
Scholarship 86
Newhouse Scholarship Program 275
Print and Graphics Scholarships Foundation 174
Printing Industry Midwest Education Foundation
Scholarship Fund 175
QualityBath.com Scholarship Program 120
Support Creativity Scholarship 117
TLMI 2 Year College Degree Scholarship
Program 262
TLMI 4 Year College Degree Scholarship
Program 262
Vectorworks Design Scholarship 117
Visual and Performing Arts Achievement
Awards 121
Woodward Scholarship 172

Health Administration

Aboriginal Health Careers Bursary 139
Alice L. Haltom Educational Fund 145
American Indian Nurse Scholarship
Program 278
American Legion Auxiliary Department of
Colorado Past Presidents' Parley Health Care
Professional ScholarshipNurses
Scholarship 125
AvaCare Medical Scholarship 100
BHW Women in STEM Scholarship 107
Continental Society, Daughters of Indian Wars
Scholarship 188
Developmental Disabilities Scholastic
Achievement Scholarship for College Students
who are Lutheran 195
Harry J. Morris, Jr. Emergency Services
Scholarship 261
HCN/Apricity Resources Scholars Program 83
Health Care Profession Scholarship 195
HIMSS Foundation Scholarship Program 277
Intermountain Medical Imaging Scholarship 125
Jerman-Cahoon Student Scholarship 276
Medical Scrubs Collection Scholarship 104
New England Employee Benefits Council
Scholarship Program 78
Novus Biologicals Scholarship Program 101
Pacific Health Workforce Award 277
Pacific Mental Health Work Force Award 277
Professional Advancement Scholarship 276
R&D Systems Scholarship 101
Royce Osborn Minority Student Scholarship 276
Scholarship for Students Pursuing a Business or
STEM Degree 80
Society for Health Systems Scholarship 241
StraightForward Media Medical Professions
Scholarship 198
Tocris Bioscience Scholarship 102

Health and Medical Sciences

$1,500 STEM Scholarship 104
Aboriginal Health Careers Bursary 139
Allied Healthcare Scholarship Program 196
American Legion Auxiliary Department of
Arizona Health Care Occupation
Scholarships 279
American Legion Auxiliary Department of
Colorado Past Presidents' Parley Health Care
Professional ScholarshipNurses
Scholarship 125
American Legion Auxiliary Department of Maine
Past Presidents' Parley Nurses
Scholarship 279
American Legion Auxiliary Department of
Michigan Medical Career Scholarship 279
American Legion Auxiliary Department of
Minnesota Past Presidents' Parley Health Care
Scholarship 279

American Legion Auxiliary Department of Texas
Past Presidents' Parley Medical
Scholarship 279
American Legion Department of Maryland Math-
Science Scholarship 99
Amy Hunter-Wilson, MD Scholarship 285
Annual Healthcare and Life Sciences
Scholarship 142
Arizona Professional Chapter of AISES
Scholarship 237
A.T. Anderson Memorial Scholarship
Program 105
AvaCare Medical Scholarship 100
Barbara A. Horwitz and John M. Horowitz
Undergraduate Research Awards 139
BHW Women in STEM Scholarship 107
CANFIT Nutrition, Physical Education and
Culinary Arts Scholarship 190
Continental Society, Daughters of Indian Wars
Scholarship 188
Crohn's & Colitis Foundation of America Student
Research Fellowship Awards 281
Cynthia E. Morgan Memorial Scholarship Fund,
Inc. 248
Developmental Disabilities Scholastic
Achievement Scholarship for College Students
who are Lutheran 195
Edith M. Allen Scholarship 209
Elizabeth and Sherman Asche Memorial
Scholarship Fund 93
Endowment Fund for Education Grant 171
Foundation for Seacoast Health Scholarships 282
Frances L. Booth Medical Scholarship sponsored
by LAVFW Department of Maine 283
Franz Stenzel M.D. and Kathryn Stenzel
Scholarship Fund 283
Galactic Unite Bytheway Scholarship 111
Harry J. Morris, Jr. Emergency Services
Scholarship 261
Health Careers Scholarship 197
Health Care Profession Scholarship 195
Health Professions Preparatory Scholarship
Program 137
HIMSS Foundation Scholarship Program 277
Indian Health Service Health Professions Pre-
graduate Scholarships 108
Intermountain Medical Imaging Scholarship 125
The Jackson Laboratory College Scholarship
Program 108
Jerman-Cahoon Student Scholarship 276
Ketamine Clinics of Los Angeles Scholarship
Program 138
Leidos STEM Scholarship 96
Linda Craig Memorial Scholarship presented by
St. Vincent Sports Medicine 284
Mary McMillan Scholarship Award 207
Medical School Scholarship 194
Medical Scrubs Collection Scholarship 104
Morton B. Duggan, Jr. Memorial Education
Recognition Award 280
National Athletic Trainers' Association Research
and Education Foundation Scholarship
Program 283
NIH Undergraduate Scholarship Program for
Students from Disadvantaged
Backgrounds 101
Northern Alberta Development Council
Bursary 205
Novus Biologicals Scholarship Program 101
Overdose Attorney Scholarship 281
Pacific Health Workforce Award 277
Pacific Mental Health Work Force Award 277
Physicians for Rural Areas Assistance
Program 282
Platinum Educational Group Scholarships Program
for EMS, Nursing, and Allied Health 102

Professional Advancement Scholarship 276
R&D Systems Scholarship 101
Royce Osborn Minority Student Scholarship 276
Ruth Shaw Junior Board Scholarship 281
Scholarship for Students Pursuing a Business or
STEM Degree 80
Scholarships for Disadvantaged Students
Program 284
Sepracor Achievement Award for Excellence in
Pulmonary Disease State Management 280
The Society for the Scientific Study of Sexuality
Student Research Grant 105
Society of Pediatric Nurses Educational
Scholarship 161
Spence Reese Scholarship 237
StraightForward Media Medical Professions
Scholarship 198
Straight North STEM Scholarship 81
Student Opportunity Scholarship 212
Student Research Scholarship 285
Thelma Orr Memorial Scholarship 278
Tocris Bioscience Scholarship 102
United Nations Association of Connecticut
Scholarship 124
William and Dorothy Ferrell Scholarship 207

Health Information Management/ Technology

$1,500 STEM Scholarship 104
AHIMA Foundation Student Merit
Scholarship 285
Alice L. Haltom Educational Fund 145
American Legion Auxiliary Department of
Colorado Past Presidents' Parley Health Care
Professional ScholarshipNurses
Scholarship 125
AvaCare Medical Scholarship 100
BHW Women in STEM Scholarship 107
Cynthia E. Morgan Memorial Scholarship Fund,
Inc. 248
Developmental Disabilities Scholastic
Achievement Scholarship for College Students
who are Lutheran 195
Health Care Profession Scholarship 195
HIMSS Foundation Scholarship Program 277
Intermountain Medical Imaging Scholarship 125
Jerman-Cahoon Student Scholarship 276
Leidos STEM Scholarship 96
Medical Scrubs Collection Scholarship 104
National Athletic Trainers' Association Research
and Education Foundation Scholarship
Program 283
Novus Biologicals Scholarship Program 101
Pacific Health Workforce Award 277
Pacific Mental Health Work Force Award 277
Professional Advancement Scholarship 276
R&D Systems Scholarship 101
Robert V. McKenna Scholarships 183
Royce Osborn Minority Student Scholarship 276
Scholarship for Students Pursuing a Business or
STEM Degree 80
Society for Health Systems Scholarship 241
StraightForward Media Medical Professions
Scholarship 198
Straight North STEM Scholarship 81
Tocris Bioscience Scholarship 102
UltrasoundTechnicianSchools.com
Scholarship 286

Heating, Air-Conditioning, and Refrigeration Mechanics

A.T. Anderson Memorial Scholarship
Program 105
BHW Women in STEM Scholarship 107
EGIA Foundation Scholarship Program 287
Rees Scholarship Foundation HVACR and Water
Heating Technician Program 287

SWE Region E Scholarship *159*
SWE Region H Scholarships *159*
SWE Region J Scholarship *159*
Sylvia W. Farny Scholarship *236*
Technical Minority Scholarship *161*
TE Connectivity Excellence in Engineering
    Scholarship *160*
Ted G. Wilson Memorial Scholarship
    Foundation *166*
TiMOTION Engineering and Excellence
    Scholarship *167*
Transit Hall of Fame Scholarship Award
    Program *162*
Undergraduate STEM Research
    Scholarships *110*
Vermont Space Grant Consortium *92*
Vertical Flight Foundation Scholarship *126*
Virginia Counts/Betty Irish SWE for Life
    Scholarship *343*
Whitley Place Scholarship *114*
Women Forward in Technology Scholarship
    Program *108*
YouthForce 2020 Scholarship Program *117*

Meteorology/Atmospheric Science

$1,500 STEM Scholarship *104*
Allegheny Mountain Section Air & Waste
    Management Association Scholarship *250*
Astronaut Scholarship *107*
A.T. Anderson Memorial Scholarship
    Program *105*
Automotive Women's Alliance Foundation
    Scholarships *71*
AWG Ethnic Minority Scholarship *200*
AWG Maria Luisa Crawford Field Camp
    Scholarship *111*
AWG Salt Lake Chapter (SLC) Research
    Scholarship *111*
Barry M. Goldwater Scholarship and Excellence in
    Education Program *107*
BHW Women in STEM Scholarship *107*
Davis Scholarship for Women in STEM *111*
Eckenfelder Scholarship *141*
Father James B. Macelwane Annual Award *251*
Florida Space Research Program *131*
HENAAC Scholarship Program *100*
Janet Cullen Tanaka Geosciences Undergraduate
    Scholarship *112*
Leidos STEM Scholarship *96*
Lone Star Rising Career Scholarship *200*
Minnesota Space Grant Consortium Scholarship
    Program *131*
Minority Scholarship Program *141*
NASA Idaho Space Grant Consortium Scholarship
    Program *109*
NASA Rhode Island Space Grant Consortium
    Undergraduate Research Scholarship *132*
Osage Chapter Undergraduate Service
    Scholarship *112*
Rogers Family Scholarship *143*
Scholarship for Students Pursuing a Business or
    STEM Degree *80*
Science Ambassador Scholarship *107*
SSPI International Scholarships *134*
Straight North STEM Scholarship *81*
Susan Ekdale Memorial Field Camp
    Scholarship *201*
Women Forward in Technology Scholarship
    Program *108*

Military and Defense Studies

AFCEA STEM Majors Scholarships for
    Undergraduate Students *106*
AFIO Undergraduate and Graduate
    Scholarships *98*
BHW Women in STEM Scholarship *107*
HORIZONS Scholarship *346*

Jerry McDowell Fund *156*
Moody Research Grants *99*
National Military Intelligence Association
    Scholarship *346*
SSPI International Scholarships *134*

Museum Studies

Adele Filene Student Presenter Grant *118*
AWG Ethnic Minority Scholarship *200*
AWG Salt Lake Chapter (SLC) Research
    Scholarship *111*
Lone Star Rising Career Scholarship *200*
Moody Research Grants *99*
Osage Chapter Undergraduate Service
    Scholarship *112*
Stella Blum Student Research Grant *118*
Susan Ekdale Memorial Field Camp
    Scholarship *201*

Music

Bach Organ and Keyboard Music
    Scholarship *351*
Charlotte Plummer Owen Memorial
    Scholarship *216*
Dr. Earl James Fahringer Performing Arts
    Scholarship *121*
Dorchester Women's Club Music
    Scholarship *347*
Douglas W. Mummert Scholarship *173*
Elaine Rendler-Rene Dosogne-Georgetown
    Chorale Scholarship *349*
Gladys C. Anderson Memorial Scholarship *347*
GMBS-3rd Place Instrumental Scholarship *348*
GMBS-Bill Baker/Hans Starreveld
    Scholarship *348*
GMBS-Ray Eberle Vocal Scholarship *348*
Hartford Jazz Society Scholarships *348*
Houston Symphony Ima Hogg Competition *349*
Houston Symphony League Concerto
    Competition *349*
Jack J. Isgur Foundation Scholarship *211*
Jim McKay Memorial Scholarship *258*
Llewellyn L. Cayvan String Instrument
    Scholarship *348*
Martha Ann Stark Memorial Scholarship *216*
Mike Wallace Memorial Scholarship *258*
MuSonics Scholarship *349*
National Academy of Television Arts and Sciences
    Trustees' Linda Giannecchini
    Scholarship *258*
NPM Board of Directors Scholarship *350*
NPM Koinonia/Board of Directors
    Scholarship *350*
NPM Perrot Scholarship *350*
Oregon Catholic Press Scholarship *350*
Paluch Family Foundation/World Library
    Publications Scholarship *350*
Polish Arts Club of Buffalo Scholarship
    Foundation Trust *122*
QualityBath.com Scholarship Program *120*
Queen Elisabeth Competition *351*
Randy Falco Scholarship *259*
R.L. Gillette Scholarship *323*
Scholarship Program for Young American
    Pianists *347*
Steven C. Warner Scholarship *350*
Steven J. Finkel Service Excellence
    Scholarship *148*
Tiffany Green Operator Scholarship Award *85*
Traditional Marching Band Extravaganza
    Scholarship Award *348*
Volkwein Memorial Scholarship *216*
VSA International Young Soloists Award *351*
Willa Beach-Porter Music Scholarships *347*

Natural Resources

American Ground Water Trust-AMTROL Inc.
    Scholarship *199*
American Ground Water Trust-Baroid
    Scholarship *199*
American Ground Water Trust-Thomas Stetson
    Scholarship *199*
Arizona Hydrological Society Scholarship *200*
Arizona Professional Chapter of AISES
    Scholarship *237*
Association of California Water Agencies
    Scholarships *106*
Association of State Dam Safety Officials
    (ASDSO) Senior Undergraduate
    Scholarship *140*
A.T. Anderson Memorial Scholarship
    Program *105*
AWG Ethnic Minority Scholarship *200*
AWG Maria Luisa Crawford Field Camp
    Scholarship *111*
AWG Salt Lake Chapter (SLC) Research
    Scholarship *111*
AWRA Richard A. Herbert Memorial
    Scholarship *352*
BHW Women in STEM Scholarship *107*
Bill Mason Scholarship Fund *212*
B.O.G. Pest Control Scholarship Fund *141*
California Groundwater Association
    Scholarship *298*
Charles A. Holt Indiana Wildlife Federation
    Endowment Scholarship *253*
Charles P. Bell Conservation Scholarship *252*
Clair A. Hill Scholarship *106*
Demonstration of Energy and Efficiency
    Developments Educational Scholarship *154*
Demonstration of Energy and Efficiency
    Developments Student Internship *154*
Demonstration of Energy and Efficiency
    Developments Student Research Grants *162*
Demonstration of Energy and Efficiency
    Developments Technical Design Project *154*
Donald A. Williams Scholarship Soil Conservation
    Scholarship *91*
Eckenfelder Scholarship *141*
Edward R. Hall Scholarship *91*
George A. Hall/Harold F. Mayfield Award *103*
HENAAC Scholarship Program *100*
Janet Cullen Tanaka Geosciences Undergraduate
    Scholarship *112*
Jerry McDowell Fund *156*
J. Fielding Reed Undergraduate Soil and Plant
    Sciences Scholarship *200*
Jim Bourque Scholarship *207*
Life Member Montana Federation of Garden Clubs
    Scholarship *202*
Lone Star Rising Career Scholarship *200*
Minority Scholarship Program *141*
NASA Idaho Space Grant Consortium Scholarship
    Program *109*
National Network for Environmental Management
    Studies Fellowship *256*
Native American Natural Resource Research
    Scholarship *353*
Osage Chapter Undergraduate Service
    Scholarship *112*
Outdoor Writers Association of America - Bodie
    McDowell Scholarship Award *174*
Paul A. Stewart Awards *103*
Rockefeller State Wildlife Scholarship *325*
Rogers Family Scholarship *143*
Russell W. Myers Scholarship *143*
South Dakota Board of Regents Bjugstad
    Scholarship *91*
Straight North STEM Scholarship *81*
Susan Ekdale Memorial Field Camp
    Scholarship *201*

Timothy L. Taschwer Scholarship *144*
Tocris Bioscience Scholarship *102*
USDA/1994 Tribal Scholars Program *96*
VASWCD Educational Foundation Inc.
Scholarship Awards Program *354*
Wildlife Leadership Awards *354*
William L. Cullison Scholarship *354*
Women Forward in Technology Scholarship
Program *108*

Natural Sciences
$1,500 STEM Scholarship *104*
ACEC-Florida Scholarship *239*
AFIO Undergraduate and Graduate
Scholarships *98*
American Chemical Society Scholars
Program *153*
American Legion Department of Maryland Math-
Science Scholarship *99*
Association of California Water Agencies
Scholarships *106*
Association of State Dam Safety Officials
(ASDSO) Senior Undergraduate
Scholarship *140*
A.T. Anderson Memorial Scholarship
Program *105*
AWG Ethnic Minority Scholarship *200*
AWG Maria Luisa Crawford Field Camp
Scholarship *111*
AWG Salt Lake Chapter (SLC) Research
Scholarship *111*
AWG Undergraduate Excellence in Paleontology
Award *106*
Barbara A. Horwitz and John M. Horowitz
Undergraduate Research Awards *139*
Barry M. Goldwater Scholarship and Excellence in
Education Program *107*
Battery Division Student Research Award
Sponsored by Mercedes-Benz Research &
Development *155*
Beulah Frey Environmental Scholarship *252*
BHW Women in STEM Scholarship *107*
Bill Mason Scholarship Fund *212*
B.O.G. Pest Control Scholarship Fund *141*
Charles P. Bell Conservation Scholarship *252*
Clair A. Hill Scholarship *106*
Donald A. Williams Scholarship Soil Conservation
Scholarship *91*
Eckenfelder Scholarship *141*
Edward R. Hall Scholarship *91*
Elizabeth and Sherman Asche Memorial
Scholarship Fund *93*
Environmental Protection Scholarship *142*
HENAAC Scholarship Program *100*
Janet Cullen Tanaka Geosciences Undergraduate
Scholarship *112*
J. Fielding Reed Undergraduate Soil and Plant
Sciences Scholarship *200*
Jim Bourque Scholarship *207*
John M. Murphy Scholarship *357*
Leidos STEM Scholarship *96*
Lone Star Rising Career Scholarship *200*
Medical Scrubs Collection Scholarship *104*
Minnesota Space Grant Consortium Scholarship
Program *131*
Minority Scholarship Program *141*
NASA Idaho Space Grant Consortium Scholarship
Program *109*
National Space Grant Consortium
Scholarships *110*
Native American Natural Resource Research
Scholarship *353*
Novus Biologicals Scholarship Program *101*
Paul W. Ruckes Scholarship *179*
R&D Systems Scholarship *101*

Scholarship for Students Pursuing a Business or
STEM Degree *80*
Science Ambassador Scholarship *107*
Sehar Saleha Ahmad and Abrahim Ekramullah
Zafar Foundation Scholarship *110*
Straight North STEM Scholarship *81*
Susan Ekdale Memorial Field Camp
Scholarship *201*
Tocris Bioscience Scholarship *102*
United Nations Association of Connecticut
Scholarship *124*
Wildlife Leadership Awards *354*
Women Forward in Technology Scholarship
Program *108*
Youth Activity Fund Grants *103*

Near and Middle East Studies
AFIO Undergraduate and Graduate
Scholarships *98*
BHW Women in STEM Scholarship *107*
Hub Foundation Scholarships *88*
ISF National Scholarship *104*
United Nations Association of Connecticut
Scholarship *124*

Neurobiology
$1,500 STEM Scholarship *104*
Al & Williamary Viste Scholarship *99*
Annual Healthcare and Life Sciences
Scholarship *142*
A.T. Anderson Memorial Scholarship
Program *105*
AvaCare Medical Scholarship *100*
Barbara A. Horwitz and John M. Horowitz
Undergraduate Research Awards *139*
Barry M. Goldwater Scholarship and Excellence in
Education Program *107*
BHW Women in STEM Scholarship *107*
Cynthia E. Morgan Memorial Scholarship Fund,
Inc. *248*
HENAAC Scholarship Program *100*
Intermountain Medical Imaging Scholarship *125*
Ketamine Clinics of Los Angeles Scholarship
Program *138*
Leidos STEM Scholarship *96*
Medical Scrubs Collection Scholarship *104*
NIH Undergraduate Scholarship Program for
Students from Disadvantaged
Backgrounds *101*
Novus Biologicals Scholarship Program *101*
R&D Systems Scholarship *101*
Scholarship for Students Pursuing a Business or
STEM Degree *80*
Science Ambassador Scholarship *107*
Straight North STEM Scholarship *81*
Tocris Bioscience Scholarship *102*
Women Forward in Technology Scholarship
Program *108*

Nuclear Science
$1,500 STEM Scholarship *104*
2017 Tailor Made Lawns Scholarship Fund *96*
American Chemical Society, Rubber Division
Undergraduate Scholarship *105*
American Legion Department of Maryland Math-
Science Scholarship *99*
American Society of Naval Engineers
Scholarship *106*
Arizona Hydrological Society Scholarship *200*
A.T. Anderson Memorial Scholarship
Program *105*
Barry M. Goldwater Scholarship and Excellence in
Education Program *107*
BHW Women in STEM Scholarship *107*
HENAAC Scholarship Program *100*
Jerry McDowell Fund *156*

Leidos STEM Scholarship *96*
Minnesota Space Grant Consortium Scholarship
Program *131*
NASA Idaho Space Grant Consortium Scholarship
Program *109*
NIH Undergraduate Scholarship Program for
Students from Disadvantaged
Backgrounds *101*
Novus Biologicals Scholarship Program *101*
R&D Systems Scholarship *101*
Scholarship for Students Pursuing a Business or
STEM Degree *80*
Science Ambassador Scholarship *107*
Straight North STEM Scholarship *81*
Tocris Bioscience Scholarship *102*
United Nations Association of Connecticut
Scholarship *124*
Women Forward in Technology Scholarship
Program *108*

Nursing
$1,500 STEM Scholarship *104*
Aboriginal Health Careers Bursary *139*
Agnes Naughton RN-BSN Fund *365*
Al & Williamary Viste Scholarship *99*
American Indian Nurse Scholarship
Program *278*
American Legion Auxiliary Department of
Arizona Nurses' Scholarships *361*
American Legion Auxiliary Department of
California Past Presidents' Parley Nursing
Scholarships *361*
American Legion Auxiliary Department of
Colorado Past Presidents' Parley Health Care
Professional ScholarshipNurses
Scholarship *125*
American Legion Auxiliary Department of Idaho
Nursing Scholarship *361*
American Legion Auxiliary Department of Iowa
M.V. McCrae Memorial Nurses Merit
Award *361*
American Legion Auxiliary Department of Maine
Past Presidents' Parley Nurses
Scholarship *279*
American Legion Auxiliary Department of
Michigan Medical Career Scholarship *279*
American Legion Auxiliary Department of
Missouri Past Presidents' Parley
Scholarship *362*
American Legion Auxiliary Department of North
Dakota Past Presidents' Parley Nurses
Scholarship *362*
American Legion Auxiliary Department of Ohio
Past Presidents' Parley Nurses
Scholarship *362*
American Legion Auxiliary Department of Oregon
Nurses Scholarship *362*
American Legion Auxiliary Department of
Pennsylvania Past Department Presidents'
Memorial Scholarship *363*
Annual Healthcare and Life Sciences
Scholarship *142*
Associate Degree Nursing Scholarship
Program *368*
A.T. Anderson Memorial Scholarship
Program *105*
AvaCare Medical Scholarship *100*
Bachelor of Science Nursing Loan Repayment
Program *368*
Bachelor of Science Nursing Scholarship
Program *368*
Back to School Nursing Scholarship
Program *363*
BHW Women in STEM Scholarship *107*
Breakthrough to Nursing Scholarships for Racial/
Ethnic Minorities *366*

Occupational Safety and Health

Oceanography

Oncology

Williams Law Group Opportunity to Grow
Scholarship *119*

Public Health

Annual Healthcare and Life Sciences
Scholarship *142*
AvaCare Medical Scholarship *100*
Continental Society, Daughters of Indian Wars
Scholarship *188*
Elizabeth and Sherman Asche Memorial
Scholarship Fund *93*
Florida Environmental Health Association
Educational Scholarship Awards *249*
Health Care Profession Scholarship *195*
Intermountain Medical Imaging Scholarship *125*
The Jackson Laboratory College Scholarship
Program *108*
Medical Scrubs Collection Scholarship *104*
National Environmental Health Association/
American Academy of Sanitarians
Scholarship *249*
New England Employee Benefits Council
Scholarship Program *78*
NIH Undergraduate Scholarship Program for
Students from Disadvantaged
Backgrounds *101*
Novus Biologicals Scholarship Program *101*
Platinum Educational Group Scholarships Program
for EMS, Nursing, and Allied Health *102*
R&D Systems Scholarship *101*
Recovery Village Healthcare Scholarship *197*
The Society for the Scientific Study of Sexuality
Student Research Grant *105*
South Carolina Public Health Association Public
Health Scholarships *397*
Tocris Bioscience Scholarship *102*

Public Policy and Administration

AFIO Undergraduate and Graduate
Scholarships *98*
American Legion Auxiliary Department of
Arizona Wilma Hoyal-Maxine Chilton
Memorial Scholarship *170*
CBC Spouses Education Scholarship *98*
Douglas W. Mummert Scholarship *173*
Harriet Irsay Scholarship Grant *120*
Harry S. Truman Scholarship *394*
Jeffrey L. Esser Career Development
Scholarship *75*
Kansas Federation of Republican Women
Scholarship *288*
Media Plan Case Competition *88*
Minorities in Government Finance
Scholarship *75*
National JACL Headquarters Scholarship *94*
New England Employee Benefits Council
Scholarship Program *78*
Recovery Village Healthcare Scholarship *197*
Washington Crossing Foundation
Scholarship *395*
Washington State Association for Justice
American Justice Essay & Video
Scholarship *189*
Whitley Place Scholarship *114*
William and Dorothy Ferrell Scholarship *207*

Radiology

$1,500 STEM Scholarship *104*
Al & Williamary Viste Scholarship *99*
Allied Healthcare Scholarship Program *196*
A.T. Anderson Memorial Scholarship
Program *105*
Cynthia E. Morgan Memorial Scholarship Fund,
Inc. *248*
Health Care Profession Scholarship *195*
Jerman-Cahoon Student Scholarship *276*

Leidos STEM Scholarship *96*
Medical School Scholarship *194*
Medical Scrubs Collection Scholarship *104*
Novus Biologicals Scholarship Program *101*
Platinum Educational Group Scholarships Program
for EMS, Nursing, and Allied Health *102*
Professional Advancement Scholarship *276*
R&D Systems Scholarship *101*
Royce Osborn Minority Student Scholarship *276*
Siemens Clinical Advancement Scholarship *378*
Tocris Bioscience Scholarship *102*
UltrasoundTechnicianSchools.com
Scholarship *286*

Real Estate

AIET Minorities and Women Educational
Scholarship *400*
Appraisal Institute Education Trust Education
Scholarships *400*
C.A.R. Scholarship Foundation Award *400*
Illinois Real Estate Educational Foundation
Academic Scholarships *400*
New Jersey Association of Realtors Educational
Foundation Scholarship Program *400*
Thomas F. Seay Scholarship *400*

Recreation, Parks, Leisure Studies

AFRS Student Scholarship *401*
AHLEF Annual Scholarship Grant Program *267*
American Hotel & Lodging Educational
Foundation Pepsi Scholarship *189*
Bill Mason Scholarship Fund *212*
Ecolab Scholarship Program *267*
Hyatt Hotels Fund for Minority Lodging
Management *268*
Incoming Freshman Scholarships *268*
Rama Scholarship for the American Dream *268*
Rogers Family Scholarship *143*
Russell W. Myers Scholarship *143*
Ruth Abernathy Presidential Scholarship *401*
The Walter J. Travis Memorial Scholarship and
The Walter J. Travis-Rudy Zocchi Memorial
Scholarship *118*

Religion/Theology

Developmental Disabilities Scholastic
Achievement Scholarship for College Students
who are Lutheran *195*
Ed E. and Gladys Hurley Foundation
Scholarship *402*
Elaine Rendler-Rene Dosogne-Georgetown
Chorale Scholarship *349*
Funk Family Memorial Scholarship *402*
GIA Pastoral Musicians Scholarship *402*
Hub Foundation Scholarships *88*
La-Philosophie.com Scholarship *104*
Leonard M. Perryman Communications
Scholarship for Ethnic Minority Students *177*
MuSonics Scholarship *349*
National Association of Pastoral Musicians
Members' Scholarship *402*
NPM Koinonia/Board of Directors
Scholarship *350*
Oregon Catholic Press Scholarship *350*
Paluch Family Foundation/World Library
Publications Scholarship *350*
Scholarships for Education, Business and
Religion *147*
The Society for the Scientific Study of Sexuality
Student Research Grant *105*
Student Opportunity Scholarship *212*

Science, Technology, and Society

$1,500 STEM Scholarship *104*
AEG Foundation Marliave Fund *199*
AIAA Foundation Undergraduate
Scholarships *127*

Arizona Hydrological Society Scholarship *200*
Association of State Dam Safety Officials
(ASDSO) Senior Undergraduate
Scholarship *140*
A.T. Anderson Memorial Scholarship
Program *105*
Automotive Women's Alliance Foundation
Scholarships *71*
Barbara A. Horwitz and John M. Horowitz
Undergraduate Research Awards *139*
Battery Division Student Research Award
Sponsored by Mercedes-Benz Research &
Development *155*
BHW Women in STEM Scholarship *107*
Carrol C. Hall Memorial Scholarship *213*
Donald A. Williams Scholarship Soil Conservation
Scholarship *91*
Eckenfelder Scholarship *141*
Galactic Unite Bytheway Scholarship *111*
Gulf Coast Hurricane Scholarship *159*
H.H. Dow Memorial Student Achievement Award
of the Industrial Electrolysis and
Electrochemical Engineering Division of the
Electrochemical Society Inc *156*
HIMSS Foundation Scholarship Program *277*
International Technology Education Association
Undergraduate Scholarship in Technology
Education *210*
The Jackson Laboratory College Scholarship
Program *108*
Jerry McDowell Fund *156*
JROTC Scholarship *403*
Jules Cohen Scholarship *218*
LastPass STEM Scholarship *109*
Leatrice Gregory Pendray Scholarship *127*
Lone Star Rising Career Scholarship *200*
Louis F. Wolf Jr. Memorial Scholarship *175*
Materials Processing and Manufacturing Division
Scholarship *228*
Math, Engineering, Science, Business, Education,
Computers Scholarships *146*
NASA Idaho Space Grant Consortium Scholarship
Program *109*
NASA Rhode Island Space Grant Consortium
Outreach Scholarship for Undergraduate
Students *338*
Native American Leadership in Education
(NALE) *146*
Novus Biologicals Scholarship Program *101*
R&D Systems Scholarship *101*
R&D Systems Scholarship Program *405*
Robert V. McKenna Scholarships *183*
Society for Technical Communication Scholarship
Program *175*
Steven J. Muir Scholarship *160*
Straight North STEM Scholarship *81*
Student Paper Award *175*
Thomas H. Dunning, Sr., Memorial
Scholarship *183*
Timothy L. Taschwer Scholarship *144*
TMS Extraction & Processing Scholarship *228*
TMS Functional Materials Gilbert Chin
Scholarship *228*
TMS/International Symposium on Superalloys
Scholarship Program *229*
TMS/Light Metals Division Scholarship
Program *229*
TMS Outstanding Student Paper Contest-
Undergraduate *229*
TMS/Structural Materials Division
Scholarship *229*
Tocris Bioscience Scholarship *102*
Tuskegee Airmen Scholarship *134*
Undergraduate STEM Research
Scholarships *110*

Civic, Professional, Social, or Union Affiliation

Reserve Officers Association

Henry J. Reilly Memorial Scholarship-High School Seniors and First Year Freshmen *452*

Henry J. Reilly Memorial Undergraduate Scholarship Program for College Attendees *452*

Retail, Wholesale and Department Store Union

Alvin E. Heaps Memorial Scholarship *452*

Service Employees International Union

SEIU Jesse Jackson Scholarship Program *452*

SEIU John Geagan Scholarship *453*

SEIU Moe Foner Scholarship Program for Visual and Performing Arts *123*

SEIU Nora Piore Scholarship Program *453*

SEIU Scholarship Program *453*

Sigma Alpha Mu Foundation

Undergraduate Achievement Awards *453*

Young Scholars Program *453*

Sigma Chi Fraternity

Sigma Chi Foundation - General Undergraduate Scholarship *453*

Slovenian Women's Union of America

Slovenian Women's Union of America Scholarship Foundation *454*

Society for Human Resource Management

SHRM Foundation Student Scholarships *297*

Society of Motion Picture and Television Engineers

Louis F. Wolf Jr. Memorial Scholarship *175*

Student Paper Award *175*

Society of Pediatric Nurses

Society of Pediatric Nurses Educational Scholarship *161*

Society of Physics Students

Society of Physics Students Leadership Scholarships *392*

Society of Physics Students Outstanding Student in Research *392*

Society of Physics Students Peggy Dixon Two-Year College Scholarship *393*

Society of Women Engineers

SWE Region E Scholarship *159*

SWE Region H Scholarships *159*

SWE Region J Scholarship *159*

Virginia Counts/Betty Irish SWE for Life Scholarship *343*

Soil and Water Conservation Society

Donald A. Williams Scholarship Soil Conservation Scholarship *91*

Melville H. Cohee Student Leader Conservation Scholarship *454*

SOKOL, USA

SOKOL, USA/Milan Getting Scholarship *453*

Springfield Newspaper 25-Year Club

Horace Hill Scholarship Fund *438*

Tau Kappa Epsilon

Bruce B. Melchert Scholarship *394*

Carrol C. Hall Memorial Scholarship *213*

Charles J. Trabold Scholarship *454*

Francis J. Flynn Memorial Scholarship *213*

Harry J. Donnelly Memorial Scholarship *82*

J.D. Williams Scholarship *455*

J. Russel Salsbury Memorial Scholarship *455*

Miles Gray Memorial Scholarship *455*

Steven J. Muir Scholarship *160*

Thomas H. Dunning, Sr., Memorial Scholarship *183*

Timothy L. Taschwer Scholarship *144*

W. Allan Herzog Scholarship *82*

Tennessee Education Association

TEA Don Sahli-Kathy Woodall Sons and Daughters Scholarship *214*

TEA Don Sahli-Kathy Woodall STEA Scholarship *214*

Texas Association of Broadcasters

Texas Association of Broadcasters - Belo Scholarship *176*

Texas Association of Broadcasters - Bonner McLane Scholarship *313*

Texas Association of Broadcasters - Tom Reiff Scholarship *313*

Texas Association of Broadcasters - Two-year/Technical School Scholarship *176*

Texas Association of Broadcasters - Undergraduate Scholarship *176*

Texas Association of Broadcasters - Vann Kennedy Scholarship *177*

Transportation Club International

Alice Glaisyer Warfield Memorial Scholarship *421*

Denny Lydic Scholarship *445*

Texas Transportation Scholarship *421*

Transportation Clubs International Charlotte Woods Scholarship *421*

Transportation Clubs International Ginger and Fred Deines Canada Scholarship *421*

Transportation Clubs International Ginger and Fred Deines Mexico Scholarship *421*

United Daughters of the Confederacy

United Daughters of the Confederacy Undergraduate Scholarships *455*

United Food and Commercial Workers

James A. Suffridge United Food and Commercial Workers Scholarship Program *455*

United States Society on Dams

United States Society on Dams Student Scholarship Award *168*

USA Water Ski

American Water Ski Educational Foundation Scholarship *436*

Utility Workers Union of America

Utility Workers Union of America Scholarship Awards Program *456*

Vermont-NEA

Vermont-NEA/Maida F. Townsend Scholarship *215*

Veterans of Foreign Wars or Auxiliary

Frances L. Booth Medical Scholarship sponsored by LAVFW Department of Maine *283*

United States Submarine Veterans Inc. National Scholarship Program *456*

Western Fraternal Life Association

Western Fraternal Life National Scholarship *456*

Wisconsin Association for Food Protection

WAFP Memorial Scholarship *456*

Women in Aviation, International

Airbus Leadership Grant *457*

The Boeing Company Career Enhancement Scholarship *136*

Delta Air Lines Aircraft Maintenance Technology Scholarship *136*

Delta Air Lines Aviation Maintenance Management/Aviation Business Management Scholarship *136*

Delta Air Lines Engineering Scholarship *136*

Keep Flying Scholarship *136*

Women in Aviation, International Achievement Awards *457*

Women in Corporate Aviation Career Scholarships *457*

Women Military Aviators Dream of Flight Scholarship *137*

Wright Chapter, Women in Aviation, International, Elisha Hall Memorial Scholarship *137*

Women in Logistics

Women in Logistics Scholarship *152*

Wyoming Farm Bureau

Livingston Family - H.J. King Memorial Scholarship *457*

Wyoming Farm Bureau Continuing Education Scholarships *457*

Wyoming Farm Bureau Federation Scholarships *457*

Corporate Affiliation

Employment/ Volunteer Experience

Impairment

Location of Study

Classic Scholarships *607*

Clunker Junker Cash for Cars and College Scholarship *227*

Finally Sold Impact Maker Scholarship *563*

Frank S. Land Scholarship *458*

Greenhouse Scholars *571*

Hagan Scholarship *572*

HENAAC Scholarship Program *100*

Idaho Governor's Cup Scholarship *465*

Idaho Nursery and Landscape Association Scholarships *292*

Idaho Opportunity Scholarship *573*

Jules Cohen Scholarship *218*

Korean-American Scholarship Foundation Western Region Scholarships *523*

LastPass STEM Scholarship *109*

Lori Rhett Memorial Scholarship *468*

Milton Fisher Scholarship for Innovation and Creativity *598*

Minority Students in Veterinary Medicine Scholarship *510*

Morrow & Sheppard College Scholarship *319*

NASA Idaho Space Grant Consortium Scholarship Program *109*

National Association for Campus Activities Scholarships for Student Leaders *468*

National Make It With Wool Competition *257*

Pedro Zamora Young Leaders Scholarship *676*

Residential Construction Management Scholarship *185*

Residential Design Scholarship *115*

Sustainable Residential Design Scholarship *115*

SWE Region J Scholarship *159*

Touchmark Foundation Nursing Scholarship *374*

Two Ten Footwear Foundation Scholarship *471*

Two Ten Foundation Footwear Design Scholarship *607*

United States Senate Youth Program *626*

U.S. Army ROTC Four-Year College Scholarship *492*

U.S. Army ROTC Four-Year Historically Black College/University Scholarship *492*

U.S. Army ROTC Four-Year Nursing Scholarship *364*

U.S. Army ROTC Guaranteed Reserve Forces Duty (GRFD), (ARNG/USAR) and Dedicated ARNG Scholarships *494*

U.S. Army ROTC Military Junior College (MJC) Scholarship *492*

Wayne C. Cornils Memorial Scholarship *148*

WICHE's Western Undergraduate Exchange (WUE) *610*

Women in Architecture Scholarship *116*

You Deserve It! Scholarship *600*

Illinois

2017 ValuePenguin Scholarship *708*

AbbVie Immunology Scholarship *483*

AG Bell College Scholarship Program *472*

Annual CGTrader Scholarship *643*

Army ROTC Green to Gold Scholarship Program for Two-Year, Three-Year and Four-Year Scholarships, Active Duty Enlisted Personnel *491*

Army (ROTC) Reserve Officers Training Corps Two-, Three-, Four-Year Campus-Based Scholarships *492*

Beacon Scholarship for Rural America *555*

Benson & Bingham Annual Scholarship *316*

Cathay Bank Foundation Scholarship Program *552*

CBC Spouses Education Scholarship *98*

CBC Spouses Performing Arts Scholarship *383*

CBC Spouses Visual Arts Scholarship *120*

Chick Evans Scholarship for Caddies *653*

Classic Scholarships *607*

Clunker Junker Cash for Cars and College Scholarship *227*

Finally Sold Impact Maker Scholarship *563*

Floyd R. Cargill Scholarship *477*

Frank S. Land Scholarship *458*

Gala Nursing Scholarships *367*

Golden Apple Scholars of Illinois *210*

Grant Program for Dependents of Police, Fire, or Correctional Officers *459*

Greenhouse Scholars *571*

Hagan Scholarship *572*

HENAAC Scholarship Program *100*

Higher Education License Plate (HELP) Program *574*

Illinois AMVETS Service Foundation Scholarship *574*

Illinois CPA Society Accounting Scholarship Program *76*

Illinois National Guard (ING) Grant Program *489*

Illinois Real Estate Educational Foundation Academic Scholarships *400*

Illinois Society of Professional Engineers/Melvin E. Amstutz Memorial Award *240*

Illinois Special Education Teacher Tuition Waiver (SETTW) Program *574*

Illinois Veteran Grant (IVG) Program *502*

Indiana Health Care Policy Institute Nursing Scholarship *368*

Jules Cohen Scholarship *218*

LastPass STEM Scholarship *109*

Milton Fisher Scholarship for Innovation and Creativity *598*

Minority Students in Veterinary Medicine Scholarship *510*

Minority Teachers of Illinois (MTI) Scholarship Program *521*

Monetary Award Program (MAP) *574*

Morrow & Sheppard College Scholarship *319*

National Association for Campus Activities Scholarships for Student Leaders *468*

National Defense Transportation Association, Scott Air Force Base-St. Louis Area Chapter Scholarship *588*

National Make It With Wool Competition *257*

One Million Degrees Scholarship Support Program *594*

PAPA Scholarship & Safety Foundation *133*

Pedro Zamora Young Leaders Scholarship *676*

Promise of Nursing Scholarship *367*

Residential Construction Management Scholarship *185*

Residential Design Scholarship *115*

Sonne Scholarship *368*

Sustainable Residential Design Scholarship *115*

SWE Region H Scholarships *159*

Tese Caldarelli Memorial Scholarship *468*

Thomas F. Seay Scholarship *400*

Township Officials of Illinois Scholarship Program *607*

Two Ten Footwear Foundation Scholarship *471*

Two Ten Foundation Footwear Design Scholarship *607*

United States Senate Youth Program *626*

U.S. Army ROTC Four-Year College Scholarship *492*

U.S. Army ROTC Four-Year Historically Black College/University Scholarship *492*

U.S. Army ROTC Four-Year Nursing Scholarship *364*

U.S. Army ROTC Guaranteed Reserve Forces Duty (GRFD), (ARNG/USAR) and Dedicated ARNG Scholarships *494*

U.S. Army ROTC Military Junior College (MJC) Scholarship *492*

Women in Architecture Scholarship *116*

Woodward Scholarship *172*

You Deserve It! Scholarship *600*

Zagunis Student Leader Scholarship *622*

Indiana

2017 ValuePenguin Scholarship *708*

21st Century Scholarship *575*

AbbVie Immunology Scholarship *483*

Adult Student Grant *575*

AG Bell College Scholarship Program *472*

American Legion Family Scholarship *432*

Annual CGTrader Scholarship *643*

Anthony Munoz Scholarship Fund *551*

Army ROTC Green to Gold Scholarship Program for Two-Year, Three-Year and Four-Year Scholarships, Active Duty Enlisted Personnel *491*

Army (ROTC) Reserve Officers Training Corps Two-, Three-, Four-Year Campus-Based Scholarships *492*

Beacon Scholarship for Rural America *555*

Benson & Bingham Annual Scholarship *316*

CBC Spouses Education Scholarship *98*

CBC Spouses Performing Arts Scholarship *383*

CBC Spouses Visual Arts Scholarship *120*

Charles A. Holt Indiana Wildlife Federation Endowment Scholarship *253*

Chick Evans Scholarship for Caddies *653*

Child of Deceased or Disabled Veteran *575*

Child of Purple Heart Recipient or Wounded Veteran *575*

Children and Spouse of Indiana National Guard *489*

Children and Spouse of Indiana National Guard Program *575*

Children and Spouse of Public Safety Officers Program *575*

Classic Scholarships *607*

Clunker Junker Cash for Cars and College Scholarship *227*

Finally Sold Impact Maker Scholarship *563*

Frank O'Bannon Grant Program *575*

Frank S. Land Scholarship *458*

Greenhouse Scholars *571*

Hagan Scholarship *572*

HENAAC Scholarship Program *100*

Indiana Broadcasters Foundation Scholarship *305*

Indiana Health Care Policy Institute Nursing Scholarship *368*

Indiana National Guard Tuition Supplement Grant *489*

Indiana Purple Heart Recipient Program *502*

Indiana Retired Teachers Foundation Scholarship *210*

Jules Cohen Scholarship *218*

LastPass STEM Scholarship *109*

Linda Craig Memorial Scholarship presented by St. Vincent Sports Medicine *284*

Milton Fisher Scholarship for Innovation and Creativity *598*

Minority Students in Veterinary Medicine Scholarship *510*

Mitch Daniels Early Graduation Scholarship *576*

Morrow & Sheppard College Scholarship *319*

National Association for Campus Activities Scholarships for Student Leaders *468*

National Defense Transportation Association, Scott Air Force Base-St. Louis Area Chapter Scholarship *588*

National Guard Extension Scholarship *489*

National Guard Tuition Supplement Grant *490*

National Make It With Wool Competition *257*

Next Generation Hoosier Educators Scholarship *576*

Part-Time Grant Program *576*

United States Senate Youth Program *626*
U.S. Army ROTC Four-Year College Scholarship *492*
U.S. Army ROTC Four-Year Historically Black College/University Scholarship *492*
U.S. Army ROTC Four-Year Nursing Scholarship *364*
U.S. Army ROTC Guaranteed Reserve Forces Duty (GRFD), (ARNG/USAR) and Dedicated ARNG Scholarships *494*
U.S. Army ROTC Military Junior College (MJC) Scholarship *492*
Women in Architecture Scholarship *116*
You Deserve It! Scholarship *600*
Zagunis Student Leader Scholarship *622*

Puerto Rico
2017 ValuePenguin Scholarship *708*
AG Bell College Scholarship Program *472*
Annual CGTrader Scholarship *643*
Army ROTC Green to Gold Scholarship Program for Two-Year, Three-Year and Four-Year Scholarships, Active Duty Enlisted Personnel *491*
Army (ROTC) Reserve Officers Training Corps Two-, Three-, Four-Year Campus-Based Scholarships *492*
Benson & Bingham Annual Scholarship *316*
CBC Spouses Education Scholarship *98*
CBC Spouses Performing Arts Scholarship *383*
CBC Spouses Visual Arts Scholarship *120*
Classic Scholarships *607*
Clunker Junker Cash for Cars and College Scholarship *227*
HENAAC Scholarship Program *100*
Jules Cohen Scholarship *218*
Pedro Zamora Young Leaders Scholarship *676*
Residential Design Scholarship *115*
SelectBlinds.com 2019 $1000 College Scholarship *600*
Sustainable Residential Design Scholarship *115*
Two Ten Footwear Foundation Scholarship *471*
Two Ten Foundation Footwear Design Scholarship *607*
U.S. Army ROTC Four-Year College Scholarship *492*
U.S. Army ROTC Four-Year Historically Black College/University Scholarship *492*
U.S. Army ROTC Four-Year Nursing Scholarship *364*
U.S. Army ROTC Guaranteed Reserve Forces Duty (GRFD), (ARNG/USAR) and Dedicated ARNG Scholarships *494*
U.S. Army ROTC Military Junior College (MJC) Scholarship *492*
You Deserve It! Scholarship *600*

Rhode Island
2017 ValuePenguin Scholarship *708*
AbbVie Immunology Scholarship *483*
AG Bell College Scholarship Program *472*
Annual CGTrader Scholarship *643*
Army ROTC Green to Gold Scholarship Program for Two-Year, Three-Year and Four-Year Scholarships, Active Duty Enlisted Personnel *491*
Army (ROTC) Reserve Officers Training Corps Two-, Three-, Four-Year Campus-Based Scholarships *492*
Beacon Scholarship for Rural America *555*
Benson & Bingham Annual Scholarship *316*
CBC Spouses Education Scholarship *98*
CBC Spouses Performing Arts Scholarship *383*
CBC Spouses Visual Arts Scholarship *120*
Classic Scholarships *607*
Clunker Junker Cash for Cars and College Scholarship *227*

Finally Sold Impact Maker Scholarship *563*
Frank S. Land Scholarship *458*
Greenhouse Scholars *571*
Hagan Scholarship *572*
HENAAC Scholarship Program *100*
Jules Cohen Scholarship *218*
Korean-American Scholarship Foundation Northeastern Region Scholarships *523*
LastPass STEM Scholarship *109*
Maine State Grant Program *564*
Milton Fisher Scholarship for Innovation and Creativity *598*
Minority Students in Veterinary Medicine Scholarship *510*
Morrow & Sheppard College Scholarship *319*
NASA Rhode Island Space Grant Consortium Outreach Scholarship for Undergraduate Students *338*
NASA Rhode Island Space Grant Consortium Undergraduate Research Scholarship *132*
NASA RISGC Science En Espanol Scholarship for Undergraduate Students *132*
NASA RISGC Summer Scholarship for Undergraduate Students *132*
National Association for Campus Activities Scholarships for Student Leaders *468*
National Make It With Wool Competition *257*
New England Employee Benefits Council Scholarship Program *78*
New England Regional Student Program-Tuition Break *589*
Norton E. Salk Scholarship *117*
Patricia W. Edwards Memorial Art Scholarship *122*
Pedro Zamora Young Leaders Scholarship *676*
Residential Construction Management Scholarship *185*
Residential Design Scholarship *115*
Roothbert Fund Inc. Scholarship *599*
Seol Bong Scholarship *531*
Sustainable Residential Design Scholarship *115*
Two Ten Footwear Foundation Scholarship *471*
Two Ten Foundation Footwear Design Scholarship *607*
United States Senate Youth Program *626*
U.S. Army ROTC Four-Year College Scholarship *492*
U.S. Army ROTC Four-Year Historically Black College/University Scholarship *492*
U.S. Army ROTC Four-Year Nursing Scholarship *364*
U.S. Army ROTC Guaranteed Reserve Forces Duty (GRFD), (ARNG/USAR) and Dedicated ARNG Scholarships *494*
U.S. Army ROTC Military Junior College (MJC) Scholarship *492*
Women in Architecture Scholarship *116*

South Carolina
2017 ValuePenguin Scholarship *708*
AbbVie Immunology Scholarship *483*
AG Bell College Scholarship Program *472*
Annual CGTrader Scholarship *643*
Army ROTC Green to Gold Scholarship Program for Two-Year, Three-Year and Four-Year Scholarships, Active Duty Enlisted Personnel *491*
Army (ROTC) Reserve Officers Training Corps Two-, Three-, Four-Year Campus-Based Scholarships *492*
Beacon Scholarship for Rural America *555*
Benson & Bingham Annual Scholarship *316*
Casualty Actuaries of the Southeast Scholarship Program *642*
CBC Spouses Education Scholarship *98*
CBC Spouses Performing Arts Scholarship *383*

CBC Spouses Visual Arts Scholarship *120*
Classic Scholarships *607*
Clunker Junker Cash for Cars and College Scholarship *227*
Finally Sold Impact Maker Scholarship *563*
Frank S. Land Scholarship *458*
Greenhouse Scholars *571*
Hagan Scholarship *572*
HENAAC Scholarship Program *100*
Jules Cohen Scholarship *218*
Korean-American Scholarship Foundation Southern Region Scholarships *523*
LastPass STEM Scholarship *109*
Milton Fisher Scholarship for Innovation and Creativity *598*
Minority Students in Veterinary Medicine Scholarship *510*
Morrow & Sheppard College Scholarship *319*
National Association for Campus Activities Scholarships for Student Leaders *468*
National Association for Campus Activities South Student Leadership Scholarships *468*
National Make It With Wool Competition *257*
Palmetto Fellows Scholarship Program *602*
Pedro Zamora Young Leaders Scholarship *676*
Polly Holliday Scholarship *123*
Promise of Nursing Scholarship *367*
Rama Scholarship for the American Dream *268*
Residential Construction Management Scholarship *185*
Residential Design Scholarship *115*
SCACPA Educational Fund Scholarships *81*
South Carolina HOPE Scholarship *602*
South Carolina Need-Based Grants Program *602*
South Carolina Tourism and Hospitality Educational Foundation Scholarships *193*
Sustainable Residential Design Scholarship *115*
Ted G. Wilson Memorial Scholarship Foundation *166*
Triangle Pest Control Scholarship *82*
Two Ten Footwear Foundation Scholarship *471*
Two Ten Foundation Footwear Design Scholarship *607*
United States Senate Youth Program *626*
U.S. Army ROTC Four-Year College Scholarship *492*
U.S. Army ROTC Four-Year Historically Black College/University Scholarship *492*
U.S. Army ROTC Four-Year Nursing Scholarship *364*
U.S. Army ROTC Guaranteed Reserve Forces Duty (GRFD), (ARNG/USAR) and Dedicated ARNG Scholarships *494*
U.S. Army ROTC Military Junior College (MJC) Scholarship *492*
Women in Architecture Scholarship *116*
You Deserve It! Scholarship *600*

South Dakota
2017 ValuePenguin Scholarship *708*
AbbVie Immunology Scholarship *483*
AG Bell College Scholarship Program *472*
American Legion Department of Minnesota Memorial Scholarship *433*
Annual CGTrader Scholarship *643*
Army ROTC Green to Gold Scholarship Program for Two-Year, Three-Year and Four-Year Scholarships, Active Duty Enlisted Personnel *491*
Army (ROTC) Reserve Officers Training Corps Two-, Three-, Four-Year Campus-Based Scholarships *492*
Beacon Scholarship for Rural America *555*
Benson & Bingham Annual Scholarship *316*
CBC Spouses Education Scholarship *98*
CBC Spouses Performing Arts Scholarship *383*

SelectBlinds.com 2019 $1000 College Scholarship 600

Terry Fox Humanitarian Award 470

You Deserve It! Scholarship 600

New Brunswick

AG Bell College Scholarship Program 472

Annual CGTrader Scholarship 643

Benson & Bingham Annual Scholarship 316

Bill Mason Scholarship Fund 212

Canada Iceland Foundation Scholarship Program 615

Clunker Junker Cash for Cars and College Scholarship 227

Dr. Ernest and Minnie Mehl Scholarship 511

Leo J. Krysa Family Undergraduate Scholarship 208

National Association for Campus Activities Scholarships for Student Leaders 468

SelectBlinds.com 2019 $1000 College Scholarship 600

Terry Fox Humanitarian Award 470

You Deserve It! Scholarship 600

Newfoundland

AG Bell College Scholarship Program 472

Annual CGTrader Scholarship 643

Benson & Bingham Annual Scholarship 316

Bill Mason Scholarship Fund 212

Canada Iceland Foundation Scholarship Program 615

Clunker Junker Cash for Cars and College Scholarship 227

Dr. Ernest and Minnie Mehl Scholarship 511

Leo J. Krysa Family Undergraduate Scholarship 208

SelectBlinds.com 2019 $1000 College Scholarship 600

Terry Fox Humanitarian Award 470

Undergraduate General Scholarship 328

You Deserve It! Scholarship 600

Northwest Territories

AG Bell College Scholarship Program 472

Annual CGTrader Scholarship 643

Benson & Bingham Annual Scholarship 316

Bill Mason Scholarship Fund 212

Clunker Junker Cash for Cars and College Scholarship 227

Dr. Ernest and Minnie Mehl Scholarship 511

SelectBlinds.com 2019 $1000 College Scholarship 600

Terry Fox Humanitarian Award 470

You Deserve It! Scholarship 600

Nova Scotia

AG Bell College Scholarship Program 472

Annual CGTrader Scholarship 643

Benson & Bingham Annual Scholarship 316

Bill Mason Scholarship Fund 212

Canada Iceland Foundation Scholarship Program 615

Clunker Junker Cash for Cars and College Scholarship 227

Dr. Ernest and Minnie Mehl Scholarship 511

Leo J. Krysa Family Undergraduate Scholarship 208

SelectBlinds.com 2019 $1000 College Scholarship 600

Terry Fox Humanitarian Award 470

Two Ten Foundation Footwear Design Scholarship 607

You Deserve It! Scholarship 600

Nunavut

SelectBlinds.com 2019 $1000 College Scholarship 600

Ontario

AG Bell College Scholarship Program 472

Annual CGTrader Scholarship 643

Benson & Bingham Annual Scholarship 316

Bill Mason Scholarship Fund 212

Canada Iceland Foundation Scholarship Program 615

Clunker Junker Cash for Cars and College Scholarship 227

Dr. Ernest and Minnie Mehl Scholarship 511

Leo J. Krysa Family Undergraduate Scholarship 208

National Association for Campus Activities Mid Atlantic Higher Education Research Scholarship 211

National Association for Campus Activities Mid Atlantic Scholarship for Student Leaders 468

National Association for Campus Activities Northern Plains Region Scholarship for Student Leaders 152

National Association for Campus Activities Scholarships for Student Leaders 468

SelectBlinds.com 2019 $1000 College Scholarship 600

Terry Fox Humanitarian Award 470

Tese Caldarelli Memorial Scholarship 468

Zagunis Student Leader Scholarship 622

Prince Edward Island

AG Bell College Scholarship Program 472

Annual CGTrader Scholarship 643

Benson & Bingham Annual Scholarship 316

Bill Mason Scholarship Fund 212

Clunker Junker Cash for Cars and College Scholarship 227

Dr. Ernest and Minnie Mehl Scholarship 511

Leo J. Krysa Family Undergraduate Scholarship 208

SelectBlinds.com 2019 $1000 College Scholarship 600

Terry Fox Humanitarian Award 470

You Deserve It! Scholarship 600

Quebec

AG Bell College Scholarship Program 472

Annual CGTrader Scholarship 643

Benson & Bingham Annual Scholarship 316

Bill Mason Scholarship Fund 212

Canada Iceland Foundation Scholarship Program 615

Clunker Junker Cash for Cars and College Scholarship 227

Dr. Ernest and Minnie Mehl Scholarship 511

Leo J. Krysa Family Undergraduate Scholarship 208

National Association for Campus Activities Scholarships for Student Leaders 468

SelectBlinds.com 2019 $1000 College Scholarship 600

Terry Fox Humanitarian Award 470

You Deserve It! Scholarship 600

Saskatchewan

AG Bell College Scholarship Program 472

Annual CGTrader Scholarship 643

Benson & Bingham Annual Scholarship 316

Bill Mason Scholarship Fund 212

Canada Iceland Foundation Scholarship Program 615

Clunker Junker Cash for Cars and College Scholarship 227

Dr. Ernest and Minnie Mehl Scholarship 511

Leo J. Krysa Family Undergraduate Scholarship 208

National Association for Campus Activities Northern Plains Region Scholarship for Student Leaders 152

National Association for Campus Activities Scholarships for Student Leaders 468

SelectBlinds.com 2019 $1000 College Scholarship 600

Terry Fox Humanitarian Award 470

U.S. Army ROTC Guaranteed Reserve Forces Duty (GRFD), (ARNG/USAR) and Dedicated ARNG Scholarships 494

You Deserve It! Scholarship 600

Yukon

AG Bell College Scholarship Program 472

Annual CGTrader Scholarship 643

Benson & Bingham Annual Scholarship 316

Bill Mason Scholarship Fund 212

Clunker Junker Cash for Cars and College Scholarship 227

SelectBlinds.com 2019 $1000 College Scholarship 600

Terry Fox Humanitarian Award 470

You Deserve It! Scholarship 600

Military Service

Air Force

2017 Nurture for Nature Scholarship 483

Air Force ROTC College Scholarship Type 1 486

Airmen Memorial Foundation Scholarship 487

Armed Forces Communications and Electronics Association ROTC Scholarship Program 179

Chief Master Sergeants of the Air Force Scholarship Program 487

General Henry H. Arnold Education Grant Program 486

Military Award Program (MAP) 487

Montgomery GI Bill Selected Reserve 487

Resident Tuition for Active Duty Military Personnel 487

Smart Kitchen Improvement Scholarship by Kitchen Guides 477

US Veterans Magazine Scholarship 487

Veterans Education (VetEd) Reimbursement Grant 485

Air Force National Guard

2017 Nurture for Nature Scholarship 483

Airmen Memorial Foundation Scholarship 487

Alabama National Guard Educational Assistance Program 488

Chief Master Sergeants of the Air Force Scholarship Program 487

Children and Spouse of Indiana National Guard 489

CSM Vincent Baldassari Memorial Scholarship Program 489

General Henry H. Arnold Education Grant Program 486

Illinois National Guard (ING) Grant Program 489

Indiana National Guard Tuition Supplement Grant 489

Kentucky National Guard Tuition Award 490

Louisiana National Guard State Tuition Exemption Program 490

Military Award Program (MAP) 487

Montgomery GI Bill Selected Reserve 487

National Guard Extension Scholarship 489

National Guard Tuition Supplement Grant 490

North Carolina National Guard Tuition Assistance Program 490

Ohio National Guard Scholarship Program 490

Postsecondary Educational Gratuity Program 491

Reserve Education Assistance Program 488

Smart Kitchen Improvement Scholarship by Kitchen Guides 477

State Tuition Assistance 488

USAA Scholarship 489

US Veterans Magazine Scholarship 487

Veterans Education (VetEd) Reimbursement Grant 485

Army

2017 Nurture for Nature Scholarship 483

American Legion Auxiliary Department of Kentucky Laura Blackburn Memorial Scholarship 491

Armed Forces Communications and Electronics Association ROTC Scholarship Program 179

Army Officers Wives Club of the Greater Washington Area Scholarship 491

Army ROTC Green to Gold Scholarship Program for Two-Year, Three-Year and Four-Year Scholarships, Active Duty Enlisted Personnel 491

Army (ROTC) Reserve Officers Training Corps Two-, Three-, Four-Year Campus-Based Scholarships 492

Army ROTC Study.com Scholarship 493

Military Award Program (MAP) 487

Montgomery GI Bill Selected Reserve 487

Resident Tuition for Active Duty Military Personnel 487

Smart Kitchen Improvement Scholarship by Kitchen Guides 477

Society of Daughters of the United States Army Scholarships 493

U.S. Army ROTC Four-Year College Scholarship 492

U.S. Army ROTC Four-Year Historically Black College/University Scholarship 492

U.S. Army ROTC Four-Year Nursing Scholarship 364

U.S. Army ROTC Military Junior College (MJC) Scholarship 492

USAWOA Scholarship Foundation 493

US Veterans Magazine Scholarship 487

Veterans Education (VetEd) Reimbursement Grant 485

Women's Army Corps Veterans' Association Scholarship 493

Army National Guard

2017 Nurture for Nature Scholarship 483

Alabama National Guard Educational Assistance Program 488

Army ROTC Study.com Scholarship 493

Children and Spouse of Indiana National Guard 489

Connecticut Army National Guard 100% Tuition Waiver 494

CSM Vincent Baldassari Memorial Scholarship Program 489

Illinois National Guard (ING) Grant Program 489

Indiana National Guard Tuition Supplement Grant 489

Kentucky National Guard Tuition Award 490

Louisiana National Guard State Tuition Exemption Program 490

Military Award Program (MAP) 487

Montgomery GI Bill Selected Reserve 487

National Guard Extension Scholarship 489

National Guard Tuition Supplement Grant 490

New Jersey Army National Guard Tuition Waiver 495

North Carolina National Guard Tuition Assistance Program 490

Ohio National Guard Scholarship Program 490

Postsecondary Educational Gratuity Program 491

Reserve Education Assistance Program 488

Smart Kitchen Improvement Scholarship by Kitchen Guides 477

Society of Daughters of the United States Army Scholarships 493

State Tuition Assistance 488

Treadwell/Pringle Scholarships 494

USAA Scholarship 489

U.S. Army ROTC Four-Year College Scholarship 492

U.S. Army ROTC Four-Year Historically Black College/University Scholarship 492

U.S. Army ROTC Four-Year Nursing Scholarship 364

U.S. Army ROTC Guaranteed Reserve Forces Duty (GRFD), (ARNG/USAR) and Dedicated ARNG Scholarships 494

U.S. Army ROTC Military Junior College (MJC) Scholarship 492

USAWOA Scholarship Foundation 493

US Veterans Magazine Scholarship 487

Veterans Education (VetEd) Reimbursement Grant 485

Coast Guard

2017 Nurture for Nature Scholarship 483

College Student Pre-Commissioning Initiative (CSPI) 485

Doran/Blair Scholarships 439

Fleet Reserve Association Education Foundation Scholarships 496

Ladies Auxiliary of the Fleet Reserve Association Scholarship 444

Military Award Program (MAP) 487

Montgomery GI Bill Selected Reserve 487

Sam Rose Memorial Scholarship 444

Smart Kitchen Improvement Scholarship by Kitchen Guides 477

Tailhook Educational Foundation Scholarship 496

Treadwell/Pringle Scholarships 494

US Veterans Magazine Scholarship 487

Veterans Education (VetEd) Reimbursement Grant 485

General

2017 Boyk Law Veteran Scholarship 501

2017 Nurture for Nature Scholarship 483

2018 PDFelement $1000 Scholarship 486

AcadGild Merit-Based Scholarships 472

American Legion Auxiliary Department of Alabama Scholarship Program 497

American Legion Auxiliary Department of California General Scholarship 497

American Legion Auxiliary Department of California Past Presidents' Parley Nursing Scholarships 361

American Legion Auxiliary Department of Idaho Nursing Scholarship 361

American Legion Auxiliary Department of Iowa Children of Veterans Merit Award 497

American Legion Auxiliary Department of Iowa Harriet Hoffman Memorial Merit Award for Teacher Training 206

American Legion Auxiliary Department of Iowa M.V. McCrae Memorial Nurses Merit Award 361

American Legion Auxiliary Department of Kentucky Mary Barrett Marshall Scholarship 497

American Legion Auxiliary Department of Maine Daniel E. Lambert Memorial Scholarship 497

American Legion Auxiliary Department of Maine Past Presidents' Parley Nurses Scholarship 279

American Legion Auxiliary Department of Michigan Medical Career Scholarship 279

American Legion Auxiliary Department of Michigan Memorial Scholarship 498

American Legion Auxiliary Department of Michigan Scholarship for Non-Traditional Student 498

American Legion Auxiliary Department of Minnesota Scholarships 498

American Legion Auxiliary Department of Missouri Lela Murphy Scholarship 430

American Legion Auxiliary Department of Missouri National President's Scholarship 430

American Legion Auxiliary Department of Missouri Past Presidents' Parley Scholarship 362

American Legion Auxiliary Department of Nebraska Ruby Paul Campaign Fund Scholarship 430

American Legion Auxiliary Department of North Dakota National President's Scholarship 460

American Legion Auxiliary Department of North Dakota Past Presidents' Parley Nurses Scholarship 362

American Legion Auxiliary Department of Ohio Continuing Education Fund 499

American Legion Auxiliary Department of Ohio Department President's Scholarship 499

American Legion Auxiliary Department of Ohio Past Presidents' Parley Nurses Scholarship 362

American Legion Auxiliary Department of South Dakota College Scholarships 431

American Legion Auxiliary Department of South Dakota Senior Scholarship 431

American Legion Auxiliary Department of South Dakota Thelma Foster Scholarship for Senior Auxiliary Members 431

American Legion Auxiliary Department of Texas General Education Scholarship 499

American Legion Auxiliary Department of Texas Past Presidents' Parley Medical Scholarship 279

American Legion Auxiliary Department of Utah National President's Scholarship 431

American Legion Auxiliary Department of Wisconsin Della Van Deuren Memorial Scholarship 431

American Legion Auxiliary's Children of Warriors National Presidents' Scholarship 498

American Legion Auxiliary Spirit of Youth Scholarship for Junior Members 498

American Legion Department of Idaho Scholarship 432

American Legion Department of Maine Children and Youth Scholarship 500

American Legion Department of Minnesota Memorial Scholarship 433

AMVETS National Ladies Auxiliary Scholarship 436

Charles L. Bacon Memorial Scholarship 433

Children of Veterans Tuition Grant 504

Daniel E. Lambert Memorial Scholarship 500

Disabled Veterans Scholarship 475, 485

Erman W. Taylor Memorial Scholarship 206

Explosive Ordnance Disposal Memorial Scholarship 463

Guy M. Wilson Scholarships 500

Henry J. Reilly Memorial Scholarship-High School Seniors and First Year Freshmen 452

Henry J. Reilly Memorial Undergraduate Scholarship Program for College Attendees 452

Illinois Veteran Grant (IVG) Program 502

Indiana Purple Heart Recipient Program 502

Institute for Nursing Scholarship 372

James V. Day Scholarship 432

Kansas Educational Benefits for Children of MIA, POW, and Deceased Veterans of the Vietnam War 503

Lillie Lois Ford Scholarship Fund 501

Louisiana Department of Veterans Affairs State Educational Aid Program 503

Matthews & Swift Educational Trust Scholarship 444

M.D. Jack Murphy Memorial Nurses Training Scholarship 363

Military Award Program (MAP) 487

Military Dependent's Scholarship Program 501

Military Order of the Purple Heart Scholarship 504

Minnesota Legionnaires Insurance Trust Scholarship 433

Montgomery GI Bill Active Duty 501

Montgomery GI Bill Selected Reserve 487

National Military Family Association's Military Spouse Scholarships 504

New Jersey War Orphans Tuition Assistance 504

New Mexico Wartime Veterans Scholarship 505

New York Vietnam/Persian Gulf/Afghanistan Veterans Tuition Awards 505

North Carolina Veterans Scholarships Class I-A 506

North Carolina Veterans Scholarships Class I-B 506

North Carolina Veterans Scholarships Class II 506

North Carolina Veterans Scholarships Class III 506

North Carolina Veterans Scholarships Class IV 506

NYS Regents Awards for Children of Deceased and Disabled Veterans 505

Ohio American Legion Scholarships 434

Ohio War Orphan & Severely Disabled Veterans' Children Scholarship Program 506

POW-MIA Tuition Benefit Program 505

Rees Scholarship Foundation Veterans Program 287

Reserve Education Assistance Program 488

Retired Enlisted Association Scholarship 507

Scholarship for Disabled Veterans 478

Scholarships for Children and Spouses of Deceased or Disabled Veterans 502

Scholarships for Military Children 501

Scholarships for Orphans of Veterans 505

Sleep Sherpa Scholarship Program 484

Smart Kitchen Improvement Scholarship by Kitchen Guides 477

Survivors and Dependents Educational Assistance (Chapter 35)-VA 502

The Titan Web Agency Bi-Annual Scholarship Program 484

TonaLaw Veteran's Scholarship 507

Tuition and Fee Exemption for Indiana Purple Heart Recipients 503

Tuition and Fee Exemption for the Child(ren) of a Disabled Veteran or POW/MIA or Purple Heart Recipients 503

US Veterans Magazine Scholarship 487

Veterans Dependents Educational Benefits-Maine 503

Veterans Education (VetEd) Reimbursement Grant 485

Veterans Tuition Credit Program-New Jersey 505

Veterans United Foundation Scholarship 508

Vietnam Veterans Award-Wyoming 507

Virginia Military Survivors and Dependents Education Program 508

Wells Fargo Veterans Scholarship Program 507

Willa Beach-Porter Music Scholarships 347

William D. and Jewell W. Brewer Scholarship Trusts 500

Women's Jewelry Associations Veterans Grant 508

Marine Corps

2017 Nurture for Nature Scholarship 483

Armed Forces Communications and Electronics Association ROTC Scholarship Program 179

Ladies Auxiliary of the Fleet Reserve Association Scholarship 444

Marine Corps Tankers Association, John Cornelius/Max English Scholarship 509

Military Award Program (MAP) 487

Sam Rose Memorial Scholarship 444

US Veterans Magazine Scholarship 487

Navy

2017 Nurture for Nature Scholarship 483

Anchor Scholarship Foundation 509

Armed Forces Communications and Electronics Association ROTC Scholarship Program 179

Gamewardens of Vietnam Scholarship 509

Had Richards UDT-SEAL Memorial Scholarship 510

Ladies Auxiliary of the Fleet Reserve Association Scholarship 444

Military Award Program (MAP) 487

Naval Special Warfare Scholarship 510

Sam Rose Memorial Scholarship 444

UDT-SEAL Scholarship 510

United States Submarine Veterans Inc. National Scholarship Program 456

US Veterans Magazine Scholarship 487

Wings Over America Scholarship Foundation 510

Nationality or Ethnic Heritage

Australian

Lemberg Law American Dream $1,250 Undergraduate Scholarship *524*

OLM Malala Yousafzai Scholarship 2017-2018 *122*

Belgian

Lemberg Law American Dream $1,250 Undergraduate Scholarship *524*

OLM Malala Yousafzai Scholarship 2017-2018 *122*

Black, Non-Hispanic

2017 Nurture for Nature Scholarship *483*

5 Strong Scholars Scholarship *511*

ABCNJ Leadership Impact Scholarship *534*

AcadGild Merit-Based Scholarships *472*

Actuarial Diversity Scholarship *300*

AFSCME/UNCF Union Scholars Program *98*

Agnes Jones Jackson Scholarship *445*

AICPA Scholarship Award for Minority Accounting Students *511*

AIET Minorities and Women Educational Scholarship *400*

Al-Ben Scholarship for Academic Incentive *157*

Al-Ben Scholarship for Professional Merit *157*

Al-Ben Scholarship for Scholastic Achievement *157*

Amelia Kemp Scholarship *539*

American Chemical Society Scholars Program *153*

American Physical Society Corporate-Sponsored Scholarship for Minority Undergraduate Students Who Major in Physics *391*

Architects Foundation Diversity Advancement Scholarship *113*

Arts Council of Greater Grand Rapids Minority Scholarship *121*

Audre Lorde Scholarship Fund *539*

AWG Ethnic Minority Scholarship *200*

BESLA Scholarship Legal Writing Competition *317*

Bishop Joseph B. Bethea Scholarship *518*

Black EOE Journal Scholarship *517*

Blanche Ford Endowment Scholarship Fund *534*

Boule' Foundation Scholarship *534*

Breakthrough to Nursing Scholarships for Racial/Ethnic Minorities *366*

CANFIT Nutrition, Physical Education and Culinary Arts Scholarship *190*

Carole Simpson Scholarship *310*

CBCF Louis Stokes Health Scholars Program *516*

CBC Spouses Education Scholarship *98*

CBC Spouses Performing Arts Scholarship *383*

CBC Spouses Visual Arts Scholarship *120*

Charles S. Brown Scholarship in Physics *391*

CIC/Anna Chennault Scholarship *170*

City of Chicago Scholarship *534*

ClothingRIC.com Annual Student Scholarship *515*

College Student Pre-Commissioning Initiative (CSPI) *485*

Colorado Legal Group Fund *515*

Cynthia Denise Robinson Horton Scholarship *534*

Davis Scholarship for Women in STEM *111*

Deborah L. Vincent/FAHRO Education Scholarship *535*

Dell Corporate Scholars Program *168*

Delta Air Lines New York Scholarships *535*

Dinwiddie Family Foundation Scholarship *535*

Discover Financial Services Scholarship *82*

Diverse Voices in Storytelling Scholarship *177*

Diversity Abroad Achievement Scholarship *512*

Dr. Dan J. and Patricia S. Pickard Scholarship *516*

Dr. Pepper Snapple Group Scholarship *535*

Ed Bradley Scholarship *310*

Edith M. Allen Scholarship *209*

EDSA Minority Scholarship *523*

Edward M. Nagel Endowed Scholarship *151*

Epsilon Sigma Alpha Foundation Scholarships *517*

Essay Writing Contest by EssayHub *474*

Galactic Unite Bytheway Scholarship *111*

GE/LULAC Scholarship *149*

GM/LULAC Scholarship *241*

Hallie Q. Brown Scholarship *526*

Harvey Washington Banks Scholarship in Astronomy *391*

HCN/Apricity Resources Scholars Program *83*

Herbert Lehman Scholarship Program *526*

Home Improvement Scholarship by Home Improvement Solutions *520*

Homus Scholarship Program *477*

Hyatt Hotels Fund for Minority Lodging Management *268*

IABA Scholarship *521*

Jackie Robinson Scholarship *466*

Jay Charles Levine Scholarship *535*

Joseph N. Boakai Sr. Higher Education Scholarship *537*

Judith McManus Price Scholarship *427*

Julianne Malveaux Scholarship *204*

KAT Team Foundation Scholarship *535*

Ken Inouye Scholarship *312*

Kroger Michigan Scholarship *535*

LAGRANT Foundation Scholarship for Graduates *85*

LAGRANT Foundation Scholarship for Undergraduates *85*

Leidos STEM Scholarship *96*

Leonard M. Perryman Communications Scholarship for Ethnic Minority Students *177*

Lorenzo Felder Scholarship *462*

Malki Museum Scholarship *525*

Martha Dudley LPN/LVN Scholarship *370*

Martin Luther King, Jr. Memorial Scholarship *208*

Master's Scholarship Program *158*

Maureen L. & Howard N. Blitman, P.E., Scholarship to Promote Diversity in Engineering *166*

Mays Family Scholarship Fund *535*

Michael P. Anderson Scholarship in Space Science *391*

Minorities in Government Finance Scholarship *75*

Minority Affairs Committee Award for Outstanding Scholastic Achievement *153*

Minority Scholarship Program *141*

Minority Students in Veterinary Medicine Scholarship *510*

Minority Student Summer Scholarship *112*

Minority Teacher Incentive Grant Program *209*

Minority Teachers of Illinois (MTI) Scholarship Program *521*

Minority Undergraduate Retention Grant-Wisconsin *538*

MSCPA/NABA Scholarship *74*

NACME Scholars Program *243*

NASCAR Wendell Scott Sr. Scholarship *83*

National Black McDonald's Owners Association Hospitality Scholars Program *83*

National Dental Association Foundation Colgate-Palmolive Scholarship Program (Undergraduates) *197*

National Press Club Scholarship for Journalism Diversity *308*

National Scholarship *526*

National Society of Black Physicists and Lawrence Livermore National Library Undergraduate Scholarship *391*

Nevada-UNCF Scholarships *536*

Northwest Journalists of Color Scholarship *84*

NSBE Corporate Scholarship Program *230*

Ohio News Media Foundation Minority Scholarship *86*

OLM Malala Yousafzai Scholarship 2017-2018 *122*

Oracle Community Impact Scholarship *183*

The Ossie Davis Legacy Award Scholarship *89*

Pacific Northwest Scholarship *536*

Palm Beach Association of Black Journalists Scholarship *309*

Panda Cares--UNCF Scholars Program (Phase I) *536*

Pennsylvania State Employees Combined Campaign Scholarship (SECA) *536*

Philadelphia Association of Black Journalists Scholarship *309*

Public Relations Society of America Multicultural Affairs Scholarship *87*

Rama Scholarship for the American Dream *268*

Ray Charles Endowed Scholarship *536*

Richard S. Smith Scholarship *517*

Rodney Thaxton/Martin E. Segal Scholarship *525*

Ronald E. McNair Scholarship in Space and Optical Physics *391*

Ron Brown Scholar Program *530*

Rowling, Dold & Associates LLP Scholarship *73*

Royce Osborn Minority Student Scholarship *276*

Ryder System Charitable Foundation Scholarship Program *151*

Scholarship for Engineering Education for Minorities (MSEE) *518*

Scholarship for Ethnic Minority College Students *209*

Scholarship for Minority High School Students *209*

S. D. Bechtel Jr. Foundation Engineering Scholarship *243*

Sidney M. Aronovitz Scholarship *525*

Sleep Sherpa Scholarship Program *484*

Smart Kitchen Improvement Scholarship by Kitchen Guides *477*

Source Supply Scholarship *532*

StraightForward Media Minority Scholarship *533*

Taylor Michaels Scholarship Fund *467*

TEA Don Sahli-Kathy Woodall Minority Scholarship *214*

Technical Minority Scholarship *161*

Texas Black Baptist Scholarship *534*

Thurgood Marshall College Fund *526*

The Titan Web Agency Bi-Annual Scholarship Program *484*

Transtutors Scholarship 2017-18 *534*

UNCF/Alliance Data Scholarship and Internship Program *88*

UNCF/Carnival Corporate Scholars Program *151*

UNCF/Koch Scholars Program *536*

UNCF-Northrop Grumman Scholarship *184*

UNCF/Travelers Insurance Scholarship *151*

The United Health Foundation/NMF Diverse Medical Scholars Program *469*

Unmet NEED Grant Program *527*

UPS Scholarship for Minority Students *442*

USA Funds Scholarship *536*

USAWOA Scholarship Foundation *493*

Voya UNCF Male Initiative *536*

La Unidad Latina Foundation Dream
Scholarship *524*

La Unidad Latina Foundation National
Scholarship *524*

Lemberg Law American Dream $1,250
Undergraduate Scholarship *524*

Mas Family Scholarship Award *149*

Northwest Journalists of Color Scholarship *84*

OLM Malala Yousafzai Scholarship 2017-
2018 *122*

Latvian

Lemberg Law American Dream $1,250
Undergraduate Scholarship *524*

OLM Malala Yousafzai Scholarship 2017-
2018 *122*

Lebanese

Lemberg Law American Dream $1,250
Undergraduate Scholarship *524*

Northwest Journalists of Color Scholarship *84*

OLM Malala Yousafzai Scholarship 2017-
2018 *122*

Lithuanian

Lemberg Law American Dream $1,250
Undergraduate Scholarship *524*

OLM Malala Yousafzai Scholarship 2017-
2018 *122*

Mexican

Automotive Women's Alliance Foundation
Scholarships *71*

Fleming/Blaszcak Scholarship *158*

La Unidad Latina Foundation Dream
Scholarship *524*

La Unidad Latina Foundation National
Scholarship *524*

Lemberg Law American Dream $1,250
Undergraduate Scholarship *524*

Minority Students in Veterinary Medicine
Scholarship *510*

Northwest Journalists of Color Scholarship *84*

OLM Malala Yousafzai Scholarship 2017-
2018 *122*

Transportation Clubs International Ginger and
Fred Deines Mexico Scholarship *421*

Mongolian

Lemberg Law American Dream $1,250
Undergraduate Scholarship *524*

Northwest Journalists of Color Scholarship *84*

OLM Malala Yousafzai Scholarship 2017-
2018 *122*

New Zealander

Lemberg Law American Dream $1,250
Undergraduate Scholarship *524*

OLM Malala Yousafzai Scholarship 2017-
2018 *122*

Pacific Health Workforce Award *277*

Pacific Mental Health Work Force Award *277*

Nicaraguan

La Unidad Latina Foundation Dream
Scholarship *524*

La Unidad Latina Foundation National
Scholarship *524*

Lemberg Law American Dream $1,250
Undergraduate Scholarship *524*

OLM Malala Yousafzai Scholarship 2017-
2018 *122*

Norwegian

King Olav V Norwegian-American Heritage
Fund *119*

Lemberg Law American Dream $1,250
Undergraduate Scholarship *524*

Nancy Lorraine Jensen Memorial
Scholarship *160*

OLM Malala Yousafzai Scholarship 2017-
2018 *122*

Polish

Lemberg Law American Dream $1,250
Undergraduate Scholarship *524*

OLM Malala Yousafzai Scholarship 2017-
2018 *122*

Polish Arts Club of Buffalo Scholarship
Foundation Trust *122*

Polish Heritage Scholarship *530*

Portuguese

Cabrillo Civic Clubs of California
Scholarship *514*

Lemberg Law American Dream $1,250
Undergraduate Scholarship *524*

OLM Malala Yousafzai Scholarship 2017-
2018 *122*

PALCUS National Scholarship Program *530*

Rumanian

Lemberg Law American Dream $1,250
Undergraduate Scholarship *524*

OLM Malala Yousafzai Scholarship 2017-
2018 *122*

Russian

Lemberg Law American Dream $1,250
Undergraduate Scholarship *524*

OLM Malala Yousafzai Scholarship 2017-
2018 *122*

Scandinavian

Lemberg Law American Dream $1,250
Undergraduate Scholarship *524*

OLM Malala Yousafzai Scholarship 2017-
2018 *122*

Scottish

Lemberg Law American Dream $1,250
Undergraduate Scholarship *524*

OLM Malala Yousafzai Scholarship 2017-
2018 *122*

St. Andrews of the State of New York Graduate
Scholarship Program *531*

St. Andrew's Society of Washington DC
Founders' Scholarship *531*

St. Andrew's Society of Washington DC
Scholarships *531*

Slavic/Czech

First Catholic Slovak Ladies Association College
Scholarships *439*

Lemberg Law American Dream $1,250
Undergraduate Scholarship *524*

OLM Malala Yousafzai Scholarship 2017-
2018 *122*

Spanish

Lemberg Law American Dream $1,250
Undergraduate Scholarship *524*

OLM Malala Yousafzai Scholarship 2017-
2018 *122*

Sub-Saharan African

Lemberg Law American Dream $1,250
Undergraduate Scholarship *524*

Northwest Journalists of Color Scholarship *84*

OLM Malala Yousafzai Scholarship 2017-
2018 *122*

Swedish

Lemberg Law American Dream $1,250
Undergraduate Scholarship *524*

OLM Malala Yousafzai Scholarship 2017-
2018 *122*

Swiss

Lemberg Law American Dream $1,250
Undergraduate Scholarship *524*

Medicus Student Exchange *533*

OLM Malala Yousafzai Scholarship 2017-
2018 *122*

Pellegrini Scholarship Grants *533*

Swiss Benevolent Society of Chicago
Scholarships *533*

Swiss Benevolent Society of San Francisco
Scholarships *533*

Syrian

Lemberg Law American Dream $1,250
Undergraduate Scholarship *524*

Northwest Journalists of Color Scholarship *84*

OLM Malala Yousafzai Scholarship 2017-
2018 *122*

Turkish

Lemberg Law American Dream $1,250
Undergraduate Scholarship *524*

Northwest Journalists of Color Scholarship *84*

OLM Malala Yousafzai Scholarship 2017-
2018 *122*

Ukrainian

Lemberg Law American Dream $1,250
Undergraduate Scholarship *524*

OLM Malala Yousafzai Scholarship 2017-
2018 *122*

U.S. Colonial

Community College STEM Scholarships *110*

Vietnamese

Lemberg Law American Dream $1,250
Undergraduate Scholarship *524*

Northwest Journalists of Color Scholarship *84*

OLM Malala Yousafzai Scholarship 2017-
2018 *122*

Welsh

Lemberg Law American Dream $1,250
Undergraduate Scholarship *524*

OLM Malala Yousafzai Scholarship 2017-
2018 *122*

Yemeni

Lemberg Law American Dream $1,250
Undergraduate Scholarship *524*

National American Arab Nurses Association
Scholarships *369*

Northwest Journalists of Color Scholarship *84*

OLM Malala Yousafzai Scholarship 2017-
2018 *122*

Religious Affiliation

Residence

You Deserve It! Scholarship *600*

Kansas

2018 Open Essay Competition *608*
AG Bell College Scholarship Program *472*
Beacon Scholarship for Rural America *555*
Classic Scholarships *607*
College Access Program (CAP) Grant *578*
Debt.com Scholarship *561*
Duck Brand Duct Tape "Stuck at Prom" Scholarship Contest *573*
Early Childhood Development Scholarship *578*
Finally Sold Impact Maker Scholarship *563*
Frank S. Land Scholarship *458*
Greater Cincinnati HSF Scholarship *520*
Hagan Scholarship *572*
Health Professions Preparatory Scholarship Program *137*
Indian Health Service Health Professions Pregraduate Scholarships *108*
Kansas Federation of Republican Women Scholarship *288*
Kansas Nurses Foundation *211*
Kentucky Educational Excellence Scholarship (KEES) *578*
Kentucky National Guard Tuition Award *490*
Kentucky Tuition Grant (KTG) *578*
Milton Fisher Scholarship for Innovation and Creativity *598*
Minority Students in Veterinary Medicine Scholarship *510*
National Don't Text and Drive Scholarship *570*
National Make It With Wool Competition *257*
OnlinePsychologyDegrees.com Education Scholarships *595*
Panda Cares—UNCF Scholars Program (Phase I) *536*
RehabCenter.net *598*
Sales Professionals-USA Scholarship *150*
Tombow's Create Your Best Work Art Scholarship *123*
Tortoise Young Entrepreneurs Scholarship *606*
Two Ten Footwear Foundation Scholarship *471*
Two Ten Foundation Footwear Design Scholarship *607*
Western Fraternal Life National Scholarship *456*
You Deserve It! Scholarship *600*

Kentucky

2018 Open Essay Competition *608*
AG Bell College Scholarship Program *472*
The Alberta C. Kaufman Scholarship *577*
American Legion Auxiliary Department of Kentucky Laura Blackburn Memorial Scholarship *491*
Anthony Munoz Scholarship Fund *551*
Beacon Scholarship for Rural America *555*
Blue Grass Energy Academic Scholarship *553*
Classic Scholarships *607*
Debt.com Scholarship *561*
Department of Veterans Affairs Tuition Waiver-KY KRS 164-507 *577*
Duck Brand Duct Tape "Stuck at Prom" Scholarship Contest *573*
Environmental Protection Scholarship *142*
Finally Sold Impact Maker Scholarship *563*
Frank S. Land Scholarship *458*
GO Grant *580*
Hagan Scholarship *572*
Health Professions Preparatory Scholarship Program *137*
Indian Health Service Health Professions Pregraduate Scholarships *108*
Inter-County Energy Scholarship *576*
Jackson Energy Scholarship Essay Contest *577*
Kentucky Society of Certified Public Accountants College Scholarship *77*

Kentucky Transportation Cabinet Civil Engineering Scholarship Program *165*
Levy Law Offices Cincinnati Safe Driver Scholarship *579*
Logan Telephone Cooperative Educational Scholarship *580*
Milton Fisher Scholarship for Innovation and Creativity *598*
Minority Students in Veterinary Medicine Scholarship *510*
National Don't Text and Drive Scholarship *570*
National Make It With Wool Competition *257*
OnlinePsychologyDegrees.com Education Scholarships *595*
Polly Holliday Scholarship *123*
RehabCenter.net *598*
Rockefeller State Wildlife Scholarship *325*
Salt River Electric Scholarship Program *600*
Shelby Energy Cooperative Scholarships *601*
Sidney B. Meadows Scholarship Endowment Fund *293*
Sr. Mary Jeannette Wess, S.N.D. Scholarship *470*
Taylor Opportunity Program for Students Honors Award *580*
Taylor Opportunity Program for Students Opportunity Level *581*
Taylor Opportunity Program for Students Performance Award *581*
Taylor Opportunity Program for Students Tech Award *581*
Tolliver Annual Nursing Scholarship *369*
Tombow's Create Your Best Work Art Scholarship *123*
Two Ten Footwear Foundation Scholarship *471*
Two Ten Foundation Footwear Design Scholarship *607*
You Deserve It! Scholarship *600*

Louisiana

2018 Open Essay Competition *608*
AG Bell College Scholarship Program *472*
Agnes Freyer Gibbs Scholarship Fund *581*
Beacon Scholarship for Rural America *555*
Broadcast Scholarship Program *424*
Chet Jordan Leadership Award *581*
Classic Scholarships *607*
Debt.com Scholarship *561*
Dixie Youth Scholarship Program *562*
Duck Brand Duct Tape "Stuck at Prom" Scholarship Contest *573*
Ed E. and Gladys Hurley Foundation Scholarship *402*
Finally Sold Impact Maker Scholarship *563*
Frank S. Land Scholarship *458*
Gulf Coast Hurricane Scholarship *159*
Guy P. Gannett Scholarship Fund *582*
Hagan Scholarship *572*
Health Professions Preparatory Scholarship Program *137*
Indian Health Service Health Professions Pregraduate Scholarships *108*
Joseph W. Mayo ALS Scholarship Fund *582*
Louisiana Department of Veterans Affairs State Educational Aid Program *503*
Louisiana National Guard State Tuition Exemption Program *490*
Lydia R. Laurendeau Scholarship Fund *582*
Maine State Grant Program *564*
Maine Vietnam Veterans Scholarship Fund *582*
Milton Fisher Scholarship for Innovation and Creativity *598*
Minority Students in Veterinary Medicine Scholarship *510*
National Don't Text and Drive Scholarship *570*

OnlinePsychologyDegrees.com Education Scholarships *595*
Patriot Education Scholarship Fund *582*
RehabCenter.net *598*
Ronald P. Guerrette FFA Scholarship Fund *101*
Sidney B. Meadows Scholarship Endowment Fund *293*
Society of Louisiana CPAs Scholarships *81*
Timothy S. and Palmer W. Bigelow, Jr. Scholarship *247*
Tombow's Create Your Best Work Art Scholarship *123*
Two Ten Footwear Foundation Scholarship *471*
Two Ten Foundation Footwear Design Scholarship *607*
Western Fraternal Life National Scholarship *456*
You Deserve It! Scholarship *600*

Maine

2018 Open Essay Competition *608*
AG Bell College Scholarship Program *472*
American Legion Auxiliary Department of Maine Daniel E. Lambert Memorial Scholarship *497*
American Legion Auxiliary Department of Maine Past Presidents' Parley Nurses Scholarship *279*
American Legion Department of Maine Children and Youth Scholarship *500*
Annual Liberty Graphics Art Contest *579*
Blessed Leon of Our Lady of the Rosary Award *530*
Classic Scholarships *607*
Daniel E. Lambert Memorial Scholarship *500*
Debt.com Scholarship *561*
Duck Brand Duct Tape "Stuck at Prom" Scholarship Contest *573*
EMBARK-Support for the College Journey *581*
Finally Sold Impact Maker Scholarship *563*
Foundation for Seacoast Health Scholarships *282*
Frances L. Booth Medical Scholarship sponsored by LAVFW Department of Maine *283*
Frank S. Land Scholarship *458*
Graphic Communications Scholarship Fund of New England *275*
Health Professions Preparatory Scholarship Program *137*
Indian Health Service Health Professions Pregraduate Scholarships *108*
The Jackson Laboratory College Scholarship Program *108*
James V. Day Scholarship *432*
Leo J. Krysa Family Undergraduate Scholarship *208*
Maine Manufacturing Career and Training Foundation Scholarship *131*
Maine Restaurant Association Education Foundation Scholarship Fund *192*
Maine Rural Rehabilitation Fund Scholarship Program *90*
Maine Society of Professional Engineers Vernon T. Swaine-Robert E. Chute Scholarship *228*
Maine State Society Foundation Scholarship *582*
Minority Students in Veterinary Medicine Scholarship *510*
National Don't Text and Drive Scholarship *570*
National Make It With Wool Competition *257*
New England Employee Benefits Council Scholarship Program *78*
New England Regional Student Program-Tuition Break *589*
OnlinePsychologyDegrees.com Education Scholarships *595*
PAMAS Restricted Scholarship Award *450*
Parker-Lovejoy Scholarship *597*
Ravenscroft Family Award *530*

American Legion Auxiliary Department of Oregon
Spirit of Youth Scholarship 430
American Legion Department of Oregon High
School Oratorical Contest 549
Audria M. Edwards Scholarship Fund 596
Beacon Scholarship for Rural America 555
Blind or Deaf Beneficiary Grant Program 483
Cady McDonnell Memorial Scholarship 412
Classic Scholarships 607
Debt.com Scholarship 561
Dimitri J. Ververelli Memorial Scholarship for
Architecture and/or Engineering 240
Dr. Michael Dorizas Memorial Scholarship 519
Dr. Peter A. Theodos Memorial Graduate
Scholarship 519
Duck Brand Duct Tape "Stuck at Prom"
Scholarship Contest 573
Ernest Alan and Barbara Park Meyer Scholarship
Fund 595
Finally Sold Impact Maker Scholarship 563
Ford Opportunity Program 567
Ford ReStart Program 567
Ford Scholars Program 567
Founders Scholarship 519
Frank S. Land Scholarship 458
Franz Stenzel M.D. and Kathryn Stenzel
Scholarship Fund 283
Friends of Bill Rutherford Education Fund 595
Hagan Scholarship 572
Health Professions Preparatory Scholarship
Program 137
Hispanic Metropolitan Chamber
Scholarships 520
Indian Health Service Health Professions Pre-
graduate Scholarships 108
Jackson Foundation Journalism Scholarship
Fund 309
Law Enforcement and Criminal Justice College
Scholarship Program 189
Mary E. Horstkotte Scholarship Fund 595
Milton Fisher Scholarship for Innovation and
Creativity 598
Minority Students in Veterinary Medicine
Scholarship 510
National Don't Text and Drive Scholarship 570
National Make It With Wool Competition 257
Nicholas S. Hetos, DDS, Memorial Graduate
Scholarship 519
NLN Ella McKinney Scholarship Fund 373
OAB Foundation Scholarship 174
OAIA Scholarship 79
OnlinePsychologyDegrees.com Education
Scholarships 595
Oregon Student Access Commission Employee
and Dependents Scholarship 595
Pacific Northwest Scholarship 536
Paideia Scholarship 440
Panda Cares—UNCF Scholars Program (Phase
I) 536
Pennsylvania Chafee Education and Training
Grant Program 596
Pennsylvania State Grant Program 596
Peter Crossley Memorial Scholarship 595
Postsecondary Educational Gratuity
Program 491
Pride Foundation Scholarship Program 598
Ready to Succeed Scholarship Program 597
RehabCenter.net 598
Rube and Minah Leslie Educational Fund 595
Salem Foundation Ansel & Marie Solie
Scholarship 482
Sehar Saleha Ahmad and Abrahim Ekramullah
Zafar Foundation Scholarship 110
Teacher Education Scholarship 212
Tombow's Create Your Best Work Art
Scholarship 123

Touchmark Foundation Nursing Scholarship 374
Two Ten Footwear Foundation Scholarship 471
Two Ten Foundation Footwear Design
Scholarship 607
Western Fraternal Life National Scholarship 456
You Deserve It! Scholarship 600

Palau
SelectBlinds.com 2019 $1000 College
Scholarship 600

Pennsylvania
2018 Open Essay Competition 608
AG Bell College Scholarship Program 472
Allegheny Mountain Section Air & Waste
Management Association Scholarship 250
American Legion Auxiliary Department of
Pennsylvania Past Department Presidents'
Memorial Scholarship 363
American Legion Auxiliary Department of
Pennsylvania Scholarship for Dependents of
Disabled or Deceased Veterans 545
American Legion Auxiliary Department of
Pennsylvania Scholarship for Dependents of
Living Veterans 546
American Legion Department of Pennsylvania
High School Oratorical Contest 549
Aviation Council of Pennsylvania Scholarship
Program 128
Beulah Frey Environmental Scholarship 252
Careers Through Culinary Arts Program Cooking
Competition for Scholarships 190
Christopher Demetris Scholarship 519
Classic Scholarships 607
Debt.com Scholarship 561
Duck Brand Duct Tape "Stuck at Prom"
Scholarship Contest 573
Eric J. Gennuso and LeRoy D. (Bud) Loy, Jr.
Scholarship Program 153
Finally Sold Impact Maker Scholarship 563
Frank S. Land Scholarship 458
Health Professions Preparatory Scholarship
Program 137
Indian Health Service Health Professions Pre-
graduate Scholarships 108
John Lepping Memorial Scholarship 579
Joseph P. Gavenonis College Scholarship (Plan
I) 434
Leo J. Krysa Family Undergraduate
Scholarship 208
Minority Students in Veterinary Medicine
Scholarship 510
National Don't Text and Drive Scholarship 570
National Make It With Wool Competition 257
New York Women in Communications
Scholarships 591
OnlinePsychologyDegrees.com Education
Scholarships 595
Panda Cares—UNCF Scholars Program (Phase
I) 536
Pellegrini Scholarship Grants 533
Pennsylvania Burglar and Fire Alarm Association
Youth Scholarship Program 469
Pennsylvania Federation of Democratic Women
Inc. Annual Scholarship Awards 449
Pennsylvania State Employees Combined
Campaign Scholarship (SECA) 536
Philadelphia Association of Black Journalists
Scholarship 309
Project BEST Scholarship 451
RehabCenter.net 598
Robert W. Valimont Endowment Fund Scholarship
(Part II) 417
Ronald Lorah Memorial Scholarship 419
Roothbert Fund Inc. Scholarship 599
St. Andrew's Society of Washington DC
Founders' Scholarship 531

St. Andrew's Society of Washington DC
Scholarships 531
Seol Bong Scholarship 531
Society of Women Engineers-Twin Tiers Section
Scholarship 182
Ted Bricker Scholarship 408
Tombow's Create Your Best Work Art
Scholarship 123
Two Ten Footwear Foundation Scholarship 471
Two Ten Foundation Footwear Design
Scholarship 607
Unmet NEED Grant Program 527
Western Fraternal Life National Scholarship 456
You Deserve It! Scholarship 600
Young Christian Leaders Scholarship 540

Puerto Rico
AG Bell College Scholarship Program 472
Classic Scholarships 607
Debt.com Scholarship 561
Duck Brand Duct Tape "Stuck at Prom"
Scholarship Contest 573
Leo J. Krysa Family Undergraduate
Scholarship 208
Minority Students in Veterinary Medicine
Scholarship 510
Panda Cares—UNCF Scholars Program (Phase
I) 536
RehabCenter.net 598
SelectBlinds.com 2019 $1000 College
Scholarship 600
Tombow's Create Your Best Work Art
Scholarship 123
Two Ten Footwear Foundation Scholarship 471
Two Ten Foundation Footwear Design
Scholarship 607
You Deserve It! Scholarship 600

Rhode Island
2018 Open Essay Competition 608
AG Bell College Scholarship Program 472
Andrew Bell Scholarship 599
Bach Organ and Keyboard Music
Scholarship 351
Blessed Leon of Our Lady of the Rosary
Award 530
Carl W. Christiansen Scholarship 80
Cheryl A. Ruggiero Scholarship 80
Classic Scholarships 607
Debt.com Scholarship 561
Duck Brand Duct Tape "Stuck at Prom"
Scholarship Contest 573
Finally Sold Impact Maker Scholarship 563
Frank S. Land Scholarship 458
Graphic Communications Scholarship Fund of
New England 275
Health Professions Preparatory Scholarship
Program 137
Indian Health Service Health Professions Pre-
graduate Scholarships 108
J. D. Edsal Scholarship 87
Leo J. Krysa Family Undergraduate
Scholarship 208
Minority Students in Veterinary Medicine
Scholarship 510
National Don't Text and Drive Scholarship 570
National Make It With Wool Competition 257
New England Employee Benefits Council
Scholarship Program 78
New England Regional Student Program-Tuition
Break 589
PAMAS Restricted Scholarship Award 450
Patricia W. Edwards Memorial Art
Scholarship 122
Pierre H. Guillemette Scholarship 414
Ravenscroft Family Award 530
RehabCenter.net 598

Utah

Vermont

Virginia

CANADA

Alberta

British Columbia

Manitoba

New Brunswick

Newfoundland

Northwest Territories

Talent/Interest Area

NOTES

NOTES

NOTES

NOTES

NOTES

NOTES

NOTES

NOTES

NOTES

NOTES